# LEGAL ETHICS, PROFESSIONAL RESPONSIBILITY, AND THE LEGAL PROFESSION

**Gregory C. Sisk**
*Laghi Distinguished Chair in Law*
*University of St. Thomas School of Law (Minnesota)*

**Susan Saab Fortney**
*Professor of Law*
*Texas A&M University School of Law*

**Charles Gardner Geyh**
*John F. Kimberling Professor of Law*
*Indiana University Maurer School of Law*

**Neil W. Hamilton**
*Holloran Center Founding Director and Professor of Law*
*University of St. Thomas School of Law (Minnesota)*

**William D. Henderson**
*Professor of Law and Val Nolan Faculty Fellow*
*Indiana University Maurer School of Law*

**Vincent R. Johnson**
*South Texas Professor of Law*
*St. Mary's University School of Law*

**Katherine R. Kruse**
*Professor of Law*
*Mitchell Hamline School of Law*

**Stephen L. Pepper**
*Professor of Law*
*University of Denver Sturm College of Law*

**Melissa H. Weresh**
*Dwight D. Opperman Distinguished Professor of Law*
*Drake University Law School*

**HORNBOOK SERIES®**

Printed in the United States of America

**ISBN:** 978-1-63460-511-3

# General Foreword

This book sounds with alternating choruses in different keys, not an exquisite melody vocalized by a solitary singer. Many valuable treatises and casebooks on professional responsibility are written with an overarching theme that weaves together each passage so that each individual contribution reads as part of a unified and fully integrated arrangement. This is not one of them.

Rather, we believe the distinctive character of this single volume is that it presents a range of perspectives on most of those subjects central to a fundamental understanding of lawyer professional ethics and responsibility. This book looks at the subject of lawyer ethics through multiple lenses, touches the topics with several different hands, and speaks with a diversity of voices, while remaining reasonably comprehensive in coverage for the inquiring student or lawyer.

At the core of any treatment of professional responsibility, this one included, remain the doctrinal subjects of disciplinary rules, malpractice liability, and judicial ethics, which indeed make up the larger share of the volume. The "blackletter law," however, must be evaluated in a larger context. Thus, this hornbook also addresses the practical consequences of the real-world changes in the market for legal services, the philosophical and jurisprudential implications of ethics for lawyers, and professional formation and professionalism. Each of these parts is separately-authored, with a separate byline for proper credit (or blame as the case may be).

Part One on "The Legal Profession and Legal Services: Nature and Evolution," is authored by William D. Henderson, Professor of Law and Val Nolan Faculty Fellow at the Indiana University Maurer School of Law. The practice of law is undergoing a structural change, with declining markets for traditional lawyer skills and the demand by clients for better, faster, and cheaper legal products and services. The sea change reflects an urgent need for legal services that can keep pace with the demands of a rapidly globalizing world. To thrive in the years to come, lawyers and law firms will need to become entrepreneurial, more efficient, and less expensive through collaboration, technology, and specialization. These changes in turn raise important issues of professional responsibility, especially for the American legal profession.

Part Two on "The Philosophy of Legal Ethics" is co-authored by Stephen L. Pepper, Professor of Law at the University of Denver Sturm College of Law, and Katherine R. Kruse, Professor of Law at the Mitchell-Hamline School of Law. The professional duties of lawyers to clients, to the legal system, and to society, have theoretical foundations in moral, political, and jurisprudential theory. This chapter explores the theories and critiques that underlie client-centered duties, strike a balance between client-centered and public duties, and shape the form and function of the lawyer-client relationship.

Part Three on "Development Toward Professionalism and the Formation of an Ethical Professional Identity to Become an Effective Lawyer" is jointly authored by Neil W. Hamilton, the Holloran Professor of Law and Founding Director of the Holloran Center for Ethical Leadership in the Professions at the University of St. Thomas School of Law (Minnesota), and Melissa H. Weresh, Dwight D. Opperman Distinguished Professor of Law at the Drake University Law School. A thorough understanding of professionalism begins in law school and, ideally, continues to grow through practical experience. This chapter explores the journey of professional identity development and formation. It begins with an analysis of the historical development and current ideal of professionalism in the legal community. Practical and valuable consequences of professional identity formation, including lawyer well-being and efficacy, are considered. The chapter concludes with an examination of current instructional trends in professional identity formation in law school and law practice.

Part Four on "Legal Ethics and the Practice of Law" is authored by Gregory C. Sisk, the Pio Cardinal Laghi Distinguished Chair in Law at the University of St. Thomas School of Law (Minnesota). Nearly every element of an attorney's legal practice is governed by formal ethics rules enforceable by professional discipline and other standards applied by courts. This part of the hornbook addresses the substance of those ethical obligations as applied to practicing lawyers. Topics include the creation and termination of the attorney-client relationship, advertising for and solicitation of clients, attorney fees and funding of legal services, duties to effectively represent clients, the duty to protect confidential information and the attorney-client privilege, the duty of loyalty and conflicts of interest, duties to organizational clients, duties of ethical advocacy, duties to those other than clients, duties as an evaluator or third-party neutral, and duties as a managing or supervising attorney.

Part Five on "Legal Malpractice" is co-authored by Susan Saab Fortney, Professor of Law at Texas A&M University School of Law, and Vincent R. Johnson, South Texas Professor of Law at St. Mary's University School of Law. Many lawyers are more concerned about their civil liability exposure than the risk of disciplinary liability. Despite this concern, lawyers often do not recognize the type of conduct that may subject them to civil liability. This chapter discusses various theories of liability, defenses, and remedies, as well as the anatomy of a malpractice case. It also provides guidance on how lawyers can take steps to lower their malpractice exposure. It concludes with a discussion of legal malpractice insurance and the proper course of action when lawyers discover their own malpractice.

Part Six on "Judicial Ethics and the Conduct of Judges" is authored by Charles Gardner Geyh, the John F. Kimberling Professor of Law at the Indiana University Maurer School of Law. With rare exception, judges are lawyers who are members of the bar, and as such remain subject to the rules of professional conduct discussed in Part 4. Judges, however, are a unique subset of lawyers who are called upon to serve, not as representatives of or advocates for others, but as impartial and independent arbiters of law. Hence, a separate body of rules is needed to regulate judicial ethics—rules of importance not only to lawyers who become judges, but to lawyers who practice before judges and must be familiar with the ethical constraints under which judges operate. This part begins by exploring core principles of judicial ethics. It then discusses the rules that govern judges' conduct on the bench, before turning to the rules that regulate judges' extrajudicial and political activities.

---

## RECOMMENDED CITATION

For those citing to this book, we recommend attribution to the individually-authored part as being most accurate. For example, the most appropriate citation format would look like this: Susan Saab Fortney & Vincent R. Johnson, Legal Malpractice § 5-1.1, in *Legal Ethics, Professional Responsibility, and the Legal Profession* (West Academic Publishing, 2018).

# Individual Author Prefaces and Acknowledgments

The foundation for my contribution to this hornbook on the rules of ethics governing lawyers was laid through my two decades of law school teaching and writing on professional responsibility and then my service as the Reporter for the Iowa Rules of Professional Conduct Drafting Committee, when that state became one of the last to adopt the Model Rules of Professional Conduct (and only after significant debate on both format and substance). Especially through my work on that drafting committee, I studied troves of court decisions on legal ethics; diligently attempted to remain abreast of developments in the American Bar Association, American Law Institute, and the states, and shared that information in a useable way for practicing lawyers on the committee; studied the rules in even greater detail than I had previously in twenty years of teaching; read nearly every page of several leading treatises and other books on professional responsibility (as well as a host of articles in law reviews and bar journals); and talked regularly with innumerable friends and colleagues in the practicing bar.

My initial foray into a book on lawyer ethics came with authoring a state-specific treatise on *Iowa Lawyer and Judicial Ethics*, with now-Chief Justice Mark Cady of the Iowa Supreme Court as my co-author (writing the section on Iowa judicial ethics), a volume that is updated every year by Thomson-Reuters in the Iowa Practice Series (and from which considerable material has been adapted with permission from Thomson-Reuters into this present work). For that practical reason, readers will find some Iowa-centric features to what follows. Beyond convenience for the author, my ongoing work and reading in the professional ethics field has confirmed that adopting more examples from Iowa cases than any other single state venue is eminently justifiable. As Lucian Pera observed in assigning box scores early after the Ethics 2000 project, Iowa and Nebraska were essentially tied among the states in most closely following the revisions to the ABA Model Rules. *See* Lucian T. Pera, *Grading ABA Leadership on Legal Ethics Leadership: State Adoption of the Revised ABA Model Rules of Professional Conduct*, 30 Okla. City U. L. Rev. 637 (2005). Moreover, by longstanding practice, not only does nearly every significant lawyer disciplinary case come before the Iowa Supreme Court, but that court renders a full opinion, frequently including a thorough canvassing of professional responsibility authorities across the nation when resolving a controverted question. When encountering a legal ethics problem, the Iowa Supreme Court is more likely than any other state court to have addressed that issue in a real-world setting with a considered analysis, making that court more of a national leader in this field than has heretofore been recognized.

By its nature as the section of this hornbook devoted to the rules of lawyer ethics, my contribution focuses primarily upon the codified set of rules that constitute mandatory authority for ethical attorney behavior in the American jurisdictions that admit lawyers to practice. At the same time, and consistent with some of the other contributions to this volume, I hope that what follows strikes an appropriate balance between offering commentary on the formal rules of professional conduct and encouraging students and practitioners to think seriously about ethical and moral behavior beyond the text of rules. Contrary to what some may say pessimistically about the state of our profession, I remain convinced, and my work with and observation of lawyers in multiple states only strengthens that confidence, that it truly is possible to be a good person *and* a good lawyer. However, the goal of leading the good life as a lawyer may be achieved only if each practitioner makes a commitment to the highest values of the profession and refuses to subordinate his or her own moral principles to exigencies of practice. On the last day of class each year in my professional responsibility course, I exhort my students to remember the words of Georges Bernanos: "Try to be the kind of man [or woman] of whom the child you once were would not be ashamed."

While I have taken steps to promote accuracy and a reasonable degree of comprehensiveness in this section on the rules of lawyer ethics, errors both substantive and typographical undoubtedly have crept through and issues of ethical importance unquestionably have been neglected. Moreover, when the rules have not directed a precise answer to an ethical problem, I often have shared my own reasoning to a conclusion. Because legal ethics applies within every field of law and area of practice,[1] and because I could not hope to be an expert on the universality of the field of human activity that we call "the law," I have less confidence in my commentary on some matters than on others. Indeed, my sense of accomplishment in finishing my work on this book is balanced by a sense of inadequacy, because so much more could be said on each topic, many topics are left unaddressed, and my own understanding pales in comparison to the collective body of scholarly work on professional responsibility. As I've said before in writing a treatise, by the nature of any general overview written by a fallible human being, there is the possibility of over-simplification and the certainty of omission.

If the reader discovers an error of substance or detail, including typographical or citation errors, I would appreciate being notified so as to correct the mistake in future editions. If I have failed to address a matter of importance that should be added in a future edition, please suggest it to me. And if the reader thinks that my ethical analysis is mistaken, I likewise invite expression of alternative perspectives on points of controversy, whether I ultimately am persuaded or not. I may be reached at gcsisk@ stthomas.edu.

A number of people generously reviewed at least some portion of this contribution or earlier published works from which it is derived and offered their comments and corrections (speaking only for themselves and not for any agency, organization, or law firm with which they are affiliated). Moreover, none of these people should be held responsible for the views expressed here, much less any errors I have made. At the grave risk of missing someone, I wish to acknowledge and thank Martin Begleiter, Matthew Doré, Greta Fails, Stephen Gillers, Bruce Green, Neil Hamilton, Peter Joy, Rory Little, Andrew Kahl, Chris Luzzie, Julie Potorff, Douglas Richmond, Rodney Uphoff, and Maura Strassberg, as well as others whose names are not listed here. For helping keep me grounded in the simple realities and dedicated professionalism of law practice in the heartland by taking the time to discuss common and emerging issues in professional responsibility, I am grateful to Chief Justice Mark Cady and Justices Brent Appel, Edward Mansfield, and David Wiggins of the Iowa Supreme Court; Justices Barry Anderson, Anne McKeig, David Lillehaug, and David Stras of the Minnesota Supreme Court; Director Nicholas (Tré) Critelli and Assistant Director Tara van Brederode of the

---

[1] MILTON C. REGAN, EAT WHAT YOU KILL 4 (U. Mich. Press, 2006) (astutely explaining that "how lawyers identify, frame, and resolve ethical questions" requires "sensitivity" to "the particular fields in which they practice").

Iowa Office of Professional Regulation; and Direct Susan Humiston and Assistant Director Patrick Burns of the Minnesota Office of Lawyers Professional Responsibility. I also wish to acknowledge the cite-checking, proof-reading, and general research and editorial assistance of Molly Beckius, Lee Bennin, Dane Knudsen, Erin Larsgaard, Olivia Luther, Kacie Phillips, and Shana Tomenes, then students at the University of St. Thomas School of Law. For assistance on earlier works that are integrated and adapted in part into this volume, I also appreciate the work of Pamela Abbate, Erin Collins, Christian Eichenlaub, Elizabeth Malay, and Anna Petosky, all law graduates of the University of St. Thomas School. Of course, I alone remain responsible for any errors that remain, for all opinions expressed, for the wisdom or foolishness of any commentary offered, and for the substance of all matters discussed.

Without the generous permission of Thomson-Reuters-West to adapt chapters and sections from my ongoing state-specific treatise *Iowa Lawyer and Judicial Ethics* published and updated each year as part of the Iowa Practice series and also available on Westlaw, my contribution to this present volume would not have been possible. I have also integrated considerable material from prior law review writing, including Gregory C. Sisk & Pamela J. Abbate, *The Dynamic Attorney-Client Privilege*, 23 Georgetown Journal of Legal Ethics 201 (2010), and Gregory C. Sisk, *The Legal Ethics of Real Evidence: Of Child Porn on the Choirmaster's Computer and Bloody Knives Under the Stairs*, 89 Washington Law Review 819 (2014).

Having taught Professional Responsibility for many years to law students at more than one law school using the casebook, *Regulation of Lawyers* (Wolter Kluwer, 10th ed., 2015) authored by Stephen Gillers of New York University School of Law, the manner in which I approach many of the subjects likely has been influenced by Professor Gillers in more ways than mere citations could fully capture. The most comprehensive commentary on the Model Rules of Professional Conduct is *The Law of Lawyering* authored by Professors Geoffrey C. Hazard, Jr. (who was a reporter for the Model Rules of Professional Conduct) and W. William Hodes, and now joined by Peter R. Jarvis as it is updated each year by Wolter Kluwer. *Modern Legal Ethics* (West Pub., 1986), by Professor Charles W. Wolfram (who was also the reporter for the *Restatement of the Law Governing Lawyers*) remains an indispensable source of information and analysis. In addition, I benefited greatly from the cogent, readable, and thoughtful discussion found in the volume titled *Professional Responsibility—A Student's Guide*, which is authored by Professors Ronald D. Rotunda and John S. Dzienkowski and is updated annually by West Academic Publishing. For the classic and masterful presentation of legal ethics from the perspective of zealous advocacy, reference always should be made to the work of the late Professor Monroe H. Freedman, who joined with Professor Abbe Smith in authoring *Understanding Lawyers' Ethics* (Lexis-Nexis, 4th ed., 2010). Beyond the many citations, and not a few quotations, to these various treatises that follow, they also served as sources to which I regularly turned for background reading and research. Sadly, during work on this book, we lost Professor Freedman, and then just as we reached the page proof stage, Professors Hazard and Rotunda passed. These three were giants in the field, whose legacies will carry us forward throughout this new century.

As always, my work and life are dedicated to my patient and ever-supportive wife, Mindy, and my bright-eyed and bright-minded daughter, Caitlin, without whom life would not be worth living.

GREGORY C. SISK
LAGHI DISTINGUISHED CHAIR IN LAW
UNIVERSITY OF ST. THOMAS
SCHOOL OF LAW (MINNESOTA)

---

At Texas A&M University School of Law the following students provided valuable assistance on research and editing: Tyla Evans, Mengyuan Fang, and Grant Moore. I thank Texas A&M University, Dean Andrew Morriss and Interim Dean Thomas Mitchell for supporting the book project. I also appreciate the hard work and contributions of my co-author, Professor Vincent R. Johnson. We appreciate West Academic giving us permission to adapt material from other books that we have published

SUSAN SAAB FORTNEY
TEXAS A&M UNIVERSITY
SCHOOL OF LAW
FORT WORTH, TEXAS

---

It takes a village to assemble a hornbook, and I'd like to thank those in my neighborhood. I have been blessed with a cohort of wonderful research assistants. Priya Purohit did everything and then some, hunting down and digesting a daunting array of cases for Chapter 6-2 and 6-3, discussing those cases with me across innumerable conversations, and editing all three chapters for style and format. Chris Hanewald did his usual, fine work in assembling cases and materials for Chapter 6-1. And Sabienne Brutus, Cody Vaughn and Kaelyne Yumul Wietelman had the thankless job of checking the citations for accuracy and completing the final manuscript edit—tasks they completed to near perfection. In addition, I have been fortunate in the extreme to have an administrative assistant who borders on the miraculous: Rita Eads kept the project files organized, formatted and reformatted my chapters, and proofread the work at critical junctures along the way. Finally, thanks to Professors Jim Alfini and Dana Remus, whose thoughts and guidance have informed my perspective on many of the issues I discuss here.

CHARLES GARDNER GEYH
JOHN F. KIMBERLING PROFESSOR OF LAW
INDIANA UNIVERSITY
MAURER SCHOOL OF LAW

---

At St. Mary' s University, preparation of the manuscript for Part 5, which deals with legal malpractice law, was ably assisted by several law students: Yamirla E. Chavez, Cali Marie Franks, Jessica Marie Manka, Marco Miguel Muñoz Castello, Julie Polansky

Bell, Cody Hearrell, Kathryn Kluge, Monique Rae Wimberly, and especially Robert Derner. They improved the draft in many ways, working under tight deadlines. Dean Stephen M. Sheppard provided generous support for the work on this project.

VINCENT R. JOHNSON
SOUTH TEXAS PROFESSOR OF LAW
ST. MARY'S UNIVERSITY SCHOOL OF LAW
SAN ANTONIO, TEXAS

# Summary of Contents


Page

GENERAL FOREWORD ..... III

INDIVIDUAL AUTHOR PREFACES AND ACKNOWLEDGMENTS ..... VII

**PART ONE. THE LEGAL PROFESSION AND LEGAL SERVICES: NATURE AND EVOLUTION**

**CHAPTER 1-1. THE STRUCTURE OF THE LEGAL PROFESSION ..... 3**
§ 1-1.1 The Two Hemispheres of Law Practice ..... 3
§ 1-1.2 How the Segments Have Changed over Time ..... 4
§ 1-1.3 Challenges of Law Practice Serving People ..... 6

**CHAPTER 1-2. THE PROBLEM OF LAGGING LEGAL PRODUCTIVITY ..... 9**
§ 1-2.1 Cost Disease ..... 9

**CHAPTER 1-3. THE FUTURE OF THE LEGAL PROFESSION ..... 19**
§ 1-3.1 A Structural Shift ..... 19

**PART TWO. THE PHILOSOPHY OF LEGAL ETHICS**

**CHAPTER 2-1. FOUNDATIONS OF THE LAWYER'S ROLE ..... 27**
§ 2-1.1 The Function of Lawyers—Their Role in Society ..... 27
§ 2-1.2 Professional Ethics ..... 28
§ 2-1.3 Role Specific Morality ..... 30
§ 2-1.4 Can a Good Person Be a Good Lawyer: The Controversy over a Lawyer's Role Specific Morality ..... 34

**CHAPTER 2-2. JURISPRUDENCE AND THE LAWYER'S ROLE: LOOKING TO AN UNDERSTANDING OF LAW—RATHER THAN TO MORALITY—FOR THE SOURCE OF LAWYERS' ETHICAL RESTRAINT ..... 41**
§ 2-2.1 Introduction ..... 41
§ 2-2.2 The Jurisprudential Turn ..... 41
§ 2-2.3 Natural Law Theory ..... 42
§ 2-2.4 Legal Positivism ..... 43

**CHAPTER 2-3. MORAL COUNSEL AND THE GAP BETWEEN LAW AND MORALITY ..... 45**

**CHAPTER 2-4. THE CORPORATION AS CLIENT—AMORAL ETHICS SQUARED ..... 49**

**CHAPTER 2-5. MORAL REMAINDERS ..... 53**

## PART THREE. DEVELOPMENT TOWARD PROFESSIONALISM AND THE FORMATION OF AN ETHICAL PROFESSIONAL IDENTITY TO BECOME AN EFFECTIVE LAWYER

**CHAPTER 3-1. PROFESSIONALISM AND PROFESSIONAL IDENTITY .......... 57**
§ 3-1.1 Why Development Toward Professionalism and the Formation of an Ethical Professional Identity Is Important ..........57
§ 3-1.2 Understanding the Formation of an Ethical Professional Identity in the Context of the Historical and Sociological Development of Professionalism and Professional Formation ..........58
§ 3-1.3 Understanding the Formation of an Ethical Professional Identity in the Context of the ABA's Model Rules and Reports and the Understanding of Exemplary Lawyers ..........68
§ 3-1.4 Comparison of the Competencies Defining an Ethical Professional Identity from the Model Rules, the ABA Reports and Exemplary Lawyers with the Professional-Formation Competencies That Legal Employers and Clients Want ..........78

**CHAPTER 3-2. THE IMPORTANCE OF STRESS MANAGEMENT IN THE FORMATION OF AN ETHICAL PROFESSIONAL IDENTITY .......... 81**
§ 3-2.1 Sources of Stress for Lawyers ..........81
§ 3-2.2 Values, Needs, Motivation, and Well-Being ..........87
§ 3-2.3 Impact of Public Service ..........88
§ 3-2.4 Importance of Organizational Ethical Culture ..........90

**CHAPTER 3-3. PROFESSIONAL IDENTITY FORMATION AND THE LAW SCHOOL CURRICULUM .......... 93**
§ 3-3.1 The Learning Outcomes That Law Faculties Are Adopting on the Ethical Professional Formation of Each Student ..........93
§ 3-3.2 Defining the Stages of Growth for a Commitment to Professional Development Learning Outcome (From Novice to Advanced Beginner to Competent to Expert) ..........96
§ 3-3.3 The General Principles That Should Guide the Development of Effective Curriculum to Foster Each Student's Ethical Professional Identity ..........101
§ 3-3.4 What Can We Learn About Professional-Identity Formation from MBA Education? ..........104

## PART FOUR. LEGAL ETHICS AND THE PRACTICE OF LAW

**CHAPTER 4-1. SOURCES OF LEGAL ETHICS AND THE LAW OF LAWYERING .......... 111**
§ 4-1.1 A Brief History of Professional Ethics for American Lawyers ..........111
§ 4-1.2 The Restatement of the Law Governing Lawyers ..........117
§ 4-1.3 The Courts: Sanctions, Disqualification, and Legal Malpractice Liability ..........119
§ 4-1.4 Criminal, Dishonest, and Discriminatory Conduct ..........125
§ 4-1.5 A Brief Outline of Lawyer Discipline ..........131
§ 4-1.6 Lawyer Disciplinary Jurisdiction, Multijurisdictional Practice of Law, and Choice of Law ..........141

**CHAPTER 4-2. ADVERTISING FOR AND SOLICITATION OF CLIENTS: INFORMATION ABOUT LEGAL SERVICES** ..... **157**
§ 4-2.1 Introduction to Lawyer Advertising and Solicitation ..... 157
§ 4-2.2 History of Lawyer Advertising and Solicitation ..... 158
§ 4-2.3 The Lawyer's Duty Not to Make a False or Misleading Statement About Professional Services ..... 160
§ 4-2.4 Advertising or Informing About Legal Services ..... 163
§ 4-2.5 The Prohibition on Direct Solicitation of Prospective Clients ..... 185
§ 4-2.6 Prohibition of "Pay-to-Play" Political Contributions in Exchange for Legal Work ..... 193

**CHAPTER 4-3. THE ATTORNEY-CLIENT RELATIONSHIP: BEGINNING TO END** ..... **195**
§ 4-3.1 Duties to Prospective Clients ..... 195
§ 4-3.2 Creation and Nature of the Attorney-Client Relationship ..... 202
§ 4-3.3 Scope of Representation ..... 213
§ 4-3.4 Allocating Decision-Making Authority Between Client and Lawyer ..... 219
§ 4-3.5 Client with Diminished Capacity ..... 222
§ 4-3.6 Ending the Representation ..... 228
§ 4-3.7 Sale of a Law Practice and Effect on Clients ..... 238

**CHAPTER 4-4. FUNDING OF LEGAL SERVICES: FEES, COMPENSATION, AND FEE SHIFTING** ..... **247**
§ 4-4.1 Funding of Legal Services: Introduction ..... 247
§ 4-4.2 Reasonableness and Legality of Fees ..... 248
§ 4-4.3 The Lawyer's Duty to Communicate the Basis for and Rate of a Fee to the Client ..... 256
§ 4-4.4 Advanced Fee Deposits and the Illegitimacy of "Nonrefundable Retainers" ..... 258
§ 4-4.5 Division of Fees Among Lawyers ..... 260
§ 4-4.6 Payment of Fees by Persons Other than Clients ..... 262
§ 4-4.7 Fee Disputes ..... 263
§ 4-4.8 Fee Shifting: Recovering Legal Fees from Another Party ..... 263

**CHAPTER 4-5. DUTIES TO EFFECTIVELY REPRESENT THE CLIENT** ..... **273**
§ 4-5.1 The Lawyer's Duty to Competently Represent the Client ..... 273
§ 4-5.2 Counseling Through Candid, Moral, and Lawful Advice ..... 278
§ 4-5.3 Diligence and Zealous Representation ..... 286
§ 4-5.4 The Duty to Keep the Client Informed ..... 291
§ 4-5.5 The Duty of a Fiduciary to Put the Client First ..... 295
§ 4-5.6 The Duty to Safeguard Client Funds and Property ..... 297

**CHAPTER 4-6. DUTIES TO PROTECT CONFIDENTIALITY OF CLIENT INFORMATION** ..... **305**
§ 4-6.1 The Fundamental Principle of Confidentiality ..... 305
§ 4-6.2 Confidentiality: Scope and Pervasive Principles in the Rules ..... 309
§ 4-6.3 The Attorney-Client Privilege ..... 312
§ 4-6.4 Attorney Work Product ..... 333
§ 4-6.5 Lawyer's Duty to Safeguard Confidential Information ..... 335

§ 4-6.6 Exceptions to Confidentiality Under Rule 1.6 ..... 338

**CHAPTER 4-7. DUTIES OF LOYALTY: CONFLICTS OF INTEREST AND PROFESSIONAL INDEPENDENCE ..... 357**

§ 4-7.1 The General Standard for Conflicts of Interest: Duty of Loyalty and to Protect Confidentiality ..... 357
§ 4-7.2 Checking for Conflicts and Withdrawal for Conflict ..... 359
§ 4-7.3 Lawyer Conflicts with a Client ..... 360
§ 4-7.4 Concurrent Client Conflicts ..... 375
§ 4-7.5 Successive Client Conflicts ..... 399
§ 4-7.6 Imputation of Conflicts of Interest Within a Firm ..... 404
§ 4-7.7 Informed Consent by Client to Conflict ..... 413
§ 4-7.8 Special Conflicts Rules for Government Employees, Judges, Arbitrators, Mediators, and Third-Party Neutrals ..... 421
§ 4-7.9 Maintaining Professional Independence ..... 430

**CHAPTER 4-8. DUTIES TO ORGANIZATION/ENTITY CLIENTS ..... 443**

§ 4-8.1 Introduction to Lawyers and Organization/Entity Clients ..... 443
§ 4-8.2 Responsibilities During the Formation of an Entity ..... 444
§ 4-8.3 Confidentiality and Attorney-Client Privilege for a Private Entity Client ... 445
§ 4-8.4 Protecting the Entity's Attorney-Client Relationship from Outside Interference (The "No-Contact" Rule for Entities) ..... 454
§ 4-8.5 The Lawyer Responding to the Client's Duly-Authorized Constituents ..... 458
§ 4-8.6 The Lawyer's Responsibilities When Unlawful Conduct or Internal Dissension Arises Within an Organization ..... 460
§ 4-8.7 Dual Representation of Organization and Individual Constituent ..... 468
§ 4-8.8 Government Clients ..... 470

**CHAPTER 4-9. DUTIES OF ETHICAL ADVOCACY ..... 475**

§ 4-9.1 Introduction to Ethics and Advocacy ..... 475
§ 4-9.2 The Classic Tension Between the Duty of the Zealous Advocate and the Officer of the Court ..... 476
§ 4-9.3 Ethical Duties in Presenting Claims or Contentions in Litigation ..... 481
§ 4-9.4 Duties to Advance the Resolution of Disputes ..... 486
§ 4-9.5 Duties of Truthfulness and Candor by Lawyer Before the Tribunal ..... 493
§ 4-9.6 Obtaining, Discovering, and Preserving Evidence for Civil Proceedings ..... 500
§ 4-9.7 Ethical Issues Regarding Collection and Retention of Evidence in Criminal Proceedings ..... 532
§ 4-9.8 Duties Regarding Presentation of Evidence ..... 567
§ 4-9.9 Behavior During and After Trial ..... 587
§ 4-9.10 The Advocate-Witness Rule ..... 594
§ 4-9.11 Extrajudicial Statements by Lawyer ..... 601
§ 4-9.12 The Heightened Ethical Duties of Lawyers for the Sovereign Government—With Special Attention to Prosecutors ..... 617
§ 4-9.13 The Duties of the Advocate in Nonadjudicative Proceedings ..... 646

**CHAPTER 4-10. DUTIES AS EVALUATOR OR THIRD-PARTY NEUTRAL.... 649**

§ 4-10.1 Introduction: The Lawyer's Roles as Evaluator and Third-Party Neutral ..... 649

§ 4-10.2 The Lawyer's Role as Evaluator ....... 649
§ 4-10.3 The Lawyer's Role as Third-Party Neutral ....... 653

**CHAPTER 4-11. RESPECT FOR OTHER PERSONS ....... 657**
§ 4-11.1 Introduction: The Lawyer's Duties to Respect the Rights and Dignity of Other Persons ....... 657
§ 4-11.2 The Lawyer's Duty of Truthfulness ....... 658
§ 4-11.3 Communications with a Represented Person ....... 663
§ 4-11.4 Communications with an Unrepresented Person ....... 675

**CHAPTER 4-12. DUTIES OF A LAWYER IN A LAW FIRM ....... 679**
§ 4-12.1 Introduction to the Responsibilities of a Lawyer in a Law Firm ....... 679
§ 4-12.2 The Responsibilities of a Managing or Supervising Lawyer over Other Lawyers ....... 680
§ 4-12.3 The Responsibilities of a Subordinate Lawyer ....... 684
§ 4-12.4 The Responsibilities of a Managing or Supervising Lawyer over Nonlawyer Assistants ....... 685

**CHAPTER 4-13. PUBLIC-REGARDING ACTIVITIES, DUTIES, AND RIGHTS ....... 689**
§ 4-13.1 Lawyer Responsibilities on Bar Admission and Discipline ....... 689
§ 4-13.2 Lawyer Involvement in Law Reform ....... 695
§ 4-13.3 Lawyer Commentary on Judges, Legal Officers, and Candidates for Judicial or Legal Office ....... 698
§ 4-13.4 Providing Legal Services to the Disadvantaged ....... 703

**PART FIVE. LEGAL MALPRACTICE**

**CHAPTER 5-1. INTRODUCTION TO LEGAL MALPRACTICE LAW ....... 715**
§ 5-1.1 The Role and Nature of Legal Malpractice Law ....... 715
§ 5-1.2 The Rise in Legal Malpractice Law ....... 716
§ 5-1.3 The Costs of Legal Malpractice ....... 718
§ 5-1.4 Overview of the Theories of Liability ....... 719
§ 5-1.5 Consequences of Classifying Theories of Liability ....... 720
§ 5-1.6 Status of the Plaintiff ....... 723
§ 5-1.7 Differentiating Malpractice and Discipline ....... 724

**CHAPTER 5-2. NEGLIGENCE ....... 727**
§ 5-2.1 Duty to Exercise Reasonable Care ....... 727
§ 5-2.2 Breach of Duty ....... 741
§ 5-2.3 Causation ....... 772

**CHAPTER 5-3. BREACH OF FIDUCIARY DUTY ....... 789**
§ 5-3.1 Lawyers as Fiduciaries ....... 789
§ 5-3.2 The "Substantial Factor" Test for Factual Causation ....... 792
§ 5-3.3 Disclosure Obligations ....... 793
§ 5-3.4 Fee Forfeiture ....... 796
§ 5-3.5 Aiding and Abetting a Breach of Fiduciary Duty ....... 799
§ 5-3.6 Intra-Firm Fiduciary Duties ....... 804

**CHAPTER 5-4. LIABILITY TO NONCLIENTS** .......... **809**
§ 5-4.1 Modern Nonclient Litigation .......... 809
§ 5-4.2 Fraud on Clients and Nonclients .......... 814
§ 5-4.3 Negligent Misrepresentation .......... 826
§ 5-4.4 Deceptive Trade Practices Acts .......... 833
§ 5-4.5 Claims Based on Representation of Fiduciaries .......... 835
§ 5-4.6 Funds and Property of Nonclients .......... 835
§ 5-4.7 Intended Beneficiaries .......... 837
§ 5-4.8 Duties to Co-Counsel .......... 841
§ 5-4.9 Liability Related to Litigation .......... 842
§ 5-4.10 Securities Law Violations .......... 846
§ 5-4.11 Fair Debt Collections Practices .......... 848

**CHAPTER 5-5. REMEDIES FOR LEGAL MALPRACTICE** .......... **851**
§ 5-5.1 Compensatory Damages .......... 851
§ 5-5.2 Punitive Damages .......... 859
§ 5-5.3 Restitution .......... 866

**CHAPTER 5-6. DEFENSES AND OBSTACLES TO RECOVERY** .......... **867**
§ 5-6.1 In General .......... 867
§ 5-6.2 Defenses Based on the Plaintiff's Conduct .......... 868
§ 5-6.3 Privileges and Immunities Based on the Defendant's Conduct .......... 874
§ 5-6.4 Defenses Arising by Operation of Law .......... 878

**CHAPTER 5-7. VICARIOUS LIABILITY** .......... **901**
§ 5-7.1 The Role of Vicarious Liability .......... 901
§ 5-7.2 Law Firm Practice .......... 901
§ 5-7.3 Other Associations That Expose Lawyers to Liability .......... 914

**CHAPTER 5-8. LEGAL MALPRACTICE INSURANCE** .......... **929**
§ 5-8.1 The Importance of Legal Malpractice Insurance .......... 929
§ 5-8.2 What Coverage Is Available .......... 932
§ 5-8.3 The Anatomy of a Policy .......... 933
§ 5-8.4 Handling Claims and Potential Claims .......... 940
§ 5-8.5 Dealing with Clients When Lawyers Commit Malpractice .......... 942

**PART SIX. JUDICIAL ETHICS AND THE CONDUCT OF JUDGES**

**CHAPTER 6-1. REGULATING JUDICIAL CONDUCT GENERALLY—FEATURES AND PRINCIPLES** .......... **951**
§ 6-1.1 Modern Judicial Ethics and Codes of Judicial Conduct .......... 951
§ 6-1.2 Judicial Discipline in the State Courts .......... 952
§ 6-1.3 Judicial Discipline in the Federal Courts .......... 953
§ 6-1.4 Core Values: Impartiality, Independence, and Integrity .......... 955
§ 6-1.5 Foundational Rules .......... 958

**CHAPTER 6-2. REGULATING JUDICIAL CONDUCT ON THE BENCH** .......... **963**
§ 6-2.1 Responsibilities Related to Maintaining Fitness for Judicial Service .......... 963
§ 6-2.2 Responsibilities Related to the Use of Judicial Independence and Power .......... 968

§ 6-2.3 Responsibilities Related to Preserving Judicial Impartiality and Fairness .......... 973
§ 6-2.4 *Ex Parte* Communications .......... 981
§ 6-2.5 Judicial Disqualification .......... 986

**CHAPTER 6-3. REGULATING JUDICIAL CONDUCT OFF THE BENCH—EXTRAJUDICIAL AND POLITICAL ACTIVITIES .......... 1011**
§ 6-3.1 Extrajudicial Conduct .......... 1011
§ 6-3.2 Political Activities .......... 1020

TABLE OF CASES .......... 1027

TABLE OF STATUTES .......... 1043

TABLE OF RULES .......... 1045

TABLE OF RESTATEMENTS .......... 1053

INDEX .......... 1057

# Table of Contents

Page


GENERAL FOREWORD .................... III

INDIVIDUAL AUTHOR PREFACES AND ACKNOWLEDGMENTS .................... VII

**PART ONE. THE LEGAL PROFESSION AND LEGAL SERVICES: NATURE AND EVOLUTION**

**CHAPTER 1-1. THE STRUCTURE OF THE LEGAL PROFESSION .................... 3**

§ 1-1.1 The Two Hemispheres of Law Practice .................... 3
§ 1-1.2 How the Segments Have Changed over Time .................... 4
§ 1-1.3 Challenges of Law Practice Serving People .................... 6

**CHAPTER 1-2. THE PROBLEM OF LAGGING LEGAL PRODUCTIVITY .................... 9**

§ 1-2.1 Cost Disease .................... 9
§ 1-2.1(a) Higher Profits for Those Servicing Large Organizational Clients .................... 10
§ 1-2.1(b) Organizational Clients Searching for Substitutes to Traditional Law Firms .................... 10
§ 1-2.1(c) Waning Demand Among Individual Clients .................... 14
§ 1-2.1(d) Impact of Legal Economy on Law School Enrollments .................... 15

**CHAPTER 1-3. THE FUTURE OF THE LEGAL PROFESSION .................... 19**

§ 1-3.1 A Structural Shift .................... 19
§ 1-3.1(a) The Future of Dispute Resolution for Individuals .................... 20
§ 1-3.1(b) The Way Forward Is Multidisciplinary .................... 22

**PART TWO. THE PHILOSOPHY OF LEGAL ETHICS**

**CHAPTER 2-1. FOUNDATIONS OF THE LAWYER'S ROLE .................... 27**

§ 2-1.1 The Function of Lawyers—Their Role in Society .................... 27
§ 2-1.2 Professional Ethics .................... 28
§ 2-1.3 Role Specific Morality .................... 30
§ 2-1.4 Can a Good Person Be a Good Lawyer: The Controversy over a Lawyer's Role Specific Morality .................... 34

**CHAPTER 2-2. JURISPRUDENCE AND THE LAWYER'S ROLE: LOOKING TO AN UNDERSTANDING OF LAW—RATHER THAN TO MORALITY—FOR THE SOURCE OF LAWYERS' ETHICAL RESTRAINT .................... 41**

§ 2-2.1 Introduction .................... 41
§ 2-2.2 The Jurisprudential Turn .................... 41
§ 2-2.3 Natural Law Theory .................... 42
§ 2-2.4 Legal Positivism .................... 43

**CHAPTER 2-3. MORAL COUNSEL AND THE GAP BETWEEN LAW AND MORALITY .................... 45**

CHAPTER 2-4. THE CORPORATION AS CLIENT—AMORAL ETHICS SQUARED ..... 49

CHAPTER 2-5. MORAL REMAINDERS ..... 53

PART THREE. DEVELOPMENT TOWARD PROFESSIONALISM AND THE FORMATION OF AN ETHICAL PROFESSIONAL IDENTITY TO BECOME AN EFFECTIVE LAWYER

CHAPTER 3-1. PROFESSIONALISM AND PROFESSIONAL IDENTITY ..... 57
§ 3-1.1 Why Development Toward Professionalism and the Formation of an Ethical Professional Identity Is Important ..... 57
§ 3-1.2 Understanding the Formation of an Ethical Professional Identity in the Context of the Historical and Sociological Development of Professionalism and Professional Formation ..... 58
§ 3-1.2(a) Law as a Learned Profession ..... 58
§ 3-1.2(b) Understanding the Importance of the Professional-Formation Competencies to Effectiveness in the Practice of Law ..... 63
§ 3-1.3 Understanding the Formation of an Ethical Professional Identity in the Context of the ABA's Model Rules and Reports and the Understanding of Exemplary Lawyers ..... 68
§ 3-1.3(a) The ABA's Model Rules of Professional Conduct ..... 69
§ 3-1.3(b) Elements of an Ethical Professional Identity Defined in the ABA and Conference of Chief Justice Reports ..... 71
§ 3-1.3(b)(1) The Stanley Commission Report in 1986 ..... 71
§ 3-1.3(b)(2) The MacCrate Report in 1992 ..... 72
§ 3-1.3(b)(3) The Haynsworth Report in 1996 ..... 72
§ 3-1.3(b)(4) The Conference of Chief Justices' National Action Plan on Lawyer Conduct and Professionalism in 1999 ..... 73
§ 3-1.3(c) Exemplary Lawyers' Understanding of the Elements of an Ethical Professional Identity—Results of a 2012 Study ..... 74
§ 3-1.3(d) Synthesis of the Key Elements of an Ethical Professional Identity from the Model Rules, the Three ABA Reports, the CCJ National Action Plan, and the Study of Exemplary Lawyers ..... 76
§ 3-1.4 Comparison of the Competencies Defining an Ethical Professional Identity from the Model Rules, the ABA Reports and Exemplary Lawyers with the Professional-Formation Competencies That Legal Employers and Clients Want ..... 78

CHAPTER 3-2. THE IMPORTANCE OF STRESS MANAGEMENT IN THE FORMATION OF AN ETHICAL PROFESSIONAL IDENTITY ..... 81
§ 3-2.1 Sources of Stress for Lawyers ..... 81
§ 3-2.1(a) External Pressure of Law Practice ..... 82
§ 3-2.1(a)(1) Workload ..... 82
§ 3-2.1(a)(2) Financial Strain ..... 83
§ 3-2.1(a)(3) Adversarial Atmosphere ..... 83
§ 3-2.1(a)(4) Perception of Low Decision Latitude ..... 84
§ 3-2.1(b) Internal Traits of Lawyers ..... 85
§ 3-2.1(b)(1) Perfectionistic ..... 85

§ 3-2.1(b)(2) Competitive ....85
§ 3-2.1(b)(3) Extrinsically Motivated ....86
§ 3-2.2 Values, Needs, Motivation, and Well-Being ....87
§ 3-2.3 Impact of Public Service ....88
§ 3-2.4 Importance of Organizational Ethical Culture ....90

**CHAPTER 3-3. PROFESSIONAL IDENTITY FORMATION AND THE LAW SCHOOL CURRICULUM .... 93**
§ 3-3.1 The Learning Outcomes That Law Faculties Are Adopting on the Ethical Professional Formation of Each Student ....93
§ 3-3.2 Defining the Stages of Growth for a Commitment to Professional Development Learning Outcome (From Novice to Advanced Beginner to Competent to Expert) ....96
§ 3-3.3 The General Principles That Should Guide the Development of Effective Curriculum to Foster Each Student's Ethical Professional Identity ....101
§ 3-3.4 What Can We Learn About Professional-Identity Formation from MBA Education? ....104

**PART FOUR. LEGAL ETHICS AND THE PRACTICE OF LAW**

**CHAPTER 4-1. SOURCES OF LEGAL ETHICS AND THE LAW OF LAWYERING .... 111**
§ 4-1.1 A Brief History of Professional Ethics for American Lawyers ....111
§ 4-1.1(a) Evolution of Professional Ethics Rules Within a Self-Regulating Bar ....111
§ 4-1.1(b) From Canons to Code to Rules ....112
§ 4-1.1(c) The Nearly-Complete Transition from the Code to the Model Rules ....114
§ 4-1.1(d) Rules of Ethics, Professional Morality, and Character ....116
§ 4-1.2 The Restatement of the Law Governing Lawyers ....117
§ 4-1.3 The Courts: Sanctions, Disqualification, and Legal Malpractice Liability....119
§ 4-1.3(a) Judicial Sanctions ....119
§ 4-1.3(b) Disqualification of a Lawyer in Litigation ....120
§ 4-1.3(c) Legal Malpractice Liability ....122
§ 4-1.4 Criminal, Dishonest, and Discriminatory Conduct ....125
§ 4-1.4(a) Criminal Conduct ....125
§ 4-1.4(b) Dishonesty, Fraud, Deceit, and Misrepresentation ....126
§ 4-1.4(c) Discrimination and Harassment ....127
§ 4-1.5 A Brief Outline of Lawyer Discipline ....131
§ 4-1.5(a) A Central Body for Receiving, Evaluating, and Investigating Ethical Complaints Against Lawyers ....132
§ 4-1.5(b) Preparation for and Formal Hearing on Prosecuted Complaint ....134
§ 4-1.5(c) Standard of Proof and Issue Preclusion ....135
§ 4-1.5(d) Confidentiality and Immunity in Disciplinary Proceedings ....136
§ 4-1.5(e) Decision by Hearing Panel or Officer and Further Review ....137
§ 4-1.5(f) Types of Sanctions and Factors in Evaluating the Appropriate Sanction ....137
§ 4-1.5(f)(1) Private Admonition ....138
§ 4-1.5(f)(2) Public Reprimand or Censure ....139

§ 4-1.5(f)(3) Suspension .......... 139
§ 4-1.5(f)(4) Disbarment or License Revocation .......... 140
§ 4-1.5(f)(5) Probation .......... 141
§ 4-1.6 Lawyer Disciplinary Jurisdiction, Multijurisdictional Practice of Law, and Choice of Law .......... 141
§ 4-1.6(a) Introduction to Disciplinary Jurisdiction, Multijurisdictional Practice, and Choice of Law .......... 141
§ 4-1.6(b) Multijurisdictional Practice of Law .......... 143
§ 4-1.6(b)(1) Temporary Practice in Association with State Lawyer .......... 143
§ 4-1.6(b)(2) Temporary Practice Before a Tribunal—Admission *Pro Hac Vice* .......... 144
§ 4-1.6(b)(3) Alternative Dispute Resolution Proceeding Related to Lawyer's Home Practice .......... 145
§ 4-1.6(b)(4) Other Temporary Services Incidental to Lawyer's Home Practice .......... 146
§ 4-1.6(b)(5) House Counsel for an Entity .......... 148
§ 4-1.6(b)(6) Legal Services Authorized by Federal or Other Law .......... 148
§ 4-1.6(b)(7) Legal Services Following a Major Disaster .......... 149
§ 4-1.6(c) Disciplinary Jurisdiction .......... 150
§ 4-1.6(d) Choice of Law for Exercise of Disciplinary Authority .......... 152
§ 4-1.6(d)(1) Choice of Law for Conduct Before a Tribunal .......... 153
§ 4-1.6(d)(2) Choice of Law for Other Matters .......... 153
§ 4-1.6(d)(3) Choice of Law Agreements .......... 155

**CHAPTER 4-2. ADVERTISING FOR AND SOLICITATION OF CLIENTS: INFORMATION ABOUT LEGAL SERVICES .......... 157**
§ 4-2.1 Introduction to Lawyer Advertising and Solicitation .......... 157
§ 4-2.2 History of Lawyer Advertising and Solicitation .......... 158
§ 4-2.3 The Lawyer's Duty Not to Make a False or Misleading Statement About Professional Services .......... 160
§ 4-2.4 Advertising or Informing About Legal Services .......... 163
§ 4-2.4(a) General Authorization of Lawyer Advertising .......... 163
§ 4-2.4(b) Advertising by Broadcast Media .......... 164
§ 4-2.4(c) Communication by Internet Including Web Pages and Social Media .......... 168
§ 4-2.4(d) Advertising by Mail .......... 169
§ 4-2.4(d)(1) The History of Regulation of Lawyer Direct Mail .......... 169
§ 4-2.4(d)(2) Targeted Mail to Persons Known to Need Legal Services .......... 170
§ 4-2.4(e) Regulation of Style and Emotional Appeal .......... 172
§ 4-2.4(f) Communicating Fields of Practice and Specialization .......... 174
§ 4-2.4(f)(1) History of Identification of Practice Areas and Specialization .......... 174
§ 4-2.4(f)(2) Communicating Practice in Particular Fields of Law .......... 174
§ 4-2.4(f)(3) Communicating Certification as a Specialist .......... 175
§ 4-2.4(g) Firm Name .......... 176
§ 4-2.4(g)(1) Firm Designation by Lawyer Names .......... 177
§ 4-2.4(g)(2) Firm Designation by Trade Name .......... 178
§ 4-2.4(g)(3) Claims of Partnership or Association .......... 179

§ 4-2.4(h) Advertising Disclaimers 180
§ 4-2.4(h)(1) Decline of General Advertising Disclaimers 180
§ 4-2.4(h)(2) Disclaimers for Advertising Suggesting Lawsuits 180
§ 4-2.4(h)(3) Disclaimers for Advertising on Fees 180
§ 4-2.4(i) Taking Personal Responsibility for Lawyer Advertising 181
§ 4-2.4(j) The General Prohibition on Paying for Referrals 181
§ 4-2.4(k) Exceptions to the Prohibition on Paying for Referrals 182
§ 4-2.4(k)(1) Paying the Costs of Advertising 182
§ 4-2.4(k)(2) Legal Service Plans 183
§ 4-2.4(k)(3) Qualified Lawyer Referral Service 184
§ 4-2.4(k)(4) Non-Profit Lawyer Referral Service 184
§ 4-2.4(k)(5) Purchasing a Law Practice 185
§ 4-2.4(k)(6) Reciprocal Professional Referral Agreements 185
§ 4-2.5 The Prohibition on Direct Solicitation of Prospective Clients 185
§ 4-2.5(a) The Purpose and Nature of the Prohibition on Direct Solicitation 185
§ 4-2.5(b) Exemptions from the Direct Solicitation Prohibition 187
§ 4-2.5(b)(1) Solicitation to Lawyers 187
§ 4-2.5(b)(2) Solicitation to Family and Close Friends 187
§ 4-2.5(b)(3) Solicitation to Current, Former, and Prospective Clients 187
§ 4-2.5(c) Communications with Members of a Class or Potential Class in Litigation 188
§ 4-2.5(d) Direct Solicitation for Public Interest Purposes 189
§ 4-2.5(e) Participation in a Legal Services Plan That Solicits Membership 190
§ 4-2.5(f) Public Communications by the Lawyer About Legal Topics 191
§ 4-2.6 Prohibition of "Pay-to-Play" Political Contributions in Exchange for Legal Work 193

**CHAPTER 4-3. THE ATTORNEY-CLIENT RELATIONSHIP: BEGINNING TO END 195**
§ 4-3.1 Duties to Prospective Clients 195
§ 4-3.1(a) Overview of the Lawyer's Responsibilities to Prospective Clients 195
§ 4-3.1(b) Defining the Prospective Client 196
§ 4-3.1(c) The Prospective Client and Confidentiality 197
§ 4-3.1(d) The Prospective Client and Conflicts of Interest 198
§ 4-3.1(e) Controlling the Prospective Client's Disclosure of Information or Obtaining an Advance Waiver of a Conflict 200
§ 4-3.2 Creation and Nature of the Attorney-Client Relationship 202
§ 4-3.2(a) Elements for Establishing the Attorney-Client Relationship 202
§ 4-3.2(b) Business Relationships and Law-Related Services 203
§ 4-3.2(b)(1) Categorizing Law Practice and Law-Related Services 204
§ 4-3.2(b)(2) Services Constituting the Practice of Law by a Lawyer 204
§ 4-3.2(b)(3) Unrelated Business Activities by a Lawyer 208
§ 4-3.2(b)(4) Defining Law-Related Services by a Lawyer 208
§ 4-3.2(b)(5) Law-Related Services Provided as Part of a Law Practice 209
§ 4-3.2(b)(6) Law-Related Services Provided Distinct from a Law Practice 210
§ 4-3.2(c) Lawyer Responsibility for Misunderstanding About Relationship 212
§ 4-3.3 Scope of Representation 213
§ 4-3.3(a) Introduction to Scope of the Representation 213

§ 4-3.3(b) Agreements to Limit the Scope of Representation ....214
§ 4-3.3(c) "Unbundled Legal Services" and Assisting *Pro Se* Litigants ....215
§ 4-3.3(d) Collaborative Lawyering Agreements ....216
§ 4-3.3(e) Reasonableness of Scope Limitation ....218
§ 4-3.4 Allocating Decision-Making Authority Between Client and Lawyer ....219
§ 4-3.5 Client with Diminished Capacity ....222
§ 4-3.5(a) Maintaining an Attorney-Client Relationship with and Respecting the Dignity of Persons with Diminished Capacity ....222
§ 4-3.5(b) Taking Legal Action to Protect the Interests of the Client with Diminished Capacity ....224
§ 4-3.5(b)(1) Evaluating Client's Capacity and Whether to Take Protective Action ....224
§ 4-3.5(b)(2) Considering Whether to Seek a Guardian ....225
§ 4-3.5(b)(3) Person or Guardian as Client ....226
§ 4-3.5(b)(4) Representing Children ....226
§ 4-3.5(b)(5) Acting Contrary to Client's Wishes ....227
§ 4-3.5(b)(6) Emergency Situation ....227
§ 4-3.5(b)(7) Confidentiality When Representing Client with Diminished Capacity ....228
§ 4-3.6 Ending the Representation ....228
§ 4-3.6(a) The Ordinary Conclusion of the Representation ....228
§ 4-3.6(b) Termination of the Lawyer by the Client ....229
§ 4-3.6(b)(1) The Near-Absolute Right of the Client to Terminate the Lawyer ....229
§ 4-3.6(b)(2) Wrongful Discharge Claims by In-House Counsel and Law Firm Employees ....230
§ 4-3.6(c) Termination by the Lawyer ....234
§ 4-3.6(c)(1) Mandatory Withdrawal (or Decline) ....234
§ 4-3.6(c)(2) Permissive Withdrawal ....234
§ 4-3.6(d) Protecting the Client's Interest upon Withdrawal ....237
§ 4-3.7 Sale of a Law Practice and Effect on Clients ....238
§ 4-3.7(a) Background and Overview on Sale of a Law Practice ....238
§ 4-3.7(b) Termination of Seller's Practice upon Sale of a Law Practice ....240
§ 4-3.7(c) Valuing the Law Practice and Paying the Sale Price ....241
§ 4-3.7(d) Selling the Entire Practice or Practice Area ....243
§ 4-3.7(e) Notice to Clients and Protection of Confidentiality ....245
§ 4-3.7(f) Fees Charged to Clients May Not Be Increased ....246

**CHAPTER 4-4. FUNDING OF LEGAL SERVICES: FEES, COMPENSATION, AND FEE SHIFTING ....247**
§ 4-4.1 Funding of Legal Services: Introduction ....247
§ 4-4.2 Reasonableness and Legality of Fees ....248
§ 4-4.2(a) The Objective Standard of a Reasonable Fee and Expenses ....248
§ 4-4.2(b) Hourly Billing ....249
§ 4-4.2(b)(1) Nature and Reasonableness ....249
§ 4-4.2(b)(2) Honesty in Fee Billing ....251
§ 4-4.2(c) Contingency Fees ....252
§ 4-4.2(c)(1) The Legitimacy of the Contingency Method for Legal Fees ....252

§ 4-4.2(c)(2) The Reasonableness Standard Applied to Contingency Fees ....253
§ 4-4.2(c)(3) Contingency Fee Agreements Must Be in Writing ....254
§ 4-4.2(c)(4) Prohibition of Contingency Fees in Criminal and Domestic Relations Cases ....254
§ 4-4.2(d) Flat Fees ....255
§ 4-4.3 The Lawyer's Duty to Communicate the Basis for and Rate of a Fee to the Client ....256
§ 4-4.4 Advanced Fee Deposits and the Illegitimacy of "Nonrefundable Retainers" ....258
§ 4-4.4(a) Advance Fee Deposits and Refunding of Unearned Fees ....258
§ 4-4.4(b) A Retainer for Lawyer Availability ....258
§ 4-4.4(c) The Illegitimacy of a "Nonrefundable Special Retainer" ....259
§ 4-4.5 Division of Fees Among Lawyers ....260
§ 4-4.6 Payment of Fees by Persons Other than Clients ....262
§ 4-4.7 Fee Disputes ....263
§ 4-4.8 Fee Shifting: Recovering Legal Fees from Another Party ....263
§ 4-4.8(a) Introduction to Attorney's Fee Shifting ....263
§ 4-4.8(b) Eligibility for a Fee Award—Prevailing Party Status ....264
§ 4-4.8(c) Measuring the Fee Award ....265
§ 4-4.8(c)(1) The Road to the Lodestar Approach ....265
§ 4-4.8(c)(2) Hours Reasonably Expended ....266
§ 4-4.8(c)(3) A Reasonable Hourly Rate ....269
§ 4-4.8(c)(4) Adjustment to the Lodestar ....270
§ 4-4.8(c)(5) Compensation for Delay in Receipt of Fees ....272
§ 4-4.8(c)(6) Fees for Fees ....272

**CHAPTER 4-5. DUTIES TO EFFECTIVELY REPRESENT THE CLIENT .... 273**
§ 4-5.1 The Lawyer's Duty to Competently Represent the Client ....273
§ 4-5.1(a) The Fundamental Expectation of Professional Competence ....273
§ 4-5.1(a)(1) General Standard of Competence ....273
§ 4-5.1(a)(2) Attaining Competence in a New Area ....274
§ 4-5.1(a)(3) Associating with a Lawyer of Established Competence ....275
§ 4-5.1(b) The Need for Expertise in Certain Fields of Law ....276
§ 4-5.1(c) Lawyer Mistakes, Personal Problems, and Competence ....277
§ 4-5.2 Counseling Through Candid, Moral, and Lawful Advice ....278
§ 4-5.2(a) Counseling a Client Within the Expanding Scope of Law Practice ....278
§ 4-5.2(b) Candid Advice and Moral Deliberation ....279
§ 4-5.2(b)(1) Offering Forthright Advice and a Frank Evaluation ....279
§ 4-5.2(b)(2) Moral Engagement with Client ....280
§ 4-5.2(b)(3) Professional Humility and Assistance by Other Professionals ....283
§ 4-5.2(c) Counseling a Client on the Requirements of the Law While Not Assisting a Client in Fraudulent or Criminal Conduct ....284
§ 4-5.3 Diligence and Zealous Representation ....286
§ 4-5.3(a) Diligence and Zealousness on Behalf of the Client ....286
§ 4-5.3(b) Diligent Action to Protect Rights of the Client ....286
§ 4-5.3(c) Diligent Action to Avoid Unnecessary Anxiety to the Client ....287

§ 4-5.3(d) Protecting the Client in Event of Lawyer's Death, Disability, or Suspension ....288
§ 4-5.3(e) Zealous Advocacy, Professionalism, and Civility ....288
§ 4-5.4 The Duty to Keep the Client Informed ....291
§ 4-5.4(a) The Duty to Communicate as Respect for the Client ....291
§ 4-5.4(b) The Duty to Communicate with the Client to Affirm Client's Authority ....292
§ 4-5.4(c) The Duty to Maintain Regular Communication and Respond to Client Inquiries ....293
§ 4-5.4(d) Confirming the Lawyer Will Not Assist in Violating the Law or Professional Expectations ....294
§ 4-5.4(e) Withholding Information from a Client ....294
§ 4-5.5 The Duty of a Fiduciary to Put the Client First ....295
§ 4-5.6 The Duty to Safeguard Client Funds and Property ....297
§ 4-5.6(a) Safekeeping and Separating Client Funds and Property ....297
§ 4-5.6(b) Accounting for and Delivering Client Funds and Property ....299
§ 4-5.6(c) Disputes Regarding Funds or Property Held by the Lawyer ....299
§ 4-5.6(c)(1) Disputes Between Lawyer and Client over Funds or Property Held by the Lawyer ....299
§ 4-5.6(c)(2) Disputes Between Client and Third Person over Funds or Property Held by the Lawyer ....301

**CHAPTER 4-6. DUTIES TO PROTECT CONFIDENTIALITY OF CLIENT INFORMATION .... 305**
§ 4-6.1 The Fundamental Principle of Confidentiality ....305
§ 4-6.2 Confidentiality: Scope and Pervasive Principles in the Rules ....309
§ 4-6.3 The Attorney-Client Privilege ....312
§ 4-6.3(a) The Special Evidentiary Immunity Given to Attorney-Client Communications ....312
§ 4-6.3(b) The Elements of the Attorney-Client Privilege ....313
§ 4-6.3(b)(1) Seeking Legal Advice ....314
§ 4-6.3(b)(2) Involving a Professional Legal Advisor ....320
§ 4-6.3(b)(3) Communication Relating to Legal Advice ....321
§ 4-6.3(b)(4) Made in Confidence ....322
§ 4-6.3(b)(5) By Client or Lawyer ....323
§ 4-6.3(b)(6) Protected at Client's Insistence ....324
§ 4-6.3(b)(7) Protected from Disclosure by Client or Lawyer ....324
§ 4-6.3(b)(8) Unless Waived by the Client ....324
§ 4-6.3(b)(9) Joint Client Privilege and Joint Defense Doctrine ....325
§ 4-6.3(c) Exceptions to the Attorney-Client Privilege ....326
§ 4-6.3(c)(1) Crime-Fraud Exception ....327
§ 4-6.3(c)(2) Identity of Client and Payment of Fees ....329
§ 4-6.3(c)(3) Lawyer-Client Disputes and Lawyer Self-Defense ....329
§ 4-6.3(c)(4) Exceptions to Confidentiality Under Ethics Rules and the Independent Protection of the Attorney-Client Privilege ....330
§ 4-6.4 Attorney Work Product ....333
§ 4-6.5 Lawyer's Duty to Safeguard Confidential Information ....335
§ 4-6.5(a) General Duty to Safeguard Confidential Information ....335
§ 4-6.5(b) Use of Modern Communications Technology ....335

§ 4-6.5(c) Inadvertent Disclosure ....337
§ 4-6.6 Exceptions to Confidentiality Under Rule 1.6 ....338
§ 4-6.6(a) Exceptions as Narrow Departures from Confidentiality ....338
§ 4-6.6(b) Lawyer and Client on the Lawyer's Decision to Disclose ....340
§ 4-6.6(b)(1) Disclosing to the Client the Ethical Qualifications on Confidentiality ....340
§ 4-6.6(b)(2) Consulting with Client Before Lawyer's Disclosure Pursuant to a Confidentiality Exception ....342
§ 4-6.6(c) To Prevent Death or Bodily Harm ....342
§ 4-6.6(d) To Prevent or Rectify Substantial Economic Harm ....345
§ 4-6.6(d)(1) History, Controversy, and Overview of Economic Harm Exceptions ....345
§ 4-6.6(d)(2) Strict Standards for Application of Economic Harm Exceptions ....347
§ 4-6.6(d)(3) When the Permission to Disclose Economic Harm Becomes a Mandatory Duty ....348
§ 4-6.6(d)(4) Counseling the Client Before Disclosure ....352
§ 4-6.6(e) To Obtain Legal Advice About Lawyer Compliance with Ethics Rules ....352
§ 4-6.6(f) For Lawyer Self-Defense and Fee Collection ....353
§ 4-6.6(g) To Comply with Other Law or Court Order ....354
§ 4-6.6(h) To Check for Conflicts of Interest ....355

**CHAPTER 4-7. DUTIES OF LOYALTY: CONFLICTS OF INTEREST AND PROFESSIONAL INDEPENDENCE ....357**
§ 4-7.1 The General Standard for Conflicts of Interest: Duty of Loyalty and to Protect Confidentiality ....357
§ 4-7.2 Checking for Conflicts and Withdrawal for Conflict ....359
§ 4-7.3 Lawyer Conflicts with a Client ....360
§ 4-7.3(a) Introduction to Lawyer-Client Conflicts ....360
§ 4-7.3(b) Business Transactions with Clients ....361
§ 4-7.3(c) Use of Confidential Information to the Disadvantage of the Client ....364
§ 4-7.3(d) Gifts from Clients and Preparation of Instruments Giving Gifts ....365
§ 4-7.3(e) Literary and Media Rights About Representation ....366
§ 4-7.3(f) Financial Assistance to a Client ....367
§ 4-7.3(f)(1) The General Prohibition on Giving or Loaning Money for Living Expenses or Otherwise to a Client ....367
§ 4-7.3(f)(2) Advancing Court Costs and Litigation Expenses ....369
§ 4-7.3(g) Compensation from a Person Other than the Client ....369
§ 4-7.3(h) Agreements to Limit or Settle Malpractice Claims ....370
§ 4-7.3(i) Acquiring a Property Interest in a Client's Claim ....371
§ 4-7.3(j) Sexual Relations with a Client ....372
§ 4-7.3(k) Family or Romantic Relationship with Lawyer for Adverse Party ....373
§ 4-7.3(*l*) Imputation of Lawyer-Client Conflicts ....374
§ 4-7.4 Concurrent Client Conflicts ....375
§ 4-7.4(a) Introduction to Client-Client Concurrent Conflicts ....375
§ 4-7.4(b) Direct Adversity Conflicts of Interest ....375
§ 4-7.4(b)(1) Nature and Purpose of the Direct Adversity Conflict Rule ....375

§ 4-7.4(b)(2) Clients Engaged in Economic Competition ..... 377
§ 4-7.4(c) Materially-Limited Representation Conflicts of Interest ..... 377
§ 4-7.4(c)(1) Nature of the Materially-Limited Conflict Rule ..... 377
§ 4-7.4(c)(2) Lawyer Personal Interest Conflicts ..... 379
§ 4-7.4(c)(3) Representing Multiple Clients in a Criminal Matter ..... 381
§ 4-7.4(c)(4) Representing Multiple Clients in Civil Litigation ..... 383
§ 4-7.4(c)(5) Aggregate Settlement of Claims Involving Multiple Clients ..... 386
§ 4-7.4(c)(6) Representing Multiple Clients in a Non-Litigation Matter ..... 389
§ 4-7.4(c)(7) Joint Representation, Withdrawal or Termination, and Confidentiality ..... 390
§ 4-7.4(c)(8) Conflicts of Interest in the Insurance Defense Context ..... 392
§ 4-7.4(c)(9) Positional Conflicts of Interest ..... 397
§ 4-7.5 Successive Client Conflicts ..... 399
§ 4-7.5(a) Introduction to the Successive Conflict Rule ..... 399
§ 4-7.5(b) Successive Conflicts When the Matters Are the Same ..... 399
§ 4-7.5(c) Successive Conflicts When the Matters Are Substantially Related ..... 400
§ 4-7.5(d) Changing a Current Client into a Former Client: The "Hot Potato" Scenario ..... 402
§ 4-7.5(e) The Prohibition on Using or Revealing Confidential Information from a Former Client Representation ..... 403
§ 4-7.6 Imputation of Conflicts of Interest Within a Firm ..... 404
§ 4-7.6(a) The General Rule of Imputed Disqualification to All Lawyers in a Law Firm ..... 404
§ 4-7.6(b) Imputed Disqualification When a Lawyer Joins or Leaves a Law Firm (The Migrating Lawyer) ..... 406
§ 4-7.6(b)(1) Whether the Incoming Lawyer Is Personally Disqualified ..... 406
§ 4-7.6(b)(2) Ethical Screening of a Personally-Disqualified Lawyer to Avoid Imputed Disqualification ..... 407
§ 4-7.6(b)(3) Removal of Imputed Disqualification When Personally-Prohibited Lawyer Leaves the Firm ..... 411
§ 4-7.7 Informed Consent by Client to Conflict ..... 413
§ 4-7.7(a) Introduction to Informed Consent Conflict Waivers ..... 413
§ 4-7.7(b) The Meaning of Informed Consent to Waive a Conflict ..... 416
§ 4-7.7(c) Client Consent Confirmed in Writing ..... 417
§ 4-7.7(d) The Continuing Duty of Competent and Diligent Representation ..... 418
§ 4-7.7(e) Nonconsentable Conflicts ..... 418
§ 4-7.7(f) Advance Conflict Waivers ..... 420
§ 4-7.8 Special Conflicts Rules for Government Employees, Judges, Arbitrators, Mediators, and Third-Party Neutrals ..... 421
§ 4-7.8(a) Special Conflict Rules for Former and Current Government Employees ..... 421
§ 4-7.8(a)(1) Conflict of Interest Rules for Former Government Officers and Employees ..... 421
§ 4-7.8(a)(2) Imputed Disqualification in Context of Former Government Officers and Employees ..... 425
§ 4-7.8(a)(3) Conflict of Interest Standard for Current Government Officers and Employees ..... 427

§ 4-7.8(b) Special Conflict Rules for Former and Current Judges, Law Clerks, Arbitrators, Mediators, and Third-Party Neutrals ............................ 428
§ 4-7.8(b)(1) Conflict of Interest Rules for Former Judges, Law Clerks, Arbitrators, Mediators, and Third-Party Neutrals................. 428
§ 4-7.8(b)(2) Conflict of Interest Rules for Current Judges, Law Clerks, Arbitrators, Mediators, and Third-Party Neutrals................. 429
§ 4-7.9 Maintaining Professional Independence....................................................... 430
§ 4-7.9(a) Avoiding Financial Entanglements with Nonlawyers ........................ 430
§ 4-7.9(b) The Prohibition on Sharing Legal Fees with Nonlawyers ................. 431
§ 4-7.9(b)(1) The General Rules Prohibiting Sharing Legal Fees with Nonlawyers............................................................................ 431
§ 4-7.9(b)(2) The Exception for Payments by a Firm to Estate or Survivors of a Deceased Lawyer ............................................ 431
§ 4-7.9(b)(3) The Exception for Payment of the Purchase Price of Sale of a Practice of a Deceased Lawyer............................................ 432
§ 4-7.9(b)(4) The Exception for a Compensation or Retirement Plan for Nonlawyer Employees .......................................................... 432
§ 4-7.9(b)(5) The Exception for Sharing Court-Awarded Fees with Nonprofit Organizations........................................................ 433
§ 4-7.9(c) The Bar on Practicing Law with Nonlawyers..................................... 436
§ 4-7.9(c)(1) The Traditional (and Persisting) Bar on Practicing in a Partnership or Through Other Business Associations Including Control by Nonlawyers ........................................... 436
§ 4-7.9(c)(2) Employing Other Professionals and Assistants....................... 437
§ 4-7.9(c)(3) Lawyer Employed by Client as House Counsel ...................... 438
§ 4-7.9(d) The Prohibition on Restricting Right to Practice .............................. 438
§ 4-7.9(d)(1) The General Prohibition on Law Firm Agreements Restricting the Right to Practice and the Exception for Retirement Benefits............................................................... 438
§ 4-7.9(d)(2) The Prohibition on Settlement Agreements Restricting a Lawyer's Right to Practice......................................................... 441

**CHAPTER 4-8. DUTIES TO ORGANIZATION/ENTITY CLIENTS.................... 443**
§ 4-8.1 Introduction to Lawyers and Organization/Entity Clients............................ 443
§ 4-8.2 Responsibilities During the Formation of an Entity..................................... 444
§ 4-8.3 Confidentiality and Attorney-Client Privilege for a Private Entity Client ... 445
§ 4-8.3(a) Determining Who Speaks for the Client for Purposes of the Privilege........................................................................................ 445
§ 4-8.3(a)(1) Identifying the Client for Privileged Communications ........... 446
§ 4-8.3(a)(2) Identifying the Client for Authority to Waive the Privilege ... 448
§ 4-8.3(b) Denying the Privilege to Ordinary Business Matters (The Ruse Abuse) ............................................................................................ 449
§ 4-8.4 Protecting the Entity's Attorney-Client Relationship from Outside Interference (The "No-Contact" Rule for Entities) ........................................ 454
§ 4-8.4(a) Defining "Represented Person" for Entities in Applying the "No-Contact" Rule ................................................................................... 454
§ 4-8.4(b) Contacting Former Employees of an Entity........................................ 456

§ 4-8.4(c) Limitations on Communications with Current or Former Constituents of an Entity ..... 457
§ 4-8.4(c)(1) Not Suggesting Lawyer Neutrality ..... 458
§ 4-8.4(c)(2) Not Violating Organization's Rights (Confidentiality) ..... 458
§ 4-8.5 The Lawyer Responding to the Client's Duly-Authorized Constituents ..... 458
§ 4-8.6 The Lawyer's Responsibilities When Unlawful Conduct or Internal Dissension Arises Within an Organization ..... 460
§ 4-8.6(a) Introduction to the Problem of Constituent Misconduct Threatening the Organization ..... 460
§ 4-8.6(b) Triggering the Lawyer's Duty to Proceed in the Best Interests of the Organization ..... 461
§ 4-8.6(b)(1) Lawyer's Knowledge of Illegal Conduct ..... 461
§ 4-8.6(b)(2) Corporate Constituent Acting in Violation of Law ..... 461
§ 4-8.6(b)(3) Substantial Injury Is Likely ..... 462
§ 4-8.6(c) Addressing the Problem Within the Organizational Structure ..... 462
§ 4-8.6(d) Disclosing Confidential Information to Correct the Problem ..... 464
§ 4-8.6(e) Prohibition on Disclosure by Lawyer Retained to Investigate or Defend ..... 465
§ 4-8.6(f) Lawyer's Responsibility When Discharged or Withdrawing ..... 466
§ 4-8.6(g) The Problem of the Miscreant Constituent and the Lawyer's Duty of Diligence to the Organization ..... 466
§ 4-8.6(h) The Lawyer's Responsibilities When Serious Conflicts Arise Among Constituents of the Organization ..... 467
§ 4-8.7 Dual Representation of Organization and Individual Constituent ..... 468
§ 4-8.8 Government Clients ..... 470
§ 4-8.8(a) The Lawyer's Responsibilities to a Government or Public Office Client ..... 470
§ 4-8.8(b) The Attorney-Client Privilege in the Government Context ..... 471
§ 4-8.8(c) Identifying the Government Client and Litigating Authority ..... 472

**CHAPTER 4-9. DUTIES OF ETHICAL ADVOCACY ..... 475**
§ 4-9.1 Introduction to Ethics and Advocacy ..... 475
§ 4-9.2 The Classic Tension Between the Duty of the Zealous Advocate and the Officer of the Court ..... 476
§ 4-9.3 Ethical Duties in Presenting Claims or Contentions in Litigation ..... 481
§ 4-9.3(a) Presenting Only Meritorious Claims and Contentions in Civil Litigation ..... 481
§ 4-9.3(b) Putting the Prosecution to Its Proof in Criminal Proceedings ..... 484
§ 4-9.4 Duties to Advance the Resolution of Disputes ..... 486
§ 4-9.4(a) Expediting Litigation and Avoiding Unreasonable Delay ..... 486
§ 4-9.4(b) Conduct Prejudicial to the Administration of Justice ..... 487
§ 4-9.4(b)(1) General Conduct Prejudicial to the Administration of Justice ..... 487
§ 4-9.4(b)(2) Manifestations of Bias Prejudicial to the Administration of Justice and Not Constituting Legitimate Advocacy ..... 488
§ 4-9.4(c) Using Means That Are Intended Solely to Embarrass, Delay, or Burden Another Person ..... 490
§ 4-9.4(c)(1) Seeking Advantage by Humiliating, Degrading, or Oppressing Another ..... 490

§ 4-9.4(c)(2) Threatening or Promising to Withhold Report of Criminal Wrongdoing.....491
§ 4-9.5 Duties of Truthfulness and Candor by Lawyer Before the Tribunal.....493
§ 4-9.5(a) Truthfulness as a Fundamental Expectation and Candor as a Special Requirement in Certain Situations.....493
§ 4-9.5(b) Duty of Truthfulness When Lawyer Makes Statements of Fact.....494
§ 4-9.5(c) Limited Duty of Candor When Lawyer Makes Legal Arguments.....495
§ 4-9.5(d) Duty of Candor When Lawyer Participates in an *Ex Parte* Proceeding.....497
§ 4-9.5(e) Duty of Lawyer to Obey Court Rules and Rulings, Unless Openly Challenging Validity.....499
§ 4-9.6 Obtaining, Discovering, and Preserving Evidence for Civil Proceedings.....500
§ 4-9.6(a) General Duties on Access to Evidence in Civil Matters.....500
§ 4-9.6(b) Ethical Duties of Proper Requests and Responses in Civil Discovery.....501
§ 4-9.6(b)(1) General Ethical Expectations in Discovery.....501
§ 4-9.6(b)(2) Requests for Discovery.....502
§ 4-9.6(b)(3) Responses to Discovery.....503
§ 4-9.6(c) Preservation of Potential Evidence.....503
§ 4-9.6(c)(1) Overview of the Law of Spoliation of Evidence.....504
§ 4-9.6(c)(2) Destruction of Documents Pursuant to a Document Retention Policy.....507
§ 4-9.6(c)(3) 2015 Amendment to the Federal Rules of Civil Procedure on Preservation of Electronically-Stored Information (ESI).....507
§ 4-9.6(c)(4) The Duty of Counsel in Preserving and Producing Evidence in Discovery.....510
§ 4-9.6(d) Prohibition on Using Methods of Obtaining Evidence That Violate Another's Legal Rights.....512
§ 4-9.6(e) Lawyer's Obligations on Unsolicited Receipt of Another's Privileged or Confidential Materials.....515
§ 4-9.6(e)(1) Distinguishing Unsolicited Receipt from Encouraged Procurement of Protected Materials.....515
§ 4-9.6(e)(2) Lawyer's Receipt of Inadvertently Transmitted Protected Materials.....516
§ 4-9.6(e)(3) Lawyer's Receipt of Protected Materials Taken by Another Without Authority.....520
§ 4-9.6(e)(4) The Problem of Metadata.....526
§ 4-9.6(f) Covert Activity to Investigate Violations of the Law or Gather Intelligence.....528
§ 4-9.6(g) General Duty Not to Request Another Person to Withhold Information from Another Party.....531
§ 4-9.7 Ethical Issues Regarding Collection and Retention of Evidence in Criminal Proceedings.....532
§ 4-9.7(a) Introduction to Ethical Issues Regarding Evidence in Criminal Matters.....532
§ 4-9.7(b) The Law on the Duty to Preserve Evidence.....534
§ 4-9.7(b)(1) A Summary of State Laws on Obstruction of Justice.....534
§ 4-9.7(b)(2) The Traditional Federal Approach to Obstruction of Justice: §§ 1503 and 1512.....536

§ 4-9.7(b)(3) Anticipatory Obstruction of Justice: Sarbanes-Oxley § 1519 ..... 537
§ 4-9.7(b)(4) Safe Harbor for Legal Representation ..... 541
§ 4-9.7(b)(5) Treatment of Contraband That Is Not Evidence in a Reasonably Anticipated Proceeding ..... 542
§ 4-9.7(b)(6) Advising the Client in a Situation of Uncertainty ..... 547
§ 4-9.7(c) The Law on Observation and Examination of Evidence ..... 549
§ 4-9.7(c)(1) Defense Lawyer Observing Evidence Without Taking Possession ..... 549
§ 4-9.7(c)(2) Defense Lawyer's Right to Examine Evidence ..... 550
§ 4-9.7(c)(3) Disposition of Evidence by the Defense Lawyer After Examination ..... 553
§ 4-9.7(c)(4) Preserving Confidentiality if Defense Lawyer Deliver Evidence to Law Enforcement ..... 557
§ 4-9.7(d) Evidence Delivered to Defense Lawyer ..... 558
§ 4-9.7(e) The Tricky Problem of Contraband ..... 561
§ 4-9.7(f) Defense Lawyer's Retention of Evidence with Contingent Notice to Law Enforcement ..... 564
§ 4-9.7(f)(1) The Mistaken Notion That a Lawyer Has a General Duty to Deliver Evidence to Law Enforcement ..... 564
§ 4-9.7(f)(2) The Gillers Solution: An Evidence Registry ..... 565
§ 4-9.7(f)(3) Other Approaches Toward Evidence After Examination ..... 566
§ 4-9.8 Duties Regarding Presentation of Evidence ..... 567
§ 4-9.8(a) The Prohibition on Presenting What Is Known to Be False Evidence and the Problem of Client Perjury ..... 567
§ 4-9.8(a)(1) The Problem of Client Perjury ..... 568
§ 4-9.8(a)(2) The Narrative Statement Approach ..... 569
§ 4-9.8(b) Discretion to Decline to Present What Is Reasonably Believed to Be False Evidence ..... 570
§ 4-9.8(c) Duty to Take Remedial Measures to Correct False Evidence Notwithstanding Confidentiality ..... 571
§ 4-9.8(d) The Standard of Knowledge as Applied to the False Evidence Problem ..... 574
§ 4-9.8(e) How to Take Reasonable Steps to Remedy False Evidence ..... 576
§ 4-9.8(f) The Duration of the Duty to Remedy False Evidence ..... 578
§ 4-9.8(g) Closing Thoughts on the Rule Mandating Disclosure of False Evidence, Including Client Perjury ..... 579
§ 4-9.8(h) Duty to Counteract Client Fraudulent or Criminal Conduct Before the Tribunal ..... 580
§ 4-9.8(i) Witness Preparation Versus Witness Coaching ..... 581
§ 4-9.8(j) Improper Inducements to a Witness ..... 585
§ 4-9.9 Behavior During and After Trial ..... 587
§ 4-9.9(a) Disruptive Behavior at Trial ..... 587
§ 4-9.9(b) Improper Allusions and Expression of Personal Opinions by Lawyer ..... 588
§ 4-9.9(b)(1) Improper Allusions to Inadmissible Evidence by Lawyer ..... 588
§ 4-9.9(b)(2) Improper Personal Vouching and Opinions by Lawyer ..... 589
§ 4-9.9(c) Improper Influence on a Tribunal ..... 589
§ 4-9.9(d) *Ex Parte* Communications with a Tribunal (Judge or Jury) ..... 590

§ 4-9.9(e) Communications with Jury After Discharge ....................................592
§ 4-9.10 The Advocate-Witness Rule ....................................594
§ 4-9.10(a) The Advocate-Witness Rule and Avoiding Confusion of the Lawyer's Role ....................................594
§ 4-9.10(b) The "Necessary Witness" Standard for the Advocate-Witness Rule ....................................596
§ 4-9.10(c) Exceptions to the Advocate-Witness Rule ....................................598
§ 4-9.10(c)(1) Uncontested Issues ....................................598
§ 4-9.10(c)(2) Nature and Value of Legal Services ....................................598
§ 4-9.10(c)(3) Substantial Hardship on the Client ....................................599
§ 4-9.10(d) Conflicts of Interest Arising from a Lawyer's Testimony as a Witness ....................................599
§ 4-9.11 Extrajudicial Statements by Lawyer ....................................601
§ 4-9.11(a) Introduction: Balancing the Right to Freedom of Expression Against the Right to a Fair Trial ....................................601
§ 4-9.11(b) The Prohibition on Extrajudicial Statements Likely to Prejudice an Adjudicative Proceedings ....................................603
§ 4-9.11(b)(1) The Standard of a Substantial Likelihood of Material Prejudice ....................................603
§ 4-9.11(b)(2) The Likelihood of Prejudice and the Nature of the Proceeding ....................................604
§ 4-9.11(c) The Prejudicial Impact of Types of Statements ....................................605
§ 4-9.11(c)(1) Statements Least Likely to be Prejudicial ....................................605
§ 4-9.11(c)(2) Statements Raising Greatest Risk of Prejudice ....................................606
§ 4-9.11(c)(3) Special Risk Posed by Statements Made by Prosecutors ....................................609
§ 4-9.11(d) The Right of Reply to Correct Prejudice Caused by Another ....................................612
§ 4-9.11(e) Other Duties and Factors Implicated by Extrajudicial Statements ....................................614
§ 4-9.11(f) The Lawyer's Responsibility for Prejudicial Extrajudicial Statements by Others ....................................616
§ 4-9.12 The Heightened Ethical Duties of Lawyers for the Sovereign Government—With Special Attention to Prosecutors ....................................617
§ 4-9.12(a) Introduction to the Ethical Responsibilities of the Prosecutor and Government Litigator ....................................617
§ 4-9.12(a)(1) The Duty of a Prosecutor to "Do Justice" ....................................617
§ 4-9.12(a)(2) The Heightened Expectation for the Government Civil Litigator in Competence and Candor ....................................619
§ 4-9.12(a)(3) Federal Government Lawyers and State Ethics Rules ....................................621
§ 4-9.12(b) The Prosecutor's Ethical Duties in Charging and Investigation ....................................622
§ 4-9.12(c) The Government Lawyer's Duty to Respect the Rights of Others, Especially the Right to Counsel ....................................624
§ 4-9.12(c)(1) Prosecutor's Duties to an Unrepresented Accused ....................................624
§ 4-9.12(c)(2) The "No-Contact" Rule as Applied to Law Enforcement Investigations by Government Lawyers ....................................626
§ 4-9.12(c)(3) Interception by the Government of Privileged Communications ....................................632
§ 4-9.12(c)(4) Demand by Government of Waiver of Privileged Communications—The Corporate Investigation Scenario ....................................633

§ 4-9.12(c)(5) Restrictions on Issuance by Prosecutors of Subpoenas to Lawyers....636
§ 4-9.12(d) Prosecutor's Duties of Disclosure....640
§ 4-9.12(d)(1) Prosecutor's Duty to Disclose Exculpatory and Mitigating Evidence....640
§ 4-9.12(d)(2) Prosecutor's Duties Regarding Wrongful Convictions....642
§ 4-9.12(e) Closing Thoughts: The Prosecutor's General Duty of Candor and Protection of the Truth-Finding Function in Court....644
§ 4-9.13 The Duties of the Advocate in Nonadjudicative Proceedings....646

**CHAPTER 4-10. DUTIES AS EVALUATOR OR THIRD-PARTY NEUTRAL.... 649**
§ 4-10.1 Introduction: The Lawyer's Roles as Evaluator and Third-Party Neutral....649
§ 4-10.2 The Lawyer's Role as Evaluator....649
§ 4-10.2(a) General Principles of Lawyer of Evaluation of Client Matters....649
§ 4-10.2(b) Preparation of Client Evaluation for Use by Another Person....650
§ 4-10.2(c) Ethical Duties When Evaluation Is Adverse to the Client....651
§ 4-10.2(d) Confidentiality and Evaluation of Client Matter....652
§ 4-10.2(e) Other Ethical and Legal Duties Regarding Client Evaluation....653
§ 4-10.3 The Lawyer's Role as Third-Party Neutral....653

**CHAPTER 4-11. RESPECT FOR OTHER PERSONS.... 657**
§ 4-11.1 Introduction: The Lawyer's Duties to Respect the Rights and Dignity of Other Persons....657
§ 4-11.2 The Lawyer's Duty of Truthfulness....658
§ 4-11.2(a) The Lawyer's Basic Duty of Truthfulness in Dealings with Others....658
§ 4-11.2(b) The Lawyer Must Avoid False Statements of Material Fact or Law to Others....659
§ 4-11.2(c) The Lawyer Must Avoid Assisting the Client in Crime or Fraud....661
§ 4-11.3 Communications with a Represented Person....663
§ 4-11.3(a) The "No-Contact" Rule: Protecting the Attorney-Client Relationship from Outside Interference....663
§ 4-11.3(b) Communications Between Represented Persons....665
§ 4-11.3(c) The No-Contact Rule Applies Only When Lawyer Is Representing a Client....667
§ 4-11.3(d) The No-Contact Rule Applies Only to Communications on the Subject of Representation....667
§ 4-11.3(e) The No-Contact Rule Applies Only When the Lawyer Knows the Person Is Represented....669
§ 4-11.3(f) Consent by Represented Person's Counsel to Contact by Another Lawyer....670
§ 4-11.3(g) Exceptions to the No-Contact Rule....671
§ 4-11.3(g)(1) Consent by the Person's Lawyer....671
§ 4-11.3(g)(2) Authorized by Law....672
§ 4-11.3(g)(3) Court Order....672
§ 4-11.3(h) The No-Contact Rule and the Right to Petition Government....673
§ 4-11.4 Communications with an Unrepresented Person....675
§ 4-11.4(a) Avoiding Suggestion of Lawyer's Neutrality....675
§ 4-11.4(b) Correcting Misunderstanding About Lawyer's Role....676

§ 4-11.4(c) Giving of Legal Advice by Lawyer ....... 676

**CHAPTER 4-12. DUTIES OF A LAWYER IN A LAW FIRM ....... 679**
§ 4-12.1 Introduction to the Responsibilities of a Lawyer in a Law Firm ....... 679
§ 4-12.2 The Responsibilities of a Managing or Supervising Lawyer over Other Lawyers ....... 680
§ 4-12.2(a) The Duty of a Managing or Supervising Lawyer on Ethical Guidance of Other Lawyers ....... 680
§ 4-12.2(a)(1) The Duty of a Managing Lawyer in a Firm ....... 680
§ 4-12.2(a)(2) The Duty of a Supervising Lawyer ....... 681
§ 4-12.2(a)(3) Reasonable Efforts to Ensure Ethical Conduct ....... 681
§ 4-12.2(a)(4) Managing or Supervising Lawyer Responsibility Is Not Vicarious Liability ....... 682
§ 4-12.2(b) Lawyer Responsibility for the Misconduct of Another Lawyer ....... 683
§ 4-12.3 The Responsibilities of a Subordinate Lawyer ....... 684
§ 4-12.4 The Responsibilities of a Managing or Supervising Lawyer over Nonlawyer Assistants ....... 685

**CHAPTER 4-13. PUBLIC-REGARDING ACTIVITIES, DUTIES, AND RIGHTS ....... 689**
§ 4-13.1 Lawyer Responsibilities on Bar Admission and Discipline ....... 689
§ 4-13.1(a) The Duty to Report Professional Misconduct ....... 689
§ 4-13.1(a)(1) Protecting the Legal Profession by Reporting Misconduct ....... 689
§ 4-13.1(a)(2) Required Knowledge of Violation for Duty to Report ....... 690
§ 4-13.1(a)(3) Duty to Report When Violation Raises Substantial Question on Fitness ....... 690
§ 4-13.1(b) Confidentiality as an Exception to the Duty to Report ....... 690
§ 4-13.1(c) Protection of Information Gained Within an Approved Lawyers Assistance Program ....... 692
§ 4-13.1(d) Duty of Candor with Respect to Regulation of the Bar ....... 693
§ 4-13.1(e) The Privilege Against Self-Incrimination, Confidentiality, and Unlawful Demands ....... 694
§ 4-13.1(e)(1) Privilege Against Self-Incrimination ....... 694
§ 4-13.1(e)(2) Client Confidentiality ....... 694
§ 4-13.1(e)(3) Lawful Demand for Information ....... 695
§ 4-13.2 Lawyer Involvement in Law Reform ....... 695
§ 4-13.2(a) Lawyer's General Freedom to Engage in Law Reform Notwithstanding Client Interest ....... 695
§ 4-13.2(b) Law Reform Activities and Conflicts of Interest ....... 696
§ 4-13.2(c) Client's Right to Discharge Lawyer Based on Law Reform Activities ....... 697
§ 4-13.2(d) Duty of Lawyer to Law Reform Organization ....... 697
§ 4-13.3 Lawyer Commentary on Judges, Legal Officers, and Candidates for Judicial or Legal Office ....... 698
§ 4-13.3(a) The Value of Informed Commentary by Lawyers on Legal Officers and Judges ....... 698
§ 4-13.3(b) The Disciplinary Standard of Knowing Falsity or Reckless Disregard for Truth ....... 699
§ 4-13.3(c) Lawyer Speech in the Courtroom About Judges ....... 701

§ 4-13.3(d) Limiting Discipline to False Factual Statements About Legal Officers or Judges ....702
§ 4-13.4 Providing Legal Services to the Disadvantaged ....703
§ 4-13.4(a) The Moral Obligation and Professional Responsibility to Provide Pro Bono Legal Services ....703
§ 4-13.4(b) Aspirational Expectations for Pro Bono Legal Services ....705
§ 4-13.4(c) Providing Short-Term Limited Pro Bono Services and Conflict of Interest Rules ....706
§ 4-13.4(d) The Lawyer's Duty to Accept Appointment to Represent a Client Absent Good Cause ....708
§ 4-13.4(d)(1) Court Appointment of Lawyer to Represent a Person ....708
§ 4-13.4(d)(2) Good Cause to Decline Appointment ....709
§ 4-13.4(e) Lawyer Serving in Governance with a Legal Services Organization and Recusal in Matters Raising a Conflict of Interest ....711

## PART FIVE. LEGAL MALPRACTICE

**CHAPTER 5-1. INTRODUCTION TO LEGAL MALPRACTICE LAW .... 715**
§ 5-1.1 The Role and Nature of Legal Malpractice Law ....715
§ 5-1.2 The Rise in Legal Malpractice Law ....716
§ 5-1.3 The Costs of Legal Malpractice ....718
§ 5-1.4 Overview of the Theories of Liability ....719
§ 5-1.4(a) Culpability ....719
§ 5-1.4(b) Differentiating Claims in the Same Lawsuit ....719
§ 5-1.5 Consequences of Classifying Theories of Liability ....720
§ 5-1.5(a) Pleadings and Proof ....720
§ 5-1.5(b) Scope of Liability ....721
§ 5-1.5(c) Defenses ....721
§ 5-1.5(d) Legal Malpractice Insurance ....722
§ 5-1.5(e) Vicarious Liability ....722
§ 5-1.5(f) Remedies ....723
§ 5-1.5(g) Discharge in Bankruptcy ....723
§ 5-1.6 Status of the Plaintiff ....723
§ 5-1.7 Differentiating Malpractice and Discipline ....724
§ 5-1.7(a) Purposes and Prosecutor ....724
§ 5-1.7(b) Procedures and Decision-Makers ....725
§ 5-1.7(c) Application of Ethics Rules ....725

**CHAPTER 5-2. NEGLIGENCE .... 727**
§ 5-2.1 Duty to Exercise Reasonable Care ....727
§ 5-2.1(a) To Whom Is a Duty Owed? ....727
§ 5-2.1(a)(1) Three Kinds of Attorney-Client Relationship ....728
§ 5-2.1(a)(1)(A) Court Appointment ....728
§ 5-2.1(a)(1)(B) Express Agreement ....729
§ 5-2.1(a)(1)(C) Inadvertent Clients ....729
§ 5-2.1(a)(1)(C)(i) Common Scenarios ....729
§ 5-2.1(a)(1)(C)(ii) Request for Legal Services ....730
§ 5-2.1(a)(1)(C)(iii) Reasonable Reliance ....731
§ 5-2.1(a)(1)(C)(iv) Prevention ....732

§ 5-2.1(a)(2) Appearance Before a Tribunal ....733
§ 5-2.1(a)(3) Attorney-Client Relationship Based on Estoppel ....734
§ 5-2.1(a)(4) Voluntary Assumption of Duty ....734
§ 5-2.1(a)(5) Prospective Clients....735
§ 5-2.1(a)(6) Class Members ....736
§ 5-2.1(b) Scope of Representation ....736
§ 5-2.1(b)(1) Defining the Scope of Representation....737
§ 5-2.1(b)(2) Changes in the Scope of Representation ....737
§ 5-2.1(b)(3) Unreasonable Limits on the Scope of Representation....738
§ 5-2.1(b)(4) Responsibility for Closely Related Matters....738
§ 5-2.1(b)(5) Termination of the Attorney-Client Relationship....739
§ 5-2.1(b)(5)(A) Post-Termination Loyalty ....740
§ 5-2.1(b)(5)(B) Termination of Authority ....741
§ 5-2.2 Breach of Duty ....741
§ 5-2.2(a) The Standard of Care ....742
§ 5-2.2(a)(1) Specialists....743
§ 5-2.2(a)(2) Representations of Greater Competence ....743
§ 5-2.2(a)(3) Disclosure of Inexperience....744
§ 5-2.2(a)(4) Malpractice by Laypersons....744
§ 5-2.2(a)(5) Lawyers with Disabilities....745
§ 5-2.2(b) No Good Faith Defense....746
§ 5-2.2(c) Risk Balancing and Economic Analysis ....746
§ 5-2.2(d) Specific Duties....747
§ 5-2.2(d)(1) Competence ....748
§ 5-2.2(d)(2) Duty to Recommend a Specialist....748
§ 5-2.2(d)(3) Diligence ....749
§ 5-2.2(e) Exercise of Judgment ....749
§ 5-2.2(e)(1) Room for Discretion....749
§ 5-2.2(e)(2) The "Mere Error of Judgment" Fallacy ....750
§ 5-2.2(e)(3) Unsettled Questions....751
§ 5-2.2(e)(4) Novel Theories, Trends, and Other Jurisdictions....752
§ 5-2.2(f) Expert Testimony ....752
§ 5-2.2(f)(1) Necessary to Establish the Standard of Care ....752
§ 5-2.2(f)(2) Exception for Obvious Negligence....753
§ 5-2.2(f)(3) Expert Affidavit Requirements....754
§ 5-2.2(f)(4) Admissibility of Expert Testimony ....755
§ 5-2.2(f)(5) Geographic Frame of Reference for Expert Testimony ....756
§ 5-2.2(f)(5)(A) No Locality Rule ....757
§ 5-2.2(f)(5)(B) International Legal Malpractice....757
§ 5-2.2(f)(6) The Role of Legal Malpractice Experts....759
§ 5-2.2(f)(6)(A) Duties and Compensation....759
§ 5-2.2(f)(6)(B) Independence Versus Partisanship....760
§ 5-2.2(f)(6)(C) Non-Testifying Experts ....761
§ 5-2.2(f)(6)(D) Honesty and Effectiveness ....762
§ 5-2.2(g) Expert Testimony on Causation ....762
§ 5-2.2(g)(1) Sometimes Permitted....762
§ 5-2.2(g)(2) Sometimes Required ....763
§ 5-2.2(g)(3) Sometimes Prohibited....764
§ 5-2.2(h) Experts' Reliance on Ethics Rules ....764

§ 5-2.2(i) Experts' Ignorance of Ethics Rules ....765
§ 5-2.2(j) Experts' Inconsistency with Ethics Rules ....765
§ 5-2.2(k) Conclusory Expert Testimony ....766
§ 5-2.2(*l*) Expert Witness Liability ....766
§ 5-2.2(m) Negligence *Per Se* in Legal Malpractice ....766
§ 5-2.2(m)(1) How Statutes Set the Standard of Care ....767
§ 5-2.2(m)(2) Statutes Disclaiming a Civil Cause of Action ....767
§ 5-2.2(m)(3) Restatement Position on Statutory Standards ....768
§ 5-2.2(m)(4) Statutes Imposing Duties Not Unique to Lawyers ....768
§ 5-2.2(n) Informed Consent in Legal Malpractice ....769
§ 5-2.3 Causation ....772
§ 5-2.3(a) Factual Causation ....772
§ 5-2.3(a)(1) The "But For" Test ....772
§ 5-2.3(a)(1)(A) Difficult to Establish ....773
§ 5-2.3(a)(1)(B) Proving an Alternative Would Have Occurred ....774
§ 5-2.3(a)(1)(C) Prior Judge and Jury May Not Testify ....775
§ 5-2.3(a)(1)(D) The "But For" Test and Multiple Tortfeasors ....775
§ 5-2.3(a)(1)(E) Independently Sufficient Causes ....776
§ 5-2.3(a)(2) "Trial Within a Trial" Analysis ....776
§ 5-2.3(a)(2)(A) Factual Complexity ....777
§ 5-2.3(a)(3) The "More Favorable Result" Standard ....778
§ 5-2.3(a)(4) Loss of a Chance ....778
§ 5-2.3(a)(5) Shifting the Burden of Proof on Causation ....780
§ 5-2.3(a)(6) Tortious Spoliation of Causation Evidence ....781
§ 5-2.3(a)(6)(A) Legitimate Destruction of Evidence ....782
§ 5-2.3(a)(7) Concerted Action Liability ....782
§ 5-2.3(b) Proximate Causation ....783
§ 5-2.3(b)(1) In General ....783
§ 5-2.3(b)(2) Superseding Causation and Shifting Responsibility ....784
§ 5-2.3(b)(2)(A) Intervening Negligent Conduct ....784
§ 5-2.3(b)(2)(B) Failure by the Client to Discover Malpractice ....785
§ 5-2.3(b)(2)(C) Subsequent Counsel's Failure to Act ....785

**CHAPTER 5-3. BREACH OF FIDUCIARY DUTY .... 789**
§ 5-3.1 Lawyers as Fiduciaries ....789
§ 5-3.1(a) A Different Point of Reference ....789
§ 5-3.1(b) Fiduciary Duty Versus Negligence ....789
§ 5-3.1(c) Disloyalty Versus Lack of Care ....790
§ 5-3.1(d) Similarities to Negligence ....791
§ 5-3.1(e) Differences from Negligence ....792
§ 5-3.2 The "Substantial Factor" Test for Factual Causation ....792
§ 5-3.2(a) No Speculation ....793
§ 5-3.3 Disclosure Obligations ....793
§ 5-3.3(a) "Absolute and Perfect Candor" ....793
§ 5-3.3(b) How Negligence Duties and Fiduciary Duties Mesh ....795
§ 5-3.3(c) Limits on Disclosure Obligations ....795
§ 5-3.4 Fee Forfeiture ....796
§ 5-3.4(a) To Prevent Unjust Enrichment ....796
§ 5-3.4(b) Causation of Harm Is Not Required ....796

§ 5-3.4(c) Clear and Serious Breach of Duty ....797
§ 5-3.4(d) Does Forfeiture Require Fiduciary Breach? ....798
§ 5-3.5 Aiding and Abetting a Breach of Fiduciary Duty ....799
§ 5-3.5(a) A Dangerous Theory of Liability ....799
§ 5-3.5(b) Two Very Different Varieties ....799
§ 5-3.5(c) Tort Principles on Aiding and Abetting ....800
§ 5-3.5(d) Evidence of Knowing Assistance ....801
§ 5-3.5(e) Evidence of Substantial Assistance ....801
§ 5-3.5(f) Privileges and Defenses ....802
§ 5-3.5(g) Implications for Corporate Policy Making ....803
§ 5-3.6 Intra-Firm Fiduciary Duties ....804
§ 5-3.6(a) Duties of Partners and Other Law Firm Principles ....805
§ 5-3.6(b) Duties of Associates ....805
§ 5-3.6(c) Movement Between Firms ....806
§ 5-3.6(d) Post-Employment Restrictive Covenants ....807

**CHAPTER 5-4. LIABILITY TO NONCLIENTS .... 809**
§ 5-4.1 Modern Nonclient Litigation ....809
§ 5-4.1(a) The Privity Obstacle ....810
§ 5-4.1(b) Exceptions to Privity ....811
§ 5-4.1(c) Statutory Limits on Nonclient Liability ....812
§ 5-4.1(d) Successors-in-Interest ....813
§ 5-4.1(d)(1) Bankruptcy Trustees and Estate Executors or Administrators ....813
§ 5-4.1(d)(2) Mergers and Sales of Assets ....813
§ 5-4.1(d)(3) Receivers ....814
§ 5-4.2 Fraud on Clients and Nonclients ....814
§ 5-4.2(a) Basic Principles of the Law Governing Fraud ....814
§ 5-4.2(a)(1) Common Law Remedies and Other Consequences ....814
§ 5-4.2(a)(2) The Elements of Fraud ....815
§ 5-4.2(a)(2)(A) Special Pleading and Proof Requirements ....816
§ 5-4.2(a)(3) Scienter ....816
§ 5-4.2(a)(3)(A) Knowledge of Falsity ....816
§ 5-4.2(a)(3)(B) Reckless Disregard for the Truth ....816
§ 5-4.2(a)(4) Materiality and Types of Misrepresentation ....818
§ 5-4.2(a)(4)(A) Words Written or Oral ....818
§ 5-4.2(a)(4)(A)(i) Words of Qualification ....819
§ 5-4.2(a)(4)(B) Conduct ....819
§ 5-4.2(a)(4)(C) Liability for Nondisclosure ....819
§ 5-4.2(a)(4)(C)(i) Fiduciary Duty to Speak ....819
§ 5-4.2(a)(4)(C)(ii) Half-Truths ....820
§ 5-4.2(a)(4)(C)(iii) Facts Basic to the Transaction ....820
§ 5-4.2(a)(4)(C)(iv) Facts Not Reasonably Discoverable ....820
§ 5-4.2(a)(4)(D) Misrepresentations by Lawyers About Credentials or Experience ....821
§ 5-4.2(a)(5) Opinion Versus Fact ....821
§ 5-4.2(a)(5)(A) "Puffing" ....821
§ 5-4.2(a)(5)(B) Implicit Statements of Fact ....822
§ 5-4.2(a)(5)(C) State of Mind ....822

§ 5-4.2(a)(5)(D) Statements of Law ....... 823
§ 5-4.2(a)(6) Justifiable Reliance ....... 824
§ 5-4.2(a)(6)(A) Statements Known to Be False ....... 824
§ 5-4.2(a)(6)(B) Danger Signals ....... 824
§ 5-4.2(a)(6)(C) Failure to Doubt ....... 824
§ 5-4.2(a)(6)(D) Contractual Disclaimers of Reliance ....... 825
§ 5-4.2(a)(7) Intent to Induce Reliance ....... 825
§ 5-4.2(a)(8) Resulting Damages ....... 825
§ 5-4.2(a)(9) Liability for Aiding and Abetting Fraud ....... 826
§ 5-4.3 Negligent Misrepresentation ....... 826
§ 5-4.3(a) *Restatement (Second) of Torts* § 552 ....... 827
§ 5-4.3(a)(1) Relationship to Voluntary Assumption of Duty ....... 828
§ 5-4.3(b) Limits on the Scope of Liability for Misrepresentation ....... 828
§ 5-4.3(b)(1) Scope of Liability for Fraud ....... 828
§ 5-4.3(b)(1)(A) Commercial Documents ....... 828
§ 5-4.3(b)(1)(B) Public Filings ....... 829
§ 5-4.3(b)(1)(C) Special Reason to Expect Reliance ....... 829
§ 5-4.3(b)(2) Scope of Liability for Negligent Misrepresentation ....... 830
§ 5-4.3(b)(2)(A) The “Near Privity” View ....... 830
§ 5-4.3(b)(2)(B) The Restatement’s “Limited Group” View ....... 831
§ 5-4.3(b)(2)(C) Summary ....... 832
§ 5-4.3(c) Negligent Misrepresentation Based on Silence ....... 832
§ 5-4.3(d) Plaintiff’s Negligence as a Defense ....... 833
§ 5-4.4 Deceptive Trade Practices Acts ....... 833
§ 5-4.4(a) Applicability to Lawyers ....... 833
§ 5-4.4(b) Advantages over Common Law ....... 834
§ 5-4.4(c) DTPA Suits by Nonclients ....... 835
§ 5-4.5 Claims Based on Representation of Fiduciaries ....... 835
§ 5-4.6 Funds and Property of Nonclients ....... 835
§ 5-4.7 Intended Beneficiaries ....... 837
§ 5-4.7(a) Invalid Wills ....... 837
§ 5-4.7(a)(1) Minority View ....... 837
§ 5-4.7(b) Insurers ....... 838
§ 5-4.7(c) Other Intended Beneficiaries ....... 839
§ 5-4.8 Duties to Co-Counsel ....... 841
§ 5-4.8(a) Protecting Fee Interests ....... 841
§ 5-4.9 Liability Related to Litigation ....... 842
§ 5-4.9(a) Malicious Prosecution and Malicious Use of Process ....... 843
§ 5-4.9(a)(1) Elements ....... 843
§ 5-4.9(a)(2) Terminology ....... 844
§ 5-4.9(a)(3) Advice of Counsel Defense and Related Claims Against Lawyers ....... 844
§ 5-4.9(b) Tortious Involvement with Litigation ....... 845
§ 5-4.9(c) Insurer Subrogation Claims ....... 845
§ 5-4.10 Securities Law Violations ....... 846
§ 5-4.10(a) “Aiding and Abetting” and “Scheme” Liability ....... 847
§ 5-4.10(b) Claims Under State Law ....... 847
§ 5-4.11 Fair Debt Collections Practices ....... 848

**CHAPTER 5-5. REMEDIES FOR LEGAL MALPRACTICE ... 851**
§ 5-5.1 Compensatory Damages ... 851
§ 5-5.1(a) No Speculation ... 851
§ 5-5.1(b) Proximately Caused Losses ... 853
§ 5-5.1(c) Emotional Distress Damages ... 853
§ 5-5.1(d) Harm to Reputation ... 854
§ 5-5.1(e) Attorney's Fees as Compensatory Damages ... 854
§ 5-5.1(e)(1) Attorney's Fees Incurred in the Malpractice Action ... 855
§ 5-5.1(e)(2) Attorney's Fees Incurred in Earlier Representation ... 855
§ 5-5.1(e)(3) Attorney's Fees Not Recovered in Earlier Litigation ... 856
§ 5-5.1(e)(4) Attorney's Fees Incurred to Remedy or Mitigate Malpractice ... 856
§ 5-5.1(f) Adjustments to Damages ... 857
§ 5-5.1(f)(1) Reduction to Present Value ... 857
§ 5-5.1(f)(2) Prejudgment Interest ... 857
§ 5-5.1(f)(3) Amounts That Would Have Been Spent on Contingent Fees ... 858
§ 5-5.1(f)(4) Quantum Meruit Offset for the Value of Services Rendered ... 858
§ 5-5.1(g) Collectability ... 858
§ 5-5.2 Punitive Damages ... 859
§ 5-5.2(a) State Law Limitations ... 859
§ 5-5.2(a)(1) Caps and Bans on Punitive Damages ... 860
§ 5-5.2(a)(2) Partial Forfeiture to the State ... 861
§ 5-5.2(b) Federal Constitutional Limitations ... 861
§ 5-5.2(b)(1) BMW of North America v. Gore ... 861
§ 5-5.2(b)(2) State Farm Mutual Automobile Insurance v. Campbell ... 862
§ 5-5.2(b)(3) Subsequent Supreme Court Cases ... 864
§ 5-5.2(c) Limitations on Punitive Awards in Legal Malpractice Cases ... 864
§ 5-5.2(d) Vicarious Liability for Punitive Damages ... 865
§ 5-5.2(e) Liability for "Lost Punitive Damages" ... 866
§ 5-5.3 Restitution ... 866

**CHAPTER 5-6. DEFENSES AND OBSTACLES TO RECOVERY ... 867**
§ 5-6.1 In General ... 867
§ 5-6.2 Defenses Based on the Plaintiff's Conduct ... 868
§ 5-6.2(a) Contributory Negligence, Comparative Negligence, and Comparative Fault ... 868
§ 5-6.2(b) Avoidable Consequences and the Failure to Mitigate ... 869
§ 5-6.2(c) Unlawful Conduct ... 870
§ 5-6.2(c)(1) A Defense in Many Guises ... 870
§ 5-6.2(c)(2) Exoneration or Innocence Requirement in Criminal-Defense Malpractice ... 872
§ 5-6.2(c)(2)(A) Lesser Included Offenses ... 873
§ 5-6.2(c)(2)(B) Sentencing Errors ... 873
§ 5-6.2(c)(2)(C) Limits on the Unlawful Conduct Defense ... 873
§ 5-6.3 Privileges and Immunities Based on the Defendant's Conduct ... 874
§ 5-6.3(a) The Absolute Judicial Proceedings Privilege (Litigation Privilege) ... 874
§ 5-6.3(b) Attorney Immunity ... 876

§ 5-6.3(c) Absolute Privilege for Truth ..... 877
§ 5-6.3(d) Qualified Privileges ..... 877
§ 5-6.3(e) Immunity of Public Defenders and Appointed Lawyers ..... 877
§ 5-6.4 Defenses Arising by Operation of Law ..... 878
§ 5-6.4(a) Malpractice Statutes of Limitations ..... 879
§ 5-6.4(a)(1) Accrual of the Cause of Action ..... 881
§ 5-6.4(a)(1)(A) Occurrence Rule ..... 881
§ 5-6.4(a)(1)(B) Damage Rule ..... 881
§ 5-6.4(a)(2) Tolling ..... 882
§ 5-6.4(a)(2)(A) Discovery Rule ..... 883
§ 5-6.4(a)(2)(B) Continuous Representation Rule ..... 885
§ 5-6.4(a)(2)(B)(i) Determining Continuity ..... 886
§ 5-6.4(a)(2)(C) Fraudulent Concealment ..... 887
§ 5-6.4(a)(2)(D) Agreement of the Parties ..... 887
§ 5-6.4(a)(2)(D)(i) Shortening the Filing Period ..... 887
§ 5-6.4(a)(2)(E) Pendency of Other Litigation ..... 888
§ 5-6.4(a)(2)(F) Equitable Estoppel ..... 888
§ 5-6.4(a)(2)(G) The Continuing Tort Doctrine ..... 889
§ 5-6.4(a)(3) Statutes of Repose ..... 889
§ 5-6.4(b) Non-Assignability of Legal Malpractice Claims ..... 890
§ 5-6.4(c) Joint Liability and Reimbursement ..... 891
§ 5-6.4(c)(1) Allocation of Fault to Other Persons ..... 891
§ 5-6.4(c)(2) Contribution ..... 892
§ 5-6.4(c)(3) Indemnity ..... 893
§ 5-6.4(c)(4) Claims Involving Successive Counsel or Co-Counsel ..... 894
§ 5-6.4(d) Releases and Covenants Not to Sue ..... 895
§ 5-6.4(d)(1) Settlement with the Defendant ..... 895
§ 5-6.4(e) Arbitration Agreements ..... 896
§ 5-6.4(f) SLAPP Laws ..... 898
§ 5-6.4(g) Judicial Estoppel ..... 899

**CHAPTER 5-7. VICARIOUS LIABILITY ..... 901**
§ 5-7.1 The Role of Vicarious Liability ..... 901
§ 5-7.2 Law Firm Practice ..... 901
§ 5-7.2(a) The Vicarious Liability of Law Firms ..... 902
§ 5-7.2(a)(1) Ordinary Course of Firm Business ..... 903
§ 5-7.2(a)(1)(A) Intended to Benefit the Firm ..... 903
§ 5-7.2(a)(1)(B) Normal Risks Incidental to the Practice of Law ..... 904
§ 5-7.2(a)(2) Actual and Apparent Authority ..... 905
§ 5-7.2(b) Procedural Issues Related to Claims Against Firms ..... 907
§ 5-7.2(c) Liability of Partners in General Partnerships ..... 908
§ 5-7.2(d) Liability of Principals in Limited Liability Law Firms ..... 908
§ 5-7.2(d)(1) Practice in Professional Corporation ..... 908
§ 5-7.2(d)(2) Practice in Limited Liability Companies and Limited Liability Partnerships ..... 910
§ 5-7.3 Other Associations That Expose Lawyers to Liability ..... 914
§ 5-7.3(a) Referral Fee Arrangements ..... 914
§ 5-7.3(a)(1) Joint Responsibility and Joint Ventures ..... 915
§ 5-7.3(a)(2) Negligent Referral ..... 916

§ 5-7.3(b) Co-Counsel Arrangements and Other Outside Counsel ....919
§ 5-7.3(c) Of Counsel Arrangements ....920
§ 5-7.3(d) Office-Sharing Arrangements ....921
§ 5-7.3(d)(1) Partnership by Estoppel ....922
§ 5-7.3(d)(2) Partnership in Fact ....923
§ 5-7.3(d)(3) Joint Venture ....923
§ 5-7.3(e) Temporary Lawyers ....924
§ 5-7.3(f) Nondelegable Duties ....925
§ 5-7.3(g) Assisting Non-Lawyers in the Practice of Law ....927

**CHAPTER 5-8. LEGAL MALPRACTICE INSURANCE .... 929**
§ 5-8.1 The Importance of Legal Malpractice Insurance ....929
§ 5-8.1(a) Mandatory Coverage ....930
§ 5-8.1(b) Disclosure Requirements ....931
§ 5-8.2 What Coverage Is Available ....932
§ 5-8.3 The Anatomy of a Policy ....933
§ 5-8.3(a) Declarations Page ....933
§ 5-8.3(b) Insuring Agreements ....934
§ 5-8.3(b)(1) Claims for Money Damages Arising from the Rendition of Legal Services to Others ....934
§ 5-8.3(b)(2) Duty to Defend ....935
§ 5-8.3(b)(3) Liability Limits and Self-Liquidating Policies ....935
§ 5-8.3(b)(4) Named Insured and Other Insureds ....936
§ 5-8.3(c) Policy Exclusions ....936
§ 5-8.3(c)(1) Exclusions Eliminating Coverage Not Intended to Be Provided ....936
§ 5-8.3(c)(2) Exclusions Targeting Extraordinary Risks ....938
§ 5-8.3(c)(3) Exclusions Relating to Moral or Illegal Risks ....938
§ 5-8.3(d) Policy Conditions That Affect Coverage ....939
§ 5-8.4 Handling Claims and Potential Claims ....940
§ 5-8.4(a) Consult Counsel ....940
§ 5-8.4(b) Disclosure Under Model Rule 1.6 ....940
§ 5-8.4(c) In-Firm Attorney-Client Privilege ....941
§ 5-8.4(d) Prompt Notice to Insurer ....941
§ 5-8.5 Dealing with Clients When Lawyers Commit Malpractice ....942
§ 5-8.5(a) Determining Whether There Is a Duty to Disclose Errors ....942
§ 5-8.5(b) What Information Should Be Disclosed ....945
§ 5-8.5(c) Avoid Breaching the Cooperation Clause ....945
§ 5-8.5(d) Consequences of Nondisclosure ....946
§ 5-8.5(e) Evaluating Remedial Action and Withdrawal ....947

**PART SIX. JUDICIAL ETHICS AND THE CONDUCT OF JUDGES**

**CHAPTER 6-1. REGULATING JUDICIAL CONDUCT GENERALLY— FEATURES AND PRINCIPLES .... 951**
§ 6-1.1 Modern Judicial Ethics and Codes of Judicial Conduct ....951
§ 6-1.2 Judicial Discipline in the State Courts ....952
§ 6-1.3 Judicial Discipline in the Federal Courts ....953

§ 6-1.4 Core Values: Impartiality, Independence, and Integrity ... 955
§ 6-1.4(a) Judicial Impartiality ... 956
§ 6-1.4(b) Judicial Independence ... 957
§ 6-1.4(c) Judicial Integrity ... 957
§ 6-1.5 Foundational Rules ... 958
§ 6-1.5(a) The Duty to Comply with the Law ... 958
§ 6-1.5(b) The Duty to Promote Public Confidence and Avoid Appearances of Impropriety ... 959
§ 6-1.5(c) The Duty to Avoid Abusing the Prestige of Judicial Office ... 961

**CHAPTER 6-2. REGULATING JUDICIAL CONDUCT ON THE BENCH ... 963**
§ 6-2.1 Responsibilities Related to Maintaining Fitness for Judicial Service ... 963
§ 6-2.1(a) Competence and Diligence ... 963
§ 6-2.1(b) Demeanor ... 966
§ 6-2.2 Responsibilities Related to the Use of Judicial Independence and Power ... 968
§ 6-2.2(a) The Duty to Uphold and Apply the Law ... 968
§ 6-2.2(b) The Duty to Resist External Influences on Judicial Conduct ... 971
§ 6-2.3 Responsibilities Related to Preserving Judicial Impartiality and Fairness ... 973
§ 6-2.3(a) Judicial Bias ... 973
§ 6-2.3(a)(1) Bias Toward Specific People ... 973
§ 6-2.3(a)(2) Bias Toward Classes of People ... 974
§ 6-2.3(b) Respecting Parties' Rights to Be Heard ... 976
§ 6-2.3(c) Public Statements on Pending and Future Cases ... 978
§ 6-2.3(c)(1) Comments on Pending and Impending Cases ... 978
§ 6-2.3(c)(2) Pledges or Promises Concerning Future Cases ... 980
§ 6-2.4 *Ex Parte* Communications ... 981
§ 6-2.4(a) In General ... 981
§ 6-2.4(b) Prohibited Communications ... 983
§ 6-2.4(c) *Ex Parte* Investigations ... 985
§ 6-2.5 Judicial Disqualification ... 986
§ 6-2.5(a) Introduction to Disqualification ... 986
§ 6-2.5(b) Disqualification Standards ... 988
§ 6-2.5(b)(1) Overview of Standards and Their Interpretation ... 988
§ 6-2.5(b)(2) When Impartiality Might Reasonably Be Questioned ... 990
§ 6-2.5(b)(2)(A) Judicial Conduct ... 991
§ 6-2.5(b)(2)(B) Extrajudicial Conduct ... 995
§ 6-2.5(b)(3) Specific Grounds ... 999
§ 6-2.5(b)(3)(A) Personal Bias ... 999
§ 6-2.5(b)(3)(B) Personal Knowledge of Disputed Facts ... 1000
§ 6-2.5(b)(3)(C) Relatives as Parties, Attorneys, or Witnesses ... 1001
§ 6-2.5(b)(3)(D) Judge Was a Lawyer or Affiliated with a Lawyer in the Proceeding ... 1002
§ 6-2.5(b)(3)(E) Economic or Other Interest in the Proceeding ... 1003
§ 6-2.5(b)(3)(F) Campaign Support and Commitments ... 1006
§ 6-2.5(c) Disqualification Procedure ... 1008

**CHAPTER 6-3. REGULATING JUDICIAL CONDUCT OFF THE BENCH—EXTRAJUDICIAL AND POLITICAL ACTIVITIES** ..... **1011**
§ 6-3.1 Extrajudicial Conduct ..... 1011
§ 6-3.1(a) Extrajudicial Conduct: General Obligations ..... 1011
§ 6-3.1(b) Governmental Activities ..... 1012
§ 6-3.1(c) Avocational Activities ..... 1014
§ 6-3.1(d) Business Activities ..... 1017
§ 6-3.1(e) Gifts ..... 1018
§ 6-3.2 Political Activities ..... 1020

TABLE OF CASES ..... 1027

TABLE OF STATUTES ..... 1043

TABLE OF RULES ..... 1045

TABLE OF RESTATEMENTS ..... 1053

INDEX ..... 1057

# LEGAL ETHICS, PROFESSIONAL RESPONSIBILITY, AND THE LEGAL PROFESSION

# Part One

## THE LEGAL PROFESSION AND LEGAL SERVICES: NATURE AND EVOLUTION

### By William D. Henderson

### INTRODUCTION TO PART ONE

As this volume is being written, the legal profession is undergoing a significant transformation. Thus, the author has the challenge of either writing about the past nature of legal practice—the one that roughly correlates with the pop culture view of lawyering as presented in television and films—or a future legal industry where the only certainty is a significant break from the past and a large influx of professionals who are not formally trained as lawyers.

As a middle ground, this chapter relies upon social science research and other sources of data to describe the composition of the legal profession as it has existed over the last full generation of lawyers. Next, the chapter discusses the problem of lagging legal productivity, which appears to be the primary driver for the structural changes we are witnessing. Finally, the chapter turns to the future and focuses on the emergence of a new and more complex legal industry that is growing up within and around the traditional legal profession. To effectively meet the legal needs of clients and broader society, lawyers will be collaborating with a wide range of professionals from other disciplines. This process is likely to alter what it means to be a lawyer, as one-on-one client counseling and courtroom advocacy will become a smaller part of how law school graduates earn their living.

### RECOMMENDED CITATION FOR PART ONE

For those citing to Chapters 1-1 through 1-3 in Part One, we recommend attribution to this individually-authored part as being most accurate. For example, the most appropriate citation format to the first section in this part would look like this: William D. Henderson, The Legal Profession and Legal Services: Nature and Evolution § 1-1.1, in *Legal Ethics, Professional Responsibility, and the Legal Profession* (West Academic Publishing, 2018).

# Chapter 1-1

# THE STRUCTURE OF THE LEGAL PROFESSION

## By William D. Henderson

*Table of Sections*

§ 1-1.1 The Two-Hemispheres of Law Practice
§ 1-1.2 How the Segments Have Changed over Time
§ 1-1.3 Challenges of Law Practice Serving People

## § 1-1.1 THE TWO HEMISPHERES OF LAW PRACTICE

Two of the most important and informative studies of the legal profession were conducted by scholars affiliated with the American Bar Foundation (ABF) and are commonly referred to as the Chicago Lawyers I and II studies.[1] Chicago Lawyers I was based on the randomized sample of approximately 800 Chicago lawyers drawn in the year 1975. One of the study's most salient findings was that the legal profession had functionally divided into two "hemispheres," one serving individuals and small businesses and the other working for large organizational clients such as corporations. Which hemisphere a lawyer served turned out to be a remarkably strong proxy for the lawyer's income, home zip code, law school attended, ethnicity, religion, and bar association and social club memberships. The researchers described these two groups as hemispheres not only because each composed roughly half the profession, but also because their professional interests and networks seldom overlapped. "Only in the most formal of senses," Heinz and Laumann said, "do the two types of lawyers constitute one profession."[2]

In 1995, the same core researchers conducted Chicago Lawyers II, which substantially replicated the original study based on a new sample of roughly 800 Chicago lawyers. Over the intervening two decades, the portion of the bar serving organizational clients had expanded dramatically due to the growing legal needs of corporate clients. The term "hemisphere," as in half, was longer accurate description, as the amount of time that lawyers devoted to organizational clients had increased to double that spent on personal and small-business clients.

This change in time allocation and professional focus corresponded with changes in law firm structure and pay. Between 1975 and 1995, the typical Chicago law firm increased in size from 27 to 141 lawyers. Further, large law firms comprised a growing segment of the Chicago bar. In 1975, roughly 5 percent of Chicago lawyers began their

---

1 JOHN P. HEINZ & EDWARD O. LAUMANN, CHICAGO LAWYERS: THE SOCIAL STRUCTURE OF THE BAR (Rev. Ed. 1994) ("Chicago Lawyers I"); JOHN P. HEINZ ET AL., URBAN LAWYERS: THE NEW SOCIAL STRUCTURE OF THE BAR 6–7 (2005) ("Chicago Lawyers II").

2 HEINZ ET AL., *supra* note 1, at 29.

careers in firms of 100 or more lawyers. By 1995, that figure had increased to 19 percent.[3] Not surprisingly, the compensation of large firm associates and partners increased dramatically during this period. After adjusting for inflation, the average income of lawyers in Chicago's largest law firms grew from $144,985 in 1975 to $271,706 in 1995. The median incomes in all other practice settings, with the exception of in-house counsel, remained flat or declined.

In the Chicago Lawyers II study, the most economically challenged group of lawyers were solo practitioners, who disproportionately serve individuals through personal injury, family law, criminal defense, and trusts-and-estates work. In 1975, the median income of a solo practitioner in the Chicago sample was $99,159 (in 1995 dollars). By 1995, this figure had plummeted to $55,000. Further, 32 percent of the solo practitioners were working a second job in 1995 compared with only 2 percent in 1975. These figures are bleak and suggest that a substantial portion of the bar is under considerable stress. Professor Benjamin Barton recently compiled statistics on the income of solo practitioners and, drawing upon IRS records, found that average income for this group was only $46,560 in 2010, reflecting a decline in real income of 37 percent since the mid-1980s.[4]

## § 1-1.2 HOW THE SEGMENTS HAVE CHANGED OVER TIME

The two-hemisphere framework is a very useful lens to understand the changes that are occurring within the legal profession and the broader legal industry. Every five years, the U.S. Census Bureau's Economic Census conducts a detailed survey of U.S. employers called the Economic Census that breaks down the nation's economic activity along several dimensions. For the last two data collection cycles (in 2007 and 2012), the analysis has tabulated total receipts for businesses providing legal services based on class of customer. Drawing upon these data, **Figure 1** below compares total spending on legal services in 2007 and 2012 based on whether the client was an individual versus a business:

---

[3] We know from other data sources that by 2008, nearly one of four law school graduates would begin their careers working in law firms with 100 or more lawyers. *See* NALP, Trends in Graduate Employment (1985–2008), online at https://www.nalp.org/july09trendsgradempl (last visited Nov. 10, 2017) (calculated based on percentage of gradates working in firms and, within that group, percentage of grads working in firms of 100 or more lawyers). Due to its rapid growth and high salary, this sector came to be known as "BigLaw."

[4] *See* BENJAMIN H. BARTON, GLASS HALF FULL: THE DECLINE AND REBIRTH OF THE LEGAL PROFESSION 15 (2010).

**Figure 1. Dollars Spent on Legal Services, 2007 and 2012, by Type of Client**

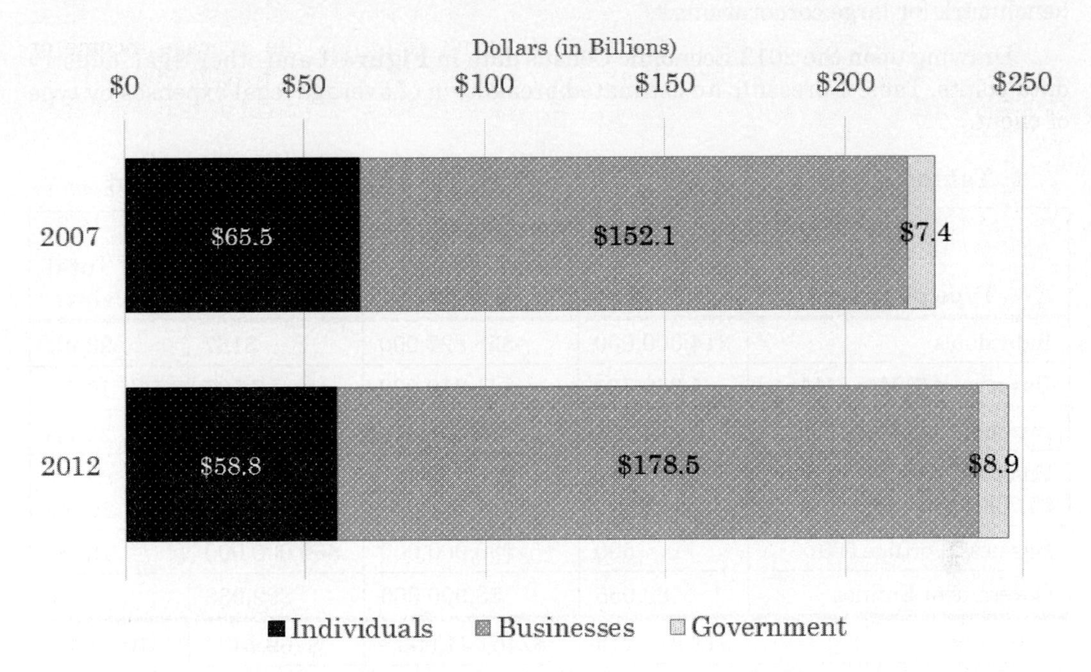


The most striking feature of **Figure 1** is that over a relatively short five-year span, the total dollar amount for legal services allocated to individual clients declined by nearly $7 billion. During the same time, the amount allocated to private sector organizational clients increased by more than $26 billion. Although these trend lines can be viewed as an extension of the findings for the Chicago Lawyers I and II studies, the actual *shrinkage* of the individual legal sectors market suggests that the legal profession is in the midst of a structural shift that is destined to challenge, and eventually change, popular perceptions about the nature of legal work and how lawyers and other legal professionals earn a living.

The divergent economic challenges facing the individual versus the organizational hemisphere is made more concrete by calculating the average legal spending based on type of client. According to U.S. Census Bureau statistics, in 2012, law firms collected $246.1 billion in revenues,[5] of which 23.9% was allocated to individual clients. In 2012, the U.S. population was 314 million people, which translates into $187 legal budget per year, which is less than the value of one hour of a U.S. lawyer's time.[6] In contrast, 72.5% of all law firm receipts came from private sector organizational clients.[7] According to the Statistics of US Business (SUSB), in 2012 there were 5.7 million U.S. businesses,[8] which translates to $31,315 per year per organization on legal expenses. This equates to 0.55%

[5] The U.S. government classifies businesses using the North American Industrial Classification System (NAICS). Law firms are classified as NAICS 541110, Offices of Lawyers.

[6] According to a report published by Clio, a widely adopted cloud-based matter management and billing software for solo and small firm practitioners, the average hourly rate for a U.S. lawyer in May 2017 was $260. In 2012, the figure was approximately $220. *See* 2017 CLIO LEGAL TRENDS REPORT 29 (2017), available online at https://www.clio.com/2017-legal-trends-report/#download.

[7] This figure combines both for-profit (70.8%) and non-profit (1.7%) organizations.

[8] *See* 2012 SUSB Annual Data Tables by Establishment Industry, online at https://www.census.gov/data/tables/2012/econ/susb/2012-susb-annual.html.

of total business receipts, which is a significantly higher percentage than 0.3% benchmark for large corporations.[9]

Drawing upon the 2012 Economic Census data in **Figure 1** and other legal industry data points, Table 1 presents an estimated breakdown of average legal expenses by type of client.

**Table 1—Breakdown of 2012 Law Firms Receipts by Type of Client**

| Type of Client | Number | Total Receipts for Legal Services | Avg. Payment per Client | % of Total Receipts |
|---|---|---|---|---|
| Individuals | 314,000,000 | $58,827,000 | $187 | 23.9% |
| Business: < $1M to $5M | 5,359,731 | $41,310,000 | $7,707 | 16.8% |
| Business: < 5M to $100M | 344,037 | $65,604,000 | $774,910 | 26.7% |
| Business: < 100M to $4.75B | 21,892 | $41,500,000 | $1,895,670 | 16.9% |
| Business: Fortune 500 | 500 | $30,000,000 | $60,000,000 | 12.2% |
| Government Entities | 89,055 | $8,900,000 | $99,938 | 3.6% |
| | 319,815,215 | $246,141,000 | $769.64 | 100.0% |

**Source:** Data from US Census Bureau with calculations done by Legal Evolution PBC

The data in **Table 1** suggest that serving individuals and small business clients, who need lawyers only occasionally and have limited means to pay them (rows one and two above), will require a significantly different business model than law firms that service large corporate clients.

## § 1-1.3 CHALLENGES OF LAW PRACTICE SERVING PEOPLE

A 2017 study by Clio, a technology company that provides cloud-based matter management and time-keeping software for primarily solo and small firms, provides a window on the challenges of running a "main street" law practice. The study sample, which was based on timekeepers from 60,000 law firms billing over 10 million hours of time in 2016 totaling more the $2.56 billion, showed that the typical lawyer was performing approximately 2.3 hours of legal work per day. Of that amount, only 82% was actually billed to clients; and of the amount billed, only 86% was being collected—the equivalent of 1.6 hours. At $250 per hour, this amounts to a mere $400 a day. Of the remaining six hours left in the work day, 33% was focused on business development and 48% on administrative tasks, such as generating and sending bills, configuring technology, and collections.[10] These are bleak statistics.

The average matter in the Clio system was worth approximately $2,500.[11] To build a financially successful law practice based on high-volume, low-stakes matters likely

[9] *See* William Henderson & Evan Parker, *Your Firm's Place in the Legal Market*, AMERICAN LAWYER (Dec. 2015) at 104 (reporting 0.3% of revenues were allocated to external spend (i.e., law firms) based upon a sample of 2,500 large corporate clients over multiple industries from 2010 to 2015).

[10] *See* Clio, *supra* note 6, at 13.

[11] *See id.* at 8 (calculated from total dollars billed (~$2.56 billion) divided by number of matters (1.03 million matters)).

requires a large investment in marketing and technology along with significant business acumen and managerial ability—resources and skills sets that few lawyers possess. Yet, under the ethics rule promulgated by the American Bar Association, lawyers must be the exclusive owners of any business that engages in the practice of law.[12] This regulatory constraint, which exists in some form in all 50 states, may be the primary reason why the segment of the bar serving individuals has entered a period of decline.

Ironically, as the work of lawyers tilts more toward business clientele with the significant financial resources to pay legal fees, many of the largest clients—with legal budgets of tens of millions dollars per year—are seeking ways to control their legal expenses. This pressure is building because of the sheer complexity of the highly regulated and interconnected global economy. Although this pressure is experienced by lawyers and their clients as a problem of cost, the root cause is likely the problem of lagging legal productivity.

---

[12] *See* MODEL RULES OF PROF'L CONDUCT R. 5.4(d) (American Bar Ass'n, 2016) [hereafter "MODEL RULE 5.4"] ("(d) A lawyer shall not practice with or in the form of a professional corporation or association authorized to practice law for a profit, if: (1) a nonlawyer owns any interest therein . . . .).

# Chapter 1-2

# THE PROBLEM OF LAGGING LEGAL PRODUCTIVITY

**By William D. Henderson**

*Table of Sections*

§ 1-2.1 Cost Disease

## § 1-2.1 COST DISEASE

One of the most distinguishing features of modern society is quantum leaps forward in technology that consistently produce better and less expensive goods. Yet, the same productivity gains are seldom present for activities that are highly labor intensive, such as education, healthcare, or legal services. The impact of differential rates of productivity gain has the effect of making labor-intensive services, in relative sense, more expensive.

The author offers the following real-world example, which he often shares with legal audiences to illustrate the conundrum. Between 1997 and 2014, the author bought three new cars—a 1997 minivan, a 2003 sedan, and a 2014 sedan. Each vehicle corresponded to a new phase in his life: the starting of family, the need for a second car to accommodate a two-income household, and the need for a third car his a teenage daughter received upon getting her driver's license. Among the three cars, the 2014 model was arguably the best, as it received the highest ratings from Consumer Reports. What do all three of these cars have in common? Remarkably, despite being separated by 17 years, they all cost $23,000. Yet, during this time period, the author, who earned his living in the government, legal, and education sectors, experienced a four-fold increase in earnings. Effectively, the vast majority of the productivity gains of the automotive industry were reaped not by the autoworkers or the automakers, but by consumers, including those of us working in sectors that underwent little or no productivity growth.

This phenomenon is what economists refer to a "cost disease." It was first noted by the economists William Baumon and William Bowen in a book about the economics of the performing arts, observing, "Human ingenuity has devised ways to reduce the labor necessary to produce an automobile, but no one has yet succeeded in decreasing the human effort expended at a live performance of a 45 minute Schubert quartet much below a total of three man-hours."[1] Despite this constraint on productivity, Baumon and Bowen observed that the wages of musicians continue to rise.

The primary effect of cost disease is that relative prices in labor-intensive activities goes up, particularly if the labor must be performed by highly skilled and educated professionals. This undoubtedly includes fields like medicine, education, and law. Yet, the pressures of cost disease can also result in waning demand for a labor-intensive service, or alternatively, a vigorous search for cost-effective substitutes. In the legal

[1] WILLIAM J. BAUMOL & WILLIAM G. BOWEN, PERFORMING ARTS: THE ECONOMIC DILEMMA 164 (1966).

marketplace circa 2017, we see evidence of all three responses, the impact of which varies dramatically based upon the type of client.

### § 1-2.1(a) Higher Profits for Those Servicing Large Organizational Clients

Since the mid 1980s, the American Lawyer has chronicled the financial performance of the nation's largest law firms in ordinal ranking based on total gross revenues and profits. In 2012, on the 25th anniversary of the "AmLaw 100," the following statistics described the changes that had occurred among the nation's 100 largest law firms:

- Total gross revenues increased from $7.2 billion to $71.0 billion (+886%)
- Total lawyer headcounts went from 26,000 to 86,272 (+231% rise).
- Average profits per partner (PPP) of an Am Law 100 firm grew from $325,000 to $1.48 million (+355%).

During this same time period, the Consumer Price Index climbed a 205% while the GDP increased 235%. Although the overall pie of the U.S. economy was growing, the nation's largest law firms have been getting a proportionately larger slice.[2]

In more recent years, large law firm profitability has continued to climb.[3] Based on 2016 fiscal year, the average profits per partner at an AmLaw 100 firm reached $1.66 million, up 3% from 2015.[4] Although profits remain high, the overall demand for corporate legal services, as measured by lawyer hours in major law firms, has been relatively flat for the last several years.[5] This flat demand is occurring because large corporate clients have been seeking out alternatives to the traditional large law firms.

### § 1-2.1(b) Organizational Clients Searching for Substitutes to Traditional Law Firms

Somewhat ironically, the biggest source of competition are clients themselves through the growth of in-house corporate legal departments.[6] As shown in the Figure 2 below, since 1997, when the U.S. Bureau of Labor Statistics began tracking these data, the number of lawyers working directly for businesses has increased 7.5 faster than lawyers working for private law firms. In 1997, approximately 35,000 lawyers were working in-house; by 2016, this figure reached more 105,000, which is more lawyers than currently work in the domestic offices of the nation's 200 largest law firms.[7] Indeed, since

---

[2] *See* William D. Henderson, *AmLaw 100 at 25*, AMERICAN LAWYER (June 2012).

[3] *See* Casey Sullivan, *How Partner Profits Have Changed Over 10 Years*, BLOOMBERG BIGLAW BUSINESS, Aug. 18, 2016, online at https://biglawbusiness.com/how-partner-profits-have-changed-over-10-years/.

[4] *See* David Lat, *The 2017 Am Law 100: A Turning Point for BigLaw?*, ABOVE THE LAW, Apr. 27, 2017, online at https://abovethelaw.com/2017/04/the-2017-am-law-100-a-turning-point-for-biglaw/.

[5] *See* James W. Jones, et al., 2017 Report on the State of the Legal Market (Georgetown Law, Center for the Study of the Legal Profession 2017) ("Overall, the past decade has been a period of stagnation in demand growth for law firm services, decline in productivity for most categories of lawyers, growing pressure on rates as reflected in declining realization, and declining profit margins.").

[6] *See, e.g.*, Jacob Gershman, *Law Firms Face New Competition—Their Own Clients*, WSJ LAW BLOG, Sept. 15, 2014, online at https://blogs.wsj.com/law/2014/09/15/law-firms-face-new-competition-their-own-clients/.

[7] *See* William D. Henderson, *The Paradox of the Client-Driven Market*, NATIONAL LAW JOURNAL, Oct. 4, 2017 (presenting statistics on the growth of in-house lawyers), online at http://www.law.com/sites/almstaff/2017/10/04/the-paradox-of-the-client-driven-market/.

2005, the number of lawyers employed in federal, state, and local government has been growing at a faster rate that of lawyers working in private law firms—both groups have increased by approximately 26,000 employed lawyers, despite the government sector starting at a much lower base (105,000 versus 355,000).

**Figure 2. Percentage Change in Number of Employed Lawyers by Practice Setting, 1997–2016**

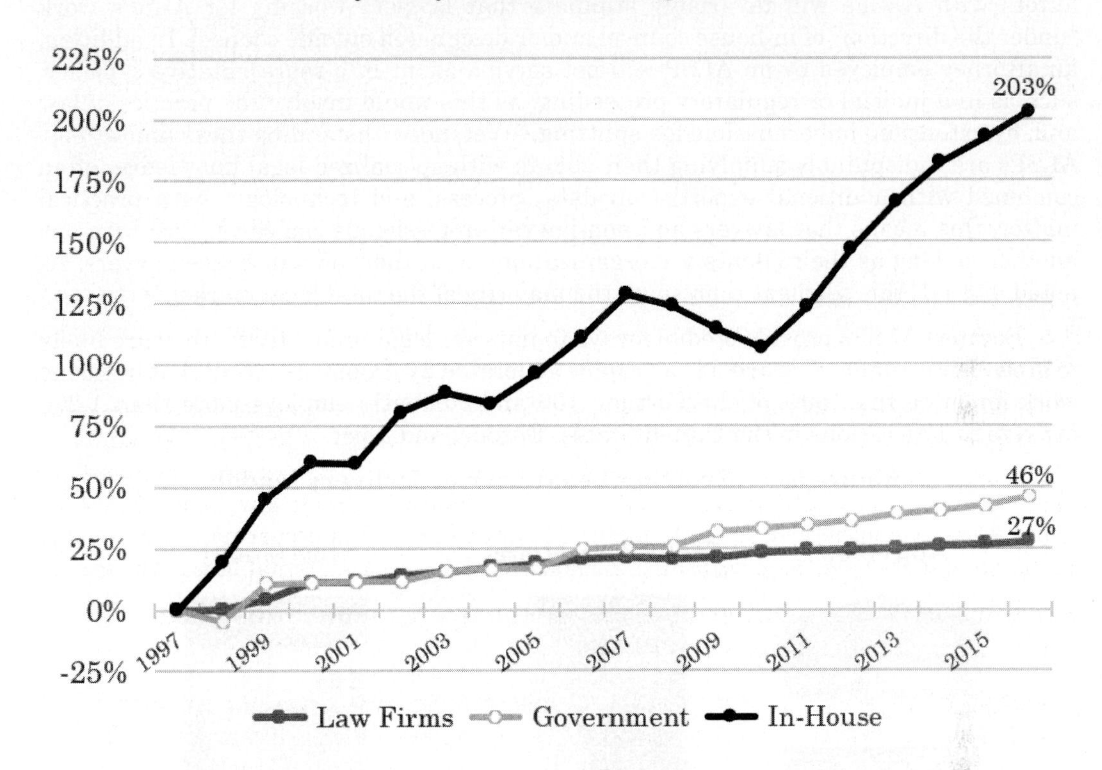


**Source:** Data from U.S. Bureau of Labor Statistics, calculations by Legal Evolution PBC

A second source of competition for traditional law firms are alternative legal service providers (ALSP), which includes companies such as Axiom, UnitedLex, Integreon, QuisLex, Pangea3 (now part of Thomson Reuters, Elevate, and many others). In most cases, these are private corporations run by a mix of lawyers and business executives and financed by non-lawyer investors, including some of the nation's most prominent venture capital and private equity funds.[8] This movement began in the mid-2000s with legal process outsourcers who specialized in large document review projects connected with the proliferation of electronically stored information (ESI). Yet, it now extends to tranches of legal work connected with sophisticated corporate transactions. In each case, the legal work is performed by lawyers who are employees of a corporation, though the corporation itself is funded and controlled by outside non-legal investors.

[8] For an in-depth discussion of this topic, see William D. Henderson, *Efficiency Engines: How Managed Services are Building Systems for Corporate Legal Work*, ABA JOURNAL, June 2017, at 38.

The prior section of this chapter discussed the legal profession's prohibition on non-lawyers having an equity interest in a business engaged in the practice of law.[9] How can this be reconciled, then, with the growth of ALSPs? Basically, ALSPs serve organizational clients in which a lawyer in the client legal department, or lawyer in a law firm, is responsible for supervising the legal work of the ALSPs, including oversight sufficient to ensure compliance with applicable legal ethics rules.[10] Thus, engagement letters with ALSPs will invariably stipulate that lawyers working for ALSPs work "under the direction" of in-house counsel and/or designated outside counsel. In addition, an attorney employed by an ALSP will not serve a client in a representative capacity, such as in a judicial or regulatory proceeding, as this would involve the practice of law and, by extension, impermissible fee-splitting.[11] Yet, notwithstanding these limitations, ALSPs are indisputably supplying their clients with specialized legal knowledge, often combined with additional expertise in data, process, and technology. As a practical matter, this means that lawyers and non-lawyer professionals can co-venture with one another as long as their clients are organizations with their own in-house lawyers. As noted in § 1-1, this segment represents the majority of the total legal market.[12]

Because ALSPs provide credible ways to improve legal productivity, they are likely to grow. For example, **Figure 3** is a graphic generated by Axiom, an ALSP that has done work for more than 50% of the Fortune 100 and currently employs more than 1,200 lawyers in 17 locations in the United States, Europe, and Asia.

**Figure 3. Evolving Legal Service Delivery Model**

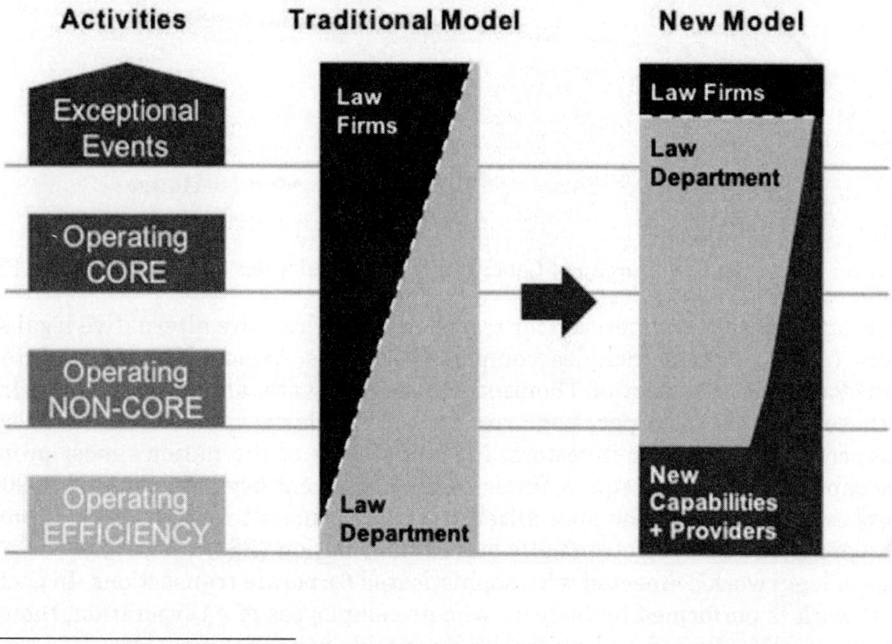

[9] *See* § 1-1.3 & note 12, *supra*, and accompanying text.

[10] *See* Henderson, *Efficiency Engines*, *supra* note 8 at 40 (noting that managed service provides are "attorney-to-attorney businesses" where the attorneys who perform the work "work under the direction of in-house counsel or outside legal counsels").

[11] *See* MODEL RULE 5.4 ("(d) A lawyer shall not practice with or in the form of a professional corporation or association authorized to practice law for a profit, if: (1) a nonlawyer owns any interest therein . . .").

[12] *See id.* at 40 ("The addressable market for [ALSPs] is the same market pursued by the AmLaw 200").

This graphic is used by Axiom professionals to explain the changing legal market to current and prospective clients. Its core message is that the legal work of large corporate clients is segmented into four categories, with ALSPs being dominant in the operating efficiency segment but also playing a role in the other three categories. In contrast, under the New Model, law firms are limited to the exceptional events segment.

Although readers might discount **Figure 3** as an aspirational sales tools of an ambitious company, at least some sophisticated corporate clients view the legal market in essentially identical terms. **Figure 4** is a depiction of how the head of outside counsel management at the mega-retailer Walmart views the past, present, and future of the litigation work he is charged with managing.[13]

**Figure 4. Allocation of Litigation Work Based on Complexity and Risk Factors**

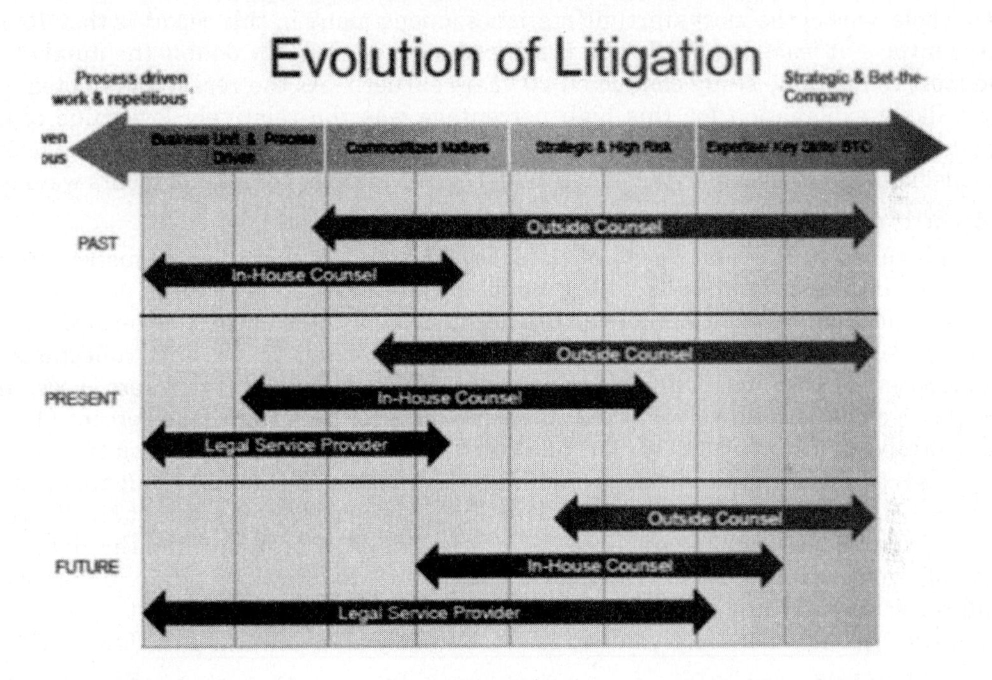


The steady growth and influence of ALSPs is one of the main reasons that the lexicon on law has subtly shifted from discussions of the legal profession to a dialogue on the changing legal industry. Noted one investment banker who has experience funding legal technology and service companies, "If law firms themselves can't have outside investors, the market will continue to chip away at every part of a law firm that is not the pure provision of legal advice. . . . Anything that can be provided legally by a third party will be."[14]

---

[13] *See* Bill Henderson, *Generalizing About Clients (013)*, LEGAL EVOLUTION, July 6, 2017 (presenting chart generated by Alan Bryan, Senior Associate GC of Legal Operations and Outside Counsel Management), online at https://www.legalevolution.org/2017/07/generalizing-about-clients-013/.

[14] *See* Barbara Rose, *Law, the Investment*, ABA JOURNAL (Sept. 2010) (quoting Nick Baughan of Marks Baughan & Co.).

### § 1-2.1(c) Waning Demand Among Individual Clients

At the same time that sophisticated organizational clients are responding to rising legal costs by searching out substitutes to traditional law practice, a growing proportion of ordinary citizens are entering the civil justice system without being represented by a lawyer.

This disturbing trend was recently documented in a major study conducted by the National Center for State Courts (NCSC).[15] The study was based on all civil matters in ten large urban counties that were disposed in those counties over a one-year period.[16] Collectively, this amounted to 925,344 cases, or approximately 5% of the total civil case load nationally. Because there is a wide range of organizational structures among the 50 states, the sample was designed to include a mix of general jurisdiction, limited jurisdiction, and single-tier systems, thus making it roughly representative of the nation as a whole. One of the most startling statistics among many in this report is that 76% of cases involve at least one party who is self-represented, roughly double the number for the most comparable study conducted 20 years earlier.[17] As the researchers noted, the most likely explanation for this high percentage was the relatively low value of the underlying claim. Of the 227,812 cases that resulted in a non-zero monetary judgment, the median value was a mere $2,441. Further, three-quarters of all judgments were less than $5,100.

A breakdown of cases by type of claim revealed a picture of the civil justice system that was dramatically at odds with a public debate that tends to focus on large jury awards and high-stakes commercial litigation. For example, nearly two-thirds of all cases (64%) were contract cases, with over half involving either debt collections or landlord/tenant disputes. Only seven percent (7%) of the sample were tort cases, and only one percent (1%) involved a real property dispute. Less than four percent (4%) of cases involved an adjudicated resolution, with bench trials (31,015) vastly outnumbering jury trials (1,109). Further, large awards were very rare, with only 357 judgments more than $500,000 and only 165 more than $1 million. The report cited a recent NCSC study that calculated the median cost per side of litigating a case, from filing through trial, ranging from $43,000 for an automobile tort case to $122,000 for a professional malpractice case. Thus, the authors concluded, "in many cases, the cost of litigation likely outstrips the monetary value of the case shortly after initiating the lawsuit."[18]

The present reality is a strange one. In 2013, litigants filed nearly 17 million civil cases in state courts compared to roughly 260,000 in U.S. District Courts.[19] Yet, the organized bar, through various state and federal organizations, does not appear to be mobilizing itself to address the large and growing problem of ordinary citizens being forced to fend for themselves in state court disputes. Instead, we observe individual

---

[15] *See* PAULA HANNAFORD-AGOR JD, SCOTT GRAVES & SHELLEY SPACEK MILLER, THE LANDSCAPE OF CIVIL LITIGATION IN STATE COURTS (National Center for State Courts 2015) [hereafter "LANDSCAPE STUDY"] (building sample based on the July 1, 2012 to June 30, 2013 time period).

[16] The counties were Maricopa County (Phoenix, AZ), Santa Clara County (San Jose, CA), Miami-Dade County (Miami, FL), Oahu County (Honolulu, HI), Cook County (Chicago, IL), Marion County (Indianapolis, IN), Bergen County (Hackensack, NJ), Cuyahoga County (Cleveland, OH), Allegheny County (Pittsburgh, PA), Harris County (Houston, TX).

[17] *See* LANDSCAPE STUDY, *supra* note 15, at 31.

[18] *See* LANDSCAPE STUDY, *supra* note 15, at 25, citing Paula L. Hannaford-Agor & Nicole L. Waters, *Estimating the Cost of Civil Litigation*, 20(1) CASELOAD HIGHLIGHTS 1, 2013.

[19] *See* NCSC COURT STATISTICS PROJECT, EXAMINING THE WORK OF STATE COURTS, 2013 (2015).

lawyers are trying to earn a living from the shrinking pool of clients that can bear the full cost of a lawyer's services—and often without much success.[20] Is there a point in the future when the organized bar will assert itself as voice of a self-regulating profession? At present, that voice is absent, to the detriment of not only lawyers, but the ordinary citizens and our political institutions.

### § 1-2.1(d) Impact of Legal Economy on Law School Enrollments

In recent years, the perception of law as a secure and stable career path has changed dramatically, due at least in part to negative media coverage of law school graduates with high debt loads struggling to find entry-level employment.[21] This in turn has dramatically affected law school enrollments. As shown in **Figure 5**, the number of law school graduates has tumbled from a high-water mark of 46,776 in 2013 to a projected 33,658 in 2019—28 percent drop over six years.

**Figure 5. Number of Law Graduates from ABA-Accredited Law Schools, 1973 to 2019**

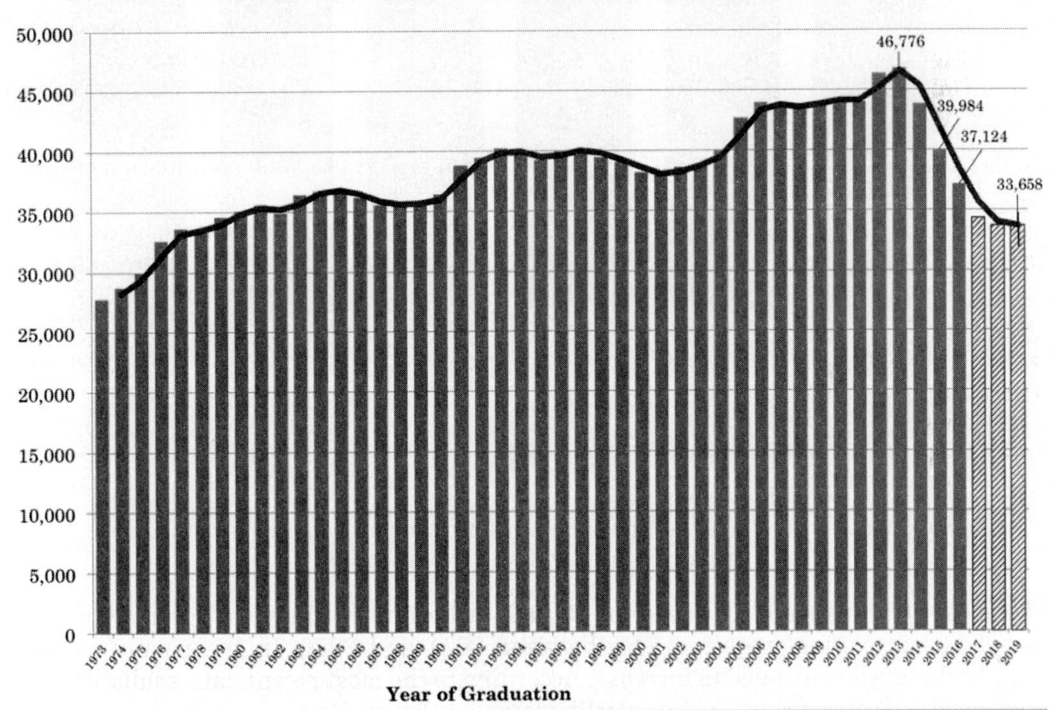


**Source:** Data from ABA Section of Legal Education and Admissions to the Bar; graph generated by Legal Evolution PBC

---

[20] *See* § 1-1.3 & notes 10–11 and accompanying text (discussing solo and small firm lawyers struggling to find paid legal work).

[21] *See, e.g.*, Noam Schieber, *An Expensive Law Degree, and No Place to Use It*, N.Y. TIMES, June 19, 2016, at BU1. Editorial Board, *The Law School Debt Crisis*, N.Y. TIMES, Oct. 25, 2015, at SR8; Steven Harper, Too Many Law Students, Too Few Legal Jobs, N.Y. TIMES, Aug. 25, 2015, at A19; Joe Palazzolo, *Law Grads Face a Brutal Job Market*, WALL ST. J., June 25, 2012; Nathan Koppel, *Bar Raised for Law-Grad Jobs*, WALL ST. J., May 5, 2010.

Current law school enrollments are now at a 40-year low. Although the drop in enrollments began in the fall of 2010 when the largest law firms cut their entry-level hiring in response to the 2008–09 financial crisis, there is reason to believe that change in hiring is permanent rather than cyclical. **Figure 6** summaries the number of full-time / long-term entry-level jobs taken by law school graduates that were either bar passage required or in which the JD is considered an advantage (e.g., regulatory compliance, management consulting, investment banking business, etc.).

**Figure 6. Bar Passage Required and JD Advantage Jobs, Full-Time / Long-Term, 2011 to 2016**

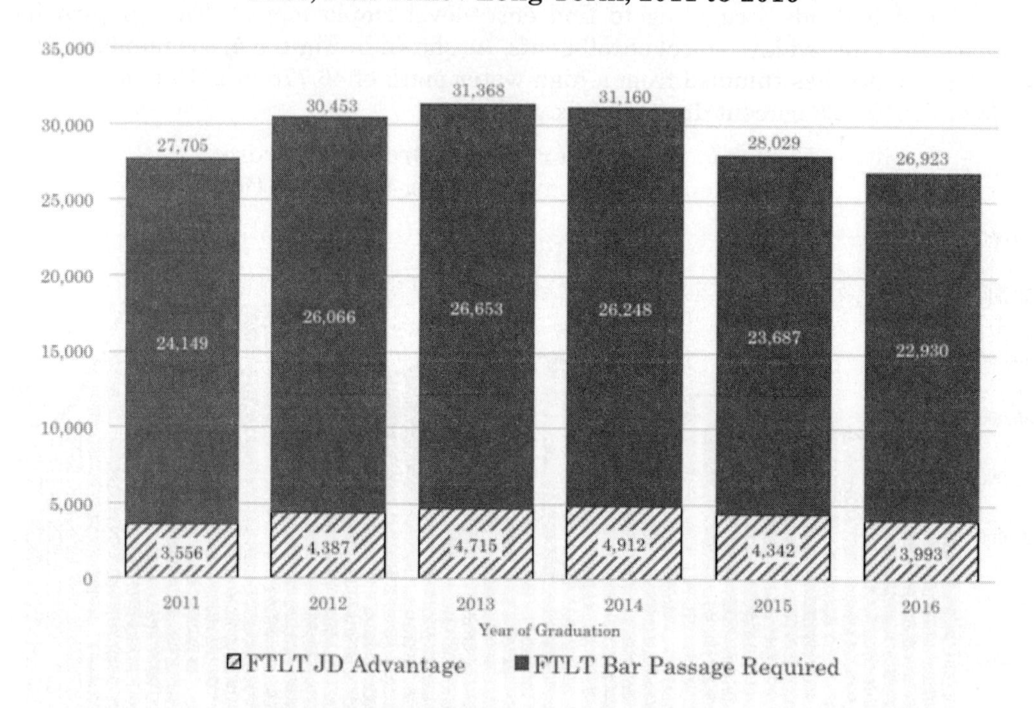


**Source:** Data from ABA Section of Legal Education and Admissions to the Bar; graph generated by Legal Evolution PBC

The most striking trend in these job data is a decline in the total number of jobs, including bar passage-required jobs, between 2011 and 2016. In the meantime, law school debt levels continued to increase. According to the most recent data available from Law School Transparency, a non-profit watchdog group that monitors the cost and employment outcomes of law school graduates, the average level of debt of a 2010 graduate was $100,346. Despite a period of intense competition for students that involved significant tuition discounting in the form of scholarships, the average debt load for the class of 2015 increased to $118,741.[22]

An important question to ask is whether other types of professional schools are experiencing similar turmoil. Figure 7 compares the number of administrations of the LSAT to the administrations of the GMAT, which is the admission test required to be admitted into most MBA programs. It appears that the attractions of these two

[22] *See* Law School Transparency, Law School Financing, online at https://www.lawschooltransparency.com/reform/projects/Law-School-Financing/.

professional degrees are closely correlated. Further, both appear to be on a similar downward slide. In contrast, as shown in Figure 8, the number of applications to law schools are moving in the opposite direction of applications to medical schools.

**Figure 7. GMAT Versus LSAT Administrations, 2004 to 2016**

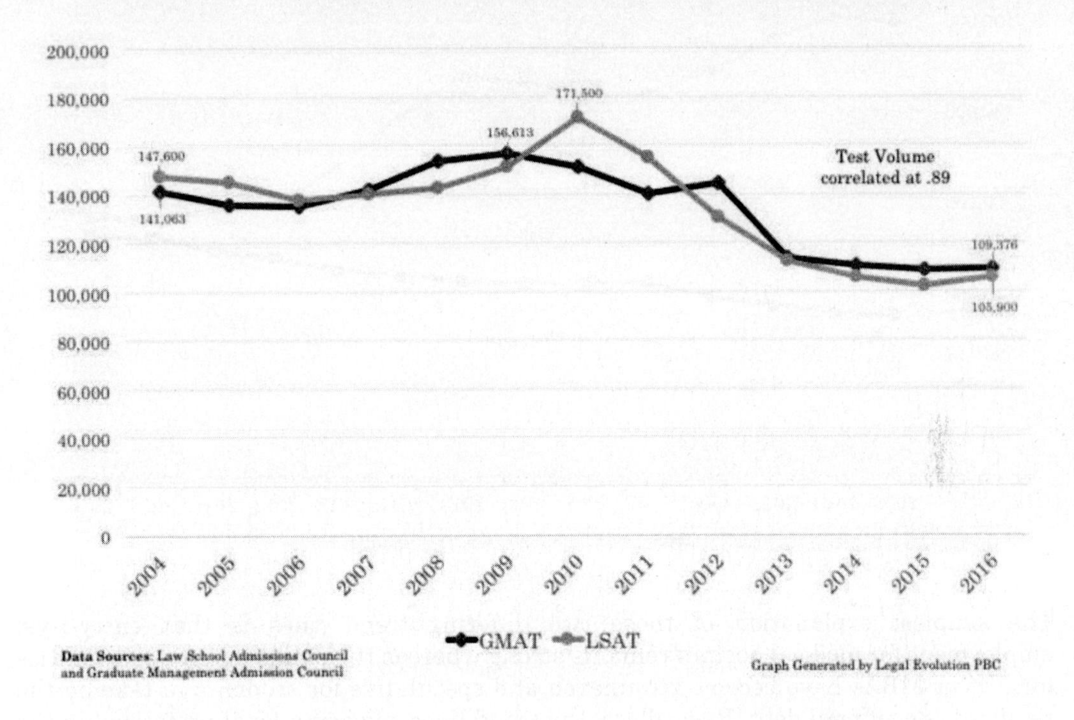

**Figure 8. Applicants to Law School Versus Medical School, 2003 to 2016**

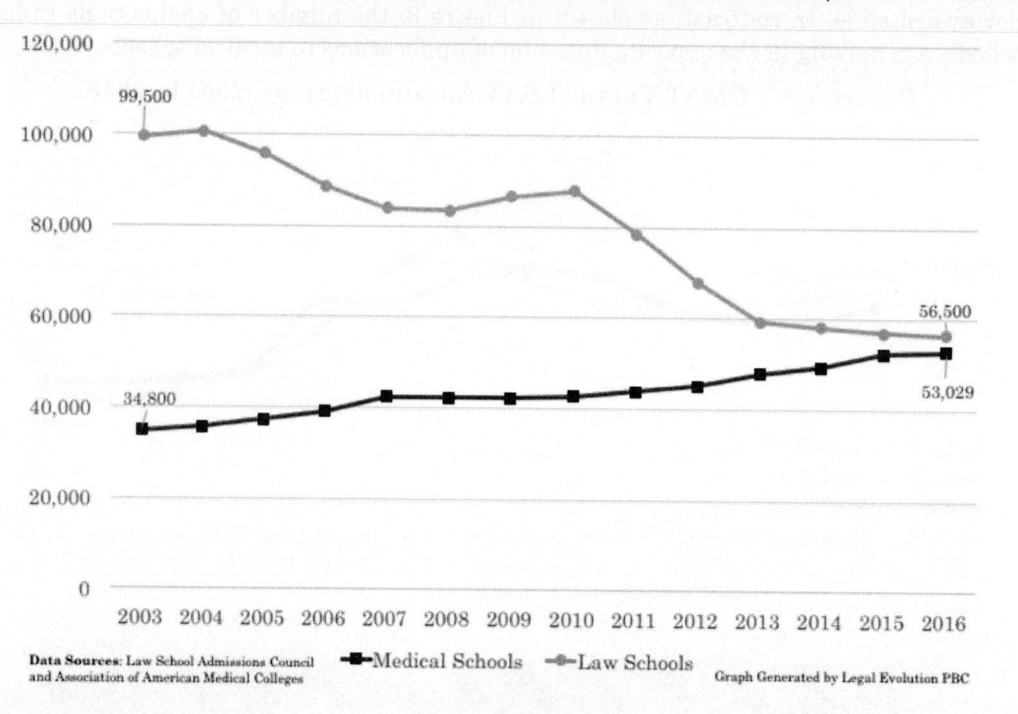


The simplest explanation of these two differing trend lines is that entry-level employment for medical doctors remains strong whereas the employment opportunities for JDs or MBAs have become too uneven and speculative for students to take on the required educational debt. Regardless, the trend lines suggest a legal profession in the midst of a major upheaval.

# Chapter 1-3

# THE FUTURE OF THE LEGAL PROFESSION

## By William D. Henderson

*Table of Sections*

§ 1-3.1 A Structural Shift

## § 1-3.1 A STRUCTURAL SHIFT

As documented in the prior two sub-chapters, the U.S. legal services market appears to be in the midst of a profound structural transformation, which in turn is reshaping the careers and livelihood of practicing lawyers. What is driving this change? As this chapter is being written, there is very little consensus.[1] Further, these is paucity of a vigorous dialogue taken up by the profession's traditional leaders, such as managing partners of major law firms, law school deans, or members of the state and federal judiciary. For the most part, the profession appears to be in a reactive mode, reluctant to carefully examine the viability and functioning of institutions that have provided economic security, privilege, and prestige to its members for several generations. Particularly for leaders, it is difficult to ask questions about difficult problems if you are unable to provide convincing answers that point to realistic solutions.

Regarding this reticence, Professor Richard Susskind would go so far as it to call it "denial," the first stage in a three-part change process.[2] In the second stage, which Susskind claims is now beginning and is likely to last for a decade or perhaps longer, the traditional work of lawyers will be redesigned and "re-sourced" in order to capture gains in quality, efficiency, and timeliness of delivery. Often these changes will be premised on the deployment of lower cost labor in combination with sophisticated technology. In the third state, the legal field enters a period of "disruption" based on advances of technology that substantially replace large tranches of work traditionally performed by lawyers.

---

1 Although there is not consensus on this issue, the leading commentator is the British lawyer, consultant, professor, and futurist Richard Susskind. *See, e.g.*, RICHARD SUSSKIND, TOMORROW'S LAWYERS: AN INTRODUCTION TO YOUR FUTURE (2nd ed. 2017).

2 *See id.* at 86.

**Figure 9. Susskind's Three Stages of Change**

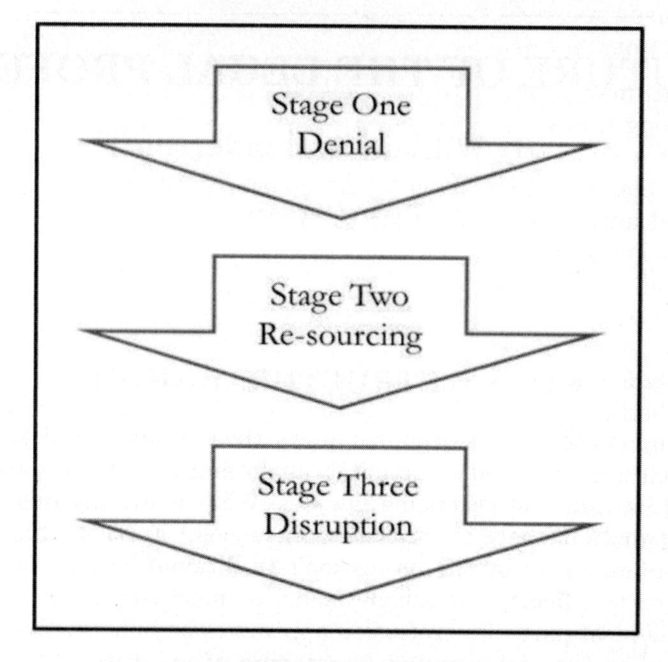


**Source:** Richard Susskind, Tomorrow's Lawyers (2nd ed. 2017) Fig. 8.1

Although Susskind is likely right that the work of lawyers is headed into a period of long-term disruption, readers of a book on the legal profession (lawyers, law students, and legal educators) are likely faced with the immediate practical problem of understanding the challenges of the current legal economy and, from there, formulating an effective strategy to adapt.

Based on the data and analysis presented in the earlier sections, the author offers two potentially helpful observations. First, notwithstanding the turmoil in the entry-level legal job market and the financial challenges of solo and small firm practice, modern civilization's future depends upon well-functioning and inclusive institutions for solving legal problems. It is hard to overstate the importance of legal knowledge, training, and experience to the period we are entering. Second, the retooling of old institutions, or the construction of new ones, will require those with legal skill and knowledge to work collaboratively with professionals from other disciplines, such as system engineers, technologists, industrial designers, process and operations experts, data scientists, marketers, financials, and behavioral and organizational psychologists. In short, the centrality of lawyer as advocate and counselor is destined to shrink.

### § 1-3.1(a) The Future of Dispute Resolution for Individuals

As noted earlier, the surge in self-represented litigants in state courts is due to a mismatch between the value of the claims being made and the cost of traditional adversarial proceedings.[3] Closing this gap requires new methods of dispute resolution

---

[3] *See* § 1-2.1(c), *supra* (reporting that 76% of civil disputes involve at least one self-represented party and that the median non-zero monetary judgment is less than $2,500).

that are far less expensive for aggrieved parties yet result in reasonably fair and equitable outcomes.[4] As a practical matter, this means designing systems that require little or no input from lawyers.

Although this may sound radical, our modern digital society has already traveled a long distance along this path. For example, the entire credit card industry could not function without a system for promptly resolving disputes that the vast majority of cardholders and merchants believe is reliable and fair. What has evolved is a highly standardized and automated process for managing millions of disputes per year that operates "almost lawyer-free."[5] Likewise, the world of online commerce relies upon a simple, swift, and predictable mechanism for resolving disputes between buyers and sellers. Thus companies like eBay and Paypal resolve over 90 percent of their disputes based upon automated online dispute resolution (ODR) processes that require no action or input by system administrators.[6] Interestingly, empirical research done at eBay discovered that settlements that flowed from the ODR process increased the parties' loyalty to eBay marketplace.[7] eBay's dispute resolution methodology, in turn, became the basis for Modria, an online dispute resolution company that targeted higher value disputes. One of its most significant uses has been property assessment tax disputes, enabling municipalities to outsource their tax court, reducing the cost of operations while improving convenience and satisfaction for its citizenry.

In 2016, the Civil Resolution Tribunal (CRT) in the province of British Columbia in Canada became the first government judicial body to implement mandatory ODR process. Pursuant to the Civil Resolution Tribunal Act of 2012,[8] the CRT has jurisdiction over all civil disputes involving monetary claims of less than $5,000 (defined as small claims) and all disputes involving strata (i.e., condominium) owners.

Remarkably, with the exception of a limited number of cases involving primarily minors or persons with impaired capacity, the CRT system does not permit the use of lawyers. Instead, parties with a potential dispute are required to explore a series of self-help solutions via a self-help portal (called "explorations"). Thereafter, once a formal dispute is initiated, the online platform provides a potential process for reaching negotiated settlements with little CRT resources. If the parties are unable to reach an agreement via on the online tools, the matter is escalated to a case manager who sets deadlines for responses and serves as an informal mediator. If the case manager is unable to facilitate a resolution, he or she issues a non-binding evaluation of the case and helps prepare it for formal adjudication. With the consent of the parties, the facilitator can also serve as a member of the tribunal that decides the dispute. All CRT

---

[4] What is fair and equitable? The author suggest a comparison with imperfect results of our current system rather than an idealized version of justice.

[5] Andrew P. Moriss, Ph.D., & Jason Korosec, J.D., *Private Dispute Resolution in the Card Context: Structure, Reputation, and Incentives*, 1 J.L. ECON. & POL'Y 393, 401 (2005).

[6] *See* Pablo Cortez, Online Dispute Resolution Services: A Selected Number of Case Studies, 20 COMPUTER & TELECOM. L. REV. 172 (2014).

[7] *See* Colin Rule, C. Rule, *Quantifying the Economic Benefits of Effective Redress: Large E-Commerce Data Sets and the Cost-Benefit Case for Investing in Dispute Resolution*, 34 U. ARK. LITTLE ROCK L. REV. 767, 772 (2012) (documenting that users who settled disputes through eBay's ODR process were, on average, more likely to increase their usage of the platform over the next three months compared to users who had not experienced a dispute).

[8] *See* Civil Resolution Tribunal Act, [SBC 2012] Chapter 25, online at http://www.bclaws.ca/civix/document/id/complete/statreg/12025_01.

adjudicated disputes result in a published decision, which is made available to the public via a searchable database.

The CRT formally launched in June of 2016. Although it has only been operational for slightly more than one year, the online platform has logged approximately 20,000 explorations,[9] with 35% of the strata users and 50% of the small claims users completing the online exploration process. Of these 20,000 users, approximately 13 percent go on to initiate a formal dispute. The most common outcome is a negotiated resolution (45%) followed by default judgments (23%). Of these cases, only 9% have resulted in a formal adjudication, with an average resolution time of four to six months. The CRT had adopted a continuous improvement methodology to improve user satisfaction. However, the even the initial statistics are encouraging, with 75 percent of users indicating they agree/strongly agree that CRT process was easy to understand; 81% that the online application was easy to use; 93% that the CRT staff treated them fairly; and 78% that the facilitation process was fair. As the CRT gains more experience and improves, the plan is to include a wider range of disputes and to increase the jurisdictional limit to $25,000 and eventually to $50,000.[10]

The key insight here is that the administration of justice is being improved by engineering lawyers out of the process. It is noteworthy that the digital platform for the CRT was built by PWC, a global accounting and consulting firm. In the UK, plans are underway to launch an ODR process for low value civil claims, defining low value as controversies under £25,000 (approximately $34,000).[11] Based on the data presented earlier in this chapter, such a system would likely sweep in a substantial majority of civil disputes that are currently in the state court system.

What does it mean for the legal profession when the legal system is *designed* to resolve legal disputes without the aid of licensed lawyers? Because three-quarters of disputes in state court already involve at least one unrepresented party, such a system is likely inevitable. If ODR materially improves access to justice for ordinary citizens, do lawyers have a professional obligation to lobby for and help construct such systems? These are questions that the organized bar needs to answer to retain its legitimacy in the administration of justice.

### § 1-3.1(b) The Way Forward Is Multidisciplinary

The crux of the legal profession's current challenges is a mismatch between the labor-intensive nature of traditional legal services and clients' ability or willingness to pay. Further, this mismatch grows more acute with the passage of time. To the extent that members of the legal profession fail to directly confront and solve this mismatch, they lose the ability to control their own destiny. What makes this transition especially difficult, however, is that lawyers are unable to navigate it on their own. Instead they need to collaborate with professionals from other disciplines to redesign how legal problems are managed and solved.

The core economic problem is illustrated in Figure 10 and reflects a steady historical progression. Until the early 20th century, virtually all lawyers were generalists. As the

---

[9] 10,800 strata disputes between June 2016 and October 2017 (approximately 17 months); and 8,900 small claim disputes between June 2017 and October 2017 (approximately five months).

[10] *See* Civil Resolution Tribunal, Presentation at the Forum on Legal Evolution, Chicago, IL, Nov. 9, 2017, online at https://forum.legalevolution.org/program/.

[11] *See* https://www.judiciary.gov.uk/reviews/online-dispute-resolution/.

nation transitioned from an agrarian to an industrial economy, the work of lawyers became more complex. Corporations required more sophisticated methods of finance. In turn, the growing power and influence of corporate enterprise spawned the rise of the administrative state and new forms of regulation that would ultimately be tested in the courts. Lawyers responded to this growing complexity by organizing themselves into law firms, thus enabling division of labor and specialization. Yet, as the industrial state has expanded beyond national borders and given way to an information-based, interconnected, and globalized economy, lawyers have exhausted the benefits that can be achieved through lawyer specialization and division of labor. Going forward, managing legal complexity will increasingly require the integration of non-legal disciplines and methodologies. Hence, the future of law is multidisciplinary.

**Figure 10. Relationship Between Legal Complexity and Economic Growth**

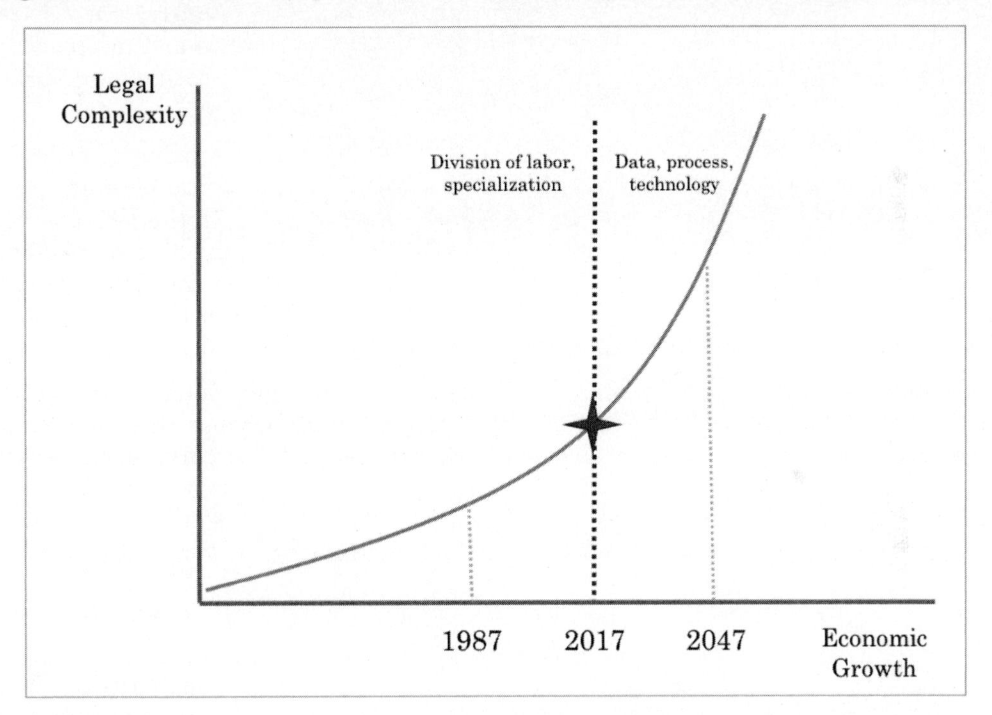


This interdependency of lawyers with other professionals is fundamentally new to the legal profession. Further, it is destined to alter status hierarchies among professionals. To the extent that lawyers try to preserve traditional labor-intensive approaches to legal problem-solving, they will lose influence. Yet, to the extent they adopt new methodologies grounded in data, process, and technology, the nature of legal work changes in ways that raise the question, "what does it mean to be a lawyer?" This is a complex question that will answered over the course of the next generation.

# Part Two

## THE PHILOSOPHY OF LEGAL ETHICS

**By Stephen Pepper and Katherine R. Kruse**

### RECOMMENDED CITATION FOR PART TWO

For those citing to Chapters 2-1 through 2-5 in Part Two, we recommend attribution to this individually-authored part as being most accurate. For example, the most appropriate citation format to the first section in this part would look like this: Stephen Pepper & Katherine R. Kruse, The Philosophy of Legal Ethics § 2-1.1, in *Legal Ethics, Professional Responsibility, and the Legal Profession* (West Academic Publishing, 2018).

# Chapter 2-1

# FOUNDATIONS OF THE LAWYER'S ROLE

**By Stephen Pepper and Katherine R. Kruse**

*Table of Sections*

§ 2-1.1 The Function of Lawyers—Their Role in Society
§ 2-1.2 Professional Ethics
§ 2-1.3 Role Specific Morality
§ 2-1.4 Can a Good Person Be a Good Lawyer: The Controversy over a Lawyer's Role Specific Morality

## § 2-1.1 THE FUNCTION OF LAWYERS—THEIR ROLE IN SOCIETY

Lawyers provide access to law in all its variety and ubiquity. On one side of the spectrum they facilitate cooperation, both large scale and small, both complicated and relatively simple. They create and facilitate corporations, partnerships, and various other forms of organization both for profit and non-profit enterprises. They facilitate our organization and activity by structuring cooperation among both such entities and individuals through negotiating and creating contracts and contractual relationships: for building something; for employment relationships; for the governance and operation of an ongoing entity; for purchases, sales, leases; and so on through the great variety and flexibility of legal devices. They create forms of ownership and sharing (the condominium, the condominium association), entities and contractual relations for debt and financing (the debenture, various corporate forms). In this function they create private law—the rules of creation and operation for these various legal entities—based upon the public law that limits and channels the permissible and the impermissible. On the basis of this aspect of their work lawyers have been called architects of order, and we might also think of them as engineers of cooperation. Lawyers will structure and effectuate corporate mergers, acquisitions and dispositions; they will similarly structure and effectuate the adoption of a child; they will assist a small or large business in creating a corporation or partnership. They help create, manage and use long and short term forms of cooperation, structuring the relations of persons from individuals through small groups to thousands of employees or shareholders.

On the other side of the spectrum, lawyers define and structure our disputes, negotiate resolutions, and represent clients through a trial if prior resolution is not effectuated. Courts are the mechanism for the resolution of disputes that cannot otherwise be resolved, and only lawyers are licensed to represent others in court. Law determines both the procedures by which these disputes are to be resolved (procedural law) and the substantive law that determines the resolution (the rules and principles of contract, property, tort, crime, labor law, and so on). Lawyers are, or become, experts in both to enable the ultimate resolution of the dispute, either by agreement, or, if that fails, by court resolution—or, more frequently as time goes on, by a private substitute for court resolution: mediation or arbitration. They facilitate and structure the resolution of disagreements, from the relatively large scale of a corporate antitrust disagreement to the small scale of a family divorce.

In the middle of the spectrum lawyers provide their clients with knowledge of the law and the limits and opportunities it provides: wage and hour laws, securities law, criminal and property law, contract and corporation, and on and on. Lawyers are the medium through which our law is effectuated, the channel through which we come to know the law and be guided, limited and assisted by it. And they are also inventive in both creating new legal mechanisms and agreements and in devising new usages for those already in existence.

## § 2-1.2 PROFESSIONAL ETHICS

A criminal defendant doesn't have the knowledge and skill to defend herself, and yet the proceeding is surely one of the most consequential of her life. The public doesn't have the knowledge or skill to know if the prosecutor is competent or skilled, yet effective criminal prosecution is an important aspect of public welfare. The situation is similar for the client who needs a will, the businesswoman or union that needs a contract, the corporation in need of transaction agreements and the documents to effectuate them, or advice about the design and effectuation of a merger or divestiture. The matter may be of substantial importance—sometimes quite crucial—but those in need of the service do not have the ability to judge the quality or effectiveness of the work. An additional factor in the consumer's vulnerability is the fact that the lawyer is charging for the service, making a living from this work the quality of which the client ordinarily cannot evaluate. And this is the defining hallmark of professional services generally. If you have a severe ache in your abdomen, should you be concerned about an ulcer, a heart attack, appendicitis? Or might it be just indigestion? For this you need the advice of a physician. The design and drawings for the construction of the new house you have decided to build: Are they sufficient, competent; well done, badly done? For this you need the help of an architect. You want to have an estate plan and a will to determine where the accumulated fruits of your labor will go upon your death. For this you need the help of a lawyer.

Professionals are generally understood to have a special ethical obligation to their patients, clients or customers for the three reasons these situations exemplify. First, the service provided is often particularly important from either the societal or personal point of view (and frequently from both). Second, competence in providing the service requires very extensive education and experience, high intellectual ability, and often substantial interpersonal skills. Third, the client, patient or customer is paying for the needed service and the professional is making a living from providing it, creating an economic conflict of interest. Professional services are often of special importance from a societal or personal perspective, but due to the complexity and extensive educational background needed, it ordinarily is impossible or impractical for the recipient to effectively evaluate the adequacy or quality of the service—thus rendering the client or patient vulnerable in relation to the superior knowledge of the professional.[1] "In sum, (1) the client or

---

[1] The following seven characteristics help define the concept of a profession:

1. A profession is a means of making a living.
2. A profession is based on specialized knowledge, training, and ability, often requiring intellectual labor and many years of higher education.

patient often has a strong need for something he cannot understand or evaluate effectively; (2) the professional is making a living from that need; and, as a result, (3) is in a position to exploit the client or patient's vulnerability for personal profit."[2] For example, in regard to the ache in the abdomen mentioned above, if the surgeon recommends surgery, is it because you are in need of it, with serious risks if you do not have it; or is it because the surgeon makes substantially more money from surgery than with an alternate treatment? (And would you feel more comfortable in the recommendation if the physician were your family practitioner or an internist who would not profit directly from a choice of surgery rather than the surgeon who will?) Consider an example from a prominent lawyers' ethics course book:

> Novak . . . has agreed to represent a plaintiff in a personal injury suit for a . . . contingent fee of one-third of the amount recovered. The other side has offered, before Novak begins work, to pay his client $15,000. Based on what he knows about the case, Novak believes the actual damages that a jury would award would be more like $60,000, but it would take him about 200 hours of work to recover that amount, and, of course, the client might not recover anything at all. Novak has concluded that it is best to recommend to the client that he accept the $15,000 immediately so that Novak can pocket a $5,000 fee with little effort and go on to the next case.[3]

If the lawyer provides this recommendation without fully informing the client of the reasons and the alternative which might well serve the client better ($45,000 dollars later rather than $10,000 now), the lawyer will have exploited the client's lack of understanding to serve her own interest, not the client's—a paradigm of the risks presented by the professional relationship. The situation is similar with the client who needs a will, the business woman or union that needs a contract: the matter may be of very substantial importance or consequence, but the person or the entity does not have the ability to judge the quality of the will, the contract, or the corporate or transaction documents the lawyer has prepared. And the lawyer is making a living from this work, charging for a product the quality of which the buyer ordinarily cannot evaluate.

---

> 3. The services rendered by the professional based upon this foundation of knowledge and ability, are necessary to individuals at various points in their lives and are frequently of the utmost personal concern (for example, services relating to physical health, liberty, religious salvation, or psychological well-being).
> 4. Because of the specialized knowledge involved, the quality of the services rendered by the professional is untestable from the perspective of the layman. The individual *needs* the service, but is unable to evaluate it, and therefore the individual is *vulnerable* in relation to the professional.
> 5. The profession holds a monopoly on a service frequently needed by individuals, and as a result wields significant economic power.
> 6. The profession is largely self-regulated in determining and administering the qualifications for membership and in policing professional activities.
> 7. Part of the self-regulation usually includes ethical prescriptions that articulate a service orientation.
>
> The seven characteristics add up to a pervasive economic conflict of interest between the professional and those who need (and pay for) his services.

Stephen Pepper, *The Lawyer's Amoral Ethical Role: A Defense, a Problem, and Some Possibilities*, 1986 AM. B. FOUND. RES. J. 613, 615 (1986).

[2] Stephen Pepper, *Three Dichotomies in Lawyers' Ethics (With Particular Attention to the Corporation as Client)*, 28 GEO. J. LEGAL ETHICS 1069, 1074–75 (2015).

[3] THOMAS D. MORGAN & RONALD D. ROTUNDA, PROFESSIONAL RESPONSIBILITY: PROBLEMS AND MATERIALS 100 (10th ed. 2008).

This vulnerability in regard to something society considers important generates the need for a special ethic beyond that of the market. The ordinary norm of "caveat emptor" is not acceptable. The licensed professional is not allowed to exploit the vulnerable patient, client, or customer to the greatest extent possible under the market conditions, but instead is required to put the interests of the patient, client or customer first. Service is understood to be the primary purpose of the professional (providing high quality access to medical care, to the law, to architectural services), not profit. Profit (the business aspect of the professional's work) is understood to be necessary (the professional must make a living in order to be available to provide the necessary service) but it is not supposed to be primary. This is the underlying ethic of the professions: putting the interests of the client, patient, student or customer first and putting the interests of the professional (doctor, lawyer, teacher) second.[4]

## § 2-1.3 ROLE SPECIFIC MORALITY

One's place, function, task, or role in a situation, in a relationship or in society more generally, often has a significant effect on the general understanding of one's moral obligations. The underlying professional ethic described in the section above is the foundation of the generally accepted role specific morality of the professions. In a classic 1975 essay Richard Wasserstrom developed this concept in regard to the lawyer's ethical role. In explaining role specific morality he provided two examples. Parents, he noted, are expected to be partial toward their children, to prefer them to others, to care for them more, to allocate assets to them in a way not justifiable in light of the greater needs of many other children in the world. There may be many starving children in the world, but it is considered morally justifiable for the parent to devote the clear majority of her resources for the benefit of her very well fed children and relatively little for the benefit of those who have nothing. For non-related persons this radical preference for particular children in light of the far greater needs and vulnerability of many others would be

---

[4] Two substantial caveats or difficulties must be noted.

1. What occupations or trades qualify as "professions" or "professional" is controversial. There are often substantial economic benefits to being a member of a formal profession, even given the purported obligation to put client/patient/customer interests first. Under the seven definitional elements at note 1 above, the profession has a limited entry monopoly on providing a service necessary to a substantial part of the population. (For example, are business executives or managers professionals in this limited understanding of a profession? They do not meet the requirements of the seven elements, yet they often speak and think of themselves as "professionals." *See* RAKESH KHURANA, FROM HIGHER AIMS TO HIRED HANDS: THE SOCIAL TRANSFORMATION OF AMERICAN BUSINESS SCHOOLS AND THE UNFULFILLED PROMISE OF MANAGEMENT AS A PROESSION (2007)).
2. Among economists and sociologists there is substantial skepticism as to the reality of the professional claim. Looking at those seven definitional aspects, as alluded to in note 1 above, the structure can be seen as a design for potential exploitation as much as a limit or prevention of such exploitation. The professions purport to be designed to protect the consumer of legal, medical or architectural services—and the state licenses and regulates the professions with this as the premise—but many social scientists perceive the reality as quite different.

And there is a third difficulty which ought to be noted before moving on. With regard to lawyers' ethics there is a significant counter-vision that has been influential for some time. Some empirical work on lawyers and their clients suggests that the model of a vulnerable client sketched above is incorrect, and the more usual situation is a relatively weak and economically dependent lawyer serving a stronger, dominating client. The image called up under this vision is that of the client as a large corporation with a lot of legal business, sophisticated and demanding management, and a corporate profit ethic instead of a humane conscience; juxtaposed against a lawyer in a much smaller economic unit (albeit perhaps, a large, profitable law firm), dependent upon that client for a substantial chunk of his or her livelihood. *See* Stephen Pepper, *Applying the Fundamentals of Lawyers' Ethics to Insurance Defense Practice*, 4 CONN. INS. L. J. 27, 44–45 (1997) and sources cited therein.

morally dubious; for parents it is expected and the moral norm. "[I]t is the nature of role-differentiated behavior that it often makes it both appropriate and desirable for the person in a particular role to put to one side considerations of various sorts—and especially various moral considerations—that otherwise would be relevant if not decisive." Wasserstrom's second example was the role-specific morality of scientists. The job of the scientist is to discover and develop new knowledge; but how that knowledge is used, what its consequences are, is not the moral responsibility of the scientist who discovered or developed it. Knowledge can be used for good or ill, but that decision is for others—by agreement or regulation, by government or a private group or agency. It is appropriate for scientists to learn and reveal sub-atomic physics, including fission and fusion, even if that can lead to the development of vastly destructive bombs. It is good to understand how to clone cells and how embryos can be controlled and manipulated, even if that knowledge has the potential for monstrous uses. How that knowledge is used and limits to be placed on its use are not the responsibility of the scientist who is engaged in discovery; that responsibility lies elsewhere—with government or private agreement or private agencies.[5]

Wasserstrom may have chosen these particular examples because the role specific morality of the lawyer is often understood as analogous in some significant ways to that of both the parent and the scientist. Lawyers prefer their clients much as parents prefer their children. The lawyer's allegiance is to the client and she is to put the client's interests above all other interests—even if that causes injury to others. (Obligations to others, including the lawyer's own interests, are considered suspect, possible violations of the ethical obligation to avoid conflicts of interest.[6]) And, even more than the typical work of the scientist, the lawyer's assistance to the client at least sometimes is likely to cause harm to others. This is a quite pointed difficulty for lawyers. All professionals share the obligation to put the client's or patient's interest first, to not exploit the client or patient for the benefit of the professional. For lawyers this obligation entails a second, morally more problematic obligation. For doctors, providing access to and assistance in medical care is almost always a clear moral good—it helps the patient and does no one any significant harm.[7] For lawyers helping clients, however, providing a benefit to the client not infrequently involves a quite specific detriment to a third party or to society more generally. The most obvious example is litigation: prevailing for the client usually means someone else loses. Transactions often have this same aspect, either for one of the parties or externalities caused to others. Sometimes these detriments are morally problematic. So long as the conduct is within the confines of relevant law and legal regulation, the limited societal role of the lawyer—to provide access to the law—is considered a moral justification for what otherwise might well be considered morally unjustifiable conduct or consequences.

---

[5] Richard Wasserstrom, *Lawyers as Professionals: Some Moral Issues*, 5 HUM. RTS. 1, 3–5 (1975).

[6] On the lawyer's duty to avoid conflicts of interest under the ethics rules, see Part Four of this book, Gregory C. Sisk, Legal Ethics and the Practice of Law, ch. 4-7. On civil liability for client disloyalty, see Part Five of this book, Susan Saab Fortney & Vincent R. Johnson, Legal Malpractice §§ 5-3.1 to 5-3.3.

[7] At least that is the case if the focus is on the individual patient. An ethic that requires doing that which is best for the individual patient without regard to cost arguably has led (under s system of cost spreading and cost sharing through insurance and some government subsidy) to a system which is too costly, wasteful and eventually likely unsustainable.

Keeping in mind that the general function of the legal profession is to provide access to law and facilitating its use (including access to legal mechanisms such as the corporate form of enterprise, and facilitating their use), consider the following chart.

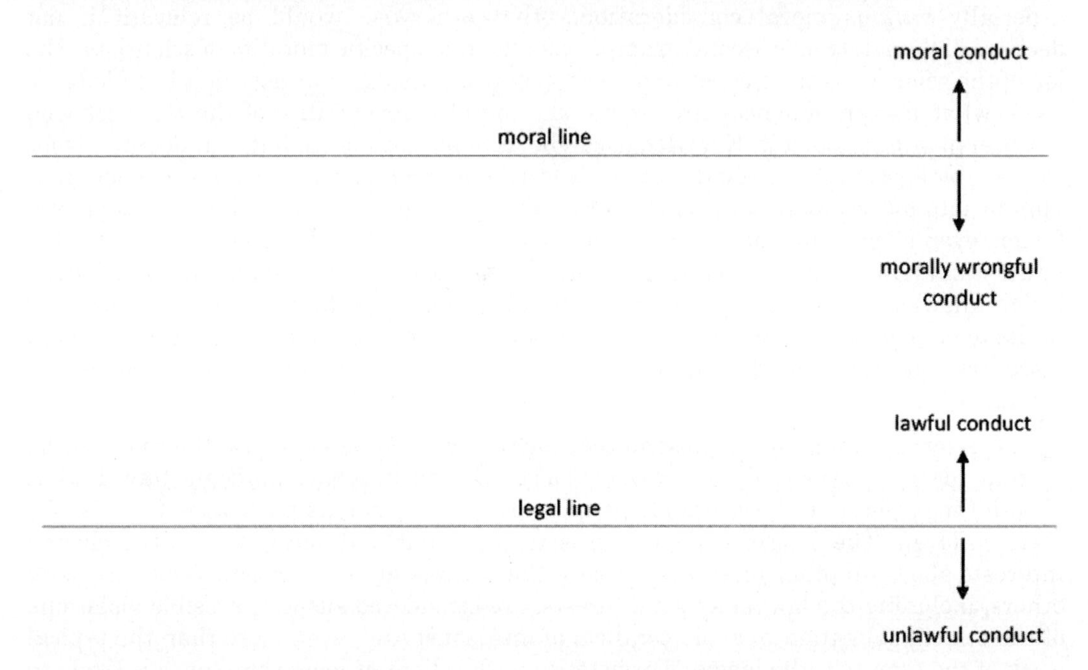


If both the conduct and the goal the lawyer is facilitating are lawful—that is, above the legal line in the illustration—the generally understood obligation of the lawyer is to provide the legal knowledge and mechanisms to assist. If that lawful conduct is morally problematic, that is, arguably below the moral line on the illustration, then fulfilling the generally understood role of the lawyer is morally problematic in that particular instance. Conduct between the lines is both lawful *and* morally problematic.

There are many well-known examples of conduct that falls between the two lines in this way:

(1) Imagine a client, corporate or individual, consulting a lawyer concerning a debt the client admits: the funds were transferred to and used by the client, a promise was made to the creditor to repay. The creditor is now seeking repayment and threatening possible suit if the funds are not forthcoming. Looking into the matter the lawyer discovers a valid legal defense, the statute of frauds or a statute of limitations. Given that the client admits having borrowed the money and made a promise to repay, the purposes of neither of these possible defenses is served by defeating repayment in this situation. Both our ordinary moral understanding and the substantive law of contract support an obligation to repay, but the possible defenses—for reasons quite inapposite to the facts of the situation—will prevent legal enforcement of this obligation. (The defenses would be what is often referred to as a technicality: the reasons for or purposes of the statute of frauds or statute of limitations would not be served by their application in this particular situation.) If suit is brought and the lawyer pleads one of the statutes as a defense, the conduct would fall in the problematic area illustrated by the chart: above the legal line (each

of the defenses is a clear legal right of the client), but below the moral line (refusing to pay a genuine debt and reneging on the promise would usually be considered to constitute a moral wrong).[8]

(2) In the course of litigation the lawyer knows a particular witness is telling the truth in regard to a possibly determinative aspect of the matter. The lawyer also knows that a skillful cross-examination is likely to cause some or all of the jurors to conclude that the witness is not telling the truth. The cross examination will implicitly assert that the witness is lying, that is assert a falsehood about the integrity and honesty of the person testifying. Lying in this way about someone in something significant normally would be considered a moral wrong—below the moral line on the chart. But cross examination is a legal right of the client, and the lawyer's obligation is to effectuate the client's legal rights, to provide effective access to the law. Thus, conducting the cross examination is clearly above the legal line. Another example of the awkward situation where the lawyer's conduct is between the lines.

(3) A criminal defense lawyer often will represent a client she knows is in fact guilty; that is, the evidence is clear that the client is guilty under the elements of the substantive criminal law, or the client has admitted the criminal conduct under circumstance that suggest she is being truthful. The lawyer, however, may know of a basis for defeating the prosecution aside from the substantive criminal law. The evidence may have been obtained through an interview in the absence of a Miranda warning to the suspect; evidence may have been obtained unlawfully as the result of an unconstitutional search or seizure; or evidence may have resulted from listening in on the conversation between lawyer and client, violating the lawyer-client privilege. By providing access to and effectuating the client's legal rights in such circumstances the lawyer can free a person who in fact committed the crime and is guilty under the substantive law. In such situations the lawyer's conduct in freeing the client will often function as facilitation for future crime and harm to future victims because violent criminals have a high likelihood of being recidivists, that is, they are likely to engage again in criminal conduct. Freeing a substantively guilty person and thus quite possibly facilitating harm to a future victim of a crime by that person would appear to many of us to be morally wrongful conduct. From this perspective the lawyer's conduct is above the legal line on the chart—she is fulfilling the professional role of providing access to the law and following the ethical

---

[8] We are assuming here that the debtor is able to pay the debt without hardship. It is true that repayment of a debt is not always unambiguously the morally correct thing to do. The disagreement a few years ago over the ethical propriety of strategic mortgage default is a good example. It arises from the unease associated with breaching the contract and not repaying what is owed balanced against factors that suggest the situation is quite different than the "just debt" scenario depicted above: the expectation of the parties may not have included further repayment beyond giving up the home upon default, and there may be far less than clean hands on the part of the financial institutions that initiated and now hold the debt. Stephen Pepper, *The Lawyer Knows More Than the Law*, 90 TEX. L. REV. 691, 700 n. 49–50 (2012). James R. Hagerty, *Is Walking Away from Your Mortgage Immoral?*, WSJ.COM (Dec. 17, 2009), http://blogs.wsj.com/developments/2009/12/17/is-walking-away-from-your-mortgage-immoral/ (examining the moral debate over strategic mortgage default and presenting arguments both in favor of and against strategic default). *Compare* Brent T. White, *Underwater and Not Walking Away: Shame, Fear, and the Social Management of the Housing Crisis*, 45 WAKE FOREST L. REV. 971, 972 (2010) (contending that while financial institutions and the government behave "irrespective of concerns about morality or social responsibility," homeowners wrongly allow fear and shame to prevent them from strategic mortgage default); Curtis Bridgeman, *The Morality of Jingle Mail: Moral Myths About Strategic Default*, 46 WAKE FOREST L. REV. 123, 144–45 (2011) (urging homeowners not to default on their mortgages because they should feel bound by a moral obligation to pay their just debts).

obligation of the lawyer to serve the client's interests—but the conduct is also, at least arguably, below the moral line on the chart.

In each of these situations the lawyer's conduct is ordinarily understood as morally justified by the lawyer's role in society: providing the client with access to her legal rights and facilitating use of that which the law makes generally available. But in each case this role justified conduct by the lawyer—role specific morality—appears to be facilitating or effectuating a moral wrong.

## § 2-1.4 CAN A GOOD PERSON BE A GOOD LAWYER: THE CONTROVERSY OVER A LAWYER'S ROLE SPECIFIC MORALITY

Thus the lawyer's job, her societal function, at least sometimes entails conduct that would otherwise be considered morally wrongful. The fundamental question in lawyers' ethics is: because the conduct is genuinely part of the job, does the general role or function which the lawyer serves render morally justifiable actions which would otherwise be evaluated as morally wrongful? Does the lawyer's role somehow cancel out the wrongfulness? Reneging on the debt ordinarily would be considered a moral wrong. Is a lawyer's knowing effectuation of that result not a moral wrong because it is part of the lawyer's rightful role in society to provide the client with access to her legal rights? Calling someone a liar when you know they are not, particularly in a very public and formal venue, would normally be considered a morally wrongful thing to do. Is it not morally wrongful for the lawyer because of her assigned role in the resolution of disputes through litigation? Almost all lawyers at some times in their careers must work their way through these situations, a problem summed up with the simple question: Can a good person also be a good lawyer?[9] Or, to the contrary, to be a good lawyer must one sometimes be a bad person? In other words, are the ethics of lawyering—the role specific morality—fundamentally different from and, in some instances, inconsistent with, ordinary morality?

The traditional[10] understanding of lawyer ethics answers these questions in the affirmative: yes, the role specific morality of the lawyer does provide a justification for conduct that would otherwise be evaluated as morally wrongful; yes, a good person can also be a good lawyer. This view came to be referred to as the "standard conception" or the "dominant view," summarized by three principles.

1. *Principle of Partisanship*: The lawyer must act out of exclusive concern with the legal interests of clients. She is permitted to disregard the interest of affected third parties and the public interest, if it would be in the client's interests to do so, and if the law permits the violation in question of the third party or public interest.

[9] Charles Fried, *The Lawyer as Friend: The Moral Foundations of the Lawyer-Client Relation*, 85 YALE L.J. 1060, 1060–61 (1976).

[10] By "traditional" we mean from the early to mid-twentieth century on. Some would dispute this characterization. *See, e.g.*, Thomas L. Shaffer, *The Unique, Novel, and Unsound Adversary Ethic*, 41 VAND. L. REV. 697, 699–703 (1988); Thomas L. Shaffer, *The Legal Ethics of Radical Individualism*, 65 TEX. L. REV. 963, 986–90 (1987).

2. *Principle of Neutrality*: The lawyer should not consider the morality of the client's cause, nor the morality of particular actions taken to advance the client's cause, as long as both are lawful.

3. *Principle of Nonaccountability*: If the lawyer adheres to the first two principles, neither third party observers nor the lawyer herself should regard the lawyer as a wrongdoer, in moral terms.[11]

Monroe Freedman provided a clear explication of what this understanding meant in practice in his 1975 book, Lawyers Ethics in an Adversary System.[12] As the title suggests, Professor Freedman found the justification for this ethic in the model of litigation; and more particularly criminal defense. His paradigm was the criminal defendant, an individual faced with the full force of the state attempting to take away his or her freedom. Noting that the adversary process "has its foundation in respect for human dignity," Freedman observed that

> a trial is far more than a search for truth, and the constitutional rights that are provided by our system of justice may well outweigh the truth-seeking value—a fact which is manifest when we consider that these rights and others guaranteed by the Constitution may well impede the search for truth rather than further it.[13]

The Sixth Amendment to the Constitution provides a right to the assistance of counsel; the Fifth provides the right to not incriminate oneself. Putting those two together: the lawyer must get all the relevant information possible from the client in order to provide effective assistance, but the lawyer's knowledge of that information (since it came from the client protected by the Fifth Amendment) cannot be used to harm the client.[14]

Freedman did not shy away from the hard examples to which this understanding leads. Our second example above—cross-examining a truthful witness—was elaborated in a full chapter of his book, with the context being the cross-examination of a truthful rape victim to suggest that she was lying. The Fifth Amendment protects the client from being harmed by the information he has revealed to the lawyer, which presumably has led to the lawyer's knowledge of the client's guilt. The Sixth Amendment guarantees the assistance of a lawyer in conducting the cross examination. The conduct is thus above the legal line in our chart above—the criminal defendant has a constitutional right to confront witnesses against him—but suggesting in a formal public forum that the young woman is lying about being raped when the lawyer is quite sure she is telling the truth

---

[11] W. BRADLEY WENDEL, LAWYERS AND FIDELITY TO LAW 7, 29 (2010) (citing Murray Schwartz, *The Professionalism and Accountability of Lawyers*, 66 CALIF. L. REV. 669, 672–75 ("standard conception") and William H. Simon, *The Ideology of Advocacy: Procedural Justice and Professional Ethics*, 1978 WIS. L. REV. 29 (1978) ("dominant view")). It was the "standard conception" in 1978, when denominated as such by Prof. Schwartz and continues to be the "dominant" conception to the present, as articulated recently by Prof. Gillers:

> [T]o work diligently to achieve a client's goals within the bounds of the law and professional conduct rules. No more, no less . . . Are they willing to work injustice? This may be an uncomfortable question, but it is not a hard one. Lawyers are agents of their clients before the law and their clients' fiduciaries. They are not agents of the justice system or of justice.

Stephen Gillers, *How to Make Rules for Lawyers: The Professional Responsibility of the Legal Profession*, 40 PEPP. L. REV. 365, 368 (2013).

[12] Monroe Freedman, LAWYERS ETHICS IN AN ADVERSARY SYSTEM (1975).

[13] *Id.* at 2.

[14] Monroe Freedman, *Personal Responsibility in a Professional System*, 27 CATH. U. L. REV. 191, 192 n. 3 (1978). In this article Professor Freedman expanded on the rationale for his client focused justification for the adversary ethic.

appears to be an egregious moral wrong. Freedman argues that our respect for the dignity of the accused—as instantiated in his constitutional rights—justifies such conduct, justifies the lawyer's role-specific morality. Although the criminal defendant was his model, Freedman's explication of the lawyers' ethical obligation was not limited to this context—the "standard conception" applied to all litigation, not just criminal defense, and to all lawyering work, not just litigation. It applies to the corporate lawyer providing counsel in the privacy of the office. Thus, in the chapter on "counseling the client," he provides the example of accurate advice about the law which has the effect of encouraging the client to violate that law.[15]

Freedman's justification of the lawyer's ethical role based upon the vulnerability and need of the criminal defendant was a weakness in regard to lawyer conduct outside of that particular sphere. Wasserstrom was convinced that the "amoral behavior of the *criminal* defense lawyer is justifiable," but was "undecided" in regard to all the other contexts of lawyering conduct.[16] He articulated four caveats about the lawyer's "amoral role," the first of which noted that

> the arguments that support the role-differentiated amorality of the lawyer on institutional grounds can succeed only if the enormous degree of trust and confidence in the institutions themselves is itself justified. . . [W]e are . . . entitled to be quite skeptical both of the fairness and of the capacity for self-correction of our larger institutional mechanisms, including the legal system. To the degree to which the institutional rules and practices are unjust, unwise or undesirable, to that same degree is the case for the role-differentiated behavior of the lawyer weakened if not destroyed.[17]

"The Adversary System Excuse" by David Luban, probably the best known and most effective critique of the "standard conception," approached the question from this direction.[18] As the title indicates, Luban was unpersuaded that the "adversary system" "excused" what would otherwise be considered morally wrongful conduct (under the criteria of what he referred to as "ordinary morality.") The essay systematically and thoroughly canvasses the arguable justifications for assisting lawful but morally wrongful client conduct (the area between the lines on the chart above) and for the most part finds them insufficient.[19] Professor Luban first considers as a justification for the adversary system (and derivatively, for lawyer's ethics) that it is the best way to discover

---

[15] The example is a client who closes a store on Sundays in compliance with a Sunday closing law. The client is "suffering a crippling decline in sales" because, "less than a mile away, in the adjoining state, several discount stores operate on Sunday." When the lawyer informs the client that the penalty for violation of the statute is only $25.00 for each day of violation, the client chooses to stay open on Sundays. The lawyer's accurate advice about the law has led to an intentional violation of that law. Freedman, *supra* note 12, at 59–60. For an exploration of this kind of problem, see Stephen Pepper, *Counseling at the Limits of the Law: An Exercise in the Jurisprudence and Ethics of Lawyering*, 104 YALE L.J. 1545 (1995). Among many other examples, that article provides the illustration of legal advice to a corporation that has the effect of encouraging possibly harmful water pollution. *Id.* at 1551.

[16] Wasserstrom, *supra* note 5, at 4, 10.

[17] Wasserstrom *supra* note 5, at 10–11.

[18] David Luban, *The Adversary System Excuse, in* THE GOOD LAWYER 83, 83–122 (David Luban ed., 1983). Echoing Wasserstrom's first caveat, the first substantive section is headed "Institutional Excuses." *Id.* at 85. The essay had been circulating in photocopied format for quite a few years before its publication. One of the authors of this chapter remembers obtaining and reading it in his first years as a law professor, struggling to understand lawyers' professional ethics as he taught the basic required Legal Profession course.

[19] The exception is criminal defense—in that context Luban agrees with Wasserstrom that there is institutional justification. *Id.* at 91–93.

the underlying truth so that disputes may be resolved as the substantively law would direct.[20] In litigation one has two biased sides presenting evidence and argument not with the goal of determining the truth, but with the goal of prevailing in a legal dispute. The party charged with making the decision (judge, or jury, or both) is for the most part passive: biased parties are active and directive, the decision-maker can only look at what is presented. This does not seem like the most effective way to determine the truth. It is quite different from the scientific method, a system specifically designed to determine truth, not to resolve disputes (the purpose of litigation).

Litigation, primarily designed to resolve disputes according to the substantive law, is also designed to do so in a way that protects important individual rights and societal interests other than accurate dispute resolution. Thus, many mixed and conflicting values and goals are served in our litigation system, and while truth is one of the foremost, it is not the highest or primary. Among those other values are the dignity of persons, fairness to those involved in the dispute being resolved, and—often protecting those values—the rights of those involved in the process. Evidence obtained in a way prohibited by the Constitution cannot be used at trial, even if accurate and helpful in determining the truth (the 4th Amendment); a criminal defendant cannot be required to testify against herself (the 5th Amendment). The lawyer-client, doctor-patient, and priest-penitent privileges similarly keep out evidence that may be quite reliable and helpful in resolving the dispute according to the substantive law, but we value the good done by those relationships more than we value truth in litigation. Luban turns next to the protection of such legal rights as a justification for the adversary system. His critique here rests primarily on the fact that lawyers do not see their task as defending rights or protecting values—their goal is to win.[21] If in doing so they impinge on the rights of others or detract from these values, that is not their primary concern as they understand it. So the active parties in litigation are not so much concerned with rights.[22] What the essay does not pause to consider is the possibility that litigation might be an effective compromise between the value of finding the truth (thus serving the purpose of resolving disputes according to the substantive law at issue) and the many other rights and interests we value.

Luban's argument continues in this fashion, presenting other previously articulated justifications for the traditional understanding and finding each separately inadequate or unpersuasive.[23] Somewhat surprisingly, Luban's ultimate conclusion is that the adversary system itself *is* justifiable, but just barely so, and mostly through inertia: we

---

[20] *Id.* at 93–97. A lawyer's obligation to truth and candor is a very complicated subject. *See, e.g.*, Stephen Pepper, *Why Confidentiality?*, 23 LAW & SOCIAL INQUIRY 331 (1998).

[21] "Lawyers themselves do not see the point of what they do as defending their clients' legal rights, but as using the law to get their clients what they want." Luban, *supra* note 18, at 99.

[22] *Id.* at 97–100.

> My legal rights are *everything I am in fact legally entitled to* not *everything the law can be made to give*. . . Every lawyer knows tricks of the trade that can be used to do opponents out of their legal deserts—using delaying tactics, for example, to make it too costly for an opponent without much money to prosecute a lengthy suit even though the law is on his or her side.

*Id.* at 98.

[23] Professor Simon, in his groundbreaking article took a somewhat similar path. He suggested three possible justifications for the "ideology of advocacy" and found each ineffective. Simon, *supra* note 11, at 39, 61, 91.

have it, it functions, and there is nothing better that we know of.[24] This minimal justification means that the adversary system (the institutional justification for the "amoral role" or the "standard conception") has little weight. It justifies only very minor moral wrongs. If the wrong is significant, the institutional justification is insufficient, and the lawyer should follow the guide of ordinary morality and not the lawyer's obligation to pursue the client's lawful aims through lawful means.[25]

In response to Wasserstrom's doubts and Luban's critique, one of the authors of this chapter suggested a defense of the traditional, client-centered, role-specific lawyer's ethic premised on values and understandings far broader than the adversary system. This understanding was structured roughly as follows:[26]

> First, access to law for the citizenry, for each individual, is of special importance. Like access to medical care, it can be seen as a fundamental good. And, unlike medical care, law is fundamentally public—it is created by various institutions of government, intended to be available to all, to regulate, facilitate and limit the conduct of all. (We are talking here of law in a far broader sense than just resolution of disputes—the litigation system. We are talking of the creation of agreements for the creation of businesses, for real estate transactions, for transactions of all sorts; for the creation of various forms of co-operation such as partnerships and corporations; for the creation of trusts and wills, for knowledge of our wage and hour rights or obligations; for knowledge about all sorts of law and legal devices, both that which limit and that which facilitate, and very often that which facilitates but with defined limits and channels.)
>
> Second, individual autonomy is a strong social value: "the belief that liberty and autonomy are a moral good, that free choice is better than constraint, that each of us wishes, to the extent possible, to make our own choices rather to have them made for us."[27] The first two premises are thus linked closely together: access to law, a fundamental public good, is of special importance partly because of its facilitation of individual autonomy. But access to law, and thus full exercise of one's autonomy, is usually dependent on the assistance of one trained in and knowledgeable about the law—a lawyer. Again this is similar to medicine: most of us can't reliably diagnose our medical problems, and we can't rely on our spouses or friends to perform the surgery we might need.
>
> Therefore the third premise: for reliable and trustworthy access to law (and the consequent exercise of our autonomy) very frequently we need the

[24] Luban, *supra* note 18, at 113–17. Luban has recently reiterated his continued agreement with this position. David Luban and W. Bradley Wendel, *Philosophical Legal Ethics: An Affectionate History*, 30 GEO. J. LEGAL ETHICS 337 (2017).

[25] The adversary system possesses only the slightest moral force, and thus appealing to it can excuse only the slightest moral wrongs. Anything else that is morally wrong for a nonlawyer to do on behalf of another person is morally wrong for a lawyer to do as well. The lawyer's role carries no moral privileges and immunities. . . When moral obligation conflicts with professional obligation, the lawyer must become a civil disobedient.

Luban, *supra* note 18, at 117–18.

[26] Pepper, *supra* note 1, at 613.

[27] *Id.* at 616–17.

assistance of a lawyer, just as we usually need a doctor for access to medical care.[28]

And the fourth premise is that the law to which we all have access should be the same law, not a particular form of the law determined by the individual lawyer through whom we are obtaining access. If law is a public good intended to be available to all, intended to guide, channel and facilitate all, then each client—each citizen—should receive the same version of the law regardless of the particular lawyer through whom that access is achieved. It would seem to fundamentally undermine the uniformity of law and equality of access for each lawyer to screen access to law through their own individual moral filter.

If the conduct is above the legal line on our chart above, then equal access to law for the citizenry, for each of us, suggests that the legal profession should provide access to that law even if it is below the moral line on the chart.

> For the lawyer to have moral responsibility for each [lawful] act he or she facilitates, for the lawyer to have a moral obligation to refuse to facilitate that which the lawyer believes to be immoral, is to substitute lawyers' beliefs for individual autonomy and diversity. Such a screening submits each to the prior restraint of the judge/facilitator and to rule by an oligarchy of lawyers.[29]

In other words, the law to which one has access ought not depend on the moral understanding of the particular lawyer one consults. The law is public and general; moral perception is more individual and private. The individual lawyer's private moral perception ought not determine the individual client's access to the public good that is the law.

This understanding is based on (1) the purpose and function of the professions in general and (2) the basic role of the legal profession to provide access to the law (concepts described in subsections 2-1.1 and 2-1.2 above). As such, the justification was far broader and deeper than just the adversary system, and thus avoided much of the critique based upon the adversary system justification.

> In the usual justification of the lawyer's amoral role, the model is adjudication, and there is a difficult stretch adapting and applying this to the lawyer's office. In this [defense], the model is the office lawyer advising about the law and implementing client goals through legally available devises, and one need not stretch to apply that model to litigation. Litigation is simply one of the available devices for implementing goals, like trust or a corporation.[30]

Wasserstrom was "undecided" about the lawyer's "amoral" role in providing access to the law. As we have seen, Luban thought it justified, but just barely so. Because the justification was so weak, Luban thought lawyers should be guided by ordinary morality in most situations where there was a conflict between it and service to the client's interests. The understanding just sketched, to the contrary, suggests that the

[28] It would be more precise to say that we need the assistance of someone with professional training and knowledge—perhaps a paraprofessional such as a nurse practitioner or a legal assistant or paralegal. And not infrequently the assistance of a lawyer—or access to legal information and guidance—may come indirectly, through the state medical association (and its monthly magazine) or through the labor union or through some other civic or private organization.

[29] *Id.* at 617.

[30] *Id.* at 621–22.

justification (equal access to the law) is a strong one, and cases of "conscientious objection" to the role should be relatively rare. In cases of conflict, lawyers should ordinarily serve the client's access to the law.[31] The professional ethics of each practicing lawyer are, to some extent, determined by where that lawyer falls on this spectrum.

---

[31] *Id.* at 632–33. Pepper did point to other possibilities for ameliorating the problem of facilitating morally wrongful access to law, primary among them a conversation and counseling between lawyer and client concerning the morality of the matter. *Id.* at 630–31. *See also* Stephen Pepper, *Lawyers' Ethics in the Gap Between Law and Justice*, 40 S. TEX. L. REV. 181 (1999). This chapter will consider that possibility in § 2-3 below.

# Chapter 2-2

# JURISPRUDENCE AND THE LAWYER'S ROLE: LOOKING TO AN UNDERSTANDING OF LAW—RATHER THAN TO MORALITY—FOR THE SOURCE OF LAWYERS' ETHICAL RESTRAINT[1]

**By Stephen Pepper and Katherine R. Kruse**

*Table of Sections*

§ 2-2.1 Introduction
§ 2-2.2 The Jurisprudential Turn
§ 2-2.3 Natural Law Theory
§ 2-2.4 Legal Positivism

---

## § 2-2.1 INTRODUCTION

By the mid-1990s, the academic field of theoretical legal ethics had settled into a sort of deadlock. The professional role of lawyers was assumed to permit—if not require—lawyers to take an amoral, instrumentalist view of the law. The Legal Realist jurisprudence, that law was nothing more than predictions about its likely enforcement, defined the "bounds of the law" that defined how far lawyers could go in pursuing their clients' interests. Because this jurisprudence brought no normative content to the law, it was not effective in balancing private and public interests. Therefore, legal ethicists searched for a way for lawyers to reign in occasional excessive self-interest of clients. They settled in one way or another on a moral role for lawyers—that lawyers should incorporate ordinary morality considerations as a constraint on their professional role.[2]

## § 2-2.2 THE JURISPRUDENTIAL TURN

Legal ethics scholars then began to turn from moral theory to jurisprudential theory, challenging the idea that the "bounds of the law" were necessarily defined by Legal Realist jurisprudence.[3] Instead, legal ethicists began to argue that law has moral content. In some cases, the moral content is built right into the definition of law. The ethical duty of lawyers is not to incorporate their personal morality into their advice to clients, but to properly interpret the law. Proper interpretation of the law will include public values.

---

[1] This section of the chapter is based upon Katherine R. Kruse, *The Jurisprudential Turn in Legal Ethics*, 53 ARIZ. LAW REV. 493 (2011).

[2] *Id.* at 498–505.

[3] *Id.* at 506.

This "jurisprudential turn in legal ethics" presents an attractive alternative to a moral values approach to legal ethics because it provides limits that spring directly from lawyers' professional duties rather than from appeals to personal morality.[4] The interpretation of law is a matter of professional expertise; it falls squarely within the scope of lawyers' decision-making authority in the lawyer-client relationship. By appealing to the public norms within the law, the lawyer can both avoid the dangers of moral overreaching with vulnerable clients and also gain traction with more powerful clients.[5]

## § 2-2.3 NATURAL LAW THEORY

William Simon was the first theorist to articulate a jurisprudential argument that lawyers' pursuit of their clients' interests were limited, not by their personal moral beliefs, but by the public morality inherent in the law. Simon argued that the basic guiding principle of legal ethics was that "lawyers should take those actions that, considering the relevant circumstances of the particular case, are most likely to promote justice."[6] Justice, in Simon's theory, is not a moral judgment of the lawyer about what was fair or right. Rather, it is an interpretation of what the law requires, drawing on traditional legal sources and methods. For that reason, he says that "justice" is synonymous with "legal merit."[7]

The idea that law is synonymous with justice suggests a natural law jurisprudence. Simon's theory of legal ethics leans heavily on the jurisprudential theory of Ronald Dworkin, who argues that the law consists not only of rules but includes the underlying principles that weave the rules together. Dworkin argues that the rules of positive law are held together by a coherent set of underlying principles of justice and fairness that are immanent in the law. Dworkin sees the interpretation of law as the writing of an unfolding narrative account of underlying principles that provide the most coherent explanation for the rules of law and the best justification for those rules.[8]

According to Dworkin, even if the law is silent on its face about how it should apply in a particular case, it is possible for jurists to discover a "right answer" about what the law says by reference to the underlying principles that form the substructure on which the system of laws is built. When judges decide cases, they participate in "constructive interpretation" of the principles that explain and justify the law. They "assume that the law is structured by a coherent set of principles of justice, fairness, and procedural due process," and they choose interpretations that both fit past decisions and "form part of a coherent theory justifying the network as a whole."[9] Dworkin distinguishes this type of legal interpretation—which he calls "law as integrity"—from both positivism and from a more pragmatic style of reasoning that looks only to what decision would make good public policy.[10]

William Simon's reliance on Dworkin's jurisprudence fulfills the promises that legal ethics makes to both the public and to clients: that the "bounds of the law" will protect

---

[4] *Id.* at 505–08.

[5] *Id.*

[6] WILLIAM H. SIMON, THE PRACTICE OF JUSTICE: A THEORY OF LAWYERS' ETHICS 138 (1998).

[7] *Id.*

[8] RONALD DWORKIN, LAW'S EMPIRE (1986).

[9] *Id.* at 243–45.

[10] *Id.*

the public interest by limiting over-zealous partisanship; and that the limits on partisanship will reflect objective criteria rather than the personal or political views of lawyers. Under Simon's view, lawyers who refuse to advance unjust claims or refrain from over-zealous tactics do not impose their personal moral views on their clients; they simply judge such claims and tactics to be legally invalid. Because clients are not entitled to pursue legally invalid claims, lawyers remain consistent with rule-of-law values.[11] In effect, this view draws the legal line (the bottom line on our chart in sub-section 2-1.3 above) up to or close to the moral line. Lawyers do not risk moral overreaching with vulnerable clients. And, lawyers can gain traction with more powerful clients by advising their clients that the law—interpreted according to its background values and underlying principles—simply does not permit the lawyers to pursue morally questionable claims.

However, the capacity to deliver on these promises rides on the ability of the Dworkian conception of law to determine true or correct answers. Without the premise that Dworkian interpretation yields a "right answer" or "best interpretation" of law most of the time, the implications are troubling. If there really is a right or best interpretation of the "bounds of the law," lawyers' judgments should roughly converge, and clients should get the same answer no matter which lawyer they hire. However, if law does not form a coherent system of justice capable of delivering "right" or "best" answers, there remains substantial leeway for lawyers to exercise personal judgment as they contemplate the question of what justice requires of them in each case. To many observers, Simon's conclusions as to what the "law" or "justice" require appear to reflect Simon's personal moral understandings rather than any clearly determinable interpretation of law—and this seems a major weakness of his suggested approach to lawyers' ethics.[12]

## § 2-2.4 LEGAL POSITIVISM

The competing jurisprudential camp that has emerged within legal ethics—which relies on legal positivism—rejects the premise that the law is woven together in a coherent system of underlying principles of justice and fairness. Rather, it views society as being characterized by deep and irreconcilable moral pluralism. Legal scholar Brad Wendel and philosopher Tim Dare have each advanced a positivist jurisprudence of lawyering.[13] They rely on a professional duty to respect the authority of positive law because law provides a framework for coordinated social activity in the face of deep and persistent normative disagreement in society. They argue that positive law deserves respect—even from those who disagree with its substance—because neutral lawmaking procedures transform the competing demands of underlying moral controversy into agreed-upon criteria of legality. Under the interpretive criteria of legal positivism, the important feature of law is not that it is necessarily fair or just.[14] Members of a morally pluralistic society will remain in hopeless disagreement about questions of justice and

---

[11] Simon, *supra* note 6, at 38–39, 140.

[12] Stephen Pepper, *Integrating Morality and Law in Legal Practice: A Reply to Professor Simon*, 23 GEO. J. LEGAL ETHICS 1011, 1012 n. 7 (2010); David Luban, *Reason and Passion in Legal Ethics*, 51 STAN. L. REV. 873, 895–96 (1999); THOMAS L. SHAFFER & ROBERT F. COCHRAN JR., LAWYERS, CLIENTS, AND MORAL RESPONSIBILITY 40–41 (2d ed. 2009).

[13] *See generally* TIM DARE, THE COUNSEL OF ROGUES?: A DEFENCE OF THE STANDARD CONCEPTION OF THE LAWYER'S ROLE (2009); W. BRADLEY WENDEL, LAWYERS AND FIDELITY TO LAW (2010).

[14] DARE, *supra* note 13, at 59–63; WENDEL, *supra* note 13, at 94–98, 114.

fairness.[15] What matters is that law can be identified as authoritative by features that are independent of its moral content—what H.L.A. Hart would call "rules of recognition."[16]

The "rules of recognition" for lawyers include the shared interpretive practices of the legal community, which preclude gamesmanship and sharp practices that toy with the ordinary meaning of law. They reject the Legal Realist idea that law is whatever you can get away with, or whatever a corrupt local official is likely to do. Lawyers, in their view, are enforcers of the plain and intended meaning of the law. Wendel, for example, would reshape lawyers' duties to their clients around clients' *legal entitlements*—defined as "what the law, properly interpreted, actually provides" for a client, rather than pursuit of client interests.[17] Dare rejects the idea that lawyers have a professional duty to "hyper-zealously" pursue every advantage for a client, including looking for ways to get around the law. Instead, he focuses professional duty on the "mere-zealous" pursuit of legal interests.[18]

The positivists would also preclude lawyers from inserting their moral judgments into legal representation by "dress[ing] up moral advice as a judgment about what the law permits."[19] The legal positivists criticize the Dworkian style of interpretation as providing lawyers with too much license to interpret the underlying principles of justice and fairness and to substitute their personal morality for what law actually says. This understanding of lawyers' ethics thus provides input only in firming up or drawing the lower (legal) line on our chart above. It provides limits on how one interprets law—limits on stretching or distorting law—but it does not otherwise answer what was articulated above as the central ethical problem of the practice of law: the gap between morality and law, the difficult fact that some of what is lawful is morally wrongful.

---

[15] WENDEL, *supra* note 13, at 87.

[16] H.L.A. HART, THE CONCEPT OF LAW 141–47 (2d ed. 1994).

[17] WENDEL, *supra* note 13, at 59.

[18] DARE, *supra* note 13, at 76.

[19] WENDEL, *supra* note 13, at 159.

# Chapter 2-3

## MORAL COUNSEL AND THE GAP BETWEEN LAW AND MORALITY

### By Stephen Pepper and Katherine R. Kruse

When the lawyer assists the client with conduct between the two lines on our chart—conduct that is within the law but nonetheless morally problematic—a real possibility arises that neither the client nor the lawyer will understand herself as responsible for the moral dimension of the situation. Consider the second of the three examples provided to illustrate the gap between that which is lawful and that which is morally justifiable.[1] When the lawyer cross-examines the truthful witness in a way to suggest that he is in fact lying, the lawyer is doing something that would be considered morally wrongful if it were done outside of the context or role of the lawyer. She is suggesting in a very public and formal context that the witness is lying when she knows that he is not. She is in effect lying about something important: the veracity of another person.[2] The lawyer will very likely think of this conduct as not her moral responsibility. To the contrary, the lawyer will see herself as fulfilling the lawyer's basic role of providing access to the law. The client has a constitutional right to confront witnesses against him but cannot do so effectively without the assistance of a lawyer. His constitutional rights also include the assistance of a lawyer to effectuate that cross-examination. The lawyer will almost certainly see herself as the instrument for effectuation of the client's legal rights, not as a moral wrongdoer.[3] Role morality provides the moral justification for what—without the role—we would characterize as moral wrongdoing. In the lawyer's view the moral responsibility for the cross-examination rests with the law and with the client. But the client is likely to perceive this misleading cross-examination as just a part of the lawyer's job—and thus the lawyer's responsibility. From the client's perspective, the distasteful cross-examination to suggest that which is not true is the lawyer's idea, conducted by the lawyer as the lawyer chooses to proceed. The client is likely to see it as simply part of what happens in litigation, which the client isn't controlling and doesn't know much about. Thus both lawyer and client can quite plausibly point to the other in regard to moral responsibility. In this way the morally problematic aspect of the cross-examination can disappear—neither sees it as their choice or obligation.

Consider also the first example of the gap provided above: the client admits a just debt to a third party, but the lawyer discovers a legal defense to that debt through the statute of frauds or a statute of limitations. Under the law of contract and under ordinary moral understandings the debt is owed and ought to be repaid, but the law will not require that repayment. The lawyer will likely perceive any moral wrong involved in

---

[1] *See supra* § 2-1.3.

[2] A frequently provided and very troubling example is the situation of the criminal defense lawyer in a rape case trying to create reasonable doubt on the part of some members of the jury by cross-examining the victim in a way that suggests she consented to the sexual encounter when the lawyer knows that in fact she did not.

[3] *See* sub-section 2-5 below on "Moral Remainders" for a brief consideration of how the conduct can be both at the same time.

failing to repay such a debt as the client's choice and the client's responsibility. And the client, in turn, may well see the law as excusing any moral obligation she has to repay. Conflating the lack of legal obligation with the lack of moral obligation, the client may well think: "My lawyer told me that there is no need to pay; I'm not obligated to pay." Or, "the law says that I'm not obligated to repay." As with the cross-examination, it is easy and understandable for client and lawyer each to place responsibility for the injustice on the other.[4] In such a situation no one take's moral responsibility—the lawyer's role-specific obligation to provide access to the law has resulted in an elision of moral responsibility.

One partial remedy for this problem lies in the possibility of moral dialogue and moral counsel between lawyer and client.[5] The lawyer in these situations might engage in a conversation with the client which points out not only the legal possibilities but also the moral implications.[6] The lawyer can explain the possibility of the cross-examination of the truthful witness or the possible defense to the debt. But the lawyer could also point out that such conduct might be morally problematic. The lawyer would be elaborating the difference between something to which the client has a legal right and that which is the morally right thing to do. The client has a legal right to the cross-examination or to assert the statute of limitations or statute of frauds defense, but it is quite possible that exercising such rights might be morally wrongful. (In other words, a legal right does not equate to a moral right.)[7]

One reason supporting such a conversation is that it is disrespectful to the client to assume her preferences and interests, to assume that she prefers the most possible money or the most possible freedom. It is disrespectful to assume that she wants to avoid paying the debt by using the statute of limitations. Likewise, it is disrespectful to the litigation client to assume that she wishes to win the lawsuit at the expense of putting an honest, innocent witness through the ordeal of a cross-examination falsely, but plausibly, charging dishonesty.[8] But such a conversation is difficult for many lawyers to imagine and hard to accomplish, partly because the standard law school curriculum does not include work on the skills of counseling. To be effective in both providing access to

---

[4] One of the pioneering works in the literature of lawyers' ethics summarized the problem:

> The upshot is that a man whose business it is to act for others finds himself, in his dealings on his client's behalf with outsiders, acting on a lower standard than he would if he were acting for himself, and lower, too, than any standard his client himself would be willing to act on, lower, in fact, than anyone on his own.

Charles P. Curtis, *The Ethics of Advocacy*, 4. STAN. L. REV. 3, 6 (1951).

[5] For more on moral engagement between the lawyer and client under the ethics rules, see Part Four of this book, Gregory C. Sisk, Legal Ethics and the Practice of Law, § 4-5.2(b)(2).

[6] Model Rule 2.1 states such conversations are permitted. MODEL RULES OF PROF'L RESPONSIBILITY r. 2.1 (AM. BAR ASS'N 2016).

[7] At least one scholar, one of the authors of this chapter, has suggested that such a conversation ought to be part of the professional ethical obligations of a lawyer:

> When the gap between law and justice is significant it ought to be part of the lawyer's ethical responsibility to clarify to the client that he or she has a moral choice in the matter. The lawyer ought to be held responsible for ensuring that the client knows that, in the lawyer's opinion, there is a gap between law and justice, and that it is the client—not the law and not the lawyer—who is primarily responsible for injustice if it occurs.

Stephen Pepper, *Lawyers' Ethics in the Gap Between Law and Justice*, 40 S. TEX. L. REV. 181, 190 (1999) (emphasis deleted). *See also* Katherine R. Kruse, *The Jurisprudential Turn in Legal Ethics,* 53 ARIZ. LAW REV. 493 (2011); Katherine R. Kruse, Beyond Cardboard Clients in Legal Ethics, 23 GEO. J. LEGAL ETHICS 103 (2010).

[8] Pepper, *supra* note 7, at 193.

law and bringing to bear a moral dimension, the lawyer needs to be gentle, honest and not overbearing; yet also clear. In such conversations the lawyer risks being intimidating or overreaching with less powerful clients and being intimidated or ignored by more powerful clients.[9]

[9] The lawyer also risks being off-putting or appearing self-righteous. For further elaboration of the difficulties of such conversations, and guidance in whether and how to have such conversations, see *id.* at 192–204; THOMAS L. SHAFFER & ROBERT F. COCHRAN JR., LAWYERS, CLIENTS, AND MORAL RESPONSIBILITY 40–41 (2d ed. 2009); Kruse, *supra* note 7.

# Chapter 2-4

# THE CORPORATION AS CLIENT—AMORAL ETHICS SQUARED

## By Stephen Pepper and Katherine R. Kruse

One of the premises upon which *professional* ethics is based is the understanding that patients and clients are vulnerable in relation to their doctors or lawyers, architects or accountants. The client or patient has a problem or a need, the professional can provide the necessary assistance, but the knowledge or processes involved are beyond the understanding of the customer. This renders the client, patient, customer vulnerable in relation to the professional. Because ordinary market norms such as *caveat emptor* leave the client subject to economic exploitation by the professional in this way, the special ethical obligations of professionalism are imposed on those considered professionals.[1] Large corporations, however, are usually not vulnerable in relation to their lawyers in this way. In fact, the vulnerability would seem to go the other way: even very large, multi-city or multinational law firms are small in relation to many of their major corporate clients, and often the law firms are economically dependent upon their large clients. Thus one of the premises underlying a special professional ethic seems far less applicable to large corporations. It is the special professional obligation to provide access to the law that justifies assisting conduct between the lines on our chart, conduct that is lawful but morally wrongful. But the lack of vulnerability on the part of corporations (at least large ones) appears to substantially undercut this justification for aiding such conduct on the part of such actors.

The other side of the coin of the lack of vulnerability on the part of corporations is that they are usually far more powerful than individuals. The corporate form is created and designed for the aggregation of capital, including both material capital and human capital. This aggregation of financial, material and human capital dwarfs that of individuals and provides corporations with power exponentially greater than the vast majority of individuals. For this reason the scope of the wrongdoing that a corporation can do when engaged in conduct above the legal line but below the moral line on our chart is far greater and of far more concern than when the client in an actual person. These two aspects of corporate power thus undermine the ordinary justification for a special client-subservient professional ethic in two ways: (1) most large corporations are not vulnerable or at risk in relation to their lawyers' knowledge and sophistication (and therefore not in need of special protection from their lawyers), and (2) large corporations' vast resources and powers makes them a special risk to others and to society.[2] (Why, one might ask, would professionals have an ethical obligation to assist such actors in lawful but morally wrongful conduct?)

A third aspect of the corporate situation also suggests that it may be more typical for the client to be the source of possible moral wrongdoing rather than the party in need of protection from it. Corporations do not have the range and complexity of motivations,

---

1 *See supra* § 2-1.2 for an explication of professional ethics.

2 Stephen Pepper, *Three Dichotomies in Lawyers' Ethics (With Particular Attention to the Corporation as Client)*, 28 GEO. J. LEGAL ETHICS 1069, 1079–80 (2015).

emotions, and restraints on conduct that individuals have; they do not have the variety of ethical motivation and perception of individuals. Both by law and pursuant to the intentions the shareholders and management (and also the general social and political understanding) the primary goal of a for-profit corporation is shareholder value or profit. Money—or its equivalent in some form—is the primary, and often sole, goal or purpose of corporations. This is a quite limited and impoverished set of values compared to that of most natural persons. Corporations don't have friends or spouses; they don't have the many feelings, emotions, likes and dislikes, goals and desire for a meaningful life that individuals have.

Corporations, of course, can only act through the actual persons responsible for their management. But the executives and managers of corporations are charged by law and contract with serving this same limited set of goals and values. We have noted above that lawyers have a role-specific morality: they are to provide their clients with access to the law and facilitation in the use of the law. If doing so leads to morally problematic consequences, that is the concern of the client not of the lawyer acting as lawyer. Corporate managers have a similar role-specific morality: they are to serve the corporation in maximizing value or profit for the shareholders. That is the goal that directs their conduct—everything else is subservient—a distant second in rank, including moral concerns. When the lawyer serves the corporate manager in providing access to the law, she does so under her limited (some describe it as amoral) ethical role. And what that manager is seeking through the law is also limited by her role—maximizing material value. In the situation of lawyers serving corporations we thus have amoral roles squared: the lawyer's role leaves out ordinary morality; the manager's role leaves out ordinary morality. Decisions are being made, conduct is occurring, without either lawyer or executive understanding ordinary morality as an essential part of their decision-making process or professional obligation.[3] And often the artificial entity for whom this is being done wields a huge amount of power while lacking an ordinary human conscience.

This is a basic contemporary problem of corporate legal practice: the current ethic of deferring to client interests and choice when combined with the reality of a powerful corporate client without a human sensibility or conscience may make it particularly likely that lawyers will assist in morally dubious or wrongful conduct by their corporate clients.[4] Corporations as clients therefore present a very substantial risk in regard to the facilitation of conduct between the two lines on our chart.[5] The rules of lawyers' professional ethics directed particularly to corporations do not address this problem. They are focused on authority within the corporation (from whom should the lawyer take direction), possible conflicts of interest within the corporate entity, and the possibility of wrongdoing by corporate constituents that might result in "substantial injury" to the corporation.[6] The philosophy of legal ethics has also, for the most part, not addressed the

---

[3] *Id.* at 1080–81.

[4] *Id.* at 1081–82.

[5] *See infra* § 2-1.3 (chart) on p. 32.

[6] MODEL RULES OF PROF'L RESPONSIBILITY r. 1.13 (AM. BAR ASS'N 2016). On the lawyer's duties to organization clients under the ethics rules, see Part Four of this book, Gregory C. Sisk, Legal Ethics and the Practice of Law, ch. 4-8.

problem of the corporation as a different kind of client presenting a different risk and has not developed ethical approaches or limits designed to address this problem.[7]

[7] *See* Pepper, *supra* note 2 (some tentative thoughts on possible ameliorative limits and approaches for this problem and further references).

# Chapter 2-5

# MORAL REMAINDERS

## By Stephen Pepper and Katherine R. Kruse

In the course of a lawyer's work most decisions are not morally problematic. The decision to represent a plaintiff in a personal injury suit, or either of the parties in a dispute over a commercial lease, usually will present little in the way of moral difficulty. Negotiating or drafting a business contract between two relatively equal business entities will not ordinarily present a difficult moral question. Occasionally, however, a lawyer's legal practice will present a moral problem, and this is the situation with which this chapter has been primarily concerned. Assume that a practicing lawyer has concluded, as most have, that a professional role specific morality justifies providing legal assistance in lawful conduct that is morally problematic, that is conduct between the lines on our chart in Section 2-1.3 above. Such a lawyer has concluded that the legal profession's role of providing equal, morally neutral access to the law justifies effectuating a statute of limitations or statute of frauds defense even when the client has admitted to her that the debt is just and owed (our first example in Section 2-1.3).[1] Taking the second example from that section above, the lawyer has chosen to cross-examine a witness known to be truthful in a way to suggest he is lying, effectuating the client's legal right to confront witnesses. In addition to providing access to the law, the lawyer in each case is also effectuating a moral wrong. A debt that is justly owed will not be repaid, a moral wrong to the creditor. An implicit public assertion will be made that an honest person is a liar—a moral wrong to that person.

Two moral wrongs have occurred. But our social and political systems understand these wrongs as justified by the moral good of access to the law, and for this moral good to be available lawyers must effectuate that access. Despite this justification—and despite its general acceptance—the moral wrong remains. The witness has been publicly defamed and hurt; the debtor has lost money to which she was entitled both morally and under the law of contract. The concept of a "moral remainder" is helpful in regard to understanding the dual nature of such a situation: the conduct is morally justified, but nonetheless a moral wrong has occurred, it remains.[2] And it remains as the moral responsibility of the lawyer. She must be able to keep in her mind and conscience these two contradictory understandings: she has provided morally justifiable facilitation in the use of the law, but she has also committed a moral wrong. We generally have concluded as a society that the first overbalances the second, that the first justifies the second. But it does not eliminate it. And it is important for the lawyer to remember and be conscious of the fact that the moral wrong remains. It is important because it assists the lawyer in not becoming calloused to the wrongs he or she may be effectuating; and to keep the wrongs in mind is to keep the possibility of ameliorating or even avoiding them in mind. It is a way to help the lawyer remain a good person while also being a good lawyer.

---

1 Under Professor Wendel's appeal to positive law—the client's "legal entitlements"—this would clearly be part of the client's legal entitlement even if morally wrongful. *See* section 2-2.4 above.

2 For a discussion of moral remainders in the practice of law see W. BRADLEY WENDEL, LAWYERS AND FIDELITY TO LAW 7, 169–75 (2010). Wendel takes the term from Bernard Williams: ". . . the moral remainder, the uncancelled moral disagreeableness . . ." *Id.* at n. 64.

# Part Three

## DEVELOPMENT TOWARD PROFESSIONALISM AND THE FORMATION OF AN ETHICAL PROFESSIONAL IDENTITY TO BECOME AN EFFECTIVE LAWYER

**By Neil W. Hamilton and Melissa H. Weresh**

### RECOMMENDED CITATION FOR PART THREE

For those citing to Chapters 3-1 through 3-3 in Part Three, we recommend attribution to this individually-authored part as being most accurate. For example, the most appropriate citation format to the first section in this part would look like this: Neil W. Hamilton and Melissa H. Weresh, Development Toward Professionalism And The Formation of An Ethical Professional Identity To Become An Effective Lawyer § 3-1.1, in *Legal Ethics, Professional Responsibility, and the Legal Profession* (West Academic Publishing, 2018).

# Chapter 3-1

# PROFESSIONALISM AND PROFESSIONAL IDENTITY

**By Neil W. Hamilton and Melissa H. Weresh**

*Table of Sections*

§ 3-1.1 Why Development Toward Professionalism and the Formation of an Ethical Professional Identity Is Important

§ 3-1.2 Understanding the Formation of an Ethical Professional Identity in the Context of the Historical and Sociological Development of Professionalism and Professional Formation

§ 3-1.3 Understanding the Formation of an Ethical Professional Identity in the Context of the ABA's Model Rules and Reports and the Understanding of Exemplary Lawyers

§ 3-1.4 Comparison of the Competencies Defining an Ethical Professional Identity from the Model Rules, the ABA Reports and Exemplary Lawyers with the Professional-Formation Competencies that Legal Employers and Clients Want

## § 3-1.1 WHY DEVELOPMENT TOWARD PROFESSIONALISM AND THE FORMATION OF AN ETHICAL PROFESSIONAL IDENTITY IS IMPORTANT

As a law student or new lawyer you are embarking on a noble career with a rich history. As you enter the profession it is important to understand how professional identity formation has been influenced by the history of the profession and the development of regulatory provisions relating to ethics and professionalism. You should also be aware that developing an ethical professional identity will be essential to your success. This chapter will therefore make clear that each law student and lawyer should develop over a career toward professionalism and the formation of an ethical professional identity because:

(1) clients and legal employers value what we will describe in the next section as the professional-formation competencies and these competencies lead to professional effectiveness; and

(2) an ultimate goal of professionalism and professional identity formation is that lawyers are worthy of client and public trust.

It is highly in each law student's and lawyer's enlightened self-interest to develop and demonstrate the professional-formation competencies that clients and legal employers want and which in turn generate client and public trust and positive reputational capital, particularly in the lawyer's own professional work, but also in the unique contribution of the profession itself which leads the public to see value in legal services.

Beyond these enlightened self-interest reasons, each law student and lawyer should grow toward professionalism and the formation of an ethical professional identity in order to be worthy of client and public trust with respect to our role in the justice system. For example, the first sentence of the Preamble of the Model Rules of Professional Conduct articulates three societal roles in the justice system for each lawyer that are in some tension with each other (a polarity), and each lawyer grows over time toward an ethical professional identity in understanding and living out all three roles: "A lawyer, as a member of the legal profession, is a representative of clients, an officer of the legal system, and a public citizen having special responsibility for the quality of justice." Understanding the historical development of professional identity formation, including its regulatory history, as well as the current expectations of clients and legal employers, is an essential step in professional identity formation.

This chapter traces a variety of influences on our understanding of professional identity formation, concluding that there is substantial convergence regarding what it means to be an ethical, effective lawyer. Law is considered one of the learned professions and a historical and sociological lens reinforces certain unique characteristics of an ethical professional identity. Therefore, in Section 3-1.2(a) we review historical and sociological underpinnings of professionalism and professional identity formation. We then turn our attention to more modern studies of professional identity formation, considering expectations that various constituencies have of lawyers and, specifically, what characteristics contribute to lawyer effectiveness. In Section 3-1.2(b) we review material gleaned from empirical studies asking respondents (including both newly licensed and more experienced lawyers as well as legal employers) to identify lawyer effectiveness factors. Sections 3-1.3 explores how the regulation of lawyers impacts professional identity development, and how an ethical professional identity is essential to client and public trust. In Section 3-1.4 we take the opportunity to compare the historical, sociological, empirical and regulatory threads of emphasis on ethical professional identity. In that section, we are reminded as we view professional identity formation through these interdisciplinary lenses that there a great deal of consistency between the expectations that the public, legal employers, and lawyers themselves have set for an ethical professional identity.

## § 3-1.2 UNDERSTANDING THE FORMATION OF AN ETHICAL PROFESSIONAL IDENTITY IN THE CONTEXT OF THE HISTORICAL AND SOCIOLOGICAL DEVELOPMENT OF PROFESSIONALISM AND PROFESSIONAL FORMATION[1]

A firm appreciation of professional identity development in the legal profession is facilitated by a cursory review of the historical and sociological understanding of law as a learned profession and the social contract of the profession with society.

### § 3-1.2(a) Law as a Learned Profession

Law has historically been considered among the "learned professions," including medicine and the clergy.[2] Professions are typically distinguished from other occupations

---

[1] This section is based, in part, on Melissa H. Weresh, *I'll Start Walking Your Way, You Start Walking Mine: Sociological Perspectives on Professional Identity Development and Influence of Generational Differences,* 61 S. CAR. L. REV. (2009).

[2] Edward D. Re, *Professionalism for the Legal Profession,* 11 FED. CIRCUIT B.J. 683, 684 (2001–2002). Re notes "[l]awyers have derived great pleasure and pride in being members of one of the historic and learned professions along with the clergy and medicine, which have been traditionally regarded as professions

on the basis of several overriding features. According to Dean Roscoe Pound of Harvard Law School, "[t]he term refers to a group . . . pursuing a learned art as a common calling in the spirit of public service-no less a public service because it may incidentally be a means of livelihood. Pursuit of the learned art in the spirit of a public service is the primary purpose."[3] In describing how professions differ from other occupations, one court explained:

> A profession is not a business. It is distinguished by the requirements of extensive formal training and learning, admission to practice by a qualifying licensure, a code of ethics imposing standards qualitatively and extensively beyond those that prevail or are tolerated in the marketplace, a system for discipline of its members for violation of the code of ethics, a duty to subordinate financial reward to social responsibility, and, notably, an obligation on its members, even in nonprofessional matters, to conduct themselves as members of a learned, disciplined, and honorable occupation. These qualities distinguish professionals from others whose limitations on conduct are largely prescribed only by general legal standards and sanctions, whether civil or criminal.[4]

The American Bar Association (ABA) Commission on Professionalism identified four elements that distinguish a profession from other occupations.[5] Recognizing that lawyers enjoy special societal privileges, including the ability to control licensing, the ABA concluded that certain assumptions distinguish law as a profession from other occupations.[6] First, the "practice requires substantial intellectual training and the use of complex judgments."[7] Second, because "clients cannot adequately evaluate the quality of the service, they must" place their trust in lawyers.[8] Third, "the client's trust presupposes that the practitioner's self-interest is overbalanced by devotion to serving both the client's interest and the public good."[9] Fourth, lawyers are self-regulating, requiring that the profession be "organized in such a way as to assure the public and the courts that its members are competent, do not violate their client's trust, and transcend

---

throughout the centuries." *See also* Bruce Beesley, *The Profession and Business of Law*, 16 NEVADA LAWYER 4, Oct. 2008. Beesley notes:

> Historically, there were only three learned professions: theology, law and medicine. These professions were considered 'callings,' requiring specialized knowledge, long and intensive preparation in the skills and methods of the professions, and training in the underlying historic principles. The professions were tightly controlled through formal organizations or concerted opinion of the members. These factors operated to maintain high standards of achievement and conduct by members of the professions, whose primary purpose was to provide service to the public.

[3] Commission on Professionalism, Am. Bar Ass'n, Report: ". . . *In the Spirit of Public Service": A Blueprint for the Rekindling of Lawyer Professionalism*, reprinted in 112 F.R.D. 243, 261 (1986) (quoting ROSCOE POUND, THE LAWYER FROM ANTIQUITY TO MODERN TIMES 5 (1953)) [hereinafter Stanley Commission Report]. *See also* Anne Colby and William M. Sullivan, *Formation Of Professionalism and Purpose: Perspectives from the Preparation for the Professions Program*, 5 U. ST. THOMAS L.J. 404, 405 (2008) (noting general agreement in defining characteristics of a profession and concluding that "[p]rofessions involve (at least) a commitment to serve the interests of clients and the welfare of society; bodies of specialized knowledge and skill; and procedures through which the professional community provides oversight of entry into the profession and quality in both practice and professional training.").

[4] *Lincoln Rochester Trust Co. v. Freeman (In re Estate of Freeman)*, 311 N.E.2d at 483.

[5] Stanley Commission Report, *supra* note 3, at 261–62.

[6] *Id.* at 261.

[7] *Id.*

[8] *Id.*

[9] *Id.*

their own self-interest."[10] Thus, advanced education and training, self-regulation and discipline under a formal code of performance, and a fiduciary obligation to elevate the public good over the self-interest of the individual professional are overriding themes which distinguish members of a profession.[11]

These attributes of professional life are related to and dependent upon one another. The specialized skills that distinguish members of a profession require members of the profession to self-license and to self-regulate. The justification for self-regulation is tied to the distinctive skills set—only individuals within the profession have the expertise to evaluate the conduct of other members.[12] This autonomy is justified by and dependent upon the profession's elevation of the public good over its own self-interest. The attributes of professional life coalesce to form a social contract relationship with the public. This social contract is based on trust, fidelity, and assurance and it justifies the profession's authority to devise and enforce a code of conduct. The historical framework of the legal profession's social contract can be summarized as follows:

> Since the late 1800s, the peer-review professions in the United States, including the legal profession, have gradually worked out stable social contracts with the public in both custom and law. The public grants a profession autonomy to regulate itself through peer review, expecting the profession's members to control entry into and continued membership in the profession, to set standards for how individual professionals perform their work so that it serves the public good in the area of the profession's responsibility, and to foster the core values and ideals of the profession.[13]

In return, each member of the profession and the profession as a whole agree to meet certain correlative duties to the public: to maintain high standards of minimum competence and ethical conduct to serve the public purpose of the profession and to discipline those who fail to meet these standards; to promote the core values and ideals of the profession; and to restrain self-interest to some degree to serve the public purpose

---

[10] *Id.* at 261–62.

[11] *See also Chase Scientific Research, Inc. v. NIA Group, Inc.*, 749 N.E.2d 161 (2001). In evaluating whether insurance agents and brokers are considered professional groups, the court noted:

> The qualities shared by such [professional] groups guide us in defining the term 'professional.' In particular, those qualities include extensive formal learning and training, licensure and regulation indicating a qualification to practice, a code of conduct imposing standards beyond those accepted in the marketplace and a system of discipline for violation of those standards. Additionally, a professional relationship is one of trust and confidence, carrying with it a duty to counsel and advise clients.

*Id.* at 166 (citations omitted). The court concluded that brokers and agents are not professionals because they are not required to complete specialized training, are not bound by an enforceable standard of conduct, and are not required to provide guidance and advice based on a "special relationship of trust and confidence." *Id.* at 167.

[12] As one author explains:

> One of the most persuasive arguments in favour of self-regulation is that an occupational group has evolved over time and developed a specialized body of knowledge which makes members of the group experts. Because the knowledge these members have is so specialized, it would be difficult and expensive for the government to determine and monitor standards of practice for the profession. It is therefore thought that members of a profession are in the best position to set standards and to evaluate whether they have been met.

Glen E. Randall, *Understanding Professional Self-Regulation* <http://www.paramedicsofmanitoba.ca/uploaded/web/pdf/Understanding%20Professional%20Self-Regulation.pdf>.

[13] Neil Hamilton, *Professionalism Clearly Defined*, 18 No. 4 PROF. LAW. 4, 4–5 (2008).

of the profession.[14] A professional community can then be commonly understood to manifest three distinguishing qualities: 1) members of the community have acquired a distinctive skill set; 2) members regulate entry into, and conduct within, the community; and 3) members enjoy and are bound by relationship of trust with the public based upon the commitment by professional members to elevate the public good over self-interest.[15]

Of course, these assertions about professionalism are not without criticism. In his book, *The Vanishing American Lawyer*, Thomas Morgan asserts that "Law in America is not a profession—and that's a good thing."[16] Morgan traces developments since the

---

[14] *Id. See also* MAGALI SARFATTI LARSON, THE RISE OF PROFESSIONALISM: A SOCIOLOGICAL ANALYSIS (University of California Press, 1977). In his sociological examination of professions, Larson identified three dimensions of the "ideal-type of profession." *Id.* at x (citations omitted.) First, there is a cognitive dimension, which is "centered on the body of knowledge and techniques which the professionals apply in their work, and on the training necessary to master such knowledge and skills." *Id.* The second dimension is the normative dimension which "covers the service orientation of professionals, and their distinctive ethics, which justify the privilege of self-regulation granted them by society." *Id.* The third dimension is evaluative and "implicitly compares professions to other occupations, underscoring the professions' singular characteristics of autonomy and prestige." *Id.* Larson concludes that "[t]he distinctiveness of the professions appears to be founded on the combination of these general dimensions. These uncommon occupations tend to become 'real' communities, whose members share a relatively permanent affiliation, an identity, personal commitment, specific interests, and general loyalties." *Id.*

[15] While these three qualities or attributes seem to accurately identify and distinguish the learned professions, scholars have identified additional ones applicable to the legal community. In *Professionalism, It's No Joke*, Charles E. McCallum noted the following seven attributes:

1. Dedication to serving clients before self[;] . . .
2. Dedication to serving the public interest[;] . . .
3. Honesty and integrity[;] . . .
4. Dedication to excellence[;] . . .
5. Practice in context[;] . . .
6. A specialized body of knowledge and skills freely shared with other professionals[;] . . .[and]
7. Adherence to ethical rules and participation in self-regulation.

Charles E. McCallum, *Professionalism, It's No Joke,* 16 BUS. L. TODAY 43, 45–46 (Feb. 2007).

Timothy P. Terrell and James H. Wildman identify six values associated with the legal professional tradition, including

1. An Ethic of Excellence[;] . . .
2. An Ethic of Integrity: A Responsibility To Say "No"[;] . . .
3. A Respect for the System and Rule of Law: A Responsibility To Say "Why"[;] . . .
4. A Respect for Other Lawyers and Their Work[;] . . .
5. A Commitment to Accountability[;] . . .
6. A Responsibility for Adequate Distribution of Legal Services.

Timothy P. Terrell and James H. Wildman, *Rethinking "Professionalism,"* 41 EMORY L.J. 403, 424–32 (1992) (emphasis omitted).

[16] THOMAS D. MORGAN, THE VANISHING AMERICAN LAWYER 66 (2010) [hereinafter Morgan, Vanishing Lawyer]. Morgan is not alone in his condemnation of the rhetoric of professionalism, Gillian Hadfield catalogues the type and breadth of criticism regarding the system and proffered justification of lawyer ethical regulation:

> Few commentators, outside of the practicing bar and the judiciary, find much to recommend in the modern system of professional regulation of lawyers. While the topic (to date) has attracted only a small share of scholarly attention, justifications for the traditional exclusive control exercised by the bar and judiciary over the practice of law have drawn withering critiques from several directions for decades. Bill Simon called for the abandonment of legal professionalism thirty years ago and again in the wake of the savings and loan crisis of the late 1980s and the Enron debacle of 2001, emphasizing the failure of self-regulation and the absence of justification for corporate attorney-client privilege in particular. Deborah Rhode has for almost three decades assailed the failure of the profession to put aside self-interest and live up to its obligation to promote access to the justice system and the interests of consumers of legal services, particularly personal (as opposed to business) legal services. Both Rick Abel and Deborah Rhode made the argument twenty-five years ago that the American Bar Association (ABA) is inherently incapable of producing any

1970s that have significantly altered the practice of law including, for example, increased globalization, increased subject matter complexity, increased numbers of lawyers, and increased technological complexity.[17] These are business realities that affect traditional understandings of professionalism.

Morgan's principal concern is that the distinction between a profession and a business has been used to enhance the social recognition and prestige of lawyers (especially in contrast to "business") and this in turn justifies opposition to business efficiency initiatives responding to the realities above. This opposition is inhibiting the delivery of legal services at a higher quality and lower price which would make access to justice more affordable.[18] Morgan thus concludes by recognizing that law can be perceived, in part, as reflecting business attributes as opposed to professionalism distinctions, asserting that "[t]here was nothing about professional status that made it less important for lawyers to deliver services of higher quality and at a lower price than one's competition, [ ] just as there was nothing about business that required losing sight of the public interest."[19] Morgan has a very good point that the competencies that create trust between a service provider and a customer are the same in business as in a profession. These competencies are explored further in Chapter 3-1.2(b).

Some sociologists have made arguments similar to those of Morgan that professionalism serves the interests of lawyers rather than the interests of society or clients. For example, Debra J. Schleef writes "[a] number of sociologists posit that professionalism itself is an ideology that serves the self-interest of lawyers or other professionals, rather than the interests of society or clients. These scholars view professional actors as making conscious efforts to perpetuate an ideology of expert knowledge that legitimates their privilege and professional dominance."[20]

---

> regulations save those that promote the interests of lawyers. Stephen Gillers offered a scathing critique in 1985 of the ABA's (then) new Model Rules of Professional Conduct, concluding that "[t]he lawyers who approved the Rules looked after their own." Twenty years ago David Luban called for the deregulation of routine legal services (such as completion of forms, drafting and probating of wills, uncontested divorces) and argued that the attorney-client privilege and related duties of confidentiality (a lynchpin of the bar's justification for key elements of its regulatory regime) were not justified in the organizational (corporate) context. In a careful history of regulation of the unauthorized practice of law (UPL) completed for the American Bar Foundation in 1980, Barlow Christensen reached the "shocking" conclusion that UPL restrictions were no longer defensible. David Wilkins raised serious questions in 1992 about the validity of the bar's defense of self-regulation based on professional independence and unique bar expertise to judge lawyers' conduct. Anthony Kronman saw no hope for the recovery of lawyerly ideals through self-regulation in the face of modern corporate legal practice in his plaint for the "lost lawyer" in 1993: any lawyer seeking those ideals has no alternative, he counseled, than to "stay clear of the . . . large-firm practice." Jonathan Macey called for the abandonment of self-regulation of the profession after Enron. Benjamin Barton has recently argued that the judicial protection of lawyer self-governance is one among many examples of how the judiciary systematically favors the private interests of lawyers. There is thus no shortage of scholarly critique.

Gillian K. Hadfield, *Legal Barriers to Innovation: The Growing Economic Cost of Professional Control over Corporate Legal Markets*, 60 STAN. L. REV. 1689, 1690–91 (2008) (citations omitted).

[17] *See generally* MORGAN, VANISHING LAWYER, *supra* note 16.

[18] Thomas D. Morgan, *Inverted Thinking About Law As A Profession or Business*, 2016 J. OF PROF. LAW. 115, 125. *See also* Neil Hamilton, *The Profession and Professionalism Are Dead?: A Review of Thomas Morgan, the Vanishing American Lawyer*, PROF. LAW., 2010, at 14.

[19] *Id.* at 127.

[20] DEBRA J. SCHLEEF, MANAGING ELITES: PROFESSIONAL SOCIALIZATION IN LAW AND BUSINESS SCHOOLS, 5 (Rowman and Littlefield Publishers, Inc., 2006).

Notwithstanding some criticism of proffered definitions of and justifications for professionalism, scholars who seek to define and justify professionalism ideals tend to emphasize the following characteristics: 1) a distinct code of ethics; 2) a distinct and unique skill set; 3) a system of self-regulation; 4) public trust; and 5) self-interest overbalanced by a commitment to the public good. We see these themes revisited in our subsequent sections, which trace professional formation competencies as defined in various ethical codes and as evidenced in the traits of exemplary lawyers.

### § 3-1.2(b) Understanding the Importance of the Professional-Formation Competencies to Effectiveness in the Practice of Law

While historically, the legal profession and legal scholars have done virtually no empirical research to define the factors that contribute to lawyer effectiveness,[21] we are beginning to see more research to help us understand which competencies are most needed for lawyer effectiveness. For example, Educating Tomorrow's Lawyers (ETL) published a substantial empirical study in 2016 where ETL asked respondents to identify the competencies, skills, characteristics and qualities that new lawyers need to be ready for practice. ETL worked with focus groups in various practice areas to identify a list of 147 possible significant items to include in the survey and distributed the survey through bar organizations in 37 states to over 780,000 lawyers, ultimately receiving 24,137 survey responses.

For each item the survey asked the respondent to identify whether the item was: (1) necessary in the short term; (2) must be acquired over time; (3) advantageous but not necessary; and (4) not relevant. The items that respondents rated "necessary in the short term" would be the group that the respondents believed the new law graduate needs immediately on beginning practice.

The data below indicate the percentage of all 24,137 responses from across all practice areas and geographies that answered that the item was "necessary in the short term." To make the data more understandable in relation to an ethical professional identity, we grouped the various "necessary in the short term" competencies into umbrella categories of Trustworthiness, Relationship Skills Including Respect for Others and Responsiveness, Strong Work Ethic/Diligence, and Common Sense/Good Judgment. The numbers to the left of the competency indicate the relative ranking of that competency as "necessary in the short term" out of the 147 possible competencies. The number to the right of each competency is the percentage of the respondents who indicated it is "necessary in the short term."

**Table 1—Educating Tomorrow's Lawyers' Data on Competencies "Necessary in the Short Term" for Law Graduates[22]**

**Trustworthiness**

1. Keep confidentiality (96%)
3. Honor commitments (94%)
4. Trustworthiness/Integrity (92%)

---

21 William Henderson, *A Blueprint for Change*, 40 PEPP. L. REV. 461, 498 (2013).

22 Alli Gerkman et al, Educating Tomorrow's Lawyers, FOUNDATIONS FOR PRACTICE SURVEY, THE WHOLE LAWYER AND THE CHARACTER QUOTIENT (2016).

15. Take individual responsibility (82%)
18. Strong moral compass (79%)

**Relationship Skills Including Respect for Others and Responsiveness**

2. Arrive on time (95%)
5. Treat others with respect (92%)
6. Listen attentively and with respect (92%)
7. Respond promptly (91%)
17. Emotional regulation and self-control (80%)
20. Exhibit tact and diplomacy (78%)

**Strong Work Ethic/Diligence**

8. Strong work ethic (88%)
9. Diligence (88%)
10. Attention to detail (88%)
11. Conscientiousness (86%)

**Common Sense/Good Judgment** (85%, this was 12th).

Note that Research the Law was 13th (84%), Intelligence was 14th (84%), Speak Professionally was 16th (80%), and Write Professionally was 19th (78%).

A number of the most important competencies "necessary in the short term" are what we call the *professional-formation competencies* (note that ETL calls these competencies "the character quotient"). These are values, virtues, and habits that can be developed over a career and include the competencies related to trustworthiness (keep confidentiality, honor commitments, trustworthiness/integrity, take individual responsibility, and strong moral compass), the competencies related to respect for others and relationship skills (arrive on time, treat others with respect, listen attentively, respond promptly, emotional regulation and self-control, and exhibit tact and diplomacy), the competencies related to strong work ethic/diligence (strong work ethic, diligence, attention to detail, and conscientiousness) and common sense/good judgment.

Other empirical research that helps us to understand the importance of the professional-formation competencies to legal employers includes four surveys of legal employers in Minnesota in 2013 and 2014 to capture the competencies considered most important in a hiring decision by those legal employers (on a scale from 0 as "not considered" to 5 as "critically important").[23] The table below shows the averages of those four surveys. (The legal employers surveyed included the 14 largest law firms of 67–740 lawyers, 23 small law firms of 2–9 lawyers, 18 county attorney's offices, and all 6 regional legal aid offices.)

[23] Neil Hamilton, *Changing Markets Create Opportunities: Emphasizing the Competencies Legal Employers Use in Hiring New Lawyers (Including Professional Formation/Professionalism)*, 65 S. CAR. L.REV. 547, 557 (2014).

**Table 2—Relative Importance of Different Competencies in the Decision to Hire a New Lawyer: Average Ratings Across Four Surveys of Legal Employers in Minnesota**

| | **Very Important to Critical Important** | |
|---|---|---|
| | **Competency** | **Average Significance** |
| 1. | Integrity/honesty/trustworthiness | 4.76 |
| 2. | Good judgment/common sense/problem solving | 4.63 |
| 3. | Analytical skills: identify legal issues from facts, apply the law, and draw conclusions | 4.37 |
| 4. | Initiative/ambition/drive/strong work ethic | 4.33 |
| 5. | Effective written/oral communication skills | 4.33 |
| 6. | Dedication to client service/responsiveness to client (1st for legal aid offices) | 4.29 |
| 7. | Commitment to firm/department/office and its goals and values | 4.25 |
| 8. | Initiates and maintains strong work and team relationships (4th for county attorneys) | 4.14 |
| | **Important to Very Important** | |
| | **Competency** | **Average Significance** |
| 9. | Integrity/honesty/trustworthiness | 3.91 |
| 10. | Legal competency/expertise/knowledge of the law | 3.87 |
| 11. | Ability to work independently (6th for small firms and 7th for county attorneys) | 3.83 |
| 12. | Commitment to professional development toward excellence | 3.68 |
| 13. | Strategic/creative thinking | 3.66 |
| 14. | Research skills (9th for large firms)<br>Note that for large firms, Business development/marketing/client retention was ranked the 15th most important competency, and for small firms this was ranked 14th most important, but this competency was not included in the county attorney and legal aid office surveys.) | 3.62 |
| 15. | Inspires confidence (8th for large firms) | 3.60 |
| 16. | Seeks feedback/responsive to feedback (12th for small firms and 11th for county attorneys) | 3.53 |
| 17. | Stress/crisis management | 3.45 |
| 18. | Leadership | 3.10 |
| 19. | Negotiation skills | 3.10 |

| Somewhat Important to Important | | |
|---|---|---|
| | Competency | Average Significance |
| 20. | Pro bono, community, bar association involvement | 2.48 |
| 21. | Delegation, supervision, mentoring | 2.37 |

Both the ETL data and the data on the competencies that legal employers value emphasize the professional-formation competencies like trustworthiness/integrity, initiative/strong work ethic/diligence, relationship skills including dedication and responsiveness to client, and good judgment/common sense). Legal employers also value and want commitment to professional development toward excellence and the habit of actively seeking feedback and reflection.

In another empirical study in 2011–12, the National Conference of Bar Examiners conducted a web-based survey of newly licensed lawyers (licensed within the last three years) who were practicing in a variety of practice settings and geographic areas.[24] The survey asked what skills, abilities, and knowledge domains are significant to the newly licensed lawyer. The new lawyers ranked several of the professional-formation competencies as very significant. For example, they ranked "professionalism" 5th, conscientiousness in terms of paying attention to detail 2nd, meeting time deadlines 12th, diligence, 20th, relationship skills like listening, 3rd, knowing when to ask a question, 10th, interpersonal skills, 13th and common sense/good judgment 17th.

Although there are few empirical studies on how clients define the values, virtues, capacities, and skills of an effective lawyer, we do have one rigorous empirical study of what competencies lawyers as clients would want if they were hiring a lawyer. In 2003, Professors Marjorie M. Shultz and Sheldon Zedeck at the University of California at Berkeley identified 26 factors important for lawyer effectiveness by interviewing people from five stakeholder groups associated with Berkeley Law: alumni, students, faculty, clients, and judges.[25] They asked questions such as "If you were looking for a lawyer for an important matter for yourself, who would you identify, and why?" and "What qualities and behavior would cause you to choose that attorney?" The 26 factors important to lawyer effectiveness that emerged from the interviews are shown in Table 3.

The Shultz-Zedeck study did not list the 26 lawyer effectiveness factors in order of importance so for comparative purposes, Table 3 lists the 26 lawyer effectiveness factors using the same umbrella categories as Table 1 on the Educating Tomorrow's Lawyers' competencies "necessary in the short term."

**Table 3—Shultz-Zedeck List of 26 Lawyer Effectiveness Factors**

**Trustworthiness**

- Integrity/honesty
- Self-development

[24] Steven Nettles & James Hellrung, A STUDY OF THE NEWLY LICENSED LAWYER 1 (2012).

[25] Marjorie M. Shultz & Sheldon Zedeck, *Predicting Lawyer Effectiveness: Broadening the Basis for Law School Admission Decisions*, 36 LAW & SOC. INQUIRY 620, 629 (2011).

**Relationship Skills**

- Building relationships with clients and providing advice and counsel
- Developing relationships within the legal profession
- Networking and business development
- Listening
- Able to see the world through the eyes of others
- Community involvement and service
- Organizing and managing others
- Evaluation, development and mentoring of others

**Strong Work Ethic/Diligence**

- Passion/engagement
- Diligence
- Stress management

**Common Sense/Good Judgment**

- Problem solving
- Practical judgment
- Creativity and innovation

**Technical Competencies**

- Analysis and reasoning
- Researching the law
- Fact finding
- Questioning and interviewing
- Influencing and advocating
- Writing
- Speaking
- Strategic planning
- Organizing and managing one's own work
- Negotiation

The few other empirical studies of how clients assess the effectiveness of lawyers nearly all focus on how in-house counsel for corporate clients assess the effectiveness of outside counsel. So again, the data set focuses essentially on what competencies lawyers as clients want from another lawyer. The central theme of these corporate-client studies is that exceptional effectiveness moves beyond excellent technical competence toward excellent *relationship skills* demonstrating (1) a strong understanding of the client's business and needs, (2) good judgment and problem solving in light of that understanding of the client, (3) strong responsiveness to the client, and (4) a focus on cost-effective solutions that provide value to the client.

A general principle of empirical research is to use a variety of quantitative and qualitative research methods and triangulate to determine if the results of different inquiries converge on similar findings or themes. The higher degree of convergence among the findings, the higher degree of confidence we have that the data are accurately pointing to the importance of the professional-formation competencies for effectiveness in the practice of law.

We can see substantial convergence among the ETL data on what competencies are "necessary in the short term" for law graduates, the data on what early career lawyers think are the most important competencies, the data on the competencies that legal employers value, and the Shultz/Zedeck lawyer effectiveness factors data. Table 4 sets forth where the data sets converge.

**Table 4—Convergence of the Professional-Formation Competencies That Legal Employers and Clients Value and Want**

- Trustworthiness and integrity
- Initiative/strong work ethic/diligence
- Relationship skills including respect for others, understanding of and responsiveness to client, and listening
- Good judgment/common sense
- Commitment to professional development toward excellence including the habit of actively seeking feedback and reflection

It is highly in each law student's and lawyer's enlightened self-interest to develop and demonstrate the professional formation competencies that legal employers and clients want. Note particularly that this section's emphasis on the importance of trustworthiness and integrity to legal employers and clients matches up with the legal profession's social contract emphasis on the foundational importance of client and public trust in individual lawyers and in the profession. The next section explores how the professional-formation competencies that legal employers and clients want overlap with the concept of an ethical professional identity in the context of the ABA's Model Rules of Professional Conduct and ABA professionalism reports and the understanding of an ethical professional identity of exemplary lawyers in practice.

## § 3-1.3 UNDERSTANDING THE FORMATION OF AN ETHICAL PROFESSIONAL IDENTITY IN THE CONTEXT OF THE ABA'S MODEL RULES AND REPORTS AND THE UNDERSTANDING OF EXEMPLARY LAWYERS

Beyond the enlightened self-interest reasons discussed above, each law student and lawyer should grow toward the formation of an ethical professional identity in order to be worthy of client and public trust with respect to our role in the justice system. The ABA Model Rules of Professional Conduct, ABA reports on professionalism and the values and core principles of the profession, and empirical research on how exemplary lawyers understand the formation of an ethical professional identity help define the elements of an ethical professional identity.

### § 3-1.3(a) The ABA's Model Rules of Professional Conduct

The Model Rules articulate both:

a. **a floor of conduct** below which the profession and the courts will discipline a lawyer (and thus maintain the public trust in the profession and the individual members of the profession); and

b. **the ideals and core principles of the profession** that each lawyer should grow into over a career.

- The first sentence of the Preamble to the Model Rules articulates three societal roles in the justice system for every lawyer. "A lawyer, as a member of the legal profession, is a representative of clients, an officer of the legal system, and a public citizen having special responsibility for the quality of justice." These three roles are in some tension with each other and the first sentence is essentially an invitation to grow toward an ethical professional identity in understanding and keeping the three roles in proper tension.

- The Preamble's Paragraph 7 states "A lawyer should strive to attain the highest level of skill, to improve the law and the legal profession, and to exemplify the legal profession's ideals of public service."

- Paragraph 5 urges "A lawyer should demonstrate respect for the legal system and all who serve it, including judges, other lawyers, and public officials."

- Paragraph 6 asks that "a lawyer should seek improvement of the law, access to the legal system, the administration of justice and the quality of the service rendered by the legal profession," and gives special emphasis that "a lawyer should be mindful of deficiencies in the administration of justice and of the fact that the poor, and sometimes persons who are not poor, cannot afford adequate legal assistance. Therefore all lawyers should devote professional time and resources and use civic influence to ensure equal access to our system of justice for all those who because of economic or social barriers cannot afford or secure adequate legal counsel."

- It is also very important to note that the Model Rules leave vast areas for a lawyer's discretion and professional judgment on difficult ethical issues regarding responsibilities to clients, to the legal system, to the quality of justice, to the lawyer's interest in being an ethical person, and the lawyer's own self-interest in making a satisfactory living. The Preamble's paragraph 9 recognizes that "difficult ethical issues" can arise from conflicts among these responsibilities. Paragraph 9 continues to say that "Within the framework of these Rules, however, **many difficult issues of professional discretion** can arise. Such issues must be resolved through the exercise of sensitive professional and moral judgment guided by the basic principles underlying the Rules."

- The Preamble's Paragraph 8 provides that "a lawyer is also guided by personal conscience and the approbation of professional peers."

- The Model Rules do not specifically address a major goal of every student and lawyer to achieve self-sufficiency except for Paragraph 9 of the Preamble. "Virtually all difficult ethical problems arise from a conflict between a lawyer's responsibilities to clients, to the legal system and to the lawyer's own interest in remaining an ethical person while earning a satisfactory living."[26]

- The Model Rules recognize that clients also face many difficult ethical issues, and a lawyer should provide independent judgment and render candid advice to help the client think through decisions that affect others. The comments to Rule 2.1 note "Advice couched in narrow legal terms may be of little value to a client, especially where practical considerations, such as cost or effects on other people, are predominant .... It is proper for a lawyer to refer to the relevant moral and ethical considerations in giving advice." The lawyer is not imposing the lawyer's morality on the client, rather the "relevant moral and ethical considerations" clearly include understanding the client's own tradition on responsibility to others and helping the client to think through the issues from the client's own tradition.[27]

- Paragraphs 10 to 12 of the Preamble outline the social contract among the members of the legal profession and society whereby the society grants lawyers autonomy to govern themselves, and, in return, the members of the profession agree to meet correlative personal and collegial peer-review duties to the society.[28] Paragraph 12 specifically states "a lawyer is responsible for observance of the Rules of Professional Conduct" and "a lawyer should also aid in securing their observance [of the Rules] by other lawyers." It ends with the caution that "neglect of these responsibilities compromises the independence of the profession and the public interest which it serves."[29] The importance of the legal profession's social contract is analyzed further in Section 3-1.3(b) below.

All these paragraphs of the Preamble taken together implicitly define the elements of an ethical professional identity by calling on each lawyer to do the following:

(1) to hold in proper tension the lawyer's roles as a representative of clients, an officer of the legal system, and a public citizen having special responsibility for the quality of justice;

(2) to comply with the *ethics of duty*—the minimum standards of competency and ethical conduct set forth in the Rules of Professional Conduct;[30]

(3) to encourage other lawyers to be accountable for compliance with the Rules and ultimately to hold them accountable;

---

[26] This sentence in the Preamble's 9th paragraph parallels the emphasis in the Preamble's first sentence on the lawyer as the representative of clients and officer of the legal system, but then adds both a lawyer's interest in living as an ethical person and the lawyer's self-interest in making a satisfactory living. In my view, this sentence in the Preamble's 9th paragraph should have included also the ethical problems created by conflicts with the lawyer's responsibilities as a public citizen responsible for the quality of justice.

[27] For further discussion of moral deliberation between the attorney and client, see Part Four of this book, Gregory C. Sisk, Legal Ethics and the Practice of Law § 4-5.2(b).

[28] *Id.* ¶¶ 10–12. Some scholars discussed at note 18 *supra* argue that the social contract calling for some restraint on self-interest on which professionalism is based no longer exists in the profession (or in the alternative, that it never existed). Russell Pearce offers a Middle Range Approach between the professionalism and the business paradigms that rejects both licensing and exclusive lawyer self-policing, but permits the organized bar to control lawyer certification. Russell Pearce, *The Professionalism Paradigm Shift: Why Discarding Professional Ideology Will Improve the Conduct and Reputation of the Bar*, 70 N.Y.U. L. REV. 1229, 1272 (1995).

[29] MODEL RULES OF PROF'L CONDUCT, Preamble ¶ 12 (2007). For further discussion of pro bono services to the disadvantaged, see Part Four of this book, Gregory C. Sisk, Legal Ethics and the Practice of Law § 4-13.4.

[30] LON L. FULLER, THE MORALITY OF LAW 3–9 (Yale U. Press, rev. ed., 1969).

(4) to foster in him or herself and other lawyers the *ethics of aspiration*—the core values and ideals of the profession, including internalizing the highest standards for the lawyer's professional skills and ethical conduct.[31]

(5) to develop and be guided also by personal conscience including the development of "professional and moral judgment," and the meaning of being an "ethical person" in deciding all the "difficult issues of professional discretion" that arise in the practice of law; and

(6) to do public service to improve justice, particularly to provide service to the disadvantaged.

### § 3-1.3(b) Elements of an Ethical Professional Identity Defined in the ABA and Conference of Chief Justice Reports

Over the past 30 years, the major reports of both the ABA and the Conference of Chief Justices on professionalism and the values of the profession as well as the Preamble to the Model Rules have stated the major elements of an ethical professional identity including the correlative duties of the social contract for each lawyer.

#### *§ 3-1.3(b)(1) The Stanley Commission Report in 1986*

The ABA formed the Stanley Commission in the mid-1980s in light of the growing concern of bar leaders, judges and lawyers both that the profession was moving "away from the principles of professionalism," and that this shift in professionalism was "so perceived by the public."[32] The Stanley Commission Report adopts a definition of professionalism that former Harvard Dean Roscoe Pound first penned in 1953:

> The term refers to a group. . .pursuing a learned art as a common calling in the spirit of public service—no less a public service because it may incidentally be a means of livelihood. Pursuit of the learned art in the spirit of a public service is the primary purpose.[33]

The Stanley Commission also included traits that distinguish a profession from other occupations. A profession is:

> An occupation whose members have special privileges, such as exclusive licensing, that are justified by the following assumptions: (1) That its practice requires substantial intellectual training and the use of complex judgments; (2) That since clients cannot adequately evaluate the quality of the service, they must **trust** those they consult; (3) That the client's **trust** presupposes that the practitioner's self-interest is overbalanced by devotion to serving both the client's interest and the public good; and (4) That the occupation is self-regulating—that is, organized in such a way as to assure the public and the courts that its members are competent, do not violate their client's **trust**, and transcend their own self-interest.[34]

---

31 *Id.*

32 *Stanley Commission Report, supra* note 3, at 248.

33 *Id.* at 261.

34 *Id.* (emphasis added).

### *§ 3-1.3(b)(2) The MacCrate Report in 1992*

The 1992 ABA MacCrate Report adds to the understanding of professionalism through a focus on professional skills and professional values.[35] The report includes both a Statement of Fundamental Lawyering Skills and a Statement of Fundamental Values of the Profession. The Fundamental Lawyering Skills include:

1. Problem Solving;
2. Legal Analysis and Reasoning;
3. Legal Research;
4. Factual Investigation;
5. Communication (oral and written);
6. Counseling;
7. Negotiation;
8. Litigation and ADR Procedures;
9. Organization and Management of Legal Work; and
10. Recognizing and Resolving Ethical Dilemmas (principally focused on the Rules of Professional Conduct).[36]

The four Fundamental Values of the Profession are:

1. Providing Competent Representation;
2. Striving to Promote Justice, Fairness and Morality (including pro bono service to the disadvantaged);
3. Striving to Improve the Profession; and
4. Undertaking Continuing Professional Self-development (including continuing reflection to learn from experience).[37]

### *§ 3-1.3(b)(3) The Haynsworth Report in 1996*

In the mid-1990s, the ABA built on the Stanley Commission Report and the MacCrate Report with the 1996 Haynsworth Report to "better inculcate a higher sense of professionalism among American lawyers."[38] The Haynsworth Report's definition of professionalism particularizes Pound's 1953 definition to the specific context of the legal profession:

> A professional lawyer is an expert in law pursuing a learned art in service to clients and in the spirit of public service; and engaging in these pursuits as part of a common calling to promote justice and public good.[39]

---

[35] *An Educational Continuum, Report of the Task Force on Law Schools and the Profession: Narrowing the Gap,* 1992 A.B.A. SEC. LEGAL EDUC. AND ADMISSIONS TO THE B., LEGAL EDUC. AND PROF. DEV. [hereinafter *MacCrate Report*].

[36] *Id.* at 138–140.

[37] *Id.* at 140–141.

[38] *Teaching and Learning Professionalism,* 1996 A.B.A SEC. LEGAL EDUC. AND ADMISSIONS TO THE BAR, REPORT OF THE PROFESSIONALISM COMM. at 1 [hereinafter *Haynsworth Report*].

[39] *Id.* at 6.

In addition to the definition, the Report includes lists of essential characteristics of the professional lawyer and supportive elements.

> The essential characteristics of the professional lawyer are: (1) learned knowledge; (2) skill in applying the applicable law to the factual context; (3) thoroughness of preparation; (4) practical and prudential wisdom; (5) ethical conduct and integrity; and (6) dedication to justice and the public good.
>
> Supportive elements include: (1) formal training and licensing; (2) maintenance of competence; (3) zealous and diligent representation of clients' interests within the bounds of law; (4) appropriate deportment and civility; (5) economic temperance; (6) subordination of personal interests and viewpoints to the interests of clients and the public good; (7) autonomy; (8) self-regulation; (9) membership in one or more professional organizations; (10) cost-effective legal services; (11) capacity for self-scrutiny and for moral dialogue with clients and other individuals involved in the justice system; and (12) a client-centered approach to the lawyer-client relationship which stresses trust, compassion, respect, and empowerment of the client.[40]

### *§ 3-1.3(b)(4) The Conference of Chief Justices' National Action Plan on Lawyer Conduct and Professionalism in 1999*

Despite the efforts of the ABA in 1986, 1992, and 1996, concerns about a perceived decline in lawyer professionalism and the decline's effect on public confidence in the legal profession and the justice system remained. In response to the continuing concerns, the Conference of Chief Justices (CCJ) adopted the National Action Plan on Lawyer Conduct and Professionalism in January of 1999.[41] The CCJ's National Action Plan defines professionalism with an aspirational focus.

> Professionalism is a much broader concept than legal ethics. For the purposes of this report, professionalism includes not only civility among members of the bench and bar, but also competence, integrity, respect for the rule of law, participation in pro bono and community service, and conduct by members of the legal profession that exceeds the minimum ethical requirements. Ethics rules are what a lawyer must obey. Principles of professionalism are what a lawyer should live by in conducting his or her affairs. Unlike disciplinary rules that can be implemented and enforced, professionalism is a personal characteristic. The bench and the bar can create an environment in which professionalism can flourish, and these recommendations are intended to assist in that endeavor. But it is the responsibility of individual judges and lawyers to demonstrate this characteristic in the performance of their professional and personal activities.[42]

The Action Plan emphasizes the role of personal conscience in achieving professionalism. "Professionalism ultimately is a personal, not an institutional characteristic. . . . No disciplinary system can enforce professionalism and no amount of exhortation by judges and bar leaders can instill it where it does not already exist. The

---

[40] *Id.* at 6–7.

[41] CONFERENCE OF CHIEF JUSTICES COMMITTEE ON PROFESSIONALISM AND LAWYER COMPETENCE, A NATIONAL ACTION PLAN ON LAWYER CONDUCT AND PROFESSIONALISM VII (1999) [hereinafter *Action Plan*].

[42] *Id.* at 2.

vast majority of lawyers possess this characteristic to some degree or another. But far too many have allowed their sense of professionalism to become dormant. The institutional framework of the legal community can create a climate in which professionalism can flourish, but individual lawyers must be the ones to cultivate this characteristic in themselves."[43]

The Action Plan also emphasizes the importance of peer-review and the responsibility of all lawyers to "not tolerate unethical or unprofessional conduct by their fellow lawyers."[44] Last the Action Plan asks each lawyer to "exemplify the ideal of the lawyer-statesman—that is, a professional who devotes his or her judgment and expertise to serving the public good, particularly through participation in pro bono and community service activities."[45]

### § 3-1.3(c) Exemplary Lawyers' Understanding of the Elements of an Ethical Professional Identity—Results of a 2012 Study

Hamilton and Monson reviewed all Minnesota county and the state of Minnesota bar association websites to identify professionalism award winners in the period 2001–2011. After compiling a list of 45 professionalism award winners, we randomly selected twelve lawyers and all twelve lawyers agreed to participate in an interview supplemented with follow-up questions. The twelve exemplary lawyers all agreed on some key elements defining their understanding of an ethical professional identity.[46] These are set forth in Table 5.

---

[43] *Id.* at 7.

[44] *Id.* at 7.

[45] *Id.*

[46] Neil Hamilton & Verna Monson, *Ethical Professional (Trans)Formation: Themes From Interviews About Professionalism With Exemplary Lawyer*, 52 SANTA CLARA L. REV. 921, 948–57 (2012).

**Table 5—Major Themes from Exemplary Lawyers on the Meaning of an Ethical Professional Identity**

| |
|---|
| Moral core or moral compass, including:<br>• deep sense of responsibility to others<br>• trustworthiness in relationships with others (including clients, colleagues, the profession, the justice system, and broader society)<br>• honesty with self and others as an important basis of trust |
| Counseling the client, including:<br>• giving independent judgment<br>• candid and honest counsel informed by the lawyer's moral core<br>• lawyer as facilitator in helping the client to identify the client's long-term interest, growth, or movement towards healing and forgiveness |
| Ongoing reflection and learning (1) from mistakes or losses and (2) about the limitations of the status quo of legal practice, including:<br>• professional setbacks (i.e., failing to meet internalized standards of excellence or losing important cases)<br>• personal setbacks (i.e., experiencing depression or loss of loved ones)<br>• alternative methods of practice (e.g., mediation)<br>• the limitations of the justice system in serving the poor or oppressed, or imbalances of power |
| Self-assessment of how the meaning of professionalism has evolved:<br>• continuous dynamic growth in understanding and internalizing the meaning of professionalism (including reflection and learning from mistakes) |

An important finding of these studies is that a student's or practicing professional's understanding of professional formation depends upon the person's stage of development. Exemplars understand ethical professional identity or professionalism in a qualitatively more complex, or expert manner, than do early-career lawyers and entering law students.[47] Later discussion in Chapter 3-3 on a professional-identity-formation curriculum will emphasize that the curriculum has to engage each student at the student's current developmental stage. A student can eventually grow over a career toward the internalization of a later-stage understanding of professional formation. Our exemplars' understanding of an ethical professional identity or professionalism represents a high level of competence or expertise, providing law schools and bar associations with a clear benchmark to use in defining levels of stage development of an ethical professional identity.[48]

---

[47] For example, the understanding of ethical professional identity of both entering law students and early-career lawyer is explained in two articles. Verna Monson & Neil Hamilton, *Entering Law Students' Conception of an Ethical Professional Identity,* 35 J. LEGAL PROF. 385 (2011) and Verna Monson & Neil Hamilton, *Ethical Professional (Trans)Formation: Early-Career Lawyers Make Sense of Professionalism,* 8 UNIV. ST. THOMAS L.J. 129 (2011).

[48] *Id.* at 963. The literature in medical education is especially informative about the concepts and processes of defining and measuring professional competencies. For example, see Ronald M. Epstein & Edward

### § 3-1.3(d) Synthesis of the Key Elements of an Ethical Professional Identity from the Model Rules, the Three ABA Reports, the CCJ National Action Plan, and the Study of Exemplary Lawyers

A synthesis of the Model Rules, the major ABA reports, the Conference of Chief Justices National Action Plan and the exemplary lawyers' study to define an ethical professional identity results in five common principles that each lawyer:

a. Agrees to comply with the ethics of duty—the minimum standards for the lawyer's professional skills and ethical conduct set by the Rules;[49]

b. Strives to realize, over a career, the ethics of aspiration—the core values and ideals of the profession including internalizing the highest standards for the lawyer's professional skills and ethical conduct;[50]

c. Continues to grow in personal conscience (a deep sense of responsibility to clients and the legal system and trustworthiness) over his or her career including the importance of the habit of seeking feedback and reflection;[51]

---

M. Hundert, *Defining and Assessing Professional Competence*, 287 JAMA 226, 226 (2002), and also see David C. Leach, *Competence is a Habit*, 287 JAMA 243, 243–44 (2002).

[49] All the professionalism definitions stress that a minimum level of competence is necessary. The Stanley Commission Report speaks of lawyering as a "learned art" and notes that it requires substantial intellectual training. *Stanley Commission Report, supra* note 3, at 10. The MacCrate Report stresses the necessity of providing competent representation. *MacCrate Report, supra* note 35, at 140. The Haynsworth Report notes the requirement by including the essential skills of learned knowledge and skill in applying the applicable law to the factual context. *Haynsworth Report, supra* note 38, at 6–7. It also includes "maintenance of competence" in its supportive elements. *Id.* The CCJ National Action Plan includes "competence." *Action Plan, supra* note 41, at 2. The Model Rules' Preamble specifically requires a lawyer to observe the Model Rules. MODEL RULES OF PROF'L CONDUCT, Preamble ¶¶ 7, 12, 14. Rule 8.3 states that it is professional misconduct to violate the Rules which include Rule 1.1 on competence and Rule 1.3 on diligence. MODEL RULES OF PROF'L CONDUCT R. 8.3, R. 1.1, R. 1.3.

[50] In the language of Dean Roscoe Pound, each lawyer should pursue the law as a "learned art in the spirit of a public service." *Stanley Commission Report, supra* note 3, at 10. Three of the four Fundamental Values of the Profession noted in the MacCrate Report spell out ideals that a lawyer should seek (*to which a lawyer should aspire*)—(1) striving to promote justice, fairness and morality, (2) striving to improve the profession, and (3) undertaking professional self-development. *MacCrate Report, supra* note 35, at 125. The Haynsworth Report mixes minimum standards and aspirational ideals on its two lists of essential characteristics and supportive elements for the professional lawyer. *Haynsworth Report, supra* note 38, at 6–7. The CCJ National Action Plan is particularly forceful in stating that professionalism requires lawyers to exceed the minimum ethical standards. *Action Plan, supra* note 41, at 6–7. The Preamble to the Model Rules of Professional Conduct states directly that "a lawyer should strive to attain the highest level of skill, to improve the law and the legal profession, and to exemplify the legal profession's ideals of public service." MODEL RULES OF PROF'L CONDUCT, Preamble ¶ 7 (2007).

[51] The MacCrate Report, the Haynsworth Report, the CCJ National Action Plan, and the Preamble to the Model Rules of Professional Conduct emphasize that a lawyer must continue to grow in personal conscience. The MacCrate Report emphasizes that the primary sources of ethical rules include, "A lawyer's personal sense of morality." *MacCrate Report, supra* note 35, at 204. The Haynsworth Report includes both an essential characteristic that a lawyer must demonstrate ethical conduct and integrity, and a supportive element that a lawyer should develop the capacity for self-scrutiny and for moral dialogue with clients and other individuals involved in the justice system. *Haynsworth Report, supra* note 38, at 6–7. The National Action Plan defines professionalism as a personal characteristic that each lawyer must cultivate in him or herself. *Action Plan, supra* note 41, at 6. The Preamble specifically provides that a lawyer is also guided by personal conscience and sensitive professional and moral judgment. MODEL RULES OF PROF'L CONDUCT, Preamble ¶¶ 7, 9 (2007). The Preamble to the ABA Model Code of Professional Responsibility is also explicit. "Each lawyer must find within his [or her] own conscience the touchstone against which to test the extent to which actions should rise above minimum standards." MODEL CODE OF PROF'L RESPONSIBILITY, Preamble ¶ 4 (1969). The introduction to the Restatement of the Law Third, The Law Governing Lawyers, provides, "other constraints, such as ideals and habits of morality, will often guide the conduct of a good person who also aspires to serve

d. Agrees both to hold other lawyers accountable for meeting the minimum standards set forth in the Rules and to encourage them to realize core values and ideals of the profession;[52] and

e. Agrees to act as a fiduciary where his or her self-interest is overbalanced by devotion to serving the client and the public good in the profession's area of responsibility: justice.[53]

   i. Devotes professional time to serve the public good, particularly by representing pro bono clients;[54] and

   ii. Undertakes a continuing reflective engagement, over a career, on the relative importance of income and wealth in light of the other principles of professionalism.

---

as an honorable public-spirited lawyer, and much more powerfully and pervasively than merely legal obligations. A good lawyer is also guided by ideals of professionalism and by an understanding of sound professional practice. Extensive consideration of such non-legal factors is not undertaken here. However they have obvious significance in a good lawyer's life and in the self-concept of the profession." 1 RESTATEMENT (THIRD) OF THE LAW GOVERNING LAWYERS INTRO. 3 (2000).

[52] Self-regulation is another common theme of these definitions of professionalism. Members of the profession are responsible for building healthy peer communities. The Stanley Commission Report notes that self-regulation is a defining characteristic of the profession, which has a responsibility to protect the public. *Stanley Commission Report, supra* note 3, at 10, 37. The MacCrate Report also notes that a lawyer is a member of a self-governing profession. *MacCrate Report, supra* note 35, at 141 and 205–6. The Haynsworth Report lists self-regulation as a supportive element to professionalism. *Haynsworth Report, supra* note 38, at 7. The CCJ National Action Plan provides that lawyers "should not tolerate unethical or unprofessional conduct by their fellow lawyers." *Action Plan, supra* note 41, at 7. The Model Rules' Preamble speaks at length of the self-regulation of the legal profession and the profession's social contract with society. "A lawyer should also aid in securing their observance [of the Rules] by other lawyers." MODEL RULES OF PROF'L CONDUCT, Preamble ¶¶ 10–12 (2007). The Preamble also stresses the responsibilities that are implicated by self-regulation and notes that the profession risks loss of its autonomy if its members fail in their duties. *Id.*

[53] The Stanley Commission Report states, "The client's trust presupposes that the practitioner's self-interest is overbalanced by devotion to serving both the client's interest and the public good." *Stanley Commission Report, supra* note 3, at 261. The Haynsworth Report builds on Dean Roscoe Pound's definition of professionalism and emphasizes that a professional lawyer pursues "a learned art in service to clients and in the spirit of public service." The Report's supportive elements include the subordination of personal interests and viewpoints to the interests of the clients and the public good. *Haynsworth Report, supra* note 38, at 6–7. Paragraph 1 of the Model Rules Preamble calls on each lawyer to hold in tension three major roles: (1) a representative of clients; (2) an officer of the legal system; and (3) a public citizen having special responsibilities for the quality of justice. MODEL RULES OF PROF'L CONDUCT, Preamble ¶ 1 (2007).

[54] Public service is an important element to all these professionalism definitions. Each lawyer should devote professional time to serve the public good, particularly by representing pro bono clients. "In the spirit of public service" is part of the title of the Stanley Commission Report. *Stanley Commission Report, supra* note 3 at 243. The MacCrate Report stresses that a lawyer should contribute to the profession's responsibility to represent pro bono clients. *MacCrate Report, supra* note 35, at 140. The Haynsworth Report's definition of professionalism retains the common phrase of "in the spirit of public service" and lists cost-effective legal services as a supportive element. *Haynsworth Report, supra* note 38, at 7. The CCJ National Action Plan exhorts lawyers to devote their judgment and expertise to the public good, particularly through participation in pro bono and community service activity. *Action Plan, supra* note 41, at 7. The Model Rules' Preamble also notes "As a public citizen, a lawyer should seek improvement of the law, access to the legal system, the administration of justice and the quality of service rendered by the legal profession. . . .[A]ll lawyers should devote professional time. . . .for all those who. . . .cannot afford or secure adequate legal counsel." MODEL RULES OF PROF'L CONDUCT, Preamble ¶ 6 (2007).

## § 3-1.4 COMPARISON OF THE COMPETENCIES DEFINING AN ETHICAL PROFESSIONAL IDENTITY FROM THE MODEL RULES, THE ABA REPORTS AND EXEMPLARY LAWYERS WITH THE PROFESSIONAL-FORMATION COMPETENCIES THAT LEGAL EMPLOYERS AND CLIENTS WANT

The competencies defining an ethical professional identity from the Model Rules, the ABA Reports, and exemplary lawyers set forth in Part 3-1.3 above seem abstract without practical day-to-day significance for many students and early-career lawyers at earlier stages of their professional development. On the other hand, the professional-formation competencies that legal employers and clients want defined in Part 3-1.2(b) above have an immediate practical enlightened self-interest importance for law students and early-career lawyers.

There is a substantial overlap between the professional-formation competencies of Part 3-1.2(b) that legal employers and clients want and the ethical professional identity competencies of Part 3-1.3 defined by the profession. Table 6 explores the overlap.

**Table 6—Comparison of the Competencies Defining an Ethical Professional Identity in Part 3-1.3 with the Competencies that Legal Employers and Clients Want in Assessing the Effectiveness of a New Lawyer in Part 3-1.2(b)**

| Ethical Professional Identity Competencies from Part 3-1.3. | Professional-Formation Competencies that Legal Employers Want (Beyond Technical Legal Skills) from Part 3-1.2(b). |
|---|---|
| Agrees to Comply with Ethical Codes | • Implicit that Law Student and Lawyer is Rules Compliant |
| Strives to Realize Over a Career the Core Values and Ideals of the Profession Including Excellence at the Lawyer's Technical Legal Skills | • Commitment to Professional Development Toward Excellence including the Habit of Actively Seeking Feedback and Reflection<br>• Initiative/Strong Work Ethic/ Diligence |
| Continues to Grow in Personal Conscience Including a Deep Sense of Responsibility to Clients and the Legal System and Trustworthiness Over Career Including the Habit of Seeking Feedback and Reflection | • Trustworthiness/Integrity<br>• Relationship Skills including Respect for Others, Understanding of and Responsiveness to Client, and Listening<br>• Good Judgment<br>• Initiative/Strong Work Ethic/ Diligence<br>• Commitment to Professional Development Toward Excellence including the Habit of Actively Seeking Feedback and Reflection |

| | |
|---|---|
| Agrees to Hold Other Lawyers Accountable for Compliance with the Ethical Codes and to Encourage Other Lawyers to Realize the Profession's Core Values and Ideals | |
| Agrees to Act as a Fiduciary Where Self-Interest is Over-Balanced by Dedication to Serving the Client and the Public Good in the Area of Justice<br>a. Providing Pro Bono Work<br>b. Undertaking Continuing Reflection on the Question How Much is a Satisfactory Living? | |

Note in Table 6 that the ethical-professional identity competencies on the left side of Table 6 above go beyond the enlightened self-interest competencies that legal employers want on the right side of Table 6. particularly with respect to encouraging other lawyers to realize the ideals and core values of the profession, holding other lawyers accountable for compliance with the ethical codes, and restraining self-interest to serve the client and the public good (including pro bono). This shows how, beyond the enlightened self-interest reasons of developing the professional-formation competences that legal employers want (the right side of Table 6) each law student and lawyer should also grow toward the formation of an ethical professional identity on the left side of Table 6 in order to be worthy of client and public trust with respect to our role in the justice system. The concept of trustworthiness in the individual lawyer and in the profession itself to serve the client and the legal system is foundational to the legal profession's social contract explored in Chapter 3-1.1, to the competencies that clients and legal employers want explored in Chapter 3-1.2 and to the Model Rules, the ABA Reports on professionalism, and exemplary lawyers' understanding of professionalism explored in Chapter 3-1.3.

# Chapter 3-2

# THE IMPORTANCE OF STRESS MANAGEMENT IN THE FORMATION OF AN ETHICAL PROFESSIONAL IDENTITY

**By Melissa H. Weresh**

*Table of Sections*


§ 3-2.1 Sources of Stress for Lawyers
§ 3-2.2 Values, Needs, Motivation, and Well-Being
§ 3-2.3 Impact of Public Service
§ 3-2.4 Importance of Organizational Ethical Culture


In a recently-issued report from the National Task Force on Lawyer Well-Being [hereinafter Lawyer Well-Being Report], studies revealed that lawyers and law students are experiencing challenges to well-being, defined in the report as "a continuous process whereby lawyers seek to thrive in each of the following areas: emotional health, occupational pursuits, creative or intellectual endeavors, sense of spirituality or greater purpose in life, physical health, and social connections with others."[1] The Lawyer Well-Being Report acknowledges the connection between lawyer well-being and professional identity development, emphasizing that "[w]ell-functioning executive capacities are needed to make good decisions and evaluate risks, plan for the future, prioritize and sequence actions, and cope with new situations."[2] The Lawyer Well-Being Report offers varied and valuable recommendations to improve lawyer well-being, identifying a variety of strategies to be employed by various stakeholders.

In order to provide a foundation for understanding challenges to well-being, this section identifies some of the sources of stress for lawyers. It then examines aspects of a positive ethical professional identity, demonstrating that certain values, needs, and motivation can positively impact lawyer well-being.

## § 3-2.1 SOURCES OF STRESS FOR LAWYERS[3]

Rosa Flores and Rose Marie Arce revealed that "[l]awyers ranked fourth when the proportion of suicides in that profession is compared to suicides in all other occupations in the study population (adjusted for age)."[4] Moreover, the Lawyer Well-Being Report revealed that lawyers and law students are experiencing depression, substance abuse,

---

[1] National Task Force on Lawyer Well-Being, *The Path to Lawyer Well-Being: Practical Recommendations for Positive Change* 9 (2017) [hereinafter *Lawyer Well-Being Report*].

[2] *Id.* at 8–9 (acknowledging that "lawyer well-being influences ethics and professionalism").

[3] Section 3-2.1 is based, in part, on Melissa H. Weresh, *The Chicken or the Egg? Public Service Orientation and Lawyer Well-Being,* 36 UALR L. Rev. 463 (2014).

[4] Rosa Flores & Rose Marie Arce, *Why Are Lawyers Killing Themselves?,* CNN U.S. (Jan. 20, 2014, 2:42 (PM)) http://www.cnn.com/2014/01/19/us/lawyer-suicides/index.html?sr=sharebar_facebook.

anxiety, and stress.[5] Some sources of stress for lawyers are associated with the practice itself.[6] For example, studies point to external, environmental burdens associated with law practice,[7] such as the workload, financial strain, and adversarial atmosphere of law practice. In addition to practice-related stress, lawyers may share certain internal attributes that unique to the profession and that predispose them to depression,[8] such as lawyers' propensity to be perfectionistic, competitive, and extrinsically motivated.

These categories are explored below in an effort to more fully understand the pressures. Having then provided a foundation for the challenges, this section then explores how aspects of a positive professional identity can contribute to lawyer well-being.

### § 3-2.1(a) External Pressure of Law Practice

Law practice is uniquely stressful. In addressing why lawyers suffer disproportionately from depression, Patrick Schiltz evaluated the external pressures associated with law practice and pointed to three forces: the hours, the money, and the "game."[9] These aspects can be more broadly considered as the workload associated with law practice, financial pressure, the competitive and adversarial nature of law practice, and the perception of some lawyers that they have limited control over decisions.

#### *§ 3-2.1(a)(1) Workload*

With regard to workload, Schiltz explains, "[i]n every study of the career satisfaction of lawyers of which I am aware, in every book or article about the woes of the legal profession that I have read, and in every conversation about life as a practicing lawyer that I have heard, lawyers complain about the long hours they have to work."[10] Working long hours is necessitated in part by other aspects of law practice, including increased reliance on technology and the complexity and depth of legal work.[11] "[N]ew technology creates an unrelenting and faster work pace. Also, the law is overwhelmingly complex today. Changing legal standards make it difficult to know how to advise clients, and courts render so many decisions that it is not easy to understand what the law actually is."[12] Contributing to the workload stress is the fact that lawyers are hard-working individuals. The Lawyer Well-Being Report reveals research supporting the conclusion

---

[5] *Lawyer Well-Being Report, supra* note 1 at 7.

[6] Flores and Arce, *supra* note 4. Flores and Arce explored stresses associated with law practice that, while similar in some ways to pressure in other professions or vocations, include aspects that are unique to the legal profession. They note one lawyer's depiction of law practice stress:

> A lawyer has conflict. He's got his clients, he's got other lawyers, he's got the opposition lawyers, he's got insurance companies, judges, jurors, and he's got the bar association," said [one lawyer], who has faced disciplinary charges himself. "They will take the most minor little thing. And they will turn it into a problem for a lawyer.

*Id.*

[7] *See* Patrick J. Schiltz, *On Being a Happy, Healthy, and Ethical Member of an Unhappy, Unhealthy and Unethical Profession,* 52 VAND. L. REV. 871, 895–906 (1999).

[8] *See, e.g.,* Susan Daicoff, *Articles Lawyer, Know Thyself: A Review of Empirical Research on Attorney Attributes Bearing on Professionalism,* 46 AM. U. L. REV. 1337, 1390 (1997).

[9] Schiltz, *supra* note 7 at 888–906.

[10] *Id.* at 889–90 (citations omitted).

[11] Joan E. Mounteer, *Depression Among Lawyers,* COLO. LAW., Jan. 2004, at 35, 36 (indicating that attorneys work long hours due to technological changes and complex legal questions).

[12] *Id.* (citations omitted).

that "about a quarter of lawyers are workaholics, which is more than double that of the 10 percent rate estimated for U.S. adults generally."[13]

The excessive workload associated with law practice can also be isolating. As one author observes, "the increase in the number of lawyers likely has led to increased competition *and diminishing personal relationships with other lawyers*."[14] In fact, the Lawyer Well-Being Report specifically recommends that legal employers "actively combat social isolation and encourage interconnectivity," noting that "[s]ocial support from colleagues is an important factor for coping with stress and preventing negative consequences like burnout."[15]

While Schiltz notes that lawyers in large law firms are among the least happy,[16] and those lawyers likely have higher billable hour requirements, law practice generally presents a demanding workload.[17] The stress and pressure associated with long hours, together with the isolating features of law practice, have the potential to have a harmful effect on lawyer well-being.

#### *§ 3-2.1(a)(2) Financial Strain*

The financial strain of law practice can also take a toll on lawyer well-being. For recent graduates, the burden of law school debt has been widely criticized. In *Law School Debt and the Practice of Law*, the Committee on Legal Education and Admission to the Bar of the New York State Bar Association observed that "financial pressures have been identified as contributing to transgressions of ethical proscriptions and as contributing to the disturbing erosion of professionalism in the practice of law."[18] One federal judge reflected, "[t]he personal, financial and professional pressures new lawyers now face are unprecedented in my experience. I graduated law school debt free. In contrast, many of our new bar members are burdened with crushing debt. This economic burden forces many to make choices driven largely by economic circumstances."[19]

#### *§ 3-2.1(a)(3) Adversarial Atmosphere*

Law practice is uniquely challenging in its adversarial and competitive nature, which places additional pressure on lawyers. "Even a cursory glance at the real world problems of lawyering highlights just how stressful the fast-paced, demanding life of a

---

[13] *Lawyer Well-Being Report*, *supra* note 1 at 32 (citations omitted).

[14] Mounteer, *supra* note 11 (emphasis added).

[15] *Lawyer Well-Being Report*, *supra* note 1 at 32 (citations omitted). The report emphasizes, "Socializing helps individuals recover from work demands and can help stave off emotional exhaustion. It inhibits lawyers feeling isolated and disconnected, which helps with firm branding, messaging, and may help reduce turnover." *Id.*

[16] Schiltz, *supra* note 7 at 886 (citations omitted) (noting that " '(l)awyers in large law firms are often among the least happy.' ").

[17] In fact, the Lawyer Well-Being Report recommends that legal employers monitor workload by conducting evaluations of policies and practiced related to well-being, including an assessment of availability and vacation expectations. *Lawyer Well-Being Report*, *supra* note 1 at 59–60.

[18] New York State Bar Association Committee on Legal Education and Admission to the Bar, *Law School Debt and the Practice of Law 2* (citing Leonard E. Gross, *The Public Hates Lawyers: Why Should We Care?*, 29 SETON HALL L. REV. 1405, 1419 (1999); Marvin Hirshman, *BEWARE! Examples of Conduct Which Will Invite the Attorney Grievance Commission to Inquire and/or Seek Further Investigation*, MD. B.J., Mar./Apr. 2001, at 59 (listing "Financial problems that affect one's practice")), *available at* http://www.nycbar.org/pdf/report/lawSchoolDebt.pdf.

[19] William F. Downes, *The Indispensable Profession*, WYO. LAW., Apr. 2012, at 24, 26 ("This new generation of lawyers is as talented as any which preceded it, but they are in trouble. We may not be able to help pay off their loans, but perhaps we can offer advice about managing personal finances.").

lawyer can be. The legal profession is often characterized as aggressive, adversarial, and competitive. Lawyers and judges are notorious for working excessive hours throughout their professional lives."[20]

Flores and Arce focused on the adversarial nature of law practice as contributing to depression and stress.[21] They observe, however, that while "[t]here are a lot of high stress professions,"[22] law practice is somewhat unique. Physicians, for example, have stress, but they do not perform in an adversarial environment. "[W]hen the surgeon goes into the surgical suite to perform his surgery, they don't send another physician in to try to kill the patient. You know, they're all on the same team trying to do one job. In the legal profession, adversity is the nature of our game."[23]

The adversarial system also represents a zero-sum game. "A zero-sum game is a familiar occurrence. It is an endeavor in which the net result is zero. For every gain by one side, there is a counterbalancing loss by the other."[24] Finally, there are concerns that civility in the profession may be declining, further undermining lawyer well-being.[25] "Chronic incivility is corrosive. It depletes energy and motivation, increases burnout, and inflicts emotional and physiological damage. It diminishes productivity, performance, creativity, and helping behaviors."[26]

#### *§ 3-2.1(a)(4) Perception of Low Decision Latitude*

The psychological perception of low decision latitude, coupled with the high-pressure environment of law practice, may also contribute to lawyer stress and dissatisfaction. "Decision latitude refers to the number of choices one has or, as it turns out, one believes one has. Workers in occupations that involve little or no control are at risk for depression and for poor physical health."[27] Studying the relationship between decision latitude and high-pressure environments, researchers found that individuals with "high job demand combined with low decision latitude . . . had a much higher incidence of coronary disease and depression."[28] The study revealed that junior associates fall into this situation and, coupled with the isolation of practice, they may be more prone to depression and dissatisfaction.[29] The Lawyer Well-Being Report

---

[20] Brent Hale, *Why Are So Many Lawyers Depressed?*, UTAH B.J., Feb. 2008, at 16.

[21] Flores & Arce, *supra* note 4.

[22] *Id.*

[23] *Id.*

[24] Martin E.P. Seligman et al., *Why Lawyers Are Unhappy*, 23 CARDOZO L. REV. 33, 46 (2001).

[25] *Lawyer Well-Being Report*, *supra* note 1 at 15 (noting "[c]ivility appears to be declining in the legal profession.").

[26] *Id.*

[27] Seligman, et al., *supra* note 24 at 41–42 (citations omitted).

[28] *Id.* at 42.

[29] *Id.* (citations omitted). The authors observe that:

> Associates often have little voice or control over their work, only limited contact with their superiors, and virtually no client contact. Instead, for at least the first few years of practice, many remain cloistered and isolated in a library (or behind a computer screen), researching and drafting memos.
>
> In these high-pressure, low decision latitude positions, the associates are likely candidates for negative health effects, such as higher rates of heart disease; and for higher divorce rates. These same associates are, not surprisingly, candidates for early departure from law firms; they are therefore often the object of "retention bonuses." Not surprisingly, many young lawyers who do

acknowledged the impact of low decision latitude on well-being, noting that "[p]ractices that rob lawyers of a sense of autonomy and control over their schedules and lives are especially harmful to their well-being. Research studies show that high job demands paired with a lack of a sense of control breeds depression and other psychological disorders."[30] The Report therefore recommended that stakeholders including lawyers and legal employers review "how long-standing structures of the legal system, organizational norms, and embedded expectations,"[31] including addressing how deadlines, extension of trial dates, and expectations of availability could be modified to better enhance lawyers' sense of control.[32]

Thus, the workload, financial strain, and competitive, adversarial environment that enhances the perception of low decision latitude together may constitute external pressures associated with law practice that contribute to lawyer dissatisfaction and depression. Internal traits of lawyers should also be considered.

### § 3-2.1(b) Internal Traits of Lawyers

In addition to the external pressures of law practice, internal attributes that are distinctive to the legal population may impact lawyer dissatisfaction and depression. Many lawyers can be characterized as perfectionistic, competitive, and extrinsically motivated. These traits may distinguish many lawyers and may make them more prone to depression and suicide.

#### *§ 3-2.1(b)(1) Perfectionistic*

There are certain stereotypical characteristics that distinguish lawyers. Susan Daicoff asserts, "[t]he lawyer stereotype is to some degree consistent with the empirical research on lawyer attributes. Lawyers are likely to be more achievement-oriented, more aggressive, and more competitive than other professionals and people in general."[33] Noting that judges and lawyers tend to "hold themselves to a higher standard," one author explained, "[s]imilar to health care professionals, many judges and lawyers go into their respective fields in an attempt to help others and to make a difference in society."[34] But the lawyer's responsibility to counsel clients can be overwhelming: "Sometimes, the pressure to provide the right answers or to be the pinnacle of morality can cause emotional strife. This may turn into depression for lawyers and judges . . . ."[35]

#### *§ 3-2.1(b)(2) Competitive*

Similarly, addressing the high rate of suicide and depression among lawyers, the director of the Washington-based American Association of Suicidology noted that "the competitiveness and perfectionism that make good lawyers—and the lack of fulfillment many lawyers feel in practicing law—put them at high risk of alcoholism, drug use,

---

> leave firms early choose alternative legal careers, such as legal aid or assistant district attorney, where the pay is considerably lower but the decision latitude is considerably greater.

*Id.* (citations omitted).

[30] *Lawyer Well-Being Report*, *supra* note 1 at 16.

[31] *Id.* at 17.

[32] *Id.*

[33] Daicoff, *supra* note 8, at 1390.

[34] Richard J. Kay & Nathan M. Comerford, *Help Me, I'm Depressed: A Look at the Definition of Depression and Resistance to Treatment among Lawyers and Judges,* Mich. B.J., Sept. 2009, at 55.

[35] *Id.*

depression and suicide."[36] Daicoff further reveals that "lawyers' needs for achievement and their competitiveness can cause workaholism and perfectionism."[37] Daicoff observes that "[i]n law practice, these traits may easily become maladaptive."[38] While "workaholism and perfectionism . . . are at first rewarded by professional and financial success, thus satisfying lawyers' drives for achievement, dominance, money, and prestige[,] [t]hese behaviors can, when used in the extreme, however, result[ ] in stress, interpersonal difficulties, and substance abuse."[39]

#### *§ 3-2.1(b)(3) Extrinsically Motivated*

The motivation orientation of lawyers may also impact well-being. Numerous studies indicate "that pursuit of the 'extrinsic' goals which are common in Western culture, and which are embedded particularly deep in the culture of most law schools and law firms, does not produce a good life and in fact can very well undermine it. These studies consistently demonstrate that, to the extent such goals are primary in a person's life, she will experience decreased life satisfaction compared to people with other primary goals."[40]

Ken Sheldon and Lawrence Krieger have studied the degree to which lawyers tend to be extrinsically motivated.[41] They found this may not be an attribute characteristic of lawyers, but one that develops as a result of the law school or practice environment. Sheldon and Krieger measured the values and motivation of students as they entered law school, and then again later during their legal education.[42] They noted that students arrive at law with "healthy well-being, values, and motives—stronger, in fact, than a large undergraduate sample. Within six months, however, the law students experienced marked decreases in well-being and life satisfaction and marked increases in depression, negative affect, and physical symptoms."[43] More importantly, "their overall motivation and valuing patterns shifted in undesirable (external/extrinsic) directions, with particular increases in the valuing of image and appearance and decreases in altruism and community orientation."[44] Those changes were directly and negatively related to diminished well-being.

In sum, lawyers may be more susceptible to depression and suicide because of external forces unique to the practice of law, including a heavy workload, financial strain, and an overly adversarial atmosphere. As a group, law students and lawyers may

---

[36] Andrew Wolfson, *Rash of Kentucky lawyer suicides concerns colleagues: Varied reasons cited for deaths in recent years; bar president urges lawyers to watch out for each other*, THE COURIER-JOURNAL (Jun 3, 2013).

[37] Daicoff, *supra* note 8, at 1418.

[38] *Id.*

[39] *Id.* (citations omitted).

[40] Lawrence S. Krieger, *Institutional Denial About the Dark Side of Law School, and Fresh Empirical Guidance for Constructively Breaking the Silence*, 52 J. LEGAL EDUC. 112, 212 (2002) [hereinafter Krieger, *Institutional Denial*] ("Subjects who identified money, image, or influence as important for life satisfaction consistently experienced the *lowest* well-being in the study. By contrast, persons whose primary goal content was "intrinsic"—toward personal growth, intimacy, and community integration—experienced significantly greater well-being.").

[41] *See generally* Lawrence S. Krieger, *The Most Ethical of People, The Least Ethical of People: Proposing Self-Determination Theory to Measure Professional Character Formation*, 8 U. ST. THOMAS L.J. 168 (2011) [hereinafter Krieger, *Most Ethical*].

[42] Krieger, *Institutional Denial*, *supra* note 40, at 122.

[43] *Id.*

[44] *Id.* at 123.

be predisposed to depression based on certain attributes within the cohort, including perfectionism, competitive nature, and extrinsic motivation. Having a backdrop on the state of lawyer well-being and some of the causes of unhappiness, the discussion now turns to the role of professionalism and the potential relationship between the public service orientation of professionalism and the depression crisis in the legal academy.

## § 3-2.2 VALUES, NEEDS, MOTIVATION, AND WELL-BEING

In spite of the foregoing challenges, there are several studies that demonstrate a positive correlation between attorney professionalism and well-being.

Lawrence Krieger has used Self-Determination Theory (SDT) to study lawyer well-being. SDT uses empirical measures "to determine causes of, and contributions to, positive aspects of human experience, including positive mood/affect, life satisfaction, sense of purpose, and effective performance."[45] SDT studies the relationship between defined fundamental needs, values, and motivations. Psychological needs include autonomy, competence, and relatedness to others."[46] Values include "self-understanding/growth, intimacy with others, helping others, and being in/building community."[47] Finally, SDT asserts that "two "internal" or "autonomous" motivations for behavior—intrinsic and identified motivation—[ ]support psychological health and well-being."[48]

Krieger asserts that "[a]ll of the primary SDT domains appear to strongly predict core propensities for ethical and professional behaviors."[49] With regard to the psychological needs, Krieger explains autonomy, the "quality of coherence between one's perceived 'self,' one's values, and one's chosen actions defines autonomy within the context of SDT,"[50] is closely associated with integrity—"the character quality of adhering to moral principles and speaking the truth that one knows."[51] This SDT need is therefore centrally related to ethics and professionalism, because trustworthiness, an aspect of integrity "implicates many dimensions of ethics and professionalism, including those involving candor before the court, fair dealing, truthfulness, and trust between lawyers."[52] Competence is related to professionalism because "a professional obviously must be capable and effective."[53] Finally, the relatedness need is associated with professionalism because of the interpersonal skills and relationships associated with law practice. Krieger explains that "[s]ocial sensitivity, honesty, decency, respectfulness, thoughtfulness, and consideration are necessary for relations in life generally, just as for professional relations. Thus, we would predict that high satisfaction of the relatedness need would predict positive relations with other lawyers and clients."[54]

---

[45] Krieger, *Most Ethical, supra* note 41 at 171 (2011) (citations omitted).

[46] *Id.* (noting that self-esteem, while also a need that promotes well-being, does not appear to effect motivation or performance).

[47] *Id.* at 172.

[48] *Id.* at 173.

[49] *Id.* at 174.

[50] Krieger, *Most Ethical, supra* note 41 at 174 (citations omitted).

[51] *Id.*

[52] *Id.* (explaining that autonomy is "the most important of the three basic psychological needs, since people must have a well-defined sense of self, feel intimately connected to themselves, and express their core values in daily life in order to function in a consistent way and with a sense of security and grounding").

[53] *Id.* at 175.

[54] *Id.*

Values and motivation are closely related to needs, and predict professional qualities. Krieger notes that the desires for self-understanding, growth, and meaning in life suggest and individual who is interested in self-improvement and an interest in "pursuits that express the other intrinsic values (i.e., doing one's best, having close friendships, helping others, being in community), resulting in positive professional behaviors while fulfilling the individual's core needs."[55] The values of intimacy, aspiration to help others, and community mindedness implicate professional characteristics, such as a "service, rather than selfish orientation."[56]

In *What Makes Lawyers Happy?: A Data-Driven Prescription to Redefine Professional Success*,[57] Lawrence S. Krieger and Kennon M. Sheldon demonstrated a positive relationship between the needs, values, and motivations in SDT and happiness and well-being in lawyer populations. Specifically, the authors demonstrate that "[e]xperiences of autonomy (including authenticity), relatedness to others, and competence most strongly predicted attorney well-being . . . These large correlations indicate that well-being co-occurs with these factors so robustly that it may not be possible to experience thriving without relative satisfaction of all of these needs."[58] Other indicators of well-being included the ability to choose "work for internally motivated reasons,"[59] "[a]utonomy-supportive supervision of attorneys at the work place (provision of understanding, respect, and choices, as opposed to control),"[60] and intrinsic values.[61]

Sheldon and Kreiger did note that their findings were consistent with happiness research in the general population. In other words, lawyers do not differ in terms of what makes them happy and satisfied.[62] The authors concluded, "[s]imply stated, there is nothing in these data to suggest that attorneys differ from other people with regard to their prerequisites for feeling good and feeling satisfied with life."[63]

## § 3-2.3 IMPACT OF PUBLIC SERVICE[64]

As noted above, the relatedness need, together with the values of intimacy with others, helping others, and being in/building community, predict professional behaviors. These, in turn, are related to well-being. Service is a critical component of these needs and values.

---

[55] *Id.*

[56] *Id.* at 176. (noting that "[h]elpful community-mindedness further requires consideration of the needs of others, and tends to moderate a lawyer's adversarial behavior—contributing to a harmonious and effective professional community").

[57] Lawrence S. Krieger & Kennon M. Sheldon, Ph.D., *What Makes Lawyers Happy?: A Data-Driven Prescription to Redefine Professional Success*, 83 GEO. WASH. L. REV. 554, 617–19 (2015) [hereinafter Krieger & Sheldon, *What Makes Lawyers Happy?*].

[58] *Id.* at 617–18 (citations omitted).

[59] *Id.* at 618.

[60] *Id.*

[61] *Id.*

[62] *Id.* at 621. Sheldon and Krieger noted that "lawyers are often considered to think and act differently than others," which could suggest "the possibility that lawyers, whether by nature or through training, may respond differently than other people to psychological and external factors that typically generate well-being in the general population." *Id.* The authors concluded that this was not the case and that lawyers do not differ from the general population with regard to happiness and satisfaction.

[63] *Id.*

[64] This section is based, in part, on Melissa H. Weresh, *The Chicken or the Egg? Public Service Orientation and Lawyer Well-Being*, 36 U. ARK. LITTLE ROCK L. REV. 463, 478–80 (2014).

"Happiness research is unambiguous in showing that students who volunteer to help people in need are generally made happier by the experience."[65] There are many medical and psychological studies that demonstrate a positive relationship between well-being and giving behavior, defined in ways ranging from a giving perspective, to service, to volunteerism, to altruism. Medical research has established a positive relationship between volunteering and well-being.[66] Moreover, psychologists have identified "the need for nurturing social relationships or civic participation" as attributes of a happy life.[67]

Service or altruism may also have an established, positive impact on mental health.[68] One study explains that "[w]ell-being consists of feeling hopeful, happy, and good about oneself, as well as energetic and connected to others."[69] The study demonstrated a positive relationship between the well-being of retirees who engaged in volunteer work.[70] "Volunteers scored significantly higher in life satisfaction and will to live and had fewer symptoms of depression, anxiety, and somatization. Because there were no differences in demographic and other background variables between the groups, the researchers concluded that volunteer activity helped explain these mental health benefits."[71] In another study, researchers confirmed "that volunteering is highly associated with greater health and happiness, while other forms of altruistic behavior, such as donations of money or donations of blood, are not."[72]

There does appear to be a positive relationship between altruism, or giving behavior, and well-being. In terms of some of the stresses related to law practice, "[a]ltruism results in deeper and more positive social integration, distraction from personal problems and the anxiety of self-preoccupation, enhanced meaning and purpose as related to well-being, a more active lifestyle that counters cultural pressures toward isolated passivity, and the presence of positive emotions such as kindness that displace harmful negative emotional states."[73]

---

[65] Nancy Levit & Douglas O. Linder, *Happy Law Students, Happy Lawyers,* 58 SYRACUSE L. REV. 351, 369 (2008).

[66] *See* Deborah Maranville, *Infusing Passion and Context into the Traditional Law Curriculum Through Experiential Learning*, 51 J. LEGAL EDUC. 51, 55 (2001) ("[F]requent volunteering has significant health benefits, ranging from decreasing depression to alleviating headaches and back pain to increasing longevity.") (citing Allan Luks & Peggy Payne, THE HEALING POWER OF DOING GOOD: THE HEALTH AND SPIRITUAL BENEFITS OF HELPING OTHERS (Fawcett Columbine, 1991)). *See generally* Stephen G. Post, *Altruism, Happiness, and Health: It's Good to Be Good,* INT'L J. BEHAV. MED., Vol. 12, No. 2 (2005).

[67] Richard Delgado and Jean Stefancic, *Can Lawyers Find Happiness*, 58 SYRACUSE L. REV. 241, 249–50 (2008) (citing Robert N. Bellah et al., *Habits of the Heart* 167–213 (1985) and Peter H. Huang & Jeremy A. Blumenthal, *Positive Law and Policy, in* ENCYCLOPEDIA OF POSITIVE PSYCHOLOGY 730 (Shane J. Lopez ed., 2009)).

[68] John Wilson & Marc Musick, *The Effects of Volunteering on the Volunteer*, 62 LAW & CONTEMP. PROBS. 141, 150 (1999) ("[V]arious studies of the effect of volunteering on mortality . . . all point in the same direction—that volunteer work does help people live longer.").

[69] Post, *supra* note 66, at 68.

[70] *Id.*

[71] *Id.*

[72] Francesca Borgonovi, *Doing well by doing good. The relationship between formal volunteering and self-reported health and happiness*, 66 SOC. SCI. & MED. 2321, 2331 (June 2008). Exploring whether there was a causal relationship, the authors conclude that "the positive association that exists between volunteering and health is not causal and is most likely to be driven by reverse causality, self-selection and omitted variable bias. On the other hand, we suggest that at least in the case of religious volunteering the relationship between volunteering and happiness is the result of a positive causal effect of volunteering." *Id.*

[73] Post, *supra* note 66, at 70 (concluding that "[i]t is entirely plausible, then, to assert that altruism enhances mental and physical health").

The Lawyer Well-Being Report acknowledges the positive impact of a service orientation, encouraging legal employers to "emphasize a service-centered mission."[74] The Report notes, "[a]t its core, law is a helping profession. This can get lost in the rush of practice and in the business aspects of law. Much research reflects that organizational cultures that focus chiefly on materialistic, external rewards can damage well-being and promote a self-only focus."[75] In contrast, "[w]hen organizational values evoke a sense of belonging and pride, work is experienced as more meaningful. Experiencing work as meaningful is the biggest contributor to work engagement—a form of work-related well-being."[76]

## § 3-2.4 IMPORTANCE OF ORGANIZATIONAL ETHICAL CULTURE

Organizational ethical culture bears a relationship to both the ethical behavior of individuals and to individual well-being. " 'Organizational ethical culture' typically describes a broad range of formal and informal organizational practices, positions, and routines that collectively influence employees' behavior regarding ethics."[77] Ethical culture and ethical climate, or "the aggregation of employees' perceptions of what their organization values or embodies with regard to ethics,"[78] are related to ethical behavior. Specifically, where employees have a perception of a self-interested organizational climate there is a likelihood of unethical behavior.[79] In contrast, "climates perceived as focused on care for multiple stakeholders (i.e., a benevolent climate) and adherence to ethical rules (i.e., a principled climate) are linked to reductions in unethical outcomes."[80] Ethical leadership is also an important influence on ethical behavior and employee satisfaction[81] and can further have a positive impact on well-being.[82]

Business scholars have studied the relationship between "meaningful work" and positive professional behavior. Meaningful work is characterized as "purposeful and significant."[83] "[T]here is often an implicit logic in this literature that meaningfulness involves a sort of "fit" or alignment between the individual and the tasks, jobs, or work he or she performs. That is, to the degree that work fulfills one's needs or matches one's values and beliefs, then work is often seen as meaningful."[84] Some of the research on meaningful work relates back to the basic needs described above in terms of authenticity, as it "focuses an individual's beliefs, or needs, or values," and demonstrates "that how

---

[74] *Lawyer Well-Being Report, supra* note 1 at 33.

[75] *Id.*

[76] *Id.* at 34 (citations omitted).

[77] Gary R. Weaver, *Encouraging Ethics in Organizations: A Review of Some Key Research Findings*, 51 AM. CRIM. L. REV. 293, 302–03 (2014).

[78] *Id.* at 303.

[79] *Id.* at 303 (noting "employee perceptions of a self-interested (i.e., egoistic) climate are most clearly linked with higher levels of unethical behavior and other normally negative outcomes").

[80] *Id.*

[81] *Id.* at 309 (citations omitted) (associated ethical leadership behavior with a variety of positive organizational outcomes, including improved employee satisfaction and a reduction in unethical behavior).

[82] *Lawyer Well-Being Report, supra* note 1 at 13 (noting that "[l]eaders can create and support change through their own demonstrated commitment to core values and well-being in their own lives and by supporting others in doing the same").

[83] Christopher Michaelson, Michael G. Pratt, Adam M. Grant, and Craig P. Dunn, *Meaningful Work: Connecting Business Ethics and Organization Studies*, 121 J. Bus. Ethics 77, 79 (2014).

[84] *Id.*

an individual views him or herself (i.e., her or his identity) strongly influences how she or he views his or her work."[85] Autonomy and self-growth are also implicated as scholars have identified characteristics of meaningful work as "work that is 'freely entered into,' 'allows the worker to exercise her autonomy and independence,' 'enable[s] the worker to develop her rational capacities,' 'provides a wage sufficient for physical welfare,' 'supports the moral development of employees,' and 'is not paternalistic.' "[86]

Attributes of meaningful work, including integrity/authenticity, autonomy, relatedness, and motivation[87] correlate with Krieger's study of lawyers' well-being and life satisfaction, and the relationship of those attributes to professionalism.[88] Krieger notes that "lawyers who find interest and meaning in their work are much more likely to be happy than others."[89] Meaningful work has a positive connection to ethical organizational culture. "[E]mpirical work has linked meaningful work to important work outcomes such as job satisfaction, work motivation, engagement, and performance, citizenship behaviors, and attachment to occupations and organizations."[90]

---

[85] *Id.*

[86] *Id.* at 82 (citations omitted).

[87] *See* Blake A. Allan, Kelsey L. Autin and Ryan D. Duffy, *Self-Determination and Meaningful Work: Exploring Socioeconomic Constraints*, FRONT. PSYCHOL., 02 February 2016.

> Studies suggest that intrinsic motivation plays a key role in meaningful work and related constructs. One hypothesis is that engaging in intrinsically motivated work behavior creates congruence between work behaviors and one's self-concept, which results in feelings of meaningfulness. Despite the limited number of studies in this area, existing research supports this idea. For example, found significant correlations between intrinsic motivation and meaningful work, and found that higher levels of state and trait curiosity at work led to greater perceptions of meaningfulness, more frequent growth-oriented behavior, and higher levels of life satisfaction.

*Id.* (citations omitted).

[88] Krieger & Sheldon, *What Makes Lawyers Happy?, supra* note 57 at 622.

[89] *Id.* at 622.

[90] Michaelson et al., *supra* note 83 at 79.

# Chapter 3-3

# PROFESSIONAL IDENTITY FORMATION AND THE LAW SCHOOL CURRICULUM

**By Neil W. Hamilton and Melissa H. Weresh**

*Table of Sections*

§ 3-3.1 The Learning Outcomes That Law Faculties Are Adopting on the Ethical Professional Formation of Each Student
§ 3-3.2 Defining the Stages of Growth for a Commitment to Professional Development Learning Outcome (From Novice to Advanced Beginner to Competent to Expert)
§ 3-3.3 The General Principles That Should Guide the Development of Effective Curriculum to Foster Each Student's Ethical Professional Identity
§ 3-3.4 What Can We Learn About Professional-Identity Formation from MBA Education?

## § 3-3.1 THE LEARNING OUTCOMES THAT LAW FACULTIES ARE ADOPTING ON THE ETHICAL PROFESSIONAL FORMATION OF EACH STUDENT

ABA accreditation standard 302 requires all law schools to establish learning outcomes that include competency in "(a) knowledge and understanding of substantive and procedural law; (b) legal analysis and reasoning, legal research, problem solving, and written and oral communication in the legal context; [and] (c) the exercise of proper professional and ethical responsibilities to clients and the legal system. . . ."[1] While learning outcomes must be in place by the end of the 2017–18 academic year, ABA accreditation site teams visiting schools in the 2016–17 academic year will be reporting on the progress a law school is making in establishing learning outcomes.[2]

A first question is to what degree are law schools creating learning outcomes that give further definition to Standard 302(c)'s competency in "the exercise of proper professional and ethical responsibilities to clients and the legal system"? As of January 20, 2017, 70 out of the 205 ABA-accredited law schools had posted learning outcomes on the school's website.[3] Of these 70 law schools, 21 have adopted essentially the minimum

---

[1] *Managing Director's Guidance Memorandum*, A.B.A. SEC. LEGAL EDUC. & ADMISSIONS TO THE BAR (June 1 2015), https://www.americanbar.org/content/dam/aba/administrative/legal_education_and_admissions_to_the_bar/governancedocuments/2015_learning_outcomes_guidance.authcheckdam.pdf.

> "Learning outcomes must consist of clear and concise statements of knowledge that students are expected to acquire, skills students are expected to develop, and values that they are expected to understand and integrate into their professional lives." *Id.* at 4 (citing Accreditation Standard 302(c)).

[2] *Id.* at 6. "Learning outcomes for the school's overall program of legal education must appear in those places on its website and in its publications where the law school describes its mission and its curriculum." *Id.* at 4.

[3] These data from a January 15, 2017 survey of law school websites have been updated from an earlier Oct. 15, 2016 version published in a Mercer Law Journal symposium. *See* Neil Hamilton, *Off-the-Shelf Formative Assessments to Help Each Student Develop Toward a Professional Formation/Ethical Professional*

Standard 302(c) learning outcome that students will be competent in "the exercise of proper professional and ethical responsibilities to clients and the legal system,"[4] while 49 have adopted learning outcomes that go beyond the minimum of Standard 302(c) and further define "professional and ethical responsibilities to clients and the legal system" to include "values that students are expected to understand and integrate into their professional lives."[5]

Of the forty-nine law schools:

1. thirty-one have a learning outcome that includes competency in the value of providing pro bono legal services to the disadvantaged;
2. twenty-six law schools have adopted a version of a learning outcome that includes the competency of demonstrating understanding and integration of pro-active self-evaluation and professional development toward excellence at the competencies needed to serve clients and the legal system (self-directed learning);[6]
3. twenty-six law schools have adopted a version of a learning outcome that includes the competency of professionalism, high or the highest ethical standards, a personal code of ethics, or the internalization of values grounded in morality or faith;
4. twenty-four law schools include the competency of teamwork/effective collaboration;
5. twenty-three include a learning outcome that students develop self-awareness and cross-cultural competency to work with those of diverse backgrounds;
6. thirteen law schools include integrity/honesty in professional life;
7. nine include the competency of good judgment;
8. nine include the competency of improving the profession/legal system;
9. seven include the competency of active listening; and
10. six include the competency of leadership.

If these same proportions hold true when all 201 ABA-accredited law schools post learning outcomes, approximately 90 law schools will have adopted a competency in

---

*Identity Learning Outcome of an Internalized Commitment to the Student's Own Professional Development,* 67 MERCER L. REV. 687, 689 (2017). For this January 15, 2017 survey, Professor Jerry Organ, Professor Neil Hamilton and Holloran Center coordinator reviewed together and discussed all the data collected from law school websites. We decided that statements that a law school was introducing law students to a particular competency or listed a particular competency in list of possible examples of competencies a student might study or was giving law students "an opportunity" to develop a particular competency did not meet the requirements of a learning outcome that each student must understand and demonstrate a particular competency. Hamilton's earlier articles had reported higher numbers of law schools with posted learning outcomes applying a less rigorous standard.

[4] 2016–2017 ABA STANDARDS AND RULES at Standard 302(c). Note that this Standard 302(c) language is ambiguous whether these "professional and ethical responsibilities to clients and the legal system" require more than competency in meeting the minimum standards of the law of lawyering.

[5] *Managing Director's Guidance Memorandum, supra* note 1, at 4. The number of schools with these various learning outcomes exceeds 53 because several schools have learning outcomes which address more than one of these aspects of professional formation.

[6] Note that the Interpretation 302–1 for ABA Standard 302 includes "self-evaluation" as one of the "other professional skills" that a law school faculty may include in its learning outcomes. 2016–2017 ABA STANDARDS AND RULES at Interpretation 302–1.

understanding the value of pro bono legal services. Seventy-six schools will have adopted learning outcomes both on self-directed learning and on professionalism/high ethical standards/personal code of ethics. Seventy will have adopted a teamwork learning outcome, and sixty-seven will have adopted a cross-cultural competency learning outcome. Thirty-nine will have adopted integrity as a learning outcome.

It is possible to synthesize two major themes from the 49 law schools that have adopted learning outcomes stating values beyond the minimum required by ABA Standard 302(c). A first clear theme is that the meaning of the competency of "the exercise of proper professional and ethical responsibilities to clients and the legal system" can be further defined by asking students to demonstrate understanding and integration of pro-active self-evaluation and professional development toward excellence at the competencies needed to serve clients and the legal system.[7]

To see a second clear theme, first observe that the meaning of the competency of "the exercise of proper professional and ethical responsibilities to clients and the legal system" is further clarified in the learning outcomes that law schools are adopting that ask students to demonstrate understanding and integrating values and skills like:

(1) pro bono service to the disadvantaged;

(2) professionalism/high ethical standards/an ethical professional identity/moral core/personal code of ethics;

(3) teamwork/effective collaboration

(4) self-awareness and cross-cultural competency;

(5) integrity/honesty;

(6) active listening; and

(7) leadership.

Stepping back from the values and skills numbered 1–7 above, we can see that they are relational in nature, and build on the relational values and skills that the student brought to law school. The second clear theme is that law schools adopting learning outcomes like the values and skills numbered 1–7 above are essentially asking each student to demonstrate continuing growth over time from high short-term self-interest and low responsibility to others that would most likely have been the case earlier in life toward an internalized deep responsibility and service to clients and the legal system. The values and skills numbered 1–7 above build on and flow from an internalized deep responsibility and service to others that is applied specifically to clients and the legal system. These two major clear themes are learning outcomes that define the formation of an ethical professional identity beyond the minimum Standard 302(c) competency of "the exercise of proper professional and ethical responsibilities to clients and the legal system."

---

[7] This is self-directed learning defined as "a process in which individuals take the initiative, with or without the help of others, in diagnosing their learning needs, formulating learning goals, identifying the human and material resources for learning, choosing and implementing appropriate learning strategies, and evaluating learning outcomes." MALCOLM KNOWLES, SELF-DIRECTED LEARNING: A GUIDE FOR LEARNERS AND TEACHERS 18 (Association Press, 1975). *See also*, Michael Hunter Schwartz, *Teaching Law Students to be Self-Regulated Learners*, 2003 MICH. ST. DCL L. REV. 447 (2003). Self-directed learning builds on a foundation of ongoing self-evaluation.

The learning outcomes the faculties are adopting rarely mention trustworthiness in the individual lawyer and the profession which Chapters 3-1.1 through 3-1.3 discuss as foundational with respect to the profession's social contract, the competencies that clients and legal employers want, and the understandings of professionalism in the Model Rules, the ABA Reports, and research on exemplary lawyers. However trustworthiness in a professional services provider like a lawyer is built on demonstrated competence and reliability of the professional's work, the relational skills of the professional, and the professional's demonstration of deep care for the person served (the client).[8] Both clear themes in the learning outcomes faculties have adopted, an internalized commitment to professional development toward excellence and an internalized deep responsibility and service to the clients and the legal system, build trustworthiness.

## § 3-3.2 DEFINING THE STAGES OF GROWTH FOR A COMMITMENT TO PROFESSIONAL DEVELOPMENT LEARNING OUTCOME (FROM NOVICE TO ADVANCED BEGINNER TO COMPETENT TO EXPERT)

If legal education follows the model of medical education, once the law schools have defined learning outcomes, the next step is that the faculty must develop a series of benchmarks or stage-development performance levels (from novice to expert) for each competency included in the faculty's learning outcomes. Medical education calls these benchmarks "milestones."[9] Milestones define specific stage-appropriate goals to aid in the internalization, evaluation, and assessment of the competencies. The American Council for Graduate Medical Education website notes that "for accreditation purposes, the milestones are competency-based developmental outcomes (e.g., knowledge, skills, attitudes, and performance) that can be demonstrated progressively by residents and fellows from the beginning of their education through graduation to the unsupervised practice of their specialties."[10] These Milestones, developed in collaboration with the American Board of Medical Specialties certifying boards, medical-specialty organizations, program-director associations, and residents, are "a natural progression of the work on the six competencies."

Overall, the Milestones reflect the Dreyfus and Dreyfus model of development from novice to expert shown in Figure 1 below:

[8] NEIL HAMILTON, ROADMAP: THE LAW STUDENT'S GUIDE TO PREPARING AND IMPLEMENTING A SUCCESSFUL PLAN FOR MEANINGFUL EMPLOYMENT 80–83 (ABA Book Publishing, 2015).

[9] This section is borrowed from my earlier article, Neil Hamilton & Sarah Schaefer, *What Legal Education Can Learn From Medical Education About Competency-Based Learning Outcomes Including Those Related to Professional Formation (Professionalism)*, 29 GEORGETOWN J. LEGAL ETHICS 399, 415–16 (2016).

[10] "Milestones," ACGME, https://www.acgme.org/acgmeweb/tabid/430/ProgramandInstitutionalAccreditation/NextAccreditationSystem/Milestones.aspx.

**Figure 1**

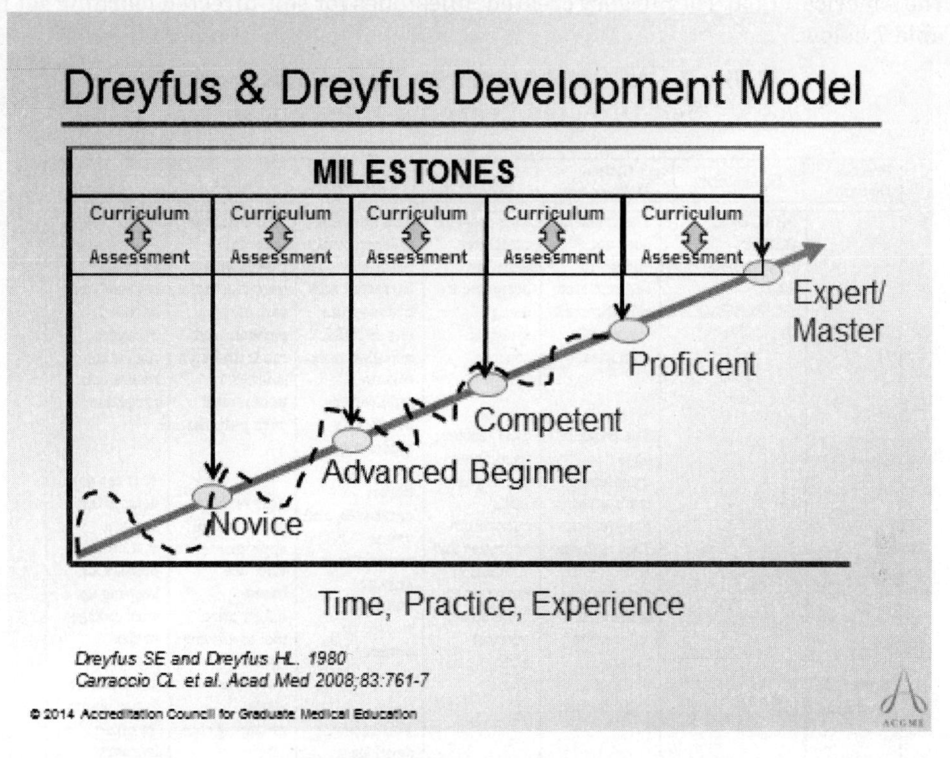


As indicated in Figure 1, for each competency the law faculty has included in its learning outcomes, the faculty would also define milestones to create a guide for the level of the particular competency that a law student should be expected to have achieved at a particular time in the student's matriculation. The milestones map progression as a student continues his or her education.

For example, for a learning outcome that each student demonstrates understanding and integration of pro-active professional development (self-directed learning) toward excellence at the competencies needed to serve clients and the legal system, the scholarship on self-directed learning is very helpful to define the relevant stages of development or milestones toward later stages of development on this learning outcome. Self-directed learning has been defined as "a process in which individuals take the initiative, with or without the help of others, in diagnosing their learning needs, formulating learning goals, identifying the human and material resources for learning, choosing and implementing appropriate learning strategies, and evaluating learning outcomes."[11] "It is widely accepted that self-directed learning promotes adult learning success in both academia and practice work."[12]

---

[11] MALCOLM KNOWLES, SELF-DIRECTED LEARNING: A GUIDE FOR LEARNERS AND TEACHERS 18 (Association Press, 1975). *See also*, Michael Hunter Schwartz, *Teaching Law Students to be Self-Regulated Learners*, 2003 MICH. ST. DCL L. REV. 447 (2003).

[12] Stefanie Boyer et al., *The Moderating Effect of the Self-Directed Learning Measurement Tool: A User's Guide,* 10 INT'L J. SELF-DIRECTED LEARNING 21, 21 (Nov. 2, 2013). Research in multiple science domains indicates that teaching students to self-monitor improves students' learning. *See, e.g.*, SUSAN A. AMBROSE ET AL., HOW LEARNING WORKS: SEVEN RESEARCH-BASED PRINCIPLES FOR SMART TEACHING 198 (Jossey-Bass, 2010).

To give a specific example, the American Council for Graduate Medical Education and the American Board of Surgery created milestones for self-directed learning set forth in Table 7 below.

**Table 7—ACGME/American Board of Surgery Self-Directed Learning Milestones**

| Practice Domain | Competency | Critical Deficiencies | LEVEL 1 | LEVEL 2 | LEVEL 3 | LEVEL 4 |
|---|---|---|---|---|---|---|
| Self-directed Learning | PRACTICE-BASED LEARNING AND IMPROVEMENT | The resident does not engage in self-initiated, self- directed learning activities.<br><br>The resident does not complete simulation assignments. This resident is frequently absent for scheduled simulation exercises without a valid excuse. | This resident completes learning assignments using multiple sources.<br><br>This resident participates in assigned skills curriculum activities and simulation exercises to build strong surgical skills. | This resident independently reads the literature and uses sources (e.g. SCORE modules, peer-reviewed publications, practice guidelines, textbooks, library databases, and online materials) to answer questions related to patients.<br><br>This resident develops a learning plan based on feedback with some external assistance.<br><br>This resident identifies gaps in personal technical skills and works with faculty members to develop a skills leaning plan. | This resident looks for trends and patterns in the care of patients and reads and uses sources to understand such patterns.<br><br>This resident can select an appropriate evidence-based information tool to answer specific questions while providing care.<br><br>This resident independently practices surgical skills in a simulation environment to enhance technical ability. | This resident participates in local, regional, and national activities, and/or self-assessment programs.<br><br>This resident demonstrates use of a system or process for keeping up with changes in the literature, and initiates assignments for other learners.<br><br>This resident leads surgical skills experiences for students and residents and participates in skills curriculum development. |

Another model of the stages or milestones of student development of self-directed learning, adapted from Gerald Grow, is shown in Table 8 below.

**Table 8—Developmental Stages of Self-Directed Learning[13]**

| | **Student Characteristics** |
|---|---|
| **Dependent Stage** | • Assumes passive role with respect to professional self-development<br>• Lacks interest in developing competencies except minimum required by external authority<br>• Does not generally want or seek feedback into strengths and weaknesses<br>• May react negatively to such feedback<br>• Depends on external authority for explicitly direction and validation |
| **Interested Stage** | • Can see self-interest in professional self-development<br>• May recognize weaknesses, but motivation to improve is principally externalized<br>• Responds reasonably to questions and feedback on strengths and weaknesses<br>• Is willing to engage mentors/coaches in goal-setting and implementation strategies<br>• Shows some initiative and persistence to learn competencies |
| **Involved Stage** | • Is committed to professional self-development<br>• Identifies strengths and weaknesses in development of competencies<br>• Responds positively to and reflects on feedback concerning strengths and weaknesses and how to improve<br>• Seeks insight from mentors and coaches in goal-setting and implementation<br>• Is internalizing motivation to learn new knowledge and skills continuously<br>• Is internalizing standard of excellence at all competencies<br>• Shows substantial persistence in learning competencies |
| **Self-Directed** | • Is intrinsically motivated to professional self-development and learning new knowledge and skills over a career<br>• Actively identifies both strength and weaknesses in development and sets goals and creates and executes implementation plans<br>• Proactively develops mentor and coach relationships and proactively seeks help and feedback from mentors and coaches |

[13] Adapted from Gerald O. Grow, *Teaching Learners to be Self-Directed,* 41 ADULT EDUC. Q. 125, 129 (1991). *See* Neil Hamilton, *A Professional Formation/Professional Challenge: Many Students Need Help With Self-Directed Learning,* 27 REGENT U. L. REV. 225, 231–32 (2015).

| | |
|---|---|
| | • Reflects on feedback and responds to feedback appropriately<br>• Knows when and how to seek help<br>• Actively seeks challenges<br>• Has internalized standard of excellence at all competencies |

Table 9 shows a model of a milestones stage-development model for an internalized deep responsibility and service to the clients and the legal system.[14]

**Table 9—Developmental Stages of an Internalized Responsibility to Clients and the Legal System[15]—a Foundational Element of an Ethical Professional Identity**

| | Student Characteristics |
|---|---|
| **Level 1** | a. Has self-awareness of own values/first principles regarding responsibilities and service to others.<br>b. Has had previous experiences in terms of responsibility to others on matters important to them, and has reflected on how the previous experience is relevant to the practice of law. |
| **Level 2** | a. Demonstrates knowledge of basic legal ethics principles and is able to identify legal ethical issues in hypothetical situations.<br>b. Demonstrates understanding of the profession's core values and ideals including the importance and priority of responsibility to the client and the legal system, for example with respect to trustworthiness. |
| **Level 3** | a. Consistently recognizes legal ethical issues in the most common and frequent experiential situations and is able to discuss, analyze, and manage such issues.<br>b. Demonstrates progress, in the most common and frequent experiential situations, with respect to integration into student's ethical identity of the profession's core values and ideals including the importance and priority of responsibility to the client and the legal system, for example with respect to trustworthiness (an ethical professional identity). |
| **Level 4** | a. Is consistently able to effectively recognize, discuss, analyze and manage legal ethical issues in complicated and challenging experiential situations. |

[14] *See* Neil Hamilton, *Professional-Identity/Professional-Formation/Professionalism Learning Outcomes: What We Can Learn About Assessment From Medical Education?*, 13 U. ST. THOMAS L.J. (forthcoming 2017) http://ssrn.com/abstract=2962461.

[15] This table is adapted from "Table 1. Four Selected General Milestones in the Next Accreditation System," *in* Thomas Nasca et al., *The Next GME Accreditation System—Rationale and Benefits,* NEW ENG. J. MED. 1, 3 (Feb. 22, 2012), https://www.acgme.org/acgmeweb/Portals/0/PDFs/NAS/NEJMfinal.pdf. Note that the Milestones in the original table, which were developed by an ACGME expert panel, reflected the following expected levels of performance that the evaluator assesses: level 2, typical graduating medical student; levels 3 and 4, resident during the program; level 5, graduating resident; level 6, advanced, specialist resident or practicing physician. *See also* "The Diagnostic Radiology Milestone Project," ACGME, http://www.acgme.org/Portals/0/PDFs/Milestones/DiagnosticRadiologyMilestones.pdf?ver=2015-11-06-120532-380, at 10.

| | |
|---|---|
| | b. Demonstrates consistent integration into student's ethical identity in complicated and challenging experiential situations of the profession's core values and ideals including the importance and priority of responsibility to the client and the legal system, for example with respect to trustworthiness. |
| **Level 5** | a. Is exemplary in effectively recognizing, discussing, analyzing and managing legal ethical issues in complicated and challenging experiential situations.<br>b. Demonstrates exemplary continuing growth, leadership, and mentorship in all situations in integrating the profession's core values and ideals including the importance and priority of responsibility to the client and the legal system, for example with respect to trustworthiness. |

## § 3-3.3 THE GENERAL PRINCIPLES THAT SHOULD GUIDE THE DEVELOPMENT OF EFFECTIVE CURRICULUM TO FOSTER EACH STUDENT'S ETHICAL PROFESSIONAL IDENTITY[16]

A number of general principles to guide curricular design to foster student development toward professional-identity learning outcomes emerge from a recent analysis of empirical research on these principles from four perspectives.[17] These perspectives include a synthesis of the five Carnegie Foundation for the Advancement of Teaching Studies of higher education for the professions; a synthesis of the empirical studies on effective curriculum coming out of the research on the Four Component Model in moral psychology; a synthesis of principles from *How Learning Works: Seven Research-Based Principles for Smart Teaching;* and a synthesis of what medical education has learned about the most effective professional-formation curriculum.

A comparison of all four research perspectives indicates agreement among them that an effective professional-formation curriculum should include the principles in Table 10 below.

**Table 10—General Agreement That an Effective Professional-Formation Curriculum Should:**

1. take into account that students are at different developmental stages of growth and engage each student at the student's present developmental stage;

2. provide repeated opportunities for reflection on the responsibilities of the profession and reflective self-assessment in general;[18]

---

[16] Some of this section is borrowed from Neil Hamilton, *Off-the-Shelf Formative Assessments to Help Each Student Develop Toward a Professional Formation / Ethical Professional Identity Learning Outcome of an Internalized Commitment to the Student's Own Professional Development*, 68 MERCER L. REV. 687 (2017).

[17] Neil Hamilton & Jerome Organ, *Thirty Reflection Questions to Help Each Student Find Meaningful Employment and Develop an Integrated Professional Identity (Professional Formation)*, 83 TENN. L. REV. 843, 874 (2016).

[18] The habit of self-assessment and reflection is foundational for students and practicing lawyers to identify areas for further professional development and become effective career-long learners. Sami Shaban et al., *Factors Influencing Medical Students' Self-Assessment of Examination Performance Accuracy: A United Arab Emirates Study*, 29 EDUC. FOR HEALTH 75, 76 (2016).

3. emphasize experiential learning, feedback on the student's performance, and reflection; and

4. emphasize coaching.[19]

In addition, one of the four research perspectives suggests that an effective professional-formation curriculum should include the principles in Table 11 below.

**Table 11—An Effective Professional-Formation Curriculum Should Also:**

5. provide experiences that create cognitive dissonance/optimal conflict with the student's current developmental stage on either of the professional-formation learning outcomes;

6. provide instruction that helps the student understand how new knowledge and skills are building on the student's prior knowledge and competencies (the student's existing narrative);

7. provide instruction that helps each student understand how the professional-formation curriculum is helping the student achieve his or her goals; and

8. give effective feedback, especially through mentoring and coaching, that tells each student where the student is developmentally relative to the stated learning outcome and what specifically the student needs to do to improve in order to make progress toward later stages of development.

One additional principle to guide curricular design on professional-formation learning outcomes is unique to legal education. There is growing empirical evidence that legal education's paradigm for professional success tends to undermine the well-being of many students.[20] For many students, legal education's reward system's emphasis on ranking, competitive achievement, status credentials, and money tends to undermine the key intrinsic values that contribute to a student's or lawyer's well-being: self-understanding/growth; intimacy with others; helping others; and being in/building community.[21] This growing body of research on the negative impact of legal education on well-being for many students leads to a ninth principle for curricular design that an effective professional-formation curriculum should:

9. consider carefully the impact of the curricular design, including formative assessment, on student well-being.

With respect to curricular design of formative professional-formation assessments in particular, we need to add the five additional important principles set forth in Table 12 to evaluate the effectiveness of assessments.

---

[19] "A coach is generally understood to mean a senior professional who guides a student by questioning the student about issues of importance in the work, helping the student to identify goals, creating a plan to achieve the goals, and providing constructive feedback." Neil W. Hamilton, Verna E. Monson & Jerome M. Organ, *Encouraging Each Student's Personal Responsibility for Core Competencies Including Professionalism,* 21 PROF. LAW. 1, 12 (2012). A mentor is a professional who has a relationship with the student and is someone from whom the student can seek advice. "In general a mentor gives advice when asked, and a coach proactively asks questions." *Id.*

[20] *See* Lawrence S. Krieger & Kennon M. Sheldon, *What Makes Lawyers Happy?: A Data-Driven Prescription to Redefine Professional Success,* 83 GEO. WASH. L. REV. 554, 566–69 (2015); Lawrence S. Krieger, *The Most Ethical of People, The Least Ethical of People: Proposing Self-Determination Theory to Measure Professional Character Formation,* 8 U. ST. THOMAS L.J. 168, 184–86 (2011).

[21] *See* Krieger & Sheldon, *supra* note 20, at 566–69; Krieger, *supra* note 20, at 184–86.

### Table 12—Effective Formative Assessments on Professional-Formation Learning Outcomes Should Also:

10. consider carefully the validity[22] and reliability[23] of the assessment while realizing that validity and reliability are of highest concern if the test is a high-stakes norm-referenced assessment, of significant concern if the test measure complex cognitive constructs, and of more moderate concern if the test is fostering interpersonal and communication abilities and self-reflection;[24]

11. consider carefully that formative self-assessments are particularly challenging because many people, particularly poor performers in comparison with their peers, are not particularly accurate at self-assessment and tend to have a higher impression of their knowledge and skills than is the reality;[25]

12. give weight to whether the students, faculty and staff, and legal employers will understand and see clear value to them from a particular assessment;

13. create a progression of curricular modules and assessments to foster each student's growth toward the next stage of development for these professional-identity learning outcomes; and

14. consider, in a time of scarce resources, how to minimize the total cost of the assessment in terms of (1) student time, (2) instructor time, (3) out-of-pocket costs to purchase the assessment and any expert debrief an assessment may require.

The first principle above in Table 10—that a professional-formation curriculum including formative assessments should take into account that students are at different developmental stages and engage each student at the student's present developmental stage—is the most foundational principle to guide curricular design. This chapter calls

---

[22] Validity: Although people tend to talk about an assessment tool or measure as "validated," and many commercially available tests or measures claim to be "validated," validity is instead an ongoing process. Validity is not a characteristic of a test or a measure but a characteristic of the data. Construct validity explores whether a test is measuring what it claims to measure. Content validity explores what subject-matter experts view as important or valid within a test or assessment. Predictive validity looks at how well scores on a test predicted some type of outcome, such as whether LSAT scores predict class grade rank at the end of law school. Through replication of studies, validity accrues.

Neil Hamilton & Verna Monson, Legal Education's Ethical Challenge: Empirical Research on How Most Effectively to Foster Each Student's Professional Formation (Professionalism), 9 U. ST. THOMAS L.J. 325, 386–87 (2011).

[23] Reliability. Reliability contributes to the overall validity of a test or measure. Reliability is estimated by looking at how similar items on a survey or measure correlate or how different versions of a test or measure given at the same time or some weeks or months apart correlate. If researchers are coding narrative data or rating responses using a scale, reliability between coders can be calculated. The widely accepted definition of sufficient reliability of a test or measure is a number—with a coefficient of approximately .80. Reliability is increased by controlling conditions in which students are given the assessment, limiting the length of the interview or survey to avoid fatigue and distraction, and training raters or coders. *Id.*

[24] *Id.*

[25] *See* Joyce Ehrlinger et al., *Why the Unskilled Are Unaware: Further Explorations of (Absent) Self-Insight Among the Incompetent*, 105 ORGAN. BEHAV. HUM. DECIS. PROCESS 98 (Jan. 2008, No. 1) ("People are typically overly optimistic when evaluating the quality of their performance on social and intellectual tasks. In particular, poor performers grossly overestimate their performances because their incompetence deprives them of the skills needed to recognize their deficits."); Susan Zvacek et al., *Accuracy of Self-Assessment Among Graduate Students in Mechanical Engineering,* PROCEEDINGS OF 2015 INT'L CONF. ON INTERACTIVE COLLABORATIVE LEARNING (Sept. 20–24, 2015) at 1 and 3 (confirming the Dunning-Kruger effect that low-performing students tend to overestimate their abilities and high-performing students tend to underestimate theirs).

principle 1 "go where they are and engage the students there." For example, this first principle means that the faculty at each school with a learning outcome relating to self-directed learning needs to assess where the students are developmentally with respect to this learning outcome. Data from four law schools indicate that approximately 50% of the 1L students are self-assessing at one of the two earlier stage of self-directed learning.[26] Since these early-stage students by definition are more passive and less likely to take advantage of elective engagements, faculty and staff need to act as co-educators on a **required** curriculum to address this learning outcome.

Curricular design principles 7 and 9 outlined above in Tables 2 and 3 also build off principle 1 and are very important foundations. Principle 7 is to provide instruction that helps each student understand how the curriculum is helping the student achieve her goals, and principle 9 is to consider carefully the impact of the curricular design on student well-being. Essentially principles 7 and 9 are further elaborations of Principle 1 and "go where they are and engage students there."

The data available indicate that the vast majority of law students have a post-graduation goal of passing the bar and gaining meaningful employment. For example, in August, 2015 and again in August, 2016, the author asked fall semester 2L students (who must take Professional Responsibility in the 2L year) "what are the professional goals you would like to achieve by six months after graduation?" Students report that the most important goals are meaningful employment and passing the bar. However if half or more of the students are at earlier stages of development on self-directed learning, many students do not know how to use their time in law school most effectively to achieve their goals.

A synthesis of principles 1, 7 and 9 together indicates that faculty and staff should be intentionally transparent in their communication with students to help them understand how the faculty's learning outcome of demonstrating pro-active professional development and the curriculum fostering this outcome are major bridges to help the student achieve her goal of meaningful employment.

## § 3-3.4 WHAT CAN WE LEARN ABOUT PROFESSIONAL-IDENTITY FORMATION FROM MBA EDUCATION?

Instruction in professional identity development in business schools differs largely from that in medical (included the discussion above) and law schools. This is due, in part, to the fact that there is no accreditation requirement associated with such instruction. Moreover, there is no uniform code of ethics applicable to businesses.[27] There is also the

---

[26] Neil Hamilton & Jerome Organ, *supra* note 17, at 859. Note that there is a self-report bias in this type of research because, "[i]n general, research participants want to respond in a way that makes them look as good as possible;" they want to respond in ways they consider "socially desirable." *See* Stewart I. Donaldson & Elisa J. Grant-Vallone, *Understanding Self-Report Bias in Organizational Behavior Research*, 17 J. BUS. & PSYCHOL. 245, 247 (2002). The true proportion of 1L students at the two earlier stages of self-directed learning is probably significantly higher than 50%.

[27] Thomas T. Piper, Mary C. Gentile, & Sharon Daloz Parks, CAN ETHICS BE TAUGHT?: PERSPECTIVES, CHALLENGES, AND APPROACHES AT HARVARD BUSINESS SCHOOL (Harvard Business School, 1993).

> Frank Pierson, in a companion report for the Carnegie Corporation, observed that an important influence shaping the work of business schools is the increasing attention being given to the social responsibilities of business enterprises. Formal standards embodied in law and governmental regulations are but one aspect of this development. Even more pervasive are the informal rules and obligations which the community expects business to meet, whether they involve dealings at national, state, or local levels. No one would argue that there is a clear and precise code of conduct applicable to business in its relations with representatives of government, unions, suppliers,

challenge that business ethics involves both the ethics and ethical culture of the organization as well as the ethics of the individual manager. Some business schools incorporate ethics into stand-alone course, while others incorporate ethics-related teaching throughout the curriculum. In *Can Ethics Be Taught?: Perspectives, Challenges, and Approaches at Harvard Business School*, authors described a comprehensive model of professionalism instruction under development at the time at Harvard Business School, which was guided by the following "program beliefs:"

> Belief 1: *Ethics is as much an attitude as it is a set of skills and knowledge.*
>
> Belief 2: *Outstanding leaders, organizations, and practice should be emphasized.*
>
> Belief 3: *The focus should be on decision making with all its complexity and ambiguity, not on issues of ethics or social responsibility in isolation.*
>
> Belief 4: *Immediate intervention is important.*
>
> Belief 5: *A broad integrative program is needed.*
>
> Belief 6: *Surround the community with opportunities to discuss leadership, ethics, and corporate responsibility.*
>
> Belief 7: *Faculty encouragement and development are as important as student development, at least during the first five to seven years.*
>
> Belief 8: *Strong, visible commitment by the dean and senior faculty leaders is essential.*[28]

There are skeptics about the effectiveness of MBA education's efforts concerning ethical professional identity formation. Some business ethics MBA professors question the efficacy of efforts to foster professional identity in light of the many public management scandals in the financial sector and the short-term profit maximization model that is featured in graduate business education. In his book *From Higher Aims to Hired Hands: The Social Transformation of American Business Schools and the Unfulfilled Promise of Management as a Profession* (2007), Harvard business school professor Rakesh Khurana observes

> The loss of this historical meta-narrative of management as a profession—a narrative that had placed managers at the center of the corporation and made them the primary link between the narrower concerns of business and the broader ones of society—is, I believe, the root cause of the inchoateness and drift that, more than 125 years after the establishment of the Wharton School and nearly 100 years after the founding of Harvard Business School characterizes much contemporary business education. The effects of this loss, in turn, are visible all around those of us who teach in business schools today."[29]

---

> stockholders, rival firms, and the like, but the norms within which employers operate are nonetheless real.

*Id.* at 9 (citing Frank C. Pierson et al., The Education of American Businessmen: A Study of University-College Programs in Business Administration (New York: McGraw-Hill, 1959).

[28] *Id.* at 119–38.

[29] RAKESH KHURANA, FROM HIGHER AIMS TO HIRED HANDS: THE SOCIAL TRANSFORMATION OF AMERICAN BUSINESS SCHOOLS AND THE UNFULFILLED PROMISE OF MANAGEMENT AS A PROFESSION 368–69 (Princeton U. Press, 2007).

For a member of a peer-review profession, Khurana emphasizes, work is more than a market exchange; it is, rather, a source of meaning and identity within a community of like-minded practitioners.[30] In sum, discipline and self restraint to some degree to preserve the good name of the professional community and advance the public good are hallmarks of a "profession."[31]

Key differences between business school professional identity development and the educational approach taken and law and medical schools are further highlighted in the following excerpt from *Teaching Professionalism: A Tale of Three Schools*.[32]

> *The Business School Case for Professionalism Education*
>
> The concept of "business professionalism" is more difficult to define than for either medicine or law. To a large degree, this difficulty stems from the fact that business schools do not teach professionalism in the sense recognized by physicians or lawyers. "Business" is not a traditional guild-based profession, charged with its own self-regulation. Rather, business school graduates go into fields as diverse as the students themselves. As such, there is no monolithic, agreed-upon concept of business professionalism.
>
> Yet business schools do offer courses in leadership, social responsibility, and nonprofit management, each of which embodies the notion that the business community is part of a larger social framework and should conform to certain standards of behavior and carry out its obligations to the public: in short, an ethic of professionalism. For decades, the business community has embraced the concept of "corporate social responsibility." Often criticized for its vagueness, this concept suggests that corporations should take the broader interests of society into account when charting a particular course of action. A corporation accounting for the "interests of society" stands in stark contrast to the views of many lawyers and economists, who argue that the only interests that should be taken into account are those of the shareholders (Friedman 1970). Yet, the ethic of corporate social responsibility is, in many ways, the analog of the altruism model taught in medical schools and the pro bono spirit espoused in many law schools. Indeed, data from Christensen et al. (2007) show that the majority of top business schools in the United States teach some form of ethics or corporate social responsibility in their curricula. Of the world's top 50 business schools, a full 84% require students to take at least one course addressing either ethics or corporate social responsibility. And if the definition of an ethics course or corporate social responsibility course is expanded to include topics such as sustainability and corporate leadership, each of the top 50 schools requires at least one such course. Much of the drive for inclusion of such courses into the mandatory curriculum comes from students themselves, perhaps spurred in part by recent corporate accounting scandals (Adler 2002).
>
> Indeed, organizations explicitly devoted to engendering an ethic of social responsibility within the business community are flourishing. One of the largest of these organizations, Net Impact, has seen explosive membership

---

[30] *Id.* at 374.

[31] *Id.*

[32] Nirav Shah, Jeffrey Anderson, & Holly J. Humphrey, *Teaching Professionalism: A Tale of Three Schools*, 51 PERSPECTIVES IN BIOLOGY AND MEDICINE 535, 541–42 (2008).

growth over the past 15 years, to over 20,000 members today. The organization strives to "make a positive impact on society by growing and strengthening a community of new leaders who use business to improve the world" (Net Impact 2008). Notably, much of the demand driving the growth of such organizations comes from business school students themselves. Each chapter is largely student-driven and assists the business community in finding socially conscious ways to achieve their business goals. At the University of Chicago Graduate School of Business, student membership in the local Net Impact chapter has more than doubled in the past three years alone. And the number of solo chapters of Net Impact worldwide has gone from six in 1993 to 159 chapters today. This suggests that most of the demand for professionalism exposure in the young business community is coming from the students themselves and not being imposed by the business schools, a stark contrast to medical professionalism education, where in some schools students report "professionalism fatigue."

# Part Four

# LEGAL ETHICS AND THE PRACTICE OF LAW

## By Gregory C. Sisk

## INTRODUCTION TO PART FOUR

Nearly every element of an attorney's legal practice is regulated by formal ethics rules enforceable by professional discipline, governed by standards applied by courts, and guided by statements of the law governing lawyers.[1] This part of the hornbook addresses the substance of those ethical obligations as applied to practicing lawyers. The topics addressed in Part Four include advertising for and solicitation of clients, the creation and termination of the attorney-client relationship, attorney fees and funding of legal services, the duty to effectively represent clients, the duty to protect confidential information and the attorney-client privilege, the duty of loyalty and conflicts of interest, duties to organizational clients, duties of ethical advocacy, duties as an evaluator or third-party neutral, respect for persons other than clients, duties as a managing or supervising attorney, and public-regarding activities by lawyers.

The Preamble to the Model Rules of Professional Conduct links the rules, which have the force of law and establish standards to which lawyers must conform, to the diverse roles and multiple responsibilities of lawyers in our system of justice and in our society. As stated in Paragraph 1 of the Preamble, the rules are grounded in the conception of the lawyer as both "a representative of clients" and "an officer of the legal system and a public citizen having special responsibility for the quality of justice."

As outlined in Paragraphs 2 through 6 of the Preamble to the Model Rules, lawyers serve as advisors, who translate the generality of the law into specifically-applicable information for their clients; as advocates, who zealously assert the interests and promote the positions of their clients; as negotiators, who seek "a result advantageous to a client" while dealing honestly with others; as evaluators, who investigate and report on legal affairs; as third-party neutrals, who resolve or assist parties to resolve a dispute; and as persons who even while acting outside of a professional capacity remain subject to high standards of integrity. When undertaking professional responsibilities, the lawyer must be competent, be diligent, communicate regularly with a client, maintain client confidentiality, conform to the requirements of the law, refrain from abusing legal process, and "demonstrate respect for the legal system and those who serve it."

The Preamble in Paragraph 6 also emphasizes that a lawyer is an officer of the court and a public citizen, who should contribute her legal knowledge and expertise toward reforming the law and improving the administration and the quality of justice. The "lawyer should further the public's understanding of and confidence in the rule of law and the justice system." And the lawyer should devote her professional skills to ensure greater access to the legal system for those who cannot afford counsel. In addition, the

---

[1] When the term "ethics" is used in this part of the book, it "denote[s] the rules of professional conduct under which lawyers practice" and other legal standards of professional ethics, rather than ethics as a subject of moral philosophy. *See* W. BRADLEY WENDEL, LAWYERS AND FIDELITY TO LAW 19 (Princeton U. Press, 2010). When moral questions beyond formal ethics rules are raised in this part of the book, they tend to be explicitly identified as such.

lawyer has a special responsibility to the profession into which she has been admitted, to participate in the self-governance of the bar and to work to preserve the independence of the legal profession.

As recognized in Paragraph 9 of the Preamble, while the Rules of Professional Conduct "prescribe terms for resolving" many of the conflicting responsibilities that arise in the practice of law, the lawyer still must "exercise . . . sensitive professional and moral judgment guided by the basic principles underlying the Rules." Accordingly, while complying with the rules and with other legal requirements, Paragraph 7 directs the lawyer to be "guided by personal conscience and the approbation of professional peers." In an aspirational statement, the Preamble exhorts the lawyer to "strive to attain the highest level of skill, to improve the law and the legal profession and to exemplify the legal profession's ideals of public service."

## RECOMMENDED CITATION FOR PART FOUR

For those citing to Chapters 4-1 through 4-13 in Part Four, we recommend attribution to this individually-authored part as being most accurate. For example, the most appropriate citation format to the first section in this part would look like this: Gregory C. Sisk, Legal Ethics and the Practice of Law § 4-1.1, in *Legal Ethics, Professional Responsibility, and the Legal Profession* (West Academic Publishing, 2018).

# Chapter 4-1

# SOURCES OF LEGAL ETHICS AND THE LAW OF LAWYERING

By Gregory C. Sisk

*Table of Sections*


§ 4-1.1 A Brief History of Professional Ethics for American Lawyers
§ 4-1.2 The Restatement of the Law Governing Lawyers
§ 4-1.3 The Courts: Sanctions, Disqualification, and Legal Malpractice Liability
§ 4-1.4 Criminal, Dishonest, and Discriminatory Conduct
§ 4-1.5 A Brief Outline of Lawyer Discipline
§ 4-1.6 Lawyer Disciplinary Jurisdiction, Multijurisdictional Practice of Law, and Choice of Law


## § 4-1.1 A BRIEF HISTORY OF PROFESSIONAL ETHICS FOR AMERICAN LAWYERS

### § 4-1.1(a) Evolution of Professional Ethics Rules Within a Self-Regulating Bar

Lawyers are members of one of the four original learned professions (law, medicine, theology, and the professoriate):

> The historical characteristics of the learned professions were: (1) the pursuit of a learned art through formalized education and extensive training; (2) a commitment to a distinctive ideal of public service which imposes ethical demands, to which ordinary citizens are not subject, to restrain self-interest and to use the special knowledge and skills gained for the common good; and (3) professional autonomy obtained from self-regulation. . . . Essentially, society and members of a learned profession form a social compact whereby the members of a profession agree to restrain self-interest, to promote ideals of public service, and to maintain high standards of performance while the society in return allows the profession substantial autonomy to regulate itself through peer review.[1]

As part of that "social compact," rules on legal ethics have largely been developed within the self-regulation regime of the profession, today supervised by the highest judicial body in a jurisdiction.

The bar as an organized profession plays another vital role in our society: it serves as an intermediary in protecting the citizen against the power of government.[2] Although

1 Neil Hamilton & Sandra Francis, *Inside the Iowa Lawyer's Oath*, IOWA LAWYER, June, 2000, at 15.

2 Neil W. Hamilton, *The Future of Callings—An Interdisciplinary Summit on the Public Obligations of Professionals into the Next Millennium*, 25 WM. MITCHELL L. REV. 45, 52–53 (1999).

the bar is subject to regulation by the federal and state governments—primarily through the judicial branch which itself is removed to some degree from direct political control—the legal profession must remain independent if it is to achieve that integral role as the sentinel for liberty.

We must remain eternally vigilant against attempts by government to co-opt lawyers into political functionaries under the guise of public responsibilities or to interfere with the attorney-client relationship and thereby undermine the ability of citizens with the assistance of counsel to resist the overreaching of government. For these reasons, Professor Stephen Carter "urges the professions to celebrate and preserve a radical autonomy from the culture and the government."[3]

### § 4-1.1(b) From Canons to Code to Rules

Law was one of the last professions to adopt a written code of ethics in the United States.[4] Our counterparts in the American medical profession committed ethical standards to a written code a half century before lawyers did.[5] Although customary and reputational expectations of legal practice and behavior had long prevailed,[6] it was not until the past century that a common and codified model for ethical practice was proposed for lawyers in the United States.[7]

The very first somewhat formal code for attorneys in any region of this country was adopted in Alabama in 1887,[8] consisting of a list of canons for lawyers that were largely drawn from a famous essay on ethics published in 1854 by Pennsylvania judge George Sharswood.[9] At the urging of establishment figures within the legal profession early in the twentieth century, the American Bar Association (ABA) proposed the first national model—the Canons of Ethics—in 1908.[10] Ultimately, the Canons were adopted by all but 13 states and the District of Columbia.[11] Although apparently intended to be a genuine disciplinary code,[12] the ABA Canons were treated by most states as guidelines rather than as directly enforceable rules.[13]

---

[3] *Id.* at 52 (describing remarks of Stephen Carter).

[4] CHARLES W. WOLFRAM, MODERN LEGAL ETHICS § 2.6.1 (West, 1986) ("Law was among the last of the professions to adopt a common code of behavior.").

[5] *Id.*

[6] *See generally* Russell G. Pearce & Eli Wald, *Rethinking Lawyer Regulation: How a Relational Approach Would Improve Professional Rules and Roles*, 2012 MICH. ST. L. REV. 513, 516–18 (describing ethical guidelines in the first generation of lawyer ethics scholars as offering "a distinctively relational understanding of lawyer's ethics" situated in a "web of relationships" among lawyers and clients in the community in which ethical reputation was essential to professional success).

[7] WOLFRAM, *supra*, § 2.6.2.

[8] GEOFFREY C. HAZARD, JR. & DEBORAH L. RHODE, THE LEGAL PROFESSION: RESPONSIBILITY AND REGULATION 108 (3d ed. 1994); RONALD D. ROTUNDA & JOHN S. DZIENKOWSKI, PROFESSIONAL RESPONSIBILITY: A STUDENT'S GUIDE § 1–1(b) (American Bar Ass'n, 2013–2014); ROBERT H. ARONSON & DONALD T. WECKSTEIN, PROFESSIONAL RESPONSIBILITY IN A NUTSHELL 20 (West, 2d ed. 1991). On the Sharswood essay and its influence on the Alabama Code, and through that on the American Bar Association's Canons of Ethics, see James M. Altman, *Considering the A.B.A.'s 1908 Canons of Ethics*, PROF'L LAWYER, 2008 Symposium Issue, at 235, 268.

[9] GEORGE SHARSWOOD, LEGAL ETHICS (T. & J.W. Johnson & Co., 5th ed. 1994).

[10] MONROE H. FREEDMAN & ABBE SMITH, UNDERSTANDING LAWYERS' ETHICS 3–4 (Lexis-Nexis, 4th ed., 2010); WOLFRAM, *supra*, § 2.6.2.

[11] HAZARD & RHODE, *supra*, at 117.

[12] Susan D. Carle, *Lawyers' Duty to Do Justice: A New Look at the History of the 1908 Canons*, 24 LAW & SOC. INQUIRY 1, 9 (1999).

[13] WOLFRAM, *supra*, at § 2.6.2.

In 1969, the ABA updated the approach of the Canons, while preserving most of the substance, through a more detailed set of rules that was titled the Model Code of Professional Responsibility.[14] With the exception of California, every state adopted the Model Code, at least in modified form.[15] The Code was distinctive in its structure. It was organized around nine Canons, each of which were divided into mandatory Disciplinary Rules and aspirational Ethical Considerations. The Canons were "statements of axiomatic norms, expressing in general terms the standards of professional conduct expected of lawyers in their relationships with the public, with the legal system, and with the legal profession."[16] The Disciplinary Rules were directly prescriptive and "state[d] the minimum level of conduct below which no lawyer can fall without being subject to disciplinary action."[17] The Ethical Considerations were "aspirational in character and represent[ed] the objectives toward which every member of the profession should strive."[18]

In 1983, the ABA significantly altered both the format and the substance of ethical rules, devising an entirely new framework for regulation of lawyers in the Model Rules of Professional Conduct.[19] In structure, the Model Rules are prepared in the format of a "Restatement" of the law.[20] Thus, the Model Rules (now) consist of 56 black-letter and mandatory Rules (and one aspirational exhortation), each of which is followed by explanatory Comments that "provide guidance for practicing in compliance with the Rules."[21] There is nothing similar in the Model Rules to the advisory Ethical Considerations found in the prior Model Code. Professor Geoffrey Hazard, the principal drafter of the Model Rules, insisted that they should be understood "as a code of legal standards, not ethics."[22] Accordingly, the Model Rules generally prescribe the foundational rules for lawyers, leaving aspirational goals to alternative venues for encouraging professionalism. The Model Rules also differ substantively from the Code, such as by including more detailed regulation of conflicts of interest and the behavior of lawyers in organizational settings.[23]

---

14 MODEL CODE OF PROF'L RESPONSIBILITY (American Bar Ass'n, 1969). *See generally* ROTUNDA & DZIENKOWSKI, *supra*, § 1–1(d).

15 HAZARD & RHODE, *supra*, at 118; WOLFRAM, *supra*, § 2.6.3.

16 MODEL CODE OF PROFESSIONAL RESPONSIBILITY, *Preliminary Statement* (American Bar Ass'n, as amended 1980).

17 *Id.*

18 *Id.*

19 MODEL RULES OF PROF'L CONDUCT (American Bar Ass'n, 1983). *See generally* ROTUNDA & DZIENKOWSKI, *supra*, § 1–1(e). The stylistic flaw in the Model Rules of Professional Conduct is the conspicuous omission of the "Oxford" or serial comma, which is an offense against clarity in legal drafting. *See* O'Connor v. Oakhurst Dairy, 851 F.3d 69, 70 (1st Cir. 2017) (ruling that, "[f]or want of a comma," a statutory listing was ambiguous in meaning). *See generally* BRYAN A. GARNER, THE REDBOOK: A MANUAL ON LEGAL STYLE 4 (West Academic Publishing, 3rd ed. 2013) ("[T[he safer practice is to use the serial comma consistently. It is never incorrect, but omitting it sometimes results in awkwardness, miscues, or even ambiguities."). As reporter for the drafting committee for the Iowa Rules of Professional Conduct, I inserted the Oxford comma, even while otherwise generally hewing to the text of the Model Rules, a stylistic improvement that was adopted by the Iowa Supreme Court when approving the new rules.

20 ARONSON & WECKSTEIN, *supra*, at 23. On the American Law Institute and the Restatement of the Law Governing Lawyers, see *infra* § 4-1.2.

21 MODEL RULES OF PROF'L CONDUCT, Scope 14 (American Bar Ass'n, 2014).

22 HAZARD & RHODE, *supra*, at 109 (citing Geoffrey C. Hazard, Jr., *Rules of Ethics: The Drafting Task,* 36 THE RECORD 77 (1981)).

23 *See* MODEL RULES OF PROF'L CONDUCT R. 1.7 to 1.13 (American Bar Ass'n, 2016).

### § 4-1.1(c) The Nearly-Complete Transition from the Code to the Model Rules

While the Model Rules were intended by the American Bar Association to immediately replace the Code, the reception to the new regime among the states was uneven and slow to reach a critical mass.[24] When the Model Rules were initially proposed by the ABA in 1983 to replace the earlier Model Code, a tide of states quickly shifted to the new regime. But the pace of adoption soon slowed, as the supposedly superseded Model Code proved surprisingly resilient with a strong core of states continuing to adhere to it. For about two decades, state supreme courts and bar associations had to choose between two competing models for regulating the conduct of attorneys—the Model Rules of Professional Conduct originally proposed in 1983 and the Model Code of Professional Responsibility originally proposed in 1969.

From the late 1990s forward, however, the trend toward the Model Rules among the remaining states accelerated, leaving the Model Code wholly in the past. With the ABA's "Ethics 2000" comprehensive review and revision of the Model Rules, resulting in many changes to the Model Rules adopted by the ABA House of Delegates in 2002,[25] the American professional ethics paradigm had moved far behind the aging Model Code.

In the 1990s, a dwindling cadre of states still adhered to the Model Code of Professional Responsibility, the former ethical system that had been superseded in 1983 by the Model Rules of Professional Conduct. As the new millennium dawned, judges and lawyers in those states came to appreciate that, if they were to stubbornly cling to a Code that had become obsolete in the nation at large, lawyers in those states would lose the opportunity to fully share in the experiences and ethical advancements of the profession at large and to benefit from the constant reevaluation and evolution of ethical standards.[26] Code states were increasingly at risk of becoming passive bystanders in national debates regarding reform of legal ethics. And there would be no turning back of the clock. As the Tennessee ethics rules revisers warned, "[a]t best, the Model Code is currently on the side of the stage and headed offstage, almost certainly never to return."[27]

By joining the community of jurisdictions that have adopted the Model Rules, lawyers facing emerging problems of professional responsibility or encountering ethical issues of first impression have a ready source of persuasive authority to which to turn. The ever-growing library of ethics committee opinions and court decisions in other states interpreting the Model Rules are available for comparison, guidance, and critique. The American Bar Association's Standing Committee on Ethics and Professional Responsibility regularly provides non-binding guidance on the meaning and application of the Model Rules through formal and informal opinions. Moreover, the decline in attention to the Code in law schools and on the bar examination presaged future

---

[24] *See* HAZARD & RHODE, *supra*, at 118; ARONSON & WECKSTEIN, *supra*, at 23.

[25] For a summary of the many revisions to the Model Rules through the Ethics 2000 project, see Margaret Colgate Love, *The Revised ABA* Model Rules of Professional Conduct: *Summary of the Work of Ethics 2000*, 15 GEO. J. LEGAL ETHICS 441 (2002).

[26] Gregory C. Sisk, *Iowa's Legal Ethics Rules—It's Time to Join the Crowd*, 47 DRAKE L. REV. 279, 285–94 (1999).

[27] Carl A. Pierce & Lucian T. Pera, *Time for a Change? The Proposed Tennessee Rules of Professional Conduct*, 34 TENN. BAR J. 23, 30 (1998).

generations of new admittees to the bar who would be unfamiliar with the Code, other than as history.

Whatever their faults, the Model Rules have the compelling advantage of being up-to-date. The Model Rules are constantly being revised, refined, and adjusted in light of emerging challenges for attorneys and new understandings of what it means to be an ethical lawyer and a true professional.

Indeed, when first promulgated by the ABA in 1983, the Model Rules already had the value of addressing professional situations or problems that either had not been adequately addressed previously or had not been anticipated by the Code drafters a decade-and-a-half earlier. For example, the Model Rules contain six rules governing the multifarious scenarios under which conflicts of interest could arise, including conflicts arising from transactions between lawyers and clients, conflicts between existing clients, successive conflicts involving former clients, conflicts created by successive government and private employment, and conflicts involving former judges or arbitrators.[28] The parallel Code provisions touched on some, but not all, of these matters[29] and thus failed to provide more complete guidance to practitioners on what is perhaps the most common ethical problem to arise in everyday legal practice. Similarly, the Code had been frequently criticized as "directed primarily to attorneys as litigators."[30] The profession has come to appreciate the diverse roles that lawyers play—as negotiators, mediators, and counselors—and the equally diverse ethical problems that arise in these areas. The Model Rules acknowledge different functions and provide direction for lawyers acting in counseling, transactional, and other non-litigation capacities.[31]

As this is written in 2017, nearly everyone today is speaking in the language of the Model Rules of Professional Conduct. All but one state follow the general pattern of the Model Rules, although each state departs from or supplements them, some more than others. California maintains its own set of ethics rules but is considering revisions that would bring it closer to the Model Rules. Even the comments to the Model Rules have attained widespread approval, being adopted formally in all but about ten states and being available as guidance in all but half a dozen. While the federal courts have independent authority to adopt rules of practice and attorney discipline,[32] most follow in substantial part the ethics rules in the state in which the court sits, which again is almost always based on the Model Rules.[33] In sum, lawyers throughout the nation need to learn the grammar and vocabulary of the rules in order to fully join in the conversation. And when ethics scholars examine recurrent professional responsibility

---

[28] MODEL RULES OF PROFESSIONAL CONDUCT R. 1.7 to 1.12 (American Bar Ass'n, 2014).

[29] *See* MODEL CODE OF PROFESSIONAL RESPONSIBILITY, Canon 5 & Disciplinary Rules 5–101 to 5–107 (American Bar Ass'n, 1980).

[30] Robert H. Aronson, *An Overview of the Law of Professional Responsibility: The Rules of Professional Conduct Annotated and Analyzed*, 61 WASH. L. REV. 823, 828 (1986).

[31] *See, e.g.*, MODEL RULES OF PROFESSIONAL CONDUCT R. 2.1 (advisor), 2.3 (evaluator), 2.4 (third-party neutral); 5.1 and 5.2 (supervisory and subordinate lawyers), 6.4 (law reform activities), Model Rules of Professional Conduct (American Bar Ass'n, 2016).

[32] For a critical analysis of federal court assertion of authority to regulate professional conduct, see Fred C. Zacharias & Bruce A. Green, *Federal Court Authority to Regulate Lawyers: A Practice in Search of a Theory*, 56 VAND. L. REV. 1303 (2003).

[33] For a succinct description of the ethics rules, attorney discipline, and other sanctions, see generally Tonia Lucio, *Standards and Regulation of Professional Conduct in Federal Practice*, 64 FED. LAWYER 50 (July 2017).

problems in the light of the meaning and application of formal rules, it is primarily the Model Rules that provide the illumination.

### § 4-1.1(d) Rules of Ethics, Professional Morality, and Character

While legal ethics practice and scholarship accepts the Model Rules of Professional Conduct as the prevailing formal set of professional standards, ethics scholars appreciate that ethical education focusing solely upon rules is morally impoverished and neglects the full richness of the professional life.

Wisely drafted ethics rules may not be sufficient for a healthy profession and moral practitioners. But they are surely necessary. Good ethics rules alone cannot make good lawyers, but bad ethics rules will undermine professionalism and moral aspiration. If a code of ethics is ambiguous, has become obsolete, fails to address emerging problems, or fails to resonate with the actual experiences and changing practices of lawyers, that code will lose the respect of the governed and breed cynicism within the profession. By contrast, a well-drafted and contemporary "corpus of rules can at least establish a common core of shared values and have an educative and uplifting effect."[34]

Still, we ask too much of any formal ethics code and too little of ourselves to expect to find within mandatory rules the roadmap to a happy and moral life and practice. Wise voices have reminded us that a set of rules, however well-constructed, cannot substitute for character and moral reasoning. Professors Robert Cochran and Teresa Collett explain: "Professional rules outline what a lawyer must do . . ., morals determine what a lawyer should do."[35]

Indeed, scholars of professional responsibility for lawyers have found that excessive attention to black-letter rules may stunt ethical growth and inhibit development of moral character.[36] The risk of a narrow focus on rules is that they will become "the boundaries of [the lawyer's] moral universe."[37] As Professors Ian Johnstone and Mary Patricia Treuthart warn, exclusive concentration on the formal disciplinary rules "sends the message that legal ethics involves no more than distinguishing permissible from impermissible conduct and that all ethical concerns can be resolved by referring to a

---

[34] *See* 1 GEOFFREY C. HAZARD, JR. & W. WILLIAM HODES, THE LAW OF LAWYERING § 203 (Aspen, 1998 Supplement); *see also* Patrick J. Schiltz, *Legal Ethics in Decline: The Elite Law Firm, the Elite Law School, and the Moral Formation of the Novice Attorney*, 82 MINN. L. REV. 705, 736–39 (1998) ("The rules are important, for they affect the conduct of lawyers (in both anticipated and unanticipated ways) and they influence the values of the profession.").

[35] ROBERT F. COCHRAN, JR. & TERESA S. COLLETT, CASES AND MATERIALS ON THE RULES OF THE LEGAL PROFESSION v (Thomson West, 1996); *see also* Geoffrey C. Hazard, Jr., *Personal Values and Professional Ethics*, 40 CLEV. ST. L. REV. 133, 133 (1992) (urging "reexamination of personal values as a fundamental resource of professional ethics" because "rules of ethics, such as those embodied in the profession's ethical codes, are insufficient guides to making the choices of action that a professional must make in practice").

[36] *See, e.g.*, THOMAS L. SHAFFER & ROBERT F. COCHRAN, JR., LAWYERS, CLIENTS, AND MORAL RESPONSIBILITY vi (West, 1994) (acknowledging the importance of disciplinary rules, but stating that "so much attention is paid to the rules that minimum standards are becoming the only standards for the profession; they are becoming the norm," thus leading the authors to present an alternative course of study of moral standards for clients and lawyers); Heidi Li Feldman, *Codes and Virtues: Can Good Lawyers Be Good Ethical Deliberators?*, 69 S. CAL. L. REV. 885, 885 (1996) (arguing that "any black letter statutory codification regulating lawyers' conduct will be flawed as an instrument of ethics for lawyers" and that "typical statutory prohibitions and permissions are likely to stunt sentimental responsiveness, a key feature of good ethical deliberation").

[37] JOSEPH G. ALLEGRETTI, THE LAWYER'S CALLING: CHRISTIAN FAITH AND LEGAL PRACTICE 16 (Paulist Press, 1996).

clear set of rules."[38] When addressing problems in ethics for lawyers in this part of the book, it sometimes will be painfully apparent that the rules say very little about what is most important.

To live a truly uplifting life in our chosen profession, a lawyer needs to remain true to his most deeply-held values. As tempting as it may be to avoid moral questions by adopting the all too-common and ultimately fictional posture of "amoral technician" in the practice of law,[39] down that road lies damnation. While the lawyer is not appointed to be a moral dictator, imposing his values upon subordinate clients,[40] neither will a lawyer find moral satisfaction by compartmentalizing his life into separate professional and personal (moral and spiritual) departments.[41] The lawyer who attempts to be one type of person in private, family, and social life (presumably a person of good character), while affecting a different and morally callous or indifferent *persona* in professional life, will find that he eventually becomes all one or the other. More often that split personality will collapse into the morally inferior of the two lives.

In the practice of law, as in any other meaningful area of human relationships, the ethical practitioner must draw deeply from the well of those same values in which we have been instructed since our youth. Chief Justice Mark Cady of the Iowa Supreme Court reminds us that "the conduct of a lawyer is not simply guided by rules of law and professional ethics," but rather "that personal values acquired as human beings remain an instructional force in the practice of law."[42]

To realize ethical progress and moral development in the practice of law, we must develop habits and disciplines of good character, in the same manner that we have done since childhood. As Professor Cochran suggests: "It may be that the problem in the legal profession is not too little attention to rules, but too little attention to character."[43] Similarly, Dean Anthony Kronman described the lawyer's wisdom—the distinctive element that defines the outstanding lawyer—as "a trait of character that one acquires only by becoming a person of good judgment, and not just an expert in the law."[44] Professor Lisa Lerman urges lawyers to become " 'reflective practitioners' who retain and develop their moral perception and their moral judgment."[45]

## § 4-1.2 THE RESTATEMENT OF THE LAW GOVERNING LAWYERS

Not all work on professional conduct proceeds under the auspices of the American Bar Association, in the form of the Model Rules of Professional Conduct, and as

---

38 Ian Johnstone & Mary Patricia Treuthart, *Doing the Right Things: An Overview of Teaching Professional Responsibility*, 41 J. LEGAL EDUC. 75, 82 (1991).

39 Richard Wasserstrom, *Lawyers as Professionals: Some Moral Issues*, 5 HUMAN RIGHTS 1, 6 (1975).

40 For more on moral deliberation and clients, see *infra* § 4-5.2(b).

41 *See* ALLEGRETTI, *supra*, at 16.

42 Mark S. Cady, *Advocating Personal Values in Advocacy*, 52 IA. LAW. 8, 8 (May 1992).

43 Robert F. Cochran, Jr., *Lawyers and Virtues: A Review Essay of Mary Ann Glendon's* A National Under Lawyer's: How the Crisis in the Legal Profession is Transforming American Society *and Anthony T. Kronman's* The Lost Lawyer: Failing Ideals of the Legal Profession, 71 NOTRE DAME L. REV. 707, 707 (1996); *see also* ALLEGRETTI, *supra*, at 100 (stating that "the best check upon the excesses of litigation is not the rules of the profession or even judicial oversight but the values and character of individual lawyers").

44 ANTHONY T. KRONMAN, THE LOST LAWYER: FAILING IDEALS OF THE LEGAL PROFESSION 2 (Harvard U. Press, 1993).

45 Lisa G. Lerman, *Teaching Moral Perception and Moral Judgment in Legal Ethics Courses: A Dialogue About Goals*, 39 WM. & MARY L. REV. 457, 486–87 (1998).

implemented in state ethics rules. The *Restatement of the Law Governing Lawyers* prepared by the American Law Institute is another authoritative source for a fully informed understanding of the ethical expectations for American lawyers. Often parallel to the Model Rules (with occasional interesting variations), the *Restatement* frequently addresses issues that arise outside of the typical disciplinary proceeding.

The American Law Institute (ALI) was founded in 1923 as an organization of leading judges, lawyers, and legal scholars, with the mission to "to promote the clarification and simplification of the law and its better adaptation to social needs, to secure the better administration of justice, and to encourage and carry on scholarly and scientific legal work."[46] Its most familiar and influential work product is found in its restatements of the law. First-year law students immediately encounter the Restatements, on such familiar topics as contracts and torts.

In the mid-1980s, Professor Geoffrey Hazard as director of the ALI and Professor Charles Wolfram initiated a project to provide further guidance on the law governing lawyers.[47] Over the following decade, Professor Wolfram as the chief reporter, along with Professors Thomas Morgan, John Leubsdorf, and Linda Mullenix, drafted sections of the new *Restatement of the Law Governing Lawyers*.[48] After ten years of work, the American Law Institute gave final approval in 1998 to the *Restatement of the Law Governing Lawyers*.[49]

The *Restatement* undertakes to provide a comprehensive description—and, in part, prescription—of the "legal constraints" upon lawyers "in discharging their several responsibilities as representatives of clients, officers of the legal system, and public citizens having special responsibilities for the quality of justice."[50] The primary purpose of the *Restatement* is to guide lawyers and judges on the law regulating their behavior in the civil context, such as actions for legal malpractice, motions to disqualify counsel, and disputes concerning attorney's fees.[51] As Professor Susan Martyn explains, the *Restatement* expansively "involve[s] rules from the law of evidence, agency, professional rules, tort and contracts."[52] And, as Professor Morgan rightly says, the illustrations that accompany the black letter law and comments "give the *Restatement* life."[53] The readability of the *Restatement*, and the illumination from the illustrations, make it an essential source for any scholar or practitioner on professional responsibility questions.

Although the *Restatement* was influenced by various lawyer codes, it was not designed to track any particular set of ethics rules. Indeed, as stated in its Foreword, the broader scope of the *Restatement* reflects the understanding that "the remedy of

[46] American Law Institute, Charter, at https://www.ali.org/about-ali/creation/.

[47] Lawrence J. Latto, *The Restatement of the Law Governing Lawyers: A View From the Trenches*, 26 HOFSTRA L. REV. 697, 701–03 (1998).

[48] Susan R. Martyn, *Judicial Reliance on the Restatement (3d) of the Law Governing Lawyers*, 6 No. 2 PROF. LAW. 8 (Feb. 1995).

[49] *ALI Completes Restatement on Lawyers, Gives Final Approval to All Sections*, ABA/BNA LAWYERS' MANUAL OF PROFESSIONAL CONDUCT: CURRENT REPORTS, May 13, 1998, at 211 [hereinafter *ALI Completes Restatement*].

[50] RESTATEMENT OF THE LAW GOVERNING LAWYERS Preface (American Law Institute, Proposed Final Draft No. 2, 1998).

[51] RESTATEMENT OF THE LAW GOVERNING LAWYERS Reporter's Memorandum at xxiv (American Law Institute, Proposed Final Draft No. 2, 1998); *ALI Completes Restatement*, *supra*, at 211.

[52] Martyn, *supra*, 6 No. 2 PROF. LAW. at 8.

[53] Thomas D. Morgan, *Conflicts of Interest in the Restatement: Comments on Professor Moore's Paper*, 10 GEO. J. LEGAL ETHICS 575, 580 (1997).

malpractice liability and the remedy of disqualification are practically of greater importance in most law practice than is the risk of disciplinary proceedings." Nonetheless, on the points of overlap, it should not be surprising that the ALI's effort to reflect the informed and deliberate consensus of the profession on professional conduct naturally bears a strong resemblance to the ethics rules regime that governs in most American jurisdictions.

Although this part of the book will highlight and often be framed by the Model Rules of Professional Conduct, the *Restatement of the Law Governing Lawyers* is also regularly cited and discussed in what follows, especially on topics on which the Model Rules are silent or on which further or different guidance is offered by the *Restatement*.

## § 4-1.3 THE COURTS: SANCTIONS, DISQUALIFICATION, AND LEGAL MALPRACTICE LIABILITY

A lawyer's failure to abide by the standards and expectations of a legal professional may lead to formal discipline for violation of rules of professional conduct[54] and to informal sanctions such as a loss of professional reputation or a personal recognition of moral failure. In addition, as discussed in this section, a lawyer appearing before a tribunal may suffer a court sanction for misconduct or disqualification from continued representation. And a lawyer faces potential civil liability for departure from the standards of professional care, including potential forfeiture of an attorney's fee.

### § 4-1.3(a) Judicial Sanctions

While the disciplinary rules adopted in a state have significant influence on the evaluation of appropriate professional conduct in court, each court has the independent power to impose appropriate sanctions for misconduct in the courtroom. Judicial rulings imposing sanctions on misbehaving lawyers in turn provide another source of law for the professional expectations for lawyers.

As an important example, under Rule 11 of the Federal Rules of Civil Procedure, an attorney who presents a pleading, written motion, or other paper to a court certifies that the allegations and other factual contentions "have evidentiary support" or are likely to have evidentiary support after a reasonable opportunity for further investigation or discovery; that denials of factual contentions are "warranted on the evidence" or are reasonably based on lack of information or belief; and that claims, defenses, and other legal contentions are "warranted by existing law or by a nonfrivolous argument for extending, modifying, or reversing existing law or for establishing new law."[55] The benchmark is that of the reasonable lawyer.[56] (The civil procedure sanction standard is directly parallel to that articulated in Rule 3.1 of the Model Rules of Professional Conduct, which expressly prohibits a lawyer from "bring[ing] or defend[ing] a proceeding" or "assert[ing] or controvert[ing]" an issue in such a proceeding, "unless there is a basis in law and fact for doing so that is not frivolous, which includes a good

---

[54] *See infra* § 4-1.5.

[55] FED. R. CIV. P. 11(b).

[56] *See* Business Guides, Inc. v. Chromatic Communications Enters., 498 U.S. 533, 550–51 (1991) (ruling that the certification of a pleading as well-founded under Rule 11 is an "objective" standard "of reasonableness under the circumstances").

faith argument for an extension, modification or reversal of existing law."[57] By design, the professional conduct rule dovetails with the court procedural rule.)

Sanctions are also available to the judge to address other abusive tactics, such as discovery misconduct,[58] improper statements to the jury, inflammatory comments in the courtroom, or impermissible denigration of opposing counsel or other parties.[59] Among these individualized sanctions are holding the lawyer in contempt of court, imposing a fine for misconduct, ordering the lawyer to pay the litigation fees and costs of the other side incurred by reason of that misconduct,[60] and disqualifying the lawyer from continuing representation in the case. (The court may also report the lawyer to the appropriate state disciplinary authorities.) The Supreme Court has held that the federal courts have "inherent powers" that are "governed not by rule or statute but by the control necessarily vested in courts to manage their own affairs so as to achieve the orderly and expeditious disposition of cases."[61]

Even if the court does not impose a penalty directly on the lawyer, the lawyer who sees a favorable judgment or jury verdict set aside by reason of the lawyer's misconduct[62] may be punished by loss of a contingent fee, the ire of a client who is left without a recovery, and perhaps a publicly-reported litigation loss.

### § 4-1.3(b) Disqualification of a Lawyer in Litigation

In addition to facing the possibility of professional discipline, the lawyer who persists in a representation despite a possible conflict of interest may encounter a motion to disqualify the lawyer from representing a particular client in a particular court or agency proceeding. In contrast with a disciplinary proceeding in which the focus is solely upon the attorney and her behavior, a request for disqualification of an attorney in ongoing litigation requires consideration as well of the equities toward the party that would be deprived of counsel of choice and the impact of the lawyer's behavior on the legal process. As a federal district court explained, "[t]he culpability of plaintiffs' counsel's alleged misconduct is an issue for the bar association's grievance committee; the issue to be determined in this forum is only whether the alleged misconduct taints

---

[57] *See infra* § 4-9.3(a).

[58] *See also infra* § 4-9.6(b), (c).

[59] *See, e.g.*, In re Katz, 476 F. Supp. 2d 572 (W.D. Va. 2007) (holding attorney in contempt for disobeying an order to cease referring to government witnesses as "liars" in summation to the jury); Clark v. Clark, 716 N.E.2d 144, 151 (Mass. Ct. App. 1999) (affirming that "the bombastic behavior of the attorney during the trial, including disparaging remarks about her opposing counsel and the judge, and her walking out of the court room during the cross-examination of her client without permission" warranted sanctions).

[60] *See* Goodyear Tire & Rubber Co. v. Haeger, 137 S. Ct. 1178, 1184 (2017) (ruling that a federal court's inherent authority to impose a sanction for bad-faith conduct by ordering payment of the other side's attorney's fees "is limited to the fees the innocent party incurred solely because of the misconduct—or to put it another way, to the fees that party would not have incurred but for the bad faith").

[61] Chambers v. NASCO, Inc., 501 U.S. 32, 43 (1991).

[62] *See, e.g.*, Tyus v. Urban Search Management, 102 F.3d 256, 261 (7th Cir. 1996) (suggesting a new trial may be appropriate when defense counsel interjected disparagement on the basis of gender, by "referring to plaintiffs' lawyer disparagingly as 'an amateur' on numerous occasions," "barking at her to 'sit down' and 'stop interfering,' " and "literally grabb[ing] papers out of her hands (all of this, we note, without any reprimand from the judge)"); Polansky v. CNA Ins. Co., 852 F.2d 626, 627 (1st Cir. 1988) (ordering a new trial in an insurance recovery case because plaintiff's counsel's "throughout his closing argument, was unable to keep his opinions and personal beliefs to himself"); People v. Hickman, 312 N.Y.S.2d 644, 644 (N.Y. App Div. 1970) (reversing a criminal conviction when prosecutor described defendant before the jury as a "junkie," "rat," and a "sculptor" with a knife).

the lawsuit to the extent that defendant's motion [for disqualification of plaintiff's counsel] need be granted."[63]

Motions to disqualify are often said to be disfavored because "disqualification has an immediate adverse effect on the client by separating him from counsel of his choice, [and because such] motions are often interposed for tactical reasons."[64] In balancing the right of the client to choose his own attorney against the public interest in maintaining high ethical standards, "a court must also be vigilant to thwart any misuse of a motion to disqualify for strategic reasons."[65] An order of disqualification is a "drastic measure which courts should hesitate to impose except when absolutely necessary."[66]

Disqualification may be necessary, however, even when the complaining party would be directly harmed by the attorney's continued involvement. Disqualification is also an appropriate exercise of the trial court's discretion when an attorney's conflict of interest (or other ethical transgression) so departs from standards of professional responsibility that the public's trust in the bar and the integrity of the legal process would be seriously undermined by the lawyer's continued participation.

A motion to disqualify is appropriately denied if untimely. As the United States Court of Appeals for the Eighth Circuit ruled in *Central Milk Producers Coop. v. Sentry Food Stores, Inc.*,[67] "[a] motion to disqualify should be made with reasonable promptness after a party discovers the facts which lead to the motion. Th[e] court will not allow a litigant to delay filing a motion to disqualify in order to use the motion later as a tool to deprive his opponent of counsel of his choice after substantial preparation of a case has been completed." If a party has "waited too long to complain" about a lawyer's or law firm's representation of the adverse party, the party will be "estopped from raising the conflict of interest at such a late date."[68]

If a lawyer or law firm is disqualified, new counsel unimpaired by the conflict will presumably be substituted. The remaining question is whether the taint of the conflict that resulted in the disqualification also infects the client files and prevents transfer of those documents to new counsel for that party. When there has been no misuse of confidential client information, most courts permit exchange of work product and allow an explanatory briefing by the departing lawyers regarding their work to replacement counsel.[69] Indeed, federal case authority places the burden on the party opposing the

---

63 Meat Price Investigators v. Iowa Beef Processors, 448 F. Supp. 1, 3 (S.D. Iowa 1977), *aff'd*, 572 F.2d 163 (8th Cir. 1978).

64 Board of Education v. Nyquist, 590 F.2d 1241, 1246 (2d Cir. 1979).

65 Bottoms v. Stapleton, 706 N.W.2d 411, 415 (Iowa 2005).

66 Freeman v. Chicago Musical Instr. Co., 689 F.2d 715, 721–22 (7th Cir. 1982); *see also* Matter of Firestorm, 916 P.2d 411, 416 (Wash. 1996) ("Disqualification of counsel is a drastic remedy that exacts a harsh penalty from the parties as well as punishing counsel; therefore, it should be imposed only when absolutely necessary.").

67 573 F.2d 988, 992 (8th Cir. 1978).

68 Sorenson v. First Wis. Nat'l Bank, 931 F.2d 19, 20 (8th Cir. 1991); *see also* State ex rel. Swanson v. 3M Co., 845 N.W.2d 808, 819 (Minn. 2014).

69 *See, e.g.*, E.E.O.C. v. Orson H. Gygi Co., Inc., 749 F.2d 620, 621–22 (10th Cir. 1984); First Wis. Mortg. Trust v. First Wis. Corp., 584 F.2d 201 (7th Cir. 1978) (en banc); International Bus. Machines Corp. v. Levin, 579 F.2d 271, 283 (3d Cir. 1978); Actel Corp. v. Quicklogic Corp., 1996 WL 297045, at *12 (N.D. Cal. 1996); Lone Star Ind., Inc. v. Southern Red-E-Mix, Inc., 1995 WL 775348, at *3 (D. Kan. 1995); Chronicle Publishing Co. v. Hantzis, 732 F. Supp. 270, 274–75 (D. Mass.), *appeal dismissed*, 902 F.2d 1028 (1st Cir. 1990).

transfer of information to replacement counsel to establish that any harm would occur.[70] As one federal court has observed:

> The courts have recognized that where an attorney has been disqualified, that attorney's present client in the pending suit will suffer the loss of experienced counsel who generally has expended considerable time and efforts in preparing and litigating the client's case. To soften the harsh impact of such a loss, new or substitute counsel has been permitted access to the work product of disqualified counsel and limited consultation with disqualified counsel for the purpose of explanation of such work product.[71]

### § 4-1.3(c) Legal Malpractice Liability

A lawyer's departure from the standard of care expected of a professional may lead to civil liability to the client harmed by the conduct. Professor John Leubsdorf recognizes that the civil claim of malpractice serves an important regulatory purpose for the profession by "delineating the duties of lawyers, creating appropriate incentives and disincentives for lawyers in their dealings with clients and others, and providing access to remedies for those injured by improper lawyer behavior."[72] The law of legal malpractice is addressed in detail subsequently in Part Five of this book authored by Professors Susan Fortney and Vincent Johnson.

Despite the origin of the attorney-client relationship through a contractual transaction, the action ordinarily will be asserted as a claim sounding in tort:

> Legal malpractice consists of the failure of an attorney "to use such skill, prudence and diligence as lawyers of ordinary skill and capacity commonly possess and exercise in the performance of the tasks which they undertake." "When such failure proximately causes damage it gives rise to an action in tort."[73]

As a claim sounding in tort, an action for legal malpractice must establish the traditional elements associated with a negligence claim, namely (1) a duty of care, which typically is established by proving the existence of an attorney-client relationship; (2) the breach of that duty of care, which in term requires defining the nature of the duty owed by the lawyer to the client; (3) proximate causation, which requires showing a reasonably close connection between the lawyer's departure from the duty of care and

---

[70] *See, e.g., Levin*, 579 F.2d at 283 (saying that "disqualification in circumstances such as these where specific injury to the moving party has not been shown is primarily justified as a vindication of the integrity of the bar" and that the "harsh effect" of the disqualification upon the client was properly ameliorated by permitting disqualified counsel to turn over work product with consultation to replacement counsel); *First Wis. Mortg. Trust*, 584 F.2d at 211 (where there is no indication of improper advantage secured, such as by use of confidential information, former counsel may provide work product to replacement counsel and "make such explication of the work product to substitute counsel as to effectuate reasonably the turnover"). *But see* In re George, 28 S.W.3d 511, 517–18 (Tex. 2000) (saying "we are not entirely satisfied by the results reached in other jurisdictions" and instead establishing "a rebuttable presumption that the work product contains confidential information").

[71] Black v. Missouri, 492 F. Supp. 848, 871 (W.D. Mo. 1980).

[72] John Leubsdorf, *Legal Malpractice and Professional Responsibility*, 48 RUTGERS L. REV. 101, 105 (1995); *see also* Susan Saab Fortney, *A Tort in Search of a Remedy: Prying Open the Courthouse Doors for Legal Malpractice Victims*, 85 FORDHAM L. REV. 2033, 2036 (2017) (urging lawyers and judges to "recognize the link between financial accountability and professionalism by supporting reforms to provide access to justice to consumers injured by lawyer misconduct").

[73] Millwright v. Romer, 322 N.W.2d 30, 32 (Iowa 1982) (quoting Neel v. Magana, Olney, Levy, Cathcart & Gelfand, 491 P.2d 421, 422–23 (Cal. 1971)).

the harm suffered by the client; and (4) damages to the claimant, which requires consideration of both the type of damages allowed for the particular cause of action and their appropriate measurement.

In a malpractice case based on negligence, the plaintiff must establish the nature of the duty of care expected of the legal professional and prove that the defendant lawyer departed from that standard. In evaluating such claims, the courts thereby articulate the professional expectations for lawyers in decisions frequently cited not only in malpractice litigation but in other matters relevant to the professional conduct of lawyers, including disciplinary proceedings.

In addition to basic questions about the lawyer's competence and professional care in handling of a matter, a malpractice action may raise issues about diligence, the scope of the lawyer's representation and the client's prerogatives on the objectives of the representation, and conflicting influences that may adversely affect the lawyer's loyal and zealous representation. Increasingly, plaintiffs are relying on agency principles to assert breach of fiduciary duty claims. Many disciplinary rules reflect how lawyers, as fiduciaries, should conduct themselves.

The Scope to the Model Rules of Professional Conduct states in Paragraph 20 that "[v]iolation of a Rule should not itself give rise to a cause of action against a lawyer nor should it create any presumption in such a case that a legal duty has been breached. . . . [The Rules] are not designed to be a basis for civil liability." Thus, simple evidence that a lawyer violated the ethical rules is not sufficient to establish liability for legal malpractice. By clarifying that something more than an ethical violation must be shown to prevail in a malpractice suit—notably proof of the existence of an attorney-client relationship between the parties and substantiation of damages proximately caused by the breach of the standard of care—the cautionary note in the Scope is unremarkable and salutary. Moreover, the casual allegation of an ethics transgression, such as the frequently interjected accusation of a conflict of interest, may too easily be levied in a legal malpractice case for the purpose of prejudicing the trier of fact, even though no actual harm is traceable to the supposed rule violation.

At the same time, this disclaimer in the Scope to the Model Rules of Professional Responsibility must be read with a grain of salt. As explained by Professor Geoffrey Hazard, a primary drafter of the Model Rules:

> These efforts [to disclaim the direct application of the ethics rules to malpractice matters] were predictably futile, however, if not fatuous. Norms stated as obligatory standards of a vocation are generally held to be evidence of the legal standard of care in practicing that vocation, or at least as a predicate for expert testimony as to what that standard is. Thus, notwithstanding the bar's attempted disclaimer in writing black-letter rules, the bar necessarily assumed unavoidable responsibilities.[74]

Indeed, the Scope itself was amended by the American Bar Association in 2002, in language to clarify that "since the Rules do establish standards of conduct by lawyers, a

[74] Geoffrey C. Hazard, Jr., *Lawyers and Client Fraud: They Still Don't Get It,* 6 GEO. J. LEGAL ETHICS 701, 718 (1993).

lawyer's violation of a Rule may be evidence of breach of the applicable standard of conduct."[75]

The *Restatement of the Law Governing Lawyers* similarly provides that, while violation of an ethical rule does not itself give rise to liability, proof of such a violation "may be considered by the trier of fact as an aid in understanding and applying" the malpractice standard of care.[76] Thus, while there may remain "room for debate as to how much weight should be given to evidence of ethics violations, there is little room for argument as to whether such evidence should be admissible."[77]

Reference by an expert witness in a legal malpractice action to the professional standards as explicated in the rules is inevitable and unavoidable to offer a fully-informed opinion.[78] Despite the disclaimer language in the Scope to the Model Rules, "it is difficult to imagine that a [legal malpractice] plaintiff's expert witness testimony would not include a reference to the [ ] Rules (presuming a violation has been established) as evidence of a breach of a standard of care."[79] After all, the ethics rules "set[ ] the standard for an attorney's conduct in any transaction in which his professional judgment may be exercised."[80]

In conclusion, as scholars have summarized, "the inference is that a reasonably prudent lawyer would not violate an ethical rule defining appropriate professional behavior. By falling below the minimal level of conduct mandated by the ethics code, an attorney breaches the professional standard of care owed to clients, and therefore may be held legally responsible for harm caused by the breach."[81] Again, in a legal malpractice suit, as contrasted with a disciplinary proceeding, breach of the standard of care as evidenced by a violation of an ethical rule is but one of the four required elements for holding the lawyer liable.

In addition to compensatory or other damages for malpractice, a lawyer who engages in a "clear and serious violation of a duty to a client destroys or severely impairs the client-lawyer relationship" and thereby forfeits a claim to compensation for that work.[82]

---

[75] For more on application of ethics rules in legal malpractice cases, see Part Five of this book, Susan Saab Fortney & Vincent R. Johnson, Legal Malpractice § 5-1.7(c).

[76] RESTATEMENT (THIRD) OF THE LAW GOVERNING LAWYERS § 52(2)(c) (American law Institute 2000).

[77] Gary A. Munneke & Anthony E. Davis, *The Standard of Care in Legal Malpractice: Do the Model Rules of Professional Conduct Define It?*, 22 J. LEGAL PROF. 33, 37, 63 n.144 (1998). *But see* Hizey v. Carpenter, 830 P.2d 646, 652–54 (Wash. 1992) (holding that a jury may be informed of the Rules of Professional Conduct by either jury instructions or by expert testimony because the ethical standards of the rules are different from the civil liability standard).

[78] On whether an expert witness in a legal malpractice case may testify as to the ethics rules, see also Part Five of this book, Susan Saab Fortney & Vincent R. Johnson, Legal Malpractice § 5-2.2(h).

[79] Carter G. Bishop, *A Tale of Two Liabilities*, 16 WM. MITCHELL L. REV. 1, 2 n.4 (1990).

[80] Cornell v. Wunschel, 408 N.W.2d 369, 377 (Iowa 1987).

[81] Munneke & Davis, *supra*, 22 J. LEGAL PROF. at 33.

[82] RESTATEMENT (THIRD) OF THE LAW GOVERNING LAWYERS § 37 cmt. b (American law Institute 2000).

# § 4-1.4 CRIMINAL, DISHONEST, AND DISCRIMINATORY CONDUCT

## § 4-1.4(a) Criminal Conduct

Bad actions have consequences. While the other standards set forth in the Model Rules of Professional Conduct describe what actions by a lawyer are required, permissible, or forbidden, Model Rule 8.4 defines the failure to comply with those rules and to uphold other specified professional expectations as "professional misconduct." Among these, Rule 8.4(b) provides that a lawyer is guilty of professional misconduct if he "commit[s] a criminal act that reflects adversely on the lawyer's honesty, trustworthiness or fitness as a lawyer in other respects."

A lawyer who commits a criminal act that in itself involves dishonesty, such as criminal fraud or the use of deceit to misappropriate funds or property, obviously stands in violation of this standard. Likewise, a lawyer who has shown such flagrant disregard for the rights and integrity of other persons as to commit a criminal act involving serious violence, such as homicide or rape, plainly has demonstrated a lack of fitness for the practice of law. What lesser forms of criminal conduct justify a professional sanction and what level of sanction would be appropriate (revocation or suspension of license versus a reprimand or admonition) require a case-by-case consideration of the circumstances, including whether there were aggravating or mitigating factors, the degree of harm caused to others, and the lawyer's history of previous professional or criminal misconduct.

Comment 2 to Model Rule 8.4 generally instructs that "a lawyer should be professionally answerable only for offenses that indicate lack of those characteristics relevant to law practice." In practice, though, courts tend to see any serious criminal offense as indicating a lawyer is not fit for continued practice.

The rule defines misconduct as the lawyer's commission of the criminal act, not whether the lawyer has been formally charged or found guilty in the criminal justice system. Thus, evidence of a lawyer's criminal behavior may be adjudicated in a disciplinary proceeding independent of criminal prosecution. Of course, when an attorney has been convicted of a crime under the high evidentiary showing of guilt beyond a reasonable doubt, that conviction ordinarily will definitively establish the lawyer's commission of that criminal act for purposes of any disciplinary proceeding.

While violation of the rules of professional conduct and the criminal law ordinarily establish professional misconduct, Comment 4 to Rule 8.4 protects a lawyer's choice to "refuse to comply with an obligation imposed by law upon a good faith belief that no valid obligation exists." Thus, Comment 4 provides that a lawyer on her own behalf or on behalf of a client may offer a "good faith challenge to the validity, scope, meaning or application of the law" including that area of law that regulates the practice of law.

While the standard expressed in the comment is one of a "good faith belief," rather than focusing directly upon the reasonableness of the lawyer's assessment of the validity of the law under challenge, good faith cannot be entirely divorced from reasonableness, especially when every lawyer necessarily holds himself out as having an educated expertise on the law. Accordingly, while a lawyer should not be disciplined for making a mistaken but colorable argument to excuse compliance with a legal obligation, the lawyer may not escape discipline for violating the law when arguments for invalidity, limited scope, or alternative meaning of the law in question are plainly frivolous. Moreover, Comment 4 should not be understood as an invitation to resort immediately to defiance of a contested legal obligation, when alternative means of challenging the validity, scope, or nature of the obligation are readily and timely available, such as seeking a judicial ruling before acting.

To claim the protection of this rule, the lawyer must be acting openly and with a clear intent to challenge the obligation,[83] as attempts to conceal the behavior, or indications that the proffered objections to the legal obligation were but an afterthought, undermine a claim of good faith.

### § 4-1.4(b) Dishonesty, Fraud, Deceit, and Misrepresentation

Rule 8.4(c) of the Model Rules of Professional Conduct generally forbids "conduct involving dishonesty, fraud, deceit or misrepresentation." Along with Rule 4.1[84] (prohibiting a lawyer from making "a false statement of material fact or law" to a person other than a client) and Rule 7.3(a) (directing the lawyer to be truthful before tribunals),[85] Rule 8.4(c) imposes a general duty of honesty on the lawyer. While the lawyer owes the client the higher and affirmative duty of candor,[86] the lawyer must refrain from outright dishonesty and deliberate deception of others.[87]

The duty under Rule 8.4(c) to refrain from "dishonesty, fraud, deceit or misrepresentation" applies whether or not the lawyer is engaged in the practice of law. The lawyer who commits civil fraud transgresses this rule and is deserving of appropriate disciplinary sanction.[88] The lawyer who knowingly defames a person with scurrilous and harmful statements violates the rule.[89]

The reference to "dishonesty" as being forbidden could be broadly read to enforce the integrity of a lawyer's conduct in all aspects from life—from not cheating when playing board games with friends and fidelity to a spouse to keeping a promise to uphold a lunch appointment and refusing to brown-nose a superior. But the purpose of the ethics rules and the textual context suggest otherwise.

First, as Professors Geoffrey Hazard and William Hodes and attorney Peter Jarvis observe, "[a] code of professional discipline should deter and punish conduct that is of special significance *to the profession*, but it should not concern itself with 'ordinary' misconduct at all."[90] The general censure of "dishonesty" in Rule 8.4(c) is not a warrant for disciplinary authorities to intrude into a lawyer's personal relationships and should not be employed as an official means to police the truthfulness of public speech.[91] When

---

[83] *See also infra* § 4-9.5(e) (discussing Rule 3.4(c) of the Model Rules of Professional Conduct, which states that "a lawyer may not "knowingly disobey an obligation under the rules of a tribunal except for an open refusal based on an assertion that no valid obligation exists").

[84] *See infra* § 4-11.2(a).

[85] *See infra* § 4-9.5(b) to (d).

[86] *See infra* § 4-5.2.

[87] *See infra* § 4-11.2(a).

[88] *See* People v. Mascarenas, 275 P.3d 1287, 1287 (O.P.D.J. Colo. 2011) (disciplining a lawyer who engaged in "an elaborate scheme to defraud the prospective purchaser of a store owned" by his wife).

[89] *See* In re Carpenter, 95 P.3d 203, 205–06 (Or. 2004) (disciplining a lawyer for a dishonest internet post implying a teacher and coach had engaged in sexual behavior with students).

[90] 2 GEOFFREY C. HAZARD, JR., W. WILLIAM HODES & PETER R. JARVIS, THE LAW OF LAWYERING § 69.02 (Aspen, 4th ed., 2016).

[91] On ethics rules and public or political speech, see *infra* §§ 4-1.4(b), (c), 4-13.3.

a lawyer is acting in a purely private and personal capacity or is speaking on public matters in a context separate from practicing law, the authority of the disciplinary authority is at its lowest ebb and constitutional principles of privacy and free speech are at their zenith.

Second, by being coupled with such other terms as "fraud," "deceit," and "misrepresentation,"[92] the term "dishonesty" in Rule 8.4(c) is best understood to refer to comparably serious breaches of the truth that have a concrete negative effect, probably in a manner that would be legally actionable by civil or criminal complaint.[93] While courts may be tempted to treat "dishonesty" in Rule 8.4(c) as a broad catch-all basis for castigating a lawyer who behaves offensively, discipline should be reserved for the kind of formal wrongdoing that reflects poorly on the person's suitability to practice law.

### § 4-1.4(c) Discrimination and Harassment

As discussed later in this book when addressing ethics in advocacy, Rule 8.4(d) of the Model Rules of Professional Conduct has long prohibited a lawyer from engaging in conduct "prejudicial to the administration of justice."[94] Before 2016, Comment 3 to Rule 8.4—adopted in most states and elevated to black letter text in several states—stated that paragraph (d) may be violated when "[a] lawyer who, in the course of representing a client, knowingly manifests, by words or conduct, bias or prejudice based upon race, sex, religion, national origin, disability, age, sexual orientation or socioeconomic status" and such actions are "prejudicial to the administration of justice." That advisory comment was limited both to when a lawyer is representing a client and when the bias or prejudice had a detrimental effect on the fair administration of justice.

In 2016, the American Bar Association adopted a new paragraph (g) to Rule 8.4 that more expansively prohibits a lawyer from engaging in discrimination or harassment, not only when representing a client but broadly related to the practice of law—on pain of professional discipline.[95] The new paragraph (g) to Rule 8.4 makes it professional misconduct for a lawyer to "engage in conduct that the lawyer knows or reasonably should know is harassment or discrimination on the basis of race, sex, religion, national origin, ethnicity, disability, age, sexual orientation, gender identity, marital status or socioeconomic status in conduct related to the practice of law."[96] Although nearly half of the states have an anti-bias rule incorporated into the professional conduct rules, the ABA Model Rules version goes further than most by extending to all professional activities (such as continuing legal education programs and bar dinners), by separating the standard for what constitutes harassment from that established in anti-discrimination law, and by expanding the list of protected categories.

***Workplace Bias Rule:*** Proponents of the new provision argue that a "workplace bias" rule is necessary to enhance equity and opportunity within the legal profession. To promote full opportunity and participation in the legal profession for those from

---

92 *See* Yates v. United States, 135 S. Ct. 1074, 1085 (2015) (ruling that the words surrounding a term in a federal statute "cabin the contextual meaning of that term" through the principle of "*noscitur a sociis*—a word is known by the company it keeps").

93 *See Carpenter*, 95 P.3d at 236 (explaining that a lawyer's harmful internet statements implying sexual misconduct by a teacher was likely to "affect the teacher's legal rights adversely").

94 *See infra* § 4-9.4(b).

95 Samson Habte, *ABA Delegates Overwhelmingly Approve Anti-Bias Rule*, 32 LAW. MAN. PROF. CONDUCT 481 (2016).

96 American Bar Ass'n, Revised Resolution 109, House of Delegate, Annual Meeting, 2016.

historically-disadvantaged groups, the new disciplinary rule applies not only to conduct representing a client and the lawyer's interaction with persons involved in the adjudicative process, but, as stated in what is now a new Comment 4, covers a lawyer "while engaged in the practice of law; operating or managing a law firm or law practice; and participating in bar association, business or social activities in connection with the practice of law."[97] Advocates explained the broader scope of the provision as addressing problems in the "extended workplace," thus making plain that discriminatory or harassing behavior excluding full participation by all at law firm social events or professional conferences are professional misconduct.[98]

***Biased Conduct and Lawyer Fitness:*** Advocates also view the rule as appropriately recognizing discriminatory conduct generally as negatively reflecting on a lawyer's fitness to be a member of the legal profession. Proponents contended that discrimination or harassment against those falling into defined protected categories also "reflect[s] adversely on the lawyer's fitness to practice law or involve[s] moral turpitude."[99] As precedent for regulating lawyer behavior beyond improper conduct directly in representation, proponents cited Model Rule 8.4(c). That rule defines professional misconduct to include any "dishonesty, fraud, deceit or misrepresentation," whether or not related to the practice of law.[100]

Opponents to what they labeled "a free-floating non-discrimination provision"[101] raised several objections, which roughly fell into five categories:

***Protecting Legitimate Advocacy:*** In response to an earlier draft of the proposed rule, concerns were raised about the chilling effect of the proposal on advocacy in cases raising issues of race, gender, or sexual orientation. In response, the final version of paragraph (g) adopted by the ABA specifies that it "does not preclude legitimate advice or advocacy consistent with these Rules."

***Effect on Accepting or Declining Clients:*** During the drafting of Rule 8.4(g), questions were raised about whether the proposal would be employed to force lawyers to accept clients from all identity or social groups, thus overriding the lawyer's traditional autonomy in selection of clients. In response, language was added to the text of the final adopted version of Rule 8.4(g) stating that the rule "does not limit the ability of a lawyer to accept, decline or withdraw from a representation in accordance with Rule 1.16."

Although some may still invoke the rule as preventing a lawyer from turning a client away based solely on membership in one of the listed protected groups, the more natural reading is that decisions to accept, decline, or terminate a client are carved out of Rule 8.4(g) by the reference to Rule 1.16. Moreover, Rule 1.16(b)(1) expressly permits a lawyer to withdraw from representation of a client for any reason when "withdrawal can be accomplished without material adverse effect on the interests of the client" (which is especially likely to be true at the outset), and Rule 1.16(b)(4) allows the lawyer to

---

[97] *See generally* Stephen Gillers, *A Rule to Forbid Bias and Harassment in Law Practice: A Guide for State Courts Considering Model Rule 8.4(g)*, 30 GEO. J. LEGAL ETHICS 195, 219 (2017).

[98] *See ABA Panel Finalizes Proposed Workplace Bias Ethics Rules*, 32 LAW. MAN. PROF. CONDUCT 355 (June 15, 2016).

[99] American Bar Ass'n, Standing Comm. on Ethics & Prof'l Responsibility, et al., Report at 10 (May 31, 2016).

[100] *See supra* § 4-1.4(b).

[101] Joint Comment Regarding Proposed Changes to ABA Model Rule of Professional Conduct 8.4 (Signed by 52 Members).

withdraw when "the client insists upon taking action that the lawyer considers repugnant or with which the lawyer has a fundamental disagreement."[102] Even if Rule 8.4(g) does not reach decisions on whether to accept or continue with a client, the practicing lawyer should be aware that state or local anti-discrimination laws may preclude retention decisions deliberately excluding clients from a protected group.

***Free Speech Concerns:*** Opponents regarded the proposal as a "departure from the historic principles of attorney regulation" by reaching lawyer conduct that is only tangentially related to the actual practice of law.[103] In this regard, they fear the rule will become unmoored from a proper focus on lawyer conduct involving representation to become "a speech code over social activities merely 'connected with the practice of law,' "[104] under which lawyers are disciplined for opinion statements that disciplinary authorities find to be offensive. Critics of Rule 8.4(g) observed that the rule could be used to discipline a lawyer who says something that someone else finds offensive at a continuing legal education event or at a table at a local bar dinner in a discussion of immigration limits, Islam or evangelical Christianity, differences between the sexes, same-sex marriage, or the "cultural causes of poverty." Rule 8.4(g) thus would be, in the words of detractors, "the new ABA speech code"[105] and unlikely to withstand constitutional challenge.[106] The Supreme Court recently emphasized those "bedrock First Amendment principles" that "[s]peech may not be banned on the ground that it expresses ideas that offend."[107]

Supporters of the rule contend that, "when lawyers communicate with each other in 'the practice of law,' they do not typically engage in public discourse" of this nature.[108] Moreover, observers suggest that prudential bar authorities will avoid pursuing charges for dubious objections to protected expressions of opinion on matters of public concern.[109]

---

[102] *See infra* § 4-3.6(c)(2). *See also* Gillers, *supra*, 30 GEO. J. LEGAL ETHICS at 232 n.125 (observing that a lawyer declining to assist a same-sex couple in adopting a child on religious grounds could cite Rule 1.16(b)(4) which allows a lawyer to withdraw from a representation which the lawyer considers repugnant or with which has a fundamental disagreement, and commenting that "[a] claim of repugnance does not even require a religious motive").

[103] Joint Comment Regarding Proposed Changes to ABA Model Rule of Professional Conduct 8.4 (Signed by 52 Members); Josh Blackman, *Reply: A Pause for State Courts Considering Model Rule 8.4(g) (The First Amendment and "Conduct Related to the Practice of Law")*, 30 GEO J. LEGAL ETHICS 241, 243 (2017) (criticizing extension of disciplinary jurisdiction to conduct with "only the most tenuous connection to representation of clients, a lawyer's fitness, or the administration of justice").

[104] Blackman, *supra*, 30 GEO J. LEGAL ETHICS at 257.

[105] Eugene Volokh, A speech code for lawyers, banning viewpoints that express 'bias,' including in law-related social activities, Volokh Conspiracy Blog, at https://www.washingtonpost.com/news/volokh-conspiracy/wp/2016/08/10/a-speech-code-for-lawyers-banning-viewpoints-that-express-bias-including-in-law-related-social-activities-2 (Aug. 10, 2016); *see also* Blackman, *supra*, 30 GEO J. LEGAL ETHICS at 243 ("Lectures given at CLE events, or dinner-time conversation at a bar-association function, would now be subject to discipline if the speaker reasonably should know someone would find it 'derogatory.' The threat of sanction will inevitably chill speech on matters of public concern.").

[106] David French, *A Speech Code for Lawyers*, NAT'L REV., at http://www.nationalreview.com/article/438906/free-speech-lawyers-american-bar-association-model-rules-professional-conduct? (Aug. 11, 2016). *See also* Letter of Ken Paxton, Attorney General of Texas, to Senator Charles Perry, Dec. 20, 2016 (offering an opinion that adoption of new Rule 8.4(g) would violate the constitutional and statutory rights of lawyers by infringing on free speech and chilling constitutionally-protected activities).

[107] Matal v. Tam, 137 S. Ct. 1744, 1751 (2017).

[108] Claudia E. Haupt, *Antidiscrimination in the Legal Profession and the First Amendment: A Partial Defense of Model Rule 8.4(g)*, 19 U. PA. J. CONST. L. ONLINE (2017).

[109] *Compare* Gillers, *supra*, 30 GEO J. LEGAL ETHICS at 235 ("Experiences teaches us that the kind of biased or harassing speech that will attract the attention of disciplinary counsel will not enjoy First Amendment protection.") *and* Haupt, *supra*, 19 U. PA. J. CONST. L. ONLINE (saying that, when lawyers engage

***Defining Discrimination and Harassment:*** Concerns were raised about whether the terms of the new standard, including the prohibited conduct of "discrimination" and "harassment," were sufficiently defined for a black-letter disciplinary rule, which a lawyer must follow at the risk of loss of the license to practice. The ABA's Standing Committee on Professional Discipline believed that the "vagueness and over-breadth" of the earlier draft proposal would make it difficult to fairly enforce and vulnerable to constitutional challenge.[110] For example, unlawful harassment in the workplace context requires several elements for establishing a hostile environment, such as that the environment is both subjectively and objectively hostile and that the harassment is sufficiently frequent and severe as to intimidate or abuse a reasonable person and thus effectively prevent work performance and employment opportunities.[111] Whether the term "harass" in new paragraph (g) to Model Rule 8.4 incorporates these elements and is subject to these limitations (which appear to be constitutionally required to prevent suppression of protected speech) is not clear. While new Comment 3 provides that "[t]he substantive law of antidiscrimination and anti-harassment statutes and case law may guide application of paragraph (g)," the report supporting the proposal took much of that back by emphasizing that such workplace discrimination law is "not necessarily dispositive in the disciplinary context."[112]

In partial response to these concerns, the final version of paragraph (g) adopted on the floor by the ABA in 2016 imposes a stricter *mens rea* requirement, stating that the lawyer must "know[ ] or reasonably should know" that the offensive conduct constitutes "harassment or discrimination."[113]

***Enforceability of New Rule:*** The ABA's Standing Committee on Professional Discipline worried generally about enforcement of the proposed workplace discrimination rule. The committee emphasized that employment discrimination law is "a complex and highly specialized area of law" that state attorney regulation authorities would find burdensome and difficult to apply and adjudicate in the context of professional disciplinary proceedings.[114] Both the Standing Committee and the Professional Responsibility Committee of the ABA Business Law Section[115] pointed to employment discrimination ethics rules in such states as New York and California that require a finding of unlawful discrimination by a lawyer in a competent tribunal (such as a court judgment on a complaint of unlawful discrimination) before a disciplinary action may be initiated.[116]

---

in "public discourse, the interests underlying speech protection counsel against an expansive interpretation of 'conduct related to the practice of law' ") *with* Blackman, *supra*, 30 GEO J. LEGAL ETHICS at 243 ("At bottom, the defenders of the model rule can only urge us to trust the disciplinary committees.").

[110] Standing Comm. on Prof'l Discipline, Comments on Draft Proposal to Amend Rule 8.4 of the ABA Model Rules of Professional Conduct at 3 (Mar. 10, 2016).

[111] *Id.* at 5; *see also* Caleb C. Wolanek, Note, *Discriminatory Lawyers in a Discriminatory Bar: Rule 8.4(g) of the Model Rules of Professional Responsibility*, 40 HARV. J.L & PUB. POL'Y. 773, 784–85 (2017) (discussing requirement that harassment be sufficiently pervasive and severe so as "look far more like physical actions than 'mere' words" to avoid constitutional prohibition on content-based regulation).

[112] American Bar Ass'n, Standing Comm. on Ethics & Prof'l Responsibility, et al., Report at 7 (May 31, 2016).

[113] *See generally* Gillers, *supra*, 30 GEO. J. LEGAL ETHICS at 217–19.

[114] Standing Comm. on Prof'l Discipline, Comments on Draft Proposal to Amend Rule 8.4 of the ABA Model Rules of Professional Conduct at 6 (Mar. 10, 2016).

[115] *Id.* at 7; Letter of Kevin R. Fisher, Chair, and Nathan Crystal, Member, of the Business Law Section Ethics Committee at 5 (Mar. 10, 2016).

[116] CAL. RULES OF PROF'L CONDUCT R. 2–400(C); N.Y. RULES OF PROF'L CONDUCT R. 8.4(g).

***Conclusion: Primary Focus on Harmful Derogatory and Harassing Behavior:*** Both proponents and opponents tend to agree on the primary target of the new Rule 8.4(g). Professor Stephen Gillers explains that the central focus on new Rule 8.4(g) is on derogatory and harassing behavior that if not arrested may "harm the justice system because they create the impression that the rule of law can be distorted by name calling grounded in identity."[117] Professor Josh Blackman agrees that sexual harassment that "would also violate well-established employment law, was [the] primary target" of the new rule.[118]

## § 4-1.5 A BRIEF OUTLINE OF LAWYER DISCIPLINE

To protect the public, especially clients, and advance the administration of justice,[119] every American jurisdiction has a set of procedures to screen those who are admitted to the practice of law and to investigate and sanction lawyers who violate the rules of ethics. States typically insist that lawyer discipline is a non-punitive protective measure. As the California Supreme Court said decades ago, the "purpose of a disciplinary proceeding is not punitive but to inquire into the fitness of the attorney to continue in that capacity for the protection of the public, the courts, and the legal profession."[120] Similarly, the Iowa Supreme Court has explained that attorney discipline is—

> not designed to punish, but rather to determine the fitness of an officer of [the] court to continue in that capacity, to insulate the courts and the public from those persons unfit to practice law, to protect the integrity of and the public confidence in our system of justice, and to deter other lawyers from engaging in similar acts or practices.[121]

Professor Leslie Levin, however, contends that "many lawyer sanctions fit within classic definitions of 'punishment' and can be justified by the traditional utilitarian justifications of punishment: incapacitation, rehabilitation, and deterrence."[122]

Professional discipline for admitted lawyers in the United States has evolved from a period of episodic and ad hoc adjudication by individual judges to a generally integrated model of evaluation and disposition by an independent central disciplinary authority under the auspices of the jurisdiction's highest court. As Professor Mary Devlin says, the different eras of discipline "can be conceptualized by tracking who has been designated as the appropriate decision-maker."[123]

In the earliest period in the United States, professional discipline generally was both initiated and disposed of by an individual judge who learned of the lawyer's behavior in the courtroom or, occasionally, in the community. If the judge concluded that the lawyer's conduct fell outside of professional ethics expectations, the judge could cite the lawyer for contempt or direct that he be removed from the rolls of lawyers admitted

---

[117] Gillers, *supra*, 30 GEO. J. LEGAL ETHICS at 223.

[118] Blackman, *supra*, 30 GEO J. LEGAL ETHICS at 248.

[119] *See* STANDARDS FOR IMPOSING LAWYER SANCTIONS, Standard 1.1 (American Bar Ass'n, 1992).

[120] Bradpiece v. State Bar of Cal., 111 Cal. Rptr. 905, 909 (1974).

[121] Committee on Prof'l Ethics & Conduct v. Borchart, 392 N.W.2d 491, 492 (Iowa 1986).

[122] Leslie C. Levin, *The Emperor's Clothes and Other Tales About the Standards for Imposing Lawyer Discipline Sanctions*, 48 AM. U. L. REV. 1, 18–19 (1998).

[123] Mary M. Devlin, THE DEVELOPMENT OF LAWYER DISCIPLINARY PROCEDURES IN THE UNITED STATES, J. OF PROF. LAWYER 359, 365 (1994).

to practice.[124] As voluntary bar associations were founded during the latter part of the nineteenth century and into the early twentieth century, professional discipline devolved on these new bodies which sought both to maintain peer review and install the bar associations as mandatory and unified professional organizations.[125] Provoked by reports of public dissatisfaction with lawyer discipline and fearing that political authorities would intervene and overturn self-regulation of the profession, a reform movement within the American Bar Association advanced the current era of unitary discipline under the control of an independent judicial branch within each state.[126]

While each state has its own system with a multitude of names for the disciplinary authorities and a persisting mix in many states of both state and local bar involvement in processing complaints,[127] general patterns may be described. Nearly all states place the ultimate authority for professional discipline into the judicial branch with supervision by bodies subject to the highest court in the jurisdiction.[128] Moreover, every system must afford procedural protections to the accused lawyer. Regarding attorney disciplinary proceedings as "adversary proceedings of a quasi-criminal nature," the Supreme Court has held that constitutional due process protections apply.[129]

This book focuses on the ethical duties of lawyers, rather than the process by which derelictions are discovered and addressed. Accordingly, the description below paints with a very broad brush and cites to general standards and procedures for discipline proposed by the American Bar Association rather than attempting to survey in any detail the variations on the theme in particular states.

### § 4-1.5(a) A Central Body for Receiving, Evaluating, and Investigating Ethical Complaints Against Lawyers

In the typical American jurisdiction, a central statewide body (often termed a disciplinary board or a professional responsibility board) or a court-appointed officer (frequently called the disciplinary counsel) appointed by the highest court serves as the point of entry to the attorney disciplinary system. This body or officer is charged with responsibility for receiving, making an initial evaluation of, and investigating complaints[130] (although some states still reply on a corps of volunteer lawyers to conduct investigations). Complaints may be received from any person (such as a lawyer's client), a law firm, a judge, or any other entity alleging that a lawyer has violated the ethical standards for practice.

After a complaint is filed, the respondent attorney is notified and directed to provide a written response within a set timeframe. One of the most common errors of lawyers subject to an ethics complaint is to fail to prepare a response, by reason of

[124] *Id.* at 359–65.

[125] *Id.* at 365–68.

[126] *Id.* at 368–80; *see also* Levin, *supra*, 48 AM. U. L. REV. at 2–4.

[127] On state lawyer disciplinary processes, see generally Debra Moss Curtis, *Attorney Discipline Nationwide: A Comparative Analysis of Process and Statistics*, 35 J. OF THE LEGAL PROF. 209 (2011).

[128] CENTER FOR PROF'L RESPONSIBILITY, AMERICAN BAR ASS'N, ANNOTATED STANDARDS FOR IMPOSING LAWYER SANCTIONS at 42–43 (American Bar Ass'n, 2015) (noting New York as an exception by granting disciplinary authority to intermediate appellate courts).

[129] In re Ruffalo, 390 U.S. 544, 550–51 (1968).

[130] MODEL RULES FOR LAWYER DISCIPLINARY ENFORCEMENT R. 2.A, 4 (American Bar Ass'n, 2001) [hereinafter MODEL RULES FOR LAWYER DISCIPLINARY ENFORCEMENT].

procrastination, embarrassment, or confusion about what to do.[131] Even if the lawyer is acquitted of the charge in the ethics complaint, failure to respond to the complaint and cooperate with the process counts as an independent violation.[132]

Not every complaint is meritorious, of course, and indeed many complaints are plainly without merit (the vast majority of complaints ultimately are dismissed). Indeed, some complaints may be facially invalid, by failing to allege what constitutes as professional misconduct,[133] lacking adequate factual support, or lodging an accusation that falls outside of professional disciplinary authorities. Disciplinary counsel reviews each complaint, along with the attorney's response, to determine whether further investigation is warranted, and typically reports to a disciplinary board. Upon receiving the lawyer's response, the disciplinary counsel or board may dismiss the complaint (giving notice to both the lawyer and the complainant) or direct further investigation.[134]

If further investigation is deemed warranted, the disciplinary counsel or board typically is granted subpoena power to compel the appearance of witnesses and the production of documents. The investigation may be conducted by the disciplinary counsel or other members or staff from the disciplinary board or, in some states, delegated to county bar associations or volunteer lawyers. Upon receipt of a report by the investigator, the board may dismiss the complaint, may have authority to impose minor discipline (such as a private admonition or public reprimand), or may prosecute a formal complaint for a formal hearing.[135]

During this early evaluation process, the attorney's responsiveness to the disciplinary counsel or board is especially important. Mark McCormick, a former justice of the Iowa Supreme Court and frequent counsel for attorneys in the disciplinary process, explains that, "[a]lthough there is no 'plea bargaining' in the disciplinary process," the attorney nonetheless is well-advised "to provide information to the ethics administrator or ethics counsel which may help bring about an acceptable resolution of a complaint."[136]

---

[131] *See* Edward J. Cleary, *Noncooperation—Making a Bad Situation Worse*, BENCH & B. OF MINN., Nov. 2000, at 20, 22 (the director of Minnesota's disciplinary authority says that the "one piece of advice I would give a lawyer who has had a complaint filed against her" is to "get past the fear and/or anger that is often a natural reaction to being made the subject of a complaint and cooperate as soon as possible," further observing that "[a]nswering in a timely manner and being forthright when a complaint is received is not only the right thing to do, it is the response that is most likely to result to the benefit of the responding attorney").

[132] *See* Disciplinary Counsel v. Wilcox, 33 N.E.3d 7, 11 (Ohio 2014); In re Ulanowski, 800 N.W.2d 785, 798 (Minn. 2011); Committee on Prof'l Ethics & Conduct v. Stienstra, 390 N.W.2d 135, 137 (Iowa 1986); Lawrence H. Averill, Jr., *The Revised Lawyer Discipline Process in Arkansas: A Primer and Analysis*, 21 U. ARK. L. REV. 13, 48–49 (1998); Paul H. Wieck II, *What Happens When an Attorney is Accused of an Ethics Violation*, IOWA LAWYER, March 2006, at 13.

[133] MODEL RULES FOR LAWYER DISCIPLINARY ENFORCEMENT R. 11.A.

[134] *Id.*, R. 4.B(1) to (2), 11.A to B.

[135] *Id.*, R. 4.B(3) to (4).

[136] Mark McCormick, *Few Ever Will Be Cited But—Lawyers Should Understand the Disciplinary Process,* IOWA LAWYER, Feb. 2000, at 18; *see also* Arnold R. Rosenfeld, *The Bar Disciplinary Process in Massachusetts: Bar Counsel's Perspective*, 79 MASS. L. REV. 180, 185 (1994) (saying that a case is more likely to be resolved quickly when the responding attorney "provides a timely, thorough, concise, and well-documented response," as contrasted with a delayed or inadequate response which "causes bar counsel to become skeptical . . . and to wonder whether there may be a sound basis" for the complaint against the lawyer).

### § 4-1.5(b) Preparation for and Formal Hearing on Prosecuted Complaint

If the disciplinary counsel or board concludes that a more severe sanction is warranted, the counsel or board will file a formal complaint with a hearing authority, variously designated as the grievance commission, hearing committee, hearing panel, or hearing officer. As a matter of due process, the complaint must be sufficiently clear to inform the lawyer of the charges and allow the lawyer to formulate a response.[137]

At this point, the disciplinary process increasingly resembles a judicial proceeding, with all the trappings of litigation, such as discovery, testimony by witnesses, resolution by a "jury" of peers, etc. The disciplinary counsel or board will prosecute the complaint,[138] but the hearing panel or officer serves as an independent and impartial body to rule on the charges.

The hearing panel typically consists of two or more lawyers along with one or more members of the public.[139] In about a third of the states, a single adjudicator or hearing officer (often a judge) presides.[140] Although part of the same central disciplinary authority as the prosecuting disciplinary counsel, the hearing panel is independent of and separate from the prosecuting officer and adjudicates the matter impartially.[141]

The lawyer subject to the disciplinary proceeding usually is entitled to conduct discovery in a manner akin to the state's civil procedure rules.[142] While the lawyer may not obtain the actual work-product of the prosecuting board or office, investigators, and administrators, written statements, transcripts, or recordings of witnesses should be disclosed.[143] The disciplinary counsel likewise may conduct discovery, but the attorney against whom the complaint is filed is not required to answer an interrogatory, request for admission, or deposition question if the answer would be self-incriminatory.[144] Either the hearing panel itself[145] or a court in the locality is empowered to issue subpoenas to compel witnesses to submit to discovery.

Both the prosecuting disciplinary counsel and the respondent attorney may present witnesses, again with the support of subpoena power.[146] An oath or affirmation is administered by the hearing panel,[147] with testimony being transcribed by a court reporter or otherwise recorded.[148] The attorney is entitled to be confronted by and to cross-examine the witnesses presented in support of the charges of professional

---

[137] MODEL RULES FOR LAWYER DISCIPLINARY ENFORCEMENT R. 11.D.

[138] *Id.*, R. 4.B(4).

[139] *See* MODEL RULES FOR LAWYER DISCIPLINARY ENFORCEMENT R. 2.A, 3.A.

[140] *See* David A. Summers, *Adjudicating Attorney Discipline: Are Panels Necessary?*, 20:2 THE PROF'L LAWYER 30 (2010).

[141] MODEL RULES FOR LAWYER DISCIPLINARY ENFORCEMENT R. 2, Commentary.

[142] *See id.*, R. 15, 18.b.

[143] *See id.*, R. 16.A.

[144] For more on the privilege against self-incrimination as it applies in the disciplinary process, see *infra* § 4-13.1(e).

[145] *See* MODEL RULES FOR LAWYER DISCIPLINARY ENFORCEMENT R. 14.B to C.

[146] *Id.*, R. 14.C.

[147] *Id.*, R. 14.A.

[148] *Id.*, R. 11, Commentary, 18.F.

misconduct. The attorney may present character evidence from a lawyer, judge, or other person by testimony or sworn affidavit.

As an alternative to the presentation of evidence at the hearing, the prosecuting officer and the respondent lawyer may enter into a stipulation as to the relevant facts including exhibits. The case thus would be submitted to the hearing panel on the basis of the stipulation, without holding a hearing, and the matter would be resolved based upon the stipulated facts and exhibits.

After the hearing or submission by stipulated facts, the parties generally are granted a reasonable time to submit post-hearing briefs and arguments.

### § 4-1.5(c) Standard of Proof and Issue Preclusion

Because of the gravity of the charge of professional misconduct and the severity of the sanction that may follow (including temporary or permanent loss of the lawyer's license to practice), the standard of proof in disciplinary proceedings is and should be greater than the simple preponderance of the evidence standard as applied in ordinary civil cases. However, because the lawyer subject to a disciplinary proceeding is not at risk of losing liberty or being disenfranchised from the privileges of ordinary citizenship (at least not by the mere fact of a professional disciplinary sanction), the stringent beyond-a-reasonable-doubt standard that is demanded in criminal cases would not reasonably apply.

Accordingly, states tend to arrive at a middle standard that "lies somewhere between the proof required in criminal cases and that required in civil cases."[149] The predominant standard of proof for establishing a case of professional misconduct is "clear and convincing evidence,"[150] although a smaller number of states apply a lesser standard such as "convincing preponderance of the evidence,"[151] "fair preponderance of the evidence,"[152] or rarely even simple "preponderance of the evidence."[153]

When the matter at issue in a disciplinary proceeding was previously adjudicated against the lawyer in a criminal or civil proceeding, where the burden of proof was greater than a mere preponderance of the evidence, the lawyer is rightly estopped from relitigating the matter in the disciplinary process. The principle of issue preclusion (traditionally known as "collateral estoppel") arises from the common-sense notion that a party in litigation should get only "one bite at the apple." "Issue preclusion prevents re-litigation of any issues that were *actually* presented in a prior lawsuit and that were *necessary* to the final judgment in that prior suit."[154] Thus, if the conduct underlying a charge of professional misconduct against the lawyer was the subject of a prior

---

[149] Committee on Prof'l Ethics & Conduct v. Garretson, 515 N.W.2d 25, 27 (Iowa 1994).

[150] MODEL RULES FOR LAWYER DISCIPLINARY ENFORCEMENT R. 18.C; *see also* In re Barach, 540 F.3d 82, 85 (1st Cir. 2008) (noting clear and convincing evidence is majority rule for lawyer discipline); STEPHEN GILLERS, REGULATION OF THE LEGAL PROFESSION 519 (Aspen Pub., 10th ed., 2015) (same). On the meaning and application of the clear and convincing standard of proof, see generally CENTER FOR PROF'L RESPONSIBILITY, AMERICAN BAR ASS'N, ANNOTATED STANDARDS FOR IMPOSING LAWYER SANCTIONS at 36–38 (American Bar Ass'n, 2015).

[151] Attorney Disciplinary Bd. v. McCuskey, 814 N.W.2d 250, 254 (Iowa 2012) (explaining this standard as less than proof beyond a reasonable doubt in a criminal case and less than clear and convincing evidence, but "more than the preponderance standard required in the usual civil case").

[152] Matter of Capoccia, 453 N.E.2d 497, 498 (N.Y. 1983).

[153] Mass. Bd. of Bar Overseers R. § 3.28.

[154] JAY TIDMARSH & ROGER H. TRANGSRUD, COMPLEX LITIGATION AND THE ADVERSARY SYSTEM 166–67 (Foundation Press, 1998).

adjudication of criminal guilt or certain types of civil liability subject to a higher standard of proof, issue preclusion may conclusively establish the matter for the disciplinary proceedings.

For issue preclusion to be applied in a disciplinary proceeding, the issue (that is, the question about the lawyer's conduct) must have been resolved in a civil proceeding that ended in a final judgment or a criminal proceeding that resulted in a finding of guilt, and the burden of proof in the prior proceeding must have been greater than that for establishing professional misconduct. When an attorney has been convicted of or pled guilty to a crime pursuant to the high evidentiary showing of guilt beyond a reasonable doubt, that outcome ordinarily establishes the commission of the acts constituting the crime for purposes of any disciplinary proceeding. Indeed, the state may regard a record of a felony conviction as conclusive evidence to suspend or remove the lawyer from practice.[155]

By contrast, because most civil lawsuits are resolved by a mere preponderance of the evidence standard, a prior judgment against a lawyer in such an action, such as being held liable in an ordinary malpractice suit, should be given no preclusive effect in a subsequent disciplinary proceeding. The prosecuting disciplinary board may not rely upon the civil judgment against the lawyer, but must instead establish the facts underlying the professional misconduct charge by the "clear and convincing" or "convincing preponderance of the evidence" standard applicable to disciplinary proceedings. However, if a civil judgment was entered upon a showing of a high standard of proof, such as proof of fraud established by clear and convincing evidence, then the lawyer may be precluded from challenging the charge of such fraud in a disciplinary hearing, assuming the requirements for issue preclusion otherwise are satisfied.

While issue preclusion when properly applied prevents the lawyer from disputing the central facts of the misconduct previously adjudicated, the lawyer should not be barred from presenting mitigating evidence that does not contradict the basic findings of misconduct.

### § 4-1.5(d) Confidentiality and Immunity in Disciplinary Proceedings

A few states mandate full transparency and thus offer public insight into each stage of the disciplinary process and regardless of the merit of the complaint against the lawyer.[156] Most states attempt to walk a tightrope between affording confidentiality to early stages of the process to avoid impairing a lawyer's reputation before any preliminary finding of serious misconduct and responding to the expressed public need for protection against miscreant lawyer. Under the American Bar Association's *Standards for Imposing Lawyer Sanctions*, the process becomes public at the point at which formal charges are presented by the disciplinary counsel after a finding of probable cause for disbarment, suspension, or public reprimand (that is, when the hearing panel process is initiated).[157] Confidentiality thus protects the reputation of the attorney when the charge of professional misconduct has been found groundless or when

---

[155] *See* MODEL RULES FOR LAWYER DISCIPLINARY ENFORCEMENT R. 19.E.

[156] OR. STATE BAR BYLAWS, art. 8, § 8.102 (2014); *see also* R.M. v. Supreme Court, 883 A.2d 369, 374–82 (N.J. 2005) (holding that confidentiality in disciplinary proceedings violated First Amendment); In re Warner, 21 So.3d 218 (La. 2009) (same).

[157] STANDARDS FOR IMPOSING LAWYER SANCTIONS, Standard 1.2 (American Bar Ass'n, 1992).

only minor misconduct is at issue.[158] In every jurisdiction, if the lawyer becomes the subject of serious disciplinary sanctions, the final decision becomes a matter of public record.[159]

To encourage those who perceive misconduct by a lawyer to take the affirmative step of making a complaint, those involved in the lawyer disciplinary process typically are afforded immunity from civil liability.[160] Thus, individuals who file complaints against lawyers with disciplinary authorities, individuals who testify in disciplinary proceedings, and members and staff of the disciplinary bodies are protected by an evidentiary rule of privilege and by immunity against threat of defamation or litigation. The immunity likewise precludes lawsuits filed against disciplinary authorities by disgruntled clients who are dissatisfied by the disposition of a complaint against their lawyers in the disciplinary process.

### § 4-1.5(e) Decision by Hearing Panel or Officer and Further Review

Following submission of the matter after an evidentiary hearing or on stipulated facts, the hearing panel or officer deliberates and renders a decision, typically in writing.[161] For each charge, the adjudicator should enter findings of fact, evaluate whether the facts demonstrate an ethical violation, and, if so, recommend appropriate disciplinary sanctions.

The hearing panel or officer typically may dismiss the complaint, issue a private admonition or public reprimand, or impose (or recommend) that the attorney's license be suspended or revoked. The hearing panel's or officer's recommendation generally is delivered to a central disciplinary body, which may accept or reject the recommendation.[162]

In nearly every jurisdiction, the hearing panel's or officer's decision is subject to further review by the highest court, which "retain[s] ultimate responsibility for all disciplinary matters."[163] In some states, the court has discretionary review, meaning that its determination not to accept further review makes the hearing panel's determination final.[164] In other states, the highest court confirms the recommendation of the adjudicator, after receiving briefing but generally without argument and a full judicial opinion. In still other states, the court conducts a full review and issues a thorough written decision whenever serious disciplinary sanctions, particularly disbarment, are recommended.

### § 4-1.5(f) Types of Sanctions and Factors in Evaluating the Appropriate Sanction

With the preeminent concern being protection of the public, the appropriate sanction against a lawyer who has been found guilty of an ethical violation depends on the seriousness of the violation, the egregiousness of the facts, the lawyer's prior record

---

158 McLaughlin v. Philadelphia Newspapers, Inc., 348 A.2d 376, 381 (Pa. 1975).

159 MODEL RULES FOR LAWYER DISCIPLINARY ENFORCEMENT R. 10.D.

160 *Id.*, R. 12.A.

161 *Id.*, R. 3.D(2).

162 *Id.*, R. 3.D, 11.E.

163 *Id.*, R. 11, Commentary.

164 *Id.*, R. 11.F.

of disciplinary misconduct, and mitigating factors. The American Bar Association's *Standards for Imposing Lawyer Sanctions* are followed as at least persuasive authority and guidelines in the substantial majority of states. Only eight states do not rely on the *Standards* even as guidelines.[165] The *Standards* are based on a four-part theoretical framework that evaluates (1) the nature of the ethical duty violated by the lawyer (whether owed to client, the public, the legal system, or the legal profession); (2) the lawyer's mental state (whether the lawyer acted intentionally, knowingly, or negligently); (3) the potential or actual injury caused by the lawyer's ethical misconduct; and (4) evidence of aggravating or mitigating circumstances.[166]

Multiple factors may weigh in favor of or against a more severe sanction: the willfulness of the ethical violation obviously militates in favor of a severe sanction, as does the invidious motive of personal gain. Dishonesty with clients and others exacerbates the misconduct. Harm to the client often warrants a more severe penalty. Multiple acts of misconduct compound the offense and justify a more critical response. A lawyer's substantial experience in the practice of law has been regarded as an aggravating factor, because the lawyer then has even less of an excuse not to be familiar with professional responsibilities. And an extensive history of disciplinary infractions merits a more severe sanction.

An important mitigating factor is the lawyer's recognition of the wrongdoing and acceptance of responsibility. That the attorney's offense was not motivated by personal gain is a mitigating factor. That a lawyer has not previously been disciplined is ordinarily a mitigating factor. The lawyer's personal problems, such as mental health or substance abuse problems, do not constitute an excuse but may be a mitigating factor that influences the severity of the sanction imposed.

### *§ 4-1.5(f)(1) Private Admonition*

Other than securing a dismissal of the disciplinary charge upon a determination that the lawyer engaged in no professional misconduct, the lightest sanction or quasi-sanction that may be received by a lawyer is that of an admonition. Indeed, a private admonition may not be regarded by every state as "discipline" for purposes of reporting the matter to other states in which an attorney is admitted for possible reciprocal discipline by that other jurisdiction.

An admonition will be imposed when, although the attorney took action that at least in retrospect was ill-advised and thus fell short of the standards expected under the rules, the attorney acted in good-faith, the violation of the rules was minor and caused little or no harm, the attorney has no significant history of professional misconduct, or there is little risk of further misconduct.[167] A non-public private admonition "should be used only 'in cases of minor misconduct, when there is little or no injury to a client, the

[165] ABA Standing Comm. on Prof. Discipline, ABA Standards for Imposing Lawyer Sanctions Comparison by Jurisdiction (Mar. 1, 2017).

[166] STANDARDS FOR IMPOSING LAWYER SANCTIONS, Standard 3.0 (American Bar Ass'n, 1992). *See generally* CENTER FOR PROF'L RESPONSIBILITY, AMERICAN BAR ASS'N, ANNOTATED STANDARDS FOR IMPOSING LAWYER SANCTIONS at xvii to xx (American Bar Ass'n, 2015).

[167] *See* MODEL RULES FOR LAWYER DISCIPLINARY ENFORCEMENT 10.A(5). *See generally* CENTER FOR PROF'L RESPONSIBILITY, AMERICAN BAR ASS'N, ANNOTATED STANDARDS FOR IMPOSING LAWYER SANCTIONS at 24–25 (American Bar Ass'n, 2015).

public, the legal system, or the profession, and when there is little likelihood of repetition by the lawyer.' "[168]

A professional admonition ordinarily is communicated privately to the attorney and thus does not appear in the public records.[169] While not in itself intended to constitute punishment, the fact of a prior admonition, particularly for the same type of conduct, will be considered in determining the appropriate sanction should the lawyer again be the subject of professional discipline.[170]

#### *§ 4-1.5(f)(2) Public Reprimand or Censure*

A public reprimand differs from that of a private admonition primarily by the fact that it is publicly reported.[171] A reprimand is a sanction considerably less severe in consequence and less condemning in pronouncement than either a suspension or license revocation. Nonetheless, the fact that the reprimand is made public means that this sanction has a genuine punitive effect by reason of the potential harm to the lawyer's professional reputation.

Professor Charles Wolfram explained that a public reprimand should be "employed for relatively innocuous, technical, or isolated violations that suggest an unusual or minor lapse of judgment rather than a more derelict state of mind."[172] A reprimand is particularly appropriate in cases of first impression, when the court or disciplinary authority has determined that the lawyer's conduct contravened the ethical expectations and thus is deserving of rebuke but nonetheless acknowledges the absence of clear guidance on the subject in the past. The reprimand is made public to serve as guidance to other members in the profession, emphasize the seriousness of ethical constraints, and protect clients.[173]

#### *§ 4-1.5(f)(3) Suspension*

When the magnitude of the professional misconduct, the harm to the client or the public, the lawyer's prior history of discipline, or other factor suggests that a public reprimand is not a sufficiently strong response, the court or disciplinary authority may impose the sanction of suspension, thereby removing the lawyer from the practice of law.[174] Next to license revocation (disbarment), suspension of a lawyer's license to practice law is the most severe of the sanctions that may be imposed for professional misconduct. Suspension may be for a specific period of time, such as six months,[175] or indefinitely.

---

[168] In re Farrar, 949 A.2d 438, 440 (Vt. 2008) (quoting Vermont court rule).

[169] *But see* Leslie C. Levin, *The Emperor's Clothes and Other Tales About the Standards for Imposing Lawyer Discipline Sanctions*, 48 AM. U. L. REV. 1, 46–49 (1998) (criticizing the "overuse" of admonitions as "valu[ing] the lawyer's reputation over the protection of the public," having little deterrent effect on the violating lawyer, and "depriv[ing] the public of useful information about whom to retain").

[170] MODEL RULES FOR LAWYER DISCIPLINARY ENFORCEMENT R. 10.A(5).

[171] *See* STANDARDS FOR IMPOSING LAWYER SANCTIONS, Standard 2.5 (American Bar Ass'n, 1992).

[172] CHARLES W. WOLFRAM, MODERN LEGAL ETHICS § 3.5.3 (West, 1986).

[173] MODEL RULES FOR LAWYER DISCIPLINARY ENFORCEMENT R. 27, Commentary. *See generally* CENTER FOR PROF'L RESPONSIBILITY, AMERICAN BAR ASS'N, ANNOTATED STANDARDS FOR IMPOSING LAWYER SANCTIONS at 69–72 (American Bar Ass'n, 2015).

[174] *See* STANDARDS FOR IMPOSING LAWYER SANCTIONS, Standard 2.3 (American Bar Ass'n, 1992). *See generally* CENTER FOR PROF'L RESPONSIBILITY, AMERICAN BAR ASS'N, ANNOTATED STANDARDS FOR IMPOSING LAWYER SANCTIONS at 55–62 (American Bar Ass'n, 2015).

[175] STANDARDS FOR IMPOSING LAWYER SANCTIONS, Standard 2.3 (American Bar Ass'n, 1992).

While the imposition of a suspension rather than a revocation offers the lawyer a meaningful opportunity for later reinstatement, the effect of the penalty upon the lawyer's professional career can be rather dramatic. Not only must the lawyer surrender his chosen means for making a living for a definite or indefinite period of time, but the lawyer typically must inform all clients of the fact of that suspension.[176] Accordingly, even should the time of suspension be short, the negative effect on the lawyer's practice and continuing relationship with clients may be severe, even aside from the reputational harm that follows a public suspension for professional misconduct.

A lawyer who practices law despite suspension commits several independent ethical violations.[177] First, the lawyer engages in the unauthorized practice of law in violation of Rule 5.5(a) of the Model Rules of Professional Conduct. Second, by falsely suggesting to clients that the lawyer is a legal practitioner, the lawyer arguably engages in deceitful and dishonest conduct in violation of Rule 8.4(c) of the Model Rules of Professional Conduct. The lawyer's representation of a client after suspension violates Rule 1.16(a) of the Model Rules of Professional Conduct, which requires a lawyer to withdraw if representation would result in a violation of the rules. And, because Rule 1.4 of the Model Rules of Professional Conduct requires a lawyer to keep the client informed about the status of the matter, the lawyer surely is obliged to inform the client that the lawyer has been suspended and can no longer represent the client.

The disciplinary authorities will not look kindly upon an attorney surreptitiously maintaining a law practice during a period of suspension, such as by using another designated attorney to hold client matters temporarily, with the prearranged understanding that the matters will be returned to the lawyer after reinstatement. However, the suspension rule in a state may not prohibit the lawyer from being employed by another attorney, law firm, or professional association—provided that the suspended lawyer only performs services that would be permissible for a layperson employed by an attorney (and presumably has no contact with clients).[178]

In addition to suspension being imposed as a sanction at the conclusion of a disciplinary proceeding, a lawyer's license may be suspended for other reasons or through other processes. For example, a lawyer may be suspended for failing to certify sufficient credits of continuing legal education; based on a determination that she is disabled and incapable of competent representation; or for such public policy reasons as failure to comply with a child support order.

### *§ 4-1.5(f)(4) Disbarment or License Revocation*

License revocation, commonly known as disbarment, is the professional equivalent of the death penalty, for it permanently removes the attorney's license to practice law.[179] While an attorney suspended from the practice of law may seek reinstatement, not all

---

[176] MODEL RULES FOR LAWYER DISCIPLINARY ENFORCEMENT R. 27.A.

[177] *See* Attorney Disciplinary Bd. v. McCuskey, 814 N.W.2d 250, 254–56 (Iowa 2012).

[178] In re Wilkerson, 834 P.2d 1356, 1362 (Kan. 1992). *But see* MODEL RULES FOR LAWYER DISCIPLINARY ENFORCEMENT R. 27 (saying that the lawyer "shall not maintain a presence or occupy an office where the practice of law is conducted," while also removing "any indicia of lawyer, counselor at law, legal assistant, law clerk or similar title").

[179] *See* STANDARDS FOR IMPOSING LAWYER SANCTIONS, Standard 2.2 (American Bar Ass'n, 1992) ("Disbarment terminates the individual's status as a lawyer.").

states allow a disbarred attorney to be readmitted to practice and no state does so with any regularity.[180]

Revocation "is reserved for the most deliberate, flagrant, and usually unlawful acts."[181] This most severe of sanctions is applied when the professional misconduct is so egregious that protection of the public and deterrence of professional wrongdoing demand removal of the lawyer from the rolls or the circumstances surrounding the offense are such as to leave no reasonable basis for believing that the lawyer could be rehabilitated to fitness for practice.

In some jurisdictions, an attorney who is the subject of a disciplinary investigation may attempt a quieter or at least less stressful termination of the proceedings by offering to surrender her license to practice. However, a lawyer who wishes to acquiesce to disbarment generally must acknowledge the nature of the allegations in the disciplinary process and confess that the material facts alleged are true or at least could not be successfully defended.[182] In sum, the lawyer who agrees to disbarment by consent essentially must plead guilty and acknowledge that she deserves the ultimate professional sanction of removal from the practice of law.[183]

#### *§ 4-1.5(f)(5) Probation*

Many states provide that a lawyer, who has fallen short of ethical standards but does not present an immediate danger to clients or the public, may be allowed to continue practicing law subject to conditions or under supervision or periodic evaluation.[184]

## § 4-1.6 LAWYER DISCIPLINARY JURISDICTION, MULTIJURISDICTIONAL PRACTICE OF LAW, AND CHOICE OF LAW

### § 4-1.6(a) Introduction to Disciplinary Jurisdiction, Multijurisdictional Practice, and Choice of Law

It is so frequently stated, and perhaps overstated, as to have become a truism—the practice of law today is increasingly an interstate practice.[185] A lawyer located in one state may represent a client in another state about a matter that involves parties or property in yet a third state. Even the lawyer who primarily represents local clients may find that a client has become involved in a dispute when visiting another state or is party to a multistate transaction. Thriving businesses must compete and engage in

---

[180] *See* CENTER FOR PROF'L RESPONSIBILITY, AMERICAN BAR ASS'N, ANNOTATED STANDARDS FOR IMPOSING LAWYER SANCTIONS at 49 (American Bar Ass'n, 2015) (maintaining that while most states allow an application for readmission after disbarment, "the presumption should be against readmission").

[181] CHARLES W. WOLFRAM, MODERN LEGAL ETHICS § 3.5.4 (West, 1986).

[182] MODEL RULES FOR LAWYER DISCIPLINARY ENFORCEMENT R. 21.D.

[183] *Id.*, R. 21, Commentary.

[184] *See* STANDARDS FOR IMPOSING LAWYER SANCTIONS, Standard 2.7 (American Bar Ass'n, 1992). *See generally* CENTER FOR PROF'L RESPONSIBILITY, AMERICAN BAR ASS'N, ANNOTATED STANDARDS FOR IMPOSING LAWYER SANCTIONS at 79–91 (American Bar Ass'n, 2015).

[185] On the growth of interstate law practice, see generally Samuel J. Brakel & Wallace D. Loh, *Regulating the Multistate Practice of Law*, 50 WASH. L. REV. 699, 699–700 (1975); H. Geoffrey Moulton, Jr., *Federalism and Choice of Law in the Regulation of Legal Ethics*, 82 MINN. L. REV. 73, 81–84 (1997); Fred C. Zacharias, *Federalizing Legal Ethics*, 73 TEX. L. REV. 335, 345–57 (1994).

transactions across state lines. Excessive barriers to interstate practice not only impair effective representation by lawyers, but also add unjustified costs to their clients.

While conducting the regular practice of law within the borders of a state is permissible only for those regularly admitted to that state's bar, Rule 5.5 of the Model Rules of Professional Conduct recognizes that there are occasions on which a client's right to the counsel of his choice or the interstate nature of a matter justifies affording limited and usually temporary permission to an out-of-state lawyer to provide legal services in the forum state. Rule 5.5 thus reduces barriers to interstate practice, while still accounting for the state's interest in ensuring the quality and ethical behavior of attorneys practicing within the borders of the state.

Paragraphs (c) and (d) of Rule 5.5 establish background principles that provide for a limited form of admission to practice.[186] The rule recognizes such quasi-licensure categories as admission *pro hac vice* before a tribunal[187] and service as in-house counsel.[188] The rule extends further to allow a lawyer admitted in another jurisdiction to provide temporary legal services when associated with local lawyer,[189] for alternative dispute resolution proceedings for which admission *pro hac vice* is not required,[190] and which arise out of or are reasonably related to the lawyer's practice in another jurisdiction.[191] If federal or state law otherwise authorizes provision of services, Rule 5.5 does not contradict that authorization.[192]

While there is considerable variation among the states in wording and elaboration on authorized practice of law within a state and accommodation to multijurisdictional practice, the vast majority of states follow the basic parameters set forth in Model Rule 5.5. In addition, following an American Bar Association model, many states allow temporary practice for out-of-jurisdiction lawyers when a major disaster has occurred. A lawyer not admitted to practice may enter the state to temporarily provide pro bono legal services to those affected by the disaster or to temporarily resume the practice of law in serving clients as part of the lawyer's practice in the home jurisdiction where the disaster occurred.[193]

For the most part, these exceptions to the general requirement that legal services be provided by those duly admitted to practice are limited not only in scope but also in duration, allowing an out-of-state lawyer to temporarily provide legal services in the state on a single occasion or for a single matter or series of matters. The general rule remains that an attorney who wishes to regularly engage in the practice of law within a particular state must be properly licensed to do so in that state.

As Professor Stephen Gillers observes, "[t]he expanded authority that Rule 5.5 confers comes at a price. A lawyer who wishes, even on a temporary basis, to provide legal services in the jurisdiction must recognize the jurisdiction's interest in disciplining

---

[186] *See infra* § 4-1.6(b).

[187] *See infra* § 4-1.6(b)(2).

[188] *See infra* § 4-1.6(b)(5).

[189] *See infra* § 4-1.6(b)(1).

[190] *See infra* § 4-1.6(b)(3).

[191] *See infra* § 4-1.6(b)(4).

[192] *See infra* § 4-1.6(b)(6).

[193] *See infra* § 4-1.6(b)(7).

him or her for misconduct in connection with those services."[194] Under Rule 8.5(a) of the Model Rules of Professional Conduct, a lawyer who provides or offers legal services in a state becomes subject to the disciplinary authority of that state.[195]

Rule 8.5 addresses the inevitable consequences that follow from the simple fact that lawyers increasingly do practice across state lines, whether licensed in more than one state or not. In light of the reality of interstate legal practice and the growing number of attorneys who are admitted in multiple states, Rule 8.5 confirms the jurisdictional authority of the particular state to discipline both those lawyers admitted to that state's bar, wherever their conduct may occur, and those lawyers not admitted in state who choose to provide or offer legal services in that state.[196]

Moreover, Rule 8.5 establishes simple and straightforward choice of law rules to determine which set of ethics rules should govern when a lawyer's professional license or conduct implicates the disciplinary authority of more than one jurisdiction.[197] Although the occasions for a true conflict—in which the ethics rules of different states or jurisdictions appear to impose contradictory duties upon a lawyer—are likely to be rare, Rule 8.5 is designed to specify the single ethical regime that governs any particular occasion of professional conduct.

## § 4-1.6(b) Multijurisdictional Practice of Law

### *§ 4-1.6(b)(1) Temporary Practice in Association with State Lawyer*

Under Rule 5.5(c)(1) of the Model Rules of Professional Conduct, a lawyer admitted to practice and in good standing in another United States jurisdiction may temporarily provide legal services within the borders of a state (or territory) when the lawyer does so in association with a lawyer admitted in that state who actively participates in the matter. As long as a lawyer regularly admitted to practice in the state is an active participant in the representation, and provided that the out-of-state lawyer's representation does not involve appearance before a tribunal (which would require admission *pro hac vice*),[198] the out-of-state lawyer's provision of legal services does not constitute the unauthorized practice of law.

Rule 5.5(c)(1) contemplates meaningful involvement in the representation by the locally-associated lawyer who, in the words of Comment 8, "share[s] responsibility for the representation of the client." In sum, when local counsel is fully associated in the provision of legal services and is not merely a passive front or mail-drop, the entry of an out-of-state lawyer to provide legal advice or other representation to a client is permitted.

Even when another lawyer admitted in the state is associated with the representation, however, the privilege granted to the out-of-state lawyer to provide legal services remains temporary in duration. If the lawyer intends to establish a sustained presence in the state, the lawyer must obtain regular admission to the state's bar. Under Rule 5.5(b), a lawyer not licensed in the state may not establish an office or "other systematic and continuous presence" in the jurisdiction for the purpose of practicing law.

---

[194] Stephen Gillers, *Lessons from the Multijurisdictional Practice Commission: The Art of Making Change*, 44 ARIZ. L. REV. 685, 715 (2002).

[195] *See infra* § 4-1.6(c).

[196] *See infra* § 4-1.6(c).

[197] *See infra* § 4-1.6(d).

[198] *See infra* § 4-1.6(b)(2).

Rule 5.5(b) clarifies that by maintaining a permanent presence in a state, through establishing an office or otherwise, or by representing that he is admitted to practice in the state, such as by targeting advertisement of legal services to potential clients in the state, an out-of-state lawyer has crossed the border and engaged in the unauthorized practice of law. Under Rule 5.5(b)(1), a lawyer who is not admitted to practice in a particular state may not "establish an office or otherwise systematic and continuous presence" in that state for the practice of law. Comment 4 explains that "[p]resence may be systematic and continuous even if the lawyer is not physically present here," thus encompassing the regular use of electronic media to create a permanent virtual presence within the state.[199]

Rule 5.5(b)(2) further prohibits an out-of-state lawyer from holding herself out to the public or otherwise representing that she is authorized to practice in the state. The rule treats such conduct as the equivalent of presence in the state and thus as constituting the unauthorized practice of law in the jurisdiction. For example, out-of-state attorneys who solicit state residents and entities, and who do not candidly disclaim admission to practice in the state, might be regarded by their affirmative advertisements as holding themselves out to the public as admitted to practice in that state. Not only may a lawyer fall into the unauthorized practice of law through such solicitations, but the lawyer may be held subject to the disciplinary jurisdiction of the state under Rule 8.5(a) by having "offer[ed] to provide any legal services in this jurisdiction."[200]

### *§ 4-1.6(b)(2) Temporary Practice Before a Tribunal—Admission* Pro Hac Vice

Under Rule 5.5(c)(2), a lawyer admitted and in good standing in another United States jurisdiction may provide legal services that are related to a pending or potential proceeding before a tribunal in another state if the lawyer (or another person that the lawyer is assisting) is or reasonably anticipates being authorized by law or order to appear before the tribunal.

The purpose of the *pro hac vice* privilege is to acknowledge the out-of-state lawyer who has a special need to represent a client on a single, generally unexpected occasion in the courts of this state. Thus, "it should be stressed that *pro hac vice* admission of an out-of-state attorney is an accommodation to be made on an infrequent basis rather than a means by which the out-of-state attorney may conduct a practice in the forum state."[201] As the Indiana Court of Appeals has explained, "pro hac vice admission should only be occasionally permitted as a courtesy towards other state bars and not as a continuing practice to avoid membership in our bar or compliance with our disciplinary rules."[202]

As the Supreme Court emphasized in *New Hampshire v. Piper*, "the decision on whether to grant *pro hac vice* status to an out-of-state lawyer is purely discretionary."[203] In a criminal case, however, under the Sixth Amendment of the United States

---

[199] *See* In re Charges of Unprofessional Conduct No. 39302, 884 N.W.2d 661, 663 (Minn. 2016) (holding by a closely-divided vote "that engaging in email communications with people in Minnesota may constitute the unauthorized practice of law in Minnesota, in violation of Minn. R. Prof. Conduct 5.5(a), even if the lawyer is not physically present in Minnesota").

[200] *See* In Re Murgatroyd, 741 N.E.2d 719, 721 (Ind. 2001).

[201] Michael A. DiSabatino, Annotation, Attorney's Right to Appear Pro Hac Vice in State Court, 20 A.L.R.4th 855, 861 (1983).

[202] Hanson v. Spolnik, 685 N.E.2d 71, 74 n.1 (Ind. Ct. App. 1997).

[203] 470 U.S. 274, 277 n.2 (1985) (citing Leis v. Flynt, 439 U.S. 438, 442 (1979) (per curiam)).

Constitution, a defendant's " 'right to the counsel of his choice includes the right to have an out-of-state lawyer admitted *pro hac vice*.' "[204]

With respect to appearance before a tribunal other than a state court or administrative agency, Rule 5.5(d)(2) permits the lawyer to provide such legal services when authorized by law or order. For example, if a federal court located in a state has granted admission, on a regular or temporary (*pro hac vice*) basis to a lawyer not admitted in the state in which that federal court sits, the rule recognizes the authority of the federal court and does not regard the lawyer's appearance and participation in such a matter as the unauthorized practice of law.

Under Rule 5.5(c)(2), if the lawyer "reasonably expects" to be authorized to appear before a tribunal, the lawyer also may provide legal services that "are in or reasonably related to a pending or potential proceeding" before that tribunal. A lawyer anticipating being admitted *pro hac vice* before a tribunal in another state may meet with the client, interview prospective witnesses, review documents, and even take depositions in the state, provided that the lawyer engages in such conduct temporarily while reasonably expecting to be admitted *pro hac vice*.

### *§ 4-1.6(b)(3) Alternative Dispute Resolution Proceeding Related to Lawyer's Home Practice*

To encourage the use of various forms of alternative dispute resolution, Rule 5.5(c)(3) allows a lawyer not admitted in a state, but in good standing in another United States jurisdiction, to provide temporary representation in a pending or potential arbitration, mediation, or other alternative dispute resolution proceeding. The permission applies only if the matter arises out of or is reasonably related to the lawyer's practice in his home jurisdiction and if the forum does not require admission *pro hac vice*.

If the matter is already pending before a tribunal in a state, and thus any alternative dispute resolution proceeding is collateral to ongoing court litigation or a contested administrative case, the out-of-state lawyer must have been admitted *pro hac vice* before he could appear before that tribunal and participate in collateral dispute resolution efforts.[205] If, however, the matter is not yet pending in a tribunal, or may never be instituted in any tribunal, such as an arbitration or mediation being conducted as a substitute for and not an adjunct to litigation, then *pro hac vice* admission is not expected and may not even be available.

When *pro hac vice* admission is not required, the rule permits a lawyer to enter a state in which the lawyer is not admitted to temporarily represent a client in or provide other legal services related to an alternative dispute resolution proceeding in this state, provided that "the services arise out of or are reasonably related to the lawyer's practice in a jurisdiction in which the lawyer is admitted to practice." Thus, if the lawyer in his home state is representing a client who happens to become involved in a dispute that gives rise to an alternative dispute resolution proceeding located in another state, the lawyer may continue his regular representation of that client by participating in that proceeding. As with the other forms of multijurisdictional practice authorized by Rule

---

[204] United States v. Gonzalez-Lopez, 399 F.3d 924, 929 (8th Cir. 2005) (quoting United States v. Ries, 100 F.3d 1469, 1471 (9th Cir. 1996), *aff'd*, 548 U.S. 140 (2006)).

[205] *See supra* § 4-1.6(b)(2).

5.5, the lawyer may not establish a "systematic and continuous presence" in the state or hold himself out to potential clients as authorized to practice to law in that state.

### *§ 4-1.6(b)(4) Other Temporary Services Incidental to Lawyer's Home Practice*

Rule 5.5(c)(4) is a catch-all provision, allowing a lawyer admitted and in good standing in another jurisdiction to provide temporary legal services in a state in which the lawyer is not admitted if those services "arise out of or are reasonably related to the lawyer's practice in a jurisdiction in which the lawyer is admitted to practice." Thus, for example, if a lawyer admitted in another state and regularly representing a particular client in that state were to enter another state temporarily to provide legal advice to or representation of that client in a transaction being negotiated or consummated there, the lawyer's provision of those services plainly would not constitute the unauthorized practice of law. In this way, an out-of-state lawyer representing a client in the lawyer's home jurisdiction may provide temporary representation when that client's interstate activities touch upon another state.

The breadth of the "catch-all" provision is debated among both courts and scholars. In the closely-divided decision *professional Conduct No. 39302,*[206] the Minnesota Supreme Court addressed whether an out-of-state lawyer could properly represent his in-laws in negotiations about an in-state judgment collection matter when the lawyer's area of practice included judgment collection matters collateral to his regular environmental law practice. The four-justice majority held that a Colorado lawyer had engaged in the unauthorized practice of law when "[b]y multiple emails sent over several months," the lawyer "advised Minnesota clients on Minnesota law in connection with a Minnesota legal dispute and attempted to negotiate a resolution of that dispute with a Minnesota attorney."[207] Because his in-laws were not Colorado residents, had no prior attorney-client relationship with him, and the matter had no interstate or federal law dimension, the majority held the Colorado lawyer's legal representation was "unrelated to his environmental law and personal-injury practice in Colorado."[208] The court explicitly rejected the suggestion that the exception for services that "arise out of or are reasonably related to the lawyer's practice" could broadly encompass "expertise in any subject matter," an interpretation the majority feared would "allow[ ] the exception to swallow the rule."[209]

The Minnesota Supreme Court's majority interpretation of the exception is consistent with the position previously expressed by the state's disciplinary officer, who had opined in a bar journal comment that the provision may "allow a Chicago attorney to represent his Chicago real estate developer client in a commercial land purchase negotiation in Minnesota. It does not, however, allow that same Chicago lawyer to represent a Minneapolis resident who is buying homestead property in Burnsville, a purely Minnesota transaction."[210] Professor W. Bradley Wendell likewise reasons that "[t]his exception does *not* permit a lawyer to represent clients with no relationship to a

---

[206] 884 N.W.2d 661 (Minn. 2016).

[207] *Id.* at 666.

[208] *Id.* at 668.

[209] *Id.* at 669.

[210] Martin Cole, *Cross-Border Practice*, Bench & Bar of Minn. (Jan. 15, 2013), at lprb.mncourts.gov/articles/Articles/Cross-Border%20Practice.pdf.

representation ongoing in the lawyer's home jurisdiction.[211] For example, he says, "a North Carolina lawyer could not handle a transaction for a South Carolina client, taking place entirely in South Carolina," even "though it is an occasional rather than continuous practice in South Carolina."

By contrast, the three-justice dissent in *In re Charges of Unprofessional Conduct No. 39302*[212] argued that the " 'reasonably related' exception in Rule 5.5(c)(4) is a *broad*, catch-all exception that is intended to exempt circumstances" such as where the out-of-state lawyer has experience in the field and was contacted by the client in his home state. In this case, the Colorado lawyer had experience in the very area of judgment collections representation, including multiple trials and filings. Moreover, the lawyer did not reach into Minnesota to attract a client, but rather the Minnesota clients (his in-laws) affirmatively sought him out for help in Colorado. Responding to the majority's argument that this interpretation allows the exception to swallow the rule, the dissent said that while the "exception is broad, it does not encompass subject matters unrelated to the lawyer's practice."

The Minnesota dissent's interpretation of the "arising-out-of-and-reasonably-related" exception finds considerable support in the *Restatement of the Law Governing Lawyers*, which includes the same exception for authorized practice by an out-of-state lawyer whose "activities arise out of or are otherwise reasonably related to the lawyer's practice."[213] Indeed, the *Restatement* includes a similar illustration in which an Illinois trust and estates lawyer, while delivering in person to Florida a codicil to a longtime client who has moved to Florida, is introduced to the client's friend who also lives in Florida and who then asks the Illinois lawyer prepare estate planning arrangements for him as well.[214] The Illinois lawyer prepares the documents in his Illinois office, frequently communicating with the Florida client by telephone and mail, and then returns to Florida for the new client to execute the documents. The *Restatement* illustration concludes that the Illinois lawyer's legal services in his field of practice on behalf of both the original client who moved to Florida and the new client he met in Florida are permissible. What appears to be pivotal to the conclusion in the *Restatement* is that lawyer's regular field of practice is involved and that the out-of-state client initiated the request for legal services, rather than the lawyer holding himself out as a lawyer in the foreign state.

Note that it is the entry of the out-of-state lawyer into the other state as a counselor or representative of a client that implicates Rule 5.5. Provision by a lawyer of legal advice to a client in that lawyer's home state, even if that advice pertains to another state's law, does not constitute the practice of law in that other state. In other words, when it comes to authority to practice law in a jurisdiction, it is not the source of the law that is determinative, but the geographic location (or virtual location) of the lawyer in providing the legal services.

As with the other forms of multijurisdictional practice approved in Rule 5.5, even when the legal services arise out of or are related to the lawyer's practice in another state, the provision of those services within the borders of the other state must be

---

[211] W. BRADLEY WENDEL, PROFESSIONAL RESPONSIBILITY: EXAMPLES & EXPLANATIONS 514 (Wolters Kluwer, 5th ed., 2016).

[212] 884 N.W.2d at 670–72 (Anderson, J., dissenting).

[213] RESTATEMENT (THIRD) OF THE LAW GOVERNING LAWYERS § 3(3) (American Law Institute, 2000).

[214] *Id.* § 3, Ill. 5.

temporary. As provided under Rule 5.5(b), a lawyer who is not admitted to practice in the state may not establish a "systematic and continuous presence in this jurisdiction for the practice of law." And, again, the prohibited regular presence in the state includes, not only a lawyer's physical presence, but the equivalent of such presence through concerted and regular use of electronic media to establish a virtual presence within the borders of the state.[215]

### *§ 4-1.6(b)(5) House Counsel for an Entity*

Under Rule 5.5(d)(1), a lawyer who is admitted and in good standing before another United States jurisdiction may provide legal services in another state to the lawyer's employer, or its organizational affiliates, provided these are not services for which that state requires admission *pro hac vice*. The lawyer who provides legal services solely to her employer is commonly described as "house counsel" or "in-house counsel." As Comment 16 explains, permitting an attorney not licensed to practice in a state nonetheless to provide legal services solely to her employer "does not create an unreasonable risk to the client and others because the employer [client] is well situated to assess the lawyer's qualifications and the quality of the lawyer's work."

If, however, a lawyer not licensed in a particular state intends to establish a more permanent presence as counsel to an entity in that state, then about two-thirds of the states require the lawyer to register as house counsel.[216] A house counsel registration rule typically covers a lawyer who does maintain an office or other systematic and continuous presence in the state as counsel for a corporation, association, or other business, educational, or governmental entity. Once so registered, the lawyer may provide the full range of legal services ordinarily provided by house counsel, including offering legal advice and representing the client in transactional matters, but may not appear on behalf of the client in a state tribunal without securing admission *pro hac vice*.

In a recent addition to paragraph (d) of Model Rule 5.5, a "foreign lawyer"—that is, a lawyer admitted "in a foreign jurisdiction"—may also serve as house counsel for a client. However, the foreign lawyer may not advise "on the law of this or another jurisdiction or of the United States." Even when given to the lawyer's employer, any advice on the law of an American jurisdiction must be given directly to the employer by, or be based upon advice given to the house counsel by, "a lawyer who is duly licensed and authorized by the jurisdiction to provide such advice."

### *§ 4-1.6(b)(6) Legal Services Authorized by Federal or Other Law*

Under Rule 5.5(d)(2), a lawyer who is admitted and in good standing before another United States jurisdiction may provide such legal services within another state as are authorized by federal or state law. If a federal or state statute, court rule, or judicial precedent allows someone who is not licensed as a lawyer in a state to offer certain kinds of services that otherwise could be considered legal in nature, then the provision of those services by someone who happens to be a lawyer admitted in another jurisdiction would not constitute the unauthorized practice of law.

---

[215] *See supra* § 4-1.6(b)(1).

[216] *See* American Bar Ass'n, Center for Prof'l Responsibility, Corporate Admissions Standards, at http://www.americanbar.org/groups/professional_responsibility/committees_commissions/commission_on_multi jurisditional_practice/mjp_uplchart.html.

As examples under state law, states typically authorize the preparation of tax returns by accountants; preparation of certain legal documents incident to real estate transactions by realtors; and limited representation by nonlawyer victim counselors in domestic violence and sexual assault matters. As examples under federal law, an attorney need not be licensed in a particular state before practicing before a federal agency such as the Merit Systems Protection Board,[217] a federal government attorney is not obliged to obtain a license from a state before practicing federal law in that state,[218] and an attorney whose practice is limited to federal immigration matters need not be admitted to a particular state bar.[219]

### *§ 4-1.6(b)(7) Legal Services Following a Major Disaster*

When a community has suffered a major disaster, residents of that community may be in desperate need of legal services, a need that could be addressed at least in part by out-of-state lawyers willing to provide pro bono services. In addition, the affected community's lawyers may find themselves temporarily exiled to surrounding states, while desiring to resume legal services for their clients from the lawyers' home jurisdiction where the disaster occurred. If strictly applied, a state's unauthorized practice of law rules would preclude provision of such legal services within the borders of that state, because it is the geographic location of the lawyer that constitutes the practice of law within a particular state.

In the wake of Hurricanes Katrina and Rita in 2005, which devastated the gulf regions of Louisiana, Mississippi, and Alabama, the American Bar Association in 2007 approved a model court rule to ease restrictions on practice of law across state borders after a major disaster. The rule encourages pro bono legal services to persons affected by a major disaster and allows lawyers forced to flee from their home jurisdiction by a major disaster to resume the practice of law temporarily in a different location.[220] As of 2016, nearly half of the states had adopted such a rule, with many others considering it.

After a major disaster has occurred, a lawyer not admitted to practice there may enter the state to temporarily provide pro bono legal services to those affected by a disaster or to temporarily practice law in serving clients as part of the lawyer's existing practice in his home jurisdiction where the disaster occurred. The determination of the existence of a major disaster will be made by the highest court of the jurisdiction in which the disaster occurred.[221]

First, the special rule allows lawyers not admitted in a state to provide pro bono services to those who have experienced a major disaster in the state or to persons displaced to the state by a major disaster in another state.[222] Pro bono services must be provided under the assignment and supervision of an established not-for-profit bar

---

[217] Augustine v. Dept. of Veterans Affairs, 429 F.3d 1334, 1339–42 (Fed. Cir. 2005).

[218] 28 C.F.R. 77.2(h); *see Augustine*, 429 F.3d at 1341 ("[W]hile government attorneys must abide by the ethical codes of conduct of each state in which they perform their services, they do not have to be licensed by those states to practice law.").

[219] Attorney Disciplinary Bd. v. Mendez, 855 N.W.2d 156, 160 (Iowa 2014); Ill. Adv. Op. 13–08.

[220] *See* ABA Delegates Approve Model Court Rule Easing Practice Restrictions During Disaster, 2007 U.S.L.W. 2510.

[221] American Bar Ass'n, Model Court Rule on Provision of Legal Services Following Determination of Major Disaster (2007).

[222] *Id.* at (b).

association, pro bono program, or legal services program, or an organization specifically designated by the highest court in the state.

Second, the rule allows lawyers admitted to practice in another state to provide legal services in the state on a temporary basis, if those legal services "arise out of and [are] reasonably related to that lawyer's practice of law" in the jurisdiction or area of a jurisdiction where the major disaster occurred.[223] This part of the rule permits an out-of-state lawyer who has been displaced to resume her practice of law, temporarily setting up an office in another state to continue to serve clients as part of the existing practice in the home jurisdiction.

The major disaster court rule does not permit court appearances, unless the lawyer is admitted *pro hac vice* or the state's highest court grants "blanket permission" to so appear.[224]

### § 4-1.6(c) Disciplinary Jurisdiction

Under Rule 8.5(a) of the Model Rules of Professional Conduct, a lawyer admitted to practice in a particular state is, of course, fully subject to the disciplinary authority of that state, including the power to continue or terminate the lawyer's license to practice. A lawyer who is not regularly admitted to practice in a state, but who nonetheless does in fact practice law there, whether authorized or not and whether temporarily or regularly, thereby submits himself to the disciplinary jurisdiction of this state.

In confirming that a lawyer licensed in a state is subject to that state's disciplinary authority, even if the lawyer's conduct occurs elsewhere, Rule 8.5(a) is consistent with the longstanding provision for reciprocal discipline of a state's lawyers who are disciplined for professional misconduct in another jurisdiction.[225] Under reciprocal discipline, a lawyer admitted to practice in a particular jurisdiction who is the subject of professional discipline in another state or territory or in federal court presumptively will be disciplined in the same manner in that particular state as well.[226] As Professors Geoffrey Hazard and William Hodes and attorney Peter Jarvis explain, this rule "might be regarded as giving extraterritorial reach to disciplinary authorities, but licensure can also be regarded as a 'status' that states may freely regulate, even if the status is enjoyed without the state as well as within its borders."[227]

An attorney who is admitted *pro hac vice* before a court[228] or an attorney who is authorized to practice law within the state in the capacity of house counsel employed by a business, educational, or governmental entity,[229] becomes subject to the disciplinary jurisdiction of the state. While the state may not technically disbar a non-licensed attorney who engages in professional misconduct while admitted *pro hac vice* or registered as house counsel, the court may revoke admission *pro hac vice* or registration

---

[223] *Id.* at (c).

[224] *Id.* at (e).

[225] On reciprocal discipline, see generally CENTER FOR PROF'L RESPONSIBILITY, AMERICAN BAR ASS'N, ANNOTATED STANDARDS FOR IMPOSING LAWYER SANCTIONS at 102–06 (American Bar Ass'n, 2015).

[226] *See* MODEL RULES FOR LAWYER DISCIPLINARY ENFORCEMENT R. 22.

[227] 2 GEOFFREY C. HAZARD, JR., W. WILLIAM HODES & PETER R. JARVIS, THE LAW OF LAWYERING § 70.03 (Aspen, 4th ed., 2016).

[228] *See supra* § 4-1.6(b)(2).

[229] *See supra* § 4-1.6(b)(5).

as house counsel, preclude such admission or registration in the future, or refer the lawyer for reciprocal discipline in his home jurisdiction.

Beyond confirming a state's disciplinary authority over those lawyers who are formally admitted to full or limited practice, Rule 8.5(a) extends disciplinary jurisdiction over any attorney who "provides or offers to provide legal services" in the jurisdiction. If a lawyer not licensed in the state engages in temporary and limited practice as authorized by Rule 5.5,[230] she may be disciplined for violation of the state's Rules of Professional Conduct. In addition, an out-of-state lawyer who offers to provide legal services in the state, such as by targeting advertising toward potential clients located in the state, has submitted to that disciplinary authority.[231] An out-of-state lawyer who engages in the unauthorized practice of law also comes under the disciplinary authority of that state.

Given that such lawyers are neither admitted to regular practice nor granted formal permission for temporary practice *pro hac vice* or by registration as house counsel, the state cannot withdraw any privileges (although a lawyer's professional misconduct certainly would be a matter of record in the event of a future application for regular admission, admission *pro hac vice*, or registration as house counsel). However, the court could enjoin a lawyer who engaged in professional misconduct while temporarily practicing law in a state from continued legal practice there. And, again, the court may refer the matter for reciprocal discipline in the lawyer's home jurisdiction. In *Attorney Disciplinary Board v. Carpenter*,[232] the Iowa Supreme Court explained that, through its equitable powers, its "authority to discipline non-Iowa licensed attorneys includes the ability to fashion practice limitations through our injunctive and equitable powers that are equivalent to license suspension, disbarment, or other sanctions related to an attorney's license."

A brief note is in order regarding disciplinary authority for federal government lawyers who primarily practice in federal court. The Citizens Protection Act of 1998 makes state ethics rules and local federal rules applicable to federal government attorneys:

> An attorney for the Government shall be subject to State laws and rules, and local Federal court rules, governing attorneys in each State where such attorney engages in that attorney's duties, to the same extent and in the same manner as other attorneys in that State.[233]

Thus, a federal government attorney is bound by the professional conduct rules that have been adopted in the state or states where he practices.

---

[230] *See supra* § 4-1.6(b).

[231] Margaret Raymond, *Inside, Outside: Cross-Border Enforcement of Attorney Advertising Restrictions*, 43 AKRON L. REV. 801, 803, 810, 815 (2010) (observing that Rule 8.5 "could certainly be interpreted to permit imposing discipline on a lawyer who has advertised in a jurisdiction on the ground that such advertising amounted to an 'offer to provide' services in the jurisdiction," but that states with stricter regulation on lawyer advertising have not enforced those rules against out-of-state lawyers, thereby putting their own lawyers at a competitive disadvantage).

[232] 781 N.W.2d 263, 269–70 (Iowa 2010).

[233] 28 U.S.C. § 530B.

### § 4-1.6(d) Choice of Law for Exercise of Disciplinary Authority

Rule 8.5(b) of the Model Rules of Professional Conduct sets forth choice of law rules to determine which jurisdiction's ethical regime should govern when either the lawyer is licensed in more than one state (or territory) or the professional conduct implicates more than one state (or territory). Paragraph (b) of Rule 8.5 is not a jurisdictional limitation on disciplinary authority, and indeed paragraph (a) of the same rule confirms that any lawyer licensed or practicing law in a state is subject to that state's disciplinary authority. Rather, when a lawyer is potentially subject to conflicting ethical rules from more than one jurisdiction, Rule 8.5(b) creates the framework for determining which rule from which jurisdiction establishes the substantive principles of professional ethics that apply in a particular case.

The supposed variation of disciplinary codes from state to state is frequently identified as a troublesome obstacle to conscientious, efficient, and ethical practice by attorneys representing interstate concerns. One commentator well-summarized the arguments of those deprecating the "balkanization" of ethical regulation of lawyers in America:

> According to the rhetoric of the organized bar, the increasing diversity in conduct rules and the growth of multijurisdictional practice have created an "increasingly serious problem" that poses "grave difficulties" for multistate practitioners. Lawyers' inability to determine in advance which of several inconsistent rules might later be applied to their conduct "undermines compliance with legal ethics codes." Commentators, lamenting the "critical level of interstate disparity in professional ethics," complain that lawyers' "ability to find guidance in a single state's code of conduct has virtually disappeared," explain that law firms are "bedeviled" by conflicting standards that might apply to a team of multiply-admitted practitioners working on a single transaction, and predict that inconsistency in state ethics rules will harm the attorney-client relationship.[234]

However, Professor Geoffrey Moulton concludes that these "calls to alarm" are exaggerated, that few state ethical rules are in direct and irreconcilable conflict, and that inconsistencies in applicable disciplinary standards are unlikely to create irresolvable problems when applied to real-world situations rather than cleverly crafted hypotheticals. Moreover, he reminds us that, even today, "the work of many (or even most) lawyers is confined to one state."[235]

Given the substantial and growing harmony among the states on legal ethics with the widespread adoption of the American Bar Association's Model Rules of Professional Conduct, subject to mostly minor variations from state to state, a true conflict of laws is unlikely to arise in most cases and the outcome ordinarily will not turn on disparities in ethical regimes.

Nonetheless, should a lawyer actually be caught in a situation where the ethical rules of multiple jurisdictions point in different directions, Comment 3 to Rule 8.5 explains that paragraph (b) is designed to ensure that "any particular conduct of a lawyer

---

[234] H. Geoffrey Moulton, Jr., *Federalism and Choice of Law in the Regulation of Legal Ethics*, 82 MINN. L. REV. 73, 99–100 (1997).

[235] *Id.* at 83.

shall be subject to only one set of rules of professional conduct." Moreover, by establishing simple rules that focus on the state in which the conduct occurred or had its predominant effect, Rule 8.5(b) strikes a balance between the disciplinary interests of the states involved and the lawyer's reasonable expectations.[236]

### *§ 4-1.6(d)(1) Choice of Law for Conduct Before a Tribunal*

Under Rule 8.5(b)(1), "for conduct in connection with a matter pending before a tribunal, the rules of the jurisdiction in which the tribunal sits" apply to the professional conduct, "unless the rules of the tribunal provide otherwise." Accordingly, if a lawyer is litigating a case before a particular state court, then the professional conduct rules of that state apply, regardless of the lawyer's state of licensure.

If a lawyer admitted in State A is practicing before the courts of State B, then the ethical rules of State B apply, to the extent of any divergence from State A's ethical rules. When practicing before federal tribunals, the lawyer must identify the ethical rules adopted by the federal tribunal, which may be the rules of the state in which the federal court sits, the federal court's own independently-promulgated rules, or some combination of the two.[237]

When a proceeding before a tribunal is anticipated, but the matter is not yet before the tribunal so as to be subject to its rules, the matter is evaluated by the alternative choice of law provision in Rule 8.5(b)(2).

### *§ 4-1.6(d)(2) Choice of Law for Other Matters*

For nonadjudicative matters or those not yet submitted to a tribunal, Rule 8.5(b)(2) directs application of "the rules of the jurisdiction in which the lawyer's conduct occurred," unless "the predominant effect of the conduct is in a different jurisdiction," in which case the rules of that other jurisdiction will apply. In cases of continuing uncertainty, the rule provides that the lawyer shall not be disciplined if the lawyer's conduct conformed to the ethical rules "of a jurisdiction in which the lawyer reasonably believes the predominant effect of the lawyer's conduct will occur." Thus, if the court finds that reasonable lawyers could disagree as to where the predominant effect of the lawyer's conduct will be felt, then the lawyer's expectation in that regard will receive appropriate deference.

To illustrate the workings of the rule for nonadjudicative matters, consider the potentially significant differences between the confidentiality rules of Iowa and the bordering state of South Dakota. Under Rule 1.6(c) of the Iowa Rules of Professional Conduct, a lawyer is *required* to disclose confidential information "to the extent the lawyer reasonably believes necessary to prevent imminent death or substantial bodily harm."[238] By contrast, South Dakota permits a lawyer to reveal confidential information

---

[236] *See, e.g.*, In re Disciplinary Action Against Overboe, 745 N.W.2d 852, 861–62 (Minn. 2008) (holding that, for a lawyer admitted to practice in Minnesota and North Dakota, (1) when he deceptively labeled a personal bank account as a trust account to avoid claims by judgment creditors, the North Dakota rules would apply because the account was in a North Dakota bank and judgment creditors were in North Dakota, but (2) when he made misrepresentations to and failed to cooperate with the Minnesota disciplinary authority, Minnesota rules would apply as the predominant effects were in Minnesota).

[237] W. BRADLEY WENDEL, PROFESSIONAL RESPONSIBILITY: EXAMPLES & EXPLANATIONS 6 (Wolters Kluwer, 5th ed., 2016) (listing three approaches that federal courts may take, by adopting (1) the ABA Model Rules, (2) the rules of the forum state, or (3) "adopt idiosyncratic rules that are not necessarily the same as the ABA or state version of the disciplinary rules").

[238] IOWA RULES OF PROF'L CONDUCT R. 32:1.6(c).

only "to prevent the client from committing a criminal act that the lawyer believes is likely to result in imminent death or substantial bodily harm."[239] Thus, Iowa mandates disclosure when the threat of death or serious bodily harm is imminent and regardless of the source of that threat, while South Dakota permits (but does not mandate) disclosure to prevent imminent death or substantial bodily harm and only grants such permission when that harm to a person will result from the client's criminal act.[240]

Suppose that a lawyer either licensed or practicing in both Iowa and South Dakota were to learn from a client of an imminent threat to human life that either was not related to anticipated criminal activity (which might include threats of self-harm by the client, if suicide is not regarded as a criminal act) or at least would not result from a criminal act committed by the client (as opposed to someone else). In either circumstance, the lawyer would be prohibited from disclosing that information under the South Dakota confidentiality rule, while the lawyer would be affirmatively required to disclose the information as necessary to prevent the death under the Iowa confidentiality rule. In sum, if such an admittedly unlikely scenario did present itself, a lawyer licensed or practicing in both states would find it impossible to simultaneously comply with both ethical directives.

Under Rule 8.5(b)(2), the lawyer in this scenario would be obliged to conform to the ethics rule of the state in which the predominant effect of the lawyer's conduct would occur, which presumably would be the state where a person faced the imminent threat of death (as it is difficult to imagine a more "predominant effect" of professional conduct than the loss of human life by the failure of the lawyer to act to prevent it). If the person at risk of death were located in South Dakota, the lawyer would be barred from disclosing the information (although if ever a moral case for civil disobedience could be justified, violating confidentiality to save a human life would surely be that case).[241] If the person at risk of death instead were located in Iowa, the lawyer not only would be permitted but compelled to disclose the information to prevent that loss of life. If the person at risk of death were located in neither South Dakota nor Iowa, then one could make a reasonable argument either for focusing upon the place where the lawyer's conduct occurred, which presumably would be where the lawyer was acting as counsel on behalf of the client whose confidential information would be disclosed, or perhaps the third jurisdiction where the person at risk is located. If both choices are regarded as reasonable, then the lawyer's expectation about the predominant effect of her conduct would govern. Of course, in the unlikely event that a lawyer were ever faced with this dilemma, the

---

[239] S.D. RULES OF PROF'L CONDUCT R. 1.6(b)(1). Wisconsin, another state that borders Iowa, also has a confidentiality rule relating to prevention of death or substantial bodily harm that appears to conflict with Iowa's mandatory disclosure rule. While Wisconsin, like Iowa, does require disclosure of information when human life is threatened, Wisconsin restricts that disclosure to circumstances where the threat of harm is attributable to the client's criminal (or fraudulent) conduct. *See* WIS. SUP. CT. RULE 20:1.6(b) (providing that a lawyer is required to reveal confidential information "to the extent the lawyer reasonably believes necessary to prevent the client from committing a criminal or fraudulent act that the lawyer reasonably believes is likely to result in death or substantial bodily harm"). However, Wisconsin more broadly permits (but does not mandate) disclosure of confidential information "to prevent reasonably likely death or substantial bodily harm," regardless of the source of the threat. *Id.* 20:1.6(c). Thus, a lawyer could avoid violating either rule by permissively disclosing under the Wisconsin rule the information that is mandated under the Iowa rule. If a lawyer deliberately or mistakenly chose not to disclose, the lawyer would stand in violation of the Iowa rule but remain within the bounds of discretion under the Wisconsin rule.

[240] On the exception to confidentiality to prevent death or bodily harm, see *infra* § 4-6.6(c).

[241] *See* Russell G. Pearce, *To Save a Life: Why a Rabbi and a Jewish Lawyer Must Disclose a Client Confidence*, 29 LOY. L.A. L. REV. 1771, 1776–79 (1996).

location of both client and person at risk probably would be the same, making the applicable jurisdiction even more plain.

### *§ 4-1.6(d)(3) Choice of Law Agreements*

As added by the American Bar Association in 2013, Comment 5 to Rule 8.5 states: "With respect to conflicts of interest, in determining a lawyer's reasonable belief under paragraph (b)(2), a written agreement between the lawyer and client that reasonably specifies a particular jurisdiction as within the scope of that paragraph may be considered if the agreement was obtained with the client's informed consent confirmed in the agreement."

---

Once the applicable ethical rule of the governing jurisdiction is determined through the choice of law analytical framework set forth in paragraph (b) of Rule 8.5, that jurisdiction's rule of professional conduct then establishes the standard for all potential disciplinary actions in all jurisdictions that have disciplinary authority over the lawyer. As Comment 6 to Rule 8.5 explains, "[i]f two admitting jurisdictions were to proceed against a lawyer for the same conduct, they should, in applying [Rule 8.5(b)], identify the same governing ethics rules."

# Chapter 4-2

# ADVERTISING FOR AND SOLICITATION OF CLIENTS: INFORMATION ABOUT LEGAL SERVICES

**By Gregory C. Sisk**

*Table of Sections*

§ 4-2.1 Introduction to Lawyer Advertising and Solicitation
§ 4-2.2 History of Lawyer Advertising and Solicitation
§ 4-2.3 The Lawyer's Duty Not to Make a False or Misleading Statement About Professional Services
§ 4-2.4 Advertising or Informing About Legal Services
§ 4-2.5 The Prohibition on Direct Solicitation of Prospective Clients
§ 4-2.6 Prohibition of "Pay-to-Play" Political Contributions in Exchange for Legal Work

## § 4-2.1 INTRODUCTION TO LAWYER ADVERTISING AND SOLICITATION

The legal profession traditionally prohibited all forms of lawyer advertising and imposed strict regulations on solicitation beyond the lawyer's circle of friends and social connections. These restrictions were seen as upholding the professional image of lawyers. Over time, more and more lawyers resisted the advertising ban, arguing lawyers were left at an economic disadvantage and citizens were left at legal risk because they were denied information about legal rights. The advertising restrictions came under constitutional challenge when the Supreme Court recognized commercial speech as protected under the First Amendment.

Today, under the Model Rules of Professional Conduct, lawyer advertising is forthrightly accepted (even if not universally admired). Regulation of advertising now is more narrowly focused on preventing false or misleading communications. By contrast, direct solicitation of clients by lawyers remains forbidden, with limited exceptions. Under the Model Rules, the lawyer must avoid false or misleading communications about legal services;[1] may advertise legal services through written, mailed, recorded, electronic, broadcast, or internet communications;[2] may communicate about fields of practice and specialization;[3] and may indicate professional status through firm names, letterhead, and other professional designations.[4] However, the lawyer may not engage

[1] *See infra* § 4-2.3.

[2] *See infra* § 4-2.4(a) to (e).

[3] *See infra* § 4-2.4(f).

[4] *See infra* § 4-2.4(g).

in direct solicitation of prospective clients[5] and may not employ political contributions to obtain a government legal engagement or appointment for legal services by a judge.[6]

While the formal regulations on advertising of legal services have been relaxed considerably over the years, what is permissible for a lawyer in terms of marketing schemes and what is wise in terms of building a long-term successful career in the profession may not be synonymous. Nicholas Critelli, a former state bar president, advises that "[t]he shortsighted lawyer who engages in sanctioned but unrestrained and undignified public advertising" may suffer damage to his reputation with colleagues and judges that outweighs any temporary financial advantage.[7] The matter of lawyer advertising has largely moved away from the regime of government regulation to the realms of professional reputation and individual character.

## § 4-2.2 HISTORY OF LAWYER ADVERTISING AND SOLICITATION

Before 1977, most states maintained an outright prohibition of solicitation and advertising by lawyers.[8] The practice of lawyer advertising was condemned by the organized bar as crass and commercial, beneath the dignity of the legal professional, and likely to undermine respect for lawyers and for the judicial system of which lawyers are an integral part.[9] Furthermore, on the view that the choice of a lawyer should be based upon her character and reputation, promotion of legal services like other consumer products was considered to be inherently deceptive to the public. Direct solicitation—commonly deprecated as "ambulance chasing"—was beyond the pale. During this period, the only acceptable means of marketing legal services beyond bar association referral programs was word of mouth from satisfied clients, admiring colleagues in the bar, or contacts developed through the lawyer's civic and social activities.

In 1977, everything—or nearly everything—changed. In *Bates v. State Bar of Arizona*, the Supreme Court held that commercial speech by lawyers is entitled to a limited but meaningful level of protection under the Free Speech Clause of the First Amendment.[10] The Court questioned the assertion that lawyer advertising would diminish the reputation of attorneys, refused to place any weight on professional etiquette, and rejected the argument that advertising by lawyers "inevitably will be

---

[5] *See infra* § 4-2.5.

[6] *See infra* § 4-2.6.

[7] Nicholas V. Critelli, Jr., *An Assessment of the Changes—Supreme Court Proposes Liberalized Ad Rules*, IOWA LAW., Sept. 2001, at 11.

[8] *See generally* James M. Altman, *Considering the A.B.A.'s 1908 Canons of Ethics*, 2008 J. PROF. L. 235, 320–26 (2008) (discussing the general prohibitions against advertising and solicitation in the ABA's 1908 Canons of Ethics, which were not superseded until 1970 by the 1969 Model Code of Professional Responsibility). There is evidence, however, that in the nineteenth century and earlier in America, lawyer advising was accepted or at least little remarked upon. *See* Geoffrey C. Hazard, Jr., Russell G. Pearce & Jeffrey W. Stempel, *Why Lawyers Should be Allowed to Advertise: A Market Analysis of Legal Services*, 58 N.Y.U. L. REV. 1084, 1085 n.2 (1983). On the history and evolution of lawyers advertising rules in Iowa, a state which maintained stricter regulation longer than most, see Gregory C. Sisk & Ellen Yee, *Lawyer Advertising in Iowa After 2012*, 62 DRAKE L. REV. 549 (2014).

[9] *See* Altman, *supra*, 2008 J. PROF. L. at 320–22 (explaining how the ABA's 1908 Canons of Ethics "marked a major change in American legal ethics" by prohibiting the previously accepted practice of lawyer advertising because, by the beginning of the 20th century, "it was commonly believed that a lawyer who acted like a tradesman in getting a client . . . would be less likely to act 'professionally' in representing that client").

[10] 433 U.S. 350, 383 (1977).

misleading."[11] The *Bates* Court instead concluded that "[a] rule allowing restrained advertising would be in accord with the bar's obligation to 'facilitate the process of intelligent selection of lawyers, and to assist in making legal services fully available.' "[12] Indeed, the Court highlighted the words of an Arizona state court judge who had dissented below, arguing that "the case should [be] framed in terms of 'the right of the public as consumers and citizens to know about the activities of the legal profession,' rather than as one involving merely the regulation of a profession."[13]

While the Supreme Court in *Bates* extended constitutional protection to lawyer communications with the public as promoting informed choices about legal services, the states are still permitted to restrain advertising that is false, deceptive, or misleading. Reasonable restrictions may be placed on the time, place, and manner of lawyer advertising.[14] Under the Court's commercial-speech doctrine, as articulated in *Central Hudson Gas & Electric Corp. v. Public Service Commission*, advertising about a lawful activity may be regulated by the government only if (1) the governmental interest is substantial, (2) the regulation directly and materially advances that government interest, and (3) the regulation is narrowly drawn.[15]

Although the door to lawyer advertising was opened in *Bates*—and opened widely—the states have retained a significant role in protecting the public from deceptive communications.[16] In *In re R. M. J.*,[17] the Court acknowledged that "[t]he public's comparative lack of knowledge, the limited ability of the professions to police themselves, and the absence of any standardization in the 'product' renders advertising for professional services especially susceptible to abuses that the States have a legitimate interest in controlling."

While the rules restricting advertising by lawyers have been greatly relaxed in the decades since *Bates*, the prohibition of personal solicitation of prospective clients, with whom the lawyer has no prior relationship, remains rather absolute.[18]

Shortly after *Bates*, the Supreme Court strongly affirmed the constitutional validity of the traditional ban on personal solicitation in its 1978 decision in *Ohralik v. Ohio State Bar Association*.[19] The case involved solicitation by a lawyer of an injured person in a hospital shortly after an accident—the classic "ambulance-chasing" scenario. Subsequently, in *Zauderer v. Office of Disciplinary Counsel*,[20] the Supreme Court again characterized face-to-face solicitation as "a practice rife with possibilities for overreaching, invasion of privacy, the exercise of undue influence, and outright fraud." The "coercive force of the personal presence of a trained advocate" and the "pressure on

---

11 *Id.* at 368–73.

12 *Id.* at 377 (quoting MODEL CODE OF PROF'L RESPONSIBILITY, Ethical Consideration 2–1 (American Bar Ass'n, 1976)).

13 *Id.* at 358 (citation omitted) (quoting In re Bates, 555 P.2d 640, 648 (Ariz. 1976) (Holohan, J., dissenting)).

14 *Id.* at 383–84.

15 Cent. Hudson Gas & Elec. Corp. v. Pub. Serv. Comm'n. of N.Y., 447 U.S. 557, 566 (1980).

16 *See infra* § 4-2.3.

17 In re R.M.J., 455 U.S. 191, 202 (1982).

18 *See infra* § 4.2-5.

19 436 U.S. at 449, 457–67.

20 471 U.S. 626, 641 (1985).

the potential client for an immediate yes-or-no answer to the offer of representation" justifies strong controls on this form of solicitation.[21]

In 1993, in *Edenfield v. Fane*,[22] the Supreme Court struck down Florida's ban on in-person solicitation of clients by certified public accountants as a violation of the First Amendment when communicating truthful, nondeceptive information about lawful commercial transactions. The Court distinguished *Ohralik* on the grounds that (1) unlike a CPA, a lawyer is "a professional trained in the art of persuasion," and (2) the "typical client of a CPA is far less susceptible to manipulation than the young accident victim in *Ohralik*."[23] Still, the Court held that solicitation was a form of speech entitled to some constitutional protection. Moreover, certain language in *Edenfield*—particularly the statement that " '[b]road prophylactic rules in the area of free expression are suspect' "[24] and the emphasis that "the clients in *Ohralik* were approached at a moment of high stress and vulnerability"[25]—could be cited to support an argument for a less absolute prohibition in the area of lawyer solicitation and in favor of regulations that focus on the circumstances of the solicitation.[26]

Nonetheless, leading commentators suggest that the *Edenfield* holding is not likely to cause "the Supreme Court [to] reverse field and clothe real-time lawyer solicitations for pecuniary gain with the same constitutional protection as advertising generally."[27]

## § 4-2.3 THE LAWYER'S DUTY NOT TO MAKE A FALSE OR MISLEADING STATEMENT ABOUT PROFESSIONAL SERVICES

Rule 7.1 of the Model Rules of Professional Conduct establishes the general standard for all communications by a lawyer about legal services to any listener: statements may not be "false or misleading." This standard well-comports with the Supreme Court's ruling in *Bates v. State Bar of Arizona*,[28] which extended constitutional free speech protection to advertising of legal services and ruled that "[a]dvertising that is false, deceptive, or misleading of course is subject to restraint." Rule 7.1 applies not only to communications that constitute lawyer advertising as such, but any statement by a lawyer about legal services.

As Professors Geoffrey Hazard and William Hodes and attorney Peter Jarvis emphasize, "[w]hen a lawyer makes a statement to which Rule 7.1 applies, that

[21] *Id.* at 642.

[22] 507 U.S. 761, 763, 766–77 (1993).

[23] *Id.* at 775.

[24] *Id.* at 777.

[25] *Id.* at 775–76.

[26] *See* 48 ROBERT P. SCHUWERK & LILLIAN HARDWICK, HANDBOOK OF TEXAS LAWYER AND JUDICIAL ETHICS: TEXAS PRACTICE SERIES § 12.03 (Thomson-Reuters, 2016) (observing that all of the rationales in *Edenfield* for overturning an absolute prohibition on solicitation by CPAs, except for the lawyer's skills as a trained advocate, would apply to lawyer solicitation, and speculating that the future may see a movement toward "a differential solicitation standard depending on the context in which the solicitation occurred"); MONROE H. FREEDMAN & ABBE SMITH, UNDERSTANDING LAWYERS' ETHICS § 11.14 (LexisNexis 4th ed. 2010) (arguing generally that, even under the lowest level of constitutional protection, a lawyer "who can show that her solicitation did not in fact involve evils like misrepresentation, overreaching, or harassment cannot properly be disciplined").

[27] 2 GEOFFREY C. HAZARD, JR., W. WILLIAM HODES & PETER R. JARVIS, THE LAW OF LAWYERING § 61.03(Aspen, 4th ed., 2016).

[28] 433 U.S. 350, 383 (1977); *see supra* § 4-2.2.

statement must be scrupulously accurate."[29] Beyond being literally truthful, however, a lawyer must not deceive the target of the communication through clever indirection or by concealing qualifying factors. Even a statement that is true may be misleading because additional information is omitted that is necessary to place the statement in context for a more complete understanding. Rule 7.1 expressly condemns a statement that "omits a fact necessary to make the statement considered as a whole not materially misleading."

Comment 2 to Rule 7.1 explains that a statement may be misleading "if there is a substantial likelihood that it will lead a reasonable person to formulate a specific conclusion about the lawyer or the lawyer's services for which there is no reasonable factual foundation." Thus, a statement by a lawyer about legal services is false or misleading if it is likely to create an unjustifiable expectation in the mind of the person hearing it. Indeed, while this language is no longer to be found in Model Rule 7.1, more than a dozen states continue to expressly prohibit a statement by a lawyer that "is likely to create an unjustified expectation about results" that may be achieved by the lawyer for the client.[30]

States traditionally have disfavored advertisements relating to the quality of a lawyer's services, under the view that qualitative claims about a lawyer's professional abilities were unverifiable. Direct prohibition of claims of quality services persist in a few states. Alabama, for example, requires lawyer advertising to contain the disclaimer that "[n]o representation is made that the quality of the legal services to be performed is greater than the quality of legal services performed by other lawyers."[31]

However, the courts increasingly have invalidated state regulations of lawyer advertising that impose a blanket prohibition on statements that relate to quality or past results and have rejected arguments that such advertising is inherently misleading. In *Alexander v. Cahill*,[32] the United States Court of Appeals for the Second Circuit upheld a First Amendment challenge to a New York rule prohibiting lawyer advertising that included client testimonials about still pending matters. While acknowledging that testimonials may mislead "if they suggest that past results indicate future performance," the court concluded that "not all testimonials do so, especially if they include a disclaimer."[33] In *Public Citizen, Inc. v. Louisiana Attorney Disciplinary Board*,[34] the Fifth Circuit struck down a Louisiana regulation that prohibited lawyering advertising about "past success or results obtained," holding that "[t]he evidence is insufficient to show that unverifiable claims in the targeted speech are so likely to be misleading that

---

29 2 GEOFFREY C. HAZARD, JR., W. WILLIAM HODES & PETER R. JARVIS, THE LAW OF LAWYERING § 59.04 (Aspen, 4th ed., 2016).

30 *See, e.g.*, ALASKA RULES OF PROF'L CONDUCT R. 7.1(b); ARIZ. RULES OF PROF'L CONDUCT R. 7.1(b); ARK. RULES OF PROF'L CONDUCT R. 7.1(b); COLO. RULES OF PROF'L CONDUCT R. 7.1(b); GA. RULES OF PROF'L CONDUCT R. 7.1(a)(2); HAW. RULES OF PROF'L CONDUCT R. 7.1(b); IDAHO RULES OF PROF'L CONDUCT R. 7.1(b); KAN. RULES OF PROF'L CONDUCT R. 7.1(b); MICH. RULES OF PROF'L CONDUCT R. 7.1(b); MO. RULES OF PROF'L CONDUCT R. 7.1(b); MONT. RULES OF PROF'L CONDUCT R. 7.1(b); NEV. RULES OF PROF'L CONDUCT R. 7.1(b); N.H. RULES OF PROF'L CONDUCT R. 7.1(b); N.J. RULES OF PROF'L CONDUCT R. 7.1(a)(2); N.D. RULES OF PROF'L CONDUCT R. 7.1(b); S.C. RULES OF PROF'L CONDUCT R. 7.1(b); S.D. RULES OF PROF'L CONDUCT R. 7.1(c)(2); UTAH RULES OF PROF'L CONDUCT R. 7.1(b).

31 ALA. RULES OF PROF'L CONDUCT R. 7.2(e).

32 598 F.3d 79 (2d Cir. 2010).

33 *Id.* at 92.

34 632 F.3d 212, 221–23 (5th Cir. 2011). *But see* In re PRB Docket No. 2002.093, 868 A.2d 709, 712 (Vt. 2005) ("Direct claims of expertise that are not truthful and factually verifiable . . . may be prohibited or restricted as unduly misleading.").

a complete prohibition is appropriate." Florida's former blanket prohibition on advertising past results likewise was invalidated in federal court.[35]

While an outright prohibition on all claims by lawyers regarding a level of quality or ability is constitutionally dubious, such claims remain fully subject to the general bar against communications that are "false or misleading." In *Bates v. State Bar of Arizona*,[36] the Supreme Court alluded to the "peculiar problems" associated with advertising claims about the quality of legal services and observed that "[s]uch claims probably are not susceptible of precise measurement or verification and, under some circumstances, might well be deceptive or misleading to the public, or even false." Nevada, for example, anticipates and allows statements "describing or characterizing the quality of the lawyer's services," but demands that such statements must be "subject to proof of verification."[37]

Assertions about quality often involve what Professors Geoffrey Hazard and William Hodes and attorney Peter Jarvis describe as "use of a lawyer's 'track record' as a selling point."[38] Given that "[m]any factors other than lawyer skill contribute to the result in any case," they explain that a lawyer's claims of ability "based upon results are especially likely to be misleading."[39] Thus, a lawyer who chooses to tout victories should (in addition to considering whether such boasts violate client confidentiality) include warnings that past results cannot predict the future.[40] Here too, Nevada's rule may lead the way, saying that a lawyer who refers to past successes must have been the lead counsel in the matter or primarily responsible—and still must make a disclaimer "that past results do not guarantee, warrant, or predict future cases."[41]

When a lawyer makes an outright promise or guarantee in communicating about legal services with prospective clients, the promise must be kept. Thus, many states specifically say that a lawyer who advertises a particular fee must then honor the advertised fee.[42] Even when not stated expressly, a lawyer's failure to perform services at the advertised fee plainly has engaged in deceptive advertising.

As with communications in general, context often matters greatly. Rule 7.1 applies with particular force to communications or advertisements to the general public that market a lawyer's legal services, recognizing that the necessarily-abbreviated nature of such messages means that subjective descriptions and claims of quality are more likely to mislead members of the public who are considering retention of a lawyer. By contrast, Rule 7.1 should not be a tool for over-scrutinizing the content of exchanges among professional colleagues at a bar convention or conversations by the lawyer with clients

---

[35] Rubenstein v. Florida Bar, 72 F. Supp. 3d 1298, 1311–18 (S.D. Fla. 2014).

[36] *Bates*, 433 U.S. at 366.

[37] NEV. RULES OF PROF'L CONDUCT R. 7.2(g).

[38] 2 GEOFFREY C. HAZARD, JR., W. WILLIAM HODES & PETER R. JARVIS, THE LAW OF LAWYERING § 59.07 (Aspen, 4th ed., 2016).

[39] *Id.*

[40] *See* N.Y. Ethics Op. 2015–7; 2012 N.C. Op. 1.

[41] NEV. RULES OF PROF'L CONDUCT R. 7.2(i).

[42] *See, e.g.*, ALA. RULES OF PROF'L CONDUCT R. 7.2(f); ARIZ. RULES OF PROF'L CONDUCT R. 7.2(d)(4); CAL. RULES OF PROF'L CONDUCT R. 7.2(Standard)(16); CONN. RULES OF PROF'L CONDUCT R. 7.2(g); FLA. RULES OF PROF'L CONDUCT R. 4–7.14(b)(5); MISS. RULES OF PROF'L CONDUCT R. 7.2(b); NEV. RULES OF PROF'L CONDUCT R. 7.2(f); N.Y. RULES OF PROF'L CONDUCT R. 7.2(m) & (n); PENN. RULES OF PROF'L CONDUCT R. 7.2(h)(2); S.C. RULES OF PROF'L CONDUCT R. 7.2(g); S.D. RULES OF PROF'L CONDUCT R. 7.2(g)(2); TEX. RULES OF PROF'L CONDUCT R. 7.04(i).

or prospective clients (who already have approached the lawyer) in the law office, assuming the statements made are not affirmatively false and misleading. The face-to-face nature of communications between the lawyer and those with whom the lawyer has already formed at least a nascent relationship not only reduces (or eliminates) the risk of improper influence, but also makes it more likely that the lawyer's statements will be placed in sufficient context during the course of ongoing discussions so as not to be misleading.

## § 4-2.4 ADVERTISING OR INFORMING ABOUT LEGAL SERVICES

### § 4-2.4(a) General Authorization of Lawyer Advertising

Rule 7.2(a) of the Model Rules of Professional Conduct authorizes a lawyer to "advertise services through written, recorded or electronic communication, including public media." Comment 1 explains that "organized information campaigns in the form of advertising" may "assist the public in learning about and obtaining legal services."

A lawyer may advertise through traditional print media, such as newspapers, periodicals, trade journals, and advertising shoppers. The simple listing in the telephone book may well remain the most common form of advertising or communication with the public about a lawyer's or law firm's services. As a form of "written" communication, as well as a type of "public media," advertising on billboards also is permitted.

Traditional electronic media, such as radio and television, may also be employed. Lawyer advertising on broadcast media has been subject to the greatest restrictions in the past and still is targeted for special rules in some states today.[43] The hosting of a web site by a lawyer or law firm is a form of advertising that is also authorized.[44] In addition, direct mail or email no longer is regarded as a type of personal solicitation but is treated simply as a particular form of advertising.[45]

Comment 2 to Rule 7.2 speaks to the substance of lawyer advertising, offering a non-exclusive list of information that may be disseminated, including lawyer's name and firm; address, email, website and telephone number; kinds of legal services; the lawyer's fee; foreign language ability; references; and, with consent, names of clients regularly represented.

The authorization of lawyer advertising found in Rule 7.2(a) is conditioned by the general proviso in Rule 7.1 that "[a] lawyer shall not make a false or misleading communication about the lawyer or the lawyer's services."[46]

Because Rule 7.2 is directed at advertising used by lawyers to procure clients, it does not apply when a lawyer is simply recognized, even as a professional, in other contexts. A lawyer appropriately may be identified by name and as a lawyer when campaigning for public office; when serving as a director or officer in business, civic, professional, and political organizations; and when authoring legal publications.

---

[43] *See infra* § 4-2.4(c).

[44] *See infra* § 4-2.4(e).

[45] *See infra* § 4-2.4(d)(1).

[46] *See supra* § 4-2.3.

### § 4-2.4(b) Advertising by Broadcast Media

As Professor John Watkins has observed, "[t]oday, television advertisements for legal services are as common as those for health clubs, home centers, and discount department stores—and every bit as tacky."[47] The average lawyer cringes when he sees television commercial depictions of advertising lawyers in a junkyard, surfacing from the water in scuba diving gear, appearing as a "rebel lawyer" in a cowboy costume, or hyped by celebrities.[48]

Nonetheless, severe restrictions on lawyer advertising through broadcast media would be vulnerable to challenge under the Supreme Court's line of commercial free speech decisions. The Court generally affords constitutional protection to the communication of accurate information in lawyer advertising.[49] Moreover, because many people, especially those of middle- and low-income, receive much of their information through electronic media, strict restrictions on broadcast advertising may significantly impede useful information about legal rights and the availability of legal services.

When it comes to radio and television broadcast media, the State of Iowa long had a deserved reputation for maintaining exceptionally stringent rules regarding lawyer advertising. Before 2013, the Iowa lawyer ethics rules provided that information could be communicated over radio or television "only by a single nondramatic voice, not that of the lawyer, and with no other background sound," and a television advertisement could not display anything other than the words in print being read by the "announcer." Under those restrictions, the viewer of lawyer television advertising in Iowa would see nothing beyond printed words scrolling across the screen and hear nothing other than a solitary voice speaking in a style that, while perhaps not a monotone, included very little inflection. And that voice could be anyone *except* the very lawyer whose legal services were being offered. Not surprisingly, few Iowa lawyers bothered to advertise by radio or television, given that, in the words of Dean Margaret Raymond, the Iowa rules had "taken all the fun out of lawyer ads."[50]

The Iowa State Bar Association justified tight controls on television advertising by lawyers because of the negative effects of such advertising on public perceptions of the legal profession.[51] In a 1983 study commissioned by the bar association, a randomly selected sample of Iowans from one urban county, were asked to evaluate the characteristics of lawyers, both before and then after the participants were shown a

---

[47] John J. Watkins, *Lawyer Advertising, the Electronic Media, and the First Amendment*, 49 ARK. L. REV. 739, 739 (1997).

[48] *See id.* at 739–40.

[49] *See* Mylene Brooks, *Lawyer Advertising: Is There Really a Problem?*, 15 LOY. L.A. ENT. L.J. 1, 20–26 (1994); Judith L. Maute, *Scrutinizing Lawyer Advertising and Solicitation Rules Under Commercial Speech and Antitrust Doctrine*, 13 HASTINGS CONST. L.Q. 487, 515–20 (1986); Bernadette Miragliotta, *First Amendment: The Special Treatment of Legal Advertising*, 1990 ANN. SURV. AM. L. 597, 621–27 (1992). *But see* Watkins, *supra*, 49 ARK. L. REV. at 775–82 (concluding that judicial precedent upholding strict constraints on television advertising apparently remain good law, but are "rather fragile precedents" and such constraints are questionable as a matter of policy).

[50] Margaret Raymond, *Inside, Outside: Cross-Border Enforcement of Attorney Advertising Restrictions*, 43 AKRON L. REV. 801, 802 (2010); *see also* W. BRADLEY WENDEL, PROFESSIONAL RESPONSIBILITY: EXAMPLES & EXPLANATIONS 462 (Wolters Kluwer, 5th ed., 2016) (saying that television ads subject to such restrictions "will be pretty doggone boring").

[51] Jim Rossi & Mollie Weighner, *An Empirical Examination of the Iowa Bar's Approach to Regulating Lawyer Advertising*, 77 IOWA L. REV. 179, 222–23 (1991) (describing Iowa State Bar Association study); Watkins, *supra*, 49 ARK. L. REV. at 772–73 (1997).

series of television advertisements by lawyers. With respect to each character trait, the rating fell precipitously after viewing lawyer advertising: trustworthiness (from 71% to 14%), professionalism (from 71% to 21%), honesty (from 65% to 14%), and dignity (from 45% to 14%).

A subsequent study in 1991 by Jim Rossi and Mollie Weighner, then two law students at the University of Iowa, compared the perceptions of lawyers by members of the public in Wisconsin (where television advertising by lawyers was common) and Iowa (where television advertising by lawyers was uncommon due at least in part to strict regulations).[52] On every attribute surveyed, on a scale of 1 to a high score of 7, the Iowa public held more favorable views about lawyers than did the Wisconsin public: honesty (Iowa 4.60 to Wisconsin 4.11), competency (Iowa 4.91 to Wisconsin 4.55), helpfulness (Iowa 4.78 to Wisconsin 4.30), effectiveness (Iowa 4.72 to Wisconsin 4.43), and reliability (Iowa 4.70 to Wisconsin 4.22). Whether these varying perceptions were entirely attributable to the single variable of lawyer advertising was doubtful, but the results were consistent with the hypothesis that the dignity of the profession may be harmed by lawyer advertising.

By contrast, the American Bar Association Commission on Advertising in its review of the research found no support for the claim that lawyer advertising on television significantly affects the public image of lawyers. The ABA Commission concluded in 1995 that "print advertising is not inherently more dignified than television advertising."[53] And the style of the advertising may make a difference in public perception of lawyers, but not necessarily in the predicted direction. Participants in an ABA study perceived lawyers as significantly less honest after viewing non-dramatic and informative "talking head" television commercials for legal services, while they found lawyers to be significantly more intelligent after watching "stylish" commercials with actors and dramatizations.[54]

On lawyer television advertising, the sharply differing opinions among lawyers and judges in the 1980s (and perhaps among some still today) were well-represented in the contrasting majority and dissenting opinions of the Iowa Supreme Court in a series of decisions in the 1980s addressing the constitutional challenge to Iowa lawyering advertising rules.

In *Committee on Professional Ethics & Conduct v. Humphrey*,[55] a majority of the Iowa Supreme Court upheld the stringent Iowa rules on lawyer advertising on broadcast media, finding a substantial government interest in "fostering rational, intelligent, and voluntary decision making in determining the need for legal services and selecting a lawyer." Justice Harris writing for the majority concluded that the Iowa prohibitions on background sound, visual displays, and dramatic elements merely removed "the tools which would manipulate the viewer's mind and will."[56] The Iowa Supreme Court reaffirmed approval of the broadcast advertising restrictions after the *Humphrey* case was remanded by the United States Supreme Court for further consideration. In this

---

[52] Rossi & Weighner, *supra*, 77 IOWA L. REV. at 232–55.

[53] AMERICAN BAR ASS'N COMM'N ON ADVERTISING, LAWYER ADVERTISING AT THE CROSSROADS 81–82 (1995).

[54] William E. Hornsby, Jr. & Kurt Schimmel, *Regulating Lawyer Advertising: Public Images and the Irresistible Aristotelian Impulse*, 9 GEO. J. LEGAL ETHICS 325, 347–56 (1996) (reporting details of ABA study).

[55] 355 N.W.2d 565, 571 (1984), *judgment vacated*, 472 U.S. 1004 (1985).

[56] *Humphrey*, 355 N.W.2d at 571.

second *Humphrey* opinion, the majority reinforced its negative appraisal of electronic media advertising as "tolerat[ing] much less deliberation by those at whom it is aimed" because "[b]oth sight and sound are immediate" and "in a flash they are gone without a trace."[57]

In a special concurrence, Chief Justice Reynoldson highlighted what he saw as the dangers that would unfold if less-restrained television advertising by lawyers were allowed. In his view, the profession's task of policing misleading and fraudulent communications by lawyers would be made all the more difficult by unrestricted broadcast advertising, as "the sights, color, sounds, subliminal messages, and not-so-hidden persuaders of commercial television advertising were added to the burden."[58] Fearing especially the potential for a decline in respect for the courts, Reynoldson argued that "[s]olemn forums for the litigation of cases whose lawyer-officers resemble carnival barkers at the doors scarcely can avoid being viewed as carnivals, or at least, places where justice is bought and sold as in any marketplace."[59]

Justice Larson, joined by Justice McCormick, dissented in *Humphrey* both before and after remand from the United States Supreme Court. In his original dissent, Justice Larson accurately described "the restrictions on *technique*" imposed by the Iowa television advertising rules as "in fact a prescription for dullness, prohibiting all background music, dramatization, and other methods of stimulating viewer interest."[60] And the television commercials at issue in *Humphrey* were hardly melodramatic in nature or likely to entrance an audience through use of high-end production techniques and innovative use of technology. Indeed, these broadcast advertisements, as Justice Larson noted, could also "be characterized as dull by today's standards."[61] In one of the commercials, a physician looking at an x-ray commented that he has "see[n] firsthand, injuries caused by the neglect of others," and that a person suffering such an injury "should be talking to a lawyer." In another commercial, set in a bowling alley, two bowlers noted that one team was a man short because "he was injured through the negligence of others," and these bowlers concluded that the teammate should talk to a lawyer and that the choice of a lawyer "will be important."

Justice Larson contended that these commercials were protected by the First Amendment because they served the vital public interest of informing people "about the nature of their legal rights and the means of pursuing them."[62] Each of the commercials at issue in *Humphrey* conveyed the message that if someone is injured by another, the law might provide a remedy, and the advertisements explained how someone could contact a law firm. Justice Larson noted "[t]he potential for these 'slice of life' commercials to inform the public about other general matters," such as consumer rights, the value of a will, or the wisdom of obtaining legal representation in contract matters, such as when purchasing a house.[63] When *Humphrey* returned to the Iowa Supreme

---

[57] 377 N.W.2d 643, 646 (Iowa 1985). *But see* Bernadette Miragliotta, *First Amendment: The Special Treatment of Legal Advertising*, 1990 ANN. SURV. AM. L. 597, 626–27 (1992) (saying that television advertisement viewers have "the opportunity to reflect and consider their options" before contacting an attorney and retain "ultimate control over the flow of information").

[58] *Humphrey*, 377 N.W.2d at 649 (Reynoldson, C.J., concurring specially).

[59] *Id.* at 650.

[60] *Humphrey*, 355 N.W.2d at 572 (Larson, J., dissenting).

[61] *Humphrey*, 377 N.W.2d at 654 (Larson, J., dissenting).

[62] *Humphrey*, 355 N.W.2d at 575 (Larson, J., dissenting).

[63] *Humphrey*, 377 N.W.2d at 655 (Larson, J., dissenting).

Court after remand by the United States Supreme Court, Justice Larson in his second dissent concluded that Iowa's extremely stringent rules regarding broadcast advertising could not satisfy the constitutional requirement that less restrictive measures be implemented if possible, rather than imposing an outright prohibition.[64] Saying that Iowa's rules had "a virtual stranglehold on lawyer advertising,"[65] Justice Larson said that it was "undisputed that the effect of these limitations on technique is to substantially diminish the effectiveness of any television advertising."[66]

Those words proved to be prophetic. The strict and stark limitations on what could be displayed and said in an Iowa television advertisement made use of that medium by lawyers so unattractive that it was rarely employed in Iowa during the next quarter century. The practical effect of silencing an entire medium for communication about legal services arguably confirmed the constitutional infirmity of these stringent rules. As one commentator stated at that point in time, "any regulation that excludes the use of the most powerful and persuasive instruments of mass communication is necessarily inconsistent with, and in derogation of, the public's right to know."[67]

In 2012, the Iowa Supreme Court accepted the recommendation of a study committee to abandon the severe restrictions on broadcast advertising of lawyer services.[68] Through its adoption of Comment 3 to Model Rule 7.2, Iowa now acknowledges that "[t]elevision, the internet, and other forms of electronic communication are now among the most powerful media for getting information to the public, particularly persons of low and moderate income; prohibiting television, internet, and other forms of electronic advertising, therefore, would impede the flow of information about legal services to many sectors of the public."

Nonetheless, a handful of states continue to impose special restrictions on use of broadcast media for lawyer advertising. Those restrictions range from relatively modest limitations or required disclaimers to an outright ban on use of dramatization. On the modest end of the range, California, Missouri, Montana, Nevada, New York, North Carolina, Rhode Island, and Utah require disclosure if actors are used to portray a lawyer or client or if fictionalized scenes are depicted,[69] with Florida barring use of any "celebrity" spokesperson.[70] Going a step further, Arizona, Louisiana, Pennsylvania, South Dakota, and Texas demand that the person portraying a lawyer on electronic

---

[64] *Id.* at 655–58; *see also Zauderer*, 471 U.S. at 648 (saying that Ohio had failed to establish "that the potential abuses associated with the use of illustrations in attorneys' advertising cannot be combated by any means short of a blanket ban").

[65] *Humphrey*, 377 N.W.2d at 657 (Larson, J., dissenting).

[66] *Humphrey*, 355 N.W.2d at 572 (Larson, J., dissenting).

[67] Michael Schein, Comment, *Commercial Speech and the Limits of Legal Advertising*, 58 OR. L. REV. 193, 218 (1979); *see also* Alexander v. Cahill, 598 F.3d 79, 94 (2d Cir. 2010) (invalidating prohibition of irrelevant techniques in lawyering advertising and rejecting the argument that potential clients might be misled by "gimmicks" such as those used by the challenging lawyers in portraying themselves on a television ad as "giants towering above local buildings," able to "run to a client's house so quickly that they appear as blurs," and as "provid[ing] legal assistance to space aliens").

[68] Gregory C. Sisk & Ellen Yee, *Lawyer Advertising in Iowa After 2012*, 62 DRAKE L. REV. 549, 560–64 (2014).

[69] CAL. RULES OF PROF'L CONDUCT R. 1–400(Standards)(13); MO. RULES OF PROF'L CONDUCT R. 4–7.1(i); MONT. RULES OF PROF'L CONDUCT R. 7.1(i); NEV. RULES OF PROF'L CONDUCT R. 7.2(b); N.Y. RULES OF PROF'L CONDUCT R. 7.1(c)(4); N.C. RULES OF PROF'L CONDUCT R. 7.1(b); R.I. RULES OF PROF'L CONDUCT R. 7.1(c); UTAH RULES OF PROF'L CONDUCT R. 7.2(b).

[70] FLA. RULES OF PROF'L CONDUCT R. 4–7.15(c).

media actually be a lawyer at the advertising law firm.[71] On the far end of the spectrum, Arkansas and New Jersey appear to stand alone in prohibiting any "dramatization."[72] New Jersey broadly outlaws use of "drawings, animations, dramatizations, music, or lyrics" in lawyer advertising, perhaps the most intrusive regulation of broadcast media use by lawyers that remains in effect in any state.

### § 4-2.4(c) Communication by Internet Including Web Pages and Social Media

Subject to the general requirement that communications not be "false or misleading,"[73] lawyers may make use of the internet including social media to advertise about legal services. Indeed, a lawyer may participate in social media or internet blogging—including discussion of events and experiences in legal practice and description of practice area—that would not constitute advertising, because the primary purpose of the communication is not to attract new clients or suggest availability for professional employment.[74] However, if social media is used for a real-time exchange with a layperson to market social services, the interaction likely constitutes prohibited solicitation,[75] rather than permissible advertising.

As the most prominent example of an internet presence, most law firms and lawyers have established a web site. By communicating information about the law firm or lawyer largely for the purpose of attracting clients, such firm web pages do constitute a form of lawyer advertising. The lawyer and law firm have a considerable degree of freedom in developing an informational web site, provided that the information is accurate. Thus, if the web page simply offers general (and truthful) information about the lawyer's legal services or practice area or about a field of law, it should occasion little concern under today's broad lawyer advertising rules. If, however, the lawyer through the web site should invite the submission of confidential information or respond to inquiries by suggesting specific answers to particular legal problems, these statements could be regarded as offering legal advice and thereby creating an attorney-client relationship with the person.[76]

Importantly, the lawyer who offers legal advice to a person, either in person or by electronic communications, may thereby create an attorney-client relationship and be responsible for the legal affairs of the assumed client.[77] As Professor Catherine Lanctot writes, "[i]nadvertent creation of an attorney-client relationship is an area that has also been affected by technological changes."[78] The "mythical 'cocktail party' "—at which a lawyer creates a professional relationship by offering advice to a layperson—is "far more likely" today to arise in "an online context." As Lanctot wisely warns, "understand that

---

[71] ARIZ. RULES OF PROF'L CONDUCT R. 7.2(e); LA. RULES OF PROF'L CONDUCT R. 7.2(c)(1)(J); PENN. RULES OF PROF'L CONDUCT R. 7.2(f); S.D. RULES OF PROF'L CONDUCT R. 7.2(h); TEX. RULES OF PROF'L CONDUCT R. 7.02(a)(7), 7.04(g).

[72] ARK. RULES OF PROF'L CONDUCT R. 7.2(e); N.J. RULES OF PROF'L CONDUCT R. 7.2(a).

[73] *See supra* § 4-2.3.

[74] *See* N.Y. Ethics Op. 2015–7; Cal. St. Bar, Formal Op. 2016–196. *See also infra* § 4-2.5(f).

[75] On solicitation, including by real-time electronic communication, see *infra* § 4-2.5.

[76] For further discussion of the possible responsibilities that may be assumed by a lawyer when communicating through the internet, social media, or email with prospective clients, see *infra* § 4-3.1(e).

[77] For more on misunderstandings concerning the creation and scope of an attorney-client relationship, see *infra* § 4-3.2(c).

[78] Catherine J. Lanctot, *Becoming a Competent 21st Century Legal Ethics Professor: Everything You Always Wanted to Know About Technology (But Were Afraid to Ask)*, 2015 J. PROF. LAW. 75, 88.

an attorney who provides specific legal advice to a lay person on-line could later be held to have created an attorney-client relationship with that person, depending on the level of specificity and the degree of reasonable reliance, and they must be warned that on-line disclaimers alone might not suffice to avoid this result."[79]

## § 4-2.4(d) Advertising by Mail

### *§ 4-2.4(d)(1) The History of Regulation of Lawyer Direct Mail*

Under today's Rules of Professional Conduct, marketing of legal services by a lawyer through the mail (including email and recorded telephone messages) is not subject to greater regulation than lawyer advertising in general. As a specific application of the general requirement that lawyer communications about legal services not be false or misleading in nature, Rule 7.3(c) provides that a lawyer who uses direct mail or email to appeal to persons who are known to have a specific need for legal services must be prominently identified as advertising.

The rules regarding direct mail advertising by lawyers traveled a considerable distance in the decades after the ban on lawyer advertising was lifted in 1977. When state ethics rules were initially revised to permit limited advertising by lawyers, to comply with the Supreme Court's commercial free speech decision in *Bates v. State Bar of Arizona*,[80] the newly-allowed forms of communication about legal services generally did not include direct mail to specific individuals. A lawyer's targeting of a direct letter to a potential client was then regarded by many states as carrying the same dangers of invasion of privacy and overreaching[81] as are present with in-person solicitation by lawyers, which has always been and remains prohibited under the rules.[82]

In 1988, in *Shapero v. Kentucky Bar Association*,[83] the Supreme Court held that an attorney's proposed direct mailing to homeowners who had a foreclosure suit filed against them constituted constitutionally-protected commercial speech. The Court overturned a Kentucky state rule that had permitted mailing by lawyers to the general public, but prohibited mailings that were directed to a specific recipient thought to need legal services for a particular matter. The Court ruled that "the State may not constitutionally ban a particular letter on the theory that to mail it only to those whom it would most interest is somehow inherently objectionable."[84]

The *Shapero* Court rejected the analogy of targeted direct-mail to prohibited in-person solicitation of clients, the latter of which involves "the coercive force of the personal presence of a trained advocate" and "the pressure on the potential client for an immediate yes-or-no answer to the offer of representation."[85] Reasoning that "the mode

---

[79] *Id.*

[80] 433 U.S. 350, 383 (1977). On the history of lawyer advertising after *Bates v. State Bar of Arizona*, see *supra* § 4-2.2.

[81] *See* 2 GEOFFREY C. HAZARD, JR. & W. WILLIAM HODES, THE LAW OF LAWYERING § 57.5 (Aspen, 3d ed., 2008) (discussing early reaction of organized bar to direct mail, even after *Bates*).

[82] *See supra* § 4-2.2 and *infra* § 4-2.5(a).

[83] 486 U.S. 466, 469–78 (1988).

[84] *Id.* at 473–74.

[85] *Id.* at 475 (quoting Zauderer v. Office of Disciplinary Counsel, 471 U.S. 626, 642 (1985)).

of communication makes all the difference," the Court observed that a letter "can readily be put in a drawer to be considered later, ignored, or discarded."[86]

Subsequently in 1995, in *Florida Bar v. Went for It, Inc.*,[87] the Supreme Court by a 5–4 vote upheld a short "blackout period" on the use of direct mail by lawyers, which precluded contacting personal injury or wrongful death clients within 30 days of an accident. The Court held that this limited time restriction on direct mail was "reasonably well tailored to [the Florida Bar's] stated objective of eliminating targeted mailings whose type and timing are a source of distress to Floridians, distress that has caused many of them to lose respect for the legal profession."[88]

Under *Shapero* and *Florida Bar*, direct mail, even that which is targeted to accident victims or other persons experiencing an episode that could give rise to the need for legal services, may not be banned, but the state may impose reasonable time, place, and manner regulations. About a third of the states do impose a "cooling off" period, typically 30 days, after a traumatic event such as a disaster or an accident before a lawyer may target an affected person with a mailing, telephone call, or email. Congress also enacted a 45-day waiting period after airline accidents before a lawyer or other interested parties (thus including the airline and insurance agents) may make an "unsolicited communication" to a victim or family members.[89] Whether these time restrictions would be sustained today by the Supreme Court under evolving commercial speech doctrine under the First Amendment is far from certain.

During the 1980s and 1990s, states gravitated toward an approach that treated a lawyer's use of direct mail to the general public as a form of advertising, while regarding mailings aimed toward identified persons believed to have specific legal problems as a somewhat disfavored form of solicitation. While outright prohibition of such targeted mailings was no longer possible, states adopted strict regulations for mail communications aimed at a specific audience believed to need particular legal services. Some states instituted a clearance procedure for mailings that were addressed to persons or groups who might need specific legal services because of a condition or occurrence known to the lawyer. Other states required the lawyer to submit a copy of the communication to the state bar or supreme court.

Today, as reflected in Rule 7.3(c) of the Model Rules of Professional Conduct, mail sent to members of the public generally is regarded as advertising, subject to the basic restrictions in Rule 7.1 and 7.2. Direct mail or email sent to persons known to be in need of particular legal services need only be identified as an advertisement through an "Advertising Material" disclaimer.

### *§ 4-2.4(d)(2) Targeted Mail to Persons Known to Need Legal Services*

When an ordinary person who has little familiarity with lawyers and the legal system receives a letter from a lawyer or a law firm, she may feel a degree of anxiety or mistakenly believe that a response is necessary.[90] If the letter further adverts to a

---

[86] *Id.* at 475–76.

[87] 515 U.S. 618, 620–33 (1995).

[88] *Id.* at 633.

[89] 49 U.S.C. § 1136(g)(2).

[90] *See* Shapero v. Kentucky Bar Ass'n, 486 U.S. 466, 481–82 (1988) (O'Connor, J., dissenting) ("Unsophisticated citizens, understandably intimidated by the courts and their officers, may therefore find it

particular episode in the life of the recipient, such as an automobile accident, a death in the family, an arrest, marital separation, or even a positive event like a home purchase, that person may also be embarrassed or regard the communication as an unwelcome intrusion upon her privacy.[91] In sum, some people finding themselves in the kind of situation that may give rise to legal problems will be apprehensive or unhappy to receive an uninvited contact from a lawyer.

Nonetheless, the fact that the condition or occurrence apparently has become known to others (including the advertising lawyer), often because it has been a matter of public record or the subject of a news report, usually means that the recipient has a lesser expectation of privacy about the matter.[92] Given that commercial enterprises, such as insurance brokers, banks, and service-providers, regularly send mail to those who have experienced major life events, yet another letter, even one from a lawyer, is unlikely to add much to the intrusion. Moreover, the self-interest of the lawyer sending the letter should result in a restrained style of communication, because the advertising lawyer will not expand his or her clientele by offending the recipients.

Importantly, many persons who have a genuine need for legal services because of something that has happened in their lives may not be aware of their legal rights, know how to secure legal representation, or have any sense of the costs of legal services. An advertising communication from a lawyer may provide necessary information at a crucial time.

Assuming that the lawyer has not engaged in unseemly tactics to discover the person's condition or the occurrence (which would be independently unethical for other reasons), it should be sufficient that the lawyer's letter to the potential client known to have a need for legal services be clearly identified as nothing other than an advertisement. The recipient should then appreciate that a mailing is not a formal legal document and does not demand more serious attention.

Accordingly, Rule 7.3(c) of the Model Rules of Professional Conduct states that a lawyer who addresses direct mail or email to "anyone known to be in need of legal services in a particular matter" must include the words "Advertising Material" on the outside of the envelope for a mailing and at the beginning and ending of any recorded or electronic communication.

Even if not directly required by disciplinary rule (and a few states do require the lawyer to document or even disclose how the determination was made),[93] the thoughtful lawyer should make reasonable efforts to ensure that he has the facts right before sending a direct message. If the recipient of targeted mail has not, in fact, suffered the asserted condition or experienced the claimed occurrence, then receipt of a letter from a lawyer, even one labeled as an advertisement, that identifies the person as having that condition or experiencing that occurrence may be unsettling. If, for example, a person were to receive a personally-addressed letter from a lawyer suggesting that the recipient

---

much more difficult to ignore an apparently 'personalized' letter from an attorney than to ignore a general advertisement").

[91] For anecdotal examples of individuals outraged by direct-mail solicitations by lawyers shortly after tragic events, see Florida Bar v. Went for It, Inc., 515 U.S. 618, 627–28 (1995).

[92] *Cf. Shapero*, 486 U.S. at 476 (saying the invasion of privacy, "if any, occurs when the lawyer discovers the recipient's legal affairs, not when he confronts the recipient with the discovery").

[93] *See, e.g.*, ARIZ. RULES OF PROF'L CONDUCT R. 7.3(c)(4); S.C. RULES OF PROF'L CONDUCT R. 7.3(c); TENN. RULES OF PROF'L CONDUCT R. 7.3(c)(6).

had been involved in an automobile accident, had been arrested on a particular charge, or may be suffering an undiagnosed injury from a product—but the assertion in the letter is mistaken—the recipient understandably might be disturbed. The recipient either may mistakenly fear that she actually has a previously-unrealized legal problem[94] or may feel compelled to investigate how she came to be so associated with that condition or event and to take action to correct that misperception. Thus, a lawyer who casually and without some effort at confirmation (such as checking both name and address information in the public record or news report) directs a targeted missive about a condition or occurrence to the wrong person may thereby cause a degree of harm simply by the posting of a letter.

The lawyer's own self-interest is a strong deterrent against direct mail or email that refers to a specific situation without reasonable investigation because a mistake is likely to alienate a potential client. Moreover, the lawyer's general duty not to make "false or misleading" communications under Rule 7.1 precludes the lawyer from knowingly or recklessly suggesting that the targeted person has a particular problem without some basis for believing it to be true. In addition, the continued requirement of a prominent disclaimer that the letter or email is merely "Advertising Material" should alleviate the potential anxiety of the person who receives it and was mistakenly included in the targeted group.

Finally, that a lawyer is permitted by Rule 7.3 to use targeted mail as a form of advertising is not an invitation to adopt unscrupulous methods to dig up personal information about people so as to prepare a specially-tailored solicitation about legal services. Espionage directed at hospital or other private records, for example, is serious misconduct. The lawyer who has employed deceptive or unlawful means to investigate the identities and circumstances of people who may have a need for legal services is deserving of disciplinary sanction.

### § 4-2.4(e) Regulation of Style and Emotional Appeal

In language that once was typical of state ethics rules,[95] advertising rules in the 1980s frequently demanded that information about legal services be "presented in a dignified style" and discouraged resort to "emotional appeals."

---

[94] *See* Shapero v. Kentucky Bar Association, 486 U.S. 466, 476 (1988) (noting that "an inaccurately targeted letter could lead the recipient to believe she has a legal problem that she does not actually have," but saying such "isolated abuses or mistakes" did not justify a total ban on direct mail).

[95] *See* Lori B. Andrews, *Lawyer Advertising and the First Amendment*, 6 A.B.A. FOUND. RESEARCH J. 967, 1010 (1981) (identifying 28 states as of 1981 that required lawyer advertising to be "dignified"). Today, no state appears to maintain a general rule that lawyer advertising be presented in a dignified manner. New Jersey allows certified attorneys to "make dignified use of the area of practice designation." N.J. GEN. APPLICATION R. 1:39–6. And three states, while not imposing such a general requirement, specify that advertising about prepaid legal services or a lawyer referral service must be presented in a dignified manner. FLA. STAT. LAWYER REFERRAL STANDARDS & GUIDELINES, Standard 8; GA. CODE ANN. § 33–35–12; MISS. CODE ANN. § 83–49–19.

Whether an insistence upon "dignity" in lawyer advertising could survive the extension of constitutional free speech protection to lawyer advertising is doubtful.[96] In *Zauderer v. Office of Disciplinary Counsel*,[97] the Supreme Court commented:

> More fundamentally, although the State undoubtedly has a substantial interest in ensuring that its attorneys behave with dignity and decorum in the courtroom, we are unsure that the State's desire that attorneys maintain their dignity in their communications with the public is an interest substantial enough to justify the abridgement of their First Amendment rights.[98]

Because the attorney in *Zauderer* had not been directly disciplined for the supposed lack of "dignity" in the advertisement at issue in the case or the illustration that accompanied it, the quoted passage may fall short of a dispositive holding.[99] Nonetheless, the Supreme Court's skeptical comments about dignity as a basis for regulating the content of a lawyer's message strongly suggests that a state's preference for decorous lawyer representations is not a state interest that will justify direct controls on the style of a lawyer's communication with the public.

In the recent prominent decision of *Alexander v. Cahill*,[100] the United States Court of Appeals for the Second Circuit invalidated a New York regulation prohibiting advertisements that rely on irrelevant techniques, saying that "[q]uestions of taste or effectiveness in advertising are generally matters of subjective judgment." A "dignity" stipulation might also prove vulnerable to challenge as being too vague and subjective to serve as a legitimate standard by which to police speech by lawyers.[101]

Moreover, prior instructions to lawyers not to "rely on emotional appeal" in advertisements were not only troublingly vague but difficult to reconcile with the general purpose of advertising and the right to raise difficult subjects. Any effective marketing strategy is designed to elicit a favorable response from the listener and thus to produce a positive sentiment about the lawyer who is the subject of the advertisement. A lawyer should not worry that she may violate an ethical prohibition through efforts to encourage the public (by appropriately non-misleading and verifiable communications) to feel good about the advertising lawyer. Nor should a lawyer be inhibited from raising sensitive topics when communicating with the public about legal services, which may include making people aware of potential harm that they may suffer from defective products, reminding members of the public of their civil rights and the dangers of governmental or societal oppression, or describing the nature of potential or pending litigation on controversial subjects. Even if the presentation of this information has the effect of

---

[96] *See* 2 GEOFFREY C. HAZARD, JR., W. WILLIAM HODES & PETER R. JARVIS, THE LAW OF LAWYERING § 59.09 (Aspen, 4th ed., 2016). (saying that the "undignified" standard is the "kind of vague and subjective criteria [that] could not long survive the Supreme Court's application of the commercial speech doctrine to lawyer advertising"); Rodney A. Smolla, *Lawyer Advertising and the Dignity of the Profession*, 59 ARK. L. REV. 437, 454–57 (2006) (criticizing the "dignity of the profession" rationale for restricting lawyer advertising and saying that "[t]he regulation of lawyer advertising on the grounds that it is demeaning to the profession raises profound First Amendment difficulties").

[97] 471 U.S. 626 (1985).

[98] *Id.* at 647–48.

[99] *See id.* at 635 n.5, 647.

[100] 598 F.3d 79, 93 (2d Cir. 2010).

[101] RONALD D. ROTUNDA & JOHN S. DZIENKOWSKI, PROFESSIONAL RESPONSIBILITY: A STUDENT'S GUIDE § 7.2–2 ((American Bar Ass'n, 2013–2014) (saying efforts to prohibit "undignified" lawyer advertising "are typically unconstitutional and fruitless, because questions of effectiveness and taste in advertising are matters of 'speculation and subjective judgment' ") (quoting MODEL RULES OF PROFESSIONAL CONDUCT R. 7.2, cmt. 1)).

provoking strong emotional reactions in some listeners, that potential response cannot be the measure of what is permissible.

While the prior adjuration against "emotional appeal" likely was limited in application to deliberate attempts to arouse passions and prejudices, unless an advertising stratagem departed so far from communication of information as to be deceptive in appeal to emotions and prejudices, deciding what was legitimate and what crossed the line would be in the subjective eye of the beholder.

In general, the legal profession has abandoned attempts to police the style of lawyer advertising. Comment 3 to Rule 7.2 of the Model Rules of Professional Conduct places restrictions "against 'undignified' advertising" among those prohibitions that some jurisdictions have maintained in the past. Instead, the comment now acknowledges, "[q]uestions of effectiveness and taste in advertising are matters of speculation and subjective judgment."

## § 4-2.4(f) Communicating Fields of Practice and Specialization

### *§ 4-2.4(f)(1) History of Identification of Practice Areas and Specialization*

Before 1977, advertising by an attorney of areas of practice or specialization was subject to the same general prohibition that applied to all forms of lawyer advertising.[102] After the door to attorney advertising was opened by the Supreme Court's commercial free speech decision in *Bates v. State Bar of Arizona*,[103] some states continued for a time to bar or strictly regulate lawyers from noting their areas of practice or referring to certified specialties. Many state bars considered references to practice specialities as the equivalent of impermissible claims of superior quality and thus as inherently misleading to the public.

Subsequent to *Bates*, the Supreme Court in two decisions found that an attorney has a constitutionally-protected right to communicate accurate and non-misleading information about practice areas and certification as a specialist. In *In re R.M.J.*,[104] the Court overturned discipline of a lawyer that Missouri had imposed because he had not precisely used language from the list of approved practice areas in the state ethics rules, instead describing his practice as involving "real estate," rather than "property," and "contracts," where the state list included no such field. In *Peel v. Attorney Registration & Disciplinary Commission*,[105] a plurality of the Supreme Court held that a state may not bar a lawyer from advertising that he is a "certified trial specialist" by the National Board of Trial Advocacy, concluding that such a truthful statement was not "actually or inherently misleading."

### *§ 4-2.4(f)(2) Communicating Practice in Particular Fields of Law*

Under Rule 7.4(a) of the Model Rules of Professional Conduct, "[a] lawyer may communicate the fact that the lawyer does or does not practice in particular fields of law." Indeed, as confirmed by Comment 1 to Rule 7.4, the lawyer may also communicate

---

[102] On the history of lawyer advertising, see *supra* § 4-2.2.

[103] 433 U.S. 350, 383 (1977).

[104] 455 U.S. 191, 196–207 (1982).

[105] 496 U.S. 91, 110–11 (1990) (plurality).

accurate information that she *specializes* in a field of law (although a statement that the lawyer is "certified" as a specialist receives separate treatment in the rule).[106]

A lawyer's statements that he practices or specializes in a particular field of law must not be false or misleading under the general proscription in Rule 7.1.[107] When lawyers holds themselves out as practicing in a defined field, and especially if they describe themselves as specialists, the public assumes a higher level of experience, knowledge, or expertise. In most states the lawyer claiming a practice concentration or specialty need not spend a certain number of hours concentrating in the field or establish a specific number of hours devoted to studying the field. Nonetheless, the lawyer surely should have some legitimate basis for the assertion. Indeed, the lawyer who claims to be a specialist arguably should be held to a higher standard of care in the event of a claim for professional malpractice.[108]

A case that arose in Iowa illustrates the real harm that can follow from "false claims of expertise." In *Committee on Professional Ethics & Conduct v. Morris*,[109] the attorney listed immigration law as one of his areas of practice in a yellow-page advertisement, which attracted the attention of a Canadian citizen who was seeking to remain in the United States as a temporary worker. The attorney, who actually had little experience in immigration law, failed to timely prepare and file the necessary application. As a result, despite assurances from her attorney that all was in order, the client was arrested at her place of work, was temporarily jailed, and had to leave the country.

Under Rule 7.4(b), an attorney who has been admitted to practice before the United States Patent and Trademark Office, which requires the attorney to possess a scientific educational background and pass a demanding examination, may identify himself by the designation "Patent Attorney" or something "substantially similar." Even during the era when the ethics rules generally prohibited advertising a lawyer's certification as a specialist, designation as a patent lawyer had been accepted a special exception.

Under Rule 7.4(c), an attorney engaged in admiralty practice may use the designation "Admiralty," "Proctor in Admiralty," or a "substantially similar designation." Admiralty law also was historically recognized as a legitimate practice specialty, even during the era of more restrictive regulation of lawyer communications about practice areas.

### *§ 4-2.4(f)(3) Communicating Certification as a Specialist*

In *Peel v. Attorney Registration & Disciplinary Commission of Illinois*,[110] the Supreme Court on First Amendment grounds overturned discipline of a lawyer for accurately stating on his letterhead that he was a "Certified Civil Trial Specialist" by the National Board of Trial Advocacy. Justice Stevens for a plurality of four justices wrote approvingly of the certification standards of National Board of Trial Advocacy (NBTA) as "objective and demanding."[111] The NBTA standards were described as

---

[106] *See infra* § 4-2.4(f)(3).

[107] On the general prohibition of false or misleading communications about legal services, see *supra* § 4-2.3.

[108] On specialists and a possible higher standard of care in legal malpractice cases, see Part Five of this book, Susan Saab Fortney & Vincent R. Johnson, Legal Malpractice § 5-2.2(a)(1).

[109] 490 N.W.2d 806, 806–10 (Iowa 1992).

[110] 496 U.S. 91, 99–111 (1990).

[111] *Id.* at 95.

involving specified trial experience, continuing legal education, a demonstration of writing skills, and passage of a day-long examination.

Although acknowledging that a "sham" certification by an organization that failed to inquire into a lawyer's fitness or that awarded certificates indiscriminately for a price would be misleading to the public, the plurality in *Peel* believed that state disciplinary authorities would be able to "distinguish[ ] between certifying boards that are bona fide and those that are bogus."[112] While rejecting an absolute ban on a lawyer from disclosing certification as a specialist, the plurality suggested that a state "might consider screening certifying organizations or requiring a disclaimer about the certifying organization or the standards of a specialty."[113] Justice Marshall, who concurred separately in the judgment in *Peel*, concluded that a claim of certification was potentially misleading and thus a state "may enact measures other than a total ban to prevent deception or confusion," such as a required disclaimer or explanation.[114]

Rule 7.4(d) of the Model Rules of Professional Conduct permits a lawyer to identify herself as a specialist when (1) certified by an organization approved by a state authority or the American Bar Association and (2) the certifying entity is clearly identified in the communication. A few states authorize a state entity, such as a commission, to approve certifying organizations, while others defer to the American Bar Association.

A substantial minority of states take the further step of requiring a disclaimer by the lawyer advertising certification as a specialist that the state itself does not certify specialists. In *Peel*, the Supreme Court specifically suggested that a state properly could "require[e] a disclaimer about the certifying organization or the standards of a specialty."[115] These disclosures may prevent members of the public from placing excessive weight on a lawyer's certification as a specialist in a field of practice, when such certification is not required for a lawyer to provide legal services in most areas of practice (with certain exceptions, such as the patent bar).

### § 4-2.4(g) Firm Name

The choice of a firm name itself is a communication. The designation of a firm name thereby implicates the general rule that communications about legal services not be false or misleading.[116] Rule 7.5 of the Model Rules of Professional Conduct requires a lawyer to select a firm name, letterhead, or professional designation that accurately identifies the lawyer or lawyers involved.

Under Rule 7.5, the lawyer's choices are essentially three: (1) designating a firm by the names of all or some of its present, retired, or deceased members; (2) using the name that appears on the lawyer's current license to practice (for a solo practitioner); or (3) using a trade name.

---

[112] *Id.* at 109.

[113] *Id.* at 110.

[114] *Id.* at 116 (Marshall, J., concurring in the judgment).

[115] *Peel*, 496 U.S. 91, 110 (1990) (plurality); *see also id.* at 116 (Marshall, J., concurring in the judgment) (agreeing that a disclaimer could be required to prevent deception of the public).

[116] On the general prohibition of false or misleading communications about legal services, see *supra* § 4-2.3.

### *§ 4-2.4(g)(1) Firm Designation by Lawyer Names*

The most common professional designation, and in the past the only designation permitted to lawyers engaged in practice for a profit, is the use of the name of the lawyer or the name of multiple lawyers in a law firm. When a law firm is designated by names, those names must be the actual present or past lawyer members of the firm or its predecessor. As Comment 1 to Rule 7.5 states, "it is misleading to use the name of a lawyer not associated with the firm or a predecessor of the firm, or the name of a nonlawyer."

The firm may include the names of all lawyers in the firm or it may choose to limit the firm name to that of a single lawyer or small set of lawyers, provided those lawyers are or were practicing in the firm or its predecessor. When the name of a departed lawyer is included, there should be what Comment 1 calls a "continuing succession in the firm's identity." Thus, if a law firm closed or a lawyer whose name was included in the firm name moves to another professional setting (as contrasted with retiring or dying), a law firm may not make use of those lawyer names.[117]

For purposes of preserving a particular lawyer's name within the firm name, a period of disability or a temporary leave of absence for something other than practicing law in another setting (such as volunteer, political, or teaching positions that do not involve practicing law) should not interrupt the connection so as to require removal of the name, at least assuming an intended return by the lawyer to the firm or retirement from any law practice in the not-too-distant future.

The names of deceased or retired members of the firm or a predecessor firm also fall within the continuing line of succession. While the rule does not specifically so say, the prohibition on false or misleading firm names presumably means that the firm may claim an association only with those now-departed lawyers who maintained their association with the law firm to the very end of their legal careers. If a partner leaves the law firm, even after many years of association with it, for an in-house position at a corporation, even if it is a corporate client of the firm such that the firm will continue to have a relationship with the lawyer, the emigrating lawyer should not be continued in the firm name. Likewise, if a retired lawyer later resumes a law practice with another firm or as a sole practitioner, the continuing line of succession should be regarded as broken and his name thus would have to be removed from the firm name. By contrast, if a retired lawyer takes up a second career late in life, but one unrelated to the practice of law, the continuing line of succession presumably remains unbroken and the person's name may be perpetuated in the firm name.

If the law firm has offices in more than one jurisdiction, Rule 7.5(b) allows the firm to retain the same name in each location. But if the firm lists the names of lawyers working in a particular office, such as on a professional announcement or letterhead, there must be an indication of those lawyers who are not admitted to practice in the jurisdiction where the particular office is located.

If a lawyer in the firm is elected or appointed to public office, then under Rule 7.5(c), the lawyer's name must be removed from the law firm name, as well as from any communications about the firm, during any period in which the lawyer is not actively

---

[117] *See* Ashtabula Cty. Bar Ass'n v. Brown, 86 N.E.3d 269 (Ohio 2017) (imposing discipline on an attorney who included a former partner who was then a state supreme court justice in his law firm name, even though the two had ceased practicing together 20 years before).

and regularly practicing with the firm. Accordingly, if the public office demands the full- or nearly full-time attention of the lawyer, so that she has ceased to be an active and regular member of the firm, the firm may no longer proclaim that lawyer's association with the firm, either directly or indirectly. The rule thus ensures that the law firm name remains accurate in description, preventing a law firm from asserting a continuing formal relationship with a person who holds a full-time public office, especially that of a judge.[118]

If, however, the public office is part-time and allows the holder to continue to engage in the private practice, and the lawyer in fact does continue to be a genuine participant in the law firm's practice, the law firm may retain that lawyer's name in the firm name.

### *§ 4-2.4(g)(2) Firm Designation by Trade Name*

Traditionally, a law firm or lawyer could not practice under a trade name, which was regarded as inherently misleading. In the past, the only permissible means of designating a law firm was by the traditional listing of names of present or past attorneys, as discussed above. Today, in most (but not quite all) states, a trade name may be used as long as it is not misleading, such as by falsely suggesting an affiliation with government or charitable organizations. A couple of states continue to prohibit the use of trade names for law firms as inherently misleading.[119]

More than thirty years ago, in *Friedman v. Rogers*,[120] the Supreme Court held that a state prohibition on the use of trade names for an optometry practice was constitutionally permissible. The Court opined that a trade name might mislead customers about who is associated with the office and who would perform professional services, referring to the "ill-defined associations of trade names with price and quality information." The Court characterized this limitation as an incidental restraint on speech given alternative avenues for advertising. The Court further noted that use of trade names would allow a professional to escape a deservedly-negative reputation by simply adopting a new trade name, one that was disassociated with his own name.

Whether the Supreme Court's *Friedman* ruling would be sustained today as applied to lawyers under present commercial free speech law is uncertain. Two federal court of appeals decisions went in opposite directions in ruling on First Amendment challenges to state restrictions on use of trade or nicknames by law firms. In *Alexander v. Cahill*,[121] the United States Court of Appeals for the Second Circuit struck down a New York rule which, while not prohibiting use of trade names altogether, barred using "a nickname, moniker, motto or trade name that implies an ability to obtain results in a matter." The court held that the state had "failed to provide evidence that consumers have, in fact, been misled by the sorts of names and promotional devices targeted by" the lawyer advertising restriction.[122] By contrast, in *Public Citizen, Inc. v. Louisiana Attorney Disciplinary Board*,[123] the Fifth Circuit upheld a nearly identical Louisiana regulation.

---

[118] *See id.* (characterizing as a significant aggravating factor for discipline that a lawyer had a "selfish motive" for using a state supreme court justice's name in the firm name, thereby using the "prestige" of the justice's position "to enhance his own reputation").

[119] *See, e.g.*, IND. RULES OF PROF'L CONDUCT R. 7.5(b); OHIO RULES OF PROF'L CONDUCT R. 7.5(a); TEX. RULES OF PROF'L CONDUCT R. 7.5(a).

[120] 440 U.S. 1, 12–16 (1979).

[121] 598 F.3d 79, 94–95 (2d Cir. 2010).

[122] *Id.* at 95.

[123] 632 F.3d 212, 224–26 (5th Cir. 2011).

Distinguishing the Second Circuit's *Alexander* decision, the Fifth Circuit explained that the state, through surveys to the public and of state lawyers and focus group discussions, had demonstrated that "advertisements containing these mottos misled the public, improperly promised results, and implied that the advertising lawyers could manipulate Louisiana courts."[124] Notably, however, both regulations applied only to trade names stating or implying an ability to obtain results, and neither absolutely prohibited the use of all trade names.

Under Rule 7.5(a) of the Model Rules of Professional Conduct, lawyers and law firms are permitted to use non-deceptive trade names. The rule provides that "[a] trade name may be used by a lawyer in private practice if it does not imply a connection with a government agency or with a public or charitable legal services organization" and is not otherwise false or misleading as prohibited by Rule 7.1.

Comment 1 to Rule 7.5 warns about the kinds of trade names that may be misleading. If a private firm uses a trade name with a geographical designation, such as "Chicago Legal Clinic," consumers might mistake that for a public legal aid agency. While the trade name is not prohibited, the comment suggests that "an express disclaimer that it is a public legal aid agency may be required to avoid a misleading implication." Similarly, although not stated in the comment, the phrase "Legal Aid" is so well-known that it probably should be reserved for non-profit legal aid agencies.

### *§ 4-2.4(g)(3) Claims of Partnership or Association*

Any representation by a lawyer regarding partnership or similar association with another lawyer must of course be truthful. Thus, if a lawyer adopts a firm name that includes the names of other lawyers or posts an office sign that links together the names of multiple lawyers, the public may assume that the lawyers are practicing together in a partnership or association.

Under Rule 7.5(d) of the Model Rules of Professional Conduct, a lawyer may "state or imply that they practice in a partnership or other organization only when that is the fact." As Comment 2 explains, lawyers who share office facilities, but are not in fact associated with each other in a law firm, "may not denominate themselves as, for example, 'Smith and Jones,' for that title suggests that they are practicing law together in a firm." Clients or other persons should not be misled about the professional status of the lawyer and his relationship with other lawyers.

As Comment 2 to Rule 1.0 of the Model Rules says in defining "law firm," the mere fact that two or more lawyers share office space, even if they "occasionally consult or assist each other," does not make them members of a law firm or implicate the Rule 7.5(d) standard for truthful association. On the other hand, a group of lawyers may be found to have formed a law firm through behavior or representations, even without a formal agreement. For example, lawyers may be regarded as practicing within a law firm if they not only office together, but hold themselves out to the public as a firm or association or if they conduct themselves as a firm through a regular practice of joint representation of clients or by allowing mutual access to confidential client information.[125]

---

[124] *Id.* at 225.

[125] *See* Brady v. Starke, 517 S.W.3d 28, 34–36 (Mo. Ct. App. 2017) (affirming trial court's ruling that two lawyers were in the same firm and that "to the general public, there was no visible way to distinguish

## § 4-2.4(h) Advertising Disclaimers

### *§ 4-2.4(h)(1) Decline of General Advertising Disclaimers*

In the immediate aftermath of the Supreme Court's ruling upholding the constitutional right of lawyers to advertise,[126] many recalcitrant states imposed stringent and often lengthy disclaimers. Because of these unwieldy requirements, communication of even basic information generally was limited to traditional forms of advertisement that afforded sufficient space to lay out each of the required disclaimers in the size of type mandated by a rule. Thus, having the law firm or lawyer name appear on the uniforms of a youth baseball team sponsored by the lawyer or firm or otherwise being listed as a contributor to a civic charity was impossible because of the demanding disclaimer requirements.

In most states, and under the Model Rules of Professional Conduct, general advertising disclaimers are eliminated, and lawyer advertising is subject only to the general prohibition on communications that are "false or misleading."

### *§ 4-2.4(h)(2) Disclaimers for Advertising Suggesting Lawsuits*

In *Zauderer v. Office of Disciplinary Counsel*,[127] the Supreme Court upheld as constitutionally protected a lawyer's advertisement that addressed a specific legal problem and that invited potential clients to consider taking legal action against the manufacturer of a defective product. The Court pointedly rejected the "traditional justification" for prohibiting such advertisements—"the fear that lawyers will 'stir up litigation.' "[128] Given that litigation is a legitimate and accepted means by which to resolve disputes and vindicate rights in this society, making injured persons aware of their legal rights and thereby facilitating their access to legal redress is a positive public good. Accordingly, the Court held that an attorney could not be prevented from engaging in "truthful and nondeceptive advertising [that] had a tendency to or did in fact encourage others to file lawsuits."[129]

Nonetheless, while few states persist in doing so today, a required disclaimer to potential clients that advancing meritless litigation could have consequences might still pass constitutional muster.

### *§ 4-2.4(h)(3) Disclaimers for Advertising on Fees*

In *Zauderer*, the Supreme Court specifically approved a state requirement that a lawyer advertising the handling of litigation on a contingent fee basis must disclose the potential liability for courts costs and other expenses, as the Court believed the omission of that information would be misleading.[130] While most states have abandoned detailed disclaimer rules, a state could (and a couple do)[131] require a lawyer advertising the availability of contingent fees to disclose how the fee is calculated.

---

separate entities," where the lawyers shared space in a building with a single sign, a common entrance and reception area, shared staff to greet clients, and provided no indication the lawyers were unaffiliated).

[126] *See supra* § 4-2.2.

[127] 471 U.S. 626, 642–47 (1985).

[128] *Id.* at 642.

[129] *Id.* at 643.

[130] *Zauderer*, 471 U.S. at 652.

[131] *See, e.g.*, CONN. RULES OF PROF'L CONDUCT R. 7.2(f); S.D. RULES OF PROF'L CONDUCT R. 7.2(g)(iii).

In any event, a lawyer who handles matters on a contingency fee basis certainly will need to provide greater detail about that fee basis either in the advertising itself or at the outset of any communication with a prospective client who responds to that advertising.[132]

### § 4-2.4(i) Taking Personal Responsibility for Lawyer Advertising

A lawyer or law firm must take personal and identified responsibility for any advertising that it disseminates. Under Rule 7.2(c) of the Model Rules of Professional Conduct, "[a]ny communication made pursuant to this Rule shall include the name and office address of at least one lawyer or law firm responsible for its content." Ensuring that the reader understands the communication as created by the lawyer or firm that is being promoted comports with the basic expectation that such communications be not misleading.

### § 4-2.4(j) The General Prohibition on Paying for Referrals

A lawyer ordinarily may not accept employment from another person or an organization that promotes the lawyer's legal services in return for compensation by the lawyer. Because a lawyer remains subject to restrictions on the manner in which he may advertise or solicit potential clients for legal services, the lawyer likewise may not employ another to engage in advertising or solicitation that is forbidden to the lawyer. Because a lawyer may not share fees earned for legal work with nonlawyers, for fear that the lawyer's professional independence may be undermined,[133] a lawyer likewise may not make payments to a nonlawyer for assistance in procuring that legal work. Just as a lawyer may not become financially beholden to others in a manner that would compromise the lawyer's professional judgment, the lawyer may not become economically dependent upon other persons or entities that channel legal work to the lawyer for a "finder's fee."

Professors Ronald Rotunda and John Dzienkowski explain that this anti-referral rule fits closely together with the rules prohibiting sharing of legal fees with a nonlawyer and practicing law in an organization in which a nonlawyer has an ownership interest:

> These provisions seek to minimize the third party influences that could affect a representation of a client. Formal arrangements in which lawyers give money or other things of value to third persons for recommending the lawyer's services implicate similar concerns. In addition, the rules reflect a fear that if third persons could receive funds for funneling cases to lawyers, those individuals could be tempted to violate the advertising rules and those violations could be difficult to police.[134]

Accordingly, Rule 7.2(b) of the Model Rules of Professional Conduct provides generally that "[a] lawyer shall not give anything of value to a person for recommending the lawyer's services." As discussed below, there are several exceptions ranging from payment of advertising costs to participation with a legal service plan. But the general rule remains that a lawyer should not be using intermediaries, especially those paid by

---

[132] *See infra* § 4-4.2(c)(3).

[133] *See infra* § 4-7.9(b).

[134] RONALD D. ROTUNDA & JOHN S. DZIENKOWSKI, PROFESSIONAL RESPONSIBILITY: A STUDENT'S GUIDE § 7.2–3(a) (American Bar Ass'n, 2013–2014).

the lawyer or which operate for commercial profit, to refer potential clients to the lawyer or the lawyer's associates.

### § 4-2.4(k) Exceptions to the Prohibition on Paying for Referrals

#### *§ 4-2.4(k)(1) Paying the Costs of Advertising*

While a payment to a newspaper or broadcast company for the cost of advertising may in a formal sense constitute a payment to a person for recommending the lawyer's services, Rule 7.2(b)(1) specifically excludes such payments from the general prohibition on procured referrals. The lawyer's constitutionally-protected and rule-authorized right to advertise would mean very little if the lawyer could not pay what the rule calls "the reasonable costs of advertisements or communications."

Thus, a lawyer may pay for the costs of directory listings; newspaper ads; television, radio, and internet advertising; and fees for sponsorships. In addition, as confirmed in Comment 5 to Rule 7.2, a lawyer may compensate persons "who are engaged to provide marketing or client development services, such as publicists, public-relations personnel, business-development staff and website designers."

Comment 5 also allows a lawyer to pay another for generating client leads, although that person may not actually recommend the lawyer to the possible clients who are identified. Nor may that person create any "reasonable impression" that she has analyzed the potential client's legal problems in selecting "which lawyer should receive the referral." In addition, the lawyer must not compensate that nonlawyer by sharing legal fees, a practice that compromises the independence of the lawyer.[135] If the fee paid to the lead generator turns directly on the person's retention of the lawyer for particular legal services then it would appear to be the equivalent of impermissible sharing of fees with a nonlawyer.[136]

While not directly addressed under the rule itself, a lawyer should be wary of paying members of the press for publicity in a news story. The general prohibition on false or misleading communications under Rule 7.1[137] would be violated by the lawyer who engaged in the deceptive practice of presenting to the public what appears to be an impartial news report but instead is nothing but a paid infomercial. Moreover, Rule 7.2(c) requires the lawyer or law firm to take personal responsibility for advertising.[138] A communication that falsely purported to be generated by a news organization but that actually amounted to nothing more than advertising would run afoul of this limitation as well.

None of this precludes a lawyer from being the subject of a positive news article, even one involving the provision of legal services. When consistent with other limitations in the rules (such as those precluding disclosure of confidential information[139] and restricting extrajudicial statements by a lawyer involved in a current litigation

---

[135] *See infra* § 4-7.9(b).

[136] *See* Alberto Bernabe, *Avvo Joins the Legal Market; Should Attorneys Be Concerned?*, 104 GEO. L.J. ONLINE 184, 194–95 (2016); *see also* N.J. Advisory Comm. on Prof'l Ethics, Op. No. 732 (2017); Ohio Bd. of Prof'l Conduct, Op. No. 2016–3 (2016); S.C. Ethics Advisory Op. 16–06 (2016); Penn. Bar Ass'n, Legal Ethics & Prof'l Resp. Comm. Formal Op. 2016–200 (2016).

[137] *See supra* § 4-2.3.

[138] *See supra* § 4-2.4(i).

[139] *See infra* §§ 4-6.1 to 4-6.6.

matter[140]), the lawyer may cooperate by responding to a reporter's questions and sharing other information with the news media. Moreover, a law firm or lawyer may issue a press release or engage a public relations firm to bring the activities or accomplishments of lawyers to the attention of the news media in the hope that a favorable news story might follow.

A lawyer or law firm may prepare an in-house newsletter or other notices about professional developments, provided that such publications are candidly acknowledged to be produced by the lawyer or law firm. If the newsletter or notice will be sent only to other lawyers or to clients, then it likely is not subject to the advertising and solicitation rules. If the publication is to be distributed to the general public or to others, then the distribution counts as an advertising, which is subject to the general provisions of Rule 7.2.

### *§ 4-2.4(k)(2) Legal Service Plans*

As originally envisioned, legal service plans would expand access to legal services by those in the broad middle class of our society, who are not eligible for government-subsidized legal aid services but yet are not sufficiently wealthy to easily afford legal counsel.[141] Through a legal service plan, a membership group—such as a labor union, trade association, or church organization—may provide access to legal services as a benefit to its members. Or an insurance company may allow a consumer to spread out the risk of the need for legal services by paying a set premium that creates an entitlement to a certain level of legal services contingent on certain events.

The entity setting up the plan may make an arrangement with a particular lawyer, firm, or group of lawyers or firms to provide such legal services within the terms and for the purposes of the plan (commonly called the closed-plan). Alternatively, the plan may provide a certain level of benefits to members or beneficiaries who may apply those benefits to any legal service provider (the open-plan). The plan may offer a period of free consultation with a lawyer, a discounted fee for services, a particular range of services, or full coverage.

Rule 7.2(b)(2) refrains from detailed prescriptions of what constitutes a qualified legal service plan. Instead the rule and comments focus on the limited form of compensation that may be provided by the lawyer to the plan and on the lawyer's duty to ensure appropriate behavior by the legal service plan in communicating with the public.

*First*, Rule 7.2(b)(2) limits transfers of money from the lawyer to a legal service plan to the "usual charges." In this way, the rule precludes any arrangement by which the legal service plan profits directly from the lawyer's provision of legal services. While the legal service plan may charge consumers with set fees or premiums for the legal service plan coverage, the legal service plan may not receive a percentage or other share of any fees that the lawyer obtains from the client for legal services beyond those directly covered by the plan. In other words, any profit that is realized by the legal service plan must not be directly attributable to the professional services performed by the lawyer, as opposed to fees to obtain membership in the plan itself.

---

[140] *See infra* § 4-9.11.

[141] For further background on legal service plans, types of plans, and regulation of such plans, see generally CHARLES W. WOLFRAM, MODERN LEGAL ETHICS § 16.5 (West 1986).

*Second*, as emphasized in Comment 7 to Rule 7.2, the "lawyer who accepts assignments or referrals from a legal service plan or referrals from a lawyer referral service must act reasonably to assure that the activities of the plan or service are compatible with the lawyer's professional obligations." Thus, the lawyer must verify that the legal service plan does not make false or misleading statements and does not engage in direct solicitation of the type that would be in violation of Rule 7.3.[142] If a member of the legal service plan engages the lawyer, that person receiving the legal services must be recognized as the client (and not the legal service plan entity), and the lawyer may not permit the legal service plan to control the lawyer's performance of legal services.[143]

### *§ 4-2.4(k)(3) Qualified Lawyer Referral Service*

A lawyer may also pay the "usual charges" to a qualified lawyer referral service. Comment 6 to Rule 7.2 explains that to be "qualified," such a lawyer referral service must be approved by an appropriate regulatory authority. As the comment says, the purpose of such approval is to ensure that such a referral service benefits the general consumer through "unbiased referrals to lawyers with appropriate experience in the subject matter of the representation and afford other client protections, such as complaint procedures or malpractice insurance requirements."

The classic example of a qualified lawyer referral service is one operated or sponsored by the bar association. Because such a bar association referral service is open without discrimination to any member, does not operate as a for-profit entity, and does not engage in inappropriate advertising or solicitation to procure clients, the concerns about abusive promotional conduct by commercial referral services are not present. Participation in a commercial referral service not approved by the jurisdiction's highest court or bar would likely not pass muster.[144]

### *§ 4-2.4(k)(4) Non-Profit Lawyer Referral Service*

A lawyer may also pay the "usual charges" to a non-profit lawyer referral service. While a "qualified" lawyer referral service must be approved by a regulatory authority, a genuine non-profit referral service need not obtain such an approval. However, under Comment 6 to Rule 7.2, a non-profit lawyer referral service must satisfy the same expectation that it operates as a "consumer-oriented organization[ ] that provide[s] unbiased referrals to lawyers with appropriate experience in the subject matter of the representation and afford[s] other client protections, such as complaint procedures or malpractice insurance requirements."

Non-profit legal assistance programs presumably fall outside of the general rule prohibiting a lawyer from requesting recommendation of employment. Without the potentially distorting effect of the profit motive, a referral from a non-profit legal assistance program is unlikely to raise troubling questions about how potential clients were attracted or compromise the independence of the lawyer who receives the referrals. Thus, as examples, a lawyer may participate with and accept referrals from a legal aid

---

[142] *See supra* § 4-2.2 and *infra* § 4-2.5(a). On Rule 7.3(d) as allowing a lawyer to participate with a legal service plan that uses direct contacts to solicit memberships for the plan, see *infra* § 4-2.5(e).

[143] On the duty of the lawyer to maintain independence of professional judgment and not allow a person who recommends or pays the lawyer to render legal services to another to control the lawyer's professional judgment, see *infra* § 4-7.3(g).

[144] *See* Ohio Adv. Op. 2016–3.

office, a public defender office, a military legal assistance office, and similar non-profit organizations, even if the lawyer will not perform the legal services pro bono.

#### *§ 4-2.4(k)(5) Purchasing a Law Practice*

When a lawyer purchases a law practice, as authorized by Rule 1.17 of the Model Rules of Professional Conduct,[145] the payment by the buying lawyer for the practice and its good will effectively obtains a recommendation of the lawyer's services to prospective clients. Although the clients of the existing practice being sold retain the right to transfer their legal matters to another lawyer, the sale-of-law-practice rule requires written notice by the selling lawyer to the clients about the transfer of the practice to another lawyer. As a practical matter, many clients will remain with the practice after the transfer to the buying lawyer.

Because the rules recognize the legitimacy of a sale of a law practice, subject to safeguards, Rule 7.2(b)(3) specifically excludes payments for a law practice under Rule 1.17 from the anti-referral prohibitions.

#### *§ 4-2.4(k)(6) Reciprocal Professional Referral Agreements*

In language added in 2002 to Rule 7.2 of the Model Rules of Professional Conduct, a lawyer may enter into a reciprocal referral arrangement with another lawyer or a nonlawyer professional. While not involving a payment as such—and indeed any payment solely for a referral remains prohibited[146]—a lawyer may enter into a reciprocal agreement with another lawyer or a nonlawyer professional to refer clients. A valuable consideration does exist, of course, but it is limited to the undertaking that each party to the agreement will refer clients or customers to the other.

Under Rule 7.2(b)(4), the client being referred must be notified of the existence and nature of the reciprocal referral arrangement. In addition, the referral agreement may not be exclusive (that is, the lawyer may refer clients to someone else as appropriate). The nonexclusivity rule preserves the independent judgment of the lawyer, so that if another professional would be "a better choice" for a client, the lawyer will so advise the client and send him in a direction outside the referral agreement.[147]

This addition by the American Bar Association to the Model Rules has received a decidedly mixed response thus far among the states, only about half of which have adopted Rule 7.2(b)(4).

## § 4-2.5 THE PROHIBITION ON DIRECT SOLICITATION OF PROSPECTIVE CLIENTS

### § 4-2.5(a) The Purpose and Nature of the Prohibition on Direct Solicitation

In contrast with liberalized advertising rules over the past several decades, the prohibition on personal solicitation of prospective clients remains nearly absolute.

---

[145] *See supra* § 4-3.7.

[146] *See supra* § 4-2.4(j) and *infra* § 4-4.5.

[147] RONALD D. ROTUNDA & JOHN S. DZIENKOWSKI, PROFESSIONAL RESPONSIBILITY: A STUDENT'S GUIDE § 7.2–3(f) (American Bar Ass'n, 2013–2014).

Rule 7.3(a) of the Model Rules of Professional Conduct states simply (with limited exceptions) that "[a] lawyer shall not by in-person, live telephone or real-time electronic contact solicit professional employment when a significant motive for the lawyer's doing so is the lawyer's pecuniary gain." Thus, the bar against direct contact covers solicitations that are conducted by the lawyer in-person, by live telephone (that is, other than by recorded telephone message), and by "real-time electronic" communications. Real-time electronic communication presumably includes exchanges by text dialogue through social media such as instant messaging, internet chat rooms, and real-time internet video, when used by the lawyer to encourage the targeted person to engage his or her legal services. Email, however, would not ordinarily be regarded as real-time electronic communication, as it typically is regulated as a form of direct mail under Rule 7.3(c).[148]

Accordingly, as said in Comment 2 to Rule 7.3, whenever communication is in a form that involves a direct back-and-forth exchange by the lawyer with a prospective client—what the comment describes as "the private importuning of the trained advocate in a direct interpersonal encounter"—the "situation is fraught with the possibility of undue influence, intimidation and over-reaching."

In *Ohralik v. Ohio State Bar Association*,[149] the Supreme Court explained that, "[u]nlike a public advertisement, which simply provides information and leaves the recipient free to act upon it or not, in-person solicitation may exert pressure and often demands an immediate response, without providing an opportunity for comparison or reflection."[150] Especially when a person is unsophisticated, injured, or otherwise distressed, "the overtures of an uninvited lawyer" may be intrusive, an invasion of privacy, and directed at a person vulnerable to improper influence.[151] Because "[o]ften there is no witness other than the lawyer and the lay person whom he has solicited, rendering it difficult or impossible to obtain reliable proof of what actually took place," and to allow states to prevent these serious harms before they occur, the Court upheld general prohibitions on personal solicitation by lawyers as appropriate "prophylactic measures."[152]

Subsequently, in *Zauderer v. Office of Disciplinary Counsel*,[153] the Supreme Court again characterized face-to-face solicitation as "a practice rife with possibilities for overreaching, invasion of privacy, the exercise of undue influence, and outright fraud." The "coercive force of the personal presence of a trained advocate" and the "pressure on the potential client for an immediate yes-or-no answer to the offer of representation" justifies strong controls on this form of solicitation.[154]

Situations may arise in which a person has an urgent need to retain legal counsel to secure rights, preserve evidence, and avoid being pressured into poor decisions by others.[155] Alternative means remain available for conveying information about legal

---

[148] On direct mail or email advertising, see *supra* § 4-2.4(d)(1).

[149] 436 U.S. 447, 457–67 (1978).

[150] *Id.* at 457.

[151] *Id.* at 464–67.

[152] *Id.* at 465–66.

[153] 471 U.S. 626, 641 (1985).

[154] *Id.* at 642.

[155] *See generally* MONROE H. FREEDMAN & ABBE SMITH, UNDERSTANDING LAWYERS' ETHICS ch. 12 (LexisNexis, 2d ed., 2002) (referring provocatively to "the professional responsibility to chase ambulances" and

services to persons in need, including advertising and direct mailing or emailing, which is liberally permitted under the rules of most states and may even be targeted toward persons who face a situation that gives rise to a specific need for legal services.[156]

Moreover, a lawyer acting alone or through a bar association or other professional organization is not restrained from making a direct personal or telephonic contact with a person who is in dire need of legal services, provided that the lawyer does so as a public service and not with the design of securing a client for herself. As Justice Powell wrote in *Ohralik*,[157] "[t]he Rule does not prohibit a lawyer from giving unsolicited legal advice; it proscribes the acceptance of employment resulting from such advice."

## § 4-2.5(b) Exemptions from the Direct Solicitation Prohibition

Under Rule 7.3(a), communications with certain categories of persons are exempted from the proscription on direct solicitation, namely another "lawyer" and those with whom the lawyer "has a family, close personal, or prior professional relationship."

While the potential for abuse through direct personal contact by the lawyer is mitigated with respect to these categories of persons, it may not disappear. For that reason, Rule 7.3(b) withdraws permission to the lawyer to make a direct contact when "the target of the solicitation has made known to the lawyer a desire not to be solicited by the lawyer; or . . . the solicitation involves coercion, duress or harassment."

### *§ 4-2.5(b)(1) Solicitation to Lawyers*

Communications or solicitations for professional employment between lawyers are excluded from the regulations on direct contact in most states. When one lawyer offers legal services to another lawyer, the familiarity of the prospective client with the nature of legal practice greatly reduces the risk that the recipient of the communication will be misled or improperly influenced in the choice of counsel. Nonetheless, more than a third of the states include no exception from the direct solicitation rule for communications to other lawyers.

### *§ 4-2.5(b)(2) Solicitation to Family and Close Friends*

A lawyer hardly may be expected to remain silent about his professional work or to refuse to offer suggestions about legal problems to those persons in the lawyer's own family or the lawyer's inner social circle.

### *§ 4-2.5(b)(3) Solicitation to Current, Former, and Prospective Clients*

When a lawyer is communicating with an existing client, even for the purpose of offering additional legal services, the client already has retained the lawyer and a fiduciary relationship exists requiring honesty in communications by the lawyer. This preexisting relationship removes these communications from the common category of solicitations to prospective clients.

Likewise, when the recipient of the communication is a former client, that is someone who previously had retained the lawyer, the prior relationship and the

---

arguing that direct solicitation which does not involve misrepresentation or undue influence should not be disciplined).

[156] *See supra* § 4-2.4(d)(1).

[157] 436 U.S. at 458.

familiarity of the parties with each other reduces the risk of undue or misleading influence by the lawyer. In this situation, the lawyer and client already have a history and an established professional relationship, even if the relationship is not active at the moment. The lawyer also has continuing fiduciary responsibilities that attend to a former client, such as the perpetual duty to maintain confidentiality[158] and the duty to decline to represent another person adverse to the former client in the same or a substantially related matter.[159] Indeed, even when a representation has been concluded, a lawyer may have a legitimate reason to speak directly with the former client about a development in the law or a new factual discovery that might affect the results of the prior representation or justify reopening the matter.

When a prospective client already has contacted the lawyer, either on the client's own initiative or in response to a valid form of advertising or contact by the lawyer, then at least a fledgling or limited professional relationship exists.[160] A response by the lawyer to a request from a prospective client for further information is not subject to the direct contact rules. In such an instance, the matter has passed beyond the initial contact stage, which was the point of greatest danger that a member of the public would be pushed toward the lawyer by misleading information or undue influence. The continuing dialogue between the client and the lawyer, even though actual retention has not yet occurred, has advanced to the stage that a more flexible interchange is appropriate, free from the rigid framework of direct contact restrictions.

### § 4-2.5(c) Communications with Members of a Class or Potential Class in Litigation

Once a class has been certified for class action litigation, the attorney who is designated as counsel for that certified class has an attorney-client relationship with every member of the class, although that relationship is atypical in that the attorney often does not have a personal relationship with each class member. Class counsel should not be restricted from contacting members of the class as clients or offering legal advice to them as clients about the pending class action litigation.

When communicating with the unnamed members of the class with whom the attorney does not have a formal contract or personal attorney-client relationship, however, the class counsel should not attempt to secure an unfair advantage, such as soliciting separate and personal attorney-client contracts from class members for additional financial advantage to the lawyer. As Professor Charles Wolfram concluded:

> There seems little reason, other than partisan advantage, to resist a rule that would leave the class' lawyer free to contact members of the class for any purpose, but should regard with suspicion any individual contracts to pay the lawyer an amount in addition to the award made out of the class recovery.[161]

When a lawyer has been properly retained by a client who has a legitimate interest in obtaining joinder by other persons to a potential class action, the lawyer may make appropriate communications with potential class members, including contacts made before certification of a class or even before a suit has been filed (subject of course to any

[158] On the lawyer's duty of confidentiality with respect to a former client, see *infra* § 4-7.5(e).

[159] On the successive conflict rules for former clients, see *infra* § 4-7.5.

[160] On the lawyer's duties to a prospective client, see *supra* § 4-3.1(c) to (d).

[161] CHARLES W. WOLFRAM, MODERN LEGAL ETHICS § 14.2.5 (West, 1986).

limitations on communications with potential class members imposed by court rules or court order).[162]

A lawyer representing an individual whose rights (or defenses) may be best secured in the context of a class action joined by others must be granted some freedom of action in communicating with other persons who potentially could join as additional plaintiffs or defendants in the putative class. By virtue of conducting necessary fact investigation prior to filing a lawsuit, the lawyer might well contact witnesses who also might be potential class members. Or the lawyer's client may know of other persons in a similar situation. If the lawyer's personal contact with such a person is carefully limited to exploring the facts and circumstances that bear on the suitability of that person for being joined to the action, and any communications are limited to suggesting such joinder, then the contact should be permissible.

However, given the general prohibition in Rule 7.3(a) on solicitation to obtain professional employment, contacts by a lawyer representing a client with other persons in a potential class should be limited to the purpose of obtaining their joinder, not soliciting direct employment by those contacted. The courts have recognized the possibility for abuse by lawyers in communication with potential class members, specifically "solicitation of direct representation of class members who are not formal parties" and "solicitation of funds and agreements to pay fees."[163] If the person contacted by the lawyer about joinder should initiate discussion about possibly retaining the lawyer as well, the lawyer may respond and accept employment that follows. Otherwise, the lawyer should be careful to conform to court limitations on contacts with potential class members and limit such communications to possible joinder with an existing client whose rights or defenses would be strengthened by such joinder.

### § 4-2.5(d) Direct Solicitation for Public Interest Purposes

Under Rule 7.3(a) of the Model Rules of Professional Conduct, the proscription on direct solicitation by a lawyer is limited to "when a significant motive for the lawyer's doing so is the lawyer's pecuniary gain." This qualifying language is intended to clarify that the anti-solicitation rule does not apply to associations and messages protected under the Free Speech Clause of the First Amendment of the United States Constitution, such as solicitation of individuals by public interest organization lawyers to participate in public interest litigation. When a lawyer is asking a citizen to join a cause through legal action, rather than seeking a client to advance the lawyer's financial interests, the protection of the First Amendment is at its apex.

---

[162] *See generally* Gulf Oil Co. v. Bernard, 452 U.S. 89, 99–104 (1981) (ruling that a trial court has broad discretion to enter appropriate orders governing the conduct of parties and counsel in class actions, including addressing abuses in communications directed at potential class members, but that a court should not routinely impose "a communications ban that interferes with the formation of a class or the prosecution of a class action in accordance" with the procedural rules).

[163] *See* A.J. ex rel. L.B. v. Kierst, 56 F.3d 849, 858 n.9 (8th Cir. 1995) (stating that "courts and scholars have recognized as potentially hazardous in class action suits" the following kinds of abuses: "(1) solicitation of direct representation of class members who are not formal parties; (2) solicitation of funds and agreements to pay fees; (3) solicitation by defendants of requests to opt out; and (4) communications with class members that misrepresent the status or effect of the pending action"). *But see* Vignaroli v. Blue Cross of Iowa, 360 N.W.2d 741 (Iowa 1985) (holding that letters that not only solicited potential class members to participate in the litigation but also solicited contribution of funds from potential class members toward expenses and costs of litigation did not violate "class action rules" and thus did not justify refusing to certify the class, although the solicitations apparently did not seek agreement to pay legal fees and the court did not discuss solicitation limitations in ethics rules).

In *In re Primus*,[164] a decision rendered on the very same day as *Ohralik v. Ohio State Bar Association*,[165] the Supreme Court rejected South Carolina's application of its anti-solicitation rule to an American Civil Liberties Union lawyer who by letter had offered free legal representation to poor women who wished to challenge the legality of a sterilization program for welfare mothers. When a lawyer is acting to further "political and ideological" goals, the Court held that the First Amendment extends protection to communications that otherwise would constitute forbidden "solicitation."[166] Indeed, the Court found that this solicitation of clients by the ACLU lawyer involved the exercise of "core First Amendment rights."[167]

Although *Primus* involved a written solicitation (but one that was a follow-up to an initial in-person meeting by the lawyer with a group of women) and the Court thus noted that there was thus no "significant opportunity for overreaching or coercion," the Court also reaffirmed its earlier decision in *NAACP v. Button*.[168] In *Button*, the Supreme Court had upheld the constitutional rights of civil rights lawyers to directly contact potential clients for school desegregation litigation. In *Primus*, the Court refused to distinguish *Button* on the supposed ground that the lawyers there had played only a small role in solicitation, instead emphasizing that the record confirmed that "NAACP staff attorneys were involved in the actual solicitation efforts."[169] Accordingly, unless the solicitation "in fact is misleading, overbearing, or involves other features of deception or improper influence,"[170] the protection of political or ideological activity by non-profit public interest organizations should extend to both written and personal communications with members of the public.

### § 4-2.5(e) Participation in a Legal Services Plan That Solicits Membership

Legal service plans promise to expand access to legal services by allowing consumers to spread out the risk by paying a premium or set fee to an insurance company or a membership organization in return for being able to obtain certain level of legal services. The Model Rules of Professional Conduct permit a lawyer to participate with legal service plans by paying the usual fees, making direct contacts with representatives of such plans, and by associating with plans that use in-person or telephone contacts to solicit members.

*First*, as discussed previously,[171] under Model Rule 7.2(b)(2), notwithstanding the general rule that a lawyer may not pay someone else for referrals, the lawyer may "pay the usual charges of a legal service plan." While the lawyer may not permit the legal service plan to profit directly from the lawyer's provision of legal services to a client by sharing legal fees, the lawyer may pay appropriate charges to participate with the plan. The lawyer also must ensure that he maintains professional independence and that the person receiving the services is recognized as the client.

---

[164] 436 U.S. 412 (1978).

[165] 436 U.S. 447 (1978). *See supra* § 4-2.5(b).

[166] *Primus*, 436 U.S. at 414–39.

[167] *Id.* at 432.

[168] 371 U.S. 415, 421–22, 428–30 (1963).

[169] *Primus*, 436 U.S. at 425 n.16.

[170] *See id.* at 438.

[171] *See supra* § 4-2.4(k)(2).

*Second*, as stated in Comment 7 to Model Rule 7.3, the lawyer may make direct contacts with the representatives of organizations or groups seeking to establish a legal service plan, notwithstanding the general prohibition on in-person, live telephone, or real-time electronic solicitation of clients. The lawyer may notify such representatives of the lawyer's availability to participate in such a plan, details concerning the plan, and what services the lawyer or law firm is willing to offer. The comment explains that "[t]his form of communication is not directed to people who are seeking legal services for themselves. Rather, it is usually addressed to an individual acting in a fiduciary capacity seeking a supplier of legal services for others who may, if they choose, become prospective clients of the lawyer."

*Third*, under Rule 7.3(d), "a lawyer may participate with a prepaid or group legal service plan operated by an organization not owned or directed by the lawyer that uses in-person or telephone contact to solicit memberships or subscriptions for the plan from persons who are not known to need legal services in a particular matter covered by the plan." Subject to several important qualifications, then, the lawyer may work with a legal service plan that itself engages in direct contacts to promote the legal service plan.

The lawyer may not own or direct the legal service plan that engages in such in-person or telephone contacts to solicit memberships or subscriptions. In this way, the rule prevents a lawyer from circumventing the prohibition on direct solicitations of clients by creating a legal service plan that really is the alter ego of the lawyer or the lawyer's law firm.

Any in-person or telephone solicitations by the legal service plan must be directed to the general public, to members of the organizations, or to a group of people identified as other than those known to need legal services in a particular matter. In contrast with the permission granted by Rule 7.3(c) to send mail or e-mails as advertising material to persons known to be in need of legal services in a particular matter,[172] no in-person or telephone contact may be made by a legal service plan with persons who are known to need legal services for a particular matter covered by the plan. When a person is known to need legal services for a particular matter, any direct solicitation creates great risks of abuse, even when the lawyer is not making the solicitation directly. A legal service plan that targets individuals that have been identified as needing legal services in a particular matter is operating in a manner fraught with risks of coercion and harassment. A lawyer may not cooperate with such an organization.

And, importantly, the in-person or telephone solicitations by a legal service plan must be made for the purpose of securing additional members or subscribers, not to sell directly the lawyer's legal services. The permitted direct solicitation must be made to promote the plan itself, not as a referral service for the lawyer. Otherwise, the purported legal service plan would be acting as the lawyer's specific agent in making direct solicitations that the lawyer is forbidden to make personally.

### § 4-2.5(f) Public Communications by the Lawyer About Legal Topics

A lawyer appropriately may provide general legal information through the lawyer's participation in public education activities and through public speaking and writing or blogging about the law, not designed to directly solicit clients or specifically-tailored to

---

[172] *See supra* § 4-2.4(d)(1).

solve individual legal problems. Because of our legal education, practice experience, expertise in fields of law, and professional commitment to public service, we as lawyers are encouraged to participate in public dialogue about legal issues and controversies and to contribute to public education about the legal system. Indeed, as the California bar has rightly concluded, when a lawyer publicly speaks about legal matters, such as blogging on site that is not integrated into the attorney or firm's professional web site, the lawyer is not engaged in a communication subject to lawyer advertising rules, unless the blog suggests the lawyer's availability for professional employment, either directly (by inviting consultation) or implicitly (such as repeated blog posts extolling the lawyer's professional successes).[173]

A lawyer who speaks publicly (or writes in print media or blogs or comments on the internet) about legal topics may agree to undertake representation of a client, even if the client was attracted to or became aware of the lawyer based upon the lawyer's participation in public discourse (and even if that effect of the public speaking or writing is reasonably anticipated).

Underlying the above discussion is the assumption that a lawyer's communication on a legal topic is a genuine civic-minded presentation at a legitimate public forum and not disguised as a means of gaining direct access to individuals to solicit employment by providing answers to specific legal problems experienced by particular persons. If rather than being invited by an organization to speak about a legal topic, the lawyer instead has generated the speaking engagement by making advance contacts with potentially interested persons who may have legal needs, those very contacts may constitute solicitation.

In addition, the lawyer who speaks or writes publicly should be careful not to volunteer answers to or be drawn into a discussion about individual legal problems during that presentation or publication. In a presentation about an area of the law, the speaker or writer may offer examples to illustrate a point and may appropriately address specific types of legal issues that have or could arise (and indeed this very book does both of those things in abundance). But the lecturer or author should not be understood to be advising any individual listener or reader about the possible answer to her personal legal problem (and that of course goes for this book as well).

The temptation to move beyond a generally-oriented discussion of the law and toward the giving of individual legal advice is especially great when a lawyer speaking on a legal topic accepts questions from the audience or when a lawyer responds to comments to blog posts or uses other social media to engage in a back-and-forth exchange. Not infrequently, a question will be framed in terms of the audience member's personal situation so as to invite suggestions from the speaker about the legal implications that might follow. The safest course of action may be to simply decline to answer the question. As Professor Catherine Lanctot rightly warns, lawyers should "understand that an attorney who provides specific legal advice to a layperson online could later be held to have created an attorney-client relationship with that person, depending on the level of specificity and the degree of reasonable reliance, and [lawyers] must be warned that online disclaimers alone might not suffice to avoid this result."[174]

---

[173] Cal. St. Bar, Formal Op. 2016–196.

[174] Catherine J. Lanctot, *Becoming a Competent 21st Century Legal Ethics Professor: Everything You Always Wanted to Know About Technology (But Were Afraid to Ask)*, 2015 J. PROF'L LAWYER 75, 88.

Alternatively, a lawyer receiving an individually-tailored question at a public presentation or on-line could preface any further comments by explaining that the lawyer may not provide individual legal advice to members of the audience and that any such advice would require careful consideration of all the facts. The lawyer then might offer some general thoughts for the audience as a whole about the broader topic that was implicated by the question.

If a person does approach the lawyer after the presentation and seeks the lawyer's legal counsel regarding a personal legal issue or problem—at that person's own initiative and not by the lawyer's importuning—the lawyer may accept employment and thereby create an attorney-client relationship. To avoid even the appearance of direct solicitation and allow the person to act with deliberation rather than in the immediate aftermath of the seminar or presentation, the lawyer should ask the person to schedule an appointment to discuss the matter further another day.

## § 4-2.6 PROHIBITION OF "PAY-TO-PLAY" POLITICAL CONTRIBUTIONS IN EXCHANGE FOR LEGAL WORK

Rule 7.6 of the Model Rules of Professional Conduct—the so-called "pay to play" prohibition—is a relatively recent addition to the formal standards of ethics, but one that so far has little following among the states. The rule was adopted by the American Bar Association in 2000 to respond to concerns in some jurisdictions that lawyers were being importuned to make political campaign contributions to candidates for judicial or public office in exchange for promised referrals of lucrative governmental legal work, notably in the municipal bond field.[175] As Professors Geoffrey Hazard and William Hodes and attorney Peter Jarvis explain, "[t]he *quid pro quo* is virtually never stated explicitly; yet, those who contribute to the government official or judge's campaigns often turn out to be the ones who are awarded the most legal, underwriting, or advisory work."[176]

Under Model Rule 7.6, a lawyer or law firm is forbidden to accept government legal work or an appointment to representation by a judge if it was preceded by a political contribution made or solicited from others by the lawyer or law firm "for the purpose of obtaining or being considered for that type of legal engagement or appointment." The mere fact that a lawyer has made a contribution to a successful political campaign and then subsequently obtains government legal work does not establish a violation of this rule. What is prohibited under the rule is a political contribution designed to produce the reward of legal employment, that is, when the lawyer or law firm attempts to corruptly influence public action through political campaign contributions (whether or not the contribution is accepted by or even known to the candidate).[177] As Comment 1 to Rule 7.6 states, "the integrity of the profession" is undermined if the public perceives that government legal work is awarded on the basis of political contributions rather than the qualifications of the lawyer or law firm.

---

[175] On the history of Rule 7.6, see generally Brian C. Buescher, *ABA Model Rules 7.6: The ABA Pleases the SEC, But Does Not Solve Pay to Play*, 14 GEO. J. LEGAL ETHICS 139, 140–151 (2000).

[176] 2 GEOFFREY C. HAZARD, JR., W. WILLIAM HODES & PETER R. JARVIS, THE LAW OF LAWYERING § 64.02 (Aspen, 4th ed., 2016).

[177] If the candidate is aware of the contributor's purpose when accepting the contribution and the promise of legal employment is made not merely implicit but explicit, then the exchange arguably amounts to a bribe of a public official, which Comment 6 to Rule 7.6 confirms would constitute a violation as well of Rule 8.4(b) by constituting a criminal act that reflects adversely on the lawyer's fitness for practice. *See supra* § 4-1.4(a).

As Comment 5 states, the rule articulates a basic "but-for" causation test, that is, the rule applies when, "but for the desire to be considered for the legal engagement or appointment, the lawyer or law firm would not have made or solicited the contributions." As with other questions of mental state relating to professional conduct, the comment explains that whether a lawyer or law firm made or solicited a contribution with the forbidden motive may be determined by "an examination" of the surrounding "circumstances." If, for example, a lawyer or law firm were to make a contribution or series of contributions to a candidate for state attorney general, county supervisor, or city council, that was "substantial in relation to other contributions," which was followed by "an award of the legal engagement," an inference could be drawn that the contribution had been made for the purpose of securing the engagement. Of course, as the comment observes, other factors may contradict that inference, such as evidence that the lawyer or law firm made the contribution "to further a political, social, or economic interest or because of an existing personal, family, or professional relationship with a candidate."

At the time this was written in 2017, fewer than ten states had adopted Rule 7.6. Whether this reflects approval of "pay-to-play" campaign contribution schemes involving lawyers and judges or public officials is doubtful. The apparent disinterest among the states likely flows from hesitations about whether a widespread problem exists in the particular jurisdiction justifying a formal solution and whether such a rule evaluating the motive behind a campaign contribution is enforceable.

# Chapter 4-3

# THE ATTORNEY-CLIENT RELATIONSHIP: BEGINNING TO END

**By Gregory C. Sisk**

*Table of Sections*

§ 4-3.1 Duties to Prospective Clients
§ 4-3.2 Creation and Nature of the Attorney-Client Relationship
§ 4-3.3 Scope of Representation
§ 4-3.4 Allocating Decision-Making Authority Between Client and Lawyer
§ 4-3.5 Client with Diminished Capacity
§ 4-3.6 Ending the Representation
§ 4-3.7 Sale of a Law Practice and Effect on Clients

---

## § 4-3.1 DUTIES TO PROSPECTIVE CLIENTS

### § 4-3.1(a) Overview of the Lawyer's Responsibilities to Prospective Clients

Lawyers always have had professional responsibilities to those with whom an attorney-client relationship is being contemplated. Most importantly, the information shared with the attorney by a would-be client was entitled to at least some of the protections of confidentiality, including the attorney-client privilege, even if the lawyer and client subsequently decided not to consummate an attorney-client relationship.

However, the theoretical basis for extending these protections, the scope or extent to which the protections applied, and the nature of the relationship between the lawyer and the putative client was uncertain. Was a quasi-attorney-client relationship to be implied for the limited purpose of initial consultation? Were the lawyer's professional responsibilities to a mere potential client limited in scope when a full-fledged attorney-client relationship did not result? How far did the rules about confidentiality and conflict of interest extend to the person who explored representation but who did not become a client represented by the lawyer?

In 2002, the American Bar Association amended the Model Rules of Professional Conduct to add Rule 1.18 to directly address these questions by creating the special category of the "prospective client." All but a couple of states have adopted Rule 1.18. As the New Jersey Supreme Court has well-explained, Rule 1.18 "seeks to strike a delicate balance between a client's right to protect communications made in the context of a consultation precedent to the actual retention of a lawyer, and the lawyer's right to be free to represent clients without being unduly restricted by the yoke of short-lived consultations that do not ripen into an attorney-client relationship."[1]

---

[1] O Builders & Assocs. v. Yuna Corp., 19 A.3d 966, 968 (N.J. 2011).

Under this rule, the lawyer's obligation to protect confidential information applies to information shared by the prospective client, even if an attorney-client relationship is not formed.[2] The lawyer's duty of loyalty attaches to the prospective client as well. However, the conflict of interest constraints upon the lawyer are more limited, in recognition that the relationship between a lawyer and a prospective client itself is limited to the discrete purpose of considering a representation that ultimately was not undertaken.[3] Because a lawyer's interaction with a prospective client may restrict her ability to represent other parties by reason of the conflict of interest constraint, the lawyer may wish to adopt measures designed to control the information received from a prospective client during an initial consultation. Alternatively, the lawyer may seek an advance consent from the prospective client that receipt of information will not prevent the lawyer from representing another party in the matter.[4]

### § 4-3.1(b) Defining the Prospective Client

Under Rule 1.18(a) of the Model Rules of Professional Conduct, the "prospective client" is defined as "[a] person who consults with a lawyer about the possibility of forming a client-lawyer relationship with respect to a matter." Because the rule applies only when there is a fair prospect that the representation will be undertaken, not every person who chooses to share information with a lawyer comes within the protections of this rule. As Comment 2 to Rule 1.18 explains, a genuine "prospective client" is the person who has a "reasonable expectation that the lawyer is willing to discuss the possibility of forming a client-lawyer relationship."

If a person confronts a lawyer unexpectedly, on the street or at a social gathering, and blurts out information of a confidential nature, the setting may negate any reasonable expectation that the lawyer was prepared to consider formation of an attorney-client relationship (unless the lawyer invited or proves responsive to the advance). The person who unilaterally imposes information upon a lawyer by an email or letter, which was not encouraged by the lawyer's advertising or invitation to send information through a web site, does not ordinarily have a rational basis to believe that such an imposition will set the stage for creation of an attorney-client relationship.[5]

Moreover, the person who discloses information to a lawyer but "is not genuinely seeking legal advice or legal services from the lawyer" and "instead has the purpose of disqualifying the lawyer (or his firm) from being engaged by an opposing party thought to be lurking in the wings" certainly does not qualify as a legitimate prospective client.[6] Comment 2 excludes from the definition of "prospective client" the "person who communicates with a lawyer for the purpose of disqualifying the lawyer." This odious practice of "taint shopping"[7] should not be tolerated by the court if and when a motion to disqualify the targeted lawyer later is filed.

When a person has a reasonable basis for believing that the lawyer might undertake the representation, and the lawyer engages in an initial consultation with that person,

---

2 *See infra* § 4-3.1(a).

3 *See infra* § 4-3.1(d).

4 *See infra* § 4-3.1(e).

5 *See also infra* § 4-3.1(e).

6 1 GEOFFREY C. HAZARD, JR., W. WILLIAM HODES & PETER R. JARVIS, THE LAW OF LAWYERING § 23.04 (Aspen, 4th ed., 2016).

7 *See* Ill. Adv. Op. 12–18; N.Y.C. Ethics Op. 2006–2.

the prospective client deserves certain protections. This client is entitled to confidentiality for the information shared with the lawyer and the assurance that the lawyer will not subsequently accept an adverse representation that could cause significant harm to the person. Because discussions with a prospective client ordinarily are "limited in time and depth" and leave both parties free to proceed no further, Comment 1 to Rule 1.18 explains that "prospective clients should receive some but not all of the protection afforded clients."

### § 4-3.1(c) The Prospective Client and Confidentiality

For a prospective client and lawyer to fully explore the possibility of a representation on a particular matter, the client ordinarily must share information sufficient for the lawyer to understand the nature of the matter, to evaluate whether the lawyer is competent and interested in undertaking responsibility for the matter, and to advise the client as to potential expenses and alternative courses of action. As discussed below, the lawyer may want to carefully control the prospective client's disclosure of information, so as to preserve greater flexibility in terms of representing other, especially existing, clients.[8] The lawyer may wish to avoid learning about the client's assessment of the substance of the matter or other sensitive information until after conducting a preliminary conflicts-check.

If the lawyer does engage in a more involved substantive discussion with the prospective client, however, the information shared by the client becomes confidential within the meaning of Rule 1.6 of the Model Rules of Professional Conduct,[9] and, indeed, falls within the attorney-client privilege.[10] A person consulting with a lawyer about possible representation is entitled to the fundamental guarantee of confidentiality. The prospective client thus may share private thoughts and relate sensitive information secure in the knowledge that what has been shared will be safeguarded and will not be used by the lawyer against the prospective client.

Under Rule 1.18(b), "[e]ven when no client-lawyer relationship ensues, a lawyer who has learned information from a prospective client shall not use or reveal that information, except as Rule 1.9 would permit with respect to information of a former client." Under Rule 1.9(c), a lawyer may not (1) use confidential information "to the disadvantage of the former client," unless the rules so permit or require as to a client (that is, one of the various exceptions to confidentiality apply) or "the information has become generally known;" or (2) disclose confidential information unless the rules so permit or require as to a client (that is, one of the exceptions to confidentiality applies).[11]

In sum, if the lawyer and prospective client do not consummate a full-fledged attorney-client relationship, the lawyer's duty to protect confidential information is the same as that owed a former client, but not quite as robust as that which applies to a present client (where the lawyer must protect confidentiality even if the information has become generally known).

---

8 *See infra* § 4-3.1(e).

9 *See infra* § 4-6.2.

10 *See infra* § 4-6.3(b)(2).

11 *See infra* § 4-7.5(e).

### § 4-3.1(d) The Prospective Client and Conflicts of Interest

The prospective client is owed not only the safeguard of confidentiality for information shared with the lawyer,[12] but also a limited degree of loyalty from the lawyer with whom the person consults about possible representation. However, as Professors Geoffrey Hazard and William Hodes and attorney Peter Jarvis explain, "[b]ecause the relationship between a prospective client and a lawyer by definition never reaches the stage where the duty of loyalty attaches with full force," the rule "imposes a less stringent regime on the lawyer than where actual clients and former clients are involved."[13] Although the guarantee of confidentiality extended to a prospective client is directly parallel to that owed to a former client, the conflict of interest protections given to a prospective client are similar to but more limited than those afforded to a full-fledged former client.

Under Rule 1.18(c), a lawyer generally may not "represent a client with interests materially adverse to those of a prospective client in the same or a substantially related matter if the lawyer received information from the prospective client that could be significantly harmful to that person in the matter." While Rule 1.9 prohibits a lawyer from representing a client adverse to a former client "in the same or a substantially related matter,"[14] Rule 1.18(c) bars such an adverse representation only if the lawyer also had obtained confidential information from the prospective client that would be "significantly harmful" if used against the prospective client.

Thus, while Rule 1.9 is designed to preclude any exploration into the specific nature of material confidential information that had been available to the lawyer when representing the former client,[15] Rule 1.18 sanctions an evaluation of the importance and harmful quality of confidential information that was actually obtained by the lawyer from a prospective client. As the New Jersey Supreme Court articulated the standard in *O Builders & Associates v. Yuna Corp.*,[16] with respect to the information obtained from a prospective client who did not thereafter enter into a full-fledged attorney-client relationship and then later faces the lawyer representing an adverse party, "the harm suffered must be prejudicial in fact to the former prospective client within the confines of the specific matter in which disqualification is sought, a determination that is exquisitely fact-sensitive and -specific."

Because an initial consultation with a prospective client ordinarily is limited in time and depth of discussion, the lawyer is somewhat less likely to obtain information that would be both significant and harmful to the prospective client. However, where the lawyer and prospective client have engaged in a more extensive substantive discussion of the matter, the lawyer may have learned information that is both significant and would be harmful if employed against the prospective client. If so, the lawyer then is disqualified from undertaking another representation materially adverse to the prospective client when the matter is the same or substantially related in nature.

---

[12] *See supra* § 4-3.1(c).

[13] 1 GEOFFREY C. HAZARD, JR., W. WILLIAM HODES & PETER R. JARVIS, THE LAW OF LAWYERING § 23.06 (Aspen, 4th ed., 2016).

[14] *See infra* § 4-7.5.

[15] *See infra* § 4-7.5(c).

[16] 19 A.3d 966, 977 (N.J. 2011).

However, Rule 1.18(d)(1) permits the lawyer to avoid what otherwise would be disqualifying by obtaining "informed consent, confirmed in writing" from both the prospective client and the client that would be affected by the lawyer's continuing representation adverse to the prospective client. A prospective client may not be amenable to such an arrangement if approached after-the-fact when the lawyer or another lawyer in the firm wishes to represent another adverse party. In advance, however, Comment 5 to Rule 1.18 invites the lawyer to "condition a consultation with a prospective client on the person's informed consent that no information disclosed during the consultation will prohibit the lawyer from representing a different client in the matter." Indeed, the lawyer also may ask the prospective client to agree that the lawyer will not be restrained from subsequent use of any confidential information received from the prospective client.

In obtaining consent to what otherwise would be an impermissible conflict of interest, the lawyer must make sure that the prospective client understands that his disclosure of confidential information during the consultation will not protect the client from subsequent adverse representation or even, if so agreed, adverse use. Under such circumstances, the prospective client should be advised that he may wish to be somewhat circumspect in what is revealed during the consultation (and that may be an understatement).

In addition, while disqualification regarding a prospective client generally extends to all lawyers in the firm, Rule 1.18(d)(2) allows other lawyers in the firm to avoid that imputed conflict of interest by taking measures to screen out the individual lawyer who received the information from the prospective client.

***Taking Reasonable Measures:*** Under Rule 1.18(d)(2), the law firm may avoid imputed disqualification only if "the lawyer who received the information took reasonable measures to avoid exposure to more disqualifying information than was reasonably necessary to determine whether to represent the prospective client." If the firm thereby limits the information that it receives, as Professors Ronald Rotunda and John Dzienkowski explain, then "the lawyers are more likely to comply with the screening requirements, and the prospective client is more likely to be comfortable with the screening procedure."[17] If the firm fails to establish clear guidelines for controlling the information received from prospective clients before deciding whether to accept retention by the person, or the lawyer conducting the client interview fails to adhere to such guidelines, the screening exception is withdrawn. Disqualification then is imputed throughout the firm, regardless of whether the personally-disqualified lawyer were to be excluded from the ongoing or subsequent representation adverse to the prospective client.

***Timely Screened:*** Under Rule 1.18(d)(2)(i), the lawyer who received the confidential information from the prospective client (and who thus is personally disqualified) must be "timely screened from any participation in the matter" and must be "apportioned no part of the fee" from that representation.[18] In addition to the use of ethical screening to avoid imputed disqualification when an individual lawyer in the firm has a conflict of interest in the context of the lawyer moving from one firm to another,[19]

---

17 RONALD D. ROTUNDA & JOHN S. DZIENKOWSKI, PROFESSIONAL RESPONSIBILITY: A STUDENT'S GUIDE § 1.18–2 (American Bar Ass'n, 2013–2014).

18 For further discussion of ethical screening, see *infra* §§ 4-7.6(b)(2), 4-7.8(a)(2).

19 *See infra* § 4-7.6(b)(2).

Rule 1.18 specifically permits effective use of a screen in the context of the prospective client.

***Written Notice:*** Under Rule 1.18(d)(2)(ii), written notice must be promptly given to the prospective client that the firm has established a screen to exclude the disqualified lawyer from participation in the matter. With proper measures to control receipt of information, screening of the disqualified lawyer, and notice to the prospective/former client, other lawyers in the firm may undertake an adverse representation in a matter that is the same or substantially related to the matter about which the prospective client consulted with the disqualified lawyer.

### § 4-3.1(e) Controlling the Prospective Client's Disclosure of Information or Obtaining an Advance Waiver of a Conflict

Because a lawyer's encounter with a prospective client may lead to disqualification from representing any other client, including an existing client, in the same or a substantially related matter, the lawyer has good reason to try to arrange a consultation with a potential client in a manner that limits the information received. Under Rule 1.18(c), a lawyer is disqualified from representing another client adverse to the prospective client in the same or a substantially related manner only if the lawyer received confidential information that "could be significantly harmful" to the prospective client.[20] Thus, while it is not necessary to prevent the prospective client from sharing any substantive information, which may be impractical if the lawyer is to intelligently evaluate whether representation is appropriate or possible, the lawyer may wish to control receipt of information that is significant and harmful.

To begin with, as mentioned earlier, the protections of Rule 1.18 may be invoked only by a genuine prospective client when there was a reasonable expectation that the lawyer with whom information was being shared might undertake the representation.[21] If an overeager would-be client thrusts unsolicited information upon a lawyer, who has not done anything to invite that information or facilitate that communication, no fair basis exists for believing the lawyer has welcomed the information or the opportunity to explore possible retention. If a person mails or emails confidential information, or leaves confidential information on the law office answering machine, but the lawyer has done nothing to encourage members of the public so to communicate with the lawyer, the sender or caller cannot reasonably anticipate that the lawyer will take the case. Rule 1.18 does not extend to a person who launches confidential missives against an unsuspecting lawyer in a misguided effort to secure legal representation by ambush.

By contrast, a lawyer or a law firm may invite members of the public to contact a law office, through lawyer advertising that asks readers to call and leave a message at a telephone number or by maintaining a web site in which interested persons are expressly invited to send an email to the law firm about a legal problem. Then the information that is received may not be regarded as unsolicited, and the reasonableness of the sender's expectation that an attorney-client relationship will be formed may increase.[22] Comment 2 provides that a lawyer likely is obliged to extend the protections of Rule 1.18 for a prospective client "if a lawyer, either in person or through the lawyer's advertising in

---

[20] *See supra* § 4-3.1(d).

[21] *See supra* § 4-3.1(b).

[22] *See* ABA Comm. on Ethics and Prof'l Responsibility, Formal Op. 10–457 (2010) ("Websites that invite inquiries may create a prospective client-lawyer relationship under Rule 1.18.").

any medium, specifically requests or invites the submission of information about a potential representation without clear and reasonably understandable warnings and cautionary statements that limit the lawyer's obligations, and a person provides information in response."

For these reasons, the lawyer or law firm that invites email or telephonic contacts by the public would be well-advised to include disclaimers on the firm web site or telephone answering machine.[23] Having a passive web page or simply listing the emails of attorneys in the firm does not constitute such an invitation, nor would simply having an answering machine in a law firm where the firm had not through advertising or the answering machine message affirmatively invited sharing information.[24]

Although some law offices include a warning on a web page that information sent may not be confidential, that declaration may go too far and could risk the loss of the attorney-client privilege for the information so transmitted, even if the lawyer later does accept representation of the client. Moreover, simply disclaiming that an attorney-client relationship is created by sending a message may not be sufficient to excuse the lawyer from being obliged to protect the information as confidential and to decline any representation adverse to that person.

Professor David Hricik suggests that the appropriate disclaimer is to advise the person who would send an email that receipt of the information by the firm will not preclude the firm from representing another party in the matter.[25] With respect to email sent through a firm web site, he further suggests that obtaining affirmative consent from the sender is the safest course, by structuring the web site so that the disclaimer opens up and a button accepting the terms must be clicked before an email may be transmitted. Professor Hricik suggests the following click wrap consent message:

> By clicking "accept", you agree that we may review any information you transmit to us. You recognize that our review of your information, even if it is highly confidential and even if it is transmitted in a good faith effort to retain us, does not preclude us from representing another client directly adverse to you, even in a matter where that information could and will be used against you.[26]

A similar disclaimer could be included in the message of a telephone answering system at a law firm and, for more sophisticated systems, the caller could be required to press a button to indicate acceptance before being able to leave a message.

Of course, a lawyer may conclude that such disclaimers or warnings are too likely to dissuade prospective clients and might impair the persuasiveness of lawyer advertising. The lawyer may choose to simply "accept the opportunity cost,"[27] potentially receive significantly harmful confidential information from a prospective client, and bear

---

[23] For an insightful analysis of this issue, see David Hricik, *To Whom It May Concern: Using Disclaimers to Avoid Disqualification by Receipt of Unsolicited E-Mail from Prospective Clients*, 16 PROF'L LAW. No. 3, at 4 (2005).

[24] ABA Comm. on Ethics and Prof'l Responsibility, Formal Op. 10–457 (2010) (saying that a website describing the work of the law firm and its lawyers and including contact information does not thereby alone "create a reasonable expectation that the lawyer is willing to discuss a specific client-lawyer relationship").

[25] Hricik, *supra*, 16 PROF'L LAW. at 5.

[26] *Id.* at 6.

[27] *See* RONALD D. ROTUNDA & JOHN S. DZIENKOWSKI, PROFESSIONAL RESPONSIBILITY: A STUDENT'S GUIDE § 1.18–1(c) (American Bar Ass'n, 2013–2014).

the consequence of potential disqualification from representing other or existing clients in the same or a related matter.

When a prospective client has arrived at the law office for an initial face-to-face consultation with the lawyer, the need to control the receipt of information becomes even more important. The fact of an actual meeting with the lawyer plainly confirms the person's reasonable expectation that an attorney-client relationship is being contemplated. The lawyer thus should begin the meeting by asking the client not to discuss the substance of the matter before providing background information about the other parties to the matter. Indeed, a better practice is to have the prospective client fill out a form with questions that elicit carefully limited information about the other parties involved, while allowing no space to share confidential details. The lawyer thus has the opportunity to conduct at least a quick conflicts check before allowing the conversation to progress into the sensitive substance of the prospective client's legal problems. If the lawyer learns very early in the consultation that the party adverse to the prospective client is a client of the lawyer or the lawyer's firm and then terminates the consultation before significantly harmful information is shared, the lawyer or firm may continue to represent the existing client even on the same or a substantially related matter.

If, however, the lawyer fails to inquire about the other parties involved in the matter before continuing the consultation with the prospective client; does make such an inquiry but then either fails to recognize a conflict with an existing client or neglects to interrupt the consultation to check for a conflict with an existing client before the prospective client reveals information to the lawyer; or otherwise asks for and receives confidential information from the prospective client, then the lawyer assumes responsibilities to protect confidentiality and avoid conflicts of interest.

Remember, however, under Rule 1.18(d)(2), that if the interviewing lawyer has made "reasonable efforts" to limit the information received to only that "reasonably necessary to determine whether to represent the prospective client," then even when the prospective client volunteers more extensive information than the lawyer sought, other lawyers in the law firm may avoid disqualification from representing an existing or new client adverse to the prospective client on the same or a substantially related matter by adopting the ethical screening procedures discussed previously.[28]

## § 4-3.2 CREATION AND NATURE OF THE ATTORNEY-CLIENT RELATIONSHIP

### § 4-3.2(a) Elements for Establishing the Attorney-Client Relationship[29]

The attorney-client relationship is created when (1) a person seeks legal advice or services from an attorney, and (2) the attorney agrees to or actually does provide legal advice or services or knows that the person is reasonably relying on the lawyer to provide that advice or services.[30]

---

[28] *See supra* § 4-3.1(e).

[29] For more on the kinds of attorney-client relationship, see Part Five of this book, Susan Saab Fortney & Vincent R. Johnson, Legal Malpractice § 5-2.1(a).

[30] RESTATEMENT (THIRD) OF THE LAW GOVERNING LAWYERS § 14 (American Law Institute, 2000); Disciplinary Counsel v. Lee, 49 N.E.3d 1255, 1262 (Ohio 2016); Hopper v. Frank, 16 F.3d 92, 95 (5th Cir. 1994) (quoting *Restatement*); Pine Island Farmers v. Erstad & Reimer, 649 N.W.2d 449, 449, 448 (Minn. 2002);

In most cases, the attorney-client relationship is formed through a written or oral contract in which each party knowingly and explicitly consents to the representation. However, a formal contract or even the payment of a retainer is not necessary to create an attorney-client relationship as the relationship may be implied from the parties' conduct. The existence of an attorney-client relationship may be proven by evidence of detrimental reliance by the client on the lawyer, particularly where the attorney, aware of the reliance "does nothing to negate it."[31]

If a layperson, relying on an attorney's professional status, entrusts the attorney with confidential information or obtains counsel on legal obligations or problems, and if the attorney fails to affirmatively dissuade that person from confiding or placing trust in the attorney, then the attorney should not be heard later to deny the existence of an attorney-client relationship. For this reason, experienced practitioners advise lawyers "to send *non-engagement letters* when we decide not to take on a matter; letters that inform the prospective client—in no uncertain terms—that we are not going to handle the matter we discussed."[32]

### § 4-3.2(b) Business Relationships and Law-Related Services

The creation of an attorney-client—as contrasted with a personal, business, or some other—relationship turns on the legal nature of the subject of the transaction. Although special ethical duties of disclosure and fair dealing apply to the lawyer who engages in a business transaction with a client,[33] a lawyer who engages in a transaction with a person with whom there is no existing professional relationship does not assume professional responsibilities to that person. Thus, for example, the lawyer who sells her house or used car to a stranger has not created an attorney-client relationship simply because of the fact irrelevant to that transaction that the seller also has a professional career. Likewise, if a lawyer owns or operates an independent non-legal business, that he keeps scrupulously separate from the legal practice, the customers of that separate business are not the beneficiaries of an attorney-client relationship.

However, as discussed in detail below, if a lawyer engages in a line of business activity that is closely related to the professional work of the attorney, then disclaiming an attorney-client relationship may be more difficult. As identified by the Kansas Supreme Court, the "principal culprit" targeted here "is the possibility that the person for whom the law-related services are performed fails to understand that the services may not carry with them the protections normally afforded as part of the client-lawyer relationship."[34]

Rule 5.7 of the Model Rules of Professional Conduct, adopted by all but a handful of states, subjects the attorney to professional ethical standards when providing "law-related services." Law-related services include those matters that may be performed collateral to a legal practice, such as accounting, financial planning, or consulting

---

Kurtenbach v. TeKippe, 260 N.W.2d 53 (Iowa 1977); DeVaux v. American Home Assur. Co., 444 N.E.2d 355, 357 (Mass. 1983); McCabe v. Arcidy, 635 A.2d 446, 449 (N.H. 1993).

[31] *Kurtenbach*, 260 N.W.2d at 56.

[32] Lawrence J. Fox, *Non-Engaging, Engaging, and Disengaging Clients*, LITIGATION, Summer, 2010, at 18, 18. On ethical duties to prospective clients, see *supra* § 4-3.1.

[33] *See infra* § 4-7.3(b).

[34] In re Rost, 211 P.3d 145, 156 (Kan. 2009).

services.[35] Unless the lawyer both performs those services in a manner distinctly separate from the legal practice and "take[s] reasonable measures to ensure that a person obtaining the law-related services knows that the services are not legal services," as stated in Rule 5.7(a)(2), the traditional protections of the attorney-client relationship will attach.

### *§ 4-3.2(b)(1) Categorizing Law Practice and Law-Related Services*

Lawyers not only engage in the practice of law, strictly defined, but regularly offer to provide clients with additional and related services, ranging from the routine (such as word-processing performed by secretaries) to the specialized (such as accounting services performed by in-house accountants or lawyers holding accounting licenses). A lawyer may also have an ownership interest in another enterprise or engage in other businesses or commercial activities, which may or may not have any actual or potential connection to the practice of law.

When additional services are offered by a lawyer or additional business ventures are operated by a lawyer, the ethical question that arises concerns the extent to which the demanding rules of professional conduct that are properly imposed upon a lawyer in her professional capacity should be extended as well to the lawyer when engaged in those other activities. When the service that is offered by a lawyer appears to be ancillary to a law practice, and the lawyer has not taken affirmative steps to separate the activity from her practice of law, the client should be affirmed in the reasonable expectation that the lawyer will perform those additional services in a manner that fully comports with the lawyer's professional duties to protect confidential information, avoid conflicts of interest, maintain professional independence, and ethically advertise for clients.

For purposes of the ethics rules, a lawyer's service or business activities may fall into three categories:

***Practice of Law:*** The lawyer's activity may constitute the practice of law, in which case the application of the Rules of Professional Conduct is straightforward.

***Unrelated Business Activities:*** The lawyer's additional activity may be so plainly disassociated from the practice of law that it would be regarded by any reasonable observer as an unrelated business to which professional ethics standards have no logical or direct application.

***Law-Related Services:*** The service offered by the lawyer may be of the kind that, while not constituting the formal practice of law, is closely associated with legal services or frequently offered as part of a law practice. For this last category, which is termed "law-related services" under Rule 5.7 of the Model Rules of Professional Conduct, the application of the lawyer ethics standard will depend upon the extent to which the lawyer has linked those services to the law practice or instead has carefully separated them from the offering of legal services.

### *§ 4-3.2(b)(2) Services Constituting the Practice of Law by a Lawyer*

When a lawyer is engaged in the practice of law, the application of the ethics rules to every element of that practice is obvious. It is important for a lawyer to appreciate what services constitute the "practice of law" when performed by a lawyer, a determination that may not be directly parallel to what would constitute the

[35] *See infra* § 4-3.2(b).

unauthorized practice of law if engaged in by someone without a law license. To be sure, if the professional service is of a kind that is reserved only to lawyers, such that a nonlawyer offering the same service would run afoul of the rules prohibiting the unauthorized practice of law,[36] then performance of such services by a lawyer manifestly constitutes the practice of law. But, in addition, some services that may be offered by nonlawyers move into the category of law practice when taken up by a lawyer.

Some services performed by lawyers—such as drafting most legal documents, preparing a will, and advocating in court—cannot legitimately be offered by someone without a law license in most states under most circumstances. But other services with a strong legal flavor—such as preparation of tax returns, preparing certain documents incident to a real estate transaction, and lobbying the legislature on legally-permeated matters—may be performed by nonlawyers. All of these activities, however, may be regarded as the practice of law in at least some jurisdictions when performed by lawyers.

Accordingly, no matter how carefully a lawyer might try to separate these particular activities from her regular law practice, they remain the practice of law and the lawyer's performance of such services remains fully subject to the Rules of Professional Conduct. For example, a lawyer who maintains one place of business that is denominated as a "law office" and another place of business that is designated as "tax preparation service" should still be regarded as practicing law in both locations, just as would a lawyer who maintains an office on one side of town in which the lawyer represents tenants in disputes with landlords and another office on the other side of town in which lawyer conducts a personal injury litigation practice.

As an illustration of the significance of recognizing such work as law practice, although one on which the courts remain divided on proper classification, a lawyer who prepares a tax return has provided a legal service that should fall within both the ethical duty of maintaining confidentiality and the attorney-client privilege.[37]

Some courts have refused to extend the privilege to communications made between a client and lawyer for the purpose of preparing a tax return, as contrasted with tax planning counsel by a lawyer, concluding that tax return preparation is not a legal professional service.[38] Most prominently, one federal court of appeals in *United States v. Frederick* declared that preparation of a tax return is accountants' work and, even when performed by a lawyer, still rises to nothing more than "lawyers . . . doing nonlawyers' work."[39] To hold otherwise, the court said, would allow a taxpayer "by hiring a lawyer to do the work that an accountant, or other tax preparer, or the taxpayer himself or herself,

---

[36] Although every state forbids the "unauthorized practice of law," and the power of admission to the bar necessarily includes the power to define the practice of law, few states have articulated an all-inclusive definition. Rather cases involving unauthorized practice of law tend to be resolved on particular facts, focusing on whether the activity involves the exercise of professional judgment or affects the legal rights of a third person. As one court has stated, the "essence of the professional judgment of the lawyer" is "the educated ability to relate the general body and philosophy of law to a specific legal problem of a client." Commission on Unauthorized Practice of Law v. Sturgeon, 635 N.W.2d 679, 681–82 (Iowa 2001).

[37] On the attorney-client privilege and the scope of legal services, see *infra* § 4-6.3(b)(1).

[38] *See* United States v. Willis, 565 F. Supp. 1186, 1189–90 (S.D. Iowa 1983); *see also* PAUL R. RICE, ATTORNEY-CLIENT PRIVILEGE IN THE UNITED STATES § 7.24 (2d ed. 1999) (finding that courts are divided on whether tax return preparation, as contrasted with tax planning, is legal assistance entitled to the protection of the privilege); Maura I. Strassberg, *Privilege Can Be Abused: Exploring the Ethical Obligation to Avoid Frivolous Claims of Attorney-Client Privilege*, 37 SETON HALL L. REV. 413, 473 n.268 (2007) (noting disagreement among courts on whether communications involving a lawyer's preparation of a tax return are protected by the privilege).

[39] 182 F.3d 496, 500 (7th Cir. 1999).

normally would do, to obtain greater protection from government investigators than a taxpayer who did not use a lawyer as his tax preparer would be entitled to."[40]

Other courts, more appropriately, have ruled that "[p]reparation of a return by an attorney pursuant to a bona fide attorney-client relationship is sufficiently within his professional legal competence to be subsumed by the privilege."[41] Even the simple preparation of a tax return may readily become the occasion for providing valuable legal advice about characterization of items, the justifiability of exemptions and deductions under the internal revenue code, and the possibility of legal proceedings. Precisely because tax matters are such fertile ground for legal issues and disputes, communications about tax return activity presumptively fall within the attorney-client privilege.[42]

Affording the privilege to tax preparation by lawyers as a legal service does mean, as the *Frederick* court apprehended, that a taxpayer who retains a lawyer for tax return work receives the benefit of the privilege, while a taxpayer who hires an accountant does not. By the same token, the home buyer who retains a lawyer to assist with a real estate transaction, rather than using a real estate agent, receives the benefit of the privilege.[43] Likewise, the manufacturer who retains a lawyer to conduct or supervise an environmental audit for regulatory compliance, rather than an engineer or other professional, thereby secures the advantage of the privilege.[44] As still another example, the employer who retains a lawyer to prepare an employee handbook or a sexual harassment policy would receive the benefit of the privilege, while the employer who uses a human resources professional or relies on her own understanding does not.[45]

---

[40] *Id.*

[41] United States v. Schmidt, 360 F. Supp. 339, 347 (M.D. Pa. 1973); *see also* Colton v. United States, 306 F.2d 633, 637 (2d Cir. 1962) ("There can, of course, be no question that the giving of tax advice and the preparation of tax returns . . . are basically matters sufficiently within the professional competence of an attorney to make them prima facie subject to the attorney-client privilege."); United States v. Merrell, 303 F. Supp. 490, 492 (N.D.N.Y. 1969) ("It appears that the attorney-client privilege is applicable to the preparation of tax returns and the giving of tax advice.").

[42] The Reporter's Note to the *Restatement of the Law Governing Lawyers* finds the tax preparation example to be difficult for application of the attorney-client privilege because "decisions disagree whether routine tax-return preparation services constitute legal services covered by the privilege." RESTATEMENT (THIRD) OF THE LAW GOVERNING LAWYERS § 72 rptr's note (American Law Institute, 2000). The comments to the *Restatement* include an illustration involving preparation of a tax return by a lawyer under which "[t]he trier of fact may, but need not, infer that Client's purpose was not that of obtaining legal assistance." *Id.* cmt. c, ill.2. However, as described in that illustration, Lawyer prepares simple tax returns "without discussing any issues with Client," Client "has never discussed with Lawyer any legal question concerning taxes or return preparation, nor has Lawyer offered such advice," and "Client pays Lawyer on a per-form basis and in an amount comparable to what nonlawyer tax preparers charge." *Id.* Thus, in that peculiar illustration, nearly every possible legal dimension has been drained from the activity—a scenario not likely to be commonly encountered in real-world exchanges between lawyers and clients.

[43] *See, e.g.*, Cedrone v. Unity Sav. Ass'n, 103 F.R.D. 423, 427–29 (E.D. Pa. 1984) (applying privilege to communications between client and lawyers retained to handle real estate transaction); Skorman v. Hovnanian of Fla., Inc., 382 So. 2d 1376, 1378 (Fla. Dist. Ct. App. 1980) (holding that all correspondence between the client and lawyer relative to a real estate transaction was privileged).

[44] *See* Olen Properties Corp. v. Sheldahl, Inc., No. CV 91-6446-WDK (Mcx), 1994 WL 212135, at *1 (C.D. Cal., Apr. 12, 1994) (holding that consultant's environmental audit, which was prepared "to gather information for [the company's] attorneys to assist the attorneys in evaluating compliance with relevant laws and regulations," and thus had "been prepared for the purpose of securing an opinion of law," was privileged and need not be produced in discovery).

[45] Richard W. Painter, *The Moral Interdependence of Corporate Lawyers and Their Clients*, 67 S. CAL. L. REV. 507, 537–38 (1994).

In the same way, when tax return work is being performed by a diligent lawyer (rather than an accountant or other nonlawyer), the lawyer's legal expertise and experience may lead her to identify and address legal issues that others would not appreciate, as is true in so many other areas of law where the services being performed by the lawyer are not forbidden to nonlawyers.

To be sure, under the longstanding doctrine that underlying facts are not privileged, the financial data submitted by the client for tax return preparation would not be insulated from discovery. Indeed, information conveyed to the lawyer for the very purpose of being included in the tax return would not be privileged because the lawyer was intended to be a conduit in transmitting that set of information to the government tax agency.[46] Thus, when a lawyer prepares a simple tax return by merely inputting financial data received from the client, the privilege has no significant reach and fears of abusive invocation are overstated.

However, as soon as the exchange between lawyer and client moves beyond financial data that is to be directly transmitted to the government on the tax return, such as correspondence about how to characterize an item of income or whether the requirements for taking a particular deduction are met, every reason is present to protect these communications with the privilege. Even if the actual preparation of the tax return were regarded as a law-related accounting service, rather than the direct performance of legal services, the privilege should cover all aspects of that tax return work other than the non-privileged underlying financial data, simple work-sheets based solely on that data, and information that is included in the return.[47] As one tax attorney has perceptively written:

> With few exceptions, when a taxpayer/client follows an attorney's advice with respect to tax issues, that advice will in some fashion ultimately be reflected on the taxpayer/client's tax returns filed with the government. In this sense, almost all tax law advice is, in some regard, associated with return preparation activities.[48]

Accordingly, tax preparation by a lawyer is not a law-related business but the practice of law itself. Wherever the lawyer conducts that work—whether in the same building as other law practice work or not—the Rules of Professional Conduct govern.

---

[46] United States v. Lawless, 709 F.2d 485, 487 (7th Cir. 1983) ("[I]f the client transmitted the information so that it might be used on the tax return, such a transmission destroys any expectation of confidentiality. . . .").

[47] *See, e.g.*, Colton v. United States, 306 F.2d 633, 637 (2d Cir. 1962) (holding that, even though the information transmitted by the client to be included in the tax return is not privileged, "the privilege is still available to [the taxpayer] to the extent of permitting him to withhold any particular confidential papers which were 'specifically prepared by the client for the purpose of consultation with his attorney' and any of the [law] firm's memoranda and worksheets 'to the extent of any unpublished expression made by an attorney therein of confidences which had passed between him and his clients' " (quoting trial judge)); United States v. Schlegel, 313 F. Supp. 177, 178–80 (D. Neb. 1970) (holding that information provided by the client to the lawyer that was included in the tax return was not privileged, along with the pre-existing financial books and records, but that other oral conversations and written communications created "solely for the purpose of delivery to his attorney for the preparation of his return" remained within the privilege).

[48] Claudine Pease-Wingenter, *Does the Attorney-Client Privilege Apply to Tax Lawyers?: An Examination of the Return Preparation Exception to Define the Parameters of the Privilege in the Tax Context*, 47 WASHBURN L.J. 699, 699 (2008).

### *§ 4-3.2(b)(3) Unrelated Business Activities by a Lawyer*

When a lawyer has an ownership interest or engages in a business that by its nature, as well as its operation, is wholly unrelated to the practice of law, the ethics rules that apply only to a lawyer in his professional capacity have no application.

For example, that the owner or operator of a restaurant happens to be a lawyer does not mean that that confidentiality protection attaches to dinnertime conversations, that diners are owed a duty of loyalty, or that advertising for the restaurant must comply with the restrictions on lawyer advertising. To be sure, if the lawyer were to take an activity that ordinarily is unrelated and connect it directly to a law practice, such as by operating a restaurant as an in-house cafeteria for the lawyer's law firm, professional responsibilities would then be implicated, such as a duty to ensure that those employed within the restaurant understand the need to maintain confidentiality with respect to legal subjects discussed by the lawyers while eating in the law firm cafeteria. In most circumstances, however, the consumer who patronizes a restaurant, hotel, clothing store, car dealership, construction company, or other business that would not commonly be linked to the practice of law does not expect that professional ethics standards will govern the business activities.

Even if the matter is wholly unrelated to the practice of law, if a lawyer enters into a business transaction with a person who is also a legal client, the lawyer must ensure that the transaction and terms are fair, that client has been fully informed in writing as to the terms, that the client has been given an opportunity to obtain independent legal counsel, and that the client has consented in writing.[49] In addition, whether acting in a professional, business, or personal capacity, a lawyer remains bound to uphold certain basic ethical principles, such as refraining from "conduct involving dishonesty, fraud, deceit or misrepresentation"[50] and not "commit[ting] a criminal act that reflects adversely on the lawyer's honesty, trustworthiness or fitness as a lawyer in other respects," both pursuant to Rule 8.4 of the Model Rules of Professional Conduct.[51]

### *§ 4-3.2(b)(4) Defining Law-Related Services by a Lawyer*

Under Rule 5.7(b) of the Model Rules of Professional Conduct, "[t]he term 'law-related services' denotes services that might reasonably be performed in conjunction with and in substance are related to the provision of legal services, and that are not prohibited as unauthorized practice of law when provided by a nonlawyer."

*First*, law-related services are those that "might reasonably be performed in conjunction" with a law practice, that is, they are the kind of services that reasonably could be integrated with legal services as part of a holistic law practice.

*Second*, law-related services must be "related" in "substance" to the provision of legal services, that is, the content of the affiliated services as actually provided is somehow connected to the subject of the legal services that are simultaneously offered.

---

[49] *See infra* § 4-7.3(b).

[50] *See supra* § 4-1.4(a).

[51] *See supra* § 4-1.4(a).

*Third*, law-related services are those that might be performed by laypersons without violating the rules against unauthorized practice of law.[52]

Nearly every law office offers some ancillary services that fall within the category of "law-related services," such as secretarial services, copying services, etc. Because these services are related to the law practice and are offered in conjunction with legal services, the lawyer must take reasonable steps to ensure that the employees who perform such services conduct themselves in a manner compatible with professional obligations, such as maintaining confidentiality with respect to documents being typed or duplicated.[53] As the practice of law grows ever more complex and the needs of clients expand, the nature of law-related services has broadened beyond those that were traditionally and routinely offered in any law office. As explained in Comment 9 to Rule 5.7, law-related services today include such things as "title insurance, financial planning, accounting, trust services, real estate counseling, legislative lobbying, economic analysis, social work, psychological counseling, tax preparation, and patent, medical or environmental consulting."

When a lawyer offers law-related services, rather than having those services performed by independent contractors, the application of professional ethics to that activity turns upon whether the services are associated with or kept distinctly separate from the law practice, as discussed below.

#### *§ 4-3.2(b)(5) Law-Related Services Provided as Part of a Law Practice*

When a service is offered as an element of a law practice, then by definition it is a law-related service. Because of the association with the performance of legal services, that law-related service must be conducted in a manner that fully comports with the Rules of Professional Conduct. Under Rule 5.7(a)(1), the ethics rules apply directly and with full force when the lawyer provides law-related services "in circumstances that are not distinct from the lawyer's provision of legal services to clients."

Law-related services that have been integrated with the practice of law most obviously are provided "in circumstances that are not distinct" from the lawyer's practice of law. When such services are offered within a unified law practice, then performance of law-related services is regarded as an integral part of that practice of law.

As Professors Geoffrey Hazard and William Hodes and attorney Peter Jarvis explain:

> Inasmuch as lawyers in these situations are held fully accountable *as lawyers*, even when providing nonlegal services, the effect of Rule 5.7(a) is to enhance client consumer protection and to negate any advantage that lawyers might otherwise seek by recharacterizing their activities as something other than the practice of law. When the Rule applies, lawyers cannot transform client (or even nonclients) into mere customers in a *caveat emptor* world.[54]

---

[52] As discussed earlier, some services that may be performed by a nonlawyer nonetheless constitute the actual practice of law (and not merely law-related services) when engaged in by a lawyer. *See supra* § 4-3.2(b)(2).

[53] On the lawyer's responsibility to ensure that nonlawyer assistants comply with professional expectations, see *infra* § 4-12.4.

[54] 1 GEOFFREY C. HAZARD, JR., W. WILLIAM HODES & PETER R. JARVIS, THE LAW OF LAWYERING § 51.03 (Aspen, 4th ed., 2016).

Or, as the Arizona Supreme Court put it nearly thirty years ago before Rule 5.7 was adopted, "the lawyer generally takes his license with him when he enters into any relationship to provide a client with what the client may reasonably believe are law-related services."[55]

When law-related services are offered in the context of an integrated practice, or where the appearance of such integration exists because the law-related services are not offered distinctly from legal services, the client appropriately will expect that confidentiality will be maintained and loyalty will be extended. Even when the person receives only the law-related services, without directly being the recipient of legal counseling or representation, the lawyer remains bound to behave ethically as though performing professional services. Indeed, the very fact that law-related services are not offered separately from legal services makes it difficult for the recipient to appreciate that law-related services are something different in kind from legal services. For that reason, the lawyer must conduct herself as though such services are one and the same. The lawyer also must be careful to adhere to other ethics rules, such as ensuring that any marketing of law-related services offered as part of the law practice is conducted in compliance with the limitations on lawyer advertising and solicitation.[56]

### *§ 4-3.2(b)(6) Law-Related Services Provided Distinct from a Law Practice*

When a lawyer or an entity controlled by the lawyer is offering a law-related service, the client may be confused as to whether the full panoply of professional obligations attaches, given both the identity of the service-provider (a lawyer or lawyer-controlled entity) and the nature of the service (one that is reasonably performed in conjunction with and is related in substance to the provision of legal services). For these reasons, the burden rests on the lawyer to carefully differentiate the law-related service from the practice of law, if the lawyer wishes to avoid strict application of the rules of legal ethics. If the association between the law-related service and the law practice is indefinite, by reason of either the structure of the services or the lawyer's failure to fully explain the matter, the client then is entitled to expect full adherence by the lawyer to professional responsibilities.

In other words, the presumption is that a lawyer offering law-related services remains subject to the Rules of Professional Conduct, unless the circumstances under which the services are offered *and* the explanatory measures taken by the lawyer are sufficient to apprise the client that the services are not legal services and that the protections of the attorney-client relationship will not be afforded.

Under Rule 5.7(a), a lawyer remains subject to the Rules of Professional Conduct when law-related services are provided (1) "in circumstances that are not distinct from the lawyer's provision of legal services to clients," or (2) "in other circumstances by an entity controlled by the lawyer individually or with others if the lawyer fails to take reasonable measures to assure that a person obtaining the law-related services knows that the services are not legal services and that the protections of the client-lawyer relationship do not exist."

*First*, to fall outside of the strictures of the legal ethics rules, it is necessary (but not sufficient) that the law-related services be provided in circumstances that are "distinct

---

[55] Matter of Pappas, 768 P.2d 1161, 1167 (Ariz. 1988).

[56] *See supra* Ch. 4-2.

from the lawyer's provision of legal services to clients." If, as discussed previously, the law-related services have been integrated within a unified law practice, or appear to be so combined given the absence of a clear differentiation, then the standards of legal ethics plainly apply.

While Rule 5.7(a)(1) does not explain what makes circumstances "distinct" for separate provision of law-related services, the reference in Rule 5.7(a)(2) to "an entity controlled by the lawyer individually or with others" as marking distinct circumstances suggests that provision of services through another entity is expected. Comment 4 to Rule 5.7 likewise suggests that the dividing line involves law-related services being provided "through an entity that is distinct from that through which the lawyer provides legal services."

However, given that the American Bar Association revised subparagraph (a)(2) of Rule 5.7 in 2002 by deliberately removing the term "separate" as a preface to "entity," this distinct arrangement need not be altogether removed from the law practice. Comment 3 indicates that arranging the provision of law-related services through "different support staff" (that is, different from those personnel who assist the lawyer in the provision of legal services) may be sufficient.

Still, whether conducted through a separate entity or as a discrete function within the law firm, the manner in which the law-related services are structured must establish a clear line of demarcation from the law practice. This signals to the outsider that the law-related services are indeed being offered in circumstances "distinct" from the practice of law.

*Second*, even when law-related services are provided under circumstances distinct from the provision of legal services, Rule 5.7(a)(2) requires the lawyer to take "reasonable measures" to ensure that the recipient of those services understands that they are not legal services. The lawyer must communicate that no attorney-client relationship has been created with the attendant protections of confidentiality, loyalty, and professional independence.

In some cases, if the law-related business has been established in a manner that plainly separates the lawyer as a professional from its operation (such as not identifying the lawyer as an owner or operator) and through a structure wholly disassociated from any law practice (such as in a physically-separate location), then the organization of the business may itself be sufficient to avoid any possible misunderstanding. In most circumstances, the lawyer will need to inform the recipient directly and forthrightly about the distinct nature of the law-related services and the inapplicability of professional standards. As Comment 7 recognizes, how much explanation is necessary will depend on both the circumstances, that is, how distinct the law-related services are from the law practice, and the sophistication of the person in use of legal services. Comment 6 to Rule 5.7 advises that the "communication should be made before" any transaction for such law-related services and "preferably should be in writing". Moreover, if the recipient of law-related services is also a client of the lawyer in the provision of legal services, the constraints of Rule 1.8(a) regarding business transactions with a client apply.[57]

---

[57] *See infra* § 4-7.3(b).

Under some circumstances, no degree of effort by the lawyer to maintain and articulate a distinction between the practice of law and law-related services may be availing. As recognized in Comment 8 to Rule 5.7, when a lawyer simultaneously provides legal services and law-related services with respect to the very same matter, they may become "so closely entwined that they cannot be distinguished from each other." In such a case, the lawyer's own conduct must comply with the Rules of Professional Conduct, and the lawyer must appropriately train nonlawyer assistants to behave by the same ethical standards.

When law-related services are offered in a manner sufficiently separate from the legal practice, both in structure and by admonition of the lawyer to the recipient, then the provision of law-related services may be conducted in the same manner as would another business enterprise operated by a lawyer that has no relationship to a law practice.

Consider, for example, a lawyer who offers accounting services or owns a copying and printing business—services that by their nature could be conjoined with a law practice and thus that fall within the general category of law-related services:

*First*, the lawyer must operate the business in a manner distinct from the law practice, such as through a different structure or at a separate location.

*Second*, the lawyer must take reasonable measures to disabuse any customer from the mistaken notion that these are legal services or result in the formation of an attorney-client relationship, such as by avoiding any identification of the lawyer with the separate business or through direct and unambiguous disclaimers.

If those efforts at detachment are effective, then the lawyer is not obliged (by legal ethics standards at least) to protect the confidentiality of client documents or to advertise the business under the constraints that apply to lawyer advertising. As Comment 11 to Rule 5.7 admonishes, however, other "principles of law external" to the ethics rules still may apply, such as the law of agency or the rules governing other professions, which may afford some protection for confidentiality and against conflicts of interest separate from the Rules of Professional Conduct.

### § 4-3.2(c) Lawyer Responsibility for Misunderstanding About Relationship

To the extent of any reasonable confusion about the existence of an attorney-client relationship, and its nature and scope, the lawyer as the professional in dealing with a layperson is responsible to clarify the situation.[58] When there is a question as to the existence of an attorney-client relationship, the attorney "is dealing in an area in which he is expert and the client is not and as to which the client must necessarily rely on the attorney."[59] If the client indicates that she is operating under the mistaken assumption that the representation is more expansive than the lawyer intends, the lawyer must explain the reasonable bounds of the retention.[60]

[58] On client misunderstandings about and reasonable reliance concerning an attorney-client relationship, see Susan R. Martyn, *Accidental Clients*, 33 HOFSTRA L. REV. 913, 919–20 (2005).

[59] Westinghouse Electric Corp. v. Kerr-McGee Corp., 580 F.2d 1311, 1317 (7th Cir. 1978) (quoting Udall v. Littell, 366 F.2d 668, 676 (D.C. Cir. 1966)).

[60] On scope of representation, see *infra* § 4-3.3.

When a lawyer has had a relationship of trust with a client, having provided legal advice on a variety of or similar matters, the client may develop a reasonable expectation that the lawyer continues to have professional responsibility for the client's affairs even after conclusion of a particular matter. Accordingly, the lawyer may be held to continuing professional responsibilities unless the lawyer carefully communicates the termination of the relationship and disavows such a relationship should the client indicate that he believes it to be ongoing.[61]

The Model Rules of Professional Conduct show considerable solicitude for the nonlawyer with respect to confusion that may attend communications with a lawyer. For example, when dealing with unrepresented laypeople, Rule 4.3 provides that "[w]hen the lawyer knows or reasonably should know that the unrepresented person misunderstands the lawyer's role in the matter, the lawyer shall make reasonable efforts to correct the misunderstanding."[62] Comment 1 to the rule explains that a layperson, "particularly one not experienced in dealing with legal matters, might assume that a lawyer is disinterested in loyalties . . . even when the lawyer represents [another] client." The ethics rules warn against misunderstandings about a lawyer's role by even an opposing unrepresented party. So much more should an attorney take responsibility for describing the nature and parameters of the relationship with those who indeed are being or have been advised or assisted by the lawyer on some matter.[63]

## § 4-3.3 SCOPE OF REPRESENTATION

### § 4-3.3(a) Introduction to Scope of the Representation[64]

The lawyer is responsible only for those matters on which the client engages the lawyer's legal services. The lawyer is not obliged to provide legal advice regarding a client's other existing or potential legal matters that are not included within the professional engagement. For a matter unrelated to the representation, the lawyer and client have not extended the attorney-client relationship.

With respect even to the specific legal matter that is the basis of the attorney-client relationship, the lawyer and client may agree to circumscribe the range of the engagement and thereby set the outer boundary of the lawyer's responsibilities. Rule 1.2(c) of the Model Rules of Professional Conduct expressly authorizes a lawyer to "limit the scope of the representation if the limitation is reasonable under the circumstances and the client gives informed consent."

Thus, for example, when representing a client who has been injured by another, the attorney and the client could agree that the attorney will be responsible only for negotiating with an insurance company, but will not file any lawsuit. However, the lawyer remains obliged to inform the client of the option of seeking legal redress in court, even if the initiation of litigation would be left to the client or another lawyer.

Even when the scope of representation has been limited, the lawyer's duty to fully inform the client before obtaining consent to the limitation means that the client should

---

61 On termination of the attorney-client relationship, see *infra* § 4-3.6.

62 *See infra* § 4-11.4.

63 For more on creation of an attorney-client relationship by advising, including by online communications, see *supra* § 4-2.4(c).

64 For more on the scope of representation in legal malpractice cases, see Part Five of this book, Susan Saab Fortney & Vincent R. Johnson, Legal Malpractice § 5-2.1(b).

be informed of other legal problems and legal options closely related to the representation.

### § 4-3.3(b) Agreements to Limit the Scope of Representation

Under Rule 1.2(c) of the Model Rules of Professional Conduct, the lawyer and the client may agree to reasonable limitations on the scope of the representation. The rule thus allows the lawyer and the client to control the nature, extent, and purpose of the relationship as it is being created.[65] When the client is informed about the consequences of such a limitation and consents, the lawyer may specify the types of legal services to be provided or the scope of the matters that fall within the representation. The limitation on the scope of the representation may be established through the engagement contract or by offering the terms of services which the client accepts.

To some extent, lawyers and clients always have had the power to limit the scope of representation and indeed some limitation on scope has been implicit. Thus, for example, retention of the lawyer by a client to handle a tax matter or to create a business association would not have been understood to encompass additional legal services by a lawyer regarding the client's domestic relations problems (absent a further retention by the lawyer for that separate purpose). Rule 1.2(c), however, goes a step further by expressly authorizing a limited representation with respect to a particular subject matter.

Comment 6 to Rule 1.2 offers some illustrations of limited scope agreements, including limitation of representation by a lawyer retained by an insurer to matters that fall within the insured's insurance coverage; a representation limited in scope by the likewise "limited objectives" of the client for the representation; and limitations that "exclude actions that the client thinks are too costly or that the lawyer regards as repugnant or imprudent."

For example, a client may request the lawyer's assistance to make a demand upon another person or raise an objection to action taken by another against him, but nonetheless have an understanding with the lawyer that the client is disinclined to pursue litigation if the demand or objection is unsuccessful. A business client may wish to explore the legal consequences of a new business strategy, while reserving the right not only to decide whether to implement the proposal but also to retain a different lawyer for the next stage of the plan.[66]

Before entering into a limited scope representation, the lawyer must obtain informed consent from the client. Thus, under Rule 1.0(e) of the Model Rules of Professional Conduct, the lawyer is obliged to ensure that the client appreciates the "material risks of and reasonably available alternatives to" the limitation. The lawyer is responsible to clearly communicate the nature of the limitation, so that the client knows what is, and even more important what is not, being provided in terms of legal services.[67] What is adequate in terms of information and explanation will of course depend on the circumstances and on the experience of the person in legal matters. A person of sophistication and experience generally needs less of an explanation. By contrast, a

---

[65] For more on the creation and existence of the lawyer-client relationship, see *supra* § 4-3.2.

[66] *See* STEPHEN GILLERS, REGULATION OF LAWYERS: PROBLEMS OF LAW AND ETHICS 98 (Wolters Kluwer 8th ed. 2009).

[67] On the lawyer's responsibility for ambiguity regarding the attorney-client relationship, see *supra* § 4-3.2(c).

person who has not previously or has only infrequently used legal services, who is not well-educated, or who otherwise demonstrates a lack of understanding or confidence deserves a more thorough explanation by the lawyer who is attempting to secure consent to a defined limitation on the legal services.

While the lawyer is not obliged to provide legal services beyond the defined scope of the representation, when the lawyer is aware of other matters that are closely related, the duty to obtain informed consent includes the duty to notify the client about those matters and offer a warning about the possible loss of rights if other representation is not obtained.

For example, as a California court ruled in *Nichols v. Keller*,[68] a lawyer who undertakes representation of an injured worker for the limited purpose of seeking workers compensation for the injury should advise the client of the possibility that a personal injury lawsuit could be maintained against a third-party responsible for the injury, such as the manufacturer of equipment used in the workplace. The lawyer should explain that the client's failure to take timely action could result in the barring of a lawsuit by reason of the statute of limitations, even though the lawyer has made clear that she will not undertake the representation of the worker in any such claim against a third-party.

### § 4-3.3(c) "Unbundled Legal Services" and Assisting *Pro Se* Litigants

Some have cited Rule 1.2(c) of the Model Rules of Professional Conduct as having particular value in allowing lawyers to provide limited services to *pro se* litigants, such as consulting or drafting legal documents, but not providing a full representation in court. Rule 1.2(c) should be understood to permit this "unbundling of legal services" and allow an attorney to provide limited services to otherwise *pro se* litigants, provided that informed consent is obtained and the scope of the representation is clearly defined.

To be sure, this approach is not without risks and consequences. The lawyer would be responsible for the quality of the limited work provided, such as drafted pleadings or motions. But that work product then might be presented and argued by a *pro se* litigant in a manner that undermines those arguments or that reflects a failure to fully appreciate the nature of the document or its contents. Moreover, the lawyer remains obliged to ensure that any litigation document drafted or presentation made before a tribunal was in pursuit of a valid, non-frivolous claim or argument.[69] In the event of an unfortunate result in litigation, an attempt to untangle the different segments of legal work to determine whether blame falls upon the lawyer's drafting work, the litigant's *pro se* advocacy, or the simple weakness of the case on the merits may prove to be a knotty endeavor.

For purposes of the conflict of interest rules,[70] a person receiving a limited scope representation is a client, even if the scope of representation is narrow and discrete. Under Rule 6.5 of the Model Rules of Professional Conduct, the conflict of interest rules and the imputed disqualification of other lawyers in a law firm are relaxed—applying only if the lawyer actually knows of a conflict of interest when providing the legal advice

---

[68] *See* Nichols v. Keller, 19 Cal. Rptr. 2d 601 (Cal. App. 1993).

[69] On the requirement to present only meritorious claims and contentions, see *infra* § 4-9.3(a).

[70] *See infra* §§ 4-7.1 to 4-7.5.

or assistance in completing forms—when a lawyer provides short-term limited representation under the auspices of a qualified pro bono program.[71]

To encourage lawyers to provide circumscribed assistance to *pro se* litigants, both to enhance access to justice and to assist the courts in addressing claims by unrepresented parties, some states have adopted specific rules to facilitate "unbundled" legal services. Maine and New Hampshire provide that a lawyer may enter a "limited appearance" in court on behalf of a client, although a lawyer who signs a pleading in Maine may not thereafter limit representation.[72] Iowa revised its rules of civil procedure so that a lawyer preparing litigation documents in a limited scope representation would be permitted to rely upon a *pro se* litigant's representation of the facts, unless the lawyer has reason to believe they are false or insufficient, in which case an independent investigation would be required.[73] The Iowa lawyer who undertakes to "ghost write" litigation documents must reveal to the tribunal and opposing counsel the lawyer's limited involvement in the matter.[74]

While Iowa is not alone in demanding that a lawyer drafting legal documents take open responsibility for that work,[75] the American Bar Association's Standing Committee on Ethics and Professional Responsibility takes the position that a lawyer may provide legal assistance to *pro se* litigants without disclosure.[76] While a few states require full disclosure by name of an attorney who drafts a litigation document for an otherwise *pro se* litigant, other states allow the *pro se* litigant to file such documents without any indication of lawyer participation or by a notation of lawyer participation without identifying the lawyer by name.[77]

### § 4-3.3(d) Collaborative Lawyering Agreements

In an effort to reduce the adversarial character of legal disputes and to preserve a healthier ongoing relationship in circumstances where the parties must continue to interact with each other after disposition of the matter (such as a marriage dissolution involving child custody arrangements), the collaborative lawyering movement proposes

---

[71] *See infra* § 4-13.4(c).

[72] MAINE RULES OF PROF'L CONDUCT R. 1.2(c); N.H. RULES OF PROF'L CONDUCT R. 1.2(f).

[73] IOWA R. CIV. P. R. 1.423(2).

[74] IOWA R. CIV. P. R. 1.423(1); *see also* Board of Prof'l Ethics & Conduct v. Lane, 642 N.W.2d 296, 299 (Iowa 2002) (characterizing as dishonest and deceitful the conduct of "ghost-writing attorneys who 'author pleadings and necessarily guide the course of the litigation with unseen hand' " (quoting Johnson v. Bd. of County Comm'rs, 868 F. Supp. 1226, 1231 (D. Colo. 1994), *aff'd in part and disapproved in part,* 85 F.3d 489 (10th Cir. 1996)); *see also* Iowa Supreme Court Attorney Disciplinary Bd. v. Rauch, 746 N.W.2d 262, 266 (Iowa 2008) (chastising an attorney who accepted a client's case after being suspended and who "tried to hide his involvement by omitting his name on the motion" and confirming that "[g]hostwriting a court document is a 'deliberate evasion of the responsibilities imposed on an attorney' ").

[75] *See* Duran v. Carris, 238 F.3d 1268, 1272 (10th Cir. 2001) (ruling that ghostwriting of legal filings constitutes misrepresentation to the court); Johnson v. Board of County Comm'rs, 868 F. Supp. 1226, 1231 (D. Colo. 1994) (characterizing as dishonest the conduct of ghost-writing attorneys who "author pleadings and necessarily guide the course of the litigation with unseen hand"), *aff'd in part and disapproved in part,* 85 F.3d 489 (10th Cir. 1996).

[76] ABA Comm. on Ethics and Prof'l Responsibility, Formal Op. 07–446 (2007); *see also* Debra Lyn Bassett, *Characterizing Ghostwriting,* 5 ST. MARY'S J. ON LEGAL MALPRACTICE & ETHICS 286 (2016); Ira P. Robbins, *Ghostwriting: Filling in the Gaps of Pro Se Prisoners' Access to the Courts,* 23 GEO J. LEGAL ETHICS 271 (2010); Jona Goldschmidt, *In Defense of Ghostwriting,* 29 FORDHAM URB. L.J. 1145 (2002).

[77] *See generally* FIA Card Services, N.A. v. Pichette, 116 A.3d 770, 782–83 (R.I. 2015); *see also* Robbins, *supra,* 23 GEO. J. LEGAL ETHICS at 273 (arguing that lawyer ghostwriting of pleadings for prisoners would help "provide pro se prisoners with the access to the courts that law and justice require").

a method of dispute resolution in which the lawyers and clients on both sides agree in advance to avoid litigation and to work cooperatively and openly with each other toward an amicable settlement.

At "[t]he heart of the collaborative lawyering process is the Participation Agreement," under which each party commits to negotiating a settlement and agrees that the lawyers involved in the cooperative settlement process will be disqualified from continuing representation of the parties if the matter should proceed to litigation.[78] This "disqualification stipulation—that written commitment to resolution without litigation—is the essential core of the process."[79] As Professor James Lawrence explains, "[b]y contracting away their right to continue their respective relationships into litigation, both the attorneys and clients have increased the stakes in the negotiation process and make a real commitment to settlement."[80]

Because the lawyer's role in the collaborative law process is non-adversarial (although the lawyer is not a third-party neutral[81] but continues to represent a client) and because the lawyer must agree in advance not to continue to represent the client (that is, to withdraw), some have questioned whether this process is consistent with the requirements of zealous advocacy and the limitations on the lawyer's power to withdraw under the professional conduct rules.

However, the comments to Rule 1.2 suggest that such a limitation on the scope of the representation, if knowingly consented to by the client, would be reasonable. Comment 6 to Rule 1.2 notes that "[a] limited representation may be appropriate because the client has limited objectives for the representation," which arguably includes the informed decision by the client to restrict the scope of the representation to achievement of a collaborative settlement. The comment also confirms that "the terms upon which representation is undertaken may exclude specific means that might otherwise be used to accomplish the client's objectives," which would appear to sanction an ex ante decision to avoid litigation and restrict the lawyer's legal services to those which advance an amicable settlement. If the representation is limited to settlement negotiations, then the lawyer's agreement not to represent the client should the matter proceed to litigation does not entail a promise to withdraw so much as an advance acknowledgment that, by the agreed-upon terms of the representation, the lawyer's services simply are concluded at the point when settlement no longer is reasonably attainable.

Thus, an agreement to participate in a collaborative lawyering process would appear to be within what Comment 7 calls the "substantial latitude" afforded by Rule 1.2 to limit the scope of a representation. The American Bar Association's Standing Committee on Ethics and Professional Responsibility, as well as the majority of state bar opinions to address the subject, have concluded that collaborative law practice is a permissible form of limited scope representation.[82]

---

[78] Lawrence, *supra*, 17 OHIO ST. J. ON DISP. RESOL. at 432; *see also* Larry R. Spain, *Collaborative Law: A Critical Reflection on Whether a Collaborative Orientation Can be Ethically Incorporated into the Practice of Law*, 56 BAYLOR L. REV. 141, 143 (2004) (outlining the elements of a collaborative law model of practice).

[79] Sheila M. Gutterman, *Collaborative Family Law—Part II*, 30 COLO. LAWYER 57, 57 (Dec. 2001).

[80] James K.L. Lawrence, *Collaborative Lawyering: A New Development in Conflict Resolution*, 17 OHIO ST. J. ON DISP. RESOL. 431, 432 (2002).

[81] On the role of the lawyer when serving as a third-party neutral, see *infra* § 4-10.3.

[82] ABA Comm. on Ethics and Prof'l Responsibility, Formal Op. 07–447 (2007) (citing state ethics opinions).

However, in August, 2011, the American Bar Association's House of Delegates, by a nearly two-to-one margin, rejected a resolution to endorse uniform state legislation setting standards for collaborative lawyering.[83] While the provision to disqualify the lawyers if the matter proceeds to litigation was criticized by several, the primary fear appeared to be that setting standards by uniform law would invite state legislatures to regulate attorneys.[84]

Whether participation in a collaborative lawyering process, and limitation of the scope of representation for such participation, is "reasonable under the circumstances" as required by Rule 1.2(c) depends on the lawyer's evaluation of the situation, a thoughtful consideration of the client's needs, and a reasonable conviction that the collaborative process is likely to succeed. The client must provide informed consent, meaning that the lawyer must explain the collaborative lawyering process to the client, clarify the roles of the participants, contrast this process with the traditional or adversarial approach to representation in legal disputes, fully inform the client of the alternatives including litigation, and describe the consequences that would follow from the lawyer's disqualification in continued representation of the client should the matter proceed to litigation.[85]

### § 4-3.3(e) Reasonableness of Scope Limitation

Rule 1.2(c) of the Model Rules of Professional Conduct permits limiting the scope of the representation only "if the limitation is reasonable under the circumstances." Comment 7 confirms that "the lawyer and client [are afforded] substantial latitude to limit the representation."

The limitation becomes unreasonable if it effectively renders the legal advice unreliable or leaves the client unavoidably exposed to serious risks. As an example from Comment 7, while it may be appropriate for a lawyer and client to agree that general advice concerning an uncomplicated legal problem might be provided through a simple telephone consultation, "the time allotted" for that conversation must be adequate so that the information provided is sufficiently complete to justify the client's reliance upon the advice.

Similarly, as Professor Stephen Gillers comments, "it would be unreasonable to accept the defense of a criminal case on the understanding that the lawyer will not do any investigation or make any pretrial motions."[86] While offering to assist a *pro se* civil litigant with discrete segments of a matter or by preparing certain documents may be a reasonable limitation on scope, the nature of a criminal case and the liberty interests at stake make it presumptively unreasonable for a lawyer to agree to dissect a criminal defense into pieces.

---

[83] *ABA Nixes Model Collaborative Law, Wants Law Graduates to Be "Practice Ready,"* 27 LAW. MAN. PROF. CONDUCT 524 (2011).

[84] *But see* Stephen Gillers, *How to Make Rules for Lawyers: The Professional Responsibility of the Legal Profession*, 40 PEPPERDINE L. REV. 365, 391–96 (2013) (discussing the objections to the collaborative lawyering resolution at the ABA meeting and saying we should be "wary of arguments based on the source of a regulation [that is, from the legislature rather than by court rule] because they can be invoked selectively to disguise opposition to substance" of the proposal).

[85] *See* Spain, *supra*, 56 BAYLOR L. REV. at 160–62; New Jersey Ethics Op.699, at 4–5 (2005).

[86] STEPHEN GILLERS, REGULATION OF LAWYERS: PROBLEMS OF LAW AND ETHICS 94 (Wolters Kluwer 8th ed. 2009).

At least outside of the unique scenario of unbundling of legal services into discrete portions on the civil side, a lawyer "may not so severely limit the services to be provided that it results in providing an incompetent representation to the client."[87]

Some legal matters by their nature must be handled by the legal professional in full—or not at all.

## § 4-3.4 ALLOCATING DECISION-MAKING AUTHORITY BETWEEN CLIENT AND LAWYER

Rule 1.2(a) of the Model Rules of Professional Conduct addresses the usually straightforward, but sometimes difficult and sensitive, question of how the authority to make decisions about the legal representation should be allocated between the client and the lawyer. In other words, the question here is who gets to "call the shots"—and on what.

In most instances, the client and the attorney either work collaboratively or have established a clear understanding between them regarding their respective realms of authority. However, the attorney-client relationship is not always harmonious. And, even when the client has not affirmatively sought a decisionmaking role with respect to a particular matter, the lawyer should be careful not to usurp appropriate client authority on matters that properly fall within the client's domain.

The problem then is to devise an approach that ensures that the client's autonomy is respected on matters of singular importance to the client, while protecting the lawyer from being second-guessed when exercising the professional expertise that a lawyer brings to bear on a legal problem. And that dividing line between client self-determination and lawyer authority must be drawn in a reasonably objective manner if the crossing of that boundary could be a basis for disciplinary action.

Rule 1.2(a) allocates decision-making authority to the client concerning the "objectives of the representation" and to the lawyer on "the means by which they are to be pursued," while requiring the lawyer to consult with (but not requiring submission to) the client as to those means. The rule essentially adopts an ends-means division.

While not every matter that arises during a representation can neatly be placed into either an objectives or means category,[88] finding a superior alternative delineation for respective client-lawyer authority that can be enforced as a disciplinary rule has proven unavailing.[89] Moreover, by requiring that the lawyer consult with the client about the means proposed to achieve the objectives, the rule ensures that the client will be informed about the manner in which the representation is proceeding and thus be given an opportunity to object.[90] The *Restatement of the Law Governing Lawyers* proposes that

[87] Patrick R. Burns, *Ethical Issues in Pro Bono Work*, MINN. LAWYER, Jan. 5, 2004.

[88] W. BRADLEY WENDEL, PROFESSIONAL RESPONSIBILITY: EXAMPLES & EXPLANATIONS 57 (Wolters Kluwer, 5th ed., 2016) (explaining that "there is not a strict, binary either/or distinction between ends and means," such that a "decision can be more ends-like or more means-like").

[89] *Cf.* Nancy J. Moore, *"Why is There No Clear Doctrine of Informed Consent for Lawyers?"*, 47 U. TOLEDO L. REV. 133, 157–58 (2015) (resisting suggestion of *Restatement (Third) of the Law Governing Lawyers* § 21 that a client "may instruct the lawyer" on all matters, including means, saying the matter is not "so simple" and the question of how to balance the interests and allocating decision-making "involves highly contested issues that . . . should not be resolved by fiat").

[90] On the duty to communicate with the client and keep the client reasonably informed, see *infra* § 4-5.4(a) to (c).

the client and lawyer "may agree which of them will make specified decisions" and that the "client may instruct a lawyer during the representation."[91] The comment to the *Restatement* emphasizes that the "lawyer is not required to carry out an instruction that the lawyer reasonably believes to be contrary to professional rules or other law," and if the client persists in a wrongful instruction, the lawyer would need to withdraw.[92] In any event, the client ordinarily retains the ultimate power to control the relationship by discharging or threatening to discharge the lawyer,[93] while the lawyer ordinarily may withdraw if there is a fundamental disagreement with the client.[94]

As Professors Geoffrey Hazard and William Hodes and attorney Peter Jarvis explain, "[t]he lawyer 'shall abide' by the client's desires with respect to objectives, because realization of those objectives is the very reason the client-lawyer relationship was established in the first place."[95] As part of this client authority, the client has the power to define the objectives of the representation, which may not always be the simple goal of success in litigation or a transaction.

Rule 1.2(a) explicitly places certain decisions under the client's exclusive authority. The client in civil litigation has the right to decide whether to settle a matter and on what basis. After being fully informed by the lawyer, the client who is a criminal defendant alone must make the intensively personal decision whether to plead guilty, as well as the choices whether to testify or waive a jury trial.[96] Of course, these specific illustrations do not describe the universe of client objectives, which again depend upon the circumstances and the purpose of the client in retaining the lawyer. (If the client appears to be suffering from diminished capacity, which thus may impair the client's ability to make decisions regarding the objectives of the representation, the lawyer should look to the provisions of Model Rule 1.14.[97])

After soliciting the client's views through consultation (other than on trivial matters or when consultation is not feasible), the lawyer has the power to choose the means that should be employed to advance the representation. As Comment 2 to Rule 1.2 states, "[c]lients normally defer to the special knowledge and skill of their lawyer with respect to the means to be used to accomplish their objectives, particularly with respect to technical, legal and tactical matters." Indeed, "if lawyers are to function as professionals,

---

[91] RESTATEMENT (THIRD) OF THE LAW GOVERNING LAWYERS § 21(1), (2) (American Law Institute, 2000).

[92] *Id.*, cmt. d.

[93] On discharge by the client, see *infra* § 4-3.6(b)(1). Even in a criminal case in which a court wishes to or has appointed counsel, the defendant has the right to reject counsel and insist on self-representation. Faretta v. California, 422 U.S. 806, 819–21 (1975).

[94] On withdrawal by the lawyer, see *infra* § 4-3.6(c)(2).

[95] 1 GEOFFREY C. HAZARD, JR., W. WILLIAM HODES & PETER R. JARVIS, THE LAW OF LAWYERING § 6.04 (Aspen, 4th ed., 2016).

[96] *See also* STANDARDS FOR CRIMINAL JUSTICE: DEFENSE FUNCTION, Standard 4–5.2(b) (American Bar Ass'n, 2015) (advising that decisions to be made by the criminal defendant client include whether to proceed without counsel, what pleas to enter, whether to accept a plea offer, whether to cooperate with or provide substantial assistance to the government, whether to waive jury trial, whether to testify in her own behalf, whether to speak at sentencing, whether to appeal, and any other decision determined in that jurisdiction to belong to the client). *But see* Gabriel J. Chin, *Pleading Guilty Without Client Consent*, 57 WM. & MARY L. REV. 1309, 1312, 1319 (2016) (arguing that "defense counsel are, and should be, authorized to negotiate and conclude plea bargains to which their clients have not agreed when a client faces catastrophic sentencing consequences by irrationally refusing a reasonable plea" and contending such a "shift in authority is probably good for clients and for the legal system").

[97] *See infra* § 4-3.5.

they must be given broad freedom of action" in selecting the legal means to achieve those objectives, "without the chilling effect of threatened second-guessing."[98]

In civil litigation, for example, the lawyer has to be able to bring professional judgment to bear on questions of legal strategy, such as the way to frame a pleading, how to conduct and respond to discovery, whether to file dispositive motions, and what legal claims or defenses should be emphasized and argued. In a criminal defense case, the lawyer ordinarily (consistent with client objectives) will decide how to present exhibits, which witnesses should testify, when to object and just as importantly when not to object to evidence or questions asked of witnesses by the prosecutor. Unless time or other circumstances make it unreasonably difficult, the lawyer should consult with the client about the means to be used in pursuing the client's litigation objectives. But as an earlier comment to Rule 1.2 correctly stated, the lawyer is not required to employ particular measures "simply because a client may wish that the lawyer do so."

Moreover, in some situations, consultation with the client simply is not possible, and the lawyer must maintain the freedom to act. As Professors Ronald Rotunda and John Dzienkowski observe, for example:

> In the middle of a trial, the lawyer cannot consult with her client on matters such as whether to object to a question that the other lawyer has asked on the grounds that it may violate the hearsay rules. By the time the lawyer explained the hearsay rule, its various exceptions, and the benefits and risks of presenting an objection, the opposing lawyer would have moved on to other witnesses and the particular question will have become ancient history.[99]

Indeed, Rule 1.4(a)(2) of the Model Rules of Professional Conduct requires that the lawyer "reasonably consult with the client about the means by which the client's objective are to be accomplished." What is "reasonable" turns of course on circumstances (including time-constraints and setting) and significance (the likely importance of the matter to the client). Furthermore, Rule 1.2(a) confirms that the "lawyer may take such action on behalf of the client as is impliedly authorized to carry out the representation," which at least allows the lawyer "to take such innocuous actions as making calls and drafting letters to schedule routine interviews and depositions without first obtaining the client's approval."[100]

When the strategy chosen to pursue a matter may have significant non-legal consequences, an earlier comment to Rule 1.2 recognized that "a clear distinction between objectives and means sometimes cannot be drawn." Professor W. Bradley Wendel perceptively contends that "[a]s a matter becomes more central to the client's interests, it should be considered as having more of an ends-like quality."[101] Professor Nancy Moore persuasively argues that "most clients would not want their lawyer to act unilaterally—that is, without first receiving the client's permission—if that action

---

[98] 1 GEOFFREY C. HAZARD, JR. & W. WILLIAM HODES, THE LAW OF LAWYERING: A HANDBOOK ON THE MODEL RULES OF PROFESSIONAL CONDUCT § 1.2:202 (2d ed. 1998).

[99] RONALD D. ROTUNDA & JOHN S. DZIENKOWSKI, PROFESSIONAL RESPONSIBILITY: A STUDENT'S GUIDE § 1.2–2(a) (American Bar Ass'n, 2013–2014); *see also* Rodney J. Uphoff & Peter B. Wood, *The Allocation of Decisionmaking Between Defense Counsel and Criminal Defendant: An Empirical Study of Attorney-Client Decisionmaking*, 47 KAN. L. REV. 1, 9 (1998) ("Time, common sense, and respect for professional autonomy simply preclude the client from making all strategic decisions.").

[100] Moore, *supra*, 47 U. TOLEDO L. REV. at 144.

[101] WENDEL, *supra*, at 57.

entails either significant risk, substantial expense, or the potential for serious harm to third persons."[102] Thus, for example, the client may be reluctant to subject a third person, such as a child, to examination and cross-examination as a witness in litigation. While the identification of witnesses ordinarily would be a matter of legal means reserved to the lawyer, the client's concerns for the interests of other persons arguably places a limitation on the objectives of the representation.[103] Even when the lawyer has professional authority to make a decision, Professor Rodney Uphoff advises, especially in a criminal defense representation, that "lawyers locked in a strategic impasse with a defendant analyze and balance four factors—the client's capacity for making an informed choice, the reasons for the client's proposed choice, the degree of harm facing the client, and the likelihood of that harm occurring—before deciding how to act."[104]

In general, the lawyer and client should work collaboratively on the direction of the representation. On questions of means, as Comment 2 to Rule 1.2 suggests, the lawyer generally may assume responsibility for technical and legal tactical issues, but should defer to the client regarding questions that fall into or border upon objectives, such as "the expense to be incurred and concern for third persons who might be adversely affected."

Again, a client who remains "perturbed about the tactical choices of his lawyer can simply fire the lawyer."[105] And as Comment 2 to Rule 1.2 states, if the lawyer and client fundamentally disagree on means, the lawyer may withdraw. But, under the black letter law of Rule 1.2(a) that distinguishes between "objectives" and "means," the lawyer should not be disciplined for making competent choices on matters falling with the realm of professional judgment.

## § 4-3.5 CLIENT WITH DIMINISHED CAPACITY

### § 4-3.5(a) Maintaining an Attorney-Client Relationship with and Respecting the Dignity of Persons with Diminished Capacity

Many members of our society experience, permanently or temporarily, conditions that limit their ability to engage in social and economic interactions or make informed decisions about their living arrangements, physical and mental health, and finances. Children (especially of tender age), the elderly in declining health, persons with

---

[102] *Id.* at 153.

[103] *But see* Rodney J. Uphoff, *Who Should Control the Decision to Call a Witness: Respecting a Criminal Defendant's Tactical Choices*, 68 U. CIN. L. REV. 763, 834 (2000) (concluding, in context of decision whether to call a witness in a criminal case, that the defendant client generally should "be afforded the right to be foolish or wrong," but that in some instances "conscientious counsel" should weigh such factors as the client's capacity, the client's reasons, and the degree and likelihood of harm is great and likely to occur "and override the defendant's strategic wishes"); STANDARDS FOR CRIMINAL JUSTICE: DEFENSE FUNCTION, Standard 4–5.2(d) (American Bar Ass'n, 2015) (advising that "strategic and tactical decisions should be made by [criminal] defense counsel, after consultation with the client where feasible and appropriate," including the decisions on "what witnesses to call" and "whether and how to conduct cross-examination").

[104] Uphoff, *supra*, 68 U. CIN. L. REV. at 799; *see also* Todd A. Berger, *The Constitutional Limits of Client-Centered Decision Making*, 50 U. RICH. L. REV. 1089, 1093, 1124–27 (2016) (arguing, in criminal cases, that "the Sixth Amendment's guarantee of effective assistance of counsel may be violated when defense counsel acquiesces to a client's strategic demands" and criticizing the rulings of most courts that a criminal defendant is estopped from bringing an ineffective assistance of counsel claim if the lawyer accepts the client's demands on a strategic decision).

[105] 1 GEOFFREY C. HAZARD, JR. & W. WILLIAM HODES, THE LAW OF LAWYERING § 1.2:202 (Aspen, 3d ed., 2005).

permanent mental or physical disabilities, and people who are incapacitated for a period of time due to injury or illness may have a diminished capacity to understand and participate as a client when receiving legal services from a lawyer.

That a client needing legal services has diminished capacity is not, however, a general invitation to the lawyer to paternalistically assume the power to determine what is in the client's best interests or to disregard client autonomy concerning the objectives of the representation.[106] Most persons of diminished capacity are able to participate at some level and with some degree of effectiveness in making important decisions about their lives. These clients deserve the respect, the necessary patience, and the sensitive counseling of their lawyers in doing so.

Rule 1.14(a) of the Model Rules of Professional Conduct encourages the lawyer "as far as reasonably possible" to "maintain a normal client-lawyer relationship" with a client of diminished capacity. As Comment 6 to the rule explains:

> In determining the extent of the client's diminished capacity, the lawyer should consider and balance such factors as: the client's ability to articulate reasoning leading to a decision, variability of state of mind, and ability to appreciate consequences of a decision; the substantive fairness of a decision; and the consistency of a decision with the known long-term commitments and values of the client.

To the extent that the client is able to participate in the representation, the lawyer must afford the client the dignity of making important decisions and defining the objectives of the representation. This need not be an all-or-nothing evaluation. If the client is able to understand and evaluate some matters, but not others, the lawyer should accept the client's directions on those subjects as to which the client is competent, while taking protective measures with respect to other subjects.[107]

The lawyer who undertakes representation of a person with diminished capacity must be prepared to devote greater personal attention, provide more detailed and repeated explanations, consult with other important persons in the client's life, and accommodate the disabilities of the client.[108] Allowing the client to bring along family members or friends to the meeting with the lawyer may give the client comfort and confidence, as well as allow the assistance of those who know the person and better understand her communications.[109] Each situation must be addressed in light of the individual circumstances of the person involved, with a general presumption in favor of allowing the client the dignity of self-determination to the extent possible.

Professors Geoffrey Hazard and William Hodes and attorney Peter Jarvis explain that the "chief mission" of Rule 1.14(a) "is simply to ensure that lawyers adequately think through the difficult problems associated with representation of clients with some

---

[106] On the client's authority to make decisions concerning the objectives of the representation, see *supra* § 4-3.4.

[107] On taking protective measures for a client with diminished capacity, see *infra* § 4-3.5(b).

[108] On representing an individual with diminished capacity, see generally David A. Green, *"I'm Ok—You're Ok": Educating Lawyers to "Maintain a Normal Client-Lawyer Relationship" with a Client with a Mental Disability*, 28 J. LEGAL PROF. 65 (2004); Stanley S. Herr, *Representation of Clients with Disabilities: Issues of Ethics and Control*, 17 N.Y.U. REV. L. & SOC. CHANGE 609 (1989–1990).

[109] On the protection of confidentiality when necessary third persons are present, which may include family and friends as appropriate, see *infra* § 4-6.3(b).

form of diminished capacity."[110] Lawyers acting reasonably and in good faith under such difficult circumstances should not fear disciplinary sanction, although "a lawyer who is oblivious to the special needs of clients with diminished capacity could be disciplined" under the rules.[111]

## § 4-3.5(b) Taking Legal Action to Protect the Interests of the Client with Diminished Capacity

### *§ 4-3.5(b)(1) Evaluating Client's Capacity and Whether to Take Protective Action*

When any attempt at maintaining a normal attorney-client relationship is futile because the client simply is incapable of meaningful participation in the representation, "an especially heavy and delicate responsibility falls upon [the client's] lawyer."[112] If important interests are at stake or the bodily or financial health of a severely incapacitated person is seriously at risk and the person is not capable of making decisions on his own behalf, Rule 1.14(b) authorizes the lawyer to "take reasonably necessary protective action, including consulting with individuals or entities that have the ability to take action to protect the client and, in appropriate cases, seeking the appointment of a guardian ad litem, conservator, or guardian."[113]

If the client retains any capacity to communicate, the lawyer should be hesitant to so intervene, as the typical lawyer lacks the medical expertise to make a determination as to a client's competence.

And the lawyer must be careful not to elevate her own view of what is in the client's best interests as the standard of what constitutes competent reasoning by the client. As the American Bar Association's Standing Committee on Ethics and Professional Responsibility reminds lawyers: "A client who is making decisions that the lawyer considers to be ill-considered is not necessarily unable to act in his own interest, and the lawyer should not seek protective action merely to protect the client from what the lawyer believes are errors in judgment."[114] In *Disciplinary Proceeding Against Eugster*,[115] the Washington Supreme Court suspended (and the dissent would have disbarred) a lawyer who filed a guardianship petition against his own client without a reasonable inquiry into her capacity and after she had resisted his advice and retained new counsel. The court admonished that "[a] lawyer's decision to have her client declared incompetent is a serious act that should be taken only after an appropriate investigation and careful, thoughtful deliberation."[116]

Moreover, even if the client is less than competent as to some matters, the lawyer's authority under Rule 1.14(b) is limited to those actions necessary to relieve the incapacitated client from being "at risk of substantial physical, financial or other harm."

---

[110] 1 GEOFFREY C. HAZARD, JR., W. WILLIAM HODES & PETER R. JARVIS, THE LAW OF LAWYERING § 19.04 (Aspen, 4th ed., 2016).

[111] *Id.*

[112] *See* State v. Aumann, 265 N.W.2d 316, 318 (Iowa 1978).

[113] *See generally* Barry Kozak, *The Forgotten Rule of Professional Conduct—Representing a Client With Diminished Capacity*, 49 CREIGHTON L. REV. 827, 850 (2016).

[114] ABA Comm. on Ethics and Professional Responsibility, Formal Op. 96–404 (1996).

[115] 209 P.3d 435 (Wash. 2009).

[116] *Id.* at 452.

The lawyer should not override the client's wishes other than as absolutely necessary, erring in the direction of protecting the client's autonomy to the extent possible.

Still, when the client truly is not competent to make pertinent decisions on her own behalf, and perhaps even is incapable of communicating with the lawyer, the lawyer may need to intervene with affirmative action to protect the client's best interests when important rights or safety is in peril. As Professors Hazard and Hodes and attorney Peter Jarvis put it, "the problem then becomes one of *ascertaining* what those best interests are."[117]

### *§ 4-3.5(b)(2) Considering Whether to Seek a Guardian*

In the past, cases involving diminished capacity to the point of apparent incompetence tended to be reflexively resolved by asking whether a guardian or other legal representative should be appointed. The presumption sometimes appeared to be in favor of seeking a guardian in cases where the client could not act in his own best interests. In some cases, such as when the client's incapacity is severe and likely to be permanent, an extensive or continuous series of decisions will have to be made, or the client is incapable of securing for his personal safety and procuring the daily necessities of life, and particularly if the client's family or caregivers agree, asking the court to appoint a guardian or other legal representative may well be the best course of action. In certain situations, such as when a person is incapable of making reasonably necessary financial transactions on his own behalf, or litigation is to be pursued on behalf of a minor, appointment or identification of a legal representative may be required.

But involuntary appointment of a guardian is far from an unalloyed virtue. The client may be embarrassed by the very initiation of the appointment proceeding and be further humiliated by being subjected to examination. If a guardian is appointed, the daily life and personal relationships of the client may be further disrupted. The client's last residual measure of personal independence and dignity may be sacrificed, with little corresponding benefit. The person appointed as guardian may have conflicting interests or be unfaithful in handling finances.[118] The client may find it burdensome to terminate the guardianship when the immediate need passes or when the client is recovering from a disability. And the expenses of the legal representative may be charged against the client's already dwindling assets. In sum, guardianship "is a drastic measure, and has significant aspects that are not benign."[119]

For these reasons, while directing that appointment of a guardian be sought in appropriate cases, Rule 1.14 encourages the lawyer for a client with diminished capacity to consider various alternatives. As less intrusive measures, Comment 5 suggests "consulting with family members, using a reconsideration period to permit clarification or improvement of circumstances, using voluntary surrogate decisionmaking tools such as durable powers of attorney, or consulting with support groups, professional services, adult-protective agencies or other individuals or entities that have the ability to protect

---

[117] 1 GEOFFREY C. HAZARD, JR., W. WILLIAM HODES & PETER R. JARVIS, THE LAW OF LAWYERING § 19.03 (Aspen, 4th ed., 2016).

[118] *See* MARGARET JASPER, GUARDIANSHIP, CONSERVATORSHIP AND THE LAW 1 (Oceana, 2008) ("An improperly conducted . . . conservatorship can result in fraud and thievery, and can jeopardize the health and safety of the ward or conservatee, particularly when non-family members are appointed as . . . conservators;" cited in In re Wyatt's Case, 982 A.2d 396, 407 (N.H. 2009)).

[119] Hellen W. Gunnarsson, *The Challenge of Representing Mentally Impaired Clients*, 92 ILL. B.J. 518, 521 (2004).

the client." Moreover, when taking protective action, the comment says that the "lawyer should be guided by such factors as the wishes and values of the client to the extent known, the client's best interests and the goals of intruding into the client's self-determination to the least extent feasible, maximizing client capacities and respecting the client's family and social connections."

Humility should be the watch word of the day. The lawyer must be careful not to substitute her own personal views or presume too readily to act in disregard for the expressed desires of the client, not because the client is manifestly incompetent and the client's preference is irrational, but because the lawyer simply does not agree with the client's choices or regards them as laden with emotion.

### *§ 4-3.5(b)(3) Person or Guardian as Client*

If a guardian or legal representative should be appointed, Comment 4 to Rule 1.14 explains that "the lawyer should ordinarily look to the representative for decisions on behalf of the client." The thinking behind this comment appears to be that, once a guardian is appointed, the lawyer-client relationship ordinarily exists between the lawyer and the guardian, with the guardian having authority to determine the best interests of the ward. However, as Dean Nina Kohn and Catheryn Koss have pointedly observed, the comments to Rule 1.14 are "self-contradictory" and confusing,[120] with Comment 2 pointing in a different direction and saying that "[e]ven if the person has a legal representative, the lawyer should as far as possible accord the represented person the status of a client."

The American College of Trust and Estate Counsel (ACTEC) suggests that the answer turns on whether the lawyer has a prior relationship with the client, in which case the lawyer should work to maintain a direct relationship with duties to the client.[121] By contrast, if the lawyer is retained by the guardian to perform services on behalf of the person, then ordinarily the lawyer has an attorney-client relationship with the fiduciary.

### *§ 4-3.5(b)(4) Representing Children*

When a lawyer represents a minor, Comment 4 to Rule 1.14 says that whether the lawyer should answer to the parents as the child's "natural guardians may depend on the type of proceeding or matter in which the lawyer is representing the minor." If the lawyer represents the minor in a personal injury suit against a third party, for example, the parents presumably will have the best interests of the child at heart.

By contrast, if the lawyer is appointed to represent a child in a proceeding to terminate parental rights, or in a child custody determination, the parents' interests may be in conflict with the child's best interests, requiring the lawyer to ensure independence in decision-making. However, the answer also turns on the expectations and standards in that state for lawyers representing a child in parental termination of disputed child custody cases. Not every state follows the strict separation of the lawyer for the child and a guardian ad litem that is recommended by the American Academy of

---

[120] Nina A. Kohn & Catheryn Koss, *Lawyers for Legal Ghosts: The Legality and Ethics of Representing Persons Subject to Guardianship*, 91 WASH. L. REV. 581, 615–16 (2016).

[121] AM. COLL. OF TR. & ESTATE COUNSEL, COMMENTARIES ON THE MODEL RULES OF PROFESSIONAL CONDUCT, at ACTEC COMMENTARY ON MRPC 1.14 (5th ed. 2016), at http://www.actec.org/publications/commentaries.

Matrimonial Lawyers (AAML).[122] In the view of the AAML, the child's lawyer should "represent[ ] what the child client desires and not what the lawyer thinks is best for the child."[123]

Even in jurisdictions that depart from the AAML approach and expect the lawyer to advocate the child's best interests, the lawyer must consult with and fully consider the child's wishes and explanations, to the extent the child is able to express them. Although a minor almost inevitably has major deficits in understanding a situation and appreciating consequences, "[a] lawyer for children should always assume that she can learn a great deal from interaction with the client, whatever the child's age or level of maturity."[124] Indeed, the lawyer must "remain open to being persuaded herself by the child's concrete reasons for a particular decision."[125]

### *§ 4-3.5(b)(5) Acting Contrary to Client's Wishes*

When vital to protect the fundamental rights of an incompetent client, the lawyer may have to take action that is contrary to the expressed wishes of the client. As emphasized above, the lawyer should long hesitate to do so, reserving this option for the case in which the benefit to the client is great and there is little or no downside.

For example, if the lawyer has been retained to obtain social security disability benefits on behalf of an indigent person, who later becomes mentally disturbed and requests that the application be withdrawn, the lawyer may proceed with the application if the lawyer reasonably concludes that the client's disability has precluded competent judgment and the receipt of disability benefits is necessary to the future well-being, or even survival, of the client.

As another example, in *State v. Aumann*,[126] the Iowa Supreme Court held that it was proper for a criminal defense lawyer to prosecute an appeal challenging the trial court's determination that the defendant was competent to stand trial and should not be acquitted as insane, even though the arguably incompetent client refused to appeal and said that he desired to be incarcerated. In *Aumann*, the court commended "counsel's lonely defense of the rights of his client," and held that the determination "to pursue this appeal against what may well have been the misguided wishes of defendant was eminently proper."[127]

### *§ 4-3.5(b)(6) Emergency Situation*

Under extreme and exigent circumstances, a lawyer who has not previously established an attorney-client relationship with an incapacitated person is authorized to take legal steps to avert an imminent crisis. Comment 9 to Rule 1.14 states that, "[i]n

---

[122] American Academy of Matrimonial Lawyers, *Standards for Representing Children in Custody and Visitation Proceedings* (2009). On the variation among the states and "navigating" the attendant "ethical minefield," see generally Bruce A. Boyer, *Representing Child-Clients with "Diminished Capacity": Navigating an Ethical Minefield*, 24:1 THE PROF'L LAWYER (2016).

[123] Mary Kay Kisthardt & Barbara Handschu, *The Changing Role of a Child's Attorney*, NAT'L L. J., Nov. 16, 2009, at 12, 29.

[124] Peter Margulies, *Lawyering for Children: Confidentiality Meets Context*, 81 ST. JOHN'S L. REV. 601, 626 (2007).

[125] *Id.* at 608.

[126] 265 N.W.2d 316, 318–19 (Iowa 1978).

[127] *Id.* at 319. *See generally* Rodney J. Uphoff, *The Role of the Criminal Defense Lawyer in Representing the Mentally Impaired Defendant: Zealous Advocate or Officer of the Court?*, 1988 WIS. L. REV. 65 (1988).

an emergency where the health, safety or a financial interest of a person with seriously diminished capacity is threatened with imminent and irreparable harm, a lawyer may take legal action on behalf of such a person," if the lawyer reasonably believes that no other person is available to protect the person's interests. The legal measures taken should be limited to those "reasonably necessary to maintain the status quo or otherwise avoid imminent and irreparable harm."

Reflecting that a true emergency existed and the lawyer was not taking advantage of the situation for selfish gain, Comment 10 concludes that, "[n]ormally, a lawyer would not seek compensation for such emergency actions taken." Once the crisis has passed, the lawyer should take steps to normalize the attorney-client relationship or implement other protective measures.

#### *§ 4-3.5(b)(7) Confidentiality When Representing Client with Diminished Capacity*

When taking actions to protect the interests of a person with diminished capacity, the lawyer is authorized under Rule 1.14(c) to reveal confidential information, "but only to the extent reasonably necessary to protect the client's interests." In consulting with family members and other persons to determine the best interests of the client, the lawyer may need to provide some explanation of the client's condition and situation.

However, the lawyer should be circumspect, refuse to share any information with persons likely to act adversely to the client, and reveal only that limited information necessary to accomplish the purpose. Importantly, the lawyer should keep foremost in mind the serious risks that may follow ill-advised disclosures, such as the use by others of information about the client's incapacity to institute proceedings for involuntary commitment.

## § 4-3.6 ENDING THE REPRESENTATION

### § 4-3.6(a) The Ordinary Conclusion of the Representation

Most attorney-client relationships come to a natural end with the conclusion of the representation. If the matter on which the client engaged the lawyer has been completed, with the end of the litigation or the consummation of the transaction, then the representation reaches a finale as well.

However, if the lawyer has represented the client on other matters and has a longstanding relationship with the client, the client may reasonably expect that the relationship is an ongoing one, even if no matter is presently underway. If the client's understanding of a continuing relationship is reasonable, and if the lawyer fails to clearly communicate to the contrary, then the lawyer has continuing professional responsibilities, including the strict limitations on adverse representation of another client even on unrelated matters.[128]

If the lawyer instead wishes to preserve his options in accepting future clients under the successive conflict of interest rules,[129] the lawyer should conclude each representation with a clear communication documenting that the relationship has been terminated.

---

[128] *See infra* § 4-7.4(b)(1).

[129] *See infra* § 4-7.5.

## § 4-3.6(b) Termination of the Lawyer by the Client

### *§ 4-3.6(b)(1) The Near-Absolute Right of the Client to Terminate the Lawyer*

The attorney-client relationship is a uniquely confidential and fiduciary one, in which the client extends personal trust to the lawyer, is encouraged to share the most intimate of secrets with the lawyer, and delegates authority to the lawyer to take actions that may have great significance for the life, prosperity, and even liberty of the client. For these reasons, when the client's faith in the lawyer is deeply shaken, the relationship ordinarily cannot continue. A lawyer should not be permitted to foist her professional services upon an unwilling recipient. If the trust that is at the heart of the attorney-client relationship is lost, the client generally must be permitted to end the relationship and be able to do so at no penalty.

Accordingly, it is black-letter law that the client may discharge the lawyer for any reason or for no reason.[130] This principle is reinforced by Rule 1.16(a)(3) of the Model Rules of Professional Conduct, which mandates that the lawyer "withdraw from the representation of a client if . . . the lawyer is discharged."

The client's right to select his own counsel, including termination of prior counsel, is further protected through the rules against restrictive covenants that would limit a lawyer's right to practice after withdrawing from a law firm,[131] the proscription of settlement agreements that would restrict the lawyer's right to practice,[132] and the prohibition in several states on nonrefundable special retainers by which a lawyer would be permitted to retain an advance payment should the client discharge the lawyer before the work is completed.[133] Anti-competitive constraints on the availability of legal counsel and financial penalties on the client's exercise of the right to seek different counsel are strongly disfavored.

Although the client's right to terminate the attorney-client relationship is often described as absolute, there is a key limitation on client choice. In a matter pending before a tribunal, the lawyer may be required to obtain permission before withdrawing. And that permission may be denied by the tribunal if it would be disruptive to the process, such as when a request to withdraw is offered on the eve of trial.[134] Under Rule 1.16(c), if a lawyer is not granted permission to withdraw, he "shall continue representation notwithstanding good cause for terminating the representation."

A criminal defendant does not have an unqualified right to refuse the assistance of counsel being made available or to insist upon substitution of counsel. When an indigent criminal defendant has an appointed lawyer, she must show sufficient cause to justify the appointment of substitute counsel. In determining whether to grant a request for substitute counsel, the trial court must balance the defendant's right to counsel of choice against the public interest in the prompt and efficient administration of justice. "[W]hen

---

[130] *See* Petition for Distribution of Attorney's Fees, 870 N.W.2d 755, 760–61 (Minn. 2015) (holding that client's "right to terminate is an implied term of contract" and thus that discharging the lawyer "with or without cause" cannot be a breach of contract).

[131] *See infra* § 4-7.9(d)(1).

[132] *See infra* § 4-7.9(d)(2).

[133] *See infra* § 4-4.4.

[134] *See* Harris v. State, 224 So. 3d 76, 78–80 (Miss. 2017) (upholding criminal contempt citation of lawyer who refused to participate in a trial when the court denied his request to withdraw on the morning of his client's trial because he believed he would not be paid); *see also* In re Kiley, 947 N.E.2d 1, 6 (Mass. 2001).

faced with a total breakdown in communication" between the lawyer and a criminal defendant, the trial court's failure to appoint new counsel may "constitute a denial of counsel in violation of the Sixth Amendment" right to counsel.[135] However, the court will not permit "a defendant to manipulate the right to counsel to delay or disrupt the trial," such as through last-minute requests for substitution as a delaying tactic.[136]

Because the trial court has the power to protect the integrity of its proceedings, the court may appoint standby counsel to be available if the defendant requests assistance, even if the criminal defendant insists on proceeding *pro se*, although that lawyer may not interfere with the defendant's actual control of the defense.[137] In a formal ethics opinion, the American Bar Association's Committee on Ethics & Professional Responsibility insists that "[t]he notion that the client-lawyer relationship can be created absent consent by on or behalf of a client—or acquiescence amounting to consent—is foreign to the concepts in the Rules."[138] Because appointment of a standby lawyer is thus not "a true 'representation,' " in the committee's view, the lawyer's legal obligation arises only from the tribunal's authority to make the appointment, and the lawyer's "ethical duties are limited to complying with the rules defining a lawyer's obligations to persons other than a client."[139] However, should the criminal defendant actually make use of the appointed lawyer's services, by seeking advice or accepting substantial participation in the defense, the defendant thereby may have consented to creation of a lawyer-client relationship.[140]

### *§ 4-3.6(b)(2) Wrongful Discharge Claims by In-House Counsel and Law Firm Employees*

When a lawyer is engaged in private practice and is retained by a client, the near-absolute rule is that the client may discharge the lawyer for any or no reason. When the lawyer is an employee of the client (as in-house counsel) or of a law firm or similar association practicing law (as an associate or staff attorney), the question arises whether a different result should follow when employment law otherwise would permit an employee to maintain an action for wrongful discharge.

Suppose, hypothetically, that an in-house counsel were fired by a corporation for properly refusing to assist in presentation of perjured testimony or for disclosing confidential information as necessary to remedy a perjurious statement. Given the public policy favoring truthful testimony in court proceedings, might an attorney-employee pursue legal action for wrongful discharge based on the public policy exception, even though the effect is to penalize the client-employer for terminating its legal counsel?

Interesting authority on the wrongful discharge question exists in two states almost next door to each other—Illinois and Minnesota—although those authorities point in opposite directions:

---

[135] United States v. Lott, 310 F.3d 1231, 1250 (10th Cir. 2002).

[136] State v. Lopez, 633 N.W.2d 774, 779 (Iowa 2001); *see also* United States v. White, 529 F.2d 1390, 1393 (8th Cir. 1976).

[137] McKaskle v. Wiggins, 465 U.S. 168, 176–78 (1984).

[138] ABA Comm. on Ethics & Prof'l Responsibility, Formal Op. 07–448 (2007).

[139] *Id.*

[140] *Id.*

In *Herbster v. North American Company for Life & Health Insurance*,[141] the Illinois Court of Appeals held that a former inside corporate counsel was not entitled to a cause of action for retaliatory discharge. The court said that it could not "separate [the attorney's] role as an employee from his profession" because his duties for the corporation had been legal in nature.[142]

Subsequently, the Illinois Supreme Court also declined to extend a cause of action for retaliatory discharge to in-house corporate counsel in *Balla v. Gambro, Inc.*,[143] reasoning that attorneys must understand that at certain times in their legal careers they may have to forgo monetary gain in order to uphold the integrity of the legal profession. The *Balla* court held that "extending the tort of retaliatory discharge to in-house counsel would have an undesirable effect on the attorney-client relationship," particularly in chilling communications between the employer-client and the in-house counsel and in risking the disclosure of confidential information.[144] Furthermore, because the tort of retaliatory discharge is a narrow exception to the doctrine of at-will employment and is justified only to the extent necessary to advance important public policies, the Illinois Supreme Court concluded that the ethical responsibilities apprehended by every lawyer are sufficient to protect the public interest without expanding the exception.

In sum, the Illinois courts regard the ethical expectations for in-house corporate counsel as identical to those of attorneys engaged in private practice and refuse to distinguish between the employee role and the legal counsel role of an in-house attorney.

In some contrast, in *Nordling v. Northern States Power Company*,[145] the Minnesota Supreme Court recognized a general theory of a wrongful discharge by an in-house attorney, when the employee asserts breach of an employment contract. The court viewed the corporate counsel's employment-related role as distinct from the attorney-client relationship and less likely to implicate ethical standards:

> The fact remains . . . that the in-house attorney is also a company employee, and we see no reason to deny the job security aspects of the employer-employee relationship if this can be done without violence to the integrity of the attorney-client relationship. For matters of compensation, promotion, and tenure, inside counsel are ordinarily subject to the same administrative personnel supervision as other company employees. These personnel arrangements differ from the traditional scenario of the self-employed attorney representing a client; and these differences are such, we think, that the elements of client trust and attorney autonomy are less likely to be implicated in the employer-employee aspect of in-house counsel status.[146]

However, while approving a breach of contract claim, the Minnesota court expressed skepticism about a retaliatory discharge theory for in-house counsel, although finding it unnecessary to decide the question in *Nordling* because any claim of retaliatory discharge was not well-founded under the circumstances of that case. The court

---

[141] 501 N.E.2d 343 (Ill. App. Ct. 1986).

[142] *Id.* at 345–46.

[143] 584 N.E.2d 104, 110 (Ill. 1991).

[144] *Id.* at 109–10; *see also* Ausman v. Arthur Andersen, 810 N.E.2d 566, 571–72 (Ill. Ct. App. 2004).

[145] 478 N.W.2d 498, 502 (Minn. 1991).

[146] *Id.*

expressed concern that "[a] retaliatory discharge claim is more likely to implicate the attorney-client relationship, raising issues not only of divulging client confidences, but confidences that relate to client wrongdoing."[147]

Subsequently, in *Kidwell v. Sybaritic, Inc.*,[148] the Minnesota Supreme Court rejected by a divided vote a former in-house counsel's suit against the corporate-client-employer for termination in violation of whistle-blower statute. The plurality stated that the lawyer's report of illegality to superiors was part of his job duties in bringing the client back into legal compliance and thus he was not "blowing the whistle" by exposing illegality as would be protected under the statute.[149] The concurrence reasoned that the lawyer had breached fiduciary duties by disclosing client confidences outside the authorization of Rule 1.6 and thus forfeited any right to recovery.[150] The dissent argued the evidence supported a jury verdict for a successful claim under the whistle-blower statute.[151]

The courts thus are divided on whether a cause of action for wrongful discharge (of any nature) may be maintained by a lawyer employed by the client, although the trend appears to be in the direction of permitting such suits under at least some circumstances.[152]

A comment to the *Restatement of the Law Governing Lawyers* argues that "[b]ecause of the importance of [an in-house] lawyer's role in assuring law compliance, the public policy that supports a remedy for such discharges is at least as strong in the case of lawyers as it is for other employees."[153] Moreover, as Professor Sally Weaver argues, "the actions of individual employees, and not the corporation itself, frequently create the ethical dilemmas that in-house attorneys must confront."[154] Thus, encouraging the in-house lawyer to take steps necessary to prevent misconduct by entity employees or officers, including protecting the lawyer's employment rights, may well-serve the interests of the entity itself and its legitimate constituents.

In addition or alternatively, it may be possible to separate some aspects of the employer-employee relationship from the attorney-client relationship. Inside attorneys for business and government entities might be allowed to protect their employment interests, especially when the employment aspects are governed by pay scales and personnel policies similar to those of other employees within the organization, without thereby endangering or unduly upsetting the continuation of the attorney-client

---

[147] *Id.* at 504.

[148] 784 N.W.2d 220 (Minn. 2010).

[149] *Id.* at 229–31 (Gildea, J.).

[150] *Id.* at 231–34 (Magnuson, J., concurring in the result).

[151] *Id.* at 239–42 (Anderson, J., dissenting).

[152] RONALD D. ROTUNDA & JOHN S. DZIENKOWSKI, PROFESSIONAL RESPONSIBILITY: A STUDENT'S GUIDE § 1.16–3 (American Bar Ass'n, 2013–2014); *see also* Alex B. Long, *Retaliatory Discharge and the Ethical Rules Governing Lawyers*, 79 U. COLO. L. REV. 1043, 1048 (2008) (outlining that the majority of courts "have been willing, in theory, to recognize" retaliatory discharge claims by attorneys against employers, although several court decisions have "either imposed limitations on such claims or prohibited them altogether"); Elizabeth Cohen, *Wrongful Discharge Claims by Former In-House Attorneys Gain Acceptance*, 29 LAW. MAN. PROF. CONDUCT 661 (2013) (stating that "[m]ost jurisdictions" now permit retaliatory discharge actions by in-house attorneys to protect the public interest).

[153] RESTATEMENT (THIRD) OF THE LAW GOVERNING LAWYERS § 32, cmt. b (American Law Institute, 2000).

[154] Sally R. Weaver, *Client Confidences in Disputes Between In-House Attorneys and Their Employer-Clients: Much Ado About Nothing—or Something?*, 30 U.C. DAVIS L. REV. 483, 489–90 (1997).

relationship on other matters.[155] Furthermore, courts that have recognized a cause of action to enforce the employment rights of in-house counsel have offered a remedy in damages, rather than insisting that the employer-client must actually reinstate the attorney.

On the other hand, the traditional fiduciary understanding of the attorney-client relationship sometimes means that a lawyer must accept a financial disadvantage when necessary to preserve professional standards—one of which has been the client's unfettered right to terminate the lawyer, regardless of future financial consequences to the lawyer. Moreover, the Model Rules of Professional Conduct do not make any distinction between attorneys in private practice and those employed by their clients in terms of the ethical standards to which they must adhere. An attorney whose private practice has become financially dependent upon the business received from a single valuable client would not be able to prevent that client from choosing instead to retain another lawyer, even if the client's reasons for doing so were distasteful or inequitable. The consequences of lost employment suffered by a terminated in-house counsel arguably is more a difference in degree than in kind from that experienced by the lawyer in private practice who loses clients. Finally, one might reasonably conclude that the best approach toward enhancing the role and reputation of house counsel is to insist upon their adherence to the same ethical standards that govern all other lawyers, including full respect for the autonomy of clients in selecting counsel.[156]

In contrast with relief for the house counsel who has been discharged by the employer-client, allowing the employee lawyer who has been wrongfully discharged from a law firm or other association of lawyers engaged in the practice of law to seek legal relief would not implicate the same sensitive concerns of respect for the attorney-client relationship and client autonomy in selection of counsel.[157] Permitting a fired lawyer to bring an action against a law firm alleging discharge in retaliation for insisting upon compliance with ethical standards would be warranted by holding, as Professors Geoffrey Hazard and William Hodes and attorney Peter Jarvis argue, that "the employment was subject to the condition that all parties would abide by" the ethics rules, which should be regarded as "impliedly incorporated into every law firm employment contract."[158]

---

[155] *See generally* Rachel S. Arnow Richman, *A Cause Worth Quitting For? The Conflict Between Professional Ethics and Individual Rights in Discriminatory Treatment of Corporate Counsel*, 75 IND. L.J. 963, 989–93, 1000–03 (2000).

[156] *But see* Weaver, *supra*, 30 U.C. DAVIS L. REV. at 534 (arguing that "the extension of a meaningful cause of action for retaliatory discharge to in-house attorneys may be necessary for in-house attorneys to maintain the very independence from their clients that is necessary to support their status as professionals").

[157] *See* RONALD D. ROTUNDA & JOHN S. DZIENKOWSKI, PROFESSIONAL RESPONSIBILITY: A STUDENT'S GUIDE § 1.16–3 (American Bar Ass'n, 2013–2014) (saying that a law firm or similar legal organization discharging an employed lawyer "does not have the rights of a client but only the rights of an employer").

[158] 1 GEOFFREY C. HAZARD, JR., W. WILLIAM HODES & PETER R. JARVIS, THE LAW OF LAWYERING § 21.05 (Aspen, 4th ed., 2016) (referring to arguments adopted by New York Court of Appeals in Wieder v. Skala, 609 N.E.2d 105 (N.Y. 1992)). *But see* Jacobson v. Knepper & Moga, P.C., 706 N.E.2d 491, 493–94 (Ill. 1998) (refusing to allow an attorney to sue a law firm for retaliatory discharge on grounds that "the attorney's ethical obligations serve to adequately protect the public interest" and thus make it "unnecessary to expand the limited and narrow tort of retaliatory discharge to the employee attorney").

### § 4-3.6(c) Termination by the Lawyer

#### *§ 4-3.6(c)(1) Mandatory Withdrawal (or Decline)*

Under Rule 1.16(a) of the Model Rules of Professional Conduct, a lawyer must decline representation or withdraw from representation if "(1) the representation will result in violation of the Rules of Professional Conduct or other law; (2) the lawyer's physical or mental condition materially impairs the lawyer's ability to represent the client; or (3) the lawyer is discharged."

Each of these three grounds for mandatory removal of a lawyer from representation is an essential element of the enforcement mechanism for upholding other ethical standards.

***Avoiding Violation of the Rules of Professional Conduct:*** If the lawyer is to faithfully abide by such directives as avoiding a conflict of interest,[159] refusing to assist a client's fraud or crime,[160] and pursuing only meritorious claims or defenses,[161] the lawyer may be obliged to withdraw to interrupt a representation that would be infected by a conflict or to prevent complicity in client wrongdoing.

***Impaired Competence:*** Because the lawyer has an independent duty to provide competent representation to the client,[162] the obligation to withdraw when a physical or mental condition materially impairs the representation is but a specific application of the preceding duty to withdraw to avoid violation of the rules.

***Discharge by the Client:*** The duty to withdraw when the lawyer has been discharged upholds the client's near-absolute right to terminate the lawyer for any or no reason.[163]

Even under circumstances where withdrawal is mandated, Rule 1.16(c) requires the lawyer who is representing a client before a tribunal to "comply with applicable law requiring notice to or permission of a tribunal when terminating a representation." If the tribunal denies that permission, the lawyer "shall continue representation notwithstanding good cause for terminating the representation."

As Comment 3 to the rule notes, the lawyer may be left in a difficult position if the lawyer is obliged to withdraw because the client demands that the lawyer engage in unprofessional conduct, the court requests an explanation for the requested withdrawal, and the lawyer is prevented from providing a full explanation by reason of confidentiality. Under such circumstances, the comment suggests that "[t]he lawyer's statement that professional considerations require termination of the representation ordinarily should be accepted [by the tribunal] as sufficient."

#### *§ 4-3.6(c)(2) Permissive Withdrawal*

***Withdrawal Without Adverse Effect:*** As a general rule, under Rule 1.16(b)(1) of the Model Rules of Professional Conduct, a lawyer may withdraw from representation of

---

159 *See infra* ch. 4-7.

160 *See infra* §§ 4-9.8(h), 4-11.2(b).

161 *See infra* § 4-9.3(a).

162 *See infra* § 4-5.1.

163 *See supra* § 4-3.6(b)(1).

a client whenever "withdrawal can be accomplished without material adverse effect on the interests of the client."

When the client would not be harmed by the lawyer's withdrawal (other than, of course, the possible need for the client at some non-exigent point to find substitute counsel), the lawyer is granted broad and flexible discretion in deciding whether to continue to represent a client. The remaining provisions in the rule for permissive withdrawal by the lawyer allow the lawyer under certain specified circumstances to terminate the relationship, even when that withdrawal is to the detriment of the client. But, again, if the client's interest will not be materially and adversely affected, the lawyer has no need to invoke these other provisions or to make any particular case for the withdrawal. Still, as noted further below, the lawyer who withdraws without substantial reason should be held to have forfeited any claim for compensation from the abandoned client.

***Other Reasons for Permissive Withdrawal:*** Even if material adverse effect to the client's interests may result, and thus option (1) is not available, Rule 1.16(b) permits (but does not require) the lawyer to withdraw if:

(2) the client persists in a course of action involving the lawyer's services that the lawyer reasonably believes is criminal or fraudulent;

(3) the client has used the lawyer's services to perpetrate a crime or fraud;

(4) the client insists upon taking action that the lawyer considers repugnant or with which the lawyer has a fundamental disagreement;

(5) the client fails substantially to fulfill an obligation to the lawyer regarding the lawyer's services and has been given reasonable warning that the lawyer will withdraw unless the obligation is fulfilled;

(6) the representation will result in an unreasonable financial burden on the lawyer or has been rendered unreasonably difficult by the client; or

(7) other good cause for withdrawal exists.

Although not open-ended, the list of grounds for permissive withdrawal under the rule is fairly expansive and offers a generous series of justifications for a lawyer who seeks to exit from continued representation of a client. Most of these grounds are unremarkable and consistent with longstanding professional expectations, such as allowing a lawyer to withdraw if the lawyer fears that the client's persistent course of conduct may be criminal or fraudulent, if the lawyer discovers that the client has abused the lawyer's services to perpetuate a crime or fraud, if the client has refused to comply with obligations to the lawyer (most commonly consisting of a failure to pay fees for legal services), or if the client's behavior has made the representation unreasonably difficult.

***Repugnant Action or Fundamental Disagreement:*** Rule 1.16(b)(4) allows the lawyer to withdraw if the client insists upon taking action that the lawyer considers "repugnant or with which the lawyer has a fundamental disagreement." This permission appears somewhat narrower than the provision in the former Model Code of Professional Responsibility, which only allowed withdrawal (in a non-litigation matter) if the client insisted upon a course of action that was "contrary to the judgment and advice of the lawyer."[164] By limiting withdrawal based upon disputes with the client as to the best course of action to those matters that provoke "repugnan[ce]" in the lawyer or which reflect a "fundamental disagreement," the new rule should discourage a lawyer from using the threat of withdrawal to coerce a client to take a step, such as accepting or rejecting a settlement, that the lawyer deems merely unwise.[165] When the lawyer finds himself seriously at odds with the client, a considered exercise in moral engagement between the attorney and client, allowing each to explain or reconsider the moral implications of a proposed course of action, may restore health to the attorney-client relationship and avert its termination.

***Unreasonable Financial Burden:*** Rule 1.16(b)(6) allows the lawyer to withdraw if "the representation will result in an unreasonable financial burden on the lawyer," At first glance, this might seem to open the exit door to a lawyer who desires to abandon a client, even if the client would suffer some harm, whenever the representation proves to be less profitable than the lawyer had hoped or than the lawyer could acquire by undertaking another matter for a different client. To be sure, if the withdrawal can be accomplished without any adverse effect upon the client, then the lawyer apparently would be permitted to withdraw under Rule 1.16(b)(1) for any reason, including the self-centered reason of comparative financial benefits. Moreover, the Ethics 2000 revision of Rule 1.16 declined to adopt an "unforeseen" prerequisite for invoking this withdrawal provision.[166] Nonetheless, when the client would suffer a detriment by withdrawal, the financial reversal that is required before allowing the lawyer to leave the client in the lurch should be correspondingly great.

That the lawyer at midcourse in the representation discovers that the representation is unlikely to be as remunerative as the lawyer had hoped at its commencement does not ordinarily amount to "an unreasonable financial burden on the lawyer." As the Massachusetts Supreme Court commented in *In re Kiley*,[167] [a] lawyer's miscalculation of the time or resources necessary to represent a client, the likelihood of success, or the amount of damages 'is usually a dubious ground' for withdrawal, because lawyers are better able than clients to forecast these matters."

This provision should be reserved for the situation in which, due to unanticipated or exceptional demands by the representation in terms of lawyer time (thus preventing work on other matters) or expenses incurred, continuation of the representation would result in a severe economic dislocation to the lawyer's practice. While we may praise the lawyer who heroically continues representation of a client despite financial devastation to her practice or a dramatic decline in the lawyer's standard of living, demanding such an extreme sacrifice at the penalty of disciplinary sanction may simply be asking too much. Similarly, if developments during the course of the matter sharply revise downward the likelihood of success or a substantial recovery, then "there comes a time

---

[164] MODEL CODE OF PROF'L RESPONSIBILITY, Disciplinary Rule 2–110(C)(1)(e) (American Bar Ass'n, 1980).

[165] *See* Rusinow v. Kamara, 920 F. Supp. 69, 72 (D. N.J. 1996) ("Sudden disenchantment with a client or a cause is no basis for withdrawal. Those who cannot live with risk, doubt and ingratitude should not be trial lawyers.").

[166] Margaret Colgate Love, *The Revised ABA Model Rules of Professional Conduct: Summary of the Work of Ethics 2000*, 15 GEO. J. LEGAL ETHICS 441, 461 (2002).

[167] 947 N.E.2d 1, 8 (Mass. 2011) (quoting 1 GEOFFREY C. HAZARD, WILLIAM W. HODES & PETER R. JARVIS, LAW OF LAWYERING § 20.9 (Wolters Kluwer, 3d ed. 2001 & Supp.2005)).

when even the most vigorous representation cannot succeed and the costs will far exceed any recovery."[168]

***Permission to Withdraw by Tribunal:*** The permissions for withdrawal granted to the lawyer under Rule 1.16(b) are conditioned under paragraph (c) by the lawyer's duty to "comply with applicable law requiring notice to or permission of a tribunal when terminating a representation."[169] If the lawyer is representing a client in a proceeding and the tribunal denies that permission, the lawyer "shall continue representation notwithstanding good cause for terminating the representation." Indeed, when permission from a tribunal to withdraw is required, the lawyer's duty of candor[170] demands acknowledgment to the client that a motion to the tribunal must be made along with an honest assessment of the likelihood that the tribunal will grant the motion.[171]

***Compensation After Withdrawal:*** What constitutes "good cause" under Rule 1.16 for permissive withdrawal may not always prove synonymous with what constitutes "good cause" for a lawyer to claim compensation for services provided prior to the withdrawal or to insist on sharing in the proceeds of a subsequent favorable recovery obtained by the client with new counsel. As the Kentucky Supreme Court held in *Lofton v. Fairmont Specialty Insurance Managers, Inc.*:[172]

> [T]he "good faith" or "good cause" or a comparable basis for withdrawing as counsel under [Rule] 1.16(b) does not translate into a comparable justification or "good cause" to be entitled to *quantum meruit* compensation for past services. They are two entirely different standards, with a much lower threshold to withdraw from the case than to withdraw with *quantum meruit* compensation.[173]

In holding that a lawyer may recover the reasonable value of services provided before withdrawal for "good cause," the Minnesota Supreme Court in *Petition for Distribution of Attorney's Fees*[174] explained that "[g]enerally, good cause requires that the attorney establish the client has engaged in culpable conduct and the attorney has not, and that the attorney's continued representation of the client would violate the attorney's ethical obligations."[175]

### § 4-3.6(d) Protecting the Client's Interest upon Withdrawal

Under Rule 1.16(d), the lawyer who withdraws, whether by mandate or by choice, "shall take steps to the extent reasonably practicable to protect a client's interests, such

---

[168] Smith v. R.J. Reynolds Tobacco Co., 630 A.2d 820, 832 (N.J. Super. 1993).

[169] *See also* supra § 4-3.6(b)(1) to (2).

[170] *See infra* § 4-5.2(b).

[171] *See* Attorney Disciplinary Bd. v. Vandel, 889 N.W.2d 659, 665 (Iowa 2016) (disciplining an attorney who threatened to withdraw in a child visitation and support case unless the client made an additional payment and doing so without informing the client that a motion to withdraw must be made along with the likelihood that the judge would grant or deny the motion).

[172] 367 S.W.3d 593 (Ky. 2012).

[173] *Id.* at 596.

[174] 870 N.W.2d 755, 765 (Minn. 2015) (suggesting that "good cause" may include the reasons for mandatory withdrawal under Rule 1.16(a) and "some of the reasons" for permissive withdrawal under Rule 1.16(b)).

[175] *See also* RESTATEMENT (THIRD) OF THE LAW GOVERNING LAWYERS § 37 (American Law Institute, 2000) (stating that a lawyer may be required to forfeit a fee for "engaging in clear and serious violation of duty to a client," meaning that complete forfeiture is reserved for serious violations of ethical duty).

as giving reasonable notice to the client, allowing time for employment of other counsel, surrendering papers and property to which the client is entitled and refunding any advance payment of fee or expense that has not been earned or incurred."

Whether the lawyer is pleased to be escaping from the representation or chagrined that the client has discharged him or that he is required to withdraw for another reason, the lawyer's responsibility to the client continues until the lawyer has taken reasonable steps to ensure that his extrication from the matter can be accomplished with the least disruption to the client. At a minimum, the lawyer must provide prompt notice to the client of the withdrawal, advise the client that he needs to hire new counsel, and return any advance fees paid that were not earned and any papers or other property entrusted to the lawyer by the client. Until withdrawal is properly made, or the client obtains other representation, the lawyer has a continuing ethical duty to protect the client's interests, including ensuring that filing deadlines are met and that court appearances are made.[176]

Under the last sentence of Rule 1.16(d), the lawyer may "retain papers relating to the client to the extent permitted by law." As confirmed by Comment 9 to Rule 1.16, this language refers to the proper exercise by the lawyer of the statutory retaining lien over the client file in order to secure payment of the lawyer's fees.

Nonetheless, a lawyer should not apply an attorney's lien in a matter that prejudices the immediate needs of the client. Indeed, a couple of states by rule expressly preclude a lawyer from refusing to share materials in the client's file because of nonpayment when it would prejudice the client.[177] A lawyer should not withhold those portions of the client's file that the client or the client's new counsel need to take imminent action to protect the client's interests (such as court documents pertinent to ongoing litigation). In any event, no wise lawyer would wish to withhold documents arguably vital to an ongoing representation and thereby risk later being charged in the context of a professional malpractice suit with having sabotaged the outcome.

## § 4-3.7 SALE OF A LAW PRACTICE AND EFFECT ON CLIENTS

### § 4-3.7(a) Background and Overview on Sale of a Law Practice

The traditional view that prevailed until fairly recently was that a law practice was not a going business concern that could be sold by one lawyer to another.[178] Under this conception, which was grounded in the ideal that the practice of law was a profession and not a business, a lawyer offered unique professional services separately to each individual client. Any "good will" of the law practice was attributable to the personal reputation of that lawyer based upon those personally-provided professional services and could not be transferred to anyone else. Accordingly, when the lawyer retired or died, nothing remained of the law practice, other than the tangible real property and personal property of the law office, that could be sold for a price by a retiring lawyer or by the estate of a deceased lawyer. As another basis for prohibiting the sale of a law practice,

---

[176] *See* In re Ulanowski, 800 N.W.2d 785, 795 (Minn. 2011) (disciplining an attorney who "withdrew from representing a client with cognitive and memory issues less than three weeks before trial and the client did not obtain substitute counsel for the trial").

[177] *See, e.g.*, ARIZ. RULES OF PROF'L CONDUCT R. 1.16(d); MASS. RULES OF PROF'L CONDUCT R. 1.17(e)(7).

[178] *See generally* CHARLES W. WOLFRAM, MODERN LEGAL ETHICS § 16.2.1 (West 1986) (discussing situation prior to adoption of new rule permitting sale of law practice); 1 GEOFFREY C. HAZARD, JR., W. WILLIAM HODES & PETER R. JARVIS, THE LAW OF LAWYERING § 22.03 (Aspen, 4th ed., 2016).

the profession strongly resisted the suggestion that the lawyer's clients were commodities that could be traded to another.

In practical reality, of course, a law practice understood as a collection of continuing legal matters and including the good will developed by the lawyer's success in practice does accumulate value over time. And unless that value is both substantial and is capable of being transferred, at least in part, there would never be a willing buyer for a law practice, and the question of whether a practice could be sold would become moot. Nor is it necessary to treat each client matter as a piece of merchandise in order to allow the law practice as a whole to be transferred. Other safeguards for protecting client interests, preserving client confidentiality, and confirming the client's freedom to select other counsel can be adopted, short of an absolute prohibition on the sale of a law practice. For that matter, permitting the transfer of a law practice may be an effective means of ensuring that the sole practitioner's clients will receive continuing professional attention after the lawyer retires or dies.

The traditional rule prohibiting the sale of a practice discriminated primarily against the sole practitioner.[179] The lawyer who practiced in association with others in a law firm effectively was able to transfer a client matter to other partners or associates in the law firm upon retirement or death, although each client still retained the freedom to move the matter elsewhere. Upon withdrawal from a firm, the lawyer is ethically permitted to receive a payment from the firm for her partnership share. The value of the share may be based, not only on the lawyer's actual monetary investment into the firm, but also on the growth of that investment as measured by the firm's income, which thus reflects the good will value of that lawyer's contribution to the law firm. Moreover, upon retirement from practice in association with other lawyers, the retiring lawyer could receive retirement benefits from the law firm, which might be based on the value of the retiring partner's contribution to the firm.[180]

The rule prohibiting any sharing of legal fees with nonlawyers was then[181] and remains subject to an exception allowing the payment of money over a reasonable period of time by a law firm to the estate or survivors of a deceased lawyer.[182] This rule exception not only permits a death benefit or continuation of retirement benefits, but effectively permits a law firm to agree in advance to pay the purchase price for assuming the departed lawyer's portfolio of legal work.

Rule 1.17 of the Model Rules of Professional Conduct now permits sale of a law practice,[183] as well as a particular practice area,[184] with written notice to clients who then have an opportunity to object.[185]

---

[179] *See* 1 GEOFFREY C. HAZARD, JR., W. WILLIAM HODES & PETER R. JARVIS, THE LAW OF LAWYERING § 22.02 (Aspen, 4th ed., 2016); RONALD D. ROTUNDA & JOHN S. DZIENKOWSKI, PROFESSIONAL RESPONSIBILITY: A STUDENT'S GUIDE § 1.17–1 (American Bar Ass'n, 2013–2014).

[180] On the payment of retirement benefits to a lawyer, including permission to restrict the lawyer's practice after retirement, see *infra* § 4-7.9(d)(1).

[181] MODEL CODE OF PROF'L RESPONSIBILITY, Disciplinary Rule 3–102(A)(1) (American Bar Ass'n, 1980).

[182] *See infra* § 4-7.9(b)(2).

[183] *See infra* § 4-3.7(d).

[184] *See infra* § 4-3.7(d).

[185] *See infra* § 4-3.7(e).

### § 4-3.7(b) Termination of Seller's Practice upon Sale of a Law Practice

Under Rule 1.17(a) of the Model Rules of Professional Conduct, the lawyer selling a law practice or practice area must "cease[ ] to engage in the private practice of law, or in the area of practice that has been sold," in either "the geographic area" or "in the jurisdiction" in which "the practice has been conducted." Because the very purpose of the provision allowing the sale of a law practice is to facilitate the transfer of the practice upon the lawyer's cessation of active practice, and because continued practice by the seller in competition with the buyer would essentially deprive the buyer of the benefit of the bargain, the selling lawyer must terminate his law practice upon the sale.

This practice restriction, however, is subject to several limitations, both those stated in the text of Rule 1.17 and those confirmed in the accompanying comments:

***Ceasing Private Practice:*** The text refers to cessation of the "private practice" of law, which as confirmed by Comment 3 to Rule 1.17 means that the lawyer remains free to accept employment as a lawyer for a government agency, with a legal services entity, or as in-house counsel to an organization.

***Selling and Ceasing Area of Practice:*** Because the rule now permits a lawyer to sell a discrete area of practice without selling the entire law practice,[186] Rule 1.17(a) provides that the lawyer who sells a practice area is obliged only to cease practice in that particular area. Thus, a lawyer may transfer one area of practice to another lawyer, while continuing to practice in other distinct fields of practice.

***Ceasing Practice in Geographic Area or Jurisdiction:*** The Model Rule offers to each state alternative language that requires the lawyer to either cease the private practice of law only in "the geographic area" or more broadly "in the jurisdiction" in which the practice has been conducted. The states are divided between those in which the lawyer must withdraw from practice throughout the jurisdiction and those which allow the seller and buyer to agree to the geographic area within which the selling lawyer must cease practice. As Comment 4 explains, under the first option, the selling lawyer may continue in the practice of law—including practicing in the same area of law—in another geographic area of the state (presumably one in which the selling lawyer will not be practicing in direct competition with the lawyer who purchased the law practice or practice area).

***Unanticipated Changes:*** Comment 2 provides an escape hatch from permanent withdrawal from the practice, when the lawyer encounters "an unanticipated change in circumstances." Thus, for example, if a lawyer sells her practice when appointed as a judge, but later suffers defeat in a retention election or resigns from the judiciary, the lawyer should be permitted to resume private practice. Given the well-recognized vicissitudes of political life, when a law practice is sold by a lawyer standing for election to political office, one might question whether subsequent electoral defeat is truly an "unanticipated change in circumstances." The political candidate might be well-advised to refrain from disposing of the law practice under Rule 1.17 until political victory appears certain. By contrast, the political office holder who despite the benefits of incumbency is turned out of office presumably would be allowed to return to the practice of law when tenure in public office is interrupted.

---

[186] *See infra* § 4-3.7(e).

***Temporary Continued Affiliation:*** As an exception of sorts to the cessation of practice mandate, the selling and buying lawyers might agree that the seller would maintain some type of limited professional affiliation with the purchaser for a short while after the transfer of the practice. Encouraging a positive mentoring relationship between the typically older and retiring seller and the typically younger buyer would be in the interests of the lawyers and the affected clients.

The American Bar Association's Standing Committee on Ethics and Professional Responsibility opines that Rule 1.17's requirement that the selling lawyer cease to practice law "does not preclude the seller from assisting the buyer or buyers in the orderly transition of active client matters for a reasonable period of time after the closing of the sale."[187] Under this opinion, the selling lawyer may not take on new client matters, but "the transition of pending or active client matters from a selling lawyer or firm to a purchasing lawyer or firm need not be immediate or abrupt."

***Death or Disability of Selling Lawyer:*** As the most permanent cessation of law practice imaginable, a lawyer who dies obviously has satisfied the termination of practice condition. Although the text of Rule 1.17 speaks in terms of "[a] lawyer or law firm" selling a law practice or practice area, Comment 13 states that the rule also applies "to the sale of a law practice of a deceased, disabled or disappeared lawyer." Rule 5.4(a)(2) of the Model Rules of Professional Conduct confirms this application, by providing as an exception to the prohibition on sharing fees with nonlawyers, that "a lawyer who purchases the practice of a deceased, disabled, or disappeared lawyer may, pursuant to the provisions of Rule 1.17, pay to the estate or other representative of that lawyer the agreed-upon purchase price."[188]

### § 4-3.7(c) Valuing the Law Practice and Paying the Sale Price

Rule 1.17 does not address the valuation of the law practice or practice area for purposes of sale, instead leaving the sale price to be negotiated by the buyer and seller in an arm's-length transaction. However, other provisions in the rules—specifically the provision governing how legal fees may be divided between lawyers and the general prohibition on sharing legal fees with nonlawyers—raise doubts about the propriety of a future profit-sharing arrangement as the means by which to purchase a law practice. The answer, however, is not certain,[189] and post-sale profit-sharing arrangements apparently are common.[190]

If the seller, whether the retiring lawyer or the lawyer's estate, sells the practice for a set price, this price may be paid by the buying lawyer immediately or over a reasonable period of time without infringing upon any ethical expectations. Even if the purchase price will be paid to a nonlawyer, such as the estate of a deceased lawyer or the legal representative or guardian of a disabled or missing lawyer, Rule 5.4(a)(2) expressly provides that the bar on sharing legal fees with a nonlawyer does not prevent "pay[ing]

---

[187] ABA Comm. on Ethics and Professional Responsibility, Formal Op. 468 (2014).

[188] *See infra* § 4-7.9(b)(3).

[189] *See* RONALD D. ROTUNDA & JOHN S. DZIENKOWSKI, PROFESSIONAL RESPONSIBILITY: A STUDENT'S GUIDE § 5.4-1(c) ((American Bar Ass'n, 2013–2014) (expressing uncertainty about whether a nonlawyer such as an estate or survivor could sell a law practice and structure it to involve future payments for many years without violating the rule against sharing fees with nonlawyers).

[190] *See* Susan A. Berson, *For Sale: LwFrm-GrtDeal*, A.B.A.J., Mar. 2015, at 34, 40 (describing "an earn-out" measured by the amount of legal business done during a set time period after the sale or by a percentage of clients retained as a "common deal structure").

to the estate or other representative of [the selling] lawyer the agreed-upon purchase price."[191] In addition, when the purchase price is a fixed figure and is paid at once or in structured installments, the payment plainly should not be considered the equivalent of fee-splitting with another lawyer subject to the limitations in Rule 1.5(e).[192]

If, however, the sale price were to be set as a percentage of future profits of the practice for a defined period of time after the transfer of the law practice, other ethical limitations may well be implicated and the legitimacy of the arrangement thus may be questioned. Payments under such an arrangement would be calculated based upon the future performance of legal services and the earnings achieved thereby by the buying lawyer after the sale of the practice or practice area. A stronger argument then can be made that the effect is to divide or share legal fees for the performance of legal services with a lawyer outside the firm (if the selling lawyer receives the future profit-percentage payments) or with a nonlawyer (if the selling lawyer's estate or representative receives the profit-sharing payments).

On the one hand, whether the purchase price for the sale of a law practice is fixed at a set dollar figure or measured as a share of future profits, the price obviously will be determined in substantial part by the predicted future success of the practice or practice area after the sale.[193] In other words, the price arrived at through negotiation between the buyer and the seller will reflect the appraisal of each as to what the practice is worth in terms of its likely ability to show a profit in future years.

Furthermore, because the entire practice or practice area must be sold under Rule 1.17(b), a sale price that is pegged to future profits of the practice as a whole might not be viewed as the direct sharing of legal fees earned in any particular matter, whether paid to a selling lawyer or to nonlawyers in an estate. In any event, Rule 5.4(a)(2) excepts payment of the "agreed-upon purchase price" for the sale of a law practice from the traditional prohibition on sharing fees with nonlawyers. And, because one of the conditions for selling a law practice is that the selling lawyer has ceased to engage in the private practice of law, or in that practice area, the concerns underlying the limitations on division or sharing of fees—that outside persons will interfere with or direct the buying lawyer's exercise of professional judgment—may be less likely to arise in this particular context.

On the other hand, when the sale price is to be paid as a share of the future profits of the law practice being sold, the selling lawyer or the nonlawyer representatives of that lawyer thereby will receive the direct benefits of an ongoing practice of law. To begin with, as Comment 1 to Rule 1.17 states, "[c]lients are not commodities that can be purchased and sold at will." In contrast with an evaluation of the value of a practice or practice area as a whole in setting a fixed purchase price, a profit-sharing arrangement arguably means that every dollar earned in performance of legal services for a particular client is being split on a percentage basis with the selling lawyer or nonlawyer. By allowing the selling lawyer or lawyer-representative to buy "a piece of the action"

---

[191] *See infra* § 4-7.9(b)(2).

[192] *See infra* § 4-4.5.

[193] *See* N.Y. Bar Ass'n Comm. on Prof'l Ethics, Op. 961 (2013) (reasoning that an arrangement to pay the selling lawyer a percentage of contingent fees for the firm's existing and related clients was permitted as part of the "good will" acquired by the buying lawyer, provided the arrangement is limited in duration and amount).

measured by a share of fees earned in each client matter, the individual client matter appears to be a more central part of the bargain.

Moreover, the prohibition on sharing legal fees with nonlawyers established in Rule 5.4(a) certainly would preclude a lawyer from paying a set percentage of overall law office revenues to an outside person or entity, even though the distribution were based on profits from all legal services performed during a particular period rather than on a particular legal matter.

While Rule 5.4(a)(2) does include an exception for payment to a lawyer's estate or representative for a practice sale under Rule 1.17, the exception literally is for payment of "the agreed-upon purchase price." This term arguably denotes payment of a set price rather than establishment of an ongoing profit-sharing arrangement based upon future provision of legal services.

Importantly, while the selling lawyer or the lawyer's estate or representatives may not have direct control over the provision of legal services, a profit-sharing arrangement does grant an ongoing financial stake in the firm's practice to outsiders. This arrangement thus carries the attendant risks of improper solicitations and referrals to the firm to enhance its profits, attempts to influence the direction of the firm, a presumed right to examine the firm books and information about client matters to ascertain the actual profits earned each period, etc. These are the very dangers that the ethical constraints on dividing or sharing fees, especially with nonlawyers, are designed to arrest. Moreover, the lingering connection by the seller with the practice that is inherent in a profit-sharing arrangement may be difficult to reconcile with the stated condition in Rule 1.17 that the sale of a practice must be accompanied by a termination of practice by the selling lawyer.

As a final comment, a profit-sharing arrangement for purchasing a legal practice appears to be contrary to the expectation that all fee transactions and relationships between a lawyer and a client should be thoroughly transparent from the client's standpoint. If the lawyer is forwarding a regular share of the fees to an outside person, the client is entitled to know of that arrangement. Even if this were characterized as the equivalent of division of a legal fee between lawyers under Rule 1.5(e), the client would be entitled to grant or withhold consent.[194]

Moreover, because the buying lawyer has performed the legal services, to allow a share of the fee to be diverted to the seller seems inappropriate, unless the seller retains accountability to the client. If the arrangement results in distribution of a portion of the client's fee to a nonlawyer, the ethical concern is even greater. From the client's perspective, learning that an outside person has an ongoing financial interest in the client's legal matter may raise understandable concerns about the lawyer's loyalty and devotion to the client's interest alone, as well as confidentiality about the client matter.

### § 4-3.7(d) Selling the Entire Practice or Practice Area

Rule 1.17(b) allows the sale of a law practice, provided that "[t]he entire practice, or the entire area of practice, is sold to one or more lawyers or law firms." Thus, the Model Rule permits a lawyer to sell, not only an entire practice, but a practice area, and to sell

[194] *See infra* § 4-4.5.

that practice or practice area to more than a single purchaser. However, a handful of states continue to require that a law practice be sold in its entirety.[195]

In the majority of states following the Model Rule, an attorney who no longer wishes to continue practice in a particular field—because she wishes to wind down a practice in contemplation of eventual retirement, wishes to concentrate an ongoing practice in other area, or simply no longer has an interest in maintaining a particular field of practice—may transfer that practice area while preserving the right to practice law in other respects within that same geographic area or jurisdiction.

Moreover, should a particular practice area attract a willing buyer while other practice areas do not, the selling lawyer would be permitted to conclude the sale at least of those practice areas that can be transferred, while then retaining responsibility for those practice areas that are not sold. From the client's perspective, the provision for separate sale of a practice area to a lawyer with a particular interest in that field of practice "increases the chance that knowledgeable counsel will continue to serve them after the sale."[196]

Whether the entire practice or a particular practice area is being sold, the rule continues to demand that the practice or area must be sold in its entirety. The rule does not permit the sale of individual client matters or segments of a practice area. The parties to the sale may not "skim off" the more lucrative elements of a practice, leaving the remaining clients unserved or left to find new counsel on their own.

While the rule does not define what constitutes a "practice area," Comment 5 to Rule 1.17 suggests the definition is flexible, contemplating, for example, that a lawyer could sell "the estate planning portion of the practice but remain in the practice of law by concentrating on probate administration." However, a seller and buyer may not define a practice area so thinly as to effectively trade individual client matters. Again, to protect the clients involved, the practice or practice area must be transferred in its entirety. As Comment 6 explains, this expectation is satisfied even if "a particular client matter" cannot be accepted by the purchaser due to a conflict of interest.

Rule 1.17(b) also permits a practice or practice area to be sold to more than one purchaser, thus not requiring that the law practice in its entirety be transferred to a single purchaser. The law practice or even an individual practice area may be divided among several purchasers, subject of course to the requirement that, at the end, the entire practice or practice area has been transferred so that all clients within that practice or practice area will be served.

Although the provision for selling a practice area to more than one buyer effectively might permit some single client matters to be transferred to a single buyer, each client remains protected by having the right to object, as discussed below,[197] and by the continuing requirement that the entire practice area consisting of all client matters in that area be included in the sale. When the practice or practice area is being sold to more

---

[195] *See, e.g.*, GA. RULES OF PROF'L CONDUCT R. 1.17(b); MD. RULES OF PROF'L CONDUCT R. 19-301.17(a)(2); MICH. RULES OF PROF'L CONDUCT R. 19–301.17; MINN. RULES OF PROF'L CONDUCT R. 1.17(a)(1); N.J. RULES OF PROF'L CONDUCT R. 1.17; OHIO RULES OF PROF'L CONDUCT R. 1.17(a); S.C. RULES OF PROF'L CONDUCT R. 1.17(b).

[196] 1 GEOFFREY C. HAZARD, JR., W. WILLIAM HODES & PETER R. JARVIS, THE LAW OF LAWYERING § 22.02 (Aspen, 4th ed., 2016).

[197] *See infra* § 4-3.7(e).

than one lawyer or law firm, the sale should be arranged in such a manner that the closing of the sale results in a complete transfer of the entire practice area.

### § 4-3.7(e) Notice to Clients and Protection of Confidentiality

While the traditional rule prohibiting the sale of a law practice has been overturned, it remains true that an individual client matter is not a commodity that may be sold or traded at the lawyer's option. Each client retains proper control over his client matter, which may not be transferred to, or even disclosed to, another lawyer without the client's explicit or implicit consent. To affirmatively protect the client's right to select his own legal counsel, the sale of a law practice may not go through without advance notice to each client and an opportunity to object or to direct transfer of the file to another lawyer. Likewise, the selling lawyer's duty to protect confidential information remains in effect. Without advance notice and an opportunity to object, the client's file may not be disclosed to the buying lawyer.

Under Rule 1.17(c), the selling lawyer must give written notice to each of her clients regarding (1) "the proposed sale," (2) "the client's right to retain other counsel or to take possession of the file," and (3) "the fact that the client's consent to the transfer of the client's files will be presumed if the client does not take any action or does not otherwise object within 90 days of receipt of the notice." In this way, both the client's autonomy in choice of legal counsel and entitlement to protection of confidential information are preserved.

Importantly, the buying lawyer may not be given access to any client-specific information prior to completion of this advance notice and opt-out procedure. The selling lawyer's duty of confidentiality precludes disclosure of confidential information regarding the clients during the negotiation of the sale and at any time prior to expiration of the 90-day period during which a client may object to the transfer. To preserve confidentiality, the required notice is to be sent by the selling lawyer (or if necessary, due to the death or disability of the selling lawyer, by the selling lawyer's estate or representative).

If the client responds to the notice by expressly consenting to the transfer of the matter to the buying lawyer, then transfer of that matter obviously is approved. If the client responds by objecting to the transfer of the matter, by making arrangements to take possession of his own file, or by retaining other counsel who in turn notifies the selling lawyer, then that client matter may be neither disclosed nor transferred to the buying lawyer. If the client does not respond, because the client has no objection or perhaps is unconcerned about choice of counsel because the matter is not active at present, then after 90 days the client's consent to the transfer of the file will be presumed. (The buying lawyer's assumption of the matter is subject, of course, to any court rules requiring approval of substitution of counsel for litigation matters.) If the client subsequently should decide to seek other counsel or simply terminate any representation or retention of client files by the buying lawyer, the sale of the law practice does not impair the client's absolute right to terminate representation.[198]

Despite reasonable efforts, the selling lawyer may be unable to provide notice of the sale to some individual clients, such as a client for whom a will had been prepared and which has been retained by the law office but who has moved and not left a forwarding

[198] *See supra* § 4-3.6(b)(1).

address. When notice cannot be given, the buying lawyer may not simply accept the transfer of the client matter or file. Under Rule 1.17(c), "representation of that client may be transferred to the purchaser only upon entry of an order so authorizing by a court having jurisdiction." As explained by Comment 8, the "court can be expected to determine whether reasonable efforts to locate the client have been exhausted, and whether the absent client's legitimate interests will be served by authorizing the transfer of the file so that the purchaser may continue the representation." To further protect the confidentiality of that absent client, the selling lawyer may not disclose information, except to the court in camera and then only to the extent necessary to obtain an order authorizing transfer of the file.

### § 4-3.7(f) Fees Charged to Clients May Not Be Increased

Rule 1.17(d) of the Model Rules of Professional Conduct states, without equivocation or qualification, that "[t]he fees charged clients shall not be increased by reason of the sale."

The lawyer who buys a law practice simply may not increase fees to the selling lawyer's clients for open matters that were part of the transferred law practice.[199] As Comment 10 says, "[e]xisting arrangements between the seller and the client as to fees and the scope of the work must be honored by the purchaser." Of course, as with any new clients that the buying lawyer adds to the practice, existing clients who seek to retain the lawyer for new matters must enter into new fee arrangements with that lawyer.

A few states expressly provide an exception to the general rule that the purchaser must honor the seller's fee arrangement. These alternative state rules allow the purchaser to refuse to undertake the representation of the seller's client unless that client agrees to pay the same fee that the purchaser regularly charges other clients for similar services.[200]

---

[199] *See* 1 GEOFFREY C. HAZARD, JR., W. WILLIAM HODES & PETER R. JARVIS, THE LAW OF LAWYERING § 22.08 (Aspen, 4th ed., 2016) (explaining 2002 revision of Rule 1.17 of the Model Rules of Professional Conduct "to eliminate the authority of the purchasing lawyer to raise fees in open matters").

[200] *See, e.g.*, GA. RULES OF PROF'L CONDUCT R. 1.17(d); MASS. RULES OF PROF'L CONDUCT R. 1.17(c); MICH. RULES OF PROF'L CONDUCT R. 1.17(b); MO. RULES OF PROF'L CONDUCT R. 4–1.17(d); OHIO RULES OF PROF'L CONDUCT R. 1.17(d).

# Chapter 4-4

# FUNDING OF LEGAL SERVICES: FEES, COMPENSATION, AND FEE SHIFTING

**By Gregory C. Sisk**

*Table of Sections*

§ 4-4.1 Funding of Legal Services: Introduction
§ 4-4.2 Reasonableness and Legality of Fees
§ 4-4.3 The Lawyer's Duty to Communicate the Basis for and Rate of a Fee to the Client
§ 4-4.4 Advanced Fee Deposits and the Illegitimacy of "Nonrefundable Retainers"
§ 4-4.5 Division of Fees Among Lawyers
§ 4-4.6 Payment of Fees by Persons Other than Clients
§ 4-4.7 Fee Disputes
§ 4-4.8 Fee Shifting: Recovering Legal Fees from Another Party

## § 4-4.1 FUNDING OF LEGAL SERVICES: INTRODUCTION

Unless one comes to the practice of law with independent wealth, a lawyer has to make a living by providing legal services. While pro bono representation is a professional expectation and moral aspiration,[1] few lawyers are able to devote their entire practice to such non-remunerative work. Many lawyers are compensated through a salary, whether as a lawyer in a government office, an in-house lawyer for a client corporation or other entity, or a staff lawyer for a legal services or public interest organization that receives funding from another source. Most lawyers, however, are compensated by fees for service paid either directly by the client or indirectly by someone else on the client's behalf. In addition, in so-called fee-shifting cases, a lawyer may be compensated by an award of attorney's fees to the client from the opposing party after the client prevails in litigation.

When a lawyer is paid a fee for legal services, the lawyer is not acting in an unregulated marketplace.[2] But, rather, the lawyer is ethically obliged to meet a general standard of reasonableness and comply with various other limitations designed to protect the person paying that legal fee. That standard and those limitations are addressed in this chapter.

---

1 *See infra* § 4-13.4(a).

2 For more on the need for a "special [professional] ethics beyond that of the market," see Part Two of this book, Stephen Pepper & Katherine R. Kruse, The Philosophy of Legal Ethics, § 2-1.2.

## § 4-4.2 REASONABLENESS AND LEGALITY OF FEES

### § 4-4.2(a) The Objective Standard of a Reasonable Fee and Expenses

The attorney-client relationship is created when a person seeks legal advice or assistance from an attorney, and the attorney agrees to or actually does provide the desired legal advice or assistance.[3] A formal contract or even the payment of a fee is not necessary to create an attorney-client relationship as the relationship may be implied from the parties' conduct. Nonetheless, payment of a fee by the person seeking legal services is a powerful indicator that an attorney-client relationship has been formed.[4]

Rule 1.5(a) of the Model Rules of Professional Conduct prohibits the lawyer from making an agreement for, charging, or collecting an "unreasonable fee." The rule thus establishes a basic and objective standard of reasonableness for measuring the appropriate size of a lawyer's fee for a matter or segment of a matter. The rule also sets forth a customary set of factors to be considered in evaluating the reasonableness of a fee:

- the time and labor required, the novelty and difficulty of the questions involved, and the skill requisite to perform the legal service properly;
- the likelihood, if apparent to the client, that the acceptance of the particular employment will preclude other employment by the lawyer;
- the fee customarily charged in the locality for similar legal services;
- the amount involved and the results obtained;
- the time limitations imposed by the client or by the circumstances;
- the nature and length of the professional relationship with the client;
- the experience, reputation, and ability of the lawyer or lawyers performing the services; and
- whether the fee is fixed or contingent.

"[N]o single factor controls the reasonableness of a fee;[5] "all factors will not be relevant in every case";[6] and "the weight accorded each factor depends on the circumstances of each particular case."[7] Nor is the listing of factors in Model Rule 1.5(a) exclusive; courts may consider other factors in appropriate cases.[8]

A lawyer charging a legal fee also must comply with any restrictions imposed by other law. Thus, a fee that might appear reasonable in amount is nonetheless improper

---

[3] On creation of the attorney-client relationship, see *supra* § 4-3.2.

[4] STEPHEN GILLERS, REGULATION OF LAWYERS: PROBLEMS OF LAW AND ETHICS 82 (9th ed. 2012) ("But even though a client-lawyer relationship can arise without a payment, the fact of payment is pretty good evidence of one.").

[5] Heng v. Rotech Med. Corp., 720 N.W.2d 54, 65 (N.D. 2006); *see also* Rodriguez v. Ancona, 868 A.2d 807, 814 (Conn. Ct. App. 2005) ("When awarding attorney's fees, the court must consider all of the factors and not seize on one to the exclusion of the others.").

[6] Township of W. Orange v. 769 Assocs., LLC, 969 A.2d 1080, 1088 (N.J. 2009); *see also* In re Jardine, 289 P.3d 516, 523 (Utah 2012) (same).

[7] McCabe v. Arcidy, 635 A.2d 446, 452 (N.H. 1993).

[8] WiFiLand, LLP v. Hudson, 100 A.3d 450, 459 (Conn. Ct. App. 2014); *Township of W. Orange*, 969 A.2d at 1088.

if charged or collected in violation of provisions regulating the fee for particular legal services, such as statutory or court rule limitations on the timing and amount of fees for probate matters.

In addition to the standard of reasonableness applying to the amount of fees, Rule 1.5(a) requires that the expenses relating to the representation that are to be charged to the client must also be reasonable in nature and amount. Comment 1 to Rule 1.5 addresses the question of seeking reimbursement from the client for the costs of services performed in-house, such as copying, telephone charges, etc. These costs are to be measured either by "a reasonable amount to which the client has agreed in advance or by charging an amount that reasonably reflects the actual costs incurred by the lawyer."[9] In sum, the lawyer should not turn the provision of in-house collateral services, from copying to electronic research fees, into an independent profit center producing large returns beyond the actual costs that the lawyer or law firm bears for providing such services.[10]

Moreover, a lawyer should not charge clients for a significant number of hours at high lawyer rates for work "not requiring legal training or other professional skills and commonly performed at a much lower cost" by non-lawyers.[11] When a necessary non-legal task is undertaken for a client that is incidental but connected to legal services and does not involve a proportionally significant fee, the lawyer presumably may charge for that work as time that otherwise would be spent on legal work, much as a lawyer may charge a client for necessary travel time. However, when those non-legal services are recurring and result in a substantial charge to the client, the lawyer should arrange for (or allow the client to arrange for) those services by others at appropriate market rates. Thus, for example, a lawyer who spends a few minutes on clerical work when completing legal services on a document, such as finalizing a word-processed document or quickly preparing an envelope for mailing, may reasonably include that charge in legal services. But a lawyer who chooses to forgo hiring a secretary and performs all clerical work may not charge a lawyer's fee for general secretarial work.

## § 4-4.2(b) Hourly Billing

### *§ 4-4.2(b)(1) Nature and Reasonableness*

While experiments with alternative means of paying legal fees have been increasing in popularity in recent years, "[s]till, the billable hour reigns."[12] In the corporate field, for example, studies suggest that alternative fee arrangements have risen above ten percent of matters,[13] meaning that the hourly rate remains the default approach and,

---

[9] *See also* ABA Comm. on Ethics & Prof'l Responsibility, Formal Op. 93–379 (1993).

[10] *See id.* ("[I]n the absence of an agreement to the contrary, it is impermissible for a lawyer to create an additional source of profit for the law firm beyond that which is contained in the provision of professional services themselves.").

[11] Attorney Disciplinary Bd. v. Laing, 832 N.W.2d 366, 373 (Iowa 2013).

[12] Leigh McMullan Abramson, *Is the Billable Hour Obsolete?*, THE ATLANTIC, Oct. 15, 2015, at http://www.theatlantic.com/business/archive/2015/10/billable-hours/410611/; *see also* Susan Saab Fortney, *The Billable Hours Derby: Empirical Data on the Problems and Pressure Points*, 33 FORDHAM URB. L.J. 171, 172 (2005) (referring to hourly billing "as the dominant billing method used by non-contingency attorneys").

[13] Frank Strong, Law Firm Bill Rates Rising? Update on Key Legal Spend Metrics, Lexis-Nexis Business of Law Blog, at http://businessoflawblog.com/2015/01/legal-spend-metrics/.

indeed, is often an element of such alternative arrangements as a blended hourly rate for all attorneys working on a matter or a capped fee.[14]

When a lawyer has adopted the traditional billable hour approach, "[a] formula is necessary to translate the relevant factors into terms of dollars and cents."[15] What is called the "lodestar" fee in fee-shifting cases[16] is derived by multiplying a reasonable hourly rate by the number of hours reasonably expended on the representation. The factors set forth in Rule 1.5(a) serve as the guiding components for determining what time was reasonably so devoted and what constitutes a reasonable hourly rate for the attorney.

Beyond simply (and honestly)[17] documenting the actual hours that were spent working on a matter, an attorney who bills by the hour should exercise "billing judgment,"[18] that is, the lawyer should make "a good faith effort to exclude . . . hours that are excessive, redundant, or otherwise unnecessary."[19] Thus, the lawyer should not charge the client when, as examples, the hours devoted were excessive for the particular task or proceeding; the time spent was excessive because an attorney lacked expertise in an area and devoted too much time developing familiarity with the topic; the hours spent were excessive because a partner performed tasks that could more appropriately have been delegated to an associate; the time was unproductive, for example, because associates received insufficient direction by partners; or the hours expended were duplicative, for example, where multiple attorneys representing the same party engaged in parallel efforts yielding a single legal document.[20]

Moreover, clients are increasingly demanding that attorneys specifically account for the time devoted to legal representation. With the advent of the personal computer, detailed time records by individual attorneys are more easily maintained and thus are coming to be the conventional expectation, at least for sophisticated clients or when the matter involved is substantial.

With respect to hourly billing, what constitutes a reasonable hourly rate for an individual attorney will depend on a multiplicity of factors, including the attorney's level of skill, reputation in the community, experience in practice, and expertise in the subject matter, as well as the undesirability of the case.[21]

---

[14] ALM Legal Intelligence, Speaking Different Languages: Alternative Fee Arrangements for Law Firms and Legal Departments 10 (April 2012), at http://almlegalintel.com/Surveys/AFAreport.

[15] *See* Copeland v. Marshall, 641 F.2d 880, 890 (D.C. Cir. 1980) (en banc) (discussing what constitutes a reasonable fee under the federal fee-shifting statute for Title VII employment discrimination suits).

[16] *See infra* § 4-4.8(c).

[17] On honesty in fee billing, see *infra* 4-4.2(b)(2).

[18] *See Copeland*, 641 F.2d at 891.

[19] *See* Hensley v. Eckerhart, 461 U.S. 424, 434 (1983) ("Counsel for the prevailing party [in a fee-shifting matter] should make a good faith effort to exclude from a fee request hours that are excessive, redundant, or otherwise unnecessary, just as a lawyer in private practice ethically is obligated to exclude such hours from his fee submission.").

[20] For authority on excessive or duplicative hours in the context of fee-shifting cases, see *infra* § 4-4.8(c)(2).

[21] For authority on calculating a reasonable hourly rate in the context of fee-shifting cases, see infra § 4-4.8(c)(3).

### *§ 4-4.2(b)(2) Honesty in Fee Billing*

To be reasonable under Rule 1.5(a), the fee charged by the lawyer must not only appear reasonable in amount, but have been calculated by accurate and honest methods. A fee based upon false documentation, a departure from the rate or basis communicated to the client,[22] or other dishonest method is, by definition, an unreasonable fee. Moreover, dishonest billing violates the lawyer's duty of truthfulness under Rule 8.4(c) of the Model Rules of Professional Conduct, which applies with special force to the client who confides in and reposes fiduciary trust in the lawyer. As Professor Charles Wolfram confirms, "[c]ourts have insisted that lawyers be entirely honest in discussing fees with clients."[23]

A lawyer should never claim more hours than actually were worked.[24] The recording of hours worked and the subject matter should be maintained contemporaneously. A re-created billing record made later in time will almost invariably be inaccurate. Inflated time and expense billings constitute fraud upon the party who receives the bill.

Moreover, when a particular fee arrangement is being established between an attorney and a client, the attorney must reveal any billing policies or practices that otherwise would mislead the client. Of course, disclosure by the lawyer and acquiescence by the client will not save an attorney's fee billing policy from being found unethical if its application results in an unreasonable fee. When "the fee is unconscionably large and involves individuals who may lack effective information and bargaining power, courts are not deterred in finding the fee excessive by the fact that the client has consented."[25]

Sadly, several scholars studying the legal profession have found that deception in fee billing is not uncommon.[26] Attorneys have not always been meticulous in keeping accurate and contemporaneous time records, and attorney billing practices too frequently fail to comport with standards of reasonableness and full disclosure to clients. Scholars long have pointed to high billable hour expectations in elite law firms as effectively pressuring harried associates to pad bills and overwork legal matters.[27] With corporate clients increasingly conducting audits of legal billing, the ability of large metropolitan law firms to run up fees may be more constrained. Unsophisticated clients in areas such as family law, bankruptcy, and probate may be more vulnerable today to unscrupulous billing practices. In any event, the prevalence of bad practices in some regions of the country or sectors of the legal profession cannot change or lower the ethical standard.

---

[22] On communicating the basis for or rate of the fee to the client, see *infra* § 4-4.3.

[23] CHARLES W. WOLFRAM, MODERN LEGAL ETHICS § 9.3.1 (West, 1986).

[24] *See* ABA Comm. on Ethics & Prof'l Responsibility, Formal Op. 93–379 (1993) (declaring unethical the "practice of billing several clients for the same time or work product").

[25] WOLFRAM, *supra*, at § 9.3.1.

[26] *See* Douglas R. Richmond, *For a Few Dollars More: The Perplexing Problem of Unethical Billing Practices by Lawyers*, 60 S.C. L. REV. 63 (2008); Douglas R. Richmond, *Professional Responsibility and the Bottom Line: The Ethics of Billing*, 20 S. ILL. U. L.J. 261 (1996); James P. Schratz, *Billing Guidelines and Fee Disputes: A Case Law Review*, 18 TRIAL DIPLOMACY J. 159, 159 (1995); William G. Ross, *The Ethics of Hourly Billing by Attorneys*, 44 RUTGERS L. REV. 1, 12–22 (1991); Lisa G. Lerman, *Lying to Clients*, 138 U. PA. L. REV. 659, 705–20, 749–53 (1990).

[27] Susan Saab Fortney, *The Billable Hours Derby: Empirical Data on the Problems and Pressure Points*, 33 FORDHAM URB. L.J. 171, 177–78 (2005); David B. Wilkins & G. Mitu Gulati, *Reconceiving the Tournament of Lawyers: Tracking, Seeding, and Information Control in the Internal Labor Markets of Elite Law Firms*, 84 VA. L. REV. 1581, 1594 (1998).

Some commentators and courts have singled out, as particularly susceptible to abuse and churning, the practice of "minimum billing increments"—such as charging for two-tenths of an hour (i.e., twelve minutes) for every action by the lawyer even if the actual time expended, say in leaving a telephone message, was about a minute.[28] One commentator characterizes minimum billing increments as a "practice that can lead to artificially large billable hour totals."[29] Another ethics scholar reports that, while attorneys differ on the legitimacy of the practice, billing clients a minimum time period for work that takes less time "account[s] in part for the startlingly large numbers of hours that many attorneys manage to record."[30] At the very least, a lawyer ought not use a minimum billing increment approach unless it is fully disclosed to the client, the increment selected is truly minimal in size, and the lawyer regularly exercises billing judgment[31] to eliminate excessive billing for a series of small tasks that should be measured together within a single increment.

## § 4-4.2(c) Contingency Fees

### *§ 4-4.2(c)(1) The Legitimacy of the Contingency Method for Legal Fees*

Both to discourage unnecessary recourse to litigation and to reduce distracting influences upon a lawyer's professional judgment by having a personal stake in the outcome, the ethics rules generally prohibit a lawyer from purchasing or otherwise obtaining a financial interest in a client's matter.[32] In the United States, a longstanding and important exception to this general principle has been acceptance of the contingency method for charging an attorney's fee. Contingent fees, which ordinarily are based upon a percentage of recovery, are recognized as an appropriate and ethical means of attorney compensation because this method enhances access to legal services by people who otherwise could not afford it and encourages lawyers to take cases in which there is a substantial risk of loss. Rule 1.5(c) of the Model Rules of Professional Conduct specifically states that "[a] fee may be contingent on the outcome of the matter for which the service is rendered."

Although contingency fees are most commonly employed by attorneys handling personal injury claims, in which the fee will be calculated as a percentage of the recovery (if any), the method is appropriate in other contexts as well. Thus, a lawyer and client might agree to a "reverse contingency" fee, which is based upon the amount of money the client as a defendant saves in the resolution of a dispute. In a transactional matter, a fee could be made contingent upon achieving a particular objective or obtaining a set price

---

[28] Richmond, *supra*, 20 S. ILL. U. L.J. at 269; *see also* Republican Party of Minn. v. White, 456 F.3d 912, 920 (8th Cir. 2006) (reducing an attorney's fee request when the firm billed in minimum quarter-hour increments, which means that "even short phone calls lasting only five minutes or less would automatically be billed for fifteen minutes," finding that overbilling for conferences in person or by telephone may have occurred, and agreeing that "quarter-hour increment billing is less reliable than tenth-hour billing and risks bill inflation").

[29] Richmond, *supra*, 20 S. ILL. U. L.J. at 269; *see also* Schratz, *supra*, 18 TRIAL DIPLOMACY J. at 165–66 (reaching same conclusion).

[30] Ross, *supra*, 44 RUTGERS L. REV. at 59.

[31] *See* Board of Prof'l Responsibility v. Casper, 318 P.3d 790, 795–96 (Wyo. 2014) (ruling that, while "[u]se of billing with minimum time increments does not necessarily result in an unreasonable fee," the lawyer's practice of "billing fifteen minutes for such tasks as signing subpoenas, stipulated orders, and one-page letters demonstrated a complete failure to exercise business judgment, which would have required her to write off unproductive, excessive, or redundant hours"). On billing judgment, see *supra* § 4-4.2(b)(1).

[32] *See infra* § 4-7.3(i).

or savings, assuming the amount can be reasonably ascertained without resorting to mere speculation.

### *§ 4-4.2(c)(2) The Reasonableness Standard Applied to Contingency Fees*

As Comment 3 to Rule 1.5 states, "[c]ontingent fees, like any other fees, are subject to the reasonableness standard of paragraph (a) of this Rule." For the litigation case in which the risk of loss is significant, the use of a substantial contingency fee—one-third of recovery is common—is unremarkable. When the case is especially demanding in terms of attorney time and resources and the risk of loss is greater than normal, a larger contingency fee may be reasonable.

However, if the risk of loss in a matter was never substantial or the ultimate recovery proves to be astronomically high, a contingency fee may be inappropriate or should be measured by a smaller percentage of the recovery.[33] As a comment to the *Restatement of the Law Governing Lawyers* explains, the amount of a contingent fee may be unreasonable if "there was a high likelihood of substantial recovery by trial or settlement, so that the lawyer bore little risk of nonpayment," or if "the client's recovery was likely to be so large that the lawyer's fee would clearly exceed the sum appropriate to pay for services performed and risks assumed."[34] For example, if the lawyer, by reason of her substantial experience, recognizes that the client is likely to obtain a positive result through a quick settlement, meaning that the lawyer will devote little time to the matter and bears little or no risk of being left without a fee, the typical one-third contingency fee would be unreasonable under the circumstances.

In making the reasonableness assessment of a contingent fee, the evaluator ordinarily should avoid an unfair examination made from "a position of hindsight, [which] suggests that the litigation was simple and that the chances for success were good."[35] When considering the appropriate compensation for the risk of loss achieve through a contingency fee, the circumstances generally must be evaluated based on the facts as known to the attorney and client at the time the contingent fee agreement was signed. Furthermore, contingency fees should be evaluated on their own terms, not by a strict comparison with what an hourly billing would have produced. The reasonableness of a contingency fee cannot be determined by simply looking at the size of the fee in comparison to the amount of work performed by the attorney. The degree of risk assumed by the lawyer at the outset of the representation ordinarily is the crucial factor.

Nonetheless, commentators and many courts insist that even a contingent fee agreement that was "reasonable when made may be rendered unreasonable by subsequent events."[36] As the New York Court of Appeals observed, in unusual circumstances, fee agreements "that are not unconscionable at inception may become

---

[33] *See* Committee on Legal Ethics v. Tatterson, 352 S.E.2d 107, 108 (W. Va. 1986) ("In the absence of any real risk, an attorney's purportedly contingent fee which is grossly disproportionate to the amount of work required is a 'clearly excessive fee' within the meaning of [the disciplinary rule].").

[34] RESTATEMENT (THIRD) OF THE LAW GOVERNING LAWYERS § 35, cmt. c (American Law Institute, 2000); *see also* RONALD D. ROTUNDA & JOHN S. DZIENKOWSKI, PROFESSIONAL RESPONSIBILITY: A STUDENT'S GUIDE § 1.5–1(c) (American Bar Ass'n, 2013–2014).

[35] Committee on Prof'l Ethics & Conduct v. McCullough, 468 N.W.2d 458, 461 (Iowa 1991); *see also* State ex rel. Oklahoma Bar Ass'n v. Flaniken, 85 P.3d 824, 827 (Okla. 2004) (rejecting a "proposed 'hindsight' test" for measuring the reasonableness of a contingency fee).

[36] Douglas R. Richmond, *Turns of the Contingent Fee Key to the Courthouse Door*, 65 BUFF. L. REV. 915, 937–38 & n.117 (2017) (citing, for example, In re Powell, 953 N.E.2d 1060, 1063–64 (Ind. 2011); Berra v. Springer & Steinberg, P.C., 251 P.3d 567, 572 (Colo. Ct. App. 2010)).

unconscionable in hindsight."[37] In particular, the magnitude of the result against which the plaintiff's contingent fee is typically calculated cannot be known until the final disposition, at which point a measurement that appeared reasonable at the outset may prove outrageous if applied without qualification to an outsized recovery.

### *§ 4-4.2(c)(3) Contingency Fee Agreements Must Be in Writing*

Rule 1.5(c) of the Model Rules of Professional Conduct directs that "[a] contingent fee agreement shall be in a writing signed by the client." While Rule 1.5 does not demand any written documentation in the context of other forms of legal fees (although a writing is preferred),[38] a written and signed agreement is mandated in the context of a contingent fee.

Contingent fee agreements must be reduced to writing because of the inherent complexity in the calculation of such fees, the greater risk of misunderstanding or confusion by clients regarding the basis of such fees (particularly in terms of deduction of expenses), and the greater danger of overreaching by a lawyer in negotiating a contingent fee arrangement given its complexity when compared to a simple hourly or fixed fee. As Professors Geoffrey Hazard and William Hodes and attorney Peter Jarvis note, "[t]he requirement of a written agreement is significant not only for disciplinary purposes, but also for assuring the enforceability of the agreement. Thus, a lawyer who has not reduced such an agreement to writing will most likely be limited to recovery in *quantum meruit*, and may be precluded from recovering any fee at all."[39]

Under Rule 1.5(c), the signed written contingency fee agreement "shall state the method by which the fee is to be determined, including the percentage or percentages that shall accrue to the lawyer in the event of settlement, trial or appeal; litigation and other expenses to be deducted from the recovery; and whether such expenses are to be deducted before or after the contingent fee is calculated." Moreover, the written agreement must specify whether the client is responsible for expenses even if the client is not the prevailing party, that is, whether the client's liability for the expenses is, like the fee, contingent on the outcome of the matter.[40] Finally, under the rule, when the matter is concluded, the lawyer must provide a full accounting to the client through "a written statement stating the outcome of the matter and, if there is a recovery, showing the remittance to the client and the method of its determination."

### *§ 4-4.2(c)(4) Prohibition of Contingency Fees in Criminal and Domestic Relations Cases*

Consistent with longstanding ethical expectations, Rule 1.5(d) of the Model Rules of Professional Conduct prohibits the use of contingent fee arrangements in certain domestic relations matters and in all criminal cases.

***Domestic Relations Matters:*** The prohibition on contingency fees in domestic relations matters is grounded in the "fundamental public policy" of preserving the

---

[37] In re Lawrence, 23 N.E.3d 965, 978 (N.Y. 2014).

[38] *See infra* § 4-4.3.

[39] 1 GEOFFREY C. HAZARD, JR., W. WILLIAM HODES & PETER R. JARVIS, THE LAW OF LAWYERING § 9.16.1 (Aspen, 4th ed., 2016) (cross-reference omitted).

[40] On making the client responsibility for expenses contingent on the outcome, see *infra* § 4-7.3(f)(2).

"marital relationship."[41] Given the sensitive nature of these matters and the human relationships involved, allowing an attorney to premise a legal fee upon the termination of a marriage or obtaining a pecuniary award attendant to dissolving that marital relationship is contrary to public policy.

Under Model Rule 1.5(d)(1), a lawyer may not charge "any fee in a domestic relations matter, the payment or amount of which is contingent upon the securing of a divorce or upon the amount of alimony or support, or property settlement in lieu thereof."

Interestingly, the Model Rule does not by its express terms prohibit a fee that is contingent on securing child custody. While not necessarily contingent on termination of the marriage (as the parties may remain married but separated and still need to arrange child custody), the spectacle of a lawyer having a fee-based incentive to press one human being to secure possession of another renders such a financial arrangement at least suspect. The *Restatement of the Law Governing Lawyers* specifically states that a fee may not be made "contingent on a specified result" in "a proceeding concerning custody of a child."[42] Some states by ethics rules likewise specify the invalidity of a fee contingent on child custody;[43] and at least one court has found such an arrangement to violate public policy.[44]

As confirmed in Comment 6 to Rule 1.5, the rule does not preclude use of contingency fees in post-judgment actions to secure payments due under child support, alimony, or other financial orders by the court. Post-decree actions to collect on past-due payments, for spousal or child support, are actions to enforce a judgment debt and therefore do not fall within the prohibition on contingent fees in domestic relations matters. Once a domestic relations matter has been concluded with a court decree, the concerns about human relations underlying the general prohibition on contingent fees in such cases are mitigated. Moreover, a contingent fee provides the lawyer with an incentive to assist an impecunious client in collecting past-due payments, which advances the strong public interest in ensuring the payment of child support.

***Criminal Cases:*** Under Rule 1.5(d)(2), a lawyer may not charge "a contingent fee for representing a defendant in a criminal case." Although the reason for the ban in criminal cases is not always as clearly stated or well understood as the domestic relations prohibition, the primary concern appears to be that a contingent fee might introduce inappropriate conflicts of interest. If, for example, the lawyer contracted to receive a fee only upon achieving an acquittal or dismissal of the criminal charges, the lawyer would have a financial disincentive to encourage the client to accept an otherwise fair and reasonable offer from the prosecution to plead guilty to a lesser charge.

### § 4-4.2(d) Flat Fees

A fixed or "flat fee" is a single fee that embraces all services to be performed by the lawyer, whether the work be relatively simple or complex and protracted. Assuming the overall amount is reasonable based on the projected scope of the legal services to be performed when the agreement is reached, the client ordinarily must pay the full

---

[41] Rogers v. Webb, 558 N.W.2d 155, 157 (Iowa 1997); Oklahoma Bar Ass'n v. Fagin, 848 P.2d 11, 13–14 (Okla. 1992).

[42] RESTATEMENT (THIRD) OF THE LAW GOVERNING LAWYERS § 35(1)(b) (American Law Institute, 2000).

[43] *See, e.g.*, IND. RULES OF PROF'L CONDUCT R. 1.5(d)(1); MD. RULES OF PROF'L CONDUCT R. 1.5(d)(1); N.Y. RULES OF PROF'L CONDUCT R. 1.5(d)(5); WIS. RULES OF PROF'L CONDUCT R. 1.5(d)(1).

[44] Maxwell Schuman & Co. v. Edwards, 663 S.E.2d 329 (N.C. Ct. App. 2008).

amount. And the lawyer is obliged to complete the work without requesting further compensation, even if the lawyer's estimate as to the time required proves mistaken (absent some unforeseeable development that significantly changes the nature and scope of the representation).

The primary questions that arise when a flat fee are charged is when the fee is earned and when the lawyer may collect the fee. If the client makes a payment toward a flat fee prior to the completion of the services, that payment could be considered an advance that must be deposited into the trust account and only withdrawn when earned, as with any other advance fee payment.[45] If regarded as an advance fee deposit, then difficult questions could arise about the point in time at which a lawyer who has performed some but not all of the contemplated services may withdraw all or part of a flat fee paid in advance.

Two neighboring states illustrate the diverse approaches to these questions that persist among the states,[46] although they both agree that a flat fee may not be made nonrefundable prior to completion of legal services:[47]

In Iowa, "a flat fee is an advance fee that is earned when the services are *completed* and therefore requires deposit in a client trust account coupled with a contemporaneous accounting to the client prior to withdrawal of such fees from the trust account."[48] Iowa court rules permit the client and lawyer to "agree as to when, how, and in what proportion the lawyer may withdraw funds" as the services are performed, provided that the arrangement "reasonably protect[s] the client's right to a refund of unearned fees if the lawyer fails to complete the services or the client discharges the lawyer."[49]

Next door in Minnesota, the flat fee "may be paid in whole or in part in advance of the lawyer providing the services," and if paid in advance, "a flat fee shall be considered to be the lawyer's property upon payment of the fee" and thus may not be deposited in the client trust account.[50] However, advance payment of a flat fee may be made only pursuant to a written agreement, which notifies the client of the right to discharge the lawyer and to a refund of all or part of the client's payment if the legal services have been completed.[51] Importantly, even though the immediately paid flat payment need not be deposited into the trust account, the lawyer may not suggest to the client or treat the payment as nonrefundable.

## § 4-4.3 THE LAWYER'S DUTY TO COMMUNICATE THE BASIS FOR AND RATE OF A FEE TO THE CLIENT

As stated in Rule 1.5(b) of the Model Rules of Professional Conduct, except when a lawyer has "regularly represented" a client and will be charging "the same basis or rate,"

---

[45] On advance fee deposits, see *infra* § 4-4.4(a).

[46] On whether a flat fee is earned on receipt or must be placed into a trust fund, see generally Douglas R. Richmond, *Understanding Retainers and Flat Fees*, 34 J. LEGAL PROF. 113, 132 (2009).

[47] *See id.* at 142 (emphasizing that, even if regarded as earned on receipt, a flat fee should never be described as non-refundable). On the legitimacy of nonrefundable fees, see *infra* § 4-4.4(c).

[48] Attorney Disciplinary Bd. v. Piazza, 756 N.W.2d 690, 698 (Iowa 2008).

[49] IOWA COURT RULE 45.10(3).

[50] MINN. RULES OF PROF'L CONDUCT R. 1.5(b)(1).

[51] *Id.*, R. 1.5(b)(1)(iv) to (v).

the lawyer is obliged to communicate the "scope of the representation[52] and the basis or rate of the fee and expenses for which the client will be responsible." This communication is to be made either before or within a reasonable time after commencing the representation. As Professors Geoffrey Hazard and William Hodes and attorney Peter Jarvis wisely advise, "[o]ne of the best ways to minimize the risk that a client will find a legal bill an unpleasant surprise is open discussion of fees and expenses in advance."[53]

While the Model Rules of Professional Conduct do not require the lawyer to present information about a non-contingent fee in writing, Rule 1.5(b) expresses a preference for communicating fee information to the client in writing.[54] The optional suggestion made in Rule 1.5 is not necessarily that the fee agreement itself be reduced to writing, much less be signed by the client. Rather, a general written explanation, in the form of a law firm brochure or otherwise, of the manner in which fees for legal services and attendant expenses are to be calculated would be sufficient for this purpose. The lawyer who chooses not to provide written notice of the fee, a practice that is more understandable when the fee is fixed and simple and the matter is small and likely to be resolved quickly, still must clearly communicate the fee basis or rate to the client. Moreover, if the lawyer does not provide written confirmation of fee information, the presumption should be in favor of the client's reasonable understanding if a dispute later arises about fees. Indeed, at least nine states depart from Model Rule 1.5 and require a written fee agreement or other written notification of the fee, at least above a minimal amount.[55]

If the fee basis or rate is changed during the course of the representation, that must also be communicated to the client. Where a firm periodically adjusts the hourly rate for lawyers, and advance warning that such adjustments may be made has been given to the client, notification of a reasonable increase in the hourly rate is unremarkable.[56] Under other circumstances, agreements that change the basis or rate of the fee in midstream are viewed with "great suspicion;" "modifications of existing fee agreements are usually suspect because of the fiduciary nature of the client-lawyer relationship."[57]

While a revised fee arrangement is not void and may be sustained if fairly made with the full knowledge and understanding of the client, there is presumption of unfairness given that the client likely has come to be dependent on the lawyer's services and may suffer adverse consequences if forced to seek new counsel to avoid an increase in fees for legal services. And, as a general rule, a lawyer may not withdraw or threaten to withdraw to coerce a client to accept an increase above a previously agreed-upon fee rate.[58]

---

[52] On limiting the scope of the representation and obtaining informed consent from the client, see *supra* § 4-3.3.

[53] 1 GEOFFREY C. HAZARD, JR., W. WILLIAM HODES & PETER R. JARVIS, THE LAW OF LAWYERING § 9.02 (Aspen, 4th ed., 2016).

[54] *See also* STANDARDS FOR CRIMINAL JUSTICE: DEFENSE FUNCTION, Standard 4–3.4(c) (American Bar Ass'n, 2015) (advising in criminal case that "the amount, rate, and terms of the fee should be promptly communicated to the client, in clear terms and in writing").

[55] *See, e.g.*, ALASKA RULES OF PROF'L CONDUCT R. 1.5(b); ARIZ. RULES OF PROF'L CONDUCT R. 1.5(b); COLO. RULES OF PROF'L CONDUCT R. 1.5(b); CONN. RULES OF PROF'L CONDUCT R. 1.5(b); N.J. RULES OF PROF'L CONDUCT R. 1.5(b); PENN. RULES OF PROF'L CONDUCT R. 1.5(b); W. VA. RULES OF PROF'L CONDUCT R. 1.5(b); WIS. RULES OF PROF'L CONDUCT R. 1.5(b)(1).

[56] ABA Comm. on Ethics & Prof'l Responsibility, Formal Op. 11–458 (2011).

[57] CHARLES W. WOLFRAM, MODERN LEGAL ETHICS § 9.2.1 (West, 1986).

[58] *Id.*

## § 4-4.4 ADVANCED FEE DEPOSITS AND THE ILLEGITIMACY OF "NONREFUNDABLE RETAINERS"

### § 4-4.4(a) Advance Fee Deposits and Refunding of Unearned Fees

If a client should tender payment toward a lawyer's fee other than after performance of legal services and presentation of a bill for completed work, the lawyer is obliged to ensure that these client funds are segregated in a trust account until earned and that any unearned fees are refunded to the client. In sum, a fee paid in advance of performance of legal services is a deposit not yet earned and which must be held in trust separate from the lawyer's personal or firm account.[59]

Under court rules in each jurisdiction, a lawyer must deposit a client's advance fee and expense payments into a client trust account maintained at an appropriate financial institution. Withdrawal of funds from the trust account before the lawyer's fee has been earned or expenses incurred constitutes misappropriation (that is, theft) of client funds, for which severe disciplinary sanctions such as license revocation are typically imposed. As discussed in more detail subsequently in this book, Rule 1.15 of the Model Rules of Professional Responsibility also requires that the lawyer safeguard client funds, which includes an advance deposit for future legal services, by segregating such funds into an account kept separate from the lawyer's personal funds.[60] Every state supplements Rule 1.15 with typically mind-numbing minutiae about appropriate financial institutions, interest-bearing accounts, maintenance of records, audits, etc.

A lawyer may regularly withdraw payments from the client trust account as the fee is earned or expenses are incurred. The lawyer simultaneously must notify the client in writing of the time, amount, and purpose of any withdrawal of the fee or expense, together with a complete accounting. For example, as discussed above,[61] the traditional charge for legal services has been hourly billing, under which the fee is based upon the number of hours reasonably expended by the lawyer multiplied by a reasonable hourly rate. If a lawyer engages in hourly billing for legal services, the lawyer may withdraw advance payment funds from the trust account periodically in direct connection to the number of hours worked at the hourly rate charged.

Any advance payment for the performance of contemplated legal services must to be refunded if the work is not performed, whether because the lawyer withdraws or the client discharges the lawyer.

### § 4-4.4(b) A Retainer for Lawyer Availability

A lawyer properly may collect a "general retainer" or an "engagement retainer,"[62] which is a fee for agreeing to make legal services available to the client if and when needed during a specified time period. A general retainer is charged for the lawyer's

---

[59] *See* Alberto Bernabe, *Avvo Joins the Legal Market; Should Attorneys Be Concerned?*, 104 GEO. L.J. ONLINE 184, 203 (2016) (observing that Avvo's new legal service program involves prepayments by clients to the company before legal services are performed and that "Avvo seems to suggest that the fact that the fee is paid in advance exempts a lawyer from having to place the money in a trust account," while "[i]n fact, the accepted rule is exactly the opposite").

[60] *See infra* § 4-5.6(a).

[61] *See supra* § 4-4.2.

[62] *See* RESTATEMENT (THIRD) OF THE LAW GOVERNING LAWYERS § 34 cmt. e (American Law Institute, 2000).

continued availability, that is, the lawyer promises to maintain the ability to turn immediately to the client's work as a priority should it prove necessary and not to accept retention by any other potential client whose interests would be in conflict with the client paying the retainer. As Professor Lester Brickman has explained, a general retainer "is an option contract; the fee is earned by the attorney when paid since the attorney is entitled to the money regardless of whether he actually performs any services for the client."[63] "In reality," as Douglas Richmond has observed, "general retainers are quite rare and few lawyers enjoy the professional reputation, or have the specialized practice, which allows them to charge general retainers."[64]

Because the general retainer is not a payment for the performance of services, but rather is compensation for the lawyer's promise of availability, the fee is earned by the lawyer at the time the retainer is paid and thus should not be deposited into a client trust account. The general retainer is not an advance deposit against future legal services, which instead would be separately calculated and charged should the lawyer actually be called upon by the client to perform legal services in the future.

### § 4-4.4(c) The Illegitimacy of a "Nonrefundable Special Retainer"

Jurisdictions universally permit the traditional (if rare) general retainer paid to assure the lawyer's continued availability. But most states preclude a lawyer from charging a "nonrefundable special retainer"—a fee charged for the performance of contemplated services, paid in advance of performance of those services, and purportedly not refundable to the client. Indeed, because this "special retainer" does not secure the lawyer's availability but rather is to be applied as payment for the lawyer's work on the matter, calling this arrangement a "retainer" is a misnomer.[65] Instead, through this device, a lawyer attempts to convert an advance deposit toward as yet unearned fees into a nonrefundable payment.

As discussed above,[66] if a payment for contemplated services is made to the lawyer prior to the performance of services, it then constitutes an "advance fee payment." It must be deposited into a client trust account and may be withdrawn by the lawyer only when earned as services are performed. An advance payment always is refundable to the client if not earned through the performance of services, notwithstanding any contrary agreement between the lawyer and client.

Several states have followed the lead of the New York Court of Appeals in expressly rejecting any arrangement for payment of fees by which a lawyer could avoid the duty to refund advance payments that were not subsequently earned by the performance of legal services. In *Matter of Cooperman*,[67] the New York court held that a nonrefundable

---

63 Lester Brickman, *The Advance Fee Payment Dilemma: Should Payments be Deposited to the Client Trust Account or to the General Office Account*, 10 CARDOZO L. REV. 647, 649 n.13 (1989); *see also* Douglas R. Richmond, *Understanding Retainers and Flat Fees*, 34 J. LEGAL PROF. 113, 116 (2009).

64 Richmond, *supra*, 34 J. LEGAL PROF. at 140.

65 Cluck v. Commission for Lawyer Discipline, 214 S.W.3d 736, 740 (Tex. 2007) (" 'If a fee is not paid to secure the lawyer's availability and to compensate him for lost opportunities, then it is a prepayment for services and not a true retainer.' " (quoting Tex. Comm. on Prof'l Ethics Op. 432 (1986))).

66 *See supra* § 4-4.4(a).

67 591 N.Y.S.2d 855, 856 (N.Y. 1993); *see also* Board of Professional Ethics & Conduct v. Apland, 577 N.W.2d 50, 57–58 (Iowa 1998); ARIZ. RULES OF PROF'L CONDUCT R. 1.5(d)(3); COLO. RULES OF PROF'L CONDUCT R. 1.5(g); MINN. RULES OF PROF'L CONDUCT R. 1.5(b)(3). *See generally* Lester Brickman & Lawrence Cunningham, *Nonrefundable Retainers: Impermissible Under Fiduciary, Statutory and Contract Law*, 57 FORDHAM L. REV. 149, 189–90 (1988).

fee arrangement improperly limits the unqualified right of the client to terminate the lawyer, by essentially holding the client hostage through the economic disincentive of discharging the lawyer only at the cost of forfeiting the fee payment. In these states, whether styled as a "special retainer," a nonrefundable flat fee, or a minimum fee, funds received from the client before legal services are performed constitute an advance fee payment that is subject to refund if services are not fully performed.

Not every state expressly prohibits what is designated a nonrefundable fee, although sometimes with the qualification that the lawyer must refund a portion of the fee if representation is not completed,[68] which is really just another way of saying that the fee is not truly nonrefundable. Vermont forthrightly authorizes "a nonrefundable fee that is earned before any legal services are rendered" or a "guaranteed minimum" fee, that will "be deemed earned regardless of whether the client terminates the representation."[69] The authorized nonrefundable fee in Vermont must be reasonable in amount, and the client must be notified in writing that the fee is nonrefundable along with the scope of availability or services that client will receive for the fee.

## § 4-4.5 DIVISION OF FEES AMONG LAWYERS

The legal profession historically imposed strict restrictions on division of fees charged to a client among lawyers who were not associated inside the same law firm. Within a law firm, lawyers could divide fees among themselves on any basis they chose. Thus, a "rainmaker" might obtain the matter from a client but delegate performance of all legal services to other lawyers in the firm, while still being allocated a substantial share of that fee, without the client being consulted or the disciplinary rules being implicated. But if two lawyers from different firms represented a single client in a particular matter, the ethics rules of old strictly regulated the means and method by which they divided the resulting fee.

This historical rule against so-called "fee splitting" exhibited what Professors Ronald Rotunda and John Dzienkowski call "a general distaste towards commercial methods of obtaining clients."[70] The ethics rules thus prevented a lawyer from acting as a referring intermediary and thereby collecting any part of the fee earned. Referral or forwarding fees were never permitted. Under Disciplinary Rule 2–107(A) of the former Model Code of Professional Responsibility,[71] fee division among lawyers outside of a firm was allowed only if the client consented to the employment of another lawyer, full disclosure was made that the fee would be divided, and the fee was divided in *direct proportion* to the services performed and the responsibilities assumed.

The Model Rules of Professional Conduct allow more generally for fee-splitting among lawyers who accept full responsibility for the venture. Under Rule 1.5(e), attorneys who are not in the same firm have greater freedom to divide the fee, specifically including a division other than in proportion to services performed. But that freedom comes at the price of accepting greater responsibility for the representation. Under Rule 1.5(e)(1), lawyers not in the same firm are offered two alternative mechanisms for allocating the fee among them. First, the fee may be divided "in proportion to the services

---

68 *See* Ohio Adv. Op. 2016–1.

69 VT. RULES OF PROF'L CONDUCT R. 1.5(f).

70 RONALD D. ROTUNDA & JOHN S. DZIENKOWSKI, PROFESSIONAL RESPONSIBILITY: A STUDENT'S GUIDE § 1.5–4 (American Bar Ass'n, 2013–2014).

71 MODEL CODE OF PROF'L RESPONSIBILITY, Disciplinary Rule 2–107(A) (American Bar Ass'n, 1980).

performed by each lawyer," which was the sole method permitted under the prior Code. Second, the fee may be divided otherwise if "each lawyer assumes joint responsibility for the representation."

This assumption of "joint responsibility for the representation" when the fee is not divided proportionally is a critical element of the more permissive arrangement under Rule 1.5(e). By contrast with the prior prohibition on non-proportional division of a fee, the "joint responsibility" provision quite adequately protects and indeed more strongly promotes the client's interest. Rather than forbidding any division of fees unrelated to the proportion of work performed by the respective lawyers, the rule ensures that the client will have the benefit of multiple attorneys who are responsible for the representation in every sense and responsible for each other.

A lawyer obtaining a client may not simply pocket a finder's fee and walk away. As Comment 7 to Rule 1.5 explains, each lawyer takes on "financial and ethical responsibility for the representation as if the lawyers were associated in a partnership." Professors Geoffrey Hazard and William Hodes describe these lawyers as "becom[ing] parties to a kind of ad hoc partnership or joint professional venture for purposes of the representation in question."[72] Not only does each lawyer become vicariously liable for professional negligence by the other lawyer in the same manner as does any ordinary partner in a law firm in a malpractice suit, but each lawyer also assumes the ethical duties that partners have under Rule 5.1 of the Model Rules of Professional Conduct to make "reasonable efforts" to ensure that appropriate measures are in place that give reasonable assurance of ethical conduct by other lawyers.[73]

Accordingly, under both substantive law and the disciplinary rules, each lawyer has a reason to remain involved in the representation, at least to the extent of being regularly informed and making some general efforts to monitor the work of the other lawyers involved. For these reasons, any attorney thinking about entering into a non-proportionate fee division with another lawyer in a different firm should think carefully about the meaningful responsibilities that would be assumed and the potential consequences that could follow. Moreover, saying that "implicit" in the joint responsibility requirement of the rule "is the concept that the referring lawyer who divides a legal fee has undertaken representation of the client," the American Bar Association's Standing Committee on Ethics and Professional Responsibility emphasizes that the conflict of interest rules apply to the referring lawyer.[74]

Rule 1.5(e)(2) further provides that the client must "agree to the arrangement, including the share each lawyer will receive," and that agreement must be confirmed in writing. Thus, the client must consent to the participation of all lawyers involved and to the share of the fee to be received by each lawyer. And, of course, Rule 1.5(e)(3) requires that the total fee remain reasonable, thus linking the fee-splitting provision back to the general reasonableness standard stated in Rule 1.5(a).[75]

When a fee division has been properly arranged, the attorney who receives the payment must deposit the money in a trust account and is accountable to the other

---

[72] 1 GEOFFREY C. HAZARD, JR. & W. WILLIAM HODES, THE LAW OF LAWYERING § 8.2 (Aspen, 3d ed., 2014).

[73] *See infra* § 4-12.2(a).

[74] ABA Comm. on Ethics & Prof'l Responsibility, Formal Op. 464 (2013).

[75] *See supra* § 4-4.2(a).

attorney to share the fee as agreed. As stated by the American Bar Association's Standing Committee on Ethics and Professional Responsibility, "Model Rules 1.15(a) and 1.15(d) require that the receiving lawyer hold the funds in an account separate from the lawyer's own property, appropriately safeguard the funds, promptly notify the other lawyer who holds an interest in the fee of receipt of the funds, promptly deliver to the other lawyer the agreed upon portion of the fee, and, if requested by the other lawyer, provide a full accounting."[76]

Although the Model Rule approach is widely followed today, it has not become universal. A few states have not adopted Rule 1.5(e), meaning that a referral fee remains expressly or implicitly prohibited.[77] (However, since two lawyers could always agree to join in partnership and share fees within the firm, which effectively is accomplished under Rule 1.5(e) for the duration of the joint matter, the efficacy of an outright prohibition is questionable.) Moreover, California remains an outlier in permitting a straightforward referral fee—without any requirement of joint responsibility—provided that the total fee charged to the client remains reasonable.[78]

Note that Rule 1.5(e) addresses only the question of division of fees among those licensed to practice law. The general prohibition on sharing of legal fees with nonlawyers continues in effect under Rule 5.4(a) of the Model Rules of Professional Conduct.[79] The American Bar Association's Standing Committee on Ethics and Professional Responsibility has explained that a lawyer who is working with a lawyer practicing in a jurisdiction that permits sharing legal fees with nonlawyers does not violate Rule 1.5(e) or Rule 5.4(a) by dividing fees with that other lawyer.[80] In such a circumstance, the lawyer in a Model Rules jurisdiction has only divided fees with another lawyer; any further sharing of that fee inside the law firm by the other lawyer with non-lawyers is not attributable to the Model Rules jurisdiction lawyer.

## § 4-4.6 PAYMENT OF FEES BY PERSONS OTHER THAN CLIENTS

Although most lawyers are compensated directly by their clients for professional services in most matters, payment of legal fees frequently is made by third persons, such as family members, an employer, or a liability insurer. As discussed further in terms of a possible conflict of interest that impairs the lawyer's independent judgment,[81] receiving payment of legal fees from someone other than the client is appropriate, provided that the lawyer remembers that his professional obligations, including the duty of loyalty and protection of confidential information, are owed solely to the client.

Rule 1.8(f) of the Model Rules of Professional Conduct provides that "[a] lawyer shall not accept compensation for representing a client from one other than the client unless: (1) the client gives informed consent; (2) there is no interference with the lawyer's independence of professional judgment or with the client-lawyer relationship; and (3)

[76] ABA Comm. on Ethics & Prof'l Responsibility, Formal Op. 475 (2016).

[77] *See* COLO. RULES OF PROF'L CONDUCT R. 1.5(e).

[78] CAL. RULES OF PROF'L CONDUCT R. 2–200; *see also* MICH. RULES OF PROF'L CONDUCT R. 1.5(e); OR. RULES OF PROF'L CONDUCT R. 1.5(d).

[79] *See infra* § 4-7.9(b).

[80] ABA Comm. on Ethics & Prof'l Responsibility, Formal Op. 464 (2013).

[81] *See infra* § 4-7.3(g).

information relating to representation of a client is protected" by confidentiality under Rule 1.6.

## § 4-4.7 FEE DISPUTES

Although a lawyer generally transgresses no disciplinary rule by using appropriate debt collection methods to collect an unpaid fee from a client or by instituting a lawsuit against a client for fees, the profession long has viewed fee disputes with clients as unseemly. Ethical Consideration 2–23 of the former Model Code of Professional Responsibility counseled that "[a] lawyer should be zealous in efforts to avoid controversies over fees with clients and should attempt to resolve amicably any differences on the subject."[82] Comment 9 to Rule 1.5 of the Model Rules of Professional Conduct also invites lawyers to submit fee disputes to arbitration or mediation procedures that may be established by the bar.

And if the distasteful nature of squabbles about fees were not enough, knowing that clients frequently respond to suits for fees with counterclaims for legal malpractice is a practical deterrent to most lawyers considering whether to formally pursue a fee claim. If despite these sobering warnings a lawyer still wishes to pursue a collection action against a client for payment of fees, it is not unethical to do so.

The best way to resolve a fee dispute of course is to avoid having one in the first place. Fee dispute prevention is advanced by clearly communicating with the client about fees at the outset of the representation and regularly and honestly billing the client for fees earned. The very purpose behind the requirement that fee agreements be communicated clearly to clients,[83] and that contingency agreements be in writing,[84] is to forestall future misunderstandings about fees between lawyers and clients, which among other things may have a detrimental effect upon ongoing representation. Whether required or not, the lawyer should take seriously the expressed preference for confirming the fee arrangement in writing. Without being reduced to writing, confusion may persist regarding the precise nature of the fee or even the scope or objectives of the representation.

## § 4-4.8 FEE SHIFTING: RECOVERING LEGAL FEES FROM ANOTHER PARTY

### § 4-4.8(a) Introduction to Attorney's Fee Shifting

The traditional rule on attorney's fees in litigation—called the "American Rule"—holds that each party must bear its own legal expenses.[85] As the Supreme Court has explained, " '[o]ur basic point of reference' when considering the award of attorney's fees is the bedrock principle known as the 'American Rule': Each litigant pays his own attorney's fees, win or lose, unless a statute or contract provides otherwise."[86] A court may award attorney's fees only if there is express statutory authorization for shifting

[82] MODEL CODE OF PROF'L RESPONSIBILITY, Ethical Consideration 2–23 (American Bar Ass'n, 1980).

[83] *See supra* § 4-4.3.

[84] *See supra* § 4-4.2(c)(2).

[85] Alyeska Pipeline Service Co. v. Wilderness Soc'y, 421 U.S. 240, 247 (1975). *See generally* John Leubsdorf, *Toward a History of the American Rule on Attorney Fee Recovery*, 47 LAW & CONTEMP. PROBS. 9 (1984).

[86] Hardt v. Reliance Standard Life Ins. Co., 560 U.S. 242, 252–53 (2010).

fees or if one of the few traditional common-law exceptions (such as bad faith) to the American Rule applies.

In theory, the American Rule is an imposing obstacle to an award of attorney's fees against the losing party in litigation. In modern-day reality, the American Rule has been whittled away by an ever-growing list of statutory exceptions,[87] running the gamut from employment discrimination claims under Title VII of the Civil Rights Act of 1964[88] to environmental protection statutes.[89]

When a party and counsel attempt to collect attorney's fees from an opponent in civil litigation where fee-shifting is authorized, two basic questions must be asked and answered. First, is the fee petitioner eligible for fees, for which the general standard is that the party must have prevailed in the litigation. Second, how is the award to be measured, for which today the general measure is that of the "lodestar" (hours spent multiplied by an hourly rate). For purposes of this book on professional responsibility, the second inquiry is highlighted, as it runs parallel to the standard of reasonableness for a fee charged to a paying client.[90]

### § 4-4.8(b) Eligibility for a Fee Award—Prevailing Party Status

The classic test of eligibility for an award under fee-shifting statutes is whether the plaintiff has "prevailed" in the case.[91] In *Hanrahan v. Hampton*,[92] the Supreme Court ruled that to qualify as a "prevailing party," the party seeking fees must have attained "some relief on the merits of his claim." Success on procedural, evidentiary, or most preliminary matters, no matter how significant at the moment, generally is not sufficient to prevail. There must have been some judicial determination of "the substantial rights of the parties,"[93] such that the plaintiff can "point to a resolution of the dispute which changes the legal relationship between itself and the defendant."[94] A technical or hypothetical victory that has no beneficial effect for the plaintiff will preclude a finding of prevailing party status.[95]

In *Texas State Teachers Association v. Garland Independent School District*,[96] the Supreme Court rejected a test for prevailing party status that required a party to prevail on the "central issue" in the litigation and not merely upon significant secondary issues. The Court adopted a general rule that, to be a prevailing party under fee-shifting

---

[87] For a multi-volume treatise also available on the LexisNexis network, see MARY FRANCES DERFNER & ARTHUR D. WOLF, COURT AWARDED ATTORNEY FEES (Matthew-Bender & Co., LexisNexis Group, 2015, Kevin Shirey, revisor). For a discussion of the general fee-shifting issues, and in the specific context of suits involving the federal government, see GREGORY C. SISK, LITIGATION WITH THE FEDERAL GOVERNMENT § 7.7 (West Academic Publishing, 2016).

[88] 42 U.S.C. § 2000e–5(k).

[89] *See, e.g.*, Clean Water Act, 33 U.S.C. §§ 1365(d), 1369(b)(3); Clean Air Act, 42 U.S.C. §§ 7604(d), 7607(f).

[90] On the reasonableness standard for fees, see *supra* § 4-4.2(a).

[91] For more on the prevailing party test, as well as the entitlement standard that is pertinent under some fee-shifting statutes, see GREGORY C. SISK, LITIGATION WITH THE FEDERAL GOVERNMENT § 7.7(b) to (c) (West Academic Publishing, 2016).

[92] 446 U.S. 754, 757–59 (1980) (per curiam).

[93] *Id.* at 758.

[94] Texas State Teachers Ass'n v. Garland Indep. Sch. Dist., 489 U.S. 782, 792 (1989).

[95] Rhodes v. Stewart, 488 U.S. 1, 4 (1988).

[96] 489 U.S. at 789–92.

statutes, a litigant need only succeed on "any significant issue in [the] litigation which achieve[d] some of the benefit the parties sought in bringing suit."

The case need not have gone to trial and resulted in a judgment before attorney's fees may be awarded. A party obtaining a favorable settlement that is approved and enforceable by the court has prevailed for purposes of fee eligibility.[97] However, in *Buckhannon Board & Care Home, Inc. v. West Virginia Dept. of Health & Human Resources*,[98] the Supreme Court emphasized that to qualify as a "prevailing party," the party must have been awarded some relief by a court. The Court, by a five-to-four vote, rejected the "catalyst theory," whereby a plaintiff would be regarded as prevailing if the lawsuit brought about a voluntary change in the defendant's conduct. The *Buckhannon* Court majority explained that "[a] defendant's voluntary change in conduct, although perhaps accomplishing what the plaintiff sought to achieve by the lawsuit, lacks the necessary judicial *imprimatur* on the change." Accordingly, as a prerequisite to an award of attorney's fees, there generally must be a court-ordered change in the legal relationship between the plaintiff and the defendant, such as a judgment on the merits or a settlement agreement enforced through a consent decree.

## § 4-4.8(c) Measuring the Fee Award

Assuming that a statutory or common-law basis exists for fee-shifting, and that the party is eligible an award, the next step is to calculate the amount of the fee award. As the Supreme Court observed in *Pennsylvania v. Delaware Valley Citizens' Council for Clean Air*,[99] most fee-shifting statutes authorize an award of a "reasonable" fee. The issue, then, the Court stated, is the "proper measure for determining the 'reasonableness' of a particular fee award." As outlined below, the evaluation of the proper fee award for fee-shifting purposes runs directly parallel to what is a reasonable fee (typically an hourly-rate fee) charged to a paying client.[100]

### *§ 4-4.8(c)(1) The Road to the Lodestar Approach*

With the advent of the age of attorney's fee-shifting in the 1970s, the courts struggled to devise a rational and practical method for calculating a reasonable fee and accounting for appropriate elements in measurement. Two approaches, derived from cases in two different circuits, evolved and competed for allegiance among the lower federal courts.

The United States Court of Appeals for the Fifth Circuit articulated a test for calculation of fees under Title VII of the Civil Rights Act in *Johnson v. Georgia Highway Express, Inc.*[101] In *Johnson*, the court directed District Courts to base fee awards on twelve factors (drawn from ethics rules), including the time and labor required, the novelty and difficulty of questions, the skills needed, the customary fee in the community, the results obtained, and several other criteria. However, as the Supreme Court later observed, the *Johnson* factors provided "very little actual guidance" to the District Courts on the concrete calculation of a fee award in a particular factual

---

[97] Maher v. Gagne, 448 U.S. 122, 129 (1980).

[98] 532 U.S. 598, 603–05 (2001).

[99] 478 U.S. 546, 562 (1986).

[100] On the reasonableness standard for fees, see *supra* § 4-4.2(a).

[101] 488 F.2d 714, 717–19 (5th Cir. 1974).

setting.[102] One critic of the *Johnson* factors explained that "[t]he fundamental problem with an approach that does no more than assure that the lower courts will consider a plethora of conflicting and at least partially redundant factors is that it provides no analytical framework for their application."[103] As the District of Columbia Circuit commented, "[s]imply to articulate those twelve factors . . . does not itself conjure up a reasonable dollar figure in the mind of a district court judge. A formula is necessary to translate the relevant factors into terms of dollars and cents."[104]

Accordingly, the courts gravitated toward the more practical fee-setting formula developed by the Third Circuit. In *Lindy Brothers Builders, Inc. v. American Radiator & Standard Sanitary Corp. (Lindy I)*,[105] and its successor case, *Lindy II*,[106] the Third Circuit devised a formula "that considered all the relevant factors but eliminated the redundancy and imprecision that many ha[d] identified in other fee-setting schemes."[107] Under the *Lindy* rule, the heart of the analysis is the "lodestar" fee, established by multiplying a reasonable hourly rate by the number of hours reasonably expended on the lawsuit.[108] The lodestar figure provides "the only reasonably objective" starting point for "valuing an attorney's services." To determine "the total reasonable value of an attorney's services," the *Lindy* rule then contemplated an increase or decrease in the lodestar fee to account for additional factors. Thus, the *Lindy* rule set forth a two-step process: first, the District Court calculated the "lodestar," by determining the hours reasonably spent and multiplying that figure by a reasonable hourly rate; second, the court could adjust the lodestar upward for factors such as the contingency risk that the case might be lost and upward or downward based upon the quality of the work done on the case.

The first and central step of the *Lindy* rule—the "lodestar" method—has plainly prevailed in fee-shifting doctrine (although, as we will see, without upward adjustments at the second step of the analysis).[109] The Supreme Court has "adopted the lodestar approach as the centerpiece of attorney's fee awards."[110] The basic concept of the "lodestar" is simple: the value of an attorney's work on a case is measured by (1) the number of hours that were reasonably expended on the litigation, multiplied by (2) a reasonable hourly rate.

### *§ 4-4.8(c)(2) Hours Reasonably Expended*

In general, an attorney is allowed compensation for time spent on any activity reasonably associated with the pursuit of the plaintiff's action for relief. This includes necessary administrative proceedings, pre-litigation activities, travel time, appellate work, post-judgment enforcement work, and time spent obtaining the attorney's fee award.

---

[102] Pennsylvania v. Delaware Valley Citizens' Council for Clean Air, 478 U.S. 546, 563 (1986).

[103] Samuel R. Berger, *Court Awarded Attorneys' Fees: What is "Reasonable,"* 126 U. PA. L. REV. 281, 286–87 (1977).

[104] Copeland v. Marshall, 641 F.2d 880, 890 (D.C. Cir. 1980) (en banc).

[105] 487 F.2d 161 (3d Cir. 1973) (*Lindy I*).

[106] 540 F.2d 102 (3d Cir. 1976) (en banc) (*Lindy II*).

[107] *Copeland*, 641 F.2d at 890 (citing *Lindy I* and *II*).

[108] *Lindy I*, 487 F.2d at 167–69; *Lindy II*, 540 F.2d at 112–18.

[109] *See infra* § 4-4.8(c)(4).

[110] Blanchard v. Bergeron, 489 U.S. 87, 94 (1989).

***Time Records:*** An attorney seeking a fee must document the hours for which compensation is sought. The Supreme Court has long declared a strong preference for contemporaneously recorded time records.[111] A growing number of federal Courts of Appeals have announced that contemporaneous time records are a prerequisite to any application for attorney's fees.[112] However, a smaller number of federal courts permit an attorney to reconstruct time records after the fact, if proven to be accurate.[113]

***Specifying Billing Activities:*** The time records submitted by the petitioning attorney must provide information about the activities on which those hours were expended. Just as private paying clients increasingly demand that attorneys specifically account for the time devoted to legal representation, courts today expect greater specificity in time records submitted to support a fee petition. The fee petitioner "has the burden of establishing the reasonableness of its fee request . . . and supporting documentation must be of sufficient detail and probative value to enable the court to determine with a high degree of certainty that such hours were actually and reasonably expended."[114] A party requesting an award of fees must present contemporaneous time records that "specify the name of each attorney working on the file, the date the work was done, the hours spent, and the nature of the work performed."[115]

With the advent of the personal computer and now specialized billing software, detailed time records by individual attorneys are more easily maintained and thus have become the standard. Vague time entries such as "legal research," "trial prep," "met w/ client,"[116] "Telephone conference with [name] regarding various matters," "reviewing email from [name] re numerous issues,"[117] or time records that do not specify "the subject matter of a meeting, telephone conference or the work performed during hours billed,"[118] are likely to be rejected as inadequate. Inadequate documentation and failure to designate the nature of work performed is a common basis for reduction of a fee award.[119]

***Billing Judgment:*** Documenting the hours spent is only the first step. As the District of Columbia Circuit explained:

> Compiling raw totals of hours spent, however, does not complete the inquiry. It does not follow that the amount of time actually expended is the amount of time reasonably expended. In the private sector, "billing judgment"

---

111 Webb v. Board of Educ., 471 U.S. 234, 238 n.6 (1985).

112 *See, e.g.*, Scott v. City of New York, 643 F.3d 56, 57 (2d Cir. 2011) (per curiam) (the requirement of contemporaneous time records "is essentially a hard-and-fast-rule 'from which attorneys may deviate only in the rarest of cases' "); Sheets v. Salt Lake City, 45 F.3d 1383, 1391 (10th Cir. 1995); Community Heating & Plumbing, Inc. v. Garrett, 2 F.3d 1143, 1145 (Fed. Cir. 1993); Grendel's Den, Inc. v. Larkin, 749 F.2d 945, 952 (1st Cir. 1984).

113 *See, e.g.*, Gagnon v. United Technisource, Inc., 607 F.3d 1036, 1044 (5th Cir. 2010) (holding that failure to provide contemporaneous records "does not preclude an award of fees per se" where attorney produced detailed affidavits and invoices); Kline v. City of Kansas City, 245 F.3d 707, 708–09 (8th Cir. 2001); Jean v. Nelson, 863 F.2d 759, 772 (11th Cir. 1988), *aff'd*, 496 U.S. 154 (1990). *But see* In re Apex Oil Co., 297 F.3d 712, 718 (8th Cir. 2002) (saying that review of a fee award was "hindered" by the attorney's failure to keep contemporaneous time records).

114 Role Models America, Inc. v. Brownlee, 353 F.3d 962, 970 (D.C. Cir. 2004).

115 Mikes v. Straus, 274 F.3d 687, 706 (2d Cir. 2001).

116 H.J. Inc. v. Flygt Corp., 925 F.2d 257, 260 (8th Cir. 1991).

117 Fabi Const. Co. v. Secretary of Labor, 541 F.3d 407, 411 (D.C. Cir. 2009).

118 In re Meese, 907 F.2d 1192, 1204 (D.C. Cir. 1990).

119 *But see* Imwalle v. Reliance Medical Products, Inc., 515 F.3d 531, 554 (6th Cir. 2008) (saying Sixth Circuit has "held that explicitly detailed descriptions are not required," at least when billing entries are "read in the context of the billing statement as a whole and in conjunction with the timeline of the litigation").

is an important component in fee setting. It is no less important here. Hours that are not properly billed to one's client also are not properly billed to one's adversary pursuant to statutory authority.[120]

Accordingly, as the Supreme Court held in *Hensley v. Eckerhart*,[121] the attorney petitioning for an award of fees should make a "good faith effort to exclude from a fee request hours that are excessive, redundant, or otherwise unnecessary, just as a lawyer in private practice ethically is obligated to exclude such hours from his fee submission."

***Disallowing Hours:*** The court may disallow compensation for certain hours for a variety of reasons,[122] such as by finding that hours devoted were excessive for the particular task or proceeding involved;[123] that time spent was excessive because an attorney lacked expertise in an area and devoted too much time developing familiarity with the topic;[124] that hours devoted were excessive because a partner performed tasks that could more appropriately have been delegated to an associate;[125] that time expended was nonproductive, for example, because associates received insufficient direction by partners;[126] that hours expended were duplicative, for example, where attorneys representing the same party engaged in parallel efforts;[127] or that the lawyers engaged in "egregious overlitigation" by "persistent[ly] tilting at wildmills" and thereby "unreasonably or unnecessarily litigating issues that were hopeless, peripheral, or otherwise extraneous."[128]

As the Seventh Circuit has observed,[129] the reviewing court should appreciate that time legitimately spent may not always advance the ball: "It's not unexpected that some legal research will prove fruitless on an ultimately successful claim, and a prevailing party may in appropriate circumstances recover for time spent going down roads that seemed promising but turn out to be dead ends." At the same time, as the court explains, the court should be familiar with the litigation and be able to differentiate between "research [ ] likely to contribute to a successful claim" and "lawyers' projects [that] were needlessly esoteric."

Moreover, as the First Circuit has observed, "the assignment of multiple attorneys to a single set of tasks should be regarded with 'healthy skepticism.' "[130] At the same time, " '[c]areful preparation often requires collaboration and rehearsal,' " which may require attention from more than one attorney, "especially in response to complex legal issues that are fiercely defended." In sum, as the First Circuit has also acknowledged,

---

[120] Copeland v. Marshall, 641 F.2d 880, 891 (D.C. Cir. 1980) (en banc).

[121] 461 U.S. 424, 434 (1983).

[122] On hours spent on unsuccessful or non-fee claims in a suit in which other claims fall under a fee-shifting statute, see GREGORY C. SISK, LITIGATION WITH THE FEDERAL GOVERNMENT § 7.7(d)(2) (West Academic Publishing, 2016).

[123] *See, e.g.*, Cooper v. U.S. R.R. Retirement Bd., 24 F.3d 1414, 1417–18 (D.C. Cir. 1994); Environmental Defense Fund, Inc. v. Reilly, 1 F.3d 1254, 1258–60 (D.C. Cir. 1993); Grendel's Den, Inc. v. Larkin, 749 F.2d 945, 953–54 (1st Cir. 1984).

[124] Action on Smoking and Health v. Civil Aeronautics Bd., 724 F.2d 211, 223 (D.C. Cir. 1984).

[125] Kronfeld v. Transworld Airlines, Inc., 129 F.R.D. 598, 602–603 (S.D.N.Y. 1990).

[126] *Copeland*, 641 F.2d at 902–03.

[127] *See, e.g.*, Evans v. Port Authority of New York and New Jersey, 273 F.3d 346, 362–63 (3d Cir. 2001); Davis Cty. Solid Waste Management & Energy Recovery Special Service v. U.S. Environmental Protection Agency, 169 F.3d 755, 761 (D.C. Cir. 1999); *Action on Smoking and Health*, 724 F.2d at 222.

[128] United States v. One Star Class Sloop Sailboat, 546 F.3d 26, 40–42 (1st Cir. 2008).

[129] Montanez v. Simon, 755 F.3d 547, 555 (7th Cir. 2014).

[130] Castaneda-Castillo v. Holder, 723 F.3d 48, 80 (1st Cir. 2013).

given "the complexity of modern litigation, the deployment of multiple attorneys is sometimes an eminently reasonable tactic."[131]

This is a case-by-case determination. The hours reasonably required to handle a matter will vary according to the novelty of the legal theories, the difficulty of the legal and factual issues, the complexity of the case, and the nature of the opposition.

### *§ 4-4.8(c)(3) A Reasonable Hourly Rate*

As the Supreme Court held in *Blum v. Stenson*,[132] the reasonable hourly rate is the charge for legal services that prevails in the market for the relevant community. The reasonable hourly rate for an individual attorney will depend on a multiplicity of factors, including the attorney's level of skill, reputation in the community, experience in practice, and expertise in the subject matter, as well as the desirability (or lack thereof) of the case. In sum, the court must attempt to determine what the market for legal services in that community would bear for that attorney's work performed on an hourly basis.[133]

***Attorney's Billing Rate:*** The petitioning attorney's billing rate charged to paying clients, if the attorney has a billing rate, is "important substantiating evidence of the prevailing community rate;"[134] it serves at least as a good starting point.[135] Indeed, a few federal Courts of Appeals have held that an attorney's actual billing rate is the presumptively appropriate figure, irrespective of whether the prevailing market average would lead to a higher or lower rate.[136] Other circuits have refused to regard billing rates as occupying such a central place in the calculation, concluding that the measure of a reasonable fee is the prevailing market rate in the community and that the ordinary billing rate serves at most as a relevant factor in establishing the market figure.[137]

***Other Evidence of Prevailing Market Rate:*** In the absence of an actual billing rate, as with attorneys in non-profit public interest organizations or attorneys who generally work on a contingent fee basis, or as further evidence of prevailing market rates,[138] "the next best evidence" of the market rate is "evidence of rates similarly experienced attorneys in the community charge paying clients for similar work and evidence of fee awards the attorney has received in similar cases."[139] The petitioning party may submit affidavits from other attorneys not affiliated with the case. The affidavit may state the rate that the outside attorney, with comparable experience and

---

[131] Gay Officers Action League v. Puerto Rico, 247 F.3d 288, 297 (1st Cir. 2001).

[132] 465 U.S. 886, 895 (1984).

[133] Henry v. Webermeier, 738 F.2d 188, 195 (7th Cir. 1984).

[134] National Ass'n of Concerned Veterans v. Secretary of Defense, 675 F.2d 1319, 1326 & n.7 (D.C. Cir. 1982).

[135] Maldonado v. Houstoun, 256 F.3d 181, 184–85 (3d Cir. 2001). *See also* United States v. One Star Class Sloop Sailboat, 546 F.3d 26, 40 (1st Cir. 2008) ("[T]he rate that private counsel actually charges for her services, while not conclusive, is a reliable indicium of market value.").

[136] *See, e.g.*, Uphoff v. Elegant Bath, Ltd., 176 F.3d 399, 407 (7th Cir. 1999); Scales v. J.C. Bradford & Co., 925 F.2d 901, 909–10 (6th Cir. 1991); Shakopee Mdewakanton Sioux Community v. City of Prior Lake, 771 F.2d 1153, 1160 (8th Cir. 1985).

[137] *See, e.g.*, Welch v. Metropolitan Life Ins. Co., 480 F.3d 942, 946 (9th Cir. 2007); Mendenhall v. National Transp. Safety Bd., 213 F.3d 464, 471 (9th Cir. 2000); Starrett v. Wadley, 876 F.2d 808, 825 (10th Cir. 1989); Save Our Cumberland Mountains, Inc. v. Hodel, 857 F.2d 1516, 1518–24 (D.C. Cir. 1988) (en banc).

[138] Robinson v. Equifax Information Services, LLC, 560 F.3d 235, 246 (4th Cir. 2009) (stating that the attorney's own "affidavit, standing alone, is not sufficient evidence of the prevailing market rates").

[139] Pickett v. Sheridan Health Care, 664 F.3d 632, 640 (7th Cir. 2011).

expertise, customarily charges for handling similar matters or may offer an expert opinion based on personal knowledge of the rates charged by other lawyers with similar ability in the community for similar litigation.[140] Alternatively, or in addition, the court may consider the amounts awarded by other courts to counsel with comparable experience in other similar cases,[141] the hourly rate charged by defense counsel (a factor not relevant when government-salaried lawyers are the defense counsel),[142] or surveys of lawyers about billing rates charged in the community.[143]

***Relevant Community:*** In determining what constitutes the "relevant community" for setting the hourly rate, the federal Courts of Appeals generally follow a "forum rule," subject to exceptions when a showing is made to justify hiring out-of-town counsel at a higher rate.[144]

In *Farmers Cooperative Co. v. Senske & Son Transfer Co.*,[145] the Eighth Circuit held that, even though the case had been transferred from one federal district to another, the "relevant community" for "determining the hourly rates is the place where the case was tried." In *Arbor Hill Concerned Citizens Neighborhood Association v. Albany County*,[146] the Second Circuit stated a presumption that "a reasonable, paying client would in most cases hire counsel from within his district," which may be rebutted in "the unusual case" if the fee petitioning party demonstrates the reasonableness of a decision to retain an out-of-district (and presumably higher rate) lawyer.

Most federal Courts of Appeals will depart from the forum rule and award fees outside the local rate when the client is unable by "diligent, good faith efforts" to find local counsel[147] or when only counsel outside the district has the "special expertise" necessary for the case.[148] The Second Circuit, in *Simmons v. New York City Transit Authority*,[149] has required a stringent showing to rebut the forum rule presumption of the forum rule, demanding evidence "persuasively establishing that a reasonable client would have selected out-of-district counsel because doing so would likely (not just possibly) produce a substantially better net result."

### *§ 4-4.8(c)(4) Adjustment to the Lodestar*

Although the lodestar concept has taken a firm hold in fee-shifting jurisprudence, the Supreme Court has largely rejected the additional element of an upward adjustment

---

[140] *National Ass'n of Concerned Veterans*, 675 F.2d at 1325–26; Davis v. City & Cty. of San Francisco, 976 F.2d 1536, 1547 (9th Cir. 1992), *vacated in part on other grounds*, 984 F.2d 345 (9th Cir. 1993).

[141] Chalmers v. City & Cty. of Los Angeles, 796 F.2d 1205, 1214 (9th Cir. 1986), *as amended*, 808 F.2d 1373 (9th Cir. 1987); *National Ass'n of Concerned Veterans*, 675 F.2d at 1325 & n.7.

[142] Arriola v. Harville, 781 F.2d 506, 512 (5th Cir. 1986); Gomez v. Gates, 804 F. Supp. 69, 77 (C.D. Cal. 1992).

[143] Grendel's Den, Inc. v. Larkin, 749 F.2d 945, 956, 958 (1st Cir. 1984); Agster v. Maricopa Cty., 486 F. Supp. 2d 1005, 1014 (D. Ariz. 2007).

[144] *See generally* Maureen Carroll, *Reclaiming the Private Attorney General* (August 10, 2015) (recognizing that most courts interpret the relevant community for the prevailing market "as the *local* community in which the action was filed," but arguing that, given "the broad geographic scope of modern legal practice," it "it makes increasingly little sense to ask whether a fee-shifting plaintiff could find a competent attorney in her local community").

[145] 572 F.3d 492, 500 (8th Cir. 2009).

[146] 522 F.3d 182, 183–85, 191 (2d Cir. 2008); *see also* Westmoreland Coal Co. v. Cox, 602 F.3d 276, 290 n.12 (4th Cir. 2010) (citing *Arbor Hills* rule).

[147] Snider v. City of Cape Girardeau, 752 F.3d 1149, 1159 (8th Cir. 2014).

[148] Bywaters v. United States, 670 F.3d 1221, 1233–34 (Fed. Cir. 2012).

[149] 575 F.3d 170, 172 (2d Cir. 2009).

or multiplier.[150] In every case brought before it, the Court has adhered to the lodestar figure as the touchstone of a reasonable fee, ruling that other factors were either subsumed within the lodestar calculation or were not a legitimate basis for enhancing a fee award.[151] The Court apparently has adopted the lodestar, without upward adjustments or multipliers (with the exception of compensation for delay in non-government cases)[152] as the sole measure of attorney's fees under fee-shifting statutes. Although the Court has declined to rule out the possibility of a justifiable enhancement in a "rare" or "exceptional" case, the Court has never found such a case.

While closing the door on upward adjustments of the lodestar, the Supreme Court emphatically has retained the option of adjusting the fee downward to reflect a plaintiff's limited success. Indeed, the Court has said that the degree of success obtained is "the most critical factor" in determining the reasonableness of a fee award.[153] Unfortunately, the Court has provided little guidance on when less than perfect success triggers an adjustment or on how partial success should affect the lodestar figure.[154]

In *Hensley v. Eckerhart*,[155] the Supreme Court ruled that "[w]here a plaintiff has obtained excellent results, his attorney should recover a fully compensatory fee," and further stated that "the fee award should not be reduced simply because the plaintiff failed to prevail on every contention raised in the lawsuit." Moreover, the Court firmly resisted reduction of the lodestar according to a mathematical ratio that compares the number of issues upon which the plaintiff actually prevailed with the total number of issues in the case. Success in a case is not a mathematical, but rather a qualitative question, requiring an evaluation of not only the number of claims or issues, but also the nature and significance of the relief.

Thus, while the lodestar is the presumptive measure of the reasonable fee, at some unspecified breaking point a plaintiff's success may fall to a level where a reduction of the overall fee is appropriate. Plainly, a plaintiff need not aspire to perfection to avoid a reduction; an "excellent result" is sufficient to assure a full fee recovery.[156] On the other end of the spectrum, when the plaintiff has attained a mere technical victory without corresponding public benefit, the fee applicant may expect a significant reduction or total disallowance of the fee. In between, however, there would seem to be a wide range of

---

[150] For more on upward and downward adjustments to the lodestar, see GREGORY C. SISK, LITIGATION WITH THE FEDERAL GOVERNMENT § 7.7(d)(4) to (d)(5) (West Academic Publishing, 2016).

[151] *See, e.g.*, City of Burlington v. Dague, 505 U.S. 557, 560–67 (1992)(ruling that the lodestar may never be adjusted upward to compensate for the contingent risk of loss, reasoning that an enhancement for contingency "would likely duplicate in substantial part factors already subsumed in the lodestar"); Pennsylvania v. Delaware Valley Citizens' Council for Clean Air, 478 U.S. 546, 565 (1986) (rejecting enhancement for superior quality of representation in an environmental case and stating that upward adjustments are permissible only in "rare" and "exceptional" cases).

[152] *See infra* § 4-4.8(c)(5).

[153] Farrar v. Hobby, 506 U.S. 103, 114 (1992); Hensley v. Eckerhart, 461 U.S. 424, 436 (1983).

[154] *See generally* Dan B. Dobbs, *Reducing Attorneys' Fees for Partial Success: A Comment on Hensley and Blum*, 1986 WIS. L. REV. 835, 844–62, 869–71.

[155] 461 U.S. 424, 435 & n.11 (1983).

[156] *Id.*, 435–36 (1983); *see also* Isabel v. City of Memphis, 404 F.3d 404, 416 (6th Cir. 2005) ("[A] reduction in attorney fees [awarded to a prevailing plaintiff] is to be applied only in rare and exceptional cases where specific evidence in the record requires it.").

possible outcomes, ranging from cases of rather substantial success on most claims or issues to cases of distinctly "partial or limited success."[157]

### *§ 4-4.8(c)(5) Compensation for Delay in Receipt of Fees*

Even in routine litigation, there may be a significant delay between the date on which legal services are performed and the date on which a fee is awarded. The Supreme Court has held that "an appropriate adjustment for delay in payment—whether by the application of current rather than historic hourly rates or otherwise—is within the contemplation of" fee-shifting statutes.[158]

### *§ 4-4.8(c)(6) Fees for Fees*

Just as fees are available for work performed in bringing the case on the merits to a successful conclusion, compensation also is available for legal fees incurred in applying for and securing an award of fees—what is sometimes called "fees for fees."[159] In *Commissioner v. Jean*,[160] the Supreme Court held that fee-shifting statutes "favor[ ] treating a case as an inclusive whole, rather than as atomized line-items." The Court also recognized that requiring a prevailing party to bear the cost of fee litigation could effectively dissipate the value of any fee award on the merits, thereby resurrecting the same financial disincentive to pursuing a judicial remedy that the fee-shifting statute was intended to eliminate. Accordingly, the Court held that fees may be awarded for the attorney's time in preparing and litigating a fee application.

As with a fee application for work performed on any other aspect of the case, the reasonableness of the fee award sought with respect to time spent on the fee application must reflect the results obtained in seeking the fee award. Thus, if a party achieves only limited success in the fee phase of the litigation, the court may reduce the fee award for those legal services.[161]

---

[157] *See* Barfield v. New York City Health and Hospitals Corp., 537 F.3d 132, 152 (2d Cir. 2008) ("Both 'the quantity and quality of relief obtained,' as compared to what the plaintiff sought to achieve as evidenced in her complaint, are key factors in determining the degree of success achieved.").

[158] Missouri v. Jenkins, 491 U.S. 274, 284 (1989) (authorizing compensation for delay against state government).

[159] American Fed. of Gov. Employees v. Federal Labor Relations Auth., 994 F.2d 20, 21 (D.C. Cir. 1993).

[160] 496 U.S. 154, 161–64 (1990).

[161] Anthony v. Sullivan, 982 F.2d 586, 589–90 (D.C. Cir. 1993); Nanetti v. University of Illinois, 944 F.2d 1416, 1420–21 (7th Cir. 1991).

# Chapter 4-5

# DUTIES TO EFFECTIVELY REPRESENT THE CLIENT

**By Gregory C. Sisk**

*Table of Sections*


§ 4-5.1 The Lawyer's Duty to Competently Represent the Client
§ 4-5.2 Counseling Through Candid, Moral, and Lawful Advice
§ 4-5.3 Diligence and Zealous Representation
§ 4-5.4 The Duty to Keep the Client Informed
§ 4-5.5 The Duty of a Fiduciary to Put the Client First
§ 4-5.6 The Duty to Safeguard Client Funds and Property


## § 4-5.1 THE LAWYER'S DUTY TO COMPETENTLY REPRESENT THE CLIENT

### § 4-5.1(a) The Fundamental Expectation of Professional Competence

#### *§ 4-5.1(a)(1) General Standard of Competence*

As demonstrated by priority of place as Rule 1.1, with this requirement being stated as the very first precept of the Rules of Professional Conduct, professional competence is a fundamental expectation for every lawyer. The rule "requires the legal knowledge, skill, thoroughness and preparation reasonably necessary for the representation." Lawrence Fox describes the concept of competence as "embrac[ing] all of those requirements our profession has established to entrust the affairs of others in the hands of qualified fiduciaries."[1]

Professional education and state licensing are designed to ensure the public that those who are authorized to practice law possess the basic knowledge and skills to be competent. Continuing legal education and other informal means allow a lawyer to remain abreast on developments in the law generally or in a field of practice. A lawyer must also be current on practical developments that affect the competent practice of law, including necessary technology skills to effectively protect confidential information and communicate securely in the digital age.[2]

Possession of competent professional faculties in the abstract is not enough. The lawyer then must use that legal training and the skills that have been developed through

[1] *See* Lawrence J. Fox, *North Dakota Bar Speech 2014 Mart Vogel Lecture on Professionalism and Legal Ethics*, 90 N.D. L. REV. 441, 454 (2014).

[2] *See generally* Andrew Perlman, *The Twenty-First Century Lawyer's Evolving Ethical Duty of Competence*, 22:4 PROF'L LAWYER 1 (2014). On the duty of competence as applied to protecting confidential information with modern technology, see *infra* § 4-6.5(b).

experience to competently perform the particular representation. Competence thus demands the preparation necessary to the specific task at hand and thorough attention in performing the work.

As outlined in Comment 1, the extent of preparation and the amount of the lawyer's time and concentration that are demanded by the representation depend on various factors, including the complexity of the matter, the lawyer's general background as well as specific experience in the area of law, and the significance of the matter. When more is at stake for the client in the representation, as recognized in Comment 5, the preparation necessary may be more painstaking and the attention that the lawyer must devote may be greater. Thus, the need for preparation entails diligence as well, which is addressed later.[3] The lawyer and the client may also agree to limit the scope of the representation, as discussed earlier,[4] which will more narrowly define the matters for which the lawyer is responsible.

### *§ 4-5.1(a)(2) Attaining Competence in a New Area*

As affirmed in Comment 2 to Rule 1.1, a lawyer may competently perform services in an area of law or with respect to a particular type of legal problem that she has not encountered before. Although practice specialties or concentrations continue to grow and some areas of practice demand special training or experience,[5] the average lawyer presumptively may develop competence on most subjects through adequate preparation. As long as the requisite competence to handle the matter may be attained through reasonable preparation and study, the lawyer ethically may undertake the representation. The measuring rod of competence is that of the reasonably able and effective attorney, with general professional education and experience, who diligently devotes herself to scholarly study of the governing legal principles and to development of the practice skills necessary. Of course, if the lawyer is unwilling or unable to dedicate the necessary time and concentration to develop competence in the new area, she should not accept the representation or should withdraw.[6]

Through legal education and ongoing experience, attorneys develop general competence in such skills as reading, understanding, and synthesizing case law; examining and interpreting statutes and regulations; investigating facts and evaluating evidence; and advocating positions and presenting arguments to judges and juries. Thus, when a lawyer encounters a new field of case law, a new statute or regulation, or a new fact-bound area of human activity, the average lawyer ordinarily can, with reasonable diligence, attain a general level of competence. Upon entering the new legal realm, the attorney typically will find herself in familiar surroundings of precedent, codified text, evidentiary standards, and required skills of persuasion. Differences between a new field and the lawyer's previous areas of practice will tend to arise at the level of detail. The transition into the new practice area may be all the more manageable because of the similarities and parallels at the level of generality.

---

3 *See infra* § 4-5.3.

4 *See supra* § 4-3.3.

5 *See infra* § 4-5.1(b).

6 *See* State ex rel. Counsel for Discipline v. Orr, 759 N.W.2d 702, 709 (Neb. 2009) ("caution[ing] general practitioners against taking on cases in areas of law with which they have no experience, unless they are prepared to do the necessary research to become competent in such areas or associate with an attorney who is competent in such areas").

To be sure, the attorney who is a neophyte to an area of practice probably cannot aspire to mastery of the new field during the pendency of a single representation. The standard is not one of expertise, but rather of competence. The fact that a client might have received superior representation from a more experienced attorney or an expert in the field (if such a lawyer had been available and if the client had been willing to pay the higher rate such a lawyer likely would have charged) by no means raises any presumption that the lawyer of general competence has provided or will provide inferior representation.

If the amount of preparation and study necessitated by a new matter is modest, the time devoted to the preparation is properly charged to the client, assuming the rate charged by the lawyer does not suggest expertise in the field. With any new matter, even in an area in which the lawyer has substantial experience, a certain amount of time is necessary to come up to speed, and ordinarily such preparation time is billable. Moreover, a lawyer new to a field presumably would bill at a lower hourly rate, to "make up for the self-education aspect of work by an inexperienced lawyer."[7]

If, however, a lawyer is required to engage in substantial background preparation and study because the lawyer lacks prior experience and training in an area, the lawyer may not expect the client to pay for such extensive education,[8] at least when other lawyers already possessing competence in that field are available. While the lawyer still may undertake the representation if that preparation and study will make him competent, all or most of the preparation time should be excluded from the bill for legal services. And it is important that the lawyer make sure that he does not neglect the client matter while engaging in the study necessary to handle it competently.[9]

### *§ 4-5.1(a)(3) Associating with a Lawyer of Established Competence*

Alternatively, a lawyer may provide competent representation through association or consultation with another lawyer of established competence in the field. If the lawyer with expertise or experience in the field actually enters into an association for the representation, then she also assumes responsibility for the matter.[10] If the original lawyer retains or contracts with another lawyer, then as Comments 6 and 7 to Rule 1.1 remind, the lawyer should have "informed consent" from the client, "reasonably believe that the other lawyers' services will contribute to the competent and ethical representation of the client," and agree with the other lawyer about the scope of representation and allocation between them of responsibilities. If instead, a lawyer consults with another lawyer with expertise or experience in the field, such as by asking questions and seeking general advice, the responsibility for ensuring that the questions asked and answers received are sufficient to establish competence to handle the particular representation remains with the asking lawyer.

---

[7] Schilling v. Community Mem. Gen. Hosp., 110 F.R.D. 377, 378 (N.D. Ill. 1986).

[8] *See* Cloward v. Shinseki, No. 09–3771E, 2011 WL 2110008, at *2 (Vet. App. May 27, 2011) (saying that the lawyer's "extensive effort to learn the law is commendable," but that "it is not properly billable to a client"); Estate of Larson, 694 P.2d 1051, 1059 (Wash. 1985) ("Reason and fairness compel us to observe that clients should not be expected to pay for the education of a lawyer when he spends excessive amounts of time on tasks which, with reasonable experience, become matters of routine.").

[9] *See* Committee on Prof'l Ethics & Conduct v. Pracht, 505 N.W.2d 196, 198 (Iowa 1993) ("No client should be made to suffer through an attorney's learning curve.").

[10] For discussion of division of the fee when lawyers not in the same firm associate on a matter, see *supra* § 4-4.5.

### § 4-5.1(b) The Need for Expertise in Certain Fields of Law

Comment 1 to Model Rule 1.1 recognizes that "[e]xpertise in a particular field of law may be required in some circumstances." When a lawyer would be unable to achieve a basic level of proficiency sufficient to handle the case through reasonable preparation and study, the lawyer should not accept the representation or should withdraw and suggest that the client retain an expert in the area. Certain fields of law, as well as certain areas of practice not defined by a legal specialty, may be sufficiently complex as to be well beyond the facility of a reasonably competent and experienced generalist lawyer. Fields of law that always or often demand specialization include patent law and taxation.

The need for expertise turns, not upon practice area categories or the label of a field as a specialty, but rather upon whether the average lawyer could develop competence with reasonable preparation and study. Indeed, a particular matter may demand representation by or association with an expert, even if the matter does not fit neatly within a specialized field of law.

As but one such example in the court advocacy context, major class action litigation is notoriously complicated.[11] Its complexity and controversy has caused it to be denominated by some as the "Frankenstein monster" of civil procedure.[12] The class action procedure "permits a lawsuit to be brought by or against large numbers of individuals or organizations whose interests are sufficiently related so that it is more efficient to adjudicate their rights or liabilities in a single action than in a series of individual proceedings."[13] Because of the need to protect the interests of absent parties and resolve in a single proceeding the rights and obligations of a multitude of individuals or entities, procedural complexities and special procedures abound within this format.[14]

Under Federal Rule of Civil Procedure 23,[15] a number of procedural prerequisites must be satisfied before a matter may proceed as a class action, including whether there is an identifiable class, whether the representatives are members of the class, whether the class is so large that joinder is impracticable, whether there are questions of law or fact common to all members of the class, whether the claims or defenses of the representatives of the class are typical of other class members, and whether the representatives of the class will adequately represent the interests of absent class members.[16] In addition, "[b]ecause class actions embrace the rights of so many persons and often present highly complex issues to resolve, the courts must use special procedures to manage or control the litigation in a way to assure fair representation of

---

[11] The late-Charles Alan Wright, a giant in scholarship on federal court practice, characterized the rules on class actions as "extremely complicated." CHARLES A. WRIGHT, LAW OF FEDERAL COURTS § 72, at 508 n.9 (West Pub. Co., 5th ed., 1994).

[12] *See* Eisen v. Carlisle & Jacquelin, 391 F.2d 555, 571 (2d Cir. 1968) (Lumbard, C.J., dissenting) (characterizing litigation, because of its complexity and length, as a "Frankenstein monster posing as a class action").

[13] JACK H. FRIEDENTHAL, MARY KAY KANE & ARTHUR R. MILLER, CIVIL PROCEDURE § 16.1 (Thomson-West, 4th ed., 2005).

[14] Arthur R. Miller, *Of Frankenstein Monsters and Shining Knights: Myth, Reality, and the "Class Action Problem,"* 92 HARV. L. REV. 664, 677 (1979) ("The procedural complexities that can emerge under rule 23 are extraordinarily variegated in character.").

[15] FED. R. CIV. P. 23.

[16] *See generally* JACK H. FRIEDENTHAL, MARY KAY KANE & ARTHUR R. MILLER, CIVIL PROCEDURE § 16.2 (Thomson-West, 4th ed., 2005).

all the interests involved."[17] Adequate notice must be provided to absent class members of the pendency of the action, in a manner reasonably calculated to reach them, to allow them to appear or opt-out of the litigation.[18] The court may issue special orders to determine the course of proceedings and direct the manner in which evidence or arguments are presented.[19] Finally, to protect the interests of the absent class members, any dismissal or settlement of the case must be submitted to and approved by the court.[20] In sum, a major class action is not the place for the disorganized, the faint-hearted, or the novice.

When the class action format of a lawsuit raises complex procedural issues of its own, the assistance of an attorney already possessing expertise in the multiple areas of the underlying substantive law and the procedural framework may be required. Indeed, courts frequently consider the class counsel's experience with and expertise in the field of law or in class action litigation when determining whether the representation is sufficiently adequate to justify certification of the case as a class action.[21] This does not mean that every non-expert lawyer is incompetent to handle every class action. If the class action aspect is relatively straightforward, such as where the defendant does not resist certification or the number of class members is manageable, then the matter may remain within the facility of an attorney of ordinary lawyerly knowledge and skill. As always, the standard is whether the subject matter, even when combined with other legal complexities in the case, remains accessible to the attorney of reasonable ability and professional experience devoting diligent effort to the matter.

### § 4-5.1(c) Lawyer Mistakes, Personal Problems, and Competence

A lawyer may make a negligent mistake during a representation, and even be held liable for that mistake, without appropriately being subject to disciplinary sanction. An adverse outcome in a single malpractice suit ordinarily should not give rise to disciplinary proceedings, unless the matter involved misconduct beyond an isolated example of simple professional negligence. Although a lawyer's inadvertent departure from the standard of care on even one occasion may technically be a violation of the competency requirement of Model Rule 1.1, being subject to civil liability for any resulting harm usually is sufficient to address an anomalous error. Formal discipline should be reserved for the lawyer who exhibits outrageous incompetence or has demonstrated a pattern of behavior that suggests a lack of competence rather than a simple mistake.

When a lawyer is found to have committed gross incompetence in handling client matters, the ineptitude discovered frequently is more attributable to problems in the lawyer's personal life than to a lack of legal ability or training. If an attorney no longer is able to devote professional attention to client matters due to abuse of alcohol or drugs, severe emotional instability, or distraction because of family or other personal problems, then the lawyer simply is no longer competent. Until the lawyer has resolved the problem or received effective treatment, the impaired lawyer should decline future representations and ensure that existing matters are transferred to another lawyer.

---

[17] *Id.* § 16.5.

[18] *Id.* § 16.6.

[19] *Id.* § 16.5.

[20] *Id.* § 16.7.

[21] *See id.* § 16.2.

## § 4-5.2 COUNSELING THROUGH CANDID, MORAL, AND LAWFUL ADVICE

### § 4-5.2(a) Counseling a Client Within the Expanding Scope of Law Practice

In the modern world, lawyers act in multiple capacities to protect the legal interests of their clients and provide comprehensive counseling about the nature and requirements of the law. Lawyers continue to play the traditional role of the advocate, zealously asserting the interests and promoting the positions of their clients in court or another forum. With the increasing omnipresence of the law, lawyers serve as general advisors, translating the "essential generality of the law"[22] into specifically applicable information so that clients may conform their behavior to the expectations of the law, plan for the future, or invoke the protections of the law.

In undertaking these professional responsibilities, the lawyer is held to a standard of competence,[23] which today often requires more than formal legal training and facility with the traditional sources and processes of the law. While rendering legal advice and assistance remains at the heart of the lawyer's distinct professional role, legal counsel frequently is of value only when integrated with the lawyer's evaluation of other factors of practical, economic, emotional, or moral importance to the client.[24] As one federal court of appeals remarked:

> The complete lawyer may well promote and reinforce the legal advice given, weigh it, and lay out its ramifications by explaining: how the advice is feasible and can be implemented; the legal downsides, risks and costs of taking the advice or doing otherwise; what alternatives exist to present measures or the measures advised; what other persons are doing or thinking about the matter; or the collateral benefits, risks or costs in terms of expense, politics, insurance, commerce, morals, and appearances.[25]

To be such a "complete lawyer," the attorney must be a jack-of-all-trades—or at least sufficiently grounded in the real-world circumstances of the clients being served. Legal advice offered in the abstract, formulated in the splendid isolation of a law library and drawing only on the texts and sources of the legal discipline,[26] may fail to connect with the client's need for relevant guidance that leads to an informed decision.[27] "[I]n today's litigious, regulated, complicated world," Professor Michele DeStefano says, "lawyers sometimes have to look outside the box to form legal opinions."[28]

---

[22] *See* ROBERT H. ARONSON & DONALD T. WECKSTEIN, PROFESSIONAL RESPONSIBILITY IN A NUTSHELL 4 (West 2d ed. 1991) ("Of great importance to a law-abiding society is the role that lawyers play in individualizing the essential generality of the law.").

[23] *See supra* § 4-5.1(a).

[24] *See also infra* § 4-6.3(b)(1).

[25] In re Erie County, 473 F.3d 413, 419 (2d Cir. 2007).

[26] *See* Katherine R. Kruse, *Beyond Cardboard Clients in Legal Ethics*, 23 GEO. J. LEGAL ETHICS 103, 127 (2010) (advocating a "client-centered approach" under which lawyers "unlearn the professional habit of 'issue-spotting' their clients and to approach their clients as whole persons who are more than the sum of their legal interests").

[27] *See* Gregory C. Sisk & Pamela J. Abbate, *The Dynamic Attorney-Client Privilege*, 23 GEO. J. LEGAL ETHICS 201, 218–24 (2010).

[28] Michele DeStefano Beardslee, *The Corporate Attorney-Client Privilege: Third Rate Doctrine for Third Party Consultants*, 62 SMU L. REV. 727, 730 (2009).

## § 4-5.2(b) Candid Advice and Moral Deliberation

### *§ 4-5.2(b)(1) Offering Forthright Advice and a Frank Evaluation*

Together with advocacy on behalf of the client, the most important and traditional role of the lawyer is as confidential and candid advisor to the client. The lawyer may evaluate the client's prospects for success in litigation or a transaction, advise the client regarding the legal and other implications of certain situations, assist the client to make intelligent decisions regarding important life matters, counsel the client to comply with regulatory and other legal requirements, and dissuade the client from engaging in fraud or other wrongful acts.

Indeed, one of the primary justifications for the attorney-client privilege is to allow the client to confide fully in her lawyer so that the lawyer has the information necessary to advise the client about what the law demands and to encourage the client to consider the morally appropriate course of action.[29] As discussed below, when addressing the lawyer's obligation not to assist the client in fraudulent or criminal behavior,[30] lawyers regularly advise and successfully persuade their clients not to embark upon or persist in legally wrongful conduct, thus producing a powerful public benefit by enhancing a confidential private relationship.

Although a lawyer often shifts back and forth between advocacy and counseling roles during the course of a representation, the lawyer's responsibilities to the client as an advisor under Rule 2.1 of the Model Rules of Professional Conduct should be recognized as different in meaningful ways from the lawyer's role as an advocate for the client. When the lawyer advocates the client's case to a judge or adverse party in litigation, to a regulator regarding legal compliance, or to those on the other side of a transaction, the lawyer presents that case in the most favorable light, short of being deceptive,[31] and may advance any colorable argument about the facts or the law.[32] By contrast, under Rule 2.1, the lawyer is admonished to be absolutely "candid" and to exercise "independent professional judgment" when advising a client.[33] As Professor Deborah Rhode writes, "lawyers, as fiduciaries for clients, have a moral obligation to provide informed, independent, and disinterested legal advice."[34]

As Comment 1 to Rule 2.1 frames it, when communicating inside the confidential seclusion of the attorney-client relationship, the lawyer has a duty to provide "straightforward advice expressing the lawyer's honest assessment." Even when plausible arguments are available to advocate the client's case before a tribunal or regulator, the lawyer must provide the client with a frank evaluation of the prospects

---

[29] *See infra* § 4-6.1. *See also* Part Two of this book, Neil W. Hamilton & Melissa H. Weresh, Development Toward Professionalism and the Formation of an Ethical Professional Identity to Become an Effective Lawyer, § 3-1.3(a).

[30] *See infra* § 4-5.2(c).

[31] On the lawyer's duty of honesty in statements to a tribunal and to another party, see *infra* §§ 4-9.5, 4-11.2. On the duty of candor and of disclosure obligations in legal malpractice cases, see Part Five of this book, Susan Saab Fortney & Vincent R. Johnson, Legal Malpractice § 5-3.3(a).

[32] *See infra* § 4-9.3.

[33] *See* W. Bradley Wendel, *Government Lawyers in the Trump Administration*, 69 HASTINGS LAW JOURNAL 275, 331–32 (2017) (saying that the law of lawyering "envisions a highly fiduciary role in which lawyers use reasonable care and effort to provide accurate, unbiased advice to clients, who then are responsible for deciding how to proceed").

[34] Deborah L. Rhode, *Moral Counseling*, 75 FORDHAM L. REV. 1317, 1319 (2006).

and about the concrete risks that might arise should a negative outcome result. Without such information, the client cannot make an intelligent decision about whether his position is sufficiently robust to justify continued litigation, resistance to regulation, or refusal of an offer. Few things are more likely to cause resentment by the client (and perhaps provoke a malpractice claim) than overpromising by the lawyer who paints too rosy a picture.

Likewise, when advising the client about the requirements of the law, the lawyer should not simply tell the client what the client may wish to hear or distort the message so as to support the client's preferences. Instead, the lawyer must acknowledge uncertainties and forthrightly warn of the dangers that may be realized if the client's choice should prove imprudent or if the lawyer's hopeful prognostication about the law's demands or the outcome of litigation should prove mistaken. To be sure, as Comment 1 to Rule 2.1 suggests, the lawyer may need "to sustain the client's morale," which may require sensitivity in the style or manner of presentation, but "a lawyer should not be deterred from giving candid advice by the prospect that the advice will be unpalatable to the client."

Importantly, however uncomfortable it may be, the lawyer must be prepared to tell the client when he has engaged in legally wrongful conduct. As Professor Richard Painter writes, "[w]hen a lawyer refuses to confront a client and insist that a wrong be rectified, the lawyer may send an unintended message: The wrong is more theoretical than real and the client's actions are not serious enough to compel correction."[35]

### *§ 4-5.2(b)(2) Moral Engagement with Client*

As Rule 2.1 affirmatively states, "[i]n rendering advice, a lawyer may refer not only to law but to other considerations such as moral, economic, social and political factors, that may be relevant to the client's situation." Professor Charles Wolfram observes that "[t]he failure of lawyers to appreciate that they deal here with emotions, human values, beliefs, secret hopes and fears, prejudices, all of the aspects of humanity, is probably the single most important reason for client dissatisfaction with legal services."[36]

If we as lawyers are to well serve our clients as whole persons and affirm their full dignity as moral beings, we should be ready to engage in moral, economic, social, and political reflection with our clients. In so doing, we must not usurp the client's authority to determine the objectives of the representation,[37] by assuming a posture of moral superiority, or by neglecting to consult with or refer the client to others, including other professionals, who may have greater competence in counseling the client on a particular matter.[38] As lawyers, we also must be mindful of our limits. Clients come to us because we are experts in the law, not because of our training as therapeutic counselors, mental health professionals, theologians, or moral philosophers. Nonetheless, the lawyer should collaborate with the client in bringing to bear the client's own moral vision as properly pertinent to the representation.

---

[35] Richard W. Painter, *The Moral Interdependence of Corporate Lawyers and Their Clients*, 67 S. CAL. L. REV. 507, 568 (1994).

[36] CHARLES W. WOLFRAM, MODERN LEGAL ETHICS § 13.2.1 (West, 1986).

[37] *See supra* § 4-3.4.

[38] *See infra* § 4-5.2(b)(3).

Rule 2.1 emphatically confirms that the lawyer properly may invoke the moral element of the counseling role. The lawyer who assumes the morally-bankrupt role of legal technician has not fully embraced the vital role of an advisor to a client.

What lawyers do on behalf of clients may have consequences, which are sometimes profound, for others. Thus, the objectives adopted by clients and the legal means employed by lawyers necessarily have moral resonance. The lawyer and the client may engage in mutual moral deliberation, in which they act cooperatively toward accomplishing the good. In this collaboration, the lawyer does not impose the lawyer's moral values upon the client but seeks to ensure that the client draws on the client's own deepest moral principles in realizing a legal outcome.[39] While no self-respecting and morally-sensitive lawyer may descend into the position of being a hired gun for the client, neither does conscious acceptance of moral responsibility for professional behavior justify assuming a posture of moral dictator. Ideally, the attorney-client relationship should be recognized as "a common moral community in which each has responsibilities to the other."[40]

For the lawyer to neglect the moral dimension of the representation may well constitute indifferent neglect of the client's true interests.[41] Morally detached lawyering could result in damage to family relationships, harm to stakeholders or employees of a business, damage to the natural environment, or failure to account for an elderly client's moral and religious beliefs in drafting a medical directive. By failing to enter into a moral dialogue, the lawyer is bereft of vital information about the client, the client's true nature, and the client's genuine desires, resulting in an artificial separation of the client's legal interests from the client's moral aspirations. How can the lawyer truly know the client and thereby purport to advance that client's wellbeing if the lawyer never asks by what moral compass the client directs her path?

The lawyer who chooses the role of legal paladin probably will not transgress any disciplinary rule in most instances,[42] however impoverished that role may be in terms of the satisfying professional life. But as Dean Robert Vischer explains, a lawyer's

---

[39] Robert F. Cochran, Jr., *Introduction: Three Approaches to Moral Issues in Law Office Counseling, in Symposium: Client Counseling and Moral Responsibility*, 30 PEPP. L. REV. 591, 599 (2003) (stating that, by asking the client to consider the effect of alternatives on other people, the lawyer does not impose values on the client, but "calls on clients to draw on their own sources of moral values"). Writing from the perspective of the "client-centered" movement, which traditionally has been skeptical of moral dialogue as "especially intrusive and arguably outside of the lawyer's professional expertise," Professor Katherine Kruse envisions moral dialogue "as an elaborate process of helping the client clarify her own values." Katherine R. Kruse, *Fortress in the Sand: The Plural Values of Client-Centered Representation*, 12 CLINICAL L. REV. 369, 431–32 (2006). In some contrast with the position I have taken in this section, Kruse believes "thicker notions of the lawyer-client relationship as a friendship or mutual search for the good are both unrealistic and inappropriate goals for legal representation" and is particularly resistant to any behavior by lawyers that appears to be "moral instruction." Katherine R. Kruse, *Engaged Client-Centered Representation and the Moral Foundations of the Lawyer-Client Relationship*, 39 HOFSTRA L. REV. 577, 589 (2011).

[40] JOSEPH G. ALLEGRETTI, THE LAWYER'S CALLING: CHRISTIAN FAITH AND LEGAL PRACTICE 45 (Paulist Press, 1996).

[41] *See* Katherine R. Kruse, *Beyond Cardboard Clients in Legal Ethics*, 23 GEO. J. LEGAL ETHICS 103, 103 (2010) (rejecting the construction of "cardboard clients" who are "one dimensional figures interested only in maximizing their legal and financial interests").

[42] *See* MODEL R. PROF'L CONDUCT R. 2.1, cmt. 3 (American Bar Ass'n, 2016) (saying that when "a client experienced in legal matters" seeks "purely technical advice," that request may be accepted "at face value" by the lawyer, although stating that "[w]hen such a request is made by a client inexperienced in legal matters, however, the lawyer's responsibility as advisor may include indicating that more may be involved than strictly legal considerations").

misguided adoption of a morally-detached and legally-exclusive approach to the client's representation—

> foregoes any opportunity by the client to correct the lawyer's misperception of the client's operative moral claims and it tends to allow clients to avoid coming to terms with the moral content of any arguably legal course of conduct. Especially in cases where the governing legal directives are ambiguous or otherwise indeterminate, attorneys become tools for facilitating morally problematic conduct, even in contexts where the client may not have deliberately embraced the moral claims embodied therein or where the client would have benefited from being pressed on the wisdom of those claims.[43]

To be blunt, then, a lawyer who fails to engage in a moral discussion with the client, at least on matters of significance with obvious moral implications, simply is not doing his job. Moral awareness is not at war with the traditional expectation of the lawyer to be a zealous advocate for the client. Professor Gerald Postema argues that a lawyer is not only authorized to raise moral issues with the client, the lawyer has a professional responsibility to do so:

> [C]ut off from sound moral judgment, the lawyer's ability to do his job well—to determine the applicable law and effectively advise his clients—is likely to be seriously affected. . . . [T]he lawyer who must detach professional judgment from his own moral judgment is deprived of the resources from which arguments regarding his client's legal rights and duties can be fashioned. In effect, the ideal of neutrality and detachment wars against its companion ideal of zealous pursuit of client interests.[44]

Again, Rule 2.1 of the Model Rules of Professional Conduct is an express reminder of the importance of holistic counseling. As Professors Geoffrey Hazard and William Hodes and attorney Peter Jarvis emphasize, this provision is "more than merely permissive;" it "should be read as active encouragement for lawyers to provide more broadly based and richer professional advice."[45] Comment 2 to Rule 2.1 reinforces the value of moral deliberation to the client:

> Advice couched in narrow legal terms may be of little value to a client, especially where practical considerations, such as cost or effects on other people, are predominant. Purely technical legal advice, therefore, can sometimes be inadequate. It is proper for a lawyer to refer to relevant moral and ethical considerations in giving advice. Although a lawyer is not a moral advisor as such, moral and ethical considerations impinge upon most legal questions and may decisively influence how the law will be applied.

Importantly, the rules-sanctioned encouragement to engage in moral deliberation with the client is subject to the vital qualification (explicit in the old Model Code of Professional Responsibility) that "the decision whether to forego legally available objectives or methods because of non-legal factors is ultimately for the client and not for"

---

[43] Robert K. Vischer, *Legal Advice as Moral Perspective*, 19 GEO. J. LEGAL ETHICS 225, 229 (2006).

[44] Gerald J. Postema, *Moral Responsibility in Professional Ethics*, 55 N.Y.U. L. REV. 63, 79 (1980).

[45] 1 GEOFFREY C. HAZARD, JR., W. WILLIAM HODES & PETER R. JARVIS, THE LAW OF LAWYERING § 25.05 (Aspen, 4th ed., 2016).

the lawyer."[46] As Professor Stephen Pepper reminds us, whether a client chooses to make a moral choice "not to exercise her legal right is the client's choice and the result is the client's responsibility."[47]

In addition, our approach to matters must be attentive to context and to the individual situations of our clients.[48] Professor Robert Cochran suggests that the lawyer "may need to empower the weak client, but "assert herself with the strong client."[49] Due to greater vulnerability and potential imbalance of power, discussions with a criminal defendant must be approached sensitively so as to preserve the client's autonomy and dignity. By contrast, the risk of undue moral influence is much less when dealing with sophisticated clients in non-exigent circumstances. As Professor Neil Hamilton also notes, clients come to us "at different stages of development in terms of ethical sensitivity, moral reasoning and judgment, moral motivation and moral character and courage."[50] Different approaches for different relationships and people must be adopted. Nuance and sensitivity, together with respect for the dignity of the other, remains essential. Moral deliberation is a two-way street, moreover, in which we should be open to and learn from the client.

By the nature of such advice, confidentially transmitted by a lawyer in a fiduciary relationship with a client, moral counseling rarely comes to public attention. Whether or not the client accepts moral advice, or even that it was given, ordinarily is a protected confidence within the attorney-client relationship. In your author's admittedly anecdotal experience, moral deliberation between lawyers and clients, colored of course by legal concepts and traditions, is a naturally-occurring and common phenomenon. On probably thousands of occasions each day somewhere in this country, lawyers and clients reach consensus that a questionable course of action should be avoided, on moral grounds or by reason of legal limitations or both. We rarely hear about such conclusions reached in a confidential environment. Instead, the episodes that come to public attention are those hopefully less typical cases where the client steamed ahead regardless of moral or legal concerns, with inadequate counseling by the lawyer or even with the lawyer's encouragement, only to enter into troubled and scandalous waters.

#### *§ 4-5.2(b)(3) Professional Humility and Assistance by Other Professionals*

As Professor Lynn Wardle writes in the particular context of family law practice, the lawyer should recognize "the limits of the law and legal solutions" and appreciate as well "the potential value of other professions and professionals."[51] Comment 4 to Model Rule 2.1 encourages us to consider whether a matter falls into "the domain of another profession. Family matters can involve problems within the professional competence of

---

[46] MODEL CODE OF PROF'L RESPONSIBILITY, Ethical Consideration 7–8 (American Bar Ass'n, 1980); *see also* Rhode, *supra*, 75 FORDHAM L. REV. at 1331 ("[T]o give moral advice is not to impose it.").

[47] Stephen L. Pepper, *Lawyers' Ethics in the Gap Between Law and Justice*, 40 S. Tex. L. Rev. 181, 190–92 (1999).

[48] *See id.* at 192–96.

[49] Cochran, *supra*, 30 PEPP. L. REV. at 600.

[50] Neil W. Hamilton, *The Moral Dilemma of Counseling the Powerful*, MINN. LAWYER, Jan. 24, 2005.

[51] Lynn D. Wardle, *Counselors and Gatekeepers: The Professional Responsibilities of Family Lawyers in Divorce Cases*, 79 UMKC L. REV. 417, 426 (2010).

psychiatry, clinical psychology or social work; business matters can involve problems within the competence of the accounting profession or of financial specialists."[52]

We lawyers tend to overestimate our expertise in a wide range of matters, including those beyond the legal realm. Humility is the watchword in knowing when to refer a client to another professional for additional help.

### § 4-5.2(c) Counseling a Client on the Requirements of the Law While Not Assisting a Client in Fraudulent or Criminal Conduct

One of the most valuable services provided by a lawyer to her client is to advise the client regarding the limits of the law and to counsel the client not to take actions that would transgress those limits.[53] As noted previously,[54] on likely thousands of occasions every day, lawyers in this country inform their clients that a proposed course of action would be improper. And clients usually accede to that legal advice and refrain from illegal conduct.

Because of the confidential nature of the attorney-client relationship,[55] we seldom hear about these common episodes in which legal advice has the salutary effect of promoting respect for and obedience to the law. Instead, we are more likely to learn about those atypical occasions in which a lawyer failed to properly advise a client to abide by the constraints of the law, or even facilitated the client's wrongdoing, with disastrous results. When such reports appear in the news, as when a corporate official is indicted for criminal wrongdoing and it is alleged that corporate counsel was complicit, the public is left with the mistaken impression that lawyers frequently fail to uphold their legal responsibilities and regularly allow legal advice to be perverted to an illicit end.

If a lawyer is to gain the confidence of the client and thereby be in a position to counsel the client to behave according to the limits of the law, the lawyer must be authorized to discuss the nature of those legal obligations and to describe the line between lawful and unlawful conduct without fear that such advice might later be regarded as assisting the client to violate the law. Moreover, sometimes the law is anything but clear, and the client's lawful course uncertain. In such uncharted territory, the lawyer appropriately may provide what clarification is possible without later being accused of leading the client into law-breaking.[56]

Rule 1.2(d) of the Model Rules of Professional Conduct emphasizes that "a lawyer may discuss the legal consequences of any proposed course of conduct with a client." Moreover, the rule further affirms that a lawyer "may counsel or assist a client to make a good faith effort to determine the validity, scope, meaning or application of the law." Rule 1.2 thus allows the lawyer to represent the client in challenging the validity of a

---

[52] On integrating other professionals into the legal representation as a collaboration to best understand and serve the client, see generally Spencer Rand, *Hearing Stories Already Told: Successfully Incorporating Third Party Professionals into the Attorney-Client Relationship*, 80 TENN. L. REV. 1 (2012).

[53] On the lawyer's duty to provide candid advice to the client, see *supra* § 4-5.2(b).

[54] *See supra* § 4-5.2(b)(2).

[55] *See infra* §§ 4-6.1 to 4-6.6.

[56] *See infra* § 4-9.7(b)(6).

law or in questioning the scope and application of that law to a particular action by the client.[57]

However, Rule 1.2(d) stresses that "[a] lawyer shall not counsel a client to engage, or assist a client, in conduct that the lawyer knows is criminal or fraudulent." Moreover, Rule 1.4(a)(5) of the Model Rules of Professional Conduct expressly directs the lawyer who knows that the client "expects assistance" not permitted under the ethics rule or the law to explain the limits on the lawyer's conduct. As Comment 9 to Rule 1.2 explains, a lawyer may not, in the guise of "presenting an analysis of legal aspects of questionable conduct," take the affirmative and unacceptable step of "recommending the means by which a crime or fraud might be committed with impunity." A lawyer may not escape responsibility for assisting illegal conduct by saying that she simply provided information about the scope and requirements of the law, when "the lawyer [has] conveyed to the client the idea that by adopting a particular course of action he may successfully defraud some one or impede the administration of justice."[58]

The fact that the client, contrary to the lawyer's intent or reasonable expectation, uses legal advice to perform a wrongful act does not make the lawyer a party to that illegal conduct. At the same time, a lawyer may not offer legal information that the lawyer knows will be misused or that could serve no legitimate purpose other than to promote violation of the law. Professor Robert Schuwerk and attorney Lillian Hardwick suggest that "[t]he touchstone in this area is whether the lawyer believes, after reasonable inquiry, that the client could not have a lawful purpose for seeking the advice in question."[59] As Professor Stephen Pepper writes, a lawyer may not provide "legal advice the client may use for clearly criminal conduct involving concrete harm to third parties. The classic example is the client who asks which South American countries have no extradition treaty with the United States covering armed robbery or murder."[60] Under such unusual circumstances, the lawyer's conduct crosses the line from legal advice to illegal assistance.

If the lawyer learns that the client's wrongful conduct is already underway, the lawyer may not allow his legal services to be used to facilitate that conduct. As discussed later,[61] the lawyer who discovers client wrongdoing after the fact may be obliged to withdraw from the representation, may also be required to disaffirm opinions or documents that the lawyer had prepared believing them to be proper but later realizes are being or have been used toward a criminal or fraudulent end, and may be permitted or required to disclose confidential information to prevent or correct the accomplishment of an illicit end by the client when the lawyer's legal services have been used in furtherance of crime or fraud.

---

57 For discussion of a lawyer's good faith challenge to the validity, scope, or application of a legal obligation to the lawyer, see *supra* § 4-1.4(a).

58 In re Bullowa, 229 N.Y.S. 145, 153 (N.Y. App. Div. 1928).

59 48 ROBERT P. SCHUWERK & LILLIAN HARDWICK, HANDBOOK OF TEXAS LAWYER AND JUDICIAL ETHICS: TEXAS PRACTICE SERIES § 6.02 (Thomson-Reuters, 2016).

60 Stephen L. Pepper, *Counseling at the Limits of the Law: An Exercise in the Jurisprudence and Ethics of Lawyering*, 104 YALE L.J. 1545, 1551 (1995).

61 *See infra* §§ 4-6.6(d), 4-9.8(c) to (h), 4-11.2(c).

## § 4-5.3 DILIGENCE AND ZEALOUS REPRESENTATION

### § 4-5.3(a) Diligence and Zealousness on Behalf of the Client

The requirement of diligence expressed in Rule 1.3 of the Model Rules of Professional Conduct speaks not only to the lawyer's reasonable expedition in bringing a legal matter to conclusion but also to her dedication in advancing the interests of the client. The duty of zealous advocacy, which was enshrined as one of the nine canons of professional ethics in the former Model Code of Professional Responsibility[62] and remains explicit in the rules of a couple of states,[63] is preserved through Comment 1 to Model Rule 1.3: "A lawyer must also act with commitment and dedication to the interests of the client and with *zeal in advocacy* upon the client's behalf" (emphasis added). Comment 1 further reads, "[a] lawyer should pursue a matter on behalf of a client despite opposition, obstruction or personal inconvenience to the lawyer, and take whatever lawful and ethical measures are required to vindicate a client's cause or endeavor."

When the lawyer is incapable of proceeding against opposition, or fails to appreciate what measures are necessary to advance the client's interests, then her lack of diligence also manifests as lack of competence.[64] And if the lawyer allows her own interests, or the interests of others, to suppress the lawyer's zeal on behalf of the client, the resulting neglect is attributable to a conflict of interest, which is independently prohibited by the rules.[65]

Competence alone is not the measure of effectiveness, and avoiding a conflict of interest does not ensure zealous advocacy. By requiring reasonable diligence, Rule 1.3 asks the lawyer to bring vitality and devotion to the project, similar to that which the lawyer would bring to bear if the matter were the lawyer's own. (At the same time, the lawyer must retain a degree of objectivity and emotional distance so as to provide independent and candid advice to the client.[66])

While no disciplinary rule can enjoin enthusiasm upon a lawyer, a loss of professional passion for serving clients is a danger sign. The lawyer who is not energetically engaged in his practice is at greater risk of falling into patterns of procrastination and neglect, which most certainly are grounds for discipline.

### § 4-5.3(b) Diligent Action to Protect Rights of the Client

The diligent lawyer ensures that the rights of the client are protected through timely action, whether by prompt interjection of an objection, timely filing of a lawsuit or other litigation document, punctual responses to offers made by other parties, etc. The repeated failure to do so constitutes professional neglect. For a disciplinary sanction to attach, neglect involves more than making an isolated mistake, and usually involves a pattern of indifference and multiple failures to conscientiously perform legal duties on behalf of the client.

---

[62] MODEL CODE OF PROF'L RESPONSIBILITY, Canon 7 (American Bar Ass'n, 1980) ("Canon 7—A Lawyer Should Represent a Client Zealously Within the Bounds of the Law.").

[63] *See, e.g.*, D.C. RULES OF PROF'L CONDUCT R. 1.3(a); MASS. RULES OF PROF'L CONDUCT R. 1.3.

[64] On competence, see *supra* § 4-5.1.

[65] *See infra* ch. 4-7.

[66] On the duty of candid advice to the client, see *supra* § 4-5.2(b).

As Comment 3 to Model Rule 1.3 warns, "[a] client's interests often can be adversely affected by the passage of time or the change of conditions; in extreme instances, as when a lawyer overlooks a statute of limitations, the client's legal position may be destroyed." An attorney's failure to file suit on behalf of a client within the statute of limitations is perhaps the classic example of neglect. Other litigation examples of neglect that may prejudice the rights of a client include failure to accomplish proper service after filing a lawsuit; failure to comply with discovery requests; failure to respond to a motion to dismiss; failure to appear at a court hearing; allowing a lawsuit to be dismissed for want of prosecution; and failing to meet appellate deadlines such as those for filing the brief and record.

An attorney's neglect of duties to a client might be compared to the malpractice of "a surgeon who, without transferring responsibility, drops his scalpel and abandons his patient in the course of an operation."[67] While the Model Rules of Professional Conduct do not expressly punish "neglect" as such, several rules address a lawyer's dilatory conduct, including Rule 1.3 on diligence, Rule 1.4 on keeping the client reasonably informed,[68] and Rule 3.2 on expediting litigation.[69] Indeed, a lawyer's abandonment, procrastination, or other neglect may result in being found in violation of all of these rules and perhaps others.

When an attorney does fall into a pattern of neglect, more often than not serious personal problems are present, as discussed previously in the section on competence.[70] If an attorney no longer is able to diligently attend to client matters due to abuse of alcohol or drugs, depression, severe emotional instability, or simple distraction because of family or other personal problems, then the lawyer should decline future representations and ensure that existing matters are transferred to another lawyer.

### § 4-5.3(c) Diligent Action to Avoid Unnecessary Anxiety to the Client

While neglect of a matter that results in the client's loss of a substantive right is aggravated professional misconduct, a failure of diligence that causes no concrete harm to a client is not to be excused.[71]

As Comment 3 to Rule 1.3 says, "[p]erhaps no professional shortcoming is more widely resented than procrastination."[72] To the lawyer, a client matter may be nothing more than another piece of work that helps the lawyer to make a living. To the client, the matter may be the source of great emotional distress, in which every delay prolongs the anxiety and uncertainty.

---

[67] Committee on Prof'l Ethics Conduct v. Freed, 341 N.W.2d 757, 759 (Iowa 1983); *see also* Attorney Grievance Comm'n v. Garrett, 46 A.3d 1169, 1177 (2012) (saying that "an attorney's failure to take fundamental steps in furthering a client's matter qualifies as neglect and inattentiveness to a client's interest").

[68] *See infra* § 4-5.4(b) to (c).

[69] *See infra* § 4-9.4(a).

[70] *See supra* § 4-5.1(c).

[71] *See* Board of Prof'l Ethics & Conduct v. Sullins, 648 N.W.2d 127, 133 (Iowa 2002) ("Neglect may be proven without evidence of monetary harm.").

[72] *See also* In re Smith, 659 N.E.2d 896, 902 (Ill. 1996) (quoting comment).

### § 4-5.3(d) Protecting the Client in Event of Lawyer's Death, Disability, or Suspension

No one can truly "go it alone" in life or the practice of law. We all need time away from the office to be refreshed. However healthy we are today, we all are at risk of becoming disabled, even if temporarily. Some of us, unfortunately, will be suspended from the practice of law, requiring relinquishment of professional responsibilities for a time. And all of us will come to the end of this life, likely not at a time of our own choosing.

Because of the inevitability that we cannot be on call for our clients at all times, and the likely prospect that during the course of a career we will be forced to step away from our practice for a period, diligence requires that the lawyer make plans to ensure that a client's interests are not seriously compromised in that eventuality. For attorneys who practice in a firm or with other lawyers in an organization, arranging for another to watch over client matters and take timely action as necessary may be relatively straightforward. But even in such a setting, the lawyer together with the firm or organization should develop a clear plan, so that partners in the firm or other lawyers in the organization would become aware of the need to and would know how to gain access to client files for matters being handled by the lawyer.

For the sole practitioner, Comment 5 to Rule 1.3 suggests that the lawyer should "prepare a plan, in conformity with applicable rules, that designates another competent lawyer to review client files, notify each client of the lawyer's death or disability, and determine whether there is a need for immediate protective action." Rule 1.17 of the Model Rules of Professional Conduct permits sale of a law practice, including sale by the estate or survivors of a deceased lawyer,[73] which also may help ensure that clients of a deceased lawyer receive continuing professional attention.

### § 4-5.3(e) Zealous Advocacy, Professionalism, and Civility

While zealous advocacy is a hallmark of our profession, an excess of zeal can lead us astray and cause us to lose our independence and detachment of professional judgment, leading even the finest lawyer to take imprudent steps that, in a quieter moment of reflection, would be appreciated as veering dangerously close to or crossing the line of professional propriety. A lawyer who too readily attributes malicious motives to an opponent or the opponent's counsel may be tempted to engage in questionable behavior toward that adversary. The lawyer must firmly resist the mind-set that "when it is 'the little guy' versus a 'big guy,' " a little deviation from high ethical standards may be justified.[74] Adopting an attitude of professionalism, beyond the letter of the ethics rules, is likely to provide a safe harbor for the prudent lawyer.

Over the past several decades, conferences of judges and leaders in the bar have become concerned that the profession is drifting "away from the principles of professionalism" and that this decline increasingly is "perceived by the public."[75] In 1999, the Conference of Chief Justices, representing the highest courts of every state, adopted

---

[73] *See supra* § 4-3.7(a) to (b).

[74] Board of Professional Ethics & Conduct v. Wanek, 589 N.W.2d 265, 270 (Iowa 1999).

[75] COMMISSION ON PROFESSIONALISM, ABA, ". . .IN THE SPIRIT OF PUBLIC SERVICE:" A BLUEPRINT FOR THE REKINDLING OF LAWYER PROFESSIONALISM v (ABA 1986).

a "National Action Plan on Lawyer Conduct and Professionalism."[76] The plan defined "professionalism" in this way:

> Professionalism is a much broader concept than legal ethics.... [P]rofessionalism includes not only civility among members of the bench and bar, but also competence, integrity, respect for the rule of law, participation in pro bono and community service, and conduct by members of the legal profession that exceeds minimum ethical requirements. Ethics rules are what a lawyer *must* obey. Principles of professionalism are what a lawyer *should* live by in conducting his or her affairs. Unlike disciplinary rules that can be implemented and enforced, professionalism is a personal characteristic. The bench and the bar can create an environment in which professionalism can flourish, . . . [b]ut it is the responsibility of individual judges and lawyers to demonstrate this characteristic in the performance of their professional and personal activities.[77]

Civility does not mean constrained advocacy nor does it mean that a lawyer should hesitate to call those who have wronged a client to account for that conduct. But a clear articulation of another's misconduct or a strongly-stated charge that a person failed to uphold an obligation need not and should not involve unnecessarily disparaging words that deprive another person of dignity. An accused criminal defendant's alleged crimes should not be described before the tribunal in vague or euphemistic terms nor should a prosecutor refrain from detailing to the jury the depraved nature of egregious acts. But even a criminal defendant who stands convicted beyond a reasonable doubt of a heinous crime should not be characterized as less than human or as the equivalent of an animal.[78] Much less should parties to a civil case or witnesses in any matter be subjected to humiliation. The unvarnished truth should be told by the lawyer, as painful as that sometimes may be for others, but name-calling and gratuitous insults are never justified. Courtesy is not an indication of weakness, but rather an affirmation of our professional calling.

While these standards and other exhortations toward professionalism and civility are aspirational, rather than stating disciplinary imperatives that must be obeyed, these principles are not merely precatory. Indeed, Comment 1 to Rule 1.3 of the Model Rules of Professional Conduct explains that "[t]he lawyer's duty to act with reasonable diligence does not require the use of offensive tactics or preclude the treating of all persons involved in the legal process with courtesy and respect." In this way, the rules create space for the development of a culture of civility. No attorney may excuse adoption of offensive tactics or use of unduly sharp language as the expected, must less the required, actions of a zealous advocate for a client. Professor Albert Alschuler similarly emphasizes that "[a] lawyer's duty of faithful representation does not justify his or her departure from ordinary social norms of civility and fair dealing."[79]

A lawyer should develop the virtue of civility, particularly showing respect for all other persons encountered during the representation of a client, for four basic reasons:

---

[76] COMMITTEE ON PROFESSIONALISM AND LAWYER COMPETENCE, CONFERENCE OF CHIEF JUSTICES, A NATIONAL ACTION PLAN ON LAWYER CONDUCT AND PROFESSIONALISM (1999).

[77] *Id.* at 19.

[78] On judicial sanctions for inflammatory comments in the courtroom, see *supra* § 4-1.3(a).

[79] Albert W. Alschuler, *How to Win the Trial of the Century: The Ethics of Lord Brougham and the O.J. Simpson Defense Team*, 29 MCGEORGE L. REV. 291, 319 (1998).

First, it is simply the right thing to do, not only when we are engaged in the practice of law but *especially* when we are so engaged. The traditional religions of the Western World teach that every person is created in the image and likeness of God,[80] which confers a sacred character on every human being. Modern human rights principles similarly maintain the dignity of every person, irrespective of origin, nationality, gender, race, age, or any other characteristic and regardless of what that person has done. If we as lawyers are to affirm the inherent dignity of every person, we must regard with respect all other persons, including the opposing party, the lawyer advocating for the other side, law firm and court staff, and the judge. Should we allow human dignity to be degraded by our behavior as lawyers, we thereby undermine the foundations of any concept of justice and the rule of law.

Second, no lawyer can be effective and successful in practice or experience a satisfactory life in the law without drawing upon the experiences and wisdom of other members of our profession. New lawyers need mentors, and experienced lawyers need colleagues. The kind of lawyer who would serve as a mentor and encourage us as a colleague is also the kind of lawyer who will abhor and refuse to be associated with a lawyer of tawdry reputation. By behaving in an unprofessional manner, a lawyer builds walls that leave him isolated within the profession. And the lawyer who becomes professionally and socially isolated is well on the way to disciplinary trouble.

Third, when we as lawyers behave offensively, especially in public, we bring disrepute upon our profession. This is an injury that we suffer collectively as lawyers. When we are admitted into this profession, we immediately benefit from a tradition of service and a public reputation for intelligence, leadership, and advocacy skills. Most of us in the legal profession can think of many occasions in which our words at a public meeting have been given greater weight by virtue of our professional standing or can recall the times that we were offered opportunities to lead an organization or spearhead a project because we were lawyers. Those lawyers who poison the well through their selfish vitriol and petulant behavior harm us all. And because they too are members of this profession, they injure themselves as well.

Fourth, if a culture of civility is to be created within the legal profession, lawyers and judges must be committed to teach those lawyers who demonstrate disrespect and incivility that such conduct is not effective. A lawyer may obtain a momentary advantage by employing offensive tactics, through intimidation of another participant in the process or by simple aversion in which others surrender an interest to avoid the abuse. But the day of reckoning will come, perhaps not through disciplinary sanction, but through an impaired ability to function effectively due to diminished reputation.

Lawyers love to tell "war stories," so the tale of the unprofessional barrister is likely to make the rounds at the bar convention, the law school class reunion, or the continuing legal education program. The day will come when that lawyer will need or desire the cooperation of another lawyer, who quite understandably will be reluctant to extend any courtesy in light of the asking lawyer's reputation for incivility. Likewise, judges have long memories, and also have been known to share a story with their colleagues. The lawyer who develops a reputation for sharp conduct or disrespect toward other persons in the courtroom will find that her credibility and persuasiveness before the bench has fallen.

---

[80] *See* GENESIS 2:26.

To be sure, that a lawyer has betrayed expectations for professional courtesy in the past is no legitimate basis for another lawyer to refuse to cooperate when the law so requires (such as through timely response to discovery requests) or for a judge to withhold a judgment to which that lawyer's client is entitled. But much of what a lawyer in representing a client may request of another lawyer or seek of a judge falls within the realm of discretion, in which the lawyer being asked to accommodate the asking lawyer or the judge being asked to enter a ruling may choose whether to grant or deny the request. The lawyer who develops a reputation for incivility should not expect that discretionary requests will be positively received.

## § 4-5.4 THE DUTY TO KEEP THE CLIENT INFORMED

### § 4-5.4(a) The Duty to Communicate as Respect for the Client

No matter how competently and diligently we perform legal services, we do not uphold our professional responsibility if we keep our clients in the dark, failing to communicate regularly and responding promptly to reasonable client inquiries. And yet, consistently for decade after decade, the most common complaint made by clients to disciplinary authorities is that their lawyer will not respond to telephone calls or fails to tell them anything for months at a time.

The attorney-client representation is an agency relationship, thus requiring by its very nature that the lawyer "receive instructions from the client, report back on progress, and seek further direction as new options become available."[81] The duty of candor in providing advice[82] is parallel to a duty of candor "to disclose information without request, as well as a duty to respond honestly when an inquiry is made."[83]

Regular consultation with the client is a matter of basic respect. Robert Caine, a member of the New York bar who learned from his experience as a litigant as well, offers this rebuke to a profession that has developed a reputation of failing to be responsive to the client's need and desire to be informed:

> There is something wrong with us lawyers . . . when we can't realize the harm we're doing to our clients and to the public, the heartache and frustration and pain we cause to others because we fail to attend civilly and promptly to the needs of other for communication. If we can't take care of a client properly, which includes communication with the client, we shouldn't accept the retainer. No excuses are acceptable, except honest illness, death or other *real* emergencies. In other businesses, if you don't deliver properly and courteously, you don't get paid or you lose the customer, or both. Why don't we at a minimum tell our secretaries or paralegals to call the client, explain what the delay is, determine what the client's concerns are, and give and receive messages.[84]

---

[81] 1 GEOFFREY C. HAZARD, JR., W. WILLIAM HODES & PETER R. JARVIS, THE LAW OF LAWYERING § 8.02 (Aspen, 4th ed., 2016).

[82] *See supra* § 4-5.2(b)(1).

[83] Vincent R. Johnson, *"Absolute and Perfect Candor" to Clients*, 34 ST. MARY'S L.J. 737, 738 (2003).

[84] Robert S. Caine, A Lawyer's View of Being a Litigant, Letter, N.Y.L.J., May 16, 1994, at 2, *reprinted in* STEPHEN GILLERS, REGULATION OF LAWYERS: PROBLEMS OF LAW AND ETHICS 82 (8th ed. 2009).

### § 4-5.4(b) The Duty to Communicate with the Client to Affirm Client's Authority

Without communication by the lawyer, the client cannot participate in the representation. It is that simple.

If the lawyer fails to keep the client informed, the client is effectively excluded from the representation, which in itself violates professional expectations. As recognized in Rule 1.4(a)(2) and (3) of the Model Rules of Professional Conduct, the lawyer's duty to respect the client's autonomy—both to abide by the client's decisions regarding the objectives of the representation and to consult with the client about the means by which those objectives are to be realized[85]—cannot be upheld unless the client is kept reasonably informed about the material developments in the representation. Thus, for example, because the client has the right to decide whether to settle a civil matter or whether to plead guilty to a criminal charge, the lawyer must promptly notify the client of an offer of settlement or a proposed plea bargain, unless the client previously has delegated authority to the lawyer regarding what would or would not be an acceptable offer or plea proposal. Even as to those legal and tactical decisions for which the lawyer generally retains authority, the lawyer still is obliged to reasonably consult with the client about the means to be employed to achieve the client's objectives.[86] For this reason as well, regular communication with the client must be maintained.

In addition, the Model Rules of Professional Conduct require consent by a client in several circumstances, including whether to disclose confidential information[87] and whether to accede to representation that otherwise would or might constitute a conflict of interest.[88] The client consent required under the rules is "informed consent," which Model Rule 1.0(e) says means the client must possess the information necessary to evaluate "the material risks of and reasonably available alternatives to the proposed course of conduct." As Rule 1.4(a)(1) recognizes, the lawyer must share with the client all the information that is materially pertinent to making the decision. And that information must be provided punctually so that the client may determine in a timely manner whether to grant or withhold the required consent.

As should be apparent, transmitting raw data to the client may not satisfy the lawyer's responsibility to communicate with the client, especially if the client is not a sophisticated user of legal services. As contemplated by Rule 1.4(b), the lawyer must devote the time necessary and make a reasonable effort to explain the nature of the information so that the client may, in the words of Comment 5, "participate intelligently in decisions concerning the objectives of the representation and the means by which they are to be pursued, to the extent the client is willing and able to do so."[89]

---

[85] *See supra* § 4-3.4.

[86] *See supra* § 4-3.4.

[87] *See infra* § 4-6.2.

[88] On client consent to conflicts of interest, see *infra* § 4-7.7.

[89] For discussion of the patience that a lawyer must have to explain matters to a client with diminished capacity, see *supra* § 4-3.5.

### § 4-5.4(c) The Duty to Maintain Regular Communication and Respond to Client Inquiries

The lawyer's duty to maintain a regular dialogue with the client is not limited to those matters on which the client has the authority to make a decision, on which consultation with the client must occur, or as to which informed consent from the client must be obtained. Whether or not any action by the client is required or anticipated, the lawyer has a continuing responsibility under Rule 1.4(a)(3) to "keep the client reasonably informed about the status of the matter." While the duty to communicate with the client applies whether or not the client specifically inquires, the lawyer has a specific duty as well under Rule1.4(a)(4) to promptly comply with the client's "reasonable requests for information."[90] The *Restatement of the Law Governing Lawyers* is directly parallel, saying that a "lawyer must keep a client reasonably informed about the matter" and "must promptly comply with a client's reasonable requests for information."[91]

These obligations to supply the client with regular status reports and to promptly comply with client requests for information are limited by the standard of reasonableness, which in turn depends upon the circumstances. If the client insists upon daily reports on a matter when the lawyer has explained that no developments will occur for several months, or if the client demands that the lawyer provide copies of file documents on an instantaneous basis when not necessary, the lawyer does not violate Rule 1.4 by offering periodic reports on a less frequent basis or by explaining that documents will be provided within a few days. However, even when a matter appears to be dormant and the point at which a new development will occur cannot be predicted, the client should not be left for months at a time without any assurance of lawyer attention to the matter. The lawyer should provide periodic updates, even if only to explain that no new developments have occurred. And a client who does ask for information that the lawyer possesses ordinarily is entitled to receive it within a fairly short timeframe.

In sum, as a matter of courtesy, as well as ethical obligation, the lawyer should maintain continuous and regular communication with the client, even if limited to the transmission of periodic status reports in matters that progress slowly despite the diligent efforts of the lawyer. Phone calls and emails ordinarily should be returned the same day, preferably by the lawyer, but at least by someone on the lawyer's staff who can provide an informed response or assure the client that the lawyer soon will respond. Every significant document created by the lawyer or received by the lawyer regarding the representation should be timely forwarded to the client. Conferences should be scheduled with clients when necessary to explain the meaning of information received, documents forwarded, or developments.

---

[90] *See also* In re Garrison, 894 N.W.2d 339, 341–43 (Neb. 2017) (imposing discipline on a lawyer who responded to repeated questions about the progress of personal injury case with such statements as "relax," "I will take care of it," "this is complicated," and "I can't explain the whole process").

[91] RESTATEMENT (THIRD) OF THE LAW GOVERNING LAWYERS § 20 (American Law Institute, 2000); *see also* Vincent R. Johnson, *"Absolute and Perfect Candor" to Clients*, 34 ST. MARY'S L.J. 737, 740, 747 (2003) (explaining that the reasonable standard for measuring required disclosure applies as well in malpractice suits).

### § 4-5.4(d) Confirming the Lawyer Will Not Assist in Violating the Law or Professional Expectations

Rule 1.4(a)(5) directs the lawyer to "consult with the client about any relevant limitation on the lawyer's conduct when the lawyer knows that the client expects assistance not permitted by the Rules of Professional Conduct or other law." This provision requires the lawyer to warn a client who appears to be seeking legal advice for an improper purpose "that lawyers are not for hire as accomplices."[92]

In this respect, Rule 1.4(a)(5) dovetails with Rule 1.2(d), which provides that "[a] lawyer shall not counsel a client to engage, or assist a client, in conduct that the lawyer knows is criminal or fraudulent." In the prior discussion of Rule 1.2(d), this book addressed the crucial difference between counseling a client regarding the obligations of the law and improperly communicating the means by which to evade legal obligations.[93]

### § 4-5.4(e) Withholding Information from a Client

Rarely may a lawyer assume the paternalistic posture of concealing information from a client as supposedly in the client's best interest. Indeed, the circumstances that would justify hiding something from the client are so unusual that the reference to such exceptional circumstances in the last comment to Rule 1.4 "might be misunderstood and perhaps would be better left unsaid."[94]

Comment 7 suggests that a lawyer may be justified in delaying transmission of information to a client "when the client would be likely to react imprudently to an immediate communication." The comment also states that a lawyer might withhold information when the client would be harmed by hearing it, evidenced for example by "a psychiatric diagnosis of a client when the examining psychiatrist indicates that disclosure would harm the client." A comment to the *Restatement of the Law Governing Lawyers* likewise observes that a psychiatric report might be withheld if "serious harm" to the client might result, but emphasizes that withholding of information from the client is proper only under "conditions of extreme necessity."[95] In addition, if a court order, such as a protective order in civil litigation restricting access to certain information only to counsel, expressly precludes disclosure to a client, the lawyer of course must abide by that decree.

Whatever words of exigency are adopted, the circumstances justifying non-disclosure that are raised in Comment 7 to rule 1.4 are unusual, and the permission to withhold information should be narrowly construed. The comment is not a license to a lawyer to use control of information to manipulate the client into avoiding decisions that the lawyer believes are unwise. Thus, as Professors Geoffrey Hazard and William Hodes and attorney Peter Jarvis warn, a lawyer may not withhold information simply because

---

[92] 1 GEOFFREY C. HAZARD, JR., W. WILLIAM HODES & PETER R. JARVIS, THE LAW OF LAWYERING § 6.03 (Aspen, 4th ed., 2016).

[93] *See supra* § 4-5.2(c).

[94] 1 GEOFFREY C. HAZARD, JR., W. WILLIAM HODES & PETER R. JARVIS, THE LAW OF LAWYERING § 8.06 (Aspen, 4th ed., 2016).

[95] RESTATEMENT (THIRD) OF THE LAW GOVERNING LAWYERS § 46 cmt. c (American Law Institute, 2000).

the lawyer "fears the client will make an 'imprudent' decision *about the subject of the representation*, such as accepting an inadequate settlement offer."[96]

On most occasions when a lawyer may be tempted to withhold information from a client, no excuse is available. Sadly, one of the most common motivations for concealing developments from a client is to hide the lawyer's lack of diligence:[97]

> No profession or calling is immune from members who undertake responsibilities they later become unable or unwilling to discharge. Often in such situations the neglect precipitates a coverup of the "check's in the mail" variety. The "white lie" then evolves into a whole course of imagined performance. When the story inevitably collapses the result ranges from embarrassment all the way to professional disgrace. This discredited conduct never made sense. Any casual observer could not help discerning that more effort was usually expended in the coverup than would have been required to punctually attend to the professional responsibility. The public, which is obviously ill served by such conduct, can take heart. Modern business records and all that comes with the computer age increasingly render coverup attempts impossible. The fact that the truth will soon be known should discourage the habit of inattention to professional responsibilities.[98]

## § 4-5.5 THE DUTY OF A FIDUCIARY TO PUT THE CLIENT FIRST[99]

While not every aspect of the attorney-client relationship fully implicates this dimension, the relationship often and correctly is referred to as a fiduciary one. As one practitioner puts it in plain and simple language, the lawyer must remember that "the relationship isn't about you." While lawyers are important, of course, "we aren't the focus of the relationship—the client is."[100]

A comment to the *Restatement of the Law Governing Lawyers* emphasizes:

> A lawyer is a fiduciary, that is, a person to whom another person's affairs are entrusted in circumstances that often make it difficult or undesirable for that other person to supervise closely the performance of the fiduciary. Assurances of the lawyer's competence, diligence, and loyalty are therefore vital.[101]

When a lawyer performs legal services, the diligence and skill that he brings to the task must adhere to a professional standard of care. Even more so, when the lawyer protects confidential information and exercises loyal and independent judgment uninfected by conflicting interests or the lawyer's own self interest, the lawyer's responsibilities are distinctly fiduciary in nature. In these matters, the trust of the client is directly at stake.

---

[96] 1 GEOFFREY C. HAZARD, JR., W. WILLIAM HODES & PETER R. JARVIS, THE LAW OF LAWYERING § 8.06 (Aspen, 4th ed., 2016).

[97] On the duty of diligence, see *supra* § 4-5.3.

[98] Board of Professional Ethics & Conduct v. Kelly, 577 N.W.2d 648, 649 (Iowa 1998).

[99] On breach of fiduciary duty in legal malpractice cases, see Part Five of this book, Susan Saab Fortney & Vincent R. Johnson, Legal Malpractice ch. 5-3.

[100] DAVID KEMPSTON, THAT'S WHY THEY CALL IT PRACTICING LAW 1 (2017).

[101] RESTATEMENT (THIRD) OF THE LAW GOVERNING LAWYERS § 16, cmt. b (American Law Institute, 2000).

Although the black letter text of the Model Rules of Professional Conduct seldom speaks in terms of fiduciary duty, outside of the context of client property,[102] the concept quietly permeates the ethical rules. The clearest expression may be found in Comment 17 to Rule 1.8, addressing attorney-client sexual relationships, which says expressly: "The relationship between lawyer and client is a fiduciary one in which the lawyer occupies the highest position of trust and confidence."

Then-Chief Judge Benjamin Cardozo of the New York Court of Appeals famously described the fiduciary duty in this way:

> Many forms of conduct permissible in a workaday world for those acting at arm's length, are forbidden to those bound by fiduciary ties. A trustee is held to something stricter than the morals of the market place. Not honesty alone, but the punctilio of an honor the most sensitive, is then the standard of behavior. As to this there has developed a tradition that is unbending and inveterate.[103]

That "punctilio of an honor" applies to the lawyer as well. As but one example of its "unbending and inveterate" tradition, the lawyer has an ethical duty arising from the fiduciary responsibility to report her own malpractice to the client, at least if the client would not readily recognize that a default in professional judgment had occurred.[104]

The lawyer's fiduciary responsibilities are most likely to be center-stage when confidentiality, loyalty, and safeguarding of client assets are at issue. Breach of fiduciary duty cases typically involve (1) knowing or reckless conflicts of interest, in which the lawyer has manifestly compromised his loyalty to the client by preferring the lawyer's own interests or the interests of another person; (2) deliberate or reckless disclosure or misuse of confidential information, most egregiously for purposes of self-dealing, which betrays the client's trust in the lawyer; or (3) appropriation of the client's assets, that is, stealing from the client, which of course includes diversion of client funds from the trust fund into the lawyer's personal account before the fee has been earned. As a federal appellate court has said, "the attorney owes a fiduciary duty to his client and must serve the client's interests with the utmost loyalty and devotion."[105]

While knowing misappropriation of client assets obviously constitutes intentional misconduct, not every technical violation of the conflict of interest rules or inadvertent disclosure of confidential information rises to the level of a breach of fiduciary duty.[106] Conflict of interest problems can be difficult to manage and hard to perceive, especially when a legal matter involves multiple entities and arises in the context of complex business transactions or litigation. Similarly, confidential information may be disclosed by mistake, through a misdirected communication or a careless statement in a document or conversation.

---

[102] *See infra* § 4-5.6.

[103] Meinhard v. Salmon, 164 N.E. 545, 546 (N.Y. 1928).

[104] RESTATEMENT (THIRD) OF THE LAW GOVERNING LAWYERS § 20, cmt. c (American Law Institute, 2000) ("If the lawyer's conduct of the matter gives the client a substantial malpractice claim against the lawyer, the lawyer must disclose that to the client."). *See generally* Benjamin P. Cooper, *The Lawyer's Duty to Inform His Client of His Own Malpractice*, 61 BAYLOR L. REV. 174 (2009). On the duty to disclose errors for legal malpractice liability, see Part Five of this book, Susan Saab Fortney & Vincent R. Johnson, Legal Malpractice § 5-5.2.

[105] In re Gonzalez, 773 A.2d 1026, 1031 (D.C. 2001).

[106] On conflicts of interest, see *infra* ch. 4-7.

But when deliberate or reckless misconduct is alleged involving the compromise of the lawyer's duty of loyalty to the client or an abuse of the client's confidences, the violation is appropriately characterized as a breach of the lawyer's fiduciary duty. A lawyer who fails to uphold the client's entitlement to independent professional judgment, not merely by a technical infringement of the conflict of interest rules but in a manner that constitutes self-dealing or demonstrates clear bias toward the interests of another, has betrayed a fiduciary relationship. And few things are more harmful to public trust in the legal profession than an attorney's unauthorized revelation of the confidences or secrets entrusted in him by one of his clients.

## § 4-5.6 THE DUTY TO SAFEGUARD CLIENT FUNDS AND PROPERTY

### § 4-5.6(a) Safekeeping and Separating Client Funds and Property

One of the core fiduciary duties of a lawyer is to safeguard the property that the lawyer receives from the client or from other sources but that belongs to the client or to third persons. Property received from a client may include funds to be applied to a transaction, a payment in satisfaction of a judgment or settlement, an advance deposit against attorney's fees, valuable documents to be analyzed, or property of evidentiary value. Under Rule 1.15(a) of the Model Rules of Professional Conduct, "[a] lawyer shall hold property of clients or third persons that is in a lawyer's possession in connection with a representation separate from the lawyer's own property." The lawyer therefore must keep the property in a secure location and segregate those assets from the lawyer's own property.

As Iowa Supreme Court Justice David Harris once remarked,[107] "[i]n generations past it was not uncommon for lawyers to conduct their professional fiscal affairs from, and to hold clients' funds in, an office safe." Today, as directed in Rule 1.15(a), the lawyer is obliged to place funds into a separate trust account maintained in a financial institution, typically according to a mind-numbing set of detailed court rules addressing what financial institutions may be used, interest-bearing accounts, maintenance of records, audits to be performed, etc.

When the funds received from a particular client or third person are nominal in amount or likely to be held only for a very short time-period, no positive net interest earnings payable to the client or third person ordinarily would be achieved by establishing a separate trust account. Because of the small size of the deposit or the short duration it would be held, the financial institution would not separately calculate and pay interest on that deposit. Moreover, the service charges for a separate account established for such a small amount of money likely would exceed any interest earned. Under such circumstances, states typically require the lawyer to deposit the funds into a pooled interest-bearing trust account, the accrued interest of which is paid by the financial institution to a state commission. The state then typically applies the interest earned on pooled accounts to law-related programs on the administration of justice, education about the law, student scholarships, and grants to organizations providing legal services to the poor.[108]

---

[107] Board of Professional Ethics & Conduct v. Bribriesco, 573 N.W.2d 37, 38 (Iowa 1997).

[108] *See* Brown v. Legal Foundation of Washington, 538 U.S. 216, 240 (2003) (holding that a state law requiring client funds "that could not otherwise generate net earnings for the client" to be deposited in an

When a lawyer receives an advance deposit against fees for future legal services, the lawyer is obliged to place those funds into the separate trust account.[109] When the lawyer receives funds from another source, such as settlement or judgment funds, the lawyer must deposit the share that belongs to the client directly into the trust account.

If the lawyer receives other property from the client, such as documents or securities, the lawyer likewise is obliged to ensure that these items are kept secure and eventually are returned to the client. Such property should be identified, cataloged, and held in a secure location that also is physically separated from the lawyer's property. While the office safe may still have residual use for temporarily holding certain valuables and for safekeeping sensitive documents, the lawyer ordinarily should place client securities and other valuable or negotiable documents into a bank safe deposit box that is separately maintained for client property.

As noted, Rule 1.15(a) requires that client funds and those of third persons be deposited into a trust account. Rule 1.15(b) prohibits depositing the lawyer's own funds into the trust account other than for the purpose and in the limited amount necessary to pay bank service charges on that account. Rule 1.15(c) requires that client payments in advance toward legal fees and expenses be placed into the trust account and withdrawn only when fees are earned and expenses are incurred.

One of the shortest paths toward disbarment is for a lawyer to improperly withdraw client funds from a trust account. When a lawyer misappropriates (or, in plain English, *steals*) unearned funds from the trust account, even with the asserted intent of replenishing the account (i.e., taking a "loan" from the trust account), the state disciplinary authority invariably responds with one of the more severe disciplinary sanctions, presumptively disbarment.[110] If commingling of funds was a negligent mistake,[111] the client suffered no financial loss,[112] or perhaps if the lawyer had a colorable future claim to funds taken from the trust fund,[113] then *some* leniency may be appropriate. If, however, the lawyer has improperly converted client funds to the lawyer's own use, revocation of the lawyer's license is a likely consequence.

The common theme running through Model Rule 1.15 is that funds and property belonging to others must be kept scrupulously separate from the lawyer's own funds and property. Not only is this proscription on commingling designed to keep the lawyer

"Interest on Lawyer Trust Account" does not constitute a "regulatory taking," and the state's transfer of those interest earnings on such pooled accounts to a public use does not violate the Fifth Amendment Just Compensation Clause because the client has suffered no pecuniary loss).

[109] *See also supra* § 4-4.4(a).

[110] *See* In re Rhoades, 740 N.W.2d 574, 579 (Minn. 2007) (stating that misappropriation of client funds "is particularly serious misconduct and usually warrants disbarment absent clear and convincing evidence of substantial mitigating factors").

[111] In re Davenport, 794 A.2d 602, 603–04 (D.C. Ct. App. 2002).

[112] Attorney Disciplinary Bd. v. D'Angelo, 710 N.W.2d 226, 236 (Iowa 2006); North Carolina St. Bar v. Talford, 556 S.E.2d 344, 354 (N.C. Ct. App. 2001).

[113] *See, e.g.*, Attorney Disciplinary Bd. v. Thomas, 844 N.W.2d 111, 117 (Iowa 2014) (explaining that license will not be revoked when an attorney has a colorable future claim to the funds, but when the evidence shows the attorney had no such colorable future claim to trust accounts converted for personal use, the attorney's license will be revoked); In re Haar, 698 A.2d 412 (D.C. 1997) (suspending rather than disbarring lawyer for "negligent misappropriation of entrusted funds" where the lawyer had a good faith, mistaken belief he was authorized to take funds); Matter of Helmer, 634 N.E.2d 56, 67 (Ind. 1994) (ruling that a lawyer's acts were "more culpable" because he improperly withdrew client funds to which he had no colorable entitlement).

honest, but it is intended to protect the client's property from inadvertent misappropriation and from being levied against by the lawyer's own creditors.

### § 4-5.6(b) Accounting for and Delivering Client Funds and Property

The lawyer not only must safeguard and segregate client or third person funds and property, but also must be prepared to account for and timely deliver the funds or property to the client or other person entitled to them. Under Model Rule 1.15(d), the lawyer must:

(1) "promptly notify the client or third person" when the lawyer has received the funds or property in which that client or third person has an interest;

(2) "promptly deliver to the client or third person any funds or other property that the client or third person is entitled to receive" (unless the law, a dispute regarding interests in the funds or property,[114] or an agreement with the client justify delaying such delivery); and

(3) "promptly render a full accounting regarding such property," if the client or third person so requests.

In sum, the lawyer is obliged to provide a full accounting to the client of the funds (that is, itemizing the amounts held and any deductions for fees or expenses) and to promptly disburse sums received, for example, from a settlement or an estate to a client or other persons entitled to those funds.

The duty to deliver property to the client includes not only funds and items received, but, absent the client's permission to retain them and assuming the client is current in payment of fees,[115] the original of those documents generated by the lawyer for the client (such as deeds, mortgages, original notices, pleadings, contracts, or wills). Just as with other client property, the client ordinarily is entitled to return of the file or transfer of the file to new counsel.[116]

### § 4-5.6(c) Disputes Regarding Funds or Property Held by the Lawyer

#### *§ 4-5.6(c)(1) Disputes Between Lawyer and Client over Funds or Property Held by the Lawyer*

Under Rule 1.15(e) of the Model Rules of Professional Conduct, if a lawyer in the course of representation comes into possession of property (which includes funds) "in which two or more persons (one of whom may be the lawyer) claim interests, the property shall be kept separate by the lawyer until the dispute is resolved." Disputes involving claims by third persons upon funds or property held by the lawyer are discussed below.[117] With respect to disputes between a lawyer and a client, typically concerning the amount of the lawyer's fee that may be deducted from an advance fee deposit by the client or

[114] *See infra* § 4-5.6(c).

[115] On the retaining lien over a client's file to secure payment of fees, see *infra* § 4-5.6(c)(1).

[116] On duties in returning the client file and questions of ownership of its contents, see CNA, Resolving Disputes Regarding the Client File (which includes a state-by-state appendix), at https://www.cna.com/web/wcm/myconnect/7ccd123f-8775-44a5-979e-3ef3430bfbeb/Resolving_Disputes_Regarding_Client_File.pdf?MOD=AJPERES&CONVERT_TO=url&CACHEID=7ccd123f-8775-44a5-979e-3ef3430bfbeb.

[117] *See infra* § 4-5.6(c)(2).

from a payment received in resolution of a dispute, the rule allows the lawyer to retain the funds in a trust account and thereby maintain a degree of security over those funds. The rule does not permit the lawyer either to take personal possession of the disputed amount or to hold the entire payment hostage to obtain an advantage over the client in resolution of the dispute.

In *In re Jones*,[118] the Louisiana Supreme Court ruled that placing funds into the lawyer's operating account despite knowledge of a fee dispute "amounts to conversion of client funds" and therefore concluded "the appropriate baseline sanction is disbarment." Similarly, in *Attorney Disciplinary Board v. Rhinehart*,[119] the Iowa Supreme Court held that a lawyer violated Rule 1.15 by disbursing settlement funds in the trust account to himself, despite knowing there was a dispute about the amount of attorney's fees to which he was entitled: "In the face of this dispute, rather than keeping the fees in a separate account until the dispute was resolved as is required under the rule, [the lawyer] paid the fees out to himself." The court rejected the lawyer's "attempted rationalization" that he was entitled to pay the funds to himself because the clients had not been willing "to engage in a dialog with him regarding the dispute."

The lawyer may assert a lien against these funds only when the lawyer has a legitimate claim to the payment of fees or expenses from legal services.[120] Moreover, under Model Rule 1.15(e), the lawyer may not withhold the entire amount pending resolution of the dispute, but must distribute that portion of the funds to the client that is not in dispute.

The attorney's retaining and charging liens against funds are subject to significant limitations:

First, funds delivered by the client to the lawyer for a designated purpose, such as to pay a settlement, a judgment, or complete a transaction, are not subject to a lien. Especially given the ethical duty of the lawyer "to take no action that would prejudice or otherwise impede the lawful objectives of his client," "it is unthinkable that a lawyer would satisfy a fee bill out of funds entrusted by a client for the express purpose of settling a lawsuit."[121]

Second, if another creditor should obtain a security interest in or attempt to garnish the same funds, the lawyer's lien is available only to secure those fees and expenses already incurred and thus cannot justify holding on to the funds to secure future anticipated legal fees. The amount secured by the lawyer's retaining lien becomes fixed at the time that a question of priority between the lawyer and another claimant arises.[122]

Third, while the lien may be imposed not only against funds but also against other property, such as the client's file, the lawyer may not withhold the file against an unpaid

[118] 952 So.2d 673, 680–81 (La. 2007).

[119] 827 N.W.2d 169, 182 (Iowa 2013).

[120] On the attorney's retaining lien, see generally Samson Habte, *The Law and Ethics of Attorneys' Retaining Liens*, 29 LAW. MAN. PROF. CONDUCT 449 (2013).

[121] Committee on Professional Ethics & Conduct v. Nadler, 445 N.W.2d 358, 361 (Iowa 1989). *Cf.* State ex rel. Oklahoma Bar Ass'n v. Cummings, 863 P.2d 1164, 1171, 1174–1175 (Okla. 1993) (holding that "[w]hen entrusted with money for a specific purpose [to pay court reporter's fee for a deposition] a lawyer must not allow his claimed fee for services rendered to conflict with his duties as a fiduciary").

[122] In re On-Line Services Ltd., 324 B.R. 342, 346–47 (8th Cir. 2005).

fee bill if to do so would prejudice the client in an ongoing matter, such as when the client has retained new counsel to handle a pending lawsuit.[123]

### *§ 4-5.6(c)(2) Disputes Between Client and Third Person over Funds or Property Held by the Lawyer*

When a lawyer holds funds (or other property) in trust for a client and a third person asserts a claim to those funds, the lawyer must consider both the directions of the client and the legal force of the claim made by the third person.

In many instances, the wishes of the client and the claim of the third person will be in harmony. When, for example, the client in a personal injury action agrees in advance that a particular amount or share of an expected settlement or judgment payment is to be distributed to another, such as a hospital or medical provider or an insurer that provided or covered medical treatment to the client, the lawyer ordinarily will proceed to distribute the funds between the client and the third person or entity in accordance with that understanding.

However, if the client has not consented to a distribution that includes another person, or if the client expressly countermands a prior instruction and orders the lawyer to distribute the full sum to the client, the lawyer then must evaluate any competing claims in light of the substantive law of property rights and security interests. When another person makes a claim upon funds held in trust, the lawyer does not become an impartial arbiter between the parties. The lawyer remains responsible and answerable to the client, absent confirmation by a third person of a properly-presented and secured claim of interest in specific property or funds.

If property or funds being held by the lawyer in trust plainly belong as matter of vested property rights to a third person, such that no genuine dispute exists regarding ownership, the lawyer of course must transfer that property or funds to the rightful owner regardless of the client's contrary preferences. A lawyer may not assist a client in conversion of the property of others. A firm and vested claim of a right by a third person in that property held by a lawyer on behalf of a client would exist, for example, when there has been a formal transfer of title, such as occurs in connection with a real estate or personal property transaction. Likewise, if a third person has placed a lien on funds held by a lawyer and the underlying dispute is resolved in favor of the third person, the lawyer must honor that ripened property interest. As a hopefully less common example, if a client were to present the lawyer with property stolen from another, the lawyer of course must return that property to the rightful owner.[124]

Similarly, if a check is received by the lawyer that is made out jointly to the client and a third person, the lawyer may negotiate that check (by depositing it into the trust account) only with the legitimate endorsement of both. Because the joint-payee nature of the check confirms that both have common property interests in the funds, the lawyer must respond to the compatible directions of both the client and the third person in distributing them. If a dispute arises as to what portion of the jointly-owned funds should be distributed to which person, Rule 1.15(e) directs the lawyer to hold the funds separate until the dispute is resolved. Pending that resolution, the rule says "[t]he lawyer shall

---

[123] *See supra* § 4-3.6(d).

[124] *See also infra* § 4-9.7(d).

promptly distribute all portions of the property as to which the interests are not in dispute."

The mere fact that a third person wishes to be paid from funds held by a lawyer for a client, even if the third person asserts a cognizable obligation by the client, does not necessarily rise to the level of a plausible claim of an actual interest in those particular funds or property. For example, in *Gianetti v. Gerardi,*[125] a Connecticut court held, that, after receiving funds from the dog owner's insurance carrier to settle the personal injury lawsuit for a child's dog-bite, the child's lawyer had no duty to distribute any portion of the funds to the doctor who had provided medical services to the child. Where there was no judgment concerning disposition of the funds, no perfected lien against the funds, and the parties had not reached an agreement on payment of those funds to the doctor, the lawyer properly delivered the insurance proceeds to the client.

When the lawyer is holding funds given to the lawyer by the client or received by the lawyer in a payment designated for the client, and a third person asserts that the client is indebted to that person and that the debt should be satisfied from those specific funds held by the lawyer, the law of secured transactions must be consulted to determine whether a genuine dispute exists as to a specific interest in the funds.[126] A third person who is a general creditor of the client has no claim of right to possession of any particular funds. Even if the client has agreed to transfer an anticipated payment to a third person, that promise alone does not create a security interest in the funds on behalf of the third person that permits the lawyer to disregard a client's subsequent directive to distribute those funds differently.

In other words, that the client is contractually obligated to make a payment to another, and even has agreed to make that payment from funds presently or soon to be held by a lawyer, does not by itself create a direct property interest by that other person in those funds. While the failure to apply the funds as so promised may constitute a breach of contract, the client's insistence upon taking possession of funds not subject to a lien or other property interest is not a conversion.[127] As Professors Geoffrey Hazard and William Hodes and attorney Peter Jarvis conclude, "[o]nly when there is such a perfected interest might it be said that failure to recognize the third party's interest is a species of fraud upon creditors or fraud upon the rendering court."[128]

If a third person has perfected a security interest in the funds received by the lawyer, the lawyer may not release the claimed portion of those funds to the client and thereby disregard the obstacle imposed by law. For example, as presented in Comment 4 to Rule 1.15, if a client's creditor has obtained a lien on funds recovered in a personal injury action, and if "the third-party claim is not frivolous under applicable law, the lawyer must refuse to surrender the property to the client until the claims are

---

[125] 44 A.3d 911, 918–19 (Ct. Super. Ct. 2010).

[126] *See* Attorney Grievance Com'n v. Levin, 69 A.3d 451, 460–061 (Md. Ct. App. 2013) (holding a lawyer violated Rule 1.15(e) by distributing settlement funds to a client as to which another party had obtained a writ of garnishment, because the lawyer had been obliged to keep the funds separate until any dispute on amount owed was resolved).

[127] RESTATEMENT (THIRD) OF THE LAW GOVERNING LAWYERS § 45, cmt. d (American Law Institute 2000) ("If a lawyer holds property belonging to one person and a second person has a contractual or similar claim against that person but does not claim to own the property or have a security interest on it, the lawyer is free to deliver the property to the person to whom it belongs").

[128] 1 GEOFFREY C. HAZARD, JR., W. WILLIAM HODES & PETER R. JARVIS, THE LAW OF LAWYERING § 20.06 (Aspen, 4th ed., 2016).

resolved."[129] For example, under typical state law, an employer or insurance company that paid workers' compensation benefits to an injured employee, a hospital that furnished medical care or other services to an injured person, and a state agency that paid for medical care to a person under a medical assistance program may obtain a lien against any recovery obtained by the injured person against third parties. If such a lien is perfected by proper notice, the lawyer must retain those funds and not distribute them to the client (or the third person or entity) until any underlying dispute is resolved.

In addition, if the lawyer is party to an advance agreement concerning how funds are to be distributed, and the client has so consented, thus placing the lawyer in the role as an escrow agent, then the lawyer must fulfill those terms.

[129] *See also* RONALD D. ROTUNDA & JOHN S. DZIENKOWSKI, PROFESSIONAL RESPONSIBILITY: A STUDENT'S GUIDE § 1.15–1(e) (American Bar Ass'n, 2013–2014).

# Chapter 4-6

# DUTIES TO PROTECT CONFIDENTIALITY OF CLIENT INFORMATION

**By Gregory C. Sisk**

*Table of Sections*


§ 4-6.1 The Fundamental Principle of Confidentiality
§ 4-6.2 Confidentiality: Scope and Pervasive Principles in the Rules
§ 4-6.3 The Attorney-Client Privilege
§ 4-6.4 Attorney Work Product
§ 4-6.5 Lawyer's Duty to Safeguard Confidential Information
§ 4-6.6 Exceptions to Confidentiality Under Rule 1.6


## § 4-6.1 THE FUNDAMENTAL PRINCIPLE OF CONFIDENTIALITY

When teaching law students in the professional responsibility class each year, the author of this part of the hornbook emphasizes that the first duty of the lawyer is to protect the client's confidences. Perhaps no other element of the attorney-client relationship is as fundamental as the sacred obligation of the lawyer to keep the confidences of her client. Indeed, in a multi-year study of 24,000 attorneys conducted by the Institute for the Advancement of the Legal System, lawyers listed keeping information confidential as the first foundational skill in the professionalism category.[1]

As attorneys, we serve as agents and advocates seeking to advance the legal objectives of our clients, but we also serve as confidants in whom our clients may repose trust. Because our clients are guaranteed confidentiality, they are willing to share their most private thoughts and relate the most sensitive and embarrassing information, safe in the knowledge that what has been shared will be safeguarded and not be used against them by the lawyer.[2]

The confidential nature of the attorney-client relationship is the foundation for everything that the lawyer does. If the lawyer is to effectively and fairly represent the client—rich or poor, confident or vulnerable, well-educated or working class, sophisticated in legal affairs or unfamiliar with the legal system—the lawyer must be able to instill trust. Confidentiality is the cornerstone of that trust.

If the lawyer is to be able to counsel clients to do the right thing, legally and morally, the lawyer must have full access to information from the client. The free flow of

1 Institute for the Advancement of the American Legal System, Foundations for Practice, at http://iaals.du.edu/foundations/reports/whole-lawyer-and-character-quotient/analysis-results-survey-category.

2 Matter of Priest v. Hennessy, 409 N.E.2d 983, 985 (N.Y. 1980).

information depends on the assurance of confidentiality.[3] Thus, the traditional ethical directive to the lawyer to maintain the client's confidences and the additional security given to attorney-client communications through the testimonial/evidentiary attorney-client privilege[4] fortify the vital professional purposes of building a strong attorney-client relationship and ensuring that the lawyer obtains the information necessary to serve the client well.

Confidentiality is also a matter of venerable moral principle, long established in the moral, philosophical, and theological, as well as legal, traditions of the Western world. Placing the matter in moral and religious context, Professors Abbe Smith and William Montross observe:

> Confidentiality is also an essential component of the virtue of fidelity. To serve a client faithfully, one must provide a refuge for the client by steadfastly maintaining his or her confidences and secrets, regardless of the circumstances. Of course, the centrality of confidentiality in ministering to another in need has roots in Judeo-Christian teachings.[5]

In the Jewish tradition, the *Torah* admonishes each person not to be a "talebearer" among the community.[6] The great rabbi, Maimonides, who codified the Jewish law during the twelfth-century, further elucidated the moral grievance of sharing confidential communications, even when the account is truthful: "Who is a tale-bearer? One who carries reports and goes from one person to another and says, 'so-and-so said this' or 'such-and-such have I heard about so-and-so.' Even if he tells the truth, [the tale-bearer] destroys the world."[7]

Under Jewish teaching, the principle of confidentiality may be set aside only when a commandment of greater importance intervenes, such as the imperative duty to uphold the "absolute spiritual value of life."[8] Indeed, under extreme circumstances, a Jewish lawyer might argue that an unduly strict confidentiality rule that precluded disclosure of information necessary to prevent serious harm to others would constitute an impermissible burden on the free exercise of religion "by creating an unnecessary conflict between his professional obligations and his religious beliefs."[9]

In the Christian tradition, confidentiality very early was given a prominent place among the special responsibilities of those called to the professions. Considering the clergy, which along with the law became one of the original professions, many readers

---

[3] *But see* William H. Simon, *Attorney-Client Confidentiality: A Critical Analysis*, 30 GEO. J. LEGAL ETHICS 447, 447 (2017) (contending it is "unlikely that the confidentiality norms induce greater client disclosure").

[4] On the attorney-client privilege, see *infra* § 4-6.3.

[5] Abbe Smith and William Montross, *The Calling of Criminal Defense*, 50 MERCER L. REV. 443, 525–26 (1999).

[6] LEVITICUS 19:16 ("Thou shalt not go up and down as a talebearer among thy people.").

[7] *Hilkhot De'ot* ch. 7:2, in THE BOOK OF KNOWLEDGE: FROM THE MISHNAH TORAH OF MAIMONIDES 14 (H.M. Russell & Rabbi J. Weinberg trans., 1981).

[8] Arthur Gross Schaefer & Peter S. Levi, *Resolving the Conflict Between the Ethical Values of Confidentiality and Saving a Life: A Jewish View*, 29 LOY. L.A. L. REV. 1761, 1767 (1996); *see also* Russell G. Pearce, *To Save a Life: Why a Rabbi and a Jewish Lawyer Must Disclose a Client Confidence*, 29 LOY. L.A. L. REV. 1771, 1776–79 (1996). Indeed, the second half of the same verse from the Torah that forbids being a talebearer also says: "[N]either shalt thou stand idly by the blood of thy neighbor: I am the Lord." LEVITICUS 19:16.

[9] Alex Kozinski & Leslie A. Hakala, *Keeping Secrets: Religious Duty vs. Professional Obligation*, 38 WASHBURN L.J. 747, 748 (1999).

will be familiar with the "seal of confession," by which a priest in the Catholic, Eastern Orthodox, or Anglican traditions is barred from revealing a sacramental confession under any circumstances. Betrayal by a priest of the sanctity of communications during the Sacrament of Reconciliation remains one of the few transgressions that results in automatic excommunication from the Catholic Church.[10] Catholic teaching also affirms the weight of confidentiality in other professional settings:

> *Professional secrets*—for example, those of political office holders, soldiers, physicians, and lawyers—or confidential information given under the seal of secrecy must be kept, save in exceptional cases where keeping the secret is bound to cause very grave harm to the one who confided it, to the one who received it or to a third party, and where the very grave harm can be avoided only by divulging the truth. Even if not confided under the seal of secrecy, private information prejudicial to another is not to be divulged without a grave and proportionate reason.[11]

In addition to personal morality and religious principle, Professors Geoffrey Hazard and Williams Hodes and attorney Peter Jarvis establish that confidentiality has a solid moral base in the nature of a free society. Confidentiality, they explain, "creates a zone of privacy that cannot be breached by a too-inquisitive government, and thus enhances the autonomy and individual liberty of citizens."[12] Professor Maura Strassberg adds that "[t]he promise of confidentiality further enhances individual autonomy by permitting effective use of legal expertise in determining a lawful means to individual ends."[13]

The primordial moral canon of confidentiality has set itself deep into the foundational bedrock of our culture. While the law does not extend formal protection to every relationship, we nonetheless accept as a basic expectation that we ought not freely share the dreams or regrets that our family members and friends share with us in private. Even when an individual has participated in a criminal conspiracy, and thus obviously has no moral or legal expectation that the wrongful communications will be held secure (and instead has a moral duty to reveal the planned misconduct), a social stigma tends to attach to the person who is viewed as a "snitch."

How much more so, then, do we regard with deserved opprobrium those such as lawyers and physicians who have a professional obligation to protect confidential information and yet violate that trust by trading upon valuable secrets for private gain or by sharing embarrassing stories about others for personal amusement. Indeed, the lawyer who appropriates the confidential information of the client toward improper ends

---

[10] *See* CODEX IURIS CANONICI (Code of Canon Law) c.1398 (Canon Law Society of America trans., 1983). On the seal of confession, see generally Anthony Cardinal Bevilacqua, *Confidentiality Obligation of Clergy from the Perspective of Roman Catholic Priests*, 29 LOY. L.A. L. REV. 1733 (1996).

[11] CATECHISM OF THE CATHOLIC CHURCH ¶ 2491 (2d ed. 1997).

[12] 1 GEOFFREY C. HAZARD, JR., W. WILLIAM HODES & PETER R. JARVIS, THE LAW OF LAWYERING § 10.02 (Aspen, 4th ed., 2016); *see also* SISSELA BOK: ON THE ETHICS OF CONCEALMENT AND REVELATION 119–21 (Pantheon Books 1982) (stating that the "first and fundamental premise" for confidentiality is "that of individual autonomy over personal information," thus respecting individuals and maintaining privacy); ELIZABETH NEIL, RITES OF PRIVACY AND THE PRIVACY TRADE 19 (Mcgill-Queen's U. Press, 2001) (describing "privacy and autonomy of thought" as the "necessary components of psychological self-identity").

[13] Maura Strassberg, *Taking Ethics Seriously: Beyond Positivist Jurisprudence in Legal Ethics*, 80 IOWA L. REV. 901, 947 (1995).

has not only violated the rules of professional conduct but also may be civilly liable for breach of fiduciary duty.[14]

For these professional and moral reasons, the legal profession always has jealously guarded the sacred principle of confidentiality. Yet confidentiality has never been absolute. When the client abuses the attorney-client relationship by seeking legal advice for the purpose of defrauding another or violating the law, for example, the privilege otherwise attaching to client communications is lost and the lawyer may be required to reveal those discussions by court order or subpoena (whether or not the lawyer is permitted to voluntarily disclose that information).[15] In addition, simple fairness or imperative reasons of public interest may justify disclosure of client information as necessary, for example, so that a lawyer may defend herself against a charge of wrongdoing[16] or may take action to prevent a client from causing serious harm to another.[17]

While a vigorous debate continues within the legal profession as to exactly which exigent circumstances justify disclosure of client confidences and how the balance between public interest and fiduciary trust should be struck, nearly everyone agrees that exceptions to confidentiality should be few in number and narrow in application. Unless carefully calibrated to address a serious and otherwise irreparable harm, a proviso that loosens the obligation of confidence might cause far more harm to the attorney-client relationship than could be justified by any projected public benefit resulting from disclosure.

In general, allowing the free flow of information between a lawyer and a client, protected by confidence, is more likely to produce socially-desirable benefits than would be achieved by placing the lawyer in a whistle-blowing role against his own client. As Supreme Court Justice Byron White once observed: "As a practical matter, if the client knows that damaging information could more readily be obtained from the attorney following disclosure than from himself in the absence of disclosure, the client would be reluctant to confide in his lawyer and it would be difficult to obtain fully informed legal advice."[18] Likewise, Lawrence Fox reminds us that, if the client learns that any discussion will not be held confidential, "the flow of information is cut off and the lawyer loses the opportunity to remonstrate with the client, one of the more valuable benefits confidentiality confers on the profession."[19] In this regard, lawyers also must be encouraged to think beyond legal technicalities and must be able to elicit conversations with clients about other aspects that are strongly connected to the legal core and to do so with the secure knowledge that the exchange is protected by that powerful species of confidentiality grounded in the attorney-client privilege.[20]

---

[14] On the lawyer-client relationship as fiduciary in nature, see *supra* § 4-5.5.

[15] On the inapplicability of the attorney-client privilege when legal services are sought in furtherance of a crime, see *infra* § 4-6.3(c)(1).

[16] *See infra* §§ 4-6.3(c)(3), 4-6.6(f).

[17] *See infra* § 4-6.6(c) to (d).

[18] Fisher v. United States, 425 U.S. 391, 403 (1976).

[19] Lawrence J. Fox, *It's All in the Atmosphere*, 62 FORDHAM L. REV. 1447, 1448 (1994). *But see* Norman W. Spaulding, *Compliance, Creative Deviance, and Resistance to Law: A Theory of the Attorney-Client Privilege*, 2013 J. PROF'L LAW. 135, 135, 169 (criticizing the modern justification of attorney-client confidentiality as promoting law compliance and arguing that confidentiality also allows lawyers to counsel clients to engage in "creative deviance" and "resistance" to the law).

[20] *See infra* § 4-6.3(b)(1), (3).

When clients are able to share information in a confidential setting, the lawyer is more likely to learn about unwise actions taken in the past or contemplated for the future and thus be able to advise the client to take the morally appropriate, as well as legally justified, course.[21] On what are probably thousands of occasions each day in this country, wise legal advisors counsel their clients to avoid going down a questionable path, to put right past wrongs, to tell the truth. Because those communications are confidential, we never hear about most of them. Yet if we too readily subordinate the principle of confidentiality and too frequently allow or even require lawyers to reveal what their clients tell them or what the lawyers have learned through the representation, the flow of information will dry up, and so then will the opportunity for lawyers to uphold their professional role as counselors.

## § 4-6.2 CONFIDENTIALITY: SCOPE AND PERVASIVE PRINCIPLES IN THE RULES

Rule 1.6(a) of the Model Rules of Professional Conduct articulates the general rule that the lawyer must safeguard confidential information by stating a prohibition on disclosure of such information without consent or other authorization and by defining what constitutes confidential information that receives the protection. As Professor Peter Rofes well-summarizes, the scope of confidential information under the rule is quite broad:

> Rule 1.6(a) makes clear that . . . lawyers have an obligation to refrain from revealing *all* "information relating to representation of a client" that their clients have not consented to have revealed. The comments and comparison sections to Rule 1.6 underscore the remarkable breadth of the confidentiality notion, explicitly noting, among other things, that the confidentiality label attaches irrespective of the source of the information, irrespective of whether the client has requested the lawyer to respect the privacy of the information, and irrespective of whether dissemination of the information would cause harm to the client.[22]

As Comment 3 to Rule 1.6 emphasizes, "[t]he confidentiality rule, for example, applies not only to matters communicated in confidence by the client but also to all information relating to the representation, whatever its source."[23] The duty to protect confidential information is perpetual, as Comment 20 confirms, continuing after the attorney-client relationship has ended. Indeed, Rule 1.9(c)(1) generally prohibits disclosure or use of confidential information to the disadvantage of a former client.[24]

In contrast with Disciplinary Rule 4–101(A) of the former Model Code of Professional Responsibility,[25] information is classified as confidential under Rule 1.6(a) whether or not the client has requested that the information be kept secret, whether or not the lawyer in her own judgment might regard the information as embarrassing or

---

21 On the lawyer's duty to provide candid advice to the client, see *supra* § 4-5.2(b).

22 Peter K. Rofes, *Another Misunderstood Relation: Confidentiality and the Duty to Report*, 14 GEO. J. LEGAL ETHICS 621, 627–28 (2001).

23 On the attorney-client privilege protecting communications, see *infra* § 4-6.3.

24 *See infra* § 4-7.5(e).

25 MODEL CODE OF PROF'L RESPONSIBILITY, Disciplinary Rule 4–101 (American Bar Ass'n, 1980) (defining non-privileged "secrets" as "other information gained in the professional relationship that the client has requested be held inviolate or the disclosure of which would be embarrassing or would be likely to be detrimental to the client").

detrimental to the client, and whether or not the information was gained during the course of (as opposed to before or after) the attorney-client relationship. In setting the parameters of confidentiality, then, Rule 1.6(a) establishes a more forceful presumption in favor of confidentiality than did the former Disciplinary Rule 4–101(A), which extended protection only to information that the client requested be "held inviolate" or that would be "embarrassing" or "likely to be detrimental" if revealed.[26] Under Rule 1.6(a), if the information relates to the representation, which covers everything that the lawyer learns about the client that has even a tangential connection to the objectives of the representation, then the lawyer is obliged to guarantee its protection.[27]

Under Rule 1.6(a), the lawyer is permitted to disclose confidential information only if the client gives informed consent, the disclosure is "impliedly authorized in order to carry out the representation," or the disclosure is permitted by Rule 1.6(b). (The exceptions to confidentiality are discussed separately below.[28])

The primary and typical basis for disclosure of confidential information is permission of the client, either directly or impliedly. Before a client is asked to permit disclosure of information, the attorney should make certain that the client has granted informed consent. As directed by Rule 1.0(e), the client must be afforded "adequate information and explanation about the material risks of and reasonably available alternatives to the proposed course of conduct." When disclosure appears innocuous and the client well-understands the nature of the information and effect of revelation, little explanation may be required. When the information is of greater value or the consequences of its release are likely to be more significant, the explanation to be given by the lawyer appropriately will be more extensive.

In addition, unless the client instructs otherwise or special circumstances indicate to the contrary, the client will be presumed to have authorized those disclosures of information that are necessary for the lawyer in pursuing the objectives of the representation. As Comment 5 to Rule 1.6 explains, "a lawyer may be impliedly authorized to admit a fact that cannot properly be disputed or to make a disclosure that facilitates a satisfactory conclusion to a matter." The *Restatement of the Law Governing Lawyers* similarly speaks of such impliedly authorized disclosures as those that the lawyer "reasonably believes" will "advance the interests of the client in the representation."[29] Still, the lawyer should remain in regular communication with the client[30] so as not to overstep the bounds here.

Unless the client has indicated that only designated lawyers within a law firm may have access to information, a lawyer also is impliedly authorized to share client confidential information with other persons in the law firm as necessary to perform the

---

[26] On the contrast between Disciplinary rule 4–101 and Rule 1.6(a), see generally 1 GEOFFREY C. HAZARD, JR., W. WILLIAM HODES & PETER R. JARVIS, THE LAW OF LAWYERING § 10.16 (Aspen, 4th ed., 2016).

[27] On the lawyer's duty to take appropriate measures to protect confidential information, see *infra* § 4-6.4.

[28] *See infra* § 4-6.6(c) to (g).

[29] RESTATEMENT (THIRD) OF THE LAW GOVERNING LAWYERS § 61 (American Law Institute, 2000).

[30] On the duty to keep the client informed, see *supra* § 4-5.4.

representation and to ensure that the firm complies with other obligations, such as maintaining a process to check for potential conflicts of interest.[31]

Rule 1.6 of the Model Rules of Professional Conduct establishes the foundational expectation that the lawyer protect client confidences, defines the broad scope of confidentiality, and sets forth several permissive provisions for lawyer disclosure of confidential information. The fundamental principle of confidentiality permeates the application of the rest of the rules as well.

Among the other rules that also implicate confidentiality most directly are the following:

- Rule 1.9(c) prohibits the lawyer from using confidential information to the disadvantage of a former client or revealing information relating to the representation of a former client.[32]
- Rule 1.13(c) permits the lawyer for an organization client to reveal confidential information in the extreme situation where a person within the organization has engaged in unlawful behavior, which the highest authority within the organization has failed to address, and the lawyer reasonably believes that such disclosure is necessary to prevent substantial injury to the organization.[33]
- Rule 3.3 requires the lawyer to take reasonable remedial measures, including if necessary disclosure of information otherwise protected by Rule 1.6, when the lawyer comes to know that material evidence presented to a tribunal was false or that a person has engaged or will engage in criminal or fraudulent conduct with respect to the adjudicatory proceeding.[34]
- Rule 3.4(a) prohibits a lawyer from unlawfully obstructing another party's access to evidence or unlawfully altering, destroying, or concealing potential evidence, which in turn requires consideration of the bounds of confidentiality as it relates to the lawyer's knowledge about such evidence and its location.[35]
- Rule 4.1(b) forbids a lawyer from knowingly "fail[ing] to disclose a material fact to a third person when disclosure is necessary to avoid assisting a criminal or fraudulent act by a client," when permitted by Rule 1.6.[36]
- Rule 4.2, which limits the authority of a lawyer to make an *ex parte* contact with a person represented by another lawyer, is accompanied by Comment 7 which emphasizes that while the rule permits *ex parte* contact with former constituents of an entity, "[i]n communicating with a current or former constituent of an organization, a lawyer must not use methods of obtaining evidence that violate the legal rights of the organization," that is, privileged or other protected information.[37]

---

31 Indeed, using client information in a manner that doesn't endanger the privilege or prejudice the client to conduct a conflicts check is now an exception to the confidentiality rule under the Model Rules of Professional Conduct. *See infra* § 4-6.6(h).

32 *See infra* § 4-7.5(e).

33 *See infra* § 4-8.6(d).

34 *See infra* § 4-9.8.

35 *See infra* §§ 4-9.6 to 4-9.8.

36 *See infra* §§ 4-6.6(d), 4-11.2(c).

37 *See infra* § 4-8.4.

- Rule 4.4(a) directs the lawyer not to use "methods of obtaining evidence that violate the legal rights of" a third person, which accompanying Comment 1 confirms includes "unwarranted intrusions into privileged relationships, such as the client-lawyer relationship" and which thus prohibits the lawyer from attempting to obtain from employees or agents of an entity any information that is protected by the attorney-client privilege or work-product doctrine.[38]
- Rule 5.3 requires lawyers to properly manage and supervise nonlawyer assistants by taking reasonable measures to uphold professional obligations, which Comment 2 emphasizes includes "the obligation not to disclose information relating to the representation of the client."[39]
- Rules 8.1(b)[40] and 8.3(c)[41] confirm that the lawyer's responsibility to cooperate with admissions or disciplinary authorities and to report the professional misconduct of another lawyer or judge does not supersede the obligation to protect client confidences.

## § 4-6.3 THE ATTORNEY-CLIENT PRIVILEGE

### § 4-6.3(a) The Special Evidentiary Immunity Given to Attorney-Client Communications

The attorney-client privilege attaches to a special subset of confidential information, consisting of communications between the lawyer and the client that are entitled to be held immune from legal process. While the lawyer generally is obliged to protect all information relating to the representation and not voluntarily disclose such information,[42] the lawyer nonetheless is required to respond to a lawful subpoena or court order that seeks information outside the parameters of a legally-recognized privilege.[43] By sharp contrast, the lawyer should not be forced to divulge the substance of communications falling within a privilege and indeed must take appropriate steps to assert and competently advance a privilege in response to any request.[44] Thus, the contents of direct communications between an attorney and a client constitute a specially-protected category of confidential information.

The attorney-client privilege "is one of the oldest recognized privileges for confidential communications."[45] To protect the honor of the legal advisor in providing confidential counsel to a client, the attorney-client privilege as a matter of the law of evidence arose in the English common law in the sixteenth and seventeenth centuries.[46] When the United States became an independent nation, early case law confirms that the

---

[38] *See infra* § 4-9.6(d).

[39] *See infra* § 4-12.4.

[40] *See infra* § 4-13.1(e).

[41] *See infra* § 4-13.1(b).

[42] *See supra* § 4-6.2.

[43] On the lawyer's duty to disclose information when required by law, see *infra* § 4-6.6(g).

[44] On the lawyer's duty to act competently to protect confidential information, see *infra* § 4-6.5.

[45] Swidler & Berlin v. United States, 524 U.S. 399, 403 (1998).

[46] PAUL R. RICE, ATTORNEY-CLIENT PRIVILEGE IN THE UNITED STATES § 1.3 (Thomson-West, updated 2012); Geoffrey C. Hazard, Jr., *An Historical Perspective on the Attorney-Client Privilege*, 66 CAL. L. REV. 1061, 1070 (1978); James A. Gardner, *A Re-Evaluation of the Attorney-Client Privilege*, 8 VILL. L. REV. 279, 289 (1963).

"privilege transferred relatively unchanged to the new republic."[47] In the present-day, the privilege remains one of the most universally-recognized, frequently-asserted, and carefully protected means of preserving the trust between a lawyer and a client, whether the client be a natural person or an organization.[48]

In the modern world, with the expansion of the law, the occasions for seeking legal advice and assistance have increased. Moreover, as legal directives overlap with non-legal considerations, the lawyer and client should be free to address a problem in a creative and integrated manner, with the privilege granting a unified protection to the deliberations. As Professor Katherine Kruse writes about a client-centered approach to representation, "the focus on understanding clients' objectives more broadly and holistically tends to break down the barriers between legal and non-legal strategies for addressing clients' problems."[49]

Importantly, if we wish to encourage lawyers to engage in moral deliberation with their clients,[50] lawyers must be able to assure clients that this moral exchange is confidential, a protection secured by the attorney-client privilege. If we want lawyers to be morally and ethically grounded, then we must assure lawyers that their introduction of social, political, business, and economic factors, as well as moral principles, into a discussion with legal clients will not have the perverse effect of removing the protection of the privilege.

An attorney-client privilege that adjusts dynamically to the changing scope of the practice of law and that facilitates a robust moral dialogue between the attorney and the client best serves the public interest in obedience to the law and social justice.[51]

### § 4-6.3(b) The Elements of the Attorney-Client Privilege

The traditional formulation of the attorney-client privilege contained eight elements:

> (1) Where legal advice of any kind is sought (2) from a professional legal adviser in his capacity as such, (3) the communications relating to that purpose, (4) made in confidence (5) by the client, (6) are at his insistence permanently protected (7) from disclosure by himself or by the legal adviser, (8) except the protection be waived.[52]

While satisfaction of all eight elements traditionally was necessary to invoke the privilege, these elements are somewhat overlapping and partially redundant.[53] Moreover, the law has evolved to modify some of the elements, for example, including prospective as well as actual clients within the protection[54] and extending coverage not

---

[47] RICE, *supra*, § 1.12.

[48] On the attorney-client privilege for corporations and other organizations, see *infra* § 4-8.3.

[49] Katherine R. Kruse, *Beyond Cardboard Clients in Legal Ethics*, 23 GEO. J. LEGAL ETHICS 103, 128 (2010).

[50] On counseling, including moral factors, see *supra* § 4-5.2.

[51] *See infra* § 4-6.3(b)(1).

[52] 8 JOHN H. WIGMORE, EVIDENCE § 2290 (McNaughton rev. 1961).

[53] The *Restatement of the Law Governing Lawyers* describes the attorney-client privilege as having four elements: "(1) a communication (2) made between privileged persons (3) in confidence (4) for the purpose of obtaining or providing legal assistance for the client." RESTATEMENT (THIRD) OF THE LAW GOVERNING LAWYERS § 68 (American Law Institute, 2000).

[54] *See infra* § 4-6.3(b)(2).

only to communications by a client to a lawyer but also the lawyer's communications to the client.[55]

### *§ 4-6.3(b)(1) Seeking Legal Advice*

The client's pursuit of legal advice triggers the privilege. When a person contacts a lawyer with the purpose of obtaining legal counsel, the communications that ensue are privileged.

By contrast, when a person contacts a lawyer for extra-legal purposes or communicates with a lawyer for reasons other than seeking legal advice to a legitimate end, the privilege does not attach or may be lost. Conversations with people who happen to be lawyers do not come under the shield of confidentiality unless those conversations are a prelude to or part and parcel of a legal representation. Thus, chewing the fat with a friend or fishing buddy or chatting with a business acquaintance or neighbor will not be afforded the privilege, unless that person also is seeking the lawyer's legal advice. Moreover, if rather than seeking legitimate legal advice, the client intends to pervert the legal representation toward an illicit end, the attorney-client privilege is forfeited. The crime-fraud exception to the privilege is discussed separately below.[56]

Notwithstanding these exceptions and limitations, when a client or prospective client talks with a lawyer, the substance of those communications presumptively are privileged. After all, the types of matters that today come within the scope of legal representation may be very broad indeed, because the expansion of legal standards and the growth of government regulation has left very few aspects of human activity and relationships untouched by law. Even persons not contemplating litigation, considering a transaction, or seeking preparation of a legal document nonetheless may seek the advice of a lawyer about the legal implications of various dimensions of human behavior.

As the practice of law emerged in England as one of the original professions,[57] lawyers acted primarily as barristers in court, advocating on behalf of their clients at trials before judges and juries.[58] Early in the history of the profession, attorneys and solicitors also became valued for their skills in drafting elemental legal documents such as pleadings, deeds, wills, and trusts.[59] Beginning in the middle of the nineteenth century, lawyers in America moved in greater numbers beyond the courtroom to prosper as commercial lawyers in the post-Civil War economic boom. As corporate businesses flourished, lawyers became business as well as legal advisors and drafted specialized documents such as corporate charters, financial agreements, and tax avoidance plans.[60]

---

[55] *See infra* § 4-6.3(b)(5.

[56] *See infra* § 4-6.3(c)(1).

[57] On the law as a profession and vocation, see generally Neil W. Hamilton, *The Future of Callings—An Interdisciplinary Summit on the Public Obligations of Professionals into the Next Millennium*, 25 WM. MITCHELL L. REV. 45 (1999). For a general discussion of what it means to say that the law is a "profession," see RONALD D. ROTUNDA & JOHN S. DZIENKOWSKI, PROFESSIONAL RESPONSIBILITY: A STUDENT'S GUIDE § 1–6 (American Bar Ass'n, 2013–2014).

[58] GEOFFREY C. HAZARD, JR. & DEBORAH L. RHODE, THE LEGAL PROFESSION: RESPONSIBILITY AND REGULATION 21 (Foundation Press, 3d ed. 1994); Charles L. Brieant, *Is It the End of the Legal World as We Know It?*, 20 PACE L. REV. 21, 23 (1999).

[59] *Id.*

[60] LAWRENCE FRIEDMAN, A HISTORY OF AMERICAN LAW 633–35 (Touchstone Books, 2d ed. 1985); Brieant, *supra*, 20 PACE L. REV. at 23.

In the latter part of the twentieth century, as the world of human activity became more complex, so also did the law.[61] By the turn of the century, for a growing number of Americans, it had become "extremely difficult to navigate through the legal web that surrounds their lives."[62] In turn, the attorney's practice has expanded from trying cases in a courtroom to providing general advice to clients about the legal risks and advantages of proposed projects, contemplated actions, and planned relationships. As the law has grown to pervade nearly every nook and cranny of human society, the role of lawyers has magnified within the business and economic world, with attorneys structuring deals, negotiating contracts, advising on regulatory compliance, and consulting on environmental matters. Beyond the fast-changing economic situation, social and cultural revolutions have required lawyers to play expanding roles and offer additional or even interprofessional services in fields like family and elder law that directly affect personal well-being, health, values, and intimate relationships.

As a result of extraordinary economic and social changes and the complementary complexities in the law, the range of services offered by today's lawyers to their clients is far broader and more diverse than at any previous time in the history of the legal profession. Although the place and responsibility of the lawyer were once "fairly well defined,"[63] the lawyer's professional role can no longer be delineated with precision. The line between legal and non-legal matters can no longer be easily drawn. As one commentator has observed, in years past, "one could distinguish with relative ease between 'legal' matters on which the lawyer focused and 'business' matters that were the province of the client."[64] The line between legal and non-legal subjects has become increasingly blurred, and a lawyer is "almost as likely to be focusing on economic, scientific, financial, or political questions as on strictly legal issues."[65]

At the same time that economic and social upheavals have provoked an expansion of the law and changes in the scope of legal practice, the legal profession has been engaged in a concerted effort, led by both members of the practicing bar and legal academics, to rediscover the traditional role of the lawyer as moral counselor.[66] Rule 2.1 of the Model Rules of Professional Conduct encourages lawyers to "refer not only to the law but to other considerations such as moral, economic, social and political factors, that may be relevant to the client's situation." Professional responsibility scholars and bar association leaders today are emphasizing, confirming, and enhancing the longstanding and commendable integration of legal directives with moral principles when lawyers counsel clients.

Appreciating the attorney-client privilege as dynamic in nature requires that we open our eyes to the changes in the services provided by lawyers as part of legal

---

[61] James W. Jones, *The Challenge of Change: The Practice of Law in the Year 2000*, 41 VAND. L. REV. 683, 684–85 (1988).

[62] Soha F. Turfler, Note, *A Model Definition of the Practice of Law: If Not Now, When? An Alternative Approach to Defining the Practice of Law*, 61 WASH. & LEE L. REV. 1903, 1904 (2004) ("[W]e are all subject in our social and working lives, to a body of legal rules and principles that is so vast, diverse, and complicated that no one can understand their full applicability and impact." (citing RICHARD SUSSKIND, THE FUTURE OF LAW: FACING THE CHALLENGES OF INFORMATION TECHNOLOGY 13 (Oxford U. Press, 1996))).

[63] *See* James W. Jones, *The Challenge of Change: The Practice of Law in the Year 2000*, 41 VAND. L. REV. 683, 684 (1988).

[64] *Id.*

[65] *Id.* at 684–85.

[66] On moral deliberation with a client, see *supra* § 4-5.2(b).

representation in today's society.[67] While the mere fact that a lawyer offers a service does not animate a sterile non-legal matter into a living legal representation, the law of privilege cannot ignore the transformation and expansion of the practice of law in the modern world. And when legal and non-legal elements intersect—whether because of the growing interconnection of law and economics in modern law practice or through the traditional synthesis of law and morality in the lawyer's guidance of clients—the lawyer must be able to offer clients legal advice and services in a complete and coordinated manner. The shield of the attorney-client privilege for these communications is essential to encourage such comprehensive counseling for a client's multifaceted problems.

The integration of law and other advice has social value as well. As Professor Neil Hamilton reminds us, "[o]ur profession plays a critical role in fostering and maintaining the foundation of moral capital on which trust in the economic system or in any individual enterprise rests."[68] Indeed, a lawyer for a client on a transactional or other matter who fails to advise a client on business-related risks so that the client may make an informed business decision is at risk of malpractice liability.[69]

Even certain services that may be performed by nonlawyers nonetheless constitute the practice of law when performed by lawyers.[70] In the past, for example, communications made to a lawyer for the purpose of preparing a tax return, rather than obtaining tax planning advice, were not always regarded as sufficiently related to the practice of law to come within the privilege.[71] However, the simple preparation of a tax return may readily become the occasion for providing valuable legal advice, because that tax return work is being performed by a diligent lawyer (rather than an accountant or other nonlawyer), who by reason of legal expertise and experience may identify legal issues that others would not appreciate.[72]

When a matter with any legal dimension is brought to a lawyer and subjected to the lawyer's professional examination, even in the process of performing services that could be performed by nonlawyers, the animating purpose of the privilege may be realized by encouraging the client to freely share all relevant information so that the lawyer may explore any legal implications. When a client specifically chooses a lawyer to provide services, rather than another service-provider, the client appropriately expects and is entitled to receive the benefits of the professional relationship. As examples, the client

---

[67] *See* Gregory C. Sisk & Pamela J. Abbate, *The Dynamic Attorney-Client Privilege*, 23 GEO. J. LEGAL ETHICS 201 (2010).

[68] Neil W. Hamilton, *Counseling the Post-Enron Corporation Using the Lawyer's Independent Professional Judgment*, 14:2 THE PROF'L LAWYER 24 (2003).

[69] *See* Peterson v. Katten Muchin Rosenman, LLP, 792 F.3d 789, 791 (7th Cir. 2015) (rejecting any "bright line" between "business advice and legal advice").

[70] *See supra* § 4-3.2(b)(2).

[71] *See* United States v. Willis, 565 F. Supp. 1186, 1189–90 (S.D. Iowa 1983); *see also* PAUL R. RICE, ATTORNEY-CLIENT PRIVILEGE IN THE UNITED STATES § 7.24 (Thomson-West, 2012). (finding that courts are divided on whether tax return preparation, as contrasted with tax planning, is legal assistance entitled to the protection of the privilege); Maura I. Strassberg, *Privilege Can Be Abused: Exploring the Ethical Obligation to Avoid Frivolous Claims of Attorney-Client Privilege*, 37 SETON HALL L. REV. 413, 473 n.268 (2007) (noting disagreement among courts on whether communications involving a lawyer's preparation of a tax return are protected by the privilege).

[72] The specific information related to the lawyer for the very purpose of being included in the tax return would not be privileged, of course, because the lawyer was intended to be a conduit in transmitting that information to the government tax agency. PAUL R. RICE, ATTORNEY-CLIENT PRIVILEGE IN THE UNITED STATES § 7.25 (Thomson-West, 2012); *see also infra* § 4-6.3(b)(6) (discussing whether the client intended information to be kept confidential).

who chooses a lawyer to prepare a tax return or to negotiate contract terms[73] is entitled to the benefit of the privileges and protections that attach to the lawyer-client relationship.

If a lawyer has performed services for a client in the context of a legal practice (as distinguished from a separate business, even if law-related),[74] the presumption should be that the client genuinely was seeking legal advice and that any communications with the attorney are within the privilege.[75] When a lawyer undertakes to assist a client in a matter that may have legal implications, the introduction of an attorney-client relationship changes the environment in a manner that invites the protection of the privilege. The lawyer is able to bring to bear his legal training to provide legal advice as appropriate, or even to confirm that the law does not exact any additional obligations, and the client naturally expects that a confidential and fiduciary relationship has been created with a member of the legal profession.

Lest a non-legal element become the tail that wags the dog, a clear and significant nexus between attorney-client communications and legal advice or assistance is rightly expected. In classifying the character of the communication, the crucial inquiry is whether the client approaches the lawyer with the intent to obtain legal counsel, even if other dimensions of a matter are addressed as well.[76]

For purposes of determining whether the content of a communication comes within the privilege, courts frequently have described the standard as whether a communication is "primarily" or "predominantly" legal in nature, that is, designed to elicit, provide, or facilitate legal advice or assistance.[77] Such a test should not be applied in a mechanical manner through a quantitative measure of whether legal or non-legal topics take up more space in the communications. Nomenclature such as "primary" or "predominant" to describe the legal purpose test may tempt some lawyers or judges to conduct a subjective, post hoc, and mechanical quantification of the legal versus non-legal elements of a matter or communication.[78]

---

[73] *See* Oasis Int'l Waters, Inc. v. United States, 110 Fed. Cl. 87, 101 (2013) ("An attorney's focus during contract negotiations on achieving the most financially advantageous outcome for his or her client does not transform the attorney's communications into unprotected, business advice.").

[74] On law-related activities performed by a lawyer, see *supra* § 4-3.2.

[75] *See* Diversified Indus., Inc. v. Meredith, 572 F.2d 596, 610 (8th Cir. 1977) ("[A] matter committed to a professional legal adviser is *prima facie* so committed for the sake of the legal advice which may be more or less desirable for some aspect of the matter, and is therefore within the privilege unless it clearly appears to be lacking in aspects requiring legal advice." (quoting 8 JOHN HENRY WIGMORE, EVIDENCE § 2296 (McNaughton rev. 1961))).

[76] *See* Harrington v. Freedom of Information Comm'n, 144 A.3d 405, 417 (Ct. 2016) (quoting parallel passage from Sisk & Abbate, *supra*, 23 GEO. J. LEGAL ETHICS at 219–20).

[77] *See, e.g.*, In re Grand Jury, 475 F.3d 1299, 1304 (D.C. Cir. 2007); In re Spalding Sports Worldwide, Inc., 203 F.3d 800, 805–06 (Fed. Cir. 2000); Loctite Corp. v. Fel-Pro, Inc., 667 F.2d 577, 582 (7th Cir. 1981); Se. Pa. Transp. Auth. v. CaremarkPCS Health, L.P., 254 F.R.D. 253, 258 (E.D. Pa. 2009); Rossi v. Blue Cross & Blue Shield, 540 N.E.2d 703, 706 (N.Y. 1989). *But see* In re Kellogg, Brown & Root, Inc., 756 F.3d 754, 758–60 (D.C. Cir. 2014) (holding, in context of internal corporate investigation, that the privilege attached not only when the sole purpose of a communication was to obtain legal advice but when that is "one of the significant purposes").

[78] A proposal to change the attorney-client privilege test "from the predominate purpose test to the significant amount test" would be an improvement because the new approach would ensure protection when the matter or communications had a substantial legal nexus. *See* Mark C. Van Deusen, Note, *The Attorney-Client Privilege for In-House Counsel When Negotiating Contracts*, 39 WM. & MARY L. REV. 1397, 1439 (1998); *see also* Amber Stevens, Comment, *An Analysis of the Troubling Issues Surrounding In-House Counsel and the Attorney-Client Privilege*, 23 HAMLINE L. REV. 290, 316–19 (1999) (proposing that courts should "consistently apply an expanded version of the predominant purpose test, the significant purpose test"). Nonetheless, the

If the appropriately integrated evaluation of legal and non-legal factors were denied protection from disclosure because a later observer decided that the non-legal factors somehow outweighed the legal factors on a numerical scale, the purpose of the privilege in encouraging laypeople to obtain legal advice and learn how to comply with legal rules would be undermined. Even assuming we were able to precisely calculate that the purpose or content of a communication was 55 or 60 percent business and 45 or 40 percent legal, the privilege should be preserved when such factors are fused together in the lawyer's provision of legal advice or assistance. The essential question for the court reviewing a claim of privilege is one of animating motive and qualitative significance, not of comparative volume.[79]

Courts instead generally apply a qualitative approach, asking whether the purported purpose in seeking legal advice or assistance was a sincere and meaningful element of the overall exchange. In *In re Ford Motor Co.*,[80] one federal court of appeals upheld the protection of the privilege over corporate committee meeting minutes by emphasizing that the matter was "infused with legal concerns." The court concluded that the client had "secur[ed] legal advice," even though the ultimate decision may have been "driven . . . principally by profit and loss, economics, marketing, public relations, or the like." Likewise, in *In re Erie County*,[81] another federal court of appeals explained that the gravamen of a communication should not "be ascertained by quantification or classification of one passage or another;" rather, "it should be assessed dynamically and in light of the advice being sought or rendered." As yet another federal court of appeals emphasized in *In re Kellogg, Brown & Root, Inc.*,[82] it is "not correct for a court to presume that a communication can have only one primary purpose. It is likewise not correct for a court to try to find *the* one primary purpose in cases where a given communication plainly has multiple purposes."

In light of how the inquiry is undertaken by the courts, the judicial examination of the motivation and substance behind a communication for which the protection of the attorney-client privilege is sought might better be described as a "genuine and material legal purpose test." By this test, the court explores whether the request for legal advice or assistance was *genuine* and the legal dimension was *material*.[83]

When the purpose and content of a communication are indeed genuinely and materially related to a legal matter, the privilege attaches to the communication as a whole. As the New York Court of Appeals explained in its oft-cited decision in *Rossi v. Blue Cross & Blue Shield*, "[s]o long as the communication is primarily or predominantly

---

proposed "significant purpose" test shares the same defect as the original by lending itself to artificial quantitative applications, such as by inviting judges to "determine if twenty percent of a discussion is about legal issues as opposed to determining whether forty-five percent or sixty percent of a discussion involves legal advice." *See* Van Deusen, *supra*, at 1437. The attorney-client privilege should protect the confidentiality of sincere requests for legal advice or assistance when a matter has a meaningful and non-incidental legal dimension, regardless of mathematical proportions.

[79] *See, e.g.*, Southeastern Pa. Transp. Auth. v. Caremark PCS Health, L.P., 254 F.R.D. 253, 260 (E.D. Pa. 2009); Allied Irish Banks, 252 F.R.D. 163, 170 (S.D.N.Y. 2008).

[80] 110 F.3d 954, 966 (3d Cir. 1997).

[81] 473 F.3d 413, 420–21 (2d Cir. 2007).

[82] 756 F.3d 754, 759–60 (D.C. Cir. 2014).

[83] Gregory C. Sisk & Pamela J. Abbate, *The Dynamic Attorney-Client Privilege*, 23 GEO. J. LEGAL ETHICS 201, 220–23 (2010); *see also* In re Kellogg, Brown & Root, Inc., 756 F.3d 754, 760 (D.C. Cir. 2014) (saying "the test boils down to whether obtaining or providing legal advice was one of the significant purposes of the attorney-client communication").

of a legal character, the privilege is not lost merely by reason of the fact that it also refers to certain nonlegal matters."[84] A party asserting the protection of the privilege for a written communication must justify the claim on a document-by-document basis[85] (and oral conversations about which evidence is sought would need to be addressed in succession as well). Once the party has provided a description of the document or conversation and made the basic showing that legal and non-legal elements are "inextricably intertwined,"[86] the lawyer and client should not ordinarily be required to meticulously parse out the threads of an interwoven dialogue into privileged and unprivileged categories.[87]

In general, when a genuine and material legal purpose is shown to have stimulated the communication, the lawyer and client should not be required to segregate particular elements of an intermixed set of messages. In an exceptional case, when a strand of the conversation was unrelated to the legal representation and formed a discursion that would not naturally unfold within a professional dialogue between a lawyer and a client, that discrete passage may be subject to disclosure.[88] The exacting and detailed segregation of privileged from unprivileged portions of an otherwise integrated communication and the redaction of the privileged sections while disclosing the remainder is a process that generally should be reserved to the situation in which the overwhelming purpose of the communication was non-legal and thus the legal advice is an incidental element of the communication.[89]

The client cannot develop a trusting relationship with the lawyer if the client lives in fear that any minor digression during a meeting with the lawyer may no longer be secret. And the lawyer cannot effectively obtain the information necessary to the representation if the lawyer must constantly interrupt to warn that the conversation is moving outside the strict boundaries of the legal representation and thus could fall outside the privilege. A holistic approach to legal representation requires a fair degree

---

[84] Rossi v. Blue Cross & Blue Shield, 540 N.E.2d 703, 706 (N.Y. 1989); *see also* United States v. United Shoe Mach. Corp., 89 F. Supp. 357 (D. Mass. 1950) (Judge Wyzanski) ("[T]he privilege of nondisclosure is not lost merely because relevant nonlegal considerations are expressly stated in a communication which also includes legal advice.").

[85] *See* FED. R. CIV. P. 26(b)(5)(A) ("When a party withholds information otherwise discoverable by claiming that the information is privileged or subject to protection as trial-preparation material, the party must (i) expressly make the claim; and (ii) describe the nature of the documents, communications, or tangible things not produced or disclosed—and do so in a manner that, without revealing information itself privileged or protected, will enable other parties to assess the claim."); PAUL R. RICE, ATTORNEY-CLIENT PRIVILEGE IN THE UNITED STATES § 11.7 (Thomson-West, 2012) ("An index of privilege claims—occasionally referred to as a privilege log—is a compilation of information about documents requested during pretrial discovery for which a privilege claim has been asserted." (footnote omitted)).

[86] *See* In re Vioxx Prod. Liab. Litig., 501 F. Supp. 2d 789, 798 (E.D. La. 2007) (quoting and adopting report of Special Master Paul Rice).

[87] *See* In re Spalding Sports Worldwide, Inc., 203 F.3d 800, 806 (Fed. Cir. 2000) (when the "overall tenor" of a document involves legal consultation, the court should not "dissect the document to separately evaluate each of its components"); Bodega Investments, Inc. v. United States, No. 08 Civ. 4065(RMB)(MHD), 2009 WL 1456642, at *5 (S.D.N.Y. May 14, 2009); Sealy Mattress Co. v. Sealy Inc., 1987 WL 12500, at *3 (Del. Ch. June 19, 1987) (ruling that, where a "letter contains an admixture of business and legal advice that is not readily divisible into separate categories," "any effort to parse the advice which is 'legal' from that which is 'business' would be hazardous at best"). *But see* Lugosch v. Congel, No. Civ. 1:00-CV-0784, 2006 WL 931687, at *14 (N.D.N.Y. Mar. 7, 2006) (arguing that when both legal and non-legal advice has been given, "a court may have to parse not only the words but their intent in order to glean the authentic purpose of the communication").

[88] On the possible abuse of the attorney-client privilege in the business setting, see *infra* § 4-8.3(b).

[89] *See* Harrington v. Freedom of Information Comm'n, 144 A.3d 405, 417 (Ct. 2016) (quoting parallel passage from Sisk & Abbate, *supra*, 23 GEO. J. LEGAL ETHICS at 223).

of freedom of conversational topics, a liberty which in turn can be assured to the client only by the protection of the privilege.

As every practicing lawyer learns from experience, what may seem tangential to the client often provides important and legally significant context to the evaluation by a trained legal professional.[90] Thus, the lawyer must be able to draw the client out and fully explore the matter, including going down what may turn out to be a conversational dead-end in order to provide an informed legal representation.[91]

Moreover, the attorney-client privilege may be effectively destroyed if a lawyer and a client are forced to explain why and how particular words or sentences uttered or written during the course of legal counseling are sufficiently connected to the objectives of the representation. Again, when the case has been made that the communication includes integrated evaluation of multiple factors, legal and non-legal, lawyers and clients rarely ought to be put in the position of having to extract supposedly non-privileged elements from an otherwise privileged set of communications.[92]

#### *§ 4-6.3(b)(2) Involving a Professional Legal Advisor*

The attorney-client privilege ordinarily attaches to the attorney-client relationship, that is, when the lawyer as a duly-licensed legal practitioner has been retained to perform legal services. Thus, a person who seeks or obtains legal or quasi-legal advice from someone that the person knows or should know is not admitted to the practice of law, such as a real estate broker or an accountant, does not gain the protection of the attorney-client privilege.

Suppose that a client seeks the legal advice of a person that the client reasonably believes to be admitted to the practice of law, but who deceives the client about that status and instead is a suspended or disbarred lawyer (or perhaps even someone who had never been admitted to the bar). The client defrauded by that counterfeit lawyer should not suffer the further injury of losing the attorney-client privilege.[93]

In a case involving a trademark infringement claim by Gucci America, Inc. against Guess?, Inc., Gucci's in-house counsel had allowed his bar membership to fall into inactive status, unbeknownst to the company.[94] When the opposing party Guess?, Inc. discovered the counsel's inactive bar status, it demanded that the company produce all communications involving him, arguing that they were not protected by the privilege because the counsel was not a licensed lawyer. The magistrate judge's ruling that the privilege did not attach and the documented communications must be disclosed received

---

[90] *See* Swidler & Berlin v. United States, 524 U.S. 399, 409 (1998) ("[A] client may not know at the time he discloses information to his attorney whether it will later be relevant to a civil or a criminal matter, let alone whether it will be of substantial importance."); In re Ampicillin Antitrust Litig., 81 F.R.D. 377, 385 n.10 (D.D.C. 1978) ("By 'relevance of the communication to a particular legal problem,' the Court does not intend to imply that a communication will only be protected if it, in fact, contains information necessary to the decision-making process for a particular legal problem, because such an *Ex post facto* approach would discourage full disclosure by an employee who may not know what information is necessary.").

[91] *See* Upjohn Co. v. United States, 449 U.S. 383, 390–91 (1981) ("The first step in the resolution of any legal problem is ascertaining the factual background and sifting through the facts with an eye to the legally relevant.").

[92] *See also supra* § 4-6.3(b)(3).

[93] *See* PAUL R. RICE, ATTORNEY-CLIENT PRIVILEGE IN THE UNITED STATES § 3.13 (Thomson-West, 2012) (addressing attachment of privilege when legal advice is given by an imposter consulted by a person with a reasonably mistaken belief that he was a lawyer).

[94] Gucci America, Inc. v. Guess?, Inc., No. 09 Civ. 4373(SAS), 2011 WL 9375 (S.D.N.Y. Jan. 3, 2011).

considerable attention in the legal press. However, the district judge set aside the magistrate's ruling and granted Gucci's motion for a protective order over these documents. Citing other decisions, the district court invoked the "undisputed" exception when a client reasonably believed the person with whom the client is communicating is a lawyer.[95] The district court held that, under a reasonable belief rather than a due diligence test, the client reasonably believed that the in-house counsel was a lawyer and was not obliged to continually check whether the lawyer had maintained active membership in the bar.

The privilege traditionally attached only when the client actually had retained the lawyer and thereby created an attorney-client relationship. Today, a lawyer is forthrightly obliged to extend certain professional considerations to a prospective client, notably including protection of confidential information, even if retention of the lawyer by that client is never consummated.[96] Moreover, it should be remembered that a formal contract or even the payment of a retainer is not necessary to create an attorney-client relationship, as the relationship may be implied from the parties' conduct and even established by evidence of the client's detrimental reliance on the attorney.[97] If a layperson relies on an attorney's professional status by entrusting the attorney with confidential information or by obtaining counsel on legal matters, and the attorney fails to affirmatively dissuade that person from confiding or placing trust in the attorney, then the attorney should not be heard later to deny the existence of an attorney-client relationship nor should the client be denied the benefit of the privilege.

### *§ 4-6.3(b)(3) Communication Relating to Legal Advice*

The attorney-client privilege attaches to the contents of communications between a lawyer and a client. The privilege does not reach the underlying facts as to which those communications relate, the lawyer's mere observations of the client's appearance or mannerisms in a non-communicative sense, or documents or materials that did not record or otherwise refer to the substance of such protected communications. Unless the privilege is lost or waived, the lawyer must never be called as a witness to testify to the substance of a communication with a client, nor may the client be compelled to relate the nature of her reports to the lawyer. But the client is not excused from responding to a lawful request for information about the client's conduct or for information within the client's knowledge or control by the mere fact that the client had communicated that information to a lawyer. While the client may not be asked what she told her lawyer about an event, the client may appropriately be examined concerning the underlying event—unless of course the client has another legitimate objection to the question (such as the constitutional privilege against self-incrimination).

In addition, as addressed above,[98] it is the client's intent to obtain legal advice that animates the privilege. Thus, communications that in their content are unrelated to the proper procurement of legal advice fall outside the protection afforded by the privilege.

---

[95] *Id.* at *2.

[96] MODEL RULES OF PROF'L CONDUCT R. 1.18 (American Bar Ass'n, 2016) (providing that, even if no attorney-client relationship is created, the lawyer "shall not use or reveal" information learned from a prospective client); RESTATEMENT (THIRD) OF THE LAW GOVERNING LAWYERS §§ 15, 70 (2000) (discussing lawyer's duties to prospective clients and stating that communications with prospective clients are privileged). On the duty of confidentiality owed to a prospective client, see *supra* § 4-3.1(c).

[97] On creation of the attorney-client relationship, see *supra* § 4-3.2.

[98] *See supra* § 4-6.3(b)(1).

As discussed below,[99] the privilege of course is forfeited when communications are made for an illegitimate purpose. Likewise, communications between a lawyer and client that are clearly extraneous to any legal representation do not obtain the shield of the privilege.

As also discussed previously,[100] unless the conversation is wholly unrelated to the representation and would not naturally occur within the relationship, a lawyer and client ought not be required to segregate those particular elements of a set of communications that relate directly to the legal objective of the representation from those that do not.[101]

### *§ 4-6.3(b)(4) Made in Confidence*

The privilege is lost, or really never comes into being, if the communication is not made in secret. When the communication is made in a setting where no reasonable expectation of privacy exists or where unnecessary third persons are present, the communication simply was not confidential in nature and the privilege does not attach.[102] Thus, for example, if the lawyer and the client exchange sensitive information while sitting in the public area of a crowded restaurant, where anyone could overhear the conversation, the necessary expectation of confidentiality is missing.

In the past few years, several courts have denied the protection of the attorney-client privilege to communications sent by an employee through an employer's computer network or prepared on an employer's computer to an outside lawyer. If the company policy grants the employer the right to access electronic messages and files, the privilege may be denied for electronic communications between an employee and a lawyer as not having been made in confidence.[103] As a California appellate court put it: "The e-mails sent via company computer under the circumstances of this case were akin to consulting her lawyer in her employer's conference room, in a loud voice, with the door open, so that any reasonable person would expect that their discussion of her complaints about her employer would be overheard by him."[104] The American Bar Association's Standing Committee on Ethics and Professional Responsibility has directed lawyers to warn clients of the risk of sending electronic communications where there is a significant risk that a third party may gain access, with specific reference to the scenario of an employee using an employer's computer system.[105]

---

[99] *See infra* § 4-6.3(c)(1).

[100] *See supra* § 4-6.3(b)(1).

[101] *See* Gregory C. Sisk & Pamela J. Abbate, *The Dynamic Attorney-Client Privilege*, 23 GEO. J. LEGAL ETHICS 201, 223 (2010).

[102] *See* People v. Harris, 456 N.Y.S.2d 694, 697 (N.Y. 1982).

[103] *See, e.g.*, Peerenboom v. Marvel Entertainment, LLC, 50 N.Y.S.3d 49 (N.Y. App. Div. 2017); Aventa Learning, Inc. v. K12, Inc., 830 F. Supp. 2d 1083, 1107–10 (W.D. Wash. 2011); Holmes v. Petrovich Dev. Co., 119 Cal. Rptr. 3d 878, 883, 893–99 (Cal. Ct. App. 2011); Scott v. Beth Isr. Med. Ctr. Inc., 847 N.Y.S.2d 436, 438–41 (N.Y. Sup. Ct. 2007); Kaufman v. Sungard Inv. Sys., No. 05-CV-1236, 2006 WL 1307882, at *4 (D.N.J. May 9, 2006). For a discussion of cases involving employees using employer technology to communicate with lawyers, see Gregory C. Sisk & Nicholas Halbur, *A Ticking Time Bomb? University Data Privacy Policies and Attorney-Client Confidentiality in Law School Settings*, 2010 UTAH L. REV. 1277, 1286–95.

[104] Holmes v. Petrovich Dev. Co., 119 Cal. Rptr. 3d 878, 883 (Cal. Ct. App. 2011).

[105] ABA Comm. on Ethics & Prof'l Responsibility, Formal Op. 11–459 (2011).

Likewise the privilege is vitiated by the presence of an unnecessary third person, again because privacy is absent.[106] However, the presence of a third person who is reasonably necessary for the providing of the legal services does not destroy the privilege.[107] Members of the lawyer's staff assisting in the matter share the lawyer's confidentiality.[108] While the presence of the client's family members ordinarily may not be regarded as necessary, the supportive attendance of the parent of a minor child or a relative or friend of a person with diminished capacity at the lawyer interview should not vitiate the privilege.[109]

### *§ 4-6.3(b)(5) By Client or Lawyer*

Under the traditional formulation, communication by the client to the lawyer, rather than by the lawyer to the client, appeared to realize the protection of the privilege. For practical reasons, however, the dubious limitation of the privilege to the client's half of the conversation has withered away.[110] As the Pennsylvania Supreme Court said in joining the majority of states upholding a two-way privilege, "we agree with those courts which have recognized the difficulty in unraveling attorney advice from client input and stressed the need for greater certainty to encourage the desired frankness."[111] Even under the traditional understanding, if revelation of the lawyer's advice would have indirectly revealed the client's communications, the privilege attached.

Given that the lawyer's advice almost invariably is responsive to the requests and explanations of the client, and thus revelation of that advice necessarily discloses the client's thoughts and understandings as conveyed to the lawyer, the privilege is properly recognized straightforwardly as adhering to both sides of the conversation between the lawyer and the client. Professors Geoffrey Hazard and Williams Hodes and attorney Peter Jarvis confirm the modern understanding that privilege includes "both up and downstream communications,"[112] as does the *Restatement of the Law Governing Lawyers*.[113]

---

[106] *See, e.g.*, United States v. Gann, 732 F.2d 714, 722–23 (9th Cir. 1983) (statements made over the phone to attorney while in the presence of police officers searching defendant's house were admissible because he knew or should have known the communication was not confidential); State v. Craney, 347 N.W.2d 668, 678–79 (Iowa 1984) (homicide defendant's telephone confession to his lawyer was made in presence of police officer).

[107] *See* People v. Osorio, 550 N.Y.S.2d 612, 614–15 (1989).

[108] *See also* Charles Gardner Geyh, Judicial Ethics and the Conduct of Judges § 6-2.4(a) (discussing parallel understanding that a judge's communications with their clerks, staff, and fellow judges are not in violation of the general judicial duty to avoid *ex parte* communications).

[109] Jeffrey A. Parness, *The Presence of Family Members and Others During Attorney-Client Communications:* Himmel's *Other Dilemma*, 25 LOY. U. CHI. L.J. 481, 492 (1994) (arguing that " '[c]ommon sense' suggests that individual clients of attorneys often face 'particularly trying' times and may require the presence of family members or friends during attorney-client communications so that professional legal services can be rendered effectively"); *see also supra* § 4-3.5(a).

[110] Dean John Henry Wigmore in his famous treatise said that it had been "always assumed" in earlier cases and "seldom been brought into question" that the attorney's communications, as well as the client's, were within the privilege. 8 JOHN HENRY WIGMORE, EVIDENCE § 2320 (McNaughton rev. 1961).

[111] Gillard v. AIG Ins. Co., 15 A.3d 44, 57 (Pa. 2011); *see also* United States v. Christensen, 828 F.3d 763, 802 (9th Cir. 2016) (holding that the federal attorney-client privilege is a "two-way street").

[112] 1 GEOFFREY C. HAZARD, JR., W. WILLIAM HODES & PETER R. JARVIS, THE LAW OF LAWYERING § 10.07.1 (Aspen, 4th ed., 2016).

[113] RESTATEMENT (THIRD) OF THE LAW GOVERNING LAWYERS § 69, cmt. i (American Law Institute, 2000).

### *§ 4-6.3(b)(6) Protected at Client's Insistence*

As discussed further below with respect to waiver,[114] the client controls the privilege. If the client does not wish certain matters that are communicated to the lawyer to be held in confidence, then the privilege either never comes into being or is waived.

When the client communicates with the lawyer in a setting in which privacy reasonably would be expected, the privilege presumably attaches, whether or not the client or the lawyer interrupts the conversation to specifically confirm the expectation that the communications will be kept secret. By contrast, if the lawyer acts as a mere conduit for transmitting information to another or is directed to place the information into the public record, such as by a court filing, then the client's communication to the lawyer or vice-versa was never intended to be held in confidence.[115]

Importantly, absent client consent or waiver, the privilege has no expiration date.[116]

### *§ 4-6.3(b)(7) Protected from Disclosure by Client or Lawyer*

Absent voluntarily-granted and informed consent by the client or waiver, the privilege protects the communication from disclosure whether the request for the information is directed to the client or to the lawyer. While, again, the client's knowledge about the facts or circumstances underlying the matter is not immunized by the attorney-client privilege, the client must be asked directly about those matters and not asked to relate what the client said to his lawyer about those facts or circumstances.[117] If the client is present when arguably privileged communications are introduced into evidence, and neither the client nor the lawyer enter an objection, the privilege is deemed waived. If the client is not present, the lawyer has a duty to raise an objection on the client's behalf.

### *§ 4-6.3(b)(8) Unless Waived by the Client*

Even if all the necessary requisites for invoking the special protection of the attorney-client privilege are present, the privilege may be lost by waiver, either because the client voluntarily and knowingly surrenders the privilege or because the client takes an action that effectively surrenders the shield of confidentiality. If, for example, the client takes the stand and testifies about communications with a lawyer "in an attempt to secure some advantage by reason of transactions between himself and his counsel," then the lawyer may be "called by the other side to give his account of the matter."[118]

Voluntary disclosure by a client of the contents of a privileged communication, at least when the disclosure is offered to the client's advantage in a judicial proceeding,[119] may count as a waiver as to all other communications on that same subject. If part of

---

[114] *See infra* § 4-6.3(b)(8).

[115] *See generally* 1 GEOFFREY C. HAZARD, JR., W. WILLIAM HODES & PETER R. JARVIS, THE LAW OF LAWYERING § 10.07.9 (Aspen, 4th ed., 2016).

[116] *See* Swidler & Berlin v. United States, 524 U.S. 399, 402–11 (1998) (holding that the attorney-client privilege survives the client's death).

[117] *See* Upjohn v. United States, 449 U.S. 383, 395–96 (1981).

[118] Knigge v. Dencker, 72 N.W.2d 494, 499 (Iowa 1955); *see also* United States v. Bilzerian, 926 F.2d 1285, 1292 (2d Cir. 1991).

[119] XYZ Corp. v. United States, 348 F.3d 16, 24–26 (1st Cir. 2003) (holding that an extrajudicial disclosure of confidential attorney-client communications does not imply a broad subject matter waiver if the client does not use that disclosure to its advantage).

the information is disclosed, thereby placing it directly in issue, the client may not withhold the remainder which may be necessary to place the whole in proper context. The client may not exercise a "selective waiver of the privilege," which "may lead to the inequitable result that the waiving party could waive its privilege for favorable advice while asserting its privilege on unfavorable advice," thereby using the privilege "as both a sword and a shield."[120] However, for an "at-issue" waiver to be found, "a party must *rely* on privileged advice from his counsel to make his claim or defense."[121] Moreover, a waiver as to one subject does not constitute a waiver as to another subject.

### *§ 4-6.3(b)(9) Joint Client Privilege and Joint Defense Doctrine*

Under the so-called "joint client" doctrine or exception to the attorney-client privilege, when two or more persons jointly consult with the same lawyer (or law firm) to represent them on a matter of common interest, neither person may invoke the privilege to prevent disclosure by the lawyer of communications to the other person and neither person may waive the privilege of the other client.[122] "Thus, when the same attorney acts for two parties, the communications are privileged from third persons in the controversy, but not in a subsequent controversy between the two parties."[123]

When involving multiple clients represented by the same lawyer or law firm, the joint-client privilege rule is not an exception to the privilege, because the communications remain privileged as to the outside world. Rather, this rule reflects the practical understanding that the lawyer's common duty to zealously represent both clients necessarily means that all material information relating to the representation must be fully shared by the lawyer with both clients, including communications made by one client to the lawyer outside the presence of the other client. Because both clients are entitled to be kept fully informed by the lawyer,[124] the lawyer may not keep a secret on behalf of one client that would be contrary to the interest of the other client.[125] As Comment 31 to Rule 1.7 of the Model Rules of Professional Conduct says, "the lawyer has an equal duty of loyalty to each client, and each client has the right to be informed of anything bearing on the representation that might affect that client's interests and the right to expect that the lawyer will use that information to that client's benefit." And one client may not invoke the privilege against the other, should they become adversaries as to this matter in the future. Again, importantly, the privilege in the joint-client scenario remains robust as applied to strangers to the attorney-client relationship.

---

[120] In re EchoStar Communications Corp., 448 F.3d 1294, 1301 (Fed. Cir. 2006); *see also* State v. Tensley, 249 N.W.2d 659, 661 (Iowa 1977) (saying it would be "unfair to permit [a party] to elicit favorable aspects of the communications without permitting [the other party] to elicit unfavorable aspects" in a case involving psychiatric expert who examined defendant at request of lawyer for purposes of testifying to his mental condition at a criminal trial).

[121] In re County of Erie, 546 F.3d 222, 229 (2d Cir. 2008). On the question of when a party may lose protection of the privilege by placing otherwise confidential advice in issue, see generally Douglas R. Richmond, *The Frightening At-Issue Exception to the Attorney-Client Privilege*, 121 PENN ST. L. REV. 1 (2016).

[122] RESTATEMENT (THIRD) OF THE LAW GOVERNING LAWYERS § 75 (American Law Institute, 2000); Anten v. Superior Court, 183 Cal. Rptr. 3d 422, 423 (Cal. Ct. App. 1974). *See generally* Amy Foote, Note, *Joint Defense Agreements in Criminal Prosecutions: Tactical and Ethical Implications*, 12 GEO. J. LEGAL ETHICS 377 (1999).

[123] Brandon v. West Bend Mut. Ins. Co., 681 N.W.2d 633, 639 (Iowa 2004); *see also* Gottlieb v. Wiles, 143 F.R.D. 241, 247 (D. Colo. 1992).

[124] *See supra* § 4-5.4(b) to (c).

[125] On treatment of confidential information in multiple client representations, including when a client would be harmed if information is shared with another client, see *infra* § 4-7.4(c).

To uphold effective assistance of counsel for criminal defendants, the courts have recognized what is variably referred to as the "joint defense doctrine," "common interest rule," or "allied lawyer setting"[126] to extend the privilege protection to multiple parties represented by separate lawyers who coordinate strategy and share confidential information in a united front pursuing a common legal interest.[127] In other words, despite revealing information to a third party, the common interest of the parties defeats a waiver of the attorney-privilege as to those outside the joint defense or allied lawyer context.

Courts have upheld the common interest rule to protect information confidentially shared by clients with allied lawyers in the civil context as well.[128] The protection arises most naturally in civil litigation, such as where separately-represented parties are make the same or similar claims or are jointly defending against a claim. To encourage entities "to seek legal advice in planning their affairs to avoid litigation as well as in pursuing it,"[129] the common interest rule is sensibly extended to joint ventures with a shared legal interest where the parties do not anticipate litigation.[130] The common interest rule, like the attorney-client privilege itself,[131] does not cover joint activities that are merely commercial in nature.[132] Nonetheless, when persons or entities need advice on the legal dimension of transaction, joint venture, or merger, the efficient choice of cooperation between allied lawyers is deserving of confidentiality protection.[133]

### § 4-6.3(c) Exceptions to the Attorney-Client Privilege

Whether viewed as the failure to establish a necessary element or instead as an exception, communications by persons with those who are not lawyers, communications made for purposes other than the proper seeking of legal advice (whether non-legal or criminal or fraudulent in nature), or communications conducted in circumstances where confidentiality could not reasonably be expected do not obtain the protection of the attorney-client privilege.[134] Importantly, however, the privilege "is not subject to an

---

[126] *See* Susan K. Rushing, Note, *Separating the Joint-Defense Doctrine From the Attorney-Client Privilege*, 68 TEX. L. REV. 1273, 1276–77 (1990) (arguing the joint defense doctrine should be recognized as a separate privilege rather than as an extension of the attorney-client privilege).

[127] *See* United States v. McPartlin, 595 F.2d 1321, 1336–37 (7th Cir. 1979); Schaeffler v. United States, 806 F.3d 34, 40–43 (2d Cir. 2015); Hunydee v. United States, 355 F.2d 183 (9th Cir. 1965).

[128] *See generally* 1 DAVID M. GREENWALD, ROBERT R. STAUFFER & ERIN R. SCHRANTZ, TESTIMONIAL PRIVILEGES § 1:105 (Thomson-Reuters, 3d ed., 2015). *But see* Grace M. Giesel, *End the Experiment: The Attorney-Client Privilege Should Not Protect Communications in the Allied Lawyering Setting*, 95 MARQ. L. REV. 475, 477–79 (2012) (contending that the attorney-client privilege should not extend to communications that are not between a lawyer and that lawyer's own client and any benefit from the privilege in the allied lawyer setting is "outweighed by the damage done to the truth-finding mission of the justice system").

[129] SCM Corp. v. Xerox Corp., 70 F.R.D. 508, 513 (D. Conn. 1976).

[130] United States v. BDO Seidman, 492 F.3d 806, 815–16 (7th Cir. 2007); In re Regents of University of Cal., 101 F.3d 1386, 1390–91 (Fed. Cir. 1996). *But see* Ambac Assur. Corp. v. Countrywide Home Loans, Inc., 36 N.Y.S.3d 838, 848 (N.Y. 2016) (divided court concluding that "the policy reasons for keeping a litigation limitation on the common interest doctrine outweigh any purported justification for doing away with it").

[131] *See supra* § 4-6.3(b)(1).

[132] Fox News Network, LLC v. U.S. Dep't of Treas., 739 F. Supp. 2d 515, 563 (S.D.N.Y. 2010) ("The interest must be a common legal interest, not merely a common commercial interest.").

[133] *See* United States v. United Technologies Corp., 979 F. Supp. 108, 112 (D. Conn. 1997) (applying common interest privilege when members of a consortium developed "a common legal strategy regarding the tax structure" of the enterprise to limit tax liability).

[134] *See supra* § 4-6.3(b).

exception simply because a private litigant, government agency, or other third party claims an important need to know what the client discussed with an attorney."[135]

### *§ 4-6.3(c)(1) Crime-Fraud Exception*

If rather than seeking legitimate legal advice, the client solicits information and services from the lawyer in order to facilitate criminal or fraudulent conduct, the attorney-client privilege is forfeited.[136]

> It is a mistaken notion to think that an attorney has the right to assist in the perpetration of a fraud, and a mistaken notion to think that one having in mind the perpetration of a fraud or a crime can safely entrust this knowledge to an attorney any more than to anybody else.[137]

When the client is engaged in criminal or fraudulent conduct, and is using legal services in an effort to advance or conceal that behavior (with or without the attorney's knowledge), the illegitimacy of the objective prevents formation of an authentic attorney-client relationship with the attendant protection of the privilege.[138] Importantly, for the privilege to be lost, the client must pervert the attorney-client relationship toward the proscribed end.

To prevent misuse of this exception to improperly gain access to privileged information, the party seeking the communication "has the burden of making a *prima facie* showing that the communications were in furtherance of an intended or present illegality," as well as proof that "there is some relationship between the communications and the illegality."[139]

As Professors Geoffrey Hazard and William Hodes and attorney Peter Jarvis emphasize, "the exception only applies where the communication is intended to or actually does advance the client's illicit purpose; providing after-the-fact evidence of the crime or fraud is insufficient."[140] Of course, a person who retains legal counsel to provide a defense to past crimes or fraud is entitled to the protection of the privilege. Nor does revelation by the client of an intent to commit a future crime, assuming the communication does not in itself exploit the legal representation to advance the criminal intent, remove the privilege.[141] Although the lawyer may have discretion or even be required to disclose to law enforcement or other persons the client's intent to cause harm to another person, through an exception to confidentiality under Rule 1.6 of the Model Rules of Professional Conduct or state ethics rules,[142] the persistence of the privilege

---

[135] *Report of the American Bar Association's Task Force on the Attorney-Client Privilege*, 60 BUS. LAW. 1029, 1032 (2005).

[136] United States v. Zolin, 491 U.S. 554, 562–63 (1989).

[137] State v. Kirkpatrick, 263 N.W. 52, 55 (Iowa 1935).

[138] *See* Fred C. Zacharias, *Harmonizing Privilege and Confidentiality*, 41 S. TEX. L. REV. 69, 78 (1999) ("The theory of the crime-fraud principle is that a client who uses a lawyer to further an ongoing or future crime is not, in fact, using the lawyer as a lawyer.").

[139] In re Grand Jury Proceedings (The Corporation), 87 F.3d 377, 380 (9th Cir. 1996).

[140] 1 GEOFFREY C. HAZARD, JR., W. WILLIAM HODES & PETER R. JARVIS, THE LAW OF LAWYERING § 10.11 (Aspen, 4th ed., 2016)).

[141] *See* Newman v. State, 863 A.2d 321, 335–36 (Md. 2004) (citing numerous federal and state cases).

[142] *See infra* § 4-6.6(c) (discussing the exceptions in Rule 1.6(b)(1) and (c) regarding disclosure to prevent death or substantial bodily harm).

would preclude the lawyer from being called to testify against the client regarding that communication.[143]

The deliberate misuse of legal services by a client in furtherance of a crime or fraud, which thereby vitiates the privilege, should be carefully differentiated from the pursuit of legal advice by a client regarding the legality of a proposed course of action that the lawyer then determines would be criminal or fraudulent. The latter is covered by the privilege to encourage people to obtain the assistance of lawyers in conforming their behavior to the requirements of the law. Moreover, when the contours of the law are unclear, or when the law appears to force a client into a difficult choice among options none of which may be plainly lawful, the client is entitled to the candid provision of information by the lawyer.[144]

The mark of distinction between the perversion of legal services to an illicit end and the commendable seeking of legal counsel about the boundaries of the law may be found in how the client responds to the legal advice, whether with appropriate acceptance of the legal limitations or intransigent insistence upon realizing an illegal end. Another important indicator of legitimacy is whether the client has been forthright in seeking legal counsel about the matter, as contrasted with deceiving the lawyer about the client's conduct while using the legal representation to avoid detection of misconduct. For this reason, the *Restatement of the Law Governing Lawyers* maintains that the attorney-client privilege is lost only if the client, after obtaining the lawyer's advice, actually accomplishes the unlawful purpose, that is, commits the crime or engages in a criminal attempt.[145]

The United States Court of Appeals for the Third Circuit in *In re Grand Jury Matter #3*[146] reversed a district court's ruling that allowed the government to show the grand jury an inadvertently disclosed email that the target had received from his lawyer suggesting retroactive correction of tax records and which the client forwarded to his accountant but without taking further action. Applying the crime-fraud exception to the parallel work product doctrine, the court found the "use-in-furtherance" requirement, which "provides a key safeguard against intrusion into the attorney-client relationship," to be lacking. The court explained:

> To illustrate, if a client approaches a lawyer with a fraudulent plan that the latter convinces the former to abandon, the relationship has worked precisely as intended. We reward this forbearance by keeping the work-product protection intact. If, by contrast, the client uses work product to further a fraud, the relationship has broken down, and the lawyer's services have been "misused."[147]

[143] On the relationship between exceptions to confidentiality under the rules and the independent protection of the attorney-client privilege, see *infra* § 4-6.3(c)(4).

[144] *See* Peter A. Joy & Rodney J. Uphoff, *"What Do I Do With the Porn on My Computer?": How a Lawyer Should Counsel Clients About Physical Evidence*, 54 AM. CRIM. L. REV. 751, 757 (2017). *See also infra* § 4-9.7(b)(6).

[145] RESTATEMENT (THIRD) OF THE LAW GOVERNING LAWYERS § 82(a) (American Law Institute, 2000) (providing that the client's unlawful purpose must be "later accomplished" for the privilege not to apply). Comment c to Section 82 of the *Restatement* explains that "accomplished" includes not only taking actions that result in criminal harm but also actions taken that constitute a criminal attempt even if the criminal end is frustrated.

[146] 847 F.3d 157 (3rd Cir. 2017).

[147] *Id.* at 165–66.

### *§ 4-6.3(c)(2) Identity of Client and Payment of Fees*

Traditionally, the attorney-client privilege did not extend to the fact that an attorney-client relationship was established, the identity of the client, or the payment of fees by the client, under the reasoning that these were facts that the lawyer observed, rather than communications made by the client to the lawyer.[148]

However, if revealing the client's identity would "chill the willingness of citizens to approach a lawyer's office" by indirectly revealing the substance of a privileged communication, then the privilege may be preserved.[149] If disclosing that a particular person sought legal advice would allow others, such as law enforcement, to combine knowledge of that now-revealed identity with other information and thereby construct a basis for pursuing adverse action against the client, such as criminal prosecution, then the presumption that mere identity is not privileged has been overcome. In such instances, the essential purpose of the privilege in encouraging persons to seek legal advice would be promoted by preserving anonymity.

In theory, if the mere existence of a fee arrangement likewise would have the effect of revealing the very nature of the representation in a manner that redounded to the detriment of the client, the privilege might extend to the payment of the fee. However, the courts have rejected the argument that this theory excuses a lawyer who receives payment from a client of more than $10,000 in cash from making the required report to the Internal Revenue Service.[150]

### *§ 4-6.3(c)(3) Lawyer-Client Disputes and Lawyer Self-Defense*

When the legal services provided by the lawyer become a matter of controversy with the client, the lawyer is permitted to defend the quality and nature of her work, including relating the content of communications with the client as necessary to that defense. The traditional rule was that the lawyer could use client confidential information only in a dispute with the client, such as defense to an accusation of malpractice or a suit to collect fees, on the understanding that the client had either waived the privilege by putting confidential information in dispute or could not justly assert the privilege to the direct disadvantage of the lawyer.[151] Bolstered by the parallel exception to confidentiality under ethics rules,[152] the courts have extended the privilege exception to cover situations in which the lawyer must use confidential information to defend against a charge of wrongdoing by a third party, such as a lawsuit against the lawyer alleging fraudulent conduct in conjunction with client representation[153] or in responding to professional disciplinary authorities on a complaint of unethical conduct.[154]

---

[148] *See* Humphreys, Hutcheson & Moseley v. Donovan, 755 F.2d 1211, 1219 (6th Cir. 1985); Howell v. Jones, 516 F.2d 53, 58 (5th Cir. 1975).

[149] American Standard Inc. v. Pfizer Inc., 828 F.2d 734, 745 (Fed. Cir. 1987).

[150] *See generally* 1 GEOFFREY C. HAZARD, JR., W. WILLIAM HODES & PETER R. JARVIS, THE LAW OF LAWYERING § 10.12 (Aspen, 4th ed., 2016).

[151] *See generally* First Fed. Sav. & Loan Ass'n v. Oppenheim, Appel, Dixon & Co., 110 F.R.D. 557, 560–61 (S.D.N.Y. 1986).

[152] *See infra* § 4-6.6(f).

[153] *See* Meyerhofer v. Empire Fire & Marine Ins. Co., 497 F.2d 1190, 1194–96 (2d Cir. 1974); *Oppenheim, Appel, Dixon & Co.*, 110 F.R.D. at 561–68.

[154] *See* People v. Robnet, 859 P.2d 872, 878–79 (Colo. 1993).

### *§ 4-6.3(c)(4) Exceptions to Confidentiality Under Ethics Rules and the Independent Protection of the Attorney-Client Privilege*

As will be the subject of considerable discussion below,[155] Rule 1.6(b) of the Model Rules of Professional Conduct articulates certain exceptions to confidentiality, permitting disclosure of information that the lawyer otherwise is ethically-bound to hold as confidential. In narrow circumstances, Rules 3.3[156] and 4.1[157] require the lawyer to reveal information, again including information that otherwise would be confidential under Rule 1.6, when necessary to prevent or correct client fraud against a tribunal or another person.

By their terms, these exceptions in the rules apply to disclosure by the lawyer from that general category of ethically-protected confidential information, which is broadly defined in Rule 1.6(a). While this nearly all-encompassing category of ethically-protected confidential information certainly includes the lawyer's communications with the client, it more broadly covers all information held by the lawyer that is related to the representation.[158] By contrast, as explained above,[159] the attorney-client privilege attaches to a special subset of that confidential information, protecting only those communications between the lawyer and the client that are entitled to be held immune from legal process and that may not be adduced as evidence against the client.[160] Confidential material thus is broadly defined, but subject to several exceptions and may not be entitled to any immunity from legal process, while privileged information is more narrowly classified (attaching only to certain communications between the lawyer and client), but is subject to fewer exceptions and does provide immunity from legally-compelled disclosure.

Because privileged communications fall within the broader category of ethically-protected confidential information, the question naturally arises as to whether an exception under the rules for disclosure of confidential information should also be understood to permit or require the lawyer to disclose information falling within the subset of privileged material, and, if so, how this authorization squares with the purpose of the privilege.

For the limited purposes and by generally non-evidentiary means for and by which disclosure is allowed under the rules, the exceptions to confidentiality in Rules 1.6, 3.3, and 4.1 do apply with equal force to that subset of confidential information that consists of communications between the lawyer and client. Given that the most important information concerning a representation ordinarily is obtained by the lawyer through communications with the client or is inextricably intertwined with such communications, the exceptions to confidentiality in the rules would have little effect if such information were regarded, not only as being privileged against evidentiary use, but also as shielded from ethically-permitted or ethically-required disclosure. Thus, for example, a lawyer's knowledge about the risk of serious harm to another typically will have been generated from the client's statements to the lawyer, meaning that any

---

[155] *See infra* § 4-6.6.

[156] *See infra* § 4-9.8(c) to (h).

[157] *See infra* §§ 4-6.6(d)(3), 4-11.2(c).

[158] *See supra* § 4-6.2.

[159] *See supra* § 4-6.3(a).

[160] *See supra* § 4-6.3(b).

disclosure of that information to save a person from death or substantial bodily harm or substantial economic injury necessarily requires sharing information that was received from what may be a privileged attorney-client communication. However, as explained below, unless an exception to confidentiality in the ethics rules aligns with an exception to the attorney-client privilege, any disclosure by the lawyer is limited to non-testimonial revelation for an extra-evidentiary purpose.

Understanding that the attorney-client privilege is designed to provide an immunity from legally-compelled process to provide evidence or testimony,[161] the exceptions to confidentiality set forth in the Model Rules of Professional Conduct that allow sharing of certain information are *not* exceptions to the attorney-client privilege. That a lawyer may be permitted or even required under the rules to divulge client confidences, including sharing information obtained through communications with a client, for the limited purposes of preventing or correcting a serious harm or advancing some other important interest, does not necessarily mean that the lawyer may be called as a witness in a legal proceeding or otherwise be required to provide evidence that would be admissible against the client. The exceptions in the ethics rules do not and cannot direct introduction of attorney-client communications into evidence in any proceeding or allow inquiry about such communications through any legally-compelled process. Unless an exception to confidentiality under the rules is co-extensive with a recognized exception to the attorney-client privilege, the lawyer is authorized by a confidentiality exception in the rules to disclose information only in the manner and to the extent necessary to prevent or correct the harm or achieve the other stated purpose—but not to testify or give evidence against the client.

However, if the attorney-client privilege does not attach or has been vitiated, as for example when the lawyer's advice has been abused by the client in furtherance of fraudulent or criminal conduct, then an exception to confidentiality under the rules may be parallel with an exception to the statutory and common-law privilege. When the privilege fails, the lawyer not only may be allowed or required by the ethics rules to disclose information to prevent harm, but the attorney may be called to give testimony or other evidence regarding the substance of those non-privileged attorney-client communications.

Two not-so-hypothetical scenarios serve to illustrate the point that the exceptions to confidentiality in the rules (allowing sharing of confidential client information) may or may not correspond to exceptions to the attorney-client privilege (allowing testimony or evidence about lawyer-client communications):

First, suppose that a lawyer were to learn from a confidential dialogue with his client that the client intends to commit a violent attack on someone, but the client has not used legal advice in furtherance of that unlawful objective so as to vitiate the privilege. Under Rule 1.6(b)(1) of the Model Rules, the lawyer would be permitted to disclose the information if the anticipated attack were reasonably certain to result in death or substantial bodily harm.[162] After revealing the planned attack in a manner designed to prevent the harm, the lawyer would not be free nor could he be compelled to

---

[161] *See* PAUL R. RICE, ATTORNEY-CLIENT PRIVILEGE IN THE UNITED STATES § 2.2 (Thomson-West, 2012) (explaining that, when the elements of the privilege have been satisfied and no exception to the privilege applies, "communications between the attorney and client will be protected" and further that "this protection is absolute").

[162] *See infra* § 4-6.6(f).

testify as a witness against the client in a subsequent criminal prosecution. The testimonial/evidentiary privilege would remain intact. The lawyer might be permitted (and perhaps required in some states) to share information gleaned from attorney-client communications with the target of the planned attack or with law enforcement, but the privilege against introduction of the lawyer's revelation into evidence would not be abrogated

In *Newman v. State*,[163] a lawyer in a divorce and child custody matter disclosed his client's threats either to kill her own children and frame her estranged husband for the murder or to hire a hitman to kill her husband, relying on the ethics rule permitting disclosure of confidential information to prevent death or substantial bodily harm. At the subsequent criminal prosecution of the woman for conspiracy to commit murder and other felonies, the trial court over objections required the lawyer to testify against his former client, relating what he had disclosed to prevent the criminal harm (and more). On appeal, the Maryland Court of Appeals correctly ruled that the lawyer's disclosure under the ethics rule exception to confidentiality did not defeat the defendant's assertion of attorney-client privilege at the criminal trial nor did the crime-fraud exception apply because the lawyer's legal advice was not used in furtherance of any criminal conduct.[164] Because the lawyer therefore should not have been required to testify, the conviction was reversed and the case remanded for a new trial. As the Maryland court ruled in *Newman v. State*, a disclosure under the ethics rule—

> is not sufficient to obviate the attorney-client privilege and admit the statements as evidence against the attorney's client, not only because of the chilling effect of the obverse, but also because it pits the attorney, as advocate and adviser, against the client, when the client is charged with a crime. To permit a Rule 1.6 disclosure to destroy the attorney-client privilege and empower the attorney to essentially waive his client's privilege without the client's consent is repugnant to the entire purpose of the attorney-client privilege in promoting candor between attorney and client.[165]

Second, and by contrast, if a lawyer were to learn that her client had used the lawyer's legal advice in furtherance of a fraudulent scheme that if undisclosed would cause substantial injury to another person's financial interests, the lawyer would be permitted (and perhaps required) under Rules 1.6(b)(2) and (3) and 4.1(b) to disclose the information as necessary to prevent the harm from being realized.[166] And because the

---

[163] 863 A.2d 321 (Md. 2004).

[164] *Id.* at 328–37; *see also* Purcell v. District Attorney, 676 N.E.2d 436, 437–41 (Mass. 1997) (ruling that, while the lawyer under ethics rules properly revealed to law enforcement threats made by the client while consulting the lawyer that the client would burn down his apartment building, the trial court erroneously denied the lawyer's motion to quash a subpoena to testify regarding those incriminating statements in a prosecution of the client for attempted arson because the crime-fraud exception to the attorney-client privilege did not apply as the communications were not for the purpose of assisting or furthering the threatened criminal conduct); In re Grand Jury Investigation, 902 N.E.2d 929 (Mass. 2009) (holding that, while an attorney properly exercised discretion to warn that a client had made angry and threatening statements against a judge, that the statements remained privileged and the attorney could not be compelled to testify about the statements in a grand jury investigation of the client). *See also* State ex rel. Ash v. Swope, 751 S.E.2d 751, 756–57 (W. Va. 2013) (holding that an attorney must testify in a subsequent criminal case about the client's death threat when the client expressly ordered the attorney to convey the threat to the judge and parties in open court, which thus waived confidentiality and put the statement outside the attorney-client privilege).

[165] *Newman*, 836 A.2d at 333.

[166] *See infra* § 4-6.6(d).

client had used legal advice in furtherance of fraud or crime, the privilege would be lost and the lawyer could choose to or be compelled to be a witness against the client.[167]

The United States Court of Appeals for the Ninth Circuit in *In re Grand Jury Proceedings*[168] upheld a subpoena to the attorney for the target of a grand jury investigation when "evidence independent of the communications between the client and the lawyer" made the required prima facie showing to the trial court that the client had used legal service "in furtherance of the ongoing unlawful scheme."[169] Even then, because no showing was made that the lawyer "knowingly participated in any criminal activity," the court required the lawyer to testify only as to factual matters, "but upheld her refusal to testify to 'opinion work product' or 'mental impressions' formulated in the course of her representation."[170]

## § 4-6.4 ATTORNEY WORK PRODUCT

When an opposing party in litigation seeks information related to the lawyer's representation of a client, certain materials sought may be protected by the work-product doctrine, as well as or instead of the attorney-client privilege. In contrast with communications between a client and lawyer, which are privileged, the rules of civil procedure provide a high but not absolute measure of protection to the attorney's work-product, that is, the attorney's preparation of notes and reports and accumulation of materials in anticipation of litigation. A federal court of appeals recently described the work product protection as a "complement to the attorney-client privilege" that "preserves the confidentiality of legal communications prepared in anticipation of litigation."[171]

Strictly speaking, the work-product doctrine is a protection or immunity against discovery and not a privilege. The work-product protection may be pierced when the opposing party shows sufficient need for the information,[172] while the attorney-client privilege may not be breached simply because someone else asserts a compelling need for the information. In this respect, the work-product doctrine is less powerful than the attorney-client privilege. However, the work-product doctrine is more encompassing than the attorney-client privilege. As one federal appellate court has explained: "Unlike the attorney-client privilege, which protects all communications whether written or oral, work-product immunity protects documents and tangible things, such as memorandums, letters, and e-mails."[173]

The work-product doctrine is designed to protect the "mental processes of the attorney."[174] To serve that purpose, the doctrine necessarily applies not only to those documents that directly reveal the lawyer's opinions (although this element receives the highest protection), but also to the lawyer's preparation and assembling of other documents and materials, recording or referring to factual observations, interviews of witnesses, inquiries made, etc. The examination of these materials might provide clues

---

[167] *See supra* § 4-6.3(c)(1).

[168] 867 F.2d 539 (9th Cir. 1989).

[169] *Id.* at 541.

[170] *Id.*

[171] In re Grand Jury Matter #3, 847 F.3d 157, 165 (3rd Cir. 2017).

[172] *See* FED. R. CIV. P. 26(b)(3).

[173] In re Echostar Communications Corp., 448 F.3d 1293, 1301 (Fed. Cir. 2006).

[174] United States v. Nobles, 422 U.S. 225, 238 (1975).

about the lawyer's evaluation of matters and strategy. Moreover, this collected body of materials constitutes the tangible result of the lawyer's efforts, upon which an opponent should not be permitted to piggy-back.

The pertinent federal discovery rule extends a nearly insuperable level of protection against "disclosure of the mental impressions, conclusions, opinions, or legal theories of an attorney or other representative of a party concerning the litigation"[175] (what is sometimes called "opinion work-product"). The work-product rule also bars access without a showing of substantial need to other "documents and tangible things" that have been "prepared in anticipation of litigation"[176] (which are sometimes called "factual work-product").[177]

In the landmark decision of *Hickman v. Taylor*,[178] the Supreme Court explained:

> In performing his various duties . . . it is essential that a lawyer work with a certain degree of privacy, free from unnecessary intrusion by opposing parties and their counsel. Proper preparation of a client's case demands that he assemble information, sift what he considers to be the relevant from the irrelevant facts, prepare his legal theories and plan his strategy without undue and needless interference. That is the historical and the necessary way in which lawyers act within the framework of our system of jurisprudence to promote justice and to protect their clients' interests. This work is reflected, of course, in interviews, statements, memoranda, correspondence, briefs, mental impressions, personal beliefs, and countless other tangible and intangible ways—aptly though roughly termed . . . as the "work product of the lawyer." Were such materials open to opposing counsel on mere demand, much of what is now put down in writing would remain unwritten. An attorney's thoughts, heretofore inviolate, would not be his own. Inefficiency, unfairness and sharp practices would inevitably develop in the giving of legal advice and in the preparation of cases for trial. The effect on the legal profession would be demoralizing. And the interests of the clients and the cause of justice would be poorly served.

Under Rule 26(b)(3) of the Federal Rules of Civil Procedure, which is tracked in most states, materials prepared "in anticipation of litigation" are protected from discovery, unless the party seeking the information demonstrates a "substantial need for

---

[175] FED. R. CIV. P. 26(b)(3)(B).

[176] *Id.* 26(b)(3)(A).

[177] *See, e.g.*, S.E.C. v. Treadway, 229 F.R.D. 454, 456 (S.D.N.Y. 2005) (ruling that even if elements of notes could be considered "factual work product" from which the "mental impressions, conclusions, opinions, or legal theories of an attorney" could be redacted, the party seeking the notes still had not made the required showing to obtain discovery); Shook v. City of Davenport, 497 N.W.2d 883, 889 (Iowa 1993) (holding that, even if a party seeking discovery had made a substantial need showing, the trial court should separate out opinion from factual work-product and permit disclosure only of the factual material), *overruled on other grounds*, Wells Dairy, Inc. v. American Indus. Refrigeration, Inc., 690 N.W.2d 38 (Iowa 2004); State ex rel. Erie Ins. Property & Cas. Co. v. Mazzone, 625 S.E.2d 355, 361–62 (W.Va. 2005) (ruling that opinion work product has near absolute immunity from discovery while factual work product may be obtained by the still high showing of substantial need). *But see* Brown v. Superior Court, 670 P.2d 725, 735 (Ariz. 1983) (holding that, while "afforded greater protection," even mental impressions and opinions may be discoverable in an unusual case of substantial need and where the state of mind is directly at issue on the merits of the claim, such as an accusation of bad faith). *But see* Fidelity & Deposit Co. of Maryland v. McCulloch, 168 F.R.D. 516, 524 (E.D. Pa. 1996) (rejecting the *Brown* decision and characterizing discovery request for mental impressions in a bad faith case as a "fairly remarkable proposition").

[178] 329 U.S. 495, 510–11 (1947).

the materials to prepare [party's case] case and cannot, without undue hardship, obtain their substantial equivalent by other means."[179]

## § 4-6.5 LAWYER'S DUTY TO SAFEGUARD CONFIDENTIAL INFORMATION

### § 4-6.5(a) General Duty to Safeguard Confidential Information

Because information related to the representation is broadly protected as confidential,[180] every lawyer must institute appropriate measures within his law practice to safeguard client information. Indeed, Rule 1.6(c) of the Model Rules of Professional Conduct now expressly mandates making "reasonable efforts to prevent the inadvertent or unauthorized disclosure of, or unauthorized access to, information relating to the representation of a client."

The lawyer must ensure that venues for confidential communications are available and maintained as private when necessary, that both traditional hard-copy and electronic information are well-secured within the office, that access to information by those not so entitled is precluded, that information-gathering activities are designed with preservation of confidentiality in mind, and that the lawyer responds vigorously and promptly to assert client confidentiality whenever information is sought by others to which a colorable objection may be made. As Comment 19 to Rule 1.6 anticipates, when information is of greater sensitivity, a confidentiality agreement so requires, or the client demands additional measures, special security measures may need to be implemented.

As an essential part of the lawyer's supervisory responsibility over nonlawyer assistants under Rule 5.3 of the Model Rules of Professional Conduct,[181] the lawyer must give appropriate instructions to employees about professional obligations, specifically and especially including the duty to safeguard protected information about clients. Likewise, when a lawyer or law firm delegates support service work to an outside company, the managerial and supervisory lawyers in the firm must adopt appropriate measures to ensure that the independent contractors also understand and adhere to professional ethical standards.[182] For example, when using an outside computer maintenance company, the American Bar Association's Standing Committee on Ethics and Professional Responsibility advises that the law firm must "ensure that the company has in place, or will establish, reasonable procedures to protect the confidentiality" of law firm computer files.[183]

### § 4-6.5(b) Use of Modern Communications Technology

Modern communications technology certainly does introduce a greater risk of inadvertent disclosure of confidential information through erroneous transmission to unintended recipients, as addressed below.[184] However, the prudent use of such means

---

179 FED. R. CIV. P. 26(b)(3)(A).

180 *See supra* § 4-6.2.

181 *See infra* § 4-12.4.

182 ABA Comm. on Ethics & Prof'l Responsibility, Formal Op. 08–451 (2008) (discussing the obligation lawyers have when outsourcing legal or nonlegal support services).

183 ABA Comm. on Ethics & Prof'l Responsibility, Formal Op. 95–398 (1995) (discussing the access of nonlawyers to a lawyer's computer files).

184 *See infra* § 4-6.5(c).

of communication, including cellular telephones and electronic mail (email), ordinarily is sufficiently secure that extraordinary precautions need not be made beyond the usual office procedures designed to ensure that access is limited to those permitted access to confidential information. Comment 19 to Rule 1.6 provides that the lawyer's duty to "take reasonable precautions to prevent the information from coming into the hands of unintended recipients" does "not require that the lawyer use special security measures if the method of communication affords a reasonable expectation of privacy."

The American Bar Association's Standing Committee on Ethics and Professional Responsibility and most states addressing this matter concluded early on that because the expectation of privacy for email is no less reasonable than the expectation of privacy for ordinary telephone calls, and because the unauthorized interception of an electronic message is a violation of federal criminal law, a lawyer would not violate Rule 1.6 by communicating with a client using email services over the internet, without encryption or specific client consent.[185] Similarly, now that most cellular telephones use digital technology, which is harder to intercept than ordinary wired or "land-line" telephones, the use of such technology for attorney-client conversations should be understood to comport with reasonable expectations of privacy to preserve confidences. Moreover, interception of cellular telephone communications also is a violation of federal criminal law, thus enhancing the expectation of privacy.[186] More recently, the Standing Committee has confirmed the same approach for the growing diversity of electronic means of communicating and exchanging documents with clients, which is that the lawyer must make "reasonable efforts to prevent inadvertent or unauthorized access."[187]

Both ABA opinions emphasize that enhanced security measures, such as encryption, are appropriate for extraordinarily sensitive matters or in exceptional circumstances where the threat of cyber intrusion is greater.

Just as a lawyer must take reasonable measures to prevent others in the office from eavesdropping upon a telephone conversation, so should the lawyer ensure that password protection is used to prevent intrusion into electronic records and transmissions. Wireless internet access should include use of firewalls and passwords to deter hacking into computers or interception of wireless communications.[188] Likewise, the lawyer should use a reputable internet service provider who maintains appropriate security over email servers. When disposing of computer disks and drives containing confidential information, including records of electronic transmissions, the lawyer should see that disks are properly destroyed and drives are wiped clean, using readily-available and inexpensive software that permanently overwrites data or destroys the key to encrypted disks and drives.

---

[185] *See, e.g.*, ABA Comm. on Ethics and Prof'l Responsibility, Formal Op. 99–413 (1999); Alaska Bar Ass'n Ethics Comm. Op. 98–2 (1998); Illinois State Bar Ass'n Advisory Op. on Prof'l Conduct 96–10 (1997); Massachusetts Bar Ass'n Comm. on Prof'l Ethics Op. 00–1 (2000); Minnesota Lawyers Prof'l Responsibility Bd. Op. 19 (1999); North Dakota State Bar Ass'n Ethics Comm. Op. 97–09 (1997); *see also* American Bar Association Resolution 98A119A (Aug. 4, 1998) (affirming that lawyer-client electronic-mail communications should be accorded the same expectations of privacy and confidentiality as those accorded to traditional means of communication). *See generally* David Hricik, *E-mail and Client Confidentiality: Lawyers Worry Too Much About Transmitting Client Confidences by Internet E-mail*, 11 GEO. J. LEGAL ETHICS 459 (1998).

[186] *See* RONALD D. ROTUNDA & JOHN S. DZIENKOWSKI, PROFESSIONAL RESPONSIBILITY: A STUDENT'S GUIDE § 1.6–2(c) (American Bar Ass'n, 2013–2014).

[187] ABA Comm. on Ethics and Prof'l Responsibility, Formal Op. 477 (2017).

[188] *See generally* Andrew Perlman, *The Twenty-First Century Lawyer's Evolving Ethical Duty of Competence*, 22:4 PROF'L LAWYER 1 (2014).

### § 4-6.5(c) Inadvertent Disclosure

Although modern communications technology ordinarily is adequately secure for confidential communications between a lawyer and client, such means do pose a greater risk of accidental transmission to an unintended recipient.[189] While this problem is nothing new, as witnessed by past episodes involving inadvertent mailing or faxing of confidential or privileged documents to opposing counsel, electronic communications make it possible to send a message or document containing confidential information to the wrong person by a simple push of a button. Nearly every user of email has had the unpleasant experience at some point of sending a personal message to a friend only to discover, sometimes to great embarrassment, that it had also been mistakenly transmitted to a larger group. When the same accidental dissemination occurs with respect to a confidential communication intended only for a client, and especially when the unintended recipient is an adversary of the client, questions arise as to whether the disclosure effectively waives the attorney-client privilege and as to the professional responsibilities of the recipient of the misdirected communication.

Similarly, in the context of electronic discovery in civil litigation, a substantial risk of inadvertent disclosure of privileged or work-product protected information arises from the sheer volume of documents that may be involved. As one federal district court observed in the leading case of *Hopson v. City of Baltimore*,[190] because "electronic document discovery may encompass hundreds of thousands, if not millions, of electronic records that are potentially discoverable," "to insist in every case upon 'old world' record-by-record pre-production privilege review, on pain of subject matter waiver, would impose upon parties costs of production that bear no proportionality to what is at stake in the litigation." Even if counsel does make extensive efforts to identify all documents that may be subject to privilege or other protection, it may be impossible to guard against every inadvertent disclosure.

A small number of courts previously regarded any voluntary disclosure of confidential communications as a waiver of the attorney-client privilege, even if the disclosure was inadvertent and regardless of the precautions taken by the lawyer.[191] Today, Professors Ronald Rotunda and John Dzienkowski find that the "general trend in the law is to hold that the attorney-client privilege is not waived by inadvertent disclosure if the lawyer and client take *reasonable* precautions to guard against inadvertent disclosures."[192]

As confirmation of the national trend, in 2008, Congress unanimously enacted a new Rule 502 of the Federal Rules of Evidence. The rule provides that disclosure of a communication or information covered by the attorney-client privilege or work product protection does not operate as a waiver if the disclosure is "inadvertent" and if the disclosing party took "reasonable steps to prevent disclosure" and then "promptly took reasonable steps to rectify the error" after the party learns or should have learned of the

---

[189] *See generally* Paula Schaefer, *Technology's Triple Threat to the Attorney-Client Privilege*, 2013 J. PROF'L LAWYER 171 (2013).

[190] 232 F.R.D. 228, 244 (D. Md. 2005).

[191] *See, e.g.*, In re Sealed Case, 877 F.2d 976, 980 (D.C. Cir. 1989).

[192] RONALD D. ROTUNDA & JOHN S. DZIENKOWSKI, PROFESSIONAL RESPONSIBILITY: A STUDENT'S GUIDE § 1.6-2(b) (American Bar Ass'n, 2013–2014). *See generally* Hopson v. City of Baltimore, 232 F.R.D. 228 (D. Md. 2005).

disclosure.[193] The Advisory Committee on Evidence Rules for the federal courts, which drafted the new rule, understood it to reflect the majority view in both the federal and state courts.[194] As enacted by Congress, this new federal rule regarding privilege waivers is binding on state courts as well with respect to disclosures made in federal court or federal administrative proceedings.[195]

The fact is that even the most diligent of lawyers, or their assistants, will make mistakes. No ethical regime or sensible approach to confidentiality could expect each lawyer to personally and carefully screen every email address used in every email message in the office, together with the content of each message and electronic document to ensure that any confidential element has been eliminated. No more would we would expect the lawyer to inspect the addressed envelopes of every piece of mail leaving the office or the telephone numbers dialed when a legal assistant is sending a facsimile message.

If the lawyer has established a reasonable system for protecting information in the office and has instructed others in the office on the importance of maintaining confidences (including taking precautions against inadvertent disclosure), the occasional error ought not be treated in a manner that is harmful to clients or punitive toward their lawyers. To be sure, the unintended recipient of a misdirected communication cannot be expected to wipe her memory upon discovering that confidential information had mistakenly been sent[196] nor should that innocent recipient be punished for another lawyer's mistake by being disqualified. However, the inadvertent disclosure of information generally should not be regarded as a waiver of the attorney-client privilege so as to permit further use of that information or its introduction into evidence.[197]

## § 4-6.6 EXCEPTIONS TO CONFIDENTIALITY UNDER RULE 1.6

### § 4-6.6(a) Exceptions as Narrow Departures from Confidentiality

The core of attorney-client confidentiality remains robust in the United States, notwithstanding some redefinition and limited expansion of exceptions under the Model Rules of Professional Conduct. The criminal defendant who confesses past wrongdoing to the lawyer may be assured that the information remains protected, subject to incursion only if that defendant subsequently introduces false evidence or testimony to a tribunal.[198] The business client who seeks to learn the limits of the law and is prepared to conform his, her, or its behavior to those limits need not fear any breach of the wall of confidentiality. Moreover, as has been discussed above with respect to each of the exceptions, the lawyer's discretion or obligation to disclose ordinarily is limited to extraordinary circumstances in which serious harm is reasonably certain to occur or has

---

[193] FED. R. EVID. 502(b).

[194] Proposed Rule 502(b) of Federal Rules of Evidence, Committee on Rules of Practice and Procedure, United States Judicial Conference, Report of the Advisory Committee on Evidence Rules (May 15, 2006).

[195] FED. R. EVID. 502(b), (f).

[196] *See* Doca Co. v. Westinghouse Elec. Co., Civ. No. 04–1951, 2011 WL 2182439 (W.D. Pa. June 3, 2011) (holding that an attorney who received a timeline prepared for counsel on the background facts of the lawsuit—privileged material that was inadvertently disclosed by the opponent—was not thereafter precluded from seeking discovery of other non-privileged facts, such as what happened at those meetings, simply because the existence of those meetings had been revealed by the mistakenly produced privileged document).

[197] On the professional responsibilities of the lawyer who receives confidential information that was inadvertently disclosed or improperly obtained by a third party, see *infra* § 4-9.6(e).

[198] *See infra* § 4-9.8(c) to (g).

resulted. The exceptions to confidentiality remain few and continue to be narrowly drawn.

In sum, the promise of confidentiality offered by the lawyer to the client continues to be as good as gold, excepting only those rare circumstances where the client's own persistence along a wrongful path or other disturbing potential for great harm tarnishes that expectation of confidentiality.[199]

The occasions for application of exceptions to confidentiality are few; the circumstances justifying disclosure are narrow; when disclosure is allowed (or required) a compelling (or at least arguably compelling) public interest is present.[200] The heart of the confidentiality principle still beats steadfastly.

At the same time, whenever significant changes are made in the governing rules that touch upon a central element of the professional relationship, such as the fundamental principle of confidentiality, the risk arises that harm to the principle may be realized through misunderstanding or unanticipated consequences.

*First*, if lawyers were mistakenly and paternalistically to assume that the new exceptions or clarifications added over the past two decades open the door widely to disclosure of confidential information whenever the lawyer in his own judgment thinks employment of that information would be useful to protect the interests of the client or other persons, then the security of confidential information would be seriously threatened. The enlarged discretion conferred upon lawyers by the new provisions is carefully circumscribed, allowing the lawyer to reveal confidential information without client consent only in cases of necessity and only to avoid or remedy reasonably certain and significant harm. The newer provisions do not grant the lawyer a roving warrant to reveal confidential information as he sees fit, nor do the rules convert the lawyer into a judge against the interests of his own client. The presumption still stands against disclosure of confidential information.

Each lawyer should carefully read Rule 1.6 of the Model Rules of Professional Conduct (and Rules 3.3 and 4.1) and the governing parallel rules in the jurisdiction of admission. The lawyer should be clear as to what the rules do and do not say, not assuming that the changes regarding confidentiality are as profound and wide-sweeping as some reports might have suggested. Moreover, one of the new exceptions to confidentiality helpfully enhances the opportunity for lawyers to deliberate more carefully and more completely before choosing to divulge a client confidence. Although it was implicit under past practice, the rule now expressly authorizes a lawyer to reveal confidential information to secure the advice of another lawyer about compliance with the rules,[201] which of course would include advice as to the permissions and obligations regarding disclosure of confidential information. Except in emergency situations, a lawyer would be well-advised to seek the counsel of other well-regarded lawyers before determining to take the momentous step of disclosing a client confidence without the client's consent and adverse to the client's interests.

---

[199] On disclosure to the client of the exceptions to confidentiality, see *infra* § 4-6.6(b)(1).

[200] On the nature of and justifications for the exceptions to attorney-client confidentiality, see generally Susan R. Martyn, *In Defense of Client-Lawyer Confidentiality . . . and Its Exceptions*, 81 NEB. L. REV. 1320, 1330–56 (2003).

[201] *See supra* § 4-6.6(e).

*Second*, there remains the possibility that an exception to confidentiality will prove in practice to have the deleterious results feared by opponents, either because these new provisions fail of their purpose in protecting the public or because they weaken the cornerstone of confidentiality more substantially than the drafters anticipated. On the one hand, as noted above, a proper understanding of the exceptional circumstances for application of these provisions should reduce the occasions for misuse. On the other hand, if lawyers do find that these exceptions are invoked, or at least potentially implicated, more frequently than anticipated, lawyers may find it awkwardly necessary to warn clients that information shared may not be protected.[202] Lawyers also may strive to avoid becoming aware of unpleasant facts so as to avoid the problem (although this is not likely to be a wise course of action and indeed could be contrary to the lawyer's duty of diligence).

If we, as a profession, find that enlarged exceptions to confidentiality have the effect of diminishing the flow of information from clients, then no disclosure to the public to remedy past harm would be possible, thus defeating the public interest purpose of the rule. In such an event, the lawyer also would be left without the necessary information to well represent and counsel the client.

*Finally*, as with any set of rules, their effectiveness and integrity depend not only upon what the text says but also upon the informed discretion of lawyers in applying those rules and the wise judgment of the courts in interpreting those rules in the context of each case.

## § 4-6.6(b) Lawyer and Client on the Lawyer's Decision to Disclose

### *§ 4-6.6(b)(1) Disclosing to the Client the Ethical Qualifications on Confidentiality*

Knowing that lawyers regularly assure a client that communications will be kept confidential, scholars continue to debate whether the lawyer has a duty to alert the client to the existence of exceptions to that confidentiality and whether such a warning should be issued at the outset or may instead be issued when events occur that implicate an exception to confidentiality.[203]

Some scholars insist that the lawyer's general duty to keep the client informed mandates an initial disclosure that complete confidentiality cannot be promised. These scholars maintain that the lawyer must acknowledge the boundaries of confidentiality at the earliest point, thus allowing the client to decide whether even to engage representation if doing so would place the lawyer in a position to obtain and perhaps later disclose confidential information.[204] Because "some clients might find the exceptions material to determining which confidences to share with an attorney," Professor Lee Pizzimenti argues that "[a]ttorneys may deprive those clients of information critical to intelligent decisionmaking if they fail to apprise clients of those exceptions, thereby limiting client's ability to choose rationally whether to confide in

---

[202] *See infra* § 4-6.6(b)(1).

[203] *See generally* Elisia M. Klinka & Russell G. Pearce, *Confidentiality Explained: The Dialogue Approach to Discussing Confidentiality With Clients*, 48 SAN DIEGO L. REV. 157 (2011).

[204] Fred C. Zacharias, *Harmonizing Privilege and Confidentiality*, 41 S. TEX. L. REV. 69, 108–09 (1999); Lee A. Pizzimenti, *The Lawyer's Duty to Warn Clients About Limits on Confidentiality*, 39 CATH. U. L. REV. 441, 450 (1990).

counsel."[205] Pizzimenti clarifies that the lawyer at the outset should not provide the client "with an equivalent of a law school education by explaining all the nuances of confidentiality rules," but rather provide "a general explanation of the duty of confidentiality and its major exceptions" so that the client may "ask intelligent questions as specific confidentiality issues arise."[206]

In some contrast regarding the necessary extent of the initial disclosure, Professors Stephen Ellmann, Robert Dinerstein, Isabelle Gunning, Katherine Kruse, and Ann Shalleck suggest an initial statement that "ordinarily" everything the client tells the lawyer is confidential, while acknowledging there are "some exceptions" that will be explained if "it turns out to be necessary as we go along."[207] If "a confidentiality exception [comes into] view," because the limits of confidentiality become a potential issue in the representation, then the lawyer would explain the exception.[208] In sum, the lawyer would make a general reference to unspecified exceptions to confidentiality at the outset of the representation, together with an equally general assurance of confidentiality, which would be followed by more specific description of exceptions if they should become pertinent to the evolving representation.

In your author's view, a lawyer's decision to reveal confidential information contrary to the client's wishes should be understood as a departure from the normal progression of a legal representation.[209] With that in mind, the lawyer who chooses not to begin a consultation with a "Miranda" type warning[210] that the client's communications may be used against her in exceptional circumstances is unlikely to cross a formal ethical line. Nonetheless, as a means of building a stronger relationship with the client, the lawyer's forthright admission that confidentiality is not without boundaries may enhance client trust by the very virtue of the lawyer's broaching the matter.

Elisia Klinka and Professor Russell Pearce propose raising confidentiality limits beginning with the initial consultation, by generally explaining the nature of confidentiality and by identifying the basic exceptions, "while at the same time encouraging dialogue regarding the exceptions. We urge lawyers to address their mistrust of clients and their fear of clients' mistrust through honesty and dialogue."[211] By generally identifying the nature of the exceptions in a dialogue, the Klinka-Pearce approach "seeks to strike a balance between providing sufficient information for the client to participate knowledgeably in the lawyer-client relationship without providing so much information that the client is overwhelmed."[212] By framing the matter as an invitation to a dialogue, rather than as a warning with detailed explanation of the

---

[205] Pizzimenti, *supra*, CATH. U. L. REV. at 450.

[206] *Id.* at 485.

[207] STEPHEN ELLMANN, ROBERT D. DINERSTEIN, ISABELLE GUNNING, KATHERINE R. KRUSE & ANN C. SHALLECK, LAWYERS AND CLIENTS: CRITICAL ISSUES IN INTERVIEWING AND COUNSELING 251 (West Academic Publishing, 2009).

[208] *Id.* at 252–53.

[209] *See supra* § 4-6.6(a). *But see* Klinka & Pearce, *supra*, 48 SAN DIEGO L. REV. at 158 (provocatively characterizing a lawyer's assurance to clients that everything is confidential as "a lie").

[210] In criminal procedure, the rule established in *Miranda v. Arizona*, 384 U.S. 436 (1966), requires that law enforcement advise a suspect being taken into custody of his rights, specifically the right to remain silent, that anything said can be used against him, and of the right to legal counsel.

[211] Klinka & Pearce, *supra*, 48 SAN DIEGO L. REV. at 196.

[212] *Id.*

exceptions, Klinka and Pearce highlight the collaborative relationship with the client.[213] In this way, they hope that "[t]he lawyer's willingness to share information on confidentiality exceptions at the commencement of the relationship indicates that the lawyer trusts and respects the client. The lawyer's honesty and commitment to dialogue maximizes the chance that the client will trust the lawyer and honestly share information."[214]

#### *§ 4-6.6(b)(2) Consulting with Client Before Lawyer's Disclosure Pursuant to a Confidentiality Exception*

When the lawyer is authorized and has decided to disclose confidential information, the lawyer's revelation ordinarily should occur only after consultation with the client about alternative means to achieve the purpose served by the exception to confidentiality. In all events, the disclosure should be limited to the extent necessary to achieve that purpose.

As discussed above with respect to the client crime-fraud exceptions,[215] when the lawyer is considering disclosure of confidential information to prevent or rectify harm to another, or to comply with a legal requirement, the lawyer generally should offer the client the opportunity to make the disclosure instead. In this way, the client's dignity is preserved in some measure, and the client may be better perceived or even receive mitigating treatment by being the source of the disclosure. On occasion, however, the imminence of the anticipated harm, or the fact that the lawyer is using confidential information to defend herself against the client's allegations of wrongdoing, will make prior consultation impossible or impractical.

In any event, the lawyer should disclose only so much information as necessary to achieve the purpose and only to those persons necessary. That an exception to confidentiality allows disclosure of some information does not excuse the lawyer from a continuing duty to safeguard other confidential information that need not be disclosed. And on no occasion should a lawyer use the exception for another purpose, such as threatening the permitted (but not required) disclosure of confidential information in order to secure an advantage against the client.

### § 4-6.6(c) To Prevent Death or Bodily Harm

The late-Professor Monroe Freedman, a nationally-recognized and zealous advocate on behalf of the principle of confidentiality and a strong opponent of most proposals to carve out exceptions to confidentiality, nonetheless long argued for broad discretion by a lawyer to reveal confidential information when necessary to prevent a person's death or serious bodily harm:

> The most compelling reason for a lawyer to divulge a client's confidence is to save a human life. There are two reasons to require divulgence in such a case. First, the value at stake, human life, is of unique importance. Second, the occasions on which a lawyer's divulgence of a client's confidence is the only thing that stands between human life and death are so rare that a requirement

---

[213] On a collaborative relationship between attorney and client in the advising context, see *supra* § 4-5.2(b).

[214] Klinka & Pearce, *supra,* 48 SAN DIEGO L. REV. at 197.

[215] *See supra* § 4-6.6(d)(4).

of divulgence would pose no threat to the systemic value of lawyer-client trust.[216]

The author of this part of the book also has written that "[c]onfidentiality cannot be justified when the life or substantial health of another is at serious and imminent risk."[217] Six states have taken what I once described as "the more enlightened approach of actually *mandating* disclosure when necessary to prevent death or serious bodily harm, whether by criminal means or otherwise."[218] As discussed below, however, most states have made such a disclosure permissive, which I have since come to conclude is the more prudential path, lest lawyers facing difficult situations be subjected to second-guessing after-the-fact.

It does not appear that any state has actually enforced a mandatory rule of disclosure in a disciplinary action against an attorney who had failed to report information necessary to prevent death or substantial bodily harm. This may confirm that the occasions truly are rare when a lawyer's disclosure is all that stands between another person and an appointment with death. Or perhaps disciplinary authorities in those minority of states with mandatory disclosure rules have appropriately hesitated to question difficult judgments made by lawyers in complex human dramas in which certainty both as to the facts and the degree of risk is frequently elusive.

As followed in most states, Rule 1.6(b)(1) of the Model Rules of Professional Conduct authorizes, but does not require, the lawyer to reveal confidential information "to the extent the lawyer reasonably believes necessary" to "prevent reasonably certain death or substantial bodily harm." In the past, Disciplinary Rule 4–101(C)(3) of the former Model Code of Professional Responsibility permitted the lawyer's disclosure only of the "intention of the client to commit a crime and the information necessary to prevent the crime."[219] While a handful of states still include "criminal" as the modifier for this permission to disclosure, the provision in Model Rule 1.6(b)(1) for disclosure to preserve life and physical integrity applies whether or not the anticipated harm would constitute a crime. Thus, for example, "[b]y removing the need to have a client crime, a client suicide will always fit within the rule, even if the state does not treat suicide as a crime."[220] In

[216] MONROE H. FREEDMAN, UNDERSTANDING LAWYERS' ETHICS 102–03 (Matthew Bender 1990); *see also* Arthur Gross Schaefer & Peter S. Levi, *Resolving the Conflict Between the Ethical Values of Confidentiality and Saving a Life: A Jewish View*, 29 LOY. L.A. L. REV. 1761, 1766–67 (1996) (saying that "saving a life takes precedence over preserving a confidential communication"); Maura Strassberg, *Taking Ethics Seriously: Beyond Positivist Jurisprudence in Legal Ethics*, 80 IOWA L. REV. 901, 923–24, 940–48 (1995).

[217] Gregory C. Sisk, *Iowa's Legal Ethics Rules—It's Time to Join the Crowd*, 47 DRAKE L. REV. 279, 309 (1999).

[218] *Id.* at 308. For the six states mandating disclosure of information to prevent death or substantial bodily harm, whether or not resulting from criminal wrongdoing, see CONN. RULES OF PROF'L CONDUCT R. 1.6(b); FLA. RULES OF PROF'L CONDUCT R. 1.6(b)(2); IOWA RULES OF PROF'L CONDUCT R. 32:1.6(c); N.J. RULES OF PROF'L CONDUCT R. 1.6(b)(1); N.D. RULES OF PROF'L CONDUCT R. 1.6(b); VT. RULES OF PROF'L CONDUCT R. 1.6(b)(1). In addition, Wisconsin requires revealing confidential information "to the extent the lawyer reasonably believes necessary to prevent the client from committing a criminal or fraudulent act that the lawyer reasonably believes is likely to result in death or substantial bodily harm." WIS. RULES OF PROF'L CONDUCT R. 20:1.6(b). Virginia requires reporting information to prevent a crime generally, which presumably would include risks to death and bodily harm from criminal wrongdoing. *See* VA. RULES OF PROF'L CONDUCT R. 1.6(c)(1).

[219] MODEL CODE OF PROF'L RESPONSIBILITY, Disciplinary Rule 4–101(C)(3) (American Bar Ass'n, 1980).

[220] RONALD D. ROTUNDA & JOHN S. DZIENKOWSKI, PROFESSIONAL RESPONSIBILITY: A STUDENT'S GUIDE § 1.6-12(e)(2) (American Bar Ass'n, 2013–2014).

fact, the threat of death or substantial bodily injury need not be attributable to the client at all. Instead, the trigger for the exception is the risk of harm, not its source.

Under the rule, if the anticipated "death or substantial bodily harm" is "reasonably certain," the lawyer who so "reasonably believes" is allowed discretion on whether to act, at least immediately, to reveal client confidences to prevent the harm. By adopting the standard of the lawyer's "reasonable belief" as to whether disclosure is necessary to prevent death or substantial bodily harm, the rule directs that the circumstances be evaluated from the perspective of the lawyer at the time and not through hindsight distorted by the unfortunate tragedy that death or substantial bodily harm did subsequently occur. As Professors Geoffrey Hazard and William Hodes and attorney Peter Jarvis comment with respect to the definition of states of mind in Model Rule 1.0, "there are gradations in the firmness and clarity with which a lawyer, like anyone else, can perceive relevant facts in a kaleidoscope of events."[221]

When a client makes threatening statements about a third-party to his lawyer—comments typically made in a burst of anger or to vent stress[222]—the lawyer in most circumstances should not file a report with law enforcement, which would create burdens on law enforcement, impose unnecessary concerns or fears on others, and undermine the lawyer-client relationship. While the lawyer should not let any threat of violence pass without cautioning the client, and receiving reassurance from the client that no actual harm is intended, the permission to disclose is reserved for those situations in which a reasonable lawyer would believe, based upon familiarity with the client and knowledge of the circumstances, that this threat is something more than the common episode of client frustration being vehemently expressed.

Perhaps the most common scenario implicating this exception will not be when a client genuinely threatens physical harm to another person, but rather when the client may be a danger to herself. Lawyers in such situations should be given ample room to make judgments about how best to evaluate the person, how to involve other professionals better able to judge the mental state of the client, and how to preserve the lawyer-client relationship if possible. Moreover, mental health professionals report that it is notoriously difficult to predict whether an individual actually will carry through on a threat of self-harm.

It already is difficult to encourage lawyers to undertake representation of persons with diminished capacity or who are emotionally vulnerable,[223] even though they may be the ones who most desperately need legal assistance. Those heroic lawyers, often in legal aid offices, who represent the most emotionally troubled and disadvantaged in our society, should not be second-guessed by disciplinary authorities for what in hindsight might appear to be a less than perfect handling of a thorny client representation.

---

[221] 1 GEOFFREY C. HAZARD, JR., W. WILLIAM HODES & PETER R. JARVIS, THE LAW OF LAWYERING § 1.23 (Aspen, 4th ed., 2016).

[222] *See* In re Grand Jury Investigation, 902 N.E.2d 929, 933 (Mass. 2009) (saying that clients need to be given "breathing room to express frustration and dissatisfaction with the legal system and its participants" and that the "expression of such sentiments" even "may serve as a springboard for further discussion regarding a client's legal options").

[223] On representation of clients with diminished capacity, see *supra* § 4-3.5.

## § 4-6.6(d) To Prevent or Rectify Substantial Economic Harm

### *§ 4-6.6(d)(1) History, Controversy, and Overview of Economic Harm Exceptions*

Subparagraphs (b)(2) and (b)(3) of Rule 1.6 of the Model Rules of Professional Conduct are the most recent and have been among the more controversial of the exceptions to confidentiality. These two overlapping provisions authorize the disclosure of confidential information when the lawyer reasonably believes such revelation is necessary, not only to prevent, but also to mitigate or rectify reasonably certain and substantial injury to the financial or property interests of others caused by the client's fraud or crime and in furtherance of which the lawyer's services were used.

These straightforwardly are "whistle-blower" provisions. In the narrow circumstances of client crime or fraud to which these provisions apply, the lawyer's authority to disclose the information necessary to prevent economic harm generally runs directly adverse to the client's interest and in favor of third persons outside the attorney-client relationship. Because lawyers rightly resist being placed in the position of adjudging their clients guilty of misconduct and then turning the clients in to the authorities or another party, any provision that appears to introduce such an expectation naturally will meet with resistance from large segments of the practicing bar.

The controversy surrounding these provisions was illustrated by their tenuous reception by the American Bar Association. In 2001, proposed paragraph (b)(2) was soundly rejected by a substantial margin by the American Bar Association's (ABA) House of Delegates, in the wake of which, proposed paragraph (b)(3) was then withdrawn.[224] At the August 2003 meeting of the House of Delegates, paragraphs (b)(2) and (b)(3) were reconsidered and then adopted by the slim margin of 218–201.[225] In fact, before the narrow approval of paragraph (b)(3) in 2003 after its withdrawal in the face of certain defeat only two years before, the ABA had twice previously (in 1983 and 1991) turned away similar proposals to authorize disclosure of confidential information to rectify financial injury from past wrongdoing.[226] The impetus for the reversal of position by the ABA in 2003 lay in the corporate scandals of Enron, WorldCom, and Tyco, in which lawyers failed to prevent and even facilitated financial irregularities.

Even before the ABA adoption of subparagraph (b)(3) in 2003, eighteen states permitted disclosure of client confidences to correct past fraudulent or criminal harm.[227] As of 2015, about two-thirds of the states have incorporated subparagraph (b)(3) or something like it into their respective ethical regimes.[228]

---

[224] *See generally* 1 GEOFFREY C. HAZARD, JR., W. WILLIAM HODES & PETER R. JARVIS, THE LAW OF LAWYERING §§ 1.18, 10.34 (Aspen, 4th ed., 2016).

[225] *Model Rules: ABA Amends Ethics Rules on Confidentiality, Corporate Clients, to Allow More Disclosure*, 19 ABA/BNA LAWYER'S MANUAL ON PROFESSIONAL CONDUCT 672 (Aug. 13, 2003).

[226] *See* Maura Strassberg, *Taking Ethics Seriously: Beyond Positivist Jurisprudence in Legal Ethics*, 80 IOWA L. REV. 901, 923–24, 939–40 (1995).

[227] E. Norman Veasey, *The Ethical and Professional Responsibilities of the Lawyer for the Corporation in Responding to Fraudulent Conduct by Corporate Officers or Agents*, 70 TENN. L. REV. 1, 18 (2002).

[228] *See* Center for Professional Responsibility, American Bar Ass'n, Comparison of State Confidentiality Rules, ABA Model Rule 1.6 (b) (2) and (3): Revealing Confidential Information in Cases of Financial Harm (Chart) (May 2015), at http://www.americanbar.org/content/dam/aba/administrative/professional_responsibility/mrpc_1_6b2_3.pdf.

Subparagraph (b)(2) of Rule 1.6 is the *prevent-future-economic-harm exception* to confidentiality, authorizing the lawyer to disclose confidential information when the lawyer reasonably believes it necessary "to prevent the client from committing a crime or fraud that is reasonably certain to result in substantial injury to the financial interests or property of another and in furtherance of which the client has used or is using the lawyer's services."

As a future-oriented measure, subparagraph (b)(2) is not a meaningful departure from past professional expectations. Disciplinary Rule 4–101(C)(3) of the former Model Code of Professional Responsibility provided that "[a] lawyer may reveal . . . [t]he intention of the client to commit a crime and the information necessary to prevent the crime."[229] Although subparagraph (b)(2) of Model Rules 1.6 permits disclosure to prevent fraudulent, as well as criminal, conduct, the kind of deliberate misrepresentation that constitutes fraud almost invariably constitutes criminal behavior as well. Importantly, because subparagraph (b)(2) permits disclosure only when the lawyer's services have been used "in furtherance" of the crime of fraud, this provision is somewhat narrower than former Disciplinary Rule 4–101(C)(3), which appeared to permit disclosure to prevent a future crime whether or not the attorney-client relationship had been abused (a position still taken in about one-third of the states).

Subparagraph (b)(3) of Rule 1.6 is the *rectify-past-economic-harm exception* to confidentiality, authorizing the lawyer to disclose confidential information when the lawyer reasonably believes it necessary "to prevent, mitigate or rectify substantial injury to the financial interests or property of another that is reasonably certain to result or has resulted from the client's commission of a crime or fraud in furtherance of which the client has used the lawyer's services."

By authorizing a lawyer to reveal confidential information not only to prevent future financial harm by fraud or crime, but also to uncover past wrongdoing by the client during the course of the representation, subparagraph (b)(3) is a new entry into the exceptions to confidentiality that are recognized in the Model Rules of Professional Conduct. The Code of Professional Responsibility did not permit a lawyer to (voluntarily) disclose confidential information about a client's past wrongdoing, whether the misconduct caused economic harm or not and whether the behavior was criminal or not. Indeed, when a client confessed to a lawyer that he had committed a past wrong, criminal or civil, the protection of confidentiality had been at its zenith (and still today remains absolute in most circumstances where the client has not also made actual use of the attorney-client relationship to advance the illegitimate scheme).

Yet subparagraph (b)(3) is not wholly unprecedented because its authorization of disclosure runs parallel to the longstanding crime-fraud exception to the attorney-client privilege.[230] The alignment between the confidentiality and privilege exceptions is further confirmed by the careful restriction of the permission to disclose in both subparagraphs (b)(2) and (3) to those situations in which the lawyer's services were or are being used "in furtherance" of the client's crime or fraud. Still, the crime-fraud exception to the attorney-client privilege removed the protection of the privilege when invoked as an objection to an inquiry from others (such as parties in civil litigation or law enforcement and prosecutors in criminal cases), but did not in itself allow or impose

---

[229] MODEL CODE OF PROF'L RESPONSIBILITY, Disciplinary Rule 4–101(C)(3) (American Bar Ass'n, 1980).

[230] *See supra* § 4-6.3(c)(1).

any duty on the lawyer to blow the whistle on the client. Furthermore, as discussed below,[231] when paragraphs (b)(2) and (3) of Rule 1.6 are read together with Rule 4.1(b), the prevent and rectify economic harm disclosure provisions may be elevated from the permissive into the mandatory category, thus introducing a new obligation for the lawyer to disclose client confidences, even without being asked.

### *§ 4-6.6(d)(2) Strict Standards for Application of Economic Harm Exceptions*

Whether perceived to be new and unfamiliar or accepted as a natural evolutionary development from the crime-fraud exception to the attorney-client privilege, the provisions in subparagraphs (b)(2) and (3) of Rule 1.6 allowing lawyer disclosure to prevent or rectify economic harm caused by client wrongdoing are reserved for extraordinary circumstances. The standards for application of subparagraphs (b)(2) and (3) are stringent, involving multiple layers of constraint before confidentiality may be subordinated by the lawyer.

Disclosure is permitted only if—

(1) the lawyer believes it *reasonably necessary*

(2) to *prevent, mitigate, or rectify*

(3) *substantial injury* to the financial or property interests of another

(4) that is *reasonably certain* to result

(5) from the planned or past commission by the client of a *crime or fraud*

(6) in *furtherance* of which the client has or is using the *lawyer's services*.

Under these exacting prerequisites, the lawyer is empowered to act only when harm is reasonably certain to occur and the lawyer finds it reasonably necessary to disclose confidential information to prevent that harm. The lawyer further must conclude that the injury to economic interests would be substantial in degree. The harm that is to be prevented or rectified must be attributable to the client's criminal or fraudulent behavior—that is, deliberate, misconduct—and not reflect mere negligence or error.

As perhaps the "most important feature" of these subparagraphs,[232] the lawyer must have discovered that the legal services he is or has been providing to the client were perverted to an illicit end, that is, the client actually has abused the attorney-client relationship to advance the crime or fraud, as contrasted with the client merely telling the lawyer of past misconduct or unlawful future plans. As Professors Geoffrey Hazard and William Hodes and attorney Peter Jarvis caution, "unless there is initially unwitting lawyer *involvement* in the client's wrongdoing, the lawyer is bound to maintain silence."[233]

To be sure, the circumstances justifying application of subparagraphs (b)(2) and (3) are by no means abstract or theoretical, as revealed by unfortunate episodes receiving public attention in which all the elements of these provisions have been present. Nonetheless, the rule places emphasis on reasonable certainty of harm and on a

---

[231] *See infra* § 4-6.6(d)(3).

[232] 1 GEOFFREY C. HAZARD, JR., W. WILLIAM HODES & PETER R. JARVIS, THE LAW OF LAWYERING § 10.34 (Aspen, 4th ed., 2016).

[233] *Id.*

reasonable belief by the lawyer that disclosure is necessary to correct the harm. The rule is further restricted to circumstances of fraud and crime to which the lawyer's service have been misappropriated. Thus, read as a whole and in context, Rule 1.6 affirms a continuing and general presumption in favor of continued confidentiality absent extraordinary circumstances.

### *§ 4-6.6(d)(3) When the Permission to Disclose Economic Harm Becomes a Mandatory Duty*

Read and applied separately, the exceptions to confidentiality set forth in Rule 1.6(b) are entirely permissive in nature, as indicated by the deliberate use of the word "may." Thus, subparagraphs (b)(2) and (3) of Rule 1.6 permit, but do not themselves require, the lawyer to reveal information to prevent, mitigate, or rectify substantial injury to the financial interests or property of another that is reasonably certain to result or has resulted from the client's commission of a crime or fraud "in furtherance of which" the client has used or is using the lawyer's services.

However, those permissive provisions in Rule 1.6 must now be read together with Rule 4.1(b) of the Model Rules of Professional Conduct, which forbids a lawyer from knowingly "fail[ing] to disclose a material fact to a third person when disclosure is necessary to avoid assisting a criminal or fraudulent act by a client."[234] The duty imposed in Rule 4.1(b) is expressly mandatory in nature, but the scope of that duty has been limited by confidentiality. Rule 4.1(b) states that revelation is not required when "disclosure is prohibited by rule 1.6." Yet precisely because subparagraphs (b)(2) and (3) of Rule 1.6 now *do* authorize revelation of confidential information to prevent or rectify economic harm caused by fraud or crime, disclosure is no longer "prohibited" by Rule 1.6 when those exceptions to confidentiality are triggered.

In other words, with the amendments to Rule 1.6(b) that were approved by the American Bar Association in 2003, confidentiality no longer stands as an obstacle to the duty to disclose under Rule 4.1(b), at least under certain (perhaps most) circumstances. As Professors Ronald Rotunda and John Dzienkowski explain:

> When Rule 4.1(b) is mandatory unless limited by Rule 1.6, the expansion of permissive disclosure in Rule 1.6 will lead to mandatory disclosure under Rule 4.1(b) to third persons in the context of financial crimes likely to cause substantial injury.[235]

Accordingly, when the stringent requisites for *both* Rule 1.6(b)(2) or (3) *and* Rule 4.1(b) are present in a case,[236] the lawyer is *required*, and not merely authorized, to make the disclosure. Somewhere in the combined operation of subparagraphs (b)(2) and (3) of Rule 1.6 and of Rule 4.1(b) may be found a newly vitalized and mandatory duty to disclose information about client fraud or crime, although this remains an area of professional responsibility that is still evolving. The parameters of that duty consequently remain uncertain.[237] And, of course, for the one-third of the states that has

---

[234] *See infra* § 4-11.2(b).

[235] RONALD D. ROTUNDA & JOHN S. DZIENKOWSKI, PROFESSIONAL RESPONSIBILITY: A STUDENT'S GUIDE § 4.1–3 (American Bar Ass'n, 2013–2014).

[236] *See infra* § 4-11.2(c).

[237] *Compare* John A. Humbach, *Shifting Paradigms of Lawyer Honesty*, 76 TENN. L. REV. 993, 1010 (2009) ("By modifying Rule 1.6, the ABA has taken the lid off the pot in Rule 4.1(b).") *with* Peter A. Jarvis & Trisha M. Rich, *The Law of Unintended Consequences: Whether and When Mandatory Disclosure Under Model*

not adopted all or part of 1.6(b)(2) and (3),[238] a mandatory duty to disclose cannot be extrapolated from the interaction of these separate provisions.

Because these rules were adopted by the American Bar Association at different times and their potential interaction may have not been fully appreciated, subparagraphs 1.6(b)(2) and (3) of Rule 1.6 are not fully integrated in language and style with Rule 4.1(b).[239] Rule 1.6(b)(2) and (3) may be invoked only when the lawyer's services were used "in furtherance" of the client's crime or fraud, while Rule 4.1(b) applies only when the lawyer's silence about a material fact would amount to "assisting a criminal or fraudulent act by the client." Given that both rules are triggered by lawyer involvement (presumably unwitting, at least at the start) with the client's wrongdoing, these provisions would appear to operate in tandem under many circumstances, although they are not perfectly congruent.

Whether Rule 1.6(b) will prove in practical application to work hand in glove with Rule 4.1(b) is not yet certain. Nonetheless, as developed further below, because of the uncertain parameters of the mandatory duty to disclose in Rule 4.1(b), together with the practical need for a lawyer whose services have been perverted toward illicit ends to extricate herself from the situation and avoid even an accusation of complicity, the prudent lawyer may well decide to exercise the discretion granted in Rule 1.6(b)(2) and (3) to disclose, even if an argument may be made against mandatory disclosure under Rule 4.1(b).

Because the American Bar Association thus far has failed to coordinate the two rules and clarify the extent of interrelationship, one may postulate circumstances under which one rule would appear to operate separately from the other, although whether such a difference in application was intended by the rules drafters is not elucidated in the rules or the comments.

For example, subparagraphs (b)(2) and (3) of Rule 1.6 grant permission to disclose a client's confidence only when the economic harm to result from the client's fraud or crime is both "reasonably certain" in terms of likelihood and "substantial" in terms of degree. By contrast, Rule 4.1(b) imposes no harm measurement limitations on the lawyer's duty to reveal information when necessary to avoid assisting a client's crime or fraud. Thus, if the harm anticipated to the other person is not "substantial" or if it is not pecuniary in nature, then subparagraphs (b)(2) and (3) of Rule 1.6 do not authorize disclosure. Even then, however, because a lawyer is obliged by Rule 1.2(d) not to assist the client in conduct known to the lawyer to be criminal or fraudulent and because the substantive law of the jurisdiction may demand that the lawyer take steps necessary to avoid being an accomplice in the client's fraud or crime, the lawyer may be obliged to reveal confidential information in order "to comply with other law," for which disclosure now authorized is under subparagraph (b)(6) of Model Rule 1.6.[240]

Thus, while a roundabout analysis is required to arrive at the conclusion, it now may be that the supposed confidentiality limitation in Rule 4.1(b) will rarely if ever apply to excuse a lawyer from making a disclosure that is necessary to avoid assisting the

*Rule 4.1(b) Trumps Discretionary Disclosure Under Model Rule 1.6*, 44 HOFSTRA L. REV. 421, 422, 437 (2015) (arguing that "Model Rule 4.1(b) does not expressly trump permissive disclosure under Model Rule 1.6(b)").

[238] *See supra* § 4-6.6(d)(1).

[239] *See generally* 2 GEOFFREY C. HAZARD, JR., W. WILLIAM HODES & PETER R. JARVIS, THE LAW OF LAWYERING § 40.02 (Aspen, 4th ed., 2016).

[240] *See infra* § 4-6.6(g).

client's fraud. Even if a textual argument could be made for avoiding compelled disclosure, lawyers may be reluctant to take the chance of being found complicit in client wrongdoing, by virtue of having concealed information necessary to correct a client misrepresentation that the lawyer previously had transmitted or had endorsed expressly or implicitly by participation in the matter.

One also may imagine a scenario under which permission to disclose information would be granted under subparagraphs (b)(2) and (3) of Rule 1.6, but the mandatory duty to disclose under Rule 4.1(b) would not be triggered, thus leaving the exceptions to confidentiality entirely discretionary in nature. Suppose that a lawyer had provided background advice to a client, who subsequently misused that information to facilitate criminal or fraudulent conduct that may cause or already has caused reasonably certain and substantial injury to the financial or property interests of another. In other words, the client's misconduct has unfolded in such a way that the lawyer's purely advisory role is unknown to the injured party and thus the lawyer has not sufficiently participated in the matter so as to even be accused of having made or endorsed a false or misleading representation or otherwise having assisted in the client's fraud. As Comment 9 to Rule 1.2 states, "that a client uses advice in a course of action that is criminal or fraudulent of itself [does not] make a lawyer a party to the course of action."

In such an instance, the lawyer's passive counseling role may not rise to the level of involvement necessary to constitute the kind of "assistance" in a crime or fraud that would implicate Rule 4.1(b) and its mandatory duty of disclosure. Still, because the lawyer's advice in this scenario would have been used by the client in furtherance of the fraud or crime, and assuming again that economic harm to another is reasonably certain and substantial, subparagraphs (b)(2) and (3) of Rule 1.6 would permit (but not require) disclosure.

Again, although one can postulate hypothetical situations in which Rule 1.6(b)(2) and (3) would operate independently of Rule 4.1(b), and vice-versa, the foregoing analysis fairly could be criticized as overly formalistic. When a lawyer does discover that a client has used the legal representation to carry out a fraudulent or criminal scheme, the requisite elements of both Rule 1.6(b)(2) and (3) and Rule 4.1(b) will typically be present. The wise lawyer should be wary of relying upon too fine distinctions about degree of lawyer participation to justify a refusal to disclose client wrongdoing, when the lawyer's own counsel (contrary to the lawyer's design) has materially advanced the client's illicit purposes.

To ensure compliance with the duty of disclosure imposed by Rule 4.1(b), and with sober appreciation of the force of the substantive civil law of fraud and criminal law regarding accomplices,[241] the lawyer may be well-advised "to reveal the fraud at an earlier point" so as to avoid the later "necessity of a formal defense, which may be costly in terms of both money and reputation."[242]

---

[241] Indeed, Professors Geoffrey Hazard and William Hodes and attorney Peter Jarvis suggest a "saving" construction of Rule 4.1(b) that embraces the exception in Rule 1.6(b)(6) allowing disclosure of confidential information "to comply with other law." By mandatory operation of the substantive law of fraud, they contend, Rule 4.1(b) "*cannot* exclude correcting a client's fraudulent misrepresentations from the ambit of responsible lawyering." 2 GEOFFREY C. HAZARD, JR., W. WILLIAM HODES & PETER R. JARVIS, THE LAW OF LAWYERING § 40.02 (Aspen, 4th ed., 2016).

[242] *Id.* § 40.07.

To be sure, as discussed above and later in this book,[243] both Rule 1.6(b)(2) and (3) and Rule 4.1(b) are reserved for the extraordinary circumstance when the lawyer becomes aware of manifest client misconduct to which the lawyer has unwittingly contributed. If the client has sought the lawyer's advice regarding past wrongdoing, in which the lawyer's legal services played no facilitating role, then the lawyer's duty of confidentiality remains intact and neither Rule 1.6(b)(2) and (3) nor Rule 4.1(b) are implicated. Indeed, a client securing representation from a lawyer to defend against charges of such past wrongdoing is one of the classic situations for which confidentiality is designed and should be zealously guarded. Likewise, if the client reveals plans for future misconduct, but the lawyer's advice has not and will not be diverted to facilitate that behavior (and thus the lawyer simply has no participation in the illicit scheme), then the lawyer has no duty under Rule 4.1(b) to disclose the client's misconduct because the lawyer has remained separate from it. At that point, as stated in Comment 3 to Rule 4.1, the lawyer "can avoid assisting a client's crime or fraud by withdrawing from the representation." For the same reason, subparagraphs (b)(2) and (3) of Rule 1.6 would not permit disclosure.

But the closer the lawyer has been drawn in to the client's illegitimate scheme through perversion of the attorney-client relationship by the client, whether the lawyer discovers the client's misuse of legal counsel before or after the fact, and the farther that the crime or fraud has progressed toward its illicit objectives, the more the lawyer should be motivated to aggressively disengage himself from the matter and disassociate himself from any perception of complicity. In this respect, Rules 1.6(b)(2) and (3) and 4.1(b) dovetail with the lawyer self-defense exception to confidentiality in subparagraph (b)(5) of Rule 1.6, which is discussed below.[244] As Professors Geoffrey Hazard and William Hodes and attorney Peter Jarvis suggest, "the lawyer's right to make disclosure [of client fraud or crime] *at the outset* is the lawyer's best protection" from being later accused of complicity in the fraudulent or criminal scheme.[245]

Unfortunately, as the foregoing discussion demonstrates, the complicated and uncertain interplay between Rule 1.6(b)(2) and (3) and Rule 4.1 has not yet been coordinated by the ethics rules drafters in the American Bar Association.[246] When an affirmative duty is imposed upon the lawyer, at the risk of a disciplinary penalty for failure to uphold it, discovery of that duty should not depend upon a careful inter-textual analysis of uncoordinated provisions, and the scope of that duty should not be ambiguous. Even worse, describing Rule 1.6(b)(2) and (3) as permissive exceptions to confidentiality is somewhat misleading to the casual reader, given the sometimes mandatory nature of these disclosures when integrated with Rule 4.1(b). Likewise, the supposed confidentiality condition on the application of Rule 4.1(b) is increasingly misleading, given that the expansion of exceptions to confidentiality in Rule 1.6(b) has left that condition with diminishing effect.

---

[243] *See supra* § 4-6.6(d)(2)) and *infra* § 4-11.2(c).

[244] *See infra* § 4-6.6(f).

[245] 1 GEOFFREY C. HAZARD, JR., W. WILLIAM HODES & PETER R. JARVIS, THE LAW OF LAWYERING § 10.34 (Aspen, 4th ed., 2016).

[246] Indeed, the Rule 4.1 versions adopted by a couple of states resolve the ambiguity by expressly overriding the confidentiality protection and mandating disclosure to avoid assisting a criminal or fraudulent act by the client. *See* MD. RULES OF PROF'L CONDUCT R. 19–304.1(b) (providing that duties under the rule apply "even if compliance requires disclosure of information otherwise protected" by Rule 1.16); N.J. RULES OF PROF'L CONDUCT R. 4.1(b) (same).

Accordingly, renewed attention by the American Bar Association to clarify and reconcile these provisions is suggested.

#### *§ 4-6.6(d)(4) Counseling the Client Before Disclosure*

Under both subparagraphs (b)(2) and (3) of Rule 1.6, the lawyer's discretion or obligation to reveal the confidential information should be exercised only after discussion with and counseling of the client, at least when possible and absent exigent circumstances. If the economic harm has not yet been imposed, then as Comment 7 to Rule 1.6 observes, the client "can, of course, prevent such disclosure by refraining from the wrongful conduct." If the lawyer does not discover the fraud or crime until after it has been accomplished by the client, then as Comment 8 explains, "[a]lthough the client no longer has the option of preventing disclosure by refraining from the wrongful conduct, there will be situations in which the loss suffered by the affected person can be prevented, rectified or mitigated."

Still, disclosure by the lawyer may be avoided if the client is willing to come clean and attempt to resolve the matter. Indeed, when the lawyer explains that she is authorized to disclose the information in any event, and thus that the truth will be revealed, the client may see the practical benefit, if not the moral responsibility, of having that truth be heard from the client's own mouth.

### § 4-6.6(e) To Obtain Legal Advice About Lawyer Compliance with Ethics Rules

A welcome addition to the Model Rules of Professional Conduct is the explicit invitation in Rule 1.6(b)(4) to the lawyer to "secure legal advice about the lawyer's compliance with these Rules" when appropriate. The rule expressly grants permission to share confidential information as reasonably believed necessary to obtain well-informed advice.

This exception to confidentiality for purposes of obtaining legal advice from another lawyer has long been understood to exist implicitly. Given that the lawyer so consulted was under the same duty to maintain confidentiality, disclosing client confidences to that lawyer posed little risk of a wider disclosure adverse to the client. Moreover, the consultation could also be justified as effectively adding yet another lawyer to the client's legal team (although the lawyer so consulted may have regarded only the lawyer seeking advice as the actual client, and the client's consent to participation of another attorney arguably was required). In any event, what was implicit is now explicit.

By expressly authorizing a lawyer to disclose confidential information in seeking legal advice on compliance with the ethics rules, Rule 1.6(b)(4) encourages each lawyer to recall that he is part of a community of practitioners. Lawyers too need counsel. New lawyers need mentors.[247] Even veteran attorneys benefit from drawing on the experiences and wisdom of other lawyers in our profession.

Disclosing confidential information that could identify a client, even for the salutary purpose of ensuring ethical professional behavior, should be done only under circumstances in which there is an expectation of privacy (and thus not through open discussion at a bar convention or casual conversation during a cocktail party) and where

---

[247] *See* Julie A. Oseid, *When Big Brother is Watching [Out For] You: Mentoring Lawyers, Choosing a Mentor, and Sharing Ten Virtues From My Mentor*, 59 S.C. L. REV. 393 (2008).

the lawyer offering the legal advice accepts the responsibility to maintain the confidences.

### § 4-6.6(f) For Lawyer Self-Defense and Fee Collection

Under Rule 1.6(b)(5), a lawyer may disclose confidential information as the lawyer reasonably believes necessary "to establish a claim or defense on behalf of the lawyer in a controversy between the lawyer and the client, to establish a defense to a criminal charge or civil claim against the lawyer based upon conduct in which the client was involved, or to respond to allegations in any proceeding concerning the lawyer's representation of the client."

Whenever the lawyer's conduct is the subject of a pending or anticipated charge of professional misconduct in a disciplinary proceeding, civil liability arising from the representation of a client, or criminal prosecution based upon conduct involving a client, the lawyer is permitted to respond, including making use of confidential information as necessary to do so. As Professors Monroe Freedman and Abbe Smith say, "[b]y analogy to the privilege against self-incrimination, it is too much to demand self-destruction by remaining silent in the face of false accusations."[248]

This "Lawyer Self-Defense" provision has been a traditional exception to confidentiality, and is parallel to the similar exception to the attorney-client privilege.[249]

Under Comment 10 to Rule 1.6, the lawyer is not required to wait until actual commencement of a civil lawsuit, criminal prosecution, or disciplinary proceeding; the lawyer may respond "when an assertion" of the lawyer's complicity in wrongdoing is made. Professors Freedman and Smith have criticized this commentary gloss as suggesting that a lawyer could reveal confidential information whenever a prosecutor or reporter asserts possible wrongdoing by the lawyer.[250] To preclude such an abuse of the exception by a nervous or unduly risk-averse lawyer, any preemptive exercise of lawyer self-defense should be restricted to the situation where the third person making the "assertion" is in a position to and is seriously contemplating initiation of formal litigation, prosecution, or professional disciplinary action. The lawyer may seek to preempt a reasonably anticipated lawsuit, criminal prosecution, or disciplinary hearing by presenting exculpatory evidence in advance to those persons who have the power to institute such proceedings.

The lawyer may use confidential information only when necessary to respond to actual or anticipated formal charges of wrongdoing, that is, accusations of misconduct presented in the form of civil litigation, criminal prosecution, or another legal proceeding (such as a disciplinary investigation). The lawyer may not betray client confidences to respond to newspaper reports, television and radio commentators, or cocktail party gossip, even if the lawyer's reputation unfairly suffers thereby. Likewise, a lawyer may not disclose confidential information to respond to a client's negative review of the lawyer's service on internet sites.[251] As an element of the fiduciary relationship that

---

[248] MONROE H. FREEDMAN & ABBE SMITH, UNDERSTANDING LAWYERS' ETHICS § 5.07[10] (LexisNexis 4th ed. 2010).

[249] *See supra* § 4-6.3(c)(3).

[250] MONROE H. FREEDMAN & ABBE SMITH, UNDERSTANDING LAWYERS' ETHICS § 5.07[10] (LexisNexis 4th ed. 2010).

[251] *See* People v. Isaac, 2016 WL 6124510 (Colo. O.P.D.J. 2016) (disciplining lawyer for disclosing client information about criminal offenses in responding to negative review on the internet); Minn. Lawyers Prof'l Responsibility Bd., Op. 24 (2016) (explaining a lawyer may not disclose client confidences in response to

lawyers assume on behalf of their clients, silently suffering "the slings and arrows of outrageous fortune"[252]—when injured within the informal venues of society—is a professional obligation. Even if the client proves to be the source of the negative chatter in media or social circles, the lawyer may not retaliate with use of client confidences.

When a lawyer is permitted to reveal client confidential information in self-defense, the door is not thereby opened to indiscriminate and wide-ranging disclosure. Only those aspects of the confidential information that bear on the matter at hand and that offer a legal defense to the lawyer should be revealed, while the lawyer carefully protects other confidential information relating to that representation.[253] And the proper forum for such revelation is the venue for the legal proceeding, as well of course in communications with other parties to that proceedings (such as through discovery, in efforts to encourage a prosecutor not to bring or to dismiss charges, etc.). General disclosure to the public does not serve this purpose.

Rule 1.6(b)(5) also permits a lawyer to use confidential information as the lawyer reasonably believes necessary "to establish a claim or defense on behalf of the lawyer in a controversy between the lawyer and the client," which includes not only responding defensively to a claim of malpractice by the client, but also presenting an affirmative claim by the lawyer to collect attorney's fees. Comment 11 to Rule 1.6 justifies this aspect of the rule as "express[ing] the principle that the beneficiary of a fiduciary relationship may not exploit it to the detriment of the fiduciary."

Although this permissive exception raises the potential of blackmail by the lawyer,[254] by threatening to expose the client's affairs as a means of extorting payment of a sincerely disputed fee, the permission to disclose confidential information is limited to that which demonstrates that a fee is owed for work performed. Furthermore, information disclosed to obtain payment of a fee should be revealed by the lawyer in the form and venue least likely to bring broader attention to the client matter. One would expect that any true episode of blackmail by the lawyer would receive severe sanction in the disciplinary process.

## § 4-6.6(g) To Comply with Other Law or Court Order

Rule 1.6 of the Model Rules of Professional Conduct as an ethical standard may be superseded by other law and, if so, the lawyer may be obliged to reveal information according to that law. Indeed, because confidential client information that falls outside of the attorney-client privilege[255] is not protected against compelled disclosure, even though the lawyer may not voluntarily reveal it, the lawyer may be required to respond to lawful discovery requests, prosecutorial subpoenas, and other forms of legal process that do not intrude upon privileged communications.

---

comments on an internet review site); Tex. St. Bar Prof'l Ethics Committee, Op. 662 (2016) (advising that a lawyer may respond in a restrained manner to negative internet reviews by a client but may not disclose confidential information); N.Y. St. Bar Ass'n Op. 1032 (2014) (stating lawyer may not disclose client confidential information to respond to client criticism on lawyer rating website).

[252] *See* WILLIAM SHAKESPEARE, HAMLET, act 3, sc. 1.

[253] *See* Rosen v. N.L.R.B., 735 F.2d 564, 576 (D.C. Cir. 1984); United States v. Sindona, 636 F.2d 792, 804 (2d Cir. 1980).

[254] MONROE H. FREEDMAN & ABBE SMITH, UNDERSTANDING LAWYERS' ETHICS § 5.07[10] (LexisNexis 4th ed. 2010); Daniel R. Fischel, *Lawyers and Confidentiality*, 65 U. CHI. L. REV. 1, 11 (1998).

[255] On the attorney-client privilege, see *supra* § 4-6.3.

If the request directed to a lawyer seeks access to that which is a privileged attorney-client communication, the lawyer must resist it.[256] Even when the information sought is not privileged, the lawyer may be justified in raising objections based upon the work-product doctrine;[257] constitutional limitations on law enforcement intrusion into the attorney-client relationship; court rules, holdings, or other standards limiting the issuance of prosecutorial subpoenas to criminal defense lawyers;[258] or simply because the requests should be directed to the client rather than the lawyer. When a colorable objection can be made to a request or demand for confidential information, the lawyer should raise it and competently advocate it.

If, however, the objection is overruled and a court order is issued requiring divulgence of the information, Model Rule 1.6(b)(6) confirms that the lawyer acts in conformance with ethical responsibilities when complying with that court order. Even while the court order compelling disclosure is being appealed, if the order is not stayed, the lawyer is not obliged to risk a contempt citation to protect a client confidence.

### § 4-6.6(h) To Check for Conflicts of Interest

As the most recent change to the exceptions to confidentiality, Rule 1.6(b)(7) of the Model Rules of Professional Conduct authorizes the lawyer to use confidential information "to detect and resolve conflicts of interest arising from the lawyer's change of employment or from changes in the composition or ownership of a firm, but only if the revealed information would not compromise the attorney-client privilege or otherwise prejudice the client."

While this exception facilitates a lawyer's efforts to identify conflict of interests when the lawyer is switching firms or when two firms are considering a merger, the permission to use confidential information is limited in content and strictly restricted to where the client would not be harmed. Thus, while the lawyer ordinarily does not need to obtain client consent to disclose such basic information as the client's identity and the type of matter involved, the information disclosed should be quite limited and may be used only to detect and resolve conflicts.

Moreover, even though the other lawyers with whom the information is shared are also bound to protect its further dissemination, the lawyer may not share information if the attorney-client privilege would be compromised or if the client's interests would be harmed. Thus, if a client has shared sensitive information such that even a summary of the client matter would be embarrassing or could be used against the client, then the limited permission to use the information in the rule is withdrawn.

---

[256] *See* ABA Comm. on Ethics & Prof'l Responsibility, Formal Op. 473 (2016) (explaining the steps that a lawyer must take when receiving a subpoena or other compulsory process for confidential documents, including raising any reasonable grounds against disclosure when instructed by the client or if the client is unavailable).

[257] *See supra* § 4-6.

[258] *See generally* 1 GEOFFREY C. HAZARD, JR., W. WILLIAM HODES & PETER R. JARVIS, THE LAW OF LAWYERING § 10.52 (Aspen, 4th ed., 2016).

# Chapter 4-7

# DUTIES OF LOYALTY: CONFLICTS OF INTEREST AND PROFESSIONAL INDEPENDENCE

## By Gregory C. Sisk

*Table of Sections*


§ 4-7.1 The General Standard for Conflicts of Interest: Duty of Loyalty and to Protect Confidentiality

§ 4-7.2 Checking for Conflicts and Withdrawal for Conflict

§ 4-7.3 Lawyer Conflicts with a Client

§ 4-7.4 Concurrent Client Conflicts

§ 4-7.5 Successive Client Conflicts

§ 4-7.6 Imputation of Conflicts of Interest Within a Firm

§ 4-7.7 Informed Consent by Client to Conflict

§ 4-7.8 Special Conflicts Rules for Government Employees, Judges, Arbitrators, Mediators, and Third-Party Neutrals

§ 4-7.9 Maintaining Professional Independence


---

## § 4-7.1 THE GENERAL STANDARD FOR CONFLICTS OF INTEREST: DUTY OF LOYALTY AND TO PROTECT CONFIDENTIALITY

Whether representation of a client in a particular matter constitutes a conflict of interest—by reason of the lawyer's responsibilities to other clients or persons or the lawyer's self-interest—is the most common ethical question encountered by the average lawyer. As Professor Charles Wolfram writes, "the transcendent importance of conflicts rules for practicing lawyers can hardly be doubted."[1]

Rule 1.7(a) of the Model Rules of Professional Conduct states that a "conflict of interest" is present when either "(1) the representation of one client will be directly adverse to another client; or (2) there is a significant risk that the representation of one or more clients will be materially limited by the lawyer's responsibilities to another client, a former client or a third person or by a personal interest of the lawyer." The *Restatement of the Law Governing Lawyers* similarly defines a conflict as when "there is a substantial risk that the lawyer's representation of the client would be materially and adversely affected by the lawyer's own interests or by the lawyer's duties to another current client, a former client, or a third person."[2]

---

[1] Charles W. Wolfram, *Ethics 2000 and Conflicts of Interest: The More Things Change . . .*, 70 TENN. L. REV. 27, 27 (2002).

[2] RESTATEMENT (THIRD) OF THE LAW GOVERNING LAWYERS § 121 (American Law Institute, 2000).

The lawyer is responsible to ascertain whether she has a conflict of interest that requires the lawyer to decline representation at the start or withdraw from representation as it continues.[3]

When a conflict of interest question is raised, two central elements of the attorney-client relationship are potentially implicated: loyalty and confidentiality:

***Loyalty to the Client:*** Loyalty is the first concern, which requires the lawyer to ask whether conflicting duties to another client, a former client, or another person, or attention to the lawyer's own self-interest, would impair the lawyer's professional allegiance to the client.[4] "The law treats a client's right to an attorney's loyalty as a kind of 'absolute' right."[5] Through the lawyer's fidelity, the client is induced to trust the lawyer in taking action on behalf of the client. The lawyer's exercise of independent professional judgment for the benefit of the client is guaranteed by ensuring that the lawyer is not compromised by a conflict of interest. Accordingly, if a lawyer's conflicting responsibilities to others or to the lawyer's personal interests would dilute the lawyer's loyalty to any client, the lawyer is precluded from accepting or continuing that representation.

***Protecting Client Confidentiality:*** Preservation of utmost confidentiality with respect to a client matter is the second concern implicated by a possible conflict of interest. The lawyer must ask whether he is able to fully protect the confidentiality of each client, while advancing the interests of every other client. One of the lawyer's most important fiduciary duties is to maintain the confidences of the client. At the same time, a lawyer must be a diligent and zealous advocate[6] and has a duty to keep the client informed about matters material to the representation.[7] A lawyer who simultaneously represents clients with conflicting interests, especially when the matters are related, may come into possession of information that ought to be maintained as confidential to one client but which would be of significant value in the representation of the other. In that way, because of the conflict of interest, the lawyer's essential duties of confidentiality and of diligent and informed representation would be at war with each other.

***Difficulty of Conflict Problems:*** While the test for a conflict of interest, as expressed in the Model Rules, may appear simple in theory, it can be anything but straightforward in application. To be sure, certain conflicts of interest are obvious based on the manifest adversity of the parties or because of the unmistakable effect of the competing influences upon the lawyer's representation. These clearly impermissible representations tend to be those that attract the attention of disciplinary authorities.[8]

---

[3] *See* Heninger & Heninger v. Davenport Bank & Trust, 341 N.W.2d 43, 49 (Iowa 1983) ("When a client retains an attorney, the responsibility is on the attorney to ascertain whether he has a conflict of interest or other ethical impediment to acceptance of the employment; the responsibility is not on the client to investigate and decide that question for the attorney.").

[4] On "role specific morality" and the lawyer's allegiance to the client, see also Part Two of this book, Stephen Pepper & Katherine R. Kruse, The Philosophy of Legal Ethics, § 2-1.3.

[5] Perl v. St. Paul Fire & Marine Ins. Co., 345 N.W.2d 209, 212 (Minn. 1984).

[6] *See supra* § 4-5.3(a).

[7] *See supra* § 4-5.4(a) to (c).

[8] *See* WILLIAM J. WERNZ, MINNESOTA LEGAL ETHICS 1188 (Minn. St. Bar Ass'n, 6th ed., 2016) ("Conflicts are rarely subject to public discipline, unless they are part of a larger pattern of misconduct or they involve aggravating circumstances, such as a conflict between the lawyer's and client's interests, resulting in a loss to a client.").

Other conflicts of interest, however, can be difficult to perceive initially and complicated to respond to once discovered, especially when the matter involves multiple entities and when the problem arises in the context of complex interactions. A lawyer who proceeds in reasonable good faith in the sometimes treacherous realm of conflicts of interest, but who then stumbles in a thorny situation, should not be too readily castigated for miscalculating.

## § 4-7.2 CHECKING FOR CONFLICTS AND WITHDRAWAL FOR CONFLICT

While a conflict of interest can arise unexpectedly during the course of a representation, every lawyer must try to avoid accepting a representation infected with an impermissible conflict of interest by instituting an appropriate procedure in the law office designed to check for conflicts when considering a new matter. An intake process by which to detect and resolve conflicts of interest when considering new representations is among the most basic policies that every law firm must have in place.[9]

The conflicts check system should include records of every present and prior representation, as well as a record of communications with prospective clients for whom representation was not undertaken.[10] At a minimum, these records should include the names of clients (which ideally would also include the names of those associated with the client, at least in terms of the representation, e.g., family members, insurers paying the cost of legal services, constituents of entities, etc.), the names of adverse parties, and a brief description of the matter. These records should be regularly updated, because the nature of a matter may change with the addition of parties or an expansion in the scope of the representation. When a new lawyer joins the firm, information regarding the matters that she brings into the firm, as well as those that the lawyer handled previously, should be added into the records.

When a conflict emerges after the representation has begun, Comment 4 to Rule 1.7 of the Model Rules of Professional Conduct advises that "the lawyer ordinarily must withdraw from the representation,"[11] unless all of the affected clients have consented.[12] The comment further states that, "[w]here more than one client is involved, whether the lawyer may continue to represent any of the clients is determined both by the lawyer's ability to comply with duties owed to the former client and by the lawyer's ability to represent adequately the remaining client or clients, given the lawyer's duties to the former client."[13] If, for example, the lawyer possesses confidential information from one client that may be used to the advantage of another client, the lawyer may not continue representation of the latter and thereby violate the continuing duty to the former client to protect confidential information.

---

[9] In terms of the responsibilities of managing and supervising lawyers to establish appropriate office policies for the ethical guidance of lawyers in a firm, see *infra* § 4-12.2(a).

[10] On conflicts of interest and communications with prospective clients, see *supra* § 4-3.1(d) to (e).

[11] On withdrawal to avoid violate of the rules, see *supra* § 4-3.6(c)(1).

[12] On informed consent by a client to a conflict, see *infra* § 4-7.7.

[13] *See also infra* § 4-7.4(c)(4), (c)(7).

## § 4-7.3 LAWYER CONFLICTS WITH A CLIENT

### § 4-7.3(a) Introduction to Lawyer-Client Conflicts

Certain situations, interests, or interactions are ethically charged and imperil the attorney's loyalty and exercise of independent judgment on behalf of the client—business transactions with clients,[14] solicitation of gifts from clients,[15] obtaining literary or media rights regarding the representation,[16] extending financial assistance to the client,[17] accepting compensation from someone other than the client,[18] attempting to secure a limitation on malpractice liability or uncounseled settlement of a malpractice claim from a client,[19] acquiring a propriety interest in the plaintiff's claim,[20] engaging in a sexual relationship with a client,[21] and representing a client adverse to a person who is represented by a lawyer related to the lawyer or with whom the lawyer is romantically involved.[22]

In many or most of these instances, application of the basic principles underlying conflict of interest analysis—particularly evaluation of whether the representation would be materially limited by the lawyer's responsibilities to another person or by the lawyer's personal interests[23]—would lead to the conclusion that the representation should not be undertaken or continued. Nonetheless, because of the well-understood risks involved, the frequency with which these matters arise in the practice of law, the significance of the harm to clients that may result if the lawyer missteps, and the value of tailored analysis to a particular problem, these matters receive special attention in Rule 1.8 of the Model Rules of Professional Conduct.

With respect to some matters, Rule 1.8 imposes a per se prohibition on conduct rather than leaving each case to be individually resolved by application of general conflict of interest principles.[24] We might imagine situations in which, as examples, a lawyer's preparation of a document granting the lawyer a testamentary gift from the client,[25] a lawyer's offering of money to a needy client for living expenses,[26] or even a lawyer's initiation of a sexual relationship with a client[27] might not take unfair advantage of the client or be certain to compromise the lawyer's independence of judgment. But the drafters of Rule 1.8 reached the judgment that the risks involved in such matters are simply are too high and the dangers to professional ethics inherent in such behavior are simply too great to permit any but the narrowest of exceptions.

---

[14] *See infra* § 4-7.3(b).

[15] *See infra* § 4-7.3(d).

[16] *See infra* § 4-7.3(e).

[17] *See infra* § 4-7.3(f).

[18] *See infra* § 4-7.3(g).

[19] *See infra* § 4-7.3(h).

[20] *See infra* § 4-7.3(i).

[21] *See infra* § 4-7.3(j).

[22] *See infra* § 4-7.3(k).

[23] *See supra* § 4-7.1 and *infra* § 4-7.4(c).

[24] *See* Richard W. Painter, *Advance Waiver of Conflicts*, 13 GEO. J. LEGAL ETHICS 289, 290 (2000) (explaining that because lawyers are fiduciaries for their clients, some ethics provisions establish immutable rules that may not be varied by agreement with the client).

[25] *See infra* § 4-7.3(d).

[26] *See infra* § 4-7.3.

[27] *See infra* § 4-7.3(j).

By contrast, certain other interactions by a lawyer with a client may be suspect in nature and generally are inadvisable, such as entering into a business transaction with a client[28] or undertaking representation of a client with whom the lawyer has a preexisting sexual relationship,[29] and yet are not absolutely forbidden under the rule but instead are subject to stringent limitations.

Still other actions by a lawyer are neither forbidden nor questionable, but should be taken with special care or subject to limitations. The lawyer may accept payment of legal fees by an insurer or family member other than the client, but only with the client's consent, when there is no interference with the lawyer's independence of judgment, and when client confidences are protected.[30] The lawyer may settle a malpractice claim with a client, but only if the client is represented by other counsel or is advised of the desirability of seeking and given a reasonable opportunity to seek independent counsel.[31]

Each of these subjects is addressed further below.

### § 4-7.3(b) Business Transactions with Clients

While not prohibited altogether under Rule 1.8(a) of the Model Rules of Professional Conduct, an attorney who chooses to combine the distinct roles of loyal counselor and business participant is skating on thin ice and will receive little sympathy from the courts if the ice should break underneath. As the Iowa Supreme Court lamented in *Committee on Professional Ethics & Conduct v. Postma*,[32] the court has "done [its] best to discourage business ventures between attorneys and their clients. The client is in a vulnerable position when the attorney's personal interests compete with the client's." The New York Court of Appeals warned in *Greene v. Greene*,[33] that "the relationship between an attorney and his client is a fiduciary one and the attorney cannot take advantage of his superior knowledge and position."

Under Rule 1.8(a), "[a] lawyer shall not enter into a business transaction with a client" unless (1) "the transaction and terms on which the lawyer acquires the interest are fair and reasonable to the client;" (2) those transaction terms "are fully disclosed and transmitted in writing in a manner that can be reasonably understood by the client;" (3) "the client is advised in writing of the desirability of seeking . . . the advice of independent legal counsel on the transaction;" (4) "the client is . . . given a reasonable opportunity to seek the advice of independent legal counsel on the transaction;" and (5) the client gives "informed consent" to the transaction in a signed writing.

The lawyer entering into a business transaction with a client must make full and honest disclosures about the proposed transaction and its terms, including the foreseeable risks to the client and the benefits to be obtained by the lawyer. The disclosure must be made in a manner that is understandable to the client and must be presented in writing, so as to impress upon the client the importance of the matter. The lawyer's advice to the client regarding the nature and wisdom of the terms of the transaction must be the same that would be given to a client looking to a lawyer for

---

[28] *See infra* § 4-7.3(b).

[29] *See infra* § 4-7.3(j).

[30] *See infra* § 4-7.3(g).

[31] *See infra* § 4-7.3(h).

[32] 430 N.W.2d 387, 391 (Iowa 1988).

[33] 436 N.E.2d 496, 499 (N.Y. 1982).

protection, not the truthful but reserved and circumscribed messages typically directed to an opposing person in an arm's-length transaction.

The lawyer also must recommend, again in writing, that the client obtain independent counsel to advise on the legal consequences of the transaction. Because "a passing suggestion" that the client should consult another lawyer communicates little, the lawyer must explain the possibility of divided loyalties and why the client may benefit from independent counsel.[34] Under Rule 1.8(a), the lawyer's persuasive and persistent insistence that the client should obtain independent counsel need not be pressed to the point of actually demanding the intervention of separate counsel as a condition to the transaction. However, because independent representation of the client is an important factor in evaluating whether the transaction was fair and reasonable to the client, declining to go forward without independent counsel for the client may well be the most prudent course of action. In any event, the lawyer must delay consummation of the transaction for an appropriate time, allowing the client to consider the need for and, if the client so chooses, to arrange for advice from independent counsel.

Under Rule 1.8(a), the client also must "give[ ] informed consent, in a writing signed by the client, to the essential terms of the transaction and the lawyer's role in the transaction, including whether the lawyer is representing the client in the transaction." The danger that the client's trust in the lawyer will be abused is heightened when the lawyer not only enters into a transaction with a client but undertakes to play what Comment 3 to Rule 1.8 calls the "dual role" of "both legal adviser and participant in the transaction."[35] In such an instance, as the comment observes, the risks increase "that the lawyer will structure the transaction or give legal advice in a way that favors the lawyer's interests at the expense of the client." Indeed, because the lawyer's personal interests are in competition with the client's interests, the lawyer has another conflict of interest that also must be disclosed to the client and for which informed consent by the client must be obtained.[36] In addition to full disclosure about the transaction terms, the lawyer "must disclose not only the attorney's adverse interest, but also the effect it will have on the exercise of his professional judgment."[37]

Even with full disclosure, a recommendation that an independent counsel be consulted, and written client consent, the attorney remains obliged as a fiduciary and a loyal agent to put the client's interests ahead of her own.[38] Especially when the client is not represented by independent counsel, an attorney entering into a transaction with a client must provide the client with the type of disinterested advice that the client would

---

[34] Matter of Smyzer, 527 A.2d 857, 862 (N.J. 1987).

[35] *See also* Panel Matter No. 87–22, 425 N.W.2d 824, 827 (Minn. 1988) (reprimanding a lawyer for lending money to a client without warning the client of potential conflicts between the attorney's dual roles as attorney and creditor).

[36] On informed consent to a conflict of interest, see *infra* § 4-7.7.

[37] Committee on Prof. Ethics & Conduct v. Humphreys, 524 N.W.2d 396, 399 (Iowa 1994); *see also* Weiss v. Statewide Grievance Committee, 633 A.2d 282, 288 (Conn. 1993) (observing that clients were unable to tell whether the attorney's actions were motivated by his interest as counsel or his interest as an investor when he advised the clients against the sale of their company).

[38] Anglo-Dutch Petroleum Int'l Inc., v. Greenberg Peden, P.C., 352 S.W.3d 445, 450 (Tex. 2011) ("Because a lawyer's fiduciary duty to a client covers contract negotiations between them, such contracts are closely scrutinized.").

have received from the lawyer if the lawyer were representing the client in "a transaction . . . with a stranger."[39]

And, under Rule 1.8(a), the lawyer must ensure that "the transaction and terms on which the lawyer acquires the interest are fair and reasonable to the client." If the lawyer profits while the client suffers a loss, the presumption should be that the transaction was not "fair and reasonable to the client." Even where there is no fraud or undue influence, "the agreement may be invalid if it appears that the attorney 'got the better of the bargain', unless he can show that the client was fully aware of the consequences and that there was no exploitation of the client's confidence in the attorney."[40] In sum, a business transaction by a lawyer with a client is most likely to be sustained when it proves mutually advantageous to all.

The requirements of Model Rule 1.8(a) apply not only to ordinary business transactions with clients, but whenever a lawyer "knowingly acquire[s] an ownership, possessory, security or other pecuniary interest adverse to a client." For example, if the attorney becomes a participant in the corporation by purchasing or otherwise obtaining an equity interest and simultaneously advises the corporation on legal matters in which the attorney has a personal interest, the attorney must make the required disclosures, advise the client to obtain independent counsel, and counsel the client to take those actions that are most advantageous for the client, even if those steps would be detrimental to the lawyer's personal interests. The attorney remains obliged as a loyal counselor and fiduciary advisor to put the client's interests ahead of the lawyer's own.

The rule encompasses those arrangements by which a lawyer accepts stock or ownership in a client's business in lieu of fees, because the lawyer under such circumstances has entered into a business transaction with the client.[41] Likewise, when a lawyer becomes a creditor of the client, the parties have divergent interests as the lawyer may be tempted to put his financial interests ahead of the client's best interests.

However, as confirmed by Comment 1 to Rule 1.8, "the Rule does not apply to standard commercial transactions between the lawyer and the client for products or services that the client generally markets to others, for example, banking or brokerage services, medical services, products manufactured or distributed by the client, and utilities' services." When the lawyer is receiving routine services on the same terms as other members of the public, the lawyer cannot obtain any unfair advantage over the client and complying with the disclosure and consent requirements are impractical and unnecessary.

Although framed under the rule as a restriction on interactions with current clients, the former client's reasonable expectation that her lawyer will act to protect that person and will provide disinterested professional judgment will linger for a period after termination of the attorney-client relationship. The client's trust in the lawyer as a confidant and fiduciary is not something that can be turned on and off like a water faucet.

---

[39] Committee on Prof'l Ethics & Conduct v. Carty, 515 N.W.2d 32, 35–36 (Iowa 1994); *see also* Goldman v. Kane, 329 N.E.2d 770, 773 (Mass. Ct. App. 1975).

[40] Greene v. Greene, 436 N.E.2d 496, 499 (N.Y. 1982).

[41] *See* ABA Standing Comm. on Ethics & Prof'l Responsibility, Formal Op. 00–418 (2000); Passante v. McWilliam, 62 Cal. Rptr. 2d 298 (Ct. App. 1997).

For this reason, the rule governing business transactions "is applicable as long as the influence arising from an attorney-client relationship continues."[42]

### § 4-7.3(c) Use of Confidential Information to the Disadvantage of the Client

Confidentiality is one of the most fundamental elements of the attorney-client relationship.[43] Because our clients are guaranteed confidentiality, they are willing to share their most private thoughts and relate the most sensitive information, secure in the knowledge that what has been shared will be safeguarded and will not be used by the lawyer against the client. For that reason, Rule 1.6 of the Model Rules of Professional Conduct enjoins the lawyer to safeguard confidential information and prohibits disclosure of such information without consent or other authorization.[44]

While Rule 1.6 establishes the duty not to *disclose* confidential information, Rule 1.8(b) creates the parallel duty not to *use* confidential information against a current client (and Rule 1.9(c)(1) imposes a similar duty with respect to former clients).[45] Under Rule 1.8(b), "[a] lawyer shall not use information relating to representation of a client to the disadvantage of the client unless the client gives informed consent, except as permitted or required by these rules."

When the lawyer converts confidential information into a tool that is used to the detriment of the client, the betrayal is not only one of confidentiality, but also of fidelity. As Comment 5 to Rule 1.8 explains, use of information to the disadvantage of the client, whether to benefit the lawyer or a third person, "violates the lawyer's duty of loyalty." The prohibition applies even if the lawyer is able to use the information without disclosure.

In two cases, the Iowa Supreme Court suspended lawyers who gained knowledge of their clients' financial affairs and subsequently used that information to solicit funds from the clients or former clients, in one case for investment in a business venture in which the lawyer was involved[46] and in the other case to obtain a personal loan.[47] While the clients and former clients in those cases did experience financial loss or other inconvenience as a result of the lawyers' conduct, the violation occurred when the information was used to the disadvantage of the client, even before any economic harm was suffered.

By its express terms and as confirmed in Comment 5, Rule 1.8(b) does not prohibit the lawyer's use of confidential information when it is not to the disadvantage of the client. However, while non-disadvantageous use of confidential information may not constitute professional misconduct, such conduct might well constitute a breach of duty under the law of agency. As Professors Ronald Rotunda and John Dzienkowski warn, the lawyer who relies upon the rule and comment "for a safe harbor will find (when a court, pursuant to the law of agency, orders an accounting to the client for any profits

---

42 In re Neville, 708 P.2d 1297, 1302 (Ariz. 1985).

43 *See supra* § 4-6.1.

44 *See supra* ch. 4-6.

45 *See infra* § 4-7.5(e).

46 Board of Prof'l Ethics & Conduct v. Sikma, 533 N.W.2d 532, 536 (Iowa 1995).

47 Board of Prof'l Ethics & Conduct v. Walters, 603 N.W.2d 772, 775 (Iowa 1999).

made) that this harbor is heavily mined."[48] Under both the *Restatement of the Law of Agency*[49] and the *Restatement of the Law Governing Lawyers*,[50] an agent/lawyer may not use confidential information of a principal/client for pecuniary gain and must account to the principal/client for any profits earned from the use of that confidential information.

### § 4-7.3(d) Gifts from Clients and Preparation of Instruments Giving Gifts

Under Rule 1.8(c), "[a] lawyer shall not solicit any substantial gift from a client, including a testamentary gift." This rule applies not only to the solicitation of gifts to be made directly to the lawyer, but also to asking the client to make gifts to those who are related to the lawyer, which the rule defines as consisting of "a spouse, child, grandchild, parent, grandparent or other relative or individual with whom the lawyer or the client maintains a close, familial relationship."

As with many of the provisions in Rule 1.8, this bar on soliciting gifts is designed to prevent overreaching by the lawyer for personal gain in the context of a fiduciary relationship. "Few infractions can be calculated to so enrage the public, or to undermine its confidence in the profession, than for a lawyer to use his or her considerable influence to acquire personal ownership of the property of a trusting client."[51]

While the rule does not preclude a lawyer from accepting a gift from a client, such as the payment of a bonus for high-quality legal services, the lawyer must not seek such a reward. Moreover, the lawyer must be careful to avoid any undue influence on the client, even that which is not intended, which may cause the client to be overly solicitous toward and unwisely generous to the lawyer. Comment 6 to Rule 1.8 suggests that acceptance of a substantial gift should "meet[ ] general standards of fairness." By framing the prohibition as being against the solicitation of a "substantial" gift, Rule 1.8(c) does not apply to such common and unremarkable events as the mutual solicitation and exchange of modest gifts on a holiday or a person's birthday.

When provision of the gift to a lawyer requires execution of a legal instrument, such as a will including a bequest of a substantial amount to the lawyer, the lawyer is ethically barred from having solicited the gift and from participation in the preparation of the document (even when the idea for the gift originated with the client). Rule 1.8(c) further states that the lawyer may not "prepare on behalf of a client an instrument giving the lawyer or a person related to the lawyer any substantial gift." While the lawyer is not precluded from accepting a testamentary gift, assuming no undue influence in procuring it, neither the lawyer nor any other lawyer in the law firm may prepare the document.

If the client is determined to carry forward that intent, she must be directed to find separate and independent legal counsel. The lawyer must "take extreme pains to distance" himself from anything to do with the gift instrument, so that "[a]ll professional

---

[48] RONALD D. ROTUNDA & JOHN S. DZIENKOWSKI, PROFESSIONAL RESPONSIBILITY: A STUDENT'S GUIDE § 1.8–3 (American Bar Ass'n, 2013–2014).

[49] RESTATEMENT (THIRD) OF THE LAW OF AGENCY § 8.05 (American Law Institute, 2006).

[50] RESTATEMENT (THIRD) OF THE LAW GOVERNING LAWYERS § 60 (American Law Institute, 2000).

[51] Board of Prof'l Ethics & Conduct v. Winkel, 541 N.W.2d 862, 864 (Iowa 1995); *see also* Discipline of Mattson, 651 N.W.2d 278, 287 (S.D. 2002) (disciplining an attorney who acting as legal advisor to his 90-year-old uncle advised him to reduce the estate by gift-giving of over half of the estate to the attorney and his wife while the uncle was still living).

advice and legal work in such an undertaking . . . come from an independent lawyer of the client's, not the initial lawyer's, choosing."[52]

Comment 8 to Rule 1.8 explains that this prohibition on preparation of an instrument making a gift to the lawyer or a related person "does not prohibit a lawyer from seeking to have the lawyer or a partner or associate of the lawyer named as executor of the client's estate or to another potentially lucrative fiduciary position." The propriety of such appointments instead is governed by the general rules on conflicts of interest and requires informed consent by the client.

The sole exception in Rule 1.8(c) to the bar on solicitation of substantial gifts and preparation of instruments making a gift is when "the lawyer or other recipient of the gift is related to the client." For purposes of the exception, the rule again defines "related" person as encompassing "a spouse, child, grandchild, parent, grandparent or other relative or individual with whom the lawyer or the client maintains a close, familial relationship." Thus, for example, a lawyer would be permitted to draft a will for the lawyer's spouse or other close relative, even though the document would include testamentary gifts to the drafting lawyer or to other relatives of the lawyer. When there is a close family relationship, such a testamentary gift is natural and the risk of undue influence is alleviated (although not eliminated in every case).[53]

### § 4-7.3(e) Literary and Media Rights About Representation

Under Rule 1.8(d) of the Model Rules of Professional Conduct, "[p]rior to the conclusion of representation of a client, a lawyer shall not make or negotiate an agreement giving the lawyer literary or media rights to a portrayal or account based in substantial part on information relating to the representation." During the course of a representation, the lawyer may not solicit or accept the right to tell the client's story by book, film, or other media.

In addition to concerns about overreaching by a lawyer in securing an agreement from a client to grant literary or media rights, this prohibition is grounded in the inescapable conflict of interest that a lawyer would have between taking the actions that best advance the client's cause through the exercise of disinterested professional judgment and taking those actions that most enliven the story and thereby enhance the value of literary and media rights to the lawyer's personal and financial benefit.[54] The only person that the lawyer should have in mind during the representation is the client, not the potential audience that might be attracted to purchase a book or a ticket to a movie.

Rule 1.8(d) permits the lawyer to obtain literary or movie rights after the conclusion of the representation, at which point the lawyer's ability to shape the representation to enhance the appeal of the tale presumably has come to an end. However, if such rights are obtained in the immediate aftermath of the representation—when the lawyer's

---

[52] *Winkel*, 541 N.W.2d at 864; *see also* Disciplinary Action Against Boulger, 637 N.W.2d 710, 712 (N.D. 2001) (explaining rule as designed to ensure the client receives detached advice from a lawyer with no interest in the matter).

[53] Magee v. State Bar, 374 P.2d 807, 813 (Cal. 1962) (stating there is nothing improper about an attorney drawing wills for family members where the attorney receives a reasonable testamentary gift).

[54] *See* Matter of Henderson, 2017 WL 1161019, 78 N.E.3d 1092 (mem.) (Ind. Jan. 13, 2017) (disciplining a prosecutor for negotiating through a literary agent to write a book while prosecuting a murder case and quoting the hearing officer as saying that the prosecutor thereby "compromised his independent judgment by securing his personal interests").

professional influence over the client remains strong—the lawyer would be obliged to comply with the directives of Rule 1.8(a) concerning business transactions with a client.[55]

In addition, before using information relating to the representation, which is protected as confidential under Rule 1.6, the lawyer must obtain informed consent from the client or former client. In this respect, the lawyer must be aware of and explain to the client that the client's grant of permission to reveal some privileged matters relating to a representation may constitute a waiver of the attorney-client privilege.[56] As Professors Ronald Rotunda and John Dzienkowski warn:

> [L]awyers must assess the risk that portrayal rights may waive some or all of the privilege and therefore expose the client to enhanced civil liability based upon the same facts as the lawyer's criminal representation. At a minimum, the lawyer needs to disclose such risk to the former client. In some cases, the increased risk may be so great that the lawyer should refrain from seeking portrayal rights from the client.[57]

In addition, as Comment 9 to Rule 1.8 clarifies, "[p]aragraph (d) does not prohibit a lawyer representing a client in a transaction concerning literary property from agreeing that the lawyer's fee shall consist of a share in ownership in the property." Because the literary property is the subject of the representation, rather than the representation being the potential subject of the literary rights, the dangers addressed by the rule are not present. However, as with any business transaction with a client, the lawyer must comply with Rule 1.8(a),[58] and because this arrangement is a form of a contingency fee, the lawyer must comply with Rule 1.5(c).[59]

## § 4-7.3(f) Financial Assistance to a Client

### *§ 4-7.3(f)(1) The General Prohibition on Giving or Loaning Money for Living Expenses or Otherwise to a Client*

With the exception of court costs and litigation expenses,[60] Rule 1.8(e) of the Model Rules of Professional Conduct provides that "[a] lawyer shall not provide financial assistance to a client in connection with pending or contemplated litigation." When a client has retained a lawyer for litigation-related services,[61] the lawyer may not offer or provide living expenses to the client—such as rent payments, money for groceries, or coverage of child-care expenses—nor offer assistance with medical bills or other financial obligations of the client. As confirmed by Comment 10 to Rule 1.8, this bar extends not only to outright monetary payments, but also to "making or guaranteeing loans" to

[55] *See supra* § 4-7.3(b).

[56] *See* In re Von Bulow, 828 F.2d 94 (2d Cir. 1987) (holding that consent to disclosure of privileged communications in a book about a criminal prosecution constituted a limited waiver of the privilege for purposes of a subsequent civil liability action).

[57] RONALD D. ROTUNDA & JOHN S. DZIENKOWSKI, PROFESSIONAL RESPONSIBILITY: A STUDENT'S GUIDE § 1.8–5 (American Bar Ass'n, 2013–2014).

[58] *See supra* § 4-7.3(b).

[59] *See supra* § 4-4.2(c).

[60] *See infra* § 4-7.3(f)(2).

[61] Because Rule 1.8(e) bars financial assistance only "in connection with pending or contemplated litigation," a lawyer is not prohibited from extending a loan to a client who has retained the lawyer for non-litigation services, although such a loan would be subject to the requirements of paragraph (a) of Rule 1.8 regarding business transactions with clients. *See supra* § 4-7.3(b).

clients for living or other non-litigation expenses.[62] That a lawyer insists that the payment to a client was made with charitable or humanitarian motives is not an excuse, nor is the financial need of the client a factor in the application of the rule.[63] Small courtesies, such as picking up the bill at a restaurant after the lawyer and client have shared a meal or a modest gift at a holiday, do not run afoul of this constraint.

According to Comment 10, the purposes behind this prohibition are that such financial assistance "would encourage clients to pursue lawsuits that might not otherwise be brought and because such assistance gives lawyers too great a financial stake in the litigation." In addition, if lawyers were permitted to offer stipends or loans for client living expenses, we might see the unseemly spectacle of some lawyers competing for clients, particularly in personal injury cases, by touting their greater generosity, thus effectively buying clients by upfront payments with the hope of both reimbursement and a profit through successful prosecution of a claim.

A few states depart from the general prohibition on advancing or guaranteeing loans for living expenses, although generally limited to extraordinary circumstances and only when the client remains ultimately responsible for those expenses. For example, Minnesota, Montana, and North Dakota authorize guaranteeing a loan for basic living expenses when "reasonably needed to enable the client to withstand delay in litigation that would otherwise put substantial pressure on the client to settle a case because of financial hardship rather than on the merits."[64] To address the concerns behind the general prohibition, Minnesota, Montana, and North Dakota provide that the client must be ultimately responsible for the guaranteed loan (that is, the duty to repay the loan may not be made contingent on the outcome) and the lawyer may not promise such financial assistance prior to being retained. Also designed to "avoid situations in which a client is compelled by exigent financial circumstances to settle a claim on unfavorable terms," the District of Columbia rule allows directly advancing living expenses, although without saying that repayment may not be made contingent.[65] Similarly, Louisiana allows financial assistance to a client "who is in necessitous circumstances" that would "adversely affect the client's ability to initiate and/or maintain the cause for which the lawyer's services were engaged"—but such financial assistance may not be promised before retention or be publicized and advertised.[66] Alabama and Mississippi allow both (1) directly advancing living expenses or (2) guaranteeing a loan, the repayment of which may not be made contingent. Alabama allows such assistance in an "emergency," while Mississippi permits assistance in an amount up to $1500 "under dire and necessitous circumstances."[67] California more generously allows the lawyer *after* employment to make a loan for personal expenses. The client must promise in writing to repay, but

---

[62] *See also* RESTATEMENT (THIRD) OF THE LAW GOVERNING LAWYERS § 36(2) & cmt. c (American Law Institute, 2000); Committee on Prof'l Ethics & Conduct v. Humphreys, 524 N.W.2d 396, 398 (Iowa 1994).

[63] *But see* Philip G. Schrag, *The Unethical Ethics Rules: Nine Ways to Fix Model Rule of Professional Conduct 1.8(e)*, 28 GEO. J. LEGAL ETHICS 39, 40, 66–70 (2015) (saying that "[b]ecause of its indifference to the humanitarian or charitable impulses of lawyers and its harsh effects on indigent clients, Rule 1.8(e) stands out as an unethical ethics rule" and proposing revisions such as limitation to contingent fees, application only to loans, and exemption for pro bono cases).

[64] MINN. RULES OF PROF'L CONDUCT R. 1.8(e)(3); MONT. RULES OF PROF'L CONDUCT R. 1.8(e)(3); N.D. RULES OF PROF'L CONDUCT R. 1.8(e)(3).

[65] D.C. RULES OF PROF'L CONDUCT R. 1.8(d)(2).

[66] LA. RULES OF PROF'L CONDUCT R. 1.8(d)(4).

[67] ALA. RULES OF PROF'L CONDUCT R. 1.8(e)(3); MISS. RULES OF PROF'L CONDUCT R. 1.8(e)(2).

California does not otherwise specify the circumstances under which such a loan may be made.[68]

### *§ 4-7.3(f)(2) Advancing Court Costs and Litigation Expenses*

Under Rule 1.8(e)(1) of the Model Rules of Professional Conduct, "a lawyer may advance court costs and expenses of litigation," which has been a longstanding practice, particularly in plaintiff's personal injury representation. The rule further permits the lawyer to make the repayment of such costs and expenses "contingent on the outcome of the matter."

Although the former Model Code of Professional Responsibility required that "the client remain[ ] ultimately liable for such expenses,"[69] the reality has always been that many clients are not economically able to repay expenses if the litigation should fail. For that reason, lawyers seldom would try to collect such expenses from clients in the aftermath of a defeat in court. Rule 1.8(e)(1) of the Model Rules of Professional Conduct thus brings the text of the rule into coordination with practice by allowing the lawyer to make costs and expenses—like the attorney's fee—contingent on the outcome of the litigation.[70]

The lawyer should understand, however, that this is merely a contractual option; the lawyer is not obliged to agree that repayment of courts costs and litigation expenses be made contingent and indeed has no ethical obligation to make that option available to the client at the time of retention.

In addition, under Rule 1.8(e)(2), when the client is "indigent," the lawyer is authorized to "pay court costs and expenses of litigation on behalf of the client." Through this provision, the lawyer not only may advance costs and expenses, but also may agree to absorb those costs and not impose them upon the client, even out of any subsequent recovery. Such litigation-related expenses may be paid outright by the lawyer on behalf of indigent clients with no expectation for later reimbursement.

## § 4-7.3(g) Compensation from a Person Other than the Client

Although most lawyers are compensated directly by their clients for professional services in most matters, it is nonetheless common for someone other than the client to pay a lawyer's fees. A parent may pay the legal fees for the representation of a son or daughter. An employer may cover the cost of representation for an employee in a matter related to the business. A liability insurer may pay the costs of defending an insured against a claim of liability covered by the insurance policy.[71]

Receiving payment of legal fees from someone other than the client is appropriate, provided that the lawyer remembers that her professional obligations, including the duty of loyalty and protection of confidential information, are owed solely to the client.

Rule 1.8(f) of the Model Rules of Professional Conduct provides that "[a] lawyer shall not accept compensation for representing a client from one other than the client unless:

---

[68] CAL. RULES OF PROF'L CONDUCT R. 4–210(A).

[69] MODEL CODE OF PROF'L RESPONSIBILITY, Disciplinary Rule 5–103(B) (American Bar Ass'n, 1980).

[70] For discussion of contingency fees, as well as the requirement of a written agreement that explains the measure of the fee and whether expenses are to be deducted before or after the contingent fee is calculated, see *supra* § 4-4.2(c).

[71] On conflicts of interest in the insurance defense context, see *infra* § 4-7.4(c)(8).

(1) the client gives informed consent; (2) there is no interference with the lawyer's independence of professional judgment or with the client-lawyer relationship; and (3) information relating to representation of a client is protected as required by Rule 1.6." Paragraph (f) is parallel to and reinforced by Rule 5.4(c), which provides that "[a] lawyer shall not permit a person who recommends, employs, or pays the lawyer to render legal services for another to direct or regulate the lawyer's professional judgment in rendering such legal services."

Under Rule 1.8(f), the lawyer must ensure the client understands that the payment of legal fees is being made by another, that the source of that compensation does not affect the confidential nature of the attorney-client relationship or alter the client's entitlement to the lawyer's unimpaired loyalty, and that the client agrees. Even with the client's consent, Rules 1.8(f) and 5.4(c) allow the lawyer to proceed only if the lawyer is confident that his independence of professional judgment will not be compromised and that client confidences will be preserved.

If the third-party payee should interfere with the representation or the lawyer is unable to maintain independence of judgment because of the lawyer's susceptibility to the influence of that third-party, then the lawyer is ethically unable to undertake or continue the representation. Comment 12 to Rule 1.8 advises that "if there is significant risk that the lawyer's representation of the client will be materially limited by the lawyer's own interest in the fee arrangement or by the lawyer's responsibilities to the third-party payer (for example, when the third-party payer is a co-client)," then the lawyer must either withdraw or obtain informed consent, not merely to the payment arrangement, but also to the conflict of interest itself from all clients as provided under Rule 1.7(b).

While the client consent requirement of Rule 1.8(f) may literally apply to lawyers who are publicly-compensated, such as a public defender in a criminal case or a legal services group in a civil case, the risk that the lawyer's independent judgment may be threatened in such contexts is minimal. In recognition, at least one state has advised in a unique comment to its rule that, while the lawyer "must disclose the fact that the lawyer is being compensated through public funding or that legal services are being provided as part of a legal aid organization," the client will not be expected to formally consent to that payment arrangement.[72]

### § 4-7.3(h) Agreements to Limit or Settle Malpractice Claims

Under Rule 1.8(h)(1) of the Model Rules of Professional Conduct, a lawyer may not "make an agreement prospectively limiting the lawyer's liability to a client for malpractice unless the client is independently represented in making the agreement."

The general prohibition against a malpractice immunity agreement prevents overreaching by the lawyer, preserves the incentive of civil accountability for the lawyer to maintain competent representation (especially given that professional discipline for neglect is unlikely to be imposed based upon an isolated incident of professional error), safeguards the client's right to seek redress and be made whole for any harm caused by a lawyer's departure from the professional standard of care, and avoids the appearance that the lawyer indirectly (or directly for that matter) may be seeking the client's acquiescence to substandard legal services.

---

[72] IOWA RULES PROF'L CONDUCT 32:1.8 cmt. 12a.

In unusual circumstances, presumably when a client wishes to obtain low-cost and limited scope legal services in a peculiar situation, a client independently represented by counsel (such as in-house counsel for a corporation) may agree to hold the lawyer harmless from a claim for malpractice.

Comment 14 clarifies that Rule 1.8(h)(1) does not preclude an agreement to arbitrate a legal malpractice claim nor does it prevent a lawyer from practicing in the form of a limited-liability entity, "provided that each lawyer remains personally liable to the client for his or her own conduct" and the law firm provides any required notice to the client or maintains liability insurance.

While a lawyer generally may not seek exoneration of malpractice liability in advance of performing legal services, the lawyer quite appropriately may seek to settle a claim after the fact, subject to ethical limitations designed to protect the client from undue influence by the lawyer. When the lawyer has engaged in professional negligence to the harm of the client, and the lawyer's efforts to correct the error have proved unavailing, the lawyer unavoidably has a personal conflict of interest when approaching the client with a proposal to remedy the harm by settling a potential or actual malpractice claim. Because the client now has a claim against the lawyer, the lawyer and the client are adversaries on this matter with clearly divided interests. Yet because of the continuing or recently-terminated attorney-client relationship, the client still may repose trust in the lawyer and not fully appreciate that the lawyer's suggestion of an equitable resolution does not reflect the lawyer's disinterested and loyal advice to a client.

Accordingly, Rule 1.8(h)(2) permits the lawyer to settle a claim or potential claim for malpractice liability with an unrepresented client or former client only if "that person is advised in writing of the desirability of seeking and is given a reasonable opportunity to seek the advice of independent legal counsel in connection therewith."

In *Committee on Professional Ethics & Conduct v. Nadler*,[73] a lawyer representing a minor who had been injured in an automobile accident failed to file the personal injury lawsuit on behalf of the minor and his parents within the statute of limitations. Although the lawyer told the clients that the lawsuit had not been filed and that the statute of limitations had run, which certainly was better than hiding or providing a false excuse for the error, the court underscored that "he did not alert them of their possible malpractice claim nor did he advise them to seek the advice of another attorney."[74] Instead, he offered to pay the clients the sum of $1,900, which he considered to be the value of the claim they had lost due to his professional negligence. That figure was well below the $35,500 amount that a court later awarded in the clients' successful action for legal malpractice against the lawyer. For this improper effort to limit his malpractice liability, as well as other episodes of professional misconduct, the Iowa Supreme Court suspended the lawyer's license indefinitely.

## § 4-7.3(i) Acquiring a Property Interest in a Client's Claim

Rule 1.8(i) of the Model Rules of Professional Conduct directs that "[a] lawyer shall not acquire a proprietary interest in the cause of action or subject matter of litigation

---

[73] 467 N.W.2d 250, 252–55 (Iowa 1991).

[74] *Id.* at 252; *see also* Matter of Blackwelder, 615 N.E.2d 106, 107 (Ind. 1993) (disciplining an attorney who missed filing date and then obtained a covenant not to sue from clients in exchange for a bankruptcy filing and while failing to advise clients in advance to consult independent counsel).

the lawyer is conducting for a client." In other words, the lawyer may not purchase an ownership interest in a client's lawsuit. As Professor Robert Schuwerk and attorney Lillian Hardwick cogently summarize, "[t]he profession's position has long been that a lawyer, as litigator, should represent a client in the litigation and not become a party to the litigation."[75] Comment 16 explains that Rule 1.8(i) "is designed to avoid giving the lawyer too great an interest in the representation."

By precluding the lawyer from having a direct stake by way of ownership in the outcome of the litigation, the rule inhibits the lawyer from promoting litigation for self-interest rather than the actual interest of a client; helps the lawyer to maintain sufficient detachment to give the client candid and disinterested advice; protects the client's right to terminate the representation of the lawyer[76] (which may be complicated if the lawyer is a co-party on the claim); denies the lawyer any control over the client's decision as to whether to accept a settlement[77] (which the lawyer might obtain as a part owner of the claim); and generally avoids the conflicts of interest that may arise when the lawyer is a potentially competing claimant alongside the client.

The rule is subject to two express exceptions, which otherwise would constitute the prohibited taking of a proprietary interest in the litigation. First, under Rule 1.8(i)(1), the lawyer is permitted to "acquire a lien authorized by law to secure the lawyer's fee or expenses."[78] Second, under Rule 1.8(i)(2), the lawyer may "contract with a client for a reasonable contingent fee in a civil case." The reasonableness of contingency fees is governed by Rule 1.5(c).[79] Rule 1.8(e) also permits the lawyer to advance court costs and litigation expenses and make them contingent on the outcome of the litigation.[80]

### § 4-7.3(j) Sexual Relations with a Client

When a person needs the assistance or counsel of a lawyer, he often is troubled and in a vulnerable position, experiencing a personal crisis such as dissolution of marriage, death of a loved one, disabling injury, financial ruin, or criminal charges.[81] Even when the lawyer is being retained for a less stressful purpose, the lawyer ordinarily holds a position of significant influence and possesses great apparent authority, inviting trust and confidence and creating a fiduciary responsibility for a legal professional.

For a lawyer to exploit the client's vulnerability or the lawyer's status and power to obtain sexual favors from a client is a despicable act and an abusive betrayal of trust that justifies the most severe disciplinary penalty. Even when the client initiates a sexual relationship or appears to reciprocate the lawyer's solicitation, the development of an intimate relationship generally deprives a lawyer of that loyal but detached judgment that is essential to diligent and successful representation. Moreover, as Comment 17 to Rule 1.8 of the Model Rules of Professional Conduct warns, "a blurred line between the professional and personal relationships may make it difficult to predict

---

[75] 48 ROBERT P. SCHUWERK & LILLIAN HARDWICK, HANDBOOK OF TEXAS LAWYER AND JUDICIAL ETHICS: TEXAS PRACTICE SERIES § 6.08 (Thomson-Reuters, 2016).

[76] On the client's right to terminate the lawyer, see *supra* § 4-3.6.

[77] On the client's right to decide on settlement, see *supra* § 4-3.4.

[78] *See supra* § 4-5.6(c)(1).

[79] *See supra* § 4-4.2(c).

[80] *See supra* § 4-7.3(f)(2).

[81] *See* MODEL CODE OF PROF'L RESPONSIBILITY, Ethical Consideration 5–25 (American Bar Ass'n, 1980) (saying that overreaching by a lawyer "presents an even greater danger to the client seeking advice in times of personal crisis such as divorce, death of a loved one, or when facing criminal charges").

to what extent client confidences will be protected by the attorney-client evidentiary privilege, since client confidences are protected by privilege only when they are imparted in the context of the client-lawyer relationship."

For these reasons, Rule 1.8(j) prohibits a lawyer from having "sexual relations with a client unless a consensual sexual relationship existed between them when the client-lawyer relationship commenced." As Comment 17 to Rule 1.8 states, "because the client's own emotional involvement renders it unlikely that the client could give adequate informed consent," this presents a conflict of interest that cannot be avoided by client consent. The danger to the attorney-client relationship has been deemed too great, in terms of the likelihood and magnitude of harm, as well as the delicate nature of potential injury, to allow any room for a lawyer to attempt to justify such behavior. Moreover, any appraisal by the lawyer of the risk of harm is unlikely to be objective given the personal nature of a romantic or sexual interaction.

The prohibition on sexual relations presumably extends to those who essentially are in the position of the client, such as the controlling agent of an entity or a guardian of a person with diminished capacity. Comment 19 clarifies that "[w]hen the client is an organization, paragraph (j) of this Rule prohibits a lawyer for the organization (whether inside counsel or outside counsel) from having a sexual relationship with a constituent of the organization who supervises, directs or regularly consults with that lawyer concerning the organization's legal matters."[82]

The only exception to the per se prohibition, and it is a limited and not always-available exception, is when the sexual relationship predates the creation of the attorney-client relationship. As Comment 18 explains, "[i]ssues relating to the exploitation of the fiduciary relationship and client dependency are diminished when the sexual relationship existed prior to the commencement of the client-lawyer relationship." Even then, the comment warns that the lawyer must consider whether the existence of an ongoing sexual relationship will impair the attorney-client relationship. The lawyer who is engaged in an intimate relationship with a client should continually evaluate the situation and err on the side of terminating the representation if it would be materially limited.

Under Rule 1.8(k), a lawyer's sexual relationship with a client is not one of those special conflicts that are imputed to other lawyers in a law firm. Unless the other lawyers would be materially limited in their representation because of their relationship with that lawyer or because of interference by the disqualified lawyer with the representation, in which case a conflict would arise under the general standard, other lawyers may represent a client or client representative that is involved in an intimate relationship with a particular lawyer in the firm.

### § 4-7.3(k) Family or Romantic Relationship with Lawyer for Adverse Party

When a lawyer marries or has a romantic relationship with another lawyer, there is the prospect that these lawyers will find themselves on opposite sides of a matter, or that the law firms with which they are associated will be paired against each other. Likewise, when multiple members of a family are engaged in the practice of law in

[82] *See also* Matter of Bergman, 382 P.3d 455, 458, 462 (Kan. 2016) (suspending a lawyer for, among other disciplinary violations, engaging in a secret sexual affair with a senior executive of a corporation for which the lawyer was outside counsel).

different law firms within the same geographic region, they may represent clients whose interests are adverse to each other. Whether these relationships create a conflict of interest and present the risk that confidential information may be revealed depends very much on how the law practices are structured, that is, whether they maintain strict isolation of professional activity from their personal lives, such as whether legal work is conducted at home, client files are brought home, etc.

Because of the risk of divided loyalties, Rule 1.8(i) of the Model Rules of Professional Conduct before 2002 provided that "[a] lawyer related to another lawyer as parent, child, sibling or spouse shall not represent a client in a representation directly adverse to a person whom the lawyer knows is represented by the other lawyer except upon consent by the client after consultation regarding the relationship."[83] Although that particular language was removed in 2002 from Rule 1.8, the basic principle is preserved in Comment 11 to Rule 1.7. That comment provides that "each client is entitled to know of the existence and implications of the relationship between the lawyers before the lawyer agrees to undertake the representation," and states that a lawyer related to another lawyer as parent, child, sibling, or spouse "ordinarily may not represent a client in a matter where that lawyer is representing another party, unless each client gives informed consent."

Because a family relationship conflict is no longer listed in Rule 1.8, it also then would not be included in the imputation of conflicts in Rule 1.8(k). Thus, the fact that a lawyer representing a client is married, is related to, or has romantic relationship with a lawyer who is a member of the law firm representing the adverse party, but the related lawyer is not personally involved in the representation, does not create a conflict of interest. In theory, then, the lawyer would not be obliged even to inform the client of her relationship with a lawyer associated with the opposing party's law firm, much less obtain informed consent. The prudent lawyer, however, would at least disclose the matter to the client, lest the client learn of the relationship in another way and suspect that the lawyer had deliberately concealed it, thereby damaging the trust of the client in the lawyer.

### § 4-7.3(*l*) Imputation of Lawyer-Client Conflicts

With the sole exception of the personal conflicts of a lawyer having a sexual relationship with a client, each of the conflict scenarios addressed under Rule 1.8 of the Model Rules of Professional Conduct is imputed to every lawyer in the law firm through Rule 1.8(k).[84]

For example, if one lawyer within a firm represents an individual or entity as a client, then any other lawyer in the firm who enters into a business transaction with that client must satisfy the requirements of Rule 1.8(a), even if that lawyer is not assigned to perform legal services for that client. As another example, the ban on a lawyer preparing a testamentary instrument under which the lawyer would receive a substantial bequest may not be circumvented by having another lawyer in the office draft the document. Likewise, the prohibitions on using confidential information to the disadvantage of a client, negotiating literary or media rights to a client's story relating to the representation, advancing living expenses to clients, and acquiring a proprietary

[83] MODEL R. PROF'L CONDUCT R. 1.8(i) (American Bar Association, 2001).

[84] On the general rule of imputed disqualification to all lawyers associated in practice, see *infra* § 4-7.6(a).

interest in the client's claim are binding, not only upon the particular lawyer who is handling the representation for that client, but on every other lawyer associated with the law firm.

## § 4-7.4 CONCURRENT CLIENT CONFLICTS

### § 4-7.4(a) Introduction to Client-Client Concurrent Conflicts

Rule 1.7(a) of the Model Rules of Professional Conduct states that a "conflict of interest" is present when either—

> (1) the representation of one client will be directly adverse to another client; or
>
> (2) there is a significant risk that the representation of one or more clients will be materially limited by the lawyer's responsibilities to another client, a former client or a third person or by a personal interest of the lawyer.

***Direct Adversity Conflicts:*** Under Rule 1.7(a)(1), a lawyer may not represent one client directly adverse to another client, even if the separate matters on which the lawyer represents the respective clients are wholly unrelated.[85]

***Material Limitation Conflicts:*** Under Rule 1.7(a)(2), a lawyer may not represent a client if the lawyer's independence of judgment is likely to be compromised, that is, "the representation of one or more clients will be materially limited," by the lawyer's conflicting responsibilities to another client.[86]

The lawyer is responsible to ascertain whether he has a conflict of interest that requires the lawyer to decline representation at the start or withdraw from representation as it continues.[87]

### § 4-7.4(b) Direct Adversity Conflicts of Interest

#### *§ 4-7.4(b)(1) Nature and Purpose of the Direct Adversity Conflict Rule*

Under Rule 1.7(a)(1) of the Model Rules of Professional Conduct, a lawyer must decline retention or withdraw when "the representation of one client will be directly adverse to another client." The direct-adversity conflict rule is simple and its purpose is evident. A lawyer may not represent one present client against another present client.

This rule of course encompasses that most dramatic of direct-adversity conflicts, in which a lawyer undertakes to represent opposing sides to the same controversy or transaction.[88] But the rule applies as well when the lawyer represents one client adverse to another client, even on a matter that is entirely unrelated to the matter on which the lawyer simultaneously represents that other client. "A client who learns that his or her lawyer is also representing a litigation adversary, even with respect to a matter wholly unrelated to the one for which counsel was retained, cannot long be expected to sustain

---

[85] *See infra* § 4-7.4(b).

[86] *See infra* § 4-7.4(c).

[87] *See supra* § 4-7.2.

[88] *See also* In re Hankey, 821 N.W.2d 839, 840 (N.D. 2012) (observing that the clients' interests "were inescapably adverse" when the lawyer "undertook dual representation of an alleged perpetrator and alleged victim of the crimes of aggravated assault and terrorizing"). Under Rule 1.7(b)(3), when the lawyer would be representing clients on opposite sides of the same litigation or proceeding before a tribunal, the direct-adversity conflict is not consentable, that is, may not be accepted by the clients through waiver. *See infra* § 4-7.7(e).

the level of confidence and trust in counsel that is one of the foundations of the professional relationship."[89]

The direct-adversity rule covers any adversarial representation, whether the lawyer is appearing for one client in bringing a court action against another client, the lawyer is representing one client in a transactional negotiation with another client, or even when the lawyer is representing one client in a proceeding and another client will take the stand as an adverse witness and thus be subject to cross-examination by the lawyer. The strict prohibition on direct-adversity conflicts protects the legal profession from the cynicism that naturally arises when a client learns that his own counsel in one matter is at the same time working to defeat the client's objectives in another matter.

As a case model of the reasons for the direct-adversity rule and a poignant illustration of the real and even personal harm that it may cause, consider *Board of Professional Ethics & Conduct v. Winkel*.[90] A lawyer had been retained by a man named Reimers and his wife to represent them in a bankruptcy proceeding. After the bankruptcy petition had been filed and while negotiations with creditors were ongoing, Reimers suffered extensive injuries in an automobile collision with an uninsured motorist named Sweers, who likely was at fault because he ran a stop sign. Anticipating a lawsuit, Sweers retained this same lawyer to prepare his defense. Having apparently failed to conduct any conflicts check, the lawyer did not learn that his bankruptcy client Reimers was the very person injured by his new client Sweers, until he received a letter from Reimer's personal injury lawyer. As the Iowa Supreme Court later observed, the contrast between the lawyer's and the client's "reactions to this state of affairs is telling."[91] Believing that Reimers had been more demanding in the bankruptcy matter, and having already spent several hours representing Sweers in the automobile accident matter, the lawyer unilaterally withdrew from the bankruptcy proceeding, leaving Reimers and his wife to negotiate the unresolved issues on their own. Reimers, who had just been released from the hospital and was out of work, stated that his "initial reaction was anger" and then he "felt very betrayed and let down."[92]

Although Reimers was able to finalize the negotiations with creditors on his own, the matter was greatly complicated by his injury, the loss of his vehicle due to damage in the accident, his mounting medical bills, and of course his lawyer's abandonment. To add insult to injury (as well as constituting yet another violation of the ethics rules), the lawyer subsequently deposed Reimers in the personal injury litigation and inquired whether Reimers had driven his motorcycle to the deposition. Because reaffirmation of Reimers's motorcycle debt had been an issue in the bankruptcy proceeding, the lawyer's use of this confidential information against his client was outrageous. Reimers was stunned by the conduct of his own bankruptcy lawyer in raising this matter, and in any event, Reimers had been too severely injured to drive any vehicle to the deposition. As the court concluded, the lawyer's "startling indifference" to his rejected client's problems "demonstrates the impaired judgment and betrayal of loyalty" that underlies the conflict of interest rule.[93]

---

[89] Flatt v. Superior Court, 885 P.2d 950, 956 (Cal. 1994).

[90] 599 N.W.2d 456, 457 (Iowa 1999).

[91] *Id.* at 458.

[92] *Id.*

[93] *Id.* at 459.

#### *§ 4-7.4(b)(2) Clients Engaged in Economic Competition*

While the direct-adversity rule applies not only to litigation but also to clients who are on opposite sides of a transaction or negotiation, it does not bar representation of clients who are simply engaged in economic competition against each other. As Comment 6 to Rule 1.7 explains, "simultaneous representation in unrelated matters of clients whose interests are only economically adverse, such as representation of competing economic enterprises in unrelated litigation, does not ordinarily constitute a conflict of interest and thus may not require consent of the respective clients."

By this understanding, a lawyer who has developed a concentration in an area of practice that serves primarily or exclusively clients from a particular sector of the economy does not ordinarily run afoul of the conflict of interest rules by offering those services to multiple commercial clients who are in competition with each another. A lawyer who has developed expertise and demonstrated a facility for representing restaurants in negotiating franchise agreements with national chains or with gasoline service stations in complying with environmental regulations generally may provide those legal services to several restaurants or gas stations, including those located in and competing within the same community.

Under the general duty of loyalty, however, a lawyer may not assist one commercial client in achieving an objective that would be directly detrimental to another client, such as seeking a change in zoning laws that effectively would put the other commercial client out of business or negotiating exclusive contractual rights that would prefer one client over another in a particular market.[94]

Moreover, under the overriding duty to protect client confidentiality, the lawyer who comes into possession of sensitive proprietary information about one commercial client may be stricken with a conflict of interest. Suppose the lawyer learns that one commercial client is economically troubled, while representing a competing commercial client and on a matter that would be directly and materially advanced by access to that confidential information.

In sum, while ordinary economic competition may not make clients directly adverse, under certain circumstances, the lawyer's responsibilities to one client may materially limit the representation that can be provided to an economic-competing client.

### § 4-7.4(c) Materially-Limited Representation Conflicts of Interest

#### *§ 4-7.4(c)(1) Nature of the Materially-Limited Conflict Rule*

Under Rule 1.7(a)(2) of the Model Rules of Professional Conduct, a lawyer must decline retention or withdraw when "there is a significant risk that the representation of one or more clients will be materially limited by the lawyer's responsibilities to another client, a former client or a third person or by a personal interest of the lawyer." The *Restatement of the Law Governing Lawyers* similarly states that "[a] conflict of interest is involved if there is a substantial risk that the lawyer's representation of the client would be materially and adversely affected by the lawyer's own interests or by the

[94] On conflicts of interest arising between economically-competing entities, see Charles W. Wolfram, *Competitor and Other "Finite Pie" Conflicts*, 36 HOFSTRA L. REV. 539, 550–55 (2007); Charles W. Wolfram, *Ethics 2000 and Conflicts of Interest: The More Things Change . . .*, 70 TENN. L. REV. 27, 38–39 (2002).

lawyer's duties to another current client, a former client, or a third person."[95] The rule requires the lawyer to consider not only whether a materially-limiting influence is present, but also whether there is a substantial potential that such a conflicting factor may emerge.

An impermissible conflict of interest is not established by the mere possibility that a divergence of influences may arise that in turn will divide or compromise the lawyer's loyalty—a possibility is inherent in nearly every human interaction. As Comment 8 to Rule 1.7 states, "[t]he critical questions are the likelihood that a difference in interests will eventuate and, if it does, whether it will materially interfere with the lawyer's independent professional judgment in considering alternatives or foreclose courses of action that reasonably should be pursued on behalf of the client."

The materially-limited representation conflict rule states an objective standard for conflict of interest analysis, although the lawyer's subjective state of mind may confirm the existence of a conflict that otherwise might not be recognized. The rule calls for an objective evaluation of those interests that pose a significant risk of impairing the loyalty of a reasonable lawyer, rather than (or in addition to) a subjective exploration of what is in the heart of the professional. If the reasonable outside observer would conclude that a lawyer would be materially limited in the representation of a client due to the conflicting influences of other persons or the lawyer's own self-interest, then an impermissible conflict of interest is present.

To be sure, if an outside observer failed to detect a compromising influence or would regard the influence as less than materially limiting, the lawyer nonetheless may not continue with the representation if she appreciates that loyalty to the client has been or likely will be compromised in a material way. Moreover, if, based on personal characteristics or atypical circumstances, the lawyer would respond against the client's interests to an influence that a reasonable outside person might find insignificant, the lawyer still is faced with a conflict of interest because the lawyer's independence of professional judgment has been subverted.

On the other hand, while a lawyer who consciously acknowledges being influenced by a contrary interest obviously has a conflict (whether another person would be so influenced or not), sincerity of belief that one is not so influenced does not necessarily suffice to avoid a conflict if a reasonable observer would regard the influence as a grave threat to professional detachment. Consider the situation of a lawyer who is retained by a client to file suit against a company in which the lawyer's life savings are invested or to bring an action for fraud and punitive damages against the lawyer's parents or spouse. That this lawyer might profess a higher calling to the role of the advocate and insist that her devotion to the professional ideal is beyond corruption—and indeed that the lawyer might be sincere in so proclaiming[96]—would not change the conclusion that the lawyer was disabled by a conflict of interest that required her withdrawal. The conflict rules were written with the ordinary lawyer in mind and cannot be applied with the assumption that some may be so noble as to resist even the greatest temptation to favor another's or the lawyer's own interest over that of a client.

---

[95] RESTATEMENT (THIRD) OF THE LAW GOVERNING LAWYERS § 121 (American Law Institute, 2000).

[96] On whether the lawyer's sincere belief on managing an ethical problem comports with behavioral psychology reality, see Jennifer K. Robbennolt & Jean R. Sternlight, *Behavioral Legal Ethics*, 45 ARIZ. ST. L.J. 1107, 1117 (2013) ("[P]eople commonly make inaccurate forecasts of their own future emotions and behavior—and, thus, may predict that they will act ethically when this is not necessarily so.").

### *§ 4-7.4(c)(2) Lawyer Personal Interest Conflicts*

Under Rule 1.7(a)(2), a lawyer has a conflict of interest if there is "a significant risk" that a representation "will be materially limited" by "a personal interest of the lawyer." A personal interest conflict may consist of anything from the lawyer's investment in an entity that is adverse to the client, to a family or romantic relationship with the attorney on the opposing side,[97] and on to the lawyer's political beliefs or extreme personal antipathy toward a client.[98] If a lawyer is being recruited for legal employment by a party or by an attorney for a party who stands in opposition to the client, the lawyer's desire to make himself attractive to the potential employer is likely to weaken the lawyer's continuing loyalty to the client. When a lawyer becomes implicated in alleged client wrongdoing, such that the lawyer becomes at personal risk of a criminal charge or civil liability, the lawyer is unlikely to be able to continue to provide the client with advice that reflects selfless and detached judgment.

In addition, when a lawyer has arguably made a professional error and the client's interests would best be advanced by challenging that error, the lawyer's personal interests in defending her actions may come into conflict with the client's interests.

While a conflict would arise when a client's goal can no longer be pursued without challenging the lawyer's effectiveness or professional work, a conflict of interest does not invariably erupt whenever an attorney makes a mistake in handling a matter. Even the best of attorneys might lapse in practice, ranging from typographical errors in documents to poorly framed questions in discovery to missed court deadlines. Fortunately, most such lawyer errors may be corrected and therefore result in no continuing prejudice to the client. When the lawyer reasonably believes that an error may be corrected, either immediately or by requesting relief from a court, the interests of the lawyer and the client often remain congruent. Similarly, no disqualifying conflict arises when the lawyer has made a mistake that does no concrete harm to the client.

When, however, efforts to correct the error have been unsuccessful or when the client should attack the lawyer's work to secure relief, the divergence in objectives gives rise to an insuperable conflict. Thus, when "there is a non-frivolous malpractice claim" against the lawyer, there is then " 'a substantial risk that the lawyer's [continuing] representation of the client would be materially and adversely affected by' his own interest in avoiding malpractice liability."[99]

In a truly astounding example, when a life was literally at stake, the case of *Christeson v. Roper*[100] stands out. Two lawyers who had been appointed to represent a death row inmate in federal post conviction proceedings failed to even meet with their client until nearly eleven months after the appointment—and six weeks after the one-year statute of limitations for filing a petition for habeas corpus had passed. They finally

---

[97] *See also supra* § 4-7.3(k).

[98] While a lawyer who has already accepted retention by a client should hesitate to refuse continued representation based upon the lawyer's personal dislike of the client, the lawyer is permitted by Rule 1.16(b) to withdraw if withdrawal can be accomplished without material adverse effect on the interests of the client or if the client insists upon taking action that the lawyer considers "repugnant or with which the lawyer has a fundamental disagreement." *See supra* § 4-3.6(c)(2).

[99] Leonard v. Dorsey & Whitney, 553 F.3d 609, 629 (8th Cir. 2009) (quoting RESTATEMENT (THIRD) OF THE LAW GOVERNING LAWYERS §§ 121, 125 (American Law Institute, 2000)).

[100] 135 S. Ct. 891, 892–93 (2015). The author of this part of the book was one of the legal ethics professors who joined the amicus brief of the Ethics Bureau at Yale in support of the petition for a writ of certiorari in *Christeson*.

filed the petition some four months late, which then was denied as untimely. Nearly seven years later, these two procrastinating attorneys consulted with two experts in capital cases, who "immediately noticed a glaring problem," namely that the only hope for the death row client was to request equitable tolling of the statute of limitations based on these two lawyers' "own malfeasance in filing to file timely the habeas petition."[101] The new consulting attorneys, with the support of the inmate, filed a motion for substitution of counsel. The defaulting lawyers not only resisted the substitution,[102] but defended their actions in miscalculating the due date for the petition and characterized their own client's potential argument for equitable tolling as "ludicrous."[103] As said by amicus, "it is troubling beyond explanation that these lawyers, in effect, argued in support of their client's execution."[104]

After the district court refused to substitute these new conflict-free counsel who offered their services and then the court of appeals affirmed in a short order, the Supreme Court summarily reversed and held that the death row petitioner was entitled to substitute counsel who could present a request to reopen the judgment and seek equitable tolling of the period for filing a habeas petition.[105] Calling the conflict of interest for the two lawyers "obvious," the Court emphasized that the standard for tolling the statute of limitations for the habeas petition was " 'serious instances of attorney misconduct.' "[106] "Advancing such a claim would have required [the two lawyers] to denigrate their own performance," an argument the Court explained counsel could not "reasonably be expected to make" as it "threatens their professional reputation and livelihood."[107]

In general, if the lawyer has a personal stake, interest, belief, position, or relationship that might compromise his independent professional judgment on behalf of a client, a conflict of interest exists and the lawyer may not proceed, at least without informed consent by the client. When the personal interest is sufficiently compelling in its influence that the lawyer could not "reasonably believe" that he would still "be able to provide competent and diligent representation" to the client, as required by Rule 1.7(b)(1), then the conflict is nonconsentable.

As discussed previously, certain personal interest conflicts are regarded as so likely to impair the lawyer's loyalty to the client as to merit special treatment or even be subject to a per se prohibition, such as the limitations on doing business with a client[108] and the prohibition on preparing an instrument giving the lawyer or a relative a substantial gift.[109] Ordinary personal interest conflicts, as well as those arising from a sexual relationship between a lawyer and client, are not imputed to other lawyers in the law firm. However, those conflicts addressed in Rule 1.8 apply, not only to the lawyer

---

[101] *Id.*

[102] Petition for a Writ of Certiorari at 11, Christeson v. Roper, 135 S. Ct. 891 (2015).

[103] *Christeson*, 135 S. Ct. at 894–95.

[104] Brief of the Ethics Bureau at Yale, Legal Ethics Professors and Capital Habeas Corpus Practitioners as Amicus Curiae in Support of Petition at 10, Christeson v. Roper, 135 S. Ct. 891 (2015).

[105] *Christeson*, 135 S. Ct. at 895–96.

[106] *Id.* at 894–95 (quoting Holland v. Florida, 560 U.S. 631, 651–52 (2010)).

[107] *Id.* at 894.

[108] *See supra* § 4-7.3(b).

[109] *See supra* § 4-7.3(d).

personally involved, but to all lawyers with whom that lawyer is associated.[110] Moreover, if the lawyer with a personal interest conflict may interfere with the representation, or if other lawyers in the firm will be significantly influenced by or solicitous toward that lawyer's personal situation or view, then a material limitation of representation conflict exists for those other lawyers in the firm, whether the disqualification is formally imputed or not.

While not strictly required in every case, ethical screening of the personally disqualified lawyer may be advisable even when vicarious disqualification does not extend to other lawyers in the firm. Such a step would help ensure that the personal interest of that single lawyer has no influence upon the behavior of other lawyers within the firm and prevent improper access to confidential information that might be disclosed or used at a disadvantage to the firm's client.

### *§ 4-7.4(c)(3) Representing Multiple Clients in a Criminal Matter*

Especially given the substantial liberty interest at stake and based upon painful experience with the frequency of problems in this context, Comment 23 to Rule 1.7 warns that "[t]he potential for conflict of interest in representing multiple defendants in a criminal case is so grave that ordinarily a lawyer should decline to represent more than one codefendant."[111] As one court observed:

> It will generally be found when two or more are accused of a serious crime, that their interests are to some extent divergent. Often the question will arise as which was the planner of the crime, which took the leading part, or in many other ways each may desire to attempt to throw the onus upon the other. Separate lawyers for separate defendants may not in all cases prove an unmixed blessing; the result may be attempts by each to cast the blame upon the other, to the profit of the prosecution. But it is settled that where there may be adverse interests, each defendant is entitled to separate representation.[112]

A lawyer attempting to juggle responsibilities to multiple criminal defendants may be unable to strike separate plea agreements, may be unable to determine which theory of the case and supporting evidence best supports one or the other client's defense, and cannot even consider offering the testimony of one defendant against the other in return for a reduced sentence or immunity.

Nonetheless, representation by a single lawyer (or law firm) of joint criminal defendants (in the same or separate trials) is not prohibited outright by the Model Rules, and there may be occasions in which the unified defense and common front against the prosecution is to the benefit of both clients. Nonetheless, the American Bar Association's *Standards for Criminal Justice* advise that informed written consent should be obtained from each client, which should be made on the record before the court "with appropriate inquiries by counsel and the court."[113]

---

[110] *See infra* § 4-7.6(a). On the imputation of conflicts under Rule 1.8, with the exception of a sexual relations conflict, see *supra* § 4-7.3(*l*).

[111] *See also* STANDARDS FOR CRIMINAL JUSTICE: DEFENSE FUNCTION, Standard 4–1.7(d) (American Bar Ass'n, 2015) (generally advising criminal defense counsel or counsel associated in practice "should not undertake to represent more than one client in the same criminal case").

[112] State v. Karsten, 72 N.W.2d 463, 466 (Iowa 1955).

[113] STANDARDS FOR CRIMINAL JUSTICE: DEFENSE FUNCTION, Standard 4–1.7(e) (American Bar Ass'n, 2015).

Moreover, multiple client conflicts of interest in the criminal context may arise in ways other than being retained by more than one defendant to the same charge. Notably, a lawyer may find that another client being simultaneously represented on a different matter ends up on the witness list for the prosecution. This type of conflict becomes particularly disturbing when the lawyer's other client is a key witness for the prosecution against the lawyer's criminal defendant client.

Conflicts arising from multiple representation in a criminal case may not emerge or may not be discovered until late in the proceeding, the client or lawyer may fail to object, or the trial court may refuse the request to appoint new counsel. Thus, the primary question facing the courts has been when the conviction of a defendant should be reversed on the ground that a conflict of interest impaired the effectiveness of the defense.

Under the Sixth Amendment to the United States Constitution, a criminal defendant is guaranteed effective assistance of legal counsel. Under the classic test of *Strickland v. Washington*,[114] to overturn a conviction on the basis of ineffective assistance of counsel, the accused ordinarily must show "a reasonable probability that, but for counsel's unprofessional errors, the result of the proceeding would have been different." In other words, in the typical case, demonstrating that the lawyer's performance of her legal duties fell below the professional standard of care is not sufficient to reverse a conviction. The convicted defendant must further establish that she was prejudiced by having been wrongly convicted, that is, had the defendant received an effective legal defense, she is likely to have been acquitted.

However, when the lawyer's deficiency in representing a criminal defendant was attributable to a conflict of interest—which thus deprived the defendant of the lawyer's undivided loyalty—the Supreme Court has reduced the showing demanded for overturning a conviction, by directing an automatic reversal in some circumstances and by requiring a lesser showing of injury in other circumstances. Three basic scenarios have presented themselves: (1) where the client or lawyer raised a conflict of interest objection and the trial court refused to investigate; (2) where neither the client nor the lawyer raised any objection, but the trial court knew or should have known that a conflict existed and yet failed to inquire; and (3) where no one raised an objection and the trial court had no reasonable basis to suspect a conflict, but the defendant asserts after conviction that his counsel had been disabled by a conflict of interest.

First, when the attorney is forced by the trial court (through denial of a motion to withdraw) to represent conflicting interests, over the lawyer's objection, it is presumed that the conflict of interest infected the defense and the conviction will be reversed without the necessity of any showing of prejudice by the defendant.[115] Thus, regardless of whether particular prejudice is shown and even when the defendant was clearly guilty (that is, the evidence of guilt was overwhelming), automatic reversal is mandated when the trial court improperly required joint or dual representation despite a conflict of interest and over a timely objection.

Second, when the trial court "knows or reasonably should know that a particular conflict exists," the judge has the duty to inquire into the propriety of the defense

[114] 466 U.S. 668, 694 (1984).

[115] Holloway v. Arkansas, 435 U.S. 475, 488 (1978).

counsel's representation of the criminal defendant.[116] If it is found, either on appeal or after further investigation on remand, that an actual conflict had existed which infected the representation, then prejudice will also be presumed. However, if neither the defendant nor defense counsel alerted the court to the possible conflict, the automatic reversal rule does not apply and the defendant must demonstrate that an actual conflict affected the lawyer's performance.[117]

Third, when the trial court did not know or have reason to know of a conflict or mistakenly concluded there was no conflict, then "to establish a violation of the Sixth Amendment, a defendant who raised no objection at trial must demonstrate that an actual conflict of interest adversely affected his lawyer's performance."[118] Importantly, while the defendant must show that the conflict had a concrete and negative effect upon the lawyer's exercise of professional judgment, the defendant is not obliged to satisfy the higher *Strickland* test by proving that the result of the trial likely would have been different but for the lawyer's divided loyalty.

In sum, demonstration of an actual (and not merely possible) conflict of interest will lead to an automatic reversal of the conviction when the lawyer or client had objected or when the judge knew or reasonably should have known of the conflict. By contrast, in the "non-notice" case where no objection was raised and the trial court had no basis to know that a conflict existed (or when the trial court performed an inquiry and found no conflict), a supposedly higher showing must be made that the conflict had an adverse effect on the lawyer's performance.

In most cases, there is unlikely to be a practical difference between the two showings. The identification of an actual conflict of interest typically will involve a demonstration that the conflict had an effect upon the lawyer's exercise of judgment. Evidence of the latter may be what indicates the presence of the former.[119] However, there may be some cases where, because of the manifest divided loyalties of the lawyer, an actual conflict does exist, even though it is difficult to establish that any particular choice made by the lawyer was infected by the conflict. In this type of case, reversal will follow only when an objection was ignored or the trial court abused discretion in failing to investigate the facts underlying what the judge knew or should have known posed a serious risk of impaired loyalty.

#### *§ 4-7.4(c)(4) Representing Multiple Clients in Civil Litigation*

While joint or dual representation in a criminal matter generally is inadvisable, representation of multiple clients (on the same side) in civil litigation is not only common but frequently makes good sense. Whenever more than one client is being represented, there almost always is some risk that the interests of the clients may diverge at some point. But the benefits of coordinated representation and presenting a united front against any adversary, as well as the reduced costs achieved by sharing the same counsel, may justify multiple representation when the risk of a disruptive conflict

---

[116] Cuyler v. Sullivan, 446 U.S. 335, 347 (1980).

[117] Mickens v. Taylor, 535 U.S. 162, 170–76 (2002).

[118] *Cuyler*, 446 U.S. at 348.

[119] *See* Stevenson v. Newsome, 774 F.2d 1558, 1561–62 (11th Cir. 1985) ("It must be demonstrated that "the attorney 'made a choice between alternative courses of action . . . . If he did not make such a choice, the conflict remained hypothetical.' ").

appears small. Professor Teresa Collett outlines the factors to be weighed from the perspectives of both clients and lawyers:

> The choice between individual and joint representation has significant consequences for both the clients and the lawyer. For clients, individual representation promises undivided attorney loyalty, maximum informational and decisional privacy, and minimal threat of disqualification or premature withdrawal by counsel. Joint representation, on the other hand, offers pooled information and resources, as well as a common commitment to the collective interests of all.
>
> For attorneys, individual representation frees them from the competing claims for loyalty that are often inherent in multiple representation. They need only consider and consult with the single client, and act according to his or her directions. Joint representation requires more of the lawyer. Communicating with joint clients is more demanding, not only because there are more clients, but also because the information that must be communicated increases with each client's response. Coordination of the clients' positions increases the demands on the lawyer's skills, yet often enhances the reliability of the lawyer's assessments of the chances of any particular strategy's success.[120]

While there are distinct advantages to joint representation of parties on the same side in civil litigation, the lawyer may proceed only if it is apparent that the parties are reasonably congenial and dedicated to a common objective. If the danger that a conflict of interest will develop is significant, the lawyer may not continue the representation. If the clients manifest animosity toward each other, if there is a significant prospect that they will stake out adverse positions or even assert claims against each other, if one client appears likely to seek more favorable treatment from the lawyer, or if one client wishes to withhold confidential information from the other, the lawyer ordinarily may not undertake or continue the representation.

For example, in *Bottoms v. Stapleton*,[121] a minority shareholder brought an action against a limited liability company and its majority shareholder which sought damages for breach of fiduciary duty and conversion and dissolution of the company. The minority shareholder moved to disqualify the opposing counsel for simultaneously representing both the company and the majority shareholder. The court explained that the focus is "on the degree of risk that a lawyer will be unable to fulfill his or her duties to both clients."[122] The court found that the interests of the company and the majority shareholder were not adverse in the present posture of the litigation, and that there was no "substantial evidence that the defendants' interests will likely become adverse, particularly given the fact that one defendant is a limited liability company and the other defendant holds the controlling interest in the company."[123] For that reason, the court concluded there was no significant potential for a divergence of interests interposing a present conflict of interest.

---

[120] Teresa Stanton Collett, *The Promise and Peril of Multiple Representation*, 16 REV. LITIG. 567, 583 (1997).

[121] 706 N.W.2d 411 (Iowa 2005).

[122] *Id.* at 416. On the general standard for a materially-limited representation conflict of interest, see *supra* § 4-6.3(a).

[123] *Bottoms*, 706 N.W.2d at 418–19.

While any simultaneous representation carries with it some possibility of differing interests arising at some point in the future, the crucial question to be asked under Model Rule 1.7(a)(2) is whether there is "a significant risk" that the lawyer's representation of one of the clients will be "materially limited" by the lawyer's responsibilities to the other client. Comment 23 to Rule 1.7 outlines possible conflicts that could arise in multiple representation cases, including "substantial discrepancy in the clients' testimony," "incompatibility in positions in relation to an opposing party," and "substantially different possibilities of settlement" of the matter.

When the commonality of interests among the multiple clients is high and the likelihood of any conflict arising between them is insignificant, Rule 1.7 does not demand that the lawyer obtain consent from each client to the shared representation. By contrast, if there is a significant risk that the clients' interests will diverge at some point (and especially if that divergence already exists), even on what appear to be minor or subsidiary points, such that the lawyer's loyalty would be divided, a present conflict of interest would exist. In that event, the lawyer may commence or undertake the representation only if informed consent from the clients may be obtained.[124]

Whether or not the risk of future separation of interests is sufficiently great as to mandate seeking informed consent at the outset, it is advisable in every case of multiple representation to consult with the clients; to raise the possibility of divided loyalty should differences arise along the way toward the common objective; to further explore the possibility that the clients may divide along one or another potential fault line as the representation progresses; to discuss how confidential information will be treated[125] and to explain that when two or more persons jointly consult with the same lawyer (or law firm), neither person may invoke the attorney-client privilege to prevent disclosure by the lawyer of communications to the other person;[126] and to consider what steps should be taken to reconcile any conflict that should emerge or how to terminate the representation if the conflict proves unmanageable.

In addition, as addressed below,[127] a conflict of interest may emerge when the lawyer is representing multiple parties and an offer is made or received for an aggregate settlement, that is, a settlement in which all parties must join or the offer is withdrawn. The lawyer may participate in making an aggregate settlement only with the informed consent of all clients in a signed writing.

Even if the potential for a future conflict falls below the threshold of significance, the lawyer and clients should carefully consider the harm that could be realized if an unexpected conflict were to emerge. As Comment 29 to Model Rule 1.7 states, "the result can be additional cost, embarrassment, and recrimination," and the lawyer ordinarily will "be forced to withdraw from representing all of the clients."

---

[124] On informed consent to a conflict, see *infra* § 4-7.7.

[125] On treatment of confidential information in multiple client situations, see also *infra* § 4-7.4(c) 4-7.4(c)(6) to (7).

[126] *See supra* § 4-6.3(c).

[127] *See supra* § 4-7.4(c)(5).

### *§ 4-7.4(c)(5) Aggregate Settlement of Claims Involving Multiple Clients*

Inherent in representation of multiple clients as parties in a civil lawsuit or as defendants in a criminal proceeding[128] is the possibility that the opposing party may offer to settle the claim or to plea bargain on the condition that two or more of the lawyer's clients consent to the disposition.

In civil litigation, an offer for an aggregate settlement may propose a simultaneous and conclusive disposition of all claims by all parties, thus meaning that the proposed resolution of the dispute depends upon agreement by all of the lawyer's multiple clients.[129] In other words, an offer for aggregate settlement is an all-or-nothing proposition; refusal by any single party constitutes a rejection of the whole and the litigation therefore would continue as to all parties, even those who favored the settlement. By contrast, settlement by individual offer and separate resolution of some or all of a group of claims does not raise the same conflict concerns.[130] It is the "characteristics of interdependency which define an aggregate settlement."[131]

Similarly, in a criminal prosecution, the prosecutor might offer an aggregate plea bargain arrangement, under which all defendants being jointly charged would enter the same plea of guilty or nolo contendere and receive a designated sentence. If any single defendant insisted upon proceeding to trial, the prosecutor would take the case to trial against all defendants.

In an aggregate resolution of a civil or criminal matter, the lawyer representing multiple parties faces a conflict of interest because the lawyer has an equal duty of loyalty to each client and must provide balanced and candid counseling to each client on the advisability of the proposal. This balance may be difficult or impossible if the interdependent proposal is more advantageous to one client than to another.

For these reasons, Rule 1.8(g) of the Model Rules of Professional Conduct provides that "[a] lawyer who represents two or more clients shall not participate in making an aggregate settlement of the claims of or against the clients, or in a criminal case an aggregated agreement as to guilty or nolo contendere pleas, unless each client gives informed consent, in a writing signed by the client."

Importantly, the lawyer is not prohibited from negotiating for an aggregate settlement or plea bargain, whether by initiating such an offer or responding to it, but

---

[128] On the conflict of interest implications for representation of multiple parties in criminal and civil litigation, see *supra* § 4-7.4(c)(3) and (4) respectively.

[129] The aggregate settlement rule applies to any proposed resolution that involves more than one of the lawyer's clients and is conditioned on joint acceptance of the settlement offer, even if the proposal may not apply to all of the lawyer's clients. Thus, if an interdependent settlement were proposed that resolved claims made by two of three plaintiffs represented by the same lawyer, the requirements of the aggregate settlement rule apply to the lawyer in offering or responding to the settlement of the claims by those two clients.

[130] Where a settlement offer does not include any condition, that is settlement is "individually negotiated and each client is free to settle or not as that client chooses," the proposal is not in the aggregate and subject to the special limitations of the rule. Peter R. Jarvis & Trisha M. Rich, *Defining Aggregate Settlements: The Road Not to Take*, 23:4 PROF. LAW. 45, 48 (2016) (criticizing suggestion that mere commonality of factual or legal issues implicates aggregate settlement rule). On controversies about what constitutes an aggregate settlement, as contrasted with a non-interdependent group settlement, see Lynn A. Baker, *Aggregate Settlements and Attorney Liability: The Evolving Landscape*, 44 HOFSTRA L. REV. 291, 306–10 (2015).

[131] Tilzer v. Davis, Bethune & Jones, L.L.C., 204 P.3d 617, 628 (2009) (citing PRINCIPLES OF THE LAW OF AGGREGATE LITIGATION § 3.16 (American Law Institute, 2009)).

the lawyer must obtain advance consent from each of the clients.[132] Moreover, the required client consent must be informed, meaning that each client must be given a full explanation of the benefits and disadvantages of the proposal, as well as being advised of any constraints on the lawyer and the lawyer's counsel by reason of divided loyalty.[133] Rule 1.8(g) further provides that "[t]he lawyer's disclosure shall include the existence and nature of all the claims or pleas involved and of the participation of each person in the settlement." The lawyer may not withhold any information, such as by declining to tell one client the nature or amount of the offer to another client.

In Formal Opinion 06–438, the Standing Committee on Ethics and Professional Responsibility of the American Bar Association directed the lawyer to disclose the following information, "at a minimum," to each client with respect to a proposed aggregate settlement or plea agreement:

- The total amount of the aggregate settlement or the result of the aggregated agreement.
- The existence and nature of all of the claims, defenses, or pleas involved in the aggregate settlement or aggregated agreement.
- The details of every other client's participation in the aggregate settlement or aggregated agreement, whether it be their settlement contributions, their settlement receipts, the resolution of their criminal charges, or any other contribution or receipt of something of value as a result of the aggregate resolution. For example, if one client is favored over the other(s) by receiving non-monetary remuneration, that fact must be disclosed to the other client(s).
- The total fees and costs to be paid to the lawyer as a result of the aggregate settlement, if the lawyer's fees and/or costs will be paid, in whole or in part, from the proceeds of the settlement or by an opposing party or parties.
- The method by which costs (including costs already paid by the lawyer as well as costs to be paid out of the settlement proceeds) are to be apportioned among them.[134]

Because each client has the right to accept or reject any settlement or plea bargain,[135] the rule protects the client's autonomy and prevents the lawyer from taking any one-sided actions or offering imbalanced advice that undermines the client's freedom to make this choice and do so intelligently. That a majority of the claimants in a civil

---

[132] Comment 13 to Rule 1.8 indicates that the aggregate settlement rule does not apply in the peculiar context of class-action suits, reasoning that "[l]awyers representing a class of plaintiffs or defendants, or those proceeding derivatively, may not have a full client-lawyer relationship with each member of the class," apparently suggesting that the lawyer for a class does not have the same duty of completely undivided loyalty to each individual as contrasted with a general duty of loyalty to the class. The comment instead directs lawyers representing a class to "comply with applicable rules regulating notification of class members and other procedural requirements designed to ensure adequate protection of the entire class."

[133] On the required disclosures by the lawyer in an aggregate settlement situation, see generally Lynn A. Baker & Charles Silver, *The Aggregate Settlement Rule and Ideals of Client Service*, 41 S. TEX. L. REV. 227, 229–30 (1999). On informed client consent to conflicts of interest, see *infra* § 4-7.7.

[134] ABA Comm. on Ethics & Prof'l Responsibility, Formal Op. 06–438 (2006). For a critique of the required elements of disclosure, see Lynn A. Baker, *Aggregate Settlements and Attorney Liability: The Evolving Landscape*, 44 HOFSTRA L. REV. 291, 322–23 (2015).

[135] *See supra* § 4-3.4.

lawsuit may favor settlement, for example, does not authorize the lawyer to accept the settlement on behalf of all clients or to override the objections of the dissenting client. Client autonomy is further safeguarded under Rule 1.8(g) by requiring that the client's agreement to an aggregate disposition be confirmed by the client's signature to a written consent agreement.

Whether multiple clients may agree in advance, through an informed consent agreement, to abide by a majority or super-majority vote as to an aggregate settlement, thus surrendering the individual right to withhold consent, is a matter of controversy. The text of the rule does not authorize such a majority-rules arrangement, and the courts to address the matter have rejected the permissibility of such a waiver.[136]

The American Law Institute's *Principles of the Law of Aggregate Litigation*, approved in 2009, recommend that advance waivers of the aggregate settlement rule be approved under certain circumstances. Under Section 3.17(b) of the *Principles*, when the lawyer has explained the alternatives, a claimant may agree in advance to be bound by a substantial majority vote of all claimants to an aggregate settlement.[137] In Comment b, the reporters of the new principles argue that the current rule prohibiting advance consent "empower[s] individual holdout claimants to exercise control over a proposed settlement and to demand premiums in exchange for approval."[138]

In response, Professor Nancy Moore, who was reporter for the American Bar Association's Ethics 2000 project to revise the Model Rules of Professional Conduct, defends the aggregate settlement rule as necessary to "protect[ ] clients against the risks of inadequate settlements and unfair allocations."[139] Thus, for example, a super-majority of claimants with less serious injuries would not be able to impose a binding settlement for an equally-divided and inadequate amount upon other claimants with more serious injuries. Rejecting the argument that hold-outs have veto power, Moore observes that the rule requires only that each client give informed consent to a settlement, that defendants are unlikely to demand unanimity before agreeing to settle, and that "[n]othing prevents the lawyer from negotiating a tentative settlement agreement that will become binding only as to those clients who accept its terms after the required full disclosure."[140]

An aggregate settlement may be further complicated for a lawyer representing multiple civil plaintiffs if the proposal is for the defendant to pay a total amount without specifying how it is to be allocated among the plaintiffs. Because the lawyer may not play favorites among the clients, the lawyer may be placed in a difficult or impossible position in determining how to divide the proceeds. But as Professor Lynn Baker writes, Rule 1.8(g) affirms that "the plaintiff's attorney *may* ethically participate in the 'making' of such settlement, including allocating a limited settlement fund."[141] Through informed consent by the clients, ideally obtained at the beginning of the representation and thus

---

[136] *See* Tax Auth., Inc. v. Jackson Hewitt, Inc., 898 A.2d 512, 518–22 (N.J. 2006) (listing cases).

[137] PRINCIPLES OF THE LAW OF AGGREGATE LITIGATION § 3.17 (American Law Institute, 2010).

[138] *Id.* § 3.17 cmt. b.

[139] Nancy J. Moore, *The American Law Institute's Draft Proposal to Bypass the Aggregate Settlement Rule: Do Mass Tort Clients Need (or Want) Group Decision Making*, 57 DEPAUL LAW REVIEW 395, 401, 410 (2008).

[140] *Id.* at 402–03.

[141] Lynn A. Baker, *Aggregate Settlements and Attorney Liability: The Evolving Landscape*, 44 HOFSTRA L. REV. 291, 317 (2015).

before the issue arises, the clients presumably could agree to a particular method or mechanism for allocating settlement dollars, based upon a reasonably objective formula or evaluation by outside and neutral experts.[142]

### *§ 4-7.4(c)(6) Representing Multiple Clients in a Non-Litigation Matter*

Even more so than in civil litigation, representation of multiple parties with a common goal in a non-litigation matter may make eminent sense for all concerned, ensuring the efficient and expeditious completion of the task at an affordable cost to the clients. Entrepreneurs and investors frequently select a single lawyer to assist in selection and creation of a new business organization;[143] a husband and wife typically will retain a single lawyer for estate planning and preparation of testamentary documents;[144] and parties who have agreed upon the terms of a transaction may seek a single lawyer to draft the necessary documents. In these and similar situations, depending on the actual circumstances and personalities involved, representation by a single lawyer or law firm makes it possible for multiple clients to achieve a common objective without hiring multiple lawyers for overlapping and redundant work at much greater expense. In addition, retaining a common lawyer may "promote[ ] a less adversarial atmosphere among parties who have already agreed that their interests are largely harmonious."[145]

As with other multiple representation situations, however, the lawyer must be careful to examine the clients and the circumstances and make a well-considered prognostication about the prospects that the interests of the clients will divide as matters progress. Even in those instances in which it does not appear at the outset that a division of interests is likely to emerge, and thus where an actual conflict (defined under Rule 1.7(a)(2) to include those situations where there is a significant risk of material limitation in the future)[146] does not presently exist, the wise lawyer nonetheless will counsel all parties about the possibility, however remote, that the lawyer's loyalty to all clients might be impaired and of the consequences should that occur. In other words, even if not required because a division of interests appears unlikely, seeking informed consent by the clients pursuant to Rule 1.7(b) is a sensible procedure.[147]

In addition to protecting both the lawyer and the clients should a conflict later emerge, adopting such a protective approach should assist the lawyer, through what she learns in conversations with the clients, to make a better-informed and more-refined assessment of the risks that the representation may be materially-limited in the future. In addition, discussing the possibility of future conflicts also allows the clients to better

---

[142] *Scc* RONALD D. ROTUNDA & JOHN S. DZIENKOWSKI, PROFESSIONAL RESPONSIBILITY: A STUDENT'S GUIDE § 1.8–8 (American Bar Ass'n, 2013–2014) (observing that some personal injury lawyers with multiple clients establish a point system by which a physician assigns points for each possible injury which then is used to create a fractional formula for allocating settlement proceeds, although saying that it is uncertain whether such a system would satisfy Rule 1.8(g)).

[143] For discussion of the lawyer's responsibilities regarding the formation of an entity, see *infra* § 4-8.2, and 5 MATTHEW G. DORÉ, IOWA PRACTICE SERIES: BUSINESS ORGANIZATIONS § 2.1 (Thomson Reuters 2017).

[144] For discussion of some of the special conflict of interest problems involved in estate planning and representing fiduciaries, see RONALD D. ROTUNDA & JOHN S. DZIENKOWSKI, PROFESSIONAL RESPONSIBILITY: A STUDENT'S GUIDE § 1.7–6(a) (American Bar Ass'n, 2013–14); Martin D. Begleiter, *The Gambler Breaks Even: Legal Malpractice in Complicated Estate Planning Cases*, 20 GA. ST. U. L. REV. 277, 343–67 (2003).

[145] 1 GEOFFREY C. HAZARD, JR., W. WILLIAM HODES & PETER R. JARVIS, THE LAW OF LAWYERING § 12.14 (Aspen, 4th ed., 2016).

[146] *See supra* § 4-7.4(c)(1).

[147] On waiver of conflicts, including multiple representation scenarios, see *infra* § 4-7.7.

understand the situation and, not incidentally, to appreciate the need to adhere to a common agenda if the joint representation is to succeed.

### *§ 4-7.4(c)(7) Joint Representation, Withdrawal or Termination, and Confidentiality*

Under what Lucian Pera calls the "fundamental principle" of joint representation, the lawyer must always "treat all joint clients equally in all respects, including loyalty, confidentiality, communication, and decision making."[148] Likewise, in parallel terms, when the lawyer can no longer uphold responsibilities to all clients in an equal manner, a conflict has interrupted the relationship.

If a conflict of interest is apparent at the beginning, or arises during the course of a joint representation, the clients may be able to consent to continued representation, thus waiving the conflict under Model Rule 1.7(b).[149] If the parties are not "fundamentally antagonistic to each other," Comment 28 to Rule 1.7 states that "common representation is permissible where the clients are generally aligned in interest even though there is some difference in interest among them."

By focusing on the mutual interests of the parties, while avoiding becoming mired in the differences among them, the lawyer may be able to achieve the general purpose despite a division that otherwise might constitute a materially-limited representation conflict of interest within the meaning of Rule 1.7(a)(2). Especially in a non-litigation matter, where none of the clients are actually opposing each other in an adversarial proceeding, Professors Geoffrey Hazard and William Hodes and attorney Peter Jarvis describe the lawyer as "acting as a facilitator" and "engaged in 'advocacy' only in the limited sense of urging jointly represented clients to heed the advice and to come to a mutually beneficial agreement or to adjust an essentially cooperative relationship that has become strained."[150]

However, if an unavoidable conflict emerges, the continuation of an attorney-client relationship in the ongoing matter with any of the individual clients is, to put it mildly, problematic. Because any separated client is now a former client entitled to the protections of the former client conflict rule,[151] the lawyer may not continue representing another of the multiple clients in any manner that would be adverse in any matter that is the same or a substantially related. Only if the continued representation for the remaining client would not be adverse in posture against the now-former client may the lawyer go forward.

Consent to continued representation of some but not all of the original jointly-represented clients may be possible, either at the time of withdrawal/termination or in advance,[152] assuming an informed consent by the separated client and that no confidential information obtained from that former client will be used against him.[153] But as Comment 29 to Rule 1.7 of the Model Rules of Professional Conduct wisely warns,

---

[148] Lucian T. Pera, *The Ethics of Joint Representation*, 40:1 LITIGATION, Fall, 2013, at 45.

[149] *See infra* § 4-7.7.

[150] 1 GEOFFREY C. HAZARD, JR., W. WILLIAM HODES & PETER R. JARVIS, THE LAW OF LAWYERING § 12.21 (Aspen, 4th ed., 2016).

[151] *See infra* § 4-7.5.

[152] *See* RESTATEMENT (THIRD) OF THE LAW GOVERNING LAWYERS § 121, Comment e(i) (American Law Institute, 2000).

[153] On advance conflict waivers, see *infra* § 4-7.7(f).

"[o]rdinarily, the lawyer will be forced to withdraw from representing all of the clients if the common representation fails."

In every multiple representation, the lawyer should address the question of confidential information to clarify that the lawyer will not withhold pertinent information obtained from one client from the other clients and to explain that, if the parties later should have a parting of the ways, neither person may invoke the attorney-client privilege to prevent disclosure by the lawyer of communications to the other person.[154] Professor Richard Zitrin strongly encourages lawyers in multiple client representations to disclose how client confidentiality will be treated:

> Clients have come to expect that lawyers will strictly protect every confidence, and they will still expect it, even if they are co-plaintiffs in a personal injury case, or both sides in a contract negotiations, or the parties to an "uncontested" dissolution. But allowing such parties to tell their mutual lawyer anything which can be held in confidence vis-à-vis the other party inevitably asks for trouble. It is almost impossible to maintain, for example, "his" secrets as against "her," and "hers" as against "him," with the parties feeling mistrust, knowing that the lawyer may know something they don't. This may doom efforts to cooperate before they've begun. The best solution is to agree—in advance—that, among multiple clients, there shall be no confidences. Should the client insist on blurting out a "confidence," however, the lawyer may be required to withdraw.[155]

If, during the course of the representation, the lawyer should discover that disclosure of information about one client to another client would harm the interests of the client who is the subject of that information, the lawyer likely has come up hard against an insuperable conflict of interest. On the one hand, because of the duty to keep each client fully informed,[156] the lawyer may not maintain clandestine side arrangements whereby the material secrets of one client are kept from another client being represented in that same matter. Nor is it likely that the lawyer could legitimately secure an agreement allowing certain secrets specific to one client to be concealed from the other client.[157] Obtaining informed consent to such an advance conflict waiver would be nearly impossible, either because the lawyer and clients would be unable to anticipate what specially-classified information is likely to surface during the representation or because fully informing the other client of the risks on that client's interests posed by withholding the information would be difficult to accomplish without disclosing the very thing that is to be kept secret for the benefit of the first client. On the other hand, because the lawyer has a duty of confidentiality and loyalty to each client, the lawyer may not simply proceed with the representation and openly disclose all information received to both clients. Unless an exception to confidentiality is properly invoked,[158] the lawyer simply cannot become the source of harmful information about a client.

---

[154] *See supra* § 4-6.3(b)(9).

[155] Richard A. Zitrin, *Risky Business . . . Representing Multiple Interests*, [Cal. State Bar] ETHICS HOTLINER, Vol. I, No. 1 (Winter 1992–93), in RICHARD A. ZITRIN & CAROL M. LANGFORD, LEGAL ETHICS IN THE PRACTICE OF LAW 181, 182 (2d ed., Lexis-Nexis (2001).

[156] *See supra* 4-5.4.

[157] On client consent to conflicts of interest including advance conflict waivers, see *infra* § 4-7.7.

[158] On exceptions to confidentiality, see *supra* § 4-6.6.

For these reasons, the American Bar Association's Standing Committee on Ethics and Professional Responsibility advises that the lawyer who "comes to understand that disclosure to one client would be harmful to the other client's interest" ordinarily must withdraw from representing one or both clients, while maintaining the confidence.[159] A comment to the *Restatement of the Law Governing Lawyers* suggests that the lawyer may make a "noisy withdrawal" by at least warning the client from whom information was withheld "that a matter seriously and adversely affecting that person's interests has come to light, which the other co-client refuses to permit the lawyer to disclose."[160]

### *§ 4-7.4(c)(8) Conflicts of Interest in the Insurance Defense Context*

The triangular relationship among a liability insurance company, an insured, and the lawyer retained by the insurance company to defend the insured is ripe with the potential for conflicts of interest. To be sure, the insurer and insured relationship ordinarily is congenial, with both united in the common purpose of avoiding or limiting liability. Nonetheless, between the date on which a claim is presented against the insured and the day of final disposition, the insured and the insurer may diverge on whether to settle, may dispute whether the claim is covered by the policy, and may disagree on how any litigation is to proceed. If interests of insured and insurer do divide, the lawyer must decide—within ethical boundaries—to whom he should answer.

Under basic conflict of interest principles stated in Rule 1.7, as well as the particular directive of Rule 1.8(f) that applies when a lawyer accepts compensation from someone other than the client,[161] the lawyer hired by the insurer to defend an insured would be obliged to devote her professional loyalty, diligence, and judgment to the insured client. In addition, under Rule 5.4(c), the lawyer may not permit a person who pays a lawyer to represent another to direct or regulate the lawyer's professional judgment in performing those legal services. How these basic principles apply to the insurer-insured relationship, complicated as it is by the insured's promise of cooperation[162] and conveyance of the power to control the defense through the insurance contract, has confounded practitioners and professional responsibility scholars.

***Identifying the Client(s):*** As Professor Nathan Crystal frames the question, when a lawyer is hired by an insurance company to defend an insured, "all authorities recognize the insured as a client, so the issue is whether the insurer should also be treated as a client."[163] While most (but not all)[164] courts regard both the insured and the insurer as clients, "the modern view"[165] appears to be that the lawyer's "paramount

---

[159] ABA Comm. on Ethics and Prof'l Responsibility, Formal Op. 08–450 (2008).

[160] RESTATEMENT (THIRD) OF THE LAW GOVERNING LAWYERS § 60, Comment *l* (American Law Institute, 2000).

[161] *See supra* § 4-7.3(g).

[162] *See* RESTATEMENT OF THE LAW OF LIABILITY INSURANCE § 29 (Tentative Draft No. 1, 2016) (American Law Institute, 2016) (saying that "the insured has a duty to cooperate with the insurer," including providing "reasonable assistance" in "investigation and settlement" and "defense of the action").

[163] Nathan Crystal, *Solving the Problem of the Insurance Defense Triangle*, S.C. LAWYER, Nov. 2013, at 9.

[164] *See* Pine Island Farmers v. Erstad & Reimer, 649 N.W.2d 449, 449, 452 (Minn. 2002) (holding "that defense counsel hired by an insurer to defend against its insured represents the insured," but that the insurer may be added as a co-client in the absence of a conflict and with express consent by the insured).

[165] Finley v. Home Ins. Co., 975 P.2d 1145, 1153 (Haw. 1998).

interest"[166] and "duty of loyalty"[167] is to the insured. Under this majority view, the insurer is a joint[168] but subsidiary client,[169] at least if there is no immediate conflict between the insurer and insured.[170]

Under the *Restatement of the Law Governing Lawyers*, when the insurer designates a lawyer for the insured, the insured becomes the client and the lawyer does not automatically assume responsibility with the insurance company.[171] The lawyer may, however, create an attorney-client relationship with the insurer as well, in the ordinary way that such a relationship comes into existence. Similarly, the American Bar Association's Standing Committee on Ethics and Professional Responsibility states that whether the lawyer represents only the insured *or* both the insured and the insurer (for all or part of the matter) turns on the retention contract.[172]

In any event, and unavoidably, the lawyer hired to represent the insured maintains a simultaneous relationship with the insurer as well, because the insurer both pays for the insurance defense and may be vicariously liable if the insured is held responsible in the underlying lawsuit. Moreover, the insurer has important contractual rights under its agreement with the insured, granting the insurer certain authority with respect to settlement of the case and even to control the defense.[173]

***Conflict of Interest Controversies in Insurance Defense:*** Traditionally, conflict of interest controversies in the insurance context arise, *first*, when the insured has an interest in settling to avoid a potential judgment beyond the policy limits, while the insurance company might prefer taking the matter to trial rather than accepting a settlement to the full extent of the policy limits, and, *second*, when the insurance company has reserved the right to dispute coverage for the insured or may have a policy defense. As Professor Tom Baker puts it, "the conflicts of interest that draw our attention to the insurance defense lawyer arise out of an incomplete transfer from insured to company of what I will call 'claim risk.' "[174]

In addition, and *third*, conflict of interest objections have been raised in recent years because insurance companies, in the natural desire to contain the costs of legal defense, increasingly have established guidelines for management of litigation. Lawyers not

---

[166] Feliberty v. Damon, 72 N.Y.2d 112, 120, 531 N.Y.S.2d 778, 527 N.E.2d 261, 265 (N.Y. 1988).

[167] Mutual of Enumclaw Ins. Co. v. Dan Paulson Const., Inc., 169 P.3d 1, 8 (Wash. 2007); *see also* Lifestar Response of Ala, Inc. v. Admiral Ins. Co., 17 So.3d 200, 217 (Ala. 2009) (saying the insured is the "primary" client); Purdy v. Pacific Auto. Ins. Co., 203 Cal. Rptr. 524, 533–34 (Cal. Ct. App. 1984) (same).

[168] *But see* Stephen L. Pepper, *Applying the Fundamentals of Lawyers' Ethics to Insurance Defense Practice*, 4 CONN. INS. L.J. 27, 47 (1997) (arguing that the ethics rules "require substantial 'informed consent' by the insured before a joint client status would be ethically acceptable").

[169] *But see* Charles Silver & Kent Syverud, *The Professional Responsibilities of Insurance Defense Lawyers*, 45 DUKE L.J. 255, 335–389 (1995) (rejecting the primary client preference for the insured when the insurer is also jointly represented per a retainer agreement).

[170] Nevada Yellow Cab Corp. v. Eighth Judicial Dist. Court ex rel. County of Clark, 152 P.3d 737, 742 (Nev. 2007); *see also* Hartford Ins. Co. of Midwest v. Koeppel, 629 F. Supp.2d 1293, 1300 (M.D. Fla. 2009) (ruling that the same attorney may represent both insured and insurer if their interests are not adverse).

[171] RESTATEMENT (THIRD) OF THE LAW GOVERNING LAWYERS § 134, Comment f (American Law Institute, 2000).

[172] ABA Comm. on Ethics & Prof'l Responsibility, Formal Op. 96–403 (1996).

[173] *See generally* Thomas D. Morgan, *What Insurance Scholars Should Know About Professional Responsibility*, 4 CONN. INS. L.J. 1 (1997–98); RONALD D. ROTUNDA & JOHN S. DZIENKOWSKI, PROFESSIONAL RESPONSIBILITY: A STUDENT'S GUIDE § 1.7–6(n)(1) (American Bar Ass'n, 2013–2014).

[174] Tom Baker, *Liability Insurance Conflicts and Defense Lawyers: From Triangles to Tetrahedrons*, 4 CONN. INS. L.J. 101, 102 (1997).

surprisingly have resisted such cost containment guidelines as interfering with professional judgment or improperly requiring divulgence to the insurer of confidential information about the insured.

***Settlement and Policy Limits:*** In most cases where a defense is provided under a liability insurance policy, the interests of the insurer and the insured are well-aligned in a common defense, as each wishes to avoid being held liable on the claim made against the insured. When the claim falls entirely within the limits of the liability insurance policy, and when the insurer does not dispute coverage, the interests ordinarily are in near-perfect congruence (absent a reputational concern by the insured which creates a non-monetary disincentive to settle). Under such circumstances, if the insurer foolishly refuses a settlement with the result that a higher amount is awarded at trial, the insurer remains responsible for the full amount and the client has not been financially disadvantaged by the insurer's exercise of settlement control.

But if the claim is for an amount beyond the policy limits, so that the insured remains at risk of being left personally responsible for some or all of a judgment against the insured, the interest of the insured in obtaining a settlement that falls within the policy limits and the interest of the insurer in avoiding or reducing disbursements may create a conflict between them. Under such circumstances, the insured may eagerly wish to settle for any amount within the policy limits, thereby avoiding any possibility that the insured will have to dig into his own pockets to pay a judgment. From the insurance company's standpoint, a proposed settlement for the full amount of the policy limits is financially indistinguishable from a judgment after trial for (or above) the full policy limits, other than the additional defense costs that might be incurred in litigating the matter through trial. Given that unpalatable choice, the insurance company may be inclined to reject a proposed settlement and instead seek to defeat the claim (or reduce the amount of damages) at trial.

When the insured and insurer differ on the desirability of settlement, the insurance company has a good faith obligation to the insured to fairly consider a settlement proposal from the opposing side.[175] The 2016 tentative draft of the new *Restatement of the Law of Liability Insurance* states that the insurer has a duty to "make reasonable settlement decisions," which is described as that which "would be made by a reasonable person who bears the sole financial responsibility for the full amount of the potential judgment."[176] Toward this end, the insurer must exercise good faith in its dealing with the insured, listen to the candidly-expressed advice of counsel hired for the insured's defense, and fully and fairly consider each settlement proposal.[177] If the insurer makes

[175] Unauthorized Practice of Law Committee v. American Home Assur. Co., Inc., 261 S.W.3d 24, 41 (Tex. 2008); Fetch v. Quam, 623 N.W.2d 357, 361 (N.D. 2001); Hartford Acc. & Indem. Co. v. Aetna Cas. & Sur. Co., 792 P.2d 749, 752 (Ariz. 1990).

[176] RESTATEMENT OF THE LAW OF LIABILITY INSURANCE § 24(1) to (2) (Tentative Draft No. 1, 2016) (American Law Institute, 2016); *see also* Schwartz v. Liberty Mut. Ins. Co., 539 F.3d 135, 142 (2d Cir. 2008) ("[T]he insurer must conduct itself as though it alone were liable for the entire amount of the judgment."); Cowden v. Aetna Cas. & Sur. Co., 134 A.2d 223, 228 (Pa. 1957) ("[T]he predominant majority rule is that the insurer must accord the interest of its insured the same faithful consideration it gives its own interest."). *But see* Kim V. Marrkand, *Duty to Settle: Why Proposed Sections 24 and 27 Have No Place in a Restatement of the Law of Liability Insurance*, 68 RUGTERS L. REV. 201, 203, 206–07 (2015) (criticizing the draft *Restatement* as "driven by a narrative that large insurers advance their own interests at the expense of relatively powerless small policy holders" and arguing that "the newly-envisioned 'duty to make reasonable settlement decisions' " is a departure from the implied duty of good faith and fair dealing which is breached by a showing of bad faith).

[177] Henke v. Iowa Home Mutual Casualty Co., 97 N.W.2d 168, 173 (Iowa 1959); *see also* Johnson v. American Family Mut. Ins. Co., 674 N.W.2d 88, 90 (Iowa 2004).

a reasonable and honest determination that the action may be defeated or a judgment held within the policy limits, the insurer may reject the settlement and proceed to trial, even if this decision later proves to be a mistake in judgment. By contrast, if the insurer breaches the duty to make a good faith or reasonable settlement decision, the insurer becomes liable for the full judgment, including that which exceeds the policy limits.[178]

The lawyer's responsibility is to honestly advise the insured client regarding the wisdom of the settlement and to share that assessment with the insurance company. Under Rule 2.3(a) of the Model Rules of Professional Conduct, a lawyer on behalf of the client may prepare "an evaluation of a matter affecting a client for the use of someone other than the client," which may not omit reference to a material fact that would make the evaluation misleading or fraudulent.[179] To the extent of disagreement, the lawyer should be an advocate for the insured, not the insurance company, although obviously the lawyer must consider and so advise the insured that cooperation and amicable relations with the insurer are essential to secure its endorsement of a favorable settlement.[180]

***Disputes Concerning Coverage:*** If the insurance company has reserved the right to challenge the coverage of the policy or may assert a policy defense, the lawyer must not assist in the insured's effort to avoid coverage or gather information that would be adverse to the insured's interest in the dispute[181] (even though the lawyer is being compensated by the insurance company). As the American Bar Association's Standing Committee on Ethics and Professional Responsibility has advised, the insurer's contractual rights do not "undermine[ ] the insured's right to expect that the lawyer will abide by Rule 1.6 and withhold from the carrier information relating to the representation that is damaging to the insured's interests under the policy."[182] Nor may the lawyer allow her professional judgment to be affected by that disagreement between the insured and the insurer.

In cases where such coverage conflicts are present at the commencement of the matter, the insurer may be well-served by allowing the insured to select independent

[178] *See* RESTATEMENT OF THE LAW OF LIABILITY INSURANCE § 27 (Tentative Draft No. 1, 2016) (American Law Institute, 2016) ("An insurer that breaches the duty to make reasonable settlement decisions is subject to liability for the full amount of damages assessed against the insured in the underlying legal action, without regard to the policy limits, as well as any other foreseeable harm caused by the insurer's breach of the duty."); Medical Mut. Liability Ins. Soc. v. Evans, 622 A.2d 103, 114 (Md. Ct. App. 1993) ("[T]he majority rule is that the measure of damages in a bad faith failure to settle case is the amount by which the judgment rendered in the underlying action exceeds the amount of insurance coverage.").

[179] On preparing an evaluation for the use of someone other than a client, see *infra* § 4-10.2. On an insured's lawyer sharing information with the insurer regarding possible settlement, see Jean Fleming Powers, *Advantages of the One-Client Model in Insurance Defense*, 45 N.M. L. REV. 79, 104 (2014).

[180] *But see* Silver & Syverud, *supra*, 45 DUKE L.J at 299 (contending that when a possible settlement is within the policy limits, the insurance defense lawyer "has no duty to advise or act for the insured on settlement, period").

[181] RESTATEMENT OF THE LAW OF LIABILITY INSURANCE § 14(1)(b(1) (Tentative Draft No. 1, 2016) (American Law Institute, 2016) (stating that the defense counsel must "protect from disclosure to the insurer any information of the insured that is protected by attorney-client privilege, work-product immunity, or a defense lawyer's duty of confidentiality under rules of professional conduct, if that information could be used to benefit the insurer at the expense of the insured"). *But see* Charles Silver & William T. Barker, *The Treatment of Insurers' Defense-Related Responsibilities in the Principles of the Law of Liability Insurance: A Critique*, 68 RUTGERS L. REV. 83, 109 (2015) (arguing that the insurer is "presumptively entitled to the information because [insurance] policies typically require an insured to cooperate in the defense and to give a sworn statement at an insurer's request").

[182] ABA Comm. on Ethics and Prof'l Responsibility, Formal Op. 08–450 (2008); *see also* Paradigm Ins. Co. v. Langerman Law Offices, 24 P.3d 593, 598 (Ariz. 2001).

counsel, thus avoiding any later accusation that insurer-selected defense counsel may have favored the insurance company's interest with respect to any dispute with the insured. Indeed, if the conflict is plain from the outset,[183] courts have recognized that the insured has the right to assume control of the defense[184] and obtain independent counsel at the insurer's expense (at least when the insurer's designated counsel could manipulate the particular outcome to take the resolution outside of policy coverage).[185]

***Cost-Containment Guidelines:*** As an effort to control the costs of litigation, many insurance companies have adopted cost-containment litigation guidelines, which may regulate the manner in which the insurer-designated lawyer is to handle a case. Such guidelines may direct that certain activities or even legal research be performed by nonlawyers, require that the lawyer obtain permission from the insurer to take depositions or employ experts, dictate how and when certain tasks such as discovery will be undertaken, and even limit the lawyer's written communications to the insured.

Some lawyers engaged in insurance defense work have resisted these cost-containment guidelines, arguing that such instructions create a conflict with the lawyer's professional and ethical responsibilities to the client. Most prominently on this side of the debate, the Montana Supreme Court sustained those objections, ruling "that the requirement of prior approval fundamentally interferes with defense counsels' exercise of their *independent* judgment, as required by Rule 1.8(f), M.R.Prof.Conduct. Further, prior approval creates a substantial appearance of impropriety in its suggestion that it is insurers rather than defense counsel who control the day to day details of a defense."[186]

By contrast, other scholars and authorities point to the insured's conveyance of litigation control to the insurer through the policy contract as "entitl[ing] the company to make all decisions that a defendant in litigation ordinarily makes."[187] On this view, the policy contract "assigns control to the best litigation manager"—that is, the insurance company.[188] While the *Restatement of the Law Governing Lawyers* concurs that the lawyer may appropriately take direction from a third-person such as an insurer "on whom the client has contractually conferred the power of direction," the *Restatement*

---

[183] *See* RESTATEMENT OF THE LAW OF LIABILITY INSURANCE § 10 cmt. c (Tentative Draft No. 1, 2016) (American Law Institute, 2016) (explaining that in some cases "the divergence [over policy coverage] may lead to a conflict of interest that is sufficiently acute that the insurer no longer has the right to defend, but rather must provide the insured an independent defense").

[184] Nandorf, Inc. v. CNA Ins. Companies, 479 N.E.2d 988, 991–92 (Ill. Ct. App. 1985).

[185] Federal Ins. Co. v. MBL, Inc., 160 Cal. Rptr. 3d 910, 919–20 (Cal. Ct. App. 2013); RESTATEMENT OF THE LAW OF LIABILITY INSURANCE § 16 (Tentative Draft No. 1, 2016) (American Law Institute, 2016) (stating that when the insurer has given notice that it contents coverage and "the action could be defended in a manner that would benefit the insurer at the expense of the insured, the insurer must provide an independent defense of the action").

[186] In re Rules of Prof'l Conduct, 2 P.3d 806, 815 (Mont. 2000); *see also* State Farm Mut. Auto. Ins. Co. v. Traver, 980 S.W.2d 625, 634 (Tex. 1998) (Gonzalez, J., concurring in part and dissenting in part) (expressing fear that "these efforts at cost containment compromise a lawyer's autonomy and independent judgment on the best means for defending an insured" and that "measures designed to produce a no-frills defense can easily result in only a token defense").

[187] Charles Silver, *Does Insurance Defense Counsel Represent the Company or the Insured?*, 72 TEX. L. REV. 1583, 1613 (1994); *see also* James M. Fischer, *Insurer-Policyholder Interests, Defense Counsel's Professional Duties, and the Allocation of Power to Control the Defense*, 14 CONN. INS. L.J. 21, 27 (2008) (same).

[188] Silver, *supra*, 72 TEX. L. REV. at 1613; *see also* RESTATEMENT OF THE LAW OF LIABILITY INSURANCE § 10 cmt. b (Tentative Draft No. 1, 2016) (American Law Institute, 2016) (stating that "insurers have greater capacity to direct the defense of a legal action than all but the most sophisticated insureds").

further demands that the lawyer also obtain consent from the insured client.[189] However, "when there appears to be no substantial risk that a claim against a client-insured will not be fully covered by an insurance policy pursuant to which the lawyer is appointed and is to be paid," the consent contemplated by the *Restatement* need be nothing more than "acquiescence of the client-insured to an informative letter to the client-insured at the outset of the representation."[190]

While the matter remains controversial, when there is not otherwise a conflict based on policy coverage disputes, a lawyer likely may comply with cost-containment guidelines that do not materially interfere with the lawyer's independence of professional judgment or excessively regulate the details of the lawyer's performance.[191] For example, in a special comment to the Iowa Rules of Professional Conduct, the Iowa Supreme Court directed:

> Where a lawyer has been retained by an insurer to represent the insured pursuant to the insurer's obligations under a liability insurance policy, the lawyer may comply with reasonable cost-containment litigation guidelines proposed by the insurer if such guidelines do not materially interfere with the lawyer's duty to exercise independent professional judgment to protect the reasonable interests of the insured, do not regulate the details of the lawyer's performance, and do not materially limit the professional discretion and control of the lawyer.[192]

### *§ 4-7.4(c)(9) Positional Conflicts of Interest*

During the course of a litigation practice,[193] the typical lawyer will find himself making opposing and even contradictory legal arguments—although ordinarily at different times and in different cases. A lawyer may plead for a strict application of the statute of limitations in one case on behalf of a defendant, while later contending for delayed accrual or equitable tolling of a statute of limitations in another case on behalf of a plaintiff. When seeking to introduce damaging evidence against an opposing party at trial, the lawyer naturally may invoke the truth-finding purpose of the adversarial process, while inveighing against supposedly disfavored evidentiary constraints like the attorney-client privilege or the work-product doctrine. When seeking to exclude damaging evidence against the lawyer's own client at trial, the lawyer instead will sing the praises of privilege and of work-product in protecting the attorney-client relationship, facilitating the counseling by lawyers of their clients in a confidential setting, and allowing an attorney the necessary privacy to prepare a case.

Being able to argue both sides of an issue is one of the skills of the advocate. And when those conflicting arguments are separated in time and made in distinct matters, no conflict of interest problem typically is presented.

---

[189] RESTATEMENT (THIRD) OF THE LAW GOVERNING LAWYERS § 134, cmts. d, f (American Law Institute, 2000).

[190] *Id.*

[191] Utah Ethics Op. 02–03 (2002); *see also* RESTATEMENT (THIRD) OF THE LAW GOVERNING LAWYERS § 134, cmt. f, illus. 5 (American Law Institute, 2000) (advising that a lawyer may accept the insurer's direction to limit expenses, such as forgoing additional depositions, when the lawyer would not thereby violate the duty to provide competent representation).

[192] IOWA RULES OF PROF'L CONDUCT R. 32:1.7 cmt. 13a.

[193] On positional conflicts of interest and the lawyer's participation in law reform activities that contradict a client's views or interests, see *infra* § 4-13.2.

A problem may arise, however, when the position taken in one case on behalf of one client may have a negative effect upon a different client's interest in another case. As the most obvious example, if the same appellate court were to schedule arguments on the same day in two cases raising the identical issue of law, which is central to the outcome in those cases, a lawyer could not argue one side of the issue in one case and then, but a few minutes later, return to the podium to present the opposing argument in the other case. Not only would the lawyer's credibility before the court be severely weakened—the recognition that a good lawyer can argue both sides of an issue goes only so far—but the expectation of loyalty to which each client is entitled would be annihilated. Indeed, the lawyer's loyalty is likely to be impaired, finding herself advocating more powerfully for the side of the issue that is associated with the more favored client or attempting to accommodate both clients by presenting the arguments in an understated way that may spare the feelings of one client but only at the expense of weakening the case of the other.[194]

Comment 24 to Rule 1.7 of the Model Rules of Professional Conduct strikes a practical balance on this question of what are called "positional" conflicts of interest. No conflict of interest is created by "[t]he mere fact that advocating a legal position on behalf of one client might create precedent adverse to the interests of a client represented by the lawyer in an unrelated matter." Thus, the mere prospect that a precedent for a current client might someday be adverse to another client in an entirely unrelated matter ought to give little pause to the lawyer. Moreover, when separate cases are being litigated in different jurisdictions, the disposition of an issue in one case typically will have no effect upon the other case.

However, there are cases of heightened legal significance or public attention that are more likely to culminate in leading appellate decisions that are will have a meaningful persuasive impact in other jurisdictions. As Comment 24 suggests, "when a decision favoring one client will create a precedent likely to seriously weaken the position taken on behalf of the other client," the risk is high that the "lawyer's action on behalf of one client will materially limit the lawyer's effectiveness in representing another client in a different case." The paradigmatic example of such precedential impact would be where the lawyer on behalf of one client has asked the court of final resort in the jurisdiction to render a decision on an issue that will become a binding, and significantly adverse, precedent to another client being represented by the lawyer (or someone else in the law firm) in another case.

Comment 24 to Rule 1.7 identifies several factors that may be relevant to the positional conflict question: "where the cases are pending, whether the issue is substantive or procedural, the temporal relationship between the matters, the significance of the issue to the immediate and long-term interests of the clients involved and the clients' reasonable expectations in retaining the lawyer." Professor John Dzienkowski suggests similar and additional factors to be considered, including the directness of the legal conflict and its importance to the representations; whether confidential information will be used or disclosed in advocating the conflicting positions;

---

[194] John Dzienkowski, *Positional Conflicts of Interest*, 71 TEXAS L. REV. 457, 485 (1993) ("A lawyer or firm involved in a positional conflict of interest may consciously or subconsciously 'soft-pedal' one client's legal arguments because of favoritism for the other client. A lawyer may consciously decide to de-emphasize or forgo, for a variety of reasons, an argument that poses a positional conflict of interest.").

the type, potential magnitude, and likelihood of harm to the clients; and whether the client notifies the lawyer that the client feels very strongly about this legal issue.[195]

## § 4-7.5 SUCCESSIVE CLIENT CONFLICTS

### § 4-7.5(a) Introduction to the Successive Conflict Rule

With respect to "successive conflicts"—that is, when the interests of an existing client conflict with those of a former client—the Model Rules of Professional Conduct have the considerable virtue of giving specific textual direction that was missing under the prior Model Code of Professional Responsibility. No practical or principled purpose is served in forbidding a lawyer from ever acting adversely to a former client's interest, even though the representation may be long past and the current matter may bear no resemblance to the prior work. Under Rule 1.9(a) of the Model Rules of Professional Conduct, "[a] lawyer who has formerly represented a client in a matter shall not thereafter represent another person in the same or a substantially related matter in which that person's interests are materially adverse to the interests of the former client unless the former client gives informed consent, confirmed in writing."

When a representation has been concluded, the attorney is disqualified from representing a current client adversely to a former client in the "same or a substantially related matter." (A similar, but slightly diluted, test applies to a prospective client, as to whom a lawyer contemplated but did not consummate a full attorney-client relationship. Under Rule 1.18, a lawyer "shall not represent a client with interests materially adverse to those of a prospective client in the same or a substantially related matter if the lawyer received information from the prospective client that could be significantly harmful to that person in the matter."[196])

In the concurrent client conflict context, the prohibition on representing a client when the lawyer has a conflict of interest serves both to guarantee the undivided loyalty of the lawyer to each client and to ensure that confidential information is protected and is not either disclosed or used against one client but to the advantage of another client, third person, or the lawyer. In the successive conflict of interest scenario, the duty of loyalty does persist beyond the end of a representation to the extent of forbidding a lawyer from undermining the very work performed in that prior representation.[197] In general, however, the lawyer's fidelity to a former client becomes increasingly attenuated as time passes. Thus, the primary purpose of the former client disqualification rule is to protect against adverse use of confidential information from the past client to the advantage of a current client.

### § 4-7.5(b) Successive Conflicts When the Matters Are the Same

The former client conflict rule applies most directly when a lawyer or law firm is said to have "switched teams" and now stands opposite the very same party in the very

---

[195] *Id.* at 508–20.

[196] *See supra* § 4-3.1(e).

[197] *See* STEPHEN GILLERS, REGULATION OF LAWYERS: PROBLEMS OF LAW AND ETHICS 147–48 (Wolters Kluwer, 10th ed. 2015) (illustrating that a lawyer may not demonstrate disloyalty to a former client in attempting in a new representation "to undo" the very thing, that is, the "specific objective" of the former representation, whether or not the lawyer uses confidential information); 1 GEOFFREY C. HAZARD, JR., W. WILLIAM HODES & PETER R. JARVIS, THE LAW OF LAWYERING § 14.09 (Aspen, 4th ed., 2016) (saying that a lawyer is not "later allowed to attack his own work product," which is characterized as "fouling his own nest").

same matter. Fortunately, such a blatant violation of fiduciary loyalty responsibilities to a client is rare—but not rare enough.

In *Doe v. Perry Community School District*,[198] the Iowa Supreme Court ordered the disqualification of a law firm when one of the lawyers for the plaintiffs in a civil suit alleging sexual abuse of a student by a teacher had moved to the law firm that was representing the defendant school district. Thus, the relatedness of the prior matter to the current one was indisputable. Nor was the lawyer's involvement in the representation of the plaintiffs insubstantial, as he had advised on whether to file suit, prepared the pleading with access to all of the case file, entered a court appearance, and maintained regular telephone calls with the plaintiffs. Then, after another lawyer took over, he withdraw and moved his employment to the new firm.

As the *Doe* court pointedly observed, the lawyer's new law "firm now stands as adversary against the [plaintiffs] in the very litigation in which [the lawyer] first served as their trusted attorney."[199] Although the side-switching lawyer apparently was not directly participating in the new law firm's defense of the school district, the law firm took no steps to screen him until after the plaintiffs had moved to disqualify the law firm.[200]

In a criminal case, in which the changing-representation lawyer did continue to be directly engaged in representation, the Louisiana Court of Appeal reversed the criminal conviction of a mother and her live-in boyfriend charged with homicide in the apparent beating death of her five-month-old boy. In *State v. Tensley*,[201] a lawyer initially had been appointed to represent both of the defendants and had confidential communications with both about evidence in the case. After the lawyer was removed from representing the mother, he continued to represent the boyfriend, including conducting a cross-examination of the mother at trial, eliciting admissions that she had told the police she did not believe her boyfriend had hurt the child and that she was aware of injuries to the child's legs. Here too, it was obvious that the "successive" representation involved the same matter, or more accurately, "dual representation of parties to the very crime at hand."[202]

As the *Tensley* court said in reversing the mother's conviction, the lawyer had been "allowed to switch clients and take an adversarial role against" his now-former client, "culminat[ing] in the ghastly unrestrained" cross-examination of the mother, during which any competent lawyer would seek to impose blame by "emphasizing the mother as dominant custodian for the child's care."[203]

### § 4-7.5(c) Successive Conflicts When the Matters Are Substantially Related

Even if the present matter is not the "same" as the prior matter, that is, the matters are not identical, an impermissible successive conflict of interest is present if the matter on which the lawyer previously represented a former client is "substantially related" to

[198] 650 N.W.2d 594, 597–601 (Iowa 2002).

[199] *Id.* at 599.

[200] On screening to avoid disqualification of a law firm when a personally-disqualified lawyer joins the firm, see *supra* § 4-7.6(b)(2).

[201] 955 So.2d 227, 240–46 (La. Ct. App. 2007).

[202] *Id.* at 245.

[203] *Id.* at 246.

the matter on which the lawyer now represents a current client adverse to that former client. The *Restatement of the Law Governing Lawyers* defines a matter as being "'substantially related' to an earlier matter if . . . there is a substantial risk that representation of the present client will involve the use of information acquired in the course of representing the former client, unless that information has become generally known."[204]

Comment 3 to Rule 1.9 of the Model Rules of Professional Conduct describes the "substantial relationship" analysis as based on an objective evaluation of the risk to confidentiality, providing two examples:

> Matters are "substantially related" for purposes of this Rule if they involve the same transaction or legal dispute or if there otherwise is a substantial risk that confidential factual information as would normally have been obtained in the prior representation would materially advance the client's position in the subsequent matter. For example, a lawyer who has represented a businessperson and learned extensive private financial information about that person may not then represent that person's spouse in seeking a divorce. Similarly, a lawyer who has previously represented a client in securing environmental permits to build a shopping center would be precluded from representing neighbors seeking to oppose rezoning of the property on the basis of environmental considerations; however, the lawyer would not be precluded, on the grounds of substantial relationship, from defending a tenant of the completed shopping center in resisting eviction for nonpayment of rent.

If the prior matter was of such a nature that the kind of information that normally would be shared by a client with his legal counsel for that representation would now be relevant to the present representation of an adverse client, then the matters are substantially related.[205] The "factual bases of the two representations" are evaluated by considering with respect to the prior representation "what information and facts ought to have been or would typically be disclosed in such a relationship."[206] As Professors Geoffrey Hazard and William Hodes and attorney Peter Jarvis summarize, the substantial relationship test today has become "in large measure a judgment as to whether the former client's confidences are at risk of being turned against him."[207]

A party seeking to disqualify an attorney who previously handled a substantially related matter for that party is not required to identify the confidential information that was shared, or even show that any confidences or secrets actually were divulged to the attorney. Requiring such a showing would undermine the very confidentiality that the rule is designed to protect. Instead, as said in an accompanying comment in the

---

[204] RESTATEMENT (THIRD) OF THE LAW GOVERNING LAWYERS § 132 (American Law Institute 2000); *see also* Westinghouse Electric Corp. v. Gulf Oil Corp., 588 F.2d 221, 224 (7th Cir. 1978) (stating that the existence of a substantial relationship "turns on the possibility, or appearance thereof, that confidential information might have been given to the attorney"); Reardon v. Marlayne, 416 A.2d 852 (N.J. 1980) (holding that a substantial relationship between matters exists where the "adversity between the interests of the attorney's former and present clients has created a climate for disclosure of relevant confidential information").

[205] *See* Analytica, Inc. v. NPD Research, Inc., 708 F.2d 1263, 1266 (7th Cir. 1983) (ruling that a lawyer should be disqualified "if the lawyer could have obtained confidential information in the first representation that would have been relevant in the second").

[206] Koch v. Koch Ind., 798 F. Supp. 1525, 1536 (D. Kan. 1992); Bowers v. Ophthalmology Group, 733 F.3d 647, 652 (6th Cir. 2013) (quoting *Koch*).

[207] 1 GEOFFREY C. HAZARD, JR., W. WILLIAM HODES & PETER R. JARVIS, THE LAW OF LAWYERING § 14.07 (Aspen, 4th ed., 2016).

*Restatement*, "[w]hen the prior matter involved litigation, it will be conclusively presumed that the lawyer obtained confidential information about the issues involved in the litigation."[208] Under the imputed disqualification rule stated in Rule 1.10 of the Model Rules of Professional Conduct, it also is presumed that confidential information possessed by one lawyer has been shared with every other lawyer in the firm.[209]

Nor does it matter that the information presumptively acquired by the lawyer in the prior matter might be discoverable by the former client's adversary in the current litigation—assuming that counsel knew what to ask for (and recognizing that the lawyer for that former client would have such inside knowledge, uniquely useful in discovery). Even if the material falls outside of the attorney-client privilege, the lawyer's duty to preserve confidential information extends much further than protecting privileged communications. Under Rule 1.6(a), a lawyer is forbidden to reveal any "information relating to the representation of a client unless the client gives informed consent, the disclosure is impliedly authorized in order to carry out the representation or the disclosure is permitted" under exceptions to confidentiality.[210]

However, if the information that was confidentially obtained in the prior representation has, in the words of Comment 3 to Rule 1.9, "been rendered obsolete by the passage of time," then disqualification in a successive representation may not be appropriate. Similarly, if the information has become generally known, such as through public disclosure by the prior client, then it may no longer be confidential in any meaningful sense.[211]

### § 4-7.5(d) Changing a Current Client into a Former Client: The "Hot Potato" Scenario

When clients are concurrently represented by a lawyer, the lawyer may not represent one present client against another present client, even when the simultaneous but adverse representations of the clients by the lawyer are unrelated to each other.[212] If a former client is the party adverse to the lawyer's present client, however, the lawyer may go forward, provided that the matters are not substantially related. Thus, whether the adverse party is an existing or a former client may be dispositive in a conflict of interest dispute. For that reason, a lawyer may have an incentive to frame the adverse party as—or even transform the adverse party into—a former client.

When a lawyer is retained for a single and discrete matter, which has been concluded, the natural presumption would be that the attorney-client relationship had ended, although the lawyer may wish to confirm as much through a clear communication to the client. However, when a lawyer has had an extended relationship of trust with a client, having provided legal advice on a variety of or several similar matters, the client may develop a reasonable expectation that the lawyer continues to have professional responsibility for the client's affairs even after conclusion of a particular matter. Accordingly, the lawyer may be held to continuing professional responsibilities unless the lawyer carefully communicates the termination of the relationship and disavows

---

[208] RESTATEMENT (THIRD) OF THE LAW GOVERNING LAWYERS § 132 Comment d(iii) (American Law Institute, 2000).

[209] *See infra* § 4-7.6(a).

[210] *See supra* § 4-6.2.

[211] State ex rel. Swanson v. 3M Co., 845 N.W.2d 808, 817 (Minn. 2014).

[212] *See supra* § 4-7.4(b)(1).

such a relationship should the former client indicate that he believes it to be ongoing. To the extent of any reasonable confusion about whether there is a continuing attorney-client relationship, the lawyer, as the professional in dealing with a layman, is responsible to clarify the situation.[213]

If a lawyer wishes to preserve her options in accepting future clients, the lawyer should conclude each representation with a polite letter explaining that the relationship has been terminated. If the lawyer instead chooses to maintain a connection with the client, even if the lawyer is not presently doing any legal work for that client, then the lawyer may find that she is unable to accept or continue a representation adverse to that client because of the more stringent concurrent conflict of interest rules.

When a lawyer finds himself in a situation where one present client offers a remunerative representation that would be adverse to another present client, and the new opportunity would be unrelated to that other representation, the lawyer may be tempted to drop the latter client like a "hot potato."[214] If the adverse party could be re-characterized as a former client, the lawyer then could invoke the more favorable (to the *lawyer*) substantial relationship test of Rule 1.9 to permit undertaking the more attractive representation adverse to that person.

But such an unseemly attempt to suddenly convert an existing client for whom legal services are not completed into a former client almost certainly will be rejected by the courts. As Professor Charles Wolfram explains, loyalty considerations come directly into play with respect to the "hot-potato" doctrine, which "sharply limits the ability of a lawyer to withdraw prematurely from a representation in order to take on the representation of an adversary of the now-former client."[215]

### § 4-7.5(e) The Prohibition on Using or Revealing Confidential Information from a Former Client Representation

The duty to protect confidential information relating to the representation of a client is part of the sacred trust of every lawyer.[216] Aside from whether a representation constitutes a successive conflict of interest, whether the matters are related or not, or even whether the lawyer would be representing a client in so acting, a lawyer simply may not misappropriate confidential information and use it to the disadvantage of a former client or disclose it without permission of the former client or as allowed by an exception to confidentiality under the rules.

Under Rule 1.9(c) of the Model Rules of Professional Conduct, the lawyer is expressly prohibited from (1) using confidential information "to the disadvantage of the former client," unless the lawyer has permission under the rules or "the information has become generally known," and (2) "reveal[ing] information relating to the representation" except as permitted under the rules. In general, then, the lawyer may

---

[213] *See supra* § 4-3.2(c). On termination of the lawyer's services, see *supra* § 4-3.6.

[214] *See* Picker Int'l, Inc. v. Varian Assocs., Inc., 670 F. Supp. 1363, 1365 (N.D. Ohio 1987) ("A firm may not drop a client like a hot potato, especially if it is in order to keep happy a far more lucrative client."). On the "hot potato" doctrine, including questions of its scope when the law firm did not cause the conflict or the client discharges the law firm rather than the firm withdrawing, see generally John Leubsdorf, *Conflicts of Interest: Slicing the Hot Potato Doctrine*, 48 SAN DIEGO L. REV. 251 (2011).

[215] Charles W. Wolfram, *Former-Client Conflicts*, 10 GEO. J. LEGAL ETHICS 677, 681 (1997).

[216] *See supra* ch. 4-6.

neither use nor reveal confidential information relating to the representation of a former client.

When information about a former client is a matter of widespread awareness, the lawyer is not barred from using that public information in representing a later client or otherwise, even though the information otherwise would fall within the purview of confidentiality, which broadly attaches under Rule 1.6 to all information "relating to the representation," regardless of the source of the information or whether it is generally known.[217]

By the text of the rule, however, appropriate use by the lawyer of generally known information about a former client is distinguished from the lawyer's affirmative revelation of that information. Even when information about the former client appears to have been widely disseminated, the lawyer generally should not be a source of its further distribution. Especially when the information is sensitive in nature, the former client should not have to bear the ignominy and embarrassment of having her own former lawyer confirming the nature and accuracy of the information.

However, when information is entirely in the public domain and is not personal or sensitive in nature, such as basic and widely available information about the nature of a business entity, the situation may be different. To strictly prohibit a lawyer from ever referring to such general facts about a former client in a future and unrelated representation—on the theory that the information still falls within the broad circle of confidentiality because it was related to the prior representation—would be an artificial application of the rule beyond what it presumably was intended to accomplish and without reasonable justification. Moreover, because Rule 1.9(c) plainly would permit the lawyer's use of the information about the former client, as having "become generally known," that permission implicitly might include such limited disclosure as necessary to make meaningful and concrete use of the information.

## § 4-7.6 IMPUTATION OF CONFLICTS OF INTEREST WITHIN A FIRM

### § 4-7.6(a) The General Rule of Imputed Disqualification to All Lawyers in a Law Firm

One of the venerable and cardinal principles within the field of conflicts of interest is that if one lawyer in the law firm has a conflict of interest, then every lawyer in the law firm has a conflict of interest. This is the so-called "imputed disqualification" rule codified in Rule 1.10(a) of the Model Rules of Professional Conduct. The duty of loyalty is owed to the client by the entire firm, regardless of which individual lawyer is assigned by the firm to handle the representation. Likewise, during the period in which a client is being represented by the law firm,[218] it is presumed that confidential information possessed by one attorney has been shared with every other attorney in the firm, thus meaning that knowledge is imputed as well.

---

[217] *See supra* § 4-6.2.

[218] In certain circumstances, when the lawyer who represented the client has terminated association with the law firm, or when a lawyer who was associated with a law firm representing a client leaves the firm and joins a new firm, disqualification is imposed on the firm or the migrating lawyer respectively only if they possess actual rather than merely imputed knowledge of confidential matters. *See infra* § 4-7.6(b)(3).

Although different attorneys within the firm may be involved with separate client representations and be handling different matters, the general rule for conflicts of interest analysis is that if one attorney in a firm would be ethically-precluded from undertaking a matter, that conflict is imputed to every other attorney in the firm. Because of this "imputed disqualification" rule, if one attorney in a firm is representing a particular client, then no other attorney in the firm may represent another client in a matter directly adverse to that client or under circumstances where, if the same lawyer were handling both matters, the lawyer would be materially limited in that representation by reason of responsibilities to another client, former client, or third person.[219] Likewise, if any lawyer in the law firm would be prohibited from undertaking a new representation because it would be adverse to a former client in the same or a substantially related matter,[220] then no other lawyer in the firm may do so.

As Comment 1 to Rule 1.10 states, the term "firm" is broadly defined for purposes of the Model Rules of Professional Conduct. Under Rule 1.0(c), this reference to a legal practice entity "denotes a lawyer or lawyers in a law partnership, professional corporation, sole proprietorship or other association authorized to practice law; or lawyers employed in a legal services organization or the legal department of a corporation or other organization." The imputed disqualification rule thus applies not only to every lawyer in the traditional office law firm, but also to all lawyers within any association or entity, which includes corporate counsel in a legal department and attorneys in a legal aid office. (As indicated by the cross-reference to Rule 1.11 in Rule 1.10(d), the per se disqualification rule does not extend to government offices.[221] Nonetheless, associated lawyers in a government office may be directly disqualified if a conflict affecting one of their colleagues is of such a nature that office relationships or other influences would materially limit the representation of those other lawyers in the office.)

As an exception to the imputed disqualification rule, Rule 1.10(a)(1) does not extend disqualification to other lawyers in the law firm when "the prohibition is based on a personal interest of the disqualified lawyer and does not present a significant risk of materially limiting the representation of the client by the remaining lawyers in the firm." When a lawyer is barred from accepting a representation by reason of purely personal interests, such as relationships with or investments in persons or entities on the other side of the matter,[222] other lawyers in the law firm ordinarily will not be similarly influenced or limited in zealous and loyal representation of a client. However, the exception to vicarious disqualification for personal interest conflicts is not unbounded. If other lawyers in the firm would extend such solicitude to the personally-conflicted lawyer and that lawyer's personal interest that those lawyers would be inhibited in providing diligent and uncompromised representation to a client, then the personal interest conflict would become a firm conflict as well.

Moreover, the reference to non-imputed "personal interest" conflicts in Rule 1.10 is not a cross-reference to the list of specific conflicts of interest addressed in Rule 1.8, such

---

219 On the general principles regarding direct adversity and materially-limited representation conflicts, see *supra* §§ 4-7.1, 4-7.2, 4-7.4(b).

220 On conflicts involving former clients, see *supra* §§ 4-7.5, 4-7.6.

221 On conflicts in a government law office, see *infra* § 4-7.8(a)(3).

222 For discussion of personal conflicts of interests and conflicts involving a lawyer's relationship to a lawyer representing an adverse party, see *supra* §§ 4-7.4(c)(2), 4-7.3(k).

as the limitations on doing business with a client[223] or the prohibition on preparing an instrument for a client to give a substantial gift to a lawyer or a relative of the lawyer,[224] which indeed are imputed to other lawyers in the firm under Rule 1.8(k).[225]

Rule 1.10 has only indirect application to nonlawyers within a law firm who may have a conflict of interest by reason of some connection to the parties or the matter. By direct force, paragraph (a) of Rule 1.10 applies only to lawyers who are disqualified as lawyers, with imputation of that disqualification to associated lawyers. As Comment 4 to Rule 1.10 states, if a paralegal, secretary, or law clerk is prohibited from being involved with the matter, the lawyers in the law firm are not similarly disqualified. Likewise, if a lawyer should be excluded from involvement with a matter because of events occurring before admission to the bar, such as work performed for another law firm while working as a law clerk during law school, that disqualification is not automatically extended to other lawyers within the firm. Nonetheless, as Comment 4 suggests, "[s]uch persons . . . ordinarily must be screened from any personal participation in the matter to avoid communication to others in the firm of confidential information that both the nonlawyers and the firm have a legal duty to protect."[226]

## § 4-7.6(b) Imputed Disqualification When a Lawyer Joins or Leaves a Law Firm (The Migrating Lawyer)

### *§ 4-7.6(b)(1) Whether the Incoming Lawyer Is Personally Disqualified*

As provided in Rule 1.10(a) of the Model Rules of Professional Conduct, when a lawyer is associated with other lawyers in a law firm, the knowledge of one lawyer is imputed to every other lawyer in the firm, thus meaning that confidential information possessed by one lawyer is regarded as being accessible to every other lawyer in the firm.[227]

However, when a lawyer departs from a law firm, he "sheds the 'taint' of imputed disability at the old firm's door."[228] The lawyer takes with him only that knowledge about clients that the lawyer actually possessed, not that which was presumed by imputation when the lawyer previously practiced in that firm. If the lawyer did not personally participate in a client matter, and did not otherwise acquire confidential information, then even if the lawyer leaves a firm that represents a client on one side of a dispute and joins a firm that represents a client on the other side of that same matter, the lawyer individually has not changed sides.

Under Rule 1.9(b), "[a] lawyer shall not knowingly represent a person in the same or a substantially related matter in which a firm with which the lawyer formerly was associated had previously represented a client" when the current representation would be "materially adverse to that person" and when the "lawyer had acquired information protected" as confidential about that person. As Comment 5 to Rule 1.9 explains:

---

[223] *See supra* § 4-7.3(b).

[224] *See supra* § 4-7.3(d).

[225] *See supra* § 4-7.3(*l*).

[226] For further discussion of ethical screening, see *infra* §§ 4-7.6(b)(2), 4-7.8(a)(2).

[227] *See supra* § 4-7.6(a).

[228] 1 GEOFFREY C. HAZARD, JR., W. WILLIAM HODES & PETER R. JARVIS, THE LAW OF LAWYERING § 15.11 (Aspen, 4th ed., 2016).

Thus, if a lawyer while with one firm acquired no knowledge or information relating to a particular client of the firm, and that lawyer later joined another firm, neither the lawyer individually nor the second firm is disqualified from representing another client in the same or a related matter even though the interests of the two clients conflict.

Rule 1.9(b) applies to the situation where the person was represented by the law firm with which the lawyer was formerly associated, while Rule 1.9(a) applies where the individual lawyer had personally represented that person as a former client. If the newly associated lawyer did not personally participate in the representation of the client at the former law firm (and thus would not be disqualified under paragraph (a)) and the lawyer did not otherwise obtain confidential information material to the matter (and thus would not be disqualified under paragraph (b)), then that lawyer is not personally prohibited from representing a client adversely to that person who is being represented by the lawyer's previous firm. Because in that scenario the incoming lawyer neither participated personally nor obtained confidential information about a client represented by the lawyer's previous firm and thus is not personally disqualified, there also is no conflict to impute to the other lawyers in the new law firm.

In such cases, the question naturally arises as to how to determine whether a migrating lawyer previously associated with a firm did or did not acquire confidential information about a client who had been represented by that firm. Comment 6 to Rule 1.9 suggests that the answer generally will turn on the manner in which lawyers worked together at the former firm. If the firm was operated in an open way, typical of many smaller law firms, such that each lawyer has "general access" to all client files and "regularly participate[s] in discussions" of client matters with other lawyers, then the lawyer will be presumed to have acquired information about all such clients. If instead a law firm is divided into separate areas, by practice, office location, or internal structure, such that a lawyer has access to only to a "limited number" of client files and participates only in discussions with other lawyers about those particular matters, then Comment 6 states that it may be "inferred that such a lawyer in fact is privy to information about the clients actually served but not those of other clients."

In all events, the burden of proof is properly placed on the lawyer to establish that she did not, in fact, acquire confidential information about the person who is now adverse to a client represented by the lawyer's new law firm.

### *§ 4-7.6(b)(2) Ethical Screening of a Personally-Disqualified Lawyer to Avoid Imputed Disqualification*

Rule 1.10(a) states the general rule of imputed disqualification that applies to private law firms—if one lawyer is disqualified, all are disqualified. With respect to the matter of vicarious disqualification, the most common and controversial question to arise in recent years has been whether an attorney who has become newly associated with a firm carries the taint of disqualification to the firm for everything that the lawyer has previously done in her practice.[229] Although the subject of heated debate within the bar, the trend has been to allow a law firm to screen out the migrating attorney from participation in a particular matter and thereby avoid imputed disqualification based

[229] Imputation to other lawyers in the new firm is only an issue, of course, if the entering lawyer himself is personally-disqualified. On the subject of personal prohibition when a lawyer is leaving a firm, see *supra* § 4-7.6(b)(1).

upon the clients represented in the newly-associated attorney's prior practice. While the majority of states now allow such ethical screening, especially after the Model Rules of Professional Conduct were revised to permit it, a substantial minority of states adhere to the traditional rule that imputed disqualification may not be so avoided.

Traditionally, the disciplinary rules did not allow for ethical screening for the migrating lawyer. For many decades, ethical screening was authorized only in the context of former public officers and government employees under Rule 1.11,[230] and in the context of former judges, adjudicative officers, law clerks, arbitrators, mediators, and other third-party neutrals under Rule 1.12.[231]

As discussed further below, in 2009, the American Bar Association adopted changes to Rule 1.10 of the Model Rules of Professional Conduct allowing a law firm to avoid firm-wide disqualification by use of an ethical screen in the particular context of the migrating lawyer. Under Rule 1.10(a)(2), the disqualified lawyer who is entering the law firm must be "timely screened" from the matter involving his former client, and the lawyer may not be apportioned any of the fee on the matter.[232] The disqualified lawyer's former client must be given prompt written notice, which describes the screening procedures, affirms that the firm is in compliance with Rule 1.10(a)(2), explains that review of the firm's use of screening may be available before a tribunal, and promises to respond promptly to any questions. This certification of compliance with the rule and with screening procedures must be provided to the former client at "reasonable intervals" if the former client so requests and when screening is terminated (presumably at the conclusion of the matter).

Because there are competing considerations when disqualification is imputed to other lawyers, reasonable and principled leaders of the bar and scholars come down differently on how far to extend what Professors Geoffrey Hazard and William Hodes and attorney Peter Jarvis descriptively label "the circle of imputation."[233]

On one side lies the client's interest in choice of counsel, an interest that the Model Rules of Professional Conduct promote in many respects, including the prohibition on the use of nonrefundable fee arrangements by which a lawyer penalizes a client for discharging the lawyer to seek alternative counsel[234] and the rule proscribing non-competition agreements that restrict a lawyer's freedom to practice law.[235] When the imputed disqualification rule is applied to an entire law firm by virtue of a conflict of interest involving a single lawyer, a prospective client not only is foreclosed from selecting that particular lawyer, but is excluded from considering retention of all other lawyers associated with the personally-prohibited lawyer.[236] Moreover, because a conflict of interest may not be discovered at the outset of a representation, or may not emerge until an unanticipated development occurs at a later point in time, "a client may expend

---

[230] *See infra* § 4-7.8(a)(2).

[231] *See infra* § 4-7.8(b)(1).

[232] *See also infra* § 4-7.8(a)(2).

[233] 1 GEOFFREY C. HAZARD, JR., W. WILLIAM HODES & PETER R. JARVIS, THE LAW OF LAWYERING § 15.03 (Aspen, 4th ed., 2016).

[234] *See supra* § 4-4.4.

[235] *See infra* § 4-7.9(d).

[236] 1 GEOFFREY C. HAZARD, JR., W. WILLIAM HODES & PETER R. JARVIS, THE LAW OF LAWYERING § 15.03 (Aspen, 4th ed., 2016).

considerable time and money pursuing a case with lawyers from a certain law firm, only to have the entire firm disqualified later on."[237]

In addition, the vicarious conflict of interest rule inhibits the movement of lawyers from one law firm to another. Some lawyers may be permanently locked in place because their past representation portfolio would create too much disruption if each such conflict would be imputed to every other lawyer in a prospective firm. Lawyers who are dismissed from employment, such as junior associates who are laid-off during difficult economic times, may have difficulty securing a position because conflicts traced to their work at the former law firm would not only disqualify them personally but be extended to every other lawyer at a new firm. And if a law firm does accept the opportunity to associate with a new lawyer, but that lawyer carries the taint of disqualification to every lawyer in that firm, the firm may well have to withdraw from representation of longstanding clients, thus exacting a cost not only upon the firm, but upon individuals and entities that have come to rely upon the firm for legal services and who have developed a trusting relationship with the firm's lawyers.

On the other side, the fundamental principles of professional loyalty to and protection of confidential information about clients previously represented by a lawyer or law firm must be considered.[238] For these reasons, as well as the public interest in the integrity of the civil justice system, a lawyer may not "switch sides" and transfer her legal services from one client to the adverse party. While the degree of reasonable concern is debated, these principles are implicated to a greater or lesser extent when a specific lawyer may not have personally switched sides but has moved to a new law firm that is now adverse to the former client. Especially in the case of an individual (rather than a business entity) client who was represented on a personal (rather than commercial) matter, the transition of a lawyer who was involved in the matter from a firm on one side of a case to a firm on the other side of the case may be unsettling and appear to be a betrayal of both loyalty and confidentiality.[239] Even if the migrating lawyer is subjected to an ethical screen and excluded from involvement in the ongoing matter at the new law firm, these concerns (or at least their appearance) may not be significantly alleviated.

Moreover, not everyone is convinced that facilitating "the lawyer's interest in being able to freely move from firm to firm in response to the most lucrative offer" justifies the attendant risks to the former client's interest in maintaining confidentiality or the public perception of the adversary system of justice.[240] Finally, for ethical screening to be accepted as a cure to imputed disqualification, we would have to trust that the very lawyers who otherwise would be disqualified will perform as honest legal physicians scrupulously committed to a quarantine against any exposure to infected information.[241]

---

[237] *Id.*

[238] *See* Lawrence J. Fox, The ABA's Role in Writing Ethics Rules: A Sacred Trust, in A CENTURY OF LEGAL ETHICS: TRIAL LAWYERS AND THE ABA CANONS OF PROFESSIONAL ETHICS at 229, 230 (ABA, Lawrence J. Fox, Susan R. Martyn & Andrew S. Pollis, eds., 2009) (labeling the proposal to allow ethical screening under Rule 1.10 as "a frontal assault on client loyalty and commitment").

[239] *See* Susan R. Martyn & Lawrence J. Fox, *Screening? Consider the Clients*, THE PRACTICAL LITIGATOR, July, 2008, at 47, 58–59 (arguing that, seen from the client's point of view, the movement of a lawyer to a new law firm and the implementation of screening, amounts to a "betrayal" of the client).

[240] *See* Neil W. Hamilton & Kevin R. Coan, *Are We a Profession or Merely a Business?: The Erosion of the Conflicts Rules Through the Increased Use of Ethical Walls*, 27 HOFSTRA L. REV. 57, 63 (1998).

[241] *But see* Robert A. Creamer, *Lateral Screening After Ethics 2000*, THE PROFESSIONAL LAWYER (Symposium Issue) 85, 86–88 (2006) (reporting that the Ethics 2000 Commission learned that actual cases of

The question then is whether ethical screening, if carefully applied and appropriately limited, may advance the client's right to counsel of the client's choice and facilitate the lawyer's evolving association with other lawyers—without threatening the right of former clients to unqualified protection of confidential information and to that degree of loyalty owed to a former client. On this question, the commentators, the courts, and various jurisdictions have been divided.

Many federal courts approved the concept of ethical screening to avoid imputed disqualification in the "migrating lawyer" context in at least some contexts.[242] Although "the balance of views among the states on the issue of screening is constantly shifting," one 2007 study found that "nearly half of the states" had allowed screening under at least some circumstances to avoid disqualification when a lawyer changes firms.[243] The American Law Institute's *Restatement of the Law Governing Lawyers* permits the use of ethical screening to avoid imputed disqualification in both the government-to-private-sector and the private firm-to-firm employment transitions, although strictly limiting the use of ethical screening to the narrow situation where the "confidential ... information communicated to the personally prohibited lawyer is unlikely to be significant" in the matter.[244]

After rejecting ethical screening for migrating lawyers as recently as 2001, and voting to indefinitely postpone an ethical screening proposal in 2008, the American Bar Association's House of Delegates formally approved ethical screening for lawyers changing law firms in February, 2009 by a vote of 226–191 (54 to 46 percent).[245] The House of Delegates turned away an alternative proposal that would have allowed screening only if the lawyer involved "had neither substantial involvement nor material information relating to the matter."

As amended, Rule 1.10 of the Model Rules of Professional Conduct now includes an ethical screening exception to the general rule that conflicts of interest are imputed to

---

abuses by lawyers—such as revealing confidential information or complaints of harm by former clients about lateral lawyers who were screened—are largely non-existent).

[242] *See, e.g.*, Hempstead Video, Inc. v. Incorporated Village of Valley Stream, 409 F.3d 127, 138 (2d Cir. 2005) ("We see no reason why, in appropriate cases and on convincing facts, isolation—whether it results from the intentional construction of a 'Chinese Wall,' or from de facto separation that effectively protects against any sharing of confidential information—cannot adequately protect against taint."); Cromley v. Lockport Bd. of Educ., 17 F.3d 1059 (7th Cir. 1994) (denying disqualification where the plaintiff's lawyer joined a law firm representing a defendant in ongoing litigation and the new law firm through screening process rebutted the presumption that confidential information was shared); Manning v. Waring, Cox, James, Sklar & Allen, 849 F.2d 222, 226 (6th Cir. 1988) (although "the quarantined lawyer was privy to confidential information received from the former client now seeking disqualification of the lawyer's present firm" in a substantially related matter, screening mechanisms have been found efficacious to rebut the presumption that confidences were shared and disqualification may be avoided if appropriate screening is demonstrated); EZ Paintr Corp. v. Padco, Inc., 746 F.2d 1459, 1462 (Fed. Cir. 1984) (applying Eighth Circuit law); Panduit Corp. v. All States Plastic Mfg. Co., 744 F.2d 1564, 1580–81 (Fed. Cir. 1984) (applying Seventh Circuit law); Schiessle v. Stephens, 717 F.2d 417, 421 (7th Cir. 1983); Cheng v. GAF Corp., 631 F.2d 1052, 1059 (2d Cir. 1980), *vacated on jurisdictional grounds*, 450 U.S. 903 (1981).

[243] Joan C. Rogers, *Conflicts of Interest: Imputed Disqualification*, 23 LAWYERS' MANUAL ON PROF. CONDUCT 647 (Dec. 26, 2007).

[244] RESTATEMENT (THIRD) OF THE LAW GOVERNING LAWYERS § 124 (American Law Institute 2000). Because of this limitation, which has not been followed by courts or incorporated into those rules approving ethical screening in the migratory lawyer context, the Restatement approach has been described as "so stingy" that it is unlikely in practice to ever result in successful removal of imputation. *See* 1 GEOFFREY C. HAZARD, JR. & W. WILLIAM HODES, THE LAW OF LAWYERING § 14.9 (Aspen, 3d ed., 2010).

[245] ABA Delegates Modify Conflicts Rule, Allow Screens When Lawyers Change Firms, 77 U.S.L.W. 2508 (2009).

all lawyers in a law firm. Under Rule 1.10(a), the other lawyers in the firm are not disqualified when the individual lawyer who is personally disqualified under Rule 1.9 is "timely screened from any participation in the matter and is apportioned no part of the fee therefrom," written notice with specified information is promptly given to the former client "to ascertain compliance" with screening requirements, and "certifications of compliance" are regularly provided if the former client so requests.

As of 2016, 32 states and the District of Columbia follow the Model Rules or otherwise allow for ethical screening in the context of lateral movement of lawyers.[246] However, 18 states continue to impute disqualification when any lawyer in the firm is personally disqualified, whether or not joining the firm in a lateral move from another firm, without any avoidance by ethical screening.

In addition, as contemplated by Rule 1.10(c) of the Model Rules of Professional Conduct, a client may waive the application of vicarious disqualification, provided the consent was fully informed and is confirmed in writing.[247] In such a case, erection of an ethical screen may be a valuable or even essential means of enforcing the waiver agreement in a manner that ensures no exchange, inadvertent or deliberate, of confidential information between the personally-prohibited lawyer and the other lawyers in the firm handling the matter. Indeed, when the client makes an informed waiver of such a conflict, imputed disqualification may be consensually lifted in situations other than those involving a migrating lawyer.

When the clients involved have consented, and the screen is implemented as soon as the conflict is identified, the establishment of a screening process to implement that agreement reinforces the legitimacy of the waiver.[248] Such a screening approach ensures that the client's or former client's legitimate concerns about confidentiality are satisfied, while the law firm may continue the simultaneous representation without breaching its professional obligations.

### *§ 4-7.6(b)(3) Removal of Imputed Disqualification When Personally-Prohibited Lawyer Leaves the Firm*

Under Rule 1.10(b) of the Model Rules of Professional Conduct, when a lawyer whose representation of a client created or would have created a conflict of interest has left a law firm, the disqualification may depart with that lawyer under certain circumstances, thereby allowing other lawyers in the firm to undertake representation of a client adverse to the interests of a client that previously had been represented by the formerly-associated lawyer. When "a lawyer has terminated an association with a firm," Rule 1.10(b) provides that "the firm is not prohibited from thereafter representing a person with interests materially adverse to those of a client represented by the formerly associated lawyer and not currently represented by the firm."

However, the rule directs that the disqualification imputed from the representation of the formerly associated lawyer remains in place if "(1) the matter is the same or substantially related to that in which the formerly associated lawyer represented the

[246] State Adoption of Lateral Screening Rule, at http://www.americanbar.org/content/dam/aba/administrative/professional_responsibility/lateral_screening.pdf.

[247] On informed consent in the context of waiver of conflicts of interest, see *infra* § 4-7.7.

[248] *See* Central Milk Producers Coop. v. Sentry Food Stores, 573 F.2d 988, 991–93 (8th Cir. 1978) (denying motion for disqualification where, with approval of opposing parties, a firm adopted screening procedures to insulate conflicted attorney from case).

client; and (2) any lawyer remaining in the firm has information [which is protected as confidential] that is material to the matter." In other words, even though the lawyer who represented the client has separated from the law firm, the remaining lawyers in the law firm may not represent a new client adverse to the past client represented by the now-departed lawyer if the representations are the same or substantially related (that is, the successive conflict standard of Rule 1.9 would apply) and if material confidential information had been shared with other lawyers who are still associated with the firm.

Rule 1.10(b) is more easily applied to remove imputed disqualification in the situation where the personally-prohibited lawyer had carried in the disqualification when migrating into the law firm and then carried out the disqualification by later migrating out of the law firm. When the formerly-associated lawyer had represented the client before joining the law firm, but did not continue representation of that client during the period of association with the firm, then the chances are greater that the lawyer will not have shared any confidential information relating to that representation with other lawyers in the firm.

As an example, the case of *Sorci v. District Court*[249] involved an assistant county attorney with prosecutorial responsibility for child welfare cases, who subsequently became executive director of a non-profit organization providing legal assistance to children—including children in many of the same cases in which she previously had been involved as a government attorney. Still later, this attorney resigned her position with the organization after controversy arose as to whether the organization's attorneys should be disqualified from representing children in the many hundreds of cases in which she formerly had public responsibilities. Although the Iowa Supreme Court affirmed the initial order of disqualification of the organization's attorneys from all pending cases in which the executive director had previously acted as counsel to the state, the court held that the imputed disqualification to other attorneys in the organization was lifted when the former assistant county attorney resigned as the organization's executive director. Subject to the confirmation that no confidential information had been acquired by any remaining lawyers in the association, the court understood Rule 1.10(b) to "thus permit removal of imputation once *any* personally prohibited lawyer leaves her new firm."[250]

In theory, the rule would also permit a law firm to avoid the continuing effect of vicarious disqualification even though the formerly-associated lawyer had represented the client during the lawyer's tenure with the law firm. Indeed, Comment 5 to Rule 1.10 states that this rule "applies regardless of when the formerly associated lawyer represented the client." In practice, however, when the lawyer had represented that client during association with the firm—and thus the client at that time was a client not only of the lawyer individually but of the firm itself—the probability that material confidential information was shared in one way or another with other lawyers in the firm increases significantly. Lawyers practicing in association with other lawyers regularly draw upon their colleagues to assist in a representation; frequently discuss the matter with the other lawyers, even if informally; may prepare and store documents and records where other lawyers in the firm have at least some access; and often provide

---

[249] 671 N.W.2d 482, 494–97 (Iowa 2003). The *Sorci* case, including the removal of disqualification upon the lawyer's departure from the non-profit association, is discussed at length at *infra* § 4-7.8(a)(1).

[250] *Sorci*, 671 N.W.2d at 496 n.3.

reports or other information about a client matter to the other lawyers in the firm for purposes of firm management and distribution of income.

When a client previously was represented during the very period of time in which the lawyer directly handling the matter was associated with the firm, a fair presumption should exist that other lawyers in the firm at the time acquired confidential information. A burden should be placed on the firm to demonstrate that none of the remaining lawyers within the firm in fact acquired confidential information that would be material to the matter upon which the firm seeks to represent a client adverse to the client represented by the formerly-associated lawyer. That burden might be sustained by showing, for example, (1) that the now-departed lawyer had been engaged in an isolated practice (at least as to that client) even inside the firm, (2) that an entire practice area of a firm has separated from the firm and thus simultaneously removed all lawyers involved with the matter, or (3) that due to the passage of time or other changes in the firm personnel, none of the lawyers having any involvement with the matter still remain.

If no lawyer still associated with the firm possesses any material confidential information about that person or entity, Rule 1.10(b) regards that client of the formerly-associated lawyer as simply a non-client from the perspective of the law firm as re-constituted in the wake of the lawyer's departure. Accordingly, the law firm is not limited in undertaking representation of a client adverse to the interests of the formerly-associated lawyer's client, even if the matter is the same or substantially related to that in which the departed lawyer represented his client.

## § 4-7.7 INFORMED CONSENT BY CLIENT TO CONFLICT

### § 4-7.7(a) Introduction to Informed Consent Conflict Waivers

As the United States Court of Appeals for the Eighth Circuit explained in *United States v. Agosto*,[251] "[a] facet of the right to counsel of choice is the [party's] ability to waive [its] right to the assistance of counsel unhindered by a conflict of interest, provided that waiver is knowing and intelligent." Under Rule 1.7(b) of the Model Rules of Professional Conduct, a client may consent to representation by the lawyer notwithstanding the existence of a direct-adversity conflict[252] or a material-limitation-on-representation conflict[253] under the following conditions:

(1) the lawyer reasonably believes that the lawyer will be able to provide competent and diligent representation to each affected client;

(2) the representation is not prohibited by law;

(3) the representation does not involve the assertion of a claim by one client against another client represented by the lawyer in the same litigation or other proceeding before a tribunal; and

(4) each affected client gives informed consent, confirmed in writing.

Consent by the client to representation under such circumstances is commonly termed a "conflict waiver." The term, "conflict waiver," may be somewhat misleading, for no client may be asked to consent to acutely impaired representation that is disabled by

[251] 675 F.2d 965, 969–70 (8th Cir. 1982).

[252] *See supra* § 4-7.4(b).

[253] *See supra* § 4-7.4(c).

a lawyer's divided loyalties. As developed further below,[254] Rule 1.10(b)(1) demands that the lawyer always remain able "to provide competent and diligent representation" to the client. A conflict waiver may be accepted by the client when a formal conflict of interest exists or when a reasonable outside observer would identify conflicting influences, but the individual lawyer who will represent the particular client remains sufficiently uncompromised by competing demands that the client will receive competent and diligent representation, that is, effective and zealous advocacy, from the lawyer.

Although this is by no means an exclusive list, the following are a few common scenarios in which, despite an apparent conflict, the client might appraise the situation in the light of fully disclosed information by the lawyer and decide to accept the lawyer's continued representation, while the lawyer might reasonably anticipate remaining able to provide high quality and largely unconstrained and disinterested professional services for that client:

***Lawyer Personal Interests:*** A lawyer might have a personal affiliation[255] or an investment with an adverse party[256] that a reasonable outside observer would regard as likely to materially limit the lawyer's ability to provide independent legal advice to the client, but which the lawyer reasonably believes will not affect competent and diligent representation (and the client concurs). For example, if a lawyer were retained to pursue a claim against a social club of which the lawyer was a member or against a corporation whose shares of stock were included as a minimal part of the lawyer's investment portfolio, the lawyer might reasonably believe that these were inconsequential personal interests that would not influence her judgment, and, after being informed of the risks, the client might agree.

***Unrelated Matters:*** A lawyer may wish to represent a client in a dispute or in litigation, but then find that he represents the adverse party on an unrelated matter.[257] While this situation may present little or no risk that confidential information would be shared (because of the lack of a relationship between the matters), it nonetheless constitutes an impermissible direct-adversity conflict because it disturbs the expectation of each client to unfettered loyalty. The lawyer, however, could go forward if both clients are willing to consent and if the lawyer believes he may provide diligent representation to both separately.

Where one or the other client is a commercial entity and where the matters involved are not sensitive or personal, the clients may be willing to accede and the lawyer may feel comfortable and confident in affording zealous advocacy to both in their continuing and separate matters. However, because the nature of the conflict is directly adverse—and actions taken to promote one client are directly to the disadvantage of the other—the lawyer should hesitate before continuing, even with client consent. The lawyer probably should not proceed when the matter has become intensely personal to either client, as feelings of betrayed loyalty are especially likely to arise in such instances.

***Imputed Disqualification:*** When another lawyer in the same law firm represents a different client who now appears as an adverse party in a dispute in which the lawyer

---

[254] *See infra* § 4-7.7(d).

[255] On conflicts arising from a lawyer's relationship with the lawyer representing another party, see *supra* § 4-7.3(k).

[256] On personal interest conflicts, see *supra* § 4-7.7(d).

[257] On direct adversity conflicts, even in unrelated matters, see *supra* § 4-7.4(b)(1).

has been representing a client, the lawyer would be prevented from accepting or continuing that representation because of imputed disqualification.[258] However, because the different lawyers in the law firm may have little or no interaction with each other, and because confidential information could be screened so that it would not be shared with the other firm lawyer on the other matter, the parties may be willing to consent to the conflict and thereby remove the effects of imputed disqualification in order for each to retain their preferred counsel.

As with other conflicts of interest, imputed conflicts may be waived by the client under Rule 1.10(c), which refers to the conditions for such waivers as set forth in Rule 1.7(b). For the waiver to be proper, the client must give informed consent, confirmed in writing, and the lawyer must reasonably believe that, notwithstanding the conflict that otherwise would be imputed, the lawyer will be able to provide competent and diligent representation to each affected client.

***Joint Representation:*** A lawyer representing multiple clients in a civil transaction or civil litigation,[259] where the parties have a common objective, may need to, or be well-advised to, obtain informed consent of the clients regarding the possibility of interests diverging during the course of the representation, such as different positions being taken in negotiation or settlement[260] or even the possibility of cross-claims being submitted against a party on the same side of a lawsuit.

As part of the process of obtaining informed consent by each client to the conflict of interest, the lawyer may also seek to prevent or at least contain potential conflicts of interest by limiting the scope of the joint representation. Such a limitation may exclude from the outset any duty to provide professional services by the lawyer on those matters outside the common objective of the clients and thus that could divide the lawyer's loyalty among the clients.

Under Rule 1.2(c) of the Model Rules of Professional Conduct, the lawyer and the client are expressly authorized to adopt reasonable limitations on the scope of the representation.[261] Here too, the lawyer must obtain informed consent from the client, ensuring that the client appreciates the "material risks of and reasonably available alternatives to" the limitation.[262] Assuming informed consent, the clients being jointly represented by the lawyer might agree that the lawyer would not advise or represent any client regarding potential claims they might have against each other. Or the lawyer would prepare documents recording the agreed-upon terms of a transaction but would not advise the clients in their negotiation with each other about those terms.

As Comment 32 to Rule 1.7 admonishes, when a lawyer seeks to adjust the relationship between the clients as part of a conflict waiver, "the lawyer should make clear that the lawyer's role is not that of partisanship normally expected in other circumstances and, thus, that the clients may be required to assume greater responsibility for decisions than when each client is separately represented." The lawyer must explain to the clients that certain issues that might be identified or interests that

---

[258] *See supra* § 4-7.6(a).

[259] On joint representation in civil litigation and in non-litigation matters, see *supra* § 4-7.4(c)(4), (6). On joint representation in creation of an entity, see *infra* § 4-8.2.

[260] On aggregate settlement conflicts, see *supra* § 4-7.4(c)(5).

[261] *See supra* § 4-7.7(d).

[262] On informed consent, see *supra* § 4.01(d).

might be advocated should each client have independent counsel will be disregarded by the lawyer in a representation limited to the common objective of the clients.

### § 4-7.7(b) The Meaning of Informed Consent to Waive a Conflict

By the definition of "informed consent" in Rule 1.0(e) in the Model Rules of Professional Conduct, the lawyer is obliged not only to notify the client of his right to grant or withhold consent, but the lawyer also must provide "adequate information and explanation about the material risks of and reasonably available alternatives to the proposed course of conduct." When "informed consent" is required, the attorney is obliged to obtain an affirmative expression of consent by the person and may not merely assume consent from silence, although consent may be inferred from the person's subsequent conduct.

When entering into a conflict waiver agreement with a client, a lawyer is obliged to fully disclose the nature and significance of the conflict or potential conflict to the client. Under Rule 1.0(e), "informed consent" "denotes the agreement by a person to a proposed course of conduct after the lawyer has communicated adequate information and explanation about the material risks of and reasonably available alternatives to the proposed course of conduct." The informed consent requirement ensures that the client has the information and understanding necessary to participate in the representation and to intelligently make any important decision that is reserved to the client.[263] For this reason, "[t]he acquiescence of a client without informed consent is tantamount to no consent at all."[264]

While the lawyer is not required to inform the client about those matters as to which the client is already fully informed, Comment 6 to Rule 1.0 warns that "a lawyer who does not personally inform the client or other person assumes the risk that the client or other person is inadequately informed and the consent is invalid." What is "adequate" in terms of information and explanation will of course depend on the circumstances, on the experience of the person in legal matters and with respect to the matter at hand, and on whether the person is independently represented by counsel. Thus, a person of sophistication and experience generally needs less of an explanation and indeed, as Comment 6 observes, a person who is separately represented by independent counsel presumably has been adequately informed when consent is given. By contrast, a person who has not previously or has only infrequently used legal services, who is not well-educated, or who otherwise demonstrates a lack of understanding or confidence deserves a more thorough explanation by the lawyer who is attempting to secure consent.

Simply warning the client that there are conflicts and seeking consent is insufficient.[265] Rather, the lawyer must fully disclose the possible effect of the conflict on the representation, reveal the other relationship or interest that creates the conflict, describe the hazards to the lawyer's loyalty and performance posed by the conflict, and explain how independent counsel might address those problems differently. Professor Charles Wolfram says that the "interests of the lawyer or other client that provoke the

---

[263] *But see* Jennifer K. Robbennolt & Jean R. Sternlight, *Behavioral Legal Ethics*, 45 ARIZ. ST. L.J. 1107, 1132–34 (2013) (expressing doubt, based on behavioral psychology, that disclosure is an effective remedy to the conflict of interest problem).

[264] Selby v. Revlon Consumer Products Corp., 6 F. Supp. 2d 577, 582 (N.D. Tex. 1997).

[265] Ransburg Corp. v. Champion Spark Plug Co., 648 F. Supp. 1040, 1045–46 (N.D. Ill. 1986) (rejecting as full disclosure the casual disclosure of the fact of adverse representation without any explanation of its significance).

conflict should be fully and candidly explained. The conversation should contain sufficient detail and supporting analysis so that the client can comprehend the ways in which the interests of each are or may be in conflict."[266]

When the lawyer is representing multiple clients and a conflict is anticipated or later emerges, Comment 18 to Rule 1.7 suggests that the information provided to the clients "must include the implications of the common representation, including possible effects on loyalty, confidentiality and the attorney-client privilege and the advantages and risks involved." A comment to the pertinent section of the *Restatement of the Law Governing Lawyers* provides a more complete list of topics for evaluation:

> In a multiple-client situation, the information normally should address the interests of the lawyer and other client giving rise to the conflict; contingent, optional, and tactical considerations and alternative courses of action that would be foreclosed or made less readily available by the conflict; the effect of the representation or the process of obtaining other clients' informed consent upon confidential information of the client; any material reservations that a disinterested lawyer might reasonably harbor about the arrangement if such a lawyer were representing only the client being advised; and the consequences and effects of a future withdrawal of consent by any client, including, if relevant, the fact that the lawyer would withdraw from representing all clients. Where the conflict arises solely because a proposed representation will be adverse to an existing client in an unrelated matter, knowledge of the general nature and scope of the work being performed for each client normally suffices to enable the clients to decide whether or not to consent.[267]

As part and parcel of the client's right to terminate representation by the lawyer for any or no reason,[268] a client also may revoke the consent to a conflict of interest. Comment 21 to Rule 1.7 advises:

> Whether revoking consent to the client's own representation precludes the lawyer from continuing to represent other clients depends on the circumstances, including the nature of the conflict, whether the client revoked consent because of a material change in circumstances, the reasonable expectations of the other clients and whether material detriment to the other clients or the lawyer would result.

### § 4-7.7(c) Client Consent Confirmed in Writing

Rule 1.7(b)(4) of the Model Rules of Professional Conduct requires that any conflict waiver reflect the "informed consent" of each affected client, "confirmed in writing."

As a means of validating that informed consent, the rule also requires that the client consent be "confirmed in writing," which Rule 1.0(b) defines as a "writing by the person or a writing that a lawyer promptly transmits to the person confirming an oral informed consent." Comment 20 to Rule 1.7 states that "[i]f it is not feasible to obtain or transmit the writing at the time the client gives informed consent, then the lawyer must obtain or transmit it within a reasonable time thereafter."

---

[266] CHARLES W. WOLFRAM, MODERN LEGAL ETHICS § 7.2.4 (West 1986).

[267] RESTATEMENT (THIRD) OF THE LAW GOVERNING LAWYERS § 122, cmt. (c)(i) (American Law Institute, 2000).

[268] *See infra* § 5.16(b)(1).

The comment further emphasizes that the requirement of a writing is no substitute for a full disclosure by the lawyer of the risks and advantages in proceeding with the representation, which ordinarily should be presented in a face-to-face conversation with the client. Instead, as Comment 20 clarifies, the purpose of the writing is to "impress upon clients the seriousness of the decision the client is being asked to make and to avoid disputes or ambiguities that might later occur in the absence of a writing."

### § 4-7.7(d) The Continuing Duty of Competent and Diligent Representation

Some lawyers have the mistaken impression that obtaining the client's blessing is sufficient to overcome any conflict of interest, regardless of the actual effect that the conflicting influence may have upon the quality of the lawyer's representation. Under this fallacious understanding, if the client knows that the lawyer is operating under a professional disability by reason of a conflict and yet is willing to proceed, then the conflict may be waived with the client apparently being reconciled to any negative consequences.

Quite to the contrary, the provision in Rule 1.7 of the Model Rules of Professional Conduct allowing consent to a conflict is conditioned on the stipulation that, notwithstanding the apparent or formal existence of a conflict, the lawyer remains ready and able to provide legal services that exhibit undiluted professional quality and sufficiently independent judgment that the client receives conscientious advice and reliable protection of the client's interests.

Rule 1.7(b)(1) mandates that the lawyer "reasonably believe[ ] that the lawyer will be able to provide competent and diligent representation to each affected client." As Professor Charles Wolfram stated, language in ethics rules requiring that the lawyer be able to adequately represent the client despite the conflict is "an emphatic insistence that consent be relied upon only if it is objectively clear that the threat to the lawyer's independent judgment is minimal."[269] Full disclosure to and informed consent from the client serves the purpose of warning the client of the risks inherent in the arrangement. Nonetheless, the attorney must also be personally satisfied and reasonably confident that she will be able to uphold the responsibilities of a competent and diligent representative, that is, a zealous advocate for the interests of the client.

### § 4-7.7(e) Nonconsentable Conflicts

Not every conflict of interest may be waived by a client; indeed, most probably cannot be so avoided. Certain conflicts are circumstantially nonconsentable, while other conflicts are per se nonconsentable.

Circumstances may conspire to make a conflict nonconsentable. The lawyer then must decline the representation or, if it has already commenced, the lawyer must withdraw (assuming permission of the court if the matter is before a tribunal).[270] As explained above,[271] under Rule 1.7(b)(1), when the lawyer does not "reasonably believe" that he "will be able to provide competent and diligent representation to each affected client," then the lawyer may not proceed regardless of any supposed consent by the

---

[269] CHARLES W. WOLFRAM, MODERN LEGAL ETHICS § 7.2.3 (West, 1986).

[270] On mandatory withdrawal when representation would result in violation of an ethical rule, see *supra* § 4-3.6(c)(1).

[271] *See supra* § 4-7.7(d).

client. The interests of the affected clients may be too severely in tension to allow the lawyer reasonably to provide effective counsel to each of them. Or, as the comment to the *Restatement of the Law Governing Lawyers* advises, the lawyer's "personal circumstances" may irredeemably impair representation, such as when "the lawyer has such strong feelings of friendship toward one or two prospective joint clients that the lawyer could not provide adequate representation to the other client."[272]

In addition, because any consent by the client must be fully informed,[273] if the lawyer is unwilling to reveal and fully explain the nature of the conflict, or is unable to do so because a complete explanation would require disclosing confidential information about another client without permission, then consent cannot be secured.

By direct provision of the rule, certain conflicts are removed from the consent option, even if one theoretically could imagine a circumstance under which the conflict could be managed or the lawyer and client otherwise could agree to continue a representation. Under Rule 1.7(b)(2) and (b)(3), when the representation is prohibited by law and when the lawyer would be representing clients on opposite sides of the same litigation or proceeding before a tribunal, these conflicts are not consentable, that is, the lawyer's continued representation may not be accepted by the clients through waiver.

***Prohibited by Law:*** Under Rule 1.7(b)(2), as a condition on informed consent, the representation must not be one that is "prohibited by law." In many states, joint representation of criminal defendants in a capital murder case is not permitted under any circumstances.[274] As another example, federal employees are barred by federal statute for two years from representing a client on a matter that was within the broad scope of the employee's "official responsibility as such officer or employee."[275] Even if the federal agency involved purported to offer consent, the federal criminal statute prohibiting the representation could not be overridden by administrators.

***Both Sides in Litigation:*** Rule 1.7(b)(3) directs that a conflict for which client consent is sought must "not involve the assertion of a claim by one client against another client represented by the lawyer in the same litigation or other proceeding before a tribunal." Comment 17 to Rule 1.7 explains that such conflicts are nonconsentable "because of the institutional interest in vigorous development of each client's position when the clients are aligned directly against each other in the same litigation or other proceeding before a tribunal." Professor W. Bradley Wendel observes that "process integrity" is compromised when a lawyer seeks to represent clients adverse to each other in the same litigation.[276] This would be like, he says, "a person trying to play both white and black in chess." Not only would the game simply "not work right," but "[i]nvariably, she would start to favor white or black, even if only subconsciously."

The comment further observes that "[w]hether clients are aligned directly against each other within the meaning of this paragraph requires examination of the context of the proceeding." Certainly, a lawyer may not represent both the plaintiff and the

---

[272] RESTATEMENT (THIRD) OF THE LAW GOVERNING LAWYERS § 122, cmt. g(iv) (American Law Institute, 2000).

[273] *See supra* § 4-7.7(c).

[274] RESTATEMENT (THIRD) OF THE LAW GOVERNING LAWYERS § 122, cmt. g(i) (American Law Institute, 2000).

[275] 18 U.S.C. § 207(a)(2)(B).

[276] W. BRADLEY WENDEL, PROFESSIONAL RESPONSIBILITY: EXAMPLES & EXPLANATIONS 312 (Wolters Kluwer, 5th ed., 2016).

defendant in litigation. And when parties nominally on the same side of a dispute direct claims against each other, such as cross-claims between defendants, the same lawyer may not represent both defendants, at least with respect to those cross-claims.

### § 4-7.7(f) Advance Conflict Waivers

As stated in Comment 22 to Rule 1.7 of the Model Rules of Professional Conduct, the requirements for client consent apply, not only when a client agrees to waive a conflict after it has arisen, but also to lawyer-client agreements to consent to a conflict that may appear in the future. Thus, an attorney and client may by advance agreement arrange their relationship so as to limit the effect of future anticipated conflicts of interest. In a formal ethics opinion, the American Bar Association's Standing Committee on Ethics and Professional Responsibility agreed that Rule 1.7 now "permits effective consent to a wider range of future conflicts" than was previously accepted.[277]

By virtue of the requirement of informed consent under Rule 1.7(b), the validity of a prospective waiver will depend on the extent to which a client could have reasonably appreciated the nature of the risk and thus given an intelligent assent to the waiver. If the advance conflict waiver is fairly specific in identifying the type of other clients that may be involved or the nature of the matters involved, such as when, in the words of Comment 22, "the client agrees to consent to a particular type of conflict with which the client is already familiar, then the consent ordinarily will be effective with regard to that type of conflict." By contrast, Comment 22 warns, "[i]f the consent is general and open-ended, then the consent ordinarily will be ineffective, because it is not reasonably likely that the client will have understood the material risks involved."

Even when the waiver language is broad in scope, the comment suggests it may be upheld "if the client is an experienced user of the legal services involved and is reasonably informed regarding the risk that a conflict may arise." An advance conflict waiver is especially likely to be approved if the client was represented by independent counsel in negotiating the waiver agreement or if the waiver is limited to future conflicts that are unrelated to the subject matter of the representation.

Therefore, specificity in identifying the anticipated conflict, limitation to representations that are unrelated to the lawyer's present or former representation of the consenting client, sophistication of the client, and independent legal counsel are important factors in measuring the effectiveness of an advance conflict waiver. These factors need not all be present, of course, and indeed any one may be sufficient to uphold a waiver, depending on the circumstances. If the waiver is detailed and limited in scope, the chances are greater that client consent will be proven to have been made with sufficient disclosure and understanding. If the client is particularly sophisticated in the use of legal services, and almost certainly if the client had the benefit of separate legal counsel on the matter,[278] even an open-ended waiver may pass muster. On the other end of the spectrum, as Professor Richard Painter writes, "blanket waivers by

---

[277] ABA Comm. on Ethics & Prof'l Responsibility, Formal Op. 05–436 (2005).

[278] *See* Richard W. Painter, *Advance Waiver of Conflicts*, 13 GEO. J. LEGAL ETHICS 289, 312 (2000) (saying that, "[b]ecause separate representation can make such a substantial difference," that factor should be "a starting place for determining whether advance waivers are enforceable," such that a waiver's reasonableness should only be subject to question if "the waiver is ambiguous or the client was not independently represented at the time the waiver was given").

unsophisticated clients may reflect asymmetry of information and unequal bargaining power between lawyers and clients."[279]

While the attorney-client relationship is indeed a special one including fiduciary responsibilities, the principle that one who knowingly and deliberately enters into an agreement should be bound by its terms is not to be abandoned in the context of conflict waivers. The courts should intervene to prevent exploitation of unsophisticated individuals by the superior knowledge of their counsel. But sophisticated persons or entities and experienced consumers of legal services, especially if represented by separate attorneys (including in-house counsel) on the meaning and wisdom of a conflict waiver, should not be heard to complain, unless the conflict that arises is wholly unanticipated or the waiver is truly ambiguous in its application.[280] Having entered into an agreement to secure the advantage of legal services from a lawyer or law firm subject to a negotiated conflict waiver, the client should not be permitted to disavow that agreement because that client later perceives a strategic advantage in disqualifying the lawyer or law firm from representing an opposing party when the conflict anticipated in the waiver subsequently arises.

Where an advance conflict waiver is designed to avoid the effect of imputed disqualification within a law firm, the parties frequently condition the required client consent upon establishment within the law firm of an ethical screen that prevents any exchange of confidential information between the separate teams of lawyers that are handling the matters for the different clients.[281] The client's informed consent "to a future conflict, without more, does not constitute the client's informed consent to the disclosure or use of the client's confidential information against the client."[282]

## § 4-7.8 SPECIAL CONFLICTS RULES FOR GOVERNMENT EMPLOYEES, JUDGES, ARBITRATORS, MEDIATORS, AND THIRD-PARTY NEUTRALS

### § 4-7.8(a) Special Conflict Rules for Former and Current Government Employees

#### *§ 4-7.8(a)(1) Conflict of Interest Rules for Former Government Officers and Employees*

Many lawyers spend a period of time in public service—prosecuting crimes, representing government agencies in litigation, serving as general counsel for government agencies, advising public officers about law or policy, or serving in elected or appointed public office. While some lawyers remain in government employment for their entire careers, other lawyers revolve back and forth between private practice and public responsibilities.

---

[279] *Id.* at 289.

[280] *See* Galderma Laboratories, L.P. v. Actavis Mid Atlantic LLC, 927 F. Supp. 2d 390, 394 (N.D. Tex. 2013) (upholding a general and open-ended advance conflict waiver by "a highly sophisticated client who is a regular user of legal services and was represented by its own counsel" when agreeing to the waiver). On advance conflict waivers by clients with both business and legal sophistication, along with review by independent counsel, see generally Peter Jarvis, David Lewis, Allison Rhodes & Calon Russell, *A "Safe Harbor" for Future Conflicts Waivers*, 29 LAW. MAN. PROF. CONDUCT 384 (2013).

[281] On ethical screens and conflicts of interest, see *supra* § 4-7.6(b)(2).

[282] ABA Comm. on Ethics & Prof'l Responsibility, Formal Op. 05–436 (2005).

When a lawyer takes on public responsibilities, she assumes duties of fidelity and confidentiality to the public. To uphold those continuing duties of public responsibility, the former public officer or government employee must carefully separate her prior public actions on specific matters from later legal representation of private clients after entering private practice. A lawyer who was intimately involved in adopting a policy, making a decision, or advocating a position on behalf of the government with respect to a discrete matter involving identifiable parties may not later convert the work that was performed for the public interest toward a private end and may not purloin the confidences that were received in public service to promote the interests of a private client.

Rule 1.11(a) of the Model Rules of Professional Conduct sets the basic standard, that a former public officer or government employee[283] may not (1) use or reveal confidential information relating to the representation of a former government client,[284] and (2) may not represent a client (either in private practice or in another government practice) "in connection with a matter in which the lawyer participated personally and substantially as a public officer or employee, unless the appropriate government agency gives its informed consent, confirmed in writing, to the representation." By this rule, the lawyer is prevented from exploiting a public position to make herself more attractive to future employers in the private sector, later seeking to subvert the decision made or position advocated when the lawyer was engaged in public service, and abusing confidential information obtained in government employment.

The rule applies only to those "matters" that involved some kind of particularized position, action, or disposition by the former public officer or government employee with respect to a specific person, entity, or group of persons, as contrasted with governmental activities or policymaking that are more general in scope or application. Rule 1.11(e) defines "matter" as "any judicial or other proceeding, application, request for a ruling or other determination, contract, claim, controversy, investigation, charge, accusation, arrest or other particular matter involving a specific party or parties." Professors Geoffrey Hazard and William Hodes described the rule as making "a distinction between matters of general policy, on the one hand, and specific matters involving identifiable parties and particularized facts on the other."[285] The government employee or public officer engaged in proposing, drafting, or enacting legislation or rules or in developing general policy positions is less likely to be able to curry the kind of particular favor with specific private interests with which the rule is concerned. Such activities fall outside of the special regulation of conflicts found in Rule 1.11(a).

The disqualification under Rule 1.11(a) attaches only when the lawyer participated "personally," that is, directly in the matter when serving in a public position, not merely when he served in the same governmental office as other officers or employees who handled the matter. Moreover, the lawyer's participation must have been "substantial,"

---

[283] The special conflict of interest standards in Rule 1.11 apply only to lawyers who are or have served as public officers or government employees and not to lawyers engaged in private practice who are retained by a government entity. *See* RONALD D. ROTUNDA & JOHN S. DZIENKOWSKI, PROFESSIONAL RESPONSIBILITY: A STUDENT'S GUIDE § 1.11–3(a) (American Bar Ass'n, 2013–2014). When a private lawyer is retained by a government client, the ordinary conflict of interest rules apply.

[284] On the general prohibition on disclosure or use of confidential information relating to representation of a former client, see *supra* § 4-7.5(e).

[285] 1 GEOFFREY C. HAZARD, JR. & W. WILLIAM HODES, THE LAW OF LAWYERING § 15.2 (Aspen, 3d ed., 2005).

something beyond routinely forwarding a document or taking a purely ministerial action that involved no exercise of discretion. Substantial participation would include court appearances, interviews of clients or witnesses, preparation of litigation documents, discussions of strategy, etc.[286] The disqualification may be removed if the appropriate government agency, after being informed of all pertinent aspects of the lawyer's prior governmental involvement and anticipated private representation, provides consent and that consent is confirmed in writing. The rule applies not only when the lawyer had acted for the government in a legal capacity (as legal counsel representing a government client), but also to actions or decisions made, or participated in, when serving as a "public officer or employee."

Rule 1.11(c) further prohibits a lawyer who formerly served in the government from employing confidential government information against a third party. During the course of public service, a person may gain access to information about members of the public "obtained under governmental authority" and which the government (1) "is prohibited by law from disclosing to the public" or (2) "has a legal privilege not to disclose and which is not otherwise available to the public." Under basic principles of confidentiality, the person who served as a government lawyer would be barred from making use of or disclosing information that is confidential with respect to the government client.

This rule applies as well to information that is confidential with respect to a third party (not only the government) and that may have been obtained by the former public officer or government employee in a capacity other than as a lawyer for the government. To eliminate any possibility that such information will be abused, by removing any incentive to employ it, Rule 1.11(c) bars the former public officer or government employee who acquired confidential information about a person from "represent[ing] a private client whose interests are adverse to that person in a matter in which the information could be used to the material disadvantage of that person."

In *Sorci v. District Court*,[287] the Iowa Supreme Court considered the ethical obligations of a former government lawyer. An assistant county attorney, with responsibility for intake of cases involving state intervention on behalf of children in need of assistance, subsequently accepted a position as executive director of a non-profit organization providing legal assistance to children. In her former capacity as assistant county attorney, this lawyer had reviewed, signed, and filed more than 1,000 petitions, working closely with case workers, medical personnel, and other professionals to determine when the state should intervene on behalf of children at risk, seek termination of parental rights, or apply for temporary removal of children from their homes. Moreover, it appears that she had access to confidential information, such as the names of otherwise anonymous reporters of child abuse, that could not be disclosed to other parties.

The non-profit Youth Law Center provides legal representation to children, with its attorneys regularly being appointed to serve as guardians ad litem for children. When the former assistant county attorney was hired as executive director of the center, no

---

[286] *See* United States v. Feuchtener, No. 2:16-cr-00100-GMN-CWH (D. Nev. Nov. 3, 2016) (disqualifying a former federal prosecutor who joined the defense team in a child pornography case after participating in discussions of the case while in the United States Attorney's office, which went beyond "pleasantries or curious banter" to include "substantive, detailed conversations about the strengths and weaknesses of the case, possible defenses which should be anticipated, the weight of the evidence, credibility of witnesses, whether further investigation could be helpful, etc.").

[287] 671 N.W.2d 482, 485–88 (Iowa 2003).

ethical screen was erected. She had open access to files regarding cases in which she had been involved while in public service, heard and participated in conversations with other staff about such cases, and on at least one occasion was approached for consultation concerning a matter she had handled in the county attorney's office.[288] Under these circumstances, the trial court ordered that Youth Law Center attorneys be disqualified from representing children in any pending case in which the executive director had acted as counsel for the state.

In *Sorci*, the Iowa Supreme Court affirmed the disqualification.[289] Speaking to the former assistant county attorney's past governmental duties, the court ruled that "[a]dvising a client, authoring correspondence or reports, signing a pleading, and appearing at a hearing each involve substantial responsibility." The court explained that the prohibition on accepting representation in a matter over which the lawyer had substantial responsibility while employed as a government lawyer prevents "the treachery of switching sides" in an ongoing matter,[290] protects confidential information from being jeopardized, and removes any suspicion that a lawyer may have conducted government work in such a way as to acquire future employment. Moreover, public trust in the legal system would be undermined if the lawyer were allowed to play different roles and represent different parties in the same ongoing matter, especially when the earlier role was one with significant public responsibilities.[291] However, the Iowa Supreme Court ruled in *Sorci* that the imputed disqualification to other attorneys in the Youth Law Center had been lifted when the former assistant county attorney later resigned as executive director of the center, although the center was obliged to affirm by

---

[288] Attorney Disciplinary Bd. v. Johnson, 728 N.W.2d 199, 202 (Iowa 2007) (reporting in context of subsequent disciplinary case that the attorney also had appeared at two hearings as guardian ad litem in two separate juvenile cases in which she previously had substantial participation as an assistant county attorney).

[289] *See Sorci*, 671 N.W.2d. at 492–93.

[290] *Id.* at 496. In a contested child welfare case, the position of the state may be adverse to or congruent with the positions taken by the child or the parents. In any event, Rule 1.11 disqualifies the former government lawyer "even in so-called 'congruent interest' situations, where the later representation does not involve opposing the government or 'switching sides.' " *See* 1 GEOFFREY C. HAZARD, JR., W. WILLIAM HODES & PETER R. JARVIS, THE LAW OF LAWYERING § 16.03 (Aspen, 4th ed., 2016). In Sorci, while the positions of the county attorney's office in seeking removal of the children from their homes and that of the center's guardian ad litems in representing children in parental termination cases often (but not invariably) might have been congruent, the facile transfer of the lawyer from representing one party to a discretely different party in the same matter raised an appearance of impropriety and potential distrust by both the public and other participants in the fairness of the legal system.

[291] *Sorci*, 671 N.W.2d at 493–94. The court in *Sorci* declined to accept an offered waiver of the conflict of interest by the Department of Human Services, which the former assistant county attorney regarded as her client. *Id.* at 494. Under Rule 1.11(a), a conflict arising by reason of the lawyer's personal and substantial participation in the matter as a public officer or government employee may be waived by the appropriate government agency. Because the attorney in *Sorci* had been employed as a prosecutor, both the client government agency and the county attorney's office would appear to have been the appropriate government agencies from which consent would have been required. Thus, even if the client agency were to have no objection in such a case, the county attorney's office might have a different view about the propriety of a lawyer's transition from representation of a public entity to a private interest in the same matter (or perhaps the county attorney's office would have granted approval given the nature of guardian ad litem representation as being in the public interest). In any event, when a former government officer or employee has gained confidential government information about a person within the meaning of Rule 1.11(c)—such as knowledge about anonymous reporters of child abuse—no consent to the use of that confidential information is possible and ethical screening of the disqualified lawyer is the only means by which to avoid imputation of the conflict to the entire firm.

affidavit in each case that no confidential government information had been shared by the departing lawyer.[292]

Rule 1.11 establishes the conflict of interest standards for former government officers and employees entering into private practice as a matter of lawyer ethics, which are enforced through professional discipline. The rule of course does not supersede government ethics statutes, often enforced by criminal penalties, that may place similar or additional restraints on the behavior of former government employees.[293] For example, in language that overlaps with but is stricter than Rule 1.11, the federal statute that regulates conflicts of interest for persons who have left federal government service establishes the following limitations, among others: (1) permanently barring representation by a former federal employee in a particular matter involving specific parties in which the United States has a direct and substantial interest and in which the employee participated "personally and substantially;"[294] and (2) placing a two-year restriction on representation by the former federal employee regarding matters that were within the broader scope of the employee's "official responsibility as such officer or employee."[295]

#### *§ 4-7.8(a)(2) Imputed Disqualification in Context of Former Government Officers and Employees*

Under Rule 1.11(b), when a former public officer or government employee is disqualified from representation by reason of a conflict of interest under paragraph (a) (that is, due to having participated personally and substantially in the matter while in public office or employment),[296] then every other lawyer in the law firm is likewise disqualified. Rule 1.11(c) similarly prohibits a law firm with which a former government officer or employee is associated from undertaking or continuing a representation of a client when that representation would be adverse to a person about whom the lawyer obtained confidential government information, if that information could be used to the material disadvantage of that person.

However, the rule allows the law firm to avoid the imputation of disqualification by screening the personally-prohibited former government officer or employee from any participation in the representation. As discussed previously with respect to Rule 1.10 of the Model Rules of Professional Conduct, ethical screening has also been approved in the rules to avoid imputed disqualification in the "migrating lawyer" context.[297] As Comment 4 to Rule 1.11 explains, the special provisions for screening or waiver of the conflict in the context of former public officers and government employees "are necessary to prevent the disqualification rule from imposing too severe a deterrent against entering public service."

Under Rule 1.11(b), when the individual former government officer or employee is disqualified by reason of personal and substantial participation in a matter during public

---

[292] *Sorci*, 671 N.W.2d at 494–97. On removal of imputation upon departure of a personally-prohibited lawyer from a firm, see also *supra* § 4-7.6(b)(3).

[293] On federal ethics regulations of current and former government employees and lawyers, see GREGORY C. SISK, LITIGATION WITH THE FEDERAL GOVERNMENT § 1.03(c) (West Academic Publishing, 2016).

[294] 18 U.S.C. § 207(a)(1).

[295] 18 U.S.C. § 207(a)(2)(B).

[296] *See supra* § 4-7.8(a)(1).

[297] *See supra* § 4-7.6(b)(2).

service, other lawyers in the firm may still undertake or continue the representation only if (1) "the disqualified lawyer is timely screened from any participation in the matter," (2) the disqualified lawyer "is apportioned no part of the fee" from the matter, and (3) "written notice is promptly given to the appropriate government agency to enable it to ascertain compliance with the provisions of this rule."

*First*, in the definitional provision of Rule 1.0(k), ethical screening "denotes the isolation of a lawyer from any participation in a matter through the timely imposition of procedures within a firm that are reasonably adequate under the circumstances to protect information that the isolated lawyer is obligated to protect under these Rules or other law." To be effective, a formal screening process must be set in place as soon as the need is or should be anticipated. A screen that is belatedly cobbled-together as a tardy response to an anticipated motion to disqualify will not pass muster.

*Second*, the disqualified lawyer must not participate in the fee for the legal services in that particular matter. The purpose of this limitation is to deprive the disqualified lawyer of any direct financial stake in the matter that might create an incentive to evade the ethical screen and provide assistance to the other lawyers in the firm that are handling the matter. Comment 6 to Rule 1.11 explains that "[t]hese paragraphs do not prohibit a lawyer from receiving a salary or partnership share established by prior independent agreement, but that lawyer may not receive compensation directly relating the lawyer's compensation to the fee in the matter in which the lawyer is disqualified."

*Third*, as soon as practicable, the law firm must provide notice that an ethical screen has been established to the government agency with which the disqualified lawyer had previously been affiliated so that the agency may determine whether the rule has been complied with and be in a position to raise an objection to the firm's representation or its screening methods. However, while notice must be given to the government agency, the agency's consent to the screening is not required to make the screening effective in dissipating the imputed conflict of interest.

Under Rule 1.11(c), when a lawyer has been disqualified because she possesses confidential government information about a third person who now is adverse to the law firm's client, other lawyers in the firm may undertake or continue the representation if (1) the disqualified lawyer is timely screened, and (2) the disqualified lawyer is apportioned no part of the fee. Because the party in interest in such a case is the person about whom the lawyer has confidential government information, Rule 1.11(c) includes no provision for giving notice to the government agency. Nor does it provide for notice to the third party as to whom the confidential government information pertains. Professors Geoffrey Hazard and William Hodes and attorney Peter Jarvis suggest "[t]he notice requirement was omitted so that the private party would not be tipped off in advance" of the legal action being contemplated against that party.[298] Indeed, because that person may not be aware that the government possesses the information, requiring notice to the third party would violate the duty to protect the government's confidential information. Instead, the rule places the burden of compliance directly on the lawyer and law firm involved (where it always rests in any event), on penalty of professional discipline, not to mention the possible application of other civil and criminal statutes governing protection of confidential government information.

---

[298] 1 GEOFFREY C. HAZARD, JR., W. WILLIAM HODES & PETER R. JARVIS, THE LAW OF LAWYERING § 16.11 (Aspen, 4th ed., 2016).

### *§ 4-7.8(a)(3) Conflict of Interest Standard for Current Government Officers and Employees*

Rule 1.11(d) establishes conflict of interest standards for a lawyer who is currently serving as a government officer or employee. First, the lawyer serving in a public position is obliged to comply with the general conflict of interest standards set forth in Rules 1.7 and 1.9 of the Model Rules of Professional Conduct. Thus, a lawyer in public service may not represent two clients who are directly adverse to each other and may not proceed when there is a significant risk that the lawyer's responsibilities to other or former clients or other persons or to the lawyer's personal interests would materially limit the representation.[299] Second, and likewise, the government lawyer may not represent a government officer or entity adverse to a former client (such as a client represented during a prior period of private practice) in the same or a substantially related matter.[300]

Beyond the general conflict standards, Rule 1.11(d)(2) regulates the behavior of the lawyer as a government employee or public officer in two particular ways designed to ensure that the lawyer is acting in the public interest and is not influenced by private concerns:

***Prior Participation During Nongovernmental Practice:*** The lawyer presently serving in government may not participate in a matter in which he previously had participated personally and substantially while in private practice or nongovernmental employment, unless the government agency gives informed consent, confirmed in writing.

As with the former government officer or employee who enters into private practice,[301] "participation" includes not only legal representation as a government lawyer, but other actions or decisions as a government officer or employee that pertain to a matter involving a specific party or parties. When the lawyer previously had participated in the same matter in prior private practice while representing a private client or working for a private entity, there naturally is a concern that the lawyer may carry forward that private influence and manifest loyalty to a prior client when formulating a public position on or resolution of the matter.

After being informed of the nature of the lawyer's participation while in private practice or nongovernmental employment, including advice from the lawyer regarding any risk of continuing influence from that prior participation, the government agency as a representative of the public interest may waive the objection—which must be confirmed in writing—and thereby permit the lawyer to be involved in the matter.

***Negotiating for Private Employment:*** Rule 1.11(d)(2) generally prohibits the lawyer in public service from negotiating for private employment with any party that is involved in a matter in which that lawyer is participating personally and substantially in a public role. The risk is manifest that the lawyer serving as a government officer or employee will be improperly influenced when seeking to obtain employment with a private person or entity that has an interest in that matter.

The rule contains an exception for a law clerk to a judge, other adjudicative officer, or arbitrator, allowing those assistants to negotiate for private employment as permitted

---

299 *See supra* § 4-7.4(c).

300 *See supra* § 4-7.5.

301 *See supra* § 4-7.8(a)(1).

by and subject to the limitations in Rule 1.12(b) (which requires notification of the judge, adjudicator, or arbitrator).[302]

When a lawyer currently serving as a public officer or government employee is disqualified from participation in a matter under Rule 1.11(d), the conflict is not imputed to other lawyers, officers, or employees within the government agency.[303] However, Comment 2 to Rule 1.11 suggests that "ordinarily it would be prudent to screen such [disqualified] lawyers."

### § 4-7.8(b) Special Conflict Rules for Former and Current Judges, Law Clerks, Arbitrators, Mediators, and Third-Party Neutrals

#### *§ 4-7.8(b)(1) Conflict of Interest Rules for Former Judges, Law Clerks, Arbitrators, Mediators, and Third-Party Neutrals*

Rule 1.12 of the Model Rules of Professional Conduct largely corresponds with Rule 1.11 and essentially extends to former and present judges and quasi-judicial officers the same conflict of interest standards that apply to former public officers and government employees under Rule 1.11.[304] The purpose of these standards is to ensure that judicial and quasi-judicial officers exercise their authority with faithful attention to the public interest and not to curry favor with those who may offer future employment or subsequent remunerative retention.

Under Rule 1.12(a), a lawyer is forbidden to represent a client "in connection with a matter in which the lawyer participated personally and substantially as a judge or other adjudicative officer or law clerk to such a person or as an arbitrator, mediator or other third-party neutral, unless all parties to the proceeding give informed consent, confirmed in writing." The rule applies not only to those who render a decision on the merits of a dispute—specifically judges, other adjudicative officers (including administrative law judges, magistrates, and special masters), and arbitrators—but also to mediators and other third-party neutrals (such as settlement commissioners associated with a court) who facilitate the voluntary resolution of disputes by the parties.[305]

Rule 1.12(d) creates an exception for "[a]n arbitrator selected as a partisan of a party in a multimember arbitration panel," who is not prohibited from subsequently representing the party on whose behalf he or she was selected as a partisan arbitration panel member.

As with the parallel provision in Rule 1.11 for former public officers and government employees,[306] the disqualification under Rule 1.12(a) attaches only when the lawyer participated "personally," that is, directly in the matter while serving in a judicial or quasi-judicial capacity. As Comment 1 to Rule 1.12 explains, if a judge was a member of

---

302 *See infra* § 4-7.8(b)(2).

303 *See* People v. Shari, 204 P.3d 453, 459 (Colo. 2009) ("[A] government attorney's individual conflicts are not imputed to the entire government agency for which he works.").

304 *See supra* § 4-7.8(a).

305 *See* RONALD D. ROTUNDA & JOHN S. DZIENKOWSKI, PROFESSIONAL RESPONSIBILITY: A STUDENT'S GUIDE § 1.12–1(c) (American Bar Ass'n, 2013–2014) (explaining revisions by the American Bar Association of Model Rule 1.12 to include mediators and third-party neutrals).

306 *See supra* § 4-7.8(a)(1).

a multi-member court, the mere fact that the matter was pending before another judge does not disqualify the former judge. Moreover, the lawyer's former participation as a judge, adjudicative officer, arbitrator, or mediator in the matter must have been "substantial," something beyond remote awareness or incidental administrative responsibilities that did not affect the merits. However, it is not necessary that the former judge have presided over the final disposition of the matter to be disqualified. For example, a judge who presides over a criminal defendant's initial appearance, explaining the defendant's rights and making a probable cause determination, has exercised substantial responsibility for the matter and thereafter is disqualified from representing anyone in that matter. However, the disqualification may be removed if all of the parties in the proceeding, after being informed of all pertinent aspects of the lawyer's prior involvement and anticipated representation, give their informed consent (confirmed in writing).

When a former judicial officer, law clerk, arbitrator, mediator, or other third-party neutral officer is disqualified from representation under Rule 1.12(a), then every other lawyer in the law firm is likewise disqualified. However, under Rule 1.12(c), other lawyers in the firm may undertake or continue the representation if (1) "the disqualified lawyer is timely screened from any participation in the matter," (2) the disqualified lawyer "is apportioned no part of the fee" from the matter, and (3) "written notice is promptly given to the parties and any appropriate tribunal to enable them to ascertain compliance with the provisions of this rule."[307]

### *§ 4-7.8(b)(2) Conflict of Interest Rules for Current Judges, Law Clerks, Arbitrators, Mediators, and Third-Party Neutrals*

While the conduct of present judicial officers is primarily governed by the Model Code of Judicial Conduct,[308] Rule 1.12 of the Model Rules of Professional Conduct extends the limitation on negotiating for future employment[309] to current judges and adjudicative officers, as well as to arbitrators, mediators, and other third-party neutrals. Rule 1.12(b) precludes a lawyer from negotiating for employment with "any person who is involved as a party or as lawyer for a party in a matter in which the lawyer is participating personally and substantially as a judge or other adjudicative officer or as an arbitrator, mediator or other third-party neutral."

No provision is made for consent by any party, presumably because the conflict of interest involved by a judge or quasi-judicial officer in negotiating for employment with a party or lawyer in the very matter presently being adjudicated or evaluated is so manifest that it simply would be impossible to maintain any independence of judgment in such a situation and because the injury to the public perception of the integrity of the judicial process would be too severe.

The ban on negotiating for future employment with a party or lawyer involved in a matter in which the judge or quasi-judicial officer participated is lifted upon the conclusion of the matter. At that point the judge, arbitrator, or mediator no longer has any power to exercise any discretion in favor of that party or lawyer.[310]

---

[307] *See supra* § 4-7.8(a)(2).

[308] *See infra* Charles Geyh, Judicial Ethics and the Conduct of Judges, Part Six of this book.

[309] *See supra* § 4-7.8(a)(3).

[310] *See* 1 GEOFFREY C. HAZARD, JR., W. WILLIAM HODES & PETER R. JARVIS, THE LAW OF LAWYERING § 17.07 (Aspen, 4th ed., 2016).

By contrast with the strict prohibition that applies to judges and other quasi-judicial officers, Rule 1.12(b) permits "[a] lawyer serving as a law clerk to a judge or other adjudicative officer [to] negotiate for employment with a party or lawyer involved in a matter in which the law clerk is participating personally and substantially, but only after the law clerk has notified the judge or other adjudicative officer." Because the law clerk is not the primary decisionmaker, his influence on the outcome of the matter is somewhat attenuated. More importantly, when properly notified, the judge or other adjudicative officer for whom the law clerk is working may exercise the necessary supervision to prevent any corruption of the judicial process.

Rule 1.12(b) by its terms requires only that a law clerk notify the judge or adjudicative officer that he is negotiating for employment with a party or lawyer involved in a matter in which the clerk is participating, not that the law clerk obtain the permission of that judge or adjudicative officer. Nonetheless, the judge or adjudicative officer, in her capacity as employer of the law clerk, has the power to instruct the law clerk to refrain from further negotiations or direct that the law clerk be removed from further involvement with the pertinent matter. The judge may also permit the law clerk to proceed, while thereafter regarding the law clerk's assistance in the matter with appropriate skepticism and conducting more careful independent review.

## § 4-7.9 MAINTAINING PROFESSIONAL INDEPENDENCE

### § 4-7.9(a) Avoiding Financial Entanglements with Nonlawyers

The legal profession traditionally has been extremely wary of financial arrangements with nonlawyers—specifically the sharing of fees generated by the practice of law[311] and the formation of a law practice in which nonlawyers have an ownership or managerial role[312]—apprehending such relationships as likely to undermine the professional independence of the lawyer. Moreover, as Professors Ronald Rotunda and John Dzienkowski explain, "[b]ecause the Rules do not apply to nonlawyers . . ., the bar would have a difficult time regulating the legal profession if nonlawyers working outside of law firms had an incentive to profit from the practice of law."[313]

When a nonlawyer obtains a financial stake in the professional services offered by the lawyer, the nonlawyer may solicit or refer clients, interfere in the lawyer's relationship with clients, or attempt to influence the professional conduct of the lawyer. Not only may such a financial entanglement with a layperson create a conflict of interest for the lawyer, but the layperson's activities designed to enhance the shared profits of the lawyer may transgress other ethical norms of the profession, such as limits on solicitation or the unauthorized practice of law.

A lawyer who practices law in a setting where she is subordinate to or must share managerial authority with a layperson thereby may become subject to the regulation or control of a person who is not bound by the ethical standards of the profession. The lawyer's independent exercise of professional judgment may be compromised by entering

---

[311] *See infra* § 4-7.9(b).

[312] *See infra* § 4-7.9(c).

[313] RONALD D. ROTUNDA & JOHN S. DZIENKOWSKI, PROFESSIONAL RESPONSIBILITY: A STUDENT'S GUIDE § 5.4–1(a) (American Bar Ass'n, 2013–2014) (addressing the purpose behind the prohibition on sharing fees with laypersons).

into a partnership with nonlawyers or practicing law through a corporation or other association in which nonlawyers are owners, shareholders, directors, or officers.

### § 4-7.9(b) The Prohibition on Sharing Legal Fees with Nonlawyers

#### *§ 4-7.9(b)(1) The General Rules Prohibiting Sharing Legal Fees with Nonlawyers*

One of the longstanding rules of legal practice is that a lawyer may not share any legal fee or any part of a legal fee with a nonlawyer, with very limited exceptions. Rule 5.4(a) of the Model Rules of Professional Conduct states simply and directly that "[a] lawyer or law firm shall not share legal fees with a nonlawyer" (subject to four specified exceptions). As stated in Comment 1 to Rule 5.4, this limitation is intended "to protect the lawyer's professional independence of judgment."

If the lawyer in the course of providing legal services becomes financially dependent on or entangled with a person who is not subject to the ethical rules of the legal profession, the incentives for both to enhance the profit-sharing operations of the law practice may encourage unscrupulous behavior by one or the other or result in disruption of the intimate and confidential attorney-client relationship. A layperson who expects to receive a share of the lawyer's fees (in the nature of a finder's fee) might solicit clients for the lawyer in inappropriate ways. A nonlawyer who enters into a joint venture with a lawyer—providing for the splitting of legal fees—might have an incentive to engage in the unauthorized practice of law by providing inexpert legal advice to clients before referring them to the lawyer. Thus, for example, if a lawyer entered into a fee-splitting arrangement with an accountant, under which each would be paid on the basis of time devoted to the client's problem, the accountant might seek to increase his share of the fee by spending additional time to provide advice that extends beyond financial matters and into the legal realm that appropriately belongs to the licensed lawyer.

The rule prohibiting sharing fees with nonlawyers also serves to protect the client's expectation that the professional relationship is solely with the lawyer and that no undisclosed third persons will have a stake in the matter or will participate in the representation.

In Rule 5.4, there are four exceptions to this proscription on sharing legal fees with laypersons: (1) for payment of death benefits to a lawyer's estate or survivors,[314] (2) for payment of the purchase price for a law practice to a lawyer's estate or representatives,[315] (3) for a compensation or retirement plan for nonlawyer employees,[316] and (4) to share court-awarded legal fees with a nonprofit organization that had employed, retained, or recommended employment of the lawyer in the matter.[317]

#### *§ 4-7.9(b)(2) The Exception for Payments by a Firm to Estate or Survivors of a Deceased Lawyer*

As the first exception to the proscription on sharing fees with nonlawyers, under Model Rule 5.4(a)(1, "an agreement by a lawyer with the lawyer's firm, partner, or

[314] *See infra* § 4-7.9(b)(2).

[315] *See infra* § 4-7.9(b)(3).

[316] *See infra* § 4-7.9(b)(4).

[317] *See infra* § 4-7.9(b)(5).

associate may provide for the payment of money, over a reasonable period of time after the lawyer's death, to the lawyer's estate or to one or more specified persons."

Under this exception, the law firm or the lawyer's partners or associates may pay a death benefit to the deceased lawyer's estate or survivors, continue to pay retirement benefits in the nature of a death benefit, or buy out the deceased lawyer's equity interest in the firm (that is, effectively purchasing the deceased lawyer's share of the practice).

#### *§ 4-7.9(b)(3) The Exception for Payment of the Purchase Price of Sale of a Practice of a Deceased Lawyer*

As a second exception to the bar on splitting of legal fees with nonlawyers, under Rule 5.4(a)(2), "a lawyer who purchases the practice of a deceased, disabled, or disappeared lawyer may, pursuant to the provisions of Rule 1.17, pay to the estate or other representative of that lawyer the agreed-upon purchase price."

Rule 1.17 of the Model Rules of Professional Conduct permits the sale of a law practice, the purchase price for which may be paid to the estate or nonlawyer representatives in the case of a deceased, missing, or disabled lawyer.[318]

#### *§ 4-7.9(b)(4) The Exception for a Compensation or Retirement Plan for Nonlawyer Employees*

As a third exception to the bar on a lawyer splitting fees with a nonlawyer, under Rule 5.4(a)(3), "a lawyer or law firm may include nonlawyer employees in a compensation or retirement plan, even though the plan is based in whole or in part on a profit-sharing arrangement." Because employees within the law office are subject to the direct supervisory control of the lawyer,[319] and because a profit-sharing arrangement is based on the overall business performance of the office rather than linked to specific fees attributable to a particular client matter, the risks inherent in the sharing of legal fees with laypersons are substantially mitigated in this particular context.

The general prohibition on sharing legal fees with nonlawyers does indeed apply to lay employees within the office, just as it does to outside persons. Still, a lawyer of course may compensate nonlawyer assistants, even though the funds to pay those employees are earned by the lawyer through the practice of law. That an employee is paid from the general revenues of the law office is no more an example of fee-sharing than is the purchase of office supplies from a merchant simply because the funds used for that purchase also came generally from the fees collected for legal services. Nor is a lawyer prevented from paying a bonus to a nonlawyer employee based upon quality of performance or time committed to work.

In addition, because of the express exception to the rule in Rule 5.4(a)(3), a lawyer also may extend a retirement plan or an incentive compensation system to nonlawyer employees that is measured in whole or in part as a share of overall profits for the law office during a set period of time. However, a lawyer may not enter into an arrangement whereby a nonlawyer, whether employed by the lawyer or not, would receive a portion

---

[318] *See supra* § 4-3.7. On whether provision for payment of the purchase price by a share of future profits of the practice violates the rule prohibiting sharing of legal fees with nonlawyers, see *supra* § 4-3.7(c).

[319] On the lawyer's responsibilities to take appropriate steps to ensure compliance with ethical standards by nonlawyer assistants, see *infra* § 4-12.4.

of the specific legal fees earned in a particular matter,[320] because that would improperly grant a layperson a direct stake in an individual client matter.

### *§ 4-7.9(b)(5) The Exception for Sharing Court-Awarded Fees with Nonprofit Organizations*

Under Rule 5.4(a)(4) of the Model Rules of Professional Conduct, as revised in 2002, "a lawyer may share court-awarded legal fees with a nonprofit organization that employed, retained, or recommended employment of the lawyer in the matter."

This subject has received substantial attention in recent years because of the "exponential increase in attorney's fee shifting statutes"[321]—that is, the shifting of legal fees from the prevailing party to the losing party in litigation[322]—and the increased participation of nonprofit organizations in pursuing public interest litigation for which court awards of attorney's fees have become an important source of funding. In many jurisdictions, attorneys who are employed by or take referrals from public interest organizations are expected to or even contractually obliged to turn over any fees the lawyers are awarded to the organization.

Drawing upon decisions upholding the constitutional right of civil rights lawyers and lawyers associated with other ideological organizations to seek clients for public interest litigation outside the constraints of state anti-solicitation rules,[323] some have argued that the First Amendment of the United States Constitution extends protection "for financial arrangements between lawyers and public interest organizations whenever those arrangements are integral to an organization's purposes."[324]

While the Supreme Court has not directly addressed the constitutional validity of the no-fee-sharing rule as applied to public interest organizations, the Court in *In re Primus*[325] held that an attorney could not be disciplined for soliciting clients for public interest litigation and further observed that she had no pecuniary motive in doing so because any fee award would have gone directly to "the central fund" of the American Civil Liberties Union. The *Primus* Court emphasized:

> [I]n a case of this kind there are differences between counsel fees awarded by a court and traditional fee-paying arrangements which militate against a presumption that ACLU sponsorship of litigation is motivated by considerations of pecuniary gain rather than by its widely recognized goal of vindicating civil liberties. Counsel fees are awarded in the discretion of the

---

[320] *See, e.g.*, Trotter v. Nelson, 684 N.E.2d 1150, 1155 (Ind. 1997) (for purposes of the exception to the rule barring sharing of legal fees with nonlawyers, "a profit-sharing plan with a nonlawyer may not be tied to the receipt of a particular legal fee"), *overruled on other grounds*, Liggett v. Young, 877 N.E.2d 178 (Ind. 2007); Matter of Anonymous Member of South Carolina Bar, 367 S.E.2d 17, 28 (S.C. 1988) (when the "method of computing the bonus compensation payments was dependent upon the attorney fees awarded in specific cases processed," the payments did not constitute a permissible profit-sharing compensation plan for law firm employees); *see also* ABA Comm. on Ethics & Prof'l Responsibility, Informal Op. 1440 (1979) (saying that an attorney may fashion a profit-sharing plan for his nonlawyer employees so long as the measure of compensation "relates to the net profits and business performance of the firm, and not to the receipt of particular fees").

[321] GREGORY C. SISK, LITIGATION WITH THE FEDERAL GOVERNMENT 444 (West Academic Publishing, 2016).

[322] Roy D. Simon, Jr., *Fee Sharing Between Lawyers and Public Interest Groups*, 98 YALE L.J. 1069, 1070–71 (1989).

[323] *See supra* § 4-2.5(d).

[324] Simon, *supra*, 98 YALE L.J. at 1121.

[325] 436 U.S. 412, 430–31 & n.24 (1978).

court; awards are not drawn from the plaintiff's recovery, and are usually premised on a successful outcome; and the amounts awarded often may not correspond to fees generally obtainable in private litigation. . . . Although such benefit to the organization may increase with the maintenance of successful litigation, the same situation obtains with voluntary contributions and foundation support, which also may rise with ACLU victories in important areas of the law. That possibility, standing alone, offers no basis for equating the work of lawyers associated with the ACLU or the NAACP with that of a group that exists for the primary purpose of financial gain through the recovery of counsel fees.[326]

Moreover, without directly addressing the fee-sharing question, the Supreme Court and other federal courts regularly have awarded attorney's fees directly to nonprofit organizations for legal services performed by staff attorneys.[327] At least one court has found such fee-sharing to be constitutionally-protected. A federal district court in Missouri issued a permanent injunction enjoining application of the fee-sharing bar in that state to prevent an affiliate of the American Civil Liberties Union from requiring that staff attorneys turn over court-awarded fees to the organization.[328]

Responding to these developments, the American Bar Association's Committee on Ethics and Professional Responsibility issued a formal opinion in 1993 stating that "[i]t is not ethically improper for a lawyer who undertakes a pro bono litigation representation at the request of a non-profit organization that sponsors such pro bono litigation to share, or agree in advance to share, with the organization court-awarded fees resulting from the representation."[329] A majority of the committee concluded that precluding sharing of court-awarded fees with nonprofit organizations was not necessary to accomplish the purposes underlying the rule prohibiting sharing fees with nonlawyers because (1) the entity involved is a nonprofit organization and thus has no economic incentive to interfere in the lawyer's relationship with a client, (2) the fees are court-awarded from the opposing party, thus eliminating any risk that the client will be burdened with excessive fees, and (3) the fees awarded are the result of successful pursuit of litigation that is recognized as serving a public purpose. One member of the ABA committee dissented, arguing that this exception contravened the plain language prohibiting a lawyer from sharing legal fees with a nonlawyer then found in Model Rule 5.4 (which at that time included no express exception for non-profit organizations) and further questioning the conclusion "that lawyers working for or with not-for-profit organizations are inherently less likely to be pressured by lay parties for whom they work, and that not-for-profit organizations do not pose the same threats as others in fee-sharing arrangements."[330]

---

[326] *Id.* at 430–31.

[327] *See, e.g.*, Blum v. Stenson, 465 U.S. 886, 891–95 (1984) (holding that an award of attorney's fees to a nonprofit legal services organization should be measured by prevailing market rates); McLean v. Arkansas Bd. of Educ., 723 F.2d 45, 47 (8th Cir. 1983).

[328] Susman v. Missouri, No. 91-4429-CV-C-5 (W.D. Mo. June 1, 1992) (effectively overturning American Civil Liberties Union/Eastern Missouri Fund v. Miller, 803 S.W.2d 592 (Mo. 1991)).

[329] ABA Comm. on Ethics and Prof'l Responsibility, Formal Op. 93–374 (1993). On developments in the Model Rules with respect to this issue, see generally RONALD D. ROTUNDA & JOHN S. DZIENKOWSKI, PROFESSIONAL RESPONSIBILITY: A STUDENT'S GUIDE § 5.4–1(e) (American Bar Ass'n, 2013–2014).

[330] ABA Comm. on Ethics and Prof'l Responsibility, Formal Op. 93–374 (1993) (dissent).

Subsequently, in the revisions to the Model Rules of Professional Conduct that were proposed as part of the "Ethics 2000" project, the American Bar Association in 2002 adopted new language in paragraph (a)(4) of Model Rule 5.4 that expressly permits sharing court-awarded attorney's fees with a nonprofit organization. The Commission on Evaluation of the Rules of Professional Conduct (the "Ethics 2000 Commission") concluded that "the threat to independent professional judgment is less here than in circumstances where a for-profit organization is involved."[331]

However, of the 47 states and the District of Columbia that have conducted a review of ethics rules following the Ethics 2000 revision of the Model Rules and as of 2016, fourteen have chosen not to add paragraph (a)(4) of Model Rule 5.4.[332]

As an example that arose prior to the Ethics 2000 revision of the Model Rules, the Rhode Island Supreme Court rejected a specific invitation to approve a similar exception and issued an opinion explaining why it had declined the request. The court reasoned that if a nonprofit organization were to receive any part of a fee or enter into an agreement to share in the legal fees earned by an attorney, that organization would be engaged in the unauthorized practice of law.[333] The court also expressed its "concern[ ] that the proposed rule changes could encourage the scurrilous practice of ambulance chasing by enterprising individuals masquerading as public-need-nonprofit corporations."[334] Such counterfeit public interest groups then could negotiate with lawyers to represent litigants and engage whomever would share the highest portion of any later-received fee award with the nonprofit corporation.

The court also rejected the argument that the no-fee-sharing rule impaired the First Amendment rights of cooperating attorneys who volunteer their services to a nonprofit organization. The Rhode Island Supreme Court noted that "any pro bono attorney whose efforts have resulted in a court-awarded counsel fee can, if he or she wishes, make a voluntary financial donation" to a nonprofit organization, even though that fee may not be exacted from the lawyer pursuant to a prior fee-sharing agreement.[335]

Subsequently, the United States District Court for the District of Rhode Island held that the state's prohibition on fee-sharing with lawyers was preempted by federal civil rights laws as applied to a non-profit organization (the American Civil Liberties Union), because it would "frustrate" one of the purposes of the federal statutes in "attracting competent counsel to pursue civil rights litigation on behalf of indigent people."[336] The federal court suggested that the bar on sharing court-awarded fees with a non-profit organization that pursued civil rights litigation might also violate the free speech protections of the First Amendment, but found it unnecessary to resolve that question

[331] American Bar Association, Ethics 2000 Commission Final Report, Reporter's Explanation Memo, Rule 5.4 (2002).

[332] *See* American Bar Association, Center for Professional Responsibility, Charts Comparing Individual Professional Conduct Model Rules as Adopted or Proposed by States to ABA Model Rules, Rule 5.4, available at http://www.americanbar.org/content/dam/aba/administrative/professional_responsibility/mrpc_5_4.pdf. These fourteen states are Alabama, Connecticut, Georgia, Indiana, Iowa, Kentucky, Louisiana, Mississippi, South Carolina, Texas, Utah, Virginia, Washington, and Wyoming. Oklahoma did not adopt paragraph (a)(4) but added the same concept into a comment.

[333] In re Rule Amendments, 815 A.2d 47, 49–53 (R.I. 2002).

[334] *Id.* at 50.

[335] *Id.* at 51.

[336] Inmates of The Rhode Island Training School v. Martinez, 465 F. Supp. 2d 131, 141 (D.R.I. 2006) (interpreting 42 U.S.C. §§ 1983, 1988).

given the court's conclusion that federal law preempted application of the rule in that case.

The Rhode Island Supreme Court then revised the rules to permit sharing of a fee award with a referring non-profit and tax-exempt organization if the proceeding advanced one of the purposes for which the organization is tax-exempt and the fee sharing is approved by the tribunal.[337]

### § 4-7.9(c) The Bar on Practicing Law with Nonlawyers

#### *§ 4-7.9(c)(1) The Traditional (and Persisting) Bar on Practicing in a Partnership or Through Other Business Associations Including Control by Nonlawyers*

Elsewhere in the world, legal services by lawyers are offered in a variety of multidisciplinary practice forms, with major accounting firms playing a substantial role in the legal market.[338] Advocates for alternative structures of law firms, including shared control, partnership, and investment by nonlawyers, contend that more flexibility would enhance access to justice by more people, facilitate easier access by firms to available funding, strengthen the delivery of services by integration with other professional services, and thereby provide more cost-effective and higher quality services.[339]

When the question is raised whether an American lawyer may practice law in partnership with a nonlawyer or through a corporate entity or other business organization in which a layperson is an owner or director, the traditional answer and the prevailing answer in nearly every state today is emphatically "no." Under Rule 5.4(b) and (d) of the Model Rules of Professional Conduct, a lawyer may not practice law in any arrangement under which a layperson holds a position of authority or control so as to intrude into the lawyer's relationship with a client or to control or direct the lawyer's exercise of professional judgment.

Rule 5.4(b) states that a lawyer may not "form a partnership with a nonlawyer if any of the activities of the partnership consist of the practice of law." Rule 5.4(d) prohibits the lawyer from practicing through "a professional corporation or association authorized to practice law for a profit" if (1) "a nonlawyer owns any interest" in the entity, other than the temporary ownership of an interest by the fiduciary representative of a lawyer's estate; (2) "a nonlawyer is a corporate director or officer" or holds a similar position in another association; or (3) "a nonlawyer has the right to direct or control the professional judgment of a lawyer."

Rule 5.4(d) applies only to corporations or associations that "practice law for a profit." Thus, a lawyer may practice law through a public agency or through a non-profit association in which nonlawyers participate as officials, directors, or officers in

---

[337] R.I. RULES OF PROF'L CONDUCT R. 5.4(a)(4).

[338] Center for the Study of the Legal Profession, Georgetown Law, 2015 Report on the State of the Legal Market 11 (2015), at http://www.law.georgetown.edu/academics/centers-institutes/legal-profession/upload/FINAL-Report-1-7-15.pdf.

[339] *See* ABA Comm'n on the Future of Legal Services, Issues Paper Regarding Alternative Business Structures at 7–9 (Apr. 8, 2016). For further discussion of the trend among business organizations toward alternative legal services providers, see also Part One of this book, William D. Henderson, The Legal Profession and Legal Services: Nature and Evolution, §§ 1-1.3, 1-2.1(b), 1-3.1(b).

determining how legal services will be provided to or on behalf of members of the public or beneficiaries under the public interest mission of the non-profit association.

In the overwhelming majority of states, a lawyer in the private practice of law may not be placed in a practice setting where a person without legal training and a law license, and who thus is not accountable under the ethics standards of the legal profession, possesses the power to determine how legal services will be marketed and offered, how a lawyer will interact with a client, what advice a lawyer may give to a client, how legal services will be billed, etc.

The District of Columbia is often cited as an exception because it does permit a nonlawyer professional to have a financial interest or exercise managerial authority in a law firm. But the D.C. rule does not allow the law firm to offer nonlegal professional services other than to assist in the delivery of legal services and further demands the nonlawyer participants to be actively involved in the firm, thereby precluding outside passive investment in a law firm by nonlawyers.[340]

While the American Bar Association's Ethics 20/20 Commission circulated a discussion draft in 2011 of possible revisions to Rule 5.4 of the Model Rules of Professional Conduct similar to the D.C. rule (with the addition of a percentage cap on nonlawyer participants so as to maintain lawyer control),[341] the Commission ultimately decided not to move forward with the proposal.[342] When the subsequent ABA Commission on the Future of Legal Services started to open the door again, it was quickly closed shut in 2016 as opposition emerged.[343] Indeed, earlier in 2016, the American Bar Association's House of Delegates adopted a resolution on regulatory objectives for legal services that reaffirmed "existing ABA policy prohibiting non lawyer ownership of law firms."[344]

In sum, the so-called "Multidisciplinary Practice of Law," in which lawyers and professionals in other disciplines would join together as equal partners or their equivalents in a combined practice organization, remains unauthorized in the United States.[345]

### *§ 4-7.9(c)(2) Employing Other Professionals and Assistants*

A lawyer may employ another professional, such as a certified public accountant or a medical practitioner, to serve as part of the legal team, but only when that person remains a subordinate of the lawyer and is not placed into either a superior or co-equal

---

[340] D.C. RULES OF PROF'L CONDUCT R. 5.4(b) & cmts. 7 to 8; *see also* Jacoby & Meyers, LLP v. Presiding Justices, 852 F.3d 178, 182 (2d Cir. 2017) (ruling that New York regulations prohibiting outside investment by non-lawyers in a law firm "are adequately supported by state interests and have too little effect on the attorney-client relationship" to offend First Amendment constitutional rights).

[341] ABA Comm'n on Ethics 20/20, Discussion Paper on Alternative Law Practice Structures (Dec. 2, 2011).

[342] ABA Comm'n on the Future of Legal Services, Issues Paper Regarding Alternative Business Structures at 2 (Apr. 8, 2016).

[343] Samson Habte, ABA Futures Report Calls For Change, Draws Critics, 32 LAW. MAN. PROF. CONDUCT 521 (2016).

[344] American Bar Ass'n, Resolution 105, ABA Model Regulatory Objectives for the Provision of Legal Services (Feb. 2016).

[345] On the history of the ethics rules precluding nonlawyer ownership in law practice firms, the prevalence of such structures in other countries, and the arguments for and against approval of multidisciplinary practice, see generally Louise Lark Hill, *The Preclusion of Nonlawyer Ownership of Law Firms: Protecting the Interest of Clients or Protecting the Interest of Lawyers?*, 42 CAP. U. L. REV. 907 (2014).

position of authority, such as a partner, shareholder, or co-director of a law firm. Likewise, a lawyer may hire a nonlawyer as an office administrator to whom certain managerial responsibilities are delegated, as long as that person remains subject to the ultimate control of the lawyers in the firm and is properly trained and supervised to ensure compliance with ethical expectations.[346]

#### *§ 4-7.9(c)(3) Lawyer Employed by Client as House Counsel*

A lawyer may be hired as an employee of a client, thus taking on the role of "house counsel." Although the nonlawyer employer obviously has substantial authority over the lawyer-employee,[347] that authority is being exercised by the client rather than by another layperson who interposes herself as an intermediary between a lawyer and client. The proscription on practicing law in a business form in which laypersons hold such positions as partners, owners, or directors is designed to prevent interference by a layperson with the attorney-client relationship, a concern that is not present when the lawyer practices law as a direct employee of the client. While the house counsel appropriately takes certain directions from the employer-client, the lawyer remains responsible to comply with the ethical expectations of the profession and, under Rule 1.13, the lawyer has certain responsibilities to the entity by which the lawyer is employed that call for the exercise of independent professional judgment.[348]

### § 4-7.9(d) The Prohibition on Restricting Right to Practice

#### *§ 4-7.9(d)(1) The General Prohibition on Law Firm Agreements Restricting the Right to Practice and the Exception for Retirement Benefits*

***The General Prohibition on Practice Restrictions:*** Under Rule 5.6(a) of the Model Rules of Professional Conduct, "[a] lawyer shall not participate in offering or making . . . a partnership, shareholders, operating, employment, or other similar type of agreement that restricts the right of a lawyer to practice after termination of the relationship, except an agreement concerning benefits upon retirement." When a lawyer departs from a law firm or similar association, the lawyer may not be constrained by a non-competition agreement that either would prevent the lawyer from continuing to practice in the geographic area or would preclude the lawyer from accepting retention by former clients of the firm.

As Comment 1 to Rule 5.6 explains, "[a]greements restricting the right of lawyers to practice after leaving a firm not only limits their professional autonomy but also limits the freedom of clients to choose a lawyer." Professors Geoffrey Hazard and William Hodes and attorney Peter Jarvis likewise describe the rule as "designed to protect present and potential clients from a diminution of their ability to choose counsel" and "to protect both individual lawyers and clients from illegitimate anticompetitive practices that will distort the market and ultimately drive up the price of legal services."[349] The

---

[346] On the managerial or supervisory lawyer's responsibilities for nonlawyer assistances, see *infra* § 4-12.4.

[347] On the termination of the in-house counsel by the client-employer, see *supra* § 4-3.6(b)(2).

[348] *See infra* ch. 4-8.

[349] 2 GEOFFREY C. HAZARD, JR., W. WILLIAM HODES & PETER R. JARVIS, THE LAW OF LAWYERING § 50.02 (Aspen, 4th ed., 2016); *see also* Neil W. Hamilton, *Are We a Profession or Merely a Business? The Erosion of Rule 5.6 and the Bar Against Restrictions on the Right to Practice*, 22 WM. MITCHELL L. REV. 1409, 1413 (1996) (saying that "the history of the rule reveals that its purpose is to ensure the freedom of clients to select counsel of their choice").

rule applies not only to a practice-restriction covenant in a law firm partnership or other organizational agreement but also to any employment contract by any employer in which the lawyer would be forced to accept a condition on subsequent law practice.

Critics point out that law firms typically make substantial investments in the training, development, and marketing of firm lawyers, who thereby receive considerable benefits from affiliation with the firm, but the rule strictly prohibiting non-competition measures leaves law firms "unable to protect themselves from the loss of assets that they help create."[350] If law firms instead were able to impose reasonable financial penalties on departing lawyers who would compete with the firm, the firms could "preserve firm-specific capital" and resist market pressures to promote professionalism values, notably "a cooperative law firm culture."[351] Professor Milton Regan contends that reasonable "competition penalties can help firms achieve economic success that makes possible the promotion of a firm culture that reconciles the different values of professionalism."[352]

Unless and until changed, however, the rule plainly bars such restrictions and leaves little wiggle room. As one longtime ethics practitioner writes:

> Law firm partners are sometimes determined to prevent lawyers who leave the firm from "poaching" the firm's clients. Defendants are sometimes determined that they will never have to face plaintiff's counsel again. When told that the Rules thwart these desires, partners and defendants will sometimes insist, "Be creative, find a way around these Rules!" Lawyers should realize that the opportunities for creative bypasses of Rule 5.6 are few and the opportunities for discipline and unenforceable contracts are many.[353]

By the text of Rule 5.6(a) and by a reference in a comment, there are two exceptions to this general prohibition on non-competition agreements:

***Retirement Benefit Restrictions:*** Under Rule 5.6(a), an agreement "concerning benefits upon retirement" may include a covenant restricting practice. Thus, as a condition to continuing receipt of retirement benefits paid by the law firm, the retiring lawyer may be obliged to remain in retirement or at least not return to the practice of law in competition with the firm paying the ongoing benefits. A comment to the *Restatement of the Law Governing Lawyers*, which also bars law firm agreements restricting the right to practice, says that the exception for retirement benefits "is supportable because it only minimally interferes with the ability of clients to choose counsel freely, given the lawyer's intent to retire from practice."[354]

Retirement benefits must be distinguished from "other payments made to departing lawyers that represent their interest in the firm's capital account or in uncollected or undistributed earned income."[355] Thus, for example, a firm may not suspend payments to buy-out a departing partner's interest or other compensation because he enters into a

---

[350] Milton C. Regan, Jr., *Law Firms, Competition Penalties, and the Values of Professionalism*, 13 GEO. J. LEGAL ETHICS 1, 3 (1999).

[351] *Id.* at 4, 62.

[352] *Id.* at 73.

[353] WILLIAM J. WERNZ, MINNESOTA LEGAL ETHICS 1085 (Minn. St. Bar Ass'n, 6th ed., 2016).

[354] RESTATEMENT (THIRD) OF THE LAW GOVERNING LAWYERS § 13, cmt. b (American Law Institute, 2000).

[355] Donnelly v. Brown, Winick, Graves, Gross, Baskerville, Schoenebaum & Walker, 599 N.W.2d 677, 683 (Iowa 1999) (Ternus, J., concurring specially).

competing practice[356] or insist on payment to the firm of any fees earned from clients taken by a departing lawyer.[357] A law firm may neither directly enforce a non-competition covenant against a withdrawing lawyer nor indirectly restrict the practice of law by imposing a monetary penalty upon a departing lawyer who establishes a competing practice or represents former firm clients.

A law firm might try to evade the prohibition on practice-restrictive covenants by formulating a variety of forms of future payments as retirement benefits, when in reality they are payments for a lawyer's equity share, deferred compensation, or other earned but not yet distributed amounts. A bona fide retirement plan has been defined as " 'a systematic arrangement established by an employer for guaranteeing an income to employees upon retirement according to definitely established rules with or without employee contributions but usu[ally] funded.' "[358]

Professor Robert Hillman focuses on whether the purpose of the plan is to fund a lawyer's retirement, as evidenced by the existence of minimum age and service requirements, separate provisions addressing withdrawal of the lawyer for purposes of retirement and withdrawal for other purposes, and provision for payments over an extended period.[359] If the payments truly are retirement benefits, their continued payment by the law firm may be conditioned on any restriction of whatever scope on the future practice of the lawyer receiving them.

***Restriction on Sale of Practice:*** Comment 3 to Rule 5.6 states that the rule does not apply to "restrictions that may be included in the terms of the sale of a law practice pursuant to Rule 1.17." Given that the sale of a law practice includes a transfer of the selling lawyer's good will to the buying lawyer, if the selling lawyer were to resume practice in the same geographic or practice area, the benefit of the bargain would be denied to the buying lawyer. Moreover, one of the foundational premises for the sale of a law practice under Rule 1.17 is that the selling lawyer is ceasing to engage in the private practice of law at least in that practice area and that geographic area or jurisdiction,[360] such that a restrictive covenant in the sale agreement would simply confirm what the text of the rule requires.

---

[356] Jacob v. Norris, McLaughlin & Marcus, 607 A.2d 142, 149–50 (N.J. 1992); Anderson v. Aspelmeier, Fisch, Power, Warner & Engberg, 461 N.W.2d 598, 600–02 (Iowa 1990); Cohen v. Lord, Day & Lord, 551 N.Y.S.2d 157, 158–60 (N.Y. 1989). *But see* Howard v. Babcock, 863 P.2d 150, 157–60 (Cal. 1993) (allowing reasonable imposition of costs against a departing partner who competes with the former firm).

[357] Law Offices of Palagi v. Howard, 747 N.W.2d 1, 13 (Neb. 2008) (finding void as against public policy an employment agreement that, while not directly restricting a departing lawyer from practicing in competition with the firm, provided that any fees earned from clients taken by the departing lawyer would be owed to the firm; saying that "[b]ecause the client's freedom of choice is the paramount interest the ethics rules attempt to serve, courts reason that any disincentive to competition is as detrimental to the public interest as an outright prohibition on competition").

[358] *Donnelly*, 599 N.W.2d at 682 (quoting WEBSTER'S THIRD NEW INT'L DICTIONARY 1939 (unbr. ed. 1986)).

[359] ROBERT W. HILLMAN, HILLMAN ON LAWYER MOBILITY § 2.3.5, at 2:89 to 2:91 (2d ed. Supp. 1999); *see also* Borteck v. Riker, Danzig, Scherer, Hyland & Perretti LLP, 844 A.2d 521, 527–29 (N.J. 2004) (referring to "sufficient indica of a bona fide retirement plan" and citing Hillman factors); Robert W. Hillman, *Ties That Bind and Restraints on Lawyer Competition: Restrictive Covenants as Conditions to the Payment of Retirement Benefits*, 39 IND. L. REV. 1, 10–13 (2005); ABA Comm. on Ethics & Prof'l Responsibility, Formal Op. 06–444 (2006) (same).

[360] *See supra* § 4-3.7(b).

### *§ 4-7.9(d)(2) The Prohibition on Settlement Agreements Restricting a Lawyer's Right to Practice*

Under Rule 5.6(b) of the Model Rules of Professional Conduct, "[a] lawyer shall not participate in offering or making . . . an agreement in which a restriction on the lawyer's right to practice is part of the settlement of a client controversy."

When an attorney has well-represented a client in a dispute with another party, the opposing party and its counsel may be tempted to offer a settlement proposal that not only resolves the current dispute but which also precludes that attorney from future representation of other clients against the same party or with respect to the same type of claim. By removing that lawyer who has developed an intimate familiarity with the subject and the parties, the party could hope to avoid or diminish future litigation and attendant losses.

Rule 5.6(b), however, plainly proscribes such an agreement as a matter of professional ethics.[361] Moreover, any such restrictive covenant in a settlement agreement presumably would be void as against public policy.[362] Rule 5.6(b) expressly protects the right of other persons with similar claims to their choice of legal counsel, including the preservation of access to a lawyer who has developed experience and expertise by previously handling similar claims or claims against a particular party.

Importantly, Rule 5.6(b) not only prevents consummation of an agreement that restricts a lawyer's right to practice, but also bars a lawyer from "offering" such an agreement. Accordingly, the lawyer who offers such a settlement proposal is subject to disciplinary sanction, even if the opposing counsel properly refuses the offer and advises his client that such a settlement provision would be void.[363] By even proposing such a limitation, the offering lawyer wrongly encourages the opposing counsel to violate the ethics rules and places that lawyer in the awkward position of having to explain to the client why such an agreement would be illegitimate.

---

[361] *See* In re Hager, 812 A.2d 904, 917–19 (D.C. 2002) (disciplining attorney for agreeing not to represent any current or future plaintiffs against manufacturer as part of settlement).

[362] *See, e.g.*, Jarvis v. Jarvis, 12 Kan.App.2d 799, 758 P.2d 244 (1988); Cardillo v. Bloomfield 206 Corp., 988 A.2d 136, 140 (N.J. Super. 2010).

[363] *See* Adams v. BellSouth Telecommunications, Inc., No. 96-2473-CIV, 2001 WL 34032759, at *3 (S.D. Fla. Jan. 29, 2001) (disciplining defendant's attorneys based on finding that, "it is clear that while Plaintiffs' counsel originally suggested a practice restriction as part of an overall settlement, [defendant's] attorneys seized on the concept and aggressively negotiated for its inclusion in any overall settlement of Plaintiffs' claims," with the design of obtaining " 'finality' for their client by preventing the filing of similar future suits by Plaintiffs' counsel"); In re Zaruba, 177 N.J. 564 (2003) (disciplining an attorney for a civil defendant for offering an agreement to restrict practice as part of a settlement in violation of Rule 5.6(b)).

# Chapter 4-8

# DUTIES TO ORGANIZATION/ENTITY CLIENTS

**By Gregory C. Sisk**

*Table of Sections*


§ 4-8.1 Introduction to Lawyers and Organization/Entity Clients
§ 4-8.2 Responsibilities During the Formation of an Entity
§ 4-8.3 Confidentiality and Attorney-Client Privilege for a Private Entity Client
§ 4-8.4 Protecting the Entity's Attorney-Client Relationship from Outside Interference (The "No-Contact" Rule for Entities)
§ 4-8.5 The Lawyer Responding to the Client's Duly-Authorized Constituents
§ 4-8.6 The Lawyer's Responsibilities When Unlawful Conduct or Internal Dissension Arises Within an Organization
§ 4-8.7 Dual Representation of Organization and Individual Constituent
§ 4-8.8 Government Clients


## § 4-8.1 INTRODUCTION TO LAWYERS AND ORGANIZATION/ENTITY CLIENTS

Lawyers regularly are called upon to represent various types of organizations as clients—corporations, partnerships, labor unions, government agencies, and other business, societal, and government entities. Entity clients are entitled to the same respect for client autonomy over the objectives of the representation,[1] the same protection of confidential information,[2] and the same loyalty undivided by conflicts of interest[3] as the lawyer must extend to any other client.[4] The lawyer representing an organization owes professional allegiance to the organization and not to its individual constituents, although the lawyer ordinarily is expected to respond to the lawful directions of the duly authorized constituents of the organization.

While the law may recognize an organization as having separate existence and legal personality for purposes of entering into transactions or becoming a party to litigation, such an artificial entity nonetheless must act through human agents.[5] At times, those agents may not be of one mind, thus making it vitally important that the lawyer know who is authorized to speak for the entity and to direct the legal representation. A person associated with the organization may have personal interests that diverge from those of

---

1 *See supra* § 4-3.4.

2 *See supra* ch. 4-6 and *infra* § 4-8.3(a).

3 *See supra* §§ 4-7.1 to 4-7.8.

4 On the lawyer for the corporation and the problems of professional independence, conflicts of interest, and the stresses and tensions inherent in that role, see generally E. Norman Veasey & Christine T. Di Guglielmo, *Tensions, Stresses, and Professional Responsibilities of the Lawyer for the Corporation*, 62 BUSINESS LAWYER 1 (2006).

5 Commodity Futures Trading Comm'n v. Weintraub, 471 U.S. 343, 348 (1985) ("As an inanimate entity, a corporation must act through agents.").

the organization, or, in extreme situations, may engage in improper conduct that endangers the organization. In addressing these matters, the lawyer is obliged to ensure that the interests of the organization are protected above those of its constituents.

## § 4-8.2 RESPONSIBILITIES DURING THE FORMATION OF AN ENTITY

As discussed in later sections of this chapter, Rule 1.13 of the Model Rules of Professional Conduct directs the lawyer to be faithful to the organization as the client and provides general guidance on professionally appropriate responses to some of the problems that may arise during representation of an ongoing entity. The rule does not, however, address the lawyer's responsibilities during the creation of an entity, that is, at the stage where the entity remains nascent and unformed.

At the formation stage, multiple persons may be involved in selecting the organization's structure, providing financing for the start-up operation, developing the mission of the organization, anticipating a role in management or product and service development, etc. While each putative constituent of the future entity could retain separate counsel, retention of a single lawyer or law firm to assist in the formation of the entity is not unusual. The lawyer's undertaking of such a unitary representation is not and should not be regarded as invariably constituting an impermissible conflict of interest. Rather, joint representation should be recognized as a legitimate and appropriate part of the lawyer's role with respect to newly-formed entities, as long as all parties provide informed consent to the lawyer's common representation should there be a substantial risk that interests may divide.[6]

Professor Matthew Doré writes that whether the lawyer is seen as representing only the planned entity or instead as representing multiple clients, joint representation is appropriate provided that the lawyer makes sure the various constituents "understand [the lawyer's] role and seek their own counsel if they desire it."[7] With respect to entities organized for business purposes, Doré further explains:

> Many practitioners attempt to perform their role at the business formation stage consistently with [the] ethical rule [regarding conflicts of interest], acting not as a zealous advocate for any one business participant, but rather as a facilitator who helps all participants come to agreement on pertinent business organization issues.[8]

Or, as Justice Louis Brandeis described the work to negotiate differences among parties to a joint venture, the attorney may seek to act as "lawyer for the situation."[9] At this stage, the lawyer's role is to bring all participants with a common interest to a point of convergence with respect to the formation of the enterprise. By acting "as a facilitator who helps all participants come to agreement on pertinent . . . organization issues,"[10] the

---

[6] On joint representation in a non-litigation context and consent to conflicts, see *supra* §§ 4-7.4(c)(6) to (7), 4-7.7.

[7] 5 MATHEW G. DORÉ, IOWA PRACTICE SERIES: BUSINESS ORGANIZATIONS § 2:1 (Thomson-Reuters 2017).

[8] *Id.*

[9] *See* Geoffrey C. Hazard, Jr., *Lawyer for the Situation*, 39 VAL. U. L. REV. 377 (2004).

[10] DORÉ, *supra*, § 2.1.

lawyer behaves in accordance with ethical expectations, as long as all parties consent and no conflict has ripened into an irresolvable dispute.

Because the entity is not yet in existence,[11] and because the multiple clients or putative constituents participating in its conception may not have identical interests, the lawyer must disclose to each person the potential for conflict of interest problems and obtain that person's individual and informed consent to the representation.[12] Some advise that the lawyer in obtaining informed consent must also urge the participants to obtain independent counsel.[13] If these persons later have a falling-out before the entity has been brought into being, and because the lawyer is unable to take sides due to the lawyer's equal responsibilities to each, a conflict of interest may emerge in a manner that cannot be managed and thus that requires the lawyer to withdraw. However, unless there is a substantial likelihood that a conflict will arise that prevents the lawyer from providing competent and diligent representation to all participants, the lawyer may undertake the representation with the informed consent of each. The fact that an insurmountable conflict later arises does not itself suggest that the joint representation arrangement was improper at the outset.

In sum, the lawyer's facilitation of an emerging business enterprise or other organization through unified representation of multiple constituents transgresses no ethical limitations (provided informed consent is obtained and zealous representation of all persons involved is not interrupted by a divergence of interests). Representation by a single lawyer or law firm of a collection of persons forming a joint venture ought to be encouraged, because it enhances economic and public service opportunities and makes it possible for people to bring a new project into being without hiring multiple lawyers for overlapping and redundant work at much greater expense.

## § 4-8.3 CONFIDENTIALITY AND ATTORNEY-CLIENT PRIVILEGE FOR A PRIVATE ENTITY CLIENT

### § 4-8.3(a) Determining Who Speaks for the Client for Purposes of the Privilege

No less than any other client, the organization client is entitled to the lawyer's fiduciary protection of confidential information. Under Rule 1.6(a) of the Model Rules of Professional Conduct,[14] the lawyer's duty to maintain confidentiality is broadly extended to all "information relating to the representation of a client." Thus, whether the lawyer for the organization has gathered information through communications with organization personnel or instead has discovered information from other sources, the broad scope of confidentiality under the rules applies with full force here. Accordingly, in most respects, the lawyer's responsibility to safeguard information relating to representation of an organization client is the same as that for a client who is a natural person.

---

[11] *But see* Paul R. Tremblay, *The Ethics of Representing Founders*, 8 WM. & MARY BUS. L. REV. 267, 273 (2017) (observing that when the business is already active, "the lawyer most likely represents the partnership as an entity and not the individual founders").

[12] See *generally id.* at 285–266. On informed consent to joint representation generally, see *supra* § 4-6.4.

[13] LAWRENCE J. FOX & SUSAN R. MARTYN, THE ETHICS OF REPRESENTING ORGANIZATIONS: LEGAL FICTIONS FOR CLIENTS 151 (Oxford U. Press, 2009).

[14] *See supra* § 4-6.2.

In two important ways, however, the lawyer's responsibility to protect confidential information requires an evaluation peculiar to the nature of the organization client: (1) identifying the "client" for purposes of the attorney-client privilege; and (2) determining who within the organization may consent to disclosure of confidential information:

### *§ 4-8.3(a)(1) Identifying the Client for Privileged Communications*

The lawyer must identify who is the "client" for purposes of the special sub-species of confidential information that falls within the nigh-absolute attorney-client privilege.[15] While the lawyer generally is obliged to protect all information relating to the representation and not voluntarily disclose such information,[16] the lawyer nonetheless is required to respond to a lawful subpoena or court order seeking information outside the parameters of the privilege. By contrast, the lawyer may not be compelled through legal process to divulge the substance of communications falling within the privilege. Thus, the contents of communications between an attorney and a client constitute a specially-protected subset of confidential information.[17]

Comment 2 to Rule 1.13 of the Model Rules of Professional Conduct articulates a remarkably broad understanding of confidentiality for communications by a lawyer with the constituents and employees of the organization:

> When one of the constituents of an organizational client communicates with the organization's lawyer in that person's organizational capacity, the communication is protected by Rule 1.6. Thus, by way of example, if an organizational client requests its lawyer to investigate allegations of wrongdoing, interviews made in the course of that investigation between the lawyer and the client's employees or other constituents are covered by Rule 1.6.

This comment refers to information protected as confidential under Rule 1.6, rather than under the attorney-client privilege as such. Nonetheless, the specific reference to an investigation by a lawyer favorably regards the lawyer's efforts to obtain information from organization constituents for purposes of providing legal advice. This emphasis on confidentiality attaching to direct communications by a lawyer with a variety of persons within the organization is consistent with an understanding that the privilege extends to these interviews as well.

The attorney-client privilege plainly protects communications between a lawyer and a client organization. Every court has agreed that the attorney-client privilege covers at a minimum communications between organization counsel and those constituents of the organization who have decision-making power regarding the legal representation and those who constitute speaking agents for the entity (and thus whose statements would constitute an evidentiary admission against the organization). A tiny group of states go no further, adhering to a narrow "control group" test.[18] The substantial majority of courts extend the privilege one significant step further to cover corporate constituents who have taken actions that might be imputed to the organization (and thus whose conduct directly implicates the organization's need for legal counsel and representation).

---

[15] On the attorney-client privilege generally, see *supra* § 4-6.3.

[16] *See supra* §§ 4-6.2, 4-6.5.

[17] *See supra* § 4-6.3.

[18] *See* Bridgeview Health Care Ctr., Ltd. v. State Farm Fire & Cas. Co., 10 N.E.3d 902, 908–09 (Ill. 2014); N.M. RULES OF PROF'L CONDUCT R. 4.2.

However, the courts have differed on whether the privilege also extends to organization employees who are without authority to decide or speak on behalf of the entity or otherwise to bind the entity, who are not alleged to have engaged in any conduct that may be imputed to the organization, and who thus may be characterized as mere witnesses to a matter. This question tends to arise when a lawyer for the organization conducts an investigation of an episode (such as an incident that may give rise to later litigation) or looks into a pattern of behavior (such as suspected wrongdoing by persons within the entity). For these purposes, the lawyer for the organization client may conduct interviews with employees who, while not themselves having taken questionable actions or created any potential basis for liability, may have observed what occurred.

For purposes of the federal attorney-client privilege, the Supreme Court in *Upjohn Co. v. United States*[19] held broadly that, when employees are directed by corporate superiors to talk with corporate counsel about topics falling generally within the subject matter of their employment and the information is being gathered to assist corporate counsel in devising appropriate legal advice to the corporation, those communications with employees are privileged. As Professor Michael Paulsen explains, "[t]he reason a broad band of communications to counsel are treated as privileged is because it will enable counsel to give legal advice to the corporation concerning possible courses of conduct to pursue, in light of the information gathered."[20] The *Upjohn* "subject matter" approach, which is the majority view among the states as well, is also reflected in the *Restatement of the Law Governing Lawyers*.[21]

A distinct minority of state courts have concluded that this "subject matter" test for entity attorney-client privilege sweeps too broadly, covering employees who do not stand as alter egos of the entity. In the Arizona Supreme Court's decision in *Samaritan Foundation v. Goodfarb*[22]—later overturned by the state legislature[23]—the court explained this alternative approach in this way:

> where someone other than the employee initiates the communication, a factual communication by a corporate employee to corporate counsel is within the corporation's privilege if it concerns the employee's own conduct within the scope of his or her employment and is made to assist the lawyer in assessing or responding to the legal consequences of that conduct for the corporate client. This excludes from the privilege communications from those who, but for their status as officers, agents or employees, are witnesses.[24]

---

[19] 449 U.S. 383, 389–97 (1981).

[20] Michael Stokes Paulsen, *Who "Owns" the Government's Attorney-Client Privilege?*, 83 MINN. L. REV. 473, 496 (1998).

[21] RESTATEMENT (THIRD) OF THE LAW GOVERNING LAWYERS § 73 (American Law Institute, 2000) (saying that, for an organizational client, "the attorney-client privilege extends to a communication" that "concerns a legal matter of interest to the organization" and is shared only with those agents of the client who facilitate the communication and "other agents of the organization who reasonably need to know of the communication in order to act for the organization").

[22] 862 P.2d 870 (Ariz. 1993).

[23] The Arizona Legislature subsequently overturned the *Samaritan Foundation* ruling, essentially adopting the *Upjohn* approach and extending the privilege to a communication by an employee or agent of the organization to the organization's legal counsel "[f]or the purpose of obtaining information in order to provide legal advice to the entity or employer or to the employee, agent, or member." ARIZ. REV. ST. § 12–2234(B)(2).

[24] *Samaritan Foundation*, 862 P.2d. at 880; *see also* Martin v. Workers' Comp. Appeals Bd., 69 Cal.Rptr.2d 138, 147 (Cal. App. 1997) ("We conclude that when an employee's only connection is as an independent witness, not as a co-defendant or as the natural person to speak for the employer, such statements do not become privileged just because they are given for transmittal to the employer's attorney in preparation

In any event, the differences between the majority *Upjohn* rule and the minority approach are likely to manifest in relatively rare situations. The attorney-client privilege immunizes only the substance of the communications between the attorney and client and ordinarily does not permit concealing the underlying facts. When law enforcement, prosecutors, or opposing parties seek information from organization employees or agents who were merely witnesses, these persons may be questioned directly, either through informal interviews if permitted[25] or by means of such legal processes as an oral deposition or court testimony. Only in the exceptional situation where, as was the case in *Samaritan Foundation*,[26] the organization employee no longer recalls the material elements of the event or matter in question when it later becomes the subject of litigation, would there even arguably be a basis for requesting access to organization counsel's contemporaneous notes about inquiries directed to those employees as part of a preliminary investigation by the lawyer.

### *§ 4-8.3(a)(2) Identifying the Client for Authority to Waive the Privilege*

Because rights respecting confidential information, including the substance of privileged communications, belong to the client, the organization client is entitled to waive confidentiality and share information or to authorize the lawyer to share information, as the organization so chooses. The Supreme Court has observed that this power to waive the privilege "rests with the corporation's management and is normally exercised by its officers and directors."[27]

The lawyer must determine who within the organization has the authority to decide whether to maintain or waive confidentiality, which in turn requires that the lawyer develop a working understanding of the organization's nature and structure. This, of course, is the level of understanding that the lawyer must secure in any event to properly follow her general duty to respond to the duly authorized constituents of the entity. The determination may be a little more complicated when the disclosure of the information, although arguably in the best interests of the organization, would be contrary to the interests of the constituent to whom the lawyer ordinarily reports. In that circumstance, the lawyer may need to seek a decision on disclosure from a higher authority within the organization. Whenever necessary to avoid confusion, the lawyer should emphasize to the constituents and employees of the entity that the confidential nature of communications made to the lawyer is within the sole control of the organization. Statements made by those within the organization may be secreted or openly revealed at the option of the organization.

As discussed below,[28] Rule 1.13(c) of the Model Rules of Professional Conduct grants the lawyer for an entity carefully circumscribed authority to disclose confidential

---

for litigation."); Keefe v. Bernard, 774 N.W.2d 663, 672 (Iowa 2009) (ruling that if "a corporate employee is interviewed as a 'witness' to the actions of others, the communication should not be protected by the corporation's attorney-client privilege").

[25] On contacts with organization employees without the consent of the lawyer for the organization, see *infra* § 4-8.4.

[26] *Samaritan Foundation*, 862 P.2d at 873, 880–81 (allowing discovery in a medical malpractice suit of summaries of interviews with hospital personnel conducted at hospital counsel's direction shortly after an operating room incident in which a child's heart stopped, after those persons could not recall at depositions two-years later what had happened, and holding these interview summaries were not privileged because these particular employees were merely fact witnesses).

[27] Commodity Futures Trading Comm'n v. Weintraub, 471 U.S. 343, 348 (1985).

[28] *See infra* § 4-8.6.

information when necessary to protect the best interests of the organization client against serious harm by reason of the misconduct of a person within the organization. Importantly, this permissive exception to the lawyer's duty to protect confidential information is, from the perspective of the organization, self-regarding only and not other-regarding. While Rule 1.6 contains exceptions that authorize (and even mandate) the lawyer to disclose confidential information as necessary to prevent or mitigate harm to someone other than the client,[29] Rule 1.13(c) permits disclosure only as designed to benefit the organization.

### § 4-8.3(b) Denying the Privilege to Ordinary Business Matters (The Ruse Abuse)

In two particular business contexts presenting a blend of legal and non-legal roles and matters, courts and commentators have been especially worried that the attorney-client privilege may be abused: (1) where in-house counsel to a business association wears two hats (both lawyer and business executive); and (2) where ordinary business communications appear to be routinely channeled through a lawyer. In these situations, courts worry that the practice of addressing the message to the lawyer may actually be "a ruse through which business rather than legal matters were being communicated."[30]

Even in these two particular business contexts, the potential for abuse is best addressed by careful application of the prerequisites for and exceptions to the privilege itself, rather than by narrowly defining the nature of the lawyer's role or artificially constraining the topics that may be considered by the lawyer and client in addressing a legal matter.[31] Courts should hesitate to enunciate general rules restricting the application of the privilege to in-house counsel or presuming that communications with lawyers that contain business information or considerations fall outside the privilege.

***Corporate In-House Counsel:*** Difficulties in identifying "what role the attorney was fulfilling arise most frequently in cases involving in-house counsel who may perform a number of functions for the corporation, only some of which place them in the role of legal advisor."[32] As the late Paul Rice summarized the state of the law on privilege in the federal courts:

> [T]he unstated operating presumption in situations involving outside retained counsel with limited responsibilities to the client (e.g., strictly legal capacity as opposed to business responsibilities because of a corporate position that he holds), is that the consultations were held for the purpose of obtaining legal advice or assistance. The same presumption does not apply to in-house counsel because of the many nonlegal responsibilities in-house counsel assumes (whether given a separate position and title or not).[33]

---

[29] *See supra* § 4-6.6(c) to (d).

[30] PAUL R. RICE, ATTORNEY-CLIENT PRIVILEGE IN THE UNITED STATES § 7.2 (Thomson-West, 2012).

[31] On the dynamic nature of the attorney-client privilege applied to matters related to legal advice, see *supra* § 4-6.3(b)(1).

[32] Andritz Sprout-Bauer, Inc. v. Beazer E., Inc., 174 F.R.D. 609, 633 (M.D. Pa. 1997); *see also* Rossi v. Blue Cross & Blue Shield, 540 N.E.2d 703, 705 (N.Y. 1989) (noting that the "day-today involvement" of in-house attorneys for a company "may blur the line between legal and non-legal communications").

[33] PAUL R. RICE, ATTORNEY-CLIENT PRIVILEGE IN THE UNITED STATES § 7.1 (Thomson-West, 2012) (footnotes omitted). *But see* Grace M. Giesel, *The Legal Advice Requirement of the Attorney-Client Privilege: A Special Problem for In-House Counsel and Outside Attorneys Representing Corporations*, 48 MERCER L. REV. 1169, 1175 (1997) (criticizing "the anticorporation and anti-in-house counsel bias which is obvious in many

Thus, in the limited context of inside corporate counsel, "[t]he overlap between 'business' advice and 'legal' advice requires a pragmatic approach" in determining whether the privilege covers all or some of the communication.[34] The fact that the in-house counsel may be regularly involved with nearly every aspect of the business enterprise cannot be a device for immunizing every such communication from outside discovery.[35]

Nonetheless, in making the fact-intensive determination of whether the privilege should apply, courts should be mindful of the necessarily expanded role of corporate counsel in the modern legal and regulatory environment. Moreover, as the *Restatement of the Law Governing Lawyers* emphasizes in a comment, the privilege "applies without distinction to lawyers who are inside legal counsel or outside legal counsel for an organization."[36] Accordingly, if non-legal components of a communication are intertwined with genuine and material requests for legal advice from corporate counsel, whether in-house or outside, the privilege should attach. But if corporate attorneys were "acting principally as business advisors giving only *incidental* legal advice," then the protection of the attorney-client privilege may not come into play.[37] Only when "any legal advice was overshadowed by non-legal information" should the court be more inclined to find that the privilege has been relinquished.[38]

***Funneling Documents Through Counsel:*** The potential for abuse of the attorney-client privilege similarly arises in the inappropriate practice of funneling all company documents and correspondence through counsel (whether in-house or outside) in an attempt to transform routine business communications into privileged attorney-client communications. As Paul Rice wrote in his treatise, "[m]any courts fear that businesses will immunize internal communications from discovery by placing legal counsel in strategic corporate positions and funneling documents through counsel (*viz.* addressing documents to the lawyers with copies being sent to the employees with whom communications were primarily intended)."[39] Courts understandably and appropriately refuse to accept the expediency of copying the lawyer on routine business correspondence and memoranda as sufficient to raise the shield of privilege over the entire content of such ordinary business documents.[40]

---

courts' opinions" on attorney-client privilege); Amber Stevens, Comment, *An Analysis of the Troubling Issues Surrounding In-House Counsel and the Attorney-Client Privilege*, 23 HAMLINE L. REV. 290, 309 (1999) (arguing that "courts have shown a bias towards corporations and in-house counsel when they examine in-house counsel's communications" and critically noting "some courts appear to presume corporate abuse of the privilege or that the communication contains primarily business advice").

[34] ABB Kent-Taylor, Inc. v. Stallings & Co., Inc., 172 F.R.D. 53, 55 (W.D.N.Y. 1996).

[35] *But see* E. Norman Veasey & Christine T. Di Guglielmo, *The Tensions, Stresses, and Professional Responsibilities of the Lawyer for the Corporation*, 62 BUS. LAW. (Nov. 2006), at 27 ("It is not clear, however, that in-house counsel offer business advice more frequently than do outside counsel, suggesting that courts should not be more skeptical of the legal nature of a communication simply because it involved in-house counsel.").

[36] RESTATEMENT (THIRD) OF THE LAW GOVERNING LAWYERS § 73 cmt. i (American Law Institute, 2000).

[37] In re Westinghouse Elec. Corp. Uranium Contracts Litig., 76 F.R.D. 47, 57 (W.D. Pa. 1977) (emphasis added); *see also* United States v. Int'l Bus. Machines Corp., 66 F.R.D. 206, 212 (S.D.N.Y. 1974) (saying that the attorney-client privilege does not apply "to incidental legal advice given by an attorney acting outside the scope of his role as attorney").

[38] *See* In re Brand Name Prescription Drugs Antitrust Litig., No. 94 C 897, 1995 WL 354268, at *3 (N.D. Ill. 1995).

[39] PAUL R. RICE, ATTORNEY-CLIENT PRIVILEGE IN THE UNITED STATES § 7.2 (Thomson-West 2012).

[40] *See, e.g.*, United States v. Segal, No. 02-CR-112, 2004 WL 830428, at * 3 (N.D. Ill. 2004) ("A prudent corporation will seek legal advice with respect to most corporate decisions, but the inclusion of general counsel does not transform all business discussions into attorney-client privileged communications."); Tri-State Equip.

Even in these two business contexts, the combination of business advice with legal counsel emphatically does not undermine the privilege, if the communication's purpose truly is to gain or provide legal assistance.[41] The central inquiry should be whether there is a logical relationship between the non-legal components of the communication and the legal nucleus of the subject on which advice or assistance is sought from the attorney.[42] "Business advice, unrelated to legal advice, is not protected by the privilege even though conveyed by an attorney to the client."[43] But if a genuine and material link to the legal matter on which advice is sought is indeed present, discussions between the lawyer and client of other aspects of a matter, including business ramifications and moral considerations, should not remove the privilege from the communication. If the contours of the privilege are drawn too narrowly, the lawyer and the client will be unduly constrained, not only in the practical integration of business factors with legal options, but also in engaging in moral deliberation about the right course to take.[44]

Importantly, the traditional prerequisites for and exceptions to the attorney-client privilege are well-suited to exclude abusive applications. Cases in which the privilege should be withheld can be adequately addressed by looking to the basic elements of the privilege itself,[45] without narrowly defining the scope of the practice of law or permitting intrusion into privileged communications that include non-legal as well as genuine legal components:

- ***Underlying Facts Not Privileged:*** "The privilege only protects disclosure of communications; it does not protect disclosure of the underlying facts by those who communicated with the attorney[.]"[46] Thus, witnesses to events, raw data, and pre-existing information typically are subject to unobstructed discovery. Especially when the underlying factual evidence has been "generated through studies and collected through observation" of data that was "obtained from sources other than the client,"[47] a claim of privilege is misplaced, whether or not the data is transmitted to the lawyer or research is supervised by the lawyer. By contrast, if a scientific report " 'put[s] in usable form information obtained from the client,' " and if the "report was connected intimately to the

v. United States, No. CIVS-94-1033-EJG-PAN, 1996 WL 376340, at *2 (E.D. Cal. 1996) (saying that, in evaluating whether the privilege attached, a business may not "conduct its ordinary business through lawyers to hide its affairs from light of day"); Jack Winter, Inc. v. Koratron Co., 54 F.R.D. 44, 47 (N.D. Cal. 1971) ("[C]orporate dealings are not made confidential merely by funnelling them routinely through an attorney.").

41 *See* Kramer v. Raymond Corp., Civ. No. 90–5026, 1992 WL 122856, at *1 (E.D. Pa. 1992) ("Because in-house counsel may play a dual role of legal advisor and business advisor, the privilege will apply only if the communication's primary purpose is to gain or provide legal assistance."). On the primary legal purpose test, and how it has been applied and should be understood, see *supra* § 4-6.3(b)(1).

42 *See, e.g.*, Burton v. R.J. Reynolds Tobacco Co., 177 F.R.D. 491, 497 (D. Kan. 1997) (denying the privilege for correspondence among counsel for tobacco companies regarding special projects for research, where the party did "not point to any specific evidence, however, that the documents were created to give legal advice instead of for general business purposes, nor do the documents themselves evidence the necessary link").

43 In re CFS-Related Sec. Fraud Litig., 223 F.R.D. 631, 635 (N.D. Okla. 2004).

44 *See supra* §§ 4-6.3(a), 4-6.3(b)(1).

45 On the elements of the attorney-client privilege, see *supra* § 4-6.3(b).

46 Upjohn Co. v. United States, 449 U.S. 383, 395 (1981).

47 United States Postal Serv. v. Phelps Dodge Ref. Corp., 852 F. Supp. 156, 162 (E.D.N.Y. 1994) (finding that documents recording factual data collected by consultants did not "reveal[ ] any confidential communications by the defendants or their attorneys to the consultants").

rendering of legal advice," the contents should receive the protection of the privilege.[48]

- ***Client's Ultimate Decision Not Privileged:*** Even though informed and perhaps influenced by a lawyer's advice, the client's ultimate decision based on that advice is not privileged. Because the client is not necessarily bound by the lawyer's suggestions, the general rule is that "[r]evealing client actions or decisions would disclose neither the substance of the recommendation nor the content of the client's privileged communications upon which the decision/actions were based."[49]
- ***Preexisting Documents Not Privileged:*** While written communications between a lawyer and client (and among those who are part of the legal team) may be privileged in nature, "preexisting documents or documents which were not created as communications to the attorney . . . do not become privileged merely by virtue of being forwarded to the lawyer."[50] The "preexisting document rule" thus underscores that only documents created for the purpose of communicating with the lawyer about the legal representation fall within the privilege.
- ***Privilege Lost if Communication Is Not Confidential:*** For the privilege to attach, the communication must be treated by the participants in a manner consistent with its asserted confidentiality.[51] If a communication is broadly disseminated beyond those agents of the client who are authorized to make decisions, speak for the client, or otherwise have a need to know, then the communication either is not privileged in the first instance because it was not held confidential or the privilege is lost due to waiver by disclosure.[52]
- ***Crime-Fraud Exception to Privilege:*** Under the crime-fraud exception to the attorney-client privilege,[53] if a client, rather than seeking legitimate legal advice, solicits information and services from a lawyer in order to facilitate

---

[48] Olson v. Accessory Controls & Equip. Co., 757 A.2d 14, 24, 28 (Conn. 2000) (quoting Federal Trade Comm'n v. TRW, Inc., 628 F.2d 207, 212 (D.C. Cir. 1980)); *see also* Andritz Sprout-Bauer, Inc. v. Beazer E., Inc., 174 F.R.D. 609, 635–36 (M.D. Pa. 1997) (holding that documents "explaining or interpreting technical data so as to allow counsel to provide legal advice" were protected by the privilege). For further analysis of the *Olson* case, and its contrast with *Phelps Dodge*, see generally Rebecca Fiechtl, *Know When to Hold 'Em: Minimizing Disclosure of Corporate Environmental Information*, 31 ENVTL. LAW. 951, 962–63 (2001).

[49] PAUL R. RICE, ATTORNEY-CLIENT PRIVILEGE IN THE UNITED STATES § 5.14 (Thomson-West, 2012).

[50] 7 JAMES A. ADAMS & JOSEPH P. WEEG, IOWA PRACTICE SERIES: EVIDENCE § 5.504:10 (Thomson-West 2005); *see also* Fisher v. United States, 425 U.S. 391, 403–04 (1976) ("This Court and the lower courts have thus uniformly held that pre-existing documents which could have been obtained by court process from the client when he was in possession may also be obtained from the attorney by similar process following transfer by the client in order to obtain more informed legal advice.").

[51] *See* Allied Irish Banks, 252 F.R.D. 163, 168 (S.D.N.Y. 2008) (" 'Generally, communications made between a [client] and counsel in the known presence of a third party are not privileged.' " (quoting People v. Osorio, 549 N.E.2d 1183, 1185 (N.Y. 1989))).

[52] *See* Fed. Trade Comm'n v. GlaxoSmithKline, 294 F.2d 141, 147 (D.C. Cir. 2002); United States v. Jones, 696 F.2d 1069, 1072 (4th Cir.1982); Se. Pa. Transp. Auth. v. CaremarkPCS Health, L.P., 254 F.R.D. 253, 258 (E.D. Pa. 2008).

[53] *See* United States v. Zolin, 491 U.S. 554, 563 (1989) ("It is the purpose of the crime-fraud exception to the attorney-client privilege to assure that the 'seal of secrecy' between lawyer and client does not extend to communications 'made for the purpose of getting advice for the commission of a fraud or crime;' " (citations omitted)).

criminal or fraudulent conduct, the attorney-client privilege is forfeited.[54] As a state court said seventy years ago, "[i]t is a mistaken notion to think that an attorney has the right to assist in the perpetration of a fraud, and a mistaken notion to think that one having in mind the perpetration of a fraud or a crime can safely intrust this knowledge to an attorney any more than to anybody else."[55] However, the crime-fraud exception is "a limited one."[56] The exception is implicated "only when there is probable cause to believe that the communications with counsel were intended in some way to facilitate or to conceal the criminal [or fraudulent] activity."[57] And, as Professors Geoffrey Hazard and William Hodes and attorney Peter Jarvis say, "the exception only applies where the communication is intended to or actually does advance the client's illicit purpose; providing after-the-fact evidence of the crime or fraud is insufficient."[58]

Accordingly, for courts to allow legitimate access to business information undeserving of privileged protection, it is not necessary to constrict the scope of the attorney-client privilege in a myopic manner that fails to appreciate the expanded nature of the modern practice of law or that would discourage business clients from seeking the integrated legal and ethical assistance of lawyers.

When a matter with a meaningful legal dimension is brought to a lawyer and subjected to the lawyer's professional examination, the animating purpose of the attorney-client privilege is realized by encouraging the lawyer and the client to fully explore any legal implications in an integrated fashion. If today's lawyer is to be effective in a legal representation, and thoroughly competent in the modern sense of having expertise, training, and experience that may extend beyond knowledge of legal texts, doctrines, and procedures, then the lawyer's performance or supervision of additional services directly related to the practice of law should be recognized as within the lawyer's professional capacity. Communications between lawyers and clients about those allied matters, as well as strictly legal issues, deserve the sound and reliable protection of the attorney-client privilege.[59]

---

[54] *See, e.g.,* State *ex rel.* Humphrey v. Philip Morris Inc., 606 N.W.2d 676, 691 (Minn. Ct. App. 2000) (referring to the trial court ruling that the tobacco companies "had engaged in criminal and fraudulent conduct by failing to conduct research into the safety of tobacco products and failing to warn consumers about research that did support negative conclusions and that [the tobacco companies'] attorneys acted in furtherance of this conduct"); In re A.H. Robins Co., 107 F.R.D. 2, 14–15 (D. Kan. 1985) (applying the crime-fraud exception when the manufacturer of a contraceptive device "failed to adequately test the Dalkon Shield before marketing it; attempted to develop hard evidence which misrepresented the nature, quality, safety and efficacy of the Dalkon Shield; ignored the mounting evidence against the Dalkon Shield, with knowledge of the potential harm caused by the product; relied upon invalid studies in an effort to refute or ignore the dangers potentially caused by the Dalkon Shield; and attempted, with the assistance of counsel, to devise strategies to cover up Robins' responsibilities and lessen its liability with respect to the Dalkon Shield").

[55] State v. Kirkpatrick, 263 N.W. 52, 55 (Iowa 1936).

[56] Olson v. Accessory Controls & Equip. Co., 757 A.2d 14, 31 (Conn. 2000).

[57] In re Grand Jury Subpoenas Duces Tecum, 798 F.2d 32, 34 (2d Cir. 1986).

[58] 1 GEOFFREY C. HAZARD, JR., W. WILLIAM HODES & PETER R. JARVIS, THE LAW OF LAWYERING § 10.11 (Aspen, 4th ed., 2016).

[59] *See also supra* § 4-6.3(b)(1).

## § 4-8.4 PROTECTING THE ENTITY'S ATTORNEY-CLIENT RELATIONSHIP FROM OUTSIDE INTERFERENCE (THE "NO-CONTACT" RULE FOR ENTITIES)

### § 4-8.4(a) Defining "Represented Person" for Entities in Applying the "No-Contact" Rule

Rule 4.2 of the Model Rules of Professional Conduct states: "In representing a client, a lawyer shall not communicate about the subject of the representation with a person the lawyer knows to be represented by another lawyer in the matter, unless the lawyer has the consent of the other lawyer or is authorized to do so by law or a court order." This "no-contact" rule prevents a lawyer representing a client from interfering with the attorney-client relationship between another lawyer and that lawyer's client, guards against inadvertent or uncounseled disclosure of confidential information by a layperson whose lawyer is not present, and precludes a lawyer from obtaining a statement from a represented party that would constitute an admission for purposes of evidentiary rules.[60]

When an entity retains legal counsel, that represented organization is also entitled to the protections of the no-contact rule. As Professors Ronald Rotunda and John Dzienkowski put it, "[a] corporation or other entity only speaks through flesh and blood agents."[61] To apply the no-contact rule in the context of an entity client, we must determine which individual constituents of the entity should be regarded as its alter ego for purposes of the prohibition on *ex parte* communication by other lawyers who represent a client in a dispute or transaction with that entity.

The courts have gravitated toward a pragmatic approach on the entity question, one that practically accounts for the factors underlying the no-contact rule.[62] The primary animating purposes of the no-contact rule are to prevent interference with or influence upon a layperson who has authority to make decisions regarding the representation and to prevent inadvertent disclosure of confidential information when the person's lawyer is not present. With respect to an entity, those purposes are fairly achieved by precluding another person's lawyer from having access to those individuals within a represented organization who regularly interact with the lawyer in obtaining legal advice for the entity, those whose actions are the subject of the present representation, and those who may bind the organization by their acts or statements. By this pragmatic approach, identifying the constituents who constitute the organizational client for application of the no-contact rule essentially becomes a question of agency law.

The leading decision on the application of the no-contact rule to a represented entity is that of the New York Court of Appeals in *Niesig v. Team I*.[63] The court began by observing that "[i]n litigation only the entity, not its employee, is the actual named party; on the other hand, corporations act solely through natural persons, and unless some employees are also considered parties, corporations are effectively read out of the [no-contact] rule."[64] The court rejected a "blanket rule" that would encompass all corporate

---

[60] *See infra* § 4-11.3.

[61] RONALD D. ROTUNDA & JOHN S. DZIENKOWSKI, PROFESSIONAL RESPONSIBILITY: A STUDENT'S GUIDE § 4.2–6(a) (American Bar Ass'n, 2013–2014).

[62] 2 GEOFFREY C. HAZARD, JR., W. WILLIAM HODES & PETER R. JARVIS, THE LAW OF LAWYERING § 41.07 (Aspen, 4th ed., 2016).

[63] 559 N.Y.S.2d 493 (N.Y. 1990).

[64] *Id.* at 496.

employees as "clos[ing] off avenues of informal discovery of information that may serve both the litigants and the entire justice system by uncovering relevant facts, thus promoting the expeditious resolution of disputes."[65] Instead, the New York court concluded that "[t]he test that best balances the competing interests, and incorporates the most desirable elements of the other approaches, is one that defines 'party' to include corporate employees whose acts or omissions in the matter under inquiry are binding on the corporation (in effect, the corporation's 'alter egos') or imputed to the corporation for purposes of its liability, or employees implementing the advice of counsel."[66] By contrast, the *Niesig* court said, employees who were merely witnesses to the event as to which the entity is sued may be contacted.[67]

Comment 7 to Rule 4.2 of the Model Rules of Professional Conduct generally endorses the basic pragmatic or agency approach. The comment states that the no-contact rule "prohibits communications with a constituent of the organization who supervises, directs or regularly consults with the organization's lawyer concerning the matter or has authority to obligate the organization with respect to the matter or whose act or omission in connection with the matter may be imputed to the organization for purposes of civil or criminal liability."

Under some formulations of the pragmatic or agency approach, the no-contact rule could apply as well to those individuals whose statements on behalf of the organization would constitute an admission by the entity as a party for purposes of evidentiary rules.[68] By this reasoning, the no-contact rule would encompasses most or all persons whose statements would be regarded as an evidentiary admission by the entity itself for purposes of escaping the hearsay exclusion, even if the entity remained able to explain and contradict that statement in presentations to the trier-of-fact.

Such a broad sweep for the no-contact rule is hard to justify under Model Rule 4.2. In the Ethics 2000 revisions to the American Bar Association's Model Rules of Professional Conduct, the pertinent comment to Rule 4.2 was revised to delete language referring to a person "whose statement may constitute an admission on the part of the organization." The reporter's notes for the Ethics 2000 project explain this deletion as intended to prevent an open-ended reading of the no-contact rule as "prohibiting communication with any person whose testimony would be admissible against the organization as an exception to the hearsay rule."[69] Similarly, the *Restatement of the Law Governing Lawyers* precludes *ex parte* contacts with an organization's constituents "if a statement of the employee or other agent, under applicable rules of evidence, would

---

[65] *Id.* at 497.

[66] *Id.* at 498.

[67] *Id.* at 498–99.

[68] *See Niesig*, 559 N.Y.S.2d at 498 (holding that the no-contact rule also covers "employees with 'speaking authority' for the corporation, and employees who are so closely identified with the interests of the corporate party as to be indistinguishable from it"); Jon S. Herreman, Note, *The Scope of the Disciplinary Rules Prohibiting* Ex Parte *Communication in a Corporate Context*, 40 DRAKE L. REV. 861, 866–76, 888 (1991) (urging Iowa to adopt a modified "binding admission" test for the no-contact rule to protect corporations from damaging disclosures).

[69] Reporter's Explanation of Changes, Model Rule 4.2, ABA Comm'n on Evaluation of the Rules of Prof'l Conduct (Ethics 2000 Commission) (2001); *see also* Carl A. Pierce, *Variations on a Basic Theme: Revising the ABA's Revision of Model Rule 4.2 (Part I)*, 70 TENN. L. REV. 121, 177–79 (2002) (explaining revision of comments).

have the effect of *binding* the organization with respect to proof of the matter."[70] As Professor Carl Pierce writes, "[p]recluding contact whenever a constituent's statement may be admissible would, in practical effect, prohibit communication with any employee who, as an employee, acquired relevant information about a claim by or against the organization."[71]

In other words, by this interpretation of Model Rule 4.2 and the words of the *Restatement*, an entity's agent who is not otherwise within the scope of the no-contact rule (because she regularly consults with the lawyer or her actions would be imputed to the entity) would come within its constraints only if that agent's statement would genuinely *bind* the organization in the manner of a stipulation or a pleading admission. Rather than a mere evidentiary admission, a binding statement would be one that the entity could not disavow or attempt to overcome by a contrary evidentiary showing.

Concerns about a lawyer inappropriately extracting refutable evidentiary admissions from organization employees might be effectively arrested by simply excluding such statements from evidence or refusing to allow the statement to be attributed to the entity itself. Importantly, as discussed below, a lawyer who is permitted to communicate with a present or former employee of an entity is forbidden to seek information from the employee that is protected by the attorney-client privilege or work-product protection for the entity.[72]

When a constituent of an organization is a lawyer-employee and is acting as a lawyer for the organization, that is, a house counsel, communications with that person do not fall under the constraints of Rule 4.2. The Standing Committee on Ethics and Professional Responsibility of the American Bar Association confirmed that a lawyer who is representing a client in a matter that involves an organization generally may communicate with the organization's inside counsel about the subject of the representation, without obtaining the prior consent of the entity's outside counsel.[73] The risks of possible overreaching by a lawyer, undue influence in extracting a decision, interference in the attorney-client relationship, and inadvertent disclosure of confidential information are not typically present with such lawyer-to-lawyer contacts. Of course, as the committee recognized, in-house counsel is always free to refer any inquiries to its outside counsel.

## § 4-8.4(b) Contacting Former Employees of an Entity

The policy considerations underlying the "no-contact" rule—to avoid exploitation of lay persons by a lawyer for purposes of obtaining settlement or other concessions and to prevent interference with the attorney-client relationship—"have marginal relevance when the communication is between an attorney and a former employee of an organization."[74] Moreover, an absolute bar on *ex parte* communications with former employees would discourage informal and inexpensive discovery of information. In a case involving application of the no-contact rule to former employees of a corporate entity, a federal district court ruled:

---

[70] RESTATEMENT (THIRD) OF THE LAW GOVERNING LAWYERS § 100(c) (American Law Institute, 2000) (emphasis added).

[71] Pierce, *supra*, 70 TENN. L. REV. at 179.

[72] *See infra* § 4-8.4(c).

[73] ABA Comm. on Ethics and Professional Responsibility, Formal Op. 06–443 (2006).

[74] Cram v. Lamson & Sessions Co., 148 F.R.D. 259, 260 (S.D. Iowa 1993).

> These policy considerations [underlying the no-contact rule] substantially impact the cost and delay of federal civil litigation. First, if all *ex parte* communications with an opposing party's former employees are prohibited, counsel's attempts at engaging in informal discovery will be sharply curtailed. In most cases, counsel will not have informal access to witnesses with important knowledge of critical facts. Counsel will be unable to access the merits of a case inexpensively and quickly by contacting these witnesses . . . . Formal discovery, in turn, can create protracted and quarrelsome discovery disputes which consume finite judicial resources.[75]

If the cloak of silence is cast too widely over fact witnesses, the no-contact rule loses its tether to underlying principles of client protection and becomes simply an excuse for interfering with an opponent's case preparation. Accordingly, as Comment 7 to Rule 4.2 states, "[c]onsent of the organization's lawyer is not required for communication with a former constituent." Of course, when a former employee is represented by her own legal counsel, that person becomes "plainly off limits" under the no-contact rule.[76]

A few courts have concluded that, while *ex parte* contacts with former employees of a corporate party are not improper per se, certain types of former employees raise special problems.[77] In *Camden v. Maryland*,[78] a federal trial court disqualified an attorney and ruled that a lawyer may not have *ex parte* contact with a former employee "when the lawyer knows or should know that the former employee has been extensively exposed to confidential client information of the other interested party." In *MMR / Wallace Power & Ind. v. Thames Assocs.*,[79] another federal court disqualified a firm for talking with a "confidential former employee" of the opposing party. In both the *Camden* and *MMR / Wallace* cases, the former employee interviewed by opposing counsel had been intimately involved in the very case being litigated and had disclosed (or apparently disclosed) extensive information about litigation strategy and even corporate counsel's appraisal of the strength of the case.

The pertinent comment to Rule 4.2 quoted above does not suggest any direct limitation on *who* may be contacted among former employees, although the *topics* for conversation may not include inquiry into privileged or otherwise protected information (as discussed below).[80]

### § 4-8.4(c) Limitations on Communications with Current or Former Constituents of an Entity

Even when an attorney representing a client adverse to an entity is permitted to conduct *ex parte* interviews with a current or former employee or other constituent of a

---

75 *Id.* at 26. On the benefits of informal fact-finding and an argument that Rule 4.2 overly restricts such efforts, see Geoffrey C. Hazard, Jr. & Dana Remus Irwin, *Toward a Revised 4.2 No-Contact Rule*, 60 HASTINGS L.J. 797, 805 (2009).

76 Terra Int'l, Inc. v. Mississippi Chem. Corp., 913 F. Supp. 1306, 1315 (N.D. Iowa 1996).

77 *See* Porter v. Arco Metals Co., 642 F. Supp. 1116, 1118 (D. Mont. 1986) (barring *ex parte* communications with former managerial employees if they had had responsibilities concerning the subject matter of the litigation).

78 910 F. Supp. 1115, 1116, 1122 (D. Md. 1996).

79 764 F. Supp. 712 (D. Conn. 1991).

80 *See infra* § 4-8.4(c); *see also* Cram v. Lamson & Sessions Co., 148 F.R.D. 259, 266 (S.D. Iowa 1993) (placing no restrictions on *ex parte* contact with former employees, but leaving open the possibility that the corporation could obtain a protective order if it could "produce sufficient evidence that privileged communications may be divulged by the former employees during *ex parte* communications").

represented organization, the attorney remains subject to other ethical rules that constrain the manner in which the contact is made and the scope of the discussion:

#### *§ 4-8.4(c)(1) Not Suggesting Lawyer Neutrality*

A lawyer making contact with an entity's former employee who does not have his own legal counsel must comply with Rule 4.3 of the Model Rules of Professional Conduct. That rule directs that a lawyer dealing with an unrepresented person must not suggest or imply that the lawyer is "disinterested," must make "reasonable efforts" to correct any misunderstanding that the person may have about "the lawyer's role in the matter," and must not provide legal advice to a person whose interests are in conflict with the lawyer's client ("other than the advice to secure counsel").[81] The lawyer may not leave the former employee with the impression that the lawyer is obliged to protect that person's interests and must correct any misapprehension by the former employee that the lawyer is a neutral observer rather than an advocate for an interested party.

The lawyer may offer appropriate legal advice to the former employee if that person's interests are congruent with those of the lawyer's client. However, the lawyer must refrain from counseling the former employee about her conduct or the consequences of testifying as a witness if the former employee's interests are incompatible with those of the lawyer's client.[82]

#### *§ 4-8.4(c)(2) Not Violating Organization's Rights (Confidentiality)*

Comment 7 to Rule 4.2 admonishes that "[i]n communicating with a current or former constituent of an organization, a lawyer must not use methods of obtaining evidence that violate the legal rights of the organization," which is a reference to the restrictions under Rule 4.4(a).[83] In particular, if present or former organizational employees or agents have information protected by the attorney-client evidentiary privilege, the lawyer may not deliberately seek to uncover such protected information. In *Cram v. Lamson & Sessions Co.*,[84] a federal district court ruled that, even when *ex parte* contact is permitted under the no-contact limitation, "an attorney communicating with the former employees of the opposing party may not inquire into privileged attorney-client communications because '[a]ny privilege existing between the former employee and the organization's counsel belongs to the organization, and can only be waived by the organization.' "[85]

### § 4-8.5 THE LAWYER RESPONDING TO THE CLIENT'S DULY-AUTHORIZED CONSTITUENTS

Rule 1.13(a) of the Model Rules of Professional Conduct states that "[a] lawyer employed or retained by an organization represents the organization acting through its

---

[81] *See infra* § 4-11.4.

[82] *See infra* § 4-11.4.

[83] On the general prohibition on discovery methods that violate legal rights of others, see *infra* § 4-9.6(d).

[84] 148 F.R.D. 259 (S.D. Iowa 1993).

[85] *Id.* at 266 (quoting Sequa Corp. v. Lititech, Inc., 807 F. Supp. 653, 668 (D.Colo.1992)); *see also* Wis. St. Bar Prof'l Ethics Comm., Op. E-07-01 (2007) (stating that a lawyer who contacts a constituent of a represented organization "must not ask any questions reasonably likely to elicit information that the lawyer knows or reasonably should know is privileged and, if necessary, should caution the unrepresented constituent not to reveal such information").

duly authorized constituents." This simple statement, which generally articulates the professional responsibilities arising from representation of an entity, has two essential elements. First, the rule emphasizes that the lawyer's professional attention should be devoted to the interests of the organization. Second, the rule explains that the lawyer fulfils these responsibilities by responding to the duly authorized constituents of that organization.

It sometimes has been said that the lawyer for an organization is ethically bound to act in the "best interests" of the organization. To the extent this advice is merely a reminder that the lawyer is to promote the wellbeing of the organization and must not prefer the interests of the individual persons affiliated with the organization, the statement is salutary. If this statement instead were misunderstood to suggest that the lawyer is generally empowered to calculate the "best interests" of the organization as the lawyer sees it—in other words, allowing the lawyer to commit professional efforts toward the lawyer's self-defined end—Rule 1.13(a) should disabuse the lawyer of that sense of professional aggrandizement.

As is true with clients who are natural persons, the organization client is entitled to decide for itself what constitutes its own "best interests" regarding the objectives of the representation. While every lawyer is encouraged to initiate a moral dialogue when counseling a client,[86] the choice among lawful objectives is reserved to the client.

And an organization makes decisions concerning the legal representation through its "duly authorized constituents." The lawyer thus must learn the nature of the organization by which he has been retained or employed, including the lines of authority and delegations of power within the organization. When the lawyer has appropriately advised the constituent with proper authority to make a decision regarding the legal representation, the lawyer ordinarily is obliged to comply with the decision and treat that decision as properly attributed to the organization itself.

Only under extreme circumstances, discussed further below,[87] when an officer, employee, or other person engages in unlawful conduct that is likely to cause substantial injury to the organization, may a lawyer proceed in the manner that he independently concludes is necessary to safeguard the "best interest" of the entity. And even then the lawyer's professional discretion is constrained.

In carrying out the representation, and being responsive to such "duly authorized constituents" as directors, officers, employees, members, and shareholders, the lawyer regularly should remind those persons that the lawyer is counsel for the entity and does not represent any of these persons in their individual capacities (unless the lawyer is engaged in dual representation of both the organization and the constituent).[88] When the lawyer responds to the directive of a person within the organization who has the authority to make a decision regarding the legal representation, the lawyer is acting to advance the organization's interest as expressed through its agent and not to satisfy the interests of the individual decision-maker.

Especially if the occasion should arise in which the lawyer knows or reasonably should know that the interests of the organization have become adverse to that of a constituent with whom the lawyer is dealing, Rule 1.13(f) directs the lawyer to "explain

---

86 *See supra* § 4-5.2(b).

87 *See infra* § 4-8.6.

88 On dual representation of the organization and an individual constituent, see *infra* § 4-8.8.

the identity of the client." In such an instance, to avoid any misunderstanding by the person involved,[89] the lawyer must underscore that she represents and takes directions from the organization as an entity and is not responsible to protect the interests of the individual officer, director, employee, or shareholder. Indeed, the lawyer is forbidden to prefer any constituent's personal desires over and against the interests of the organization as properly declared through the organization's chain-of-command.

Thus, for example, if the president of an organization comes to be at odds with the governing board of directors, the counsel for the organization must carefully clarify to all concerned that the lawyer's direction must be taken from the board (assuming the board is the duly authorized governing body of the entity). While the lawyer may communicate with the president on behalf and at the direction of the board of directors, the lawyer must refrain from offering any legal advice to the president on those points of separation and dispute with the board (or on any personal matter or obligation). As necessary to avoid misunderstanding, Comment 10 to Rule 1.13 directs the lawyer to advise any constituent with a personal interest adverse to the organization that she may wish to obtain separate legal counsel on that matter.

## § 4-8.6 THE LAWYER'S RESPONSIBILITIES WHEN UNLAWFUL CONDUCT OR INTERNAL DISSENSION ARISES WITHIN AN ORGANIZATION

### § 4-8.6(a) Introduction to the Problem of Constituent Misconduct Threatening the Organization

As is true with any human enterprise, the persons who make up an organization may not always agree on the course of action to take, may battle for control of the entity, or may even find themselves in fundamental disagreement on matters crucial to the survival of the entity. While the lawyer's responsibilities as counsel to the entity certainly are made more difficult in such circumstances, the fundamental principle remains that the lawyer must respond to the organization's decisions as expressed through its duly authorized constituents.

By contrast with ordinary instances of disagreement or conflict among entity constituents, when a lawyer in the course of representation[90] encounters the extreme scenario of a person within the organization who is planning or has engaged in misconduct that is likely to cause serious harm to the organization, Rule 1.13(b) to (d) of the Model Rules of Professional Conduct directs the lawyer to take such counteractive measures as the lawyer concludes are reasonably necessary to protect the "best interest" of the organization.

---

[89] On the corporate lawyer's duties to clarify her representational role when conducting internal corporate investigations, especially in light of federal prosecutorial guidelines encouraging voluntary disclosure of privileged information, see *infra* § 4-9.12(c)(4). On the lawyer's responsibilities concerning the misunderstandings of laypersons regarding whether an attorney-client relationship has been created, see *supra* § 4-3.2(c).

[90] *See* Christopher J. Motz, Note, *Officious Meddler or Ethical Advocate? Corporate Counsel's Model Rule 1.13 Obligation to Report Up the Ladder: Defining "Related to the Representation,"* 10 U. ST. THOMAS L.J. 352, 362 (2012) (arguing that "the category of what might trigger up-the-ladder reports under Rule 1.13" is narrowly restricted "to only those things relating to the actual work assignment or specific task of the attorney").

Even under such acute circumstances, Rule 1.13(b) presumes that the lawyer will act within the ordinary chain-of-command to seek resolution of the problem. Only if the highest authority within the organization defaults in its responsibilities to protect the entity from serious harm by a miscreant constituent is the lawyer authorized to disclose confidential information if reasonably necessary to prevent the injury.

In all events, Rule 1.13 directs the lawyer to be responsive to and guided by the "best interest" of the organization, rather than the interests of any individual constituents within the organization or persons outside the organization (although the interests of others, especially if they may be injured by fraudulent behavior, may require certain professional actions under the provisions of other rules).[91]

### § 4-8.6(b) Triggering the Lawyer's Duty to Proceed in the Best Interests of the Organization

Rule 1.13(b) provides in the first sentence:

> If a lawyer for an organization knows that an officer, employee or other person associated with the organization is engaged in action, intends to act or refuses to act in a matter related to the representation that is a violation of a legal obligation to the organization, or a violation of law that reasonably might be imputed to the organization, and that is likely to result in substantial injury to the organization, then the lawyer shall proceed as is reasonably necessary in the best interest of the organization.

Each part of this complex sentence must be unpacked to reveal the extraordinary nature of the problem being addressed:

#### *§ 4-8.6(b)(1) Lawyer's Knowledge of Illegal Conduct*

Rule 1.13(b)'s directive that the lawyer must choose how to proceed in the best interests of the organization is activated only if the lawyer knows that a person within the organization has engaged or intends to engage in what amounts to illegal misconduct. Under Rule 1.1, the word "knows" means that the person has "actual knowledge of the fact in question," which here would be the past or anticipated misconduct.

The lawyer's mere suspicion of illegal behavior by another is not sufficient to trigger the lawyer's duty to act, although a concrete basis for suspicion presumably would prompt the diligent lawyer[92] to investigate further, which in turn may produce actual knowledge. The lawyer may not act in willful disregard for the clues that he finds or the direction in which such evidence leads.

#### *§ 4-8.6(b)(2) Corporate Constituent Acting in Violation of Law*

Before the special duty of Rule 1.13(b) takes effect, the lawyer must learn that someone associated with the organization has acted, is acting, or will act in a manner relating to the organization that is "a violation of a legal obligation to the organization, or a violation of law that reasonably might be imputed to the organization."

---

[91] *See supra* § 4-6.6 and *infra* § 4-11.2(a).

[92] On lawyer's duty of diligence, see *supra* § 4-5.3.

That the lawyer questions the wisdom of a constituent's course of action, or even believes such a measure is likely to result in injury to the organization, gives no warrant to the lawyer to take extraordinary steps to preempt that action (although, to the extent that the matter falls within the lawyer's province as legally-related, a good lawyer might counsel a contrary course or perhaps bring the matter to the attention and seek the advice of higher authority within the corporation). Nor does Rule 1.13(b) necessarily apply to the situation discussed below in which constituents of the organization have fallen into such serious discord that the survival of the entity is in doubt.[93]

Again, only if the lawyer knows that the conduct of the person or persons at issue contravenes the directives of the law—that is, rises to the level of law-breaking behavior—is Rule 1.13(b) implicated.

#### *§ 4-8.6(b)(3) Substantial Injury Is Likely*

The lawyer's duty to proceed as is reasonably necessary in the best interest of the organization comes into play only if the lawyer believes the misconduct is "likely to result in substantial injury to the organization." Minor or technical violations of the law that are unlikely to have much, if any, consequence to the organization do not justify extraordinary measures.

Of course, the lawyer should offer appropriate legal advice designed to arrest any legal delinquency and should appreciate that a pattern of lawlessness in small things may add up to something more significant and eventually set in motion the duties of Rule 1.13(b).

### § 4-8.6(c) Addressing the Problem Within the Organizational Structure

Even if all the foregoing prerequisites are present, and the lawyer thus has an ethical duty to take appropriate corrective action, the lawyer's authority to proceed in the best interest of the organization is circumscribed. In particular, the lawyer is directed to work within the organizational structure and its chain-of-command to address the problem of constituent misconduct. Rule 1.13(b) provides in its second sentence:

> Unless the lawyer reasonably believes that it is not necessary in the best interest of the organization to do so, the lawyer shall refer the matter to higher authority in the organization, including, if warranted by the circumstances, to the highest authority that can act on behalf of the organization as determined by applicable law.

On some occasions, the lawyer may conclude it is not necessary to escalate the controversy by complaining to the next level of the entity. As Comment 4 to Rule 1.13 suggests, the lawyer instead may decide "to ask the constituent to reconsider the matter; for example, if the circumstances involve a constituent's innocent misunderstanding of law and subsequent acceptance of the lawyer's advice."

Indeed, as part of the lawyer's basic responsibilities to the entity, the lawyer should take "a sensible preventive law approach" and regularly counsel constituents about their

---

[93] *See infra* § 4-8.6(h).

legal responsibilities in advance, so as to discourage misconduct before it occurs.[94] Moreover, the existence of "the formal up-the-ladder reporting requirement" may "provide counsel with the leverage to cause the [entity] constituents to 'do the right thing.' "[95]

In some instances, however, because of the seriousness of the illegality, the imminence of the harm, or the intransigence of the miscreant constituent, the lawyer will need to refer the matter to higher authority within the organization. In bringing the constituent's wrongdoing to the attention of superiors within the entity, the lawyer should take appropriate steps to protect the organization, such as minimizing the chance that confidential information will be disclosed outside of the organization.

The lawyer's responsibility under Rule 1.13(b) to proceed as is reasonably necessary in the best interest of the organization, upon discovering unlawful conduct by a constituent that threatens serious harm to the entity, will be fully satisfied in most cases by bringing the matter to the attention of the governing body within the organization.

Not incidentally, this duty to report misconduct up the organizational ladder aligns with, although it does not precisely parallel, the statutory duties of the corporate lawyer under the federal Sarbanes-Oxley Act of 2002,[96] which was enacted in the wake of Enron, WorldCom, Tyco, and other notorious corporate scandals. Under regulations adopted by the Securities and Exchange Commission, a lawyer who has "evidence" that a "material violation" of federal or state securities laws or regulations has occurred or is about to occur must directly refer the matter to the chief legal officer or chief operating officer of the business organization and, if the violation is not remedied, then to higher authority in the corporation.[97]

Reporting up-the-chain ordinarily should be sufficient to secure the necessary corrective action—and achieve that correction within the organization structure. As Professors Geoffrey Hazard and Williams Hodes and attorney Peter Jarvis anticipate:

> This is because people at the top of most corporations or unions or other organizations have no interest in shielding fraud by lower echelon personnel, and a strong interest to avoid doing so. Most high-ranking officials are law-abiding, and require the same of their subordinates, a few spectacular recent examples to the contrary notwithstanding. These officials do not want the legal grief involved in responding to investigations of wrongdoing, let alone the pain

[94] *See* Lyman Johnson & Rob Ricca, *(Not) Advising Corporate Officers About Fiduciary Duties*, 42 WAKE FOREST L. REV. 663, 665, 689 (2007) (arguing in corporate context that "[i]f lawyers are to report 'potential' or 'ongoing' breaches of fiduciary duty, a sensible preventive law approach to governance reform demands that lawyers first advise officers as to the existence and scope of those fiduciary duties," but finding in a survey of corporate lawyers "that many lawyers do not provide full-bodied fiduciary duty advice to officers in their capacity as officers at all").

[95] E. Norman Veasey & Christine T. Di Guglielmo, *The Tensions, Stresses, and Professional Responsibilities of the Lawyer for the Corporation*, 62 BUS. LAW. 1, 21 (Nov. 2006).

[96] Pub. L. No. 107–204, 116 Stat. 745 (codified as amended in scattered sections of 11, 15, 28 and 29 U.S.C.).

[97] 17 C.F.R. Part 205. For an excellent and detailed, but still succinct, description of the securities lawyer's obligations under Sarbanes-Oxley, see W. BRADLEY WENDEL, PROFESSIONAL RESPONSIBILITY: EXAMPLES & EXPLANATIONS 112–16 (Wolters Kluwer, 5th ed., 2016).

of actual litigation or prosecution. And if top management is typically risk averse, independent directors are even more so.[98]

### § 4-8.6(d) Disclosing Confidential Information to Correct the Problem

If the lawyer fails in the effort to provoke corrective action by higher authority within the organization, then Model Rule 1.13(c) authorizes, but does not command, the lawyer to take the additional step of disclosing confidential information to outsiders to prevent injury to the entity. In other words, if "reporting up" within the organization to higher authority proves unsuccessful, the lawyer has circumscribed authority to "report out" from the organization to outsiders.[99]

Here too, Model Rule 1.13 appears parallel to regulations adopted by the Securities and Exchange Commission under the Sarbanes-Oxley Act of 2002,[100] which authorize (but do not mandate) a lawyer who has "evidence" that a "material violation" of federal or state securities laws or regulations to report the matter out to regulators if necessary to prevent harm to the company.[101]

However, precisely because the report-out option is permissible and not mandatory under the Sarbanes-Oxley regulations, a lawyer would be authorized to take this step only if the state ethics rules also permitted the action. Thus, in the substantial minority of states that have not adopted the Model Rule 1.13(c) reporting-out provision,[102] non-complicit lawyers in securities matters could not claim permission to disclose confidential information to securities regulators,[103] instead having to withdraw from the representation.

For the majority of states that follow Model Rule 1.13, permission is granted, but only under exceptional circumstances. If after receiving the lawyer's report of law-breaking by a constituent and the risk of substantial injury to the organization, the "highest authority" within the organization endorses the reported misconduct by the offending constituent, fails to address it in a timely and appropriate manner, or refuses to address or even acknowledge the problem, then that "highest authority" will have been proven fatally defective on this crucial matter. In light of the governing body's abysmal failure to uphold its duty to protect the organization, the lawyer is granted the exceptional discretion to go beyond the organization structure and seek the assistance of outsiders in resolving the problem.

---

[98] 1 GEOFFREY C. HAZARD, JR., W. WILLIAM HODES & PETER R. JARVIS, THE LAW OF LAWYERING § 18.15 (Aspen, 4th ed., 2016).

[99] W. BRADLEY WENDEL, PROFESSIONAL RESPONSIBILITY: EXAMPLES & EXPLANATIONS 111 (Wolters Kluwer, 5th ed., 2016) ("Remember that reporting out is permissive ('may reveal'), while reporting up is mandatory ('shall refer the matter to a higher authority').").

[100] Pub. L. No. 107–204, 116 Stat. 745 (codified as amended in scattered sections of 11, 15, 28 and 29 U.S.C.).

[101] 17 C.F.R. Part 205.

[102] *See, e.g.*, CAL. RULES OF PROF'L CONDUCT R. 3–600(C); FLA. RULES OF PROF'L CONDUCT R. 4–13; N.Y. RULES OF PROF'L CONDUCT R. 1.13(c). *See generally* N.Y. Cnty. Lawyers' Ass'n Formal Op. 746 (2013).

[103] At least a lawyer could not do so based on the Sarbanes-Oxley regulation or the state version of Rule 1.13, but the lawyer might be able to invoke a self-defense exception to confidentiality, see *supra* § 4-6.6(f), to avoid being prosecuted or held liable for a securities violation committed by other company constituents contrary to the lawyer's advice.

Rule 1.13(c) permits the lawyer to disclose confidential information "but only if and to the extent the lawyer reasonably believes necessary to prevent substantial injury to the organization." The lawyer might report the intramural misconduct to an outside law enforcement or regulatory body that would force the entity to comply with the law. Or, in the case of a corporation, the lawyer might report the matter to shareholders who might be able to intervene and save the organization from itself.

It must be emphasized that the lawyer's permissive authority to disclose confidential information, for the purpose of provoking an outside intervention, is only for the benefit of the entity.[104] This is *not* a "whistle-blower" provision. Instead, to use the label coined by Professor George Harris, Rule 1.13(c) contemplates a "loyal disclosure" in the interest of the entity.[105] As confirmation of "the inward looking and client-protecting nature" of Rule 1.13, Professors Geoffrey Hazard and William Hodes and attorney Peter Jarvis characterize such extramural disclosures "as a last-ditch effort to rescue *the client* from suffering substantial injury due to lawbreaking activities ratified (or ignored) even by the highest authority in the organization."[106]

Indeed, given the failure of the organization's governing body to take curative action on its own—which is an abdication of that body's fundamental responsibilities—the lawyer's disclosure of confidential information under the extreme circumstances contemplated in Rule 1.13(c) might be regarded less as an exception to the confidentiality principle than as a waiver by the organization itself acting through its lawyer as a substitute agent for the defective governing body.

However, while Rule 1.13 does not oblige the lawyer to disclose confidential information other than to assist the organization, other provisions in the rules do permit and may even require disclosure of confidential information to prevent or rectify fraudulent or criminal behavior by a client, whether an organization or an individual, that may cause serious financial harm to another. Rule 4.1(b) of the Model Rules of Professional Conduct, which forbids a lawyer from knowingly "fail[ing] to disclose a material fact when disclosure is necessary to avoid assisting a criminal or fraudulent act by a client," when read together with the exceptions in Rule 1.6(b)(2) and (3), which permit disclosure to prevent or rectify substantial financial harm caused by a client's criminal or fraudulent behavior, effectively requires disclosure of confidential information in narrow circumstances.[107]

### § 4-8.6(e) Prohibition on Disclosure by Lawyer Retained to Investigate or Defend

When the lawyer has been retained by the organization "to investigate an alleged violation of law, or to defend the organization or an officer, employee or other constituent associated with the organization against a claim arising out of an alleged violation of law," Rule 1.13(d) withdraws the permission granted to the lawyer under Rule 1.13(c) to

[104] *See* Pang v. International Document Servs., 356 P.3d 1190, 1201 (Utah 2015) ("It is true that when in-house attorneys report illegal conduct to their superiors, the public reaps incidental benefits from corrective action the company might undertake to comply with the law. But rule 1.13 regulates conduct that is, at its core, a private matter between attorneys and their clients, not one of broad public concern.").

[105] George C. Harris, *Taking Entity Theory Seriously: Lawyer Liability for Failure to Prevent Harm to Organization Clients Through Disclosure of Constituent Wrongdoing*, 11 GEO. J. LEG. ETHICS 597, 600 (1988).

[106] 1 GEOFFREY C. HAZARD, JR., W. WILLIAM HODES & PETER R. JARVIS, THE LAW OF LAWYERING § 18.02 (Aspen, 4th ed., 2016).

[107] *See supra* § 4-6.6(d)(3) and *infra* § 4-11.2(a).

disclose confidential information to those outside the organization for the purpose of protecting the organization.

Thus, when the representational role is limited to conducting a fact-finding investigation within the organization or is for the specific purpose of defending the organization or its constituents against a charge of unlawful misconduct,[108] the lawyer does not have permission to bypass the organization's chain-of-command and disclose confidential information outside the organization. As Comment 7 to Rule 1.13 explains, "[t]his is necessary in order to enable organizational clients to enjoy the full benefits of legal counsel in conducting an investigation or defending against a claim." Note that the lawyer hired to investigate or defend the organization is not relieved of the responsibilities outlined in Rule 1.13(b) to report findings about misconduct to those in higher authority within the entity.

### § 4-8.6(f) Lawyer's Responsibility When Discharged or Withdrawing

Under Rule 1.13(e), the lawyer's responsibilities under Rule 1.13(b) do not evaporate altogether because the lawyer has been or believes that she has been discharged or the lawyer chooses to withdraw from the representation of the entity.[109] Indeed, that the duty to report is a continuing one may even help the lawyer keep her job (or retain the entity client), despite antipathy toward the lawyer by those entity constituents who are the subject of the lawyer's negative report up-the-ladder of the organization.

If the lawyer reasonably believes that she has been discharged from representation because of the corrective actions that the lawyer has taken in response to unlawful conduct by a constituent that threatens substantial injury to the organization, or if the lawyer chooses to withdraw from representing the entity, Rule 1.13(e) nonetheless requires the lawyer to take reasonable steps "to ensure that the organization's highest authority is informed of the lawyer's discharge or withdrawal." The rule is designed to make sure that the entity's governing body is informed of the state of affairs or at least placed on notice that something may be awry. And because the lawyer may inform miscreant constituents that this reporting duty survives any termination of the representation, those offending persons may be less likely to try to force the lawyer out as a means of silencing objections to their conduct.

### § 4-8.6(g) The Problem of the Miscreant Constituent and the Lawyer's Duty of Diligence to the Organization

Most of the directives in Rule 1.13(b) to (e) tell the lawyer to do exactly what a lawyer for an organization ought to do anyway, animated by the core principle that the lawyer is responsible to organization itself as the actual client. Thus, even in the substantial minority of states that have not adopted all of the provisions of Rule 1.13, the lawyer's responsibilities in most respects may not be materially different from those clarified and expressed in Rule 1.13 of the Model Rules of Professional Conduct.

The lawyer should insist that every person within the organization comply with the clear directives of the law; should refuse to tolerate the illegal behavior of any constituent; should seek assistance from a higher authority within the organization

---

[108] On limitations on the scope of representation generally, see *supra* § 4-3.3.

[109] On the question of whether an employed house counsel for an entity may bring an action for wrongful discharge, see *supra* § 4-3.6(b)(2).

when someone within the entity has engaged or is engaging in misconduct (or for that matter should consult with superiors within the organization whenever the matter is sufficiently important to warrant referral); and should reserve extraordinary measures to protect the organization from harm, such as disclosure of confidential information to outsiders, for the anomalous circumstance in which the organization's governing body proves utterly inadequate to the task. Even aside from Rule 1.13, the lawyer has a professional duty to protect the entity against the wrongful acts of its constituents, as failure to do so places the lawyer at the risk not only of disciplinary action, but also of civil liability.[110] When understood in this way, what appears at first glance to be an extraordinary set of provisions in Rule 1.13, instead articulates a basic expectation of due diligence by the lawyer who represents an organization.

Attorney Lawrence Fox and Professor Susan Martyn are not as sanguine about the implications of a rule that also permits a lawyer to disclose confidential information outside the organization, even if restricted to the extraordinary circumstance where that disclosure is believed necessary to protect the organization client itself from the harmful misconduct of its constituents. They rightly worry that the report-out permission of Model Rule 1.13 could lead a judge to overreach and adopt "the guardian angel view of how lawyers' obligations should be defined."[111] They properly remind lawyers for organizations that "it is very rare that a lawyer will know more about the business and mission of the organization than those in control."

The provisions of Rule 1.13, designed as they are to assist the lawyer in protecting the interests of the organization, can be effective only if the lawyer is morally- and ethically-grounded. If, instead, as Mark Sargent described the behavior of lawyers in corporate scandals, "moral priorities . . . often seemed to disappear into a smog of expediency, rationalization, willful blindness and slavish obedience to the wishes of self-interested managers who purported to speak for the corporate client,"[112] then no formal rule can save the day. In the end, there is no substitute for professional independence, ethical reasoning, and a willingness by the lawyer to engage in moral deliberation with the client.

### § 4-8.6(h) The Lawyer's Responsibilities When Serious Conflicts Arise Among Constituents of the Organization

If an organization should dissolve into infighting among its constituents, the lawyer must be especially careful to identify precisely who is entitled to speak for and make decisions on behalf of the organization. As directed by Rule 1.13(a), the lawyer must respond to the entity client as embodied in the person or body within that organization that has lawful governing authority.[113] In addition, the lawyer should be wary of

---

[110] *See* FDIC v. O'Melveny & Meyers, 969 F.2d 744, 748–51 (9th Cir. 1992), *rev'd on other grounds*, 512 U.S. 79 (1994); *see also* Mark A. Sargent, *Lawyers in the Perfect Storm*, 43 WASHBURN L.J. 1, 30 (2003). For a discussion of defenses that may be available to the lawyer when malpractice claims are asserted in such contexts, see Matthew G. Doré, *Presumed Innocent? Financial Institutions, Professional Malpractice Claims, and Defenses Based on Management Misconduct*, 1995 COLUM. BUS. L. REV. 127.

[111] LAWRENCE J. FOX & SUSAN R. MARTYN, THE ETHICS OF REPRESENTING ORGANIZATIONS: LEGAL FICTIONS FOR CLIENTS 71–77 (Oxford U. Press, 2009); *see also* Lawrence J. Fox, *Can Confidentiality Survive Enron, Arthur Andersen, and the ABA?*, 34 STETSON L. REV. 147, 157 (2004) (expressing concern that by granting lawyers permission to disclose, "it will not be a very big step for somebody to come along and assert that lawyers should be liable for failing to do it").

[112] Mark A. Sargent, *Lawyers in the Moral Maze*, 49 VILL. L. REV. 867, 872 (2004).

[113] *See supra* § 4-8.5.

becoming enmeshed in internal strife by offering legal advice to conflicting parties or by becoming a partisan among battling constituents with apparently equal claim to control the organization. Especially at a point of such turmoil within an organization, the attorney must diligently comply with paragraph Rule 1.13(f) by reminding all within the organization that the lawyer's representation is solely of the entity and that the lawyer's advice is intended only for those persons or bodies authorized to decide for the entity. The lawyer must disavow any representational responsibilities to those with interests adverse to the organization and advise them to obtain independent legal counsel.

When the constituents of an organization enter into disputation among themselves, the lawyer for an organization understandably may seek to be the oil on troubled waters. With a wise counselor, who carefully makes clear his ultimate allegiance to the entity and who takes great pains to avoid any misunderstanding about that loyalty among the participants—and when there is reason to believe that the dispute can be managed or resolved—such an approach may prevent the unraveling of the enterprise and such counseling services may redound to the benefit of all. However, as Professor Geoffrey Hazard has warned:

> Playing God is a tricky business. It requires skill, nerve, detachment, compassion, ingenuity, and the capacity to sustain confidence. When mishandled, it generates the bitterness and recrimination that results when a deep trust has been betrayed. Perhaps above all, it requires good judgment as to when such intercession can be carried off without unfairly subordinating the interests of one of the parties or having later to abort the mission.[114]

When attempting to facilitate an amicable resolution among warring constituents in an organization, the lawyer faces the dangers that she will fail to maintain a clear identification as the counsel only for the organization and that she will overstay the professional sojourn after irresolvable conflicts of interest have emerged that prevent faithful responsiveness to the entity through its duly-authorized constituents. As stressed repeatedly here, the lawyer for an entity is obliged to uphold the interests of the corporation as a whole, not preferring the interests of one or another constituent above the interests of others. Once the lawyer starts to behave as an intermediary among disputing constituents, by offering suggestions and nurturing trust and confidence among the players, it may become increasingly difficult for the lawyer to clearly separate the role of facilitation from that of offering legal advice and thereby developing an attorney-client relationship with individual members.

Finally, if the lawyer does not exercise prudence in abandoning the peacemaking effort when all hope is lost, the lawyer's continuing participatory role may materially limit the lawyer's ability to continue to represent the organization client and require that he withdraw from further representation of any and all elements, collectively and separately, of the entity.

## § 4-8.7 DUAL REPRESENTATION OF ORGANIZATION AND INDIVIDUAL CONSTITUENT

Under Rule 1.13(g) of the Model Rules of Professional Conduct, a lawyer for an organization may also choose to represent directors, officers, employees, members, shareholders, or other constituents, who then become additional clients, subject to

[114] GEOFFREY C. HAZARD, JR., ETHICS IN THE PRACTICE OF LAW 65 (Yale U. Press, 1978).

conflict of interest limitations. In such a case, the lawyer has entered into what is commonly called a "dual representation," in which the lawyer simultaneously assumes the full range of professional responsibilities to both the organization and to the individual person within the organization.[115]

As is true with any attorney-client relationship, the lawyer must loyally and zealously represent each client—organization and individual—and safeguard the confidential information of each. While dual representation is permitted by the rule, it bears risks for the lawyer because the interests of the constituent may become adverse to those of the organization (or vice-versa), in which case the lawyer could be disqualified from continuing to represent either. The extent of the risk depends upon the purpose of the representations undertaken for the constituent, as well as the nature of the entity:

If the representations are unrelated, such as where a lawyer representing a corporation also agrees to represent a corporate officer or employee in a lawsuit arising from a personal automobile accident or undertakes to draft a will or prepare documents involving the purchase of a home for the officer or employee, then the potential that a conflict of interest will arise is reduced. Even if a conflict later does arise, the lawyer may be able to avoid being disqualified from both representations. Of course, even if the representations are unrelated, when both representations are current, the lawyer may not represent one client adversely to the other.[116]

If the representations are related, such as simultaneously representing both an organization and one of its constituents as co-litigants in a lawsuit involving the same allegations, then the crucial question is the likelihood that the interests of the organization as to the conduct and outcome of the lawsuit may diverge at some point from the personal interests of the constituent.[117] In many instances, maintaining a united defense of both the organization and its members may be appropriate, effective, and cost-efficient. In other instances, the organization may wish at some point to jettison the officer or employee and point the finger at that person as primarily responsible, which thus makes continued dual representation impossible. Moreover, the attorney has a duty of confidentiality to both the corporation and the individual, which means that the attorney may not "interrogat[e] one client to benefit another client" or disclose any such "privileged communications to third parties without [the individual client's] consent."[118] Of course where the organization is a closely held corporation, and thus the interests of the entity and constituent may be more closely parallel, dual representation of a principal is less likely to provoke a conflict with the organization.

If the constituent and the organization should become directly adverse in the very matter upon which the lawyer is engaged in dual representation, in that one or the other has or is about to commence litigation or introduce a cross-claim against the other, such a conflict is irresolvable and the lawyer ordinarily may not continue to represent

---

[115] On representation of multiple clients in civil litigation and the conflict of interest implications, see *supra* § 4-7.4(c)(4).

[116] On the rule prohibiting representing one current client adverse to another, see *supra* § 4-7.4(b).

[117] On joint representation of clients in civil litigation, see *supra* § 4-7.4(c)(4).

[118] United States v. Nicholas, 606 F. Supp. 2d 1109, 1119–20 (C.D. Cal. 2009) (criticizing a law firm—that represented both a corporation and the chief financial officer on separate but related matters involving stock options—for interviewing the officer without his informed written consent to the potential conflict and then disclosing his statements to government regulators and prosecutors).

either.[119] While the lawyer might attempt to anticipate and avoid the need to withdraw from representing the organization after a conflict emerges, Lawrence Fox and Professor Susan Martyn warn that this is "a prospective waiver that can always be challenged later as not sufficiently well informed."[120]

In the absence of direct adversity, the conflict inquiry is whether there is a significant risk that the representation of the constituent (or the organization) will be materially limited by the lawyer's responsibilities to the organization (or the constituent).[121] If the risk of a material limitation is significant but either not yet become concrete or the conflict is manageable, simultaneous representation may continue if both parties give informed consent and the lawyer reasonably believes that she will be able to provide competent and diligent representation to each.[122] Under Rule 1.13(g), when consent to dual representation is required under the conflict rules, "the consent shall be given by an appropriate official of the organization other than the individual who is to be represented, or by the shareholders."

While each case of an arguably emerging conflict of interest must be decided on its own facts, the lawyer who is contemplating dual representation of an organization and a constituent must evaluate the likelihood that a conflict will develop. The lawyer ought to think carefully about whether the dual representation is wise, even if ethically permitted at the moment, in light of those risks. Moreover, the lawyer who becomes associated with a particular constituent through dual representation, even on unrelated matters, may face a difficult or even untenable situation should that person later engage in misconduct that harms the entity[123] or become a partisan to infighting among the constituents of the organization.[124]

Finally, the lawyer representing a constituent of an organization may not counsel or assist the person to behave in an unlawful manner with respect to the organization or its other constituents. The lawyer's professional obligation to counsel compliance with legal requirements applies of course to any lawyer for any type of client and applies to a lawyer for a constituent whether or not the lawyer also represents the organization. For example, as stated in the *Restatement of the Law Governing Lawyers*, "[i]f the lawyer represents as a client . . . the constituent owing fiduciary duties [to the entity or another constituent], the lawyer may not counsel or assist a breach of any fiduciary obligation owed by the constituent to the organization."[125]

## § 4-8.8 GOVERNMENT CLIENTS

### § 4-8.8(a) The Lawyer's Responsibilities to a Government or Public Office Client

The basic principles and attendant duties with respect to organization clients stated in Rule 1.13 of the Model Rules of Professional Conduct apply in full measure to

[119] LAWRENCE J. FOX & SUSAN R. MARTYN, THE ETHICS OF REPRESENTING ORGANIZATIONS: LEGAL FICTIONS FOR CLIENTS 19 (Oxford U. Press, 2009).

[120] *Id.* at 153.

[121] *See supra* § 4-7.4.

[122] *See supra* § 4-7.7.

[123] *See supra* § 4-8.6.

[124] *See supra* § 4-8.6(h).

[125] RESTATEMENT (THIRD) OF THE LAW GOVERNING LAWYERS § 96, cmt. g (American Law Institute, 2000).

government lawyers who represent public entities or offices. The government lawyer's client may be a specific agency, a branch of government, or the government as a whole. In addition, government lawyers may have broader obligations on behalf of the public interest to question the conduct or policy choices of officials within a client agency or other governmental entity in a manner and for a purpose beyond that found in the private attorney-client relationship. The Model Rules of Professional Conduct do not supersede that authority or responsibility.

In particular, the government lawyer is bound by the core principle of Rule 1.13, which means that the lawyer represents the governmental entity—however defined—and not a particular individual even if that person is the lawyer's supervisor. Thus, for example, attorneys in the United States Department of Justice or in a state attorney general's office are responsible to the offices of the United States Attorney General or the state Attorney General respectively, not to the person who happens to hold the office at the moment. Of course, most of the time that is a distinction without a difference. When an official or supervisor is the duly authorized official to make decisions for that government office, the subordinate government lawyer properly responds to the directives of that official. But in the hopefully rare instance when an individual office-holder has engaged in wrongdoing, the government lawyer's allegiance belongs to the office and the lawyer may not protect or excuse wrongdoing by the person who holds it.

### § 4-8.8(b) The Attorney-Client Privilege in the Government Context

In the course of criminal investigations during the Clinton Administration by separate independent counsels, two federal appellate courts upheld the basic principle that the government lawyer's responsibility goes beyond the person of the office-holder and attaches to higher government authority charged with protecting the public interest. In separate cases, these courts ruled that the attorney-client privilege could not be invoked to prevent official White House lawyers (as contrasted with President Clinton's personal legal counsel) from being called to testify or to produce documents involving communications with the president about his alleged criminal wrongdoing.[126] When a government lawyer learns through communications with a government official of possible criminal misconduct, neither the lawyer nor the government official may rely on the attorney-client privilege to shield such information from disclosure to a grand jury.

While these two decisions may be faulted for framing the issue primarily as whether a government attorney-client privilege existed at all in the context of a criminal investigation, the outcome is better understood as simply confirming that the government entity itself, as the lawyer's ultimate client, is entitled to control the attorney-client privilege. Given the basic rule that the attorney-client privilege is owned by the client, the government lawyer may be compelled to disclose otherwise privileged information if called upon to do so by that government client, when acting through a legally-authorized constituent, whether or not such disclosure is in the personal interests of the government officer to whom the lawyer ordinarily reports. As the United States Court of Appeals for the Ninth Circuit held recently in rejecting the argument that the former governor of Oregon could personally invoke the privilege for consultations with

---

[126] In re Lindsey, 158 F.3d 1263, 1267–78 (D.C. Cir. 1998); In re Grand Jury Subpoena, 112 F.3d 910, 915–21 (8th Cir. 1997).

state government attorneys about whether he had a conflict of interest that could lead to personal liability: "Government lawyers, like the elected officials they assist, are public servants, and their client is the government, not officeholders in their personal capacities."[127]

In other words, the conclusion for the government lawyer is the same as it would be for the corporate lawyer who is directed by a board of directors to waive the attorney-client privilege and disclose to a government regulator or other outside parties the substance of communications with a corporate officer, whether or not that individual officer would so desire that revelation.[128]

By contrast, when someone outside the government seeks access to confidential communications between a government lawyer relating to representation of a government client, the attorney-client privilege protects the substance of that communication from outside interference.[129] In *United States v. Jicarilla Apache Nation*,[130] the Supreme Court explained that "[t]he objectives of the attorney-client privilege apply to governmental clients." Unless a particular law directs otherwise, "the Government may invoke the attorney-client privilege in civil litigation to protect confidential communications between Government officials and Government attorneys."[131]

### § 4-8.8(c) Identifying the Government Client and Litigating Authority

One of the distinctive characteristics of government lawyers, at both the state and federal level, is the heightened responsibility or authority that they may possess with respect to decisions on whether to litigate, how to manage the litigation, what issues to raise, and whether to settle.

By federal statute,[132] authority regarding the initiation and the conduct of litigation is centralized in the Attorney General of the United States and thus in the United States Department of Justice.[133] Congress explained this statutory directive as intended to ensure "a unity of decision, a unity of jurisprudence in the executive law of the United States."[134]

Accordingly, as legal counsel for a government party, the Department of Justice has largely plenary control over the litigation above and beyond that of its client agencies and departments. In the private sector, if a client orders an attorney to file a motion or an appeal or to raise a particular claim or argument, and the attorney fails to do so for reasons other than ethical limitations, the client may have a malpractice claim against

---

[127] In re Grand Jury Subpoena, No. 15–35434 (9th Cir. 2016).

[128] For a detailed examination and critique of the *Lindsey* and *Grand Jury Subpoena* cases, and an argument that the government attorney-client privilege should be analogized to that which exists for a corporation, see generally Michael Stokes Paulsen, *Who "Owns" the Government's Attorney-Client Privilege?*, 83 MINN. L. REV. 473 (1998).

[129] In re Erie, 473 F.3d 413, 418 (2d Cir. 2007); Oasis Int'l Waters, Inc. v. United States, 110 Fed. Cl. 87, 97 (2013).

[130] 564 U.S. 162, 169–70 (2011).

[131] *Id.* at 170.

[132] *See, e.g.*, 28 U.S.C. §§ 516, 519.

[133] *See generally* GREGORY C. SISK, LITIGATION WITH THE FEDERAL GOVERNMENT § 1.2 (West Academic Publishing, 2016).

[134] Cong. Globe, 41st Cong., 2d Sess. at 3036 (1870).

the attorney. By contrast, the Department of Justice is in charge of both litigation strategy and litigation objectives, including which actions to bring, which claims to assert, and which arguments to make, with the advice—but not the control—of the client agency. Moreover, in the private sector, if the client does not like the advice that an attorney gives or the work that he performs, the client can discharge the attorney and seek new counsel. By contrast, federal government entities are "captive clients" who are unable to "fire" the Department of Justice as litigation counsel.[135]

This is not to say that the relationship between federal Department of Justice lawyers and the officers and general counsel for the client agency is an adversarial one for the most part. In general, agency counsel and Department of Justice litigating attorneys work together closely and cooperatively. Although the agency officials technically are not in charge of the litigation, they may be more familiar with the agency practices implicated by the lawsuit, as well as with the actual facts of the case, and thus their advice is taken seriously by the litigating government lawyers. But if there is disagreement, the Department of Justice has authority to make the final decision regarding litigation objectives and means.

The authority of the typical state attorney general to represent the state in litigation likewise is broad, although the state attorney general's independence of judgment against that of a client agency is sometimes more circumscribed than the federal Attorney General. The pertinent constitutional provisions, statutes, and regulations in each state must be consulted to determine the extent of the attorney general's litigating authority, whether plenty in nature or limited in some instances by the preferences of a state agency.

Importantly, whatever may be the standards and practices regarding litigating authority and the powers of the government lawyer acting under the Attorney General of the United States or the attorney general of a state, they are left undisturbed by the Model Rules of Professional Conduct. Although from time to time some commentators have suggested using the ethics rules to set restrictions on the powers of government lawyers with respect to client agencies, the rule drafters have thus far refused to be so paternalistic or to intrude into an area that has its own set of rules and statutory limits. Thus, Paragraph 18 of the Scope of the Model Rules of Professional Conduct expressly acknowledges that government lawyers may have authority to make decisions that ordinarily would be reserved to clients, such as whether to settle and whether to appeal. The paragraph concludes by saying: "These rules do not abrogate any such authority."

Similarly, both Paragraph 18 of the Scope and Comment 9 to Rule 1.13 of the Model Rules of Professional Conduct explain that conflict of interest principles cannot be extrapolated directly from the private to the governmental context. Thus, the government lawyer's client may be a specific agency, a branch of government, or the government as a whole. The government lawyer may have the authority to question the conduct of officials within a client agency or other governmental entity in a manner and for a purpose beyond that which would occur in the private attorney-client relationship. The ethics rules do not limit that authority.

The District of Columbia bar, which has a very large membership of lawyers for government at both the federal and District of Columbia level, makes even more specific

---

[135] Susan M. Olson, *Challenges to the Gatekeeper: The Debate Over Federal Litigating Authority*, 68 JUDICATURE 71, 73 (1984).

and explicit that legal and regulatory standards for government practice are not inconsistent with or undermined by the ethics rules. Thus, the D.C. version of Rule 1.2 states that a "government lawyer's authority and control over decisions concerning the representation may, by statute or regulation, be expanded beyond the limits" that otherwise reserve decisions on the objectives to the client.[136] Similarly, a comment to the D.C. general rule on conflicts of interests explains that it is "not intended to apply to conflicts between agencies or components of government (federal, state, or local) where the resolution of such conflicts has been entrusted by law, order, or regulation to a specific individual or entity."[137]

[136] D.C. RULES OF PROF'L CONDUCT R. 1.2(d).

[137] *Id.* R. 1.7 cmt. 35.

# Chapter 4-9

# DUTIES OF ETHICAL ADVOCACY

## By Gregory C. Sisk

*Table of Sections*


§ 4-9.1 Introduction to Ethics and Advocacy
§ 4-9.2 The Classic Tension Between the Duty of the Zealous Advocate and the Officer of the Court
§ 4-9.3 Ethical Duties in Presenting Claims or Contentions in Litigation
§ 4-9.4 Duties to Advance the Resolution of Disputes
§ 4-9.5 Duties of Truthfulness and Candor by Lawyer Before the Tribunal
§ 4-9.6 Obtaining, Discovering, and Preserving Evidence for Civil Proceedings
§ 4-9.7 Ethical Issues Regarding Collection and Retention of Evidence in Criminal Proceedings
§ 4-9.8 Duties Regarding Presentation of Evidence
§ 4-9.9 Behavior During and After Trial
§ 4-9.10 The Advocate-Witness Rule
§ 4-9.11 Extrajudicial Statements by Lawyer
§ 4-9.12 The Heightened Ethical Duties of Lawyers for the Sovereign Government—With Special Attention to Prosecutors
§ 4-9.13 The Duties of the Advocate in Nonadjudicative Proceedings


---

## § 4-9.1 INTRODUCTION TO ETHICS AND ADVOCACY

This chapter addresses the ethical foundations for one of the lawyer's most prominent roles, that of an advocate on behalf of a client. The advocate stands as an intermediary between the client and the government or another private party and zealously advances the client's interests in an adversary system.[1] While diligently and vigorously presenting the client's case, the lawyer simultaneously must adhere to legal and ethical limits, as abuse of the legal process cannot be justified as serving the client's interest. The ethical standards draw "the line dividing zealous advocacy from sharp—and unethical—practice."[2]

The lawyer advocate must present only valid claims and contentions, the understanding of which varies by civil and criminal context.[3] The advocate has certain duties to advance the dispute toward resolution, including expediting the litigation;[4]

---

[1] *See* Murray L. Schwartz, *The Zeal of the Civil Advocate*, 1983 AM. B. FOUND. RES. J. 543, 548–50 (characterizing the criminal defense lawyer as "the archetype of the advocate in the adversary system").

[2] *See* Board of Prof'l Ethics & Conduct v. Wanek, 589 N.W.2d 265, 266 (Iowa 1999) (describing attorney's conduct in litigation as having "crossed the line dividing zealous advocacy from sharp—and unethical—practice").

[3] *See infra* § 4-9.3.

[4] *See infra* § 4-9.4.

eschewing obstructive means that have no purpose other than to embarrass, delay, or burden another;[5] and avoiding conduct prejudicial to the administration of justice.[6] A lawyer has a general duty of truthfulness before a tribunal, including truthful representations to the court and others,[7] refusing to offer false evidence,[8] and taking remedial measures if later learning of such falsity.[9] The lawyer is bound to obey legal requirements of fairness and respect for the rights of others in discovering, obtaining, preserving, and using evidence.[10] To uphold the impartiality of the tribunal, the lawyer must generally avoid *ex parte* contacts with the adjudicator.[11] The lawyer has a duty to respect the decorum of the tribunal and avoid improper trial tactics.[12] The lawyer must refrain from extrajudicial statements that are substantially likely to materially prejudice an adjudicative proceeding.[13] A lawyer must uphold the special responsibility of promoting justice when acting as a prosecutor or government litigator.[14] The lawyer generally must not combine the inconsistent roles of advocate and witness.[15] And the lawyer must conform to ethical expectations when serving as an advocate in nonadjudicative proceedings.[16]

## § 4-9.2 THE CLASSIC TENSION BETWEEN THE DUTY OF THE ZEALOUS ADVOCATE AND THE OFFICER OF THE COURT

On the first day of Professional Responsibility class each year, the author of this part of the book outlines for law students the timeless tension or clash of interests that lies at the heart of much of advocacy ethics.[17] For illustrative (and entertainment) purposes, it is framed as the "Vince Lombardi Doctrine versus the Superman Principle." In common terms, this is the ineliminable competition between the role of the zealous advocate and the officer of the court.

On one side of this classic dilemma lies the lawyer's traditional expectation of nearly-unrestrained loyalty in promoting the interests of the client against others and achieving the goals of the client. Vince Lombardi, the coach of the Green Bay Packers when they dominated national football during the 1960s, is remembered (perhaps

5 *See infra* § 4-9.4(c).

6 *See infra* § 4-9.4(c).

7 *See infra* § 4-9.5.

8 *See infra* § 4-9.8.

9 *See infra* § 4-9.8.

10 *See infra* §§ 4-9.6, 4-9.7.

11 *See infra* § 4-9.5(d).

12 *See infra* § 4-9.9(b).

13 *See infra* § 4-9.11.

14 *See infra* § 4-9.12.

15 *See infra* § 4-9.10.

16 *See infra* § 4-9.13.

17 Although framed differently, scholars may recognize this dilemma as parallel to the debate about role morality in the field of moral philosophy as applied to the professions. *See* DAVID LUBAN, LAWYERS AND JUSTICE: AN ETHICAL STUDY 105–16 (Princeton U. Press, 1988); ALAN GOLDMAN, THE MORAL FOUNDATIONS OF PROFESSIONAL ETHICS 1–33, 90–155 (Rowman & Littlefield, 1980); Richard Wasserstrom, Roles and Morality, *in* THE GOOD LAWYER: LAWYERS' ROLES AND LAWYERS' ETHICS 24–27 (Rowman & Allenh, David Luban, ed., 1983). For more on a lawyer's role specific morality, see Part Two of this book, Stephen Pepper & Katherine R. Kruse, The Philosophy of Legal Ethics, § 2-1.4.

mistakenly) for coining the sports credo: "Winning isn't everything. It's the only thing."[18] Extrapolating this "Vince Lombardi Doctrine" into the lawyer-client context, we find the most extreme version of zealous advocacy, that winning the client's case is the sole purpose of legal representation.[19]

Perhaps the most eloquent (and certainly most often quoted) statement of the zealous advocate concept was that of Lord Henry Brougham at the adultery trial before the House of Lords of Queen Caroline in 1820. In his defense of Queen Caroline, Brougham alluded to his possession of evidence that would remove the kingdom into chaos; in particular, he was aware of rumors that the king himself had engaged in adulterous affairs and, more significantly, that the king had entered into a secret marriage with a Roman Catholic which, if publicly revealed, would have caused him to lose his crown.[20] After a speech that included the following passage, Brougham succeeded in persuading the government to drop the charges. He said:

> [A]n advocate, in the discharge of his duty, knows but one person in all the world, and that person is his client. To save that client by all means and expedients, and at all hazards and costs to other persons, and, amongst them, to himself, is his first and only duty; and in performing this duty he must not regard the alarm, the torments, the destruction which he may bring upon others. Separating the duty of a patriot from that of an advocate, he must go on reckless of consequences, though it should be his unhappy fate to involve his country in confusion.[21]

The duty of zealous advocacy was enshrined as one of the nine canons of professional ethics in the American Bar Association's Code of Professional Responsibility: "Canon 7—A Lawyer Should Represent a Client Zealously Within the Bounds of the Law." The succeeding Model Rules of Professional Conduct, interestingly, do not include an explicit statement of this duty in the text of any rule. However, the concept is preserved in the first comment following Rule 1.3: "A lawyer must also act with commitment and dedication to the interests of the client and with *zeal in advocacy* upon the client's behalf" (emphasis added).

On the other side of this classic conflict of duties lies the equally-venerable portrayal of the lawyer as serving the public interest and morally bound to uphold certain public-regarding goals even during the representation of a private client.[22] Given that this

---

[18] THOMAS TUTKO & WILLIAM BURNS, WINNING IS EVERYTHING AND OTHER AMERICAN MYTHS 4 (Macmillan, 1976). Coach Lombardi claimed that he had been misquoted and had said something very different: "Winning isn't everything—but making the effort to win is." *Id.*

[19] *See* ALAN DERSHOWITZ, THE BEST DEFENSE xv (Random House, 1982) ("Once I decide to take a case, I have only one agenda: I want to win.").

[20] CHARLES W. WOLFRAM, MODERN LEGAL ETHICS 580 & n.82 (West, 1986); DAVID MELLINKOFF, THE CONSCIENCE OF A LAWYER 188–89 (West, 1973).

[21] *Id.* For an interesting debate between leading modern professional responsibility scholars about whether Lord Brougham's statement reflected his considered and continuing views about the proper role of the advocate or whether he later in life expressed regret about the words he had spoken, compare Monroe H. Freedman, *Henry Lord Brougham, Written by Himself*, 19 GEO. J. LEGAL ETHICS 1213 (2006) (arguing that Brougham never repudiated his classic statement about zealous advocacy) with Fred C. Zacharias & Bruce A. Green, *"Anything Rather Than a Deliberate and Well-Considered Opinion—Henry Lord Brougham, Written by Himself*, 19 GEO. J. LEGAL ETHICS 1221 (2006) (citing Brougham's later writings as indicating that his statement had not been intended as a learned disquisition on the role of the advocate).

[22] *See* WILLIAM H. SIMON, THE PRACTICE OF JUSTICE: A THEORY OF LAWYERS' ETHICS 9, 140 (Harvard U. Press, 1998) (criticizing the adversarial process and proposing the "basic maxim" that the lawyer should take those actions most "likely to promote justice," that is, a "justice-oriented" standard of professional ethics);

purported goal is to seek "truth, justice, and the American way," this approach may facetiously be referred to as the "Superman Principle." Translating this understanding of public duty into the legal context, we find the role of the lawyer as an officer of the court. Although the origin of the term "officer of the court" is "murky," it apparently derives from a special licensure for legal advocates or the delegation of advocacy powers to an agent of the Crown in the English courts many centuries ago.[23] As Professor W. Bradley Wendel puts it, a lawyer's fidelity to the law serves the public interest, making the lawyer "a quasi-public official—an 'officer of the court' as that term is generally understood in legal ethics."[24]

As with the duty of zealous advocacy, modern expressions of the officer of the court concept may be found in multiple authoritative sources. For example, noted American jurist Benjamin Cardozo, in words later approvingly quoted by the Supreme Court,[25] stated: "[A lawyer admitted to practice w]as received into that ancient fellowship for something more than private gain. He became an officer of the court, and, like the court itself, an instrument or agency to advance the ends of justice."[26] Similarly, the American Bar Association and the Association of American Law Schools, in a Joint Statement on Professional Responsibility in 1958 offered this vision of the lawyer: "The lawyer's highest loyalty . . . runs, not to persons, but to procedures and institutions. The lawyer's role imposes on him a trusteeship for the integrity of those fundamental processes of government and self-government upon which the successful functioning of our society depends."[27]

In addition to the client-centered demands for zealous advocacy (the Vince Lombardi Doctrine) and the public-regarding expectations for an officer of the court (the Superman Principle), there is a third position—the attorney's self-interest—that we could characterize as the "Ebenezer Scrooge Factor." In that way, we could reformulate this ethical tension from a tug-of-war between two competing ideals into a triangle of interests. However, while every lawyer must earn a living to remain an effective member of the profession, a more self-serving desire to milk the client for money or to otherwise use the client and her matter to the attorney's advantage plainly is not a positive ethical goal. While the risk that a lawyer will act for self-interest is a practical concern, and one with which aspects of the ethics rules are directly applicable, it does not create a moral tension. The ethical dilemma inherent in the system of rules and the practice of law

---

DEBORAH L. RHODE, IN THE INTERESTS OF JUSTICE: REFORMING THE LEGAL PROFESSION 58 (Oxford U. Press 2000) (arguing that lawyers must "accept personal moral responsibility for the consequences of their professional actions," including making "decisions as advocates in the same way that morally reflective individuals make any ethical decision," by giving weight to client interests but also assessing "their obligations in light of all the societal interests at issue in particular practice contexts"); Harry L. Subin, *The Criminal Lawyer's "Different Mission": Reflections on the "Right" to Present a False Case*, 1 GEO J. LEGAL ETHICS 125, 125–26 (1987) (arguing that a lawyer, including a criminal defense attorney, is obliged as an "officer of the court" to assist the tribunal in arriving at a "truthful verdict" or at least refrain from "truth defeating devices"); *see also* W. BRADLEY WENDEL, LAWYERS AND FIDELITY TO LAW 8–9 (Princeton U. Press, 2010) (framing the public-regarding duty of lawyers as distinct from a "call for lawyers to assume direct responsibility for justice or the public interest" and instead as grounded in "fidelity to law," which a lawyer should regard as "worthy of being taken seriously, interpreted in good faith with due regard to its meaning, and not simply seen as an obstacle standing in the way of the client's goals").

[23] Eugene R. Gaetke, *Lawyers as Officers of the Court*, 42 VAND. L. REV. 39, 42 (1989).

[24] *See* WENDEL, *supra*, at 210.

[25] Theard v. United States, 354 U.S. 276, 281 (1957).

[26] Karlin v. Culkin, 162 N.E. 487, 489 (N.Y. 1928) (Cardozo, C.J.).

[27] Lon L. Fuller & John D. Randall, *Professional Responsibility: Report of the Joint Conference*, 44 A.B.A. J. 1159, 1162 (1958).

remains a two-sided conflict between the client-centric approach and the public-regarding demands.

How, then, might we reconcile the perpetual conflict between the duty of zealous advocacy on behalf of the client's interests and the responsibility of the officer of the court to the system of justice? Three possible answers suggest themselves, although not all three are equally satisfying from a moral perspective and the more simple of these answers are wanting.

First, one might assume an absolutist posture, in one direction or the other. Indeed, some trial lawyers adopt zealous advocacy as the sole criterion for legal representation. In so doing, they deny any duty as an officer of the court or any responsibility for the consequences to others that flow from their partisan advocacy. As committed disciples of the Vince Lombardi Doctrine, they contend that the adversary process entitles the trial lawyer to do everything (within some legal bounds) necessary to prevail—and that it is the obligation of the other side to do the same. By contrast, a few judges at least on occasion appear to have adopted the Superman Principle, believing that lawyers first and foremost must behave as officers of the court, working cooperatively (and even altruistically) to reach the truth, even when such an approach works directly against the interests of their clients.

No serious ethical system, however, countenances such an absolutist approach without any nuance or attention to context, in which the interests of one or the other party or the command of an abstract principle complete fealty. Neither do the formal rules permit a lawyer to neglect either the interests of client or the demands of the justice system.

It must be acknowledged, however, that the prominent roles of lawyers in the criminal justice system make the strongest case for enshrinement of these opposites as ethically-justifiable visions of advocacy. For the criminal defense counsel, what Professor Abbe Smith calls a "lawyering paradigm" that makes "zealous advocacy and the maintenance of client confidence and trust . . . paramount"[28] is enormously attractive and should allow few exceptions or qualifications. For the criminal prosecutor, Professor Fred Zacharias "advocated development of the general 'do justice' maxim for prosecutors."[29]

Second, one might place various elements of representation into separately labeled boxes, whereby some aspects of legal practice fall into the box labeled "Zealous Advocacy" while other aspects are collected into the "Officer of the Court" box. In many respects, the Model Rules of Professional Conduct reflect a considered attempt to do precisely that. As an over-general description, a few discrete provisions of the rules impose an obligation akin to that of an officer of the court, while everything else is left to the general regime of zealous advocacy. While a lawyer acting primarily as a client-centered advocate would remain within the constraints of the rules in most instances, there are a few black-letter rules that do establish public-regarding duties, often in ways that engender continuing controversy (as with duties of disclosure regarding client confidences when necessary to

[28] Abbe Smith, *The Difference in Criminal Defense and the Difference It Makes*, 11 J. L. & PUB. POLICY 83, 89 (2003).

[29] Rory K. Little, *Proportionality as an Ethical Precept for Prosecutors in Their Investigative Role*, 68 FORDHAM L. REV. 723, 757 (1999) (citing Fred C. Zacharias, *Structuring the Ethics of Prosecutorial Trial Practice: Can Prosecutors Do Justice?*, 44 VAND. L. REV. 45, 50, 109 (1991)).

serve certain public interests). In other words, this second answer to the tension is at least partially and formally correct.

The lawyer who adopts the second resolution to this tension as his personal solution likely will avoid falling into formal professional misconduct. Unfortunately, while sorting ethical issues into boxes appeals to the legal formalists among us (and the author of this part counts himself among them), the rules do not—and simply cannot—offer a roadmap out of all of the moral quandaries into which the legal practitioner may fall. While the categorical division of ethical problems manifested in the rules are a fallback or default position, and sometimes may prove to offer the best resolution we can find under difficult circumstances, we cannot thereby elide engaging with clients and adversaries about moral as well as legal responsibilities.[30]

Third, we could and should acknowledge that the tension between the moral claims of clients and of the justice system (and others) is inescapable and cannot be avoided. In fact, the attempt to sidestep or ignore moral claims, such as by adopting the falsely-neutral position of legal technician, has unavoidable moral implications of its own. Rather than seeking to escape from the moral tension, we need to develop the practical wisdom necessary to strike the appropriate balance in a particular matter and context.

The formal disciplinary rules, quite appropriately given their limited purpose, do not direct particular answers to many moral problems, but neither do they preclude lawyers and their clients from seeking such answers. Indeed, the Preamble to the American Bar Association's Model Rules of Professional Conduct recognizes the multiple and simultaneous roles of and demands upon the lawyer: "A lawyer, as a member of the legal profession, is a representative of clients, an officer of the legal system and a public citizen having special responsibility for the quality of justice."

When difficult questions of professional ethics and moral behavior arise during the practice of law, we may not always be able to arrive at a consensus as to the objectively *right* answer, but through experience and sensitive engagement with the problems, we should find that some answers are *better* than others. This approach requires us to fully understand the issues and to consider all factors. We must sympathetically understand the conflicting arguments.[31] With an appreciation for the principles underlying the formal rules, which may constrain many of the choices available to us, and a commitment to call upon deeper moral values, we then are better equipped to reach that better answer.

Finally, as legal professionals seek to be constantly sensitive to matters of both legal ethics and moral values, we must remember that we are never alone. Our clients ought to be regarded not merely as the subjects of our practices but as full partners in the representation and in moral deliberation.[32] Reminding lawyers that they are moral actors is not an invitation to moral imperialism by attorneys, by which lawyers would

---

[30] *See supra* § 4-5.2(b).

[31] *See* Andrew M. Perlman, *A Behavioral Theory of Legal Ethics*, 90 IND. L.J. 1639, 1640 (2015) (observing that zealous "partisanship distorts objectivity" and encouraging lawyers encountering ethical problems in advocacy to seek "second opinions" from colleagues or ethics committees).

[32] *See supra* § 4-5.2(b).

impose their own answers to every problem.[33] Moral deliberation is a two-way discussion with our clients, in which the client ordinarily is entitled to the final say.

## § 4-9.3 ETHICAL DUTIES IN PRESENTING CLAIMS OR CONTENTIONS IN LITIGATION

### § 4-9.3(a) Presenting Only Meritorious Claims and Contentions in Civil Litigation

As Comment 1 to Rule 3.1 of the Model Rules of Professional Conduct states, "[t]he advocate has a duty to use legal procedure for the fullest benefit of the client's cause, but also a duty not to abuse legal procedure." While an advocate is permitted to pursue every tenable factual and legal assertion that advances the client's position, Rule 3.1 expressly prohibits a lawyer from "bring[ing] or defend[ing] a proceeding" or "assert[ing] or controvert[ing]" an issue in such a proceeding, "unless there is a basis in law and fact for doing so that is not frivolous, which includes a good faith argument for an extension, modification, or reversal of existing law."

The rule generally benefits the lawyer's own client and certainly protects the opposing party, as well as serving to strengthen the legal justice system. Because "frivolousness is often closely related to incompetence,"[34] Model Rule 3.1 reminds the lawyer of her obligation of competence under Model Rule 1.1, which in turn "requires the legal knowledge, skill, thoroughness, and preparation reasonably necessary for the representation."[35] (However, even if interposing a baseless argument appears to benefit a client because it may cause delay or may not effectively be counteracted by an adversary, or when a difficult client insists upon such an action, the lawyer is not justified in crossing that ethical line.[36]) Because a party may be oppressed, emotionally or financially, by having to respond to non-meritorious assertions, the rule imposes this duty of minimal fairness toward opponents in litigation.

And abuse of the legal process also injures the public interest in fair and just resolution of disputes. As Professor Maura Strassberg writes, "[t]he use of scarce judicial resources by frivolous claims and defenses slows the judicial process. This, in turn, hurts the quality of justice for both civil and criminal litigants, as justice merely delayed for some is justice lost for others."[37]

By forbidding the lawyer to offer an assertion that is "frivolous," Rule 3.1 adopts an objective measure of what constitutes a legitimate or tenable factual or legal position. The benchmark is that of the reasonable lawyer. The standard announced here in a

---

[33] *See also* Part Two of this book, Stephen Pepper & Katherine R. Kruse, The Philosophy of Legal Ethics, § 2-1.4 ("The individual lawyer's private moral perception ought not determine the individual client's access to the public good that is the law.").

[34] 2 GEOFFREY C. HAZARD, JR., W. WILLIAM HODES & PETER R. JARVIS, THE LAW OF LAWYERING § 30.07 (Aspen, 4th ed., 2016).

[35] *See supra* § 4-3.4.

[36] *See* People v. Forsyth, 292 P.3d 1248, 1253–54 (Colo. O.P.D.J., Sup. Ct. 2012) (ruling that if a client insists on making a frivolous contention, the lawyer must withdraw); In re Martinez, 393 B.R. 27, 34 (Bank. D. Nev. 2008) (citing Rule 3.1 and noting that the lawyers "took the passive approach to client representation, seemingly doing whatever the client requested, regardless of whether it was reasonable or justified by the facts"); Board of Prof'l Ethics & Conduct v. Wanek, 589 N.W.2d 265, 270 (Iowa 1999) (stating that "client pressure" does "not justify the assertion of an unwarranted legal position").

[37] Maura I. Strassberg, *Privilege Can Be Abused: Exploring the Ethical Obligation to Avoid Frivolous Claims of Attorney-Client Privilege*, 37 SETON HALL L. REV. 413, 427 (2007).

disciplinary rule for evaluating whether a claim, defense, or other argument is frivolous is directly parallel to that articulated in rules of civil procedure applied to presentation by a lawyer of a motion, pleading, or other paper to the court. Under Rule 11 of the Federal Rules of Civil Procedure, an attorney who presents a pleading, written motion, or other paper to a court certifies that the allegations and other factual contentions "have evidentiary support," or are likely to have evidentiary support after a reasonable opportunity for further investigation or discovery; that denials of factual contentions are "warranted on the evidence" or are reasonably based on lack of information or belief; and that claims, defenses, and other legal contentions are "warranted by existing law or by a nonfrivolous argument for extending, modifying, or reversing existing law or for establishing new law."[38] By design, the ethics rule dovetails with the procedural rule.

The duty not to present meritless claims or arguments under Model Rule 3.1 incorporates the expectation that the lawyer has made "reasonable inquiry," a standard that should be familiar to every lawyer practicing in civil litigation. The legitimacy of the position advocated by the lawyer must be considered in light of the particular circumstances and the information that should have been uncovered by a reasonable prior investigation.[39] The reasonableness of the inquiry into the facts and law by a lawyer—

> may depend on such factors as the time available to the signor for investigation; whether the signor had to rely on a client for information as to the facts underlying the pleading, motion, or other paper; whether the pleading, motion, or other paper was based on a plausible view of the law; or whether the signor depended on forwarding counsel or another member of the bar.[40]

The lawyer should understand that "a reasonable inquiry into fact ordinarily requires more than exclusive reliance on the client's statement of the facts."[41] If the lawyer is able through reasonable investigation to explore the circumstances underlying the client's story, the lawyer should do so and should not proceed without some minimal substantiation of the factual foundation (although a full examination of the evidence may await formal discovery).[42] When objective evidence directly contradicts the client's account, and the client offers no plausible explanation, or when the client's representations are inconsistent in material respects, the lawyer may not frame a case around what is plainly a fable. On some occasions, however, the client's report to the lawyer about what happened, who was involved, and what was said by whom is the only or the best source of information available to the lawyer at the time, even if the adversary party (if she should be asked) unsurprisingly denies those assertions. Absent clear

---

[38] FED. R. CIV. P. 11(b). *See* Business Guides, Inc. v. Chromatic Communications Enters., 498 U.S. 533, 550–51 (1991) (ruling that the certification of a pleading as well-founded under Rule 11 is an "objective" standard "of reasonableness under the circumstances").

[39] *See* Eastway Constr. Corp. v. City of New York, 762 F.2d 243, 253–54 (2d Cir. 1985) (stating that whether an adequate investigation has been made for purposes of Rule 11 is judged by an objective reasonableness standard).

[40] Century Prods., Inc. v. Sutter, 837 F.2d 247, 250–51 (6th Cir. 1988).

[41] Edward W. Remsburg & Steven K. Gaer, *General Overview of Federal Rule of Civil Procedure 11*, 38 DRAKE L. REV. 261, 274 (1988–89).

[42] *See* Mark S. Cady, *Curbing Litigation Abuse and Misuse: A Judicial Approach*, 36 DRAKE L. REV. 483, 491 (1986–87) (explaining that the sanction rule "falls far short of requiring a compilation of all supporting evidence and law prior to filing").

unreliability in the client's statements, "a lawyer not only is permitted to take a client's statements as true, but is required by the duty of zealousness to advocate them."[43]

In evaluating the reasonableness of a pleading or other presentation as of the time of filing, the court must "avoid using the wisdom of hindsight" gained" by what is later learned through discovery or evidence at trial.[44]

However, when circumstances do change during the course of litigation, the lawyer must be prepared to "in good faith, back[ ] off."[45] Even if a claim or defense, or other position asserted or to which a response was made, was initially justified, a lawyer may not persist in asserting or controverting an issue unless the lawyer continues to have a non-frivolous basis for so doing. As a matter of professional responsibility, Model Rule 3.1 does impose a "continuing duty voluntarily to dismiss claims or abandon defenses that have become frivolous."[46] In addition, a lawyer who fails to withdraw a filing that has lost any reasonable standing would be responsible for an unjustified delay in the disposition of the matter and thus would violate Model Rule 3.2 for failing to make "reasonable efforts to expedite litigation."[47]

The objective standard of frivolousness applies to legal as well as factual positions. With respect to legal arguments, the essential question is whether a reasonable court could find the offered legal analysis to be at least colorable. Professors Geoffrey Hazard and William Hodes and attorney Peter Jarvis warn that "overuse of the charge of frivolousness would chill not only the zeal but the creativity of lawyers who operate on the leading edge of legal development."[48] Even if a position cannot be sustained under the current state of the law, the position is not frivolous under the language of Rule 3.1 if it reflects a "good faith argument for an extension, modification or reversal of existing law."

A legal position that lacks any support in law may be every bit as frivolous as would be a factual position that is entirely unsupported by evidence. When the contrary legal proposition is well-settled and has become "black letter law" free from serious doubt or dispute or when the courts have firmly, consistently, and recently rejected a position, no reasonable lawyer may continue to assert the position on the thin rationalization that the law is always subject to change or based on the foolish hope that some judge (perhaps due to inadvertent error) might accept the argument.[49] Still, judges should be chary of demanding too tight a connection between a legal argument and direct precedential support. Especially on controversial questions of law, the judge or judicial officer considering the issue as a matter of either professional discipline or court sanction must be careful to avoid the temptation of viewing his own opinion on the legal merits as the

---

[43] 2 GEOFFREY C. HAZARD, JR., W. WILLIAM HODES & PETER R. JARVIS, THE LAW OF LAWYERING § 30.05 (Aspen, 4th ed., 2016).

[44] Advisory Committee Note, 97 F.R.D. 165, 199 (1983).

[45] *See* Board of Prof'l Ethics & Conduct v. Wanek, 589 N.W.2d 265, 270 (Iowa 1999).

[46] 2 GEOFFREY C. HAZARD, JR., W. WILLIAM HODES & PETER R. JARVIS, THE LAW OF LAWYERING § 30.15 (Aspen, 4th ed., 2016).

[47] *See supra* § 4-9.4(a). *See also* 2 GEOFFREY C. HAZARD, JR., W. WILLIAM HODES & PETER R. JARVIS, THE LAW OF LAWYERING § 31.02 (Aspen, 4th ed., 2016) (observing that Rule 3.2 complements Rule 3.1, "because a consequence of frivolous litigating tactics is that they also cause unwarranted delays").

[48] 2 GEOFFREY C. HAZARD, JR., W. WILLIAM HODES & PETER R. JARVIS, THE LAW OF LAWYERING § 30.12 (Aspen, 4th ed., 2016).

[49] On the lawyer's duty under Rule 3.3(a)(2) to disclose "legal authority in the controlling jurisdiction known to the lawyer to be directly adverse to the position of the client and not disclosed by opposing counsel," see *infra* § 4-9.5(c).

measure of manifest reasonableness.[50] That a legal argument is wrong, even if the judge reviewing the question believes strongly that it is wrong, does not necessarily mean that it is frivolous and deserving of professional discipline or sanction.[51]

Chief Justice Mark Cady of the Iowa Supreme Court offers the following advice for lawyers seeking to expand the boundaries of the law:

> [I]t is advisable for attorneys to approach a claim for extension or creation of law with a degree of candor and honesty. An attorney should show that his or her homework has been done. Existing law and precedent should not be ignored, but explained. Policy considerations should be carefully constructed and authority from other jurisdictions should be recognized. An attorney cannot embark on a course to change or modify the law with a cavalier attitude, but must do so with respect and recognition of the prevailing law and strong grounds to forge a change. If a good faith, forthright attitude is shown, sanctions will likely be avoided.[52]

### § 4-9.3(b) Putting the Prosecution to Its Proof in Criminal Proceedings

While forbidding a lawyer from presenting a frivolous argument in litigation, Model Rule 3.1 carefully clarifies that "[a] lawyer for the defendant in a criminal proceeding, or the respondent in a proceeding that could result in incarceration, may nevertheless so defend the proceeding as to require that every element of the case be established."

By this provision applicable to a criminal case or a proceeding in which incarceration of the client may result (such as certain juvenile proceedings), the lawyer may put the prosecution to its proof, even if there is no non-frivolous basis for interposing a defense. Because the prosecution has a constitutionally-mandated duty to prove guilt beyond a reasonable doubt,[53] the defendant may resist the charges and refuse to acquiesce. The lawyer's assistance in such a defense is consistent with and indeed compelled by the lawyer's professional and ethical responsibilities.

That the prosecution may be obliged to prove every element of the charges beyond a reasonable doubt does not mean, however, that the defense lawyer is permitted to affirmatively contradict the prosecution's case with false evidence or by interposing frivolous defenses. The lawyer's duty of candor to the tribunal precludes making any false statement to the court or offering any evidence that the lawyer knows to be fraudulent.[54] Thus, while the lawyer must extend reasonable loyalty and trust to the

---

[50] *See* Lawrence M. Grosberg, *Illusion and Reality in Regulating Lawyer Performance: Rethinking Rule 11*, 32 VILL. L. REV. 575, 635 (1987) (observing that, in deciding whether to impose sanctions under Federal Rule of Civil Procedure 11, "[t]here seems to be an ineluctable pressure on judges to reinforce the propriety of their initial legal determinations by extending them a step further, thus concluding that their legal analysis is so correct and perhaps even self-evident that anybody but a fool, an incompetent lawyer, or one misusing the courts should have reached the same conclusion").

[51] *See* Mark S. Stein, *Rule 11 in the Real World: How the Dynamics of Litigation Defeat the Purpose of Imposing Attorney Fee Sanctions for the Assertion of Frivolous Legal Arguments*, 132 F.R.D. 309, 316 (1990) (stating that, in considering whether to impose sanctions under Federal Rule of Civil Procedure 11 for an allegedly frivolous legal argument, "a judge's perception of whether an argument is so wrong as to be sanctionable may become clouded" and the judge "may be impelled to proclaim the frivolousness of a position as a means of emphasis, just like a lawyer").

[52] Cady, *supra*, 36 DRAKE L. REV. at 498.

[53] Mullaney v. Wilbur, 421 U.S. 684, 691–703 (1975); In re Winship, 397 U.S. 358, 361–64 (1970).

[54] *See infra* § 4-9.8.

client, if the lawyer knows that a particular fact is or is not true, the lawyer may not permit the defendant or a witness for the defendant to testify falsely to the contrary. The criminal defense lawyer should forcefully direct the jury's attention to omissions and weaknesses in the prosecution's case, for the purpose of suggesting the presence of reasonable doubt. But the lawyer ideally should frame any contrary narrative that the lawyer knows to be fictitious as the only conclusion permitted under the evidence (viewed of course in light of the standard of reasonable doubt),[55] rather than as a forthright assertion of a false story.[56] Nor may the lawyer invoke frivolous legal objections as part of the defense.

Following a conviction, appellate counsel for a criminal defendant should raise and brief nonfrivolous arguments for reversal or for a change in sentence. In *Anders v. California*,[57] the Supreme Court held:

> [Appointed appellate counsel's] role as advocate requires that he support his client's appeal to the best of his ability. Of course, if counsel finds his case to be wholly frivolous, after a conscientious examination of it, he should so advise the court and request permission to withdraw. That request must, however, be accompanied by a brief referring to anything in the record that might arguably support the appeal. A copy of counsel's brief should be furnished the indigent and time allowed him to raise any points that he chooses; the court—not counsel—then proceeds, after a full examination of all the proceedings, to decide whether the case is wholly frivolous. If it so finds it may grant counsel's request to withdraw and dismiss the appeal insofar as federal requirements are concerned, or proceed to a decision on the merits, if state law so requires. On the other hand, if it finds any of the legal points arguable on their merits (and therefore not frivolous) it must, prior to decision, afford the indigent the assistance of counsel to argue the appeal.[58]

This "unique" *Anders* approach applies only when the appeal is "wholly frivolous," and the *Anders* brief is to be filed only when the lawyer is therefore moving to withdraw.[59] However, as the United States Court of Appeals for the Eighth Circuit has said, "there is no provision for including '*Anders* issues' in a merits brief. Either the issue is meritless and should not be included in a merits brief, or the issue has merit and should be vigorously argued."[60]

---

[55] *See* W. BRADLEY WENDEL, LAWYERS AND FIDELITY TO LAW 192–93 (Princeton U. Press, 2010) (arguing that while deceptive tactics generally contradict a proposed lawyer duty of fidelity to law, a criminal defense lawyer "may cobble together, out of bits of storytelling material that are themselves true, a story that persuades the jury to draw an inference that is false" because "it is the only effective way for criminal defense lawyers to put the state to its proof, and require the prosecution to prove its case beyond a reasonable doubt").

[56] *See* Todd A. Berger, *The Ethical Limits of Discrediting the Truthful Witness: How Modern Ethics Rules Fail to Prevent Truthful Witnesses From Being Discredited Through Unethical Means*, 99 MARQ. L. REV. 283, 314–15 (2015) (arguing that a criminal defense lawyer may ethically present "the false-implication and evidence-reflects closing arguments," which "only ask the jury to draw reasonable inferences based entirely on the existence of admissible evidence, without ever explicitly telling the jury something the defense attorney knows to be untrue," but may not present a "false-story closing argument [that] more strongly presents the defense theory in story form through a series of affirmative statements that defense counsel knows to be untrue").

[57] 386 U.S. 738 (1967).

[58] *Id.* at 744.

[59] United States v. Meeks, 639 F.3d 522, 528–29 n.2 (8th Cir. 2011).

[60] *Id.*

## § 4-9.4 DUTIES TO ADVANCE THE RESOLUTION OF DISPUTES

### § 4-9.4(a) Expediting Litigation and Avoiding Unreasonable Delay

Few things are more frustrating to parties entangled in litigation or more injurious to the public perception of a fair and just legal system than dilatory tactics and interminable delay in the disposition of lawsuits. Rule 1.2 instructs the lawyer to "act with reasonable diligence and promptness in representing a client."[61] Many cases in which delays multiply are sadly attributable to the lawyer's neglect in attending to her own client's case. In that case, the lawyer's misconduct likely causes harm to everyone involved in the process, including the lawyer's own client, the opposing party, and the judicial system.[62]

Rule 3.2 of the Model Rules of Professional Conduct takes the matter a step further, by directing that the lawyer may not unreasonably prolong the process, even if the lawyer's own client is not harmed by, or perhaps even benefits from, the delay. Rule 3.2 directs lawyers to "make reasonable efforts to expedite litigation consistent with the interests of the client."

The expectation enforced upon the lawyer by Rule 3.2 is to make "reasonable efforts" to expedite the litigation and to do so as "consistent with the interests of the client." Depending on the nature and complexity of the matter, a period of time, perhaps a fairly substantial interval, will be necessary to thoroughly prepare for the litigation. The unavoidable delays attendant to investigation and discovery, submission of preliminary matters or motions to the court, etc. are accepted as a necessary part of the litigation process. Moreover, because every party and every lawyer is entitled to a healthy and balanced life, scheduling matters or seeking a continuance of a proceeding to reasonably accommodate a party's or lawyer's work-load, family needs, or even a well-deserved vacation is not a violation of this ethical objective.

At some point, however, as the matter lags, as postponements increase, as excuses proliferate, or as a pattern of deliberate delay emerges, the lawyer's conduct crosses the line from reasonable deferral to unjustified obstruction of the fair and punctual resolution of the litigation. In addition, the attorney's failure to comply with court deadlines is a clear violation of the duty to make reasonable efforts to expedite litigation, even if the client is not harmed as a result.

Although the lawyer's duty to expedite litigation is qualified by the lawyer's proper attention to the interests of the client, delay for delay's sake to achieve a financial gain (or avoid a financial loss) at the expense of the opponent, or simply to postpone the day of reckoning cannot justify dragging out the litigation.

---

[61] *See supra* § 4-5.3.

[62] *See* Attorney Disciplinary Bd. v. Lesyshen, 712 N.W.2d 101, 105 (Iowa 2006) ("not[ing] the dilatory handling of client matters is a disservice not only to the client but also to the judicial system"); Busik v. Levine, 307 A.2d 571, 575 (N.J. 1973) (stating that, because "tort litigation is a major demand upon the judicial system," "[d]elay in the disposition of those cases has an impact upon other litigants who wait for their turn, and upon the taxpayers who support the system.").

## § 4-9.4(b) Conduct Prejudicial to the Administration of Justice

### *§ 4-9.4(b)(1) General Conduct Prejudicial to the Administration of Justice*

Under Rule 8.4(d) of the Model Rules of Professional Conduct, a lawyer commits professional misconduct by engaging in "conduct that is prejudicial to the administration of justice." This rule attaches to lawyer conduct that inappropriately disrupts the legal process, unjustifiably impairs the ability of a participant in the process to effectively present a case, improperly impedes progress of the matter (such as by failing to timely file necessary court documents or not complying with court deadlines), or perverts the disposition of a matter.

While some forms of conduct prejudicial to the administration of justice, such as bribing a judge or juror or presenting false evidence,[63] are independently wrongful, the specific prohibition in Model Rules 8.4(d) on prejudicial conduct focuses attention on the impact of such behavior upon the parties and the public in terms of their confidence in the justice system. As examples, a lawyer's false notarization of a client's signature on court documents "hampered the efficient operation of the court by occupying its attention and resources in considering whether the purported signatures of [the client] were authentic,"[64] and a lawyer's falsification of certificates attached to discovery requests sent to opposing counsel "waste[ed] judicial resources" through a "completely unnecessary hearing about a collateral matter completely unrelated to the merits of the underlying lawsuit."[65] An attorney's failure to appear at trial is obviously prejudicial to the administration of justice because "an attorney plays such an integral role in the judicial process that without his presence the wheels of justice must, necessarily, grind to a halt."[66]

In addition, acts that viewed in isolation may not appear improper or may not appear to rise to the level of professional misconduct, may be found to be a violation of Rule 8.4(d) when reviewed in fuller context and thereby revealed to be part of a series of related actions, such as a pattern of discovery abuse in civil litigation. Repeated failures to respond to discovery requests, forcing regular resort to motions to compel production even of documents that plainly are discoverable, prejudices the administration of justice.[67] A lawyer's unprofessional behavior while defending the deposition of a client that makes it difficult or impossible for the examining attorney to ask questions and obtain un-coached answers from the client witness may be conduct prejudicial to the administration of justice.

At the same time, Model Rule 8.4(d) is not a warrant for disciplinary authorities to impose penalties upon a maverick lawyer who uses unorthodox (but lawful and ethical) means to pursue client interests or who is a gadfly that irritates institutions or public

---

[63] On the duty of the lawyer not to present false evidence, see *infra* § 4-9.8.

[64] Attorney Disciplinary Bd. v. Palmer, 825 N.W.2d 322, 324–24 (Iowa 2013); *see also* Matter of McCann, 669 A.2d 49, 56 (Del. 1995) (submitting falsified documents to a court is prejudicial to the administration of justice).

[65] Attorney Disciplinary Bd. v. McGinness, 844 N.W.2d 456, 465 (Iowa 2014).

[66] Murphy v. State, 416 A.2d 748, 753 (Md. Ct. App. 1980).

[67] *See* In re Disciplinary Action Against Moe, 851 N.W.2d 868, 870–71 (Minn. 2014) (failure to respond to discovery requests and to a court order compelling discovery was conduct prejudicial to the administration of justice). On the lawyer's duty to make a reasonably diligent effort to comply with a legally proper discovery request by an opposing party, see *infra* § 4-9.6(b).

figures to provoke reform. Nor, as discussed both immediately below[68] and later with respect to criticisms of public officials and judges,[69] is this an appropriate means by which to enforce ideals of professional courtesy and civility through the formal sanction of discipline. In adopting paragraph (d) of Rule 8.4, the delegates to the American Bar Association's House of Delegates insisted that it would be employed against "violations of well-understood norms and conventions of practice only."[70]

### *§ 4-9.4(b)(2) Manifestations of Bias Prejudicial to the Administration of Justice and Not Constituting Legitimate Advocacy*

Before 2016, Comment 3 stated that Rule 8.4(d) may be violated when "[a] lawyer who, in the course of representing a client, knowingly manifests, by words or conduct, bias or prejudice based upon race, sex, religion, national origin, disability, age, sexual orientation or socioeconomic status" and such actions are "prejudicial to the administration of justice." In 2016, Rule 8.4 of the Model Rules of Professional Conduct was amended by the American Bar Association to add a new paragraph (g) to Rule 8.4 that expansively prohibits a lawyer from engaging "in conduct that the lawyer knows or reasonably should know is harassment or discrimination on the basis of race, sex, religion, national origin, ethnicity, disability, age, sexual orientation, gender identity, marital status or socioeconomic status in conduct related to the practice of law." The application of Rule 8.4(g) to non-litigation conduct has been addressed previously in this book.[71]

Both as part of the general duty not to engage in conduct prejudicial to the administration of justice in Model Rule 8.4(d) and now as part of the broader prohibition on discriminatory and harassing behavior in Rule 8.4(g), a lawyer engages in professional misconduct when representing a client by demonstrating bias or prejudice in a manner that has a detrimental effect on the fair administration of justice. As previously expressed in a comment and now stated in the text of Model Rule 8.4(g), the prohibition on harassment or discrimination on the stated bases "does not preclude legitimate advice or advocacy consistent with these Rules."[72]

Judges, magistrates, and disciplinary authorities considering these matters have the difficult task of simultaneously ensuring (1) that manifestations of bias by a lawyer do not undermine the pursuit of justice, (2) that chastising true misconduct not devolve into the Sisyphean and unduly intrusive project of policing civility through the formal rules of discipline, and (3) that legitimate advocacy not be chilled through misuse of this provision in a manner that weakens zealous advocacy and threatens freedom of expression on issues of public importance.

***Prejudicial Manifestation of Bias:*** A judge or magistrate presiding over a proceeding, or a disciplinary authority reviewing conduct that had allegedly undermined fair proceedings should be aggressive in rooting out the use of bias in litigation (both in

---

[68] *See infra* § 4-9.4(b)(2).

[69] *See infra* § 4-13.3.

[70] 2 GEOFFREY C. HAZARD, JR. & W. WILLIAM HODES, THE LAW OF LAWYERING § 65.6 (Aspen, 3d ed., 2005).

[71] *See supra* § 4-1.4(c).

[72] In the context of advocacy in criminal cases, Comment 5 to the Rule 8.4 states that "[a] trial judge's finding that peremptory challenges were exercised on a discriminatory basis does not alone establish a violation of paragraph (g)."

discovery and in the courtroom) and in similar proceedings as a means to appeal to a fact-finder or to weaken the effectiveness of opposing advocacy.

In *Matter of Schiff*,[73] a New York court addressed an attorney's conduct during a deposition in which he "showered [a female opposing attorney] with sexist obscenities, partly off the record and partly on the record, in pursuance of a generally obstructive pattern of conduct." The court found that this attorney, "without provocation, chose to degrade and disparage his adversary by using dirty, discriminating gutter language offensively directed to harass her because of her gender." Refusing to regard such "humiliating and reprehensible sexual harassment" as a " 'rite of passage' which must be silently endured," the court issued a public censure and advised that the discipline would have been more severe but for the attorney's unblemished record and youth. In *People v. Sharpe*,[74] the Colorado Supreme Court imposed a public censure on a prosecuting attorney, who in the hallway outside the courtroom told the counsel for Hispanic criminal defendants that the prosecutor did not "believe either one of those chili-eating bastards."[75] In *Sonksen v. Legal Services Corp.*,[76] the Iowa Supreme Court censured an attorney who filed an appellate brief "replete with the most offensive racism and cruel sarcasm about the poor," describing the opposing parties as "members of the black underclass" and "ignorant psychopaths" who sought "to be relocated into municipal public housing so that they might suck at the teat of the welfare state forever."

Invocations of raw bias, such as those illustrated above, in the lawyer's public role in advocating a case should not be tolerated.

***Professionalism/Civility Not Enforceable by Disciplinary Rule:*** While not hesitating to admonish true manifestations of bias, no judicial officer or disciplinary official can ensure that the parties and their counsel always behave with the highest standards of courtesy and civility. Serious breaches of civility, whether manifesting bias or not, that have a concrete and prejudicial impact on the administration of justice should be challenged and sanctioned when necessary. But affirmative demands for professional courtesy at the risk of formal disciplinary action are misplaced.

As the Conference of Chief Justices stated in its "National Action Plan on Lawyer Conduct and Professionalism" in 1999, "[u]nlike disciplinary rules that can be implemented and enforced, professionalism is a personal characteristic .... No disciplinary system can enforce professionalism . . ."[77]

Judges, lawyers, and other participants in the legal process should work to create a culture of professionalism and civility, by modeling appropriate behavior, by ensuring that those who betray our expectations of civility and professionalism learn that such conduct is not effective, and by mentoring newly admitted members of the bar. Frequently-adopted standards of professionalism are aspirational and are not to be used as a basis for court sanctions nor to add to the requirements of the disciplinary rules.

---

[73] Docket No. HP 22/92 (Feb. 2, 1993), Departmental Disciplinary Committee, First Judicial Department, New York State Supreme Court, reprinted in STEPHEN GILLERS, REGULATION OF LAWYERS: PROBLEMS OF LAW AND ETHICS 533–35 (10th ed. 2015).

[74] 781 P.2d 659 (Colo. 1989).

[75] On the prosecutor's ethical duty to refrain from insults and denigrating comments, see also *infra* § 4-9.12(e).

[76] 389 N.W.2d 386, 389 (Iowa 1986).

[77] COMMITTEE ON PROFESSIONALISM AND LAWYER COMPETENCE, CONFERENCE OF CHIEF JUSTICES, A NATIONAL ACTION PLAN ON LAWYER CONDUCT AND PROFESSIONALISM 2, 14 (1999).

Professionalism, in other words, primarily must be attained by inspiration, not the threat of punishment.

***Protecting Legitimate Advocacy and Freedom of Speech:*** Abusive invocations of the ethics rules to silence or hamper advocacy or dialogue on issues that implicate gender, race, sexual orientation, or other characteristics must be promptly and firmly rejected. Rule 8.4(d) and (g) are designed to protect those involved in the civil or criminal justice process from bigoted statements or falsely stereotypical references to categories of people that are unrelated to the merits of the case and that have no purpose other than to appeal to possible prejudices held by a fact-finder or to shatter the confidence of parties or attorneys subjected to such manifestations of bias.

Neither paragraph (d) nor paragraph (g) of Rule 8.4 should be mistaken for a speech code that distorts or inhibits public debate, including arguments presented to the courts, or that imposes a form of orthodoxy in viewpoint about political, social, or cultural matters.[78] Thus, for example, an accusation of impermissible manifestation of bias under Rule 8.4 would be out of place if applied to the speech of advocates in the public square or before the bench on either side of such controverted questions as the use of affirmative action on the basis of race in education or employment, appropriate accommodations for the disabled in public facilities, or whether requests for religious accommodations regarding services for same-sex marriages should be recognized by law.

## § 4-9.4(c) Using Means That Are Intended Solely to Embarrass, Delay, or Burden Another Person

### *§ 4-9.4(c)(1) Seeking Advantage by Humiliating, Degrading, or Oppressing Another*

Litigation is not for the faint-hearted or the thin-skinned. The fact that a disagreement has persisted beyond labors toward amicable resolution and has been elevated to the subject of a formal legal action often signals a matter in which feelings are running high and the underlying facts and conduct of the parties are sharply disputed. Because accusations of wrongdoing, such as criminal charges or claims for civil liability, are at the heart of many lawsuits, a sense of grievance and injustice on one side and feelings of persecution or unfairness on the other side are often present. That personal liberty (in a criminal case) or financial assets or family relationships (in civil cases) may be at stake may also heighten the tension and exacerbate the antipathy that the litigants feel toward each other. To fully investigate the matter and forthrightly submit the case in its fullest context to the trier of fact may require the lawyer to insist that parties and witnesses respond to pointed questions about sensitive or embarrassing matters, such as integrity, personal behavior or vices, patterns of conduct, relationships with other persons, etc.

Rule 4.4(a) of the Model Rules of Professional Conduct directs, in pertinent part, that, "[i]n representing a client, a lawyer shall not use means that have no substantial purpose other than to embarrass, delay, or burden a third person."

As a matter of collaborative moral deliberation, a lawyer and the client may choose to forgo certain courses of action or areas of inquiry in order to lessen the wounds to

---

[78] *See supra* § 4-1.4(c).

another that otherwise may be dealt by the litigation process.[79] Nonetheless, a lawyer does not cross the ethical line by zealously pursuing legitimate areas of inquiry, presenting relevant and material evidence, and advocating a well-founded position, even though the unfortunate result may be to embarrass, distress, or intrude upon the private lives of other parties or witnesses.

The ethical line is drawn at the point where the lawyer's questioning and advocacy go beyond explorations of significant points of controversy that are necessary to advance a legitimate claim or defense and instead seek unseemly advantage by humiliating, degrading, or oppressing another human being. For example, a lawyer was disbarred for repeatedly issuing dozens of unenforceable out-of-state subpoenas in some two dozen cases that had no substantial purpose other than to embarrass or burden.[80] A lawyer's question at a deposition suggesting a court-appointed parenting consultant in child visitation case had previously been accused of sexual misconduct with a minor was without any basis and was intended to embarrass and humiliate.[81] An attorney was disciplined for asking a witness during a deposition in a false arrest lawsuit about his sexual orientation and whether he had Alzheimer's when he said that he could not recall something.[82]

Professor Robert Schuwerk and attorney Lillian Hardwick suggest as a touchstone that, "[i]f the means employed appear to have been chosen primarily for their destructive impact on the party affected, the conduct violates the 'no substantial purpose' test."[83]

Likewise, while a lawyer should not refrain from using legitimate litigation tools to secure material evidence, seek judicial relief, and schedule litigation-related events, interposing such devices solely for the purposes of causing delay[84] or burdening another person is improper.

### *§ 4-9.4(c)(2) Threatening or Promising to Withhold Report of Criminal Wrongdoing*

Under Disciplinary Rule 7–105 of the former Model Code of Professional Responsibility, a lawyer was forbidden to "present, participate in presenting, or threaten to present criminal charges solely to obtain an advantage in a civil matter."[85] A handful of states maintain a similar prohibition on promising to forbear in reporting a crime as negotiation leverage for a civil settlement.[86]

The Model Rules of Professional Conduct include no similar express prohibition. Because of this deliberate omission, the American Bar Association's Standing Committee on Ethics and Professional Responsibility advised that the Model Rules do not prohibit a lawyer from using the possibility of presenting criminal charges against the opposing

---

[79] On moral deliberation between the lawyer and client, see generally *supra* § 4-5.2(b).

[80] Attorney Grievance Comm'n v. Mixter, 109 A.3d 1 (Md. Ct. App. 2015).

[81] In re Disciplinary Action Against Kurzman, 871 N.W.2d 753, 755–56 (Minn. 2015).

[82] In re Hammer, 718 S.E.2d 442, 444 (S.C. 2011).

[83] 48 ROBERT P. SCHUWERK & LILLIAN HARDWICK, HANDBOOK OF TEXAS LAWYER AND JUDICIAL ETHICS: TEXAS PRACTICE SERIES § 9.04 (Thomson-Reuters, 2016).

[84] On the general duty to expedite litigation and avoid unnecessary delay, see *supra* § 4-9.4(a).

[85] MODEL CODE OF PROF'L RESPONSIBILITY, Disciplinary Rule 7–105 (American Bar Ass'n, 1980).

[86] *See, e.g.*, GA. RULES OF PROF'L CONDUCT R. 3.4(h); IDAHO RULES OF PROF'L CONDUCT R. 4.4(a)(3), (4); KY. RULES OF PROF'L CONDUCT R. 3.4(f); MAINE RULES OF PROF'L CONDUCT R. 3.1(b); OR. RULES OF PROF'L CONDUCT R. 3.4(g); TENN. RULES OF PROF'L CONDUCT R. 4.4(a)(2); TEX. RULES OF PROF'L CONDUCT R. 4.4(b)(1).

party to obtain relief in a civil matter. Under the ABA opinion, a lawyer may agree "to refrain from presenting" those charges in a settlement agreement, "provided that the criminal matter is related to the client's civil claim, the lawyer has a well-founded belief that both the civil claim and the criminal charges are warranted by the law and the facts, and the lawyer does not attempt to exert or suggest an improper influence over the criminal process."[87]

When the potential criminal complaint concerns the same subject as the actual or potential civil action (such as a claim for return of or reimbursement for stolen property or compensation for an assault and battery), when the recovery is limited to the fair value of the harm (as opposed to obtaining a bonus in exchange for silence), when the lawyer has calmly offered restraint in reporting the crime rather than forcefully threatening the opposite, and when the lawyer does not also offer to destroy physical evidence of the possible crime or suggest false testimony,[88] the lawyer's conduct should be found ethically appropriate. When, for example, a lawyer represents a merchant who has discovered thefts by an employee or a customer, the lawyer's assistance in quietly arranging for return of the item or payment by the offending person, with the understanding that the authorities will not then be notified of the theft, would be a sensible alternative resolution that involves no abuse of the criminal justice system or harm to the public interest in obedience to the law.

The lawyer should exercise caution in alluding to possible criminal charges in an overly aggressive effort to extract an arguably excessive recovery from another party. As Professors Ronald Rotunda and John Dzienkowski warn, "[i]f the lawyer's threats amount to criminal extortion under state law, then . . . Rule 8.4(b) would apply, for that provision prohibits a lawyer from committing a criminal act that reflects adversely on honesty, trustworthiness or fitness as a lawyer in other respects."[89]

For example, in *Attorney Disciplinary Board v. Stowers*,[90] the Iowa Supreme Court found that a lawyer had engaged in extortion by sending emails threatening to injure another's professional reputation unless that person made a large charitable contribution in the name of the lawyer's wife. The court rejected the lawyer's argument that he had the right to make the threat as leverage to obtain a settlement of a claim. Because the lawyer had never mentioned the claim in the threatening communications and, as the lawyer knew or reasonably should have known, the statute of limitations barred the claim, the court concluded the lawyer was not pursuing settlement of claim but rather "sought to vindicate a personal grudge."[91]

By contrast, when the victim of a wrong has a well-founded claim that the wrong is not only tortious but criminal in character, thus giving rise to a claim of "right" under the typical extortion statute, and if the victim's lawyer seeks no more in recovery from the wrongdoer than the amount to which the lawyer reasonably concludes the victim is entitled, the lawyer's forthright raising of the prospect of criminal charges and

---

[87] ABA Comm. on Ethics & Prof'l Responsibility, Formal Op. 92–363 (1992).

[88] Disciplinary Action Against Kennedy, 864 N.W.2d 342, 348–49, 354 (Minn. 2015) (disciplining an attorney for offering to change the client's testimony in a criminal case in exchange for favorable settlement of a civil claim, over a dissent that viewed the lawyer as instead offering that the client might choose not to testify).

[89] RONALD D. ROTUNDA & JOHN S. DZIENKOWSKI, PROFESSIONAL RESPONSIBILITY: A STUDENT'S GUIDE § 4.4–1(b) (American Bar Ass'n, 2013–2014).

[90] 823 N.W.2d 1, 14–15 (Iowa 2012).

[91] *Id.* at 15.

suggesting that a complaint be withheld if the matter is settled would appear to be neither a crime nor a violation of the standards of professional responsibility in many (but not all) states.[92]

## § 4-9.5 DUTIES OF TRUTHFULNESS AND CANDOR BY LAWYER BEFORE THE TRIBUNAL

### § 4-9.5(a) Truthfulness as a Fundamental Expectation and Candor as a Special Requirement in Certain Situations

With "[f]undamental honesty" as "the base line" for the legal profession,[93] the Model Rules of Professional Conduct repeatedly enjoin honesty upon the lawyer, by requiring truthfulness by the lawyer when representing a client in transactions (including non-adjudicative matters) with others under Model Rule 4.1;[94] by generally forbidding "conduct involving dishonesty, fraud, deceit or misrepresentation" under Model Rule 8.4(b);[95] and by demanding that the lawyer speak the truth before tribunals under Model Rule 7.3(a).[96]

At the same time, the lawyer remains a zealous advocate and is not generally expected to take the affirmative step of leading adversaries or even courts toward a conclusion adverse to the client, especially in criminal proceedings in which the government is put to its proof. As Professor Bruce Green explains:

> [B]eing *truthful* is different from being *candid*. One might speak truthfully, believing everything one says to be true, but not say everything that matters. If one discloses all the relevant information, one is candid. To make a false statement is to lie, but to withhold relevant information—to fail to be candid—is to be reticent.[97]

In this respect, Green observes that, "[w]hile truthfulness is the rule for lawyers, candor is the exception."[98]

While a criminal defense lawyer may not lie to the judge or jury, she is not expected to candidly divulge confidential information that might correct a misimpression.[99] While the lawyer may not knowingly present false evidence to the tribunal,[100] she may cross-examine a truthful prosecution witness with the goal of undermining credibility, even if the effect is to mislead the trier-of-fact.[101] (As discussed later, the prosecutor is bound by

---

92 *See* 2 GEOFFREY C. HAZARD, JR., W. WILLIAM HODES & PETER R. JARVIS, THE LAW OF LAWYERING § 43.04 (Aspen, 4th ed., 2016).

93 Committee on Prof'l Ethics & Conduct v. Bauerle, 460 N.W.2d 452, 453 (Iowa 1990); *see also* In re Kahil's Case, 773 A.2d 647, 648 (N.H. 2001) (saying "it is the responsibility of every attorney at all times to be truthful").

94 *See infra* § 4-11.2.

95 *See supra* § 4-1.4(a).

96 *See infra* § 4-9.5(b) to (d).

97 Bruce A. Green, *Candor in Criminal Advocacy*, 44 HOFSTRA L. REV. 1105, 1108 (2016).

98 *Id.* at 1109.

99 *See* AMERICAN BAR ASS'N, STANDARDS FOR CRIMINAL JUSTICE: DEFENSE FUNCTION, Standard 4–1.4(a) (4th ed. 2015) ("In light of criminal defense counsel's constitutionally recognized role in the criminal process, defense counsel's duty of candor may be tempered by competing ethical and constitutional obligations.").

100 *See infra* § 4-9.8.

101 Monroe H. Freedman, *Professional Responsibility of the Criminal Defense Lawyer: The Three Hardest Questions*, 64 MICH. L. REV. 1469, 1474–75 (1966).

special ethical principles, including a heightened expectation of candor.[102]) Similarly, provided the result is not to advance a frivolous claim or defense or commit fraud, a lawyer in civil litigation is not obliged to be forthcoming with information beyond that which was properly sought in discovery.[103]

Literal honesty and transparent frankness are simply not the same. In particular, given that truth and rightfulness are frequently disputed in litigation, the lawyer should not be put into the position of presuming to judge his own client.

With this in mind, the ethics rules "narrowly define situations"[104] in which the lawyer is impressed with the more exacting duty of "candor," that is, being required to disclose the full set of information necessary for a fair decision by another. As pertinent to the litigation context, the lawyer is required to disclose mandatory legal authority in the jurisdiction, even if that position is contrary to her client's interests.[105] The lawyer's zealous advocacy must also be suppressed and candid disclosure must follow when the lawyer engages in the peculiar activity of making an *ex parte* contact with an adjudicator.[106]

### § 4-9.5(b) Duty of Truthfulness When Lawyer Makes Statements of Fact

Rule 3.3(a)(1) of the Model Rules of Professional conduct provides that "[a] lawyer shall not knowingly . . . make a false statement of fact or law to a tribunal or fail to correct a false statement of material fact or law previously made to the tribunal by the lawyer."

The lawyer does not vouch for the authenticity of the evidence submitted at trial[107] (although the lawyer may not knowingly present false evidence[108] and must take remedial action should the lawyer learn that false evidence has been presented[109]). Nor is the lawyer held to have guaranteed the accuracy of factual allegations made in pleadings, which are understood to be a presentation of the client's assertions (although the lawyer must verify that factual allegations have some evidentiary support and are not frivolous in nature).[110]

However, as Comment 3 to Rule 3.3 states, "an assertion purporting to be on the lawyer's own knowledge, as in an affidavit by the lawyer or in a statement in open court, may properly be made only when the lawyer knows the assertion is true or believes it to be true on the basis of a reasonably diligent inquiry." Lawyers frequently make statements to a tribunal, offering an explanation for a delay, providing background for a request for judicial discretion, describing the status of the case, or explaining the

---

[102] *See infra* § 4-9.12(e).

[103] *See infra* § 4-9.6.

[104] Green, *supra*, 44 HOFSTRA L. REV. at 1110.

[105] *See infra* § 4-9.5(c).

[106] *See infra* § 4-9.5(d).

[107] Matter of Disciplinary Proceedings Against Riley, 882 N.W.2d 820, 842 (Wis. 2016) (plurality).

[108] *See infra* § 4-9.8(a) to (b).

[109] *See infra* § 4-9.8(c) to (h).

[110] *See supra* § 4-9.3(a).

lawyer's actions. Such statements must be scrupulously honest and not misleading if the judge or other judicial officer is to be able to trust the lawyer.[111]

In *Committee on Professional Ethics & Conduct v. Ramey*,[112] involving criminal prosecution of a police officer for theft of property seized during execution of a search warrant, the prosecutor represented to the court that he personally had verified the serial numbers of bills of currency that would be introduced as exhibits during the trial and guaranteed that those numbers would match a serialized list of currency that had been earlier inventoried in the investigation. The prosecutor thereby assured the court that proper chain-of-custody had been maintained over the evidence and that the currency had not been altered. During foundational testimony for admission of the first bill as an exhibit, the serial number was found not to match any number on the list. When confronted with his assurances, the prosecutor claimed that he had forgotten being informed that there was such a discrepancy, conceded that he had never personally compared the bills with the list as he had claimed, and admitted that he had personally guaranteed that they would match.

On its review of the subsequent disciplinary proceeding, the Iowa Supreme Court in *Ramey* described the conduct as "unacceptable," even assuming the prosecutor had failed to recall the discrepancy, that he had not made the statement in order to secure improper admission of the exhibit, and that he had not intended to deceive the court. As Professor Peter Henning observes, because the attorney's honesty is so important, "courts will sanction lawyers for dishonest acts that have no effect on the determination of the truth."[113]

In considering what disciplinary sanction should be imposed, the court in *Ramey* said that "[t]he crucial question is whether the false statement was: (1) deliberately misleading so as to call for disbarment; (2) made in reckless disregard of the true facts so as to call for not less than license suspension; or (3) negligently made during the confused heat of trial."[114] Concluding that the "the case falls somewhere between the first situation and the second," the court ultimately settled upon suspension of the prosecutor's license as the appropriate sanction.[115]

### § 4-9.5(c) Limited Duty of Candor When Lawyer Makes Legal Arguments

When making statements about the law to the tribunal, the lawyer likewise is obliged to speak the truth, when the statement may be evaluated as objectively truthful or not. When the lawyer asserts that the law directly and unequivocally speaks to a point, the lawyer violates Rule 3.3(a)(1) of the Model Rules of Professional Conduct if the lawyer knowingly misrepresents the force of that law. Consider, for example, the lawyer who assures the court that the statute of limitations for a cause of action is a certain period of years, although the lawyer knows the limitations period to be otherwise. As another example, suppose the lawyer asserts that a controlling appellate decision bars

---

[111] On the prosecutor's heightened duty to speak truthfully in representations to the court, see also *infra* § 4-9.12(e).

[112] 512 N.W.2d 569, 569–72 (Iowa 1994).

[113] Peter J. Henning, *Lawyers, Truth, and Honesty in Representing Clients*, 20 NOTRE DAME J.L. ETHICS & PUB. POL'Y 209, 243 (2006).

[114] *Ramey*, 512 N.W.2d at 570.

[115] *Id.*

admission of certain evidence, when the lawyer knows that the decision says nothing of the kind or fails to directly address the question. In either instance, the lawyer has made a false statement about the law no different in nature than a false statement of fact.[116]

Many propositions of law are anything but clear and unequivocal, either as to what the rule of law directs or how it applies to a particular situation. When the answer to a legal question is uncertain, the lawyer may offer any legal arguments that are not frivolous[117] and those arguments should not be treated as an affirmative declaration subject to falsification. As long as the lawyer does not falsely represent that the binding legal authorities are more explicit or certain than their texts plausibly permit, the lawyer's legal advocacy should be measured by objective reasonableness and not by a misplaced standard of what is true.

However, the lawyer's duty of candor in making legal arguments is somewhat more demanding than with respect to factual representations in terms of what must be disclosed to the tribunal. The lawyer presenting a fact-based case to the trier-of-fact is not ordinarily obliged to volunteer the existence of evidence or alternative theories that cast doubt upon the client's preferred account of the facts,[118] unless the factual contention is frivolous because it lacks any reasonable basis,[119] the failure to disclose a particular fact effectively would constitute a misrepresentation,[120] or the lawyer is under a duty to reveal even adverse material facts such as when presenting a matter to a judge in an *ex parte* proceeding.[121] By contrast, the lawyer presenting legal argumentation has an affirmative duty to volunteer binding legal authority even when it may contravene the legal position the lawyer is advocating: "Failure to acknowledge *controlling* authority [in the jurisdiction], even in—perhaps especially in—a quest to overturn or modify that precedent is *not* 'zealous advocacy,' nor is it merely intellectual dishonesty; it is instead a failure to satisfy the minimum ethical standards for attorneys in this state."[122]

Under Rule 3.3(a)(2) of the Model Rules of Professional Conduct, the lawyer "shall not knowingly . . . fail to disclose to the tribunal legal authority in the controlling jurisdiction known to the lawyer to be directly adverse to the position of the client and not disclosed by opposing counsel."[123] While it may be wise strategy to acknowledge adverse persuasive authority from other jurisdictions that the court is likely to uncover, the rule demands disclosure only of legal authority in the "controlling jurisdiction," that is, those codified or judicial sources that have authority as directly-governing statutes,

---

[116] *See also* Attorney Disciplinary Bd. v. Sporer, 897 N.W.2d 69, 84–6 (Iowa 2017) (concluding a lawyer violated Rule 3.3(a)(1) by finding that the lawyer's position was not only objectively unreasonable as matter of law but that the lawyer did not subjectively believe his own position, as the court found "it hard to accept the notion that an experienced lawyer would believe [an opposing lawyer's] secretary dispatched on a routine mission of picking up legal documents had the authority to bind a client to the terms of a settlement agreement, particularly one in which a party was required to surrender a substantial legal claim").

[117] On the prohibition against making frivolous legal contentions, see *supra* § 4-9.3(c).

[118] *See* RONALD D. ROTUNDA & JOHN S. DZIENKOWSKI, PROFESSIONAL RESPONSIBILITY: A STUDENT'S GUIDE § 3.3–3(b) (American Bar Ass'n, 2013–2014) (explaining that "[i]t is not always necessary, or even permissible, to volunteer adverse facts when appearing before a tribunal," unless the failure to disclose a fact would effectively be a misrepresentation).

[119] On the duty to present only those factual contentions that have a reasonable basis, see *supra* § 4-9.3(b).

[120] *See infra* § 4-11.2(c).

[121] *See infra* § 4-9.5(d).

[122] McPherson v. Apfel, 110 F. Supp. 2d 1162, 1171 (N.D. Iowa 2000).

[123] *See also* AMERICAN BAR ASS'N, STANDARDS FOR CRIMINAL JUSTICE: DEFENSE FUNCTION, Standard 4–1.4(c) (4th ed. 2015) (same).

regulations, rules, or precedential rulings in the particular federal, state, or other jurisdiction in which the tribunal is situated.

As Professors Ronald Rotunda and John Dzienkowski stress, the rule "does *not* speak of 'controlling authorities," but rather more broadly refers to "legal authority in the controlling jurisdiction."[124] The standard for what must be disclosed is whether the legal authority is "directly adverse" to the client's position, not whether it is actually decisive and directly controls the outcome of the case. Relying on an early ethics opinion, Professors Geoffrey Hazard and William Hodes and attorney Peter Jarvis suggest that "right note on this issue" is to ask "whether the omitted authorities 'would be considered important by the judge sitting on the case,' or whether the judge might consider himself 'misled' if he remained unaware of them."[125]

Judge Mark Drummond suggests that lawyers would be wise to disclose legal authority that is even arguably adverse, as "nothing is more impressive than the advocate who comes into court" citing adverse as well as favorable decisions.[126] Such a forthright practice not only enhances the lawyer's reputation with the court, but has the persuasive effect of indicating that the lawyer is not overly concerned about apparently negative authority (as evidenced by the lawyer's very acknowledgment of such authority) and confirms the lawyer's reliability (as having done the homework of thoroughly researching the question.

The obligation of the lawyer under Model Rule 3.3(a)(2) is to acknowledge the legal authority if opposing counsel has failed to do so, not to surrender to that authority if a reasonable basis for escape remains. Having disclosed its existence, the lawyer not only may, but as a zealous advocate *must*, offer every reasonable argument for why adverse legal authority should be distinguished, limited, overruled, or overridden.

### § 4-9.5(d) Duty of Candor When Lawyer Participates in an *Ex Parte* Proceeding

One of the fundamental premises of our adversarial system of legal justice is that each party to a matter is entitled to be heard before a neutral magistrate so that a balanced presentation of both sides to the case will be made. Ordinarily, an *ex parte* communication by a party with the judge is forbidden as destructive of procedural fairness and undermining public confidence in the impartiality of the judiciary. As discussed subsequently, Rule 3.5(b) of the Model Rules of Professional Conduct prohibits a lawyer from communicating *ex parte* with a judge unless authorized to do so by law or a court order.[127] Under narrow circumstances, such as when a party seeks an emergency restraining order, a lawyer may be permitted to appear before a judge or other judicial officer without the presence of the opposing party or that party's representative.

On those rare occasions when an *ex parte* communication with a judge or other judicial officer is allowed, Rule 3.3(d) of the Model Rules of Professional Conduct imposes

---

[124] RONALD D. ROTUNDA & JOHN S. DZIENKOWSKI, PROFESSIONAL RESPONSIBILITY: A STUDENT'S GUIDE § 3.3–2 (American Bar Ass'n, 2013–2014).

[125] 2 GEOFFREY C. HAZARD, JR., W. WILLIAM HODES & PETER R. JARVIS, THE LAW OF LAWYERING § 32.09 (Aspen, 4th ed., 2016) (quoting ABA Comm. on Ethics and Professional Responsibility, Formal Op. 280 (1949)).

[126] Mark A. Drummond, *What Judges Want*, LITIGATION, Summer, 2005, at 3–4; *see also* 2 GEOFFREY C. HAZARD, JR. & W. WILLIAM HODES, THE LAW OF LAWYERING § 29.11 (Aspen, 3d ed., 2009) (saying that "many lawyers believe that surfacing adverse precedent is a good tactic, for it permits taking the wind out of an opponent's sails").

[127] *See infra* § 4-9.9(d).

a special duty of candor upon the lawyer, because the adversarial truthfinding function is hampered by the absence of the other party who would be expected to present the opposing side. Rule 3.3(d) provides that, "[i]n an ex parte proceeding, a lawyer shall inform the tribunal of all material facts known to the lawyer that will enable the tribunal to make an informed decision, whether or not the facts are adverse." In order that the judge may obtain a better understanding of the underlying facts so as to accord the absent party fair consideration when rendering a judicial decision, Comment 14 to Rule 3.3 says that the lawyer for the represented party who appears *ex parte* must "make disclosures of material facts known to the lawyer and that the lawyer reasonably believes are necessary to an informed decision."

When an *ex parte* contact with an adjudicator is authorized, the lawyer has a duty to give the full flavor of the matter to the judge, identifying all affected persons, describing the nature of the dispute, outlining the circumstances that led to the dispute, and fairly summarizing the likely factual narrative that would be offered by the opposing party. Lest the judge be deceived about the genuine nature of the matter, all material facts must be disclosed, including facts that are adverse to the lawyer's client in seeking the *ex parte* relief.

While the lawyer may not have a duty to actively seek out evidence that would be harmful to the client's case, the lawyer may not withhold critical information that is within the lawyer's personal knowledge nor may the lawyer remain in willful ignorance of obvious circumstances. And if the lawyer's factual understanding remains cloudy despite reasonable prior investigation,[128] the confused state of the case should be forthrightly acknowledged, as the judge may conclude that such a "muddled situation call[s] for a contested hearing."[129]

While the lawyer who chooses to make an *ex parte* application is bound to reveal all material information, even that which otherwise would be confidential, the lawyer is not required to reveal information that is actually privileged, which the lawyer reasonably believes would not be subject to discovery or subpoena by reason of an evidentiary privilege such as that afforded to attorney-client communications.[130]

In addition to disclosing the material facts about the underlying merits as relevant to the *ex parte* relief being sought, the lawyer must also disclose material information about the procedural status of the case, including whether the absent party is represented by counsel and whether or not that counsel was given reasonable advance notice about the *ex parte* proceeding.

Even in an *ex parte* proceeding, the lawyer remains an advocate for the client. As Professors Geoffrey Hazard and William Hodes and attorney Peter Jarvis explain, "[o]nce counsel has made full disclosure of all material facts, she is of course free to argue the case with full vigor."[131]

---

[128] On the duty of reasonable prior inquiry before making a presentation to the court, see *supra* § 4-9.3.

[129] Committee on Prof'l Ethics & Conduct v. Zimmerman, 354 N.W.2d 235, 237 (Iowa 1984).

[130] *See* RESTATEMENT (THIRD) OF THE LAW GOVERNING LAWYERS § 112, cmt. b (American Law Institute, 2000) (stating that "the rule of the Section does not require the disclosure of privileged evidence").

[131] 2 GEOFFREY C. HAZARD, JR., W. WILLIAM HODES & PETER R. JARVIS, THE LAW OF LAWYERING § 32.22 (Aspen, 4th ed., 2016).

### § 4-9.5(e) Duty of Lawyer to Obey Court Rules and Rulings, Unless Openly Challenging Validity

Rule 3.4(c) of the Model Rules of Professional Conduct states that a lawyer may not "knowingly disobey an obligation under the rules of a tribunal except for an open refusal based on an assertion that no valid obligation exists."

By generally directing the lawyer to obey court rules, Rule 3.4(c) is unremarkable and is parallel to many other provisions in the rules that also demand the lawyer to be law-abiding. For example, Model Rule 8.4 broadly requires a lawyer to comply with various legal requirements, including conformance to the Rules of Professional Conduct; not committing criminal acts; refusing to engage in such unlawful conduct as fraud and misrepresentation; and refraining from sexual harassment and unlawful discrimination. Rule 1.2(d) forbids a lawyer from "counsel[ing] a client to engage, or assist[ing] a client, in conduct that the lawyer knows is criminal or fraudulent."[132] Consistent with these other provisions, Rule 3.4(c) makes plain that the lawyer's duty to comply with the various obligations imposed by law encompasses those procedural and other requirements that are codified in the rules of a court or other tribunal or that are the subject of a court order issued pursuant to the rules of the tribunal.

As with other provisions in the ethics rules that impose a professional duty to abide by legal requirements, Rule 3.4(c) excuses a lawyer (in terms of potential disciplinary sanction but not necessarily in terms of the procedural and other sanctions that may attend disobedience of a court rule or order) when the lawyer forthrightly (and presumably with good-faith and a reasonable basis) denies that a valid obligation exists. Rule 1.2(d) similarly affirms that a lawyer "may counsel or assist a client to make a good faith effort to determine the validity, scope, meaning, or application of the law."[133] Comment 6 to Model Rule 8.4 also recognizes a lawyer's choice to "refuse to comply with an obligation imposed by law upon a good faith belief that no valid obligation exists."[134] Rule 3.4(c) authorizes a lawyer to question the application or validity of a court rule or court order as well.

To claim the protection of this rule, the lawyer must make an "open refusal," thus acting with candor and clarity in challenging the obligation even while simultaneously declining to comply with it. As the Utah Supreme Court has ruled, "an attorney must either obey a court order or alert the court that he or she intends to not comply with the order."[135] When a lawyer surreptitiously violates an obligation stated in a court rule or order, the attempt to conceal the behavior undermines any claim of good faith and weakens the credibility of the lawyer's challenge to the validity of the obligation.[136] Nor may a lawyer invoke this exception belatedly when charged with disobedience, as the rule demands open refusal from the outset if a lawyer's non-compliance with the obligation is to be treated as other than professional misconduct. Moreover, if alternative

---

[132] *See supra* § 4-5.2(c).

[133] *Id.*

[134] *See supra* § 4-1.4(a).

[135] Matter of Discipline of Gilbert, 379 P.3d 1247, 1256 (Utah 2016).

[136] *See* Attorney Disciplinary Bd. v. Stowers, 823 N.W.2d 1, 9 (Iowa 2013) (refusing to accept a lawyer's "open refusal" defense to contemptuous violation of a protective order for confidential information, quoting the commission's conclusion that the lawyer "by sending the threatening private emails, did not act openly in court but rather 'proceeded vigilante-style to use threats of embarrassment, disbarment, and prosecution to extra-judicially seek remedies' ").

means are readily available by which to test the validity of the obligation, such as by asking for reconsideration by the judge or through an appeal to a reviewing court, immediate resort to disobedience would be unnecessary and thus not in good faith.

While a lawyer may not disobey a judicial order or court rule with impunity, when the lawyer openly refuses to accept the validity of an obligation, Rule 3.4(c) does mark a shift in the enforcement mechanism. Under Rule 3.4(c), when a lawyer openly resists compliance with a judicial order or court rule, claiming the order or rule is invalid, responsibility for enforcing the judicial obligation has been moved away from the *professional disciplinary process* and returned back to the *tribunal*, whose order or rule has been placed in question and which has the power to impose sanctions for violation of a court order or rule or even to hold the disobedient lawyer in contempt.

Provided that the lawyer "open[ly] refus[es]" to comply "based on an assertion that no valid obligation exists," as stated in Model Rule 3.4(c), the lawyer's noncompliance with a court order or rule should not be punished as professional misconduct.[137] Instead, the validity of the judicial obligation, and the consequences that should attach to the lawyer's violation of a court order or rule if that validity is confirmed, are now left to the judicial process.[138] Again, the question is not whether court orders and rules are enforceable against the disobedient lawyer, even the lawyer who openly refuses to comply in good faith, but rather where the venue should be located for that enforcement and what means of enforcement should be employed. Under Rule 3.4(c), when a lawyer openly refuses to comply with a judicial action by asserting that no valid obligation exists, enforcement responsibilities have been returned to the tribunal (where they always have resided).[139]

## § 4-9.6 OBTAINING, DISCOVERING, AND PRESERVING EVIDENCE FOR CIVIL PROCEEDINGS

### § 4-9.6(a) General Duties on Access to Evidence in Civil Matters

Rule 3.4(a) of the Model Rules of Professional Conduct forbids a lawyer to "unlawfully obstruct another party's access to evidence or unlawfully alter, destroy or conceal a document or other material having potential evidentiary value." The rule further provides that "[a] lawyer shall not counsel or assist another person to do any such act."

Comments 1 and 2 to Rule 3.4 explain these proscriptions are necessary to ensure "[f]air competition in the adversary system" and to uphold the important procedural "right of an opposing party, including the government, to obtain evidence through discovery or subpoena."

---

[137] *But see* In Matter of Sklar, No. 13-O-14606, at 9 (Cal. St. Bar 2016) (applying California statutory rule, Cal. Bus. & Prof. Code § 6103, that does not contain an open refusal exception akin to Model Rule 3.4 to impose discipline on a lawyer, saying she could not "disregard court orders because she believes they are invalid, even if she has a personal good faith reason to do so").

[138] *See* 48 ROBERT P. SCHUWERK & LILLIAN HARDWICK, HANDBOOK OF TEXAS LAWYER AND JUDICIAL ETHICS: TEXAS PRACTICE SERIES § 8.04 (Thomson/West, 2016) (explaining that while open refusal to obey an obligation under a court rule or order is an exception to the professional conduct rule, "[a] lawyer operating under this exception can of course be subject to sanctions imposed by the tribunal itself").

[139] *See* 2 GEOFFREY C. HAZARD, JR., W. WILLIAM HODES & PETER R. JARVIS, THE LAW OF LAWYERING § 33.08 (Aspen, 4th ed., 2016) (explaining that while "[c]ontempt may sometimes be an appropriate remedy [for a lawyer's refusal to comply with a court rule or ruling] . . . disciplinary action is generally not taken as long as the lawyer acted openly and in good faith"). *See generally id.*, § 33.11.

As a diligent and zealous advocate, the lawyer may and should raise plausible objections to requests for discovery. But if legal resistance by a lawyer to a request or demand for documents or other evidence proves unsuccessful, the lawyer must comply with such lawful requests and may not inappropriately impede access to the evidence.

## § 4-9.6(b) Ethical Duties of Proper Requests and Responses in Civil Discovery

### *§ 4-9.6(b)(1) General Ethical Expectations in Discovery*

> Nowhere is watching the line between truth and aggressive lawyering more important than in conducting discovery. Tactics that might go too far when conducted in the open do far more damage when carried out in shadows .... Questionable allegations in pleadings, unfair questions in cross-examination, and dubious arguments to the court or jury are visible to opposing counsel and can often be exposed or countered. But when a document never comes to light because a request for production was construed too narrowly, or a witness shades his testimony as a result of some adroit behind-the-scenes coaching, the actors in the system who might serve as counterweights—opposing counsel, the court, even jurors—have less to work with. The basic factual script from which the entire drama proceeds has been altered in deeper ways, and more violence has been done to the truth.[140]

Rule 3.4(d) of the Model Rules of Professional Conduct provides that, "[i]n pretrial procedure," the lawyer shall not "make a frivolous discovery request or fail to make reasonably diligent effort to comply with a legally proper discovery request by an opposing party." Through Rule 26(g) of the Federal Rules of Civil Procedure, followed in substantial part by most states, a lawyer making a discovery request or response certifies:

> (A) with respect to a disclosure, it is complete and correct as of the time it is made; and
>
> (B) with respect to a discovery request, response, or objection, it is:
>
> (i) consistent with these rules and warranted by existing law or by a nonfrivolous argument for extending, modifying, or reversing existing law, or for establishing new law;
>
> (ii) not interposed for any improper purpose, such as to harass, cause unnecessary delay, or needlessly increase the cost of litigation; and
>
> (iii) neither unreasonable nor unduly burdensome or expensive, considering the needs of the case, prior discovery in the case, the amount in controversy, and the importance of the issues at stake in the action.[141]

Through these two provisions, the lawyer is obliged to participate responsibly in discovery both as a matter of professional ethics and as a matter of court rule.[142] And

---

[140] Martin J. Siegel, *Zealous Advocacy v. Truth*, LITIGATION, Fall, 2006, at 31.

[141] FED. R. CIV. P. 26(g).

[142] On the framework for civil discovery and ethical responsibilities, see generally Paula Schaefer, *Attorneys, Document Discovery, and Discipline*, 30 GEO. J. LEGAL ETHICS 1 (2017).

because discovery ordinarily takes place without "constant judicial intervention," these "important principles of fair play [must be vindicated] in the largely private world of civil discovery . . . . The rules of discovery must necessarily be largely self-enforcing."[143]

In sum, both on the part of the requesting attorney and on the part of the responding attorney, "a spirit of cooperation and forthrightness during the discovery process is necessary for the proper functioning of modern trials."[144] As Professor Paula Schaefer writes, discovery misconduct that transgresses ethical limitations "generally falls into one of two categories: (1) misleading an opposing party, and (2) intentionally or negligently failing to perform a duty owed to an opposing party."[145]

### *§ 4-9.6(b)(2) Requests for Discovery*

When seeking information in civil discovery, a lawyer ethically may propound a discovery request only when it is well-founded, that is, at least arguably relevant and not subject to a discovery limitation. Given the generally broad scope of discovery,[146] a request is likely to cross an ethical line (as opposed to a prudential line) only when it plainly seeks irrelevant, privileged, or otherwise protected information or when the volume of the discovery requests becomes so large and disproportionate to the nature of the case as to indicate these requests are designed to harass and oppress.

While a lawyer who makes unnecessarily broad requests may lose credibility with the judge when seeking to compel discovery and thus is likely to see the scope of discovery restricted by the court, the lawyer ordinarily may rely upon the responding party to seek to control the scope of discovery by raising appropriate objections or seeking a protective order.

However, as of 2015, Rule 26(b)(1) expressly defines the scope of permissible discovery as not only that which is relevant and non-privileged but also is "proportional to the needs of the case, considering the importance of the issues at stake in the action, the amount in controversy, the parties' relative access to relevant information, the parties' resources, the importance of the discovery in resolving the issues, and whether the burden or expense of the proposed discovery outweighs its likely benefit."[147] We may expect in the coming years considerably greater attention by federal courts to the question of proportionality, especially as related to electronically-stored information (the

---

[143] Poole ex rel. Elliott v. Textron, Inc., 192 F.R.D. 494, 507 (D. Md. 2000) (quoting Hopei Garments (Hong Kong), Ltd. v. Oslo Trading Co., 1988 WL 25139 (S.D.N.Y. 1988)).

[144] Washington State Physicians Ins. Exchange & Ass'n v Fisons Corp., 858 P.2d 1054, 1077 (Wash. 1993); *see also* Poole ex rel. Elliott, 192 F.R.D. 494, 507 (D. Md. 2000) (saying that the discovery rules "rely on the honesty and good faith of counsel in dealing with adversaries").

[145] Schaefer, *supra*, 30 GEO. J. LEGAL ETHICS at 26.

[146] *See* Sentis Grp., Inc. v. Shell Oil Co., 763 F.3d 919, 926 (8th Cir. 2014) (explaining that discovery is not "limited to material that might be deemed relevant and admissible at trial, but also serves as an "investigatory tool intended to help litigants gain an understanding of the key persons, relationships, and evidence in a case and . . . the veracity of those persons and purported evidence, even if the evidence discovered is later deemed not admissible").

[147] FED. R. CIV. P. 26(b)(1). Before 2015, similar language was located in Rule 26(b)(2)(C) of the Federal Rules of Civil Procedure, which directed the court to limit discovery if "the burden or expense of the proposed discovery outweighs its likely benefit, considering the needs of the case, the amount in controversy, the parties' resources, the importance of the issues at stake in the action, and the importance of the discovery in resolving the issues." Proportionality as a factor in the scope of permissible discovery has a long history in the procedural rules.

preservation of which is discussed below),[148] which may set further ethical markers for lawyers in discovery requests directed to an opponent in litigation.

By operation of Rule 3.4(c), which requires a lawyer to obey court rules, limitations on appropriate discovery established in the procedural rules may not properly be circumvented by a lawyer seeking to discover evidence. For example, as Professors Geoffrey Hazard and William Hodes and attorney Peter Jarvis suggest, "[i]nasmuch as the Federal Rules of Civil Procedure . . . provide detailed protocols for taking discovery of an opposing party's expert witnesses, while barring any discovery with respect to non-testifying experts except under exceptional circumstances," then "informal and *ex parte* 'debriefing' " of an opposing party's expert "must be considered to be prohibited, at least by clear implication."[149] *Ex parte* contacts with the other party's expert witnesses, either for purposes of gathering information outside the discovery process or attempting to convert the expert to the opposing side, is improper conduct that may justify disqualification of the offending lawyer. Other extra-judicial conduct that offends ethical limitations on gathering evidence for civil matters is discussed below.[150]

#### *§ 4-9.6(b)(3) Responses to Discovery*

When responding to a discovery request, the lawyer must make "a reasonable effort to assure that the client has provided all the information and documents . . . responsive to the discovery demand."[151]

> Counsel need not conduct an exhaustive investigation, but only one that is reasonable under the circumstances. Relevant circumstances may include: (1) the number and complexity of the issues; (2) the location, nature, number and availability of potentially relevant witnesses or documents; (3) the extent of past working relationships between the attorney and the client, particularly in related or similar litigation; and (4) the time available to conduct an investigation.[152]

In responding to discovery requests, "it is ultimately the lawyer's responsibility to preserve potentially relevant evidence, including that maintained in electronic format," meaning that a lawyer cannot delegate to the client in a "wholesale fashion" the tasks of identifying, gathering, reviewing, and disclosing documents.[153] While plausible and legitimate objections to discovery requests are part of the adversarial process in the realm of civil discovery and reflect appropriate zealous advocacy, obstructionist objections to discovery violate ethical expectations because a frivolous resistance cannot be characterized as a "reasonably diligent effort" to comply with a discovery request.

### § 4-9.6(c) Preservation of Potential Evidence

When litigation is reasonably anticipated, the party must institute a "litigation hold" and preserve relevant evidence, with the party's counsel then assuming an ethical

---

148 *See infra* § 4-9.6(c)(1) to (3).

149 2 GEOFFREY C. HAZARD, JR., W. WILLIAM HODES & PETER R. JARVIS, THE LAW OF LAWYERING § 33.09 (Aspen, 4th ed., 2016).

150 *See infra* § 4-9.6(d) to (g).

151 Advisory Committee Notes to 1983 Amendments to Federal Rule of Civil Procedure 26(g).

152 St. Paul Reinsurance Co., Ltd. v. Commercial Financial Corp., 198 F.R.D. 508, 516 n.3 (N.D. Iowa 2000) (citing Dixon v. Certainteed Corp., 164 F.R.D. 685, 691 (D. Kan. 1996)).

153 Paul D. Weiner & Mary Kay Brown, *Navigating the New E-Discovery Rules*, LITIGATION, Winter, 2007, at 30.

duty to monitor and oversee compliance with that litigation hold.[154] Especially in the era of electronically-stored information, the lawyer must diligently evaluate the situation, understand the client's storage of information, and carefully monitor the client's actions. The consequence of error in this sensitive area may extend beyond professional discipline[155] to include sanctions by the court that in extraordinary instances may include an adverse spoliation instruction to a jury.

### *§ 4-9.6(c)(1) Overview of the Law of Spoliation of Evidence*

Most states and courts require preservation of evidence only when the actor believes that a proceeding is pending or about to be commenced.[156] In general, then, most state laws prohibit the concealment or destruction of evidence that would be relevant either to an existing proceeding or to a future proceeding that is almost certain to be filed.[157] By contrast, if potential evidence is lost or destroyed before a party should have reasonably anticipated litigation, and thus before a party had a duty to preserve the evidence, the party has committed no wrong.[158]

As a matter of common law, state courts long have emphasized that deliberate destruction of evidence in advance of imminent litigation is improper and may result in a spoliation inference:

> It is a well established legal principle that the intentional destruction of or the failure to produce documents or physical evidence relevant to the proof of an issue in a legal proceeding supports an inference that the evidence would have been unfavorable to the party responsible for its destruction or nonproduction. The nonproduction, alteration, or destruction of evidence is commonly referred to as spoliation. When established, the inference is regarded as an admission by conduct of the weakness of the party's case. The inference is imposed both for evidentiary and punitive reasons. The evidentiary value of the inference is derived from the common sense observation that a party who destroys a document with knowledge that it is relevant to litigation is likely to have been threatened by the document. Additionally, an inference serves to deter parties from destroying relevant evidence.
>
> . . . However, the inference can only be based upon the intentional destruction of evidence. It is not warranted if the disappearance of the evidence is due to mere negligence, or if the evidence was destroyed during a routine procedure.[159]

---

[154] Zubulake v. UBS Warburg LLC, 229 F.R.D. 422, 432 (S.D.N.Y. 2004). *See generally* Nathan M. Crystal, *Ethical Responsibility and Legal Liability of Lawyers for Failure to Institute or Monitor Litigation Holds*, 43 AKRON L. REV. 715 (2010).

[155] *See* Paula Schaefer, *Attorneys, Document Discovery, and Discipline*, 30 GEO. J. LEGAL ETHICS 1, 25 (2017) (arguing court sanctions alone is insufficient "to address pervasive discovery misconduct" and the regular use of professional discipline would likely make sure that attorneys "get the message and change").

[156] *See* Ricardo G. Cedillo & David Lopez, *Document Destruction in Business Litigation From a Practitioner's Point-of-View: The Ethical Rules vs. Practical Realities*, 20 ST. MARY'S L.J. 637, 644 (1989).

[157] For more on state law on destruction of evidence in the criminal context, see *infra* § 4-9.7(b)(1).

[158] *See* Marshall v. Dentfirst, P.C., 313 F.R.D. 691, 697 (N.D. Ga. 2016) (denying plaintiff's motion for spoliation sanctions where a former employee's browsing history and emails on an office computer were not shown to still be existing when the defendant reasonably should have anticipated litigation).

[159] Phillips v. Covenant Clinic, 625 N.W.2d 714, 718–19 (Iowa 2001); *see also* State v. Vasquez, 230 S.W.3d 744, 754 (Tex. App. 2007); Courtney v. Big O Tires, Inc., 87 P.2d 903, 933 (Idaho 2003); California Civil Jury Instructions (BAJI) 2.03 ("Willful Acts to Preclude Use of Evidence: If you find that a party willfully

Several federal courts have expounded on spoliation of evidence in the challenging context of electronically-stored information (ESI). As a civil procedure treatise puts it, the "explosion of ESI causes a raft of problems for 'E-discovery' " because of the volume, variety, and volatility of ESI.[160] In these ESI cases, questions have arisen on both the front-end about the duty to preserve records and on the back-end about the appropriate response by a court when records that should have been preserved are found to have been destroyed.

As the United States Court of Appeals for the Fourth Circuit ruled, "[t]he duty to preserve material evidence arises not only during litigation but also extends to that period before the litigation when a party reasonably should know that the evidence may be relevant to anticipated litigation."[161] Professor A. Benjamin Spencer identifies the "[t]wo key parameters" for this duty to preserve evidence as—

> the trigger for the duty and its scope. The *trigger* refers to the point in time at which an individual or entity can be said to be under the duty to preserve. *Scope* refers to the identification of materials and information that must be preserved pursuant to the duty and to whom the duty attaches.[162]

***Trigger:*** The *trigger* for a duty to preserve evidence is the reasonable anticipation of litigation,[163] which demands some concrete basis for fearing a specific lawsuit that goes beyond a "general concern over litigation"[164] or the "mere existence of a dispute."[165] The identification of that point in time when a party is placed on notice of impending litigation unavoidably requires a contextual, case-by-case, fact-specific judgment of what a reasonable person would expect under the circumstances. Spencer advises that the duty to preserve likely is triggered by letters from prospective adversaries that threaten litigation[166] or otherwise places a party with certain and specific notice of impending litigation;[167] a pre-litigation "hold" notice from an adversary, demanding that certain evidence be preserved;[168] notice of an incident in which substantial harm has or may

---

[suppressed] [,] [altered] [,] [damaged] [,] [concealed] [, or] [destroyed] evidence in order to prevent its being used in this trial, you may consider that fact in determining what inferences to draw from the evidence."); Charles W. Adams, *Spoliation of Evidence: Sanctions Versus Advocacy*, 18 MICH. TELECOMM. TECH. L. REV. 1, 12 (2011) ("The circumstantial evidence of intentional spoliation of evidence supports both the evidentiary and punitive components for an adverse inference. In contrast, the negligent loss of computer files would not support an inference concerning their probable content.").

160 GENE R. SHREVE, PETER RAVEN-HANSEN & CHARLES GARDNER GEYH, UNDERSTANDING CIVIL PROCEDURE § 10.03 (Lexis-Nexis, 5th ed. 2013).

161 Silvestri v. Gen. Motors Corp., 271 F.3d 583, 591 (4th Cir. 2001); *see also* Kronisch v. United States, 150 F.3d 112, 126 (2d Cir. 1998).

162 A. Benjamin Spencer, *The* Preservation Obligation*: Regulating and Sanctioning Pre-Litigation Spoliation in Federal Court*, 79 FORDHAM L. REV. 2005, 2007 (2011); *see also* SHREVE, RAVEN-HANSEN & GEYH, *supra*, § 10.03[a], at 331 (describing the two questions as "*when* does a duty to preserve attach, and *what* evidence must be preserved").

163 Zubulake v. UBS Wartburg LLC, 220 F.R.D. 212, 217 (S.D.N.Y. 2003).

164 Realnetworks, Inc. v. DVD Copy Control Ass'n, 264 F.R.D. 517, 526 (N.D. Cal. 2009).

165 Goodman v. Praxair Servs., Inc., 632 F. Supp. 2d 494, 510 (D. Md. 2009).

166 Spencer, *supra*, 79 FORDHAM L. REV. at 2008–10; *see also Goodman*, 632 F. Supp. 2d at 511 (referring to a letter that "openly threatens litigation"); Turner v. United States, 736 F.3d 274, 282 (4th Cir. 2013) (finding a duty to preserve was not triggered when the plaintiff failed to send defendants "a document preservation letter, or any other correspondence threatening litigation").

167 *See* AAB Joint Venture v. United States, 75 Fed. Cl. 432, 441–42 (2007) ("The letter did not provide Defendant with the requisite certainty or specificity of impending litigation, nor did it apprise Defendant of the scope of the claims which would be filed.").

168 Spencer, *supra*, 79 FORDHAM L. REV. at 2008.

occur;[169] or, from a prospective plaintiff's standpoint, consulting or retaining a lawyer or suffering a substantial loss.[170] In the absence of any pre-litigation objections or demand for action, the duty to preserve evidence is certainly triggered by service of the lawsuit.[171]

***Scope:*** The *scope* of the duty to preserve evidence has been described in a leading federal court decision as extending to all records, documents, and items that the party "knows, or reasonably should know, is relevant in the action, is reasonably calculated to lead to the discovery of admissible evidence, is reasonably likely to be requested during discovery and/or is the subject of a pending discovery request."[172] In particular, files and emails held by "key players" in the events that provoke or may lead to litigation and that relate in any way to the dispute must be maintained.[173]

By virtue of professional education and experience, the lawyer has a special role in ensuring that the client understands what constitutes and properly preserves relevant evidence.[174] The determination of "what was potentially relevant" should not be left to the discretion of the client; "what might be potentially relevant to a person trained in law might not be relevant to a lay person."[175]

***Sanctions:*** When the duty to preserve evidence has been breached, the remaining question is what sanction or other response is justified. Outlining the issues in general terms, the Sedona Working Group on Electronic Document Retention and Production (a think-tank of interested judges, lawyers, academics, and experts) advised in 2007:

> Sanctions, including spoliation findings, should be considered by the court only if it finds that there was a clear duty to preserve, a culpable failure to preserve and produce relevant electronically stored information, and a reasonable probability that the loss of the evidence has materially prejudiced the adverse party.[176]

Consistent with state court decisions cited earlier, the substantial majority of the federal Courts of Appeals to address the question reserve the most severe sanctions—dismissal, default judgment, or an adverse inference spoliation instruction to the jury—for cases in which a party intentionally destroyed evidence.[177] As one federal court of

---

[169] *Id.* at 2010; *see also* Jones v. Staübli Motor Sports Div. of Staubli American Corp., 897 F. Supp. 2d 599, 608 (S.D. Ohio 2012) (ruling that "[i]n the face of such a serious accident, [in which a member of the pit crew for a race car was injured when the refueling equipment spilled gasoline as it was disconnected], it was all but obvious that litigation was within the realm of possibility").

[170] Spencer, *supra*, 79 FORDHAM L. REV. at 2011; *see also* Innis Arden Golf Club v. Pitney Bowes, Inc., 257 F.R.D. 334, 340 (D. Conn. 2009) (concluding that a duty to preserve arose when plaintiff retained counsel in connection with potential legal action but had not yet identified responsible parties).

[171] *See* Nacco Materials Handling Group, Inc. v. Lilly Co., 278 F.R.D. 395, 403 (W.D. Tenn. 2011).

[172] *Zubulake*, 220 F.R.D. at 217 (footnotes omitted).

[173] *Id.*; Goodman v. Praxair Servs., Inc., 632 F. Supp. 2d 494, 512–13 (D. Md. 2009).

[174] *See infra* § 4-9.6(c)(4).

[175] Clark Constr. Grp. v. City of Memphis, 229 F.R.D. 131, 136–37 (W.D. Tenn. 2005).

[176] THE SEDONA CONFERENCE WORKING GRP. ON ELEC. DOCUMENT RETENTION & PROD., THE SEDONA PRINCIPLES, SECOND EDITION: BEST PRACTICES RECOMMENDATIONS & PRINCIPLES FOR ADDRESSING ELECTRONIC DOCUMENT PRODUCTION, Principle 14, at 70 (2007), at https://www.paed.uscourts.gov/documents/procedures/The%20Sedona%20Principles.pdf.

[177] Micron Technology, Inc. v. Rambus Inc., 645 F.3d 1311, 1326–27 (Fed. Cir. 2011); United States v. Laurent, 607 F.3d 895, 902 (1st Cir. 2010); Mann v. Taser, Int'l, Inc., 588 F.3d 1291, 1310 (11th Cir. 2009); Faas v. Sears, Roebuck & Co., 532 F.3d 633, 644 (7th Cir. 2008); Henning v. Union Pac. R.R. Co., 530 F.3d 1206, 1220 (10th Cir. 2008); Greyhound Lines, Inc. v. Wade, 485 F.3d 1032, 1035 (8th Cir. 2007); Condrey v. SunTrust Bank of Ga., 431 F.3d 191, 203–05 (5th Cir. 2005); Med. Lab. Mgmt. Consultants v. Am. Broad. Co.,

appeals explained, "[t]he ultimate focus for imposing sanctions for spoliation of evidence is the intentional destruction of evidence indicating a desire to suppress the truth."[178] As discussed below, a recent amendment to the Federal Rules of Civil Procedure has codified this approach in the federal courts.

### *§ 4-9.6(c)(2) Destruction of Documents Pursuant to a Document Retention Policy*

Destruction of records according to a reasonable, established, and consistently followed procedure for document retention-destruction is not improper, provided of course that it is not reasonably known at the time of the destruction that particular records are relevant to a pending or anticipated proceeding.[179] Rather than being motivated to remove adverse evidence from business files, a business may reasonably adopt such a policy to avoid the costs and burdens of storing documents, maintaining massive numbers of electronic files, and of searching for documents and electronic files in response to discovery requests if unanticipated litigation should later emerge.[180]

By statute or regulation, however, certain business records—such as employment records, audit information for publicly-held companies, occupational hazard information, information regarding imports, etc.[181]—must be retained for a period of time, regardless of whether any litigation is anticipated.

Importantly, as discussed above, "once a party reasonably anticipates litigation, it has a duty to suspend any routine document purging system that might be in effect and to put in place a litigation hold to ensure the preservation of relevant documents—failure to do so constitutes spoliation."[182]

### *§ 4-9.6(c)(3) 2015 Amendment to the Federal Rules of Civil Procedure on Preservation of Electronically-Stored Information (ESI)*

In recent years, the Judicial Conference has adopted changes to the Federal Rules of Civil Procedure that affect the scope of discovery generally and discovery of electronically-stored information (ESI) in particular in the federal courts. While many of the pertinent proposed changes are focused on the proportionality of discovery[183] due to

---

306 F.3d 806, 824 (9th Cir. 2002); Brewer v. Quaker State Oil Ref. Corp., 72 F.3d 326, 334 (3d Cir. 1995); Vodusek v. Bayliner Marine Corp., 71 F.3d 148, 156 (4th Cir. 1995).

[178] Greyhound Lines, Inc. v. Wade, 485 F.3d 1032, 1035 (8th Cir. 2007); *see also* Flagg v. City of Detroit, 715 F.3d 165, 177–78 (6th Cir. 2013).

[179] *See* State v. Langlet, 283 N.W.2d 330, 333 (Iowa 1979) (approvingly citing a federal decision holding that destruction of records under routine procedures well in advance of service of interrogatories seeking information from such records is not spoliation of evidence).

[180] *See* Daniel S. Hapke, Jr., *Developing and Implementing Records Retention Programs in Business Organizations*, in RECORDS RETENTION MANUAL (American Corp. Counsel Ass'n, 1st ed. Supp. 1995) ("The occasional presence of a 'smoking gun' in documents produced is not what motivates a business to implement a document retention and destruction program. Rather, it is the administrative burden and cost of searching through mounds of paper and electronic files in response to each request.") (quoted in Christopher Cotton, Note, *Document Retention Programs for Electronic Records: Applying a Reasonableness Standard to the Electronic Era*, 24 J. CORP. L. 417, 421 n.32 (1999)).

[181] Cotton, *supra*, 24 J. CORP. L. at 419 & n.22; A. Benjamin Spencer, *The Preservation Obligation: Regulating and Sanctioning Pre-Litigation Spoliation in Federal Court*, 79 FORDHAM L. REV. 2005, 2006 (2011); Christopher R. Chase, *To Shred or Not to Shred: Document Retention Policies and Federal Obstruction of Justice Statutes*, 8 FORDHAM J. CORP. & FIN. L. 721, 725 & n.23 (2003).

[182] Rambus, Inc. v. Infineon Tech. AG, 220 F.R.D. 264, 281 (E.D. Va. 2004).

[183] *See supra* § 4-9.6(b).

the costs of producing electronic data, past and proposed changes addressing the nature of the duty to preserve and the consequences for destruction of records and data more directly implicate the party's and the lawyer's ethical duties.

***Routine Loss of ESI:*** In 2006, the Judicial Conference adopted a new paragraph (e) of Rule 37 of the Federal Rules of Civil Procedure, although this change disappeared with the 2015 changes addressed below. The 2006 amendment addressed the routine loss of ESI in the ordinary course of operations.[184] ESI may be lost by overwriting and modification of data that occurs by normal use of computer systems. Every time that a computer is turned on, certain data is lost as files are deleted by the operating system and disk space is made available for over-writing. Moreover, routine deletion of emails and recycling of backup tapes or other media is efficient and frequently automatically scheduled. And, of course, electronic data in addition to emails may be more intentionally and permanently removed from systems pursuant to an established document retention procedure.[185]

Under the 2006 version of Rule 37(e), a court was precluded, absent exceptional circumstances, from imposing civil discovery sanctions "on a party for failing to provide electronically stored information lost as a result of the routine, good-faith operation of an electronic information system."[186] The Committee on Rules of Practice and Procedure of the United States Judicial Conference explained that:

> Even when litigation is anticipated, it can be very difficult to interrupt or suspend the routine operation of computer systems to isolate and preserve discrete parts of the information they overwrite, delete, or update on an ongoing basis, without creating problems for the larger system. Routine cessation or suspension of these features of computer operation is also undesirable; the result would be even greater accumulation of duplicative and irrelevant data that must be reviewed, making discovery more expensive and time-consuming .... Using an example from current technology, many large organizations routinely recycle hundreds of backup tapes every two or three weeks; placing a hold on the recycling of these tapes for even short periods can result in hundreds of thousands of dollars of expense. Similarly, the regular purging of e-mails or other electronic communications is necessary to prevent a build-up of data that can overwhelm the most robust electronic information systems.[187]

However, as a civil procedure treatise advises, while the 2006 version of Rule 37(e) provided "a safe harbor of sorts," that "harbor is lined with shoals."[188] When considering metadata that is lost during good faith operation of electronic systems, Rule 37(e) accepted that such modification of electronic data is unavoidable and that routine operations ordinarily need not be suspended to prevent alteration of metadata. But because this "safe harbor" applies only to "good faith operation," the party's duties may

---

[184] Administrative Office of the U.S. Courts, Federal Rules of Civil Procedure: Adoption and Amendments to Civil Rules (April 12, 2006).

[185] *See supra* § 4-9.6(c)(2).

[186] FED. R. CIV. P. 37(e).

[187] Administrative Office of the U.S. Courts, Federal Rules of Civil Procedure: Adoption and Amendments to Civil Rules (April 12, 2006).

[188] GENE R. SHREVE, PETER RAVEN-HANSEN & CHARLES GARDNER GEYH, UNDERSTANDING CIVIL PROCEDURE § 10.03[a] (Lexis-Nexis, 5th ed. 2013).

change when either litigation is reasonably anticipated or a potential adversary asks for preservation of evidence. In such an instance, the direct destruction of evidence through a document retention policy must be placed on hold. Moreover, when metadata is relevant or when there is reason to believe that backup media will be important, then the party may have a duty to intervene even into the routine operation of the informational system.[189]

***Curative Measures and Sanctions for Failure to Preserve Information:*** Effective at the end of 2015, paragraph (e) of Rule 37 was completely revised, focusing less on the duty to preserve than on the consequences for failing to do so.[190] The Advisory Committee on Civil Rules for the United States Judicial Conference chose not to propose a rule either specifically or generally stating when and how information must be preserved and instead focused on sanctions, as a so-called "back-end" rule.[191] The committee explained that "[b]y articulating what would be 'reasonable' [for purposes of avoiding serious sanctions, the rule] might cast a long shadow over preservation without purportedly directly to regulate it."[192] Moreover, as considerations for determining whether to impose sanctions, the proposed rule would "provide general guidance for parties contemplating their preservation obligations."[193]

Under new Rule 37(e)(1), "[i]f electronically stored information that should have been preserved in the anticipation or conduct of litigation is lost because a party failed to take reasonable steps to preserve it, and it cannot be restored or replaced through additional discovery," then the court may order curative measures "no greater than necessary to cure the prejudice."[194] While the rule is not more specific, the preservation duty has been breached under Rule 37(e) only if the party "failed to take reasonable steps to preserve" the evidence. While the 2006 safe harbor for ESI "lost as a result of the routine, good-faith operation of an electronic information system" has been removed from the text of Rule 37(e), such "routine, good faith" operations presumably may be considered in evaluating whether "reasonable steps" were taken.

In terms of curative measures, the new Rule 37(e)(1) first speaks to whether additional discovery could restore or replace the otherwise lost evidence. Thus, discovery could be permitted of ESI that is not reasonably available, such as backup tapes that are expensive to restore, or create substitute information. If additional discovery is not possible or feasible, then the responsible party may be prevented from presenting certain evidence; the parties may be permitted to present evidence and argue to the jury about the lost ESI; or jury instructions may be to help the jury evaluate the significance of the lost information—provided such instructions are not the equivalent of an adverse-inference instruction.[195]

---

[189] *See* FED. R. CIV. P. 37 advisory committee note (2006) ("Good faith in the routine operation of an information system may involve a party's intervention to modify or suspend certain features of that routine operation to prevent the loss of information, if that information is subject to a preservation obligation.").

[190] For the history of and an overview to the 2015 amendment to Rule 37(e), see Scott O. Brien, Note, *Analog Solutions: E-Discovery Spoliation Sanctions and the Proposed Amendments to FRCP 37(e)*, 65 DUKE L.J. 151 (2015).

[191] Judicial Conference Committee on Rules of Practice & Procedure, Memorandum at 14, Preliminary Draft of Proposed Amendments to the Federal Rules of Bankruptcy and Civil Procedure (August 2013).

[192] *Id.*

[193] *Id.* at 17.

[194] FED. R. CIV. P. 37(e) (2016).

[195] *See* 2015 Advisory Comm. Notes, Fed. R. Civ. P.

However, under the new Rule 37(e)(2), the most severe sanctions may be imposed or an adverse-inference jury instruction may be given only if the party's actions in failing to preserve evidence were willful. The rule states that "only upon finding that the party acted with the intent to deprive another party of the information's use in the litigation" may these more draconian measures be imposed.[196] If such deliberate wrongdoing is established, then the court may "(A) presume that the lost information was unfavorable to the party; (B) instruct the jury that it may or must presume the information was unfavorable to the party; or (C) dismiss the action or enter a default judgment."[197]

As the advisory committee acknowledged when proposing the rule,[198] new Rule 37(e)(2) specifically overturns the Second Circuit's decision in *Residential Funding Corp. v. DeGeorge Financial Corp.*,[199] which allowed imposition of sanctions on a showing of mere negligence in failing to preserve information. In general, actual sanctions such as an adverse inference spoliation instruction to the jury (as contrasted with other curative measures) would be available only on a showing that the person who failed to preserve had acted deliberately.

### *§ 4-9.6(c)(4) The Duty of Counsel in Preserving and Producing Evidence in Discovery*

As outlined in one of the leading federal court decisions on preservation of ESI, the lawyer's ethical obligations with respect to preserving and producing evidence in civil litigation are threefold: (1) giving timely notice of the duty to preserve documents and physical evidence because litigation is reasonably anticipated; (2) clearly instructing the party about the nature and scope of that obligation, which means directly contacting the key players and fully understanding the data system so as to ensure that relevant electronic information is retained;[200] and (3) regularly monitoring the client's retention and production of evidence to assist the client's compliance.[201] As Professor Paula Schaefer writes, the lawyer's efforts are essential to avoid deletion of information "by a client who does not understand the legal obligation to preserve it and consequences of failing to do so or who is willing to take the chance."[202]

***Timely Notice of "Litigation Hold":*** Once the lawyer comes on the scene—either as in-house counsel for an enterprise or as outside counsel retained when litigation has ensued or is imminent—he must work with the party to provide timely notice to all constituents about the need to preserve documents and electronic data that is relevant to the matter. Thus, at the outset of the litigation, or earlier if counsel is involved and

---

[196] FED. R. CIV. P. 37(e)(2) (2016).

[197] *Id.* 37(e)(2)(A) to (C).

[198] Judicial Conference Committee on Rules of Practice & Procedure, Memorandum at 14, Preliminary Draft of Proposed Amendments to the Federal Rules of Bankruptcy and Civil Procedure (August 2013).

[199] 306 F.3d 99 (2d Cir. 2002).

[200] *See* Nathan M. Crystal, *Ethical Responsibility and Legal Liability of Lawyers for Failure to Institute or Monitor Litigation Holds*, 43 AKRON L. REV. 715, 720–21 (2010).

[201] Zubulake v. UBS Warburg LLC, 229 F.R.D. 422, 431–36 (S.D.N.Y. 2004); *see also* In re Ethicon, Inc. Pelvic Repair Sys. Prod. Liability Litig., 299 F.R.D. 502, 521 (S. D. W. Va. 2014).

[202] *See* Paula Schaefer, *Attorneys, Document Discovery, and Discipline*, 30 GEO. J. LEGAL ETHICS 1, 15 (2017).

reasonably anticipates litigation, the lawyer must issue a "litigation hold" to prevent loss or destruction of data and take affirmative steps to preserve information.[203]

***Clear Instructions on Duty to Preserve Evidence:*** The lawyer must ensure that the significance and scope of the duty to preserve evidence is impressed on the party and its constituents in a clear and detailed manner.[204] To accomplish this, the lawyer must have a solid understanding of the underlying dispute so that she appreciates what is relevant and can identify the key players for direct contact, explanation of the duty to preserve, and identification of information that each such person possesses.[205]

So that the instructions are targeted and specific as well as sufficiently encompassing, the lawyer "must become fully familiar with her client's document retention policies, as well as the client's data retention architecture. This will invariably involve speaking with information technology personnel, who can explain system-wide backup procedures and the actual (as opposed to theoretical) implementation of the firm's recycling policy."[206] Being so informed, the lawyer can speak intelligently with each key player about how her active files are stored and then inspect "all potential sources of information."[207]

***Regular Monitoring of Production of Preserved Evidence:*** As the federal district court emphasized in *Zubulake v. UBS Warburg LLC*, "[a]t the end of the day . . . the duty to preserve and produce documents rests on the party."[208] The court well understood that "[a] lawyer cannot be obliged to monitor his client like a parent watching a child."[209] But "it is *not* sufficient to notify all employees of a litigation hold and expect that the party will then retain and produce all relevant information. Counsel must take affirmative steps to monitor compliance so that all sources of discoverable information are identified and searched."[210]

To begin with, "[t]he litigation hold should be periodically re-issued so that new employees are aware of it, and so that it is fresh in the minds of all employees."[211] Next, as relevant active files are identified, the lawyer should instruct that they be preserved for later production if called for in discovery, either by electronic copy to the lawyer or segregation in a separate folder on a computer desktop.[212] Throughout this process, effective communication with and regular de-briefing of the party's technology personnel is crucial.[213]

---

[203] *Zubulake*, 229 F.R.D. at 431, 433; *see also* Nacco Materials Handling Group, Inc. v. Lilly Co., 278 F.R.D. 395, 403 (W.D. Tenn. 2011) (because of the failure to issue a written company-wide hold after service of the complaint, the company "did not take any steps to prevent emails from being deleted, or to prevent data from being overwritten, or to identify and preserve backup tapes").

[204] *Zubulake*, 229 F.R.D. at 432–33.

[205] *Id.* at 432–33.

[206] *Id.* at 432.

[207] *Id.* at 432.

[208] *Id.* at 436.

[209] *Id.* at 433.

[210] *Id.* at 432; *see also* Rodman v. Safeway, Inc., No. 11-cv-03003-JST, 2016 WL 5791210, at *3 (N.D. Oct. 4, Cal. 2016) (imposing sanctions where the lawyer provided no meaningful assistance to the corporation's marketing director in searching a computer drive, even though he had no experience in conducting such a search and kept no record of the search and searched only document titles and not contents).

[211] *Zubulake*, 229 F.R.D. at 433.

[212] *Id.* at 434.

[213] *Id.* at 434.

### § 4-9.6(d) Prohibition on Using Methods of Obtaining Evidence That Violate Another's Legal Rights

Beyond the formal processes of civil discovery, a lawyer handling a litigation matter appropriately may conduct an informal investigation into the underlying facts and circumstances, such as by visiting the location of an incident, interviewing witnesses, reviewing documents, etc. In this way, the lawyer can evaluate the merits of the case in advance of the anticipated litigation so as to ensure that claims made[214] and defenses asserted will be meritorious and also may act to preserve evidence for later use in the litigation.

When acting outside the formal process of civil discovery, the lawyer must be careful to abide by legal and ethical restrictions on access to persons and property and to respect the legal rights of others from whom information and materials may be taken or solicited or about whom information may be sought. (Other provisions of the Model Rules of Professional Conduct address the lawyer's ethical responsibilities when using the tools of civil discovery to obtain evidence in a litigation matter.[215])

Rule 4.4(a) of the Model Rules of Professional Conduct provides, in pertinent part, that "a lawyer shall not . . . use methods of obtaining evidence that violate the legal rights" of a third person. However valuable a particular piece of evidence might be to the lawyer's representation of a client, and even if a party in litigation were entitled to obtain that evidence through discovery, a lawyer may not become a legal vigilante acting to procure that evidence by improper means. Even when documents sought by a lawyer are not privileged or otherwise protected, participating in or encouraging surreptitious and unlawful schemes to obtain properly discoverable materials is not acceptable conduct for a lawyer. As an obvious example, that a party may be entitled to production of certain documents from a company hardly gives that party's lawyer license to burglarize the company's offices—or to encourage others to do so—to secure those documents.

In *Lipin v. Bender*,[216] a lawyer's client, who was also an employee of the lawyer, covertly removed and copied the opponent's documents that she saw sitting on a table in a hearing room, while opposing counsel was distracted with discovery arguments. While the lawyer had not initially been aware of this misappropriation, he subsequently condoned the theft by reviewing and using the copied documents. As a sanction, the court dismissed the client's lawsuit, saying that, "regardless of whether the documents were privileged, the highly improper manner in which they were obtained, combined with their subsequent use by plaintiff's counsel to defendants' detriment, constitutes a sufficient basis for the court's action."[217]

Special care and affirmative cautionary steps must be taken by the lawyer when an *ex parte* contact with another person could result in improper revelation of confidential information, which thus would violate the legal rights of another party. For example,

---

[214] *See supra* § 4-9.3.

[215] *See supra* § 4-9.6(a).

[216] 597 N.Y.S.2d 340 (N.Y. App. Div. 1993), *aff'd*, 620 N.Y.S.2d 744, 644 N.E.2d 1300 (1994).

[217] *Id.* at 343; *see also* Perna v. Electronic Data Syst. Corp., 916 F. Supp. 388 (D. N.J. 1995) (dismissing a plaintiff's claim when the plaintiff examined and copied work product documents in the defense counsel's briefcases left in the plaintiff's office while the lawyers took a lunch break during document inspection in civil discovery, which improper conduct was reported in this case by the plaintiff's own counsel); In re Johnson, 835 N.W.2d 628 (Minn. 2013) (disciplining an attorney for "opening the mail of the opposing party in a case without authorization").

while the no-contact rule in Rule 4.2 of the Model Rules of Professional Conduct generally does not preclude *ex parte* contact with former employees or officers of an entity,[218] the lawyer should be careful not to extract from such persons material that is privileged for the entity. Even when *ex parte* contact is permitted under the no-contact limitation, "an attorney communicating with the former employees of the opposing party may not inquire into privileged attorney-client communications because '[a]ny privilege existing between the former employee and the organization's counsel belongs to the organization, and can only be waived by the organization.' "[219] This restriction on the scope of exploration by the investigating lawyer applies not only to receipt of privileged documents but to oral inquiries into the substance of privileged communications.

For a lawyer to deliberately invade privileged communications involving the opposing party and its legal counsel would be to compromise the very integrity of the adversarial process and would justify severe judicial and disciplinary sanctions.[220] The prudent and ethically-responsible lawyer should never put himself in the position of prying into communications involving another party and that party's counsel, and then presuming to conduct a self-interested and secret in-house "privilege review"—outside the purview of the court—to justify the solicitation, retention, and use of those communications.

In *Arnold v. Cargill, Inc.*,[221] a federal court disqualified a plaintiff's law firm in an employment discrimination case, because the law firm had contacted a retired management employee of the defendant who had worked with defendant's legal counsel, obtained from him documents recording privileged communications with the defendant's legal counsel about employment discrimination law and prior cases, and concealed the possession of those documents. The court concluded that, "the spirit of ethical standards in this district, if not the letter of the rules, prohibits an attorney from conducting her own privilege review of documents belonging to a corporation" that the lawyer was planning to sue and then retaining the documents without notifying the privilege holder.[222]

In addition to prohibiting outside intrusion into those relationships specially protected by an evidentiary privilege, the *Restatement of the Law Governing Lawyers* instructs that "[a] lawyer communicating with a nonclient . . . may not seek to obtain

---

[218] *See supra* § 4-8.4(b).

[219] Cram v. Lamson & Sessions Co., 148 F.R.D. 259, 266 (S.D. Iowa 1993) (quoting Sequa Corp. v. Lititech, Inc., 807 F. Supp. 653, 668 (D.Colo.1992)); *see also* Clark v. Beverly Health & Rehabilitation Servs., Inc., 797 N.E.2d 905, 911 (Mass. 2003) (citing Rules 4.2 and 4.4 in ruling that counsel interviewing former employees "must also be careful to avoid violating applicable privileges or matters subject to appropriate confidences or protections"); Wis. St. Bar Prof'l Ethics Comm., Op. E-07-01 (2007) (stating that a lawyer who contacts a constituent of a represented organization "must not ask any questions reasonably likely to elicit information that the lawyer knows or reasonably should know is privileged and, if necessary, should caution the unrepresented constituent not to reveal such information").

[220] *See* In re Meador, 968 S.W.2d 346, 351 (Tex. 1998) (saying that "a lawyer who uses privileged information improperly obtained from an opponent potentially subverts the litigation process"); MMR/Wallace Power & Indus., Inc. v. Thames Assocs., 764 F. Supp. 712, 728 (D. Conn. 1991) (disqualifying counsel and saying that, while the court was "concerned about interfering with [the client's] right to freely select counsel of its choice, that concern is outweighed by [the opposing party's] interest in a trial free from the risk that confidential information has been used against it and in the public's interest in the integrity of the judicial process itself").

[221] No. 01–2086, 2004 Westlaw 2203410 (D. Minn. Sept. 24, 2004); *see also* Clark v. Superior Court, 125 Cal. Rptr. 3d 361, 373–76 (Cal. Ct. App. 2011) (disqualifying a law firm that reviewed and used opponent company's privileged document provided by the client who was a former employee of the company).

[222] *Arnold*, 2004 Westlaw 2203410 at *10.

information that the lawyer reasonably should know the nonclient may not reveal without violating a duty of confidentiality to another imposed by law."[223] While the *Restatement*'s proscription certainly covers improper attempts to obtain privileged information from unauthorized sources, it further encompasses solicitation of information that a person is obliged to maintain as confidential by other law, such as proprietary information gained by an employee or former employee about a business operation that is confidential under common-law agency doctrine.[224] The *Restatement* thus confirms the direction of Rule 4.4(a), which prohibits obtaining evidence by improper means.

When a lawyer has employed improper investigative tactics, the seriousness of the lawyer's misconduct will not be significantly mitigated by the plea that the information could have been obtained or should have been disclosed through discovery. In *E.E.O.C. v. Hora, Inc.*,[225] a federal court disqualified a plaintiff's attorney in an employment discrimination case, who had been contacted by an administrative assistant to the defendant's general manager, who in turn was gathering information about defendant's employees and management so as to secretly assist the plaintiff. With the encouragement of the plaintiff's attorney, this administrative assistant provided copies of confidential, but apparently non-privileged, business and personnel documents. The court rejected the argument that the discoverability of documents excused the lawyer's improper receipt of the opponent's confidential documents, ruling that the lawyer should have discouraged transfer of confidential materials "outside the normal rules and channels of discovery."[226]

The harm caused to the legal rights of another party is greatest when improper methods of obtaining evidence have the effect of circumventing the important protections for privilege, work-product, and other confidential information afforded through the civil discovery process. By using the formal process of discovery, rather than surreptitious means that procure arguably confidential information of dubious provenance, both parties are alerted to the potentially protected, even privileged, nature of the information sought and thereby have a fair opportunity to raise an objection and seek a judicial ruling either precluding or limiting the discovery allowed. Obtaining evidence by improper means bypasses that judicial safeguard.[227]

---

[223] RESTATEMENT (THIRD) OF THE LAW GOVERNING LAWYERS § 102 (American Law Institute, 2000).

[224] *Id.* cmt. b; *see also* Chamberlain Group v. Lear Corp., 270 F.R.D. 392, 398 (N.D. Ill. 2010) (stating, that "[e]ven in the absence of privilege," "it is generally 'an improper litigation tactic to use a disgruntled employee to secretly obtain non-public internal business documents from an opposing party' " (quoting Glynn v. EDO Corp., No. JFM-07-01660, 2010 WL 3294347, at *5 (D. Md. Aug. 20, 2010))). On the fiduciary duty of former employees or agents to preserve the confidential information of their employers or principals under Iowa statutes and common-law, see Economy Roofing & Insulating Co. v. Zumaris, 538 N.W.2d 641, 647–48 (Iowa 1995); Kendall/Hunt Publishing Co. v. Rowe, 424 N.W.2d 235 (Iowa 1988); Central States Indus. Supply, Inc. v. McCoullough, 279 F. Supp. 2d 1005, 1042–43 (N.D. Iowa 2003).

[225] 2005 Westlaw 1387982 (E.D. Pa. June 8, 2005).

[226] *Id.* at *3.

[227] *See* In re Shell Oil Refinery, 143 F.R.D. 105, 108 (E.D. La. 1992) (stating that the surreptitious receipt of defendant's proprietary documents from an employee "has effectively circumvented the discovery process and prevented [defendant] from being able to argue against production").

## § 4-9.6(e) Lawyer's Obligations on Unsolicited Receipt of Another's Privileged or Confidential Materials

### *§ 4-9.6(e)(1) Distinguishing Unsolicited Receipt from Encouraged Procurement of Protected Materials*

The question of what a lawyer should do when receiving unsolicited materials that appear to reflect privileged or confidential communications of another person, particularly when it reveals the strategy of an opposing party in litigation, has long been a subject of practical concern to the bar. This question has arisen with some regularity in the practice of law (and became more common with the ease of electronic transmissions).[228] The question also has been the topic of theoretical debate, as it implicates the sometimes opposing principles of zealous advocacy on behalf of a client and of respect for the legal rights of others and particularly for the integrity of another's attorney-client relationship.[229]

The following two subsections address this question in the related but arguably different contexts of materials that were inadvertently sent[230] and materials that were stolen or disclosed without authority.[231] The discussion culminates with the suggestion that proper respect for the legal rights of others and the importance of attorney-client confidentiality oblige the receiving lawyer not to further examine and use materials that the lawyer has reason to know are privileged or protected as work-product.

To be sharply contrasted with a lawyer's receipt of truly unsolicited materials, in which the lawyer genuinely is an innocent recipient and the only question thus is proper disposition of what has been unexpectedly received, is the situation in which the lawyer either directly procures or indirectly encourages unauthorized disclosure of another's privileged or protected communications. The lawyer who takes affirmative action to acquire materials that the lawyer reasonably should know are protected by privilege or otherwise (such as work-product) has violated Rule 4.4(a) of the Model Rules of Professional Conduct by "us[ing] methods of obtaining evidence that violate the legal rights of" a third person.[232]

As previously discussed,[233] a lawyer exceeds the bounds of appropriate evidentiary investigation if the lawyer interviews a person who is or has been an employee or agent of that represented person and inquires into the substance of privileged communications, whether or not that inquiry actually results in disclosure of documents. Nor may the lawyer cultivate a person who had or has inside access to the privileged communications or confidential materials of another, reap the inevitable fruits of a distribution of such information from that person, and thereafter claim to have been the mere recipient of an unsolicited disclosure of privileged information. The lawyer who communicates with a person that the lawyer reasonably should know has had access to privileged communications, whether oral or documentary, is obliged to forthrightly caution that person not to reveal those communications (unless the person is unrepresented and

---

[228] *See supra* § 4-6.5(c).

[229] On the tension between the lawyer's duty as zealous advocate and as officer of the court, see *supra* § 4-9.2.

[230] *See infra* § 4-9.6(e)(2).

[231] *See infra* § 4-9.6(e)(3).

[232] *See supra* § 4-9.6(d).

[233] *See supra* §§ 4-8.4(c) and *infra* § 4-9.6(d).

authorized to waive the privilege). Accordingly, the question of proper disposition by a lawyer of unsolicited privileged or otherwise confidential materials arises only in those cases where the lawyer has played no role in bringing about the disclosure, but instead has been the unexpected and innocent recipient.

The potentially privileged communications of one's opponent are rightly regarded as the third-rail of professional responsibility. If one deliberately touches that third-rail and the power happens to be off (that is, the privilege does not attach), the lawyer who has procured materials outside the formal discovery process has been extraordinarily lucky and may escape harm. But if the power is on (that is, the privilege does attach), then purposely grasping that third-rail and receiving the jolt of uninsulated exposure to an opponent's privileged communications could prove devastatingly injurious and perhaps fatal to the lawyer's continuing representation in that matter.[234]

### *§ 4-9.6(e)(2) Lawyer's Receipt of Inadvertently Transmitted Protected Materials*

When a lawyer is the passive recipient of materials that were sent by another party or party's lawyer, the lawyer cannot be expected to wipe away from memory what she sees on initial review nor can the lawyer be punished for innocent acceptance of those materials.[235] However, upon learning that the materials were privileged and mistakenly delivered, the receiving lawyer must alert the sender and may not conceal the possession of those materials. Rule 4.4(b) of the Model Rules of Professional Conduct provides that "[a] lawyer who receives a document or electronically stored information relating to the representation of the lawyer's client and knows or reasonably should know that the document or electronically stored information was inadvertently sent shall promptly notify the sender." Beyond expressly requiring notification so that the sender is made aware that confidential materials were inadvertently disclosed, the rule leaves the question of proper disposition of those materials to the substantive law of the jurisdiction.

In 1992, the American Bar Association's (ABA) Standing Committee on Ethics and Professional Responsibility, in Formal Opinion 92–368, opined that when a lawyer receives materials that "on their face appear to be subject to the attorney-client privilege or are otherwise confidential," the receiving lawyer has three obligations: (1) to refrain from further examination of the materials; (2) to notify the sending lawyer of the receipt of the materials; and (3) to "abide by the instructions" of the sending lawyer (whether to destroy or return the materials).[236] A federal court later endorsed this approach as reflecting "common sense and a high sensitivity toward ethics and the importance of attorney-client confidentiality and privilege."[237]

In 2002, the ABA amended Model Rule 4.4(b) to expressly provide a partial answer to the problem of inadvertent disclosure of confidential information by requiring the receiving lawyer to notify the sender, as discussed above. The rule, however, is silent on

---

[234] *See also* D.C. Bar Op. 318 (2002) (stating that "a receiving lawyer proceeds at his own risk if indicia of a privileged document do exist and there is not a reasonable basis to conclude that the privilege has been waived").

[235] *See supra* § 4-6.5(c).

[236] ABA Comm. on Ethics and Prof'l Responsibility, Formal Op. 92–368 (1992).

[237] Resolution Trust Corp. v. First of America Bank, 868 F. Supp. 217, 220 (W.D. Mich. 1994).

the question of what the receiving lawyer should do with the materials after such notification.

In 2005, the ABA's Committee on Ethics and Professional Responsibility withdrew Formal Opinion 92–368 on the basis that, other than obliging the receiving lawyer to notify the sender, the proper disposition of inadvertently-received materials was no longer subject to resolution by application of the Model Rules of Professional Conduct.[238] Comment 2 to Rule 4.4 likewise states that "[w]hether the lawyer is required to take additional steps, such as returning the original document or electronically stored information, is a matter of law beyond the scope of these rules, as is the question of whether the privileged status of a document or electronically stored information has been waived."

Accordingly, these important questions remain to be resolved by general principles of substantive law and legal ethics beyond the text of the rules.

As discussed previously in the chapter on attorney-client confidentiality,[239] the "general trend in the law is to hold that the attorney-client privilege is not waived by inadvertent disclosure if the lawyer and client have taken *reasonable* precautions to guard against inadvertent disclosures."[240] Because the client controls the privilege,[241] an isolated episode of erroneous transmission to an unintended recipient should not strip away the privilege.

As for the recipient lawyer's handling of those materials after notification, while ABA Formal Opinion 92–368 may no longer reflect the formal position of the ABA in terms of a strict interpretation of the Model Rules of Professional Conduct, that opinion itself had acknowledged that "[a] satisfactory answer to the question posed cannot be drawn from a narrow, literalistic reading of the black letter of the Model Rules."[242] Formal Opinion 92–368 was primarily an explication of general principles of professional responsibility, informed by underlying substantive law, and thus continues to have substantial persuasive force. The Preamble to the Model Rules of Professional Conduct notes that "[t]he rules do not . . . exhaust the moral and ethical considerations that should inform a lawyer, for no worthwhile human activity can be completely defined by legal rules."

In opining that the lawyer receiving an inadvertent transmission of confidential materials should leave them unexamined and return them to the sending lawyer, Formal Opinion 92–368 emphasized the vital importance of attorney-client confidentiality, as reflected in the protections provided by the rules and the law of attorney-client privilege. According to the committee, such other potentially competing factors as zealous advocacy on behalf of a client "pale[ ] in comparison to the importance of maintaining confidentiality."[243] The "loss of confidentiality is a very high penalty to pay for a mere

---

[238] ABA Comm. on Ethics and Prof'l Responsibility, Formal Op. 05–437 (2005).

[239] *See supra* § 4-6.5(c).

[240] RONALD D. ROTUNDA & JOHN S. DZIENKOWSKI, PROFESSIONAL RESPONSIBILITY: A STUDENT'S GUIDE § 1.6–2(b) (American Bar Ass'n, 2013–2014).

[241] In re Seagate Tech., LLC, 497 F.3d 1360, 1372 (Fed. Cir. 2007) ("The attorney-client privilege belongs to the client, who alone may waive it."); United States v. Merida, 828 F.3d 1209–10 (10th Cir. 2016) (holding that the privilege for an entity client belongs to the entity and not an individual officer).

[242] ABA Comm. on Ethics and Prof'l Responsibility, Formal Op. 92–368 (1992).

[243] *Id.*; *see also* Paula Schaefer, *The Future of Inadvertent Discovery: The Lingering Need to Revise Professional Conduct Rules*, 66 MD. L. REV. 195, 236 (2010) (arguing for an ethical duty to protect the contents of inadvertently disclosed confidential information because "the profession's faith in confidentiality is a

slip," particularly when the party paying that "price" ordinarily is not the sending lawyer but the party.[244] Moreover, the opinion stated, expecting the receiving lawyer to return the documents unexamined "achieves a high level of professionalism which can only redound to the lawyer's benefit."[245]

The ABA committee further drew from the common law of bailments, which imposes a constructive bailment upon a person who obtains mistaken possession of another's property:

> When possession of personal property of another is acquired and held under circumstances where the recipient, on principles of justice, ought to keep it safely and restore or deliver it to the owner, as, for example where possession has been acquired accidentally, gratuitously, through mistake, or by agreement since terminated for some other purpose than bailment, the law, irrespective of any actual meeting of the minds, any voluntary undertaking, or any reasonable basis for implying mutual benefit, imposes on the recipient the duties and obligations of a bailee. Such bailments are known as constructive and involuntary bailments, and ordinarily the party in possession of the property is regarded as a gratuitous bailee.[246]

In sum, the law of bailment supports the imposition of a duty on a lawyer who assumes possession and control over mistakenly-sent confidential documents to return those materials to the rightful owner. Return of the property to the rightful owner of course is an essential component of any bailment.

ABA Formal Opinion 92–368 continues to be followed by bar associations and state ethics rules[247] and by a growing number of courts.[248] Professor Peter Henning suggests

---

professional conduct issue"); N.Y. County Law. Ass'n, Comm. on Prof'l Ethics Formal Op. 730 (2002) (opining that "it is appropriate that all lawyers share responsibility for ensuring that the fundamental principle that client confidences be preserved—the most basic tenet of the attorney-client relationship—is respected when privileged information belonging to a client is inadvertently disclosed").

[244] ABA Comm. on Ethics and Prof'l Responsibility, Formal Op. 92–368 (1992).

[245] *Id.*

[246] *Id.* (quoting 8 Am. Jur. 2d *Bailments* § 64 (1980)); *see also* Trina Jones, *Inadvertent Disclosure of Privileged Information and the Law of Mistake: Using Substantive Legal Principles to Guide Ethical Decision Making*, 48 EMORY L.J. 1255, 1316–27 (1999) (concluding that the receiving lawyer generally has a duty to return a misdirected privileged communication, at least when the disclosure was plainly inadvertent, based upon analogy to the evolving doctrine of unilateral mistake in contract law, by which "courts have rescinded or canceled contracts in unilateral mistake cases if the mistake either was known or should have been known to the other party or if enforcement of those contracts would be unconscionable").

[247] *See, e.g.*, Cal. Formal Op. 2013–188; HAW. RULES OF PROF'L CONDUCT R. 4.4(b)(1); Iowa State Bar Ass'n, Opinion 15–02 (2015); LA. RULES OF PROF'L CONDUCT R. 4.4(b); ME. RULES OF PROF'L CONDUCT R. 4.4(b); N.H. RULES OF PROF'L CONDUCT R. 4.4(b); N.J. RULES OF PROF'L CONDUCT R. 4.4(b); N.Y. County Law. Ass'n, Comm. on Prof'l Ethics Formal Op. 730 (2002); TENN. RULES OF PROF'L CONDUCT R. 4.4(b); Tenn. Bd. Prof'l Responsibility Formal Ethics Op. 2004-F-150; Va. Ethics Op. 1702 (1997) (overturning earlier contrary ethics opinion); WIS. RULES OF PROF'L CONDUCT R. 4.4(c). *But see* Oregon Formal Op. 2005–150 (stating that Rule 4.4 by its direct terms does not require the recipient to return the document, which is a question beyond the scope of the rules); Massachusetts Bar Ass'n Ethics Op. 99–4 (1999) (saying that zealous advocacy requires the lawyer to resist opposing counsel's request to return the document and requires the lawyer to urge the tribunal to reject a claim of privilege).

[248] *See, e.g.*, Rico v. Mitsubishi Motors Corp., 171 P.3d 1092, 1094 (Cal. 2007) (holding that an attorney who received opposing counsel's work-product through inadvertence was obliged not to read or make use of it further once its content became apparent and instead notify opposing counsel to resolve the situation, and upholding disqualification of the attorney for failure to take such steps); Employer's Reinsurance Corp. v. Clarendon Nat. Ins. Co., 213 F.R.D. 422, 430 (D. Kan. 2003) (finding policies underlying ABA Formal Op. 92–368 to be "instructive"); United States ex rel. Bagley v. TRW, Inc., 204 F.R.D. 170, 182 n.17 (C.D. Cal. 2001); Transportation Equipment Sales Corp. v. BMY Wheeled Vehicles, 930 F. Supp. 1187, 1188 (N.D. Ohio 1996);

that "[a]n inadvertent disclosure is a mistake that should not affect the outcome of the proceeding, and lawyers who use or communicate the information are not acting authentically by taking advantage of the lapse."[249]

As a recent indication of the national trend, the Supreme Court in 2006 approved a revision of the Federal Rules of Civil Procedure that specifically addresses the proper disposition by the receiving lawyer when confidential materials are accidentally disclosed to the opposing side during discovery of documents and electronic data in federal litigation.[250] Rule 26(b)(5)(B) provides:

> Information Produced. If information produced in discovery is subject to a claim of privilege or of protection as trial-preparation material, the party making the claim may notify any party that received the information of the claim and the basis for it. After being notified, a party must promptly return, sequester, or destroy the specified information and any copies it has; must not use or disclose the information until the claim is resolved; must take reasonable steps to retrieve the information if the party disclosed it before being notified; and may promptly present the information to the court under seal for a determination of the claim. The producing party must preserve the information until the claim is resolved.[251]

Finally, even if return of the confidential document were not required under state law or court rules, the accompanying comment to Rule 4.4 empowers the lawyer to choose the course that best accords with the expectations of professionalism and to refuse to take unfair advantage of the opposing party's mistake. Comment 3 to Rule 4.4 reads:

> Some lawyers may choose to return a document or delete electronically stored information unread, for example, when the lawyer learns before receiving it that it was inadvertently sent. Where a lawyer is not required by applicable law to do so, the decision to voluntarily return such a document or delete electronically stored information is a matter of professional judgment ordinarily reserved to the lawyer.

As discussed previously,[252] references to aspirational standards of professionalism or to professional judgment in the rules or the comments are not merely high-minded rhetoric. By embedding these principles of professionalism in the rules or comments, the rules create space for the development of a culture of civility. While an attorney may not be disciplined for failing to comply with an aspirational standard, neither may the attorney excuse unprofessional conduct as the expected, much less the required, actions of a zealous advocate for a client.

---

State Compensation Ins. Fund v. WPS, Inc., 82 Cal.Rptr.2d 799 (Cal. App. 1999); Resolution Trust Corp. v. First of America Bank, 868 F. Supp. 217 (W.D. Mich. 1994).

[249] Peter J. Henning, *Lawyers, Truth, and Honesty in Representing Clients*, 20 NOTRE DAME J.L. ETHICS & PUB. POL'Y 209, 238 (2006); *see also* Schaefer, *supra*, 66 MD. L. REV. at 239 (arguing that the bar should not "acquiesc[e] to receiving attorneys refusing to return [inadvertently disclosed confidential documents], making notes as they dissect and analyze its contents, and forwarding it to others").

[250] *See* Andrew Perlman, *The Parallel Law of Lawyering in Civil Litigation*, 79 FORDHAM L. REV. 1965, 1965 (2011) (observing that this rule of civil procedure "now increasingly governs lawyers' conduct" as "parallel law" that effectively supersedes the more limited Model Rule).

[251] FED. R. CIV. P. 26(b)(5)(B); *see also* FED. R. CIV. P. 45(e)(2)(B) (providing same protections for privileged materials and work-product inadvertently disclosed in response to a subpoena).

[252] *See supra* § 4-5.3(e).

As the Virginia State Bar Association's Standing Committee on Legal Ethics concluded in addressing the lawyer's duty when receiving an inadvertent transmittal of confidential information, "[a] 'use whatever you have, no matter how you got it' rule may reflect the rules of the marketplace," but " '[h]igher standards should prevail in the practice of law.' "[253]

### *§ 4-9.6(e)(3) Lawyer's Receipt of Protected Materials Taken by Another Without Authority*

When a lawyer has affirmatively procured, solicited, or accepted an offer to receive delivery of another's privileged or otherwise confidential information, and thereby has actively participated in the deprivation of another's legal rights, the lawyer has violated the proscription in paragraph (a) of Rule 4.4 against "use [of] methods of obtaining evidence that violate the legal rights of such a person."[254]

When instead the lawyer has unexpectedly and without encouragement received materials that the lawyer reasonably should know are confidential and under circumstances that indicate the materials were shared by someone without authority to disclose them, Rule 4.4 does not dictate a direct answer to the question of the receiving lawyer's obligations.

Nonetheless, the principles underlying Rule 4.4(b) provide some direction and the nearly-sacred protection attendant to privileged communications suggest a disposition consistent with maintaining confidentiality. And the underlying substantive law of bailments and regarding receipt of stolen property (as well as ethics rules governing disposition of property owned by another) solidify that conclusion.

A lawyer may receive another's privileged or otherwise protected materials from a diverse cast of interlopers who in turn may gain unauthorized access to such materials in a variety of ways. A law firm secretary may steal client files, a traitor in the opposing side's legal team may leak inside information, a corporate spy may conduct an espionage operation against a competitor, a burglar may rob an executive's home, an angry spouse or family member may take confidential papers, a car prowler may take a lawyer's or client's briefcase from a locked car, a computer hacker may break into a server, a disgruntled ex-employee or other agent may steal documents or data as he goes out the door, or a well-intended whistleblower may divulge confidential information in an attempt to reveal or prevent actual or suspected wrongdoing.

Barring an implicit waiver by reason of an abject failure by the owner to maintain any semblance of protection over confidential materials, misappropriation of privileged documents by a wrongdoer would not fairly be held to undermine the continued protection of the attorney-client privilege.[255] At the same time, another lawyer's passive,

---

[253] Virginia Ethics Op. 1702 (1997) (quoting Gunter v. Virginia State Bar, 385 S.E.2d 597, 600 (Va. 1989)); *see also* Tom Galbraith, *Lawyer Behavior for Survival and Elegance*, LITIGATION, Fall, 2006, at 8, 14 (saying that the "elegant lawyer," that is, a lawyer upholding high professional standards, who receives a letter containing privileged communications that was accidentally misaddressed or who obtains privileged material inadvertently produced in discovery, would stop reading the document, notify the opposing counsel, and either return the document or seek judicial review to determine whether a claim of privilege is proper).

[254] *See supra* § 4-9.6(d) to (e).

[255] *See* RESTATEMENT (THIRD) OF THE LAW GOVERNING LAWYERS § 79, cmt. g ill. 4 (American Law Institute, 2000) (stating that a burglar's theft of an attorney's files, including confidential client communications, which were examined by the police after the burglar was arrested, was not a voluntary waiver of the attorney-client privilege); 6 JAMES A. MOORE, ET. AL, MOORE'S FEDERAL PRACTICE § 26.49[5][e]

unsolicited receipt of improperly-acquired materials does not constitute professional misconduct, although how that lawyer acts after receiving the information remains the crucial question. When a lawyer receives an opposing party's confidential information under "suspicious circumstances," the lawyer is, at a minimum, obliged to notify the opposing party of the lawyer's possession of that confidential information—while review and use of that confidential information may result in discipline, disqualification in litigation, and other sanctions or liability.[256]

In 1994, the American Bar Association's (ABA) Committee on Ethics and Professional Responsibility issued Formal Opinion 94–382,[257] which advised:

> A lawyer who receives on an unauthorized basis materials of an adverse party that she knows to be privileged or confidential should, upon recognizing the privileged or confidential nature of the materials, either refrain from reviewing such materials or review them only to the extent required to determine how appropriately to proceed; she should notify her adversary's lawyer that she has such materials and should either follow instructions of the adversary's lawyer with respect to the disposition of the materials, or refrain from using the materials until a definitive resolution of the proper disposition of the materials is obtained from a court.[258]

Even more so than in the instance of inadvertent disclosure of confidential information by a lawyer to the opposing side, the committee viewed the unauthorized transmission of confidential information as deleterious to the precious attorney-client privilege and thus as imposing preventive duties on the receiving lawyer. The committee stated that "a party should be able to protect its proprietary interests, as in the case of confidential materials, and its privileges, as in the case of material falling within the attorney-client privilege, despite the unauthorized efforts of others to undermine or sabotage them."[259] Still, recognizing that in some instances the receiving lawyer may have a legitimate claim that the document should have been disclosed in discovery or that the document was received from someone acting under the authority of a whistleblower statute, the committee directed that in the case of dispute, the recipient

(Matthew-Bender, 3d ed. 2005) ("The attorney-client privilege is not waived through public disclosure of a stolen privileged document.").

[256] *See* Castellano v. Winthrop, 27 So.3d 134, 136–37 (Fla. Ct. App. 2010) (holding that a law firm representing a mother in a domestic relations matter that received from the mother, under "very, very suspicious circumstances," a flash drive containing the father's privileged and other confidential information and that then proceeded to review and use those files without notice had thereby gained "an unfair informational or tactical advantage" requiring that the firm be disqualified, make their computers available to a third-party inspection to confirm deletion of the files, and indemnify the father for any damages caused by improper use of his privileged information); *see also* Clark v. Superior Court, 125 Cal. Rptr. 3d 361, 373–76 (Cal. Ct. App. 2011) (holding that as soon as the law firm saw that its client, a former employee, had provided documents involving communications between an attorney and the opposing company, the firm should have stopped reviewing the documents and notified the opposing party about its possession of the apparently privileged documents). *But see* Tex. State Bar Prof'l Ethics Comm., Op. 664 (2016) (although "caution[ing] that a lawyer's conduct upon receipt of another party's confidential information may have material consequences for the client, including the possibility of procedural disqualification," opining that "b]ecause the Texas Disciplinary Rules are silent regarding the duty of a lawyer who receives an opponent's confidential information, a lawyer who thereafter fails to notify the opposing party does not necessarily violate those Rules").

[257] ABA Comm. on Ethics and Prof'l Responsibility, Formal Op. 94–382 (1994).

[258] *Id.*

[259] *Id.*

should refrain from further review or use until a definitive resolution of the proper disposition of the materials has been obtained from the pertinent court.[260]

In 2002, the American Bar Association amended Rule 4.4(b) to expressly provide that, when a lawyer has received an inadvertent disclosure of confidential information, the receiving lawyer must notify the sending lawyer. Because Rule 4.4(b) mandates notification when the lawyer has received an inadvertent disclosure, while not speaking directly to the situation of an unauthorized disclosure, the ABA's Committee on Ethics and Professional Responsibility issued Formal Opinion 06–440 in 2006 to withdraw Formal Opinion 94–382, which was now regarded as addressing a subject that falls outside the scope of the rules.[261] As likewise stated in Comment 2 to Rule 4.4, "this Rule does not address the legal duties of a lawyer who receives a document or electronically stored information that the lawyer knows or reasonably should know may have been inappropriately obtained by the sending person." That important question instead remains to be resolved by general principles of professional responsibility and the underlying substantive law of the jurisdiction.

However, in Formal Opinion 06–440, the ABA Committee on Ethics and Professional Responsibility was careful to explain to the reader that the withdrawal of Formal Opinion 94–382 was not intended as a commentary on the validity of that opinion's analysis of what may be expected under other sources of law. Formal Opinion 06–440 modestly describes itself as but a formal interpretation of Rule 4.4(b), while emphasizing that "the Rules do not exhaust the moral and ethical considerations that should inform a lawyer."[262] The 2006 opinion positively acknowledges that the principles cited in Formal Opinion 94–382—namely "the protection of confidentiality, the inviolability of the attorney-client privilege, the law governing bailments and missent property, and general considerations of common sense, reciprocity, and professional courtesy"—must be part of "the broader perspective that may guide a lawyer's conduct in the situations addressed in those opinions."[263]

And, indeed, despite its withdrawal by the ABA committee, Formal Opinion 94–382 remains the leading and most widely-followed authority on this ethical problem. Both before and after the ABA amended Model Rule 4.4 in 2002, nearly every court to address the question, especially in the federal judiciary, has adopted the approach of Formal Opinion 94–382.[264]

While not speaking directly to the question, Rule 4.4(b) does shed some light on the matter through its clear directive that the lawyer receiving an inadvertent disclosure must at least alert the opposing lawyer that privileged or otherwise confidential

---

[260] *Id.*

[261] ABA Comm. on Ethics and Prof'l Responsibility, Formal Op. 06–440 (2005).

[262] *Id.*

[263] *Id.*

[264] *See, e.g.*, Chamberlain Group v. Lear Corp., 270 F.R.D. 392, 398 (N.D. Ill. 2010); S.E.C. v. Brady, 2006 WL 2880444, at *15 (N.D. Tex. 2006); Knitting Fever, Inc. v. Coats Holding Ltd., 2005 WL 3050299, at *4 (E.D.N.Y.,2005); Maldonado v. New Jersey ex rel. Administrative Office of Courts, 225 F.R.D. 120, 138 (D. N.J. 2004); Arnold v. Cargill, Inc., 2004 Westlaw 2203410, at *10 (D. Minn. Sept. 24, 2004); Richards v. Jain, 168 F. Supp.2d 1195, 1200–01 (W.D. Wash. 2001); In re Meador, 968 S.W.2d 346, 349 (Tex. 1998); Weeks v. Samsung Heavy Industries, Ltd., 1996 WL 288511, at *3 (N.D. Ill. 1996).

documents were received.[265] If the rules demonstrate such solicitude for the attorney-client privilege that a lawyer who receives privileged documents must disclose that receipt—even when the receipt is due to the fault of the opposing lawyer (or party) in mistakenly forwarding them—how much more so then should the rules be understood to require disclosure of such receipt when the receiving lawyer knows that the privilege has been violated by the wrongful act of a dishonest intermediary. While Rule 4.4(b) may not apply of its own direct force, given the textual limitation to the matter of inadvertent rather than unauthorized disclosures, the theme of fair notice to an opponent applies with even greater force when the opponent has been a victim of an unauthorized disclosure.

Moreover, as discussed above,[266] a lawyer is forbidden to seek privileged information from present or former organizational employees or agents who have privileged information. Given that unauthorized disclosures of confidential information frequently originate with present or former employees or agents of an entity, this strengthens the conclusion that a lawyer receiving what is likely a privileged or work-product document from a suspicious source should not take control over the document and use that information to the disadvantage of the rightful holder of the privilege.

Nor is invocation of an unqualified duty of zealous advocacy likely to support a contrary vision of professional responsibilities. As stated by one commentator with respect to the related question of receipt of confidential materials inadvertently disclosed, one may "zealously represent our clients and give no quarter," but "still expect appropriate professional behavior from both our colleagues and adversaries."[267]

In addition, substantive law provides a compelling basis to conclude that a lawyer may not simply hold and use privileged or other confidential information that has been misappropriated from a person or entity. To begin with, as discussed previously with respect to the receipt of inadvertently disclosed materials,[268] the law of bailments generally imposes a constructive bailment when a party takes possession of property under circumstances when the recipient knows that the property has been separated from its rightful owner. Such a bailment entails at least a duty to return the property. Surely that principle would apply with as much or more force when a lawyer receives property, here in the form of documents or electronic data, that the lawyer has reason to know was stolen from another.

In the context of misappropriated materials, the protective principles of bailment law are bolstered and supplemented by the criminal law prohibiting one from knowingly receiving stolen property without taking appropriate action to return the property to the rightful owner. Whether in a civil or criminal representation, or for that matter even when no litigation is anticipated, a lawyer has no more legal right than any other person to accept and store stolen property, which would include documents or data that had

---

[265] *See Chamberlain Group*, 270 F.R.D. at 398 ("Many courts, this Court included, fail to see why this same duty to disclose [inadvertent receipt of confidential information to the opposing party] should cease where confidential documents are sent intentionally and without permission.").

[266] *See supra* § 4-9.6(d).

[267] Bertram Perkel, Letters, *"Errant Fax" Argument Proves Too Simplistic*, LEGAL TIMES, Feb. 6, 1995, at 33 (criticizing the ethical "poverty" of the position that one could control and use confidential material inadvertently sent by another lawyer).

[268] *See supra* § 4-9.6(e).

been illegally misappropriated. There is no "zealous advocate" defense to a charge of receipt of stolen property.

Since professional standards demand more of a lawyer than simply avoiding the commission of a crime, the presence of facts that place a lawyer on reasonable notice that received materials were stolen presumably carries a duty to investigate further and, if the misappropriation is confirmed, to promptly notify the rightful owner and return the stolen property. As the District of Columbia Bar Association stated in addressing the question of a lawyer's receipt of a privileged document that may have been stolen or taken without authorization from another: "[I]f a lawyer receives what appears to be a privileged document under highly suspicious circumstances, such as from a client or other person who says with a wink, 'don't ask me how I got this,' the prudent receiving lawyer, would make further inquiry prior to reviewing or using the document."[269] And if and when the lawyer does learn that privileged or otherwise confidential materials were purloined, professional expectations surely do not permit the lawyer to secretly hold on to those stolen documents or use them against the rightful owner.

Rule 1.15 of the Model Rules of Professional Conduct may also become relevant when documents, recordings, or electronic data come into the lawyer's possession that belong as a matter of property right to another party.[270] Rule 1.15(d), which requires a lawyer to safeguard the property of others, states that—

> Upon receiving funds or other property in which a client or third person has an interest, a lawyer shall promptly notify the client or third person. Except as stated in this Rule or otherwise permitted by law or by agreement with the client, a lawyer shall promptly deliver to the client or third person any funds or other property that the client or third person is entitled to receive and, upon request by the client or third person, shall promptly render a full accounting regarding such property.

While Rule 1.15 allows a lawyer to retain property pending resolution of a genuine dispute between the client and a third person who makes a claim to that specific property, when the property being held by the lawyer plainly belongs as matter of property rights to a third person, the lawyer of course must transfer that property to the rightful owner regardless of the client's contrary preferences.[271] A lawyer may not assist a client in conversion of the property of others or become a depository of stolen property. For that reason, when a lawyer takes possession of another's property, and the right of that other person's ownership is not disputed, Rule 1.15(d) requires the lawyer to promptly deliver it.[272]

Accordingly, when a lawyer receives confidential materials that he has reason to believe was taken from another party by a person who did not have authority to remove the documents or waive confidentiality, the lawyer may not deliberately conceal, retain,

---

[269] D.C. Bar Op. 318 (2002).

[270] *See* Brian S. Faughnan & Douglas R. Richmond, *Model Rule 1.15: The Elegant Solution to the Problem of Purloined Documents*, 26 LAW. MAN. PROF. CONDUCT 623 (2010) (agreeing that Rule 1.15 imposes professional responsibilities on lawyers who receive documents improperly taken from another, characterizing Rule 1.15 as "offer[ing] an elegant answer" to the problem).

[271] *See supra* § 4-5.6(c)(2).

[272] *See* D.C. Bar Op. 318 (2002) (opining that, when a lawyer receives a privileged document from a client or other person that may have been stolen or taken without authorization from an opposing party, Rule 1.15 requires the lawyer to notify the proper owner and promptly return the property).

or use those stolen documents to the disadvantage of that other party. This conclusion is grounded in the civil law of bailments, the criminal law regarding the receipt of stolen goods, and the ethical rule on the lawyer's duty to deliver another's property, as well as on fundamental expectations of professional responsibility regarding respect for the legal rights of others and protection of attorney-client confidentiality against outside intrusion. Even if a lawyer should innocently and passively receive privileged or otherwise protected documents that were sent unexpectedly by an interloper under circumstances that suggest misappropriation, the lawyer may not simply take hold of those materials, mine them for information, and conceal their possession from the opposing party.

Proper solicitude for attorney-client confidentiality and respect for the legal rights of other persons does not leave a lawyer without recourse if she should discover that another party has engaged in spoliation of evidence or has withheld information that now has come into the hands of another person. When a genuine whistleblower appears on the scene, with information about wrongful conduct or the improper withholding of materials that should have been disclosed in discovery, some appropriate means must be available to the lawyer for securing that information and thereby upholding the integrity of the truth-finding function of the litigation process. When a lawyer has a reasonable basis for believing that a "smoking gun" document exists or that documents have been improperly withheld, and then learns that another person has such documents (albeit having been wrongfully procured by that person), the lawyer must be able to take some step to protect that evidence.

In such an instance, one typically effective and ethically-safe course for the lawyer is to refuse to engage in surreptitious conversations with the person holding arguably privileged or otherwise confidential information and to refuse to accept any documents, while proceeding openly with targeted civil discovery. As one federal court has explained, when disqualifying a plaintiff's attorney who had encouraged a clerical employee for the defendant to forward confidential (but arguably discoverable) documents, "[a]t a minimum," the attorney "should have considered awaiting the institution of proper discovery procedures."[273] The court observed that the attorney had "violated her adversaries' legal rights that permit an appropriately calculated and sometimes negotiated flow of information through the traditional discovery process."[274] For example, by seeking a deposition of the person holding the information, and openly requesting any documents that this person may possess through a subpoena duces tecum, the matter would be brought to light in a formal and adversarial setting. The opposing party would thereby be allowed the deserved opportunity to raise objections to the inquiry or disclosure of documents, to which the lawyer may respond with arguments for exceptions to privilege or work-product as appropriate. Importantly, those objections would be addressed by the court prior to any revelation of the contents of such communications or documents to the lawyer who seeks them.

If the court determines that the testimony or documents are discoverable, the evidence would have been both preserved and now may be safely reviewed. If instead the court determines that the materials, in whole or in part, are privileged or otherwise protected as work-product, the lawyer at least will have carefully kept himself removed from any participation in obtaining the documents and from any exposure to another's

---

[273] E.E.O.C. v. Hora, Inc., 2005 Westlaw 1387982, at *13 (E.D. Pa. June 8, 2005).

[274] *Id.* at *9.

privileged or protected materials, thus pretermitting any question about professional misconduct or potential disqualification in the litigation.[275]

Similarly, as an equally forthright and ethically-proper approach, the lawyer seeking the information could ask that any potentially privileged documents or other materials be delivered in a sealed envelope, not to the lawyer directly, but to a legitimate intermediary, preferably the court but perhaps another well-respected lawyer who is independent of the parties, together with simultaneous notice by the lawyer to the opposing party and the court. Through this method as well, if the court then determines that access is appropriate because the documents are discoverable, the lawyer will obtain the evidence sought. If the court decides otherwise, the lawyer again is protected from improper contact with privileged or otherwise protected materials.

By having the materials delivered to the court or another independent person as an intermediary, no questions could be raised about whether the lawyer encouraged any improper dissemination of stolen documents[276] or obtained inappropriate access to confidential information. Along these lines, the New York State Bar Association, in a formal ethics opinion, advised that, when a lawyer had learned from a former employee of the law firm for the opposing party that documents may have been altered, the lawyer should not seek additional information from the employee if it "would exploit the adversary's confidences or secrets," but instead should seek judicial guidance.[277]

### *§ 4-9.6(e)(4) The Problem of Metadata*

Growing attention has been drawn in the practitioner literature and ethics opinions to the problem of unknowing transmission of electronic documents that contain "metadata." Metadata is hidden information about the creation and revision of documents that is generated by word-processing software programs. Most metadata is innocuous and conveys little information, merely showing the dates on which a document was created or revised and who authored the document. However, if software options for tracking document changes or inserting comments were used during development of a document, a lawyer could inadvertently disclose metadata that traces earlier revisions to a document or contains critical evaluations expressed by electronic comments in the margins. In the worst case scenario, a lawyer thereby could reveal the client's ultimate position or negotiation strategy in settlement communications or a transactional offer.

In principle, the unintended revelation of client confidences through metadata in an electronic document is but another example of the general problem of inadvertent disclosure of privileged information.[278] Thus, consistent with its position on the professional implications of a lawyer's receipt of inadvertently disclosed information

---

[275] *See* Ackerman v. National Property Analysts, Inc., 887 F. Supp. 510, 518 (S.D.N.Y. 1993) (saying, in disqualifying plaintiffs' counsel, that the court "must presume" that former in-house counsel for the defendants had disclosed confidential information because plaintiffs' counsel "had taken no steps to insulate itself" from the protected information).

[276] *See* ABA Comm. on Ethics & Prof'l Responsibility, Formal Op. 94–382 (1994) (suggesting that the receiving lawyer resort to judicial remedies because "the receipt of [confidential materials] may give rise to accusations by an adversary that the materials were, in fact, solicited by the receiving lawyer").

[277] N.Y. St. Bar Ass'n, Comm. on Prof'l Ethics, Formal Op. 700 (1998); *see also* ABA Formal Op. 94–382 (1994) (advising the lawyer receiving apparently privileged or confidential materials as to which there is a dispute to "refrain[ ] from using the material until a definitive resolution of the proper disposition of the materials is obtained from a court").

[278] *See* Andrew M. Perlman, *The Legal Ethics of Metadata Mining*, 43 AKRON L. REV. 785, 786 (2010) (saying "the issue is simply a variation of the oft-examined problem of inadvertently disclosed documents").

generally,[279] the American Bar Association's Committee on Ethics and Professional Responsibility in Formal Opinion 06–442 concluded that Model Rule 4.4(b) requires only that the receiving lawyer provide notice of the receipt of inadvertently disclosed metadata but "set[s] no other specific restrictions on the receiving lawyer's conduct."[280] Those jurisdictions to issue opinions about the ethics of mining for metadata by the receiving lawyer have pointed in opposite directions (with the majority forbidding it).[281]

While the same standards that govern other instances of inadvertent disclosure should apply to unconscious revelation and discovery of metadata, practical considerations make application of those standards arguably different in the metadata context:

*First*, while a lawyer who inadvertently discloses confidential information does not ordinarily waive the client's attorney-client privilege, the premise remains that the lawyer and client had taken reasonable precautions to prevent inadvertent disclosure.[282] In the recent past, many lawyers remained unaware of the problem of metadata, which is insidious by reason of its hidden nature. Thus, a lawyer transmitting an electronic document to another party genuinely may not have any knowledge, at that time or a later date, that confidential information was inadvertently disclosed. Professor David Hricik argued that, "until it is clear that lawyers beyond those in the largest or most sophisticated firms know about embedded data, the courts and bar associations should hold that the transmission of embedded data is either per se or presumptively inadvertent transmissions."[283]

However, as time passes, a plea of ignorance about the problem of metadata becomes more difficult to sustain. Moreover, erasing metadata is relatively easy for most documents (and transmission of hard copies avoids the problem entirely). Accordingly, a lawyer in the future may not be found to have acted with reasonable care to guard against inadvertent disclosure if he fails to have in place a considered practice of scrubbing metadata from sensitive documents that are to be electronically transmitted to those outside of the attorney-client relationship. Even at that point in time, however, a lawyer who does have a sound system in place for erasing metadata may accidentally transmit a particular document without metadata being removed, which then should fall comfortably within the general rule that the privilege is not thereby lost.

*Second*, with respect to privileged documents or passages inadvertently included in a set of documents delivered to another party, the receiving lawyer ordinarily should be excused in deciding to review the document, at least until such point at which the privileged nature of the material and its inadvertent disclosure become apparent. Thus,

---

[279] *See supra* § 4-9.6(e)(2) (discussing ABA Comm. On Ethics and Prof'l Responsibility, Formal Op. 05–437 (2005)).

[280] ABA Comm. On Ethics and Prof'l Responsibility, Formal Op. 06–442 (2006).

[281] *Compare* Colorado Ethics Op. 119 (2008) (allowing review by receiving lawyer of metadata in electronic documents), Maryland Ethics Op. 2007–09 (2006) (same), District of Columbia Ethics Op. 341 (2007) (same), and Tex. Ethics Op. 665 (2016) (same) *with* Alabama Ethics Op. 2007–02 (2007) (forbidding review by receiving lawyer of metadata in electronic documents), Arizona Ethics Op. 07–03 (2007) (same); Florida Ethics Op. 06–02 (2006 (same), Maine Ethics Op. 196 (2008) (same), and New York State Ethics Op. 749 (2004) (same). *See generally* Melissa H. Weresh, *Nope, It's Metadata*, IOWA LAWYER, Feb., 2009, at 22–23.

[282] *See supra* §§ 4-6.5(c), 4-9.6(e)(2).

[283] David Hricik, *Mining for Embedded Data: Is It Ethical to Take Intentional Advantage of Other People's Failures*, 8 N.C. J. L. & TECH. 231, 247 (2007). *But see* Ronald D. Rotunda, *Applying the Revised ABA Model Rules in the Age of the Internet: The Problem of Metadata*, 42 HOFSTRA L. REV. 175, 229–30 (2013).

as previously discussed,[284] in the typical case, the lawyer who receives an inadvertent disclosure of privileged information cannot be expected to wipe her memory upon discovering that confidential information had mistakenly been sent nor should that innocent recipient be punished for another lawyer's mistake. Along these lines, Comment 2 to Rule 4.4 states: "Metadata in electronic documents creates an obligation under this Rule only if the receiving lawyer knows or reasonably should know that the metadata was inadvertently sent to the receiving lawyer." However, hidden metadata in an electronic document will never be seen by the receiving lawyer unless she consciously determines to search for it. Thus, the receiving lawyer's discovery of the inadvertently disclosed information will be the product of what some observers regard as the unseemly practice of deliberately mining for confidential metadata.[285]

While the problem of inadvertent disclosure of privileged information through metadata could arise in the context of civil litigation discovery, such as when a document includes hidden comments by a lawyer offering legal advice, the issue is more likely to arise outside of the discovery process when a lawyer creates a document that is designed for transmission to an opposing party, such as an offer for settlement or in a transactional negotiation. Indeed, in the context of civil discovery, when a document is sought by the opposing party, removal of metadata so as to conceal earlier versions of the document may well be spoliation of evidence.[286] Even if privileged information is included in the metadata of a document that is responsive to a discovery request, the proper procedure is for the lawyer to openly acknowledge the existence of the document with the metadata and to assert the attorney-client privilege as an objection to its disclosure.

Finally, the responsible lawyer having been alerted to the existence of metadata in electronic documents should learn how to remove it when appropriate. Word-processing software programs include methods, either in the program itself or as an addition, by which sensitive hidden data may be removed from the final version of a document. In addition, most metadata (but not all) may be removed by saving a word-processing document into another format, such as "portable document format" (pdf) or "rich text format" (rtf). The time to learn about hidden electronic data and how to remove it is before the problem arises through an embarrassing, even if not harmful, revelation to another person.

### § 4-9.6(f) Covert Activity to Investigate Violations of the Law or Gather Intelligence

As a classic example of lawyer participation with covert investigations of suspected violations of the law, a lawyer in private practice in Oregon pretended to be a

---

[284] *See supra* § 4-6.5(c).

[285] Maine Ethics Op. 196 (2008) ("Not only is the attorney's conduct dishonest in purposefully seeking by this method to uncover confidential information of another party, that conduct strikes at the foundational principles that protect attorney-client confidences, and in doing so it clearly prejudices the administration of justice."); Ala. Ethics Op. 2007–02 (2007) ("The mining of metadata constitutes a knowing and deliberate attempt by the recipient attorney to acquire confidential and privileged information in order to obtain an unfair advantage against an opposing party."); *see also* Hricik, *supra*, 8 N.C. J. L. & TECH. at 231 (saying that "it is dishonest by a lawyer to actively look for embedded data"). *But see* Colorado Ethics Op. 119 (2008) ("[T]here is nothing inherently deceitful or surreptitious about searching for metadata"); Rotunda, *supra*, 42 HOFSTRA L. REV. at 176 ("Lawyers who worry over what to do about disclosing documents, including the metadata within documents, should take care not to make the disclosures in the first place, unless the documents have forensic value so that removing metadata will unlawfully alter evidence.").

[286] On the lawyer's duties with respect to evidence, including avoiding spoliation, see *infra* § 4-9.7.

chiropractor in a 1994 telephone conversation with an officer of a private company in an effort to obtain information about suspected medical insurance fraud. In *In re Gatti*,[287] the Oregon Supreme Court held that the lawyer's conduct violated disciplinary rules regarding deceit, misrepresentation, and false statements. The Oregon disciplinary rules at issue in *Gatti* were parallel to Rule 8.4(c) of the Model Rules of Professional Conduct, which provides that it is professional misconduct to "engage in conduct involving dishonesty, fraud, deceit or misrepresentation."

Law enforcement, government regulatory officials, and other organizations were concerned that the Oregon decision could undermine even legitimate undercover operations, which regularly are supervised by prosecutors[288] and other lawyers and which necessarily involve a degree of deception. In response to the concerns raised about the *Gatti* decision, the Oregon Supreme Court subsequently adopted a new provision to that state's ethics rules specifically permitting lawyer supervision of lawful covert activity to investigate suspected violations of civil or criminal law or of constitutional rights.[289]

At about the same time as Oregon episode, a federal judge in New Jersey, in *Apple Corps. Ltd. v. International Collectors Society*,[290] concluded that Rule 8.4(c) of the New Jersey Rules of Professional Conduct did not apply when private lawyers posed as consumers to investigate suspected violation of a contempt order limiting the marketing of stamps bearing the image of "The Beatles" rock band. The court ruled that Rule 8.4(c) "does not apply to misrepresentations solely as to identity or purpose and solely for evidence-gathering purposes."[291] The court further explained:

> Undercover agents in criminal cases and discrimination testers in civil cases, acting under the direction of lawyers, customarily dissemble as to their identities or purposes to gather evidence of wrongdoing. This conduct has not been condemned on ethical grounds by courts, ethics committees or grievance committees. This limited use of deception, to learn about ongoing acts of wrongdoing, is also accepted outside the area of criminal or civil-rights law enforcement. The prevailing understanding in the legal profession is that a public or private lawyer's use of an undercover investigator to detect ongoing violations of the law is not ethically proscribed, especially where it would be difficult to discover the violations by other means.[292]

As likewise suggested by Douglas Richmond, the "better argument" is that Rule 8.4(c) in prohibiting deceitful conduct by lawyers is "not intended to apply to lawyers' use of undercover investigators."[293]

---

[287] 8 P.3d 966 (Ore. 2000).

[288] For a discussion of undercover investigations by government lawyers and the implications for the rule prohibiting communications by a lawyer with a represented person, see *infra* § 4-9.12(c)(2).

[289] OR. RULES OF PROF'L CONDUCT R. 8.4(b).

[290] 15 F. Supp. 2d 456 (D. N.J. 1998).

[291] *Id.* at 475.

[292] *Id.*

[293] Douglas R. Richmond, *Deceptive Lawyering*, U. CINN. L. REV. 577, 596 (2005). On the definition of dishonesty, fraud, deceit, and misrepresentation in Rule 8.4(c), see also *supra* § 4-1.4(b).

Under the explicit approval of such covert activity in Oregon by its ethics rules,[294] in Utah by an ethics opinion,[295] and in Alaska and Iowa by a comment to the ethics rule,[296] a lawyer may supervise, participate in, or advise clients about conducting lawful covert activity to investigate suspected violations of civil or criminal law or of constitutional rights, as well as engage in lawful intelligence-gathering to find evidence of such violations. In these jurisdictions, "covert activity" is defined as the gathering of information on unlawful activity through the use of misrepresentations or other subterfuge. As stated in Oregon rule, before a lawyer may support or participate in such covert activity, he must have a "good faith" belief that "there is a reasonable possibility that unlawful activity has taken place, is taking place or will take place in the foreseeable future." The approval of covert activity in these jurisdictions is not limited to attorneys in law enforcement or prosecutor's offices, but applies to private attorneys as well when attempting to detect ongoing violations of the law.[297]

Under this approach, which may also be implicitly permitted under the Model Rules of Professional Conduct, covert activity or intelligence-gathering must be otherwise lawful. Attorneys have no special privilege to engage in behavior, such as trespass or breaking-and-entering, other espionage methods that would be unlawful, or extortionate threats.[298] Moreover, while a lawyer engaged in covert activity or intelligence-gathering may not thereby violate Model Rule 8.4(c), the lawyer still must comply with other applicable provisions of the Model Rules of Professional Conduct, such as those that constrain a lawyer's contact with a represented person[299] or that forbid intrusion into privileged relationships, such as by acquisition of confidential information.[300]

Finally, while appropriate use of covert means against others to promote the interests of the lawyer's client in detecting illegal conduct should be acceptable under the rules, turning those same undercover methods against a client and thus betraying the fiduciary trust placed by client in the lawyer would constitute an especially egregious violation of the prohibition in Model Rule 8.4(c) against conduct involving dishonesty or deceit. In *Committee on Professional Ethics & Conduct v. Mollman*,[301] the court suspended an attorney who, to secure leniency in a prosecution against the attorney for drug possession, had agreed with law enforcement to wear a concealed microphone to record an incriminating conversation with a person, who was a friend and a former client, about past drug use. Although the person being targeted by this undercover operation was not presently a client in any matter and, during the recorded conversation, the attorney expressly disclaimed any intent to act as that person's counsel in the

---

[294] OR. RULES OF PROF'L CONDUCT R. 8.4(b).

[295] Utah Ethics Advisory Opinion No. 02–05 (Mar. 18, 2002).

[296] ALASKA RULES OF PROF'L CONDUCT R. 8.4, cmt. (adopting Oregon and Utah approach in comment); IOWA RULES OF PROF'L CONDUCT R. 32:8.4, cmt. 6 (same). *See generally* Peter A. Joy & Kevin C. McMunigal, *Different Rules for Prosecutors?*, CRIM. JUS., Fall, 2016, at 48, 49–50.

[297] *See* Barry Temkin, *Deception in Undercover Investigation: Conduct-Based vs. Status-Based Ethical Analysis*, 32 SEATTLE U. L. REV. 123, 155–56 (2008) (citing Sisk's Iowa legal ethics treatise and categorizing the Iowa comment as adopting an approach that is not limited to law enforcement officers and thus, as discussed in the article, is conduct-based rather than status-based).

[298] *See* In re Crossen, 880 N.E.2d 352, 371–75 (Mass. 2008) (disbarring an attorney who sought to find evidence of a judge's bias by staging a sham employment interview of the judge's former law clerk and further used "enticing, false information in the pressured context of a 'job interview,' including "threatening and deceptive" methods that " 'border[ed] on outright extortion' ").

[299] *See infra* § 4-9.12(c)(2).

[300] *See supra* § 4-9.6(d).

[301] 488 N.W.2d 168 (Iowa 1992).

ongoing drug investigation, the court emphasized that the attorney "was able to draw incriminating statements" out of this friend and former client "precisely because their conversation centered on the legal implications" of their past behavior and because the person looked to the lawyer "for guidance, if not legal advice, on these matters."[302]

### § 4-9.6(g) General Duty Not to Request Another Person to Withhold Information from Another Party

Rule 3.4(f) of the Model Rules of Professional Conduct states that a lawyer should not "request a person other than a client to refrain from voluntarily giving relevant information to another party."

A person who has witnessed an event or otherwise possesses information that is relevant to a controversy generally has no obligation to voluntarily share that information with anyone (although she may be required to divulge information by a subpoena or other legal compulsion). Nonetheless, by virtue of the professional commitment to the truth-finding function of the legal process, a lawyer ordinarily should not advise a potential witness to exercise that right to silence and refuse to share information with another party. That such a person may be free to withhold information does not permit the lawyer to play an obstructive role by encouraging such reticence in order to deprive other parties of equal access to a potential witness.[303] Nor should a lawyer suggest that a witness flee from the jurisdiction or conceal her existence, thereby depriving other parties of the opportunity to interview the witness during the typical informal investigation that precedes any formal discovery process.

The prohibition set forth in Model Rule 3.4(f) is subject to two exceptions:

*First*, the lawyer may properly advise the lawyer's own client not to speak to others, especially an opposing party, as part of the appropriate control over information and the manner of its disclosure in a legal representation.

*Second*, a lawyer may advise another person to withhold information if (1) "the person is a relative or an employee or other agent of a client," and (2) "the lawyer reasonably believes that the person's interests will not be adversely affected by refraining from giving such information."

Because of the close relationship that such persons have with the client—as a relative, employee, or agent—the lawyer appropriately may encourage them to cooperate with the client in controlling access by outsiders to information. Comment 4 to Rule 3.4 explains that "a lawyer [may] advise employees of a client to refrain from giving information to another party, for the employees may identify their interests with those of the client."

The permission granted to the lawyer to encourage the client and close associates of the client to withhold information is conditioned, however, on the lawyer's reasonable determination that the person's interests will not be adversely affected. The lawyer should consider the possibility that refusal to cooperate in a law enforcement investigation might lead to the person being charged with obstruction of justice or denied

[302] *Id.* at 170–71.

[303] *See* Matthew Rosengart, *Preparing Witnesses for Trial: A Post-Moussaoui Primer for Federal Litigators*, FED. LAW. (Nov.–Dec. 2007), at 40 ("Although it is customary and proper for a witness to decline to speak with opposing counsel, it is generally a choice that must be made by the witness, and absent unusual circumstances, counsel should not counsel a witness not to do so.").

leniency in criminal charges.[304] Similarly in a civil matter, resistance to requests for information by an opposing party could lead to that person being named as an additional party to anticipated or ongoing litigation.

## § 4-9.7 ETHICAL ISSUES REGARDING COLLECTION AND RETENTION OF EVIDENCE IN CRIMINAL PROCEEDINGS

### § 4-9.7(a) Introduction to Ethical Issues Regarding Evidence in Criminal Matters

> [T]he legal responsibility imposed upon lawyers who learn of the existence of tangible evidence of a completed crime in the course of an attorney-client relationship is complex and far from settled. Moreover, a lawyer can be faced with a host of conflicting important obligations to balance, including the duty to preserve client confidences, investigate the case, and maintain an allegiance to the system of justice as an officer of the court.[305]

Rule 3.4(a) of the Model Rules of Professional Conduct forbids a lawyer to "unlawfully obstruct another party's access to evidence or unlawfully alter, destroy or conceal a document or other material having potential evidentiary value." The rule further provides that "[a] lawyer shall not counsel or assist another person to do any such act."

When law enforcement or prosecutorial authorities investigating or prosecuting an alleged violation of the law present a lawful claim of access to evidence, the lawyer for a client is obliged to properly respond to that request and not to unlawfully obstruct access to, alter, destroy, or conceal that evidence. As a diligent and zealous advocate, the lawyer may and should assert non-frivolous grounds for quashing a subpoena from law enforcement. The lawyer may be justified in raising objections based on the attorney-client privilege; the privilege against self-incrimination; constitutional limitations on law enforcement intrusion into the attorney-client relationship; and court rules, holdings, or other standards limiting the issuance of prosecutorial subpoenas to criminal defense lawyers.[306] When a colorable objection can be made to a request or demand for confidential information, the lawyer should raise and competently advocate it.

The more difficult questions tend to arise when law enforcement is not directly seeking evidence from the lawyer, but rather the lawyer has come to know about or has come into contact with evidence that may pertain to a crime. Again, Model Rule 3.4(a) declares that it is professional misconduct for a lawyer to "unlawfully obstruct another party's access to evidence or unlawfully alter, destroy or conceal a document or other material having potential evidentiary value." The key word here is "unlawfully," which

---

[304] *See* Matter of Alcantara, 676 A.2d 1030, 1034–35 (N.J. 1995) (disciplining a lawyer who attempted to persuade two co-defendants not to testify against the lawyer's client, saying the lawyer "could not reasonably have believed that advising [the co-defendants] to take the Fifth Amendment and not to testify truthfully would benefit them," given that "then the prosecutor would have been free not to make a lenient recommendation at sentencing").

[305] Wemark v. State, 602 N.W.2d 810, 816 (Iowa 1999).

[306] On government subpoenas to criminal defense counsel, see *infra* § 4-9.12(c)(5), and 1 GEOFFREY C. HAZARD, JR., W. WILLIAM HODES & PETER R. JARVIS, THE LAW OF LAWYERING § 10.52 (Aspen, 4th ed., 2016).

appears twice in the sentence. As Stephen Gillers observes, this rule "offer[s] no help" and simply "yields to the law. If it's legal, it's ethical. If not, not."[307]

The criminal defense lawyer must be a zealous advocate, protect the client's right against self-incrimination, and maintain confidentiality in representing a client. Accordingly, the lawyer is entitled—nay, professionally mandated—to prevent others from gaining access to or information about the location of documents, objects, or other materials that are or were in the possession of the client—unless such efforts would amount to "unlawfully obstruct[ing] another party's access to evidence."

Moreover, a lawyer may properly counsel a client to dispossess herself from documents, objects, or materials that are associated with wrongful behavior or that in themselves are wrongfully possessed (contraband). But, again, the lawyer's forward duties to shield the client's affairs from prying eyes and to advise the client regarding disposal of effects come to a screeching halt if the conduct would be "unlawful."

So where then is that legal line with respect to physical evidence? The Model Rules of Professional Conduct buck that question by referring the professional to the substantive law of the applicable sovereign, federal or state. And the law of evidentiary preservation, especially in the context of federal criminal law, is opaque. Congress has responded to corporate scandals by imposing stricter duties to preserve potential evidence.[308] And, while some general themes can be drawn from judicial opinions, the case law does not address every situation and is not readily accessible to the lawyer who must decide what to do with potential real evidence under exigent circumstances.[309]

The risk-averse lawyer understandably might sail for the safe harbor of advising the client to save everything forever and to generously reveal everything once an investigation is underway.[310] But that lawyer then would be deceived. The lawyer's duties of zealous advocacy and confidentiality cannot be so readily surrendered, even if the alternatives provoke anxiety. Indeed, in an era of growing awareness that law enforcement crime labs may lack competent training and rigorous scientific standards, criminal defense lawyers may have a duty to conduct or arrange for independent forensic testing of real evidence. In sum, trimming sails and dropping anchor at the dock of law enforcement may deprive the client of effective assistance of counsel.

In the discussion that follows, three themes are advanced, which should lead the way to a reasonable conclusion in difficult cases:

---

[307] Stephen Gillers, *Guns, Fruits, Drugs, and Documents: A Criminal Defense Lawyer's Responsibility for Real Evidence*, 63 STAN. L. REV. 813, 818 (2011).

[308] *See infra* § 4-9.7(b)(3).

[309] Gillers, *supra*, 63 STAN. L. REV at 816 (saying that "it is impossible to make sense of those authorities," because court "[r]ulings are confusing and inconsistent, ignore constitutional or other rights, impede return of stolen property, and endanger the public"); *see also* Regina v. Murray, 2000 O.J. No. 2182, 48 O.R. (3d 544), ¶ 149 (Ontario Superior Ct. of Justice, 2000) (Canadian judge comments pointedly in an obstruction of justice case that a criminal defense solicitor who concealed incriminating video tapes prior to trial "made only a token effort to find out what his obligations were" with respect to physical evidence of a crime, but "had he done careful research he might have remained confused").

[310] *See* Greta Fails, *The Boundary Between Zealous Advocacy and Obstruction of Justice after Sarbanes-Oxley*, 68 N.Y.U. ANN. SURV. AM. L. 397, 421 (2012) (warning that the "over-criminalization of previously innocent conduct" creates "an incentive structure that pits lawyers' interests in self-preservation against their clients' interests"); Bruce A. Green, *The Criminal Regulation of Lawyers*, 67 FORDHAM L. REV. 327, 366 (1998) (noting that "a cautious lawyer might derive the lesson that his own interests, if not those of the client, may be best served by avoiding conduct that, although lawful, could be misconstrued as an attempt to conceal or destroy incriminating material").

***Criminal Defense Lawyer May Need to Engage with Physical Evidence:*** The lawyer's professional duty to the client may require her to learn of, examine, and perhaps take possession of real evidence, while striving to remain zealously loyal to the client and maintain confidentiality in the face of uncertain legal demands.[311] In other words, the professionally responsible and effective lawyer may not be able to avoid engagement with real evidence and the ethical dilemma that may attach with that engagement. When making these difficult decisions in the present environment of legal uncertainty, criminal defense lawyers acting in good faith should be given ample breathing room, without facing the prospect of criminal prosecution or disciplinary charges.

***The Duty to Preserve Evidence Is Triggered by Reasonable Anticipation of Investigation or Proceeding:*** The criminal defense lawyer's ethical obligation to preserve or disclose evidence is not triggered unless a criminal investigation or another proceeding is reasonably anticipated in the foreseeable future.[312] That a document or object conceivably may be relevant to a possible dispute that could arise at some point in the future should not impose a duty to preserve that item or result in the destruction being characterized as obstruction of justice or evidence tampering. In advising a client on the duty to preserve or the right to destroy, the criminal defense lawyer's professional judgment about whether an investigation or proceeding may be reasonably anticipated should ordinarily be respected.[313]

***Criminal Defense Lawyer May Not Make It Harder—or Easier—for Law Enforcement to Find Physical Evidence:*** While the lawyer (and client) may be prohibited from taking certain actions that make discovery of evidence by law enforcement substantially more difficult, the lawyer (or client) is not obliged to make such revelation any easier. A lawyer's engagement with real evidence does not become wrongful just because law enforcement subsequently fails to find that evidence in a criminal investigation. In particular, a criminal defense lawyer's right and duty to examine real evidence should not be transmuted into a general obligation to then deliver it to law enforcement when returning evidence to its original location or possessor is possible.[314]

## § 4-9.7(b) The Law on the Duty to Preserve Evidence

### *§ 4-9.7(b)(1) A Summary of State Laws on Obstruction of Justice*

There is variation among the states on obstruction of justice or tampering with evidence.[315] Nonetheless, as discussed below, the conscious contemplation of an official proceeding or investigation—and not merely the remote possibility of such—appears to be a nearly universal expectation before a person's destruction or alteration of what might have been evidence is regarded as criminal.

---

[311] *See infra* § 4-9.7(c).

[312] *See* JAMIE S. GORELICK, STEPHEN MARZEN, LAWRENCE SOLUM & ARTHUR BEST, DESTRUCTION OF EVIDENCE § 7.1 (Wolters Kluwer, 2014) ("The better view . . . is that destruction of evidence is unethical and in violation of the prohibition of conduct prejudicial to the administration of justice when the evidence is relevant to a reasonably foreseeable or pending legal proceeding, even if the destruction does not violate a criminal law.").

[313] *See infra* § 4-9.7(b)(4).

[314] *See infra* § 4-9.7(c)(3).

[315] On state obstruction of justice statutes, see generally JAMIE S. GORELICK, STEPHEN MARZEN, LAWRENCE SOLUM & ARTHUR BEST, DESTRUCTION OF EVIDENCE §§ 5.6 to 5.10 (Wolters Kluwer, 2014).

In most states, the imminent prospect of a proceeding or investigation is placed at the forefront of the criminal evaluation by focusing on the person's knowledge or belief about the existence or likelihood of an official proceeding or investigation.[316] For example, state statutes may refer to an official proceeding or investigation as "pending or . . . about to be instituted";[317] or as "pending or in progress";[318] or may prohibit destruction of something that "is about to be produced in evidence upon any trial, inquiry, or investigation."[319] The Model Penal Code prohibits tampering with evidence, which is defined as "alter[ing], destroy[ing], conceal[ing] or remov[ing] any record, document or thing with purpose to impair its verity or availability" in "an official proceeding or investigation" that the person believes "is pending or about to be instituted."[320] In these states, then, intentional destruction or alteration of evidence is criminal conduct if there is an actual or imminent proceeding or at least one that " 'could readily have been contemplated' under the circumstances of the case."[321] Indeed, some states incorporate the prospect of a proceeding into the ethical duty of the lawyer in the state version of ethics Rule 3.4(a).[322]

Other state criminal statutes demand proof that the person who destroyed or altered evidence acted with the specific intent to impede a proceeding or investigation, without referring directly to pendency or imminence. For example, an Iowa statute prohibits destroying, altering, or concealing evidence that would be admissible in a criminal trial, if done "with intent to prevent the apprehension or obstruct the prosecution or defense of any person."[323] By classifying such conduct as criminal obstruction of justice when done with intent to prevent "apprehension," as well as when designed to obstruct prosecution or defense of a person, this statute effectively integrates the anticipation of a future criminal investigation or proceeding into the *mens rea* for the crime.

A handful of states simply and generally prohibit obstruction of justice.[324] For example, the pertinent Maryland statute states that "[a] person may not, by . . . corrupt means, obstruct, impede, or try to obstruct or impede the administration of justice in a court of the State."[325] Because this statute prohibits acting by "corrupt means," which the federal courts interpret to mean conscious knowledge that one is engaging in

---

[316] Peter A. Joy & Kevin C. McMunigal, *Incriminating Evidence—Too Hot to Handle?*, CRIM. JUST., Summer 2009, at 42, 43 (explaining that most states follow the Model Penal Code approach by requiring the person charged with tampering of evidence to have believed an official proceeding was pending or about to be instituted).

[317] *See, e.g.*, FLA. STAT. § 918.13(1).

[318] *See, e.g.*, TEX. PENAL CODE ANN. § 37.09(a).

[319] CAL. PENAL CODE § 135.

[320] MODEL PENAL CODE § 241.7(1) (American Law Institute, 1962). More than a dozen states have statutes directly based on the Model Penal Code, GORELICK, MARZEN, SOLUM & BEST, *supra*, § 5.8, and most follow the general approach, Peter A. Joy & Rodney J. Uphoff, *"What Do I Do With the Porn on My Computer?": How a Lawyer Should Counsel Clients About Physical Evidence*, 54 AM. CRIM. L. REV. 751, 768 (2017).

[321] People v. Mercedes, 756 N.Y.S.2d 735, 738 (N.Y. Crim. Ct. 2003).

[322] *See, e.g.*, D.C. RULES OF PROF'L CONDUCT R. 3.4(a) (stating the lawyer's duties with respect to evidence as applying "if the lawyer reasonably should know that the evidence is or may be the subject of discovery or subpoena in any pending or imminent proceeding"); GA. RULES OF PROF'L CONDUCT R. 3.4(a) (stating the lawyer's duties with respect to evidence as applying when "the lawyer knows or reasonably should know [the evidence] is relevant to a pending or reasonably foresseable proceeding").

[323] IOWA CODE § 719.3.

[324] GORELICK, MARZEN, SOLUM & BEST, *supra*, § 5.7.

[325] MD. CODE ANN. CRIM. LAW § 9–306.

wrongdoing,[326] these statutes place a heavy burden of proof on the prosecution. When there is no reasonable prospect of a criminal prosecution at the point in time that a document or item is destroyed, proof of "corrupt" motivation becomes impossible. Moreover, when construing parallel language in a federal statute,[327] the courts have held that "administration of justice" means that the destruction of evidence must relate to a pending judicial proceeding.[328]

### *§ 4-9.7(b)(2) The Traditional Federal Approach to Obstruction of Justice: §§ 1503 and 1512*

Federal criminal law regarding preservation of evidence traditionally adhered to the expectation that a proceeding must be pending or imminent before a duty would arise to preserve physical items or documents.[329] The original federal obstruction of justice statute, 18 U.S.C. § 1503, sometimes called the Omnibus Clause, generally prohibits "corrupt[ ] ... endeavors to influence, obstruct, or impede, the due administration of justice."[330]

This criminal statute has long been interpreted by the Supreme Court to apply only when some judicial proceeding, such as a grand jury, is actually pending and the defendant had notice of that proceeding; the mere existence of a law enforcement investigation or the possibility of a future proceeding is insufficient to characterize an individual's conduct as an obstruction of justice under § 1503.[331] For a criminal conviction under § 1503, "the act must have a relationship in time, causation, or logic with the judicial proceedings" and "the endeavor must have the 'natural and probable effect' of interfering with the due administration of justice."[332]

Somewhat more broadly, although ultimately limited by judicial construction, another federal obstruction of justice statute, 18 U.S.C. § 1512(b), prohibits "corruptly persuad[ing] another person, or attemp[ting] to do so," "with intent to . . . alter, destroy, mutilate, or conceal an object with intent to impair the object's integrity or availability for use in an official proceeding."[333] Section 1512 further specifies that "an official proceeding need not be pending or about to be instituted at the time of the offense."[334] Subsequently, subsection (c) was added to § 1512 to clarify that an actor obstructs justice

---

[326] *See* GORELICK, MARZEN, SOLUM & BEST, *supra*, § 5.7 (predicting these state statutes will be interpreted consistently with traditional federal obstruction of justice statutes).

[327] 18 U.S.C. § 1503 (prohibiting a person from "corruptly" "obstruct[ing], or imped[ing]" "the due administration of justice").

[328] *See supra* § 4-9.7(b)(2); GORELICK, MARZEN, SOLUM & BEST, *supra*, § 5.3.

[329] On federal obstruction of justice statutes, see generally Gregory C. Sisk, *The Legal Ethics of Real Evidence: Of Child Porn on the Choirmaster's Computer and Bloody Knives Under the Stairs*, 89 WASH. L. REV. 819, 830–40 (2014).

[330] 18 U.S.C. § 1503(a). On the Omnibus Clause, see generally Justin Alexander Kasprisin, *Obstruction of Justice*, 47 AM. CRIM. L. REV. 847, 849–65 (2010); Kimberley A. Schaefer & John S. Schowengerdt, *Obstruction of Justice*, 43 AM. CRIM. L. REV. 763, 765–80 (2006); Kyle R. Taylor, Note, *The Obstruction of Justice Nexus Requirement After* Arthur Andersen *and Sarbanes-Oxley*, 93 CORNELL L. REV. 401, 406–09 (2008).

[331] United States v. Aguilar, 515 U.S. 593, 598–99 (1995); Pettibone v. United States, 148 U.S. 197, 206–07 (1893).

[332] *Aguilar*, 515 U.S. at 599.

[333] 18 U.S.C. § 1512(b)(2)(B). *See generally* Kasprisin, *supra*, 47 AM. CRIM. L. REV. at 877–79; Schaefer & Schowengerdt, *supra*, 43 AM. CRIM. L. REV. at 780–92.

[334] 18 U.S.C. § 1512(f)(1).

if he directly performs the obstructive activity rather than encouraging others to do so.[335] The provision thus extends obstruction of justice to when a person "corruptly . . . alters, destroys, mutilates, or conceals a record, document, or other object, or attempts to do so, with the intent to impair the object's integrity or availability for use in an official proceeding."[336]

In *Arthur Andersen LLP v. United States*,[337] the Supreme Court reversed the § 1512 conviction of an accounting firm for having directed employees to destroy documents, holding that the statutory requirement that the defendant have acted "knowingly" and "corruptly" demanded "proof of consciousness of wrongdoing."[338] The Court further rejected the government's argument that the statute required no showing that the actor's encouragement to destroy documents was motivated by the anticipation of a proceeding:

> It is . . . one thing to say that a proceeding "need not be pending or about to be instituted at the time of the offense," and quite another to say a proceeding need not even be foreseen. A "knowingly . . . corrup[t] persuade[r]" cannot be someone who persuades others to shred documents under a document retention policy when he does not have in contemplation any particular official proceeding in which those documents might be material.[339]

As the Supreme Court said quite recently about a statute forbidding "corruptly" obstruction of the administration of internal revenue, the government must show that either an actual "proceeding was pending at the time defendant engaged in the obstructive conduct or, at the least, was then reasonably foreseeable by the defendant."[340]

### *§ 4-9.7(b)(3) Anticipatory Obstruction of Justice: Sarbanes-Oxley § 1519*

***Removing the Direct Link to a Pending or Imminent Proceeding or Investigation:*** As part of the Corporate and Criminal Fraud Accountability Act of 2002, commonly known as the Sarbanes-Oxley Act,[341] Congress enacted a new criminal statute demanding preservation of documents and items relevant to a federal matter and removing the requirement of a direct connection to a pending or imminent investigation or judicial proceeding:

> Whoever knowingly alters, destroys, mutilates, conceals, covers up, falsifies, or makes a false entry in any record, document, or tangible object with the intent to impede, obstruct, or influence the investigation or proper administration of any matter within the jurisdiction of any department or agency of the United States or any case filed under title 11 [bankruptcy], or in relation to or

---

[335] Taylor, *supra*, 93 CORNELL L. REV. at 423.

[336] 8 U.S.C. § 1512(c)(1).

[337] 544 U.S. 696 (2005).

[338] *Id.* at 704–07.

[339] *Id.* at 707–08; *see also* Julie R. O'Sullivan, *The Federal Criminal "Code" is a Disgrace: Obstruction Statutes as Case Study*, 96 J. CRIM. L. & CRIMINOLOGY 643, 706 (2006) (lauding the Supreme Court's "insist[ence] that there be consciousness of wrongdoing before a defendant can be convicted" for obstruction of justice under § 1512, but pointedly commenting that the fact this "should even have been an issue, let alone one that had to be litigated all the way to the Supreme Court, speaks volumes about the deficiencies of the federal [criminal] 'code' ").

[340] Marinello v. United States, ___ S. Ct. ___, 2018 WL 140242 (U.S. Mar. 21, 2018).

[341] Pub. L. No. 107–204, 116 Stat. 800 (2002) (codified at 18 U.S.C. § 1519).

contemplation of any such matter or case, shall be fined under this title, imprisoned not more than 20 years, or both.[342]

Section 1519 was enacted in the aftermath of corporate financial and accounting scandals and designed to make corporate fraud easier to detect by preventing destruction of documents and electronic records.[343] In *Yates v. United States*,[344] a commercial fisherman was convicted under § 1519 for throwing overboard undersized grouper fish as obstructing an investigation into catching fish under the legal size limit. In reversing the conviction, the Supreme Court read the term "tangible object" in § 1519 in the context of the accompanying words "record" and "document" to apply only to destruction of evidence related to record-keeping. A plurality of the Court held that a "tangible object" within the meaning of § 1519 "is better read to cover only objects one can use to record or preserve information, not all objects in the physical world,"[345] while a concurring justice agreed that the term " 'tangible object' should mean something similar to records or documents."[346] Thus, § 1519 does not apply to obstruction of justice involving other types of physical evidence.[347]

For our present purposes in addressing the duty to preserve evidence, the most important feature of § 1519 is that it does not directly link the forbidden conduct of altering or destroying evidence to the pendency of an investigation, much less the imminence of a judicial proceeding. As the Supreme Court observed in *Yates*, § 1519 "covers conduct intended to impede any federal investigation or proceeding, including one not even on the verge of commencement."[348] The Senate Report accompanying the 2002 legislation clarified that § 1519 was designed to eliminate "any technical requirement" that "tie[d] . . . obstructive conduct to a pending or imminent proceeding or matter."[349]

As Dana Hill has described it, § 1519 prohibits "anticipatory obstruction of justice,"[350] that is, conduct that occurs before the actors know of a specific investigation or proceeding but nonetheless undertaken with an intent to obstruct. For that reason, some courts have held that a nexus to a specific federal investigation is not a predicate to the charge,[351] much less that the person destroying or altering evidence believed that the actions were likely to succeed in obstructing an investigation.[352] Nonetheless, to have acted with the specific intent to impede or obstruct, "the defendant must have been

---

[342] 18 U.S.C. § 1519. On federal obstruction of justice statutes, see generally Gregory C. Sisk, *The Legal Ethics of Real Evidence: Of Child Porn on the Choirmaster's Computer and Bloody Knives Under the Stairs*, 89 WASH. L. REV. 819, 830–40 (2014).

[343] *See* Greta Fails, *The Boundary Between Zealous Advocacy and Obstruction of Justice after Sarbanes-Oxley*, 68 N.Y.U. ANN. SURV. AM. L. 397, 402 (2012).

[344] 135 S. Ct. 1074 (2015).

[345] *Id.* at 1081.

[346] *Id.* at 1090 (Alito, J., concurring in the judgment).

[347] *See* United States v. McRae, 795 F.3d 471, 477–78 (5th Cir. 2015) (overturning conviction under § 1519 for burning a body and car to hide a homicide as not being related to records or documents).

[348] *Id.* at 1087.

[349] S. REP. NO. 107–146, at 14–15 (2002).

[350] Dana E. Hill, Note, *Anticipatory Obstruction of Justice: Pre-Emptive Document Destruction Under the Sarbanes-Oxley Anti-Shredding Statute, 18 U.S.C. § 1519*, 89 CORNELL L. REV. 1519, 1523 (2004).

[351] United States v. Kernell, 667 F.3d 746, 753 (6th Cir. 2012).

[352] United States v. Yielding, 657 F.3d 688, 712 (8th Cir. 2011); United States v. Gray, 642 F.3d 371, 377 (3d Cir. 2011).

aware of the pending or contemplated matter or investigation."[353] As the Supreme Court held very recently with respect to an internal revenue obstruction statute, to ensure fair warning of what is unlawful, the proceeding or administrative investigation that was allegedly obstructed by the defendant "must at least be in the offing."[354]

***Reasonable Anticipation Integrated into* Mens Rea *for § 1519:*** While "a link between a defendant's conduct and an imminent or pending official proceeding" may not be a predicate fact that must be proven under § 1519,[355] reasonable anticipation of an investigation presumably has been integrated into the *mens rea* element. As the United States Court of Appeals for the Fifth Circuit noted, a "plausible" construction that "gives effect to the statute's language as a whole" is to "read[ ] intent into every clause."[356] Indeed, the legislative history emphasizes that "the intent required is the intent to obstruct, not some level of knowledge."[357]

One cannot intend to obstruct an investigation or act in "contemplation" of an investigation unless one anticipates an investigation.[358] The mere fact that the destruction of a document or object has the collateral effect of obstructing a federal investigation or administration is not sufficient; the statute expressly requires proving that the charged party had the specific intent of causing such obstruction. When a criminal investigation is only conceivable but remains speculative, destruction of documents or objects that provide evidence of criminal wrongdoing should not implicate § 1519.[359]

Lest innocent conduct be subject to prosecution, Greta Fails argues that § 1519 "should be construed to contain a nexus requirement," by which "[d]efendants need to have foreseen a potential future proceeding that their conduct could possibly obstruct to have violated the obstruction statutes."[360] Further, construing § 1519 to require proof of corrupt intent by the charged defendant will "prevent overcriminalization" of conduct

---

353 United States v. Perraud, 672 F. Supp. 2d 1328, 1350 (S.D. Fla. 2009).

354 Marinello v. United States, ___ S. Ct. ___, 2018 WL 140242 (U.S. Mar. 21, 2018).

355 *Gray*, 642 F.3d at 377; *see also id.* at 378 n.5 ("By its plain terms, however, § 1519 does not require the existence of an 'official proceeding.' ").

356 United States v. McRae, 702 F.3d 806, 837 (5th Cir. 2012), *overturned on other grounds*, 795 F.3d 471 (5th Cir. 2015).

357 148 CONG. REC. S7,418–19 (daily ed. July 26, 2002) (statement of Sen. Leahy).

358 *See* United States v. Fattah, 223 F. Supp. 3d 336, 371–72 (E.D. Pa. 2016) (granting motion to acquit of charges under § 1519, saying that while "[w]e acknowledge that § 1519 does not require the existence of an investigation at the time that the document is falsified," the government must "prove that a defendant acted to impede an investigation or did so in relation to or in contemplation of an investigation" and the government presented no evidence that the defendants "knew of or even contemplated any investigation whatsoever, be it federal or otherwise").

359 *See* S. REP. NO. 107–146, at 27 (2002) ("[Section 1519] should not cover the destruction of documents in the ordinary course of business, even where the individual may have reason to believe that the documents may tangentially relate to some future matter within the conceivable jurisdiction of an arm of the federal bureaucracy.").

360 Fails, *supra*, 68 N.Y.U. ANN. SURV. AM. L. at 433; Taylor, *supra*, 93 CORNELL L. REV. at 432 (arguing that the courts should continue "the trend toward a broadly applicable nexus requirement"); *see also* Marinello v. United States, ___ S. Ct. ___, 2018 WL 140242 (U.S. Mar. 21, 2018) (holding that a broad interpretation of an internal revenue obstruction statute would "risk the lak of fair warning and related kinds of unfairness" and thus requiring the government to "show (among other things) that there is a 'nexus' between the defendant's conduct and a particular administrative proceeding").

that may serve multiple purposes, only one of which is the forbidden intent to obstruct an investigation or matter.[361]

In *United States v. Yielding*,[362] the Eighth Circuit explained that § 1519 would apply not only when the "defendant acts directly" with respect to "a pending matter," but when a defendant acts "with intent to obstruct a foreseeable investigation of a matter within the jurisdiction of a federal agency [that] has not yet commenced."[363] As the court explained, without a sharp focus on the specific intent to obstruct an investigation, § 1519 would reach plainly innocent conduct, such as routine destruction of documents.[364] In other words, § 1519 does not criminalize behavior that purportedly "obstructs" a remotely possible investigation.[365] Thus, as well stated by the Eighth Circuit, § 1519 by applying to acts "in contemplation" of an investigation "refer[s] to a matter that was not yet pending but which the defendant envisioned or anticipated."[366]

Moreover, § 1519 likely would be unconstitutionally vague, unless "construed as requiring proof that defendant acted with specific, wrongful intent."[367] Although interpreting a different obstruction of justice statute, the Supreme Court's observation in *Arthur Andersen* that a person cannot intend to obstruct a proceeding that would "not even be foreseen"[368] remains enlightening in this respect. By confining the operation of § 1519 to circumstances where the wrongful nature of the act is obvious, and thus where conscious knowledge of wrongdoing by the defendant is established directly or indirectly, concerns about overbreadth in § 1519 diminish.

In any event, we could hardly countenance the prospect that a person interfering with a document or object becomes a felon based merely on awareness that an investigation "might begin at some point in the future."[369] Applied so broadly, § 1519 would exceed all bounds of fair notice and sweep within its criminal designation a host of perfectly legitimate acts. To criminally convict a person when she could not reasonably have contemplated that an action would obstruct an objectively foreseeable investigation or proceeding is the essence of strict criminal liability. As Professor Herbert Wechsler wrote sixty years ago, "[t]o condemn when fault is absent is barbaric."[370]

---

[361] United States v. Kernell, 667 F.3d 746, 754 (6th Cir. 2012) (stating that the intent to obstruct language in § 1519 "subsumes the [corrupt intent] requirement"); *McRae*, 702 F.3d at 838 (referring to *Kernell's* suggestion "that there is 'no dispute' that criminal liability under § 1519 requires some corrupt intent").

[362] 657 F.3d 688 (8th Cir. 2011).

[363] *Id.* at 711.

[364] *Id.* (stating that without requiring specific intent to obstruct an investigation, "then the statute would forbid innocent conduct such as routine destruction of documents that a person consciously and in good faith determines are irrelevant to a foreseeable federal matter").

[365] *See McRae*, 702 F.3d at 837–38 (saying the court was "receptive to [defendant's] well-presented argument" that § 1519 might be vague if applied where "[t]he connection between the defendant's conduct and an investigation might be so remote . . . that the statute punishes innocent conduct").

[366] *Yielding*, 657 F.3d at 714.

[367] United States v. Stevens, 771 F. Supp. 2d 556, 562 (D. Md. 2011).

[368] Arthur Andersen LLP v. United States, 544 U.S. 696, 707–08 (2005).

[369] *See Kernell*, 667 F.3d at 755.

[370] Herbert Wechsler, *A Thoughtful Code of Substantive Law*, 45 J. CRIM. L. CRIMINOLOGY & POLICE SCI. 524, 528 (1955).

### *§ 4-9.7(b)(4) Safe Harbor for Legal Representation*

Professor Rodney Uphoff perceptively observes that "the mere threat of criminal prosecution or disciplinary sanctions may well chill some defense lawyers from taking action that a zealous advocate ought to be willing to take in defending a client."[371]

For that reason, presumably, the chapter in Title 18 of the United States Code containing the obstruction of justice statutes establishes an affirmative defense peculiar to lawyers. Section 1515(c) provides: "This chapter does not prohibit or punish the providing of lawful, bona fide, legal representation services in connection with or anticipation of an official proceeding."[372] This "rather opaque defense to the crime,"[373] offers no further elucidation on what constitutes "lawful, bona fide" legal representation. As long as the lawyer does not know that the client's objectives are unlawful, he should not be chilled from zealous representation of a client, including advice regarding the destruction of documents or items that the lawyer has no reason to believe are relevant to a proceeding or investigation that may be reasonably anticipated.

When a lawyer is the target of a prosecution for obstruction of justice, the jury should be instructed that bona fide legal representation without an improper purpose is a complete defense.[374] The jury should be told that a lawyer's "purpose to zealously represent his client is fully protected by the law."[375] And, as the Ninth Circuit held in *United States v. Kellington*,[376] a lawyer defending himself against a charge of obstruction of justice for assisting a client in destroying items is entitled to present "expert testimony on the lawyer's ethical obligations [as] relevant to establish the lawyer's intent and state of mind."

In *United States v. Stevens*,[377] a federal district court took the unusual but commendable step of interrupting the prosecution of a lawyer for obstruction of justice and ordering acquittal for charges based on the lawyer's legal advice to a client. While the court acknowledged that some of the responses made by the pharmaceutical company to the Food and Drug Administration were imperfect, the in-house counsel had directed the drafting of those statements as legal advice and in good faith reliance on the advice of other internal and outside lawyers. In an earlier ruling, the court held that "the most reasonable reading" of § 1519 "imposes criminal liability only on those who were conscious of the wrongfulness of their actions," because otherwise § 1519 would "reach inherently innocent conduct, such as a lawyer's instruction to his client to withhold documents the lawyer in good faith believes are privileged."[378]

---

[371] Rodney J. Uphoff, *The Physical Evidence Dilemma: Does ABA Standard 4–4.6 Offer Appropriate Guidance?*, 62 HASTINGS L.J. 1177, 1188 (2011).

[372] 18 U.S.C. § 1515(c).

[373] Stephen Gillers, *Guns, Fruits, Drugs, and Documents: A Criminal Defense Lawyer's Responsibility for Real Evidence*, 63 STAN. L. REV. 813, 818 (2011).

[374] *See* United States v. Mintmire, 507 F.3d 1273, 1277, 1293–94 (11th Cir. 2007) (approvingly quoting jury instructions).

[375] *Id.*

[376] 217 F.3d 1084, 1098 (9th Cir. 2000); *see also* United States v. Kloess, 251 F.3d 941, 949 (11th Cir. 2001) (approving expert testimony on legal ethics in obstruction case against lawyer).

[377] Bench Ruling, Crim. No. RWT-10-694, at 5 (D. Md. May 10, 2011); *see generally* Greta Fails, *The Boundary Between Zealous Advocacy and Obstruction of Justice after Sarbanes-Oxley*, 68 N.Y.U. ANN. SURV. AM. L. 397, 413–30 (2012) (discussing the *Stevens* case).

[378] United States v. Stevens, 771 F. Supp. 2d 556, 561 (D. Md. 2011).

The judge in *Stevens* "carved out a specific role for the judiciary"[379] in preventing prosecutorial overreach by targeting lawyers for obstruction of justice charges:

> The institutional problem that causes me a great concern is that while lawyers should not get a free pass, the Court should be vigilant to permit the practice of law to be carried on, to be engaged in, and to allow lawyers to do their job of zealously representing the interests of their client. Anything that interferes with that is something that the court system should not countenance.[380]

In sum, § 1515(c) provides a safe harbor for lawyers, requiring the government to disprove the lawful and bona fide nature of the lawyer's representation beyond a reasonable doubt. When a lawyer has advised or acted to destroy that which was evidence, but under circumstances where an investigation was not reasonably anticipated, then the court should presume that lawful purposes were in mind. The court should demand that the government present concrete evidence that the lawyer should have anticipated an investigation and was acting with an improper purpose.

### *§ 4-9.7(b)(5) Treatment of Contraband That Is Not Evidence in a Reasonably Anticipated Proceeding*

When a thing is illegal to even possess—that is, *contraband*—the lawyer's conflicting obligations regarding potential evidence become exquisitely complicated.

When a lawyer receives from a client an item that is contraband, and "where there is no pending case or investigation relating to this evidence," the American Bar Association for many years advised through the 1993 *Standards for Criminal Justice* that "counsel may suggest that the client destroy it," as long as "such destruction is clearly not in violation of any criminal statute."[381] Thus, the lawyer was expected to consult appropriate criminal codes to determine whether contraband that is not evidence in a pending or imminent criminal proceeding or investigation may be destroyed lawfully. Revisions in the 2015 *Standards for Criminal Justice* likewise encourage courts and legislatures to allow destruction of contraband, "[w]hen defense counsel reasonably believes that contraband does not relate to a pending criminal investigation or prosecution."[382]

By contrast, the Reporter's Notes to the American Law Institute's *Restatement of the Law Governing Lawyers*, characterize the ABA's position as "problematical," because "[c]ontraband is both property that may be illegal to possess and evidence that may be illegal to destroy."[383] No citation in the notes to cases or statutes supports this conclusion. These notes suggests that a lawyer should "read the ABA's standard with caution."[384]

---

[379] Greta Fails, *The Boundary Between Zealous Advocacy and Obstruction of Justice after Sarbanes-Oxley*, 68 N.Y.U. ANN. SURV. AM. L. 397, 419 (2012).

[380] *Stevens*, Bench Ruling, Crim. No. RWT-10-694, at 10.

[381] STANDARDS FOR CRIMINAL JUSTICE: DEFENSE FUNCTION, Standard 4–4.6(d) (American Bar Ass'n, 1993).

[382] STANDARDS FOR CRIMINAL JUSTICE: DEFENSE FUNCTION, Standard 4–4.7(j)(ii) (American Bar Ass'n, 2015).

[383] RESTATEMENT (THIRD) OF THE LAW GOVERNING LAWYERS § 119 rptr. note (American Law Institute, 2000).

[384] *Id.*

Consistent with the ABA *Standards*, Dean Norman Lefstein opined that "[f]rom a policy standpoint . . . the attorney who destroys contraband should not be prosecuted, because his or her action will have divested the client of the contraband and thus deprived the client of its use or the possibility of sale or gift to another."[385] For example, while penalizing the possession of child pornography, findings enacted as part of a federal criminal statute set out Congress's reasoning that "prohibiting the possession and viewing of child pornography will encourage the possessors of such material to rid themselves of or destroy the material, thereby helping to protect the victims of child pornography and to eliminate the market for the sexual exploitative use of children."[386] Given that the continued existence of the contraband is the greater evil, preventing ongoing possession of the contraband by the client[387] and removing the items from circulation through destruction is the common-sense solution.[388]

Contraband that is or could be evidence in a pending, imminent, or reasonably anticipated criminal investigation or official proceeding may not be destroyed, just as other evidence of a crime may not properly be destroyed. As a rough guideline, the greater the quantity of the contraband material and the less amenable it is to easy destruction, the more likely it may be that the contraband material is relevant as evidence. Thus, the lawyer probably should not instruct a client to destroy an illegal weapon or large quantities of illegal narcotics.[389] Such items pose heightened public safety concerns and proper disposal of such items will be difficult. Moreover, the nature or quantity of these objects are more likely to indicate a connection to a criminal enterprise that has come to the attention of the authorities and may be the subject of an ongoing criminal investigation.

Notwithstanding that he acted within what should have been accepted as the permissible range of professional discretion (even if unwise), a lawyer who advised a client on handling of contraband consistent with the above discussion was indicted for his troubles. In *United States v. Russell*,[390] leaders in a church parish discovered child pornography on a laptop belonging to the longtime choirmaster. Having no reason to believe that the choirmaster had abused any person at the parish, church leaders wanted to avoid any further embarrassment by quietly dismissing him. Before taking that step, they sought the advice of legal counsel. Because possession of child pornography is illegal, the lawyer advised that the hard-drive be destroyed to remove the child

[385] Norman Lefstein, *Incriminating Physical Evidence, the Defense Attorney's Dilemma, and the Need for Rules*, 64 N.C. L. REV. 897, 935 n.188 (1986).

[386] Child Pornography Prevention Act, Pub. L. No. 104–208, § 121(1)(12), 110 Stat. 3009, 3009–27 (1996).

[387] *See* United States v. Angle, 234 F.3d 326, 339–40 & n.15 (7th Cir. 2000) (describing as interesting the defendant's argument that his deletion of child pornography computer files meant that he did not knowingly continue to possess them, but noting also the government's response that the files were still retrievable because the disk had not been reformatted, although finding it unnecessary to decide the question because not all of the files had been deleted).

[388] STANDARDS FOR CRIMINAL JUSTICE: DEFENSE FUNCTION, Standard 4–4.6 cmt. (American Bar Ass'n, 1993) ("The social benefit accomplished by the destruction and discontinued circulation of such items outweighs any hypothetical social costs stemming from the fact that these items have been rendered unavailable to serve as evidence in future criminal investigations or prosecutions.").

[389] On instructing a client about the legal implications of evidence or potential evidence, see *infra* § 4-9.7(b)(6).

[390] 639 F. Supp. 2d 226 (D. Conn. 2007). On the *Russell* case, see generally Gregory C. Sisk, *The Legal Ethics of Real Evidence: Of Child Porn on the Choirmaster's Computer and Bloody Knives Under the Stairs*, 89 WASH. L. REV. 819, 842–61 (2014).

pornography. Indeed, the lawyer was willing to perform that task for them.[391] Unbeknownst to the lawyer and the church leaders, the now-dismissed choirmaster was under investigation by federal law enforcement for distribution of child pornography (and, indeed, a host of other crimes). When federal authorities discovered that the lawyer had destroyed the computer hard-drive, he was indicted for obstruction of justice.[392] Facing a jail term of 20 years, the lawyer agreed to plead guilty to a lesser offense and be placed on probation, rather than maintain a defense that he had acted appropriately.[393]

Consider a variation on the *Russell* scenario that may help to demonstrate that the prosecution for obstruction of justice in that case contravenes fair expectations for professional obligations. Suppose that, instead of being approached by the church leaders, a lawyer had been engaged by the choirmaster himself who desired to extricate himself from an addiction to pedophiliac material. Imagine that this hypothetical choirmaster came to our hypothetical lawyer, bringing with him the laptop containing the child pornography. The choirmaster admits that he has a problem and that he has been downloading child pornography but insists that he has not himself abused any child or created any of the obscene material. Based on the choirmaster's narrative, the lawyer has no reason to believe that a criminal investigation has targeted him.[394] The choir director then explains that he has begun psychological counseling and now wishes to separate himself entirely from the child pornography by removing his cache of such files, just as an alcoholic would rid himself of any alcohol in his house.

Certainly the lawyer in such a hypothetical circumstance must not betray the client and report him to law enforcement, which would be antithetical to the fiduciary attorney-client relationship and an egregious breach of professional confidentiality.[395] Moreover, given the "basic human right not to assist the government in causing one's own destruction,"[396] the client is not obliged to self-report nor is the lawyer ethically obliged to encourage him to do so (ordinarily, quite the opposite). At the same time, the lawyer cannot tell the client to simply hold on to the child pornography-tainted computer, not only because it would be detrimental to the client's mental recovery but also because the continued possession of such contraband is illegal. And the lawyer cannot take the laptop and turn it over to law enforcement, given the ease with which computer forensics would identify the owner. As Professor Stephen Gillers writes, surrender of the laptop to law enforcement "would certainly seal the choirmaster's fate," which is an "unacceptable" solution.[397]

Many of us at some point in our lives engaged in moral wrongdoing that might also have constituted criminal misconduct, but reached a turning point and determined to

---

[391] *See* Sisk, *supra*, 89 WASH. L. REV. at 844–45.

[392] *Id.* at 846–50.

[393] *Id.* at 850–51.

[394] *See* Stephen Gillers, *Guns, Fruits, Drugs, and Documents: A Criminal Defense Lawyer's Responsibility for Real Evidence*, 63 STAN. L. REV. 813, 867 (2011) (describing this variation on the *Russell* case and noting that, at the time of the hypothetical meeting, "the choirmaster might never have become the focus of an investigation").

[395] *See* Counsel for Discipline v. Tonderum, 840 N.W.2d 487, 491–92 (Neb. 2013) (suspending a lawyer indefinitely for disclosing to the prosecution confidential information about criminal charges against a former client).

[396] *See* Stuart Green, *Uncovering the Cover-Up Crimes*, 42 AM. CRIM. L. REV. 9, 32 (2005).

[397] STEPHEN GILLERS, REGULATION OF LAWYERS: PROBLEMS OF LAW AND ETHICS 435 (Aspen, 9th ed. 2012).

leave that past behind. Once making that decision, abandonment or destruction of the accouterments of a criminal lifestyle may be undertaken, not to conceal evidence in anticipation of a criminal investigation, but to avoid embarrassment and make a clean break.

The courts should long hesitate to read an obstruction of justice statute to effectively forbid a person from ever turning away from past misdeeds and shutting the door by discarding the residue of that past life. To be sure, once an investigation is underway or is reasonably anticipated, it may be too late and steps taken at that point to hide, destroy, or alter that which may constitute evidence of criminal wrongdoing are more difficult to separate from an intent to impede the investigation.

But when an investigation is only a possibility from the perspective of the actor, with no awareness of law enforcement interest or objective reason to believe a specific investigation into this matter will be forthcoming, then a person should be encouraged to make a break from a criminal past. An individual's admirable resolve to separate from wrongdoing by tossing aside the instruments and forbidden objects of that wrongdoing should not readily be characterized as the equivalent of a specific intent to obstruct justice.

The primary lesson that Professor Gillers draws from the *Russell* episode is that, "even when a lawyer honestly believes that destruction of potential evidence is lawful, the lawyer should not be the one to do it."[398] In other words, the lawyer might counsel the client to destroy the material in appropriate circumstances, but the lawyer should not undertake to do it herself.

For several reasons, this is good advice:

First, if the lawyer advises the client that destruction is legitimate or simply advises about the legal consequences in uncertain circumstances[399]—but leaves any action to the client—the lawyer's counsel likely will remain confidential. Indeed, because destroying an item is not something that falls within the typical understanding of legal services, the lawyer is well advised to confine her participation to providing legally-informed advice to the client about whether the item constitutes evidence, whether it may be lawfully destroyed, and what are the legal consequences for a choice that the client makes.

Second, if the client subsequently should be charged with criminal wrongdoing for destroying the item, the lawyer could be called as a witness for the defense, outlining the legal advice given and perhaps strengthening the argument that the destruction of the evidence was not undertaken by the client with the wrongful intent to obstruct justice.

Third, the lawyer's direct participation in destroying an item connected to the client's felonious wrongdoing does open the door to a charge of misprision of a felony, which is the lesser offense to which the attorney in *Russell* pled. Even if there is no reason to anticipate any criminal investigation or proceeding, thus precluding a

[398] Gillers, *supra*, 63 STAN. L. REV. at 816. *But see* STANDARDS FOR CRIMINAL JUSTICE: DEFENSE FUNCTION, Standard 4–4.7(j)(ii) (American Bar Ass'n, 2015) (encouraging adoption of procedures whereby "counsel may take possession of the contraband and destroy it" when counsel "reasonably believes that contraband does not relate to a pending criminal investigation or prosecution").

[399] *See infra* § 4-9.7(b)(6).

legitimate accusation of an intent to obstruct justice, destroying proof of another's commission of a felony might be seen as literally falling under the misprision statute.[400]

And, fourth, law enforcement attention is less likely to be drawn to the lawyer who merely advises but does not act.

To be sure, the question remains whether the destruction of the item is lawful, whether performed by the lawyer or client, and thus whether an investigation or proceeding is reasonably foreseeable. Rule 3.4(a) of the Rules of Professional Conduct admonishes a lawyer not to "unlawfully alter, destroy or conceal a document or other material having potential evidentiary value," but further states that "[a] lawyer shall not counsel or assist another person to do any such act." If it is illegal to destroy an item because it constitutes real evidence, it is illegal for the lawyer to be complicit in the destruction by directly instructing the client to do it.[401] For that reason, the lawyer who is uncertain about the demands of the law (and blamelessly so given the murkiness of the legal standards) and thus advises the client about the legal consequences in a context of uncertainty has acted properly.[402]

At least one federal court of appeals, in an unpublished decision, goes to the furthest extreme by decrying any destruction of what could possibly be evidence as obstruction of justice: "It is beyond dispute that ordering the erasure of a hard drive containing child pornography, the very possession of which violates federal law, falls within the intended reach of § 1519."[403] Except, of course, that it is anything but "beyond dispute" that destruction of child pornography is illegal when the prospect of a criminal investigation is low and thus the destruction cannot reasonably be characterized as intended to obstruct justice.

The prosecution of the lawyer in *Russell* plainly was designed to send a chilling message to lawyers from the government.[404] And the message was that a lawyer in possession of evidence of someone's wrongdoing must report that person to prosecutors—or turn over the incriminating material, which is the same thing—even if the lawyer has no concrete and objective reason to believe the person is coming under criminal investigation.[405] As the Connecticut Criminal Defense Association argued as amicus in the *Russell* case:

---

[400] *See* 18 U.S.C. § 4 (prohibiting one who has "knowledge of the actual commission of a [federal] felony" from concealing and failing to "make known" the felony to appropriate authorities). This statute has been read to require "an affirmative act to conceal the underlying felony" and construed not to "apply when a person destroys evidence of his or her own crime." Peter A. Joy & Rodney J. Uphoff, *"What Do I Do With the Porn on My Computer?": How a Lawyer Should Counsel Clients About Physical Evidence*, 54 AM. CRIM. L. REV. 751, 762, 767 (2017).

[401] *See* Evan A. Jenness, *Ethics and Advocacy Dilemmas—Possessing Evidence of a Client's Crime*, CHAMPION, Dec. 2010, at 16, 18 (arguing that a suggestion to the client to destroy evidence is an "even worse" choice).

[402] *See infra* § 4-9.7(b)(6).

[403] United States v. Atkinson, 532 F. App'x 873, 875 (11th Cir. 2013).

[404] *See* Greta Fails, *The Boundary Between Zealous Advocacy and Obstruction of Justice after Sarbanes-Oxley*, 68 N.Y.U. ANN. SURV. AM. L. 397, 429 (2012) ("Commentators largely condemned [Russell's] prosecution as retribution and prosecutorial overreach.").

[405] *See* Evan T. Barr, *'Russell': Prosecuting Defense Counsel for Obstruction*, N.Y.L.J., Nov. 21, 2007, at 2 (advising that, in light of the *Russell* court's failure to dismiss, lawyers who come into possession of "questionable material" should "assume the worst, and contact the authorities right away, rather than face the dilemma of being blamed either for retaining or destroying the contraband in question").

> If attorneys are forced to incriminate their clients in an effort to avoid being charged with obstruction of justice themselves, zealous advocacy becomes impossible, the attorney-client relationship becomes imperiled, and the careful balance of our adversarial system is disrupted.[406]

The appropriate solution, then, is to balance (A) the lawyer's need to uphold her duties to a client without fear that any misstep will lead to a criminal conviction and loss of a professional license against (B) the public interest in preventing someone from knowingly or recklessly destroying evidence that would be relevant in prosecuting an offender. And that line is best drawn by a presumption, consistent with the heightened burden of proof in a criminal charge of obstruction of justice, that a lawyer acts legitimately in handling or counseling destruction of documents or items unless there is a clear signal of a foreseeable criminal investigation that a reasonable lawyer would recognize. The courts should permit a prosecution for obstruction of justice against a lawyer representing a client to proceed only if convinced that a jury could find beyond a reasonable doubt that the lawyer had anticipated an investigation and acted directly to impede it.

### *§ 4-9.7(b)(6) Advising the Client in a Situation of Uncertainty*

Every lawyer should appreciate that legal responsibilities with respect to potential real evidence may present a moving target, with important new and expanding statutes on obstruction of justice being enacted and with fresh court rulings being rendered. To add to the uncertainty, the legal obligations regarding preservation of and access to real evidence vary not only by the underlying area of activity and by the jurisdiction whose laws govern, but often depend as well on the circumstances under which the lawyer comes into contact with the evidence, on the likelihood that an investigation or proceeding will follow, the nature of the evidence and its forensic characteristics, and perhaps even on the notoriety of the alleged criminal activity.

The lawyer may face a situation in which any action the client takes with respect to potential evidence may violate some legal precept. If a criminal investigation is uncertain but not wholly speculative, the case may fall on the line as to whether destruction of the evidence would be obstruction of justice. Questions may arise as to whether contraband, such as illegal narcotics or child pornography, may be lawfully destroyed, whether or not an investigation or proceeding may be reasonably anticipated. If the client does destroy the contraband, he may be engaging in obstruction of justice or may be exacerbating the illegality of contraband possession. But if the client does not destroy the contraband, he persists in a state of illegal possession and runs the risk that someone else—a family member or co-worker—will discover the object or material and bring about a criminal investigation that otherwise would not have unfolded.

Professors Peter Joy and Rodney Uphoff consider this type of evidentiary dilemma and persuasively conclude that the lawyer is "permitted to give an honest opinion about the likelihood of those legal consequences under whatever course of conduct the client might select."[407] While being careful not to directly instruct the client to take a particular

---

[406] Brief for Connecticut Criminal Defense Lawyers Association as Amicus Curiae Supporting Defendant's Motions to Dismiss the Indictment at 3, United States v. Russell, No. 3:07-cr-00031-AHN (D. Conn. July 2, 2007).

[407] Peter A. Joy & Rodney J. Uphoff, *"What Do I Do With the Porn on My Computer?": How a Lawyer Should Counsel Clients About Physical Evidence*, 54 AM. CRIM. L. REV. 751, 757 (2017).

step when all choices are legally dubious, the lawyer may address the likelihood that destruction of the evidence or contraband would resolve the problem and the sanctions that would attach if such destruction was wrongful as contrasted with the criminal penalties for being charged with possession.[408] "[A]dvising a client of risks of various courses of action," Joy and Uphoff observe, is "expressly permitted" under Rule 1.2 of the Model Rules of Professional Conduct.

Model Rule 1.2(d) prohibits a lawyer from "counsel[ing] a client to engage, or assist a client, in conduct that the lawyer knows is criminal or fraudulent," but simultaneously states that "a lawyer may discuss the legal consequences of any proposed course of conduct with a client."[409] Comment 9 to Model Rule 1.2 draws "a critical distinction between presenting an analysis of legal aspects of questionable conduct and recommending the means by which a crime or fraud might be committed with impunity."

In this regard, Professor Stephen Pepper begins with the "first rule or principle" that "the client has a presumptive right to know the law governing his or her situation."[410] He reads the "line drawn" in Rule 1.2(d) as "between directing, suggesting, or assisting in criminal or fraudulent conduct, on the one hand, and providing information about the law ('legal consequences') on the other."[411]

Indeed, Professor Renee Newman Knake argues that a lawyer's counsel to a client is protected by the Free Speech Clause of the United States Constitution and "that legal advice may be constitutionally restricted in only very limited circumstances."[412] As she writes, "[t]he role of an attorney in navigating and, when necessary, challenging the law is a critical component of American democratic government."[413] In *Milavetz, Gallop & Milavetz, P.A. v. United States*,[414] the Supreme Court considered a constitutional challenge to a statute prohibiting a lawyer (and others) from advising a client to take on more debt "in contemplation" of declaring bankruptcy.[415] The Court narrowly construed the statute to preclude only "misconduct designated to manipulate the protections of the bankruptcy system" and thus prohibiting the lawyer from "advising a debtor to incur more debt because the debtor is filing for bankruptcy, rather than for a valid purpose."[416] The Court cited to Model Rule 1.2(d) in concluding that "the inhibition of frank discussion serves no conceivable purpose" under the bankruptcy statute.[417]

With this in mind, Professors Joy and Uphoff properly interpret Model Rule 1.2(d) as "clearly allow[ing] a lawyer to give a client full and candid advice of the legal predicament that the client finds herself, so the client can make an informed choice as

---

[408] *Id.* at 770.

[409] *See supra* § 4-5.2(c). *See also* CRIMINAL JUSTICE STANDARDS: DEFENSE FUNCTION, Standard 4–3.8(b) (American Bar Ass'n, 2016) (stating that "defense counsel may discuss the legal consequences of a proposed course of conduct with a client, and may counsel or assist a client in a good faith effort to determine the validity, scope, meaning, or application of the law").

[410] Stephen L. Pepper, *Counseling at the Limits of the Law: An Exercise in the Jurisprudence and Ethics of Lawyering*, 104 YALE L.J. 1545, 1609 (1995).

[411] *Id.* at 1588.

[412] Renee Newman Knake, *Attorney Advice and the First Amendment*, 68 WASH. & LEE L. REV. 639, 641–42 (2011); *see also* Pepper, *supra*, at 1598–99 ("[A] client has a clear interest in, and perhaps even an entitlement to, knowledge of the law that governs her.").

[413] *Id.* at 642–43.

[414] 559 U.S. 229 (2010). On *Milavetz*, see generally Knake, *supra*, 68 WASH. & LEE L. REV. at 649–52.

[415] 11 U.S.C. § 526(a)(4).

[416] *Milavetz*, 559 U.S. at 243.

[417] *Id.* at 246.

to how to proceed."[418] In the sometimes tricky context of evidence, contraband and otherwise, "no lawyer should face criminal or ethics charges merely for providing clients good-faith advice designed to give them a full and honest appraisal of their options."[419] Drawing in Professor Knake's constitutional analysis, the government may prohibit "attorney advice directing a client to engage in criminal or fraudulent activity," but may *not* ban "advice *about* criminal or fraudulent activity, an important distinction."[420] At the very least, the safe harbor designed by Congress for legal representation in the federal obstruction statute was designed to protect the lawyer in offering good faith advice to a client about the legal consequences.[421]

## § 4-9.7(c) The Law on Observation and Examination of Evidence

Assuming that the documents or items involved in a case are indeed evidence that is potentially relevant to a reasonably anticipated investigation or proceeding,[422] the next set of questions concerns the ethical duties of a lawyer in observing or examining that evidence. Accepting that the real evidence may not be destroyed, which would constitute obstruction of justice, we must consider the lawyer's responsibilities when observing evidence without removing it or taking possession, after taking possession of evidence for examination, and when receiving evidence from the client or a third person, as well as the tricky problem of examining contraband evidence.

### *§ 4-9.7(c)(1) Defense Lawyer Observing Evidence Without Taking Possession*

When a lawyer takes actual possession of real evidence, even temporarily, special responsibilities attach, as discussed below.[423] By contrast, when the lawyer learns about the location of evidence through a client communication, even if followed up by passive observation, the attorney-client privilege protects against disclosure.[424] The lawyer for a client may observe evidence in its original condition, such as by verifying that an item truly exists at a particular location or by taking photographs at the scene of a crime, at least if the lawyer takes appropriate steps to avoid altering characteristics of the scene. In sum, when based on a client's description of events or circumstances, the lawyer's knowledge and attendant observations short of taking possession of real evidence are protected by the attorney-client privilege.

In the classic "Buried Bodies Case" from Lake Pleasant, New York, a person charged with murder confidentially confessed to his lawyers that he had also committed other murders and left the bodies of the victims in a wooded area, which he described to the lawyers.[425] One of the lawyers visited the scene and found skeletal remains, which he photographed. The lawyers kept the crimes, as well as the location of the bodies, secret for many months, only revealing this information when calling the client to testify to the

---

[418] Peter A. Joy & Rodney J. Uphoff, *"What Do I Do With the Porn on My Computer?": How a Lawyer Should Counsel Clients About Physical Evidence*, 54 AM. CRIM. L. REV. 751, 779 (2017).

[419] *Id.* at 789.

[420] Knake, *supra*, 68 WASH. & LEE L. REV. at 694.

[421] *See supra* § 4-9.7(b)(4) (discussing 18 U.S.C. § 1515(c)).

[422] *See supra* § 4-9.6(b).

[423] *See infra* § 4-9.7(c)(2) to (d).

[424] Wemark v. State, 602 N.W.2d 810, 816 (Iowa 1999); Clutchette v. Rushen, 770 F.2d 1469, 1473 (9th Cir. 1985).

[425] *See* CHARLES W. WOLFRAM, MODERN LEGAL ETHICS § 12.6.1 (West, 1986).

additional murders in support of an insanity defense at the client's murder trial. When one of the lawyers was indicted for a violation of a state statute requiring anyone knowing of the death of a person to report it to authorities to afford a decent burial, the trial court dismissed the charges on the ground that the lawyer's silence was required by the attorney-client privilege.[426]

While the New York appellate court affirmed the dismissal of the indictment, it expressed unease about whether the attorney-client privilege covered the situation, saying that the lawyer's protection of the client's interest ought to be balanced against "basic human standards of decency" and "due regard to the need that the legal system accord justice to the interests of society and its individual members."[427] However, the New York State Bar Association ethics committee opined that the lawyers were obliged under the ethics rules not to reveal the information because it was the result of the client's confidential communication.[428] In the ensuing forty years, the consensus among scholars and other observers has been that the state bar ethics committee reached the correct result, which is that the observation of evidence in its original location by a lawyer pursuant to a client's confidential communication falls comfortably within the privilege.

### *§ 4-9.7(c)(2) Defense Lawyer's Right to Examine Evidence*

A lawyer representing an actual or potential criminal defendant "has the same privilege as a prosecutor to possess and examine [physical evidence] for the lawful purpose of assisting in the trial of criminal cases."[429] As the Iowa Supreme Court stated in *Wemark v. State*,[430] "[i]f the defense lawyer does not take possession of the instrument of the crime, there can be no opportunity to have it examined for any evidence that may be critical to the defense."

The *Restatement of the Law Governing Lawyers* states that a lawyer properly may take possession of physical evidence of a client crime "to examine it and subject it to tests that do not alter or destroy material characteristics of the evidence."[431] Accordingly, a lawyer who is not reasonably familiar with and prepared to adhere to standards for collection and examination of evidence—including modern forensic techniques, preserving and avoiding contamination of evidence, establishing the chain of custody, etc.—should not remove evidence from its original location or conduct tests of the items.

Because taking possession of real evidence could lead to disclosure to the prosecution, even if law enforcement would not otherwise have discovered it, defense counsel should acquire real evidence only if "*they believe the client's defense genuinely requires it*."[432] Indeed, commentators advise that "a lawyer can avoid some subsequent

---

[426] People v. Belge, 372 N.Y.S.2d 798 (Cnty. Ct. 1975), *aff'd*, 376 N.Y.S.2d 771 (N.Y. App. Div. 1975), *aff'd*, 359 N.E.2d 377 (N.Y. 1976).

[427] *Belge*, 376 N.Y.S.2d at 772.

[428] N.Y. State Bar Ass'n Comm. on Prof'l Ethics, Op. 479 (1978).

[429] RESTATEMENT (THIRD) OF THE LAW GOVERNING LAWYERS § 119 cmt. b (American Law Institute, 2000).

[430] 602 N.W.2d 810, 817 (Iowa 1999).

[431] RESTATEMENT (THIRD) OF THE LAW GOVERNING LAWYERS § 119(1) (American Law Institute, 2000).

[432] Norman Lefstein, *Incriminating Physical Evidence, the Defense Attorney's Dilemma, and the Need for Rules*, 64 N.C. L. REV. 897, 931 (1986) (emphasis in original); *see also* Peter A. Joy & Rodney J. Uphoff, *"What Do I Do With the Porn on My Computer?": How a Lawyer Should Counsel Clients About Physical Evidence*, 54 AM. CRIM. L. REV. 751, 755 n.24 (2017) (same).

legal and ethical dilemmas by refusing to take possession of evidence of a client's crime."[433]

Today, however, a lawyer's right to independent examination of real evidence takes on heightened importance as the infirmities of state and county crime laboratories become increasingly manifest[434] and national efforts to heighten laboratory standards appear to be stalled.[435] A series of public scandals involving law enforcement-affiliated crime labs—from the St. Paul, Minnesota police department crime lab to the North Carolina State Bureau of Investigation crime lab—have revealed a troubling absence of standard procedures, faulty testing techniques, the failure to acknowledge when initial test results could not be confirmed, a general "pro-prosecution bias," and poorly trained staff with a "woeful ignorance of basic scientific principles."[436] A 2009 study of public forensics labs by the National Academy of Sciences reported:

> [T]he quality of forensic practice in most disciplines varies greatly because of the absence of adequate training and continuing education, rigorous mandatory certification and accreditation programs, adherence to robust performance standards, and effective oversight. These shortcomings obviously pose a continuing and serious threat to the quality and credibility of forensic science practice.[437]

Even before evidence arrives at the crime lab, police may fail to properly collect, handle, and preserve it[438]—or even fraudulently manufacture or plant evidence.[439]

For many reasons, then, defense counsel should hesitate to accept any forensic findings by law enforcement. Effective assistance of counsel for a criminal defendant, as expected under the Sixth Amendment, may mandate independent scientific testing of evidence.[440]

Indeed, if it truly is the case that a criminal defense lawyer has the same privilege to examine the evidence as does a prosecutor, then the defense lawyer should also have the right to conduct or arrange for laboratory tests of the evidence, even if such testing may affect the characteristics of the evidence. When appropriate forensic examination of real evidence will unavoidably degrade the evidence or change its characteristics, the

---

[433] Peter A. Joy & Kevin C. McMunigal, *Incriminating Evidence—Too Hot to Handle?*, CRIM. JUST., Summer 2009, at 55.

[434] *See* Rodney Uphoff, *Convicting the Innocent: Aberration or Systemic Problem?*, 2006 WIS. L. REV. 739, 782–83. On the prevalence of flawed forensic evidence in wrongful convictions, see generally BRANDON L. GARRETT, CONVICTING THE INNOCENCE: WHERE CRIMINAL PROSECUTIONS GO WRONG (Harvard U. Press, 2011).

[435] *See* Spencer S. Hsu, *Sessions Orders Justice Dept. to End Forensic Science Commission, Suspend Review Policy*, WASH. POST, Apr. 10, 2017 (reporting that the attorney general "will end a Justice Department partnership with independent scientists to raise forensic science standards and has suspended an expanded review of FBI testimony across several techniques that have come under question, saying a new strategy will be set by an in-house team of law enforcement advisers").

[436] Mark Hansen, *A String of Shoddy, Suspect and Fraudulent Results has Put Forensics Labs under the Microscope*, A.B.A. J., Sept. 2013, at 45, 46–50.

[437] NATIONAL ACADEMY OF SCIENCES, STRENGTHENING FORENSIC SCIENCE IN THE UNITED STATES: A PATH FORWARD 6 (2009).

[438] Uphoff, *supra*, 2006 WIS. L. REV. at 782 (referring to the "Myth" that "the Police Properly Collect, Handle, Preserve, and Analyze Forensic Evidence").

[439] *See* Alex Kozinski, *Criminal Law 2.0*, 44 GEO. L.J. ANN. REV. CRIM. PROC. iii, x (2015) (providing examples of cases where "the police manipulated or concealed evidence").

[440] *See* STANDARDS FOR CRIMINAL JUSTICE: DEFENSE FUNCTION, Standard 4–4.1(d) (American Bar Ass'n, 2015).

criminal defense lawyer nonetheless should be permitted to conduct those tests. No principle of law requires that a criminal defense lawyer defer to or grant priority to law enforcement-affiliated crime labs. Prosecutors should not later be heard to insist that a defense lawyer should have immediately surrendered the evidence, refrained from any testing, and abjectly deferred to state or county crime laboratories that may or may not be competent to perform the task.

In sum, contrary to the conventional wisdom held by many lawyers, law enforcement does not hold a legal monopoly on the finding and examination of evidence. While a defense lawyer may not invade a crime scene that is under the control of law enforcement, that lawyer is not prohibited from visiting the crime scene beforehand or afterward.

To be sure, the criminal defense lawyer may take a risk of being accused of improper behavior or of obstruction of justice if she visits a crime scene, examines and tests evidence, and the evidence is thereby necessarily or inadvertently altered. When law enforcement personnel improperly handle or incompetently test evidence, they rarely need fear an obstruction of justice charge. But a criminal defense attorney or investigator may well come under greater scrutiny and be extended little benefit of the doubt.

Not surprisingly, criminal defense lawyers are leery about engagement with real evidence, at least prior to examination by law enforcement. For practical reasons, including the sad possibility of overzealous reaction by prosecutors, this is understandable. But reticence is not legally compelled and, indeed, zealous advocacy for a criminal defendant may require such engagement, as uncomfortable as it may make the criminal defense lawyer.

In 2015, the American Bar Association approved revisions to Standard 4–4.7 of the *Standards for Criminal Justice* that more affirmatively recognize the criminal defense lawyer's right to conduct independent forensic examination and testing of physical evidence.[441] Under Standard 4–4.7, a lawyer who "determines that effective representation of the client requires that such physical evidence be submitted for forensic examination and testing" would be permitted to go forward. The lawyer would be expected to follow procedures for handling the evidence that "ensure its integrity" and to "avoid, whenever possible, consumption of the item" so that the evidence could later be tested or examined by the prosecution.[442] If a test of the evidence would "entirely consume the item or destroy the prosecution's opportunity and ability to re-test the item," then a criminal defense lawyer would be obliged to notify the prosecution to allow an opportunity to object and ask for judicial relief.[443]

If the forensic testing by the criminal defense team does change or alter material characteristics of real evidence, then the defense lawyer might be required to share the laboratory results or at least confirm that testing was done, at the appropriate time.[444] However, notification of forensic testing should be expected only when law enforcement appropriately and independently obtains the evidence. If law enforcement would not find

---

[441] *Id.*, Standard 4–4.7(g).

[442] *Id.*, Standard 4–4.7(g)(i) to (ii).

[443] *Id.*, Standard 4–4.7(g)(iv) to (v).

[444] *Cf.* Rodney J. Uphoff, *The Physical Evidence Dilemma: Does ABA Standard 4–4.6 Offer Appropriate Guidance?*, 62 HASTINGS L.J. 1177, 1211 (2011) ("If testing will use up the entire sample, however, and then [the lawyer] decides to test anyway, she is obligated to reveal the results to the authorities even if doing so might prove incriminating.").

the evidence for reasons other than the lawyer's interference (such as a failure to search the original location), then law enforcement should not receive the windfall of defense counsel's diligent work in conducting a test of the evidence—unless, of course, the defense intends to use the evidence as exculpation, in which case early disclosure is probably wise.

Under the 2015 revision of the ABA Standard, a criminal defense lawyer who planned to conduct testing that would consume or destroy the evidence altogether would be required to give advance notice to the prosecution. Given that consumptive testing would deprive the prosecution of any opportunity to conduct its own tests, such a notice requirement tends to uphold fair and equal treatment in the adversarial process. Under similar circumstances, law enforcement presumably has a similar duty of advance notice to defense counsel when forensic testing would consume or destroy physical evidence. Circumstances are not always parallel, of course; law enforcement may need to conduct testing before a suspect has been identified or when exigencies of public safety are present.

When a criminal defense lawyer's examination or testing of evidence has not consumed the item, but some characteristics necessarily have been altered at least to the extent of indicating the evidence was handled, the defense lawyer is under no such duty to provide advance notification. Indeed, the criminal defense lawyer should not be obliged to confirm the existence of the real evidence or that non-consumptive testing was performed unless and until law enforcement has independently discovered the evidence in its original location or from the original possessor.

### *§ 4-9.7(c)(3) Disposition of Evidence by the Defense Lawyer After Examination*

After a lawyer has taken possession of real evidence of a potential crime for examination or testing, the crucial remaining question regards proper disposition of that evidence.[445] And on this point, the authorities are in conflict.

Comment 2 to Rule 3.4 of the Model Rules of Professional Conduct is equivocal, saying that the "law *may* require the lawyer to turn the evidence over to the police or other prosecuting authority, *depending on the circumstances*" (emphasis added). A few state court decisions suggest the lawyer must turn over real evidence to the government after testing,[446] but these courts arrive at that conclusion with little analysis and without careful evaluation of defense counsels' professional responsibilities and defendants' constitutional rights.[447] Other authority allows an attorney to return evidence to the source.[448]

In the course of preparing the *Restatement of the Law Governing Lawyers*, the drafters at the American Law Institute began with one position, but ended with another. A tentative draft of the *Restatement* would have allowed the lawyer "to return the evidence to the site from which it was taken, when that can be accomplished without

---

[445] For more on the lawyer's retention of real evidence, see *infra* § 4-9.7(f).

[446] *See* Peter A. Joy & Kevin C. McMunigal, *Incriminating Evidence—Too Hot to Handle?*, CRIM. JUST., Summer 2009, at 45.

[447] Norman Lefstein, *Incriminating Physical Evidence, the Defense Attorney's Dilemma, and the Need for Rules*, 64 N.C. L. REV. 897, 918 (1986).

[448] Hitch v. Superior Court, 708 P.2d 72, 78 (Ariz. 1985) (en banc).

destroying or altering material characteristics of the evidence."[449] However, in the final version of the *Restatement of the Law Governing Lawyers*, the provision allowing return of the item to the site from which it was taken was deleted. The *Restatement* instead states that, after possession, "the lawyer must notify prosecuting authorities of the lawyer's possession of the evidence or turn the evidence over to them."[450]

Notwithstanding this change in language to this *Restatement* section, the accompanying comment notes that some decisions "allude[ ] to an additional option—returning the evidence to the site from which it was taken, when that can be accomplished without destroying or altering material characteristics of the evidence," although the comment suggests that approach "will often be impossible."[451] Professors Ronald Rotunda and John Dzienkowski similarly argue that—

> [i]n light of advances in forensic science, it is hard to imagine how a lawyer could return physical evidence to the scene of the crime without leaving the lawyer's DNA on the evidence or without feeling the need to remove fingerprints and other indicia of the lawyer's possession of the evidence. Such conduct would constitute tampering or altering the evidence.[452]

Notwithstanding these understandably cautious views, the option of returning the evidence to its source after examination ought to be presumptively and generally available.[453] Law enforcement would not be disadvantaged and would have every fair and reasonable opportunity to discover the evidence at its original location. When the evidence is promptly returned to its original place, even after the lawyer has examined it, the situation is restored to what it would have been had the lawyer merely been informed of the location (which of course imposes no duty of disclosure).[454] While a lawyer may have "no right to make the police officer's job more difficult with respect to the discovery of physical evidence,"[455] the lawyer also has no duty to make the police officer's job any easier. As Professor Stephen Gillers writes, "[t]he [ethical] rules don't transform the lawyer for a private client into an arm of the state."[456]

Moreover, the defendant's constitutional right against self-incrimination is not adequately preserved if a lawyer who examines evidence must thereafter deliver it up to law enforcement.[457] Even if the real evidence is not a document that amounts to a

---

[449] RESTATEMENT OF THE LAW GOVERNING LAWYERS § 179 (American Law Institute, Tentative Draft No. 8, 1997).

[450] RESTATEMENT (THIRD) OF THE LAW GOVERNING LAWYERS § 119(2) (American Law Institute, 2000); *see also* 1 GEOFFREY C. HAZARD, JR., W. WILLIAM HODES & PETER R. JARVIS, THE LAW OF LAWYERING § 10.46 (Aspen, 4th ed., 2016) (arguing that, while mandatory disclosure "run[s] counter to the tradition of client loyalty, any other rule would inevitably degenerate into a race between the police and a suspect's lawyer to be first to take possession of evidence").

[451] RESTATEMENT (THIRD) OF THE LAW GOVERNING LAWYERS § 119 cmt. c (American Law Institute, 2000).

[452] RONALD D. ROTUNDA & JOHN S. DZIENKOWSKI, PROFESSIONAL RESPONSIBILITY: A STUDENT'S GUIDE § 3.4–2(a) footnote (American Bar Ass'n, 2013/2014).

[453] Gregory C. Sisk, *The Legal Ethics of Real Evidence: Of Child Porn on the Choirmaster's Computer and Bloody Knives Under the Stairs*, 89 WASH. L. REV. 819, 857–59 (2014).

[454] Lefstein, *supra*, 64 N.C. L. REV. at 929.

[455] 2 GEOFFREY C. HAZARD, JR., W. WILLIAM HODES & PETER R. JARVIS, THE LAW OF LAWYERING § 33.06 (Aspen, 4th ed., 2016).

[456] STEPHEN GILLERS, ESSENTIALS: REGULATION OF THE LEGAL PROFESSION 243 (Aspen, 2009).

[457] Stephen Gillers, *Guns, Fruits, Drugs, and Documents: A Criminal Defense Lawyer's Responsibility for Real Evidence*, 63 STAN. L. REV. 813, 824–29 (2011).

testimonial statement, and thus is not itself protected by the Fifth Amendment right against self-incrimination, the Supreme Court in *Fisher v. United States*[458] observed that the act of producing evidence has "communicative aspects of its own, wholly aside from" the nature of the paper or item.[459] Thus, as the Court held in *United States v. Hubbell*,[460] the Fifth Amendment is implicated when the act of production "could provide a prosecutor with a 'lead to incriminating evidence,' or 'a link in the chain of evidence needed to prosecute.' "[461] Indeed, two members of the *Hubbell* Court found historical evidence "that the Fifth Amendment privilege protects against the compelled production not just of incriminating testimony, but of any incriminating evidence."[462]

To compel an attorney who has examined evidence, which the attorney uncovered through the client's confidential communication, to then pass it on to law enforcement is constitutionally dubious. In that scenario, the accused has been degraded into "the deluded instrument of his own conviction."[463] As Professors Monroe Freedman and Abbe Smith emphasize, a criminal "defendant's *constitutional* privilege against self-incrimination [is] safeguarded by his *constitutional* right to counsel."[464] At the very least, as Professor Kevin Reitz rightly insists, "[t]here should be no constitutional tariff upon the act of obtaining counsel."[465]

To be sure, in many or most cases that involve real evidence other than documents, it may be impossible to return physical evidence to the original location without some alteration of material characteristics at the site, if not in the evidence itself. Under the *Restatement*, the lawyer who has taken possession of physical evidence of a client crime for examination would be obliged to notify the prosecuting authorities that the lawyer has the evidence or to directly turn the evidence over to those authorities. But the conclusion reached by the *Restatement* does not logically follow. As Gillers writes, the "breadth" of the *Restatement* mandate to deliver evidence to law enforcement is "astonishing."[466]

To begin with, if the forensic properties of the site or the evidence itself have been altered by the criminal defense lawyer exercising the right to examine the evidence, then that change in characteristics will have occurred whether the lawyer returns the evidence to its original location or instead delivers it to law enforcement. The question is not whether there are changes caused by the lawyer's appropriate examination but what should be done to apprise law enforcement of such changes. Thus, the real issue is whether, when, and how law enforcement should be notified of those changes in the

---

[458] 425 U.S. 391 (1976).

[459] *Id.* at 410. On the privilege against self-incrimination as preventing a suspect from being compelled to produce real evidence where production would authenticate evidence, admit that it exists, or show the suspect had control over it, see generally Kevin R. Reitz, *Clients, Lawyers and the Fifth Amendment: The Need for a Projected Privilege*, 41 DUKE L.J. 572, 642–45 (1991).

[460] 530 U.S. 27 (2000).

[461] *Id.* at 41–42 (citation omitted).

[462] *Id.* at 49 (Thomas, J., concurring).

[463] Culombe v. Connecticut, 367 U.S. 568, 581 (1961) (quoting 2 WILLIAM HAWKINS, PLEAS OF THE CROWN 595 (8th ed. 1824)).

[464] MONROE FREEDMAN & ABBE SMITH, UNDERSTANDING LAWYERS' ETHICS § 6.16 (LexisNexis 4th ed. 2010).

[465] Reitz, *supra*, 41 DUKE L.J. at 650.

[466] Gillers, *supra*, 63 STAN. L. REV. at 848.

evidence so that law enforcement is not disadvantaged by the lawyer's otherwise proper examination.

Ordering that the lawyer deliver real evidence to law enforcement after examination ensures both that law enforcement will gain access to the evidence, which may or may not otherwise have occurred, and that law enforcement will know that the lawyer had been an intervening player, which thus explains any changes in forensic characteristics. The government may be entitled to the latter, but not the former. If there is a way to fairly ensure that lawyer-caused changes in forensic characteristics come to the attention of law enforcement if and when it finds evidence, then there is no reason to give law enforcement the windfall of delivery of evidence that it would not have found on its own. Again, given that the lawyer's knowledge about the real evidence and its location frequently comes from a confidential communication to the lawyer, simply delivering the evidence to law enforcement in every case punishes the client for the confidential communication and discourages defense counsel from exercising the important right to examine evidence. In sum, imposing a general and unqualified duty of delivery of examined evidence to the government contravenes basic principles of professional responsibility as well as a criminal defendant's constitutional right against self-incrimination and constitutional entitlement to effective assistance of counsel.

As discussed below,[467] Professor Gillers proposes a new registry system that would allow lawyers to retain evidence while giving law enforcement access to that evidence if an investigation later is directed against the client and law enforcement is unaware of the lawyer's retention. In any event, the lawyer who examines evidence should be permitted to return it to the original location, notwithstanding forensic consequences (at least as long as the lawyer acted with reasonable care in compliance with expectations of forensic science).

In most instances, the lawyer could simply attach a note or label to the real evidence, perhaps encased in clear plastic like the common desktop paper-weight. The plastic casing would serve to hold down the note, so it does not blow away, and to protect it from the elements. The note would inform law enforcement that, if the evidence should be discovered, that the lawyer conducted forensic testing and that the examination necessarily made changes in the site or evidence. And if the original location of the evidence is the client's home or place of business, the lawyer will be informed if a search is conducted, at which point the lawyer might be obliged to explain any alteration. In neither case has the lawyer caused an obstruction of the investigation, much less had the requisite specific intent to do so. Instead, the lawyer would be prepared to offer appropriate assistance to the investigation through the sharing of information if and when that investigation successfully uncovers the evidence.

In any event, the option to replace evidence plainly is appropriate when the item does not contain any material forensic characteristics that could be altered. In particular, real evidence includes not only physical objects, but also documents and computer data. Documents and electronic data ordinarily may be returned to the original location, such as a client's office files or computer archives, without affecting any evidentiary characteristics (and assuming the client has been appropriately counseled about the law against improper concealment or destruction of evidence).

---

[467] *See infra* § 4-9.7(f).

Whatever might be the correct disposition of evidence under other circumstances, when even temporary possession of the evidence by the lawyer has operated to deny lawful discovery of the evidence by law enforcement, the lawyer then probably should be obliged to disclose the evidence to law enforcement. For example, if the lawyer was holding the evidence at the very point in time that a search warrant was executed at the client's home or that police searched the site where the item was originally located, then returning the item to its original location afterward is effectively a form of concealment.

If, contrary to the above analysis, a jurisdiction does insist that disclosure of real evidence to law enforcement must follow any possession of it, then the lawyer ordinarily would have to avoid any examination beyond the most passive observation. As Professor Rodney Uphoff predicts, "[z]ealous defense lawyers will be extremely reluctant to take possession of evidentiary items at all, if doing so always requires disclosure to the authorities."[468] And, as discussed previously, the lawyer thereby may be unable to effectively prepare for the defense and must rely on dubious law enforcement-controlled forensics testing.

### *§ 4-9.7(c)(4) Preserving Confidentiality if Defense Lawyer Deliver Evidence to Law Enforcement*

If the lawyer must deliver real evidence to the authorities, the ABA's *Standards for Criminal Justice* as revised in 2015 recommend that "the prosecution should be prohibited from presenting testimony or argument identifying or implying the defense as the source of the evidence," except where the defense objects to introduction of such evidence for lack of foundation.[469] When possible, and when it matters, the lawyer should arrange for anonymous delivery through another person or perhaps the local bar association,[470] an ingenious option put into practice by the District of Columbia Office of Bar Counsel.[471] But if the lawyer has removed the item from a location that itself has evidentiary value, then failing to disclose as much could be regarded as concealing evidence (which is all the more reason to permit the item to be returned to the original location[472]).

If anonymous delivery is not available or practically effective, the prosecution and the lawyer should make appropriate arrangements for introduction and authentication of the evidence in a manner that preserves client confidences as much as possible. As suggested in the comment to the *Restatement of the Law Governing Lawyers*, to avoid prejudice to the client and to preserve attorney-client confidentiality, the material or items should be admitted into evidence at the trial "without improperly revealing the source of the evidence to the finder of fact."[473]

Still, the value of such arrangements for the client should not be overstated, nor should the duty to deliver to law enforcement be casually accepted on the assumption

---

[468] Rodney J. Uphoff, *The Physical Evidence Dilemma: Does ABA Standard 4–4.6 Offer Appropriate Guidance?*, 62 HASTINGS L.J. 1177, 1213 (2011).

[469] STANDARDS FOR CRIMINAL JUSTICE: DEFENSE FUNCTION, Standard 4–4.7(j)(ii) (American Bar Ass'n, 2015).

[470] Rodney J. Uphoff, *The Physical Evidence Dilemma: Does ABA Standard 4–4.6 Offer Appropriate Guidance?*, 62 HASTINGS L.J. 1199, 1221 (2011).

[471] *See* D.C. RULES OF PROF'L CONDUCT R. 3.4, cmt. 5.

[472] *See supra* § 4-9.7(c)(3).

[473] RESTATEMENT (THIRD) OF THE LAW GOVERNING LAWYERS § 119, cmt. c (American Law Institute, 2000).

such protections in introduction of evidence will mitigate harm to the defendant. As Professor Stephen Gillers notes, withholding the identity of the source of the item "may be small comfort to the client if the thing itself must be turned over and can implicate the client in a crime (e.g., if it's the victim's wallet containing the client's fingerprints)."[474]

In the classic California case of *People v. Meredith*,[475] based on a confidential communication by the client with the lawyer, an agent of the lawyer retrieved a wallet, which had belonged to the victim of a robbery and homicide, from a burn barrel located near the defendant's home. The lawyer examined the contents of the wallet to confirm it was the victim's. He then turned it over to the police. By removing it from the original location, the lawyer of course had altered the evidence; it was as if the wallet "bore a tag bearing the words 'located in the trash can by [defendant's] residence,' " and the lawyer, "by taking the wallet, destroyed this tag."[476] Thus, under those circumstances, the prosecutor was entitled to bring to the jury's attention that the wallet had been found in that particular location. In an important footnote, the California Supreme Court advised:

> [T]he defendant may be willing to enter a stipulation which will simply inform the jury as to the relevant location or condition of the evidence in question. When such a stipulation is proffered, the prosecution should not be permitted to reject the stipulation in the hope that by requiring defense counsel personally to testify to such facts, the jury might infer that counsel learned those facts from defendant.[477]

### § 4-9.7(d) Evidence Delivered to Defense Lawyer

Even when a lawyer has not affirmatively taken possession of real evidence of a possible crime to examine it, such evidence nonetheless may find its way into the lawyer's hands by being delivered to the lawyer by a client or another person.

A lawyer should not counsel another person, whether a client or otherwise, to remove evidence from its original location if to do so would effectively destroy or alter the evidence, including forensic characteristics that a trained criminal investigator could discover. Thus, for example, the lawyer should not direct a client to return to the scene of a crime and carry away objects that were present there, even for the purported purpose of examining the object in the lawyer's office, because such removal probably could not be accomplished without altering material characteristics of the scene or the evidentiary object. If the lawyer wishes to exercise the right to examine the evidence,[478] the lawyer herself should make proper arrangements for doing so.

By contrast, if the evidence is already in the client's immediate possession or is located in a place where it may be retrieved without changing evidentiary qualities (such as the client's home or office), the lawyer may ask to see it or ask the client to retrieve it. For example, the lawyer may ask the client to take documents out of the client's files

---

[474] STEPHEN GILLERS, ESSENTIALS: REGULATION OF THE LEGAL PROFESSION 249 (Aspen, 2009).

[475] 631 P.2d 46 (1981).

[476] *Id.* at 53.

[477] *Id.* at 54 n.8; *see also* RESTATEMENT (THIRD) OF THE LAW GOVERNING LAWYERS § 119 cmt. c (American Law Institute, 2000) ("The parties may also agree that the tribunal may instruct the jury, without revealing the lawyer's involvement, that an appropriate chain of possession links the evidence to the place where it was located before coming into the lawyer's possession.").

[478] *See supra* § 4-9.7(c)(2).

for delivery to the lawyer for examination and to make copies. If the client did remove evidence from the scene (perhaps prior to receiving a lawyer's contrary advice) or the evidence has always been in the client's possession, and the client then delivers it to the lawyer, the lawyer may accept temporary possession of that evidence for examination purposes as discussed above.[479] Disposition of the evidence afterward is a more complex question, as addressed above and below.[480]

When the lawyer has received evidence from a client or other person, the 1993 version of the American Bar Association's *Standards for Criminal Justice* stated that the lawyer may be permitted to return the evidence to the person who delivered it, while counseling that person regarding the illegality of concealing, altering, or destroying that evidence after taking it back.[481] The 2015 *Standards* say that defense counsel may return evidence if he "reasonably determines" there is no legal obligation to do otherwise and then the lawyer must act "consistently with ethical and other rules and law."[482] The lawyer must seriously impress upon the client or other person who brought the evidence to the lawyer that hiding the item, destroying it, or changing its evidentiary characteristics might constitute obstruction of justice, assuming that the item has potential evidentiary value to a reasonably anticipated criminal proceeding. In explaining to a client the legal consequences of retaining or destroying the evidence, the lawyer may also offer "any good-faith arguments for contesting the validity or applicability of the law to the client's situation."[483]

However, leading authorities place important limitations on the lawyer's ability to return evidence to the person who delivered it:

***Rightful Owner:*** The evidence can be returned to the person who delivered it only if that person also is the rightful owner or possessor.[484] If a client or other person delivers to the lawyer material that not only is evidence of a crime but which has been taken from another, such as stolen property, the lawyer is obliged to see that these materials are either presented to law enforcement or are restored to the rightful owner from whom they were wrongfully taken (which can be accomplished anonymously).[485]

Not only is retention of stolen goods a crime, but it could be criminal misconduct for "the lawyer, once having taken possession of the goods, to return them to the thief."[486] Professors Geoffrey Hazard and William Hodes and attorney Peter Jarvis state that the lawyer has "no right to delay return of the fruits of crime to their rightful owners."[487]

---

[479] *See supra* § 4-9.7(c)(2).

[480] *See supra* § 4-9.7(c)(3) and *infra* § 4-9.7(f).

[481] STANDARDS FOR CRIMINAL JUSTICE: DEFENSE FUNCTION, Standard, Standard 4–4.6(b) (American Bar Ass'n, 1993).

[482] STANDARDS FOR CRIMINAL JUSTICE: DEFENSE FUNCTION, Standard 4–4.7(i) (American Bar Ass'n, 2015).

[483] Peter A. Joy & Kevin C. McMunigal, *Incriminating Evidence—Too Hot to Handle?*, CRIM. JUST., Summer 2009, at 44.

[484] *See* D.C. RULES OF PROF'L CONDUCT R. 3.4(a) (providing that when a lawyer receives physical evidence that belongs to someone other than the client, "the lawyer shall make a good faith effort to preserve it and to return it to the owner").

[485] STANDARDS FOR CRIMINAL JUSTICE: DEFENSE FUNCTION, Standard, Standard 4–4.6 cmt. (American Bar Ass'n, 1993).

[486] RESTATEMENT (THIRD) OF THE LAW GOVERNING LAWYERS § 45 cmt. f (American Law Institute, 2000).

[487] 2 GEOFFREY C. HAZARD, JR., W. WILLIAM HODES & PETER R. JARVIS, THE LAW OF LAWYERING § 33.06 (Aspen, 4th ed., 2016).

***Fear of Destruction:*** Even when the person who delivered the evidence to the lawyer is the rightful possessor, the 1993 *ABA Standards* advised that the lawyer may not return the evidence to that person if the lawyer reasonably fears that evidence will be unlawfully destroyed or altered.[488] If the lawyer has reason to believe that the client or other person will not treat the evidence with respect, then 1993 Standard 4–4.6(c) stated that the lawyer may not return it to the source heedless to its likely destruction or concealment. In most cases involving an ordinary street crime then, the lawyer would not act reasonably in returning evidence plainly indicating illegal conduct, such as the instrumentalities of the crime or clothing stained with blood, to the apparent perpetrator, who almost certainly would conceal or destroy it.

But the assumption that the lawyer's fear of possible destruction by another, even over the lawyer's contrary advice, imposes a duty to retain the evidence should be questioned. The lawyer had no public-regarding duty to accept the evidence in the first instance, even for temporary examination. And the lawyer "does not have a corresponding duty to preserve incriminating evidence not in her possession or control."[489] Since returning it to the person who delivered it to the lawyer initially would simply restore the status quo that existed before taking temporary possession, one should wonder why the lawyer would be obliged to retain it even though she reasonably fears that it may be destroyed.[490] To be sure, the lawyer should counsel the person to whom it is returned about the legal duty to preserve and not conceal evidence (under the law of obstruction of justice). But the lawyer's temporary examination of the evidence should not so easily be converted into a duty to take permanent possession of it, even to prevent its destruction or concealment by someone else—especially if the (mistaken) conventional assumption prevails that a lawyer taking possession of evidence must then deliver it to law enforcement.

In any event, when a business client has shared documents with the lawyer that are arguably relevant to an alleged financial crime, returning the documents with the instruction that they should be placed back in the client's files is appropriate, at least provided the lawyer has a reasonable basis for believing the client will comply. In addition, the lawyer could retain copies of those documents, with the client's understanding that, should the client conceal or destroy them, the lawyer *might* be obliged to provide those copies to law enforcement. With respect to any real evidence and for the purpose of memorializing the matter in the event of later inquiry, the 1993 ABA *Standards for Criminal Justice* directed the lawyer to prepare a written record for the lawyer's files of the item and its return to the source.[491]

***Risk of Harm:*** Under the 1993 ABA *Standards for Criminal Justice*, the lawyer should not return an item to the client or other person if the lawyer "reasonably fears

---

[488] STANDARDS FOR CRIMINAL JUSTICE: DEFENSE FUNCTION, Standard, Standard 4–4.6(c) (American Bar Ass'n, 1993); *see also* Hitch v. Superior Court, 708 P.2d 72, 78 (Ariz. 1985) (en banc) ("[I]f the attorney reasonably believes that evidence will not be destroyed, he may return it to the source, explaining the laws on concealment and destruction."). The 2015 *Standards* allow counsel to take possession of evidence when counsel fears that the evidence would be destroyed, but does not appear to impose such a requirement. STANDARDS FOR CRIMINAL JUSTICE: DEFENSE FUNCTION, Standard 4–4.7(d)(i) (American Bar Ass'n, 2015).

[489] Rodney J. Uphoff, *The Physical Evidence Dilemma: Does ABA Standard 4–4.6 Offer Appropriate Guidance?*, 62 HASTINGS L.J. 1199, 1203 (2011).

[490] Stephen Gillers, *Guns, Fruits, Drugs, and Documents: A Criminal Defense Lawyer's Responsibility for Real Evidence*, 63 STAN. L. REV. 813, 847 (2011).

[491] STANDARDS FOR CRIMINAL JUSTICE: DEFENSE FUNCTION, Standard, Standard 4–4.6(b) (American Bar Ass'n, 1993).

that return of the item to the source will result in physical harm to anyone."[492] Thus, for example, the lawyer understandably will be reluctant to return a weapon to a client if the lawyer has a reasonable basis to believe that the weapon has been or may be used in a crime. Toxic substances, even if legal to possess, likewise ought not be left in the hands of a person without appropriate training and equipment to handle them safely.

***Contraband:*** For obvious reasons and as discussed below,[493] the lawyer ordinarily may not simply return contraband items to a client for continued possession, because the client's restored possession of the item may be unlawful.

If the lawyer must turn over real evidence to law enforcement when it cannot be returned to the person who delivered it, then the lawyer generally should decline to accept such evidence in the first instance. By declining to accept evidence, the lawyer takes on no responsibility for its preservation or disposition,[494] and thus no conceivable duty to act against the client's interests by handing the evidence over to law enforcement. To be sure, the lawyer ought to warn the continuing possessor about the consequences of retaining or destroying it and the legal significance of evidence.

Whenever the lawyer is unable to return items to the source or to the rightful owner and is obliged to deliver the item to law enforcement, the lawyer ought to take steps to protect the client's confidentiality by withholding information about the source of the evidence.[495] As Professor Charles Wolfram observes, while courts frequently have obliged lawyers to turn over evidence to law enforcement, "courts have drawn the line at the turn-over obligation . . . and have generally protected the lawyer's information about the source of the incriminating evidence if that source is the lawyer's client."[496] As the Washington Supreme Court stated in *State v. Olwell*,[497] an early decision on this subject, "the state, when attempting to introduce such evidence at the trial, should take extreme precautions to make certain that the source of the evidence is not disclosed in the presence of the jury and prejudicial error is not committed."

### § 4-9.7(e) The Tricky Problem of Contraband

Both the American Bar Association (in the *Standards for Criminal Justice*) and the American Law Institute (in comments to the pertinent section of the *Restatement of the Law Governing Lawyers*) take the position that a lawyer may take temporary possession of contraband as part of his professional duties in representing a client. The *Standards for Criminal Justice* generally permit a lawyer to take possession of an item of physical evidence for, among others reasons, "when defense counsel reasonably believes that examining or testing such evidence is necessary for effective representation of the client."[498] While the lawyer then has a duty to either destroy the item or notify law enforcement when the item is contraband,[499] the initial reception of it for examination falls under the general permissive rule. The *Restatement* comment states that as long as

---

[492] *Id.*

[493] *See infra* § 4-9.7(e).

[494] Gillers, *supra*, STAN. L. REV. at 855–56.

[495] *See supra* § 4-9.7(c)(3).

[496] CHARLES W. WOLFRAM, MODERN LEGAL ETHICS § 12.3.5 (West, 1986).

[497] 394 P.2d 681, 685 (1964).

[498] STANDARDS FOR CRIMINAL JUSTICE: DEFENSE FUNCTION, Standard 4–4.7(d)(v) (American Bar Ass'n, 2015).

[499] *See id.*, Standard 4–4.7(d)(iv), (i), (j)(ii).

the lawyer's possession of materials is for the purposes of examining or testing physical evidence of a possible client crime, "criminal laws that generally prohibit possession of contraband or other evidence of crimes are inapplicable to the lawyer."[500]

Provided the lawyer holds it for a short duration and only to confirm its nature, this is a sensible approach. Indeed, with respect to most items, that the item truly is contraband would not be certain until after some objective examination, even if it appears from a first-glance to be an item the possession of which is prohibited. Thus, what appears to be cocaine could be an innocuous white powder; what appears to be child pornography could be depictions of a young-looking adult.

The more difficult question is what to do with the contraband after examination. The conventional wisdom is that when "an object is contraband . . . the obligation to turn it over to law enforcement is self-executing, and no prosecution motion or court order is required."[501] But the *ABA Standards for Criminal Justice* are more nuanced, saying that defense counsel may take possession "when such evidence is contraband and counsel may lawfully take possession of it in order to destroy it."[502] Moreover, the *Standards* encourage courts and legislatures to adopt procedures so that "[w]hen defense counsel reasonably believes that contraband does not relate to a pending criminal investigation or prosecution, counsel may take possession of the contraband and destroy it."[503]

In a professional disciplinary proceeding, the Montana Supreme Court approved a lawyer's taking possession of contraband for purposes of examination. In the case of *In re Olson*,[504] a lawyer for a criminal defendant accused of possession of child pornography was contacted by the client's mother who suggested there were items in the client's apartment that the lawyer should view. The lawyer went the apartment and took possession of photographs, which depicted naked young children in erotic poses. Although the lawyer testified that he did not believe the photographs constituted child pornography, the court later stated that it was "difficult . . . to comprehend how anyone would not 'know' that these are examples of child pornography."[505] Nonetheless, even assuming the photographs were child pornography, the court concluded that the lawyer had engaged in no misconduct, recognizing that he "had a duty to conduct an investigation on behalf of his client and prepare a defense."[506]

With the disciplinary commission in *Olson* characterizing the lawyer's conduct as "a 'text book example' of the type of functioning expected of defense counsel,"[507] it is important to outline the careful steps this conscientious professional took in handling this contraband.[508] First, from the apartment scene, the items were tagged and sealed

---

[500] RESTATEMENT (THIRD) OF THE LAW GOVERNING LAWYERS § 119 cmt. b (American Law Institute, 2000).

[501] Evan A. Jenness, *Ethics and Advocacy Dilemmas—Possessing Evidence of a Client's Crime*, CHAMPION, Dec. 2010, at 18.

[502] STANDARDS FOR CRIMINAL JUSTICE: DEFENSE FUNCTION, Standard 4–4.7(d)(iv) (American Bar Ass'n, 2015).

[503] *Id.*, Standard 4–4.7(j)(ii).

[504] 222 P.3d 632, 634 (Mont. 2009). For a thoughtful and complete discussion of *Olson*, see Uphoff, *supra*, 62 HASTINGS L.J. at 1204–09.

[505] *Olson*, 222 P.3d at 638.

[506] *Id.*

[507] *Id.* at 637.

[508] Uphoff, *supra*, 62 HASTINGS L.J. at 1204 (describing *Olson* as an example of "the conscientious criminal defense lawyer when dealing with contraband").

and then were securely locked in the lawyer's office.[509] Second, the lawyer obtained an *ex parte* protective order from a state judge authorizing him to retain possession of the items, in the event someone might consider them to be contraband.[510]

While *Olson* stands as solid precedent for the proposition that a lawyer may take temporary possession of contraband evidence to examine it as part of a criminal defense investigation, the decision is unclear about what should happen afterward. In *Olson*, the lawyer retained the evidence in his office (sealed and under lock) until a replacement lawyer later took over the case and delivered the photographs to the prosecution.[511] The dissent insisted that the evidence should have been made available to the prosecutor and that the lawyer had wrongly concealed it.[512] The majority sidesteps the question of when, if ever, a lawyer should disclose the evidence. The court stated that the lawyer did not, "at that point in the proceedings" have a duty to turn over the information and concluded there was "no evidence in this record of [the lawyer's] intent to tamper with or fabricate physical evidence."[513]

With respect to the proper disposition of the evidence after examination, the circumstances presented in the *Olson* case may be unusual. The evidence could not be returned to the apartment, not only because that might be restoring someone to wrongful possession of contraband, but because the client apparently remained in jail and the landlord was evicting her from the apartment.[514] The police had already searched and released the apartment, without taking the subject photographs.[515] And during the successful federal prosecution of the client, the photographs were never used, as most of those photographs had already been found elsewhere and were simply unnecessary to prosecute and convict.[516] In sum, as Professor Rodney Uphoff concludes in his thoughtful dissection of the *Olson* case, "the authorities already had full access to this evidence and, for whatever reason, decided not to take possession of the items."[517] Thus, *Olson* cannot be cited in general support for a lawyer taking permanent possession of evidence, contraband or not, at least without steps to ensure that law enforcement could find the evidence through an ordinary investigation.

When a lawyer does conclude that contraband must be delivered to law enforcement, the lawyer should act carefully and with forethought. To avoid transporting such material with the possibility that it might be lost or that the lawyer would be stopped while holding it, the lawyer probably should not attempt a direct delivery to law enforcement and should instead notify authorities to come to the lawyer's office to secure the contraband evidence.

---

[509] *Olson*, 222 P.3d at 638.

[510] *Id.* at 635.

[511] *Id.* at 635–36.

[512] *Id.* at 640 (Nelson, J., dissenting).

[513] *Id.* at 638.

[514] *Id.* at 634.

[515] *Id.*

[516] *Id.* at 636.

[517] Uphoff, *supra*, 62 HASTINGS L.J. at 1207.

## § 4-9.7(f) Defense Lawyer's Retention of Evidence with Contingent Notice to Law Enforcement

### *§ 4-9.7(f)(1) The Mistaken Notion That a Lawyer Has a General Duty to Deliver Evidence to Law Enforcement*

The unexamined assumption has been that a lawyer may not retain possession of evidence of a crime beyond the time reasonably necessary to examine and test it. As this presumption is often expressed, the lawyer should not become "a depository for criminal evidence."[518] Moreover, as discussed previously,[519] the prevailing but largely unexamined precedent holds that the lawyer must turn over real evidence to the prosecution, even if received directly from a client.[520]

Professor Stephen Gillers, writing in an essential article on this subject, submits that on this question, "the courts have it wrong."[521] The "nearly unanimous belief" that a lawyer who takes possession of real evidence either for examination or because it was delivered by someone (and return was not proper or possible) must thereafter deliver it directly to law enforcement is simply "wrong."[522]

*First*, the assumption that law enforcement is entitled to receipt of evidence that it would not otherwise have discovered on its own is impossible to square with zealous advocacy by a defense lawyer as a professional responsibility, protection of the confidentiality of client communications, the client's constitutional right against self-incrimination, and the guarantee to defendants of effective assistance of counsel.[523] To be sure, the real evidence itself—that is, the object—is not protected by privilege. But the client's description of where the evidence is located certainly is privileged,[524] as is the client's communicative act of delivering evidence to his lawyer and any forced act of production by the lawyer to law enforcement.[525]

---

[518] State v. Olwell, 64 Wash.2d 828, 833, 394 P.2d 681, 684 (1964).

[519] *See supra* § 4-9.7(c)(3).

[520] *See* Morrell v. State, 575 P.2d 1200, 1210–11 (Alaska 1978). *But see* D.C. RULES OF PROF'L CONDUCT R. 3.4 cmt. 7 (stating that when the lawyer has received physical evidence for examination or testing, the lawyer may return the property to the client, unless it would be contraband or belongs to someone else). For a powerful critique of the assumption that a criminal defense lawyer must deliver evidence to the prosecution, as stated in decisions such as *Olwell* and *Morrell*, see Kevin R. Reitz, *Clients, Lawyers and the Fifth Amendment: The Need for a Projected Privilege*, 41 DUKE L.J. 572, 584–613 (1991).

[521] Stephen Gillers, *Guns, Fruits, Drugs, and Documents: A Criminal Defense Lawyer's Responsibility for Real Evidence*, 63 STAN. L. REV. 813, 846 (2011).

[522] *Id.*; *see also* Regina v. Murray, 2000 O.J. No. 2182, 48 O.R. (3d 544), ¶ 120 (Ontario Superior Ct. of Justice, 2000) (Canadian judge observes in an obstruction of justice case against a criminal defense solicitor who concealed incriminating video tapes prior to trial that the judge was "not entirely clear why there exists this almost universal view that incriminating physical evidence must go to the prosecution," and further commenting it "does not follow [that] because concealment of incriminating physical evidence is forbidden there is always a corresponding positive obligation to disclose").

[523] *See supra* § 4-9.7(c)(3).

[524] *See supra* § 4-9.7(c)(1).

[525] STEPHEN GILLERS, ESSENTIALS: REGULATION OF THE LEGAL PROFESSION 242 (Aspen, 2009); *see also* Norman Lefstein, *Incriminating Physical Evidence, the Defense Attorney's Dilemma, and the Need for Rules*, 64 N.C. L. REV. 897, 903 (1986). ("It follows that if a client actually gives evidence to an attorney while seeking legal advice, the attorney-client privilege should protect the information implicitly communicated by the client's act, namely, the fact that the client has possessed the evidence.").

In sum, the criminal defendant's right to have counsel investigate and examine real evidence[526] is compromised, and probably must be abandoned, if the lawyer knows that exercising that right will redound to the client's detriment when the evidence afterward must be laid at the doorstep of the prosecution.[527] But, as Professor Kevin Reitz puts it, suspects in criminal matters should not be penalized for hiring lawyers who then "must behave as government agents or informants, providing client-incriminating evidence and information to prosecutors."[528]

*Second*, imposing a mandatory duty of delivery after the lawyer takes possession of real evidence is not in the public interest, even aside from the criminal defendant's constitutional privilege and right to effective representation that includes a full defense investigation. When real evidence is at risk of being destroyed, when an item may pose a public danger (such as a loaded gun left in a public place), or when stolen property may disappear beyond recovery, the lawyer who takes possession of that real evidence and thereby preserves, disarms, and returns it has served a genuine public service.[529] But, as Professor Stephen Gillers writes, "[b]y commanding turnover whenever a lawyer chooses to receive and cannot (or is not allowed) to return an item, the courts discourage lawyers from protecting these public interests if doing so will harm their clients."[530]

### *§ 4-9.7(f)(2) The Gillers Solution: An Evidence Registry*

On the question of handling of physical evidence, we encounter the apparently conflicting goals of (1) preventing the harm to the state's criminal investigation that may result if the lawyer effectively conceals evidence by taking possession against (2) the lawyer's duty as a zealous advocate which may require taking possession of evidence to test and preserve it but to do so in a manner that does not betray the client. The difficulty lies in finding a resolution that accommodates both interests—neither allowing the lawyer to withdraw the evidence from any possibility of discovery nor requiring the lawyer who properly examines evidence to simply hand it over to law enforcement.

For those few cases in which the lawyer cannot return the evidence and law enforcement does not know the identity of the lawyer for the suspect, the solution proposed by Professor Stephen Gillers is creation of a new evidence registry.[531] The lawyer would record that she represented a client, thereby notifying law enforcement of that representation if and when the client comes under investigation. As previously proposed by Professor Kevin Reitz, law enforcement would serve a court approved subpoena on the lawyer, who then would be obliged to either turn over any real evidence being held that is identified by law enforcement with reasonable particularity or seek court suppression of the subpoena or search.[532]

The elegance of the Gillers solution lies in its simultaneous respect for the premises that "neither the client nor the Government [should be left] worse off than he or it would be if the evidence had remained in the client's or a third person's possession or in a

---

[526] *See supra* § 4-9.7(c)(2).

[527] *See supra* § 4-9.7(c)(3).

[528] Reitz, *supra*, 41 DUKE L.J. at 573.

[529] Gillers, *supra*, 63 STAN. L. REV. at 848–51.

[530] *Id.* at 851.

[531] *Id.* at 862.

[532] Reitz, *supra*, 41 DUKE L.J. at 655–58; Gillers, *supra*, 63 STAN. L. REV. at 861–62.

location known to the lawyer (e.g., the loaded gun in the woods)."[533] If law enforcement never conducts an investigation or never searches for the evidence (or perhaps never searches in the right location), then the real evidence remains undiscovered and the client's communication with the lawyer remains sealed. But if law enforcement does conduct an investigation that would uncover the evidence, the lawyer's retention of it does not amount to concealment and the lawyer is then obliged to respond lawfully to a subpoena.

However, in our imperfect world, the wisdom of a solution does not translate into the likelihood of its adoption. Because the current expectation that a lawyer cough up any evidence retained for examination or not returnable to the source produces a windfall to the government, law enforcement agencies and prosecutors may well resist any alternative. And even if a state or two does act to establish a registry, the patchwork of differing expectations among the states (and the federal government) will leave many a lawyer dangling from an ethical noose, especially if a matter extends across state borders or if the choice of state or federal criminal jurisdiction cannot be readily predicted.

### *§ 4-9.7(f)(3) Other Approaches Toward Evidence After Examination*

In meantime, however, there are other ways by which we could move in the direction of upholding professional responsibilities without improperly impeding law enforcement:

*First,* the mistaken presumption that a lawyer may not return evidence to its original location, even if forensic characteristics have been altered, should be overturned. As discussed earlier, as long as the lawyer provides some type of notice at the location itself as to the availability of a forensics report, the lawyer has acted properly to examine evidence and has taken no action to obstruct any criminal investigation.[534]

*Second,* if a lawyer does choose to take the bold step of openly retaining evidence in the confident expectation that the client will certainly know if any search or subpoena is directed at the client, then the lawyer should be permitted to act at that time to notify law enforcement that evidence is being held and not be accused of concealment.

In either event, the lawyer should create a record that the purpose of holding the evidence is not concealment, such as by creating a contemporaneous written document explaining the decision made to retain the evidence, the lawyer's plan for ensuring that he will be alerted to any search or interrogation of the client as a suspect, and how law enforcement would be notified at the appropriate time. And the lawyer probably should ensure that this record is confidentially shared with other respected lawyers in the community who can later vouch that these steps were considered professional judgments and not post hoc inventions after being caught holding the evidence.

Returning to the subject of obstruction of justice discussed earlier,[535] this is a specific intent crime. And the federal criminal statute includes a safe harbor for actions taken by a lawyer in representing a client in a proceeding.[536] As one state court puts it, "[t]he main rationale for the rule requiring disclosure of the fruits and instrumentalities of the crime when taken into possession by the lawyer is that a lawyer must not impede

---

[533] *See* Gillers, *supra*,63 STAN. L. REV. at 829, 863–64.

[534] *See supra* § 4-9.7(c)(3).

[535] *See supra* § 4-9.7(b)(3).

[536] *See supra* § 4-9.7(b)(4).

or inhibit the discovery of evidence by the state."[537] Thus, a lawyer who forthrightly acts by holding evidence in a manner that does not conceal it from law enforcement if and when an investigation is actually initiated and a search or subpoena is forthcoming is not legitimately subject to prosecution and has contravened no ethical constraint.[538] However, unless the courts act to suspend abusive prosecutions, lawyers understandably will be reluctant to boldly act as zealous advocates with respect to possession of real evidence.

*Finally*, as Professor Norman Lefstein advises, "retention of physical evidence by counsel should be the exceptional case, not an everyday event."[539] A lawyer who chooses to retain real evidence undertakes a weighty responsibility, although that may simply follow from the increasingly weighty responsibilities of criminal defense lawyers in an era where missteps may draw prosecutorial attention and public forensics labs are of dubious reliability.

As noted earlier, the lawyer certainly must treat the evidence in accordance with reasonable forensic standards and with careful documentation of the chain of evidence. As the 2015 Standards of Criminal Justice direct, "[c]ounsel should maintain the evidence separately from privileged materials of other clients, and preserve it in a manner that will not impair its evidentiary value."[540] The lawyer must ensure that evidence is stored in a secure manner, both to ward against abuse by employees and the possibility of theft by outsiders. And the passage of time must also be addressed, including what happens if many months or years go by without a criminal investigation (that is, when does the duty to retain rather than destroy the evidence expire), the lawyer retires (that is, how is deposited evidence transferred to other stewards), or the evidence is perishable and deteriorates while being held.

## § 4-9.8 DUTIES REGARDING PRESENTATION OF EVIDENCE

### § 4-9.8(a) The Prohibition on Presenting What Is Known to Be False Evidence and the Problem of Client Perjury

Rule 3.3(a)(3) of the Model Rules of Professional Conduct prohibits a lawyer from "offer[ing] evidence that the lawyer knows to be false."[541]

Even if the false representation will be made by someone else, so that it does not come out of the lawyer's own mouth, the lawyer may not participate in or condone false testimony by another. Notwithstanding the client's wishes, the lawyer must refuse to offer a forged document into evidence or to call to the stand a witness who the lawyer knows will present perjured or other false testimony.

If the client intends to testify falsely or wants the lawyer to introduce false evidence, Comment 6 to Model Rule 3.3 advises the lawyer to "seek to persuade the client" otherwise, but if the client persists, the lawyer simply "must refuse to offer the false

---

[537] Wemark v. State, 602 N.W.2d 810, 816 (Iowa 1999).

[538] *See* Bruce A. Green, *The Criminal Regulation of Lawyers*, 67 FORDHAM L. REV. 327, 361 (1998) ("For example, a lawyer who puts evidence in a drawer with the intent to safeguard it until it must be produced presumably would not be guilty of obstruction, while a lawyer who engaged in the same conduct with the intent of hiding the evidence permanently from criminal investigators probably would be.").

[539] Lefstein, *supra*, 64 N.C. L. REV. at 933.

[540] STANDARDS FOR CRIMINAL JUSTICE: DEFENSE FUNCTION, Standard 4–4.7(i) (American Bar Ass'n, 2015).

[541] On the standard of knowledge as applied to false evidence, see *infra* § 4-9.8(d).

evidence." The comment further suggests that if "only a portion" of anticipated testimony would be false, the lawyer may allow the witness to take the stand but "must not elicit or otherwise permit the witness to present the testimony that the lawyer knows to be false."

As noted immediately above, the lawyer is forbidden to "offer evidence that the lawyer knows to be false" under Model Rule 3.3(a)(3). Model Rule 3.4(b) emphasizes (although it hardly seems necessary to do so) that the lawyer also may not participate in manufacturing false evidence. The lawyer obviously may not either offer fabricated materials on behalf of the client's own case or deliver counterfeit evidence to another person in the hope that it will be accepted as genuine, with the result that litigation may be averted or the evidence may be adopted by another party to present in its case.

### *§ 4-9.8(a)(1) The Problem of Client Perjury*

Professors Ronald Rotunda and John Dzienkowski suggest that "[t]he best way to 'prevent' the crime of perjury or fraud is to tell the client that if the client testifies falsely, the lawyer will reveal it to the judge."[542] Even in a criminal case where the burden of proof lies heavily on the prosecution and the client's liberty or even life may be at stake, the defendant has no right to present perjured testimony in his defense. In *Nix v. Whiteside*,[543] the Supreme Court held that a lawyer's forceful and successful persuasion of a criminal defendant not to testify falsely, by threatening to disclose perjury to the court, did not violate the defendant's constitutional entitlement under the Sixth Amendment of the United States Constitution to the effective assistance of counsel.

However, the problem of client perjury in a criminal setting is not always easily addressed. The accused has a constitutional right to testify,[544] which means that the lawyer ultimately may not prevent a client who plans to testify falsely from taking the stand if the client insists, even after cautionary warnings from the lawyer about the wrongfulness of perjury and the lawyer's ethical duties (including disclosure) if it occurs. Moreover, the lawyer's duty to remedy a criminal defendant's false testimony is an extraordinary departure from the general duty of confidentiality (and is not followed in every jurisdiction). This affirmative duty to expose otherwise confidential information poses significant problems for effective criminal defense advocacy, and certainly is reserved to exceptional circumstances where the falsity of the defendant's testimony is manifest.[545] Thus, while a criminal defense lawyer plainly should remonstrate with the defendant who insists on false testimony, the direct threat to reveal the matter to the tribunal is not universally regarded as an appropriate response to this difficult situation.

---

[542] RONALD D. ROTUNDA & JOHN S. DZIENKOWSKI, PROFESSIONAL RESPONSIBILITY: A STUDENT'S GUIDE § 3.3–5(a) (American Bar Ass'n, 2013–2014); *see also* Ellen Yaroshefsky, *My Client, The Cooperator, Lied: Now What?*, 7 OHIO ST. J. CRIM. L. 659, 662 (2010) (saying that a lawyer counseling a client who is tempted to offer false testimony has an "ethical obligation" to be "a steadfast, thoughtful, zealous advocate and counsel the client diligently and, hopefully, persuasively").

[543] 475 U.S. 157, 173–75 (1986). For an analysis of *Nix v. Whiteside*, explaining the limited scope of its constitutional ruling and arguing that it leaves policy choices about ethical obligations of lawyers facing client perjury to the states, see Brent R. Appel, *The Limited Impact of* Nix v. Whiteside *on Attorney-Client Relations,* 136 U. PA. L. REV. 1913 (1988).

[544] *See* Rock v. Arkansas, 483 U.S. 44, 49–53 (1987). On the right to testify in one's own defense as fundamental and not waivable by counsel or the court, see generally Owens v. United States, 483 F.3d 48, 58 (1st Cir. 2007) (listing cases); United States v. Gillenwater, 717 F.3d 1070, 1079–80 (9th Cir. 2013); and Rodney J. Uphoff, *Who Should Control the Decision to Call a Witness: Respecting a Criminal Defendant's Tactical Choices*, 68 U. CINN. L. REV. 763, 784–89 (2000).

[545] *See infra* § 4-9.8(c) to (g).

In the typical case, the client will positively respond to the lawyer's counsel that the client must testify truthfully. Even if the client initially intimates that he may do otherwise, the lawyer's strongly-stated admonition that perjury is wrongful and perhaps that the ethical rules may require the lawyer to disclose the perjury to the tribunal ordinarily will suffice to arrest the client's inclination to stray from the manifest truth. In sum, the lawyer seldom will be confronted by a client who truly insists upon testifying in a manner that the lawyer knows to be false. If the client assures the lawyer that the client will testify truthfully, the lawyer may rely upon that assurance and allow the client to take the stand in all good conscience. Should the client thereafter betray that assurance or surprise the lawyer with false testimony, the lawyer then may have a duty to take reasonable remedial measures to correct the false evidence, as discussed below.[546]

### *§ 4-9.8(a)(2) The Narrative Statement Approach*

Comment 7 to Model Rule 3.3 explains that the ethical responsibilities of the lawyer under the rule are subordinate to the court's instructions in a criminal case. If the lawyer tries to prevent or discourage the defendant from taking the stand because the lawyer knows that the defendant intends to present perjured testimony, the lawyer must accede to the court's contrary direction. Moreover, the comment suggests, if the court allows the accused to testify by giving a "narrative statement," the lawyer must acquiesce.

The so-called "narrative statement" approach developed as a means by which a lawyer could permit a defendant who insisted upon testifying falsely to take the stand and tell her story uninterrupted by questions on direct examination, which proponents argued would satisfy the lawyer's ethical obligations because the lawyer would not have actually elicited any perjured statements.[547] Viewing the requirement of disclosure of anticipated client perjury to the tribunal as fomenting confusion and uncertainty in the courtroom, as well as damaging the relationship between defense counsel and the defendant, some commentators suggested the narrative approach as a workable alternative.[548]

Critics fault the narrative approach as failing to uphold the lawyer's responsibilities either to the tribunal or to the client. Professors Rotunda and Dzienkowski argue that, even if the defendant testifies by narrative, the lawyer nonetheless remains sufficiently involved that the duty to correct the false testimony persists and disclosure to the tribunal is still required.[549] Professors Geoffrey Hazard, William Hodes, Monroe Freedman, Abbe Smith, and attorney Peter Jarvis contend that narrative approach is harmful to the client.[550] As Professor Jay Sterling Silver observes, the lawyer's silence and refusal to ask questions, as well as the lawyer's failure to dignify the defendant's

---

[546] *See infra* § 4-9.8(c) to (g).

[547] Norman Lefstein, *Client Perjury in Criminal Cases: Still in Search of an Answer*, 1 GEO J. LEGAL ETHICS 520, 551 (1988) ("The narrative approach thus serves to accommodate the tension that exists between a defendant's constitutional right to testify and the duty of counsel not to offer false testimony, especially since counsel's involvement with the narrative does not constitute suborning perjury.").

[548] *Id.* at 550–51.

[549] RONALD D. ROTUNDA & JOHN S. DZIENKOWSKI, PROFESSIONAL RESPONSIBILITY: A STUDENT'S GUIDE § 3.3–5(e) (American Bar Ass'n, 2013–2014). On the duty to correct false evidence, see *infra* § 4-9.8(e) to (h).

[550] 2 GEOFFREY C. HAZARD, JR., W. WILLIAM HODES & PETER R. JARVIS, THE LAW OF LAWYERING § 32.17:2 (Aspen, 4th ed., 2016); MONROE H. FREEDMAN & ABBE SMITH, UNDERSTANDING LAWYERS' ETHICS § 6.07 (LexisNexis 4th ed. 2010).

testimony by commenting on it during later summation, "telegraph[s]" to the jury that the lawyer believes his own client has testified falsely.[551]

Comment 7 to Model Rule 3.3 specifically refers to the narrative approach and suggests that a lawyer must comply with a court's directive in that regard. But it is not clear whether this comment language should be read as merely acknowledging the possibility that a judge might employ this approach or as indicating affirmative approval of the practice in criminal cases. Comment 7 reads: "In some jurisdictions, however, courts have required counsel to present the accused as a witness or to give a narrative statement if the accused so desires, even if counsel knows that the testimony or statement will be false." The slightly disparaging acknowledgment that "some jurisdictions" have directed use of the narrative statement could be read to distance the American Bar Association from any suggestion of approval.[552]

The narrative statement approach, as imperfect as it may be, nonetheless falls within the trial court's discretion when facing an impossible situation in a criminal case in which the lawyer properly resists cooperating with the defendant who wishes to testify falsely and yet the defendant insists upon her constitutional right to testify. To be sure, because Model Rule 3.3(a)(3) requires the lawyer to take reasonable remedial measures to correct material false evidence offered by "the lawyer's client," and not only that evidence directly offered by the lawyer, the lawyer's duty to rectify or inform the tribunal that the client has testified falsely remains,[553] regardless of the fact that the perjury occurred in the context of a narrative statement. Still, given that a trial court presumably would order that a defendant be allowed to testify by narrative statement only when the accused's lawyer already has effectively indicated that the lawyer anticipates perjured testimony, the court likely must respond by permitting the case to be submitted to the jury for its own evaluation of the accused's narrative presentation.

Even when the court has directed that the defendant be permitted to present a narrative, the lawyer may not rely upon any testimony that the lawyer knows to be false when presenting closing arguments, as awkward as that reticence may be and despite the negative implications that the jury may infer from the lawyer's omission.

### § 4-9.8(b) Discretion to Decline to Present What Is Reasonably Believed to Be False Evidence

Rule 3.3(a)(3) of the Model Rules of Professional Conduct confers discretion on the lawyer to decline to offer evidence to the tribunal that the lawyer "reasonably believes is false."

While the lawyer is prohibited from presenting evidence that the lawyer *knows* is false,[554] the lawyer may choose whether or not to present evidence that the lawyer reasonably *believes* is false. If the lawyer chooses to submit the evidence and allow the

---

[551] Jay Sterling Silver, *Truth, Justice, and the American Way: The Case Against the Client Perjury Rules*, 47 VAND. L. REV. 338, 421 (1994).

[552] *But see* Nathan M. Crystal, *False Testimony by Criminal Defendants: Still Unanswered Ethical and Constitutional Questions*, 2003 U. ILL. L. REV. 1529, 1547–49 (suggesting that the revisions to Rule 3.3 and the comments foreshadow greater use of the narrative solution to the problem of client perjury in criminal cases).

[553] *See* Matter of Disciplinary Proceedings Against Riley, 882 N.W.2d 820, 835 (Wis. 2016) (plurality) ("The duty to take remedial measures does not arise only when the lawyer has affirmatively elicited the false testimony through pointed questions."). On the duty to correct false evidence when the lawyer later comes to know of its falsity, see *infra* § 4-9.8(c) to (g).

[554] *See supra* § 4-9.8(a).

trier of fact to make the determination of its validity, the lawyer has not transgressed the duty of candor to the tribunal because the lawyer did not know the evidence to be false. If, however, the lawyer chooses to withhold the evidence, either because of the lawyer's ethical qualms or because the lawyer sees the submission of gravely dubious evidence as likely to undermine the case or the advocate's credibility, the lawyer may not be accused of failing to exercise appropriate diligence or zealousness on behalf of the client.[555]

However, the lawyer should not fall into the misconceived role of being a judge against his own client's interests by withholding potentially important evidence that is merely doubtful but as to which the lawyer has no reasonable belief that it is false. As Professors Geoffrey Hazard and William Hodes observe, "[p]erfectly legitimate evidence is often of unknown reliability. It is the function of the trier of fact, not the advocate, to resolve the issue of reliability."[556]

Moreover, as Comment 9 to Model Rule 3.3 states:

> Because of the special protections historically provided criminal defendants . . . this Rule does not permit a lawyer to refuse to offer the testimony of such a client where the lawyer reasonably believes but does not know that the testimony will be false. Unless the lawyer knows the testimony will be false, the lawyer must honor the client's decision to testify.[557]

### § 4-9.8(c) Duty to Take Remedial Measures to Correct False Evidence Notwithstanding Confidentiality

In addition to enjoining the lawyer to speak the truth before tribunals and not to knowingly offer false evidence, Rule 3.3 of the Model Rules of Professional Conduct further imposes the responsibility on the lawyer to correct false statements or false evidence presented to the tribunal by the lawyer, the lawyer's client, or a witness called by the lawyer. Importantly, the lawyer's obligation under Model Rule 3.3 to take reasonable remedial measures with respect to statements or evidence that the lawyer comes to know is false is mandatory, even when the only effective remedy is disclosure of confidential or privileged information to the tribunal.

That the lawyer is obliged to be truthful with the court and that the lawyer must encourage the client to be truthful in representations in the proceedings are neither new nor controversial precepts. However, because Rule 3.3 reverses (at least in part) the prior expectations under the prior Model Code of Professional Responsibility—under which the principle of attorney-client confidentiality was elevated above the duty to correct client untruths—this particular aspect of Rule 3.3 has been one of the more controversial elements of the Model Rules regime. Indeed, even now more than three decades after initial adoption of the Model Rules, several states hesitate or forthrightly decline to impose a duty of disclosure of confidential information in criminal cases.[558]

---

[555] On the duty of diligence and zealous advocacy, see *supra* § 4-5.3(a).

[556] 2 GEOFFREY C. HAZARD, JR. & W. WILLIAM HODES, THE LAW OF LAWYERING § 29.8 (Aspen, 3d ed., 2009).

[557] On the criminal defendant's right to testify, see *supra* § 4-9.8(a).

[558] *See, e.g.*, ALA. RULES OF PROF'L CONDUCT R. 3.3, cmt.; D.C. RULES OF PROF'L CONDUCT R. 3.3(b) & cmt.8; MD. RULES OF PROF'L CONDUCT R. 19–303, cmts. 7 to 11; MASS. RULES OF PROF'L CONDUCT R. 3.3, cmt.11; MISS. RULES OF PROF'L CONDUCT R. 3.3, cmt.; N.D. RULES OF PROF'L CONDUCT R. 3.3(a)(3) & cmts. 10 to 11; VA. RULES OF PROF'L CONDUCT R. 3.3(a)(4) & cmt. 11; *see also* Ore. Bar Formal Op No. 2005–34.

For the substantial majority of jurisdictions that have adopted the Model Rules of Professional Conduct, Rule 3.3 directs that a lawyer, who discovers that a client has committed fraud upon a tribunal in a proceeding that is not yet concluded, must take reasonable remedial measures, including if necessary disclosure to the tribunal. Unlike the standard under the prior Model Code of Professional Responsibility, even when the lawyer's knowledge of a client's perjury or other fraud on the court has been obtained through a privileged communication, the lawyer is not excused from the duty to disclose the information.

The problem of client perjury (as the classic example of false evidence being submitted to a tribunal) has been an intractable one for the legal profession and has led people of wisdom and good faith to reach diametrically opposed conclusions.[559] The client perjury dilemma, especially in criminal cases, presents in the most poignant manner the ever-present tension in the legal profession between the ideal of the attorney as an officer of the court and the role of the attorney as a zealous advocate of the client.[560] As common ground, nearly all agree that a lawyer may not knowingly elicit false testimony, that a client should be dissuaded from committing perjury, and that a client who has falsely testified should be urged to rectify the perjury.[561] However, there is no consensus on how to respond when the lawyer is surprised by the client's false testimony or when the client confesses afterward that she prevaricated on the witness stand.

On the officer of the court side of the debate,[562] advocates of mandatory disclosure by the attorney to the tribunal "have argued that non-disclosure of perjury is a taint on a lawyer's character and an affront to the court's dignity."[563] Arguing that "the truth-seeking elements of a trial must remain paramount in order to preserve the integrity of our adversary system of justice," proponents compare the duty to reveal client perjury to

---

[559] *Compare* RONALD D. ROTUNDA & JOHN S. DZIENKOWSKI, PROFESSIONAL RESPONSIBILITY: A STUDENT'S GUIDE § 3.3–5 (American Bar Ass'n, 2013–2014) (defending duty to disclose client perjury in Model Rule 3.3); and Jeffrey L. Dunetz, *Surprise Client Perjury: Some Questions and Proposed Solutions to an Old Problem*, 29 N.Y.L. SCH. L. REV. 407 (1984) (advocating duty to disclose client perjury) *with* MONROE H. FREEDMAN & ABBE SMITH, UNDERSTANDING LAWYERS' ETHICS ch. 6 (LexisNexis 4th ed. 2010) (opposing duty of disclosure); Ernest F. Lidge, III, *Client Perjury in Tennessee: A Misguided Ethics Opinion, an Amended Rule, and a Call for Further Action by the Tennessee Supreme Court*, 63 TENN. L. REV. 1 (1995) (same); and Jay Sterling Silver, *Truth, Justice, and the American Way: The Case Against the Client Perjury Rules*, 47 VAND. L. REV. 339 (1994) (same). *See also* 2 GEOFFREY C. HAZARD, JR. & W. WILLIAM HODES, THE LAW OF LAWYERING § 29.15 (Aspen, 3d ed., 2009) (generally supporting the duty of disclosure of false evidence or fraud on the tribunal, but stating that Professor Hazard has "concluded that requiring a criminal defense lawyer to disclose *client* perjury is an excessive and unrealistic expectation"); Geoffrey C. Hazard, Jr., *The Client Fraud Problem as a Justinian Quartet: An Extended Analysis*, 25 HOFSTRA L. REV. 1041 (1997) (same).

[560] *See* CHARLES W. WOLFRAM, MODERN LEGAL ETHICS § 12.5 (West 1986) ("A lawyer faced with perjurious testimony by a client or friendly witness confronts the choice between client interest and social interest in a most poignant form."); Brent R. Appel, *The Limited Impact of* Nix v. Whiteside *on Attorney-Client Relations,* 136 U. PA. L. REV. 1913, 1916–17 (1988) (describing the client perjury problem as implicating the contrasting models of the attorney as "officer of the court" and as the client's "alter ego"). On this classic tension between the officer of the court and the zealous advocate ideals, see *supra* § 4-9.2.

[561] Lidge, *supra*, 63 TENN. L. REV. at 6–7 (describing "general, although not unanimous, agreement on a few points").

[562] *See* Matter of Disciplinary Proceedings Against Riley, 882 N.W.2d 820, 842–43 (Wis. 2016) (plurality) (declaring that the lawyer has a duty to disclose testimony by a client that is knowingly false because the lawyer "is not just a zealous advocate on behalf of a client, but also an officer of the court, who bears obligations to assist the court in its search for the truth").

[563] *Id.* at 9 (describing position of advocates of mandatory disclosure).

the lawyer's responsibility to prevent threats or bribes to witnesses or jurors.[564] As suggested in Comment 11 to Model Rule 3.3, the failure to disclose would mean that the lawyer essentially "cooperate[s] in deceiving the court, thereby subverting the truth-finding process which the adversary system is designed to implement."

On the zealous advocacy side, opponents contend that forcing revelation of client confidences "transform[s] the attorney from an advocate to a whistleblower."[565] A mandatory disclosure rule discourages clients from entrusting their lawyers with confidential information. It also tempts the lawyer to avoid the problem by remaining deliberately ignorant and avoiding investigation so that he will never actually "know" that a client has given false testimony, thereby impairing effective representation performed after thorough investigation and with full understanding of the client's story.[566] Some further argue that the lawyer's appropriation of incriminating statements by the client for use in disclosing client perjury to the tribunal would violate the Fifth Amendment privilege against self-incrimination, especially when the client was not warned in advance that her statements to the lawyer might be used against the client.[567]

The proper resolution of the client perjury dilemma was a point of striking divergence between the Model Rules of Professional Conduct and the Model Code of Professional Responsibility. Disciplinary Rule 7–102(B)(1) of the former Model Code prohibited the lawyer from disclosing a client's confessed perjury to the court when the lawyer had learned of the untruthful testimony through a privileged communication.[568] Under the former Code, the lawyer, of course, could not knowingly offer or use perjured testimony or other false evidence.[569] But the lawyer who learned of the client's perjury after-the-fact or was surprised by it during the trial was bound to uphold the attorney-client privilege, in the same manner as the lawyer's privileged knowledge of other past wrongdoing by a client.[570] Although the attorney was not to reveal a client's admission to the lawyer of perjury or other fraud on the tribunal, by reason of the attorney-client

---

[564] *See* Dunetz, *supra*, 29 N.Y.L. SCH. L. REV. at 426–27; *see also* Nix v. Whiteside, 475 U.S. 157, 174–75 (1986) (comparing, in dicta, the duty to prevent or reveal client perjury to the duty to rectify bribes or threats to witnesses or jurors).

[565] Lidge, *supra*, 63 TENN. L. REV. at 3.

[566] *See* MONROE H. FREEDMAN & ABBE SMITH, UNDERSTANDING LAWYERS' ETHICS §§ 6.08, 6.17 to .19 (LexisNexis 4th ed. 2010); Wayne D. Brazil, *Unanticipated Client Perjury and the Collision of Rules of Ethics, Evidence, and Constitutional Law*, 44 MO. L. REV. 601, 641–42 (1979); Lidge, *supra*, 63 TENN. L. REV. at 9–11.

[567] FREEDMAN & SMITH, *supra*, § 6.16; *see also* Nathan M. Crystal, *False Testimony by Criminal Defendants: Still Unanswered Ethical and Constitutional Questions*, 2003 U. ILL. L. REV. 1529, 1565–71 (noting the constitutional questions, especially under due process and the privilege against self-incrimination, that remain unanswered regarding defense counsel action to prevent or rectify false testimony by a criminal defendant).

[568] *See* MODEL CODE OF PROF'L RESPONSIBILITY, Disciplinary Rule 7–102(B)(1) (American Bar Ass'n, 1980) ("A lawyer who receives information clearly establishing that [h]is client has, in the course of the representation, perpetrated a fraud upon a person or tribunal shall promptly call upon his client to rectify the same, and if his client refuses or is unable to do so, he shall reveal the fraud to the affected person or tribunal, except when the information is protected as a privileged communication.").

[569] *See* MODEL CODE OF PROF'L RESPONSIBILITY, Disciplinary Rule 7–102(A)(4) (American Bar Ass'n, 1980).

[570] During the period in which the American Bar Association's Model Code of Professional Responsibility was in effect in most jurisdictions, the ABA Standing Committee on Ethics and Professional Responsibility had interpreted Disciplinary Rule 7–102(B)(1) as precluding the lawyer's disclosure of client fraud, not only when learned in a privileged communication, but whenever the information was confidential, that is, information gained during the course of the representation other than through a client communication. ABA Comm. on Ethics and Professional Responsibility, Formal Op. 341 (1975). In any event, a lawyer who comes to know of a client's perjured testimony is most likely to learn of its falsity through the client's confidential confession or through inconsistent statements made by the client during privileged communications.

privilege, the Code directed the attorney to withdraw if the client refused to rectify the falsity with the tribunal or person affected.[571]

By contrast, Rule 3.3 of the Model Rules of Professional Conduct takes the opposite stance by mandating that the attorney disclose the client's perjury to the court, notwithstanding that the lawyer may have learned of it through a privileged communication. In a formal ethics opinion, the American Bar Association's Standing Committee on Ethics and Professional Responsibility confirmed that Model Rule 3.3 "represent[s] a major policy change" from the Code of Professional Responsibility because the duty to disclose a client's perjury would no longer be excused by client confidentiality.[572] The committee concluded that the attorney's duty under Rule 3.3 to take "reasonable remedial measures" to correct the fraud indeed does mandate revealing his client's perjury directly to the court.

Under the Model Rules standard, the public interest in the integrity of proceedings is given priority over attorney-client confidentiality. Accordingly, under Rule 3.3(a)(3) and (c) of the Model Rules of Professional Conduct, if the attorney discovers after the fact that the client or a witness has offered perjured testimony or false evidence, the lawyer is required to disclose that information to the tribunal, even if the information would otherwise be a client confidence. Rule 3.3(a)(3) thus imposes a whistleblowing duty on lawyers to report client wrongdoing that undermines the integrity of the adjudicative process during the course of the lawyer's representation of a client before a tribunal. Under Rule 3.3(c), that mandatory duty of disclosure prevails over the lawyer's duty to protect confidential information related to the representation of the client.[573]

### § 4-9.8(d) The Standard of Knowledge as Applied to the False Evidence Problem

The duty of the lawyer to prevent false evidence from being offered to the tribunal and to take reasonable remedial measures to correct false evidence after-the-fact is triggered only when the lawyer "knows" the evidence is false. Rule 3.3(a)(3) directs the lawyer not to "offer evidence that the lawyer knows to be false." This subparagraph further directs the lawyer to take corrective measures with respect to material evidence when "the lawyer comes to know of its falsity." Comment 8 to Rule 3.3 emphasizes that "a lawyer's reasonable belief that evidence is false" does not mandate withholding the evidence.[574] Moreover, the comment urges the lawyer to "resolve doubts about the

---

[571] For an analysis consistent with this understanding of the Code of Professional Responsibility regarding the responsibilities of lawyers to preserve client confidentiality while taking other steps to prevent the presentation of false evidence, see State v. Hischke, 639 N.W.2d 6, 11 (Iowa 2002) (Carter, J., concurring specially) (while majority found it unnecessary to address whether revelation to the court of proposed client perjury was proper because that issue was not raised on appeal, concurring justice opined that the lawyer should attempt to dissuade the client from false testimony, attempt a quiet withdrawal if unsuccessful in persuading the client, and not invite false testimony in questioning of client if not permitted to withdraw, but that the lawyer should not breach confidentiality by disclosing suspected perjury to the court).

[572] ABA Comm. on Ethics and Professional Responsibility, Formal Op. 353 (1987).

[573] *See* 2 GEOFFREY C. HAZARD, JR., W. WILLIAM HODES & PETER R. JARVIS, THE LAW OF LAWYERING § 32.03 (Aspen, 4th ed., 2016) (describing Rule 3.3 as a "trumping" rule because it imposes duties with which the lawyer must comply even if compliance requires disclosure of information otherwise protected as confidential).

[574] *See also* Matter of Disciplinary Proceedings Against Riley, 882 N.W.2d 820, 842 (Wis. 2016) (plurality) (saying that the rule "does not make an attorney the guarantor of the factual accuracy of everything that is said by a client or other witness called by the attorney," but rather, the "attorney's obligation arises only when the attorney has actual knowledge of the falsity and only when the false testimony is material to the proceeding").

veracity of testimony or other evidence in favor of the client." At the same time, the comment observes that a lawyer's knowledge that evidence is false "can be inferred from the circumstances," and that "the lawyer cannot ignore an obvious falsehood." In sum, Model Rule 3.3 imposes the duties to prevent or correct false evidence only when the lawyer "knows" the evidence is false, and Model Rule 1.0(f) defines "knows" as "denot[ing] actual knowledge of the fact in question."

As Professor Ellen Yaroshefsky writes, "[f]ew lawyers ever obtain the requisite 'actual knowledge' of client intended or completed perjury that triggers the rule's obligation."[575] Professor Nathan Crystal suggests that a criminal defense lawyer would have actual knowledge that a defendant intends to (or did) testify falsely when the defendant confesses to the lawyer that the testimony is false, when the defendant admits certain facts to the lawyer that contradicts the testimony, or when facts known to the lawyer from independent investigation are inconsistent with the defendant's testimony.[576] The Connecticut Supreme Court emphasized in *State v. Chambers*[577] that—

> an attorney, before invoking the rule, must act in good faith and have a firm basis in objective fact. Conjecture or speculation that the defendant intends to testify falsely would not be enough. Nor would mere inconsistencies in the evidence or in the defendant's version of events translate to actual knowledge, even though they may raise concerns in counsel's mind.[578]

The lawyer should not draw inferences against the client nor readily interpret loose language or venting by a client to signal an intent to commit perjury.[579]

The knowledge standard that triggers the lawyer's duties under Rule 3.3 is appropriately high. The lawyer, especially when representing a client against the prosecutorial power of the government, should not lightly question her client's veracity. Absent exceptional circumstances and a solid factual foundation that forces a contrary conviction, the lawyer properly presumes that the client has testified truthfully. The lawyer should not assume the role of judge or jury against her own client. As criminal defense attorney B. John Burns writes, "[t]he credibility of the defendant's testimony should, in most cases, be measured by the jury, not by his or her own advocate."[580] Moreover, we should be mindful of "the vast cultural gulf separating most criminal defense attorneys and their clients," which can "impede mutual understanding" about the nature and veracity of the client's proposed or given testimony.[581]

---

[575] Ellen Yaroshefsky, *My Client, The Cooperator, Lied: Now What?*, 7 OHIO ST. J. CRIM. L. 659, 659 (2010).

[576] Nathan M. Crystal, *False Testimony by Criminal Defendants: Still Unanswered Ethical and Constitutional Questions*, 2003 U. ILL. L. REV. 1529, 1534–37.

[577] 994 A.2d 1248 (Conn. 2010).

[578] *Id.* at 1259 n.13.

[579] *See* Florida Bar v. Knowles, 99 So.2d 918, 922 (Fla. 2012) (disciplining a lawyer for improperly notifying the state's attorney that her client would lie to the immigration court based on the plainly insufficient basis that the client had mentioned "that she would do anything, including lying in court, to avoid deportation").

[580] 4A B. JOHN BURNS, IOWA PRACTICE SERIES: CRIMINAL PROCEDURE § 39:5 (Thomson-West 2012); *see also* State v. Whiteside, 272 N.W.2d 468, 470 (Iowa 1978) ("[A] lawyer's task is not to determine guilt or innocence, but only to present evidence so that others—either court or jury—can do so.").

[581] Jay Sterling Silver, *Truth, Justice, and the American Way: The Case Against the Client Perjury Rules*, 47 VAND. L. REV. 339, 390 (1994).

In his concurring opinion in *Nix v. Whiteside*,[582] Justice Stevens suggested that what may appear "pellucidly clear" to an appellate court, which has the distinct advantage of reviewing the evidence after the facts have been sifted at trial by another judge, may have been anything but certain when viewed from the perspective of a trial lawyer evaluating "mixtures of sand and clay" in preparing for trial. Even when the client's story has changed, Justice Stevens warned that "[a] lawyer's certainty that a change in his client's recollection is a harbinger of intended perjury—as well as judicial review of such apparent certainty—should be tempered by the realization that, after reflection, the most honest witness may recall (or sincerely believe he recalls) details that he previously overlooked."[583]

## § 4-9.8(e) How to Take Reasonable Steps to Remedy False Evidence

Rule 3.3(a)(3) of the Model Rules of Professional Conduct requires the lawyer, who has come to know of the falsity of evidence offered by the "lawyer, the lawyer's client, or a witness called by the lawyer," to take "reasonable remedial measures, including, if necessary, disclosure to the tribunal."

Although disclosure to the tribunal may be necessary, revelation by the lawyer should not be the option of first resort. As Comment 10 to Rule 3.3 advises, the lawyer should begin by "remonstrat[ing] with the client confidentially", explaining the lawyer's ethical duty to protect the integrity of the proceeding and seeking the "client's cooperation" in withdrawing or otherwise correcting false statements or evidence. In addition to emphasizing the wrongfulness of perjury or other misleading representations, the lawyer may suggest to the client that the correction will be better received if coming from the client and that it may be possible to make the correction in a manner that mitigates any negative effect on the client's interests. Many clients will accept their lawyers' advice and agree to rectify the false evidence, particularly if their lawyers have spelled out the consequences of failing to do so, namely that the lawyer will disclose the client's false testimony or other evidence.

If the client refuses to cooperate with the lawyer in disclosing or otherwise correcting the false evidence, the lawyer may not voluntarily continue to represent the client. To concretely disassociate himself from any fraud upon the tribunal, the lawyer ordinarily should seek permission of the tribunal to withdraw. Nonetheless, even though the advocate ordinarily must request such permission, withdrawal is unlikely to be an effective remedy when false evidence has been submitted to the tribunal and the client resists its correction. As Comment 10 to Rule 3.3 acknowledges, "[i]f withdrawal from the representation is not permitted or will not undo the effect of the false evidence, the advocate must make such disclosure to the tribunal as is reasonably necessary to remedy the situation." Because the silent withdrawal of the lawyer from the representation is unlikely to fully rectify the situation, disclosure to the tribunal of the false evidence almost invariably must follow. And, again, Rule 3.3(c) makes plain that the duty of disclosure preempts the protection of confidentiality under Rule 1.6.[584]

Once the lawyer has disclosed the nature of the problem to the tribunal, the lawyer's ethical obligations have been satisfied. As Comment 10 states, "[i]t is for the tribunal

[582] 475 U.S. 157, 190 (1986) (Steven, J., concurring in the judgment).

[583] *Id.* at 191.

[584] *See supra* § 4-9.8(c).

then to determine what should be done—making a statement about the matter to the trier of fact, ordering a mistrial, or perhaps nothing." If the lawyer is not permitted to withdraw, as frequently will be the case,[585] the lawyer must continue with the representation. If the tribunal also chooses to allow the case to proceed without taking any further action, which often may be the only reasonable course for the tribunal, especially in a criminal case, the lawyer may not exploit the perjured testimony or other false evidence by making any further use of it in arguments to the trier of fact or otherwise.

In a criminal case, the tribunal confronted with a lawyer's disclosure of false evidence, especially client perjury, faces a difficult choice, in which choosing to allow the matter to go forward to resolution by the jury frequently will be the best or least-worst option. In a jury trial, the lawyer's disclosure should be presented to the judge in a sidebar, outside the presence or hearing of the jury. Because the jury thus will not have been tainted by learning of the lawyer's contradiction of the evidence submitted on behalf of the lawyer's own client, declaration of a mistrial by the tribunal may be unnecessary. Still, because the lawyer's disclosure may be seen by the client as a grave betrayal, resulting in a serious and irreparable loss of trust, a mistrial may be necessary for that reason, although such a complete breakdown of the attorney-client relationship may not be "an inevitable result."[586] By contrast, if a criminal prosecution was being tried to the bench, and the lawyer is forced to disclose the falsity of evidence over the client's objection, a mistrial appears unavoidable.[587] Not only has the lawyer become a (non-testifying) witness against the client before the trier of fact, but the lawyer and client may find themselves in irreconcilable conflict about the fundamental facts, making continued representation impossible.

If a mistrial is not declared in a criminal case, the judge may direct such corrective measures, if any, as are appropriate and feasible under the circumstances. The prosecution might be allowed a continuance to conduct further investigation or be allowed to present additional witnesses to rebut the false evidence. Witnesses may be recalled to undergo further examination or cross-examination. However, the judge in a criminal case may not instruct the jury to disregard the accused's testimony or to find a particular fact to have occurred or not to have occurred, because the prosecution bears the burden of establishing all of the elements of the charge beyond a reasonable doubt.[588]

Nor may the defendant's lawyer be forced or permitted to testify as a witness against her own client, or otherwise provide evidence of privileged communications that could be used against the client, even if the lawyer has been permitted to withdraw. As Professors Geoffrey Hazard and William Hodes observe, the lawyer usually will know of the falsity of the client's testimony or other evidence "because it does not jibe with other information the lawyer gained during the confidential relationship."[589] While

[585] MONROE H. FREEDMAN & ABBE SMITH, UNDERSTANDING LAWYERS' ETHICS § 6.06 (LexisNexis 4th ed. 2010) (noting that motions by lawyers to withdraw are commonly denied, as the judge responds by saying that the situation is understood but that the next lawyer would face the same difficulty, so the lawyer simply must proceed as best as the lawyer can).

[586] 2 GEOFFREY C. HAZARD, JR. & W. WILLIAM HODES, THE LAW OF LAWYERING § 29.21 (Aspen, 3d ed., 2009).

[587] *Id.*

[588] *See* Mullaney v. Wilbur, 421 U.S. 684, 691–703 (1975); In re Winship, 397 U.S. 358, 361–64 (1970).

[589] 2 GEOFFREY C. HAZARD, JR. & W. WILLIAM HODES, THE LAW OF LAWYERING § 29.21 (Aspen, 3d ed., 2009).

information imparted by the client to the lawyer that directly facilitated the crime of perjury would fall within the crime-fraud exception to the attorney-client privilege,[590] Professors Hazard and Hodes note that the information that typically would alert the lawyer to the falsity of evidence ordinarily would have been received earlier in the representation and not for the purpose of advancing perjury.[591] "A client's confession to her lawyer that she was in fact guilty, for example, would be privileged, even if she later decided that she was going to lie about her guilt."[592]

That a lawyer may be permitted or required under the Model Rules of Professional Conduct to divulge client confidences—including disclosing information obtained through communications with a client, for the purposes of preventing or correcting a serious harm or for some other important purpose such as preserving the integrity of a judicial proceeding—does not ordinarily mean that the lawyer may be called as a witness or otherwise be required to provide evidence that would be admissible in court against the client.[593] Unless an exception to confidentiality under the rules (such as the Rule 3.3 duty to disclose false evidence) is directly co-extensive with an exception to the attorney-client privilege, the lawyer is authorized or required to share information only in the manner and to the extent necessary to prevent or correct the harm or achieve the designed purpose, but not to testify or give evidence against the client. When an exception to confidentiality stated in the ethics rules does not align with an exception to the attorney-client privilege, the lawyer's duty of disclosure is limited to extra-evidentiary forms, namely sharing the information with the appropriate person or authorities.

In sum, the exception to confidentiality in Rule 3.3 does not permit introduction of attorney-client communications into evidence through lawyer testimony or permit inquiry about those communications as part of the presentation of evidence before any tribunal, absent a recognized exception to the privilege itself.

### § 4-9.8(f) The Duration of the Duty to Remedy False Evidence

When a professional disciplinary rule imposes an affirmative duty, which the lawyer fails to uphold only at the risk of a disciplinary penalty for failure, the scope or duration of the obligation should not be left open-ended. Model Rule 3.3(c) provides that the lawyer's duties of candor in representations to the tribunal, to refrain from presenting false evidence, and to take reasonable remedial measures to protect the tribunal from false evidence or other criminal or fraudulent conduct related to the proceeding "continue to the conclusion of the proceeding."

Because these duties articulated by the rule are connected to the nature of the representation in an adjudicative matter before a tribunal, the rule clarifies that the lawyer's duty regarding correction of perjury, fraud, or other offenses to the administration of justice continues only while the proceeding itself continues and thus while "the lawyer can be said to have contributed to the court's being led astray."[594]

---

[590] On the crime-fraud exception to privilege, see *supra* § 4-6.3(c)(1).

[591] 2 GEOFFREY C. HAZARD, JR. & W. WILLIAM HODES, THE LAW OF LAWYERING § 29.21 (Aspen, 3d ed., 2009).

[592] *Id.*

[593] *See supra* § 4-6.3(c)(4).

[594] 2 GEOFFREY C. HAZARD, JR., W. WILLIAM HODES & PETER R. JARVIS, THE LAW OF LAWYERING § 32.03 (Aspen, 4th ed., 2016).

Comment 13 to Model Rule 3.3 fixes the conclusion of the proceeding at the point "when a final judgment in the proceeding has been affirmed on appeal or the time for review has passed."

In sum, the lawyer's responsibilities with respect to the representation before the tribunal appropriately begin and end with the adjudicative matter for which the lawyer was retained and do not persist into the infinite future.

### § 4-9.8(g) Closing Thoughts on the Rule Mandating Disclosure of False Evidence, Including Client Perjury

When states moved to an ethics regime patterned on the Model Rules of Professional Conduct, they were forced to confront a sharp difference in ethical direction and underlying policy on the persistent problem of client perjury. Each jurisdiction had to choose whether to adhere to the Model Code of Professional Responsibility elevation of attorney-client confidentiality to a position of superior protection or instead to incorporate the Model Rules mandate for disclosure of client perjury as necessary to protect the integrity of the tribunal.[595]

Whatever answer was given would be controversial, as the problem of client perjury is one where some regard anything less than full disclosure as the lawyer suborning perjury, while others regard the cure of revelation as being worse than the disease of falsity. Nor was any answer likely to achieve more than grudging acceptance within the bar, as those on both sides of the scholarly debate have acknowledged that they remain less than satisfied with their own positions and even persons with strongly-held views have changed their positions over the years.[596] And, in the end, some commentators suggest that the issue has become unduly inflated in importance, as few criminal defendants who go to trial are acquitted, whether they lie on the stand or not, and thus a disclosure rule "would affect the outcome in an insignificant number of cases."[597]

Perhaps the most sensible approach is to resist any utopian impulses and accept that any resolution for this intractable problem will do little more than provide some general direction for lawyers and judges who face what we may hope is an uncommon if not rare scenario. Although lawyers, particularly those in the criminal defense bar, may regularly encounter situations where they suspect or even reasonably believe that a client's story is less than fully truthful, the American Bar Association's Standing Committee on Ethics and Professional Responsibility anticipated that the disclosure duty under Rule 3.3 would be seldom invoked because it will be "the unusual case where the lawyer does know" about client perjury.[598]

---

[595] On states that have not adopted the Model Rules approach to the client perjury dilemma, see *supra* § 4-9.8(c).

[596] *See* MONROE H. FREEDMAN & ABBE SMITH, UNDERSTANDING LAWYERS' ETHICS § 6.20 (LexisNexis 4th ed. 2010) (acknowledging that the authors "are less than fully satisfied" with their position in opposition to a disclosure rule in the case of client perjury, and noting that Professor Geoffrey Hazard, who had strongly supported Rule 3.3, had come to believe that requiring "a criminal defense lawyer to 'blow the whistle' on client perjury is futile or counterproductive" (citing Geoffrey C. Hazard, Jr., *The Client Fraud Problem as a Justinian Quartet: An Extended Analysis*, 25 HOFSTRA L. REV. 1041, 1060 (1997))).

[597] Nathan Crystal, *Confidentiality Under the Model Rules of Professional Conduct*, 30 KAN. L. REV. 215, 242 (1982); *see also* Brent R. Appel, *The Limited Impact of* Nix v. Whiteside *on Attorney-Client Relations,* 136 U. PA. L. REV. 1913, 1937 (1988) (saying that a duty of disclosure will impact few actual cases because "[o]nly rarely will a lawyer know both that the proposed testimony is false and that the client is determined to offer the false testimony at trial").

[598] ABA Comm. on Ethics and Professional Responsibility, Formal Op. 353 (1987).

When that unusual criminal case does arise, we should leave ample room for the lawyers involved, and the judges who receive a report of client perjury, to make the best of a difficult situation. They must struggle to uphold their obligations of integrity, while avoiding a mistrial if feasible; attempt if possible to salvage the attorney-client relationship from irretrievable breakdown despite a compelled disclosure; protect the attorney-client privilege as much as possible by ensuring that the lawyer's disclosure is limited to a side-bar with the judge and counsel outside the presence of the jury; and be careful not to trespass upon the constitutional rights afforded to a criminal defendant to testify in his own defense and to having the charges evaluated by a jury. We should resist the temptation to be too specific in setting guidelines that must govern every case, regardless of circumstances, or to engage in second-guessing of those who are on the front-lines.

We all might do well to learn from the hard-won experience and later reassessment of federal district Judge Marvin E. Frankel, who had been the most prominent advocate of the adamant position that truth-finding must be the paramount value in the litigation process[599] and who later was the primary architect of the mandatory disclosure directive that was incorporated into Rule 3.3 of the Model Rules.[600] Several years later, after leaving the bench and returning to the practice of law, he acknowledged that, despite the mandatory disclosure duty in the rules, "no evidence suggests that there has been a notable increase in truth-telling in the courthouse."[601] He further admitted, "[t]he more I see of life and the practice of law, the more justifiable I find the stance that we really ought not be called upon to 'know' when someone's story is false."[602] While rules about client perjury are "easily stated," he lamented, they are "only the beginning of daunting perplexities."[603] In the end, he wisely suggested, recognizing that "we are not omniscient remains a sound perception and a legitimate comfort in these situations."[604]

## § 4-9.8(h) Duty to Counteract Client Fraudulent or Criminal Conduct Before the Tribunal

Together with the advocate's duty of candor to the tribunal, in speaking truthfully and refusing to present or to acquiesce in the presentation of false evidence, Rule 3.3(b) of the Model Rules of Professional Conduct requires the lawyer to take "reasonable remedial measures" when the lawyer representing a client in that proceeding "knows that a person intends to engage, is engaging, or has engaged in criminal or fraudulent conduct related to the proceeding." The duty to take "reasonable remedial measures" includes the duty to disclose the matter to the court if necessary to rectify the situation. As with the lawyer's discovery that false evidence has been presented to the tribunal,[605] the duty of disclosure with respect to fraudulent or criminal conduct relating to the proceeding applies under paragraph (c) of Rule 3.3 "even if compliance requires disclosure of information" otherwise protected as confidential under Model Rule 1.6.

---

599 MARVIN E. FRANKEL, PARTISAN JUSTICE (Hill & Wang, 1980); Marvin E. Frankel, *The Search for Truth: An Umpireal View*, 123 U. PA. L. REV. 1031 (1975).

600 On Judge Frankel's role and later change of position, see MONROE H. FREEDMAN & ABBE SMITH, UNDERSTANDING LAWYERS' ETHICS § 6.21 (LexisNexis 4th ed. 2010).

601 Marvin Frankel, *Partisan Justice: A Brief Revisit*, LITIGATION, Summer, 1989, at 43, 44.

602 *Id.*

603 *Id.* at 43.

604 *Id.* at 44.

605 *See supra* § 4-9.8(c) to (g).

As Rule 3.3(a)(3) addresses the presentation of false evidence in the proceeding, which of course is a form of fraud upon the tribunal and when done knowingly constitutes a crime, Rule 3.3(b) is addressed to other forms of criminal or fraudulent conduct that undermine the integrity of the adjudicative process. Comment 12 to Rule 3.3 provides such examples as "bribing, intimidating or otherwise unlawfully communicating with a witness, juror, court official or other participant in the proceeding, unlawfully destroying or concealing documents or other evidence or failing to disclose information to the tribunal when required by law to do so."

The lawyer again not only must refrain from assisting such wrongful misconduct but, upon obtaining knowledge that such activities have occurred or are underway, must take those measures necessary to counteract the deleterious effects upon the proceeding, including disclosure to the tribunal as necessary.

### § 4-9.8(i) Witness Preparation Versus Witness Coaching

Rule 3.4(b) of the Model Rules of Professional Conduct forbids a lawyer to "counsel or assist a witness to testify falsely." While a lawyer obviously may not suborn perjury by a witness, that is, advise a witness to knowingly testify falsely, Rule 3.4(b) extends beyond such extreme misconduct and further prohibits a lawyer from manipulating a witness to testify falsely, even if the influence is applied with subtlety and in such a manner that the witness believes he is telling the truth.

The practical difficulty presented by a broad application of the venerable principle against tampering with a witness is that even the most sincerely-conducted preparation of a witness by a lawyer may have the unintended, but often unavoidable, effect of not merely refreshing but altering the witness's recollection. Moreover, too many lawyers regularly prepare a witness by aggressive means and repeated rehearsals that inevitably changes the witness's memory and understanding of past events.[606]

On the one hand, as we are taught by scientific studies of the psychology of memory, every time a person recalls a past event, she actually "reconstruct[s] the memory . . . colored by succeeding events, increased understanding, a new context, suggestions by others, other people's recollections."[607] Thus, when a person is asked yet again to recall a past event, even without being asked suggestive questions, the person may be "either supplementing or falsifying the data of perception," "without being in the least aware."[608]

On the other hand, the diligent lawyer must thoroughly prepare witnesses to be presented on behalf of the client's cause, particularly when that witness is also the lawyer's client, in order to ensure that all of the necessary information has been extracted and the witness has been alerted to the kinds of questions likely to be asked

---

[606] *See* Bruce A. Green, *"The Whole Truth?": How Rules of Evidence Make Lawyers Deceitful*, 25 LOYOLA L.A. L. REV. 699, 704–05 (1992) (explaining that "by apprising their witnesses of the law relevant to the case and of the statements made by others, as well as by asking questions in a suggestive manner, lawyers cause witnesses to recall things differently from how they originally perceived them; by rehearsing their witnesses' testimony, lawyers make witnesses inordinately certain of the quality of their recollection").

[607] ELIZABETH LOFTUS, MEMORY: SURPRISING NEW INSIGHTS INTO HOW WE REMEMBER AND WHY WE FORGET 169 (Addison-Wesley Pub. Co., 1980). On the psychology of memory as relevant to preparing witnesses, see generally MONROE H. FREEDMAN & ABBE SMITH, UNDERSTANDING LAWYERS' ETHICS § 7.06 (LexisNexis 4th ed. 2010).

[608] FREDERICK C. BARTLETT, REMEMBERING: A STUDY IN EXPERIMENTAL AND SOCIAL PSYCHOLOGY 14 (Cambridge U. Press, 1967).

on both direct- and cross-examination.[609] The comments accompanying the witness preparation section of the *Restatement of the Law Governing Lawyers* advise that preparation of a witness appropriately includes:

> discussing the role of the witness and effective courtroom demeanor; discussing the witness's recollection and probable testimony; revealing to the witness other testimony or evidence that will be presented and asking the witness to reconsider the witness's recollection or recounting of events in that light; discussing the applicability of law to the events in issue; reviewing the factual context into which the witness's observations or opinions will fit; reviewing documents or other physical evidence that may be introduced; and discussing probable lines of hostile cross-examination that the witness should be prepared to meet. Witness preparation may include rehearsal of testimony.[610]

In light of the unavoidable conflict between the lessons of psychology regarding the effect on accurate memory that attends any interview of a witness and the important professional duty of the lawyer to prepare witnesses, Professors Monroe Freedman and Abbe Smith well state the problem:

> The lawyer's dilemma, therefore, is that if she fails to probe the client's memory, important facts may be lost; but if she tells the client that a particular fact is important and why it is important, she may induce the client to "remember" the fact even if it did not occur. Furthermore, since the client's memory is inevitably going to be affected by reconstruction consistent with self-interest, a client who has a misunderstanding of her own legal interest could be psychologically inclined to remember in a way that is not only inconsistent with her case, but also inaccurate.[611]

How then is the ethically-responsible lawyer supposed to *prepare* a witness, without improperly *coaching* a witness? No easy answer is available, but some food for ethical thought may be served to the conscientious lawyer:

***Begin with the Witness's Own Story:*** The lawyer should begin an interview with a client or a witness in a manner that allows the person to tell the story without being prompted or led by the lawyer. After hearing this narrative, the lawyer ordinarily will need to follow-up by asking pointed and even skeptical questions, seeking more detailed information, probing the background of the story, exploring the context and circumstances of the witness's observations, assessing the witness's level of confidence about each element of the narrative, and even testing or challenging the accuracy of the

---

[609] *See* DeVoss v. State, 648 N.W.2d 56, 64 (Iowa 2002) (saying that "[a]ttorneys certainly have the right to prepare their witnesses," and "[i]t would be foolhardy not to"); People v. McGuirk, 245 N.E.2d 917, 922 (Ill. Ct. App. 1969) ("An attorney is bound by the testimony of his witnesses and there is nothing improper in refreshing their memories before they take the stand. Reviewing their testimony before trial makes for better direct examination, facilitates the trial and lessens the possibility of irrelevant and perhaps prejudicial interpolations."); Hamdi & Ibrahim Mango Co. v. Fire Ass'n of Philadelphia, 20 F.R.D. 181, 183 (S.D.N.Y. 1957) (explaining that in a witness preparation conference, "counsel will usually, in more or less general terms, ask the witness the same questions as he expects to put to him on the stand," review documents in a complex case "both for the purpose of refreshing the witness' recollection and to familiarize him with those which are expected to be offered in evidence," as "[t]his sort of preparation is essential to the proper presentation of a case and to avoid surprise"). On witness preparation in practice, see generally John S. Applegate, *Witness Preparation*, 68 TEX. L. REV. 277, 286–324 (1989).

[610] RESTATEMENT (THIRD) OF THE LAW GOVERNING LAWYERS § 116, cmt. b (American Law Institute, 2000).

[611] FREEDMAN & SMITH, *supra*, § 7.07.

client's (or the witness's) account.[612] Still, the fact that the person began the session by speaking in his own voice and by offering a reconstruction of memory that is undirected by the lawyer provides some minimal protection against undue influence by the lawyer. As one thoughtful litigator suggests, "[h]aving searched their memories and committed to their relevant recollections, prospective witnesses are less likely to adopt other versions or claim lack of recall because they believe it is expected or helpful."[613]

In sum, eliciting the witness's story by narrative at the beginning of the interview, even as a prelude to a more thorough preparation that includes challenging questions, makes it somewhat more likely that the testimony ultimately offered will retain a meaningful resemblance to the client's unadulterated recollection.

***Think About Purpose of Preparation:*** Professor Richard Wydick urges the lawyer to "continuously think about whether there is a legitimate purpose for the next question or the next statement."[614] Before asking a follow-up question of a client or witness during preparation, the lawyer should engage in candid self-examination and confirm in the lawyer's own mind that the subject of the question and the manner in which it will be raised is truly intended to draw out further information or appropriately encourage the client or witness to reconsider the accuracy of a perception, rather than designed to suggest a different answer by the client or witness that would better advance the representation.[615] In this respect, Professor Charles Wolfram suggests that "[t]he line between legitimate and disreputable preparation is largely one of the lawyer's intentions."[616]

Moreover, if an attorney does cross the ethical line and succeeds in supplanting the witness's narrative with the lawyer's preferred story, there is a substantial risk that this "sandpapering" of the witness's memory will be exposed at trial. One federal court acknowledged that "[t]he line is not easily drawn between proper review of the facts and refreshment of the recollection of a witness and putting words in the mouth of the witness or ideas in his mind."[617] However, the same court observed that "[s]ome protection is afforded to a party against such abuses by permitting him to question the witness on cross-examination about prior conversations with counsel."[618] Former Assistant United States Attorney Hank Shea warns that "[m]any witnesses will defer to an attorney's claim of superior knowledge of the facts when alone with the attorney but will revert to their original view" under cross-examination.[619] If the witness then points to the lawyer as the source of the changed story, judicial sanctions, ethical discipline, and even criminal charges for suborning perjury or obstructing justice could follow.[620] As veteran federal prosecutor Patrick Fitzgerald has suggested, with respect to witness

---

[612] *See* Stephen M. Goldman & Douglas A. Winegardner, *The Anti-False Testimony Principle and the Fundamentals of Ethical Preparation of Deposition Witnesses*, 59 CATH. U. L. REV. 1, 23 (2009) ("The rules do not require that lawyers adopt the completely passive posture of a potted plant when hearing how their clients or witnesses describe events that they perceived.").

[613] Martin J. Siegel, *Zealous Advocacy v. Truth*, LITIGATION, Fall, 2006, at 31, 33.

[614] Wydick, *supra*, 7 CARDOZO L. REV. at 52.

[615] *See* Applegate, *supra*, 68 TEX. L. REV. at 308 (discussing the abusive problem of "suggestive questioning during witness preparation").

[616] CHARLES W. WOLFRAM, MODERN LEGAL ETHICS § 12.4.3 (West, 1986).

[617] Hamdi & Ibrahim Mango Co. v. Fire Ass'n of Philadelphia, 20 F.R.D. 181, 183 (S.D.N.Y. 1957).

[618] *Id.*

[619] Hank Shea, Ethical Witness Preparation: How to Make the Witness Own His or Her Testimony (and Keep the Lawyer Out of Trouble) (Oct. 19, 2007).

[620] *Id.*

preparation, "never say anything to a witness that you would not want to see on the front page of the *New York Times*."[621]

***Avoid Excessive Preparation:*** While the zealous advocate will naturally be diligent in preparing a witness, too much of an appropriate thing may become an inappropriate thing. The lawyer should not be overly persistent on a particular point where the witness has adhered to a position or statement that the lawyer regards as unfavorable, returning repeatedly to a subject long past the point of any legitimate effort to uncover information that the witness genuinely may recall, preparing written instructions that have the effect of substituting the lawyer's preferred narrative for that of the witness, or rehearsing the witness's testimony excessively to script exactly what the witness is to say and how to say it.[622] By over-emphasis and excessive attention, preparatory activities may overwhelm the witness's autonomy, with the result that the testimony ceases to be that of the witness and becomes instead that of the lawyer with the witness being only a mouthpiece.[623]

***Encourage Witness to Tell the Truth:*** The lawyer should tell the witness to tell the truth and should "[r]epeat this admonition often, especially when the witness is not your client and your discussions are therefore not protected by the attorney-client privilege."[624] Emphasizing the importance of testifying truthfully is not only an ethical mandate but may also have some effect of reducing unintended influence on the witness to tailor the story toward what the witness believes the lawyer wishes or the circumstances suggest is better.

In the end, the lawyer engaged in ethically-appropriate witness preparation should be seeking to develop the witness's own story, although to be sure it will be better refreshed, more thoroughly examined, and more articulately presented. Still, it should be the witness's story and not one composed by the lawyer. While it may often be difficult to divine,[625] "[a]n attorney must respect the important ethical distinction between discussing testimony and seeking improperly to influence it."[626]

---

[621] Patrick J. Fitzgerald, *Thoughts on the Ethical Culture of a Prosecutor's Office*, 84 WASH. L. REV. 11, 22 (2009).

[622] *See* Applegate, *supra*, 68 TEX. L. REV. at 343 (saying that "polishing, scripting, and rehearsing (especially repeated rehearsing) seem undesirable"). *Cf.* Committee on Prof'l Ethics & Conduct v. LaPointe, 415 N.W.2d 617, 619–20 (Iowa 1987) (imposing discipline on an attorney who attempted to influence his girlfriend's anticipated testimony regarding an assault he committed upon her by, among other things, preparing what the court called an "ill-advised 'refresher' document" that instructed her to testify the assault had been in self-defense, that she exaggerated the truth, and that she had benefited from her relationship with the attorney, and by the attorney's persistence in talking with her about her anticipated testimony).

[623] *See* State ex rel. Abner v. Elliott, 706 N.E.2d 765, 768 (Ohio 1999) (refusing to overturn a judge's instruction to the jury in a suit against asbestos manufacturers that plaintiff's attorneys had "informed plaintiff [and co-workers] that it would be to their advantage for them to name as many of the defendants' products as possible during their depositions," after an inappropriate plaintiff preparation document had surfaced in another case and after the plaintiff failed to comply with a discovery order to disclose witness preparation documents in the case or submit to the judge for in camera inspection).

[624] Matthew Rosengart, *Preparing Witnesses for Trial: A Post-Moussaoui Primer for Federal Litigators*, FED. LAW. (Nov.–Dec. 2007), at 38.

[625] *See* Applegate, *supra*, 68 TEX. L. REV. at 279 (saying that "the line between preparing and prompting (or 'coaching,' the usual term of opprobrium) is rarely clear even for most scrupulous").

[626] *See* Geders v. United States, 425 U.S. 80, 90 n.3 (1976).

### § 4-9.8(j) Improper Inducements to a Witness

As part and parcel of the prohibition on encouraging a witness to testify falsely, Rule 3.4(b) of the Model Rules of Professional Conduct forbids a lawyer from "offer[ing] an inducement to a witness that is prohibited by law."

The manifest concern underlying this proscription is that the lawyer's offer of financial or other incentives to a witness may cause that witness to slant her testimony, consciously or otherwise, in the direction of the party that offers the inducement. Whether or not such an inducement was intended by the lawyer as a bribe in exchange for false testimony, the witness nonetheless may be influenced by the prospect of the reward and thus the veracity of the witness may be compromised. Indeed, even when a particular payment to a witness is permitted, Professors Roger Haydock, David Herr, and Jeffrey Stempel suggest that tactical considerations may make the payment inadvisable: "A witness who receives substantial reimbursement may appear to a fact finder to be biased in favor of the party who paid the money."[627]

In an extreme case, where the inducement is plainly designed to influence the substance of witness testimony in a criminal proceeding, a lawyer's offer of compensation may constitute criminal tampering with a witness. In *Committee on Professional Ethics & Conduct v. Halleck*,[628] a lawyer who offered restitution to the victim of a crime was convicted of witness tampering, as the evidence showed that the payment was offered to sway the witness's testimony in favor of the lawyer's client in the theft case. As the court explained, "[t]he vice in this case was not in offering restitution but in using it as leverage to attempt to influence the witness to assist in chilling or hindering the prosecution of [the lawyer's] client."[629]

Rule 3.4(b) bars only those payments to a witness that are "prohibited by law." An expert witness may be compensated for his time spent in evaluating a matter, developing an opinion, and preparing for and testifying to that opinion, together with any expenses incurred by the expert. But the expert witness may not be compensated based upon the content of the opinion itself or paid a bonus for reaching the "right" result. In this regard, Comment 3 to Rule 3.4 observes that "it is improper to pay an expert witness a contingent fee."

With ordinary fact witnesses, Comment 3 to Rule 3.4 explains that "it is not improper to pay a witness's expenses." Thus, a fact witness may be reimbursed for expenses incurred in participating in a proceeding, such as travel and lodging costs. Several states specifically approve compensation to witnesses for both expenses and for lost time in preparing for, attending, and delivering testimony.[630] The American Bar

---

[627] ROGER S. HAYDOCK, DAVID F. HERR & JEFFREY W. STEMPEL, FUNDAMENTALS OF PRETRIAL LITIGATION 70 (West Group, 5th ed., 2001).

[628] 325 N.W.2d 117, 118 (Iowa 1982).

[629] *Id.* at 118; *see also* Disciplinary Counsel v. Doumbas, 76 N.E.3d 1185, 1186–88 (Ohio 2017) (suspending a lawyer who was convicted of bribery after "civil settlements" were offered by co-counsel to sexual assault victims as purportedly showing the client had made restitution for purposes of sentencing, where the evidence indicated the "monetary settlements . . . were contingent upon [the victims'] making requests that the sentencing judge not impose jail time" and where the lawyer had been found complicit).

[630] *See, e.g.,* GA. RULES OF PROF'L CONDUCT R. 3.4(b)(3); IOWA RULES OF PROF'L CONDUCT R. 32:3.4, cmt. 3; HAW. RULES OF PROF'L CONDUCT R. 3.4(c); MASS. RULES OF PROF'L CONDUCT R. 3.4(g); N.Y. RULES OF PROF'L CONDUCT R. 3.4(b); OR. RULES OF PROF'L CONDUCT R. 3.4(b); PA. RULES OF PROF'L CONDUCT R. 3.4(b); TENN. RULES OF PROF'L CONDUCT R. 3.4(h); TEX. RULES OF PROF'L CONDUCT R. 3.4(b); VA. RULES OF PROF'L CONDUCT R. 3.4(c).

Association's Standing Committee on Ethics and Professional Responsibility interprets the Model Rules as permitting compensation of an ordinary witness for the time spent preparing for and testifying.[631] Under the ABA opinion, compensation is not limited to circumstances in which the witness has actually suffered a loss of income, such as lost wages while absent from a job, because payment for the value of the time lost may be made to an unemployed or retired individual.[632]

The ABA committee directs the lawyer to "determine the reasonable value of the witness's time based on all relevant circumstances,"[633] a test that Professors Ronald Rotunda and John Dzienkowski aptly describe as "none too clear" and one that could "invite less scrupulous lawyers to, in effect, pay witnesses for the content of their testimony."[634] To avoid any suggestion that a payment amounts to an improper inducement to the witness to testify in a particular manner, the ethically-responsible lawyer should seek an objective measure for compensation of a witness, which typically will be found by reference to the witness's hourly compensation or equivalent in her work or employment or, for individuals who are not presently employed, by reference to wages for the individual's former occupation or for the kind of work for which the individual has been trained or would be qualified.

In addition, as a commonly-accepted practice, prosecutors may offer a criminal defendant immunity or a reduction in sentence in exchange for testifying about the conduct of another criminal defendant (commonly referred to as "turning state's evidence").[635] Professors Rotunda and Dzienkowski explain that the courts have allowed such inducements "because their purpose is not to change the content of the testimony but simply to get information that, realistically, would not otherwise normally be given."[636] In any event, the trier of fact is entitled to be informed about any such arrangement by a prosecutor with a witness because such inducements may well undermine the credibility of the witness.[637]

By contrast, a prosecutor who offers a similar inducement to arrange for the absence of a witness—thereby directly subverting the truth-finding function of the criminal justice system—has offered an unlawful inducement in violation of Rule 3.4(b).[638]

---

[631] ABA Comm. on Ethics and Prof'l Responsibility, Formal Op. 96–402 (1996).

[632] *See also* N.Y. St. Bar Comm. On Prof'l Ethics Op No. 668 (1994).

[633] *Id.*, see also RESTATEMENT (THIRD) OF THE LAW GOVERNING LAWYERS § 117(1) (American Law Institute, 2000) (allowing compensation of a witness for "the reasonable value of the witness's time spent in providing evidence").

[634] RONALD D. ROTUNDA & JOHN S. DZIENKOWSKI, PROFESSIONAL RESPONSIBILITY: A STUDENT'S GUIDE § 3.4–3(c) (American Bar Ass'n, 2013–2014).

[635] *See* Edwards v. State, 25 P.3d 142, 143–44 (Kan. Ct. App. 2001) (finding no violation of Rule 3.4(b) forbidding unlawful inducement when a prosecutor entered into a plea bargain with the defendant's accomplice in exchange for his testimony).

[636] RONALD D. ROTUNDA & JOHN S. DZIENKOWSKI, PROFESSIONAL RESPONSIBILITY: A STUDENT'S GUIDE § 3.4–3(d) (American Bar Ass'n, 2013–2014).

[637] On the prosecutor's duty to disclose exculpatory and mitigating evidence to the defense in a criminal case, including evidence that tends to impeach a witness, see *infra* § 4-9.10.

[638] *See* In re Disciplinary Proceedings Against Bonet, 29 P.3d 1242, 1248–49 (Wash. 2001) (finding a violation of Rule 3.4(b) where a prosecutor promised not to charge a witness in exchange for the witness's agreement to invoke the right against self-incrimination and refuse to testify in criminal case).

## § 4-9.9 BEHAVIOR DURING AND AFTER TRIAL

### § 4-9.9(a) Disruptive Behavior at Trial

Rule 3.5(d) of the Model Rules of Professional Conduct admonishes a lawyer not to "engage in conduct intended to disrupt a tribunal."

The rule should never be abused as a basis to enforce a standard of tepid civility that inhibits a lawyer from zealous representation and speaking the uncomfortable truth. Drawing attention to injustice and making a clear record of wrongdoing may be disruptive to the status quo, but it should not be characterized as behavior having no purpose other than an intent to disrupt a tribunal.

By contrast, insults, name-calling, unjustified personal attacks, obscene remarks, outbursts, temper tantrums, intoxication, and rude or flagrantly offensive gestures will not be tolerated in the courtroom. The improper means by which a contemptuous lawyer may disrupt proceedings before a tribunal are, sadly, limited only by the capacity of human imagination for mischief.[639] A trial may sometimes be dramatic, but as one court warns, "lawyers who turn a courtroom into theater will be on the outside looking in for a long time."[640]

Again, it must be emphasized that, while deliberate misconduct and serious breaches of protocol by a lawyer that are designed to cause a prejudicial disruption in the proceedings are both punishable by contempt and serve as a basis for professional discipline, Rule 3.5(d) does not impose a duty of good manners and courtesy at the penalty of disciplinary sanction.[641] As Professors Geoffrey Hazard and William Hodes and attorney Peter Jarivs comment, "while a discourteous advocate brings the system of justice into disrepute [and, your author would add, undermines the persuasiveness of his or her own case by that discourtesy], judges should be made of sufficiently stern stuff to survive affronts to their personal dignity."[642]

Nor should Rule 3.5(d) be invoked against a lawyer who simply upholds his professional obligation to make a case, complete the record, or preserve an issue for later appellate review. When an impatient or petulant judge refuses to permit or strongly discourages a lawyer from recording an objection or making an offer of proof, the lawyer must firmly and calmly persevere, without losing his temper or raising the temperature further by resorting to insulting language. The lawyer must ensure that the matter is made a part of the record and that the judge's interference with the lawyer's proper advocacy on behalf of the client is clearly reflected in the transcript of the proceedings. In *In re McConnell*,[643] the Supreme Court ruled that "[t]he arguments of a lawyer in presenting his client's case strenuously and persistently cannot amount to a contempt of court so long as the lawyer does not in some way create an obstruction which blocks the judge in the performance of his judicial duty."

---

[639] *See generally Trial Conduct: Courtroom Speech and Conduct,* 27 LAW. MAN. PROF. CONDUCT 617 (2011).

[640] Matter of Daniels, 570 A.2d 416, 427 (N.J. 1990).

[641] *See also supra* § 4-9.4(b) (addressing the aspirations for professionalism, while explaining that the ideals of professional courtesy and civility may not be enforced through the formal sanction of professional discipline).

[642] 2 GEOFFREY C. HAZARD, JR., W. WILLIAM HODES & PETER R. JARVIS, THE LAW OF LAWYERING § 34.09 (Aspen, 4th ed., 2016).

[643] 370 U.S. 230, 236 (1962).

### § 4-9.9(b) Improper Allusions and Expression of Personal Opinions by Lawyer

When a litigation matter proceeds to trial, the lawyer ordinarily is an advocate for a client, not a witness testifying to truth of events based upon personal knowledge.[644] The lawyer serves as a conduit for evidence, seeking the admission of evidence and presenting the testimony of others, rather than as the source of an evidentiary submission.

Yet the influence of the lawyer upon the trier of fact, especially when the case is tried to a jury of laypersons, may be substantial by virtue of the lawyer's constant presence in the courtroom, status as an educated professional, and authoritative role in the proceedings. Thus, the unscrupulous lawyer may have an opportunity to insinuate improper impressions into the minds of the jury. When the lawyer in the presence of the jury comments upon or even hints at the existence of evidence that has been refused admission, presumes to personally vouch for the truth of evidence or testimony submitted on behalf of the lawyer's client, or offers personal editorial comments about elements of the case, the lawyer crosses the line between advocacy of the client's cause and an improper personal investment in the case.

Rule 3.4(e) of the Model Rules of Professional Conduct provides that it is misconduct for a lawyer

> in trial, [to] allude to any matter that the lawyer does not reasonably believe is relevant or that will not be supported by admissible evidence, assert personal knowledge of facts in issue except when testifying as a witness, or state a personal opinion as to the justness of a cause, the credibility of a witness, the culpability of a civil litigant, or the guilt or innocence of an accused.

#### *§ 4-9.9(b)(1) Improper Allusions to Inadmissible Evidence by Lawyer*

If the rules of evidence are to be given full force, the evidentiary inadmissibility of certain matters as irrelevant, the product of hearsay, immunized by privilege, etc. may not properly be circumvented by a lawyer's allusions, direct or veiled, to such materials. Not only are references to excluded evidence a basis for a mistrial, because of the prejudicial effect on the jury, but such misconduct may justify a contempt citation against the lawyer as well as professional discipline. While a lawyer who has a colorable argument for the admission of evidence is entitled to seek its admission, including submission of physical evidence or documents or examination of witnesses during the course of the trial (when the matter has not been excluded by a prior motion in limine), the lawyer must be willing to abide by the common expectation that extensive argument about evidentiary admissibility ordinarily should occur outside the presence of the jury. And the lawyer must not attempt to sabotage court rulings that exclude a matter from evidence.

When a matter is plainly inadmissible, the lawyer must not resort to what Professors Geoffrey Hazard and William Hodes and attorney Peter Jarvis call those "common 'tricks of the trade,' namely the deliberate asking of improper questions [typically in an attempt to elicit answers that reveal privileged or otherwise inadmissible matters] that are then withdrawn if the other side objects, and alluding to matter that

---

[644] On the Advocate-Witness Rule generally barring a lawyer from simultaneously advocating to the court and jury and testifying as a witness, see *infra* 4-9.10.

will *not* be supported by admissible evidence, hoping that the trier of fact will not be able to 'un-ring the bell,' even after the court gives a cautionary instruction."[645] Similarly, as Professor Charles Wolfram notes, "a lawyer who has no reason to believe that a matter is subject to proof may not, by pursuing the matter in examining a witness or in arguing to the court, attempt to create the impression that the matter is factual."[646]

#### *§ 4-9.9(b)(2) Improper Personal Vouching and Opinions by Lawyer*

Unless the lawyer has personal knowledge of facts and is testifying as a witness, in which case the lawyer ordinarily may not simultaneously appear as an advocate in that proceeding,[647] the lawyer must not personally vouch for the truthfulness of facts testified to by a witness or otherwise presented into evidence.[648] This does not mean, of course, that the lawyer may not argue the evidence or rely upon evidence admitted when offering a summation to the trier of fact. The lawyer must distinguish between zealous argumentation and personal verification, always maintaining some distance between commentary on or highlighting of certain evidence and a suggestion of personal knowledge of the facts in issue.

Similarly, the lawyer must steer clear of offering a personal opinion about the merits of the case, the credibility of a witness, the culpability of a party in civil litigation, or the guilt or innocence of a defendant to a criminal prosecution. It is improper to vouch for the truthfulness (or lack thereof) of a witness "whether the personal belief is purportedly based on knowledge of facts not possessed by the jury, counsel's experience in similar cases, or any ground other than the weight of the evidence at the trial."[649]

Again, the lawyer certainly may be appropriately forceful and enthusiastic in arguing the case, including encouraging the trier of fact to perceive the evidence as leading in a particular direction. Thus, for example, the lawyer properly may draw attention to underlying factors and apparent motivations and contradictions that suggest a witness has not testified truthfully, and indeed may openly invite the trier of fact to question the credibility of that witness. But the lawyer must stop short of announcing the lawyer's own judgment on the matter, thereby merging the lawyer's personality into the case.

### § 4-9.9(c) Improper Influence on a Tribunal

The decision-maker, whether judge or jury, is obliged to decide an adjudication matter based upon the governing law and the evidence presented in an adversarial setting. Accordingly, a lawyer's efforts to convince the tribunal to rule in favor of the lawyer's client should be directed primarily toward the thorough discovery and submission of admissible evidence, accompanied by zealous (but non-frivolous) advocacy about the meaning and application of the pertinent law.

---

[645] 2 GEOFFREY C. HAZARD, JR., W. WILLIAM HODES & PETER R. JARVIS, THE LAW OF LAWYERING § 33.13 (Aspen, 4th ed., 2016).

[646] CHARLES W. WOLFRAM, MODERN LEGAL ETHICS § 12.1.2 (West, 1986).

[647] For discussion of the conflict between the role of the advocate and that of a witness, see *infra* § 4-9.10.

[648] On the prosecutor's heightened duty not to personally vouch for witnesses or evidence, see also *infra* § 4-9.12(e).

[649] State v. Williams, 334 N.W.2d 742, 744 (Iowa 1983).

When a lawyer's attempts to influence a judge or jury go beyond references to the evidence and appeals to the law, as well as the exercise of legitimate advocacy techniques that enhance the lawyer's persuasiveness and the client's credibility, the lawyer's advocacy may cross an ethical line. The Model Rules of Professional Conduct prohibit, as examples, allusions by a lawyer to irrelevant or inadmissible matters,[650] assertions by the lawyer of personal knowledge or personal opinions,[651] use of means by the lawyer designed only to embarrass or burden a witness or party,[652] or manifestations of bias by the lawyer[653] when appearing before a tribunal. When an attempt to sway a judge or jury further crosses the line of legality, the lawyer stands at risk of both legal (perhaps criminal) penalties and professional sanction.

Rule 3.5(a) of the Model Rules of Professional Conduct prohibits a lawyer from "seek[ing] to influence a judge, juror, prospective juror or other official by means prohibited by law." This ethical provision is designed to arrest corrupt influences upon the tribunal, such as offering a bribe for a favorable ruling or threatening violence to prevent an unfavorable ruling. As Professors Ronald Rotunda and John Dzienkowski explain, given that the conduct prohibited is already illegal, "[t]he purpose of this rule is to make clear that the lawyer who engages in such conduct must fear not only the sanctions that other law imposes but also the sanction of losing his or her license to practice law."[654]

### § 4-9.9(d) *Ex Parte* Communications with a Tribunal (Judge or Jury)

The American adjudicatory system is generally premised on the ideal that the search for the truth and the wise interpretation and development of the law are best advanced through an adversarial process. Each party submits evidence and presents legal argument, while simultaneously testing the evidence presented and challenging the legal arguments made by the opposing side.

Thus, a lawyer who speaks privately with a judge or juror about the merits of the case, without giving the opposing lawyer an opportunity to participate, ordinarily commits a serious offense against justice. When a lawyer for one party communicates surreptitiously with a judge or juror in a manner that may influence the outcome of the adjudication, the other party has been deprived of its due process right to be heard. And the confidence of the public in the impartiality of the tribunal may be compromised.

Accordingly, Rule 3.5(b) of the Model Rules of Professional Conduct prohibits a lawyer from "communicat[ing] ex parte with [a judge, juror, prospective juror, or other official] unless authorized to do so by law or court order." (And the judge who accepts an *ex parte* interaction with a lawyer likely runs afoul of the parallel prohibition under the Code of Judicial Conduct.[655])

---

[650] *See supra* § 4-9.9(b)(1).

[651] *See supra* § 4-9.9(b)(2).

[652] *See supra* § 4-9.4(c).

[653] *See* supra § 4-9.4(b)(2).

[654] RONALD D. ROTUNDA & JOHN S. DZIENKOWSKI, PROFESSIONAL RESPONSIBILITY: A STUDENT'S GUIDE § 3.5–1 (American Bar Ass'n, 2013–2014).

[655] For discussion of ex parte communications under the Code of Judicial Conduct, see *infra* Charles Geyh, Judicial Ethics and the Conduct of Judges § 6-2.4.

The exceptions to the prohibition against *ex parte* contacts with a judge are few and typically involve exigent circumstances, such as obtaining a restraining order to protect against the threat of imminent violence or obtaining a search warrant as part of a criminal investigation.

On those unusual occasions on which an *ex parte* communication with a judge is permitted, Model Rule 3.3(d) places the ethical burden on the lawyer to "inform the tribunal of all material facts known to the lawyer that will enable the tribunal to make an informed decision, whether or not the facts are adverse." Precisely because the absent party has no opportunity to present an opposing perspective, the lawyer communicating *ex parte* with a judge has a special duty of candor.[656]

While social and professional exchanges between a lawyer and a judge unrelated to a matter pending before a tribunal are common and generally accepted, "[t]here is simply no legitimate reason for a lawyer to have private contact with a juror before or during the trial."[657] Thus, while the prohibition on *ex parte* contact with a tribunal generally should be understood to constrain only the subject of discussion between a lawyer and a judge, the rule ordinarily should be applied to strictly bar any communications by a lawyer with a juror (other than a brief and courteous greeting if the two should happen to meet in the courthouse hallway or on the street).[658]

When a lawyer and judge meet in a social or professional context, their professional training and the independent ethical responsibilities that attach to each presumably will cause them to be circumspect in the choice of conversational topics. Moreover, the judge, as a member of the profession and experienced in adjudication, is unlikely to be influenced by ordinary social and professional interactions with a lawyer, even if the lawyer is excessively ingratiating during the encounter.

By contrast, when a lawyer speaks privately with a juror, the juror typically is in a more vulnerable position, not fully appreciating the ethical limitations on appropriate exchanges and more likely to be flattered by and respond favorably to the lawyer's attention, even if the conversation does not move directly into forbidden territory. Moreover, public confidence in the integrity of the jury system requires that "the jury work[ ] in a controlled environment, untouched by any influence other than that properly permitted by the trial judge."[659]

To illustrate and contrast the different ethical expectations that should govern *ex parte* communications by a lawyer with a judge and those by a lawyer with a jury member, consider the ordinary social setting in which the subject of the pending matter is not broached:

A lawyer who has a matter pending before a particular judge at trial or on appeal may well find herself seated at the same table with that judge at a bar association or other professional or social event. For either to take advantage of this event to make even an indirect reference to the merits of the pending adjudication matter would be both unethical and in extremely poor taste. However, the lawyer and judge may feel

---

656 *See also supra* § 4-9.5(d).

657 2 GEOFFREY C. HAZARD, JR., W. WILLIAM HODES & PETER R. JARVIS, THE LAW OF LAWYERING § 34.03 (Aspen, 4th ed., 2016).

658 *See* Colosimo v. Pennsylvania Elec. Co., 486 A.2d 1378, 1381 (Pa. Super. 1984) ("Certainly a new trial is not warranted where an attorney acknowledges a juror in an elevator or says hello at a ball game.").

659 Hobson v. Wilson, 737 F.2d 1, 48 (D.C. Cir. 1984).

quite comfortable, and appropriately so, in discussing other subjects, including other legal topics and recent developments involving the courts. Indeed, if the bar and the bench are to maintain a positive relationship, regular interactions between lawyers and judges are to be encouraged, even recognizing the inevitability that some of the lawyers involved in such bench-bar conferences will have matters pending before some of the participating judges.

By contrast, suppose that lawyers for a defendant in civil litigation stop for dinner at a restaurant after a day at trial. As it happens, one of the jurors is sitting at the bar and insists upon buying a round of drinks for the lawyers. After receiving the drinks, the lawyers are introduced by the juror to other patrons in the bar "and they all conversed about various subjects," but the pending trial apparently was not discussed. The events described above were those in *Omaha Bank v. Siouxland Cattle Co-op.*[660] The court ruled that the trial court abused its discretion in failing to remove this juror, saying:

> The juror's offer of drinks and the lawyers' acceptance was clearly misconduct by all of them. [The juror], in speaking to the lawyers and offering and buying them drinks, violated the standard admonition given by the court to refrain from contact with the lawyers involved in the case. The bank's lawyers violated their ethical obligation prohibiting communication with a juror during trial unless it is in the course of official proceedings.[661]

Even accepting that the trial was never the topic of conversation, the court described the case as involving "gross impropriety" and compromising the independence of the jury.[662]

## § 4-9.9(e) Communications with Jury After Discharge

Each year at the Drake University Law School, regular first-year classes are suspended for a week so that law students may participate in a trial practicum, attending each day's proceedings in an actual civil or criminal jury trial that is conducted in the school's teaching courtroom.[663] In your author's experience during the years in which I taught there, the most compelling part of this unique program was the final act, in which those jurors who were willing (which usually was all or most of them) returned after the verdict to meet with the law students, share their impressions, and answer questions. The jurors often identified which witnesses they found most (and least) credible, which arguments by the lawyers were most (and least) persuasive, which advocacy styles by the lawyers they found most (and least) attractive, which elements of the trial were satisfying and which were irritating, how they understood and applied the judge's instructions, how they collectively reasoned through to a verdict, and how they handled the emotional stress of, for example, deciding whether to find an individual guilty of a serious felony, such as murder. By participating in this program, soon-to-be lawyers obtain a rare inside look at the manner in which lay members of a jury evaluate the facts, apply the law, and reach a verdict.

The finest advocates are those who constantly test their skills and learn from experience. When it comes to education about how to best appeal to a jury, the lawyer is likely to find no better teacher than the members of an actual jury that decided (or

---

[660] Omaha Bank v. Siouxland Cattle Co-op., 305 N.W.2d 458, 461 (Iowa 1981).

[661] *Id.*

[662] *Id.* at 463.

[663] *See* Russell E. Lovell, II, *Trial Practicum Integral to First-Year Law School Curriculum*, JUDICATURE, Nov.–Dec. 2006.

reached a mistrial in) a case in which the lawyer participated. After the jury has been discharged and the lawyer's *ex parte* contact thus no longer may influence the verdict, a lawyer may wish to interview members of the jury and discover what elements of the case and what aspects of the lawyer's advocacy were successful in persuading a juror and what was not. As a lesser motivation, the lawyer may also wish to verify with members of the jury that they did not engage in any misconduct in reaching a verdict, although the courts generally refuse to allow evidence gathered from such interviews (or otherwise) to impeach a jury verdict.[664] For these reasons, a lawyer ordinarily acts appropriately in requesting to speak with members of the jury after the proceeding is concluded and the jury has been discharged.

Under Rule 3.5(c) of the Model Rules of Professional Conduct, the lawyer is not required to ask permission of the court before conducting an interview with a willing member of the discharged jury. However, Model Rule 3.5(c) places three important constraints on the general consent extended to a lawyer to speak with members of the jury after discharge.

*First*, Rule 3.5(c) (1) bars such communications when they are "prohibited by law or court order." The lawyer must comply with the directions of the judge, which may preclude any communications with the discharged jury in certain cases of great sensitivity or where the jurors have asked not to be contacted, may require the lawyers to wait a period of time until the jurors have had an opportunity to recover from an emotional ordeal, or may limit the scope of questions that may be asked of jurors.

Importantly, in contrast with the permissive approach of Model Rule 3.5(c) the "[f]ederal courts have generally disfavored post-verdict interviewing of jurors."[665] Many state court systems are similarly restrictive.[666]

*Second*, Rule 3.5(c)(2) precludes a lawyer from attempting to interview a juror when "the juror has made known to the lawyer a desire not to communicate." The lawyer's interest in speaking with a juror to improve advocacy or investigate the jury verdict remains subordinate to the juror's right to personal privacy.

*Third*, Rule 3.5(c)(3) directs the lawyer in communicating with a juror not to engage in "misrepresentation, coercion, duress or harassment." Despite the natural enthusiasm

---

[664] *See* Pena-Rodriguez v. Colorado, 137 S. Ct. 855, 864–65 (2017) (explaining that the general no-impeachment rule serves to "promote[ ] full and vigorous discussion by providing jurors with considerable assurance that after being discharged they will not be summoned to recount their deliberations, and they will not otherwise be harassed or annoyed by litigants seeking to challenge the verdict," but finding a constitutional exception when compelling evidence of juror statements indicates racial animus); United States v. Connolly, 341 F.3d 16, 34 (1st Cir. 2003) ("[Federal Rule of Evidence 606(b) codifies the 'near-universal and firmly established common-law rule' that prohibits admission of juror testimony to impeach a jury verdict," thereby promoting "finality, maintaining the integrity of the jury system, encouraging frank and honest deliberations, and the protection of jurors from subsequent harassment by a losing party." (quoting Tanner v. United States, 483 U.S. 107, 117 (1987))); Long v. Brusco Tug & Barge, Inc., 368 P.3d 478, 480 (Wash. 2016) ("Central to our jury system is the secrecy of jury deliberations. Courts are appropriately forbidden from receiving information to impeach a verdict based on revealing the details of the jury's deliberations."); Weatherwax v. Koontz, 545 N.W.2d 522, 523–26 (Iowa 1996) (emphasizing that evidence is rarely admissible to impeach a jury verdict, explaining that matters involving the jury's reasoning process are said to inhere in the verdict, and thus may not be the basis for a challenge to a verdict, while questions concerning outside influences that improperly were introduced into the deliberations may be examined, although being further disinclined to allow impeachment of a verdict after the jury has been discharged).

[665] Haeberle v. Texas Intern. Airlines, 739 F.2d 1019, 1021 (5th Cir. 1984).

[666] *See* People v. Giuca, No. 8166/2004, 2009 WL 901526, at *8–9 (N.Y. Sup. Ct. Apr. 1, 2009) (discussing approaches of several states).

of the partisan for a case or urgency of the lawyer in exploring the reasons for an unfavorable outcome, the lawyer must be scrupulous and reasonably gentle in communicating with a juror, not misleading the juror as to the lawyer's purpose or imposing upon the juror who is reluctant to speak about a matter.

## § 4-9.10 THE ADVOCATE-WITNESS RULE

### § 4-9.10(a) The Advocate-Witness Rule and Avoiding Confusion of the Lawyer's Role

The advocate-witness rule holds that a lawyer may not simultaneously serve both as the advocate on behalf of a client and as a witness in a litigation matter. If the lawyer is to be a witness, then he must step aside as the client's lawyer. This longstanding disqualification rule is now codified in Rule 3.7 of the Model Rules of Professional Conduct.

While the advocate-witness rule in the past was sometimes framed as avoiding a potential conflict of interest, it is understood today as designed primarily to prevent a confusing conflict of roles.[667] Whether a lawyer's testimony creates a conflict of interest with a client largely depends on whether the substance of that testimony supports the client's case or undermines it.[668] But whenever a lawyer appears in the courtroom as an advocate on behalf of a client, and then steps out of the well of the court and into the witness box to testify, the line is blurred between the role of a zealous advocate in presenting the case most favorably to the client and the role of a sworn witness to testify to the truth.

"The most cogent rationale for the advocate-witness rule rests on protection of the fact-finding process."[669] Allowing a lawyer to wear two hats—that of advocate and that of witness—during the same proceeding would likely be confusing to the trier-of-fact. A jury of laypersons may be unable to clearly see the crucial line between statements by a witness that are evidence and statements by an advocate that are merely argument.[670] As one federal court explained, "[h]aving seen the attorney take an oath on the witness stand, the jury might accord testimonial weight to his closing arguments, or might simply place undue weight on the testimony of a court officer."[671] Likewise, Comment 2

---

[667] RESTATEMENT (THIRD) OF THE LAW GOVERNING LAWYERS § 108, Reporter's Note (American Law Institute, 2000) (stating that the Code "treated the advocate-witness problem primarily as one of conflicts of interest," while the Model Rules "treat the advocate-witness issue more generally as a problem of managing advocacy"); *see also* National Child Care, Inc. v. Dickinson, 446 N.W.2d 810, 812 (Iowa 1989) (saying that the rule "does not directly focus on conflicts of interest between attorney and client, but at preventing harm to the client because of a conflict inherent in the attorney's dual role as advocate and witness"); Presnick v. Esposito, 513 A.2d 165, 167 (Conn. Ct. App. 1986) (stating the reasons for the rule as including the public policy concern that "permitting an attorney who is trying a case also to be a witness in establishing its facts will visit on the legal profession public distrust and suspicion arising from the attorney's dual role").

[668] *See infra* § 4-9.10(d).

[669] 48 ROBERT P. SCHUWERK & LILLIAN HARDWICK, HANDBOOK OF TEXAS LAWYER AND JUDICIAL ETHICS: TEXAS PRACTICE SERIES § 8:8 (Thomson/West, 2016).

[670] *See* United States v. Jones, 600 F.3d 847, 862 (7th Cir. 2010) ("The rule recognizes the danger that an attorney might not be a fully objective witness, as well as the risk that a jury could confuse the two roles when deciding how much weight to accord to a testifying attorney's statements.").

[671] MacArthur v. Bank of New York, 524 F. Supp. 1205, 1208 (S.D.N.Y. 1981); *see also* Nelson v. Hartford Ins. Co., No. CV 11-162-M-DWM, 2012 WL 761965, at *4 (D. Mont, Mar. 8, 2012) ("[W]here an attorney has observed or participated in events giving rise to facts disputed at trial, a jury may misinterpret his questions or summation as testimony conveying his own version of those events;" internal quotation marks and citation omitted).

to Model Rule 3.7 states that "[i]t may not be clear whether a statement by an advocate-witness should be taken as proof or as an analysis of the proof."

A judge is more likely to appreciate the difference between the two roles, and the risks addressed by the advocate-witness rule are thus mitigated when the trier of fact is the judge. The rule nonetheless applies as well to cases tried to the bench and thus in which the judge is asked to weigh the credibility of the lawyer as a witness.[672]

The advocate-witness rule also reinforces the proscriptions placed on the lawyer when acting as an advocate in Rule 3.4(e) of the Model Rules of Professional Conduct against such improper trial tactics as asserting "personal knowledge of facts in issue" or stating a "personal opinion" about "the credibility of a witness."[673] As a lawyer for a client at trial, the advocate serves as a conduit for evidence, by seeking the admission of evidence and presenting the testimony of others, rather than being the source of evidence. But if the lawyer is permitted to move back-and-forth between the roles of advocate and witness, the lawyer will be in a position at some points in the trial to personally vouch for the truth of evidence, while at other times the lawyer will be constrained from offering a personal opinion. The trier of fact may find it difficult or impossible to separate these strands of lawyer statements before the tribunal. As Ethical Consideration 5–9 of the former Model Code of Professional Responsibility stated, "[a]n advocate who becomes a witness is in the unseemly and ineffective position of arguing the lawyer's own credibility."[674]

To avoid the possibility of being disqualified from courtroom advocacy on behalf of the client, the prudent lawyer who conducts preliminary investigations into matters that may be litigated or contemplates personal participation in a client's activities will shape his professional behavior to account for the disqualifying effect of the advocate-witness rule:

***Conducting Investigations:*** When investigating the circumstances underlying ongoing or anticipated litigation or when interviewing a witness, a lawyer must be careful not to put herself in a position where the lawyer is the sole witness to observed facts or uttered statements by others that become central to the litigation.[675] The simple solution for the investigating lawyer is to examine physical items or locations and speak to witnesses only when someone else, such as a legal assistant, law clerk, or investigator, is also present. If the condition of a physical item, the appearance of a location, or a witness's statement later assumes evidentiary importance, either to be directly presented through testimony or to contradict and impeach a witness who says otherwise, the assistant, clerk, or investigator may then be called to the stand, rather than the lawyer.

---

[672] *See* United States v. Johnston, 690 F.2d 638, 644 (8th Cir. 1982) (saying the argument that the advocate-witness rule does not apply to a proceeding tried to a judge rather than a jury "asks for too much" and noting that the judge then must choose between the credibility not only of the parties but also of one of the lawyers who simultaneously is an advocate).

[673] *See supra* § 4-9.9(b).

[674] MODEL CODE OF PROF'L RESPONSIBILITY, Ethical Consideration 5–9 (American Bar Ass'n, 1980).

[675] *See* STANDARDS FOR CRIMINAL JUSTICE: DEFENSE FUNCTION, Standard 4–4.3(f) (American Bar Ass'n, 2015) (explaining that, while "[a]n interview of routine witnesses (for example, custodians of records) should not require a third-party observer," the lawyer who "reasonably anticipate[s]" the "the need for corroboration of an interview" should make sure to bring along "another trusted and credible person" and "should avoid being alone with foreseeably hostile witnesses").

***Participating in Client Activities:*** When considering whether to become an active participant in a client's activities, such as by accepting a position on a client entity's board of directors, the lawyer must be aware that she could thereby become a necessary fact witness in later litigation regarding business decisions or other conduct by the client, in which case the lawyer would be unable to advocate for the client in the courtroom. The advocate-witness rule is one more reason for a lawyer to carefully maintain professional independence and a degree of distance from the client so as to be able to provide disinterested legal advice and preserve the ability to appear as an advocate on behalf of the client without conflict or constraint.

With respect to the scope of disqualification in the "advocate-witness" situation, Model Rule 3.7 focuses upon the potentially confusing effect of the same lawyer simultaneously acting as an advocate and as a witness in the same proceeding. Accordingly, and in contrast with the former Model Code of Professional Responsibility,[676] the lawyer-witness's disqualification is no longer imputed to other lawyers in the same law firm. Under Rule 3.7(b), a lawyer may continue to "act as advocate in a trial in which another lawyer in the lawyer's firm is likely to be called as a witness," unless that testimony would create a conflict of interest.

### § 4-9.10(b) The "Necessary Witness" Standard for the Advocate-Witness Rule

Under Rule 3.7(a) of the Model Rules of Professional Conduct, "[a] lawyer shall not act as advocate at a trial in which the lawyer is likely to be a necessary witness" (subject to certain exceptions).[677] In determining when a lawyer must take the stand and testify, while simultaneously being required to withdraw from representation of the client as an advocate, Rule 3.7 adopts the fairly stringent standard of the "necessary witness."

Under the former Model Code of Professional Responsibility, when a conflict appeared to exist or might exist between being an advocate and being a witness, the lawyer's duties varied according to the point in time in which the problem arose (before or after retention) and on whether the lawyer was to be called as a witness for or against the client. First, a lawyer was generally directed not to "accept employment in contemplated or pending litigation if it is known or it is obvious that a member of the lawyer's firm ought to be called as a witness."[678] Second, a lawyer generally was required to withdraw as counsel if the lawyer "learns or it is obvious that he or a member of his firm ought to be called as a witness on behalf of the client."[679] Third, a lawyer could continue representation if the "lawyer learns or it is obvious that the lawyer or member of the firm may be called as a witness other than on behalf of the client . . . until it is apparent that the testimony is or may be prejudicial to the client."[680]

By contrast, Rule 3.7(a) of the Model Rules of Professional Conduct adopts a uniform standard for the advocate-witness rule, regardless of who calls the lawyer to the stand, focusing on whether the lawyer "is likely to be a *necessary* witness" (emphasis added).

---

[676] MODEL CODE OF PROF'L RESPONSIBILITY, Disciplinary Rules 5–102 (American Bar Ass'n, 1980).

[677] For the exceptions to the advocate-witness rule, see *infra* § 4-9.10(c).

[678] MODEL CODE OF PROF'L RESPONSIBILITY, Disciplinary Rule 5–101(D) (American Bar Ass'n, 1980).

[679] *Id.* Disciplinary Rule 5–102(A).

[680] *Id.* Disciplinary Rule 5–102(B).

Although the language expressing the standard for disqualification under the advocate-witness rule differs ("ought to be called as a witness" versus "necessary witness"), the pertinent provisions of the Model Code of Professional Responsibility and of Rule 3.7 of the Model Rules of Professional Conduct are roughly parallel.[681] Drafting notes indicate that the "ought to be called" language of the Code was objectionable to the Model Rules drafters "because it did not sufficiently confine itself to instances in which the lawyer's testimony was 'necessary.' "[682] Professor Geoffrey Hazard, reporter for the Model Rules drafting committee, states that the Code's language was "vague" and "overbroad" because the term "ought" to testify had been read by some courts to require "disqualification if the lawyer's testimony was little more than relevant and admissible."[683] He explains that the text of Rule 3.7 is "more carefully crafted," applying only when the advocate is "likely" to be a "necessary" witness.[684] He emphasizes that "a lawyer does not become 'necessary' merely because an opposing party asserts that the lawyer has knowledge that might be relevant, or calls him to the stand."[685] Still, the adoption of "necessary" as the operative term in Rule 3.7 has been understood by other observers as simply clarifying the manner in which the former Code's "ought to be called" provision was appropriately applied.[686] Writing during the Code era and while Rule 3.7 was in the drafting stage, Professor Richard Wydick found that "[m]ost courts interpret 'ought to be a witness' to mean that the lawyer is a 'necessary' or 'indispensable' witness—the lawyer is the only person available to testify about a crucial fact."[687]

Accordingly, before a lawyer may be disqualified under the advocate-witness rule as now articulated in Rule 3.7, the lawyer must be a primary and not merely cumulative witness about a substantial matter that is of meaningful consequence to the fair disposition of the litigation. The lawyer who is a "necessary witness" ordinarily will be the only individual having personal knowledge about evidence that is not merely relevant but that bears directly on a controverted issue that a reasonable person would regard as pivotal in resolving the dispute. If the lawyer's testimony would be merely helpful or supplementary, the lawyer properly may avoid the witness stand and continue as an advocate with the client's approval. The client's choice of counsel ought not lightly be defeated.

When the lawyer truly would be a "necessary witness" on his own client's behalf, the lawyer may not avoid the effect of the advocate-witness rule by declining to take the stand and thus withholding significant supportive evidence. In *State v. Vanover*,[688] which arose under the former Code of Professional Responsibility, the Iowa Supreme

---

[681] *See* Richard C. Wydick, *Trial Counsel as Witness: The Code and the Model Rules*, 15 U.C. DAVIS L. REV. 651, 702 (1982) ("[O]n the printed page, Rule 3.7 strongly resembles its predecessors in the Code.").

[682] CHARLES W. WOLFRAM, MODERN LEGAL ETHICS § 7.5.2 (West, 1986).

[683] 2 GEOFFREY C. HAZARD, JR., W. WILLIAM HODES & PETER R. JARVIS, THE LAW OF LAWYERING § 36.04 (Aspen, 4th ed., 2016).

[684] *Id.*

[685] *Id.*

[686] *See* Erik G. Luna, *Avoiding a "Carnival Atmosphere": Trial Court Discretion and the Advocate-Witness Rules*, 18 WHITTIER L. REV. 447, 459 (1997) (stating that "tribunals and practitioners have found little difference between the advocate-witness provisions in the Model Code and the Model Rules" and that "the discrepancy in language ['ought to be called as a witness' versus 'likely to be a necessary witness'] has been viewed as rhetorical rather than purposeful").

[687] Richard C. Wydick, *Trial Counsel as Witness: The Code and the Model Rules,* 15 U.C. DAVIS L. REV. 651, 666 (1982).

[688] 559 N.W.2d 618 (Iowa 1997).

Court ruled that the advocate-witness rule prevented a party from being put to the choice of obtaining the attorney's valuable testimony and benefiting from the attorney's continued representation: "All doubt is resolved in favor of the attorney's testimony and against the attorney's representation."[689] While the client usually may obtain other effective counsel, the client " 'cannot obtain substitute testimony for a counsel's relevant personal knowledge.' "[690] Accordingly, the client may not waive the protections of the advocate-witness rule by agreeing not to call the lawyer as a necessary witness.[691]

## § 4-9.10(c) Exceptions to the Advocate-Witness Rule

Under Model Rule 3.7, there are three exceptions to the general bar against dual roles of advocate and witness being played by a lawyer:

### *§ 4-9.10(c)(1) Uncontested Issues*

First, under Model Rule 3.7(a)(1), the lawyer is not disqualified from serving as an advocate if the lawyer's "testimony relates to an uncontested issue." Comment 3 to Rule 3.7 explains that the harmful "ambiguities" posed by simultaneously serving as advocate and witness are "purely theoretical" when an issue is uncontested and thus the tribunal need not make a decision as to which position is more persuasive or has greater evidentiary support.

Although this exception is not limited to testimony about ancillary matters or formalities, it is most likely to be invoked in such circumstances as when a lawyer signs an affidavit testifying to the accuracy of documents being attached to a motion or relates under oath the circumstances underlying a request for a routine exercise of judicial discretion such as a continuance.

### *§ 4-9.10(c)(2) Nature and Value of Legal Services*

Second, under Model Rule 3.7(a)(2), the lawyer may continue to represent a client when "the testimony relates to the nature and value of legal services rendered in the case."

This exception ordinarily applies when a lawyer seeks payment under circumstances where court approval is required or submits on behalf of the client a petition for an award of attorney's fees against an opponent at the conclusion of a proceeding.[692] The attorney must provide, typically through a sworn affidavit, information about time records, activities on which that time was expended, and hourly rates. By no means are such requests invariably uncontested, and indeed fee petitions are often subject to a rigorously adversarial process. Thus, in contrast with the exception for uncontested issues, the lawyer's credibility as a witness may play a role in the disposition of a fee petition. Nonetheless, Comment 3 to Rule 3.7 states that "permitting the lawyers to testify avoids the need for a second trial with new counsel to resolve" the attorney's fee issue. Moreover, as the comment observes, the judge has "first-hand

---

[689] *Id.* at 632; *see also* People v. Passillas-Sanchez, 214 P.3d 520, 527 (Colo. App. 2009) (holding there was an unwaivable conflict between a lawyer's role as an advocate and as a critical witness because his failure to testify on behalf of a criminal defendant left "defendant as the only remaining source of 'critical and outcome determinative information' ").

[690] *Vanover*, 559 N.W.2d at 632 (quoting MacArthur v. Bank of New York, 524 F. Supp. 1205, 1209 (S.D.N.Y. 1981)).

[691] *Id.*

[692] On awards of attorney's fees in fee-shifting cases, see *supra* § 4-4.8.

knowledge" about fees for legal services and thus has less need to use the "adversary process to test the credibility of the testimony."[693]

### *§ 4-9.10(c)(3) Substantial Hardship on the Client*

Third, under Model Rule 3.7(a)(3), the lawyer may avoid the advocate-witness rule when "disqualification of the lawyer would work substantial hardship on the client."

In a case of claimed hardship as an exceptional circumstance, the interests of the client in avoiding loss of counsel of choice must be balanced against the interests of the tribunal and the opposing party in avoiding the confusion inherent in the dual roles of witness and advocate. Comment 4 to Rule 3.7 explains that "[w]hether the tribunal is likely to be misled or the opposing party is likely to suffer prejudice depends on the nature of the case, the importance and probable tenor of the lawyer's testimony, and the probability that the lawyer's testimony will conflict with that of other witnesses." When the lawyer's testimony is central to the litigation, when the underlying facts are hotly contested, and when the matter is being tried before a jury which is more likely to be confused by the lawyer's attempt to testify and advocate simultaneously, the advocate-witness rule is more likely to apply, even if the client is harmed by the loss of chosen counsel.

If the client or lawyer should have anticipated that the lawyer would probably be a necessary witness, a claim of hardship is less likely to be availing because they could have made alternative arrangements at an earlier stage. But if the opposing side could reasonably foresee the need to call the lawyer as a necessary witness, and yet did not alert the lawyer and the lawyer was not at fault in failing to anticipate the problem, the client ordinarily should not be deprived of the counsel on which the client has come to rely because the opposing party sandbagged the lawyer with a subpoena to testify at the last minute.

Finally, because Rule 3.7 does not apply to other lawyers associated in the law firm, the availability of co-counsel in the firm to undertake courtroom duties as advocate for the client frequently will mitigate hardship on the client by reason of the testifying lawyer's disqualification.

## § 4-9.10(d) Conflicts of Interest Arising from a Lawyer's Testimony as a Witness

Even when a lawyer would not be disqualified by direct operation of the advocate-witness rule itself, or even though another lawyer in the firm is ready to appear as the client's counsel in the courtroom, both the testifying lawyer and the law firm may still be disqualified from continued representation of a client by the emergence of a conflict of interest related to the lawyer's anticipated or actual testimony. Rule 3.7(b) of the Model Rules of Professional Conduct allows a lawyer to act as an advocate in a trial in which another lawyer in the firm is likely to be called as a witness only if a conflict of interest does not exist under Rules 1.7 and 1.9 of the Model Rules of Professional Conduct.[694]

---

693 *See also* United States v. Metropolitan Dist. Comm'n, 847 F.2d 12, 18 (1st Cir. 1988) (saying that, in evaluating a fee petition, the judge may " 'draw[ ] on his own experience and wisdom [in] deciding whether the time spent on each phase was in excess of a reasonable amount' " (quoting Gabriele v. Southworth, 712 F.2d 1505, 1507 (1st Cir. 1983))).

694 On conflicts of interest, see generally *supra* §§ 4-7.1, 4-7.2, 4-7.4(b) to (c), 4-7.5, 4-7.6.

Whenever a lawyer testifies as a witness while that same lawyer or another lawyer in the same firm simultaneously serves as an advocate in the proceeding, some loss of credibility or persuasiveness usually occurs because the trier-of-fact likely will learn that the testifying lawyer is not a disinterested witness. If a lawyer testifies as a witness on behalf of a client being represented in court by another lawyer in the firm, the opposing party is entitled to direct the tribunal's attention to the lawyer-witness's personal and professional association with the lawyer-advocate. The lawyer's appreciation of this potentially unfavorable perception may cause the lawyer to suggest alternative counsel for the client as tactically wise. Nonetheless, absent an indication that the loss of persuasiveness is likely to be severe and jeopardize the client's case, or that the lawyer's credibility as witness will be seriously impeached, this strategic consequence alone would not ordinarily pose an impermissible conflict of interest.

However, if the testifying lawyer will be called as a necessary witness by either side and her truthful testimony is likely to be adverse to the client, a conflict of interest is unavoidably presented.[695] The conflict of interest is especially acute if the lawyer will testify in a manner sharply at odds with the testimony of the client. The client's expectation of loyalty[696] cannot be reconciled with the prospect of the client suffering through the negative effect of harmful, or even contradictory, testimony being adduced when the client's own lawyer (or another lawyer in the same firm, which is nearly the same thing) takes the stand.

While the advocate-witness rule applies only to current counsel for a client, if a lawyer's anticipated testimony is likely to be damaging to a former client, and either arises in the same or a substantially related matter as that on which the lawyer previously represented the client or will involve disclosing information held confidential as to that former client, the lawyer would be disqualified from proceeding under the successive conflict of interest standard.[697]

While the disqualification imposed by the advocate-witness rule itself is not extended beyond the individual witness-lawyer to associated lawyers,[698] the general rule of imputed disqualification does attach to a conflict of interest that arises because a lawyer has become a necessary witness and the lawyer's testimony will be harmful to the client.[699] If the client wishes to retain the services of the law firm, notwithstanding that damaging testimony is likely to be presented to the tribunal by a particular lawyer in the firm, and the circumstances are such that the harm to the client's case would not be substantially mitigated by selection of other available and qualified counsel, the client may provide informed consent to that continued representation. That informed consent must be given pursuant to the general rules governing when consent to a conflict is

---

[695] Some states expressly preclude a lawyer from acting as an advocate if another lawyer in the firm will testify other than "on behalf" of the client and do so in a manner that "may be prejudicial" to the client. *See* N.Y. RULES OF PROF'L CONDUCT R. 3.7(b)(1); OR. RULES OF PROF'L CONDUCT R. 3.7(c); VA. RULES OF PROF'L CONDUCT R. 3.7(b). This language is held over from the Model Code of Professional Responsibility, which provided that if "a lawyer learns or it is obvious that he or a lawyer in his firm may be called as a witness other than on behalf of his client, he may continue the representation until it is apparent that his testimony may be prejudicial to his client." MODEL CODE OF PROFESSIONAL RESPONSIBILITY, Disciplinary Rule 5–102(B) (American Bar Ass'n, 1980).

[696] On the lawyer's duty of loyalty to the client, see *supra* § 4-7.1.

[697] On duties owed to a former client, see *supra* § 4-7.5.

[698] *See supra* § 4-9.10(a).

[699] *See supra* § 4-7.6.

permitted, the disclosures that must be made to the client, and how the consent must be confirmed.[700]

## § 4-9.11 EXTRAJUDICIAL STATEMENTS BY LAWYER

### § 4-9.11(a) Introduction: Balancing the Right to Freedom of Expression Against the Right to a Fair Trial

When a lawyer enters the courthouse and represents a client in an adjudication before a tribunal, the lawyer's freedom of speech inside the courtroom is significantly curtailed by the lawyer's professional responsibilities to the client and to the tribunal.[701] Under the Model Rules of Professional Conduct, for example, the lawyer may not allude to irrelevant or inadmissible matters at trial,[702] assert personal knowledge or personal opinions at trial,[703] engage in *ex parte* communications with the judge or members of the jury,[704] engage in conduct intended to disrupt the tribunal,[705] use means designed only to embarrass or burden a witness or party,[706] or manifest bias.[707]

When the lawyer exits the courthouse, the professional duties of decorum, respect for the evidentiary and procedural rules of the tribunal, and regard for the fairness of the proceeding do not fade away altogether.[708] However, outside the courtroom, constraints on the lawyer's public speech must be carefully balanced with other rights, especially freedom of expression, and other interests, especially the client's justifiable concern in countering the harmful effects of negative publicity:

On the one hand, the lawyer as a citizen retains a constitutionally-protected right of free speech, even while representing a client, and, further, may better uphold the client's own right of expression by speaking on the client's behalf or assisting the client to more effectively do so.[709] The lawyer as an advocate for the client may also have an obligation to correct or supplement the public understanding of a pending matter and thereby reduce prejudicial publicity that may negatively affect the client either inside or outside the courtroom.[710] Writing on this point for a plurality of the Supreme Court in *Gentile v. State Bar of Nevada*,[711] Justice Kennedy said:

---

[700] On client consent to a conflict of interest, see *supra* § 4-7.7.

[701] On the lawyer's freedom of speech in and outside of court, see *supra* § 4-1.4(c) and *infra* § 4-13.3.

[702] *See supra* § 4-9.9(b)(1).

[703] *See supra* § 4-9.9(b)(2).

[704] *See supra* § 4-9.9(d).

[705] *See supra* § 4-9.9(a).

[706] *See supra* § 4-9.4(c).

[707] *See supra* § 4-9.4(b)(2).

[708] *See* Scott M. Matheson, Jr., *The Prosecutor, the Press, and Free Speech*, 58 FORDHAM L. REV. 865, 893 (1990) ("Lawyers cannot communicate with jurors outside the courtroom before or during trial and advocate the case. Why should they be able to advocate a case publicly when jurors or prospective jurors might hear them?").

[709] Government lawyers, as agents of the government, have lesser rights of freedom of speech and thus are subject to greater constraints on extrajudicial speech by ethical rule. *See infra* § 4-9.11(c)(3).

[710] *See* Michele DeStefano Beardslee, *Advocacy in the Court of Public Opinion Installment One: Broadening the Role of Corporate Attorneys*, 22 GEO. J. LEGAL ETHICS 1159 (2009) (advocating the role of lawyers in managing public relations because a company's valuable reputation may be damaged by the way a legal controversy is portrayed in the media, even if the company technically prevails in a legal dispute).

[711] 501 U.S. 1030 (1991). For further discussion of the *Gentile* case, see *infra* § 4-9.11(d).

> An attorney's duties do not begin inside the courtroom door. . . . Just as an attorney may recommend a plea bargain or civil settlement to avoid the adverse consequences of a possible loss after trial, so too an attorney may take reasonable steps to defend a client's reputation and reduce the adverse consequences of indictment, especially in the face of a prosecution deemed unjust or commenced with improper motives. A defense attorney may pursue lawful strategies to obtain dismissal of an indictment or reduction of charges, including an attempt to demonstrate in the court of public opinion that the client does not deserve to be tried.[712]

In addition, the public has a general interest in the subject matter of litigation proceeding in the public court system, which may be undermined if the participating lawyers, who may be the most experienced and informed participants in the legal process, are enjoined to absolute silence.

On the other hand, the lawyer as a professional and participant in the legal process has an obligation to preserve the right to a fair trial, which may be severely compromised by prejudicial extrajudicial statements, especially when they are attributed to a lawyer who by virtue of his participation may be seen as having greater authority or may have enhanced credibility through his presumed access to inside information. As one court insisted:

> When one is admitted to the bar he embraces certain ethical considerations and restrictions not required or expected of laymen which experience has indicated will be of benefit to the public if lawyers are required to obey them. One of these ethical rules, broadly stated, is that disputes should be tried by lawyers in court where limiting safeguards are available and not in the public news media.[713]

As outlined in Comment 1 to Rule 3.6 of the Model Rules of Professional Conduct, the ethical limitations on extrajudicial statements are designed to "strike a balance between protecting the right to a fair trial and safeguarding the right of free expression." The rule generally prohibits those extrajudicial statements by a lawyer that have a substantial likelihood of materially prejudicing an adjudicative proceeding,[714] while expressly allowing statements about certain matters that are either unlikely to cause prejudice or for which there is a strong public interest in disclosure.[715] The rule further allows a lawyer a right of fair response to protect a client against prejudicial publicity initiated by another person or party.[716] Recognizing the greater risk of harm posed by prejudicial publicity to the fair trial of a criminal defendant, Rule 3.8(f) of the Model Rules places additional constraints and responsibilities on prosecutors with respect to extrajudicial statements.[717]

---

[712] *Gentile*, 501 U.S. at 1043; *see also* Margaret Tarkington, *Lost in the Compromise: Free Speech, Criminal Justice, and Attorney Pretrial Publicity*, 66 FLA. L. REV. 1873 (2014) (observing that only by "a response to the charges" can a defendant and her counsel "timely salvage the reputation of the accused before family, friends, and associates").

[713] In re Porter, 521 P.2d 345, 349 (Ore. 1974).

[714] *See infra* § 4-9.11(b).

[715] *See infra* § 4-9.11(c)(1).

[716] *See infra* § 4-9.11(d).

[717] *See infra* § 4-9.11(c)(3).

## § 4-9.11(b) The Prohibition on Extrajudicial Statements Likely to Prejudice an Adjudicative Proceedings

### *§ 4-9.11(b)(1) The Standard of a Substantial Likelihood of Material Prejudice*

Rule 3.6(a) of the Model Rules of Professional Conduct provides:

> A lawyer who is participating or has participated in the investigation or litigation of a matter shall not make an extrajudicial statement that the lawyer knows or reasonably should know will be disseminated by means of public communication and will have a substantial likelihood of materially prejudicing an adjudicative proceeding in the matter.[718]

The rule thus applies to a lawyer who is a participant (typically by representing a client)[719] in an adjudicative proceeding, who makes a statement about that proceeding which the lawyer knows or reasonably should know will be publicized, and who knows or reasonably should know that the statement is substantially likely to cause material prejudice to the proceeding.

The central and constitutionally-validated criterion for what constitutes an impermissible extrajudicial statement under Model Rule 3.6(a) turns on whether the lawyer knows or reasonably should know that there is a "substantial likelihood of materially prejudicing an adjudicative proceeding." The nature of the proceeding[720] and the content of the statements[721] are significant factors in evaluating the likelihood of material prejudice to the proceeding. In addition, factors in evaluating the risk of prejudice include the location in which the public statements were disseminated (whether close to or some distance away from the venue where the trial will occur), the timing of the statement (whether made long before or close to the date of the trial),[722] and the actual effect on the decisionmaker (whether the jurors or prospective jurors were affected by the statement).[723]

Model Rule 3.6(a) applies only when the lawyer knows or reasonably should know that the statement will be publicly disseminated. If the lawyer has taken reasonable

---

[718] The District of Columbia states the test as whether the statement creates "a serious and imminent threat" of prejudice to the proceeding, D.C. RULES OF PROF'L CONDUCT R. 3.7(a), while New Mexico speaks of "a clear and present danger of prejudicing the proceeding," N.M. RULES OF PROF'L CONDUCT R. 16–306(A)(2).

[719] *See* In re Goode, 821 F.3d 553, 558 (5th Cir. 2016) (explaining that restrictions on extrajudicial statements apply beyond the lawyers who are counsel of record and include lawyers "associated" with the case, such as those involved with trial preparation and who confer with counsel for the parties).

[720] *See infra* § 4-9.11(b)(2).

[721] *See infra* § 4-9.11(c)(1) to (3).

[722] *See* Gentile v. Nevada State Bar, 501 U.S. 1030, 1044 (1991) (plurality opinion) (observing that a "statement which reaches the attention of the venire on the eve of *voir dire* might require a continuance or cause difficulties in securing an impartial jury, and at the very least could complicate the jury selection process," but that "exposure to the same statement six months prior to trial would not result in prejudice, the content fading from memory long before the trial date").

[723] *See* Board of Prof'l Ethics & Conduct v. Visser, 629 N.W.2d 376, 382 (Iowa 2001) (looking "to the facts surrounding the statements at the time they were made" and "the *ex post* evidence that relates to the likelihood of prejudice," the court observed the resulting newspaper article was published many miles away from where the trial was held, was published more than two years before trial, and none of the jurors at trial had heard of the parties); Matter of Hinds, 449 A.2d 483, 486 (N.J. 1982) ("We further hold that the determination of whether a particular statement is likely to interfere with a fair trial involves a careful balancing of factors, including consideration of the status of the attorney, the nature and timing of the statement, as well as the context in which it was uttered.").

steps to ensure that a statement is being made to the client or another person in a confidential setting, then the surreptitious or unanticipated interception of that statement by another who is in a position to publicize it will not expose the lawyer to disciplinary sanction.[724]

By contrast, the lawyer who agrees to be interviewed by a reporter, who issues a press release, or who holds a press conference is obviously engaged in direct public dissemination through means designed to attract news media attention. In such circumstances, the lawyer should be regarded as intending that every word uttered be transmitted to a broader public. Likewise, the lawyer who cleverly offers provocative comments about the proceeding, in a pretense of speaking *sotto voce* but within the obvious hearing of a representative of the news media, knows or reasonably should know that the statement will be publicly disseminated. And the lawyer involved in the proceeding who offers commentary on social media ordinarily should anticipate further distribution of the remarks.[725]

By the terms of Rule 3.6(a), only those attorneys who are, or have been, involved in the investigation or litigation of the matter are subject to the rule. As Comment 3 to Rule 3.6 explains, restrictions on the speech of other lawyers would be unjustified because "the public value of informed commentary is great and the likelihood of prejudice to a proceeding by the commentary of a lawyer who is not involved in the proceeding is small." To be sure, an uninvolved lawyer making public comments might highlight sensitive information in an unfairly prejudicial manner, although he may be less motivated to do so given the absence of any personal stake in the outcome of the matter. While prejudice may be heightened when the public speaker is a participant in the matter with presumed inside information, the lawyer commentator has no participatory role in the proceeding and thus should be understood as an outside observer. In any event, when a lawyer is speaking as an informed citizen, rather than as an officer of the court who is involved in the proceeding, the right of free expression is at its apex.[726]

### *§ 4-9.11(b)(2) The Likelihood of Prejudice and the Nature of the Proceeding*

Because the projected danger occasioned by irresponsible extrajudicial statements is that of harm to the fair and impartial disposition of a matter before a tribunal, the likelihood of harm and the justifiability of constraints on public statements will depend on the circumstances, including the nature of the proceeding. As Comment 6 to Model Rule 3.6 states, "[c]riminal jury trials will be most sensitive to extrajudicial speech."

By far, the greatest threat targeted by Rule 3.6 is that the prospective jury pool for or the actual jury panel in a criminal case may be tainted by reason of prejudicial publicity, especially through attention being drawn to matters that likely would be inadmissible at trial or by commentary that tends to inflame public antipathy against

---

[724] *See* 2 GEOFFREY C. HAZARD, JR., W. WILLIAM HODES & PETER R. JARVIS, THE LAW OF LAWYERING § 35.04 (Aspen, 4th ed., 2016) (saying that "there could be no violation if the lawyer had no way of knowing that a newspaper reporter had through subterfuge gained access to what was supposed to be a private meeting, or if his email program was hacked").

[725] STANDARDS FOR CRIMINAL JUSTICE: DEFENSE FUNCTION, Standard 4–1.10(a) (American Bar Ass'n, 2015) (observing that public communication and media includes social media).

[726] *But see* STANDARDS FOR CRIMINAL JUSTICE: DEFENSE FUNCTION, Standard 4–1.10(i) (American Bar Ass'n, 2015) (advising that lawyer uninvolved in a matter "should make reasonable efforts to be well-informed about the facts of the matter and the governing law" and "should not offer commentary regarding the specific merits of an ongoing prosecution or investigation, except in a rare case to address a manifest injustice and counsel is reasonably well-informed about the relevant facts and law").

the defendant. By contrast, civil jury trials may be less sensitive to extrajudicial statements, although the kinds of cases that attract news media attention may be precisely those in which a similar risk of prejudice to the jury is presented, such as when a case involves scandalous facts, when allegations of serious misconduct have been levied, or when the public statements highlight prejudicial subjects that would be withheld from the jury at trial.

By contrast, the fairness of non-jury proceedings ordinarily will not be endangered by extrajudicial statements. As a comment to the *Restatement of the Law Governing Lawyers* affirms, "[j]udicial officers are expected to be immune from the influences of inadmissible evidence and similar sources of information and from the potentially distorting effects of inflamed public opinion."[727] Thus, for example, lawyers should be understood to have carte blanche permission to speak with the news media about the substance and issues of an appellate case that they plan to or have briefed or argued (at least if the case is unlikely to be tried before a jury on remand). Not only is there no legitimate risk that appellate judges will be influenced by media reports, but the fact that the case is pending before that court suggests that it is a matter on which greater public understanding about the legal process would be especially worthwhile.

Finally, largely for reasons other than the prejudicial effect on the decisionmaker by extrajudicial publicity, Comment 2 to Model Rule 3.6 admonishes, "[s]pecial rules of confidentiality may validly govern proceedings in juvenile, domestic relations and mental disability proceedings, and perhaps other types of litigation." The lawyer of course must comply with such rules when they are in effect for a particular proceeding.[728]

## § 4-9.11(c) The Prejudicial Impact of Types of Statements

### *§ 4-9.11(c)(1) Statements Least Likely to be Prejudicial*

Not every public statement by a participating lawyer about a pending litigation matter carries the potential for undermining the fairness of the trial. In addition, the public interest in being informed about the legal system or in being warned about threats to public safety may outweigh opposing concerns and justify public disclosures.

Although not intended to be an exhaustive list of permissible public statements, Rule 3.6(b) of the Model Rules of Professional Conduct expressly authorizes certain statements to be made by a lawyer:

> (1) the claim, offense or defense involved and, except when prohibited by law, the identity of the persons involved;
>
> (2) information contained in a public record;
>
> (3) that an investigation of a matter is in progress;
>
> (4) the scheduling or result of any step in litigation;
>
> (5) a request for assistance in obtaining evidence and information necessary thereto;

---

727 RESTATEMENT (THIRD) OF THE LAW GOVERNING LAWYERS § 109 cmt. b (American Bar Ass'n, 2000).

728 *See supra* § 4-9.5(e).

(6) a warning of danger concerning the behavior of a person involved, when there is reason to believe that there exists the likelihood of substantial harm to an individual or to the public interest; and

(7) in a criminal case, in addition to subparagraphs (1) through (6):

(i) the identity, residence, occupation and family status of the accused;

(ii) if the accused has not been apprehended, information necessary to aid in apprehension of that person;

(iii) the fact, time and place of arrest; and

(iv) the identity of investigating and arresting officers or agencies and the length of the investigation.

In addition to clarifying appropriate further detail on these permissible statements (such as specifying "the general length and scope of the investigation, and the identity of the investigating officer or agency"), the American Bar Association's *Standards for Criminal Justice* suggest that a prosecutor ordinarily may release "the identity of the victim, where the release of that information is not otherwise prohibited by law or would not be harmful to the victim."[729]

Notably omitted from this approved list of particulars is the provision that was found in the former Model Code of Professional Responsibility allowing a prosecutor to reveal "[a]t the time of seizure, a description of the physical evidence seized, other than a confession, admission, or statement."[730] When Model Rule 3.6 was substantially revised by the American Bar Association in 1994, the drafting committee's "Model Code Comparison" that accompanied the rule explained that revelation of seized evidence "may be substantially prejudicial" and observed that such seizures "are frequently the subject of pretrial suppression motions whose success would be undermined by disclosure of the suppressed evidence to the press."[731]

To be sure, the results of a search pursuant to a warrant may be a matter of public record, and public record information ordinarily could be the subject of a permissible public statement. However, republication of the description of seized items by a prosecutor, especially when the admissibility of the seized material is being disputed or when the seizure included embarrassing materials that are not relevant to the actual charges later brought, could taint the prospective jury pool by drawing attention to a matter that should be excluded from their knowledge and consideration.[732]

### *§ 4-9.11(c)(2) Statements Raising Greatest Risk of Prejudice*

Although the authoritative text of Model Rule 3.6 does not contain a list of impermissible prejudicial statements (parallel to the approved statements in Rule 3.6(b)), Comment 5 to Rule 3.6 offers guidance to lawyers by providing a list of "certain

---

[729] STANDARDS FOR CRIMINAL JUSTICE: FAIR TRIAL AND PUBLIC DISCOURSE, Standard 8–2.2(b) (American Bar Ass'n, 2013).

[730] MODEL CODE OF PROF'L RESPONSIBILITY, Disciplinary Rule 7–107(C)(7) (American Bar Ass'n, 1980).

[731] *See* Model Code Comparison, Rule 3.6, Model Rules of Professional Conduct (American Bar Ass'n, 1994).

[732] *See* N.J. Advisory Comm. on Prof'l Ethics Op. 731 (2017) (advising that "the public display of drugs, weapons, or other contraband seized during a criminal investigation" by the prosecutor would be improper extrajudicial statements in violation of Rules 3.6 and 3.8).

subjects that are more likely than not to have a material prejudicial effect on a proceeding, particularly when they refer to a civil matter triable to a jury, a criminal matter, or any other proceeding that could result in incarceration." Several states continue to list topics especially likely to cause prejudice to fair trial in the text of the rule itself.[733] The subjects suggested in the Model Rule 3.6 Comment as being presumptively harmful to a fair trial are:

(1) the character, credibility, reputation or criminal record of a party, suspect in a criminal investigation or witness, or the identity of a witness, or the expected testimony of a party or witness;

(2) in a criminal case or proceeding that could result in incarceration, the possibility of a plea of guilty to the offense or the existence or contents of any confession, admission, or statement given by a defendant or suspect or that person's refusal or failure to make a statement;

(3) the performance or results of any examination or test or the refusal or failure of a person to submit to an examination or test, or the identity or nature of physical evidence expected to be presented;

(4) any opinion as to the guilt or innocence of a defendant or suspect in a criminal case or proceeding that could result in incarceration;

(5) information that the lawyer knows or reasonably should know is likely to be inadmissible as evidence in a trial and that would, if disclosed, create a substantial risk of prejudicing an impartial trial; and

(6) the fact that a defendant has been charged with a crime, unless there is included therein a statement explaining that the charge is merely an accusation and that the defendant is presumed innocent until and unless proven guilty.

Consistent with concerns about statements manifesting bias in a matter before a tribunal,[734] the American Bar Association's *Standards for Criminal Justice* direct that a prosecutor should avoid risking prejudice by making a statement regarding "the identity, race, ethnicity, creed, religion, or sexual orientation . . . of prospective witnesses other than the victim, and the race, ethnicity, creed, religion, [or] sexual orientation . . . of the victim."[735] The defense lawyer is also advised to avoid commenting on "the identity, race, ethnicity, creed, religion, or sexual orientation . . . of alleged victims or prospective witnesses."[736]

While a public statement by a participating lawyer on one of the sensitive matters included on this presumptively-forbidden list is more likely to violate Rule 3.6, whether the ethical line has actually been crossed in a particular case will require a circumstantial evaluation of the likely prejudicial effect of the statement.

---

[733] *See* ALA. RULES OF PROF'L CONDUCT R. 3.7(b); IND. RULES OF PROF'L CONDUCT R. 3.7(d); MICH. RULES OF PROF'L CONDUCT R. 3.7(a); MISS. RULES OF PROF'L CONDUCT R. 3.7(a); N.H. RULES OF PROF'L CONDUCT R. 3.7(b); N.Y. RULES OF PROF'L CONDUCT R. 3.7(b); TEX. RULES OF PROF'L CONDUCT R. 3.07(b); WASH. RULES OF PROF'L CONDUCT R. 3.7 Appendix; WIS. RULES OF PROF'L CONDUCT R. 3.7(b).

[734] *See supra* § 4-9.4(b)(2).

[735] STANDARDS FOR CRIMINAL JUSTICE: FAIR TRIAL AND PUBLIC DISCOURSE, Standard 8–2.2(a)(vii) (American Bar Ass'n, 2013).

[736] *Id.*, Standard 8–2.3(a)(v).

Reviewing the topics collected in the presumptively-forbidden list from Comment 5 to Model Rule 3.6, they tend to fall into two general categories of public statements that pose a greater danger to a fair trial, most especially in the context of an anticipated criminal jury trial:

***Potential Evidentiary Matters:*** Extrajudicial statements pose a particular danger of prejudice if they may imprint into the minds of the prospective jury pool or members of the jury panel particular items of information that may or may not be admitted into evidence. These matters include a criminal defendant's confession, a criminal defendant's refusal to make a statement, the results of an examination or test or a defendant's refusal to submit to a particular test, the likely testimony of a party or witness, or the nature of physical items that may be introduced at trial.

Public commentary about these potential evidentiary materials is peculiarly likely to undermine a fair trial when their validity or admissibility is likely to be challenged. As the Supreme Court held in *Sheppard v. Maxwell*,[737] "[t]he exclusion of such evidence in court is rendered meaningless when the news media make it available to the public."

For that reason, the rule restricting extrajudicial statements is more likely to attach to public statements that highlight prejudicial information that would not be admissible into evidence when the litigation matter is ultimately brought to trial before a jury. As Comment 1 to Rule 3.6 states, "[i]f there were no such limits [on extrajudicial statements], the result would be the practical nullification of the protective effect of the rules of forensic decorum and the exclusionary rules of evidence." This prejudicial effect is especially troubling in the context of criminal proceedings. But it is relevant in the civil jury context as well, such as if information about insurance coverage or other settlements is made public and thus more likely to be learned by members of the prospective jury.

But even if formal admissibility into evidence is not the subject of a likely contest, the foreshadowing of what testimony will be heard or physical items will be presented at a criminal trial may prove to be mistaken when the actual presentation of evidence and testimony unfolds at trial.

Thus, prior extrajudicial statements about these matters increase the possibility that the jury will be influenced by what they have heard about supposed observations by witness or physical evidence that exists, outside the courtroom and beyond what is formally introduced into evidence.

***Derogatory Statements About the Criminal Defendant:*** Public statements that emphasize derogatory information about a person being charged with a criminal offense may serve to enhance public antipathy toward the defendant, making it more difficult to receive a fair and unbiased hearing from a jury once empaneled. In addition to being generally inadmissible at trial, and thus being objectionable material for public exploitation on that basis, information about the character, reputation, or criminal record of a defendant or expressions of an opinion as to the defendant's guilt or innocence are likely to shift the weight of public opinion against the defendant. Beyond the general constraints on prejudicial extrajudicial statements in Rule 3.6, Rule 3.8(f) imposes a stricter limitation on prosecutors, requiring that they "refrain from making extrajudicial

---

[737] 384 U.S. 333, 360 (1966).

comments that have a substantial likelihood of heightening public condemnation of the accused."[738]

When a lawyer is contemplating a public statement about a litigation matter in which she is participating, the lawyer should carefully consider what may appropriately be said and identify in advance what subjects should be avoided. During the course of an interview with a reporter, and especially if the lawyer holds a press conference, a member of the media may inquire about a matter as to which the lawyer should hesitate to offer a comment. The lawyer may also be swept up in the excitement of media attention and unintentionally slide from permissible statements to improper and prejudicial remarks. Even when a particular public statement is generally permitted, the lawyer must be wary of straying from a legitimate message into forbidden territory.

When a particular subject already has attracted considerable public attention, such as media reports about evidence excluded from admission in a criminal case or prior settlements of similar claims with respect to a civil case, the risk of prejudice through lawyer commentary on that subject is certainly mitigated—but it may not disappear altogether. Even when a subject has been reported in newspaper stories and television news broadcasts, a participating lawyer's commentary may renew the attention and intensify the publicity, particularly because the lawyer may be regarded by both media outlets and the listening public as a particularly authoritative source and as having the informed perspective of an inside participant in the ongoing matter. Accordingly, when a matter is sensitive and likely to be excluded from evidence and argument before a jury, the lawyer should be circumspect in public statements about it.

### *§ 4-9.11(c)(3) Special Risk Posed by Statements Made by Prosecutors*

Like any lawyer participating in the investigation or litigation of a matter, a prosecutor is directed under Rule 3.6 of the Model Rules of Professional Conduct to "not make an extrajudicial statement that the lawyer knows or reasonably should know will be disseminated by means of public communication and will have a substantial likelihood of materially prejudicing an adjudicative proceeding in the matter."[739] Concerns about and restrictions on prejudicial public statements are especially likely to be justified in the context of a criminal jury trial, for fear that the jury pool may be tainted through attention being drawn to matters that likely would be inadmissible at trial or by commentary that tends to inflame public antipathy against the defendant.[740]

The kinds of public statements that are presumptively harmful under Rule 3.6 are those likely to undermine the fairness and integrity of a criminal trial, such as comments by participating lawyers on the credibility or reputation of a defendant or witness, speculation on the possibility of a guilty plea, the existence or contents of a confession, the performance or results of any examination or test or the refusal or failure of a person to submit to such a test or examination, and opinions on the guilt or innocence of an accused.[741] Moreover, beyond the potential effect on a criminal proceeding, a prosecutor's unnecessarily condemnatory statements about a person cause immediate and lasting

[738] *See infra* § 4-9.11(c)(3).

[739] *See supra* § 4-9.11(c)(1) to (2).

[740] *See supra* § 4-9.11(b)(2).

[741] *See supra* § 4-9.11(c)(2).

harm to that person's reputation, damage that even a later acquittal may do little to mitigate.

When the person making a public statement about a criminal investigation or a criminal proceeding holds the powerful and prestigious position of a criminal prosecutor, the prospect is greater that the person's words will be reported by the news media and that they will be given great weight by the listening public. As the Maryland Court of Appeals said in *Attorney Grievance Commission v. Gansler*,[742] when reprimanding a prosecutor for extrajudicial statements about a defendant's confession and the prosecutor's decision to offer a plea bargain, prosecutors' "unique role and extensive access to information lends a degree of credibility to their speech that an ordinary citizen's speech may not usually possess." Because of the enormous respect that the public ordinarily has for prosecutors, a prosecutor's failure to be discrete and careful in public statements poses a heightened risk of injury to the cause of justice. The ethics rules thus place an elevated responsibility on prosecutors to avoid contributing to prejudicial publicity about a criminal matter. In addition, as a public employee and an agent of the government, a prosecutor enjoys lesser constitutional protection for speech and thus is properly subject to greater constraints.[743]

While the restrictions on extrajudicial statements by prosecutors are designed primarily to mitigate prejudice to the jury pool and harm to the reputation of the defendant, "they serve another salutary purpose by preventing the prosecutor from locking himself into a view from he cannot deviate without losing face politically."[744] Given the prosecutor's continuing ethical duty to evaluate whether the charge has sufficient evidentiary support,[745] the prosecutor must maintain a degree of professional detachment that allows her to objectively assess whether new information produced by a continuing investigation, laboratory results, pre-trial discovery, or shared by the defendant's counsel justifies going forward with the prosecution. The prosecutor who has gone on the public record asserting the strength of the prosecution's case or condemning the supposed wrongdoing of the defendant will find it more difficult to admit mistakes, acknowledge that previously expressed opinions were misguided, adjust to changed circumstances, and withdraw charges that have become unwarranted.[746]

In addition, a policy of not commenting outside of court documents on investigations, even when a criminal charge is not filed, is an "important protection

---

[742] Attorney Grievance Comm'n v. Gansler, 835 A.2d 548, 559 (Md. Ct. App. 2003).

[743] *See* Garcetti v. Ceballos, 547 U.S. 410, 421 (2006) (holding, in the context of a prosecutor who was disciplined for writing memoranda arguing that a charge should be dismissed for governmental misconduct, "[w]hen public employees make statements pursuant to their official duties, the employees are not speaking as citizens for First Amendment purposes, and the Constitution does not insulate their communications from employer discipline"). *But see* R. Michael Cassidy, *The Prosecutor and the Press: Lessons (Not) Learned From the Mike Nifong Debacle,* 71 LAW & CONTEMP. PROBS. 67, 71–79 (2008) (arguing that elected prosecutors have robust First Amendment rights to speak to the media about law enforcement priorities, how the prosecutor is handling public duties, and potential dangers to the public).

[744] Deborah Jeffrey, *How Prosecutors Go Bad*, LEGAL TIMES, Aug. 6, 2007, at 45; *see also* Margaret Tarkington, *Lost in the Compromise: Free Speech, Criminal Justice, and Attorney Pretrial Publicity*, 66 FLA. L. REV. 1873, 1905 (2014) (noting that "a prosecutor's pretrial publicity can wed him to the charges despite even overwhelming evidence that develops to the contrary").

[745] *See supra* § 4-9.12(b).

[746] *See* Anna Stoley Persky, *Aggressive Justice*, A.B.A. J., May 2010, at 36, 38–39 (quoting former United States Attorney Joseph diGenova as saying that overzealous prosecutorial behavior follows when the Department of Justice calls a "campaign du jour" that brings media attention to the effort to stop a type of crime, so that prosecutors have "invested too much" to hold back from aggressively seeking victory at all costs).

against abuse of a very grave nature."[747] As former prosecutor and now United States Senator Sheldon Whitehouse explains, "[t]he danger of a prosecutor who can't make a case nevertheless smearing an individual with investigative information is a real one."[748] Derogatory information about a defendant should be limited to the four corners of the charging document. "The obvious corollary," White emphasizes, is "no charges, no derogatory information."[749]

Accordingly, superimposed over the general requirements of Rule 3.6, Rule 3.8(f) imposes an additional limitation directed toward those lawyers who discharge the singular responsibilities of a criminal prosecutor: "except for statements that are necessary to inform the public of the nature and extent of the prosecutor's action and that serve a legitimate law enforcement purpose, [a prosecutor shall] refrain from making extrajudicial comments that have a substantial likelihood of heightening public condemnation of the accused." The *Restatement of the Law Governing Lawyers* advances the identical standard for prosecutors in their public statements.[750]

Whenever a prosecutor speaks in a public forum or for public dissemination about a particular criminal investigation or case that is still pending, he should carefully consider whether each remark comports with the standards of Rules 3.6 and 3.8(f) that it not be improperly prejudicial, whether the statement serves to promote better public understanding of the legal system, whether the message properly explains actions being taken by the prosecutor's office without being unduly argumentative, and whether an announcement advances an articulable and meaningful law enforcement purpose, rather than simply heaping further opprobrium on an accused. The prudent prosecutor chooses to do most of his talking in the courtroom, especially at the trial date draws near, speaking for public attribution only to dispassionately explain the legal process and the steps being taken by the prosecution (in an educational and informational manner); to seek the public's assistance when evidence and witnesses are being sought; to calmly assure the public that a danger has passed (but threading the ethical needle by not opining directly on the guilt of the accused); or to alert the public that a danger exists (such as when a suspect in an ongoing crime wave has not yet been identified or an armed and dangerous fugitive remains at large).

Patience may also carry its own reward. When a prosecutor wishes to educate the public about the criminal justice process, explain or defend the considered decisions made at each stage of the prosecution, and take appropriate credit for securing a just conviction, the optimum time for doing so may be at the successful conclusion of a prosecution. Once the criminal trial has reached its natural end with a verdict, disposition of post-trial motions, and a sentence, at least when the prosecutor reasonably believes that the prospects for an appellate reversal and retrial are small (and in any event would not occur until many months or years later), the restrictions on extrajudicial statements in Rules 3.6 and 3.8(f) are then lifted. At that point, the prosecutor may fully describe the events and actions leading to the institution of criminal charges and occurring during the course of the prosecution and may do so in broader context, subject only to special rules of confidentiality (such as attach to grand jury proceedings or a juvenile matter).

---

[747] Sheldon Whitehouse, *Prosecutors Ought to Put Up or Shut Up*, NAT'L L.J., Nov. 7, 2016, at 26.

[748] *Id.*

[749] *Id.*

[750] RESTATEMENT (THIRD) OF THE LAW GOVERNING LAWYERS § 109(2) (American Law Institute, 2000).

### § 4-9.11(d) The Right of Reply to Correct Prejudice Caused by Another

A lawyer's client, who is a party to a pending or imminent proceeding before a tribunal, may suffer significant adverse effects by prejudicial extrajudicial publicity, through insinuation of misleading or false information into the minds of potential or actual jury members or by negative effects on the person in social life or business activities. As Professors Peter Joy and Kevin McMunigal wryly observe, "[o]ur criminal justice system presumes innocence, but human beings rarely do."[751] When the damaging publicity has originated with someone other than the client, the principles of fairness and reciprocity argue for a right to respond publicly to correct the public understanding, introduce new information that places matters in better context, and remind the public that any allegations made are not yet proven in court.

In *Gentile v. Nevada State Bar*,[752] the Supreme Court considered a case in which the owner of a warehouse company, which was used by the police to store narcotics and other items for undercover operations, was charged with stealing drugs and money from the police vault. Prior to indictment, the prosecution and police had made regular statements to the press, praising the police officers who had access to the vault, clearing the police officers of any wrongdoing after an internal investigation, and saying that the focus of the investigation was on the defendant, including references to the defendant's supposed relationships with unsavory persons and his refusal to take a polygraph test.[753] To counter this negative publicity, the defendant's counsel held a press conference shortly after the indictment saying that, once the case went to trial, the evidence would establish that the defendant was innocent and was being used as a "scapegoat" to cover-up police corruption in the community.[754] Even after the press conference, as Justice Kennedy later characterized matters, "the repetitive publicity" that had been orchestrated by law enforcement made it "difficult to come to any conclusion but that the balance [of the prejudicial effect] remained in favor of the prosecution."[755] When the case went to trial, evidence indeed was presented suggesting that police officers with direct access had stolen the money and drugs, resulting in the acquittal of the defendant.[756] Nonetheless, defense counsel then was reprimanded by the state bar for violating the extrajudicial publicity rule.

In *Gentile*, the Supreme Court overturned discipline of the defense attorney, holding that the state's extrajudicial publicity rule was void for vagueness in the context of the Free Speech Clause of the First Amendment because the rule failed to clearly define the "safe harbor" of what statements were permissible.[757] Justice Kennedy, writing for a majority of the Court, ruled that imposing discipline on this attorney for responding to

---

[751] Peter A. Joy & Kevin C. McMunigal, *The Ethics of Talking to the Media*, in MEDIA COVERAGE IN CRIMINAL JUSTICE CASES: WHAT PROSECUTORS AND DEFENDERS SHOULD AND SHOULD NOT SAY ch. 2 (Andrew E. Taslitz, ed., ABA, 2013).

[752] 501 U.S. 1030 (1991).

[753] *Id.* at 1039–41.

[754] *Id.* at 1059–60.

[755] *Id.* at 1046.

[756] *Id.* at 1047–48.

[757] *Id.* at 1033–34, 1048–49.

such pretrial publicity offended First Amendment principles because the limitations imposed by the rule were unduly vague.[758]

In 1994, in response to *Gentile*, the American Bar Association revised Rule 3.6 of the Model Rules of Professional Conduct to provide a specific exception to the bar on prejudicial extrajudicial publicity for attorneys responding on behalf of clients to prejudicial publicity generated by another person.[759] Rule 3.6(c) creates a "safe harbor" that allows a lawyer to respond on behalf of a client to undue prejudice from adverse publicity initiated by someone other than the lawyer or the client.

As a matter of fair response, Rule 3.6(c) states that "a lawyer may make a statement that a reasonable lawyer would believe is required to protect a client from the substantial undue prejudicial effect of recent publicity not initiated by the lawyer or the lawyer's client." The response is limited to that which reasonably serves to counter the adverse publicity, and should not be the source of a new form of prejudicial publicity on an aspect of the case unrelated to the publicity that prompted the response. The rule provides that the responsive statement "shall be limited to such information as is necessary to mitigate the recent adverse publicity."

For criminal cases, the American Bar Association's recently-revised *Standards for Criminal Justice* recognize a right to "respond to public statements from any source in order to protect a client's legitimate interests."[760] However the *Standards* appear to foreclose the defense right to respond when that response would create a "substantial likelihood of materially prejudicing a criminal proceeding, in which case defense counsel should approach the prosecutor or the Court for relief."[761] To be sure, the lawyer might be wise to raise the question with the prosecutor, perhaps requesting a joint statement to create or balance the record. The lawyer probably should bring a damaging extrajudicial commentary to the attention of the court to perhaps prevent future harmful comments adverse to the defendant or to consider other curative measures such as a change of venue or jury instructions. Still, while the defense lawyer's response to offset prejudicial statements by others should indeed be limited to that necessary to mitigate the damage, neither the practicalities of the situation nor the protections of the Constitution should demand that the defense lawyer invariably depend on the grace of the prosecutor or be satisfied with the limited remedies available to the judge.

When a lawyer sees a client suffering from the effects of prejudicial publicity generated by others, it is asking too much to expect that lawyer to refrain from taking appropriate steps on behalf of her client to respond and strive for some balance in public perception. A criminal defense lawyer whose client is the subject of daily stories suggesting guilt that emanate from the police or prosecution, or a corporate lawyer whose client is subjected to attacks by others talking to the media about its supposed improper activities or business practices, should not be left helpless from assisting the

---

[758] *Id.* at 1048–54. Other federal courts had held Disciplinary Rule 7–107 of the former Model Code of Professional Responsibility to be an unconstitutional constraint of First Amendment rights of freedom of speech. *See, e.g.*, Hirschkop v. Snead, 594 F.2d 356 (4th Cir. 1979) (en banc); Chicago Council of Lawyers v. Bauer, 522 F.2d 242 (7th Cir. 1975); Shadid v. Jackson, 521 F. Supp. 85 (E.D. Tex. 1981).

[759] 2 GEOFFREY C. HAZARD, JR., W. WILLIAM HODES & PETER R. JARVIS, THE LAW OF LAWYERING § 35.02 (Aspen, 4th ed., 2016).

[760] STANDARDS FOR CRIMINAL JUSTICE: DEFENSE FUNCTION, Standard 4–1.10(f) (American Bar Ass'n, 2015).

[761] *Id.*

client in a response that would level the playing field for a fair trial and alleviate the damage to the client's public reputation.

Even if the statement made by the opposing lawyer that created the prejudicial climate was authorized under Model Rule 3.6(b), the lawyer remains entitled to respond under Rule 3.6(c) as necessary to protect the client from a meaningful prejudicial effect. Indeed, even if the injury to a fair trial or to reputation is attributable solely to the news media, without the active involvement of other parties or direct participants in the matter before the tribunal, the rule guarantees a right of fair response. When such a fair response is justified due to prejudicial publicity generated by another, the lawyer frequently is the best person to make or guide that response, owing to the lawyer's greater understanding of the legal issues and greater skills in advocacy.[762]

Notably, the ABA *Standards for Criminal Justice* also permit a criminal defense lawyer to "participate in the formulation of a response" when "the mere filing of a criminal charge is likely to cause grave harm to the defendant's business, career, employment, or financial condition prior to the resolution of the criminal case."[763] The response designed to "mitigate the harm" may include accurate statements about "the performance of any examinations or tests, or the defendant's willingness to submit to an examination or test;" "the nature of physical evidence expected to be presented;" and "the identity, expected testimony, or credibility of prospective witnesses."[764]

### § 4-9.11(e) Other Duties and Factors Implicated by Extrajudicial Statements

***Potential Harm to Client's Case:*** The lawyer who elects to make a public statement (or advises a client to do so) about pending or imminent litigation in which the lawyer is participating should be aware of possible negative results that may follow after a poor choice of words, an inadvertent remark, or an inaccurate declaration that is disseminated to the public. As Professors Peter Joy and Kevin McMunigal warn, "[p]ublic statements by a client might reveal confidential information and top off the prosecutor to the defense's trial strategy. Public statements may also create evidentiary admissions and generate useful impeachment material for cross-examination, such as a prior inconsistent statement or a false exculpatory statement."[765]

In addition to the potential impact on the client's case, and beyond the risk of disciplinary sanctions for running afoul of the limitations on prejudicial extrajudicial statements in Model Rule 3.6, other consequences may attach to the lawyer's conduct:

***Accuracy in Public Statements:*** A lawyer must be scrupulously accurate in public statements about an imminent or pending proceeding.[766] A seriously flawed

---

[762] *See* MONROE H. FREEDMAN & ABBE SMITH, UNDERSTANDING LAWYERS' ETHICS § 4.09 (LexisNexis 4th ed. 2010) (stating that "[i]t could be disastrous . . . for an unskilled [criminal] defendant to confront the cacophony and confusion of a press conference," and thus that "[d]efense counsel, by virtue of her knowledge about the case and her training as an advocate, is frequently the most appropriate person to speak publicly on behalf of the defendant").

[763] STANDARDS FOR CRIMINAL JUSTICE: FAIR TRIAL AND PUBLIC DISCOURSE, Standard 8–2.3(c) (American Bar Ass'n, 2013).

[764] *Id.*

[765] PETER A. JOY & KEVIN C. MCMUNIGAL, DO NO WRONG: ETHICS FOR PROSECUTORS AND DEFENDERS 64 (American Bar Ass'n, 2009); *see also* Tarkington, supra, 66 FLA. L. REV. at 1893 (explaining that a criminal defense lawyer must obtain client consent to the disclosure of confidential information to the press).

[766] *See* Michele DeStefano Beardslee, *Advocacy in the Court of Public Opinion Installment Two: How Far Should Corporate Attorneys Go?*, 23 GEO. J. LEGAL ETHICS 1119, 1134 (2010) (suggesting that, because

statement to the public certainly heightens the potential for a prejudicial effect on the decisionmaker. Beyond the danger of a prejudicial effect on the imminent or pending proceeding that lies at the heart of the restrictions imposed in Rule 3.6, Rule 8.4(c) imposes an independent duty on the lawyer not to engage in conduct that involves "dishonesty" or "misrepresentation."[767]

In *Board of Professional Ethics & Conduct v. Visser*,[768] the Iowa Supreme Court held that a lawyer's public statements to a newspaper reporter challenging the merits of a recently-filed lawsuit against the lawyer's client were not reasonably likely to affect the fairness of the litigation and thus did not cross the ethical line with respect to extrajudicial statements. However, the court reprimanded the lawyer for making a misrepresentation, because one of the statements made to the reporter was "only partially true."[769] Although the court did not expressly link the reprimand with the nature of the statement as an extrajudicial comment on pending litigation, the context appears crucial to the disposition.

In *United States v. Aversa*,[770] a federal prosecutor issued a press release accusing the defendant of money laundering by structuring deposits into a bank account, which the release said "is usually done for purposes of tax evasion, drug dealing or organized crime." Although perhaps literally true, the statement implied the defendant was hiding illicit funds even though the prosecutor knew the defendant instead was attempting to conceal assets should his wife seek a divorce. Although declining to hold the United States liable for slander, the court described the statement as "false, misleading, self-serving, unjust, and unprofessional" and referred the matter for disciplinary investigation.[771]

A lawyer who makes a public comment as a citizen, rather than as an officer of the court while representing a client, would not ordinarily be subject to professional discipline based on the incompleteness or even the inaccuracy of a contribution to public debate.[772] But when a public statement is made by a lawyer as representative of a client to advance the client's interests, and especially when the statement is made publicly with respect to a pending litigation matter, the lawyer is subject to a heightened duty of care and expectation of accuracy. The alternative, of course, is to refrain from public comment and confine statements to the judicial process.

***Defamation Liability:*** The lawyer who speaks publicly opens himself up to the possibility of legal action should those statements be deemed defamatory by another person. A lawyer's statements made in connection with a proceeding before a tribunal—such as pleadings, affidavits, hearings, trials, briefs, motions, conferences, and other communications preliminary to the proceeding—are absolutely privileged.[773] A lawyer is not subject to suit, for defamation or otherwise, based upon such statements. However,

---

"[l]awyers' contribution to unfair, deceitful media communication around legal controversies poses risks above and beyond lawyer professionalism," standards should be established to control misleading statements by lawyers to the media about legal controversies).

767 *See supra* § 4-1.4(b).

768 629 N.W.2d 376 (Iowa 2001).

769 *Id.* at 383.

770 99 F.3d 1200, 1204 (1st Cir. 1996).

771 *Id.* at 1222.

772 On the lawyer's freedom of speech in and outside of court, see *supra* § 4-1.4(c) and *infra* § 4-13.3.

773 *See* RESTATEMENT OF LAW (SECOND) OF TORTS § 586 (American Law Institute, 1977).

the privilege or immunity does not cover a lawyer's statements during the course of an interview with a newspaper reporter, even if the lawyer simply describes the allegations or arguments in the litigation.[774]

The lawyer who chooses to step outside of the courtroom and away from judicial supervision to make a public statement—by issuing a press release, submitting to an interview with a reporter, or calling a press conference—assumes responsibility for the legal consequences that may follow.

### § 4-9.11(f) The Lawyer's Responsibility for Prejudicial Extrajudicial Statements by Others

Under Rule 3.8(f) of the Model Rules of Professional Conduct, a prosecutor in a criminal case shall "exercise reasonable care to prevent investigators, law enforcement personnel, employees or other persons assisting or associated with the prosecutor in a criminal case from making an extrajudicial statement that the prosecutor would be prohibited from making under Rule 3.6 or this Rule."[775]

For those persons who are associated with the prosecutor as employees of or subject to disciplinary supervision by the prosecutor's office, this is merely a specific application of the general rule stated in Rule 5.3 of the Model Rules of Professional Conduct that managerial and supervisory lawyers must make reasonable efforts to ensure that all nonlawyer assistants behave in a manner compatible with the lawyer's professional obligations.[776] That a prosecutor is obliged to ensure that those working in her office understand and obey professional constraints on extrajudicial statements should be unremarkable.

For those persons who assist a prosecutor but who are not employed by or subject to the disciplinary supervision of the prosecutor's office, the prosecutor's duty to "exercise reasonable care" to prevent others from making prejudicial public statements becomes a duty of clear notice and appropriate education. At the federal level, investigation and prosecution of federal crimes often occur under the unified authority of the Department of Justice and thus law enforcement personnel ordinarily are subject to direct control and supervision by lawyers who hold a professional responsibility to ensure that their behavior comports with professional standards.[777] By contrast, state and county prosecutors frequently have little or no supervisory control over the police who investigate crimes. In that situation, Comment 6 to Rule 3.8 explains that "[o]rdinarily, the reasonable care standard will be satisfied if the prosecutor issues the appropriate cautions to law-enforcement personnel and other relevant individuals."

---

[774] *See, e.g.*, Bochetto v. Gibson, 860 A.2d 67 (Pa. 2004); Kurczaba v. Pollock, 42 N.E.2d 425, 441–42 (Ill. Ct. App. 2000); Kennedy v. Zimmermann, 601 N.W.2d 61, 65–66 (Iowa 1999); Kennedy v. Canon, 82 A.2d 54, 58–59 (Md. Ct. App. 1962).

[775] *See also* STANDARDS FOR CRIMINAL JUSTICE: FAIR TRIAL AND PUBLIC DISCOURSE, Standard 8–3.1(a) (American Bar Ass'n, 2015) (stating that "law enforcement officers and employees of law enforcement agencies should not make, cause to be made, condone or authorize the making of a public extrajudicial statement that a lawyer would be prohibited from making" under standards prohibiting prejudicial extrajudicial statements).

[776] *See infra* § 4-12.4.

[777] *See* Panel *Discussion: The Regulation and Ethical Responsibilities of Federal Prosecutors*, 26 FORDHAM URBAN L.J. 737, 762 (1999) (remarks of Mark F. Pomerantz) (observing that the United States Attorney's office has "some success" in addressing leaks from the Federal Bureau of Investigation, but that "[i]t is vastly more difficult to clamp down on" another agency involved in a particular investigation with which the office does "not have regular contact").

Guidance provided by prosecutors to law enforcement and other personnel to comply with Rule 3.8(f) should not be perfunctory nor suggest that the standards regarding extrajudicial publicity are less important because the rules are not directly enforceable against nonlawyers outside the prosecutor's direct supervision. The prosecutor's message should highlight that these standards were adopted by the courts as important protections to ensure a fair, just, and honorable criminal justice system. While law enforcement personnel who are not lawyers are not subject to professional discipline for failure to comply with these rules, good faith observance (or the lack thereof) by law enforcement to the guidelines established in Rules 3.6 and 3.8 presumably would be a factor to be considered by a court when ruling on a criminal defendant's motion for a change of venue or for a mistrial due to prejudicial publicity.

While the Model Rules do not directly impose a parallel requirement on criminal defense lawyers[778] and lawyers participating in other proceedings to similarly control the conduct of their associates and assistants, the expectation undoubtedly stands. Rule 8.4(a) of the Model Rules of Professional Conduct defines professional misconduct as including "knowingly assist[ing] or induc[ing] another to" violate the Rules. Rule 5.3 directs the managing or supervising lawyer to make "reasonable efforts" to ensure that nonlawyer assistants uphold the "professional obligations of the lawyer."[779]

## § 4-9.12 THE HEIGHTENED ETHICAL DUTIES OF LAWYERS FOR THE SOVEREIGN GOVERNMENT—WITH SPECIAL ATTENTION TO PROSECUTORS

### § 4-9.12(a) Introduction to the Ethical Responsibilities of the Prosecutor and Government Litigator

#### *§ 4-9.12(a)(1) The Duty of a Prosecutor to "Do Justice"*

Given their immense power over the freedom and even the lives of others and because they represent the sovereign public interest,[780] prosecutors have special and heightened ethical responsibilities. Or at least they should.

"A prosecutor has the responsibility of a minister of justice and not simply that of an advocate," states the first comment to Rule 3.8 of the Model Rules of Professional Conduct. In *Berger v. United States*,[781] the Supreme Court said of the federal prosecutor:

> The United States Attorney is the representative not of an ordinary party to a controversy, but of a sovereignty whose obligation to govern impartially is as

[778] The American Bar Association's *Standards for Criminal Justice* do direct criminal defense counsel to "exercise reasonable care to prevent investigators, employees, or other persons assisting or associated with the defense from making an extrajudicial statement or providing non-public information that defense counsel would be prohibited from making or providing under this Standard or other applicable rules or law." STANDARDS FOR CRIMINAL JUSTICE: DEFENSE FUNCTION, Standard 4–1.10(e) (American Bar Ass'n, 2015).

[779] *See infra* § 4-12.4.

[780] *See* Bruce A. Green, *Why Should Prosecutors "Seek Justice"?*, 26 FORDHAM URBAN L.J. 607, 625–34 (1999) (discussing the justifications for the prosecutor's duty to seek justice as "rooted in the prosecutor's power" and "in the prosecutor's professional role as a representative of the sovereign," and concluding the second rationale is the stronger because, "[w]ith respect to the criminal law, a sovereign's overarching objective in this country . . . is to 'do justice' "); PETER A. JOY & KEVIN C. MCMUNIGAL, DO NO WRONG: ETHICS FOR PROSECUTORS AND DEFENDERS 13–18 (American Bar Ass'n, 2009) (describing the rationales for treating prosecutors differently as the government's interest in justice, protecting against abuse of power, asymmetry of resources, public confidence in the justice system, and promoting open government).

[781] 295 U.S. 78 (1935).

compelling as its obligation to govern at all; and whose interest, therefore, in a criminal prosecution is not that it shall win a case, but that justice shall be done. As such, he is in a peculiar and very definite sense the servant of the law, the twofold aim of which is that guilt shall not escape or innocence suffer. He may prosecute with earnestness and vigor—indeed, he should do so. But, while he may strike hard blows, he is not at liberty to strike foul ones. It is as much his duty to refrain from improper methods calculated to produce a wrongful conviction as it is to use every legitimate means to bring about a just one.[782]

In contrast with the ordinary advocate who is accountable primarily to a single client, "a prosecutor owes a duty to the defendant as well as to the public."[783] Quoting the *Standards for Criminal Justice*, the Minnesota Supreme Court has described the prosecutor as "a minister of justice whose obligation is to guard the rights of the accused as well as to enforce the rights of the public."[784] For this reason, the Iowa Supreme Court has described prosecutors as having "a dual function."[785] In addition to speaking on behalf of those who seek justice for the wrongdoing of another, the prosecutor has a responsibility to see that true justice is done by rightly identifying the accused and in assuring that the defendant enjoys a fair trial and is extended every right protected by statute or constitution. Thus, prosecutors "should keep in mind their obligation to the accused at every stage of the proceeding."[786]

Many of the ethical requirements set forth in the Model Rules of Professional Conduct apply with special force to prosecutors, as the injury to the integrity of public justice and the danger that innocent persons will be unjustly deprived of liberty is heightened in such a context.[787] As discussed above, prosecutors are subject to additional restrictions on extrajudicial statements, that they refrain from making extrajudicial statements that heighten public condemnation of the accused and exercise reasonable care to prevent prejudicial extrajudicial statements by law enforcement.[788] Rule 3.8 of the Model Rules of Professional Conduct further emphasizes the special responsibilities of a prosecutor in a criminal case, establishing specific mandates that a prosecutor bring only charges that are supported by probable cause;[789] that prosecutors make reasonable efforts to ensure that persons unrepresented by counsel be advised of and given the opportunity to obtain counsel and that prosecutors not deprive unrepresented accused persons of important pretrial rights;[790] that prosecutors disclose exculpatory and mitigating information and information indicating a reasonable likelihood of a wrongful conviction;[791] and that prosecutors not subpoena criminal defense lawyers before a grand

---

[782] *Id.* at 88; *see also* STANDARDS FOR CRIMINAL JUSTICE: PROSECUTION FUNCTION, Standard 3–1.2(b) (American Bar Ass'n, 2015) ("The primary duty of the prosecutor is to seek justice within the bounds of the law, not merely to convict."). *But see* Abbe Smith, *Can You Be a Good Person and a Good Prosecutor?*, 14 GEO. J. LEGAL ETHICS 355 (2001) (complaining that the concept of seeking justice "could not be more ambiguous and subject to multiple interpretations").

[783] State v. Graves, 668 N.W.2d 860, 870 (Iowa 2003).

[784] State v. Penkaty, 708 N.W.2d 185, 196 (Minn. 2006) (quoting STANDARDS FOR CRIMINAL JUSTICE: PROSECUTION FUNCTION, Standard 3–1.1 cmt. 3.7 (American Bar Ass'n, 1979)).

[785] State v. Webb, 244 N.W.2d 332, 333 (Iowa 1976).

[786] *Graves*, 668 N.W.2d at 870.

[787] *See infra* § 4-9.12(e).

[788] *See supra* §§ 4-9.11(c)(3), 4-9.11(f).

[789] *See infra* § 4-9.12(b).

[790] *See infra* § 4-9.12(c)(1).

[791] *See infra* § 4-9.12(d).

jury or other proceeding absent a reasonable belief that the information is not privileged, that the evidence sought is essential, and that there is no other feasible alternative to obtain the evidence.[792] In addition, although both the underlying context and the resulting legal constraints appear to grant more latitude to prosecutors, prosecutors also may not interfere with the attorney-client relationship through improper *ex parte* contacts with criminal defendants known to be represented by counsel.[793]

The prosecutor's broader duty to seek justice extends beyond the rules and beyond what could be captured in an enforceable disciplinary standard. As Professor Laurie Levenson writes, a prosecutor "seeking justice often must go beyond the boundaries of the law in an effort to create informal procedures for justice that will apply when the law is silent."[794] Whether a prosecutor's office becomes a ministry of justice or instead a gathering of prosecutorial overlords ultimately turns on the culture of the office even more than the constitutional constraints and the limits of formal ethical rules.

### *§ 4-9.12(a)(2) The Heightened Expectation for the Government Civil Litigator in Competence and Candor*

In addition to those government lawyers employed to bring and prosecute criminal charges, many government lawyers represent units of government in civil litigation. Government lawyers handling civil litigation also have heightened ethical expectations.[795]

Professor Bruce Green argues that, just as it is well established that prosecutors must "seek justice" in criminal cases, so also government lawyers in civil litigation have a "distinctive professional role."[796] Because the client government agency or official "owes fiduciary duties to the public," Green suggests that the government lawyer "owes some derivative duties to the public."[797] Thus, in some contrast with the standard of zealous advocacy and the partisan nature of the lawyer's role on behalf of private clients, the government lawyer has "public-regarding obligations" and should not "assert every plausible claim or defense, or [ ] otherwise engage in every method permitted by law to prevail in litigation."[798] Like government lawyers in criminal prosecution, government lawyers in civil litigation should refrain from "bringing 'bad' or undeserving cases,"[799] which Green articulates as a higher standard than merely avoiding taking frivolous positions. In addition, government lawyers should be more restrained than private lawyers in exploiting legal and factual errors made by the court or the opposing party.[800]

---

[792] *See infra* § 4-9.12(c)(5).

[793] *See infra* § 4-9.12(c)(2).

[794] Laurie L. Levenson, *Working Outside the Rules: The Undefined Responsibilities of Federal Prosecutors*, 26 FORDHAM URBAN L.J. 553, 553 (1999).

[795] *See generally* GREGORY C. SISK, LITIGATION WITH THE FEDERAL GOVERNMENT § 1.3(c) (West Academic Publishing, 2016).

[796] Bruce A. Green, *Must Government Lawyers "Seek Justice" in Civil Litigation?*, 9 WIDENER J. PUB. L. 235, 239–40 (2000). *But see* W. Bradley Wendel, *Government Lawyers in the Trump Administration*, 69 HASTINGS LAW JOURNAL 275, 294 (2017) (questioning the proposition that government lawyers have greater public-regarding responsibilities beyond the "distinctive ethical obligations" of prosecutors).

[797] Green, *supra*, 9 WIDENER J. PUB. L. at 269–70.

[798] *Id.* at 270–74.

[799] *Id.* at 240–41.

[800] *See also* Duncan Webb, *Keeping the Crown's Conscience: A Theory of Lawyering for Public Sector Counsel*, 5 N.Z. J. PUB. & INT'L L. 243 (2007) (arguing that "the legal advisers of a public sector entity ought to

Douglas Letter, formerly Director of the Appellate Staff of the Civil Division at the United States Department of Justice, argues that government attorneys should begin from very different premises in how the case is litigated along the path to settlement or judgment:

> One . . . recurring dilemma [is that] regarding the duty of the public service attorney when opposing counsel make mistakes that could be remedied if the opposing attorneys were aware of them. That this dilemma even arises reveals that the Justice Department has a very different role from the private firm representing a private client. On several occasions of which I am aware government attorneys have notified opposing counsel of technical problems so that they can be fixed before jurisdictional limits make a remedy impossible. This action would be obvious malpractice if followed while representing a private party.[801]

This perspective on the role of the government lawyer is not without skeptics and critics. That the government attorney might be tempted to pull punches with a sympathetic opponent is characterized as an "unwarranted restraint" by Michael Cardozo, formerly Corporation Counsel for the City of New York, who argues this is "also a disservice to the government entity the attorney represents."[802] Unless the government lawyer is given "a special constitutional or statutory duty to represent the public interest," Cardozo argues that the government lawyer in the adversarial system must play by the rules, but "owe[s] it to the tax-payer to play to win."

Similarly, Professor Catherine Lanctot argues that in applying mandatory ethical codes, government lawyers are subject to the same standards as other members of the bar and are fully entitled to serve as zealous advocates on behalf of the government.[803] With respect to raising technical defenses, candor to the courts, and presentation of weak (but not frivolous) arguments, she concludes that—

> under the Model Code and the Model Rules, the government lawyer may represent the government client the same way that a private lawyer represents a private client. . . . In short, the ethical codes draw no distinctions between the duty of the government lawyer and the duty of the private lawyer to defend a civil case zealously.[804]

Lanctot emphasizes that, because private practitioners are permitted to provide moral advice to clients, and because "the duty to consider the public good is a duty of all public servants, not just lawyers," the government lawyer may discuss with the government client the issues of justice and fairness. Still, Lanctot concludes that government lawyers have little leeway to implement their personal view of justice or the public interest:

> As government officials and as lawyers representing clients, government lawyers should participate in this decision-making process. Ultimately,

act differently than a lawyer who is acting for private clients" because they act on behalf of the government and the "government deals on behalf of the citizens").

[801] Douglas Letter, *Lawyering and Judging on Behalf of the United States: All I Ask for is a Little Respect*, 61 GEO. WASH. L. REV. 1295, 1300 (1993).

[802] Michael A. Cardozo, *The Conflicting Ethical, Legal, and Public Policy Obligations of the Government's Chief Legal Officer*, 22:3 PROF'L LAW. at 4, 7–8 (2014).

[803] Catherine J. Lanctot, *The Duty of Zealous Advocacy and the Ethics of the Federal Government Lawyer: The Three Hardest Questions*, 64 S. CAL. L. REV. 951, 957–58, 985–86, 1015 (1991).

[804] *Id.* at 957–58.

however, in the American political system, the decision as to which governmental action will benefit "the people" or "the public interest" is vested in elected officials or those to whom they have delegated their decision-making authority. Once that policy decision has been made, the government lawyer may ethically defend it, even if the lawyer believes that the public interest may not be served by that decision. The government lawyer, after all, is not employed by the federal government to represent personal interests, and it is virtually impossible for anyone to determine where a neutral view of the "public interest" ends and one's own personal opinions begin.[805]

At the end of the day, the courts do have higher expectations for government lawyers appearing in court. Former District of Columbia Circuit Chief Judge Patricia Wald outlines that "higher standard" as including a higher level of competence, greater candor with the court, credibility by virtue of the attorney's enthusiasm for and confidence in the position advocated, a greater concern for civility, and consistency in government positions taken before the courts.[806] In one oft-cited federal appellate decision, *Freeport-McMoRan Oil & Gas Co. v. FERC*,[807] the court issued a published opinion to counter the "remarkable" assertion by the commission's attorney at oral argument "that government attorneys ought not be held to higher standards than attorneys for private litigants." The court insisted that the traditional principle that prosecutors have greater ethical obligations "appl[ies] with equal force to the government's civil lawyers."[808] The court chastised the government lawyer for having failed more diligently to appreciate that the case was moot and to take steps "to avoid needless litigation."[809]

#### *§ 4-9.12(a)(3) Federal Government Lawyers and State Ethics Rules*

Enacted to counter occasional suggestions by the United States Department of Justice that federal attorneys might sometimes be subject to federal rules of practice that supersede state ethical rules (typically patterned after the Model Rules of Professional Conduct), the Citizens Protection Act of 1998 (commonly known as the McDade Act) makes state ethics rules and local federal rules applicable to federal government attorneys:

> An attorney for the Government shall be subject to State laws and rules, and local Federal court rules, governing attorneys in each state where such attorney engages in that attorney's duties, to the same extent and in the same manner as other attorneys in that State.[810]

Thus, a federal government attorney is bound by the professional conduct rules that have been adopted in the state or states where he practices.

---

[805] *Id.* at 1015; *see also* W. Bradley Wendel, *Government Lawyers in the Trump Administration*, 69 HASTINGS LAW JOURNAL 275, 332 (2017) ("Government lawyers do not have an open commission to serve the public interest; they are agents who must carry out the lawful instructions of their principal.").

[806] Patricia M. Wald, *"For the United States": Government Lawyers in Court*, 61 LAW & CONTEMP. PROBS. 107, 109–10, 119–27 (Winter 1998).

[807] 962 F.2d 45, 46 (D.C. Cir. 1992).

[808] *Id.* at 47.

[809] *Id.* at 46.

[810] 28 U.S.C. § 530B.

### § 4-9.12(b) The Prosecutor's Ethical Duties in Charging and Investigation

Professors Monroe Freedman and Abbe Smith described the powerful and devastating consequences of becoming the subject of a formal accusation of criminal wrongdoing by criminal information or indictment:

> The defendant's reputation is immediately damaged, frequently irreparably, regardless of an ultimate acquittal. Anguish and anxiety become a daily presence for the defendant and for the defendant's family and friends. The emotional strains of the criminal process have been known to destroy marriages and to cause alienation or emotional disturbance among the accused's children. Also, the financial burden can be enormous. A criminal charge may well result in loss of employment because of absenteeism due to pretrial detention, attendance at hearings and the trial, or simply because the accused has been named as a criminal defendant. The trial itself, building up to the terrible anxiety during jury deliberations, is a harrowing experience.[811]

Appreciating that the prosecutor's discretionary power to charge a person with a crime involves the discharge of a solemn responsibility, Rule 3.8(a) of the Model Rules of Professional Conduct directs that a prosecutor in a criminal case "refrain from prosecuting a charge that the prosecutor knows is not supported by probable cause." "[A] prosecutor's decision whether or not to dismiss a charge, like a prosecutor's decision whether or not to prosecute, 'lies at the heart of the prosecutorial function.' "[812] Even when an indictment is brought by a grand jury, the prosecutor retains ultimate responsibility and "has authority, and sometimes a responsibility, to move for dismissal of an indictment."[813]

The prosecutor must take personal responsibility for ensuring that the evidence then reasonably available justifies bringing to bear the awesome powers of the state in prosecuting an individual for an alleged crime. A prosecutor may not simply accept the complaint of an alleged victim or the judgment of the police; "prosecutors have an affirmative, independent responsibility to review the evidence and, if necessary, seek additional evidence."[814] The rule that a charge be supported by probable cause states a continuing duty,[815] meaning that the prosecutor must continually evaluate and reconsider whether the charge continues to have sufficient evidentiary support in the light of new information produced by continuing investigation, pretrial discovery, or developments at trial.

The American Bar Association's recently-revised *Standards for Criminal Justice* place even greater emphasis on the importance of evidentiary sufficiency to support a criminal charge and expect a higher showing by the prosecutor to assure its legitimacy

---

[811] MONROE H. FREEDMAN & ABBE SMITH, UNDERSTANDING LAWYERS' ETHICS § 10.04 (LexisNexis 4th ed. 2010).

[812] Altman v. Kelly, 28 F. Supp.2d 50, 53 (D. Mass. 1998) (quoting Guzman-Rivera v. Rivera-Cruz, 55 F.3d 26, 31 (1st Cir.1995), and upholding absolute immunity from tort liability for discretionary prosecutorial decision).

[813] State v. Iowa Dist. Ct., 568 N.W.2d 505, 509 (Iowa 1997).

[814] Bruce A. Green, *Why Should Prosecutors "Seek Justice"?*, 26 FORDHAM URB. L.J. 607, 640–41 (1999).

[815] *See* Hans P. Sinha, *Prosecutorial Ethics: The Charging Decision*, THE PROSECUTOR (Sept.–Oct. 2007), at 37 (stating that the term " 'refrain' [in Rule 3.8(a)] should be given a broader reading so as to include the institution of and the continuing prosecution of cases").

than does Model Rule 3.8(a). Rule 3.8(a) prohibits a prosecutor from prosecuting a charge only if the prosecutor "knows" it is not supported by probable cause. As Professors Ronald Rotunda and John Dzienkowski suggest, the requirement in the Model Rule "that a prosecutor have knowledge about the lack of probable cause makes it unlikely that this provision will serve as a basis for discipline in the vast majority of cases."[816] The *Standards for Criminal Justice* state that a prosecutor should seek or file a charge "only if the prosecutor *reasonably believes* that the charges are supported by probable cause, that admissible evidence will be sufficient to support conviction beyond a reasonable doubt, and that the decision to charge is in the interests of justice" (emphasis added).[817]

A prosecutor should not be permitted to proceed with outrageous ignorance about the supporting facts and evidence or with unreasonable irrationality in charging anyone with a criminal offense, then resting on the excuse that the prosecutor did not actually "know" that probable cause was missing. Given that a reasonably competent and prudent prosecutor will conduct a diligent inquiry into the basis for a proposed charge, the enhanced expectation in the *Standards for Criminal Justice* should be satisfied as a matter of course in an ethically-responsible prosecutor's office.

A prosecutor's formal ethical responsibility is satisfied by ensuring that every criminal charge is supported by probable cause. And a disciplinary charge cannot legitimately be premised upon the mere fact of a later acquittal because the trier of fact concluded there was a reasonable doubt about guilt.

However, conscientious prosecutors follow a higher standard than merely having evidence supporting a prima facie case before they exercise the awesome power of advancing a criminal charge against a fellow citizen. Professor John Kaplan reported many decades ago that in his experience as a federal prosecutor, the "first and most basic standard" is that a prosecutor is not morally justified in pursuing a prosecution unless she is "personally convinced" that the accused is guilty of the charged offense.[818] Carl Lowenson argues more pointedly that, while probable cause may be enough to obtain an arrest or search warrant—

> any prosecutor who indicts based solely on probable cause—perhaps in the hope that the defendant will plead guilty or that more evidence will turn up by trial—exhibits a woeful disregard for the rights of the accused, the purposes of the criminal justice system, the limited resources of the prosecutor's office, and probably the prosecutor's own career.[819]

---

[816] RONALD D. ROTUNDA & JOHN S. DZIENKOWSKI, PROFESSIONAL RESPONSIBILITY: A STUDENT'S GUIDE § 3.8–2(a) (American Bar Ass'n, 2013–2014).

[817] STANDARDS FOR CRIMINAL JUSTICE: PROSECUTION FUNCTION, Standard 3–4.3(a) (American Bar Ass'n, 2015) (emphasis added).

[818] John Kaplan, *The Prosecutorial Discretion—A Comment*, 60 NW. U. L. REV. 174, 1768–79 (1965); *see also* United States Attorneys' Manual §§ 9–27.200(B), 9–27.220(A) (2016) (stating that probable cause is "a threshold consideration only" and that "[t]he attorney for the government should commence or recommend Federal prosecution if he/she believes the person's conduct constitutes a Federal offense and that the admissible evidence will probably be sufficient to obtain and sustain a conviction"); Laurie L. Levenson, *Working Outside the Rules: The Undefined Responsibilities of Federal Prosecutors*, 26 FORDHAM URBAN L.J. 553, 558 (1999) (saying that, "[m]orally," prosecutors should consider the public interest and "their personal sense of the defendant's culpability for the crime, including the prosecutor's individual assessment of the credibility of witness' testimony, the accuracy of evidence and the need to punish the defendant for his actions").

[819] Carl H. Lowenson, *The Decision to Indict*, 24 LITIGATION 13 (1997); *see generally* MONROE H. FREEDMAN & ABBE SMITH, UNDERSTANDING LAWYERS' ETHICS §§ 10.04 to 10.05 (LexisNexis, 4th ed. 2010).

Again, the *ABA Standards of Criminal Justice*, which are cited as a guide in Comment 1 to Model Rule 3.8, advise that a prosecutor "is not obliged to file or maintain all criminal charges which the evidence might support," exercising discretion to decline to prosecute based on such factors, among several others, as "the prosecutor's doubt that the accused is in fact guilty," "the extent or absence of harm caused by the offense," and "whether the authorized or likely punishment or collateral consequences are disproportionate in relation to the particular offense or the offender."[820]

For many decades, "the perceived wisdom was that prosecutors prosecute and investigators investigate."[821] The reality today, especially in the federal system, is that prosecutors and law enforcement agents work together from an early stage, planning and implementing an investigation and selecting targets and methods. In some respects, this is commendable, as the legally-educated prosecutor may help guide investigators to respect the rights of those being investigated and those charged. Other aspects of this intertwining of prosecutorial and investigation functions are more troubling, as the prosecutor may become so invested as to be unable to make an independent judgment about pursuing charges. As Professor Daniel Richman asks, "Can a prosecutor who really sees himself as a partner of the agents in developing a case at some point later step back and make the kinds of decisions about, not just what is winnable, but what is right and appropriate in a particular case?"[822]

Professor Rory Little has advanced a proposed set of ethical rules directing prosecutors to "engage in an analysis of proportionality in choosing which investigative steps to pursue, and how aggressively to pursue them."[823] Prosecutors thus would be obliged to reconsider overbroad subpoenas for documents that impose considerable burdens and expenses on business enterprises, akin perhaps to the newly-emphasized rule of proportionality adopted in the federal rules for civil discovery.[824] Similarly, prosecutors in authorizing a search warrant would have to consider "the extent of the intrusion or the impact on the target or on other, innocent, occupants of the space to be searched."[825]

## § 4-9.12(c) The Government Lawyer's Duty to Respect the Rights of Others, Especially the Right to Counsel

### *§ 4-9.12(c)(1) Prosecutor's Duties to an Unrepresented Accused*

To prevent overreaching by trained advocates bearing the authority of the government when dealing with an unrepresented person and to prevent interference with an actual or imminent attorney-client relationship, Rule 3.8(b) and (c) of the Model Rules of Professional Conduct requires a prosecutor to take reasonable steps to facilitate access to counsel by an accused and prohibits a prosecutor from procuring a waiver of important pretrial rights from an unrepresented accused. Professor Bruce Green

---

[820] STANDARDS FOR CRIMINAL JUSTICE: PROSECUTION FUNCTION, Standard 3–4.4(a) (American Bar Ass'n, 2015).

[821] *Panel Discussion: The Expanding Prosecutorial Role from Trial Counsel to Investigator and Administrator*, 26 FORDHAM URBAN L.J. 679, 681 (1999) (remarks of Daniel C. Richman).

[822] *Id.*

[823] Rory K. Little, *Proportionality as an Ethical Precept for Prosecutors in Their Investigative Role*, 68 FORDHAM L. REV. 723, 752 (1999).

[824] On proportionality in civil discovery, see *supra* § 4-9.6(b).

[825] Little, *supra*, 68 FORDHAM L. REV. at 755.

explains these special ethical responsibilities which rest upon prosecutors as part of their unique professional obligation to "seek justice":[826]

> Lawyers in civil practice may exploit their superior skill and expertise in dealing with unrepresented adversaries, as long as their role is clear and they do not suggest that they are disinterested. Prosecutors, in contrast, must make efforts to assure that an unrepresented criminal defendant is aware of the right to counsel and has opportunities to obtain counsel, and, in dealing with unrepresented defendants, prosecutors may not seek to obtain waivers of important pretrial rights.[827]

Thus, for example, the American Bar Association's *Standards for Criminal Justice* advise that, other than following the general rules in dealing with an unrepresented person[828] and not intimidating or attempting to influence the truthfulness of a witness,[829] a criminal defense attorney is not required, "when interviewing a witness, to caution the witness concerning possible self-incrimination or a right to independent counsel."[830] By contrast, and especially when dealing with an accused, a prosecutor does have the affirmative duty to both advise of and effectively facilitate the accused's right to counsel.

Model Rule 3.8(b) states that a prosecutor in a criminal case shall "make reasonable efforts to assure that the accused has been advised of the right to, and the procedure for obtaining, counsel and has been given reasonable opportunity to obtain counsel." While law enforcement officers ordinarily will have advised a person taken into custody of the right to legal counsel, including appointed counsel if he is unable to afford legal representation, the prosecutor has an independent duty to ensure that this advice has been given, that the steps required to obtain that counsel have been explained, and that the person is allowed the time and ability to secure legal counsel. Even if it is unclear under particular circumstances whether the person is constitutionally entitled to the so-called *Miranda* warning on the right to counsel,[831] Professors Geoffrey Hazard and William Hodes and attorney Peter Jarvis explain that Rule 3.8(b) "requires a prosecutor to take a reasonably generous view of these matters, rather than to exact every possible advantage from an unrepresented person before counsel becomes available."[832]

Rule 3.8(c) provides that a prosecutor in a criminal case shall "not seek to obtain from an unrepresented accused a waiver of important pretrial rights, such as the right to a preliminary hearing." Although pretrial rights ordinarily may be waived, Rule 3.8(c) forbids a prosecutor from seeking to extract such a waiver from an accused who does not have the benefit of counsel. As with Rule 3.8(b), Rule 3.8(c) means that a prosecutor may not profit from an accused's lack of counsel by securing a possible advantage, whether or not that conduct would cross a constitutional line.

---

[826] On the prosecutor's general duty to do justice, see *supra* § 4-9.12(a)(1).

[827] Bruce A. Green, *Why Should Prosecutors "Seek Justice,"* 26 FORDHAM URB. L.J. 607, 615–16 (1999).

[828] *See infra* § 4-11.4.

[829] *See supra* § 4-9.8(j).

[830] STANDARDS FOR CRIMINAL JUSTICE: DEFENSE FUNCTION, Standard 4–4.3(g) (American Bar Ass'n, 2015).

[831] *See* Miranda v. Arizona, 384 U.S. 436 (1966).

[832] 2 GEOFFREY C. HAZARD, JR., W. WILLIAM HODES & PETER R. JARVIS, THE LAW OF LAWYERING § 37.05 (Aspen, 4th ed., 2016).

The rule, however, is subject to certain practical limits based on the choice of the accused, the preliminary stage of a criminal investigation, and perhaps the nature of a charge:

*First*, some criminal defendants will choose to represent themselves, in which case the prosecutor has no choice but to deal directly with the accused. Comment 2 confirms that Rule 3.8(c) does not apply "to an accused appearing *pro se* with the approval of the tribunal." Once the court has confirmed that the criminal defendant has made a knowing, voluntary, and intelligent waiver of the right to legal counsel, the prosecutor may interact directly with that person, including negotiations that involve waiver of rights. The prosecutor remains subject to the general limitations of Model Rule 4.3 on dealings with unrepresented persons, meaning that the prosecutor must not state or imply that she is disinterested and must not give legal advice to the accused.[833] The prosecutor may inform the accused of the terms of any proposed agreement or plea bargain and may explain the prosecutor's own view of the governing law as applicable to such a proposal.

*Second*, as Comment 2 states, Rule 3.8(c) does not forbid "the lawful questioning of an uncharged suspect who has knowingly waived the rights to counsel and silence." Rule 3.8(c) is not intended to interfere with a criminal investigation or interrogation of a suspect before criminal proceedings are initiated by charge or indictment, provided that any custodial interrogation is conducted pursuant to constitutional limitations, including advice of the right to counsel and silence. If the suspect is represented by counsel at the time of the pre-charge contact, the prosecutor's communications with that person are subject to the limitations of Model Rule 4.2, as applicable to a law enforcement investigation.[834]

In addition, a strict prohibition on prosecutorial negotiations with an unrepresented person unless and until a tribunal has approved appearing *pro se* could be impractical when applied to minor offenses, as to which the risk of harm from prosecutorial overreaching is at its lowest ebb. In many localities in the United States, simple misdemeanors are resolved by plea negotiations directly between a prosecutor and an unrepresented accused, before any opportunity for the court to approve the defendant's self-representation. Indeed, one state has adopted comment language clarifying that Rule 3.8(c) "does not apply to a defendant charged with a simple misdemeanor for which the prosecutor reasonably believes the defendant will not be incarcerated."[835]

#### *§ 4-9.12(c)(2) The "No-Contact" Rule as Applied to Law Enforcement Investigations by Government Lawyers*

Rule 4.2 of the Model Rules of Professional Conduct states: "In representing a client, a lawyer shall not communicate about the subject of the representation with a person the lawyer knows to be represented by another lawyer in the matter, unless the lawyer has the consent of the other lawyer or is authorized to do so by law or a court order." This rule, often called the "no-contact" rule,[836] prevents a lawyer representing a client from interfering with the attorney-client relationship between another lawyer and that lawyer's client, guards against inadvertent or uncounseled disclosure of confidential

---

[833] *See infra* § 4-11.4.

[834] *See infra* § 4-9.12(c)(2).

[835] IOWA RULES PROF'L CONDUCT 32:3.8 cmt. 2.

[836] *See infra* § 4-11.3.

information by a layperson whose lawyer is not present, and precludes a lawyer from obtaining a statement from a represented party that would constitute an admission under evidentiary rules.

Government lawyers engaged in law enforcement and conducting an investigation of criminal or civil wrongdoing frequently seek to interview or engage in other communications with persons who are or may be represented by counsel.[837] For example, when government lawyers are participating in or supervising covert surveillance or undercover investigations of suspected criminal enterprises, those lawyers or the undercover operatives acting at the lawyer's direction must make contact with those suspected of illegal activity. While the targets of such investigations may include individuals or entities who have retained standing counsel, notifying that counsel in advance obviously would stymie the investigation, destroy any undercover element of the operation, and alert suspects who are under surveillance. As Professors Ronald Rotunda and John Dzienkowski colorfully describe it:

> In pursuing crime the Government does not limit itself to behavior expected in your grandmother's drawing room. It uses sting operations, bait to trap a criminal, decoys, stoolies, and undercover operatives.[838]

While communications with such a person after she has been arrested or charged with an offense are narrowly circumscribed by both constitutional limitations and by the no-contact rule, non-custodial communications before indictment in the course of both overt and covert law enforcement investigations have long been understood to fall within the "authorized by law" exception.[839] Accordingly, a criminal suspect may not evade otherwise legitimate use by government law enforcement of surveillance, informants, or undercover operations by retaining counsel before or while carrying on criminal activities.

Comment 5 to Model Rule 4.2 states that "[c]ommunications authorized by law may also include investigative activities of lawyers representing governmental entities, directly or through investigative agents, prior to the commencement of criminal or civil enforcement proceedings." Given the public interest in law enforcement, courts (primarily the federal courts) regularly have concluded that lawyers employed in government law enforcement agencies are not barred from appropriate investigative contacts with criminal suspects, who have not yet been arrested (or otherwise taken into custody) or charged (by information or indictment), merely because they had a lawyer on retainer.[840]

---

[837] For discussion of contacts by a prosecutor or law enforcement agents under prosecutor supervision with represented criminal defendants to investigate allegations of criminal wrongdoing other than the offense on which the defendant has been arrested or charged, see *infra* § 4-11.3(d).

[838] RONALD D. ROTUNDA & JOHN S. DZIENKOWSKI, PROFESSIONAL RESPONSIBILITY: A STUDENT'S GUIDE § 4.2–1(b) (American Bar Ass'n, 2013–2014).

[839] On the "authorized by law" exception to the no-contact rule, see *infra* § 4-11.3(g).

[840] *See* United States v. Carona, 660 F.3d 360, 366 (9th Cir. 2011) ("It would be antithetical to the administration of justice to allow a wrongdoer to immunize himself against such undercover operations simply by letting it be known that he has retained counsel."); United States v. Plumley, 207 F.3d 1086, 1095 (8th Cir. 2000) (holding that the ethical rule " 'does not require government investigatory agencies to refrain from any contact with a criminal suspect because he or she previously had retained counsel' " (quoting United States v. Dobbs, 711 F.2d 84, 86 (8th Cir. 1983))); United States v. Balter, 91 F.3d 427, 436 (3d Cir. 1996) (listing cases); United States v. Ryans, 903 F.2d 731, 739 (10th Cir. 1990) (holding that the no-contact rule does not apply at all to "the investigative phase of law enforcement"). *See generally* RONALD D. ROTUNDA & JOHN S.

However, one federal appellate decision, although quite narrow in actual holding, set the stage for a controversy that for a time overshadowed the larger domain of common ground on this question. In *United States v. Hammad*,[841] the United States Court of Appeals for the Second Circuit established a narrow limitation on the government's pre-arrest or pre-charge criminal investigation authority, holding that it was improper for a prosecutor to issue a counterfeit subpoena "to create a pretense that might help the informant elicit admissions from a represented suspect."[842] The court thus effectively found that the no-contact rule was violated when the government fraudulently enlisted the support of the judicial branch, through the issuance of a sham subpoena purporting to be an exercise of court authority, in an effort to trick a suspect into an admission as part of an undercover operation.[843] Even on that point—whether the government engages in illegitimate deception by using a fake subpoena in an undercover operation—the Second Circuit appears to stand alone, as both the Ninth Circuit and the Third Circuit have found the use of false documents such as a fake subpoena or subpoena attachments to be legitimate "props" used to "bolster" the credibility of an undercover agent in inducing a suspect to make incriminating statements.[844]

Notwithstanding the unique circumstances giving rise to the *Hammad* decision, the United States Department of Justice reacted aggressively to the ruling and attempted to wholly exempt federal government lawyers from the constraints of the no-contact rule by asserting that federal law overrides state ethics rules and that state rules may not control federal law enforcement authorities. In 1989, Attorney General Richard Thornburgh issued a memorandum asserting that state ethics rules did not apply to Department of Justice attorneys and their investigators so as to limit their communications with a represented person, until that person had been indicted.[845] In 1994, Attorney General Janet Reno issued a Department rule, codified in the Code of Federal Regulations, that similarly purported to "preempt [as a matter of federal law] the entire field of [state ethics] rules concerning" contacts by federal government attorneys with represented persons.[846]

Because the Department of Justice sought to excuse government lawyers from compliance with ethics rules in the states in which they were licensed, the Department's efforts encountered severe criticism and strong resistance from the Conference of Chief Justices representing all state supreme courts. Ultimately, in 1998, Congress enacted a

---

DZIENKOWSKI, PROFESSIONAL RESPONSIBILITY: A STUDENT'S GUIDE § 4.2–1(b) (American Bar Ass'n, 2013–2014).

[841] 858 F.2d 834 (2d Cir. 1988).

[842] *Id.* at 839.

[843] *See* United States v. DeVillio, 983 F.2d 1185, 1192 (2d Cir. 1993) (explaining *Hammad* decision as turning upon the use by prosecutors of a pretend subpoena); United States v. Grass, 239 F. Supp. 2d 535, 543 (M.D. Pa. 2003) (saying that *Hammad* was "more concerned with curbing prosecutorial skullduggeries than it was with preventing the use of government informants to obtain incriminating statements from parties represented by counsel in the pre-indictment non-custodial setting").

[844] United States v. Carona, 660 F.3d 360, 365–66 (9th Cir. 2011); United States v. Martino, 825 F.2d 754, 760 (3d Cir. 1987).

[845] On the history of this dispute, see generally STEPHEN GILLERS, REGULATION OF LAWYERS: PROBLEMS OF LAW AND ETHICS 126–29 (Aspen, 8th ed. 1998); STEPHEN GILLERS & ROY D. SIMON, REGULATION OF LAWYERS: STATUTES AND STANDARDS 281–83 (Aspen 2009); Geoffrey C. Hazard, Jr. & Dana Remus Irwin, *Toward a Revised 4.2 No-Contact Rule*, 60 HASTINGS L.J. 797, 807–09 (2009); Carl A. Pierce, *Variations on a Basic Theme: Revising the ABA's Revision of Model Rule 4.2 (Part I)*, 70 TENN. L. REV. 121, 123–38 (2002).

[846] 28 C.F.R. § 77.12 (1995) (superseded).

statute (commonly-known as the McDade Act) that subjects government attorneys to state laws and rules, as well as federal court rules, that govern attorney conduct.[847]

Lost for a time within this turf battle between the Department of Justice and the state supreme courts over ethics regulation of federal government lawyers was the longstanding and continuing consensus among the courts that the government indeed was generally authorized by law, within the meaning of the no-contact rule itself, to conduct law enforcement investigations that involved communications with represented persons before arrest or charge.[848] The *Hammad* decision, which had initiated the firestorm, acknowledged that career criminals cannot hire "house counsel" to immunize themselves from investigation and further stated:

> This Court has recognized that prosecutors have a responsibility to perform investigative as well as courtroom-related duties in criminal matters . . . . As we see it, under [the predecessor to Rule 4.2], a prosecutor is "authorized by law" to employ legitimate investigative techniques in conducting or supervising criminal investigations, and the use of informants to gather evidence against a suspect will frequently fall within the ambit of such authorization.[849]

Accordingly, under the "authorized by law" exception to Rule 4.2, a government lawyer conducting an otherwise legitimate law enforcement investigation may directly, or through persons acting at the lawyer's direction or under the lawyer's supervision (such as law enforcement agents, undercover operatives, and informants), communicate with a suspected law-breaker who is known to be represented by a lawyer. This communication is permissible only before that person has been taken into custody (by arrest or otherwise), criminally charged (by information or indictment), or named as a defendant in civil litigation brought by the government to enforce the law.

In this way, the public interest is served in assuring that legitimate law enforcement investigations are conducted under appropriate legal supervision, while the right of the individual to counsel is protected by rigorously restricting communications with represented persons after arrest, criminal charge, or service or filing of a civil complaint. The "authorized by law" exception for government investigations applies, not only to criminal investigations, but also to civil law enforcement, in which government lawyers investigate allegedly unlawful conduct that may be penalized under federal regulatory powers or through civil litigation.

A contrary approach that would handicap law enforcement investigations whenever supervised by government lawyers would have detrimental consequences, not only for effective policing of unlawful conduct, but for the rule of law as applied to such investigations. It must be remembered that the no-contact rule applies only to lawyers. Thus, Rule 4.2 applies in the context of a criminal investigation only if government

---

[847] 28 U.S.C. § 530B. *See supra* § 4-9.12(a)(3).

[848] *See* National Association of Criminal Defense Lawyers' Comment on Proposed Changes to ABA Rule 4.2 (1998) (acknowledging that federal appellate courts have held that non-custodial, pre-indictment communications are permissible under Rule 4.2 or that the rule does not apply to such communications and that "[r]outine undercover investigative communications have been authorized by every court to look at the issue").

[849] *Hammad*, 858 F.2d at 839; *see also* United States v. Scozzafava, 833 F. Supp. 203, 209 (W.D.N.Y. 1993) (stating that "[t]he *Hammad* court clearly intended that prosecutors be able to utilize undercover informants in a pre-indictment, non-custodial situation, in the absence of some egregious misconduct suggestive or pretense or unfair dealing which would disqualify the Government's behavior from reliance upon the 'authorized by law' exception" to the no-contact rule).

lawyers are involved. If covert and other law enforcement investigation activities were unduly constrained by an overly strict application of the no-contact rule to government lawyers, the simple and likely answer would be to take law enforcement investigations away from supervision by lawyers. If lawyers were removed from participation in such investigations, leaving them instead to be conducted solely by nonlawyer investigators, the application of the no-contact rule would fall away. In that event, however, the casualties would include the loss of the salutary effects of lawyer supervision over law enforcement investigations, which is likely to better protect the legal and constitutional rights of those being investigated and to assure that legitimate techniques produce admissible evidence.

Application of the "authorized by law" exception to law enforcement investigations does not mean that government lawyers are held to different ethical standards than other lawyers for purposes of the no-contact rule. Every lawyer is bound by the same set of ethical rules, but the appropriate standard may depend upon the context. The Model Rules of Professional Conduct appropriately account differently for different actors in different situations. No sensible ethical regime fails to account for the varying circumstances and constraints facing the lawyer. The alternative of forcing all people into the same box regardless of context would be ineffective and unjust. Nor is it accurate to characterize such special rules and exceptions as granting an unfair preference or privilege to a particular type of practice or practitioner. Provisions for context-specific treatment in the rules are not based on the person of the acting lawyer, but rather upon the circumstances and the lawyer's distinctive role in that circumstance.

In this regard, the Model Rules of Professional Conduct repeatedly and properly recognize the special context of criminal defense practice and accordingly provide for certain exceptions and unique treatment. For example, while Rule 3.1 generally prohibits lawyers from presenting a frivolous argument or defense, the rule carves out an exception for criminal defense lawyers by saying that this rule does not prevent a lawyer from requiring the prosecution to prove every element of an offense.[850] As another example, Rule 3.6(c) allows lawyers, with criminal defense lawyers particularly in mind, to make a responsive public statement on behalf of a client in order to alleviate the prejudice created by statements made to the press or otherwise published in the media about the client.[851] By contrast, prosecutors are granted less leeway, as they are constrained by Rule 3.8(f) to avoid any public statement that might heighten public condemnation of an accused.[852] As a final example, a criminal defense lawyer, while not being permitted to unlawfully conceal information and being required to comply with discovery rules in the jurisdiction, has no general duty to volunteer adverse information and, by reason of privilege and work-product, is permitted to withhold much information from the prosecution. Under Rule 3.8(d), however, a prosecutor must disclose to the defense all evidence or information "that tends to negate the guilt of the accused or mitigates the offense."[853]

With respect to the application of the no-contact rule to law enforcement investigations in which government lawyers participate, the circumstances and context shift the balance somewhat and temporarily in the other direction. Comment 5 to Rule

---

[850] *See supra* § 4-9.3(b).

[851] *See supra* § 4-9.11(d).

[852] *See supra* § 4-9.11(c)(3).

[853] *See infra* § 4-9.12(d).

4.2 and the caselaw upholding the investigatory exception to the no-contact rule acknowledge the unique setting of pre-arrest and pre-charge law enforcement investigations, recognizing that prosecutors and other government lawyers, by reason of their special public responsibilities, must be authorized to conduct law enforcement investigations. Because of this set of circumstances not ordinarily faced by other lawyers, and the unique public interest in effective law enforcement, government lawyers are permitted to participate in or supervise law enforcement investigations that involve contact with criminal suspects and those suspected of civil wrongdoing, including those who have retained lawyers.

Once a represented person has been taken into custody, charged, or named as defendant to a government-initiated civil proceeding, the pendulum swings heavily back in favor of a stricter application of the no-contact rule. Even when exigent circumstances arguably justify allowing a government lawyer to make an *ex parte* contact with a represented person after arrest, charge, or civil complaint, the government should seek judicial permission through the "court order" exception to the no-contact rule.[854] Communications without the consent or knowledge of the person's counsel may be appropriate under rare circumstances, such as when there is a risk of death or bodily harm (that is, the person is a threat to another or is at risk himself), or when a represented person initiates communication with the government because he does not believe counsel is acting in his best interest. To protect the person's constitutional rights and prevent interference with the attorney-client relationship, a judicial officer should review whether the proposed communication is justified under the circumstances and whether the represented person has voluntarily, knowingly, and intelligently waived the rights to remain silent and to counsel. Given the availability of *ex parte* and summary proceedings before a judge or magistrate (similar to those involved in securing a search warrant), requiring court permission is a minimal burden and should not be an insuperable obstacle to prompt action when necessary.

Moreover, despite a general acceptance that law enforcement covert activity before arrest or charge may fall outside the general parameters of the no-contact rule, some authority remains that especially overt interference with the attorney-client relationship may become so egregious as to remove the conduct from the authorized-by-law exception. In *United States v. Koerber*,[855] a federal district court suppressed a defendant's incriminating statement where the federal prosecutor, on the eve of indictment and without notice to the defendant's attorney, authorized federal law enforcement agents to "initiate[ ] overt communications with Defendant rather than pursuing the investigation through use of an undercover informant . . . or through other covert means." Agents used scripted questions "designed to induce Defendant, who was the target of their investigation and whom prosecutors intended to indict, to waive attorney-client privilege and to reveal potential trial strategy." In *State v. Miller*,[856] the Minnesota Supreme Court acknowledged that "legitimate investigative processes may go forward without violating [the no-contact rule] even when the target of the investigation is represented by counsel," but then found that the process in that case went "beyond fair and legitimate investigation and [was] so egregious" that exclusion of the defendant's statement to a law enforcement officer was necessary. In that case, the criminal investigation followed

---

[854] On the "court order" exception, see *infra* § 4-11.3(g).

[855] 966 F. Supp. 2d 1207, 1214, 1229 (D. Utah 2013).

[856] 600 N.W.2d 457, 461–62, 466–68 (Minn. 1999).

a prior civil investigation where all knew the defendant was represented by counsel. The government lawyer interviewed the individual at the scene during execution of a search warrant, and the individual's attorney asked that the interview be ended and then was blocked by law enforcement from entering the premises to talk with his client, with the knowledge and acquiescence of the prosecutor. These circumstances, which "went beyond appropriate and commonly accepted investigatory activity of police," were so "egregious" as to "impair[ ] the fair administration of justice."[857]

### *§ 4-9.12(c)(3) Interception by the Government of Privileged Communications*

While certain pre-arrest and non-custodial *ex parte* contacts with a suspect by government lawyers or their agents may be permissible in a law enforcement investigation as "authorized by law,"[858] the government may not intercept the privileged communications of a person with his lawyer (absent a proper warrant based on probable cause that the communications themselves are in furtherance of illegal conduct). As the Washington Supreme Court has stated:

> The Sixth Amendment guarantees a criminal defendant the right to assistance of counsel, which includes the right to confer privately with that counsel. State intrusion into those private conversations is a blatant violation of a foundational right. We strongly condemn "the odious practice of eavesdropping on privileged communication between attorney and client."[859]

In *Wolff v. McDonnell*,[860] the Supreme Court described the Sixth Amendment right for prisoners as designed to "protect the attorney-client relationship from intrusion in the criminal setting."[861] Because " 'an accused does not enjoy the effective aid of counsel if he is denied the right of private consultation with him,' " the right of confidential communications by a criminal defendant with his lawyer is "nearly sacrosanct."[862] Accordingly, "[w]hen the government deliberately interferes with the confidential relationship between a criminal defendant and defense counsel, that interference violates the Sixth Amendment right to counsel if it substantially prejudices the criminal defendant."[863]

Beyond the constitutional implications in criminal cases,[864] the government lawyer who participates in or knowingly acquiesces in conduct by government agents designed

---

[857] *Id.* at 467.

[858] *See supra* § 4-9.12(c)(2).

[859] State v. Fuentes, 318 P.3d 257, 258 (Wash. 2014) (quoting State v. Cory, 382 P.2d 1019, 1023 (Wash. 1963)).

[860] 418 U.S. 539 (1974).

[861] *Id.* at 576.

[862] Nordstrom v. Ryan, 762 F.3d 903, 910 (9th Cir. 2014) (quoting Coplon v. United States, 191 F.2d 749, 757 (D.C. Cir. 1951)).

[863] Williams v. Woodford, 384 F.3d 567, 584–85 (9th Cir.2004); *see also* United States v. Danielson, 325 F.3d 1054, 1069 (9th Cir. 2003) (when a government agent obtains privileged information from the defense, "[i]t is clear . . . that the government improperly interfered with [the defendant's] attorney-client relationship.").

[864] *See, e.g.*, State v. Lenarz, 22 A.3d 536, 539–40, 551–52 (Conn. 2011) (presuming prejudice and dismissing a conviction where the prosecutor received and read "voluminous written materials containing detailed discussions of the defendant's trial strategy" found in a search of the defendant's computer); Morrow v. Superior Court, 36 Cal.Rptr.2d 210, 212 (Cal. Ct. App. 1994) ("Where the prosecutor uses the courtroom as a place to eavesdrop upon privileged attorney-client communications which results in the acquisition of confidential information, the conscience of the court is shocked and dismissal is the appropriate remedy.").

to secure privileged information has violated fundamental expectations of a professional. The lawyer who acquires materials that the lawyer reasonably should know are protected by privilege violates Rule 4.4(a) of the Model Rules of Professional Conduct by "us[ing] methods of obtaining evidence that violate the legal rights of" a third person.[865] When that lawyer is a prosecutor who has deliberately intruded into the attorney-client privilege as a representative of the sovereign government that is constitutionally obliged to respect the right to counsel, the lawyer deserves more than a mere rebuke or slap on the hand.

### *§ 4-9.12(c)(4) Demand by Government of Waiver of Privileged Communications—The Corporate Investigation Scenario*

The federal government's still-evolving policy of demanding that corporations suspected of criminal fraud disclose information—perhaps including privileged attorney-client communications from internal investigations—to receive credit for cooperation has engendered considerable controversy over the past two decades.

Deputy Attorney General Larry Thompson in 2003 issued a binding directive to federal lawyers (the "Thompson Memo") that, when evaluating whether a corporation had sufficiently cooperated with a government investigation to avoid indictment, "the prosecutor may consider the corporation's willingness to identify the culprits within the corporation, including senior executives; to make witnesses available; to disclose the complete results of its internal investigation; and to waive attorney-client and work product protection."[866]

Together with earlier statements and ongoing practices, the position of the U.S. Department of Justice fostered a "culture of waiver," in which corporations believed that affirmatively waiving the attorney-client privilege and sharing privileged documents and results of internal investigations was essential to avoid criminal charges that could destroy the business entity. Given the coercive nature of the prosecutorial demand, the voluntariness of a waiver of the privilege was doubtful.[867] Even more worrisome, individual officers and employees who had been interviewed by corporate counsel in internal investigations could find that their forthright and cooperative statements were later forwarded to prosecutors to be used against them in a criminal case. Even a warning to individuals by corporate counsel that they represented the corporation and not its constituents was unlikely to alert these individuals that their responses to questions from counsel might effectively waive Fifth Amendment rights against self-incrimination.[868]

Facing an avalanche of criticism from a diverse set of critics—from legal academics and civil liberties advocates to the American Bar Association and members of

---

[865] *See supra* §§ 4-9.6(d), 4-9.6(e)(1).

[866] Memorandum from Larry D. Thompson, Deputy Att'y Gen., to Heads of Department Components, United States Attorneys, on Principles of Federal Prosecution of Business Organizations, at 6 (Jan. 20, 2003). On the series of memoranda from the Department of Justice on charging criteria for and cooperation by corporate targets of government investigations, see generally Adam Rahman, *Cooperation and Its Discontents: The Constitutional and Policy Implications of the DOJ's War on Corporate Crime*, 14 GEO. J.L. & PUB. POL'Y, 323 (2016).

[867] LAWRENCE J. FOX & SUSAN R. MARTYN, THE ETHICS OF REPRESENTING ORGANIZATIONS: LEGAL FICTIONS FOR CLIENTS 123 (Oxford U. Press, 2009).

[868] On the impact of the culture of waiver on the rights of individuals, see generally Sarah Helene Duggin, *The McNulty Memorandum, the KPMG Decision and Corporate Cooperation: Individual Rights and Legal Ethics*, 21 GEO. J. LEGAL ETHICS 341, 402 (2008).

Congress[869]—the Department of Justice in 2006 revised its charging criteria to clarify that a waiver for privileged communications was not required for a corporation to be regarded as cooperating. Deputy Attorney General Paul McNulty circulated a new memorandum (the "McNulty Memo") stating that "[w]aiver of attorney-client and work product protections is not a prerequisite to a finding that a company has cooperated in the government's investigation."[870] The memo instructed prosecutors that such a waiver may be requested only if "there is a legitimate need for the privileged information"—not merely that it would be "desirable or convenient"—as shown by importance of the information to the investigation, the unavailability of alternative means of seeking the information, and the amount of voluntary disclosure already provided, as well as considering the "collateral consequences to the corporation of such a waiver."[871] Moreover, privileged information that is "purely factual" may be obtained only by written authorization from the United States Attorney in consultation with the Assistant Attorney General for the Criminal Division (at Main Justice), and privileged advice to the corporation may be "only be sought in rare circumstances" with authorization from the Deputy Attorney General.[872]

The directives of the McNulty Memo were subsequently emphasized in revisions to the *United States Attorneys' Manual*, which now recites that the "attorney-client privilege and the attorney work product protection serve an extremely important function in the American legal system" and reiterates that waiving these protections "has never been a prerequisite under the Department's prosecution guidelines for a corporation to be viewed as cooperative."[873] Instead, the *Manual* insists, federal prosecutors seek only "the facts known to the corporation about the putative criminal misconduct under review."[874]

Critics were not mollified, contending that even with the McNulty Memo clarification, prosecutors continued to push for waivers or for internal investigation information that effectively waived the attorney-client privilege. In addition to undermining the attorney-client privilege, lawyers and scholars warned that aggressive prosecutorial conduct may be counterproductive, as corporate counsel would be stymied in obtaining candid responses from officers and employees when investigating possible wrongdoing. As one commentator summed up, "[t]he premium placed on unbridled disclosure frustrates the purposes of the attorney-client privilege by chilling full and frank communication between lawyers and the companies they represent."[875] The central purpose of the privilege in encouraging clients to seek legal advice to comport their conduct to the requirements of the law[876] would be thwarted if corporate officers

---

[869] Paul J. Larkin, Jr. & John-Michael Seibler, *All Stick and No Carrot: The Yates Memorandum and Corporate Criminal Liability*, 46 STETSON L. REV. 7, 20–21 (2016). In addition, a federal court dismissed an indictment against corporate employees because prosecutors coerced the corporation to cut-off payment of defense costs to individual employees, ruling that this was "part of a broader pattern of government misconduct that shocks the conscience and violated their right to substantive due process." United States v. Stein, 495 F. Supp. 2d 390, 409 (S.D.N.Y. 2007).

[870] Memorandum from Paul J. McNulty, Deputy Att'y Gen., to Heads of Department Components, United States Attorneys, on Principles of Federal Prosecution of Business Organizations, at 8 (Dec. 12, 2006).

[871] *Id.* at 8–9.

[872] *Id.* at 9–10.

[873] United States Attorneys' Manual § 9–28.710 (2016).

[874] *Id.*

[875] Rahman, *supra*, 14 GEO. J. LEGAL ETHICS at 332.

[876] *See supra* §§ 4-6.1, 4-6.3(a).

and employees begin to regard communications with corporate counsel as posing serious risks to their well-being and even their liberty.

After a period of nearly a decade in which the debate continued to simmer on low flame, the controversy was brought back to full boil with the 2015 issuance of new prosecutorial guidelines by Deputy Attorney General Sally Yates (the "Yates Memo"). Titled "Individual Accountability for Corporate Wrongdoing," the memo highlighted the need for corporations to share full information about individual behavior before receiving credit for cooperation.[877] In an accompanying speech, Yates said that "if a company wants any credit for cooperation," then "[i]t's all or nothing. No more picking and choosing what gets disclosed. No more partial credit for cooperation that doesn't include information about individuals."[878]

Although the Justice Department insisted that nothing had changed in terms of demands for waivers of the attorney-client privilege, Yates predecessor as Deputy Attorney General sharply criticized the "all-or-nothing" approach and said it will discourage corporations from even attempting to cooperate.[879] As practitioners Michael Kelly and Ruth Mandelbaum explain:

> From our experience, when employees receive an interview request, most worry more about their job security than their potential exposure to a federal criminal investigation. If the Justice Department dramatically increases the number of prosecutions of individuals, more employees will decline to participate in interviews even if that decision potentially jeopardizes their jobs.[880]

With the change of administration in 2017, as this book was being completed, the future of the Yates memo and Justice Department guidance on investigations of corporate wrongdoing remained uncertain. Out-going Deputy Attorney General Yates expressed optimism that her policy would continue and stated her expectation that "when companies enter into high-dollar resolutions with the Justice Department, you'll see a higher percentage of those cases accompanied by criminal or civil actions against the responsible individuals."[881] As of mid-2017, the Trump Justice Department had not yet revealed any new approach as debate continued about whether the previous policies would remain, be revised, or be rejected.[882]

In the wake of the Yates Memo, corporate counsel will have to be crystal clear to constituents about their role as attorney for the corporation and more emphatic in denying any solicitude for the individual officers and employees. As discussed previously, a lawyer for an entity should regularly remind constituents that the lawyer is counsel for the entity and does not represent any of these persons in their individual capacities.[883] And if the lawyer knows or reasonably should know that the interests of

---

[877] Memorandum from Sally Q. Yates, Deputy Att'y Gen., to Heads of Dep't Components and U.S. Attorneys, *Individual Accountability for Corporate Wrongdoing* (Sept. 9, 2015).

[878] Speech by Sally Q. Yates, U.S. Deputy Attorney General, available at https://www.justice.gov/opa/speech/deputy-attorney-general-sally-quillian-yates-delivers-remarks-new-york-university-school.

[879] Katelyn Polantz, *DOJ's "Yates Memo" Goes Too Far, Former Deputy AG Says*, NAT'L L.J., Nov. 20, 215).

[880] Michael P. Kelly & Ruth E. Mandelbaum, *Are the Yates Memorandum and the Federal Judiciary's Concerns About Over-Criminalization Destined to Collide?*, 53 AM. CRIM. L. REV. 899, 936 (2016).

[881] C. Ryan Barber, *Yates Ponder Facts of Namesake Memo*, NAT'L L.J., Dec. 5, 2016, at 23.

[882] Sam Skolnik, *Memo Faces Uncertain Fate Under Trump, Attorneys Say*, ABA/BNA LAWYERS' MANUAL OF PROFESSIONAL CONDUCT: CURRENT REPORTS, June 14, 2007.

[883] *See supra* § 4-8.5.

the organization have become adverse to that of a constituent, Rule 1.13(f) of the Model Rules of Professional conduct directs the lawyer to "explain the identity of the client."[884] Indeed, corporate practitioners are advising that "[i]t would be prudent to add to the standard *Upjohn* warnings [that is, warnings during corporate investigations that communications are privileged for the benefit of the corporation] some language informing the interviewee that the corporation may choose to cooperate with the government, and that in so doing, the corporation may reveal information developed in the interview to the government."[885]

The important questions about core ethical concepts such as attorney-client privilege presented by federal prosecution guidelines for corporate wrongdoing do not readily translate into enforceable ethical strictures for individual government lawyers. The Department of Justice policy may be justly criticized as improperly coercing corporate leaders and lawyers into undermining the rights of individual employees and, in cases of heavy-handed prosecutorial behavior, may provoke a judicial rebuke and even dismissal of charges. Yet it has been unlikely that the policy itself clearly transgresses professional ethical duties in a manner that would result in a disciplinary charge against a government lawyer who acts on it.

However, that threshold for disciplinary enforcement may have been reached by the Yates Memorandum, which aggressively directs prosecutors to induce corporate agents, including their counsel, to investigate the behavior of individual corporate employees toward the end of turning them in as law-breakers. By effectively deputizing corporate investigators as agents of the federal government,[886] a supervising federal prosecutor may need to regard the internal corporate investigator as an alter ego. The prosecutor may thereby assume the obligation to ensure that the inside corporate investigator upholds the special ethical duties imposed on a prosecutor, including the duty to affirmatively advise and assist targets in exercising the right to counsel.[887] Indeed, corporate counsel may be ahead on that score, as "many companies will feel compelled to ensure employees suspected of wrongdoing have access to separate attorneys much earlier in an investigation."[888]

### *§ 4-9.12(c)(5) Restrictions on Issuance by Prosecutors of Subpoenas to Lawyers*

When a prosecutor obtains a subpoena addressed to a lawyer that seeks delivery by the lawyer of evidence regarding the client or requires the lawyer to submit to a testimonial examination about a client matter, there is a grave risk of destructive interference with the attorney-client relationship.[889] By forcing the lawyer to disclose

---

[884] On the lawyer's responsibilities concerning the misunderstandings of laypersons regarding whether an attorney-client relationship has been created, see *supra* § 4-3.2(c).

[885] G. Douglas Jones & Christopher J. Nicholson, *The Rules Have Just Changed: DOJ Issues New Guidelines Targeting Individuals in Corporate Investigations*, 77 ALA. LAW. 264, 272 (2016).

[886] *See* Larkin & Seibler, *supra*, 46 STETSON L. REV. at 9 (observing that the Yates Memo "forces corporations to become deputies in the government's investigation").

[887] *See supra* § 4-9.12(c)(1).

[888] Kelly & Mandelbaum, *supra*, 53 AM. CRIM. L. REV. at 909–10.

[889] *See* United States v. Perry, 857 F.2d 1346, 1347 (9th Cir. 1988) (observing that "[a]mong the perceived costs" of government-issued subpoenas to criminal defense lawyers "are the potential loss of a client's choice of counsel should the latter be compelled to testify at the trial and the potential chilling effect upon the client's trust in his counsel's loyalty"); Baylson v. Disciplinary Bd., 975 F.2d 102, 112 (3d Cir. 1992) (saying that the "court is not unmindful of the serious problems associated with the practice of government prosecutors

information that may be adverse to the client, a conflict of interest may be introduced as the client will feel betrayed by his confidential advisor. Even if a formal conflict of interest does not emerge, the compelled conversion of the lawyer from an advocate into a witness creates a potential conflict in roles, possibly disqualifying the lawyer from continued representation of the client before a tribunal under the advocate-witness rule codified in Rule 3.7 of the Model Rules of Professional Conduct.[890] Moreover, even assuming the lawyer exercises due diligence to avoid revelation of privileged client communications,[891] placing a lawyer in the unfamiliar position of responding to hostile questions by a prosecutor enhances the possibility of an inadvertent disclosure of information that is protected by the attorney-client privilege.

At the same time, the existence of an attorney-client relationship does not exempt a lawyer from generally-applicable legal responsibilities, does not excuse a lawyer from the duty of every citizen to render testimony as a witness when necessary and as to non-privileged matters, and does not allow a lawyer to conceal non-privileged evidence. A prosecutor or a grand jury acting at a prosecutor's suggestion must be permitted to seek evidence from a lawyer when there is good reason to believe the lawyer has taken possession of physical or documentary evidence from a client or other person[892] or when the lawyer's performance of legal services has been perverted by a client to facilitate an obstruction of justice or to commit another crime and the lawyer possesses essential and non-privileged information about the client's conduct.[893] For example, in *In re Grand Jury Subpoena*,[894] the court denied an attorney's motion to quash a prosecutor's subpoena, holding that the government had made a prima facie showing that legal advice had been provided in furtherance of illegal or fraudulent activity, specifically for the client to use offshore banks and corporations to hide money as part of a mail fraud scheme. Accordingly, while prosecutorial discretion to issue subpoenas to lawyers may be appropriately limited to avoid unnecessary intrusions into the attorney-client relationship, lawyers cannot be granted general immunity from the operation of the investigative and evidentiary processes.

In an attempt to balance competing interests or values, Rule 3.8(e) of the Model Rules of Professional Conduct provides that a prosecutor in a criminal case shall—

> not subpoena a lawyer in a grand jury or other criminal proceeding to present evidence about a past or present client unless the prosecutor reasonably believes:
>
> (1) the information sought is not protected from disclosure by any applicable privilege;
>
> (2) the evidence sought is essential to the successful completion of an ongoing investigation or prosecution; and

---

subpoenaing attorneys to testify about past or present clients before grand juries," with citation to *Perry*, and suggesting a federal rule limiting such subpoenas may be appropriate).

[890] *See supra* § 4-9.12.

[891] On the lawyer's general duty to safeguard confidential information, including the responsibility to respond vigorously and promptly to assert client confidentiality whenever information is sought by others to which a colorable objection may be made, see *supra* § 4-6.5.

[892] On the lawyer's responsibilities with respect to physical evidence of criminal conduct by a client, see *supra* § 4-9.7.

[893] On the crime-fraud exception to the attorney-client privilege, see *supra* § 4-6.3(c)(1).

[894] 132 F. Supp. 2d 776, 777–80 (S.D. Iowa 2000).

(3) there is no other feasible alternative to obtain the information.

In sum, under Model Rule 3.8(e), a prosecutor should not compel a lawyer to disclose information about a client unless the information sought is likely to fall within an exception to the attorney-client privilege,[895] the evidence is truly necessary to the successful completion of an investigation or prosecution, and there is no other reasonably available means by which to obtain the information (such as by issuing the subpoena directly to the lawyer's client or obtaining a warrant to search the client's premises). One federal court of appeals has described the rule as "[e]mbodying the well-honored principle of professional conduct that thou shalt not interfere with the attorney-client relationship without a showing of cause."[896]

Ever since the predecessor to Rule 3.8(e) was added in 1990 by the American Bar Association (ABA) to the Model Rules of Professional Conduct, federal prosecutors have objected to the use of professional disciplinary rules to control prosecutorial or grand jury discretion on the issuance of subpoenas. They argue that the rule improperly invades the province of the federal courts in defining the scope of federal privileges and violates the independence of the grand jury and the secrecy of its proceedings.[897]

The judicial response has been mixed:

Two federal appellate courts, one of which was sharply divided, disapproved the application to federal prosecutors of an ethics rule that required prior judicial approval before issuance of subpoenas to lawyers.[898] The judicial pre-approval requirement, which was formerly a feature of Model Rule 3.8, was deleted by the ABA in 1995.[899]

Most recently, another federal appellate court, in a divided decision, considered a challenge by the federal government to a state rule of professional conduct, which included no requirement of prior judicial approval but which did restrict prosecutorial discretion in subpoenaing an attorney to compel evidence about a past or present client. The Tenth Circuit in *United States v. Supreme Court of New Mexico*,[900] held that the rule was enforceable against federal prosecutors with respect to criminal proceedings, but was preempted by federal law relative to federal prosecutors' issuance of attorney subpoenas in grand-jury context. The majority cited Supreme Court decisions construing

---

[895] On the attorney-client privilege and its exceptions, see *supra* § 4-6.3.

[896] United States v. Colorado Supreme Court, 189 F.3d 1281, 1288 (10th Cir. 1999); *see also* State v. Gonzalez, 234 P.2d 1, 12 (Kan. 2010) (saying that, by limiting permissible use of a subpoena to an attorney to cases of genuine need, the ethical rule "communicate[s] a general unwillingness" to intrude on the attorney-client relationship).

[897] For a scholarly presentation of federal prosecutors' objections to limitations by state ethics rules on subpoena authority, see Frank O. Bowman, III, *A Bludgeon by Any Other Name: The Misuse of "Ethical Rules" Against Prosecutors to Control the Law of the State*, 9 GEO. J. LEGAL ETHICS 665, 684–721 (1996). For the argument that "[t]he vision of lawyering embodied in ethics rules purporting to restrict the fact-gathering authority of federal law enforcement officials conflicts with positive law as well as with considerations of ordinary morality," see Roger C. Cramton & Lisa K. Udell, *State Ethics Rules and Federal Prosecutors: The Controversies Over the Anti-Contact and Subpoena Rules*, 53 U. PITT. L. REV. 291 (1992).

[898] Stern v. U.S. Dist. Court, 214 F.3d 4, 13–23 (1st Cir. 2000) (holding, over a dissent by three judges from denial of the petitions for rehearing en banc, that the federal district court lacked the power to adopt the Massachusetts ethics rule requiring an adversarial proceeding and judicial pre-approval for issuance of attorney subpoenas); Baylson v. Disciplinary Bd., 975 F.2d 102, 111–12 (3d Cir. 1992) (holding that a Pennsylvania ethics rule which required a prosecutor to obtain prior judicial approval before issuing a subpoena to a lawyer violated the Supremacy Clause of the United States Constitution).

[899] RONALD D. ROTUNDA & JOHN S. DZIENKOWSKI, PROFESSIONAL RESPONSIBILITY: A STUDENT'S GUIDE § 3.8–2(d) (American Bar Ass'n, 2013–2014).

[900] 839 F.3d 888, 893 (10th Cir. 2016).

the Grand Jury Clause of the Fifth Amendment to the Constitution as instructing that, "for federal grand juries to properly carry out their investigative role, there must be no more than minimal limitations placed on the kinds of evidence that they can consider."[901] Acknowledging that Congress in the McDade Act holds federal lawyers subject to the professional ethics rules of the state of practice,[902] the Tenth Circuit said it was "compel[led] . . . to insist" that Congress "speak more clearly" before placing a significant burden "on grand juries' constitutionally authorized investigative functions."[903] The dissent argued that the federal preemption argument failed because Congress through the McDade Act had instructed federal prosecutors to obey state ethics rules.[904] Holding that the rule on issuance of attorney subpoenas is not inconsistent with the provision for indictment in the Grand Jury Clause, the dissent viewed the ethics rule as merely instructing prosecutors "of their of their professional duty when issuing subpoenas to third-party lawyers in criminal cases."[905]

Given that the guidelines in Model Rule 3.8(e) parallel those adopted in most prosecutor's offices, the application of the rule should occasion little or no controversy in most circumstances. Nonetheless, for most state and federal prosecutors, the rule provides only non-binding guidelines. Only about half of the states have adopted Model Rule 3.8(e), not including several populous states, meaning that neither state nor federal prosecutors are bound by these express conditions on issuing a subpoena to a lawyer.[906]

With respect to federal prosecutors, even if Model Rule 3.8(e) has not been adopted in the jurisdiction of practice or has been held preempted in part by the courts as applied to grand jury proceedings, the Department of Justice's *United States Attorneys' Manual* leads to the same end. The *Manual* acknowledges "the potential effects upon an attorney-client relationship that may result from the issuance of a subpoena to an attorney for information relating to the attorney's representation of a client;" states that the "need for the information must outweigh the potential adverse effects upon the attorney-client relationship;" and requires prior approval of attorney subpoenas by the Assistant Attorney General for the Criminal Division at Main Justice in Washington, D.C.[907]

The guidelines in the *Manual*, which are largely coextensive with the factors articulated in Rule 3.8(e), are (1) "[t]he information sought shall not be protected by a valid claim of privilege;" (2) "[a]ll reasonable attempts to obtain the information from alternative sources shall have proved to be unsuccessful;" and (3) in a criminal case, "there must be reasonable grounds to believe that a crime has been or is being committed, and that the information sought is reasonably needed for the successful completion of the investigation or prosecution" and, in that respect, "[t]he subpoena must not be used to obtain peripheral or speculative information."[908] The *United States Attorneys' Manual* further directs that "[t]he subpoena shall be narrowly drawn and

---

[901] *Id.* at 926.

[902] 28 U.S.C. § 530B. *See supra* § 4-9.12(a)(3).

[903] *Supreme Court of New Mexico*, 839 F.3d at 927.

[904] *Id.* at 930 (Tymkovich, C.J., concurring in part and dissenting in part).

[905] *Id.* at 930–31.

[906] *See* American Bar Ass'n Center for Prof'l Responsibility, Variations of the ABA Model Rules of Professional Conduct, Rule 3.8(e) (May 6, 2015), at http://www.americanbar.org/content/dam/aba/administrative/professional_responsibility/mrpc_3_8_e.pdf.

[907] United States Attorneys' Manual § 9–13.410(A), (C) (2016).

[908] *Id.* § 9–13.410(C).

directed at material information regarding a limited subject matter and shall cover a reasonable, limited period of time."[909]

## § 4-9.12(d) Prosecutor's Duties of Disclosure

### *§ 4-9.12(d)(1) Prosecutor's Duty to Disclose Exculpatory and Mitigating Evidence*

Under Rule 3.4(a) of the Model Rules of Professional Conduct, a lawyer representing a client in litigation may not "unlawfully obstruct another party's access to evidence or unlawfully alter, destroy or conceal a document or other material having potential evidentiary value."[910] And under Model Rule 3.4(d), a lawyer must not "fail to make reasonably diligent effort to comply with a legally proper discovery request by an opposing party."[911] However, the typical advocate ordinarily has no affirmative obligation to volunteer evidence that is potentially harmful to the client's case.

As part of the prosecutor's dual function, which entails duties not only to the public but also to the accused,[912] a prosecutor in a criminal case is compelled by both professional ethics and constitutional mandate to disclose exculpatory and mitigating information to the defense. Rule 3.8(d) of the Model Rules of Professional Conduct provides that a prosecutor shall

> make timely disclosure to the defense of all evidence or information known to the prosecutor that tends to negate the guilt of the accused or mitigates the offense, and, in connection with sentencing, disclose to the defense and to the tribunal all unprivileged mitigating information known to the prosecutor, except when the prosecutor is relieved of this responsibility by a protective order of the tribunal.[913]

In *Brady v. Maryland*,[914] the Supreme Court held that the government is required to disclose exculpatory information to protect a criminal defendant's due process rights. But whether prosecutors have universally integrated this constitutional responsibility into their standards of behavior is highly debated. In a dissent from the denial of a petition for rehearing en banc, then-Chief Judge Alex Kozinski of the United States Court of Appeals for the Ninth Circuit wrote that there is an "epidemic of *Brady* violations abroad in the land,"[915] an assertion he repeated in a law review article[916] that has also received great attention in the criminal law community of both practitioners

---

909 *Id.*

910 *See supra* § 4-9.7.

911 *See supra* § 4-9.6(b).

912 *See supra* § 4-9.12(a).

913 The American Bar Association's Standards for Criminal Justice take the expectation one step further and oblige the prosecutor to disclose exculpatory information not only to defense counsel but to a grand jury considering whether there is probable cause to indict: "A prosecutor with personal knowledge of evidence that directly negates the guilt of a subject of the investigation should present or otherwise disclose that evidence to the grand jury." STANDARDS FOR CRIMINAL JUSTICE: PROSECUTION FUNCTION, Standard 3–4.6(e) (American Bar Ass'n, 2015); *see also* D.C. RULES OF PROF'L CONDUCT R. 3.8(g) (directing prosecutor "to bring to the attention of the grand jury material facts tending to substantially negate the existence of probable cause").

914 373 U.S. 83, 87 (1963).

915 United States v. Olsen, 737 F.3d 625, 626 (9th Cir. 2013) (Kozinski, C.J., dissenting from denial of rehearing en banc).

916 *See* Alex Kozinski, *Criminal Law 2.0*, 44 GEO. L.J. ANN. REV. CRIM. PROC. iii, viii (2015) (providing examples of cases where "the police manipulated or concealed evidence").

and scholars. Two top officials at the U.S. Department of Justice responded in a letter to the journal, contending that the judge "goes too far in casting aspersions on the men and women responsible for the administration of justice in this country" and that the federal government has the "capacity to self-correct in the (very small) minority of cases when someone falls short."[917]

The ethical standard articulated in Model Rule 3.8(d) appears to be somewhat broader than the government's constitutional mandate to reveal exculpatory evidence under *Brady v. Maryland*. The prosecutor's constitutional duty of disclosure is limited to evidence that is deemed material to guilt or punishment,[918] while the ethics rule does not expressly include a materiality requirement.[919] Nonetheless, a majority of the few states addressing the question have been wary of holding prosecutor's to an ethical duty of disclosure that differs from the legal standard under the Constitution or court rule.[920]

In any event, when addressing the materiality requirement of the *Brady* rule, the Supreme Court advised in *United States v. Agurs*[921] that "[b]ecause we are dealing with an inevitably imprecise standard, and because the significance of an item of evidence can seldom be predicted accurately until the entire record is complete, the prudent prosecutor will resolve doubtful questions in favor of disclosure." And in *Smith v. Cain*,[922] the Court warned that reversal will follow from a failure to disclose if "the likelihood of a different result is great enough to 'undermine[ ] confidence in the outcome of the trial.' " The *Agurs* Court emphasized that, unlike the standard for ineffective assistance of defense counsel,[923] the victim of prosecutorial misconduct in withholding exculpatory information does not have "the severe burden of demonstrating that newly discovered evidence probably would have resulted in acquittal."[924]

Model Rule 3.8(d) is best read to instruct "the prudent prosecutor" to avoid even the temptation of making self-serving judgment as to whether evidence that "tends to negate the guilt of the accused or mitigates the offense" is sufficiently material to fall within the duty of disclosure. As the American Bar Association's Standing Committee on Ethics and

---

917 Letter of Andrew D. Goldsmith, Assoc. Dep'y Att'y Gen. & John F. Walsh, U.S. Att'y for D. of Colo. to Geo. L.J., Nov. 4, 2015, at 1.

918 *Brady*, 373 U.S. at 87.

919 *See* ABA Comm. on Ethics and Prof'l Responsibility, Formal Op. 09–454 (2009) (stating that Rule 3.8(d) "requires the disclosure of evidence or information favorable to the defense without regarding to the anticipated impact of the evidence or information on a trial's outcome"). *See generally* Bruce A. Green, *Prosecutors' Ethical Duty of Disclosure in Memory of Fred Zacharias*, 48 SAN DIEGO L. REV. 57 (2011).

920 Oklahoma Bar Ass'n v. Ward, 353 P.3d 509, 521 (Okla. 2015) (construing Rule 3.8(d) in a "manner consistent with the scope of disclosure required by applicable law"); In re Riek, 834 N.W.2d 384, 390 (Wis. 2013) (rejecting the ABA opinion stating a higher ethical standard than *Brady*, saying that "[d]isparate standards are likely to generate confusion and could too easily devolve into a trap for the unwary"). *But see* In re Kline, 113 A.3d 202, 213 (D.C. 2015) (following the ABA opinion approach and holding that the ethical rule "requires a prosecutor to disclose all potentially exculpatory information in his or her possession regardless of whether that information would meet the materiality requirements" of the *Brady* line of cases); Disciplinary Action Against Feland, 820 N.W.2d 672, 678 (N.D. 2012) (rejecting the materiality standard for wrongful conviction cases and holding for disciplinary rule purposes that a "prosecutor's ethical duty to disclose all exculpatory evidence to the defense does not vary depending upon the strength of the other evidence in the case").

921 427 U.S. 97, 108 (1976).

922 132 S. Ct. 627, 630 (2012) (quoting Kyles v. Whitley, 514 U.S. 419, 434 (1995)).

923 *See* Strickland v. Washington, 466 U.S. 668, 694 (1984) (ruling that to overturn a conviction on the basis of ineffective assistance of counsel in violation of the Sixth Amendment, the accused ordinarily must show "a reasonable probability that, but for counsel's unprofessional errors, the result of the proceeding would have been different"); *see also supra* § 4-7.4(c)(3).

924 *Agurs*, 427 U.S. at 111.

Professional Responsibility states, "[t]he rule requires prosecutors to disclose favorable evidence so that the defense can decide on its utility."[925]

This ethical expectation is solidified by the *Standards for Criminal Justice* recently revised by the American Bar Association. The pertinent standard states that "[a]fter charges are filed if not before, the prosecutor should diligently seek to identify all information in the possession of the prosecution or its agents that tends to negate the guilt of the accused, mitigate the offense charged, impeach the government's witnesses or evidence, or reduce the likely punishment of the accused if convicted."[926] Confirming that this ethical expectation does not turn on the prosecutor's self-centered and subjective evaluation of materiality, the standard emphasizes that this duty applies "regardless of whether the prosecutor believes it is likely to change the result of the proceeding."[927]

Rule 3.8(d) applies only to exculpatory or mitigating evidence that is "known to the prosecutor."[928] Thus, while a prosecutor will not be excused for deliberately withholding evidence that tends to undermine the offense or supports a reduced sentence, Rule 3.8(d) is not a trap for the unwary nor a prescription for perfection. A prosecutor should not be subject to discipline because an extraneous piece of arguably exculpatory or mitigating evidence is later discovered in some government file but which had not been found by or recognized at the time by the prosecutor as falling within a disclosure duty. This does not forgive the prosecutor for willful ignorance about the information that is contained in the records and evidence gathered by the government. As the Supreme Court said in *Kyles v. Whitley*,[929] the constitutional *Brady* disclosure rule "means that the individual prosecutor has a duty to learn of any favorable evidence known to the others acting on the government's behalf in the case, including the police."

Rule 3.8(d) allows a prosecutor to withhold exculpatory or mitigating evidence "when the prosecutor is relieved of this responsibility [of disclosure] by a protective order of the tribunal." If disclosure of the information would be harmful to an individual or the public interest, such as information about confidential informants, the prosecutor may seek judicial authority to withhold or redact that information. The court then will determine whether the need for the information to ensure a fair trial or fair sentence for the accused overrides the purpose of protecting a person or interest from potential harm by disclosure.

### *§ 4-9.12(d)(2) Prosecutor's Duties Regarding Wrongful Convictions*

Consistent with the prosecutor's pre-conviction duty to disclose exculpatory or mitigating evidence, a prosecutor has an ethical duty to disclose, investigate, and take appropriate remedial action when she learns of evidence indicating that a person may

[925] ABA Comm. on Ethics and Prof'l Responsibility, Formal Op. 09–454 (2009).

[926] STANDARDS FOR CRIMINAL JUSTICE: PROSECUTION FUNCTION, Standard 3–5.4(a) (American Bar Ass'n, 2015).

[927] *Id.*, Standard 3–5.4(c). *See generally* Ellen Yaroshefsky, *Prosecutorial Disclosure Obligations*, 62 HASTINGS L.J. 1321, 1334–37 (2011).

[928] *See* ABA Comm. on Ethics and Prof'l Responsibility, Formal Op. 09–454 (2009) (explaining that the prosecutor is not required "to conduct investigations for favorable evidence that may possibly exist but of which they are unaware").

[929] 514 U.S. 419, 437 (1995); *see also* Kozinski, *supra*, 44 GEO. L.J. ANN. REV. CRIM. PROC. at xxviii ("Yet the government's disclosure obligation extends to information that is in the hands of investigators and places an affirmative obligation on prosecutors to become aware of exculpatory evidence that is held by others acting on the government's behalf.").

have been wrongly convicted of a crime.[930] In 2008, the American Bar Association amended Rule 3.8 to add new paragraphs (g) and (h):

> (g) When a prosecutor knows of new, credible and material evidence creating a reasonable likelihood that a convicted defendant did not commit an offense of which the defendant was convicted, the prosecutor shall:
>
> (1) promptly disclose that evidence to an appropriate court or authority, and
>
> (2) if the conviction was obtained in the prosecutor's jurisdiction,
>
> (i) promptly disclose that evidence to the defendant unless a court authorizes delay, and
>
> (ii) undertake further investigation, or make reasonable efforts to cause an investigation, to determine whether the defendant was convicted of an offense that the defendant did not commit.
>
> (h) When a prosecutor knows of clear and convincing evidence establishing that a defendant in the prosecutor's jurisdiction was convicted of an offense that the defendant did not commit, the prosecutor shall seek to remedy the conviction.[931]

The states have been slow thus far to adopt paragraphs (g) and (h) to Rule 3.8, with fewer than half adopting these provisions or variations on them.[932]

If a prosecutor's duties regarding wrongful convictions are to have force, they must be accompanied by a duty to preserve information and evidence regarding criminal cases, even after conviction and affirmance of the conviction.[933] The *Standards for Criminal Justice* say the prosecutor should "make reasonable efforts" to preserve "relevant materials during and after a criminal case."[934] While the *Standards* limit the time for preservation in felony cases "until post-conviction litigation is concluded or time-limits have expired," which could be problematic if new forensic technology is later developed or new evidence comes forward, the *Standards* do demand preservation of information in death penalty cases until the last possible moment, that is "until the penalty is carried out or is precluded."[935]

---

[930] *See* Imbler v. Pachtman, 424 U.S. 409, 427 n.25 (1976) ("[A]fter a conviction the prosecutor also is bound by the ethics of his office to inform the appropriate authority of after-acquired or other information that casts doubt upon the correctness of the conviction.").

[931] *See generally* Bruce A. Green & Ellen Yaroshefsky, *Prosecutorial Discretion and Post-Conviction Evidence of Innocence*, 6 OHIO ST. J. CRIM. L. 467 (2009).

[932] *See* American Bar Ass'n Center for Prof'l Responsibility, Variations of the ABA Model Rules of Professional Conduct, Rule 3.8(g) and (h) (Sept. 21, 2016), at http://www.americanbar.org/content/dam/aba/administrative/professional_responsibility/mrpc_3_8_g_h.pdf.

[933] *See* Alex Kozinski, *Criminal Law 2.0*, 44 GEO. L.J. ANN. REV. CRIM. PROC iii, xv (2015) (observing that overturning a wrongful conviction is very difficult, in part because evidence in non-physical crime cases "may well [be] discarded . . . after the conviction becomes final").

[934] STANDARDS FOR CRIMINAL JUSTICE: PROSECUTION FUNCTION, Standard 3–5.5(a) (American Bar Ass'n, 2015).

[935] *Id.*, Standard 3–5.5(c).

### § 4-9.12(e) Closing Thoughts: The Prosecutor's General Duty of Candor and Protection of the Truth-Finding Function in Court

Special ethical rules designed for prosecutors are discussed above in this section and in the earlier discussion of the special duty of prosecutors to "refrain from making extrajudicial comments that have a substantial likelihood of heightening public condemnation of the accused."[936] In addition, many of the general ethical requirements for advocates in the Model Rules of Professional Conduct apply (or should apply) with special force to prosecutors.[937] When a prosecutor exceeds the bounds of legitimate advocacy, the injury to the integrity of public justice and the danger that innocent persons will be unjustly deprived of liberty is aggravated. Professors Peter Joy and McMunigal explain that when "prosecutorial standards do differ from those governing other lawyers, it is typically in degree rather than in kind."[938] But that difference in degree is meaningful.

The courts and disciplinary authorities thus should regard as particularly grave any professional misconduct when committed by a prosecutor in the course of prosecuting a case against a defendant,[939] such as dishonesty before a tribunal;[940] an appeal to prejudice;[941] methods that have no purpose other than to embarrass or burden

---

[936] *See supra* § 4-9.11(c)(3).

[937] *See supra* § 4-9.12(a)(1).

[938] PETER A. JOY & KEVIN C. MCMUNIGAL, DO NO WRONG: ETHICS FOR PROSECUTORS AND DEFENDERS 3 (American Bar Ass'n, 2009).

[939] *See* Bruce Green & Ellen Yaroshefsky, *Prosecutorial Accountability 2.0*, 92 NOTRE DAME L. REV. 51, 52, 78–79, 114 (2016) (observing that in recent years "there has been increased acceptance of the argument that prosecutorial misconduct is widespread and systemic," bringing a more aggressive approach toward prosecutors by disciplinary agencies and courts).

[940] *See supra* § 4-9.5; *see also* United States v. Kojayan, 8 F.3d 1315, 1322 (9th Cir. 1993) (holding that a prosecutor's statement during trial that a witness did not testify because he had invoked the privilege against self-incrimination, while withholding the information that the witness had entered a cooperation agreement to testify truthfully, was such prejudicial prosecutorial misconduct as to violate due process and require reversal of the conviction).

[941] *See supra* § 4-9.4(b)(2); *see also* Bennet v. Stirling, 842 F.3d 319, 321 (4th Cir. 2016) (overturning death sentence where prosecutor made "[t]he most egregious appeals to racial prejudice . . . in his closing argument," referring to the defendant as "King Kong," a "caveman," and "[t]he beast of burden"); People v. Sharpe, 781 P.2d 659 (Colo. 1989) (censuring prosecutor, who in the hallway outside the courtroom told the counsel for Hispanic criminal defendants that the prosecutor did not "believe either one of those chili-eating bastards").

another;[942] improper vouching for or against the credibility of a witness;[943] or improper argument before the jury.[944]

The core of the prosecutor's ethical duty may be located in a "heightened duty of candor"[945] united with a public-regarding responsibility for the truth-finding function of the criminal justice system. As Professor Bruce Green says, "prosecutors are expected to volunteer relevant factual and legal information in various situations where other attorneys, and certainly criminal defense lawyers, might legitimately remain reticent."[946] This duty of candor merges into a dedication to the search for the truth in the courtroom. While a criminal defense lawyer has a duty as an advocate to undermine the prosecution's case, including through cross-examination of truthful witnesses,[947] the prosecutor is forbidden from discrediting the witness presenting truthful testimony.[948] Indeed, the prosecutor must never present evidence or make statements to the jury that he actually knows to be false, but it is also improper for a prosecutor "to present to the jury statements or inferences" that he "has very strong reason to doubt."[949]

Explaining the vital importance of ethical culture for prosecutors, Judge Alex Kozinski writes:

> While most prosecutors are fair and honest, a legal environment that tolerates sharp prosecutorial practices gives important and undeserved career advantages to prosecutors who are willing to step over the line, tempting others to do the same. Having strict rules that prosecutors must follow will thus not merely avoid the risk of letting a guilty man free to commit other crimes while an innocent one languishes his life away, it will also preserve the integrity of

---

[942] *See supra* § 4-9.4(c); *see also* In re Campbell, 199 P.3d 776, 777–80 (Kan. 2009) (concluding that a prosecutor had no substantial purpose other than to embarrass when, after determining not to file any charge of sexual assault, he insisted on showing to parents of minors who had attended a party photographs of their children consuming alcohol and of a minor girl partially clothed and engaged in sexual intercourse with another minor, even over objections by the girl's mother).

[943] *See supra* § 4-9.9(b)(2); *see also* United States v. Trujillo, 376 F.3d 593, 607–08 (6th Cir.2004) (defining improper vouching as when the prosecutor "plac[es] the prestige of the office of the United States Attorney behind that witness"); United States v. Nanny, 745 F. Supp. 475, 482–84 (M.D. Tenn. 1989) (granting mistrial where a prosecutor not only vouched for the credibility of witnesses but "also attempted to invoke the name of the United States Government to show that the Government's witnesses were unbiased"); Gaby v. State, 949 N.E.2d 870, 880–81 (Ind. Ct. App. 2011) (reversing conviction where a prosecutor told the jury she was "confident" they would reach the same conclusion on guilt as the prosecutor and police and that she would not bring charges she believed to be false); State v. Martens, 521 N.W.2d 768, 772 (Iowa Ct. App. 1994) (observing that it is especially improper for a prosecutor to personally vouch for evidence as this "may induce the jury to trust the judgment of the prosecutor rather than their view of the evidence since the prosecutor's opinion carries the imprimatur of the Government").

[944] *See* United States v. Maloney, 755 F.3d 1044 (9th Cir. 2014) (en banc) (reversing conviction where a prosecutor alluded to supposed inculpatory fact not in evidence in closing argument). For a catalog in one state of prosecutorial misconduct in summations before the jury, see generally Peder B. Hong, Summation at the Border: Serious Misconduct in Final Argument in Criminal Trials, 20 HAMLINE L. REV. 43, 43–55 (1996).

[945] *See* STANDARDS FOR CRIMINAL JUSTICE: PROSECUTION FUNCTION, Standard 3–1.4(a) (American Bar Ass'n, 2015).

[946] Bruce A. Green, *Candor in Criminal Advocacy*, 44 HOFSTRA L. REV. 1105, 1116 (2016).

[947] *See supra* § 4-9.5(a).

[948] *See* PETER A. JOY & KEVIN C. MCMUNIGAL, DO NO WRONG: ETHICS FOR PROSECUTORS AND DEFENDERS 14 (American Bar Ass'n, 2009); Bruce A. Green, *Why Should Prosecutors "Seek Justice,"* 26 FORDHAM URB. L.J. 607, 631–32 (1999).

[949] United States v. Reyes, 577 F.3d 1069, 1077 (9th Cir. 2009).

the prosecutorial process by shielding principled prosecutors from unfair competition from their less principled colleagues.[950]

## § 4-9.13 THE DUTIES OF THE ADVOCATE IN NONADJUDICATIVE PROCEEDINGS

Lawyers serve as advocates for their clients, not only in the traditional litigation venue of the courtroom and other judicial forums, but also before rule-making and policy-making governmental bodies in formal but nonadjudicative proceedings. Appreciating the importance of the lawyer's advocacy role before such governmental entities and the need for guiding ethical standards, Rule 3.9 of the Model Rules of Professional Conduct provides that "[a] lawyer representing a client before a legislative body or administrative agency in a nonadjudicative proceeding shall disclose that the appearance is in a representative capacity and shall conform to the provisions of Rules 3.3(a) through (c), 3.4(a) through (c), and 3.5."

As Comment 1 to Model Rule 3.9 explains, when a legislative or administrative body is acting in a rule-making or policy-making capacity, that is, as a formal decision-making body, a lawyer is bound to "present facts, formulate issues and advance argument" with integrity and in conformity with the applicable rules of procedure of that forum. Toward those ends, Rule 3.9 incorporates those ethical rules on advocacy that are well-suited for this type of non-adjudicative forum. Specifically, these are the duties not to make false statements of law or fact and not to present false evidence as stated in Model Rule 3.3 (excepting only that provision in Rule 3.3(d) governing forms of *ex parte* relief that are not applicable in the legislative or administrative context);[951] to allow access to and preservation of evidence, not to falsify evidence or tamper with a witness, and to obey the procedural rules of the forum as directed by Model Rule 3.4 (but not including those ethical duties stated in Rule 3.4 that are more specific to litigation, such as duties involving pretrial discovery, appropriate statements at trial, etc.);[952] and to refrain from improper influences on the decisionmaker and disruption of proceedings as set forth in Model Rule 3.5.[953]

The ethical rules of the advocate regarding expedition of litigation, extrajudicial statements, the advocate-witness rule, and the special responsibilities of a criminal prosecutor are not referenced in Rule 3.9, because they are generally inapposite to the context of nonadjudicative legislative and administrative venues. In addition, as Professors Ronald Rotunda and John Dzienkowski explain, the prohibition in Model Rule 3.1 against making frivolous legal arguments[954] is not incorporated into Rule 3.9 because, "in politics, it is standard operating procedure to design arguments that appeal to emotion and may not necessarily follow the rules of logic."[955]

As part of the lawyer's duty of candor with a legislative or administrative body, Rule 3.9 requires that the lawyer "disclose that the appearance is in a representative

---

[950] *See* Alex Kozinski, *Criminal Law 2.0*, 44 GEO. L.J. ANN. REV. CRIM. PROC. iii, xxvi (2015) (providing examples of cases where "the police manipulated or concealed evidence").

[951] *See supra* § 4-9.8.

[952] *See supra* §§ 4-9.5(e), 4-9.6(a) to (b), 4-9.8(a), 4-9.8(i) to (j), 4-9.9(b).

[953] *See supra* § 4-9.9.

[954] *See supra* § 4-9.3(a).

[955] RONALD D. ROTUNDA & JOHN S. DZIENKOWSKI, PROFESSIONAL RESPONSIBILITY: A STUDENT'S GUIDE § 3.9–3 (American Bar Ass'n, 2013–2014).

capacity." A lawyer's representation of a client in an adjudicative proceeding is made obvious when an appearance is entered before a tribunal. But a lawyer appearing before a legislative or administrative body in a nonadjudicative proceeding to argue for or against a proposed rule or policy may not be recognized as speaking on behalf of someone else, rather than expressing her own views as an interested citizen.

While Rule 3.9 emphasizes the lawyer's ethical responsibilities toward the governmental entity before which the lawyer advocates in a nonadjudicative proceeding, the lawyer's ethical duties to the client in such a representation should be noted as well. As discussed previously,[956] when a lawyer offers services with a strong legal flavor—such as preparation of tax returns, preparing certain documents incident to a real estate transaction, and lobbying the legislature on legally-permeated matters—the lawyer likely is engaged in the practice of law, even if those activities may also be performed by nonlawyers. Thus, for example, when a lawyer acts as a lobbyist before a legislative or administrative agency, she is bound by the higher professional standards applicable to lawyers, even though nonlawyers also may serve as lobbyists and are not similarly bound. The lawyer thus must recognize professional ethical duties to a client with respect to confidentiality, competence, and conflicts of interest.

Finally, targeted as it is to the context of formal government venues for rule- or policy-making, Model Rule 3.9 does not apply to lawyer advocacy that is directed toward legislative or administrative entities in distinctly different circumstances:

*First*, under Rule 1.0(m) of the Model Rules of Professional Conduct, the term "tribunal" includes not only a court, but also "a legislative body, administrative agency or other body acting in an adjudicative capacity." Rule 1.0(m) further explains that a legislative, administrative, or other entity acts in "an adjudicative capacity" "when a neutral official, after the presentation of evidence or legal argument by a party or parties, will render a binding legal judgment directly affecting a party's interests in a particular matter." Accordingly, when a lawyer is representing a client before a legislative or administrative tribunal acting to resolve an adjudicative dispute, the lawyer must comply with the full panoply of ethical rules governing the advocate found in Rules 3.1 through 3.8 of the Model Rules of Professional Conduct and as discussed in this chapter of the book.

*Second*, as explained in Comment 3 to Model Rule 3.9, the rule applies only to the lawyer's advocacy with respect to "an official hearing or meeting of a governmental agency or a legislative body to which the lawyer or the lawyer's client is presenting evidence or argument." When, instead, a lawyer represents a client in a "bilateral transaction" with a government agency, such as negotiating a government contract; applying for a license or other privilege; or assisting a client in complying with a reporting requirement, such as the filing of an income tax return, the provisions of Rule 3.9 do not apply. Nor does Rule 3.9 apply when a lawyer is representing a client who is under investigation by a government agency, such as a regulatory agency that is examining whether the client is in compliance with the law. As Comment 3 clarifies, with respect to such matters, the lawyer's duties are prescribed by those ethical rules that address the lawyer's responsibilities when dealing with nonlawyers.[957]

---

[956] *See supra* § 4-3.2(b)(2).

[957] *See infra* ch. 4-10.

# Chapter 4-10

# DUTIES AS EVALUATOR OR THIRD-PARTY NEUTRAL

**By Gregory C. Sisk**

*Table of Sections*

§ 4-10.1 Introduction: The Lawyer's Roles as Evaluator and Third-Party Neutral
§ 4-10.2 The Lawyer's Role as Evaluator
§ 4-10.3 The Lawyer's Role as Third-Party Neutral

## § 4-10.1 INTRODUCTION: THE LAWYER'S ROLES AS EVALUATOR AND THIRD-PARTY NEUTRAL

In addition to the traditional roles of a counselor[1] to and an advocate[2] for a client in litigation, transactions, or other legal matters, a lawyer may be retained to evaluate the client's policies or conduct for the benefit of third person or may serve as a third-party neutral to impartially facilitate the resolution of disputes. This chapter addresses the roles of the lawyer as the author of an evaluation of a matter affecting a client which will be used by and relied upon by third persons;[3] and as a third-party neutral, such as an arbitrator or mediator, who is charged with assisting other persons who are not clients to reach a resolution of a dispute or other matter.[4]

## § 4-10.2 THE LAWYER'S ROLE AS EVALUATOR

### § 4-10.2(a) General Principles of Lawyer of Evaluation of Client Matters

Lawyers frequently are charged with evaluating a client's situation, such as considering whether the client's affairs or future plans comply with the law; appraising the effectiveness of the client's procedures or policies to ensure regulatory compliance or reduce the risk of liability; estimating the prospects for success on a claim against another party; assessing whether the client is likely to be held liable to another party and the scope of that liability; reporting on the client's potential exposure for not-as-yet asserted claims against the client; confirming the authority of the client to enter into a particular transaction; or offering an opinion on the validity of the client's title to real property.

When the lawyer performs such an evaluation for the sole and confidential benefit of the client, the lawyer is acting as an advisor, as to which Rule 2.1 of the Model Rules

---

1 *See supra* § 4-5.2.

2 *See supra* ch. 4-9.

3 *See infra* § 4-10.2.

4 *See infra* § 4-10.3.

of Professional Conduct directs the lawyer to be "candid" and to exercise "independent judgment" when advising a client.[5]

However, if the lawyer's evaluation of the client or the client's affairs is to be used by someone other than the client—such as a financial institution in granting credit, an insurer in providing insurance coverage, or another party as a condition to completing a transaction—the lawyer must adjust her continuing responsibilities to the client to simultaneously uphold certain ethical responsibilities to the third person (whether or not the lawyer assumes any legal duty to that third person). Throughout the process of preparing and reporting the evaluation, the lawyer remains a representative of the client, subject to the foundational ethical rules governing the attorney-client relationship. In discharging these responsibilities to both the client and the third party, the lawyer does not take on an impartial and independent role, such as that of a mediator or third-party neutral.[6]

In setting forth the ethical responsibilities of a lawyer in evaluating a matter affecting a client for the use of another person, Rule 2.3 of the Model Rules of Professional Conduct primarily provides a specific application of and reminder about ethical principles drawn from other provisions in the rules:

With respect to the client, the lawyer's preparation of an evaluation for and dissemination of information to a third person—especially confidential information the disclosure of which may be detrimental to the client's interest—implicates the lawyer's duties under Rule 1.6 to protect confidential client information[7] and under Rule 1.7 to avoid conflicts of interest by reason of incompatible responsibilities to others.[8]

With respect to the third person who receives the evaluation, the lawyer under Rule 1.2(d) may not assist a client in conduct that the lawyer knows is criminal or fraudulent,[9] and under Rule 4.1 may not knowingly make a false statement of fact or law or fail to disclose a material fact when necessary to avoid assisting the client in a criminal or fraudulent act.[10]

With these implications in mind, Rule 2.3 is designed to confirm that the lawyer appropriately may undertake an evaluation of a matter affecting the client. The rule requires the lawyer to obtain the informed consent of the client when that evaluation "is likely to affect the client's interests materially and adversely." The rule also reminds the lawyer of the continuing duty to protect confidential information except as authorized for the particular purpose of reporting on the evaluation.

## § 4-10.2(b) Preparation of Client Evaluation for Use by Another Person

Rule 2.3(a) approves as ethically permissible the preparation by a lawyer of "an evaluation of a matter affecting a client for the use of someone other than the client." However, as Comment 3 to Rule 2.3 observes, an evaluation of the client or matters relating to the client that is intended for the information of or use by someone other than

---

5 *See supra* § 4-5.2(b).

6 On the ethical responsibilities of a mediator and other third-party neutrals, see *infra* § 4-10.3.

7 *See supra* ch. 4-6.

8 *See supra* ch. 4-7.

9 *See supra* § 4-5.2(c).

10 *See infra* § 4-11.2.

the client "involves a departure from the normal client-lawyer relationship" and thus "careful analysis of the situation is required." For that reason, Rule 2.3(a) directs the lawyer to ensure that she is satisfied that undertaking this activity is "compatible with other aspects of the lawyer's relationship with the client." Professor Charles Wolfram explains this compatibility requirement as meaning "that the evaluator must be able to exercise relative independence in performing the role of evaluator."[11]

For example, Comment 3 suggests that a lawyer who is acting as an advocate in defending a client against a charge of fraud ordinarily would not be able to simultaneously perform an appropriately disinterested evaluation for others in the same or a related transaction. At the very least, the lawyer's dual role as both advocate/advisor to the client and evaluator must be revealed to the third person so that the third person may weigh the reliability of the resulting report.

When the preparation of a report is unlikely to generate any adverse effect upon the client, the lawyer is not obliged to seek the client's formal consent to the undertaking. Furthermore, when the client has specifically retained the lawyer to prepare the report or otherwise directed the lawyer to do so, release of the report to the intended third person recipient ordinarily would be a disclosure of confidential information that, as stated in Rule 1.6(a) of the Model Rules of Professional Conduct, is "impliedly authorized in order to carry out the representation."

Still, precisely because the preparation by the lawyer of an evaluation for the purpose of its use by someone other than the client is, as Comment 3 to Rule 2.3 says, "a departure from the normal client-lawyer relationship" and because it does in fact involve release of otherwise confidential information, the prudent lawyer will ensure that the client appreciates the significance of the report.

### § 4-10.2(c) Ethical Duties When Evaluation Is Adverse to the Client

When, as anticipated by Rule 2.3(b), "the lawyer knows or reasonably should know that the evaluation is likely to affect the client's interests materially and adversely," the lawyer encounters a tension in responsibilities and may not proceed with the evaluation without express approval and intelligently-given consent by the client.[12] In such an instance, the lawyer is placed in the difficult position of retaining a duty of loyalty to the client while being asked to prepare a report that, once received by a third person, is likely to undermine that client's interests. Under such circumstances, the rule provides that "the lawyer shall not provide the evaluation unless the client gives informed consent."

In a case where the preparation of the report is likely to affect the client's interests in a material and adverse manner, the lawyer must consult with the client about the potential effects of the report, explore whether there are any alternative means of preparing and providing a report that may limit the adverse effect (without being dishonest or deceptive), and consider whether the evaluation should be abandoned. When the risk of material and adverse harm to the client is limited in degree or by

---

[11] CHARLES W. WOLFRAM, MODERN LEGAL ETHICS § 13.4.2 (West, 1986).

[12] *See also* RESTATEMENT (THIRD) OF THE LAW GOVERNING LAWYERS § 95(2) (American Law Institute, 2000) (stating that if the lawyer's evaluation "is reasonably likely to affect the client's interests materially and adversely," the lawyer must obtained informed consent from the client).

comparison to the benefits to be obtained, the client may choose to authorize the report to a third person notwithstanding its negative elements.

In addition, as an exercise of moral reasoning,[13] the client may determine that release of the report and forthright disclosure of information relating to the matter being evaluated is the proper approach, even if detrimental consequences may follow.

Or the evaluation may be required by a government regulation or a contractual obligation, in which case the client has little choice but to approve its preparation and dissemination.

In any event, the lawyer must examine these questions with the client and must abide by the client's decision as to whether the evaluation should continue. While the attorney may never cooperate with the client in falsifying any aspect of an evaluation, the attorney ordinarily may (and sometimes must) choose to discontinue the evaluation project, thus meaning that no report, truthful or otherwise, will be disseminated.

In some instances, as explained in Comment 4 to Rule 2.3, the scope or terms of the evaluation may be limited, such that "certain issues or sources may be categorically excluded" from the report. The lawyer who is aware of a material fact that makes other representations in the report misleading and fraudulent in nature may not omit reference to that material fact or agree to a limitation on the scope of the evaluation that conceals the essential information. However, if the evaluation is confined to a particular topic, such as the validity of title to real property that is the subject of a proposed transaction, the lawyer ordinarily would not be required to reveal negative but unrelated information about the client, such as that the client has a troubled history or has failed to comply with contractual obligations in the past.[14] However, as Comment 4 states, any limitations on the scope of the report "that are material to the evaluation should be described in the report."

### § 4-10.2(d) Confidentiality and Evaluation of Client Matter

Paragraph (c) of Rule 2.3 provides that "[e]xcept as disclosure is authorized in connection with a report of an evaluation, information relating to the evaluation is otherwise protected" under Rule 1.6. As Professors Geoffrey Hazard and William Hodes and attorney Peter Jarvis explain, this paragraph "simply provides a reminder, if any were needed, that evaluations under Rule 2.3 constitute a departure from the normal rules of confidentiality—a departure authorized by the client, either explicitly or

---

[13] On moral deliberation with a client, see *supra* § 4-5.2(b)(2).

[14] *See, e.g.*, Geaslen v. Berkson, Gorov & Levin, Ltd., 581 N.E.2d 138, 140–45 (Ill. App. Ct. 1991) (holding that while the attorney for the client-purchaser had a duty of care in preparing an opinion letter regarding the legal authority of the purchaser to enter the transaction and the legal validity and effect of the agreement, the attorney was not obliged to investigate and disclose to the seller other matters beyond the scope of the opinion, specifically the purchaser-client's negative legal, credit, and financial history), *aff'd in part and rev'd in part on other grounds*, 613 N.E.2d 702 (Ill. 1993); Fortson v. Winstead, McGuire, Sechrest & Minick, 961 F.2d 469, 472–75 (4th Cir. 1992) (holding that, even if lawyers representing general partners knew of the negative financial health of the real estate partnership, the lawyers had no duty to disclose those matters to the limited partner investors when the lawyers' legal opinion was limited in scope to the tax implications of the transaction and the letter expressly disclaimed any financial disclosures). However, if the lawyer knows that the client will use the evaluation to advance a fraudulent or criminal scheme, even if the report itself is legitimate and non-deceptive when viewed in isolation, then the lawyer would be prohibited under Rule 1.2(d) from assisting that conduct. *See supra* § 4-5.2(c) and *infra* § 4-11.2(c). When the lawyer learns that the client's wrongful conduct is already underway, the lawyer may not allow his legal services to be used to facilitate that conduct.

impliedly."[15] While the client has authorized release of confidential information as necessary to the report of the evaluation (and thus also has waived the attorney-client privilege to that extent), the exception to the protection of confidentiality is limited and does not extend beyond that necessary to the report. As Hazard, Hodes, and Jarvis state, the release of confidential information "should be no greater than authorized in order to carry out the evaluation fairly and competently."[16]

### § 4-10.2(e) Other Ethical and Legal Duties Regarding Client Evaluation

When an evaluation is made by the lawyer for the intended use of a third person, a legal duty (in addition to the ethical responsibility) may or may not arise. As Comment 3 to Rule 2.3 states, "[t]hat legal question is beyond the scope of this rule." When a non-client has relied on the report to his detriment, the substantive law of each state determines whether the lawyer may be held liable for negligent preparation of the report (despite the lack of privity between the lawyer and a person who is not a client) or for fraud by having made a false statement or by withholding material information. The *Restatement of the Law Governing Lawyers* directs that the lawyer preparing such an evaluation "must exercise care" when the third person is invited to rely on it and does so rely.[17]

In terms of legal ethics, the lawyer is bound as a matter of the duty of competence under Rule 1.1 to apply "the legal knowledge, skill, thoroughness and preparation reasonably necessary" to the task.[18] The lawyer also is obliged under Rule 4.1 neither to "make a false statement of material fact or law to a third person" nor to "fail to disclose a material fact when disclosure is necessary to avoid assisting a criminal or fraudulent act by a client."[19]

Finally, Comment 6 to Rule 2.3 addresses the situation where the lawyer is not directly preparing the evaluation but is asked to respond to a question by the client's financial auditor about the legal situation of the client. An auditor might inquire as to the legality of securities issued by the client or the client's liability exposure in pending or potential claims. The comment directs the lawyer to follow the procedures set forth in the American Bar Association Statement of Policy Regarding Lawyers' Responses to Auditors' Requests for Information, which was adopted by that organization in 1975.

## § 4-10.3 THE LAWYER'S ROLE AS THIRD-PARTY NEUTRAL

Although the role of the third-party neutral is not unique to lawyers and may be "the most radical departure from the lawyer's traditional role" as an advocate and client representative,[20] lawyers increasingly are serving in this capacity. As Comment 1 to Rule 2.4 of the Model Rules of Professional Conduct observes, alternative dispute resolution has become "a substantial part of the civil justice system" and, not

---

15 1 GEOFFREY C. HAZARD, JR., W. WILLIAM HODES & PETER R. JARVIS, THE LAW OF LAWYERING § 27.07 (Aspen, 4th ed., 2016).

16 *Id.*

17 RESTATEMENT (THIRD) OF THE LAW GOVERNING LAWYERS §§ 51(2), 95(3) (American Law Institute, 2000).

18 *See supra* § 4-5.1(a).

19 *See infra* § 4-11.2(c).

20 Carrie Menkel-Meadow, *The Lawyer as Problem Solver and Third-Party Neutral: Creativity and Non-Partisanship in Lawyering*, 72 TEMPLE L. REV. 785, 803 (1999).

surprisingly, with their legal training and experience, lawyers often are called upon to facilitate the voluntary settlement of dispute among parties, to evaluate the strengths and weaknesses of the various claims presented by the parties in an effort to encourage such a voluntary resolution, or to make an arbitrated decision that is binding upon the parties. Rule 2.4 is designed to confirm the lawyer's neutral and non-representative role under such circumstances and to ensure that the lawyer clarifies the impartial character of that role to any participants who might misunderstand.

A lawyer who serves as an arbitrator, mediator, conciliator, settlement commissioner, or other third-party neutral is engaged in a professional activity and remains subject to professional standards of ethics. But the lawyer is not acting in a role that involves representation of a client. Instead, the lawyer assumes a position of general neutrality as to all parties, acting disinterestedly and equitably either to resolve (in the case of an arbitrator) or to facilitate the voluntary resolution by the parties (in the case of a mediator, conciliator, or other third-party neutral) of a dispute that has arisen among the participants in the dispute resolution process.

While nonlawyers also serve as arbitrators, mediators, or other third-party neutrals, a lawyer acting in such a capacity is more likely to find that other persons who participate in the process, particularly parties who are not represented by counsel, are confused about the nature of the lawyer's role. By reason of the lawyer's professional status and the common perception of lawyers as serving as zealous and confidential representatives of their clients, a participant may mistakenly believe that the lawyer-arbitrator or lawyer-mediator will offer advice with special solicitude for the interests of that participant or will carefully protect as confidential any information shared by the participant.

Rule 2.4(b) provides that "[a] lawyer serving as a third-party neutral shall inform unrepresented parties that the lawyer is not representing them." And when "the lawyer knows or reasonably should know that a party does not understand the lawyer's role in the matter," then the rule directs the lawyer to "explain the difference between the lawyer's role as a third-party neutral and a lawyer's role as one who represents a client."

When a lawyer serves as an arbitrator, thus having the ultimate authority to resolve the dispute between the parties, either by acting alone or as a member of a panel, the lawyer assumes responsibilities similar to that of a judge. These expectations include maintaining impartiality (unless selected as a partisan of a party on a multimember arbitration panel), avoiding *ex parte* communications with the parties, etc.

Although Rule 2.4 does not speak to these other ethical responsibilities, they are enforced indirectly through constraints on the lawyers participating in the arbitration because the rules imposing ethical duties with respect to a tribunal[21] apply with full force to an arbitration proceeding, given that Rule 1.0(m) of the Model Rules of Professional Conduct defines "tribunal" to include "an arbitrator in a binding arbitration proceeding." Accordingly, those provisions in the Model Rules of Professional Conduct that establish the responsibilities of lawyers when representing a client in adjudication apply not only to the traditional litigation process in the court system but also to that formal if private means of adjudication known as binding arbitration. In addition, a lawyer serving as an arbitrator should be familiar with the formal requirements under which an arbitration decision will be recognized and enforced, such as those found in the

---

[21] *See supra* ch. 4-9.

Federal Arbitration Act.[22] Comment 2 to Rule 2.4 also encourages arbitrators to refer to pertinent codes of ethics for that role, such as the Code of Ethics for Arbitration in Commercial Disputes prepared by a joint committee of the American Bar Association and the American Arbitration Association.

When a lawyer serves as a mediator or other third-party neutral, charged with facilitating the voluntary resolution of the dispute by the parties, the lawyer still retains considerable power, even though the mediator or third-party neutral can neither decide nor force a decision upon the parties. As Professors Richard Zitrin and Carol Langford explain, mediators "control both the process and the flow of information between the parties," including "deciding how and when to break up into caucuses" and "determining when to reveal information to each side, and how much to reveal."[23]

Because of the significant power and influence that a lawyer enjoys when serving as a facilitator, the simple direction in Rule 2.4 that the lawyer should avoid any misunderstanding by participants about the lawyer's neutral role hardly describes the whole of the lawyer-mediator's ethical responsibilities. Nor does reference to the distinctly different position of the arbitrator shed much light. Mediation is not a proceeding before a "tribunal" under Rule 1.0(m), and the ethical constraints on lawyers in adjudication do not apply as readily to a mediation proceeding. For example, in contrast with strict limitations placed on interactions with a judge or arbitrator, the parties to a mediation may well be encouraged to engage in *ex parte* communications with the mediator and the mediator may accept those communications in confidence. Beyond inclusion of mediators among the professional roles that are subject to the special conflict of interest rules applicable to other judicial and quasi-judicial officers in Rule 1.12,[24] the Model Rules of Professional Conduct provide very limited guidance on the duties and ethical constraints upon mediators.

Comment 2 to Rule 2.4 reminds lawyer-neutrals that they may be subject to court rules or other laws. For example, lawyers generally engaged in mediation should consult the Model Standards of Conduct for Mediators jointly prepared by the American Bar Association, the American Arbitration Association, and the Society of Professionals in Dispute Resolution. As said by one of the founders of the alternative dispute resolution movement, Professor Carrie Menkel-Meadow, professional standards for those serving as neutrals include "disclosure of conflicts of interests, transparency of decision methods and processes, fair compensation (and generally no contingent fees), 'neutrality' (or non-bias, impartiality, or, preferably, 'fairness' and no prejudgment for the parties) and *adhered-to promises* of confidentiality, advice-giving or other contractually agreed to terms."[25]

---

[22] 9 U.S.C. §§ 1–16.

[23] RICHARD A. ZITRIN & CAROL M. LANGFORD, LEGAL ETHICS IN THE PRACTICE OF LAW 623 (2d ed., Lexis-Nexis, 2001).

[24] *See supra* § 4-7.8(b).

[25] Carrie Menkel-Meadow, *Maintaining ADR Integrity*, 27 ALTERNATIVES TO THE COST LITIG. 1 (2009).

# Chapter 4-11

# RESPECT FOR OTHER PERSONS

## By Gregory C. Sisk

*Table of Sections*


§ 4-11.1 Introduction: The Lawyer's Duties to Respect the Rights and Dignity of Other Persons
§ 4-11.2 The Lawyer's Duty of Truthfulness
§ 4-11.3 Communications with a Represented Person
§ 4-11.4 Communications with an Unrepresented Person


## § 4-11.1 INTRODUCTION: THE LAWYER'S DUTIES TO RESPECT THE RIGHTS AND DIGNITY OF OTHER PERSONS

The lawyer's primary ethical responsibilities are directed to clients, with whom the lawyer has a fiduciary relationship demanding loyalty and confidentiality.[1] The lawyer also has important and defined duties (1) to the legal system, such as truthfulness before a tribunal;[2] refusing to offer false evidence,[3] and taking remedial measures if later learning of such falsity; and generally refraining from conduct prejudicial to the administration of justice;[4] and (2) to the legal profession and society, including the duty to report professional misconduct by other lawyers;[5] and the moral obligation and professional responsibility to provide pro bono legal services.[6]

Many of these ethical duties also preserve the rights and uphold the dignity of third persons. As part of the lawyer's obligation to the truth-finding functions of the justice system, a lawyer may assert only valid claims and contentions against others;[7] and must obey legal requirements in discovering, obtaining, preserving, and using evidence, including respecting privileged communications.[8] A level of respect for the rights and dignity of other persons is woven into many of the ethical restrictions on a lawyer's behavior.

A lawyer representing a client has limited duties to other persons, who often stand at arm's length from or even in opposition to the client. When such other-regarding duties are imposed on the lawyer, they tend to fall into three general categories: (1) a duty of fundamental honesty, in the sense of being truthful (but not necessarily being affirmatively candid with someone other than the client); (2) a duty to respect the right of others to legal representation, both by refusing to interfere with the attorney-client

---

1 *See supra* § 4-5.5.

2 *See supra* § 4-9.5.

3 *See supra* § 4-9.8.

4 *See supra* § 4-9.4(c).

5 *See infra* § 4-13.1(a).

6 *See infra* § 4-13.4(a).

7 *See supra* § 4-9.3.

8 *See supra* §§ 4-9.6, 4-9.7.

relationship and by avoiding misunderstandings of legal solicitude when dealing with unrepresented persons; and (3) a duty to respect the inherent dignity of other persons.

Previously in this part of the book, we have encountered ethical duties that fit into the category of respect for the dignity of others. In advocacy, the duty to avoid means that have no purpose other than to embarrass another is transgressed when the lawyer seeks unseemly advantage by humiliating, degrading, or oppressing another human being.[9] In both advocacy[10] and now by a new rule prohibiting manifestation of bias in any aspect of the practice of law,[11] a lawyer may not harmfully denigrate other persons through illicit discrimination or harassment. Each of these rules reminds a lawyer that, even in the heat of hard-fought litigation or other disputes, conduct that denies the essential dignity of each human being has no place in professional life.

In this chapter, we further address the lawyer's responsibilities to other persons that fit into the other two categories, namely the general duty of truthfulness to third persons;[12] the duty not to interfere with another person's relationship with an attorney by improperly communicating on the matter of the representation with that person outside the presence of her own attorney;[13] and the duty to be careful in dealing with unrepresented persons to avoid an impression of disinterest or a misunderstanding of the lawyer's role.[14]

## § 4-11.2 THE LAWYER'S DUTY OF TRUTHFULNESS

### § 4-11.2(a) The Lawyer's Basic Duty of Truthfulness in Dealings with Others

A lawyer owes more than mere honesty to a client, having an affirmative duty to keep the client fully informed and candidly counseled.[15] For persons other than clients, the lawyer is obliged to refrain from outright dishonesty and deliberate deception. "[I]t is the responsibility of every attorney at all times to be truthful,"[16] when representing a client in transactions or in advocacy. Multiple provisions in the Model Rules of Professional Conduct mandate honesty or prohibit dishonesty, including Rule 8.4(c) which generally forbids "conduct involving dishonesty, fraud, deceit or misrepresentation;"[17] Rule 3.3(a) which demands that the lawyer speak the truth before tribunals;[18] and Rule 4.1 which forbids false statements and which is the focus of this section of the hornbook.[19]

To again quote the nuanced explanation of Professor Bruce Green that was included in the earlier discussion on truthfulness in advocacy[20]:

---

[9] *See supra* § 4-9.4(c).

[10] *See supra* § 4-9.4(b).

[11] *See supra* § 4-1.4(c).

[12] *See infra* § 4-11.2.

[13] *See infra* § 4-11.3.

[14] *See infra* § 4-11.4.

[15] *See supra* § 4-5.2.

[16] In re Kahil's Case, 773 A.2d 647, 648 (N.H. 2001).

[17] *See supra* § 4-1.4(c).

[18] *See supra* § 4-9.5(b) to (d).

[19] *See infra* § 4-11.2.

[20] *See supra* 4-9.5(a).

> [B]eing *truthful* is different from being *candid*. One might speak truthfully, believing everything one says to be true, but not say everything that matters. If one discloses all the relevant information, one is candid. To make a false statement is to lie, but to withhold relevant information—to fail to be candid—is to be reticent.[21]

In this respect, Green observes that, "[w]hile truthfulness is the rule for lawyers, candor is the exception."[22] In sum, a lawyer ordinarily need not volunteer information to a third person, but when the lawyer does speak, he may not lie.

Under Rule 4.1(a) of the Model Rules of Professional Conduct, a lawyer is prohibited from making "a false statement of material fact or law" to a person other than a client. Under Rule 4.1(b), the lawyer is forbidden to remain silent when failure to disclose "a material fact" would assist a criminal or fraudulent act by the client. The obligation of disclosure imposed by Rule 4.1(b) is lifted when revelation would violate a duty of confidentiality under Rule 1.6.[23] However, as discussed at some length previously and again below,[24] the addition of new exceptions to confidentiality in Rule 1.6 has drained some, perhaps most, of the force from the confidentiality qualification to the mandatory duty to disclose stated in Rule 4.1(b).

### § 4-11.2(b) The Lawyer Must Avoid False Statements of Material Fact or Law to Others

In *Hansen v. Anderson, Wilmarth & Van Der Maaten*,[25] the Iowa Supreme Court declared that, "[b]ecause of confidentiality prohibitions, a lawyer may generally refuse to provide information without breaching any duty. However, once the lawyer undertakes to provide information, that lawyer has a duty to provide the information truthfully." In describing the facts alleged in the *Hansen* case, one scholar has said that "[h]onorable mention in any rouges' gallery of attorney misrepresentation belongs to an Iowa transactional attorney who helped a client fabricate corporate documents so that the client could sell a business which he never owned."[26] After the true owners of the corporation appeared and successfully asserted their right to compensation for transfer of the business entity, the defrauded buyers filed a malpractice suit against their own lawyer for failing to discover the seller's lack of authority. The buyers' lawyer in turn sought indemnity from the lawyer for the putative seller who had prepared the counterfeit corporate documents. In holding that the lawyer for the defrauded buyers could obtain indemnification from the opposing lawyer who had perpetrated the fraud, the Iowa court in *Hansen* approved the black-letter proposition "that a lawyer who makes fraudulent misrepresentations to a nonclient, including a lawyer representing another client, is subject to liability when the other elements of that tort are satisfied."[27]

---

[21] Bruce A. Green, *Candor in Criminal Advocacy*, 44 HOFSTRA L. REV. 1105, 1108 (2016).

[22] *Id.* at 1109.

[23] *See supra* ch. 4-6.

[24] *See supra* § 4-6.6(d)(3) and *infra* § 4-11.2(c).

[25] 630 N.W.2d 818, 825 (Iowa 2001).

[26] Barry R. Temkin, *Misrepresentation by Omission in Settlement Negotiations: Should There be a Silent Safe Harbor?*, 18 GEO. J. LEGAL ETHICS 179, 194 (2004).

[27] *Hansen*, 630 N.W.2d at 825 (adopting the approach of the RESTATEMENT (THIRD) OF THE LAW GOVERNING LAWYERS § 98 (American Law Institute, 2000)).

Rule 4.1(a) of the Model Rules of Professional Conduct confirms this fundamental expectation of honest dealing by a lawyer when communicating with third persons. The rule provides that the lawyer shall not "make a false statement of material fact or law to a third person." Although the duty to refrain from making a false statement is somewhat broader than the duty to avoid a fraudulent misrepresentation, outright dishonesty regarding a material element ordinarily will constitute fraud as well. Moreover, while a lawyer ordinarily is not obliged to share information at all with a third person, if she does choose to speak, the statement must be sufficiently complete as to not be deliberately misleading. As noted in Comment 1 to Rule 4.1, "[m]isrepresentations can also occur by partially true but misleading statements or omissions that are the equivalent of affirmative false statements." Because the rule confines the lawyer's duty of honesty to truthful statements about "material" facts, the professional obligation of veracity extends only to those factual matters that would be significant and induce reasonable reliance by the other person.

The primary purpose of Model Rule 4.1(a) is to ensure accuracy in factual representations, thus requiring an appreciation of the distinction between statements about facts, which must be made truthfully, and expressions of opinion, which are not regulated by this rule. This in turn requires evaluation of the circumstances under which the statements were made and the expectations held by the persons involved.

In particular, when parties are engaged in negotiations about a business transaction or settlement of a dispute, a certain degree of puffery and exaggeration is expected as part of the back and forth haggling. As Comment 2 to Rule 4.1 explains:

> Under generally accepted conventions in negotiation, certain types of statements ordinarily are not taken as statements of material fact. Estimates of price or value placed on the subject of a transaction and a party's intentions as to an acceptable settlement of a claim are ordinarily in this category, and so is the existence of an undisclosed principal except where nondisclosure of the principal would constitute fraud.

The Standing Committee on Ethics and Professional Responsibility of the American Bar Association explains that, consistent with Rule 4.1(a), "a lawyer may downplay a client's willingness to compromise, or present a client's bargaining position without disclosing the client's 'bottom-line' position, in an effort to reach a more favorable resolution."[28] As Professors Monroe Freedman and Abbe Smith have explained, given the "expected and accepted norms of behavior within a group," to call a "lawyer's posturing a lie" in such a context is "simply silly."[29]

Because the lawyer's duty in such a setting is truthfulness within the conventions of the dialogue, not a duty of candor, a lawyer has no duty to volunteer that she has failed to find any eyewitness to an event. But neither may the lawyer falsely tell the opposing side that she had found such an eyewitness.[30] However, withholding of information may sometimes taint the entire expression as dishonest. The lawyer for a plaintiff in a wrongful discharge case may not hide the fact the plaintiff has found new

[28] ABA Comm. on Ethics and Prof'l Responsibility, Formal Op. 06–439 (2006).

[29] Monroe H. Freedman & Abbe Smith, *Misunderstanding Lawyers' Ethics*, 108 MICH. L. REV. 925, 930 (2010).

[30] *See* ABA Comm. on Ethics and Prof'l Responsibility, Formal Op. 06–439 (2006).

employment at a higher salary because that fact would make any claim for continuing lost wages fraudulent.[31]

Rule 4.1(a) also brings statements about "law" within the lawyer's duty of truthfulness, although the comments provide no further explication on this obligation. Given that the focus of Rule 4.1 is upon accuracy in representations, the statements about the law that fall within this prohibition presumably are those that are concrete in expression and that can be objectively evaluated as actually true or false.

A lawyer who offers his opinion about a disputed legal issue or the likelihood of success in a legal proceeding does not violate Rule 4.1(a), even if the lawyer's prediction about the law and its application or the outcome of litigation later prove to be exaggerated or mistaken. Nor is Rule 4.1(a) designed to discourage frivolous legal positions taken in litigation, which instead is governed by Model Rule 3.1.[32] Rather, Rule 4.1(a) should be held to apply only to those statements about the law that are equivalent to a statement of fact—such as a declaration that a corporate entity has been properly incorporated, that the statute of limitations is or is not about to run on a dispute that is the subject of negotiation, that a proposed transaction or element of a transaction is clearly lawful or illegal, or that a proposed clause in a contract is or is not prohibited by law—and about which the lawyer has deliberately prevaricated in an effort to mislead another as to the law's requirements.

As with statements of fact, conventions in negotiation are relevant here, such that, for example, a lawyer would not violate this rule by making "overstatements or understatements of the strengths or weaknesses of a client's position in litigation or otherwise."[33]

Finally, Rule 4.1(a) focuses on statements by the lawyer himself, rather than those made by the client (which are addressed in Rule 4.1(b) and discussed further in the next subsection). Of course, the lawyer's own statements frequently will be a transmission or endorsement of statements by the lawyer's client, to which Rule 4.1(a) certainly applies.

### § 4-11.2(c) The Lawyer Must Avoid Assisting the Client in Crime or Fraud

While Model Rule 4.1(a) commands honesty in affirmative statements by the lawyer, Rule 4.1(b) precludes silence by the lawyer when it has the effect of assisting the client in the commission of a crime or fraud. Under Rule 4.1(b), the lawyer must "disclose a material fact when disclosure is necessary to avoid assisting a criminal or fraudulent act by a client, unless disclosure is prohibited by Rule 1.6." Similarly, Rule 1.2(d) of the Model Rules of Professional Conduct directs that "[a] lawyer shall not counsel a client to engage, or assist a client, in conduct that the lawyer knows is criminal or fraudulent."[34]

Whether the client has engaged in conduct that constitutes a crime or fraud turns upon the substantive civil and criminal law of the jurisdiction and the federal government. Under Rule 1.0(d) of the Model Rules of Professional Conduct, the term "fraud" "denotes conduct that is fraudulent under the substantive or procedural law of the applicable jurisdiction and has a purpose to deceive." In its most basic sense,

---

[31] *See* Cal. St. Bar Standing Comm. on Prof'l Responsibility & Conduct, Formal Op. 2015–194.

[32] *See supra* § 4-9.3(a).

[33] ABA Comm. on Ethics and Prof'l Responsibility, Formal Op. 06–439 (2006).

[34] *See supra* § 4-5.2(c).

"[d]eliberate action that misleads another is fraud, and a lawyer may not counsel or assist a client in such conduct."[35]

Importantly, Rule 4.1(b) is implicated only if the lawyer has become involved (presumably unwittingly) in the client's criminal or fraudulent scheme, in such a way that the lawyer would be "assisting" the client by remaining silent after discovery of the client's wrongdoing.[36] If the lawyer never discovers the client's criminal or fraudulent behavior, then the lawyer cannot take action to avoid assisting the client's wrongdoing. The oblivious lawyer also lacks the necessary scienter to later be held legally responsible as an accomplice in the plot, although the fact finder might not accept the lawyer's disclaimer of knowledge and negligence liability might attach in the unusual case in which the lawyer had additional responsibilities to someone other than the miscreant client. In other words, Rule 4.1(b) applies when the lawyer's legal services have been appropriated by the client to advance the crime or fraud, when the lawyer learns of the misconduct at a point in time when the illegal act may be prevented, and when the informed lawyer's failure to take such preventive measures would amount to assistance by the lawyer.[37]

If the lawyer has never become involved in the client's misconduct, remaining solely in the background as an advisor (assuming the lawyer of course has not advised the client directly as to how to accomplish the wrongdoing) or being retained only after the fact to represent the client in responding to charges of misconduct, the duty to disclose stated in Rule 4.1(b) does not attach. But if the lawyer has been present when the client makes a false statement to another, has participated in negotiations during which deliberately misleading representations were made by the lawyer or the client (even if the lawyer did not learn of the deceptive nature of the statements until later), or has prepared documents for the client that were used to facilitate the crime or fraud, then the lawyer should extricate herself from the situation. Frequently, the only effective means for the lawyer to separate herself from the client's fraud will be to disclose the false or deceptive nature of the communications, that is, to reveal the material facts necessary to remove or counter the false or deceptive effect of those statements.

Under Rule 4.1(b), the lawyer's duty to disclose information to avoid assisting the client's crime or fraud long has been limited by the potentially conflicting duty to maintain client confidentiality which is protected under Rule 1.6.[38] However, as Professors Ronald Rotunda and John Dzienkowski explain:

> When Rule 4.1(b) is mandatory unless limited by Rule 1.6, the expansion of permissive disclosure in Rule 1.6 will lead to mandatory disclosure under Rule 4.1(b) to third persons in the context of financial crimes likely to cause substantial injury.[39]

---

[35] 2 GEOFFREY C. HAZARD, JR., W. WILLIAM HODES & PETER R. JARVIS, THE LAW OF LAWYERING § 40.06 (Aspen, 4th ed., 2016).

[36] *See* Attorney Disciplinary Bd. v. Haskovec, 869 N.W.2d 554, 559 (Iowa 2015) (quoting GREGORY C. SISK & MARK S. CADY, IOWA PRACTICE SERIES: LAWYER AND JUDICIAL ETHICS § 8.1(d) (Thomson Reuters 2015)).

[37] *See also supra* § 4-6.3 (discussing the crime-fraud exception to the attorney-client privilege) and *supra* § 4-6.6(d) (discussing the exceptions to confidentiality to prevent or rectify economic harm caused by the client's crime or fraud in furtherance of which the lawyer's services were used).

[38] *See supra* ch. 4-6.

[39] RONALD D. ROTUNDA & JOHN S. DZIENKOWSKI, PROFESSIONAL RESPONSIBILITY: A STUDENT'S GUIDE § 4.1–3(a) (American Bar Ass'n, 2013–2014).

In 2003, the American Bar Association added new exceptions to confidentiality in Rule 1.6 that allow disclosure to prevent or rectify economic harm when the client has used the legal services to further criminal or fraudulent conduct[40] and that permit disclosure to comply with other law (which includes the laws of fraud and criminal complicity).[41] And, as a longstanding exception to Rule 1.6, a lawyer may use confidential information to defend himself against a charge of wrongdoing.[42] Accordingly, ever fewer circumstances remain under which the lawyer's duty in Rule 4.1(b) to disclose information to avoid assisting client crime or fraud would be constrained by a conflicting duty to maintain client confidences.

Moreover, even if a lawyer learning of a crime or fraud by a client could offer a formal argument to resist mandatory disclosure under Rule 4.1(b), the lawyer may be well-advised to invoke the permissive exceptions to confidentiality in Rule 1.6(b)(2) and (3) to share the information.[43] In this way, the lawyer may fully extricate himself from the client's fraudulent or criminal conduct, thus reducing the chances of being charged, even mistakenly, with complicity.

The complex and uncertain interaction between Rule 4.1(b) and the Rule 1.6 exceptions to confidentiality to prevent or rectify economic harm caused by client crime or fraud—as well as the exceptions to confidentiality for lawyer self-defense and to comply with other law in Rule 1.6(b)(5) and (6)—is addressed at length in the earlier part of this book addressing confidentiality.[44]

## § 4-11.3 COMMUNICATIONS WITH A REPRESENTED PERSON

### § 4-11.3(a) The "No-Contact" Rule: Protecting the Attorney-Client Relationship from Outside Interference

Rule 4.2 of the Model Rules of Professional Conduct states: "In representing a client, a lawyer shall not communicate about the subject of the representation with a person the lawyer knows to be represented by another lawyer in the matter, unless the lawyer has the consent of the other lawyer or is authorized to do so by law or a court order."

This rule, often called the "no-contact" rule,[45] prevents a lawyer representing a client from interfering with the attorney-client relationship between another lawyer and that lawyer's client, guards against inadvertent or uncounseled disclosure of confidential information by a layperson whose lawyer is not present, and precludes a lawyer from obtaining a statement from a represented party that would constitute an admission for purposes of evidentiary rules. "The rule exists to protect the represented person from 'the supposed imbalance of legal skill and acumen between the lawyer and the party litigant.' "[46]

---

[40] *See supra* § 4-6.6(d).

[41] *See supra* §§ 4-6.6(d)(3), 4-6.6(g).

[42] *See supra* §§ 4-6.6(d)(3), 4-6.6(f).

[43] *See supra* § 4-6.6(d)(3).

[44] *See supra* § 4-6.6(d)(3).

[45] Carl A. Pierce, *Variations on a Basic Theme: Revising the ABA's Revision of Model Rule 4.2 (Part I)*, 70 TENN. L. REV. 121, 122 n.2 (2002).

[46] Board of Prof'l Ethics & Conduct v. Herrera, 626 N.W.2d 107, 113 (Iowa 2001) (quoting Massiah v. United States, 377 U.S. 201, 211 (1964) (White, J., dissenting)).

Professor Stephen Gillers identifies several risks that are guarded against by the rule:

- getting a damaging admission from the represented person;
- learning a fact or getting a document she would not learn or get if counsel were present;
- winning a concession in the matter or learning the client's true position in negotiation;
- learning the client's strategy or gaining information protected by the attorney-client privilege or the work-product doctrine;
- weakening the represented person's resolve by casting doubt on the strength of his position; and
- driving a wedge between the represented person and her lawyer.[47]

Rule 4.2 prohibits an attorney from communicating with another represented party if four elements are present:

(1) The communication occurs while the attorney is representing a client.[48]

(2) The communication concerns the subject of the other attorney's representation.[49]

(3) The attorney knows that the person with whom he is communicating is represented by counsel on the subject of the communication.[50]

(4) The other lawyer has not consented or the communication is not otherwise authorized by law.[51]

Each of these four elements is discussed further below.

The represented person may not waive the application of the no-contact rule; only the person's lawyer may do so. Comment 3 to Rule 4.2 emphasizes that "[t]he Rule applies even though the represented person initiates or consents to the communication." As Professor Carl Pierce explains, this comment "provides a useful warning to lawyers that they must silence the represented person who calls them no matter how badly that person wants to talk."[52]

The rule's protective purpose can be achieved only by insisting that the represented person's lawyer must be the sole source for any legitimate consent to ex parte communications with that lawyer's client. "[T]he ethical responsibility rests with the attorney and not the layman."[53] Because the rule is designed to prevent lawyer overreaching, purported consent from the represented party that was extracted by the

---

[47] STEPHEN GILLERS, REGULATION OF LAWYERS: PROBLEMS OF LAW AND ETHICS 77 (Wolters-Kluwer, 10th ed. 2015); *see also* Pierce, *supra*, 70 TENN. L. REV. at 139–47 (discussing the purpose of the no-contact rule).

[48] *See infra* § 4-11.3(c).

[49] *See infra* § 4-11.3(d).

[50] *See infra* § 4-11.3(e).

[51] *See infra* § 4-11.3(f).

[52] Carl A. Pierce, *Variations on a Basic Theme: Revising the ABA's Revision of Model Rule 4.2 (Part III)*, 70 TENN. L. REV. 643, 645 (2003).

[53] Monceret v. Bd. of Prof'l Responsibility, 29 S.W.3d 455, 461 (Tenn. 2000); Attorney Disciplinary Bd. v. Box, 715 N.W.2d 758, 764 (Iowa 2006) (quoting *Monceret*).

communicating lawyer is void. In this respect, the no-contact rule is "paternalistic" in nature,[54] applying with full force even if the represented person purports to consent.

Violations of the no-contact rule by a lawyer often result in severe sanctions. In addition to the ever-present possibility that professional discipline will be visited upon the lawyer for a violation of the rule, a common response by a court when a lawyer has improperly communicated with a represented party is to disqualify the offending lawyer and the lawyer's entire law firm from continuing to represent their own client in that matter.[55] In addition, any agreement negotiated by a lawyer directly with a represented person whose lawyer is not present and without permission may be voided.[56]

### § 4-11.3(b) Communications Between Represented Persons

The no-contact rule does not prohibit or directly constrain exchanges between represented persons, that is, between the clients when unaccompanied by their lawyers. In some circumstances, such as when the represented persons have ongoing family or business relationships, continued contacts outside the presence of their lawyers may be unavoidable. While Comment 4 to Rule 4.2 warns that a lawyer may not make a prohibited communication through "the acts of another,"[57] the comment simultaneously advises that the "[p]arties to a matter may communicate directly with each other, and a lawyer is not prohibited from advising a client concerning a communication that the client is legally entitled to make." Thus, for example, the lawyer's client ordinarily may speak ex parte with the opposing party about the merits of the case, the wisdom of settlement, etc., and may receive the benefit of his lawyer's counsel about those subjects prior to and with the particular purpose of approaching the opposing party.

The line between appropriate client-to-client communications and inappropriate lawyer communications with a represented person through the medium of another person presumably is crossed at the point in which a client's communication with the opposite party becomes so strongly directed by the lawyer that the client has become nothing more than a mouthpiece of the lawyer. Locating that ethical line has been a subject of controversy.[58]

Under one approach to the question, the removal of the lawyer from the meeting largely suffices to take a client-to-client conversation outside of Rule 4.2. The "no-contact" rule primarily wards against the undue influence that a lawyer may project through her perceived authority, by virtue of legal education and the lawyer's persuasive powers as a trained and experienced advocate. If the lawyer is not present, even if the

---

[54] *See* ABA Comm. on Ethics and Prof'l Responsibility, Formal Op. 95–396 (1995) (acknowledging that "not allowing the represented person to waive the Rule's protection may be seen as paternalistic").

[55] *But see* Geoffrey C. Hazard, Jr., & Dana Remus Irwin, *Toward a Revised 4.2 No-Contact Rule*, 60 HASTINGS L.J. 797, 800–01 (2009) (arguing that, "in the absence of actual or apparent injury," judges should consider an admonition or referring the matter to a disciplinary authority rather than disqualification).

[56] RONALD D. ROTUNDA & JOHN S. DZIENKOWSKI, PROFESSIONAL RESPONSIBILITY: A STUDENT'S GUIDE § 4.2–2(c) (American Bar Ass'n, 2013–2014).

[57] In addition, Rule 5.3(a) of the Model Rules of Professional Conduct requires a lawyer to "make reasonable efforts to ensure" that the conduct of those employed or retained "is compatible with the professional obligations of the lawyer." *See infra* § 4-12.4. Accordingly, a lawyer may not evade the restrictions of the no-contact rule through use of a nonlawyer assistant as the messenger. PETER A. JOY & KEVIN C. MCMUNIGAL, DO NO WRONG: ETHICS FOR PROSECUTORS AND DEFENDERS 121 (American Bar Ass'n, 2009).

[58] *See generally* Carl A. Pierce, *Variations on a Basic Theme: Revising the ABA's Revision of Model Rule 4.2 (Part II)*, 70 TENN. L. REV. 321, 335–43 (2003).

lawyer has directed her client in some detail in how to approach the other represented party, then the principal concerns embodied in Rule 4.2 may be mitigated.

In Formal Opinion 11–461,[59] the American Bar Association's Standing Committee moved rather strongly in this direction by opining that "a lawyer may give substantial assistance to a client regarding a substantive communication with a represented adversary."[60] Under this opinion, a lawyer could initiate the idea of a meeting between the clients and then advise his own client on "the subjects or topics to be addressed, issues to be raised and strategies to be used." The lawyer could even draft a document that the client would ask the other party to sign, although Formal Opinion 11–461 says that the lawyer must advise the client to encourage the other party to consult counsel before entering an obligation and should include conspicuous language in any draft agreement "warn[ing] the other party to consult with his lawyer before signing the agreement."

By contrast, others have insisted that the ethical line for Rule 4.2 is crossed when a lawyer scripts the conversation that will unfold between the clients or prepares legal documents for the lawyer's client to present to the opposing side for signature.[61] In direct response to the ABA opinion, for example, the Minnesota Office of Lawyers Professional Responsibility stated that, under Rule 4.2, a lawyer "*may not* script any such communication [between clients] or draft an agreement to be presented to the adverse person, even at the client's request."[62] The author of a treatise on *Minnesota Legal Ethics* cogently argues that "Opinion 11–461 is so permissive that it would subvert the basic purpose of Rule 4.2, viz. protecting represented clients, especially vulnerable clients, from other lawyers' overreaching."[63]

In any event, a client's contacts with the opposing party would be unlikely in ordinary circumstances to undermine the protective purposes of the no-contact rule, even after an advance briefing (that is not overly scripted) by the client's lawyer.[64] If a lawyer is particularly concerned that her client may be swayed by the advances of the opposing party, the lawyer certainly may instruct the client not to speak with the opposing party and may maintain regular connections with the client to counteract any undesirable

---

59 ABA Comm. on Ethics and Prof'l Responsibility, Formal Op. 11–461 (2011).

60 *See also* RESTATEMENT (THIRD) OF THE LAW GOVERNING LAWYERS § 99(2) (American Law Institute, 2000) (stating that the rule "does not prohibit the lawyer from assisting the client in otherwise proper communication by the lawyer's client with a represented nonclient").

61 *See, e.g.*, In re Pyle, 91 P.3d 1222, 1228–29 (Kan. 2004) (holding that Rule 4.2 was violated when a lawyer prepared an affidavit that his client would ask the opposing party to sign); Cal. Comm. on Prof'l Resp. and Conduct, Formal Op. 1993–131 ("An attorney is . . . prohibited from scripting the questions to be asked or statements to be made in the communications or otherwise using the client as a conduit for conveying to the represented opposing party words or thoughts originating with the attorney."); *see also* Attorney Disciplinary Bd. v. Schmidt, 796 N.W.2d 33, 37–40 (Iowa 2011) (saying, when a lawyer drafted a consent decree in a marriage dissolution proceeding for the lawyer's client to take to her husband for him to sign, that the lawyer "cannot circumvent rule [Rule 4.2] by having his client do what he cannot do, especially when a no-contact order exists prohibiting the parties from contacting each other").

62 Martin A. Cole, Director, Minn. Office of Lawyers Prof'l Responsibility, *Scripting Contacts With Represented Persons*, BENCH & BAR OF MINN., Nov. 2011; *see also* James Podgers, *On Second Thought: Changes Mulled Re ABA Opinion on Client Communications Issue*, ABA J., Jan. 2012.

63 WILLIAM J. WERNZ, MINNESOTA LEGAL ETHICS 934 (Minn. St. Bar Ass'n, 6th ed., 2016).

64 *See* Pierce, *supra*, 70 TENN. L. REV. at, 344 (2003) (agreeing that the lawyer may counsel the client with respect to a communication with another represented person, because "the presumed capacity of the lawyer to take advantage of the represented person" will be "greatly diminished when the lawyer has to stay in the background").

influences. But that other person violates no ethical constraint by initiating communications that are not otherwise improper.

### § 4-11.3(c) The No-Contact Rule Applies Only When Lawyer Is Representing a Client

With respect to the first element of the no-contact rule, Rule 4.2 prohibits an attorney from communicating with another represented person only if the communication occurs while the attorney is representing a client. It is the lawyer's role as a representative of a client that poses the danger that the lawyer may be motivated when communicating with a represented person to overreach and interfere with the other attorney-client relationship. By contrast, if the lawyer is not representing a client on the matter on which the layperson is represented by other counsel, the communicating lawyer has no potentially adverse interest and presumably a lesser motive to separate that person from good legal counsel.

In particular, the limitation of the no-contact rule to circumstances in which the lawyer is representing a client enables a person who may be dissatisfied with a lawyer or with a lawyer's advice to interview and secure a new lawyer or to seek a second opinion from another lawyer, without either the person or the lawyer having to obtain permission from the person's present lawyer.

### § 4-11.3(d) The No-Contact Rule Applies Only to Communications on the Subject of Representation

With respect to the second element of the no-contact rule, Rule 4.2 prohibits an attorney from communicating with another represented person only if the communication concerns the subject of the other attorney's representation. While a lawyer ought to be chary of striking up any conversation with an opposing party without that person's lawyer being present, as conversations have a way of meandering into dangerous territory, the rule does not attach unless and until the subject of the representation arises. If a lawyer representing a client comes into contact with another person represented on the matter in a social or business setting, the lawyer is not barred from discussing other matters, provided that the lawyer scrupulously steers the conversation away from the forbidden topic. Likewise, if a lawyer is at a meeting with the opposing party and his counsel and that party's lawyer steps out of the room for a moment, the lawyer need not assume a posture of ill-mannered silence, but may appropriately extend ordinary courtesies and engage in casual conversation about the news of the day, the weather, or other innocuous topics without running afoul of the rule.

That a person is represented on one matter does not prevent a lawyer representing a client on another matter from communicating with that person. As an important example, courts have allowed prosecutors (and law enforcement officials acting under the supervision of prosecutors)[65] to contact represented criminal defendants to investigate allegations of criminal wrongdoing other than the offense on which the defendant has been arrested or charged.[66] Such a communication is ethically-permissible

---

[65] For further discussion of the no-contact rule as applied to law enforcement investigations and particularly undercover operations, see *supra* § 4-9.12(c)(2).

[66] *See, e.g.*, Texas v. Cobb, 532 U.S. 162 (2001) (holding that the Sixth Amendment right to counsel attaches only to charged offenses and thus communications with a criminal defendant about uncharged conduct do not violate the Constitution, without commenting on application of professional conduct rules); United States v. Johnson, 352 F.3d 339 (8th Cir. 2003) (holding that testimony by a jailhouse informant, who

only if it is designed to gather evidence for use regarding the subject matter of that separate investigation and does not seek to gather evidence regarding the subject matter of the pending criminal proceeding on which the defendant is represented. In some instances, the criminal activity being investigated may be remote in time and place from the conduct that is the subject of the charge (and on which the defendant is represented). Government investigators may also communicate with a defendant to investigate additional or different violations of the law that consist of offenses against the administration of justice or obstruction of justice in the very matter in which the defendant is charged, which might include bribes to a judge or jurors, violence against or attempts to intimidate witnesses or jurors,[67] or unlawful flight to avoid prosecution.

However, under the no-contact rule, a government lawyer or someone acting under her direction to investigate other crimes may not ask questions that are likely to elicit information about the pending criminal charge or proceeding. Nor does the possibility of excluding any incriminating statements from evidence at trial[68] justify the reckless solicitation of information from a represented defendant in a manner likely to lead to discussion of the charged offense. For that reason, the government lawyer investigating additional criminal conduct should refrain from communicating with a represented criminal defendant about closely related, even if technically different, wrongful conduct,[69] which line of inquiry is likely to cause the exchange to cross the ethical line. Examples of dubious contacts include questioning a represented person arrested for unlawful possession of a controlled substance about the illegal distribution of that substance and discussing other unsolved burglaries with a person who has been charged with a particular burglary.[70]

In addition, a government lawyer engaged in a law enforcement matter has an ethical obligation to be familiar with constitutional standards regarding the questioning of individuals who have been taken into custody or who have been charged with an offense. For example, under *Massiah v. United States*,[71] a criminal defendant's Sixth

---

had acted under the direction of the government in talking with a defendant in custody and under indictment, could be admitted without restriction against the criminal defendant with respect to new charges filed in a second indictment, without violating defendant's Fifth Amendment right against self-incrimination and Sixth Amendment right to counsel); United States v. Crawford, 60 Fed. Appx. 520, 535–36 (6th Cir. 2003) (unpublished opinion) (holding that the government lawyer did not violate the no-contact rule in contacting a represented criminal defendant about other conduct, namely conspiracy to tamper with a witness); United States v. Ford, 176 F.3d 376, 379–80, 382 (6th Cir. 1999) (holding that placement of an informant in the cell of a defendant charged with money laundering and gambling offenses to investigate threats that represented defendant had allegedly made against a prosecutor, a juror, and witnesses did not violate either the Sixth Amendment right to counsel or Rule 4.2).

[67] *Ford*, 176 F.3d at 379–82; *Crawford*, 60 Fed. Appx. at 535–36.

[68] *Cf.* Maine v. Moulton, 474 U.S. 159, 180 (1985) (holding that "incriminating statements pertaining to pending charges are inadmissible at the trial of those charges, not withstanding the fact that the police were also investigating other crimes, if, in obtaining this evidence, the State violated the Sixth Amendment by knowingly circumventing the accused's right to the assistance of counsel").

[69] *See* State v. Prieto-Rubio, 376 P.3d 255, 256 (Ore. 2016) (holding that a prosecutor exceeded the legitimate scope of questioning of a defendant charged with sexual abuse about other sexual abuse offenses because "the charged and uncharged offenses were so closely related that it was reasonably foreseeable that questioning defendant about the uncharged offenses would elicit incriminating evidence about the charged offense").

[70] In this respect, the no-contact rule, as a matter of professional ethics, may impose somewhat greater restrictions on contacts by government lawyers with represented criminal defendants than does the United States Constitution, as the Sixth Amendment right not to be questioned without counsel attaches only to charged offenses and does not extend to uncharged crimes that are factually related. *See* Texas v. Cobb, 532 U.S. 162 (2001).

[71] 377 U.S. 201, 206 (1964).

Amendment right to counsel is violated when government agents "deliberately elicit" incriminating words from the defendant in the absence of defense counsel about conduct that has been charged in an indictment. A government lawyer engages in professional misconduct if she questions an individual outside the presence of the individual's lawyer in a manner that subverts clearly established constitutional limitations on the interrogation of persons who are in custody or who have been charged with an offense.[72]

### § 4-11.3(e) The No-Contact Rule Applies Only When the Lawyer Knows the Person Is Represented

With respect to the third element of the no-contact rule, Model Rule 4.2 prohibits an attorney from communicating with another represented person only if the communicating attorney knows that the person with whom he is communicating is represented by counsel on the subject of the communication. As Comment 8 to Rule 4.2 explains, the communication bar is raised only when "the lawyer has actual knowledge of the fact of the representation."

However, the comment clarifies that "such actual knowledge may be inferred from the circumstances," and "[t]hus, the lawyer cannot evade the requirement of obtaining the consent of counsel by closing eyes to the obvious." As Professor W. Bradley Wendel offers by way of example, "after a mass disaster such as an airplane crash, it is obvious that the airline will retain counsel to help it deal with the inevitable litigation; for a lawyer to say she didn't 'know' the airline was represented by counsel strains credibility."[73]

Moreover, even if the lawyer initiates a conversation in excusable ignorance that the other person is represented by counsel on the matter, Comment 3 to Rule 4.2 warns that "[a] lawyer must immediately terminate communication with a person if, after commencing communication, the lawyer learns that the person is one with whom communication is not permitted by this Rule."

In *Attorney Disciplinary Board v. Box*,[74] the Iowa Supreme Court issued a public reprimand to a lawyer who, while representing a man who had an interest in purchasing real estate from his elderly aunt, met at his office with and supervised execution of real estate sale documents between the nephew and aunt, despite having earlier been notified by letter that another attorney was representing the aunt. The lawyer justified the communications on the basis that the other lawyer's letter indicated he was representing the aunt only with respect to a will and trust, not any real estate matters, and that the woman further had insisted she would speak to whatever lawyer she chose, thereby supposedly renouncing the other lawyer's representation.[75] Because the letter from the aunt's attorney not only mentioned the will and trust, but also stated that the lawyer represented her on "other personal matters" and emphasized that any contacts should be made with him and not the client, the court found that the "letter clearly speaks to contacts with [the aunt] on matters arising in the future."[76]

---

[72] On the government lawyer's duty to respect the legal rights of an accused, see *supra* § 4-9.6(d).

[73] W. Bradley Wendel, Professional Responsibility: Examples & Explanations 68 (Wolters Kluwer, 5th ed., 2016).

[74] 715 N.W.2d 758 (Iowa 2006).

[75] *Id.* at 761–65.

[76] *Id.* at 763.

As for the aunt's purported renunciation of continuing representation by the other lawyer, the court in *Box* explained that the protective purpose of the no-contact rule would be seriously undermined if a mere statement by a person that she may speak to whomever she pleases were regarded as an effective waiver of the rule.[77] While a person is entitled to discharge her lawyer, and then proceed as an unrepresented party in meeting with a lawyer and his client, the court insisted that the lawyer must "verif[y] that this has been done before [he] makes contact with a previously represented party."[78] In sum, when the lawyer knows that a person has been represented by a lawyer, and circumstances do not clearly indicate that the representation has been terminated, the lawyer is directed to verify the status of the matter "by a simple telephone call."[79]

When the represented person is an entity, such as a corporation, the no-contact rule requires identifying which constituents of the entity count as its alter ego for this purpose. As discussed earlier in the chapter on entity clients,[80] under the pragmatic approach applied by most jurisdictions, the no-contact rule precludes gaining access to those individuals within a represented organization who regularly interact with the lawyer in obtaining legal advice for the entity, those whose actions are the subject of the present representation, and those who may bind the organization by their acts or statements.

Determining whether a person is continuing to be represented by counsel, such that the no-contact rule attaches, may be problematic in the context of an individual who is receiving specific legal services from a lawyer under a limited scope agreement, but who otherwise is proceeding *pro se*. Under the rubric of "unbundling of legal services," an attorney may provide limited services to otherwise *pro se* litigants, provided that informed consent is obtained and the scope of the representation is clearly defined as required by Rule 1.2(c).[81] A person receiving only limited representation from a lawyer should be considered to be unrepresented for purposes of the no-contact rule, unless the opposing lawyer knows of or has been provided with a written notice of appearance or other written notice by the person's lawyer. Several states provide this guidance expressly in the text of the state no-contact rule.[82]

### § 4-11.3(f) Consent by Represented Person's Counsel to Contact by Another Lawyer

With respect to the fourth element of the no-contact rule, Rule 4.2 allows an attorney to communicate with a person represented by another lawyer if that other lawyer has so consented or the communication is authorized by law or a court order. If the represented person's counsel should grant permission for the other lawyer to speak with his client, the lawyer's consent amounts to a waiver of the protections of the no-contact rule. (The "authorized by law" and "court order" exceptions to the no-contact rule

---

[77] *Id.* at 764. On the requirement that only the person's lawyer may consent to a communication under Rule 4.2, see *supra* § 4-11.3(a).

[78] *Box*, 715 N.W.2d at 765.

[79] *Id.*

[80] *See supra* § 4-8.4(a).

[81] On "unbundled legal services" and *pro se* litigants, see *supra* § 4-3.3(c).

[82] *See, e.g.*, IOWA RULES OF PROF'L CONDUCT R. 32:4.2(b), FLA. RULES OF PROF'L CONDUCT R. 4.2(b); MAINE RULES OF PROF'L CONDUCT R. 4.2(b); MONT. RULES OF PROF'L CONDUCT R. 4.2(b); N.H. RULES OF PROF'L CONDUCT R. 4.2(b); UTAH RULES OF PROF'L CONDUCT R. 4.2(b).

are addressed separately below.[83]) When a client is represented by more than one lawyer on the same matter, consent from any single lawyer is sufficient (as coordination among a group of lawyers representing a single client on the same matter is the responsibility of those lawyers).

The occasions for application of the lawyer consent provision are likely to be few, and the scope of the ex parte discussion for which permission is granted is likely to be carefully limited in most circumstances. In the ordinary context, any lawyer worth her salt will refuse to allow an opposing attorney to gain unsupervised access to the client, recognizing the danger that the other attorney may extract an admission, procure inside information about legal strategy, or exert influence over the client.

Nonetheless, one can readily imagine circumstances in which limited consent would reasonably be granted, thereby partially lifting the communication bar. For example, a represented person's lawyer might authorize another lawyer to accept a direct delivery of documents from that represented person or might authorize the opposing attorney to visit the client's place of business to examine documents. In either case, the prudent lawyer would instruct that the opposing attorney may speak with the represented person only for the limited purposes of confirming that the correct documents are being delivered or to receive directions to the specific location within the person's business facility where documents responsive to a discovery request are stored, while strictly forbidding any substantive discussion about the subject of the representation.

In special situations, a broader scope of consent may be granted as appropriate or even necessary to accomplish the task. For example, suppose that a business transaction needs to be negotiated on an expedited basis, but the client's lawyer is unavailable and the client is a capable and experienced business-person. In that case, the lawyer might authorize the opposing party and its lawyer to negotiate directly with the client. As another example, consider the situation where a criminal defendant has pleaded guilty and entered into a cooperation agreement with the prosecution, thus seeking to qualify for a reduced sentence through assisting the investigation and prosecution of another criminal actors. In that event, the defendant's counsel ordinarily will consent to fairly open-ended and regular communications by government lawyers with the defendant. Both so that the government may effectively obtain assistance through open access to the cooperating defendant and so that the defendant's counsel need not schedule a joint meeting whenever law enforcement needs to interview the defendant or prepare him for testimony, defense counsel often agree to allow government lawyers and those under their supervision to work directly with the defendant.

## § 4-11.3(g) Exceptions to the No-Contact Rule

By its express terms, Rule 4.2 of the Model Rules of Professional Conduct articulates three exceptions to the no-contact rule:

### *§ 4-11.3(g)(1) Consent by the Person's Lawyer*

As discussed immediately above, the proscription on communications with a represented person is lifted if "the lawyer has the consent of the other lawyer."[84] This

---

[83] *See infra* § 4-11.3(g), (h).

[84] *See supra* § 4-11.3(f).

consent proviso is not so much an exception to the application of the no-contact rule as it is a definition of the scope of the prohibition and a means for a waiver of its restrictions.

### *§ 4-11.3(g)(2) Authorized by Law*

Under Rule 4.2, a lawyer may speak directly with a represented person when "authorized to do so by law." A communication with a represented person is authorized under Rule 4.2 if permitted by legal authority, such as in the exercise of a constitutional or other legal right. Lawyers also may rely on judicial precedent that authorizes a lawyer to contact persons without permission of the represented person's lawyer.

An example of the former, discussed below, is the important constitutional entitlement of a person, acting directly or through a representative, to express an opinion to or petition for a redress of grievances to government officials, even though such officials or the government entity in which they serve may be represented by a lawyer on the subject matter.[85] An example of the latter, as discussed previously in the chapter on ethics in advocacy,[86] may found in the judicial decisions generally allowing a government lawyer conducting or supervising a law enforcement investigation to communicate with a suspect before commencement of civil or criminal proceedings.

### *§ 4-11.3(g)(3) Court Order*

Rule 4.2 authorizes a lawyer who wishes to communicate with a represented person to ask for authorization through a "court order." As explained by Comment 6 to Rule 4.2, the court order exception to the no-contact rule may apply either (1) when a lawyer is "uncertain whether a communication with a represented person is permissible," or (2) when "exceptional circumstances" would justify "a communication that would otherwise be prohibited by this Rule, for example, where communication with a person represented by counsel is necessary to avoid reasonably certain injury."

As Professor Carl Pierce sums it up: "If unsure, ask a judge!"[87] Out of an abundance of ethical caution, a lawyer who believes that he is permitted to communicate with a particular person may be reluctant to engage in self-help and instead may seek the assistance of the court, knowing that judicial imprimatur will remove any risk that the lawyer later would be accused of professional misconduct. Thus, for example, if a lawyer is uncertain whether a particular corporate employee or other constituent may be contacted without the permission of the entity's lawyer,[88] the lawyer may be well-advised to seek clarification from the court. As another example, if a criminal defendant says that he wishes to discharge legal counsel and speak directly to the prosecutor, but there is reason to doubt whether the waiver of counsel is voluntarily and knowingly made, the prosecutor may wish to obtain judicial approval before continuing communications.

The "court order" exception also provides a safeguard against unthinking and rigid application of the no-contact rule in a manner contrary to other important interests or in a situation where the purposes of the rule are not implicated or are greatly weakened in application. For example, a court might find good cause to authorize a communication with the represented person without notice to or consent of that person's lawyer if

---

[85] *See infra* § 4-11.3(h).

[86] *See supra* § 4-9.12(c)(2).

[87] Carl A. Pierce, *Variations on a Basic Theme: Revising the ABA's Revision of Model Rule 4.2 (Part III)*, 70 TENN. L. REV. 643, 669 (2003).

[88] On the application of the no-contact rule to entities, see *supra* § 4-8.4.

necessary to protect against a risk of death or bodily harm to either the represented person or another. Likewise, if a represented criminal defendant wishes to speak with the prosecutor and does not wish her lawyer to be notified of or be present during that communication (perhaps for fear that the lawyer is beholden to a co-defendant or even an accomplice to a criminal conspiracy), the court, upon ex parte application by the government lawyer, may authorize the communication if the court finds that the represented person is making a voluntary and informed waiver of her rights to remain silent and to be represented by counsel.[89]

As another example, leading commentators suggest that, because class members other than the named representatives may have an indeterminate status or an attenuated relationship with class counsel, defense counsel in a class action might obtain a court order allowing direct contact with those unnamed class members in an appropriate case and subject to appropriate limitations.[90]

In exercising authority to allow access under the "court order" exception to Rule 4.2, the court may place limitations upon the scope or timing of the conversations or set out other instructions as a condition of the court's permission.

### § 4-11.3(h) The No-Contact Rule and the Right to Petition Government

The former Model Code of Professional Responsibility provided:

> In an adversary proceeding, a lawyer shall not communicate, or cause another to communicate, as to the merits of the cause with a judge or an official before whom the proceeding is pending, except:
>
> (1) In the course of official proceedings in the cause.
>
> (2) In writing if he promptly delivers a copy of the writing to opposing counsel or to the adverse party if he is not represented by a lawyer.
>
> (3) Orally upon adequate notice to opposing counsel or to the adverse party if he is not represented by a lawyer.
>
> (4) As otherwise authorized by law . . . .[91]

This provision ensured that a lawyer representing a client in a dispute with a government body could, with certain restrictions, continue to communicate with elected public officials, as any constituent or citizen is entitled to do. At least one state has

---

[89] *See also supra* § 4-9.12(c)(2).

[90] *See, e.g.*, 2 GEOFFREY C. HAZARD, JR., W. WILLIAM HODES & PETER R. JARVIS, THE LAW OF LAWYERING § 41.04 (Aspen, 4th ed., 2016); RONALD D. ROTUNDA & JOHN S. DZIENKOWSKI, PROFESSIONAL RESPONSIBILITY: A STUDENT'S GUIDE § 4.2–2(b) (American Bar Ass'n, 2013–2014). Under an opinion of the American Bar Association's Standing Committee on Ethics and Professional Responsibility, before the class is certified, counsel for both plaintiff and defense may contact persons who may in the future become members of the class, subject to the ethical duties of lawyer's in dealing with unrepresented persons. ABA Comm. on Ethics & Prof'l Responsibility, Formal Op. 77–445 (2007); *see also* Vincent R. Johnson, *The Ethics of Communicating with Putative Class Members*, 17 REV. LITIG. 497, 507 (1998) ("Absent a judicial determination that a class should be certified, there is no basis for concluding that an unnamed potential member of a class, who has never been in contact with the lawyer seeking to certify the class, should be treated as having a lawyer."). *But see* Debra Lyn Bassett, *Pre-Certification Communication Ethics in Class Actions*, 36 GA. L. REV. 353, 405 (2000) (arguing that for putative class members the "courts should substitute the current presumption of non-representation with a presumption of representation" to protect their legal rights).

[91] MODEL CODE OF PROF'L RESPONSIBILITY, Disciplinary Rule 7–110(B) (American Bar Ass'n, 1980).

preserved the same approach as the former Code in its rule,[92] and several states have more broadly added language to their versions of Rule 4.2 confirming that the no-contact prohibition does not apply to communications with public officers or bodies.[93]

While this government-access confirmation has not been incorporated directly into the text of Rule 4.2 of the Model Rules of Professional Conduct, Comment 5 states that "[c]ommunications authorized by law may include communications by a lawyer on behalf of a client who is exercising a constitutional or other legal right to communicate with the government." Moreover, the American Bar Association's Standing Committee on Professional Ethics and Conduct "agree[d] that the no-contact rule must not be applied so as to frustrate a citizen's right to petition, exercised by direct communication with government decision makers, through a lawyer."[94]

Given the compelling public interest in ensuring a citizen's access to governmental decisionmakers, as well as the constitutional right under the First Amendment of the United States Constitution to petition the government for redress of grievances, Rule 4.2 should not be read to prevent a lawyer representing a person involved in a dispute with or seeking action from a governmental body from communicating directly with elected or appointed government officials, even without the permission or presence of the counsel for that government official or body.

Although it is not certain that such can be constitutionally mandated, the lawyer communicating with a government officer or body should give the government's legal counsel reasonable notice of the communication, by sending copies of written communications or giving prior notice of proposed meetings.[95] Through such notice, the government's lawyer has the opportunity to advise the public official of the status of the matter at issue and about the potential legal consequences of any statement or action by the public official.[96]

A lawyer representing a client may also communicate with governmental decisionmakers in the course of official proceedings, such as a public hearing (e.g., by a legislative committee) or a public meeting (e.g., a city council meeting), without either prior notice to or consent of the governmental body's counsel.[97]

The "authorized by law" exception to Rule 4.2, which allows a lawyer to speak on behalf of a client directly with a governmental official, should be limited to circumstances

---

[92] N.C. RULES OF PROF'L CONDUCT R. 4.2(b).

[93] *See, e.g.*, CAL. RULES OF PROF'L CONDUCT R. 2–100(C)(1); D.C. RULES OF PROF'L CONDUCT R. 4.2(d); MD. RULES OF PROF'L CONDUCT R. 19–304.2(c); *see also* UTAH RULES OF PROF'L CONDUCT R. 4.2(d)(3) (allowing communication with government parties unless litigation is "pending or imminent" and with "elected officials on policy matters" afterward).

[94] ABA Comm. on Ethics & Prof'l Responsibility, Formal Op. 97–408 (1997).

[95] *See* 2 GEOFFREY C. HAZARD, JR., W. WILLIAM HODES & PETER R. JARVIS, THE LAW OF LAWYERING § 41.11 (Aspen, 4th ed., 2016) (describing the approach that allows lawyer to communicate with a government official notwithstanding objection by agency counsel, but requiring notification of the contact to agency counsel, as "a reasonable compromise"). *But see* RONALD D. ROTUNDA & JOHN S. DZIENKOWSKI, PROFESSIONAL RESPONSIBILITY: A STUDENT'S GUIDE § 4.2–2(b) (American Bar Ass'n, 2013–2014) (arguing that nothing in Rule 4.2 requires that a lawyer, in exercising First Amendment rights, must give government counsel advance notice of contacts with government officials).

[96] *See* ABA Comm. on Ethics & Prof'l Responsibility, Formal Op. 97–408 (1997) (saying that the advance notice "afford[s] an opportunity for consultation between government counsel and the officials on the advisability of their entertaining the communication").

[97] For the lawyer's duties when advocating before a government body in a nonadjudicative context to disclose the lawyer's representative capacity and act with integrity toward the body, see *supra* § 4-9.13.

where that official is being approached as a decisionmaker in a position to take action on the matter being presented by the lawyer (even if that matter is the subject of litigation).

By contrast, when a government official or employee may be a witness in litigation, the lawyer's contact with that person is governed by the ordinary standard of the no-contact rule (or, if the government official or employee is unrepresented, by the standard of Model Rule 4.3).[98] Moreover, a lawyer who is representing a party to an administrative proceeding being adjudicated by an agency tribunal is generally prohibited under Model Rule 3.5 from engaging in any ex parte communication with the agency adjudicators.[99]

## § 4-11.4 COMMUNICATIONS WITH AN UNREPRESENTED PERSON

In representing a client, a lawyer often must deal with persons who do not have their own counsel, such as interviewing a witness who has not retained a lawyer, negotiating a transaction with a person who is not represented, or being involved in litigation with a *pro se* litigant. In such situations, the lawyer has a good reason to communicate directly with the unrepresented person—and often has no choice but to do so.

However, because a lawyer is a trained advocate with an educated understanding of the law, a lawyer may overreach or mislead a unrepresented person by making an assertion about the law that the layperson wrongly assumes to be an authoritative and impartial description of legal obligation. As Comment 1 to Rule 4.3 of the Model Rules of Professional Conduct explains, "[a]n unrepresented person, particularly one not experienced in dealing with legal matters, might assume that a lawyer is disinterested in loyalties or is a disinterested authority on the law even when the lawyer represents a client."

Rule 4.3 provides clarification as to how a lawyer should comport him or herself when speaking with persons who have not retained legal counsel:

### § 4-11.4(a) Avoiding Suggestion of Lawyer's Neutrality

Rule 4.3 directs that the lawyer must not "state or imply that the lawyer is disinterested." When a lawyer represents a client, the lawyer is properly obliged as a zealous advocate to advance that client's interests. Accordingly, as a matter of integrity, while representing a client, the lawyer must never suggest to another person that the lawyer is a neutral observer, that the lawyer is an impartial authority on the law, or that the lawyer will protect that person's interests even if doing so would conflict with the interests of the lawyer's client.

For example, when a lawyer is interviewing a non-client witness or preparing such a person for testimony, the lawyer must be careful not to intimate that the lawyer is representing the witness or that the lawyer's primary concern is for the well-being of the witness rather than to promote the interests of the client. Even more so when dealing with a self-represented opponent in litigation or a person on the other side of an arm's

---

[98] *See infra* § 4-11.4.

[99] *See supra* § 4-9.9(d).

length transaction, the lawyer should never suggest that the client's interests are not preeminent in the lawyer's thinking and actions.

### § 4-11.4(b) Correcting Misunderstanding About Lawyer's Role

Under Rule 4.3, "[w]hen the lawyer knows or reasonably should know that the unrepresented person misunderstands the lawyer's role in the matter, the lawyer shall make reasonable efforts to correct the misunderstanding." Not only is the lawyer directed not to suggest or imply that the lawyer is disinterested, but if the unrepresented person still fails to appreciate the lawyer's role as a partisan advocate, the lawyer must clarify matters, even if the lawyer has not contributed to the unrepresented person's misunderstanding.

For example, when a lawyer is representing an entity, such as a corporation or other business association, the lawyer regularly should remind directors, officers, employees, members, and shareholders that the lawyer is counsel for the entity and does not represent any of these persons in their individual capacities (unless the lawyer is engaged in dual representation of both the organization and the constituent).[100] Especially if the occasion should arise in which the lawyer for an entity knows or reasonably should know that the interests of the organization have become adverse to that of a constituent with whom the lawyer has been dealing, the lawyer must underscore that she represents and takes directions from the organization as an entity and is not responsible to protect the interests of the individual officer, director, employee, or shareholder.[101] Indeed, corporate counsel participating in internal investigations are advised to issue a "corporate *Miranda* warning" to those that they interview, advising employees that they represent the corporation, that the interview is for the purpose of providing legal advice to the corporation, and that, while the communication may be covered by the attorney-client privilege, the privilege belongs to and may be surrendered by the company.[102]

As another example, when a lawyer speaks directly with an unrepresented person who is or may be the target of legal action by the lawyer's client, the lawyer's failure to disclose that possibility unavoidably means that "the unrepresented person misunderstands the lawyer's role in the matter" within the meaning of Rule 4.3.[103]

### § 4-11.4(c) Giving of Legal Advice by Lawyer

Rule 4.3 provides that a lawyer shall not "shall not give legal advice to an unrepresented person, other than the advice to secure counsel, if the lawyer knows or reasonably should know that the interests of such a person are or have a reasonable possibility of being in conflict with the interests of the client."

With respect to the provision of legal advice, Comment 2 explains that "[t]he Rule distinguishes between situations involving unrepresented persons whose interests may be adverse to those of the lawyer's client and those in which the person's interests are

---

[100] On dual representation of an organization and an individual constituent, see *supra* § 4-8.8.

[101] *See also supra* §§ 4-8.5, 4-8.6(h).

[102] Michael M. Farhang & Daniel L. Weiss, *Corporate Miranda Warnings: Defining Your Role and Avoiding Pitfalls in Internal Company Investigations*, LITIGATION, Spring 2010, at 21, 21–22. *See supra* § 4-9.12(c)(4).

[103] 2 GEOFFREY C. HAZARD, JR. & W. WILLIAM HODES, THE LAW OF LAWYERING § 39.4 (Aspen, 3d ed., 2005) (saying that "[i]n the case of a potential civil defendant, . . . a lawyer communicating with such a person would be required to disclose the fact that he contemplated filing a lawsuit").

not in conflict with the client's." When the interests of the unrepresented person are compatible with those of the client, the lawyer is not forbidden from offering legal advice, although even then the lawyer should be careful that his elucidation of the law does not leave the mistaken impression that the lawyer is acting for any reason other than the best interests of the client. Indeed, if a lawyer offers legal advice to a layperson, but fails to clarify the nature of the relationship and disclaim any professional obligation to that person, an attorney-client relationship might be implied from the circumstances.[104]

To build on the example given above,[105] the lawyer who is interviewing a non-client witness or preparing such a person for testimony may provide legal explanations about the effect of the testimony, its admissibility as a matter of evidence, and the potential consequences for the witness in testifying, but the lawyer regularly should remind the witness that the lawyer must place the client's interests at the forefront.

If it should become apparent that the witness may suffer adverse consequences by testifying favorably to the lawyer's client—such as exposing himself to a criminal charge or liability by self-inculpatory statements—then the interests of the witness have come into conflict with those of the lawyer's client. At that point, the lawyer may not appropriately offer legal advice to the witness, because advising the witness to testify may seriously compromise the witness's interest, while explaining the privilege against self-incrimination or the possibility of immunity may compromise the client's interest in obtaining the benefit of that favorable testimony. In such an instance, the lawyer must refrain from legal explanations other than the advice to the witness to obtain independent legal counsel.

Under Rule 4.3, when the lawyer does "know[ ] or reasonably should know that the interests of [the unrepresented person] are or have a reasonable possibility of being in conflict" with those of the lawyer's client, the lawyer must refrain from offering any legal advice. As Comment 2 to Rule 4.3 states, "the possibility that the lawyer will compromise the unrepresented person's interests is so great that the Rule prohibits the giving of any advice, apart from the advice to obtain counsel."

This prohibition on offering legal counsel to an unrepresented person whose interests are in conflict with the lawyer's client does not necessarily impose a duty of silence upon the lawyer. If the other person is acting *pro se* in litigation or going without representation in the negotiation of a transaction, the lawyer must continue to deal with that person. The lawyer's client should not be deprived of the lawyer's services by the opposing party's choice to proceed without legal counsel. Nor is the lawyer forbidden to express a legal opinion or advocate the client's position concerning the obligations or direction of the law, provided the lawyer plainly discloses that she is speaking as an advocate for the client and not as an advisor to the unrepresented person (and regularly cautions the person to seek independent legal counsel). As Comment 2 explains, "[s]o long as the lawyer has explained that the lawyer represents an adverse party and is not representing the person, the lawyer may inform the person of the terms on which the lawyer's client will enter into an agreement or settle a matter, prepare documents that

[104] On the implication of an attorney-client relationship from the parties' conduct, if the layperson detrimentally relies upon the lawyer's counsel, see *supra* § 4-3.2(a). On the lawyer's responsibility for avoiding misunderstandings regarding the existence or nature of the attorney-client relationship, see *supra* § 4-3.2(c).

[105] *See supra* § 4-11.4(a).

require the person's signature and explain the lawyer's own view of the meaning of the document or the lawyer's view of the underlying legal obligations."

# Chapter 4-12

# DUTIES OF A LAWYER IN A LAW FIRM

**By Gregory C. Sisk**

*Table of Sections*

§ 4-12.1 Introduction to the Responsibilities of a Lawyer in a Law Firm
§ 4-12.2 The Responsibilities of a Managing or Supervising Lawyer over Other Lawyers
§ 4-12.3 The Responsibilities of a Subordinate Lawyer
§ 4-12.4 The Responsibilities of a Managing or Supervising Lawyer over Nonlawyer Assistants

## § 4-12.1 INTRODUCTION TO THE RESPONSIBILITIES OF A LAWYER IN A LAW FIRM

A lawyer has ethical responsibilities that arise from the manner, arrangements, structure, associations, and affiliations through which the lawyer engages in the practice of law and provides legal and other services. This chapter addresses the responsibilities of the lawyer as a partner, manager, and supervisor of other lawyers;[1] the responsibilities of a subordinate lawyer to comply with ethical duties;[2] and the responsibilities of a lawyer regarding nonlawyer assistants.[3]

While the pertinent provisions of the Model Rules of Professional Conduct refer generically to a law "firm" or a "partner," Rule 1.0 explains this as a term of art that has a broader meaning than the ordinary usage of these words and encompasses modern additions or parallels to the traditional law firm and partner.

Rule 1.0(c) states that the reference to a legal practice entity as a "firm" "denotes a lawyer or lawyers in a law partnership, professional corporation, sole proprietorship or other association authorized to practice law; or lawyers employed in a legal services organization or the legal department of a corporation or other organization." In sum, the term includes not only the traditional office law firm with partners and associates, but also covers any association of lawyers in the practice of law and includes corporate counsel practicing in a legal department as well as attorneys working together in a legal aid office.

The related term of "partner" is defined in Rule 1.0(g) as "denot[ing] a member of a partnership, a shareholder in a law firm organized as a professional corporation, or a member of an association authorized to practice law." Thus, not every lawyer practicing with a "firm" is a "partner" of the firm, but only those who hold a position of membership, which thus entails certain supervisory or managerial responsibilities.

---

[1] *See infra* § 4-12.2.

[2] *See infra* § 4-12.3.

[3] *See infra* § 4-12.4.

## § 4-12.2 THE RESPONSIBILITIES OF A MANAGING OR SUPERVISING LAWYER OVER OTHER LAWYERS

### § 4-12.2(a) The Duty of a Managing or Supervising Lawyer on Ethical Guidance of Other Lawyers

When a lawyer practices together with other lawyers in a law firm or similar organization, she takes on responsibilities with respect to the conduct of those other lawyers, not only in terms of potential tort and contract liability, as always has been the case, but also potential disciplinary sanction. Supervising or managing lawyers within a law firm have a duty to take certain steps to protect clients and the public from misconduct by other lawyers in the firm.

Importantly, the supervisory steps taken by leaders in the law firm determine the ethical culture of the firm, which may have a greater effect on the ethical behavior of the firm's lawyers than anything set forth in the words of the Model Rules of Professional Conduct.[4]

#### *§ 4-12.2(a)(1) The Duty of a Managing Lawyer in a Firm*

Under Rule 5.1(a) of the Model Rules of Professional Conduct, a lawyer with managerial authority in a firm is required to "make reasonable efforts to ensure that the firm has in effect measures giving reasonable assurance that all lawyers in the firm conform to the Rules of Professional Conduct." The lawyer-partner or lawyer-manager thus has an affirmative responsibility for the ethical climate of the firm, being obliged to see that reasonable measures have been implemented in the firm to encourage ethical practice and to guard against professional misconduct.[5] Moreover, when partners in a law firm have reason to believe one of their own suffers from mental impairment by reason of mental illness, substance abuse, or the advances of age, they have a duty to watch closely for violation of ethics rules and duties to clients.[6] Again, by virtue of the expansive definition of "law firm" in Rule 1.0(c), Rule 5.1(a) applies, not only to partners in traditional law firms, but also to managing lawyers in corporate and government legal departments and in legal service organizations.

The rule as adopted in nearly all states does not, however, extend disciplinary standards to the law firm as an entity, instead leaving supervising responsibility with the individual partner or managing lawyer. New York and New Jersey stand alone in allowing for professional discipline of the law firm as a whole; while such remedies as suspension and disbarment are inapplicable to a firm, the discipline may include censure and fines.[7]

---

4 *See* Jennifer K. Robbennolt & Jean R. Sternlight, *Behavioral Legal Ethics*, 45 ARIZ. ST. L.J. 1107, 1165 (2013) ("The ethical culture of a firm, company, agency, or practice group is an important determinant of how ethically the attorneys within that entity will behave.").

5 *See* MILTON C. REGAN, EAT WHAT YOU KILL 358–60 (U. Mich. Press, 2006) (explaining that a law firm must both have an "ethical infrastructure"—"formal policies and procedures, as well as cultural norms"—and "reinforce it with an organizational ethos that clearly places value on meeting ethical responsibilities").

6 *See* 2013 N.C. Ethics Op. 8.

7 N.J. RULES OF PROF'L CONDUCT R. 5.1(a); N.Y. RULES OF PROF'L CONDUCT R. 5.1(a), (c). For a debate on expanding discipline to law firms, compare Ted Schneyer, *Professional Discipline for Law Firms?*, 77 CORNELL L. REV. 1 (1992) (arguing that enforcement of disciplinary rules on supervisory duties against a firm is appropriate because it may be difficult to determine which particular supervising attorney is at fault and, indeed, no single lawyer may be responsible as the problem may lie in the firm's "ethical infrastructure") with

### *§ 4-12.2(a)(2) The Duty of a Supervising Lawyer*

Parallel to the duty of a managerial lawyer who has a responsibility for the law firm as a whole, a lawyer who has direct supervisory authority over another lawyer is required under Rule 5.1(b) to "make reasonable efforts to ensure that the other lawyer conforms to the Rules of Professional Conduct." The supervisory lawyer may not take a hands-off approach as to subordinates, but must exercise reasonable oversight that encourages attention to ethical requirements and is designed to detect actual or incipient misconduct.

### *§ 4-12.2(a)(3) Reasonable Efforts to Ensure Ethical Conduct*

What constitutes "reasonable efforts" and appropriate "measures giving reasonable assurance" of ethical deportment by all lawyers in the firm are not expressly defined in the rule or the accompanying comments. Comment 2 to Rule 5.1 refers to certain basic policies and procedures that every law firm must have in place, namely an intake process by which to detect and resolve conflicts of interest when considering new representations, a calendaring process to ensure that necessary actions are taken in pending matters, a system to properly account for client funds and property,[8] and a practice for properly supervising inexperienced attorneys.

Beyond those basic expectations, Rule 5.1(a) does not impose a one-size-fits-all approach to internal ethical procedures or policies upon law firms. Thus, as Comment 3 to Rule 5.1 anticipates, for a small firm, "informal" approaches to ensuring adherence to ethical standards may be appropriate. In a large firm, or in practice settings in which difficult ethical problems frequently arise, "more elaborate" safeguards may be expected, including formal written procedures or detailed rules of governance on particular matters. Firms, whether large or small, may also rely on continuing legal education in professional ethics. In any practice context, partners or other managerial lawyers should ensure that all lawyers in the firm have ready access to and are encouraged to regularly review the governing Rules of Professional Conduct in that jurisdiction.

Professors Jennifer Robbennolt and Jean Sternlight emphasize that the law firm as an organization must "monitor" the professional conduct of its lawyers:

> Given the very human ways in which people can fall prey to ethical temptations, entities should not assume that attorneys are behaving ethically, but should instead develop systems to provide checks on behavior—whether by using software to monitor billing patterns, having colleagues double-check what discovery or due diligence is produced, reviewing how attorneys conduct negotiations, or monitoring how attorneys prepare their clients for depositions or trial. It is most important to monitor situations in which attorneys, due to cognitive or temporal depletion or structural temptations, are most likely to engage in ethical misconduct.[9]

---

Julie Rose O'Sullivan, *Professional Discipline for Law Firms? A Response to Professor Schneyer's Proposal*, 16 GEO. J. LEGAL ETHICS 1 (2002) (questioning the case for firm liability as a "fair or effective" means of "furthering the aims of professional discipline" and raising concern that "such a rule may actually undermine *individual* ethical incentives rather than furthering attorney accountability").

[8] *See also supra* § 4-5.6.

[9] Jennifer K. Robbennolt & Jean R. Sternlight, *Behavioral Legal Ethics*, 45 ARIZ. ST. L.J. 1107, 1180 (2013).

Many firms also designate a senior partner or committee as in-house ethics counsel to whom lawyers may refer ethical questions.[10] Highlighting the importance of in-firm counsel, the American Bar Association in 2013 endorsed the coverage of the attorney-client privilege to lawyers' discussions with in-house counsel about issues arising from a client representation.[11]

### *§ 4-12.2(a)(4) Managing or Supervising Lawyer Responsibility Is Not Vicarious Liability*

A partner or a lawyer with comparable managerial authority is generally accountable for the ethical atmosphere of the firm, and a lawyer with direct supervisory authority over another lawyer has a closer responsibility to encourage ethical conduct and monitor the behavior of a subordinate attorney. A managerial or supervisory lawyer does not thereby become a guarantor against any and every ethical violation by other lawyers in the firm.

If, for example, a lawyer in the firm is discovered to have defrauded a client by dishonest billing for fees, the managerial lawyer with responsibility for the firm or a supervisory lawyer with responsibility for the acting lawyer would not be guilty of professional misconduct if that managerial or supervisory lawyer had made reasonable efforts to institute appropriate measures or maintain supervision, even though such efforts unfortunately failed to prevent that particular episode of misconduct. No set of policies or procedures or supervisory practices can guarantee that every lawyer in the firm will invariably behave with utmost rectitude.

Even if the efforts made by the managing or supervisory lawyer are found to have been less than reasonable, the disciplinary infraction would be for neglectful ethical management or supervision, rather than direct disciplinary responsibility for the fraudulent billing of the other lawyer in the example above. In other words, Rule 5.1(a) and (b) establish an independent professional duty for proper ethical management and supervision, separate from underlying misconduct by another lawyer in the firm.[12] The

[10] On the ethical obligations of an "ethics counsel" within a law firm, including that the in-house counsel typically represents the law firm as an entity and not the individual lawyers who consult with the counsel, see ABA Comm. on Ethics and Prof'l Responsibility, Formal Op. 08–453 (2008). On the trend, especially within larger law firms, toward appointing in-house counsel on ethics matters and on the ethical implications of this development, see generally Elizabeth Chambliss, *The Professionalization of Law Firm In-House Counsel*, 84 N.C. L. REV. 1515 (2006); Elizabeth Chambliss & David B. Wilkins, *The Emerging Role of Ethics Advisors, General Counsel, and Other Compliance Specialists in Large Law Firms*, 44 ARIZ. L. REV. 559 (2002); Peter R. Jarvis & Mark J. Fucile, *Inside an In-House Legal Ethics Practice*, 14 NOTRE DAME J.L. ETHICS & PUB. Pol'y 103 (2002). For a readable explanation of the practical value of a designated ethics counsel from the perspective of a particular state, see Chuck Lundberg, *Why Your Firm Needs an Ethics Partner. Now.*, MINN. BENCH & BAR, Dec. 2016, at 28.

[11] *See* Joan C. Rogers, *ABA Formally Backs Attorney-Client Privilege for Consults with Law Firms' Inside Counsel,* 29 LAW. MAN. PROF. CONDUCT 553 (2013). *See generally* William T. Barker, *May a Law Firm Have Privileged Communications with In-House Counsel Regarding a Current Client?*, 51 TORT TRIAL & INS. PRAC. L.J. 777 (2016). On the attorney-client privilege inside a firm in legal malpractice cases, see Part Five of this book, Susan Saab Fortney & Vincent R. Johnson, Legal Malpractice § 5-4.4(a)(2).

[12] *See* In re Phillips, 244 P.3d 549, 554 (Ariz. 2010) (holding that the hearing officer "clearly understood and correctly applied the law by carefully not conflating vicarious liability with managerial and supervisory liability"); In re Anonymous Member of S.C. Bar, 552 S.E.2d 10, 12 (S.C. 2001) (explaining that "vicarious liability is *not* the issue" but rather "whether the supervising attorney violated Rule 5.1 by failing to satisfy the ethical responsibilities of a partner or supervisory lawyer in relation to the other supervised attorney's misconduct").

fact of underlying misconduct by another lawyer may (or may not) suggest inadequacies in firm management or lawyer supervision.

A managerial or supervisory lawyer is not to be held directly responsible through the disciplinary process for the ethical wrongdoing of an individual lawyer within the firm, unless that managerial or supervisory lawyer has ordered, ratified, or knew of and failed to address the wrongful conduct, as addressed immediately below. At the same time, managing or supervising lawyers who "attempt to shield themselves from any direct liability under Rule 5.1(c) by distancing themselves from attorneys under their direct supervisory authority may find themselves guilty of a failure to properly supervise under Rule 5.1(b)."[13]

### § 4-12.2(b) Lawyer Responsibility for the Misconduct of Another Lawyer

Under Rule 5.1(c)(1) of the Model Rules of Professional Conduct, a lawyer becomes responsible for the behavior of another lawyer if the lawyer "orders or, with knowledge of the specific conduct, ratifies the conduct involved." In either instance of ordering or ratifying, the lawyer has become a direct participant in the conduct. Ratification in this context suggests something active, such as affirmative expression of approval to the lawyer who plans to engage in misconduct or endorsement of the lawyer's behavior to a third person, while knowing of the specific nature of the conduct being so ratified.

A lawyer who becomes an accomplice of another lawyer who violates the Rules of Professional Conduct quite naturally becomes fully responsible for that violation, even though another lawyer may have been the direct agent of the violation. Indeed, Rule 8.4(a) also incorporates complicity within the definition of professional misconduct, by prohibiting a lawyer from "knowingly assist[ing] or induc[ing] another to" violate the ethics rules, or violating the rules "through the acts of another." Rule 5.1(c)(1) applies to any lawyer, regardless of the prior relationship between them or whether the lawyer has managerial or supervisory responsibility for the other lawyer, although it would be unusual for a lawyer without a managerial, supervisory, or at least association relationship to be in a position to order or ratify misconduct.

Under Rule 5.1(c)(2), a managerial or supervisory lawyer who comes to "know[ ] of the conduct at a time when its consequences can be avoided or mitigated," but who then "fails to take reasonable remedial action," likewise is held directly responsible for the misconduct. Although Rule 5.1(c)(2) extends responsibility beyond the typical accessory situation of Rule 5.1(c)(1), this is not vicarious disciplinary liability because the managerial or supervisory lawyer is only being held personally responsible for his own failure in supervision that effectively facilitated the other lawyer's misconduct.[14]

A lawyer who comes to know of another lawyer's professional misconduct does not ordinarily become directly responsible (although the lawyer may have a duty to report that wrongdoing to disciplinary authorities under Rule 8.3[15] and may have a moral obligation to take some action). But the lawyer who has assumed a managerial or supervisory role is appropriately held accountable when learning of an associated or

[13] In re Anonymous Member of S.C. Bar, 552 S.E.2d 10, 14 (S.C. 2001).

[14] On the difference between managerial or supervisory responsibility and vicarious liability, see *supra* § 4-12.2(a)(4).

[15] *See infra* § 4-13.1.

subordinate lawyer's misconduct at a point in time in which the harm can be prevented or mitigated. Under those circumstances, the managerial or supervisory lawyer is obliged to take "reasonable remedial action."

As explained in Comment 5 to Rule 5.1, what constitutes appropriate "remedial action" for a managerial lawyer who has more general responsibility for other lawyers in a firm "would depend on the immediacy of that lawyer's involvement and the seriousness of the misconduct." For a supervisory lawyer, who has a closer connection to the misbehaving subordinate, a greater duty to intervene and correct the problem would arise.

## § 4-12.3 THE RESPONSIBILITIES OF A SUBORDINATE LAWYER

Rule 5.2(a) of the Model Rules of Professional Conduct makes clear that every lawyer, whether or not acting at the direction of another and regardless of position within the hierarchy of an organization, is "bound by the Rules of Professional Conduct." The subordinate lawyer maintains an independent duty to be competent and practice ethically,[16] including taking "an active role in seeking supervision" to uphold those expectations.[17] The so-called "Nuremberg Defense," that one was "just following orders," is not available to the lawyer who has violated a plain directive of the rules.

Rule 5.2(b) offers a very narrow exception to the lawyer's personal and non-delegable duty to follow the ethics rules, affording a subordinate lawyer limited protection when he "acts in accordance with a supervisory lawyer's reasonable resolution of an arguable question of professional duty."[18] The narrow application of Rule 5.2(b) is made more apparent when one considers that even the supervisory lawyer is less likely to be subject to discipline if the question of professional responsibility is sufficiently arguable that reasonable people could disagree as to the correct resolution.[19] As Professors Geoffrey Hazard and William Hodes and attorney Peter Jarvis remark, "if the matter is indeed debatable, then even the supervisory lawyer may be found not to have violated the Rules of Professional Conduct if the choice is later determined to have been wrong."[20] Douglas Richmond explains that, when internal debate is concluded on a difficult ethics question, "[i]t is generally acceptable for subordinate lawyers to let their supervisors decide close ethical questions because lawyers occupying supervisory or leadership roles commonly have more experience and greater professional knowledge on which to draw."[21]

---

[16] *See generally* Douglas R. Richmond, *Professional Responsibilities of Law Firm Associates*, 45 BRANDEIS L.J. 199 (2007).

[17] Nancy M. Maurer & Robert Seibel, *Addressing Problems of Power and Supervision in Field Placements*, 17 CLINICAL L. REV. 145, 163 (2010).

[18] For a critique of Rule 5.2(b) as undermining the responsibility of "every lawyer to stop and consider the propriety of his actions," see Carol M. Rice, *The Superior Orders Defense in Legal Ethics: Sending the Wrong Message to Young Lawyers*, 32 WAKE FOREST L. REV. 887, 890 (1997).

[19] *See* Andrew M. Perlman, *The Silliest Rule of Professional Conduct: Model Rule 5.2(b)*, 19:3 THE PROF'L LAWYER 14, 14, 16 (2009) (characterizing this provision as "the silliest rule of professional conduct" that "applies to a vanishingly small set of cases" because "if the supervising attorney does not deserve discipline in this kind of case, it is hard to argue that the subordinate needs any protection").

[20] 2 GEOFFREY C. HAZARD, JR., W. WILLIAM HODES & PETER R. JARVIS, THE LAW OF LAWYERING § 46.04 (Aspen, 4th ed., 2016).

[21] Douglas R. Richmond, *Academic Silliness About Model Rule 5.2(b)*, 19:3 THE PROF'L LAWYER 15, 19 (2009).

If the directive of the rules is clear and thus not subject to reasonable disputation, then Rule 5.2(b) has no application and the subordinate lawyer remains bound by the rule, notwithstanding the contrary command of a superior. The lawyer must "do the right thing," even if the lawyer faces the loss of her position (although compelled compliance with the ethics rules may provide the subordinate a basis for challenging an adverse personnel action within the law firm).[22] In this regard, as Professor W. Bradley Wendel warns, "[a]n implicit corollary of this rule" is that the subordinate lawyer has a responsibility to "*do your own research into the law governing lawyers*," because only then can the lawyer know whether the supervising lawyer's direction is reasonable or not.[23]

## § 4-12.4 THE RESPONSIBILITIES OF A MANAGING OR SUPERVISING LAWYER OVER NONLAWYER ASSISTANTS

In language directly parallel to that in Rule 5.1 of the Model Rules of Professional Conduct regarding the responsibilities of managerial and supervisory lawyers for other lawyers in the law firm,[24] Rule 5.3 obliges managerial and supervisory lawyers to make reasonable efforts to ensure that all nonlawyer assistants in the firm behave in a manner compatible with the lawyer's professional obligations. The ethical integrity of any law office is dependent in substantial part upon the ethical behavior of nonlawyer administrators, secretaries, paralegals, receptionists, or other assistants, especially but not only in terms of their access to confidential information.

As with Rule 5.1 which addresses the responsibilities of managerial and supervisory lawyers for the ethical conduct of other lawyers in the firm, Rule 5.3 and the accompanying comments do not set forth specific measures that must be taken in every law firm to ensure ethical behavior by nonlawyer assistants. However, the rule and comments do make plain that a lawyer may not simply hope that the right course of action will be obvious to nonlawyers or that ethical expectations will be absorbed by each assistant through osmosis simply because they are present in a law office. Indeed, the expected level of supervision over and instruction of nonlawyer assistants necessarily is higher than for another lawyer in the firm, as nonlawyers lack the professional training of a lawyer and are not themselves subject to disciplinary action.

Accordingly, a deliberate and considered plan of instruction and supervision of nonlawyer assistants is necessary,[25] with particular attention to the obligation not to disclose confidential information. Moreover, the lawyer must establish appropriate office policies and procedures designed to provide reasonable assurance that legal assistants will continue to satisfy professional expectations and to detect problems at the earliest possible stage.[26] Asking all employees to sign a confidentiality agreement is a wise and salutary measure as well, both as a reminder that confidentiality is a continuing

---

[22] On the potential cause-of-action for a discharged attorney action against a law firm alleging discharge in retaliation for insisting upon compliance with ethical standards, see *supra* § 4-3.6(b)(2).

[23] W. BRADLEY WENDEL, PROFESSIONAL RESPONSIBILITY: EXAMPLES & EXPLANATIONS 477 (Wolters Kluwer, 5th ed., 2016).

[24] *See supra* § 4-12.2.

[25] *See* Disciplinary Action Against Kellington, 852 N.W.2d 395, 403 (N.D. 2014) (finding a violation of Rule 5.3 for a lawyer's "failure to properly train her assistants," who received no orientation or training or policy or procedure manuals).

[26] *See also supra* § 4-6.5(a).

obligation and a direct means of enforcement should a person violate confidentiality after departing from the office.

The lawyer's duties of appropriate instruction and supervision under Rule 5.3 apply not only to nonlawyer assistants employed within the law office, but also to independent contractors offering services either in or outside the office. If a law firm delegates word-processing, duplication, or filing services to independent contractors, the managerial and supervisory lawyers in the firm must adopt appropriate measures to ensure that these persons also understand and adhere to professional ethical standards.[27] Speaking specifically to use of an outside computer maintenance company, the American Bar Association's Standing Committee on Ethics and Professional Responsibility advises that the law firm must "ensure that the company has in place, or will establish, reasonable procedures to protect the confidentiality" of law firm computer files.[28]

While there can be no substitute for a substantial level of internal instruction and supervision by the lawyer over nonlawyer assistants, continuing education programs offered by bar associations and other organizations (such as associations for legal administrators and legal assistants) may play a valuable role in helping legal assistants to appreciate professional standards and to learn about effective means for administering or facilitating the operation of a law practice so as to enhance compliance with ethical expectations.

As with Rule 5.1 regarding the responsibilities of managerial and supervisory lawyers for other lawyers in a firm,[29] the general ethical duty imposed by Rule 5.3 upon the managerial or supervisory lawyer with respect to legal assistants is to make reasonable efforts to ensure ethical compliance, not to guarantee appropriate behavior by legal assistants. If the lawyer has taken reasonable steps in instruction and supervision, but the legal assistant nonetheless engages in misconduct, the lawyer does not become vicariously responsible under the disciplinary rules (although she may well be civilly liable as a principal for the misconduct of a legal assistant as an agent). By contrast, if the managing lawyer does not properly supervise the legal assistant, or fails to investigate when indications of misconduct are brought to his attention, then the lawyer is subject to discipline, even though the lawyer is not directly held ethically responsible for the misconduct.[30]

Under two circumstances, however, a lawyer does become directly culpable under the disciplinary rules for the conduct of a legal assistant that would be a violation of the ethics rules if engaged in by a lawyer. First, under Rule 5.3(c)(1), a lawyer becomes responsible for the behavior of a legal assistant if the lawyer "orders or, with knowledge of the specific conduct, ratifies the conduct involved." Second, under Rule 5.3(c)(2), a managerial or supervisory lawyer who comes to "know[ ] of the [legal assistant's] conduct at a time when its consequences can be avoided or mitigated," but who then "fails to take reasonable remedial action," is held directly responsible for the misconduct. Further explanation of direct responsibility for managerial or supervisory lawyers, in the parallel

---

[27] On the ethical obligations of lawyers when outsourcing legal or nonlegal support services, see ABA Comm. on Ethics and Prof'l Responsibility, Formal Op. 08–451 (2008).

[28] ABA Comm. on Ethics and Prof'l Responsibility, Formal Op. 95–398 (1995).

[29] *See supra* § 4-12.2(a).

[30] *See* In Matter of Discipline of Donohue, No. 69228, 2016 WL 4079666, at 1–2 (Nev. 2016) (finding a violation of Rule 5.3 by a lawyer who allowed a paralegal access to funds and financial information and failed to investigate complaints that the paralegal was stealing from clients).

context of responsibility for other lawyers in a law firm, may be found in that earlier discussion.[31]

[31] *See supra* § 4-12.2(b).

# Chapter 4-13

# PUBLIC-REGARDING ACTIVITIES, DUTIES, AND RIGHTS

**By Gregory C. Sisk**

*Table of Sections*


§ 4-13.1 Lawyer Responsibilities on Bar Admission and Discipline
§ 4-13.2 Lawyer Involvement in Law Reform
§ 4-13.3 Lawyer Commentary on Judges, Legal Officers, and Candidates for Judicial or Legal Office
§ 4-13.4 Providing Legal Services to the Disadvantaged


## § 4-13.1 LAWYER RESPONSIBILITIES ON BAR ADMISSION AND DISCIPLINE

### § 4-13.1(a) The Duty to Report Professional Misconduct

#### *§ 4-13.1(a)(1) Protecting the Legal Profession by Reporting Misconduct*

If the legal profession is to preserve its integrity, it must maintain an effective and regularly-exercised means of self-regulation, including removal from the profession of those individuals who have shown a lack of fitness through professional misconduct. If lawyers prove incapable of policing their own ranks, the executive or legislative branches may intervene. If the profession loses independence from the political branches of government, the lawyer's ability to act with zealous regard for the rights of the citizenry may be weakened. For these reasons, a lawyer has a moral and a formal duty, as well as a self-interested incentive, to report the observed wrongdoing of other members of our profession, so that the disciplinary process may be invoked to protect the public from those practitioners who are not fit to maintain a legal practice.

In addition, the duty to report ethical misconduct "implies a duty by the subject attorney not to frustrate that process."[1] Thus, a lawyer commits an independent infraction if she seeks to dissuade others from filing a report of misconduct or discourages them from cooperating with a disciplinary investigation.[2] Indeed, some states expressly state that a lawyer may not attempt to negotiate an agreement or settle a matter on the condition that disciplinary conduct not be reported to the authorities.[3] In any event, an

---

1 Board of Prof'l Ethics & Conduct v. Miller, 568 N.W.2d 665, 667 (Iowa 1997); *see also* In re Kline, 311 P.3d 321, 391 (Kan. 2013) ("[B]ecause lawyers are a self-regulating profession, cooperation and honesty during the disciplinary process is crucial").

2 People v. Olson, No. 15PDJ062, 2016 WL 5076078, at *12 (Colo. O.P.D.J. July 25, 2016) (disciplining a lawyer who discouraged his former wife to testify at his disciplinary hearing by telling her to ignore the subpoena and asked her to "soften" her description of domestic violation); In re Eicher, 661 N.W.2d 354, 365 (S.D. 2003) ("The duty to report disciplinary violations also embraces a responsibility not to frustrate the reporting by others or dissuading others from cooperating in disciplinary investigations.").

3 *See* CONN. RULES OF PROF'L CONDUCT R. 8.3(a); HAW. RULES OF PROF'L CONDUCT R. 8.3(d).

attempt to obstruct the disciplinary process also constitutes conduct prejudicial to the administration of justice under Rule 8.4(d), as the "administration of justice" plainly includes the disciplinary process designed to ensure the integrity of the legal profession.

Rule 8.3(a) of the Model Rules of Professional Conduct codifies that obligation. The reporting duty is limited to those violations that truly are known to, and not merely suspected by, the reporting lawyer; to episodes that raise serious questions about the lawyer's fitness to practice; and does not override lawyer's duty to maintain client confidences.[4]

#### *§ 4-13.1(a)(2) Required Knowledge of Violation for Duty to Report*

By providing that the duty arises when the lawyer has come to "know" that another lawyer has violated the rules, Rule 8.3(a) incorporates the definition of "knows" from Rule 1.0(f) as "denot[ing] actual knowledge of the fact in question." Thus, the lawyer must have more than a subjective belief that misconduct may have occurred. Rather, the duty to report arises when the lawyer has a firm factual basis, typically grounded in personal knowledge, upon which to conclude that a violation has taken place, although absolute certainty is not necessary before the reporting requirement is triggered.

Rule 8.3(b), which imposes a duty to report the misconduct of judges, is directly parallel to Rule 8.3(a), in likewise expressing an affirmative duty to report violations by judges that are known to the lawyer.

#### *§ 4-13.1(a)(3) Duty to Report When Violation Raises Substantial Question on Fitness*

Rule 8.3(a) limits the duty to report another lawyer's misconduct to a violation of the rules "that raises a substantial question as to that lawyer's honesty, trustworthiness or fitness as a lawyer in other respects." Rule 8.3(b) similarly limits the duty to report a judge's misconduct to a matter "that raises a substantial question as to the judge's fitness for office." Comment 3 to Rule 8.3 explains that a duty to report every violation of the rules would be "unenforceable" and that the reporting obligation should be limited "to those offenses that a self-regulating profession must vigorously endeavor to prevent."

In making this judgment, however, the lawyer should consider whether what appeared to be an insignificant violation might instead be part of a larger pattern of misconduct. The lawyer should be aware that what might appear to be an insubstantial or technical violation could be the first manifestation of a lawyer's personal problems infecting the practice of law, for which an early intervention by the disciplinary authorities could be salutary.

### § 4-13.1(b) Confidentiality as an Exception to the Duty to Report

Under Rule 8.3(c) of the Model Rules of Professional Conduct, the duty to report misconduct by a lawyer or judge does not require disclosure of information that is protected under attorney-client confidentiality. The reporting requirement does not supersede the lawyer's more fundamental duty to preserve confidential information,[5] absent the client's informed consent to any disclosure.

---

[4] On the confidentiality exception to the duty to report, see *infra* § 4-13.1.

[5] *See supra* §§ 4-6.1 to 4-6.2.

Given the breadth of and high priority given to protection of client confidences, the confidentiality exception to the reporting requirement often suspends the mandatory obligations of Rule 8.3(a) and (b).[6] Under Rule 1.6(a), a lawyer has an obligation to refrain from disclosing any "information relating to representation of a client" that the client has not consented to reveal. Comment 3 to Rule 1.6 observes that "[t]he confidentiality rule, for example, applies not only to matters communicated in confidence by the client but also to all information relating to the representation, whatever its source."

Lawyers ordinarily will learn of the misconduct of other lawyers during the course of representation of a client. Accordingly, knowledge of another lawyer's misconduct "almost always" will fall within the realm of confidential information.[7] There will be exceptions to this pattern, such as when the lawyer observes misconduct while not representing a client, learns of misconduct through a confession by a colleague,[8] or discovers that a partner or associate within the same firm has misappropriated funds. But, most of the time, the lawyer's authority to report misconduct by another will depend upon the client's willingness to consent to that disclosure. Disclosure should be obtained only after the client has been fully informed of the consequences, which may include the client's need to testify in a disciplinary proceeding or public attention being attracted to the matter in the event of a successful prosecution of the offending lawyer for misconduct.

In some cases, the client may be quite willing, even eager, to authorize her lawyer to report misconduct by another lawyer. However, clients, even those who have pursued malpractice actions against a former lawyer, often are exhausted by the conclusion of litigation, inclined to leave a painful experience in the past, and reluctant to serve as a witness in the disciplinary process.

Nonetheless, Comment 2 to Rule 8.3 says that "a lawyer should encourage a client to consent to disclosure where prosecution [of the professional misconduct] would not substantially prejudice the client's interests." While the client is entitled to make the final decision on whether to waive confidentiality, and should be fully informed as to the processes that may follow a complaint to disciplinary authorities, the lawyer should also explain the importance of the disciplinary process and the value of that process in protecting other persons from being subjected to similar misconduct. Moreover, the lawyer's willingness to serve as a supporting friend to the client during the disciplinary process—presumably at no additional cost to the client but as the lawyer's contribution to enhancement of our profession—may make the client more willing to pursue a complaint directly or authorize the necessary disclosure for the lawyer to do so.

The well-known lawyer-reporting-duty decision of the Illinois Supreme Court in *In re Himmel*[9] does not, given the unusual circumstances of that case, contradict the

---

[6] On the breadth of the confidentiality exception to the reporting requirement, as well as the reasons that confidentiality takes priority, see generally Peter K. Rofes, *Another Misunderstood Relation: Confidentiality and the Duty to Report*, 14 GEO. J. LEGAL ETHICS 621 (2001).

[7] *See* STEPHEN GILLERS, REGULATION OF LAWYERS: PROBLEMS OF LAW AND ETHICS 536 (10th ed., Wolters Kluwer, 2015).

[8] Matter of Riehlmann, 891 So.2d 1239 (La. 2005) (a former prosecutor confessed to a lawyer friend that he had suppressed exculpatory evidence in a prior case resulting in an innocent man being sentenced to death).

[9] 533 N.E.2d 790, 791–94 (Ill. 1988). On the *Himmel* case, see generally Ronald Rotunda, *The Lawyer's Duty to Report Another Lawyer's Unethical Violations in the Wake of* Himmel, 1988 U. ILL. L. REV. 977.

traditional understanding that client confidentiality supersedes the reporting requirement. In any event, *Himmel* was not an application of the particular standard of confidentiality now articulated in Rule 8.3(c). In *Himmel*, the lawyer on behalf of a client suing a former lawyer for misappropriation of client money proceeded to negotiate a settlement under which the miscreant lawyer agreed, not only to refund the money converted, but to pay a much larger sum. In return, the client agreed not to report the former lawyer's misconduct to disciplinary or law enforcement officials. Because the lawyer and client thus accepted a direct payment in exchange for silence about criminal misconduct, they had committed the crime of compounding under state law.[10] Moreover, the client had surrendered the attorney-client privilege under the unusual circumstances of the case: conversations in the presence of unnecessary third persons, communications with an insurance company, an apparent prior initial report to disciplinary authorities, and the filing of the civil suit. Accordingly, as Professors Geoffrey Hazard and William Hodes and attorney Peter Jarvis caution, "*In re Himmel* was an important case in that the court took the reporting requirement seriously as an independent element of the law of lawyering and forced the profession to do likewise. It should not be read, however, as a radical departure, heralding a new era of routine reports to the disciplinary authority."[11]

Notwithstanding *Himmel* with its unusual and egregious facts, Rule 8.3(c) of the Model Rules of Professional Conduct today expressly states that the lawyer's superior duty is to protect all confidential client information, and not only that subset of information that is subject to the attorney-client privilege.

### § 4-13.1(c) Protection of Information Gained Within an Approved Lawyers Assistance Program

Every state bar association has created a program to encourage lawyers suffering from substance abuse or other addictive behavior to seek counseling and treatment. Such lawyer assistance programs allow lawyers to share their stories to provide support and personal evidence of successful recovery from addictive behavior. To ensure the success of the program, and to encourage lawyers to seek help, confidentiality must be guaranteed.

In recognition of the great value of these programs, Rule 8.3(c) of the Model Rules of Professional Conduct does not require disclosure of information regarding potential misconduct by lawyers or judges that was gained by a lawyer participating in the program. As Comment 5 to Rule 8.3 says, without such an exception from the reporting requirement, "lawyers and judges may hesitate to seek assistance from these programs, which may then result in additional harm to their professional careers and additional injury to the welfare of clients and the public."

Accordingly, when a lawyer serving as a counselor or involved with a group session at an approved lawyer assistance program learns of behavior by a lawyer that may constitute professional misconduct, the duty to report imposed by Rule 8.3 is suspended.

---

[10] On the question of a lawyer participating in an agreement to withhold a criminal complaint as part of settlement of a controversy, provided there is a fair recovery and not a bonus payment for silence, see *supra* § 4-9.4(c).

[11] 2 GEOFFREY C. HAZARD, JR., W. WILLIAM HODES & PETER R. JARVIS, THE LAW OF LAWYERING § 68.11 (Aspen, 4th ed., 2016).

### § 4-13.1(d) Duty of Candor with Respect to Regulation of the Bar

Rule 8.1 of the Model Rules of Professional Conduct imposes a duty of candor on lawyers and applicants for admission to the bar. They are expected to be truthful in making statements, have an affirmative duty to volunteer information to correct a misapprehension, and maintain an obligation to cooperate with lawful demands for information by admissions or disciplinary authorities.

Evaluation of applications for admission to the bar and the professional disciplinary process are "the twin pillars of self-regulation by the legal profession."[12] Admission to the bar is restricted to those who possess the necessary legal education, have good moral character, and demonstrate fitness. For those already so admitted, professional misconduct may be investigated and prosecuted. In these ways, the lawyer admissions and disciplinary authorities seek to ensure that those who hold themselves out to the public as legal counselors have excellent qualifications and superior standards of character and behavior. If the admissions and disciplinary authorities, under the supervisory review of the courts, are to uphold these vital gatekeeping responsibilities, they must receive accurate information from those who are members of, or seek membership in, our profession.

Because honesty is one of the hallmarks of the professional,[13] Rule 8.1 as applied to lawyers is chiefly a reminder that the admissions and disciplinary processes depend upon the forthright cooperation of all members of our profession. The rule, however, is also extended to those in transition to bar membership, namely those who are applying for admission to the bar. If a person knowingly makes a false statement while seeking admission to the bar, that deceit is not only a basis for denying admission, but also for later disciplinary sanction if the person should be admitted. For a lawyer, the duties in Rule 8.1 apply not only to those admissions or disciplinary matters that involve the lawyer's own qualifications, character, or conduct, but also to representations made (or information possessed) about others who are seeking admission to the bar or are subject to the disciplinary process and about whom the lawyer has knowledge. Again, the rule is designed not only to insist upon candor by those directly subject to evaluation in the admission or disciplinary process, but also to encourage every lawyer to participate in the self-regulation of our profession.

Under Rule 8.1(a), applicants for admission to the bar and lawyers are forbidden from knowingly making a false statement of material fact with respect to an application for admission or a disciplinary matter. A prohibition against deliberate deceit is unremarkable, if sadly necessary.

Rule 8.1(b) goes a significant step farther and imposes affirmative obligations both (1) to volunteer information when necessary "to correct a misapprehension" that the person knows has arisen, and (2) to respond to a "lawful demand" for information from admissions or disciplinary authorities. The affirmative duty to correct a misapprehension applies even if the lawyer or applicant has no responsibility for the original misunderstanding[14] (although typically the misapprehension will be

---

[12] 2 GEOFFREY C. HAZARD, JR., W. WILLIAM HODES & PETER R. JARVIS, THE LAW OF LAWYERING § 66.02 (Aspen, 4th ed., 2016).

[13] *See supra* § 4-9.5(a).

[14] 2 GEOFFREY C. HAZARD, JR., W. WILLIAM HODES & PETER R. JARVIS, THE LAW OF LAWYERING § 66.05 (Aspen, 4th ed., 2016).

attributable to the lawyer's or applicant's own prior statements). The prohibition against knowingly failing to respond to requests for information by the admissions and disciplinary officials is a somewhat self-enforcing one, because such a failure likely will result in denial of admission to the bar or a sanction for non-cooperation with the disciplinary process.

### § 4-13.1(e) The Privilege Against Self-Incrimination, Confidentiality, and Unlawful Demands

No exception could be accepted to the duty not to make a false statement of material fact in an admissions or disciplinary matter. Nonetheless, the affirmative duties to volunteer information to correct a misapprehension that has arisen and to respond to a request by admissions or disciplinary authorities are subject to several exceptions:

#### *§ 4-13.1(e)(1) Privilege Against Self-Incrimination*

As Comment 2 to Rule 8.1 explains, the rule must surrender to the constitutional privilege against self-incrimination protected by the Fifth Amendment to the United States Constitution. In *Spevak v. Klein*,[15] the Supreme Court held that a lawyer may not be required to incriminate himself at the risk of professional discipline. While the attorney is obliged to respond to a complaint or request for information from the attorney disciplinary authorities, the attorney against whom a professional misconduct complaint is filed is not required to answer an interrogatory, request for admission, or deposition question if the answer would be self-incriminatory. The privilege against self-incrimination must be openly and timely asserted,[16] and the invocation must be limited to matters that reasonably could call for an incriminating answer.[17]

#### *§ 4-13.1(e)(2) Client Confidentiality*

As is true with respect to the lawyer's duty to report misconduct by a lawyer or judge under Rule 8.3(c),[18] the lawyer's duty to volunteer information and respond to requests by admissions and disciplinary authorities under Rule 8.1(b) does not require disclosure of information that is protected as confidential by Rule 1.6 or by the attorney-client privilege. Again, the general duty to provide information to admissions or disciplinary authorities does not supersede the lawyer's more fundamental duty to protect confidential information absent client consent.

While this confidentiality exception applies most obviously, as Comment 3 to Rule 8.1 recognizes, to "a lawyer representing an applicant for admission to the bar, or representing a lawyer who is the subject of a disciplinary inquiry or proceeding," it reaches further. If a lawyer is called as a witness in a disciplinary proceeding against another lawyer, the lawyer may not disclose information that is subject to client confidentiality, either by affirmative statement or in response to a question. The lawyer who is the actual respondent to a professional misconduct complaint is authorized by the self-defense exception to Rule 1.6(b)(5) to use confidential information when necessary "to respond to allegations in any proceeding concerning the lawyer's representation of

---

[15] 385 U.S. 511, 514 (1967).

[16] In re Warburgh, 644 F.3d 173, 177 n.3 (2d Cir. 2011).

[17] In re Holliday, 15 So.3d 82, 94 (La. 2009) ("[T]he protection of the Fifth Amendment must be confined to instances where the witness has reasonable cause to apprehend danger from a direct answer.").

[18] *See supra* § 4-13.1(c).

the client."[19] By contrast, a lawyer who appears only as a witness and who is not charged with misconduct may not invoke the self-defense exception to confidentiality, although the disciplinary authorities presumably could subpoena the lawyer's client to obtain the information directly.[20]

#### *§ 4-13.1(e)(3) Lawful Demand for Information*

By the terms of Rule 8.1(b), the duty to respond to a request by admissions or disciplinary authorities arises only with respect to a "lawful demand." If the demand by the authorities for information is unlawful, such as by requesting disclosure of political beliefs or associations contrary to First Amendment rights of free expression, by inquiring into matters of physical or mental health in a manner that violates the federal Americans with Disabilities Act,[21] or by otherwise improperly extending beyond what the law authorizes, the applicant or lawyer is not obliged to respond, although raising an objection and explaining the reason for non-response ordinarily would be expected.

## § 4-13.2 LAWYER INVOLVEMENT IN LAW REFORM

### § 4-13.2(a) Lawyer's General Freedom to Engage in Law Reform Notwithstanding Client Interest

Many lawyers admirably participate in legal reform efforts, seeking to bring about a more just society by advocating changes in the law or improvements in the administration of the law through public education and contributions to public debate; drafting or commenting on proposed court or agency rules, legislation, or other potentially authoritative sources of law (such as the influential *Restatements of the Law* adopted by the American Law Institute); writing articles or books that promote reform of the law; preparing amicus curiae briefs on behalf of public interest organizations; and legislative or agency lobbying.

When a lawyer acts as a public citizen or participates with a law reform organization, the lawyer ordinarily is not representing a client and the ethics rules thus do not apply as straightforwardly or as strictly to that conduct.

While the lawyer has a duty of loyalty to a client, that loyalty does not entail an obligation to adopt the ideology or political views of that client. Rule 1.2(b) of the Model Rules of Professional Conduct confirms that "[a] lawyer's representation of a client, including representation by appointment, does not constitute an endorsement of the client's political, economic, social or moral views or activities." Accordingly, a lawyer ordinarily remains free to take positions on public issues or become involved in legal reform work without being obliged to espouse the views of a client or consider how proposed changes in the law might affect a client.

To confirm that the conflict of interest rules generally do not apply in this context, Rule 6.4 of the Model Rules of Professional Conduct states that "[a] lawyer may serve as a director, officer or member of an organization involved in reform of the law or its administration notwithstanding that the reform may affect the interests of a client of the lawyer." Thus, a lawyer need not conduct a conflicts check whenever the lawyer

---

[19] *See supra* § 4-6.6(f).

[20] 2 GEOFFREY C. HAZARD, JR., W. WILLIAM HODES & PETER R. JARVIS, THE LAW OF LAWYERING §§ 66.07 to 66.08 (Aspen, 4th ed., 2016).

[21] 42 U.S.C. §§ 12101–213.

speaks or participates as a public citizen with respect to law reform. Nor does a client who is unhappy with the lawyer's law reform activities ordinarily have a legitimate complaint that the lawyer has breached a formal professional duty. A lawyer is entitled to a sphere of political freedom in which to participate as a citizen in public life, without being accountable to a client who may disagree with or even be affected by a law reform proposal but which does not directly harm an ongoing representation.

### § 4-13.2(b) Law Reform Activities and Conflicts of Interest

When a lawyer advocates a change in the law that would negatively impact a client, an appearance could arise that the lawyer thereby has a conflict of interest with the complaining or affected client. In some circumstances, the representation may be materially harmed such that a true conflict of interest has arisen that requires the lawyer's withdrawal.

As Comment 1 to Rule 6.4 cautions, "[i]n determining the nature and scope of participation in [law reform] activities, a lawyer should be mindful of obligations to clients under other Rules, particularly Rule 1.7."

A conflict of interest may emerge if (1) a lawyer advances a proposed reform or change in the law that directly contradicts the client's objectives in an ongoing representation or (2) if the lawyer's involvement in a law reform activity has changed the lawyer's attitude toward that client in a manner that would undermine the representation or that compromises the lawyer's ability to represent the client. In other words, a conflict of interest could arise by reason of the lawyer's non-representational law reform activities in two particular ways: (1) a concrete injury to the representation by reason of the lawyer's public association with advocacy contrary to the material interests of a client; or (2) a personal conflict of interest created by the lawyer's growing antipathy to the client generated by the lawyer's law reform efforts which thus impairs the lawyer's ability to provide zealous and diligent representation.

First, if the lawyer becomes publicly associated with a position antithetical to that of the client on a subject directly related to the representation, the lawyer's representation may be weakened and the client's faith in the lawyer may be shaken. A comment to the American Law Institute's *Restatement of the Law Governing Lawyers* states that "a lawyer may not publicly take a policy position that is adverse to the position of a client that the lawyer is currently representing if doing so would materially and adversely affect the lawyer's representation of the client in the matter."[22] For example, if a lawyer represents a casino on regulatory compliance while simultaneously becoming prominently involved in a campaign to abolish gambling in the state, the lawyer's reform activity necessarily injures the representation given that the lawyer is effectively working to destroy the client's business through changes in the law.

Second, under Rule 1.7(a)(2), a lawyer has a conflict of interest if there is "a significant risk" that a representation "will be materially limited" by "a personal interest of the lawyer." If a lawyer has a personal stake, interest, belief, position, or relationship that might compromise her independent professional judgment on behalf of a client,[23] a

---

[22] RESTATEMENT (THIRD) OF THE LAW GOVERNING LAWYERS § 125, cmt. 3 (American Law Institute, 2000). *See generally* John Dzienkowski, *Positional Conflicts of Interest*, 71 TEXAS L. REV. 457, 535 (1993) ("The focus of inquiry in a positional conflict between a present client and a law reform activity should be the potential injury to the client representation.").

[23] On personal conflicts of interest, see *supra* § 4-7.4(c)(2).

conflict of interest exists and the lawyer may not proceed, at least without informed consent by the client. When the personal interest is sufficiently compelling in its influence that the lawyer could not "reasonably believe" that she would still "be able to provide competent and diligent representation" to the client, as required by Rule 1.7(b)(1), then the conflict is nonconsentable.[24]

Even if the circumstances do not create an objective conflict of interest from the perspective of an outside observer—and Rule 6.4 disclaims a conflict of interest based solely on a lawyer's general participation in a law reform activity—a lawyer nonetheless has an impermissible personal conflict of interest if the lawyer's personal beliefs and activities undermine the lawyer's continuing loyalty to the client. Suppose that a lawyer represents the owner of a gun shop on transactions with suppliers and tax matters, while simultaneously pursuing law reform proposals to restrict the private ownership of firearms. If the lawyer, during the course of the lawyer's reform activities, were to develop repugnance toward firearms retailers, regarding them as unsavory weapons dealers whose trade harms society, a conflict of interest may arise, and the lawyer may be unable to continue representation of that client.

### § 4-13.2(c) Client's Right to Discharge Lawyer Based on Law Reform Activities

The client's prerogative on choice of counsel remains an important qualification on a lawyer's freedom to engage in law reform exercises. While the client generally may not assert professional misconduct because the lawyer advocates a position in the public square that does not correspond to the preferred views of the client, the client is entitled to discharge the lawyer if the client is offended by the lawyer's conduct or statements in the lawyer's personal or public life. As a general rule, a client may discharge the lawyer for any reason or for no reason.[25]

The attorney-client relationship is a uniquely confidential and fiduciary one. The client extends personal trust to the lawyer, is encouraged to share the most intimate of secrets with the lawyer, and delegates authority to the lawyer to take actions that may have great significance for the life, prosperity, and even liberty of the client. If the trust that is at the heart of the attorney-client relationship is lost, the client generally must be permitted to end the relationship and be able to do so at no penalty. While a lawyer ordinarily commits no professional misconduct by undertaking law reform activities with which a client disagrees, the lawyer still may not foist his professional services upon an unwilling recipient.

In sum, because of the fiduciary and confidential nature of the attorney-client relationship, the client may insist upon choosing a different lawyer with whose expressed views the client is more comfortable, even though the client may not as a matter of formal obligation impose a worldview or perspective upon the lawyer.

### § 4-13.2(d) Duty of Lawyer to Law Reform Organization

Rule 6.4 also creates a professional duty on the part of the lawyer with respect to the law reform organization in which the lawyer participates. Recognizing that a lawyer's relationship with and loyalty to a client may influence the lawyer's attitude

---

[24] On the continuing duty of competent and diligent representation, despite supposed client consent to a conflict, see *supra* § 4-7.4(c)(2).

[25] *See supra* § 4-3.6(b)(1).

(positively or negatively) toward a legal reform proposal being considered by an organization, Rule 6.4 imposes an enforceable duty of disclosure on the lawyer.

Under Rule 6.4, "[w]hen the lawyer knows that the interests of a client may be materially benefitted by a decision in which the lawyer participates" as part of a law reform organization, the lawyer must "disclose that fact" to the organization, "but need not identify the client." While the rule does not require the lawyer to recuse himself from such decisions, the mandated disclosure ensures that other participants in the decision are aware of the lawyer's affiliation with that client and can take it into account in considering the persuasiveness of the lawyer's views expressed on the law reform issue before the organization.

The law reform organization remains free to adopt more stringent constraints to reduce outside influences on law reform activities, including demanding greater disclosure or requiring a lawyer to recuse herself from decisions affecting client interests. This is a matter of internal concern for the organization rather than a subject for professional discipline.

## § 4-13.3 LAWYER COMMENTARY ON JUDGES, LEGAL OFFICERS, AND CANDIDATES FOR JUDICIAL OR LEGAL OFFICE

### § 4-13.3(a) The Value of Informed Commentary by Lawyers on Legal Officers and Judges

Rule 8.2(a) of the Model Rules of Professional Conduct directs a lawyer not to "make a statement that the lawyer knows to be false or with reckless disregard as to its truth or falsity concerning the qualifications or integrity of a judge, adjudicatory officer or public legal officer, or of a candidate for election or appointment to judicial or legal office." Similarly, the *Restatement of the Law Governing Lawyers* provides that "[a] lawyer may not knowingly or recklessly make publicly a false statement of fact concerning the qualifications or integrity of an incumbent of a judicial office."[26]

When commenting on the qualifications and integrity of a particular public official charged with responsibility for the administration of justice, a lawyer's prevarications may have deleterious consequences both for the morale of public officials and for public respect for the law. When a lawyer impugns the basic credentials or character of a judge or other legal official such as the attorney general, a prosecutor, or a public defender, and does so with reckless disregard for the truth, public confidence may be undermined in the administration of justice. If candidates for a judicial or other legal office are subjected to character or credential assassination by those who knowingly or recklessly level false accusations of past misconduct or fact-based ineptitude, people of good character and qualifications will be less willing to be considered for such positions.

At the same time, the judicial branch of government is hardly immune from criticism in a free society. "Ethical rules that prohibit false statements impugning the integrity of judges . . . are not designed to shield judges from unpleasant or offensive criticism, but to preserve public confidence in the fairness and impartiality of our system of justice."[27] Even less so should legal officers in the political branches of government be

---

[26] RESTATEMENT (THIRD) OF THE LAW GOVERNING LAWYERS § 114 (American Law Institute, 2000).

[27] Standing Comm. on Discipline of the U.S. Dist. Ct. v. Yagman, 55 F.3d 1430, 1437 (9th Cir. 1995).

heard to complain too readily about the rough-and-tumble style of political disputation in American society.

With their advanced legal education and greater familiarity with the substance and process of the law, lawyers are especially well-positioned to provide an informed critique of the legal system and its participants.[28] A lawyer may have an honest and intelligently-formed—but negative—appraisal of a candidate for judicial or other legal office. Or, after reasonable inquiry, a lawyer may reach a sincere conclusion that a judicial or other legal officer has failed in a material way to uphold the expectations of that office. That lawyer should be encouraged to appropriately share that opinion or information so that those unfit for office are not selected, those who have abused such an office are disciplined or removed, and the legal system may be reformed. As Professor Charles Wolfram wrote, "[i]f lawyers were reluctant to call public attention to judicial shortcomings, most incompetent or corrupt judges would probably remain unchastened on the bench."[29]

Especially when speaking other than as a representative of a party in a particular case,[30] a lawyer has the same fundamental right of freedom of speech as do other citizens. Public debate about legal actors should not be unduly chilled nor should an official orthodoxy as to acceptable viewpoints about judicial and legal matters be imposed by the very judicial and legal officials who may be the subject of criticism. Disciplinary authorities must be quite restrained when considering disciplinary action against public lawyer speech.

### § 4-13.3(b) The Disciplinary Standard of Knowing Falsity or Reckless Disregard for Truth

In the celebrated First Amendment case of *New York Times Co. v. Sullivan*,[31] the Supreme Court held that a statement about a public official may be punished only if the statement was both false and made with "actual malice." The Court termed "actual malice" as a statement made either with knowledge that it was false or with reckless disregard as to its truth or falsity. By prohibiting statements about judicial or other public officers "that the lawyer knows to be false or with reckless disregard as to its truth or falsity," the drafters of Rule 8.2(a) of the Model Rules of Professional Conduct apparently intended to adopt the free speech standard articulated in *New York Times v. Sullivan*.[32]

Nonetheless, while the "reckless disregard" standard in the *New York Times* case with respect to defamation of public officials "requires more than a departure from reasonably prudent conduct,"[33] the majority of states have concluded that "the interests protected by the disciplinary system call for a test less stringent than the *New York*

---

[28] Hancock v. Board of Prof'l Responsibility, 447 S.W.3d 844, 854 (Tenn. 2014) (saying that "attorneys are in the best position to know the 'character and efficiency of our judges' ").

[29] CHARLES W. WOLFRAM, MODERN LEGAL ETHICS § 11.3.2 (West, 1986).

[30] For discussion of the lawyer's duty to avoid conduct that disrupts a proceeding before at tribunal, which includes a necessary measure of decorum, see *supra* § 4-9.9(a). For a discussion of limitations on extrajudicial speech by a lawyer who is representing a party when such speech may materially prejudice an adjudicative proceeding, see *supra* § 4-9.11.

[31] 376 U.S. 254, 279–80 (1964).

[32] *See* 2 GEOFFREY C. HAZARD, JR., W. WILLIAM HODES & PETER R. JARVIS, THE LAW OF LAWYERING §§ 67.02, 67.04 (Aspen, 4th ed., 2016).

[33] Harte-Hanks Comm., Inc. v. Connaughton, 491 U.S. 657, 688 (1989).

*Times* standard."[34] The New York Court of Appeals protested that the *New York Times* "subjective" standard "would immunize all accusations, however reckless or irresponsible, from censure as long as the attorney uttering them did not actually entertain serious doubts as to their truth."[35] The Supreme Judicial Court of Massachusetts argued that while a different standard may apply to "free and public debate in our society," greater regulation of attorney speech "is essential to the orderly and judicious presentation of cases in a court room."[36]

A few courts have suggested that the prohibition in Rule 8.2(a) should be applied less strictly in the context of such public speech as election campaigning than to statements made in the course of litigation.[37] In *Attorney Grievance Commission v. Stanalonis*,[38] the Maryland Court of Appeals declined to find that a candidate for judicial office had violated Rule 8.2 through an exaggerated description of an opponent's position on an issue. The court observed that, even if the objective test for Rule 8.2 is normally applied, "there is a significant argument that a subjective test should be applied in an election context, in light of the 'core' First Amendment values at stake."[39] As the Maryland court observed, "there inevitably is some imprecision in language used during the heat of a political campaign," and "campaign flyers are not appellate briefs."[40] Given the Supreme Court's repeated admonition that speech about candidates for public office, including judicial candidates, is "at the core of our First Amendment freedoms,"[41] restrictions on speech in an election context through professional discipline rules are especially vulnerable to constitutional challenge.

Even assuming a standard less strict than that stated in *New York Times*, the United States Court of Appeals for the Sixth Circuit held the Kentucky version of Rule 8.2(a) unconstitutional as applied to a lawyer's public criticism of a state commission's investigation of alleged fund-raising violations by a legislator. In *Berry v. Schmidt*,[42] a lawyer protested the closure of a state legislative ethics commission to the public and media, while the legislator was permitted to remain, as giving "grave cause for some to speculate that the deck was stacked." After a lengthy investigation by the Inquiry Commission of the Kentucky Bar Association, disciplinary charges were dismissed. Nonetheless, the commission issued a warning letter finding that the lawyer had violated Kentucky's Rule 8.2(a) "by publicly implying that the Legislative Ethics Commission did not conduct its review appropriately." The Sixth Circuit in *Berry* ruled

---

[34] Attorney Disciplinary Bd. v. Weaver, 750 N.W.2d 71, 80–81 (Iowa 2008); *see also* In re Graham, 453 N.W.2d 313, 322 (Minn. 1990). *But see* Margaret Tarkington, *The Truth be Damned: The First Amendment, Attorney Speech, and Judicial Reputation*, 97 GEO. J. LEGAL ETHICS 1567, 1575 (2009) (arguing that "attorney speech critical of the judiciary is core political speech entitled to the fullest protection offered by the Constitution and clearly falls within *Sullivan*" and the required showing of knowledge or a reckless disregard to falsity).

[35] In re Holtzman, 577 N.E.2d 30, 43 (N.Y. 1991).

[36] In re Cobb, 838 N.E.2d 1197, 1214 (Mass. 2005).

[37] *See also* Brian G. Liegel, Note, *A Higher Bar: The Search for Restrictions on Attorney Criticism of Judges on Blogs*, 27 GEO. J. LEGAL ETHICS 689, 690 (2014) (proposing a test for Rule 8.2 that "would weigh the public utility of the criticism [of judges] against its harm to the administration of justice").

[38] 126 A-3d 6 (Md. Ct. App. 2015).

[39] *Id.* at 15; *see also* In re Charges of Unprofl Conduct, 720 N.W.2d 807, 813–15 (Minn. 2006) (suggesting, without deciding, that a subjective test for Rule 8.2 may apply in election context).

[40] *Stanalonis*, 126 A.2d at 13.

[41] Republican Party of Minn. v. White, 536 U.S. 765, 774 (2002); *see also* Williams-Yulee v. Florida Bar, 135 S. Ct. 1656, 1665 (2015) (plurality) (applying strict scrutiny to restrictions on speech of judicial candidates).

[42] 688 F.3d 290, 294–95, 302–04 (6th Cir. 2012).

that the lawyer's statement—"conveying the public's belief that the 'deck was stacked'—is opinion protected by the First Amendment." Because the lawyer was speaking as an interested member of the public, the court took "no position on whether our analysis would be different if it involved an attorney speaking during judicial proceedings."

### § 4-13.3(c) Lawyer Speech in the Courtroom About Judges

Because a judicial proceeding is a non-public forum, "lawyers' speech in trial, depositions, formal and informal pretrial proceedings (such as letters to other lawyers), and court filings may be subject to reasonable regulations."[43] Even in judicial proceedings, however, strident and arguably offensive attorney speech should not lightly be sanctioned or disciplined. Context is important. For example, courts have recognized that a lawyer challenging the impartiality of a judge, such as through a motion to recuse, necessarily must assert bias as an element of the request and should be allowed reasonable breathing room to do so when a plausible, even if mistaken, basis is present to make such a claim.[44] As the Fifth Circuit said in *United States v. Brown*,[45] "[a]ttorneys should be free to challenge, in appropriate legal proceedings, a court's perceived partiality without the court misconstruing such a challenge as an assault on the integrity of the court. Such challenges should, however, be made only when substantiated by the trial record." Similarly, the Indiana Supreme Court said in *In Re Dixon*[46] that "attorneys need wide latitude in engaging in robust and effective advocacy on behalf of their clients—particularly on issues . . . that *require* criticism of a judge or a judge's ruling." With that in mind, the court interpreted Rule 8.2(a) as "least restrictive" of critical speech "when an attorney is engaged in good faith professional advocacy in a legal proceeding requiring critical assessment of a judge or a judge's decision."

Professor Margaret Tarkington relates a rather jarring episode when judicial misconduct was passed over lightly while the attorney who called it out was heavily criticized and suspended from practice.[47] In *In re Atanga*,[48] an African-American criminal defense attorney was held in contempt for missing a hearing rescheduled on an *ex parte* request by the prosecutor, even though the trial judge was aware the attorney had a conflicting court appearance in another county. In behavior outrageous both in its extremity and racial overtones, the judge had the attorney arrested at his office and jailed. This judge then paraded the lawyer into an auxiliary jail courtroom in jail garb to respond to the contempt and represent his client in the pending motion, before an audience of prosecuting attorneys and several reporters. In a later interview with a civil liberties newsletter, the attorney offered the blunt, but under the circumstances rather restrained, assessment of the judge as "ignorant, insecure, and racist."

For his effrontery, the lawyer was suspended for a month for violating Rule 8.2 and accused by the Indiana Supreme Court of "greatly impairing" the "judicial institution"

---

[43] W. Bradley Wendel, *Free Speech for Lawyers*, HASTINGS CONST. L.Q. 305, 443–44 (2001).

[44] *See generally* Margaret Tarkington, *Attorney Speech and the Right to an Impartial Adjudicator*, 30 REV. LITIG. 849, 850 (2011) (recognizing that if client due process rights to impartial adjudication are to be meaningful, "then attorneys need to be free to fully pursue the protection of the due process right on behalf of their clients"); Margaret Tarkington, *A Free Speech Right to Impugn Judicial Integrity in Court Proceedings*, 51 B.C. L. REV. 363, 377 (2010) ("[I]n order for litigants to meaningfully assert of these rights [to judicial impartiality], attorneys must be allowed to express them.").

[45] 72 F.3d 25, 29 (5th Cir. 2006).

[46] 994 N.E.2d 1129, 1138 (Ind. 2013).

[47] Tarkington, *supra*, 97 GEO. L.J. at 1607–08.

[48] 636 N.E.2d 1253, 1255–57 (Ind. 1994) (per curiam).

by "assault[ing] the integrity of the process and the individuals called upon to make decisions."[49] The same court was rather muted in commentary on the judge's conduct, describing the requirement the attorney represent a client in jail attire as a "questionable practice."[50] As Professor Tarkington well-summarizes and appropriately deprecates, the lawyer "received a significantly harsher punishment for his speech regarding [the judge's] abuse of power than [the judge] received for the underlying abuse."[51]

### § 4-13.3(d) Limiting Discipline to False Factual Statements About Legal Officers or Judges

In or out of the courtroom, formal punishment of an attorney for speech can only be justified when applied to scurrilous factual accusations rather than hyperbolic expressions of opinion. Rule 8.2(a) of the Model Rules of Professional Conduct prohibits a lawyer from making a "statement" about "the qualifications or integrity" of a judicial or legal officer that the lawyer knows is false or that is made with reckless disregard for its truth or falsity. By its terms, then, the rule is reserved for the case in which a lawyer's allegedly false declaration is one of objective fact, the accuracy of which can be convincingly determined by an impartial fact-finder.

Thus, if a lawyer knowingly, or with reckless disregard for the truth, were to falsely accuse a judge of fairly specific and material misconduct on the bench, allege corruption activity or collusion by a judge with party actors without basis,[52] or dishonestly describe the particular training or other credentials of a candidate for judicial or other legal office, discipline may be justified. By contrast, the attorney who incorporates excessive rhetoric into a submission to a court likely will suffer the immediate sanction of undermining his persuasiveness with the tribunal, but such generally-stated and hyperbolic criticisms of a judicial decision would not justify formal discipline under the objectively-false statement standard adopted through Rule 8.2(a).[53]

When applied cautiously, the professional disciplinary process is an appropriate mechanism to address factually false statements charging specific misconduct by or deficiencies in a judge or legal officer or candidate for such office. By contrast, when a lawyer expresses a general and unfavorable view about the capabilities of an individual who holds or has been nominated for a judgeship or about the merits of a decision rendered by a court, the professional disciplinary process is the wrong venue for challenging the wisdom of the lawyer's opinion. The illegitimacy of professional discipline to define the permissible scope of lawyer viewpoints is even more clear in the

---

[49] *Id.* at 1258.

[50] *Id.* at 1257.

[51] Tarkington, *supra*, 97 GEO. L.J. at 1608.

[52] *See* Attorney Grievance Comm'n v. Frost, 85 A.3d 264, 274 (Md. 2014) ("Allegations of corruption tend to discredit the public's trust and confidence in the judiciary and judicial system.").

[53] *See, e.g.*, Standing Comm. on Discipline of the U.S. Dist. Ct. v. Yagman, 55 F.3d 1430, 1440–41 (9th Cir. 1995) (saying that criticisms by a lawyer of the quality of a judicial decision or its reasoning, such as labeling it as "intellectually-dishonest" or "result-oriented," are not susceptible to professional discipline because such statements "cannot be proved true or false by reference to a 'core of objective evidence' "); Berry v. Schmidt, 688 F.3d 290, 303–04 (6th Cir. 2012) (adopting *Yagman* standard that a lawyer's opinion may be subject to discipline only if it declares actual facts that are capable of being proven true or false); In re Green, 11 P.3d 1078, 1083–86 (Colo. 2000) (applying the actual malice test of *New York Times v. Sullivan* and concluding that an attorney's characterization of a judge as "racist and bigot" with a "bent of mind" were opinions based upon fully disclosed and uncontested facts that could not be the basis of discipline).

context of comments about a candidate who has submitted her name for elective office. Nor should a lawyer be disciplined for an unfortunate tone or rudeness in complaining about legal or judicial matters or events when the expression has not actually disrupted a judicial proceeding or concretely prejudiced the administration of justice. The formal disciplinary process cannot be the means by which professional courtesy is advanced.[54]

Especially when a lawyer is speaking outside the courtroom and is expressing himself as a citizen rather than as an advocate with respect to an ongoing litigation matter, the lawyer's opinions about the judiciary, about participants in the justice system, about a court decision, or about the legal system, as well as the manner in which the lawyer expresses those opinions, receive the full protection of the constitutional guarantees of freedom of speech. As in other areas of public life and with respect to other public controversies, the best answer to speech of poor quality ordinarily is a response with speech of higher quality. In this regard, the role of leaders in the bar is important in providing a counterpoint to poorly-informed and demagogic criticisms of the justice system.

## § 4-13.4 PROVIDING LEGAL SERVICES TO THE DISADVANTAGED

### § 4-13.4(a) The Moral Obligation and Professional Responsibility to Provide Pro Bono Legal Services

Every person who achieves success through the multiple opportunities afforded and generous public assistance offered to those of us who are raised in this prosperous society has a moral obligation to give back to her community. Understanding the legal profession as a vocation, every lawyer should embrace the moral expectation of public service that is fundamental to a profession. Prominent among these is the duty to provide legal services with no expectation of payment and thereby allow meaningful access to justice for those who otherwise could not afford representation by a lawyer.

The expectation that a lawyer will provide legal services pro bono publico (literally "for the public good") may be traced back to the very origins of the law as one of the traditional professions. Historian James Brundage reports that "medieval lawyers regarded it as one mark of their superiority to other craftsmen that they furnished their specialized skills to economically and socially disadvantaged persons without compensation."[55]

Many centuries later, the vision of public service continues to be emphasized in the foundational ethical documents of our profession. In its very first paragraph, the Preamble to the Model Rules of Professional Conduct reminds us that a lawyer, as "a member of the legal profession," becomes "a public citizen having special responsibility for the quality of justice." As a central aspect of that public responsibility, Rule 6.1 of the Model Rules of Professional Conduct states that "[e]very lawyer has a professional responsibility to provide legal services to those unable to pay."

We as members of the legal profession have a profound and distinctive responsibility to facilitate access to justice by virtue of our role, not only as stewards of the legal system,

---

[54] *See supra* § 4-1.4(c).

[55] James A. Brundage, *Legal Aid for the Poor and the Professionalization of Law in the Middle Ages*, 9 J. LEGAL HIST. 169, 175 (1988).

but as the sentinels who effectively determine who may pass into the system. As Professor Deborah Rhode aptly describes it, "[o]ur justice system is designed by and for lawyers, and anyone who attempts to navigate without counsel is generally at a disadvantage. That disadvantage is particularly great among the poor, who typically lack the skills and information necessary for effective self-representation."[56] In other words, we the lawyers have created this legal system, which appears as a confusing maze to the average person, while simultaneously insisting that only those regularly admitted to the practice of law may be trusted to offer a map or directions to those who enter the system. As the creators and the gatekeepers to the system, we then have an obligation to use our privileged position to open the door more widely through pro bono services to those who otherwise would be left outside.[57]

To be sure, the general public also has a responsibility to enhance access to justice for those who cannot afford it by providing adequate funding to legal aid programs and for indigent criminal defense. However, while those who are employed in legal aid and public defender programs are the essential backbone for legal assistance to the disadvantaged, the need can never be fully satisfied without the diligent commitment to volunteer service and financial support by those of us who have been granted the privilege of admission to the practice of law.

Professor Neil Hamilton and Lisa Brabbitt explain that the legal profession has entered into an unwritten social compact with our society:

> The members of the profession agree to restrain self-interest to serve the transcendental purpose of the profession (justice in the case of the legal profession), to promote the ideals of the profession (particularly public service), and to maintain high standards of minimum performance, while society, in return, allows the profession substantial autonomy to regulate itself through peer review.[58]

If we as a profession should fail to uphold our end of the bargain by providing equal justice, we may lose the vital autonomy that we enjoy. If we should default in our public-regarding responsibilities, and if society should respond with intrusive regulatory measures, the ultimate injury may be realized by our entire society, which depends on independent lawyers who stand apart from and, when necessary, are willing to resist those in authority who wield the powers of government.

In sum, the exercise of our professional responsibility to afford access to justice assists not only the pro bono clients who are the immediate beneficiaries of volunteer legal services, but the larger society as the justice system is strengthened and as rights and freedoms are made more secure by the continuing public service of the members of the legal profession. Indeed, "because access by the poor to legal services is a necessary

---

[56] Deborah L. Rhode, *Pro Bono in Principle and in Practice*, 53 J. LEGAL EDUC. 413, 431 (2003); *see also* DAVID LUBAN, LAWYERING AND JUSTICE: AN ETHICAL STUDY 244 (Princeton U. Press, 1988) ("It is an obvious fact . . . that all of our legal institutions (except small claims court) are designed to be operated by lawyers and not by laypersons. Laws are written in such a way that they can be interpreted only by lawyers; judicial decisions are crafted so as to be fully intelligible only to the legally trained. Court regulations, court schedules, even courthouse architecture are designed around the needs of the legal profession.").

[57] *See* 2 GEOFFREY C. HAZARD, JR., W. WILLIAM HODES & PETER R. JARVIS, THE LAW OF LAWYERING § 53.02 (Aspen, 4th ed., 2016) (describing the lawyer's pro bono duty as "one of reciprocity" given that "[l]awyers have contributed significantly to the 'legalizing' of our society").

[58] Neil Hamilton & Lisa Montpetit Brabbit, Fostering Professionalism Through Mentoring, at 9 (2006), available at http://papers.ssrn.com/sol3/papers.cfm?abstract_id=899405.

precondition to the legitimacy of the legal process, lawyers must accept a duty of service," lest lawyers be left "to retail their trade—providing legal services to paying clients—in a legal system that has lost its legitimacy."[59]

Although contributing pro bono legal services is a professional responsibility that, in the words of Comment 1 to Rule 6.1 applies to "every lawyer, regardless of professional prominence or professional work load," the framers of the Model Rules of Professional Conduct have deemed it inappropriate to define that obligation in a manner that is formally binding upon all lawyers or to enforce the ethical obligation by exercising the power of disciplinary sanction. No state has imposed a mandatory pro bono requirement, although a few states have required lawyers to report annually the number of hours contributed to pro bono legal services[60] (and many invite voluntary reporting of pro bono activities).

Thus, in contrast with the mandatory directives found elsewhere in the Rules of Professional Conduct, Rule 6.1 states that "[a] lawyer should *aspire*" (emphasis added) to provide legal services to those unable to pay.[61] Nonetheless, as Professors Geoffrey Hazard and William Hodes and attorney Peter Jarvis maintain, "the obligation is still a 'real' one, for the very lack of an enforceable duty heightens the moral duty."[62]

### § 4-13.4(b) Aspirational Expectations for Pro Bono Legal Services

As framed in the Model Rules of Professional Conduct, Rule 6.1 establishes a concrete hourly expectation for pro bono legal services contributed by each lawyer and encourages that most of those services should be directed toward the disadvantaged or those who serve them. The rule states that "[a] lawyer should aspire to render at least (50) hours of pro bono publico legal services per year." As Comment 1 acknowledges, "[i]t is recognized that in some years a lawyer may render greater or fewer hours than the annual standard specified, but during the course of his or her legal career, each lawyer should render on average per year, the number of hours set forth in this Rule." Under Rule 6.1(a), "a substantial majority" of those hours should be provided through legal services without a fee or expectation of a fee that are devoted either (1) to "persons of limited means" or (2) to "charitable, religious, civic, community, governmental and educational organizations in matters that are designed primarily to address the needs of persons of limited means."

After satisfying the primary purpose of providing uncompensated legal services those in need, a lawyer is encouraged by Rule 6.1(b) to provide additional services by (1) delivering legal services at no fee or a substantially reduced fee "to individuals, groups or organizations seeking to secure or protect civil rights, civil liberties or public rights, or charitable, religious, civic, community, governmental, and educational organizations in matters in furtherance of their organizational purposes;" (2) delivering legal services "at a substantially reduced fee to persons of limited means" (which is sometimes called

---

[59] Tigran W. Eldred & Thomas Schoenherr, *The Lawyer's Duty of Public Service: More Than Charity?*, 96 W. VA. L. REV. 367, 398 (1993/94).

[60] FLORIDA RULES OF PROF'L CONDUCT R. 6.1(d); INDIANA RULES OF PROF'L CONDUCT R. 6.7; NEVADA RULES OF PROF'L CONDUCT R. 6.1(b).

[61] *See* RONALD D. ROTUNDA & JOHN S. DZIENKOWSKI, PROFESSIONAL RESPONSIBILITY: A STUDENT'S GUIDE § 6.1–2(a) (American Bar Ass'n, 2013–2014) ("Rule 6.1 is the only Black Letter Rule that never uses the word 'shall' and only uses the word 'should.' ").

[62] 2 GEOFFREY C. HAZARD, JR., W. WILLIAM HODES & PETER R. JARVIS, THE LAW OF LAWYERING § 53.02 (Aspen, 4th ed., 2016).

"low bono" services); or (3) participating in activities for "improving the law, the legal system or the legal profession."

Finally, in addition to (but not as a substitute for) providing pro bono legal services, Rule 6.1 encourages a lawyer to "voluntarily contribute financial support to organizations that provide legal services to persons of limited means."

### § 4-13.4(c) Providing Short-Term Limited Pro Bono Services and Conflict of Interest Rules

To encourage and emphasize the importance of providing pro bono legal services to those who cannot afford representation, Rule 6.5 of the Model Rules of Professional Conduct tailors the conflict of interest rules to the unique context of short-term and limited representation through a non-profit legal assistance program in a manner that allows a lawyer to participate in this limited program without an advance conflicts checks and without constricting other lawyers in the same in their freedom to represent clients.

When volunteering to provide short-term and limited legal services in an organized pro bono program, a lawyer is precluded from participating only if she knows that the person seeking legal counsel has an interest adverse to a client represented by the lawyer or the lawyer's law firm. Afterward, the lawyer's law firm may continue to represent or may accept retention by a client whose interests are adverse to the pro bono client who received the lawyer's short-term and limited legal assistance. By relaxing the impact of conflict of interest rules in this way, "Model Rule 6.5 represents an attempt by the ABA to fortify, or at least render less difficult to fulfill, the fifty-hour pro bono commitment" established under Rule 6.1.[63]

Rule 6.5 was added to the Model Rules of Professional Conduct in 2002 as part of the revision of the rules by the American Bar Association (ABA) under the Ethics 2000 project. The reporter for the ABA's Commission on Evaluation of the Rules of Professional Conduct (the "Ethics 2000 Commission") explained that the rule was drafted in response to the—

> concern that a strict application of the conflict-of-interest rules may be deterring lawyers from serving as volunteers in programs in which clients are provided short-term limited legal services under the auspices of a nonprofit organization or a court-annexed program. The paradigm is the legal-advice hotline or pro se clinic, the purpose of which is to provide short-term limited legal assistance to persons of limited means who otherwise would go unrepresented.[64]

Moreover, the relaxation of conflict rules—making the rules apply only if the lawyer participating in the pro bono program knows of a conflict—does not pose a significant risk to pro bono clients given the restricted nature of the legal advice provided in nonprofit short-term limited legal service programs.

To take advantage of the relaxed application of conflict of interest rules while providing this kind of pro bono legal services, the lawyer must satisfy several factors

---

[63] Rachel Brill & Rochelle Sparko Current Development, *Limited Legal Services and Conflicts of Interest: Unbundling in the Public Interest*, 16 GEO. J. LEGAL ETHICS 553, 553 (2003).

[64] Reporter's Explanation of Changes, Model Rule 6.5, Comm'n on Evaluation of the Rules of Prof'l Conduct, American Bar Ass'n (2001).

that are designed to remove any profit incentive, to protect the reasonable expectations of the pro bono clients, and to reasonably facilitate the participation of volunteer lawyers in providing legal assistance to the disadvantaged:

***Genuine Pro Bono Program:*** Under Rule 6.5(a), the lawyer must act "under the auspices of a program sponsored by a nonprofit organization or court." Rule 6.5 applies only to genuine pro bono activities conducted by a legitimate non-profit organization or annexed to a judicial body. A lawyer who expects compensation for legal services should not be afforded any exception from the strict application of the conflict of interest rules. Moreover, to ensure that the program is genuinely designed to provide assistance to those of limited means and is not a marketing front for a law firm or other commercial venture, a non-profit organization or a court must sponsor the program.

***Short-Term Limited Services:*** The lawyer must provide "short-term limited legal services" to the pro bono client. The relaxation of the strict conflict of interest rules is permitted under these circumstances primarily as a matter of necessity. As Comment 1 to Rule 6.5 explains, programs that provide short-term and limited legal advice or assistance in completing forms—such as legal-advice hot lines, advice-only street clinics, or *pro se* counseling programs—"are normally operated under circumstances in which it is not feasible for a lawyer to systematically screen for conflicts of interest as is generally required before undertaking a representation."

As required by Rule 1.2(c),[65] the pro bono client receiving such services must provide informed consent to the limited nature of the legal services being provided. By expressly authorizing a program of short-term limited legal services, Rule 6.5 articulates a limited exception to the general rule of Rule 1.2(c) that a lawyer and client may limit the scope of representation only "if the limitation is reasonable under the circumstances."[66] The legal counsel provided by the lawyer ordinarily must be sufficiently complete to justify the client's reliance upon the advice, which means that some limitations on the scope of representation would not be reasonable because the condensed or unfinished nature of the relationship renders the legal advice unreliable or leaves the client exposed to serious risks. By nature, however, a pro bono advice-only or hot-line program often will provide incomplete legal services, which is justified by the view that some assistance is better than nothing. Comment 2 to Rule 6.5 explains this imperfect balance by advising that "[i]f a short-term limited representation would not be reasonable under the circumstances, the lawyer may offer advice to the client but must also advise the client of the need for further assistance of counsel."

***No Expectation of Continuing Representation:*** For these purposes, the rule directs that the lawyer must provide the short-term and limited representation "without expectation by either the lawyer or the client that the lawyer will provide continuing representation in the matter." The setting of the program, the limited scope of the representation, and the succinct manner in which the legal advice or assistance are provided ordinarily will communicate clearly that the pro bono client will receive no further assistance beyond the short-term program. If any doubt or confusion should remain, the lawyer should make plain that the legal representation will not continue beyond the immediate provision of legal advice or assistance in completing forms.

---

[65] *See supra* § 4-3.3.

[66] *See* supra § 4-3.3.

Because of the short-lived nature of the representation, there is no need for assurance that the lawyer's counsel will not be compromised in the future by a possible (but as yet unrecognized) conflict of interest. The deliberately transitory nature of the lawyer's representation of the pro bono client in such a program makes application of the full range of conflict of interest rules unnecessary to protect the quality of the legal services and the integrity of the attorney-client relationship. (If the lawyer subsequently should agree to continued representation of the pro bono client, the conflict of interest rules apply in full force to that ongoing representation.)

***No Knowledge of a Conflict of Interest:*** Under Rule 6.5(a)(1) and (a)(2), the lawyer may only provide short-term and limited representation to a pro bono client if the lawyer does not "know[ ] that the representation of the client involves a conflict of interest" (that is, that the person is adverse to the lawyer's personal interests or those of one of the lawyer's clients), and the lawyer does not "know[ ] that another lawyer associated with the lawyer in a law firm is disqualified" by reason of a conflict of interest." While the lawyer is not required to implement an extensive conflicts screening before accepting the pro bono client under these special circumstances, the lawyer may not ignore a conflict of interest about which he is aware. The lawyer thus remains obliged to exercise some vigilance in verifying that the person who is seeking the short-term and limited representation is not someone whose interests are adverse to one of the lawyer's own clients or to a client of the law firm of whom the lawyer is aware.

When the lawyer knows that the pro bono client is adverse to a client of the lawyer's or the lawyer's firm, the lawyer must decline to offer any legal advice or assistance and instead refer that person to another lawyer volunteering in the program.

***No Implied Disqualification to Other Lawyers in Firm:*** Under Rule 6.5(b), a lawyer's participation in a short-term and limited pro bono representation under a qualified program is personal to the lawyer and is not attributed to other associated lawyers in a law firm. The individual lawyer may not subsequently represent a client against the pro bono client in the same or a substantially related matter, as that would clearly violate the lawyer's duty of loyalty and confidentiality to the pro bono client. However, provided that the lawyer when providing the pro bono legal services was unaware that another lawyer in firm represented an adverse client, Rule 6.5 overrides the general rule that a conflict of interest is imputed to all other lawyers in the same firm.[67]

Thus, the lawyer's limited and short-term representation of the pro bono client does not disqualify other lawyers in the firm from continuing to represent or being retained in the future by a client whose interests are adverse to those of the pro bono client, even with respect to the same or a substantially related matter.

## § 4-13.4(d) The Lawyer's Duty to Accept Appointment to Represent a Client Absent Good Cause

### *§ 4-13.4(d)(1) Court Appointment of Lawyer to Represent a Person*

Just as a client ordinarily may select counsel of his choice, so also may an attorney ordinarily accept or reject employment by a client at the lawyer's discretion. However, just as a client's right to choice of counsel is not absolute (e.g., an indigent criminal

[67] *See supra* § 4-7.6.

defendant who receives appointed defense counsel),[68] the lawyer's freedom to decline representation of a client is not unqualified. Under Rule 6.2 of the Model Rules of Professional Conduct, "[a] lawyer shall not seek to avoid appointment by a tribunal to represent a person except for good cause." Under standard practice, courts appoint only those lawyers who have volunteered to be available for court appointments and who have demonstrated experience and competence in the type of case, and appointed lawyers typically are entitled to payment for providing legal services.

Nonetheless, as part of the lawyer's ethical aspiration to provide pro bono publico service, as well as to ensure that unpopular matters and clients are not denied access to the legal system, a lawyer should consider accepting court appointments and, arguably, may be required to accept an appointment as a professional obligation.[69]

### *§ 4-13.4(d)(2) Good Cause to Decline Appointment*

When a lawyer has been asked by a court to accept an appointment to represent a person of limited means or whose cause is unpopular, the lawyer should decline the appointment only for good cause. Rule 6.2 lists three types of good cause that would justify declining an appointment to represent a client:

***Appointment Would Violate Ethics Rules:*** Under Rule 6.2(a), the lawyer must demur if "representing the client is likely to result in violation of the Rules of Professional Conduct or other law." If the lawyer would have an impermissible conflict of interest or if the lawyer could not provide competent representation (which means that the lawyer could not attain the requisite competence to handle the matter through reasonable preparation and study),[70] the lawyer is precluded from accepting the representation. The client of an appointed attorney is no less entitled than anyone else to a lawyer who compiles fully with the Rules of Professional Conduct.

***Appointment Would Impose Unreasonable Financial Burden:*** Under Rule 6.2(b), the lawyer may avoid the appointment if "representing the client is likely to result in an unreasonable financial burden on the lawyer." A lawyer ought not refuse an appointment merely because it would be less financially rewarding than other legal employment opportunities (which will almost always be the case) or even that it will result in a net financial loss to the lawyer.

The language of Rule 6.2(b) is directly parallel to that in Rule 1.16(b)(6), which allows a lawyer to withdraw from representation of a client if "the representation will result in an unreasonable financial burden on the lawyer." In both contexts, the "unreasonable financial burden" exception should be reserved for the situation in which, due to exceptional demands by the representation in terms of lawyer time (preventing work on other matters) or expenses incurred, continuation of the representation would result in a severe economic dislocation to the lawyer's practice.[71] For example, in

[68] *See supra* § 4-3.6(b)(1).

[69] *Cf.* Mallard v. United States District Court, 490 U.S. 296, 306 n.6 (1989) (observing without deciding that a court may have inherent powers to require "an unwilling attorney to render service" by appointment to represent a client without compensation and refraining from offering "an opinion on the constitutionality of compulsory assignments," while holding in that case that the statute at issue did not authorize involuntary appointments).

[70] *See supra* § 4-5.1(a).

[71] *See supra* § 4-3.6(c)(2).

*Cunningham v. Sommerville*,[72] the West Virginia Supreme Court agreed that a lawyer employed fulltime as in-house counsel for a corporation, who likely would lose her job if required to devote substantial time to representing indigent persons, had demonstrated good cause to resist the appointments.

While we may praise the lawyer who heroically accepts an appointment to represent a client in need, despite financial devastation to the lawyer's practice or a dramatic decline in the lawyer's standard of living, demanding such an extreme sacrifice at the penalty of disciplinary sanction is simply asking too much.

***Appointment Would Be Repugnant to Lawyer:*** Under Rule 6.2(c), the lawyer may decline an appointment if "the client or the cause is so repugnant to the lawyer as to be likely to impair the client-lawyer relationship or the lawyer's ability to represent the client." This provision bears some resemblance to Rule 1.16(b)(4), which permits a lawyer to withdraw from representation if "the client insists upon taking action that the lawyer considers repugnant or with which the lawyer has a fundamental disagreement."[73] However, while Rule 1.16(b)(4) addresses attorney-client disputes that arise after retention about the appropriate course of action when the representation is underway, Rule 6.2(c) focuses upon the nature of the client or the cause at the outset of the representation.

Rule 6.2(c), in describing the kind of antipathy to a cause or client that would justify a lawyer in refusing a court appointment, speaks of a client or cause that the lawyer finds to be "repugnant." The term denotes a high degree of aversion, beyond mere disagreement on a matter of no great principle or general distaste for the person.

Accordingly, a lawyer may resist an appointment when the lawyer's antagonism to the client or to the client's cause reflects a fundamental conflict that would require the lawyer to compromise a deeply-held moral principle or a powerful personal disgust that would impair any attorney-client relationship. For example, a lawyer who believes in the sanctity of unborn human life should not be forced to betray that principle by accepting an appointment to represent a minor girl who is seeking judicial permission to have an abortion without parental notice or consent.[74] Likewise, a lawyer who has been the victim of sexual violence should not be expected to accept an appointment to represent a criminal defendant charged with rape or sexual abuse.[75]

While not clearly stated in the rule, the nature of the representation is also important, as providing legal representation to a criminal defendant, even or especially when that person is unpopular and cannot find other counsel, is essential to protect the rule of law and control the power of the state. As criminal defense lawyer Michael Tigar writes, "[t]he most despised, the most endangered defendants may be without counsel.

---

[72] 388 S.E.2d 301, 304–05 (W. Va. 1989).

[73] *See supra* § 4-3.6(c)(2).

[74] *See* Teresa Stanton Collett, *Professional Versus Moral Duty: Accepting Appointments in Unjust Civil Cases*, 32 WAKE FOREST L. REV. 635, 656–70 (1997) (concluding that "[t]he constitutional protection of the free exercise of religion, as well as the lawyer's right of free speech, requires accommodation of the lawyer's unwillingness to accept appointed representation of girls seeking judicial authorization for abortions").

[75] *See* JOHN WESLEY HALL, JR., PROFESSIONAL RESPONSIBILITY IN CRIMINAL DEFENSE PRACTICE § 9:11 (Thomson-West, 3d ed., 2011) (saying that when "[s]omething in the lawyers' past or the past of their immediate family members or close friends may make them unable to represent accused murderers, rapists, child molesters, or child pornographers," "that moral judgment should be respected, for good of all concerned").

Yet their cases, as history teaches us without any reason for doubt, are the ones most likely to have excited governmental passion in ways that make judgment fallible."[76]

By contrast, when a person seeking the appointment of counsel wishes to initiate litigation, the lawyer may legitimately consider whether pursuing that objective, in terms of the impact on other litigants or the effect on society in changing the law, contradicts the lawyer's understanding of the good society—and thus the lawyer may legitimately refuse to cooperate with that client in pursuing an objective deemed by the lawyer to be morally unsound. To be sure, under Rule 1.2(b), a lawyer may insist that an agreement to represent a client, "including representation by appointment, does not constitute an endorsement of the client's political, economic, social, or moral views or activities."[77] Nonetheless, as Professor Teresa Collett contends:

> By deciding to expend their time and legal talents in the furtherance of particular projects, claims, or defenses—lawyers undertake actions that will have foreseeable effects on the lives of particular individuals and communities. As an individual seeking to "do good and avoid evil," and as a member of a community that is enhanced by good acts and diminished by evil, a lawyer should remain free to decline representation because of the immorality of the client's objectives.[78]

### § 4-13.4(e) Lawyer Serving in Governance with a Legal Services Organization and Recusal in Matters Raising a Conflict of Interest

Continuing this same focus upon equal access to justice, Rule 6.3 of the Model Rules of Professional Conduct encourages lawyers to serve those organizations that offer legal services to the disadvantaged by accepting a position "as a director, officer, or member of a legal services organization, apart from the law firm in which the lawyer practices." In addition to requesting lawyers to volunteer their time to represent persons of limited means, legal services programs need lawyers to assist in program management and governance. A lawyer's devotion of time and talent to serve on the managing board of a legal aid or pro bono program is itself a significant form of pro bono publico service.

Legal aid programs typically offer legal assistance to those of limited means in a variety of subject matter areas—such as family law, housing, health care, income maintenance, and consumer protection matters.[79] A real and constant possibility exists that the program will accept as a client a person who stands adverse to the interests of a client represented by one of the lawyers serving on the governing body of the program. If a lawyer were to be disqualified from serving on the board of a legal services organization whenever a client had interests that conflict with those of someone being

---

[76] Michael E. Tigar, *Defending*, 74 TEX. L. REV. 101, 104 (1994).

[77] *See supra* § 4-13.2.

[78] Teresa Stanton Collett, *The Common Good and the Duty to Represent: Must the Last Lawyer in Town Take Any Case*, 40 S. TEX. L. REV. 137, 177–78 (1999); *see also* David B. Wilkins, *Race, Ethics, and the First Amendment: Should a Black Lawyer Represent the Ku Klux Klan*, 63 GEO. WASH. L. REV. 1030, 1068 (1995) ("The choice that 'I' should represent this client is inherently a moral one that must take account of predictable consequences in the real world."); Monroe H. Freedman, *Ethical Ends and Ethical Means*, 41 J. LEGAL EDUC. 55, 56 (1991) ("I do not consider the lawyer's decision to represent a client or cause to be morally neutral. Rather, a lawyer's choice of client or cause is a moral decision that should be weighed as such by the lawyer and that the lawyer should be prepared to justify to others.").

[79] *See supra* § 4-13.4(b).

served by that program, then the pool of talent for leadership positions could become very shallow. Lawyers who practice in certain fields of law, such as real estate, retail, or health law, and lawyers who practice in larger law firms with a diverse clientele would find it difficult or impossible to serve.

Accordingly, Rule 6.3 of the Model Rules of Professional Conduct states that a lawyer may continue to serve in a governance role for a legal service program, "notwithstanding that the organization serves persons having interests adverse to a client of the lawyer." Comment 1 to Rule 6.3 confirms that "[a] lawyer who is an officer or a member of such an organization does not thereby have a client-lawyer relationship with persons served by the organization." A lawyer serving as a director, officer, or member of a legal services organization does not encounter an automatically disqualifying conflict of interest simply because a client of the lawyer is adverse to a person being represented under the program.

However, Rule 6.3 recognizes that the lawyer's duty of loyalty to a present client and the lawyer's responsibility to behave with integrity toward the legal services program demand that the lawyer recuse himself from direct involvement in the specific matter that presents the adverse interests. Rule 6.3(a) directs that the lawyer "shall not knowingly participate in a decision or action of the organization . . . if participating in the decision or action would be incompatible with the lawyer's obligations to a client under Rule 1.7." Rule 6.3(b) directs the lawyer not to "knowingly participate in a decision or action of the organization . . . where the decision or action could have a material adverse effect on the representation of a client of the organization whose interests are adverse to a client of the lawyer." (Comment 2 to Rule 6.3 advises that "[i]t may be necessary in appropriate cases to reassure a client of the organization that the representation will not be affected by conflicting loyalties of a member of the board.") To ensure that lawyers serving as directors, officers, or board members recuse themselves when appropriate, and to establish procedures to separate that lawyer from further participation, the organization should adopt a written policy to provide further direction.

In sum, a lawyer serving on a board of directors for a legal assistance program is not disqualified from participating in general managerial and policymaking decisions, such as budget setting, general employee policies and supervision, and adoption of goals and initiatives, even though such actions may have the indirect effect of affording access to legal services for a person who is adverse to a client of the lawyer.

The lawyer serving in a governance capacity, however, must abstain from involvement in actions or decisions that directly and materially affect a matter that brings a client of the program into conflict with a client of the lawyer. The lawyer not only must withhold formal comment and voting at any meeting of the governing body (and probably should leave the room if the matter is addressed at a meeting, to avoid learning of any confidential information and avoid the appearance that she has any influence on that subject), but the lawyer also should carefully avoid any discussion with other board members, managers, or staff about the specific matter that involves such a representation. In this way, the lawyer serving in a governance capacity for the legal assistance program is screened from participation in any matter that the lawyer knows has brought a client of the lawyer (or presumably the lawyer's law firm) into an adverse position to a person being served by the legal services program.

# Part Five

## LEGAL MALPRACTICE

### By Susan Saab Fortney and Vincent R. Johnson

### RECOMMENDED CITATION FOR PART FIVE

For those citing to Chapters 5-1 through 5-8 in Part Five, we recommend attribution to this individually-authored part as being most accurate. For example, the most appropriate citation format to the first section in this part would look like this: Susan S. Fortney and Vincent R. Johnson, Legal Malpractice § 5-1.1, in *Legal Ethics, Professional Responsibility, and the Legal Profession* (West Academic Publishing, 2018).

# Chapter 5-1

# INTRODUCTION TO LEGAL MALPRACTICE LAW

**By Susan Saab Fortney and Vincent R. Johnson[1]**

*Table of Sections*

§ 5-1.1 The Role and Nature of Legal Malpractice Law
§ 5-1.2 The Rise in Legal Malpractice Law
§ 5-1.3 The Costs of Legal Malpractice
§ 5-1.4 Overview of the Theories of Liability
§ 5-1.5 Consequences of Classifying Theories of Liability
§ 5-1.6 Status of the Plaintiff
§ 5-1.7 Differentiating Malpractice and Discipline

---

## § 5-1.1 THE ROLE AND NATURE OF LEGAL MALPRACTICE LAW

Following admission to the practice of law, lawyers are subject to various forms of regulation, including regimes providing for professional discipline and civil liability.[2] This Part of the book examines the professional responsibility of lawyers through the lens of legal malpractice.

The civil liability of lawyers for acts and omissions committed in a professional capacity is commonly referred to as "legal malpractice."[3] Although there is no uniform consensus on the meaning of "legal malpractice," the phrase commonly describes a kind of tortious conduct.[4] Often commentaries and cases use the term "legal malpractice" to refer to negligence claims against lawyers.[5] With the increased frequency of other types of claims against lawyers, the term, "legal malpractice," generally refers to various professional liability claims against lawyers.[6] This text adopts the more expansive

---

[1] Some of the language and ideas in Part Five have been drawn from books and articles that we previously published, including SUSAN SAAB FORTNEY AND VINCENT R. JOHNSON, LEGAL MALPRACTICE LAW: PROBLEMS AND PREVENTION (West Academic Publishing, 2d ed. 2015) and VINCENT R. JOHNSON, LEGAL MALPRACTICE LAW IN A NUTSHELL (West Academic Publishing, 2d ed. 2016).

[2] "Upon admission to the bar of any jurisdiction, a person becomes a lawyer and is subject to applicable law governing such matters as professional discipline, procedure and evidence, civil remedies, and criminal sanctions." RESTATEMENT (THIRD) OF THE LAW GOVERNING LAWYERS § 1 (American Law Institute, 2000).

[3] For a discussion of remedies commonly available to clients and nonclients, see RESTATEMENT (THIRD) OF THE LAW GOVERNING LAWYERS § 6 (American Law Institute, 2000).

[4] RONALD E. MALLEN, LEGAL MALPRACTICE § 1:1 (Thomson Reuters, 2017 ed.).

[5] CHARLES W. WOLFRAM, MODERN LEGAL ETHICS § 5.6.1 at 206 (West, 1986) (using the term "legal malpractice" to refer to the common-law "right of a client to recover damages from a lawyer whose negligent performance has caused financial loss to the client").

[6] The *Restatement of the Law Governing Lawyers* uses the terms "malpractice" and "legal malpractice" to refer to theories of both professional negligence (§ 48) and breach of fiduciary duty (§ 49). RESTATEMENT (THIRD) OF THE LAW GOVERNING LAWYERS, Introductory Note, Chapter 4 (American Law Institute, 2000).

connotation, using "legal malpractice" as an umbrella term that covers various professional liability claims against lawyers, including claims alleging negligence, breach of fiduciary duty, and negligent misrepresentation.

Increasingly, scholars and practicing lawyers acknowledge the important role that malpractice concerns play in influencing lawyer conduct. As noted by the late Professor Geoffrey C. Hazard in the Foreword to the *Restatement of the Law Governing Lawyers*, "the remedy of malpractice liability and remedy of disqualification are of greater importance in most law practice than the risk of disciplinary proceedings."[7] Legal malpractice relates to three important functions of the law of lawyering by "delineating the duties of lawyers, creating appropriate incentives and disincentives for lawyers in their dealings with clients and others, and providing access to remedies for those injured by improper lawyer behavior."[8]

Traditionally, legal malpractice claims have served the "corrective justice" purpose of tort law, "identifying wrongdoers obliged to return victims to their pre-injury position."[9] Applying efficiency theory, legal malpractice rules "operate to impose accident costs to incentivize care without discouraging socially useful activities."[10] Using this analytical framework, lawyers should be held accountable for harm resulting from their professional misconduct, but liability should not sweep so broadly as to hinder the practice of law. In this sense, legal malpractice law attempts to strike a fair balance between the public's interest in consumer protection and the legal profession's need to exercise discretion to effectively represent clients.

Legal malpractice law as a substantive area of law is continuously evolving. As it does, it assumes a greater role in influencing lawyers' conduct and dealings with clients and nonclients alike.

## § 5-1.2 THE RISE IN LEGAL MALPRACTICE LAW

Courts in the United States have recognized professional liability claims against lawyers since the late eighteenth century.[11] In these early cases, recovery was only possible if clients could demonstrate that the lawyer was responsible for gross negligence.[12] Starting in the mid to late nineteenth century, several courts began to find liability for ordinary negligence.[13]

Although courts somewhat relaxed the standards and burdens for legal malpractice plaintiffs, there were not many reported legal malpractice cases until the 1970s. Summarizing data on the relative frequency of reported legal malpractice decisions in the U.S., legal malpractice expert Ronald E. Mallen notes that during the 1970s there

---

[7] Geoffrey C. Hazard, Jr. *Foreword*, RESTATEMENT (THIRD) OF THE LAW GOVERNING LAWYERS, at xxi (American Law Institute, 2000).

[8] John Leubsdorf, *Legal Malpractice and Professional Responsibility*, 48 RUTGERS L. REV. 101, 105 (1995). Professor Leubsdorf served as Associate Reporter on the American Law Institute's *Restatement (Third) of the Law Governing Lawyers*.

[9] Cristina Carmody Tilley, *Tort Law Inside Out*, 126 YALE L.J. 1320, 1326 (2017).

[10] *Id.* at 1326–27.

[11] *See* George S. Mahaffrey, Jr., *Cause-in-Fact and the Plaintiff's Burden of Proof with Regard to Causation and Damages in Transactional Legal Malpractice Matters: The Necessity of Demonstrating the Better Deal*, 37 SUFFOLK U.L. REV. 393, 400 (2004) (identifying the Supreme Court of Virginia decision in *Stephens v. White*, 2 Va. 203 (1786) as the first case of legal malpractice in the U.S.).

[12] *Id.* at 401 (stating that "American courts did not find liability for an attorney's honest mistake").

[13] *Id.*

were almost as many reported legal malpractice decisions as there were in the previous history of American jurisprudence.[14] This trend continued in the 1980s when the number of reported decisions tripled over the prior decade and in the 1990s when there was a 155 percent increase over the prior decade.[15] Mallen's data reveal that the number of reported decisions continued to increase in the new millennium with relative frequency until the curve flattened by the end of 2009.[16] Mallen concludes that this reflects "stabilization in claims frequency and not a decline."[17]

Other trend data relate to malpractice claims. Insurers and insurance brokers periodically report on claims developments. For example, the National Legal Malpractice Data Center, a body established by the ABA Standing Committee on Professional Liability, publishes studies called *The Profile of Legal Malpractice Claims.*[18] Because these studies rely on information reported by insurers that participated in the study, the reports could be viewed as a snapshot of legal malpractice claims. Anyone seeking information on claims trends should consult these studies published by the ABA.

In a 2015 article, Professors Tom Baker and Rick Swedloff analyzed the ABA claims data, as well as data from the largest insurer of large law firms in the U.S. and a summary of large claims from a leading insurance broker.[19] Based on their review, they conclude that the "quantitative data on the past thirty years of experience in lawyers' professional liability shows a pattern of relative stability."[20] Because quantitative analysis of legal malpractice may be difficult, they urge more qualitative research.[21]

Changes in the legal profession and the environment in which lawyers practice have influenced both the number of reported cases and claims, as well as the type of malpractice claims. Most notably, the areas of potential liability have expanded over the last three decades. This includes decisions relaxing standards for establishing liability for some claims and recognizing new theories of liability. For example, lawyers now face claims from more nonclients as a result of courts allowing theories of liability such as negligent misrepresentation and aiding and abetting breach of fiduciary duty. At the same time, courts may resist lawyers' efforts to summarily dismiss actions based on defenses that deprive plaintiffs of their day in court.

Another noteworthy development is that the profession, as a self-protecting trade group, has in some respects disintegrated. Previously, the "conspiracy of silence" made it difficult for aggrieved persons to retain counsel to handle a legal malpractice case because lawyers refused to criticize other lawyers. Although the economics and obstacles in legal malpractice litigation still present serious challenges for plaintiffs, lawyers

---

[14] RONALD E. MALLEN, LEGAL MALPRACTICE § 1.14 (Thomson Reuters, 2017 ed.).

[15] *Id.*

[16] *Id.*

[17] *Id.* Mallen notes that the chart tracking reported cases has not been updated because relying on "published appellate decisions is no longer a valid methodology to compare statistical trends concerning legal malpractice cases." *Id.*

[18] In 2016, the ABA Standing Committee on Lawyers' Professional Liability published its seventh study of national legal malpractice claims data, following studies in 1985, 1995, 1999, 2003, 2007, and 2011. ABA STANDING COMMITTEE ON LAWYER'S PROFESSIONAL LIABILITY, PROFILE OF LEGAL MALPRACTICE CLAIMS 2012–2015 (2016) at p. 7.

[19] Tom Baker & Rick Swedloft, *Liability Insurer Data as a Window on Lawyers' Professional Liability,* 5 UC IRVINE L. REV. 1273 (2015).

[20] *Id.* at 1314.

[21] *Id.* at 1316.

around the country now sue other lawyers, with many specializing in legal malpractice work.

Within law practice, organizational changes have also contributed to increases in the number of malpractice claims. For large and mid-size firms the expansion in the number of branch offices and lateral hires has resulted in more malpractice exposure.[22] Regardless of firm size, financial pressure to produce income may tempt lawyers to dabble in new practice areas or represent risky clients. The use of technology and the handling of electronic data exposes lawyers to daily malpractice risks.

Increased consumerism and changes in client expectations have also affected the likelihood that aggrieved persons will pursue complaints against attorneys. With the proliferation of media and fiction stories, there is "much greater public consciousness of lawyers' work."[23]

Changes in the economy also impact the number of claims asserted against lawyers. Statistics on claims reveal a short lag time between recessions and economic slumps and an increase in legal malpractice claims.[24]

Lawyers' own financial pressure can increase their malpractice exposure when they pursue actions to collect past due fees.[25] With such a collection action, the lawyer may face a compulsory counterclaim for legal malpractice.[26]

## § 5-1.3 THE COSTS OF LEGAL MALPRACTICE

Malpractice is costly for both injured persons and lawyers. Many persons who are injured by lawyers will not be able to pursue actions against the tortfeasor. Because of the dynamics and economics of legal malpractice litigation, the damages may not be enough to support a plaintiffs' attorney handling the matter on a contingent fee basis.

Even if an injured person successfully pursues a legal malpractice action, the plaintiff may not be restored to the "pre-tort" position. In most legal malpractice cases, the plaintiff will not be able to recover attorneys' fees.[27]

From the perspective of lawyers, malpractice claims can take a personal and financial toll. Legal malpractice insurance may not cover the type or amount of the claim.[28] Even when a matter is covered by insurance, the lawyer will be responsible for

---

22 *Law Firms See Rise in Malpractice Claim Frequency, Severity,* INS. J., June 27, 2013, http://www.insurancejournal.com/news/national/2013/06/27/296979.htm.

23 Geoffrey C. Hazard, Jr., *The Future of Legal Ethics*, 100 YALE L.J. 1239, 1239 (1991) (noting that newspaper, magazine, and television serials regularly cover lawyers' work).

24 *Lawyer Malpractice Claims Shift to Substance; Procedural Errors Less a Factor,* VT. B.J. & L., June, 1997 at 14 (explaining that "after a recession and the financial distress that it causes more business transactions fall apart, more [debtors] default on their loans, and there are more bankruptcies and more quarrels over assets").

25 Experts advise against suing clients to collect fees. *See, e.g.*, ABA BAR ASSOCIATION STANDING COMMITTEE ON LAWYERS' PROFESSIONAL LIABILITY, THE LAWYER'S DESK GUIDE TO PREVENTING LEGAL MALPRACTICE 60–62 (1992) (identifying "Zealous Effort to Collect a Fee" among the top ten malpractice traps to avoid).

26 *See e.g.*, David Beck, *Legal Malpractice in Texas*, 43 BAYLOR L. REV. 21, 25 (1991) (noting that under Texas civil procedure rules "a claim of legal malpractice arising out of the legal services that form the basis for a suit to recover attorneys' fees is a compulsory counterclaim").

27 *See infra* § 5-5.1(e)(1).

28 *See infra* § 5-8.2.

the deductible or retention amount under the policy. Claims may also increase future insurance premiums and may even affect the lawyer's insurability.

Malpractice claims also affect lawyers' productivity. Defendants will likely lose income when they are forced to devote time to responding to discovery and other aspects of the case.

Some monetary costs are harder to quantify. For example, serious malpractice claims may affect a lawyer's reputation and ability to attract and retain clients. When malpractice claims become public, other lawyers may also be less inclined to refer business to lawyers sued for malpractice.

In addition to these tangible costs, malpractice claims take a psychic toll. Depending on the nature of the claim and the lawyer's circumstances, malpractice claims can adversely affect a lawyer's health, relationships, and job satisfaction.

Lawyers who recognize the costs of legal malpractice to both injured persons and practitioners should be more willing to devote time and resources to preventing legal malpractice. Such risk management efforts start with understanding the bases of liability.

## § 5-1.4 OVERVIEW OF THE THEORIES OF LIABILITY

### § 5-1.4(a) Culpability

Generally speaking malpractice recovery will require some culpability on the lawyer's part. Except for claims based on contract breaches and vicarious liability, lawyers are not strictly liable for their acts and omissions. Ordinarily, a plaintiff must establish that the defendant-lawyer intended to cause harm or failed to exercise reasonable care to prevent foreseeable losses from occurring. A lawyer's lack of care can be either reckless or negligent. Compared to negligence, recklessness involves a higher degree of culpability, such as conduct reflecting extreme lack of care or conscious indifference to a known risk of harm to others. As discussed in the following section, a number of issues turn on the degree of the lawyer's culpability and the theory of liability asserted.

### § 5-1.4(b) Differentiating Claims in the Same Lawsuit

Depending on the facts and circumstances, a plaintiff may assert multiple theories of liability in the same action. This strategy enables the plaintiff to move forward, developing the plaintiff's case from different angles. Generally speaking, each separate claim should provide the basis for a plaintiff to pursue discovery related to the theory, to offer related evidence in court, and to obtain jury charges related to the theory, provided there is legally sufficient evidence related to the theory.

As discussed in the next section, the theory pursued affects issues related to the litigation and the plaintiff's ability to recover. Notably, asserting multiple theories may enable a plaintiff to obtain a judgment on one theory even if an affirmative defense can be successfully used to defeat another claim. For example, a plaintiff may want to assert both negligence and breach of fiduciary duty claims when the fiduciary duty claim has a longer limitations period and there is a risk that the negligence claim may be barred by the applicable statute of limitations.

The plaintiff's ability to successfully assert more than one theory of liability in the same action will largely depend on the facts and circumstances, as well as the applicable common and statutory law. Regardless of what theory is alleged, the prevailing method is to determine the "essence," "gist," "substance" or "real nature" of the claim.[29] With this approach, "a court may refuse to recognize the distinctions and dichotomies between and among the actions, concluding that regardless of how the cause is characterized it is essentially a tort action for malpractice."[30]

In those jurisdictions that allow multiple causes of action, it is important for the plaintiff to differentiate claims by showing that the gravamen of each claim focuses on an independent basis of liability. Specifically, the plaintiff should attempt to convince the court that the duties and facts supporting the two claims are not the same. This is illustrated in a Colorado case where the court determined that it was not error to allow a jury verdict on both breach of fiduciary duty and negligence.[31] The appellate court concluded that the negligence claim related to the duty of a reasonably prudent attorney under the same and similar circumstances, while the breach of fiduciary duty was based on an assertion of the attorney's self-interest and conflict of interest.[32]

Even in those jurisdictions that allow multiple professional liability claims to be asserted together, a defendant may ask the court to dismiss particular claims, arguing that the plaintiff is improperly attempting to "fracture" a single legal malpractice claim into multiple theories.[33] Dismissal of a claim can leave the plaintiff with no recovery when the remaining claim is barred by the applicable statute of limitations, but the dismissed claim would have survived a limitations attack. This possibility underscores the importance of both the plaintiff and defendant understanding the jurisdiction's approach to evaluating multiple claims in the same malpractice action.

## § 5-1.5 CONSEQUENCES OF CLASSIFYING THEORIES OF LIABILITY

There are various consequences associated with different theories of liability relied on by plaintiffs. The classification of a liability theory impacts a number of matters related to the litigation, including the pleadings and proof, scope of liability, affirmative defenses, insurance coverage, vicarious liability, remedies, and discharge in bankruptcy.

### § 5-1.5(a) Pleadings and Proof

For each theory of liability, a plaintiff must carefully plead and prove each element of all claims asserted. With proof, a litigant should be able to ask for a jury instruction relating to the cause of action.

The burden of proof may vary, depending on the particular claims asserted and the circumstances of the case. With negligence cases, the plaintiff must carry the burden to

---

[29] *See* RONALD E. MALLEN, LEGAL MALPRACTICE § 23:5 (Thomson Reuters, 2017 ed.) (noting that jurisdictions vary on the criteria emphasized).

[30] Roy Ryden Anderson & Walter W. Steele, *Fiduciary Duty, Tort and Contract: A Primer on the Legal Malpractice Puzzle*, 47 SMU L. REV. 235 (1994).

[31] Boyd v. Garvert, 9 P.3d 1161 (Colo. App. 2000).

[32] *Id.* at 1163.

[33] Texas courts have articulated an "anti-fracturing" rule that prohibits a malpractice plaintiff from "opportunistically transforming a claim sounding in negligence into separate non-negligence causes of action." Haase v. Abraham, Watkins, Nicols, Sorrels, Agosto and Friend, L.L.P., 404 S.W. 3d 75–82 (Tex. App. 2013).

prove claims by a preponderance of the evidence. However, in some states, the elements of a cause of action for fraud must be established by clear and convincing evidence.[34]

Depending on the theory, the burden of proof may shift to the defendant. For example, for a breach of fiduciary duty claim based on the lawyer-defendant's business transactions with clients, the court may shift to the defendant the burden of proof and treat the transactions as presumptively fraudulent,[35] or require that the lawyer demonstrate that the transaction was fair to the client.[36]

### § 5-1.5(b) Scope of Liability

As with other types of tort actions, a lawyer will have the most liability exposure to injured persons when the wrongful conduct involves highly blameworthy acts or omissions.[37] Thus, a lawyer who intentionally misrepresents a fact may be liable to a wider class of plaintiffs than a defendant who makes a merely negligent misstatement.

### § 5-1.5(c) Defenses

The theory of liability asserted also affects the available defenses. For example, under rules of contributory negligence, comparative negligence, or comparative fault, the defendant may point to the plaintiff's own negligence in defending a claim based on negligence, but not if the claim is based on intentionally tortious conduct. Whether the plaintiff's carelessness is a defense in an action alleging that a lawyer acted recklessly depends upon state law. In a breach of fiduciary duty case, a lawyer's ability to defend on the basis of the plaintiff's own lack of care may depend on the nature of the breach. Carelessness on the part of the plaintiff may be a defense if the lawyer's breach of fiduciary duty was merely negligent, but not if it was intentional.

The applicable statute of limitations will turn on the nature of the particular claim asserted. For example, the statute of limitations for breach of fiduciary duty claims may be different than the statute of limitations applicable to negligence claims. In some states, a single statute of limitations applies to all actions against lawyers based on their professional conduct, regardless of what theories of liability are alleged.[38]

If the applicable limitations period is longer for a breach of contract claim than for a tort claim, a plaintiff may try to characterize the claim as a breach of contract. Although a lawyer's duty of care may be thought of as arising out of an implied term of the client-lawyer agreement, "characterization of a claim as a contract claim or tort claim for the purposes of the statute of limitations will depend on the language, structure and policies of the jurisdiction's statutes of limitations."[39] Generally speaking, the prevailing rule is that there is no cause of action for breach of an express contract unless the wrong

---

[34] *See* Dixon v. Klenda, Mitchell, Austerman & Zuercher, L.L.C., 2013 WL 3331029, at *6 (Kan. App. 2013).

[35] *See* Ball v. Kotter, 723 F.3d 813, 826 (7th Cir. 2013).

[36] John S. Dzienkowski, *The Decline of Lawyer Independence: Lawyer Equity Investments in Clients*, 81 TEX. L. REV. 405, 446 (2002).

[37] *Cf.* RESTATEMENT (THIRD) OF TORTS: LIABILITY FOR PHYSICAL AND EMOTIONAL HARM § 33(b) (American Law Institute, 2010) (stating the rule in the context of physical harm).

[38] *See, e.g.*, FLA. STAT. ch. 95.11(4)(a) (Westlaw 2017) (providing that an action shall be commenced within two years for "An action for professional malpractice, other than medical malpractice, whether founded on contract or tort; provided that the period of limitations shall run from the time the cause of action is discovered or should have been discovered with the exercise of due diligence. However, the limitation of actions herein for professional malpractice shall be limited to persons in privity with the professional").

[39] RESTATEMENT (THIRD) OF THE LAW GOVERNING LAWYERS § 48 cmt. c (American Law Institute, 2000).

sued for breaches a specific promise.[40] Therefore, a plaintiff likely will face opposition in attempting to pursue a breach of contract to avoid the running of the statute of limitations on a negligence claim.

### § 5-1.5(d) Legal Malpractice Insurance

The pursuit of particular claims affects coverage under the defendant-lawyer's legal malpractice policies. Under legal malpractice policies insurers are obliged to provide a defense for claims covered under the policy and to indemnify the insured for covered claims. Legal malpractice policies are intended to cover insureds for claims arising out of the rendition of legal services to others, subject to policy exclusions and limitations. Common policy exclusions eliminate coverage for intentional torts. To improve the likelihood of recovering proceeds under insurance policies, plaintiffs' attorneys often include at least one covered claim, such as negligence or breach of fiduciary duty, that is not excluded under the insurance policy.

### § 5-1.5(e) Vicarious Liability

The nature of a claim will also affect whether a principal will be vicariously liable for the certain acts and omissions of agents acting on behalf of the principal.[41] Under the doctrine of *respondeat superior*, employers, such as law firms, can be held vicariously liable for harm caused by any person "who was acting in the ordinary course of the firm's business or with actual or apparent authority."[42]

In evaluating vicarious liability, distinctions can be drawn between lawyers' negligence and intentional conduct. Negligent acts and omissions in representing firm clients are generally regarded as conduct within the ordinary scope of the firm's business if the failure to exercise care involves conduct intended to benefit the firm. In contrast, conduct that does not advance firm business, such as a lawyer's entry into a business venture that is unrelated to representation of firm clients, ordinarily should not subject the firm or its principals to vicarious liability.[43] Occasionally, intentional conduct, such as knowingly representing clients with conflicting interests or padding bills, may expose the firm to vicarious liability because the conduct may fall within the "ordinary course of the firm's business," in the sense that it is part of the normal risks incidental to the operation of a law firm. Thus, the vicarious liability for asserted claims will turn on the facts and circumstances of the lawyer's conduct and its connection to firm business.

Depending on the organizational structure of the law firm, the vicarious liability of firm principals for the misconduct of other firm agents may also depend on the liability theory asserted. State law that applies to limited liability firms in most jurisdictions eliminates vicarious liability for all types of claims—meaning that a partnership creditor is not entitled to a judgment against a principal based solely on the status of the person as a principal in the firm.[44] Some statutes have not adopted this "full-shield" approach. Rather the limited liability shield in those states only applies to claims arising out or

---

[40] RONALD E. MALLEN, LEGAL MALPRACTICE § 8:27 (Thomson Reuters, 2017 ed.).

[41] In a law firm setting, agents may include lawyers who are principals in the firm and employed lawyers, as well as support staff and non-firm agents who are retained to act on behalf of the firm.

[42] *See* RESTATEMENT (THIRD) OF THE LAW GOVERNING LAWYERS § 58(1) (American Law Institute, 2000).

[43] *Id.*

[44] *See infra* § 5-7.2(d).

errors and omissions of another agent of the firm. In those jurisdictions, the theory asserted may affect the vicarious liability exposure of firm principals.[45]

### § 5-1.5(f) Remedies

The liability theories and proof asserted will affect the remedies available to a successful plaintiff. In addition to compensatory damages, proof of egregious conduct may support a punitive damages award. Fiduciary theories support claims seeking equitable remedies, such as fee forfeiture, creation of constructive trusts, or disgorgement of profits. Finally, the plaintiff's ability to recover attorneys' fees will also depend on the theory of liability.

### § 5-1.5(g) Discharge in Bankruptcy

Following an adverse malpractice judgment, a lawyer may attempt to escape liability by filing a bankruptcy petition. The ability to discharge a claim through bankruptcy will be affected by the underlying conduct of the lawyer sued for malpractice.

First, under the U.S. Bankruptcy Code, debts resulting from "willful and malicious injury by the debtor to another" are not dischargeable.[46] Thus judgments based on various intentional tort claims may not be dischargeable, but claims based on negligent conduct may be discharged. For example, a malpractice judgment is likely to be nondischargeable if the plaintiff establishes that the lawyer misappropriated funds entrusted to the lawyer. In contrast, judgments based on negligent handling of trust funds may be dischargeable.

Second, bankruptcy will not discharge a debt arising from "money, property, [or] services * * * obtained by false pretenses, a false representation, or actual fraud," or from "fraud or defalcation while acting in a fiduciary capacity, embezzlement, or larceny."[47] Thus, whether bankruptcy discharges liability for a judgment arising from misrepresentations in an opinion letter may turn upon whether the lawyer acted with scienter (knowledge of falsity or reckless disregard for the truth), and thus committed fraud,[48] or whether the errors in the letter resulted from mere negligence.

Finally, other exceptions under the Bankruptcy Code apply to specific conduct, such as securities law violations. When formulating a course of action and theories of liability, a plaintiff should recognize the various exceptions to dischargeability if the plaintiff wants to obtain a malpractice judgement that may be recoverable. Ironically, the type of culpable conduct that prevents a defendant from discharging a debt through bankruptcy may also be the type of intentional or fraudulent conduct that is likely excluded under an insurance policy that the lawyer-defendant carries.

## § 5-1.6 STATUS OF THE PLAINTIFF

The status of the plaintiff affects the lawyer's duties to the plaintiff and the claims available to the plaintiff. Clients, as opposed to nonclients, hold the best position in pursuing claims against their lawyers. While lawyers owe clients a number of duties,

---

[45] Christine Hurt, et al., BROMBERG AND RIBSTEIN ON LIMITED LIABILITY PARTNERSHIPS, THE REVISED UNIFORM PARTNERSHIP ACT, AND THE UNIFORM LIMITED PARTNERSHIP ACT (2001) § 1.01(d) (2017 ed.) (noting that in 2013 nine states retained partial-shield statutes).

[46] 11 U.S.C.A. § 523(a)(6) (Westlaw 2017).

[47] 11 U.S.C.A. § 523(a)(2)(A) & (a)(4) (Westlaw 2017).

[48] *See infra* § 5-4.2(a)(3).

lawyers owe few duties to nonclients. For example, a lawyer owes clients a duty to exercise reasonable care to protect clients' interests,[49] but owes no such general duty to nonclients.[50] However, clients and nonclients occasionally enjoy the same forms of protection from harm. A lawyer cannot deliberately deceive a person regardless of whether that person is a client.[51]

Because important questions of liability turn upon whether the plaintiff is a client or a nonclient, special rules apply to the formation of the lawyer-client relationship.[52] Other rules address protection for prospective clients who seek legal representation, but never actually become clients. That would be true, for example, if, after an initial interview with a lawyer, a prospective client decided not to hire the lawyer or if the lawyer declined the representation. Not surprisingly, a lawyer owes a prospective client some, but not all, of the duties owed to a client.[53]

## § 5-1.7 DIFFERENTIATING MALPRACTICE AND DISCIPLINE

As noted in the first section of the *Restatement of the Law Governing Lawyers*, persons admitted to law practice are "subject to applicable law governing such matters as professional discipline, procedure and evidence, civil remedies, and criminal sanctions."[54]. Depending on the facts and circumstances, a lawyer may be subject to both professional discipline and civil liability for the same conduct. For example, a lawyer who knowingly represents persons with conflicting interests may face disciplinary charges, as well as a malpractice claim. Although both disciplinary complaints and malpractice actions deal with departures from professional standards, the regimes differ in their purposes, prosecutors, procedures and application of the ethics rules.

### § 5-1.7(a) Purposes and Prosecutor

Often commentators refer to the public-protection purpose for imposing professional discipline when lawyers fail to comply with disciplinary rules that state the minimum standards for lawyers practicing in a state.[55] Lawyers who violate applicable disciplinary rules face sanctions, ranging from private reprimands to disbarment. By contrast, lawyers in civil litigation can be held liable for damages and subject to other remedies intended to restore plaintiffs to their pre-tort positions. Unlike disciplinary actions intended to protect the public in general from risks of harm by unethical practitioners, civil suits are intended to afford redress to specific persons injured by lawyers.

Related to the different purposes of the two systems is the difference in adversaries. In a disciplinary action, regulatory counsel files and prosecutes the disciplinary complaint. Persons affected by the lawyer's misconduct, such as clients, may serve as witnesses in the disciplinary matter. On the other hand, in a civil action, the counsel

---

[49] *See infra* § 5-2.1.

[50] *See infra* § 5-4.1(a).

[51] *See infra* § 5-4.2.

[52] *See infra* § 5-2.1(a)(1).

[53] *See infra* § 5-2.1(a)(5).

[54] RESTATEMENT (THIRD) OF THE LAW GOVERNING LAWYERS § 1 (American Law Institute, 2000).

[55] *See* Leslie C. Levin *The Emperor's Clothes and Other Tales About the Standards for Imposing Lawyer Discipline Sanctions*, 48 AMER. L. REV. 1, 17–18 (1998) (describing the purpose of sanctions and disciplinary standards as follows: "Three reasons are typically cited for imposing discipline on lawyers: first and foremost, protection of the public, second, protection of the administration of justice, and third, preservation of confidence in the legal profession").

hired by an injured person initiates and pursues the complaint seeking to hold the lawyer accountable for misdeeds.

### § 5-1.7(b) Procedures and Decision-Makers

State rules of disciplinary procedure govern the handling of disciplinary matters while legal malpractice cases proceed according to rules of civil procedure applicable to the court where the legal malpractice action is filed. Decisions on whether a lawyer is subject to discipline are usually made by judges or lawyers serving on disciplinary bodies. In contrast, lay persons play a more important decision-making role in civil litigation when a party elects to have a jury make determinations on contested facts.

A judge presiding over a malpractice case may refer a matter to disciplinary authorities if there is evidence that the lawyer-defendant violated applicable disciplinary rules. This type of referral may occur even if the plaintiff fails to recover damages in the malpractice action.[56] Attorneys representing parties in legal malpractice cases may have a similar obligation to report misconduct, at least after the malpractice litigation has concluded.[57]

### § 5-1.7(c) Application of Ethics Rules

Disciplinary proceedings focus on whether the respondent-lawyer violated the jurisdiction's ethics rules. In civil actions, courts use different approaches in allowing disciplinary rules to be used. One approach is to allow violations of disciplinary rules to be treated as evidence of the applicable standard of conduct. The Preamble of the ABA Model Rules of Professional Conduct and state ethics codes recognize this approach. As stated:

> Violation of a Rule should not itself give rise to a cause of action against a lawyer nor should it create any presumption in such a case that a legal duty has been breached. In addition, violation of a Rule does not necessarily warrant any other nondisciplinary remedy, such as disqualification of a lawyer in pending litigation. The Rules are designed to provide guidance to lawyers and to provide a structure for regulating conduct through disciplinary agencies. They are not designed to be a basis for civil liability. * * * Nevertheless, since the Rules do establish standards of conduct by lawyers, a lawyer's violation of a Rule may be evidence of breach of the applicable standard of conduct.[58]

In noting that violations of disciplinary rules may be considered by the trier of fact as an aid in understanding and applying the standard of care,[59] the *Restatement of the Law Governing Lawyers* uses a similar approach to that taken by the majority of courts. These courts allow experts to refer to the ethics rules when opining on the standard of care. An opinion from the South Carolina Supreme Court summarizes approaches that some courts use as follows:

> Other courts have held that ethics standards conclusively establish the duty of care and that any violation is negligence *per se*. A minority find that violation

---

[56] *See, e.g.*, Herrera v. Hark, 2007 WL 1319448, *3 (N.J. Super. Ct. App. Div.).

[57] *See* Vincent R. Johnson, *Legal Malpractice Litigation and the Duty to Report Misconduct*, 1 ST. MARY'S J. LEGAL MAL. & ETHICS 40 (2011).

[58] MODEL RULES OF PROF'L CONDUCT, Preamble and Scope (American Bar Ass'n, 2017).

[59] RESTATEMENT (THIRD) OF THE LAW GOVERNING LAWYERS § 52 (American Law Institute, 2000).

> of an ethics rule establishes a rebuttable presumption of legal malpractice. And, finally, a few courts hold that ethical standards are inadmissible in a legal malpractice case.[60]

Given the different treatment of ethics rules in legal malpractice cases, litigants must know what approach is used in the jurisdiction where the case is pending.

[60] Smith v. Haynsworth, Marion, McKay & Geurard, 472 S.W. 2d 612, 613–14 (S.C. 1996) (citations omitted).

# Chapter 5-2

# NEGLIGENCE

**By Susan Saab Fortney and Vincent R. Johnson**

*Table of Sections*

§ 5-2.1 Duty to Exercise Reasonable Care
§ 5-2.2 Breach of Duty
§ 5-2.3 Causation

## § 5-2.1 DUTY TO EXERCISE REASONABLE CARE

Negligence is the most important cause of action in the field of lawyer liability. This is true, first, because the general principles of negligence are so well established and easily adapted that they cover a wide range of the professional errors that cause harm to current or former clients. Second, negligence sometimes has important advantages over other causes of action. For example, malpractice insurance typically covers negligence claims.[1] Law firms and their principals are also routinely held liable for the negligent conduct of agents acting within the scope of a firm's business.[2] These considerations mean that a malpractice judgment or settlement won by the plaintiff based on negligence is more likely to be collectible.

Nevertheless, the elements of a negligence cause of action, and the special rules that guide the application of negligence principles in cases against lawyers, may limit a lawyer's liability.[3] As in other areas of the law, a negligence action against a lawyer has four elements: duty, breach, causation, and damages.[4] A plaintiff may recover from a lawyer for negligence only if the plaintiff has suffered damage that was caused (both factually and proximately) by the defendant's violation of a duty owed to the plaintiff. The action fails if any of the four elements of negligence is missing. This chapter explores the elements of duty, breach, and causation. The subject of damages is discussed in Chapter 5-5.

### § 5-2.1(a) To Whom Is a Duty Owed?

In areas of tort law involving physical harm, a defendant often owes a duty of care to any person foreseeably endangered by the defendant's misfeasance. As Chief Judge Benjamin N. Cardozo famously wrote in *Palsgraf v. Long Island Railroad Co.*,[5] a case involving physical injuries resulting from the explosion of a package, "the risk reasonably to be perceived defines the duty to be obeyed." However, lawyer malpractice

---

[1] *See infra* Chapter 5-8.

[2] *See infra* § 5-7.2(a).

[3] *See* Susan Saab Fortney, *A Tort in Search of a Remedy: Prying Open the Courthouse Doors for Legal Malpractice Victims*, 85 FORDHAM L. REV. 2033 (2017) (examining the challenges that face plaintiffs pursuing malpractice claims).

[4] *See* Bond v. McLaughlin, 229 So. 3d 760, 765 (Ala. 2017).

[5] 162 N.E. 99, 100 (N.Y. 1928).

rarely results in personal injury or property damage. In most cases, the harm is not physical, but purely economic. Because the economic consequences of negligence are often wide ranging, the law has traditionally been reluctant to recognize liability for negligence causing only economic harm. It is therefore not surprising that a lawyer does not owe a duty of care to every person who might foreseeably be affected by the lawyer's careless conduct. In fact, the scope of a lawyer's duties is rather tightly circumscribed.

Clearly, a lawyer owes a duty of care to a client.[6] Lawyers also owe certain duties of care to prospective clients who might become clients—that is, persons in the process of seeking legal advice.[7] Duties may also be owed by a lawyer to members of a class whose interests may be affected by class action litigation.[8] Nonclients have a difficult time stating a claim against a lawyer for negligence. Liability to nonclients is discussed in Chapter 5-4.

### *§ 5-2.1(a)(1) Three Kinds of Attorney-Client Relationship*

Clients stand in the most preferred position when it comes to lawyer liability. They are entitled to have their lawyers exercise reasonable care to protect their interests from harm. Clients therefore usually have no difficulty establishing the duty element of a negligence cause of action, provided that the alleged negligence falls within the "scope of the representation," a concept that limits the extent of duty.[9]

The critical question, then, is who actually qualifies as a "client." At one level, the answer is simple. An attorney-client relationship is created only three ways: by judicial appointment, by express agreement, and by inadvertence. According to the *Restatement*:

> A relationship of client and lawyer arises when:
>
> (1) a person manifests to a lawyer the person's intent that the lawyer provide legal services for the person; and either
>
> (a) the lawyer manifests to the person consent to do so; or
>
> (b) the lawyer fails to manifest lack of consent to do so, and the lawyer knows or reasonably should know that the person reasonably relies on the lawyer to provide the services; or
>
> (2) a tribunal with power to do so appoints the lawyer to provide the services.[10]

Thus, two of the three ways of establishing a lawyer-client relationship—court appointment and express agreement—are relatively formal and easy to recognize. However, the third type of attorney-client relationship—which is created by inadvertence—is more subtle. To that extent, it is a more dangerous theory of legal liability.

#### *§ 5-2.1(a)(1)(A) Court Appointment*

Court appointment involves the judicial exercise of official power to instruct a lawyer to render legal services to an affected individual. Through a formal process the

---

6 *See infra* § 5-2.1(a)(1).

7 *See infra* § 5-2.1(a)(5).

8 *See infra* § 5-2.1(a)(6).

9 *See infra* § 5-2.1(b).

10 RESTATEMENT (THIRD) OF THE LAW GOVERNING LAWYERS § 14 (American Law Institute, 2000).

court notifies a lawyer that the tribunal has determined that the lawyer must act to protect the interests of a specific person or group. For example, a court may appoint a lawyer to represent an indigent individual accused of a crime. In these types of cases, there is little chance that a lawyer will not understand that there is a lawyer-client relationship. However, uncertainties about who qualifies as a client may arise when a lawyer is appointed by a court as counsel to represent a class in class action litigation.[11]

*§ 5-2.1(a)(1)(B) Express Agreement*

Formalities also mark an express agreement to create an attorney-client relationship. Typically, a person requests legal services, and the lawyer, by words or conduct, manifests a willingness to provide those services. Before or within a reasonable time after commencing representation of a new client, a lawyer should communicate to the client the scope of representation and the basis or rate of fee to be charged.[12] Ideally, the obligations of the lawyer and client are embodied in a written employment contract. When a lawyer expressly consents to render legal services, a lawyer must recognize that duties follow the establishment of an attorney-client relationship. Of course, the parties to the agreement may misunderstand the scope of the lawyer's obligations to the client.[13]

Sometimes the formalities leading to client status are a bit different because a person does not deal with the lawyer directly. For example, a request for legal services may be made through an agent. Thus, in *Smith v. Patout*,[14] the plaintiff gave a power of attorney to a woman who then retained a lawyer to represent several heirs, including the plaintiff. A Louisiana appellate court found that there was nevertheless an attorney-client relationship between the lawyer and the plaintiff. Even though the plaintiff had never directly dealt with the lawyer, there was an authorized request for legal services and the lawyer agreed to represent the plaintiff's interests.[15]

*§ 5-2.1(a)(1)(C) Inadvertent Clients*

In contrast to attorney-client relationships established by court appointment or express agreement, a relationship arising from mistake may create obligations that come as an unwelcome surprise when the attorney faces a malpractice action. This is particularly true because in many instances there may be an attorney-client relationship even though no fee was agreed upon or paid. However, the attorney should not be totally surprised because, as discussed below, the attorney's conduct led the putative client to reasonably believe that the lawyer would provide services.

*§ 5-2.1(a)(1)(C)(i) Common Scenarios*

Consider three common scenarios.[16] First, some persons seeking legal advice may do so in casual settings. For example, a lawyer may be asked legal questions in an informal setting, such as a sports event or social gathering, or even online.[17] In some

---

[11] *See infra* § 5-2.1(a)(6) (discussing class members).

[12] MODEL RULES OF PROF'L CONDUCT R. 1.5(b) (American Bar Ass'n, 2017).

[13] *See infra* § 5-2.1(b) (discussing the scope of representation).

[14] 956 So. 2d 689 (La. Ct. App. 2007).

[15] *Id.* at 691.

[16] For additional illustrations and examination of issues related to inadvertent representation, see Stephen Gillers, *Virtual Clients: An Idea in Search of a Theory (With Limits)*, 42 VAL. U. L. REV. 797 (2008); Susan R. Martyn, *Accidental Clients*, 33 HOFSTRA L. REV. 913 (2005).

[17] *See* Paige A. Thomas, Comment, *Online Legal Advice: Ethics in the Digital Age*, 4 ST. MARY'S J. LEGAL MAL. & ETHICS 440, 443 (2014) ("An inherent danger lies in off-the-cuff remarks, made on the Internet, a

instances, the person making the inquiry may be seriously seeking legal guidance and discussing a matter of great importance to that person. However, the lawyer, perhaps because of the casual setting, may fail to appreciate that fact, or may even give an evasive response which induces detrimental reliance. For example, a lawyer might incautiously say, "That's a good question; let me look into it," or "I need to think about that." If the lawyer forgets about the question or otherwise fails to get back to the person making the inquiry, the lawyer may have opened the door to liability. The putative client may reasonably believe that the lawyer has taken the matter under advisement and will provide direction if there is anything the person needs to do to protect his or her interests.

A second common scenario involves the ownership of entities. For example, suppose that several physicians hire a law firm to create a limited partnership that will own and operate an ambulatory surgery center in which the physicians will be limited partners. The law firm may believe that it represents the entity that will come into being (the limited partnership), or perhaps, during the period prior to the formation of the limited partnership, the unincorporated association that reflects the common, undifferentiated interests of the physicians vis-a-vis a proposed management group. Despite the law firm's understanding, an individual physician who becomes a limited partner in the new enterprise may later allege that he or she believed that the firm represented the physician's personal financial interests in the formation of the limited partnership venture.

Another example involves owners of a small, closely-held corporation asking a law firm to provide representation regarding certain issues of legal liability. Although the firm may believe that it represented only the entity, the owners of the closely-held corporation may allege that they believed that the law firm, which was in communication with them personally, was also hired to protect their individual ownership interests.

A third common scenario relates to entity constituents, such as the officers, directors, and employees of corporations. The constituent, as a result of dealings with the company's legal counsel, may view that lawyer as a trusted legal advisor. Thus, constituents may believe that the lawyer is protecting their personal interests, and not just the interests of the corporation.

*§ 5-2.1(a)(1)(C)(ii) Request for Legal Services*

The *Restatement* is clear that in order for an attorney-client relationship to arise by reason of mistake, there must have been a request for representation. The putative client must have manifested to the lawyer the person's intent for the lawyer to provide legal services for the person.[18]

This requirement is decisive in some cases. For example, in *International Strategies Group, Ltd. v. Greenberg Traurig, LLP*,[19] an investor in a corporate venture sued the corporation's lawyer for losses sustained when the venture failed as a result of unauthorized transfers of assets. In his efforts to recoup the corporation's losses, the lawyer had urged the investor not to sue the corporation by arguing that such litigation

---

platform generally associated with distressingly low standards of research, citation and accountability. While an attorney may view these remarks as mere suggestions, if a client perceives them to be legal strategy—or worse, advice—that attorney may be at risk of a malpractice suit").

[18] RESTATEMENT (THIRD) OF THE LAW GOVERNING LAWYERS § 14(1) (American Law Institute, 2000).

[19] 482 F.3d 1 (1st Cir. 2007).

would disrupt negotiations to recover the missing funds, and that everyone would be better off if those efforts succeeded. In a subsequent suit by the investor against the lawyer (and the lawyer's present and former law firms), the First Circuit rejected an argument that the investor had become an "inadvertent" client of the lawyer. As the court's opinion explained: "Courts interpreting * * * [Massachusetts law] require concrete communication by the plaintiff requesting that the attorney represent him, or explicitly seeking individualized legal advisement."[20] The court found that the facts before it were fatally deficient because not only had there been no express request for legal services, but on at least two occasions the plaintiff had acknowledged that it was not a client. In one letter, the plaintiff's director had stated "I appreciate that you act for * * * [the corporation]" and in another he complained about "your treatment of us as third parties."[21]

*§ 5-2.1(a)(1)(C)(iii) Reasonable Reliance*

A key issue in inadvertent-client cases is often whether the putative client reasonably relied on the lawyer to provide legal services.[22] That is, was it reasonable for the person to think that the lawyer was protecting the person's own interests? In many cases, this is a hotly contested issue of fact. The issue of whether it was reasonable for the plaintiff to believe there was an attorney-client relationship will ultimately be decided by a fact finder, typically a lay jury, which may sympathize more with the plaintiff than with the malpractice defendant. In *Pete v. Anderson*,[23] the Supreme Court of Kentucky agreed that summary judgment had been improperly granted to a legal malpractice defendant because it was plausible that his conduct left a woman "with the reasonable understanding that he would pursue her minor sons' claims as well as her own."[24]

There are many factors that might bear upon whether it was reasonable for a person seeking legal services to believe that an attorney-client relationship has been created. The fact finder may want to know: Was there a written contract of employment? Who did the agreement name as the "client?" To whom were the invoices for legal services addressed and delivered? Who paid the bills? Who was listed as the "client" in the firm's filing system and conflicts-checking database? What were the oral communications between the lawyer and the putative client? What statements were made in correspondence and other written communications with the putative client and others? To whom were letters and electronic messages addressed? What did the regarding line of the letters say? Was the "client" a sophisticated person who was unlikely to misunderstand to whom representation was being provided? Did the plaintiff hire other lawyers, either in this instance or in other matters, to protect the plaintiff's interests? Did the lawyer ever appear in litigation on behalf of the putative client or tell a third party that the lawyer represented the putative client? Was the relationship between two business partners strained and characterized by distrust, such that it was unreasonable

---

[20] *Id.* at 8.

[21] *Id.* at 9.

[22] *See* RESTATEMENT (THIRD) OF THE LAW GOVERNING LAWYERS § 14(1) (American Law Institute, 2000).

[23] 413 S.W.3d 291 (Ky. 2013).

[24] *Id.* at 296–97.

for one to think that that a lawyer engaged by the other to write a partnership agreement represented them both?[25]

Facts about which the plaintiff was unaware can provide no basis for concluding that the plaintiff relied upon a lawyer for representation. For example, *H-D Transport v. Pogue*[26] was a legal malpractice suit that arose from a dispute between two partners, Diges and Hughes. According to the Idaho Supreme Court, "Diges told Hughes that he had hired an attorney [Pogue] to prepare a partnership agreement, and Pogue, Hughes and Diane Barker, the partnership bookkeeper, participated in a conference call regarding the partnership."[27] In concluding that it was not reasonable for Hughes to believe that he (and the partnership) had attorney-client relationships with Pogue, the district court noted that, "because Hughes was unaware that Pogue was paid with H-D Transport's money, the source of the funds could not have been a basis for a reasonable belief that Pogue represented H-D Transport."[28]

In some cases, it may be significant that the lawyer represented the "client" in other transactions. For example, *Geddes v. Campbell*,[29] was a dispute arising in the context of complex business transactions. Based in part on the fact that the defendant-lawyer had written a letter stating that he represented the plaintiff in a subsequent, closely-related transaction, the court found there was a question of fact as to whether the defendant represented the plaintiff in an earlier transaction.

Under the mistake theory of attorney-client relationship, it is not enough that the plaintiff seeks legal services and reasonably believes that they are being rendered. The lawyer must also have known or had reason to know that the plaintiff was relying on the lawyer to provide those services. Thus, there is one question about the state of mind of the would-be client, and another about the state of mind of the lawyer. However, the latter question is often not a great obstacle to a finding of liability. A jury willing to believe that it was reasonable for a person to have relied upon a lawyer to provide legal services will usually also be ready to find that the lawyer knew or should have known of that mistake and should have corrected it.

In *Linegar v. DLA Piper LLP (US)*,[30] the Texas Supreme Court held that an individual beneficiary of a self-directed retirement account, which was managed by a corporate trustee, had standing to bring a legal malpractice action against the trustee's law firm based on advice the firm allegedly gave to him personally regarding a loan from the retirement account to a third party. The jury found that there was an attorney-client relationship between the individual beneficiary and the firm, and that the firm's breach of duties caused harm to the individual beneficiary.[31]

### *§ 5-2.1(a)(1)(C)(iv) Prevention*

Sloppy business practices greatly increase the risk of a lawyer being held liable for failing to protect the interests of a person who claims client status under the mistake theory of liability. Employment agreements and other correspondence should clearly

[25] H-D Transp. v. Pogue, 374 P.3d 591, 596 (Idaho 2016).

[26] 374 P.3d 591 (Idaho 2016).

[27] *Id.* at 593.

[28] *Id.* at 598.

[29] 2006 WL 3352182, at *4 (Cal. Ct. App.).

[30] 495 S.W.3d 276 (Tex. 2016).

[31] *Id.* at 281.

document who is, and who is not, being represented. For example, if the parent of an injured client consults a lawyer about representation, the lawyer should clarify in writing whether the lawyer is representing (1) the client, (2) the parent, or (3) the child and the parent.

Similarly, the owners and representatives of entities should be informed—again, preferably in writing—that they are not being personally represented (unless the lawyer intends to provide representation). If written evidence disclaiming representation can be adduced in a malpractice suit, it may be given great weight by the fact finder. Tangible evidence that the lawyer took steps to clarify the lawyer's role may be a critical factor in avoiding a finding that the plaintiff was a client. Such evidence could take the form of a non-engagement letter in which the lawyer confirms that the lawyer will not be representing the individuals affiliated with the entity-client.

By contrast, evidence that the plaintiff was orally advised that he or she was not being represented is much less helpful. Whether such advice was given may be a matter of dispute. In a swearing-match between the parties, the lawyer's self-serving testimony may be unpersuasive. This may be true for no other reason than that it would have been easy for the lawyer to have documented the disclosure, thereby creating a more dependable piece of evidence. From the perspective of law and economics scholarship, it might be said that liability in these types of cases is likely to be imposed on the lawyer because the lawyer was the "cheapest cost avoider" in preventing a misunderstanding about who was being represented.

In *Sabin v. Ackerman*,[32] the Supreme Court of Iowa addressed "whether an attorney designated by an executor or administrator to assist in the administration of the estate has an independent duty to represent the personal interests of the executor or administrator." The court answered that question in the negative, but quoted the *Restatement* in cautioning that:

> In trusts and estates practice a lawyer may have to clarify with those involved whether a trust, a trustee, its beneficiaries or groupings of some or all of them are clients and similarly whether the client is an executor, an estate, or its beneficiaries. In the absence of clarification the inference to be drawn may depend on the circumstances. . . .[33]

### *§ 5-2.1(a)(2) Appearance Before a Tribunal*

The *Restatement* indicates that, insofar as concerns the "rights of third persons," "[a] lawyer who enters an appearance before a tribunal on behalf of a person is presumed to represent that person as a client."[34] However, the presumption does not apply to "litigation between lawyer and client, where the person seeking relief usually bears the burdens of persuasion and of coming forward with evidence."[35] Nevertheless, whether a lawyer appeared in court on behalf of a person would seem to be a factor relevant to the issue of whether there was an attorney-client relationship.

---

[32] 846 N.W.2d 835, 841 (Iowa 2014).

[33] *Id.* at 843 (quoting RESTATEMENT (THIRD) OF THE LAW GOVERNING LAWYERS § 14 cmt. f (American Law Institute, 2000)).

[34] RESTATEMENT (THIRD) OF THE LAW GOVERNING LAWYERS § 25 (American Law Institute, 2000).

[35] *Id.* § 25 cmt. d.

In *Gibson v. Williams, Williams & Montgomery, P.A.*,[36] a case involving pleadings signed by a lawyer who later suggested there was a scrivener's error, the Supreme Court of Mississippi held that there was a genuine issue of material fact concerning the existence of an attorney-client relationship that prevented granting summary judgment for the defendant on a legal malpractice claim. The court explained that "by signing the petition as an 'attorney for the petitioner' in a pleading to the court that listed Bobby [the legal malpractice plaintiff] as a 'petitioner,' Montgomery [the legal malpractice defendant] not only represented to Bobby that he was his attorney, but he made that same representation to the court."[37] Further, the court found that Bobby's claim of client status was supported by Rule 11 of the Mississippi Rules of Civil Procedure, which provides that "the signature of an attorney constitutes a certificate that the attorney has read the pleading or motion; that to the best of the attorney's knowledge, information, and belief there is good ground to support it."[38] The court concluded that, "in accordance with this rule, when Montgomery signed the petition as 'attorney for petitioner,' he certified to the court that this representation was true and accurate."[39]

### *§ 5-2.1(a)(3) Attorney-Client Relationship Based on Estoppel*

It might be argued that the lawyer's statements to a court or third person, purporting to represent one who later claims to have been a client, estop the lawyer from denying the existence of an attorney-client relationship. The doctrine of quasi estoppel precludes a person from asserting, to another's disadvantage, a right inconsistent with a position previously taken.[40] The doctrine applies when it would be unconscionable to allow a person to maintain a position inconsistent with one to which he acquiesced, or from which he accepted a benefit.[41] A person "may not assert a particular position in order to serve one purpose, then assert a wholly contrary position to serve another."[42] The purpose of the estoppel doctrine is to preclude an attorney from taking advantage of his or her own wrongdoing by contradicting the propriety of the lawyer's prior conduct.[43]

If a lawyer defending a malpractice claim is estopped from denying the existence of an attorney-client relationship with the plaintiff, then the lawyer cannot deny that he or she owed a duty of care to the person who was purportedly represented. A duty of care is an indispensable component of every attorney-client relationship.

### *§ 5-2.1(a)(4) Voluntary Assumption of Duty*

Voluntary assumption of duty is a concept well established in the law of torts. Under common law principles, even if a person has no duty to act, he or she can voluntarily assume a duty to exercise care by undertaking to do so by way of words or conduct.

---

[36] 186 So. 3d 836 (Miss. 2016).

[37] *Id.* at 850.

[38] *Id.*

[39] *Id.*

[40] Lopez v. Munoz, Hockema & Reed, L.L.P., 22 S.W.3d 857, 864 (Tex. 2000).

[41] *See* Beckwith v. Pennsylvania State Univ., 2015 WL 140042, at *10 (M.D. Pa.); *see also* Travelers Prop. Cas. Corp. v. Jim Walter Homes, Inc., 966 P.2d 1190, 1191 (Okla. Civ. App. 1998).

[42] Owen v. Knop, 853 S.W.2d 638, 643 (Tex. App. 1993).

[43] RONALD E. MALLEN, LEGAL MALPRACTICE § 22:69 (Thomson Reuters, 2017 ed.) (discussing advice).

While the concept of voluntary assumption of duty has been applied most frequently in cases involving physical harm,[44] it is not limited to that context. Cases have permitted the recovery of purely economic damages under voluntary assumption of duty principles.[45]

It is possible for lawyers to voluntarily assume a duty of care to protect the legal interests of persons with whom they have not entered into a contract. As the Supreme Court of Idaho stated: "There is no reason why the same rule should not apply to attorneys. An attorney can voluntarily assume a duty to a nonclient just as can an appraiser."[46]

Reliance is not an essential element of a claim based on voluntary assumption of duty. All that is necessary is that the undertaking increase the risk of harm to the plaintiff.[47]

On appropriate facts, it may be possible to circumvent the lack of a traditional attorney-client relationship by arguing that the lawyer voluntarily assumed a duty of care to the plaintiff. A court may need to address such a claim as an issue of first impression in a legal malpractice case. There appear to be no reported cases.

### *§ 5-2.1(a)(5) Prospective Clients*

Persons seeking legal services sometimes never become clients. This is true, for example, if the person elects not to hire a lawyer or if the lawyer declines the representation. Nevertheless, in the course of determining whether an attorney-client relationship will be commenced, a person seeking legal services may entrust confidential information to a lawyer. Likewise, a lawyer may provide advice relevant to the person's interests, such as a preliminary assessment of the merits of a claim or defense. Therefore, it is not surprising that the law recognizes that lawyers owe some duties to prospective clients.

According to *Restatement*:

> (1) When a person discusses with a lawyer the possibility of their forming a client-lawyer relationship for a matter and no such relationship ensues, the lawyer must:
>
> (a) not subsequently use or disclose confidential information learned in the consultation, except to the extent permitted with respect to confidential information of a client or former client * * *;
>
> (b) protect the person's property in the lawyer's custody * * *; and
>
> (c) use reasonable care to the extent the lawyer provides the person legal services.[48]

---

44 *See* RESTATEMENT (THIRD) OF TORTS: LIABILITY FOR PHYSICAL AND EMOTIONAL HARM § 43 (2012); RESTATEMENT (SECOND) OF TORTS § 324A (1965).

45 *See* Bates v. Chicago Title Co., 2013 WL 3753062, at *6–7 (Cal. Ct. App.); Valdez v. Taylor Auto. Co., 278 P.2d 91, 95 (Cal. Ct. App. 1954).

46 Taylor v. Riley, 336 P.3d 256, 272 (Idaho 2014).

47 *See* Staples v. Merck & Co., 270 F. Supp. 2d 833, 841 (N.D. Tex. 2003); *see also* Artiglio v. Corning Inc., 957 P.2d 1313, 1317 (Cal. 1998).

48 RESTATEMENT (THIRD) OF THE LAW GOVERNING LAWYERS § 15 (American Law Institute, 2000).

This means, for example, that a lawyer may be subject to liability for telling a prospective client, without qualification, that a claim has no merit, if careful research and investigation of the facts would have led to a contrary conclusion. Similarly, if a lawyer misstates the applicable statute of limitations in advising a prospective client to seek other counsel, the lawyer may be subject to liability if the misstatement induces the person to delay the search for counsel until the claim is time-barred.

Information learned from a prospective client, rather than actual client, may create conflicts of interest that disqualify the lawyer from representing certain persons in the future.[49] The conflict of interest rule relating to former prospective clients is narrower than the conflict of interest rule applicable to former (actual) clients. This makes sense because a narrower range of duties is owed to a former prospective client than to a former client.[50]

In dealing with prospective clients, limiting the scope of discussion may minimize the risks of future disqualifying conflicts of interest. Of course, regardless of whether an initial consultation is narrowly limited or wide ranging, a lawyer should track information related to the identity of a prospective client and the matters about which legal representation was discussed. Such records enable the lawyer to comply with conflict of interest rules, even if a conflict does not emerge until many years later.

#### *§ 5-2.1(a)(6) Class Members*

A lawyer appointed to represent a group of persons in class action litigation has an attorney-client relationship with the named class representatives. The lawyer also owes certain legal and ethical duties to members of the class, at least until they opt out of the lawsuit. Thus, if a law firm represents, in housing litigation, a class defined as the tenants who resided in a building on a certain date, the firm has a duty to distribute the proceeds of a judgment or settlement only to members of the class, and not to other persons who may have resided in the building on earlier occasions.[51]

However, if a potential class has not been certified as one suitable for aggregate litigation, the unnamed members of the putative class are not clients. In the usual case, those persons never requested legal services from the lawyer and no court appointed the lawyer to represent them. Thus, the potential class members do not fall within any of the three categories of attorney-client relationship discussed above.[52]

### § 5-2.1(b) Scope of Representation

A lawyer's duties to a client normally extend only as far as the scope of the representation. Thus, a lawyer who serves as general counsel to a corporation has a much greater range of potential liability than a lawyer hired by a corporation to handle only an isolated matter.

---

[49] *See* RESTATEMENT (THIRD) OF THE LAW GOVERNING LAWYERS § 15(2) (American Law Institute, 2000).

[50] *Compare* MODEL RULES OF PROF'L CONDUCT R. 1.9 (American Bar Ass'n, 2017) (addressing former client conflicts) *with id.* R. 1.18 (addressing prospective client conflicts).

[51] *See* Taylor v. Akin, Gump, Strauss, Hauer & Feld, 859 A.2d 142 (D.C. 2004).

[52] *See generally* Vincent R. Johnson, *The Ethics of Communicating with Putative Class Members*, 17 REV. LITIG. 497 (1998).

### § 5-2.1(b)(1) *Defining the Scope of Representation*

In assessing the scope of representation,[53] it is useful to focus on what services the client requested and what services the lawyer agreed to provide. Statements in the lawyer-client employment contract about the contemplated legal work are highly relevant. However, other factors also must be taken into account. These factors include the history of dealings between the parties and whether the client employed different attorneys to handle other legal matters for the client.

If the lawyer has served for a period of years as the sole, all-purpose counsel for a client, it is easier to conclude that a new matter of legal significance discussed with the lawyer was within an expanded scope of the representation, regardless of what the original lawyer-client contract stated. Similarly, if a business entity hires different lawyers from time to time, or hires multiple lawyers simultaneously to handle diverse matters, it may be difficult to prove that a new matter, even if it was called to the attention of the defendant-lawyer, was within the scope of the defendant's representation of the plaintiff. The client may have mentioned the matter just to test the lawyer's reaction, before deciding whom to hire to handle the representation.

The relative sophistication of the putative client is important. If the person is well educated and has experience in retaining and changing lawyers, there is less reason to think that the person was mistaken about whether a lawyer-client relationship was created. In contrast, if the person is inexperienced in dealing with lawyers, and to that extent more likely to depend on counsel to protect the client's interests, it is easier to believe that the person reasonably believed he or she was being represented.

### § 5-2.1(b)(2) *Changes in the Scope of Representation*

The scope of representation may change during the course of a lawyer's employment. As time passes, a client may ask a lawyer to address matters that were not contemplated at the time the employment agreement was initially signed. Thus, testimony about an expanding range of representation may persuade jurors, even if the testimony differs from the written terms of the engagement. The failure to revise the original statements about the scope of representation may mean simply that the document was not updated, rather than that the scope of representation never changed.

In *Grochocinski v. Mayer Brown Rowe & Maw LLP*,[54] the defendants argued that they were not responsible for alleged malpractice relating to litigation because their agreement with the client said that they were retained "only in connection with * * * [the client's] formation and corporate activities."[55] However, a federal court in Illinois found that there was a basis for concluding that the defendants owed a duty of care with respect to the litigation because, in fact, they provided legal advice related to the lawsuit and an e-mail from one lawyer instructed the client to feel "free to contact * * * me with any questions * * * you might have regarding the current situation."[56]

[53] For more on scope of representation, see Part Four of this book, Gregory C. Sisk, *Legal Ethics and the Practice of Law* § 4-3.3.

[54] 2007 WL 1875995 (N.D. Ill.).

[55] *Id.* at *7.

[56] *Id.*

### *§ 5-2.1(b)(3) Unreasonable Limits on the Scope of Representation*

The rules of professional conduct afford lawyers and clients broad latitude in defining the scope of representation.[57] Such a limitation is valid if it is reasonable under the circumstances and the client gives informed consent.[58] This means, for example, that the duties of a lawyer retained by an insurer to represent an insured may be limited to matters related to the insurance coverage.[59]

In *Lerner v. Laufer*,[60] a lawyer had a client sign a detailed statement acknowledging that the lawyer was reviewing a property settlement agreement only to ensure that it reflected the terms of an earlier mediation; was not advising the client on the fairness of the deal; and had not investigated the divorcing couple's assets or liabilities. In a subsequent malpractice action, a New Jersey court concluded that the lawyer did not breach the standard of care by performing no discovery or investigatory services related to the fairness of the agreement because the scope of representation had been limited to exclude those services. Relevant to whether the limited scope of representation was reasonable was the fact that there was no dispute relating to the client's competence, her general knowledge of the family's financial and personal affairs, or the voluntariness of her decision to submit to mediation.[61]

However, a limitation on duty is invalid and unenforceable if the limitation unreasonably impairs the efficacy of a lawyer's services.[62] Consider, for example, the case of a lawyer advising a client on a contract for the sale of goods to a foreign buyer. If the lawyer-client contract provides that the lawyer is not obliged to consider issues arising under international law, such as the Convention on Contracts for the International Sale of Goods, that limitation may be so unreasonable that it may not limit the lawyer's liability for failing to address such issues.[63]

In some cases, doubts about the scope of the representation are resolved against the lawyer. For example, if a lawyer unsuccessfully represents a client at trial, and no agreement has been reached as to whether the lawyer will be responsible for appealing the adverse judgment, the lawyer must consult with the client about the possibility of appeal before relinquishing responsibility for the case.[64] A contract limiting the scope of representation is construed from the standpoint of a reasonable client.[65]

### *§ 5-2.1(b)(4) Responsibility for Closely Related Matters*

Some cases hold that a lawyer's duties extend beyond the strict scope of representation and encompass closely related matters. For example, in *Geddes v.*

---

[57] *See* RESTATEMENT (THIRD) OF THE LAW GOVERNING LAWYERS § 19 (American Law Institute, 2000).

[58] MODEL RULES OF PROF'L CONDUCT R. 1.2 (American Bar Ass'n, 2017).

[59] MODEL RULES OF PROF'L CONDUCT R. 1.2 cmt. 6 (American Bar Ass'n, 2017).

[60] 819 A.2d 471 (App. Div. 2003).

[61] *Id.* at 484.

[62] *Cf.* Michele N. Struffolino, *Taking Limited Representation to the Limits: The Efficacy of Using Unbundled Legal Services in Domestic-Relations Matters Involving Litigation*, 2 ST. MARY'S J. LEGAL MAL. & ETHICS 166, 260 (2012) ("[L]imited representation is not appropriate in contested domestic-relations matters").

[63] *See generally* Vincent R. Johnson, *Legal Malpractice in International Business Transactions*, 44 HOFSTRA L. REV. 325, 337–38 (2015).

[64] *See* MODEL RULES OF PROF'L CONDUCT R. 1.3 cmt. 4 (American Bar Ass'n, 2017).

[65] *See* RESTATEMENT (THIRD) OF THE LAW GOVERNING LAWYERS § 19 cmt. c (American Law Institute, 2000).

*Campbell*,[66] the court held that if a lawyer represented an individual in connection with the sale of certain partnership property, and discovered by reading the partnership agreement that the individual owed certain fiduciary duties to others, the lawyer had a duty to advise the individual with respect to his fiduciary duties, regardless of the precise scope of the representation. The court explained:

> An attorney who undertakes one matter on behalf of a client owes a duty to consider and advise the client as to other related matters the client may be overlooking and which should be pursued to avoid prejudicing the client's interests. "[E]ven when a retention is expressly limited, the attorney may still have a duty to alert the client to legal problems which are reasonably apparent, even though they fall outside the scope of retention."[67]

Similarly, the Supreme Court of Kentucky has stated: "An attorney cannot completely disregard matters coming to his attention which should reasonably put him on notice that his client may have legal problems or remedies that are not precisely or totally within the scope of the task being performed by the attorney."[68] According to legal malpractice expert Ronald E. Mallen, "An attorney may be obligated to counsel the client even regarding collateral legal matters or, at least, alert the client to the need for legal representation."[69]

However, other cases appear to be contrary. In *AmBase Corp. v. Davis Polk & Wardwell*,[70] the New York Court of Appeals held that a law firm that successfully represented a client in a tax protest had no duty to question whether an agreement between the client and a related company could have been interpreted to relieve the client of tax liability in the dispute with the Internal Revenue Service. The court wrote:

> The retainer agreement states that AmBase has "engaged [Davis Polk] to represent [it] as agent for City Investing to resolve the tax issues currently before" the IRS. The plain language of the retainer agreement indicates that Davis Polk was retained to litigate the amount of tax liability and not to determine whether the tax liability could be allocated to another entity. Thus, the issue whether plaintiff was primarily or secondarily liable for the subject tax liability was outside the scope of its representation.[71]

### *§ 5-2.1(b)(5) Termination of the Attorney-Client Relationship*

Termination of the attorney-client relationship greatly contracts the scope of duties owed to a client. At the moment of termination, the client, who previously occupied the most preferred status, is transformed into a former client to whom only limited duties are owed. The most important of the surviving duties is continued confidentiality of client information. However, the array of duties is somewhat larger. According to the

---

66 2006 WL 3352182 (Cal. Ct. App.).

67 *Id.* at *5 (Cal. Ct. App.) (quoting Nichols v. Keller, 15 Cal. App. 4th 1672, 1684, 19 Cal. Rptr. 2d 601 (1993)).

68 Daugherty v. Runner, 581 S.W.2d 12, 17 (Ky. App. 1978); *see also* Maillard v. Dowdell, 528 So. 2d 512, 515 (Fla. Dist. Ct. App. 1988) (Schwartz, C.J., dissenting) (quoting *Daugherty* with approval); Castillo v. Massachusetts General Hosp., 649 N.E.2d 788, 790 (Mass. App. Ct. 1995) (quoting *Daugherty* with approval); Davis v. Klein, 637 N.Y.S.2d 137, 139 (N.Y. App. Div. 1996) (Sullivan, J., dissenting) (quoting *Daugherty* with approval).

69 RONALD E. MALLEN, LEGAL MALPRACTICE, § 33:4 (Thomson Reuters, 2017 ed.).

70 8 N.Y.3d 428, 866 N.E.2d 1033, 834 N.Y.S.2d 705 (2007).

71 *Id.* at 709.

*Restatement*, after a lawyer-client relationship has ended, a lawyer must also: observe obligations to a former client related to conflicts of interest, property, documents, and fee collection; refrain from further action on behalf of a former client without new authorization; convey to the former client any material communication the lawyer receives relating to the representation; and avoid taking unfair advantage of the former client by abusing knowledge or trust acquired during the representation.[72]

*§ 5-2.1(b)(5)(A) Post-Termination Loyalty*

Cases occasionally assert that a lawyer owes a former client a continuing duty of loyalty. That is certainly not true in any broad sense. A past engagement is not transformed by termination of the representation into a lifetime of far ranging obligations. For example, "attorneys have no ongoing duty to monitor the legal status of the property mentioned in a testamentary instrument."[73]

State law may impose particular obligations. For example, in Texas, a lawyer representing a new client shall not question "the validity of the lawyer's [own] services or work product for * * * [a] former client."[74]

Of course, lawyers may, and frequently do, feel moral obligations of loyalty to former clients, and often tailor their conduct in accordance therewith. Depending on the facts, solicitude for the interests of former clients may be appropriate and wholly laudable. Nevertheless, malpractice law is concerned with legal obligations, and there is no general, broad-ranging duty of loyalty to a former client that is enforceable in an action for negligence or under any other legal theory.

In *Torban v. Obermayer Rebmann Maxwell & Hippel*,[75] a lawyer revised the wills of a husband and wife to include trusts for tax-planning purposes. Although the lawyer advised the couple that all of the tax planning would be worthless unless they divided their assets, the couple, either intentionally or negligently, rejected that advice, and continued to own their assets jointly. Later, when the wife died, the couple's son, serving as executor, hired the lawyer to handle the administration of his mother's estate. After a fee dispute developed, the son alleged that the lawyer committed malpractice by failing to advise him and his father, after his mother death, about other steps his father could take to minimize estate taxes by disclaiming an interest in the mother's certificates of deposit. An appellate court in New Jersey rejected the malpractice claim. It found that the father's attorney-client relationship with the lawyer had terminated long before his wife's death, and that the attorney-client relationship between the son and the lawyer did not encompass advice about his father's estate planning, because the lawyer had been hired only to probate the mother's will. Therefore, the lawyer had no duty to provide the tax advice in question. This was true even though that information might have been useful to the son or his father and was in some sense related to the subject matter of the earlier representation. The lawyer's continuing duties to the father had greatly contracted because the attorney-client relationship with the father had ended.

---

[72] RESTATEMENT (THIRD) OF THE LAW GOVERNING LAWYERS § 33(2) (American Law Institute, 2000).

[73] Soignier v. Fletcher, 256 P.3d 730, 734 (Idaho 2011).

[74] TEX. DISCIP. RULES OF PROF'L CONDUCT R. 1.09(a)(1) (2017).

[75] 2007 WL 1827283 (N.J. Super. Ct. App. Div.).

*§ 5-2.1(b)(5)(B) Termination of Authority*

A lawyer's authority to represent a client may end for any of several reasons.[76] Authority terminates if the client discharges the lawyer; if the client dies or, in the case of an entity client, loses its capacity to function; or if the lawyer dies or becomes physically or mentally incapable of providing further representation. Authority also ends if the lawyer is disbarred or suspended from the practice of law, or is ordered by a tribunal to cease representing the client. Likewise, authority terminates if the representation has ended as provided for by the contract or because the contemplated services have been completed.

However, termination of authority to act is not the same as termination of representation. Some of the named factors that bear on the issue of authority (e.g., death of the client or lawyer) may also support the conclusion that the representation has ended. However, other considerations may be relevant. If a lawyer's engagement is limited to a specific matter, the attorney-client relationship normally terminates when the matter has been resolved.[77] In contrast, if a lawyer has represented the client in many different matters over a period of years, the client may be justified in assuming that the lawyer will continue to serve on an ongoing basis unless the lawyer gives notice of withdrawal.[78]

Harkening back to the mistake theory of attorney-client relationship,[79] it is useful to ask whether the person who was previously represented still reasonably believes that he or she is a client. If so, it may well be the case that the attorney-client relationship has not ceased, and that a wide range of duties are still owed to that person. Thus, lawyers should clearly communicate in writing the termination of the attorney-client relationship. Subsequent communications with former clients should avoid creating the impression of continuing representation.

## § 5-2.2 BREACH OF DUTY

In language consistent with that used by other courts,[80] the Michigan Court of Appeals, in *Harris v. Farmer*,[81] explained the duty of care imposed by the law of negligence in the following terms:

> An attorney is obligated to use reasonable skill, care, discretion, and judgment in representing a client and to act as would an attorney of ordinary learning, judgment, or skill under the same or similar circumstances * * *. Although an attorney has the duty to fashion a strategy so that it is consistent with prevailing * * * law, he does not have a duty to ensure or guarantee the most favorable outcome possible. * * *.[82]

---

76 *See* RESTATEMENT (THIRD) OF THE LAW GOVERNING LAWYERS § 22 (American Law Institute, 2000).

77 *See* Berry v. McFarland, 278 P.3d 407, 411 (Idaho 2012)

78 *See* MODEL RULES OF PROF'L CONDUCT R. 1.3 cmt. 4 (American Bar Ass'n, 2017); Berry v. McFarland, 278 P.3d 407, 411 (Idaho 2012).

79 *See infra* § 5-2.1(a)(1)(C).

80 *See* Thomas v. Kidani, 267 P.3d 1230, 1234 (Haw. 2011) (a lawyer has a duty "to use such skill, prudence, and diligence as lawyers of ordinary skill and capacity commonly possess and exercise in the performance of the tasks which they undertake").

81 2010 WL 395764 (Mich. Ct. App.).

82 *Id.* at *1.

Whether a lawyer breached a duty of care to the plaintiff is normally a question of fact for the jury (or for the court sitting as fact finder). However, in cases where fair minds could not differ, a court may rule as a matter of law that the defendant acted unreasonably. This may be true, for example, where a lawyer fails to file a lawsuit before the statute of limitations lapses.

Conversely, a court may sometimes rule as a matter of law that certain conduct was not negligent. In *Driftmyer v. Carlton*,[83] the court found that the record contained no evidence of foreseeable harm to a man's estate based on his naming a Defined Pension Benefit Trust as the beneficiary of his life insurance policy. The estate therefore could not maintain an action for legal malpractice against the decedent's lawyer based on the lawyer's alleged failure to recommend the establishment of a separate trust to avoid estate taxation of the life insurance proceeds.[84] *Driftmyer* is an apt reminder of the fact that negligence is the unreasonable failure to guard against foreseeable harm. If harm is not foreseeable, the failure to avoid it is not a breach of duty under negligence principles.

### § 5-2.2(a) The Standard of Care

The law of negligence sets an objective standard for evaluating the conduct of a defendant-lawyer. In the usual case, the question is simply whether the defendant did what a reasonably prudent lawyer exercising ordinary care could have done under the same or similar circumstances. Either the defendant measures up to that standard, or the defendant falls short.

An objective negligence standard makes sense from a consumer protection perspective. When any client walks into any law office, the client is guaranteed a certain objectively defined level of protection with respect to a host of important matters, such as the safeguarding of confidential information, avoidance of conflicts of interest, communication of material information, and diligence in researching legal and factual issues.

By mandating the exercise of reasonable care, the law of negligence not only protects clients who do not know what risks should be considered in hiring a lawyer, it also makes the engagement of legal representation more efficient for sophisticated clients. Every client is assured, in the absence of an agreement to the contrary, that every lawyer comes with all of the "standard equipment" that is reasonably necessary for effective and ethical legal representation. This includes, for example, knowledge of the law, legal research skills, diligent work habits, customary office practices, and conformance with professional ethics rules.

The standard of care does not require "average" performance, which would imply that lawyers in the less skillful part of the profession were necessarily negligent.[85] The benchmark for avoiding negligence liability is to act reasonably. Thus, the duty is not to be average, or better than average, but to be reasonable under the circumstances.

---

[83] 2007 WL 1229305 (Ohio Ct. App.).

[84] *Id.* at *15–16.

[85] *See* RESTATEMENT (THIRD) OF THE LAW GOVERNING LAWYERS § 52 cmt. b (American Law Institute, 2000).

### *§ 5-2.2(a)(1) Specialists*

Lawyers who specialize[86] in a particular area of the law may be held to a higher standard of care than lawyers who do not specialize. Conceptually, this has appeal because those with talent should be encouraged to use it wisely. Nevertheless, the difficulties of implementing a higher standard of care for specialists (or for others) deserves consideration. Indeed, relatively few malpractice cases talk about a higher standard of care.

In practice, it is easiest to hold specialists to a higher standard if there is some clear point of reference that can be used to articulate what a specialist knows or does that is different from, and presumably superior to, what an ordinary practitioner would know or do. For example, some states have certification processes by which lawyers earn the right to call themselves specialists. These credentialing processes typically involve either educational requirements and/or demonstrations of proficiency through examinations, performance standards, or peer review. If that is the case, the standard of care for a certified specialist could be established by producing expert testimony from another certified specialist, or by reference to the principles that are taught or tested in the credentialing process (assuming those principles are distinguishable from what ordinary lawyers know or do).

*De facto* specialization is a different matter. It may be difficult to discern the applicable standard of care if specialization means simply that a lawyer has devoted a significant percentage of his or her practice to a particular kind of work for a period of years. Would a plaintiff have to adduce expert testimony from another lawyer who devoted a similar percentage of practice to the same type of work for about the same number of years? Could an expert who has specialized in an area of the law for twenty years opine on what type of care should have been exercised by a defendant-lawyer who has specialized in the same area for one year, five years, ten years, or thirty years?

If *de facto* specialists are held to a higher standard of care, what about other groups that could be treated similarly? Should there be a higher standard of care for lawyers practicing in large law firms, or graduates of Ivy League law schools, or lawyers who have earned post-doctoral LL.M. degrees?

It is easy to see why tort law has normally eschewed fracturing the standard of care into a myriad of different measures. In the absence of a clear point of reference (such as a certification process) for articulating what the higher standard entails, the preferable course may be the one that minimizes complexity. Lawyers—regardless of where they graduated from law school, what courses they took, what degrees they earned, or what kind of firm they practice in—should be held to the standard of conduct of an ordinary, reasonably prudent lawyer under the same or similar circumstances. Rather than changing the standard of care, *de facto* specialization might simply be treated as a factor relevant to whether ordinary care was exercised.

### *§ 5-2.2(a)(2) Representations of Greater Competence*

The *Restatement* does not directly address whether specialization changes the standard of care, or is merely a factor relevant to whether the lawyer has acted in conformance with the standard of ordinary care under the circumstances. In discussing

---

[86] On the ethical rules concerning communication of specialization in an area of law, see Part Four of this book, Gregory C. Sisk, *Legal Ethics and the Practice of Law* § 4-2.4(f).

lawyers who claim to be experts or specialists, the *Restatement* commentary says that "a lawyer who represents to a client that the lawyer has greater competence * * * *is held to that higher standard.*"[87] However, that language is part of a comment entitled "[s]imilar circumstances," the first sentence of which says that "[a] lawyer's representations or disclaimers and qualifications may *constitute circumstances* affecting what a client is entitled to expect from the lawyer."[88] Therefore, representations related to concentrating or specializing in particular practice areas may be relevant in evaluating the reasonableness of conduct under the circumstances.

Holding specialists to a higher standard might not necessarily be an advantage to malpractice plaintiffs. A plaintiff may prefer to rely on an ordinary standard of care if establishing the higher standard complicates the presentation of the malpractice case, or if finding a qualified expert to testify about the higher duty of care is difficult.

#### *§ 5-2.2(a)(3) Disclosure of Inexperience*

New members of the legal profession are ordinarily held to the same standard of care as those with experience. There is no "learner's permit" for the practice of law that absolves novices from liability for mistakes that could have been avoided through the exercise of reasonable care.

The *Restatement* says that an agreement limiting the duty that a lawyer owes to a client is permissible if the client is adequately informed and the terms of the limitation are reasonable.[89] Moreover, "disclaimers and qualifications may constitute circumstances affecting what a client is entitled to expect from the lawyer."[90] However, an illustration in the *Restatement* adds that a general waiver of the duty of competence would be invalid.[91]

#### *§ 5-2.2(a)(4) Malpractice by Laypersons*

A layperson who practices law can be sued for legal malpractice. It is no defense to liability for the layperson to argue that he or she was never admitted to the practice of law.

For example, in *Buscemi v. Intachai*,[92] the defendant, a financial planner who had a legal education but was not admitted to the bar, was sued for mishandling legal issues related to the investment of guardianship funds. The defendant had told the plaintiff that he "would comply with the Supreme Court of Florida rules and regulations," and charge a cheaper fee than a lawyer.[93] A Florida appellate court held that, whether a person is a lawyer or not, one who undertakes to give legal advice, must exercise due care.[94]

---

[87] RESTATEMENT (THIRD) OF THE LAW GOVERNING LAWYERS § 52 cmt. d (American Law Institute, 2000) (emphasis added).

[88] *Id.* (emphasis added).

[89] *See* RESTATEMENT (THIRD) OF THE LAW GOVERNING LAWYERS § 19 (American Law Institute, 2000).

[90] *Id.* at § 52 cmt. d.

[91] *Id.* § 19 illus. 3.

[92] 730 So. 2d 329 (Fla. Dist. Ct. App. 1999).

[93] *Id.* at 330.

[94] *Id.*

Similarly, in *Webb v. Pomeroy*,[95] a layperson, whose brother was a lawyer, was sued for malpractice related to real property conveyancing instruments. The Kansas Court of Appeals ruled broadly that a person "in the same position as a regularly admitted practicing attorney" is "bound to the same degree of knowledge, skill, dedication, and ethical conduct as * * * [a] member of the bar."[96]

There are few reported cases holding nonlawyers liable for legal malpractice. This may change as nonlawyers are increasingly permitted to represent persons before state and federal agencies, or take on a wider range of law-related tasks for businesses. However, it is possible that the law may develop in a way that does not hold all nonlawyers to the standard of performance for lawyers, but instead liable under contract principles requiring simply that they must deliver what they promise.[97] This might not be too far different from liability under tort principles which, as noted above, say that a lawyer and client may define the scope of the representation.[98] Even under a contract standard, a person who impersonates a lawyer, or otherwise expressly or implicitly represents that he or she can deliver the same quality of services as a lawyer, might be judged by reference to the standard of care for lawyers.

Nevertheless, substituting contract remedies for tort principles might seriously erode the protection that legal malpractice law provides to clients, as well as the role that tort law plays in deterring improper practices. "Contract law offers no great repository of client protection principles, but rather an array of rules which do as much to limit obligations by lawyers to clients as to create them," and therefore "[w]eak and unsophisticated clients are unlikely to be protected by contractual principles from practitioners who are incompetent or more loyal to other interests."[99]

### *§ 5-2.2(a)(5) Lawyers with Disabilities*

There are numerous unanswered questions regarding the malpractice liability of lawyers with disabilities. One issue is whether an undisclosed disability (e.g., dyslexia or inability to mentally focus in noisy situations) affects the standard of care. In many areas of tort law, physical disabilities are taken into account in determining whether the defendant acted as a reasonably prudent person.[100] Thus, a person who is blind is required to exercise the same degree of care as a reasonably prudent person who is blind. However, mental disabilities, such as poor judgment, low intelligence, or even insanity, are generally ignored.[101] The difficulties of applying these rules to learning disabilities are apparent because it is often less than clear whether such disabilities can be categorized as exclusively or predominantly physical or mental.

---

[95] 655 P.2d 465 (Kan. App. 1982).

[96] *Id.* at 468.

[97] *See generally* THOMAS D. MORGAN, THE VANISHING AMERICAN LAWYER 77–78 (Oxford Univ. Press, 2010); Thomas D. Morgan, *Professional Malpractice in a World of Amateurs*, 40 ST. MARY'S L.J. 891, 903 (2009).

[98] *See* § 5-2.1(b)(1).

[99] Vincent R. Johnson, *Legal Malpractice in a Changing Profession: The Role of Contract Principles*, 61 CLEV. ST. L. REV. 489, 526 (2013); *id.* at 520 ("The question * * * is whether contract law principles, which are so seldom a basis for lawyer liability, might somehow play an important role in assuring that nonlawyers and lawyers who are not fully licensed are deterred from causing harm to clients and held accountable for deficient conduct. A negative answer to this query is strongly suggested by five factors, including the unrealistic prospect of clients bargaining for protection, the absence of implied warranties for services, problems of proof, limited damages, and inconsistent client treatment").

[100] *See* RESTATEMENT (THIRD) OF TORTS: LIABILITY FOR PHYSICAL AND EMOTIONAL HARM § 11(a) (2010).

[101] *Id.* § 11(c).

For consumer protection reasons, it is arguable that a lawyer's *undisclosed disability* of any kind should not play a role in a legal malpractice action. Such lawyers should be held to the same standard of care as any reasonably prudent attorney. This view would seem to be consistent with the position of the *Restatement*, which, as noted above, provides that an agreement limiting the duty that a lawyer owes to a client is permissible *if the client is adequately informed* and the terms of the limitation are reasonable.[102]

### § 5-2.2(b) No Good Faith Defense

Because negligence is concerned with conduct, not state of mind, there is no good faith defense to a negligence claim.[103] The issue is not whether the defendant tried his or her best, or undertook certain conduct in an effort to benefit the client, or honestly believed that the client's interests would be protected. Rather, the relevant inquiry is simply whether the defendant acted reasonably.

If the defendant acted reasonably, there is no liability for negligence. Thus, in the absence of an agreement to bring a retaliation claim, no matter how much or little it was worth, a lawyer is not liable for failing to assert such a claim where the undisputed facts indicate that it would not yield more than nominal damages.[104]

### § 5-2.2(c) Risk Balancing and Economic Analysis

In the law of negligence generally, the standard of care is discussed in different ways. For example, rather than asking whether the defendant acted appropriately in the anthropomorphic terms of what a reasonably prudent person would have done, courts or scholars sometimes ask whether the risks outweighed the utility of the actor's conduct.[105] Or they consider whether the burden of prevention outweighed the gravity of the threatened loss viewed in light of the probability of that harm occurring.[106]

Interestingly, balancing tests and economic analysis seem to play almost no role in legal malpractice cases. Although the reason is not clear, courts and scholars rarely speak in those terms. The relevant inquiry in evaluating whether a lawyer acted appropriately is virtually always framed in terms of reasonable care. That is, the question is whether the defendant exhibited the level of care that a reasonably prudent lawyer would exercise in the relevant geographic area.

The extent to which risk-utility calculations or other aspects of economic analysis apply (or do not apply) to legal malpractice claims has yet to be fully charted. Nevertheless, it is worth noting that such principles have occasionally played a role in *medical* malpractice litigation.

In the famous and controversial case of *Helling v. Carey*,[107] the court employed a type of economic analysis in concluding that the defendant ophthalmologist was negligent in following the customary practice of not testing persons under forty years of age for glaucoma. The court found that the test, if properly administered, would have

---

[102] *See* RESTATEMENT (THIRD) OF THE LAW GOVERNING LAWYERS § 19 (American Law Institute, 2000).

[103] *See* Cosgrove v. Grimes, 774 S.W.2d 662, 664–65 (Tex. 1989).

[104] *See* Cecala v. Newman, 2010 WL 1936384, at *1 (9th Cir.).

[105] RESTATEMENT (THIRD) OF TORTS: LIABILITY FOR PHYSICAL AND EMOTIONAL HARM § 3 cmt. e (2010).

[106] *Cf.* United States v. Carroll Towing Co., 159 F.2d 169 (2d Cir. 1947).

[107] 519 P.2d 981 (Wash. 1974).

been relatively simple, inexpensive, and dependable, and that without the test, detection of the disease at that time was virtually impossible. Mindful of the grave and devastating nature of the potential harm to the plaintiff patient (loss of vision), and of the slight burden that administering the test would have imposed, the court held that it was negligent as a matter of law for the doctor not to give the test. In economic terms, the gravity of the threatened loss, viewed in light of its probability, significantly outweighed the burden of prevention ($B < L \times P$).

Perhaps similar balancing-test arguments could be made in the legal malpractice context. For example, in *Hodges v. Carter*,[108] the lawyers representing the plaintiff in a case involving the denial of insurance coverage for losses resulting from a fire were not liable for failing to predict that a long-observed practice for serving out-of-state insurance companies with process would be held invalid. However, it might have been argued that once it was known that the insurance companies were contesting the validity of the customary procedures, the defendant-lawyers should not have gambled that the procedures would be upheld by the state high court. Instead, the lawyers should have reinitiated the suit within the approximately sixty days then available by serving process in a different manner, assuming that was possible. Viewed in terms of economic analysis, it was arguably negligent for the attorneys not to incur the slight burden of re-instituting the suit when doing so would have avoided great harm (loss of coverage) that, while unlikely (because the challenged practice was long-standing), was nevertheless a serious risk (because validity of the process had been contested). If the case had been argued in those terms, the result might have been different.

If there is a persuasive reason why balancing tests and economic analysis do not apply in the field of legal malpractice, it may relate to the need to ensure that lawyers have room to exercise judgment without fear of legal liability.[109]

### § 5-2.2(d) Specific Duties

It is difficult to identify what specific obligations are encompassed by the duty of care because virtually every aspect of a lawyer's performance could be treated as a subcategory. A lawyer's duty of reasonable care extends to all aspects of the client's representation, including, for example, interviewing, counseling,[110] research,[111] drafting,[112] investigation,[113] advocacy, litigation, and dispute resolution. "[U]pon proper proof, failure to sue the correct party may be a viable basis for a legal malpractice cause of action."[114]

---

[108] 80 S.E.2d 144 (N.C. 1954).

[109] *See infra* § 5-2.2(e) (discussing exercise of judgment).

[110] *See, e.g.*, Morris v. Hap Taylor & Sons, Inc., 301 P.3d 639, 645 (Idaho 2013) (dicta).

[111] *See* Charles Epps Ipock, *How an Obscure Tennessee Opinion Uncovers the Veil of Legal Malpractice Between Asset-Protection Trusts and the Uniform Trust Code*, 3 ST. MARY'S J. LEGAL MAL. & ETHICS 308, 318 (2013) (emphasizing the importance of thoroughly researching which jurisdiction's law will be most beneficial to a client who is establishing an asset-protection trust because "simply establishing the trust in a client's domicile may lead to malpractice").

[112] *See, e.g.*, McKay v. Walker, 369 P.3d 926, 927 (Idaho 2016) (no breach); Soignier v. Fletcher, 256 P.3d 730, 733 (Idaho 2011) (no breach).

[113] Stephen v. Sallaz & Gatewood, Chtd., 248 P.3d 1256, 1260 (Idaho 2011).

[114] Heldring v. Lundy Beldecos & Milby, P.C., 151 A.3d 634, 642 (Pa. Super. 2016).

At a general level, there are at least two overarching obligations encompassed by the duty of reasonable care: competence and diligence.[115] Competence and diligence are discussed in the following sections. Certain specific obligations, such as the duty of candor, are discussed in other parts of the text.[116]

### *§ 5-2.2(d)(1) Competence*

Competence[117] entails many things, including both knowledge and professional skills. Required knowledge may concern applicable law, legal institutions, ethical restrictions, and to some extent, human nature. The professional skills that are necessary for competent representation may relate to such routine matters as research,[118] writing, interviewing, counseling,[119] advocacy, dispute resolution, and office management.

The duty to mitigate damages is a basic principle of American law. A lawyer who fails to advise a client about the necessity of mitigating damages may be held to have violated the duty of competence. This is true because reasonably prudent lawyers would be aware of the mitigation rule and would understand how it applies to a particular set of facts.

### *§ 5-2.2(d)(2) Duty to Recommend a Specialist*

On appropriate facts, the duty of competence may require a lawyer to refer a potential client to a specialist. This may be true if the proposed representation entails a need for greater knowledge or skills than are typically possessed by an ordinary practitioner.[120]

In *Dennerline v. Atterholt*,[121] a lawyer, despite lack of relevant experience, agreed to represent a complex insurance trust. The lawyer did not consult anyone for advice, nor did he conduct research into the applicable laws. Consequently, he failed to advise the trust about the legal ramifications of operating without a certificate of registration from the state Department of Insurance. Further, the lawyer did not "even think about" a mandatory provision in the trust agreement requiring termination of the trust if it became insolvent.[122] Ultimately, the lawyer and his law firm were held liable for nearly $18 million in losses.[123]

---

[115] *See* RESTATEMENT (THIRD) OF THE LAW GOVERNING LAWYERS § 52 cmt. b (American Law Institute, 2000).

[116] *See infra* § 5-3.3 (discussing disclosure obligations).

[117] On the ethical rule requiring competence, see Part Four of this book, Gregory C. Sisk, *Legal Ethics and the Practice of Law* § 4-5.1.

[118] *See* General Nutrition Corp. v. Gardere Wynne Sewell, LLP, 2008 WL 4411951, at *2 (W.D. Pa.) ("Although a lawyer is not expected to be infallible, he or she is expected to conduct that measure of research sufficient to allow the client to make an informed decision").

[119] *See id.* ("In order for a lawyer to advise a client adequately, he or she is obligated to scrutinize any contract which the client is to execute, and thereafter must disclose to the client the full import of the instrument and any possible consequences which might arise therefrom").

[120] RESTATEMENT (THIRD) OF THE LAW GOVERNING LAWYERS § 52 cmt. d (American Law Institute, 2000).

[121] 886 N.E.2d 582 (Ind. Ct. App. 2008).

[122] *Id.* at 588.

[123] *Id.* at 586.

#### *§ 5-2.2(d)(3) Diligence*

Diligence requires timely attention to the client's affairs and reasonable persistence in addressing obstacles. Diligence also requires a lawyer to perform whatever tasks are appropriate to the representation.

The degree of diligence required of a reasonably prudent attorney varies according to many factors, including the importance of the matter, the instructions of the client, applicable deadlines, the costs entailed, customary practice among other lawyers, and the press of competing obligations which affect the time available. Ordinarily, "[a]n estate plan should be completed in a timely fashion."[124] However, if a client instructs a lawyer to draft a complex will and trust within a day because the client is gravely ill, and the instrument turns out to be invalid, the time limitation under which the lawyer was acting will be a relevant factor in determining whether reasonable care was diligently exercised.[125]

### § 5-2.2(e) Exercise of Judgment

To say that lawyers are held to an objective standard of care often defined by reference to customary professional practices is not to suggest that there is only one way to practice law and that anything else is negligence. Indeed, most legal assignments entail a degree of factual and legal complexity that makes it reasonable for the lawyer to use any of several different approaches to serving the client's needs. Therefore, the application of negligence principles to legal malpractice issues must allow room for an attorney's exercise of discretion.

For example, an "appellate attorney is not required to raise every claim of arguable legal merit in order to be an effective counsel."[126] Thus, decisions relating to which issues to raise, or whether to appeal rather than seek reconsideration of an adverse finding, will ordinarily not form the basis for a malpractice action.

Similarly, a lawyer may exercise caution by advising a client to be more concerned about the potential ramifications of felony convictions, including the loss of liberty, than about the possible civil consequences of not cooperating with the client's employer.[127] This is nothing more than a reflection of the type of judgment commonly exhibited by lawyers who need to counsel clients about the risks of making potentially incriminating statements.

#### *§ 5-2.2(e)(1) Room for Discretion*

A lawyer is negligent only if the lawyer does what no reasonably prudent lawyer could do, or fails to do what every reasonably prudent lawyer must do. Between those broad extremes, there is a wide field of discretion. Some lawyers would handle a matter one way and others would handle it another way. The mere fact that someone else would have done something differently than did the defendant is merely evidence of a divergence of opinion or practice.

---

[124] Gerry W. Beyer, *Avoid Being a Defendant: Estate Planning Malpractice and Ethical Concerns*, 5 ST. MARY'S J. LEGAL MAL. & ETHICS 224, 237 (2015).

[125] RESTATEMENT (THIRD) OF THE LAW GOVERNING LAWYERS § 52 illus. 1 (American Law Institute, 2000).

[126] Kandalaft v. Peters, 2007 WL 1138395, at *3 (Mich. Ct. App.).

[127] *See* Hopp & Flesch, LLC v. Backstreet, 123 P.3d 1176, 1185 (Colo. 2005).

The duty of competence "does not require a lawyer, in a situation involving the exercise of professional judgment, to employ the same means or select the same options as would other competent lawyers in the many situations in which competent lawyers reasonably exercise professional judgment in different ways."[128] To establish negligence, the evidence must show that no reasonably prudent lawyer could have done what the defendant did. That is, the evidence must show that the defendant's choice was unreasonable.

For example, it would be unreasonable for a lawyer not to call an expert witness in a case requiring expert testimony.[129] However, lawyers typically have discretion in deciding how many experts to call in support of a client's case. Similarly, a defense lawyer may normally elect, without risk of negligence liability, to simply cross-examine the plaintiff's expert, rather than introduce opposing expert testimony.

To establish the standard of care in legal malpractice cases, it is insufficient for experts to testify that they, personally, would have handled the matter differently than did the defendant. That is not the question. The issue is not whether someone (an expert or anyone else) could or would have done something differently, but rather whether any lawyer exercising reasonable care could have done what the defendant did.

#### *§ 5-2.2(e)(2) The "Mere Error of Judgment" Fallacy*

Judgment calls by lawyers are often not actionable. Thus, decisions relating to litigation strategies or trial tactics cannot easily be attacked in a legal malpractice action.

In *Harris v. Farmer*,[130] the plaintiff argued that the defendant-lawyer was negligent in failing to subpoena or present certain witnesses and documents. Citing precedent protecting a lawyer's' exercise of discretion and other evidence that was presented at trial, the Michigan Court of Appeals held that summary disposition was properly granted in favor of the lawyer.

In efforts to capture the idea that lawyers are not liable under negligence law for the reasonable exercise of discretion, opinions sometimes (over)state that a "mere error of judgment" does not give rise to liability. That, of course, is an imprecise and unnecessarily misleading way to formulate the rule. If an error of judgment is reasonable, there is no liability. However, if the choice made by a lawyer was the type of unreasonable choice that no lawyer could make, the fact that the lawyer was exercising judgment does not insulate the lawyer from liability. The essential question is whether the lawyer acted reasonably, not whether the lawyer's conduct involved a choice between competing alternatives.

Because reasonableness is often a disputed fact question, the judgment rule rarely resolves a malpractice claim early in the litigation. For example, in *General Nutrition Corp. v. Gardere Wynne Sewell, LLP*,[131] a law firm advised a client that it would have limited liability for damages if it terminated a contract. However, when the client was sued after it terminated the agreement, a court held that the client was liable for millions

---

[128] RESTATEMENT (THIRD) OF THE LAW GOVERNING LAWYERS § 52 cmt. b (American Law Institute, 2000).

[129] *See* Charles Toulant, *Missing Expert Report Leads to $850K Malpractice Verdict*, N.J.L.J., Jan. 30, 2017.

[130] 2010 WL 395764 (Mich. Ct. App.).

[131] 2008 WL 4411951 (W.D. Pa.).

of dollars in consequential damages because the contract predominantly involved a sale of services, rather than goods. Because that was true, the Uniform Commercial Code did not apply to preclude an award of consequential damages. In a subsequent malpractice action by the client against the law firm, alleging that the client had received improper legal advice, the law firm moved to dismiss on the ground that its advice to the client was an exercise of judgment. The firm argued that there was some basis for it to have concluded that the contract involved a sale of goods subject to the UCC. A federal court nevertheless refused to dismiss the claim. The court reasoned that the complaint properly pleaded that the law firm "breached this standard in numerous respects, for example, by assigning labor and employment attorneys to a contract case and by conducting inadequate factual and legal research."[132] The court concluded that these issues were fact-intensive and that the discovery process must run its course before the applicability of the judgment rule could be determined.

In some states, the "attorney judgment rule" is an affirmative defense.[133] In those jurisdictions, the defendant must prove that the conduct in question was a permissible exercise of discretion.

In *Bloomberg v. Kronenberg*,[134] a federal court concluded that "Ohio has explicitly refused to adopt the professional judgment rule."[135] Presumably, that means that in Ohio the focus is on whether a lawyer acted reasonably, not on whether the lawyer was choosing between alternatives.

### *§ 5-2.2(e)(3) Unsettled Questions*

If a lawyer has exercised care in addressing an unsettled question, there is no malpractice related to that aspect of the lawyer's conduct. Thus, in *Smith v. McLaughlin*,[136] the Supreme Court of Virginia held that a lawyer did not breach the obligations that he owed to a client by failing to correctly anticipate a judicial ruling on the unsettled issue of whether a settlement with one defendant in a criminal malpractice action unconditionally released the codefendants, and the effect such a ruling would have on the client's release agreement with one of the law firms or attorneys involved in the underlying criminal malpractice action. As the court explained, "[I]f an attorney exercises a 'reasonable degree of care, skill, and dispatch' while acting in an unsettled area of the law, which is to be evaluated in the context of 'the state of the law at the time' of the alleged negligence, then the attorney does not breach the duty owed to the client."[137]

Not every error by a lawyer amounts to negligence. Even reasonably prudent lawyers make mistakes. Sometimes the law is so confused or under-developed that it is not possible to predict the resolution of an unsettled question or even fully understand the import of a decision that has already been made.

However, some decisions appear to broadly insulate lawyers from malpractice liability related to unsettled legal questions. For example, in *Evans v. Hamby*,[138] a case

---

[132] *Id.* at 2.

[133] *See* Bowman v. Gruel Mills Nims & Pylman, LLP, 2007 WL 1203580, at *4 (W.D. Mich.).

[134] 2006 WL 3337467 (N.D. Ohio).

[135] *Id.* at *3.

[136] 769 S.E.2d 7 (Va. 2015).

[137] *Id.* at 14.

[138] 378 S.W.3d 723 (Ark. 2011).

raising an issue related to the retroactive application of a statute, the Supreme Court of Arkansas wrote that, "An attorney is not, as a matter of law, liable for a mistaken opinion on a point of law that has not been settled by a court of the highest jurisdiction and on which reasonable attorneys may have different opinions."[139]

Of course, a lawyer must act reasonably in consulting legal authorities and in interpreting their meaning. The better view is that debatable issues of importance cannot be ignored if a reasonably prudent lawyer would take precautions to protect the client's interests.

For example, in *L.D.G., Inc. v. Robinson*,[140] the Supreme Court of Alaska held that unsettled law did not excuse a lawyer from the duty to exercise care in defending a bar in a dram shop action. The lawyer was not immune from a legal malpractice claim based on the lawyer's failure to add a visibly intoxicated alcohol consumer as a party for apportionment of fault. This was true even though the issue of whether alcohol sellers could apportion fault to consumers in dram shop actions was unsettled. A prudent defense lawyer would have considered adding the consumer as a defendant for purposes of fault allocation.

#### *§ 5-2.2(e)(4) Novel Theories, Trends, and Other Jurisdictions*

There is a duty to be aware of novel theories of liability and defenses, trends in the law, and out-of-state precedent, but only to the extent that a reasonably prudent lawyer would be cognizant of those developments. For example, in *Darby & Darby, P.C. v. VSI Int'l, Inc.*,[141] the New York Court of Appeals held that a law firm had no duty to inform its clients about possible "advertising liability" insurance coverage for their patent infringement litigation expenses. The court noted that the basis for liability was a novel theory which, at the time, had been rejected by courts in the two states most relevant to the litigation, and was largely unrecognized by courts elsewhere. In not calling the theory to the attention of its clients, the law firm, therefore, acted reasonably and in a manner consistent with the law as it existed at the time of the representation.

### § 5-2.2(f) Expert Testimony

Expert testimony plays an important role in almost every legal malpractice lawsuit. Not surprisingly, a considerable body of law has developed relating to the necessity for, and legal sufficiency of, such evidence.

#### *§ 5-2.2(f)(1) Necessary to Establish the Standard of Care*

Although juries are usually charged with determining whether a lawyer breached a duty of care to a malpractice plaintiff, the persons sitting on juries normally have no specialized knowledge about the responsibilities of members of the legal profession. Consequently, expert testimony is generally necessary to guide the jury in understanding the standard of care as applied to the facts of the case.[142] Indeed, so

---

[139] *Id.* at 730 ("This court has never settled the issue of the retroactive application of Act 522 before its effective date. For that reason alone, it is clear to this court that Jerry Evans cannot prove that Hamby's conduct fell below the generally accepted standard of practice and proximately caused his damages. While Hamby could have advised Jerry Evans that the option to reinstate the charter may be available to him, this fact alone is too tenuous to support proximate cause for legal malpractice").

[140] 290 P.3d 215 (Alaska 2012).

[141] 739 N.E.2d 744 (N.Y. 2000).

[142] *See, e.g.*, Lorenzetti v. Enterline, 44 A.3d 922 (Del. 2012).

important is such assistance that the introduction of expert testimony is normally an essential step in securing an award of damages.[143] According to ethics expert William Hodes, "Without the assistance of expert witnesses with specialized knowledge, based on either science or experience and practice, jury verdicts would often be the result of pure whim and prejudice, or random and arbitrary decision-making."[144]

For example, it is beyond the ken of the jury whether a lawyer breached the standard of care by failing to raise on appeal issues related to double jeopardy, jury instructions, jurisdiction, and verdict consistency.[145] If such complex matters are at issue, expert testimony must be adduced to prove what the standard of care required.

### *§ 5-2.2(f)(2) Exception for Obvious Negligence*

In rare cases—where even laypersons must know that the lawyer acted improperly—expert testimony is unnecessary. Thus, there is no need for expert testimony to establish that the standard of care "would prohibit the theft of a client's settlement proceeds or fraudulent billing."[146]

Courts have held, for example, that expert testimony was not required where a client suffered a default judgment because his lawyer did "absolutely nothing to protect him;"[147] where the defendant engaged in an adulterous affair with a client's wife;[148] and where, despite a client's instruction to the defendant-lawyer to appeal a judgment, notice of appeal was not timely filed.[149]

Similarly, in *Guyton v. Hunt*,[150] an Alabama appellate court ruled that "an attorney's failure to notify a client of a [court's] ruling on a motion in time for the client to timely file an appeal constitutes a breach of the standard of care that is so apparent that expert testimony is not required."[151] In an earlier case, the Alabama Supreme Court had ruled that expert testimony was not necessary in a malpractice action where the defendant-lawyer had allegedly lied to a client about his experience by falsely stating that he had represented other clients in previous breast implant litigation.[152]

In *Dowell v. Nelissen*,[153] an Iowa appellate court held that a layperson could recognize that not filing a request to modify child support, which had been agreed upon by the plaintiff-client and his ex-wife, and not informing the plaintiff of that inaction, failed to meet the standard of reasonable care. As the court explained, "[b]asic deficiencies in legal representation do not require illumination by an expert."[154]

---

[143] *See* RESTATEMENT (THIRD) OF THE LAW GOVERNING LAWYERS § 52 cmt. g (American Law Institute, 2000).

[144] W. William Hodes, *Navigating Some Deep and Troubled Jurisprudential Waters: Lawyer-Expert Witnesses and the Twin Dangers of Disguised Testimony and Disguised Advocacy*, 6 ST. MARY'S J. LEGAL MAL. & ETHICS 180, 190 (2016).

[145] *See* Moore v. Crone, 970 A.2d 757, 760 (Conn. App. 2009).

[146] Rosier v. Fleischer, 2015 WL 3648606, at *4 (Alaska).

[147] Paul v. Gordon, 754 A.2d 851, 853 (Conn. App. 2000).

[148] *See* Pierce v. Cook, 992 So. 2d 612, 618 (Miss. 2008).

[149] *See* Global NAPs, Inc. v. Awiszus, 930 N.E.2d 1262 (Mass. 2010).

[150] 61 So. 3d 1085 (Ala. Civ. App. 2010).

[151] *Id.* at 1090.

[152] *See* Valentine v. Watters, 896 So. 2d 385, 395 (Ala. 2004).

[153] 786 N.W.2d 874 (table), 2010 WL 2384617 (Iowa Ct. App.).

[154] *Id.* at *3.

However, courts are normally quite reluctant to dispense with the necessity of expert testimony. Thus, the Connecticut Supreme Court held that its own observation during an appeal in the underlying litigation, that the client's lawyer had violated basic rules of appellate procedure, did not excuse the client from presenting expert evidence regarding the standard of care and breach of duty in a subsequent malpractice action.[155]

Professor David S. Caudill has observed that, "The notion that the formation of an attorney-client relationship is a simple question within the ordinary layperson's experience is easily challenged."[156] He therefore argues that "expert legal testimony should be allowed in certain cases to enable the jury to decide this difficult question."[157]

### *§ 5-2.2(f)(3) Expert Affidavit Requirements*

To promptly dispose of frivolous claims, a number of jurisdictions have enacted expert affidavit requirements that apply to legal malpractice actions. A plaintiff must file an affidavit of merit by an expert within a specified period of time after the commencement of litigation, or else the suit will be dismissed.

*Shamrock Lacrosse, Inc. v. Klehr, Harrison, Harvey, Branzburg & Ellers, LLP*,[158] was a malpractice action based on a lawyer's failure to ensure that renewal fees for a patent were paid. A New Jersey court found that the state's affidavit requirement applied to claims against law firms, as well as to claims against individual lawyers, and that this was true even though the firms were located out of state. However, the court vacated an order dismissing the plaintiff's claims based on lack of an affidavit because the law on these issues was unsettled and in conflict at the time the affidavit should have been filed.

Even if expert affidavit requirements are imposed, there may be exceptions. An affidavit generally is not required in the rare malpractice case where expert testimony is unnecessary. For example, in *Whalen v. DeGraff, Foy, Conway, Holt-Harris & Mealey*,[159] the plaintiff argued that the defendant firm was liable for malpractice because the outside lawyer it employed to file a notice of claim with an estate had failed to do so. In ruling that the law firm was liable for negligent supervision of the outside lawyer, a New York appellate court held that no affidavit was necessary. It was undisputed that the defendant law firm knew of the deadline for filing the notice of claim and took no steps whatsoever to ensure that the claim was filed. Therefore, the plaintiff was entitled to summary judgment as a matter of law.

Noncompliance with an affidavit requirement may not bar claims against lawyers that are rooted in obligations other than those created by the professional standard of care. Thus, in *Stoecker v. Echevarria*,[160] a New Jersey court affirmed dismissal of a legal malpractice claim because an affidavit was filed too late, but allowed a fraud claim related to a real estate transaction to go forward.

---

[155] *See* Grimm v. Fox, 33 A.3d 205 (Conn. 2012).

[156] David S. Caudill, *The Roles of Attorneys as Courtroom Experts: Revisiting the Conventional Limitations and Their Exceptions*, 2 ST. MARY'S J. LEGAL MAL. & ETHICS 136, 164 (2012).

[157] *Id.*

[158] 3 A.3d 518 (N.J. Super. App. Div. 2010).

[159] 863 N.Y.S.2d 100 (App. Div. 2008).

[160] 975 A.2d 975 (N.J. Super. App. Div. 2009).

In *Walker v. Cromartie*[161] a malpractice plaintiff argued that Georgia's expert affidavit requirement was unconstitutional because it prohibited indigent plaintiffs from pursuing actions for professional negligence due to the costs of procuring an expert affidavit, thereby violating due process, equal protection, and the right to trial. The Supreme Court of Georgia disagreed because nothing in the state statute imposed a cost or fee for filing or obtaining an expert affidavit. Rather the costs to which the appellants objected were created by private actors.

### *§ 5-2.2(f)(4) Admissibility of Expert Testimony*

Trial courts perform an important gate-keeping function in determining who is qualified to testify as an expert.[162] In general, the witness must be well acquainted, by study or experience, with the matters at issue. Under these circumstances, it is appropriate for a jury to rely on the expert's guidance because the testimony is informed and arguably trustworthy.

Judges have a duty to exclude expert testimony that is not adequately informed. In *Glaser v. Pullman & Comley, LLC*,[163] a Connecticut appellate court held that a trial judge properly found that an expert was not qualified to testify because the expert "conceded that he did not know whether Connecticut law differs from the law of other states, * * * where he is licensed to practice law, on such specific issues * * * as environmental rules * * * or how a Connecticut court would interpret 'time is of the essence' clauses."[164]

There are more than a million lawyers in the United States, and presumably not all of them are qualified to testify as legal ethics experts simply by reason of the fact that they have been licensed to practice law. Nevertheless, some lawyers are indeed ethics experts because they have studied (or perhaps helped to draft) the relevant standards of conduct, served on grievance committees, taught courses, lectured on malpractice prevention, or served as law firm in-house or outside ethics counsel.

Not surprisingly, law professors who teach courses on attorney professional responsibility frequently appear as experts in legal malpractice litigation. Generally, such faculty members are so well versed with respect to the standards of conduct for lawyers that their testimony might aid a jury in understanding what a lawyer is required to do when faced with certain facts.

Many malpractice cases involve questions of legal ethics, such as whether certain facts create a conflict of interest or have to be disclosed to a client. However, legal malpractice cases also raise issues of conduct that are not related to legal ethics. For example, the question may be whether the duty of reasonable care requires a lawyer to include a noncompetition provision in a contract between family members[165] or to ensure that a company hired to pay a structured settlement is bonded.[166] Those types of cases require special expertise not directly related to ethics, so it is likely that someone other

---

[161] 696 S.E.2d 654 (Ga. 2010).

[162] *See* David S. Caudill, *Controversial Defenses to Legal Malpractice Claims: Are Attorney-Experts Being Asked to Be Advocates?*, 5 ST. MARY'S J. LEGAL MAL. & ETHICS 312, 317 (2015) (discussing judges as gatekeepers).

[163] 871 A.2d 392 (Conn. App. Ct. 2005).

[164] *Id.* at 401.

[165] *See* Russo v. Griffin, 510 A.2d 436 (Vt. 1986).

[166] *See* Williams v. Lakin, 2007 WL 1170597 (N.D. Okla.).

than an ethics expert should testify to support those aspects of a plaintiff's claim. In many legal malpractice cases, there are multiple experts on various sides of the litigation.

### *§ 5-2.2(f)(5) Geographic Frame of Reference for Expert Testimony*

Whether a lawyer's conduct complied with the standard of care can only be determined in context, an important part of which is the geographic frame of reference.

As a general rule, lawyers are judged by a state-wide standard, because substantive and procedural law often varies from state to state, and so do the ethics rules that govern attorney conduct. Taking this approach, the Vermont Supreme Court, in *Russo v. Griffin*,[167] held that an out-of-town expert's testimony sufficiently supported a negligence claim because even though the expert was not from the same locality as the defendant, the expert was acquainted with the standard of care in the state.

Out-of-state experts sometimes testify in legal malpractice cases. However, the expert must be sufficiently familiar with the law of the jurisdiction so that the expert's testimony will assist the jury in understanding the case.[168] In *Phillips v. Wilks, Lukoff & Bracegirdle, LLC*,[169] the Supreme Court of Delaware concluded that a New Jersey lawyer was not qualified to testify about the standard of care applicable to a negligent representation claim governed by Delaware law. Although the lawyer had familiarized himself with Delaware case law, "more than a mere reading of Delaware case law was required."[170]

Virtually all state ethics rules are based, to some extent, on the American Bar Association's model codifications. In addition, the American Law Institute's *Restatement (Third) of the Law Governing Lawyers*[171] reflects legal principles that are endorsed by the law of many jurisdictions. Therefore, it is not surprising that an expert well acquainted with the ABA Model Rules of Professional Conduct[172] and the *Restatement*, and the types of issues addressed in law school professional responsibility courses, might be found capable of assisting a jury in understanding the standard of care, even if the expert does not reside in the state whose law governs the dispute.

Some areas of the law are national in scope, such as federal tax law, federal securities law, bankruptcy law, and patent law. When a case involves issues relating to these sources of law, it makes sense that the frame of reference should be national. Of course, a single case may raise multiple issues, some of which are state-based and others of which are federal. Whether a lawyer practicing federal tax law in Pennsylvania has a conflict of interest might properly be determined with reference to the Pennsylvania ethics rules, but whether particular advice for minimizing tax liability was reasonable might more appropriately be determined by reference to what lawyers practicing federal tax law throughout the United States would regard as acceptable conduct.

---

[167] 510 A.2d 436 (Vt. 1986).

[168] Crawford v. Katz, 32 A.3d 418, 427 (D.C. 2011) ("[I]n light of the nature of the malpractice claimed in this case, [the professor tendered as an expert] . . . need not be an expert both in the professional norms and ethics applicable to civil litigation in a wrongful discharge case *and* an expert on the intricacies of various types of employment law").

[169] 2014 WL 4930693 (Del.).

[170] *Id.* at *2.

[171] *See* RESTATEMENT (THIRD) OF THE LAW GOVERNING LAWYERS (American Law Institute, 2000).

[172] *See* MODEL RULES OF PROF'L CONDUCT (American Bar Ass'n, 2017).

### *§ 5-2.2(f)(5)(A) No Locality Rule*

Perhaps the most important consideration relating to geographic frame of reference is that the standard of care should not be defined in purely local terms. Embracing a locality rule raises two concerns. The first is that it may be difficult or impossible for a plaintiff with a meritorious case to recruit an expert from the town or region in which the defendant practices. In a given locality, there may be a small number of lawyers, and those lawyers may be reluctant or unwilling to testify against one another. This is the "conspiracy of silence" problem.[173]

The second concern relates to encouragement of good practices. Setting the standard of care at the local level undercuts the incentives that tort law can provide for lawyers to avoid liability by keeping pace with legal knowledge and evolving notions of professional responsibility in other geographic areas. The standard of care should be framed in geographic terms that protect consumers of legal services by tending to ensure that lawyers are not insulated from liability when practitioners in a particular area lag behind others in terms of knowledge, skills, and procedures.

Fortunately, courts have rarely applied a locality rule for measuring the performance of lawyers charged with malpractice.[174] The standard of care is ordinarily set at the state or national level.[175]

### *§ 5-2.2(f)(5)(B) International Legal Malpractice*[176]

The growing internationalization of law practice raises many questions about how the standard of care should be defined when a lawyer's work involves international treaties or the law of other nations, or when the lawyer is located in a foreign country or serves foreign clients. As yet, there is no clear consensus on these types of questions. Nevertheless, these issues are sure to be litigated in coming years.

There are numerous reported cases involving legal malpractice claims arising from international aspects of American law practice. A number of cases have involved patent law. American law firms have been sued for failing to timely file an application for foreign patent protection of an invention;[177] negligently terminating services;[178] failing

---

[173] *See* Jeffrey I.H Soffer, *A Professional (Lack of) Courtesy: The Emergence of Expert Testimony in Legal and Medical Malpractice Cases*, 5 ST. MARY'S J. LEGAL MAL. & ETHICS 346, 376 (2015) (observing that "the 'conspiracy of silence,' where there was an unspoken agreement between attorneys and physicians not to testify against one another, has largely disappeared").

[174] *But see* Brett v. Berkowitz, 706 A.2d 509, 517–18 (Del. 1998) ("[T]he requirement that medical malpractice experts be competent to testify concerning the standard of skill and care ordinarily employed in the relevant community apply equally to experts in legal malpractice cases"); Anna M. Limoges, Student Article, *Lost in the Locality Labyrinth: A Search for the Appropriate Legal Malpractice Standard Set Forth in Hamilton v. Sommers*, 61 S.D. L. REV. 108, 138 (2016) (arguing that "local considerations are always relevant in determining the result of the underlying litigation in a legal malpractice action").

[175] *See* RESTATEMENT (THIRD) OF THE LAW GOVERNING LAWYERS § 52 cmt. b (American Law Institute, 2000).

[176] Some material in this section has been drawn from: Vincent R. Johnson, *Legal Malpractice in International Business Transactions*, 44 HOFSTRA L. REV. 325 (2015).

[177] *See* Vaxiion Therapeutics, Inc. v. Foley & Lardner LLP, 593 F. Supp. 2d 1153, 1167, 1175 (S.D. Cal. 2008) (finding that there were disputed questions of fact related to the alleged untimely filing of a Patent Cooperation Treaty patent application); Kairos Sci. Inc. v. Fish & Richardson P.C., 2006 WL 171921, at *1, *17 (Cal. Ct. App.) (awarding damages).

[178] *See* Harness, Dickey & Pierce, P.L.C. v. Andrews, 2006 WL 2671039, at *13 (E.D. Mich.) (rejecting the claim because "Andrews could have had no reasonable expectation that Harness Dickey would continue to

to attach a translation to a U.S. Patent and Trademark Office filing for a Japanese client;[179] making misrepresentations regarding the availability of foreign patents;[180] and, failing to timely file an Asian patent for a pharmaceutical product.[181]

Other legal malpractice cases related to international law or international lawyering have involved allegedly defective legal advice. For example, lawyers have been sued for issuing an opinion letter erroneously assuring an Egyptian bank, which did business in New York, that a mortgage and promissory note were enforceable,[182] and for failing to advise a Dutch company that involvement by its officers in arranging a subsidiary's payment of a bribe in Panama could result in criminal liability for the company.[183]

Other suits have involved a wide variety of deficiencies related to international aspects of law practice. Lawyers have been sued for inadequately representing a foreign client in arbitration proceedings;[184] improperly structuring a stock purchase agreement and otherwise failing to properly address the enforceability of a pledge used to secure Bahamian collateral;[185] negligently handling a transaction creating a supplier/distributor relationship with a Taiwanese company;[186] failing to satisfactorily resolve the issue created when a bank refused to accept checks from the Israeli partner to a money-services business relationship;[187] and, assisting an allegedly fraudulent scheme to sell Ecuadoran water that purportedly offered medicinal benefits.[188] One legal malpractice claim grew out of a dispute over the reasonableness of fees charged in representation that involved fighting more than 1,700 subpoenas. The underlying matter involved the alleged theft of an international law firm's clients in Kazakhstan by lawyers who left the firm.[189]

In one case, Austrian clients alleged (unsuccessfully) that an American law firm had negligently provided erroneous advice. The advice related to the structure of an investment in the securities of a Russian natural gas concern, and the risk of criminal prosecution if the investment structure was deemed to be illegal.[190]

---

represent him without payment, or * * * subsidize his foreign patent portfolio by continuing to absorb the fees and costs generated by its foreign associates").

[179] *See* Seed Co. v. Westerman, 62 F. Supp. 3d 56, 59, 67 (D.D.C. 2014) (finding no breach of the duty of care).

[180] *See* Waterloov Gutter Prot. Sys. Co. v. Absolute Gutter Prot., L.L.C., 64 F. Supp. 2d 398, 418, 428 (D.N.J. 1999) (rejecting a legal malpractice claim, but allowing a common law fraud claim to go forward).

[181] *See* InKine Pharm. Co. v. Coleman, 759 N.Y.S.2d 62, 63 (App. Div. 2003) (stating that a cause of action was adequately alleged for legal malpractice causing a "substantial diminution of the value of [the plaintiff's] worldwide license to manufacture, sell and sublicense the product").

[182] *See* Arab African Int'l Bank v. Epstein, 10 F.3d 168, 170 (3d Cir. 1993).

[183] *See* Stichting Ter Behartiging v. Schreiber, 327 F.3d 173, 176–78 (2d Cir. 2003).

[184] *See* Doucakis v. Speiser, Krause, Madole, P.C., 2002 WL 1397155, at *1–2 (Tex. App.).

[185] *See* Hart v. Carro, Spanbock, Kaster & Cuiffo, 620 N.Y.S.2d 847, 848–49 (App. Div. 1995); *see also* Hart v. Carro, Spanbock, Kaster & Cuiffo, 620 N.Y.S.2d 850, 850 (App. Div. 1995) (related case).

[186] *See* Joseph DelGreco & Co., v. DLA Piper L.L.P., 535 Fed. Appx. 31 (2d Cir. 2013) (plaintiff failed to prove malpractice).

[187] *See* K.R. Exch. Servs., Inc. v. Fuerst, Humphrey, Ittleman, PL, 48 So. 3d 889, 891–92, 894–95 (Fla. Dist. Ct. App. 2010) (finding that the complaint failed to state a cause of action).

[188] *See* Ohman v. Kahn, 685 F. Supp. 1302, 1304–05, 1311 (S.D.N.Y. 1988).

[189] *See* Sokol Holdings, Inc. v. Dorsey & Whitney, LLP, 2010 WL 599330, at *3 (Del. Super. 2010) (denying a motion to amend the complaint in order to assert a legal malpractice claim).

[190] *See* GUS Consulting GMBH v. Chadbourne & Parke LLP, 2010 WL 2518538 (N.Y. App. Div.).

In *DiStefano v. Greenstone*,[191] a U.S. lawyer failed to "sustain contact" with an Italian law firm that he was using to handle an international tort claim for the plaintiff, who had been injured in Italy. As a result, the claim was not promptly filed and became time-barred. In a subsequent malpractice action, the U.S. lawyer was held liable for the full value of the lost claim, attorney's fees in the malpractice action, and other expenses.

Many American law firms operate branch offices in China. However, the Chinese government restricts the range of services that can be provided by foreign law firms.[192] In addition, there are great differences between the Chinese legal system and its American counterpart. Many would argue that China has less commitment to the Rule of Law, and that Chinese courts lack a tradition of judicial independence and are more susceptible to corruption and government influence.[193] If American legal malpractice standards apply to an American law firm representing American clients in China, it might well be argued that the firm must disclose the limits on the range of services it can provide (as well as the expense and delay that may entail for the client), as well as the special risks that a client may face in Chinese courts, including corruption, partisanship, and lack of judicial independence.

#### ***§ 5-2.2(f)(6) The Role of Legal Malpractice Experts***

Expert witnesses play a special role in legal malpractice litigation. Their job is neither zealous advocacy of a party's interests, nor determining who should win the lawsuit. Rather, the duty of an expert witness is to assist the judge and jury in understanding how the law governing lawyers applies to the facts of a dispute giving rise to a malpractice claim.

##### *§ 5-2.2(f)(6)(A) Duties and Compensation*

Ethics experts in legal malpractice litigation typically review voluminous amounts of material, such as pleadings, discovery answers, depositions, underlying documents, and court decisions relating to the case. They study this information to fully understand the facts from which the dispute arises and to identify and be prepared to discuss

---

[191] 815 A.2d 496 (N.J. Super. App. Div. 2003).

[192] REGULATION FOR THE MANAGEMENT OF REPRESENTATIVE OFFICES SET UP BY FOREIGN LAW FIRMS IN CHINA art. 15 (2001) ("A resident representative office and its representatives may engage in the following activities *not involving Chinese Legal Affairs*: (1) provide to its clients legal advice regarding the laws of the countries where the lawyers of the foreign law firm are allowed to engage in the provision of legal services, as well as advice on international conventions and international practices; (2) accept instruction from its clients or a Chinese law firm to handle the legal affairs in the countries where the lawyers of the foreign law firm are allowed to engage in the provision of legal services") (emphasis added); STIPULATIONS OF THE MINISTRY OF JUSTICE CONCERNING THE ENFORCEMENT OF THE "REGULATION FOR THE MANAGEMENT OF REPRESENTATIVE OFFICES SET UP BY FOREIGN LAW FIRMS IN CHINA" art. 32 (2002, revised 2004) ("The following acts shall be recognized as 'the matters related to laws of China' as specified in Article 15 of the Regulations [*and therefore not permitted*]: (1) Participate in litigation activities in the name of a lawyer within the territory of China; (2) Provide opinions or certifications on specific issues in contracts, agreements, articles of association, or other written documents, to which the laws of China are applicable; (3) Provide opinions or certifications on acts or events to which the laws of China are applicable; (4) Present agent comments on the application of the laws of China as an agent in arbitration activities; and (5) Go through formalities of registration, change, application, record filing, and other formalities with Chinese government authorities or other organization with administrative functions authorized under the laws and regulations").

[193] *Cf.* Vincent R. Johnson, *The Rule of Law and Enforcement of Chinese Tort Law*, 34 T. JEFFERSON L. REV. 43, 87 (2011) ("As an instrument for building the Rule of Law, the new Chinese Tort Law faces many obstacles. Among these are China's deeply entrenched practice of guanxi and political pressures favoring business interests, as well as the lack of an independent judiciary or a tradition of transparency in dealing with issues related to accident compensation").

relevant issues. Other types of experts perform similar tasks. For example, an expert on damages may need to examine the facts of the dispute to construct models for determining what consequential damages were caused by the alleged negligence.

Deciphering handwritten notes made by attorneys or others during the course of representation is often maddeningly tedious. However, doing so sometimes is the key that allows an expert to comprehend what was really going on at a particular point in time.

Ethics experts may also need to research the holdings of other cases or the writings of scholars because malpractice lawsuits frequently raise questions to which the answers are less than clear, even when viewed from an expert's perspective. All of this work takes a great deal of time. Because experts are normally paid by the hour, and contingent fees are forbidden,[194] litigating a malpractice claim can be an expensive proposition. The costs associated with hiring and working with an expert affect the economics of pursuing a legal malpractice claim.[195]

It is possible to minimize the expenses of expert testimony by engaging an expert to testify based solely in response to hypothetical questions (i.e., assumed facts that the party believes it can prove), rather than based on the expert's review of the facts of the case. For example, a lawyer can hire an expert to testify in response to a simple list of questions, such as "Is there a conflict of interest if a lawyer persuades a client to invest in a business the lawyer owns without disclosing that ownership interest to the client?" Surprisingly, expert testimony based on hypothetical questions seems to be a practice rarely used in legal malpractice litigation. Presumably, the lawyers litigating malpractice cases find it more effective to present expert witnesses who are well acquainted with the dispute and can testify about what was required under any of several competing versions of the facts and the particular circumstances of the dispute.

In the usual case, the law firm that hires a malpractice expert, as well as the client on whose behalf the expert serves, is liable for the payment of the expert's fees.[196]

*§ 5-2.2(f)(6)(B) Independence Versus Partisanship*

Although experts who appear in malpractice litigation are selected and paid for their time by the parties on whose behalf they work, experts are not merely partisans. A testifying expert has a duty to the court and to the justice system to honestly answer questions under oath, even if those answers may hurt the side of the case that has engaged the expert.

An expert's credibility may be challenged on many grounds, such as general qualifications, inadequate devotion of time to the case, or lack of access to critical documentary materials. Opposing counsel may also challenge an expert's credibility if the expert's testimony is inconsistent with what the expert has previously stated in publications, such as books or law review articles, or before tribunals on other occasions.

---

[194] *See* MODEL RULES OF PROF'L CONDUCT R. 3.4 cmt. 3 (American Bar Ass'n, 2017).

[195] Susan Saab Fortney, *A Tort in Search of a Remedy: Prying Open the Courthouse Doors for Legal Malpractice Victims*, 85 FORDHAM L. REV. 2033, 2040–2042 (2017) (suggesting that the cost of retaining an expert influences a plaintiff's attorney's decision to handle a legal malpractice case and may prevent an injured person from finding a lawyer to handle the matter on a contingency fee basis).

[196] *See* RESTATEMENT (THIRD) OF THE LAW GOVERNING LAWYERS § 30 & cmt. b (American Law Institute, 2000).

Ordinarily no attorney-client relationship exists between a legal malpractice expert and the party on whose behalf the expert has been retained. Because this is true, the conflict of interest rules contained in attorney disciplinary rules generally do not apply to the expert because the expert is not "representing" a client. Nevertheless, experts, as agents or subagents, have certain duties to their principals (the clients for whose benefit they have been hired). For example, an expert must treat information learned in the course of working on the case confidentially, unless the information has become a matter of public record or common knowledge, or some other consideration permits revelation or use.[197] Moreover, in a limited range of cases, it might be argued that a lawyer who previously served as an expert witness has a conflict of interest that materially limits the representation of a subsequent client due to obligations of continuing confidentiality owed to the person for whom the lawyer served as an expert.[198]

### *§ 5-2.2(f)(6)(C) Non-Testifying Experts*

A distinction is sometimes drawn between testifying experts (with which this discussion is concerned) and non-testifying experts who act as consultants or co-counsel. Non-testifying experts may have an attorney-client relationship with the individual on whose behalf their guidance is sought. If so, the expert is subject to the duties and restrictions normally imposed on lawyers representing clients.[199] Of course, the scope of a consulting expert's attorney-client duties may be limited, and in such cases the conduct of the expert will be judged in light of the narrowness of the engagement.

An expert who is hired to testify does not necessarily represent the client merely because testimony is never given. In *Frantz v. Hawley Troxell Ennis & Hawley LLP*,[200] a lawyer, Clark, had been retained as an expert witness to testify on behalf of Frantz, the plaintiff in an earlier legal malpractice matter. In a subsequent debt collection action, Frantz sought to disqualify Clark's law firm from representing the opposing party on conflict of interest grounds. Frantz alleged that in the earlier matter Clark's role had been "to provide consultation and expert testimony."[201] Although Clark provided a preliminary report, the "malpractice claim settled without Clark issuing a final written report, being deposed, or testifying."[202] In pressing the disqualification motion, Frantz alleged that, in the earlier legal malpractice case, Clark had "consulted on areas of the case outside of [his] expert testimony,"[203] and that his "role morphed from that of a testifying expert to that of consulting expert thereby forming an attorney-client relationship" with Frantz.[204] The bankruptcy judge presiding over the debt collection matter rejected this argument and refused to disqualify Clark's firm, concluding that Clark's "role in the malpractice litigation was solely that of a testifying expert witness" and that no attorney-client relationship was formed."[205]

---

[197] *See generally* ABA Formal Op. 97–407 (1997).

[198] *See* MODEL RULES OF PROF'L CONDUCT R. 1.7(a)(2) (American Bar Ass'n, 2017).

[199] *See* ABA Formal Op. 97–407 (1997).

[200] 383 P.3d 1230, 1232 (Idaho 2016).

[201] *Id.*

[202] *Id.*

[203] *Id.*

[204] *Id.*

[205] *Id.*

#### *§ 5-2.2(f)(6)(D) Honesty and Effectiveness*

In most malpractice cases, there are multiple competing versions of the facts that are supported by the testimony of the various witnesses. Typically, some versions of the facts favor the plaintiff and others favor the defendant. Rarely will an expert be in a position to testify that, regardless of which set of facts the jury accepts, the lawyer acted appropriately (or inappropriately). Rather, professional honesty[206] and candor to the court normally oblige an expert to admit that if the jury makes certain findings, the other side wins on particular issues.

Indeed, a lawyer will have no credibility with the jury, and will be subject to relentless (and well deserved) cross-examination, if the expert fails to concede points that should be conceded. For example, if an expert is asked to assume that the jury will find that the defendant-lawyer knowingly made a false statement of material fact to a client, the expert cannot opine that the lawyer complied with the standard of care. Intentional deception about an important matter is never consistent with a lawyer's obligations.

In many cases, there is a dispute about whether an attorney-client relationship existed between the plaintiff and defendant who are now the parties to the malpractice litigation. If an attorney-client relationship did exist, it may be clear that the lawyer breached obligations to the client. If there was no attorney-client relationship, it may be equally clear that there was no breach. An expert's testimony must reflect these realities. Knowing and admitting what must be conceded is part of the job of any honest and effective expert.

### § 5-2.2(g) Expert Testimony on Causation

The principal focus of a legal malpractice expert's work relates to establishing the standard of care and whether it was breached. However, in many jurisdictions, the law permits experts to testify about causation and damages as well.

#### *§ 5-2.2(g)(1) Sometimes Permitted*

In some states, expert testimony about the harm caused by malpractice is allowed.[207] However, whether an expert persuades a jury as to what losses resulted from unprofessional conduct probably depends upon the nature of the malpractice.

For example, suppose that a lawyer breached a duty of candor by failing to tell a client that the client was entrusting funds to a person the lawyer knew to have been previously convicted of, and incarcerated for, a felony involving financial fraud. The expert may firmly believe that the client would not have entrusted money to the former felon, and that the funds would not have been lost, had the lawyer disclosed the information to the client. A court might permit such testimony on causation of damages because it does not seem particularly speculative. On those facts, a judge may allow the testimony in order to assist the jury.

In other cases, it is harder for an expert to trace the lines of factual and proximate causation that may run between breach of duty and alleged damages. Assume that a

---

[206] *Cf.* Josiah M. Daniel, *Am I a "Licensed Liar"?: An Exploration into the Ethics of Honesty in Lawyering*, 7 ST. MARY'S J. LEGAL MAL. & ETHICS 32, 32 (2015) (tracing the history of the question of lawyer honesty).

[207] *See* RESTATEMENT (THIRD) OF THE LAW GOVERNING LAWYERS § 52 cmt. g (American Law Institute, 2000).

lawyer has serious conflicts of interest that are undisclosed and that the transaction in which the lawyer is assisting a client (say, acquisition of certain assets) fails. Although the expert may offer convincing testimony about the conflicts of interest, it may be difficult for the expert to persuade a judge or jury that the expert, based on professional knowledge and experience, knows to a reasonable degree of certainty that, but for the breach of the conflicts rules: the defendant-lawyer would have withdrawn; an independent lawyer without conflicts would have been hired; better advice or assistance would have been provided by the new, unconflicted lawyer; and the plaintiff would have been able to consummate the purchase of assets on acceptable terms. In some jurisdictions, such testimony may be permitted because the expert helps the jury to understand the case by connecting the dots between breach of duty and damages. However, in other cases, the testimony may be rejected as impermissible speculation by the expert.

Factual causation is normally established in a legal malpractice action by applying a demanding "but for" test that requires the plaintiff to prove that the harm would not have occurred if the defendant had not been negligent.[208] However, in some jurisdictions, claims for breach of fiduciary duty are actionable upon a lesser showing that the defendant-lawyer's conduct need only have been a "substantial factor" in producing harm to the plaintiff.[209] A court applying the "substantial factor" rule to the facts in the example involving undisclosed conflicts of interest, mentioned above, might extend greater latitude to an expert testifying about causation issues than in a negligence case governed by the "but for" rule.

### *§ 5-2.2(g)(2) Sometimes Required*

Some jurisdictions not only permit expert testimony on causation in legal malpractice cases, they require it, in most instances, because whether a lawyer's breach of duty causes harm is beyond the knowledge of the average layperson. For example, in *Estate of Sicotte v. Lubin & Meyer, P.C.*,[210] a law firm charged a one-third contingent fee for representing a minor without indicating that a court would ordinarily not approve a fee in excess of twenty-five percent, except "upon good cause shown." The firm also did not disclose, as required by state law, that the client had a right to be represented on a non-contingent fee basis. Nevertheless, the Supreme Court of New Hampshire dismissed the resulting malpractice claim because the plaintiff failed to produce expert testimony on whether the alleged breaches of duty caused damages.

Similarly, in *Primis Corp. v. Milledge*,[211] a default judgment was entered against the plaintiff in a suit to confirm an arbitration award. In a subsequent malpractice action, the plaintiff alleged, and the trial court found, that the defendant law firm was negligent in connection with the plaintiff's efforts to overturn the default judgment. However, the trial court also determined that the plaintiff failed to prove that the law firm's negligence caused damage. The Texas Court of Appeals agreed because no expert testimony was introduced on that issue. According to the appellate court, the plaintiff was required to prove that, with the assistance of reasonably prudent counsel, a court would have vacated or modified the arbitration award. This causation inquiry was

---

[208] *See infra* § 5-2.3(a)(1).

[209] *See infra* § 5-3.2.

[210] 157 N.H. 670, 959 A.2d 236 (N.H. 2008).

[211] 2010 WL 2103936 (Tex. App.).

beyond the common understanding of the triers of fact. Therefore, expert testimony was necessary to prove causation.

Some courts strongly reject the idea that expert testimony on causation is ordinarily required in a malpractice case. Thus, in *Bloomberg v. Kronenberg*,[212] a federal court in Ohio stated that "the overwhelming weight of authority indicates that although an expert certainly may testify regarding the issue of proximate cause in a legal malpractice cause of action, such testimony is not required."

#### *§ 5-2.2(g)(3) Sometimes Prohibited*

Some jurisdictions prohibit the introduction of expert testimony on the issue of causation, at least in certain types of cases. *Leibel v. Johnson*[213] was a legal malpractice action where, in order to determine whether the defendant had caused damages, it was necessary to try a "suit within a suit."[214] As the Supreme Court of Georgia explained:

> [T]he second jury in the malpractice case is not deciding what the first jury would have done in the underlying case had the attorney not been negligent, but only what a reasonable jury would have done had the underlying case been tried without the attorney negligence alleged by the plaintiff. The second jury does this by independently evaluating the evidence in the underlying case as it should have been presented to determine whether it believes that the plaintiff has a winning case, not by deciding whether some prior jury may or may not have believed that the plaintiff had a winning case * * *. This is a task that is solely for the jury, and that is not properly the subject of expert testimony.[215]

### § 5-2.2(h) Experts' Reliance on Ethics Rules

In forming their opinions, legal malpractice experts often rely on the text of relevant disciplinary rules. Thus, an expert will probably consider either Rule 1.8(a) of the Model Rules of Professional Conduct, or more likely the parallel disciplinary rule of the state whose law governs the dispute, when opining on whether a lawyer took unfair advantage of a client in purchasing property from the client. Such rules directly address what a lawyer should do when engaging in business transactions with clients.

For example, a Nevada ethics rule, which is identical in relevant part to ABA Model Rule 1.8, provides that "[a] lawyer shall not enter into a business transaction with a client * * * unless: (1) The transaction and terms on which the lawyer acquires the interest are fair and reasonable to the client and are fully disclosed * * *; (2) The client is advised in writing of the desirability of seeking and is given a reasonable opportunity to seek the advice of independent legal counsel on the transaction; and (3) The client gives informed consent * * *."[216] In these types of cases, the terms of a disciplinary rule are highly relevant to any assessment of what the standard of care requires.[217]

Many courts do not object to an expert's reference under oath, by title, number, or text, to disciplinary rules bearing upon the issues in a malpractice case. Moreover, even

---

[212] 2006 WL 3337467, *6 (N.D. Ohio).

[213] 728 S.E.2d 554 (Ga. 2012).

[214] *Id.* at 556.

[215] *Id.* at 556–57.

[216] NEV. RULES OF PROF'L CONDUCT R. 1.8(a) (2017).

[217] *See generally* Douglas R. Richmond, *Why Legal Ethics Rules Are Relevant to Lawyer Liability*, 38 ST. MARY'S L.J. 929 (2007).

courts that do not permit citation to specific provisions usually permit an expert to use the language of a disciplinary rule in testifying about the standard of care.[218]

Of course, there are sources of guidance other than disciplinary rules that experts should take into account. Case law, advisory ethics opinions, or scholarly writings may amplify or clarify what disciplinary rules say. Those sources may make a convincing case for why a particular rule may set an appropriate standard for discipline, but not for malpractice. An expert may freely consider these kinds of authority, and may sometimes espouse an opinion at odds with language in the state's disciplinary rules.

For example, suppose that, unlike the ABA Model Rules,[219] a state's disciplinary rule on confidentiality does not address whether a lawyer may disclose client information to a third party in the course of seeking ethics advice relating to the representation. An expert might nevertheless reasonably opine that such disclosure does not violate the standard of care because other authorities recognize the propriety of such disclosures. Of course, an expert whose opinion departs from the terms of a disciplinary rule in stating the standard of care should expect to be called upon in cross-examination to defend that position.

### § 5-2.2(i) Experts' Ignorance of Ethics Rules

While experts' reliance on ethics rules is a common practice regarded as generally acceptable, ignorance or disregard of the disciplinary rules is another matter. An expert who does not know what state disciplinary rules require might not be permitted to testify if the judge determines that the expert's opinion is not sufficiently informed to be likely to assist the jury. For example, one malpractice case arose from legal representation of a medical limited partnership in matters that involved a peer review process. A lawyer who was an ethicist at a prestigious university, and who was a highly regarded expert in medical peer review procedures, was not permitted to testify about the malpractice standard of care applicable to determining whether the defendant-lawyers had acted properly. This was true because the expert admitted that he was unacquainted with the state's disciplinary rules governing lawyers. In addition, if an expert is permitted to take the stand, testimony that ignores the terms of a relevant ethics rule may be found to be unpersuasive.[220]

### § 5-2.2(j) Experts' Inconsistency with Ethics Rules

Testimony of an expert that departs from what the disciplinary rules require may be found to be so subjective as to provide no reliable basis for a jury determination that the defendant-lawyer breached the standard of care. For example, in *Lerner v. Laufer*,[221] a lawyer agreed to provide a client with a limited scope of representation relating to the client's divorce. Despite assertions to the contrary by the client's expert in a subsequent malpractice case, a New Jersey appellate court held that the lawyer had no duty to discuss with the client the client's feelings of guilt, or how guilt might have affected the property settlement to which the client had agreed. The court found that the expert's report failed to establish "an authoritative or recognized standard of care" that rose above provisions in the state's disciplinary rules which allow a lawyer and client to limit

---

[218] *See, e.g.*, Tilton v. Trezza, 819 N.Y.S.2d 213 (Sup. Ct. 2006).

[219] *See* MODEL RULES OF PROF'L CONDUCT R. 1.6(b)(4) (American Bar Ass'n, 2017).

[220] *See* Sealed Party v. Sealed Party, 2006 WL 1207732, at *11 n.32 (S.D. Tex.).

[221] 819 A.2d 471 (N.J. Super. Ct. App. Div. 2003).

the scope of representation.[222] The court found that any obligation the lawyer had to explore the client's guilt feelings appeared to be "personal" to the expert.[223]

### § 5-2.2(k) Conclusory Expert Testimony

In order to be effective, an expert must explain the basis for the expert's opinions. Conclusory opinions may be deemed to be legally insufficient. Thus, if an expert offers little more than his or her credentials and a subjective opinion, the expert's opinion is unlikely to be competent summary judgment evidence.[224] As the Texas Supreme Court explained in *Rogers v. Zanetti*:[225]

> In order to be competent summary-judgment evidence, an expert's opinion must have a "demonstrable and reasoned basis on which to evaluate his opinion." * * *. This basis must come in the form of an answer to the question "Why": Why did the expert reach that particular opinion? * * *. An expert's familiarity with the facts is not alone a satisfactory basis for his or her opinion.[226]

### § 5-2.2(*l*) Expert Witness Liability

Although expert testimony may harm persons involved in the litigation, experts normally cannot be sued because of the widely-recognized judicial proceedings privilege (sometimes called the litigation privilege). The privilege bars a civil action for damages against persons participating in litigation (e.g., judges, jurors, and witnesses).[227] However, the privilege, as it applies to expert witnesses, may have limits. At least in theory, an expert who fails to review crucial documentary evidence, or does so carelessly, should no more be immune from suit than a lawyer who fails to prepare adequately for trial. *Mattco Forge, Inc. v. Arthur Young & Co.*,[228] held that an action by a client against its own expert was not barred by the litigation privilege. However, there is little precedent to support a theory of expert witness liability for negligence.

### § 5-2.2(m) Negligence *Per Se* in Legal Malpractice

In ordinary negligence actions, a plaintiff may be able to take a shortcut in establishing breach of duty. In a majority of jurisdictions, an unexcused violation of a legislative enactment may conclusively prove that the defendant acted unreasonably. This is called negligence *per se*, meaning negligence "in itself." Proof of the unexcused violation obviates the need for a "totality of the circumstances" inquiry into the facts surrounding the defendant's conduct. The unexcused violation of the legislative enactment establishes breach of the duty of reasonable care. Note, however, that in a minority of states, violation of a standard-setting legislative enactment is only (a)

---

[222] *Id.* at 483.

[223] *Id.* at 484.

[224] *See* Merrell Dow Pharm., Inc. v. Havner, 953 S.W.2d 706, 712 (Tex. 1997); Gillespie v. Hernden, 516 S.W.3d 541, 554 (Tex. App. 2016).

[225] 2017 WL 1553154 (Tex.).

[226] *Id.* at 7–11.

[227] *See infra* § 5-6.3(a).

[228] 5 Cal. App. 4th 392, 6 Cal. Rptr. 2d 781 (1992).

presumptive evidence of negligence[229] or (b) some evidence from which negligence may be inferred.[230] In those jurisdictions, a detailed inquiry into the facts may still be necessary to determine whether the presumption of unreasonable conduct is rebutted by other evidence or whether the permissible evidence of negligence that the violation constitutes is sufficiently strong to warrant a finding of unreasonableness in light of competing facts.

### *§ 5-2.2(m)(1) How Statutes Set the Standard of Care*

A legislative enactment may set the standard of care for a civil cause of action for either of two reasons. The first reason is that the enactment contains language making clear that one of the remedies for breach of its requirements is a civil suit for damages.[231] The second reason that an enactment may set the standard of care is that, even though it is silent as to civil liability, a court determines that it is an appropriate indicator of whether the defendant acted reasonably. In making that assessment, a court considers whether the enactment was intended to protect the class of persons of which the plaintiff was a member from the type of harm that occurred.[232] If the answer is yes on both accounts, a court may treat the statute as setting the standard of conduct of a reasonably prudent person, provided there are no good reasons to the contrary. For example, a court might decline to hold that a legislative enactment sets the standard of care if it is obsolete or vague. Likewise, the court should not hold that a statute sets the standard of care if there is evidence that the legislature intended other penalties, such as criminal or administrative fines, to be the exclusive remedy for a violation or intended that a violation of the enactment, by itself, would not trigger liability for negligence.

### *§ 5-2.2(m)(2) Statutes Disclaiming a Civil Cause of Action*

State disciplinary rules typically contain a provision, similar to one found in the Model Rules of Professional Conduct, stating that a violation of a disciplinary rule does not automatically give rise to a cause of action against a lawyer or create a presumption that a legal duty has been breached.[233] It is clear from this type of provision that the drafters of the relevant enactment did not intend for a violation of the rules to support a negligence *per se* argument.

Similarly, the rules adopted by the Securities and Exchange Commission pursuant to the federal Sarbanes-Oxley Act, that impose various duties on lawyers, expressly

---

[229] *See* RESTATEMENT (THIRD) OF TORTS: PHYSICAL AND EMOTIONAL HARM § 14 Reporters' Note cmt c (American Law Institute, 2010) ("Some states say that the violation of a statute creates a rebuttable presumption of negligence, or prima facie proof of negligence").

[230] *Id.* ("About a dozen states conclude that violation of a statute is only some evidence of negligence").

[231] *See, e.g.*, TEX. CODE CRIM. PROC. Art. 18.20 (Westlaw 2017) ("Sec. 16. (a) A person whose wire, oral, or electronic communication is intercepted, disclosed, or used in violation of this article, or in violation of Chapter 16, Penal Code, has a civil cause of action against any person who intercepts, discloses, or uses or solicits another person to intercept, disclose, or use the communication and is entitled to recover from the person: (1) actual damages but not less than liquidated damages computed at a rate of $100 a day for each day of violation or $1,000, whichever is higher; (2) punitive damages; and (3) a reasonable attorney's fee and other litigation costs reasonably incurred").

[232] *See* RESTATEMENT (THIRD) OF TORTS: LIABILITY FOR PHYSICAL AND EMOTIONAL HARM § 14 (American Law Institute, 2010).

[233] *See* MODEL RULES OF PROF'L CONDUCT Scope Note (American Bar Ass'n, 2017).

indicate that they do not create a private right of action against a lawyer or law firm.[234] Again, it seems clear that a negligence *per se* argument is foreclosed.

However, it is not true that disciplinary rules and Sarbanes-Oxley regulations play no role in legal malpractice actions. A violation of their provisions does not establish a shorthand route to a finding that the defendant acted unreasonably. Nevertheless, a plaintiff may still argue that the defendant was negligent under the usual "totality of the circumstances" test, one of the relevant factors being that the defendant violated applicable rules. So too, an expert testifying in support of the plaintiff's case may base an opinion about the standard of care in part on what legislative enactments state about the lawyer's duties, even if those enactments do not create a negligence *per se* shortcut.

### *§ 5-2.2(m)(3) Restatement Position on Statutory Standards*

Summarizing the relationship between the rules governing lawyers' conduct and the standard of care in malpractice litigation, the *Restatement* explains:

> Proof of a violation of a rule or statute regulating the conduct of lawyers:
>
> (a) does not give rise to an implied cause of action for professional negligence or breach of fiduciary duty;
>
> (b) does not preclude other proof concerning the duty of care * * * or the fiduciary duty; and
>
> (c) may be considered by a trier of fact as an aid in understanding and applying the standard of * * * [care or fiduciary duty] to the extent that
>
> > (i) the rule or statute was designed for the protection of persons in the position of the claimant and
> >
> > (ii) proof of the content and construction of such a rule or statute is relevant to the claimant's claim.[235]

### *§ 5-2.2(m)(4) Statutes Imposing Duties Not Unique to Lawyers*

Some legislative enactments applicable to lawyers may support a negligence *per se* argument. For example, a few jurisdictions have laws expressly requiring lawyers, among others, to reveal confidential information to prevent child abuse. Under this type of law, a victim who suffers harm might persuasively argue that a lawyer who failed to make a report is liable for abuse that could have been prevented because the statute was intended to prevent that type of harm to the class of persons of which the plaintiff was a member. Many states have passed security breach notification laws which require database possessors (like law firms) to protect the personal information of data subjects (including present and former clients) from unauthorized access. Database possessors must also notify data subjects when the security of their personal information has been breached. Some of these laws expressly provide for civil liability for damages.[236] Other state laws are silent on the issue of civil liability. However, in those jurisdictions, a court might conclude that a lawyer was negligent *per se* based on an unexcused violation of

---

[234] 17 C.F.R. § 205.7 (Westlaw 2017).

[235] RESTATEMENT (THIRD) OF THE LAW GOVERNING LAWYERS § 52(2) (American Law Institute, 2000).

[236] *See, e.g.*, CAL. CIV. CODE § 1798.84 (Westlaw 2017) (allowing an injured customer to "institute a civil action to recover damages").

these statutory obligations.[237] Cyber criminals often target law firms for the purpose of gaining confidential client information.[238]

## § 5-2.2(n) Informed Consent in Legal Malpractice

The doctrine of informed consent is well established in the medical malpractice field. With limited exceptions, the doctrine requires a physician to disclose to a patient the material risks of, and available alternatives to, a course of treatment. The failure to make such disclosures and obtain the patient's consent is actionable negligence if that breach causes harm. This is true regardless of whether the physician otherwise exercised care in treating the patient.

Clients, like patients, have a right to exercise extensive control over their own affairs, including their legal representation.[239] Consequently, there is no reason why the informed consent doctrine should not apply as readily to legal malpractice cases as it does in suits against physicians.

Until recently, the term "informed consent" only occasionally appeared in court opinions dealing with legal malpractice. However, the underlying idea is well established. A lawyer has a duty to communicate to a client material information relating to the client's case.[240] Failure to keep a client reasonably informed is a breach of a lawyer's duties.[241]

---

[237] *See* Vincent R. Johnson, *Cybersecurity, Identity Theft, and the Limits of Tort Liability*, 57 S.C. L. REV. 255, 268 (2005); *see also* Vincent R. Johnson, *Credit Monitoring Damages in Cybersecurity Tort Litigation*, 19 GEO. MASON L. REV. 113, 130–31 (2011) (discussing Weakley v. Redline Recovery Services, LLC, 2011 WL 1522413 (S.D. Cal.), where "[t]he court ordered the responsible attorney to pay for five years of credit monitoring to protect the plaintiff from identity theft").

[238] *See* Mark Hamblett, *Chinese Nationals Charged with Hacking Firms to Steal M&A Info*, N.J.L.J., Dec. 27, 2016; Nell Gluckman & Christine Simmons, *Cravath Admits Breach as Law Firm Hacks Go Public*, AM. LAW., Mar. 30, 2016.

[239] *Cf.* RESTATEMENT (THIRD) OF THE LAW GOVERNING LAWYERS §§ 21–22 (American Law Institute, 2000).

[240] *See id.* § 20; MODEL RULES OF PROF'L CONDUCT R. 1.4 (American Bar Ass'n, 2017); *see also* Sierra Fria Corp. v. Evans, 127 F.3d 175, 179–80 (1st Cir. 1997) ("[W]hen a client seeks advice from an attorney, the attorney owes the client 'a duty of full and fair disclosure of facts material to the client's interests.' This means that the attorney must advise the client of any significant legal risks involved in a contemplated transaction, and must do so in terms sufficiently plain to permit the client to assess both the risks and their potential impact on his situation").

[241] *See* Thomas & Wong Gen. Contractor, Inc. v. Wallace, 2010 WL 475690, at *9–10 (Ariz. Ct. App.) (finding that the record reflected sufficient evidence for the jury to find that the lawyer breached her duty by failing to disclose material information, and that a new trial should not have been granted); Rice v. Downs, 203 Cal. Rptr. 3d 555, 569–70 (Ct. App. 2016) (holding that a legal malpractice action based on failure to disclose and obtain informed consent with respect to actual and potential conflicts was not barred by an arbitration clause); Giannini, Chin & Valinoti v. Superior Court, 42 Cal. Rptr. 2d 394, 405 (Ct. App. 1995) (recognizing, in a malpractice action seeking fee disgorgement, the "attorneys' duties to obtain informed consent before engaging [in] representing a client in the face of a potential conflict of interest," and holding that summary judgment was improperly granted to the defendant-lawyer); Stanley v. Richmond, 41 Cal. Rptr. 2d 768, 774 (Ct. App. 1995) (finding that claims for professional negligence and breach of fiduciary duty were stated in an action involving failure to obtain informed written consent to a conflict of interest); *cf.* GTI Capital Holdings, L.L.C. v. Comerica Bank-California, 2008 WL 4149632, at *2 (Ariz. Ct. App.) (declining to address the plaintiffs' informed consent claim because they were not clients of the attorneys in question); Frazee v. Proskauer Rose LLP, 2016 WL 6236400, at *2 (Cal. Ct. App.) (affirming dismissal of legal malpractice claims based on failure to obtain informed consent to the terms of a settlement because plaintiff failed to prove proximate causation of damages); Lewellen v. Phillips, 2010 WL 4851362, at *5 (Cal. Ct. App.) (finding that the evidence negated the plaintiff's allegations that her lawyer badgered her into accepting the settlement agreement and failed to obtain her informed consent before it was executed).

In *Bowman v. Gruel Mills Nims & Pylman, LLP*,[242] a malpractice action, a federal court considered the obligations imposed by the Michigan counterpart to Model Rule 1.4. It concluded that regardless of whether a lawyer's decision not to press ERISA claims in a retirement benefit dispute was a protected exercise of professional discretion, that choice, as a key strategic decision, needed to be discussed with the client.

The language of "informed consent" is now deeply embedded in the law of lawyering. The Model Rules of Professional Conduct use the term "informed consent" so frequently that the term is specifically defined. "Informed consent" signals a client's agreement to a proposed course of conduct after the lawyer has adequately communicated information about the material risks and reasonably available alternatives.[243] While references to the term "informed consent" may ultimately take on a slightly different meaning in the legal malpractice context than it has in lawyer discipline, courts are likely to increasingly discuss lawyers' obligations in terms of "informed consent." This means that attention will be focused on whether or not material risks and alternatives were disclosed. In many instances, the obligation to obtain "informed consent" means that an attorney "must disclose any fact that may limit his or her ability to comply with the fiduciary obligations."[244] Moreover, a "client must be informed of any acts or events, concerning the subject matter of the retention for which the client has a right to exercise discretion or control."[245]

The informed-consent disclosure obligation is backed, in part, by the law of negligence. In making disclosures, a lawyer must act reasonably, taking into account the magnitude of the risks, the feasibility of the alternatives, and the sophistication of the client.[246] Thus, "[a] lawyer must keep a client reasonably informed about the status of a matter entrusted to the lawyer, including the progress, prospects, problems, and costs of the representation."[247]

However, the obligation to disclose material risks and obtain informed consent is also backed by the law of fiduciary duty. Thus:

> A corollary of the fiduciary obligations of undivided loyalty and confidentiality is the attorney's responsibility to promptly advise the client of any important information that may impinge on those obligations. This means that there must be complete disclosure of all information that may bear on the quality of the attorney's representation. The disclosure must include not only all material facts but also should include an explanation of their legal significance.[248]

---

[242] 2007 WL 1203580, at *5–*6 (W.D. Mich.).

[243] *See* MODEL RULES OF PROF'L CONDUCT R. 1.0(e) (American Bar Ass'n, 2017); *see also* RESTATEMENT (THIRD) OF THE LAW GOVERNING LAWYERS § 122 cmt. c(i) (American Law Institute, 2000) ("Informed consent requires that each affected client be aware of the material respects in which the representation could have adverse effects on the interests of that client"); Vincent R. Johnson, *Legal Malpractice in International Business Transactions*, 44 HOFSTRA L. REV. 325, 345–47 (2015) (discussing informed consent).

[244] RONALD E. MALLEN, 2 LEGAL MALPRACTICE § 15:26 (Thomson Reuters 2017 ed.).

[245] *Id.* (citing, among other cases, In re Russin, 462 P.2d 812 (Ariz. 1969), and Salopek v. Schoemann, 124 P.2d 21 (Cal. 1942)).

[246] *See* RESTATEMENT (THIRD) OF THE LAW GOVERNING LAWYERS § 16 cmt. c (American Law Institute, 2000) ("The lawyer must keep the client informed and consult with the client as is reasonably appropriate to learn the client's decisions"); § 20(1) (similar).

[247] *Id.* § 20 cmt.

[248] RONALD E. MALLEN, 2 LEGAL MALPRACTICE § 15:26 (Thomson Reuters, 2017 ed.).

With respect to a lawyer's liability for negligence, three issues relating to informed consent are likely to warrant attention and debate. The first concerns "materiality," since even in the medical malpractice field, only material risks and alternatives need to be disclosed. The term "materiality" has diverse meanings in different areas of the law. In many instances, it means simply that the matter is of such weight and moment that a reasonable person would take it into account in making a decision. Considering that the purpose of the informed consent doctrine is to enable clients to decide their own affairs, courts should interpret the term "material" in a manner that does not frustrate the purposes of the rule. Nevertheless, the term has limits. For example, a lawyer is not liable for failing to advise a client to assert a claim for insurance benefits for which the client is not eligible.[249] One way to explain this result is to say that the undisclosed information was not "material."

Second, exceptions to informed consent obligations should be recognized in the law of legal malpractice. In medicine, a physician need not disclose a risk if it ought to be known by everyone or is in fact known to the patient; if there is an emergency and the patient is incapable of determining whether treatment should be administered; or if full disclosure would be detrimental to the patient's care and best interests. These exceptions are narrowly construed so that they do not undercut the policies behind the informed consent doctrine. Presumably, similar exceptions will apply to informed consent rules in the legal malpractice field.

Third, it is important to remember that failure to obtain informed consent is merely evidence of breach of duty. A plaintiff suing for negligence must still prove that the breach of duty caused damages. In medical malpractice law, a large majority of courts hold that, in proving causation in an informed-consent case, the appropriate inquiry is whether a reasonable person (as opposed to the specific plaintiff) would have made a different decision if the undisclosed matter had been called to the person's attention. Courts may follow this approach in legal malpractice cases. Phrasing the inquiry in reasonable-person terms minimizes the risk that self-serving testimony by the plaintiff will distort the assessment of whether the nondisclosure did, in fact, cause damage.

However, some courts may take a different approach. In *Smith v. O'Donnell*,[250] the Texas Supreme Court allowed an executor to bring a malpractice claim against a law firm that allegedly provided bad advice to the decedent. In dicta the court stated that, "Of course, if the evidence demonstrates that * * * [the decedent] would have ignored * * * [the law firm's] advice no matter how competently provided, the malpractice claim will fail for lack of proximate causation."[251] However, the court did not definitively rule on the issue of whether a subjective or objective standard governs proof of causation in legal malpractice cases.

Consider this example: a client alleges that the defendant-lawyer failed to advise the client about the risks of submitting a dispute to arbitration, rather than trying a case in a court. Among the undisclosed risks are the facts that the arbitrators are not strictly bound by substantive law and that there is very little opportunity for judicial review of an unfavorable arbitration decision. In a legal malpractice action alleging lack of informed consent, the plaintiff will have to establish that the undisclosed matters were

---

249 *See* Abbo v. Perkins, 2007 WL 949760, at *6 (Ohio App. 2007).

250 288 S.W.3d 417 (Tex. 2009).

251 *Id.* at 421.

material and unknown to the plaintiff, that a reasonable person would not have agreed to arbitration if that information had been disclosed, and that a court of law would have rendered a decision more favorable to the client. Consequently, the plaintiff in an informed consent case faces many obstacles.

## § 5-2.3 CAUSATION

A plaintiff suing a lawyer for negligence must always prove that the lawyer's unreasonable conduct caused harm. The usual inquiry into causation has two aspects. Factual causation requires that the defendant's conduct be significantly linked to the damages the plaintiff alleges, and proximate causation requires that it be fair to hold the defendant responsible for damages factually caused. Factual and proximate causation are discussed in the following sections.

"The principles and proof of causation in a legal malpractice action do not differ from those governing an ordinary negligence case."[252] "A plaintiff need not prove causation with absolute certainty, but the evidence must establish causation beyond mere possibility or speculation."[253]

### § 5-2.3(a) Factual Causation

No matter how serious a lawyer's negligence, causation of damages is not presumed. If a new associate with no experience and inadequate supervision makes serious errors in trying a case, the plaintiff must still prove that those errors adversely impacted the result of the trial.[254]

Similarly, even if a law firm is negligent in failing to prevent a lawyer from sexualizing a lawyer-client relationship, a client cannot recover damages for losses incidental to an adverse arbitration ruling without proving that, except for the negligence, those losses would not have occurred.[255] Likewise, even if a lawyer is negligent in representing a client in divorce proceedings,[256] or failing to challenge the entry of summary judgment on a constructive discharge claim,[257] the client cannot prevail in a malpractice action unless the client can prove that he or she would have achieved a more favorable result but for the negligence.

#### *§ 5-2.3(a)(1) The "But For" Test*

Legal malpractice cases are governed by the same factual causation principles that apply in other areas of tort law.[258] Thus, the well-known "but for" test is the most common method of proving factual causation. Under that test, the plaintiff must show that but for the negligence of the defendant, harm would not have occurred. For example, "[i]n an action alleging that an attorney failed to perfect an appeal, the plaintiff must

---

[252] Rogers v. Zanetti, 518 S.W.3d 394, 402 (Tex. 2017) (quoting 1 Ronald E. Mallen, *Legal Malpractice* § 8:20 at 1029 (2017)).

[253] Rogers v. Zanetti, 518 S.W.3d 394, 411 (Tex. 2017).

[254] *See* Alexander v. Turtur & Associates, Inc., 146 S.W.3d 113 (Tex. 2004).

[255] *See* Cecala v. Newman, 2007 WL 2530369, at *6 (D. Ariz.), *aff'd*, 379 Fed. Appx. 584 (9th Cir. 2010).

[256] *See* Oakes v. Clark, 69 A.3d 371 (Del. 2013).

[257] *See* Steele v. Salb, 93 A.3d 1277, 1279 (D.C. 2014).

[258] *See* RESTATEMENT (THIRD) OF THE LAW GOVERNING LAWYERS § 53 (American Law Institute, 2000).

prove that he or she would have been successful on appeal if the appeal had properly been perfected."[259]

If a plaintiff wishes to recover damages resulting from a business transaction that allegedly failed due to a lawyer's negligence, the plaintiff must show that but for the lawyer's errant conduct the transaction would have succeeded and the losses would not have been sustained. Likewise, if the plaintiff alleges that a lawyer's failure to disclose relevant information to the client caused a lawsuit not to settle and eventually precipitated a disastrous jury verdict, the plaintiff must convince the jury that, but for the nondisclosure, there could have been a meeting of the minds on an acceptable settlement amount.[260] If such evidence is adduced, the plaintiff can then recover the difference between the lesser amount for which the case would have settled and the amount of the jury verdict.

*§ 5-2.3(a)(1)(A) Difficult to Establish*

"But for" causation is often difficult to establish. For example, in *Faber v. Herman*,[261] a divorcing couple had agreed that the wife was entitled to half of the husband's retirement benefits. However, the husband's lawyer erred, first, by drafting a stipulation that sought to implement the agreement by means not permitted by law (an immediate payment from the retirement fund based on present value), and, second, by failing to advise his client of the further steps he had taken to correct the first error (a delayed payment of a percentage of the husband's retirement benefits). Nevertheless, the Iowa Supreme Court held that the lawyer's malpractice did not cause damages because the husband had agreed to an even division of retirement benefits and that was what was ultimately achieved.

In another case, the plaintiff alleged that but for a law firm's failure to provide proper tax advice "it would not have had to maintain the multi-million dollar loss reserve on its books, creating the appearance that it had a negative net worth, which caused it to lose business opportunities and incur monetary damages."[262] However, the New York Court of Appeals found that the plaintiff failed to establish factual causation of damages. The loss reserve had been in place for years before the law firm was hired and was still carried on the books after the law firm advised the plaintiff that there was a very strong case that it had no liability for the taxes in question.[263]

Courts may logically impose a lighter causation burden of proof on a malpractice plaintiff seeking to survive a motion for summary judgment than on a plaintiff seeking to secure a favorable verdict. In *Bond v. McLaughlin*,[264] the plaintiff alleged that her attorney, McLaughlin, failed to properly contest a copy of a will that was admitted to probate, and that as a result she suffered damages. In addressing the defendant's motion for summary judgment, the Supreme Court of Alabama wrote:

---

[259] Universal Underwriters Ins. Co. v. Judge & James, Ltd., 865 N.E.2d 531, 538 (Ill. App. Ct. 2007).

[260] *Cf.* Rogers v. Zanetti, 517 S.W.3d 123, 136 (Tex. App. 2015), *aff'd,* 518 S.W.3d 394 (Tex. 2017) ("The Clients adduced no evidence raising a genuine fact issue that a settlement agreement actually would have been reached because there is no evidence proving that the same terms would have been acceptable to both the Alexanders and the Clients").

[261] 731 N.W.2d 1 (Iowa 2007).

[262] AmBase Corp. v. Davis Polk Wardwell, 834 N.Y.S.2d 705, 710 (N.Y. 2007).

[263] *Id.* at 709.

[264] 229 So. 3d 760 (Ala. 2017).

> We note that McLaughlin and the trial court in its summary-judgment order place great emphasis on the fact that Bond must ultimately prove that the result of the underlying proceeding—the will contest—"would" have been different, rather than "may" have been different. At the summary-judgment stage in the present case, it is true that Bond was required to present "substantial evidence" that the result of the underlying proceeding "would" have been different, but she did not have to present undisputed evidence or definitively prove that the result of the underlying proceeding would have been different. At this stage, Bond was required to present evidence from which the finder of fact could infer that the result of the underlying proceeding would have been different. We hold that Bond has presented such evidence.[265]

*§ 5-2.3(a)(1)(B) Proving an Alternative Would Have Occurred*

Proving causation often requires a plaintiff to show that an alternative sequence of events would have occurred but for the defendant's breach of duty. Moreover, persuasion by a preponderance of the evidence is required. The mere fact that another sequence of events *might* have occurred is insufficient to establish factual causation. Rather, it must be shown that, more likely than not, but for the lawyer's negligence, a different series of events would have taken place.

*Bristol Co., LP v. Osman*,[266] was a suit based on a law firm's alleged failure to provide proper advice about the defense of laches. A Colorado appellate court found that the portions of the plaintiff's complaint addressing causation were insufficient to support a damages award because the allegations were purely hypothetical and speculative. The complaint did not identify an actual harm, but merely "a harm that might have occurred had events unfolded differently."[267]

However, the mere fact that an alternative sequence of events involves several variables does not necessarily preclude proof of causation, if each of those variables is susceptible to proof. In *Geddes v. Campbell*,[268] a California court found that causation was not "beyond the realm of proof" or a matter of speculation where it was necessary for the plaintiff to show that, if the defendant-lawyer had advised the plaintiff to make certain disclosures to a third party, the plaintiff would have followed that advice and the third party would have agreed to a release of liability. Presumably, the plaintiff could testify about whether he would have followed the advice; the defendant could challenge that testimony or introduce contrary evidence; and the jury could resolve the issue, one way or the other. As to whether the third-person would have signed a release, the court noted simply that the person "could be questioned about whether he would have signed such a release had he known what he allegedly did not know."[269]

*Christensen & Jensen, P.C. v. Barrett & Daines*[270] was a legal malpractice case that arose from a dispute which gave rise to a landmark punitive damages ruling. In the underlying case, multiple jointly-represented co-clients rejected a $150 million settlement offer. Ultimately, they recovered a total of about only $10 million after the

---

[265] *Id.* at 767.

[266] 190 P.3d 752 (Colo. Ct. App. 2007).

[267] *Id.* at 758.

[268] 2006 WL 3352182, *7 (Cal. Ct. App.).

[269] *Id.* at *8.

[270] 194 P.3d 931 (Utah 2008).

United States Supreme Court articulated new standards, which now greatly constrain punitive damages awards.

In the subsequent malpractice case, the plaintiff (one of the former co-clients) argued first that the $150 million settlement offer would have been accepted by the co-clients if it had been better explained, and second that the plaintiff could have settled his claim individually if he had not been represented by lawyers who had a conflict of interest by representing multiple co-clients. The Utah Supreme Court rejected both arguments, finding that on neither ground could the plaintiff prove that the malpractice defendants' conduct caused damage. The $150 million settlement offer had been conditioned by the defendant in the underlying case on all co-clients joining in a request for the state supreme court to vacate an opinion which contained findings that the defendant had engaged nationally in a pattern of abusive business practices over a period of many years. The settlement offer was further conditioned on the state supreme court's vacatur of the opinion in question.

In the malpractice case, the Utah Supreme Court found that the causation standards for negligence, breach of fiduciary duty, and even breach of contract were essentially the same as applied to the facts of the dispute.[271] Thus, in order to recover, the plaintiff needed to show that, but for the breach, the plaintiff would have benefitted. However, the court concluded that the plaintiff was unable to make this showing. There was undisputed evidence that the co-clients had entered into an agreement requiring unanimity for acceptance of any settlement offer. The co-clients other than the plaintiff were adamant that they would not have settled on the terms proposed by the defendant in the underlying suit because they were more interested in preserving the disputed opinion and its findings than they were in money. Finally, there was no evidence that the defendant would have settled with the malpractice plaintiff separately.

#### *§ 5-2.3(a)(1)(C) Prior Judge and Jury May Not Testify*

If malpractice is alleged to have impacted an earlier trial, it is reasonable to consider whether it would be possible to ask the judge or jurors from the earlier case if their decisions would have been different but for the malpractice. However, this is not permitted. For reasons of judicial ethics, the judge in the earlier proceeding is not allowed to testify in the malpractice lawsuit. Testimony by the former judge would be unduly prejudicial because the prestige of the judge's judicial office would be aligned with one of the parties in the malpractice litigation. For different reasons, generally relating to impracticality, finality, and the integrity of jury deliberations, jurors from the first proceeding are also not allowed to testify about whether they would have decided the underlying case differently if the lawyer had not been negligent.

#### *§ 5-2.3(a)(1)(D) The "But For" Test and Multiple Tortfeasors*

In cases involving multiple tortfeasors, there may be more than one "but for" cause. Suppose that Lawyer #1 negligently omits important provisions from a contract, and that successor counsel, Lawyer #2, negligently fails to discover the omission at a time when it would have been possible to reform the instrument at minimal costs to the client. If the client becomes liable under the contract for onerous amounts as a result of the omitted provisions, the client can successfully sue either lawyer or both. But for Lawyer #1's omission of the provisions, the client never would have become liable under the

[271] *Id.* at 938.

contract. But for Lawyer #2's negligence, the omission would have been discovered, the contract would have been reformed, and the client would not have incurred contractual liability. The negligence of each lawyer is a factual cause of the plaintiff's harm.

*§ 5-2.3(a)(1)(E) Independently Sufficient Causes*

Authorities widely recognize that even if the "but for" test cannot be met, the defendant's conduct is a factual cause of the plaintiff's harm if the defendant's conduct was independently sufficient to cause the harm.[272] This rule applies to legal malpractice cases.[273]

Consider the following scenario: Lawyer #3 and Lawyer #4 are each asked to draft separate provisions for a complex document. Each lawyer does so negligently, and each act of negligence is sufficient to render the document invalid, causing losses to the client. Lawyer #3 does not escape liability because Lawyer #4's conduct would have precipitated the same losses, and vice versa. Because each lawyer's conduct was independently sufficient to cause the invalidity of the document, each lawyer will be held responsible even though it cannot be said that either was a "but for" cause of the damages.

***§ 5-2.3(a)(2) "Trial Within a Trial" Analysis***

Establishing factual causation requires the plaintiff to prove what would have happened if the facts had been different. In a malpractice lawsuit, this process is sometimes referred to as a "trial within a trial" or a "case within a case."

The expression is particularly apt when the alleged malpractice relates to an underlying litigation claim. The first lawsuit must be presented within the context of the malpractice action to gauge what the result would have been but for the defendant-lawyer's negligence.

For example, a malpractice plaintiff may allege that, but for the lawyer's negligence, the plaintiff would have secured a verdict—or a more favorable verdict—in the underlying action. In that case, "[a]ll the issues that would have been litigated in the previous action are litigated between the plaintiff and the plaintiff's former lawyer, with the latter taking the place and bearing the burdens that properly would have fallen on the defendant in the original action."[274] As the Supreme Court of Kentucky explained in *Osborne v. Keeney*:[275]

> When trying a suit-within-a-suit, especially when the reason for the lost claim is the expiration of the relevant statute of limitations, "all the issues that would have been litigated in the [barred] action are litigated between the plaintiff and the plaintiff's former lawyer." And, in recreating the litigation, the usual instructions that should be given in the underlying case, including any special verdict forms, are those to be used in the malpractice trial.[276]

---

[272] *Cf.* RESTATEMENT (THIRD) OF TORTS: LIABILITY FOR PHYSICAL AND EMOTIONAL HARM § 27 (American Law Institute, 2010).

[273] *Cf.* Rogers v. Zanetti, 518 S.W.3d 394, 402 (Tex. 2017) (recognizing that in cases of concurrent causation a "substantial factor," rather than "but for," rule applies, but finding the rule inapplicable to the legal malpractice dispute before the court).

[274] Suder v. Whiteford, Taylor & Preston, LLP, 992 A.2d 413, 420 (Md. 2010) (quoting RESTATEMENT (THIRD) OF THE LAW GOVERNING LAWYERS § 52 cmt. b (American Law Institute, 2000)).

[275] 399 S.W.3d 1 (Ky. 2012).

[276] *Id.* at 10–11.

However, the parties have some flexibility in deciding which issues to raise in the malpractice action. In *Suder v. Whiteford, Taylor & Preston, LLP*,[277] the Maryland Court of Appeals held that the malpractice defendant was not precluded from raising defenses which were never asserted in an earlier trial which gave rise to the malpractice claim.[278]

In *Aquino v. Kuczinski, Vila & Assoc., P.C.*,[279] the plaintiff alleged that the defendant-attorney failed to file her slip-and-fall case before the statute of limitations expired. The court held that the defendant-attorney was entitled to summary judgment because the "plaintiff failed to introduce any evidence that the casino either created the dangerous condition, or had actual or constructive knowledge of it."[280] Absent such evidence, the plaintiff could not prove that she would have prevailed on the underlying premises liability claim.

*§ 5-2.3(a)(2)(A) Factual Complexity*

One practical consequence of the "trial within a trial" process is that legal malpractice cases can be exceedingly complex. This is particularly true if the underlying matter involves a sophisticated area of law practice that is ordinarily difficult to understand even without the added issues of a legal malpractice claim. This may be true, for example, in a case where the lawyer was allegedly negligent in representing a subsidiary in a dispute with the subsidiary's parent corporation. In that situation, malpractice liability may turn on careful assessment of the actions, statements, and expectations of numerous entity representatives and stakeholders.

In some cases, conducting a trial within a trial requires the presentation of many witnesses and documents, prolonging the malpractice trial with little hope of keeping the jurors focused until a verdict can be reached. Even if all the evidence is presented, the jury may not fully comprehend the matter. Faced with these realities, some cases settle because it is unlikely that a better result will be forthcoming even if the litigation were allowed to run its course.

In order to minimize the complexity of the trial within a trial process, litigators may seek to sever the underlying action for a separate trial. Procedures in some states permit this.[281]

If the alleged malpractice relates to the mishandling of a legal malpractice case, there may be a third layer of complexity. For example, in *Smith v. McLaughlin*,[282] the court found that the legal malpractice claim before it implicated "a case (the initial criminal matter) within a case (the criminal malpractice matter) within the case (the legal malpractice matter that is now before us)."[283]

A jury can be aided in tracing the consequences of legal malpractice by the introduction of expert testimony. Indeed, states like Connecticut hold that "[i]n complex legal malpractice matters, 'expert testimony is necessary to keep the jury from

277 992 A.2d 413, 420 (Md. 2010).

278 *Id.* at 421.

279 835 N.Y.S.2d 16 (App. Div. 2007).

280 *Id.* at 20.

281 *See, e.g.*, ALA. CODE § 6–5–579 (Westlaw 2017).

282 769 S.E.2d 7 (Va. 2015).

283 *Id.* at 11.

speculating on how the client's loss or injury is *directly linked* to that which he claims was the breach of duty by the attorney.' "[284]

### *§ 5-2.3(a)(3) The "More Favorable Result" Standard*

Litigating cases is only one small part of the wide range of legal services that are provided by lawyers. If malpractice relates to transactional matters, or other types of work not involving litigation, it often makes little sense to talk of conducting a "trial within a trial" as the means for ascertaining whether alleged errors or omissions caused damages. Thus, "[w]here the injury claimed does not depend on the merits of the underlying action, * * * the case-within-a-case methodology does not apply."[285]

In such cases, the relevant question is whether, but for the negligence of the defendant-lawyer, the plaintiff would have achieved a more favorable result. Thus, as the Minnesota Supreme Court has explained, "When a case does not involve damage to or loss of a cause of action, but instead involves transactional malpractice, we have modified the but-for element to require a plaintiff to show that, 'but for defendant's conduct, the plaintiff would have obtained a more favorable result in the underlying transaction than the result obtained.' "[286]

A more favorable result can take different forms. In some cases, it means that the plaintiff would have received a better deal from a counterparty. In other cases, it means that the plaintiff would not have entered into a transaction and would therefore have avoided losses related to that transaction. These better-deal and no-deal perspectives on factual causation offer a useful reminder that not everything lawyers do plays out in courts. As the Texas Supreme Court plainly stated, "to the extent the lawyers argue that we always require a hypothetical showing of ultimate victory, they are mistaken."[287]

In addition, it is important to recall that, even when suit is filed, most cases are not resolved by a final judgment in litigation, but by settlement. In many fields, the percentage of meritorious cases that settle may be higher than 90%.

It is often fair for a plaintiff to argue that but for the defendant-lawyer's malpractice, a better settlement would have been achieved. This is true regardless of whether the claim might have failed on the merits if ruled on by a court. Cases can have real settlement value, even if the plaintiff is unlikely to prevail before a judge and jury.

Of course, a plaintiff who argues that a better settlement would have been reached had malpractice not been committed must be ready to muster persuasive evidence. A defendant is sure to argue that what would have happened, if the facts had been different, is a matter of speculation. In order to prevail, the plaintiff will have to make a compelling case. The plaintiff must prove by a preponderance of the evidence that damages were in fact suffered.

### *§ 5-2.3(a)(4) Loss of a Chance*

Loss of a chance is not a theory of factual causation, but rather a different way of looking at damages. The chance of securing a successful result is regarded as something

[284] Bozelko v. Papastavros, 147 A.3d 1023, 1032 (2016) (quoting Van Sommeren v. Gibson, 991 N.E.2d 1199, 1208 (Ohio App.2013) (emphasis in original)).

[285] Rogers v. Zanetti, 518 S.W.3d 394, 401 (Tex. 2017).

[286] Guzick v. Kimball, 869 N.W.2d 42, 50 (Minn. 2015).

[287] Rogers v. Zanetti, 518 S.W.3d 394, 405 (Tex. 2017).

important, the loss of which is a kind of damage itself. If that is true, proving factual causation is simple: all that the plaintiff must show is that, but for the defendant's tortious conduct, the valuable chance would not have been lost.

A number of states have accepted "loss of a chance" arguments in the context of medical malpractice.[288] For example, assume that a doctor negligently fails to read an x-ray that reveals cancer, and that during the period that the cancerous condition goes undetected the plaintiff's chances of survival declined from 40% to 10%. Most persons would regard the lost chance of survival as an important loss, and some states permit recovery. This may be true even if, as in the posited scenario, the patient was already more likely than not to die at the time that the initial x-ray was taken. In the subsequent action, the doctor's negligence is a "but for" cause of the lost chance of survival, rather than of the death.

Courts and scholars sometimes bristle at the mere mention of "loss of a chance" as a legitimate rationale for recovery. They fear that the doctrine is an unwise step down an ill-advised path that might lead to theories of "probabilistic causation" that lie far afield from the certainties of the "but for" rule. Few cases have expressly endorsed the loss of a chance theory in the legal malpractice context.[289] Nevertheless, the *Restatement* opines that "a plaintiff who can establish that the negligence or fiduciary breach of the plaintiff's former lawyer deprived the plaintiff of a substantial chance of prevailing and that, due to that misconduct, the results of a previous trial cannot be reconstructed, may recover for the loss of that chance in jurisdictions recognizing such a theory of recovery in professional-malpractice cases generally."[290]

There are many cases where a lawyer's negligence does indeed cause the loss of an important chance, such as where a lawyer neglects to relay a settlement offer or plea bargain that might have been accepted. In malpractice actions arising from these types of disputes, some decisions effectively recognize the loss of a chance doctrine without using the term. For example, in *Vahila v. Hall*,[291] the Supreme Court of Ohio held that, to succeed in a malpractice action, the plaintiffs were not required to show that they would have prevailed in certain civil, criminal, and administrative proceedings absent the negligence of their lawyers. The court wrote:

> [W]e reject any finding that the element of causation in the context of a legal malpractice action can be replaced * * * with a rule of thumb requiring that a plaintiff * * * prove in every instance that he or she would have been successful in the underlying matter(s) giving rise to the complaint. * * *. A strict "but for" test * * * ignores settlement opportunities lost due to the attorney's negligence.[292]

---

[288] *See* Matsuyama v. Birnbaum, 890 N.E.2d 819, 828 n.23 (Mass. 2008).

[289] For criticism of courts' refusal to apply the loss of chance doctrine in legal malpractice cases, see Benjamin H. Barton, *Do Judges Systematically Favor the Interests of the Legal Profession?*, 59 ALA. L. REV. 453, 494–96 (2008); Lawrence W. Kessler, *The Unchanging Face of Legal Malpractice: How the "Captured" Regulators of the Bar Protect Attorneys*, 86 MARQ. L. REV. 457, 474–77 (2002); and Susan Saab Fortney, *A Tort in Search of a Remedy: Prying Open the Courthouse Doors for Legal Malpractice Victims*, 85 FORDHAM L. REV. 2033, 2047 (2017).

[290] RESTATEMENT (THIRD) OF THE LAW GOVERNING LAWYERS § 52 cmt. b (American Law Institute, 2000).

[291] 674 N.E.2d 1164 (Ohio 1997).

[292] *Id.* at 1168–69 (internal quotations omitted).

Of course, if a malpractice plaintiff alleges that harm was caused by the defendant-lawyer's failure to convey a settlement offer, the plaintiff must be prepared to show that but for the negligence the case would have settled. If the plaintiff testifies "only that he would have tried to settle the case had he known about the settlement offer," the claim is likely to fail due to a lack of convincing evidence that the breach of duty caused harm.[293]

In some cases, a plaintiff may allege not that he or she lost the opportunity to settle, but lost the benefits of a trial. "[W]hen a plaintiff premises a legal-malpractice claim on the theory that he would have received a better outcome if his attorney had tried the underlying matter to conclusion rather than settling it, the plaintiff must establish that he would have prevailed in the underlying matter and that the outcome would have been better than the outcome provided by the settlement."[294]

#### *§ 5-2.3(a)(5) Shifting the Burden of Proof on Causation*

Occasionally, courts have shifted the burden of proof on the issue of causation to the malpractice defendant, at least on certain issues.[295] Shifting the burden of proof particularly makes sense if the lawyer's alleged malpractice is of a type that would naturally deprive the plaintiff of evidence relating to causation.

Under Louisiana law, a client's proof that a lawyer's negligence caused the loss of the opportunity to assert a claim creates an inference that the lost opportunity caused damages. The burden then shifts to the lawyer to establish that the client could not have succeeded on the original claim.[296]

In *Gamer v. Ross*,[297] lawyers were hired to handle personal injury actions against a landowner and an independent contractor after a boy, while in-line skating, tripped over wires and debris located on a public sidewalk. After the actions were decided adversely to the plaintiffs, the plaintiffs sued their lawyers for malpractice. The plaintiffs alleged that the lawyers were negligent in failing to conduct proper discovery. The lawyers sought summary judgment on the ground that the plaintiffs could not have succeeded in the underlying actions inasmuch as they adduced no evidence that the landowner or independent contractor caused the dangerous condition. In affirming an order denying the lawyers' request for summary judgment, a New York appellate court wrote:

> [T]his argument fundamentally misconstrue[s] the central theory of the plaintiffs' case, viz., that the defendants were negligent in failing to conduct proper discovery that would have uncovered facts sufficient to prevent the dismissal of the underlying actions. As the moving parties, the defendants bore the initial burden of establishing that the missing discovery would not have prevented the dismissal of the underlying actions. "This burden cannot be satisfied merely by pointing out gaps in the plaintiff[s]' case" * * *.[298]

---

[293] Rogers v. Zanetti, 518 S.W.3d 394, 411 (Tex. 2017).

[294] Environmental Network Corp. v. Goodman Weiss Miller, L.L.P., 893 N.E.2d 173, 175 (Ohio 2008).

[295] *See* RONALD E. MALLEN, LEGAL MALPRACTICE § 33:32 (Thomson Reuters, 2017 ed.) (discussing collectability; noting a "significant minority" of jurisdictions).

[296] *See* Prince v. Buck, 969 So.2d 641, 643 (La. Ct. App. 2007).

[297] 854 N.Y.S.2d 160 (App. Div. 2008).

[298] *Id.* at 162.

In *Baptiste v. Rohn*,[299] a federal trial court in the Virgin Islands noted that:

> [T]here is some support for the proposition that, in legal malpractice cases alleging professional negligence, the burden of proof on the issue of causation may be shifted to the defendant. For example, in California, the Court of Appeals has shifted the burden of proof to the defendant-attorney where the defendant-attorney's negligence made it "impossible" for the plaintiff-client to prove the underlying case. In *Galanek v. Wismar*, 68 Cal. App. 4th 1417 (1999), the plaintiff brought a legal malpractice action against her former attorney and his law firm based on the attorney's alleged negligent spoliation of evidence while representing the plaintiff in a products liability case against a car manufacturer—*i.e.*, the attorney failed to take reasonable steps to prevent the destruction of the car the plaintiff had been driving when she was injured.[300]

However, the *Baptiste* court found that the plaintiff had failed to demonstrate why shifting the burden of proof was appropriate on the facts before it.

In many jurisdictions, there is little precedent for shifting the burden of proof on causation to a legal malpractice defendant. In *Thomas v. Kidani*,[301] the Supreme Court of Hawaii rejected the malpractice plaintiff's argument "that under a 'fiduciary fraud' theory of liability, there is a burden shift, and instead of the plaintiff carrying the burden to show fraud, the defendant carries a burden to show that no fraud was committed."[302]

### *§ 5-2.3(a)(6) Tortious Spoliation of Causation Evidence*

Sometimes a lawyer's negligence results in the loss of evidence needed by a client to prove that the lawyer's conduct caused damages. For example, in *Fontanella v. Marcucci*,[303] a boy was injured in an automobile accident as the result of allegedly defective seatbelts. However, before the seatbelts were inspected properly, the boy's mother sold the car to her insurer, allegedly on the advice of their attorney. The automobile was subsequently destroyed, making the seatbelt evidence unavailable. Pointing to the destruction of evidence, the plaintiff filed a legal malpractice action against the former lawyer and his firm, alleging that the lawyer failed to obtain and preserve the automobile for inspection concerning the alleged seatbelt failure.[304]

A judge may use different approaches to address spoliation. A common approach is for the judge to instruct the jury that it may infer that the missing evidence hurts the spoliator and helps the opposing party. Another approach is to shift to the lawyer the burden of disproving that the lawyer's negligence caused harm to the plaintiff.[305]

For example, suppose that a lawyer deceives a client for a period of years about performing work to investigate the facts of the client's case.[306] By the time the deception is discovered, it may be too late to assemble the essential witnesses and documents. In these types of cases, if the client sues the lawyer, it is unfair to require the client to prove

---

[299] 2016 WL 1261072 (D.V.I.).

[300] *Id.* at *4.

[301] 267 P.3d 1230 (Haw. 2011).

[302] *Id.* at 1236.

[303] 877 A.2d 828 (Conn. App. 2005), *certification granted in part*, 275 Conn. 907, 882 A.2d 670 (2005), *certification withdrawn* (Mar. 13, 2006).

[304] *Id.* at 832.

[305] Galanek v. Wismar, 81 Cal. Rptr. 2d 236, 242 (Cal. App. 1999).

[306] *See* Jerista v. Murray, 883 A.2d 350, 366 (N.J. 2005).

that the underlying claim would have been won. A spoliation inference or presumption may be an appropriate remedy for this kind of misconduct, at least where the spoliation was culpable, unexcused, and clearly injurious to the client.

Some states permit sanctions or an independent tort action based on intentional or negligent spoliation of evidence. However, the trend of recent decisions favors using spoliation inferences or presumptions when that is feasible.[307] The jury is told that it may infer, or in the absence of evidence to the contrary is required to presume, that the missing evidence would have been favorable to the plaintiff. Of course, a lawyer who wrongfully destroys evidence is subject to disciplinary sanctions, as well as malpractice liability.[308]

#### *§ 5-2.3(a)(6)(A) Legitimate Destruction of Evidence*

Lawyers regularly discard material, such as handwritten notes, documents, e-mail messages, and electronic files. Prohibiting destruction of such material would essentially transform law offices into over-stocked warehouses for information that might rarely be used. Therefore, lawyers must be allowed to destroy material pursuant to a carefully crafted document retention policy. Such a policy can help protect lawyers from spoliation claims because the policy may explain why it was reasonable, rather than negligent, to discard certain papers or electronic files. Of course, when it is foreseeable that a dispute might call for information pertaining to a client, ordinary policies on document retention must give way to more careful implementation of the duty to preserve or return to the client documents and other information and property.

### *§ 5-2.3(a)(7) Concerted Action Liability*

Lawyers can be held liable for harm caused by others under concerted action principles.[309] Thus, liability may be imposed under the usual rules governing aiding-and-abetting (i.e., concerted action by assistance) and civil conspiracy (i.e., concerted action by agreement).[310] Such principles create liability for negligence and other forms of tortious conduct committed by the person the defendant assisted or with whom the defendant embarked on a common plan. However, concerted action liability generally requires proof that the defendant acted with knowledge of the other's wrongdoing.

For example, in *Go-Best Assets Ltd. v. Citizens Bank of Massachusetts*,[311] the plaintiff sought to hold a lawyer's (Goldings's) former partners liable for his theft of client funds on aiding-and-abetting principles, rather than negligence. The court affirmed a judgment in favor of the former partners because "[e]ach aiding and abetting claim requires knowledge by the defendant of the principal's wrongdoing * * * [and the evidence was insufficient to] support an inference of knowledge of an ongoing unlawful scheme."[312]

---

[307] *See* Justice Rebecca Simmons & Michael J. Ritter, *Texas's Spoliation "Presumption,"* 43 ST. MARY'S L.J. 691 (2012).

[308] *See* Karen Sloan, *Ohio Supreme Court Suspends Lawyer for Destroying Documents and Lying About It*, www.law.com, Aug. 30, 2010.

[309] *See* Vincent R. Johnson & Stephen C. Loomis, *Malpractice Liability Related to Foreign Outsourcing of Legal Services*, 2 ST. MARY'S J. LEGAL MAL. & ETHICS 262, 319 (2012) (discussing aiding and abetting).

[310] *See* RESTATEMENT (SECOND) OF TORTS § 876 (American law Institute, 1979).

[311] 947 N.E.2d 581, 594 (Mass. App. Ct. 2011).

[312] *Id.* at 597–98.

## § 5-2.3(b) Proximate Causation

The requirement of proximate causation is a policy-based inquiry into fairness. The rule holds that even if the defendant factually caused the plaintiff's harm, the defendant will not be accountable if it would be unfair to impose responsibility.

### *§ 5-2.3(b)(1) In General*

There are different ways of talking about fairness. Thus, as in other areas of tort law, a malpractice defendant's conduct may be found not to be a proximate cause of a loss that was unforeseeable[313] or not within the risks that made the defendant's conduct tortious.[314] It may also be impossible or unfair to impose liability if many intervening forces contributed to the production of the loss. Thus, it may be said that "[a] proximate cause is one that produces an injury through a natural and continuous sequence of events unbroken by any effective intervening cause."[315]

Consider the economic "meltdown" of American financial institutions between 2007 and 2009. Lawyers presumably contributed to the marketing of the sub-prime loans and financial "derivatives" that many persons say were an important cause of the crisis. If those lawyers were sued for malpractice by the entities they represented, by the successors of those entities, or by investors or lenders who suffered losses, one defense would be lack of proximate causation. The argument, presumably, would be that a collapse of the American economy on a scale approaching the Great Depression was so unforeseeable and had so many contributing causes, that it would be unfair to hold particular lawyers liable for the resulting damages. Of course, whether that is a good argument depends upon how one reads legal history. There are literally thousands of cases addressing the issue of proximate causation in tort law generally, and many address it specifically in the context of lawyer liability.

Even courts that frame proximate causation in terms of foreseeability do not require strict foreseeability of harm. Otherwise many blameworthy tortfeasors would escape liability. Rather, fairness simply requires that the defendant should have foreseen, in loose terms, harm to the class of persons of which the plaintiff is a member, and the general type of harm that in fact occurred. Differences in the manner of occurrence are generally irrelevant, as is the fact that the harm may have been greater than expected.

Some decisions have saved a lawyer from liability based on lack of proximate causation. In *TIG Ins. Co. v. Giffin Winning Cohen & Bodewes, P.C.*,[316] the Seventh Circuit determined that huge expenses incurred in fighting a discovery motion were not recoverable by an insurer in its legal malpractice action against a law firm hired to

---

[313] *See* Stanfield v. Neubaum, 494 S.W.3d 90, 97 (Tex. 2016) ("Breach of a duty proximately causes an injury if the breach is a cause in fact of the harm and the injury was foreseeable").

[314] *Cf.* RESTATEMENT (THIRD) OF TORTS: LIABILITY FOR PHYSICAL AND EMOTIONAL HARM § 29 (American Law Institute, 2010).

[315] Cleveland v. Rotman, 297 F.3d 569, 573 (7th Cir. 2002); *see also* Stanfield v. Neubaum, 494 S.W.3d 90, 98 (Tex. 2016) ("In evaluating the existence of a superseding cause, '[t]he question always is, was there an unbroken connection? Would the facts constitute a continuous succession of events so linked together as to make a natural whole, or was there some new and independent cause intervening between the wrong and the injury?' ").

[316] 444 F.3d 587 (7th Cir. 2006).

represent its insured because it was unforeseeable that a failure to produce documents would "spawn a million-dollar bill for attorney's fees."[317]

### *§ 5-2.3(b)(2) Superseding Causation and Shifting Responsibility*

The proximate causation inquiry in legal malpractice cases may also require consideration of the doctrines called "superseding causation" and "shifting responsibility." Intervening causes are actions or forces that contribute to the production of the plaintiff's harm. Sometimes intervening causes break the chain of proximate causation, in which case they are called "superseding causes." In contrast, "shifting responsibility" concerns the question of whether someone else's failure to act saves an antecedent tortfeasor from liability. Occasionally, but not often, an omission breaks the chain of proximate causation.

The operative principles in this area are much the same as they are in any tort case raising issues of proximate causation.[318] If the act or omission was foreseeable or part of the risks that made the defendant's conduct tortious, it probably will not preclude a finding of proximate causation.[319] Conversely, if the intervening act or omission was unforeseeable and not part of the risks that made the malpractice defendant's conduct tortious, it will probably be deemed a superseding cause.

Courts have held that judicial error can constitute a new and independent cause that can relieve a trial lawyer from liability for alleged malpractice, as long as the attorney did not contribute to the error and the error was not otherwise foreseeable.[320] Thus, in *Stanfield v. Neubaum*,[321] the Texas Supreme Court held a trial court's error of law on an agency issue was a new and independent cause of an adverse usury judgment, and therefore the plaintiffs could not hold their lawyers responsible in a malpractice action for the ensuing appellate litigation costs. The court emphasized that "attorneys cannot guarantee a perfectly functioning judiciary or an error-free trial * * * [and] should be responsible for harm they actually cause—not harm caused by judicial error."[322] The court concluded:

> Because the unfavorable usury judgment was reversed on the basis of a trial-court error and the record bears no evidence the Attorneys contributed to the error or that the error was reasonably foreseeable under the circumstances, any unrelated negligence of the Attorneys * * * is not the proximate cause of the * * * appellate litigation costs as a matter of law.[323]

The defendant-lawyers did not need to produce expert testimony to negate causation.

#### *§ 5-2.3(b)(2)(A) Intervening Negligent Conduct*

Even if intervening conduct is negligent, it often does not prevent a finding of proximate causation. Taking an example from the physical injury context, suppose that a driver negligently strikes a pedestrian, who then receives deficient medical care in the

---

[317] *Id.* at 592.

[318] *See* Stanfield v. Neubaum, 494 S.W.3d 90, 93 (Tex. 2016) (applying "well-established causation principles" to a legal malpractice claim).

[319] *See id.* at 98.

[320] *See id.* at 100 (citing cases from various jurisdictions).

[321] *Id.* at 104.

[322] *Id.*

[323] *Id.*

emergency room. The driver is likely to be held to be a factual and proximate cause of both the initial injuries sustained in the collision and the aggravated injuries resulting from the negligent medical treatment. As to the latter component of damages, the reasoning is likely to be that one of the risks to which the driver subjected the pedestrian was the risk of negligent medical care in an emergency room. Put somewhat differently, negligently deficient medical care is a foreseeable risk, not because it is so common that it is probable, but because it is not so rare or bizarre that it should save the driver from liability for aggravated injuries that would not have been incurred but for the driver's negligence.

The same principles apply in the field of legal malpractice. Think back to the example, above, where Lawyer #1 negligently omits important provisions from a contract, and another lawyer, Lawyer #2, negligently reviews the document and fails to discover the omission at a time when it would have been possible to reform the instrument. Lawyer #2's negligent actions do not prevent Lawyer #1 from being found to be a proximate cause of losses resulting from the lack of key provisions in the document. (Of course, Lawyer #2's negligence is also a proximate cause of the harm, since that was precisely the harm that was foreseeable if Lawyer #2 failed to exercise care in reviewing the document.)

*§ 5-2.3(b)(2)(B) Failure by the Client to Discover Malpractice*

In general, American tort law is reluctant to allow a tortfeasor to escape liability merely because someone else subsequently failed to prevent the threatened harm from occurring. Thus, a subsequent omission, even if negligent, usually does not break the chain of causation.[324]

A person who causes an automobile accident is liable for injuries resulting from the victim's loss of blood or exposure to bad weather, even if someone else could have stopped to render aid before those consequences developed. Similarly, if a lawyer inadvertently omits a critical residuary clause from a will, the lawyer may be found to have proximately caused harm to intended beneficiaries, even though the client reviewed the will before signing it and had an opportunity to detect the omission.[325]

*§ 5-2.3(b)(2)(C) Subsequent Counsel's Failure to Act*

Notwithstanding the general rule on omissions, the law sometimes holds that even if one person set the stage for harm to occur, the responsibility for preventing that harm shifted to another person. Generally, these are cases where the antecedent tortfeasor has done everything possible to prevent the risk of harm from coming to fruition or where the other person's failure to act is so unforeseeable, bizarre, or abnormal that it would be unfair to hold the initial tortfeasor liable.

In the legal malpractice context, these types of issues arise in cases where one lawyer, who acted negligently, is replaced by a second lawyer who then fails to avert the harm by identifying the problem and taking corrective action. In many situations, the second lawyer's omission does not save from liability the lawyer who initially set the stage for harm to occur.

---

[324] *See* RESTATEMENT (SECOND) OF TORTS § 452 (American Law Institute, 1965).

[325] *See* Young v. Williams, 645 S.E.2d 624, 626 (Ga. Ct. App. 2007).

Consider a variation of the example discussed above, assuming that after Lawyer #1 omits important terms from a document, successor counsel, Lawyer #2, does not review the document at all and therefore fails to discover the deficiency and seek reformation of the document. It seems quite unlikely Lawyer #2's omission will save Lawyer #1 from liability. On the stated facts, there is no reason to say that the first lawyer did everything possible to prevent the harm from coming to pass, nor is there any reason to think that Lawyer #2's omission was so unforeseeable or extraordinary that it would be unfair to hold Lawyer #1 responsible for harm caused by the missing provisions.

An important variation of the subsequent omission problem concerns failure to file suit before the statute of limitations elapses. Assume, for example, that in declining representation of a prospective client, Lawyer #5 incorrectly advises the client that the statute of limitations is longer than it actually is. Does the client's failure to seek new counsel before the claim is time-barred prevent Lawyer #5 from being liable? Probably not. Dilatory inaction is foreseeable. Or suppose that before the period for filing elapses, the client consults Lawyer #6, who declines to take the case, or hires Lawyer #7, who then neglects to file suit before it is too late. In those situations, do subsequent events break the chain of causation so that Lawyer #5 is not liable for the untimely filing of the case? Does it make any difference whether Lawyer #6 or Lawyer #7 knows what Lawyer #5 said about the statute of limitations deadline?

Some cases have focused on whether there is a new attorney on board who had a fair opportunity to file the action before the statute of limitations elapses. Those decisions "appear to have taken the position * * * that when the duty of care shifts from the original attorney to the successor, so does the liability, provided that the successor had the opportunity to undo or avert the harm precipitated by the actions or omissions of the original attorney."[326] However, even if that is the case, there is reason to distinguish situations where the client merely had the opportunity, never exercised, to engage substitute counsel before the claim became time barred. Thus, in *Lopez v. Clifford Law Offices, P.C.*, the Illinois Appellate Court held that a client's consultation with possible successor counsel, who declined to take the case before the statute of limitations expired, was not sufficient to absolve from liability a law firm that incorrectly advised a prospective client about the statute of limitations when the firm declined representation.[327]

The better view is that a client's engagement of a new lawyer does not insulate an earlier lawyer from liability for antecedent negligence that plays a substantial role in causing harm after the change of counsel. Following this approach, in *Gefre v. Davis Wright Tremaine, LLP*,[328] the Supreme Court of Alaska explained:

> DWT [the defendant law firm] urges us to adopt a rule holding that an attorney who refers a case to another attorney while time still remains on the statute of limitations cannot be liable for failing to advise a client about the statute of limitations. But we decline to adopt such a bright-line rule. Instead, as the superior court acknowledged, "Alaska follows the 'substantial factor test' of causation, which generally requires the plaintiff to show that the [harm] would not have happened 'but for' the defendant's negligence." This inquiry involves

[326] Lopez v. Clifford Law Offices, P.C., 841 N.E.2d 465, 475 (Ill. App. Ct. 2005).

[327] *Id.* at 476.

[328] 372 P.3d 256 (Alaska 2016).

determining whether "the negligent act was so important in bringing about the injury that reasonable individuals would regard it as a cause and attach responsibility to it." We have never adopted a "superseding duty" doctrine as distinct from this general proximate cause doctrine.[329]

[329] *Id.* at 262.

# Chapter 5-3

# BREACH OF FIDUCIARY DUTY


### By Susan Saab Fortney and Vincent R. Johnson


*Table of Sections*


§ 5-3.1 Lawyers as Fiduciaries
§ 5-3.2 The "Substantial Factor" Test for Factual Causation
§ 5-3.3 Disclosure Obligations
§ 5-3.4 Fee Forfeiture
§ 5-3.5 Aiding and Abetting a Breach of Fiduciary Duty
§ 5-3.6 Intra-Firm Fiduciary Duties


## § 5-3.1 LAWYERS AS FIDUCIARIES

When a lawyer's performance is examined under the law of negligence, it is clear that there is room for the professional exercise of discretion. A lawyer need only act reasonably in order to avoid liability. So long as a lawyer does not make a choice beyond the range of reasonable prudence, responsibility for damages will not be imposed.[1]

However, the lawyer-client relationship is not a mere arms-length transaction, but rather a relationship of trust and confidence. As a matter of law, the lawyer serves as the client's fiduciary. This means that lawyers must always act with clients' interests in mind, and those interests must come first.

### § 5-3.1(a) A Different Point of Reference

Does fiduciary duty law allow lawyers the same room for the professional exercise of discretion that is accorded by negligence law? This is an important question because the sound exercise of judgment in the face of uncertainty and complexity is the quintessence of good lawyering. Nevertheless, judgment can only be exercised if it is permissible for a lawyer to choose between alternatives. The answer to the question depends on how the standard of care for breach of fiduciary duty is framed, and how that standard applies.

### § 5-3.1(b) Fiduciary Duty Versus Negligence

The language of fiduciary duty is demanding. Fiduciary principles speak, for example, not of reasonable prudence and ordinary care, but of the utmost good faith, complete fair dealing, and full disclosure. At face value, the language of fiduciary duty appears to require more of a lawyer than the law of negligence. Consequently, fiduciary principles may afford less room for the professional exercise of judgment. If that is so, and if fiduciary principles are allowed to sweep too broadly in determining the obligations of lawyers, there is a risk that imposing a more demanding standard for

1 *See supra* § 5-2.2(e)(1).

performance will render negligence law largely irrelevant. With that demise, the latitude for the exercise of discretion would logically contract or disappear.

### § 5-3.1(c) Disloyalty Versus Lack of Care

The key to understanding the proper role of fiduciary principles in the governance of lawyer conduct is to ask whether the matter at issue involves a question of loyalty and trust, rather than the exercise of care (*e.g.*, competence or skill). If so, fiduciary principles apply, for those norms exist to ensure that obligations of trust are neither betrayed nor ignored. In contrast, if loyalty is not an issue, then it is likely that negligence principles are sufficient to protect clients from unnecessary harm. Negligence law applies to many aspects of modern life, and it usually provides an appropriate mechanism for balancing competing interests and creating incentives that minimize unnecessary harm.

In *Bolton v. Crowley, Hoge & Fein, P.C.*,[2] the District of Columbia Court of Appeals stated that, "the law recognizes a clear distinction between allegations of legal malpractice based on negligence (sometimes called a breach of the standard of care) and those based on breach of fiduciary duty (sometimes called breach of the standard of conduct)."[3] Mindful of that distinction, the court remanded the case before it for a more careful examination of the plaintiff's fiduciary duty claims.[4]

Issues relating to conflict of interest, confidentiality, and candor frequently involve questions of loyalty, and are examples of matters where it is appropriate to presume that fiduciary principles apply. In contrast, issues relating to knowledge of substantive law, correct drafting of documents, and adequate trial preparation often raise questions of competence and skill, rather than loyalty. To that extent, they may more properly be resolved by reference to negligence principles.

Of course, there are cases where the same course of professional conduct can raise issues of both competence and loyalty. A lawyer may violate conflict of interest rules not merely because the lawyer chooses to sacrifice the interests of a client to competing interests, but because the lawyer ignores what the rules require or fails to appreciate that they apply to particular facts. A loyal lawyer does not violate the conflict of interest rules, but neither does a competent one. Thus, in some situations, a plaintiff may properly allege that certain lawyer conduct constitutes both a breach of fiduciary duty and the tort of negligence.

However, some courts have gone to great lengths in distinguishing negligence from breach of fiduciary duty. For example, in *Lee v. Brenner, Saltzman and Wallman*,[5] lawyers purportedly represented a medical practice group and several of its physicians individually, in violation of the applicable conflict of interest rules. In a subsequent malpractice action, one of the physicians asserted a variety of claims, including, among others, legal malpractice (*i.e.*, professional negligence) and breach of fiduciary duty. A Connecticut court struck the breach of fiduciary duty claim because there was no evidence that the lawyers were dishonest or disloyal. Thus, the court distinguished between conflicts of interest arising from the lawyers' own interests, and conflicts arising among the interests of clients. Only the former, the court found, is sufficient to establish

---

[2] 110 A.3d 575 (D.C. 2015).

[3] *Id.* at 583.

[4] *Id.* at 585.

[5] 2007 WL 1600052 (Conn. Super. Ct. 2007).

a breach of fiduciary duty. The court concluded that "the plaintiff's allegations that a conflict of interest existed between the defendants' representation of the Group and its representation of the Group's individual members * * * [did] not give rise to a breach of fiduciary duty because the allegations do not suggest that the defendants were involved in fraud or self-dealing of any kind."[6] Not all courts would agree with this analysis.

The principal advantage of suing for breach of fiduciary duty as compared to negligence is that fiduciary obligations are often articulated in more demanding terms. This makes it easier for a fact finder to conclude that the lawyer fell short of what fiduciary principles require. Beyond that significant distinction, actions for breach of fiduciary duty and negligence have certain similarities and some important differences.

### § 5-3.1(d) Similarities to Negligence

In general, "the elements of a claim for breach of fiduciary duty are (1) the existence of a fiduciary duty, (2) breach of the duty, (3) causation, and (4) damages."[7] Breach of fiduciary duty is not a strict liability tort. A plaintiff alleging fiduciary breach must show that the defendant-lawyer acted negligently, recklessly, or intentionally in violating fiduciary principles. Absent proof of culpability, there is no liability for breach of fiduciary duty.

For example, suppose that a former corporate client has changed names so frequently that, in the exercise of reasonable care, the lawyer could not have detected a conflict of interest. On those facts, the lawyer is not liable for breach of fiduciary duty even if the lawyer engaged in conflicting representation during the period in which the relevant facts were unknown.

An action for breach of fiduciary duty cannot be distinguished from negligence on the ground that culpability is not required. A suit against a lawyer for breach of fiduciary duty requires at least as much culpability as a suit for the tort of negligence.

The culpability of a fiduciary breach determines whether defenses based on the plaintiff's conduct (contributory negligence, comparative negligence, or comparative fault, depending on the state) may be asserted by the lawyer-defendant.[8] If a client claims that a lawyer breached a fiduciary duty based on negligent failure to prepare settlement documents in a timely manner because the lawyer's needs were placed ahead of the client's, the client's own negligent failure to promptly inform the lawyer that an agreement was reached and that documentation was needed may constitute a total or partial defense according to state law.

Both negligence and breach of fiduciary duty actions generally require expert testimony to establish the standard of care.[9] Typically, the same expert will testify as to whether particular conduct, such as the lawyer's practices in handling client property, constituted negligence, breach of fiduciary duty, or both. An expert claiming acquaintance with the standard of care generally can be assumed to be prepared to talk about a lawyer's duty of reasonable care under negligence law, as well as the lawyer's fiduciary obligations.

---

6 *Id.* at *4.

7 First United Pentecostal Church of Beaumont v. Parker, 514 S.W.3d 214, 220 (Tex. 2017).

8 *See infra* § 5-6.2(a).

9 *See infra* § 5-2.2(f).

No useful distinction can be drawn between negligence and breach of fiduciary duty with respect to statutes of limitations. Different limitation periods may apply to the two actions. However, which statute is longer depends on the law of the jurisdiction. It is not possible to generalize. Moreover, in some jurisdictions, the same statute of limitations governs all legal malpractice claims, regardless of the theory of liability asserted.[10]

### § 5-3.1(e) Differences from Negligence

The most important distinctions between negligence and breach of fiduciary duty claims against lawyers concern proof of causation, disclosure obligations, and fee forfeiture. Those subjects are discussed in the following sections.

## § 5-3.2 THE "SUBSTANTIAL FACTOR" TEST FOR FACTUAL CAUSATION

If a legal malpractice plaintiff wishes to recover damages, the plaintiff must prove that a lawyer's negligence or breach of fiduciary duty caused harm. However, some states hold that the demanding "but for" test for factual causation, which is a basic part of a negligence cause of action,[11] does not apply to claims for breach of fiduciary duty. In those states, it is enough for a plaintiff to show that the defendant's conduct was a "substantial factor" in producing the harm for which damages are sought.[12] Because "but for" causation is often difficult to prove, the more relaxed "substantial factor" standard, if applicable, makes it considerably easier for the plaintiff to establish that the defendant should be required to pay damages for breaching fiduciary duties.

For example, it may be hard for a jury to conclude that, "but for" an undisclosed conflict of interest amounting to breach of fiduciary duty, a lawyer's efforts to negotiate a corporate merger would have been successful. However, depending on the strength of the conflict, it may be possible for the fact finder to determine that the conflict was a "substantial factor" in the failure of negotiations.

Some states apply the more lenient "substantial factor" rule only to cases involving intentional breaches of fiduciary duty.[13] Other states also apply the rule to negligent breaches of fiduciary duty. However, many states require proof of "but for" causation in breach of fiduciary duty cases.

In *Estate of Re v. Kornstein Veisz & Wexler*,[14] a case involving both negligence and breach of fiduciary duty claims, the plaintiff alleged that certain debatable advocacy tactics had caused the plaintiff to be defeated in arbitration. The court found that the evidence was insufficient to establish "but for" causation, and therefore dismissed the negligence claim.[15] However, the court further determined that certain potential conflicts of interest caused the defendants' otherwise defensible tactical decisions to take on a "more troubling gloss," which suggested that divided loyalties had contributed to the plaintiff's arbitration defeat.[16] The defendants' motion for summary judgment on the breach of fiduciary duty claim was denied because, under applicable law, the plaintiff

---

[10] *See infra* § 5-6.4(a).

[11] *See infra* § 5-2.3(a)(1).

[12] *See, e.g.*, Estate of Re v. Kornstein Veisz & Wexler, 958 F. Supp. 907, 927–29 (S.D.N.Y. 1997).

[13] *Cf.* RESTATEMENT (THIRD) OF THE LAW GOVERNING LAWYERS § 49 cmt. e (American Law Inst., 2000).

[14] 958 F. Supp. 907 (S.D.N.Y. 1997).

[15] *Id.* at 924.

[16] *Id.* at 927–28.

was only required to show that the alleged breach of fiduciary duty was a "substantial factor" in the loss at arbitration.[17]

### § 5-3.2(a) No Speculation

A jury's decision about causation must be rooted firmly in the evidence. Speculation is not permitted. The "no speculation" rule applies not just to negligence claims, but throughout the law of torts, including claims based on breach of fiduciary duty.

In *Pietrangelo v. Wilmer Cutler Pickering Hale & Dorr, LLP*,[18] a former client sued the law firm that had unsuccessfully represented him in challenging the federal "Don't Ask, Don't Tell" (DADT) statute. He complained that after he filed a petition *pro se* seeking review by the Supreme Court, his former law firm breached its fiduciary duties by filing a response brief on behalf of other plaintiffs arguing that "the Court would be better advised to defer review at this time."[19] The District of Columbia Court of Appeals rejected the former client's malpractice claim. Although he alleged that, "but for" the law firm's filing, the Supreme Court would have granted certiorari, found in his favor on the merits, and remanded the case to the federal district court, which then would have ordered his reinstatement into the military, that alleged outcome was predicated upon mere speculation.[20]

## § 5-3.3 DISCLOSURE OBLIGATIONS

What must a lawyer tell a client? This question arises thousands of times every day in law offices. If the law of negligence governs, the answer is clear. The lawyer must keep the client reasonably informed about the status of the matter, must respond to reasonable requests for information, and must provide the information reasonably necessary to enable the client to make informed decisions about the representation.[21] In other words, a lawyer must act reasonably in communicating with the client.

For example, if a lawyer learns that "precious stones" listed on a balance sheet for millions of dollars are rented, and not owned, the lawyer has a duty to tell the client that the stones are not a legitimate asset, particularly if that means that the client is insolvent.[22]

### § 5-3.3(a) "Absolute and Perfect Candor"

Fiduciary duty law sometimes sets a higher standard than the law of negligence. Indeed, incautious language in certain fiduciary duty cases purports to impose on lawyers an obligation of "absolute and perfect candor."[23] Surely this is not an accurate statement of a lawyer's disclosure obligations—at least not in every circumstance. If lawyers were routinely subject to actions for damages based on anything falling short of

---

17 *Id.* at 927–29.

18 68 A.3d 697 (D.C. 2013).

19 *Id.* at 705.

20 *Id.* at 709–10.

21 *See* RESTATEMENT (THIRD) OF THE LAW GOVERNING LAWYERS § 20 (American Law Inst., 2000).

22 *See* Dennerline v. Atterholt, 886 N.E.2d 582, 588 (Ind. Ct. App. 2008).

23 *See* State v. Saunders, 2011 WL 334299, at *5 (Ohio Ct. App. 2011) (" 'The relation between attorney and client is a fiduciary relationship of the very highest character, and bonds the attorney to most conscientious fidelity—*uberrima fides*.' * * *. *Black's Law Dictionary* defines '*uberrima fides*' as 'The most abundant good faith; absolute and perfect candor or openness and honesty; the absence of any concealment or deception, however slight.' ").

"absolute and perfect candor," they would be compelled to forego the exercise of judgment about the significance of information and forced to pass on to clients every fact learned in the course of representation, no matter how dubious, redundant, trivial, or useless.[24]

One area where legal precedent effectively requires total candor is when lawyers engage in business transactions with clients. The law is highly suspicious of such dealings because of their potential for lawyer abuse. Absent "absolute and perfect candor," courts are unlikely to uphold business transactions between lawyers and their clients.[25]

The reason that a high degree of candor is required in the context of business transactions is because the interests of lawyer and client are adverse. Whenever there is such adversity, there is reason to think that the lawyer may be less than fully faithful to the client or protective of the client's interests. Consequently, the heightened disclosure obligations under fiduciary duty law are not restricted to business transactions. They apply to other situations where the interests of lawyers and clients are at odds. This is why a lawyer must inform a client when the lawyer's negligent conduct gives the client a substantial malpractice claim.[26]

Of course, special ethics rules already govern disclosure obligations in certain contexts where the interests of lawyer and client are adverse. For example, the disciplinary rules dealing with conflicts of interest spell out in detail what types of disclosures are required to obtain informed consent.[27] Similarly, the rules already clearly specify what a lawyer must tell a client about the terms of a contingent fee agreement.[28] There is no reason to substitute an amorphous "absolute and perfect candor" standard for these types of well-developed principles that were undoubtedly formulated with lawyers' fiduciary obligations in mind. In *Gillespie v. Hernden*,[29] a Texas appellate court held that where a contingent fee contract was written, signed by the clients, and expressly described the fee agreement, the attorneys did not breach their fiduciary duties by failing to advise the clients about other sections in the disciplinary rules and Texas Government Code that govern contingent fee contracts and fee-sharing agreements.

To the extent that a rule of "absolute and perfect candor" defines a lawyer's disclosure obligations, it should be limited to contexts where the interests of lawyers and clients are adverse and where specific guidance as to what is required of a lawyer has not yet been articulated. Moreover, the culpability requirement of fiduciary duty law means that, even if, there is clear adversity between a lawyer and client, liability should not be imposed for nonnegligent nondisclosure. Though some cases use the phrase "absolute and perfect candor," their holdings usually can be explained on the ground that the lawyers who were ultimately held liable were negligent or engaged in more

---

[24] *See* Vincent R. Johnson, *"Absolute and Perfect Candor" to Clients*, 34 ST. MARY'S L.J. 737, 739 (2003).

[25] *See generally* RESTATEMENT (THIRD) OF THE LAW GOVERNING LAWYERS § 126 (American Law Inst., 2000) (discussing business transactions between a lawyer and client).

[26] *See* RESTATEMENT (THIRD) OF THE LAW GOVERNING LAWYERS § 20 cmt. c (American Law Inst., 2000); *see also* Benjamin P. Cooper, *The Lawyer's Duty to Inform His Client of His Own Malpractice*, 61 BAYLOR L. REV. 174, 214 (2009).

[27] *See, e.g.*, MODEL RULES OF PROF'L CONDUCT R. 1.7 cmt. 18, R. 1.1(e), and R. 1.1 cmt. 6 (American Bar Ass'n, 2017).

[28] *See id.* R. 1.5.

[29] 2016 WL 7234067, *11 (Tex. App.).

blameworthy conduct. Courts never impose liability for[30] damages under common law fiduciary duty principles for nonnegligent (*i.e.*, innocent) failure to communicate information. "A lawyer who has acted with reasonable care is not liable in damages for breach of fiduciary duty."[31]

### § 5-3.3(b) How Negligence Duties and Fiduciary Duties Mesh

It is possible to summarize the disclosure obligations of lawyers as follows: (1) In a broad range of situations, a lawyer is subject to a duty of reasonableness, which is to say the law of negligence. (2) In situations where the lawyer's and client's interests are adverse, as in the case of a business transaction between them, a lawyer has heightened disclosure obligations, which sometimes approach "absolute and perfect candor." (3) If applicable ethics rules (*e.g.*, the rules dealing with fees, client funds and property, and conflicts of interest) specify what must be disclosed, those provisions will be regarded by many as defining what is called for under negligence and fiduciary principles. Finally, (4) liability for damages based on common law breach of fiduciary duty should not be imposed on a lawyer for nondisclosure without proof of culpability.

### § 5-3.3(c) Limits on Disclosure Obligations

Several factors limit the disclosure obligations of lawyers. These limits apply regardless of whether negligence or fiduciary duty principles govern.

A lawyer is generally under no duty to disclose facts outside the scope of the representation[32] or information that is immaterial.[33] In addition, there is usually no obligation to tell a client what the client already knows. Thus, in *Grochocinski v. Mayer Brown Rowe & Maw LLP*,[34] a federal court in Illinois ruled that a bankruptcy trustee could not recover from lawyers for their allegedly negligent failure to disclose the risk that a third person would file suit. This was true because the bankrupt entity was already well aware that there was a looming risk of such litigation.

There is also never an obligation to disclose to one client what a lawyer is obliged to keep confidential about the representation of another client.[35] (However, the resulting conflict of interest may oblige the lawyer to withdraw.) In addition, a lawyer and client ordinarily can tailor disclosure obligations, just as they may agree on other aspects of the representation.[36] Consequently, there is normally no duty to disclose to a client

---

[30] "Other remedies such as disqualification, restitution, or injunctive or declaratory relief may be available without proof of negligence or intentional wrongdoing." RESTATEMENT (THIRD) OF THE LAW GOVERNING LAWYERS § 49 cmt. a (American Law Inst., 2000).

[31] *Id.* at § 49 cmt. d.

[32] *See* Joe v. Two Thirty Nine Joint Venture, 145 S.W.3d 150, 160 (Tex. 2004) ("While it is true that an attorney owes a client a duty to inform the client of matters material to the representation, * * * this duty to inform does not extend to matters beyond the scope of the representation.").

[33] "A fiduciary never has a duty to reveal immaterial information." Vincent R. Johnson & Shawn M. Lovorn, *Misrepresentation by Lawyers About Credentials or Experience*, 57 OKLA. L. REV. 529, 544 (2004) (citing STAR Ctrs., Inc. v. Faegre & Benson, L.L.P., 644 N.W.2d 72 (Minn. 2002)).

[34] 2007 WL 1875995 (N.D. Ill.).

[35] *Cf.* MODEL RULES OF PROF'L CONDUCT R. 1.7 cmt. 19 (American Bar Ass'n, 2017) ("For example, when the lawyer represents different clients in related matters and one of the clients refuses to consent to the disclosure necessary to permit the other client to make an informed decision, the lawyer cannot properly ask the latter to consent").

[36] *Cf.* RESTATEMENT (THIRD) OF THE LAW GOVERNING LAWYERS § 20 cmt. c (American Law Inst., 2000) ("[T]o the extent that the parties have not otherwise agreed, a standard of reasonableness under all the circumstances determines the appropriate measure of consultation").

information which the client has agreed need not be transmitted. These various factors which limit the disclosure obligations of lawyers frequently play a role in malpractice litigation.

## § 5-3.4 FEE FORFEITURE

Every client who is unhappy with a lawyer would like to recover any fees already paid to the lawyer, as well as be excused from paying any balance still due. Reflecting this reality, malpractice plaintiffs increasingly seek fee forfeiture.[37]

### § 5-3.4(a) To Prevent Unjust Enrichment

Damages and forfeiture are different remedies, but are frequently asserted together in a legal malpractice action. A claim for damages is a request for compensation for harm caused by the lawyer's misconduct. Fee forfeiture, in contrast, is essentially a request for a refund, or for forgiveness of nonpayment, because the client did not get what was bargained for, namely representation by a lawyer faithful to important duties. Forfeiture is a restitutionary remedy designed to prevent unjust enrichment of the lawyer.

The difference between damages and forfeiture is the difference between loss and gain. Damages are measured by what the plaintiff lost; forfeiture, as a form of restitution, is measured by what the defendant improperly gained.[38]

If a client is seeking a return of fees that have already been paid, the claim is sometimes called a request for fee "disgorgement." However, the term "forfeiture" is increasingly used to cover any loss of fees by a lawyer, regardless of whether those fees have yet been paid.

In response to a request for fee forfeiture, a lawyer may seek a declaratory judgment that outstanding amounts are owed. Thus, a malpractice plaintiff who does not prevail on a claim for fee forfeiture is sometimes ordered to pay amounts due under the attorney-client contract.[39]

### § 5-3.4(b) Causation of Harm Is Not Required

Importantly, fee forfeiture is available even if the plaintiff is unable to prove that the lawyer's tortious conduct caused damages.[40] The fact that fee forfeiture may be awarded even if damages are not proved is a significant remedial consideration. This is true because proving that malpractice was a factual and proximate cause of harm is often difficult or impossible. The fees paid to a lawyer, particularly if the representation was complex or extended over a long period of time, may be so great that it may be worth bringing a malpractice action to obtain forfeiture, even if it might not be possible to show that the lawyer's breach of duty caused damages.

In *First United Pentecostal Church of Beaumont v. Parker*,[41] a lawyer (Parker) learned that another lawyer for whom he had worked (Lamb) had stolen and misused the funds of a client for whom Parker had provided legal services. Parker admitted that

---

[37] *See generally* Jeff A. Webb & Blake W. Stribling, *Ten Years After Burrow v. Arce: The Current State of Attorney Fee Forfeiture*, 40 ST. MARY'S L.J. 967 (2009).

[38] *See generally* RESTATEMENT (THIRD) OF RESTITUTION & UNJUST ENRICHMENT § 49 (American Law Inst., 2011).

[39] *See* AmBase Corp. v. Davis Polk & Wardwell, 834 N.Y.S.2d 705, 708 (N.Y. 2007).

[40] *See* Burrow v. Arce, 997 S.W.2d 229, 240 (Tex. 1999).

[41] 514 S.W.3d 214 (Tex. 2017).

he breached his fiduciary duties by failing to disclose the theft to the client or investigate the matter. However, the loss of the funds had occurred before Parker learned about the theft, and was therefore not caused by his nondisclosure or failure to investigate. The Texas Supreme Court nevertheless found that a cause of action for breach of fiduciary duty was stated because the client had presented a claim for disgorgement, not just for damages.[42]

### § 5-3.4(c) Clear and Serious Breach of Duty

The *Restatement* recognizes that total or partial fee forfeiture is appropriate only in cases involving a "clear and serious violation of duty."[43] Among the factors that are relevant to the issue of forfeiture are "the gravity and timing of the violation, its willfulness, its effect on the value of the lawyer's work for the client, any other threatened or actual harm to the client, and the adequacy of other remedies."[44] Some courts also emphasize that, because "the central purpose of the equitable remedy of forfeiture is to protect relationships of trust by discouraging agents' disloyalty," an additional factor that must be given great weight in determining whether fees should be lost is "the public interest in maintaining the integrity of attorney-client relationships."[45]

With respect to fee forfeiture, there are roles to be played by both jury and judge. The jury normally decides disputed questions of fact, relating, for example, to the culpability of the lawyer's breach of duty.[46] The judge then determines whether forfeiture is appropriate, and if so, what amount of fees[47] should be lost by the lawyer.

In *Chen v. Chen Qualified Settlement Fund*,[48] the Second Circuit denied all compensation to a lawyer who had secured a multi-million dollar settlement of claims arising from birth-related injuries to a young child named David. The lawyer had submitted to the court an unexplained request for attorney's fees in excess of the statutory maximum allowed in medical malpractice cases. The court found that the evidence indicated that the lawyer had made "only limited inquiries into David's condition and the nature and extent of David's future medical needs" and "offered none of the documentation and reports necessary for the court to determine whether the settlement proposed by the parties was reasonable."[49] The appellate court concluded that "it was not an abuse of discretion for the district court to determine that * * * [the lawyer] had inadequately represented his client."[50]

Similarly, in *Rodriguez v. Disner*,[51] the Ninth Circuit ordered total fee forfeiture. It concluded that because of a serious conflict of interest, which amounted to a breach of fiduciary duty "from day one," class counsel was not entitled to any fees related to its representation of numerous class members in an antitrust suit against bar review course providers.

---

[42] *Id.* at 222.

[43] *See* RESTATEMENT (THIRD) OF THE LAW GOVERNING LAWYERS § 37 (American Law Inst., 2000).

[44] *Id.*

[45] Burrow v. Arce, 997 S.W.2d 229, 244 (Tex. 1999).

[46] *Id.* at 245.

[47] *Id.* at 246.

[48] 552 F.3d 218 (2d Cir. 2009).

[49] *Id.* at 227.

[50] *Id.*

[51] 688 F.3d 645, 651 (9th Cir. 2012).

### § 5-3.4(d) Does Forfeiture Require Fiduciary Breach?

Without dispute, a clear and serious breach of fiduciary duty can trigger the powerful remedy of fee forfeiture. However, whether negligence not amounting to breach of fiduciary duty is sufficient to warrant total or partial loss of a fee is an open question in many states.

The relevant portions of the *Restatement*, discussing what constitutes a "clear and serious violation of duty," indicate that "the source of the duty can be civil or criminal law, including, for example, the requirements of an applicable lawyer code or the law of malpractice."[52] This language seems to allow the possibility that negligence not involving disloyalty may, on appropriate facts, support an award for forfeiture.

Support for the proposition that mere negligence, not amounting to breach of fiduciary duty, is sufficient to cause loss of attorney's fees can be found in *DiStefano v. Greenstone*.[53] In *DiStefano*, an American lawyer failed to "sustain contact" with an Italian law firm that he was using to handle an international tort claim for the plaintiff. As a result, the claim was not timely filed and became time-barred. There was no evidence that the failure to sustain contact was the result of disloyalty to the plaintiff. Therefore, the case involved mere negligence. In a subsequent malpractice action against the American lawyer, the fundamental question was whether the plaintiff could recover the full value of the lost claim ($90,000) or only a reduced amount ($60,000) reflecting reduction for the one-third contingent fee the client would have had to pay if the claim had been timely prosecuted and successful. The court surveyed relevant precedent, concluding that under New Jersey law a "negligent attorney is precluded from recovering his attorney fee."[54] The court therefore allowed the plaintiff to recover the full value of the lost claim ($90,000) with no reduction for the amount that would have gone to the defendant-attorney under the fee agreement if the representation had not been negligent. Interestingly, the court, in departure from the "American rule," also allowed the plaintiff to recover compensation for attorney's fees incurred in prosecuting the malpractice action, noting that this result was not a windfall because the plaintiff had to "endure two lawsuits."[55]

Nevertheless, a plaintiff's ability to call the lawyer's breach a violation of fiduciary principles appears to be important to the success of a forfeiture claim. Most of the cases ordering forfeiture involve breaches of fiduciary duty. Moreover, the *Restatement* commentary cautions that "forfeiture is generally inappropriate when the lawyer has not done anything willfully blameworthy."[56] "Willfully blameworthy" conduct would seem to amount to disloyalty, and therefore constitute breach of fiduciary duty. In addition, "willfully blameworthy" conduct is something more than ordinary negligence. The language tends to suggest that what is required is a type of aggravated malfeasance approaching recklessness or perhaps even intentionally tortious conduct.

The decisions on fee forfeiture often emphasize that forfeiture is especially appropriate in cases involving serious breaches of trust and disloyalty. Consequently, evidence of a breach of fiduciary duty, as opposed to ordinary negligence that does not

---

[52] RESTATEMENT (THIRD) OF THE LAW GOVERNING LAWYERS § 37 cmt. c (American Law Inst., 2000).

[53] 815 A.2d 496 (N.J. Super. App. Div. 2003).

[54] *Id.* at 499.

[55] *Id.* at 499–500.

[56] RESTATEMENT (THIRD) OF THE LAW GOVERNING LAWYERS § 37 cmt. c (American Law Inst., 2000).

involve disloyalty, places a client seeking fee forfeiture in a stronger position to persuade a court that the lawyer's loss of all or part of a fee is appropriate.

## § 5-3.5 AIDING AND ABETTING A BREACH OF FIDUCIARY DUTY

Lawyers can be liable not only for breaching their own fiduciary duties, but for aiding and abetting other persons in their breaches of fiduciary duties. At one level, this is not surprising because aiding and abetting liability is a well-established, generally non-controversial, theory of tort responsibility.[57] At a different level, however, holding a lawyer liable for aiding and abetting another's breach of fiduciary duty is not only surprising but alarming. This is because the theory has the potential to greatly expand the range of persons to whom lawyers may be accountable for damages. Many clients and client representatives, such as corporate officers and directors, business partners, trustees, guardians, executors, and majority shareholders owe fiduciary duties to others. To hold a lawyer liable for aiding and abetting breaches of fiduciary duty means that, on an appropriate set of facts, a lawyer may be liable to third persons standing in a fiduciary relationship with clients or client representatives, even though those third persons were never clients of the lawyer.

### § 5-3.5(a) A Dangerous Theory of Liability

At least four things make aiding and abetting a breach of fiduciary duty a dangerous theory of lawyer liability. The first is that the relevant legal principles are not well developed. This makes it difficult for lawyers to intelligently assess the risks and plan accordingly. Second, "aiding and abetting" claims are often factually complex, typically requiring analysis of various players and diverse areas of the law from which fiduciary duties arise. To this extent, claims against lawyers for aiding and abetting breaches of fiduciary duty are more expensive to defend, unpredictable, and difficult to manage. Third, in many respects, the law of fiduciary duty is phrased in highly demanding terms (*e.g.*, "utmost good faith" and "complete fair dealing") with few clear markers for understanding the extent of attorneys' obligations. If it is easy for the fiduciary-client to fall short of obligations to others, it may also be easy for a lawyer to become liable to a third person for aiding and abetting a client's breach of fiduciary duty. Finally, a lawyer's fear of liability to a nonclient for aiding and abetting may dilute the lawyer's loyalty to the fiduciary-client.

Claims for aiding and abetting breaches of fiduciary duty are now a common feature of what might be called "entity implosion" litigation. For example, in the 2001 collapse of Enron, then one of the world's largest companies, Enron's lawyers were sued on many theories, including aiding and abetting breaches of fiduciary duty. Eventually, some of the law firms paid huge settlements to various plaintiffs. Similarly, in the malpractice cases filed following the 2007–09 Wall Street "meltdown," plaintiffs sued lawyers, asserting that they aided and abetted breaches of fiduciary duty by the officers and directors who ran the failed financial institutions.

### § 5-3.5(b) Two Very Different Varieties

The first thing to understand about claims for aiding and abetting breach of fiduciary duty is that there are two very different varieties of the claim. In one case, the

---

[57] *See* RESTATEMENT (SECOND) OF TORTS § 876(b) (American Law Inst., 1979).

claim is asserted against the lawyer by the lawyer's own client. Typically, the client is an entity, and the lawyer is alleged to have aided and abetted fiduciary breaches by constituent representatives of the entity, such as officers and directors. This is the stronger variety of the claim because lawyers owe numerous duties to their clients. There is nothing shocking about saying, for example, that a lawyer cannot assist an officer or director in harming the lawyer's entity client. Indeed, in many cases, it might be possible to forego the language of "aiding and abetting" and simply argue that the lawyer's conduct was a violation of the lawyer's own fiduciary obligations to the plaintiff client.

The second variety of aiding and abetting claim is one asserted by a non-client. Because there is no privity between the lawyer and non-client, and typically no basis for saying the lawyer personally had any legal duty to the non-client, this is the weaker variety of claim. In this type of case, the fiduciary being aided by the lawyer is normally the lawyer's client (or a representative of the lawyer's client). In that case, it may be argued that there is a privilege to represent one's client without competing obligations to third persons, and that this privilege should defeat an aiding and abetting breach of fiduciary duty claim. These kinds of privileges are discussed below. Note, however, that this kind of privilege has no role in the first type of aiding and abetting claim discussed above. In that case, the plaintiff *is* the lawyer's client.

### § 5-3.5(c) Tort Principles on Aiding and Abetting

Under general tort principles, aiding and abetting liability does not require proof of an express or tacit agreement on the part of the aider-abettor to participate in a wrongful activity in violation of the plaintiff's rights. Rather, what is necessary is that the aider-abettor knowingly provide substantial assistance to one engaged in tortious conduct. For this reason, the aiding and abetting theory of tort liability is sometimes called "concerted action by substantial assistance."[58]

Although courts differ in articulating the elements of lawyer liability for aiding and abetting a breach of fiduciary duty, the requirements are usually simple. Generally, the plaintiff must prove: (1) that the fiduciary breached a fiduciary obligation owed to the plaintiff; (2) that the breach caused damages; (3) that the lawyer knew that fiduciary obligations were being breached; and (4) the lawyer nevertheless provided substantial assistance to the fiduciary, thereby contributing to the breach.

In *Tamposi v. Denby*,[59] a federal court found that a claim was stated against an attorney and law firm for aiding and abetting a trustee's breach of fiduciary duty. The defendants were aware that the trustee was breaching her fiduciary duties by instituting a lawsuit, and directly participated in that breach by preparing for and supporting the action.

Aiding and abetting a breach of fiduciary duty is an intentional tort in the sense that it must be shown that the defendant-lawyer knew that the person being assisted was committing a breach of fiduciary duty.[60] Presumably, this classification carries with

---

[58] Halberstam v. Welch, 705 F.2d 472, 477 (D.C. Cir. 1983).

[59] 974 F. Supp. 2d 51, 61–62 (D. Mass. 2013).

[60] *Cf.* RESTATEMENT (THIRD) OF TORTS: LIABILITY FOR PHYSICAL AND EMOTIONAL HARM § 1 (American Law Inst., 2010) (discussing intent).

it all of the consequences that attach to an intentional tort, including the inapplicability of defenses based on the plaintiff's own negligent conduct.[61]

### § 5-3.5(d) Evidence of Knowing Assistance

A lawyer's knowledge of a fiduciary's breach of duty can be proved either by direct evidence (*e.g.*, e-mail messages clearly indicating what the attorney knew) or by circumstantial evidence. In the latter case, indirect evidence is pieced together to draw a conclusion as to what the defendant-lawyer must have known. For example, a lawyer's acceptance of a valuable gift from a fiduciary, who was known by the lawyer to have longstanding financial problems, may provide the basis for a jury to conclude that the lawyer knew that fiduciary obligations were being violated and that the fiduciary was improperly profiting.[62]

In the *Enron* case, there was no direct evidence of any particular attorney's knowledge of wrongful conduct by Enron's officers. However, despite the lawyers' denial of actual knowledge, circumstantial evidence suggested that the lawyers knew that fiduciary obligations were being betrayed.[63]

In contrast, in *Zazzali v. Hirschler Fleischer, P.C.*,[64] a federal court concluded that the evidence was too thin to sustain a finding that lawyers knowingly aided breaches of fiduciary duties by corporate officers and directors. Although there were numerous and glaring misstatements in the relevant private placement memoranda, there were no facts from which it could reasonably be inferred that the lawyers knew the documents contained inaccurate information.

Evidence that a lawyer knowingly assisted another lawyer in covering up the latter's theft of client funds is insufficient to impose aiding and abetting liability for the theft. This is true at least where there is no evidence that the alleged aider and abettor assisted or encouraged the theft, and no evidence that the cover-up caused any harm to the client.[65]

### § 5-3.5(e) Evidence of Substantial Assistance

*De minimis non curat lex*—the law does not concern itself with trifles. It is therefore not surprising that aiding and abetting liability will only be imposed on a lawyer who provides substantial assistance that contributes to a fiduciary breach.

The word "substantial" has different meanings in diverse areas of the law. On some occasions, a requirement of a "substantial" contribution sets a more demanding level of proof than on others. There are some court decisions that suggest that for a professional's assistance to be "substantial" for purposes of aiding and abetting liability, there must be something more than the rendition of routine professional services.[66] Whether other courts will follow the same path is doubtful.

---

[61] *See supra* § 5-1.5.

[62] *See* Chem-Age Industries, Inc. v. Glover, 652 N.W.2d 756 (S.D. 2002).

[63] *See* Report of Neal Batson, Court-Appointed Examiner, app. C, at 1–2, In re Enron Corp., No. 01–16034 (Bankr. S.D.N.Y. Nov. 4, 2003).

[64] 482 B.R. 495, 519 (D. Del. 2012).

[65] *See* First United Pentecostal Church of Beaumont v. Parker, 514 S.W.3d 214, 225 (Tex., 2017).

[66] *See* Witzman v. Lehrman, Lehrman & Flom, 601 N.W.2d 179, 189 (Minn. 1999) (involving accountants).

Routine legal services often entail knowledge of the law, critical evaluation of the facts, and the exercise of professional judgment. Such services undoubtedly can make a "substantial" contribution to a fiduciary's performance (or breach) of duties owed to others. If a lawyer renders routine legal services to a fiduciary whom the lawyer knows is breaching fiduciary obligations, courts may refuse to allow the lawyer to escape responsibility on the ground that the lawyer did not "substantially" contribute to the breach.

Presumably, the "substantial assistance" requirement is concerned with ensuring that a lawyer actually contributed to the plaintiff's harm. If what the lawyer did was minimal, irrelevant, duplicative, and of little efficacy, there may be good reason not to impose responsibility for aiding and abetting a breach of fiduciary duty. However, in other areas of the law, mere moral support that deliberately emboldens a tortfeasor in perpetrating wrongful conduct is sufficient to support a finding of aiding and abetting liability.[67] There is little justification for allowing a lawyer to escape responsibility on the ground that a contribution was insubstantial, if the lawyer knew what was at stake and acted in ways that effectively encouraged the fiduciary to betray important duties.

For purposes of determining whether a lawyer made a substantial contribution, some courts draw a distinction between acts and omissions. In *Abrams v. McGuireWoods, LLP*,[68] a federal court in Indiana wrote:

> The assistance must be active and direct, rather than passive and indirect. * * *. In other words, the defendant has to have actually done something to help, and not just helped by failing to prevent the breach.[69]

## § 5-3.5(f) Privileges and Defenses

A lawyer sued by a nonclient may attempt to defeat an aiding and abetting claim by arguing that recognition of such a claim would conflict with the lawyer's obligations to a client. Because a lawyer owes a duty of undivided loyalty to a client, the lawyer's representation of the client should not be fettered by a theory of liability that recognizes competing obligations to a nonclient. Arguably, recognizing such a claim threatens to distort the representation of the client, even if the client is serving as a fiduciary.

Of course, any such argument has limits. It is well recognized that a lawyer may not assist a client in conduct that is criminal or fraudulent.[70] Such forms of conduct can often be cast as breaches of fiduciary duty. Therefore, lawyers should not be protected from aiding and abetting liability if they knowingly assist clients in criminal or fraudulent conduct. Moreover, the lawyer-client relationship should not shield a lawyer from liability for conduct that falls outside the scope of the representation, because duties to a client generally extend no further than the scope of the representation.[71]

Mindful that a liability risk may create conflicts of interest for lawyers, some courts have recognized a privilege that may defeat a nonclient's claim against a lawyer for aiding and abetting a breach of fiduciary duty. For example, in *Reynolds v. Schrock*,[72]

---

[67] *See generally* RESTATEMENT (SECOND) OF TORTS § 876 cmt. d (American Law Inst., 1979).

[68] 2014 WL 3721950 (N.D. Ind.).

[69] *Id.* at *9.

[70] *See, e.g.*, MODEL RULES OF PROF'L CONDUCT R. 1.2(d) (American Bar Ass'n, 2017).

[71] *See supra* § 5-2.1(b).

[72] 142 P.3d 1062, 1069 (Or. 2006).

the Supreme Court of Oregon endorsed a strong qualified privilege that protects lawyers from liability for conduct within the scope of their representation that is not motivated by the lawyers' "own self-interest and contrary to their clients' interest," and that does not involve assisting clients in crime or fraud.

It is unclear whether other courts will follow the lead of the Oregon Supreme Court. In *Cantey Hanger, LLP v. Byrd*,[73] the Texas Supreme Court, in a 5–4 decision, adopted a surprising rule. In the words of the court:

> Fraud is not an exception to attorney immunity; rather, the defense does not extend to fraudulent conduct that is outside the scope of an attorney's legal representation of his client, just as it does not extend to other wrongful conduct outside the scope of representation. An attorney who pleads the affirmative defense of attorney immunity has the burden to prove that his alleged wrongful conduct, regardless of whether it is labeled fraudulent, is part of the discharge of his duties to his client.[74]

Thus, in Texas, the only question seems to be whether the conduct in question fell within the scope of the representation. How can knowing assistance of fraudulent conduct ever be part of a lawyer's duties to a client?

In other areas of tort law, courts have held that certain matters, not mentioned in *Reynolds*, such as bad faith, ill will, vindictiveness, or excessiveness, can destroy a qualified privilege.[75] Thus, it remains to be seen what role qualified privileges will play in the law governing lawyer liability for aiding and abetting breaches of fiduciary duty.

Privileges are likely to be irrelevant in cases where the plaintiff is a client and the lawyer is alleged to have aided an officer or director in breaching duties to the client. In such situations, imposing liability on the lawyer would not threaten to divert the lawyer from attention to the interests of the client, but would instead reinforce the performance of obligations the lawyer already owes to the client.

### § 5-3.5(g) Implications for Corporate Policy Making

Subjecting a lawyer to liability for aiding and abetting corporate officers and directors in conduct that may later be viewed as a breach of fiduciary duty has implications for how lawyers perform the role of corporate counsel. This is true because prudent lawyers will want to minimize their liability exposure to claims asserting this theory.

Suppose, for example, that a lawyer for a corporation is assisting a corporate division manager in closing an asset sale, and that the lawyer knows that the manager, without authority, has made certain guarantees to the purchaser. If the purchaser later successfully sues the corporation to enforce those guarantees, the corporation may seek to hold the lawyer accountable. With the benefit of hindsight, the making of unauthorized guarantees that could trigger legal liability may be viewed as a breach of fiduciary duties owed by the division manager to the corporation. Further, the work of the lawyer, perhaps in transmitting those assurances to the purchaser or embodying them in a document, may be viewed as aiding and abetting the division manager's breach

---

[73] 467 S.W.3d 477 (Tex. 2015).

[74] *Id.* at 484.

[75] *See* RESTATEMENT (SECOND) OF TORTS §§ 603–04 (American Law Inst., 1977).

of fiduciary duty. Rather than risk liability under this theory, the lawyer, upon becoming aware that the division manager lacked authority to make the guarantees, might refuse to provide further assistance for the transaction. This may be true even if the manager insisted that making the guarantees was in the best interests of the corporation and was unlikely to give rise to corporate liability. Indeed, the lawyer might not only refuse to assist the transaction, but might elect to report the matter to persons with greater authority in the corporation—that is, go "over the head" of the division manager in an effort to force the manager to take a different course.[76]

Perhaps this is not a bad result. Corporations might be better off if lawyers asked more questions about what their clients' representatives were doing before carrying out orders. In fact, it is possible to ask whether the Wall Street meltdown and the collapse of major investment banks in 2008–09 could have been avoided if lawyers had taken a more active role in challenging dubious practices, such as the marketing of subprime loans and incomprehensible financial derivatives or the use of bonus compensation arrangements which created perverse incentives.[77]

Not long ago, the established wisdom in many quarters of the legal profession was that corporate lawyers were not supposed to second guess the policy decisions of duly authorized representatives of corporate entities, such as officers and directors. However, it is sometimes easy to recast a policy decision as a breach of fiduciary duty. For example, the sale of an asset for a modest price may later be labeled as a breach of fiduciary duty by those who disagreed with the decision. The argument would be that disposing of property for inadequate consideration is a breach of fiduciary obligations.

Exposing lawyers to claims for aiding and abetting breach of fiduciary duty is likely to cause lawyers to scrutinize the conduct of their corporate clients more closely than what once was the case. This is an important change in the world of corporate lawyering, but it is a change consistent with the temper of the times. The rules enacted by the Securities and Exchange Commission pursuant to the federal Sarbanes-Oxley Act[78] and subsequent amendments to the Model Rules of Professional Conduct[79] now provide, in an increased range of circumstances, for "up the ladder" reporting of information learned by a lawyer about unlawful conduct or breaches of duty that could harm the interests of corporate clients. The purpose of such requirements is to see that those at the top of the corporate ladder have the information that is needed to ensure that corporations act lawfully and that corporate interests are protected from harm that can be caused by the unfaithful or ill-advised conduct of entity constituents.

## § 5-3.6 INTRA-FIRM FIDUCIARY DUTIES

Lawyers owe fiduciary duties not only to their clients, but to the law firms for which they work. The broad contours of these obligations are sketched below.

---

[76] *See* MODEL RULES OF PROF'L CONDUCT R. 1.13 (American Bar Ass'n, 2017) (discussing representation of entities).

[77] *See* Terry Carter, *How Lawyers Enabled the Meltdown: And How They Might Have Prevented It*, A.B.A. J., Jan. 2009, at 34.

[78] SARBANES-OXLEY ACT OF 2002, Pub. L. No. 107–204, 116 Stat. 745.

[79] *See* MODEL RULES OF PROF'L CONDUCT R. 1.13 (American Bar Ass'n, 2017).

### § 5-3.6(a) Duties of Partners and Other Law Firm Principles

Under common law principles, members of a law partnership are fiduciaries and owe important fiduciary obligations to one another. A partner may not prefer his or her economic interests to those of other partners. More specifically, a partner may not injure the partnership by establishing a competing enterprise. A partner also must disclose to the other partners facts concerning economic opportunities that relate to the partnership's business.

Some fiduciary duties can even survive the termination of a partner's relationship with a law firm. In *Friedman Siegelbaum, LLP v. Pribish*,[80] a New Jersey appellate court affirmed a judgment holding a former non-equity partner, who assured his former firm of his willingness to assist in the collection of accounts receivable, liable for breach of fiduciary duty based, in part, on his failure to turn over money that had been collected.

Of course, common law principles are only the starting point for thinking about partners' obligations. The common law has been superseded or supplemented by statutes in many states patterned on the Uniform Partnership Act and the Revised Uniform Partnership Act. Moreover, many lawyers now practice law in limited liability partnerships and limited liability companies.[81] Therefore, when talking about partners' duties, it is essential to consult pertinent legislative enactments in the relevant jurisdiction to determine whether and to what extent they alter the common law fiduciary obligations of partners and principals in other forms of business associations.

A firm's partnership agreement or other operating agreement may also define the duties of partners, members, or other principals. Of course, disputes often arise over the meaning of such documents.[82]

There are at least two special areas where partners may be charged with violating fiduciary obligations to one another. The first concerns expulsion, or, as it is sometimes called, "de-equitization." Lawyers who are forced out of a partnership sometimes assert claims for breach of fiduciary duty, as well as related claims for fraud, breach of contract, promissory estoppel, or unjust enrichment.[83] The second area, which is discussed below,[84] involves a partner's voluntary withdrawal from a firm. A departing partner may seek to take along firm clients, thus depriving the firm of a future source of revenue. The departing lawyer's solicitation of those clients may involve conduct that is an alleged breach of fiduciary obligations owed to the firm.[85]

### § 5-3.6(b) Duties of Associates

Under common law principles, associates are agents who have fiduciary obligations to the firms for which they work. There is an overarching duty of loyalty that requires an associate to act loyally for the law firm's benefit in all matters connected with the

---

[80] 2009 WL 910326, at *8 (N.J. Super. Ct. App. Div.).

[81] *See infra* § 5-7.2(d).

[82] *See, e.g.*, Nate Raymond, *Former Chadbourne Attorney Claims Partnership Agreement Permits Him to Keep Compensation*, www.law.com, Sept. 8, 2010.

[83] *See, e.g.*, Max Mitchell, *Attorney Sues Former Partner*, N.J. L.J., Nov. 28, 2016 (discussing claims for breach of contract, unjust enrichment, conversion, and a charge related to computer hacking).

[84] *See* § 5-3.6(c).

[85] For a discussion of risk management measures to avoid litigation and respect client choice, see Robert W. Hillman, *Problems and Prevention: Law Firm Management in Era of Breakups and Lawyer Mobility: Limitations and Opportunities*, 43 TEX. TECH L. REV. 449 (2011).

firm.[86] More specifically, an associate may not improperly benefit from the associate's relationship with the firm;[87] act on behalf of an adverse party;[88] divert or usurp business opportunities, or otherwise compete with the firm;[89] or misuse the firm's property or confidential information.[90] Of course, conduct consented to by a law firm is not a breach of an associate's fiduciary duties.[91]

An associate has an obligation to the employing law firm to exercise care, competence, and diligence in law firm matters.[92] An associate must also act only within the associate's scope of actual authority and must abide by the law firm's instructions.[93]

The same type of departure-based client solicitation that creates issues when partners leave the firm may also arise when associates move to another firm or start a new law office.

Unfortunately, there is some divergence between legal obligations and practice. Postings by associates on websites like Above the Law might be construed as breaches of fiduciary duty.[94]

Receipt of an undisclosed commission, bonus, or gift from a third party for performing duties owed to the firm constitutes a breach of fiduciary duty.[95] This is true even if there is no showing that the firm has been damaged.

Similarly, referring a potential firm client to another law firm in exchange for a commission is impermissible. However, fiduciary obligations are not absolute. An associate who recommends that a client engage different counsel because that is in the best interest of the client is not liable for the fee lost by the associate's firm, provided that the associate did not profit in some way based on the diversion of business.[96]

An associate who fails to disclose to a law firm that he does not have a law degree, and who thereby steals money by collecting a lawyer's salary, is liable to the firm for the improper receipt of benefits.[97]

### § 5-3.6(c) Movement Between Firms

It was once the case that most lawyers stayed with the same law firm for a lifetime. Today, that degree of loyalty and continuity is the rare exception. Lawyers are highly mobile, typically changing firms several times in a career.

A question of tremendous practical importance is whether a lawyer can invite a client the lawyer served at one firm to transfer the client's business to the lawyer at the

---

[86] *Cf.* RESTATEMENT (THIRD) OF AGENCY § 8.01 (American Law Inst., 2006).

[87] *See id.* at § 8.02.

[88] *See id.* at § 8.03.

[89] *See id.* at § 8.04.

[90] *See id.* at § 8.05.

[91] *See id.* at § 8.06.

[92] *See id.* at § 8.07.

[93] *See id.* at § 8.08.

[94] *See generally* Susan Saab Fortney, *Leaks, Lies, and the Moonlight: Fiduciary Duties of Associates to Their Law Firms*, 41 ST. MARY'S L.J. 595 (2010); Brenda Sapino Jeffreys, *Firm Files Libel Suit Against Former Employee*, TEX. LAW., Jan. 7, 2015.

[95] *Cf.* Kinzbach Tool Co. v. Corbett-Wallace Corp., 138 Tex. 565, 160 S.W.2d 509 (1942).

[96] *See* Brewer v. Johnson & Pritchard, P.C., 73 S.W.3d 193 (Tex. 2002).

[97] *See Fake Lawyer to Pay Firm Restitution*, NAT'L L.J. at 16 (Oct. 15, 2007).

next firm. The answer to the question demands careful consideration, because client solicitation in the context of moving between law firms raises issues of potential liability under disciplinary, tort, and fiduciary duty principles. Fortunately, certain once-disputed points are now the subject of consensus. Thus, the *Restatement* provides that:

> Absent an agreement with the firm providing a more permissive rule, a lawyer leaving a law firm may solicit firm clients:
>
> (a) prior to leaving the firm:
>
> (i) only with respect to firm clients on whose matters the lawyer is actively and substantially working; and
>
> (ii) only after the lawyer has adequately and timely informed the firm of the lawyer's intent to contact firm clients for that purpose; and
>
> (b) after ceasing employment in the firm, to the same extent as any other nonfirm lawyer.[98]

Although a few states continue to take a harsh view of departure-based client solicitation, a lawyer who acts in conformity with the *Restatement*'s view is unlikely to be liable for breach of fiduciary duty or tortious interference with contract or prospective advantage. Professional discipline is also unlikely because prohibitions on solicitation normally exempt communications with one's own present or former clients.[99]

### § 5-3.6(d) Post-Employment Restrictive Covenants

With respect to departure-based solicitation of clients, the most important principle is that clients have the right to decide who will provide representation going forward. Not surprisingly, agreements between lawyers purporting to determine who "owns" which client, or banning departing lawyers from competing with the former firm, are invalid.[100]

---

[98] RESTATEMENT (THIRD) OF THE LAW GOVERNING LAWYERS § 9(3) (American Law Inst., 2000).

[99] *See* MODEL RULES OF PROF'L CONDUCT R. 7.3 (American Bar Ass'n, 2017) (permitting contact with a person who has "a family, close personal, or prior professional relationship with the lawyer").

[100] *See* MODEL RULES OF PROF'L CONDUCT R. 5.6 (American Bar Ass'n, 2017) (prohibiting restrictions on the right to practice); Vincent R. Johnson, *Solicitation of Law Firm Clients by Departing Partners and Associates: Tort, Fiduciary, and Disciplinary Liability*, 50 U. PITT. L. REV. 1, 111–16 & n.226 (1988).

# Chapter 5-4

# LIABILITY TO NONCLIENTS

**By Susan Saab Fortney and Vincent R. Johnson**

*Table of Sections*

§ 5-4.1 Modern Nonclient Litigation
§ 5-4.2 Fraud on Clients and Nonclients
§ 5-4.3 Negligent Misrepresentation
§ 5-4.4 Deceptive Trade Practices Acts
§ 5-4.5 Claims Based on Representation of Fiduciaries
§ 5-4.6 Funds and Property of Nonclients
§ 5-4.7 Intended Beneficiaries
§ 5-4.8 Duties to Co-Counsel
§ 5-4.9 Liability Related to Litigation
§ 5-4.10 Securities Law Violations
§ 5-4.11 Fair Debt Collections Practices

---

## § 5-4.1 MODERN NONCLIENT LITIGATION

Lawyers may be liable to nonclients on a variety of theories. Indeed, nonclient claims pose some of the greatest malpractice risks. Highly publicized cases often involve nonclients seeking to recoup losses resulting from failed investments and business transactions. Suits by shareholders and creditors are not uncommon. In malpractice cases like those resulting from the failure of major corporations, nonclient plaintiffs have recovered millions of dollars under an array of legal theories.

Often the stakes are high. In one case, a New York law firm, which previously represented the Stanford Financial Group, was sued by investors as the result of an allegedly fraudulent $7 billion scheme related to a Caribbean bank, and paid a $35 million settlement.[1] In another case, after a California jury returned a $34.5 million compensatory damages verdict, but deadlocked on an award of punitive damages, an internationally known law firm settled with three nonclient investors who allegedly had been misled about failed real estate investments.[2]

This chapter examines the theories of nonclient liability that pose risks to lawyers and law firms. The chapter also considers the challenges that nonclients encounter in suing lawyers they never employed to provide legal services.

---

1 *See* Jim Eccleston, *Law Firm Found Responsible for Ponzi Scheme Fraud*, FINANCIAL COUNSEL (Blog), July 25, 2016, 2016 WLNR 22608174.

2 *See* Zach Winnick, *Holland & Knight Partially Settles $35 M Fraud Trial*, Law360 (Los Angeles), Apr. 24, 2012.

### § 5-4.1(a) The Privity Obstacle

It is still true, and probably always will be, that nonclients have a harder time than clients holding lawyers accountable for the losses they sustain. The explanation for this reality concerns the issue of legal duty. Discussions of that subject are often cloaked in the language of "privity." In the law of legal malpractice, "privity" means that there was an attorney-client relationship between the defendant and the plaintiff (or the plaintiff's predecessor-in-interest), and that the lawyer therefore owed the plaintiff a broad array of legally enforceable obligations.[3]

In the absence of privity, a lawyer has only limited duties to potential plaintiffs. For example, in *Gall v. Colon-Sylvain*,[4] a New York appellate court concluded that the attorney for a purchaser-borrower and a lender did not have a duty to act or give advice for the benefit of the seller's shareholder, and thus could not be held liable for breach of fiduciary duty.

In *Shoemaker v. Gindlesberger*,[5] two of the decedent's three children alleged that a lawyer had improperly drafted a will and a deed that allowed the decedent to retain an interest in a farm which had been transferred to the third child. As a result, the two other children suffered damages in the form of increased estate taxes and did not share evenly in their mother's assets, as their mother had intended. In rejecting their malpractice claim, the Ohio Supreme Court explained:

> The strict privity rule ensures that attorneys may represent their clients without the threat of suit from third parties who may compromise that representation. * * *. Otherwise, an attorney's preoccupation or concern with potential negligence claims by third parties might diminish the quality of legal services provided to the client if the attorney were to weigh the client's interests against the possibility of third-party lawsuits.[6]

*Flaherty-Wiebel v. Morris, Downing & Sherred*[7] was a typical case. A woman (Flaherty) sued the lawyer and law firm who represented her former husband (Wiebel) in drafting a pre-nuptial agreement. In rejecting the woman's claim, the Third Circuit noted that "Flaherty was represented by her own counsel during the negotiation of the pre-nuptial agreement."[8] The court concluded that, "Since Flaherty was not represented by the defendants during the negotiation of the pre-nuptial agreement, she cannot sustain a claim for legal malpractice based on their performance in drafting this agreement."[9]

The mere receipt of attorney work product is not enough to make one a client and thereby surmount the privity barrier. This is true because the *Restatement* makes clear that in order for an attorney-client relationship to arise by agreement or by mistake, there must have been a request for representation.[10] The decision in *Great American E*

---

[3] *See supra* § 5-2.1(a).

[4] 2017 WL 2454293 (N.Y. App. Div.).

[5] 887 N.E.2d 1167 (Ohio 2008).

[6] *Id.* at 1171. For a discussion of liability to nonclients for harm caused by invalid wills, see *infra* § 5-4.7(a).

[7] 384 F. App'x 173 (3d Cir. 2010).

[8] *Id.* at 176.

[9] *Id.*

[10] *See* RESTATEMENT (THIRD) OF TORTS § 14 (American Law Institute, 2000).

*& S Insurance Co. v. Quintairos, Prieto, Wood & Boyer, P.A.*[11] is illustrative. In that case, which was brought by an excess insurance carrier [Great American] against lawyers [Quintairos] hired by the primary insurance carrier to defend an insured, the Supreme Court of Mississippi wrote:

> Great American argues that Quintairos provided it with legal services when it sent Great American the case-status reports that estimated the settlement and trial values of the case. Taken as true, these case-status reports—without more—are insufficient to establish an attorney-client relationship.
>
> Great American would have us hold that an attorney employed by a primary insurance carrier—simply by providing an excess carrier with courtesy copies of its settlement evaluations—establishes an attorney-client relationship. For us to accept Great American's view would require us to ignore the realities of real-world litigation, which often involves several defendants with common interests. * * *.
>
> Because an attorney-client relationship is an essential element in a legal-malpractice claim, * * * we affirm the trial court's dismissal of any direct legal-malpractice claim against Quintairos.[12]

## § 5-4.1(b) Exceptions to Privity

Jurisdictions sometimes describe themselves as "strict privity" states in an effort to capture the idea that it is difficult—indeed, sometimes exceedingly difficult—for a nonclient to recover damages. Yet, even where "strict privity" is the rule, nonclients can successfully assert certain claims against lawyers who did not represent them.

Indeed, nonclients sometimes prevail on at least seventeen different theories of liability. Of course, there is no magic in that number. Courts and legislatures may recognize new nonclient causes of action or reject theories of liability that were once found to be meritorious. In thinking about the theories of liability which do not depend on privity, it is somewhat useful, for purposes of memory, to group the causes of action into clusters.

The first three exceptions concern the law of misrepresentation. Thus, lawyers may be liable to nonclients for fraud, for negligent misrepresentation, and for statutorily defined deceptive trade practices.

Three other exceptions relate more or less directly to fiduciary obligations. A lawyer may be responsible for harm caused to a nonclient by knowingly aiding and abetting another's breach of fiduciary duties to the nonclient; by failing to exercise care to protect a beneficiary while representing a fiduciary client; and, under some circumstances, by failing to protect property or funds in the lawyer's possession that belong to a nonclient.

A third trio of exceptions to the privity requirement concern claims by persons whose interests were once actually or apparently aligned with the interests of the lawyer or the lawyer's client. Consequently, certain actions may be brought against a lawyer by a former prospective client, by an intended third-party beneficiary of legal services for a client, or by a lawyer's former co-counsel.

---

[11] 100 So. 3d 420 (Miss. 2012).

[12] *Id.* at 424–25.

Three other theories of liability to nonclients relate to persons harmed by litigation. Thus, a lawyer may be liable to a nonclient for misuse of legal process or tortious involvement with litigation that causes the nonclient to incur attorney's fees, and to a malpractice carrier for losses it sustains as a result of the lawyer's negligence.

Two more theories of liability involve widely recognized tort actions: tortious interference with contract and intentional or reckless infliction of emotional distress. Under the first action, a lawyer can be liable to another lawyer for interfering with an existing lawyer-client relationship by persuading a client who is already represented to change law firms. Under the second action, lawyers may be liable to nonclients for intentionally or recklessly causing severe emotional distress, such as by "blatantly" lying to secure default judgment against the nonclient.[13]

Finally, three other theories of liability illustrate how statutes may create causes of action for nonclients. First, lawyers are sometimes liable to nonclients under state or federal securities laws. Second, lawyers hired to collect money may be civilly liable for violating applicable debt collection laws. Third, anti-recording statutes may make lawyers liable for certain types of invasion of privacy.[14]

Liability to former prospective clients[15] and to persons alleging that the defendant-lawyer aided or abetted a breach of fiduciary duty[16] are discussed elsewhere in this book. Several of the other main theories of liability to nonclients are explored in this chapter.

### § 5-4.1(c) Statutory Limits on Nonclient Liability

In efforts to protect lawyers from malpractice liability to persons who were never their clients, some state legislatures have passed laws limiting the theories under which responsibility may be imposed. For example, an Arkansas law limits liability to persons not in privity to "conduct that constitutes fraud or intentional misrepresentation" or conduct where the lawyer "was aware that a primary intent of the client was for the professional services to benefit or influence the particular person bringing the action."[17]

Although such laws undoubtedly set important limits on the malpractice liability of attorneys, those limits may be less restrictive than might first appear. Federal laws, such as the Fair Debt Collection Practices Act and federal securities laws, create bases of liability to nonclients which states are not free to supersede. Moreover, it remains unclear whether state legislation, such as the Arkansas statute quoted above, overrides every other form of nonclient liability under state law, such as a lawyer's liability for misuse of legal process or pursuant to state securities, anti-recording, or debt collection statutes.

---

[13] *See* Alex B. Long, *Lawyers Intentionally Inflicting Emotional Distress*, 42 SETON HALL L. REV. 55, 89 (2012).

[14] *See, e.g.*, TEX. CODE CRIM. PROC. Art. 18.20 (Westlaw 2017) ("Sec. 16. (a) A person whose wire, oral, or electronic communication is intercepted, disclosed, or used in violation of this article, or in violation of Chapter 16, Penal Code, has a civil cause of action against any person who intercepts, discloses, or uses or solicits another person to intercept, disclose, or use the communication and is entitled to recover from the person: (1) actual damages but not less than liquidated damages computed at a rate of $100 a day for each day of violation or $1,000, whichever is higher; (2) punitive damages; and (3) a reasonable attorney's fee and other litigation costs reasonably incurred.").

[15] *See supra* § 5-2.1(a)(5).

[16] *See supra* § 5-3.5.

[17] ARK. CODE. ANN. § 16–22–310 (Westlaw 2017).

## § 5-4.1(d) Successors-in-Interest

Lack of privity is not an obstacle to a malpractice action brought by certain successors to the interests of clients. This category includes bankruptcy trustees, estate executors and administrators, business entities resulting from corporate mergers, and receivers.

### *§ 5-4.1(d)(1) Bankruptcy Trustees and Estate Executors or Administrators*

If a client files for bankruptcy protection or dies, the client's trustee in bankruptcy or estate representative stands in the shoes of the client. Lack of privity therefore does not bar the trustee or representative from bringing a malpractice action related to a lawyer's prior representation of the client. The trustee or estate representative is regarded as a successor-in-interest with essentially the same rights as the client. Indeed, once a person with a malpractice claim declares bankruptcy, the bankruptcy trustee is the only party with standing to pursue the malpractice claim.[18] However, if a bankruptcy trustee abandons a legal malpractice claim, the person whose debts are discharged in bankruptcy sometimes has a right to prosecute the malpractice action, provided that the claim is not time-barred.[19]

Similarly, courts usually hold that claims on behalf of a decedent or the decedent's estate must be brought by the executor or administrator of the estate.[20] In *Smith v. O'Donnell*,[21] the executor of the estate of a husband brought a malpractice claim against a law firm which allegedly provided the husband with bad advice while he was serving as the executor of his wife's estate. The Texas Supreme Court held that it made no difference whether the alleged malpractice related to estate planning or occurred outside of the estate-planning context. The executor was permitted to sue. To hold otherwise, the court wrote, would "place us alone among the states, and would unnecessarily immunize attorneys who commit malpractice."[22]

### *§ 5-4.1(d)(2) Mergers and Sales of Assets*

If entities merge, the successor entity may assert the rights of the predecessor entities. The attorney-client relationship, and hence privity, is deemed to transfer.

However, a mere sale of assets does not make one a successor in interest.[23] In *Greene's Pressure Treating & Rentals, Inc. v. Fulbright & Jaworski, L.L.P.*,[24] a company had purchased patent rights from a seller to whom a law firm had issued an opinion letter stating that the seller's process did not infringe another patent. Because the transaction was treated as a mere sale of assets, there was no attorney-client

---

18 *See* Douglas v. Delp, 987 S.W.2d 879, 882 (Tex. 1999).

19 *See* Newman v. Enriquez, 869 N.E.2d 735 (Ohio Ct. App. 2007).

20 *See, e.g.*, Fleischman v. Horton, 2006 WL 3541780, *2 (W.D. Okla. 2006).

21 288 S.W.3d 417 (Tex. 2009).

22 *Id.* at 421.

23 *See* Greene's Pressure Treating & Rentals, Inc. v. Fulbright & Jaworski, L.L.P., 178 S.W.3d 40, 44 (Tex. App. 2005) ("Whether a prior attorney-client relationship transfers depends on whether the transaction is characterized as a merger or merely as an acquisition of assets. * * *. An attorney client relationship will transfer when a merger of two corporations takes place. * * *. In a merger, the successor organization stands in the shoes of prior management and continues the operations of the prior entity. * * *. However, when a corporate transaction is merely a sale of assets, it is not a merger, and rights and liabilities do not transfer unless expressly assumed.").

24 178 S.W.3d 40, 40 (Tex. App. 2005).

relationship between the buyer of the patented process and the law firm. Therefore, the firm did not breach a fiduciary duty by representing a different party in an action against the buyer.

The "commercial transfer of a legal malpractice claim, along with other assets and liabilities, to a successor in interest"[25] is generally allowed. This is true despite the prohibition against assignment of malpractice claims in many jurisdictions.

#### *§ 5-4.1(d)(3) Receivers*

By statute, receivers appointed to liquidate insolvent companies may assert malpractice claims against the lawyers who represented the failed institutions.[26] Thus, in the wake of the Savings and Loan Crisis in the late 1980s and early 1990s, the Federal Deposit Insurance Corporation initiated numerous suits against the lawyers who represented the defunct financial institutions.[27]

## § 5-4.2 FRAUD ON CLIENTS AND NONCLIENTS

In many respects, fraud is the most important theory under which lawyers may be liable to nonclients. This is true for several reasons. First, every state recognizes an action for fraud, so there is plenty of precedent to draw upon in crafting actions against lawyers. Second, numerous states have held lawyers liable to nonclients for fraud, and no state has ever ruled that a lawyer may deliberately defraud a person merely because of the lack of privity. Third, because legal work involves language, both written and oral, there is abundant material to cull in search of misstatements. Finally, fraud is seriously wrongful conduct, and a lawyer found to have acted fraudulently may be liable not only for compensatory damages (perhaps generously calculated by the jury because of the defendant's bad conduct), but punitive damages, too.

### § 5-4.2(a) Basic Principles of the Law Governing Fraud

In the course of human history, there has been no shortage of fraudulent conduct. Not surprisingly, there is an immense amount of case precedent dealing with the subject, and equally voluminous scholarship exploring the intricate rules and distinctions that have emerged from the courts. The following discussion merely sketches the subject, focusing on actions against lawyers.

#### *§ 5-4.2(a)(1) Common Law Remedies and Other Consequences*

At the outset, it is important to keep in mind the range of consequences that flow from fraud. In addition to a tort action for damages, fraud may trigger other remedies. Possible consequences include forfeiture of attorney's fees,[28] invalidation of a contract,[29]

---

[25] St. Luke's Magic Valley Reg'l Med. Ctr. v. Luciani, 293 P.3d 661, 666 (Idaho 2013); *cf.* Greene's Pressure Treating & Rentals, Inc. v. Fulbright & Jaworski, L.L.P., 178 S.W.3d 40, 44 (Tex. App. 2005) ("A mere transfer of assets, with no attempt to continue the pre-existing operation, does not transfer the prior attorney client relationship.").

[26] *Cf.* Dennerline v. Atterholt, 886 N.E.2d 582 (Ind. Ct. App. 2008).

[27] *See* SUSAN SAAB FORTNEY & VINCENT R. JOHNSON, LEGAL MALPRACTICE LAW: PROBLEMS AND PREVENTION 13 (West Academic Publishing, 2d ed. 2015) (discussing the savings and loan crisis).

[28] *See* RESTATEMENT (THIRD) OF THE LAW GOVERNING LAWYERS § 37 (American Law Institute, 2000) (discussing partial or complete fee forfeiture).

[29] *See* RESTATEMENT (SECOND) OF CONTRACTS § 7 cmt. b (American Law Institute, 1981).

and a suit for restitution in which recovery is based not on what the plaintiff lost (damages), but on what the defendant improperly gained (unjust enrichment).[30]

In addition, conduct that might be actionable as common law fraud sometimes forms the basis for an action that is rooted in statutory obligations. For example, in *Banco Popular North America v. Gandi*,[31] a bank alleged that a lawyer participated in a civil conspiracy to violate the Uniform Fraudulent Transfers Act. The New Jersey Supreme Court held that the lower court properly refused to dismiss the conspiracy count because the allegations indicated that the lawyer had counseled the client to transfer his assets to defraud a creditor and had facilitated the transfer.

Aside from civil liability, a lawyer's perpetration of fraud may also result in criminal prosecution[32] or professional discipline. Under Model Rule 8.4, a lawyer commits professional misconduct if the lawyer engages "in conduct involving dishonesty, fraud, deceit or misrepresentation."[33] In addition, under Model Rule 1.2, "[a] lawyer shall not counsel a client to engage, or assist a client, in conduct that the lawyer knows is criminal or fraudulent."[34] An attorney who is found to have engaged in fraudulent conduct is likely to be subject to serious disciplinary sanctions, because fraud is not a minor misstep, but a form of deliberate victimization.

Statutes sometimes alter the common law categorization of malpractice claims. For example, under the Alabama Legal Services Liability Act (ALSLA), there is only one form and cause of action against legal service providers. Thus, the requirements of the ALSLA apply to an action based on fraud.[35]

#### *§ 5-4.2(a)(2) The Elements of Fraud*

Most cases refer to liability for "fraud," although some use the term "deceit." Whichever term is used, the civil cause of action is usually defined as having five elements. The plaintiff must show that: (1) the defendant made a material misrepresentation; (2) the defendant acted with "*scienter*" (meaning knowledge of the misrepresentation's falsity or reckless disregard for its truth); (3) the misrepresentation was intended or expected by the defendant to induce reliance; (4) the plaintiff justifiably relied upon the misrepresentation; and (5) damages resulted.

To impose liability, there must be evidence to establish each of the elements of fraud. In *O'Neill v. Hernandez*,[36] a claim that lawyers committed fraud by submitting documents to a state court was dismissed by a federal court in New York because the plaintiff did not even allege that the lawyers knew the statements were false or otherwise acted with *scienter*.

---

[30] *See* RESTATEMENT (THIRD) OF RESTITUTION AND UNJUST ENRICHMENT § 13 (American Law Institute, 2011) ("(1) A transfer induced by fraud or material misrepresentation is subject to rescission and restitution. The transferee is liable in restitution as necessary to avoid unjust enrichment").

[31] 876 A.2d 253 (N.J. 2005).

[32] *See* John Council, *Dallas Lawyer Indicted for Arranging Fake Marriage for Legal Assistant*, TEX. LAWYER, July 20, 2017.

[33] MODEL RULES OF PROF'L CONDUCT R. 8.4(c) (American Bar Ass'n, 2017).

[34] *Id.* R. 1.2.

[35] *See* Yarbrough v. Eversole, 2017 WL 382295, at *3 (Ala.).

[36] 2009 WL 860647 (S.D.N.Y. 2009).

#### *§ 5-4.2(a)(2)(A) Special Pleading and Proof Requirements*

Under federal procedural rules, and similar provisions in most states, the circumstances constituting fraud must be pleaded with particularity.[37] Many states require that the elements of fraud must be proved by "clear and convincing evidence," except perhaps the damages element.[38]

### *§ 5-4.2(a)(3) Scienter*

"*Scienter*" is a highly blameworthy state of mind, entailing knowledge of falsity or reckless disregard for the truth. Thus, it is possible to establish the defendant's liability in either of two ways.

#### *§ 5-4.2(a)(3)(A) Knowledge of Falsity*

If the defendant allegedly made misrepresentations with knowledge of their falsity, the focus will be on what the defendant knew and when the defendant knew it. Suppose, for example, that a lawyer allegedly defrauded an opposing party into accepting an inadequate settlement by misrepresenting how much insurance coverage was available to the lawyer's client for purposes of covering the loss. One way that the plaintiff can prevail in an action for fraud is to show that the lawyer knew that the insurance policy had higher limits of liability when the lawyer made the statement.

Some kinds of evidence, if credited by the jury, leave little room for doubt about what a lawyer in fact knew. Such evidence might consist of e-mails, hard copy correspondence, or the deposition testimony of another lawyer. In other cases, knowledge of falsity is proven by circumstantial evidence.

#### *§ 5-4.2(a)(3)(B) Reckless Disregard for the Truth*

The second way to prove *scienter* greatly expands the range of culpable conduct that may give rise to liability for fraud. Under this alternative, a plaintiff does not need to show that the defendant knew that a representation was false, but merely that the defendant acted with reckless disregard for the truth. To understand what this means, it is important to differentiate mere negligence from recklessness. Negligence is insufficient to establish *scienter*.

Negligence is less culpable than recklessness, and involves nothing more than the failure to exercise reasonable care. Thus, the fact that a reasonably careful person would have detected the falsity of the statement uttered by the defendant does not prove that the defendant acted with *scienter*.

In contrast to negligence, recklessness is defined, in various areas of the law, either (a) objectively, as an extreme lack of care, or (b) subjectively, as conscious indifference to a known risk of serious harm.

Three examples illustrate *scienter* based on recklessness. First, a person acts with *scienter* if the person asserts something as a matter of fact, even though he or she does not know whether the assertion is true. In that case, the utterance is made with conscious disregard for whether the statement is true or false. The speaker knows that he or she does not know whether the statement is accurate. Suppose, for example, that

---

[37] *See* FED. R. CIV. P. 9(b) (2017).

[38] *See* Asen v. All American Landscape and Design, Inc., 2016 WL 921276, at *12 (Conn. Super. Ct. 2016).

a lawyer represents that a corporation is making money, even though the lawyer does not know whether it is running in the black or the red financially. The lawyer will be liable for fraud if the assertion turns out to be false and foreseeably causes damages to a person who was expected to rely on the assertion.

Second, according to the *Restatement*, a person acts with *scienter* if the person lacks the factual basis that a statement implies.[39] For example, assume that a lawyer declines a case by telling a prospective client that there are no legal grounds for bringing suit. If the lawyer implies that the lawyer's decision was based on a careful review of the law, when that was not the case, and the prospective client is dissuaded from seeking other representation for what would have been a meritorious claim, the lawyer may be liable not just for negligence, but for fraud.

In *Anthoulis v. Mastoros*,[40] a lawyer was sued by nonclients for fraud based on his conduct while representing clients in a real estate transaction. In refusing to dismiss the fraud claim, a New York court wrote:

> [L]iability will attach for statements which are intentionally made with knowledge of their falsity and to statements which are recklessly made, *particularly where there is the "pretense of knowledge where there is none."* * * * If [lawyer] Alatsas displayed checks from or on the account of Harry and Betty as evidencing their capital contributions, but he did not know or inquire as to whether such checks had actually been negotiated and deposited, such conduct could well be viewed as reckless.[41]

Third, according to the *Restatement*, a person acts with *scienter* by making a misrepresentation in which the person lacks the confidence that is stated or implied.[42] Thus, an unequivocal assurance about the tax deductibility of certain expenditures may support a fraud action if the assertion proves erroneous and there is evidence that the lawyer had doubts about how taxing authorities would rule on the issue of deductibility.

Proof of *scienter* inevitably requires evidence of the defendant's state of mind regarding the truth or falsity of the allegedly misrepresented matter. Suppose, for example, that a lawyer transmits a document containing a material misstatement of fact, but that the lawyer proves that he or she was unaware of the contents of the document and was merely acting as a courier. These facts do not support a finding that the lawyer acted with *scienter*. It might be argued that the lawyer should have known about the contents of the document because a reasonable lawyer would have inquired, but that is only negligence, which is not sufficient to establish *scienter* and liability for fraud.

In *Tevrow v. Arowolo*,[43] a former employee had embezzled money from his employers. In a resulting criminal action, the employers agreed not to oppose a sentence of probation if the former employee entered into a co-signed repayment agreement. The former employee's lawyer notarized the signatures of the co-signers who were presented by the former employee. After the former employee defaulted on the repayment agreement, the employers discovered that the co-signers were in fact imposters and that

---

[39] *See* RESTATEMENT (SECOND) OF TORTS § 526 (American Law Institute, 1977).

[40] 2007 WL 7230928 (N.Y. Sup. Ct.).

[41] *Id.* at *15 (emphasis added).

[42] *See* RESTATEMENT (SECOND) OF TORTS § 526 (American Law Institute, 1977).

[43] 2015 WL 9694315 (N.J. Super. Ct. App. Div.).

they had been deceived. Seeking to recoup their losses, the employers sued the former employee's lawyer for "legal malpractice." A New Jersey appellate court held that summary judgment was properly granted to the lawyer because the employers did not allege that the lawyer had "conspired with * * * [the former employee] to commit fraud or that he had any knowledge that the individuals purporting to be * * * [the co-signers] were imposters."[44]

### *§ 5-4.2(a)(4) Materiality and Types of Misrepresentation*

An action for fraud may be based on misleading words, conduct, or, in some cases, silence. These types of misrepresentation are discussed below.

To be actionable, a misrepresentation must be material. This simply means that the matter must be one to which a reasonable person would attach importance in making a decision, or one which the defendant knows is important to the particular plaintiff.[45] Materiality is often a question of fact. For example, in *First Arkansas Bank & Trust, Tr. v. Gill Elrod Ragon Owen & Sherman, P.A.*,[46] the Supreme Court of Arkansas declined to affirm a grant of summary judgment to a law firm that was sued for malpractice based on fraud because there was a fact issue as to whether an underlying purchase mortgage was material and therefore had to be disclosed.

#### *§ 5-4.2(a)(4)(A) Words Written or Oral*

A misrepresentation may consist of words, whether written or oral. Therefore, a real estate lawyer may be subject to liability for falsely telling a client that a contract has been signed and a deposit received.[47] Similarly, a lawyer may be liable for fraud based on backdating documents, if the misrepresented date is material.

In one case, a client sued its law firm after it settled an antitrust dispute with a rival GPS company. The client alleged that the firm had misled it by incorrectly representing that the client did not have to worry about what fees it would incur in the dispute because it could recover all of its fees and costs if it prevailed on even one aspect of its antitrust claims. In refusing to dismiss the fraud claim, the court found that there was some evidence that the client relied on the assurance and, as a result, spent "lots and lots of money."[48]

On appropriate facts, ambiguous statements and half-truths will support an action for fraud.[49] For example, a statement that a seller's title to property has been upheld by a particular court is a false representation if the speaker fails to disclose knowledge that an appeal from the decision is pending.[50]

---

44 *Id.* at *6.

45 *See* RESTATEMENT (SECOND) OF TORTS § 538 (American Law Institute, 1977).

46 427 S.W.3d 47, 53 (Ark. 2013).

47 *See* Stoecker v. Echevarria, 975 A.2d 975 (N.J. Super. Ct. App. Div. 2009).

48 *See* Kate Moser, *Quinn Emanuel Faces Trial in Dispute with Ex-Client Over $15 Million Bill*, www.law.com (June 16, 2010).

49 *See infra* § 5-4.2(a)(4)(C)(ii).

50 *Cf.* RESTATEMENT (SECOND) OF TORTS § 529 cmt. a (American Law Institute, 1977).

*§ 5-4.2(a)(4)(A)(i) Words of Qualification*

Words of qualification—such as "about," "more or less," or "roughly"—merely indicate a margin of error. They do not make a statement nonactionable. Consider the following examples involving similar, but different, statements.

If a lawyer says that the ranch being sold by a client has a thousand acres, when it only has 980 acres, there has been a misstatement of fact. If the other elements of fraud are established, the plaintiff can recover damages based on the reduced size of the property.

In contrast, if the lawyer says that the 980-acre ranch has "roughly a thousand acres," it is less clear that there has been a misrepresentation. The jury must determine if the size of the ranch was substantially as stated. If not, the representation is actionable to the extent of the deficiency.

*§ 5-4.2(a)(4)(B) Conduct*

A misrepresentation may also consist of conduct that communicates information. In *Scandrett v. Greenhouse*, a lawyer presented a release and demanded payment of a certain debt, which by prior agreement of the parties was to be paid only if the plaintiff's compensation carrier had agreed to waive its claim. The Wisconsin Supreme Court found that the lawyer, through his conduct, had fraudulently represented that the compensation carrier had been satisfied or had waived its claim.[51]

*§ 5-4.2(a)(4)(C) Liability for Nondisclosure*

In law, as in etiquette, the general rule is that silence is golden. Nondisclosure will support an action for fraud only if there is a duty to speak. There are at least four situations where such an obligation arises.

*§ 5-4.2(a)(4)(C)(i) Fiduciary Duty to Speak*

First, the law of fiduciary duty may impose an obligation to speak. This means that it is often easier for a client to base a fraud action on silence, than for a nonclient to make the same argument. Lawyers, as fiduciaries, have broad obligations to keep clients informed of material information. In contrast, nonclients stand on a very different footing. Lawyers typically do not owe fiduciary duties to nonclients.

Suppose that a lawyer involved with the management of a client's trust appoints as manager of the trust's real estate holdings a person who, unknown to the client, is a close friend of the lawyer. If the client suffers losses and the arrangement turns sour, it is easy to see how the client might allege that the lawyer is liable for fraudulent nondisclosure of material information.

In *Cummings v. Sea Lion Corp.*,[52] the Supreme Court of Alaska held that a lawyer was liable for failing to reveal to the client corporation that the lawyer would only be paid if the transaction between the corporation and a previous client of the lawyer was successful.

---

[51] 11 N.W.2d 510 (Wis. 1943).

[52] 924 P.2d 1011 (Alaska 1996).

*§ 5-4.2(a)(4)(C)(ii) Half-Truths*

The truth cannot be told in such a way as to leave a false impression. Thus, a lawyer cannot say that a property has been "sold" in an effort to trigger a person's promissory note repayment obligations, without also disclosing that the sale had no substance and was strictly pro forma.[53]

A statement may be half-true because, although accurate when made, new developments have occurred.[54] In this kind of situation, there is a duty to correct the earlier statement. The duty continues until it is no longer possible for the recipient of the original statement to avoid the harm that will be caused by reliance on the erroneous information. In *McMahan v. Greenwood*,[55] a Texas court recognized that a lawyer had a duty to correct misimpressions created by earlier statements to a nonclient.

*§ 5-4.2(a)(4)(C)(iii) Facts Basic to the Transaction*

There is a duty to disclose facts so "basic to a transaction" that nondisclosure amounts to "swindling."[56] In one case, lawyers who represented hedge funds allegedly failed to disclose to investors that the person who headed the funds was a disbarred New York lawyer who had drained a client's escrow account.[57] It could reasonably be argued that the duty to disclose basic facts applies to this sort of case.

In *Banco Popular North America v. Gandi*,[58] a lawyer's client provided a guarantee to a bank in connection with receiving a loan. In holding that the bank stated claims for fraud and negligent misrepresentation against the lawyer, who had negotiated the loan and had written an opinion letter to facilitate the transaction, the New Jersey Supreme Court explained, "given [lawyer] Freedman's knowledge of the worthlessness of the guaranty, he had a duty, in light of what he had done and what he knew, either to counsel Gandi [the client] to tell the Bank the truth and see to it that he did so or to discontinue his representation."[59]

*§ 5-4.2(a)(4)(C)(iv) Facts Not Reasonably Discoverable*

Many decisions hold that there is a duty to disclose material facts that are not reasonably discoverable. This exception reflects the limits of the rationale underlying the rule that silence is usually not actionable. The general rule creates an incentive for persons to exercise care to protect their own interests. They cannot stand by and expect others to do their work for them. They must conduct their own investigations, ask good questions, and draw reasonable conclusions. If they fail to do so, they risk incurring economic losses for which there will be no legal remedy.

However, if the relevant facts are not reasonably discoverable, no purpose would be furthered by a rule countenancing nondisclosure of material information. The potential plaintiff would simply be relegated to making an uninformed decision. To avoid this result, disclosure of facts is required if they are beyond the range of reasonable discovery.

---

[53] *See* In re Conduct of Hiller, 694 P.2d 540, 544 (Or. 1985).

[54] *See* RESTATEMENT (SECOND) OF TORTS § 551(2)(d) (American Law Institute, 1977).

[55] 108 S.W.3d 467 (Tex. App. 2003).

[56] RESTATEMENT (SECOND) OF TORTS § 551 cmt. *l* (American Law Institute, 1977).

[57] *See* Julie Kay, *Receiver in Alleged $347 Million Ponzi Scheme Sues Holland & Knight for Malpractice*, www.law.com (Sept. 2, 2009).

[58] 876 A.2d 253 (N.J. 2005).

[59] *Id.* at 268.

The cases recognizing this type of duty to disclose have generally involved claims against nonlawyers related to the sale or leasing of real property. However, there is no reason that the same rationale could not apply to other types of facts that commonly give rise to legal malpractice actions.

*§ 5-4.2(a)(4)(D) Misrepresentations by Lawyers About Credentials or Experience*

Sometimes questions arise as to whether a lawyer misrepresented his or her credentials or experience. It is possible to analyze these kinds of statements or nondisclosures under the law of fraud.[60] Some misrepresentations about qualifications or prior work history are potentially actionable. For example, in *Nason v. Fisher*,[61] a New York appellate court found that a client raised a triable issue of fact about whether a lawyer had committed constructive fraud by misrepresenting that he had experience in handling commercial partnership cases.

Of course, it is important to remember that there are alternatives to suing for fraud. In some circumstances, those alternatives may be preferable. For example, nondisclosure may sometimes be characterized as negligent failure to obtain informed consent.[62] Framing the claim as negligence, rather than fraud, may make it easier to impute the conduct to the defaulting lawyer's law firm and its principals, as well as more likely to fall within malpractice insurance coverage.

In *Aiken v. Hancock*,[63] a Texas court held that a former client's allegations that his attorney falsely represented that he was prepared to try a case, and that an expert witness was prepared to testify, were actionable under a theory of "legal malpractice." Many states equate the term "legal malpractice" with professional negligence, not with fraud.

***§ 5-4.2(a)(5) Opinion Versus Fact***

Statements of fact are more readily actionable under the law of misrepresentation than statements of opinion. Thus, it is possible to sue a lawyer for falsely stating, "we have filed the appeal," but not for inaccurately predicting, "we probably will win on appeal."

Nevertheless, a complex matrix of rules makes clear that statements of opinion are sometimes actionable. Of relevance to issues of lawyer liability are the rules dealing with "puffing," implicit statements of fact, misrepresented intentions, and statements of "law." These topics are discussed in the following sections.

*§ 5-4.2(a)(5)(A) "Puffing"*

"Puffing" is sales talk—language which casts a warm glow over a transaction, but says nothing too specific. In general, puffing is treated as a non-actionable expression of opinion. A multinational law firm with many offices probably cannot be sued by a disappointed client based simply on the fact that the firm's website touted the availability of "world class" legal services.

---

[60] *See* Vincent R. Johnson & Shawn M. Lovorn, *Misrepresentation by Lawyers About Credentials or Experience*, 57 OKLA. L. REV. 529, 536–61 (2004).

[61] 828 N.Y.S.2d 51 (App. Div. 2007).

[62] *See supra* § 5-2.2(n).

[63] 115 S.W.3d 26, 28–29 (Tex. App. 2003).

However, once a lawyer begins to assert specific facts, rather than conclusory opinions, the puffing rule affords little protection. A law firm cannot say that it has offices in three countries, if that is not true.

In some situations, statements about credentials or experience go far beyond puffing. Thus, in *Baker v. Dorfman*,[64] a lawyer was found to have engaged in resume fraud to induce a client to hire him. The Second Circuit concluded that grossly false statements gave the impression that the lawyer was an experienced litigator, although this was not true.[65]

*§ 5-4.2(a)(5)(B) Implicit Statements of Fact*

Every statement of opinion carries with it two implicit statements of fact. The first is that the maker of the statement has some factual basis for forming an opinion. The second is that the facts known to the speaker are not entirely inconsistent with the opinion expressed.

A lawyer cannot say that he or she is "good at corporate mergers and acquisitions" if the lawyer knows nothing about the subject. Nor can the lawyer make that claim if he or she has recently been held liable for malpractice based on widespread incompetence in the mergers and acquisition field.

*§ 5-4.2(a)(5)(C) State of Mind*

One's state of mind is a fact. A lawyer either does, or does not, intend to do what the lawyer states an intention of doing. It is sometimes difficult to prove that intentions were misrepresented. However, in the Digital Age, e-mails, tweets, and postings on social networking sites may provide compelling evidence about the defendant's state of mind.

---

[64] 239 F.3d 415, 422–24 (2d Cir. 2000).

[65] The court found that Dorfman admitted making the following misrepresentations:

1. "[H]e opened his own 'practice' not in 1991, as he represented to Baker, but only one month before he met Baker in 1994. * * *Prior to that time, Dorfman had done per diem work involving one appellate argument, and a handful of guardianship trials without a jury."

2. "[T]he first jury he had selected was that which heard this case against him."

3. "[H]e was not even admitted to practice law until 1992."

4. "[A]t the time he gave his resume to Baker in 1994, he was not a member of the New Jersey or Massachusetts bars despite having passed the bar exam in each of those states."

5. "[A]s of 1994, he had not yet represented a single 'health care organization as their attorney.' "

6. "[He] had not 'created' the [LL.M.] in Health Care Law at NYU, but instead had met with the dean and designed his own individual course of study."

7. "[H]e still has not completed his studies to receive the LL.M. degree from NYU."

8. "[H]e had not actually taught a course at NYU, but was a tutor."

9. "[H]e had not done any work at all for private companies concerning the Americans with Disabilities Act. . . ."

10. "[T]he 'public company' for which he had done per diem work was the Department of Juvenile Justice. . . ."

11. "[H]e had not done any work in the area of 'labor relations'. . . ."

12. "[T]he 'particularly difficult or important' cases for which he had served as 'special litigation counsel' were landlord-tenant cases that he did on a per diem basis. . . ."

13. "[A]ll of the other cases referenced in his resume were cases in which he acted on a per diem basis hired by counsel."

*Id.* at 424. The Second Circuit concluded that "Dorfman knowingly and with intent to deceive made numerous material misrepresentations concerning his experience and expertise." *Id.*

A knowingly false assertion of one's intent is actionable as fraud. For example, in *Graubard Mollen Dannett & Horowitz v. Moskovitz*,[66] a partner in a law firm orally represented that he planned to "act to ensure the future of the firm."[67] The New York Court of Appeals held that the law firm stated a claim for fraud by alleging the partner never intended to protect the firm's interests.

Similarly, in *Charnay v. Cobert*,[68] a California appellate court ruled that a client adequately pleaded claims for fraud and negligent misrepresentation by alleging that her lawyer falsely told her that she need not be concerned about escalating costs because she would recover those costs at the end of the litigation. The client argued, in part, that the lawyer made these representations despite the fact that he did not believe them.

*§ 5-4.2(a)(5)(D) Statements of Law*

Statements about what the law is, or about what is or is not legal, are sometimes treated as statements of opinion which cannot form the basis for liability. In these cases, the conclusion that the statement is not actionable usually rests on one of two contradictory rationales. On the one hand, it is said that the law is so complex that any assertion about it is a mere opinion, which no one would be justified relying upon. On the other hand, it is said that everyone is presumed to know the law, so no one could be misled by a statement about what the law is or requires.

The rule that a statement of law is not a sufficient predicate for a tort action is subject to several exceptions. First, it is reasonable for clients to rely on what their lawyers tell them. Therefore, if the other elements of fraud are met, a lawyer will rarely escape liability to a client on the ground that a statement about the law was not a misrepresentation of fact.

Second, it is sometimes reasonable and appropriate for even nonclients to rely upon a lawyer's statements. Thus, if a statement of law is uttered as an assertion of fact, it may be relied upon by the recipient, even though there is no attorney-client relationship.

For example, in *National Conversion Corp. v. Cedar Building Corp.*,[69] a document contained a false representation that the leased premises were not subject to restrictions imposed by the zoning laws. Further, the lessor dissuaded the lessee from adjourning the negotiations to verify that fact by stating unequivocally, "[we] own the property, * * * we know the area * * *, we guarantee it."[70] The New York Court of Appeals held that it would be unfair not to allow reliance on that assurance. Presumably, the result would have been the same if the statements had been made, not by the lessor, but by the lessor's lawyer. As the *Restatement (Second) of Torts* explains:

> [A] layman who asks the opinion of a lawyer on a point of law may assume that he has special knowledge of the law, and is entitled to an honest opinion from him. The layman may justifiably rely on the lawyer's opinion even though he

---

[66] 653 N.E.2d 1179 (N.Y. 1995).

[67] *Id.* at 1184.

[68] 51 Cal. Rptr. 3d 471 (Ct. App. 2006).

[69] 298 N.Y.S.2d 499 (N.Y. 1969).

[70] *Id.* at 354.

knows that the lawyer is representing a client whose interest is adverse to his own. He may, in other words, reasonably assume professional honesty.[71]

Third, a statement of law may carry with it implicit statements of fact. If a lawyer for the seller asserts that a certain property complies with building code requirements, that may be regarded as a factual assurance that the building contains a certain type of electrical wiring or plumbing.

### *§ 5-4.2(a)(6) Justifiable Reliance*

A misrepresentation will form the basis of tort liability only if it causes damages. This means, among other things, that the plaintiff must have learned of the misrepresentation and relied upon it.

#### *§ 5-4.2(a)(6)(A) Statements Known to Be False*

A person who learns that a statement is false before incurring detrimental reliance cannot recover on a fraud claim. Stated differently, if the recipient knows a statement is false, his or her best and only remedy under tort law is self-help. The recipient must forbear reliance, rather than burden the courts with a request for redress.

#### *§ 5-4.2(a)(6)(B) Danger Signals*

If there are danger signals that would place a reasonable person on notice that a statement is untrustworthy, reliance on the statement is ordinarily not justified. Rather than rely, the recipient of the statement must conduct whatever investigation is appropriate to protect his or her interests. Failure to do so bars an action for fraud.

Moreover, if a person makes an investigation of the facts, a potential fraud defendant is sure to argue (sometimes with success) that any harm that thereafter occurs was caused not by reliance on the initial misrepresentation, but by reliance on what was learned during the plaintiff's inquiry into the facts.

However, the presence of a danger signal will sometimes be disregarded. First, if the plaintiff suffers from a mental disability, the law usually will not fault the plaintiff for having failed to make an investigation that a reasonable person would have made. Second, clients are expected to trust their lawyers. Therefore, a client's failure to investigate may be more easily excused than similar conduct by a nonclient. Third, if the results of a diligent investigation are inconclusive, a plaintiff may be allowed to argue that subsequent conduct, and resulting harm, was caused, at least in part, by justifiable reliance on the defendant's earlier statements.

#### *§ 5-4.2(a)(6)(C) Failure to Doubt*

In the absence of danger signals, there is no general duty to doubt the truthfulness of a person's affirmative statement. Thus, a positive utterance may be accepted at face value.

In *Media General, Inc. v. Tomlin*,[72] there was evidence to support a jury finding that, when the purchaser of a business inquired about contingent liabilities, the seller's law firm said that a suit by a terminated employee sought only $139,000 in damages,

---

[71] RESTATEMENT (SECOND) OF TORTS § 545 cmt. d (American Law Institute, 1977) (discussing misrepresentation of law).

[72] 532 F.3d 854, 858–59 (D.C. Cir. 2008).

even though the seller had received a draft complaint in which the former employee asked for $6 million. The district court found that it was unreasonable for the purchaser to rely on the alleged misrepresentation of the magnitude of the claim because the purchaser, which was aware of a pending audit of the seller, could have asked to see the seller's letter to its auditor, which fully described the threatened litigation. Rejecting this line of analysis, the D.C. Circuit found that the purchaser was not required to make such a request to see if the seller was lying.

*§ 5-4.2(a)(6)(D) Contractual Disclaimers of Reliance*

Contracts sometimes contain language stating that one party has not relied on any statements by the other. This type of provision may preclude proof of detrimental reliance in a fraud action. However, many courts take the position that a contractual disclaimer of reliance is only one factor to consider in determining whether justifiable reliance occurred.[73]

### *§ 5-4.2(a)(7) Intent to Induce Reliance*

A misrepresentation is actionable only if it is meant to be known by the plaintiff and to induce reliance, or if reliance should reasonably be expected. For example, in *Banco Popular North America v. Gandi*,[74] the Supreme Court of New Jersey found that a lawyer was not liable for assisting a client with a fraudulent transaction because the transaction was intended to be carried out without the plaintiff's knowledge, the lawyer did not expect reliance, and no reliance, in fact, ensued.

### *§ 5-4.2(a)(8) Resulting Damages*

In the typical fraud case, an award of compensatory damages is mainly concerned with economic losses, which are commonly measured in either of two ways. Under the "contract rule," also known as the "benefit of the bargain rule," the plaintiff may recover the difference between the value of what the plaintiff was promised and the value of what was received. Under the "tort rule" or "out of pocket rule," the plaintiff recovers the difference between what the plaintiff paid and the value of what the plaintiff received.

For example, suppose that a piece of property would have been worth $200,000 if the plaintiff received what was bargained for. However, because the facts were misrepresented, the property was worth only $100,000. If the plaintiff paid $130,000 for the property, the plaintiff could recover $100,000 under the "benefit of the bargain rule," but only $30,000 under the "out of pocket rule."

Courts typically have discretion to determine which measure of damages—either the "benefit of the bargain rule" or "out of pocket rule"—applies to a particular case. Of course, the "benefit of the bargain rule" is applicable in a fraud action only if there was a contract between the parties, and only if the plaintiff can prove with reasonable certainty the value of the bargain.

Many misrepresentations relate to real property. Sometimes there are conflicting estimates as to what property would have been worth absent a misrepresentation, but clear evidence as to both what the plaintiff paid and what the plaintiff received when

---

[73] *See generally* Robert K. Wise *et al.*, *Of Lies and Disclaimers—Contracting Around Fraud*, 41 ST. MARY'S L.J. 119 (2009).

[74] 876 A.2d 253, 261–66 (N.J. 2005).

the property was resold. In that case, it may be easier to prove "out of pocket" losses with reasonable certainty, than to prove the value of the lost bargain.

#### *§ 5-4.2(a)(9) Liability for Aiding and Abetting Fraud*

Lawyers may be liable not only for committing fraud, but for aiding and abetting the fraudulent conduct of others. For example, in *Oster v. Kirschner*,[75] a law firm drafted the private placement memorandum whereby its client perpetrated a $22 million fraud on investors. In an action against the law firm, a New York appellate court concluded that "[a] plaintiff alleging an aiding-and-abetting fraud claim must allege the existence of the underlying fraud, actual knowledge, and substantial assistance."[76] On the facts of the case, the court found that these elements were adequately pleaded based on circumstantial evidence.

## § 5-4.3 NEGLIGENT MISREPRESENTATION

Numerous states recognize a cause of action for negligent misrepresentation. This theory of liability is a well-established exception to the "economic loss rule," which holds that, in some circumstances, negligence that causes purely economic losses is not actionable under tort law.[77]

Negligent misrepresentation shares many of the doctrinal features of the law of fraud. For example, the principles that govern liability for half-truths and statements of opinion in suits for fraud also generally apply to claims alleging negligent misrepresentation.

Similarly, a plaintiff suing for negligent misrepresentation must prove justifiable reliance. For example, in *Breen v. Law Office of Bruce A. Barket, P.C.*,[78] a deed was incorrectly drawn by a husband's attorney in a divorce action. A New York appellate court concluded that the husband's wife could not state a claim for negligent misrepresentation because she could not prove justifiable reliance. The facts established that the wife discovered the error, brought it to her lawyer's attention, and was advised by her lawyer to nevertheless sign the incorrect deed.

However, negligent misrepresentation differs from fraud in two key respects. First, negligent misrepresentation permits recovery of damages based on a less demanding showing of culpability than is required in fraud actions. What is needed is mere negligence as to the falsity of the misleading statement, rather than knowledge of falsity or reckless disregard for its truth. Second, negligent misrepresentation typically restricts the scope of liability more tightly than the law of fraud.

Note also that some (but not all) courts hold that a negligent misrepresentation action cannot be based on silence, and requires proof of an affirmative misstatement.[79] Further, a claim for negligent misrepresentation, unlike fraud, is subject to defenses based on the plaintiff's failure to exercise care (i.e., contributory negligence, comparative

---

[75] 2010 WL 2650532 (N.Y. App. Div.).

[76] *Id.* at *3.

[77] *See* Vincent R. Johnson, *The Boundary-Line Function of the Economic Loss Rule*, 66 WASH. & LEE L. REV. 523, 530 (2009).

[78] 862 N.Y.S.2d 50 (App. Div. 2008).

[79] *See infra* § 5-4.3(c).

negligence, or comparative fault, depending on the law of the state).[80] These various topics are discussed below.

The absence of a lawyer-client relationship is generally not an obstacle to a suit for negligent misrepresentation.[81] Therefore, this cause of action is an important weapon in the litigation arsenal of nonclients.

### § 5-4.3(a) *Restatement (Second) of Torts* § 552

The most common point of reference in the law of negligent misrepresentation is § 552 of the *Restatement (Second) of Torts*.[82] This section has been so widely endorsed and influential that, unlike most *Restatement* provisions, it is commonly referred to by number. Section 552 provides:

> One who, in the course of his business, profession or employment, or in any other transaction in which he has a pecuniary interest, supplies false information for the guidance of others in their business transactions, is subject to liability for pecuniary loss caused to them by their justifiable reliance upon the information, if he fails to exercise reasonable care or competence in obtaining or communicating the information.[83]

In *Banco Popular North America v. Gandi*,[84] a lawyer made false statements while negotiating the terms of a loan guarantee on behalf of a client, and in issuing a related opinion letter to a bank which stated, "[a]fter due investigation, we are unaware of any material matters contrary to the representations and warranties of the Borrower or the Guarantor contained in the Loan Documents."[85] Noting that the lawyer knew the true state of the financial affairs of his client because he was the architect of the client's divestiture of assets, the Supreme Court of New Jersey held that the bank properly alleged claims against the lawyer for fraud and negligent misrepresentation.

Some courts strictly interpret the language of § 552 so as to make it inapplicable to claims by certain nonclients. In *Allen v. Steele*,[86] the Supreme Court of Colorado wrote:

> [A] "business transaction" in the context of negligent misrepresentation means exactly what common understanding of the term implies: to state a claim of negligent misrepresentation, the misrepresentation must be given for the plaintiff's business or commercial purposes. Although a negligence lawsuit against another party has the potential to affect indirectly a non-client's financial or economic interests, a civil lawsuit does not involve a business or commercial relationship or transaction. Hence, we hold as a matter of law that an initial consultation to discuss a potential civil lawsuit is not sufficient to meet the element of "guidance of others in their business transactions."[87]

---

[80] *See infra* § 5-6.2(a).

[81] *See* RESTATEMENT (THIRD) OF THE LAW GOVERNING LAWYERS § 51(2) (American Law Institute, 2000).

[82] RESTATEMENT (SECOND) OF TORTS § 552(1) (American Law Institute, 1977); *see also* RESTATEMENT (THIRD) OF TORTS: LIABILITY FOR ECONOMIC HARM § 5 (American Law Institute, Tent. Draft No. 1, 2012).

[83] *Id.*

[84] 876 A.2d 253 (N.J. 2005).

[85] *Id.* at 267.

[86] 252 P.3d 476 (Colo. 2011).

[87] *Id.* at 484.

#### *§ 5-4.3(a)(1) Relationship to Voluntary Assumption of Duty*

In some respects, tort liability for negligent misrepresentation is merely a specific application of well-established tort principles governing liability for mis-performance of a voluntarily assumed duty. In *Taylor v. Riley*,[88] the issue was whether a lawyer who, as corporate counsel, issued an opinion letter stating that a stock redemption agreement did not violate the law could be held liable to a shareholder if the opinion was incorrect. The Supreme Court of Idaho concluded that, "[i]f one voluntarily undertakes to perform an act, having no prior duty to do so, the duty arises to perform the act in a non-negligent manner."[89] The court found that "[t]here is no reason why . . . [this] rule should not apply to attorneys," and that the defendant voluntarily undertook a duty of care to the plaintiff by stating in a letter, "[t]his opinion is furnished by us solely for your benefit for use in connection with the Transaction Documents and the transactions contemplated thereby; and it may not be furnished or quoted to, or relied upon, by any other person."[90]

### § 5-4.3(b) Limits on the Scope of Liability for Misrepresentation

The scope of potential liability to nonclients is more tightly circumscribed for negligent misrepresentation than for fraud. This is true because when culpability is slight (*i.e.*, when falsity is negligent, rather than intentional or reckless), imposition of broad exposure to damages would more easily offend the principle that liability should be proportional to fault. Proportionality is a fundamental policy in modern American tort law.

The rules which courts have endorsed for limiting the scope of liability for fraud differ from those which apply to negligent misrepresentation actions. The applicable legal principles are discussed below.

#### *§ 5-4.3(b)(1) Scope of Liability for Fraud*

The *Restatement* says that liability for fraud extends to persons whom the defendant "intends or has reason to expect to act or to refrain from action in reliance upon the misrepresentation."[91] To address liability issues related to indirectly disseminated fraudulent statements, the *Restatement* articulates two special rules related to commercial documents and public filings, as well as a general rule which purports to require something more than foreseeability of reliance. The following sections explore these topics.

##### *§ 5-4.3(b)(1)(A) Commercial Documents*

The *Restatement (Second) of Torts* contains a provision dealing with written misrepresentations incorporated into commercial documents. Section 532 provides, "[o]ne who embodies a fraudulent misrepresentation in an article of commerce, a muniment of title, a negotiable instrument or a similar commercial document, is subject to liability for pecuniary loss caused to another who deals with him or with a third person regarding the article or document in justifiable reliance upon the truth of the representation."[92] This *Restatement* rule is "limited to those documents or chattels that

---

[88] 336 P.3d 256, 261 (Idaho 2014).

[89] *Id.* at 272.

[90] *Id.*

[91] RESTATEMENT (SECOND) OF TORTS § 531 (American Law Institute, 1977).

[92] RESTATEMENT (SECOND) OF TORTS § 532 (American Law Institute, 1977).

are in themselves articles of commerce," and thus "does not apply to an ordinary letter misrepresenting the title to land or to a report furnished by an accountant to a corporation concerning its finances, because these documents are not to be expected to have commercial circulation."[93] An "article of commerce" is something that is offered for sale and which has a value and existence independent of the parties. Examples listed in the *Restatement* include deeds, bonds, promissory notes, and merchandise containers.

The Maryland Court of Appeals followed the *Restatement* rule in *Diamond Point Plaza Ltd. Partnership v. Wells Fargo Bank, N.A.*,[94] a case involving loan documents that were likely to be resold on the secondary market. The court concluded that a claim for fraud was not defeated by the fact that the defendant had not made the representations directly to the plaintiff.

*§ 5-4.3(b)(1)(B) Public Filings*

An action for fraud may sometimes be based on false statements contained in a public filing, if the plaintiff is a member of the class the information is intended to protect.[95] Thus, reports made by corporations required to publicly disclose their financial positions may usually be relied upon by persons making deposits or investments, as well as by those lending money to the entities in question.[96]

In some states, oil and gas well operators are required to report information to a state commission, which is then available to others doing business in the same field. If such filings contain fraudulent statements, they may be actionable by persons who suffer harm in reliance on those misrepresentations.[97]

*§ 5-4.3(b)(1)(C) Special Reason to Expect Reliance*

The official commentary to the *Restatement's* basic rule on "expectation of influencing conduct" states that a general risk of reliance—the type of risk that is inherent in virtually every misrepresentation—is an insufficient predicate for liability. Thus:

> The maker of the misrepresentation must have information that would lead a reasonable man to conclude that there is an especial likelihood that it will reach those persons and will influence their conduct * * *.[98]

Some courts have gone to great lengths to indicate that merely foreseeable reliance is an insufficient basis for a fraud action. These authorities hold that a special reason to expect reliance is necessary even in cases involving misrepresentations in documents intended for commercial circulation or in publicly filed reports.

For example, after the Enron corporation collapsed, investors sued the investment professionals who had deliberately disseminated false information to the public for the purpose of hiding the deteriorating financial condition of the company. A federal court

---

93 *Id.*

94 929 A.2d 932 (Md. 2007).

95 RESTATEMENT (SECOND) OF TORTS § 536 (American Law Institute, 1977).

96 *Id.* at § 536 cmt. e.

97 *Cf.* NationsBank of Texas, N.A. v. Akin, Gump, Hauer & Feld, L.L.P., 979 S.W.2d 385, 389–90 (Tex. App. 1998).

98 RESTATEMENT (SECOND) OF TORTS § 531 cmt. d (American Law Institute, 1977).

in Texas held that those widely disseminated fraudulent statements were not actionable. As the court explained:

> [T]o establish fraudulent intent, Plaintiffs must allege and show more than that information was available in the investment community, pursuant to industry custom, and that it was foreseeable that it would reach them; Plaintiffs must show that Plaintiffs' "reliance must be 'especially likely' and justifiable, and that the transaction sued upon must be the type the defendant contemplated."[99]

The court found that these standards were not satisfied even though the principal defendant, Merrill Lynch, had allegedly "cooked the books" by devising fraudulent transactions to mislead investors and rating agencies and had "issued through its analysts, even as Enron was descending into bankruptcy * * *, 'buy' or 'strong buy' recommendations for Enron securities, which Merrill Lynch knew would be 'widely disseminated in the financial news media.' "[100]

The wisdom of decisions like *Enron* is open to question. Why should professionals who deliberately deceive large groups of potential investors not be held liable for the losses suffered by those who are misled?[101]

### *§ 5-4.3(b)(2) Scope of Liability for Negligent Misrepresentation*

In contrast to the rules governing liability for fraud (discussed above), states adhere to one of two positions regarding the scope of liability for negligent misrepresentation. These limits on liability are often referred to as: (1) the "near privity" view and (2) the "limited group" view.

These views are important in the law of legal malpractice only with respect to claims by nonclients. Clients are owed duties of care by their lawyers under generally applicable principles of negligence law. Therefore, clients can sue their lawyers for harm caused by negligently false statements, as well as for losses caused by other forms of negligence. Lack of privity is not a problem.

In contrast, lawyers have no general obligation to exercise care to protect nonclients from harm. Liability to nonclients for negligent misrepresentation is therefore a special rule which imposes a limited duty on lawyers to exercise care to protect the pecuniary interests of nonclients. The two views, mentioned above, determine how far that limited duty of care extends. Some nonclients are beyond the scope of the obligations imposed by the law of negligent misrepresentation even if they rely on negligently false information and suffer damages.

#### *§ 5-4.3(b)(2)(A) The "Near Privity" View*

New York and a number of other states adhere to the "near privity" view on liability to persons not party to a contract with the negligent misrepresentation defendant. This view greatly limits the liability of lawyers and other professionals to persons who have not employed them. Under this type of rule, a person who has never dealt with a lawyer

---

[99] In re Enron Corporation Securities, Derivative & "ERISA" Litigation, 490 F. Supp. 2d 784, 824 (S.D. Tex. 2007).

[100] *Id.* at 787.

[101] *See* Andrew R. Simank, Comment, *Deliberately Defrauding Investors: The Scope of Liability*, 42 ST. MARY'S L.J. 253 (2010).

generally cannot sue for negligent misrepresentation, regardless of whether reliance was foreseeable.

In *Credit Alliance Corp. v. Arthur Andersen & Co.*,[102] the New York Court of Appeals explained its variation of the "near privity" view. *Credit Alliance* involved the appeals of two cases against auditors. In one case, audited financial statements had been passed indirectly to the plaintiff by the audited party. The court held there was no liability. In the other case, the auditors had frequently been in direct communication with the plaintiff. On those facts, the court held that the plaintiff could sue for negligent misrepresentation. According to the court, auditors are liable for negligent preparation of financial reports only to persons who are in privity of contract with them, or to persons whose relationship with the auditors is "so close as to approach that of privity."[103] As Judge Matthew Jasen explained:

> Before accountants may be held liable in negligence to noncontractual parties who rely to their detriment on inaccurate financial reports, certain prerequisites must be satisfied: (1) the accountants must have been aware that the financial reports were to be used for a particular purpose or purposes; (2) in the furtherance of which a known party or parties was intended to rely; and (3) there must have been some conduct on the part of the accountants linking them to that party or parties, which evinces the accountants' understanding of that party or parties' reliance.[104]

The third requirement stated above was satisfied in the second appeal because the negligently false statement was directly transmitted by the defendant to the plaintiff.

In the legal malpractice context, suppose that a corporation hires a lawyer to draft an opinion letter about the tax treatment of an investment the corporation is offering to investors. If that letter is distributed by the corporation to unknown persons who rely upon its statements, those persons will not be able to successfully sue the lawyer for negligent misrepresentation in a state with a "near privity" requirement. This is true even if the lawyer's statements were negligently false.

*§ 5-4.3(b)(2)(B) The Restatement's "Limited Group" View*

The *Restatement* view on liability to third persons for negligent misrepresentation causing purely economic losses is less demanding than the "near privity" approach.[105] According to the *Restatement*, liability for negligent misrepresentation extends only to "the person or one of a limited group of persons for whose benefit and guidance * * * [the defendant] intends to supply the information or knows that the recipient intends to supply it."[106] Moreover, under the *Restatement* rule, there is liability only where the

---

102 493 N.Y.S.2d 435 (N.Y. 1985).

103 *Id.* at 440.

104 *Id.* at 443.

105 *See* Great American E & S Ins. Co. v. Quintairos, Prieto, Wood & Boyer, P.A., 100 So.3d 420, 428 (Miss. 2012) ("In Touche Ross & Co. [v. Commercial Union Ins. Co., 514 So.2d 315 (Miss.1987)], this Court implicitly adopted the *Restatement of Torts* view of professional duty and held that an independent auditor can be held liable to "reasonably foreseeable users of the audit, who request and receive a financial statement from the audited entity for a proper business purpose, and who then detrimentally rely on the financial statement, suffering a loss, proximately caused by the auditors' negligence").

106 RESTATEMENT (SECOND) OF TORTS § 552 (American Law Institute, 1977).

reliance takes place in a transaction substantially similar to the one the defendant intended to influence or knew the recipient intended to influence.

While it is not essential that the maker of the statement know the identity of the person for whose guidance the information is supplied, it "may be vitally important" that he be aware of the "number and character of the persons to be reached and influenced, and the nature and extent of the transaction for which guidance is furnished," because those factors define the "risk of liability to which the supplier subjects himself by undertaking to give the information."[107] This requirement ensures that liability is not only based on fault, but limited in proportion to fault. Unless the defendant has access to the facts which indicate the magnitude of the harm that might result from mere negligence, and thus has the opportunity and incentive to exercise an appropriate degree of care, it is unfair to impose liability for resulting losses.

*§ 5-4.3(b)(2)(C) Summary*

In many cases, it makes a great difference to plaintiffs and defendants which view a jurisdiction follows with respect to the scope of liability for negligent misrepresentation. Unless there has been direct communication between a lawyer and a nonclient, or other conduct which evinces the lawyer's understanding of the nonclient's reliance, there is no liability for negligent misrepresentation under the "near privity" view. And, unless the nonclient was a member of a limited group who was intended to be benefitted by the representation, and unless the reliance occurred in the type and magnitude of transaction of which the defendant had been apprised, there is no liability under the *Restatement* view.

The limitations applicable to negligent misrepresentation do not apply to an action for fraud. As discussed earlier, fraud has its own demanding requirements. Nevertheless, it is generally much easier for a nonclient to recover for fraud than for negligent misrepresentation. Consequently, whether the plaintiff can obtain compensation for purely economic losses often depends upon whether the plaintiff can prove that the defendant acted with *scienter* (knowledge of falsity or reckless disregard for the truth[108]) and was not simply negligent. Even if the plaintiff proves that the defendant acted with careless falsity, an action for negligent misrepresentation may fail because the plaintiff was not within the scope of liability.

## § 5-4.3(c) Negligent Misrepresentation Based on Silence

There is an issue, not definitively resolved, as to whether an action for misrepresentation requires proof of an affirmative misstatement, as opposed to misleading silence. Some cases have held that silence is not a sufficient predicate for a negligent misrepresentation action.[109] Others hold that silence is actionable under the law of negligent misrepresentation if there is a duty to speak. Thus, in *In re Agrobiotech, Inc.*,[110] a federal court in Nevada found that "silence about material facts basic to the transaction, when combined with a duty to speak, is the functional equivalent of a [negligent] misrepresentation * * *."[111]

---

[107] *Id.* § 552 cmt. h.

[108] *See* § 5-4.2(a)(3).

[109] *See* Eberts v. Goderstad, 569 F.3d 757, 765–66 (7th Cir. 2009).

[110] 291 F. Supp. 2d 1186 (D. Nev. 2003).

[111] *Id.* at 1192.

In thinking about this issue, it may be useful to draw a distinction based on whether the plaintiff is a client or a nonclient. In some cases, whether there is a duty to disclose may depend upon the fact that the plaintiff is a client to whom fiduciary duties are owed. In contrast, those same obligations are not owed to a nonclient. Of course, some rules imposing a duty to speak are not rooted in fiduciary obligations. If the facts of the case fall within those rules, it is harder to argue that a negligent nondisclosure, even to a nonclient, is outside the range of legal liability.

### § 5-4.3(d) Plaintiff's Negligence as a Defense

Because negligent misrepresentation is merely a special kind of negligence, defenses that can be raised in any negligence action may be pleaded and proved by the defendant. Carelessness on the part of the plaintiff, which contributes to the harm for which recovery is sought, is a total or partial defense, depending on whether the state adheres to principles of traditional contributory negligence, comparative negligence, or comparative fault.[112]

In a case not involving legal malpractice, *Staggs v. Sells*,[113] the defendants' agent had incorrectly represented that a residential property was not prone to flooding. The court allowed the buyers to recover for negligent misrepresentation, but reduced the damages by 40% because the buyers had neglected to follow their appraiser's advice to have the property surveyed for the risk of this type of damage.

## § 5-4.4 DECEPTIVE TRADE PRACTICES ACTS

Every state has adopted a deceptive trade practices act (DTPA). These laws supplement the common law remedies afforded by the actions for fraud and negligent misrepresentation. In many cases, the terms of the state DTPA provide an easier or better path to recovery by relaxing or dispensing with requirements of the parallel tort actions or offering more generous compensation. Victims of deception in the field of legal services frequently allege claims for fraud, negligent misrepresentation, and violation of the DTPA as separate counts in a single malpractice action.

However, any statutory action for damages has limits. This is particularly true of DTPA laws because "reformers" in many states have lobbied successfully to restrict DTPA remedies. Consequently, the common law actions for fraud and negligent misrepresentation remain useful.

### § 5-4.4(a) Applicability to Lawyers

Some states make it difficult or impossible to sue lawyers under DTPA laws. For example, in Texas, it is hard for corporate plaintiffs to state a DTPA claim in cases involving large potential damages. The state's DTPA law does not "apply to a cause of action arising from a transaction, a project, or a set of transactions relating to the same project, involving total consideration by the consumer of more than $500,000 * * *."[114]

In addition, the Texas DTPA does not apply to "a claim for damages based on the rendering of a professional service, the essence of which is the providing of advice, judgment, opinion, or similar professional skill," unless there was: "an express

---

112 *See infra* § 5-6.2(a).

113 86 S.W.3d 219 (Tenn. Ct. App. 2001).

114 TEX. BUS. & COM. CODE § 17.49(g) (Westlaw 2017).

misrepresentation of a material fact" that cannot be characterized as advice, judgment, or opinion; a failure to disclose certain types of information intended to induce a consumer to participate in a transaction; an "unconscionable action or course of action that cannot be characterized as advice, judgment, or opinion"; or a "breach of an express warranty that cannot be characterized as advice, judgment, or opinion."[115]

In *United Genesis Corp. v. Brown*,[116] a lawyer prepared closing documents and conducted a lien search using a name for the seller of a restaurant that was provided to the lawyer by a real estate agent. The name was wrong, and therefore the search failed to reveal outstanding liens against the restaurant's equipment. The court held that the buyer could not state a claim against the lawyer under the Texas Deceptive Trade Practices Act. The lawyer's conduct consisted of omissions (*e.g.*, the failure to independently ensure the identity of the seller and that the seller owned the property), not express misrepresentations. Moreover, the court found that the misrepresentation of fact with regard to the ownership of the business was a misrepresentation by the real estate agency, not by the lawyer.

Garden-variety malpractice is not actionable under the Connecticut Unfair Trade Practices Act. "CUTPA covers only the entrepreneurial or commercial aspects of the profession of law."[117] Thus, a claim that a law firm failed to supervise a lawyer who misappropriated client funds was not actionable under the Connecticut statute because it did not involve the entrepreneurial or business aspects of the provision of legal services.[118]

However, in *Yelin v. Swartz*,[119] a federal court held that even though Pennsylvania's Unfair Trade Practices and Consumer Protection Law did not apply to attorneys engaged in the practice of law, a consumer stated a claim under that act against a lawyer and his law firm because the consumer, who was not a client of the firm, only challenged the defendants' debt-collection practices, not the adequacy of their legal representation of a client.

## § 5-4.4(b) Advantages over Common Law

DTPA laws typically require a showing of deception based on fault. However, the level of culpability that is required may be less demanding than what would be needed in a parallel tort action.

A DTPA action is sometimes subject to a relaxed causation requirement which obviates the need for a "trial within a trial," and may permit recovery of emotional distress damages that would not normally be recoverable under some common law theories of liability.[120]

Of great importance is the fact that DTPA laws often allow recovery of multiple damages (*e.g.*, treble damages to deter unconscionable conduct) and attorney's fees.

---

[115] *Id.* at § 17.49(c).

[116] 2007 WL 1341358 (Tex. App. 2007).

[117] Haynes v. Yale-New Haven Hosp., 699 A.2d 964, 973 (Conn. 1997).

[118] *See* Vanacore v. Kennedy, 86 F. Supp. 2d 42, 52 (D. Conn. 1998), *aff'd,* 208 F.3d 204 (2d Cir. 2000).

[119] 790 F. Supp. 2d 331 (E.D. Pa. 2011).

[120] *See* Latham v. Castillo, 972 S.W.2d 66 (Tex. 1998).

### § 5-4.4(c) DTPA Suits by Nonclients

It is sometimes difficult or impossible for a nonclient to state a DTPA claim because such laws typically require a plaintiff to prove that he or she was a "consumer" of legal services. However, occasional decisions have allowed recovery by persons for whom legal services were purchased by someone else.[121]

## § 5-4.5 CLAIMS BASED ON REPRESENTATION OF FIDUCIARIES

According to the *Restatement*, a lawyer is liable to a nonclient for negligence if:

(a) the lawyer's client is a trustee, guardian, executor, or fiduciary acting primarily to perform similar functions for the nonclient;

(b) the lawyer knows that appropriate action by the lawyer is necessary with respect to a matter within the scope of the representation to prevent or rectify the breach of a fiduciary duty owed by the client to the nonclient, where (i) the breach is a crime or fraud or (ii) the lawyer has assisted or is assisting the breach;

(c) the nonclient is not reasonably able to protect its rights; and

(d) such a duty would not significantly impair the performance of the lawyer's obligations to the client.[122]

Thus, if a lawyer is representing a trustee and knows that the trustee intends to embezzle trust assets, the lawyer has a duty to the beneficiary to take reasonable steps to prevent that harm from occurring.[123] However, since this form of liability is negligence-based, some courts hold that a duty of care arises not only where the lawyer knows of the fiduciary's wrongdoing, but also where the lawyer should know of the wrongdoing.[124]

## § 5-4.6 FUNDS AND PROPERTY OF NONCLIENTS

There is a well-known rule of professional conduct which recognizes that lawyers have ethical obligations to nonclients with respect to the handling or disbursement of funds or property in which nonclients have an interest. For example, Rule 1.15 of the Indiana Rules of Professional Conduct, which is identical in relevant part to Model Rule 1.15,[125] states that:

> (d) Upon receiving funds or other property in which a client or third person has an interest, a lawyer shall promptly notify the client or third person. Except as stated in this rule or otherwise permitted by law or by agreement with the client, a lawyer shall promptly deliver to the client or third person any funds or other property that the client or third person is entitled to receive and, upon

---

121 *Cf.* Perez v. Kirk & Carrigan, 822 S.W.2d 261, 268 (Tex. App. 1991).

122 In re Food Management Group, LLC, 380 B.R. 677, 708 (Bkrtcy. S.D.N.Y. 2008) (quoting *Restatement (Third) of the Law Governing Lawyers* § 51(4) (American Law Institute, 2000)).

123 *See* RESTATEMENT (THIRD) OF THE LAW GOVERNING LAWYERS § 51 illus. 5 (American Law Institute, 2000).

124 *See* Pederson v. Barnes, 139 P.3d 552, 554 (Alaska 2006) (holding that a guardian's lawyer was liable to the ward for the guardian's wrongdoing "only if the lawyer knew or had reason to know of the wrongdoing").

125 MODEL RULES OF PROF'L CONDUCT R. 1.15 (American Bar Ass'n, 2017).

request by the client or third person, shall promptly render a full accounting regarding such property.

(e) When in the course of representation a lawyer is in possession of property in which two or more persons (one of whom may be the lawyer) claim interests, the property shall be kept separate by the lawyer until the dispute is resolved. The lawyer shall promptly distribute all portions of the property as to which the interests are not in dispute.[126]

These types of state rules are enforceable in disciplinary proceedings. A violation may give rise to sanctions such as reprimand, suspension, or disbarment.

However, it is not surprising that nonclients have argued, sometimes with success, that the same professional obligations are legally enforceable, on some theory, in a civil action for damages.

In *Hsu v. Parker*,[127] a client who was injured in an auto accident executed a document entitled "Security Agreement for Medical Services," which granted a doctor "a security interest" in any and all proceeds from the client's pending personal injury action. The agreement authorized the client's lawyer, who had not prepared the assignment, "to withhold sufficient funds from any settlement, judgment, or verdict" that were due to the doctor and to pay such funds to the doctor. When the case was settled, the client instructed her lawyer to transfer all of the settlement proceeds to her and not to pay the doctor's medical fees. The Ohio Court of Appeals held that the lawyer acted improperly in following those instructions and ordered the lawyer to reimburse the doctor. However, the court did not specify the legal theory on which the lawyer was held responsible, other than to emphasize that the lawyer had knowledge of the assignment.

An attorney may be liable to a nonclient for the tort of conversion based on nonpayment of funds to which the nonclient is entitled. For example, in *Ellis v. City of Dallas*,[128] a lawyer (Ellis) represented an injured firefighter in a worker's compensation claim against the City and in a lawsuit against a third-party tortfeasor. The settlement check in the lawsuit was made payable to Ellis and his client, and Ellis knew that the City had a subrogation interest in those funds. There was some dispute about the amount to which the City was entitled, and whether the City had agreed to accept a lesser amount. However, the jury resolved those factual issues against the lawyer, and the Texas Court of Appeals affirmed a judgment holding Ellis liable for conversion based on the fact that he paid the City less than the value of its subrogation claim.

In *Smith v. Patout*,[129] a Louisiana appellate court concluded that a lawyer had a duty to provide an accounting to the plaintiff regarding funds in which the plaintiff had an interest. This was true even if the plaintiff was not a client. Because there was a

---

[126] IND. CODE ANN. Tit. 34 App. Court Rules (Civil) (Westlaw 2017); *see also* Vincent R. Johnson, *The Limited Duties of Lawyers to Protect the Funds and Property of Nonclients*, 8 ST. MARY'S J. LEGAL MAL. & ETHICS 58, 58 (2017) ("[L]awyers are obliged to protect the property interests of third persons only if they possess a 'matured legal or equitable interest' in the specific funds or property held by the lawyer. To be entitled to protection * * * a third person must be known by the lawyer to hold an interest in the relevant funds or property by way of assignment, lien, court order, judgment, statute, or letter of protection. Anything less normally will not suffice").

[127] 688 N.E.2d 1099 (Ohio Ct. App. 1996).

[128] 111 S.W.3d 161 (Tex. App. 2003).

[129] 956 So.2d 689 (La. Ct. App. 2007).

factual dispute as to whether such an accounting had occurred, the court concluded that summary judgment could not be granted to the defendant-lawyer.

In *Meisels v. Fox Rothschild, LLP*,[130] a law firm followed the instructions of its American client to disburse funds allegedly belonging to the client's London partner to entities unrelated to their planned investment. The London partner sued the law firm for aiding and abetting the American client by knowingly permitting its trust account to be used for fraudulent purposes. The court found that a cause of action was stated.

## § 5-4.7 INTENDED BENEFICIARIES

Nonclients can sometimes prevail in a malpractice action because they were intended third-party beneficiaries of a lawyer-client contract. The general rule is that a lawyer owes a duty of care to a nonclient when and to the extent that:

> (a) the lawyer knows that a client intends as one of the primary objectives of the representation that the lawyer's services benefit the nonclient;
>
> (b) such a duty would not significantly impair the lawyer's performance of obligations to the client; and
>
> (c) the absence of such a duty would make enforcement of those obligations to the client unlikely * * *.[131]

### § 5-4.7(a) Invalid Wills

A majority of courts allow the intended beneficiaries of a will to sue for harm suffered as a result of the negligent preparation of a will or otherwise negligently deficient estate planning. For example, in *Young v. Williams*,[132] a lawyer neglected to include provisions in a husband's will for distribution of real property. As a result, after the husband died, the real property was disbursed under the rules of intestate succession, and the surviving wife received only one-third of the real property, rather than all of it as the decedent had intended. Addressing applicable law, the Court of Appeals of Georgia wrote:

> [A]n attorney may owe a duty to a party who is not his client, but who is a third-party beneficiary to an agreement between the attorney and his client. For a third party to claim such a duty exists, it must clearly appear from the contract that it was intended for her benefit. The mere fact that the third party would benefit from performance of the agreement is not alone sufficient.[133]

Finding that it was clear that the decedent had hired the defendant-lawyer so that certain persons would inherit particular property upon his death, the court affirmed a judgment against the lawyer in favor of the surviving wife.

#### *§ 5-4.7(a)(1) Minority View*

On the facts of the case, the issue before the court in *Young* (discussed above) was not difficult. The defendant-lawyer admitted that the deceased husband had intended

---

[130] 2014 WL 7891590, at *1 (N.J. Super. Ct. App. Div.).

[131] Petrine v. Sinchak-Higby, 2009 WL 1530727, at *3 (Ariz. Ct. App.) (quoting *Restatement (Third) of the Law Governing Lawyers* § 51(3) (American Law Institute, 2000)).

[132] 285 Ga. App. 208, 645 S.E.2d 624 (2007).

[133] *Id.* at 625.

for the will to benefit the husband's wife in the amount that she claimed. The lawyer merely asserted (unsuccessfully) that the surviving wife could not sue him because there was no privity of contract between the wife and the lawyer. However, in many cases, the facts are less clear as to what the decedent intended. These types of uncertainties have caused a minority of courts to reject malpractice claims by estate beneficiaries.

For example, in *Barcelo v. Elliott*,[134] the Texas Supreme Court explained:

> In most cases where a defect renders a will or trust invalid, * * * there are concomitant questions as to the true intentions of the testator. Suppose, for example, that a properly drafted will is simply not executed at the time of the testator's death. The document may express the testator's true intentions, lacking signatures solely because of the attorney's negligent delay. On the other hand, the testator may have postponed execution because of second thoughts regarding the distribution scheme. * * *.
>
> * * * [Here, plaintiffs] contend that Elliott was negligent in failing to fund the trust during Barcelo's lifetime, and in failing to obtain a signature from the trustee. These alleged deficiencies, however, could have existed pursuant to Barcelo's instructions, which may have been based on advice from her attorneys attempting to represent her best interests. An attorney's ability to render such advice would be severely compromised if the advice could be second-guessed by persons named as beneficiaries under the unconsummated trust.[135]

Finding it impossible to "craft a bright-line rule that allows a lawsuit to proceed where alleged malpractice causes a will or trust to fail in a manner that casts no real doubt on the testator's intentions, while prohibiting actions in other situations," the Texas Supreme Court concluded that the greater good would be served by denying a cause of action to all beneficiaries whom the attorney did not represent.[136] Other courts have reached similar conclusions.[137]

However, the Pennsylvania Supreme Court found it possible to articulate a bright-line rule. In *Estate of Agnew v. Ross*,[138] the court wrote that "[t]o the extent the attorney has drafted testamentary documents, which have been fully executed by the testator, such documents are conclusive evidence the testator intended to benefit the named beneficiaries, * * * [but] individuals who are named only in unexecuted, consequently invalid documents * * * may not claim status as third-party beneficiaries of the legal contract between the testator and his attorney, and may not achieve a legacy through alternate means, such as a breach of contract action."[139]

### § 5-4.7(b) Insurers

An insurer who hires a lawyer to defend an insured, and who suffers losses as a result of the lawyer's negligence, is sometimes permitted to sue for malpractice on the

---

[134] 923 S.W.2d 575 (Tex. 1996).

[135] *Id.* at 578.

[136] *Id.*

[137] Baker v. Wood, Ris & Hames, P.C., 364 P.3d 872, 874 (Colo. 2016); Shoemaker v. Gindlesberger, 887 N.E.2d 1167, 1172 (Ohio 2008).

[138] 152 A.3d 247 (Pa. 2017).

[139] *Id.* at 264.

ground that the insurer was an intended beneficiary of the contract. As a federal court in West Virginia explained:

> Recognizing that the lawyer owes a duty to the insurer promotes enforcement of the lawyer's obligations to the insured. However, such a duty does not arise when it would significantly impair * * * the lawyer's performance of obligations to the insured. For example, if the lawyer recommends acceptance of a settlement offer just below the policy limits and the insurer accepts the offer, the insurer may not later seek to recover from the lawyer on a claim that a competent lawyer in the circumstances would have advised that the offer be rejected. * * *.[140]

Not all states agree that an insurer should be treated as an intended beneficiary of the lawyer-client contract. According to a federal court in Virginia:

> [While the] * * * courts of other jurisdictions generally recognize such a cause of action, they differ markedly on the theory of liability under which such a claim may be brought. In most jurisdictions, the retaining insurer may sue the law firm directly as its client. * * * [Some cases] reflect the view that a "tripartite relationship" exists among insurer, insured, and counsel, with both insurer and insured as co-clients of the firm in the absence of a conflict of interest. * * *. Some courts and the *Restatement* recognize an additional or substitute cause of action by the insurer as a non-client beneficiary of the firm's legal services. * * *. Some jurisdictions go one step further, however, and reject outright the idea of a duty owed by the firm to the insurer, contending that such a duty would compromise the law firm's loyalty to the insured. Although these rejecting jurisdictions thus preclude any direct legal malpractice liability from the firm to the insurer, they nevertheless permit the insurer to be subrogated to the insured and thus to sue the firm standing in the insured's shoes. Accordingly, despite sharp doctrinal differences regarding the relationship between the insurer and the firm it retains, nearly all jurisdictions in the United States permit some form of legal malpractice action by an insurer against the firm it retains to defend an insured.[141]

In *State & County Mutual Fire Ins. Co. v. Young*,[142] a lawyer hired to defend an insured failed to respond to discovery and dispositive motions. As a result, the insurer alleged that it was forced to settle the underlying claims for amounts in excess of their true value. The court held that since the insurer hired the lawyer, it could sue to recover its losses without any need to show additional evidence of a duty.

### § 5-4.7(c) Other Intended Beneficiaries

Lawyers are often asked by clients to furnish opinion letters assuring nonclients about legal aspects of proposed transactions, such as tax consequences or the presence of liens. The recipients of such letters qualify as intended beneficiaries of the lawyer-client relationship and may therefore sue the authoring lawyer for harm caused by the

---

[140] State & County Mutual Fire Ins. Co. v. Young, 490 F. Supp. 2d 741, 744 (N.D. W. Va. 2007) (quoting *Restatement (Third) of the Law Governing Lawyers* § 51 cmt. g (American Law Institute, 2000)).

[141] General Sec. Ins. Co. v. Jordan, Coyne & Savits, LLP, 357 F. Supp. 2d 951, 956–57 (E.D. Va. 2005); *see also infra* § 5-4.9(c) (discussing insurer subrogation claims).

[142] 490 F. Supp. 2d 741 (N.D. W. Va. 2007).

failure to exercise care.[143] In *In re Estate of Powell*,[144] the Illinois Supreme Court held that the beneficiaries of a wrongful death action were intended third-party beneficiaries who could sue for legal malpractice.[145]

Cases occasionally focus more on whether reliance was expected than on whether it was intended. For example, in *Estate of Spencer v. Gavin*,[146] a lawyer represented three interrelated estates of a mother and her two daughters. A second lawyer, who was enlisted by the first lawyer, did a small amount of work related to one of the estates, but no work at all for the other two estates. A New Jersey appellate court held that if the second lawyer learned that the first lawyer was misappropriating funds from the three estates, he could be liable to all three estates for harm caused by not disclosing that information. The estate for which the second lawyer did legal work was a client, so there were clear grounds for liability based on failure to reveal material information (such as, presumably, actions for negligence, breach of fiduciary, fraud, and negligent misrepresentation). Although the other two estates were nonclients, the court found that they too could state a claim for damages. As the court explained, "an attorney may be liable to a nonclient in certain situations where the attorney knows, or should know, that the nonclient will rely on the attorney." Because the estates of the three close family members were interrelated in terms of their disposition of assets, such reliance was to be expected.

Nevertheless, it must be emphasized that, in many cases, it is difficult for a nonclient to establish the right to sue as an intended third-party beneficiary. For example, in *Breen v. Law Office of Bruce A. Barket, P.C.*,[147] a New York court concluded, in the context of a divorce action, that a wife, who was represented by her own lawyer, was at most an incidental beneficiary of the retainer agreement between her husband and his lawyer.

In *Scott v. Burgin*,[148] the District of Columbia Court of Appeals rejected a malpractice claim against a divorce lawyer that was filed by a deceased client's fiancée because "third party claims may be sustained [only] where the plaintiffs were 'the direct and intended beneficiaries of the contracted for services.' "[149]

---

143 *See* RESTATEMENT (THIRD) OF THE LAW GOVERNING LAWYERS §§ 51(2) & 52 illus. 2 (American Law Institute, 2000).

144 12 N.E.3d 14 (Ill. 2014).

145 *Id.* at 21–22. As the court explained:

> [T]he Act creates a cause of action for pecuniary losses suffered by the deceased's spouse and next of kin by reason of the decedent's death. Yet, the decedent's beneficiaries are precluded from pursuing individual actions since a wrongful death action must be brought by and in the name of the personal representative of the deceased. Nevertheless, the Act makes clear that any amount recovered in such an action shall be for the "exclusive benefit" of the surviving spouse and next of kin. * * *. Clearly, the underlying purpose of a wrongful death action is to compensate those beneficiaries named in the action rather than the decedent's estate. Therefore, the primary purpose and intent of an attorney-client relationship between the personal representative of the deceased and the attorney who brings a wrongful death action is to benefit the decedent's beneficiaries. * * *.

*Id.* at 21.

146 946 A.2d 1051 (N.J. Super. Ct. App. Div. 2008).

147 862 N.Y.S.2d 50, 52–53 (App. Div. 2008).

148 97 A.3d 564 (D.C. 2014).

149 *Id.* at 566. As the court explained:

> [T]he "end and aim" of a divorce proceeding is the dissolution of a marriage and the distribution of marital assets * * *. The only parties directly concerned with a divorce proceeding are the married

In *Sutton v. Llewellyn*,[150] a lawyer was appointed as counsel to an elderly woman in her conservatorship proceedings. After the woman passed away, her surviving family members sued the lawyer for legal malpractice and other wrongful conduct. They alleged that the lawyer had bankrupted the estate and kept the elderly woman away from her home and family, even though the woman had allegedly wanted to move to New York to be with them. In granting judgment on the pleadings for the lawyer on the professional negligence claim, a federal court in California wrote:

> [T]he main inquiry is "whether the principal purpose of the attorney's retention [was] to provide legal services for the benefit of the plaintiff." * * *. Try as they might to characterize them otherwise, plaintiffs' allegations arise entirely from [lawyer] Nicora's performance of professional services as counsel for Rose [the elderly woman] in her conservatorship proceeding. * * *.
>
> Plaintiffs claim, however, "[t]he minute that * * * [Rose] requested the right to live with her children, plaintiffs became third party beneficiaries of the attorney-client relationship to provide legal services." * * *. This argument, while creative, is without support in case law. * * *. Finding a duty outside of the estate planning context is rare. * * *.[151]

## § 5-4.8 DUTIES TO CO-COUNSEL

Another category of nonclients who might assert claims against lawyers are other lawyers with whom they work. This includes partners or associates in one's firm, as well as lawyers outside the firm who serve as co-counsel on cases.

To a limited extent, legally enforceable obligations are owed to other lawyers. A lawyer may be liable to other members of the lawyer's firm for breach of fiduciary duties.[152] Also, lawyers who are subject to liability for malpractice may sometimes assert reimbursement claims against other lawyers seeking indemnity or contribution.[153]

However, legal duties to other lawyers must not conflict with the duties to clients. As discussed below, this may mean that one lawyer has no duty to protect the interest of another lawyer in earning a contingent fee.

### § 5-4.8(a) Protecting Fee Interests

Several cases suggest that lawyers do not have an obligation to protect the fee interests of co-counsel. Thus, in *Mazon v. Krafchick*,[154] the Supreme Court of Washington held that there are no duties between co-counsel that will allow recovery for lost or reduced prospective fees. As the court explained, "decisions about how to pursue a case must be based on the client's best interests, not the attorneys'."[155] According to the court, the "undivided duty of loyalty means that each attorney owes a duty to pursue the case

---

> couple and their minor offspring. A fiancée of either party is a complete stranger to the transaction, legally speaking, and the divorce itself does nothing to change that status. * * *.

*Id.*

[150] 2006 WL 3371623 (N.D. Cal. 2006).

[151] *Id.* at *3.

[152] *See supra* § 5-3.6.

[153] *See infra* §§ 5-6.4(c)(2) & (3).

[154] 144 P.3d 1168 (Wash. 2006).

[155] *Id.* at 1172.

in the client's best interests, even if that means not completing the case and forgoing a potential contingency fee."[156]

It might be argued that no harm would be done by recognizing a claim by co-counsel for lost fees if that claim is entirely consistent with the interests of the client. However, thus far, courts have generally not focused on whether lost-fee claims are consistent with, or adverse to, the interests of the client. Rather, they have tended to adopt black-and-white no-duty rules.

In *Beck v. Wecht*,[157] three lawyers, B, M, and W, served as co-counsel to clients in a personal injury case. The night before closing arguments at trial, with a $6 million settlement offer from the defendants on the table, the clients decided to settle. At a meeting with M and W, they instructed M to contact the defendant to arrange a settlement. However, M never followed those instructions. Then, at trial, the jury ruled for the defense.

Subsequently, the clients sued M and W for malpractice, and B sued W to recover the share of the contingent fee that he would have received if the case had been settled for $6 million. (M had already paid B a settlement.)

The California Supreme Court rejected B's claim for lost-fees. Adopting a bright-line rule, the court held that it "would be contrary to public policy to countenance actions based on the theory that co-counsel have a fiduciary duty to protect one another's prospective interests in a contingency fee."[158]

It is difficult to see how recognizing B's claim would have interfered with the representation of the client. M and W (because W was vicariously liable for M's conduct under joint venture principles) had a duty to follow their clients' instructions to settle the case. That was precisely the same argument that B was making.

## § 5-4.9 LIABILITY RELATED TO LITIGATION

A lawyer's duties run mainly to clients, not to opposing parties. Therefore, a lawyer representing a person on one side of a transaction or litigation rarely has an obligation to protect the interests of a person on the other side. Because there is usually no duty to exercise care, there is no liability. As a practical matter, this makes good sense. The undivided loyalty that a lawyer owes to a client would be greatly impaired by the easy recognition of obligations to protect a client's adversaries.

The fact that liability to adverse clients is rarely imposed does not mean such claims are not filed. In *DeFelice v. Costagliola*,[159] the buyer of a premises who later encountered furnace problems sued the seller's lawyer—apparently because the seller was unavailable to be sued, having moved from the jurisdiction. In concluding that the claim was "completely baseless," a New York court surmised that, "the theory behind bringing these baseless legal actions * * * [is] that owing to the small amount of money involved, the lawyer would pay the claim rather than engage in the cost of litigation."[160] The court

[156] *Id.*

[157] 48 P.3d 417 (Cal. 2002).

[158] *Id.* at 418.

[159] 882 N.Y.S.2d 882 (N.Y. City Civ. Ct. 2009).

[160] *Id.* at 884.

rejected the plaintiff's claim and granted the defendant-lawyer's counterclaim for damages resulting from frivolous litigation.

## § 5-4.9(a) Malicious Prosecution and Malicious Use of Process

Although many claims by opposing parties fail because of lack of duty or privilege, some claims do succeed. A lawyer may be liable to an adverse party for fraud[161] or for negligent misrepresentation.[162] Those causes of action are very significant exceptions to the general rule of no liability. Less important, because it usually fails, is the cause of action for malicious use of process (or what is sometimes called malicious prosecution). This cause of action can be brought by a nonclient against a lawyer who unsuccessfully represented a client in a lawsuit.[163]

### *§ 5-4.9(a)(1) Elements*

To recover for malicious misuse of process, a plaintiff must generally prove that (1) an underlying action was commenced by the defendant, (2) with malice, and (3) without probable cause, and that the action (4) was terminated on the merits in favor of the plaintiff and (5) caused damages. It is normally very difficult to establish all of these elements. Actions against lawyers rarely succeed because the plaintiff must prove that the lawyer knew the underlying action was baseless and that the lawyer, personally, had an improper purpose.

Spite, ill-will, or vindictiveness will generally satisfy the malice requirement. In addition, acting for an improper purpose (such as to coerce an adversary to settle a dispute or sell a piece of land) will also suffice. However, a lawyer is not liable for malicious misuse of process if the lawyer acts primarily to help the client obtain a proper adjudication of the client's claim.[164]

Lack of probable cause means that there was no reasonable basis, in law and in fact, for the defendant to believe that the claim could succeed. As stated in the *Restatement of the Law Governing Lawyers*, a "decision by a competent tribunal upholding the client's claim on the merits is ordinarily conclusive evidence of probable cause, even if it is reversed on appeal * * *."[165]

With respect to damages, some courts say that, if the underlying action was civil, the plaintiff must allege a "special grievance." Thus, the New Jersey Supreme Court explained:

> [T]he special grievance is designed to take the place of the injurious effects, including arrest, restraint, or the attendant humiliation of being held on bail, finger-printed, and photographed, that ordinarily flow from a wrongfully instituted criminal charge.[166]

---

161 *See supra* § 5-4.2.

162 *See supra* § 5-4.3.

163 *See* Colleen V. Lisowski, *Guilt by Association: How "Stand-by Co-Counsel" Exposes Attorneys to Malicious Prosecution Liability*, 3 ST. MARY'S J. LEGAL MAL. & ETHICS 284, 307 ("even miniscule participation can lead to monstrous liability, simply because of name association as counsel of record").

164 *See* RESTATEMENT (THIRD) OF THE LAW GOVERNING LAWYERS § 57(2) (American Law Institute, 2000).

165 RESTATEMENT (THIRD) OF THE LAW GOVERNING LAWYERS § 57 cmt. d (American Law Institute, 2000).

166 LoBiondo v. Schwartz, 970 A.2d 1007 (N.J. 2009).

Interference with the constitutional rights of speech, press, and petition, are among the things which establish a "special grievance."[167] However, other courts do not require proof of a special grievance and permit recovery for harm to reputation, emotional distress, expenses incurred, and interference with legally protected interests.[168]

#### *§ 5-4.9(a)(2) Terminology*

In some jurisdictions, a distinction is carefully drawn based on the criminal or civil nature of the underlying action. Misuse of criminal processes can give rise to an action for malicious prosecution.[169] In contrast, misuse of civil litigation is actionable as malicious use of process.[170] In other places, authorities use the term "malicious prosecution" to encompass misuse of civil proceedings.[171]

There are other terminological complexities. The *Restatement* differentiates between "wrongful use of civil proceedings" and "abuse of process."[172] Consequently, particular care must be exercised in reviewing precedent in this area of the law.

#### *§ 5-4.9(a)(3) Advice of Counsel Defense and Related Claims Against Lawyers*

In *LoBiondo v. Schwartz*,[173] malicious use of process claims were filed against both a client who had sued a neighbor for defamation and the client's lawyers. The defamation claim, which was ultimately found to be without merit, was based on the neighbor's opposition to the client's proposed business expansion and related requests for governmental approval. As a defense to the malicious use of process charge, the client argued that it was immune from suit because it had acted on advice of counsel. The Supreme Court of New Jersey acknowledged that advice of counsel is a long-recognized complete defense, but took care to articulate its requirements. As the court explained:

> To claim its benefit, the original plaintiff must prove that he or she relied on counsel's advice and that the advice was given after a full and fair presentation to counsel of all of the relevant facts. * * *. "Full and fair" means disclosure to counsel of all information known to the original plaintiff that could justify or militate against the filing of the proposed cause of action. * * *. In this context, if any of the facts so reported to counsel were known to the original plaintiff to be false, the advice-of-counsel defense will not operate as a shield against the claim.[174]

Satisfactory proof that the client acted on advice of counsel defeats a malicious use of process action because it proves that the client acted with probable cause in the underlying litigation.

The *LoBiondo* court further held that if, and only if, a client sued for malicious use of process raises an advice of counsel defense, the client's lawyer can be sued on the same

---

[167] *Id.* at 1012.

[168] *See* RESTATEMENT (SECOND) OF TORTS § 681 (American Law Institute, 1977).

[169] *Cf. id.* §§ 653–71.

[170] *Cf. id.* §§ 674–681B.

[171] *See* Franklin Mint Co. v. Manatt, Phelps & Phillips, LLP, 109 Cal. Rptr. 3d 143 (Cal. Ct. App. 2010).

[172] RESTATEMENT (SECOND) OF TORTS §§ 674–82 (American Law Institute, 1977).

[173] 970 A.2d 1007 (N.J. 2009).

[174] 970 A.2d at 1025.

grounds. After reviewing precedent establishing that lawyers are subject to ethical rules and penalties for frivolous litigation, and rarely have a legal duty to nonclients, the court wrote:

> Our decision to permit the nonclient to proceed against the attorney [for malicious use of process] is a limited one * * *. [W]e limit the cause of action to the circumstance in which the client has first raised the defense of advice of counsel in order to prevent the claim from being used for purposes of creating an adverse relationship between counsel and client. Because we recognize that the attorney's first duty is to zealously represent the client, and because an attorney faced with a claim of malicious use of process may as a practical matter be unable to mount a defense by reason of the bounds of confidentiality or privilege, we limit the grounds for the claim to those in which the client has already called the attorney's advice into issue. Fairness demands no less.[175]

*LoBiondo* demonstrates that in some jurisdictions, a malicious use of process claim cannot be asserted against a lawyer, unless the client has also been sued and has raised an advice of counsel defense.

### § 5-4.9(b) Tortious Involvement with Litigation

The District of Columbia imposes liability for "tortious involvement with litigation." This cause of action, which may be related in part to the tort of negligent misrepresentation, is available when a lawyer negligently (or otherwise tortiously) gives legal advice to a nonclient who is then foreseeably subjected to litigation by a third party, which is then resolved in the nonclient's favor.

The lawyer is liable to the nonclient for the amount of the attorney's fees incurred in the litigation. "The essential elements that must be established for this claim are: (1) the plaintiff must have incurred the fees in the course of prior litigation, (2) ordinarily that litigation must have occurred between the plaintiff and the third party who is not the defendant in the present action, and (3) the plaintiff must have become involved in the underlying litigation as a consequence of the defendant's tortious act."[176]

In *Perry v. Scholar*,[177] a federal court in the District of Columbia held that a claim was stated under this theory in a case where a lawyer for a pension plan allegedly gave erroneous advice to the accountant who served as the plan administration, who relied on the advice and was thereafter sued.

### § 5-4.9(c) Insurer Subrogation Claims

Some states hold that even if a malpractice insurer is not a client of a lawyer who is hired to defend an insured, the insurer can assert a claim seeking reimbursement for losses it sustains as a result of the lawyer's negligence. If the lawyer breaches duties owed to the insured, a carrier who is forced to pay higher damages may pursue the same claim against the lawyer that the client could have pursued.

Equitable subrogation is analogous to claims for indemnity and contribution. It is "one of the mechanisms by which the law of restitution and unjust enrichment will

---

[175] *Id.* at 1031.

[176] 696 F. Supp. 2d 91, 94 (D.D.C. 2010).

[177] *Id.*

reallocate the burden of a given liability from one who has originally discharged it to another whom the law considers more appropriate to bear it."[178]

In *Great American E & S Insurance Co. v. Quintairos, Prieto, Wood & Boyer, P.A.*,[179] the Supreme Court of Mississippi recognized a claim for equitable subrogation. As the court explained:

> After the estate of a former resident sued a nursing home [Shady Lawn] for negligent care, the primary insurance carrier [Royal] employed lawyers [Quintairos] to defend the suit. Because the lawyers failed to timely designate an expert witness, the settlement value of the case greatly increased, causing the nursing home's primary carrier to pay its policy limits, and its excess insurance carrier [Great American] to step in, defend the nursing home, and ultimately settle the suit. The excess carrier sued the law firm for professional negligence—both directly and under a theory of equitable subrogation. * * *.
>
> We hold that—under the facts as alleged in the complaint—the doctrine of equitable subrogation applies, and the excess carrier may, to the extent of its losses, pursue a claim against the lawyers to the same extent as the insured. We further hold that the excess carrier has failed to allege a sufficient factual basis for a direct claim of professional negligence against the law firm.[180]

Other courts reach similar results without using the term "equitable subrogation." In *Carolina Casualty Insurance Co. v. Sharp*,[181] a federal court in Ohio found that there was privity between the insurer and the insured, and that the insurer therefore had standing to bring a legal malpractice action against the lawyers hired to defend the insured.[182]

## § 5-4.10 SECURITIES LAW VIOLATIONS

Lawyers are sometimes liable to nonclients under state or federal securities laws. Under federal Rule 10b-5, it is unlawful to make "any untrue statement of a material fact or to omit to state a material fact necessary in order to make the statements made, in light of the circumstances under which they were made, not misleading * * * in connection with the purchase or sale of any security."[183]

It is difficult for a nonclient to maintain an action against a lawyer based on violation of federal securities laws. Nevertheless, some claims succeed. In *Media General, Inc. v. Tomlin*,[184] the D.C. Circuit found that a law firm which had been actively involved with concealing a contingent liability in connection with the sale of a business was subject to liability for both common law fraud and securities fraud.

---

[178] RESTATEMENT (THIRD) OF RESTITUTION AND UNJUST ENRICHMENT § 24 cmt. a (American Law Institute, 2011).

[179] 100 So. 3d 420 (Miss. 2012).

[180] *Id.* at 421–24.

[181] 940 F. Supp. 2d 569, 572–76 (N.D. Ohio 2013).

[182] *Cf. supra* § 5-4.7(b) (indicating that some states treat insurers as clients or intended third-party beneficiaries).

[183] 17 C.F.R. § 240.10b-5 (Westlaw 2017); *see also* 15 U.S.C. § 78j(b) (Westlaw 2017).

[184] 532 F.3d 854 (D.C. Cir. 2008).

### § 5-4.10(a) "Aiding and Abetting" and "Scheme" Liability

In *Central Bank of Denver, N.A. v. First Interstate Bank of Denver, N.A.*,[185] the Supreme Court ruled that there is no liability for merely aiding and abetting a violation of the federal securities laws. However, the court acknowledged that "[a]ny person or entity, including a lawyer, * * * who employs a manipulative device or makes a material misstatement (or omission) on which a purchaser or seller of securities relies may be liable as a primary violator under 10b-5, assuming all of the requirements for primary liability under Rule 10b-5 are met."[186]

Subsequently, the Supreme Court has emphasized that, in order to be recoverable, economic losses must be directly linked to a defendant's misrepresentations. In *Stoneridge Investment Partners, LLC v. Scientific Atlanta, Inc.*,[187] an action by investors against a corporation, its executives, an independent auditor, and the corporation's vendors and customers, the Supreme Court ruled that the investors had failed to show that they had relied upon deceptive behind-the-scenes behavior when purchasing stock. Thus, the court greatly limited what some authorities had called "scheme liability." The court wrote:

> ["Scheme liability"] does not answer the objection that petitioner did not in fact rely upon respondents' own deceptive conduct.
>
> Liability is appropriate, petitioner contends, because respondents engaged in conduct with the purpose and effect of creating a false appearance of material fact to further a scheme to misrepresent Charter's revenue. The argument is that the financial statement Charter released to the public was a natural and expected consequence of respondents' deceptive acts; had respondents not assisted Charter, Charter's auditor would not have been fooled, and the financial statement would have been a more accurate reflection of Charter's financial condition. * * *.
>
> In effect petitioner contends that in an efficient market investors rely not only upon the public statements relating to a security but also upon the transactions those statements reflect. Were this concept of reliance to be adopted, the implied cause of action would reach the whole marketplace in which the issuing company does business; and there is no authority for this rule.
>
> * * * [W]e conclude respondents' deceptive acts, which were not disclosed to the investing public, are too remote to satisfy the requirement of reliance. It was Charter, not respondents, that misled its auditor and filed fraudulent financial statements; nothing respondents did made it necessary or inevitable for Charter to record the transactions as it did.[188]

### § 5-4.10(b) Claims Under State Law

Lawyers can sometimes be sued under state securities laws. In *Chadbourne & Parke LLP v. Troice*,[189] the Supreme Court narrowly construed the Securities Litigation

---

[185] 511 U.S. 164 (1994).

[186] *Id.* at 191.

[187] 552 U.S. 148 (2008).

[188] *Id.* at 160–61.

[189] 134 S. Ct. 1058 (2014).

Uniform Standards Act of 1998, which forbids large securities class actions based upon violations of state law. That ruling allowed a state law class action to go forward against the law firms and insurance broker who had allegedly assisted a "fraudster" in a $7 billion Ponzi scheme.

## § 5-4.11 FAIR DEBT COLLECTIONS PRACTICES

The federal Fair Debt Collection Practices Act (FDCPA) proscribes a wide range of abusive conduct related to debt collection.[190] Persons injured by an intentional violation of its terms may maintain a civil cause of action against an offending debt collector for actual damages (including emotional distress), costs, attorney fees, and, in the case of an individual plaintiff, additional damages not exceeding $1,000.

The FDCPA restricts communications by debt collectors with debtors and third persons, and compels certain written disclosures. Section 1692c(a) provides in part:

> [A] debt collector may not communicate with a consumer in connection with the collection of any debt—(1) at any unusual time or place or a time or place known or which should be known to be inconvenient to the consumer * * * [or] (3) at the consumer's place of employment if the debt collector knows or has reason to know that the consumer's employer prohibits the consumer from receiving such communication.[191]

In addition, section 1692d provides:

> A debt collector may not engage in any conduct the natural consequence of which is to harass, oppress, or abuse any person in connection with the collection of a debt. Without limiting the general application of the foregoing, the following conduct is a violation of this section:
>
> (1) The use or threat of use of violence or other criminal means to harm the physical person, reputation, or property of any person.
>
> (2) The use of obscene or profane language or language the natural consequence of which is to abuse the hearer or reader.
>
> (3) The publication of a list of consumers who allegedly refuse to pay debts, except to a consumer reporting agency or to persons * * * [who lawfully may receive reports from such agencies].
>
> (4) The advertisement for sale of any debt to coerce payment of the debt.
>
> (5) Causing a telephone to ring or engaging any person in telephone conversation repeatedly or continuously with intent to annoy, abuse, or harass any person at the called number.
>
> (6) Except as provided in section 1692b of this title [which imposes limitations on collection of information about the location of a consumer], the placement of telephone calls without meaningful disclosure of the caller's identity.[192]

---

[190] *See* 15 U.S.C. §§ 1692a–1692k (Westlaw 2017).

[191] *Id.* § 1692c(a).

[192] *Id.* § 1692d.

The requirements of the Fair Debt Collection Practices Act apply to a lawyer or law firm that "regularly" collects debts on behalf of third parties.[193] Thus, a lawyer may be liable for the misleading nature of debt collection letters sent on a creditor's behalf.

In *Lesher v. Law Office of Mitchell N. Kay, P.C.*,[194] a federal court in Pennsylvania held that a lawyer's letter advising a debtor that payments were due was misleading in that it gave the debtor the impression that legal action would be taken if the debt was not settled. In fact, as language buried in the body of the letter pointed out, no lawyer with the firm had reviewed the circumstances of the account at the time the letter was mailed.

Some states have also enacted statutes which impose additional limitations on debt collection practices.

[193] *See* Heintz v. Jenkins, 514 U.S. 291 (1995).

[194] 2009 WL 3487795 (M.D. Pa. 2009).

# Chapter 5-5

# REMEDIES FOR LEGAL MALPRACTICE

**By Susan Saab Fortney and Vincent R. Johnson**

*Table of Sections*


§ 5-5.1 Compensatory Damages
§ 5-5.2 Punitive Damages
§ 5-5.3 Restitution


## § 5-5.1 COMPENSATORY DAMAGES

No matter how serious a lawyer's error, a malpractice plaintiff may recover damages only if the error caused harm. Thus, even if a lawyer fails to adequately investigate the facts of a case, there is no liability if the settlement the lawyer recommended was a good one.[1]

### § 5-5.1(a) No Speculation

"Actual damages are never presumed in a legal malpractice action."[2] Malpractice damages must always be proved with reasonable certainty. This means that a jury must be provided with evidence that will support a finding, without speculation, of what losses the plaintiff sustained. While this basic rule is simple, there are many ways in which plaintiffs come up short of its requirements.

In some cases, the plaintiff simply fails to introduce evidence of harm. For example, in *United Genesis Corp. v. Brown*,[3] the Texas Court of Appeals held that a conclusory assertion, unsupported by evidence, that alleged malpractice caused $75,000 in damages was insufficient to raise a fact issue to defeat the defendant's motion for summary judgment.

In other cases, the plaintiff errs by failing to link evidence of harm to the alleged malpractice. Thus, in *Talmage v. Harris*,[4] a lawyer's negligence meant that the plaintiff was unable to pursue a bad faith claim against an insurance company (United Fire) related to the destruction of a shop. In a subsequent malpractice action, the plaintiff sought to recover damages for interest he had been charged. As the United States Court of Appeals for the Seventh Circuit explained:

> Talmage's theory was that United Fire's delays and under-payments required him to carry large balances on his credit cards, for which he paid a substantial amount of interest. The only evidence Talmage offered on this point was a report from his accounting expert * * * [which] displayed and quantified the

---

[1] *See* RESTATEMENT (THIRD) OF THE LAW GOVERNING LAWYERS § 52 cmt. c (American Law Institute, 2000).

[2] Stevens v. McGuireWoods LLP, 43 N.E.3d 923, 927 (Ill. 2015).

[3] 2007 WL 1341358, *2 (Tex. App.).

[4] 486 F.3d 968 (7th Cir. 2007).

interest charges that he paid during the period after the shop was destroyed. It does not, however, segregate charges related to the reconstruction from other charges he may have incurred during that period. This evidence fell so far short of anything revealing a causal link between the interest paid and United Fire's alleged bad faith that the district court properly kept it from the jury.[5]

In some cases, there are too many unconvincing links in the causal chain to make ascertainment of damages reasonably certain. For example, in *GUS Consulting GMBH v. Chadbourne & Parke LLP*,[6] Austrian clients alleged that an American law firm had failed to properly advise them that the use of a certain business structure would expose them to criminal investigation and possible prosecution in the Russian Federation, where they were investing in natural gas operations. In rejecting the $500 million suit, a New York appellate court concluded that the plaintiffs' contention that they would have changed or ceased their use of the business structure, and would have been able to maintain and grow their business in Russia over the next six years while the Russian economy rebounded, was too speculative to support a legal malpractice claim.[7]

Similarly, in *Heritage Partners, LLC v. Stroock & Stroock & Lavan LLP*,[8] the court found that the plaintiffs' "unsupported factual allegations, speculation and conclusory statements failed to sufficiently show that but for defendant's alleged failure to advise plaintiffs to pursue Chapter 11 bankruptcy upon their default on a $47 million loan, plaintiffs would not have lost approximately $80 million in equity in the underlying condominium project."[9] The court found that the plaintiffs' calculations ignored the fact that the Attorney General would not allow the sponsor to sell any units "because it had failed to submit a plan that sufficiently stated how it would pay its arrears and other financial obligations" and failed to allege "that they had funds to even initiate bankruptcy proceedings."[10]

In some cases, proof of damages fails because there is no way of knowing what someone would have done. For example, *Rudolf v. Shayne, Dachs, Stanisci, Corker & Sauer*[11] was a malpractice action that arose from the mishandling of an auto accident claim. At the first trial, the jury was erroneously instructed on the duties of pedestrians. The result was a jury verdict for $255,000, which was reduced by 50% based on the plaintiff's comparative negligence. At a second trial intended to cure the erroneous charge, the jury was properly instructed. However, before a verdict was returned, the parties settled the case for $750,000. In the subsequent malpractice action based on the original lawyer's failure to object to the erroneous instruction, the New York Court of Appeals denied the plaintiff's request for compensatory damages for interest that could have been earned from investment of the judgment if $750,000 had been awarded at the first trial. The court reasoned that the "plaintiff's assertion that, had the proper instruction been charged, the first jury would have awarded $750,000—instead of the $255,000 it actually awarded—is pure speculation."[12]

---

[5] 486 F.3d at 975.

[6] 905 N.Y.S.2d 158 (App. Div. 2010).

[7] *Id.* at 160.

[8] 19 N.Y.S.3d 511 (App. Div. 2015).

[9] *Id.* at 512.

[10] *Id.*

[11] 867 N.E.2d 385 (N.Y. 2007).

[12] *Id.* at 838.

Similarly, in *Hand v. Howell, Sarto & Howell*,[13] the Alabama Supreme Court held that a lawyer's failure to join an alleged tortfeasor's corporate employer as a defendant in the plaintiff's personal injury lawsuit did not constitute legal malpractice. The court explained that there was no evidence indicating that any additional insurance coverage would have been available had the employer been named as a defendant, and that there was "only speculation" that the plaintiff would have secured a higher settlement if the employer had been made a party.[14]

## § 5-5.1(b) Proximately Caused Losses

Legal malpractice tort actions are subject to the usual principles of causation. In order to be recoverable, damages must have been factually and proximately caused by the defendant's tortious conduct.

The particular components of compensatory damages vary from case to case, depending on what the plaintiff lost. Thus, "[t]here is no single measure of damages" applicable to every legal malpractice case, and "the appropriate measure must be determined by [reference to] the facts and circumstances."[15]

With proper factual support, an award might include amounts for: the loss of a transaction's intended tax advantages;[16] loss of "control" of a corporation;[17] interest that could have been recovered on an underlying claim;[18] and prejudgment interest on amounts that should have been received at an earlier date.[19]

## § 5-5.1(c) Emotional Distress Damages

Compensation for emotional distress is generally not available in a legal malpractice action based on negligence. Thus, if a lawyer negligently provides incorrect advice about a child visitation order, a client ordinarily cannot recover compensation for mental anguish, even if emotional distress in fact results.[20] This is not surprising for, in the law of torts generally, negligent infliction of emotional distress is actionable only in a narrow range of cases.[21]

However, there are exceptions to the rule. For example, if emotional distress arising from a lawyer's lack of care is not just a possibility, but a special probability, compensation for emotional harm may be recoverable as an aspect of compensatory damages. This may be true, for example, if a lawyer's negligence results in a client's imprisonment.[22] In *Miranda v. Said*,[23] the court held on an issue of first impression that

---

[13] 131 So. 3d 599 (Ala. 2013).

[14] *Id.* at *605.

[15] Smith v. McLaughlin, 769 S.E.2d 7, 17 (Va. 2015).

[16] *See, e.g.*, Williams v. Lakin, 2007 WL 1170597, *3 (N.D. Okla.).

[17] *Cf.* Price v. Ragland, 966 So.2d 246 (Ala. 2007).

[18] *See* Hook v. Trevino, 839 N.W.2d 434, 451 (Iowa 2013).

[19] *See* Cadle Co. v. Sweet & Brousseau, P.C., 2007 WL 1958915 (N.D. Tex.).

[20] *See* Long-Russell v. Hampe, 39 P.3d 1015, 1019–20 (Wyo. 2002).

[21] *See* VINCENT R. JOHNSON, STUDIES IN AMERICAN TORT LAW 573–90 (Carolina Academic Press, 5th ed. 2013).

[22] *See* RESTATEMENT (THIRD) OF THE LAW GOVERNING LAWYERS § 53 cmt. g (American Law Institute, 2000).

[23] 836 N.W.2d 8 (Iowa 2013).

emotional distress damages are sometimes recoverable in legal malpractice actions arising from immigration law practice.

Emotional distress resulting from intentionally tortious conduct is more readily compensable than similar harm based on negligence. This is true because deliberate victimization of a potential plaintiff not only makes such harm more likely to result, but warrants deterrence through imposition of liability for emotional distress damages.

Malpractice claims for breach of contract seldom support an award of emotional distress damages. Such losses do not qualify as consequential damages under principles of contract law and are actionable only if there is an independent tort.

In Georgia, there is special legislation relating to emotional distress damages that must be taken into account in a legal malpractice action.[24] "The plain and explicit terms of * * * [the state] statute do not provide for evidence of a defendant's worldly circumstances to be admitted in a case in which the only injury is to a plaintiff's peace, happiness, or feelings."[25]

### § 5-5.1(d) Harm to Reputation

Damages for harm to the plaintiff's reputation are rarely available in legal malpractice actions. The critical question is whether such losses were a foreseeable and probable consequence of the defendant's conduct. This standard is more easily satisfied if the defendant intended to cause such harm, than if the defendant was merely careless. However, occasional cases permit recovery of reputation damages in actions for negligent malpractice. Thus, if it can be said that, but for a lawyer's negligence, a doctor would not have been found liable for medical malpractice, the doctor may be permitted to garner compensation for harm to his or her professional reputation.[26]

A plaintiff may also offer evidence of harm to reputation to support a claim for emotional distress damages. As explained by a Maine court: "To prove damages for emotional distress in a legal malpractice action, the plaintiff must prove economic loss and egregious actions by the attorney or harm to reputation or personal losses such as the deterioration of relationships."[27]

### § 5-5.1(e) Attorney's Fees as Compensatory Damages

Whether a malpractice plaintiff can recover attorney's fees depends on the reason they were incurred. In this regard, it is possible to distinguish at least four categories: (1) fees paid in the legal malpractice action itself; (2) fees paid in an earlier representation giving rise to the malpractice claim; (3) fees that would have been recovered in earlier litigation but for the malpractice; and (4) fees paid to remedy or mitigate the consequences of the defendant-lawyer's malpractice.

Attorney's fees falling within the first category are generally not recoverable as compensatory damages.[28] The contrary is true regarding attorney's fees falling within

---

[24] *See* GA. CODE ANN., § 51–12–6 (Westlaw 2017).

[25] Holland v. Caviness, 737 S.E.2d 669, 672 (Ga. 2013).

[26] Kirtland and Packard v. Superior Ct., 131 Cal. Rptr. 418, 421 (Cal. Ct. App. 1976).

[27] Pawlendzio v. Haddow, 2015 WL 8484384 *5 (Me. Super.), *aff'd*, 148 A.3d 713 (Me. 2016).

[28] *But see* Sande L. Buhai, *Everyone Makes Mistakes: Attorney's Fees Recovery in Legal Malpractice Suits*, 6 ST. MARY'S J. LEGAL MAL. & ETHICS 32, 32 (2016) (arguing that "the American Rule should be changed for legal malpractice suits because the attorney-client relationship is the quintessential fiduciary relationship

the last two categories, provided that the fees are reasonable. The recoverability of attorney's fees falling into the second category depends on whether the lawyer properly rendered the services that were due. These issues are discussed below.

### *§ 5-5.1(e)(1) Attorney's Fees Incurred in the Malpractice Action*

The *Restatement* notes that there are exceptions to the general rule against recovery of malpractice action attorney's fees. Thus, "many jurisdictions allow recovery of attorney's fees against a plaintiff or defendant that litigates in bad faith * * *."[29] Under Mississippi law, if a malpractice award against a lawyer includes punitive damages, attorney's fees are also recoverable.[30] In Idaho, "an action seeking to recover damages for legal malpractice is an action to recover in a commercial transaction where the legal services were not rendered for personal or household purposes," and therefore attorney's fees may be recovered.[31]

Legal malpractice may amount to a deceptive trade practice. Such a showing frequently entitles a plaintiff to an award of attorney's fees, in addition to compensatory damages.[32]

In some states, legal malpractice that constitutes a breach of contract rather than a tort will support an award of attorney's fees. For example, a Texas statute provides that "[a] person may recover reasonable attorney's fees from an individual or corporation, in addition to the amount of a valid claim and costs, if the claim is for: * * * (8) an oral or written contract."[33]

Laws in some states make a party who rejects an offer of settlement liable for the offeror's attorney's fees if the offeree proceeds to trial and ultimately obtains a less favorable judgment.[34] These laws may protect lawyers as well as legal malpractice plaintiffs. For example, in *Menchise v. Akerman Senterfitt*,[35] an estate was held liable for almost a quarter of a million dollars in attorney's fees incurred by a law firm defending a malpractice action.

"New Jersey * * * is arguably the only state where the plaintiff's cost of successfully prosecuting a legal malpractice claim is [routinely] added to the compensatory damages recovered from the negligent lawyer."[36]

### *§ 5-5.1(e)(2) Attorney's Fees Incurred in Earlier Representation*

As to attorney's fees paid in the underlying representation, courts have often denied recovery.[37] That would seem to be the appropriate result if the underlying work was properly performed. However, some cases apply the general rule barring recovery even if the lawyer's work was clearly infirm.

---

and because of the added concern of unequal information available to each party as a result of the large disparity in power").

[29] RESTATEMENT (THIRD) OF THE LAW GOVERNING LAWYERS § 53 cmt. f (American Law Institute, 2000).

[30] *See* Duggins v. Guardianship of Washington, 632 So.2d 420, 431 (Miss. 1993).

[31] Taylor v. Riley, 336 P.3d 256, 273 (Idaho 2014).

[32] *See supra* § 5-4.4.

[33] TEX. CIV. PRAC. & REM. CODE ANN. § 38.001(8) (Westlaw 2017).

[34] *See* FLA. STAT. ANN. § 768.79 (Westlaw 2017).

[35] 532 F.3d 1146 (11th Cir. 2008).

[36] Bennett J. Wasserman, *Recovering Damages in Legal Malpractice Cases*, N.J. L.J., Jan. 17, 2013.

[37] *See* Jones v. Link, 493 F. Supp. 2d 765, 771 (E.D. Va. 2007).

For example, in *Jones v Link*,[38] the defendant-lawyer had failed to object to a five-level enhancement of punishment. As a result, his client was sentenced to 36 extra months of imprisonment. The sentencing error was later corrected through post-conviction proceedings, which established that the client had received ineffective assistance of counsel. Nevertheless, a federal court in Virginia did not permit the client to recover, in a malpractice action, the attorney's fees he had paid his lawyer for the initial representation.

In many instances, the reason the lawyer is being sued for malpractice is that services were not performed or were performed badly. In those kinds of cases, in some states, unnecessary attorney's fees paid by the client should be recoverable as compensatory damages. As the Supreme Court of Alaska explained in *Gefre v. Davis Wright Tremaine, LLP*,[39] "a legal malpractice plaintiff may recover as actual damages the attorney['s] fees incurred as a result of the defendant's malpractice, so long as the plaintiff can demonstrate [he or] she would not have incurred the fees in the absence of the defendant's negligence."[40]

### *§ 5-5.1(e)(3) Attorney's Fees Not Recovered in Earlier Litigation*

Some types of claims entitle a plaintiff to recover attorney's fees in addition to other damages. Thus, if as a result of malpractice a claim is lost, one of the consequences of the lawyer's misconduct is the loss of the attorney's fees that would have been reimbursed if the claim had been successful. In these kinds of cases, the lost attorney's fees are generally compensable.

For example, in *Cadle Co. v. Sweet & Brousseau, P.C.*,[41] a federal court in Texas permitted recovery not only of the damages that the plaintiff should have recovered in a suit on a promissory note, but also the amount of attorney's fees that it paid the defendants. The court reasoned that both amounts would have been recovered in the underlying action but for the defendants' negligence.

### *§ 5-5.1(e)(4) Attorney's Fees Incurred to Remedy or Mitigate Malpractice*

Fees incurred in an effort to remedy or mitigate the consequences of a lawyer's malpractice are generally recoverable. For example, suppose that a document drafted by the lawyer is invalid and unenforceable, and that legal proceedings must be commenced to reform the document by correcting the lawyer's errors. The attorney's fees paid by the plaintiff related to the reformation will be treated as an element of consequential damages, and will be recoverable, provided they are reasonable in amount.

In *Rudolf v. Shayne, Dachs, Staniscl, Corker & Sauer*,[42] a lawyer failed to object at trial to an error in charging the jury. "The erroneous charge forced the plaintiff to hire new counsel to move to set aside the verdict * * *, pursue an appeal * * * and retain expert witnesses to testify at the second trial."[43] Finding that these steps would not have

---

[38] *Id.*

[39] 372 P.3d 256 (Alaska 2016) (quoting earlier decisions).

[40] *Id.* at 258.

[41] 2007 WL 1958915 (N.D. Tex.).

[42] 867 N.E.2d 385 (N.Y. 2007).

[43] *Id.* at 388.

been necessary but for the original lawyer's negligence, the New York Court of Appeals permitted recovery of these fees and expenses in the subsequent malpractice action.

However, it is important to be precise as to whether a client was forced to incur attorney's fees as a result of malpractice, as opposed to other factors. For example, in *Akin, Gump, Strauss, Hauer & Feld, L.L.P. v. National Development and Research,*[44] a law firm's failure to request inclusion of necessary questions in a jury charge preceded an appeal. In a subsequent malpractice action, the plaintiff sought to recover as damages the costs of appealing an adverse judgment, including the expenses of hiring law professors as consultants to focus on the jury charge. The Texas Supreme Court refused to allow recovery of attorney's fees and expenses related to the appeal generally because, even if the charge had been correct and the malpractice plaintiff had prevailed in the underlying action, the plaintiff might have been required to defend its judgment on appeal. It could not be said that but for the law firm's negligence, there would not have been an appeal. However, the court further ruled that, if properly supported by relevant evidence, the costs related to the retention of the law professors were recoverable. But for the errors in the jury charge, it would not have been necessary to hire experts to focus on the charge.

## § 5-5.1(f) Adjustments to Damages

The calculation of compensatory damages in a legal malpractice action may be adjusted for a variety of reasons. In particular, compensation for future losses is normally reduced to present value, and pre-judgment interest is often awarded to offset the lost time-value of delayed compensation for losses previously incurred. In addition, an award may be reduced to reflect the amount that the plaintiff would have spent on fees in earlier litigation that gave rise to the malpractice claim, the value of the services the defendant rendered, or the amount of a judgment that would not have been collectible. These subjects are discussed in the following sections.

### *§ 5-5.1(f)(1) Reduction to Present Value*

Legal malpractice damages are sometimes intended to compensate the plaintiff for losses that will not occur until various points in the future. This would be true, for example, if a lawyer's negligence causes the loss of periodic payments under an annuity.

As in other types of tort cases, compensation for future losses is reduced to present value. Thus, a plaintiff may not recover now the total value of future losses, but only a reduced amount which, if safely invested, would generate sufficient compensation to fully pay future losses at the date those losses would accrue.

### *§ 5-5.1(f)(2) Prejudgment Interest*

Damages in a legal malpractice action may be intended to reimburse the plaintiff for losses that accrued long before a judgment was entered. The delay in the receipt of those amounts has deprived the plaintiff of the time-value of money. To remedy this loss, prejudgment interest may be awarded in addition to the usual amounts of compensatory damages.[45]

---

[44] 299 S.W.3d 106, 122 (Tex. 2009).

[45] *See* Cadle Co. v. Sweet & Brousseau, P.C., 2007 WL 1958915 (N.D. Tex.).

In most states, the calculation of prejudgment interest is regulated by statute. Often, such awards are not a matter of entitlement, but of judicial discretion. This allows a court to take into account which party bears responsibility for delays in the litigation process. If the damages for which the plaintiff seeks prejudgment interest were not liquidated, recovery may be denied.[46] In addition, some states broadly deny recovery of prejudgment interest in legal malpractice actions.[47]

#### *§ 5-5.1(f)(3) Amounts That Would Have Been Spent on Contingent Fees*

When a successful legal malpractice action arises out of a failed tort claim, there is a question as to whether the plaintiff's recovery should be reduced to reflect the fact that had the underlying tort action succeeded, the plaintiff would have paid a substantial contingent fee. States are divided on this issue.[48] In *Hook v. Trevino*,[49] Iowa adopted what it called "the majority and better-reasoned rule reflected in the *Restatement (Third) of the Law Governing Lawyers*," which declines to impose such a setoff because the malpractice defendant never earned the fee and the malpractice plaintiff must pay a fee to the new counsel who prosecuted the malpractice action.

#### *§ 5-5.1(f)(4) Quantum Meruit Offset for the Value of Services Rendered*

Should an award of damages in a malpractice action be reduced by the value of the services the defendant-lawyer rendered? In the *Hook* case (mentioned above), the court left "open the possibility for a quantum meruit setoff from a legal malpractice recovery on an appropriate record."[50] However, the court found that no such adjustment was warranted by the facts before it. As the court explained:

> Trevino offered no expert testimony or other evidence of the reasonable value of the services he performed for Hook or how they benefited her. Hook's new counsel noted they used different experts * * * and presented live medical testimony. In addition, they had to retain a legal malpractice expert, a necessary expense to prove Trevino's negligence, but a cost that would have been avoided had the underlying tort action been prosecuted successfully against the state. Hook's ultimate recovery was delayed by years due to Trevino's negligence.[51]

### § 5-5.1(g) Collectability

In some states, a plaintiff suing with respect to malpractice committed in earlier litigation must prove that damages related to an underlying action would have been collectible.[52] Obviously, it may be hugely important to a malpractice plaintiff whether a state subscribes to this rule, and, if so, what specifically the rule requires.

Cases sometimes address the plaintiff's burden of proving collectability in detail. Thus, in *Akin, Gump, Strauss, Hauer & Feld, L.L.P. v. National Development and*

---

[46] *See, e.g.*, Yale v. Bowne, 2017 WL 527324, at *9–10 (Cal. Ct. App.).

[47] *See* Tri-G, Inc. v. Burke, Bosselman & Weaver, 856 N.E.2d 389, 412 (Ill. 2006).

[48] *See also* Baptiste v. Rohn, 2016 WL 1261072, at *7 (D.V.I.) (making no reduction, but surveying the various approaches).

[49] 839 N.W.2d 434, 437 (Iowa 2013).

[50] Hook v. Trevino, 839 N.W.2d 434, 449 (Iowa 2013).

[51] *Id.* at 449.

[52] *See, e.g.,* Williams v. Kublick, 837 N.Y.S.2d 803 (App. Div. 2007).

*Research*,[53] the Texas Supreme Court specified that "(1) the amount of damages that would have been collectible in the prior suit is the greater of the amount of a judgment for damages that would have been either paid or collected from the underlying defendant's net assets; and (2) the time at which collectability is determined is as of or after the time a judgment was first signed in the underlying case."[54] Further, the court explained, "[g]enerally, * * * the amount that would have been collectible in regard to an underlying judgment * * * will be the greater of either (1) the fair market value of the underlying defendant's net assets that would have been subject to legal process for satisfaction of the judgment as of the date the first judgment was signed or at some point thereafter, or (2) the amount that would have been paid on the judgment by the defendant or another, such as a guarantor or insurer."[55]

Some courts have emphasized that collectability is an issue only in certain kinds of malpractice cases. Thus, in *Vossoughi v. Polaschek*,[56] the Supreme Court of Iowa explained, "Collectability need not be shown if a plaintiff alleges legal malpractice directly caused actual loss; but collectability is a critical element of any legal malpractice claim alleging legal malpractice *prevented the plaintiff's recovery*."

Not all jurisdictions subscribe to the rule requiring the plaintiff to prove collectability of malpractice damages. Some states treat uncollectability of damages as an affirmative defense to be pleaded and proved by the defendant.

## § 5-5.2 PUNITIVE DAMAGES

It is very hard to obtain and sustain through appellate review a substantial award of punitive damages. Nevertheless, some types of lawyer malpractice may justify such an award.

The terms "punitive damages" and "exemplary damages" are often used interchangeably. The purpose of such an assessment is to punish and make an example of the defendant.

### § 5-5.2(a) State Law Limitations

Punitive damages (also called exemplary damages) are available only in cases of highly culpable conduct. Ordinarily, proof of mere negligence in a legal malpractice action will never support a punitive award.[57]

In some states, the standard for recovery of punitive damages is exceedingly demanding. For example, a Texas statute provides:

> (a) * * * [E]xemplary damages may be awarded only if the claimant proves by clear and convincing evidence that the harm with respect to which the claimant seeks recovery of exemplary damages results from: (1) fraud; (2) malice; or (3) gross negligence. * * *

---

[53] 299 S.W.3d 106 (Tex. 2009).

[54] *Id.* at 109.

[55] 299 S.W.2d at 114.

[56] 859 N.W.2d 643, 656 (Iowa 2015).

[57] *See* Call v. Czaplicki, 2010 WL 3001395, *8 (D. N.J. 2010); *but see* In re Tylenol (Acetaminophen) Mktg., Sales Practices and Products Liab. Litig., 144 F. Supp. 3d 680, 684–87 (E.D. Pa. 2015) ("In Alabama, only punitive damages are available in wrongful death actions, and these damages may be awarded against a defendant based on its negligent conduct").

(d) Exemplary damages may be awarded only if the jury was unanimous in regard to finding liability for and the amount of exemplary damages.[58]

Discussing the "malice" provision in this statute, the Texas Supreme Court explained in a legal malpractice case, *Smith v. O'Donnell*:[59]

> Malice has both an objective and a subjective prong; proof of malice involves an objective determination that the defendant's conduct involves an extreme risk of harm, and a subjective determination that the defendant had actual awareness of the extreme risk created by his conduct.[60]

Addressing the claim before it, which involved allegedly defective advice to an estate executor, the *Smith* court found no evidence that the defendant law firm intended to cause injury or acted with actual awareness of an extreme risk of harm. Consequently, there was no basis for an award of exemplary damages under Texas law. Of course, other states frame the requirements for an award of punitive damages in different terms.

To justify an award of punitive damages, conduct must be not only highly culpable, but clearly established. A majority of states now require clear and convincing evidence of entitlement to a punitive award.

#### *§ 5-5.2(a)(1) Caps and Bans on Punitive Damages*

Many jurisdictions have capped the amount of punitive damages that may be recovered from a defendant, either in tort actions generally or in legal malpractice suits in particular. However, these restrictions vary greatly.

For example, Alaska generally restricts a punitive award to the greater of three times compensatory damages or $500,000.[61] However, if the defendant's action is motivated by financial gain, punitive damages are limited to the greater of four times compensatory damages, four times the aggregate amount of financial gain, or $7,000,000.[62]

In Colorado, punitive damages may not exceed actual damages or, if there are aggravating circumstances, three times actual damages.[63]

In Kansas, a punitive damages award, with certain exceptions, may be no more than $5 million or the gross income of the defendant, whichever is less.[64]

In Texas, except when conduct violates selected rules in the state penal code, "[e]xemplary damages awarded against a defendant may not exceed an amount equal to the greater of: (1) (A) two times the amount of economic damages; plus (B) an amount equal to any noneconomic damages found by the jury, not to exceed $750,000; or (2) $200,000."[65]

---

[58] TEX. CIV. PRAC. & REM. CODE § 41.003 (Westlaw 2017).

[59] 288 S.W.3d 417 (Tex. 2009).

[60] *Id.* at 423.

[61] *See* ALASKA STAT. § 09.17.020(f) (Westlaw 2017).

[62] *See id.* § 09.17.020(g).

[63] COLO. REV. STAT. ANN. § 13–21–102 (Westlaw 2017).

[64] *See* KAN. STAT. ANN. § 60–3701(1)(e)–(f) (Westlaw 2017).

[65] TEX. CIV. PRAC. & REM. CODE § 41.008 (Westlaw 2017).

In Connecticut, damages awarded to punish may not exceed litigation expenses less taxable costs.[66]

A Nebraska constitutional provision precludes an award of punitive damages.[67] In Washington State, a similar rule was judicially created.[68]

Illinois expressly bans awards of punitive damages in legal malpractice cases. A state statute provides:

> In all cases, whether in tort, contract or otherwise, in which the plaintiff seeks damages by reason of legal, medical, hospital, or other healing art malpractice, no punitive, exemplary, vindictive or aggravated damages shall be allowed.[69]

#### *§ 5-5.2(a)(2) Partial Forfeiture to the State*

Some states have passed laws requiring part of any punitive damages award to be forfeited to the state. For example, an Iowa statute requires forfeiture of at least 75% of a punitive award, unless the defendant's conduct was directed specifically at the claimant.[70]

### § 5-5.2(b) Federal Constitutional Limitations

The two key decisions of the United States Supreme Court limiting awards of punitive damages are *BMW of North America, Inc. v. Gore*[71] and *State Farm Mutual Automobile Ins. Co. v. Campbell*.[72] The latter case ultimately gave rise to a legal malpractice claim.[73] Subsequent cases have explored the meaning of *Gore* and *Campbell*. These various decisions are discussed in the sections that follow.

#### *§ 5-5.2(b)(1) BMW of North America v. Gore*

In *Gore*, Justice John Paul Stevens explained for the Supreme Court:

> Elementary notions of fairness enshrined in our constitutional jurisprudence dictate that a person receive fair notice not only of the conduct that will subject him to punishment, but also of the severity of the penalty that a State may impose.[74]

With this principle in mind, *Gore* then identified three guideposts for determining whether a punitive award complies with the demands of due process. In reviewing awards, courts must consider: (1) the degree of reprehensibility of the defendant's misconduct; (2) the disparity between the actual or potential harm suffered by the plaintiff and the punitive damages award; and (3) the difference between the punitive damages awarded by the jury and the civil penalties authorized or imposed in comparable cases.

---

66 *See* Triangle Sheet Metal Works, Inc. v. Silver, 222 A.2d 220 (Conn. 1966).

67 *See* NEB. CONST. art. VII, § 5 (Westlaw 2017).

68 *See* Spokane Truck & Dray Co. v. Hoefer, 25 P. 1072 (Wash. 1891).

69 735 ILCS 5/2–1115 (Westlaw 2017).

70 *See* IOWA CODE ANN. § 668A.1(2)(b) (Westlaw 2017).

71 517 U.S. 559 (1996).

72 538 U.S. 408 (2003).

73 *See* Christensen & Jensen, P.C. v. Barrett & Daines, 194 P.3d 931 (Utah 2008).

74 517 U.S. at 574.

### *§ 5-5.2(b)(2) State Farm Mutual Automobile Insurance v. Campbell*

In *Campbell*,[75] the Supreme Court explored the meaning of *Gore*. Addressing the first guidepost, Justice Anthony Kennedy wrote for the Court that:

> [T]he most important indicium of the reasonableness of a punitive damages award is the degree of reprehensibility of the defendant's conduct." * * *. We have instructed courts to determine the reprehensibility of a defendant by considering whether: the harm caused was physical as opposed to economic; the tortious conduct evinced an indifference to or a reckless disregard of the health or safety of others; the target of the conduct had financial vulnerability; the conduct involved repeated actions or was an isolated incident; and the harm was the result of intentional malice, trickery, or deceit, or mere accident * * *. The existence of any one of these factors weighing in favor of a plaintiff may not be sufficient to sustain a punitive damages award; and the absence of all of them renders any award suspect. It should be presumed a plaintiff has been made whole for his injuries by compensatory damages, so punitive damages should only be awarded if the defendant's culpability, after having paid compensatory damages, is so reprehensible as to warrant the imposition of further sanctions to achieve punishment or deterrence * * *.[76]

Justice Kennedy then made the following points, which are paraphrased here from the opinion of the Court:

- A State cannot base an award of punitive damages on conduct that was lawful where it occurred; or, generally, on unlawful conduct that was committed outside the State's jurisdiction; or on dissimilar acts of the defendant that occurred independent of the acts upon which liability is premised; or on hypothetical claims involving injuries to third parties;[77] and
- A defendant should be punished for conduct that harmed the plaintiff, not for being an unsavory individual or business.[78]

Elaborating on the relevance of events that occurred outside the jurisdiction to a punitive damages award, Justice Kennedy explained:

- Lawful out-of-state conduct may be probative when it demonstrates the deliberateness and culpability of the defendant's action in the State where it is tortious, but that conduct must have a nexus to the specific harm suffered by the plaintiff.[79]

Addressing the significance of harm to others, Justice Kennedy acknowledged that "evidence of other acts need not be identical to have relevance in the calculation of punitive damages."[80] He further explained:

- Although "[o]ur holdings that a recidivist may be punished more severely than a first offender recognize that repeated misconduct is more reprehensible than

---

[75] State Farm Mut. Auto. Ins. Co. v. Campbell, 538 U.S. 408 (2003).

[76] *Id.* at 419.

[77] *Id.* at 421–23.

[78] *See id.* at 423.

[79] *See id.* at 422.

[80] *Id.* at 423.

an individual instance of malfeasance," in the context of civil actions courts must ensure the conduct in question replicates the prior transgressions.[81]

The *Campbell* court then turned to the second guidepost, namely the relationship between the actual or potential harm suffered by the plaintiff and the size of the punitive damages award. In terms paraphrased from the language of Justice Kennedy:

- While there are no rigid benchmarks, few awards exceeding a single-digit ratio will comply with the demands of due process.[82]
- Greater ratios may pass constitutional muster if particularly egregious conduct has resulted in only a small amount of economic damages.[83]
- However, if compensatory damages are substantial, a lesser ratio of punitive damages (perhaps only 1:1), will be the maximum that due process allows.[84]
- The wealth of a defendant, and the fact that the defendant may be punished only in rare cases, cannot justify an otherwise unconstitutional punitive damages award.[85]

The Court's single-digit ratio maxim suggests that there may be a great difference between a 9:1 ratio and a 10:1 ratio of punitive to compensatory damages. Nine to one is a single-digit ratio; ten to one is a double-digit ratio.

The third guidepost articulated in *Gore*—namely, the disparity between a punitive damages award and the civil penalties authorized or imposed in comparable cases—is typically the least useful factor in determining whether a punitive damages award violates due process. No clear rule-of-thumb has emerged. Thus, in *Campbell*, the Supreme Court said little about this consideration. Justice Kennedy wrote simply that:

> The existence of a criminal penalty does have bearing on the seriousness with which a State views the wrongful action. When used to determine the dollar amount of the award, however, the criminal penalty has less utility * * *.[86]

In overturning a multimillion dollar punitive damages award, the *Campbell* court merely noted that the award dwarfed the most relevant civil sanction under state law for the wrong in question, a $10,000 fine.[87]

*Campbell* was remanded for further proceedings consistent with the standard announced by the Supreme Court, which had opined that, in light of the substantial compensatory damages award of $1 million, the facts "likely would justify a punitive damages award at or near the amount of compensatory damages."[88] However, the Utah Supreme Court ultimately approved a generous $9,018,780.75 in punitive damages, an amount barely within the single-digit ratio articulated by the United States Supreme Court.[89]

---

[81] *Id.*

[82] *Id.* at 425.

[83] *Id.*

[84] *Id.*

[85] *Id.* at 427.

[86] *Id.* at 428.

[87] *Id.*

[88] *Id.* at 429.

[89] *See* Christensen & Jensen, P.C. v. Barrett & Daines, 194 P.3d 931, 936 (Utah 2008).

### *§ 5-5.2(b)(3) Subsequent Supreme Court Cases*

Subsequent to *Campbell*, the Supreme Court emphasized that an award of punitive damages may not be based, even in part, on a jury's desire to punish a defendant for harming nonparties. In *Philip Morris USA v. Williams*,[90] the jury, in response to the plaintiff's argument that many other smokers had been killed by the defendant's cigarettes, made a large punitive damages award to the estate of a heavy smoker. In remanding the case for further proceedings, Justice Stephen Breyer's opinion for the court explained:

> [T]he Due Process Clause prohibits a State from punishing an individual without first providing that individual with "an opportunity to present every available defense." * * *. Yet a defendant threatened with punishment for injuring a nonparty victim has no opportunity to defend against the charge, by showing, for example * * *, that the other victim was not entitled to damages * * *.
>
> * * * [T]o permit punishment for injuring a nonparty victim would add a near standardless dimension to the punitive damages equation. How many such victims are there? How seriously were they injured? Under what circumstances did injury occur? The trial will not likely answer such questions as to nonparty victims. The jury will be left to speculate * * *.
>
> * * * [W]e can find no authority supporting the use of punitive damages awards for the purpose of punishing a defendant for harming others * * *.
>
> Respondent argues that she is free to show harm to other victims because it is relevant to a different part of the punitive damages constitutional equation, namely, reprehensibility. * * *. Yet for the reasons given above, a jury may not go further than this and use a punitive damages verdict to punish a defendant directly on account of harms it is alleged to have visited on nonparties.
>
> * * *. We * * * conclude that the Due Process Clause requires States to provide assurance that juries are not asking the wrong question, i.e., seeking, not simply to determine reprehensibility, but also to punish for harm caused [to] strangers.[91]

In *Exxon Shipping Co. v. Baker*,[92] a case arising from an Alaskan oil spill, the Court held that, under federal maritime law, an award of punitive damages could not exceed the jury's substantial compensatory damages award of $507.5 million.

## § 5-5.2(c) Limitations on Punitive Awards in Legal Malpractice Cases

Like other forms of tort litigation, legal malpractice cases are subject to the limitations announced in the *Gore-Campbell* line of cases. This means, among other things, that punitive awards are unlikely to exceed compensatory damages by a factor of ten or more even in cases of highly egregious conduct, such as intentional overbilling of clients or using a Ponzi scheme to defraud investors.

---

[90] 549 U.S. 346 (2007).

[91] *Id.* at 353–55.

[92] 554 U.S. 471 (2008).

Questions sometimes arise as to whether an award of statutory damages is punitive and therefore subject to constitutional restrictions on punitive awards. In *Goldfine v. Barack, Ferrazzano, Kirschbaum & Perlman*,[93] the Illinois Supreme Court held that it was permissible to apply the civil remedies provisions of the Illinois Securities Law to calculate clients' damages in a legal malpractice action. "Those presumed damages included plaintiffs' loss of investment, plus statutory interest on their lost investments, attorney fees, and costs."[94] The court further held that such remedies did not constitute an award of punitive damages that was statutorily barred in a legal malpractice action, and that the total potential award of both statutory interest plus attorney fees did not amount to an excessive judgment in violation of the Due Process Clause.

### § 5-5.2(d) Vicarious Liability for Punitive Damages

If a law firm and or its principals are held vicariously liable for a punitive damages award based on the conduct of a lawyer in the firm, there is a risk that persons actually punished by the award will be innocent of any wrongdoing. Nevertheless, the United States Supreme Court has held that vicarious liability for punitive damages does not violate the Constitution. In *Pacific Mutual Life Ins. Co. v. Haslip*,[95] a case not involving legal malpractice, the Court explained:

> Imposing exemplary damages on the corporation when its agent commits intentional fraud creates a strong incentive for vigilance by those in a position "to guard substantially against the evil to be prevented." * * *. If * * * [an entity] were liable for such damages only upon proof that it was at fault independently, it would have an incentive to minimize oversight of its agents. Imposing liability without independent fault deters fraud more than a less stringent rule. It therefore rationally advances the State's goal [in allowing awards of punitive damages].[96]

Some states have passed statutes addressing the issue of vicarious liability for punitive damages. For example, Alaska law provides:

> In a civil action in which an employer is determined to be vicariously liable for the act or omission of an employee, punitive damages may not be awarded against the employer under principles of vicarious liability unless
>
> > (1) the employer or the employer's managerial agent (A) authorized the act or omission and the manner in which the act was performed or omission occurred; or (B) ratified or approved the act or omission after the act or omission occurred; or
> >
> > (2) the employee (A) was unfit to perform the act or avoid the omission and the employer or the employer's managerial agent acted recklessly in employing or retaining the employee; or (B) was employed in a managerial capacity and was acting within the scope of employment. * * *.[97]

---

[93] 18 N.E.3d 884 (Ill. 2014).

[94] *Id.* at 890.

[95] 499 U.S. 1 (1991).

[96] *Id.* at 14.

[97] ALASKA STAT. § 09.17.020(k) (Westlaw 2017).

### § 5-5.2(e) Liability for "Lost Punitive Damages"

A lawyer's negligence at trial may cause the plaintiff to lose not only compensatory damages, but a punitive award that would have been assessed in that litigation. This raises the question as to whether lawyers who commit litigation-related malpractice are liable for "lost punitive damages."

Some states allow malpractice plaintiffs to recover lost punitive damages as an element of compensation. However, other courts reject this approach.[98] The courts in the latter group generally reason that there is no entitlement to punitive damages; that making a merely negligent lawyer liable for a lost punitive award would punish the wrong party and exacerbate the costs of legal services and legal malpractice insurance; and that efforts to assess the size of a lost punitive award would amount to sheer speculation.[99]

## § 5-5.3 RESTITUTION

Restitution is a remedy which measures the plaintiff's entitlement to redress based not on what the plaintiff lost (damages), but on what the defendant improperly gained. Thus, a restitutionary remedy is designed to prevent unjust enrichment.

In many cases, a lawyer who commits malpractice enjoys no benefit at the plaintiff's expense. For example, the misdrafting of a will may mean that a portion of the decedent's estate goes not to A, but to B; it does not mean that the legacy in question goes to the lawyer. In this type of case, there is no basis to talk about restitution. Even though the lawyer was paid a fee for legal services, the payment was presumably made by the decedent rather than by the disappointed legatee. The lawyer has not been unjustly enriched at the expense of A, so as to give A the right to restitution.

However, in some situations, a lawyer wrongfully benefits at the plaintiff's expense. This may be true if confidential client information is misused and the lawyer thereby usurps a valuable business opportunity. In such a case, the client should be entitled to recover the value of what the lawyer gained, even though the client suffered no "out-of-pocket" losses.

For many years, the law of restitution was neglected by courts and scholars. However, the completion of the *Restatement (Third) of Restitution and Unjust Enrichment*[100] seems certain to catalyze a revival of this area of the law. Undoubtedly, restitutionary principles will find increased application in legal malpractice cases. An excellent illustration of how the law may develop is the increased prominence of claims for total or partial fee forfeiture in cases where a lawyer committed a clear and serious breach of duty.[101] Fee forfeiture is a remedy designed to prevent unjust enrichment. As noted earlier, forfeiture is generally available even if the plaintiff has not suffered provable damages.

---

[98] *See* Tri-G, Inc. v. Burke, Bosselman & Weaver, 856 N.E.2d 389 (Ill. 2006).

[99] *See* Osborne v. Keeney, 399 S.W.3d 1, 19 (Ky. 2012); RESTATEMENT (THIRD) OF THE LAW GOVERNING LAWYERS § 53 cmt. h (American Law Institute, 2000).

[100] RESTATEMENT (THIRD) OF RESTITUTION AND UNJUST ENRICHMENT (American Law Institute, 2011).

[101] *See supra* § 5-3.4.

# Chapter 5-6

# DEFENSES AND OBSTACLES TO RECOVERY

**By Susan Saab Fortney and Vincent R. Johnson**

*Table of Sections*

§ 5-6.1 In General
§ 5-6.2 Defenses Based on the Plaintiff's Conduct
§ 5-6.3 Privileges and Immunities Based on the Defendant's Conduct
§ 5-6.4 Defenses Arising by Operation of Law

## § 5-6.1 IN GENERAL

With respect to lawyer liability, defenses are as important as causes of action. Even if a lawyer has blatantly violated the standard of care and caused serious damages, a defense may defeat the plaintiff's claim or limit the extent of the defendant's liability. There are three broad categories of defenses relevant to legal malpractice claims.

The first category deals with conduct on the part of the plaintiff. This includes carelessness and unlawful conduct that contributes to the harm for which recovery is sought, as well as the plaintiff's failure to mitigate damages.

The second category of malpractice defenses relates to conduct on the part of the defendant, such as representation of a client or participation in litigation. These types of conduct may give rise to a qualified or absolute privilege which will defeat liability if the lawyer is sued by a nonclient. Also within this category are the immunities which sometimes bar actions against public defenders or court-appointed lawyers or that arise under special statutes.

The third category of malpractice defenses concerns obstacles to recovery that arise mainly by operation of law. This category encompasses statutes of limitations (including tolling under a discovery rule or a continuing representation doctrine, and caps on tolling under statutes of repose), the rules governing joint and several liability and related matters (such as indemnity, contribution, and credits for payments made by other tortfeasors), and the general non-assignability of malpractice claims. Also within this category are the rules governing arbitration agreements or settlement documents, or raising an estoppel based on allegations made by the plaintiff in earlier litigation.

These various topics, and their application to legal malpractice actions, are discussed below. Of course procedural defenses, such as lack of personal jurisdiction, may also play an important role in legal malpractice litigation.[1]

---

1 *See* Cassandra Burke Robertson, *Personal Jurisdiction in Legal Malpractice Litigation*, 6 ST. MARY'S J. LEGAL MAL. & ETHICS 2 (2016).

## § 5-6.2 DEFENSES BASED ON THE PLAINTIFF'S CONDUCT

The plaintiff's own conduct can give rise to a total or partial defense in a legal malpractice action in at least three ways. First, carelessness on the part of the plaintiff may be a defense under the doctrines of contributory negligence, comparative negligence, or comparative fault. Second, unreasonable failure to mitigate damages may reduce recovery from the defendant. Third, some forms of unlawful conduct constitute a total barrier to recovery of damages in a legal malpractice action.

### § 5-6.2(a) Contributory Negligence, Comparative Negligence, and Comparative Fault

In the vast majority of states with comparative negligence or comparative fault regimes, the plaintiff's recovery in a malpractice action may be reduced based on the plaintiff's own carelessness, if that conduct contributed to the harm for which damages are claimed. On appropriate facts, such carelessness might consist of the plaintiff's failure to read a document, supply accurate information, or carry out a lawyer's request for action that is needed to protect the client's interests.

In *Yale v. Bowne*,[2] a lawyer negligently failed to implement his client's express instruction to maintain her assets as separate property in certain trust documents. However, the California Court of Appeal affirmed a 10% reduction in the plaintiff's damages under the state's comparative fault regime because the jury had allocated 10% of the fault to the client. That finding was supported by the evidence, which showed that "[w]hen . . . [the client] read the words 'community property' in two of the deeds, she understood what that meant but she did not say anything to . . . [her lawyer] about the use of the term 'community property' or raise any other question with him about the effect of these deeds."[3]

In another case, a former professional athlete, who was represented by a law firm in the purchase of a jet, alleged that he did not understand the changing terms of the deal and that the law firm did not advise him that he would be liable for a $7 million loan. A jury returned a verdict in favor of the plaintiff, but reduced his recovery because he bore some responsibility for entering into the ill-advised transaction.[4]

In states with "modified," rather than "pure," systems of comparative negligence or comparative fault, a plaintiff is totally barred from recovery, rather than allowed a reduced recovery, if the plaintiff's share of the negligence or fault is greater than 50%. Whether a plaintiff who is exactly 50% responsible is entitled to a reduced recovery, or no recovery at all, depends on the wording of the applicable comparative negligence or comparative fault rule.

A few states (Maryland, Virginia, North Carolina, and Alabama, as well as the District of Columbia) have never adopted comparative negligence or comparative fault. They continue to adhere to the doctrine of contributory negligence. Under that rule, any negligence on the part of the plaintiff is a total bar to an action for negligence. Thus, in legal malpractice actions, any carelessness on the part of a client or other plaintiff will preclude recovery from a lawyer for professional negligence. For example, in *Lyle, Siegel,*

---

[2] 9 Cal. App. 5th 649 (2017).

[3] *Id.* at 656.

[4] *See* Karen Sloan, *Former NBA Star Wins $2 Million Legal Malpractice Judgment*, NAT'L L.J. (July 2, 2010).

*Croshaw & Beale, P.C. v. Tidewater Capital Corp.*,[5] the Supreme Court of Virginia found that there was a question of fact as to whether the actions and knowledge of a partner in the defendant law firm, who was also a 50% shareholder of the plaintiff client, could be imputed to the client. If so, the client would be barred from recovery by the state's contributory negligence rule.[6]

Carelessness (*i.e.*, negligence) on the part of a malpractice plaintiff is never a defense to an intentional tort claim. Therefore, a lawyer who steals a client's money cannot argue that the client was careless in entrusting the money to the lawyer or in monitoring the lawyer's conduct. Carelessness is also not a defense to a breach of contract claim.

### § 5-6.2(b) Avoidable Consequences and the Failure to Mitigate

A lawyer ordinarily is not liable for damages that a malpractice plaintiff could have avoided through the exercise of reasonable care after the lawyer's breach of duty caused harm. This avoidable consequences principle is sometimes referred to as the plaintiff's duty to mitigate damages.

For example, if a lawyer's negligence results in the entry of a default judgment against a client, the cost of the judgment is not compensable if it was feasible for the client to have moved to vacate the default judgment and the motion would have been granted. However, in *Grochocinski v. Mayer Brown Rowe & Maw LLP*,[7] a federal court in Illinois found that these issues were so legally and factually complex that they could not be decided on a motion for summary judgment.

Alternatively, suppose that a lawyer's malpractice subjects a client's successor-in-interest to claims by a third party, and that the successor settles those claims at an inflated price. If the defendant law firm can prove at trial that there was a collusive settlement of the underlying demands, that evidence would presumably negate causation and/or mitigate damages related to the successor's legal malpractice claim.[8]

In *McCormick International USA, Inc. v. Shore*,[9] a client (Roberta) hired a lawyer (Bokides) to represent her in her divorce from William. Under the terms of the divorce decree, William acquired all interests in the couple's business, Bear River Equipment, Inc. (Bear River), a farm equipment dealer. Roberta instructed Bokides to provide notice to McCormick International USA, Inc. (McCormick), a Bear River creditor, that she would no longer personally guarantee its advances, but such notice was never given. In a subsequent legal malpractice action Bokides argued "that Roberta failed to mitigate her damages because she did not seek to enforce the divorce decree's mandate that William hold her harmless from all Bear River debts."[10] In affirming the trial court's rejection of that argument, the Supreme Court of Idaho wrote:

> The defendant bears the burden of proving that the proposed means of mitigation were reasonable under the circumstances, could be accomplished at a reasonable cost, and were within the plaintiff's ability.* * * Proof of the latter

---

5 457 S.E.2d 28 (Va. 1995).

6 *See id.* at 32 ("contributory negligence is available as a defense in a legal malpractice action").

7 2007 WL 1875995 (N.D. Ill.).

8 *See* Smith v. O'Donnell, 288 S.W.3d 417, 422 (Tex. 2009).

9 277 P.3d 367 (Idaho 2012).

10 *Id.* at 369.

> of these three requires more than a mere suggestion that a means of mitigation exists. . . . [W]hen advancing a claim that the plaintiff failed to mitigate damages, the defendant must prove both that a means of mitigation existed and that the proposed course of mitigation would, in fact, have resulted in a reduction of the plaintiff's damages.
>
> The adage that one cannot get blood from a turnip is applicable to this appeal. The fact that Roberta had a legal right to obtain indemnification from William does not lead inexorably to the conclusion that he possessed the ability to provide such indemnification. * * *.[11]

Failure to mitigate damages is now treated as a form of comparative fault in many jurisdictions.[12]

### § 5-6.2(c) Unlawful Conduct

In recent years, many states have legislatively enacted or judicially recognized, in a wide range of circumstances, what amounts to an unlawful conduct defense. The defense goes by various names.[13] However, in general terms, it bars recovery for damages that are the direct result of knowingly participating in serious criminal or tortious conduct.

The unlawful conduct defense plays an important role in legal malpractice cases. Thus, a client who is found to have lied under oath cannot sue the lawyer who advised the client to commit perjury. Likewise, a business involved in defrauding investors may not be able to sue its lawyers for having negligently facilitated the transactions.[14]

#### *§ 5-6.2(c)(1) A Defense in Many Guises*

In some cases, the unlawful conduct defense is really an attack on the causation element of a legal malpractice claim. Courts often hold that the plaintiff's criminal conduct makes it impossible to prove that the alleged malpractice caused damages.

For example, in *Fang v. Bock*,[15] representatives of a university legal aid office were allegedly negligent in advising the plaintiff that he would not be deported if he pleaded guilty to assaulting a family member. After the plaintiff entered that plea, he was deported to China. Although the plaintiff's initial guilty plea was eventually withdrawn, and a conviction pursuant to a second guilty plea was expunged, the Supreme Court of Montana rejected the plaintiff's malpractice claim. The plaintiff alleged that as a result of the bad legal advice he was exposed to the possibility of removal from the country and had to spend large sums of money. However, the court found that the plaintiff's legal expenses and deportation predicament were the result of his own unlawful conduct, which he had admitted on two separate occasions. He would have been exposed to

---

[11] *Id.* at 371.

[12] *See* UNIFORM COMPARATIVE FAULT ACT § 1(b), 12 U.L.A. 123 (Westlaw 2017).

[13] *See* Vincent R. Johnson, *The Unlawful Conduct Defense in Legal Malpractice*, 77 UMKC L. REV. 43, 46 (2008) ("Rulings deny relief from errant attorneys under the rubric of *in pari delicto*, unclean hands, and even proximate causation.").

[14] *See* Kevin H. Michels, *The Corporate Attorney as "Internal" Gatekeeper and the In Pari Delicto Defense: A Proposed New Standard*, 4 ST. MARY'S J. LEGAL MAL. & ETHICS 318, 318 (2014) ("Attorneys can interpose an *in pari delicto* defense to corporation claims for malpractice, arguing that knowledge of the executive's wrongdoing should be imputed to the corporation and, as a result, the latter should be barred from recovery because it is 'equally or more culpable' than the failed attorney gatekeeper").

[15] 28 P.3d 456 (Mont. 2001).

removal from the country, based on his conduct, with or without the allegedly negligent advice. In cases like *Fang*, the plaintiff's unlawful conduct is not an affirmative defense that needs to be pleaded and proved by the defendant, but rather a matter which negates the causation element of the plaintiff's *prima facie* case.[16]

On other occasions, the plaintiff's unlawful conduct is treated as an affirmative defense. Thus, in some suits, the plaintiff is said to be barred from seeking recourse in the courts because the plaintiff is "*in pari delicto*" (equally at fault) with the defendant, has "unclean hands," or is a party to an illegal contract.[17] However, there is so much imprecision and questionable precedent surrounding these equitable doctrines that it is better to talk, as some courts do, in straight-forward terms about an unlawful conduct defense with clear requirements.

One of the better definitions of such a defense was offered in *Barker v. Kallash*,[18] a case not involving legal malpractice. There, the New York Court of Appeals explained that "when the plaintiff has engaged in activities prohibited, as opposed to merely regulated, by law, the courts will not entertain the suit if the plaintiff's conduct constituted a serious violation of the law and the injuries for which he seeks recovery were the direct result of that violation."[19]

It is important to remember that any formulation of the unlawful conduct defense which too readily closes the court house doors to legal malpractice claims threatens to undercut the deterrent force of tort law and its ability to discourage bad professional practices. Comparative fault principles already make it possible to reduce a plaintiff's recovery based on the plaintiff's own fault. Consequently, recognition of a total bar to recovery based on unlawful conduct is only needed if there are interests at stake so significant that they warrant full denial of judicial relief.

In general, this means only the most serious forms of unlawful conduct, knowingly committed by the plaintiff, should suffice as the predicate for an unlawful conduct defense in a legal malpractice action. The plaintiff's commission of fraud, perjury, or another grievous felony readily falls within this category. Of course, the plaintiff's knowing perpetration of serious unlawful conduct must be convincingly proven, either by prior adjudication in a criminal or civil proceeding, or in the legal malpractice action itself. Finally, the plaintiff's unlawful conduct should be a total defense to liability only if that conduct is both a factual and proximate cause of the plaintiff's injury, judged according to ordinary tort principles. To satisfy the demands of factual causation, the plaintiff's conduct must normally have been such a substantial factor that it made an indispensable contribution to the production of the harm (*i.e.*, was a but-for cause). Further, to meet the requirements of proximate causation, the harm for which the plaintiff seeks recovery must have been a foreseeable result or a direct consequence of the plaintiff's unlawful conduct.

---

[16] *Id.* at 460 (finding the plaintiff failed to prove that the alleged malpractice was a "but for" cause of the harm that he suffered).

[17] *See* In re ICP Strategic Credit Income Fund Ltd., 2017 WL 1929546 (S.D.N.Y.) (holding that the doctrine of *in pari delicto* under New York law barred liquidators' claims against a law firm for aiding and abetting a breach of fiduciary duty); *see also* Taylor v. Riley, 336 P.3d 256, 262 (Idaho 2014) (illegality doctrine inapplicable).

[18] 468 N.E.2d 39 (N.Y. 1984).

[19] *Id.* at 41 (holding that a fifteen-year-old boy who was injured while constructing a "pipe bomb" was precluded from recovering from the nine-year-old boy who supplied the gunpowder).

Nevertheless, there are many cases which apply the unlawful conduct defense in a largely free-wheeling fashion. When that happens, the defense may threaten to immunize large classes of lawyers from malpractice liability. As discussed below, this is true in numerous states with respect to malpractice arising from representation of persons accused of crime.

### *§ 5-6.2(c)(2) Exoneration or Innocence Requirement in Criminal-Defense Malpractice*

In the legal malpractice field, the unlawful conduct defense finds its clearest endorsement in the decisions requiring persons alleging defective criminal representation to first overturn their convictions and, in some states, also prove their innocence of the crimes for which they were prosecuted.[20] Although these cases do not use the term "unlawful conduct defense," they clearly seize upon the defendant's unlawful conduct to insulate lawyers from liability.

What is most striking about state exoneration or innocence requirements is how broadly they sweep. Any kind of criminal conduct (misdemeanors as well as felonies), however established (whether by plea or conviction), often wholly bars an action for professional negligence (regardless of the gravity of the lawyer's misconduct). It is easy to doubt the wisdom of these formidable obstacles to recovery for lawyer wrongdoing. Not surprisingly, exoneration and innocence requirements have been widely criticized.

To begin with, these obstacles to recovery—which are not affirmative defenses, but additional requirements in the plaintiff's *prima facie* case—are simply doctrinal overkill. If the concern is that an undeserving claim will succeed, there is little cause for worry. It is difficult for even appealing and sympathetic plaintiffs with good facts to prevail on legal malpractice claims. Presumably, it is all the more challenging for one carrying the stigma of actual or apparent criminality to do so. The difficulty of finding an attorney to initiate a malpractice action, the nature of the jury system, the demanding requirements of the "trial within a trial" causation analysis, and the rules that protect a lawyer's exercise of discretion, all conspire to defeat a malpractice claim raised by one charged with or convicted of a crime.[21]

In addition, exoneration or innocence requirements are of dubious value from the standpoint of legal deterrence. In the sphere of criminal defense work, there are virtually no formal legal mechanisms for enforcing the standards of conduct that should be observed by lawyers.[22] Requests for post-conviction relief based on ineffective assistance of counsel seldom succeed. Disciplinary sanctions against errant criminal defense lawyers are infrequently imposed. Motions for disqualification or disgorgement of fees are essentially unheard of in the world of criminal representation.

One explanation for the rush by states to adopt exoneration and innocence requirements is that this is just another effort to limit the rights of criminals and those

---

[20] *But see* Molen v. Christian, 388 P.3d 591, 596 (Idaho 2017) ("actual innocence is not an element"); Barker v. Capotosto, 875 N.W.2d 157, 168 (Iowa 2016) ("actual innocence is not a prerequisite").

[21] *See* Susan Saab Fortney, *A Tort in Search of a Remedy: Prying Open the Courthouse Doors for Legal Malpractice Victims*, 85 FORDHAM L. REV. 2033, 2045–2046 (2017) (examining the special challenges that face plaintiffs pursuing malpractice claims against criminal defense lawyers).

[22] *See* Thomas P. Sullivan & Maurice Possley, *The Chronic Failure to Discipline Prosecutors for Misconduct: Proposals for Reform*, 105 J. CRIM. L. & CRIMINOLOGY 881, 881 (2015) (describing "the distressing, decades-long absence of discipline imposed on prosecutors whose knowing misconduct has resulted in terrible injustices being visited upon defendants throughout the country").

suspected of crimes. In other words, one might argue, these requirements are just another part of the ongoing "war on crime." However, a more convincing explanation is that proponents of these rules were concerned about the risk of criminal defense attorneys, often appointed by courts and poorly compensated, being deluged with malpractice claims filed by prisoners, chilling the willingness of attorneys to represent indigent defendants.

*§ 5-6.2(c)(2)(A) Lesser Included Offenses*

Some courts hold that a plaintiff suing with respect to malpractice committed during criminal representation must prove not only innocence of the charge directly related to the malpractice, but also innocence of lesser included offenses.[23] For example, in *Sangha v. La Barbera*,[24] the defendant-lawyer was allegedly negligent in advising the plaintiff to plead guilty to felony vandalism. Subsequently, that plea was set aside when the plaintiff retained new counsel and admitted guilt to a misdemeanor vandalism charge. The California Court of Appeal rejected the plaintiff's argument that he only needed to prove innocence of the offense to which the malpractice was directly related. Consequently, the plaintiff's misdemeanor plea was an insuperable obstacle to his malpractice claim. The court quoted with approval an earlier decision which opined that "damages should only be awarded to a person who is truly free from any criminal involvement."[25]

*§ 5-6.2(c)(2)(B) Sentencing Errors*

Some jurisdictions otherwise requiring proof of actual innocence hold that the requirement does not apply to malpractice claims based on sentencing errors. For example, in *Jones v. Link*,[26] a lawyer improperly failed to object to a five-level enhancement when his client was sentenced. Thereafter, the client proved that he had received ineffective assistance of counsel, and his sentence was reduced by 36 months. In a subsequent malpractice action, the court held, in line with other jurisdictions, that it is not necessary to prove actual innocence in this kind of case because "the improper sentence was not the direct result of the plaintiff's criminal behavior, but rather, it was the proximate result of his attorney's negligence."[27]

*§ 5-6.2(c)(2)(C) Limits on the Unlawful Conduct Defense*

Some states have limited the use of unlawful conduct as a defense in tort actions. For example, in *Dugger v. Arredondo*,[28] the Texas Supreme Court held that a common law unlawful acts doctrine was not available as an affirmative defense in personal injury and wrongful death cases because "[l]ike other common law assumption of the risk defenses, it was abrogated by * * * [the state's adoption of a statutory] proportionate responsibility scheme."[29] Clarifying that point, Justice Paul Green explained, "[u]nless the requirements of the affirmative defense in section 93.001 [a statutory unlawful conduct rule with a limited scope] are satisfied, a plaintiff's share of responsibility for

---

[23] *See* Foondle v. O'Brien, 346 P.3d 970, 974 (Alaska 2015) (rule stated).

[24] 52 Cal. Rptr. 3d 640 (Cal. Ct. App. 2006).

[25] *Id.* at 647.

[26] 493 F. Supp. 2d 765 (E.D. Va. 2007).

[27] *Id.* at 770.

[28] 408 S.W.3d 825 (Tex. 2013).

[29] *Id.* at 836.

his or her injuries should be compared against the defendant's."[30] Commentators addressing legal malpractice liability have suggested that in light of cases such as *Dugger*, "[t]he day may yet come when a criminal defendant's conduct operates not as a complete bar to recovery, but as the subject of a comparative responsibility analysis by the finder of fact."[31]

## § 5-6.3 PRIVILEGES AND IMMUNITIES BASED ON THE DEFENDANT'S CONDUCT

Privileges or immunities generally fall within two broad categories: absolute and qualified. Conduct coming within the terms of an absolute privilege or immunity is wholly insulated from the risk of liability. The defendant's state of mind and the reasonableness of the defendant's conduct are generally irrelevant. In contrast, a qualified privilege or immunity is conditional, which is to say defeasible. Depending on what the defendant knows, or how or why the defendant acted, the protection of a qualified privilege or immunity may be lost.

### § 5-6.3(a) The Absolute Judicial Proceedings Privilege (Litigation Privilege)

The judicial proceedings privilege, which is sometimes called the litigation privilege, bars a wide variety of claims arising from statements made by participants in lawsuits, such as lawyers, clients, and witnesses.[32] Thus, while the privilege is frequently asserted to defeat defamation actions, it may also bar claims for fraud and intentional infliction of emotional distress.[33]

The privilege is absolute, so long as the statement in question, in a broad sense, is related to the litigation. The privilege applies not only to what is said in a courtroom, but also to depositions and pleadings, as well as certain other out-of-court utterances. This includes some statements made by lawyers before a suit is filed.[34]

Finding that courts apply an extremely liberal test in determining what statements are pertinent to litigation, and therefore protected, the United States Court of Appeals for the Second Circuit held that allegedly defamatory statements in an e-mail message relating to a fee dispute arising from litigation could not serve as the basis for a cause of action.[35]

Nevertheless, courts sometimes find that statements connected to litigation are not protected by the absolute judicial proceedings privilege. For example, in *Bochetto v. Gibson*,[36] a lawyer (Bochetto) was sued for malpractice based on conduct related to the defense of a client in quiet-title actions. In the legal malpractice action, the client (the malpractice plaintiff) was represented by a new lawyer (Gibson). The malpractice complaint alleged that Bochetto had breached fiduciary obligations by failing to disclose

---

[30] *Id.*

[31] John G. Browning & Lindsey Rames, *Proof of Exoneration in Legal Malpractice Cases: The Peeler Doctrine and Its Limits in Texas and Beyond*, 5 ST. MARY'S J. LEGAL MAL. & ETHICS 50, 133 (2014).

[32] For an examination of the reach of the litigation privilege, see Louis Lark Hill, *The Litigation Privilege: Its Place in Contemporary Jurisprudence*, 44 HOFSTRA L. REV. 401 (2015).

[33] *See* Simms v. Seaman, 69 A.3d 880, 893–907 (Conn. 2013).

[34] *See* RESTATEMENT (SECOND) OF TORTS § 586 (American Law Institute, 1977).

[35] *See* Cassuto v. Shulick, 313 Fed. Appx. 448 (2d Cir. 2009).

[36] 860 A.2d 67 (Pa. 2004).

an expert report to the client and by misconduct related to the procurement of a substitute expert report. After filing the legal malpractice complaint for his client, Gibson faxed a copy to a reporter with the *Legal Intelligencer* (Dudick). The result was the publication of a story which Bochetto claimed was false and defamatory.[37]

In Bochetto's defamation action against Gibson and his law firm, the defendants argued that the claim was barred by the judicial proceedings privilege. The Supreme Court of Pennsylvania held that absolute immunity extends only to communications which are issued in the regular course of judicial proceedings and are pertinent and material to the redress or relief the plaintiff seeks. Under this standard, Gibson's publication of the complaint to the trial court was clearly protected by the privilege. However, because Gibson's act of sending the complaint to Dudick was an extrajudicial act that occurred outside of the regular course of judicial proceedings, and was not relevant in any way to those proceedings, it plainly was not protected by the judicial proceedings privilege. The court noted, however, that liability for faxing the complaint to the reporter might be barred by a qualified privilege.[38]

The judicial proceedings privilege ordinarily applies only to claims arising from *statements* pertinent to litigation. Thus, a garden-variety malpractice claim by a client, based on a lawyer's acts or omissions during the course of a lawsuit, is not barred by the privilege. As the California Court of Appeal observed in *Kolar v. Donahue, McIntosh & Hammerton*,[39] there is no sound reason why litigators should be exempted from malpractice liability.

Nevertheless some courts envision the privilege as barring types of suits based on conduct as well as statements. For example, in *Taylor v. McNichols*,[40] the Supreme Court of Idaho wrote that "where an attorney is sued by the current or former adversary of his client, as a result of *actions* or communications that the attorney has taken or made in the course of his representation of his client in the course of litigation, the action is presumed to be barred by the litigation privilege."[41]

When the privilege is applied to statements made in litigation, it can be seen as facilitating the search for the truth and the fearless performance by participants of their respective roles in adjudication. Focusing on lawyers and the boundaries that set the limits for advocacy, the Idaho Supreme Court in *Taylor* explained:

> Application of the litigation privilege varies across jurisdictions, but the common thread found throughout is the idea that an attorney acting within the law, in a legitimate effort to zealously advance the interests of his client, shall be protected from civil claims arising due to that zealous representation. An attorney engaging in malicious prosecution, which is necessarily pursued in bad faith, is not acting in a manner reasonably calculated to advance his client's interests, and an attorney engaging in fraud is likewise acting in a manner foreign to his duties as an attorney. If an attorney engages in tortious interference with a third-party's interest out of a personal desire to harm, separate entirely from his desire to advance his client's interests, that

---

[37] *Id.* at 70.

[38] *Id.* at 73 n.15.

[39] 52 Cal. Rptr. 3d 712 (Cal. Ct. App. 2006).

[40] 243 P.3d 642 (Idaho 2010).

[41] *Id.* at 657 (emphasis added).

> attorney's conduct is not properly adjudged as occurring in the course of his representation of his client's interests.[42]

When misconduct occurs in the course of representation, judges may rely on procedural rules and the court's inherent authority to address such matters.

### § 5-6.3(b) Attorney Immunity

What some states treat as an aspect of the judicial proceedings or litigation privilege (discussed in the preceding section), other states have articulated as the doctrine of attorney immunity. In *Cantey Hanger, LLP v. Byrd*,[43] one divorce litigant "sued opposing counsel for fraud and related claims in connection with the law firm's alleged preparation of a document to effectuate the transfer of personal property awarded to its client in the [divorce] decree."[44] In holding that the claims were barred, the Texas Supreme Court, in a 5–4 decision, explained:

> This attorney-immunity defense is intended to ensure "loyal, faithful, and aggressive representation by attorneys employed as advocates." * * *. In accordance with this purpose, there is consensus among the courts of appeals that, as a general rule, attorneys are immune from civil liability to non-clients "for actions taken in connection with representing a client in litigation." * * *. Even conduct that is "wrongful in the context of the underlying suit" is not actionable if it is "part of the discharge of the lawyer's duties in representing his or her client." * * *. However, other mechanisms are in place to discourage and remedy such conduct, such as sanctions, contempt, and attorney disciplinary proceedings.[45]

In contrast to the many courts that note that there is no immunity for fraudulent conduct by a lawyer,[46] the Texas Supreme Court embraced a different rule, stating:

> Fraud is not an exception to attorney immunity; rather, the defense does not extend to fraudulent conduct that is outside the scope of an attorney's legal representation of his client, just as it does not extend to other wrongful conduct outside the scope of representation. An attorney who pleads the affirmative defense of attorney immunity has the burden to prove that his alleged wrongful conduct, regardless of whether it is labeled fraudulent, is part of the discharge of his duties to his client.[47]

It is difficult to see how fraudulent conduct can ever be within the scope of representation. Texas follows the widely embraced rule, which is also part of the *Model Rules of Professional Conduct*,[48] holding that "[a] lawyer shall not assist or counsel a client to engage in conduct that the lawyer knows is criminal or fraudulent."[49] If the *Cantey Hanger* court wanted to protect attorneys from claims by litigation adversaries,

---

[42] *Id.* at 656–57.

[43] 467 S.W.3d 477 (Tex. 2015).

[44] *Id.* at 479.

[45] *Id.* at 481–82.

[46] *See, e.g.*, Taylor v. McNichols, 243 P.3d 642 (Idaho 2010) ("an attorney engaging in fraud is * * * acting in a manner foreign to his duties as an attorney").

[47] *Id.* at 484.

[48] MODEL RULES OF PROF'L CONDUCT R. 1.2(d) (American Bar Ass'n, 2017) ("A lawyer shall not counsel a client to engage, or assist a client, in conduct that the lawyer knows is criminal or fraudulent").

[49] TEX. DISCIP. RULES OF PROF'L CONDUCT R. 1.02(c) (Westlaw 2017).

it would have been better to articulate a no-duty rule than to suggest that fraudulent conduct is sometimes within the scope of representation.

### § 5-6.3(c) Absolute Privilege for Truth

An allegedly defamatory statement may be privileged because it is substantially true. In *Pitcock v. Kasowitz, Benson, Torres & Friedman LLP*,[50] a trade publication reported that a partner had jump[ed] ship from the defendant law firm. In response, the law firm issued a press release stating that the ex-partner had been terminated because of extremely inappropriate behavior, which news reports said included suggestive comments, gender-specific jokes, and obscene gestures.[51] A New York appellate court ruled that the firm did not defame the ex-partner because the statements were substantially true.[52]

### § 5-6.3(d) Qualified Privileges

A qualified privilege arises when there is good reason for the law to encourage or permit certain types of conduct,[53] such as efforts by a lawyer to defend his or her professional reputation.[54] However, such a privilege is lost by abuse, which may occur if a person acts with an improper purpose or knowledge of a statement's falsity, or publishes a statement excessively by disseminating it to improper recipients.[55]

A lawyer has a qualified privilege to represent his or her client. Thus, a lawyer for one co-defendant can make an argument on that client's behalf even if the lawyer knows that doing so may cause harm to another, separately represented, co-defendant.[56]

### § 5-6.3(e) Immunity of Public Defenders and Appointed Lawyers

Public defenders are often protected from malpractice liability by some form of absolute or qualified statutory immunity. For example, in *Osborne v. Goodlett*,[57] the plaintiff alleged that his public defender committed malpractice by failing to interview a co-defendant and subpoena him for trial, preventing the plaintiff from testifying in his own defense, and otherwise not providing adequate representation. The Tennessee Court of Appeals found that the defendant-lawyer was absolutely immune under a state statute which provided:

---

[50] 903 N.Y.S.2d 43 (App. Div. 2010).

[51] *Id.* at 44.

[52] *Id.* at 45.

[53] *See* RESTATEMENT (SECOND) OF TORTS §§ 593–598A (American Law Institute, 1977).

[54] *See* Clement J. Hayes, Comment, *The Qualified Privilege of Texas Lawyers to Defend Their Reputations*, 5 ST. MARY'S J. LEGAL MAL. & ETHICS 192, 198 (2014) ("In general, the qualified privilege permits certain persons to make statements, or relay or report statements, that would be considered slander and libel if made by anyone else"); *but see* Laurel A. Rigertas, *How Do You Rate Your Lawyer: Lawyers' Responses to Online Reviews of Their Services*, 4 St. MARY'S J. LEGAL MAL. & ETHICS 242, 265 (2014) ("The *Restatement of the Law Governing Lawyers* states that a lawyer may only reveal client confidences 'to defend against charges that imminently threaten the lawyer or the lawyer's associate or agent with serious consequences, including criminal charges, claims of legal malpractice, and other civil actions . . . .' The *Restatement* further opines that the disclosure of confidential information in self-defense is warranted only when it constitutes a 'proportionate and restrained response to the charges' ").

[55] *See* RESTATEMENT (SECOND) OF TORTS §§ 599–605A (American Law Inst., 1977).

[56] *See* Maynard v. Caballero, 752 S.W.2d 719, 721 (Tex. App. 1988).

[57] 2005 WL 1713868 (Tenn. Ct. App.).

> State officers and employees are absolutely immune from liability for acts or omissions within the scope of the officer's or employee's office or employment, except for willful, malicious, or criminal acts or omissions or for acts or omissions done for personal gain. * * *.[58]

Moreover, the defendant in *Osborne* was further immune from suit because another statute provided in relevant part:

> No court in this state has any power, jurisdiction or authority to entertain any suit against * * * any public defender * * * with a view to reach the * * * funds or property of any public defender * * * for any act of negligence arising from the execution of * * * official duties as an employee of the district public defenders conference.[59]

However, some states, like California, have expressly ruled that public defenders are not immune from suit.[60]

Court-appointed lawyers often face greater exposure to malpractice liability than their public defender counter parts. A majority of states permit legal malpractice actions against attorneys appointed to represent criminal defendants * * * [and only] a small minority of states have statutes that provide immunity to attorneys appointed to represent indigent criminal defendants.[61]

Federal law does not provide immunity to a private lawyer appointed by a federal judge in a criminal case.[62] However, immunity may be conferred by state law. In *Mooney v. Frazier*, the Supreme Court of Appeals of West Virginia held that an attorney appointed by a federal court to represent a criminal defendant, in a federal criminal prosecution in West Virginia, has absolute immunity from purely state law claims of legal malpractice that derive from the attorney's conduct in the underlying criminal proceedings.[63]

In *Mashaney v. Board of Indigents' Defense Services*,[64] a former client whose criminal conviction was set aside because of ineffective assistance of counsel sued his trial and appellate lawyers and the governmental agency that provided the lawyers. Noting that there was no express statutory authorization for the agency to sue or be sued, the Supreme Court of Kansas held the agency lacked the capacity to be sued.[65]

## § 5-6.4 DEFENSES ARISING BY OPERATION OF LAW

Certain defenses that may be raised in a legal malpractice case arise more or less by operation of law. These include defenses related to statutes of limitations and repose, equitable and judicial estoppel, non-assignability of malpractice claims, arbitration agreements, SLAPP statutes, and the rules governing joint liability and reimbursement

---

[58] *Id.*

[59] *Id.*

[60] *See* Barner v. Leeds, 13 P.3d 704 (Cal. 2000).

[61] *See* Mooney v. Frazier, 693 S.E.2d 333 (W. Va. 2010); *see also* Ashley v. Stiller, 58 A.3d 982 (Del. 2012) (court-appointed criminal defense lawyers have qualified immunity under the State Tort Claims Act).

[62] *See* Ferri v. Ackerman, 444 U.S. 193 (1979).

[63] *See* Mooney v. Frazier, 693 S.E.2d 333, 345 (W. Va. 2010).

[64] 355 P.3d 667 (Kan. 2015).

[65] *Id.* at 672.

(including indemnity and contribution), releases, and covenants not to sue. These matters are discussed below.

### § 5-6.4(a) Malpractice Statutes of Limitations

In every case, it is vitally important for the lawyers to identify the applicable statute of limitations. Even if a defendant's malpractice is egregious, the untimely filing of a claim will wholly defeat the plaintiff's cause of action, when the defense is asserted by the defendant.

In some instances, the filing period for legal malpractice is governed by a statute expressly applicable to claims against lawyers. For example, a Louisiana statute provides:

> No action for damages against any attorney * * *, whether based upon tort, or breach of contract, or otherwise, arising out of an engagement to provide legal services shall be brought unless filed * * * within one year from the alleged act, omission, or neglect, or within one year from the date the alleged act, omission or neglect is discovered or should have been discovered * * *.[66]

However, in other cases, a general statute of limitations governs. For example, in *Channel v. Loyacono*,[67] the Mississippi Supreme Court determined that the operative statute for a legal malpractice claim was one that provided:

> All actions for which no other period of limitations is prescribed shall be commenced within three (3) years after the cause of such action accrued, and not after.[68]

Similarly, in *Bank of Saipan v. Carlsmith Ball Wichman Case & Ichiki*, the Supreme Court for the Commonwealth of the Northern Mariana Islands held that legal malpractice actions were governed by a six-year statute of limitations that was applicable to all causes of action not enumerated by the legislature.[69]

In some circumstances, a special statute of limitations applies based on the nature of the malpractice claim. Thus, the Louisiana statute quoted above does not apply in cases of fraud.[70]

The reach of a special legal malpractice statute of limitations may depend on a careful examination of the relevant facts and circumstances. For example, in *Lee v. Hanley*,[71] the Supreme Court of California interpreted a state statute (Code of Civil Procedure section 340.6 (a)) providing that, "[a]n action against an attorney for a wrongful act or omission, other than for actual fraud, arising in the performance of professional services shall be commenced within one year after the plaintiff discovers, or through the use of reasonable diligence should have discovered, the facts constituting the wrongful act or omission. . . ." The court concluded that the statute's "time bar applies to claims whose merits necessarily depend on proof that an attorney violated a

---

66 LA. REV. STAT. 9:5605(A) (Westlaw 2017).

67 954 So. 2d 415, 421 (Miss. 2007).

68 *Id.* at 420.

69 1999 WL 33992414, at *3 (N. Mar. I.).

70 LA. REV. STAT. 9:5605(E) (Westlaw 2017).

71 354 P.3d 334, 336 (Cal. 2015).

professional obligation in the course of providing professional services." As the court explained:

> In this context, a "professional obligation" is an obligation that an attorney has by virtue of being an attorney, such as fiduciary obligations, the obligation to perform competently, the obligation to perform the services contemplated in a legal services contract into which an attorney has entered, and the obligations embodied in the Rules of Professional Conduct. By contrast, * * * section 340.6(a) does not bar a claim for wrongdoing—for example, garden-variety theft—that does not require proof that the attorney has violated a professional obligation, even if the theft occurs while the attorney and the victim are discussing the victim's legal affairs. Section 340.6(a) also does not bar a claim arising from an attorney's performance of services that are not "professional services," meaning "services performed by an attorney which can be judged against the skill, prudence and diligence commonly possessed by other attorneys." * * *.[72]

Amplifying its interpretation, the court stated:

> To be sure, section 340.6(a) does not apply to claims involving an attorney's provision of services unrelated to the practice of law, such as concert promotion * * *. But the attorney-client relationship often requires attorneys to provide nonlegal professional services such as accounting, bookkeeping, and holding property in trust.[73]

The court cautioned that:

> [T]he question is not simply whether a claim alleges misconduct that entails the violation of a professional obligation. Rather, the question is whether the claim, in order to succeed, necessarily depends on proof that an attorney violated a professional obligation as opposed to some generally applicable nonprofessional obligation.[74]

Turning to the facts before it, the *Lee* court explained:

> Lee's complaint may be construed to allege that Hanley is liable for conversion for simply refusing to return an identifiable sum of Lee's money. Thus, at least one of Lee's claims does not necessarily depend on proof that Hanley violated a professional obligation in the course of providing professional services. Of course, Lee's allegations, if true, may also establish that Hanley has violated certain professional obligations, such as the duty to refund unearned fees at the termination of the representation * * * just as an allegation of garden-variety theft, if true, may also establish a violation of an attorney's duty to act with loyalty and good faith toward a client. But because Lee's claim of conversion does not necessarily depend on proof that Hanley violated a professional obligation, her suit is not barred by section 340.6(a).[75]

---

[72] *Id.* at 341–42.

[73] *Id.* at 342.

[74] *Id.* at 343.

[75] *Id.* at 344.

### *§ 5-6.4(a)(1) Accrual of the Cause of Action*

The statute of limitations begins to "run" when the plaintiff's cause of action "accrues." In each jurisdiction, accrual is normally governed by either of two different rules: an "occurrence rule" or a "damage rule."

#### *§ 5-6.4(a)(1)(A) Occurrence Rule*

In states that follow the occurrence rule, the plaintiff's cause of action accrues, and the statute of limitations begins to run, when the negligent act or omission occurs. Thus, a Connecticut statute provides that:

> No action founded upon a tort shall be brought but within three years from the date of the act or omission complained of.[76]

In *Abdelsame v. Foden de Castro*,[77] the Superior Court of Connecticut held that, under this statute, a malpractice claim alleging negligence related to obtaining a passport stamp for travel was untimely. More than three years had passed since the lawyer's allegedly wrongful acts and omissions, and there was no basis for tolling the running of the statute that would make the filing of the action timely.[78]

#### *§ 5-6.4(a)(1)(B) Damage Rule*

Some states adhere to a damage rule under which the statute of limitations does not begin to run until the lawyer's malpractice causes damage. Thus, in *Vossoughi v. Polaschek*,[79] the Supreme Court of Iowa held that the limitations period did not begin to run on a real estate vendor's malpractice claim against lawyers who prepared the sale documents until the purchaser defaulted on its contract payments. Similarly, in *Abel v. Austin*,[80] the Supreme Court of Kentucky held that a claim arising from improper settlement practices accrued only when deficient disbursements were made from the settlement fund. In these kinds of cases, the idea is that until damage has occurred, it would be impossible for the plaintiff to successfully litigate a malpractice claim because proof of damages is essential.[81]

It is sometimes difficult to pin-point when damage occurs. *Jones v. Westbrook*[82] was a case involving a lawyer's purported failure to properly document a security interest related to the sale of the client's business. The Alaska Supreme Court concluded that the client's legal malpractice claim was timely filed in 2013 under a three-year statute of limitations even though the error had occurred in 2004. The court reasoned that the client did not suffer any appreciable injury when the sale documents were signed in 2004, nor when the escrow manager first notified him in 2005 that the buyer had missed a payment, because alternative payment arrangements were made under which the client did not waive any rights. The client only suffered an appreciable injury in late 2011 when

---

[76] CONN. GEN. STATS. § 52–577 (Westlaw 2016).

[77] 2007 WL 2036849 (Conn. Super. Ct.).

[78] *See infra* § 5-6.4(a)(2) (discussing tolling).

[79] 859 N.W.2d 643, 654 (Iowa 2015).

[80] 411 S.W.3d 728, 736 (Ky. 2013).

[81] *Cf. Vossoughi*, 859 N.W.2d at 652 ("The statute of limitations cannot require legal malpractice claims to be brought while 'the record is uncertain and speculative whether a party has sustained damages' ").

[82] 379 P.3d 963, 969 (Alaska 2016).

the Internal Revenue Service (IRS) recorded liens on the physical assets causing the client to lose the ability to acquire anything greater than junior lienholder status.[83]

Similarly, in *Minnick v. Hawley Troxell Ennis & Hawley, LLP*,[84] the Idaho Supreme Court explained, "Here, the Minnicks' claim against Hawley Troxell based on the firm's failure to subordinate the deed of trust could not have begun accruing until the IRS raised subordination in the underlying tax court proceedings."[85]

In *Warnock v. Karm Winand & Patterson*,[86] the substantive issue was whether the drafting of certain letter agreements amounted to malpractice. In rejecting the defendant's statute of limitations defense, an Illinois appellate court applied the state's damage rule for determining when a cause of action accrues. The court found that damage did not occur, and the statute of limitations did not begin to run, until an adverse judgment was entered against the plaintiffs in a suit related to the letter agreements. The court reaffirmed an earlier holding that "a cause of action for legal malpractice will rarely accrue prior to the entry of an adverse judgment, settlement, or dismissal of the underlying action in which the plaintiff has become entangled due to the purportedly negligent advice of his attorney."[87]

Nevertheless, other cases have found that "damage" can occur before the entry of an adverse court ruling. For example, in *Antone v. Mirviss*,[88] a lawyer was allegedly negligent in preparing a prenuptial agreement that failed to protect his client's interest in appreciation of his premarital property. The Supreme Court of Minnesota held that the client's legal malpractice action against the lawyer accrued when the agreement took effect. Therefore, the statute of limitations began to run upon the client's marriage, rather than when the client's wife was later awarded a portion of the appreciation in a marital dissolution proceeding. As the majority explained, at the time of his marriage, the client lost the legal right to unfettered ownership in his premarital property. The fact that the full extent of the damage was not ascertainable did not mean that no damage had occurred.[89]

### *§ 5-6.4(a)(2) Tolling*

The running of the statute of limitations may be "tolled," which is to say temporarily suspended, by certain types of special circumstances. This may be true, for example, for the period during which the plaintiff is under the age of majority or suffers from mental incapacity.[90] However, it is not easy to generalize. Even with regard to these types of disabilities, the law varies from state to state.

Of particular relevance to legal malpractice actions is tolling based on lack of discovery of the lawyer's errors, continuation of the lawyer-client relationship, an agreement of the parties, or the pendency of other litigation, such as a client's pursuit of

---

[83] *Id.*

[84] 341 P.3d 580 (Idaho 2015).

[85] *Id.* at 584–85.

[86] 876 N.E.2d 8 (Ill. App. Ct. 2007).

[87] *Id.* at 15.

[88] 720 N.W.2d 331 (Minn. 2006).

[89] *Id.* at 338.

[90] *See* DeLuna v. Burciaga, 857 N.E.2d 229 (Ill. 2006).

post-conviction relief. These issues and related topics are discussed in the following sections.

*§ 5-6.4(a)(2)(A) Discovery Rule*

Most states apply a discovery rule to legal malpractice claims. In these jurisdictions, the statute of limitations generally does not begin to run until the plaintiff has discovered, or reasonably should have discovered, the lawyer's malpractice. The relevant inquiry is typically " 'highly fact-bound' and requires an evaluation of all of the circumstances, including the conduct and misrepresentations of the defendant, the reasonableness of plaintiff's reliance on the defendant, and the existence of a fiduciary relationship between the parties."[91]

In *Fogarty v. Palumbo*,[92] the Supreme Court of Rhode Island explained that state's version of the discovery rule in the following terms:

> The standard applied to this exception is objective: [I]t "requires only that the plaintiff be aware of facts that would place a reasonable person on notice that a potential claim exists." * * *. The discovery rule does not require perfect crystallization of the nature and extent of the injury suffered or a clear-cut anchoring to the allegedly negligent conduct of a defendant." * * *. Rather, a legal-malpractice plaintiff is afforded three years to commence suit from "the time that the act or acts of the malpractice should, in the exercise of reasonable diligence, have been discovered."[93]

In *Widom v. Egenberg*,[94] a lawyer was allegedly negligent in representing multiple parties to a real estate transaction and in failing to explain to the plaintiffs the consequences, under the Statute of Frauds, of not documenting in writing a side agreement for the buyers to re-convey the property to the sellers on certain terms at a future date. Although there was a six-year statute of limitations, and the malpractice action was not filed until almost eight years after the closing, a New Jersey appellate court found that, under the applicable discovery rule, the suit was not untimely. There was no reason for the plaintiffs to have known until long after the closing that they should have had independent counsel and that the side agreement should have been put into writing.[95]

Similarly, in *Viglione v. Farrington*,[96] the court found the mere fact that the plaintiff had expressed disappointment with a final divorce settlement did not mean she had discovered that the defendant-lawyer's representation of her was significantly flawed.

In *Ross v. Ihrie*,[97] a lawyer allegedly committed malpractice by incorrectly telling a client that recovery for a personal injury claim was capped by a Nevada statute at $50,000. The lawyer argued that the client had discovered the malpractice because he was dissatisfied with the lawyer's representation from "Day One." However, a federal court in Michigan rejected that contention because the "statute of limitations for legal

---

[91] BDO Seidman, LLP v. Morgan, Lewis & Bockius LLP, 89 A.3d 492, 500 (D.C. 2014).

[92] 2017 WL 2713289 (R.I. 2017).

[93] *Id.* at *5.

[94] 2006 WL 3432552 (N.J. Super. Ct. App. Div.).

[95] *Id.* at *4.

[96] 2007 WL 2302342 (N.J. Super. Ct. App. Div.).

[97] 2006 WL 3446897 (E.D. Mich. 2006).

malpractice does not begin to run just because a client is unhappy with his attorney's work."[98]

For purposes of a dispute with another party to a contract, a person is presumed to have read and understood the terms of the contract at the time of execution. However, that does not mean that the statute of limitations on a malpractice claim begins to run on the date the contract was signed. In a state with a discovery rule, the defendant-lawyer must still prove that the plaintiff actually discovered, or should have discovered, the error or omission related to the contract giving rise to malpractice liability.[99]

In some cases, a client's threat to sue or file a grievance has been found to establish that the plaintiff discovered the lawyer's malpractice, and to commence the running of the statute of limitations.[100] However, something less than a threat to initiate litigation may also amount to discovery. For example, in *Franklin Financial, Inc. v. Sandoz*,[101] the court found that a client discovered its lawyer's malpractice, and the statute of limitations began to run, when it sent the lawyer a letter detailing the lawyer's errors. This was true, the Louisiana Court of Appeal held, even though the client argued that its continuing relationship with the lawyer meant that it did not realize the full extent of the lawyer's errors.[102]

In *Channel v. Loyacono*,[103] a law firm represented clients in a mass tort action, some of whom later sued the firm for malpractice. The Mississippi Supreme Court concluded that the statute of limitations began to run once the clients suspected wrongdoing and contacted another lawyer for advice, or when the clients were approached by disaffected lawyers, who had previously been involved in the case and wanted to take over the representation.[104]

The application of a discovery rule is often a fact-intensive process. This means that while a lawyer may ultimately prevail in asserting a statute of limitations defense, it may not be possible to bring the plaintiff's malpractice action to an early termination.

For example, in *General Nutrition Corp. v. Gardere Wynne Sewell, LLP*,[105] a federal court in Pennsylvania refused to grant a motion to dismiss. Although there was evidence that the client had discovered the defendant's malpractice because it had received an expert report from a law professor, there was also conflicting evidence that the defendant law firm had continued to assure the client that its analysis of the client's potential liability to a third-party was correct, and that the firm had covered up its original error. The court concluded that it could not determine at that early stage of the proceedings that the plaintiff's claim was untimely. There was applicable law tolling the running of the statute of limitations "when the client, despite the exercise of due diligence, cannot discover the injury or its cause."[106]

---

[98] *Id.* at *6.

[99] *See* Dashiell v. Meeks, 913 A.2d 10 (Md. 2006).

[100] *See* Serou v. DeLaup, 2006 WL 3759555, at *3 (E.D. La.), *aff'd*, 244 Fed. Appx. 588 (5th Cir. 2007).

[101] 956 So. 2d 143 (La. Ct. App. 2007).

[102] *Id.* at 146.

[103] 954 So. 2d 415 (Miss. 2007).

[104] *Id.* at 422.

[105] 2008 WL 4411951 (W.D. Pa. 2008).

[106] *Id.* at *4.

Of course, the prospect of prolonged litigation increases the settlement value of a malpractice claim. The longer litigation continues, the greater the costs of mounting a successful defense, and the more a defendant may be willing to pay to resolve the claim. Thus, the plaintiff's ability to plausibly invoke the discovery rule may increase the likelihood of settlement.

*§ 5-6.4(a)(2)(B) Continuous Representation Rule*

Many states hold that the running of the statute of limitations is tolled for the period during which a lawyer continues to represent a client in the matter giving rise to the alleged malpractice. The reason for this rule is that it normally would be unreasonable to require a client, who is the victim of malpractice, to sue the client's lawyer while the representation is still in progress. If the client were compelled to file suit, the client would need to retain other counsel to present the malpractice claim. That, in itself, can be difficult, time-consuming, and expensive. In addition, the commencement of such litigation, with its attendant threat of liability and reputational harm to the defendant-lawyer, would so harm the professional relationship between the client and malpractice defendant as to make further representation difficult or impossible. Thus, the client might be forced to also hire new counsel for the underlying matter. Not only would that be burdensome, but any opportunity for the defendant-lawyer to cure the malpractice through remedial actions and good lawyering would probably be lost. The continuous representation rule alleviates these problems by delaying the necessity of filing suit.

Of course, a finding that there was no attorney-client relationship between the plaintiff and defendant undercuts any attempt by a plaintiff to rely on the continuous representation rule. For example, in *International Strategies Group, Ltd. v. Greenberg Traurig, LLP*,[107] the First Circuit concluded that there was no attorney-client relationship between a corporate investor and the corporation's lawyer. Therefore, the investor's claims against the lawyer for conversion, and for aiding and abetting fraud and breach of fiduciary duty, were time-barred. The applicable statute of limitations was three years, and more than that amount of time had passed since the investor knew or should have known of the improper transfer of funds on which the claims were based.[108]

In addition, the continuous representation rule does not toll the statute of limitations with respect to any period of time after the lawyer-client relationship has ended. Thus, there is an issue in many cases about whether the professional relationship terminated. Conduct reflecting serious tensions in a lawyer-client relationship may be found to raise a fact question about whether legal representation ended.

For example, in *Thayer v. Fuller & Henry, Ltd.*,[109] a lawyer was alleged to have committed malpractice by failing to secure, as part of an employment severance package, a release of the client's personal guaranty of a loan. Although the client later consulted another lawyer regarding whether the defendant-lawyer and law firm had committed malpractice, and sent the individual defendant a letter saying that he had lost confidence in him and did not intend to pay an outstanding bill, it was not clear that the representation had terminated. The defendants had not performed legal services for the plaintiff for a period of time, but upon receiving the plaintiff's letter responded by seeking clarification as to whether the firm should cease any further legal work. Moreover, the

---

107 482 F.3d 1 (1st Cir. 2007).

108 *Id.* at 14.

109 503 F. Supp. 2d 887 (N.D. Ohio 2007).

costs of the plaintiff's hiring and bringing substitute counsel "up to speed" were substantial. Therefore, it was for the jury to determine when the representation ended. Thus, summary judgment on statute of limitations grounds could not be granted.[110]

States differ in how they articulate the continuous representation rule. In some jurisdictions, the formulation of the rule is highly nuanced. For example, in Connecticut, a plaintiff may invoke the doctrine, and thus toll the running of the statute of limitations, only "when the plaintiff can show: (1) that the defendant continued to represent him with regard to the same underlying matter; and (2) either that the plaintiff did not know of the alleged malpractice or that the attorney could still mitigate the harm allegedly caused by that malpractice during the continued representation period."[111]

In *Abdelsame v. Foden de Castro*,[112] a court interpreting Connecticut's continuous representation rule found that the plaintiff's filing of a grievance against an attorney unequivocally indicated that the plaintiff had ceased relying on the defendant's professional and legal judgment.

Some states do not recognize a continuous representation rule as a basis for tolling.[113]

*§ 5-6.4(a)(2)(B)(i) Determining Continuity*

The continuous representation rule, by its very terms, necessitates proof that representation of the client *continued.* A lawyer's handling of discrete matters for a client at different times may fail to meet this requirement. Thus, the Second Circuit wrote:

> New York's continuous representation doctrine does not apply to a client's "continuing general relationship with a lawyer." * * *. Rather, it tolls the statute of limitations "only where the continuing representation pertains specifically to the matter in which the attorney committed the alleged malpractice."[114]

However, some courts are more lenient in determining that there has been a continuation of representation sufficient to trigger the tolling rule. For example, in *Williams v. Maulis*, the Supreme Court of South Dakota held that a lawyer's representation of the estate of a widow's deceased husband was a continuation of related services that the lawyer had rendered for the widow in negotiating a contract for deed, which was the focus of the alleged malpractice.[115]

A lawyer who is discharged by a client, but later resumes the client's representation, may decide that it would have been better not to re-commence legal services. By resuming representation after being discharged, a lawyer may be found to have extended the statute of limitations. Thus, in *Dodson v. Fishman*,[116] a California appellate court

---

[110] *Id.* at 894.

[111] DeLeo v. Nusbaum, 821 A.2d 744, 749–50 (Conn. 2003).

[112] 2007 WL 2036849 (Conn. Super. Ct.).

[113] *See* George L. Blum, Annotation, *Attorney Malpractice—Tolling or Other Exceptions to Running of Statute of Limitations*, 87 A.L.R.5th 473, § 4 (2015 Supp.) (surveying state cases that have applied or rejected the continuous-representation doctrine).

[114] Bastys v. Rothschild, 154 Fed. Appx. 260, 262 (2d Cir. 2005).

[115] 2003 S.D. 138, 672 N.W.2d 702 (2003).

[116] 2006 WL 3639746 (Cal. Ct. App.).

held that a two-month hiatus during an initial discharge did not mean that the lawyer's resumption of representation was not continuous.

*§ 5-6.4(a)(2)(C) Fraudulent Concealment*

Fraudulent concealment by a lawyer is sometimes deemed to toll the running of the statute of limitations on a malpractice claim.[117] However, this basis for tolling is often narrowly construed. In general, it is not sufficient that the lawyer merely failed to disclose the errors or omissions that allegedly constitute malpractice. Rather, the lawyer must have taken affirmative steps to conceal the malpractice by preventing its discovery.

In *Bomar v. Moser*,[118] the Supreme Court of Arkansas stated that "in order to toll the statute of limitations on the basis of fraudulent concealment, there must be (1) a positive act of fraud (2) that is actively concealed, and (3) is not discoverable by reasonable diligence." The *Bomar* court found that the first two elements of the test were satisfied because the defendant-lawyers had allegedly set up entities as shell corporations and eliminated the plaintiff's access to various accounts and financial records. As to the third element, there was a question of fact, because it was unlikely that the plaintiff, even if he had exercised his rights as a shareholder, could have discovered the fraud. Therefore, it was improper for the trial court to grant summary judgment for the defendant-lawyers on statute of limitations grounds.

*§ 5-6.4(a)(2)(D) Agreement of the Parties*

Within reasonable limits, persons may contractually agree to lengthen or shorten the statute of limitations. If the agreement is valid, a party thereto is estopped from asserting the statute of limitations as a defense.

A contract which lengthens the filing period may do so to allow more time for investigation of the facts or settlement negotiations, in the hope of avoiding the bad publicity that attends the filing of a lawsuit. That type of arrangement is referred to as a "tolling agreement."

*§ 5-6.4(a)(2)(D)(i) Shortening the Filing Period*

An agreement purporting to shorten the filing period for disputes is only valid if it allows an aggrieved party an adequate opportunity to seek legal redress.[119] For example, in *Charnay v. Cobert*,[120] a client alleged that she had been misled by her lawyer about her exposure to liability for attorney's fees in litigation. In a malpractice action alleging fraud, negligent misrepresentation, and breach of fiduciary duty, the defendant-lawyer argued that the action was barred by a provision in the lawyer-client contract stating that the client would be billed monthly, and that if the client did not object to a bill within ten days, the law firm would assume that the client did not dispute the bill's accuracy. Rejecting that contention, the California Court of Appeal wrote, "if the notice provision

---

[117] *See* Jett v. Wooten, 110 So. 3d 850, 857 (Ala. 2012) (the statute did not begin to run until the client discovered that the lawyer had not filed the actions the lawyer told her he had filed).

[118] 251 S.W.3d 234, 242 (Ark. 2007).

[119] Such an agreement may also violate disciplinary rules that prohibit a lawyer from prospectively limiting liability for malpractice unless the client is represented by independent counsel. *See* MODEL RULES OF PROF'L CONDUCT R.1.8(h)(1) (American Bar Ass'n, 2017).

[120] 51 Cal. Rptr. 3d 471 (Ct. App. 2006).

were interpreted to be an agreement to shorten the applicable limitations period, it would be unreasonable as a matter of law and thus unenforceable."[121]

#### *§ 5-6.4(a)(2)(E) Pendency of Other Litigation*

Considerations relating to judicial efficiency sometimes warrant the tolling of a malpractice statute of limitations. This is why some (but not all) states hold that a person alleging malpractice in connection with criminal representation may delay the initiation of the malpractice claim until judicial review of the underlying conviction has become final.[122] For example, in *McKnight v. Office of Public Defender*,[123] a public defender failed to advise a client of the risk that he might be deported if he pleaded guilty to certain charges. The Supreme Court of New Jersey held that the two-year statute of limitations ran from the date that the client received post-conviction relief setting aside his guilty plea.[124]

Similar considerations arise outside of the criminal practice context. In *Fontanella v. Marcucci*,[125] the victims of an auto accident alleged that their lawyers were negligent in failing to obtain and preserve evidence of alleged seatbelt failure. The court held that "because of the complexity of the legal and factual issues arising out of the spoliation of evidence relating to the product liability claim, the legal malpractice claim was not capable of being adjudicated by the judicial power until the underlying product liability claim was resolved by final judgment."[126] Therefore, the running of the statute of limitations on the plaintiff's legal malpractice and breach of contract claims was tolled during the pendency of the underlying action.[127]

Texas applies a bright-line tolling rule to a broad category of legal malpractice cases: "When an attorney commits malpractice in the prosecution or defense of a claim that results in litigation, the statute of limitations on a malpractice claim against that attorney is tolled until all appeals on the underlying claim are exhausted or the litigation is otherwise finally concluded."[128] In *Apex Towing Co. v. Tolin*,[129] the Texas Supreme Court concluded that the two-year statute of limitations only began to run when the court of appeals issued an order dismissing an appeal in the litigation that was the basis for the malpractice claim. This was true despite the fact that the plaintiff had previously hired a new attorney.[130]

#### *§ 5-6.4(a)(2)(F) Equitable Estoppel*

Some courts will toll the running of the statute of limitations under the doctrine of equitable estoppel. Generally, the defendant must have intended to deceive the plaintiff,

---

121 *Id.* at 481.

122 *See supra* § 5-6.2(c)(2).

123 962 A.2d 482 (N.J. 2008).

124 *See also* Molen v. Christian, 388 P.3d 591, 594 (Idaho 2017); Garcia v. Ball, 363 P.3d 399, 408 (Kan. 2015).

125 877 A.2d 828 (Ill. App. Ct. 2005).

126 *Id.* at 830.

127 *Id.* at 835–37.

128 Apex Towing Co. v. Tolin, 41 S.W.3d 118, 119 (Tex. 2001).

129 *Id.*

130 *See also* Stokes-Craven Holding Corp. v. Robinson, 2015 WL 5247124, at *11 (S.C.) (holding that "the statute of limitations for a legal malpractice action may be tolled until resolution on appeal of the underlying case if the client has not become aware of the injury prior to the decision on appeal").

made misrepresentations, or engaged in bad faith tactics to delay the commencement of litigation. In *Abdelsame v. Foden de Castro*,[131] the plaintiff was deported from the United States after traveling to Egypt, allegedly as the result of the defendant-lawyer's failure to properly advise him about travel and to have his passport stamped correctly. The court found the equitable tolling doctrine inapplicable to the facts of the case because there was no evidence that "the defendant intended to induce or deceive the plaintiff into believing that he could travel in and out of the United States, or that the defendant lulled the plaintiff into believing that it was not necessary for him to commence litigation, or that it was impossible for him to file a timely claim from Egypt."[132]

*§ 5-6.4(a)(2)(G) The Continuing Tort Doctrine*

The "continuing tort" doctrine occasionally plays a role in legal malpractice litigation. A continuing tort is one that is inflicted over a period of time and involves wrongful conduct that is repeated until desisted.

It is not sufficient that there are continual ill effects arising from a completed violation of the plaintiff's rights. There is only a continuing tort if the tortious conduct persists.

In cases involving a continuing tort, the plaintiff's cause of action accrues, and the statute of limitations begins to run, on the date of the last injury, or when the tortious conduct ceases. As interpreted by some courts, if suit for a continuing tort is timely filed, a jury may award damages for all of the wrongs committed during the progress of the continuing tort, even if those actions occurred many years earlier.

In *Pierce v. Cook*,[133] a lawyer represented a husband, wife, and son on a medical malpractice claim. During the course of the representation, the lawyer had an adulterous affair with the wife. In affirming a $1.5 million award for the husband on a variety of legal theories, the Mississippi Supreme Court held that the husband's claim for intentional infliction of emotional distress was not barred by a one-year statute of limitations because the lawyer had committed a continuing tort which lasted until the couple's divorce. Not only had the lawyer taken the wife on a trip to New Orleans, during which he had sexual relations with her, he also flaunted his involvement with the wife in front of her husband at a restaurant, coached the wife on what to say to her husband during a phone call, and called the husband on the phone to apologize about the situation. The court found that there was repeated wrongful conduct by the lawyer.[134]

***§ 5-6.4(a)(3) Statutes of Repose***

Some states have statutes of repose which are applicable to legal malpractice actions. A statute of repose provides that, regardless of the other calculations related to the applicable statute of limitations, a claim is barred after the passage of a certain period of time. Statutes of repose are not subject to tolling based on non-discovery. Thus, a statute of repose can extinguish a plaintiff's cause of action before the plaintiff is even aware of the need to sue.

---

131 2007 WL 2036849 (Conn. Super. Ct.).

132 *Id.* at *3.

133 992 So. 2d 612 (Miss. 2008).

134 *Id.* at 620.

In certain jurisdictions, the statute of repose is part of the same legislative provision that establishes the statute of limitations for a malpractice claim. For example, legislation in Montana provides that a legal malpractice action:

> must be commenced within 3 years after the plaintiff discovers or through the use of reasonable diligence should have discovered the act, error, or omission, whichever occurs last, but in no case may the action be commenced after 10 years of the date of the act, error, or omission.[135]

In *Snyder v. Love*,[136] the statute quoted above was applied to a case where a lawyer was allegedly negligent in drafting the terms of a will. The testator's will was executed on February 24, 1987; the testator died on November 18, 1992; the will was admitted to probate on November 25, 1992; and the malpractice complaint was filed on August 21, 2002. The Supreme Court of Montana held that the suit was time-barred because the ten-year statute of repose began to run on February 24, 1987. The court expressly rejected arguments that the running of the statute of repose was tolled by a discovery rule or by the fact that no cause of action accrued prior to the testator's death.[137]

### § 5-6.4(b) Non-Assignability of Legal Malpractice Claims

Most states hold that, for reasons of public policy, a legal malpractice claim is not assignable. Thus, a client cannot settle a claim by assigning to an adversary the right to sue the client's former lawyer. If such an assignment is made and a malpractice claim is initiated by the adversary, the client's former lawyer can usually defeat the claim by arguing non-assignability.

Legal malpractice claims cannot be transferred because permitting that practice would pose a serious threat to the justice system. An adversary could drive a wedge between a client and lawyer by offering a favorable settlement to the client at the expense of the lawyer. Ultimately, lawyers might become reluctant to represent certain types of clients, such as those who are underinsured or judgment-proof. Moreover, if a malpractice claim were assigned, the client would lose control over the litigation, but the client's lawyer would have the right to defend against the claim by revealing confidential client information.[138]

In *Kim v. O'Sullivan*,[139] the Washington State Court of Appeals refused to permit circumvention of the non-assignment rule by an agreement that the client would prosecute the malpractice claim in his own name for the benefit of the client's former adversary. The court held that the agreement was invalid and therefore the malpractice action was subject to dismissal because the adversary was the real party in interest.[140]

Most applications of the non-assignment rule are straightforward. Thus, a malpractice claim cannot be sold or given away. However, the rule against assignment is sometimes recognized in surprising ways. In *Johnson v. Hart*,[141] the Supreme Court

---

[135] MONT. CODE ANN. § 27–2–206 (Westlaw 2017).

[136] 153 P.3d 571 (Mont. 2006).

[137] *Id.* at 574.

[138] *See* MODEL RULES OF PROF'L CONDUCT R. 1.6(b)(5) (American Bar Ass'n, 2017) (discussing exceptions to confidentiality).

[139] 137 P.3d 61 (Wash. App. 2006).

[140] *Id.* at 64–65.

[141] 692 S.E.2d 239 (Va. 2010).

of Virginia considered whether the sole testamentary beneficiary of an estate, in her individual capacity, could maintain a legal malpractice action against the estate's lawyer for negligence in representing the estate. The court answered that question in the negative, reasoning that to allow such a claim would violate the principle that legal malpractice claims are not assignable.[142]

A minority of courts have declined to adopt a total prohibition on the assignment of claims for legal malpractice. "The cases from the jurisdictions in the minority generally determine that the legal malpractice action alleges a pecuniary injury similar to a property injury and does not present the concerns raised by the courts that ban the assignment of legal malpractice claims, or suggest that those concerns are overstated."[143] In *Villanueva v. First American Title Insurance Company*,[144] the Supreme Court of Georgia held that the legal malpractice allegation before it—namely, that the attorney failed to pay outstanding loans in full—alleged a purely pecuniary injury, rather than a personal tort, and that the assignment of that claim raised neither an issue of professional responsibility nor an issue of illegality.[145]

A distinction can be drawn between assigning a malpractice claim and assigning rights under a malpractice insurance policy. In some states, a law firm may settle a claim for malpractice by assigning to the plaintiff its rights against a malpractice insurer which denied coverage for the claim.[146]

### § 5-6.4(c) Joint Liability and Reimbursement

The principles of joint and several liability that apply in other tort actions typically govern responsibility for damages in legal malpractice cases. However, it is difficult to generalize about this area of the law because, in recent years, states have greatly modified the common law rules governing the liability of joint tortfeasors. The law now differs substantially from one jurisdiction to the next.[147]

#### *§ 5-6.4(c)(1) Allocation of Fault to Other Persons*

In many situations, tort defendants are now subject only to "several liability," which is individual and proportional, rather than "joint and several liability," under which a defendant may be liable for the wrongdoing of others in addition to personal wrongdoing. If liability is several, a defendant may seek to limit its responsibility for damages by having a portion of the fault which caused the plaintiff's losses allocated to one or more other persons.

In *Dennerline v. Atterholt*,[148] a law firm allegedly failed to advise a healthcare insurance trust that its lawyers had discovered that the trust was insolvent and needed to cease operations. Thereafter, the state insurance commissioner sued the firm for legal malpractice to recover millions of dollars in losses that the commission incurred when it liquidated the trust. The law firm argued that the losses were caused in whole or in part

---

[142] *Id.* at 244.

[143] Villanueva v. First Am. Title Ins. Co., 740 S.E.2d 108, 111 (Ga. 2013).

[144] *Id.* at 111.

[145] *Id.* at 112.

[146] *See* C. Ingram Co. v. Philadelphia Indem. Ins. Co., 694 S.E.2d 181 (Ga. App. 2010).

[147] *See generally* RESTATEMENT (THIRD) OF TORTS: APPORTIONMENT OF LIABILITY (American Law Institute, 2000).

[148] 886 N.E.2d 582 (Ind. Ct. App. 2008).

by various nonparties, including actuaries, a third-party administrator, the trust's management, trustees, member associations, and even the company from whom the trust purchased a computer system. The Indiana Court of Appeals recognized the theoretical viability of the law firm's comparative fault argument. However, it concluded that the jury had properly allocated 100% of the fault to the law firm because the firm failed to prove that alleged breaches of duty by the various nonparties had caused any of the damages.

### *§ 5-6.4(c)(2) Contribution*

If liability is several, there is generally no need to talk about reimbursement. No defendant pays more than its fair share because several liability is proportional. That is, a percentage of the fault is allocated to a particular defendant, and that defendant pays only that percentage of the plaintiff's damages.

However, where liability is joint and several, contribution and indemnity may be important issues. While these principles do not reduce the defendant's liability to the plaintiff, they sometimes allow a defendant to obtain reimbursement for amounts paid to the plaintiff as a result of a malpractice claim. Contribution is partial reimbursement; indemnity is total reimbursement.

Intentional tortfeasors generally have no right to contribution. In addition, many states hold that contribution cannot be obtained from a settling joint tortfeasor. In these jurisdictions (but not in all states), settlement of claims is encouraged by the fact that a tortfeasor who pays a settlement is sure that its exposure to liability is extinguished. This is true even though denying other joint tortfeasors contribution from the settling joint tortfeasor may ultimately result in an allocation of liability that is disproportionate to fault.

In every state, detailed rules govern the assertion of contribution rights. It is essential for a legal malpractice lawyer to become familiar with the applicable statutory provisions and related precedent.

Contribution is available only from a person who qualifies as a joint tortfeasor. This means that if the person from whom contribution is sought owed no duty to the plaintiff in the underlying action, contribution will be denied. For example, *Breen v. Law Office of Bruce A. Barket, P.C.*,[149] was a legal malpractice action arising from a divorce. The former wife sued her lawyers, as well as her former husband's lawyer. The former wife's lawyers then sued the former husband's lawyer for contribution or indemnification. A New York appellate court rejected the reimbursement claims because there was no theory under which the former husband's lawyer owed a duty of care to the wife or to her lawyers. Thus, with respect to whatever harm the wife allegedly suffered as a result of her own lawyers' wrongful conduct, her husband's lawyer was not a joint tortfeasor.

In contrast, *Connell, Foley & Geiser, LLP v. Israel Travel Advisory Service, Inc.*[150] involved a contribution claim against co-counsel, rather than opposing counsel. A New Jersey appellate court held that a contribution claim was validly stated, even though the

[149] 862 N.Y.S.2d 50 (App. Div. 2008).

[150] 872 A.2d 1100 (N.J. Super. Ct. App. Div. 2005).

lawyer who served as co-counsel was not admitted to practice in the state and was not named as a defendant in the malpractice action.[151]

### *§ 5-6.4(c)(3) Indemnity*

The ascendency of proportionality principles in American tort law during the past half century means that indemnification (total reimbursement) is now available only in a limited range of situations. Two such occasions are where an innocent person is held vicariously liable for the tortious conduct of another or where one person has granted another person a contractual right to indemnity. A firm's governing agreement may entitle principals within the firm to indemnity from the firm under specified circumstances. However, lawyers practicing in limited liability entities[152] may be personally immunized from reimbursement claims by applicable statutory provisions. For example, the Tennessee limited liability partnership act provides that, except with respect to liability for any person under a partner's direct supervision and control:

> An obligation of a partnership incurred while the partnership is a registered limited liability partnership, whether arising in contract, tort, or otherwise, is solely the obligation of the partnership. A partner is not personally liable, directly or indirectly, by way of contribution or otherwise, for such an obligation solely by reason of being or acting as a partner. * * *.[153]

Today, common law indemnity is generally not available to a joint tortfeasor who was personally at fault. A blameworthy joint tortfeasor has rights to reimbursement only if such rights are granted by the law of contribution. For example, in *Spencer v. Gavin*,[154] a lawyer acting as executor and administrator of three estates misappropriated their assets. A second lawyer, who did a small amount of work for one of the estates, allegedly knew about the misappropriation, but failed to disclose it. In a malpractice action by the estates, the second lawyer tried unsuccessfully to assert claims for indemnity and contribution against the first lawyer (and the first lawyer's estate, since the first lawyer had died). A New Jersey appellate court found that the second lawyer had no common law right to indemnification, presumably because this was not a case of innocent vicarious liability. The court held that if the second lawyer had actual knowledge of the wrongdoing, he had a duty to disclose that information. Furthermore, the contribution claim failed because the estate of the first lawyer had settled with the plaintiffs, and applicable state law barred contribution claims against settling joint tortfeasors. The *Spencer* court noted that the second lawyer might be entitled to a credit against any judgment eventually entered against him recognizing the fault of the settling defendants.[155]

States differ with regard to how they calculate such credits. Some jurisdictions reduce the plaintiff's judgment on a dollar-for-dollar basis calculated by reference to the exact amount previously paid by a settling joint tortfeasor. If the settling joint tortfeasor paid the plaintiff $10,000, another joint tortfeasor against whom a judgment is subsequently entered will be given credit for the plaintiff's having already received

---

151 *Id.* at 1109.

152 *See infra* § 5-7.2(d).

153 TENN. CODE ANN. § 61–1–306(c) (Westlaw 2017).

154 946 A.2d 1051 (N.J. Super Ct. App. Div. 2008).

155 *Id.* at 1072.

$10,000. Thus, if the subsequent judgment was for $100,000, the joint tortfeasor against whom it was rendered will only have to pay $90,000.

Other states hold that by settling with one of several tortfeasors, the plaintiff gives up the right to enforce a portion of a subsequent judgment. The forfeited portion is normally equivalent to the percentage of the settling joint tortfeasor's share of the fault. This percentage is not determined until the eventual trial of the case. Therefore, under this type of system, a plaintiff cannot be sure about what is being given up by entry into a pretrial settlement.

For example, suppose there are two joint tortfeasors, A and B. Assume further that the plaintiff settles with A, and a subsequent verdict against B determines that the plaintiff suffered $100,000 in damages, and that A was 40% at fault and B was 60% at fault. The plaintiff will be deemed to have given up 40% of the judgment by reason of the earlier settlement with A, and B will only have to pay $60,000. The uncertainties surrounding this approach may discourage plaintiffs from settling with potentially responsible persons, particularly with seemingly peripheral parties. In some states, there are other types of rules for calculating credits in cases where some, but not all, of the responsible parties settle before trial.

In *Powell v. Wood County Comm'n*, the Supreme Court of Appeals of West Virginia held that a statute conferring immunity on court-appointed criminal defense counsel logically required a county to indemnify appointed counsel from costs incurred in defending against a malpractice claim.[156]

### *§ 5-6.4(c)(4) Claims Involving Successive Counsel or Co-Counsel*

In many states, a lawyer responsible for malpractice may obtain contribution or indemnity from another lawyer involved in the client's representation. This is true regardless of whether the other lawyer served as predecessor counsel, co-counsel, or successor counsel.[157] Thus, if a law firm is vicariously liable for the malpractice of outside co-counsel,[158] the outside lawyer may be obliged to pay contribution or indemnity.[159]

However, a few jurisdictions have barred some types of reimbursement claims because of perceived conflicts of interest or threats to client confidences. For example, California prohibits a negligent initial lawyer from seeking reimbursement from a negligent successor lawyer.[160]

However, California holds that whether reimbursement claims should be permitted between co-counsel should be decided on a case-by-case basis. In *Musser v. Provencher*, the California Supreme Court concluded that, on the facts of the case before it, there was no danger of conflict of interest or risk to client confidences. The court therefore allowed a family law lawyer to assert a reimbursement claim against a bankruptcy lawyer who had provided erroneous information, which the family lawyer then relied upon in the client's representation.

---

[156] 550 S.E.2d 617 (W. Va. 2001).

[157] *See, e.g.*, Bolton v. Weil, Gotshal & Manges, LLP, 2005 WL 2185470 (N.Y. Sup. Ct.).

[158] *See generally* § 5.7.

[159] *See* RESTATEMENT (THIRD) OF THE LAW GOVERNING LAWYERS § 58 cmt. e (American Law Institute, 2000).

[160] *See* Musser v. Provencher, 48 P.3d 408, 412 (Cal. 2002).

## § 5-6.4(d) Releases and Covenants Not to Sue

Under traditional rules, now modified in many jurisdictions, there were two important types of settlement documents. A release given to one tortfeasor extinguished the plaintiff's rights against all joint tortfeasors. However, a covenant not to sue a tortfeasor was enforceable only by the person to whom it was given, and did not affect the plaintiff's rights against other joint tortfeasors.

There was often confusion as to the legal effect of a document which, although denominated a release, purported to reserve rights against some joint tortfeasors. This sometimes meant that a plaintiff, who thought that rights had been reserved, was unexpectedly barred from litigating a case against one wrongdoer because of an earlier settlement with another person involved in the relevant events.

To avoid ensnaring plaintiffs in the legal traps inherent to this area of the law, the *Restatement (Second) of Torts* embraces a sensible position: a valid release of one tortfeasor does not discharge others liable for the same harm, unless it is agreed that it will discharge them.[161] Under the *Restatement*, the plaintiff's intent to reserve rights need not be written and can be proved by parol evidence.

Some states go even further than the *Restatement* in attempting to prevent the inadvertent release of legal claims. For example, in *McMillen v. Klingensmith*, the Texas Supreme Court held that a settlement document releases from liability only those tortfeasors named or otherwise specifically identified in the document, and no others.[162]

### *§ 5-6.4(d)(1) Settlement with the Defendant*

Sometimes a malpractice claim is barred because there has been a related settlement of claims with the same defendant in another proceeding. For example, in *Liberty Associates v. Etkin*,[163] a client sued a lawyer for legal malpractice. Later, while the malpractice claim was pending, the lawyer's firm commenced a separate proceeding against the plaintiff for unpaid fees. After the fee dispute was settled, the lawyer successfully moved to dismiss the malpractice claim. A New York appellate court wrote:

> This action to recover damages for legal malpractice against Etkin, as a member of the Ravin Firm, arises out of the same series of transactions as the fee dispute action asserted by the Ravin Firm against the plaintiff herein for legal fees. Upon resolution of the fee dispute action, the parties, by their attorneys, executed a stipulation of dismissal with prejudice and without costs. A stipulation of discontinuance with prejudice without reservation of right or limitation of the claims disposed of is entitled to preclusive effect under the doctrine of *res judicata*.[164]

Lawyers may not secure from a client a relinquishment of claims without complying with applicable rules of legal ethics. In general, it is unethical for a lawyer to make an agreement prospectively limiting the lawyer's liability to a client for malpractice unless the client is represented by independent counsel in making the agreement.[165] Further, a

---

161 *See* RESTATEMENT (SECOND) OF TORTS (§ 885) (American Law Institute, 1979).

162 467 S.W.2d 193 (Tex. 1971).

163 893 N.Y.S.2d 564 (App. Div. 2010).

164 *Id.* at 565.

165 *See* MODEL RULES OF PROF'L CONDUCT R. 1.8(h) (American Bar Ass'n, 2017).

lawyer may not settle an existing claim with an unrepresented client or former client without advising that person in writing of the desirability of obtaining independent counsel, and allowing that person a reasonable opportunity to do so.[166] A release obtained in violation of these rules will subject a lawyer to discipline, and is likely to be deemed unenforceable by a court.[167]

### § 5-6.4(e) Arbitration Agreements

Lawyer-client contracts sometimes contain mandatory arbitration provisions. Depending on their language, such clauses may require the arbitration of malpractice claims (as opposed to, or in addition to, fee disputes). In such cases, a defendant may seek to avoid judicial review of a malpractice claim by moving for enforcement of the arbitration provision. Such requests are often granted. Courts sometimes say that "any ambiguity is construed in favor of arbitration."[168]

Whether lawyers fare better in arbitration than in court is an issue that is open to question. In many respects, the principles of legal malpractice law protect lawyers from liability. Consider, for example, the rules that permit lawyers to reasonably exercise discretion without risk of liability or that impose demanding causation requirements on malpractice plaintiffs that necessitate a trial within a trial. A lawyer who elects to include a malpractice claim arbitration provision in a lawyer-client contract cannot be sure that the usual substantive rules will be followed by the arbitrator. Moreover, if the arbitrator departs from well-established malpractice principles, there will be little opportunity to appeal a resulting adverse ruling. Consequently, choosing arbitration over litigation has risks. Arbitration may not minimize a lawyer's exposure to liability.

A court may refuse to enforce mandatory arbitration clauses because, on the particular facts, it amounts to an adhesion contract.[169] Of course, the invalidity of an arbitration agreement is never presumed. Rather, the unconscionability of the provision must be proven by the client seeking to avoid arbitration.

In *Woodroof v. Cunningham*,[170] the Court of Appeals for the District of Columbia held that a client, who was challenging the validity of an arbitration provision, "failed to prove that she was 'powerless' in her interaction with Cunningham [the defendant-lawyer] or had 'no real choice' in the contract terms."[171] As the court explained:

> Woodroof [the client] admits that her own counsel helped her select Cunningham and was present during the "engagement meeting" with Cunningham. She presented no evidence that she objected to the contract or attempted to bargain for different terms. Essentially, Woodroof failed to show "that there was no opportunity for negotiation *and* that the services could not be obtained elsewhere."[172]

---

[166] *See id.*

[167] *See* Campbell Harrison & Dagley L.L.P. v. Lisa Blue/Baron and Blue, 843 F. Supp. 2d 673, 689 (N.D. Tex. 2011), *aff'd*, Hill v. Schilling, 495 Fed. Appx. 480, 488 (5th Cir. 2012) (holding that while a release was unenforceable due to insufficient evidence that the client was fully informed of all material facts, the lawyers' attempt to secure a release was not a breach of fiduciary duty).

[168] *See* Woodroof v. Cunningham, 147 A.3d 777, 789 (D.C. 2016).

[169] *See* LaFleur v. Law Offices of Anthony G. Buzbee, P.C., 960 So. 2d 105, 110 (La. Ct. App. 2007).

[170] 147 A.3d 777 (D.C. 2016).

[171] *Id.* at 789.

[172] *Id.*

Judicial review of the enforceability of mandatory arbitration provisions takes place against the backdrop of ethical obligations imposed on lawyers for the protection of clients. "[C]ourts across the country continuously struggle with * * * whether the attorney is required to fully apprise the client of the legal consequences of such a clause."[173]

The evaluation of the ethics of mandatory arbitration agreements starts with an examination of the applicable professional conduct rules. General rule provisions to consider involve communications with clients and conflicts of interest. A more specific concern relates to whether the arbitration provision triggers the state version of Model Rule 1.8(h), addressing lawyers prospectively limiting their malpractice liability. Comment (14) following Model Rule 1.8 provides guidance on the use of arbitration agreements in stating that the rule does not "prohibit a lawyer from entering into an agreement with the client to arbitrate legal malpractice claims, provided such agreements are enforceable and the client is fully informed of the scope and effect of the agreement."[174]

A number of advisory ethics opinions address the propriety of lawyers entering agreements that require arbitration of malpractice claims. "Generally, these opinions are positive and allow lawyers to contract with their clients for pre-dispute ADR procedures."[175] These opinions may identify conditions related to the scope of the agreement and the lawyer's disclosure obligations. For example, the Supreme Court of Texas Professional Ethics Committee concluded that a lawyer's use of a malpractice arbitration clause in a fee agreement is not a *per se* unethical attempt to limit malpractice liability.[176] However, the committee noted three important constraints on the use of arbitration agreements:

> First, use of an arbitration clause that prohibits the recovery of certain otherwise allowable damages for legal malpractice would be an impermissible and unethical limitation on a lawyer's malpractice liability.
>
> Second, a lawyer may not include clearly unfair terms in an arbitration agreement, such as language giving the lawyer the sole right to select an arbitrator, requiring arbitration in a remote location, or entailing excessive costs that would effectively foreclose the client's use of arbitration.
>
> Third, a client must receive sufficient information about the differences between litigation and arbitration to permit the client to make an informed decision about the wisdom of agreeing to binding arbitration. A lawyer should normally advise an individual or small-business client about relevant costs and

---

[173] *See* Chrissy L. Schwennsen, Case Note, *Arbitration Clauses in Fee Retainer Agreements*, 3 ST. MARY'S J. LEGAL MAL. & ETHICS 330, 330–31 (2013).

[174] MODEL RULES OF PROF'L CONDUCT R. 1.8 cmt. 14 (American Bar Ass'n, 2007). *Compare* RESTATEMENT (THIRD) OF THE LAW GOVERNING LAWYERS § 54 cmt. b (American Law Institute, 2000) (stating that the provision relating to lawyers prospectively limiting their liability does not prohibit a lawyer from entering into an agreement with the client to arbitrate malpractice claims "provided that the client receives proper notice of the scope and effect of the agreement" and such agreements are enforceable under the law applicable in the jurisdiction).

[175] Kristen M. Blankley, *The Ethics and Practice of Drafting Pre-dispute Resolution Clauses*, 49 CREIGHTON L. REV. 743, 750 (2016) (noting that the states differ on the following points: whether the arbitration provision in an engagement letter triggers the requirements of Model Rule 1.8 and whether the clients are required to consult independent counsel prior to the execution of the engagement letter).

[176] TEX. ETH. OP. 586, 2008 WL 5680298.

time savings and the fact that choosing arbitration may entail waiver of significant rights, such as the right to a jury trial, reduced availability of discovery, inapplicability of the rules of evidence, and great restrictions on the right to appeal an adverse decision.[177]

Using similar analytical frameworks, courts have generally upheld arbitration provisions in agreements between lawyers and their clients. In *Hodges v. Reasonover*,[178] the Supreme Court of Louisiana found that arbitration clauses in attorney-client agreements may be enforceable, but that the one before it did not pass muster. According to the court, "an attorney must make full and complete disclosure of the potential effects of an arbitration clause," and the contract "must explicitly list the types of disputes covered by the arbitration clause, e.g., legal malpractice, and make clear that the client retains the right to lodge a disciplinary complaint."[179]

Arbitration can be expensive. Arbitrators sometimes charge hourly fees that match or exceed the billing rates of top lawyers. If a dispute will be heard by three arbitrators, the costs to the parties are all the greater. However, courts are reluctant to allow a client to escape an otherwise valid arbitration provision by pleading poverty.[180]

### § 5-6.4(f) SLAPP Laws

Lawsuits may be filed not to win, but to silence critics who may be coerced to back down rather than face the inconvenience, expense, and uncertainties of litigation. Not surprisingly, many states have sought to curb such abuses, at least insofar as they threaten to diminish discussion and resolution of public issues. These states have passed what are called SLAPP laws. The acronym is short for Strategic Lawsuits Against Public Participation.[181] Many SLAPP laws provide for early dismissal of unmeritorious claims filed to interfere with the valid exercise of the Constitutional rights of free speech and petition.

Occasionally lawyers assert that a malpractice claim is barred by a SLAPP law. However, this type of defense seldom succeeds.

For example, in *Kmart v. Lewis Brisbois Bisgaard & Smith LLP*,[182] the court found that although malpractice claims challenging the competency of legal counsel typically reference protected litigation activities, such claims are rarely subject to dismissal under California's SLAPP statute. The *Kmart* malpractice action alleged that the defendant-lawyers had improperly represented and disclosed information to a party with adverse interests. The court found that the act giving rise to the plaintiff's breach of loyalty and confidentiality claims was not the defendant-lawyers' filing of suit on behalf of the

---

[177] *Id. Compare* ABA COMM. ON PROF'L ETHICS & PRO'F RESP., FORMAL OP. 02-425 (2002) (concluding that it is permissible to include a binding arbitration provision in a retainer agreement, "provided that the client has been fully apprised of the advantages and disadvantages of arbitration and has given her informed consent to the inclusion of the arbitration provision").

[178] 103 So. 3d 1069 (La. 2012).

[179] *Id.* at 1078.

[180] *See* Max Mitchell, *Legal Mal Suit Against Bracewell Must Be Arbitrated, Despite Plaintiffs' Plea of Poverty*, LEGAL INTELLIGENCER, June 28, 2017.

[181] *See* VINCENT R. JOHNSON, ADVANCED TORT LAW: A PROBLEM APPROACH 326–28 (Carolina Academic Press, 2d ed. 2014) (discussing SLAPP laws).

[182] 2010 WL 2804360 (Cal. Ct. App.).

adverse party, but their decision to undertake a representation that allegedly violated ethical standards. Consequently, California's SLAPP law was inapplicable.

### § 5-6.4(g) Judicial Estoppel

A malpractice claim may be barred by judicial estoppel. That doctrine prohibits a party from deliberately taking inconsistent factual positions in different cases involving related matters or in different phases of the same case.

In *Jackson v. Hancock & Canada, L.L.P.*, a Texas appellate court found that former clients who had failed to identify a potential legal malpractice action as an asset in their bankruptcy proceeding were thereafter precluded from prosecuting the malpractice claim.[183]

Judicial estoppel sometimes does not bar an action because a party's later position is not clearly inconsistent with its former position. For example, in *Pike v. Mullikin*,[184] a client, who feared that his antenuptial agreement with his wife was unenforceable, negotiated a division of assets with his wife. The couple then certified to the divorce court that they were each satisfied that the agreement was a fair and equitable resolution of the divorce. The Supreme Court of New Hampshire held that the client's subsequent legal malpractice action against the lawyers who drafted the antenuptial agreement was not barred by judicial estoppel. The court reasoned that, during the divorce proceedings, the client never asserted any claims or took any position with respect to the validity of the antenuptial agreement or the adequacy of the legal services the client's lawyer rendered in connection with its drafting. The client's acknowledgment that the division of assets was fair and equitable was not clearly inconsistent with his claim that the defendants committed malpractice.[185]

[183] 245 S.W.3d 51 (Tex. App. 2007).

[184] 965 A.2d 987 (N.H. 2009).

[185] *Id.* at 990.

# Chapter 5-7

# VICARIOUS LIABILITY

By Susan Saab Fortney and Vincent R. Johnson

*Table of Sections*

§ 5-7.1 The Role of Vicarious Liability
§ 5-7.2 Law Firm Practice
§ 5-7.3 Other Associations That Expose Lawyers to Liability

## § 5-7.1 THE ROLE OF VICARIOUS LIABILITY

Depending on the circumstances, a plaintiff may pursue both direct liability claims against persons directly involved in the alleged misconduct and vicarious liability claims against others with some responsibility for the malpractice. A number of rationales are used to justify the imposition of vicarious liability. Both traditional policy justifications and economic theories reflect the principle that risk and loss should be borne along with benefit, profit, and control.[1] Referring to the several rationales proffered in support of vicarious liability, the *Restatement (Third) of Torts* notes that the most popular justification for the imposition of vicarious liability is that the costs of an agent's torts should be borne by the enterprise.[2]

Lawyers' enterprises expose them to vicarious liability risks. Whether a person practices law in a transnational firm or serves as a solo practitioner, a lawyer works with others whose misconduct may be imputed to the lawyer for civil liability purposes. This section discusses lawyers' vicarious liability, starting with issues related to law firm practice and then examining other types of relationships that may subject lawyers to malpractice claims arising from the wrongful conduct of other lawyers.

## § 5-7.2 LAW FIRM PRACTICE

Lawyers may practice as an employee or a member of a law firm constituted as a partnership, professional corporation, or similar entity.[3] By organizing in firms, lawyers seek to accomplish tasks that individuals cannot manage on their own. Through a firm structure, lawyers may achieve economies of scale (e.g., sharing space and support staff) and economies of scope by providing a range of legal services.[4] Depending on the size of the firm, clients benefit from diversification and specialization.[5]

---

1 *See* Paula J. Dailey, *All in a Day's Work: Employers' Vicarious Liability for Sexual Harassment*, 104 W. VA. L. REV. 517, 535 (2002) (surveying the range of justifications for imposing vicarious liability under tort and agency law).

2 RESTATEMENT (THIRD) OF TORTS: APPORTIONMENT OF LIABILITY § 13 (American Law Institute, 2000).

3 RESTATEMENT (THIRD) OF THE LAW GOVERNING LAWYERS § 9 (American Law Institute, 2000).

4 S.S. Samuelson, *The Organizational Structure of Law Firms: Lessons from Management Theory,* 51 OHIO ST. L.J. 645, 647–648 (1990) (describing the benefits of professionals associating together in law firms).

5 *Id.* at 648.

Economists characterize a law firm as "an organization consisting of a nexus of contracts between owners of factors of production and customers."[6] Lawyers, as agents of the firm, offer "inalienable human capital and perform services for clients."[7]

Within the firm, monitoring plays an important role in facilitating lawyer performance and minimizing the risks posed by incompetent or malfeasant lawyers. Senior lawyers (such as partners, shareholders, or senior associates) supervise the performance of more junior lawyers. The deferred ownership structure of law firms also incentivizes associates to work hard to impress their superiors and earn an invitation to be a principal in the law firm.[8]

Firm-wide policies and procedures may apply to all lawyers. Increasingly, firms of all sizes are implementing and maintaining management measures that promise to improve the quality of legal services, minimize malpractice exposure, and protect and enhance the firm's reputation.[9]

Despite risk management efforts, clients and third parties may be injured by the malpractice of a firm representative. In those situations, the injured person may seek to hold the law firm and its principals vicariously liable for harm caused by persons acting on behalf of the firm. Their ability to successfully do so will turn on a number of considerations discussed below.

### § 5-7.2(a) The Vicarious Liability of Law Firms

Determining whether a law firm will be held vicariously liable involves principles of both tort and agency law. In explaining the justification for imposing vicarious liability, a comment to the *Restatement (Third) of the Law Governing* Lawyers states that the vicarious liability of law firms and their members results from the principles of *respondeat superior* or enterprise liability.[10] The comment goes on to elaborate on the rationale as follows:

> Vicarious liability also helps to maintain the quality of legal services, by requiring not only a firm but also its principals to stand behind the performance of other firm personnel. Because many law firms are thinly capitalized, the vicarious liability of principals helps to assure compensation to those who may have claims against principals of a firm.[11]

According to the *Restatement (Third) of the Law Governing Lawyers*, a law firm is subject to civil liability for injuries legally caused to a person by any wrongful act or omission of any principal or employee of the firm who was "acting in the *ordinary course*

---

[6] *See* Susan Saab Fortney, *Am I My Partner's Keeper? Peer Review in Law Firms,* 66 U. COLO. L. REV. 329, 338 (1995).

[7] *Id.*

[8] *See* Vincent R. Johnson, *On Shared Human Capital, Promotion Tournaments, and Exponential Law Firm Growth,* 70 TEX. L. REV. 537 (1991).

[9] For a manual on law firm risk management and self-assessment questionnaires, see ANTHONY E. DAVIS & KATIE M. LACHTER, RISK MANAGEMENT: SURVIVAL TOOLS FOR LAW FIRMS (ABA Book Pub., 3rd ed. 2015).

[10] *See* RESTATEMENT (THIRD) OF THE LAW GOVERNING LAWYERS § 58 cmt. b (American Law Institute, 2000). Enterprise liability holds a master "liable for all the costs foreseeably generated by her business." Paula Daily, *Destroying the Scope of Employment,* 55 WASHBURN L.J. 637, 641–42 (2016) (reviewing the different tests for imposing liability on business enterprises).

[11] RESTATEMENT (THIRD) OF THE LAW GOVERNING LAWYERS § 58 cmt. b (American Law Institute, 2000).

*of the firm's business or with actual or apparent authority.*"[12] As captured in this *Restatement* section, liability can be based on establishing (1) that the misconduct was within the ordinary course of business or (2) that the firm actor committed the tort while acting with actual or apparent authority.

### *§ 5-7.2(a)(1) Ordinary Course of Firm Business*

Even when the firm actor did not have actual or apparent authority, the *Restatement* explains that the firm may be liable when the act was in the ordinary course of firm business. The *Restatement* then provides guidance on the meaning of "ordinary course of business." As stated:

> The ordinary course of business of a law firm includes the practice of law and various activities normally related to it. Thus, liability is imposed for legal malpractice * * * by any firm lawyer; indebtedness incurred by staff in purchasing services or supplies: misapplication of funds in the custody of the firm or its personnel * * *; and torts committed by a principal or employee while acting in the scope of employment, for example for the negligent driving of an employee who is on firm business.[13]

If the conduct is not connected to the practice of law or related activities, the conduct is not within the firm's ordinary course of business. By way of example, the *Restatement* explains that entry by a law firm principal into an unrelated business partnership that is not part of the firm's practice of law and its ancillary activities should not be treated as conduct within the ordinary course of business of the law firm.[14] Similarly, the firm should not be liable for the harm caused by nonprincipals who acted outside the scope of their employment.[15]

The scope of the ordinary course of business will depend on the firm's own activities and course of dealings. To illustrate how the breadth of the course of business will differ from firm to firm, the *Restatement* uses the illustration of a firm that regularly makes investments for clients using the client's settlement proceeds. Because of the firm's course of conduct, a fact finder may conclude that making investments for clients was conduct within the ordinary business of the firm.[16]

Although "ordinary course of business" has no fixed meaning because it depends on the firm's own activities, it may include conduct intended to benefit a law firm (e.g., advising clients, conducting litigation, or even overbilling).[17] Another approach is to consider whether the conduct was part of the normal risks of operating a law firm.

#### *§ 5-7.2(a)(1)(A) Intended to Benefit the Firm*

Under the doctrine of *respondeat superior,* liability should only be imputed to the firm if the agent's conduct was intended, at least in part, to further the business purposes

---

[12] *Id.* (emphasis added).

[13] *Id.* at cmt. d.

[14] *Id.*

[15] *Id.* (using the example of a nonlawyer firm librarian writing a will without authorization).

[16] *Id.*

[17] Vincent R. Johnson & Stephen C. Loomis, *Malpractice Liability Related to Foreign Outsourcing of Legal Services*, 2 ST. MARY'S J. LEGAL MALPRACTICE & ETHICS 262, 300 (2012).

of the principal. The *Restatement (Third) of Agency* refers to the role of intent in discussing the "scope of employment." As stated:

> An employee acts within the scope of employment when performing work assigned by the employer or engaging in a course of conduct subject to the employer's control. An employee's act is not within the scope of employment when it occurs within an independent course of conduct not intended by the employee to serve any purpose of the employer.[18]

In using this section to evaluate whether liability should be imputed to the law firm, certain activities can easily be categorized as conduct intended to benefit the law firm. For example, counseling clients and handling their affairs under the terms of an engagement letter that provides for compensation to the firm clearly is conduct that is intended to benefit the law firm. By contrast, a rogue associate who moonlights and represents her family members on a *pro bono* basis may not be engaged in conduct that is intended to benefit the law firm.[19]

In order to support a claim for vicarious liability, the plaintiff should be prepared to demonstrate that the tortfeasor's conduct was intended to directly benefit the firm. Indirect benefit should not suffice to impose liability on the law firm. This was illustrated in a case in which a plaintiff sought to hold a law firm liable for damages arising out of an automobile accident involving one of the firm's partners who was commuting to a part-time job as a municipal judge. Applying the *Restatement* standard for vicarious liability, rather than the broader enterprise liability standard imposing liability for risks incidental to an enterprise, the court concluded that the partner's commutation to his job as a municipal judge was, as a matter of law, unrelated to his law firm activities.[20]

*§ 5-7.2(a)(1)(B) Normal Risks Incidental to the Practice of Law*

Rather than relying on the rule that bases "ordinary course of business" on whether the conduct was intended to benefit the firm, a court may focus on the connection or nexus between the alleged misconduct and the employer's business. Thus, in the case of a law firm, liability could turn on the plaintiff's ability to demonstrate that the risk of tortious conduct is incidental to the practice of law. For example, a firm could be held liable for wrongful disclosure of information while handling an immigration matter for the plaintiff.[21]

In evaluating whether conduct was incidental to the practice of law, a court may not require that the firm benefit from the conduct of the firm actor. For example, a federal court, applying Connecticut law, concluded that a defendant law firm was liable for the harm that resulted when a partner misappropriated a client's funds because the partner, in the "ordinary course" of serving as the client's lawyer, received trust funds from a third party in connection with the client's sale of a business.[22] Although the firm did not

---

[18] RESTATEMENT (THIRD) OF AGENCY § 7:07(2) (American Law Institute, 2006).

[19] *See* Susan Saab Fortney, *Leaks, Lies, and the Moonlight: Fiduciary Duties of Associates to Their Law Firms*. 41 ST. MARY'S L.J. 595, 606–607 (2009) (discussing different types of moonlighting and unauthorized work by associates that may breach associates' duties to their firms).

[20] O'Toole v. Carr, 815 A.2d. 471, 474 (N.J. 2003) (relying on the *Restatement (Second) of Agency*).

[21] *See* Lunn v. Fragomen, Del Rey, Bernsen & Loewy P.C., 2006 WL 492098, at *8 (S.D. Tex.) (upholding a summary judgment because there was no evidence supporting the plaintiff's claim).

[22] Vanacore v. Kennedy, 86 F. Supp. 2d 42 (D. Conn. 1998), *aff'd*, 208 F. 3d 204 (2d Cir. 2000). For the conduct to fall within the ordinary course of a law firm's business, the acts "must have (1) been the kind of thing a law partner would do; (2) occurred substantially within the authorized time and geographic limits of

"benefit" from the funds that the partner stole, the circumstances of representation revealed that for many years the partner had represented the client through the firm.[23]

By contrast, vicarious liability should not be imposed when the tortious conduct was not incidental or an outgrowth of the practice of law. Courts often reach this conclusion when intentional torts, such as assaults, have been committed by persons connected to a law firm.[24]

Law firms sometimes escape liability for harm caused by sexual relationships between a lawyer and a client on the ground that such conduct by an employee was not intended to further the business purposes of the law firm. However, other cases have imposed liability, sometimes reasoning that such risks are incidental to the operation of a law firm.[25] The grounds for holding a law firm vicariously liable are stronger in cases where the plaintiff is a client of the firm and the existence of a lawyer-client relationship facilitated the commission of the tort.[26]

Some sex-related claims against firms may be filed by employees who allege that they were victimized by other firm employees.[27] As illustrated in a 2010 Louisiana case, the ability to establish vicarious liability may turn on the connection between the sexual misconduct and the business of the firm. In that case, a law firm clerical employee alleged that a firm lawyer raped her on the firm's premises. In addition to asserting that she was an employee, the plaintiff alleged that she was a client because the firm represented her on a *pro bono* basis, advising her on a child custody matter, and appearing for her in court. In an action against the law firm and the lawyer who allegedly committed the battery, the Louisiana Court of Appeal refused to grant summary judgment in favor of the firm because there were unresolved issues of fact as to the plaintiff's legal status and whether the firm had been negligent.[28]

In addition to pursuing a vicarious liability claim against the firm, a plaintiff may assert a direct liability cause of action. In such a claim, the plaintiff would maintain that the she was owed a duty of care and that the firm negligently failed to take reasonable steps to prevent sexual misconduct.

#### *§ 5-7.2(a)(2) Actual and Apparent Authority*

Even if the tortious conduct was not within the ordinary course of the firm's business, a firm can still be civilly liable if the wrongful act or omission was committed

---

the partnership; and (3) been motivated at least in part by a purpose to serve the partnership." *Id.* at 51 (citations omitted).

[23] *Id.* at 45.

[24] *E.g.,* Morales v. Laughlin, Falbo, Levy, & Moresi, LLP., 2016 WL 1688289, *3 (Cal. App. Apr. 25, 2016) (concluding that it was not foreseeable for the associate to end up in the opposing party's car and slap that person for sending an email to the associate's work address). By contrast, the court noted that a physical altercation between opposing counsel at a deposition could be foreseeable. *Id.*

[25] "Jurisdictions disagree about whether, under general agency law, a principal is liable for intentional torts such as assaults that an agent commits without any purpose of serving a principal whose enterprise helped create the risk of the act." RESTATEMENT (THIRD) OF THE LAW GOVERNING LAWYERS § 58 cmt. d (American Law Institute, 2000).

[26] *Id.*

[27] In 1994, a jury awarded 7.1 million dollars in punitive damages to a former Baker & McKenzie secretary who alleged that a firm partner sexually harassed her. Susan Saab Fortney, *Are Law Firm Partners Islands Unto Themselves? An Empirical Study of Law Firm Peer Review and Culture*, 10 GEO. J. LEGAL ETHICS 271 (Winter, 1997).

[28] *See* Doe v. Hawkins, 42 So. 3d 1000, 1012–13 (La. Ct. App. 2010).

by a person with actual or apparent authority.[29] Applying general agency law, a law firm (as principal) is subject to liability to a third party harmed by an agent's tortious conduct that is within the scope of the agent's actual authority or ratified by the principal.[30] In addition, the firm (as principal) may be subject to vicarious liability to a third party harmed by an agent's conduct when the agent is an employee who commits a tort while acting within the scope of employment, or the agent commits a tort when acting with apparent authority in dealing with a third party on, or purportedly on, behalf of the principal.[31]

Actual authority refers to "true authority" communicated when a principal gives an agent authority to act on the principal's behalf.[32] According to the *Restatement (Third) of Agency*, the "focal point for determining whether an agent acted with actual authority is the agent's reasonable understanding at the time the agent takes action."[33] In the context of law practice, actual authority may be conferred through a specific authorization, such as an employment agreement, or through "general understandings reflected in past practice and other circumstances."[34]

Apparent authority focuses on the communications between the principal (the firm) and the third person. Specifically, the principal is held "accountable for the results of third-party beliefs about an actor's authority to act as an agent when the belief is reasonable and is traceable to a manifestation of the principal."[35] For example, a law firm may cloak a person with apparent authority by providing the person with business cards and an office. The question of apparent authority will largely depend on whether the firm's communications to the third party under the circumstances made it reasonable for the third party to believe that the tortfeasor was acting on behalf of the law firm.[36]

Two cases involving misappropriation of funds illustrate how vicarious liability based on apparent authority turns on the firm's communications to third parties and the reasonableness of the plaintiff's belief that the putative agent was acting on behalf of the firm. On the basis of apparent authority, the court in *Myers v. Aragona* affirmed a judgment against a defendant Myers for losses suffered by the plaintiffs due to misappropriation by Gordon, another lawyer.[37] Even though no actual partnership existed between Gordon and Myers, the court concluded that Myers was estopped from denying the existence of a partnership because Myers used and allowed the use of the name "Gordon & Myers, Attorneys at Law" on settlement statements and "Law Office of

---

[29] RESTATEMENT (THIRD) OF THE LAW GOVERNING LAWYERS § 58 cmt. d (American Law Institute, 2000).

[30] RESTATEMENT (THIRD) OF AGENCY § 7.04 (American Law Institute, 2006). A principal is also subject to liability to a third party harmed by an agent's conduct when the "agent's conduct, if that of the principal, would subject the principal to tort liability." *Id.*

[31] *Id.* at § 7.03. *Restatement (Third) of Agency* also describes the liability of a principal as follows: "A principal is subject to vicarious liability for a tort committed by an agent in dealing or communicating with a third party on or purportedly on behalf of the principal when actions taken by the agent with apparent authority constitute the tort or enable the agent to conceal its commission." *Id.* at § 7.08.

[32] *Id.* at § 2.01 cmt. b. "An agent acts with actual authority when, at the time of taking action that has legal consequences for the principal, the agent reasonably believes, in accordance with the principal's manifestations to the agent, that the principal wishes the agent so to act." *Id.* at 2.01.

[33] *Id.* at § 2.01 cmt. c.

[34] RESTATEMENT (THIRD) OF THE LAW GOVERNING LAWYERS § 58 cmt. d (American Law Institute, 2000).

[35] RESTATEMENT (THIRD) OF AGENCY § 2.03 cmt. c (American Law Institute, 2006).

[36] At the same time, unauthorized statements made by a putative agent to a third party cannot create apparent authority. *Id.*

[37] 318 A.2d 263, 269 (Md. 1974).

Gordon & Myers" on letterhead.[38] Under the facts and the applicable partnership law, Myers was liable for the representations made to those who relied on them.[39]

The court in *Rouse v. Pollard* reached the opposite conclusion, refusing to hold firm partners liable for amounts embezzled by a firm lawyer.[40] In that case, the plaintiff had given the lawyer her money to invest after the lawyer represented her. The court rejected the plaintiff's attempt to hold the other partners liable on the basis of apparent authority because the partners did nothing to indicate that the lawyer had any authority to act on their behalf in investing money, an undertaking outside the practice of law.[41]

### § 5-7.2(b) Procedural Issues Related to Claims Against Firms

Substantive law and procedural rules govern who should be named as defendants when a plaintiff seeks to hold a firm and its individual partners liable for a judgment. The following describes procedural concerns related to pursuing claims against individual lawyers and their firms:

> Depending on jurisdictional rules, typically those of civil procedure, the partnership may be sued as an entity or, under the aggregate theory of partnership, which requires that each member must be sued. When jurisdiction exists over a partner, usually it exists over the partnership. The converse however may not be true, though there are different jurisdictional views based on whether partners are agents of each other.
>
> Service on each partner must meet the jurisdictional criteria concerning individuals. Generally, even under the entity theory, unless individual partners are named and served as parties, they are not personally liable for a judgment and their personal assets are not subject to execution. If the innocent partners are named, the usual rule is that the partnership assets must be exhausted before the personal assets of the individual partners.[42]

An Ohio opinion underscores the importance of knowing the jurisdiction's rules related to naming and serving defendants in legal malpractice cases. In *National Union Fire Insurance Co. of Pittsburgh, PA v. Wuerth,* the Supreme Court of Ohio held that a firm cannot commit legal malpractice directly because the firm does not engage in the practice of law.[43] According to that court, a law firm cannot be vicariously liable for malpractice unless one of its lawyers is liable for malpractice.[44] Clearly, a plaintiff should know whether the relevant jurisdiction imposes a similar requirement for naming an individual tortfeasor. Otherwise, the plaintiff may face a motion for summary judgment or motion for failure to state a claim on which relief can be granted.

An individual tortfeasor and firm can be held jointly and severally liable even though the tortfeasor-agent's conduct was within the scope of firm business. As discussed

---

[38] *Id.* at 268.

[39] *Compare* Licette Music Corp. v. Sills, Cummis, Zuckerman, Radin, Tischman, Epstein & Gross, P.A., 2009 WL 2045259 (N.J. Super. Ct. App. Div. 2009) (rejecting the plaintiff's reliance on apparent authority where there was no reliance on the defendant law firm's resources).

[40] 21 A.2d 801, 130 N.J. Eq. 204 (1941).

[41] *Id.* at 209.

[42] RONALD E. MALLEN, LEGAL MALPRACTICE § 5.4 (Thomson Reuters, 2017 ed.).

[43] 913 N.E.2d 939, 940 (Ohio 2009).

[44] *Id.* at 943.

in the next section, the vicarious liability of other firm lawyers may turn on the organizational structure of the firm.

### § 5-7.2(c) Liability of Partners in General Partnerships

When the firm is organized as a general partnership, the partners in the firm may be jointly and severally liable as a matter of partnership law. The relevant state's version of the Uniform Partnership Act (1914) or Revised Uniform Partnership Act (1993) govern the rights, duties, and liability of a partner in a general partnership. Under Section 13 of the UPA, the partnership is liable for loss or injury caused "to any person, not being a partner," for "any wrongful act or omission of any partner acting in the ordinary course of partnership business or with the authority of the co-partners."[45] Under this section, a partnership is ordinarily liable for a tort committed by one of the members acting within the scope of the firm's business, even though the persons sought to be charged did not participate in, ratify, or have knowledge of such conduct.[46] Under the UPA, each member of the partnership is liable for all partnership debts and obligations, including those arising from wrongful acts or omissions of a partner or from breaches of trust chargeable to the firm. Thus, under partnership law, a partner who has not participated in or condoned the wrongful actions of another partner (a non-participating partner) may still be liable for acts or omissions of other partners.[47]

The timing of the misconduct affects the liability of firm partners. Unless the partner assumes liability on joining a partnership, the partner is not liable for acts or omissions that occurred before the lawyer became a partner.[48] Likewise, a partner's withdrawal does not terminate the partner's responsibility for liabilities or debts that arose prior to the withdrawal.[49] As explained by a bankruptcy court in a case holding two former partners jointly and severally liable for more than $3.7 million, a "partner cannot escape liability simply by leaving the partnership after the malpractice is committed but before the client wins or settles a malpractice claim."[50]

### § 5-7.2(d) Liability of Principals in Limited Liability Law Firms

Lawyers now use different organizational structures for their firms. The following section discusses vicarious liability issues related to practice in limited liability firms.

#### *§ 5-7.2(d)(1) Practice in Professional Corporation*

The traditional structure of lawyers practicing in general partnerships began to change in the 1960s when lawyers lobbied for the ability to practice in corporations. Originally, lawyers sought to incorporate to gain tax advantages. They were successful

---

[45] For a discussion of this section, see Susan Saab Fortney, *Am I My Partner's Keeper? Peer Review in Law Firms*, 66 U. COLO. L. REV. 329, 349–50 (1996).

[46] *Id.*

[47] *See* Dennerline v. Atterholt, 886 N.E. 2d 582, 586 n. 1 (Ind. Ct. App. 2008) (referring to the defendant-partner and his law firm interchangeably because their liability for harm caused by failure to advise a client was "coextensive").

[48] RESTATEMENT (THIRD) OF THE LAW GOVERNING LAWYERS § 58 cmt. i (American Law Institute, 2000).

[49] *Id.*

[50] In re Keck, Mahin & Cate, 274 B.R. 740, 745 (Bankr. N.D. Ill. 2002).

in convincing legislatures to allow them to practice in a corporate form, commonly called a Professional Corporation or Professional Association.[51]

After elimination of the tax benefits associated with incorporation, lawyers continued to incorporate their law practices to limit their vicarious liability exposure for claims related to other members of the firm. The liability shield for shareholders in professional corporations depends on state law.[52] Although there is variation in the liability protection provided to shareholders under state law, Professor Robert W. Hillman places the jurisdictions in the following three categories:

> Many states provide shareholders of professional corporations limited liability equivalent to that available to shareholders of other corporations. At least as to law firms, however, some states make the shareholders vicariously liable as if they were partners or render shareholders jointly and severally liable within defined limited. Still, other states fall between the extreme by creating liability for the professional's own acts as well as the acts of others under the professional's supervision and control.[53]

As with the other limited liability structures discussed below, the ability of a principal (shareholder) in a professional corporation to avoid vicarious liability will depend on whether the corporation meets statutory and other requirements imposed by state law. For example, a state statute or rule may require that professional corporations maintain minimum levels of insurance if principals want to escape personal liability for harm caused by other firm actors.[54] In Illinois, the state supreme court adopted a rule requiring insurance for lawyers seeking to limit their vicarious liability by practicing in a professional corporation or other form of limited liability firm.[55]

The Illinois rule related to insurance and vicarious liability of firm principals also points to the role of the judiciary in regulating the practice of law. Specifically, the high court of a state may exercise its inherent authority to prohibit or limit lawyers' ability to escape vicarious liability, even though the state legislature provides organizational choices with limited liability for principals in the organization.[56] This was the position that the Georgia Supreme Court took in 1983 in *First Bank & Trust Co. v. Zagoria*.[57] In *Zagoria*, the court held that members of law firms will be liable for their own professional misdeeds, as well as those of the other members of the firm, with no distinction between partnerships and professional corporations. Thirteen years later, the Georgia Supreme Court reversed its position, concluding that lawyer-shareholders in a professional

---

[51] Robert W. Hillman, *Organizational Choices of Professional Service Firms: an Empirical Study,* 58 BUS. LAW. 1387, 1391 (2003).

[52] *See generally Liability of Professional Corporation of Lawyers, or Individual Members Thereof, for Malpractice or Other Tort of Another Member,* 39 A.L.R. 4th 556 (originally published in 1985).

[53] Robert W. Hillman, *Organizational Choices of Professional Service Firms: an Empirical Study,* 58 BUS. LAW. 1387, 1391–92 (2003).

[54] *E.g.*, CAL. BUS. & PROF. CODE § 6171(b) (Westlaw 2017) (requiring that a professional corporation "provide and maintain security by insurance or otherwise for claims against it by its clients for errors and omissions arising out of the rendering of professional services").

[55] Illinois Supreme Court Rule 722(b)(1) requires that firms maintain minimum insurance coverage of $100,000 per claim and $150,000 annual aggregate multiplied by the number of lawyers in the firm, provided that the firm's insurance need not exceed $5 million per claim and $10 million for all claims during the year.

[56] For an examination of the inherent powers doctrine and the likelihood of courts using it to strike down LLP protection for lawyers, see Charles W. Wolfram, *Inherent Powers in the Crucible of Lawyer Self-Protection: Reflections on the LLP Campaign*, S. TEX. L. REV. 359, 377–81 (1998).

[57] 302 S.E. 2d 674, 676 (Ga. 1983).

corporation hold the "same rights and responsibility as shareholders in other professional corporations."[58]

In those jurisdictions where courts have held that individual shareholders are not vicariously liable for the malpractice or other torts of another member of the corporation, the shareholder may still be liable if the corporation fails to observe corporate formalities. As with other corporations, a plaintiff may attempt to use this failure to pierce the corporate veil in an effort to hold all shareholders personally liable for the misconduct of another member of the professional corporation.

A plaintiff may also seek to hold individual shareholders personally liable by framing the claims as direct liability claims, as opposed to vicarious liability claims. This was the tack that the plaintiff successfully took in a dispute decided by the New Mexico Supreme Court.[59] In that case, the shareholders in the defendant firm maintained that they should not have personal liability for the claims asserted by the plaintiff. Based on the record in the trial court, the court concluded that the claims against the shareholders were not vicarious liability claims, but were direct liability claims related to the shareholders' involvement in terminating the representation of the client.[60] This approach to avoiding the liability shield is one that a plaintiff can also take in asserting claims against lawyers who practice in limited liability companies and limited liability partnerships.

#### *§ 5-7.2(d)(2) Practice in Limited Liability Companies and Limited Liability Partnerships*

As noted above, interest in incorporating could be traced to professionals' desire to take advantage of tax benefits available for incorporated entities. After these tax advantages were no longer available, lawyers around the U.S. continued to incorporate with the expectation that doing so could help limit their personal liability for the acts and omissions of other firm agents. The impediment or downside of incorporating for many lawyers in larger firms was that the creation of a separate entity could have tax consequences. Specifically, the incorporation could result in double taxation at the individual and corporate level, unless the law firm was small enough to qualify for a Subchapter S election under the Internal Revenue Code. Therefore, for decades many larger firms did not use an organizational structure to limit members' vicarious liability. This situation changed with the advent of limited liability companies (LLCs) and limited liability partnerships (LLPs).

In 1977, Wyoming passed the first LLC statute to assist a mineral concern that sought to organize a business entity offering limited liability to all equity holders, while allowing them to avoid taxation at the entity level.[61] After the Internal Revenue Service released a Revenue Ruling that concluded that the LLC under Wyoming law could be classified as a partnership (and avoid double taxation at the individual and company

---

[58] Henderson v. HSI Financial Services, Inc., 471 S.E. 2d 885, 886 (Ga. 1996). The court stated that it overruled the strict liability rule [imposing vicarious liability] "because the legislature has provided that shareholders of professional corporations are not personally liable for corporate debts except by personal conduct." *Id.*

[59] Sanders, Bruin, Coll & Worley, P.A. v. McKay Oil Corp., 943 P.2d 104 (N.M. 1977).

[60] "We hold that, as a general matter, membership or shareholder status in a professional corporation does not shield an attorney from individual liability for his own mistakes or professional misdeeds." *Id.* at 106.

[61] Susan Saab Fortney, *Seeking Shelter in the Minefield of Unintended Consequences: The Traps of Limited Liability Law Firms*, 54 WASH. & LEE L. REV. 717 722–23 (1997) (discussing the emergency of LLCs).

levels) other states passed LLC legislation.[62] The form proved to be popular because the LLC structure enabled the owner-members to limit their vicarious liability and still avoid corporate taxation.[63]

From the standpoint of the owner-members, one organizational hurdle to forming an LLC is the adoption of an operating agreement for the LLC. As with professional corporations, the equity owners (called "members" in an LLC) should observe organizational formalities and not inadvertently function as a partnership. Failure to do so may subject the members of the firm to personal liability if a plaintiff can successful pierce the LLC shield.

As compared to the LLC, the LLP has fewer organizational formalities. Simply stated, an LLP is a general partnership that has elected to operate as an LLP. The LLP form grew out of the aftermath of the savings and loan crisis and the numerous cases that the federal government brought against lawyers who represented the failed financial institutions. An outside defense counsel for one of the defendant law firms proposed a new organizational structure that was later included in legislation proposed in Texas. The legislation allowed for lawyers (and others) to convert to an LLP. When Texas first enacted the LLP, the legislation required that the LLP maintain $100,000 of liability insurance. The first LLP provisions enacted in Texas, provided a liability shield that protected partners from tort claims arising from the acts or omissions of another firm actor. The statute also provided for supervisory liability.[64]

Following the Texas legislation, the LLP form spread nationwide.[65] Although all U.S. jurisdictions have adopted LLP provisions, a few states, including California and New York, permit only professional firms to organize as LLPs.[66]

As the LLP organizational form swept across the U.S., the liability protection expanded. Statutes evolved from partial shield statutes that protected partners from vicarious liability claims based on tort-type theories to "full-shield" statutes providing partners with full protection against vicarious liability for all obligations of the firm.[67]

States impose their own requirements for registering a partnership as an LLP. In addition to the initial filing, a state may require periodic renewals. All filings must include the firm's name and designation as an LLP. "The usual requirement is that 'LLP'

---

[62] *Id.* at 722.

[63] "LLCs protect their members to the same extent as professional corporations." RONALD. E. MALLEN, LEGAL MALPRACTICE § 5:20 (Thomson Reuters, 2017 ed.).

[64] Years later, the Texas legislature amended the LLP provisions to eliminate the provisions related to insurance, financial responsibility, and supervisory liability. Amendments also expanded the liability protection to cover all debts and obligations of the partnership. Elizabeth S. Miller, *The Perils and Pitfalls of Practicing Law in a Texas Limited Liability Partnership*, 43 TEX. TECH L. REV. 563, 565 (2011).

[65] To many, the LLP is the "entity of choice" for lawyers desiring to limit their liability because the organizational form provides the vicarious liability shield without the "difficulties inherent in the other structures." RONALD. E. MALLEN, LEGAL MALPRACTICE § 5:24 (Thomson Reuters, 2017 ed.).

[66] CHRISTINE HURT, ET AL, BROMBERG AND RIBSTEIN ON LIMITED LIABILITY PARTNERSHIPS, THE REVISED UNIFORM PARTNERSHIP ACT, AND THE UNIFORM LIMITED PARTNERSHIP ACT § 1.01(e) (Wolters Kluwer, 2017 ed.) "Of the highest performing 200 law firms in the United States, 170 operate as LLPs." *Id.* (citing an AMERICAN LAWYER REPORT).

[67] *Id.* at § 1.01 (b)–1.01(d) (tracing the evolution of LLP statutes). "The march toward full-shield protection continues, and in 2013 only nine states retain partial-shield statutes. * * *. Under full shield statutes * * * the limited liability of partners in LLPs is substantially indistinguishable from that of corporate shareholders or member of LLCs." *Id.* at § 1.01(c).

(with or without periods), 'Limited Liability Partnership,' or the equivalent for 'Registered Limited Liability Partnership,' be the last letters of words in the name."[68]

Jurisdictions also use different approaches to requiring insurance or evidence of financial responsibility as a condition to obtaining limited liability protection as an LLP.[69] Some states require a specific dollar amount for the LLP.[70] Others base the amount on the number of lawyers practicing in the LLP.[71] The majority of states do not require that lawyers maintain insurance or evidence of financial responsibility.[72]

Another difference in LLP statutes relates to the treatment of supervisory liability. A number of LLP statutes expressly impose supervisory liability, providing that the limited liability structure does not affect the liability of partners or members for their own acts or the acts of those they directly supervise.[73]

Statutes imposing supervisory liability may not specify whether a partner is strictly liable for conduct of supervised attorneys, or whether the plaintiff must establish negligence or fault on the part of the supervisor.[74] Even with statutes that expressly provide for supervisory liability, questions remain on the level of supervision that gives rise to liability.[75] Given the limited guidance in the statutes, cases have turned on the court's interpretation of the statute and the facts developed in the record.[76] Basically, a court should not summarily dismiss claims against individual partners if the record supports the plaintiff's allegations implicating the supervisor in the misconduct personally or through direct supervision of the firm's operations.[77]

Various opinions illustrate how imposition of liability on a supervisor will turn on the specific statutory language and the factual record. Applying the statutory provision related to the supervisory liability of a partner in an LLP, a Texas federal court concluded that the complaint asserted no facts to support supervisory liability, finding that the complaint did not allege that the partner participated in or was even aware of the other partner's actions with regard to another partner's collection efforts that

---

[68] *Id.* at § 2.05.

[69] The insurance requirement could be set in a statute or a court rule. *E.g.*, Illinois Supreme Court Rule 722(b)(1).

[70] *E.g.*, CONN. GEN. STAT. § 34–327(e) (Westlaw 2017) (requiring $250,000).

[71] *E.g.*, N.J. Ct. R. 1:21–1C(a)(3) (requiring $100,000 per claim multiplied by the number of lawyers in the LLP, not to excel $5 million per claim).

[72] "Although common in the first generation of LLP statutes, insurance requirements have been dropped from most LLP statutes." Elizabeth S. Miller, *The Perils and Pitfalls of Practicing Law in a Texas Limited Liability Partnership*, 43 TEX. TECH L. REV. 563, 576 (2011).

[73] *E.g.*, N.Y. P'SHIP LAW § 26(c) (Westlaw 2017) (stating that partners, employees and agents of an LLP "shall be personally and fully liable and accountable for any negligent or wrongful act or misconduct committed by him or her or by any person under his or her direct supervision and control").

[74] Susan Saab Fortney, *Seeking Shelter in the Minefield of Unintended Consequences: The Traps of Limited Liability Law Firms*, 54 WASH. & LEE L. REV. 717, 731 (1997).

[75] *See id.* at 732–37 (examining questions related to supervisory liability and possible adverse effects on attorneys' willingness to collaborate and supervise others).

[76] *See* Cooke-Zwiebach v. Oziel, 962 N.Y.S. 2d 64 (N.Y. App. Div. 2013) (noting that the wording in the firm's partnership agreement did not establish as a matter of law that the defendant-partner had supervisory control over the attorney accused of misconduct and that the record failed to conclusively establish that the defendant-partner had knowledge or reason to know of the other attorney's malfeasance).

[77] *See, e.g.*, Connolly v Napoli, Kaiser & Ber, LLP, 817 N.Y.S. 2d 872 (N.Y. Sup. Ct. 2006) (refusing to dismiss claims brought by a discharged associate because the associate's allegations implicated the partners in the misconduct personally or through direct supervision of the firm's operations).

allegedly violated federal collection law.[78] As suggested by the opinion, it will not suffice for a plaintiff to allege that the partner was "aware or should have been aware" of the alleged misconduct.

Similarly, it will be difficult to establish liability by asserting that a partner had a duty to oversee firm operations. This was the position by the Connecticut court in *Kus v. Irving*.[79] In that case, the court held that two partners in a three-partner LLP law firm would not be subject to liability for the third partner's misconduct. The plaintiff alleged that the two partners violated provisions of the Connecticut disciplinary rule that requires partners to make reasonable efforts to ensure that the firm maintains reasonable measures giving reasonable assurance that all lawyers in the firm conform to the rules of professional conduct. Even if there was evidence of a violation of Rule 5.1, the court concluded that the LLP structure supersedes the rule except where the other person is under the partner's "direct supervision or control."[80]

The variations in state treatment of LLPs make generalizations difficult. To analyze the vicarious liability of members of limited liability law firms, a number of factors should be considered. First, the analysis should consider whether statute or a state rule allows lawyers to practice in the particular form of limited liability firm. Second, what types of claims are covered by the vicarious liability shield? Third, does state law impose supervisory liability?[81] Fourth, what statutory or rule requirements must be satisfied? Finally, what circumstances or conduct may jeopardize the limited liability protection of individual partners?

Starting with the organizational requirements, a partner or member of a law firm may lose the limited liability protection if there is a failure to meet the requirements for practice in an LLP. This includes some deficiency in the initial registration or renewal. If the registration or renewal is defective, a court may take the position that strict compliance is necessary and refuse to allow a partner to rely on the limited liability shield. This outcome is more likely when the noncompliance relates to public disclosures and financial responsibility.[82] This was the approach used by a Texas appellate court in a case involving an LLP's failure to carry the required insurance.[83]

Rather than strict compliance, a statute may require only "substantial compliance," or a court may excuse good faith errors. For example, in a case involving claims arising out of a partner's negligence in handling a patent-infringement settlement, the court concluded that the insurance requirement in the New Jersey Rule did not extend to the firm's windup period, and therefore did not require the firm to purchase tail insurance.[84]

---

[78] Garcia v. Jenkins/Babb LL., 2013 WL 3789830, at *7 (N.D. Tex. 2013).

[79] 736 A.2d 946, 947 (Conn. Super. Ct. 1999).

[80] *Id.*

[81] Although the vast majority of LLC statutes do not refer to supervisory liability, a number of LLP statutes provide for some degree of personal liability for conduct of supervised persons. Susan Saab Fortney, *Seeking Shelter in the Minefield of Unintended Consequences: The Traps of Limited Liability Law Firms*, 54 WASH. & LEE L. REV. 717, 730 (1997) (discussing the emergence of LLCs).

[82] CHRISTINE HURT, ET AL, BROMBERG AND RIBSTEIN ON LIMITED LIABILITY PARTNERSHIPS, THE REVISED UNIFORM PARTNERSHIP ACT, AND THE UNIFORM LIMITED PARTNERSHIP ACT § 2.07(b) (Wolters Kluwer, 2017 ed.).

[83] Edward B. Elmer, M.D., P.A. v. Santa Fe Properties, Inc., 2006 WL 3612359 (Tex. Ct. App. 2006) (refusing to allow a physician in an LLP to limit his liability for lease obligations). Although the physician carried an errors and omissions policy in his own name, the court concluded that the policy did not cover the LLP or the physician's partner. *Id.* at *2.

[84] Mortgage Grader, Inc. v. Ward & Olivo, *L.L.P.*, 139 A.3d 30, 33 (N.J. 2016).

Although violation of the rule could subject the attorney to professional discipline for violating a disciplinary rule in New Jersey, the failure to maintain insurance did not result in automatic conversion of a law firm organized as an LLP into a general partnership.[85]

In addition to attempting to demonstrate that the firm did not comply with statutory prerequisites for LLP status, a plaintiff may attempt to bust the LLP shield on other grounds.[86] First, a plaintiff may ask the court to exercise its inherent authority to regulate the legal profession and hold principals vicariously liable.[87] Such an attack would likely fail if the state high court has already addressed in case law or ruled on the vicarious liability of firm principals. Second, in states that have only addressed the vicarious liability of shareholders in a professional corporation, a plaintiff may assert that the LLP structure is misleading for lay people who believe that they are represented by a partnership in which the partners share joint and several liability.[88] To rely on such an argument, a plaintiff should be prepared to show that firm communications would lead a reasonable person to understand that all partners would be responsible for the acts and omissions of firm representatives.[89] Therefore, firms that want to rely on the LLP status to protect individual partners should avoid statements in brochures and other firm communications that would lead to reasonable expectations that all firm partners stand behind the work performed by members of the firm.

## § 5-7.3 OTHER ASSOCIATIONS THAT EXPOSE LAWYERS TO LIABILITY

Increasingly, lawyers are subject to malpractice claims related to the outside counsel.[90] A variety of relationships may subject a lawyer to liability for the misconduct of other lawyers who are not members of the lawyer's firm. These relationships include entering referral fee arrangements and associating with another lawyer who serves as "co-counsel" or "of counsel." A poorly structured and executed office-sharing arrangement might also expose a lawyer to vicarious liability claims. A lawyer may also be subject to liability for conduct of independent contractors when they handle nondelegable duties. The following analyzes liability exposure related to these associations with persons outside the lawyer's firm.

### § 5-7.3(a) Referral Fee Arrangements

Depending on the nature of the representation and the lawyer's circumstances, a prudent course of conduct may be to refer a legal matter to a person outside the lawyer's law firm. As a matter of professional responsibility, a lawyer should decline representation if the lawyer is not competent to handle the matter and the requisite level of competence cannot be achieved by reasonable study.[91] Another option is for a lawyer

---

[85] *Id.*

[86] Susan Saab Fortney, *Professional Responsibility and Liability Issues Related to Limited Liability Law Partnerships*, 39 S. TEX. L. REV. 399, 427–42 (1998) (analyzing various strategies for piercing the LLP shield).

[87] *See id.* at 427–29.

[88] *See id.* at 432–35.

[89] *See id.* at 436–39 (discussing how communications may mislead clients).

[90] John T. Lay & Child Cantey Thrasher, *Potential Liability for Attorneys Engaging Co-Counsel and Referrals*, 79 DEF. COUNSEL J. 490 (2012).

[91] MODEL RULES OF PROF'L CONDUCT, R. 1.1 cmt. 4 (American Bar Ass'n, 2017).

to refer the matter to or consult with a lawyer with established competence in the particular field in question.[92]

### *§ 5-7.3(a)(1) Joint Responsibility and Joint Ventures*

In referral situations, ABA Model Rule 1.5 and state equivalents of the model rule allow the referring lawyer to receive a portion of the fee, provided certain conditions are satisfied. Unless the division of the fee is in proportion to the services performed by each lawyer, the ethics rule requires that the total fee be reasonable and that the client agree to the arrangement, including the share each lawyer will receive, and that the client's agreement be confirmed in writing.[93]

The ethics rule also requires that both the referring lawyer and the "handling" lawyer assume "joint responsibility."[94] A comment to the rule explains that joint responsibility "entails financial and ethical responsibility for the representation as if the lawyers were associated in a partnership."[95] Thus, by complying with the requirements for receiving a fee, referring lawyers subject themselves to vicarious liability for the misconduct of handling lawyers because the lawyers voluntarily assume joint responsibility for the representation.

The *Restatement* includes a comparable "joint responsibility" requirement for referral arrangements.[96] A comment following the *Restatement* section elaborates on the meaning of "joint responsibility," stating that it means that "each lawyer can be held liable in a malpractice suit and before disciplinary authorities for the others' acts to the same extent as could partners in the same traditional partnership."[97]

Another comment suggests that the rationale for the "joint responsibility" requirement is that it encourages lawyers to refer matters to competent counsel rather than simply referring matters to lawyers who might pay large referral fees.[98] ABA and state ethics opinions point to this justification for imposing financial responsibility.[99] These opinions treat acceptance of referral fees as the assumption of responsibility to a partner in a law firm.[100] After reviewing a number of these ethics committee opinions, as well as court opinions, related to referral fees, a 2017 Colorado opinion adopted the "joint and several" or vicarious-liability test for financial responsibility.[101]

A number of courts have used joint venture law to pursue claims against lawyers in fee sharing agreements.[102] For example, in *Duggins v. Guardianship of Washington*, the plaintiff sought to hold Duggins liable following a misappropriation by Barfield, another

---

[92] *Id.* at R. 1.1 cmt 2.

[93] *Id.* at R. 1.5(d).

[94] *Id.*

[95] *Id.* R. 1.5 cmt. 7.

[96] RESTATEMENT (THIRD) OF THE LAW GOVERNING LAWYERS § 47 (American Law Institute, 2000).

[97] *Id.* at § 47 cmt. d.

[98] *Id.* at § 47 cmt. b.

[99] ABA Comm. on Ethics and Profl. Responsibility, Informal Op. 85–1514 (1985); Fla. Bar Comm. on Profl. Ethics, Op. 96–3 (1997).

[100] New York Cty. Lawyer's Assoc. Comm. on Profl. Ethics, Op. 715 (1996).

[101] Scott R. Larson, P.C. v. Grinnan, 2017 WL 2590525, at 42 (Col. App. 2017).

[102] *E.g.,* Noris v. Silver, 701 So. 2d 1238, 1241 (Fla. Dist. Ct. App. 1997). For a discussion of the features of a joint venture, see Rachel L. Bosworth, Note, *Is the Model Rule Outdated? Texas Carries Referral Fee Responsibility into the Limited Liability Era*, 84 TEX. L. REV. 509, 514 (2005).

lawyer.[103] Stating that the "intent to share both the responsibility and the profits from the representation clearly demonstrated the presence of a joint venture," the court held both lawyers liable even though Duggins had no knowledge of and did not participate in the misappropriation.[104] In *Duggins*, the court also noted that the referring lawyer may also be liable for negligent referral.[105]

In *First United Pentecostal Church of Beaumont v. Parker*,[106] the Texas Supreme Court stated that "The elements of a joint venture are (1) an express or implied agreement to engage in a joint venture, (2) a community of interest in the venture, (3) an agreement to share profits and losses from the enterprise, and (4) a mutual right of control or management of the enterprise."[107] However, the court declined in impose joint venture liability on one lawyer (Parker) for the theft of churches funds perpetrated by another lawyer (Lamb) for whom he worked. Although "Parker referred to the firm variously as 'our firm,' 'us,' and 'we've' during his sworn statement," there was "no evidence that Parker agreed with Lamb to either steal the church's money or share that money."[108] The court noted that:

> the church points out that Parker's bi-monthly paychecks may have included some of the church's money. But even if they did, that does not comprise evidence that Parker had a mutual right to control and manage the stolen money, entered into a joint venture to steal the church's money, or had an agreement with Lamb to share profits and losses from the theft of the church's money. * * * [N]one of the evidence the church points to provides support for its claim that there was an express or implied agreement by Parker to be part of a joint venture with Lamb for the purpose of stealing the church's money."[109]

### *§ 5-7.3(a)(2) Negligent Referral*

In addition to exposure for assuming joint responsibility, referring lawyers may be liable for negligence in referring a matter to another attorney. This liability could relate either to negligence associated with conduct in making the referral or negligence associated with transferring the matter to another lawyer. With respect to both types of negligent referral claims, the plaintiff would attempt to establish that the referring lawyer assumed a duty by making the referral and the lawyer should be held to a standard of a reasonable referring lawyer under the same or similar circumstances. Such claims are not based on a vicarious liability theory, but based on liability for the referring lawyer's own acts and omissions.[110]

---

[103] 632 So. 2d 420 (Miss. 1993).

[104] *Id.* at 428.

[105] *Id.* at 429.

[106] 514 S.W.3d 214 (Tex. 2017).

[107] *Id.* at 225.

[108] *Id.* at 226.

[109] *Id.*

[110] As noted in the *Restatement (Third) of the Law Governing Lawyers*, a "firm is not ordinarily liable for the acts or omissions of a lawyer outside the firm who is working with firm lawyers as co-counsel or in a similar arrangement," but can be liable for "the acts and omissions of its own principals and employees relating to the outside lawyer, for example when it undertakes to recommend or supervise the outside lawyer and does so negligently or when its lawyers advise or participate in the outside lawyer's actionable conduct." RESTATEMENT (THIRD) OF THE LAW GOVERNING LAWYERS § 58, cmt. e (American Law Institute, 2000).

A plaintiff may pursue negligent referral claims when the handling lawyer commits malpractice and does not have assets or insurance to cover the loss. When a handling lawyer commits malpractice, the client could challenge the conduct of the referring lawyer, asserting that the referring lawyer knew or should have known that the other lawyer was likely to commit malpractice.

The ability to successfully pursue such a claim first depends on whether the jurisdiction has addressed the issue of negligent referral by lawyers. Courts have reached different conclusions in determining whether an independent cause of action for negligent referral should be recognized. The following excerpt from a 2016 Minnesota opinion reviews the jurisdictional approaches used by various courts:

> [The plaintiff] urges this court to adopt the reasoning of the New Jersey federal district court, which has held that an attorney who refers a matter to another attorney has an affirmative duty to exercise care to ensure that the second attorney is competent and trustworthy. *Tormo v. Yormark,* 398 F. Supp. 1159, 1169–70 (D.N.J. 1975). In the 40 years since *Tormo,* few appellate courts have ruled on whether a cause of action exists for negligent referral by an attorney. Those that have, have taken various approaches to the issue. *See, e.g., Christensen, O'Connor, Garrison & Havelka v. State,* 97 Wash. 2d 764, 649 P.2d 839, 842 (Wash. 1982) (holding that "[r]eferring law firms are neither liable to their clients for * * * malpractice nor can they recover from the engaged law firm for such malpractice"); *Noris v. Silver,* 701 So. 2d 1238, 1241 (Fla. Dist. Ct. App. 1997) (affirming dismissal of a negligent-referral claim when the referring attorney did not know that the referred attorney would commit malpractice, but noting possibility of liability based on fee-splitting). New York courts have taken a flexible approach, concluding that liability depends on such factors as whether the referring and receiving attorneys practice in the same state or the same subject area and whether the referring attorney has an ongoing supervisory role. *Compare Broadway Maint. Corp. v. Tunstead & Schecter,* 110 A.D.2d 587, 487 N.Y.S.2d 799, 800–01 (App. Div.1985) (holding that, in the absence of assuming a supervisory role, general counsel could not be held liable for malpractice in connection with its referral to out-of-state trial counsel, who failed timely to commence a lawsuit) *with Reed v. Finkelstein, Levine, Gittlesohn & Tetenbaum,* 304 A.D.2d 329, 756 N.Y.S.2d 577, 578 (App. Div. 2003) (holding that an issue of fact existed as to referring attorneys' responsibilities in malpractice action when they practiced in the same state and specialized in that same subject area as referred attorney.)[111]

Noting that the state supreme court has the power to recognize common law doctrines and extend existing law, the Minnesota appellate court concluded that current Minnesota law does not authorize a cause of action based on a lawyer's negligent referral.[112]

In a jurisdiction in which the question has not yet been addressed, the court will likely decide the matter as a question of law.[113] In evaluating whether the tort of negligent referral should be recognized, a court may balance a number of factors

---

[111] Wells v. Mattox, 2016 WL 3223227, at *4 (Minn. Ct. App.).

[112] *Id.* at *5.

[113] Andrew W. Martin, Jr. *Legal Malpractice: Negligent Referral as a Cause of Action,* 29 CUMB. L. REV. 679, 689 (1999).

including the lawyer's ethical duties to the client, the expectations of both the client and the lawyer, and "the public policy behind having a system of referrals."[114] "Also important in the analysis are the extent to which the attorney-client relationship has developed, the knowledge of the legal needs of the prospective client, and the existence of referral fees."[115]

When a court recognizes the cause of action for negligent referral, the issues could be framed as follows:

> (1) whether the referring attorney had a duty to use reasonable care in selecting and referring a client's case to another attorney; (2) whether that attorney breached his duty of care by selecting the referred attorney; (3) whether there existed a causal connection between the alleged negligent referral and the resulting injury; and (4) whether actual loss or damage resulted from the attorney's alleged negligence.[116]

In tackling these issues, the fact determination of negligent conduct may turn on what the referring attorney knew about the attorney to whom the matter was referred. This was the crux of the court opinion in *Tormo v. Yormark*, the seminal case in which a federal court in New Jersey analyzed the tort of negligent referral.[117] In that case, a New York lawyer agreed to investigate a personal injury claim.[118] After the claim was not settled, the New York lawyer referred the matter to a New Jersey lawyer.[119] Rather than the lawyer simply relying on the fact that the New Jersey lawyer was licensed to practice law, the court indicated that the circumstances suggested that the New Jersey lawyer lacked trustworthiness, putting the New York lawyer on notice to inquire further to determine if the New Jersey attorney had improperly solicited clients.[120] Based on the record, the court concluded that a lawyer who "knowingly entrusted his client's business to a lawyer who he had reason to believe was guilty of [improper solicitation] would be clearly negligent either in making the referral at all, or in doing so without advising his client of his suspicions."[121]

As suggested by the dicta in *Tormo*, a lawyer's liability for negligent referral may depend on the totality of the circumstances relating to what the lawyer knew or should have known.[122] In a trial, the judge can instruct the jury in making their fact determination as to whether the lawyer's conduct failed to comport with the standard of care for making a referral under the circumstances.[123]

Liability may also be based on the manner in which the referral is made. Once a lawyer assumes a duty to make a referral, the lawyer can be responsible for exercising care in transferring the matter, communicating fast-approaching deadlines, and

---

[114] *Id.* at 689–90.

[115] *Id.* at 690.

[116] *Id.* at 696.

[117] 398 F. Supp. 1159 (D.N.J.1975).

[118] *Id.* at 1166.

[119] *Id.*

[120] *Id.* at 1171.

[121] *Id.*

[122] Rachel L. Bosworth, Note, *Is the Model Rule Outdated: Texas Carries Referral Fee Responsibility into the Limited Liability Era*, 84 TEX. L. REV. 509, 514 (2005).

[123] *See* RONALD E. MALLEN, LEGAL MALPRACTICE § 5:51 (Thomson Reuters, 2017 ed.) (noting that the standard of care depends upon the circumstances of the particular subject matter).

disclosing relevant information as a fiduciary.[124] Once again, the responsibilities of the lawyer will depend on the totality of the circumstances, including the extent of the lawyer's dealings with the client or prospective client and status of the representation.

### § 5-7.3(b) Co-Counsel Arrangements and Other Outside Counsel

Rather than referring an entire matter to a lawyer in another law firm, a lawyer may enter a co-counsel arrangement with the other lawyers. A lawyer may seek to co-counsel for a variety of reasons, such as associating with other lawyers with particular expertise or local connections. These co-counsel arrangements may take different forms, including principal-agent relationships and joint ventures.[125] As explained in the *Restatement (Third) of the Law Governing Lawyers*, when lawyers collaborate on a client matter, the express or implied terms of the lawyers' particular agreement of association will determine their powers, rights, and obligations with respect to one another.[126]

Absent an agreement or circumstances to the contrary, a co-counsel usually serves as an independent agent of the client.[127] Therefore, a lawyer ordinarily should not be vicariously liable for the acts or omissions of a lawyer outside the firm.[128] As explained by one legal malpractice expert, the lawyers are "fellow agents of the client, each owning the client independent duties of care, confidentiality, and loyalty."[129]

In evaluating liability issues in co-counsel arrangements, a starting point is to examine the agreement between the lawyers. "Regardless of how the first lawyer identifies co-counsel or the nature of their relationship thereafter, the first lawyer may face liability for negligent referral if the second lawyer breaches duties to the client."[130] As discussed in the previous section on negligent referral, lawyers (and their firms) may still be liable for their own acts or omissions relating to co-counsel.[131] This could occur if a lawyer undertakes to "recommend or supervise the outside lawyer and does so negligently or when its lawyers advise or participate in the outside lawyer's actionable conduct."[132]

The lawyer may also be liable for the misconduct of co-counsel when the lawyer, rather than the client, employs the co-counsel. In that event, co-counsel may function as a sub-agent of the lawyer, and the lawyer may be liable vicariously or for negligent supervision. This was the outcome in *Whalen v. DeGraff, Foy, Conway, Holt-Harris & Mealey*.[133] In that case, a New York law firm hired a Florida lawyer and his law firm to

---

[124] *See id.* (referring to North Carolina case in which the client stated a cause of action for unjust enrichment based on the lawyer's failure to disclose a referral fee).

[125] "An association for a legal matter can be a joint venture, the effect being a partnership for the particular transaction." RONALD E. MALLEN, LEGAL MALPRACTICE § 5:48 (Thomson Reuters, 2017 ed.).

[126] RESTATEMENT (THIRD) OF THE LAW GOVERNING LAWYERS § 9 cmt. h (American Law Institute, 2000).

[127] *Id.* at § 58 cmt. e.

[128] *Id.* (noting that it is "especially likely" for the second lawyer to be treated as an independent agent when that lawyer represents a client in another jurisdiction).

[129] Douglas R. Richmond, *Professional Responsibilities of Co-Counsel: Joint Venturers or Scorpions in a Bottle*, 98 KY. L.J.461,482–83 (2009–2010).

[130] *Id.* at 483.

[131] *See, e.g.,* Duggins v. Guardianship of Washington Through Huntly, 632 So. 2d 420 (Miss 1993) (liability supported by the fact that the lawyer had selected the other counsel and coordinated different aspects of the client's representation).

[132] RESTATEMENT (THIRD) OF THE LAW GOVERNING LAWYERS § 58 cmt. e (American Law Institute, 2000). (citing the *Restatement (Second) of Agency*).

[133] 53 A.D.3d 912, 863 N.Y.S.2d 100 (2008).

collect a judgment that the New York firm had obtained. In holding the New York law firm liable for the malpractice of the Florida lawyer, the court pointed to facts that indicated that the New York lawyer had retained the Florida lawyer and that the client had no contact with the Florida lawyer. Based on those facts and others revealing that the client relied on the New York firm, the court concluded that the New York firm had assumed the responsibility to collect the judgment and that the Florida attorney became a subagent of the New York firm.[134] As suggested by the *Whalen* opinion, the assumption of duties related to outside counsel may support a direct liability claim against the law firm that associated with co-counsel.

A close relationship between the lawyer and co-counsel may also subject a lawyer to special responsibilities with respect to co-counsel. Such a close relationship influenced the court's conclusion in a New Jersey case involving misappropriation by a wills and trusts lawyer.[135] In that case, the court considered the liability of the defendant, a lawyer who occupied an office in the building of the wills and trust lawyer accused of serious misconduct. Additional facts pointed to a close relationship between the two lawyers, frequent referrals, and the possibility that the defendant-lawyer may have been aware of misconduct by the wills and trusts lawyer. Based on the record, the court explained that a lawyer "who has a close and interdependent business relationship with another lawyer, and who is performing legal work for a common client at that lawyer's request, has a duty to report that lawyer if he or she develops actual knowledge that the lawyer has been stealing funds from their common client."[136]

To define their respective roles and responsibilities, lawyers should clarify in writing the division of responsibilities.[137] Doing so can avoid misunderstandings and lower the risk of liability for the malpractice of co-counsel.[138]

### § 5-7.3(c) Of Counsel Arrangements

Law firms frequently use the term "of counsel" to refer to affiliated lawyers. The *Restatement (Third) of the Law Governing Lawyers* indicates that "of counsel" refers to a lawyer who has a regular and continuing relationship with a law firm, even though the lawyer is neither a principal in the firm, nor employed on a full-time basis.[139] Although the actual structure of the continuing relationship varies from firm to firm, the ABA Committee on Ethics and Professional Responsibility described the following patterns used for "of counsel" arrangements:

1. Part-time lawyers who practice on a basis different from the "mainstream lawyers in the firm,"

---

[134] *Id.*

[135] Estate of Spencer v. Gavin, 946 A.2d. 1051, 1068–69 (N.J. Super. Cot. App. Div. 2008).

[136] *Id.* at 1069 (remanded for a determination as to whether the defendant-lawyer had actual knowledge of the other lawyer's theft of client funds, and if so, whether the breach of that duty caused damage).

[137] RONALD E. MALLEN, LEGAL MALPRACTICE § 5:47 (Thomson Reuters 2017 ed.) (suggesting that a written agreement with the client can prevent liability for the co-counsel's malpractice).

[138] *See* Douglas R. Richmond, *Professional Responsibilities of Co-Counsel: Joint Venturers or Scorpions in a Bottle*, 98 KY. L.J.461,495 (2009–2010) (noting that a carefully drafted engagement letter should defeat allegations of joint or vicarious liability based on alleged subagency or shared responsibility for a representation, although it is doubtful whether it will be effective where co-counsel must assume joint responsibility for a representation to be able to divide fees).

[139] *See* RESTATEMENT (THIRD) OF THE LAW GOVERNING LAWYERS § 123 cmt. c(ii) (American Law Institute, 2000).

2. Retired partners who do not actively practice law but remain available for occasional consultation,
3. Probationary partners-to-be, and
4. Lawyers who have attained a permanent status within a firm but do not expect to attain full partner status.[140]

For lawyers who fit one of these descriptions or who otherwise qualify as a firm agent, the firm may be held liable for the tortious conduct of the "of counsel" lawyer when the conduct occurred within the scope of firm business. As stated in the *Restatement (Third) of the Law Governing Lawyers*, a law firm and its principals are liable for the acts and omissions of lawyers serving in "of counsel" positions, provided that such conduct occurs within the scope of that relationship.[141] In addition to exposure under the *respondeat superior* doctrine, a firm may be liable for the selection or supervision of the "of counsel" attorney.

Depending on the circumstances, a plaintiff may also seek to hold a firm liable, relying on the principles of apparent authority. This was the position taken in a New Jersey case in which a firm failed to notify the plaintiff that its relationship with an "of counsel" lawyer had terminated.[142] Based on communications with the client, the appellate court reversed a summary judgment for the defendant, concluding that the firm could be liable if the client could show that the "of counsel" attorney acted negligently with the firm's apparent authority.

In short, a firm can be vicariously liable for the conduct of the "of counsel" lawyer who "acts within the actual or apparent scope of the firm's practice and for the firm."[143] Plaintiffs who do not have evidence that the "of counsel" lawyer acted with such authority, will likely face a motion for summary judgment.[144]

### § 5-7.3(d) Office-Sharing Arrangements

For a variety of reasons, lawyers enter office-sharing arrangements. Such arrangements enable lawyers to split the costs associated with running an office, while providing sources of referrals and companionship. Despite the advantages of sharing office space, such arrangements can also lead to disciplinary and malpractice liability.

First, lawyers sharing office facilities should avoid violating disciplinary rules that prohibit the use of a firm name, letterhead, or other professional designation that is false or misleading. ABA Model Rule 7.5(d) expressly states that "[l]awyers may state or imply that they practice in a partnership or other organization only when that is the fact."[145]

---

[140] ABA Comm. on Ethics and Prof'l Responsibility, Formal Op. 90–357 (1990).

[141] RESTATEMENT (THIRD) OF THE LAW GOVERNING LAWYERS § 58 cmt. c (American Law Institute, 2000).

[142] Staron v. Weinstein, 701 A.2d 1325 (N.J. Super. Ct. App. Div. 1997). In *Staron*, the "of counsel" lawyer was listed on law firm stationery and the client signed an engagement agreement that named the firm as the contracting party. *Id.* at 1326. Based on communications with the client, the New Jersey appellate court concluded that the client raised a triable issue of fact as to whether the "of counsel" lawyer acted with sufficient apparent authority to make the firm liable for his malpractice. *Id.* at 1328–29.

[143] RONALD E. MALLEN, LEGAL MALPRACTICE § 5.34 (Thomson Reuters, 2017 ed.).

[144] For an overview of legal malpractice issues related to "of counsel" lawyers, see JEAN I. BATEMAN, HAROLD G. WREN & BEVERLY J. GLASCOCK, OF COUNSEL, A GUIDE FOR LAW FIRMS AND PRACTITIONERS 107–115 (2013).

[145] Comments following ABA Model Rule 7.5 provides the following guidance on office-sharing arrangements: "Lawyers sharing office facilities, but who are not in fact partners, may not denominate

Second, lawyers may be subject to malpractice liability arising from communications and the course of dealings between lawyers sharing offices. This malpractice liability may be based on the theories related to partnership by estoppel, partnership in fact, or the lawyers functioning in an unincorporated association or joint venture.

### *§ 5-7.3(d)(1) Partnership by Estoppel*

Even though office sharers may not have intended to enter a partnership with one another, their dealings and communications with others may subject them to liability as a *de facto* partnership. Specifically, by holding themselves out as a partnership, the partners can be vicariously liable for one another under a theory of "partnership by estoppel." Relying on this theory, a client will point to communications that would lead a reasonable person to believe that the lawyers were members of the same firm and therefore should be estopped from denying the existence of a partnership.

To establish partnership by estoppel, a plaintiff generally must prove: "(1) that a lawyer held himself out as a partner; (2) that the holding out was done by the lawyer directly or with the lawyer's consent; (3) that the plaintiff had knowledge of such holding out; and (4) that the plaintiff relied on the ostensible partnership to his or her prejudice."[146] The Uniform Partnership Act and some state statutes codify the common law standards for partnership by estoppel.[147]

Although there is "no precise formula that identifies the indicia that suffice to create an apparent partnership," the primary test is "whether the attorneys led the client to believe that the representation was being provided by an entity and the client reasonably relied on the representation."[148] To determine whether the plaintiff met the burden to establish partnership by estoppel, the court examines the entire record, including references used and communications to the general public (e.g., directories and advertising) and specific communications with the plaintiff (e.g., written and oral statements).

Written and oral communications from one office sharer to the other's client may create the appearance that the office sharers practiced law as partners.[149] For example, in one case the First Circuit determined that the following communications potentially supported a finding of partnership by estoppel: one lawyer told the clients that he was "with" the other lawyers; that lawyer's name was listed alongside the other lawyers' names on a lobby directory; the lawyer used the office of the other lawyers to meet with the clients; and the other lawyers sometimes talked with the clients about their cases and assisted with aspects of their representation.[150]

Plaintiffs must also prove reliance on such communications. In *Ross v. Ihrie*, a federal court in Michigan found that a malpractice plaintiff had raised a fact issue

---

themselves as, for example, 'Smith and Jones' for that title suggests partnership in the practice of law." MODEL RULES OF PROF'L CONDUCT R. 7.5 cmt. 2 (American Bar Ass'n, 2017).

[146] Gosselin v. Webb, 242 F.3d 412, 415 (1st Cir. 2001).

[147] *E.g.*, IND. CODE ANN. 23–1–1–16 (Westlaw 2017).

[148] RONALD E. MALLEN, LEGAL MALPRACTICE § 5:11 (Thomson Reuters, 2017 ed.).

[149] *See, e.g.*, Andrews v. Elwell, 367 F. Supp. 2d 35, 42 (D. Mass. 2005) (determining that under Maryland law listings on firm letterhead and an insurance policy would satisfy the requirement that the plaintiff prove that the officer sharers held themselves out as partners).

[150] Gosselin v. Webb, 242 F.3d 412, 417 (1st Cir. 2001).

regarding partnership by estoppel.[151] The three lawyers had listed all of their names on common stationery and had used a joint name ("Ihrie, Scarfone & O'Brien") on business cards, in answering the telephone, and in lawyer-client agreements.

In some legal malpractice cases, the plaintiff is unable to prove the reliance element of partnership by estoppel. For example, in *Glazer v. Brookhouse*, the plaintiff added a retired lawyer to a pending malpractice action only upon learning that the retired lawyer was listed on firm letterhead years earlier, at the time when a trust was allegedly negligently amended.[152] In rejecting the partnership by estoppel claim, the court found that there was insufficient evidence that the plaintiff had relied on the retired lawyer's alleged participation in the partnership.[153]

#### ***§ 5-7.3(d)(2) Partnership in Fact***

The fact that there is no written partnership agreement does not necessarily mean that there is not a partnership. A partnership may exist as a result of the conduct, intention, and relationship of the parties. However, a promise or intention to share profits is usually treated as an indispensable element of partnership in fact. In *Community Capital Bank v. Fischer & Yanowitz*, a New York appellate court held that a lawyer was entitled to summary judgment in a malpractice action because there was no evidence that he agreed to share profits with another lawyer and no basis for finding a partnership by estoppel.[154]

#### ***§ 5-7.3(d)(3) Joint Venture***

Liability may arise if the office sharers were engaged in a joint venture. In discussing vicarious liability in a legal malpractice case, the Supreme Court of Appeals of West Virginia defined a joint venture as follows:

> A joint venture is "an association of two or more persons to carry out a single business enterprise for profit, for which purpose they combine their property, money, effects, skill and knowledge. It arises out of a contractual relationship between the parties. The contract may be oral or written, express or implied."[155]

Although joint ventures are frequently likened to partnerships, the court distinguished the two by explaining that a partnership relates to a general business, while a joint venture relates to a single business transaction.[156] Referring to the scope of joint venture, two commentators note: "More limited in the scope of endeavor than an ongoing partnership, '[a] joint venture has been found to exist where attorneys have agreed to share fees.' Some courts have at times insisted on a rough equivalence of responsibility, authority, and profit sharing, although others do not."[157]

A plaintiff may assert that lawyers sharing offices were engaged in a joint venture for the purpose of representing the plaintiff. As stated in an Illinois case involving

---

[151] 2006 WL 3446897, at *9 (E.D. Mich. 2006).

[152] 471 F. Supp. 2d 945, 950 (E.D. Wis. 2007).

[153] *Id.*

[154] 850 N.Y.S.2d 508 (N.Y. App. Div. 2008).

[155] Armor v. Lantz, 535 S.E.2d 737, 742 (W. Va. 2000) (involving a vicarious liability claim against local counsel).

[156] *Id.* 742–43.

[157] Vincent R. Johnson & Stephen C. Loomis, *Malpractice Liability Related to Foreign Outsourcing of Legal Services*, 2 ST. MARY'S J. LEGAL MALPRACTICE & ETHICS 262, 313–14 (2012).

attorney discipline, "it appears well accepted in other jurisdictions that where lawyers between whom no general partnership relation exists jointly undertake to represent a client in a case, they may be regarded as joint venturers, or 'special partners,' for the particular transaction."[158] Unlike a *de facto* partnership that turns on the communications relied on by the plaintiff, the existence of a joint venture focuses on the lawyers' relationship with one another and their intentions to pursue a shared business enterprise.

Partnership law in the jurisdiction may set forth the factors to be considered in evaluating the whether the lawyers functioned as a joint venture. An Illinois appellate court identified the following considerations:

> The existence of a joint venture is shown by allegations demonstrating (1) a community of interest in the purpose of the joint association, (2) a right of each member to direct and govern the policy and conduct of the other members, and (3) a right to joint control and management of the property used in the enterprise.[159]

Plaintiffs seeking to hold office sharers vicariously liable should determine the showing required to establish a joint venture under the applicable state law. This was the approach used in a Texas case in which Isabel Sloan sued attorneys Oscar Gonzalez, Eric Turton, and the Law Office of Oscar C. Gonzalez, alleging that they misappropriated $75,000 in trust funds that Turton received after settling a case on Sloan's behalf.[160] The two individual defendants shared a law office. "The jury found that Sloan had an attorney-client relationship with all three defendants" and assigned responsibility "40% to Turton, 30% to Gonzalez, and 30% to the Law Office." At the intermediate court of appeals, "Sloan argued that Gonzalez and the Law Office * * * [were] each jointly and severally liable for all damages, including those attributable to Turton's actions, because the jury found that they were all engaged in a joint enterprise and joint venture."[161] The Texas Supreme Court subsequently ruled that the court of appeals had erred by failing to address those issues. In remanding the case to the court of appeals, the high court expressed no opinion on whether the state's "proportionate-responsibility scheme supersedes common law joint-venture and joint-enterprise theories for imposing joint and several liability, and * * * left it to the court of appeals to address that issue in the first instance."[162]

### § 5-7.3(e) Temporary Lawyers

On a short-term basis, a firm may use the services of "temporary" lawyers. Typically, this is done when the firm needs to handle a matter, but does not have the personnel to do the work. This may occur when there is an unexpected vacancy or a large engagement, such as a major piece of litigation that needs a number of lawyers to assist with discovery or a large corporate transaction.

A firm may retain a temporary lawyer directly or procure the assistance through a placement agency that provides "contract lawyers." Although the degree of supervision

---

158 *In re Johnson*, 552 N.E. 2d 703 (Ill. 1989).

159 Romanek v. Connelly, 753 N.E. 2d 1062 (Ill. App. 2001).

160 *Sloan v. Law Office of Oscar C. Gonzalez, Inc.*, 479 S.W. 3d. 833 (Tex. 2016).

161 *Id.*

162 *Id.* at 835.

and support provided to the temporary lawyer varies from engagement to engagement, the temporary lawyer functions essentially as a subagent of the law firm.[163] As noted in the *Restatement (Third) of the Law Governing Lawyers*, the law firm becomes liable for the acts and omissions of the temporary agent by assigning a client's work to the lawyer.[164]

### § 5-7.3(f) Nondelegable Duties

Although lawyers are ordinarily not liable for the conduct of independent contractors they retain, liability may arise if the independent contractor performs a nondelegable duty.[165] Because few courts have stated a general rule on when a duty cannot be properly delegated,[166] it is difficult to predict what a lawyers' liability exposure is for delegating duties that may later be determined to be "nondelegable."

In *Kleeman v. Rheingold*, the New York Court of Appeals held that a law firm had a nondelegable duty to its client to exercise care in assuring proper service of legal process and, therefore, was liable for an independent contractor's negligent performance of that duty.[167] The opinion describes the professional responsibility justification for applying the nondelegable duties exception to liability for the torts of independent contracts as follows:

> The exception [for nondelegable duties] is often invoked where the particular duty in question is one that is imposed by regulation or statute * * *. However, * * * examples of nondelegable common-law duties abound * * *. [W]hether a particular duty is properly categorized as "nondelegable" necessarily entails a sui generis inquiry, since the conclusion ultimately rests on policy considerations * * *.
>
> * * * [A] duty will be deemed nondelegable when " 'the responsibility is so important to the community that the employer should not be permitted to transfer it to another' " * * *. This flexible formula recognizes that the "privilege to farm out [work] has its limits" and that those limits are best defined by reference to the gravity of the public policies that are implicated * * *.
>
> * * *. Manifestly, when an individual retains an attorney to commence an action, timely and accurate service of process is an integral part of the task that the attorney undertakes * * *. Given the central importance of this duty, our State's attorneys cannot be allowed to evade responsibility for its careful performance by the simple expedient of "farming out" the task to independent contractors.
>
> The existence of an extensive and comprehensive Code of Professional Responsibility that governs the obligations of attorneys to their clients reinforces our conclusion. Under the Code, a lawyer may not "seek, by contract or other means, to limit prospectively the lawyer's individual liability to a client

---

[163] For a discussion of how different structures may affect the ability of a firm to bill the client more than the contract rate, see ABA Comm. on Ethics and Prof'l. Responsibility, Formal Ethics Op. 00–420 (2000).

[164] RESTATEMENT (THIRD) OF THE LAW GOVERNING LAWYERS § 58 cmt. e (American Law Institute, 2000).

[165] *See id.*

[166] *See* RESTATEMENT (SECOND) OF TORTS, note preceding § 416 (American Law Institute, 1965).

[167] 614 N.E. 2d. 712, 718 (N.Y.1993).

> for malpractice" * * *. Moreover, the Code forbids lawyers from "[n]eglect[ing] legal matter[s] entrusted to [them]" * * *, enjoins them to assist in "secur[ing] and protect[ing] available legal rights" * * * and requires them to represent their clients as zealously as the "bounds of the law" permit * * *.
>
> Our conclusion is also supported by the perceptions of the lay public and the average client, who may reasonably assume that all of the tasks associated with the commencement of an action, including its formal initiation through service of process, will be performed either by the attorney or someone acting under the attorney's direction. While it may be a common practice among attorneys to retain outside agencies * * * to assist them in effecting service, that custom is not necessarily one of which the general public is aware. Even where a client is expressly made aware that a process serving agency will be retained, it is unlikely that the client will understand or appreciate that the process serving agency's legal status as an "independent contractor" could render the retained attorney immune from liability for the agency's negligence. Under established principles, the client's reasonable expectations and beliefs about who will render a particular service are a significant factor in identifying duties that should be deemed to be "nondelegable" * * *.
>
> * * *. The responsibility for achieving [the goal of timely commencement of legal actions]—and the liability for negligent failures to achieve it—must remain squarely on the shoulders of trained and licensed attorneys who, as members of a "learned profession," alone have the necessary knowledge and experience to protect their clients' rights.[168]

At least three important points can be gleaned from *Kleeman*. First, whether a duty is nondelegable depends on an assessment of the particular facts in light of public policy considerations, such as the policies favoring consumer protection, client control of the representation, enterprise responsibility, and protecting lawyers from unfair claims. Second, conduct that violates the obligations imposed by ethics rules may qualify as the breach of a nondelegable duty. Thus, lawyers may not escape their ethical responsibilities by "farming out" tasks to independent contractors. Third, the expectations of the client play a pivotal role in determining whether a lawyer may delegate a task and escape liability for its improper performance. Unless the client understands that the lawyer will be immune from liability for the outsourcing provider's negligence, public policy may require that the outsourcing lawyer be accountable for the provider's misperformance of duties.

Presumably, "nondelegable" duties includes those obligations which, if not performed properly, threaten to cause great harm. In the legal malpractice context, a lawyer's duty to disclose to the client that the lawyer is withdrawing from representation may fall within this category.[169]

The existence of a nondelegable duty might also make one lawyer liable for the conduct of another lawyer, even in the absence of an employment relationship. Suppose that lawyers from different law firms are working on a case as co-counsel, and would not ordinarily be vicariously responsible for each other's malpractice. If one of the lawyers has a nondelegable duty to convey important information to the client, that lawyer may

---

168 *Id.* at 715–17.

169 *Cf.* Staron v. Weinstein, 701 A.2d 1325, 1328 (N.J. Super. Ct. App. Div. 1997).

be found to have acted at his or her peril in relying on the other lawyer to make the communication. If the matter in question is so important that it qualifies as "nondelegable," the lawyer who entrusted the task to outside co-counsel should be responsible for the nonperformance of the task in just the same way as if he or she had hired the other lawyer to carry out that function.

Regardless of whether a law firm is vicariously liable for the conduct of an independent contractor, the firm may be liable for negligently selecting or supervising the independent contractor.[170] For example, in a New York case, the malpractice plaintiff asserted that a law firm was liable for the failure of an outside firm it employed to file a notice of claim with an estate because the duty was nondelegable.[171] In finding for the plaintiff, a New York appellate court did not expressly rule on the nondelegable duty argument because it concluded that the firm had a duty to supervise the actions of the outside lawyer and that it had taken no steps whatsoever to fulfill that obligation.

### § 5-7.3(g) Assisting Non-Lawyers in the Practice of Law

Non-lawyers who practice law face various consequences, including prosecution for violation of a criminal statute prohibiting the unauthorized practice of law.[172] Regulatory authorities may seek to enjoin the non-lawyer from continuing to practice law. Another common risk is that the clients may refuse to pay fees charged by the non-lawyer.

A non-lawyer who causes harm to a "client" while engaging in unauthorized practice may be sued for malpractice. When sued for malpractice, courts have applied the standard of care that is applicable to lawyers.[173] In actions for damages, nonlawyers will not be able to defend on the basis that they are not lawyers. Disclosing the fact that the practitioner is not a lawyer will not prevent an injured person from seeking damages for injuries caused by the nonlawyer.[174] This was the position taken by a Florida court that "affirmed a judgment for $675,000 against a financial planner for advising a client in the dissolution of a marriage, despite the fact that the defendant had disclosed that he was not licensed to practice law.[175]

Lawyers who assist non-lawyers in the practice of law may be disciplined by state regulatory authorities. In addition, lawyers who facilitate the unauthorized practice of law may be liable for aiding and abetting the non-lawyer's misconduct.[176] Rather than direct liability, a lawyer may also be subject to vicarious liability on bases discussed in § 5.7, including the doctrine of *respondeat superior*.

---

170 *See* RESTATEMENT (THIRD) OF THE LAW GOVERNING Lawyers § 58 cmt. e (American Law Institute, 2000).

171 Whalen v. DeGraff, Foy, Conway, Holt-Harris & Mealey, 863 N.Y.S.2d 100, 102 (N.Y. App. Div. 2008).

172 *See* RESTATEMENT (THIRD) OF THE LAW GOVERNING LAWYERS § 4 cmt. a (American Law Institute, 2000).

173 *See* Sande L. Buhai, *Act Like a Lawyer, Be Judged Like a Lawyer: The Standard of Care for the Unlicensed Practice of Law*, 2007 UTAH L. REV. 87, 88–89 (noting that courts have applied this standard in cases involving insurance claim adjusters, real estate brokers, paralegals, persons assisting in divorces and escrow agents, among others).

174 Buscemi v. Intachai, 730 So. 2d 329 (Fla. Dist. Ct. App. 1999).

175 *Id.* at 330.

176 *See* RESTATEMENT (SECOND) OF TORTS § 876(b) (American Law Institute, 1979).

# Chapter 5-8

# LEGAL MALPRACTICE INSURANCE

**By Susan Saab Fortney and Vincent R. Johnson**

*Table of Sections*

§ 5-8.1 The Importance of Legal Malpractice Insurance
§ 5-8.2 What Coverage Is Available
§ 5-8.3 The Anatomy of a Policy
§ 5-8.4 Handling Claims and Potential Claims
§ 5-8.5 Dealing with Clients When Lawyers Commit Malpractice

## § 5-8.1 THE IMPORTANCE OF LEGAL MALPRACTICE INSURANCE

Despite diligent efforts to prevent malpractice, practicing law poses risks to lawyers and others. Legal malpractice insurance, commonly called "lawyers professional liability insurance," is designed to help lawyers mitigate risks associated with providing legal services.

Legal malpractice insurance functions as third-party liability protection, providing coverage when lawyers' errors and omissions allegedly harm others. In exchange for policy premiums, the insurance company issues an insurance policy to the insured lawyer or law firm. The policy spells out the terms and conditions under which the insurer provides coverage to insured persons.

From the standpoint of an insured lawyer, insurance enables the lawyer to look to the insurer for assistance when a claim is covered under the policy. For a lawyer, especially a risk-averse one, this provides some comfort when the lawyer is handling work that creates malpractice exposure. This would include handling very complex transactions or venturing into new areas of practice. Even for routine law practice, policies protect the insured law firm and its lawyers when claims arise out of the acts and omissions of persons, such as paralegals, acting on behalf of the lawyer or the firm. This type of protection is especially important if the firm is thinly capitalized or if the lawyer is vicariously liable for the misconduct of other firm actors.

As discussed below, malpractice insurance also covers attorneys' fees and expenses associated with defending covered claims. Because these defense costs can be very expensive, the insurer's payment of defense costs may be as important as payments for judgments and settlements.

A related benefit is that the insurer may hire defense counsel to advise insureds in dealing with possible claims. This type of assistance, especially when provided by experienced counsel, can be invaluable in avoiding or mitigating consequences of a malpractice claim.

In addition to providing guidance in dealing with potential claims, insurers also provide general risk management assistance.[1] "[M]alpractice insurers take great pains to get law firms to comply with the ethics rules."[2]

This type of loss prevention guidance can help insureds improve firm policies and practices, proactively avoiding problems that could give rise to claims. Pointing to the role that malpractice insurers now play in influencing the conduct of lawyers, some commentators have argued for recognizing insurers as regulators of the legal profession.[3]

Most importantly, legal malpractice insurance protects clients and others who lawyers may injure. Unless a defendant-lawyer has significant non-exempt assets, a successful malpractice plaintiff may not be compensated if the lawyer does not have insurance. Lawyers fulfill their responsibilities as accountable professionals by maintaining adequate insurance to cover civil liability claims.[4] When injured persons are left without recovery, it wrongfully shifts to them the costs of lawyer misconduct, hurting the victims of malpractice and the reputation of the legal profession.

### § 5-8.1(a) Mandatory Coverage

Around the world, injured persons, as well as lawyers, are protected in jurisdictions where malpractice insurance is mandatory. For example, in many common-law countries, including Canada and Australia, regulators require that practicing lawyers carry minimum levels of insurance.[5] As explained by the Law Society of England and Wales, professional indemnity insurance is important in maintaining public confidence because insurance "increases [lawyer's] financial security and serves an important public interest function by covering civil liability claims * * * which might otherwise be uncompensated."[6]

Mandating coverage may help lawyers avoid inadvertent coverage gaps and may improve the accessibility and affordability of malpractice insurance. In the U.S., the interest in creating a source for affordable insurance prompted the state of Oregon to

---

[1] *See* Anthony E. Davis, *Professional Liability Insurers as Regulators of Law Practice,* 65 FORDHAM L. REV. 209, 220–221 (1996) (describing kinds of risk management services that insurers provide lawyers and law firms, including educational risk management programs, and reviews or audits of firm management systems).

[2] Nancy B. Rapoport, *"Nudging" Better Lawyer Behavior: Using Default Rules and Incentives to Change Behavior in Law Firms,* 4 ST. MARY'S J. LEGAL MAL. & ETHICS 42, 50 n.28 (2014).

[3] *See, e.g.,* Anthony E. Davis, *Professional Liability Insurers as Regulators of Law Practice,* 65 FORDHAM L. REV. 209, 209 (1996); George M. Cohen, *Legal Malpractice Insurance and Loss Prevention: A Comparative Analysis of Economic Institutions,* 4 CONN. INS. L. J. 305, 306 (1997–98); Tom Baker & Rick Swedloff, *Regulation by Liability Insurance from Auto to Lawyers' Professional Liability,* 60 UCLA L. REV. 1412, 1439 (2013). Based on empirical data, Professor Leslie Levin concluded that the impact of insurers on solo and small firm lawyers was limited, as compared to the impact of insurers on the conduct of lawyers in larger firms. Leslie C. Levin, *Regulators at the Margins: The Impact of Malpractice Insurers on Solo and Small Firm Lawyers,* 49 CONN. L. REV. 553 (2016).

[4] Susan Saab Fortney, *Law as a Profession: Examining the Role of Accountability,* 40 FORDHAM URB. L.J. 177, 214 (2012) (arguing that those who espouse the status of law as a profession should recognize and promote financial responsibility as a professional virtue).

[5] For a survey of mandatory insurance schemes around the world, see Jennifer Ip & Nora Rock, *Mandatory Professional Indemnity Insurance and a Mandatory Insurer: A Global Perspective,* 10 LAWPRO MAG. 2 (2011).

[6] Professional Indemnity Insurance, L. Soc'y § 2.2 (July 18, 2016), *available at* https://www.lawsociety.org.uk/Support-services/Advice/Practice-notes/Archive/Professional-indemnity-insurance/26-May-2011/.

enact a mandatory insurance program.[7] Oregon became the first state in the U.S. to enact legislation in 1978 requiring that lawyers in private practice purchase insurance.[8]

Although Oregon is the only state in the U.S. to require malpractice insurance, lawyers may be required to obtain insurance as a condition to representing clients or practicing in certain settings. For example, a corporate client or non-profit referral network might require that their lawyers carry malpractice insurance. State law or court rules may also mandate minimum levels of insurance or proof of financial responsibility for limited liability law firms.[9] Finally, insurance may be required in the disposition of a disciplinary matter, such as requiring insurance as a condition to participating in a disciplinary diversion program or as a condition of reinstatement.[10]

### § 5-8.1(b) Disclosure Requirements

Many non-lawyers may incorrectly assume that legal malpractice insurance is mandatory. To create opportunities for consumers to learn whether their lawyers carry insurance, states may adopt mandatory disclosure rules. In 2004, the ABA House of Delegates adopted a Model Court Rule on Insurance Disclosure.[11] The ABA Model Rule requires that lawyers disclose on their annual registration statement whether they maintain malpractice insurance.[12] According to a 2016 implementation chart developed by the ABA Standing Committee on Client Protection, seventeen states use the ABA approach.[13] State rules in seven states (Arkansas, California, New Hampshire, New Mexico, Ohio, Pennsylvania, and South Dakota) recognize the value of direct communication with clients, requiring that lawyers who lack insurance notify their clients. Five states (Arizona, Connecticut, Florida, Kentucky, and Texas) have decided not to adopt disclosure rules and North Carolina withdrew its disclosure rule.[14]

---

7 "The plan was originally proposed by the Oregon Bar Association and approved by the state legislature with the hope that the fund would provide lower rates, make coverage more available, and protect the public from harm by uninsured attorneys." Fredric L. Goldfein, *Legal Malpractice Insurance*, 61 TEMP. L. REV. 1285, 1296 (1988).

8 *Id.* Under statutory authority, the Oregon professional liability fund commission requires that "qualified members of the profession * * * carry professional liability insurance offered by the fund with primary liability limits of at least $200,000." ORE. REV. STAT. § 752.035 (Westlaw 2017).

9 *See, e.g.*, Ill. S. Ct. Rule 722(b)(1) (Westlaw 2017) (eliminating vicarious liability for misconduct of other firm lawyers provided that the law firm maintain "minimum insurance or proof of financial responsibility of at least $100,000 per claim and $150,000 annual aggregate, times the number of lawyers in the firm, provided that the firm's insurance not exceed $5,000,000 per claim or $10,000000 annual aggregate").

10 *E.g., In re Reinstatement of Hopewell*, 736 N.W.2d 864 (S.D. 2007).

11 The Model Rule was developed by the ABA Standing Committee on Client Protection. For the text of the rule, see https://www.americanbar.org/content/dam/aba/administrative/professional_responsibility/client pro_migrated/malprac_disc_rule.authcheckdam.pdf. The ABA Model Rule provides that the highest court of the jurisdiction will designate the means for making disclosure information available to the public.

12 *Id.* States vary on allowing public access to registration information. Some states make registration information available on a website, others require a request, and a few do not allow public access to the information. Jeffrey D. Watters, *What They Don't Know Can Hurt Them: Why Clients Should Know if Their Attorney Does Not Carry Malpractice Insurance*, 62 BAYLOR L. REV. 245, 256 (2010).

13 The following states have rules requiring disclosure on annual statements: Arizona, Colorado, Delaware, Hawaii, Idaho, Illinois, Kansas, Massachusetts, Michigan, Minnesota, Nebraska, Nevada, North Dakota, Rhode Island, Virginia, Washington, and West Virginia. ABA STANDING COMM. ON CLIENT PROTECTION, STATE IMPLEMENTATION OF THE ABA MODEL RULE ON INSURANCE DISCLOSURE, *available at*, https://www.americanbar.org/content/dam/aba/administrative/professional_responsibility/chart_implementation_of_mcrid.authcheckdam.pdf.

14 *Id.*

According to a 2016 implementation chart, six states are considering adoption of a disclosure rule.[15]

## § 5-8.2 WHAT COVERAGE IS AVAILABLE

Insurance experts note that the legal malpractice insurance market is not monolithic.[16] Lawyers shopping for malpractice insurance will discover a patchwork of different types of carriers, including commercial insurers, bar-affiliated insurers and risk retention reciprocals. The number and types of insurers reflect the cyclical nature of the market for legal malpractice insurance. With a hard market, the number of insurers typically goes down and the cost of insurance increases.

In an effort to manage their costs and contain their exposure on particular policies, malpractice insurers have changed the type of policies that they offer. Initially, professional liability insurers offered "occurrence policies" which provided coverage for an insurable event that occurred during the policy period. For legal malpractice insurers, the occurrence policy created a great deal of uncertainty in predicting losses and setting premiums because it may take many years before a lawyer's misconduct gives rise to an actual malpractice claim. This meant that insurers could not accurately evaluate the amount of money that they may need to pay out under an occurrence policy.

In order to deal with actuarial estimation problems and to control their exposure, legal malpractice insurers largely abandoned the occurrence form of policies, adopting instead the "claims-made" policy form. With the claims-made form, coverage turns on whether a claim is made during the policy period. "The notable difference between the occurrence policy and the claims-made policy is that under a claims-made policy an insured can be indemnified for an event that occurred before the policy began, as long as the event is reported during the policy period."[17] This "prior acts" coverage is an important feature of a claims-made policy. The prior acts protection provides coverage for acts and omissions that occurred prior to the inception of the policy, provided that the insured had no prior knowledge of any act or omission that could give rise to a claim.

Because coverage turns on the date of the claim, policy language should be studied to determine if the term "claim" is defined. If not defined, the rules of insurance contract construction should be applied.

Insureds should also understand if the policy requires that the claim be both made and reported during the policy period. When the policy requires that claims be both made and reported during the policy period, there is no grace period for reporting claims. Although insureds have challenged strict reporting deadlines, courts have enforced policy reporting periods.[18]

---

[15] *Id.* (identifying Maine, New Jersey, New York, South Carolina, Utah, and Vermont as states considering adoption of a disclosure rule).

[16] Tom Baker & Rick Swedloff, *Regulation by Liability Insurance: From Auto to Lawyers Professional Liability*, 60 UCLA L. REV. 1412, 1438–39 (2013) (noting that insurers focus on different markets, largely based on the number of lawyers affiliated with the insured firms).

[17] Matthew Court, *Berry & Murphy, P.C. v. Carolina Casualty Insurance Co: Malpractice Liability Insurance in the Tenth Circuit*, 88 DENV. U. L. REV. 443, 445 (2011).

[18] *E.g.*, Ashby v. Bar Plan Mut. Ins., 949 N.E.2d 307, 314 (Ind. 2011) (holding as a matter of law that a "claims made" policy provided "no coverage without [the lawyer]'s compliance with the policy's condition requiring a personal written notice from him to the company within twenty days of his receiving a claim).

From the standpoint of an insured, the most limiting aspect of a claims-made policy is that a lawyer must always have a claims-made policy in effect. If a claim is made after the expiration date of the claims-made policy, the lawyer effectively has no coverage, unless the insured reported a potential claim to the insurer when the policy was in effect. Therefore, lawyers changing practice settings or retiring should determine if they have or can obtain an extended reporting endorsement. Such an endorsement provides "tail" coverage, extending the time period that an insured has to report claims relating to acts or omissions that predated the policy expiration.[19]

## § 5-8.3 THE ANATOMY OF A POLICY

Although insurers use different approaches and formats, legal malpractice policies have four principal parts: declarations, insuring agreements, exclusions and conditions. The following discussion describes these parts, identifying various provisions of particular interest to insured lawyers.

### § 5-8.3(a) Declarations Page

The declarations page serves as the front portion of a policy that sets forth the specific terms for the policy issued to the applicant for insurance. It identifies the named insured, the policy period, the policy limits of liability on a per claim and an aggregate claim basis, and the deductibles that apply per claim and per year.

If the policy limits prior acts coverage, the declarations page will state a retroactive date. For a matter to be covered, the alleged malpractice must occur after the retroactive date. When the declarations page does not include a retroactive date, the insured has full prior acts coverage, provided that the insured did not know at the inception of the policy of an action or omission that was reasonably likely to give rise to a claim.

The declarations page should also identify any endorsements that are used to change provisions in the insurer's standard form policy issued to the insured. For example, an insured interested in coverage for punitive damages, may negotiate an endorsement that extends coverage for punitive damages (assuming that state law permits such coverage).[20]

The application for insurance may also be attached to the policy and incorporated as part of the insurance contract. Insurers underwrite policies relying on information disclosed on the application for insurance. This information includes representations about the applicant's law practice, disciplinary histories, and knowledge of acts or omissions that might give rise to a claim. If the application representations are incorporated into the policy, the insurer may seek to rescind the policy based on any material misrepresentation in the application.[21]

---

[19] RONALD E. MALLEN, LEGAL MALPRACTICE § 38:39 (Thomson Reuters, 2017 ed.).

[20] Some courts hold that insuring punitive damage awards would frustrate public policies. *See, e.g.,* Johnson & Johnson v. Aetna Cas. & Sur. Co., 667 A.2d 1087 (N.J. Super. Ct. App. Div. 1995); Peterson v. Superior Ct. of Ventura Co., 642 P.2d 1305 (Cal. 1982); Hartford Accident and Indem. Co. v. Village of Hempstead, 397 N.E.2d 737 (N.Y. 1979). Other states are to the contrary. *See* Westchester Fire Ins. v. Admiral Ins., 152 S.W.3d 172 (Tex. App. 2004) (holding, on specific facts, that coverage for punitive damages under a primary liability policy was not void as against public policy).

[21] *E.g.,* Cont'l Cas. Co. v. Law Office of Melbourne Mills, Jr., PLLC, 676 F.3d. 534 (6th Cir. 2012) (affirming the district court's decision on rescinding the policy because the lawyer failed to disclose in an application the fact that he faced disciplinary charges).

### § 5-8.3(b) Insuring Agreements

The insuring agreements set forth the scope of risk for which coverage is provided. Most broadly, the insuring agreements state who and what is covered.

#### *§ 5-8.3(b)(1) Claims for Money Damages Arising from the Rendition of Legal Services to Others*

The principal insuring agreement will state that the insurer agrees to pay all sums the insured becomes legally obligated to pay as money damages arising from the rendition of legal services. Relying on this insuring agreement, an insurer may maintain that the policy does not cover criminal, injunctive, or disciplinary actions because they do not involve claims for "money damages."

Pointing to this insuring agreement, an insurer may also decline to cover fee disputes and disciplinary action awards. In some coverage disputes, courts have agreed with the insurer, concluding that the fee dispute should not be treated as a claim for "money damages."[22] In other coverage disputes involving legal fees, courts have afforded coverage to the insured.[23] To avoid these coverage disputes, insurers have written policies to expressly define "money damages" in a way to exclude fee disputes.[24]

Another consideration is whether the claim arises out of the rendition of professional services as a lawyer to others. Under the operative language of the policy, the claim must arise out of an act or omission in rendering or failing to render legal services to others.[25] This language relates to the fact that the policy as a professional liability policy for lawyers is not designed to cover risks associated with insureds performing non-legal work, such as service as a real estate broker or an investment advisor. An insured may assume that the legal malpractice policy covers claims arising from rendering ancillary services closely related to the practice of law, such as serving as an escrow agent. The good news for insureds is that courts have been liberal in finding professional services.[26] To make it more difficult for a court to treat ancillary services as the practice of law, insurers have added policy language to specifically define "professional services."

Insurers have also added definitions of "legal services" or "professional services" to bolster their position that certain conduct is not covered because it did not arise out of the rendition of legal services to others. Focusing on the language, "to others," insurers may take the position that the insuring agreements do not cover businesses or ventures

---

[22] This was the position that an insurer successfully took in a coverage dispute involving a court-ordered refund of excessive lawyers' fees. The U.S. Court of Appeals for the Fourth Circuit concluded that the insuring agreement did not cover the matter because the fee forfeiture award did not qualify as "damages" under the ordinary meaning of the word. Friend v. Attorney Liab. Prot. Soc'y, No. 96–2862, 1997 WL 746761, at *2 (4th Cir.).

[23] *E.g.,* Perl v. St. Paul Fire and Marine Ins., 345 N.W.2d 209 (Minn. 1984) (concluding that "damages" included a forfeiture of legal fees for breach of fiduciary duty to a client).

[24] RONALD E. MALLEN, LEGAL MALPRACTICE, § 38:27 (Thomson Reuters, 2017 ed.).

[25] In a case in which the insured faced claims for unjust enrichment and restitution in connection with a personal injury action that the insured handled, the Fifth Circuit rejected the insured's argument for coverage, concluding that the claims did not allege a single professional act or omission by the insured that gave rise to the claims. Edwards v. Cont'l Cas. Co., 841 F.3d 360, 363 (5th Cir. 2016).

[26] RONALD E. MALLEN, LEGAL MALPRACTICE, § 38:23 (Thomson Reuters, 2017 ed.) (noting that a survey of legal malpractice actions shows the "wide boundaries encompassing the practice of law").

controlled by the insured lawyer. As discussed below, exclusions can also address claims relating to business enterprises controlled by an insured lawyer.

An insurer may also take the position that claims related to the running of a law firm do not qualify as claims arising out of the rendition of legal services. For example, in a 2015 case, the U.S. District Court in Massachusetts determined that the legal malpractice policy did not cover the claim alleging that the insured firm failed to provide liability insurance for a former attorney.[27] According to the court, the claim was "commercial" rather than professional.[28]

### *§ 5-8.3(b)(2) Duty to Defend*

Insuring agreements will describe the insurer's duty to defend covered claims asserted against an insured. Normally, the provisions will state that the insurer will pay attorneys' fees and other costs associated with defending the insured.

The insuring agreements may also address the insurer's right to appoint defense counsel. The agreements may describe the insured's role in consenting to a proposed settlement. If an insured rejects a settlement, the policy may limit the insurer's liability to be amount for which the claim could have been settled, plus all claims expenses incurred up to the time the insurer made the recommendation to settle.

Generally, the duty to defend arises "whenever a claim alleges facts that may fall within the specific risk defined by the policy."[29] Beyond this general proposition, jurisdictions use different rules for analyzing when the duty to defend is triggered. One approach applies the "eight corners rule" that compares the language of the complaint to the language in the policy.[30] Under this rule, the insurer has a duty to defend the entire lawsuit if the complaint assets a claim that may be covered by the policy. Other jurisdictions apply the "potentiality rule," determining whether the complaint raises a "potential for coverage."[31] Under the "potentiality rule," the insurer's analysis must look beyond the pleadings to consider any facts brought to the insurer's attention or any facts it could reasonably discover.[32]

### *§ 5-8.3(b)(3) Liability Limits and Self-Liquidating Policies*

Insuring agreements will cover terms related to the limits of liability and handling of claims expenses and defense costs. These provisions may note whether defense costs will be deducted from the limits of liability available to pay settlements and judgments. Such a provision is referred to as an "expense within limits" feature and the policy is referred to as a "self-liquidating policy." Amounts spent on the defense of a claim reduce the coverage available to pay a judgment or settlement. Since the 1980s, insurers have preferred to write self-liquidating policies to limit their total exposure under policies issued.

---

[27] Gandor v. Torus Nat'l Ins., 140 F. Supp. 3d 141, 147–48 (D. Mass. 2015).

[28] *Id.* at 148.

[29] Fredric L. Goldfein, *Legal Malpractice Insurance*, 61 TEMP. L. R. 1285, 1291 (1988).

[30] ROBERT H. JERRY, II & DOUGLAS RICHMOND, UNDERSTANDING INSURANCE LAW 798 (5th ed. 2012).

[31] *Id.* (explaining that "eight corners" refers to the four corners of the complaint compared to the four corners of the policy).

[32] *Id.* at 862.

#### *§ 5-8.3(b)(4) Named Insured and Other Insureds*

Whether there is coverage under a malpractice policy turns on whether a claim is made against a person insured under the policy. In addition to the named insured specified on the declarations page, the insuring agreements may identify classes of other insured persons, such as employed lawyers, former partners, and predecessor firms. A policy definition of "insured" can also be used to describe the classes of insured persons.

Because lawyers are changing firms with increasing frequency, the policy provisions related to "insured" persons are particularly important when it comes to coverage for the work of lawyers previously affiliated with the named insured firm. To limit coverage to claims related to the firm that is the "named insured," a policy may provide that a person only qualifies as an "insured" for legal services performed on behalf of the named insured firm or a predecessor firm.[33]

In addition to employed attorneys and principals in a firm, claims may relate to the work of contract lawyers and "of counsel" attorneys. One must study the insuring agreements to determine if these individuals qualify under the policy definition of "insured." Although the firm, as the named insured, may have coverage for vicarious liability claims related to a contract or "of counsel" lawyer, a person working in such a capacity may not be treated as "insured" if the policy definition of "insured" is limited to employees and members of the firm.

### § 5-8.3(c) Policy Exclusions

A coverage analysis starts with determining if a matter is covered under the insuring agreement. The analysis continues with determining if a policy exclusion eliminates coverage. Although policies may differ a great deal on the specific provisions included, exclusions generally fall into three categories: "(1) those eliminating coverage not intended to be provided in a legal malpractice policy; (2) those relating to extraordinary financial risks; and (3) those relating to "moral" or illegal risks."[34]

#### *§ 5-8.3(c)(1) Exclusions Eliminating Coverage Not Intended to Be Provided*

As noted above, insuring agreements limit coverage to claims arising out of an insured's conduct in rendering legal services to others. To more precisely eliminate coverage for types of claims not intended to be covered in a legal malpractice policy, insurers may include exclusions. For example, a policy may exclude coverage for bodily injury and property damage claims.

Exclusions also may address insureds serving in some capacity other than as legal counsel for a client. Various versions of exclusions clarify the insurer's position that such claims should not be covered under a legal malpractice policy. These exclusions include those that relate to claims based on or arising out of an insured's capacity as a director or officer for an entity not named in the declarations (D&O Exclusion). Insurers dissuade lawyers from serving as both a director or officer for an entity and counsel for the entity because such dual roles expose lawyers and their firms to costly conflict of interest

---

[33] For a discussion of the coverage issues related to lawyer mobility, see Susan Saab Fortney, *Insurance Issues Related to Lateral Hire Musical Chairs*, 2000 PROF. LAW. 65 and Bruce A. Campbell, *Of Greener Grass, Bigger Bucks and Open Septic Tanks . . . Law Firm Break-ups, Spin-off and Other Changes*, 61 TEX. B.J. 322 (1998).

[34] RONALD E. MALLEN, LEGAL MALPRACTICE: THE LAW OFFICE GUIDE TO PURCHASING LEGAL MALPRACTICE INSURANCE § 2:43 (David A. Grossbaum *et al.* eds.) (Thomson Reuters, 2017 ed.).

claims. The D&O exclusion clearly communicates to insureds the insurer's position that such risky claims will not be covered.

Similarly, the policy may address lawyers serving in fiduciary positions, such as guardians, trustees, administrators, executors, or similar capacities. A policy definition may state that such services are not "professional services" or exclusions may eliminate or limit coverage for lawyers acting in fiduciary capacities. Some exclusions are narrow, addressing particular fiduciary capacities, such as service as a fiduciary under the Employment Retirement Income Security Act of 1974 (ERISA) or some other law. Other policies may address dual capacity situations in which lawyers act as fiduciaries and provide legal services.[35] In those situations, the policy definition or exclusion may grant coverage for legal services provided, but state that the exercise of investment or business judgment in fiduciary capacities shall not be construed to be a "legal service." Given the different possibilities, any lawyer who serves in any fiduciary capacity should study the entire policy to determine how it handles the fiduciary work. If the legal malpractice policy does not cover the lawyer's activities, the lawyer could seek an endorsement to add the protection or purchase a separate errors and omissions policy.

Insurers commonly rely on business pursuits exclusions to eliminate coverage for business ventures of lawyers. The reach of these "business pursuits" exclusions will turn on the precise language in the exclusion. An insured would likely prefer a narrow exclusion that only addresses claims related to the conduct of the business in which the lawyer has an entrepreneurial interest, but do not exclude claims related to legal services provided in connection with the business.[36] A broader exclusion may exclude all claims related to the business enterprise, even if the claims relate to the rendition of legal services.[37]

Some business pursuits provisions are written in terms of a minimum percentage of the business owned by an insured. One California court applied such a provision that excluded coverage for claims by a business enterprise "in which the Insured owns more than a 10 percent interest, or in which any Insured is an owner, partner, or employer or which is directly or indirectly controlled, operated or managed by any Insured."[38] Even though the plaintiff claimed that the insured rendered legal advice, the court declared that there was no coverage, noting that the defendant law firm's sole equity partner managed the plaintiff-entity at the time that the malpractice action was reported to the

---

[35] *See* RONALD E. MALLEN, LEGAL MALPRACTICE § 38:60 (Thomson Reuters, 2017 ed.) (referring to a case in which the court applied a "dual capacity" policy provision that covers acts or omissions for which the insured would have been legally responsible as attorney for a fiduciary).

[36] *See* Greenberg & Covitz v. Nat'l Union Fire Ins. of Pittsburgh, 711 A. 2d 909, 913 (N.J. Super. Ct. App. Div. 1998) (concluding that a narrow business exclusion did not exclude claims related to the insured lawyer's activities as an owner of a mortgage company because some of the acts complained of involved legal services performed by the insured lawyers).

[37] In a Texas federal district court case, the court held that a business pursuits exclusion eliminated coverage for claims arising from a loan transaction involving a savings and loan association owned by the insured lawyers. In the court's opinion, the following exclusion applied, even if the insured lawyer performed legal services:

> any claim based upon or arising out of work performed by the insured * * * with respect to any * * * business enterprise or other venture* * * irrespective of whether or not any attorney-client relationship exists, unless such entity is named in the Declarations.

Home Ins. of Ind. v. Walsh, 854 F. Supp. 458, 460 (S.D. Tex. 1994).

[38] Carolina Cas. Ins. v. L.M. Ross Law Group, LLP, 108 Cal. Rptr. 3d 701, 703 (Ct. App. 2010).

insurer and a revocable trust of which the partner was both the settlor and trustee owned a majority interest in the plaintiff-entity.[39]

### *§ 5-8.3(c)(2) Exclusions Targeting Extraordinary Risks*

In writing policies and making underwriting decisions, insurers attempt to limit coverage for extraordinary risks. Insurers may decline to insure lawyers who specialize in practice areas that are deemed to be particularly risky, such those who handle mass tort or patent work. Others may attempt to avoid the risk by excluding coverage for particular types of claims. For example, a basic policy may exclude claims arising under securities laws or claims brought by regulatory agencies. With these types of exclusions insurers seek to avoid responsibility for claims that are expensive in terms of defense costs and indemnity payments.

### *§ 5-8.3(c)(3) Exclusions Relating to Moral or Illegal Risks*

Policies typically eliminate coverage for various claims related to conduct that is criminal, unlawful, or intentional. Exclusions may address specific types of conduct such as sexual harassment, commingling of client funds, or conversion. In addition to excluding claims related to specific conduct, policy provisions may exclude various types of questionable conduct that is characterized as "unlawful," "malicious," "intentional" or "wrongful." This is noteworthy because some types of unlawful or wrongful conduct may not be criminal. To determine whether the exclusion applies, coverage may turn on the alleged misconduct and the elements that a plaintiff must prove in the underlying malpractice action.[40]

Legal malpractice policies also exclude coverage for claims based on fraud and dishonest conduct.[41] Insureds should study the specific language in the specimen policies because the "fraud" or "willful acts" exclusion is "the most common basis upon which insurers reserve rights on coverage, refuse to defend an insured or deny coverage."[42] Policy language varies on the breath of the exclusion. Notably, an insured would prefer an exclusion that is limited to actual fraud or deliberately wrongful conduct.[43]

---

[39] The court applied the exclusion under the policy that provides that the insurer would not be obligated to pay any damages or claims expenses in connection with a claim by any business enterprise other than the insured law firm "in which the insured owns more than 10 percent interest, or in which any Insured is an owner partner, or employee, or which is directly or indirectly controlled, operated, or managed by any Insured." *Id.*

[40] *See* Mendel v. Home Ins., 806 F. Supp. 1206, 1210–11 (E.D. Pa. 1992) (concluding that the "deliberately wrongful acts" provision excluded coverage for a tortious interference claim because the tort requires the plaintiff to establish an "intentional and unprivileged interference"). *See also* Steadfast Ins. v. Stroock & Stroock & Lavaon LLP, 277 F. Supp. 2d 245, 252 (S.D.N.Y. 2003) (applying the "wrongful act" exclusion to claims alleging that the insured aided, abetted and conspired to breach fiduciary duties because those causes of action required actual knowledge of the wrongdoing).

[41] Common exclusion language states that the policy does not apply to "any claim based on or arising out of any dishonest, fraudulent, criminal, malicious act or omission or intentional wrongdoing by an Insured." CNA Lawyers Professional Liability Policy, Specimen Policy G118011A (8–09).

[42] RONALD E. MALLEN, LEGAL MALPRACTICE § 38:52 (Thomson Reuters, 2017 ed.).

[43] *See* Brooks, Tarlton, Gilbert, Douglas & Kressler v. U.S. Fire Ins., 832 F.2d 1358, 1370 (5th Cir. 1987) (adopting the insured's argument that the policy provisions excluding coverage for "any dishonest, fraudulent, criminal or malicious act or omission" did not apply to the constructive fraud claims asserted in the underlying action).

Otherwise, there could be a dispute related to whether the policy excludes unintentional harm or constructive fraud claims.[44]

Another concern relates to breath of the fraud exclusions and coverage for insureds who were not directly involved in the alleged wrongdoing, but subject to vicarious liability exposure for the acts or omissions of the alleged wrongdoer. If the exclusions refer to the conduct of "any insured," the exclusion might also eliminate coverage for non-participating insureds.[45] To preserve the possibility of insurance for vicarious liability claims, lawyers should purchase policies that include "innocent insured" provisions which state that the exclusion does not apply to an insured who did not personally commit, participate in, or ratify the wrongful conduct.

Although a non-participating insured may rely on "innocent partner" protection to avoid losing coverage under a fraud or dishonest conduct exclusion, a "prior knowledge exclusion" may preclude coverage. A prior knowledge exclusion states that the policy does not apply to claims arising out of acts or omissions occurring prior to the effective date of the policy if any insured at the effective date of the policy knew or could have known that such an act or omission might be expected to be the basis of a claim. "Prior knowledge" on the part of any insured, provides another common basis for insurers denying coverage. To minimize this risk, a lawyer and firm applying for insurance should take steps to discover if any person connected with the firm is aware of an error that could give rise to a claim. When a potential claim is discovered, the firm should promptly give notice under the applicable insurance policy. Failure to do so risks the possibility that an insurer could later rely on the "prior knowledge" exclusion if a claim is later made with respect to the matter that could have been discovered. Furthermore, the failure to disclose material information that is sought in an insurance application could also provide a basis for the insurer later seeking to rescind the entire policy.

### § 5-8.3(d) Policy Conditions That Affect Coverage

Professional liability policies state conditions precedent to coverage. An insured's failure to comply with or meet the policy conditions can result in the loss of coverage. Two common conditions impose duties on the insured to give notice and cooperate in the defense of claims made under the policy.

Although the language varies from policy to policy, the notice provision describes the duty of an insured to notify the insurer of claims. Some notice conditions obligate the insured to give the insurer written notice of any claim as soon as reasonably practical after learning of a claim.

The policy may then define "claim." A narrow definition of claim may refer to "demand" received by the insured for money arising out of an act or omission in rendering or failing to render legal services. A broader definition of claim could trigger the duty to

---

[44] In Perl v. St. Paul Fire & Marine Ins. Co, 345 N.W. 2d 209, 213 (Minn. 1984), the Supreme Court of Minnesota held that an exclusion related to "any dishonest, fraudulent, criminal or malicious act or omission of any Insured" did not encompass constructive fraud for breach of a fiduciary duty. *See also* RONALD E. MALLEN, LEGAL MALPRACTICE § 38:52 (Thomson Reuters, 2017 ed.) (referring to several courts that have held that an "innocent breach of fiduciary duty, which is constructive fraud, is not actual fraud").

[45] *See, e.g.*, Aragona v. St. Paul Fire & Marine Ins., 378 A.2d 1346, 1351 (Md. 1977) (concluding that the exclusion applied to claims against an insured whose partner misappropriated escrowed funds, despite the fact that the claims against the insured alleged negligence).

notify the insurer of any act, error or omission which could reasonably be expected to form the basis of a claim, even if an actual claim has not yet been made.

The notice condition commonly requires that the insured give notice "as soon as practicable." Timely notice enables the insurer to investigate the claim, assist the insured, and hire counsel to help defend the insured and mitigate losses. Late notice may prejudice the insurer's ability to do so. An insurer's denial of coverage based on the failure to give timely notice may turn on whether the jurisdiction requires that the insurer establish that it was prejudiced by the insured's delay.[46]

The cooperation condition requires that the insured assist the insurer and cooperate in defending the case. The provision may also prohibit an insured from voluntarily making payments or admitting liability without the consent of the insurer.

## § 5-8.4 HANDLING CLAIMS AND POTENTIAL CLAIMS

### § 5-8.4(a) Consult Counsel

Lawyers may react differently when they learn about the possibility of a claim or facts and circumstances that could give rise to a claim. Initially, a lawyer may react with anger, denial, shame, or fear.[47] Experts suggest that these feelings may become less acute as lawyers "get used to it" and deal more objectively with the potential malpractice concern.[48] Consulting counsel should help the lawyer objectively evaluate the situation and plan a course of action. In seeking guidance, a lawyer should retain an expert who focuses on legal ethics and malpractice matters.

### § 5-8.4(b) Disclosure Under Model Rule 1.6

When a person seeks legal advice, the information shared with counsel should be treated as confidential under ABA Model Rule 1.6(a) and state versions of the rule.[49] If the lawyer is communicating with legal counsel to facilitate the rendition of legal services, the communications should also be protected under the evidentiary privilege applicable to attorney-client communications.

In communicating with counsel and getting professional responsibility guidance, the lawyer may need to share confidential information related to the underlying representation. Under ABA Model Rule 1.6(b)(6), a lawyer may reveal confidential information to secure legal advice about the lawyer's compliance with the ethics rules.[50]

In communicating with their attorneys and others, lawyers should follow their attorneys' guidance. Depending on the circumstances, internal memoranda, and other documents may later be discoverable.

---

[46] Ronald E. Mallen & David A. Grossbaum, *The "Anatomy" of a Policy,* *in* RONALD E. MALLEN, LEGAL MALPRACTICE: THE LAW OFFICE GUIDE TO PURCHASING LEGAL MALPRACTICE INSURANCE § 3:4 (David A. Grossbaum *et al.* eds.) (Thomson Reuters, 2017 ed.) (referring to jurisdictional variations and the majority approach that requires the insurer to show a material breach and prejudice).

[47] Bruce Schafer, *Lawyers Are Like Other People,* 72 OR. ST. B. BULL. 62 (April 2012).

[48] *Id.*

[49] MODEL RULES OF PROF'L CONDUCT R. 1.6(a) (American Bar Ass'n, 2017).

[50] *Id.* at R. 1.6(b)(6).

### § 5-8.4(c) In-Firm Attorney-Client Privilege

A lawyer facing a malpractice claim should exercise caution in communicating with others about the matter. When possible, the lawyer should limit communications to those that will be treated as confidential and not subject to discovery.

If a lawyer seeks legal advice from another attorney in the lawyer's own firm (as opposed to consulting outside counsel), a question arises as to whether the attorney-client privilege will protect the in-firm communications. Dating back to the 1980s, courts often took a very restrictive view in recognizing a privilege for in-firm communications between one lawyer and another lawyer in the same firm, such as a person designated as the law firm's general counsel.[51] Since 2011, the trend has shifted with courts around the country now taking a more expansive view of the protection that should apply when the requirements for an attorney-client consultation are satisfied.[52] However, lawyers should still recognize the risks associated with discoverability when dealing with in-firm counsel or outside counsel, and take steps to protect the attorney-client privilege.[53]

### § 5-8.4(d) Prompt Notice to Insurer

When consulted, counsel may assist a lawyer in evaluating whether the lawyer is obligated to notify an insurer of a potential claim. Even when the applicable policy may not require notice, insurer involvement may help the insured in addressing or mitigating the harm and possible damages. Most importantly, an insured should recognize that failure to give prompt notice may jeopardize coverage under the policy. As noted above, the claims-made nature of a policy usually requires that a claim be reported during the applicable policy period.

Policy conditions will describe what triggers the notice requirement. It is common for a policy to require the insured to give written notice as soon as practical after the insured learned of a "claim."[54] If this approach is used, the policy may define "claim" to cover situations when an insured becomes aware of an act or omission that might reasonably be expected to be the basis of a claim under the policy. This approach may entail application of an objective standard of "what a 'reasonable attorney' should have reported under the circumstances."[55] In a coverage dispute related to the insured's failure to inform the insurer of a potential claim when an adverse decision criticized the

---

[51] *See* Susan Saab Fortney, *Are Law Firm Partners Islands Unto Themselves? An Empirical Study of Law Firm Peer Review and Culture*, 10 GEO. J. LEGAL ETHICS 271, 297–300 (1996) (discussing discoverability and the courts' refusal to extend the privilege to protect communications related to current firm clients).

[52] *See* Edward J. Imwinkelried, *Preliminary Thoughts on An Attorney-Client Privilege for Law Firms: When a Current Client Threatens to Sue the Firm for Malpractice, Does the Privilege Apply to the Firm's Consultation with In-House Counsel about the Potential Claim?* 48 VAL. U.L. REV. 715 (2014) (analyzing the split in authority and policy considerations) and Evan King & Jeffrey A. Parness, *Intra Law Firm Communications Regarding Questionable Attorney Conduct*, 5 ST. MARY'S J. LEGAL MALPRACTICE & ETHICS 2 (2014) (proposing a "road map" for how state courts should approach the privilege issue, considering both work-product and attorney-client privilege).

[53] For a survey of case law and recommendations on how to protect the privilege, see Glen R. Olson, et al., *Ethics and Internal Firm Communications Regarding Lawyer Malpractice Claims*, 45-WTR Brief 52 (2016).

[54] Courts have interpreted the phrase "as soon as practicable" to mean notice that "is prompt and reasonable under the circumstances." RONALD E. MALLEN, LEGAL MALPRACTICE: THE LAW OFFICE GUIDE TO PURCHASING LEGAL MALPRACTICE INSURANCE § 9:31 (David A. Grossbaum *et al.* eds.) (Thomson Reuters, 2017 ed.).

[55] *See* RONALD E. MALLEN, LEGAL MALPRACTICE § 38:43 (Thomson Reuters, 2017 ed.) (discussing cases in which the court applied the reasonableness standard).

insured's handling of the representation, a New York court elaborated on the reasonableness standard as follows:

> The issue is not whether or not plaintiffs actually committed malpractice, or whether they subjectively believed there was no conduct which could give rise to a claim, but whether a reasonable attorney would have expected a malpractice claim under the circumstances.[56]

Although the duty to notify the insurer will turn on facts and circumstances of the alleged claim, lawyers should recognize that failure to comply with unambiguous conditions precedent will likely vitiate coverage, unless late notice is excused or the jurisdiction requires that the insurer demonstrate that it was prejudiced by the late notice. Therefore, the safest course of action for insureds is to understand their obligations under the policy and to notify the insurer when required. This will protect coverage and provide an opportunity for the insurer to assist the insured in dealing with the potential claim.[57]

## § 5-8.5 DEALING WITH CLIENTS WHEN LAWYERS COMMIT MALPRACTICE

When a lawyer reports potential malpractice claims to an insurer, the insurer may consult the insured on steps to be taken to deal with the potential claims and liability exposure. Depending on the circumstances, the insurer may hire counsel to represent the insured, even before a claim is filed. In counseling the insured, the retained attorney and the insurer may consult the insured on the duty and advisability of disclosing potential malpractice to clients. The decision on disclosure should take into account a number of factors, including applicable ethics rules, the law in the jurisdiction, and practical and logistical consequences associated with disclosure and nondisclosure.

### § 5-8.5(a) Determining Whether There Is a Duty to Disclose Errors

Disciplinary rules and fiduciary principles require that lawyers communicate with clients and address conflicts of interest through disclosure and consent when proper.[58] Ethics opinions have referred to both the communication and conflicts rules in concluding that lawyers have a professional duty to disclose their own errors to clients.[59]

---

[56] Cass v. Am. Guarantee & Liab. Ins., 2006 WL 3359664, at *6 (N.Y. Sup. Ct.).

[57] For practical guidance on giving notice of a potential claim, see *How and When to Submit a Claim under a Professional Liability Policy*, Chapter 9, in RONALD E. MALLEN, LEGAL MALPRACTICE: THE LAW OFFICE GUIDE TO PURCHASING LEGAL MALPRACTICE INSURANCE § 9:31 (David A. Grossbaum *et al.* eds.) ((Thomson Reuters, 2017 ed.).

[58] Dating back to 1967, an ABA Informal Opinion considered the conflicts that arise when a lawyer discovers an omission in representing a client. Under the facts presented, the opinion concluded that the lawyer should withdraw from representation, after making "full disclosure to the client of all of the facts." ABA Comm. on Ethics & Prof'l Responsibility, Informal Op. 1010 (1967).

[59] *See, e.g.,* Minn. Ethics Op. 21, 2009 WL 8396588 (2009) (noting that the communication and conflicts rules are implicated when a lawyer knows that the lawyer's conduct could "reasonably be the basis for a non-frivolous malpractice claim by a current client that materially affects the client's interest"). In concluding that a lawyer has a duty to disclose to clients malpractice committed by a co-counsel, a New York State Bar Association Ethics Opinion reviewed a number of ethics opinions related to a lawyer's duty to disclose the lawyer's own malpractice. N.Y. State Bar Ass'n Comm. Prof'l Ethics, Op. 1092, 2016 WL 3355903 (2016). On the ethics rules concerning disclosure and hourly billing, see Part Four of this book, Gregory C. Sisk, LEGAL ETHICS AND THE PRACTICE OF LAW § 4-4.2(b).

Starting with the duty to communicate, ABA Model Rule 1.4 states that a lawyer shall keep a client "reasonably informed about the status of [a] matter," "promptly comply with reasonable requests for information," and "explain a matter to the extent reasonably necessary to permit the client to make informed decisions regarding the representation."[60] Asserting that clients rely on lawyers for information and explanations, clients could point to Rule 1.4 in arguing that the rule imposes on lawyers the duty to inform clients when lawyers learn that their own malpractice may harm clients.[61] This is the position that ethics opinions have taken when analyzing lawyers' duties to disclose their own misconduct.[62]

In considering a lawyer's duty to keep clients reasonably informed, the *Restatement of the Law Governing Lawyers* provides more guidance than the disciplinary rules.[63] A comment following *Restatement* § 20 addresses how this duty applies when lawyers discover their own errors in representing clients.[64] As stated:

> A lawyer must keep a client reasonably informed about the status of a matter entrusted to the lawyer, including the progress, prospects, problems, and costs of the representation (*see Restatement Second, Agency* § 381) * * *.
>
> If the lawyer's conduct of the matter gives the client *a substantial malpractice claim* against the lawyer, the lawyer must disclose that to the client. For example, a lawyer who fails to file suit for a client within the limitations period must so inform the client, pointing out the possibility of a malpractice suit and the resulting conflict of interest that may require the lawyer to withdraw.[65]

State ethics opinions have taken a similar approach in concluding that lawyers must inform their clients of significant or serious errors or omissions.[66] If only "significant or serious errors" trigger the disclosure duty, then lawyers should not be required to disclose minor errors. Arguably, they also should not be required to disclose errors or omissions that do not impact the representation or errors that are easily correctable with no adverse consequences for the client.

A Colorado Bar Association ethics opinion examines the disclosure obligations of a lawyer, referring to a spectrum of errors that may occur in representation. As stated in the opinion:

---

[60] ABA MODEL RULES OF PROF'L CONDUCT R. 1.4 (American Bar Ass'n, 2017). For an analysis of lawyers' duty of candor, see Vincent R. Johnson, *"Absolute and Perfect Candor" to Clients,* 34 ST. MARY'S L.J. 737, 773 (2003).

[61] "Rule 1.4 has been consistently interpreted by courts * * * as requiring lawyers to inform clients whenever the lawyer makes a serious error in the course of representation." Timothy J. Pierce & Salle E. Anderson, *What To Do After Making a Serious Error*. WISCONSIN LAW., 83-Feb Wis. Law 6, 7–8 (Feb. 2010).

[62] *See, e.g.,* N.J. Supreme Court Advisory Comm. on Prof'l Ethics, Op 684, 7 N.J.L.J. 544 (1998) (noting that Rule 1.4 "requires prompt disclosure in the interest of allowing the client to make informed decisions"). "Disclosure should therefore occur when the attorney ascertains malpractice may have occurred, even though no damage may yet have resulted." *Id.*

[63] RESTATEMENT (THIRD) OF THE LAW GOVERNING LAWYERS § 20 (American Law Institute, 2000) (stating that a lawyer shall keep a client reasonably informed about a matter).

[64] *Id.* at cmt. c.

[65] *Id.*

[66] *See, e.g.,* N.Y. State Bar Ass'n Comm. on Prof'l Ethics, Op. 734, 2000 WL 33347720 (2000) (noting that the lawyer has an obligation to report to the client that the lawyer has made "a significant error or omission" that may give rise to a possible malpractice claim).

> At one end are errors that * * * will likely prejudice a client's right or claim. Examples of those kinds of errors are the loss of a claim for failure to file it within a statutory limitations period or a failure to serve a notice of claim within a statutory period. The lawyer must promptly inform the client of an error of this kind, if a disinterested lawyer would conclude there was an ethical duty to do so, because the client must decide whether to appeal the dismissal of the claim or pursue a legal malpractice action. Another example is the loss of a right of appeal for failure to file a timely notice of appeal. However, * * * the lawyer should be given an opportunity to remedy the error before disclosing it to the client.
>
> At the other end of the spectrum are errors and possible errors that may never cause harm to the client, either because any resulting harm is not reasonably foreseeable, there is no prejudice to the client's right or claim, or the lawyer takes corrective measures that are reasonably likely to avoid any such prejudice. For example, missing a nonjurisdictional deadline, a potentially fruitful area of discovery, or a theory of liability or defense may constitute grounds for loss of sleep, but not an ethical duty to disclose to the client. As one commentator remarked regarding similar circumstances, "Unless there are steps that can be taken now to avoid the possibility of future harm, there is probably no immediate duty to disclose the mere possibility of lawyer error or omission." Lawyers should be given the opportunity to remedy any error before disclosing the error to the client. The later assertion of a legal malpractice claim does not mean that the allegedly negligent lawyer breached a duty to disclose the error to the client and the failure to disclose the error should not be construed as an independent claim against the lawyer. Whether a lawyer has an ethical duty to disclose depends on the facts and circumstances known to the lawyer once he or she has realized the error, not those that appear only through the prism of hindsight.
>
> In between these two ends of the spectrum are innumerable errors that do not fall neatly into either end of the spectrum and must be analyzed on an individual basis.[67]

In addition to the general expectation that lawyers keep clients reasonably informed, disciplinary rules and fiduciary principles also require that lawyers analyze and disclose to their clients information related to conflicts of interest. After making an error, lawyers' interests in protecting themselves conceivably conflict with the client's interest in independent representation that is free from compromising influences. Therefore, after discovering an error or omission that constitutes malpractice, a lawyer must determine if continued representation is proper with informed client consent. Depending on the nature and status of the representation, a lawyer may be required to withdraw because the conflicts would be deemed to be nonconsentable. At withdrawal, the lawyer could inform the client of the advisability of seeking independent counsel.[68]

---

[67] Colo. Bar. Ass'n Ethics Comm., Formal Op. 113, at 3 (2005) (modified July 18, 2015 solely to reject January 1, 2008 changes in the Rules of Professional Conduct).

[68] *See* Charles E. Lundberg, *Self-reporting Malpractice or Ethics Problems*, 60-SEP BENCH & B. MINN. 24, at 24 (noting that the conflict gives rise to an affirmative ethical disclosure obligation under Model Rule 1.7).

### § 5-8.5(b) What Information Should Be Disclosed

When lawyers determine that they want to make disclosure they must determine specifically what information should be communicated to clients. Ethics opinions differ in describing what should be disclosed to clients. The following outlines the different approaches:

> A Pennsylvania ethics opinion stated that an attorney only had a duty to disclose material developments in a case such as the dismissal of a case based on a statute of limitations issue. However, the jurisdiction is in the minority on this question.
>
> The majority of jurisdictions that have considered the question (including Minnesota, New Jersey, New York, and Wisconsin) state that a lawyer has an ethical obligation to promptly notify the client of both the failure to act and of the possible malpractice claim against the attorney* * *.
>
> A Colorado ethics opinion took a hybrid approach regarding what to disclose and stated that an "attorney need not advise the client about whether a claim for malpractice exits." However, the opinion suggested that an attorney should disclose the facts surrounding the error and inform the client that "it may be advisable to consult with an independent lawyer with respect to the potential impact of the error on the client's rights or claims." In addition, the attorney should not simply "admit liability," and should consider the impact of disclosure on their malpractice insurance coverage.[69]

Because of the sensitive nature of the disclosure and the insurance ramifications, a lawyer may wish to obtain guidance from legal counsel and the insurer before approaching the client. These experts may assist lawyers in formulating the manner and content of the disclosure. However, the lawyer should bear in mind that the interests of both the lawyer and the insurer may seriously conflict with the interests of the client, and that until the attorney-client relationship has ended the lawyer owes the client demanding fiduciary duties. Under fiduciary principles, the interests of the client must come first.

### § 5-8.5(c) Avoid Breaching the Cooperation Clause

A lawyer should recognize that disclosure of information related to a potential malpractice claim might affect coverage under the lawyer's malpractice policy. Specifically, the cooperation condition in an insurance policy may restrict an insured's ability to confess liability by stating that insureds shall not, except at their own cost, voluntarily make a payment, settlement or assume an obligation. To avoid a question as to whether disclosure would violate this clause, an insured lawyer should consult the insurer before making any disclosure.

In a reported Illinois case, an insurer unsuccessfully challenged coverage asserting that the insured violated the cooperation clause by disclosing an error.[70] In that case, the insured maintained he did not violate the policy provision that prohibited the insured

---

[69] CNA Prof'l Counsel, *To Err is Human: Managing the Disclosure of Mistakes to Clients*, 5–6 (2011), http://paragonunderwriters.com/wp-content/uploads/2013/01/105_PROfessional-Counsel-CNA_Lawyers_Error_Practice_Guide.pdf.

[70] Illinois State Bar Ass'n Mut. Ins. v. Frank M. Greenfield and Assoc., P.C., 980 N.E.2d 1120, 1127–29 (Ill. App. Ct. 2012).

from admitting liability.[71] Rather the insured asserted that he disclosed an estate planning error to fulfill his ethical duty to inform will beneficiaries of his error.[72] On appeal, the court held that the "voluntary payment" provision in the insurance policy was unenforceable because it violated public policy.[73] It is unclear whether other courts would find the court's rationale to be persuasive. To avoid such a coverage dispute, insureds should consult their insurers before disclosing errors. If consulted, an insurer may retain defense counsel to assist the insured in fulfilling ethical obligations to clients.

### § 5-8.5(d) Consequences of Nondisclosure

After discovering their own malpractice, some lawyers may take an ostrich approach, hoping that the matter may "go away" or never be discovered by clients or others. This approach to handling client affairs can have serious consequences.

First, a lawyer could face disciplinary charges for failing to keep a client reasonably informed and failing to deal with conflicts of interest. Such disciplinary action is more likely in jurisdictions with advisory ethics opinions or court opinions that specially recognize that a lawyer's duty to keep a client informed require that lawyers disclose to clients the lawyer's own malpractice. One expert suggests that the "potential discipline will increase the more egregious the conduct and the more significant the detriment to the client."[74] Lawyers who engage in a cover-up involving misrepresentation could face a suspension or disbarment.[75]

The second consequence relates to the impact of a perceived "cover-up" by the lawyer, the fiduciary who was supposed to function as a trusted advisor. A client may feel betrayed when a lawyer fails to act proactively to disclose the malpractice. This can contribute to a client (now the former client) filing a malpractice action.[76]

When sued, the failure to disclose an error can be used to portray the lawyer as a scoundrel who took advantage of a client, a person who relied on the lawyer to be honest, candid, and to put the client's interests above the lawyer's own interests. This characterization can seriously damage jurors' perceptions of the lawyer and the lawyer's conduct. Conceivably, this may contribute to jurors generally questioning the lawyer's credibility, including accurate accounts of the facts in the case.

Where a juror has some latitude in awarding damages based on the evidence, the juror's negative perspective of the lawyer based on the non-disclosure might affect the damage award. Although emotional distress damages are generally not allowed in legal malpractice damages, a plaintiff may attempt to use the non-disclosure to bolster a claim for emotional distress damages. In very serious non-disclosure cases, a plaintiff might even seek punitive damages.

---

[71] *Id.* at 1122.

[72] *Id.* at 1124.

[73] *Id.* at 1129.

[74] CNA Prof'l Counsel, *To Err is Human: Managing the Disclosure of Mistakes to Clients* 1, 6–7 (2011), *available at* http://paragonunderwriters.com/wp-content/uploads/2013/01/105_PROfessional-Counsel-CNA_Lawyers_Error_Practice_Guide.pdf.

[75] *E.g.*, Attorney Grievance Comm'n of Maryland v. Pennington, 876 A.2d 642 (Md. 2005) (lawyer disbarred after failing to disclose dismissal of client's lawsuit and inducing the client to accept settlement).

[76] *Id.* (noting that a client could not make an informed judgment without information on the circumstances and status of the case after it was dismissed with prejudice).

Another risk is that non-disclosure may extend the period in which a client may file a claim for malpractice. Depending on the jurisdiction, concealment may toll the running of the statute of limitations.

A lawyer may face a cause of action asserting a breach of fiduciary duty based on the lawyer's failure to disclose the error or omission. Those who push for recognition of such a cause of action point to clients' reliance on lawyers.[77] In addressing such claims, a court may conclude that the fiduciary nature of a lawyer's relationship with a client requires full and fair disclosure.[78] Other courts have rejected claims that assert an independent duty to disclose potential malpractice to clients.[79]

In jurisdictions that have recognized an independent cause of action, a lawyer may face a claim for fee forfeiture. This is more likely in jurisdictions that allow for fee forfeitures for clear and serious breaches of duty, without the showing of separate damages.

Finally, nondisclosure may affect a lawyer's reputation and future business development. Although other lawyers may be more forgiving, the general public may see the defendant-lawyer as untrustworthy and unethical.

### § 5-8.5(e) Evaluating Remedial Action and Withdrawal

Depending on the status of the representation and the nature of the potential malpractice, a lawyer should consider whether some remedial action is required or advisable. Before taking such steps, a lawyer should consult the client. Failure to do so could toll limitations and be treated as a desperate effort to conceal the malpractice.

Lawyers should also consider whether they have a duty to withdraw because the malpractice creates a nonconsensual conflict. Professor Benjamin P. Cooper describes the precarious position of a lawyer who believes that consent can be used to obviate the need to withdraw:

> Once the lawyer's conduct has given rise to a substantial malpractice claim by his client, his personal interests are adverse to his client's. At first blush, no conflict is apparent since both the lawyer and the client have an interest in obtaining a favorable outcome. But closer inspection reveals that the lawyer's interest is not necessarily aligned with the client's. The lawyer might want to settle the litigation quickly in order to try and hide his mistake or minimize the damages available to the client in a subsequent malpractice case. Even more likely, the lawyer might want to litigate the case to the end to vindicate his (or his law firm's) original advice while the client's interest is best served by reaching the quickest and least expense resolution of the litigation. Because

---

[77] *Compare* Benjamin P. Cooper, *The Lawyer's Duty to Inform His Client of His Own Malpractice,* 61 BAYLOR L. REV. 174, 187 (2009) *with* RONALD E. MALLEN, LEGAL MALPRACTICE § 24:11) (Thomson Reuters, 2017 ed.) (suggesting that disclosure be made if failure to do so "could reasonably be expected to prejudice the continued representation").

[78] For example, in RFF Family Partnership, LP v. Burns & Levinson, LLP, 2012 WL 6062740 (Mass. Super. Ct. 2012), at *5, the court concluded that a lawyer had a duty to disclose that he or his firm had mishandled a matter in a way that was likely to damage the client's interests. In reaching that conclusion, the court noted that a "majority of jurisdictions that have faced the question of tort liability for an attorney's concealment of a significant mistake have found such claims viable whether presented as straightforward legal malpractice or as a breach of fiduciary duty." *Id.*

[79] Leonard v. Dorsey & Whitney LLP, 553 F.3d 609, 629 (8th Cir. 2009) (concluding that there was no duty to disclose potential malpractice unless failure to disclose created a conflict of interest).

> of his tunnel vision, the attorney is not in a position to realistically evaluate the claim asserted against the client or to give independent legal advice that is in the best interest of the client. Rather, the conflicted lawyer becomes fixated on vindicating his or his firm's own position instead of acting in the best interests of the client. Indeed, one of the comments to this rule makes this clear: "If the probity of a lawyer's own conduct in a transaction is in serious question, it may be difficult or impossible for the lawyer to give a client detached advice."[80]

If a lawyer believes that the circumstances allow continuing representation of the client with informed consent, the safest course would be to require that the client consult independent counsel with respect to the consent. At a minimum, a lawyer should communicate in writing the advisability of consulting independent legal counsel.

When a lawyer withdraws, steps should be taken to protect the client's interests and make the transition a smooth one. This includes cooperating with new counsel to the extent possible.

[80] Benjamin P. Cooper, *The Lawyer's Duty to Inform His Client of His Own Malpractice*, 61 BAYLOR L. REV. 174, 185 (2009).

# Part Six

# JUDICIAL ETHICS AND THE CONDUCT OF JUDGES

## By Charles Gardner Geyh

Part Six surveys the professional responsibilities of judges. With very few exceptions, judges are lawyers: state systems, constitutions, statutes, and administrative regulations generally demand that judges be licensed to practice or otherwise be learned in the law.[1] In the federal system, to survive the gauntlet of review by the President, Senate, and American Bar Association, nominees for Article III judgeships have traditionally needed a law degree and meaningful legal experience, even though the U.S. Constitution does not require them.[2] Insofar as judges are licensed attorneys, they are subject to the same rules of professional conduct and the same disciplinary processes as other lawyers, discussed in the preceding chapters of this book. That said, with the exception of part-time judges, sitting judges are forbidden from practicing law,[3] and the rules of professional conduct are oriented toward regulating lawyers in their capacity as practitioners. Hence, except in circumstances of gross misconduct triggering the general edicts of Rule 8.4 (aimed at "maintaining the integrity of the profession") judicial conduct implicates the rules of professional conduct infrequently.

Judges, in other words, comprise a unique subset of lawyers. The rules of professional conduct seek to ensure that lawyers are ethical advocates for and advisors to their clients. Judges, in contrast, are not advocates; they are not advisors; and they do not have clients. Whereas good advocates are expected to be partial to their clients' interests, good judges are expected to be impartial, to keep their prejudices at bay, and to rule on the basis of applicable facts and law. As a consequence, judges are subject to different norms than other lawyers—norms embodied in a different code of conduct.

Part Six begins with Chapter 6-1, which fleshes out the core principles that underlie the regulation of judicial ethics, and the means by which those principles are codified and regulated. Chapter 6-2 surveys the ethics of judges' conduct on the job, in the context of the cases they decide and the courts they administer. Chapter 6-3 explores the ethics of judges' conduct off the bench, in relation to their extrajudicial activities and the political activities incident to attaining and retaining judicial office.

## RECOMMENDED CITATION FOR PART SIX

For those citing to Chapters 6-1 through 6-3 in Part Six, we recommend attribution to this individually-authored part as being most accurate. For example, the most

---

1 http://www.judicialselection.us/ (select a state; click on "selection of judges" and cursor down to "qualifications of judges").

2 For example, the American Bar Association's questionnaire for judicial nominees solicits information concerning the nominee's legal education, bar memberships, and bar admissions. AMERICAN BAR ASSOCIATION STANDING COMMITTEE ON THE FEDERAL JUDICIARY: WHAT IT IS AND HOW IT WORKS, APPENDIX II (2009), *available at* http://www.americanbar.org/content/dam/aba/migrated/scfedjud/federal_judiciary09.authcheckdam.pdf.

3 ABA MODEL CODE OF JUDICIAL CONDUCT, Rule 3.10 (2007) hereinafter MODEL CODE.

appropriate citation format to the first section in this part would look like this: Charles Gardner Geyh, Judicial Ethics and the Conduct of Judges § 6-1.1, in *Legal Ethics, Professional Responsibility, and the Legal Profession* (West Academic Publishing, 2018).

# Chapter 6-1

# REGULATING JUDICIAL CONDUCT GENERALLY—FEATURES AND PRINCIPLES

By Charles Gardner Geyh

*Table of Sections*


§ 6-1.1 Modern Judicial Ethics and Codes of Judicial Conduct
§ 6-1.2 Judicial Discipline in the State Courts
§ 6-1.3 Judicial Discipline in the Federal Courts
§ 6-1.4 Core Values: Impartiality, Independence, and Integrity
§ 6-1.5 Foundational Rules


## § 6-1.1 MODERN JUDICIAL ETHICS AND CODES OF JUDICIAL CONDUCT

There is nothing new about rules of judicial ethics. As early as the fourth century B.C.E., Plato, quoting Socrates, observed that "[f]our things belong to a judge: to hear courteously, to answer wisely, to consider soberly, and to decide impartially."[1] In the 1600s, Sir Matthew Hale, Lord Chief Justice under King Charles II, penned "Rules for His Judicial Guidance" that elaborated on the need for a judge to: remain impartial; promote just case outcomes; be diligent and forthright; remain loyal to God, king and country; and avoid personal, financial or professional entanglements in matters before the court.[2] In the modern era, however, the story of judicial ethics begins with Judge Kenesaw Mountain Landis.

In 1905, Judge Landis, a semi-professional baseball player in his youth, was appointed district judge for the northern district of Illinois. In the wake of the so-called "Black Sox" scandal of 1919, in which players on the Chicago White Sox were bribed to throw the World Series, Judge Landis was appointed the first commissioner of baseball. Landis accepted the position, which paid $42,500 annually, without resigning his judgeship or relinquishing its $7,500 salary. Questions were raised about the integrity of a judge who would neglect the duties of his judgeship by taking a second full-time job, as well as the independence and impartiality of a judge who would be motivated to interpret laws relevant to baseball in a manner favorable to his employer.[3] Although the House of Representatives initiated an impeachment inquiry, some members were concerned that Landis's conduct did not rise to the level of an impeachable crime or

---

[1] FRANKLIN PIERCE ADAMS, FPA BOOK OF QUOTATIONS 466 (1952).

[2] "VIII. That in business capital, though my nature prompt me to pity, yet to consider that there is also a pity due to the country"; "IX. That I be not too rigid in matters conscientious, where all the harm is in diversity of judgment"; "XIII. If in criminals it be a measuring cast, to incline to mercy and acquittal"; "XIV. In criminals that consist merely in words when no harm ensues, moderation is no injustice"; "XV. In criminals of blood, if the fact be evident, severity is justice."

[3] 6 Cannon's Precedents § 536 (1935).

misdemeanor.[4] In 1922 Landis rendered the issue moot by resigning his judgeship, but the episode prompted the American Bar Association to establish a Committee, then chaired by Chief Justice William Howard Taft, which eventually promulgated Canons of Judicial Ethics that the ABA adopted in 1924.[5]

A majority of the state judiciaries would later adopt the ABA Canons of Judicial Ethics, but the Canons were toothless by design—a series of hortatory pronouncements "intended to be nothing more than the American Bar Association's suggestions for guidance of individual judges."[6] In 1972, the ABA promulgated the "Model Code of Judicial Conduct," comprised of seven broadly worded canons and a series of more specific provisions underlying each canon, accompanied by a preamble which declared that "the canons and text establish mandatory standards unless otherwise indicated." The ABA substantially revised the Model Code in 1990, and again in 2007,[7] retaining and enhancing its mandatory character.[8] The number of canons in successive versions of the Model Code declined from seven, to five, to four; the issues covered, though, have remained substantially the same. In its current incarnation, Canon 1 addresses overarching principles of judicial conduct. Canon 2, in turn, concerns judicial duties; Canon 3 regulates extrajudicial activities; and Canon 4 pertains to political and campaign conduct.

The ABA Model Code is, by definition, a "model" for state supreme courts to adopt and apply to judges within their respective jurisdictions. No state has adopted the Model Code verbatim, but the supreme courts in all fifty states and the lower federal courts have adopted Codes of Conduct based on one of the three ABA Models.[9] The United States Supreme Court is thus the only court in the United States that is not subject to a code of conduct, which has been a subject of controversy.[10] As adopted, the codes serve two distinct purposes. First, the codes function as a source of guidance for judges; second, in state systems, at least, the codes function as a basis for judicial discipline, as discussed in § 6-1.2.[11]

## § 6-1.2 JUDICIAL DISCIPLINE IN THE STATE COURTS

The states have established organizations to discipline judges for misconduct defined with reference to the codes of judicial conduct described in § 6-1.1. The first modern judicial conduct commission was established in California in 1960; by 1981, all fifty states had disciplinary processes in place.[12] Over half the states provide for the

---

[4] Impeachment Charges Against Judge Kenesaw Mountain Landis, House Rep. No. 1407, 66th Cong. 3d Sess., March 2, 1921.

[5] Quoted in JOHN P. MACKENZIE, THE APPEARANCE OF JUSTICE 181–83 (1974).

[6] Robert Martineau, *Enforcement of the Code of Judicial Conduct*, 1972 UTAH L. REV. 410, 411.

[7] Charles Gardner Geyh served as co-Reporter to the ABA Commission that revised the Model Code in 2007.

[8] For example, the 1990 Model Code replaced pervasive references to what a judge "should" do in the 1972 Code, with what a judge "shall" do, to underscore the mandatory character of Code directives. ABA MODEL CODE OF JUDICIAL CONDUCT (1990).

[9] CHARLES GARDNER GEYH, JAMES J. ALFINI, STEVEN LUBET, JEFFREY L. SHAMAN, JUDICIAL CONDUCT AND ETHICS § 1.03 (5th ed. 2013).

[10] *Judicial Ethics and the Supreme Court*, N.Y. TIMES, Jan. 5, 2012, at A24, *available at* http://www.nytimes.com/2012/01/06/opinion/judicial-ethics-and-the-supreme-court.html.

[11] MODEL CODE, Preamble.

[12] *See*, Jonathan Abel, Note, *Testing Three Commonsense Intuitions About Judicial Conduct Commissions*, STANFORD L. REV. 1022, 1024 (2012) (internal citation omitted); Steven Lubet, *Judicial*

establishment of judicial conduct commissions in their constitutions; the remaining states establish such bodies by means of statute or court rule.[13]

In state systems, the disciplinary process begins with the filing of a complaint against a judge, which triggers an investigation by the Commission. If investigators find that there is probable cause to believe that misconduct has occurred and the judge does not wish to contest the matter, most jurisdictions authorize their commissions to negotiate a resolution prior to initiation of formal proceedings. Otherwise, the Commission will initiate a formal disciplinary proceeding against the judge, culminating in a hearing, a decision, and—if the Commission determines that misconduct has occurred—a proposed sanction. Available sanctions range from private reprimand, to public reprimand, to suspension, to removal from office.

A majority of states employ a single tier system, in which the Commission both investigates and adjudicates complaints. Some states, however, bifurcate their functions in one of two ways: by establishing two separate bodies—one that prosecutes and another that adjudicates; or by establishing two panels within a single body, so that the personnel who investigate/prosecute a given case will not adjudicate that same case. Nevertheless, in nearly all jurisdictions, regardless of structure, Commission determinations and proposed sanctions are subject to state supreme court review. This structure can pose a problem when a supreme court is called upon to review a disciplinary action against one of its own justices. For example, in 2013, the Wisconsin Supreme Court was unable to resolve a disciplinary action against a justice, which alleged that he had put another justice in a chokehold during a meeting in chambers, after mass-recusals left the Court without a quorum.[14] Around a dozen states have addressed this issue by arranging for special courts or otherwise different judges to review adjudications of complaints against supreme court justices.[15]

Preliminary Commission investigations are confidential in all states, as are Commission decisions to dismiss complaints in nearly all states, so as not to impugn a judge's reputation unfairly with groundless but highly publicized accusations. States vary as to when disciplinary proceedings cease to be confidential: most jurisdictions draw the line at the point when formal proceedings are commenced; others preserve confidentiality until the Commission issues a formal recommendation of discipline.

## § 6-1.3 JUDICIAL DISCIPLINE IN THE FEDERAL COURTS

In the federal system, circuit judicial councils were established in 1939 to administer the federal courts in each of the regional circuits.[16] The circuit judicial councils exercised limited informal regulatory authority over judicial conduct, until their disciplinary role was formalized in 1980, when Congress enacted the Judicial Councils

---

*Discipline and Judicial Independence*, 61 LAW & CONTEMPORARY PROBLEMS 59, 60 (1998), *available at* http://scholarship.law.duke.edu/lcp/vol61/iss3/9.

[13] *How Judicial Conduct Commissions Work* 28 JUSTICE SYSTEM J. 405, 407 (2007), *available at* http://www.ncsc.org/~/media/Files/PDF/Publications/Justice%20System%20Journal/How%20Judicial%20Conduct%20Commissions%20Work.ashx.

[14] Patrick Marley, *Justice Bradley Got More Security Before Prosser Incident; Safety Concerns Remain,* MILWAUKEE JOURNAL-SENTINEL, Feb. 13, 2013.

[15] Cynthia Gray, *Discipline of Supreme Court Justices,* 30 JUD. CONDUCT REP. 1, 4–5 (Fall, 2008).

[16] Charles Gardner Geyh, *Informal Methods of Judicial Discipline,* 142 U. PA. L. REV. 243, 261–271 (1993).

Reform and Judicial Conduct and Disability Act.[17] That Act authorized judicial councils in each of the thirteen federal circuits to investigate complaints against federal judges and administer discipline for conduct deemed "prejudicial to the effective and expeditious administration of justice."[18] The Act authorizes any person to file a written complaint with the clerk of the circuit court; alternatively, the circuit chief judge may initiate proceedings on his or her own.[19] Conduct related to the merits of judicial decisions is not subject to discipline under the Act.[20] Complaints are reviewed by the circuit chief judge. After review, the chief judge may appoint a committee to investigate the complaint, or may dismiss the complaint if the judge concludes that: (1) it is frivolous; (2) it relates to the merits of the underlying dispute; or (3) adequate, informal corrective action has been taken without the need for a formal investigation.[21] If the Chief Judge appoints an investigating committee, the committee prepares a report for the judicial council reflecting the results of its investigations and recommended sanctions, if any.[22] The judicial council may then conduct further investigation, dismiss the complaint, or take such action as it deems appropriate.[23]

Whereas discipline imposed on judges by state conduct commissions may include removal from office; in the federal system, the Constitution is generally thought to reserve the removal power to Congress and the impeachment process.[24] Consequently, the Judicial Councils Act of 1980 limits judicial councils to imposing a range of lesser sanctions, such as private and public censure, requesting a judge to retire, temporarily suspending a judge's caseload, and recommending that the House of Representatives consider initiating an impeachment investigation.[25] Council decisions are reviewable by the Judicial Conference of the United States.[26]

Whereas the states employ their codes in the service of judicial discipline, the federal system primarily uses its code as a tool for guidance. While the Judicial Conference notes that Code violations can serve as a basis for discipline,[27] the federal disciplinary system operates independently of the Code and, as previously noted, subjects judges to discipline for conduct "prejudicial to the effective and expeditious administration of the business of the courts."[28] Thus, violating an applicable canon in the Code of Conduct for U.S. Judges, while instructive, is neither necessary nor sufficient for the imposition of discipline.

---

17 Judicial Councils Reform and Judicial Conduct and Disability Act of 1980, Pub. L. No. 96–458, 94 Stat. 2035 (1980).

18 28 U.S.C. § 351(a).

19 28 U.S.C. §§ 351(a), (b).

20 *Id.* § 352(b)(1)(A)(ii).

21 *Id.* § 352(b).

22 *Id.* § 353(c).

23 *Id.* § 354(a)(1).

24 *See Judicial Tenure Act: Hearing on S. 1423 Before Subcomm. on Improvements in Judicial Machinery of the Senate Comm. on the Judiciary*, 95th Cong. 1st Sess. 61–81 (1977).

25 28 U.S.C. § 351(c)(6)(B).

26 *Id.* § 358(c).

27 JUDICIAL CONFERENCE COMMITTEE ON JUDICIAL CONDUCT AND DISABILITY, RULES FOR JUDICIAL-CONDUCT AND JUDICIAL-DISABILITY PROCEEDINGS (2008), *available at* http://www.uscourts.gov/sites/default/files/guide-vol02e-ch03.pdf.

28 *Id.*

## § 6-1.4 CORE VALUES: IMPARTIALITY, INDEPENDENCE, AND INTEGRITY

Codes of Conduct, as described in § 6-1.1, and enforced to varying degrees by disciplinary processes summarized in § 6-1.2, embrace three instrumental values core to judicial ethics: impartiality, independence, and integrity. The relevance of these values is best understood with reference to the role they play in promoting the rule of law.

In his writings on the rule of law, Aristotle opined that "[w]e do not allow a man to rule, but rational principle," because "desire . . . twists rulers even when they are the best of men"; desire, then, must be constrained by law, which Aristotle described as "intelligence without appetite."[29] For James Madison, architect of the U.S. Constitution, the challenge was to design a system of government that would subject the people—whom he did not otherwise trust—to the rule of law through a system administered by the very same people he did not trust:

> If men were angels, no government would be necessary. . . In framing a government which is to be administered by men over men, the great difficulty lies in this: you must first enable the government to control the governed; and in the next place oblige it to control itself.[30]

For Madison and his fellow framers, the solution was to divide the powers of government into three separate and independent branches, which would exercise executive, legislative and judicial powers to control the governed, and wield checks over each other to control the government itself.[31]

In this tripartite schema, the "judicial power" is the power that the Constitution delegates to courts to decide cases and controversies. The power to decide cases and controversies includes the courts' primary check on the other branches of government: the power to say what the law means, and to invalidate unconstitutional acts of the executive and legislature, through the exercise of judicial review.[32] For the exercise of judicial power, including judicial review, to be compatible with rule of law principles, the decisions judges make must be constrained by operative law. That means judges must not be so beholden to others that judges will disregard the law and do the bidding of those who control them. It also means, as Blackstone explained, that a judge must be sufficiently free from internal bias to "determine, not according to his own private judgment, but according to the known laws and customs of the land."[33]

In short, judges play their part in the rule of law through the exercise of judicial power, by applying operative facts to applicable law on a case-by-case basis, to the end of administering justice. Accepting this as the underlying objective, it is possible to identify three instrumental values essential to achieving that objective: impartiality, independence, and integrity.

---

[29] ARISTOTLE, POLITICS BOOK III XVI (Barker, Ernest, *rev'd*, Richard Stalley 1995).

[30] James Madison, *Federalist #51*, *in* THE FEDERALIST PAPERS (1961).

[31] *Id.*

[32] Marbury v. Madison, 5 U.S. 137 (1803).

[33] WILLIAM BLACKSTONE, COMMENTARIES ON THE LAWS OF ENGLAND, 69 n. 1558 (1765).

### § 6-1.4(a) Judicial Impartiality

Impartiality has been a defining feature of the judicial role dating back to Socrates, if not earlier.[34] The Oxford English Dictionary defines "impartial" as "not partial; not favouring one party or side more than another; unprejudiced, unbiased, fair, just, equitable."[35] The relevance of impartiality to the rule of law is obvious: we want judges to set their personal biases aside and uphold the law.

Social science data collected over the course of the past half-century, however, suggest that judges are subject to internal biases. Particularly, in close cases where the law is uncertain and hotly contested, the data show that judicial decision-making can be influenced by the judge's ideological predispositions and other extralegal predilections.[36] Yet to say that perfect impartiality is thus unattainable is not to gainsay the value of impartiality as an aspiration, or the need for judges to remain impartial enough to further rule of law objectives. When a conscientious judge is confronted with comparably compelling arguments for differing interpretations of fact or law, it may be inevitable that her education, life experience, and policy preferences will influence—even if only subconsciously—her views of what the facts and law are. But that is not on a par with judges going rogue and acting on their prejudices by disregarding applicable facts and law and imposing their personal preferences.

In *Republican Party of Minnesota v. White*,[37] the United States Supreme Court considered three different definitions of impartiality. The Court accepted one definition: "the lack of bias for or against either *party* to the proceeding."[38] It rejected a second definition: "lack of preconception in favor of or against a particular *legal view*,"[39] which the Court regarded as neither possible nor desirable, because learned judges should and inevitably will develop views on the meaning of laws that they are called upon to interpret and apply. Hence, a judge's predilections concerning the proper interpretation of applicable law do not ordinarily constitute an illicit form of partiality. Finally, the Court entertained the possibility of a third definition (which it deemed inapplicable to the case at hand): open-mindedness.[40] By implication, a judge whose predilections, ideological or otherwise, are so entrenched as to close her mind to the competing legal arguments she is called upon to assess, runs afoul of this third definition. The Model Code of Judicial Conduct incorporates the first and third of these variations into its definition of "impartiality:" the "absence of bias or prejudice in favor of, or against, particular parties or classes of parties, as well as maintenance of an open mind in considering issues that may come before a judge."[41]

---

[34] FRANKLIN PIERCE ADAMS, FPA BOOK OF QUOTATIONS 466 (1952) ("Four things belong to a judge: to hear courteously, to answer wisely, to consider soberly, and to decide impartially.").

[35] *Impartial*, OXFORD ENGLISH DICTIONARY, *available at* http://www.oed.com/view/Entry/92112?redirectedFrom=impartial.

[36] *See, e.g.*, Jeffrey J. Rachlinksi, Sheri Lynn Johnson, Andrew J. Wistrich & Chris Guthrie, *Does Unconscious Racial Basis Affect Trial Judges?*, 84 NOTRE DAME L. REV. 1195 (2009).

[37] 536 U.S. 765 (2002).

[38] *Id.* at 775.

[39] *Id.* at 777.

[40] *Id.* at 778.

[41] MODEL CODE, Terminology.

### § 6-1.4(b) Judicial Independence

Judicial independence is a term of myriad meanings.[42] In the context of judicial ethics, it focuses on what is often referred to as "decisional" independence—a judge's independence from inappropriate external interference with the decisions that the judge makes. Decisional independence can refer to structural features that insulate judges from external interference with their decision-making. For example, Article III, Section 1 of the U.S. Constitution guarantees federal judges tenure during good behavior and a salary that neither Congress nor the president may diminish. Other structures constrain decisional independence: most state constitutions, for example, hold judges accountable to the electorate in periodic elections. For purposes here, however, the focus is less on structure than behavior: ethical judges should disregard inappropriate external sources of influence on their decision-making—structural and otherwise—and uphold the law as they construe it to be written. Thus, for example, ethical judges should resist the temptation to make decisions that would be popular with voters but contrary to law, despite an impending election.

By necessary implication, judicial "independence" does not imply unfettered autonomy, which would liberate judges to disregard the law that independence aims for them to uphold. External constraints on judicial decision-making imposed by substantive and procedural law that promote, rather than undermine rule of law values, are not inappropriate. The ABA defines independence for purposes of the Model Code, as "a judge's freedom from influence or controls other than those established by law."[43] So defined, independence and impartiality are corollaries to each other. Whereas judicial impartiality promotes the rule of law by minimizing the influence of a judge's internal biases on her decision-making, judicial independence promotes the rule of law by minimizing extralegal, external influences on her decision-making. The two concepts are likewise intertwined: dependent judges who acquiesce to inappropriate, external influence on their decision-making are partial to those upon whom they rely.

### § 6-1.4(c) Judicial Integrity

Integrity encompasses a cluster of attributes that the Model Code defines to include "probity, fairness, honesty, uprightness, and soundness of character."[44] The relationship between basic integrity and the rule of law is obvious: the corrupt judge who sells decisions to the highest bidder does not uphold the law. Likewise, there exists a relationship between integrity, impartiality, and independence. Dishonest judges whose minds are closed by corrupt motives are partial to the outcomes that serve their private interests, while dishonest judges who flout the law in favor of their benefactors are dependent upon those benefactors.

When contemplating judicial ethics, one can defend the centrality of impartiality, independence, and integrity in relation to the rule of law, from the perspective of judges, parties, and the general public. From a judge's perspective, impartiality, independence, and integrity are intrinsic to the platonic ideal of a good or virtuous jurist who has taken an oath to uphold the law. From the perspective of parties, the right to due process of law demands an impartial, independent, and honest judge. Finally, from the general

---

[42] Charles Gardner Geyh, *Judicial Independence as an Organizing Principle,* 10 ANN. REV. OF L. & SOC. SCI. 185 (2014).

[43] MODEL CODE, Terminology.

[44] *Id.*

public's perspective, judges who are perceived to be impartial, independent, and honest arbiters of the law promote the judiciary's legitimacy. Each of these three perspectives finds expression in the Model Code of Judicial Conduct. And, significantly, the ABA Commission that promulgated the Model Code characterized independence, integrity, and impartiality, as "overarching, fundamental values that the Rules promote."[45] Hence, the Model Code begins with the Canon 1 directive that "[a] judge shall uphold the independence, integrity, and impartiality of the judiciary."[46]

## § 6-1.5 FOUNDATIONAL RULES

The Model Code of Judicial Conduct begins with Canon 1, which "articulate[s] a limited number of general, overarching principles that should govern a judge's conduct."[47] Consistent with that objective, the Canon itself paints with broad strokes: "[a] judge shall uphold and promote the independence, integrity, and impartiality of the judiciary, and shall avoid impropriety and the appearance of impropriety."[48] Subsumed within Canon 1 are three foundational rules concerning a judge's duty to obey the law, promote public confidence in the judiciary by avoiding appearances of impropriety, and not abuse the prestige of judicial office for the benefit of the judge or others.

### § 6-1.5(a) The Duty to Comply with the Law

Rule 1.1 of the Model Code of Judicial Conduct, unencumbered by commentary, states simply that: "[a] judge shall comply with the law, including the Code of Judicial Conduct."[49] The duty to "comply with the law" refers to a judge's obligation to obey the law. Thus, a garden-variety illustration of a judge disciplined for a Rule 1.1 failure to comply with the law, is *In re Weber*, wherein the Indiana Supreme Court reprimanded a judge after he pled guilty to criminal mischief and driving under the influence.[50] The judge's duty to uphold the substantive and procedural laws that the judge applies in cases the judge decides, is separately governed by Rule 2.2.

A judge's duty to comply with the law touches conduct on and off the job. On the job, the rule applies to laws that regulate judges' official conduct, such as statutes prohibiting bribery, and other forms of malfeasance.[51] The Rule seeks to regulate misconduct that undermines public confidence in the courts through misuse of office. In addition, Rule 1.1 states that the "law" includes the Code of Judicial Conduct. In this way, the Model Code makes clear in its first rule that a judge is bound by the rules that follow.

Off the job, the rule directs judges to comply with the same body of laws that govern the general population. Consistent with Canon 1's objective of promoting public confidence and discouraging the appearance of impartiality, the rule admonishes judges not to flout the very laws that they hold parties accountable for disobeying. Hence, judges have been disciplined for a wide range of criminal offenses, from the relatively minor (e.g., violation of game and wildlife laws, mutilation of trees on public land, and

---

[45] CHARLES G. GEYH AND W. WILLIAM HODES, REPORTERS' NOTES TO THE MODEL RULES OF JUDICIAL CONDUCT 19 (2009).

[46] MODEL CODE, Canon 1.

[47] GEYH & HODES, *supra* note 45 at 17.

[48] MODEL CODE, Canon 1.

[49] MODEL CODE, Canon 1, Rule 1.1.

[50] *In re* Weber, 21 N.E.3d 92 (Ind. 2014).

[51] *See, e.g.*, Mississippi Comm'n on Judicial Performance v. Teel, 863 So.2d 973 (Miss. 2004) (a judge, seeking reimbursement for payments not made, was sanctioned for embezzlement).

shoplifting) to the more serious (e.g., breaking and entering, child endangerment, and mail fraud).[52]

Whether a judge must be convicted of a crime in order to be disciplined for failing to comply with the law under Rule 1.1, however, remains an open question. More accurately perhaps, it has proved to be an unnecessary question. When an investigation reveals that a judge engaged in illegal conduct, despite the absence of arrest or conviction, the simpler course has been to discipline the judge under Rule 1.2.[53] Rule 1.2 enables disciplinary action for failure to act at all times in a manner that promotes public confidence in the integrity and impartiality of the judiciary, thereby creating an appearance of impropriety (discussed at greater length in the next section).[54] Note too, that when a judge is under criminal investigation, it may call the judge's impartiality into question and require disqualification from pending criminal cases.[55]

### § 6-1.5(b) The Duty to Promote Public Confidence and Avoid Appearances of Impropriety

Rule 1.2 of the Model Code provides that "[a] judge shall act at all times in a manner that promotes public confidence in the independence, integrity, and impartiality of the judiciary, and shall avoid impropriety and the appearance of impropriety."[56] In many ways, Rule 1.2 is the flagship of the Model Code. First, it articulates—in the broadest possible terms—a judge's ethical responsibility to promote the legitimacy of the judiciary by being mindful of how the judge acts, and also of how the public might perceive those acts. Second, the rule establishes a baseline for judicial conduct that effectively subsumes the rest of the Code. In other words, Rule 1.2 enshrines the three instrumental values core to judicial ethics: independence, integrity, and impartiality.[57] Insofar as nearly all the rules proscribe conduct deleterious to one of these three core values,[58] a

---

[52] CHARLES GARDNER GEYH, JAMES J. ALFINI, STEVEN LUBET, JEFFREY L. SHAMAN, JUDICIAL CONDUCT AND ETHICS § 10.04[2] (5th ed. 2013).

[53] *In re* Hedges, 988 N.E.2d 509 (N.Y. 2013) (a judge who admitted to sexual misconduct with a five-year old girl years before ascending the bench was removed from office, on the grounds that the admitted conduct "undermined the integrity and impartiality of the judiciary"); *In re* Turco, 970 P.2d 731 (Wash. 1999) (judge was sanctioned for act of domestic violence, despite criminal charges being dismissed, on the grounds that the conduct reflected adversely on the judge's integrity and impartiality).

[54] MODEL CODE, Rule 1.2.

[55] U.S. v. Jaramillo, 745 F.2d 1245, 1249 (9th Cir. 1984) ("[A] reasonable person with knowledge of all the facts pertaining to the nature of the indictment would question the ability of a judge facing prosecution to remain impartial as the presiding jurist in a criminal proceeding."); U.S. v. Garrudo, 869 F. Supp. 1574, 1581 (S.D. Fla. 1994) ("[T]he average person on the street will believe that if a federal judge is the subject of a pending grand jury investigation, then the [federal judge] cannot conduct criminal trials impartially."). *But see* Rippo v. State, 946 P.2d 1017, 1023 (Nev. 1997) (a federal criminal investigation of a state judge "does not by itself create an appearance of impropriety sufficient to warrant disqualification"). At a minimum, disqualification may be in order in cases where the defendant and judge are accused of similar crimes. *See* In the Matter of Frese, 789 A.2d 654 (N.J. 2002) (judge reprimanded for failing to disqualify himself from drunk driving case while proceedings against the judge for drunk driving were impending).

[56] MODEL CODE, Canon 1, Rule 1.2 (2010).

[57] *See* § 6-1.4.

[58] One can make an exception for rules relating to basic judicial competence, including the related duties of diligence and dedication, which do not clearly implicate judicial independence, impartiality, or integrity as the Code defines those terms. Hence, the Code sets competence apart from integrity, independence, and impartiality in the Preamble, which declares that "[t]he United States Legal System is based upon the principle that an independent, impartial and competent judiciary, composed of men and women of integrity, will interpret and apply the law that governs our society." MODEL CODE, Preamble (2010).

violation of a more specific rule usually implicates a violation of the broader principles embodied in Rule 1.2.

The broad scope of Rule 1.2 and its relationship to more specific rules in the remainder of the Code, enable it to serve multiple functions in disciplinary proceedings. First, it can be an add-on: by sanctioning a judge for a violation of Rule 1.2, in addition to a more specific rule, the disciplinary authority sends the message that the judge's particular misconduct was both unethical in a specific way and hurtful to public confidence in the judiciary more generally. For example, in *In re Dean*, the Iowa Supreme Court determined that a judge who arrived for work intoxicated violated the specific duties of competence and diligence under Rule 2.5, as well as the general duties imposed by Rule 1.2.[59] Similarly, in *In re Wilfong*, the West Virginia Supreme Court concluded that a judge who conducted a secret, extramarital affair with a community corrections director who frequently appeared before her simultaneously violated the general directive to avoid impropriety and its appearance, as well as the specific duties not to permit social relationships to influence her judicial conduct (Model Code Rule 2.4(b)) and to disqualify herself from proceedings in which her impartiality might reasonably be questioned (Model Code Rule 2.11(a)).[60]

Second, Rule 1.2 can be a kind of lesser-included offense. When a judge is charged with violating both a specific rule and Rule 1.2 for the same conduct, the dual charges provide the disciplinary authority with the flexibility to find that the judge appeared to act improperly, without finding that the judge actually acted improperly. Such flexibility can facilitate settlement where the underlying facts remain disputed or unclear, or soften the implications of the sanction. For example, in *In re Logan*, telephone records revealed that a judge received several calls from a county commissioner shortly after a fellow commissioner had been arrested and shortly before the judge—who had not been scheduled for arraignment duty—released the commissioner on his own recognizance.[61] The Michigan Supreme Court approved a proposed settlement wherein the judge was censured for creating an appearance of impropriety, without resolving the more serious charge that the judge misled the judicial conduct commission concerning the calls he received (which, presumably, could have led to charges of inappropriate, *ex parte* communications, as well as abusing the prestige of office for the benefit of another). In approving the lesser sanction of censure, the Court explained, "everything else being equal . . . conduct that is prejudicial to the actual administration of justice is more serious than misconduct that is prejudicial only to the appearance of propriety."[62]

Third, Rule 1.2 can be a catchall—a means to discipline judges for misconduct not otherwise proscribed in the Code. To the extent that enforcing the duty to avoid the "appearance of impropriety" risks subjecting judges to discipline for the amorphous sin of looking bad, it can be quite controversial.[63] As one scholar has observed, "a charge of appearance of impropriety raises serious due process concerns," and the "lack of specificity as to what conduct makes a judge vulnerable" to that charge is "bound to

---

[59] 855 N.W.2d 186 (Ia. 2014).

[60] 765 S.E.2d 283 (W.V. 2014).

[61] 783 N.W.2d 705 (Mich. 2010).

[62] *Id.*

[63] Raymond McKoski, *Judicial Discipline and the Appearance of Impropriety: What the Public Sees is What the Judge Gets,* 94 MINN. L. REV. 1914 (2010).

burden judges with uncertainty."[64] The Code, however, has recently been revised to address this very concern, with an explanatory comment accompanying Rule 1.2:

> The test for appearance of impropriety is whether the conduct would create in reasonable minds a perception that the judge violated this Code or engaged in other conduct that reflects adversely on the judge's honesty, impartiality, temperament, or fitness to serve as a judge.

Thus, the duty to avoid the appearance of impropriety has been tethered to the "act at all times" clause, with respect to which there has been considerably less controversy. In other words, Rule 1.2 does not subject judges to discipline for "looking bad" in arbitrary or undefined ways. Rather, an actionable "appearance of impropriety" arises when reasonable people would conclude that a judge has acted in ways that cast doubt on the judge's allegiance to the Code and the core values it embodies, to the detriment of public confidence in the courts.[65]

### § 6-1.5(c) The Duty to Avoid Abusing the Prestige of Judicial Office

Rule 1.3 of the Model Code of Judicial Conduct admonishes judges not to "abuse the prestige of judicial office to advance the personal or economic interests of the judge or others."[66] The essential point is that the judicial office is a public trust that judges should not exploit for private gain. Rule 1.3 qualifies as an overarching Canon 1 directive because it proscribes an archetypal abuse of power that undermines public confidence in the integrity of the judiciary, and because the rule (like other Canon 1 rules) applies in both judicial *and* extrajudicial settings.

In judicial settings, problems arise when judges exploit their status as judges to gain advantage for themselves or others in legal proceedings. A recurring scenario is where judges seek to fix traffic tickets, or to expedite or otherwise secure favorable treatment for themselves, their families, or friends in criminal and other proceedings.[67]

In non-judicial settings, problems arise when judges attempt to trade on their status as judges to gain personal advantage for themselves or others. Hence, judges have been disciplined for exploiting their position as sitting judges to land a role in a reality

---

[64] Leslie Abramson, *Canon 2 of the Code of Judicial Conduct,* 79 MARQ. L. REV. 949, 955 (1996).

[65] *See In re* Piper, 534 P.2d 159 (1975); Hayes v. Alabama Court of Judiciary, 437 So.2d 1276, 1278 (Ala. 1983) (explaining that judges are held to heightened standards of integrity and ethical conduct as compared to the public or even lawyers).

[66] MODEL CODE, Canon 1, Rule 1.3 (2010).

[67] *See In re* Bylsma, Order F00-1JC-024 (S. Ct. of Utah, Oct. 20, 2000) (judge reprimanded for giving the appearance of attempting to influence the outcome of a case in which the judge was personally involved); Inquiry Concerning Hyde, Decision and Order 48 Cal. 4th CJP Supp. 329 (Cal. Comm'n on Judicial Performance, Sept. 23, 2003) (judge removed for, *inter alia,* using his judicial position to obtain confidential information from restricted DMV records for the judge's personal reasons); *In re* Sharlow, Unreported Determination (N.Y. Comm'n, Mar. 22, 2005) 2005 WL 5727958 (judge censured for acting as his son's advocate in a trespass case and writing to the case's presiding justice on court stationery, thereby implicitly requesting favoritism); *In re* Schatz, 845 N.W.2d 273 (Neb. 2014) (judge publicly reprimanded for improperly intervening in a felony drunk driving case by contacting the jail and instructing jail personnel to release the defendant, the judge's friend without paying bond); *In re* Snow's Case, 674 A.2d 573 (N.H. 1996) (judge censured and suspended for six months without pay for calling police officer after officer ticketed the judge's brother); *In re* Beckham, 620 S.E.2d 69 (S.C. 2005) (judge suspended for 60 days for informing his father-in-law that he could assist with a family friend's traffic ticket).

television series;[68] when they have exploited information they acquire in court proceedings for private commercial gain;[69] when they use their titles as judges to gain leverage in business negotiations with merchants;[70] or when they solicit funds as judges from attorneys or others for charitable causes.[71]

There are circumstances in which judges may use the "prestige of office" to advance the interests of themselves or others in some sense of the phrase without running afoul of this rule. For example, judges are permitted to serve as references for their law clerks. In such circumstances, judges may be using, but not "abusing" the prestige of office to advance their clerks' interests.[72] Judges may likewise serve as personal references for friends, neighbors, service providers, and so on, but must be mindful not to identify themselves as judges if their judicial experience is irrelevant to the recommendation, and conveying such information could be interpreted as an attempt to influence the recipient. On a related note, judges may serve as character witnesses for parties in judicial or administrative proceedings as long as they are subpoenaed to do so—the subpoena serving as a means to ensure that judges are not unnecessarily exploiting their stations for the benefit of others.[73] Finally, courts have distinguished between public-spirited uses and private or personal misuses of judicial office. For example, in *In re Hecht*, the Texas Supreme Court concluded that it was inappropriate to discipline a judge for commenting favorably in a public forum on the United States Supreme Court nomination of Harriet Miers, with whom the judge was personally familiar.[74] The Court reasoned that to the extent the judge's remarks assisted Ms. Miers in securing a life-tenured position, the remarks were in furtherance of a public, not a private purpose.[75]

---

[68] Inquiry Concerning Ross 49 Cal. 4th CJP Supp. 79 (Cal. Comm'n on Judicial Performance, Nov. 16, 2005).

[69] *In re* Yaccarino, 502 A.2d 3 (N.J. 1985) (judge sought to acquire property at an unreasonably favorable price on the basis of confidential information acquired during judicial proceedings); *see also* MODEL CODE, Rule 3.5 ("A judge shall not intentionally . . . use nonpublic information acquired in a judicial capacity for any purpose unrelated to a judge's judicial duties.").

[70] In the Matter of Dumar, Unreported Determination (N.Y. Comm'n, May 18, 2004) 2004 WL 1813744.

[71] *In re* Castellano, 889 P.2d 175 (N.M. 1995). *See also* Model Rule 3.7(A)(2) (limiting a judge's authority to solicit charitable contributions to family members and fellow judges).

[72] MODEL CODE, Rule 1.3, Comment 1. Earlier versions of the Code directed judges not to "lend" the prestige of office to advance the interests of others, which created some confusion concerning the propriety of judges writing such recommendation letters, but in 2007 the term "abuse" was substituted and commentary added to clarify. CHARLES E. GEYH [SIC] AND W. WILLIAM HODES, REPORTERS' NOTES TO THE MODEL CODE OF JUDICIAL CONDUCT 22–23 (2009).

[73] MODEL CODE, Rule 3.3, Comment 1.

[74] 213 S.W.3d 547 (Tex. 2006).

[75] *Id.* at 577.

# Chapter 6-2

# REGULATING JUDICIAL CONDUCT ON THE BENCH

By Charles Gardner Geyh

*Table of Sections*

§ 6-2.1 Responsibilities Related to Maintaining Fitness for Judicial Service
§ 6-2.2 Responsibilities Related to the Use of Judicial Independence and Power
§ 6-2.3 Responsibilities Related to Preserving Judicial Impartiality and Fairness
§ 6-2.4 *Ex Parte* Communications
§ 6-2.5 Judicial Disqualification

This section concerns a judge's ethical responsibilities on the job. As explained in § 6-1.5, judges are subject to overarching ethical directives that govern both their public and private lives. Included among those overarching directives are duties to comply with the law,[1] to "act at all times" in a manner that promotes public confidence in the judiciary,[2] to avoid the appearance of impropriety,[3] and not to abuse the prestige of judicial office.[4] Insofar as those directives govern judicial (in addition to extrajudicial) conduct, they remain relevant here.

This chapter organizes a judge's ethical responsibilities on the bench into five clusters: (1) responsibilities related to maintaining a judge's fitness for judicial service; (2) responsibilities related to the use of judicial independence and power; (3) responsibilities related to preserving judicial impartiality; (4) the responsibility to avoid *ex parte* communications; and (5) the responsibility to disqualify when required.

## § 6-2.1 RESPONSIBILITIES RELATED TO MAINTAINING FITNESS FOR JUDICIAL SERVICE

The ability to perform the duties of judicial office is a defining feature of a good judge. Duties related to maintaining fitness for judicial service include competence, diligence, and temperament.

### § 6-2.1(a) Competence and Diligence

Just as the Model Rules of Professional Conduct impose duties on lawyers to "provide competent representation to a client,"[5] and to "act with reasonable diligence and promptness in representing a client,"[6] Rule 2.5 of the Model Code of Judicial Conduct

---

1 MODEL CODE, Rule 1.1.

2 MODEL CODE, Rule 1.2.

3 MODEL CODE, Rule 1.2.

4 MODEL CODE, Rule 1.3.

5 MODEL RULES OF PROFESSIONAL CONDUCT 1.1.

6 MODEL RULES OF PROFESSIONAL CONDUCT 1.3.

obligates judges to "perform judicial and administrative duties competently and diligently."[7] A comment accompanying Rule 2.5 elaborates that "competence in the performance of judicial duties requires the legal knowledge, skill, thoroughness, and preparation reasonably necessary to perform a judge's responsibilities of judicial office."[8] Diligence, in turn, is explained with reference to a duty of "prompt disposition," which "requires a judge to devote adequate time to judicial duties, to be punctual in attending court and expeditious in determining matters under submission."[9]

Incompetence spans a wide range of manifestations. One is inattentiveness. In *Matter of Halverson,* for example, the Nevada Commission on Judicial Discipline removed a judge for sleeping though parts of three trials.[10] The Commission listed the varied tasks that a judge must perform at trial, and bluntly concluded "a judge cannot hear matters when a judge is asleep."[11] The Commission took pains to add that an isolated episode of nodding off, while not good, was worse as a recurring phenomenon, which not only incapacitated the judge while she was asleep, but conveyed indifference to the proceedings.[12] Such perceived indifference undermines a judge's duty to act at all times in a manner that promotes public confidence in the integrity of the judiciary. Incompetence as manifested by inattentiveness can also arise in the context of a judge's administrative responsibilities. In *In re Disciplinary Action Against Hagar,* the North Dakota Supreme Court suspended a judge for administrative incompetence, evidenced by funds he did not deposit, final disposition reports he failed to process, and staff training he declined to authorize.[13]

Other manifestations of incompetence include gross disregard of applicable law or process due to indifference, inability, or overwork. Incompetence does not technically encompass willful refusals to uphold applicable law, which are separately regulated.[14] That said, the line that separates incompetence from deliberate failures to follow the rules can be indistinct. For example, in *Matter of Inquiry Concerning a Judge,*[15] the Georgia Supreme Court found that "in two cases . . . Judge Vaughn denied appeal bonds to criminal misdemeanor defendants, each of whom was entitled, *as a matter of law,* to be granted appeal bonds." The Court characterized the judge's actions as both "clear and convincing evidence of extreme judicial incompetence in the law," and as "blatant disregard for the law, and as such, judicial misconduct and bad faith."[16]

Diligence, in contrast to competence, focuses on neglect and delay. Extreme decision-making delays are recurring problems that aggrieved parties and their lawyers have sought to address via administrative, adjudicative, and disciplinary routes. When confronted with a delayed ruling, a lawyer's first recourse is typically administrative. Wheedling court staff about the pending ruling is aided in some jurisdictions by

---

[7] MODEL CODE, Rule 2.5(a).

[8] MODEL CODE, Rule 2.5, Comment 1.

[9] MODEL CODE, Rule 2.5, Comment 3.

[10] In the Matter of Halverson, Case No. 0801–1066, 1–28 at 6 (Nev. Comm'n on Judicial Discipline, Nov. 18, 2008), *available at* http://judicial.nv.gov/uploadedFiles/judicialnvgov/content/Discipline/Dicisions/2011-01-31_0801-1066_Halverson_FindingsofFactConclusionsofLawandImpositionofDiscpline.pdf.

[11] *Id.* at 7.

[12] *Id.*

[13] 842 N.W.2d 873 (N.D. 2014).

[14] MODEL CODE, Rule 2.2.

[15] 462 S.E.2d 728, 733–34 (Ga. 1995).

[16] *Id.* at 734.

statutory case processing time standards, which require judges to report matters pending longer than a specified time, typically sixty days (and which may subject judges with backlogged dockets to penalties).[17] When informal importuning via administrative channels fails, lawyers have sometimes sought relief for isolated cases of extreme and unjustified decision-making delay in the appellate courts via petitions for writ of mandamus.[18] Finally, decision-making delays can implicate a judge's ethical duty of diligence and culminate in disciplinary proceedings, which is the focus of this section.

The kinds of neglect and delay sufficient to violate a judge's ethical duty of diligence ordinarily arise in one of three situations: where disorganized, lazy, or willful judges are unjustifiably derelict in their duties; where otherwise conscientious judges are overwhelmed by crowded dockets; and where judges are disabled or impaired.

The dereliction of duty category includes matters of neglect in the forms of chronic tardiness and extended absences from the office. In such cases, disciplinary bodies have shied from drawing bright lines in close cases, favoring the imposition of discipline only in matters so egregious that the misconduct is obvious. For example, judges have been removed for protracted absences from work.[19] Lesser sanctions of reprimand or suspension have been imposed on judges who have been chronically late to court or absented themselves for personal reasons on multiple occasions.[20]

With respect to dereliction-driven delay, as with neglect, there are rarely bright lines; discipline is typically reserved for patterns of excessive delay.[21] For example, in *In re Disciplinary Action Against Hagar*, the North Dakota Supreme Court suspended a judge for (among other things) decision-making delay in an isolated case, but noted that the disciplinary matter arose shortly after the judge had been censured for decision-making delays in a dozen other cases.[22] With rare exception,[23] disciplinary bodies have refrained from sanctioning judges for isolated instances of delay,[24] except in circumstances so extreme that the delay implied willful misconduct.[25]

Circumstances in which delays are caused by crowded dockets that overwhelm otherwise conscientious judges present a different and difficult problem. One cannot

---

17 CHARLES GARDNER GEYH, JAMES J. ALFINI, STEVEN LUBET, & JEFFREY SHAMAN, JUDICIAL CONDUCT AND ETHICS § 6.02[2] (5th ed. 2013).

18 Charles Gardner Geyh, *Informal Methods of Judicial Discipline*, 142 U. PA. L. REV. 243, 286–94 (1993).

19 *In re* Merlo, 58 A.3d 1 (Pa. 2012) (judge removed for, among other things, being absent 30% of the time); Kennick v. Commission on Judicial Performance, 787 P.2d 591 (Cal. 1990) (judge removed for being absent from work for a four and a half month period, prior to which the judge had been absent for 96 days in the preceding twenty-two months).

20 In the Matter of Peebles (Mo. S. Ct., Mar. 29, 2013) (judge suspended, *inter alia*, for chronic tardiness); In the Matter of Vega, Findings of Fact, Conclusions of Law, and Order (Nevada Comm'n on Judicial Discipline, Aug. 29, 2013) (judge reprimanded, *inter alia*, for recessing court early on multiple occasions to attend her daughter's soccer games).

21 *In re* Cofield, 2013 WL 9866977 (Conn. Comm. Jud. Eth. 2013) (imposing a suspension for inexcusable delays in multiple cases spanning eleven months to over a year); *In re* Perez, 843 N.W. 2d 562 (Minn. 2014) (judge censured, *inter alia,* for delays in six cases).

22 842 N.W.2d 873 (N.D. 2014).

23 *See In re* Bell, 344 S.W.3d 304 (Tenn. 2011) (rejecting assertion that a pattern of delay was necessary and imposing a suspension for an inexcusable nine month delay in deciding a single case).

24 *In re* Alvino, 494 A.2d. 1014, 1016 (N.J. 1985) ("atypical" delays in two cases "were not intended to, and do not, constitute judicial misconduct").

25 *In re* Kilburn, 599 A.2d 1377, 1379 (Vt. 1991) (discipline appropriate for isolated instance of delay "so lacking in legitimate justification that it is willful").

reasonably discipline a judge for violating her duty of diligence because of decision-making delays beyond the judge's control. At the same time, the duty of diligence extends not only to judicial matters but administrative matters. A comment accompanying Rule 2.5 admonishes that "[a] judge should seek the necessary docket time, court staff, expertise, and resources to discharge all adjudicative and administrative responsibilities."[26] Judges have an ethical responsibility to administer their courts so as to maintain control of their dockets; consequently, to the extent that delays are attributable to mismanagement, judges can be subject to discipline.[27]

Lapses of diligence (and competence) can also result from disability or impairment caused by substance abuse and dementia or other mental illness. Permanent disability, of course, may necessitate removal from office.[28] Treatable disabilities, such as drug abuse or alcoholism, can be remedied by treatment, which may mitigate the need for discipline,[29] except to the extent that the court regards the impairment as voluntary.[30] To assist in the detection and treatment of disability and impairment, the Model Code imposes a duty on judges to take "appropriate action" when they have a "reasonable belief" that the performance of another judge is "impaired by drugs or alcohol, or by a mental, emotional, or physical condition."[31] The operative rule adds that "appropriate action" may include a confidential referral to a judicial assistance program.[32]

### § 6-2.1(b) Demeanor

A sound judicial temperament is a qualification for judicial service that reflects both on a judge's general fitness for judicial office, and on the judge's commitment to impartiality, as discussed further in § 6-2.3. The Model Code of Judicial Conduct declares that, "[a] judge shall be patient, dignified, and courteous to litigants, jurors, witnesses, lawyers, court staff, court officials, and others with whom the judge deals in an official capacity."[33] It would be a mistake to undervalue the need to preserve judicial demeanor and temperament as a kind of cosmetic duty to be nice or politically correct. Social science research shows that for parties in litigation, the legitimacy of court proceedings turns less on the outcome than on whether litigants felt that they were treated fairly and afforded a meaningful opportunity to be heard.[34] Hence, abusive or impatient judges who create the impression that their rulings are arbitrary or vindictive, undermine their overarching directive to "act at all times in a manner that promotes public confidence" in the judiciary.[35]

---

[26] MODEL CODE, Rule 2.5, Comment 2.

[27] *In re* Vincent, Unreported Determination (N.Y. Comm'n 1986) 1986 WL 327093 (failure to maintain complete case dockets); Inquiry Concerning Hinson, Judgment and Order (Ariz. 2009) (failure to establish a case tracking system); Mardikian v. Commission on Judicial Performance, 709 P.2d 852 (Cal. 1985) (failure to set case scheduling priorities).

[28] *In re* Williamson, 242 S.E.2d 221 (S.C. 1978).

[29] Matter of Dean, 855 N.W.2d 186 (Ia. 2014).

[30] Starnes v. Judicial Ret. & Removal Comm'n, 680 S.W.2d 922, 923 (Ky. 1984).

[31] MODEL CODE, Rule 2.14.

[32] *Id.*

[33] MODEL CODE, Rule 2.8(B).

[34] TOM R. TYLER, ET AL., SOCIAL JUSTICE IN A DIVERSE SOCIETY 82–83 (1997); Tom R. Tyler, *The Role of Perceived Injustice in Defendants' Evaluation of their Courtroom Experience*, 18 L. & SOC. REV. 51, 69–70 (1984).

[35] *See* Inquiry Concerning a Judge, No. 90–311; *In re* Perry, 586 So.2d 1054 (Fla. 1991) (approving stipulation for public reprimand of judge who "engaged in verbal abuse and intimidation of attorneys, witnesses, and parties in violation of Canons 3(A)(2) and 3(A)(3)"); *In re* Concerning Holien, 612 N.W.2d 789

The duty to be patient, dignified, and courteous does not imply a duty to display no emotion; judges are, after all, human beings who will react to what they witness in court proceedings, and efforts to purge emotion from the bench are likely to be fruitless and counterproductive to the art of adjudication.[36] Rather, the duty is a matter of degree. Hence, the Arizona Commission on Judicial Conduct reprimanded a judge who berated the victim as an "idiot" because she had recommended against incarcerating the defendant, to whom she was emotionally attached.[37] As the Commission explained, "[w]hile the judge's concerns about the defendant were entirely appropriate, his comments about and characterizations of the victim were not."[38]

Most cases imposing discipline on judges for inappropriate demeanor feature repeated displays of extreme impatience, verbal abuse, sarcasm, or aberrational conduct.[39] Lawyers to proceedings before the judge are common targets of such conduct.[40] In some cases, the judge has reacted injudiciously to a lawyer's conduct in the case at bar.[41] In other instances, the judge has reacted vindictively toward a lawyer with whom the judge had a history.[42] Parties have likewise been a frequent focus of cases concerning indecorous judicial temperament.[43] Although less common, judges have also been sanctioned for belittling witnesses (including victims)[44] and court personnel.[45]

---

(Ia. 2000) (judge removed, in part, for negative attitude displayed toward attorneys, witnesses, parties, court personnel and other judges).

[36] *See* Susan Bandes & Jeremy Blumenthal, *Emotion and the Law,* 8 ANN. REV. OF L. & SOC. SCI. 161 (2012).

[37] Arizona Comm'n on Judicial Conduct, Disposition of Complaint 13–178, Dec. 13, 2013.

[38] *Id.*

[39] *See, e.g., In re* Watson, No. 152 (Kan. Comm'n on Judicial Qualifications, Oct. 10 1995) (commission ordered judge to cease and desist from conduct that violated code requirements to be patient, dignified, and courteous to litigants and lawyers); McBryde v. Committee to Review Circuit Council Conduct & Disability Orders of the Judicial Conference of the United States, 83 F. Supp. 2d 135 (1999) (upholding reprimand, suspension of new case assignments for one year, and suspension from participation in cases involving 23 attorneys who had testified against a federal district judge by the Judicial Council of the Fifth Judicial Circuit pursuant to an investigation by a "Special Committee" that found that the judge engaged in a pattern of intemperate and abusive behavior prejudicial to the effective administration of the courts); *In re* Inquiry Concerning a Judge, 657 S.E.2d 346 (N.C. 2008) (judge censured and suspended from office for 60 days without pay for being habitually rude and condescending to those appearing before him and demonstrating an arrogant, contemptuous demeanor while presiding over court).

[40] *In re* Sullivan, Order of Censure (Nev. Comm'n on Judicial Discipline, June 21, 1993) (judge censured for a pattern of behavior that included rude treatment of court personnel, attorneys, parties, and others; use of profane language; and fits of temper and outbursts both in and out of the courtroom).

[41] Disciplinary Counsel v. Weithman, No. 2014–0544, Feb. 12, 2015 (ordering a stayed suspension against a judge for, *inter alia*, an outburst in which the judge stated, "[t]his is so goddamn simple. If you give the discovery and don't do all this bullshit, I don't have to sit here and listen to this crap . . . . Comply with discovery and shut up once in a while . . . . Stupid. All Franklin County attorneys are stupid.").

[42] *In re* Carnesoltas, 563 So.2d 83 (Fla. 1990). *See also* Re Bayly, Determination and Undertaking (District of Columbia Comm'n on Judicial Disabilities and Tenure, Mar. 11, 2008) (judge determined to be in violation of code of judicial conduct by ordering the detention of an attorney appearing before him without warrant; judge undertook to avoid any such conduct in the future).

[43] Mississippi Comm'n on Judicial Performance v. Darby, 143 So.3d 564 (Miss. 2014) (removing a Youth Court Referee, where the judge "acknowledge[d] that she was frequently and unnecessarily confrontational toward litigants . . . and that she treated litigants . . . in an abusive, belittling, impatient, unprofessional, and discourteous manner").

[44] Arizona Comm'n on Judicial Conduct, Disposition of Complaint 13–178 (Dec. 13, 2013) (referring to victim as "an idiot").

[45] *In re* Seitz, 441 Mich. 590, 495 N.W.2d 559 (1993) (judge sanctioned for unprofessional relationships with and hostile attitudes toward court employees, including encouraging secretary to be uncivil); *In re* Complaint Concerning Rice, 515 N.W.2d 53 (Minn. 1994) (judge reprimanded and suspended for 60 days for a pattern of behavior that included angry and undignified responses to staff members over a number of years).

Conduct reflecting impatience and discourtesy can amount to simple sound and fury, signifying nothing more than an injudicious temperament, which undermines the perception that those coming before the judge are being treated fairly. To the extent that impatience and discourtesy display judgmental animus, however, they can also reflect ill on the judge's impartiality, as discussed in § 6-2.3, and can give rise to arbitrary abuses of judicial power, discussed in § 6-2.2.

## § 6-2.2 RESPONSIBILITIES RELATED TO THE USE OF JUDICIAL INDEPENDENCE AND POWER

Judges wield considerable power. Power is subject to abuse. Section 6-1.5(c) discussed one form of abuse that arises when judges improperly exploit the prestige of their office to advance the interests of themselves or others, which is regulated by one of the Model Code's overarching edicts in Canon 1. This section considers two additional abuses of power that concern misuse of judicial independence. First, the instrumental values of impartiality, independence, and integrity, as described in § 6-1.4, paired with fitness for duty, as described in § 6-2.1, enable judges to wield judicial power to the end of upholding the law. Judicial independence operates on the premise that if judges are afforded a measure of protection from external threats or blandishments that could contort their judgment, they will impartially uphold the law. That premise, however, holds only if judges do not abuse their independence by substituting their personal preferences for the law; hence, the Model Code of Judicial Conduct imposes on judges a duty to "uphold and apply the law."[46] Second, this same premise holds only insofar as judges act with independence by resisting inappropriate external influences; hence, the Model Code admonishes judges not to heed "public clamor" and not to allow social, family, political, and popular influences to affect their conduct.[47] This section examines the relationship between judicial power and independence by exploring the dual ethical duties to uphold the law and to resist inappropriate, external influences.

### § 6-2.2(a) The Duty to Uphold and Apply the Law

Rule 2.2 of the Model Code states that "[a] judge shall uphold and apply the law." Superficially, this seems to be little more than a banal directive for judges to do their jobs. This seemingly trite bromide, however, addresses the inherent tension between judicial independence and accountability. As discussed in § 6-1.4(b), judicial independence, among other instrumental values, aims to promote the rule of law by insulating judges from external interference with their judgment so that they might impartially uphold the law. Decades of social science data, however, suggest that judges are subject to extralegal influences, which recent quantitative research has begun to quantify and qualify with greater precision.[48] To the extent that independence liberates judges to disregard the law, it raises the question of whether independence is more of a hindrance than a help to values surrounding the rule of law.

---

[46] MODEL CODE, Rule 2.2.

[47] MODEL CODE, Rule 2.4.

[48] JEFFREY SEGAL AND HAROLD SPAETH, THE SUPREME COURT AND THE ATTITUDINAL MODEL REVISITED (2002); LEE EPSTEIN, WILLIAM LANDES, RICHARD POSNER, THE BEHAVIOR OF FEDERAL JUDGES: A THEORETICAL AND EMPIRICAL STUDY OF RATIONAL CHOICE (2013); Gregory C. Sisk, *The Quantitative Moment and the Qualitative Opportunity: Legal Studies of Judicial Decision Making*, 93 CORNELL L. REV. 873, 876 (2008) (reviewing FRANK B. CROSS, DECISION MAKING IN THE U.S. COURTS OF APPEALS (2007)).

Setting the United States Supreme Court to one side and focusing on lower courts, if for no other reason than the fact that the Supreme Court is the only court in the United States that has not bound itself to a code of conduct, the best evidence suggests that while a judge's ideology can play a role in judicial decision-making, the law retains significant influence.[49] In close cases, when the law is unclear, extralegal influences can operate subconsciously: the cognitive theory of "motivated reasoning" suggests that when judges must choose between comparably plausible opposing legal arguments, they may subconsciously find the argument that aligns with their policy perspective more persuasive.[50] There is nothing unethical about that. Rather, ethical problems arise when a judge makes a conscious choice to disregard the law and impose her or his personal preferences. A comment accompanying Rule 2.2 explains, "[a]lthough each judge comes to the bench with a unique background and personal philosophy, a judge must interpret and apply the law without regard to whether the judge approves or disapproves of the law in question."[51]

Imposing a duty on judges to uphold and apply the law on pain of discipline raises potentially troubling judicial independence concerns. Former Tennessee Chief Justice Adolpho Birch has defined judicial independence as "the judge's right to do the right thing or, believing it to be the right thing, to do the wrong thing."[52] Birch's essential point is that judicial independence, properly understood, should afford judges the latitude to uphold the law as they understand it to be written—without fear of reprisal if they make a mistake. Accordingly, relevant commentary accompanying Rule 2.2 opines, "[w]hen applying and interpreting the law, judges sometimes make good-faith errors of fact or law. Errors of this kind do not violate this rule."[53]

As a technical matter, then, good faith errors of conscientious judges are not subject to sanction. Nominally good faith errors of incompetent judges violate the duty of competence under Rule 2.5,[54] while bad faith "errors"—better characterized as willful usurpations of power—violate a judge's duty to uphold the law under 2.2. In practice, however, the line that separates gross incompetence from bad faith is not critical insofar as both are subject to sanction.[55] The line that separates error from misconduct is another matter, because imposing discipline for error can encroach on independence. To avoid incursions on judicial independence, disciplinary bodies have sanctioned judges for failure to uphold the law only in extreme cases.

In *In re Dileo,* the New Jersey Supreme Court followed what it characterized as the practice of most jurisdictions and concluded that to justify discipline for failure to uphold the law, there must first be "clear and convincing proof of objective legal error" that is committed " 'contrary to the clear and determined law about which there is no confusion

---

49 Gregory C. Sisk & Michael Heise, *Judges and Ideology: Public and Academic Debates About Statistical Measures*, 99 NW U. L. REV. 743 (2005).

50 EILEEN BRAMAN, LAW, POLITICS, AND PERCEPTION: HOW POLICY PREFERENCES INFLUENCE LEGAL REASONING (2009).

51 MODEL CODE, Rule 2.2, Comment 2.

52 Linda Greenhouse, *Judges Seek Aid in Effort to Remain Independent,* N.Y. TIMES, Dec. 10, 1998, http://www.nytimes.com/1998/12/10/us/judges-seek-aid-in-effort-to-remain-independent.html.

53 MODEL CODE, Rule 2.2, Comment 3.

54 *See* § 6-2.1(a).

55 *See, e.g.*, Matter of Inquiry Concerning a Judge, 462 S.E.2d 728 (Ga. 1995) (characterizing the judge's conduct as both "clear and convincing evidence of extreme judicial incompetence in the law," as well as "blatant disregard for the law, and as such, judicial misconduct and bad faith").

or question as to its interpretation.' "[56] In addition, the court continued, there must be a "plus:" "the error must be 'egregious, made in bad faith, or made as part of a pattern or practice of legal error.' " In this case, the judge "forced" two brothers "to go to trial *pro se* after refusing their request for a public defender, prosecuted the case with the help of the arresting police officer, personally cross-examined the defendants, and [then] found the defendants guilty based on testimony that he himself had elicited"—procedural errors the Court deemed "egregious" enough to warrant a public reprimand.[57] Other cases are largely in accord, imposing discipline for legal error when a judge's procedural or substantive errors are isolated but egregious,[58] made in bad faith,[59] or part of a pattern.[60]

The unusual matter of California Court of Appeals Justice Stephen O. Kline illustrates the perils of bringing a disciplinary action against a judge for failing to uphold the law under circumstances in which the underlying facts are less compelling.[61] Justice Kline dissented from a court order granting a "stipulated reversal"—a practice authorized by the California Supreme Court, which allowed parties to settle their dispute on terms that disregarded or "reversed" the rulings of the court in the underlying case. In his dissent, Justice Kline explained, "I acknowledge that the opinion of the California Supreme Court in *Neary v. Regents of the University of California* requires that the motion before us be granted. I would deny the motion, however, because I cannot as a matter of conscience apply the rule announced in *Neary*."[62]

The California Commission on Judicial Performance initiated disciplinary proceedings against Judge Kline on the grounds that he violated the state corollary to Rule 2.2. The Commission explained that "in order for the commission to discipline Justice Kline it must find by clear and convincing evidence that his decision to file a dissent was legal error and that the decision was made in bad faith or for some improper motive."[63]

Kline (supported by the California Judges Association as amici) argued that he was motivated by the honest concern that stipulated reversals were destructive of judicial institutions, but the Commission concluded that the judge's sincerity, by itself, did not

---

[56] 83 A.3d 11, 27 (N.J. 2014).

[57] *Id* at 30.

[58] *In re* Moore, Case No. 33 at 5 (Ala. Ct. of the Judiciary 2003), *aff'd*, Moore v. Judicial Inquiry Comm'n of the State of Alabama, 891 So.2d 848, 853 (Ala. 2004) (suspending then-Chief Justice Moore from office for failure to uphold the law under Rule 2.2 when he refused a federal court order to remove a monument to the Ten Commandments). Re-elected in 2012, Moore now faces potential removal from office for violating Rule 2.2 when he directed the state's probate judges to refuse applications for marriage licenses by same-sex couples. *In re* Moore, Case No. 46 (Ala. Ct. of the Judiciary 2016).

[59] *In re* Matter Concerning a Judge, 462 S.E.2d 728 (Ga. 1995) (refusing to order appeal bonds in two cases was a "blatant disregard for the law, and as such, judicial misconduct and bad faith").

[60] *In re* Young, 943 N.E.2d 1276 (Ind. 2011) ("by employing a practice of imposing increased penalties against traffic-infraction litigants for exercising their trial rights so as to penalize them for doing so and to discourage others from doing so" the judge violated, *inter alia,* Rule 2.2); *In re* Bennington, 24 N.E.3d 958 (Ind. 2015) (judge removed for violating, *inter alia,* Rule 2.2, across a series of cases in which the judge abused her contempt powers, imposed a penalty in excess of the statutory maximum, unlawfully altered a plea agreement, and improperly conducted a sentencing hearing without the prosecutor present).

[61] Inquiry Concerning Kline, Decision of Order and Dismissal No. 151 (Cal. Comm'n on Judicial Performance, Aug.19, 1999).

[62] Morrow v. Hood Commun., Inc., 69 Cal. Rptr. 2d 489, 491 (Cal. Ct. App. 1997) (Kline, J., dissenting). *See also* Neary v. Regents of U. of California, 834 P.2d 119 (Cal. 1992).

[63] Inquiry Concerning Kline, Decision and Order of Dismissal No. 151, at 3 (Cal. Comm'n on Judicial Performance, Aug. 19, 1999).

justify Kline's conscious failure to follow supreme court precedent. Though Kline argued that a recent decision by the United States Supreme Court "provided good cause" to reconsider *Neary*, the Commission did not find such a claim to be "clearly persuasive." Finally, Kline defended his dissent, in part, on the grounds that the California Supreme Court would never have an opportunity to reconsider its prior ruling unless an appellate court refused to grant a proposed settlement with a stipulated reversal, in defiance of the California Supreme Court's holding in *Neary*. But the Commission was not persuaded on that point either, noting that Judge Kline could have called the issue to the California Supreme Court's attention via a "critical concurrence," and that the Court could then reconsider *Neary* on its own motion.

The Commission nevertheless dismissed the complaint. Under the totality of the circumstances, the Commission concluded that Kline's argument for a narrow exception to the *stare decisis* principle was not "so far-fetched as to be untenable." In other words, while Kline's refusal to abide by state supreme court precedent may have been erroneous, it was not "improper," and so did not warrant discipline. In so concluding, the Commission made clear that in a close case such as this, the value of independence trumped the need for discipline:

> [W]e readily reaffirm our fundamental belief in the principle of judicial independence . . . . [I]n exercising our mandate as conferred by the people, we appreciate the critical need for California judicial officers to act both independently and in conformity with the laws of the State, and we are sensitive to the substantial issues that arise when these principles clash.[64]

### § 6-2.2(b) The Duty to Resist External Influences on Judicial Conduct

At a conceptual level, one can think about judicial independence in structural and behavioral terms.[65] As a structural matter, judicial independence is promoted by formal structures that thwart external interference with the decisions of individual judges or the autonomy of the judiciary as a branch. Examples of structural independence include Article III of the U.S. Constitution, which guarantees federal judges tenure during good behavior and a salary that cannot be diminished; and state constitutions that explicitly guarantee the independence of their respective judicial branches. The presence of such structures, however, does not guarantee that judges will behave independently. For example, a federal judge may issue a ruling that yields to congressional criticism despite tenure and salary protections. Conversely, the absence of such structures does not guarantee that judges will behave dependently: for example, a state judge who is subject to reelection and hence is structurally dependent on the electorate for her continued tenure in office, may issue decisions without regard to the electorate's preferences.

The Model Code encourages behavioral independence by admonishing judges to resist inappropriate external influences on their decision-making. Rule 2.4(a) declares, "[a] judge shall not be swayed by public clamor or fear of criticism." Rule 2.4(b) adds, "[a] judge shall not permit family, social, political, financial, or other interests or relationships to influence the judge's judicial conduct or judgment." A comment accompanying Rule 2.4 explains its rationale: "[a]n independent judiciary requires that

---

[64] *Id.* at 4.

[65] Charles Gardner Geyh, *Judicial Independence as an Organizing Principle,* 10 ANN. REV. L. & SOC. SCI. 1085 (2014).

judges decide cases according to facts and law, without regard to whether particular laws or litigants are popular or unpopular with the public, the media, government officials, or the judge's friends or family."[66]

Social science suggests that judges are sometimes influenced by political interests, "public clamor," and fear of criticism. For example, one study of sentencing patterns in criminal cases found that "all else equal, the sentence by a judge whose election is imminent is likely to be about three to four-and-one-fourth months longer . . . than if the judge[ ] w[as] recently elected or retained."[67] As a practical matter, however, a rule directing judges not to be so influenced is inherently difficult to enforce. Judges are unlikely to concede that such rulings are the product of forbidden influences, both because such influences can operate subconsciously and because judges understand that those influences are improper. Furthermore, in the absence of such a concession, while there might be suspicion of inappropriate influence, there will not be any proof.

Consider, for example, a controversial case from the 1990s, in which federal district judge Harold Baer excluded evidence from a drug case on the grounds that the police had obtained the evidence illegally, in violation of the defendant's fourth amendment rights. Senate Majority Leader (and presidential candidate) Robert Dole, joined by Speaker of the House Newt Gingrich, proposed to initiate impeachment proceedings against Judge Baer if he did not reverse that ruling; meanwhile, President Bill Clinton's press secretary suggested that the President would request Baer's resignation if he did not reverse himself. On the government's motion for reconsideration, Baer reversed his ruling, but took pains then—and later—to emphasize that he had not succumbed to political pressure but had based his reversal on the merits of the motion. The Baer imbroglio focused more on the conduct of Dole, Gingrich, and Clinton, and whether such conduct unfairly threatened Judge Baer's independence. But the case also illustrates the difficulty of distinguishing proper from improper influences for purposes of applying Rule 2.4.

As a consequence, when Rule 2.4 has been brought to bear in disciplinary proceedings, evidence of improper influence is often a matter of record. In *Inquiry concerning a Judge, Gridley*, for example, the Florida Supreme Court reprimanded a judge for allowing a personal relationship to influence his judicial conduct, when he converted a criminal defendant's sentence from first to second degree murder after he struck up a personal correspondence with the defendant, and others associated with the defendant, post-conviction.[68] In *Ohio State Bar Association v. McCafferty*, the Ohio Supreme Court suspended a county judge for, *inter alia,* violating Rule 2.4. The case concerned a judge who had been convicted on multiple counts of making false statements to the FBI—including false statements understating the influence certain county public officials sought to exert over her judicial conduct.[69] Those false statements formed the basis for the court's conclusion that that the judge had been subject to the influence of the county officials in violation of Rule 2.4.[70]

---

[66] MODEL CODE, Rule 2.4, Comment 1.

[67] Gregory Huber and Sanford Gordon, *Accountability & Coercion: Is Justice Blind When it Runs for Office?*, 48 AM. J. OF POL. SCI. 247 (2004).

[68] 417 So.2d 950 (Fla. 1982).

[69] Ohio State Bar Ass'n v. McCafferty, 17 N.E.3d 521, 522 (Ohio 2014).

[70] *See id.* at 523.

## § 6-2.3 RESPONSIBILITIES RELATED TO PRESERVING JUDICIAL IMPARTIALITY AND FAIRNESS

Judicial impartiality is identified in § 6-1.4(a) as an instrumental value core to judicial ethics that promotes justice under law. And the duty to act at all times in a manner that promotes public confidence in the impartiality of the judiciary is identified in § 6-1.5(b) as a foundational rule in the Model Code of Judicial Conduct. Judicial impartiality connotes two meanings of relevance to judicial ethics: (1) open-mindedness with respect to the issues before the court, and (2) lack of bias or prejudice toward parties or classes of parties.[71] This section moves the discussion of judicial impartiality, so defined, from the philosophical and foundational to the more specific ethical responsibilities that guide a judge's conduct on the bench. Such responsibilities include the performance of judicial duties fairly, impartially, and without bias; respecting the parties' rights to be heard; and limiting public statements on pending and future cases. Two additional ethical duties relevant to preserving judicial impartiality on the job—the duties to avoid ex parte communications and to recuse from proceedings in which the judge is conflicted or her impartiality is otherwise in doubt—are considered separately in § 6-2.4 and § 6-2.5.

### § 6-2.3(a) Judicial Bias

Model Code Rule 2.2 directs judges to "perform all duties of judicial office fairly and impartially," while Rule 2.3 directs them to "perform the duties of judicial office without bias or prejudice." Insofar as the Code defines "impartiality" to mean the "absence of bias or prejudice in favor of, or against, particular parties or classes of parties," these rules cover the same turf. Insofar as impartiality is broader than the absence of bias for or against parties, because it includes "maintenance of an open mind in considering issues that may come before the judge," it is less commonly regulated by Rule 2.2, than by the "act at all times" clause of Rule 1.2, as discussed in § 6-1.5(b),[72] coupled with disqualification, as discussed in § 6-2.5.

#### *§ 6-2.3(a)(1) Bias Toward Specific People*

Forbidden bias can be directed at specific people or classes of people. With respect to specific people, impermissible "bias" does not ordinarily include the favorable or unfavorable views that a judge naturally forms with respect to parties, lawyers, or witnesses over the course of court proceedings. There is nothing improper about judges presiding over cases in which they become irritated with obstreperous witnesses, admire the performance of able attorneys, or develop negative views toward parties as the evidence against them mounts. Rather, discipline has been reserved for judges who exhibit bias or favoritism that cannot be explained as a normal response to what they have witnessed in court proceedings. Such problems can arise inexplicably, perhaps as an excessive reaction to something that transpires in the courtroom. More often, inappropriate displays of bias toward specific participants in court proceedings are attributable to relationships that develop prior to or during court proceedings.[73] Thus,

---

[71] MODEL CODE, Terminology; *see also*, discussion at § 6-1.4(a).

[72] MODEL CODE, Rule 1.2 ("A judge shall act at all times in a manner that promotes public confidence in the independence, integrity, and impartiality of the judiciary.").

[73] Note that when judges exhibit bias on the basis of such relationships, the conduct can simultaneously implicate the duty not to permit "social" or "other. . .relationships" to "influence the judge's judicial conduct or judgment." MODEL CODE, Rule 2.4(B); *see also* § 6-2.2(b).

judges have been disciplined for exhibiting bias in light of such relationships with parties[74] and attorneys,[75] including prosecutors.[76]

Rules that instruct judges to perform their duties impartially and avoid bias travel in tandem with disqualification rules, discussed in § 6-2.5. Judges cannot be faulted for the likes and dislikes they develop with respect to the particular people they meet over the course of their personal and professional relationships (the analysis changes when judges exhibit biases toward entire classes of people, which reflects badly on their fitness to serve, as discussed in § 6-2.3(a)(2)). Nor can judges be faulted for such relationships sometimes clouding their impartiality: who would blame a judge for her inability to be evenhanded in the trial of her former maid of honor? Judges *can* be faulted, however, for proceeding to hear such cases—meaning that the only reason such judges are ultimately sanctioned for exhibiting bias or favoritism is for failure to disqualify themselves.

#### *§ 6-2.3(a)(2) Bias Toward Classes of People*

The Model Code takes pains to emphasize that bias directed toward any class of people is improper, "including, but not limited to" bias or prejudice based on "race, sex, gender, religion, national origin, ethnicity, disability, age, sexual orientation, marital status, socioeconomic status, or political affiliation."[77] Simply put, judges who prejudge parties on such bases are incapable of impartially upholding the law and ill-suited to serve as judges.[78]

Among the varied bases for improper bias directed at a class of people, race and gender have been the most persistent. With respect to racial bias, continuing suspicion that African Americans were subject to disparate treatment in the courts (especially state courts) in the years following the civil rights movement, led several states, beginning in the 1980s, to establish racial bias task forces.[79] Those task forces found widespread evidence of racial bias, and recommended reforms, ranging from judicial education and training, to diversification of the bench, to revisions to codes of judicial conduct. In 1990, the Model Code of Judicial Conduct was amended to include a canon directing judges to perform their duties free from racial bias; accompanying commentary warned against bias in any form—including demeanor and body language.[80] More recent research reveals persistent racial disparities across the administration of justice, from

---

[74] *In re* Lindell-Cloud, Determination (N.Y. Comm'n on Judicial Conduct, July 14, 1995) (part-time judge censured for imposing a sentence against a former employer in retaliation for the employer firing the judge from her previous job). *In re* Crislip, 391 S.E.2d 84 (W. Va. 1990) (magistrate "attempted on several occasions to get the officer who had issued the traffic citation to withdraw it and ultimately dismissed the case" per defendant's *ex parte* request); Inquiry Concerning Wasilenko, Cal. Comm'n on Judicial Performance, 49 Cal. 4th CJP Supp. 26, Mar. 2, 2005 (retired judge barred for favoritism toward family friends).

[75] Inquiry Concerning Cardenas, Decision and Order Imposing Public Admonishment, 48 Cal. 4th CJP Supp. 167, Oct. 3, 2000 (judge admonished for creating appearance of favoritism toward attorney).

[76] *In re* Hartsfield, 722 S.E.2d 496, 498–99 (N.C. 2012) (judge suspended for arbitrarily dismissing traffic charges due to "fundamental and philosophical differences" with the assistant district attorney); Chiles, Order Disposition of Complaint 12–012 (Arizona Comm'n on Judicial Conduct, Apr. 9, 2012 (judge reprimanded for conduct creating an appearance of bias in favor of the prosecution).

[77] MODEL CODE, Rule 2.3(B).

[78] *In re* Cook, Unreported Determination (N.Y. Comm'n, Nov. 19, 1986) 1986 WL 327081 ("[R]acist remarks on and off the bench, standing alone, demonstrate. . .unfitness for judicial office.").

[79] Suellyn Scarnecchia, *State Responses to Task Force Reports on Race and Ethnic Bias in the Courts*, 16 HAMLINE L. REV. 923 (1993); *see also*, NATIONAL CENTER FOR STATE COURTS, GENDER AND RACIAL FAIRNESS-STATE LINKS, http://www.ncsc.org/Topics/Access-and-Fairness/Gender-and-Racial-Fairness/State-Links.aspx?cat=Gender%20Fairness%20Task%20Forces%20and%20Reports.

[80] ABA MODEL CODE OF JUDICIAL CONDUCT, Canon 3B(5) and commentary (1990).

arrest rates[81] to incarceration rates,[82] as well as in the imposition of capital punishment.[83] Furthermore, surveys reveal that African Americans express significantly lower rates of confidence in the impartiality of the judiciary than the general population.[84]

Racial bias subjecting judges to sanction has taken a range of forms. Judges have been disciplined for using racial slurs, including the so-called "N" word on[85] and off the bench.[86] They have been sanctioned for racially insensitive attempts at humor, for example, by asking prospective jurors of Asian or African descent (respectively) about the current price of fish heads and rice, or watermelon.[87] Judges have been also disciplined for generalizing about parties' conduct from their race, inquiring into the immigration status of Hispanic litigants,[88] by saying that the judge was "sick and tired of colored people"[89] or "[t]hese damn Puerto Ricans get away with everything,"[90] and, finally, by making categorical declarations that African American children are born out of wedlock to parents who abuse the welfare system.[91]

Gender bias, like racial bias, has been the subject of task force study.[92] In 1990, the ABA added Canon 3(B)(5) to its Model Code of Judicial Conduct, which included a prohibition on gender bias, as well as commentary (accompanying the rule) directing judges to avoid sexual harassment.[93] In 2007, when the ABA Commission that revised the Model Code of Judicial Conduct proposed to delete the specific reference to "sexual" harassment from commentary accompanying Rule 2.3—to further the goal of proscribing harassment in all forms—several Commission witnesses objected on the grounds that the move could be misconstrued as diminished concern for sexual harassment as a prevalent form of gender bias.[94] In response, the Commission amended the black-letter rule to bar judges from "manifest[ing] bias or prejudice, or engag[ing] in harassment," which the rule defined to include bias, prejudice, and harassment based on sex or gender.[95] In addition, the 2007 Code added a comment that described sexual harassment

---

[81] Brad Heath, *Racial Gap in U.S. Arrest Rates: "Staggering Disparity,"* U.S.A. TODAY, November 19, 2014.

[82] Becky Pettit & Bruce Western, *Mass Imprisonment and the Life Course: Race and Class Inequality in U.S. Incarceration*, 69 AM. SOC. REV. 151 (2004).

[83] *Id.*

[84] DAVID B. ROTTMAN, RANDALL HANSEN, NICOLE MOTT, & LYNN GRIMES, PERCEPTIONS OF THE COURTS IN YOUR COMMUNITY: THE INFLUENCE OF EXPERIENCE, RACE AND ETHNICITY, FINAL REPORT 10 (2003), available at http://www.ncjrs.gov/pdffiles1/nij/grants/201302.pdf.

[85] *In re* Agresta, 476 N.E.2d 285 (N.Y. 1985).

[86] *In re* Pearson, 386 S.E.2d 249 (S.C. 1989).

[87] Gonzalez v. Comm'n on Judicial Performance, 657 P.2d 372 (Cal. 1983).

[88] *In re* Poyfair, Wash. Jud. Disp. Op. 6691-F-153 (Wash. Comm. Jud. Cond.) 2012 WL 1952384, May 4, 2012.

[89] *In re* Cook, Unreported Determination (N.Y Comm'n, Nov. 19, 1986).

[90] *Id.*

[91] *In re* Judicial Disciplinary Proceedings Against Gorenstein, 434 N.W.2d 603 (1989).

[92] NATIONAL CENTER FOR STATE COURTS, GENDER AND RACIAL FAIRNESS-STATE LINKS, http://www.ncsc.org/Topics/Access-and-Fairness/Gender-and-Racial-Fairness/State-Links.aspx?cat=Gender%20Fairness%20Task%20Forces%20and%20Reports.

[93] ABA MODEL CODE OF JUDICIAL CONDUCT, Canon 3(B)(5) (1990).

[94] CHARLES E. GEYH [SIC] AND W. WILLIAM HODES, REPORTERS' NOTES TO THE MODEL CODE OF JUDICIAL CONDUCT 29 (2009).

[95] *Id.*

as encompassing "sexual advances, requests for sexual favors, and other verbal or physical conduct of a sexual nature that is unwelcome."[96]

Gender bias problems have tended to fall into one of two categories: conduct that demeans or disparages lawyers, parties, or others because of their gender; and conduct in the vein of unwelcome sexual advances or harassment. Examples from the former category include infantilizing female lawyers as "little girls," "babes," or "lawyerettes,[97] demeaning attempts at teasing or humor directed at women,[98] and marginalizing women as loathsome or inferior.[99] Harassment, on the other hand, must be understood with reference to the power judges wield over parties, lawyers, and court staff, where the targets of unwelcome advances may fear the consequences of objecting or resisting. Judges have been sanctioned for conduct ranging from crass remarks,[100] to persistent advances,[101] groping,[102] and preferential treatment in exchange for sexual favors.[103]

Improper bias directed against classes of people includes but is not limited to the grounds listed in Rule 2.3. For example, judges have been sanctioned for violating Rule 2.3 for evidencing bias against victims of domestic violence,[104] and for favoring parties based on their statements of religious belief and practice.[105]

### § 6-2.3(b) Respecting Parties' Rights to Be Heard

Judicial impartiality includes a procedural dimension. The judge who is biased for or against a party, or is closed-minded with respect to the issues before the court, can manifest their partiality by dispensing with or contorting the procedural protections to which parties are entitled. Hence, the Model Code of Judicial Conduct provides that "[a] judge shall accord to every person who has a legal interest in a proceeding. . .the right to be heard according to law," with the accompanying explanation that, "[t]he right to be

---

[96] MODEL CODE, Rule 2.3, Comment 4.

[97] Unreported Determination (N.Y. Comm'n, Jan. 26, 1983) 1983 WL 189803 (judge reprimanded for demeaning reference to female attorney as "little girl" after she objected to the reference); In re Barr, Opinion of Tribunal Appointed by the Supreme Court of Texas, 13 S.W. 3d 525 (Feb. 13, 1998) (judge removed, *inter alia*, for referring to female attorneys as "babes").

[98] *In re* Henderson, 343 P.3d 518 (Kan. 2015) (judge suspended, *inter alia,* for sexually offensive humor); *In re* Doolittle, Unreported Determination (N.Y. Comm'n, Jun. 13, 1985) 1985 WL 286211 (judge sanctioned for implying that female attorneys would receive preferential treatment depending on their appearance).

[99] *In re* Lewis, JC-13-042-C (N.H. Jud. Cond. Comm., Apr. 1, 2014) (judge avoided more serious sanction than reprimand, by retiring after making "disparaging comments about female attorneys," concerning "the negative effect the presence of female attorneys may have on the public's perception of the legal profession"); *In re* Greene, 403 S.E.2d 257 (N.C. 1991) (referring to organizations that assist battered women as "a one-sided, man-hating bunch of females, a pack of she-dogs"); Complaint Concerning Kirby, 354 N.W.2d 410 (Minn. 1984) (judge censured for referring to counsel as "lawyerette," and "attorney generalette").

[100] *In re* Disciplinary Proceedings Against Deming, 736 P.2d 639 (Wash. 1987) (judge removed, *inter alia*, for comments on the physical attributes of female attorneys, including a statement to a prosecutor that "I would really like to jump your bones" and a directive to a female intern that she "take [her] clothes off and bend over").

[101] *In re* Henriksen, 70 A.3d 206 (Del. 2012) (judge sanctioned for persistent efforts to establish an inappropriate, social relationship with female attorney).

[102] Public Warning of DePena, CJC No. 08-0073-MU, Texas State Comm'n on Judicial Conduct, Aug. 29, 2008) (judge warned for kissing and fondling female detention officers).

[103] *In re* Gravely, 467 S.E.2d 924 (S.C. 1996) (judge censured for soliciting sex with a litigant facing eviction in exchange for helping her stay in her home).

[104] *In re* Romano (N.Y. Aug. 7, 1998) 1998 WL 543813 (judge removed, *inter alia*, for evidencing bias against victims of domestic violence).

[105] Judicial Inquiry & Review Bd. of Supreme Court v. Fink, 532 A.2d 358 (Pa. 1987).

heard is an essential component of a fair and impartial system of justice."[106] The duty to accord parties their rights to be heard intersects with other responsibilities. For example, a judge can deny parties their right to be heard by intemperately silencing a party, contrary to the duty to be patient, dignified and courteous with litigants under Rule 2.3.[107] Similarly, a judge can deny parties their right to be heard by willfully denying them access to counsel in derogation of their duty to uphold and apply the law under Rule 2.2.[108]

Even if a judge is impartial in fact, the judge's failure to respect procedural rights can undermine the perceived impartiality of the judge with litigants, to the detriment of the court's legitimacy.[109] As discussed in § 6-2.1(a), judges are bound by a duty of diligence that subsumes a duty to administer their courts efficiently. To that end, judges are authorized by rules of procedure to facilitate the settlement of disputes.[110] In their zeal to reduce docket congestion, however, there is the risk that judges will impose undue pressure on litigants to settle their claims, to the detriment of their procedural rights.[111] Hence, Model Code Rule 2.6(b) provides that "[a] judge may encourage parties to a proceeding and their lawyers to settle matters in dispute but shall not act in a manner that coerces any party into settlement."

Settlement negotiations implicate the ethics of administering procedural justice in an additional way. The judge who oversees settlement negotiations is positioned to learn things about the parties and the strengths and weaknesses of their respective cases that would not necessarily be adduced at trial. The judge who strives to facilitate settlement may unavoidably form views about the parties and the value of the case, not from the perspective of an impartial adjudicator, but from that of a facilitator bent on ending the litigation by settlement, for whom trial may represent a perceived failure of one or both parties to acquiesce to a resolution the judge regards as reasonable. Should settlement talks fail, the judge's previous role as settlement promoter could color both her judgment and ability to perform as impartial adjudicator at trial. As a consequence, some dispute resolution scholars have argued that the tasks of overseeing settlement talks and of presiding at trial should be assigned to different people.[112] The Model Code does not insist on such explicit bifurcation, but does warn that disqualification may be necessary: "[d]espite a judge's best efforts, there may be instances when information obtained during settlement discussions could influence a judge's decision-making during trial.

---

[106] MODEL CODE, Rule 2.6(a); Comment 1.

[107] CHARLES GARDNER GEYH, JAMES J. ALFINI, STEVEN LUBET & JEFFREY SHAMAN, JUDICIAL CONDUCT AND ETHICS § 3.02[3] (5th ed. 2013) ("A judge who is impatient with a litigant runs the risk of violating the duty to accord the litigant 'full right to be heard according to law.' ").

[108] *In re* Gustafson, 756 P.2d 21 (Or. 1988) (judge's refusal to appoint defendant's choice of public defender because of personal differences with that lawyer simultaneously disregarded the law and deprived the defendant of his right to be heard).

[109] TOM R. TYLER, ET AL., SOCIAL JUSTICE IN A DIVERSE SOCIETY 82–83 (1997); Tom R. Tyler, *The Role of Perceived Injustice in Defendants' Evaluation of their Courtroom Experience*, 18 L. & SOC. REV. 51, 69–70 (1984).

[110] *See. e.g.*, Fed. R. Civ. P. 16 (authorizing pretrial conferences for the purpose of promoting settlement).

[111] Kothe v. Smith, 771 F.2d 667 (2d Cir. 1985) (imposing sanctions on defendant for failure to settle case was improper because the law does not permit "trial judges to effect settlements through coercion").

[112] Nancy Welsh, Donna Stienstra & Bobbi McAdoo, *The Application of Procedural Justice Research to Judicial Actions and Techniques in Settlement Sessions*, *in* THE MULTI-TASKING JUDGE: COMPARATIVE JUDICIAL DISPUTE RESOLUTION 60–63, 68–69, 70 (Tania Sourdin and Archie Zariski, eds., 2013); Nancy A. Welsh, *Magistrate Judges, Settlement, and Procedural Justice*, 16 NEV. L. J. 983 (2016).

And, in such instances, the judge should consider whether disqualification may be appropriate."[113]

### § 6-2.3(c) Public Statements on Pending and Future Cases

The real and perceived fairness of judicial proceedings can be affected by what the judge says or does outside the courtroom, which is why judges are subject to the overarching directive that they "act at all times" in a manner that promotes public confidence in the independence, integrity and impartiality of the judiciary.[114] The ethics of extrajudicial conduct generally, is discussed in § 6-3.1(a). However, when it comes to public comments on pending or impending cases, and pledges or promises to decide future cases in specified ways, the direct impact of extrajudicial speech on judicial duties and impartiality warrants elaboration here.

#### *§ 6-2.3(c)(1) Comments on Pending and Impending Cases*

Model Code, Rule 2.10(A) imposes significant limits on what judges can say about pending and impending cases:

> A judge shall not make any public statement that might reasonably be expected to affect the outcome or impair the fairness of a matter pending or impending in any court, or make any nonpublic statement that might substantially interfere with a fair trial or hearing.

Prohibited public statements do not include explanations of court procedure, or statements "in the course of official duties"—meaning that proscribed speech is limited to statements judges make off the bench.[115]

Nonetheless, the reach of this rule is sweeping. Rule 2.10(A) prohibits judges from not only commenting on cases pending or impending before them, but before *any* court, in any jurisdiction.[116] Thus, judges have been disciplined for appearing on television programs to comment on cases pending in other courts.[117] The rule ostensibly affords judges the wiggle-room to make public statements on pending matters that cannot "reasonably be expected to affect the outcome or impair [their] fairness." That language, however, was an innovation of the 1990 Model Code that remains in tension with deeply entrenched norms, which embrace the view that good judges let their opinions and court transcripts do the talking, and avoid gratuitous extrajudicial commentary. As Judith Kaye, Chief Judge of the New York Court of Appeals, explained:

> [T]o secure an impartial forum, even for their most vocal critics, and to assure the dignity of the judicial process, judges by and large must stay out of the fray. They do not duel with public officials about the correctness of their decisions; they do not conduct press conferences about cases; and they have no call-in

---

[113] MODEL CODE, Rule 2.6, Comment 3.

[114] MODEL CODE, Rule 1.2.

[115] MODEL CODE, Rule 2.10(D).

[116] Florida Supreme Court Comm. on Standards Governing Conduct of Judges, Op. 96–25 (1996) (surveying cases in other jurisdictions and concluding that it would be improper for a judge to serve as a paid guest on a television talk show where he would comment on topical legal questions, in part, because it would violate the state corollary to Rule 2.10(A)).

[117] *In re* Broadbelt, 146 N.J. 501 (1996).

radio and television shows to explain their rulings. They rely on their decisions, whether written or oral, to speak for themselves.[118]

The Rule anticipates that a judge will feel the greatest need to comment publicly on pending cases as a means to clarify or correct what the judge regards as mistakes or misunderstands of court rulings created by the media, the parties, the lawyers, or others. Rule 2.10(E) thus states that "a judge may respond directly or through a third party to allegations in the media or elsewhere concerning a judge's conduct in the matter," which seems to afford judges latitude to respond publicly to their critics. But the 2007 Model Code made that rule "subject to the requirements of paragraph (A)", which effectively renders paragraph E a nullity: [i]f the judge's response satisfies paragraph (A), then the judge is permitted to make the statement without recourse to paragraph (E); and if the judge's response fails to satisfy paragraph (A), then the judge is forbidden from making the statement, paragraph (E) notwithstanding.

While there are cases in which courts have declined to sanction judges for responding to their critics in pending cases, such cases remain exceptional.[119] When judges share their views on pending cases outside the courtroom, the prevailing concern remains that they can appear to be taking sides prematurely or to be overly invested in the proceeding, to the detriment of their real and perceived impartiality. Hence, judges have been disciplined for making comments to reporters criticizing a party's discovery request,[120] and holding "off the record" conversations with a reporter in the midst of a murder trial.[121]

In *United States v. Microsoft Corporation*, the District of Columbia Circuit Court of Appeals found that a trial judge's secret interviews with select reporters prior to entering final judgment on the case required the judge's disqualification.[122] During those clandestine meetings, the judge offered his views on the "credibility of witnesses, the validity of legal theories, the culpability of the defendant, [and] the choice of remedy."[123] The appellate court found that the trial judge's violations of 28 U.S.C. § 455(a), as well as Canons 2, 3(A)(4), and 3(A)(6) were "deliberate, repeated, and flagrant."[124]

In *Ligon v. City of New York*, a racial profiling case that challenged the New York Police Department's "stop and frisk" policy, the United States District Court Judge Shira A. Scheindlin participated in "a series of media interviews and public statements" while the case was pending, "purporting to respond publicly to criticism of the District Court."[125] The U.S. Court of Appeals for the Second Circuit reassigned the case to a different judge on its own initiative, concluding that the judge's statements gave rise to an appearance of impropriety.[126] The circuit court received significant criticism for its decision, and subsequently issued a second opinion explaining the reassignment. The

---

[118] Judith Kaye, *Safeguarding a Crown Jewel: Judicial Independence and Lawyer Criticism of Courts*, 25 HOFSTRA L. REV. 703, 712 (1997).

[119] *Memorandum on Ethical Constraints*, in UNCERTAIN JUSTICE, 173, 176–83. (New York: The Century Foundation Press, 2000).

[120] Inquiry Concerning a Judge (Andrews), 875 So.2d 442 (Fla. 2004).

[121] *In re* Hayes, 543 So.2d 105 (Fla. 1989).

[122] *See id.* (citing United States v. Microsoft Corp., 253 F.3d 34 (D.C. Cir. 2001)).

[123] *Id.*

[124] *Id.*

[125] Ligon v. City of New York, 538 Fed. App'x 101, 102–103 (2d Cir. 2013).

[126] *Id.*

circuit panel referenced an article that quoted the judge as stating about city officials, that "I know I'm not their favorite judge," and additional articles which reported that the judge "describes herself as a jurist who is skeptical of law enforcement, in contrast to certain of her colleagues, whom she describes as inclined to favor the government."[127] The court explained, that "interviews in which the presiding judge draws such distinctions between herself and her colleagues might lead a reasonable observer to question the judge's impartiality."[128]

### *§ 6-2.3(c)(2) Pledges or Promises Concerning Future Cases*

Rules that prohibit judges from publicly sharing their views on pending and impending litigation, as discussed in § 6-2.3(c)(1), do not apply to comments on issues the court is likely to confront at some uncertain point in the future, where the impact on the judge's real or perceived impartiality is more attenuated. In *Republican Party of Minnesota v. White*, the United States Supreme Court held that ethics rules barring judicial candidates from announcing their views on issues that may come before them later do not further the state's interest in preserving judicial impartiality and violate the candidates' first amendment freedom of speech.[129]

With respect to statements concerning future cases, as distinct from those pending or impending, Rule 2.10(B) prohibits judges from making "pledges, promises or commitments that are inconsistent with the impartial performance of the adjudicative duties of judicial office" in regard to "cases, controversies, or issues likely to come before the court." This restriction leaves room for judges to announce their views on issues likely to arise in future cases, subject to the uncertain lines that separate announcements of views from pledges, promises, or commitments, and distinguish future cases from impending ones. Although the constitutionality of Rule 2.10(B) remains uncertain after *White*,[130] one can reasonably argue that a judge who commits herself to reach a specified outcome in a future case constrains her latitude to decide that case impartially and with an open mind in ways that a judge who announces her views in a more general way does not.

For example, in *In re Kinsey*, the Florida Supreme Court found that the first amendment did not protect a judicial candidate's statement of intent to "help law enforcement by putting criminals where they belong—behind bars!"[131] The judge's pledges to victims of crime, "promising to bend over backward for them and stressing the point that she identified with them 'above all else'" adversely affected her "appearance of impartiality and fitness as a judge."[132] *The Kinsey* Court expressed particular concern for "criminal defendants" and "criminal defense lawyers," both of whom would have genuine concerns about their respective abilities to face a "fair and impartial tribunal."[133]

---

[127] Ligon v. City of New York, 736 F.3d 118, 127 (2d Cir. 2013).

[128] *Id.*

[129] Republican Party of Minnesota v. White, 536 U.S. 765 (2002); *see* discussion at § 6-3.2.

[130] Cases invalidating rules prohibiting pledges, promises, or commitments include *Duwe v. Alexander*, 490 F. Supp. 2d 968 (W.D. Wis. 2007); *North Dakota Family Alliance, Inc. v. Bader*, 361 F. Supp. 2d 1021 (D.N.D. 2005); and *Family Trust Found. of Ky. v. Wolnitzek*, 345 F. Supp. 2d 672 (E.D. Ky. 2004)). Cases upholding such rules include *In re* Kinsey, 842 So.2d 77 (Fla. 2003), *cert. denied*, 540 U.S. 825 (2003); *In re* Watson, 794 N.E.2d 1 (N.Y. 2003).

[131] 842 So.2d at 88.

[132] *Id.*

[133] *Id.* at 89.

Courts have also found that the first amendment does not guarantee judges a right to publicly endorse a political candidate.[134] In so holding, courts such as the Supreme Court of New Mexico have stated, "the prohibition against judges making political endorsements is purposefully designed to preclude judges from engaging in conduct that has the potential for creating bias or the appearance of bias for or against a party to a proceeding."[135]

## § 6-2.4 *EX PARTE* COMMUNICATIONS

### § 6-2.4(a) In General

*Ex parte* communications concern communications initiated by or with the judge about a pending or impending case that do not include all parties and their counsel. In an adversarial system, in which the judge is supposed to serve the role of a detached neutral, the prospect of the judge sidling up to one side to discuss the case outside the hearing of the other side, has the potential to implicate all three values core to judicial ethics, discussed in § 6-1.4: impartiality, integrity, and independence. First, *ex parte* discussions of pending cases with some parties but not others, exposes the judge to one-sided argumentation and those with whom the judge communicates to potential coercion, which opens the door to favoritism or animus that can undermine real and perceived impartiality. Second, *ex parte* communications initiated for the benefit of parties with whom the judge has a relationship that she allows to influence her judgment, reflect behavioral dependence.[136] Third, *ex parte* communications driven by corrupt motives to fix cases reflect a fundamental lack of integrity.

Model Code, Rule 2.9, provides that a judge "shall not initiate, permit, or consider *ex parte* communications, or consider other communications made to the judge outside the presence of other parties or their lawyers, concerning a pending or impending matter."[137] This general rule is subject to enumerated exceptions. For example, the rule against *ex parte* communications does not extend to communications for "scheduling, administrative, or emergency purposes," which the rule distinguishes from communications on "substantive matters," that directly implicate the policy concerns summarized in the preceding paragraph.[138] Even then, this exception applies only when the judge does not "reasonably believe[ ]" that the communication will advantage parties to the communication, and parties excluded are promptly notified and offered an opportunity to respond.[139]

A second all-purpose exception to the rule against *ex parte* communication is that judges may communicate with their clerks, staff, and fellow judges (except judges who are disqualified from the case or who may review the matter on appeal), on a theory similar to that which effectively defines the attorney to include the attorney's staff and

---

[134] *In re* Vincent, 172 P.3d 605 (N.M. 2007).

[135] *Id.* at 608 ("Under the specific facts of this case, [the judge's] endorsement of Mayor Standley for reelection would certainly create the appearance of bias were the mayor or anyone associated with his administration to appear before [the judge] in an actual case.").

[136] *See, e.g., In re* Vann, Pa. Jud. Disc. LEXIS 16 (2015) (finding that a magistrate judge's failure to disqualify herself from a case involving a close family friend required suspension because the judge failed to act in a neutral and detached manner when granting protection from abuse petitions and issuing arrest warrants).

[137] MODEL CODE, Rule 2.9(A).

[138] MODEL CODE, Rule 2.9(A)(1).

[139] *Id.*

colleagues for purposes of the attorney-client privilege.[140] By the same token, however, because the judge's staff is an extension of the judge, *ex parte* communications that would be improper for the judge, are improper for the judge's staff.[141] Along similar lines, judges are authorized to consult with their own counsel *ex parte*, on matters relating to the ethics of their conduct.[142]

A third general exception to the rule against *ex parte* communication is that with the consent of the parties, the judge can meet with the parties *ex parte* to facilitate settlement.[143] This exception proceeds from the premise that *ex parte* communications can facilitate settlement talks insofar as parties and their counsel may be more candid or willing to make concessions with the judge, outside the presence of opposing parties and their counsel. Such communications, however, can raise issues discussed in § 6-2.5(b)(2) if settlement talks break down and the case proceeds to trial after the judge has received information *ex parte* that could affect the judge's perceived impartiality.

A fourth general exception to the rule against *ex parte* communications is for communications "expressly authorized by law." While this is intended as a general catchall, it has acquired specific relevance in the context of the so-called "problem solving courts or "therapeutic courts" movement.[144] This movement, which began with specialized drug courts, mental health courts, and veterans' courts (and has since spilled into courts of more general jurisdiction (such as juvenile courts and family courts), seeks to respond to the legal issues that bring people into court, by addressing the chronic substance abuse or mental health problems that underlie those issues. In such courts, judges function predominantly as engaged problem-solvers, rather than detached neutrals. Because these judges work cooperatively with offenders, families, and community service-providers, their work can be complicated by traditional rules against *ex parte* communication. The Model Code acknowledges this complication, and notes that the "expressly authorized by law" exception can be triggered by rules governing problem solving court that permit *ex parte* communications.[145]

A strict reading of the rule against *ex parte* communications can sometimes be in tension with a local practice that tolerates *ex parte* communications forbidden by the traditional rule. Infractions have sometimes been excused on that basis.[146] Other courts,

---

[140] MODEL CODE, Rule 2.9(A)(3), Comment 5; *see also* Gregory C. Sisk, Legal Ethics and the Practice of Law § 4-6.2 (discussing the lawyer's implied authorization "to share client confidential information with other persons in the law firm as necessary to perform the representation"), § 4-6.3(b)(4) (explaining that the attorney-client privilege extends to members of the lawyer's staff assisting in the matter). Such personnel include court appointed receivers. *In Re* Disqualification of McGee, 937 N.E.2d 1019 (Ohio 2009).

[141] MODEL CODE, Rules 2.9(D) ("A judge shall make reasonable efforts, including providing appropriate supervision, to ensure that this Rule is not violated by court staff"); 2.12, Comment 1 ("A judge may not direct court personnel to engage in conduct on the judge's behalf. . .when such conduct would violate the Code if undertaken by the judge").

[142] MODEL CODE, Rule 2.9, Comment 7. For a discussion of the exception relevant to judges who consult *ex parte* with legal experts on questions of law at issue in their cases, see § 6-2.4(b).

[143] MODEL CODE, Rule 2.9(A)(4).

[144] For a description of problem solving courts, see http://www.ncsc.org/Topics/Alternative-Dockets/Problem-Solving-Courts/Home.aspx.

[145] MODEL CODE, Rule 2.9, Comment 4 ("A judge may initiate, permit, or consider *ex parte* communications expressly authorized by law, such as when serving on therapeutic or problem-solving courts, mental health courts, or drug courts. In this capacity, judges may assume a more interactive role with parties, treatment providers, probation officers, social workers, and others."). *See also In re* Disqualification of Giesler, 985 N.E.2d 486 (Ohio 2011). (applying rule authorizing *ex parte* communications "when administering a specialized docket").

[146] *In re* Mosley, 102 P.3d 555, 561 (Nev. 2004).

however, have rejected local practice as a defense.[147] The more coherent approach, when faced with a conflict between the rule and local practice, is to amend the rule, alter the practice, or lessen the severity of the sanction in light of the judge's good faith in following local practice, rather than to read the state-wide ethics rule to include unstated exceptions for entrenched, local deviations.

When an improper, *ex parte* communication occurs, the Rule directs the judge to "make provision promptly to notify the parties of the substance of the communication and provide the parties with an opportunity to respond."[148] With respect to willful violations that warrant discipline, such a directive may seem naïve; frequently, however, improper ex *parte* communications occur due to no fault of the judge, or, at worst, a momentary oversight on the judge's part. Consider, for example, when a party or lawyer approaches a judge outside of court and makes an unsolicited statement about the case before the judge can end the conversation, or when the judge does not recognize that an improper communication has occurred until after the conversation has ended. In such situations, if the judge notifies all parties about the improper or unsolicited communications, timely notification can address concerns that the party excluded from the conversation might otherwise have, or provide the excluded party with the information it needs to frame a request to disqualify the judge, as discussed in § 6-2.5.

### § 6-2.4(b) Prohibited Communications

Improper *ex parte* communications typically occur between the judge and attorneys, parties, witnesses, or law enforcement. Improper *ex parte* communications between judges and lawyers occur with some frequency because the opportunities for such communication are plentiful, and, often, the circumstances under which those opportunities arise are seemingly harmless. Judges have preexisting relationships with many of the local lawyers who appear before them, and become acquainted with many more who regularly appear before them. When those judges and lawyers cross paths in courthouse halls, restaurants, bar association functions, and even on social media, it is natural to engage in small talk, and equally natural for such small talk to turn to the case they have in common. Communications that simply mention the case or allude to an upcoming hearing may be harmless, but problems arise when such communications transcend idle conversation. Judges have been disciplined for communications initiated by other judges or attorneys on such issues as the merits of the case,[149] admission of evidence,[150] and next steps in the proceeding.[151] Such communications often inure to the

---

[147] Thomas v. Judicial Conduct Comm'n, 77 S.W.3d 578 (Ky. 2002).

[148] MODEL CODE, Rule 2.9(B).

[149] *In re* Complaint Against White, 651 N.W.2d 551, 562 (Neb. 2002) (finding that the "potential that a case may be remanded to a trial judge provides an additional rationale for prohibiting *ex parte* communications between the trial judge and the parties even while the matter is on appeal"); In the Matter of More, Determination (N.Y. Comm'n on Judicial Conduct, March 13, 1995) (following oral argument on a motion to dismiss, judge called the assistant district attorney and defense counsel separately to ask how he should rule); Harrington v. State, 584 N.E.2d 558, 561 (Ind. 1992) (trial court judge violated Canon 3, "forsaking his stance of neutrality" in writing letter to attorney general suggesting that attorney general file motion for rehearing of appellate decision reversing trial court).

[150] In the matter of Diamond, order (July 11, 2013) (http://www.judiciary.state.nj.us/pressrel/2013/pr130711a.pdf) (*ex parte* assistance to prosecutor on admissibility) Judicial Inquiry & Review Bd. v. Snyder, 523 A.2d 294 (Pa. 1987) (*ex parte* assistance on issues including admission of evidence).

[151] *In re* Beckham, 620 S.E.2d 69, 70, 76 (S.C. 2005) (after finding defendant guilty of criminal domestic violence, a magistrate judge reopened a case based on an *ex parte* communication with defendant's attorney and was suspended for 60 days); Roberts v. Comm'n on Judicial Performance, 661 P.2d 1064 (Cal. 1983) (en banc) (denying the contention that trial judge may participate personally in *ex parte* communications with real

benefit of the lawyer involved, but are improper regardless.[152] Recurring problems have arisen with judges who approach lawyers *ex parte* with instructions to draft prospective orders favorable to the lawyers' clients, for the judge to sign.[153]

Judges have likewise been subjected to discipline for *ex parte* communication with parties. Frequently these communications inure to the benefit of the party.[154] Such communications sometimes give rise to or result from relationships that influence the judge's conduct, which violates not only the rule against *ex parte* communications, but also Rule 2.4, which admonishes judges to avoid such influences, as discussed in § 6-2.2(b). In other cases, *ex parte* communications have worked to the disadvantage of the party involved, for example, when judges have contacted parties for the purpose of extracting guilty pleas or collecting judgments.[155]

Judges have also been subject to sanction for communications with witnesses—including victims—outside the presence of parties and counsel.[156] One limited exception to the general rule against *ex parte* communications with witnesses, concerns legal experts that judges may consult on their own initiative, which, in effect, enables judges to consult trusted law professors on thorny legal issues. Provided that the parties are afforded notice and an opportunity to object and respond, the Model Code permits judges to consult *ex parte* with a "disinterested expert on issues of law.[157] While these experts do not testify and hence are not witnesses per se, they inform the court's analysis of operative law in much the same way as expert witnesses inform the fact-finder's analysis of operative facts. The peril of such consultations is that a biased legal expert could influence the judge outside the presence of the lawyers or parties; the rule thus requires

party concerning subsequent appellate proceedings reviewing judge's order), *disapproved on other grounds*, Doan v. Commission on Judicial Performance, 902 P.2d 272 (Cal. 1995); Matter of Disciplinary Proceeding Against Aulik, 429 N.W.2d 759, 761 (Wis. 1988) (although judge and attorney were involved a chance meeting outside attorney's office building, judge violated rule against *ex parte* contact when judge informed attorney that his firm might be involved in a frivolous lawsuit, and then, later, mailed attorney a summary of his law clerk's research on that lawsuit).

[152] *In re* Starcher, 457 S.E.2d 147, 148–49 (W. Va. 1995) (judge coached the prosecutor to have some supporters "e.g., the victims . . . and some female attorneys" present in the courtroom during closing argument, to use the term "serial rapist," and to appear more emotional before the jury); *In re* Clayton, 504 So.2d 394, 395 (1987) (a judge, on four separate occasions, conducted *ex parte* proceedings with defense counsel and was publicly remanded for "assuming the role of an advocate on behalf of the defendants").

[153] Disciplinary Counsel v. Stuard, 901 N.E.2d 788 (Ohio 2009) (a judge was reprimanded for *ex parte* communications in which he asked a prosecutor to assist him in writing an opinion sentencing the defendant to death); Written Public Censure, Seventh Circuit Judicial Counsel (1985). *See* letter from Walter J. Cummings, Chief Judge of the Seventh Circuit, to Charles B. McCormick, United States Bankruptcy Court, Northern Dist. of Ill. (May 7, 1985) (a federal bankruptcy judge allowed attorneys for one party to draft the Court's rulings without any notice to the other counsel).

[154] Fletcher v. Comm'n on Judicial Performance, 968 P.2d 958, 967 (Cal. 1998) (finding that a judge who failed to disqualify himself from a narcotics possession case after making *ex parte* contact with defendant's family members committed prejudicial misconduct).

[155] *In re* Mayville, Unreported Determination (N.Y. Comm'n 1984) (a judge made multiple attempts to collect debts for local businesses, including speaking with both defendants as well as members of their families about the debts, and, in several cases, intimidating individuals into paying the disputed amounts); *In re* Yengo, 72 N.J. 425 (1977) (a judge developed a bias in favor of the complainant after meeting with the complainant prior to the defendant's arrival in court).

[156] In the Matter of McCormick, Determination (N.Y. Comm'n on Judicial Conduct, June 9, 1993) (a judge initiated *ex parte* contact with the complaining witness in order to express judge's desire that witness withdraw his complaint); *In re* Cummings, 211 P.3d 1136, 1138–39 (Alaska 2009) (finding that a district court judge, who engaged in intentional *ex parte* communications by passing multiple notes to state troopers serving as witnesses for the prosecution team, violated statutes and canons of the Code of Judicial Conduct barring the appearance of impropriety).

[157] MODEL CODE, Rule 2.9(A)(2).

judges to supply the parties with notice of the consultation and an opportunity to respond.

Finally, judges have been disciplined for *ex parte* communications with representatives from law enforcement. As with lawyers who appear before them, judges become acquainted with police officers, sheriffs, constables, parole officers, and others who play a role in the administration of justice and appear regularly in their courts. Problems arise when judges communicate with such personnel *ex parte*, for the purpose of assisting, supervising, or coordinating with law enforcement.[158]

### § 6-2.4(c) *Ex Parte* Investigations

*Ex parte* investigations concern information that judges obtain independently of the parties about a pending or impending case.[159] *Ex parte* investigations, unsupervised by the adversarial process, can lead the judge to rely on one-sided sources of information to the detriment of her impartiality. Hence, the rule governing *ex parte* investigations states that "[a] judge shall not investigate facts in a matter independently, and shall consider only the evidence presented and any facts that may properly be judicially noticed."[160] An accompanying comment adds that, "[t]he prohibition against a judge investigating the facts in a matter extends to information available in all mediums, including electronic."[161]

An important exchange on the limits of *ex parte* Internet investigation occurred between two circuit judges in *Rowe* v. *Gibson*.[162] Rowe filed a 1983 action against administrators of the state prison where he was incarcerated, alleging that they violated his Eighth Amendment right against cruel and unusual punishment by administering medication he had been prescribed for gastroesophageal reflux disease (GERD), at the wrong times or depriving him of the medication altogether. The district court granted summary judgment in light of an affidavit from Dr. Wolfe, a prison physician who testified that the medication was unnecessary and had not been administered at inappropriate times.

Judge Richard Posner, writing for the Seventh Circuit, reversed and remanded for trial, concluding that there was a genuine dispute of material fact. In the course of his opinion, Judge Posner cited Internet sources that summarized Dr. Wolfe's credentials, described GERD, discussed the relationship between eating and GERD pain, described the prescribed medication, and specified that the medication should be administered before meals. Judge David Hamilton dissented in part: "Dr. Wolfe's testimony was undisputed. We have no business reversing summary judgment based on our own, untested factual research. By doing so, the majority has gone well beyond the appropriate role of an appellate court." Judge Posner disagreed: "We are not deeming

---

[158] *In re* Reeves, Unreported Determination (N.Y. Comm'n), *aff'd*, 63 N.Y.2d 105 (1984) (a judge initiated an *ex parte* conference with a probation department employee, during which they discussed a case pending before the judge); *In re* Mullen, Unreported Determination (N.Y. Comm'n 1986) (a judge held a series of *ex parte* meetings with law enforcement officers concerning defendant's arrest; judge made numerous decisions—including quadrupling defendant's bond—based on such meetings); *In re* Ross, 428 A.2d 858 (Me. 1981) (a judge requested that a police officer file charges against a friend's son to teach the son about the dangers of speeding).

[159] Elizabeth Thornburg, *The Curious Appellate Judge: Ethical Limits on Independent Research*, 28 REV. OF LIT. 131 (2008).

[160] MODEL CODE, Rule 2.9(C).

[161] MODEL CODE, Rule 2.9, Comment 6.

[162] 798 F.3d 622 (7th Cir. 2015).

the Internet evidence cited in this opinion conclusive or even certifying it as being probably correct, though it may well be correct since it is drawn from reputable medical websites. We use it only to underscore the existence of a genuine dispute of material fact. Particularly in cases such as this, where there is a lack of "parity between the adversaries," Judge Posner was loath to "fetishize adversary procedure in a pure eighteenth-century form,"[163] which would be "heartless" and "doom the plaintiff's case regardless of the merits."[164]

*Rowe* was not a disciplinary matter and did not discuss the ethics of *ex parte* investigations *per se*. Unlike the Model Code, the Code of Conduct for U.S. Judges does not mention such investigations in its canon governing *ex parte* communications. But the majority and dissent both recognized that the factual information the majority drew from Internet sources was not so generally known or readily determined as to be subject to judicial notice; hence, had Rule 2.9 applied, the investigation would seem problematic. *Rowe* thus illustrates the temptation that the Internet creates for judges to hunt facts and right wrongs by undertaking online investigations at the expense of traditional procedural safeguards of the adversarial process that evidentiary and ethical rules seek to preserve.

## § 6-2.5 JUDICIAL DISQUALIFICATION

### § 6-2.5(a) Introduction to Disqualification

Judicial disqualification is the means by which judges who are less than impartial or whose impartiality is in doubt can be removed from a case *sua sponte* or at the request of a party. Some courts and commentators use the term "recusal" interchangeably with disqualification, while others use "recusal" when referring to judges who withdraw from cases on their own initiative. Because federal and state disqualification rules are derived from the Model Code of Judicial Conduct, which does not use the term recusal at all, the term disqualification will be used here for all purposes, except when "recusal" is embedded in quoted material.

Judicial disqualification is governed by statutes, rules, and the due process clause of the United States Constitution. It is simultaneously a procedural device that protects the rights of litigants to a fair and impartial judge, and an ethical rule that serves as a source of guidance and (in state systems, at least) articulates standards of conduct that judicial conduct commissions enforce in disciplinary proceedings. In the federal system, for example, substantially similar disqualification rules appear in two places: a procedural statute that requires judges to disqualify themselves under specified circumstances;[165] and a canon in the Code of Conduct for U.S. Judges,[166] which "is the law with respect to the ethical obligations of federal judges."[167] Insofar as the operative disqualification standards in procedural and ethical settings are functionally identical, cases applying those standards as procedural rules in litigation and ethical rules in

---

[163] *Id.*

[164] *Id.* at 630.

[165] 28 U.S.C. § 455. A second, infrequently used procedural statute, 28 U.S.C. § 144, not discussed here. For a discussion of § 144, see CHARLES GARDNER GEYH, JUDICIAL DISQUALIFICATION: AN ANALYSIS OF FEDERAL LAW 83–94 (2d ed 2010).

[166] CODE OF CONDUCT FOR U.S. JUDGES, Canon 3C.

[167] United States v. Microsoft Corp., 253 F.3d 34, 113 (D.C. Cir. 2001).

disciplinary proceedings will be discussed interchangeably here.[168] That said, the circumstances under which a judge will be reversed as opposed to disciplined for erroneous non-disqualification differ because honest error in applying disqualification standards warrants reversal, but not discipline. Discipline is typically reserved for cases of misconduct, when a judge's violation of the disqualification standards is willful or egregious.[169]

A bit of history helps to place the law of disqualification in context. Under English common law, as Blackstone described it, "the law will not suppose a possibility of bias or favour in a judge, who is already sworn to administer impartial justice."[170] Gradually, this ironclad bar to disqualification began to yield. In 1609, Sir Edward Coke declared in *Dr. Bonham's Case,* "[n]o man shall be a judge in his own case,"[171] and ruled that a judge was disqualified from presiding over cases in which he was paid from the proceeds of fines he assessed. In 1792, the U.S. Congress codified the exception from *Dr. Bonham's Case* by disqualifying district judges who were "concerned in interest," and added that judges were subject to disqualification if they were "of counsel for either party."[172] In the decades that followed, legislation expanded the grounds for disqualification to include cases in which the judge was related to a party,[173] was hearing the appeal in a matter over which the judge had presided at trial,[174] or was a material witness in the proceeding.[175] And in 1927, the United States Supreme Court added a constitutional dimension to disqualification, holding that a state judge who presided over a case, in which he had an economic interest, deprived the parties of their due process rights to an impartial judge.[176]

These emerging grounds for disqualification in the federal courts were, with exceptions, emulated by the states, and comprised a regime based on conflicts of interest: if one of the enumerated conflicts arose, the judge was disqualified regardless of whether the conflict would or would not have impaired the judge's impartiality.[177] Conversely, if an enumerated conflict did not arise, disqualification was inappropriate regardless of how partial the judge might be or appear to be.[178] English common law gradually evolved to acknowledge disqualification for bias distinct from specific conflicts of interest, but, with the exception of isolated states, American courts were slow to accept bias as a basis for disqualification.[179]

---

[168] In addition, because federal and state disqualification standards are, with exceptions explained when relevant, likewise essentially the same, federal and state cases will also be discussed interchangeably.

[169] *In re* Complaint as to the Conduct of Schenck, 870 P.2d 185 (Or. 1994). This is the basic distinction discussed in § 6-2.2(a), where willful or egregious failures to uphold operative law will subject judges to discipline, but honest errors will not.

[170] WILLIAM BLACKSTONE, III COMMENTARIES ON THE LAWS OF ENGLAND 361 (1768).

[171] Dr. Bonham's Case, 77 Eng. Rep. 646, 652 (1609).

[172] Act of May 8, 1792, ch. 36, § 11, 1 Stat. 178–79 (1792).

[173] Act of March 3, 1821, ch. 51, 3 Stat. 643 (1821).

[174] Act of March 3, 1891, ch. 23, § 21, 36 Stat. 1090 (1891).

[175] Act of March 3, 1911, ch. 231, § 20, 36 Stat. 1090 (1911).

[176] Tumey v. Ohio, 273 U.S. 510 (1927).

[177] Charles Gardner Geyh, *Why Judicial Disqualification Matters. Again.,* 30 REV. OF LITIG. 671, 677–686 (2011).

[178] John Frank, *Disqualification of Judges*, 56 YALE L.J. 605, 611–12 (1947).

[179] Comment, *Disqualification of Judges for Bias or Prejudice—Common Law Evolution, Current Status, and the Oregon Experience,* 48 OREGON L. REV. 311, 322 (1969).

In 1966, the United States Supreme Court brought ethics principles to bear in an arbitration case to the end of declaring that "any tribunal permitted by law to try cases and controversies not only must be unbiased but also must avoid even the appearance of bias."[180] In 1972, the American Bar Association took the Supreme Court's lead when promulgating a new disqualification rule for its Model Code of Judicial Conduct. The new Code directed judges to disqualify themselves when their "impartiality might reasonably be questioned," including but not limited to circumstances in which the judge "has a personal bias or prejudice concerning a party,"[181] or is subject to enumerated conflicts of interest. This new disqualification regime, summarized in § 6-2.5(b), has since been codified by Congress,[182] and included in codes of conduct adopted by the lower federal courts[183] and virtually all of the state supreme courts.[184] In 2009, the Supreme Court revisited the due process dimension of disqualification, holding that a litigant's due process rights were violated by a state supreme court justice who participated in a case after receiving campaign support from the corporate defendant's CEO, under circumstances that gave rise to a probability of bias.[185] The due process clause of the Fourteenth Amendment thus serves as a kind of backstop to state disqualification rules, limited to those unusual circumstances wherein the more rigorous Model Code-based state disqualification standards are misapplied or flouted.

## § 6-2.5(b) Disqualification Standards

### *§ 6-2.5(b)(1) Overview of Standards and Their Interpretation*

The Model Code of Judicial Conduct, as adopted by virtually all states, articulates standards for disqualification by means of a two-tier structure. Tier 1 features the general directive that a judge "shall disqualify himself or herself from any proceeding in which the judge's impartiality might reasonably be questioned. . ."[186] This general directive ends with the clause "including, but not limited to the following circumstances," which bridges the first tier to a second tier that enumerates recurring scenarios where disqualification is automatic.[187]

In the Model Code, the specific disqualification rules in Tier 2 are presumptive subsets of the general disqualification rule in Tier 1, and include the following scenarios, where disqualification is mandatory:

- The judge has a "personal bias or prejudice" concerning a party or party's lawyer;[188]
- The judge has "personal knowledge" of facts in dispute, or was a "material witness" concerning the matter;[189]

---

[180] *Commonwealth Coatings v. Continental Casualty Co.*, 393 U.S. 145 (1966).

[181] ABA MODEL CODE OF JUDICIAL CONDUCT, Canon 3(C)(1)(1972).

[182] 28 U.S.C. § 455(a).

[183] CODE OF CONDUCT FOR U.S. JUDGES, Canon 3C.

[184] The ABA Judicial Disqualification Project, *Taking Disqualification Seriously,* 92 JUDICATURE 12, 14 (2008).

[185] Caperton v. A.T. Massey Coal Co., 556 U.S. 868 (2009).

[186] MODEL CODE, Rule 2.11(A).

[187] *Id.*

[188] MODEL CODE, Rule 2.11(A)(1).

[189] MODEL CODE, Rules 2.11(A)(1); 2.11(A)(6)(c).

- The judge's relatives are parties, lawyers, or witnesses in the proceeding;[190]
- The judge is or was a lawyer in the proceeding, or was formerly affiliated with lawyers in the proceeding at specified times and in specified ways;[191]
- The judge or designated family members have an economic or other interest in the proceeding;[192]
- A party, lawyer, or law firm in the proceeding made contributions to the judge's election campaign in excess of a specified amount within a specified time-frame;[193]
- The judge made public statements that committed or appeared to commit the judge to reach a particular result in the proceeding.[194]

The disqualification standards in the federal statute are substantially similar to those in the Model Code, but differ slightly in the relationship they create between Tiers 1 and 2. The federal disqualification statute does not characterize Tier 2 scenarios as subsets of Tier 1, but as freestanding disqualification standards.[195] That allows for the possibility that under the federal statute, a judge could be subject to disqualification under Tier 2 in scenarios that would not call the judge's impartiality into question under Tier 1. For example, Tier 2 of the federal statute requires judges to disqualify themselves for financial interests "however small," which presumably includes interests so small that they could not reasonably call the judge's impartiality into question under Tier 1—which would be the case if the judge owns a single share of a corporate defendant's stock, valued at $0.75. In contrast, under Tier 2 of the Model Code, disqualifying economic interests are limited to those that would call the judge's impartiality into question under Tier 1.[196]

Disqualification standards in the federal and state judicial systems are subject to interpretative ground-rules and limitations. First, it bears emphasis that the relationship between Tiers 1 and 2, described here, makes clear that a judge is subject to disqualification when his or her impartiality might reasonably be questioned, under circumstances not specified in Tier 2 scenarios. For example, a judge must disqualify herself from a case in which her maid of honor is a party to the proceeding, on the grounds that her impartiality might reasonably be questioned under Rule 2.11(a),[197] even though none of the enumerated grounds for disqualification specified in Rule 2.11(A)(1)–(6) apply.

Second, if the basis for a disqualification claim is addressed but excluded by a Tier 2 scenario, resort to a Tier 1 claim will be unavailing. For example, Rule 2.11(A)(2)(a) provides that a judge is disqualified if specified relatives are parties to the proceeding.

---

190 MODEL CODE, Rule 2.11(A)(2)(a)–(b).

191 MODEL CODE, Rules 2.11(A)(2)(b); 2.11(A)(6)(a)–(b).

192 MODEL CODE, Rules 2.11(A)(2); 2.11(A)(2)(c).

193 MODEL CODE, Rule 2.11(A)(4).

194 MODEL CODE, Rule 2.11(A)(5).

195 Section 455(a), like MODEL CODE, Rule 2.11(a)(1) articulates the tier 1 standard that judges should disqualify themselves when their "impartiality might reasonably be questioned." Section 455(b), however, does not characterize Tier 1 as "including but not limited to" Tier 2 scenarios; rather, Section 455(b) states, with respect to Tier 2 scenarios, that the judge "shall also disqualify himself in the following circumstances."

196 *See* discussion of disqualifying economic interests in § 6-2.5(b)(3)(e).

197 *See* discussion of disqualification and personal relationships in § 6-2.5(b)(2)(B).

If a blood relative too remote to make the Rule 2.11(A)(2)(a) list is a party to the proceeding, the blood relationship will not be enough to call the judge's impartiality into question and disqualify her under Tier 1, absent additional circumstances, such as a close personal relationship.[198]

Third, the duty to disqualify when the judge's impartiality might reasonably be questioned under Rule 2.11(A), must be read in tandem with Rule 2.7, which provides that "[a] judge shall hear and decide matters assigned to the judge, except when disqualification is required." Prior to 1972, before the current, two-tier disqualification rule was promulgated, judges often spoke of a "duty to sit."[199] The duty to sit required judges to preside unless barred by an explicit disqualification rule—which in the absence of a rule requiring them to disqualify themselves when their impartiality might reasonably be questioned, meant that they had a duty to preside despite apparent bias. While the 1972 Model Code ended the duty to sit in such cases,[200] Rule 2.7 emphasizes that judges remain obligated to preside when disqualification is unnecessary. Hence, judges are directed not to use disqualification as an excuse to avoid "difficult, controversial, or unpopular issues."[201] As a consequence, when interpreting disqualification standards, the impulse to err on the side of caution and disqualify freely is blunted by the duty to decide assigned cases unless disqualification rules dictate otherwise. That duty, coupled with the presumption of impartiality that dates back to ancient English common law, establishes a default position resistant to routine disqualification.

Fourth, under unusual circumstances in which all available judges would be disqualified, the "rule of necessity" enables otherwise disqualified judges to preside, given the need for someone to administer justice.[202] If, for example, a judge files suit challenging legislation that affects the salary or benefits of all judges within the jurisdiction, the rule of necessity permits a conflicted judge to preside.[203]

### *§ 6-2.5(b)(2) When Impartiality Might Reasonably Be Questioned*

Virtually all disqualification regimes in the state and federal courts begin with the directive that judges shall disqualify themselves when their "impartiality might reasonably be questioned."[204] Disqualification, under this standard, turns on whether a reasonable person might doubt the judge's impartiality, which makes the standard one of appearance or perception.

There are at least three reasons for making perceived partiality a basis for disqualification. First, even when judges are impartial in fact, if the public reasonably perceives them to be partial, it can undermine public confidence in the impartiality

---

[198] Liteky v. United States, 510 U.S. 540, 553 (1994) (the statutory section "which addresses the matter of relationship specifically, ends the disability at the *third* degree of relationship, and that should obviously govern for purposes of § 455(a) as well").

[199] Laird v. Tatum, 409 U.S. 824, 837 (1972).

[200] H.R. Rep. No. 93–1453, at 5 (1974) (House report on 1974 amendments to the federal disqualification statute, which implemented the 1972 Model Code, indicating that the amendments ended the duty to sit).

[201] MODEL CODE, Rule 2.7, Comment 1.

[202] Pilla v. American Bar Assoc., 542 F.2d 56, 59 (8th Cir. 1976) ("[W]here all are disqualified, none are disqualified.").

[203] United States v. Will, 449 U.S. 200 (1980).

[204] The ABA Judicial Disqualification Project, *Taking Disqualification Seriously,* 92 JUDICATURE 12, 14 (2008).

courts, which, as discussed in § 6-1.5(b), is an overarching concern of judicial ethics. Second, disqualifying judges for conduct that appears partial to reasonable people obviates the impossible task of crawling inside judges' minds to determine whether they are biased in fact. Third, it is less stigmatizing for judges to concede that others might reasonably question their impartiality than concede that they are actually biased, which makes such a rule easier for judges to accept and administer.

Whether a judge's impartiality might reasonably be questioned is an objective inquiry, in which one asks whether a disinterested observer fully informed of the relevant facts would entertain a significant doubt that the judge in question was impartial.[205] It is "objective" in that disqualification is determined from the perspective of a reasonable observer, rather than from the subjective perspective of the judge; hence, disqualification may be necessary even though the judge in question subjectively feels that he or she can be fair and impartial.[206] Moreover, because a primary goal of Rule 2.11(A) is to preserve public confidence in the judiciary, the objective observer must be a reasonable outsider, who is "less inclined to credit judges' impartiality and mental discipline than the judiciary."[207] At the same time, this hypothetical observer must be thoughtful" and "well-informed,"[208] and not unreasonably suspicious, because "the disqualification decision must reflect *not only* the need to secure public confidence through proceedings that appear impartial, *but also* the need to prevent parties from too easily obtaining the disqualification of a judge, thereby potentially manipulating the system for strategic reasons, perhaps to obtain a judge more to their liking."[209]

Although Rule 2.11(A) can be brought to bear in myriad contexts, it is possible to group most of the cases into one of three basic categories: disqualification based on the judge's judicial conduct; disqualification based on the judge's extra-judicial conduct; and, disqualification based on the judge's personal relationships.

*§ 6-2.5(b)(2)(A) Judicial Conduct*

The starting point in an analysis of disqualification related to a judge's conduct on the bench, is with the so-called "extrajudicial source rule." In *United States v. Grinnell Corp.*,[210] a case predating the 1974 amendments to § 455, the United States Supreme Court observed that, "[t]he alleged bias and prejudice to be disqualifying must stem from an extrajudicial source . . . other than what the judge learned from his participation in the case."[211] The Court declined to require disqualification in that case because "[a]ny adverse attitudes that [the judge] evinced toward the defendants were based on his study

---

[205] Pepsico, Inc. v. McMillan, 764 F.2d 458, 460 (7th Cir. 1985); United States v. Sellers, 566 F.2d 884, 887 (4th Cir. 1977); Unites States v. Bayless, 201 F.3d 116, 126 (2d Cir. 2000).

[206] Appeal of Seacoast Anti-Pollution League, 482 A.2d 509 (N.H. 1984); Home Placement Serv., Inc. v. Providence Journal Co., 739 F.2d 671 (1st Cir. 1984).

[207] *In re* Mason, 916 F.2d 384, 386 (7th Cir. 1990); *see also* United States v. De Temple, 162 F.3d 279, 287 (4th Cir. 1998); *In re* Faulkner, 856 F.2d 716 (5th Cir. 1988).

[208] *In re* Mason, 916 F.2d 384, 386 (7th Cir. 1990). *See also* United States v. Jordan, 49 F.3d 152, 156 (5th Cir. 1995); O'Regan v. Arbitration Forums, Inc., 246 F.3d 975, 988 (7th Cir. 2001).

[209] *In re* Allied-Signal Inc., 891 F.2d 967, 970 (1st Cir. 1989) (Breyer, J.) (citation omitted).

[210] 384 U.S. 563 (1966).

[211] *Id.* at 583.

of the depositions and briefs which the parties had requested him to make."[212] The Court elaborated further on the extrajudicial source rule in *Liteky v. United States*.[213]

> The judge who presides at a trial may, upon completion of the evidence, be exceedingly ill disposed towards the defendant, who has been shown to be a thoroughly reprehensible person. But the judge is not thereby recusable for bias or prejudice, since his knowledge and the opinion it produced were properly and necessarily acquired in the course of the proceedings, and are indeed sometimes (as in a bench trial) necessary to completion of the judge's task.[214]

The Court extended this proposition to comments and observations that the judge made in prior judicial proceedings.[215]

The *Liteky* Court, however, took pains to qualify the extrajudicial source rule, explaining that an extrajudicial source "is the only *common* basis [for disqualification] but not the *exclusive* one."[216] Rather, the Court identified two exceptions, where disqualification may be required on the basis of a judge's remarks from the bench: (1) "if they reveal an opinion that derives from an extrajudicial source;" and (2) "if they reveal such a high degree of favoritism or antagonism as to make fair judgment impossible.[217] The former exception is not so much an exception as a recognition that evidence of preexisting, extrajudicial bias can be derived from what the judge says in the courtroom, e.g., a statement evincing racial prejudice. With respect to the latter exception, bias that "springs from the facts adduced or the events occurring at trial," the Court limited its application to actual bias that "is so extreme as to display clear inability to render fair judgment.[218]

Consistent with *Liteky* and the extrajudicial source doctrine, remarks that a judge makes during judicial proceedings in response to her observations do not ordinarily warrant disqualification. In *In re Huntington Commons Associates,* for example, the district court referred to its "predisposition... in this matter," which was "a result of things that have taken place in this very courtroom."[219] The Seventh Circuit did not regard "predisposition" of this kind as "remotely sufficient evidence of the required 'deep-seated and unequivocal antagonism that would render fair judgment impossible.' "[220] In a more extreme case, the Tenth Circuit upheld a refusal to disqualify even though the trial judge said of the defendant pretrial that, "the obvious thing that's going to happen ... is that she's going to get convicted ...."[221] The Court of Appeals believed the judge merely expressed a view of what was likely to happen from what he had observed in the

---

[212] *Id.*

[213] 510 U.S. 540 (1994).

[214] *Id.* at 550–51.

[215] *Id.* at 555 ("[O]pinions formed by the judge on the basis of facts introduced or events occurring in the course of the current proceedings, or of prior proceedings, do not constitute a basis for a bias or partiality motion. . . .").

[216] *Id.* at 551.

[217] *Id.* at 555.

[218] *Id.* at 551.

[219] *In re* Huntington Commons Assocs., 21 F.3d 157, 158 (7th Cir. 1994).

[220] *Id.* at 159 (quoting *Liteky*).

[221] United States v. Young, 45 F.3d 1405, 1414 (10th Cir. 1995).

case: "[n]othing in the remark indicates that the judge was unable or unwilling to carry out his responsibilities impartially."[222]

There are exceptions. In *Unites States v. Whitman*, the Sixth Circuit remanded the case to a different judge after the original trial judge engaged in a "lengthy harangue" of the defense attorney that "had the unfortunate effect of creating the impression that the impartial administration of the law was not his primary concern."[223] In *United States v. Antar,* the trial judge commented on the issue of restitution during sentencing, that "[m]y object in this case from day one has always been to get back to the public that which was taken from it as a result of the fraudulent activities of this defendant and others."[224] The Third Circuit ordered disqualification:

> [T]his is a case where the district judge, in stark, plain and unambiguous language, told the parties that his goal in the criminal case, from the beginning, was something other than what it should have been and, indeed, was improper. . . . It is difficult to imagine a starker example of when opinions formed during the course of judicial proceedings display a high degree of antagonism against a criminal defendant.[225]

Similarly, judges have sometimes been disqualified when they have taken actions or made statements indicating that they have become personally invested in the case. For example, the Third Circuit reversed a refusal to disqualify where the judge had written a lengthy letter responding to the petitioners' mandamus motion, "exhibit[ing] a personal interest in the litigation."[226] In *In re Johnson,*[227] the Fifth Circuit disqualified a judge who became angered with a bankruptcy trustee and held the trustee in contempt after the trustee allegedly mis-described the judge's conduct in an effort to receive a favorable court order from a different judge. During the contempt proceedings, the judge declared that he was "prejudiced in this matter," "not in the least inclined to be neutral," and would serve as "complaining witness, prosecutor, judge, jury, and executioner."[228] The Fifth Circuit concluded that the judge "considered [the party's] actions to be a personal affront to his authority," which called his impartiality into question and necessitated disqualification.[229]

Cases in which a party or lawyer make inflammatory statements that insult or attack the judge are distinguishable. In extremely rare cases, a party who makes a viable threat on the judge's life has required disqualification.[230] As a general matter, however, "a party cannot force disqualification by attacking the judge and then claim that these attacks must have caused the judge to be biased against [her]."[231]

---

[222] *Id.* at 1416. *See also* United States v. Martin, 278 F.3d 988 (9th Cir. 2002) (holding that the district court didn't abuse discretion in denying motion to disqualify where, during sentencing hearing, the judge became frustrated with the defendant and counsel, and made remarks concerning the defendant's credibility—"the . . . comments . . . may have been testy, but they do not justify a recusal").

[223] United States v. Whitman, 209 F.3d 619, 626–27 (6th Cir. 2000).

[224] United States v. Antar, 53 F.3d 568, 573 (3d Cir. 1995).

[225] *Id.* at 576.

[226] Alexander v. Primerica Holdings, Inc., 10 F.3d 155, 165 (3d Cir. 1993).

[227] 921 F.2d 585 (5th Cir. 1991).

[228] *Id.* at 587.

[229] *Id.*

[230] State v. Dalal, 438 N.J. Super. 156 (2014).

[231] FDIC v. Sweeney, 136 F.3d 216, 219 (1st Cir. 1998) (quoting 13A Charles Alan Wright & Arthur R. Miller, Federal Practice and Procedure § 3542); U.S. v. Mosby, 177 F.3d 1067 (8th Cir. 1999).

The general rule against disqualification for in-court comments on pending cases is premised on the view that reacting and responding from the bench to events as they transpire is an unavoidable part of a judge's job. Comments on pending cases gratuitously volunteered outside of court, previously discussed in § 6-2.3(c) are not on the same footing. The judge who flirts with violating the rule against public statements on pending cases often appears overly invested in the case, as a cheerleader or advocate for her ruling, to the detriment of her real or apparent impartiality. And while such comments are regulated in relationship to a judge's judicial duties because they arise in the context of cases pending before the judge, they are in certain meaningful respects, extrajudicial in character. In *United States v. Microsoft Corp.*,[232] the D.C. Circuit disqualified the trial judge because of the cumulative effect of the judge's comments on the merits of the case in a series of secret interviews with reporters throughout the course of the trial. The court explained that the judge's comments "might not have given rise to a violation of the Canons [and the disqualification statute] had he uttered them from the bench" but that "[i]t is an altogether different matter when the statements are made outside the courtroom, in private meetings unknown to the parties, in anticipation that ultimately the Judge's remarks would be reported."[233]

There are numerous examples of judges being disqualified for public comments on pending cases. In *United States v. Cooley*,[234] the Tenth Circuit reversed a refusal to disqualify in a case where the trial judge appeared on national television while the case was pending and stated that the defendants—abortion protesters—were "breaking the law."[235] In a controversial case, the Second Circuit disqualified a New York District Judge on its own initiative, on the grounds that her comments to the media called her impartiality into question. While a suit challenging the constitutionality of New York City's "stop and frisk" law (in which police were authorized to initiate random stops on city streets) was pending, the judge was reported to have told the media that she knew she was not the city's "favorite judge," and that she "describe[d] herself as a jurist who is skeptical of law enforcement, in contrast to certain of her colleagues, whom she describe[d] as inclined to favor the government.".[236] The Second Circuit concluded that a reasonable person might question the impartiality of the presiding judge when, in interviews, she "draws such distinctions between herself and her colleagues."[237]

Public comments on pending cases, however, do not inevitably require disqualification. In *United States v. Pitera*,[238] the judge gave a videotaped lecture to a government drug enforcement task force seven months before a narcotics case was tried, but after the case had already been assigned to her. In the lecture, the judge urged the assembled agents and prosecutors to take certain steps to increase prospects for conviction in narcotics cases. The Second Circuit nevertheless upheld the refusal to disqualify because the judge's lecture "included several emphatic criticisms of prosecutors that would lead a reasonable person not to question, but to have confidence in the [j]udge's impartiality."[239] In addition, the judge participated in various programs

---

[232] 253 F.3d 34 (D.C. Cir. 2001).

[233] *Id.* at 115.

[234] 1 F.3d 985 (10th Cir. 1993).

[235] *Id.* at 990.

[236] Ligon v. City of New York (*In re* Assignment of Cases), 736 F.3d 118 (2d Cir. 2013).

[237] *Id.* at 127.

[238] 5 F.3d 624 (2d Cir. 1993).

[239] *Id.* at 626.

for criminal defense lawyers, and she "commendably lectures to a variety of trial practice seminars."[240]

*Ex parte* communications, like public comments on pending cases, are problematic,[241] and can require disqualification under circumstances in which they call the judge's impartiality into question. In *Price Bros. v. Philadelphia Gear Corp.*, the Sixth Circuit remanded a case in which appellant alleged that the district judge had sent his law clerk to gather evidence, thus necessitating disqualification. The court observed that while "not every *ex parte* communication to the trial court requires reversal," the allegation here was sufficiently serious as to require a remand to determine its truth.[242] When the trial judge met *ex parte* with a panel of experts and prohibited counsel from discovering the contents of the meeting, the Seventh Circuit reversed a refusal to disqualify.[243] The Sixth Circuit, in contrast, upheld a refusal to disqualify in a similar situation involving various *ex parte* communications because the judge "explained to Plaintiffs' counsel the ministerial nature of these *ex parte* discussions before they took place" and "personally extended to Plaintiffs' counsel an invitation to attend *all* of these meetings."[244] Counsel chose not to attend, and "failed to register any objection to the meetings at that time."[245]

*§ 6-2.5(b)(2)(B) Extrajudicial Conduct*

As implied by § 6-2.5(b)(2)(A)'s discussion of the extrajudicial source doctrine, a judge is subject to disqualification for extrajudicial conduct manifesting real or apparent bias that could compromise the judge's impartiality in a case to which the judge is assigned. This category is vast in theory but small in practice. Judges are subject to the same prejudices that afflict the general population, and so, as a theoretical matter, one can speculate that judges, to no less an extent than others, have a lifetime of experiences that color and skew their judgment. As a practical matter, however, most of these extrajudicial experiences fall outside the scope of disqualifying bias, and most of the extrajudicial experiences that fall within its scope, come to light in the course of the proceedings themselves, and were previously discussed in § 6-2.5(b)(2)(A).

Two sources of extrajudicial influence that typically fall outside the scope of disqualifying bias are ideological predisposition, and group affiliation. As to ideological predisposition, "impartiality" subsumes a lack of bias toward a party, and perhaps open-mindedness toward the issues before the court, but does not require the absence of preexisting views on the legal questions that the judge must decide.[246] Thus, the fact that a judge comes to a case with preexisting views on the legal questions presented, based on prior, extrajudicial learning, is no grounds for disqualification. As the Court observed in *Liteky*: "*Some* opinions acquired outside the context of judicial proceedings

---

240 *Id.* at 627.

241 *See* § 6-2.3(c).

242 629 F.2d 444, 446 (6th Cir. 1980) (finding harmless error when the case returned to the Sixth Circuit); Price Bros. v. Philadelphia Gear Corp., 649 F.2d 416 (6th Cir. 1981).

243 Edgar v. K.L., 93 F.3d 256 (7th Cir. 1996).

244 Reed v. Rhodes, 179 F.3d 453, 468 (6th Cir. 1999).

245 *Id.*

246 Republican Party of Minnesota v. White, 536 U.S. 765 (2002).

(for example, the judge's view of the law acquired in scholarly reading) will *not* suffice" to warrant disqualification.[247]

With respect to group affiliation, it may well be the case that judges are sometimes subject to the influence of their race, gender, sexual orientation, religion, party affiliation, and so on. In the context of a given case, specific manifestations of bias in favor of one group or against another may require disqualification.[248] But group affiliation per se, is not grounds for disqualification.[249] For example, to disqualify a judge from presiding over a race discrimination case because the judge and plaintiff are both African American is problematic at multiple levels. First, it presumes that judges of African ancestry are captives to the influence of their race and incapable of ruling fairly. Second, it presumes that judges of European ancestry are somehow less subject to the influence of their race in evaluating the merits of an African American's claim. And, third, as an administrative matter, if one were to disqualify judges from presiding over cases in which people who share the judge's race, gender, ethnicity, religion, or party affiliation have an interest, it would necessitate disqualification on a massive scale.

Disqualification is required for apparent bias emanating from an extrajudicial source. In the vast majority of these cases, the perception of extrajudicial bias will be inferred from something the judge said in the course of the proceedings themselves: judges will make comments in court proceedings that imply a preexisting bias; or they will create a perception of preexisting bias through public comments on pending matters, as discussed in § 6-2.5(b)(2)(A). What that leaves is the relatively small subset of cases in which something the judge said or did before proceedings began that later comes to light in court proceedings, which calls the judge's impartiality into question. For example, in *Liljeberg v. Health Servs. Acquisition Corp.*, the Supreme Court affirmed the Fifth Circuit's reversal of a district court judge's denial of a motion to disqualify the district judge.[250] Respondent had filed a motion to disqualify the judge under 28 U.S.C. § 455(a) after learning that the judge was a board member of an entity attempting to acquire—from the petitioner—the same parcel of land in the parties' dispute.[251] The Supreme Court noted that the district judge professed to be unaware of the entity's interest in the litigation prior to the entry of judgment even though he attended board

---

[247] *Liteky*, 510 U.S. at 554.

[248] State v. Good Plume, 799 N.W.2d 717 (S.D. 2011) (although judge's use of the phrase "go native" was poorly chosen, in context, the judge's comments did not explicitly articulate racial bias or prejudice directed toward defendant); *Owens v. The University Club of Memphis*, 1998 Tenn. App. LEXIS 688 (Oct. 15, 1998) (defendant, a private club, unsuccessfully moved for disqualification of a judge because three years prior to the trial the judge had criticized the defendant—by name—for its racially restrictive membership policies. The appellate court found that the judge, at that juncture, had merely expressed his own moral convictions, and such expressions were not grounds for recusal). *But see* Peter N. Thompson and William E. Martin, *Judicial Toleration of Racial Bias in the Minnesota Justice System*, 25 HAMLINE L. REV. 236 (2002) (discussing the findings of a Racial Bias Taskforce that concluded that Minnesota courts accommodate racial bias in the courtroom because they place a higher premium on other principles).

[249] Higganbotham v. Oklahoma, 328 F.3d 638 (10th Cir. 2003); Bryce v. Episcopal Church in the Diocese of Colo., 289 F.3d 648 (10th Cir. 2002); In re Martinez-Catala, 129 F.3d 213, 221 (1st Cir. 1997) ("Former affiliations with a party may persuade a judge not to sit; but they are rarely a basis for compelled recusal."); In re Mason, 916 F.2d 384, 386 (7th Cir. 1990) ("Courts that have considered whether pre-judicial political activity is . . . prejudicial regularly conclude that it is not.").

[250] 486 U.S. 847 (1988).

[251] *Id.* at 850.

meetings where the acquisition was discussed, but concluded that under § 455(a), a reasonable suspicion that the judge was aware, was enough to require disqualification.[252]

One controversial issue concerns judges' prior attendance at educational seminars on issues relevant to pending cases that were sponsored by organizations with an interest in the case. For years, educational institutions and other organizations have hosted expense-paid educational seminars for judges on a range of issues that arise in litigation. When seminar sponsors later appear as parties before those judges in cases that litigate issues addressed by the seminars, it raises the dual questions of whether it was ethical for the judge to have attended the expense-paid event in the first place, and whether the judge is disqualified when the case arises. The ethics of judicial participation in expense paid seminars is discussed in § 6-3.1(e).

With respect to disqualification for attendance at expense-paid seminars, resolution of the issue is fact sensitive. The Third Circuit reversed a refusal to disqualify in a mass tort case where the judge attended a conference on the dangers of asbestos, funded in part by the plaintiffs' settlement fund.[253] The court concluded that a reasonable person might question the judge's impartiality because the judge "attended a predominantly pro-plaintiff conference on a key merits issue; the conference was indirectly sponsored by the plaintiffs . . . his expenses were largely defrayed by the conference sponsors," and, not insignificantly, the conference exposed him to a "Hollywood-style 'pre-screening' " of the plaintiffs' case.[254]

The Second Circuit, in contrast, upheld a refusal to disqualify in a case where the judge attended an expense-paid environmental seminar funded indirectly by Texaco shortly before a suit against Texaco that the judge had previously dismissed was remanded to his court.[255] The Second Circuit declined to disqualify the judge because Texaco's financial contribution to the organizations that hosted the seminar was minor, because the organizations that hosted the seminar were not involved in the case, and because the seminar did not address issues relevant to the litigation.

A common form of extrajudicial conduct that can require disqualification in certain circumstances is personal relationships that the judge may have with participants in court proceedings. As discussed in § 6-2.5(b)(3)(c), judges are subject to automatic disqualification under Rule 2.11(A)(2) when specified family members or blood relatives appear before them as parties or lawyers. The circumstances under which judges will be disqualified from hearing cases involving people they know but to whom they are not related, is much more limited. Judges often cannot avoid acquaintance with the underlying parties, lawyers or events giving rise to litigation, particularly in smaller communities; in such situations, courts are in accord that a reasonable person fully informed of the circumstances would not doubt the judge's impartiality. There is, however, an indistinct line, in which a judge's familiarity with a party, lawyer, or witness is so close that disqualification is necessary.

With respect to parties, courts have held that mere acquaintanceship and other distant relationships to a party are not enough to warrant disqualification. For example, courts have declined to disqualify judges who have a relationship with a shareholder

---

[252] *Id.* at 851–852.

[253] *In re* School Asbestos Litig., 977 F.2d 764 (3d Cir. 1992).

[254] *Id.* at 781–82.

[255] *In re* Aguinda, 241 F.3d 194 (2d Cir. 2001).

victimized by the defendants that ended years before the litigation began,[256] or who have had a remote but adversarial relationship with the judge's husband.[257] Courts have also declined to disqualify judges where the party served as the homeroom teacher for the judge's child[258] and, where the judge's wife served as a teacher for the party's child.[259]

Some personal relationships with parties, however, are so close as to put the judge's impartiality into question. Judges have been disqualified for: vouching for one of the defendants in a sex discrimination suit as an "honorable man" who "would never intentionally discriminate against anybody;"[260] admitting that a prior relationship with the defendant influenced the judge's decision making;[261] and where there was a publicized history of "bad blood" between the defendant and a close personal friend of the judge.[262] Courts have faulted judges who fail to disqualify themselves from a custody determination involving a close friend[263] or from a proceeding involving a colleague who assisted the judge in obtaining appointment and a pay increase.[264]

With respect to attorneys, courts have noted that "friendships among judges and lawyers are common" and "a judge need not disqualify himself just because a friend—even a close friend—appears as a lawyer."[265] There are, however, cases in which the relationship is so close as to make disqualification necessary. For example, disqualification has been deemed necessary when: the judge and prosecuting attorney planned to vacation together immediately after the trial;[266] a partner in the law firm representing one of the parties was a former law clerk and the father of a current law clerk to the judge;[267] the judge was represented in an unrelated matter by a partner in a firm that was representing a party in a case before the judge;[268] the judge had engaged in business dealings with the attorney for one of the parties;[269] and the judge's law secretary represented a party before the judge.[270]

Attorneys who previously served as law clerks to the judges before whom they appear present a recurring disqualification issue under Rule 2.11(A). On the theory that disqualifying relationships dissipate with time, the issue is often addressed by judges or courts imposing moratoriums in which judges disqualify themselves from cases in which

---

[256] United States v. Lovaglia, 954 F.2d 811, 817 (2d Cir. 1992).

[257] United States v. Morrison, 153 F.3d 34, 47–49 (2d Cir. 1998).

[258] Duncan v. Sherrill, 341 So.2d 946 (Ala. 1977) (significantly, defendants did not raise issue of bias until after judgment was entered).

[259] Berry v. Berry, 654 S.W.2d 155 (Mo. Ct. App. 1983) (judge was unaware of relationship between judge's wife and party until case was decided and motion for disqualification was made).

[260] Roberts v. Bailar, 625 F.2d 125, 127 (6th Cir. 1980).

[261] U.S. v. Toohey, 448 F.3d 542 (2nd Cir. 2006).

[262] United States v. Jordan, 49 F.3d 152 (5th Cir. 1995).

[263] *In re* Gaddis, Stipulation, Agreement, and Order of Reprimand (Wash. Comm'n on Judicial Conduct, 2004).

[264] *In re* Samay, 764 A.2d 398 (N.J. 2001).

[265] United States v. Murphy, 768 F.2d 1518, 1537 (7th Cir. 1985).

[266] Murphy, 768 F.2d 1518.

[267] Parker v. Connors Steel Co., 855 F.2d 1510 (11th Cir. 1988) (but finding non-disqualification harmless error).

[268] *In re* Cargill, 66 F.3d 1256 (1st Cir. 1995).

[269] Potashnick v. Port City Const. Co., 609 F.2d 1101 (5th Cir. 1980). *See also In re* Means, 452 S.E.2d 696 (W. Va. 1994) (finding that a judge should disqualify himself is he and an attorney appearing before him are the equal owners of all the shares of a corporation).

[270] *In re* Intemann, Unreported Determination (N.Y. Comm'n, Oct. 25, 1988).

their former clerks appear as counsel, for a specified number of years after the clerkship ended.[271] When the judge's current law clerk has a possible conflict of interest in a case before the court (if for example, the clerk's former or future employer appears as party or counsel), one court has concluded that "it is the clerk, not the judge who must be disqualified"—meaning that the conflict is avoided if the clerk is screened from participation in the case.[272]

With respect to witnesses who appear before the judge, as with parties and attorneys, simple acquaintance does not require disqualification.[273] On the other hand, in extreme cases, disqualification may be necessary. When, for example, the judge observed that that his friendship with a witness might lead him to "bend over backwards to prove he lacked favoritism," and "expressed profound doubts" about presiding, the appellate courts concluded that "such doubts should have been resolved in favor of disqualification."[274]

#### *§ 6-2.5(b)(3) Specific Grounds*

##### *§ 6-2.5(b)(3)(A) Personal Bias*

Model Code Rule 2.11(A)(1) provides that judges must disqualify themselves if they have a "personal bias or prejudice toward a party or a party's lawyer . . . in the proceeding . . . ." As a practical matter, disqualification for bias is rarely needed or utilized. Under Model Rule 2.11(A), judges must disqualify themselves when their impartiality might reasonably be questioned, including but not limited to circumstances in which they have a personal bias or prejudice under Rule 2.11(A)(1). Because it is easier and less an indictment of the judges involved to show that their impartiality might reasonably be questioned because of apparent bias, than that they were subjectively biased in fact, courts often decide bias cases without resort to Rule 2.11(A)(1).

The issue of disqualification for bias nonetheless arises, if only because courts do not always differentiate between real and reasonably perceived bias when evaluating judicial conduct. Disqualification for bias under Rule 2.11(A)(1) requires that a litigant present evidence of a "negative bias or prejudice [which] must be grounded in some personal animus or malice that the judge harbors against him."[275] The standard for determining if such bias exists is "whether a reasonable person would be convinced the judge was biased."[276] As with disqualification when a judge's impartiality might reasonably be questioned under Rule 2.11(A), disqualification for "[b]ias against a litigant must . . . arise from an extrajudicial source." Hence, adverse contempt orders and other rulings in the same case are insufficient to establish bias for disqualification

---

[271] *In re* Martinez-Catala, 129 F.3d 213, 221 (1st Cir. 1997).

[272] Byrne v. Nezhat, 261 F.3d 1075, 1101–02 (11th Cir. 2001) (quoting Hunt v. American Bank & Trust Co., 783 F.2d 1011, 1016 (11th Cir. 1986)).

[273] Fletcher v. Conoco Pipe Line Co., 323 F.3d 661 (8th Cir. 2003).

[274] United States v. Kelly, 888 F.2d 732, 745 (11th Cir. 1989).

[275] United States v. Balistrieri, 779 F.2d 1191, 1201 (7th Cir. 1985).

[276] Hook v. McDade, 89 F.3d 350, 355 (7th Cir. 1996); *see also* Collins v. Illinois, 554 F.3d 693, 697 (7th Cir. 2009); Brokaw v. Mercer County, 235 F.3d 1000, 1025 (7th Cir. 2000). Other courts have noted that the standard for finding actual bias is objective, and that "it is with reference to the 'well-informed, thoughtful and objective observer, rather than the hypersensitive, cynical and suspicious person' that the objective standard is currently established." Andrade v. Chojnacki, 338 F.3d 448, 462 (5th Cir. 2003) (quoting United States v. Jordan, 49 F.3d 152, 156 (5th Cir. 1995)).

under Rule 2.11(A)(1);[277] the opinions a judge forms in the course of current and prior judicial proceedings are "nearly exempt from causing recusal," unless they "reveal such a high degree of favoritism or antagonism as to make fair judgment impossible."[278] In *Lyell v. Renico*, the Sixth Circuit found that a trial judge violated the defendant's due process rights when the judge took over the cross-examination of the central witness in the case, interrupted prosecution multiple times using "derogatory tone and content" throughout the trial, and demonstrated "implicit disapproval of the defense counsel's theory of the case" in the aforementioned interruptions.[279] The Sixth Circuit panel noted that the trial judge's actions made a "fair trial impossible,"[280] and that such misconduct met the high standard for establishing bias under *Liteky*, wherein "a judge's misconduct at trial may be 'characterized as bias or prejudice' only if 'it is so extreme as to display clear inability to render fair judgment.' "[281]

*§ 6-2.5(b)(3)(B) Personal Knowledge of Disputed Facts*

Model Code Rule 2.11(A)(1) requires disqualification when the judge has prior knowledge of disputed facts. In a related vein, Rule 2.11(A)(6)(c) requires disqualification when the judge "was a material witness concerning the matter." Thus, for example, one court ordered disqualification when one of the judge's relatives participated in transactions relevant to the defendant's indictment and "communicated to the judge . . . material facts and her opinions and attitudes regarding those facts."[282] Another court concluded that disqualification was necessary when the judge had been a state legislator involved in legislative battles germane to a lawsuit over a state university and was "forced to make factual findings about events in which he was an active participant."[283] Likewise, where a judge had negotiated with a defendant while he was holding hostages, the appellate court found that the judge should have disqualified himself from the defendant's preliminary hearing.[284]

Conversely, when a judge simply possesses information generally available to the public, disqualification is unnecessary. One court, for example, ruled that disqualification under Rule 2.11(A)(1) was unnecessary after the judge acquired information as a courtroom spectator in another proceeding, where he "learned nothing . . . that any member of the public could not also have learned by attending the trial or reading a good newspaper account of its progress. This limited exposure is simply not the kind of *personal* knowledge of disputed evidentiary facts with which [Rule 2.11(A)(1)] is concerned."[285] The court did, however, order disqualification under the equivalent of Rule 2.11(A), because the case that the judge observed, in which the judge's son participated as counsel, was so closely related to the case at bar.[286]

---

[277] *See, e.g.*, Brokaw v. Mercer County, 235 F.3d 1000, 1025 (7th Cir. 2000).

[278] Andrade, 338 F.3d at 462 (citing Liteky, 510 U.S. at 555–56).

[279] Lyell v. Renico, 470 F.3d 1177, 1187 (6th Cir. 2006).

[280] *Id.*

[281] *Id.* at 1186 (quoting Liteky, 510 U.S. at 551 (internal quotation marks omitted)).

[282] *In re* Faulkner, 856 F.2d 716, 721 (5th Cir. 1988).

[283] United States v. Alabama, 828 F.2d 1532, 1545 (11th Cir. 1987).

[284] State v. Blackmon, 664 S.W.2d 644 (Mo. Ct. App. 1984). The Court affirmed the conviction, as the defendant did not preserve the disqualification issue for appeal and the judge's failure to disqualify himself did not bring an unjust result.

[285] *In re* Hatcher, 150 F.3d 631, 635 (7th Cir. 1998).

[286] *Id.*

*§ 6-2.5(b)(3)(C) Relatives as Parties, Attorneys, or Witnesses*

Under Model Code Rule 2.11(A)(2), judges must disqualify themselves from proceedings in which "the judge, the judge's spouse or domestic partner or a person within the third degree of relationship to either of them, or the spouse or domestic partner of such a person" is a party or closely affiliated with a party (including officers, directors, general partners, managing members, or trustees); a lawyer; or likely to be a material witness. Individuals within the "third degree of relationship," include "great-grandparent, grandparent, parent, uncle, aunt, brother, sister, child, grandchild, great-grandchild, nephew, and niece." Because the rule lists the spouses or domestic partners of listed individuals, in-laws are likewise included.

Courts have read the rule literally. For example, the rule has been interpreted not to require disqualification when the father of the judge's son-in-law was a director on the board of one of the named parties.[287] Familial relationships more remote than those requiring automatic disqualification under Rule 2.11(A)(2) will not, by themselves, subject the judge to disqualification under the general appearance of partiality standard of Rule 2.11(A).[288] In context, however, more remote familial relationships can give rise to close personal relationships that subject the judge to disqualification under Rule 2.11A. In *In re Faulkner*, the Fifth Circuit disqualified a judge from hearing a case in which his cousin had been actively involved in transactions giving rise to the defendant's indictment, because they "describe[d] their relationship as more like that of 'brother and sister."[289]

Courts have likewise given a literal construction to the rule as applied to relatives who appear as counsel in proceedings before the court. In 1993, seven members of the United States Supreme Court, each with relatives employed by law firms, issued a letter acknowledging that the federal corollary to Rule 2.11(A)(2) required disqualification when a listed family member appeared as counsel.[290] The justices reasoned, however, that Rule 2.11(A)(2) could have but did not require disqualification when a relative is affiliated with a law firm that appears before a judge.[291] That, in turn, refuted categorical assertions that a judge's impartiality might reasonably be questioned simply because a firm that employs one of the judge's relatives enters an appearance.[292] A separate concern, as to whether relatives who are profit-sharing partners at law firms that appear before the judge have an interest in the outcome of the case, thereby requiring disqualification under Rule 2.11(A) (2)(c), is discussed in § 6-2.5(b)(3)(e).

Problems can arise when parties seek to replace their counsel mid-litigation with lawyers related to the judge. Courts have authorized judges to deny such requests when made for the apparent purpose of forcing the judge's disqualification,[293] or when the judge's disqualification would cause undue delay, absent a showing of "overriding need"

---

[287] Oriental Fin. Group, Inc. v. Fed. Ins. Co., Inc., 467 F. Supp. 2d 176 (D.P.R. 2006).

[288] Liteky, 510 U.S. at 553 (the statutory section "which addresses the matter of relationship specifically, ends the disability at the *third* degree of relationship, and that should obviously govern for purposes of § 455(a) as well").

[289] *In re* Faulkner, 856 F.2d at 718.

[290] Supreme Court Statement of Recusal Policy, 114 S. Ct. (Orders Section, p.52) (1993).

[291] *Id.*

[292] *Id.*

[293] McCuin v. Texas Power & Light Co., 714 F.2d 1255, 1265 (5th Cir. 1983) ("[A] lawyer may not enter a case for the primary purpose of forcing the presiding judge's recusal.").

for the new counsel that "would trump both time delay and the loss of prior judicial activity."[294]

*§ 6-2.5(b)(3)(D) Judge Was a Lawyer or Affiliated with a Lawyer in the Proceeding*

Full time judges are prohibited from practicing law.[295] The Model Code permits judges to represent themselves *pro se*, but otherwise prohibits them from entering appearances in any forum.[296] Part-time judges are permitted to practice law, but not before the court in which they preside.[297] Hence, it is categorically improper for judges to find themselves acting as lawyers in cases assigned to their courts, and the Code makes clear that in that eventuality, disqualification is necessary.

More commonly, recently appointed judges may be assigned cases in which they formerly served as counsel to one of the parties before ascending the bench, and the Model Code requires judges to disqualify themselves when they "served as a lawyer in the matter in controversy."[298] For judges who "served in governmental employment," disqualification is required if they "participated personally and substantially as a lawyer or public official concerning the proceeding.[299]

Even more commonly, recently appointed judges may be assigned cases that were being handled by someone else in their office when they were still in practice. Here, the Code imposes more exacting disqualification standards on judges who were formerly in private practice than government service. For judges who came to the bench from private practice, the need for disqualification is automatic if the judge "was associated with a lawyer who participated substantially as a lawyer in the matter during such association."[300] If the judge was a still lawyer with the firm when the firm agreed to take the matter on, the fact that the judge had nothing to do with the matter is irrelevant—disqualification is mandatory. For judges who came to the bench from governmental service, in contrast, the need for disqualification is limited to circumstances in which, as noted in the preceding paragraph, the judge "participated personally and substantially as a lawyer or public official concerning the proceeding,[301] or "publicly expressed in such capacity an opinion concerning the merits of the particular matter in controversy."[302] One can explain this distinction, at least in part, in terms of the practical consequences that would follow if, for example, a former state attorney general was appointed to judicial office and required to disqualify herself from every case the state litigated that was pending while she was attorney general, regardless of her involvement in the case.

---

[294] Robinson v. Boeing Co., 79 F.3d 1053, 1056 (11th Cir. 1996); *see also* McCuin v. Texas Power & Light Co., 714 F.2d 1255, 1263 (5th Cir. 1983).

[295] MODEL CODE, Rule 3.10.

[296] *Id.* The Model Code creates a limited exception that permits judges to draft legal documents and offer legal advice to family members free of charge.

[297] MODEL CODE, Application, Part III.

[298] MODEL CODE, Rule 2.11(A)(6)(b).

[299] MODEL CODE, Rule 2.11(A)(6)(b).

[300] MODEL CODE, Rule 2.11(A)(6)(a).

[301] MODEL CODE, Rule 2.11(A)(6)(b).

[302] *Id.* In Williams v. Pennsylvania, 136 S.Ct. 1899 (2016), the U.S. Supreme Court concluded that a Pennsylvania Supreme Court justice deprived a criminal defendant of his Fourteenth Amendment right to due process of law by declining to disqualify himself from a case in which he had, while the district attorney decades earlier, approved the decision to pursue the death penalty against the defendant.

Some courts differ in their approach to determining when the "matter" that is before the court is the same as the matter that the judges or their former affiliates previously handled as lawyers. For example, one court has defined the same matter to include "more than the charges brought by the government," and to encompass the "defense asserted by the accused;"[303] hence, even though the charges were new, disqualification was deemed necessary because the "defense, in part at least, will consist of evidence of matters in which the judge's former partner served as lawyer."[304] Conversely, another court described "the matter in controversy" more narrowly, as referring only to "the case that is before the Court as defined by the docket number attached to that case and the pleadings contained therein."[305]

Rule 2.11(A)(6) does not bar a judge from presiding over matters in which lawyers from the judge's former firm enter an appearance, when the matter came to the firm after the judge has left. The specific circumstances surrounding a given judge's relationship with her former firm and the lawyers in it can still call the judge's impartiality into question and require disqualification under Rule 2.11A, if for example, the judge's social ties to the firm and its lawyers remain close. Hence, some judges routinely disqualify themselves from cases in which their former firms enter an appearance, for a period of years or in perpetuity.[306]

*§ 6-2.5(b)(3)(E) Economic or Other Interest in the Proceeding*

The Supreme Court has held that the due process clause of the Fourteenth Amendment to the U.S. Constitution guarantees litigants the right to an impartial judge who is unencumbered by economic conflicts of interest.[307] The Model Code of Judicial Conduct likewise subjects judges to disqualification for economic and other conflicts of interest. With respect to economic conflicts, Rule 2.11(A)(3) provides that a judge is disqualified if the judge or a member of the judge's family—including "the judge's spouse, domestic partner, parent, or child, or any other member of the judge's family residing in the judge's household"—has "an economic interest in the subject matter in controversy or in a party to the proceeding."[308] The Model Code defines "economic interest" to include "ownership of more than a *de minimis* legal or equitable interest," and defines "*de minimis*" as "an insignificant interest that could not raise a reasonable question regarding the judge's impartiality."[309] In addition, the Rule obligates judges to "keep informed about the judge's personal and fiduciary economic interests," and to "make a reasonable effort to keep informed about the personal economic interests of the judge's spouse or domestic partner and minor children residing in the judge's household."[310]

With respect to other conflicts of interest, the most recent iteration of the Model Code requires disqualification when the judge, or a member of the judge's family—defined somewhat differently to include "the judge's spouse or domestic partner, or a person within the third degree of relationship to either of them, or the spouse or domestic

---

[303] *In re* Rodgers, 537 F.2d 1196 (4th Cir. 1976).

[304] *Id.* at 1198.

[305] Blue Cross & Blue Shield of Rhode Island v. Delta Dental of Rhode Island, 248 F. Supp. 2d 39, 46 (D.R.I. 2003).

[306] McClure v. Harris, 503 F. Supp. 409, 415 (N.D. Cal. 1980).

[307] Tumey v. Ohio, 273 U.S. 510 (1927).

[308] MODEL CODE, Rule 2.11(A)(3).

[309] MODEL CODE, Terminology.

[310] MODEL CODE, Rule 2.11(B).

partner of such a person"—has "more than a *de minimis* interest that could be substantially affected by the proceeding."[311] Taken together, Rules 2.11(A)(2)(c) and 2.11(A)(3) subject a judge to disqualification for conflicts of interest, economic or otherwise, that are sufficiently significant to raise reasonable questions as to the judge's impartiality.

The federal disqualification statute is substantially similar to that in the current Model Code, but includes one critical difference that harkens back to the Model Code's 1972 predecessor.[312] With respect to a "financial interest"—the term that the federal statute uses in lieu of "economic interest" in the Model Code—the federal statute requires disqualification when the judge or a listed family member "has a financial interest in the subject matter in controversy or in a party to the proceeding,"[313] and defines "financial interest" as "ownership of a legal or equitable interest, however small."[314] Hence, for example, in federal court, judges are disqualified if they or members of their families own a single share of a corporate party's stock.[315] In state systems that follow the current Model Code, such judges are not disqualified insofar as a nominal shareholding could not reasonably call the judge's impartiality into question.[316]

"Economic" or "financial" interests in the parties or subject matter sufficient to trigger disqualification have included cases in which the judge: owned stock in a corporate party;[317] served as trustee in relation to trusts at issue in the litigation;[318] was paid fees from costs the judge assessed against parties;[319] retained a financial interest in his former law firm, whose lawyers he appointed to represent indigent defendants with public funds;[320] and was a debtor of a lawyer or party to the proceedings.[321] With respect to stock ownership, the U.S. Judicial Conference Committee on Codes of Conduct advised that it is per se disqualifying for the judge to hold stock in the parent corporation of a party that is a corporate subsidiary, given the control that a parent exercises over a subsidiary;[322] but that it is not disqualifying for the judge to hold stock in the corporate subsidiary of a party that is the subsidiary's parent corporation, unless the subsidiary could be substantially affected by the outcome of the litigation.[323] Interests deemed too

---

[311] MODEL CODE, Rule 2.11(A)(2)(c). The predecessor Model Code, promulgated in 1990, was in accord (ABA MODEL CODE OF JUDICIAL CONDUCT, Canon 3E (1990)), but the 1972 Model Code subjected judges to disqualification for *de minimis* financial interests (ABA MODEL CODE OF JUDICIAL CONDUCT, Canon 3C (1972)).

[312] ABA MODEL CODE OF JUDICIAL CONDUCT, Canon 3C (1972).

[313] 28 U.S.C. § 455(b)(4).

[314] 28 U.S.C. § 455(d)(4).

[315] *In re* Cement Antitrust Litigation, 688 F.2d 1297 (9th Cir. 1982).

[316] *See* John P. Freeman, *Appearance of Impropriety, Recusal, and the Segars-Andrews Case*, 62 S.C. L. REV. 485 (2011); Jeffrey W. Stempel, *Impeach Brent Benjamin Now!? Giving Adequate Attention to Failings of Judicial Impartiality*, 47 SAN DIEGO L. REV. 1 (2010).

[317] White v. SunTrust Bank, 538 S.E.2d 889 (Ga. Ct. App. 2000) (judge disqualified for owning $20,000 in corporate defendant's stock).

[318] Inquiry Concerning Sullivan, No. 163 (Cal. Comm'n on Judicial Performance, May 17, 2002).

[319] Taylor v. Public Convalescent Serv., 267 S.E.2d 242 (Ga. 1980).

[320] *In re* Lawrence, 335 N.W.2d 456 (Mich. 1983).

[321] *In re* Anderson, 252 N.W. 2d 592 (Minn. 1977) (judge presided over cases in which he owed the lawyers money); *In re* Yandell, 772 P.2d 807 (Kan. 1989) (judge presided over case of a bank that had held loans to the judge that were in default).

[322] In state systems that adopt the Model Code variation of Rule 2.11, stock ownership in a parent corporation could only be a disqualifying "economic interest" only if the interest was more than "*de minimis*." MODEL CODE, Terminology.

[323] Committee on Codes of Judicial Conduct Advisory Committee Op. 57: Disqualification Based on Stock Ownership in Parent Corporation of a Party or Controlled Subsidiary of a Party (Jun. 2009).

remote to constitute an economic interest have included cases in which the judge: paid utilities that could allegedly be affected by a natural gas antitrust case;[324] was one of many shareholders in a non-party, corporate victim of an alleged fraud;[325] and owned stock in a party's competitor, where the impact of the case on the competitor was "attenuated."[326]

Model Code, Rule 3.11 permits judges to hold and manage their investments, but prohibits them from engaging in financial activities that "lead to frequent disqualification." Judges can avoid frequent disqualification by divesting themselves of stock in corporate parties that make regular appearances in their courtrooms. When the judge or parties discover, after the litigation has begun, that the judge (or a member of the judge's family) holds stock in a corporate party, the federal disqualification statute enables the judge to "cure" the conflict through divestiture, provided that the judge has already "devoted substantial time to the matter," and that the judge's interest could not be "substantially affected by the outcome."[327] In state systems that follow the Model Code, disqualification can be avoided in such circumstances if the parties agree to waive disqualification, as discussed in § 6-2.5(c).

In addition to "economic" interests, Model Code Rule 2.11(A)(2)(c) requires disqualification when the judge or specified family members have "more than a *de minimis* interest that could be substantially affected by the proceeding." This section can apply in at least two situations where Rule 2.11(A)(3), governing disqualification for economic interests, does not. First, the list of family members whose interests will subject a judge to disqualification, differ between the two provisions. Thus, for example, the judge's sister (assuming that she does not live in the judge's home) is not among the family members whose economic interest in a proceeding will subject the judge to disqualification under Rule 2.11(A)(3), but is among the family members who will subject the judge to disqualification if she has an interest that "could be substantially affected by the proceeding under Rule 2.11(A)(2)(c).

Second, Rule 2.11(A)(3) applies to interests that are analogous to economic interests but may not constitute economic interests per se. One recurring issue concerns judges with relatives who work at law firms that enter appearances before those judges. As previously discussed in § 6-2.5(b)(3)(c), Rule 2.11(A)(2)(b) disqualifies judges from proceedings in which family members appear as counsel, but does not disqualify judges from presiding over cases in which partners or associates of family members enter appearances. The issue then becomes whether such family members, by virtue of their affiliation with firms that appear before the judge, have a "more than *de minimis* interest that could be substantially affected by the proceeding," under Rule 2.11(A)(2)(c). An associate does not possess such an interest, the Eighth Circuit concluded, because the judge's daughter was "a salaried employee . . . not a partner whose income is directly

---

324 *In re* New Mexico Natural Gas Antitrust Litig., 620 F.2d 794, 796 (10th Cir. 1980) (finding that a district judge's "interest" in the impact of an antitrust case on the judge's utility bill was too remote to constitute a disqualifying financial interest).

325 United States v. Rogers, 119 F.3d 1377 (9th Cir. 1997) ("stock ownership in the corporate victim of a crime cannot be deemed a financial interest in the subject matter in controversy," where the judge was one of millions of shareholders in a non-party victim of the defendant's alleged fraud).

326 Armenian Assoc. v. Cafesjian, 783 F. Supp. 2d 78, 92 (D.D.C. 2011).

327 28 U.S.C. § 455(f). *See, e.g.*, Kidder, Peabody & Co. v. Maxus Energy Corp., 925 F.2d 556 (2d Cir. 1991) (authorizing divestiture to avoid squandering "three years of the litigants' time and resources and substantial judicial efforts").

related to the profit margin of the firm and could be substantially affected by the outcome of this case."[328] With respect to family members who are partners with firms that appear before the judge, the Eighth Circuit implied that disqualification would be in order. The Fifth Circuit has agreed.[329] The Second Circuit, however, has taken the opposite view, concluding that it was "unrealistic to assume" that firm partners had a meaningful interest that could be substantially affected by the outcome of any given proceeding.[330] In a 1993 letter signed by seven members of the Supreme Court who then had lawyers within their families, the justices took a middle position.[331] In their view, when Congress disqualified judges from presiding over cases in which family members entered appearances in the disqualification statute, it could have but did not extend disqualification to appearances by the firms of those family members, which undercut the argument that such a categorical bar was intended.[332] The justices nonetheless decided that they would disqualify themselves from any case in which a relative held a partnership interest in a firm appearing before the Court, unless the Court received assurances from the firm that the relative would not share in profits derived from the case.[333]

*§ 6-2.5(b)(3)(F) Campaign Support and Commitments*

Beginning in the 1990s, judicial election campaigns became exponentially "noisier, nastier, and costlier."[334] Concerned by the pressures judicial races placed on judicial impartiality, in 1999, the American Bar Association amended the Model Code of Judicial Conduct to add Rule 2.11(a)(4), which triggered a duty to disqualify if a party or lawyer appeared before the judge who had contributed to the judge's election campaign within a period of time and in amounts that the ABA left for individual states to specify.

The Rule governing disqualification for campaign contributions was sparingly adopted by the states, and did not address what many observers regarded as a more troubling problem: the impact of independent expenditures (as opposed to direct contributions) in support of judicial campaigns. That problem was illustrated in the case of *Caperton v. A.T. Massey Coal Company*.[335] Massey lost a $50 million verdict in a West Virginia jury trial. While Massey's appeal was impending, one justice on the five-member West Virginia Supreme Court was up for reelection. Massey's CEO contributed $3 million to organizations that campaigned for the defeat of the incumbent and for the election of his challenger. The challenger prevailed, declined to disqualify himself from Massey's case, and cast the deciding vote in its favor. The plaintiff petitioned the United States Supreme Court to hear the case. To ensure a fair tribunal that satisfied due process requirements, the Court declared that disqualification is necessary when "the probability of actual bias on the part of the judge or decision-maker is too high to be

[328] *In re* Kansas Pub. Employees Ret. Sys., 85 F.3d 1353, 1364 (8th Cir. 1996).

[329] Potashnick v. Port City Construction Co, 609 F.2d 1101, 1113 (5th Cir. 1980) ("[W]hen a partner in a law firm is related to a judge within the third degree, that partner will always be 'known by the judge to have an interest that could be substantially affected by the outcome' of a proceeding involving the partner's law firm.").

[330] Pashaian v. Eccelston Properties, Ltd., 88 F.3d 77 (2d Cir. 1996).

[331] Supreme Court Statement of Recusal Policy, 114 S. Ct. (Orders Section, p.52) (1993).

[332] *Id.*

[333] *Id.*

[334] Roy A. Schotland, *Comment*, 61 LAW & CONTEMPORARY PROBLEMS 149, 150 (1998).

[335] *See* Caperton v. A.T. Massey Coal Co., 556 U.S. 868 (2009).

constitutionally tolerable."[336] Applying a probability of bias standard to the facts of the case, the majority found that the "campaign contributions—in comparison to the total amount contributed to the campaign, as well as the total amount spent in the election—had a significant and disproportionate influence on the electoral outcome."[337] In addition, it found that this "significant and disproportionate influence—coupled with the temporal relationship between the election and the pending case—" 'offer a possible temptation to the average . . . judge to . . . [l]ead him not to hold the balance nice, clear and true.' "[338] The Court therefore concluded that "[o]n these extreme facts, the probability of actual bias rises to an unconstitutional level."[339]

After *Caperton,* then, judges are subject to disqualification for the independent campaign support they receive, in "extreme" cases when the "probability of actual bias" would deprive parties of their due process rights, and somewhat less extreme cases in which the judge's "impartiality might reasonably be questioned" under Model Code Rule 2.11(A), as adopted by the states.[340] Post-*Caperton,* the ABA Standing Committee on Ethics and Professional Responsibility undertook a multi-year effort to amend 2.11(A)(4) to include independent expenditures, but failed in large part due to objections from the ABA's Judicial Division that any such a rule should be a matter of procedure, not ethics.[341]

The new politics of judicial elections have likewise generated concerns over the impact of campaign speech on judicial impartiality. In 2002, the Supreme Court ruled that judicial candidates had a First Amendment right to announce their views on issues likely to come before their courts. In 2003, the ABA responded with Rule 2.11(A)(5), which provides that judges are subject to disqualification if they make a public statement, as a judge or judicial candidate, that "commits or appears to commit the judge to reach a particular result or rule in a particular way in the proceeding or controversy." Although Rule 2.11(A)(5) arose in response to concerns over the impact of campaign promises on judicial impartiality, by its terms it is not limited to campaign-related commitments.

Several jurisdictions have adopted Rule 2.11(A)(5);[342] those that have not must evaluate the need for disqualification with reference to the general standards of Rule 2.11(A). Precedent addressing disqualification for campaign commitments is sparse, which is understandable, given that judges are under a separate ethical directive not to

---

[336] *Id.* at 877 (quoting Withrow v. Larkin, 421 U.S. 35, 47 (1975)).

[337] *Id.* at 885.

[338] *Id.* at 885 (quoting Tumey v. Ohio, 273 U.S 510, 532 (1927)).

[339] *Id.* at 887.

[340] *Id.* at 888 ("And because the States may have codes of conduct with more rigorous recusal standards than due process requires, most recusal disputes will be resolved without resort to the Constitution, making the constitutional standard's application rare."). In declining to disqualify himself from *Caperton* (heard by the Supreme Court of Appeals of West Virginia), West Virginia Justice Brent Benjamin did not apply West Virginia's corollary to Rule 2.11(A). West Virginia Code of Judicial Conduct, Canon 3E(1). Rather, he rejected an "appearance" standard in favor of an "actuality" of justice approach, pursuant to which a judge's actual impartiality was shown by the reasons for his ruling. Caperton v. A.T. Massey Coal Co., 679 S.E.2d at 223, 292–93 (W. Va. 2008) (Benjamin, J., concurring).

[341] Charles Gardner Geyh, Myles Lynk, Robert Peck, and Toni Clarke, *The State of Recusal Reform,* 18 N.Y.U. J. OF LEG. & PUB. POL. 520 (2015).

[342] The ABA Judicial Disqualification Project, *Taking Disqualification Seriously,* 92 JUDICATURE 12, 14–15 (2008).

make such commitments in the first place.[343] One illustration reported in the popular press concerned a West Virginia Justice, who, as a judicial candidate, said of tort reform legislation, the constitutionality of which was likely to come before the court, that "I will not vote to overturn it, I will not vote to change it. I will not vote to modify it."[344] He initially declined to disqualify himself from the case when it came before the court, on the grounds that "my predisposition does not equate to an actual bias," but ultimately withdrew.[345]

### § 6-2.5(c) Disqualification Procedure

Codes of conduct provide that a judge must withdraw from a case when the standards for disqualification discussed in § 6-2.5(b) are met, "regardless of whether a motion to disqualify is filed."[346] When a party moves to disqualify a judge, the motion must be filed promptly. Courts look askance at tactical delays in which disqualification requests occupy "a fallback position in the event of adverse rulings on pending matters,"[347] and so require that motions be filed expeditiously after obtaining knowledge of facts demonstrating the basis for such a claim.[348]

Often, those with greatest access to information relevant to disqualification are the judges themselves. Model Code commentary states that the judge "should disclose on the record information that the judge believes the parties or their lawyers might reasonably consider relevant to a possible motion for disqualification, even if the judge believes there is no basis for disqualification."[349]

When information that would subject a judge to disqualification comes to light—via the judge or some other source—the parties will sometimes remain confident in their judge's impartiality and feel no need to request disqualification. In such situations, the Model Code authorizes the judge to ask the parties and lawyers "to consider, outside the presence of the judge and court personnel, whether to waive disqualification."[350] The Model Code authorizes waivers of disqualification on all grounds except personal bias or prejudice;[351] the federal disqualification statute, in contrast, limits waiver to circumstances in which disqualification is based on the general standard that the judge's impartiality "might reasonably be questioned."[352]

---

[343] MODEL CODE, Rule 2.10(B) ("A judge shall not, in connection with cases, controversies, or issues that are likely to come before the court, make pledges, promises, or commitments that are inconsistent with the impartial performance of the adjudicative duties of judicial office.").

[344] Tony Mauro, *New Recusal Controversy in West Virginia High Court*, BLOG LEGAL TIMES. (Sept. 24, 2010, 4:10 PM), http://legaltimes.typepad.com/blt/2010/09/new-recusal-controversy-in-west-virginia-high-court.html.

[345] Jessica Karmasek, *Ketchum Reverse Course, Recuses Himself*, WEST VIRGINIA RECORD, September 28, 2010, http://wvrecord.com/stories/510599238-ketchum-reverses-course-recuses-himself.

[346] MODEL CODE, Rule 2.11, Comment 2.

[347] *In re* IBM Corp., 45 F.3d 641, 643 (2d Cir. 1995).

[348] Travelers Ins. Co. v. Liljeberg Enters., Inc., 38 F.3d 1404, 1410 (5th Cir. 1994); *In re* National Union Fire Ins. Co., 839 F.2d 1226, 1232 (7th Cir. 1988) ("Counsel who perceive a problem under § 455(a) must not tarry, for delay imposes heavy costs on other litigants and the judicial system.").

[349] MODEL CODE, Rule 2.11, Comment 5.

[350] MODEL CODE, Rule 2.11(C).

[351] *Id.*

[352] 28 U.S.C. § 455(a).

When a party files a motion to disqualify, the most common approach is for the subject judge to review the motion on the merits.[353] Alternatively, several states require that the motion be decided on its merits by a different judge.[354] A blended approach, adopted by a significant number of states, requires the subject judge to review the motion first for legal sufficiency (i.e., to assess whether the allegations in the motion, if true, would necessitate disqualification), but assigns another judge to rule on the merits of the motion (i.e., to ascertain whether the allegations are true).[355] Around twenty states seek to reduce the need for judges to evaluate their own impartiality or that of their colleagues, through recourse to a process known as "peremptory challenge," or "substitution" of judges. In those jurisdictions, parties are afforded a one-time opportunity to request the disqualification of their assigned judge, without showing, or in some jurisdictions even alleging, that their judge's impartiality is in doubt.[356]

If a litigant is unsatisfied with a judge's decision not to disqualify, review via appeal or writ of mandamus are generally available.[357] On appeal, the standard of review is most commonly an abuse of discretion standard.[358] Other states employ a comparably stringent "clearly erroneous" standard or its equivalent.[359] A small number of states have adopted a *de novo* standard of review.[360]

---

[353] The ABA Judicial Disqualification Project, *Taking Disqualification Seriously*, 92 JUDICATURE at 16.

[354] *Id.*

[355] *Id.*

[356] *Id.* at 15.

[357] RICHARD E. FLAMM, JUDICIAL DISQUALIFICATION: RECUSAL AND DISQUALIFICATION OF JUDGES §§ 32.1, 32.6 (2d ed. 2007).

[358] *Id.* at § 33.1.

[359] *Id.*

[360] *Id.*

# Chapter 6-3

# REGULATING JUDICIAL CONDUCT OFF THE BENCH—EXTRAJUDICIAL AND POLITICAL ACTIVITIES

**By Charles Gardner Geyh**

*Table of Sections*

§ 6-3.1 Extrajudicial Conduct
§ 6-3.2 Political Activities

---

As discussed in § 6-1.5(b), judges are under a duty to "act at all times" in a manner that promotes public confidence in the independence, integrity, and impartiality of the judiciary. That includes times when they are off the bench, because the manner in which judges conduct themselves when they are not performing the duties of judicial office can reflect on their fitness to serve as judges. Off the bench conduct can be loosely grouped into two categories: political activities, which are associated with attaining or retaining judicial office; and extrajudicial activities, which concern all other conduct unrelated to the performance of judicial duties.

## § 6-3.1 EXTRAJUDICIAL CONDUCT

The ethics of a judge's general personal conduct are regulated by Canon 1 of the Model Code of Judicial Conduct, as discussed in § 6-1. The section that follows concerns more specific subsets of extrajudicial conduct: governmental activities; avocational activities; business activities; and receiving gifts.

### § 6-3.1(a) Extrajudicial Conduct: General Obligations

Judges are under an ethical directive to act at all times in a manner that preserves their independence, integrity, and impartiality.[1] That does not mean, however, that judges are expected to cut themselves off from the rest of the world. To the contrary, meaningful life experience can be indispensable to understanding the perspectives of the parties and the circumstances giving rise to cases that judges are called upon to adjudicate. Moreover, when judges participate in the life of their communities, those communities can acquire a better appreciation for and understanding of judges and courts. Accordingly, judges are authorized to participate in extrajudicial activities,[2] and even encouraged to engage in community outreach.[3]

There are, however, risks associated with extrajudicial activities. Judges can become so preoccupied with extrajudicial priorities that they neglect their judicial duties. Their extrajudicial activities can give rise to conflicts of interest that require

---

[1] MODEL CODE, Rule 1.2.

[2] MODEL CODE, Rule 3.1.

[3] MODEL CODE, Rule 1.2, Comment 6; Rule 3.1, Comments 1 and 2.

disqualification, thereby imposing additional administrative burdens on a disqualified judge's colleagues. Some extrajudicial activities can undermine a judge's perceived impartiality, independence, or integrity. Other activities can involve inappropriate exploitation of the judge's office.

Accordingly, the Model Code of Judicial Conduct includes several general limitations on a judge's extrajudicial activities. First, judges must give priority to the duties of judicial office,[4] and "shall not. . .participate in activities that will interfere with the proper performance of the judge's judicial duties."[5] Second, judges are forbidden from engaging in activities "that will lead to frequent disqualification."[6] Third, judges are directed not to participate in activities that "would appear, to a reasonable person, to undermine the judge's independence, integrity, or impartiality."[7] Fourth, to guard against inappropriate exploitation of their offices, judges are barred from engaging in extrajudicial conduct that appears coercive,[8] or (with limited exceptions) that uses court resources.[9]

### § 6-3.1(b) Governmental Activities

Judges are public citizens who have chosen careers in government service. As such, they acquire expertise in matters affecting the courts that they may wish to share with those in a position to influence public policy; and they may have an affinity for governmental affairs generally that they would like to pursue. Opportunities for judges to participate in civic and governmental activities can arise in a variety of ways: judges may be invited to participate on governmental commissions or task forces; or, judges may be invited to testify before or consult with legislative or administrative bodies, or may seek to testify or consult on their own initiative.

Like other citizens, judges enjoy a first amendment right to speak and petition their government. Moreover, a judge's participation in governmental and civil activities can better inform governmental decision-making, improve public understanding of the courts, and promote constructive relations between the three branches of government. There are, however, several risks that ethics rules seek to manage. First, participation in such activities can divert judges from their first priority, which is to perform the duties of judicial office. Second, and more important for purposes of discussion here, judges can align themselves with causes or issues in ways that call the judges' impartiality into question. Third, judges can sometimes appear to be trading on their position to influence governmental policy.

With respect to judges serving on governmental committees, boards, or commissions, codes of conduct limit such service to bodies that concern "the law, the legal

---

[4] MODEL CODE, Rule 2.1.

[5] MODEL CODE, Rule 3.1(A).

[6] MODEL CODE, Rule 3.1(B).

[7] MODEL CODE, Rule 3.1(C).

[8] MODEL CODE, Rule 3.1(D). Concern for coercion arises when a judge calls upon others to do things in extrajudicial settings that they may feel obligated to do because of the judge's position of authority. MODEL CODE, Rule 3.1, Comment 4.

[9] MODEL CODE, Rule 3.1(E). Subsection (E) exempts "incidental" use of court resources for extrajudicial activities related to the law, the legal system and the administration of justice—an exemption consistent with the Model Code's exhortation of judges to participate in activities that promote public confidence in the administration of justice. MODEL CODE, Rule 1.2, Comment 6.

system, or the administration of justice."[10] In a similar vein, codes authorize judges to consult with or appear voluntarily before legislative and executive branch bodies on matters concerning "the law, the legal system, and the administration of justice."[11] As to appearances before governmental bodies, state and federal codes of conduct include two additional exceptions, authorizing appearances on matters in which the judge has acquired special expertise by virtue of the judge's judicial experience, and authorizing the judge to appear *pro se* on matters involving the judge or the judge's interests.[12]

Governmental bodies oversee the operation of government, which is controlled by applicable law. Read expansively, then, every governmental body is concerned with "the law;" insofar as ethics rules authorize judges to serve on or appear before governmental bodies that are concerned with matters of law, the rules arguably impose no meaningful restrictions on extrajudicial conduct. And there are examples on the less restrictive end of the spectrum in which judicial advisory committees have interpreted law broadly enough to permit judges to serve on bodies concerned with such issues as the status of women;[13] the mentally ill;[14] and juvenile corrections.[15]

Some jurisdictions, however, have read the rules more restrictively. As a federal judicial conference advisory opinion explained, "to qualify as an acceptable law-related activity, the activity must be directed toward the objective of improving the law, qua law, or improving the legal system or administration of justice, and not merely utilizing the law or the legal system as a means to achieve an underlying social, political, or civic objective."[16] The advisory opinion elaborated on this general proposition with two "formulations":

> First, permissible law-related activities are "limited to the kinds of matters a judge, by virtue of [the judge's] judicial experience, is uniquely qualified to address." . . . Second, we look to see if the beneficiary of the activity is the law or legal system itself. A permissible activity, in other words, is one that serves the interests generally of those who use the legal system, rather than the interests of any specific constituency.[17]

The principle underlying this more restrictive view is that judges can jeopardize public confidence in their impartiality when they participate in governmental affairs that align the judge with the policy agendas of specific constituencies—particularly in those affairs where their status as judges is not especially relevant. Advisory committees taking a more restrictive view have counseled judges not to serve on bodies that address a school's drug testing policy;[18] mayoral ethics;[19] or reducing the incidence of domestic violence—although, in the latter instance, the opinion authorized the judge to consult

---

[10] MODEL CODE, Rule 3.4.

[11] MODEL CODE, Rule 3.2(A).

[12] MODEL CODE, Rule 3.2(B)–(C); CODE OF CONDUCT FOR U.S. JUDGES, Canon 4A(2).

[13] Florida Judicial Ethics Advisory Op. 2004–05 (2004).

[14] Arizona Judicial Ethics Advisory Op. 90–11 (1990).

[15] *Id.*

[16] Committee on Codes of Judicial Conduct Advisory Committee Op. 93: Extrajudicial Activities Related to the Law (Jun. 2009).

[17] *Id.*

[18] Kansas Judicial Ethics Advisory Op. JE–150 (2007).

[19] Washington Ethics Advisory Comm. Op. 90–16 (1990).

with the group on domestic violence issues that concerned court business.[20] In a like vein, judges have been advised against making appearances before governmental bodies for the reform of drug laws that judges will be called upon to interpret.[21]

An exception permits judges to appear before governmental bodies *pro se*. There is nothing problematic about permitting a judge to petition the government on issues affecting the judge's property, neighborhood or other legal interests, as long as the judge does not attempt to abuse the prestige of office by appearing in her capacity as a judge, rather than a private citizen.[22] Problems have arisen, however, with the scope of this exception. The Code of Conduct for Federal Judges and earlier iterations of the Model Code of Judicial Conduct, permit judges to appear *pro se* on matters involving the judge's "interest" or "interests."[23] In 2002, the Arkansas Judicial Commission recommended that an appellate judge be admonished for a public appearance before the Arkansas Legislative Black Caucus, at which he urged the Caucus to send a "budgetary vote of no confidence" to the University of Arkansas, because of its "sorry leadership" on race-related issues.[24] The Arkansas Supreme Court concluded that the judge's appearance was inappropriate under the general standards regulating judicial appearances before governmental bodies, but declined to impose a sanction, concluding that the exception for *pro se* appearances was unconstitutionally vague because it did not define the scope of a "judge's interests" adequately to exclude the appearance in question from its scope.[25] In response, the ABA revised the Model Code in 2007 to limit the *pro se* exception to "matters involving the judge's legal or economic interests."[26]

### § 6-3.1(c) Avocational Activities

Judges are authorized to participate in activities sponsored either by "organizations. . .concerned with the law, the legal system, or the administration of justice,"[27] or by "educational, religious, charitable, fraternal, or civic organizations not conducted for profit",[28] even when these latter activities "do not involve the law."[29] With respect to such activities, however, three recurring ethical concerns are (1) that judges not exploit the prestige of their offices for the benefit of the extrajudicial activities in which they engage; (2) that they not participate in activities that will require frequent disqualification; and (3) that they not pursue avocations that undermine public confidence in their impartiality.

Judges misuse their positions to advance the interests of the organizations with which they are affiliated, if they exploit their status and power to influence others to join or make contributions to assist those organizations. Accordingly, codes of conduct impose significant restrictions on the role judges can play in fundraising. Model Code Rule 3.7

---

[20] Massachusetts Advisory Op. 2014–4.

[21] Committee on Codes of Judicial Conduct Advisory Committee Op. 93: Extrajudicial Activities Related to the Law (June 2009) ("[P]articipating in an organization lobbying for legislation to implement a particular policy pertaining to drug and alcohol abuse is not consistent with the obligations of judicial office.").

[22] MODEL CODE, Rule 3.2, Comment 3.

[23] ABA MODEL CODE OF JUDICIAL CONDUCT, Canon 4C(1) (1990); CODE OF CONDUCT FOR U.S. JUDGES, Canon 4(A)(c).

[24] Griffen v. Arkansas Judicial Discipline & Disability Comm'n, 130 S.W.3d 524 (2003).

[25] *Id.*

[26] MODEL CODE, Rule 3.2(C).

[27] MODEL CODE, Rule 3.7(A).

[28] MODEL CODE, Rule 3.7(A).

[29] MODEL CODE, Rule 3.1, Comment 1.

authorizes judges to solicit contributions for an organization "only from members of the judge's family, or from judges over whom the judge does not exercise supervisory or appellate authority."[30] As the Pennsylvania Ethics Committee explained, "advertising the judge's presence, placing the judge in a strategic position to influence potential customers or contributors, having a judge endorse a fundraising event or product, or having a judge sell tickets, may lead to effects the Code is designed to prevent."[31]

Conduct Committees thus seek to draw a line between permissible avocational activities and impermissible fundraising for those activities. For example, the New York Commission on Judicial Ethics advised that a judge "may serve as deacon of his/her church, make administrative announcements, and deliver a sermon, provided that he/she does not solicit tithes or contributions."[32] Even though judges are largely prohibited from soliciting funds themselves, the Model Code permits them to "assist[ ] such an organization or entity in planning related to fund-raising."[33] Hence, Code commentary elaborates that it is "generally permissible for a judge to serve as an usher or food preparer . . . at fundraising events" because "[s]uch activities are not solicitation and do not present an element of coercion or abuse the prestige of judicial office."[34]

Controversy has surrounded the question of whether it is appropriate for judges to serve as featured speakers at fundraising events, where the judge is effectively on the front-line of the organization's fundraising effort, even if the judge is not soliciting contributions per se. The 1990 Model Code and the Code of Conduct for U.S. judges prohibited judges from speaking at fundraising events.[35] As a consequence, United States Supreme Court Justice Clarence Thomas, and former Justice Antonin Scalia have been criticized for serving as featured speakers at Federalist Society events that arguably serve a fundraising purpose—[36] even though the Supreme Court has not adopted the Code of Conduct for U.S. judges (which, again, applies only to judges in the lower federal courts). In 2007, however, the ABA concluded that the benefits of judges sharing their insights at law related events outweighed the risk that those judges would be perceived as lending the prestige of their office to generate revenue for the sponsoring organization. Accordingly, Rule 3.7 authorizes judges "appearing at, receiving an award or other recognition at, being featured on the program of, and permitting his or her title to be used in connection with" extrajudicial events generally, and fund-raising events in particular if the event is law-related.[37]

Concerns similar to those relating to fund-raising have resulted in restrictions on the authority of judges to solicit members for organizations with which they are affiliated. Model Code Rule 3.7 authorizes judges to solicit membership on behalf of organizations concerned with law, the legal system and the administration of justice

---

[30] MODEL CODE, Rule 3.7(A)(2).

[31] 2015 WL 4926716 (PA Conf. St. Trl. Jud. Eth. Comm.).

[32] N.Y. Jud. Adv. Op. 15–92(A).

[33] MODEL CODE, Rule 3.7 (A)(1).

[34] MODEL CODE, Rule 3.7, Comment 3.

[35] MODEL CODE, Canon 4C, Commentary ("A judge must not be a speaker or guest of honor at an organization's fundraising event."); CODE OF CONDUCT FOR U.S. JUDGES, Canon 4C, Commentary ("A judge may attend fundraising events of law-related and other organizations although the judge may not be a speaker, a guest of honor, or featured on the program of such an event.").

[36] Press release, Alliance for Justice, Justices Scalia and Thomas to Attend Federalist Society Fundraising Dinner, Demonstrating Ongoing Lack of Respect for Judicial Ethics (Nov. 9, 2011), *available at* https://www.highbeam.com/doc/1G1-272011283.html.

[37] MODEL CODE, Rule 3.7(A)(4).

(even if membership includes dues that serve a fundraising purpose), but not others.[38] Permitting judges to solicit membership in law related organizations proceeds from the premise that the public would regard a judge's participation in membership solicitation on behalf of such organizations "as more natural or more appropriate than solicitation of membership in nonlaw-related organizations."[39] One could, of course, argue for the opposite conclusion, that "the potentially coercive effect of membership solicitation by a judge would less likely be felt in venues where fewer of the people involved would be lawyers."[40] The 1990 iteration of Model Code, still in place in some states, is more in accord with the latter view: it forbids membership solicitation "if the solicitation might reasonably be perceived as coercive,"[41] and adds in commentary that a judge "must not" solicit membership from persons "who are likely ever to appear before the court on which the judge serves."[42]

A separate concern is raised by judges' choice of avocational activities. Advisory Committees discourage judges from associating themselves with organizations that are likely to make regular appearances before the judge, which would require frequent disqualification.[43] Codes of Conduct explicitly prohibit judges from joining organizations that practice invidious discrimination (for example, country clubs that exclude people on the basis of race or gender), because membership in such organizations can foster the public perception that the judge shares the organization's views, to the detriment of public confidence in the judge's impartiality.[44] Even if the organization has no formal policy against admitting members of a particular group, and even if the judge is an outspoken proponent of admitting such members, retaining membership in such an organization that, in practice, excludes members of such a group, can violate the code.[45] Similarly, judges are discouraged from affiliating themselves with organizations that take "public positions on controversial topics," which "might raise a reasonable question regarding the judge's impartiality.[46]

With respect to participation in the activities of bar associations, judges must be mindful to avoid aligning themselves with causes or positions that could call their impartiality into question. That concern may counsel against judges affiliating with specialized bar associations that champion points of view on issues likely to come before the judge. Participation in general state and national bar associations, do not present a similar risk, and judges need not disqualify themselves from cases in which their bar

---

[38] MODEL CODE, Rule 3.7(A)(3).

[39] CHARLES E. GEYH [SIC] AND W. WILLIAM HODES, REPORTERS' NOTES TO THE MODEL RULES OF JUDICIAL CONDUCT 69–70 (2009).

[40] *Id.* at 69.

[41] ABA MODEL CODE OF JUDICIAL CONDUCT, Canon 4C(3)(b)(iii) (1990).

[42] *Id.* at Canon 4C, Commentary.

[43] Committee on Codes of Judicial Conduct Advisory Committee Op. 82: Joining Organizations (June 2009).

[44] MODEL CODE, Rule 3.6, Comment 1 ("A judge's membership in an organization that practices invidious discrimination creates the perception that the judge's impartiality is impaired").

[45] *In re* Paine, C.C.D. No. 11–01 at *1–2 (Comm. on Judicial Conduct & Disability of Judicial Conf. of U.S. Dec. 1, 2011), *available at* file: http://www.uscourts.gov/sites/default/files/ccd-11-01order-final-12-01-11 amended-11-17-01.pdf (while the Sixth Circuit Judicial Council, citing the judge's efforts to change the practices of the organization, found no misconduct, the Judicial Conference Committee disagreed, concluding that the judge's membership violated Canons 2A and 2C of the Code of Conduct for U.S. Judges and constituted misconduct under the Judicial Conduct and Disability Act).

[46] Committee on Codes of Judicial Conduct Advisory Committee Op. 82: Joining Organizations (June 2009).

associations enter an appearance, as long as the judge did not participate in formulating the association's position on the issue in litigation.[47] At the same time, judges are discouraged from participating in bar activities on "controversial subjects" that align the judge with narrow constituencies, which could cast doubt on the judge's impartiality.[48]

Finally, judges are permitted to engage in "educational," activities, which include speaking, teaching, and writing. Model Code commentary observes that, "[j]udges are uniquely qualified to engage in extrajudicial activities that concern the law, the legal system, and the administration of justice, such as by speaking, writing, teaching, or participating in scholarly research projects."[49] When teaching, writing, and speaking judges are subject to rules of conduct previously discussed. In addition to restrictions on extrajudicial activities generally,[50] judges should not comment publicly on pending or impending cases in their teaching or writing;[51] they should not misuse the prestige of judicial office by, for example, serving as a regular expert commentator on a television talk show,[52] and they should act at all times in a manner that promotes public confidence in their independence, integrity, and impartiality.[53] Judges are permitted to accept reasonable compensation for their speaking, teaching, and writing, provided that doing so would not lead a reasonable person to doubt their independence, integrity, and impartiality.[54] Such extrajudicial compensation is subject to periodic reporting requirements.[55]

### § 6-3.1(d) Business Activities

Ethics rules impose significant restrictions on a judge's business activities. By virtue of the nearly universal prerequisite to judicial office that judges be learned in law or licensed to practice law, the most obvious business activity in which judges would be qualified and likely to engage would be the practice of law. Codes of conduct, however, universally forbid judges from practicing law.[56] The potential for legal practice to distract from a judge's judicial duties, the risk that judges could exploit their offices to gain advantage for themselves and their clients; and the inevitability of conflicts arising for judges who are simultaneously advocates, has long been deemed intolerably great. Codes of conduct do not usually define "practice of law," which can create confusion at the margins, but it clearly bars court appearances (pro bono or otherwise),[57] being identified as attorney of record in any context,[58] or preparing legal documents for others.[59] There

---

47 Committee on Codes of Judicial Conduct Advisory Committee Op. 85: Membership and Participation in the American Bar Association (June 2009).

48 Committee on Codes of Judicial Conduct Advisory Committee Op. 85: Membership and Participation in the American Bar Association (June 2009).

49 MODEL CODE, Rule 3.1, Comment 1.

50 MODEL CODE, Rule 3.1; *see* discussion at § 6-3.1(a).

51 MODEL CODE, Rule 2.10(A); *see* discussion at § 6-2.3(c).

52 MODEL CODE, Rule 1.3; *see* discussion at § 6-1.5(c).

53 MODEL CODE, Rule 1.2; *see* discussion at § 6-1.5(b).

54 MODEL CODE, Rule 3.12.

55 MODEL CODE, Rule 3.15.

56 MODEL CODE OF JUDICIAL CONDUCT, Rule 3.10.

57 Inquiry Concerning a Judge (Henson), 414 So. 2d 579 (FL 2005) (judge removed from office for representing a defendant in a criminal proceeding); *In re* Hammons, 484 N.W. 2d 401 (Mich. 1992) (judge censured for representing a friend in a jury trial).

58 *In re* Sasso, Presentment, ACJC 2007–162, N.J. Advisory Comm. on Judicial Conduct (2007) (judge disciplined for being identified as an attorney in company documents).

59 *In re* Van Susteren, 262 N.W. 2d 133 (1978) (discipline imposed for drafting contract).

are, however, limited exceptions: part-time judges may continue to practice law, but may not make appearances before the court that they serve;[60] judges may represent themselves *pro se*;[61] and they may give legal advice to and draft and review legal documents for members of their families.[62]

Judges are likewise barred from serving as arbitrators or mediators outside the scope of their official judicial duties, unless otherwise authorized by law.[63] They are prohibited from serving in fiduciary positions (such as trustees or executors), except with respect to matters involving family members, and even then, only if doing so will not interfere with their official duties, or likely require them to appear before the courts they serve.[64] And while there is some variation among the states, judges are forbidden from serving as officers, directors or employees of for for-profit business entities, with limited exceptions for family businesses and businesses that manage family investments.[65]

Passive business activities, in contrast, are generally tolerated. Judges are permitted to manage investments and real estate holdings for themselves and members of their families.[66] Even these activities, however, are subject to restrictions: judges must avoid activities that will interfere with the performance of their judicial duties (such as when investment activities cause judges to neglect their caseloads), or create conflicts of interest that would result in frequent disqualification.[67] For example, if a lawyer who becomes a judge holds stock in a local company that makes frequent appearances in the court that the judge serves, divestiture is the appropriate solution.[68]

Judges may accept reasonable compensation for business activities in which they are authorized to engage.[69] Such compensation however, is subject to periodic reporting requirements, which add a degree of transparency that promotes public confidence in the judiciary, and provide lawyers and litigants with information that can be relevant to disqualification, insofar as activities giving rise to compensation can create conflicts of interest.[70]

### § 6-3.1(e) Gifts

Gifts present a special challenge for judges. On the one hand, people can give gifts to judges for the best of reasons—to express love, friendship, appreciation, or respect. On the other hand, people can give gifts to judges for the worst of reasons—to buy influence, invite a quid pro quo, or cultivate dependence. Moreover, people can give gifts to judges for the best of reasons that others misperceive as for the worst for reasons, to the detriment of public confidence in the judge's independence, integrity, and impartiality.

---

[60] MODEL CODE, Application, Part III A, B.

[61] MODEL CODE, Rule 3.10.

[62] MODEL CODE, Rule 3.10.

[63] MODEL CODE, Rule 3.9.

[64] MODEL CODE, Rule 3.8.

[65] MODEL CODE, Rule 3.11(B). For a discussion of state variations, see CHARLES GARDNER GEYH, JAMES J. ALFINI, STEVEN LUBET, JEFFREY L. SHAMAN, JUDICIAL CONDUCT AND ETHICS § 7.08 (5th ed. 2013).

[66] MODEL CODE, Rule 3.11(A); 3.11(B)(2), Comment 1.

[67] MODEL CODE, Rule 3.11(C).

[68] MODEL CODE, Rule 3.11, Comment 2.

[69] MODEL CODE, Rule 3.12.

[70] MODEL CODE, Rule 3.15.

For judges to decline some gifts can make them look discourteous or rude; for them to accept other gifts can make them look corrupt.

Given the ethical thicket that exchanging gifts creates, it is unsurprising that the subject is regulated by a complex web of ethics rules. There are different standards governing: gifts that judges must not accept; gifts that are acceptable and need not be reported; and gifts that are acceptable but need to be reported.

The general standard governing gifts, as reflected in Rule 3.13(A) of the Model Code of Judicial Conduct, is that a judge "shall not accept any gifts, loans, bequests, benefits, or other things of value, if acceptance . . . would appear to a reasonable person to undermine the judge's independence, integrity, or impartiality."[71] This general standard creates a baseline for gifts the judge must not accept.

The rule includes a list of gifts that are ordinarily so harmless as to be acceptable without the need to report them publicly—subject to the caveat that if a given gift runs afoul of the Rule 3.13(A) general standard, it may not be accepted. The list of presumptively unobjectionable gifts includes items of trivial value, such as greeting cards or commemorative plaques; gifts from friends, relatives, or lawyers who are so close to the judge as to require the judge's disqualification from proceedings in which they appeared regardless of the gifts; "ordinary social hospitality;" commercial opportunities or benefits available to judges on the same terms as non-judges; rewards or prizes in contests open to non-judges; scholarships and fellowships available to non-judges; complimentary books and materials supplied by publishers to judges for official use; and gifts to members of the judge's family associated with the family member's business, profession or activities, that are of incidental benefit to the judge.[72]

The gifts rule identifies additional gifts that are acceptable if they do not run afoul of the general 3.13(A) standard, but which are potentially problematic enough to require public reporting, in the same manner as compensation for extrajudicial activities.[73] Such gifts include gifts of non-trivial value associated with public testimonials (gifts of trivial value awarded as testimonials, such as commemorative plaques, need not be reported);[74] invitations to attend, without charge, events related to law, the legal system, or the administration of justice, and events unrelated to law if the invitation is extended to similarly situated non-judges; and gifts from persons whose interests, or who themselves have or are likely to come before the judge.[75]

It bears emphasis that the general standard articulated in Rule 3.13(A) operates to exclude gifts otherwise authorized by the rule. For example, Rule 3.13(C) ostensibly authorizes judges to accept gifts from lawyers and parties who appear before them, as long as those gifts are reported, but such gifts are limited to those that survive analysis under Rule 3.13(A). Thus, for example, a judge may accept a wedding gift from a friend and lawyer who appeared before the judge five years earlier but who has since retired, moved out of the state or left litigation practice: no reasonable person would think that the gift undermines the judge's integrity or impartiality under Rule 3.13(A), and if reported, the gift is acceptable under Rule 3.13(C). On the other hand, if the defendant's

---

[71] MODEL CODE, Rule 3.13(A).

[72] MODEL CODE, Rule 3.13(B).

[73] MODEL CODE, Rule 3.15.

[74] MODEL CODE, Rule 3.13(B)(2).

[75] MODEL CODE, Rule 3.13(C).

counsel gives the judge an expensive watch on the eve of trial, Rule 3.13(C) is irrelevant, because the gift does not survive analysis under 3.13(A) and must not be accepted.

One recurring issue concerns gifts to judges in the form of expense-paid seminars hosted by educational institutions or other organizations, often at desirable venues. Interest groups and journalists have derisively branded those seminars "junkets for judges," which have sometimes been underwritten by corporations, on topics of interest to those corporations in litigation.[76] Insofar as the seminar topics are law related, the basic rule governing gifts characterizes expense paid seminars as gifts a judge may accept but must report—provided that accepting such gifts would not reasonably appear to undermine the judge's integrity or impartiality.[77]

In response to concerns raised, a Model Code rule governing reimbursement or waiver of fees or charges imposes additional restrictions.[78] Under the Model Code, judges may only accept reimbursement for "reasonable and necessary" expenses actually incurred, and then, only for expenses necessary for the judge to travel to and attend the event—meaning that expenses associated with entertainment on site are excluded.[79] Moreover, commentary accompanying the rule provides additional guidance.[80] To avoid accepting waivers or reimbursements under circumstances that could call a judge's independence, integrity, or impartiality into question, judges are advised to consider: the identity of the sponsor and funding sources for the program; the purpose, content, and viewpoint of the program and its relationship to litigation before the judge; and connections between program sponsors, funding sources and parties or interests likely to appear before the judge.[81]

## § 6-3.2 POLITICAL ACTIVITIES

When discussing constitutional structure, authors often denominate the executive and legislative branches of government as "political," in contrast to the judicial branch.[82] From the perspective of those who explained the new Constitution to a fledgling nation, the judiciary was rendered distinct from the other branches government by virtue of its independence from political control, owing to the tenure and salary protections of Article III.[83] Those protections, they argued, would serve as "an excellent barrier to the encroachments and oppressions of the representative body," and were "the best expedient which can be devised in any government, to secure a steady, upright, and impartial administration of the laws."[84]

Characterizing the judiciary as "apolitical" is a misnomer in several respects. Federal judges are subject to a range of political controls, including: impeachment processes; budgetary appropriations; establishment, disestablishment and regulatory

---

76 Allison Morrow, *Spotlight on Judicial Junkets*, WALL STREET JOURNAL LAW BLOG (Mar. 29, 2013), *available at* http://blogs.wsj.com/law/2013/03/29/spotlight-on-judicial-junkets/.

77 MODEL CODE, Rule 3.13(A), (C).

78 MODEL CODE, Rule 3.14.

79 MODEL CODE, Rule 3.14(A)–(B).

80 MODEL CODE, Rule 3.14, Comment 3. The Comment is based on Committee on Codes of Judicial Conduct Advisory Committee Op. 67: Attendance at Educational Seminars (June 2009).

81 MODEL CODE, Rule 3.14, Comment 3.

82 The Federalist No. 78 (Alexander Hamilton).

83 *Id.*

84 *Id.*

oversight of lower courts; and adjustments to subject matter jurisdiction.[85] Social science data show that the decisions of federal and state judges are subject to ideological and other "political" influences.[86] And many states have been selecting their judges via popular election since the 1830s; as of today, judges are subject to some form of popular election in 38 states.[87]

Judicial ethics struggles with the resulting irony. On the one hand, judicial independence from political control remains central to the judiciary's self-identity. The lead canon in the Model Code of Judicial Conduct declares, "a judge shall uphold and promote the independence . . . of the judiciary."[88] Similarly, judges are admonished not to "be swayed by public clamor," or to permit "political . . . interests or relationships to influence the judge's judicial conduct or judgment."[89] At the same time, the vast majority of states render judges dependent on the electorate for their continuation in office, which requires judges to behave like political actors to the end of winning popular support.

Canon 4 of the Model Code of Judicial Conduct seeks to strike a balance between the judiciary's decisional independence and electoral accountability, by imposing significant restrictions on judges' political activities while relaxing restrictions during campaign seasons to accommodate judges' need to run for office. Rules 4.1 and 4.2 occupy the core of Canon 4. Rule 4.1 is, in effect, a list of prohibited activities. It applies to judges and non-judge judicial candidates alike,[90] and provides that they shall not: (1) serve as leaders in political organizations;[91] (2) make speeches for political organizations;[92] (3) publicly endorse or oppose candidates for public office;[93] (4) solicit funds for or make contributions to candidates or political organizations;[94] (5) attend events of candidates or political organizations;[95] (6) identify themselves publicly as candidates of political

---

[85] CHARLES GARDNER GEYH, WHEN COURTS AND CONGRESS COLLIDE: THE STRUGGLE FOR CONTROL OF AMERICA'S JUDICIAL SYSTEM (2006).

[86] CHARLES GARDNER GEYH, COURTING PERIL: THE POLITICAL TRANSFORMATION OF THE AMERICAN JUDICIARY (2016) (summarizing social science data).

[87] Billy Corriher, *Partisan Judicial Elections and the Distorting Influence of Campaign Cash*, Center for American Progress (Oct. 25, 2012), https://www.americanprogress.org/issues/civil-liberties/report/2012/10/25/42895/partisan-judicial-elections-and-the-distorting-influence-of-campaign-cash/.

[88] MODEL CODE, Canon 1.

[89] MODEL CODE, Rule 2.4(A)–(B).

[90] As discussed in the introduction to Section 6, states require that judges be lawyers. Lawyers are subject to codes of professional conduct that require them to abide by applicable codes of judicial conduct when they are judicial candidates. Model Rules of Professional Conduct, Rule 8.2(B).

[91] MODEL CODE, Rule 2.4(A)(1); In Matter of King, Determination (N.Y. Comm'n on Judicial Conduct, Feb. 14, 2007) (Justice of the Peace admonished for serving as chair of the local Republican Party).

[92] MODEL CODE, Rule 4.1(A)(2); Wolfson v. Concannon, 811 F.3d 1176 (9th Cir. 2016) (upholding constitutionality of Arizona corollary to Rule 4.1(A)(2) prohibiting judicial candidates making speeches for political organizations).

[93] MODEL CODE, Rule 4.1(A)(3); Wersel v. Sexton, 674 F.3d 1010 (8th Cir. 2012) (upholding constitutionality of Minnesota corollary to Rule 4.1(A)(3)).

[94] MODEL CODE, Rule 4.1(A)(4); *In re* Chappell (Ky. Judicial Conduct Comm'n, May 27, 2008) (judge reprimanded for making contribution to another candidate's campaign while the judge's appointment was pending).

[95] MODEL CODE, Rule 4.1(A)(5); *In re* Sanchez, 815 A.2d 418 (N.J. 2003) (judge reprimanded for attending political event and participating in celebration of successful candidates).

organizations;[96] (7) seek or accept endorsements of political organizations;[97] (8) solicit contributions except through their campaign committees;[98] (9) use campaign contributions for private purposes;[99] (10) use court resources in judicial campaigns;[100] (11) knowingly or recklessly make false or misleading statements;[101] (12) make public statements that could affect the fairness of pending or impending court proceedings;[102] or (13) make pledges or promises concerning future cases.[103]

Rule 4.2 then lifts some of the restrictions imposed by Rule 4.1 during campaign seasons, when judges and judicial candidates—including candidates for contested and retention elections—may: endorse and oppose candidates for the same judicial office for which they are running; attend events of candidates or political organizations; seek or accept endorsements from political organizations that are not denominated partisan; and contribute limited amounts to candidates and political organizations. The rule lifts two additional restrictions for candidates in states that select judges via partisan elections: they may identify themselves as candidates of political organizations, and they may seek and accept endorsements of partisan political organizations.

Canon 4 regulates the ethics of judges and judicial candidates by restricting what they are permitted to say and with whom they are permitted to associate, which raises first amendment questions. The American Bar Association's 1972 Model Code of Judicial Conduct included a clause in its canon governing political activities, which prohibited

---

[96] MODEL CODE, Rule 4.1(A)(6); Inquiry Concerning a Judge (Angel), 867 So.2d 379 (Fla. 2004) (Florida Supreme Court reprimanded a judge for attending and participating in partisan political gatherings and meetings).

[97] MODEL CODE, Rule 4.1(A)(7); *In re* Starcher, 501 S.E.2d 772 (W. Va. 1998) (admonishing a state supreme court justice who had personally sought the endorsement of a labor organization during his campaign, and finding him guilty of violating Canon 5(C)(2)).

[98] MODEL CODE, Rule 4.1(A)(8) Williams-Yulee v. Florida Bar, 135 S. Ct. 1656 (2015) (upholding constitutionality of Florida corollary to Rule 4.1(A)(8) rule, imposing discipline on judicial candidate for direct-mail solicitation of prospective contributors); *In re* Krouse, Stipulation, Agreement, and Order of Reprimand (Wash. Comm'n on Judicial Conduct May 5, 2005) (a judge's campaign committee solicited donations by email over the judge's signature). *But see* Weaver v. Bonner, 309 F.3d 1312 (11th Cir. 2002), *reh'g and reh'g en banc denied*, 57 F. App'x 416 (11th Cir. 2003) (the Weaver court reasoned that the fact that judicial candidates require financial support and public endorsements to run successful campaigns does not suggest that they will be partial if they are elected).

[99] MODEL CODE, Rule 4.1(A)(9); *In re* Lawrence, 335 N.W. 456 (Mich. 1983) (judge suspended for diverting campaign contributions to personal expense fund).

[100] MODEL CODE, Rule 4.1(A)(10); Comm. on Judicial Ethics, Judicial Section, State Bar of Tex., Op. 68 (1983) (affirming that judges may not use court stationery to exploit the power and prestige of the office to promote his or her candidacy).

[101] MODEL CODE, Rule 4.1(A)(11); In the Matter of Davis, Order (Ind. S. Ct., May 7, 2013) (former judicial candidate disciplined for failing to request that newspaper retract a false statement attributed to the candidate about the candidate's opponent); *In re* Chmura, 608 N.W.2d 31, 43 (Mich. 2000) (Mich. Supreme Court amended the Canon to provide simply that a candidate for judicial office "should not knowingly, or with reckless disregard, use or participate in the use of any form of public communication that is false").; Doyle v. Judicial Ret. & Removal Comm'n, 885 S.W.2d 917 (Ky. 1994) (Court reprimanded a judge for misrepresentation in a campaign advertisement, but held that two other ads, although arguably in poor taste, did not constitute misrepresentation).

[102] MODEL CODE, Rule 4.1(A)(12); *In re* Burick, 705 N.E.2d 422 (Five Judge Comm'n Appointed by Ohio Sp. Ct. 1999) (reprimanding and fining a judicial candidate for a number of violations, including: stating that an incumbent opponent was appointed by political bosses; supporting the death penalty; making a statement about a sentence imposed by opponent while the case was still pending; and making misleading statements about endorsements).

[103] MODEL CODE, Rule 4.1(A)(13); *In re* Kinsey, 842 So. 2d 77 (Fla. 2003), *cert. den'd*, 540 U.S. 825 (2003); *In re* Watson, 794 N.E. 2d 1 (N.Y. 2003). *But see*, Duwe v. Alexander, 490 F. Supp. 2d 968 (W.D. Wis. 2007)(invalidating clause on First Amendment grounds).

judges from announcing their views on disputed legal issues.[104] In 1990, when the Model Code was next amended, the "announce clause" was removed, "to be more in line with constitutional guarantees of free speech."[105] Several states, however, Minnesota included, retained the announce clause in their codes of conduct. In 2002, a closely divided United States Supreme Court invalidated Minnesota's announce clause, and declared that judicial candidates had a first amendment right to announce their views on disputed legal issues that may come before them as judges.[106] The Court interpreted the announce clause as a content-based restriction on speech. As such, it was subject to "strict scrutiny," meaning that it must be narrowly tailored to serve a compelling government interest. Minnesota argued that the announce clause served the state's interest in preserving judicial impartiality and the appearance of judicial impartiality, but the Supreme Court disagreed. If "impartiality" meant lack of bias against a party, the clause was "barely tailored" to serve that interest because it prohibited speech about issues, not parties;[107] and if impartiality meant open-mindedness, the clause was "woefully under-inclusive" because it prohibited announcements on disputed legal issues during judicial campaigns but not before or after.[108]

A judicial candidate's right to announce his or her views on a disputed legal issue does not necessarily imply a corresponding right to act upon those views as a public official, when the issue comes before the candidate later, as a judge.[109] In his concurrence in *White*, Justice Kennedy acknowledged the state's authority to establish recusal standards that could be enforced on pain of discipline.[110] This implies that states are within their rights to force the disqualification of judges who announce their views in ways that call their impartiality into question. As discussed in § 6-2.5(b)(3)(f), the American Bar Association responded to *White* by adding Rule 2.11(b)(5), which requires judges to disqualify themselves when they "while a judge or a judicial candidate . . . made a public statement . . . that commits or appears to commit the judge to reach a particular result or rule in a particular way in the proceeding . . . ."

Broadly read, *White* implies that every Code of Conduct restriction on judicial speech must survive the exacting test of strict scrutiny, which bodes ill for a host of rules limiting campaign speech and association. Narrowly construed, *White* simply invalidated the "announce clause," which few states employed, and which the Model Code of Judicial Conduct jettisoned twelve years before *White* was decided because it imposed unwarranted restrictions on the rights of judicial candidates to express their views on issues of the day. In the years that followed, the lower federal courts applied *White* to other rules in different contexts, with inconsistent results. Some courts read *White* broadly and used it to strike down rules barring judges from making pledges, promises, or commitments; prohibiting judges from personally soliciting campaign

---

104 ABA MODEL CODE OF JUDICIAL CONDUCT, Canon 7B(1)(c) (1972).

105 LISA L. MILORD, THE DEVELOPMENT OF THE ABA JUDICIAL CODE 50 (1972).

106 Republican Party of Minnesota v. White, 536 U.S. 765 (2002).

107 *Id.*

108 *Id.* at 766.

109 Charles Gardner Geyh, *The Dimensions of Judicial Impartiality,* 65 FLA. L. REV. 493, 528 (2013).

110 Republican Party of Minnesota, 536 U.S. at 794 (Kennedy, J., concurring).

funds; and engaging in various partisan activities.[111] Others adopted a narrower reading of *White* and upheld similar code restrictions on judicial conduct.[112]

In *Wolfson v. Concannon*, the Ninth Circuit, held that (1) rules prohibiting judicial candidates from personally soliciting or accepting campaign contributions did not violate First Amendment, and (2) rules prohibiting judicial candidates from soliciting funds for other candidates or publicly endorsing other candidates did not violate the first amendment.[113] Although the Ninth Circuit was careful to note that the first amendment 'requires [courts] to err on the side of protecting political speech rather than suppressing it,'[114] it found that such restraints on the political speech of judicial candidates were essential to preserving "the public's confidence that judges base rulings on law, and not on party affiliation."[115] The Seventh Circuit, too, in *Bauer v. Shephard*, found that an Indiana judicial conduct rule limiting the political activities of Indiana's judges did not run afoul of the first amendment rights of a judge who wanted to serve as "a delegate at the Indiana State Republican Convention, speak at political clubs on behalf of persons running for judicial office as Republicans, speak to students on behalf of the Republican Party, and encourage donating to the Republican Party."[116] The Court stated that even if the judge did not identify himself as a judge in such settings, the audience generally "knows who is on the bench," and "might think that judiciary is behind endorsement."[117] "The desire to prevent judges from using the prestige of office for other ends," explained the Court, "underlies a great deal of the Code of Judicial Conduct for United States Judges."[118]

In 2015, the Supreme Court revisited the constitutional validity of Code restrictions on judicial campaign speech in *Williams-Yulee v. Florida Bar*.[119] At issue in *Williams-Yulee*, was the so-called "solicitation clause," included in the Model Code and widely adopted across the states, which authorized judicial candidates to solicit campaign contributions from prospective donors through their campaign committees, but prohibited them from doing so directly, to avoid real or perceived coercion arising from candidates soliciting funds from parties or lawyers likely to appear before them later as judges.[120] In another 5–4 decision, the Supreme Court upheld the solicitation clause. The Court concluded that the solicitation clause served the compelling state interest of maintaining public confidence in the integrity of the judiciary, and was narrowly tailored to limit its impact on speech because it did not prohibit solicitation altogether but enabled candidates to solicit contributions through their campaign committees. "Judges are not politicians, even when they come to the bench by way of the ballot," the Court declared, "and a State's decision to elect its judiciary does not compel it to treat judicial

---

[111] *See* Republican Party of Minnesota v. White, 416 F.3d 738 (8th Cir. 2005); Republican Party of Minnesota v. White, 361 F.3d 1035 (8th Cir. 2004). *See also* Duwe v. Alexander, 490 F. Supp. 2d 968 (W.D. Wis. 2007).

[112] Simes v. Arkansas Judicial Discipline & Disability Comm'n, 247 S.W.3d 876 (Ark. 2007); *In re* Watson, 794 N.E.2d 1 (N.Y. 2003).

[113] 811 F.3d 1176 (9th Cir. 2016) (en banc).

[114] *Id.* at 1180 (citing Federal Election Comm'n v. Wisconsin Right to Life, Inc., 551 U.S. 449, 457 (2007)).

[115] *Id.* at 1183.

[116] 620 F.3d 704, 711 (7th Cir. 2010).

[117] *Id.* at 712.

[118] *Id.*

[119] Williams-Yulee, 135 S. Ct. at 1656.

[120] MODEL CODE, Rule 4.1(A)(8).

candidates like campaigners for political office."[121] Although this could be construed to give codes of conduct some breathing room when judges or judicial candidates raise first amendment objections to restrictions on their political activities, the Court took pains to describe this as "one of the rare cases in which a speech restriction withstands strict scrutiny."[122]

When thinking about the ethical implications of judicial campaigns, the elephant in the parlor is financial support in the form of direct contributions to the candidate and independent expenditures on the candidate's behalf, in favor of the candidate or against the candidate's opponent. Non-candidate spending in supreme court races (meaning spending by independent organizations and individuals) increased nine-fold between the 2001–02 and 2011–12 election cycles[123]; and retention election spending in state supreme court races was twenty-five times greater during the 2013–2014 cycle as compared to the 2001–2002 cycle.[124] News stories have reported on the frequency with which state supreme court justices side with those who have lent financial support to their campaigns.[125] Survey data show that the public thinks judges are influenced by the campaign support they receive, which has a deleterious effect on the court's perceived legitimacy.[126] State statutes impose limits on the size of individual contributions that judges and judicial candidates may accept, which seek to diminish the perception of influence peddling.[127] The Supreme Court has upheld the constitutionality of individual contribution limits,[128] but more recently invalidated aggregate contribution limits as a violation of contributors' first amendment freedom of speech,[129] which has left the field in a state of uncertainty.[130] Regulation of independent expenditures is even more problematic after the Supreme Court's decision in *Citizens United v. FEC*, where the Court ruled, in another 5–4 decision, that federal restrictions on independent expenditures and electioneering communications violated the First Amendment rights of those seeking to spend money in support of a candidate.[131]

As a consequence, judicial ethics has focused more on remediating the adverse effects of campaign finance on judicial integrity and impartiality after they occur. In *Caperton v. Massey Coal Company*, the Supreme Court ruled that a party's due process right to an impartial judge requires disqualification when the judge has received

---

[121] Williams-Yulee, 135 S. Ct. at 1662.

[122] Williams-Yulee, 135 S. Ct. at 1666.

[123] ALICIA BANNON, LINDA CASEY, LIANNA REAGAN, ERIC VELASCO, THE NEW POLITICS OF JUDICIAL ELECTIONS 2011–12 5 (2012), *available at* https://judicialpolitics.org/report/2012-report/.

[124] SCOTT GREYTAK, ALICIA BANNON, ALLYSE FALCE & LINDA CASEY, BANKROLLING THE BENCH: THE NEW POLITICS OF JUDICIAL ELECTIONS 2013–2014 1–99, 22 (Laurie Kinney ed., 2015), *available at* http://newpoliticsreport.org/app/uploads/JAS-NPJE-2013-14.pdf.

[125] Adam Liptak and Janet Roberts, *Campaign Cash Mirrors a High Court's Rulings* N.Y. TIMES, Oct. 1, 2006, at A1, *available at* http://www.nytimes.com/2006/10/01/us/01judges.html?_r=0.

[126] *See* JAMES L. GIBSON, ELECTING JUDGES: THE SURPRISING EFFECTS OF CAMPAIGNING ON JUDICIAL ELECTIONS (2012).

[127] Deborah Goldberg, Public Funding of Judicial Elections: The Roles of Judges and the Rules of Campaign Finance, 64 OHIO STATE L.J. 95 (2003).

[128] *See* Buckley v. Valeo, 424 U.S. 1 (1976).

[129] McCutcheon v. FEC, 134 S. Ct. 1434 (2014).

[130] Robert Barnes, *Supreme Court Strikes Down Limits on Federal Campaign Donations*, THE WASHINGTON POST, April 14, 2014, https://www.washingtonpost.com/politics/supreme-court-strikes-down-limits-on-federal-campaign-donations/2014/04/02/54e16c30-ba74-11e3-9a05-c739f29ccb08_story.html (discussing uncertain constitutionality of campaign finance restrictions after *McCutheon*).

[131] Citizens United v. Federal Election Comm'n, 558 U.S. 310, 320 (2010).

campaign support in amounts and under circumstances sufficient to create a probability of bias.[132] And the ABA has amended the Model Code of Judicial Conduct to require disqualification when judges receive campaign contributions in excess of a specified amount from parties and lawyers who appear before them.[133] For a discussion of disqualification and campaign support, *see* § 6-2.5(b)(3)(f).

---

[132] Caperton v. Massey Coal Co., 556 U.S. 868 (2009).

[133] MODEL CODE, Rule 2.11(A)(4).

# Table of Cases


A.H. Robins Co., In re, 453
A.J. ex rel. L.B. v. Kierst, 189
AAB Joint Venture v. United States, 505
ABB Kent-Taylor, Inc. v. Stallings & Co., Inc., 450
Abbo v. Perkins, 771
Abdelsame v. Foden de Castro, 886, 889
Abel v. Austin, 881
Abner, State ex rel. v. Elliott, 584
Abrams v. McGuireWoods, LLP, 802
Ackerman v. National Property Analysts, Inc., 526
Actel Corp. v. Quicklogic Corp., 121
Action on Smoking and Health v. Civil Aeronautics Bd., 268
Adams v. BellSouth Telecommunications, Inc., 441
Agnew, Estate of v. Ross, 838
Agosto, United States v., 413
Agresta, In re, 975
Agrobiotech, Inc., In re, 832
Agster v. Maricopa Cty., 270
Aguilar, United States v., 536
Aguinda, In re, 997
Agurs, United States v., 641
Aiken v. Hancock, 821
Akin, Gump, Strauss, Hauer & Feld, L.L.P. v. National Development and Research, 857, 859
Alabama, United States v., 1000
Alcantara, Matter of, 532
Alexander v. Cahill, 161, 167, 173, 178
Alexander v. Primerica Holdings, Inc., 993
Alexander v. Turtur & Associates, Inc., 772
Allen v. Steele, 827
Allied Irish Banks, P.L.C. v. Bank of America, N.A., 318, 452
Allied-Signal Inc., In re, 991
Altman v. Kelly, 622
Alvino, In re, 965
Alyeska Pipeline Service Co. v. Wilderness Soc'y, 263
Ambac Assur. Corp. v. Countrywide Home Loans, Inc., 326
AmBase Corp. v. Davis Polk & Wardwell, 739, 773, 796
American Civil Liberties Union/Eastern Missouri Fund v. Miller, 434
American Fed. of Gov. Employees v. Federal Labor Relations Auth., 272
American Standard Inc. v. Pfizer Inc., 329
Ampicillin Antitrust Litig., In re, 320
Analytica, Inc. v. NPD Research, Inc., 401
Anders v. California, 485
Anderson v. Aspelmeier, Fisch, Power, Warner & Engberg, 440
Anderson, In re, 1004
Andrade v. Chojnacki, 999
Andrews v. Elwell, 922
Andritz Sprout-Bauer, Inc. v. Beazer E., Inc., 449, 452
Angle, United States v., 543
Anglo-Dutch Petroleum Int'l Inc., v. Greenberg Peden, P.C., 362
Anonymous Member of S.C. Bar, In re, 682, 683
Anonymous Member of South Carolina Bar, Matter of, 433
Antar, United States v., 993
Anten v. Superior Court, 325
Anthony v. Sullivan, 272
Anthoulis v. Mastoros, 817
Antone v. Mirviss, 882
Apex Oil Co., In re, 267
Apex Towing Co. v. Tolin, 888
Apple Corps. Ltd. v. International Collectors Society, 529
Aquino v. Kuczinski, Vila & Assoc., P.C., 777
Arab African Int'l Bank v. Epstein, 758
Aragona v. St. Paul Fire & Marine Ins., 939
Arbor Hill Concerned Citizens Neighborhood Association v. Albany County, 270
Armenian Assoc. v. Cafesjian, 1005
Armor v. Lantz, 923
Arnold v. Cargill, Inc., 513, 522
Arriola v. Harville, 270
Arthur Andersen LLP v. United States, 537, 540
Artiglio v. Corning Inc., 735
Asen v. All American Landscape and Design, Inc., 816
Ash, State ex rel. v. Swope, 332
Ashby v. Bar Plan Mut. Ins., 932
Ashley v. Stiller, 878
Ashtabula Cty. Bar Ass'n v. Brown, 177
Atanga, In re, 701
Atkinson, United States v., 546
Attorney Disciplinary Board v. Box, 664, 669
Attorney Disciplinary Board v. Carpenter, 151
Attorney Disciplinary Board v. D'Angelo, 298
Attorney Disciplinary Board v. Haskovec, 662
Attorney Disciplinary Board v. Johnson, 424
Attorney Disciplinary Board v. Laing, 249
Attorney Disciplinary Board v. Lesyshen, 486

Attorney Disciplinary Board v. McCuskey, 135, 140
Attorney Disciplinary Board v. McGinness, 487
Attorney Disciplinary Board v. Mendez, 149
Attorney Disciplinary Board v. Palmer, 487
Attorney Disciplinary Board v. Piazza, 256
Attorney Disciplinary Board v. Rhinehart, 300
Attorney Disciplinary Board v. Schmidt, 666
Attorney Disciplinary Board v. Sporer, 496
Attorney Disciplinary Board v. Stowers, 492, 499
Attorney Disciplinary Board v. Thomas, 298
Attorney Disciplinary Board v. Vandel, 237
Attorney Disciplinary Board v. Weaver, 700
Attorney Grievance Comm'n of Maryland v. Mixter, 491
Attorney Grievance Comm'n of Maryland v. Pennington, 946
Attorney Grievance Comm'n v. Frost, 702
Attorney Grievance Comm'n v. Gansler, 610
Attorney Grievance Comm'n v. Garrett, 287
Attorney Grievance Comm'n v. Levin, 302
Attorney Grievance Comm'n v. Stanalonis, 700
Augustine v. Dept. of Veterans Affairs, 149
Aumann, State v., 224, 227
Ausman v. Arthur Andersen, 231
Aventa Learning, Inc. v. K12, Inc., 322
Aversa, United States v., 615
Bagley, United States ex rel. v. TRW, Inc., 518
Baker v. Dorfman, 822
Baker v. Wood, Ris & Hames, P.C., 838
Balistrieri, United States v., 999
Ball v. Kotter, 721
Balla v. Gambro, Inc., 231
Balter, United States v., 627
Banco Popular North America v. Gandi, 815, 820, 825, 827
Bank of Saipan v. Carlsmith Ball Wichman Case & Ichiki, 879
Baptiste v. Rohn, 781, 858
Barach, In re, 135
Barcelo v. Elliott, 838
Barfield v. New York City Health and Hospitals Corp., 272
Barker v. Capotosto, 872
Barker v. Kallash, 871
Barner v. Leeds, 878
Barr, In re, 976
Bastys v. Rothschild, 886
Bates v. Chicago Title Co., 735
Bates v. State Bar of Arizona, 158, 160, 169, 174
Bates, In re, 159
Bauer v. Shephard, 1024
Bayless, United States v., 991
Baylson v. Disciplinary Bd., 636, 638
BDO Seidman, LLP v. Morgan, Lewis & Bockius LLP, 883
BDO Seidman, United States v., 326
Beck v. Wecht, 842
Beckham, In re, 961, 983
Beckwith v. Pennsylvania State Univ., 734
Belge, People v., 550
Bell, In re, 965
Bennet v. Stirling, 644
Bennington, In re, 970
Berger v. United States, 617
Bergman, Matter of, 373
Berra v. Springer & Steinberg, P.C., 253
Berry v. Berry, 998
Berry v. McFarland, 741
Berry v. Schmidt, 700, 702
Bilzerian, United States v., 324
Black v. Missouri, 122
Blackmon, State v., 1000
Blackwelder, Matter of, 371
Blanchard v. Bergeron, 266
Bloomberg v. Kronenberg, 751, 764
Blue Cross & Blue Shield of Rhode Island v. Delta Dental of Rhode Island, 1003
Blum v. Stenson, 269, 434
BMW of North America, Inc. v. Gore, 861
Board of Education v. Nyquist, 121
Board of Professional Ethics & Conduct v. Apland, 259
Board of Professional Ethics & Conduct v. Bribriesco, 297
Board of Professional Ethics & Conduct v. Herrera, 663
Board of Professional Ethics & Conduct v. Kelly, 295
Board of Professional Ethics & Conduct v. Lane, 216
Board of Professional Ethics & Conduct v. Miller, 689
Board of Professional Ethics & Conduct v. Sikma, 364
Board of Professional Ethics & Conduct v. Sullins, 287
Board of Professional Ethics & Conduct v. Visser, 603, 615
Board of Professional Ethics & Conduct v. Walters, 364
Board of Professional Ethics & Conduct v. Wanek, 288, 475, 481, 483
Board of Professional Ethics & Conduct v. Winkel, 365, 376
Board of Professional Responsibility v. Casper, 252
Bochetto v. Gibson, 616, 874
Bodega Investments, Inc. v. United States, 319
Bolton v. Crowley, Hoge & Fein, P.C., 790
Bolton v. Weil, Gotshal & Manges, LLP, 894
Bomar v. Moser, 887
Bond v. McLaughlin, 727, 773
Borteck v. Riker, Danzig, Scherer, Hyland & Perretti LLP, 440

Bottoms v. Stapleton, 121
Bowers v. Ophthalmology Group, 401
Bowman v. Gruel Mills Nims & Pylman, LLP, 751, 770
Boyd v. Garvert, 720
Bozelko v. Papastavros, 778
Bradpiece v. State Bar of Cal., 131
Brady v. Maryland, 640
Brady v. Starke, 179
Brand Name Prescription Drugs Antitrust Litig., In re, 450
Brandon v. West Bend Mut. Ins. Co., 325
Breen v. Law Office of Bruce A. Barket, P.C., 826, 840, 892
Brett v. Berkowitz, 757
Brewer v. Johnson & Pritchard, P.C., 806
Brewer v. Quaker State Oil Ref. Corp., 507
Bridgeview Health Care Ctr., Ltd. v. State Farm Fire & Cas. Co., 446
Bristol Co., LP v. Osman, 774
Broadbelt, In re, 978
Broadway Maint. Corp. v. Tunstead & Schecter, 917
Brokaw v. Mercer County, 999, 1000
Brooks, Tarlton, Gilbert, Douglas & Kressler v. U.S. Fire Ins., 938
Brown v. Legal Foundation of Washington, 297
Brown v. Superior Court, 334
Brown, United States v., 701
Bryce v. Episcopal Church in the Diocese of Colo., 996
Buckhannon Board & Care Home, Inc. v. West Virginia Dept. of Health & Human Resources, 265
Buckley v. Valeo, 1025
Bullowa, In re, 285
Burick, In re, 1022
Burlington, City of v. Dague, 271
Burrow v. Arce, 796, 797
Burton v. R.J. Reynolds Tobacco Co., 451
Buscemi v. Intachai, 744, 927
Busik v. Levine, 486
Business Guides, Inc. v. Chromatic Communications Enters., 119, 482
Bylsma, In re, 961
Byrne v. Nezhat, 999
Bywaters v. United States, 270
C. Ingram Co. v. Philadelphia Indem. Ins. Co., 891
Cadle Co. v. Sweet & Brousseau, P.C., 853, 856, 857
Call v. Czaplicki, 859
Camden v. Maryland, 457
Campbell Harrison & Dagley L.L.P. v. Lisa Blue/Baron and Blue, 896
Campbell, In re, 645
Cantey Hanger, LLP v. Byrd, 803, 876
Caperton v. A.T. Massey Coal Co., 988, 1006, 1007, 1026
Capoccia, Matter of, 135
Cardillo v. Bloomfield 206 Corp., 441
Cargill, In re, 998
Carnesoltas, In re, 967
Carolina Cas. Ins. v. L.M. Ross Law Group, LLP, 937
Carolina Casualty Insurance Co. v. Sharp, 846
Carona, United States v., 627, 628
Carpenter, In re, 126
Carroll Towing Co., United States v., 746
Cass v. Am. Guarantee & Liab. Ins., 942
Cassuto v. Shulick, 874
Castaneda-Castillo v. Holder, 268
Castellano v. Winthrop, 521
Castellano, In re, 962
Castillo v. Massachusetts General Hosp., 739
Cecala v. Newman, 746, 772
Cedrone v. Unity Sav. Ass'n, 206
Cement Antitrust Litigation, In re, 1004
Central Bank of Denver, N.A. v. First Interstate Bank of Denver, N.A., 847
Central Hudson Gas & Elec. Corp. v. Pub. Serv. Comm'n. of N.Y., 159
Central Milk Producers Coop. v. Sentry Food Stores, Inc., 121, 411
Central States Indus. Supply, Inc. v. McCoullough, 514
Century Prods., Inc. v. Sutter, 482
CFS-Related Sec. Fraud Litig., In re, 451
Chadbourne & Parke LLP v. Troice, 847
Chalmers v. City & Cty. of Los Angeles, 270
Chamberlain Group v. Lear Corp., 514, 522
Chambers v. NASCO, Inc., 120
Chambers, State v., 575
Channel v. Loyacono, 879, 884
Chappell, In re, 1021
Charges of Unprofessional Conduct No. 39302, In re, 144, 146
Charges of Unprofessional Conduct, In re, 700
Charnay v. Cobert, 823, 887
Chase Scientific Research, Inc. v. NIA Group, Inc., 60
Chem-Age Industries, Inc. v. Glover, 801
Chen v. Chen Qualified Settlement Fund, 797
Cheng v. GAF Corp., 410
Chicago Council of Lawyers v. Bauer, 613
Chmura, In re, 1022
Christensen & Jensen, P.C. v. Barrett & Daines, 774, 861, 863
Christensen, O'Connor, Garrison & Havelka v. State, 917
Christensen, United States v., 323
Christeson v. Roper, 379, 380
Chronicle Publishing Co. v. Hantzis, 121
Citizens United v. Federal Election Comm'n, 1025
Clark Constr. Grp. v. City of Memphis, 506
Clark v. Beverly Health & Rehabilitation Servs., Inc., 513
Clark v. Clark, 120

Clark v. Superior Court, 513, 521
Clayton, In re, 984
Cleveland v. Rotman, 783
Cloward v. Shinseki, 275
Cluck v. Commission for Lawyer Discipline, 259
Clutchette v. Rushen, 549
Cobb, In re, 700
Cofield, In re, 965
Cohen v. Lord, Day & Lord, 440
Collins v. Illinois, 999
Colorado Supreme Court, United States v., 638
Colosimo v. Pennsylvania Elec. Co., 591
Colton v. United States, 206, 207
Commission on Unauthorized Practice of Law v. Sturgeon, 205
Committee on Legal Ethics v. Tatterson, 253
Committee on Professional Ethics & Conduct v. Bauerle, 493
Committee on Professional Ethics & Conduct v. Borchart, 131
Committee on Professional Ethics & Conduct v. Carty, 363
Committee on Professional Ethics & Conduct v. Garretson, 135
Committee on Professional Ethics & Conduct v. Halleck, 585
Committee on Professional Ethics & Conduct v. Humphrey, 165, 166
Committee on Professional Ethics & Conduct v. Humphreys, 362, 368
Committee on Professional Ethics & Conduct v. LaPointe, 584
Committee on Professional Ethics & Conduct v. McCullough, 253
Committee on Professional Ethics & Conduct v. Mollman, 530
Committee on Professional Ethics & Conduct v. Morris, 175
Committee on Professional Ethics & Conduct v. Nadler, 300, 371
Committee on Professional Ethics & Conduct v. Postma, 361
Committee on Professional Ethics & Conduct v. Pracht, 275
Committee on Professional Ethics & Conduct v. Ramey, 495
Committee on Professional Ethics & Conduct v. Stienstra, 133
Committee on Professional Ethics & Conduct v. Zimmerman, 498
Committee on Professional Ethics Conduct v. Freed, 287
Commodity Futures Trading Comm'n v. Weintraub, 443, 448
Commonwealth Coatings v. Continental Casualty Co., 988
Community Capital Bank v. Fischer & Yanowitz, 923
Community Heating & Plumbing, Inc. v. Garrett, 267
Concerning Holien, In re, 966
Condrey v. SunTrust Bank of Ga., 506
Conduct of Hiller, In re, 820
Conduct of Schenck, In re Complaint as to the, 987
Connell, Foley & Geiser, LLP v. Israel Travel Advisory Service, Inc., 892
Connolly v Napoli, Kaiser & Ber, LLP, 912
Connolly, United States v., 593
Continental Cas. Co. v. Law Office of Melbourne Mills, Jr., PLLC, 933
Cook, In re, 974, 975
Cooke-Zwiebach v. Oziel, 912
Cooley, United States v., 994
Cooper v. U.S. R.R. Retirement Bd., 268
Cooperman, Matter of, 259
Copeland v. Marshall, 250, 266, 268
Coplon v. United States, 632
Cornell v. Wunschel, 124
Cory, State v., 632
Cosgrove v. Grimes, 746
Counsel for Discipline v. Tonderum, 544
Counsel for Discipline, State ex rel. v. Orr, 274
Courtney v. Big O Tires, Inc., 504
Cowden v. Aetna Cas. & Sur. Co., 394
Cram v. Lamson & Sessions Co., 456, 457, 458, 513
Craney, State v., 323
Crawford v. Katz, 756
Crawford, United States v., 668
Credit Alliance Corp. v. Arthur Andersen & Co., 831
Crislip, In re, 974
Crossen, In re, 530
Culombe v. Connecticut, 555
Cummings v. Sea Lion Corp., 819
Cummings, In re, 984
Cunningham v. Sommerville, 710
Cuyler v. Sullivan, 383
Dalal, State v., 993
Daniels, Matter of, 587
Danielson, United States v., 632
Darby & Darby, P.C. v. VSI Int'l, Inc., 752
Dashiell v. Meeks, 884
Daugherty v. Runner, 739
Davenport, In re, 298
Davis Cty. Solid Waste Management & Energy Recovery Special Service v. U.S. Environmental Protection Agency, 268
Davis v. City & Cty. of San Francisco, 270
Davis v. Klein, 739
Davis, In the Matter of, 1022
De Temple, United States v., 991
Dean, In re, 960, 966
DeFelice v. Costagliola, 842
DeLeo v. Nusbaum, 886
DeLuna v. Burciaga, 882
Dennerline v. Atterholt, 748, 793, 814, 891, 908

DeVaux v. American Home Assur. Co., 203
DeVillio, United States v., 628
DeVoss v. State, 582
Diamond Point Plaza Ltd. Partnership v. Wells Fargo Bank, N.A., 829
Diamond, In the Matter of, 983
Dileo, In re, 970
Disciplinary Action Against Boulger, 366
Disciplinary Action Against Feland, 641
Disciplinary Action Against Hagar, In re, 964, 965
Disciplinary Action Against Kellington, 685
Disciplinary Action Against Kennedy, 492
Disciplinary Action Against Kurzman, In re, 491
Disciplinary Action Against Moe, In re, 487
Disciplinary Action Against Overboe, In re, 153
Disciplinary Counsel v. Doumbas, 585
Disciplinary Counsel v. Lee, 202
Disciplinary Counsel v. Stuard, 984
Disciplinary Counsel v. Weithman, 967
Disciplinary Counsel v. Wilcox, 133
Disciplinary Proceeding Against Aulik, Matter of, 984
Disciplinary Proceeding Against Eugster, In re, 224
Disciplinary Proceedings Against Bonet, In re, 586
Disciplinary Proceedings Against Deming, In re, 976
Disciplinary Proceedings Against Riley, Matter of, 494, 570, 572, 574
Discipline of Donohue, In Matter of, 686
Discipline of Gilbert, Matter of, 499
Discipline of Mattson, In re, 365
Disqualification of Giesler, In re, 982
Disqualification of McGee, In re, 982
DiStefano v. Greenstone, 759, 798
Distribution of Attorney's Fees, In re Petition for, 229, 237
Diversified Indus., Inc. v. Meredith, 317
Dixon v. Certainteed Corp., 503
Dixon v. Klenda, Mitchell, Austerman & Zuercher, L.L.C., 721
Dixon, In re, 701
Doan v. Commission on Judicial Performance, 984
Dobbs, United States v., 627
Doca Co. v. Westinghouse Elec. Co., 338
Dodson v. Fishman, 886
Doe v. Hawkins, 905
Doe v. Perry Community School District, 400
Donnelly v. Brown, Winick, Graves, Gross, Baskerville, Schoenebaum & Walker, 439
Doolittle, In re, 976
Doucakis v. Speiser, Krause, Madole, P.C., 758
Douglas v. Delp, 813
Dowell v. Nelissen, 753
Doyle v. Judicial Ret. & Removal Comm'n, 1022
Dr. Bonham's Case, 987
Driftmyer v. Carlton, 742
Dugger v. Arredondo, 873
Duggins v. Guardianship of Washington Through Huntly, 855, 916, 919
Dumar, Unreported Determination, In the Matter of, 962
Duncan v. Sherrill, 998
Duran v. Carris, 216
Duwe v. Alexander, 980, 1022, 1024
E.E.O.C. v. Hora, Inc., 514, 525
E.E.O.C. v. Orson H. Gygi Co., Inc., 121
Eastway Constr. Corp. v. City of New York, 482
Eberts v. Goderstad, 832
EchoStar Communications Corp., In re, 325, 333
Economy Roofing & Insulating Co. v. Zumaris, 514
Edenfield v. Fane, 160
Edgar v. K.L., 995
Edward B. Elmer, M.D., P.A. v. Santa Fe Properties, Inc., 913
Edwards v. Cont'l Cas. Co., 934
Edwards v. State, 586
Eicher, In re, 689
Eisen v. Carlisle & Jacquelin, 276
Ellis v. City of Dallas, 836
Employer's Reinsurance Corp. v. Clarendon Nat. Ins. Co., 518
Enron Corp., In re, 801
Enron Corporation Securities, Derivative & "ERISA" Litigation, In re, 830
Environmental Defense Fund, Inc. v. Reilly, 268
Environmental Network Corp. v. Goodman Weiss Miller, L.L.P., 780
Erie County, In re, 278, 318, 472
Erie Ins. Property & Cas. Co., State ex rel. v. Mazzone, 334
Erie, In re County of, 325
Ethicon, Inc. Pelvic Repair Sys. Prod. Liability Litig., In re, 510
Evans v. Hamby, 751
Evans v. Port Authority of New York and New Jersey, 268
Exxon Shipping Co. v. Baker, 864
EZ Paintr Corp. v. Padco, Inc., 410
Faas v. Sears, Roebuck & Co., 506
Faber v. Herman, 773
Fabi Const. Co. v. Secretary of Labor, 267
Family Trust Found. Of Ky. v. Wolnitzek, 980
Fang v. Bock, 870
Faretta v. California, 220
Farmers Cooperative Co. v. Senske & Son Transfer Co., 270
Farrar v. Hobby, 271
Farrar, In re, 139
Fattah, United States v., 539

Faulkner, In re, 991, 1000, 1001
FDIC v. O'Melveny & Meyers, 467
FDIC v. Sweeney, 993
Federal Election Comm'n v. Wisconsin Right to Life, Inc., 1024
Federal Ins. Co. v. MBL, Inc., 396
Federal Trade Comm'n v. GlaxoSmithKline, 452
Federal Trade Comm'n v. TRW, Inc., 452
Feliberty v. Damon, 393
Ferri v. Ackerman, 878
Fetch v. Quam, 394
Feuchtener, United States v., 423
FIA Card Services, N.A. v. Pichette, 216
Fidelity & Deposit Co. of Maryland v. McCulloch, 334
Finley v. Home Ins. Co., 392
Firestorm, Matter of, 121
First Arkansas Bank & Trust, Tr. v. Gill Elrod Ragon Owen & Sherman, P.A., 818
First Bank & Trust Co. v. Zagoria, 909
First Fed. Sav. & Loan Ass'n v. Oppenheim, Appel, Dixon & Co., 329
First United Pentecostal Church of Beaumont v. Parker, 791, 796, 801, 916
First Wis. Mortg. Trust v. First Wis. Corp., 121
Fisher v. United States, 308, 452, 555
Flagg v. City of Detroit, 507
Flaherty-Wiebel v. Morris, Downing & Sherred, 810
Flatt v. Superior Court, 376
Fleischman v. Horton, 813
Fletcher v. Comm'n on Judicial Performance, 984
Fletcher v. Conoco Pipe Line Co., 999
Florida Bar v. Knowles, 575
Florida Bar v. Went For It, Inc., 170, 171
Fogarty v. Palumbo, 883
Fontanella v. Marcucci, 781, 888
Food Management Group, LLC, In re, 835
Foondle v. O'Brien, 873
Ford Motor Co., In re, 318
Ford, United States v., 668
Forsyth, People v., 481
Fortson v. Winstead, McGuire, Sechrest & Minick, 652
Fox News Network, LLC v. U.S. Dep't of Treasury, 326
Franklin Financial, Inc. v. Sandoz, 884
Franklin Mint Co. v. Manatt, Phelps & Phillips, LLP, 844
Frantz v. Hawley Troxell Ennis & Hawley LLP, 761
Frazee v. Proskauer Rose LLP, 769
Frederick, United States v., 205
Freeman v. Chicago Musical Instr. Co., 121
Freeman's Estate, In re, 59
Freeport-McMoRan Oil & Gas Co. v. FERC, 621
Frese, In the Matter of, 959
Friedman Siegelbaum, LLP v. Pribish, 805
Friedman v. Rogers, 178
Friend v. Attorney Liab. Prot. Soc'y, 934
Fuentes, State v., 632
Gabriele v. Southworth, 599
Gaby v. State, 645
Gaddis, In re, 998
Gagnon v. United Technisource, Inc., 267
Galanek v. Wismar, 781
Galderma Laboratories, L.P. v. Actavis Mid Atlantic LLC, 421
Gall v. Colon-Sylvain, 810
Gandor v. Torus Nat'l Ins., 935
Gann, United States v., 323
Garcetti v. Ceballos, 610
Garcia v. Ball, 888
Garcia v. Jenkins/Babb, LL., 913
Garner v. Ross, 780
Garrison, In re, 293
Garrudo, United States v., 959
Gatti, In re, 529
Gay Officers Action League v. Puerto Rico, 269
Geaslen v. Berkson, Gorov & Levin, Ltd., 652
Geddes v. Campbell, 732, 739, 774
Geders v. United States, 584
Gefre v. Davis Wright Tremaine, LLP, 786, 856
General Nutrition Corp. v. Gardere Wynne Sewell, LLP, 748, 750, 884
General Sec. Ins. Co. v. Jordan, Coyne & Savits, LLP, 839
Gentile v. State Bar of Nevada, 601, 603, 612
George, In re, 122
Gianetti v. Gerardi, 302
Giannini, Chin & Valinoti v. Superior Court, 769
Gibson v. Williams, Williams & Montgomery, P.A., 734
Gillard v. AIG Ins. Co., 323
Gillenwater, United States v., 568
Gillespie v. Hernden, 766, 794
Giuca, People v., 593
Glaser v. Pullman & Comley, LLC, 755
Glazer v. Brookhouse, 923
Global NAPs, Inc. v. Awiszus, 753
Glynn v. EDO Corp., 514
Go-Best Assets Ltd. v. Citizens Bank of Massachusetts, 782
Goldfine v. Barack, Ferrazzano, Kirschbaum & Perlman, 865
Goldman v. Kane, 363
Gomez v. Gates, 270
Gonzalez v. Comm'n on Judicial Performance, 975
Gonzalez, In re, 296
Gonzalez, State v., 638
Gonzalez-Lopez, United States v., 145
Good Plume, State v., 996
Goode, In re, 603
Goodman v. Praxair Servs., Inc., 505, 506

Goodyear Tire & Rubber Co. v. Haeger, 120
Gosselin v. Webb, 922
Gottlieb v. Wiles, 325
Graham, In re, 700
Grand Jury Investigation, In re, 332, 344
Grand Jury Matter #3, In re, 328, 333
Grand Jury Proceedings (The Corporation), In re, 327
Grand Jury Proceedings, In re, 333
Grand Jury Subpoena, In re, 471, 637
Grand Jury Subpoenas Duces Tecum, In re, 453
Grand Jury, In re, 317
Grass, United States v., 628
Graubard Mollen Dannett & Horowitz v. Moskovitz, 823
Gravely, In re, 976
Graves, State v., 618
Gray, United States v., 538
Great American E & S Insurance Co. v. Quintairos, Prieto, Wood & Boyer, P.A., 811, 831, 846
Green, In re, 702
Greenberg & Covitz v. Nat'l Union Fire Ins. of Pittsburgh, 937
Greene v. Greene, 361, 363
Greene, In re, 976
Greene's Pressure Treating & Rentals, Inc. v. Fulbright & Jaworski, L.L.P., 813, 814
Grendel's Den, Inc. v. Larkin, 267, 268, 270
Greyhound Lines, Inc. v. Wade, 506, 507
Griffen v. Arkansas Judicial Discipline & Disability Comm'n, 1014
Grimm v. Fox, 754
Grinnell Corp., United States v., 991
Grochocinski v. Mayer Brown Rowe & Maw LLP, 737, 795, 869
GTI Capital Holdings, L.L.C. v. Comerica Bank-California, 769
Gucci America, Inc. v. Guess?, Inc., 320
Gulf Oil Co. v. Bernard, 189
Gunter v. Virginia State Bar, 520
GUS Consulting GMBH v. Chadbourne & Parke LLP, 758, 852
Gustafson, In re, 977
Guyton v. Hunt, 753
Guzick v. Kimball, 778
Guzman-Rivera v. Rivera-Cruz, 622
H.J. Inc. v. Flygt Corp., 267
Haar, In re, 298
Haase v. Abraham, Watkins, Nicols, Sorrels, Agosto and Friend, L.L.P., 720
Haeberle v. Texas Intern. Airlines, 593
Hager, In re, 441
Halberstam v. Welch, 800
Hamdi & Ibrahim Mango Co. v. Fire Ass'n of Philadelphia, 582, 583
Hammad, United States v., 628
Hammer, In re, 491
Hammons, In re, 1017
Hancock v. Board of Prof'l Responsibility, 699
Hand v. Howell, Sarto & Howell, 853
Hankey, In re, 375
Hanrahan v. Hampton, 264
Hansen v. Anderson, Wilmarth & Van Der Maaten, 659
Hanson v. Spolnik, 144
Hardt v. Reliance Standard Life Ins. Co., 263
Harness, Dickey & Pierce, P.L.C. v. Andrews, 757
Harrington v. Freedom of Information Comm'n, 317, 319
Harrington v. State, 983
Harris v. Farmer, 741, 750
Harris v. State, 229
Harris, People v., 322
Hart v. Carro, Spanbock, Kaster & Cuiffo, 758
Harte-Hanks Comm., Inc. v. Connaughton, 699
Hartford Accident and Indem. Co. v. Aetna Cas. & Sur. Co., 394
Hartford Accident and Indem. Co. v. Village of Hempstead, 933
Hartford Ins. Co. of Midwest v. Koeppel, 393
Hartsfield, In re, 974
Hatcher, In re, 1000
Hayes v. Alabama Court of Judiciary, 961
Hayes, In re, 979
Haynes v. Yale-New Haven Hosp., 834
H-D Transp. v. Pogue, 732
Hecht, In re, 962
Hedges, In re, 959
Heintz v. Jenkins, 849
Heldring v. Lundy Beldecos & Milby, P.C., 747
Helling v. Carey, 746
Helmer, Matter of, 298
Hempstead Video, Inc. v. Incorporated Village of Valley Stream, 410
Henderson v. HSI Financial Services, Inc., 910
Henderson, In re, 976
Henderson, Matter of, 366
Heng v. Rotech Med. Corp., 248
Heninger & Heninger v. Davenport Bank & Trust, 358
Henke v. Iowa Home Mutual Casualty Co., 394
Henning v. Union Pac. R.R. Co., 506
Henriksen, In re, 976
Henry v. Webermeier, 269
Hensley v. Eckerhart, 250, 268, 271
Herbster v. North American Company for Life & Health Insurance, 231
Heritage Partners, LLC v. Stroock & Stroock & Lavan LLP, 852
Herrera v. Hark, 725
Hickman v. Taylor, 334
Hickman, People v., 120
Higganbotham v. Oklahoma, 996

Hill v. Schilling, 896
Himmel, In re, 691
Hinds, Matter of, 603
Hirschkop v. Snead, 613
Hischke, State v., 574
Hitch v. Superior Court, 553, 560
Hizey v. Carpenter, 124
Hobson v. Wilson, 591
Hodges v. Carter, 747
Hodges v. Reasonover, 898
Holland v. Caviness, 854
Holland v. Florida, 380
Holliday, In re, 694
Holloway v. Arkansas, 382
Holmes v. Petrovich Dev. Co., 322
Holtzman, In re, 700
Home Ins. of Ind. v. Walsh, 937
Home Placement Serv., Inc. v. Providence Journal Co., 991
Hook v. McDade, 999
Hook v. Trevino, 853, 858
Hopei Garments (Hong Kong), Ltd. V. Oslo Trading Co., 502
Hopp & Flesch, LLC v. Backstreet, 749
Hopper v. Frank, 202
Hopson v. City of Baltimore, 337
Howard v. Babcock, 440
Howell v. Jones, 329
Hsu v. Parker, 836
Hubbell, United States v., 555
Humphrey, State ex rel. v. Philip Morris Inc., 453
Humphreys, Hutcheson & Moseley v. Donovan, 329
Hunt v. American Bank & Trust Co., 999
Huntington Commons Assocs., In re, 992
Hunydee v. United States, 326
IBM Corp., In re, 1008
ICP Strategic Credit Income Fund Ltd., In re, 871
Illinois State Bar Ass'n Mut. Ins. v. Frank M. Greenfield and Assoc., P.C., 945
Imbler v. Pachtman, 643
Imwalle v. Reliance Medical Products, Inc., 267
InKine Pharm. Co. v. Coleman, 758
Inmates of The Rhode Island Training School v. Martinez, 435
Innis Arden Golf Club v. Pitney Bowes, Inc., 506
Inquiry Concerning a Judge (Andrews), 979
Inquiry Concerning a Judge (Angel), 1022
Inquiry Concerning a Judge (Henson), 1017
Inquiry Concerning a Judge, Gridley, In re, 972
Inquiry Concerning a Judge, In re, 967
Inquiry Concerning a Judge, Matter of, 964, 969
Intemann, In re, 998
International Bus. Machines Corp. v. Levin, 121
International Bus. Machines Corp., United States v., 450
International Strategies Group, Ltd. v. Greenberg Traurig, LLP, 730, 885
Iowa Dist. Ct., State v., 622
Iowa Supreme Court Attorney Disciplinary Board v. Rauch, 216
Isaac, People v., 353
Isabel v. City of Memphis, 271
Jack Winter, Inc. v. Koratron Co., 451
Jackson v. Hancock & Canada, L.L.P., 899
Jacob v. Norris, McLaughlin & Marcus, 440
Jacobson v. Knepper & Moga, P.C., 233
Jacoby & Meyers, LLP v. Presiding Justices, 437
Jaramillo, United States v., 959
Jardine, In re, 248
Jarvis v. Jarvis, 441
Jean v. Nelson, 267
Jean, Commissioner v., 272
Jerista v. Murray, 781
Jett v. Wooten, 887
Jicarilla Apache Nation, United States v., 472
Joe v. Two Thirty Nine Joint Venture, 795
Johnson & Johnson v. Aetna Cas. & Sur. Co., 933
Johnson v. American Family Mut. Ins. Co., 394
Johnson v. Bd. of County Comm'rs, 216
Johnson v. Georgia Highway Express, Inc., 265
Johnson v. Hart, 890
Johnson, In re, 512, 924
Johnson, Matter of, 993
Johnson, United States v., 667
Johnston, United States v., 595
Jones v. Link, 855, 873
Jones v. Staübli Motor Sports Div. of Staubli American Corp., 506
Jones v. Westbrook, 881
Jones, In re, 300
Jones, United States v., 452, 594
Jordan, United States v., 991, 998, 999
Joseph DelGreco & Co., v. DLA Piper L.L.P., 758
Judicial Disciplinary Proceedings Against Gorenstein, In re, 975
Judicial Inquiry & Review Bd. of Supreme Court v. Fink, 976
Judicial Inquiry & Review Bd. v. Snyder, 983
K.R. Exch. Servs., Inc. v. Fuerst, Humphrey, Ittleman, PL, 758
Kahil's Case, In re, 493, 658
Kairos Sci. Inc. v. Fish & Richardson P.C., 757
Kandalaft v. Peters, 749
Kansas Pub. Employees Ret. Sys., In re, 1006
Karlin v. Culkin, 478
Karsten, State v., 381

Katz, In re, 120
Kaufman v. Sungard Inv. Sys., 322
Keck, Mahin & Cate, In re, 908
Keefe v. Bernard, 448
Kellington, United States v., 541
Kellogg, Brown & Root, Inc., In re, 317, 318
Kelly, United States v., 999
Kendall/Hunt Publishing Co. v. Rowe, 514
Kennedy v. Canon, 616
Kennedy v. Zimmermann, 616
Kennick v. Commission on Judicial Performance, 965
Kernell, United States v., 538, 540
Kidder, Peabody & Co. v. Maxus Energy Corp., 1005
Kidwell v. Sybaritic, Inc., 232
Kilburn, In re, 965
Kiley, In re, 229, 236
Kim v. O'Sullivan, 890
Kinsey, In re, 980, 1022
Kinzbach Tool Co. v. Corbett-Wallace Corp., 806
Kirby, Complaint Concerning, 976
Kirkpatrick, State v., 327, 453
Kirtland and Packard v. Superior Ct., 854
Kleeman v. Rheingold, 925
Kline v. City of Kansas City, 267
Kline, In re, 641, 689
Kloess, United States v., 541
Kmart v. Lewis Brisbois Bisgaard & Smith LLP, 898
Knigge v. Dencker, 324
Knitting Fever, Inc. v. Coats Holding Ltd., 522
Koch v. Koch Ind., 401
Koerber, United States v., 631
Kojayan, United States v., 644
Kolar v. Donahue, McIntosh & Hammerton, 875
Kothe v. Smith, 977
Kramer v. Raymond Corp., 451
Kronfeld v. Transworld Airlines, Inc., 268
Kronisch v. United States, 505
Krouse, In re, 1022
Kurczaba v. Pollock, 616
Kurtenbach v. Tekippe, 203
Kus v. Irving, 913
Kyles v. Whitley, 641, 642
L.D.G., Inc. v. Robinson, 752
LaFleur v. Law Offices of Anthony G. Buzbee, P.C., 896
Laird v. Tatum, 990
Langlet, State v., 507
Larson, Estate of, 275
Latham v. Castillo, 834
Laurent, United States v., 506
Law Offices of Palagi v. Howard, 440
Lawless, United States v., 207
Lawrence, In re, 254, 1004, 1022
Lee v. Brenner, Saltzman and Wallman, 790
Lee v. Hanley, 879
Leibel v. Johnson, 764
Leis v. Flynt, 144
Lenarz, State v., 632
Leonard v. Dorsey & Whitney LLP, 379, 947
Lerner v. Laufer, 738, 765
Lesher v. Law Office of Mitchell N. Kay, P.C., 849
Lewellen v. Phillips, 769
Lewis, In re, 976
Liberty Associates v. Etkin, 895
Licette Music Corp. v. Sills, Cummis, Zuckerman, Radin, Tischman, Epstein & Gross, P.A., 907
Lifestar Response of Ala, Inc. v. Admiral Ins. Co., 393
Liggett v. Young, 433
Ligon v. City of New York, 979, 980, 994
Liljeberg v. Health Servs. Acquisition Corp., 996
Lindsey, In re, 471
Lindy Brothers Builders, Inc. v. American Radiator & Standard Sanitary Corp. (Lindy I), 266
Lindy Brothers Builders, Inc. v. American Radiator & Standard Sanitary Corp. (Lindy II), 266
Linegar v. DLA Piper LLP (US), 732
Lipin v. Bender, 512
Liteky v. United States, 990, 992
LoBiondo v. Schwartz, 843, 844
Loctite Corp. v. Fel-Pro, Inc., 317
Lofton v. Fairmont Specialty Insurance Managers, Inc., 237
Logan, In re, 960
Lone Star Ind., Inc. v. Southern Red-E-Mix, Inc., 121
Long v. Brusco Tug & Barge, Inc., 593
Long-Russell v. Hampe, 853
Lopez v. Clifford Law Offices, P.C., 786
Lopez v. Munoz, Hockema & Reed, L.L.P., 734
Lopez, State v., 230
Lorenzetti v. Enterline, 752
Lott, United States v., 230
Lovaglia, United States v., 998
Lugosch v. Congel, 319
Lunn v. Fragomen, Del Rey, Bernsen & Loewy P.C., 904
Lyell v. Renico, 1000
Lyle, Siegel, Croshaw & Beale, P.C. v. Tidewater Capital Corp., 869
MacArthur v. Bank of New York, 594, 598
Magee v. State Bar, 366
Maher v. Gagne, 265
Maillard v. Dowdell, 739
Maine v. Moulton, 668
Maldonado v. Houstoun, 269
Maldonado v. New Jersey ex rel. Administrative Office of Courts, 522
Mallard v. United States District Court, 709
Maloney, United States v., 645

Mann v. Taser, Int'l, Inc., 506
Manning v. Waring, Cox, James, Sklar & Allen, 410
Marbury v. Madison, 955
Mardikian v. Commission on Judicial Performance, 966
Marinello v. United States, 537, 539
Marshall v. Dentfirst, P.C., 504
Martens, State v., 645
Martin v. Workers' Comp. Appeals Bd., 447
Martin, United States v., 993
Martinez, In re, 481
Martinez-Catala, In re, 996, 999
Martino, United States v., 628
Mascarenas, People v., 126
Mashaney v. Board of Indigents' Defense Services, 878
Mason, In re, 991, 996
Massiah v. United States, 663, 668
Matal v. Tam, 129
Matsuyama v. Birnbaum, 779
Mattco Forge, Inc. v. Arthur Young & Co., 766
Matter Concerning a Judge, In re, 970
Maxwell Schuman & Co. v. Edwards, 255
Maynard v. Caballero, 877
Mayville, In re, 984
Mazon v. Krafchick, 841
McBryde v. Committee to Review Circuit Council Conduct & Disability Orders of the Judicial Conference of the United States, 967
McCabe v. Arcidy, 203, 248
McCann, Matter of, 487
McClure v. Harris, 1003
McConnell, In re, 587
McCormick International USA, Inc. v. Shore, 869
McCormick, In the Matter of, 984
McCuin v. Texas Power & Light Co., 1001, 1002
McCutcheon v. FEC, 1025
McGuirk, People v., 582
McKaskle v. Wiggins, 230
McKay v. Walker, 747
McKnight v. Office of Public Defender, 888
McLaughlin v. Philadelphia Newspapers, Inc., 137
McLean v. Arkansas Bd. of Educ., 434
McMahan v. Greenwood, 820
McMillen v. Klingensmith, 895
McPartlin, United States v., 326
McPherson v. Apfel, 496
McRae, United States v., 538, 539
Meador, In re, 513, 522
Means, In re, 998
Meat Price Investigators v. Iowa Beef Processors, 121
Media General, Inc. v. Tomlin, 824, 846
Medical Lab. Mgmt. Consultants v. Am. Broad. Co., 506
Medical Mut. Liability Ins. Soc. v. Evans, 395
Meeks, United States v., 485
Meese, In re, 267
Meinhard v. Salmon, 296
Meisels v. Fox Rothschild, LLP, 837
Menchise v. Akerman Senterfitt, 855
Mendel v. Home Ins., 938
Mendenhall v. National Transp. Safety Bd., 269
Mercedes, People v., 535
Meredith, People v., 558
Merida, United States v., 517
Merlo, In re, 965
Merrell Dow Pharm., Inc. v. Havner, 766
Merrell, United States v., 206
Metropolitan Dist. Comm'n, United States v., 599
Meyerhofer v. Empire Fire & Marine Ins. Co., 329
Mickens v. Taylor, 383
Micron Technology, Inc. v. Rambus Inc., 506
Microsoft Corp., United States v., 979, 986, 994
Mikes v. Straus, 267
Milavetz, Gallop & Milavetz, P.A. v. United States, 548
Miller, State v., 631
Millwright v. Romer, 122
Minnick v. Hawley Troxell Ennis & Hawley, LLP, 882
Mintmire, United States v., 541
Miranda v. Arizona, 341, 625
Miranda v. Said, 853
Mississippi Comm'n on Judicial Performance v. Darby, 967
Mississippi Comm'n on Judicial Performance v. Teel, 958
Missouri v. Jenkins, 272
MMR/Wallace Power & Indus., Inc. v. Thames Assocs., 457, 513
Molen v. Christian, 872, 888
Monceret v. Bd. of Prof'l Responsibility, 664
Montanez v. Simon, 268
Mooney v. Frazier, 878
Moore v. Crone, 753
Moore v. Judicial Inquiry Comm'n of the State of Alabama, 970
Moore, In re, 970
Morales v. Laughlin, Falbo, Levy, 905
More, In the Matter of, 983
Morrell v. State, 564
Morris v. Hap Taylor & Sons, Inc., 747
Morrison, United States v., 998
Morrow v. Hood Commun., Inc., 970
Morrow v. Superior Court, 632
Mortgage Grader, Inc. v. Ward & Olivo, L.L.P., 913
Mosby, United States v., 993
Mosley, In re, 982
Mullaney v. Wilbur, 484, 577
Mullen, In re, 985

Murgatroyd, In re, 144
Murphy v. State, 487
Murphy, United States v., 998
Musser v. Provencher, 894
Mutual of Enumclaw Ins. Co. v. Dan Paulson Const., Inc., 393
Myers v. Aragona, 906
NAACP v. Button, 190
Nacco Materials Handling Group, Inc. v. Lilly Co., 506, 511
Nandorf, Inc. v. CNA Ins. Companies, 396
Nanetti v. University of Illinois, 272
Nanny, United States v., 645
Nason v. Fisher, 821
National Ass'n of Concerned Veterans v. Secretary of Defense, 269
National Child Care, Inc. v. Dickinson, 594
National Conversion Corp. v. Cedar Building Corp., 823
National Union Fire Ins. Co. of Pittsburgh, PA v. Wuerth, 907
National Union Fire Ins. Co., In re, 1008
NationsBank of Texas, N.A. v. Akin, Gump, Hauer & Feld, L.L.P., 829
Neary v. Regents of U. of California, 970
Neel v. Magana, Olney, Levy, Cathcart & Gelfand, 122
Nelson v. Hartford Ins. Co., 594
Nevada Yellow Cab Corp. v. Eighth Judicial Dist. Court ex rel. County of Clark, 393
Neville, In re, 364
New Hampshire v. Piper, 144
New Mexico Natural Gas Antitrust Litig., In re, 1005
New York Times Co. v. Sullivan, 699
Newman v. Enriquez, 813
Newman v. State, 327, 332
Nicholas, United States v., 469
Nichols v. Keller, 215, 739
Niesig v. Team I, 454
Nix v. Whiteside, 568, 573, 576
Nobles, United States v., 333
Nordling v. Northern States Power Company, 231
Nordstrom v. Ryan, 632
Noris v. Silver, 915, 917
North Carolina St. Bar v. Talford, 298
North Dakota Family Alliance, Inc. v. Bader, 980
O Builders & Assocs. v. Yuna Corp., 195, 198
O'Connor v. Oakhurst Dairy, 113
O'Neill v. Hernandez, 815
O'Regan v. Arbitration Forums, Inc., 991
O'Toole v. Carr, 904
Oakes v. Clark, 772
Oasis Int'l Waters, Inc. v. United States, 317, 472
Ohio State Bar Ass'n v. McCafferty, 972
Ohman v. Kahn, 758
Ohralik v. Ohio State Bar Association, 159, 186, 190
Oklahoma Bar Ass'n v. Fagin, 255
Oklahoma Bar Ass'n v. Ward, 641
Oklahoma Bar Ass'n, State ex rel. v. Cummings, 300
Oklahoma Bar Ass'n, State ex rel. v. Flaniken, 253
Olen Properties Corp. v. Sheldahl, Inc., 206
Olsen, United States v., 640
Olson v. Accessory Controls & Equip., Co., 452, 453
Olson, In re, 562
Olson, People v., 689
Olwell, State v., 561, 564
Omaha Bank v. Siouxland Cattle Co-op., 592
One Star Class Sloop Sailboat, United States v., 268, 269
On-Line Services Ltd., In re, 300
Oriental Fin. Group, Inc. v. Fed. Ins. Co., Inc., 1001
Osborne v. Goodlett, 877
Osborne v. Keeney, 776, 866
Osorio, People v., 323, 452
Oster v. Kirschner, 826
Owen v. Knop, 734
Owens v. United States, 568
Pacific Mutual Life Ins. Co. v. Haslip, 865
Paine, In re, 1016
Palsgraf v. Long Island Railroad Co., 727
Panduit Corp. v. All States Plastic Mfg. Co., 410
Panel Matter No. 87–22, In re Appeal of, 362
Pang v. International Document Servs., 465
Pappas, Matter of, 210
Paradigm Ins. Co. v. Langerman Law Offices, 395
Parker v. Connors Steel Co., 998
Pashaian v. Eccelston Properties, Ltd., 1006
Passante v. McWilliam, 363
Passillas-Sanchez, People v., 598
Paul v. Gordon, 753
Pawlendzio v. Haddow, 854
Pearson, In re, 975
Pederson v. Barnes, 835
Peebles, In the Matter of, 965
Peel v. Attorney Registration & Disciplinary Commission of Illinois, 174, 175, 176
Peerenboom v. Marvel Entertainment, LLC, 322
Pena-Rodriguez v. Colorado, 593
Penkaty, State v., 618
Pennsylvania v. Delaware Valley Citizens' Council for Clean Air, 265, 266, 271
Pepsico, Inc. v. McMillan, 991
Perez v. Kirk & Carrigan, 835
Perez, In re, 965
Perl v. St. Paul Fire & Marine Ins. Co., 358, 934, 939
Perna v. Electronic Data Syst. Corp., 512
Perraud, United States v., 539

Perry v. Scholar, 845
Perry, In re, 966
Perry, United States v., 636
Pete v. Anderson, 731
Peterson v. Katten Muchin Rosenman, LLP, 316
Peterson v. Superior Ct. of Ventura Co., 933
Petrine v. Sinchak-Higby, 837
Pettibone v. United States, 536
Philip Morris USA v. Williams, 864
Phillips v. Covenant Clinic, 504
Phillips v. Wilks, Lukoff & Bracegirdle, LLC, 756
Phillips, In re, 682
Picker Int'l, Inc. v. Varian Assocs., Inc., 403
Pickett v. Sheridan Health Care, 269
Pierce v. Cook, 753, 889
Pietrangelo v. Wilmer Cutler Pickering Hale & Dorr, LLP, 793
Pike v. Mullikin, 899
Pilla v. American Bar Assoc., 990
Pine Island Farmers v. Erstad & Reimer, 202, 392
Piper, In re, 961
Pitcock v. Kasowitz, Benson, Torres & Friedman LLP, 877
Pitera, United States v., 994
Plumley, United States v., 627
Polansky v. CNA Ins. Co., 120
Poole ex rel. Elliott v. Textron, Inc., 502
Porter v. Arco Metals Co., 457
Porter, In re, 602
Potashnick v. Port City Const. Co., 998, 1006
Powell v. Wood County Comm'n, 894
Powell, In re, 253
Powell, In re Estate of, 840
Poyfair, In re, 975
PRB Docket No. 2002.093, In re, 161
Presnick v. Esposito, 594
Price Bros. v. Philadelphia Gear Corp., 995
Price v. Ragland, 853
Priest, Matter of v. Hennessy, 305
Prieto-Rubio, State v., 668
Primis Corp. v. Milledge, 763
Primus, In re, 190, 433
Prince v. Buck, 780
Public Citizen, Inc. v. Louisiana Attorney Disciplinary Board, 161, 178
Public Warning of DePena, 976
Purcell v. District Attorney, 332
Purdy v. Pacific Auto. Ins. Co., 393
Pyle, In re, 666
R.M. v. Supreme Court, 136
R.M.J., In re, 159, 174
Rambus, Inc. v. Infineon Tech. AG, 507
Ransburg Corp. v. Champion Spark Plug Co., 416
Re, Estate of v. Kornstein Veisz & Wexler, 792
Realnetworks, Inc. v. DVD Copy Control Ass'n, 505
Reardon v. Marlayne, 401
Reed v. Finkelstein, Levine, Gittlesohn & Tetenbaum, 917
Reed v. Rhodes, 995
Reeves, In re, 985
Regents of University of Cal., In re, 326
Regina v. Murray, 564
Reinstatement of Hopewell, In re, 931
Republican Party of Minnesota v. White, 252, 700, 956, 980, 995, 1023, 1024
Residential Funding Corp. v. DeGeorge Financial Corp., 510
Resolution Trust Corp. v. First of America Bank, 516, 519
Reyes, United States v., 645
Reynolds v. Schrock, 802
RFF Family Partnership, LP v. Burns & Levinson, LLP, 947
Rhoades, In re, 298
Rhodes v. Stewart, 264
Rice v. Downs, 769
Rice, In re Complaint Concerning, 967
Richards v. Jain, 522
Rico v. Mitsubishi Motors Corp., 518
Riehlmann, Matter of, 691
Riek, In re, 641
Ries, United States v., 145
Rippo v. State, 959
Roberts v. Bailar, 998
Roberts v. Comm'n on Judicial Performance, 983
Robinson v. Boeing Co., 1002
Robinson v. Equifax Information Services, LLC, 269
Robnet, People v., 329
Rock v. Arkansas, 568
Rodgers, In re, 1003
Rodman v. Safeway, Inc., 511
Rodriguez v. Ancona, 248
Rodriguez v. Disner, 797
Rogers v. Webb, 255
Rogers v. Zanetti, 766, 772, 773, 776, 778, 780
Rogers, United States v., 1005
Role Models America, Inc. v. Brownlee, 267
Romanek v. Connelly, 924
Romano, In re, 976
Rosen v. N.L.R.B., 354
Rosier v. Fleischer, 753
Ross v. Ihrie, 883, 923
Ross, In re, 985
Rossi v. Blue Cross & Blue Shield, 317, 319, 449
Rost, In re, 203
Rouse v. Pollard, 907
Rowe v. Gibson, 985
Rubenstein v. Florida Bar, 162
Rudolf v. Shayne, Dachs, Stanisci, Corker & Sauer, 852, 856
Ruffalo, In re, 132
Rule Amendments, In re, 435
Rules of Prof'l Conduct, In re, 396

Rusinow v. Kamara, 236
Russell, United States v., 543, 547
Russin, In re, 770
Russo v. Griffin, 755, 756
Ryans, United States v., 627
S.E.C. v. Brady, 522
S.E.C. v. Treadway, 334
Sabin v. Ackerman, 733
Salopek v. Schoemann, 770
Samaritan Foundation v. Goodfarb, 447
Samay, In re, 998
Sanchez, In re, 1021
Sanders, Bruin, Coll & Worley, P.A. v. McKay Oil Corp., 910
Sangha v. La Barbera, 873
Sasso, In re, 1017
Saunders, State v., 793
Save Our Cumberland Mountains, Inc. v. Hodel, 269
Scales v. J.C. Bradford & Co., 269
Scandrett v. Greenhouse, 819
Schaeffler v. United States, 326
Schatz, In re, 961
Schiessle v. Stephens, 410
Schilling v. Community Mem. Gen. Hosp., 275
Schlegel, United States v., 207
Schmidt, United States v., 206
School Asbestos Litig., In re, 997
Schwartz v. Liberty Mut. Ins. Co., 394
SCM Corp. v. Xerox Corp., 326
Scott R. Larson, P.C. v. Grinnan, 915
Scott v. Beth Isr. Med. Ctr. Inc., 322
Scott v. Burgin, 840
Scott v. City of New York, 267
Scozzafava, United States v., 629
Seacoast Anti-Pollution League, Appeal of, 991
Seagate Tech., LLC, In re, 517
Sealed Case, In re, 337
Sealed Party v. Sealed Party, 765
Sealy Mattress Co. v. Sealy Inc., 319
Seed Co. v. Westerman, 758
Segal, United States v., 450
Seitz, In re, 967
Selby v. Revlon Consumer Products Corp., 416
Sellers, United States v., 991
Sentis Grp., Inc. v. Shell Oil Co., 502
Sequa Corp. v. Lititech, Inc., 458, 513
Serou v. DeLaup, 884
Shadid v. Jackson, 613
Shakopee Mdewakanton Sioux Community v. City of Prior Lake, 269
Shamrock Lacrosse, Inc. v. Klehr, Harrison, Harvey, Branzburg & Ellers, LLP, 754
Shapero v. Kentucky Bar Association, 169, 170, 172
Shari, People v., 428
Sharlow, In re, 961
Sharpe, People v., 489, 644
Sheets v. Salt Lake, City, 267
Shell Oil Refinery, In re, 514
Sheppard v. Maxwell, 608
Shoemaker v. Gindlesberger, 810, 838
Shook v. City of Davenport, 334
Sicotte, Estate of v. Lubin & Meyer, P.C., 763
Sierra Fria Corp. v. Evans, 769
Silvestri v. Gen. Motors Corp., 505
Simes v. Arkansas Judicial Discipline & Disability Comm'n, 1024
Simmons v. New York City Transit Authority, 270
Simms v. Seaman, 874
Sindona, United States v., 354
Sklar, In Matter of, 500
Skorman v. Hovnanian of Fla., Inc., 206
Sloan v. Law Office of Oscar C. Gonzalez, Inc., 924
Smith v. Cain, 641
Smith v. Haynsworth, Marion, McKay & Geurard, 726
Smith v. McLaughlin, 751, 777, 853
Smith v. O'Donnell, 771, 813, 860, 869
Smith v. Patout, 729, 836
Smith v. R.J. Reynolds Tobacco Co., 237
Smith, In re, 287
Smyzer, Matter of, 362
Snider v. City of Cape Girardeau, 270
Snow's Case, In re, 961
Snyder v. Love, 890
Soignier v. Fletcher, 740, 747
Sokol Holdings, Inc. v. Dorsey & Whitney, LLP, 758
Sonksen v. Legal Services Corp., 489
Sorci v. District Court, 412, 423
Sorenson v. First Wis. Nat'l Bank, 121
Southeastern Pennsylvania Transp. Auth. v. CaremarkPCS Health, L.P., 317, 318, 452
Spalding Sports Worldwide, Inc., In re, 317, 319
Spencer, Estate of v. Gavin, 840, 893, 920
Spevak v. Klein, 694
Spokane Truck & Dray Co. v. Hoefer, 861
St. Luke's Magic Valley Reg'l Med. Ctr. v. Luciani, 814
St. Paul Reinsurance Co., Ltd. v. Commercial Financial Corp., 503
Staggs v. Sells, 833
Standing Comm. on Discipline of the U.S. Dist. Ct. v. Yagman, 698, 702
Stanfield v. Neubaum, 783, 784
Stanley v. Richmond, 769
Staples v. Merck & Co., 735
Starcher, In re, 984, 1022
Starnes v. Judicial Ret. & Removal Comm'n, 966
Staron v. Weinstein, 921, 926
Starrett v. Wadley, 269
State & County Mutual Fire Ins. Co. v. Young, 839

State Compensation Ins. Fund v. WPS, Inc., 519
State Farm Mutual Automobile Ins. Co. v. Campbell, 861, 862
State Farm Mutual Automobile Ins. Co. v. Traver, 396
Steadfast Ins. v. Stroock & Stroock & Lavaon LLP, 938
Steele v. Salb, 772
Stein, United States v., 634
Stephen v. Sallaz & Gatewood, Chtd., 747
Stephens v. White, 716
Stern v. U.S. Dist. Court, 638
Stevens v. McGuireWoods LLP, 851
Stevens, United States v., 540, 541
Stevenson v. Newsome, 383
Stichting Ter Behartiging v. Schreiber, 758
Stoecker v. Echevarria, 754, 818
Stokes-Craven Holding Corp. v. Robinson, 888
Stoneridge Investment Partners, LLC v. Scientific Atlanta, Inc., 847
Strickland v. Washington, 382, 641
Suder v. Whiteford, Taylor & Preston, LLP, 776, 777
Sullivan, In re, 967
Supreme Court of New Mexico, United States v., 638
Sutton v. Llewellyn, 841
Swanson, State ex rel. v. 3M Co., 121, 402
Swidler & Berlin v. United States, 312, 320, 324
Talmage v. Harris, 851
Tamposi v. Denby, 800
Tanner v. United States, 593
Tax Auth., Inc. v. Jackson Hewitt, Inc., 388
Taylor v. Akin, Gump, Strauss, Hauer & Feld, 736
Taylor v. McNichols, 875, 876
Taylor v. Public Convalescent Serv., 1004
Taylor v. Riley, 735, 828, 855, 871
Tensley, State v., 325, 400
Terra Int'l, Inc. v. Mississippi Chem. Corp., 457
Tevrow v. Arowolo, 817
Texas State Teachers Ass'n v. Garland Indep. Sch. Dist., 264
Texas v. Cobb, 667, 668
Thayer v. Fuller & Henry, Ltd., 885
Theard v. United States, 478
Thomas & Wong Gen. Contractor, Inc. v. Wallace, 769
Thomas v. Judicial Conduct Comm'n, 983
Thomas v. Kidani, 741, 781
TIG Ins. Co. v. Giffin Winning Cohen & Bodewes, P.C., 783
Tilton v. Trezza, 765
Tilzer v. Davis, Bethune & Jones, L.L.C., 386
Toohey,. United States v., 998
Torban v. Obermayer Rebmann Maxwell & Hippel, 740
Tormo v. Yormark, 917, 918
Touche Ross & Co. v. Commercial Union Ins. Co., 831
Transportation Equipment Sales Corp. v. BMY Wheeled Vehicles, 518
Travelers Ins. Co. v. Liljeberg Enters., Inc., 1008
Travelers Prop. Cas. Corp. v. Jim Walter Homes, Inc., 734
Triangle Sheet Metal Works, Inc. v. Silver, 861
Tri-G, Inc. v. Burke, Bosselman & Weaver, 858, 866
Tri-State Equip. v. United States, 450
Trotter v. Nelson, 433
Trujillo, United States v., 645
Tumey v. Ohio, 987, 1003, 1007
Turco, In re, 959
Turner v. United States, 505
Tylenol (Acetaminophen) Mktg., Sales Practices and Products Liab. Litig., In re, 859
Tyus v. Urban Search Management, 120
Udall v. Littell, 212
Ulanowski, In re, 133, 238
Unauthorized Practice of Law Committee v. American Home Assur. Co., Inc., 394
United Genesis Corp. v. Brown, 834, 851
United Shoe Mach. Corp, United States v., 319
United States Postal Serv. v. Phelps Dodge Ref. Corp., 451
United Technologies Corp., United States v., 326
Universal Underwriters Ins. Co. v. Judge & James, Ltd., 773
Uphoff v. Elegant Bath, Ltd., 269
Upjohn Co. v. United States, 320, 324, 447, 451
Vahila v. Hall, 779
Valdez v. Taylor Auto. Co., 735
Valentine v. Watters, 753
Van Sommeren v. Gibson, 778
Van Susteren, In re, 1017
Vanacore v. Kennedy, 834, 904
Vanover, State v., 597
Vasquez, State v., 504
Vaxiion Therapeutics, Inc. v. Foley & Lardner LLP, 757
Vega, In the Matter of, 965
Viglione v. Farrington, 883
Vignaroli v. Blue Cross of Iowa, 189
Villanueva v. First Am. Title Ins. Co., 891
Vincent, In re, 966, 981
Vioxx Prod. Liab. Litig., In re, 319
Vodusek v. Bayliner Marine Corp., 507
von Bulow, In re, 367
Vossoughi v. Polaschek, 859, 881
Walker v. Cromartie, 755
Warburgh, In re, 694
Warner, In re, 136
Warnock v. Karm Winand & Patterson, 882

Washington State Physicians Ins. Exchange & Ass'n v Fisons Corp., 502
Waterloov Gutter Prot. Sys. Co. v. Absolute Gutter Prot., L.L.C., 758
Watson, In re, 967, 980, 1022, 1024
Weakley v. Redline Recovery Services, LLC, 769
Weatherwax v. Koontz, 593
Weaver v. Bonner, 1022
Webb v. Board of Educ., 267
Webb v. Pomeroy, 745
Webb, State v., 618
Weber, In re, 958
Weeks v. Samsung Heavy Industries, Ltd., 522
Weiss v. Statewide Grievance Committee, 362
Welch v. Metropolitan Life Ins. Co., 269
Wells Dairy, Inc. v. American Indus. Refrigeration, Inc., 334
Wells v. Mattox, 917
Wemark v. State, 532, 549, 550, 567
Wersel v. Sexton, 1021
West Orange, Township of v. 769 Assocs., LLC, 248
Westchester Fire Ins. v. Admiral Ins., 933
Westinghouse Elec. Corp. Uranium Contracts Litig., In re, 450
Westinghouse Electric Corp. v. Gulf Oil Corp., 401
Westinghouse Electric Corp. v. Kerr-McGee Corp., 212
Westmoreland Coal Co. v. Cox, 270
Whalen v. DeGraff, Foy, Conway, Holt-Harris & Mealey, 754, 919, 927
White v. SunTrust Bank, 1004
White, In re Complaint Against, 983
White, United States v., 230
Whiteside, State v., 575
Whitman, United States v., 993
Widom v. Egenberg, 883
WiFiLand, LLP v. Hudson, 248
Wilfong, In re, 960
Wilkerson, In re, 140
Will, United States v., 990
Williams v. Kublick, 858
Williams v. Lakin, 755, 853
Williams v. Maulis, 886
Williams v. Pennsylvania, 1002
Williams v. Woodford, 632
Williams, State v., 589
Williamson, In re, 966
Williams-Yulee v. Florida Bar, 700, 1022
Willis, United States v., 205, 316
Winship, In re, 484, 577
Withrow v. Larkin, 1007
Witzman v. Lehrman, Lehrman & Flom, 801
Wolff v. McDonnell, 632
Wolfson v. Concannon, 1021, 1024
Woodroof v. Cunningham, 896
Wyatt's Case, In re, 225
XYZ Corp. v. United States, 324
Yaccarino, In re, 962
Yale v. Bowne, 858, 868
Yandell, In re, 1004
Yarbrough v. Eversole, 815
Yates v. United States, 127, 538
Yelin v. Swartz, 834
Yengo, In re, 984
Yielding, United States v., 538, 540
Young v. Williams, 785, 837
Young, In re, 970
Young, United States v., 992
Zaruba, In re, 441
Zauderer v. Office of Disciplinary Counsel, 159, 169, 173, 180, 186
Zazzali v. Hirschler Fleischer, P.C., 801
Zolin, United States v., 327, 452
Zubulake v. UBS Warburg LLC, 504, 505, 510

# Table of Statutes


U.S. Const., Art. III, § 1 .......... 957
8 U.S.C. § 1512(c)(1) .......... 537
9 U.S.C. §§ 1–16 .......... 655
11 U.S.C. § 523(a)(2)(A) .......... 723
11 U.S.C. § 523(a)(4) .......... 723
11 U.S.C. § 523(a)(6) .......... 723
11 U.S.C. § 526(a)(4) .......... 548
15 U.S.C. § 78j(b) .......... 846
15 U.S.C. § 1692a–k .......... 848
18 U.S.C. § 4 .......... 546
18 U.S.C. § 207(a)(1) .......... 425
18 U.S.C. § 207(a)(2)(B) .......... 419, 425
18 U.S.C. § 1503 .......... 536
18 U.S.C. § 1503(a) .......... 536
18 U.S.C. § 1512 .......... 537
18 U.S.C. § 1512(b) .......... 536
18 U.S.C. § 1512(b)(2)(B) .......... 536
18 U.S.C. § 1512(f)(1) .......... 536
18 U.S.C. § 1515(c) .......... 541, 542, 549
18 U.S.C. § 1519 .......... 537, 538, 539, 540, 541
28 U.S.C. § 144 .......... 986
28 U.S.C. § 351(a) .......... 954
28 U.S.C. § 351(b) .......... 954
28 U.S.C. § 351(c)(6)(B) .......... 954
28 U.S.C. § 455 .......... 986
28 U.S.C. § 455(a) .......... 979, 988, 996, 1008
28 U.S.C. § 455(b)(4) .......... 1004
28 U.S.C. § 455(d)(4) .......... 1004
28 U.S.C. § 455(f) .......... 1005
28 U.S.C. § 516 .......... 472
28 U.S.C. § 519 .......... 472
28 U.S.C. § 530B .......... 151, 621, 629, 639
33 U.S.C. § 1365(d) .......... 264
33 U.S.C. § 1369(b)(3) .......... 264
42 U.S.C. § 1983 .......... 435
42 U.S.C. § 1988 .......... 435
42 U.S.C. § 2000e–5(k) .......... 264
42 U.S.C. § 7604(d) .......... 264
42 U.S.C. § 7607(f) .......... 264
42 U.S.C. §§ 12101–12213 .......... 695
49 U.S.C. § 1136(g)(2) .......... 170
Pub. L. No. 104–208 .......... 543
Pub. L. No. 107–204 .......... 463, 464, 537, 804
Pub. L. No. 96–458 .......... 954
Ala. Code § 6–5–579 .......... 777
Alaska Stat. § 09.17.020(f) .......... 860
Alaska Stat. § 09.17.020(k) .......... 865
Ariz. Rev. Stat. § 12–2234(B)(2) .......... 447
Cal. Bus. & Prof. Code § 6103 .......... 500
Cal. Bus. & Prof. Code § 6171(b) .......... 909
Cal. Civ. Code § 1798.84 .......... 768
Cal. Penal Code § 135 .......... 535
Colo. Rev. Stat. Ann. § 13–21–102 .......... 860
Conn. Gen. Stat. § 34–327(e) .......... 912
Conn. Gen. Stat. § 52–577 .......... 881
Fla. Stat. Ann. § 95.11(4)(a) .......... 721
Fla. Stat. Ann. § 768.79 .......... 855
Fla. Stat. Ann. § 918.13(1) .......... 535
Ga. Code Ann. § 33–35–12 .......... 172
Ga. Code Ann. § 51–12–6 .......... 854
735 Ill. Comp. Stat. 5/2–1115 .......... 861
Ind. Code Ann. 23–1–1–16 .......... 922
Ind. Code Ann. Tit. 34 .......... 836
Iowa Code Ann. § 668A.1(2)(b) .......... 861
Iowa Code Ann. § 719.3 .......... 535
Kan. Stat. Ann. § 60–3701(1)(e)–(f) .......... 860
La. Rev. Stat. § 9:5605(A) .......... 879
La. Rev. Stat. § 9:5605(E) .......... 879
Md. Code Ann. Crim. Law § 9–306 .......... 535
Miss. Code Ann. § 83–49–19 .......... 172
Mont. Code Ann. § 27–2–206 .......... 890
Neb. Const. art. VII, § 5 .......... 861
N.Y. P'ship Law § 26(c) .......... 912
Ore. Rev. Stat. § 752.035 .......... 931
Tenn. Code Ann. § 61–1–306(c) .......... 893
Tex. Bus. & Com. Code § 17.49(g) .......... 833
Tex. Civ. Prac. & Rem. Code § 38.001(8) .......... 855
Tex. Civ. Prac. & Rem. Code § 41.003 .......... 860
Tex. Civ. Prac. & Rem. Code § 41.008 .......... 860
Tex. Code Crim. Proc. Art. 18.20 .......... 767
Tex. Penal Code Ann. § 37.09(a) .......... 535

# Table of Rules


ABA Model Code Jud. Cond. 1.1..... 958, 963
ABA Model Code Jud. Cond. 1.2.... 959, 963, 973, 978, 1011, 1017
ABA Model Code Jud. Cond. 1.2, cmt. 6.......... 1011, 1012
ABA Model Code Jud. Cond. 1.3.... 961, 963, 1017
ABA Model Code Jud. Cond. 1.3, cmt. 1.......... 962
ABA Model Code Jud. Cond. 2.1.......... 1012
ABA Model Code Jud. Cond. 2.2.... 964, 968, 973
ABA Model Code Jud. Cond. 2.2, cmt. 2.......... 969
ABA Model Code Jud. Cond. 2.2, cmt. 3.......... 969
ABA Model Code Jud. Cond. 2.3(B)........ 974
ABA Model Code Jud. Cond. 2.3, cmt. 4.......... 976
ABA Model Code Jud. Cond. 2.4............ 968
ABA Model Code Jud. Cond. 2.4(A)(1).......... 1021
ABA Model Code Jud. Cond. 2.4(A)–(B).......... 1021
ABA Model Code Jud. Cond. 2.4(b)......... 960
ABA Model Code Jud. Cond. 2.4(B)........ 973
ABA Model Code Jud. Cond. 2.4, cmt. 1.......... 972
ABA Model Code Jud. Cond. 2.5............ 963
ABA Model Code Jud. Cond. 2.5(a)......... 964
ABA Model Code Jud. Cond. 2.5, cmt. 1.......... 964
ABA Model Code Jud. Cond. 2.5, cmt. 2.......... 966
ABA Model Code Jud. Cond. 2.5, cmt. 3.......... 964
ABA Model Code Jud. Cond. 2.6(a), cmt. 1.......... 977
ABA Model Code Jud. Cond. 2.6(b)......... 977
ABA Model Code Jud. Cond. 2.6, cmt. 3.......... 978
ABA Model Code Jud. Cond. 2.7, cmt. 1.......... 990
ABA Model Code Jud. Cond. 2.8(B)........ 966
ABA Model Code Jud. Cond. 2.9............ 981
ABA Model Code Jud. Cond. 2.9(A)........ 981
ABA Model Code Jud. Cond. 2.9(A)(1).... 981
ABA Model Code Jud. Cond. 2.9(A)(2).... 984
ABA Model Code Jud. Cond. 2.9(A)(3).... 982
ABA Model Code Jud. Cond. 2.9(A)(4).... 982
ABA Model Code Jud. Cond. 2.9(B)........ 983
ABA Model Code Jud. Cond. 2.9(C)........ 985
ABA Model Code Jud. Cond. 2.9(D)........ 982
ABA Model Code Jud. Cond. 2.9, cmt. 4.......... 982
ABA Model Code Jud. Cond. 2.9, cmt. 6.......... 985
ABA Model Code Jud. Cond. 2.9, cmt. 7.......... 982
ABA Model Code Jud. Cond. 2.10(A)..... 978, 1017
ABA Model Code Jud. Cond. 2.10(B).... 1008
ABA Model Code Jud. Cond. 2.10(D)...... 978
ABA Model Code Jud. Cond. 2.11(a)....... 960
ABA Model Code Jud. Cond. 2.11(A)..... 988, 999, 1007
ABA Model Code Jud. Cond. 2.11(a)(1).......... 989
ABA Model Code Jud. Cond. 2.11(A)(1).......... 988, 999, 1000
ABA Model Code Jud. Cond. 2.11(A)(2).......... 989, 1001
ABA Model Code Jud. Cond. 2.11(A)(2)(a)–(b).......... 989
ABA Model Code Jud. Cond. 2.11(A)(2)(b).......... 989
ABA Model Code Jud. Cond. 2.11(A)(2)(c).......... 989, 1004, 1005
ABA Model Code Jud. Cond. 2.11(A)(3).......... 1003
ABA Model Code Jud. Cond. 2.11(a)(4).......... 1006
ABA Model Code Jud. Cond. 2.11(A)(4).......... 989, 1026
ABA Model Code Jud. Cond. 2.11(A)(5).......... 989
ABA Model Code Jud. Cond. 2.11(A)(6)(a).......... 1002
ABA Model Code Jud. Cond. 2.11(A)(6)(a)–(b).......... 989
ABA Model Code Jud. Cond. 2.11(A)(6)(b).......... 1002
ABA Model Code Jud. Cond. 2.11(A)(6)(c).......... 988, 1000
ABA Model Code Jud. Cond. 2.11(B).... 1003
ABA Model Code Jud. Cond. 2.11(C).... 1008
ABA Model Code Jud. Cond. 2.11, cmt. 2.......... 1008
ABA Model Code Jud. Cond. 2.11, cmt. 5.......... 1008
ABA Model Code Jud. Cond. 2.14.......... 966
ABA Model Code Jud. Cond. 3.1.......... 1011, 1017
ABA Model Code Jud. Cond. 3.1(A)...... 1012
ABA Model Code Jud. Cond. 3.1(B)...... 1012
ABA Model Code Jud. Cond. 3.1(C)...... 1012
ABA Model Code Jud. Cond. 3.1(D)...... 1012
ABA Model Code Jud. Cond. 3.1(E)...... 1012
ABA Model Code Jud. Cond. 3.1, cmt. 1.......... 1011, 1014, 1017

ABA Model Code Jud. Cond. 3.1, cmt. 2 .... 1011
ABA Model Code Jud. Cond. 3.1, cmt. 4 .... 1012
ABA Model Code Jud. Cond. 3.2(A) .... 1013
ABA Model Code Jud. Cond. 3.2(B)–(C) .... 1013
ABA Model Code Jud. Cond. 3.2(C) .... 1014
ABA Model Code Jud. Cond. 3.2, cmt. 3 .... 1014
ABA Model Code Jud. Cond. 3.3, cmt. 1 .... 962
ABA Model Code Jud. Cond. 3.4 .... 1013
ABA Model Code Jud. Cond. 3.5 .... 962
ABA Model Code Jud. Cond. 3.6, cmt. 1 .... 1016
ABA Model Code Jud. Cond. 3.7 .... 1014, 1015
ABA Model Code Jud. Cond. 3.7(A) .... 1014
ABA Model Code Jud. Cond. 3.7(A)(1) .... 1015
ABA Model Code Jud. Cond. 3.7(A)(2) .... 1015
ABA Model Code Jud. Cond. 3.7(A)(3) .... 1016
ABA Model Code Jud. Cond. 3.7(A)(4) .... 1015
ABA Model Code Jud. Cond. 3.7, cmt. 3 .... 1015
ABA Model Code Jud. Cond. 3.8 .... 1018
ABA Model Code Jud. Cond. 3.9 .... 1018
ABA Model Code Jud. Cond. 3.10 .... 949, 1002, 1017, 1018
ABA Model Code Jud. Cond. 3.11 .... 1005
ABA Model Code Jud. Cond. 3.11(A) .... 1018
ABA Model Code Jud. Cond. 3.11(B) .... 1018
ABA Model Code Jud. Cond. 3.11(B)(2), cmt. 1 .... 1018
ABA Model Code Jud. Cond. 3.11(C) .... 1018
ABA Model Code Jud. Cond. 3.11, cmt. 2 .... 1018
ABA Model Code Jud. Cond. 3.12 .... 1017, 1018
ABA Model Code Jud. Cond. 3.13(A) ... 1019, 1020
ABA Model Code Jud. Cond. 3.13(B) .... 1019
ABA Model Code Jud. Cond. 3.13(B)(2) .... 1019
ABA Model Code Jud. Cond. 3.13(C) ... 1019, 1020
ABA Model Code Jud. Cond. 3.14 .... 1020
ABA Model Code Jud. Cond. 3.14(A)–(B) .... 1020
ABA Model Code Jud. Cond. 3.14, cmt. 3 .... 1020
ABA Model Code Jud. Cond. 3.15 .... 1017, 1018, 1019
ABA Model Code Jud. Cond. 4.1(A)(2) .... 1021
ABA Model Code Jud. Cond. 4.1(A)(3) .... 1021
ABA Model Code Jud. Cond. 4.1(A)(4) .... 1021
ABA Model Code Jud. Cond. 4.1(A)(5) .... 1021
ABA Model Code Jud. Cond. 4.1(A)(6) .... 1022
ABA Model Code Jud. Cond. 4.1(A)(7) .... 1022
ABA Model Code Jud. Cond. 4.1(A)(8) .... 1022, 1024
ABA Model Code Jud. Cond. 4.1(A)(9) .... 1022
ABA Model Code Jud. Cond. 4.1(A)(10) .... 1022
ABA Model Code Jud. Cond. 4.1(A)(11) .... 1022
ABA Model Code Jud. Cond. 4.1(A)(12) .... 1022
ABA Model Code Jud. Cond. 4.1(A)(13) .... 1022
ABA Model Code Jud. Cond. 8.2(B) .... 1021
ABA Model Code Jud. Cond. Canon 1 .... 958, 1021
ABA Model Code Jud. Cond. Canon 3B(5) .... 974
ABA Model Code Jud. Cond. Canon 3(B)(5) .... 975
ABA Model Code Jud. Cond. Canon 3(C)(1) .... 988
ABA Model Code Jud. Cond. Canon 3C .... 1004
ABA Model Code Jud. Cond. Canon 3E .... 1004
ABA Model Code Jud. Cond. Canon 4C .... 1015
ABA Model Code Jud. Cond. Canon 4C(1) .... 1014
ABA Model Code Jud. Cond. Canon 4C(3)(b)(iii) .... 1016
ABA Model Code Jud. Cond. Canon 7B(1)(c) .... 1023
ABA Model Code Jud. Cond. Preamble .... 952, 959
ABA Model Code Jud. Cond. Terminology .... 956, 957, 973, 1003, 1004
ABA Model Code Prof. Cond. Ethical Consideration 7–8 .... 283
ABA Model Code Prof. Cond. Preamble .... 76
ABA Model Code Prof. Resp. Canon 5 .... 115
ABA Model Code Prof. Resp. Disciplinary Rule 2–107(A) .... 260
ABA Model Code Prof. Resp. Disciplinary Rule 2–110(C)(1)(e) .... 236
ABA Model Code Prof. Resp. Disciplinary Rule 3–102(A)(1) .... 239
ABA Model Code Prof. Resp. Disciplinary Rule 4–101 .... 309
ABA Model Code Prof. Resp. Disciplinary Rule 4–101(C)(3) .... 343, 346
ABA Model Code Prof. Resp. Disciplinary Rule 5–101(D) .... 596

ABA Model Code Prof. Resp. Disciplinary Rules 5–101–107 ........ 115
ABA Model Code Prof. Resp. Disciplinary Rule 5–102 ........ 596
ABA Model Code Prof. Resp. Disciplinary Rule 5–102(B) ........ 600
ABA Model Code Prof. Resp. Disciplinary Rule 5–103(B) ........ 369
ABA Model Code Prof. Resp. Disciplinary Rule 7–102(A)(4) ........ 573
ABA Model Code Prof. Resp. Disciplinary Rule 7–102(B)(1) ........ 573
ABA Model Code Prof. Resp. Disciplinary Rule 7–105 ........ 491
ABA Model Code Prof. Resp. Disciplinary Rule 7–107 ........ 613
ABA Model Code Prof. Resp. Disciplinary Rule 7–107(C)(7) ........ 606
ABA Model Code Prof. Resp. Disciplinary Rule 7–110(B) ........ 673
ABA Model Code Prof. Resp. Ethical Consideration 2–1 ........ 159
ABA Model Code Prof. Resp. Ethical Consideration 2–23 ........ 263
ABA Model Code Prof. Resp. Ethical Consideration 5–9 ........ 595
ABA Model Code Prof. Resp. Ethical Consideration 5–25 ........ 372
ABA Model Code Prof. Resp. Preliminary Statement ........ 113
ABA Model Rule Lawyer Disc. Enf. 2 ........ 134
ABA Model Rule Lawyer Disc. Enf. 2.A ........ 132, 134
ABA Model Rule Lawyer Disc. Enf. 3.A ........ 134
ABA Model Rule Lawyer Disc. Enf. 3.D ........ 137
ABA Model Rule Lawyer Disc. Enf. 3.D(2) ........ 137
ABA Model Rule Lawyer Disc. Enf. 4 ........ 132
ABA Model Rule Lawyer Disc. Enf. 4.B(1)–(2) ........ 133
ABA Model Rule Lawyer Disc. Enf. 4.B(3)–(4) ........ 133
ABA Model Rule Lawyer Disc. Enf. 4.B(4) ........ 134
ABA Model Rule Lawyer Disc. Enf. 10.A(5) ........ 138, 139
ABA Model Rule Lawyer Disc. Enf. 10.D ........ 137
ABA Model Rule Lawyer Disc. Enf. 11 ........ 134, 137
ABA Model Rule Lawyer Disc. Enf. 11.A ........ 133
ABA Model Rule Lawyer Disc. Enf. 11.A–B ........ 133
ABA Model Rule Lawyer Disc. Enf. 11.D ........ 134
ABA Model Rule Lawyer Disc. Enf. 11.E ........ 137
ABA Model Rule Lawyer Disc. Enf. 11.F ........ 137
ABA Model Rule Lawyer Disc. Enf. 12.A ........ 137
ABA Model Rule Lawyer Disc. Enf. 14.A ........ 134
ABA Model Rule Lawyer Disc. Enf. 14.B–C ........ 134
ABA Model Rule Lawyer Disc. Enf. 14.C ........ 134
ABA Model Rule Lawyer Disc. Enf. 15 ........ 134
ABA Model Rule Lawyer Disc. Enf. 16.A ........ 134
ABA Model Rule Lawyer Disc. Enf. 18.b ........ 134
ABA Model Rule Lawyer Disc. Enf. 18.C ........ 135
ABA Model Rule Lawyer Disc. Enf. 18.F ........ 134
ABA Model Rule Lawyer Disc. Enf. 19.E ........ 136
ABA Model Rule Lawyer Disc. Enf. 21 ........ 141
ABA Model Rule Lawyer Disc. Enf. 21.D ........ 141
ABA Model Rule Lawyer Disc. Enf. 22 ........ 150
ABA Model Rule Lawyer Disc. Enf. 27 ........ 139, 140
ABA Model Rule Lawyer Disc. Enf. 27.A ........ 140
ABA Model Rule Prof. Cond. 1.0(d) ........ 661
ABA Model Rule Prof. Cond. 1.0(e) ........ 214, 416, 770
ABA Model Rule Prof. Cond. 1.0(m) ........ 647, 654
ABA Model Rule Prof. Cond. 1.0, cmt. 2 ........ 179
ABA Model Rule Prof. Cond. 1.1 ........ 76, 963
ABA Model Rule Prof. Cond. 1.1(e) ........ 794
ABA Model Rule Prof. Cond. 1.1, cmt. 1 ........ 276
ABA Model Rule Prof. Cond. 1.1, cmt. 4 ........ 914
ABA Model Rule Prof. Cond. 1.1, cmt. 6 ........ 794
ABA Model Rule Prof. Cond. 1.2 ........ 548, 738
ABA Model Rule Prof. Cond. 1.2(a) ........ 219
ABA Model Rule Prof. Cond. 1.2(b) ........ 695
ABA Model Rule Prof. Cond. 1.2(c) ........ 213, 214, 215, 218, 415
ABA Model Rule Prof. Cond. 1.2(d) ........ 284, 661, 802, 876
ABA Model Rule Prof. Cond. 1.2, cmt. 6 ........ 738
ABA Model Rule Prof. Cond. 1.3 ........ 76, 286, 963
ABA Model Rule Prof. Cond. 1.3, cmt. 1 ........ 286, 289
ABA Model Rule Prof. Cond. 1.3, cmt. 4 ........ 738, 741

ABA Model Rule Prof. Cond. 1.4.... 140, 769, 943
ABA Model Rule Prof. Cond. 1.4(a)(2)... 221, 292
ABA Model Rule Prof. Cond. 1.4(a)(3).... 292
ABA Model Rule Prof. Cond. 1.4(a)(5).... 285
ABA Model Rule Prof. Cond. 1.5(a) ........ 248
ABA Model Rule Prof. Cond. 1.5(b) ....... 256, 729
ABA Model Rule Prof. Cond. 1.5(c)........ 252, 254
ABA Model Rule Prof. Cond. 1.5(d) ........ 254
ABA Model Rule Prof. Cond. 1.5, cmt. 9 .................................................. 263
ABA Model Rule Prof. Cond. 1.6.... 197, 311, 327, 339, 354, 364
ABA Model Rule Prof. Cond. 1.6(a) ....... 309, 445, 651, 940
ABA Model Rule Prof. Cond. 1.6(b) ........ 330
ABA Model Rule Prof. Cond. 1.6(b)(1)... 331, 343
ABA Model Rule Prof. Cond. 1.6(b)(2)... 345, 346
ABA Model Rule Prof. Cond. 1.6(b)(3).... 345
ABA Model Rule Prof. Cond. 1.6(b)(4)... 352, 765
ABA Model Rule Prof. Cond. 1.6(b)(5).... 890
ABA Model Rule Prof. Cond. 1.6(b)(6).... 349
ABA Model Rule Prof. Cond. 1.6(b)(7).... 355
ABA Model Rule Prof. Cond. 1.6(c)......... 335
ABA Model Rule Prof. Cond. 1.7.... 418, 427, 599
ABA Model Rule Prof. Cond. 1.7–1.12.... 115
ABA Model Rule Prof. Cond. 1.7–1.13.... 113
ABA Model Rule Prof. Cond. 1.7(a) ....... 357, 375
ABA Model Rule Prof. Cond. 1.7(a)(1).... 375
ABA Model Rule Prof. Cond. 1.7(a)(2)... 377, 761
ABA Model Rule Prof. Cond. 1.7(b) ........ 413
ABA Model Rule Prof. Cond. 1.7(b)(4).... 417
ABA Model Rule Prof. Cond. 1.7, cmt. 4 .................................................. 359
ABA Model Rule Prof. Cond. 1.7, cmt. 18 ................................................ 794
ABA Model Rule Prof. Cond. 1.7, cmt. 19 ................................................ 795
ABA Model Rule Prof. Cond. 1.7, cmt. 22 ................................................ 420
ABA Model Rule Prof. Cond. 1.7, cmt. 24 ................................................ 398
ABA Model Rule Prof. Cond. 1.7, cmt. 29 ................................................ 390
ABA Model Rule Prof. Cond. 1.7, cmt. 31 ................................................ 325
ABA Model Rule Prof. Cond. 1.8.... 360, 374, 764
ABA Model Rule Prof. Cond. 1.8(a) ....... 361, 764
ABA Model Rule Prof. Cond. 1.8(d) ........ 366
ABA Model Rule Prof. Cond. 1.8(e)......... 367
ABA Model Rule Prof. Cond. 1.8(e)(1).... 369
ABA Model Rule Prof. Cond. 1.8(f).........262, 369
ABA Model Rule Prof. Cond. 1.8(g).........386
ABA Model Rule Prof. Cond. 1.8(h).........895
ABA Model Rule Prof. Cond. 1.8(h)(1)...370, 887
ABA Model Rule Prof. Cond. 1.8(i).........371, 374
ABA Model Rule Prof. Cond. 1.8, cmt. 14 ................................................897
ABA Model Rule Prof. Cond. 1.8, cmt. 17 ................................................372
ABA Model Rule Prof. Cond. 1.9....427, 599, 736
ABA Model Rule Prof. Cond. 1.9(a).........399
ABA Model Rule Prof. Cond. 1.9(c) .........403
ABA Model Rule Prof. Cond. 1.9, cmt. 3 ..................................................401
ABA Model Rule Prof. Cond. 1.10 ..........402, 408, 410, 425
ABA Model Rule Prof. Cond. 1.10(a)......404, 406
ABA Model Rule Prof. Cond. 1.10(b).......411
ABA Model Rule Prof. Cond. 1.10(c) .......411
ABA Model Rule Prof. Cond. 1.10, cmt. 1 ..................................................405
ABA Model Rule Prof. Cond. 1.11(a).......422
ABA Model Rule Prof. Cond. 1.12 ..........428, 429
ABA Model Rule Prof. Cond. 1.13....50, 444, 466, 470, 804
ABA Model Rule Prof. Cond. 1.13(a).......458
ABA Model Rule Prof. Cond. 1.13(b).......460
ABA Model Rule Prof. Cond. 1.13(c) .......448
ABA Model Rule Prof. Cond. 1.13(d).......460
ABA Model Rule Prof. Cond. 1.13(f)........636
ABA Model Rule Prof. Cond. 1.13(g).......468
ABA Model Rule Prof. Cond. 1.13, cmt. 2 ..................................................446
ABA Model Rule Prof. Cond. 1.13, cmt. 9 ..................................................473
ABA Model Rule Prof. Cond. 1.14(a).......223
ABA Model Rule Prof. Cond. 1.15 ..........258, 524, 835
ABA Model Rule Prof. Cond. 1.15(a).......297
ABA Model Rule Prof. Cond. 1.15(e).......299
ABA Model Rule Prof. Cond. 1.16 ...........128
ABA Model Rule Prof. Cond. 1.16(a)......140, 234
ABA Model Rule Prof. Cond. 1.16(a)(3).........................................229
ABA Model Rule Prof. Cond. 1.16(b)(1)..................................128, 234
ABA Model Rule Prof. Cond. 1.16(b)(4).........................................128
ABA Model Rule Prof. Cond. 1.17 ..........185, 239, 288, 432
ABA Model Rule Prof. Cond. 1.17(a).......240
ABA Model Rule Prof. Cond. 1.17(d).......246
ABA Model Rule Prof. Cond. 1.18 ..........195, 321, 736
ABA Model Rule Prof. Cond. 1.18(a).......196

ABA Model Rule Prof. Cond. 2.1...... 46, 115, 279, 282, 315, 649
ABA Model Rule Prof. Cond. 2.1, cmt. 3 .......... 281
ABA Model Rule Prof. Cond. 2.3..... 115, 650
ABA Model Rule Prof. Cond. 2.3(a) ........ 395
ABA Model Rule Prof. Cond. 2.4............ 115
ABA Model Rule Prof. Cond. 2.4, cmt. 1 .......... 653
ABA Model Rule Prof. Cond. 3.1............ 119
ABA Model Rule Prof. Cond. 3.1–3.8...... 647
ABA Model Rule Prof. Cond. 3.1, cmt. 1 .......... 481
ABA Model Rule Prof. Cond. 3.2............ 486
ABA Model Rule Prof. Cond. 3.3.... 339, 571, 574
ABA Model Rule Prof. Cond. 3.3(a)(1)... 494, 495
ABA Model Rule Prof. Cond. 3.3(a)(2).... 496
ABA Model Rule Prof. Cond. 3.3(a)(3)... 567, 568, 570, 574, 576
ABA Model Rule Prof. Cond. 3.3(b) ....... 568, 580
ABA Model Rule Prof. Cond. 3.3(c)......... 574
ABA Model Rule Prof. Cond. 3.3(d) ........ 497
ABA Model Rule Prof. Cond. 3.3, cmt. 6 .......... 567
ABA Model Rule Prof. Cond. 3.3, cmt. 7 .......... 569, 570
ABA Model Rule Prof. Cond. 3.3, cmt. 9 .......... 571
ABA Model Rule Prof. Cond. 3.4(a) ....... 500, 532, 640
ABA Model Rule Prof. Cond. 3.4(b) ....... 581, 585
ABA Model Rule Prof. Cond. 3.4(c)........ 126, 499
ABA Model Rule Prof. Cond. 3.4(d) ........ 501
ABA Model Rule Prof. Cond. 3.4(e)........ 588, 595
ABA Model Rule Prof. Cond. 3.4(f) ......... 531
ABA Model Rule Prof. Cond. 3.4, cmt. 2 .......... 553
ABA Model Rule Prof. Cond. 3.4, cmt. 3 .......... 760
ABA Model Rule Prof. Cond. 3.5(a) ........ 590
ABA Model Rule Prof. Cond. 3.5(b) ....... 497, 590
ABA Model Rule Prof. Cond. 3.5(c)......... 593
ABA Model Rule Prof. Cond. 3.5(d) ........ 587
ABA Model Rule Prof. Cond. 3.6.... 606, 609, 613
ABA Model Rule Prof. Cond. 3.6(a) ........ 603
ABA Model Rule Prof. Cond. 3.6(b) ........ 605
ABA Model Rule Prof. Cond. 3.6, cmt. 1 .......... 602
ABA Model Rule Prof. Cond. 3.7.... 594, 597, 637
ABA Model Rule Prof. Cond. 3.7(a) ........ 596
ABA Model Rule Prof. Cond. 3.7(b) ........ 599
ABA Model Rule Prof. Cond. 3.8..... 617, 618
ABA Model Rule Prof. Cond. 3.8(a) ........ 622
ABA Model Rule Prof. Cond. 3.8(b)......... 624
ABA Model Rule Prof. Cond. 3.8(c)......... 624
ABA Model Rule Prof. Cond. 3.8(d)......... 640
ABA Model Rule Prof. Cond. 3.8(e)......... 637
ABA Model Rule Prof. Cond. 3.8(f)......... 602, 616
ABA Model Rule Prof. Cond. 3.9 ............ 646
ABA Model Rule Prof. Cond. 4.1 ..... 126, 339
ABA Model Rule Prof. Cond. 4.1(a)........ 659, 660
ABA Model Rule Prof. Cond. 4.1(b)........ 348, 465
ABA Model Rule Prof. Cond. 4.2 .... 454, 513, 626, 663, 671
ABA Model Rule Prof. Cond. 4.2, cmt. 5 .......... 674
ABA Model Rule Prof. Cond. 4.2, cmt. 7 .......... 455
ABA Model Rule Prof. Cond. 4.3 ............ 458
ABA Model Rule Prof. Cond. 4.3, cmt. 1 .......... 675
ABA Model Rule Prof. Cond. 4.4(a)........ 490, 512, 515, 633
ABA Model Rule Prof. Cond. 4.4(b)......... 516
ABA Model Rule Prof. Cond. 5.1 .... 115, 261, 685
ABA Model Rule Prof. Cond. 5.1(a)......... 680
ABA Model Rule Prof. Cond. 5.1(c)(1)..... 683
ABA Model Rule Prof. Cond. 5.2 ............ 115
ABA Model Rule Prof. Cond. 5.2(a)......... 684
ABA Model Rule Prof. Cond. 5.3 ..... 335, 616
ABA Model Rule Prof. Cond. 5.3(a)......... 665
ABA Model Rule Prof. Cond. 5.4 ....... 12, 437
ABA Model Rule Prof. Cond. 5.4(a)........ 262, 431
ABA Model Rule Prof. Cond. 5.4(a)(2)..... 241
ABA Model Rule Prof. Cond. 5.4(a)(4)..... 433
ABA Model Rule Prof. Cond. 5.4(b)......... 436
ABA Model Rule Prof. Cond. 5.4(d)..... 7, 436
ABA Model Rule Prof. Cond. 5.5 ..... 142, 145
ABA Model Rule Prof. Cond. 5.5(a)......... 140
ABA Model Rule Prof. Cond. 5.5(b)........ 143, 148
ABA Model Rule Prof. Cond. 5.5(b)(1)..... 144
ABA Model Rule Prof. Cond. 5.5(b)(2)..... 144
ABA Model Rule Prof. Cond. 5.5(c)(1)..... 143
ABA Model Rule Prof. Cond. 5.5(c)(2).... 144, 145
ABA Model Rule Prof. Cond. 5.5(c)(3)..... 145
ABA Model Rule Prof. Cond. 5.5(c)(4).... 146, 147
ABA Model Rule Prof. Cond. 5.5(d)(1) .... 148
ABA Model Rule Prof. Cond. 5.5(d)(2) ... 145, 148
ABA Model Rule Prof. Cond. 5.6 ............ 807
ABA Model Rule Prof. Cond. 5.6(a)......... 438
ABA Model Rule Prof. Cond. 5.6(b)......... 441
ABA Model Rule Prof. Cond. 5.7 ..... 203, 204
ABA Model Rule Prof. Cond. 5.7(b)......... 208
ABA Model Rule Prof. Cond. 6.1 ..... 703, 705
ABA Model Rule Prof. Cond. 6.1, cmt. 1 .......... 705

ABA Model Rule Prof. Cond. 6.2............ 709
ABA Model Rule Prof. Cond. 6.3..... 711, 712
ABA Model Rule Prof. Cond. 6.4..... 115, 695
ABA Model Rule Prof. Cond. 6.5..... 215, 706
ABA Model Rule Prof. Cond. 7.1..... 160, 170
ABA Model Rule Prof. Cond. 7.1, cmt. 2............ 161
ABA Model Rule Prof. Cond. 7.2..... 170, 185
ABA Model Rule Prof. Cond. 7.2(a)........ 163
ABA Model Rule Prof. Cond. 7.2(b)........ 181
ABA Model Rule Prof. Cond. 7.2(c)........ 181
ABA Model Rule Prof. Cond. 7.2, cmt. 1............ 173
ABA Model Rule Prof. Cond. 7.2, cmt. 2............ 163
ABA Model Rule Prof. Cond. 7.2, cmt. 3............ 167, 174
ABA Model Rule Prof. Cond. 7.2, cmt. 5............ 182
ABA Model Rule Prof. Cond. 7.3............ 807
ABA Model Rule Prof. Cond. 7.3(a)....... 126, 186, 189
ABA Model Rule Prof. Cond. 7.3(c)........ 169, 170, 171
ABA Model Rule Prof. Cond. 7.3, cmt. 7............ 191
ABA Model Rule Prof. Cond. 7.4(a)........ 174
ABA Model Rule Prof. Cond. 7.4(a), cmt. 1............ 174
ABA Model Rule Prof. Cond. 7.4(d)........ 176
ABA Model Rule Prof. Cond. 7.5............ 176
ABA Model Rule Prof. Cond. 7.5(a)........ 179
ABA Model Rule Prof. Cond. 7.5(d)........ 179
ABA Model Rule Prof. Cond. 7.5, cmt. 1............ 177, 179
ABA Model Rule Prof. Cond. 7.5, cmt. 2............ 922
ABA Model Rule Prof. Cond. 7.6............ 193
ABA Model Rule Prof. Cond. 8.1............ 693
ABA Model Rule Prof. Cond. 8.2(a)....... 698, 699, 702
ABA Model Rule Prof. Cond. 8.3............ 76
ABA Model Rule Prof. Cond. 8.3(a)........ 690
ABA Model Rule Prof. Cond. 8.3(c)........ 690, 692
ABA Model Rule Prof. Cond. 8.4.... 125, 128, 129, 130, 208, 488
ABA Model Rule Prof. Cond. 8.4(a)........ 617
ABA Model Rule Prof. Cond. 8.4(b)........ 125
ABA Model Rule Prof. Cond. 8.4(b), cmt. 2............ 125
ABA Model Rule Prof. Cond. 8.4(b), cmt. 4............ 125
ABA Model Rule Prof. Cond. 8.4(c)........ 126, 140, 251, 529, 815
ABA Model Rule Prof. Cond. 8.4(d)....... 127, 487
ABA Model Rule Prof. Cond. 8.4(g)........ 128
ABA Model Rule Prof. Cond. 8.4, cmt. 3............ 127, 130
ABA Model Rule Prof. Cond. 8.5............ 143
ABA Model Rule Prof. Cond. 8.5(a)........ 143, 150
ABA Model Rule Prof. Cond. 8.5(b)........ 152
ABA Model Rule Prof. Cond. 8.5(b)(1)..... 153
ABA Model Rule Prof. Cond. 8.5(b)(2).... 153, 154
ABA Model Rule Prof. Cond. 8.5, cmt. 5............ 155
ABA Model Rule Prof. Cond. 8.5, cmt. 6............ 155
ABA Model Rule Prof. Cond. Preamble ... 70, 76, 77, 703, 725
ABA Model Rule Prof. Cond. Preamble and Scope............ 725
ABA Model Rule Prof. Cond. Scope 14.... 113
ABA Model Rule Prof. Cond. Scope Note............ 767
ABA Model Rule Prof. Resp. Canon 7..... 286
Code of Conduct for U.S. Judges, Canon 3C............ 986, 988
Code of Conduct for U.S. Judges, Canon 4A(2)............ 1013
Code of Conduct for U.S. Judges, Canon 4A(c)............ 1014
Code of Conduct for U.S. Judges, Canon 4C............ 1015
Fed. R. Civ. P. 9(b)............ 816
Fed. R. Civ. P. 11............ 119, 482, 484
Fed. R. Civ. P. 11(b)............ 119, 482
Fed. R. Civ. P. 16............ 977
Fed. R. Civ. P. 23............ 276
Fed. R. Civ. P. 26(b)(1)............ 502
Fed. R. Civ. P. 26(b)(2)(C)............ 502
Fed. R. Civ. P. 26(b)(3)............ 333, 334
Fed. R. Civ. P. 26(b)(3)(A)............ 335
Fed. R. Civ. P. 26(b)(3)(B)............ 334
Fed. R. Civ. P. 26(b)(5)(A)............ 319
Fed. R. Civ. P. 26(b)(5)(B)............ 519
Fed. R. Civ. P. 26(g)............ 501, 503
Fed. R. Civ. P. 37............ 509
Fed. R. Civ. P. 37(e)............ 508, 509
Fed. R. Civ. P. 37(e)(2)............ 510
Fed. R. Civ. P. 45(e)(2)(B)............ 519
Fed. R. Evid. 502............ 337
Fed. R. Evid. 502(b)............ 338
Fed. R. Evid. 502(f)............ 338
Fed. R. Evid. 606(b)............ 593
Ala. R. Prof. Cond. 1.8(e)(3)............ 368
Ala. R. Prof. Cond. 3.3, cmt............ 571
Ala. R. Prof. Cond. 3.7(b)............ 607
Ala. R. Prof. Cond. 7.2(e)............ 161
Ala. R. Prof. Cond. 7.2(f)............ 162
Alaska R. Prof. Cond. 1.5(b)............ 257
Alaska R. Prof. Cond. 7.1(b)............ 161
Alaska R. Prof. Cond. 8.4, cmt............ 530
Ariz. R. Prof. Cond. 1.5(b)............ 257
Ariz. R. Prof. Cond. 1.5(d)(3)............ 259
Ariz. R. Prof. Cond. 1.16(d)............ 238
Ariz. R. Prof. Cond. 7.1(b)............ 161
Ariz. R. Prof. Cond. 7.2(d)(4)............ 162
Ariz. R. Prof. Cond. 7.2(e)............ 168
Ariz. R. Prof. Cond. 7.3(c)(4)............ 171

Ark. R. Prof. Cond. 7.1(b) .......... 161
Ark. R. Prof. Cond. 7.2(e) .......... 168
Cal. R. Prof. Cond. 1–400
(Standards)(13) .......... 167
Cal. R. Prof. Cond. 2–100(C)(1) .......... 674
Cal. R. Prof. Cond. 2–200 .......... 262
Cal. R. Prof. Cond. 2–400(C) .......... 130
Cal. R. Prof. Cond. 3–600(C) .......... 464
Cal. R. Prof. Cond. 4–210(A) .......... 369
Cal. R. Prof. Cond. 7.2(Standard)(16) .......... 162
Colo. R. Prof. Cond. 1.5(b) .......... 257
Colo. R. Prof. Cond. 1.5(e) .......... 262
Colo. R. Prof. Cond. 1.5(g) .......... 259
Colo. R. Prof. Cond. 7.1(b) .......... 161
Conn. R. Prof. Cond. 1.5(b) .......... 257
Conn. R. Prof. Cond. 1.6(b) .......... 343
Conn. R. Prof. Cond. 7.2(f) .......... 180
Conn. R. Prof. Cond. 7.2(g) .......... 162
Conn. R. Prof. Cond. 8.3(a) .......... 689
D.C. R. Prof. Cond. 1.2(d) .......... 474
D.C. R. Prof. Cond. 1.3(a) .......... 286
D.C. R. Prof. Cond. 1.7, cmt. 35 .......... 474
D.C. R. Prof. Cond. 1.8(d)(2) .......... 368
D.C. R. Prof. Cond. 3.3(b) .......... 571
D.C. R. Prof. Cond. 3.3(b), cmt. 8 .......... 571
D.C. R. Prof. Cond. 3.4(a) .......... 535, 559
D.C. R. Prof. Cond. 3.4, cmt. 5 .......... 557
D.C. R. Prof. Cond. 3.4, cmt. 7 .......... 564
D.C. R. Prof. Cond. 3.7(a) .......... 603
D.C. R. Prof. Cond. 3.8(g) .......... 640
D.C. R. Prof. Cond. 4.2(d) .......... 674
D.C. R. Prof. Cond. 5.4(b) .......... 437
D.C. R. Prof. Cond. 5.4(b), cmts. 7–8 .......... 437
Fla. R. Prof. Cond. 1.6(b)(2) .......... 343
Fla. R. Prof. Cond. 4.2(b) .......... 670
Fla. R. Prof. Cond. 4–7.14(b)(5) .......... 162
Fla. R. Prof. Cond. 4–7.15(c) .......... 167
Fla. R. Prof. Cond. 4–13 .......... 464
Fla. R. Prof. Cond. 6.1(d) .......... 705
Ga. R. Prof. Cond. 1.17(b) .......... 244
Ga. R. Prof. Cond. 1.17(d) .......... 246
Ga. R. Prof. Cond. 3.4(a) .......... 535
Ga. R. Prof. Cond. 3.4(b)(3) .......... 585
Ga. R. Prof. Cond. 3.4(h) .......... 491
Ga. R. Prof. Cond. 7.1(a)(2) .......... 161
Haw. R. Prof. Cond. 3.4(c) .......... 585
Haw. R. Prof. Cond. 4.4(b)(1) .......... 518
Haw. R. Prof. Cond. 7.1(b) .......... 161
Haw. R. Prof. Cond. 8.3(d) .......... 689
Idaho R. Prof. Cond. 4.4(a)(3) .......... 491
Idaho R. Prof. Cond. 4.4(a)(4) .......... 491
Idaho R. Prof. Cond. 7.1(b) .......... 161
Ill. S. Ct. R. 722(b)(1) .......... 909, 912, 931
Ind. R. Prof. Cond. 1.5(d)(1) .......... 255
Ind. R. Prof. Cond. 1.15 .......... 835
Ind. R. Prof. Cond. 3.7(d) .......... 607
Ind. R. Prof. Cond. 6.7 .......... 705
Ind. R. Prof. Cond. 7.5(b) .......... 178
Iowa Ct. R. 45.10(3) .......... 256
Iowa R. Civ. Proc. 1.423(1) .......... 216
Iowa R. Civ. Proc. 1.423(2) .......... 216
Iowa R. Prof. Cond. 32:1.6(c) .......... 153, 343
Iowa R. Prof. Cond. 32:1.7, cmt. 13a .......... 397
Iowa R. Prof. Cond. 32:1.8, cmt. 12a .......... 370
Iowa R. Prof. Cond. 32:3.4, cmt. 3 .......... 585
Iowa R. Prof. Cond. 32:3.8, cmt. 2 .......... 626
Iowa R. Prof. Cond. 32:4.2(b) .......... 670
Iowa R. Prof. Cond. 32:8.4, cmt. 6 .......... 530
Kan. R. Prof. Cond. 7.1(b) .......... 161
Ky. R. Prof. Cond. 3.4(f) .......... 491
La. R. Prof. Cond. 1.8(d)(4) .......... 368
La. R. Prof. Cond. 4.4(b) .......... 518
La. R. Prof. Cond. 7.2(c)(1)(J) .......... 168
Maine R. Prof. Cond. 1.2(c) .......... 216
Maine R. Prof. Cond. 3.1(b) .......... 491
Maine R. Prof. Cond. 4.2(b) .......... 670
Maine R. Prof. Cond. 4.4(b) .......... 518
Md. R. Prof. Cond. 1.5(d)(1) .......... 255
Md. R. Prof. Cond. 19–301.17(a)(2) .......... 244
Md. R. Prof. Cond. 19–303, cmts. 7–11 .......... 571
Md. R. Prof. Cond. 19–304.1(b) .......... 351
Md. R. Prof. Cond. 19–304.2(c) .......... 674
Mass. Bd. of Bar Overseers R. § 3.28 .......... 135
Mass. R. Prof. Cond. 1.3 .......... 286
Mass. R. Prof. Cond. 1.17(c) .......... 246
Mass. R. Prof. Cond. 1.17(e)(7) .......... 238
Mass. R. Prof. Cond. 3.3, cmt. 11 .......... 571
Mass. R. Prof. Cond. 3.4(g) .......... 585
Mich. R. Prof. Cond. 1.5(e) .......... 262
Mich. R. Prof. Cond. 1.17(b) .......... 246
Mich. R. Prof. Cond. 3.7(a) .......... 607
Mich. R. Prof. Cond. 7.1(b) .......... 161
Mich. R. Prof. Cond. 19–301.17 .......... 244
Minn. R. Prof. Cond. 1.5(b)(1) .......... 256
Minn. R. Prof. Cond. 1.5(b)(3) .......... 259
Minn. R. Prof. Cond. 1.8(e)(3) .......... 368
Minn. R. Prof. Cond. 1.17(a)(1) .......... 244
Minn. R. Prof. Cond. 5.5(a) .......... 144
Miss. R. Civ. Proc. 11 .......... 734
Miss. R. Prof. Cond. 1.8(e)(2) .......... 368
Miss. R. Prof. Cond. 3.3, cmt. .......... 571
Miss. R. Prof. Cond. 3.7(a) .......... 607
Miss. R. Prof. Cond. 7.2(b) .......... 162
Mo. R. Prof. Cond. 4–1.17(d) .......... 246
Mo. R. Prof. Cond. 4–7.1(i) .......... 167
Mo. R. Prof. Cond. 7.1(b) .......... 161
Mont. R. Prof. Cond. 1.8(e)(3) .......... 368
Mont. R. Prof. Cond. 1.8(f) .......... 396
Mont. R. Prof. Cond. 4.2(b) .......... 670
Mont. R. Prof. Cond. 7.1(b) .......... 161
Mont. R. Prof. Cond. 7.1(i) .......... 167
Nev. R. Prof. Cond. 1.8(a) .......... 764
Nev. R. Prof. Cond. 6.1(b) .......... 705
Nev. R. Prof. Cond. 7.1(b) .......... 161
Nev. R. Prof. Cond. 7.2(b) .......... 167
Nev. R. Prof. Cond. 7.2(f) .......... 162
Nev. R. Prof. Cond. 7.2(g) .......... 162
Nev. R. Prof. Cond. 7.2(i) .......... 162
N.H. R. Prof. Cond. 1.2(f) .......... 216
N.H. R. Prof. Cond. 3.7(b) .......... 607
N.H. R. Prof. Cond. 4.2(b) .......... 670
N.H. R. Prof. Cond. 4.4(b) .......... 518
N.H. R. Prof. Cond. 7.1(b) .......... 161
N.J. Ct. R. 1:21–1C(a)(3) .......... 912

N.J. R. Prof. Cond. 1.5(b) ........................ 257
N.J. R. Prof. Cond. 1.6(b)(1) .................... 343
N.J. R. Prof. Cond. 1.17.......................... 244
N.J. R. Prof. Cond. 4.1(b) ........................ 351
N.J. R. Prof. Cond. 4.4(b) ........................ 518
N.J. R. Prof. Cond. 5.1(a) ........................ 680
N.J. R. Prof. Cond. 7.1(a)(2) .................... 161
N.J. R. Prof. Cond. 7.2(a) ........................ 168
N.J. R. Prof. Cond. 8.4(c)......................... 529
N.M. R. Prof. Cond. 4.2 .......................... 446
N.M. R. Prof. Cond. 16–306(A)(2) ........... 603
N.Y. R. Prof. Cond. 1.5(d)(5).................... 255
N.Y. R. Prof. Cond. 1.13(c) ...................... 464
N.Y. R. Prof. Cond. 3.4(b)......................... 585
N.Y. R. Prof. Cond. 3.7(b)......................... 607
N.Y. R. Prof. Cond. 3.7(b)(1).................... 600
N.Y. R. Prof. Cond. 5.1(a)......................... 680
N.Y. R. Prof. Cond. 5.1(c) ........................ 680
N.Y. R. Prof. Cond. 7.1(c)(4) .................... 167
N.Y. R. Prof. Cond. 7.2(m)....................... 162
N.Y. R. Prof. Cond. 7.2(n)........................ 162
N.Y. R. Prof. Cond. 8.4(g)......................... 130
N.C. R. Prof. Cond. 4.2(b)......................... 674
N.C. R. Prof. Cond. 7.1(b)......................... 167
N.D. R. Prof. Cond. 1.6(b)......................... 343
N.D. R. Prof. Cond. 1.8(e)(3) .................. 368
N.D. R. Prof. Cond. 3.3(a)(3) .................. 571
N.D. R. Prof. Cond. 3.3(a)(3), cmts. 10–11 ....... 571
N.D. R. Prof. Cond. 7.1(b)......................... 161
Ohio R. Prof. Cond. 1.17(a) ..................... 244
Ohio R. Prof. Cond. 1.17(d) ..................... 246
Ohio R. Prof. Cond. 7.5(a) ....................... 178
Or. R. Prof. Cond. 1.5(d).......................... 262
Or. R. Prof. Cond. 3.4(b).......................... 585
Or. R. Prof. Cond. 3.4(g).......................... 491
Or. R. Prof. Cond. 3.7(c) .......................... 600
Or. R. Prof. Cond. 8.4(b)................... 529, 530
Or. State Bar Bylaws, art. 8, § 8.102...... 136
Penn. R. Prof. Cond. 1.5(b)...................... 257
Penn. R. Prof. Cond. 3.4(b)...................... 585
Penn. R. Prof. Cond. 7.2(f)....................... 168
Penn. R. Prof. Cond. 7.2(h)(2) ................ 162
R.I. R. Prof. Cond. 5.4(a)(4) .................... 436
R.I. R. Prof. Cond. 7.1(c)......................... 167
S.C. R. Prof. Cond. 1.17(b)....................... 244
S.C. R. Prof. Cond. 7.1(b)......................... 161
S.C. R. Prof. Cond. 7.2(g)......................... 162
S.C. R. Prof. Cond. 7.3(c)......................... 171
S.D. R. Prof. Cond. 1.6(b)(1) ................... 154
S.D. R. Prof. Cond. 7.1(c)(2) ................... 161
S.D. R. Prof. Cond. 7.2(g)(2) ................... 162
S.D. R. Prof. Cond. 7.2(g)(iii).................. 180
S.D. R. Prof. Cond. 7.2(h) ....................... 168
Tenn. R. Prof. Cond. 3.4(h)...................... 585
Tenn. R. Prof. Cond. 4.4(a)(2) ................ 491
Tenn. R. Prof. Cond. 4.4(b)...................... 518
Tenn. R. Prof. Cond. 7.3(c)(6)................. 171
Tex. Discip. R. Prof. Cond. 1.02(c) .......... 876
Tex. Discip. R. Prof. Cond. 1.09(a)(1)...... 740
Tex. R. Prof. Cond. 3.07(b) ..................... 607
Tex. R. Prof. Cond. 3.4(b) ....................... 585
Tex. R. Prof. Cond. 4.4(b)(1) ...................491
Tex. R. Prof. Cond. 7.02(a)(7) .................168
Tex. R. Prof. Cond. 7.04(g).......................168
Tex. R. Prof. Cond. 7.04(i)........................162
Tex. R. Prof. Cond. 7.5(a).........................178
Utah R. Prof. Cond. 4.2(b) .......................670
Utah R. Prof. Cond. 4.2(d)(3)...................674
Utah R. Prof. Cond. 7.1(b) .......................161
Utah R. Prof. Cond. 7.2(b) .......................167
Vt. R. Prof. Cond. 1.5(f)............................260
Vt. R. Prof. Cond. 1.6(b)(1).......................343
Va. R. Prof. Cond. 1.6(c)(1) ......................343
Va. R. Prof. Cond. 3.3(a)(4).......................571
Va. R. Prof. Cond. 3.3(a)(4), cmt. 11........571
Va. R. Prof. Cond. 3.4(c)...........................585
Va. R. Prof. Cond. 3.7(b) ..........................600
Wash. R. Prof. Cond. 3.7 Appx. ...............607
W. Va. R. Prof. Cond. 1.5(b).....................257
Wis. R. Prof. Cond. 1.5(b)(1) ...................257
Wis. R. Prof. Cond. 1.5(d)(1) ...................255
Wis. R. Prof. Cond. 3.7(b).........................607
Wis. R. Prof. Cond. 4.4(c) .........................518
Wis. R. Prof. Cond. 20:1.6(b)....................343
Wis. S. Ct. R. 20:1.6(b).............................154

# Table of Restatements


Restatement (Second) of Agency § 381... 943
Restatement (Third) of Agency § 2.01.... 906
Restatement (Third) of Agency § 2.01, cmt. b ... 906
Restatement (Third) of Agency § 2.01, cmt. c ... 906
Restatement (Third) of Agency § 2.03, cmt. c ... 906
Restatement (Third) of Agency § 7.03.... 906
Restatement (Third) of Agency § 7.04.... 906
Restatement (Third) of Agency § 7.07(2) ... 904
Restatement (Third) of Agency § 7.08.... 906
Restatement (Third) of Agency § 8.01.... 806
Restatement (Second) of Contracts § 7, cmt. b ... 814
Restatement of the Law Governing Lawyers, Preface ... 118
Restatement of the Law Governing Lawyers, Reporter's Memo ... 118
Restatement (Third) of the Law Governing Lawyers, Introduction ... 77
Restatement (Third) of the Law Governing Lawyers, Introductory Note, Chapter 4 ... 715
Restatement (Third) of the Law Governing Lawyers § 1 ... 715, 724
Restatement (Third) of the Law Governing Lawyers § 3(3) ... 147
Restatement (Third) of the Law Governing Lawyers § 4, cmt. a ... 927
Restatement (Third) of the Law Governing Lawyers § 6 ... 715
Restatement (Third) of the Law Governing Lawyers § 9 ... 901
Restatement (Third) of the Law Governing Lawyers § 9(3) ... 807
Restatement (Third) of the Law Governing Lawyers § 9, cmt. h ... 919
Restatement (Third) of the Law Governing Lawyers § 13, cmt. b ... 439
Restatement (Third) of the Law Governing Lawyers § 14 ... 202, 728
Restatement (Third) of the Law Governing Lawyers § 14(1) ... 730, 731
Restatement (Third) of the Law Governing Lawyers § 14, cmt. f ... 733
Restatement (Third) of the Law Governing Lawyers § 15 ... 321, 735
Restatement (Third) of the Law Governing Lawyers § 15(2) ... 736
Restatement (Third) of the Law Governing Lawyers § 16, cmt. b ... 295
Restatement (Third) of the Law Governing Lawyers § 16, cmt. c ... 770
Restatement (Third) of the Law Governing Lawyers § 19 ... 738, 744, 746
Restatement (Third) of the Law Governing Lawyers § 19, cmt. c ... 738
Restatement (Third) of the Law Governing Lawyers § 19, illus. 3 ... 744
Restatement (Third) of the Law Governing Lawyers § 20 ... 293, 793, 943
Restatement (Third) of the Law Governing Lawyers § 20, cmt. ... 770
Restatement (Third) of the Law Governing Lawyers § 20, cmt. c ... 296, 794, 795, 943
Restatement (Third) of the Law Governing Lawyers § 21 ... 219
Restatement (Third) of the Law Governing Lawyers §§ 21–22 ... 769
Restatement (Third) of the Law Governing Lawyers § 21(1) ... 220
Restatement (Third) of the Law Governing Lawyers § 21(2) ... 220
Restatement (Third) of the Law Governing Lawyers § 21(2), cmt. d ... 220
Restatement (Third) of the Law Governing Lawyers § 22 ... 741
Restatement (Third) of the Law Governing Lawyers § 25 ... 733
Restatement (Third) of the Law Governing Lawyers § 25, cmt. d ... 733
Restatement (Third) of the Law Governing Lawyers § 30 ... 760
Restatement (Third) of the Law Governing Lawyers § 30, cmt. b ... 760
Restatement (Third) of the Law Governing Lawyers § 32, cmt. b ... 232
Restatement (Third) of the Law Governing Lawyers § 33(2) ... 740
Restatement (Third) of the Law Governing Lawyers § 34, cmt. e ... 258
Restatement (Third) of the Law Governing Lawyers § 35(1)(b) ... 255
Restatement (Third) of the Law Governing Lawyers § 35, cmt. c ... 253
Restatement (Third) of the Law Governing Lawyers § 36(2) ... 368
Restatement (Third) of the Law Governing Lawyers § 36(2), cmt. c ... 368
Restatement (Third) of the Law Governing Lawyers § 37 ... 237, 797, 814
Restatement (Third) of the Law Governing Lawyers § 37, cmt. b ... 124
Restatement (Third) of the Law Governing Lawyers § 37, cmt. c ... 798
Restatement (Third) of the Law Governing Lawyers § 45, cmt. d ... 302

Restatement (Third) of the Law Governing Lawyers § 45, cmt. f .......... 559
Restatement (Third) of the Law Governing Lawyers § 46, cmt. c .......... 294
Restatement (Third) of the Law Governing Lawyers § 47 .......... 915
Restatement (Third) of the Law Governing Lawyers § 47, cmt. b .......... 915
Restatement (Third) of the Law Governing Lawyers § 47, cmt. d .......... 915
Restatement (Third) of the Law Governing Lawyers § 48, cmt. c .......... 721
Restatement (Third) of the Law Governing Lawyers § 49, cmt. a .......... 795
Restatement (Third) of the Law Governing Lawyers § 49, cmt. d .......... 795
Restatement (Third) of the Law Governing Lawyers § 49, cmt. e .......... 792
Restatement (Third) of the Law Governing Lawyers § 51(2) .......... 653, 827, 840
Restatement (Third) of the Law Governing Lawyers § 51(3) .......... 837
Restatement (Third) of the Law Governing Lawyers § 51(4) .......... 835
Restatement (Third) of the Law Governing Lawyers § 51, cmt. g .......... 839
Restatement (Third) of the Law Governing Lawyers § 51, illus. 5 .......... 835
Restatement (Third) of the Law Governing Lawyers § 52 .......... 725
Restatement (Third) of the Law Governing Lawyers § 52(2) .......... 768
Restatement (Third) of the Law Governing Lawyers § 52(2)(c) .......... 124
Restatement (Third) of the Law Governing Lawyers § 52, cmt. b .......... 742, 748, 750, 757, 776, 779
Restatement (Third) of the Law Governing Lawyers § 52, cmt. c .......... 851
Restatement (Third) of the Law Governing Lawyers § 52, cmt. d .......... 744, 748
Restatement (Third) of the Law Governing Lawyers § 52, cmt. g .......... 753, 762
Restatement (Third) of the Law Governing Lawyers § 52, illus. 1 .......... 749
Restatement (Third) of the Law Governing Lawyers § 52, illus. 2 .......... 840
Restatement (Third) of the Law Governing Lawyers § 53 .......... 772
Restatement (Third) of the Law Governing Lawyers § 53, cmt. f .......... 855
Restatement (Third) of the Law Governing Lawyers § 53, cmt. g .......... 853
Restatement (Third) of the Law Governing Lawyers § 53, cmt. h .......... 866
Restatement (Third) of the Law Governing Lawyers § 54, cmt. b .......... 897
Restatement (Third) of the Law Governing Lawyers § 57(2) .......... 843
Restatement (Third) of the Law Governing Lawyers § 57, cmt. d .......... 843
Restatement (Third) of the Law Governing Lawyers § 58(1) .......... 722
Restatement (Third) of the Law Governing Lawyers § 58, cmt. b .......... 902
Restatement (Third) of the Law Governing Lawyers § 58, cmt. c .......... 921
Restatement (Third) of the Law Governing Lawyers § 58, cmt. d .......... 903, 905, 906
Restatement (Third) of the Law Governing Lawyers § 58, cmt. e .......... 894, 916, 919, 925, 927
Restatement (Third) of the Law Governing Lawyers § 58, cmt. i .......... 908
Restatement (Third) of the Law Governing Lawyers § 60 .......... 365
Restatement (Third) of the Law Governing Lawyers § 60, cmt. *l* .......... 392
Restatement (Third) of the Law Governing Lawyers § 61 .......... 310
Restatement (Third) of the Law Governing Lawyers § 68 .......... 313
Restatement (Third) of the Law Governing Lawyers § 69, cmt. i .......... 323
Restatement (Third) of the Law Governing Lawyers § 70 .......... 321
Restatement (Third) of the Law Governing Lawyers § 72, cmt. c, illus. 2 .......... 206
Restatement (Third) of the Law Governing Lawyers § 72, Reporter's Note .......... 206
Restatement (Third) of the Law Governing Lawyers § 73 .......... 447
Restatement (Third) of the Law Governing Lawyers § 73, cmt. i .......... 450
Restatement (Third) of the Law Governing Lawyers § 75 .......... 325
Restatement (Third) of the Law Governing Lawyers § 79, cmt. g, illus. 4 .......... 520
Restatement (Third) of the Law Governing Lawyers § 82(a) .......... 328
Restatement (Third) of the Law Governing Lawyers § 95(2) .......... 651
Restatement (Third) of the Law Governing Lawyers § 95(3) .......... 653
Restatement (Third) of the Law Governing Lawyers § 96, cmt. g .......... 470
Restatement (Third) of the Law Governing Lawyers § 98 .......... 659
Restatement (Third) of the Law Governing Lawyers § 99(2) .......... 666
Restatement (Third) of the Law Governing Lawyers § 100(c) .......... 456
Restatement (Third) of the Law Governing Lawyers § 102 .......... 514
Restatement (Third) of the Law Governing Lawyers § 102, cmt. b .......... 514

Restatement (Third) of the Law Governing Lawyers § 108, Reporter's Note .......... 594
Restatement (Third) of the Law Governing Lawyers § 109(2) .......... 611
Restatement (Third) of the Law Governing Lawyers § 109, cmt. b .......... 605
Restatement (Third) of the Law Governing Lawyers § 112, cmt. b .......... 498
Restatement (Third) of the Law Governing Lawyers § 114 .......... 698
Restatement (Third) of the Law Governing Lawyers § 116, cmt. b .......... 582
Restatement (Third) of the Law Governing Lawyers § 117(1) .......... 586
Restatement (Third) of the Law Governing Lawyers § 119(1) .......... 550
Restatement (Third) of the Law Governing Lawyers § 119(2) .......... 554
Restatement (Third) of the Law Governing Lawyers § 119, cmt. b .......... 550, 562
Restatement (Third) of the Law Governing Lawyers § 119, cmt. c .......... 554, 557, 558
Restatement (Third) of the Law Governing Lawyers § 119, Reporter's Note .......... 542
Restatement (Third) of the Law Governing Lawyers § 121 .......... 357, 378, 379
Restatement (Third) of the Law Governing Lawyers § 121, cmt. e(i) .......... 390
Restatement (Third) of the Law Governing Lawyers § 122, cmt. c(i) .......... 417, 770
Restatement (Third) of the Law Governing Lawyers § 122, cmt. g(i) .......... 419
Restatement (Third) of the Law Governing Lawyers § 122, cmt. g(iv) .......... 419
Restatement (Third) of the Law Governing Lawyers § 123, cmt. c(ii) .......... 920
Restatement (Third) of the Law Governing Lawyers § 124 .......... 410
Restatement (Third) of the Law Governing Lawyers § 125 .......... 379
Restatement (Third) of the Law Governing Lawyers § 125, cmt. 3 .......... 696
Restatement (Third) of the Law Governing Lawyers § 126 .......... 794
Restatement (Third) of the Law Governing Lawyers § 132 .......... 401
Restatement (Third) of the Law Governing Lawyers § 132, cmt. d(iii) .......... 402
Restatement (Third) of the Law Governing Lawyers § 134, cmt. d .......... 397
Restatement (Third) of the Law Governing Lawyers § 134, cmt. f .......... 393, 397
Restatement (Third) of the Law Governing Lawyers § 134, cmt. f, illus. 5 .......... 397
Restatement (Third) of the Law Governing Lawyers § 179 .......... 554
Restatement (Third) of the Law of Agency § 8.05 .......... 365
Restatement of the Law of Liability Insurance § 10, cmt. b .......... 396
Restatement of the Law of Liability Insurance § 10, cmt. c .......... 396
Restatement of the Law of Liability Insurance § 14(1)(b(1) .......... 395
Restatement of the Law of Liability Insurance § 16 .......... 396
Restatement of the Law of Liability Insurance § 24(1)–(2) .......... 394
Restatement of the Law of Liability Insurance § 27 .......... 395
Restatement of the Law of Liability Insurance § 29 .......... 392
Restatement (Third) of Restitution and Unjust Enrichment § 13 .......... 815
Restatement (Third) of Restitution and Unjust Enrichment § 24, cmt. a .......... 846
Restatement (Third) of Restitution and Unjust Enrichment § 49 .......... 796
Restatement (Second) of Torts § 324A .......... 735
Restatement (Second) of Torts § 416, Preceding Note .......... 925
Restatement (Second) of Torts § 452 .......... 785
Restatement (Second) of Torts § 526 .......... 817
Restatement (Second) of Torts § 529, cmt. a .......... 818
Restatement (Second) of Torts § 531 .......... 828
Restatement (Second) of Torts § 531, cmt. d .......... 829
Restatement (Second) of Torts § 532 .......... 828
Restatement (Second) of Torts § 536 .......... 829
Restatement (Second) of Torts § 536, cmt. e .......... 829
Restatement (Second) of Torts § 538 .......... 818
Restatement (Second) of Torts § 545, cmt. d .......... 824
Restatement (Second) of Torts § 551(2)(d) .......... 820
Restatement (Second) of Torts § 551, cmt. *l* .......... 820
Restatement (Second) of Torts § 552 .......... 831
Restatement (Second) of Torts § 552(1) .......... 827
Restatement (Second) of Torts § 552, cmt. h .......... 832
Restatement (Second) of Torts § 586 .......... 615, 874
Restatement (Second) of Torts §§ 593–598A .......... 877
Restatement (Second) of Torts §§ 599–605A .......... 877
Restatement (Second) of Torts §§ 603–604 .......... 803

Restatement (Second) of Torts §§ 674–682 ........ 844
Restatement (Second) of Torts § 681 ........ 844
Restatement (Second) of Torts § 876 ........ 782
Restatement (Second) of Torts § 876(b) ........ 799, 927
Restatement (Second) of Torts § 876, cmt. d ........ 802
Restatement (Second) of Torts § 885 ........ 895
Restatement (Third) of Torts § 14 ........ 810
Restatement (Third) of Torts: Apportionment of Liability § 13 ........ 901
Restatement (Third) of Torts: Liability for Economic Harm § 5 ........ 827
Restatement (Third) of Torts: Liability for Physical and Emotional Harm § 1 ........ 800
Restatement (Third) of Torts: Liability for Physical and Emotional Harm § 3, cmt. e ........ 746
Restatement (Third) of Torts: Liability for Physical and Emotional Harm § 11(a) ........ 745
Restatement (Third) of Torts: Liability for Physical and Emotional Harm § 14 ........ 767
Restatement (Third) of Torts: Liability for Physical and Emotional Harm § 27 ........ 776
Restatement (Third) of Torts: Liability for Physical and Emotional Harm § 29 ........ 783
Restatement (Third) of Torts: Liability for Physical and Emotional Harm § 33(b) ........ 721
Restatement (Third) of Torts: Liability for Physical and Emotional Harm § 43 ........ 735
Restatement (Third) of Torts: Physical and Emotional Harm § 14 ........ 767

# Index

## References are to Pages


ABA MODEL RULES AND REPORTS AND EXEMPLARY LAWYERS
Professionalism and Professional Identity, this index

ABSOLUTE AND PERFECT CANDOR
Malpractice, breach of fiduciary duty, 793–795

ABSOLUTE JUDICIAL PROCEEDINGS PRIVILEGE
Malpractice, 874–876

ABUSE OF PRESTIGE
Judicial ethics and conduct of judges, 961–962

ACCESS TO EVIDENCE
Evidence in civil proceedings, 500–501

ACCOUNTING
Effective representation, client funds and property, 299

ACCRUAL OF CAUSE OF ACTION
Malpractice, 881–882

ACTUAL AND APPARENT AUTHORITY
Malpractice, vicarious liability, 905–907

ADMISSION TO BAR AND DISCIPLINE
Generally, 689–695
Attorney-client privilege, 694–695
Candor with respect to regulation of bar, 693–694
Confidential information
generally, 694–695
attorney-client privilege, 694–695
reporting of professional misconduct, 690–692
Demand for information by disciplinary authorities, 695
Judges, Legal Officers and Candidates for Judicial or Legal Office, this index
Judicial Ethics and Conduct of Judges, this index
Jurisdiction, disciplinary, 150–151
Knowledge of violation, reporting of professional misconduct, 690
Lawyers assistance program, protection of information gained within, 692
Malpractice, this index
Pro Hac Vice Admission, this index
Reporting of professional misconduct
generally, 689–692
attorney-client confidentiality, 690–692
knowledge of violation, 690
substantial question on fitness raised by violation, 690
Self-incrimination, privilege against, 694
Sources of Legal Ethics and Law, this index
Substantial question on fitness raised by violation, reporting of professional misconduct, 690

ADVANCE CONFLICT WAIVERS
Generally, 420–421

ADVANCED FEE DEPOSITS
Attorneys' Fees, this index

ADVERSARIAL ATMOSPHERE
Stress management, 83–84

ADVERTISING
Generally, 157–185
Broadcast media, 164–168
Certification as specialist, 175–176
Direct mail, 169–172
Disclaimers
generally, 180–181
decline of disclaimers, 180
fees, 180–181
suggestion of lawsuit, 180
False or misleading statements, 160–163
Fees, disclaimers, 180–181
Fields of practice and specialization
generally, 174–176
certification as specialist, 175–176
history, 174
practice in particular fields of law, 174–175
Firm name
generally, 176–179
lawyer names, designation of firm by, 177–178
partnership or association, claims of, 179
trade name, designation of firm by, 178–179
First Amendment, 158–160
General authorization, 163
History, 158–160
Internet, including web pages and social media, 168–169
Lawyer names, designation of firm by, 177–178
Name of firm. Firm name, above
Partnership or association, claims of, 179
Personal responsibility for advertising, 181
Referrals, this index
Specialization. Fields of practice and specialization, above
Style and emotional appeal, regulation of, 172–174
Targeted direct mail, 169–172
Trade name, designation of firm by, 178–179

ADVICE OF COUNSEL DEFENSE
Malpractice, malicious prosecution and malicious use of process, 844–845

ADVOCACY
Generally, 475–647
Accuracy in public statements of lawyer, 614–615
Advancement of resolution of disputes
generally, 486–493

conduct prejudicial to administration of justice, 487–490
criminal wrongdoing, threat or promise to withhold report of, 491–493
embarrassment, delay or burdensome means, 490
expediting litigation and avoiding unreasonable delay, 486
freedom of speech, 490
humiliation, degradation or oppression, seeking advantage by, 490–491
manifestations of bias prejudicial to administration of justice and not constituting legitimate advocacy, 488–490
professionalism/civility, 489–490
Advocate-Witness Rule, this index
Burdensome means, advancement of resolution of disputes, 490
Candor
competence and candor of government prosecutors and other lawyers, 619–621
truthfulness and candor before tribunal, below
Charging by prosecutors, 622–624
Civility, 489–490
Competence and candor of government prosecutors and other lawyers, 619–621
Conduct prejudicial to administration of justice, 487–490
Court rules and rulings, obedience unless openly challenging validity, 499–500
Criminal proceedings, putting prosecution to its proof, 484–485
Criminal wrongdoing, threat or promise to withhold report of, 491–493
Defamation, extrajudicial statements by lawyer, 615–616
Degradation, seeking advantage by, 490–491
Delay, advancement of resolution of disputes, 490
Derogatory statements about criminal defendant, extrajudicial statements by lawyer, 608–609
Disclosures by prosecutor, 640–643
Disruptive behavior at trial, 587
"Do justice," duty of prosecutor to, 617–619
Ebenezer Scrooge Factor, 478
Embarrassment, advancement of resolution of disputes, 490
Evidence in Civil Proceedings, this index
Evidence in Criminal Proceedings, this index
Exculpatory evidence, duty of prosecutor to disclose, 640–642
Ex parte communications with tribunal, 590–592
Ex parte proceedings, truthfulness and candor before tribunal, 497–498
Expediting litigation and avoiding unreasonable delay, 486
Extrajudicial statements by lawyer
generally, 601–617
accuracy in public statements, 614–615
defamation liability, 615–616
derogatory statements about criminal defendant, 608–609
freedom of expression *vs.* fair trial, 601–602
nature of proceeding, prejudice to adjudicative proceedings, 604–605
potential evidentiary matters, 608
potential harm to client's case, 614
prejudice to adjudicative proceedings, 603–617
prosecutors, statements made by, 609–611
reply to correct prejudice caused by another, 612–614
substantial likelihood of material prejudice to adjudicative proceedings, 603–604
third persons, responsibility of lawyers for prejudicial extrajudicial statements by, 616–617
types of statements, generally, 605–611
Freedom of expression *vs.* fair trial, extrajudicial statements by lawyer, 601–602
Freedom of speech, advancement of resolution of disputes, 490
Frivolous claims and contentions, 481–485
Government prosecutors and other lawyers
generally, 617–646
charging and investigations by prosecutors, 622–624
competence and candor, 619–621
disclosures by prosecutor, 640–643
"do justice," duty of prosecutor to, 617–619
exculpatory and mitigating evidence, duty of prosecutor to disclose, 640–642
law enforcement investigations by government lawyers, "no-contact" rule, 626–632
privileged communications, interception by government, 632–633
respect for rights of others, 624–640
state ethics rules and federal government lawyers, 621
subpoenas, restriction on issuance by prosecutors to lawyers, 636–640
unrepresented accused, duties of prosecutor to, 624–626
waiver of privileged communications, demand by government for, 633–636
wrongful convictions, disclosure duties of prosecutors, 642–643
Humiliation, seeking advantage by, 490–491
Inadmissible evidence, improper allusions to, 588–589
Influence on tribunal, 589–590
Investigations by prosecutors, 622–624
Jury communications after discharge, 592–594
Law enforcement investigations by government lawyers, "no-contact" rule, 626–632
Legal arguments, truthfulness and candor before tribunal, 495–497
Meritorious claims and contentions in civil proceedings, 481–484
Mitigating evidence, duty of prosecutor to disclose, 640–642
Non-adjudicative proceedings, 646–647
Oppression, seeking advantage by, 490–491
Personal vouching and opinions by lawyer, 588–589

Prejudice to adjudicative proceedings, extrajudicial statements by lawyer, 603–617
Presentation of claims and contentions in litigation, 481–485
Presentation of Evidence, this index
Privileged communications, interception by government, 632–633
Professionalism, advancement of resolution of disputes, 489–490
Prosecutors, extrajudicial statements made by, 609–611
Reply to correct prejudice caused by another, extrajudicial statements by lawyer, 612–614
Resolution of disputes. Advancement of resolution of disputes, above
Statements of fact, truthfulness and candor before tribunal, 494–495
Subpoenas, restriction on issuance by prosecutors to lawyers, 636–640
Substantial likelihood of material prejudice to adjudicative proceedings, extrajudicial statements by lawyer, 603–604
Superman Principle, 478
Third persons, responsibility of lawyers for prejudicial extrajudicial statements by, 616–617
Trial, behavior during and after
generally, 587–594
disruptive behavior at trial, 587
ex parte communications with tribunal, 590–592
inadmissible evidence, improper allusions to, 588–589
influence on tribunal, 589–590
jury communications after discharge, 592–594
personal vouching and opinions by lawyer, 588–589
Truthfulness and candor before tribunal
generally, 493–500
court rules and rulings, obedience unless openly challenging validity, 499–500
ex parte proceedings, 497–498
legal arguments, 495–497
statements of fact, 494–495
Unrepresented accused, duties of prosecutor to, 624–626
Vince Lombardi Doctrinc, 478
Waiver of privileged communications, demand by government for, 633–636
Wrongful convictions, disclosure duties of prosecutors, 642–643
Zealous advocacy *vs.* duties as officer of court, 476–481

**ADVOCATE-WITNESS RULE**
Generally, 594–601
Client activities, participation of lawyer and, 596
Conflicts of interest arising from lawyer's testimony as witness, 599–601
Confusion of lawyer's role, 594–596
Exceptions to rule
generally, 598–599
nature and value of legal services, 598–599
substantial hardship on client, 599
uncontested issues, 598
Investigations, conduct by lawyer, 595
Nature and value of legal services, 598–599
Necessary witness standard, 596–598
Substantial hardship on client, 599
Uncontested issues, 598

**AGGREGATE SETTLEMENTS**
Conflicts of interest, claims involving multiple current clients, 386–389

**AGREEMENTS OF PARTIES**
Choice of law for disciplinary authority, 155
Malpractice, statutes of limitation, 887–888

**AIDING AND ABETTING**
Malpractice, this index

**ALTERNATIVE LEGAL SERVICE PROVIDERS (ALSP)**
Legal productivity, 11–13

**AMERICAN RULE**
Attorneys' fees, shifting of fees to another party, 263–264

**ANTICIPATORY OBSTRUCTION OF JUSTICE**
Evidence in Criminal Proceedings, this index

**APPEARANCE BEFORE TRIBUNAL**
Malpractice, duty to exercise reasonable care, 733–734

**APPEARANCE OF IMPROPRIETY**
Judicial ethics and conduct of judges, 959–961

**APPOINTMENT**
Malpractice, immunity, 877–878
Pro Bono Legal Services, this index

**APPROVAL**
Consent, this index

**ARBITRATION**
Conflicts of Interest, this index
Malpractice, 896–898

**ASPIRATIONAL EXPECTATIONS**
Pro bono legal services, 705–706

**ASSIGNMENT OF CLAIMS**
Malpractice, 890–891

**ASSISTANTS**
Professional independence, employment, 437–438

**ASSOCIATES**
Malpractice, intra-firm fiduciary duties, 805–806

**ATTORNEY-CLIENT PRIVILEGE**
Generally, 312–333
Admission to bar and discipline, 694–695
Communication by client or lawyer, 323
Communication relating to legal advice, 321–322
Crime-fraud exception
generally, 327–328
organization/entity clients, 452–453
Elements, generally, 313–326

Ethics rules and independent protection of privilege, 330–333
Exceptions
generally, 326–333
crime-fraud exception, 327–328
ethics rules and independent protection of privilege, 330–333
identity of client and payment of fees, 329
lawyer-client disputes and lawyer self-defense, 329
Identity of client and payment of fees, 329
Involving professional legal advisor, 320–321
Joint client privilege and joint defense doctrine, 325–326
Lawyer-client disputes and lawyer self-defense, 329
Made in confidence, 322–323
Malpractice, insurance, 941
Organization/Entity Clients, this index
Protected at client's insistence, 324
Protected from disclosure by client or lawyer, 324
Seeking legal advice, 314–320
Waiver by client, 324–325

**ATTORNEY-CLIENT RELATIONSHIP**
Generally, 195–246
Agreements to limit scope of relationship, 214–215
Allocation of decision-making authority, 219–222
Business relationships. Creation and nature of relationship, below
Categories of services. Creation and nature of relationship, below
Children, 226–227
Client, termination of representation by, 229–233
Collaborative lawyering agreements, 216–218
Confidentiality
diminished capacity, clients with, 228
prospective clients, duties to, 197
Conflicts of Interest, this index
Creation and nature of relationship
generally, 202–213
business relationships and law-related services, generally, 203–212
categories of services
generally, 204
law-related services, 204
practice of law, 204
unrelated business activities, 204
elements, 202–203
law practice, law-related services provided as part of or distinct from, 209–212
law-related services, 204, 208–212
misunderstandings about relationship, responsibility of lawyer for, 212–213
practice of law, 204–207
tax returns and tax planning, 205–207
unrelated business activities, 204, 208
Death, termination of private practice or area of practice upon sale of practice, 241
Diminished capacity, clients with
generally, 222–228
acting contrary to wishes of client, 227
children, 226–227
confidentiality, 228
emergency situations, 227–228
evaluation of capacity and whether to take protective action, 224–225
guardian, consideration of whether to seek, 225–226
maintenance of relationship with and respect for dignity of persons with diminished capacity, 222–224
person or guardian as client, 226
protection of interests of persons with diminished capacity, generally, 224–228
Disability, termination of private practice or area of practice upon sale of practice, 241
Emergency situations, clients with diminished capacity, 227–228
Evaluation of capacity and whether to take protective action, clients with diminished capacity, 224–225
Fees. Attorneys' Fees, this index
Financial burden, permissive withdrawal by lawyer for unreasonable, 236–237
Geographic area or jurisdiction, termination of private practice or area of practice upon sale of practice, 240–241
Guardian, consideration of whether to seek for client with diminished capacity, 225–226
Lawyer, termination of representation by, 234–237
Mandatory withdrawal or decline by lawyer, 234
Misunderstandings about relationship, responsibility of lawyer for, 212–213
Nature of relationship. Creation and nature of relationship, above
Notice to clients and protection of confidentiality, sale of law practice and effect on clients, 245–246
Permissive withdrawal by lawyer, 234–237
Prospective clients, duties to
generally, 195–202
confidentiality, 197
Conflicts of Interest, this index
control of disclosure of information or obtaining advance waiver of conflict, 200–202
prospective clients, defined, 196–197
Protection of client's interest upon withdrawal, 237–238
Reasonableness of limitation of scope of relationship, 218–219
Repugnant action or fundamental disagreement, permissive withdrawal by lawyer, 235–236
Sale of law practice and effect on clients
generally, 238–246
death or disability, termination of private practice or area of practice upon sale, 241
entire practice of area of practice, sale of, 243–245
fees charged to clients, increase in, 246
geographic area or jurisdiction, termination of private practice or area of practice upon sale, 240–241
notice to clients and protection of confidentiality, 245–246

temporary continued affiliation, termination of private practice or area of practice upon sale, 241
termination of private practice or area of practice upon sale, 240–241
unanticipated changes, termination of private practice or area of practice upon sale, 240
valuation of law practice and payment of sale price, 241–243
Scope of relationship
generally, 213–219
agreements to limit scope, 214–215
collaborative lawyering agreements, 216–218
reasonableness of scope limitation, 218–219
unbundled legal services and assisting pro se litigants, 215–216
Tax returns and tax planning, 205–207
Temporary continued affiliation, termination of private practice or area of practice upon sale of practice, 241
Termination of representation
generally, 228–238
adverse effect, permissive withdrawal by lawyer without, 234–235
client, termination by, 229–233
compensation after permissive withdrawal, 237
conflicts of interest, concurrent client conflicts, 390–392
financial burden, permissive withdrawal by lawyer for unreasonable, 236–237
lawyer, termination by, 234–237
malpractice, 739–741
mandatory withdrawal or decline by lawyer, 234
near-absolute right of client to terminate lawyer, 229–230
ordinary conclusion of representation, 228
organization/entity clients, unlawful conduct or internal dissension within organization, 466
permissive withdrawal by lawyer, 234–237
protection of client's interest upon withdrawal, 237–238
repugnant action or fundamental disagreement, permissive withdrawal by lawyer, 235–236
tribunal, withdrawal by lawyer with permission from, 237
wrongful discharge claims by in-house counsel and law firm employees, 230–233
Unanticipated changes, termination of private practice or area of practice upon sale of practice, 240
Unbundled legal services and assisting pro se litigants, 215–216
Valuation of law practice and payment of sale price, sale of law practice and effect on clients, 241–243
Wrongful discharge claims by in-house counsel and law firm employees, 230–233

**ATTORNEY IMMUNITY**
Malpractice, 876–877

**ATTORNEYS' FEES**
Generally, 247–272
Advanced fee deposits
generally, 258–260
general or engagement retainer, availability of lawyer, 258–259
nonrefundable special retainers, 259–260
refunding of unearned fees, 258
Advertising, disclaimers, 180–181
American Rule, shifting of fees to another party, 263–264
Billing judgment, shifting of fees to another party, 267–268
Communication of basis for and rate of fee, duty of lawyer, 256–257
Confidential information, fee collection by lawyer, 353–354
Contingency fees
generally, 252–255
criminal and domestic relations cases, 254–255
legitimacy of method, 252–253
malpractice, amounts that would have been spent, 858
reasonableness standard, 253–254
written agreement, 254
Criminal cases, contingency fees, 254–255
Delay in receipt of fees, shifting of fees to another party, 272
Disputes regarding fees, 263
Division of fees among lawyers, 260–262
Domestic relations cases, contingency fees, 254–255
Engagement retainer, availability of lawyer, 258–259
Flat fees, 255–256
General retainer, availability of lawyer, 258–259
Honesty in hourly billing, 251–252
Hourly billing
generally, 249–252
honesty in billing, 251–252
nature and reasonableness, 249–250
Legality. Reasonableness and legality of fees and expenses, below
Lodestar method, shifting of fees to another party, 265–266, 270–272
Malpractice, this index
Nonrefundable special retainers, 259–260
Objective standard for reasonableness and legality of fees and expenses, 248–249
Permissive withdrawal by lawyer, compensation after, 237
Prevailing market rate, shifting of fees to another party, 269–270
Prevailing parties, shifting of fees to another party, 264–265
Professional Independence, this index
Reasonableness and legality of fees and expenses
generally, 248–256
contingency fees, above
flat fees, 255–256
hourly billing, above
objective standard, 248–249

shifting of fees to another party, below
Refunding of unearned fees, 258
Retainers. Advanced fee deposits, above
Sale of law practice and effect on clients, increase in fees, 246
Shifting of fees to another party
generally, 263–272
adjustment to lodestar, 270–272
American Rule, 263–264
attorney's billing rate, 269
billing judgment, 267–268
delay in receipt of fees, compensation for, 272
disallowance of hours, 268–269
fees for application for fees, 272
hours reasonably expended
generally, 266–269
billing judgment, 267–268
disallowance of hours, 268–269
specification of billing activities, 267
time records, 267
lodestar method, 265–266, 270–272
measurement of award, 265–272
prevailing market rate, 269–270
prevailing parties, 264–265
reasonable hourly rate
generally, 269–270
attorney's billing rate, 269
prevailing market rate, 269–270
relevant community, 270
relevant community, reasonable hourly rate, 270
specification of billing activities, 267
time records, 267
Splitting of fees among lawyers, 260–262
Third persons, payment of fees by, 262–263
Time records, shifting of fees to another party, 267
Written agreement, contingency fees, 254

**AVOCATIONAL ACTIVITIES**
Judicial ethics and conduct of judges, 1014–1017

**BAD FAITH**
Malpractice, 746

**BANKRUPTCY**
Malpractice, this index

**BAR ADMISSION**
Admission to Bar and Discipline, this index

**BIAS OR PREJUDICE**
Advocacy, extrajudicial statements by lawyer, 603–617
Judicial ethics and conduct of judges, 973–976
Sources of legal ethics and law, biased conduct and lawyer fitness, 128

**BILLING JUDGMENT**
Attorneys' fees, shifting of fees to another party, 267–268

**BODILY HARM**
Confidential information, prevention, 342–344

**BROADCAST MEDIA**
Advertising, 164–168

**BURDEN OF PROOF**
Malpractice, factual causation, 780–781

**BURDENSOME MEANS**
Advocacy, advancement of resolution of disputes, 490

**BUSINESS ACTIVITIES**
Judicial ethics and conduct of judges, 1017–1018

**BUSINESS RELATIONSHIPS**
Attorney-Client Relationship, this index

**"BUT FOR" TEST**
Malpractice, this index

**CAMPAIGN SUPPORT AND COMMITMENTS**
Judicial ethics and conduct of judges, disqualification, 1006–1008

**CANDID ADVICE**
Effective Representation, this index

**CANDIDATES FOR JUDICIAL OR LEGAL OFFICE**
Judges, Legal Officers and Candidates for Judicial or Legal Office, this index

**CANDOR**
Admission to bar and discipline, candor with respect to regulation of bar, 693–694
Advocacy, this index

**CAUSATION**
Malpractice, this index

**CHICAGO LAWYERS I AND II STUDIES**
Structure of legal profession, 3–4

**CHILDREN**
Attorney-client relationship, 226–227

**CHOICE OF LAW**
Sources of Legal Ethics and Law, this index

**CIVILITY**
Advocacy, 489–490
Effective representation, 288–291

**CIVIL RESOLUTION TRIBUNAL (CRT)**
British Columbia, 21–22

**CLASS MEMBERS**
Malpractice, duty to exercise reasonable care, 736
Solicitation, 188–189

**CLEAR AND SERIOUS BREACH OF DUTY**
Malpractice, fee forfeiture for breach of fiduciary duty, 797

**CLOSE FRIENDS**
Solicitation, 187

**CO-COUNSEL**
Malpractice, this index

**COLLABORATIVE LAWYERING AGREEMENTS**
Attorney-client relationship, 216–218

**COMMERCIAL DOCUMENTS**
Malpractice, negligent misrepresentation, 828–829

**COMMON SENSE**
Professionalism and professional identity, 67

**COMMUNICATIONS**
Effective Representation, this index
Ex Parte Communications, this index
Respect for Rights and Dignity of Other Persons, this index

**COMPARATIVE NEGLIGENCE AND COMPARATIVE FAULT**
Malpractice, 868–869

**COMPENSATION**
Attorneys' Fees, this index
Malpractice, experts, 759–760
Professional independence, nonlawyer employees, 432–433

**COMPETENCE**
Advocacy, government prosecutors and other lawyers, 619–621
Effective Representation, this index
Judicial service, fitness for, 963–966
Malpractice, 748

**COMPETITIVENESS**
Stress management, internal traits of lawyers, 85–86

**CONCERTED ACTION**
Malpractice, factual causation, 782

**CONCURRENT CLIENT CONFLICTS**
Conflicts of Interest, this index

**CONFERENCE OF CHIEF JUSTICES' NATIONAL ACTION PLAN ON LAWYER CONDUCT AND PROFESSIONALISM OF 1999**
Professionalism and professional identity, 73–74

**CONFIDENTIAL INFORMATION**
Generally, 305–355
Admission to Bar and Discipline, this index
Advocacy, interception by government of privileged communications, 632–633
Attorney-Client Privilege, this index
Attorney-Client Relationship, this index
Bodily harm, prevention of, 342–344
Conflicts of interest, 355, 358
Consultation with client before disclosure, 342, 352
Court order or other law, compliance with, 354–355
Death, prevention of, 342–344
Disclosures to client regarding ethical qualifications on confidentiality, 340–342
Duty of lawyer to safeguard confidential information
- generally, 335–338
- inadvertent disclosure, 337–338
- modern communications technology, use of, 335–336

Economic harm, prevention or rectification of substantial
- generally, 345–352
- counseling of client before disclosure, 352
- history, controversy and overview, 345–347
- mandatory *vs.* permissive nature, 348–352
- strict standards for application, 347–348

Evaluators, confidentiality and evaluation of client matter, 652–653
Evidence in Civil Proceedings, this index
Exceptions
- generally, 338–355
- conflicts of interest, checking for, 355
- consultation with client before disclosure pursuant to exception, 342
- court order or other law, compliance with, 354–355
- death or bodily harm, prevention of, 342–344
- disclosures to client regarding ethical qualifications on confidentiality, 340–342
- economic harm, prevention or rectification of substantial, above
- legal advice about lawyer compliance with ethics rules, obtaining of, 352–353
- narrow departures, exceptions as, 338–340
- self-defense of lawyer and fee collection, 353–354

Fee collection by lawyer, 353–354
Fundamental principle of confidentiality, 305–309
Inadvertent disclosure, 337–338
Legal advice about lawyer compliance with ethics rules, obtaining of, 352–353
Modern communications technology, use of, 335–336
Organization/Entity Clients, this index
Presentation of evidence, remedial measures to correct false evidence notwithstanding confidentiality, 571–574
Safeguarding information. Duty of lawyer to safeguard confidential information, above
Scope and pervasive principles in rules, 309–312
Self-defense of lawyer, 353–354
Sources of legal ethics and law, discipline, 136–137
Work product of attorney, 333–335

**CONFLICTS OF INTEREST**
Generally, 357–430
Advance conflict waivers, 420–421
Advocate-witness rule, 599–601
Aggregate settlement of claims involving multiple current clients, 386–389
Arbitrators. Judges, law clerks, arbitrators, mediators and third-party neutrals, below
Business transactions with clients, 361–364
Checking for conflicts, 359
Concurrent client conflicts
- generally, 375–399
- aggregate settlement of claims involving multiple clients, 386–389
- civil litigation, representation of multiple clients in, 383–385

criminal matter, representation of multiple clients in, 381–383
direct adversity conflicts, 375–377
economic competition, clients engaged in, 377
insurance defense, below
joint representation, withdrawal or termination and confidentiality, 390–392
materially-limited representation conflicts, 377–399
non-litigation matter, representation of multiple clients in, 389–390
personal interest of lawyer, 379–381
positional conflicts of interest, 397–399
Confidential information, 355, 358
Consent. Waiver by informed consent, below
Cost-containment guidelines, insurance defense, 396–397
Costs, advancement of, 369
Coverage disputes, insurance defense, 395–396
Difficulty of conflict problems, 358–359
Direct adversity conflicts, concurrent client conflicts, 375–377
Economic competition, current clients engaged in, 377
Ethical screening of personally-disqualified lawyer, imputation of conflicts within firm, 407–411
Family relationship with lawyer for adverse party, 373–374
Financial assistance to client, 367–369
Gifts from clients and preparation of instruments giving gifts, 365–366
Government officers and employees
generally, 421–428
current government officers and employees, 427–428
former government officers and employees, 421–426
imputed disqualification of former government officers and employees, 425–426
prior participation during nongovernmental practice of current government officers and employees, 427
private employment negotiations of current government officers and employees, 427–428
"Hot potato" scenario, successive client conflicts, 402–403
Imputation of conflicts within firm
generally, 404–413
departure of personally-disqualified lawyer from firm, 411–413
ethical screening of personally-disqualified lawyer, 407–411
joining or leaving law firm - migrating lawyers, 406–413
personal disqualification of incoming lawyer, 406–407
Imputation of lawyer-client conflicts, 374–375
Imputed disqualification
former government officers and employees, 425–426
waiver by informed consent, 414–415
Informed consent. Waiver by informed consent, below
Insurance defense
generally, 392–397
conflict of interest controversies, 393–394
cost-containment guidelines, 396–397
coverage disputes, 395–396
identification of client(s), 392–393
settlement and policy limits, 394–395
Joint representation
concurrent client conflicts, 390–392
waiver by informed consent, 415–416
Judges, law clerks, arbitrators, mediators and third-party neutrals
generally, 428–430
current judges, law clerks, arbitrators, mediators and third-party neutrals, 429–430
former judges, law clerks, arbitrators, mediators and third-party neutrals, 428–429
Law clerks. Judges, law clerks, arbitrators, mediators and third-party neutrals, below
Law reform, 696–697
Lawyer-client conflicts
generally, 360–375
business transactions with clients, 361–364
court costs and litigation expenses, advancement of, 369
disadvantage of client, use of confidential information to, 364–365
family or romantic relationship with lawyer for adverse party, 373–374
financial assistance to client, 367–369
gifts from clients and preparation of instruments giving gifts, 365–366
imputation of conflict, 374–375
literary and media rights about representation, 366–367
living expenses or otherwise, prohibition on giving or loaning money to client for, 367–369
malpractice claims, agreements to limit or settle, 370–371
property interest in client's claim, acquisition of, 371–372
sexual relations with client, 372–373
third person, compensation from person other than client, 369–370
Literary rights about representation, 366–367
Litigation expenses, advancement of, 369
Living expenses or otherwise, prohibition on giving or loaning money to client for, 367–369
Loyalty to client, 358
Malpractice claims, agreements to limit or settle, 370–371
Materially-limited representation conflicts, concurrent client conflicts, 377–399
Media rights about representation, 366–367
Mediators. Judges, law clerks, arbitrators, mediators and third-party neutrals, above
Migrating lawyers, imputation of conflicts within firm, 406–413

Nonconsentable conflicts, 418–420
Non-litigation matter, representation of multiple current clients in, 389–390
Personal disqualification of incoming lawyer, imputation of conflicts within firm, 406–407
Personal interests of lawyer
concurrent client conflicts, 379–381
waiver by informed consent, 414
Positional conflicts of interest, concurrent client conflicts, 397–399
Private employment negotiations of current government officers and employees, 427–428
Pro Bono Legal Services, this index
Property interest in client's claim, acquisition of, 371–372
Prospective clients, duties to
generally, 198–200
reasonable measure, taking, 199
timely screened, 199–200
written notice, 200
Romantic relationship with lawyer for adverse party, 373–374
Settlement and policy limits, insurance defense, 394–395
Sexual relations with client, 372–373
Substantially related matters, successive client conflicts, 400–402
Successive client conflicts
generally, 399–404
confidential information from former client representation, use or reveal of, 403–404
current client changed into former client - "hot potato" scenario, 402–403
identical matters, 399–400
substantially related matters, 400–402
Termination, concurrent client conflicts, 390–392
Third-party neutrals. Judges, law clerks, arbitrators, mediators and third-party neutrals, above
Third person, compensation from person other than client, 369–370
Waiver by informed consent
generally, 413–421
advance conflict waivers, 420–421
both sides in litigation, nonconsentable conflicts, 419–420
continuing duty of competent and diligent representation, 418
imputed disqualification, 414–415
informed consent, defined, 416–417
joint representation, 415–416
nonconsentable conflicts, 418–420
personal interests of lawyer, 414
unrelated matters, 414
written confirmation of consent, 417–418
Withdrawal
generally, 359
concurrent client conflicts, 390–392
Written confirmation of waiver by consent, 417–418

CONSENT
Communications with represented person, consent by represented person's counsel to contact by another lawyer, 670–672
Conflicts of Interest, this index
Informed Consent, this index

CONSTITUTIONAL LAW
Freedom of Speech, this index
Malpractice, punitive damages, 861–864

CONTINGENCY FEES
Attorneys' Fees, this index

CONTINUING TORTS
Malpractice, statutes of limitation, 889

CONTINUOUS REPRESENTATION RULE
Malpractice, statutes of limitation, 885–887

CONTRABAND
Evidence in Criminal Proceedings, this index

CONTRACTS
Agreements of Parties, this index

CONTRIBUTION
Malpractice, 892–893

CONTRIBUTORY NEGLIGENCE
Malpractice, 868–869

COOPERATION CLAUSE
Malpractice, insurance, 945–946

COST-CONTAINMENT GUIDELINES
Conflicts of interest, insurance defense, 396–397

COSTS AND EXPENSES
Conflicts of interest, 367–369
Legal malpractice, 718–719
Legal Productivity, this index
Referrals, payment for costs of advertising, 182–183

COVENANTS NOT TO SUE
Malpractice, 895–896

COVERT ACTIVITY
Evidence in civil proceedings, investigation of violations of law or gather intelligence, 528–531

CRIME-FRAUD EXCEPTION
Attorney-Client Privilege, this index

CRIMINAL CASES
Advocacy, putting prosecution to its proof, 484–485
Contingency fees, 254–255
Evidence in Criminal Proceedings, this index

CRIMINAL CONDUCT
Advocacy, threat or promise to withhold report, 491–493
Avoidance of assistance to crime by client, 661–663
Effective representation, assistance in conduct, 284–285

Presentation of evidence, counteraction of fraudulent or criminal conduct of client before tribunal, 580–581
Sources of legal ethics and law, 125–126

**CURATIVE MEASURES**
Evidence in civil proceedings, Federal Rules of Civil Procedure on Preservation of Electronically-Stored Information, 509–510

**CURRICULUM**
Law School Curriculum, this index

**DAMAGES**
Malpractice, this index

**DEATH**
Attorney-client relationship, termination of private practice or area of practice upon sale of practice, 241
Confidential information, prevention, 342–344
Effective representation, protection of client in event of death of lawyer, 288

**DECEPTIVE TRADE PRACTICES ACTS**
Malpractice, this index

**DEFAMATION**
Advocacy, extrajudicial statements by lawyer, 615–616

**DEFENSES**
Malpractice, this index

**DEGRADATION**
Advocacy, seeking advantage, 490–491

**DELAY**
Advocacy, advancement of resolution of disputes, 490

**DELIVERY**
Effective representation, client funds and property, 299
Evidence in Criminal Proceedings, this index

**DEMEANOR**
Judicial service, fitness for, 966–968

**DEROGATORY STATEMENTS**
Advocacy, extrajudicial statements by lawyer, 608–609

**DIGNITY**
Respect for Rights and Dignity of Other Persons, this index

**DILIGENCE**
Effective Representation, this index
Judicial service, fitness for, 963–966
Malpractice, 749
Professionalism and professional identity, 64, 67

**DIMINISHED CAPACITY**
Attorney-Client Relationship, this index

**DIRECT MAIL**
Advertising, 169–172

**DISABLED PERSONS**
Attorney-client relationship, termination of private practice or area of practice upon sale of practice, 241
Effective representation, protection of client in event of disability of lawyer, 288
Malpractice, lawyers with disabilities, 745–746

**DISASTERS**
Multijurisdictional practice of law, 149–150

**DISBARMENT**
Sources of legal ethics and law, 140–141

**DISCIPLINE**
Admission to Bar and Discipline, this index

**DISCLAIMERS**
Advertising, this index
Malpractice, disclaimer of civil cause of action by statutes, 767–768

**DISCLOSURES**
Advocacy, prosecutors, 640–643
Confidential information, ethical qualifications on confidentiality, 340–342
Malpractice, this index
Organization/entity clients, unlawful conduct or internal dissension within organization, 464–466

**DISCOVERY**
Evidence in Civil Proceedings, this index

**DISCOVERY RULE**
Malpractice, statutes of limitation, 883–885

**DISCRETION**
Malpractice, 749–750

**DISCRIMINATION**
Sources of Legal Ethics and Law, this index

**DISQUALIFICATION**
Judicial Ethics and Conduct of Judges, this index

**DISRUPTIVE BEHAVIOR**
Advocacy, trials, 587

**DIVISION OF FEES**
Attorneys' fees, 260–262

**"DO JUSTICE"**
Advocacy, duty of prosecutor, 617–619

**DOMESTIC RELATIONS CASES**
Contingency fees, 254–255

**DREYFUS AND DREYFUS MODEL OF DEVELOPMENT**
Law school curriculum, 96–97

**DUTY TO DEFEND**
Malpractice insurance, 935

**EBENEZER SCROOGE FACTOR**
Advocacy, 478

**ECONOMIC CENSUS DATA**
Structure of legal profession, 4–6

**ECONOMIC COMPETITION**
Conflicts of interest, current clients engaged in competition, 377

**ECONOMIC HARM**
Confidential Information, this index

**ECONOMIC INTEREST**
Judicial ethics and conduct of judges, disqualification, 1003–1006

**EFFECTIVE REPRESENTATION**
Generally, 273–303
Accounting for client funds and property, 299
Affirmation of client's authority, communication with client, 292
Association with lawyer of established competence, competent representation, 275
Candid, moral and lawful advice
- generally, 278–285
- expanding scope of law practice, counseling within, 278
- forthright advice and frank evaluation, 279–280
- fraudulent or criminal conduct, assistance in, 284–285
- moral engagement with client, 280–283
- professional humility and assistance by other professionals, 283–284

Civility and professionalism, 288–291
Communication with client
- generally, 291–295
- affirmation of client's authority, 292
- duty to communicate, generally, 291
- maintenance of regular communication and response to client inquiries, 293
- violations of law or professional expectations, confirmation the lawyer will not assist in, 294
- withholding information from client, 295–295

Competent representation
- generally, 273–277
- association with lawyer of established competence, 275
- expertise in certain fields of law, need for, 276–277
- fundamental expectation of professional competence, 273–275
- general standard of competence, 273–274
- mistakes, personal problems and competence, 277
- new area, attaining competence in, 274–275

Criminal conduct, assistance in, 284–285
Death of lawyer, protection of client in event of, 288
Delivery of client funds and property, 299
Diligence and zealous representation
- generally, 286–291
- advocacy, 476–481
- avoidance of unnecessary anxiety to client, 287
- death, disability or suspension of lawyer, protection of client in event of, 288
- professionalism and civility, 288–291
- protection of rights of client, 286–287

Disability of lawyer, protection of client in event of, 288
Expertise in certain fields of law, need for, 276–277
Fiduciary duty to put client first, 295–297
Forthright advice and frank evaluation, 279–280
Fraudulent conduct, assistance in, 284–285
Funds and property of client, safeguarding of
- generally, 297–303
- accounting for and delivery of client funds and property, 299
- disputes regarding funds or property held by lawyer
  - generally, 299–303
  - lawyer and client, disputes between, 299–301
  - third-party and client, disputes between, 301–303
- safekeeping and separation of client funds and property, 297–299

Lawful advice. Candid, moral and lawful advice, above
Mistakes and competence, 277
Moral advice. Candid, moral and lawful advice, above
New area, attaining competence in, 274–275
Personal problems and competence, 277
Professional humility and assistance by other professionals, 283–284
Professionalism and civility, 288–291
Property of client. Funds and property of client, safeguarding of, above
Separation of client funds and property, 297–299
Suspension of lawyer, protection of client in event of, 288
Violations of law or professional expectations, confirmation the lawyer will not assist in, 294
Withholding information from client, 295–295
Zealous representation. Diligence and zealous representation, above

**EMBARRASSMENT**
Advocacy, advancement of resolution of disputes, 490

**EMERGENCY SITUATIONS**
Attorney-client relationship, clients with diminished capacity, 227–228

**EMOTIONAL APPEAL**
Advertising, 172–174

**EMOTIONAL DISTRESS**
Malpractice, 853–854

**EMPLOYMENT**
Professional independence, other professionals and assistants, 437–438
Shifting of fees to another party, employment discrimination, 264

**ENGAGEMENT RETAINER**
Attorneys' fees, 258–259

**ENTITY CLIENTS**
Organization/Entity Clients, this index

**ENVIRONMENTAL PROTECTION**
Shifting of fees to another party, 264

**EQUITABLE ESTOPPEL**
Malpractice, statutes of limitation, 888–889

**ESTATES**
Professional independence, payments by firm to estate of deceased lawyer, 431–432

**ESTOPPEL**
Malpractice, this index

**EVALUATORS**
Generally, 649–653
Adverse evaluations, 651–652
Confidentiality and evaluation of client matter, 652–653
Other ethical and legal duties, 653–653
Preparation of client evaluation for use by third person, 650–651

**EVIDENCE IN CIVIL PROCEEDINGS**
Generally, 500–532
Access to evidence, duties regarding, 500–501
Clear instructions, preservation of potential evidence, 511
Confidential materials. Unsolicited receipt of another's privileged or confidential materials, below
Covert activity to investigate violations of law or gather intelligence, 528–531
Curative measures and sanctions, Federal Rules of Civil Procedure on Preservation of Electronically-Stored Information, 509–510
Discovery, generally, 501–532
Document retention policy, destruction of documents pursuant to, 507
Federal Rules of Civil Procedure on Preservation of Electronically-Stored Information, 507–510
General ethical expectations, 501–502
Inadvertently transmitted protected materials, receipt of, 516–520
Metadata, unsolicited receipt of another's privileged or confidential materials, 526–528
Methods of obtaining evidence that violate another's legal rights, 512–514
Presentation of Evidence, this index
Preservation of potential evidence
generally, 503–511
clear instructions, duty of counsel, 511
curative measures and sanctions, Federal Rules of Civil Procedure on Preservation of Electronically-Stored Information, 509–510
document retention policy, destruction of documents pursuant to, 507
duty of counsel, 510–511
Federal Rules of Civil Procedure on Preservation of Electronically-Stored Information, 507–510
regular monitoring of production, duty of counsel, 511
sanctions for breach of duty to preserve, 506–507
scope of preservation, 506
spoliation of evidence, 504–507
trigger for duty to preserve, 505–506
Privileged materials. Unsolicited receipt of another's privileged or confidential materials, below
Requests for discovery, 502–503
Responses to discovery, 503
Sanctions for breach of duty to preserve, 506–507
Spoliation of evidence, 504–507
Third person, receipt of protected materials taken by, 520–526
Unsolicited receipt of another's privileged or confidential materials
generally, 515–528
encouraged procurement *vs.* unsolicited receipt, 515–516
inadvertently transmitted protected materials, receipt of, 516–520
metadata, 526–528
third person, receipt of protected materials taken by, 520–526
Withholding of information from another party, request of another person for, 531–532

**EVIDENCE IN CRIMINAL PROCEEDINGS**
Generally, 532–567
Anticipatory obstruction of justice. Preservation of evidence, below
Contraband
generally, 561–564
delivery of evidence to defense lawyer, 561
preservation of evidence, treatment of contraband that is not evidence in reasonably anticipated proceeding, 542–547
Delivery of evidence to defense lawyer
generally, 557–561
contraband, 561
destruction, fear of, 560
harm, fear of, 560–561
rightful owner, 559
Disposition of evidence by defense lawyer following examination, 553–557
Engagement with real evidence by defense lawyer, 534
Evidence registry, retention of evidence by defense lawyer with contingent notice to law enforcement, 565–566
Examination of evidence. Observation and examination of evidence, below
Fear of harm or destruction, delivery of evidence to defense lawyer, 560–561
Law enforcement, actions to make discovery of physical evidence easier or harder, 534
Notice to law enforcement. Retention of evidence by defense lawyer with contingent notice to law enforcement, below
Observation and examination of evidence
generally, 549–558
delivery of evidence by defense lawyer to law enforcement and preservation of confidentiality, 557–558
disposition of evidence by defense lawyer following examination, 553–557

examination of evidence by defense lawyer, 550–553
observation of evidence by defense lawyer without taking possession, 549–550
Obstruction of justice, preservation of evidence, 536–540
Presentation of Evidence, this index
Preservation of evidence
generally, 534–549
anticipatory obstruction of justice, Sarbanes-Oxley § 1519
generally, 537–540
reasonable anticipation integrated into mens rea, 539–540
removal of direct link to pending or imminent proceeding or investigation, 537–539
contraband that is not evidence in reasonably anticipated proceeding, treatment of, 542–547
obstruction of justice, 536–540
safe harbor for legal representation, 541–542
summary of state laws, 534–536
uncertain situations, advice to client in, 547–549
Reasonable anticipation of investigation or proceeding, trigger of duty to preserve evidence, 534
Retention of evidence by defense lawyer with contingent notice to law enforcement
generally, 564–567
evidence registry, 565–566
general duty to deliver evidence to law enforcement, 564–565
other approaches, 566–567
Safe harbor for legal representation, preservation of evidence, 541–542
Sarbanes-Oxley Act. Preservation of evidence, below

**EXAMINATION OF EVIDENCE**
Evidence in Criminal Proceedings, this index

**EXCULPATORY EVIDENCE**
Advocacy, duty of prosecutor to disclose, 640–642

**EXECUTORS OR ADMINISTRATORS**
Malpractice, 813

**EXEMPLARY DAMAGES**
Malpractice, this index

**EX PARTE COMMUNICATIONS**
Advocacy, 590–592
Judicial Ethics and Conduct of Judges, this index

**EX PARTE PROCEEDINGS**
Advocacy, truthfulness and candor before tribunal, 497–498

**EXPENSES**
Costs and Expenses, this index

**EXPERT TESTIMONY**
Malpractice, this index

**EXTRAJUDICIAL ACTIVITIES**
Judicial ethics and conduct of judges, disqualification for reasonable questions regarding impartiality, 995–999

**EXTRAJUDICIAL CONDUCT**
Judicial Ethics and Conduct of Judges, this index

**EXTRAJUDICIAL STATEMENTS**
Advocacy, this index

**EXTRAORDINARY RISKS**
Malpractice insurance, 938

**EXTRINSIC MOTIVATION**
Stress management, internal traits of lawyers, 86–87

**FACTUAL CAUSATION**
Malpractice, this index

**FAIR DEBT COLLECTIONS PRACTICES**
Malpractice, 848–849

**FAIRNESS**
Judicial Ethics and Conduct of Judges, this index

**FAIR TRIAL**
Advocacy, extrajudicial statements by lawyer, 601–602

**FALSE EVIDENCE**
Presentation of evidence, 567–580

**FALSE OR MISLEADING STATEMENTS**
Advertising, 160–163
Respect for rights and dignity of other persons, 659–661
Solicitation, 160–163

**FAMILY**
Conflicts of interest, relationship with lawyer for adverse party, 373–374
Solicitation, 187

**FEDERAL RULES OF CIVIL PROCEDURE ON PRESERVATION OF ELECTRONICALLY-STORED INFORMATION**
Evidence in civil proceedings, 507–510

**FEES**
Attorneys' Fees, this index

**FIDUCIARY DUTY**
Effective representation, fiduciary duty to put client first, 295–297
Malpractice, this index

**FIELDS OF PRACTICE**
Advertising, this index

**FIFTH AMENDMENT**
Philosophy of legal ethics, 35–37

**FINANCIAL ASSISTANCE**
Conflicts of interest, 367–369

**FINANCIAL BURDEN OR STRAIN**
Attorney-client relationship, permissive withdrawal by lawyer, 236–237

Pro bono legal services, 709–710
Stress management, 83

**FIRM NAME**
Advertising, this index

**FIRST AMENDMENT**
Advertising, 158–160
Solicitation, 158–160

**FITNESS FOR JUDICIAL SERVICE**
Judicial Ethics and Conduct of Judges, this index

**FLAT FEES**
Attorneys' fees, 255–256

**FORFEITURE**
Malpractice, punitive damages, 861

**FORTHRIGHT ADVICE AND FRANK EVALUATION**
Effective representation, 279–280

**FOUNDATIONS OF LAWYER'S ROLE**
Philosophy of Legal Ethics, this index

**FOURTH AMENDMENT**
Philosophy of legal ethics, 37

**FRAUD**
Avoidance of assistance to client, 661–663
Effective representation, assistance in conduct, 284–285
Malpractice, this index
Presentation of evidence, counteraction of fraudulent or criminal conduct of client before tribunal, 580–581
Sources of legal ethics and law, 126–127

**FRAUDULENT CONCEALMENT**
Malpractice, statutes of limitation, 887

**FREEDOM OF EXPRESSION**
Advocacy, extrajudicial statements by lawyer, 601–602

**FREEDOM OF SPEECH**
Advocacy, advancement of resolution of disputes, 490
Sources of legal ethics and law, discrimination and harassment, 129

**FRIVOLOUS CLAIMS AND CONTENTIONS**
Advocacy, 481–485

**FUNDS OF CLIENT**
Effective Representation, this index

**FUTURE OF LEGAL PROFESSION**
Generally, 19–23
Civil Resolution Tribunal (CRT), British Columbia, 21–22
Individuals, dispute resolution for, 20–22
Multidisciplinary future, 22–23
Online dispute resolution, 21–22
Structural shift, 19–23

**GENERAL RETAINER**
Attorneys' fees, 258–259

**GEOGRAPHIC AREA OR JURISDICTION**
Attorney-client relationship, termination of private practice or area of practice upon sale of practice, 240–241

**GIFTS**
Conflicts of interest, 365–366
Judicial ethics and conduct of judges, 1018–1020

**GOOD FAITH**
Malpractice, 746

**GOOD JUDGMENT**
Professionalism and professional identity, 67

**GOVERNMENTAL ACTIVITIES**
Judicial ethics and conduct of judges, 1012–1014

**GOVERNMENT CLIENTS**
Organization/Entity Clients, this index

**GOVERNMENT OFFICERS AND EMPLOYEES**
Conflicts of Interest, this index

**GOVERNMENT PROSECUTORS AND OTHER LAWYERS**
Advocacy, this index

**GUARDIAN**
Attorney-client relationship, consideration of whether to seek for client with diminished capacity, 225–226

**HALF-TRUTHS**
Malpractice, fraud on clients and nonclients, 820

**HANDICAPPED PERSONS**
Disabled Persons, this index

**HARASSMENT**
Sources of Legal Ethics and Law, this index

**HAYNSWORTH REPORT OF 1996**
Professionalism and professional identity, 72–73

**HONESTY**
Attorneys' fees, hourly billing, 251–252
Malpractice, experts, 762
Sources of legal ethics and law, 126–127

**"HOT POTATO" SCENARIO**
Conflicts of interest, successive client conflicts, 402–403

**HOURLY BILLING**
Attorneys' Fees, this index

**HUMILIATION**
Advocacy, seeking advantage, 490–491

**HUMILITY**
Effective representation, 283–284

**ILLEGAL RISKS**
Malpractice insurance, 938–939

**IMMORAL RISKS**
Malpractice insurance, 938–939

**IMMUNITY**
Sources of legal ethics and law, discipline, 136–137

**IMPARTIALITY**
Judicial Ethics and Conduct of Judges, this index

**IMPUTATION OF CONFLICTS**
Conflicts of Interest, this index

**IMPUTED DISQUALIFICATION**
Conflicts of Interest, this index

**INADVERTENT CLIENTS**
Malpractice, this index

**INADVERTENT DISCLOSURE**
Confidential information, 337–338

**INDEMNITY**
Malpractice, 893–894

**INDEPENDENCE**
Judicial Ethics and Conduct of Judges, this index
Professional Independence, this index

**INFORMED CONSENT**
Conflicts of Interest, this index
Malpractice, 769–772

**INNOCENCE**
Malpractice, requirement in criminal defense malpractice, unlawful conduct, 872–874

**INSURANCE**
Conflicts of Interest, this index
Malpractice, this index

**INTEGRITY**
Judicial ethics and conduct of judges, 955, 957–958

**INTENDED BENEFICIARIES**
Malpractice, this index

**INTERNAL DISSENSION**
Organization/Entity Clients, this index

**INTERNATIONAL LEGAL MALPRACTICE**
Geographic frame of reference for expert testimony, 757–759

**INTERNET**
Advertising, 168–169

**INTERVENING NEGLIGENT CONDUCT**
Malpractice, proximate causation, 784–785

**INTRA-FIRM FIDUCIARY DUTIES**
Malpractice, this index

**INVESTIGATIONS**
Advocacy, prosecutors, 622–624
Advocate-witness rule, 595

**ISSUE PRECLUSION**
Sources of legal ethics and law, discipline, 135–136

**JOINT CLIENT PRIVILEGE AND JOINT DEFENSE DOCTRINE**
Attorney-client privilege, 325–326

**JOINT LIABILITY**
Malpractice, this index

**JOINT REPRESENTATION**
Conflicts of Interest, this index

**JOINT RESPONSIBILITY AND JOINT VENTURES**
Malpractice, this index

**JUDGES, LEGAL OFFICERS AND CANDIDATES FOR JUDICIAL OR LEGAL OFFICE**
Generally, 698–703
Comments of lawyers, generally, 698–703
Courtroom speech by lawyers about judges, 701–702
Disciplinary standard of knowing falsity or reckless disregard for truth, 699–701
False factual statements, limitation of discipline to, 702–703
Value of informed commentary by lawyers, 698–699

**JUDICIAL ESTOPPEL**
Malpractice, 899

**JUDICIAL ETHICS AND CONDUCT OF JUDGES**
Generally, 949–962
Abuse of prestige of judicial office, duty to avoid, 961–962
Appearances of impropriety, duty to avoid, 959–961
Avocational activities, 1014–1017
Bias, 973–976
Business activities, 1017–1018
Campaign support and commitments, disqualification, 1006–1008
Classes of people, bias toward, 974–976
Competence, fitness for judicial service, 963–966
Compliance with law, duty of, 958–959
Conflicts of Interest, this index
Core values, 955–958
Demeanor, fitness for judicial service, 966–968
Diligence, fitness for judicial service, 963–966
Discipline
- federal courts, 953–954
- state courts, 952–953

Disqualification
- generally, 986–1009
- campaign support and commitments, 1006–1008
- economic or other interest in proceeding, 1003–1006
- extrajudicial conduct, reasonable questions regarding impartiality, 995–999
- impartiality, reasonable questions regarding, 990–999
- interpretation of standards, 988–990
- judicial conduct, reasonable questions regarding impartiality, 991–995
- personal bias, 999–1000
- personal knowledge of disputed facts, 1000
- prior status as lawyer or affiliation with lawyer in proceeding, 1002–1003
- procedure, 1008–1009

relatives as parties, attorneys or witnesses, 1001–1002
standards, generally, 988–1008
Economic or other interest in proceeding, disqualification, 1003–1006
Ex parte communications
generally, 981–986
exceptions, 981–982
ex parte investigations, 985–986
prohibited communications, 983–985, 995
External influences, duty to resist, 971–972
Extrajudicial activities
generally, 1011–1020
avocational activities, 1014–1017
business activities, 1017–1018
gifts, 1018–1020
governmental activities, 1012–1014
Extrajudicial conduct, disqualification for reasonable questions regarding impartiality, 995–999
Fairness. Impartiality and fairness, below
Fitness for judicial service
generally, 963–968
competence and diligence, 963–966
demeanor, 966–968
Foundational rules, 958–962
Gifts, 1018–1020
Governmental activities, 1012–1014
Impartiality and fairness
generally, 955–956, 973–981
bias, 973–976
classes of people, bias toward, 974–976
disqualification for reasonable questions regarding impartiality, 990–999
public statements
future cases, 980–981
pending and impending cases, 978–980, 994–995
rights of parties to be heard, respect for, 976–978
specific people, bias toward, 973–974
Independence and power
generally, 955, 957, 968–972
external influences, duty to resist, 971–972
upholding and application of law, 968–971
Integrity, 955, 957–958
Judicial conduct, disqualification for reasonable questions regarding impartiality, 991–995
Modern judicial ethics and codes of judicial conduct, 951–952
Personal bias, disqualification, 999–1000
Personal knowledge of disputed facts, disqualification, 1000
Political activities, 1020–1026
Power. Independence and power, above
Public confidence, duty to promote, 959–961
Public statements. Impartiality and fairness, above
Relatives as parties, attorneys or witnesses, disqualification, 1001–1002

**JUDICIAL SANCTIONS**
Sources of legal ethics and law, 119–120

**JURISDICTION**
Generally, 141–151
Disciplinary jurisdiction, 150–151
Multijurisdictional Practice of Law, this index
Pro hac vice admission, disciplinary jurisdiction, 150–151

**JUSTIFIABLE RELIANCE**
Malpractice, this index

**LAW CLERKS**
Conflicts of Interest, this index

**LAW FIRMS**
Generally, 679–687
Duties of lawyers in law firms, generally, 679–687
Managing or supervising lawyers
generally, 680–687
ethical guidance of other lawyers, 680–683
nonlawyer assistants, 685–687
reasonable efforts to ensure conduct, 681–682
vicarious liability, 682–683
Nonlawyer assistants, managing or supervising lawyers, 685–687
Responsibility of lawyer for misconduct of another lawyer, 683–684
Subordinate lawyers, responsibilities of, 684–685
Supervising lawyers. Managing or supervising lawyers, above
Vicarious liability, managing or supervising lawyers, 682–683

**LAWFUL ADVICE**
Effective Representation, this index

**LAW REFORM**
Generally, 695–698
Conflicts of interest, 696–697
Discharge of lawyer by client based on law reform activities, 697
General freedom of lawyer to engage in law reform notwithstanding client interest, 695–696
Law reform organization, duty of lawyer to, 697–698

**LAW SCHOOL CURRICULUM**
Generally, 93–107
Developmental stages of self-directed learning, 99–100
Dreyfus and Dreyfus model of development, 96–97
General principles to guide development of effective curriculum, 101–104
Learning outcomes, 93–96
MBA education, compared, 104–107
Milestones stage development model, 100–101
Stages of growth for commitment to professional development learning outcome, 96–101

**LAWYERS ASSISTANCE PROGRAM**
Discipline, protection of information gained within program, 692

**LEARNED PROFESSION**
Professionalism and professional identity, 58–63

Sources of legal ethics and law, 111

**LEARNING OUTCOMES**
Law school curriculum, 93–96

**LEGAL POSITIVISM**
Philosophy of legal ethics, 43–44

**LEGAL PRODUCTIVITY**
Generally, 9–18
Alternative legal service providers (ALSP), 11–13
Cost disease, generally, 9–18
Individual clients, 14–15
Large organizational clients, 10
Law school enrollments, 15–18
Substitutes to traditional law firms, 10–13

**LEGAL SERVICE PLANS**
Referrals, 183–184

**LESSER INCLUDED OFFENSES**
Malpractice, unlawful conduct, 873

**LIBEL**
Advocacy, extrajudicial statements by lawyer, 615–616

**LIMITED LIABILITY COMPANIES AND LIMITED LIABILITY PARTNERSHIPS**
Malpractice, vicarious liability, 910–914

**LITERARY RIGHTS**
Conflicts of interest, 366–367

**LIVING EXPENSES**
Conflicts of interest, prohibition on giving or loaning money to client, 367–369

**LODESTAR METHOD**
Attorneys' fees, shifting of fees to another party, 265–266, 270–272

**LOSS OF CHANCE**
Malpractice, factual causation, 778–780

**"LOST PUNITIVE DAMAGES"**
Malpractice, 866

**LOYALTY**
Generally, 357–441
Conflicts of Interest, this index
Professional Independence, this index

**MACCRATE REPORT OF 1992**
Professionalism and professional identity, 72

**MAIL**
Advertising, 169–172

**MAIN STREET LAW PRACTICE**
Structure of legal profession, 6–7

**MALICIOUS PROSECUTION AND MALICIOUS USE OF PROCESS**
Malpractice, this index

**MALPRACTICE**
Generally, 713–948
Absolute and perfect candor, breach of fiduciary duty, 793–795
Absolute judicial proceedings privilege, 874–876
Accrual of cause of action, 881–882
Actual and apparent authority, vicarious liability, 905–907
Adjustments to damages, 857–858
Admissibility of expert testimony, 755–756
Advice of counsel defense and related claims against lawyers, malicious prosecution and malicious use of process, 844–845
Agreement of parties, statutes of limitation, 887–888
Aiding and abetting
- fiduciary duty, breach of, below
- fraud on clients and nonclients, 826
- securities law violations, 847

Allocation of fault to other persons, 891–892
Appearance before tribunal, duty to exercise reasonable care, 733–734
Appointed lawyers, immunity of, 877–878
Arbitration agreements, 896–898
Assignment of claims, 890–891
Associates, intra-firm fiduciary duties, 805–806
Attorney-client privilege, insurance, 941
Attorney immunity, 876–877
Attorneys' fees
- generally, 854–857
- co-counsel, duties to, 841–842
- earlier litigation, fees not recovered in, 856
- earlier representation, fees incurred in, 855–856
- fiduciary duty, breach of, below
- malpractice action, fees incurred in, 855
- remedy or mitigation of malpractice, fees incurred to, 856–857

Avoidable consequences and failure to mitigate, 869–870
Bankruptcy
- discharge, 723
- trustees, liability to, 813

Bans on punitive damages, 860–861
Breach of duty
- generally, 741–772
- competence, 748
- diligence, 749
- expert testimony, below
- good faith defense, 746
- informed consent, 769–772
- judgment, exercise of, below
- per se negligence, below
- recommendation of specialist, duty to make, 748
- risk balancing and economic analysis, 746–747
- specific duties, generally, 747–749
- standard of care, below

Burden of proof, factual causation, 780–781
"But for" test. Factual causation, below
Caps on punitive damages, 860–861
Causation
- generally, 772–787
- expert testimony, 762–764
- factual causation, below
- fee forfeiture for breach of fiduciary duty, 796–797
- proximate causation, below

Classification of theories of liability, consequences of, generally, 720–723
Class members, duty to exercise reasonable care, 736
Clear and serious breach of duty, fee forfeiture for breach of fiduciary duty, 797
Closely related matters, responsibility for, 738–739
Co-counsel
  duties to, 841–842
  joint liability and reimbursement, 894
  vicarious liability, 919–920
Collectability of damages, 858–859
Commercial documents, negligent misrepresentation, 828–829
Common law remedies and other consequences, fraud on clients and nonclients, 814–815
Comparative negligence and comparative fault, 868–869
Compensation of experts, 759–760
Compensatory damages, 851–859
Competence, 748
Concerted action liability, factual causation, 782
Conclusory expert testimony, 766
Conditions that affect insurance coverage, 939–940
Conduct, fraud on clients and nonclients, 819
Conflicts of interest, agreements to limit or settle claims, 370–371
Constitutional limitations on punitive damages, 861–864
Consultation with counsel, insurance, 940
Contingent fees, amounts that would have been spent on, 858
Continuing torts, statutes of limitation, 889
Continuous representation rule, statutes of limitation, 885–887
Contractual disclaimers of reliance, fraud on clients and nonclients, 825
Contribution, 892–893
Contributory negligence, 868–869
Cooperation clause, insurance, 945–946
Costs of legal malpractice, 718–719
Court appointment, attorney-client relationship, 728–729
Covenants not to sue, 895–896
Credentials of lawyers, fraud on clients and nonclients, 821
Culpability, 719
Damage rule, accrual of cause of action, 881–882
Damages. Remedies, below
Deceptive trade practices acts
    generally, 833–835
  applicability to lawyers, 833–834
  common law, advantages over, 834
  nonclients, actions by, 835
Defenses and other obstacles
    generally, 721–722, 867–899
  aiding and abetting breach of fiduciary duty, 802–803
  arbitration agreements, 896–898
  assignment of claims, 890–891
  avoidable consequences and failure to mitigate, 869–870
  conduct of plaintiff, generally, 868–874
  contributory negligence, comparative negligence and comparative fault, 868–869
  exoneration or innocence requirement in criminal defense malpractice, unlawful conduct, 872–874
  joint liability and reimbursement, below
  judicial estoppel, 899
  lesser included offenses, unlawful conduct, 873
  operation of law, generally, 878–899
  privileges and immunities, below
  releases and covenants not to sue, 895–896
  sentencing errors, unlawful conduct, 873
  settlement with defendant, 895–896
  SLAPP laws, 898–899
  statutes of limitation, below
  unlawful conduct
      generally, 869–870
    exoneration or innocence requirement in criminal defense malpractice, 872–874
    lesser included offenses, 873
    limits on defense, 873–874
    sentencing errors, 873
Differentiation of claims in same lawsuit, 719–720
Diligence, 749
Disabilities, lawyers with, 745–746
Discipline *vs.* malpractice
    generally, 724–726
  ethics rules, application of, 725–726
  procedures and decision-makers, 725
  purposes and prosecutor, 724–725
Disclaimer of civil cause of action by statutes, 767–768
Disclosures
  fiduciary duty, breach of, below
  inexperience, 744
  insurance, 931–932, 940, 942–945
Discovery rule, statutes of limitation, 883–885
Discretion, room for, 749–750
Duty to defend, insurance, 935
Emotional distress, 853–854
Equitable estoppel, statutes of limitation, 888–889
Estate executors or administrators, liability to, 813
Estoppel
  attorney-client relationship, 734
  partnership by estoppel, 922–923
Ethics rules, discipline *vs.* malpractice, 725–726
Exemplary damages. Punitive damages, below
Exoneration requirement in criminal defense malpractice, unlawful conduct, 872–874
Experience of lawyers, fraud on clients and nonclients, 821
Expert testimony
    generally, 752–766
  admissibility of expert testimony, 755–756
  causation, testimony on, 762–764
  conclusory testimony, 766
  duties and compensation of experts, 759–760
  expert affidavit requirements, 754–755

geographic frame of reference, 756–759
honesty and effectiveness of experts, 762
ignorance of ethics rules, 765
inconsistency with ethics rules, 765–766
independence *vs.* partisanship of experts, 760–761
international legal malpractice, geographic frame of reference, 757–759
liability of expert witness, 766
nontestifying experts, 761
obvious negligence, exception for, 753–754
reliance on ethics rules, 764–765
role of legal malpractice experts, generally, 759–762
standard of care, establishment of, 752–753
Express agreement, attorney-client relationship, 729
Extraordinary risks, insurance, 938
Fact, partnership in, 923
Factual causation
generally, 772–782
burden of proof, shifting of, 780–781
"but for" test
generally, 772–776
difficulty to establish, 773–774
independently sufficient causes, 776
multiple tortfeasors, 775–776
prior judge and jury, testimony by, 775
proof that alternative would have occurred, 774–775
concerted action liability, 782
independently sufficient causes, "but for" test, 776
legitimate destruction of evidence, 782
loss of chance, 778–780
"more favorable result" standard, 778
multiple tortfeasors, "but for" test, 775–776
tortious spoliation of causation evidence, 781–782
trial within trial analysis, 776–778
Fair debt collections practices, 848–849
Fiduciaries, claims based on representation of, 835
Fiduciary duty, breach of
generally, 789–807
absolute and perfect candor, disclosure obligations, 793–795
aiding and abetting breach of duty
generally, 799–804
corporate policymaking, implications for, 803–804
dangerous theory of liability, 799
knowing assistance, evidence of, 801
privileges and defenses, 802–803
substantial assistance, evidence of, 801–802
tort principles, 800–801
associates, intra-firm fiduciary duties, 805–806
causation of harm, fee forfeiture, 796–797
clear and serious breach of duty, fee forfeiture, 797
corporate policymaking, implications of aiding and abetting breach of duty, 803–804
disclosure obligations
generally, 793–796
absolute and perfect candor, 793–795
limits on disclosure obligations, 795–796
negligence duties and fiduciary duties, meshing of, 795
disloyalty *vs.* lack of care, 790–791
evidence of knowing assistance or substantial assistance, aiding and abetting breach of duty, 801–802
factor test for factual causation, 792–793
fee forfeiture
generally, 796–799
causation of harm, 796–797
clear and serious breach of duty, 797
fiduciary breach, 798–799
unjust enrichment, prevention of, 796
fraud on clients and nonclients, fiduciary duty to speak, 819
intra-firm fiduciary duties
generally, 804–807
associates, 805–806
movement between firms, 806–807
partners and other law firm principals, 805
postemployment restrictive covenants, 807
knowing assistance, aiding and abetting breach of duty, 801
lawyers as fiduciaries, 789–792
negligence, similarities to and differences from, 792
negligence *vs.* fiduciary duty, 789–790
partners and other law firm principals, intra-firm fiduciary duties, 805
postemployment restrictive covenants, intra-firm fiduciary duties, 807
privileges and defenses, aiding and abetting breach of duty, 802–803
speculation, factor test for factual causation, 793
substantial assistance, aiding and abetting breach of duty, 801–802
unjust enrichment, fee forfeiture, 796
Forfeiture to state, punitive damages, 861
Fraud on clients and nonclients
generally, 814–826
aiding and abetting fraud, 826
common law remedies and other consequences, 814–815
conduct, 819
contractual disclaimers of reliance, 825
credentials or experience of lawyers, 821
damages, 825–826
elements, 815–816
facts basic to transaction, 820
facts not reasonably discoverable, 820–821
failure to doubt, justifiable reliance, 824–825
fiduciary duty to speak, 819
half-truths, 820

implicit statements of fact, 822
intent to induce reliance, 825
justifiable reliance
generally, 824–825
contractual disclaimers of reliance, 825
danger signals, 824
failure to doubt, 824–825
statements known to be false, 824
knowledge of falsity, scienter, 816
materiality and types of misrepresentation
generally, 818–821
conduct, 819
credentials or experience of lawyers, 821
facts basic to transaction, 820
facts not reasonably discoverable, 820–821
fiduciary duty to speak, 819
half-truths, 820
nondisclosure, liability for, 819–821
qualification, words of, 819
written words or oral, 818–819
nondisclosure, liability for, 819–821
opinion *vs.* fact
generally, 821–824
implicit statements of fact, 822
puffing, 821–822
statements of law, 823–824
state of mind, 822–823
puffing, 821–822
qualification, words of, 819
reckless disregard for truth, scienter, 816–818
scienter
generally, 816–818
knowledge of falsity, 816
reckless disregard for truth, 816–818
special pleading and proof requirements, 816
statements of law, 823–824
state of mind, 822–823
written words or oral, 818–819
Fraudulent concealment, statutes of limitation, 887
Funds and property of nonclients, 835–837
General partnerships, vicarious liability of partners in, 908
Geographic frame of reference, expert testimony, 756–759
Good faith defense, 746
Half-truths, fraud on clients and nonclients, 820
Honesty and effectiveness of experts, 762
Illegal risks, insurance, 938–939
Immoral risks, insurance, 938–939
Immunities. Privileges and immunities, below
Implicit statements of fact, fraud on clients and nonclients, 822
Inadvertent clients. Reasonable care, duty to exercise, below
Indemnity, 893–894
Independence *vs.* partisanship of experts, 760–761
Independently sufficient causes, "but for" test and factual causation, 776
Informed consent, 769–772
Innocence requirement in criminal defense malpractice, unlawful conduct, 872–874
Insurance
generally, 722, 929–948
available coverage, 932–933
claims for money damages arising from rendition of legal services to others, 934–935
conditions that affect coverage, 939–940
consultation with counsel, 940
contents of policies, generally, 933–940
cooperation clause, 945–946
disclosure of errors, 931–932, 940, 942–945
duty to defend, 935
extraordinary risks, 938
handling of claims and potential claims
generally, 940–942
consultation with counsel, 940
disclosure under Model Rule 1.6, 940
in-firm attorney-client privilege, 941
prompt notice to insurer, 941–942
immoral or illegal risks, 938–939
in-firm attorney-client privilege, 941
insuring agreements
generally, 934–936
claims for money damages arising from rendition of legal services to others, 934–935
duty to defend, 935
liability limits and self-liquidating policies, 935
named insured and other insureds, 936
liability limits and self-liquidating policies, 935
mandatory coverage, 930–931
named insured and other insureds, 936
nondisclosure, consequences of, 946–947
policy exclusions
generally, 936–939
coverage not intended to be provided, 936–938
extraordinary risks, 938
immoral or illegal risks, 938–939
prompt notice to insurer, 941–942
remedial action and withdrawal, evaluation of, 947–948
Intended beneficiaries
generally, 837–841
insurers, 838–839
wills, invalid, 837–838
Intent to benefit firm, vicarious liability, 903–904
Intent to induce reliance, fraud on clients and nonclients, 825
International legal malpractice, geographic frame of reference for expert testimony, 757–759
Intervening negligent conduct, proximate causation, 784–785
Intra-firm fiduciary duties. Fiduciary duty, breach of, above
Joint liability and reimbursement
generally, 891–894
allocation of fault to other persons, 891–892
contribution, 892–893

indemnity, 893–894
successive counsel or co-counsel, claims involving, 894
Joint responsibility and joint ventures
referral fee arrangements, 915–916
vicarious liability, 923–924
Judgment, exercise of
generally, 749–752
discretion, room for, 749–750
mere error of judgment, 750–751
novel theories, trends and other jurisdictions, 752
unsettled questions, 751–752
Judicial estoppel, 899
Justifiable reliance. Fraud on clients and nonclients, above
Knowledge of falsity, fraud on clients and nonclients, 816
Laypersons, malpractice by, 744–745
Lesser included offenses, unlawful conduct, 873
Liability limits, insurance, 935
Limitation of actions. Statutes of limitation, below
"Limited group" view of Restatement, negligent misrepresentation, 831–832
Limited liability companies and limited liability partnerships, vicarious liability, 910–914
Loss of chance, factual causation, 778–780
"Lost punitive damages," 866
Malicious prosecution and malicious use of process
generally, 843–845
advice of counsel defense and related claims against lawyers, 844–845
elements, 843–844
terminology, 844
Materiality and types of misrepresentation. Fraud on clients and nonclients, above
Mere error of judgment, 750–751
Mergers, liability to nonclients, 813–814
Mitigation of malpractice, 856–857, 869–870
"More favorable result" standard, factual causation, 778
Multiple tortfeasors, "but for" test and factual causation, 775–776
Nature of legal malpractice law, 715–716
"Near privity" view, negligent misrepresentation, 830–831
Negligence, generally, 727–787
Negligent misrepresentation
generally, 826–833
commercial documents, 828–829
defense based on negligence of plaintiff, 833
"limited group" view of Restatement, 831–832
limits on scope of liability, 828–832
"near privity" view, 830–831
public filings, 829
Restatement (Second) of Torts § 552, 827–828
silence, liability for, 832–833
special reason to expect reliance, 829–830
voluntary assumption of duty, relationship to, 828
Nonclients, deceptive trade practices by, 835
Nonclients, liability to
generally, 809–849
bankruptcy trustees and estate executors or administrators, 813
co-counsel, duties to, 841–842
deceptive trade practices acts, above
fair debt collections practices, 848–849
fee interests, duties to co-counsel, 841–842
fiduciaries, claims based on representation of, 835
fraud on clients and nonclients, above
funds and property of nonclients, 835–837
intended beneficiaries, above
litigation, liability related to, generally, 842–846
malicious prosecution and malicious use of process, above
mergers and sales of assets, 813–814
negligent misrepresentation, above
privity, 810–812
receivers, 814
securities law violations, below
statutory limits, 812
subrogation claims of insurers, 845–846
successors-in-interest
generally, 813–814
bankruptcy trustees and estate executors or administrators, 813
mergers and sales of assets, 813–814
receivers, 814
tortious involvement with litigation, 845
Nondelegable duties, vicarious liability, 925–927
Notice to insurer, 941–942
Novel theories, trends and other jurisdictions, 752
Obvious negligence, expert testimony, 753–754
Occurrence rule, accrual of cause of action, 881
Of counsel arrangements, vicarious liability, 920–921
Office-sharing arrangements. Vicarious liability, below
Opinion *vs.* fact. Fraud on clients and nonclients, above
Ordinary course of firm business, vicarious liability, 903–905
Partners and other law firm principals, intra-firm fiduciary duties, 805
Pendency of other litigation, statutes of limitation, 888
Per se negligence
generally, 766–769
disclaimer of civil cause of action by statutes, 767–768
duties not unique to lawyers, imposition by statutes, 768–769
Restatement position on statutory standards, 768
standard of care set by statutes, 767
Person to whom duty owed, 727–736
Pleadings and proof, 720–721
Postemployment restrictive covenants, intra-firm fiduciary duties, 807
Post-termination loyalty, 740
Prejudgment interest, 857–858

Present value, reduction of damages to, 857
Prevention of inadvertent clients, duty to exercise reasonable care, 732–733
Privileges and immunities
generally, 874–878
absolute judicial proceedings privilege, 874–876
aiding and abetting breach of fiduciary duty, 802–803
attorney immunity, 876–877
public defenders and appointed lawyers, immunity of, 877–878
qualified privileges, 877
truth, absolute privilege for, 877
Privity, liability to nonclients, 810–812
Professional corporations, vicarious liability, 908–910
Prospective clients, duty to exercise reasonable care, 735–736
Proximate causation
generally, 783–787
failure of client to discover malpractice, 785
intervening negligent conduct, 784–785
remedies, 853
subsequent counsel's failure to act, 785–787
superseding causation and shifting responsibility, 784–787
Public defenders, immunity of, 877–878
Public filings, negligent misrepresentation, 829
Puffing, fraud on clients and nonclients, 821–822
Punitive damages
generally, 859–866
caps and bans, 860–861
federal constitutional limitations, 861–864
limitations, 861–865
"lost punitive damages," 866
partial forfeiture to state, 861
state law limitations, 859–861
vicarious liability, 865
Qualified privileges, 877
Quantum meruit offset for value of services rendered, 858
Reasonable care, duty to exercise
generally, 727–741
appearance before tribunal, 733–734
class members, 736
court appointment, attorney-client relationship, 728–729
estoppel, attorney-client relationship based on, 734
express agreement, attorney-client relationship, 729
inadvertent clients, attorney-client relationship
generally, 729–733
prevention, 732–733
reasonable reliance, 731–732
request for legal services, 730–731
person to whom duty owed, 727–736
prevention of inadvertent clients, 732–733
prospective clients, 735–736
reasonable reliance, inadvertent clients, 731–732
request for legal services, inadvertent clients, 730–731
scope of representation, below
types of attorney-client relationship, 728–733
voluntary assumption of duty, 734–735
Receivers, liability to nonclients, 814
Reckless disregard for truth, fraud on clients and nonclients, 816–818
Recommendation of specialist, duty to make, 748
Reduction of damages to present value, 857
Referral fee arrangements. Vicarious liability, below
Reimbursement. Joint liability and reimbursement, above
Releases, 895–896
Remedies
generally, 723, 851–866
adjustments to damages, 857–858
attorney's fees, above
collectability, 858–859
compensatory damages, 851–859
contingent fees, amounts that would have been spent on, 858
emotional distress, 853–854
fraud on clients and nonclients, 825–826
prejudgment interest, 857–858
proximate cause of loss, 853
punitive damages, above
quantum meruit offset for value of services rendered, 858
reduction of damages to present value, 857
reputation, harm to, 854
speculation, 851–853
Remedy of malpractice, fees incurred for, 856–857
Representations of greater competence, 743–744
Reputation, harm to, 854
Request for legal services, inadvertent clients, 730–731
Restatement (Second) of Torts
negligent misrepresentation, 827–828
per se negligence, 768
Restitution, 866
Rise in legal malpractice law, 716–718
Risk balancing and economic analysis, 746–747
Role of legal malpractice law, 715–716
Sales of assets, liability to nonclients, 813–814
Scheme liability, securities law violations, 847
Scienter. Fraud on clients and nonclients, above
Scope of liability, 721
Scope of representation
generally, 736–741
changes in scope, 737
closely related matters, responsibility for, 738–739
defining scope, 737
post-termination loyalty, 740
termination of attorney-client relationship, 739–741
unreasonable limits, 738
Securities law violations
generally, 846–848
aiding and abetting and scheme liability, 847
state law claims, 847–848
Self-liquidating policies, insurance, 935

Sentencing errors, unlawful conduct, 873
Settlement with defendant, 895–896
Silence, negligent misrepresentation, 832–833
SLAPP laws, 898–899
Sources of legal ethics and law, 122–124
Specialists, 743
Special pleading and proof requirements, fraud on clients and nonclients, 816
Speculation
  remedies, 851–853
  substantial factor test for factual causation for breach of fiduciary duty, 793
Standard of care
  generally, 742–746
  disabilities, lawyers with, 745–746
  disclosure of inexperience, 744
  expert testimony, 752–753
  laypersons, malpractice by, 744–745
  per se negligence, 767
  representations of greater competence, 743–744
  specialists, 743
Statements of law, fraud on clients and nonclients, 823–824
State of mind, fraud on clients and nonclients, 822–823
Status of plaintiff, 723–724
Statutes of limitation
  generally, 879–890
  accrual of cause of action, 881–882
  agreement of parties, 887–888
  continuing torts, 889
  continuous representation rule, 885–887
  damage rule, accrual of cause of action, 881–882
  discovery rule, 883–885
  equitable estoppel, 888–889
  fraudulent concealment, 887
  occurrence rule, accrual of cause of action, 881
  pendency of other litigation, 888
  statutes of repose, 889–890
  tolling, generally, 882–889
Statutes of repose, 889–890
Subrogation claims of insurers, 845–846
Subsequent counsel's failure to act, proximate causation, 785–787
Substantial assistance, aiding and abetting breach of fiduciary duty, 801–802
Successive counsel, joint liability and reimbursement, 894
Successors-in-interest. Nonclients, liability to, above
Superseding causation and shifting responsibility, proximate causation, 784–787
Temporary lawyers, vicarious liability, 924–925
Termination of attorney-client relationship, 739–741
Theories of liability, generally, 719 et seq.
Tolling. Statutes of limitation, above
Tortious involvement with litigation, 845
Tortious spoliation of causation evidence, 781–782
Truth, absolute privilege for, 877
Unjust enrichment, fee forfeiture for breach of fiduciary duty, 796
Unlawful conduct. Defenses and other obstacles, above
Unsettled questions, 751–752
Vicarious liability
  generally, 722–723, 901–927
  actual and apparent authority, 905–907
  assisting nonlawyers in practice of law, 927
  co-counsel arrangements and other outside counsel, 919–920
  estoppel, partnership by, 922–923
  fact, partnership in, 923
  general partnerships, liability of partners in, 908
  intent to benefit firm, 903–904
  joint responsibility and joint ventures, referral fee arrangements, 915–916
  joint venture, 923–924
  law firm practice, generally, 901–914
  limited liability companies and limited liability partnerships, 910–914
  negligent referral, 916–919
  nondelegable duties, 925–927
  normal risks incidental to practice of law, 904–905
  of counsel arrangements, 920–921
  office-sharing arrangements
    generally, 921–924
    estoppel, partnership by, 922–923
    fact, partnership in, 923
    joint venture, 923–924
  ordinary course of firm business, 903–905
  procedural issues, 907–908
  professional corporations, 908–910
  punitive damages, 865
  referral fee arrangements
    generally, 914–919
    joint responsibility and joint ventures, 915–916
    negligent referral, 916–919
  temporary lawyers, 924–925
Voluntary assumption of duty
  negligent misrepresentation, 828
  reasonable care, duty to exercise, 734–735
Wills, intended beneficiaries, 837–838

**MANAGING LAWYERS**
Law Firms, this index

**MATERIALITY**
Malpractice, this index

**MEDIA RIGHTS**
Conflicts of interest, 366–367

**MEDIATION**
Conflicts of Interest, this index

**MERGERS**
Malpractice, liability to nonclients, 813–814

**METADATA**
Evidence in civil proceedings, unsolicited receipt of another's privileged or confidential materials, 526–528

**MIGRATING LAWYERS**
Conflicts of interest, imputation of conflicts within firm, 406–413

**MILESTONES STAGE DEVELOPMENT MODEL**
Law school curriculum, 100–101

**MINORS**
Attorney-client relationship, 226–227

**MISREPRESENTATION**
Sources of legal ethics and law, 126–127

**MISTAKES**
Effective representation, competence, 277

**MITIGATING EVIDENCE**
Advocacy, duty of prosecutor to disclose, 640–642

**MITIGATION**
Malpractice, 856–857, 869–870

**MORAL ADVICE**
Effective Representation, this index

**MORAL OBLIGATION**
Pro bono legal services, 703–705

**MORAL REMAINDERS**
Philosophy of legal ethics, 53

**"MORE FAVORABLE RESULT" STANDARD**
Malpractice, factual causation, 778

**MULTIJURISDICTIONAL PRACTICE OF LAW**
Generally, 141–150
Alternative dispute resolution proceeding related to lawyer's home practice, 145–146
Federal or other law, legal services authorized by, 148–149
House counsel for entity, 148
Major disaster, legal services following, 149–150
Other temporary services incidental to lawyer's home practice, 146–148
Temporary practice before tribunal - pro hac vice admission, 144–145
Temporary practice in association with state lawyer, 143–144

**MULTIPLE TORTFEASORS**
Malpractice, "but for" test and factual causation, 775–776

**NAMES**
Advertising, this index

**NARRATIVE STATEMENTS**
Presentation of evidence, false evidence and client perjury, 569–570

**NATURAL LAW THEORY**
Philosophy of legal ethics, 42–43

**"NEAR PRIVITY" VIEW**
Malpractice, negligent misrepresentation, 830–831

**NEGLIGENCE**
Malpractice, this index

**NEGLIGENT MISREPRESENTATION**
Malpractice, this index

**NEUTRALITY**
Communications with unrepresented person, 675–676
Philosophy of legal ethics, 35

**NONACCOUNTABILITY PRINCIPLE**
Philosophy of legal ethics, 35

**NONCLIENTS**
Malpractice, this index

**NONLAWYER ASSISTANTS**
Managing or supervising lawyers, 685–687

**NONPROFIT ORGANIZATIONS**
Professional independence, sharing of court-awarded fees, 433–436

**NOTICE**
Evidence in Criminal Proceedings, this index
Malpractice insurance, 941–942
Sale of law practice and effect on clients, notice to clients and protection of confidentiality, 245–246

**NOVEL THEORIES**
Malpractice, 752

**OBSERVATION OF EVIDENCE**
Evidence in Criminal Proceedings, this index

**OBSTRUCTION OF JUSTICE**
Evidence in criminal proceedings, preservation of evidence, 536–540

**OBVIOUS NEGLIGENCE**
Malpractice, expert testimony, 753–754

**OCCURRENCE RULE**
Malpractice, accrual of cause of action, 881

**OF COUNSEL ARRANGEMENTS**
Malpractice, vicarious liability, 920–921

**OFFICE-SHARING ARRANGEMENTS**
Malpractice, this index

**OPINIONS**
Malpractice, this index

**OPPRESSION**
Advocacy, seeking advantage, 490–491

**ORDINARY BUSINESS MATTERS (RUSE ABUSE)**
Organization/entity clients, confidentiality and attorney-client privilege, 449–453

**ORGANIZATIONAL ETHICAL CULTURE**
Stress management, 90–91

**ORGANIZATION/ENTITY CLIENTS**
Generally, 443–474
Attorney-client privilege. Confidentiality and attorney-client privilege, above
Confidentiality and attorney-client privilege
generally, 445–453
corporate in-house counsel, 449–450

crime-fraud exception, 452–453
determination who speaks for client for purposes of privilege, 445–449
funneling documents through counsel, 450–451
government clients, 471–472
loss of privilege if communication not confidential, 452
ordinary business matters (ruse abuse), 449–453
pre-existing documents not privileged, 452
ultimate decision of client not privileged, 452
underlying facts not privileged, 451–452
waiver of privilege, 448–449
Constituents of client, response by lawyer to, 457–459
Crime-fraud exception, confidentiality and attorney-client privilege, 452–453
Discharge of lawyer, unlawful conduct or internal dissension within organization, 466
Disclosures of information, unlawful conduct or internal dissension within organization, 464–466
Dual representation of organization and individual constituent, 468–470
Formation of entity, responsibilities during, 444–445
Former employees of entity, contacts with, 456–457
Funneling documents through counsel, confidentiality and attorney-client privilege, 450–451
Government clients
generally, 470–474
attorney-client privilege, 471–472
identification of government client and litigating authority, 472–474
Internal dissension. Unlawful conduct or internal dissension within organization, below
Knowledge of lawyer regarding illegal conduct within organization, 461
Limitations on communications with current or former constituents of entity, 457–458
Miscreant constituent and lawyer's duty of diligence to organization, 466–467
Ordinary business matters (ruse abuse), confidentiality and attorney-client privilege, 449–453
Outside interference—"no contact" rule for entities
generally, 454–457
former employees of entity, contacts with, 456–457
limitations on communications with current or former constituents of entity
generally, 457–458
neutrality of lawyer, 457
violation of organization's rights, 457
represented person, defined, 454–456
Pre-existing documents, confidentiality and attorney-client privilege, 452
Serious conflicts among constituents of organization, 467–468
Substantial injury, unlawful conduct or internal dissension within organization, 462
Ultimate decision of client, confidentiality and attorney-client privilege, 452
Underlying facts, confidentiality and attorney-client privilege, 451–452
Unlawful conduct or internal dissension within organization
generally, 459–468
addressing of problem within organizational structure, 462–464
discharge or withdrawal of lawyer, 466
disclosure by lawyer retained to investigate or defend, 465–466
disclosure of confidential information to correct problem, 464–465
knowledge of lawyer regarding illegal conduct, 461
miscreant constituent and lawyer's duty of diligence to organization, 466–467
serious conflicts among constituents of organization, 467–468
substantial injury, likelihood of, 462
triggering of lawyer's duty to proceed in best interests of organization, 461–462
violation of law by corporate constituent, 461–462
Waiver of attorney-client privilege, 448–449
Withdrawal of lawyer, unlawful conduct or internal dissension within organization, 466

**PARTISANSHIP PRINCIPLE**
Philosophy of legal ethics, 34

**PAY-TO-PLAY**
Political contributions, 158, 193–194

**PERFECTIONISM**
Stress management, internal traits of lawyers, 85

**PERJURY**
Presentation of evidence, 567–580

**PERMISSION**
Consent, this index

**PER SE NEGLIGENCE**
Malpractice, this index

**PERSONAL BIAS**
Judicial ethics and conduct of judges, disqualification, 999–1000

**PERSONAL INTERESTS**
Conflicts of Interest, this index

**PERSONAL KNOWLEDGE**
Judicial ethics and conduct of judges, disqualification, 1000

**PERSONAL PROBLEMS**
Effective representation, competence, 277

**PERSONAL VOUCHING AND OPINIONS**
Advocacy, 588–589

**PHILOSOPHY OF LEGAL ETHICS**
Generally, 25–53
Corporation as client, amoral ethics squared, 49–51
Fifth Amendment, 35–37
Foundations of lawyer's role
generally, 27–40
Fifth Amendment, 35–37
Fourth Amendment, 37
function of lawyers in society, 27–28
good person as good lawyer, 34–40
legality *vs.* morality, 32–34
neutrality principle, 35
nonaccountability principle, 35
partisanship principle, 34
professional ethics, 28–30
role specific morality, 30–40
Sixth Amendment, 35–36
Fourth Amendment, 37
Function of lawyers in society, 27–28
Gap between law and morality, 45–47
Good person as good lawyer, 34–40
Jurisprudence and lawyer's role
generally, 41–44
jurisprudential turn, 41–42
legal positivism, 43–44
natural law theory, 42–43
rules of recognition, 44
Legality *vs.* morality, 32–34
Legal positivism, 43–44
Morality *vs.* legality, 32–34
Moral remainders, 53
Natural law theory, 42–43
Neutrality principle, 35
Nonaccountability principle, 35
Partisanship principle, 34
Professional ethics, 28–30
Role specific morality, 30–40
Rules of recognition, 44
Sixth Amendment, 35–36

**PLEADINGS**
Malpractice, 720–721

**POLITICAL ACTIVITIES**
Judicial ethics and conduct of judges, 1020–1026

**POLITICAL CONTRIBUTIONS**
Generally, 158, 193–194
Pay-to-play contributions, 158, 193–194

**PREJUDGMENT INTEREST**
Malpractice, 857–858

**PREJUDICE**
Bias or Prejudice, this index

**PRESENTATION OF EVIDENCE**
Generally, 567–586
Confidentiality, remedial measures to correct false evidence notwithstanding, 571–574
Discretion to decline to present evidence reasonably believed to be false, 570–571
Duration of duty to remedy false evidence, 578–579
Excessive preparation of witness, avoidance of, 584
False evidence and client perjury, 567–580
Fraudulent or criminal conduct of client before tribunal, counteraction of, 580–581
Improper inducements to witness, 585–586
Narrative statements, false evidence and client perjury, 569–570
Remedial measures to correct false evidence, 571–574, 576–578
Standard of knowledge as applied to false evidence problem, 574–576
Truth, encouragement of witness to tell, 584
Witness preparation *vs.* witness coaching, 581–584

**PRESENT VALUE**
Malpractice, reduction of damages, 857

**PRESERVATION OF EVIDENCE**
Evidence in Civil Proceedings, this index
Evidence in Criminal Proceedings, this index

**PREVAILING MARKET RATE**
Attorneys' fees, shifting of fees to another party, 269–270

**PREVAILING PARTIES**
Attorneys' fees, shifting of fees to another party, 264–265

**PRIVATE ADMONITIONS**
Sources of legal ethics and law, discipline, 138–139

**PRIVILEGED INFORMATION**
Confidential Information, this index
Evidence in Civil Proceedings, this index

**PRIVILEGES AND IMMUNITIES**
Malpractice, this index

**PRIVITY**
Malpractice, liability to nonclients, 810–812

**PROBATION**
Sources of legal ethics and law, discipline, 141

**PRO BONO LEGAL SERVICES**
Generally, 703–712
Acceptance of appointment absent good cause
generally, 708–711
ethics rules, violation of, 709
financial burden, imposition of unreasonable, 709–710
repugnant to lawyer, appointment as, 710–711
Aspirational expectations, 705–706
Conflict of interest and service in governance with legal services organization, 711–712
Conflicts of interest and short term limited pro bono services
generally, 706–708
continuing representation, absence of expectation for, 707–708
implied disqualification to other lawyers in firm, 708
knowledge of conflict, 708
Continuing representation, absence of expectation for, 707–708
Ethics rules, violation of, 709

Financial burden, imposition of unreasonable, 709–710
Implied disqualification to other lawyers in firm, 708
Moral obligation and professional responsibility, 703–705
Repugnant to lawyer, appointment as, 710–711

**PRODUCTIVITY**
Legal Productivity, this index

**PROFESSIONAL CORPORATIONS**
Malpractice, vicarious liability, 908–910

**PROFESSIONAL INDEPENDENCE**
Generally, 430–441
Assistants, employment of, 437–438
Compensation plan for nonlawyer employees, 432–433
Employment of other professionals and assistants, 437–438
Estate of deceased lawyer, payments by firm to, 431–432
Fees, sharing with nonlawyers
generally, 431–436
compensation or retirement plan for nonlawyer employees, 432–433
estate or survivors of deceased lawyer, payments by firm to, 431–432
nonprofit organizations, sharing of court-awarded fees with, 433–436
purchase price of sale of practice of deceased lawyer, payment of, 432
Financial entanglements with nonlawyers, avoidance of, 430–431
House counsel, lawyer employed by client as, 438
Nonprofit organizations, sharing of court-awarded fees with, 433–436
Partnerships or other business associations including control by nonlawyers, 436–437
Practicing law with nonlawyers
generally, 436–438
employment of other professionals and assistants, 437–438
house counsel, lawyer employed by client as, 438
partnerships or other business associations including control by nonlawyers, 436–437
Purchase price of sale of practice of deceased lawyer, payment of, 432
Restriction of right to practice
generally, 438–441
retirement benefit restrictions, 439–440
sale of practice, restriction on, 440
settlement agreements, 441
Retirement benefit restrictions, 439–440
Retirement plan for nonlawyer employees, 432–433
Sale of practice, restriction on, 440
Settlement agreements, 441
Survivors of deceased lawyer, payments by firm to, 431–432

**PROFESSIONALISM AND PROFESSIONAL IDENTITY**
Generally, 57–79
ABA Model Rules and Reports and exemplary lawyers
generally, 68–77
Conference of Chief Justices' National Action Plan on Lawyer Conduct and Professionalism of 1999, 73–74
exemplary lawyers' understanding, 74–75
floor of conduct, 69
Haynsworth Report of 1996, 72–73
ideals and core principles, 69–71
MacCrate Report of 1992, 72
Stanley Commission Report of 1986, 71
synthesis of key elements, 76–77
Advocacy, advancement of resolution of disputes, 489–490
Common sense/good judgment, 67
Comparison of competencies defining ethical professional identity, 78–79
Conference of Chief Justices' National Action Plan on Lawyer Conduct and Professionalism of 1999, 73–74
Diligence, 64, 67
Effective representation, 288–291
Haynsworth Report of 1996, 72–73
Historical and sociological development of professionalism and professional formation
generally, 58–68
common sense/good judgment, 67
learned profession, law as, 58–63
occupation and profession, distinctions, 59–60
professional-formation competencies necessary to effectiveness, 63–68
relationship skills, 64, 67
self-licensing and self-regulation, 60
technical competencies, 67
trustworthiness, 63–64, 66
work ethic/diligence, 64, 67
Ideals and core principles, ABA Model Rules and Reports and exemplary lawyers, 69–71
Learned profession, law as, 58–63
MacCrate Report of 1992, 72
Relationship skills, 64, 67
Self-licensing and self-regulation, 60
Sociological development. Historical and sociological development of professionalism and professional formation, above
Stanley Commission Report of 1986, 71
Technical competencies, 67
Trustworthiness, 63–64, 66
Work ethic, 64, 67

**PRO HAC VICE ADMISSION**
Disciplinary jurisdiction, 150–151
Multijurisdictional practice of law, 144–145

**PROPERTY OF CLIENT**
Effective Representation, this index

**PROSPECTIVE CLIENTS**
Attorney-Client Relationship, this index
Conflicts of Interest, this index

Malpractice, duty to exercise reasonable care, 735–736
Solicitation, 187–188

PROXIMATE CAUSATION
Malpractice, this index

PUBLIC CONFIDENCE
Judicial ethics and conduct of judges, 959–961

PUBLIC DEFENDERS
Malpractice, immunity, 877–878

PUBLIC INTEREST PURPOSES
Solicitation, 189–190

PUBLIC REPRIMAND OR CENSURE
Sources of legal ethics and law, discipline, 139

PUBLIC SERVICE
Stress management, 88–90

PUBLIC STATEMENTS
Judicial Ethics and Conduct of Judges, this index

PUFFING
Malpractice, fraud on clients and nonclients, 821–822

PUNITIVE DAMAGES
Malpractice, this index

QUALIFIED PRIVILEGES
Malpractice, 877

QUANTUM MERUIT
Malpractice, offset for value of services rendered, 858

REASONABLE CARE AND REASONABLENESS
Attorneys' Fees, this index
Malpractice, this index

RECEIVERS
Malpractice, liability to nonclients, 814

RECIPROCAL PROFESSIONAL REFERRAL AGREEMENTS
Generally, 185

REFERRALS
Generally, 181–185
Costs of advertising, payment for, 182–183
Exceptions to prohibition on payment for referrals, generally, 182–185
General prohibition on payment for referrals, 181–182
Legal service plans, 183–184
Malpractice, this index
Nonprofit lawyer referral service, 184–185
Payment for referrals, generally, 181 et seq.
Purchase of law practice, 185
Qualified lawyer referral service, 184
Reciprocal professional referral agreements, 185

REFUNDS
Attorneys' fees, unearned fees, 258

REIMBURSEMENT
Malpractice, this index

RELATIONSHIP SKILLS
Professionalism and professional identity, 64, 67

RELEASES
Malpractice, 895–896

REMEDIES
Malpractice, this index

REPORTS
Admission to Bar and Discipline, this index

REPUTATION
Malpractice, 854

REQUESTS FOR DISCOVERY
Evidence in civil proceedings, 502–503

RESPECT FOR RIGHTS AND DIGNITY OF OTHER PERSONS
Generally, 657–678
Communications with represented person
  generally, 663–675
  communications between represented persons, 665–667
  consent by represented person's counsel to contact by another lawyer, 670–672
  court order, 672–673
  exceptions to no-contact rule
    generally, 671–673
    authority under law, 672
    consent by person's lawyer, 671–672
    court order, 672–673
  knowledge of lawyer that person is represented, 669–670
  "no-contact" rule, generally, 663–665
  petition of government, right regarding, 673–675
  representation of client, 667
  subject of representation, communications on, 667–669
Communications with unrepresented person
  generally, 675–678
  legal advice by lawyer, 676–678
  misunderstanding about lawyer's role, correction of, 676
  neutrality of lawyer, avoidance of suggestion of, 675–676
Consent by represented person's counsel to contact by another lawyer, 670–672
Court order, communications with represented person, 672–673
Crime by client, avoidance of assistance to, 661–663
False statements of material fact or law, avoidance of, 659–661
Fraud by client, avoidance of assistance to, 661–663
Knowledge of lawyer that person is represented, communications with represented person, 669–670
Misunderstanding about lawyer's role, communications with unrepresented person, 676
Neutrality of lawyer, communications with unrepresented person, 675–676

"No-contact" rule. Communications with represented person, above
Petition of government, right regarding, 673–675
Truthfulness
generally, 658–663
basic duty of truthfulness in dealings with others, 658–659
crime or fraud by client, avoidance of assistance to, 661–663
false statements of material fact or law, avoidance of, 659–661

**RESPONSES TO DISCOVERY**
Evidence in civil proceedings, 503

**RESTATEMENT OF LAW GOVERNING LAWYERS**
Sources of legal ethics and law, 117–119, 124

**RESTATEMENT (SECOND) OF TORTS**
Malpractice, this index

**RESTITUTION**
Malpractice, 866

**RESTRICTIVE COVENANTS**
Malpractice, intra-firm fiduciary duties, 807

**RETAINERS**
Attorneys' Fees, this index

**RETENTION OF EVIDENCE**
Evidence in Criminal Proceedings, this index

**RETIREMENT PLANS**
Professional independence, 432–433, 439–440

**REVOCATION OF LICENSE**
Sources of legal ethics and law, 140–141

**RISK BALANCING**
Malpractice, 746–747

**ROLE SPECIFIC MORALITY**
Philosophy of legal ethics, 30–40

**ROMANTIC RELATIONSHIPS**
Conflicts of interest, relationship with lawyer for adverse party, 373–374

**RULES OF RECOGNITION**
Philosophy of legal ethics, 44

**SAFE HARBOR**
Evidence in criminal proceedings, preservation of evidence, 541–542

**SALE OF LAW PRACTICE**
Attorney-Client Relationship, this index

**SANCTIONS**
Evidence in civil proceedings, 506–507, 509–510

**SARBANES-OXLEY ACT**
Evidence in Criminal Proceedings, this index

**SCHEME LIABILITY**
Malpractice, securities law violations, 847

**SCIENTER**
Malpractice, this index

**SCOPE OF REPRESENTATION**
Malpractice, this index

**SECURITIES LAW**
Malpractice, this index

**SELF-DEFENSE**
Confidential information, 353–354

**SELF-DETERMINATION THEORY**
Stress management, 87

**SELF-INCRIMINATION**
Admission to bar and discipline, 694

**SELF-LICENSING AND SELF-REGULATION**
Professionalism and professional identity, 60

**SELF-LIQUIDATING POLICIES**
Malpractice insurance, 935

**SENTENCING**
Malpractice, unlawful conduct, 873

**SETTLEMENTS**
Conflicts of interest, 386–389, 394–395
Malpractice, 895–896
Professional independence, 441

**SEXUAL RELATIONS**
Conflicts of interest, 372–373

**SHIFTING OF FEES**
Attorneys' Fees, this index

**SILENCE**
Malpractice, negligent misrepresentation, 832–833

**SIXTH AMENDMENT**
Philosophy of legal ethics, 35–36

**SLANDER**
Advocacy, extrajudicial statements by lawyer, 615–616

**SLAPP LAWS**
Malpractice, 898–899

**SOCIAL MEDIA**
Advertising, 168–169

**SOLICITATION**
Generally, 157–163, 185–193
Class members, communications with, 188–189
Close friends, solicitation to, 187
Current clients, solicitation to, 187–188
Exemptions from prohibition, generally, 187–188
False or misleading statements, 160–163
Family, solicitation to, 187
First Amendment, 158–160
Former clients, solicitation to, 187–188
History, 158–160
Lawyers, solicitation to, 187
Legal services plan that solicits membership, participation in, 190–191
Nature of prohibition, 185–187
Potential class members, communications with, 188–189
Prospective clients, solicitation to, 187–188

Public communications about legal topics, 191–193
Public interest purposes, 189–190
Purpose of prohibition, 185–187

**SOURCES OF LEGAL ETHICS AND LAW**
Generally, 111–155
Acceptance of clients, discrimination and harassment, 128–129
Agreements of parties, choice of law for disciplinary authority, 155
Biased conduct and lawyer fitness, 128
Central body for receiving, evaluating and investigating ethical complaints, 132–133
Choice of law for disciplinary authority
- generally, 141–143, 152–155
- agreements of parties, 155
- conduct before tribunal, 153
- other matters, 153–155

Conduct before tribunal, choice of law for disciplinary authority, 153
Confidentiality and immunity, discipline, 136–137
Courts
- generally, 119–124
- disqualification of lawyer in litigation, 120–122
- judicial sanctions, 119–120
- legal malpractice liability, 122–124

Criminal conduct, 125–126
Deceit, 126–127
Decision by hearing panel or officer and further review, discipline, 137
Declining of clients, discrimination and harassment, 128–129
Disbarment, 140–141
Discipline, outline of
- generally, 131–141
- central body for receiving, evaluating and investigating ethical complaints, 132–133
- confidentiality and immunity, 136–137
- decision by hearing panel or officer and further review, 137
- disbarment or revocation of license, 140–141
- Jurisdiction, this index
- preparation for and formal hearing, 134–135
- private admonitions, 138–139
- probation, 141
- public reprimand or censure, 139
- sanctions, generally, 137–141
- standard of proof and issue preclusion, 135–136
- suspension, 139–140

Discrimination and harassment
- generally, 127–131
- acceptance or declining of clients, 128–129
- biased conduct and lawyer fitness, 128
- defined, 130
- enforceability of new rule, 130
- free speech, 129
- legitimate advocacy, protection of, 128
- workplace bias rule, 127–128

Dishonesty, 126–127
Disqualification of lawyer in litigation, 120–122
Evolution of professional ethics within self-regulating bar, 111–112
Fraud, 126–127
Free speech, discrimination and harassment, 129
Harassment. Discrimination and harassment, above
History
- generally, 111–117
- canons to codes to rules, 112–116
- evolution of professional ethics within self-regulating bar, 111–112
- learned profession, 111
- rules of ethics, professional morality and character, 116–117

Issue preclusion, discipline, 135–136
Judicial sanctions, 119–120
Jurisdiction, this index
Learned profession, 111
Legal malpractice liability, courts, 122–124
Legitimate advocacy, protection of, 128
Misrepresentation, 126–127
Private admonitions, discipline, 138–139
Probation, discipline, 141
Public reprimand or censure, discipline, 139
Restatement of Law Governing Lawyers, 117–119, 124
Revocation of license, 140–141
Sanctions. Discipline, outline of, above
Standard of proof, discipline, 135–136
Suspension, discipline, 139–140
Workplace bias rule, 127–128

**SPECIALISTS AND SPECIALIZATION**
Advertising, this index
Malpractice, 743

**SPECULATION**
Malpractice, this index

**SPLITTING OF FEES**
Attorneys' fees, 260–262

**SPOLIATION OF EVIDENCE**
Evidence in civil proceedings, 504–507

**STANDARD OF CARE**
Malpractice, this index

**STANDARD OF PROOF**
Sources of legal ethics and law, discipline, 135–136

**STANLEY COMMISSION REPORT OF 1986**
Professionalism and professional identity, 71

**STATE OF MIND**
Malpractice, fraud on clients and nonclients, 822–823

**STATUTES OF LIMITATION**
Malpractice, this index

**STATUTES OF REPOSE**
Malpractice, 889–890

**STRESS MANAGEMENT**
Generally, 81–91
Adversarial atmosphere, 83–84

Competitiveness, internal traits of lawyers, 85–86
Decision latitude, perception of low, 84–85
External pressure of law practice
generally, 82–85
adversarial atmosphere, 83–84
decision latitude, perception of low, 84–85
financial strain, 83
workload, 82–83
Extrinsic motivation, internal traits of lawyers, 86–87
Financial strain, 83
Internal traits of lawyers
generally, 85–87
competitiveness, 85–86
extrinsically motivated, 86–87
perfectionism, 85
Organizational ethical culture, importance of, 90–91
Perfectionism, internal traits of lawyers, 85
Public service, impact of, 88–90
Self-determination theory, 87
Sources of stress, generally, 81–87
Values, needs, motivation and well-being, 87–88
Workload, 82–83

**STRUCTURE OF LEGAL PROFESSION**
Generally, 3–7
Chicago Lawyers I and II studies, 3–4
Economic census data, 4–6
Main street law practice, 6–7
Two hemispheres, 3–4

**STYLE**
Advertising, 172–174

**SUBORDINATE LAWYERS**
Law firms, 684–685

**SUBPOENAS**
Advocacy, restriction on issuance by prosecutors to lawyers, 636–640

**SUBROGATION**
Malpractice insurance, 845–846

**SUBSTANTIAL HARDSHIP**
Advocate-witness rule, 599

**SUBSTANTIAL INJURY**
Organization/entity clients, unlawful conduct or internal dissension within organization, 462

**SUCCESSIVE CLIENT CONFLICTS**
Conflicts of Interest, this index

**SUCCESSIVE COUNSEL**
Malpractice, joint liability and reimbursement, 894

**SUCCESSORS-IN-INTEREST**
Malpractice, this index

**SUPERMAN PRINCIPLE**
Advocacy, 478

**SUPERVISING LAWYERS**
Law Firms, this index

**SUSPENSION**
Effective representation, protection of client, 288
Sources of legal ethics and law, discipline, 139–140

**TARGETED DIRECT MAIL**
Advertising, 169–172

**TAX RETURNS AND TAX PLANNING**
Attorney-client relationship, 205–207

**TECHNICAL COMPETENCIES**
Professionalism and professional identity, 67

**TEMPORARY LAWYERS**
Malpractice, vicarious liability, 924–925

**TERMINATION OF REPRESENTATION**
Attorney-Client Relationship, this index

**THIRD-PARTY NEUTRALS**
Generally, 649, 653–655
Conflicts of Interest, this index

**THIRD PERSONS**
Advocacy, responsibility of lawyers for prejudicial extrajudicial statements, 616–617
Attorneys' fees, payment of, 262–263
Conflicts of interest, compensation from person other than client, 369–370
Evidence in civil proceedings, receipt of protected materials taken, 520–526

**TIME RECORDS**
Attorneys' fees, shifting of fees to another party, 267

**TOLLING**
Malpractice, this index

**TRADE NAME**
Advertising, designation of firm, 178–179

**TRIALS**
Advocacy, this index

**TRUSTWORTHINESS**
Professionalism and professional identity, 63–64, 66

**TRUTH AND TRUTHFULNESS**
Advocacy, this index
Malpractice, absolute privilege, 877
Respect for Rights and Dignity of Other Persons, this index

**UNJUST ENRICHMENT**
Malpractice, fee forfeiture for breach of fiduciary duty, 796

**UNLAWFUL CONDUCT**
Malpractice, this index

**VALUATION OF LAW PRACTICE**
Attorney-client relationship, sale of law practice and effect on clients, 241–243

**VICARIOUS LIABILITY**
Law firms, managing or supervising lawyers, 682–683
Malpractice, this index

**VINCE LOMBARDI DOCTRINE**
Advocacy, 478

**VOLUNTARY ASSUMPTION OF DUTY**
Malpractice, this index

**WAIVER**
Advocacy, demand by government for waiver of privileged communications, 633–636
Attorney-client privilege, 324–325
Conflicts of Interest, this index
Organization/entity clients, attorney-client privilege, 448–449

**WEB PAGES**
Advertising, 168–169

**WILLS**
Malpractice, intended beneficiaries, 837–838

**WITHDRAWAL**
Conflicts of Interest, this index

**WITHHOLDING INFORMATION FROM CLIENT**
Effective representation, 295–295

**WITNESSES**
Advocate-Witness Rule, this index

**WORK ETHIC**
Professionalism and professional identity, 64, 67

**WORKLOAD**
Stress management, 82–83

**WORKPLACE BIAS RULE**
Sources of legal ethics and law, 127–128

**WORK PRODUCT**
Confidential information, 333–335

**WRONGFUL CONVICTIONS**
Advocacy, disclosure duties of prosecutors, 642–643

**WRONGFUL DISCHARGE**
Attorney-client relationship, claims by in-house counsel and law firm employees, 230–233

**ZEALOUS REPRESENTATION**
Effective Representation, this index